Today's most **popular authors** have collaborated on this exciting new series, which combines **great literature** with remarkably **effective instruction,** bringing real writers and real tools together for real results.

Give your students

Real writers
unprecedented access to award-winning authors
(see page T2)

Real tools
remarkably effective tools for differentiated instruction
(see page T4)

Real results
built-in benchmarking to guarantee standards mastery and learning success   (see page T6)

"**This project is what I wish I'd had when I was in school . . . a resource where I could not only read really good writing, but also get a sense about how the authors actually felt!**"

—Cornelius Eady
featured unit author

TEACHER'S EDITION CONTENTS

TEACHER'S EDITION

PRENTICE HALL
LITERATURE

PENGUIN EDITION

GRADE NINE

Copyright © 2007 by Pearson Education, Inc., publishing as Pearson Prentice Hall, Boston, Massachusetts 02116. All rights reserved. Printed in the United States of America. This publication is protected by copyright, and permission should be obtained from the publisher prior to any prohibited reproduction, storage in a retrieval system, or transmission in any form or by any means, electronic, mechanical, photocopying, recording, or likewise. For information regarding permission(s), write to: Rights and Permissions Department, One Lake Street, Upper Saddle River, New Jersey 07458.

Pearson Prentice Hall™ is a trademark of Pearson Education, Inc.
Pearson® is a registered trademark of Pearson plc.
Prentice Hall® is a registered trademark of Pearson Education, Inc.

Boston, Massachusetts
Upper Saddle River, New Jersey

ISBN 0-13-131755-5

5 6 7 8 9 10   10 09 08

Real writers

Fifty-three of today's most popular writers have collaborated on this extraordinary new program.

Now your students can learn about reading, writing, and literature from the authors themselves, as they share their personal experiences, insights, and expertise while presenting key instructional concepts.

For me, this is a way of talking to kids directly, explaining to them why it's so important to be engaged in the written word.

—Lan Samantha Chang
Grade 8, Unit 6 author

Unit 6

Introduction:
Themes in American Stories

From the Author's Desk

Lan Samantha Chang
Talks About Storytelling

Lan Samantha Chang

We share our lives through the stories we tell. Long before our ancestors invented reading or writing, they were telling stories.

The Oral Tradition Is Alive and Well

Despite our reliance on written literature, media, and the Internet, we continue to pass down our experience through the spoken word. As a matter of fact, every culture has an oral trad

▲ Lan Samantha Chang has received critical acclaim for her work about the Chinese American immigrant experience.

Each **unit** in *Prentice Hall Literature* is hosted by one of the featured **authors**. Each author serves as a **guide** for your students, taking them on an unforgettable journey through the writer's world and introducing them to a universe of great literature.

Give your students unprecedented access to award-winning authors!

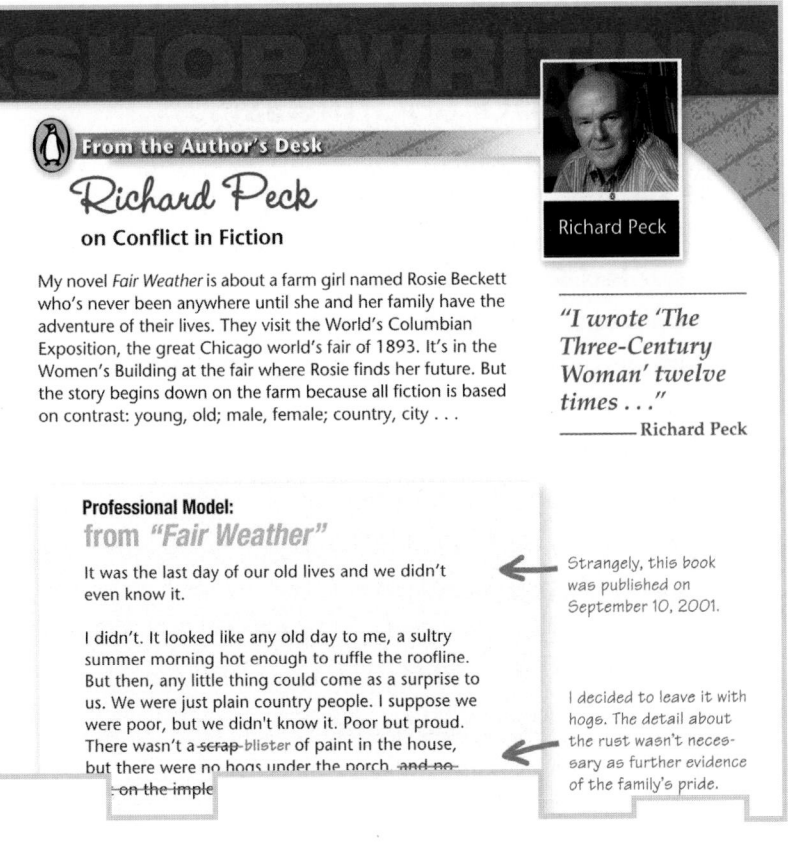

From the Author's Desk

Richard Peck
on Conflict in Fiction

My novel *Fair Weather* is about a farm girl named Rosie Beckett who's never been anywhere until she and her family have the adventure of their lives. They visit the World's Columbian Exposition, the great Chicago world's fair of 1893. It's in the Women's Building at the fair where Rosie finds her future. But the story begins down on the farm because all fiction is based on contrast: young, old; male, female; country, city . . .

Richard Peck

"I wrote 'The Three-Century Woman' twelve times . . ."
——— Richard Peck

Professional Model:
from *"Fair Weather"*

It was the last day of our old lives and we didn't even know it.

Strangely, this book was published on September 10, 2001.

I didn't. It looked like any old day to me, a sultry summer morning hot enough to ruffle the roofline. But then, any little thing could come as a surprise to us. We were just plain country people. I suppose we were poor, but we didn't know it. Poor but proud. There wasn't a ~~scrap blister~~ of paint in the house, but there were no hogs under the porch, ~~and no~~ ~~on the imple~~

I decided to leave it with hogs. The detail about the rust wasn't necessary as further evidence of the family's pride.

Each author
- hosts a unit in *Prentice Hall Literature*
- introduces a literary genre
- provides insight into the "story behind the story"
- answers questions about writing and literature from real students
- uses his or her own writing to illustrate the writing process

From the Author's Desk DVD

A corresponding video program brings your students into the writer's world, as the authors explain how their personal experiences shaped their writing and how they use the world around them to create the stories that inform, engage, and entertain readers around the world.

Real tools

Presenting: QuickTake™
instant progress monitoring
as easy as 1, 2, 3!

1 Pose questions
to the entire class

2 Students answer via
response pads

3 Results are recorded
and displayed instantly

Deliver differentiated instruction easily and seamlessly.

For every selection:

- **Leveled Reading Warm-ups**
  Brief reading passages comprising high-interest
  text and low-level Lexile™ vocabulary preteach
  essential reading skills.

- **Leveled Vocabulary Warm-ups**
  Lexiled™ word lists and activities prepare
  students for reading selections.

- **Leveled Assessment**
  Two levels of selection tests allow you to provide
  assessment targeted for different ability levels.

- **Reader's Notebook series**
  Three levels of interactive readers support
  every selection.

**Technology to help you
Plan, Teach, and Assess:**

- **TeacherEXPRESS™**
  Powerful lesson-planning, resource management,
  and standards-aligned assessment tools, all in one
  place, make class preparation quick and easy!

- **StudentEXPRESS™**
  An interactive textbook, electronic worksheets,
  and links to online activities make this the perfect
  student tool for studying or test review.

- **Exam*View*™ Test Generator**
  Create standards-aligned tests in seconds or
  customize tests to suit an individual student's needs.

Strategic pairing lets you choose your selection without skipping a skill.

A **unique organization** ensures complete skills and standards coverage while providing ample opportunity for true differentiated instruction.

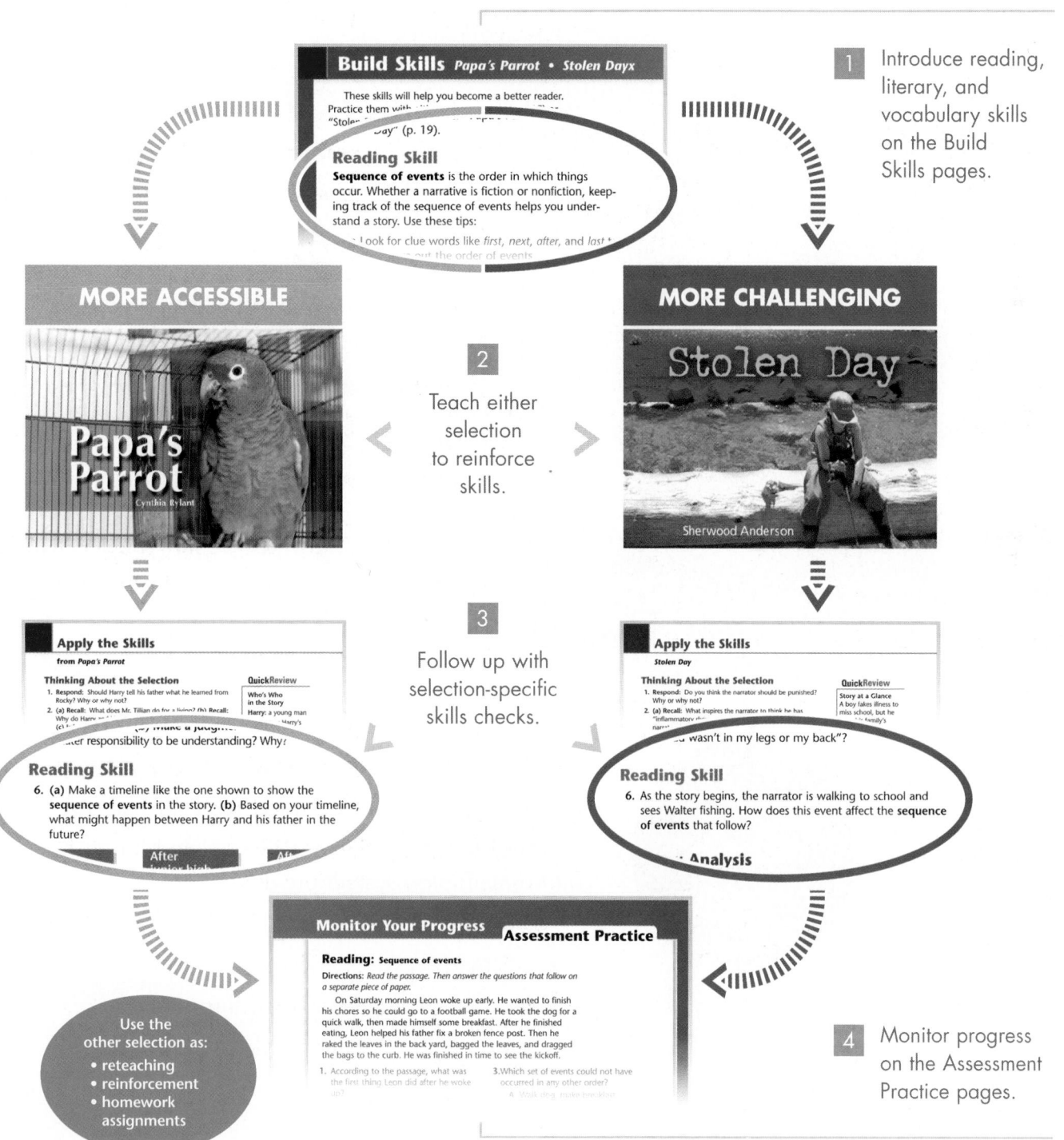

Build Skills *Papa's Parrot • Stolen Dayx*

These skills will help you become a better reader. Practice them with ... "Stolen ... Day" (p. 19).

Reading Skill
Sequence of events is the order in which things occur. Whether a narrative is fiction or nonfiction, keeping track of the sequence of events helps you understand a story. Use these tips:
· look for clue words like *first*, *next*, *after*, and *last* ...
... out the order of events

1 — Introduce reading, literary, and vocabulary skills on the Build Skills pages.

MORE ACCESSIBLE

Papa's Parrot
Cynthia Rylant

MORE CHALLENGING

Stolen Day
Sherwood Anderson

2 — Teach either selection to reinforce skills.

Apply the Skills
from *Papa's Parrot*

Thinking About the Selection
1. **Respond:** Should Harry tell his father what he learned from Rocky? Why or why not?
2. (a) **Recall:** What does Mr. Tillian do for a living? (b) **Recall:** Why do Harry ...
(c) ... ... make a judgment
... ter responsibility to be understanding? Why?

QuickReview
Who's Who in the Story
Harry: a young man
... Harry's

Reading Skill
6. (a) Make a timeline like the one shown to show the **sequence of events** in the story. (b) Based on your timeline, what might happen between Harry and his father in the future?

After junior high ...

3 — Follow up with selection-specific skills checks.

Apply the Skills
Stolen Day

Thinking About the Selection
1. **Respond:** Do you think the narrator should be punished? Why or why not?
2. (a) **Recall:** What inspires the narrator to think he has "inflammatory ... ... wasn't in my legs or my back"?

QuickReview
Story at a Glance
A boy takes illness to miss school, but he ...

Reading Skill
6. As the story begins, the narrator is walking to school and sees Walter fishing. How does this event affect the **sequence of events** that follow?
... Analysis

Monitor Your Progress   **Assessment Practice**

Reading: Sequence of events
Directions: Read the passage. Then answer the questions that follow on a separate piece of paper.
On Saturday morning Leon woke up early. He wanted to finish his chores so he could go to a football game. He took the dog for a quick walk, then made himself some breakfast. After he finished eating, Leon helped his father fix a broken fence post. Then he raked the leaves in the back yard, bagged the leaves, and dragged the bags to the curb. He was finished in time to see the kickoff.

1. According to the passage, what was the first thing Leon did after he woke ...?
3. Which set of events could not have occurred in any other order?
4. ...

4 — Monitor progress on the Assessment Practice pages.

Use the other selection as:
• reteaching
• reinforcement
• homework assignments

Real results

Catch small learning problems <u>before</u> they become big ones!

Diagnose Readiness

Brief assessments at the beginning of each part determine student readiness to learn new skills.

Monitor Progress

Assessment Practice features after each selection set check skills proficiency and make sure students are on track.

Benchmark Mastery

Frequent benchmark tests gauge standards mastery and determine whether intervention is needed.

Online Reading Intervention

Introducing: Prentice Hall Success Tracker™
Help your students make real progress!

This fully automated, interactive online diagnostic and remediation system provides

- Diagnosis and benchmarking of skills
- Customized skills practice
- At-a-glance standards reporting

See page T80 for more information.

Built-in benchmarking ensures success.

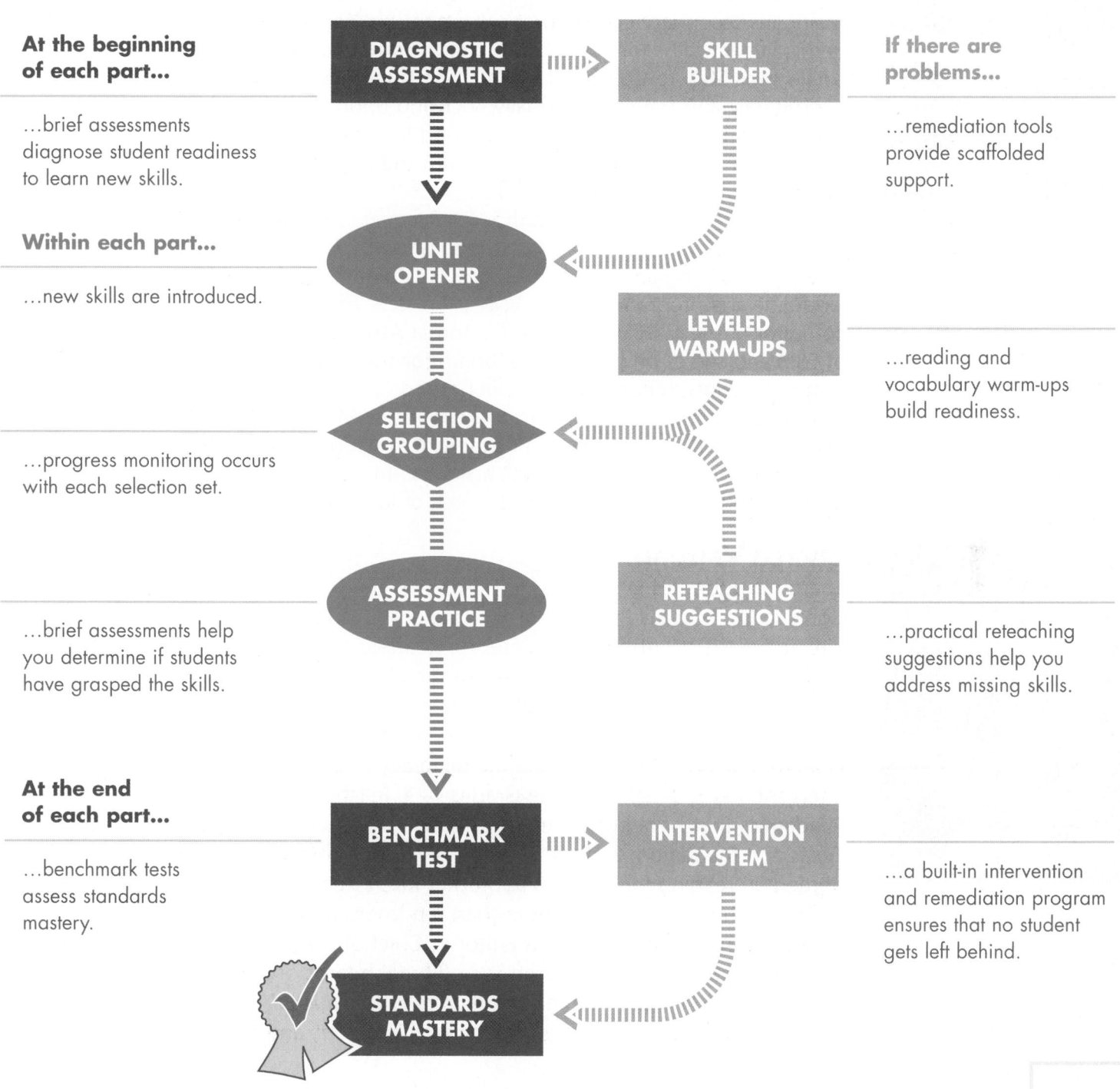

At the beginning of each part...

...brief assessments diagnose student readiness to learn new skills.

Within each part...

...new skills are introduced.

...progress monitoring occurs with each selection set.

...brief assessments help you determine if students have grasped the skills.

At the end of each part...

...benchmark tests assess standards mastery.

DIAGNOSTIC ASSESSMENT

SKILL BUILDER

UNIT OPENER

LEVELED WARM-UPS

SELECTION GROUPING

ASSESSMENT PRACTICE

RETEACHING SUGGESTIONS

BENCHMARK TEST

INTERVENTION SYSTEM

STANDARDS MASTERY

If there are problems...

...remediation tools provide scaffolded support.

...reading and vocabulary warm-ups build readiness.

...practical reteaching suggestions help you address missing skills.

...a built-in intervention and remediation program ensures that no student gets left behind.

CONTRIBUTING AUTHORS

The contributing authors guided the direction and philosophy of *Prentice Hall Literature, Penguin Edition*. Working with the development team, they helped to build the pedagogical integrity of the program and to ensure its relevance for today's teachers and students.

Kate **Kinsella**

Kate Kinsella, Ed.D., is a teacher educator in the Department of Secondary Education at San Francisco State University. She teaches coursework addressing academic language and literacy development in linguistically and culturally diverse classrooms. Dr. Kinsella maintains secondary classroom involvement by teaching an academic literacy class for adolescent English learners through the University's Step to College Program. She publishes and provides consultancy and training nationally, focusing upon responsible instructional practices that provide second language learners and less proficient readers in grades 4–12 with the language and literacy skills vital to educational mobility.

Dr. Kinsella is the program author for *Reading in the Content Areas: Strategies for Reading Success,* published by Pearson Learning and the lead program author for the 2002 Prentice Hall secondary language arts program *Timeless Voices: Timeless Themes.* She is the co-editor of the *CATESOL Journal* (California Association of Teachers of ESL) and serves on the editorial board for the *California Reader.* A former Fulbright scholar, Dr. Kinsella has received numerous awards, including the prestigious Marcus Foster Memorial Reading Award, offered by the California Reading Association in 2002 to a California educator who has made a significant statewide impact on both policy and pedagogy in the area of literacy.

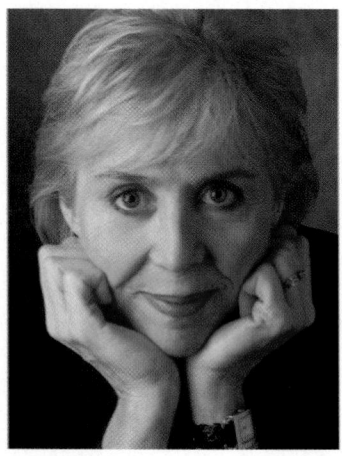

Sharon **Vaughn**

Sharon Vaughn, PH.D., is the H.E. Hartfelder/The Southland Corporation Regents Professor at the University of Texas and also director of the Vaughn Gross Center for Reading and Language Arts at the University of Texas (VGCRLA). As director of the VGCRLA, she leads more than five major initiatives, including The Central Regional Reading First Technical Assistance Center; the Three-Tier Reading Research Project; a bilingual-biliteracy (English/Spanish) intervention research study; the Grades 1– 4 Teacher Reading Academies that have been used for teacher education throughout Texas and the nation; and the creation of online professional development in reading for teachers and other interested professionals.

Dr. Vaughn has published more than ten books and over one hundred research articles. She is Editor in Chief of the *Journal of Learning Disabilities* and serves on the editorial boards of more than ten research journals, including the *Journal of Educational Psychology,* the *American Educational Research Journal,* and the *Journal of Special Education.*

Kevin **Feldman**

Kevin Feldman, Ed.D., is the Director of Reading and Intervention for the Sonoma County Office of Education and an independent educational consultant. He publishes and provides consultancy and training nationally, focusing upon improving school-wide literacy skills as well as targeted interventions for struggling readers, special needs students, and second language learners. Dr. Feldman is the co-author of the California Special Education Reading Task Force report and the lead program author for the 2002 Prentice Hall secondary language arts program *Timeless Voices: Timeless Themes.* He serves as technical consultant to the California Reading and Literature Project and the CalSTAT State Special Education Improvement Project. Dr. Feldman has taught for nineteen years at the university level in Special Education and Masters' level programs for University of California, Riverside, and Sonoma State University.

Dr. Feldman earned his undergraduate degree in Psychology from Washington State University and has a Master's Degree from UC Riverside in Special Education, Learning Disabilities, and Instructional Design. He has an Ed.D. from the University of San Francisco in Curriculum and Instruction.

Differentiated Instruction Advisor
Don **Deshler**

Don Deshler, Ph.D, is the Director of the Center for Research on Learning (CRL) at the University of Kansas. Dr. Deshler's expertise centers on adolescent literacy, learning strategic instruction, and instructional strategies for teaching content-area classes to academically diverse classes. He is the author of *Teaching Content to All: Evidence-Based Inclusive Practices in Middle and Secondary Schools,* a text which presents the instructional practices that have been tested and validated through his research at CRL.

UNIT AUTHORS

An award-winning contemporary author hosts each unit in each level of Prentice Hall Literature. *Serving as guides for your students, these authors introduce literary concepts, answer questions about their work, and discuss their own writing processes, using their works as models. Following are the featured unit authors for Grade 9.*

Elizabeth **McCracken** (b. 1966)

Unit 1: Fiction and Nonfiction Elizabeth McCracken is highly qualified as a guide for this unit, having written prize-winning fiction and nonfiction. Her first novel, *The Giant's House*, was a finalist for the National Book Award. Her non-fiction includes pieces on Charles Dickens's *Bleak House* and Victor Hugo's *The Hunchback of Notre Dame* and the personal essay "Desiderata." In both genres, she creates a lively and engaging voice.

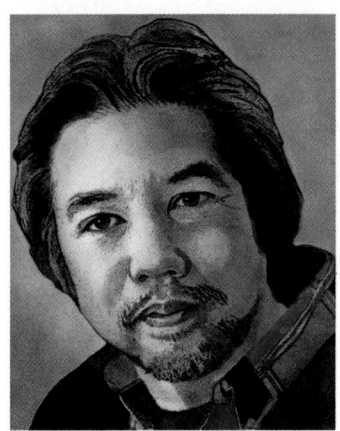

Wayson **Choy** (b. 1939)

Unit 2: Short Stories Known for his novel *The Jade Peony*, which won Canada's Trillium Book Award, and for its sequel, *All That Matters*, Wayson Choy is also devoted to the short-story form. The seed for *The Jade Peony* was a much-anthologized short story of the same name, and another story received the Best American Short Stories Award. His writing has been praised by *Maclean's* magazine for its "exquisite grace."

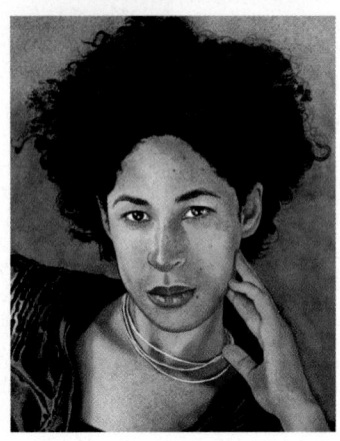

Rebecca **Walker** (b. 1969)

Unit 3: Types of Nonfiction Rebecca Walker is the ideal guide for the nonfiction unit. Her essays and articles have appeared in many magazines and publications, and her books are taught in high schools and colleges in the U.S. and Canada. When she was twenty-five, Ms. Walker was named by *Time* magazine as one of fifty influential American leaders under the age of forty. She has received awards for both her writing and her work as an advocate for young women.

Pat **Mora** (b. 1942)

Unit 4: Poetry Pat Mora, the guide for the poetry unit, has won acclaim for both writing and teaching poetry. Her many verse collections include *Agua Santa: Holy Water, Borders, Chants, Communion* and *My Own True Name: New and Selected Poems for Young Adults*. Among the prizes given to her verse are the Southwest Book Award and the Pellicer-Frost Bi-national Poetry Award.

Gary L. **Blackwood** (b. 1945)

Unit 5: Drama Though famous for his award-winning fiction and nonfiction for young adults, Gary L. Blackwood is a perfect guide for the drama unit. Half a dozen of his stage plays, including his dramatization of his novel *The Shakespeare Stealer*, have been produced and performed at the Kennedy Center in Washington, D.C., and at other well-known theaters. Mr. Blackwood has also taught classes and workshops in playwriting.

Coach Dean **Smith** (b. 1931)
with John **Kilgo** (b. 1935)

Unit 6: Themes in Literature: Heroism Coach Dean Smith is ideally suited as a guide for this unit on heroism. Throughout his career with the University of North Carolina basketball team, he was known as much for developing the character of his players as he was for his 879 career victories. With John Kilgo, a distinguished sportswriter, Smith wrote about his philosophy in *The Carolina Way*.

Unit Authors ■ *v*

PROGRAM ADVISORS

The program advisors provided ongoing input throughout the development of *Prentice Hall Literature: Penguin Edition.* Their valuable insights ensure that the perspectives of the teachers throughout the country are represented within this literature series.

Sherice Alford
Language Arts Instructor
Cape Fear Senior High School
Fayetteville, North Carolina

Leslie Ballard
State Director
North Central Association CASI
Indiana State University
Terre Haute, Indiana

Heather Barnes
Language Arts Instructor
Central Crossing High School
Grove City, Ohio

Kathryn Shelley-Barnes
District Support Specialist
Traverse City Central High School
Traverse City, Michigan

Karen C. Lilly-Bowyer
Instructional Services Assessment Team
Winston-Salem Forsyth County Schools
Winston-Salem, North Carolina

Lee Bromberger
English Department Chairperson
Mukwonago High School
Mukwonago, Wisconsin

Shawn L. Brumfield
Literacy Coach
Horace Mann Middle School
Los Angeles Unified School District
Local 3
Los Angeles, California

Susanne Buttrey
Librarian
Sycamore Middle School
Pleasant View, Tennessee

Denise Campbell
K–12 Literacy Content Coordinator
Cherry Creek School District
Centennial, Colorado

Patricia A. Cantrowitz
Language Arts Instructor (Retired)
Union-Endicott High School
Endicott, New York

Holly Carr
Language Arts Instructor
Central Crossing High School
Grove City, Ohio

Melody Renee Chalmers
Language Arts Instructor
E. E. Smith High School
Fayetteville, North Carolina

Susan Cisna
Language Arts Instructor
East Prairie Junior High School
Tuscola, Illinois

Barbra Evans-Thompson
English Department Chairperson
Westover High School
Fayetteville, North Carolina

Ebony Forte
Language Arts Instructor
Pine Forest Senior High School
Fayetteville, North Carolina

Linda Fund
Reading Specialist
Ezra L. Nolan Middle School #40
Jersey City, New Jersey

Karen Gibson, Ph.D.
Communication Arts Program Leader
Appleton Area School District
Appleton, Wisconsin

Gail Hacker
Language Arts Instructor (Retired)
North Charleston High School
North Charleston, South Carolina

Kimberly Hartman
Language Arts Instructor
Franklin Heights High School
Columbus, Ohio

Doris Sue Hawkins
Language Arts Instructor
C. W. Otto Middle School
Lansing, Michigan

Darby Holley
Language Arts Instructor
Henry L. Sneed Middle School
Florence, South Carolina

Helen Hudson
Language Arts Instructor
Crawfordsville High School
Crawfordsville, Indiana

Kathleen Keane
English Department Chairperson
Foxborough High School
Foxborough, Massachusetts

John Kiser
English Curriculum Specialist (Retired)
Charlotte-Mecklenburg Schools
Charlotte, North Carolina

Cheryl W. Lee
Language Arts Instructor
Douglas Byrd High School
Fayetteville, North Carolina

Carrie Lichtenberg
Language Arts Instructor
Highlands High School
Ft. Thomas, Kentucky

Catherine Linn
Language Arts Instructor
Palm Springs High School
Palm Desert, California

Agathaniki Locklear
District Technology Resource Teacher
Kenton County Schools
Ft. Wright, Kentucky

John Ludy
Language Arts Instructor
Fremont High School
Fremont, Indiana

Leigh L. Matthewson
Language Arts Instructor
Albuquerque Public Schools
Albuquerque, New Mexico

Sherrie McDowell
Language Arts Instructor
Central High School
Cheyenne, Wyoming

Suzanne Mitoraj
English/Language Arts Consultant
Berlin, Connecticut

Nancy Monroe
Language Arts Instructor
Bolton High School
Alexandria, Louisiana

Gail Phelps
Language Arts Instructor
Northwood Middle School
North Little Rock, Arkansas

Matthew Scanlon
K–12 Humanities Supervisor
Hackettstown Public Schools
Hackettstown, New Jersey

John Scott
Language Arts Instructor (Retired)
Hampton City Schools
Hampton City, Virginia

Jean Shope
Language Arts Instructor
Grant Middle School
Albuquerque, New Mexico

Margaret St. Sauver
Staff Development-English/Language Arts
St. Paul Public Schools
St. Paul, Minnesota

Steve Thalheimer
Language Arts Instructor
Lawrenceburg High School
Lawrenceburg, Indiana

Cathy Robbs Turner
Director of Academies
Chattanooga Central High School
Harrison, Tennessee

Sandra VanBelois
Language Arts Instructor
Jack Britt High School
Fayetteville, North Carolina

Martha Lee Wildman
Language Arts Instructor
Lynn Middle School
Las Cruces, New Mexico

Melissa Williams
Language Arts Instructor
Delsea Regional High School
Franklinville, New Jersey

Charles Youngs
HS Language Arts Curriculum Facilitator
Bethel Park High School
Bethel Park, Pennsylvania

CONTENTS IN BRIEF

vii

Unit 1 Fiction and Nonfiction

Six units per grade explore specific genres. Program pacing allows benchmarking at 3, 6, or 9 week intervals.

PART **1** Strategies for Making Predictions   21

Each unit is divided into two parts that focus on core reading and vocabulary skills. These core skills are broken out into component strategies and are developed throughout the part, enabling students to fully master them before moving on.

How does fact relate to fiction?

Leveled selection pairs let you choose text that is appropriate for your students' abilities without skipping essential skills.

Apply reading skill to informational text.

Contents ■ ix

Short Stories

Award-winning authors introduce genres and guide students through key literary concepts.

Frequent progress monitoring catches small learning problems before they become big ones.

How do we find solutions?

Unit 3

Types of Nonfiction: Essays, Articles, and Speeches

How do we gather information?

Unit 4

Poetry

PART **1** **Strategies for Reading Fluently** 561

Practice skills with either group of poems.

How do we respond to the world?

Contents ■ *xv*

Unit 5

Drama

Support genre study through comparative analysis.

How do other people see us?

Provide cross-curricular nonfiction links to literature.

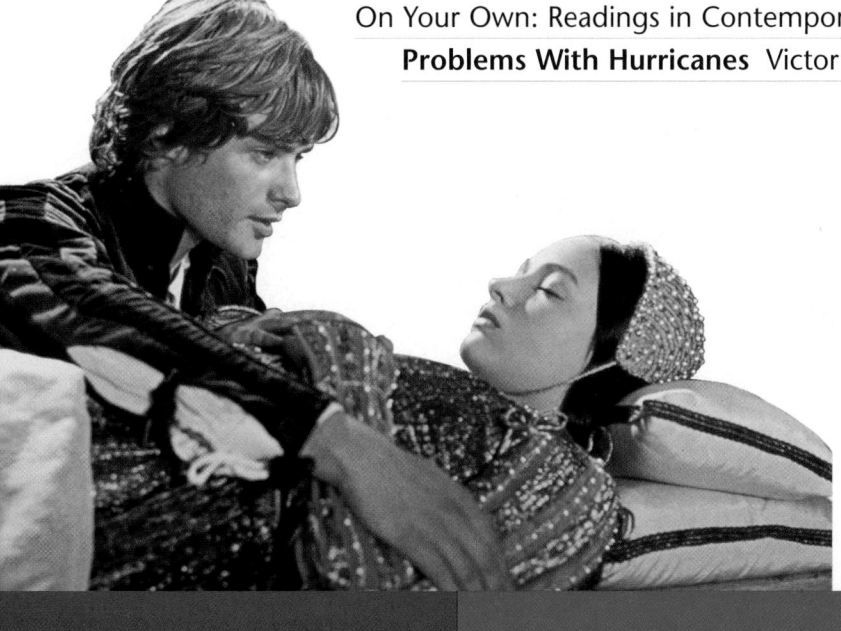

Contents ■ *xvii*

Themes in Literature

Multi-genre approach in Unit 6 connects literature across cultures.

How does our heritage help shape us?

High-interest selections encourage independent reading.

Contents ■ *xix*

SELECTIONS BY READING SKILL

Unit Three

Unit Four

(Continued on next page)

■ Unit Four (Continued from previous page)

SELECTIONS BY THEME

■ Spine Tinglers

■ Challenges and Choices

■ Moments of Discovery

■ The Lighter Side

■ Reflections on the Past, Visions of the Future

■ Hope and Aspiration

INFORMATIONAL TEXTS AND OTHER NONFICTION

■ Reading Informational Materials—Instructional Workshops

■ Additional Nonfiction—Selections by Type

■ Literature in Context—Reading in the Content Areas

A wealth of expository nonfiction is found throughout this program. Nonfiction texts are highlighted in red in the Index.

COMPARING LITERARY WORKS

xxviii ■

WORKSHOPS

■ Writing Workshops

■ Spelling Workshops

■ Communications Workshops

PRENTICE HALL LITERATURE: A RICH TRADITION OF LEARNING SUCCESS

The Research Process

Since 1988, *Prentice Hall Literature* has been at the forefront of language arts instruction, providing teachers and their students with quality instruction and assessment tools to ensure success. Each successive edition builds on the strong heritage of *Prentice Hall Literature*.

To develop the current edition of *Prentice Hall Literature*, we conducted a variety of research studies, yielding three key elements of an effective language arts program: clean, clear, non-distracting design with considerate text; systematic, consistent skills instruction; and built-in benchmarking to ensure learning success. Our research comprised these three design stages:

1 EXPLORATORY NEEDS ASSESSMENT

In conjunction with Prentice Hall authors, we conducted research to explore proven educational reading methodologies. The results of this research were incorporated into our instructional strategy and pedagogy to create a more effective literature program. This stage included

- Reading research
- Review of state standards
- Teacher interviews

2 FORMATIVE RESEARCH, DEVELOPMENT, AND FIELD-TESTING

During this phase of the research, we developed and field-tested prototype material with students and teachers. Results informed revisions to the final design and pedagogy. Formative research included

- Field testing of prototypes in classroom pilots
- Classroom observations
- Teacher reviews
- Supervisor reviews
- Educator advisory panels

3 SUMMATIVE RESEARCH, VALIDATION RESEARCH

Finally, we have conducted and will continue to conduct longer-term research under actual classroom conditions. Research at this phase includes:

- Pilot-testing
- Prepublication learner verification research
- Postpublication validation studies, including validation of test questions
- Evaluation of results on standardized tests

RESEARCH BIBLIOGRAPHY

Reading

Alexander, Patricia A., and Tamara Jetton. "Learning from Text: A Multidimensional and Developmental Perspective." *Handbook of Reading Research*, vol. 3, ed. M. L. Kamil, P. B. Mosenthal, P. D. Pearson, and R. Barr. Mahwah, NJ: Lawrence Erlbaum Associates, 2000. 285–310.

Finders, Margaret J., and Susan Hynds. *Literacy Lessons: Teaching and Learning with Middle School Students.* Upper Saddle River, NJ: Merrill, 2003.

Guthrie, John T., and Allan Wigfield. "Engagement and Motivation in Reading." *Handbook of Reading Research,* vol. 3, ed. M. L. Kamil, P. B. Mosenthal, P. D. Pearson, and R. Barr. Mahwah, NJ: Lawrence Erlbaum Associates, 2000. 403–422.

Harvey, Stephanie, and Anne Goudvis. "Determining Importance in Text: The Nonfiction Connection." In *Strategies That Work: Teaching Comprehension to Enhance Understanding.* Portland, ME: Stenhouse Publishers, 2000.

Langer, Judith. "Beating the Odds: Teaching Middle and High School Students to Read and Write Well," 1999. Center on English Learning and Achievement. May 2003. <http://cela.albany.edu/eie2/main.html>

National Reading Panel. *Teaching Children to Read: An Evidence-Based Assessment of the Scientific Research on Reading and Its Implications for Reading Instruction.* NIH Publication 00-4769. Bethesda, MD: U.S. Department of Health and Human Services, 2000.

Pressley, Michael. "What Should Comprehension Instruction Be the Instruction Of?" *Handbook of Reading Research*, vol. 3, ed. M. L. Kamil, P. B. Mosenthal, P. D. Pearson, and R. Barr. Mahwah, NJ: Lawrence Erlbaum Associates, 2000. 545–562.

Vocabulary

Baumann, J.F., and E.J. Kame'enui. *Vocabulary Instruction: From Research to Practice.* New York: Guilford Press, 2004.

Blachowicz, Camille, and Peter Fisher. *Teaching Vocabulary in All Classrooms*, 2nd Ed. Upper Saddle River, NJ: Merrill, 2002.

Coxhead, Averil. "A New Academic Word List." *TESOL Quarterly*, 2000.

Kinsella, Kate. "Strategies to Teach Academic Vocabulary." Strategies to Promote Academic Literacy for Second Language Learners Within the English Language Arts Classroom, 2005.

Kinsella, Kate, and Kevin Feldman. *Narrowing the Language Gap: The Case for Explicit Vocabulary Instruction.* New York: Scholastic, Inc., 2005.

Marzano, Robert J. "The Developing Vision of Vocabulary Instruction." *Vocabulary Instruction: From Research to Practice.* New York: Guilford Press, 2004

Differentiated Instruction

Allington, Richard L. *What Really Matters for Struggling Readers: Designing Research-Based Programs.* New York: Longman, 2001.

Armbruster, Bonnie, and Thomas H. Anderson. "On Selecting 'Considerate' Content Area Textbooks." *Remedial and Special Education*, vol. 9 (1): 47–52.

Carnine, Douglas, Jerry Silbert, and Edward J. Kame'enui. *Direct Instruction Reading. 3rd ed.* Upper Saddle River, NJ: Prentice Hall, 1997.

Deshler, Donald D., Keith B. Lenz, and Brenda R. Kissam. *Teaching Content to All: Evidence-Based Inclusive Practices in Middle and Secondary Schools.* Boston: Allyn and Bacon, 2004.

Moore, David. W., and Kathleen A. Hinchman. *Starting Out: A Guide to Teaching Adolescents Who Struggle with Reading.* Boston: Allyn and Bacon, 2003.

Vaughn, Sharon, Candace S. Bos, and Jeanne Shay Schumm. *Teaching Exceptional, Diverse, and At-Risk Students in the General Education Classroom.* Boston: Allyn and Bacon, 2002.

FIELD-TESTING OF PRENTICE HALL LITERATURE, PENGUIN EDITION

Background In May 2004, six Language Arts teachers and 133 students field-tested Grade 7 and Grade 9 prototypes. Each teacher taught the prototype with one or more classes for three weeks. The students involved in the study represented a wide range of backgrounds and ability levels.

Prentice Hall researchers and editors used a variety of tools to gather information, including classroom observation and weekly debriefings with teachers who kept weekly lesson logs to note their experiences and observations about the prototype. In addition, we reviewed the results of pre-tests and post-tests to assess students' knowledge of the skills addressed in the prototypes.

Key Findings Reaction to the prototype from both teachers and students was highly favorable. The most highly-praised features of the program included the following:

Paired Selections: Teachers liked choosing which selection to teach. They agreed that this organization was useful for differentiated instruction.

Skills Instruction: Teachers praised the systematic skills instruction in the prototype. Classroom observation, teacher lesson logs, and student post-test results confirmed student mastery of the skills taught in the prototype.

Literature Selections: Students praised the selections as "interesting" and "fun-to-read," while teachers also noted that the content of the prototype was appropriate for their students' grade and ability levels.

Unit Authors: Teachers felt the featured unit authors added value by providing the writers' insights into their works.

Program Design and Organization: Both students and teachers enjoyed the bright, vibrant pictures. Teachers also commended the ratio of text to visuals, the consistent organization, and the ease of navigation.

How Field-Testing Informed Development

Pacing The prototype included more material than could be taught in a three-week cycle.	The final product includes fewer part-level features and provides suggestions for revised pacing.
Reading Informational Materials Students and teachers commented that the prototype selection was not age-appropriate.	Editors identified selections for the feature that would be more relevant to students' everyday lives, such as articles, recipes, applications, and schedules.
Practice & Assess Questions Students and teachers told us some questions were too complicated.	Questions in the final product are direct, clear, and concise.
Vocabulary Instruction Teachers told us they wanted to see more vocabulary development.	We expanded the part vocabulary preview and review. For each selection, we developed Vocabulary Warm ups to increase the number of words taught per selection.

PRENTICE HALL LITERATURE: PROVEN TO GET RESULTS

National Effect-Size Study: Student Performance of *Prentice Hall Literature*, Users vs. Non-Users

This quasi-experimental study examined longitudinal test results of 976 closely matched user and non-user districts as a point of comparison across the same time periods and achievement tests.

Prentice Hall users performed as well or better than their counterparts, achieving approximately a 56 percent gain in the percentage of students meeting or exceeding state reading/ELA standards and a 62 percent gain in national percentile ranking after one or more years of program implementation. A sustained gain was noted in districts that have implemented the program for two or more years.

State: Colorado

Number of Districts: 10

Assessment: CSAP

State: Arizona

Number of Districts: 34

Assessment: Stanford

State: Tennessee

Number of Districts: 117

Assessment: Terra Nova

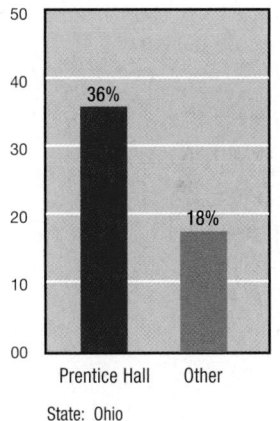

State: Ohio

Number of Districts: 43

Assessment: OPT

Learner Verification Research

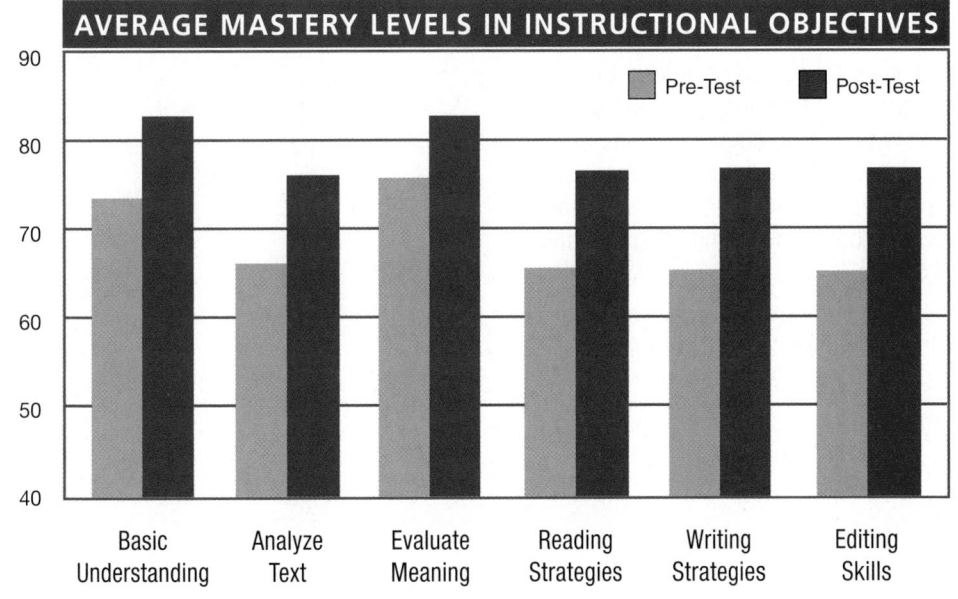

AVERAGE MASTERY LEVELS IN INSTRUCTIONAL OBJECTIVES

In a yearlong learner verification study, students using *Prentice Hall Literature* increased their mastery levels in several diagnostic skill areas for reading/language arts.

All students were tested at the start of the year with a nationally normed standardized test, the TerraNova™ Complete Battery Plus exam. At the end of the study period, students were retested with the same standardized test. Only students who completed both the pre- and post-tests were included in this analysis. All tests were scored by CTB/McGraw Hill, publisher of the TerraNova™.

PROFESSIONAL DEVELOPMENT GUIDEBOOK

The Prentice Hall contributing authors and advisors guided the pedagogical design and content of Prentice Hall Literature Penguin Edition. *Their expertise informed the development of instruction and support. In these pages, we share the authors' expertise on some of the key issues in language arts education.*

BECOMING A STRATEGIC READING TEACHER

" *It's not what you say or do that ultimately matters. It is what you get the students to do as a result of what you said and did that counts.* "

Kate Kinsella Ed.D.

Strategic Reading

Recent research suggests that skillful and strategic reading is a long-term developmental process in which "readers are simultaneously extracting and constructing meaning" through interaction with written language. In other words, successful readers know how to decode all types of words, read with fluency and expression, have well-developed vocabularies, and possess various comprehension strategies such as note-taking and summarizing to employ as the reading task demands (Snow and Sweet, 2003).

Research illustrates that virtually all students benefit from direct, systematic, and explicit instruction in reading (Baker and Gersten, 2000). There are three stages to the instructional process:

- **Instructional Frontloading** (before reading)
- **Guided Instruction** (during reading)
- **Reflection and Study** (after reading)

Instructional Frontloading

If teachers emphasize preteaching, or frontloading instruction, they will help structure learning to ensure student success. Frontloading instruction is especially critical in mixed-ability classrooms with English language learners, students with special needs, and other students performing below grade level in terms of literacy. Before reading, prepare students with the following prereading activities and instruction:

- Introduce the big concepts.
- Provide direct teaching of vocabulary necessary to comprehend key ideas.
- Build academic vocabulary.
- Build, activate, and elaborate on background knowledge.
- Pique curiosity and guide students to generate questions.
- Use launch activities that incorporate key vocabulary.

Guided Instruction

In guided instruction, the teacher models approaches for how to actively engage with the text to gain meaning. The teacher guides the students through the text using reading strategies and then guides discussion about the content using participation strategies.

Structured Accountable Responses

During the instructional frontloading and the guided instruction, it is important to ensure participation by all students in a nonthreatening environment. The following strategies are ways to structure your instruction so that all students are accountable and prepared to participate.

Use partners. Partner response increases active language use, attention, and higher order thinking during instruction.

- Choose partners, alternating ranking based on literacy/social skills.
- Assign roles—such as *A* and *B*. *"A's tell B's two things we have learned about. . . ."*
- Give a specific topic. *"What do you predict. . . ?" "What are two things we have learned about. . . . ?"*
- Allow a brief time of exchange: *"A's tell B's two things we have learned about. . . ."*
- Call on students to share with the class after they have practiced with a partner.

Write first. Writing first increases thinking, accountability, and focus. It provides you as the teacher with concrete formative feedback. Having students write before responding connects written language to oral language, and it provides an opportunity for students to target academic language.

Nominate volunteers. Choosing volunteers based on your observations during partner work or written work allows you to ensure that all students participate and succeed. Circulate and observe as students discuss or write about the topic. Ask students to share their responses with you. Then, "nominate" the students you will ask to share with the class—that is, alert the student that he or she will be sharing with the class, so that the student can practice with a partner or with you before sharing with the larger group.

PRENTICE HALL LITERATURE

Putting Research Into Practice

You can introduce the big concepts for each selection using the **Connecting to the Selection** feature in the **Student Edition**.

You will find teaching plans for instructional frontloading in the *General Resources* including plans and student pages for the following activities:

- Anticipation Guide
- KWL Chart
- Idea Wave

PRENTICE HALL LITERATURE

Putting Research Into Practice

You can use questions and prompts provided in the **Student Edition** and the **Teacher's Edition** as prompts for structured accountable responses.

Language for Active Classroom Participation

Explicitly teach students ways to express themselves in class discussions. Model the use of these phrases, and encourage students to use them in responding.

Expressing an Opinion
I think that _____
I believe that _____
In my opinion_____

Asking for Clarification
What do you mean?
Will you explain that again?
I have a question about that.

Soliciting a Response
What do you think?
Do you agree?

Individual Reporting
I discovered from_____that_____
I found out that_____
_____pointed out that

Disagreeing
I don't agree with you because
I got a different answer than you.
I see it a different way.

Affirming
That's an interesting idea.
I hadn't thought of that.
I see what you mean.

Predicting
I predict that _____
I imagine that_____
Based on_____I predict that_____

Paraphrasing and Clarifying
So you are saying that_____
In other words, you think that_____
What I hear you saying is_____

Acknowledging Ideas
My idea is related to_____'s idea.
My idea is similar to _____'s idea.
My idea builds on_____'s idea.

Partner and Group Reporting
We agreed that _____
We decided that _____
We had a different approach.
We had a similar idea.

Offering a Suggestion
Maybe we could_____
What if we_____
Here's something we might try.

Holding the Floor
As I was saying _____
What I was trying to say was_____

PRENTICE HALL LITERATURE

Putting Research Into Practice

- Questions and notes in the **Student Edition** provide frequent, regular opportunities for applying the strategies.
- In the Reading and Vocabulary Preview, in the **Student Edition**, students learn the academic vocabulary needed to write and speak about the concepts taught in the parts of the unit.

- The **Teachers' Edition** provides strategies for ensuring student participation.
- You will find teaching plans and student pages in the *General Resources* for participation strategies, including
  - Oral Cloze
  - Choral Reading
  - ReQuest

Works Cited

Gersten, Russell and Scott K. Baker. "What We Know About Effective Instructional Practices for English-Language Learners." *Exceptional Children,* Vol. 66(4), 2000. 454-470.

Snow, Catherine E. and Anne Polselli Sweet. "Reading for Comprehension." *Rethinking Reading Comprehension.* New York: Guilford Press, 2003.

ENERGIZING VOCABULARY INSTRUCTION

"Educators need to make robust intentional vocabulary instruction a high priority."

Kevin Feldman Ed.D.

Vocabulary Instruction

There is a clear consensus among literacy researchers that accelerating vocabulary growth is a vital and often neglected component of comprehensive language arts instruction (Baumann and Kame'enui, 2004). Numerous studies have documented the strong and reciprocal relationship between vocabulary knowledge and reading comprehension. Research focused on school-age second language learners similarly concludes that vocabulary knowledge is the single best predictor of their academic achievement across subject matter domains. Therefore, educators need to make robust intentional vocabulary instruction a high priority. Intensive instruction should focus on words related to central lesson concepts and high-use academic words. Academic word lists developed by researchers can help educators determine appropriate high-use academic words (Coxhead, 2000; Xue and Nation, 1984).

Big Ideas in Vocabulary Teaching

Connect
Assess students' current knowledge of the target lesson vocabulary.
Give explanations before definitions.
Use student friendly explanations.
Use language students already know.
Use examples from students' experiential realm.
Use synonyms.

Process
Have students give examples and images.
Have students use Sho w you know" sentences.
Have students generate synonyms and antonyms.

Practice
Have students use graphic organizers and webs.
Have students use the words in new contexts.

Rationale for Direct Vocabulary Instruction

Over the past two decades, mounting research has challenged traditional views regarding the role of direct teaching in vocabulary development. Numerous studies have documented the positive impact of direct, explicit vocabulary instruction on both immediate word learning and longer-term reading comprehension (Baker, Simmons, and Kame'enui, 1995; Beck, McKeown, and Kucan, 2002; Biemiller, 2004; Marzano, 2004).

PRENTICE HALL LITERATURE

Putting Research Into Practice

- You can preteach academic vocabulary in the **Reading and Vocabulary Preview** at the beginning of each part of the **Student Edition**.

- All vocabulary activities in the **Student Edition** are structured to be generative, "show you know" types of activities.

- You can develop students' expressive vocabulary for talking about the big concepts and themes of the literature with the **Connecting to the Literature** feature that precedes every selection in the **Student Edition**.

- The **Teacher's Edition** provides consistent support for introducing vocabulary at the beginning of every selection.

- The *Unit Resources* provide generative activities for all vocabulary instruction and activities.

A Powerful Teaching Routine

The following steps can be elaborated and adapted, depending on the relative importance of the words in question and the students' background knowledge.

1) **Pronounce** The first step in teaching a new term is guiding students in correctly pronouncing the word. This will support learners in decoding the word confidently, while also supporting both auditory and muscle memory (Shaywitz, 2003).

2) **Explain** Understanding a new term requires a clear explanation of the meaning, using language familiar to the students (Beck et al., 2002; Stahl, 1999). Provide a synonym to solidify the connection between the new vocabulary term and students' prior knowledge.

3) **Provide examples** Students will usually need at least two or three examples of a new term to firmly grasp the meaning of it. Moreover, these examples should be drawn from a variety of contexts, not only the one used in the reading or lesson.

4) **Elaborate** Research in cognitive psychology consistently indicates that learners understand and remember information better when they elaborate on it themselves (Marzano et al., 2001). Thus, students' understanding of new vocabulary terms is strengthened when they are given opportunities to elaborate word meanings by generating their own examples.

5) **Assess** Research, such as Baker et al., (1995) and Marzano (2004), have documented the importance of incorporating regular informal assessment into the instructional process, especially with academically diverse learners. Assessment of vocabulary involves both formative evaluation (quick checks for understanding) and summative evaluation (formal quizzes or tests).

PRENTICE HALL LITERATURE

Putting Research Into Practice

- Use the Vocabulary notes in the **Teacher's Edition** for consistent, predictable vocabulary instruction structure.

- Use the **Vocabulary Knowledge Rating Sheet** in **General Resources** to assess students' current knowledge.

- Use the **Academic Vocabulary** lessons in the **Vocabulary Preview and Review** to introduce high-frequency words.

- Use the sample sentences in the **Vocabulary Builder** feature with each selection in the **Student Edition** to preteach words.

Works Cited

Baker, Scott, Deborah C. Simmons, and Edward J. Kame'enui. *Vocabulary Acquisition: Synthesis of the Research.* (Tech. Report No. 13). Eugene: University of Oregon, National Center to Improve the Tools of Educators, 1995.

Baumann, James F., and Edward J. Kame'enui. Eds. *Vocabulary Instruction: From Research to Practice.* New York: Guilford Press, 2004.

Beck, Isabel L., Margaret G. McKeown, and Linda Kucan. *Bringing Words to Life: Robust Vocabulary Instruction Solving Problems in the Teaching of Literacy.* New York: Guilford Publications, 2002.

Biemiller, Andrew. "Teaching Vocabulary in the Primary Grades: Vocabulary Instruction Needed." Eds. J.F. Baumann and Edward J. Kame'enui. *Vocabulary Instruction: From Research to Practice.* New York: Guilford Press, 2004.

Coxhead, Averil. "A New Academic Word List." *TESOL Quarterly,* 2000.

Marzano, Robert J., Debra J. Pickering, and Jane E. Pollock. *Classroom Instruction That Works: Research-Based Strategies for Increasing Student Achievement.* Alexandria, Virginia: Association for Supervision and Curriculum Development, 2001.

Marzano, Robert J. "The Developing Vision of Vocabulary Instruction." Eds. J.F. Baumann and E.J. Kame'enui. *Vocabulary Instruction: From Research to Practice.* New York: Guilford Press, 2004.

Shaywitz, Sally E. *Overcoming Dyslexia: A New and Complete Science-Based Program for Reading Problems at Any Level.* New York: Knopf, 2003.

Stahl, Steven A. *Vocabulary Development.* Cambridge: Brookline, 1999.

Xue, Guoyi, and I. S. P. Nation. "A University Word List." *Language Learning and Communication.* Vol. 3(2), 1984, 215-229.

GIVING HOPE TO STRUGGLING READERS

> *Students with reading difficulties are very aware that they struggle. What is amazing is that despite these challenges, students are motivated to improve when given stimulating text, good instruction, and opportunities.*
>
> **Sharon Vaughn, Ph.D.**

Middle and high school students are expected to read at proficient levels and possess vocabularies and comprehension skills for understanding complex reading material. However, despite reading intervention programs during the primary grades, many students continue to experience learning problems well into their adolescent years. Many of these students experience difficulty in word recognition skills, decoding, reading fluency, and vocabulary development (Biancarosa and Snow, 2004). Moreover, besides their scant word recognition skills and poor reading fluency, students with low reading skills may demonstrate significant deficits in reading comprehension. Unfortunately, findings from previous research indicate that adolescents with reading-related learning disabilities become further behind in reading each year in school and risk losing the skills they acquired during elementary school.

Older students with reading disabilities need explicit and systematic instruction in reading. In addition, their instruction in reading is enhanced by experiences that are designed explicitly to foster vocabulary development, background knowledge, the ability to detect and comprehend relationships among verbal concepts, and the ability to actively use strategies to ensure understanding and retention of material.

Attitudes Toward Reading

In general, students with low reading skills perceive reading as a difficult, unsuccessful, and unappealing activity (McKenna, Kear, and Ellsworth, 1995). Increasingly, researchers have used qualitative studies to describe middle and high school students' reading opportunities and reader characteristics. Kos (1991), for example, explores the reasons why middle school students reading problems persist. Using a case study approach, Kos identified three reasons why middle school students make limited progress in reading.

PRENTICE HALL LITERATURE

Putting Research Into Practice

- **The Vocabulary and Reading Warm-ups** in the *Unit Resources* are explicitly designed to foster vocabulary development and build background knowledge.

- Use the *Reader's Notebook* series to enhance students' ability to actively use reading strategies taught in the **Student Edition.**

- First, although students are cognizant of their deficiencies in reading and in the instruction they have received and are motivated to improve their reading, they feel hopeless to do so in their current school situations.

- Second, reading problems may manifest themselves in stress-related behaviors and distraction from instruction.

- Third, even when students attempt to use reading strategies, they often fail to use them efficiently.

Bintz (1993) examined reasons for declining interest in reading during the middle and high school years. According to Bintz, although students' interest in school reading declines, they do not necessarily lose interest in pleasure reading and informational reading outside of school. Second, students are not nonstrategic in their approach to reading, nor do they use dysfunctional strategies. Rather, Bintz maintains, middle and high school students use different strategies for in-school and out-of-school reading. For instance, in school, students were observed using shortcut strategies to assist them in completing assignments. Outside of school, however, these students were more inclined to use higher-level strategies because the material was personally interesting. Third, students do not fit into developmental categories such as avid, passive, or reluctant readers, but instead demonstrate different literate behaviors depending on the tasks they perform, the texts they read, and the interpretive stances they adopt.

Likewise, Worthy and McKool (1996), through analysis of student interviews of sixth-grade students who were good readers but who also had negative attitudes toward reading, suggested that students' negative attitudes toward reading may be related to their limited opportunities in reading instruction. Students who indicated negative attitudes toward reading also indicated that they had limited opportunities to read independently, select reading materials, or read personally interesting materials in school. Moreover, their feelings about reading instruction and materials used in school might have distorted their opinion about reading in general and thus their willingness to read.

PRENTICE HALL LITERATURE

Putting Research Into Practice

- Use the **On Your Own** feature and the **For Further Reading** pages in the **Student Edition** to encourage independent reading.

Works Cited

Biancarosa, Gina, and Catherine E. Snow. "Reading Next—A Vision for Action and Research in Middle and High School Literacy: A Report to Carnegie Corporation of New York." Washington, DC: Alliance for Excellent Education, 2004.

Bintz, William P. "Resistant Readers in Secondary Education: Some Insights and Implications." *Journal of Reading.* Vol. 36(8), May 1993. 604-615.

Kos, Raylene. "Persistence of Reading Disabilities: The Voices of Four Middle School Students." *American Educational Research Journal.* Vol. 28(4), Winter 1991, 875-895.

McKenna, Michael C., Dennis J. Kear, and R. A. Ellsworth. "Children's Attitudes Toward Reading: A National Survey." *Reading Research Quarterly,* Vol. 30(4), 1995, 934-956.

Worthy, Jo, and S. McKool. "Students Who Say They Hate to Read: The Importance of Opportunity, Choice, and Access." Eds. Donald J. Leu, Charles K. Kinzer, and Kathleen Hinchman, *Literacies for the 21st Century: Research and Practice.* Chicago: National Reading Conference, 1996, 245-256.

MAKING THE DIFFERENCE MATTER

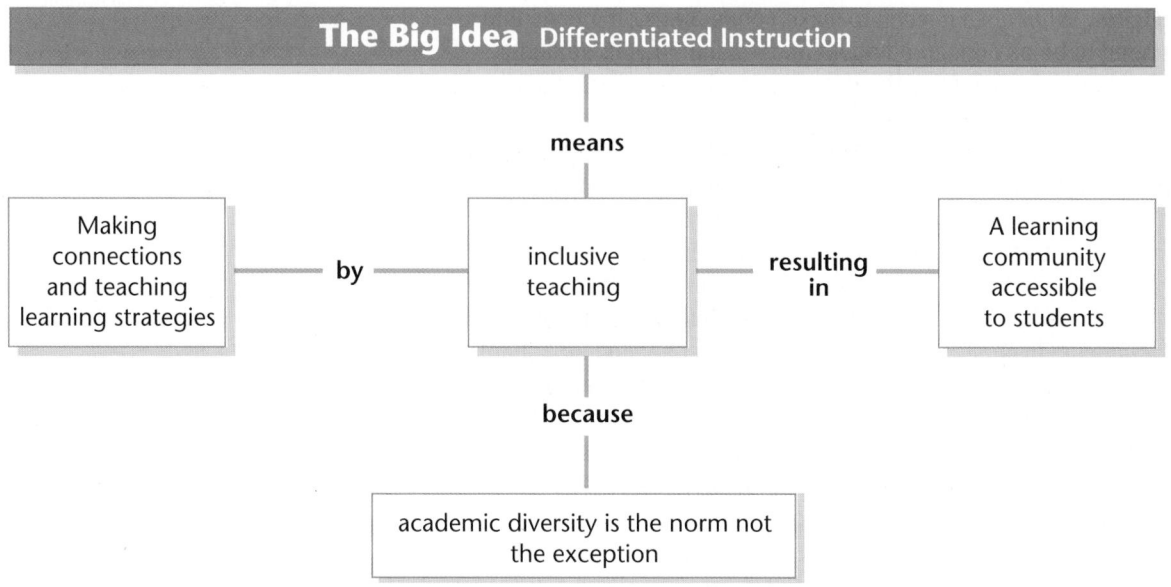

The Big Idea Differentiated Instruction

```
                              means

Making                                                      A learning
connections          by      inclusive      resulting      community
and teaching                  teaching          in         accessible
learning strategies                                         to students

                             because


                   academic diversity is the norm not
                             the exception
```

Why do we need differentiated instruction?

The wide range of academic diversity in schools today presents both a challenge and an opportunity to all teachers. Because the challenge is so great and the need to accommodate all students so urgent, we need to think about the problem of planning and teaching to include all learners in a new way.

Diversity is the norm. Thinking about diversity among students as the norm rather than as something out of the ordinary is the first step in building inclusive teaching practices. Diane Ferguson (1995) has noted that "Meaningful change will require nothing less than a joint effort to reinvent schools to be more accommodating to all dimensions of human diversity" (282). She argues that we must change our view of the school's role from one of providing educational services to one of providing educational support for learning:

> Valuing diversity and difference, rather than trying to change or diminish it so that everyone fits some ideal of similarity, leads to the realization that we can support students in their efforts to become active members of their communities....Perhaps the most important feature of support as a concept for schooling is that it is grounded in the perspective of the person receiving it, not the person providing it.

This is not to say, however, that differences should be ignored. It is important to respect differences and to incorporate them into the classroom and the curriculum, so that learning is grounded in what is familiar to students.

Don Deshler, Ph.D.

Works Cited

Ferguson, Diane L. "The Real Challenge of Inclusion: Confessions of a 'Rabid Inclusionist.'" *Phi Delta Kappan.* Vol. 77(4), 1995, 281-87.

How do we provide inclusive instruction?

Make connections. What does it mean to make connections? It means that as a teacher you need to be as concerned about understanding your students and what is important and meaningful to them as you are about understanding your content and how to teach it. Making connections means that students need to believe that what you want to teach is important and relevant to them and that you can and will help them learn. Making connections also means that you as the teacher need to believe it is worthwhile to build a learning community in your classroom, to know and understand your students well enough to make choices about content and instruction so that all students have an opportunity to learn. Every good teacher aspires to these goals, and many teachers successfully realize them. But as academic diversity among students grows in secondary schools, teachers need more support and more tools to be effective with all learners. Support can be gained, we believe, by thinking about a classroom as a learning community where teacher and students work together to ensure that everyone is learning. More tools become available with the implementation of teaching routines and learning strategies that make learning more accessible to more learners.

Understand what students already know. What students already know, or their "prior knowledge," comes not only from what students have previously learned in school, but also from their lived experiences. Lived experience includes all the differences that students bring with them into the schools, such as culture, language, ethnic background, as well as previous learning successes or failures. Valuing and using the prior knowledge of students allows teachers to link new knowledge to what students already know, thereby making learning more meaningful for students. It also allows students to construct new knowledge for themselves.

Teach learning strategies. Finally, students are more likely to make connections in learning the content in your class if they know how to learn. All good listeners use strategies to learn new things. Some students are better than others at developing strategies to learn. Inclusive teaching means that you have to take into account whether all your students are good strategic learners, and the only way to do this is to teach them—explicitly—how to use and develop learning strategies.

What is the result of differentiated instruction?

A learning community. Making connections and building a learning community in your classroom will establish an environment where learning, cooperation, and respect for differences are all valued. The "work" of this community is learning. Everyday practices and routines are based on cooperation in accomplishing this work, and the interests and learning needs of everyone in the community are taken seriously.

PROGRAM CONSULTANTS

The Prentice Hall national language arts consultants advised on many aspects of this program, particularly the professional development strand. The professional development notes in this textbook represent successful strategies acquired and applied during their many years of experience in classrooms.

Yvonne R. Cadiz
Language Arts, ESOL and Spanish teacher
Curriculum Specialist for ESOL
Hillsborough County, Tampa, Florida
Director of the MERIT Program (Multilingual Educational Resource Information and Training Program), University of South Florida

Anita Clay
District Coordinator, Gateway Institute of Technology
St. Louis, MO

Nancy McDonald
K-12 Reading Specialist Waterloo School District, Waterloo, WI Belleville School District, Belleville, WI
Title I Language Arts Teacher, 6-8
Beloit Turner Middle School, Beloit, WI
Grade 8 Language Arts Teacher
Olson Junior High School, Woodstock, IL

Jean Ripple
Language Arts Teacher, 1-10
Model Classroom for Inclusion
Pennsylvania

John R. Scannell
Teacher, 9-12 English, Writing, Acting and Drama, Debate and Public Address
Newport HS, Bellevue, WA
Lykens Jr. HS, Lykens, PA
Nazareth HS, Nazareth, PA

Kathryne Lewis Stewart
Director of Humanities Instruction
Tomball Independent School District
Tomball, Texas
Teacher/ GT Specialist
Burleson High School
Burleson Independent School District
Burleson, Texas

Joseph A. Wieczorek, PhD
Instructor, Georgetown University
College of Notre Dame
University of Maryland, Baltimore County
Howard County Public Schools, Maryland
Language Specialist, FBI

LITERATURE REVIEW PANEL

These teachers helped develop the Penguin Edition of Prentice Hall Literature by testing new selections by contemporary authors and gathering student questions for these authors to answer. The work of these teachers helped ensure that the program would be truly interactive, with a built-in dialogue between authors and students.

Sherry Abner
Two Rivers Middle School
Covington, KY

Heather Barnes
Central Crossing High School
Grove City, OH

Bonnie Bellows
Humboldt Senior High School
St. Paul, MN

Shawn L. Brumfield
Los Angeles Unified School District
Los Angeles, CA

Donna Burch
Southern Middle School
Somerset, KY

Susanne Buttrey
Sycamore Middle School
Pleasant View, TN

Denise Campbell
Cherry Creek School District
Centennial, CO

Holly Carr
Central Crossing High School
Grove City, OH

Vanessa Carroll
LBJ High School
Austin, TX

Joanne Chambers
Swiftwater Intermediate School
Swiftwater, PA

Susan Cisna
East Prairie Junior High School
Tuscola, IL

Nancy DiGasso
Pine Bush High School
Pine Bush, New York

Karen Gibson
Appleton North High School
Appleton, WI

Margaret Jan Graham
Cobb Middle School
Tallahassee, FL

Doris Sue Hawkins
C. W. Otto Middle School
Lansing, MI

Deanna Hilliard
Soddy Daisy Middle School
Soddy Daisy, TN

Helen Hudson
Crawfordsville High School
Crawfordsville, IN

Gisele Le Duc
East Lyme Middle School
Niantic, CT

Greg MacAvoy
Pine Bush High School
Pine Bush, New York

Deb Madej
Norris Middle School
Omaha, NE

Nancy Mast
Hobart Middle School
Hobart, Indiana

Nancy Monroe
Bolton High School
Alexandria, LA

Suzanne Moore
Sunrise Middle School
Clackamas, OR

Paul Putnoki
Torrington Middle School
Torrington, CT

Herb Ranlose
Zion Benton High School
Zion, IL

Robert Rarrick
Union Endicott Senior High
Endicott, NY

Margaret St. Sauver
St. Paul Public Schools
St. Paul, MN

Denise Greer Wallace
Western Valley Middle School
Phoenix, AZ

Debbie Watts
Jacobs Fork Middle School
Newton, NC

Melissa Williams
Delsea Regional High School
Franklinville, NJ 08322

Charles Youngs
Bethel Park High School
Bethel Park, PA

1 WHERE DO I START?

Right here! These pages will guide you through the program's unique organization and describe the many resources you have available to enrich your teaching. *Prentice Hall Literature, Penguin Edition* is carefully designed to make pacing, lesson planning, teaching, and assessment easier, and it provides a guaranteed path to meet standards and learning expectations.

2 HOW DO I TEACH THE UNIT?

Each of the six units focuses on a different genre. The unit is hosted by a featured contemporary author who provides an **Introduction** to the genre.

> The orange *From the Author's Desk* banner appears throughout the unit when the featured author appears.

Use the introduction to prepare your students to learn about each genre by introducing important characteristics, key concepts, and literary terms.

> Characteristics of the genre

> Literary terms

Technology

From the Author's Desk

Stimulate student interest with this engaging DVD featuring in-depth interviews with unit authors discussing unit concepts, literature, reading and writing.

Then, read the **Model Selection** by the unit author to help students apply their understanding of the literary forms and concepts to high-interest selections. Use the **Author's Insight** notes that accompany the selection to enhance students understanding of the literary concepts taught in the unit.

> Model selection by featured author

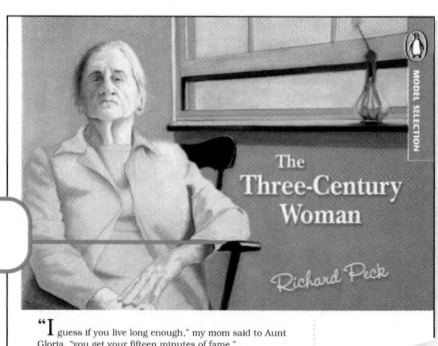

Unit 1
Introduction:
Fiction and Nonfiction

From the Author's Desk
Richard Peck
Talks About the Forms

I write **fiction**—made-up stories—because of two boys I met when I was only a kid myself. I didn't meet them in school; I'm not sure I'd have sat next to them at school. I met them in the library: Tom Sawyer and Huckleberry Finn.

I'd already met their creator, Mark Twain, in his book *Life on the Mississippi*. It appeared to be **nonfiction**, a factual account, and so I believed every word of Mark Twain's apprenticeship as a Mississippi riverboat pilot.

Reading Needed To Be Real

▲ Richard Peck has written many novels in which teenage characters show independence and individuality.

▼ Critical Viewing
How does this picture dramatize Richard Peck's assertion that "nobody but a reader ever becomes a writer"? **[Connect]**

Learning About Fiction and Nonfiction

Elements of Fiction

Fiction writing can be inspired by fact or based entirely on the fantastic. All works of fiction, regardless of their content, share certain basic elements.

- Fictional works include made-up people or animals, called **characters,** and a made-up series of events, called the **plot.**
- They take place in a time and location, or **setting,** which may or may not be real.
- Fictional writing is narrated or told by a speaker, called the **narrator.**
- Fiction is told from a certain perspective, or **point of view. First-person point of view** is the perspective of a character in the story. **Third-person point of view** is the perspective of a narrator outside the story.
- Works of fiction often include a **theme,** or message, about life.

The **Three-Century Woman**

Richard Peck

"I guess if you live long enough," my mom said to Aunt Gloria, "you get your fifteen minutes of fame."
Mom was on the car phone to Aunt Gloria. The minute Mom rolls out of the garage, she's on her car phone. It's state-of-the-

3 WHAT SHOULD I USE TO PLAN AND PREPARE?

Start your planning with the **Time and Resource Manager** before every selection set. This guide provides

- information for choosing the most appropriate selection to teach.
- a detailed lesson plan.
- suggestions for incorporating program resources into your instruction.

Accessibility at a Glance
An analysis of the factors that influence accessibility

Pacing Guide
Suggested pacing information

Resources
Suggested resources for differentiated instruction

Meeting Your Standards
Standards coverage information

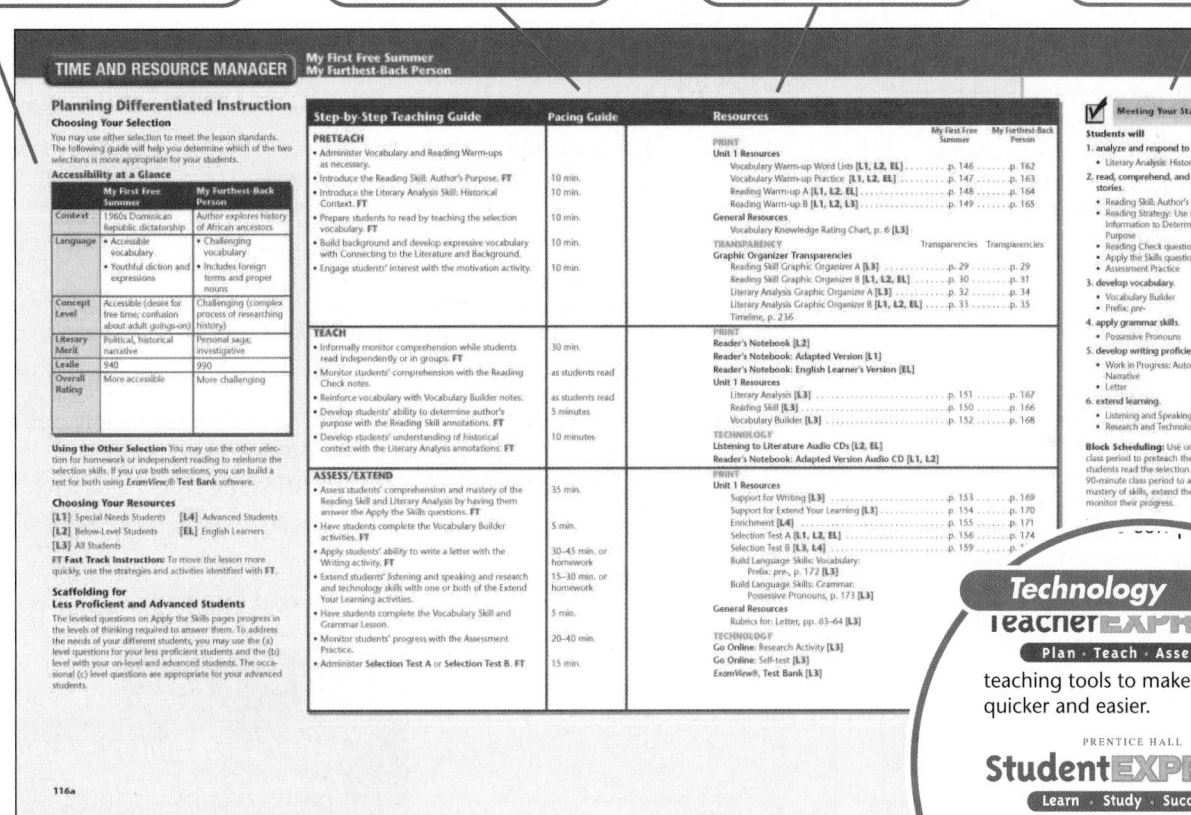

4 HOW DOES THE PROGRAM HELP ME WITH PACING?

The program is organized into three-week instructional blocks, or parts, with each part focusing on core skills and standards. This consistent organization ensures thorough skills coverage presented in manageable chunks. A benchmark test is provided for each part, allowing you to administer assessment at 3-, 6-, or 9-week intervals. This systematic, logical organization with built-in progress monitoring allows you to make sound instructional choices for your class without skipping or missing any skills or standards.

5 HOW DO I TEACH EACH PART?

A In each Part, a single reading skill is introduced, developed and assessed. Use the **Reading and Vocabulary Preview** to introduce the skill.

B Choose a selection from the **selection set** to teach and practice the core skills and strategies for the part. (See p. T53 for how to choose the most appropriate selection for your class.)

C Show your students how to apply the core reading skills to real-life reading situations with the **Reading Informational Materials** feature.

D Choose a selection from the second **selection set** to continue teaching and practicing the core skills and strategies for the part.

E Deepen students' understanding of the genre with the **Comparing Literary Works** feature, which provides students with the opportunity to analyze a specific literary element at work in two or more selections.

F Use the **Reading and Vocabulary Review** to check students' competency with the core skills before administering a benchmark or moving on to the next part.

G Use the workshops to provide opportunities for skills practice. (See p. T54 for more details).

H Develop students' ability to read independently and make their own reading choices with the **On Your Own** selection and the **For Further Reading** feature.

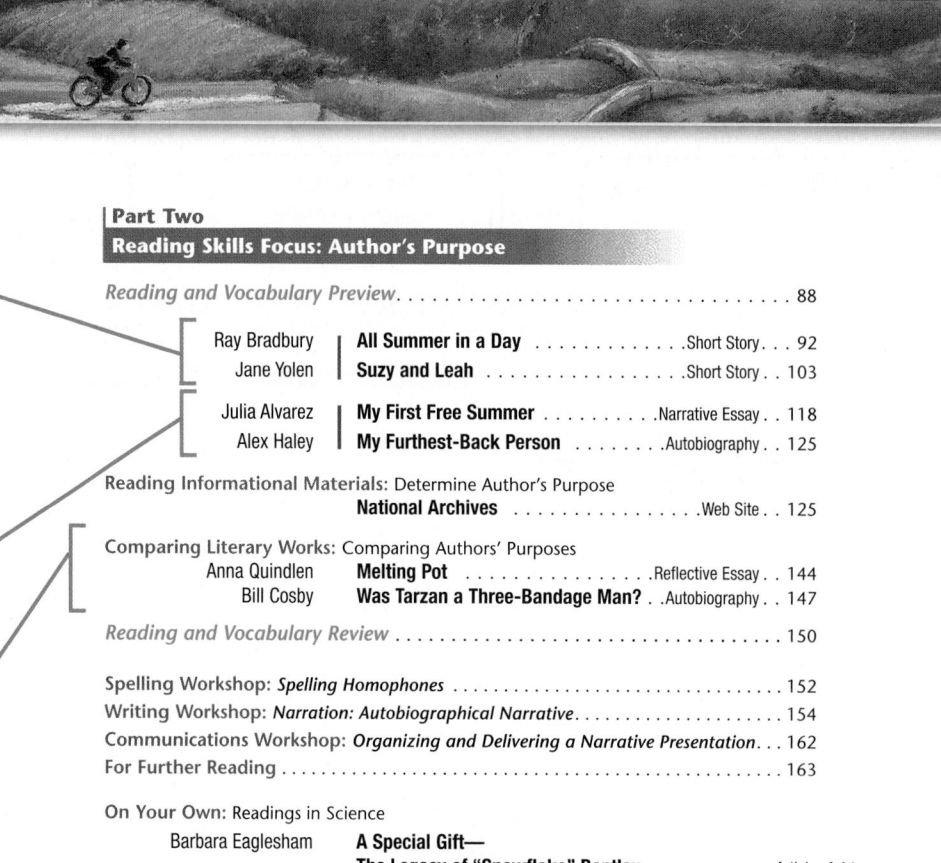

Every selection is supported by these resources:

- Skills Development Workbook
- Graphic Organizers on Transparency
- Selection Tests
- Reader's Notebook series
- Listening to Literature audio program
- Student Express
- Teacher Express

6 *Prentice Hall Literature* addresses the challenges of today's mixed ability classrooms through its unique combination of differentiated instruction, online activities, and skills support. When planning lessons for a diverse group of students, look for the Accessibility-at-a-Glance grid on the Time and Resource Manager pages. Take advantage of the following useful features:

> This grid provides a variety of qualitative measures to help you match your students to the literature that is most appropriate for them. **Context** and **language** indicate how close a selection is to your students' backgrounds and language styles. **Concept level** indicates the difficulty of the themes presented. Finally, **literary merit** highlights a selection's uniqueness.

> This chart also provides a quantitative measure of selection difficulty—the **Lexile** score. Lexile uses factors such as sentence length and vocabulary difficulty to determine a score that can help you predict student comprehension.

	Hamadi	**The Tell-Tale Heart**
Context	Contemporary American city or town	Historical: 1800s
Language	• Informal narrative • Youthful perspective	• Difficult vocabulary • Complicated sentences • Period language
Concept Level	Accessible (If you are a friend with an open mind, you'll have much support in painful times.)	Accessible (Bad deeds haunt the doer.)
Literary Merit	Cross-cultural issues; cross-generational issues	Noted Author
Lexile	670L	860L
Overall Rating	More accessible	More challenging

> Qualitative and quantitative measures are combined in the **Overall Rating**. You can use this rating as the final tool for deciding which selection is appropriate for your students.

Throughout *Prentice Hall Literature*, there are online prompts that provide Penguin author videos, supplementary author biographies, additional enrichment activities, and opportunities for self-assessment. The Web code supplied in each prompt provides a direct link to the content from the www.PHSchool.com home page.

7 HOW DO I DIFFERENTIATE INSTRUCTION?

Prentice Hall Literature provides unprecedented opportunities for differentiated instruction:

- **Teacher's Edition:** Use the strategies and techniques geared toward different reading levels and learning styles.
- **Reader's Notebooks:** Customize instruction for every selection with reading support for struggling readers and English learners.
- **Leveled Vocabulary and Reading Warm-ups:** For each selection, build background, fluency, and vocabulary.
- **Leveled Selection Tests:** Choose from two tests for each selection according to students' ability levels.
- **Graphic Organizers:** Give struggling readers additional support with completed versions of all organizers in the Student Edition.

Differentiated Instruction Solutions for All Learners

Support for Special Needs Students
Students may have difficulty understanding that the dialogue between Jean and Priscilla is imaginary. Make certain that they understand the purpose of the note at the bottom of the previous page. Then remind students that the Pilgrims were the first people from Europe to move to America and that some of them arrived on the *Mayflower*. Explain that when Jean opens the book, she imagines the Pilgrims are with her and on their way to America just as she will be one day soon.

Enrichment for Gif[...]
Ask students to consi[...]
relates to Priscilla. Ha[...]
acters with whom the[...]
them create an imagi[...]
character of their cho[...]
consider an issue or s[...]
students to choose th[...]
serious, formal, hum[...]
logue for the class.

8 WHEN DO I TEACH WRITING?

This program incorporates opportunities in every unit for both process writing and writing for assessment.

Writing Process To help students prepare for every part-level Writing Workshop, **Work-in-Progress** features appear throughout each part. These focused prewriting activities encourage students to practice pre-writing strategies such as these:

- choosing and narrowing a topic
- gathering details
- preparing a thesis statement

In each part, a **Writing Workshop** with step-by-step instruction guides students to develop their ideas into full-length compositions, addressing these key stages in the writing process:

- Prewriting
- Drafting
- Revising
- Editing and Proofreading
- Publishing and Presenting

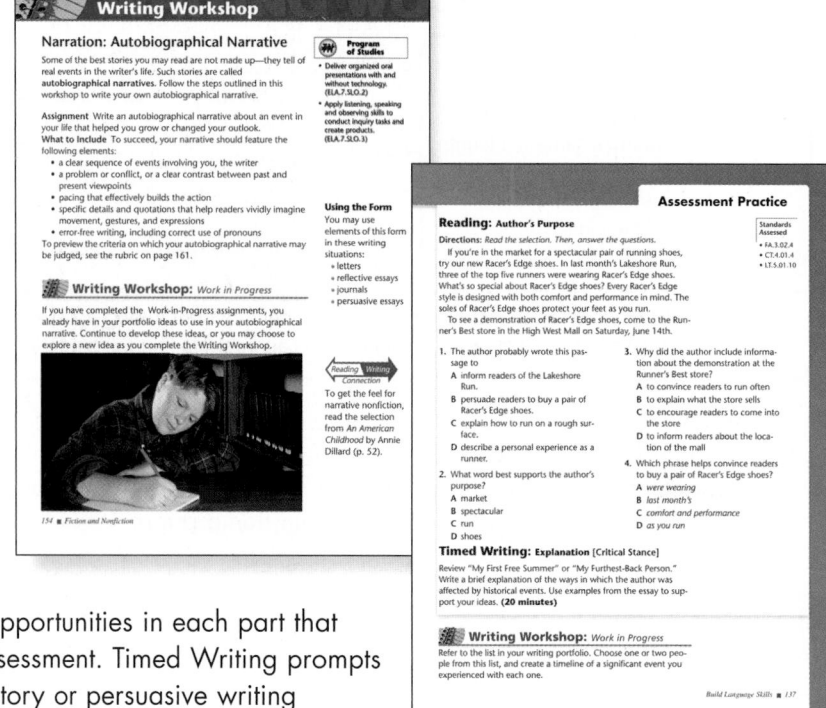

Timed Writing To address the growing call for on-demand writing, the program provides several opportunities in each part that help students practice writing for assessment. Timed Writing prompts ask students to produce brief expository or persuasive writing relating to the literature they have read.

Technology

Score student essays in seconds.

Finally, to facilitate your teaching of writing, the Prentice Hall **Online Essay Scorer** provides instant scoring and feedback, plus tips for revision. You save time, and your students become better writers!

9 HOW DO I MONITOR STUDENT PROGRESS?

Prentice Hall makes progress monitoring easy with frequent opportunities to evaluate student progress and to reteach material.

• Use the **Diagnostic Tests** at the beginning of each part to determine readiness. You will find frequent reading checks and suggestions in the Teacher's Edition for monitoring student progress during reading.

• After reading selections, use the **Selection Tests** to assess comprehension and mastery of the reading and literary analysis skills.

• As you teach the part, use the **Monitor Your Progress** pages in the standardized-test format. These appear at the end of each selection set and after the Reading Informational Material section to give students practice in applying specific skills under test-taking conditions.

• At the end of each part, use the **Reading and Vocabulary Review** to assess competency in the core skills.

• Use the **Benchmark Tests** to monitor progress at regular, frequent intervals. For your convenience, tests are provided for every part.

Technology

Monitor student progress instantly in an interactive format.

Access companion web sites for self-tests.

Use the electronic test generator to customize assessment.

10 HOW DOES *PRENTICE HALL LITERATURE* HELP ME DEVELOP AS A TEACHER?

The Teacher's Edition provides built-in professional development. Look for these special features:

• **Step-by-Step Teaching:** Margin notes provide strategies, tips, and examples for teaching skills.

• **Differentiated Instruction:** Notes provide support, strategies, and enrichment for learners of varied abilities.

• **Vocabulary Development:** A variety of strategies help you expand students' vocabulary.

• **Professional Development:** Pedagogical explanations of specific techniques enhance your effectiveness as a teacher.

T55

Unit	From the Author's Desk Featured Author	Reading and Vocabulary Skills Preview/ Review	Writing Workshop
1. **Fiction and Nonfiction**	**Elizabeth McCracken,** pp. 2, 6, 13, 14, 19, 165	**Reading:** **Make Predictions,** pp. 22, 86 **Author's Purpose,** pp. 94, 158 **Vocabulary:** Word Roots, pp. 23, 87 Word Origins, pp. 95, 159	**Autobiographical Narrative,** p. 88 **Work in Progress:** pp. 13, 19, 41, 71, 88 *Writing and Grammar Ch. 4* **Problem-and-Solution Essay,** p. 162 **Work in Progress:** pp. 117, 145, 162 *Writing and Grammar Ch. 11*
2. **Short Stories**	**Wayson Choy,** pp. 182, 186, 195, 375	**Reading:** **Make Inferences,** pp. 198, 282 **Analyze Cause and Effect,** pp. 290, 368 **Vocabulary:** Word Roots, pp. 199, 283, 291, 369	**Narration: Short Story,** p. 284 **Work in Progress:** pp. 195, 239, 265, 284 *Writing and Grammar Ch. 5* **Cause-and-Effect Essay,** p. 372 **Work in Progress:** pp. 319, 343, 372 *Writing and Grammar Ch. 10*
3. **Types of Nonfiction**	**Rebecca Walker,** pp. 386, 390, 397, 539	**Reading:** **Identify Main Idea and Supporting Details,** pp. 400, 464 **Persuasive Appeals,** pp. 472, 532 **Vocabulary:** Prefixes: *con-, com-, equi,* pp. 401, 465 Prefixes: *ante-, inter-,* pp. 473, 533	**Business Letters,** p. 466 **Work in Progress:** pp. 397, 423, 445, 466 *Writing and Grammar Ch. 15* **Persuasion: Editorial,** p. 536 **Work in Progress:** pp. 491, 513, 536 *Writing and Grammar Ch. 7*
4. **Poetry**	**Pat Mora,** pp. 550, 554, 559, 691	**Reading:** **Reading Fluently,** pp. 562, 618 **Paraphrasing,** pp. 626, 684 **Vocabulary:** Suffixes: *-able, -tion,* pp. 563, 619 Suffixes: *-age, -ism, -ize,* pp. 627, 685	**Description: Descriptive Essay,** p. 620 **Work in Progress:** pp. 559, 585, 611 *Writing and Grammar Ch. 6* **Response to Literature,** p. 688 **Work in Progress:** pp. 651, 675, 688 *Writing and Grammar Ch. 13*
5. **Drama**	**Gary L. Blackwood,** pp. 702, 706, 719, 920	**Reading:** **Summarizing,** pp. 722, 872 **Draw Conclusions,** pp. 880, 912 **Vocabulary:** Word Roots, pp. 723, 873 Word Roots, pp. 881, 913	**Exposition: How-to Essay,** p. 874 **Work in Progress:** pp. 719, 813, 851 *Writing and Grammar Resources, Writing and Grammar Ch. 3* **Research Writing: Research Report,** p. 916 **Work in Progress:** pp. 891, 916 *Writing and Grammar Ch. 12*
6. **Themes in Literature: Heroism**	**Dean Smith,** pp. 934, 938, 943, 1137	**Reading:** **Analyzing Cultural and Historical Context,** pp. 946, 1038 **Compare and Contrast,** pp. 1046, 1130 **Vocabulary:** Word Roots, pp. 947, 1039 Context Clues and Word Roots, pp. 1047, 1131	**Writing for Assessment:** **Timed Writing,** p. 1040 **Work in Progress:** pp. 943, 991, 1021, 1040 *Writing and Grammar Ch. 14* **Exposition: Comparison-and-Contrast Essay,** p. 1134 **Work in Progress:** pp. 1093, 1111 *Writing and Grammar Ch. 9*

Technology

Go Online PHSchool.com
• Author Biography
• Self-tests
• Internet Activities

From the Author's Desk DVD
Bring real writers into your classroom

ExamView QuickTake
Monitor student progress instantly

Success Tracker ONLINE
Score benchmark tests electronically for data aggregation

PH Online Essay Scorer: score essays in seconds

StudentEXPRESS PRENTICE HALL
Learn · Study · Succeed

TeacherEXPRESS PRENTICE HALL
Plan · Teach · Assess

Instant access to all program resources with the click of a mouse

Spelling Workshop	Communications Workshop	Reading Informational Materials
Content area words, p. 160 *Writing and Grammar Ch. 31, section 31.4*	**Analyzing Broadcast Media Presentations,** p. 170 *Writing and Grammar Ch. 30*	**Recipe:** Read to perform a task, p. 42 **Spanish/English Dictionaries:** Recognizing organizational features of text, p. 118
Unusual consonant groupings, p. 370 *Writing and Grammar Ch. 31, section 31.4*	**Evaluating a speech,** p. 380 *Writing and Grammar Ch. 30*	**Beach Safety Guide:** Evaluating visual aids, p. 240 **NC Transportation Museum:** Evaluating text format, p. 344
Tools for checking spelling, p. 534 *Writing and Grammar Ch. 31, section 31.4*	**Delivering a persuasive speech,** p. 544 *Writing and Grammar Ch. 30*	**NASA:** Reading for specific information, p. 446 **Lessons in Leadership:** Distinguishing fact from opinion, p. 514
Words with affixes, p. 686 *Writing and Grammar Ch. 31, section 31.4*	**Oral interpretation of literature,** p. 696 *Writing and Grammar Ch. 30*	**Careers in Robotics:** Making generalizations, p. 586 **Tornadoes Web site:** Evaluating Web sources, p. 652
Using Silent *e*, p. 914 *Writing and Grammar Ch. 31, section 31.4*	**Multimedia presentation of a research report,** p. 928 *Writing and Grammar Ch. 30*	**Atlas of Italy:** Skimming and scanning, p. 852 **Review of a Translation of Chekhov's Plays:** Evaluating credibility of an author, p. 892
Spelling on college entrance exams, p. 1132 *Writing and Grammar Ch. 31*	**Comparing media coverage,** p. 1142 *Writing and Grammar Ch. 30*	**Application for an Archaeological Dig:** Following directions, p. 1022 **Encyclopedia Entry: Detective Story:** Set a purpose for reading, p. 1094

	Selection	Page	Reading Skill	Literary Analysis	Vocabulary
UNIT INTRO	from *The Giant's House* Elizabeth McCracken	7		**Fiction and Nonfiction** pp. 2–6, 14	
	Desiderata Elizabeth McCracken	15			

PART 1 — READING FOCUS PREDICTIONS		Selection	Page	Reading Skill	Literary Analysis	Vocabulary
		Reading and Vocabulary Skills Preview and Review		**Make Predictions** p. 22		**Word Roots** p. 23
	MC	**The Washwoman** Isaac Bashevis Singer	26	**Ask Questions to Make and Verify Predictions** pp. 24, 32, 38 UR pp. 24, 40	**Narrative Essay** pp. 24, 32, 38 UR pp. 23, 39	**Word Roots** p. 40 UR p. 45
	MA	**New Directions** Maya Angelou	35			
		Reading Informational Materials Instructions: Recipes	42	**Read to Perform a Task** p. 42		
	MA	**Sonata for Harp and Bicycle** Joan Aiken	48	**Reading on to Verify Predictions** pp. 46, 58, 68 UR pp. 58, 74	**Plot and Foreshadowing** pp. 46, 58, 68 UR pp. 57, 73	**Word Roots** p. 70 UR p. 79
	MC	**The Cask of Amontillado** Edgar Allan Poe	61			
		Comparing Literary Works Checkouts Cynthia Rylant	74		**Comparing Literary Works: Point of View** pp. 72, 85	
		The Girl Who Can Ama Ata Aidoo	78			

PART 2 — READING FOCUS AUTHOR'S PURPOSE		Selection	Page	Reading Skill	Literary Analysis	Vocabulary
		Reading and Vocabulary Skills Preview and Review		**Author's Purpose** p. 94		**Word Origins** p. 95
	MA	from *A White House Diary* Lady Bird Johnson	98	**Previewing to Identify an Author's Purpose** pp. 96, 104, 114 UR pp. 117, 133	**Author's Voice and Autobiographical Writing** pp. 96, 104, 114 UR pp. 116, 132	**Word Origins** p. 116 UR p. 139
	MC	**My English** Julia Alvarez	107			
		Reading Informational Materials Spanish/English Dictionaries	118	**Recognizing the Organizational Features of Text** p. 118		
	MA	**The Secret Life of Walter Mitty** James Thurber	124	**Reflecting to Determine Author's Purpose** pp. 122, 130, 142 UR pp. 151, 167	**Character** pp. 122, 130, 142 UR pp. 150, 166	**Word Origins** p. 144 UR p. 172
	MC	**Uncle Marcos** Isabel Allende	133			
		Comparing Literary Works "If I Forget Thee, Oh Earth. . ." Arthur C. Clarke	148		**Comparing Literary Works: Theme** pp. 146, 157	
		from *Silent Spring* Rachel Carson	153			

Key: UR: Unit Resources **MA:** More Accessible **MC:** More Challenging
See Accessibility at a Glance chart on Time and Resource Manager

Skills Navigator

Writing	Grammar	Extend Your Learning	Assessment	
Writing Workshop: Work in Progress: Autobiographical Narrative p. 165 *Writing and Grammar Ch. 4*			**Research the Author** p. 20	
			Monitor Your Progress pp. 40, 70, 86	
Anecdote pp. 33, 39 UR pp. 26, 42 *Writing and Grammar Ch. 4* **Writing Workshop: Work in Progress:** Autobiographical Narrative, p. 41 *Writing and Grammar Ch. 4*	**Common Nouns and Proper Nouns** p. 40 UR p. 46 *Writing and Grammar Ch. 16, section 16.1*	**Interview Oral Presentation** pp. 33, 39 UR pp. 27, 43	**Monitor Your Progress** p. 41 **Timed Writing** Narration p. 41 **Selection Tests** UR pp. 29-34; 47–52	
			Monitor Your Progress p. 45	**Timed Writing** Explanation p. 45
Critique pp. 59, 69 UR pp. 60, 76 *Writing and Grammar Ch. 13* **Writing Workshop: Work in Progress:** Autobiographical Narrative, p. 71 *Writing and Grammar Ch. 4*	**Abstract and Concrete Nouns** p. 70 UR p. 80 *Writing and Grammar Ch. 16, section 16.1*	**Retelling Storyboard** pp. 59, 69 UR pp. 61, 77	**Monitor Your Progress** p. 71 **Timed Writing** Explanation p. 71 **Selection Tests** UR pp. 63–68; 81–86	
Writing to Compare Literary Works p. 85 *Writing and Grammar Ch. 9*			**Selection Tests** UR pp. 94–99	
			Monitor Your Progress pp. 116, 144, 158	
Journal Entry pp. 105, 115 UR pp. 119, 135 *Writing and Grammar Ch. 1* **Writing Workshop: Work in Progress:** Problem-and-Solution Essay p. 117 *Writing and Grammar Ch. 11*	**Personal and Reflexive Pronouns** p. 116 UR p. 139 *Writing and Grammar Ch. 16, section 16.2*	• **Radio Broadcast** • **Multimedia Presentation** pp. 105, 115 UR pp. 120, 136	**Monitor Your Progress** p. 117 **Timed Writing** Explanation p. 117 **Selection Tests** UR pp.122–127; 140–145	
			Monitor Your Progress p. 121	**Timed Writing** Exposition p. 121
Character Profile pp. 131, 143 UR pp. 153, 169 *Writing and Grammar Ch. 6* **Writing Workshop: Work in Progress:** Problem-and-Solution Essay p. 145 *Writing and Grammar Ch. 11*	**Pronouns: Relative, Interrogative, and Indefinite** p. 144 UR p. 173 *Writing and Grammar Ch. 16, section 16.2*	• **Scene** • **Learning Log** pp. 131, 143 UR pp. 154, 170	**Monitor Your Progress** p. 145 **Timed Writing** Explanation p. 145	**Selection Tests** UR pp. 174–179; 187–192
Writing to Compare Literary Works p. 157 *Writing and Grammar Ch. 9*			**Selection Tests** UR pp. 187–192	

Unit 2: The Short Story

	Selection	Page	Reading Skill	Literary Analysis	Vocabulary
UNIT INTRO	**The Jade Peony** Wayson Choy	187		**Short Stories** pp. 182–186	
PART 1 READING FOCUS **INFERENCES**	**Reading and Vocabulary Skills Preview and Review**		**Making Inferences** p. 198		**Word Roots** p. 199
MC	**American History** Judith Ortiz Cofer	202	**Asking Questions to Make Inferences** pp. 200, 212, 236 UR pp. 23, 39	**Conflict** pp. 200, 212, 236 UR pp. 22, 38	**Word Roots** p. 238 UR p. 44
MA	**The Most Dangerous Game** Richard Connell	215			
	Reading Informational Materials Signs and Instructions	240	**Evaluating Visual Aids** p. 240		
MA	**The Gift of the Magi** O. Henry	246	**Using Your Own Prior Knowledge and Experience to Make Inferences** pp. 244, 252, 262 UR pp. 57, 73	**Irony** pp. 244, 252, 262 UR pp. 56, 72	**Word Roots** p. 264 UR p. 78
MC	**The Interlopers** Saki	255			
	Comparing Literary Works The Man to Send Rain Clouds Leslie Marmon Silko	268		**Comparing Literary Works: Setting** pp. 266, 281	
	Old Man of the Temple R. K. Narayan	274			
PART 2 READING FOCUS **CAUSE AND EFFECT**	**Reading and Vocabulary Skills Preview and Review**		**Analyzing Cause and Effect** p. 290		**Word Roots** p. 291
MA	**The Necklace** Guy de Maupassant	294	**Asking Questions to Analyze Cause and Effect** pp. 292, 302, 316 UR pp. 117, 133	**Character and Characterization** pp. 292, 302, 316 UR pp. 132, 150	**Word Roots** p. 318 UR p. 138
MC	**Rules of the Game** Amy Tan	305			
MA	**Blues Ain't No Mockin Bird** Toni Cade Bambara	322	**Visualizing the Action to Analyze Cause and Effect** pp. 320, 330, 340 UR pp. 150, 166	**Dialogue** pp. 320, 330, 340 UR pp. 149, 165	**Word Roots** p. 342 UR p. 171
MC	**The Invalid's Story** Mark Twain	333			
	Reading Informational Materials NC Transportation Museum	344	**Evaluating Text Format** p. 344		
	Comparing Literary Works The Scarlet Ibis James Hurst	350		**Comparing Literary Works: Symbolism and Allegory** pp. 348, 367	
	The Golden Kite, the Silver Wind Ray Bradbury	362			

Key: UR: Unit Resources   **MA:** More Accessible   **MC:** More Challenging
See Accessibility at a Glance chart on Time and Resource Manager

Writing	Grammar	Extend Your Learning	Assessment
Writing Workshop: Work in Progress: Short Story p. 195 *Writing and Grammar Ch. 5*		**Research the Author** p. 196	**Selection Tests** UR pp. 8–13
			Monitor Your Progress pp. 238, 264, 282
Alternative Ending pp. 213, 237 UR pp. 25, 41 *Writing and Grammar Ch. 5* **Writing Workshop: Work in Progress:** Short Story p. 239 *Writing and Grammar Ch. 5*	**Regular Verbs** p. 238 UR p. 45 *Writing and Grammar Ch. 23, section 23.1*	• **Speech** • **Photo Essay** pp. 213, 237 UR pp. 26, 42	**Monitor Your Progress** p. 239 **Timed Writing** Interpretation p. 239 **Selection Tests** UR pp. 28–33; 46-51
			Monitor Your Progress p. 243 **Timed Writing** Persuasion p. 243
News Story pp. 253, 263 UR pp. 59, 75 *Writing and Grammar Ch. 10* **Writing Workshop: Work in Progress:** Short Story p. 265 *Writing and Grammar Ch. 5*	**Irregular Verbs** p. 264 UR p. 79 *Writing and Grammar Ch. 23, section 23.1*	• **Debate** • **Plan for an Illustrated Report** pp. 253, 263 UR pp. 60, 76	**Monitor Your Progress** p. 265 **Timed Writing** Explanation p. 265 **Selection Tests** UR pp. 62–67; 80–85
Writing to Compare Literary Works p. 281 *Writing and Grammar Ch. 9*			**Selection Tests** UR pp. 93–98
			Monitor Your Progress pp. 318, 342, 368
Written Presentation pp. 303, 317 UR pp. 119, 135 *Writing and Grammar Ch. 30* **Writing Workshop: Work in Progress:** Cause-and-Effect Essay p. 319 *Writing and Grammar Ch. 10*	**Subject/Predicate** p. 318 UR p. 139 *Writing and Grammar Ch. 20, section 20.1*	• **Monologue** • **Informative Brochure** pp. 303, 317 UR pp. 119, 135	**Monitor Your Progress** p. 319 **Timed Writing** Interpretation p. 319 **Selection Tests** UR pp. 121–126; 139–144
Informal Letter pp. 331, 341 UR pp. 152, 168 *Writing and Grammar Ch. 6* **Writing Workshop: Work in Progress:** Cause-and-Effect Essay p. 343 *Writing and Grammar Ch. 10*	**Active and Passive Voice** p. 342 UR p. 173 *Writing and Grammar Ch. 23, section 23.2*	**Dialogue Photo Collection** pp. 331, 341 UR pp. 153, 169	**Monitor Your Progress** p. 343 **Timed Writing** Description p. 343 **Selection Tests** UR pp. 155–160; 173–178
			Monitor Your Progress p. 347 **Timed Writing** Persuasion p. 347
Writing to Compare Literary Works p. 367 *Writing and Grammar Ch. 9*			**Selection Tests** UR pp. 186-191

All selections are supported in the Readers Notebooks.

	Selection	Page	Reading Skill	Literary Analysis	Vocabulary
UNIT INTRO	**Before Hip-Hop Was Hip-Hop** Rebecca Walker	391		**Types of Nonfiction** pp. 386–390	
PART 1 — READING FOCUS: **MAIN IDEA AND SUPPORTING DETAILS**	**Reading and Vocabulary Skills Preview and Review**		**Identifying Main Idea and Supporting Details** p. 400		**Word Prefixes** p. 401
MA	**A Celebration of Grandfathers** Rudolfo A. Anaya	404	**Generating Questions Prior to Reading** pp. 402, 412, 420 UR pp. 23, 39	**Author's Style** pp. 402, 412, 420 UR pp. 22, 38	**Word Prefixes** p. 422 UR p. 44
MC	**On Summer** Lorraine Hansberry	415			
MC	**The News** Neil Postman	426	**Rereading to Identify the Main Idea and Supporting Details** pp. 424, 434, 442 UR pp. 57, 73	**Expository Essay** pp. 424, 434, 442 UR pp. 56, 72	**Word Prefixes** p. 444 UR p. 78
MA	**Single Room, Earth View** Sally Ride	437			
	Reading Informational Materials NASA	446	**Reading for Specific Information** p. 446		
	Comparing Literary Works from *A Lincoln Preface* Carl Sandburg **Arthur Ashe Remembered** John McPhee	452 460		**Comparing Literary Works: Biographical Writing** pp. 450, 463	
PART 2 — READING FOCUS: **PERSUASIVE APPEALS**	**Reading and Vocabulary Skills Preview and Review**		**Analyzing Persuasive Appeals** p. 472		**Word Prefixes** p. 473
MA	**Carry Your Own Skis** Lian Dolan	476	**Rereading to Analyze and Evaluate Persuasive Appeals** pp. 474, 480, 488 UR pp. 116, 132	**Persuasive Essay** pp. 474, 480, 488 UR pp. 115, 131	**Prefixes** p. 490 UR p. 137
MC	**Libraries Face Sad Chapter** Pete Hamill	483			
MA	**"I Have a Dream"** Martin Luther King, Jr.	494	**Reading Aloud to Analyze Persuasive Techniques** pp. 492, 500, 510 UR pp. 151, 167	**Persuasive Speech** pp. 492, 500, 510 UR pp. 150, 166	**Prefixes** p. 512 UR p. 172
MC	**First Inaugural Address** Franklin D. Roosevelt	503			
	Reading Informational Materials Lessons in Leadership	514	**Distinguishing Fact from Opinion** p. 514		
	Comparing Literary Works The Talk Gary Soto **Go Deep to the Sewer** Bill Cosby	522 525		**Comparing Literary Works: Humorous Essay** pp. 520, 531	

Key: UR: Unit Resources **MA:** More Accessible **MC:** More Challenging
See Accessibility at a Glance chart on Time and Resource Manager

Writing	Grammar	Extend Your Learning	Assessment
Writing Workshop: Work in Progress: Business Letter p. 397 *Writing and Grammar Ch. 15*		**Research the Author** p. 398	**Selection Tests** UR pp. 28–33
			Monitor Your Progress pp. 422, 444, 464
Book Jacket Copy pp. 413, 421 UR pp. 25, 41 *Writing and Grammar Ch. 6* **Writing Workshop: Work in Progress:** Business Letter p. 423 *Writing and Grammar Ch. 15*	**Direct and Indirect Objects** p. 422 UR p. 45 *Writing and Grammar Ch. 20, section 20.3*	• **Panel Discussion** • **Annotated Map** pp. 413, 421 UR pp. 26, 42	**Monitor Your Progress** p. 423 **Timed Writing** Evaluation p. 423 **Selection Tests** UR pp. 28–33; 46–51
Script pp. 435, 443 UR pp. 59, 75 *Writing and Grammar Ch. 5* **Writing Workshop: Work in Progress:** Business Letter p. 445 *Writing and Grammar Ch. 15*	**Predicate Nominatives and Predicate Adjectives** p. 444 UR p. 79 *Writing and Grammar Ch. 20, section 20.3*	• **Informal Presentation** • **Journal Entries** pp. 435, 443 UR pp. 60, 76	**Monitor Your Progress** p. 445 **Timed Writing** Explanation p. 445 **Selection Tests** UR pp. 62–67; 80–85
			Monitor Your Progress p. 449 **Timed Writing** Exposition p. 449
Writing to Compare Literary Works p. 463 *Writing and Grammar Ch. 9*			**Selection Tests** UR pp. 93–98
			Monitor Your Progress pp. 490, 512, 532
Abstract pp. 481, 489 UR pp. 118, 134 **Writing Workshop: Work in Progress:** Editorial p. 491 *Writing and Grammar Ch. 7*	**Adjectives** p. 490 UR p. 139 *Writing and Grammar Ch. 18, section 18.1*	• **Persuasive Speech** • **Comparative Chart** pp. 481, 489 UR pp. 119, 135	**Monitor Your Progress** p. 491 **Timed Writing** Persuasion p. 491 **Selection Tests** UR pp. 121–126; 139–144
Proposal pp. 501, 511 UR pp. 152, 168 *Writing and Grammar Ch. 11* **Writing Workshop: Work in Progress:** Editorial p. 513 *Writing and Grammar Ch. 7*	**Adverbs** p. 512 UR p. 172 *Writing and Grammar Ch. 18, section 18.2*	• **Radio News Report** • **Annotated Source List** pp. 501, 511 UR pp. 153, 169	**Monitor Your Progress** p. 513 **Timed Writing** Evaluation p. 513 **Selection Tests** UR pp. 155–160; 173–178
			Monitor Your Progress p. 519 **Timed Writing** Analysis p. 519
Writing to Compare Literary Works p. 531 *Writing and Grammar Ch. 9*			**Selection Tests** UR pp. 186–191

	Selection	Page	Reading Skill	Literary Analysis	Vocabulary
UNIT INTRO	(Penguin) **Uncoiling a Voice** Pat Mora	555		**Poetry** pp. 550–559	
PART 1	**Reading and Vocabulary Skills Preview and Review**		**Reading Fluently** p. 562		**Suffixes** p. 563
MA	**Dream Deferred; Dreams,** Langston Hughes; **I Wandered Lonely as a Cloud**, William Wordsworth; **Meciendo/ Rocking,** Gabriela Mistral; **Sonnets on Love XIII**, Jean de Sponde	566	**Reading in Sentences** pp. 564, 574, 582 UR pp. 23, 39	**Figurative Language** pp. 564, 574, 582 UR pp. 22, 38	**Suffixes** p. 584 UR p. 44
MC	**All Watched Over by Machines of Loving Grace,** Richard Brautigan; **"Hope" is the thing with feathers— Much Madness is divinest Sense**–Emily Dickinson; **The War Against the Trees**, Stanley Kunitz	577			
	Reading Informational Materials Careers in Robotics	586	**Making Generalizations** p. 586		
MA	**Summer,** Walter Dean Myers; **The Eagle,** Alfred, Lord Tennyson; **Analysis of Baseball,** May Swenson	592	**Using Your Senses** pp. 590, 596, 608 UR pp. 57, 73	**Sound Devices** pp. 590, 596, 608 UR pp. 56, 72	**Suffixes** p. 610 UR p. 78
MC	**The Bells,** Edgar Allan Poe; **Slam, Dunk, & Hook,** Yusef Komunyakaa; **Jabberwocky,** Lewis Carroll	599			
	Comparing Literary Works **There is No Word for Goodbye,** Mary TallMountain, **Blackberry Eating,** Galway Kinnell, **Daily,** Naomi Shihab Nye	614 615 616		**Comparing Literary Works: Imagery** pp. 612, 617	
PART 2	**Reading and Vocabulary Skills Preview and Review**		**Paraphrasing** p. 626		**Suffixes** p. 627
MA	**Casey at the Bat,** Ernest Lawrence Thayer; **Fifteen,** William Stafford; **Twister Hits Houston,** Sandra Cisneros	630	**Picturing the Action** pp. 628, 636, 648 UR pp. 116, 132	**Narrative Poetry** pp. 628, 636, 648 UR pp. 115, 131	**Suffixes** p. 650 UR p. 137
MC	**The Raven,** Edgar Allan Poe; **The Horses,** Edwin Muir; **The Writer,** Richard Wilbur	639			
	Reading Informational Materials Tornadoes Web site	652	**Evaluating Web Sources** p. 652		
MA	**We never know how high we are,** Emily Dickinson; **The Road Not Taken,** Robert Frost; **Macavity: The Mystery Cat,** T.S. Eliot	659	**Breaking Down Long Sentences** pp. 657, 664, 672 UR pp. 150, 166	**Rhyme** pp. 656, 664, 672 UR pp. 149, 165	**Suffixes** p. 674 UR p. 171
MC	**Fire and Ice,** Robert Frost; **maggie and milly and molly and may,** E. E Cummings; **The Seven Ages of Man,** William Shakespeare	667			
	Comparing Literary Works **Women** Alice Walker, **Three Haiku** Bashō and Chiyojo, **I Hear America Singing**, Walt Whitman, **Sonnet 30** William Shakespeare	678 679 680 682		**Comparing Literary Works: Lyric Poetry** pp. 676, 683	

Key: UR: Unit Resources **MA:** More Accessible **MC:** More Challenging
See Accessibility at a Glance chart on Time and Resource Manager

Writing	Grammar	Extend Your Learning	Assessment
Writing Workshop: Work in Progress: Descriptive Essay p. 559 *Writing and Grammar Ch. 6*			**Research the Author** p. 560
			Monitor Your Progress pp. 584, 610, 618
Description of a Scene pp. 575, 583 UR pp. 25, 41 *Writing and Grammar Ch. 6* **Writing Workshop: Work in Progress:** Descriptive Essay p. 585 *Writing and Grammar Ch. 6*	**Preposition and Object of the Preposition** p. 584 UR p. 45 *Writing and Grammar Ch. 19, section 19.1*	• Impromptu • Speech • Soundtrack pp. 575, 583 UR pp. 26, 42	**Monitor Your Progress** p. 585 **Timed Writing** Analysis p. 585 **Selection Tests** UR pp. 28–33; 46–51
			Monitor Your Progress p. 589 **Timed Writing** Exposition p. 589
Editorial pp. 597, 609 UR pp. 59, 75 *Writing and Grammar Ch. 7* **Writing Workshop: Work in Progress:** Descriptive Essay p. 611 *Writing and Grammar Ch. 6*	**Prepositional Phrases** p. 610 UR p. 79 *Writing and Grammar Ch. 21, section 21.1*	• Dramatic Reading • Illustrated Version pp. 597, 609 UR pp. 60, 76	**Monitor Your Progress** p. 611 **Timed Writing** Analysis p. 611 **Selection Tests** UR pp. 62–67; 80–85
Writing to Compare Literary Works p. 617 *Writing and Grammar Ch. 9*			**Selection Tests** UR pp. 93–98
			Monitor Your Progress pp. 650, 674, 684
Detailed Description of a Scene pp. 637, 649 UR pp. 118, 134 *Writing and Grammar Ch. 6* **Writing Workshop: Work in Progress:** Response to Literature p. 651 *Writing and Grammar Ch. 13*	**Appositive Phrase** p. 650 UR p. 138 *Writing and Grammar Ch. 21, section 21.1*	• Dialogue • Fact Sheet pp. 637, 649 UR pp. 119, 135	**Monitor Your Progress** p. 651 **Timed Writing** Analysis p. 651 **Selection Tests** UR pp. 121–126; 139–144
			Monitor Your Progress p. 655 **Timed Writing** Evaluation p. 655
Poem pp. 665, 673 UR pp. 152, 168 *Writing and Grammar Ch. 6* **Writing Workshop: Work in Progress:** Response to Literature p. 675 *Writing and Grammar Ch. 13*	**Infinitives and Infinitive Phrases** p. 650 UR p. 173 *Writing and Grammar Ch. 21, section 21.1*	• Panel Discussion • Annotated Electronic Database pp. 665, 673 UR pp. 153, 169	**Monitor Your Progress** p. 675 **Timed Writing** Interpretation p. 675 **Selection Tests** UR pp. 155–160; 173–178
Writing to Compare Literary Works p. 683 *Writing and Grammar Ch. 9*			**Selection Tests** UR pp. 186–191

All selections are supported in the Readers Notebooks.

	Selection	Page	Reading Skill	Literary Analysis	Vocabulary
UNIT INTRO	from *The Shakespeare Stealer* Gary L. Blackwood	707		**Drama** pp. 702–706	
PART 1 — READING FOCUS **SUMMARIZING**	**Reading and Vocabulary Skills Preview and Review**		**Summarizing** p. 722		**Word Roots** p. 723
MC	*The Tragedy of Romeo and Juliet*, Act I William Shakespeare	730	**Using Text Aids** pp. 728, 754 UR p. 23	**Dialogue** pp. 728, 754 UR p. 22	**Word Roots** p. 812 UR p. 60
MC	*The Tragedy of Romeo and Juliet*, Act II	757	**Reading in Sentences to Summarize** pp. 756, 780 UR p. 39	**Blank Verse** pp. 756, 780 UR p. 38	
MC	*The Tragedy of Romeo and Juliet*, Act III	783	**Paraphrasing** pp. 782, 810 UR p. 55	**Dramatic Speeches** pp. 782, 810 UR p. 54	
MC	*The Tragedy of Romeo and Juliet*, Act IV	815	**Breaking Down Long Sentences** pp. 814, 830 UR p. 73	**Dramatic Irony** pp. 814, 830 UR p. 72	**Word Roots** p. 850 UR p. 94
MC	*The Tragedy of Romeo and Juliet*, Act V	833	**Identifying Causes and Effects** pp. 832, 848 UR p. 89	**Tragedy** pp. 832, 848 UR p. 88	
	Reading Informational Materials Atlas of Italy	852	**Skimming and Scanning** p. 852		
	Comparing Literary Works Pyramus and Thisbe Ovid **from** *A Midsummer Night's Dream* William Shakespeare	858 862		**Comparing Literary Works: Archetypal Theme** pp. 856, 871	
PART 2 — READING FOCUS **CONCLUSIONS**	**Reading and Vocabulary Skills Preview and Review**		**Drawing Conclusions** p. 880		**Word Roots** p. 881
MA	*The Inspector-General* Anton Chekhov	884	**Drawing Conclusions from Dialogue and Stage Directions** pp. 882, 888 UR p. 132	**Comedy and Dramatic Irony** pp. 882, 888 UR p. 131	**Word Roots** p. 890 UR p. 137
	Reading Informational Materials Review of a Translation of Chekhov's Plays	892	**Evaluate Credibility of an Author** p. 892		
	Comparing Literary Works from *The Importance of Being Earnest* Oscar Wilde **from** *Big Kiss* Henry Alford	898 906		**Comparing Literary Works: Satire** pp. 896, 911	

Key: UR: Unit Resources   **MA:** More Accessible   **MC:** More Challenging

See Accessibility at a Glance Chart on Time and Resource Manager

Writing	Grammar	Extend Your Learning	Assessment
Writing Workshop: Work in Progress: How-to Essay p. 719 *Writing and Grammar Resources Ch. 5*		**Research the Author** p. 720	**Selection Tests** UR pp. 8–13
			Monitor Your Progress pp. 812, 850, 872
Letter to Advice Columnist p. 755 UR p. 25 *Writing and Grammar Ch. 11* **Editorial** p. 811 UR p. 57 *Writing and Grammar Ch. 7* **Writing Workshop: Work in Progress:** How-to Essay p. 813 *Writing and Grammar Resources Ch. 3*	**Participles and Participle Phrases** p. 812 *Writing and Grammar Ch. 21, section 21.1*	• **Staged Performance** p. 755 UR p. 26 • **Annotated Flowchart** p. 781 UR p. 42 • **Film Review** p. 811 UR p. 58	**Selection Tests** UR pp. 28–33; 44–49; 62–67
Abstract p. 831 UR p. 75 *Writing and Grammar Ch. 13* **Persuasive Letter** p. 849 UR p. 91 *Writing and Grammar Ch. 7* **Writing Workshop: Work in Progress:** How-to Essay p. 851 *Writing and Grammar Resources Ch. 3*	**Gerund and Gerund Phrase** p. 850 *Writing and Grammar Ch. 21, section 21.1* UR p. 95	• **Multimedia Presentation** p. 831 UR p. 76 • **Mock Trial** p. 849 UR p. 92	**Monitor Your Progress** p. 851 **Timed Writing** Interpretation p. 851 **Selection Tests** UR pp. 78–83; 96–101
			Monitor Your Progress p. 855 **Timed Writing** Exposition p. 855
Writing to Compare Literary Works p. 871 *Writing and Grammar Ch. 9*			**Selection Tests** UR pp. 109–114
			Monitor Your Progress pp. 890, 912
Short Play pp. 883, 889 UR p. 134 *Writing and Grammar Ch. 5* **Writing Workshop: Work in Progress:** Research Report *Writing and Grammar Ch. 12*	**Main and Subordinate Clauses** p. 890 UR p. 138 *Writing and Grammar Ch. 21, section 21.1*	• **Readers Theatre Presentation** • **Informational Chart** p. 889 UR p. 135	**Monitor Your Progress** p. 891 **Timed Writing** Interpretation p. 891 **Selection Tests** UR pp. 139–144
			Monitor Your Progress p. 895 **Timed Writing** Exposition p. 895
Writing to Compare Literary Works p. 911 *Writing and Grammar Ch. 9*			**Selection Tests** UR pp. 152–157

	Selection	Page	Reading Skill	Literary Analysis	Vocabulary
UNIT INTRO	Play Hard; Play Together; Play Smart, from *The Carolina Way* Dean Smith	939		Themes in Literature: Heroism pp. 934–938	
PART 1 (READING FOCUS CULTURAL AND HISTORICAL CONTEXT)	Reading and Vocabulary Skills Preview and Review		Analyzing the Influence of Cultural and Historical Context p. 946		Word Roots p. 947
MC	from the *Odyssey*, Part 1 Homer	950	Using Background and Prior Knowledge pp. 948, 988 UR pp. 23	Epic Hero pp. 948, 988 UR pp. 22	Word Roots p. 990 UR p. 28
MC	from the *Odyssey*, Part 2 Homer	994	Identify Influences on Your Own Reading and Responses pp. 992, 1018 UR pp. 41	Epic Simile pp. 992, 1018 UR pp. 40	Word Roots p. 1020 UR p. 46
	Reading Informational Materials Application for an Archaeological Dig	1022	Following Directions p. 1022		
	Comparing Literary Works An Ancient Gesture Edna St. Vincent Millay	1028		Comparing Literary Works: Contemporary Interpretations pp. 1026, 1037	
	Siren Song, Margaret Atwood	1030			
	Prologue and Epilogue from the *Odyssey*, Derek Walcott	1032			
	Ithaca, Constantine Cavafy	1034			
PART 2 (READING FOCUS COMPARE AND CONTRAST)	Reading and Vocabulary Skills Preview and Review		Compare and Contrast p. 1046		Context Clues and Word Roots p. 1047
MA	Three Skeleton Key George G. Toudouze	1050	Generating Questions After Reading pp. 1048, 1064, 1090 UR pp. 84, 100	Protagonist and Antagonist pp. 1048, 1064, 1090 UR pp. 83, 99	Context Clues and Word Roots p. 1092 UR p. 105
MC	The Red-headed League Sir Arthur Conan Doyle	1067			
	Reading Informational Materials Encyclopedia Entry: Detective Story	1094	Set a Purpose for Reading p. 1094		
MA	There Is a Longing Chief Dan George	1100	Using Self-monitoring pp. 1098, 1102, 1108 UR pp. 118, 132	Author's Purpose and Philosophical Assumptions pp. 1098, 1102, 1108 UR pp. 117, 131	Context Clues and Word Roots p. 1110 UR p. 137
MC	Glory and Hope Nelson Mandela	1105			
	Comparing Literary Works Pecos Bill: The Cyclone Harold W. Felton	1114	Comparing Literary Works: Tall Tale and Myth pp. 1112, 1129		
	Perseus, Edith Hamilton	1121			

Key: UR: Unit Resources **MA:** More Accessible **MC:** More Challenging
See Accessibility at a Glance chart on Time and Resource Manager

Writing	Grammar	Extend Your Learning	Assessment
Writing Workshop: Work in Progress: Writing for Assessment p. 943 *Writing and Grammar Ch. 14*		**Research the Author** p. 944	**Selection Tests** UR pp. 8–13
			Monitor Your Progress pp. 990, 1020, 1038
Everyday Epic pp. 949, 989 UR pp. 25 *Writing and Grammar Ch. 5* **Writing Workshop: Work in Progress:** Writing for Assessment p. 991 *Writing and Grammar Ch. 14*	**Simple and Compound Sentences** p. 990 UR p. 29 *Writing and Grammar Ch. 21, section 21.2*	• **Improvise a Conversation** • **Illustrated Travelogue** p. 989 UR pp. 26	**Monitor Your Progress** p. 991 **Timed Writing** Explanation p. 991 **Selection Tests** UR pp. 30–35
Biography of Odysseus p. 1019 UR pp. 43 *Writing and Grammar Ch. 13* **Writing Workshop: Work in Progress:** Writing for Assessment p. 1021 *Writing and Grammar Ch. 14*	**Complex and Compound Complex Sentences** p. 1020 UR p. 47 *Writing and Grammar Ch. 21, section 21.2*	• **Director's Influence Chart** • **Debate** p. 1019 UR pp. 44	**Monitor Your Progress** p. 1021 **Timed Writing** Interpretation p. 1021 **Selection Tests** UR pp. 48–53
			Monitor Your Progress p. 1025 **Timed Writing** Persuasion p. 1025
Writing to Compare Literary Works p. 1037 *Writing and Grammar Ch. 9*			**Selection Tests** UR pp. 61–66
			Monitor Your Progress pp. 1092, 1110, 1130
Journal Entries pp. 1065, 1091 UR pp. 86, 102 *Writing and Grammar Ch. 1* **Writing Workshop: Work in Progress:** Comparison-and-Contrast Essay p. 1093 *Writing and Grammar Ch. 9*	**Commas** p. 1092 UR p. 106 *Writing and Grammar Ch. 29, section 29.2*	• **Interview** • **Oral Report** pp. 1065, 1091 UR pp. 87, 103	**Monitor Your Progress** p. 1093 **Timed Writing** Explanation p. 1093 **Selection Tests** UR pp. 89–94; 107–112
			Monitor Your Progress p. 1097 **Timed Writing** Exposition p. 1097
Letter pp. 1103, 1109 UR pp. 120, 134 *Writing and Grammar Ch. 13* **Writing Workshop: Work in Progress:** Comparison-and-Contrast Essay p. 1111 *Writing and Grammar Ch. 9*	**Colons, Semicolons and Ellipses Points** p. 1110 UR p. 138 *Writing and Grammar Ch. 29, section 29.3*	• **Panel Discussion** • **Outline** pp. 1103, 1109 UR pp. 121, 135	**Monitor Your Progress** p. 1111 **Timed Writing** Analysis p. 1111 **Selection Tests** UR pp. 123–126; 139–142
Writing to Compare Literary Works p. 1129 *Writing and Grammar Ch. 9*			**Selection Tests** UR pp. 150–155

UNIT 1

Words in italic are expressive vocabulary, presented in the Connecting to the Literature feature preceding each selection.

Program Vocabulary

Unit 3

Introduction

"Before Hip-Hop Was Hip-Hop," Rebecca Walker

palpable, bravado, lexicon, *assemble, commit, identify, persist, provoke, transmit*

PART 1	PART 2
Build Language Skills equivalent, contemplate, abstract, hence, illuminate	**Academic Vocabulary** anticipate, internal, derive, texture, signify

Selection Set 1

A Celebration of Grandfathers, Rudulfo A. Anaya	**"Carry Your Own Skis,"** Lian Dolan
perplexes, absurdity, permeate, anguish, *appreciate, clarify, demonstrate, maximize*	inevitability, potential, riddled, *attain, challenge, concentrate, display, frustrate*
"On Summer," Lorraine Hansberry	**"Libraries Face Sad Chapter,"** Pete Hamill
aloofness, melancholy, pretentious, apex, *embody, signify, react, dominate*	curtailed, medium, duration, *perceive, reveal, respond, dedicate, distribute*

Selection Set 2

"The News," Neil Postman	**"I Have a Dream,"** Martin Luther King, Jr.
compensation, temporal, revered, daunting, *analyze, rely, clarify, indicate*	hallowed, degenerate, creed, *embody, comprise, define, invoke*
"Single Room, Earth View," Sally Ride	**"First Inaugural Address,"** Franklin D. Roosevelt
articulate, novice, diffused, extrapolating, *alter, contradict, emphasize, perceive*	abdicated, evanescent, arduous, *evoke, project, render, stimulate, transform*

Comparing Literary Works

from *A Lincoln Preface*, Carl Sandburg	**"The Talk,"** Gary Soto
despotic, censure, droll, *commit, enrich, pursue, exceed, devote*	renegade, feisty, *derive, imply, react, anticipate, provoke*
"Arthur Ashe Remembered," John McPhee	**"Go Deep to the Sewer,"** Bill Cosby
legacy, enigma, lithe	lateral, interpretation

Unit 4

Introduction

"Uncoiling; A Voice," Pat Mora

spunky, *enrich, immigrate, incorporate, maintain, perceive, transform*

PART 1	PART 2
Build Language Skills considerable, deliberation, transition, concept, impact	**Academic Vocabulary** usage, emphasize, mechanism, abstract, distinct

Selection Set 1

"Dream Deferred," "Dreams," Langston Hughes; **"I Wandered Lonely as a Cloud,"** William Wordsworth; **"Meciendo/Rocking,"** Gabriela Mistral; **"Sonnets on Love XIII,"** Jean de Sponde (trans. by David R. Slavitt)	**"Casey at the Bat,"** Ernest Lawrence Thayer; **"Fifteen,"** William Stafford; **"Twister Hits Houston,"** Sandra Cisneros
deferred, pensive, *achieve, benefit, focus, maintain*	pallor, writhing, demure, *evoke, respond, reinforce, react, promote*
"All Watched Over . . .," Richard Brautigan; **"'Hope' is the thing with feathers—" "Much Madness is divinest Sense–,"**Emily Dickinson; **"The War Against the Trees,"** Stanley Kunitz "	**"The Raven,"** Edgar Allan Poe; **"The Horses,"** Edwin Muir; **"The Writer,"** Richard Wilbur
preliminaries, discerning, *maximize, interact, minimize, accelerate*	beguiling, respite, archaic, *evoke, respond, reinforce, react, promote*

Selection Set 2

"Summer," Walter Dean Myers; **"The Eagle,"** Alfred, Lord Tennyson; **"Analysis of Baseball,"** May Swenson	**"The Road Not Taken,"** Robert Frost; **"We never know how high we are,"** Emily Dickinson; **"Macavity: The Mystery Cat,"** T. S. Eliot
clasps, azure, *anticipate, coincide, displays, participate*	diverged, warp, bafflement, depravity, *challenge, compel, conform, distinguish*
"The Bells," Edgar Allan Poe; **"Slam, Dunk & Hook,"** Yusef Komunyakaa; **"Jabberwocky,"** Lewis Carroll	**"Fire and Ice,"** Robert Frost; **"maggie and milly and molly and may,"** e.e. cummings; **"The Seven Ages of Man,"** William Shakespeare
metaphysical, jibed, voluminously, palpitating, *signify, trigger, appreciate, contemplate, interprets*	suffice, languid, woeful, treble, *acquire, alter, cease, coincide, embody*

Comparing Literary Works

"There Is No Word for Goodbye," Mary Tall Mountain; **"Blackberry Eating,"** Galway Kinnell; **"Daily,"** Naomi Shihab Nye	**"Women,"** Alice Walker; **"Three Haiku,"** Bashō and Chiyojo
penalty, unbidden, shriveled, scarred, *emphasize, consume, appreciate, impact*	stout, *signify, elaborate, emerge, stress, embrace*
	"I Hear America Singing," Walt Whitman; **"Sonnet 30"** William Shakespeare
	intermission, woes, wail

UNIT 5

Introduction
from *The Shakespeare Stealer*, Gary L. Blackwood

feckless, spectral, parsimonious, rustic, *revise, clarify, illuminate, compensate, supplement, confirm*

PART 1	PART 2
Build Language Skills	**Academic Vocabulary**
condense, relevant, ambiguous, elaborate, illuminate	revise, convince, implement, strategy, compile

Selection Set 1

PART 1	PART 2
Romeo and Juliet, Act I, William Shakespeare	***The Inspector-General,*** Anton Chekhov
pernicious, augmenting, grievance, transgression, *illustrate, contrast, emphasizes, reinforces, adapt*	anonymous, trundle, discreetly, cunning, *distorts, ignore, interpret, respond, injure*
Romeo and Juliet, Act II, William Shakespeare	
procure, predominant, intercession, sallow, lamentable, unwieldy, *anticipate, obstacle, reluctant, mutual*	

Selection Set 2

PART 1	PART 2
Romeo and Juliet, Act III, William Shakespeare	
gallant, fray, martial, exile, eloquence, fickle, *comply, drastic, intense, tolerate*	
Romeo and Juliet, Act IV, William Shakespeare	
pensive, enjoined, wayward, dismal, loathsome, *intense, liberate, potential, sacrifice*	

Comparing Literary Works

PART 1	PART 2
Romeo and Juliet, Act V, William Shakespeare	**from *The Importance of Being Earnest*,** Oscar Wilde
remnants, penury, haughty, ambiguities, scourge, assess, circumstance, react, significant	allotment, assiduous, demonstrative, ignorance, *assess, confront, contradict, minimize, construct*
"Pyramus and Thisbe," Ovid; **scenes from *Romeo and Juliet*; scene from *A Midsummer Night's Dream*,** William Shakespeare	**from *Big Kiss*,** Henry Alford
lament, inevitable, *enamored, enthralled, enrich, sustain, console, transform, unify*	

UNIT 6

Introduction
"Play Hard; Play Together; Play Smart" from *The Carolina Way*," Dean Smith

tenets, *confirm, persist, illustrate, participate, dominate, signify*

PART 1	PART 2
Build Language Skills	**Academic Vocabulary**
controversy, technique, appraise, confirm, complex	cogent, significant, defect, compelling, coherent

Selection Set 1

PART 1	PART 2
from the *Odyssey*, Part 1, Homer	**"Three Skeleton Key,"** George G. Toudouze
plundered, dispatched, mammoth, assuage, bereft, ardor, insidious, *encounter, highlight, coincide, eliminate, interact*	lurched, diminution, derisive, *isolate, access, forgo, induce*
from the *Odyssey*, Part 2, Homer	**"The Red-headed League,"** Sir Arthur Conan Doyle
dissemble, incredulity, bemusing, equity, maudlin, contempt, *magnetize, marvel, confront, interrogates*	introspective, vex, formidable, *perceive, observe, differentiate, reveal*

Selection Set 2

PART 1	PART 2
	"There Is a Longing," Chief Dan George
	determination, endurance, *reinforce, contemporary, domestic, spectrum*
	"Glory and Hope," Nelson Mandela
	confer, pernicious, covenant, *derive, signify, devote, evoke*

Comparing Literary Works

PART 1	PART 2
"An Ancient Gesture," Edna St. Vincent Millay; **"Siren Song,"** Margaret Atwood; **"Prologue and Epilogue from the *Odyssey*,"** Derek Walcott; **"Ithaca,"** Constantine Cavafy	**"Pecos Bill: The Cyclone,"** Harold W. Felton
authentic, picturesque, siege, lofty, defrauded, *integrate, manifest, confront, enlighten*	usurped, skeptics, *impact, negate, illuminate, exceed, undertake*
	"Perseus," Edith Hamilton
	mortified, revelry

Academic Vocabulary

Academic vocabulary is the specialized vocabulary that appears frequently throughout academic texts in all content areas, including standardized tests and textbooks. The words on this page are culled from a variety of academic vocabulary word lists, including the work of Averil Coxhead, Jim Burke, and Xue Guoyi and I.S.P. Nation.

Prentice Hall Literature, Penguin Edition, develops academic vocabulary at each grade. In grades 6-10, selected grade-appropriate words are presented in the *Academic Vocabulary* features at the part level. In addition, they appear in the *Connecting to the Literature* element on the *Build Understanding* page before each selection. Words in boldface are taught in grade 9. Words in lightface represent related words.

abstract	**comprehend**	**distinguish**	**imply**	pursuit
abstraction	**comprise**	**distort**	**impress**	**react**
accelerate	**concentrate**	**distribute**	**indicate**	**rebel**
access	**concept**	**domestic**	indicative	rebellious
accessible	conceptual	domesticate	**induce**	**reinforce**
accomplish	**condense**	**dominate**	induction	**relevant**
achieve	**confirm**	**elaborate**	**initiate**	reliable
acquire	**conform**	elaboration	**injure**	**rely**
adapt	conformity	**elevate**	**integrate**	**render**
adaptable	**confront**	**eliminate**	integration	**respond**
adjust	confrontation	**embody**	**interact**	**reveal**
alter	**considerable**	**embrace**	**internal**	revelation
alteration	**console**	**emerge**	**interpret**	**revise**
ambiguity	**consume**	embodiment	**intervene**	**sequence**
ambiguous	consumption	**emotion**	intervention	sign
analyze	**contemplate**	**emphasize**	**invoke**	**significant**
anticipate	contemplative	**encounter**	**involve**	**signify**
appraise	**contemporary**	**enhance**	**isolate**	**simulate**
appreciate	**contradict**	**enlighten**	**justify**	**specific**
aspect	**contrast**	**enrich**	**maintain**	specify
assess	**contribute**	**equivalent**	**manifest**	**spectrum**
assist	controversial	**establish**	manifestation	**stimulate**
beneficiary	**controversy**	establishment	**maximize**	strategic
benefit	**convince**	**evoke**	**minimize**	**strategy**
categorize	debatable	**evolve**	**motivate**	**stress**
category	**debate**	**exceed**	**motive**	**sustain**
cease	**dedicate**	**expose**	**negate**	sustenance
challenge	**defect**	exposure	negation	**technique**
circumstance	**define**	**focus**	obligation	**texture**
circumstantial	deliberate	**forgo**	**oblige**	**transform**
clarification	**deliberation**	**frustrate**	**observe**	**transition**
clarify	**demonstrate**	**generate**	**obtain**	**trigger**
cogent	deniable	generation	obtainable	**trivial**
cohere	**deny**	**hence**	**participate**	trivialize
coherent	deprivation	**highlight**	**perceive**	**undertake**
coincide	**deprive**	**identify**	perception	**unify**
coincidence	derivative	**ignore**	**precipitate**	**utilize**
commit	**derive**	**illuminate**	**prohibit**	**verify**
communicate	**detect**	illumination	**project**	**vital**
compel	**devote**	**illustrate**	projection	vitality
compelling	**dictate**	illustration	**promote**	
compile	**differentiate**	**impact**	provocation	
complex	**displace**	**implement**	**provoke**	
complexity	**display**	implication	**pursue**	

Language Arts Standards-at-a-Glance

This chart provides an overview of where you'll find the general Language Arts standards addressed in *Prentice Hall Literature: The Penguin Edition*. Prentice Hall developed this list of standards based on a review of state standards across the country. For more detailed information regarding skills coverage, see the **Skills Navigator**, found on page T58, which provides an overview of the skills by selection. The **Time and Resource Manager** will show the skills breakdown for each unit of study.

Standard Course of Study for Language Arts

	UNIT 1		UNIT 2		UNIT 3		UNIT 4		UNIT 5		UNIT 6	
PART	1	2	1	2	1	2	1	2	1	2	1	2

Reading—Reflection and Response: Students will reflect upon and respond to print and non-print text.

Skill	U1P1	U1P2	U2P1	U2P2	U3P1	U3P2	U4P1	U4P2	U5P1	U5P2	U6P1	U6P2
Narrate personal scenes located effectively in time and place.						●			●		●	
Narrate personal impressions of setting and plot.	●	●			●							
Show appreciation for the significance of a personal account.					●		●					
Narrate with a personal voice.				●	●							
Show understanding of personal reaction to the text through response.		●				●	●					
React in response after careful consideration of the text.					●			●			●	
Show awareness of how personal and cultural influences affect response.											●	
Select, monitor, and modify reading strategies appropriate to situation.					●				●			●
Identify, evaluate, and analyze the impact of text components.		●		●						●	●	
Provide evidence to support understanding of response to text.	●	●				●						
Summarize key events and/or points from text in response.									●	●		
Make inferences and draw conclusions in response based on text.	●						●					
Identify and analyze influences, contexts, or biases in response.						●					●	
Make connections between works, self, and related topics in response.									●			
Analyze and evaluate the effects of author's craft and style in response.				●	●				●			
Analyze connections among ideas, concepts, characters, and experience in response.			●	●			●	●				

● *Supports standard mastery*

Standard Course of Study for Language Arts

	UNIT 1		UNIT 2		UNIT 3		UNIT 4		UNIT 5		UNIT 6	
PART	1	2	1	2	1	2	1	2	1	2	1	2
Analyze through response, elements of expressive environment found in text.	●	●										
Identify and analyze elements of expressive environment found in text in light of purpose, audience, and context.	●						●					

Research/Reading Informational Materials: Students will analyze and use informational materials to answer research questions.

	UNIT 1		UNIT 2		UNIT 3		UNIT 4		UNIT 5		UNIT 6	
	1	2	1	2	1	2	1	2	1	2	1	2
Select, monitor, and modify reading strategies appropriate to answering research questions.		●	●						●		●	
Analyze text components and evaluate impact on text and on research.		●			●							
Provide textual evidence to support understanding of and response to text in answering questions.	●			●	●							
Demonstrate comprehension of main idea and supporting details in answering research questions.					●							
Summarize key events and/or points from text for research.												●
Make inferences and draw conclusions based on text to answer research questions.	●			●								
Analyze influences, contexts, or biases in answering research questions.		●									●	
Make connections between works, self, and related topics to inform audience.						●			●			
Analyze the effects of author's craft and style in informing audience.				●				●	●			
Analyze connections among ideas, concepts, characters, and experiences to inform audience.			●								●	
Analyze elements of informational environment in text when answering research questions.			●					●				
Clearly state the subject to be defined in research question.					●			●	●			
Classify terms and identify characteristics to inform audience.						●			●			●
Organize ideas and details effectively to inform audience.				●	●					●		
Use description, comparison, and figurative language to elaborate ideas to inform audience.		●					●	●				●
Demonstrate a clear sense of audience and purpose in answering research questions.	●				●							

	UNIT 1		UNIT 2		UNIT 3		UNIT 4		UNIT 5		UNIT 6	
PART	1	2	1	2	1	2	1	2	1	2	1	2
Consider the audience's degree of knowledge in explaining procedures.			●		●				●			●
Provide complete and accurate information in explaining procedures.					●					●		
Use visuals and media to make presentations effective in explaining procedures.		●	●	●	●			●				
Use layout and design elements to enhance presentation of procedure.					●	●			●	●		
Decide upon and use appropriate methods to answer research questions.	●		●	●	●	●	●	●			●	●
Prioritize and organize the information for investigation.		●	●							●		
Incorporate effective media and technology to inform about research.		●	●	●	●	●		●				
Report the research for a specified audience.	●		●			●		●	●	●		●

Critical Reading—Analysis: Students will use critical thinking skills to analyze text structures and develop and support aruguments.

	1	2	1	2	1	2	1	2	1	2	1	2
Examine relevant reasons and evidence in argument.						●			●			
Note the progression of ideas that substantiate the argument proposal.						●			●		●	
Analyze use of language for a particular effect in argument.									●		●	●
Analyze influences, contexts, or biases in argument.					●		●		●			
Identify and analyze rhetorical strategies that support proposals.		●						●				
State clearly a personal view that is logical and coherent.				●						●		
Engage the reader's interest or curiosity through an informed opinion.										●		●
Provide relevant and convincing reasons for an informed opinion.						●						●
Use various types of evidence to support an opinion.	●					●		●				
Use appropriate and effective language, reasons, and structure to express an opinion.	●											
Select, monitor, and modify reading strategies appropriate to argumentative texts.	●				●		●		●			●
Analyze text components and evaluate impact on argumentative text.		●	●									

Standard Course of Study for Language Arts

	Unit 1		Unit 2		Unit 3		Unit 4		Unit 5		Unit 6	
PART	1	2	1	2	1	2	1	2	1	2	1	2
Provide textual evidence to support understanding of response to argumentative text.									•			•
Demonstrate comprehension of main idea and supporting details.				•					•			
Summarize key events and/or points from argumentative text.									•	•		
Make inferences, predict, and draw conclusions based on text.			•		•		•			•		
Identify and analyze influences, contexts, or biases.						•				•		
Make connections between argumentative works, self, and related topics.						•	•					
Analyze author's craft and argument style.	•			•								
Analyze connections between ideas, concepts, characters, and experiences in argumentative text.										•		•
Identify and analyze elements of argument.		•		•								

Critical Reading—Evaluation: Students will use critical thinking skills to evaluate literature and critique communication.

	Unit 1		Unit 2		Unit 3		Unit 4		Unit 5		Unit 6	
	1	2	1	2	1	2	1	2	1	2	1	2
Examine the use of strategies in a presentation to critique communication.											•	•
Apply a set of predetermined standards to critique communication.			•			•					•	
Create standards and apply them to critique presentation/product.			•			•						
Compare effective strategies used in different presentations/products.			•								•	•
Use preparation, engagement, and reflection appropriate to critique text.		•										•
Identify and use standards to critique and evaluate work.			•	•			•					
Judge different stylistic and literary devices in work.	•	•					•					
Select, monitor, and modify reading strategies appropriate to critiquing work.		•			•		•					
Analyze text components and evaluate impact on critiquing text.	•			•								•
Provide textual evidence to support understanding of critical text.			•								•	
Demonstrate comprehension of main idea and supporting details in critiquing communication.			•								•	

Standard Course of Study for Language Arts

	Unit 1		Unit 2		Unit 3		Unit 4		Unit 5		Unit 6	
PART	1	2	1	2	1	2	1	2	1	2	1	2
Summarize key events and/or points from text when critiquing communication.					●				●			
Make inferences and draw conclusions when critiquing communication.			●									
Identify and analyze influences, contexts, or biases in communication.					●						●	
Make connections between works, self, and related topics in communication.	●									●		
Analyze author's craft and style when critiquing communication.	●				●							
Analyze connections or relationships between ideas, concepts, characters, and experiences when critiquing communication.			●				●					
Analyze elements of critical environment found in text when critiquing communication.										●		●

Literary Analysis: Students will analyze, interpret, and respond to various literary genres.

	Unit 1		Unit 2		Unit 3		Unit 4		Unit 5		Unit 6	
Use reading strategies for preparation, engagement, and reflection.		●	●	●				●				●
Recognize and analyze the characteristics of literary genres.	●	●	●		●	●	●	●	●	●	●	●
Interpret literary devices.		●	●				●	●				●
Understand the importance of tone, mood, diction, and style.	●							●		●		
Explain and interpret archetypal characters, themes, and settings.				●			●	●				
Explain how point of view is developed and its effect on texts.								●	●			●
Determine a character's traits.		●	●		●							
Explain how the writer creates literary elements.	●			●					●	●		
Make thematic connections.						●	●	●				
Understand the importance of cultural and historical impact on texts.	●		●	●				●			●	
Produce responses that follow the conventions of a specific genre.	●	●						●		●		
Select, monitor, and modify appropriate to literary purpose.	●						●		●			
Analyze text components and evaluate impact on literary text.		●							●	●		

Standard Course of Study for Language Arts

	UNIT	1		2		3		4		5		6	
	PART	1	2	1	2	1	2	1	2	1	2	1	2
Provide textual evidence to support understanding of response to literary text.					•				•				•
Demonstrate comprehension of main idea and supporting details in literary texts.		•				•			•		•		
Summarize key events and/or points from literary texts.							•		•	•			
Make inferences and draw conclusions based on literary text.											•		
Analyze influences, contexts, or biases in literary text.		•			•								
Make connections between literary works, self, and related topics.									•				
Analyze and evaluate the effects of author's craft and literary style.					•						•		
Analyze connections between ideas, concepts, characters, and experiences in literary works.					•								•
Analyze elements of literary environment found in text.		•						•					•

Language—Vocabulary, Grammar, Usage, and Mechanics: Students will apply conventions of grammar and language usage.

	UNIT	1		2		3		4		5		6	
	PART	1	2	1	2	1	2	1	2	1	2	1	2
Use varying sentence types purposefully, correctly, and for specific effect.				•		•		•					
Select verb tense to show an appropriate sense of time.				•									
Apply parts of speech to clarify and edit language.		•						•					
Address clarity and style through grammar and usage.			•				•	•				•	•
Analyze the place and role of dialects and standard/nonstandard English.						•			•				
Use vocabulary strategies to discern word meanings.		•	•	•	•	•	•	•	•	•	•	•	•
Avoid fragments, run-ons, and comma splices.									•				
Select correct verbs and agreement.					•								
Use and place modifiers correctly.							•					•	
Edit for spelling and mechanics.			•		•		•	•	•			•	•

Success Tracker™ ONLINE

Catch small problems *before* they become big ones.

How it works:
Success Tracker diagnoses student readiness to learn new skills and benchmarks their progress towards standards mastery.

1 ## AT THE BEGINNING OF EACH UNIT OR PART:
- Students take Diagnostic Tests online.
- Tests measure skills necessary to successfully complete the unit.
- Tests are scored instantly and results trigger one of three levels of remediation:

High Score	=	no remediation required
Medium Score	=	Level B remediation
Low Score	=	Level A remediation

- Success Tracker provides a list of recommended remediation assignments students automatically.

2 ## AT THE END OF EACH UNIT OR PART:
- Students take Benchmark Tests online.
- Tests measure mastery of skills covered in the unit.
- Tests are scored instantly, and a list of "mastered" and "unmastered" skills are reported to the teacher.
- Remediation activities are automatically assigned, based on "unmastered" skills.
- Benchmark re-tests can be assigned online to students by the teacher, if needed.

3 ## AS YOU DOCUMENT ADEQUATE YEARLY PROGRESS (AYP):
Success Tracker's easy-to-use reporting system lets you see at a glance where students may be having trouble mastering standards. These reports give you the kind of data you need make decisions that will positively affect student performance on high-stakes tests.

Welcome to your new classroom.

PRENTICE HALL
LITERATURE

Play It Pretty for the People by Phoebe Beasley (b. 1943) takes its name from the slogan of 1940s jazz band leader and trumpet player Louis Prima. As an artist, a businesswoman, and a community activist, Beasley uses materials that she feels reflect the African American experience. This painting is a mixed media collage, incorporating paint and tissue paper. Beasley has the rare honor of being awarded two Presidential Seals for her artwork.

PENGUIN **EDITION**

Upper Saddle River, New Jersey
Boston, Massachusetts

ISBN 0-13-131717-2

2 3 4 5 6 7 8 9 10   10 09 08 07 06

Cover: *Play It Pretty for the People*, collage, Phoebe Beasley/Omni-Photo Communications, Inc.

ACKNOWLEDGMENTS

Grateful acknowledgment is made to the following for copyrighted material:

American School of Classical Studies at Athens "Bulletin: Excavations in the Athenian Agora Volunteer Program" by Staff from *The American School of Classical Studies at Athens.* Reproduced courtesy of the Trustees of the American School of Classical Studies at Athens.

Arte Público Press "A Voice" by Pat Mora from *Communion.* Copyright © 1991 by Pat Mora. Reprinted with permission of Arte Público Press.

Ballantine Books "New Road Chicken Pies from The Book Lover's Cookbook" by Shaunda Kennedy Wenger and Janet Kay Jensen from *The Book Lover's Cookbook: Recipes Inspired By Celebrated Works Of Literature And The Passages That Feature Them.* Copyright © 2003 by Shaunda Kennedy Wenger and Janet Jensen. All rights reserved.

Elizabeth Barnett, Literary executor for the Edna St. Vincent Millay Society "An Ancient Gesture" by Edna St. Vincent Millay. From *Collected Poems,* HarperCollins. Copyright © 1954, 1982 by Norma Millay Ellis. All rights reserved. Used by permission of Elizabeth Barnett, Literary executor.

Susan Bergholz Literary Services "My English" by Julia Alvarez from *Something To Declare.* Copyright © Julia Alvarez, 1998. Published by Plume, an imprint of Penguin Group (USA), in 1999. From "A Celebration of Grandfathers" by Rudolfo Anaya. Copyright © 1983 by Rudolfo Anaya. First published in *New Mexico Magazine, March 1983.* Reprinted by permission of Susan Bergholz Literary Services, New York. All rights reserved.

Gary L. Blackwood "The Shakespeare Stealer" by Gary L. Blackwood from *The Shakespeare Stealer.* Copyright © 2003 by Gary L. Blackwood. Reprinted with permission of the author.

Brandt & Hochman Literary Agents, Inc. "Sonata For Harp and Bicycle" from *The Green Flash and Other Tales of Horror* by Joan Aiken. Copyright © 1957, 1958, 1959, 1960, 1965, 1968, 1969, 1971 by Joan Aiken. "The Most Dangerous Game" by Richard Connell from *The Most Dangerous Game.* Copyright © 1924 by Richard Connell. Copyright renewed © 1952 by Louise Fox Connell. Reprinted by permission.

The Bukowski Agency "The Jade Peony" by Wayson Choy. Copyright by Wayson Choy 1977. First published in the UBC Alumni Chronicle, Vol. 34, No. 4, Winter 1979. The novel *The Jade Peony,* based on this story, is published in the United States by The Other Press. Used with permission of The Bukowski Agency.

Jonathan Clowes Ltd. on behalf of Andrea Plunket "The Red-headed League" from *The Adventures Of Sherlock Holmes* by Sir Arthur Conan Doyle. Copyright © 1996 Sir Arthur Conan Doyle Copyright Holders. Reprinted by kind permission of Jonathan Clowes Ltd., London, on behalf of Andrea Plunket, the Administrator of the Sir Arthur Conan Doyle Copyrights.

Coffee House Press "Problems With Hurricanes" by Victor Hernandez Cruz, from *Red Beans.* Copyright © 1991 by Victor Hernandez Cruz. Reprinted by permission of Coffee House Press.

Don Congdon Associates, Inc. "The Golden Kite, the Silver Wind" by Ray Bradbury from *Epoch, February 1953.* Copyright © 1953 by Epoch Associates; renewed 1981 by Ray Bradbury. Reprinted by permission of Don Congdon Associates, Inc.

Catherine Costello "There Is No Word for Goodbye" by Mary Tall Mountain from *There Is No Word For Goodbye: Poems By Mary Tall Mountain.* Copyright © 1994 by Tall Mountain Estate. Reprinted with permission of Catherine Costello. All rights reserved.

Curtis Brown, Ltd. "Uncoiling" by Pat Mora, copyright © 1995. First appeared in *Daughters of the Fifth Sun,* published by Riverhead Press. Reprinted by permission of Curtis Brown, Ltd.

The Dial Press/Dell Publishing, a division of Random House, Inc. From "The Giant's House" by Elizabeth McCracken, copyright © 1996 by Elizabeth McCracken. Used by permission of The Dial Press/Dell Publishing, a division of Random House, Inc.

(Continued on page R68, which is hereby considered an extension of this copyright page.)

CONTRIBUTING AUTHORS

The contributing authors guided the direction and philosophy of *Prentice Hall Literature: Penguin Edition.* Working with the development team, they helped build the pedagogical integrity of the program and ensure its relevance for today's teachers and students.

Kevin Feldman

Kevin Feldman, Ed.D., is the Director of Reading and Intervention for the Sonoma County Office of Education and an independent educational consultant. He publishes and provides consultancy and training nationally, focusing upon improving school-wide literacy skills as well as targeted interventions for struggling readers, special needs students, and second language learners. Dr. Feldman is the co-author of the California Special Education Reading Task Force report and the lead program author for the 2002 Prentice Hall secondary language arts program *Timeless Voices, Timeless Themes*. He serves as technical consultant to the California Reading and Literature Project and the CalSTAT State Special Education Improvement Project. Dr. Feldman has taught for nineteen years at the university level in Special Education and Master's level programs for University of California, Riverside, and Sonoma State University.

Dr. Feldman earned his undergraduate degree in Psychology from Washington State University and has a master's degree from UC Riverside in Special Education, Learning Disabilities, and Instructional Design. He has an Ed.D. from the University of San Francisco in Curriculum and Instruction.

Sharon Vaughan

Sharon Vaughn, Ph.D., is the H.E. Hartfelder/The Southland Corporation Regents Professor at the University of Texas and also director of the Vaughn Gross Center for Reading and Language Arts at the University of Texas (VGCRLA). As director of the VGCRLA, she leads more than five major initiatives, including The Central Regional Reading First Technical Assistance Center; the Three-Tier Reading Research Project; a bilingual-biliteracy (English/Spanish) intervention research study; the Grades 1–4 Teacher Reading Academies that have been used for teacher education throughout Texas and the nation; and the creation of online professional development in reading for teachers and other interested professionals.

Dr. Vaughn has published more than ten books and over one hundred research articles. She is Editor in Chief of the *Journal of Learning Disabilities* and serves on the editorial boards of more than ten research journals, including the *Journal of Educational Psychology,* the *American Educational Research Journal,* and the *Journal of Special Education.*

Kate Kinsella

Kate Kinsella, Ed.D., is a teacher educator in the Department of Secondary Education at San Francisco State University. She teaches coursework addressing academic language and literacy development in linguistically and culturally diverse classrooms. Dr. Kinsella maintains secondary classroom involvement by teaching an academic literacy class for adolescent English learners through the University's Step to College Program. She publishes and provides consultancy and training nationally, focusing upon responsible instructional practices that provide second language learners and less proficient readers in Grades 4–12 with the language and literacy skills vital to educational mobility.

Dr. Kinsella is the program author for *Reading in the Content Areas: Strategies for Reading Success,* published by Pearson Learning, and the lead program author for the 2002 Prentice Hall secondary language arts program *Timeless Voices, Timeless Themes.* She is the co-editor of the *CATESOL Journal* (California Association of Teachers of ESL) and serves on the editorial board for the *California Reader.* A former Fulbright scholar, Dr. Kinsella has received numerous awards, including the prestigious Marcus Foster Memorial Reading Award, offered by the California Reading Association in 2002 to a California educator who has made a significant statewide impact on both policy and pedagogy in the area of literacy.

Differentiated Instruction Advisor
Don Deshler

Don Deshler, Ph.D., is the Director of the Center for Research on Learning (CRL) at the University of Kansas. Dr. Deshler's expertise centers on adolescent literacy, learning strategic instruction, and instructional strategies for teaching content area classes to academically diverse classes. He is the author of *Teaching Content to All: Evidence-Based Inclusive Practices in Middle and Secondary Schools,* a text that presents the instructional practices that have been tested and validated through his research at CRL.

Introduce Unit 1

- Draw students' attention to the art-work shown here. **Ask** students: What elements in the painting represent imagination—the world of fiction? What images represent facts—the genre of nonfiction?
- **Answer:** Images of birds, flowers, butterflies, and a fragment of sheet music suggest the world of imagination. The equations, calipers, maps, diagrams, and tape measure suggest the genre of facts.

Instructional Resources

Unit 1 Resources support students in developing and mastering the unit skills and help you assess progress.

▶ **Progress Monitoring** These tests enable you to assess and monitor student progress in each part:
- **Diagnostic test**
- **Benchmark test**

▶ **Vocabulary Warm-ups** Additional vocabulary support, based on Lexile scores of vocabulary words, is provided for each selection.
- **Word List A and Practice A** provide vocabulary-building activities for students reading two grades below level.
- **Word List B and Practice B** provide vocabulary-building activities for students reading one grade below level.

▶ **Reading Warm-ups** Two Reading Warm-ups for each selection provide a context for students to apply newly learned vocabulary. Each Reading Warm-up consists of a short reading passage loosely tied to a theme in the selection. Questions and activities guide students to focus on particular vocabulary items.
- **Reading Warm-up A,** for students reading two grades below level, focuses on the vocabulary items presented in Vocabulary Warm-up A.
- **Reading Warm-up B,** for students reading one grade below level, focuses on the vocabulary items presented in Vocabulary Warm-up B.

▶ **Selection Support** These practice pages are available for each selection:
- **Reading Skills**
- **Literary Analysis**
- **Vocabulary Builder**
- **Support for Writing**
- **Support for Extend Your Learning**
- **Enrichment**

PRENTICE HALL
TeacherEXPRESS™ You may also
Plan · Teach · Assess   access these
resources on TeacherExpress.

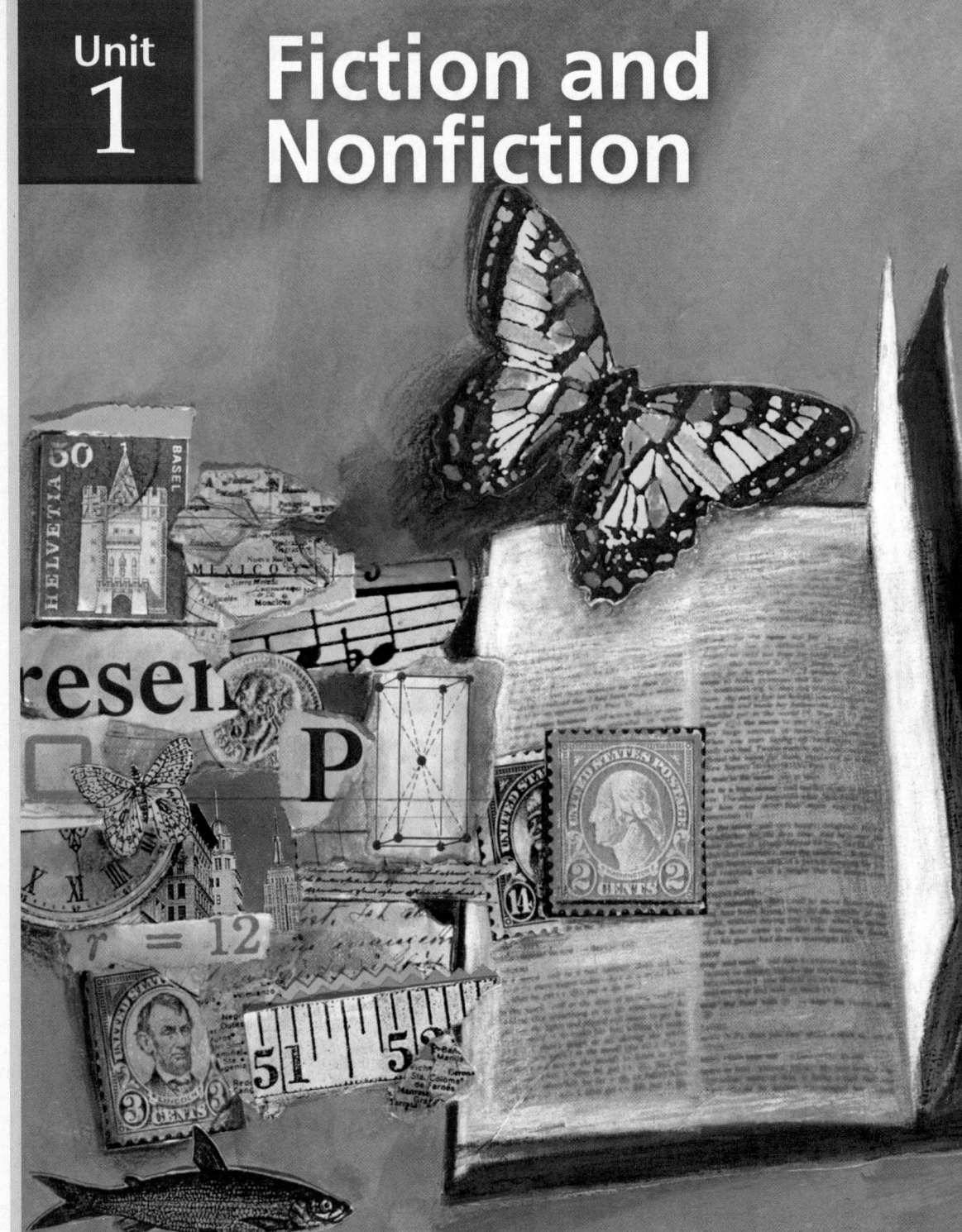

Unit 1
Fiction and Nonfiction

Assessment Resources

Program Assessment

Unit 1 Resources
   Selection Tests A and B

TeacherExpress™
   ExamView® Test Bank
   Software

Adequate Yearly Progress Monitoring Assessment

Unit 1 Resources
   Diagnostic Tests: Part 1, Part 2
   Benchmark Tests: Part 1, Part 2

Standardized Assessment

Standardized Test
   Preparation Workbook

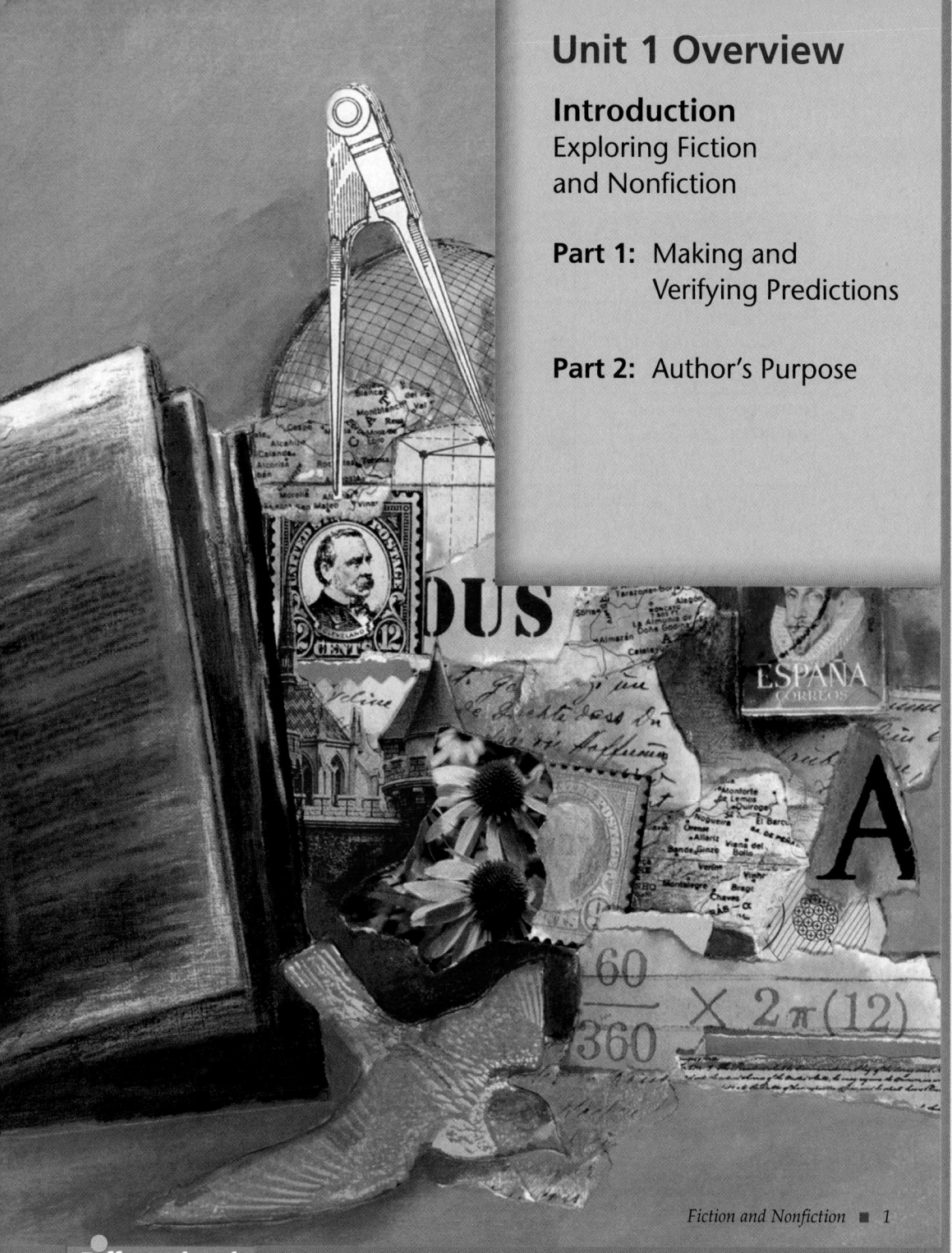

Unit 1 Overview

Introduction
Exploring Fiction
and Nonfiction

Part 1: Making and
Verifying Predictions

Part 2: Author's Purpose

Unit 1 Overview
Genre Focus

Author Elizabeth McCracken introduces the literary genres, fiction and nonfiction, with models of both. Students read and analyze examples of fiction and nonfiction.

Using the Unit Selections

Teach Skills Instructional selections are presented in sets of two. To teach the skills and meet the objectives, you need to complete only one selection in each set.

Differentiate and Reinforce Choose the selection in a set that is best suited to your students. The selections are listed by accessibility in the Differentiated Instruction box below. You may use the other selection in the set to reinforce comprehension and skills or to provide enrichment.

Integrate Skills Each selection set gives students a reading strategy, literary analysis, and vocabulary development as well as opportunities for writing about the selection, research and technology, listening and speaking, grammar, and assessment practice.

See pages 21 and 93 for an overview of the skills in each part.

Using the Unit Features

These additional reading selections give you the opportunity to apply, reinforce, and extend the unit skills.

Reading Informational Materials Students learn to analyze and evaluate informational texts.

Comparing Literary Works Students read a pair of literary works to compare the treatment of a literary element.

On Your Own Students may read this selection independently, or you may teach it actively to reinforce a unit reading skill.

See the Unit 1 Overview and Pacing Plan on the following pages.

Differentiated Instruction   Solutions for All Learners

Accessibility for Ability Levels
This chart gives a general accessibility rating to help you decide which selection is more appropriate for your students. For additional guidance on factors that affect the accessibility of each selection, see the **Time and Resource Manager** for each selection set.

	More Accessible	More Challenging
Part 1		
Set 1	New Directions	The Washwoman
Set 2	Sonata for Harp and Bicycle	Cask of Amontillado
Part 2		
Set 1	*from* A White House Diary	My English
Set 2	The Secret Life of Walter Mitty	Uncle Marcos

1

Unit 1

OVERVIEW AND PACING PLAN

Fiction and Nonfiction

Meeting Your Standards

Students will

1. **recognize and appreciate fiction and non-fiction as literary genres.**
2. **read and analyze a variety of fiction and nonfiction.**
3. **apply reading skills.**
   - Making and verifying predictions
     - Ask questions to make and verify predictions
     - Reading on to verify predictions
   - Author's Purpose
     - Previewing to identify author's purpose
     - Reflecting to determine author's purpose
4. **analyze literary elements.**
   - Narrative essay
   - Plot, conflict, foreshadowing, suspense
   - Author's voice and autobiographical writing
   - Character
5. **build vocabulary.**
   - Word roots
   - Word origins
6. **learn elements of grammar, usage, and style.**
7. **use a recursive writing process to write in a variety of forms.**
   - Autobiographical Narrative
   - Problem-and-Solution Essay
8. **read informational materials.**
   - Read to perform a task
   - Recognizing organizational features on printed text
9. **compare literary works.**
   - First-person and third-person point of view
   - Theme in fiction, nonfiction and poetry
10. **use technology to do research.**
    - Oral presentation
    - Storyboard
    - Multimedia presentation
    - Learning log
11. **develop listening and speaking skills.**
    - Interview
    - Retelling
    - Radio broadcast
    - Scene
12. **develop spelling proficiency.**

Unit Introduction and Part 1	Week 1					Week 2					Week 3				
	①	②	③	④	⑤	①	②	③	④	⑤	①	②	③	④	⑤
Introduce the Unit author: Elizabeth McCracken (p. 2).	●														
Introduce fiction and nonfiction (pp. 2–6).	●														
Teach the Model selections (pp. 7–12, 15–18).	●	●	●												
Administer the Unit 1, Part 1 Diagnostic Test.				●											
Introduce the Reading and Vocabulary Skills for Part 1 (pp. 22–23).				●											
Teach one selection from Set 1 (pp. 26–37).					●	●	●	●	●						
Teach one selection from Set 2 (pp. 48–67).							●	●	●	●					
Teach Reading Informational Materials (pp. 42–44).											●				
Teach Comparing Literary Works (pp. 72–84).												●	●		
Complete the Reading and Vocabulary Review (pp. 86–87).														●	
Have students complete the Writing Workshop (pp. 88–92).											●	●	●	●	●
Administer the Unit 1, Part 1 Benchmark Test.															●

Part 2	Week 1 ①	②	③	④	⑤	Week 2 ①	②	③	④	⑤	Week 3 ①	②	③	④	⑤
Administer the Unit 1, Part 2 Diagnostic Test.	●														
Introduce the Reading and Vocabulary Skills for Part 2 (pp. 94–95).	●														
Teach one selection from Set 1 (pp. 98–113).		●	●	●	●										
Teach one selection from Set 2 (pp. 124–141).						●	●	●	●						
Teach Reading Informational Materials (pp. 118–120).										●					
Teach Comparing Literary Works (pp. 146–156).											●	●			
Complete the Reading and Vocabulary Review (pp. 158–159).												●			
Have students complete the Writing Workshop (pp. 162–169).											●	●	●	●	●
Have students complete the Communications Workshop (p. 170).														●	
Have students complete the Spelling Workshop (pp. 160–161).														●	
Administer the Unit 1, Part 2 Benchmark Test.															●

Options for Block and Daily Scheduling

The assignments and activities in this unit planner are organized by week. You may adjust them to your daily or block schedule. The Time and Resource Managers for the selection sets give specific times to help your planning.

Options for Independent Reading

Use these independent reading options to differentiate, reinforce, and extend your instruction:

On Your Own

Students may read this selection on their own or you may use it to reteach and reinforce unit skills.

Scott McCloud, excerpt from *Understanding Comics*

For Further Reading

Have students choose and read a full-length work while working on this unit.

[L1, L2, EL] Rosa Parks with James Haskins, *Rosa Parks: My Story*

[L2] John Knowles, *A Separate Peace*

[L3] Charles Dickens, *Great Expectations*

[L4] Agatha Christie, *A Pocketful of Rye*

[L4] Authors in Depth

Rachel Carson, from *The Sea Around Us;* from *Always, Rachel;* "An Island I Remember"; from *Under the Sea-Wind*

[L1] Special Needs Students
[L2] Below-Level Students
[L3] All Students
[L4] Above-Level Students
[EL] English Learners

PRENTICE HALL
Teacher **EXPRESS**™
Plan · Teach · Assess Use this complete suite of powerful teaching tools to make lesson planning and testing quicker and easier.

ExamView® QuickTake Monitor student progress instantly.

Introduction
Fiction and Nonfiction

PRETEACH

✓ Meeting Your Standards

Students will

1. understand the characteristics, types, and purposes of fiction and nonfiction.
2. learn about author Elizabeth McCracken.
3. read and analyze an example of fiction and an example of nonfiction.
4. build vocabulary.
5. begin the process of writing an autobiographical narrative.

From the Author's Desk

❶ Introduce Elizabeth McCracken

- *The Giant's House* is former librarian Elizabeth McCracken's first novel. *Granta Magazine* recently named her one of the Best Young American Novelists.

- Use the *From the Author's Desk DVD* to introduce the author and the genre. Show Segment 1 to provide insight into McCracken's attitude toward creating fantastic characters. **Ask:** Why does McCracken like to develop extraordinary characters in her stories? **Answer:** McCracken's fascination with eccentric characters stems from having a family full of strange and eccentric people.

- Interested students might enjoy these works by Elizabeth McCracken. (We recommend that you preview them before recommending them to students.)
  - *Here's Your Hat, What's Your Hurry?*, a collection of short stories
  - *Niagara Falls All Over Again,* a novel about a comedy team

❷ Critical Viewing

Possible responses: Some students may say that it is easier to write fiction because possibilities are limited only by the writer's imagination. Others may say it is easier to write nonfiction because the writer need only discover stories, not make them up.

 From the Author's Desk

Elizabeth McCracken ❶
Talks About the Forms

Elizabeth McCracken

▲ Elizabeth McCracken has written short stories and novels about unusual and unforgettable characters.

This is how I learned the difference between fiction and nonfiction.

On my 15th birthday I walked into the local public library and demanded a job and wonder of wonders they gave me one. Good thing: most of the jobs my friends had (waitress, camp counselor, ice cream scooper) required eye contact and good balance. I had a terrific knowledge of the alphabet, and a need *not* to look people in the eye. In other words, I was a born shelver.

On-the-Job Training ❸

Fiction is prose writing that tells about imaginary characters and events; **nonfiction** is prose writing that presents information and ideas about real people, places, events, or objects.

My beat was Fiction A–SM, which was in the hallway leading from the circulation desk to the reference room. The library building was old and weird and made of lots of little rooms. Books had to be shelved where they could. Fiction SM–Z, for instance, was in the front room. The majority of shelf space was devoted to nonfiction, the way it is in most libraries.

◀ Critical Viewing This image ❷ seems to show a child learning to write. Do you think it is easier to learn to write fiction or nonfiction? Why?

2 ■ *Fiction and Nonfiction*

Teaching Resources

The following resources can be used to enrich, extend, or differentiate the instruction for the Unit Introduction and Model Selections.

Unit 1 Resources, pp. 1–14

General Resources, p. 6

Graphic Organizer Transparencies, pp. 1–2

From the Author's Desk DVD
   Elizabeth McCracken, Segments 1 and 3

Reader's Notebook

Reader's Notebook: Adapted Version

Reader's Notebook: English Learner's
   version

Listening to Literature Audio CD

Adapted Reader's Notebook Audio CD

❹ "Nonfiction was bossy"

At first I wasn't interested in nonfiction. Nonfiction was bossy. Cookbooks, history books, and auto repair manuals told you what happened or they told you what to do. You had to believe it because it was true. How could that compare to my beloved Fiction A–SM? Let's face it: I wasn't even interested in Fiction SM–Z. I shelved novels and short story collections, books with black and white skulls on the spine (mysteries) or yellow and red Young Adult stickers.

I was very slow because I kept stopping to read. Somewhere in there, I decided to write a book myself, a novel that one day would be shelved in Fiction A–SM. The only problem was what to write about: I'd had a dull, happy life.

Fiction is a piece of truth that turns lies to meaning.
from *Skin*
—Dorothy Allison

After a while I got faster, and they gave me an additional section to shelve: New Nonfiction. It turned out that I *liked* history books (the 900s), collections of essays (800s), biographies (shelved according to subject), even cookbooks (600s).

Fictional Characters With Nonfictional Cars

These books made me want to write, too. I could make up characters and then look up what kind of cars they'd drive, what kind of food they'd eat, what kind of clothes they'd wear. Even now, the first thing I do when I start a short story or a novel is to read a nonfiction book on the same subject.

More About Elizabeth McCracken

Elizabeth McCracken (b. 1966), who was a librarian before she became a full-time writer, says she misses working in the library. Her dual identity as novelist and librarian serves her well in her first novel, *The Giant's House* (1996), which depicts a relationship between a librarian and the world's tallest teenager. In explaining her fascination with eccentric characters, she has said, "I believe that most people are extraordinary."

Fast Facts

▶ McCracken was influenced at an early age by "a lot of relatives who were very serious about telling stories."
▶ She confesses that "there are probably more times than I care to admit when I giggle happily at something I've written."

From the Author's Desk: Elizabeth McCracken ■ 3

influenced by the nonfiction research she conducts before she writes.

Go Online **For:** An online video
Author Link **Visit:** www.PHSchool.com
Web Code: epe–8101
Give students this Web code for a video clip of Elizabeth McCracken.

TEACH

❸ Elizabeth McCracken Talks About the Forms
Exploring Fiction and Nonfiction

- Explore students' knowledge of fiction and nonfiction by making connections to what they know. Invite students to give examples of fiction and nonfiction books or stories that they have read.

- **Ask:** How would a nonfiction article about computers be different from a fictional story about computers?
  Possible response: A nonfiction article might tell about the history of computers or describe computers that exist today. A fictional story might tell about something that does not exist, such as a computer that governs an entire country.

- Have students read Elizabeth McCracken's discussion of fiction and nonfiction.

❹ "Nonfiction was bossy"
Discuss the Genres

- **Ask** students to name the categories of fiction and nonfiction McCracken encountered in the library and to list other types of fiction and nonfiction.
  Answer: McCracken mentions novels, short stories, mysteries, and young adult books (all fiction) and history, manuals, essays, biographies, and cookbooks (all nonfiction). Other categories of fiction include science fiction, adventure, and romance. Nonfiction might include textbooks and travel, science, or current events books.

- *Skin* Direct students' attention to the quotation from Dorothy Allison, award-winning novelist and author of short stories, poetry, and essays. *Skin* is a collection of essays on topics including literature. Point out the irony of the quotation to students. **Ask** students to restate the quotation in their own words.
  Possible response: Fiction may be "lies"—made up—but it should contain a larger truth that gives a story meaning.

- Explain to students that although McCracken's stories are fiction, many of the details, such as setting, time period, and clothing, are

3

Exploring Fiction and Nonfiction

❺ Characteristics of Fiction

❺ **Characteristics of Fiction**

- Tell students that many fictional plots focus on one of three kinds of conflict: a character in conflict with another person or persons, a character in conflict with nature, or a character with an internal conflict about an important decision or moral issue. **Ask:** What kinds of stories might result from each of these three types of plots?
Possible response: A story about an argument or a war would be an example of people in conflict with one another. An adventure story of a person trying to survive an earthquake would be a plot based on conflict with nature. A story about a person who feels guilt over a misdeed would be a story based on an internal conflict.

- Point out to students the statement that says the narrator, or point-of-view character, may or may not be part of the story. Tell students that in the excerpt from *The Giant's House* that they are about to read, the narrator appears in the story but is not the main character. Ask them to notice as they read which character is the narrator and which character the story is mostly about.

All works of fiction, no matter how long, short, simple, or complex, share certain elements.

- Fiction features **characters,** invented people who experience a series of events, called the **plot.** Characters always face a **conflict,** or problem, that sets the plot in motion.
- It occurs in a time and place, or **setting.** The setting may be real or imaginary.
- Fiction is told, or narrated, from the **point of view** of a character who may or may not be part of the story.
- It includes a **theme,** a message or an insight about life.

❻ Types of Fiction

❻ **Types of Fiction**

- Explain to students that the difference between a short story and a novel is like the difference between a simple one-act play and a complex five-act Shakespearean play.

- Explore student's knowledge of different types of fiction. Ask students to name examples of novels, novellas, and short stories that they have read.

Works of fiction can be categorized by length and complexity.

- A **novel** is a long work of fiction that is usually presented in segments called **chapters.** Novels often feature several characters, take place in multiple settings, and concern more than one conflict. In addition to the main plot, a novel may contain subplots, or separate, related stories.
- A **novella** is a work of fiction that is longer than a short story but shorter than a novel.
- A **short story** is a work of fiction that is brief enough to be read in one sitting. Short stories usually focus on one main plot that is driven by a single conflict.

❼ Critical Viewing

Possible response: The anonymous stack of closed books reveals nothing of the imaginative worlds the books contain.

▶ Critical Viewing How does
❼ the physical appearance of these books compare to the imaginative possibilities they hold? [**Compare and Contrast**]

⑧ Characteristics of Nonfiction

Works of nonfiction differ from works of fiction in several ways.

* The people, events, places, and ideas presented in nonfiction are real, not invented.
* Nonfiction is narrated by an author who is a real person.
* It presents facts, describes true-life experiences, or discusses ideas.
* Nonfiction is written for a specific **audience,** or group of readers. In addition, it addresses a clear **purpose,** or reason for writing. The audience and purpose influence the type of information a writer includes.
* **Tone,** the author's attitude toward the subject or reader, is displayed through the writer's word choice and style.

⑨ Types of Nonfiction

There are four main types, or modes, of nonfiction that are defined by their purposes.

* **Narrative** nonfiction tells stories of real-life events. Examples include autobiographies and memoirs. Some narrative nonfiction is **reflective writing,** which shares the writer's thoughts and feelings about a personal experience, an idea, or a concern. Examples include reflective essays, personal essays, and journals.
* **Expository** nonfiction informs or explains. Examples include analytical essays and research reports.
* **Persuasive** nonfiction presents reasons and evidence to convince the reader to act or think in a certain way. Examples include editorials and political speeches.
* **Descriptive** nonfiction uses details related to the senses to create mental images for the reader. Examples include character sketches and scientific observations.

Check Your Understanding

For each of the following items, indicate whether the literary work being described is more likely fiction or nonfiction. Explain your response.

1. a book about the training routine of a champion athlete
2. a politician's memories of her childhood
3. a story set on another planet in the distant future
4. an essay about a social issue

Exploring Fiction and Nonfiction ■ 5

From the Author's Desk

❶ Introduce the Selection

- Invite students to read Elizabeth McCracken's introduction to the story.

- Call students' attention to the fact that the idea for this piece of fiction evolved from a photograph of a real person: Robert Wadlow, the world's tallest man.

❷ Background

Exceptional People People who are different from the norm—especially those who are visibly, physically different—are sometimes feared, hated, or shunned. While many people struggle to fit into society, physically exceptional people face the problem at its most challenging.

❸ Connecting to the Literature

- Ask students to think about stories or movies they are familiar with that deal with a person who tries to fit in or gain acceptance in a group or community. Have them write several sentences about the plot or characters in these works.

- To develop expressive vocabulary, tell students to use at least three of the following words: *adapt, external, individual, vary.*

- To help students understand the meanings of the words they are asked to use, give them these sentences:

  1. Each *individual* brings his or her own gifts to a community.

  2. Sometimes people must *adapt* to the expectations and traditions of a community.

  3. People *vary* in the ways they react to others' differences.

  4. *External* appearances reveal very little about a person's personality.

- To further develop students' expressive vocabulary, suggest that they also use the following words in discussing the selection: *accommodate, conform, participate, significant, unique.*

Model Selection:
Fiction

From the Author's Desk
Elizabeth McCracken Introduces the excerpt from *The Giant's House*

My fiction often starts with a photograph: I stare, I get obsessed, I start to make things up.

Inspired by *The Guinness Book of World Records*

My favorite book when I was a kid was *The Guinness Book of World Records,* and every year the same picture appeared in the front: the world's tallest man, Robert Pershing Wadlow, who grew to be 8'11". The picture showed him with his father and little brother; Robert Wadlow's hair brushed the ceiling of their house.

Other than being enormous, he was ordinary looking. He wore glasses and a suit. His ears stuck out a little. There was a little chart of his ages and heights. For instance, when he was in kindergarten he was more than six feet tall.

Maybe that picture meant something to me because I was always the shortest kid in school, and that seemed something like being the tallest, but mostly I liked how ordinary it was. If you were that tall, you'd have to work hard to be ordinary. People wouldn't want to let you be normal. No matter what your real personality was, all people would see would be *tall*. They'd keep telling you that you *weren't* normal, and soon you might think the same thing.

My Main Characters and Their Conflicts

I did a little research on Robert Wadlow when I started *The Giant's House,* but mostly I wanted to make things up, to get to know *my* **characters**: James Carlson Sweatt, the World's Tallest Man, and the people who knew him.

I decided to tell the story from the **point of view** of Peggy, the town librarian, because I needed someone who would always be struggling to see both sides of James—the enormous body that needed a lot of help to get through the ordinary-sized world, and the regular, teenaged-sized personality that needed conversation and music and company.

That's the narrator's **conflict** in the book, just as James's struggle is simply to live as best as he can, considering his size.

6 ■ Fiction and Nonfiction

Vocabulary Development

Vocabulary Knowledge Rating
Create a **Vocabulary Knowledge Rating Chart** with these words from the selection:

   elusive   *pertinent*

Give students a copy. Introduce the words by reading them aloud and having students mark their rating in the Before Reading column. Urge them to be alert to these words as they read and discuss the selection, because they will rate their knowledge of the words again after they finish.

If you wish, you may tally how many students know (or think they know) a word to gauge how much instruction you need to provide. As students read, point out the words and their context.

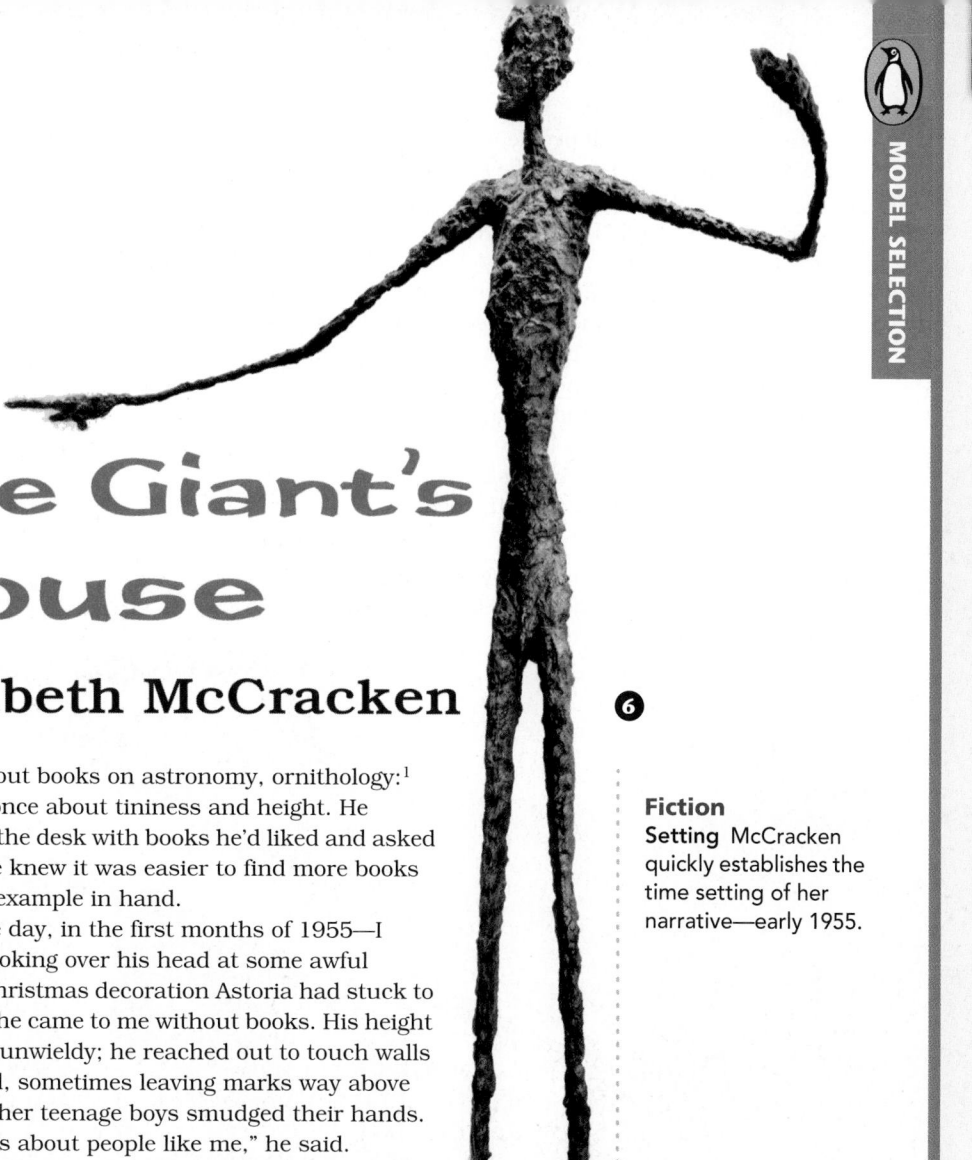

from

❹ ❺ The Giant's House

Elizabeth McCracken

James took out books on astronomy, ornithology:[1] sciences at once about tininess and height. He approached the desk with books he'd liked and asked for more—he knew it was easier to find more books with a good example in hand.

❼ Then one day, in the first months of 1955—I remember looking over his head at some awful persistent Christmas decoration Astoria had stuck to the ceiling—he came to me without books. His height had become unwieldy; he reached out to touch walls as he walked, sometimes leaving marks way above where the other teenage boys smudged their hands. "I want books about people like me," he said.

I thought I knew what he was talking about, but I wanted to be cautious. "What exactly about you?" I asked. I made myself think of all the things he could have meant: Boy Scouts, basketball players. Never jump to conclusions when trying to answer a reference question. Interview the patron.

---

1. **astronomy, ornithology** Astronomy is the study of the stars and planets. Ornithology is the study of birds.

❻
Fiction
Setting McCracken quickly establishes the time setting of her narrative—early 1955.

❽ ✓ **Reading Check**
What kind of books does James ask the librarian to find?

The Giant's House ■ 7

MODEL SELECTION

TEACH

❹ Motivation
Ask students to discuss whether it is preferable to fit in with a group or to stand out from others. Challenge students to give reasons for their opinions.

Concept Connector ➡
Students will return to these discussion points when they have completed their reading of this selection.

❺ About the Selection
Aware of his physical differences, James searches for other people like him and for ways that he can be like other people. The town librarian tries to help him in his quest and observes the growth of his character and understanding.

❻ Humanities
Man Pointing, 1947, by Alberto Giacometti
Alberto Giacometti, a Swiss sculptor and painter who gained fame in the late 1930s through the 1940s, created objects that illustrated a direct relationship to the surrounding space. Use this question for discussion:

• What does the figure's shape and posture suggest about it?
Possible response: The figure is very tall and straight, which makes it seem dramatic or proud. It is pointing forward, which suggests looking toward the future.

❼ Fiction
Setting
• Point out to students that Elizabeth McCracken tells readers when the story takes place, rather than letting them infer it from details.
• Discuss with students why it might be important that the action of the story takes place in 1955.
Possible response: The story may concern issues that were thought of differently in 1955 than they are today.

❽ Reading Check
Answer: James asks the librarian to find books about people like him.

Differentiated Instruction Solutions for All Learners

Support for Special Needs Students
Have students read the adapted version of the excerpt from *The Giant's House* in the **Reader's Notebook: Adapted Version.** They may also listen to the adapted version on the **Reader's Notebook: Adapted Version Audio CD.**

Support for Less Proficient Readers
Have students read the excerpt from *The Giant's House* in the **Reader's Notebook.** After students finish the selection in the *Reader's Notebook,* have them complete the questions and activities in the Student Edition.

Support for English Learners
Have students read the excerpt from *The Giant's House* in the **Reader's Notebook: English Learner's Version.** English learners may also read the selection as they listen to the recorded version on the **Listening to Literature Audio CD.**

7

- Point out that the mention of a card catalog is another clue to the reader that the story does not take place in modern times.

- **Ask** students in what ways computerized library catalogs are superior to older ones that used actual cards.
  Answer: Computerized library catalogs are faster and easier for most people to use. The links that computer catalogs provide make it possible to expand or narrow a search easily. A computer catalog may even suggest alternate search terms.

- Invite students to **speculate** why a person might prefer the older, less efficient version of a library catalog.
  Possible response: A person might prefer the familiarity of the system he or she first learned to use.

10 **Critical Viewing**

Possible response: Students may say that the library in the photograph seems like a "small-town" place because the building is smaller and more old-fashioned than a library in a large urban area would probably be.

"Tall people," he said.

"Tall people? Just tall people in general?"

"Very tall people. Like *me*," he said, clearly exasperated with my playing dumb. "What they do."

"Okay," I told him. "Try the card catalog. Look in the big books on the table—see those books?" I pointed. "Those are books of subject headings for the card catalog. Look under words that you think describe your topic." James was used to me doing this: I gave directions but would not pull the books off the shelf for him. My job was to show people—even people I liked—how to use the library, not to use it for them. "Dig around," I said. "Try height, try stature. Then look in the catalog for books."

He nodded, leaned on the desk, and pushed off.

An hour later he headed out the door.

10 ▼ **Critical Viewing** Does this library seem like the "small-town" place Peggy describes on page 9? Explain. **[Connect]**

9 *Elizabeth McCracken*
Author's Insight
Card catalogs have been replaced by computer catalogs. I miss them, even though computers are more efficient in almost every way.

8 ■ *Fiction and Nonfiction*

Vocabulary Development

Think Aloud: Context

Direct students' attention to the word *stature* on this page. Using a think-aloud process, model how to use context to infer the meaning of an unknown word. Say to students:

I'm going to think aloud to show you how I figure out the meaning of *stature* from its context.

James is looking for information about people like him. The librarian suggests that he search using the word *stature*.

We know that the most unusual thing about James is that he is so tall. He is likely to be looking for information about people who are tall. *Stature* may have something to do with being tall. Peggy also tells James to search using the term *height*. So I think the word *stature* refers to a person's or thing's tallness or height.

"Did you find what you needed?" I asked.

"There isn't anything," he said. "There was one book that sort of was about it, but I couldn't find it on the shelf."

"There's something," I told him. "Come back. We'll look for it together."

That night after closing, I hunted around myself. The only thing under *stature* was a book about growth and nutrition. I tried our two encyclopedias under height and found passing references. Not much.

In truth, my library was a small-town place, and this was a specialized topic. Still, I was certain I could find more. I got that familiar mania—there is information somewhere here, and I can find it, I have to. A good librarian is not so different from a prospector, her whole brain a divining rod. She walks to books and stands and wonders: here? Is the answer here? The same blind faith in finding, even when hopeless. If someone caught me when I was in the throes of tracking something <u>elusive</u>, I would have told them: but it's out there. I can feel it. God *wants* me to find it.

That night I wandered the reference department, eyed the bindings of the encyclopedias, dictionaries, atlases. James was so big I almost expected to locate him in the gazetteer.[2] I set my hands upon our little card catalog, curled my fingers in the curved handles of the drawers. Then I went to the big volumes of subject headings.

Looking under *height* and *stature* turned up nothing; *anthropometry* was not quite right. Then I realized the word I was looking for: *Giant.*

Giant described him. *Giant,* I knew, would lead me to countless things—not just the word, located in indexes and catalogs and encyclopedias, but the idea of Giant, the knowledge that the people that James wanted to read about, people who could be described as like him, were not just tall but giants. I sat in a spindle-backed chair in the reference room, waiting for a minute. Then I checked the volume of the Library of Congress headings. *Giants. See also: dwarfs.*

We did not have a book, but I found several encyclopedia entries. Nowadays I could just photocopy; but that night I wrote down the page and volume numbers, thinking I could not bear to tell him the word to look under. Most of the very tall people mentioned in the encyclopedia had worked in the circus as professional giants, so I went to our books on the circus.

The photographs showed enormous people. Not just tall, though of course they were that, often with an ordinary person posed

---

2. **gazetteer** (gaz′ ə tir′) *n.* dictionary or index of geographical names.

Vocabulary Builder
elusive (ē loo′
siv) *adj.* hard to grasp
or retain mentally

⓫ *Elizabeth McCracken*
Author's Insight
I love the word *anthropometry,* which means the measuring of human beings.

⓬ ✓Reading Check
What word does the librarian use to direct her search?

from *The Giant's House* ■ 9

⓫ Author's Insight
• Elizabeth McCracken defines the word *anthropometry* as "the measuring of human beings." **Ask** students what kind of person might use the word *anthropometry.*
Answer: *Anthropometry* is similar to scientific terms such as anthropology and geometry. It would probably be used by a scientist.

• Tell students that in the nineteenth and early twentieth centuries, anthropometry was considered very important. Some scientists believed that measurements of a person's head could reveal important aspects of their intelligence and character.

• **Ask** students whether a person's physical appearance reveals anything about that person's character. **Possible responses:** Some students may say that physical features reveal nothing about what a person is like. Other students might say that a physical feature such as large muscles might reveal that a person believes exercise or health is important.

⓬ Reading Check
Answer: The librarian uses the term "giant" to direct her search.

Differentiated
Instruction   Solutions for All Learners

Strategy for Special Needs Students
Help students understand why the librarian does not want to tell James to search for books using the word *giant.* Ask students to list words that they associate with the word and to describe giants they have heard about in stories such as "Jack and the Beanstalk." Their lists will likely include words such as *clumsy, mean, angry, stupid,* and *destructive.* Emphasize that Peggy hesitates to use the word with James because he might also have these negative associations.

Strategy for Advanced Readers
Point out this sentence: "A good librarian is not so different from a prospector, her whole brain a divining rod." Have students identify what figure of speech the author is using. They should realize that the phrase "not so different from" is equivalent to "like," and therefore the sentence contains a simile. Then, invite students to create their own similes to describe the qualities and duties of a librarian.

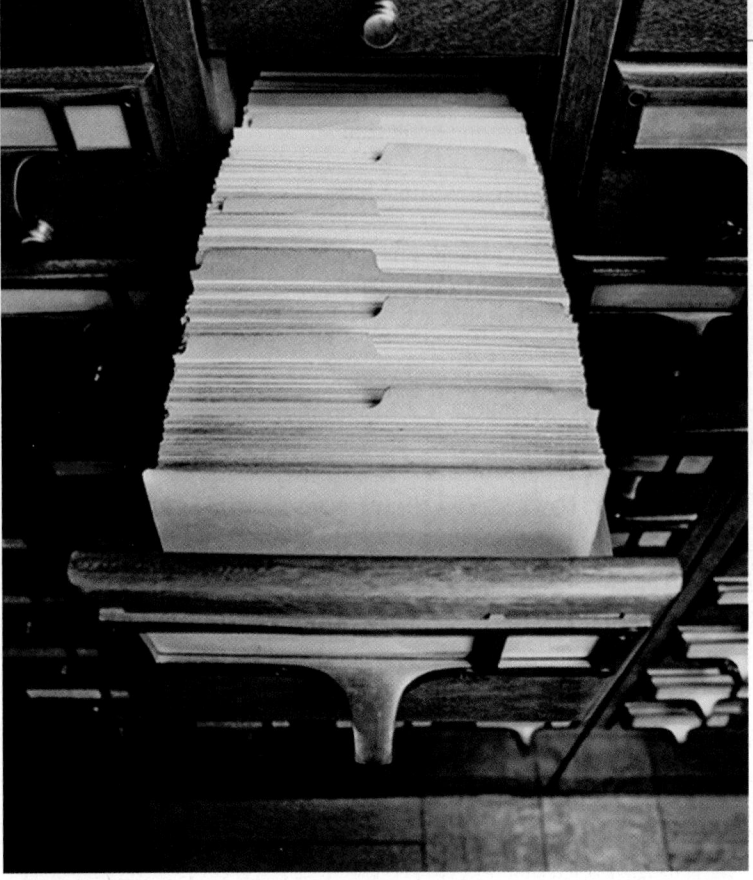

beside them. The tall people looked twice as big as the ambassador from the normal-sized, as if they were an entirely different race. The books described weak stomachs and legs and bones. Sometimes what made them tall showed in their faces: each feature looked like something disturbed in an avalanche, separate from the others, in danger of slipping off.

Anna Swann, the Nova Scotia Giantess, married Captain Bates, the Kentucky Giant. As a young woman at Barnum's Dime Museum in New York, Miss Swann had been in two fires; in the second she had to be lifted out by a crane. No ordinary over-the-shoulder rescue for a woman better than seven feet tall. She and her husband retired to Ohio, to a specially made house. Their church installed an extra-large pew.

Byrne, the Irish Giant, lived in fear of a certain doctor who lusted after his skeleton; he imagined the doctor's giant kettle ready to boil his bones.

10 ■ *Fiction and Nonfiction*

10

14 Jack Earle was over seven feet tall, traveled with the circus for years; after his retirement he wrote poetry.

I took comfort in Anna Swann and her husband. They were solid-looking people. Respectable. They'd had two children, though neither survived. The book described them as *in love*, and you could believe that from the pictures: their complementary heights were just a lovely coincidence to their love affair. I found myself that late night a little jealous of Anna Swann and her handsome, bearded captain.

The books said that giants tended to exaggerate their heights for exhibition purposes. I did not know it then, but every person I read about was shorter than James grew to be.

The worst book was called *Medical Curiosities*. I say worst now. That is hindsight. The night I looked, I thought, in fact, that it was the best book—not because it was good or even accurate, but because it had the most pages on the subject I was researching. I found it under the subject heading *Abnormalities, human*. A terrible phrase, and one I knew I could not repeat to James. It was a late-nineteenth-century medical book, described two-headed people and parasitic twins and dwarfs. And giants. Not exactly information, but interesting: giants who had enormous or usual appetites; ones who grew throughout their lives or only after adolescence; professional giants and private citizens.

So I took that book, and the circus books, marked the <u>pertinent</u> places with the old catalog cards I used for scrap, and set them aside. Ready for him, so that he did not have to look in the index, or wander through the pages at all.

"Your tall friend is here," Astoria said to me the next week. I was in my office, reading reviews. "He's looking for you."

James waited for me at the circ desk. "You said we could—"

"I looked," I said. I'd stowed the books beneath the shelf. "Try these out."

He took them to the big table in the front room. Read them.

15 **Elizabeth McCracken**
Author's Insight
I can't remember whether I've seen this book or I made it up. There are definitely books with this title, but did I have one in mind? Who knows!

Vocabulary Builder
pertinent (pʉrt´'n ənt)
adj. relevant; having a connection to the matter at hand

16
Reading Check
Under what subject heading does the librarian finally find information that will be useful to James?

from The Giant's House ■ 11

15 Author's Insight

• Explain to students that books with titles like *Medical Curiosities* do exist. **Ask:** Why do you think Elizabeth McCracken described this book in such detail?
Possible response: McCracken may have described the book to inform readers about how people like James were viewed in the past.

• Point out that the librarian changes her mind about the medical curiosities book. At first she thinks it is the best book that she has found on the subject of giants. Later, she says the same book was the worst. **Ask** students why Peggy's opinion of the book changes so drastically.
Possible response: At first, Peggy thinks it is the best book because it contains the most information about giants. Later she realizes that it is the worst book because it uses "terrible" phrases like "human abnormalities" and presents people who are different as oddities rather than individuals.

• **Ask** students: What do you think James's reaction will be to this book?
Possible responses: Students may say that James will be glad to find a book that discusses people like him. Other students may say that he will be hurt by the book's insensitivity.

16 Reading Check

Answer: The librarian finds useful information under the heading "Abnormalities, human."

Differentiated Instruction   Solutions for All Learners

Strategy for Less Proficient Readers
In order to make the stories, characters, and setting vivid for the reader, McCracken included many details in the novel. Suggest that students skim through the excerpt and highlight or make notes on only the action that is taking place. Explain to students that these notes will help them follow the plot and define the conflict. After students have outlined the plot and determined the conflict, have them reread the excerpt with more attention to the details. Tell them that the details will reveal more about the characters and their motivations.

Enrichment for Advanced Readers
Introduce the concept of foreshadowing. Explain that authors will often include details in a story that do not relate directly to the action at that point in the plot, but suggest what might happen later. The use of foreshadowing is especially common in longer works such as novels. Ask students to discuss passages in this excerpt from *The Giant's House* that might foreshadow events that will occur later in the novel. For example, what might the story about Anna Swann foreshadow?

Plot

- **Ask:** What does this passage reveal about James's feelings about his height?
  Answer: The discussion between librarian and student reveals that James is unhappy about being so tall. He is looking for a way to cure his condition, which he would not do if he felt good about his height.

- Explore with students which of the three types of conflict James appears to be having. Emphasize to students that at this point in the story it is difficult to tell. The plot might turn out to be James against other people if his schoolmates reject him. The plot might emphasize James's struggle against nature in the form of his medical condition. James might also be in conflict with himself because he may feel ashamed of this height.

18 Author's Insight

- **Ask** students why they think McCracken mentions the detail about James's interest in cards and magic tricks.
  Possible responses: Some students may say that the detail about learning magic tricks shows that James is interested in the same subjects as other boys his age. It is also possible that James wants to learn magic tricks so that he will be special for something other than his height.

- **Ask:** What is "magical" about the information that James is seeking?
  Answer: James is looking for a cure that will magically make him more like everybody else. It would take magic to make him the same size as other people because no cure for his condition exists.

Concept Connector

Have students review their discussion on the advantages and disadvantages of fitting in with or standing out from a crowd. Then have them discuss James's possible conflicts with these comments in mind. Encourage students to speculate about what James might learn about himself and others as the novel continues.

He made the sturdy chair, the same chair I'd sat in the night before, seem tiny.

Afterward he came up to me.

"How were they?" I asked. "Would you like to take them home?"

He shook his head.

"No," he said. "Thanks."

"Nothing useful here at all?"

"No," he said.

I tried to catch his eye. "Close?"

"Close. I guess." He pointed at *Medical Curiosities*. "I guess that's close."

I picked up the book and opened it to where the marker was, but he'd moved it to another page. A line drawing of a double-bodied baby looked up at me. Horrible. I snapped the book shut.

"I meant medical books," he said. "But new ones. Ones that say what goes wrong. How to cure it."

"Cures," I said. "Oh." Cures for giants? No such thing. No cure for height. Only preventive medicine. I said it as a question. "Cures? For tall people?"

"Yes," he said.

All I wanted was for him to explain it to me. It seemed presumptuous to come to any conclusions myself. I knew what he was talking about. I did. But what he wanted, I couldn't help him with.

Darla, the shelver, came rattling up with her metal cart. "Shelve these?" she said, pointing at the books. The catalog cards I'd used stuck out from the pages; James had lined them up, like a pack of cards he'd shuffled into them. "Hi, Jim," she said.

"Hi." He squinted down at her.

She stared at me; I waited for her to get back to shelving.

"Peggy. Shelve them, or not?"

"Not yet," I said. She sighed and pushed the cart off.

James stood in silence on the other side of the desk. He looked ready to leave.

"You mean how to stop growing," I said.

"Yes." Now he looked at me. "Medicine, or operations, or something."

"I'm not sure we have anything here," I said. That was a lie. I knew we didn't. "A medical library somewhere, perhaps. Or a university library. But really—" I started pulling the bookmarks from the books. I tried to sound gentle. "Really, you should ask your doctor."

"I have," he said. "I've asked a lot of doctors."

17 Fiction
Plot Peggy's attempts at research finally cause James to reveal his real quest.

18 Elizabeth McCracken
Author's Insight Earlier in the book, James comes to the library to learn how to do card and other magic tricks.

Vocabulary Development

Vocabulary Knowledge Rating
When students have completed reading and discussing the excerpt from *The Giant's House,* have them take out their **Vocabulary Rating Chart** for this selection. Read the words aloud once more and have students rate their knowledge of the words again in the After Reading column. Clarify any words that are still problematic. Have students write their own definitions or examples in the appropriate column. Encourage students to use the words in further discussion and written work about this selection. Remind them that they will be accountable for these words on the Selection Test.

19 Q. How did you decide on the details to suggest James's height, such as his reaching "out to touch walls as he walked"?

A. I had a brown paper, life-sized cutout of James on a wall of my apartment while I wrote *The Giant's House.* When I wanted to really think about what it would mean to be that tall, I got out of my chair and stood next to it. It was a very strange experience: My head came up to his waist. Most of the details came out of that.

20 Q. To what extent is the narrator acting as more than a helpful librarian?

A. Peggy is a good person, and a good librarian, but she's also lonely, needy, grasping. She needs every patron desperately, and James most of all. To get close to people she tries to be extra-helpful.

21 Q. Did you want the failure of James's library search to be symbolic?

A. I wanted to demonstrate to two characters who believed that books could solve all problems that even books can fall short, and you have to look for answers from actual people—which is, I guess, symbolic!

Student Corner

22 Q. Why didn't you use James as a narrator? Wouldn't he be more effective in conveying his own thoughts?
—Maria Seger, Bethel Park, Pennsylvania

A. One of the things I was interested in when I started the book was how who James was physically changed the people around him. Some people would be able to ignore his height and see the person inside, and others wouldn't. I didn't think I could do that in his voice. Then, once I found Peggy's voice, I got as interested in *her* thoughts as I was in his.

▨ Writing Workshop: *Work in Progress*

Autobiographical Narrative
For an autobiographical narrative you may write, list three vivid memories. Describe the visual picture you see in your mind for each of these memories. Save this Memory List in your writing portfolio.

Differentiated Instruction   Solutions for All Learners

Enrichment for Gifted/Talented Students
Suggest that students make a life-sized (8' 11") paper cutout of James and stand beside it as Elizabeth McCracken did when writing *The Giant's House.* Have students write a script for a conversation they imagine having with a person that size the first time they met. You might also suggest that students write the dialogue as if they are visiting a planet on which all the inhabitants are as tall as the paper cutout.

Strategy for Advanced Readers
To explore further how point of view affects what readers know, have students rewrite the interactions between James and Peggy with James as the narrator. Remind students that the narrator can reveal his own thoughts and feelings, but can only speculate about another person's, or infer them from that person's words or actions. Then, have students discuss how their revised versions of the scenes differ from McCracken's original versions.

Elizabeth McCracken's Insights

- Tell students that Elizabeth McCracken is frequently asked questions like these about her work. Her answers provide insight into decisions that a writer makes which create meaning in a story.

- In her comments, McCracken addresses the topics of problems or conflicts and point of view. Have students review these terms on p. 4.

19 In this answer, McCracken tells how she discovered details that would suggest James's height. **Ask** students what other details McCracken might have used to suggest the character's height.
Possible response: McCracken might have described how James looked standing next to an ordinary object such as a chair or doorway.

20 After students read this question and answer, **ask** them which of Peggy's actions show that she tries to be extra-helpful.
Possible response: Peggy tries to be extra-helpful to James by trying not to use or let him see words that might hurt him.

21 After students read this question and answer, **ask** them how the failure of the library search adds to the conflict in the story.
Possible response: The failure of the library search leaves the conflict unresolved. Peggy now knows what James's internal conflict is and this may help her think of ways to help him.

22 In this answer, McCracken discusses why the narrator is not the main character in the story. **Ask** students how Peggy's point of view helps readers better understand the story.
Possible response: Readers can share Peggy's feelings and insights as she learns about James and his unusual problems.

▨ Writing Workshop
Work in Progress

In the Work-in-Progress assignments through Part 1, students will complete activities that prepare them for the Writing Workshop on autobiographical narrative on pp. 88–92. Work with students on this brief prewriting activity. Have them save their work in their portfolios for later use.

㉓ Nonfiction

- Have students read Elizabeth McCracken's introduction to this nonfiction piece.

- Call students' attention to the terms used in discussing nonfiction: personal essay, informal tone, audience, purpose.

- Ask students to identify these elements in "Desiderata" as they read.

㉔ Background

Family History Studying genealogy, or family history and lineage, has gone from a hobby pursued by those related to nobility to an interest shared by many families. Intergenerational oral history projects and family heritage Web sites are just two of the modern manifestations of this new-found interest in the past.

㉕ Connecting to the Literature

- Ask students to write a few sentences about family stories that they would like to preserve or objects that remind them of a particular relative. Tell them to use at least three of the following words: *appreciate, correspond, enrich, generation.*

- To help students understand the meanings of the words they are asked to use, give them these sentences:

  1. If I could *correspond* with my ancestors, I would ask them about their hopes and dreams.

  2. Their stories would *enrich* my connection with the past.

  3. Many people in my *generation* don't take the time to learn about their ancestors.

  4. I think they would better *appreciate* their families if they learned about the history of other members.

- To further develop students' expressive vocabulary, suggest that they also use the following words in discussing the selection: *eloquent, rural, similar, comprehend, immigrate, prosper.*

Concept Connector ➤

Students will follow up on this activity after completing this essay.

 From the Author's Desk
Elizabeth McCracken Introduces "Desiderata"

㉔ ㉕

I write fiction naturally, but most of my nonfiction comes out of an assignment. In the case of "Desiderata," someone at my publishing house was putting together a Web site and asked me to write a **personal essay**, with an **informal tone**. My **audience**, of course, would be anyone who visited the site, and my **purpose** was to make them want to read my novel *The Giant's House.*

How to Find Subjects for Writing: Be a Snoop!

Personally, I find myself boring, but other people interest me. In other words, I'm a snoop. I like to read through other people's mail, flip through other people's photo albums, eavesdrop on other people's phone conversations. Best of all: my family's mail, my family's conversations.

I'm the youngest in my family, and it shows: I'm a bratty kid sister, always sneaking in places, always wondering what happened before I showed up. My parents were married for thirteen years before I was born! My brother was alive for two and a half years! No fair! I want to know everything, and what I don't know I'll make up.

Finding Inspiration in a Shopping List

I couldn't figure out exactly what to write about for the Web site until I looked at my grandmother's shopping list, which was taped to my computer screen. So that's what I decided to write about.

My nosiness is probably what made me a writer. I was lucky enough to have been born into a family of sentimental packrats, and before I could even read, my relatives were showing me photographs and telling me stories. I liked to hear *The Little Engine That Could,* but even better I liked to hear the story of my mother and her twin sister and their first exchange of birthday presents. They gave each other an American flag and a balloon on a stick.

The essay itself was my way of getting all that ephemera—stuff that's doomed to disappear or degrade, things that were never meant to last—in some kind of order.

Vocabulary Development

Vocabulary Knowledge Rating

Create a **Vocabulary Knowledge Rating Chart** with this word from the selection:

   vindictive

Give students a copy. Introduce the word by reading it aloud and having students mark their rating in the Before Reading column. Urge them to be alert to this word as they read and discuss the selection, because they will rate their knowledge of the word again after they finish.

If you wish, you may tally how many students know (or think they know) the word to gauge how much instruction you need to provide. As students read, point out the word and its context.

DESIDERATA

Elizabeth McCracken

㉖ ㉗

Desiderata, I learned in library science school, were the items you needed for an archive to make it useful. Useful, not complete, because there is no such thing as a complete archive. There's always a letter out there you want and need, either in someone else's collection or in an attic or just unfound. You need and want things you don't even know exist. That's how collections work.

I come from a family strong on documents. I have a small archive myself. My grandfather McCracken was a genealogist—I have his history of the McCrackens, a lovely compilation of research on early ancestors and personal remembrances of his own relatives. His wife, my grandmother, wrote stories and poems; I have copies of those, and remember once opening a drawer full of letters she wrote to God, part prayer and part daily correspondence to Someone dear. I have my grandmother Jacobson's collection of family letters; she had 11 brothers and sisters, some who wrote often and some just now and then. I have diplomas of relatives I never met. I have diaries and laundry lists. I love anything written by a relative, any evidence of what they really thought.

㉘ Elizabeth McCracken
Author's Insight
The minute I heard the word "desiderata" I knew I would try to use it in my writing. It appears in *The Giant's House*, too.

㉙ Elizabeth McCracken
Author's Insight
My grandfather edited a magazine called *The American Genealogist* for years.

Desiderata ■ 15

Differentiated Instruction   Solutions for All Learners

Support for Special Needs Students
Have students read the adapted version of "Desiderata" in the **Reader's Notebook: Adapted Version**. They may also listen to the adapted version on the **Reader's Notebook: Adapted Version Audio CD**.

Support for Less Proficient Readers
Have students read "Desiderata" in the **Reader's Notebook**. After students finish the selection in the *Reader's Notebook*, have them complete the questions and activities in the Student Edition.

Support for English Learners
Have students read "Desiderata" in the **Reader's Notebook: English Learner's Version**. English learners may also read the selection as they listen to the recorded version on the **Listening to Literature Audio CD**.

㉖ Motivation
In her introduction to "Desiderata," Elizabeth McCracken says that she is "a snoop" and likes to read her family's mail and listen to her family's conversations. Ask students whether they think their own families or other people's families are more interesting, and the reasons for their answers.

㉗ About the Selection
"Desiderata" may have originated as a writing assignment designed to entice visitors to a Web site into reading Elizabeth McCracken's novel, but its effects are much greater than that. In her essay, McCracken explores how primary sources—authentic documents from a person or an era—can alter her perceptions of people and events she thought she knew.

㉘ Author's Insight
- Tell students that the word *desiderata* is related to the word *desire*. Desiderata are items that a person desires, wants, or needs.
- **Ask** students what the desiderata might be for the curator of a museum of rock music artifacts. **Possible responses:** Students may mention costumes, sheet music, guitars or other instruments, and original lyrics.
- **Ask:** How would these items help visitors better understand the subject of rock music? **Answer:** Students should recognize that seeing these items might help visitors understand how people created the songs or memorable performances.

㉙ Author's Insight
- Point out that many people in McCracken's family were interested in writing and collecting, just as she is.
- Invite students to discuss interests that are shared by many members or different generations of their families. **Ask** how these shared interests bring the generations together. **Answer:** Shared interests give family members something to talk about and the opportunity to get to know the other person better.

- In this passage, McCracken contrasts three points of views regarding Martha: her mother's, her aunt Carolyn's, and her own.

- **Ask** students what McCracken's mother thought about Aunt Martha and her letters.
  Answer: McCracken says that her mother found Martha and her letters "lovely and slightly daffy."

- **Ask:** How would you describe Aunt Carolyn's view of Martha and her letters? How does Aunt Carolyn's point of view differ from that of McCracken's mother?
  Possible response: The words "dark" and "Dickensian" might imply that Aunt Carolyn did not like Martha or was afraid of her. Aunt Carolyn's remarks contrast sharply with the description of Martha as "lovely" and "daffy."

- Then discuss McCracken's view of Martha. **Ask:** What evidence does McCracken use to support her point of view?
  Possible response: McCracken's view of Martha and her letters is neither as positive as her mother's nor as negative as her Aunt Carolyn's. McCracken says that Martha was "at best, weird," based on stories that Martha reported in her letters.

And I read these documents fairly regularly. Besides letters from her family, my grandmother also saved letters from Martha, her children's nanny. My mother, who says she had the happiest childhood on record, remembers Martha and her letters as lovely and slightly daffy. Her twin sister, my aunt Carolyn, remembers the letters and the woman as dark and Dickensian,[1] longing for a time that never really existed. I'd always assumed that the truth was somewhere in the middle, but I have the letters and now know that Martha was, at best, weird. She wrote to my travelling grandmother that the twins—The Dollies, she called them—didn't miss her at all. She reported that she took them out to her mother's farm, and couldn't understand why the girls were so upset to be served for dinner the chicken they'd met earlier. She reported on The Dollies' toilet training as if it were grand opera, and the Dollies heroines who wanted only, desperately, to triumph.

I'm glad to know this, I think. Certainly, it's a whole different Martha than the one I knew from my mother's stories. I know Martha now because of all that she reveals of herself, not knowing she was doing it, in her letters.

Still, there are many frustrations to family papers. First of all, you may learn things you don't want to know. For instance: some of my grandmother's sisters wanted to sue the widow of one of their brothers. Even in letters from the litigious[2] sisters themselves, this comes across as merely petty and <u>vindictive</u>. There are letters that can break your heart: my Aunt Edna, writing to my grandmother, lamented how poor her health was, how the doctors told her to slow down; I know from the dates that Edna died two weeks later, of a heart attack.

But the major frustration is how incomplete everything is, how incomplete *people* are if you try to meet them this way. The great-aunt who wanted to sue only happened to write it down; maybe she gave up the idea. Maybe she was suffering otherwise—her life was continually tragic in small ways, I know that. Some of the great-aunts I barely know, because they barely wrote. Or rather, I *think* they barely wrote—my grandmother saved every letter some years, and selected letters others. Perhaps those great-aunts simply never made it into the collection.

And then there's my grandmother Jacobson herself. She was a wonderful and complex woman, an attorney and small

---

1. Dickensian of or relating to English novelist Charles Dickens (1812–1870).
2. litigious (li tij′ əs) *adj.* given to carrying out lawsuits; quarrelsome.

Vocabulary Builder
vindictive (vin dik′tiv)
adj. revengeful; inclined to seek vengeance

Vocabulary Development

Dictionary Use

Help students learn how to use a dictionary to find the meaning of unfamiliar terms.

Ask students to reread the following sentence: "The pieces of paper I have from her don't *conjure* her up at all."

Tell students to begin by turning to the "c" section of the dictionary, since *conjure* begins with the letter "c." Then have them turn to the "co" section. Model how to skim the boldface entries on the page until you locate the word *conjure*.

Have students read the definition and restate the meaning in their own words. Then suggest that students try their restated definitions in the sentence in place of the word *conjure*. They should realize that to conjure someone up is to make the person appear as if by magic. In the context of the essay, which discusses learning about a person from pieces of paper, to conjure up means to give a vivid mental picture.

businessperson who died at home at the age of 90. The pieces of paper I have from her don't conjure her up at all. Her diary (which I don't own but have read) is a very careful record of daily events, nothing more. She doesn't detail worries or doubts, and the fact is she was a worried and somewhat doubtful person. I think she knew that we'd read it, eventually, and didn't want to tell us in her diary anything she hadn't told us already.

One piece of paper I do have: a post-it note from late in her life, which she used to mark a recipe in *The Jewish Cookbook*. It says:

> coffee
> bananas
> bread
> milk
> wax beans?

and then, in the corner, written diagonally and underlined,

> *lottery ticket.*

㉛

I know that this dates to a time when she was both worried about money and had become very serious about luck. I don't know how superstitious she'd previously been, but about two years before she died, she began to see luck good and bad, in everything: she read her horoscope, her children's horoscope, the horoscope of everyone who might touch her life that day. She believed in fortune cookies. She told her own fortune playing solitaire. And she bought lottery tickets, not so much because she believed she might win but because not playing meant she did not believe that sudden good things could happen. She was a businessperson, after all: she knew what a bad investment that weekly dollar was.

I love that little green piece of paper. *Desideratum* to me, though less than ephemera[3] to anyone else.

I could tell dozens of other stories from the pages of family papers: my aunt Blanche's pell-mell record of taking care of her favorite sister, Elizabeth, who was dying of Alzheimer's; Blanche has that disease herself now, and you can see the early signs in these notes. My great-uncles' cheery letters from Europe during World War II. A letter my brother wrote to my grandmother when I was four and he was six, thanking her for a gift and then recording that I was resisting writing a thank-you note myself.

---

3. **ephemera** (e fem´ ər ə) *n.* something, often printed material, meant to last for only a short time.

Desiderata ■ 17

Nonfiction

Exposition The actual text from her grandmother's note helps the author show the kinds of pieces she has collected. Later, she explains how she finds meaning in them.

㉜ *Elizabeth McCracken*

Author's Insight Four of my grandmother's brothers served overseas. Their mother died five hours after the last, my great-uncle Gerald, came back to the family house.

㉝ ✓ **Reading Check**

What is the author's major frustration in regard to her collection of family papers?

Vocabulary for English Learners
Teach English learners the following idiomatic expressions from this essay: *strong on* (p. 15) very interested in; *daffy* (p. 16) silly or amusing; and *pell-mell* (p. 17) hectic, hurried. Ask students to use the expressions in sentences that demonstrate the words' meanings.

Strategy for Gifted/Talented Students
Give students experience in seeing how details can suggest who a character is. Provide a list of objects and notes that might be found in a person's coat pocket, such as a bus token, a business card from a computer consultant, a receipt for dry cleaning, and a shopping list that reads "spark plugs, cat food, cheesecake, vitamins." Ask students to write a description of the person who carries these items or a brief synopsis of that person's day.

㉛ Nonfiction
Exposition

- **Ask** students why McCracken would want to collect items as ordinary as grocery lists.
  Answer: McCracken is interested in the everyday lives of people in her family.

- **Ask:** What types of information might a grocery list reveal?
  Answer: A grocery list might reveal what someone liked to eat and whether he or she was wealthy enough to afford expensive items.

- Remind students that exposition is writing that explains something. **Ask:** What do the words on the note and the way they are written reveal to McCracken about her grandmother?
  Answer: The words on the note reveal that McCracken's grandmother's interest in luck made her want to buy a lottery ticket. The fact that the words are separate from the groceries on the list and are underlined reveals that the lottery ticket is important to her.

㉜ Author's Insight

- **Ask** students to describe the tone of McCracken's essay.
  Answer: The tone of the essay is conversational and nostalgic.

- Point out that in the essay, McCracken discusses her great-uncles' "cheery letters," but not the death of their mother. **Ask** how including that fact would change the tone of the essay, and why McCracken might have decided not to include it.
  Possible response: It would make the essay more serious and sad. McCracken may have decided not to include it because she had already mentioned a relative who died of Alzheimer's and did not want to talk about sad subjects only.

㉝ Reading Check

Answer: McCracken's major frustration in regard to her collection of family papers is that the collection is incomplete and does not contain all the information she would like to know.

17

Possible response: Students may say that such artifacts are meaningful not only to individuals but to society as a whole. Historical documents and images help people remember and understand the past.

35 Nonfiction

Audience

• In the introduction, McCracken says that the intended audience for this piece of nonfiction was anyone who visited her publisher's Web site. **Ask** students: Why might McCracken have chosen the topic of family and learning more about them instead of another topic such as very tall people?

Possible response: McCracken would not know who would visit the Web site. She might have wanted to choose a topic that would interest many different kinds of people. Not many people have had an experience with a very tall person, but most people have a family and are usually interested in learning more about them.

Concept Connector

Have students return to their remarks about family stories or artifacts that they believe should be preserved. Ask students to write one question they would like to ask an ancestor or to describe one family document they would like to preserve. Invite volunteers to share their ideas with the class.

⟵

Here's a last story. My father's parents were, when I knew them, quiet people. I know now that my version of them is different from anyone else's, but they were my grandparents and I never questioned who I understood them to be. After their deaths, I inherited a cherry chest-of-drawers from their house. I owned this imposing piece of furniture for a few years before I lifted some paper lining from one of the drawers and found a letter. Part of a letter, actually, written by my grandfather to my grandmother before their marriage.

It was one of the most beautiful love letters I've ever read, full of delight for her person and for their love together. It was passionate and thrilled and almost disbelieving of his great fortune, to have found her. I never imagined my grandfather, my quiet careful grandfather, was the sort of man who'd write any kind of love letter, never mind this kind. Wrong again. And my grandmother had saved it for more than fifty years. I wondered whether she took it out and reread it from time to time, or whether she'd forgotten where she'd put it.

My parents were out of town that weekend, and as it happened I'd agreed to pick them up at the airport. I brought the letter to give to my father—if it meant that much to me, I couldn't imagine what it would mean to him. And so, sitting on a bench in Logan,[4] I gave it to him. "Look what I found," I said.

"Oh," he said, perfectly pleased but not surprised. "Another letter. I'll put it with the others."

Turns out there were many more—my grandparents had written each other several times a day during their courtship. Which makes it, of course, a happier story.

35 My question is: was that letter more a *desideratum* for me, or my father? He had the collection, I didn't. Sometimes I regret giving it to him. I've forgotten the exact words my grandfather used, but it doesn't seem right to ask for someone else's love letter back. Someday I'll see it again, I know. Meanwhile, I need it and desire it. I need and desire everything that belongs to my family, and in some ways, I think, that's what I do with my days, writing fiction. I am writing love letters to diaries and post-it notes and telegrams and birthday cards. I am writing love letters to love letters.

34 ▲ **Critical Viewing**
Are letters and photos like these meaningful to society as a whole or just to individuals and families? Explain. **[Make a Judgment]**

4. **Logan** Boston's Logan International Airport, named for General Edward Lawrence Logan.

18 ■ *Fiction and Nonfiction*

Vocabulary Development

Vocabulary Knowledge Rating
When students have completed reading and discussing "Desiderata," have them take out their **Vocabulary Knowledge Rating Chart** for this selection. Read the word aloud once more and have students rate their knowledge of the word again in the After Reading column. Clarify the word if it is still problematic. Have students write their own definitions or examples in the appropriate column. Encourage students to use the word in further discussion and written work about this selection. Remind them that they will be accountable for this word on the Selection Test.

36 Q. What audience did you have in mind for this article?

A. I was asked to write an essay for my publisher's Web site when *The Giant's House* came out, and I hadn't really written nonfiction. I knew it would have to be a relatively short essay, and I knew I wanted it to be something that would (I hoped) make people want to read the novel itself. But I didn't imagine one particular person reading it. Mostly, I'm my own audience when I write (and a demanding, judgmental one at that).

37 Q. How did members of your family react to this article?

A. They liked it, I think. I say *I think* because while I try my best never to write something that would upset my family, I try hard not to worry too much about exactly what they'll think about my work—I love them and want to write about them, but if I imagined, say, my parents reading everything I wrote, I'd never write anything!

38 Q. Why is writing fiction like "writing love letters to love letters"?

A. All of those family love letters and photographs and diaries are what made me want to be a writer: I wanted to think about the family stories and do them justice. I'm grateful that my relatives are such packrats. It's been a real help to have the family documents as inspiration.

StudentCorner

39 Q. Was it hard to leave your grandfather's letter with your father, risking the possibility that you might not ever see it again?
—Meredith Kern, Oakland, New Jersey

A. It was extremely hard! Still, I know it was the right thing to do. That letter belonged with the other letters.

Writing Workshop: *Work in Progress*

Autobiographical Narrative

Choose one item from the Memory List in your writing portfolio. Build the scene you see in your mind by adding details related to other senses. Include what you heard, smelled, and felt. Save this expanded Memory List in your writing portfolio.

Assessment Resources

The following resources can be used to assess students' knowledge and skills.

Unit 1 Resources:
  Selection Test A, pp. 9–11
  Selection Test B, pp. 12–14

Go Online
Assessment Students may use the **Self-test** to prepare for **Selection Test A** or **Selection Test B.**

Elizabeth McCracken's Insights

- In these comments McCracken remarks on the purpose of the essay and its audience. Have students review these terms on p. 5.

36 In this question and answer, McCracken discusses the audience for her essay and her purpose in writing it. **Ask:** Does reading "Desiderata" make you want to read the novel *The Giant's House*? Why or why not?
Possible responses: Some students may say that the essay does not refer to the novel at all and so does not make them want to read it. Other students may say that they enjoy McCracken's writing and would like to read more of her work.

37 After students read this question and answer, point out that although McCracken may have a specific audience in mind while writing, the first person her work has to satisfy is the author herself.

38 McCracken's answer to this question addresses the connection between nonfiction and fiction. Point out that the essay discusses factual documents, but that these are some of the sources McCracken may use for details in her fiction.

39 After students read this question and answer, ask whether they agree with McCracken that her father's letter belonged with the other letters. Ask them to support their opinions with reasoning.

Writing Workshop
Work in Progress

In the Work-in-Progress assignments through Part 1, students will complete activities that prepare them for the Writing Workshop on autobiographical narrative on pp. 88–92. Work with students on this brief prewriting activity. Have them save their work in their portfolios for later use.

19

1. Students may say they feel sympathy for James because they understand how it feels to be different. Other students may say they do not sympathize with him because they do not know what it is like to be very tall.

2. (a) James hopes to find a cure for his condition. (b) James has already asked doctors whether he can be cured. (c) James feels unhappy about his plight. He wants to learn "why things go wrong" and is willing to try medicines and operations that might cure him.

3. (a) Peggy refers to her training as a librarian when she says she interviews the patron on his research topic and when she says that she should help people find information, not look it up for them. (b) Peggy looks up information for James despite the fact that it is not her job, because she cannot bring herself to say the word *giant* to him.

4. (a) **Sample answer: Research Question:** Are there cures for tall people? How do very tall people deal with their problems? **Possible Sources:** medical journal, Web site for tall people, biography of Robert Wadlow. (b) Have students support their ideas with reasoning.

5. (a) McCracken is frustrated by the fact that the archive is incomplete, and that she does not have enough information on some family members. (b) **Possible response:** McCracken writes fiction so she can make up stories that fill in the gaps left in the archives.

6. James's problem is affected by the setting of the story because physical differences were not as accepted in 1955 as they are today, there were far fewer medical treatment options, and because not much information was available in the small-town library.

7. In "Desiderata" McCracken's primary purpose is to reflect on the importance of documents and artifacts in learning about family history.

Apply the Skills

Fiction and Nonfiction

Thinking About the Selections

1. **Respond:** Do you feel sympathy for James in *The Giant's House*? Explain.

2. **(a) Recall:** What information about his condition does James hope to find? **(b) Infer:** What actions has he already taken to get this information? **(c) Describe:** Using details from the text, describe James's attitude toward his plight.

3. **(a) Recall:** Note two points at which the narrator, Peggy, refers to her training as a librarian. **(b) Analyze:** Do Peggy's efforts for James meet her criteria for being a good librarian? Explain.

4. **(a) Speculate:** Imagine that *The Giant's House* is set in the present day. Complete a chart like the one shown to list specific research sources, including the Internet and the library, that James could use to find information about his condition. **(b) Evaluate:** Discuss your chart with a classmate to identify the most valuable resource. Share your ideas with the class.

Research Question	Possible Source

5. **(a) Recall:** In "Desiderata," what are some of the frustrations McCracken experiences in "meeting" people through family papers? **(b) Speculate:** Based on this essay, why do you think McCracken became a writer of **fiction**?

Fiction and Nonfiction Review

6. How does the **setting** of *The Giant's House* affect James's problem?

7. In her **nonfiction** essay "Desiderata," is McCracken's primary purpose to persuade, to inform, or to reflect? Explain.

Research the Author

Elizabeth McCracken was a librarian before she became a writer. Using the Internet and library resources, identify other McCracken works that reveal her interest in libraries, documents, and research. Present your findings to the class in an **oral report.**

- Prepare summaries of McCracken works that touch on library work, archives, and research.
- Include quotes from McCracken's writings.

Research the Author

Students may complete this research assignment for homework.

Go Online
—Author Link

For: More information
For: More about the author
Visit: www.PHSchool.com
Web Code: epe-8101

For additional information about Elizabeth McCracken, give students this Web code. After typing in the Web code, students select *Elizabeth McCracken.*

QuickReview

Selections at a Glance

In *The Giant's House,* a young man searches for information in a small-town library.

"**Desiderata**" describes the power of ordinary writings to preserve family history.

Go Online
—Assessment
For: Self-test
Visit: www.PHSchool.com
Web Code: epa-6101

Fiction: literary narratives about imagined people and events

Nonfiction: literary works that present information about real people, events, or ideas

Setting: the time and place in which a story takes place

Unit 1
Part 1
Making and Verifying Predictions

Skills You Will Learn

Literary Analysis: *Narrative Essay*
Reading Skill: *Ask Questions to Make Predictions*

Reading Skill: *Read to Perform a Task*

Literary Analysis: *Plot, Foreshadowing, and Suspense*
Reading Skill: *Read On to Verify Predictions*

Literary Analysis: *Point of View*

Literature You Will Read

Make Predictions ■ *21*

Differentiated Instruction — Solutions for All Learners

Resources for Monitoring Progress

Unit 1 Resources
    Unit 1, Part 1 Diagnostic Test, pp. 16–18
    Unit 1, Part 1 Benchmark Test,
    pp. 102–107

Reading Kit

Success Tracker

Skills Overview
Reading Skill: Making and Verifying Predictions
- Ask questions to make and verify predictions
- Reading on to verify predictions

Vocabulary Development
- Word Roots

Literary Analysis
- Narrative Essay: significant details
- Plot and Conflict: rising action, climax, falling action, resolution, foreshadowing

Writing
- Autobiographical Narrative
- Work in Progress, pp. 13, 19, 41, 71

Monitoring Progress

Diagnose: Before you begin Part 1, administer the **Diagnostic Test** for Unit 1, Part 1. This test will identify students' level of readiness for the reading and vocabulary skills in Part 1. Use the **Interpretation Guide** for the Diagnostic Test to determine which students need help with prerequisite skills before beginning Part 1.

Preteach and Prepare: Use the information indicated in the **Interpretation Guide** to help students build prerequisite skills. In addition, prepare students by using the **Vocabulary Warm-up** activities and the **Reading Warm-up** activities as necessary for each selection set.

Teach: Use the instructional plan and resources provided to teach the skills and selections.

Assess: After students have completed Part 1, administer the **Benchmark Test** for Unit 1, Part 1. The test results will indicate which skills students have mastered and those on which they need more work.

Reteach: Use the Interpretation Guide to determine the appropriate reteaching pages from the **Reading Kit.**

Intervention: The prerequisite and reteaching pages are also available in the **Success Tracker.**

Introduce the Reading Skill

- Introduce the reading skill: making predictions. Draw students' attention to the definition. Point out that writers provide clues in the text that allow readers to ask questions and make predictions. Tell students that making predictions about the reading is one way for a reader to get involved in the text and to make sense of the text.

- Tell students that when they predict they should consider each character's personality and what information he or she knows. Tell students to also look for places where the author hints at future events.

Model the Reading Strategy

- Model how asking questions based on details allows students to make meaningful predictions. Write this sentence on the board.

Waiting patiently under the tree, the leopard crouched as the playful cub approached.

Then **ask** these questions:

What will the leopard do?

What will the cub do?

Answer: Based on the leopard's stance, it will attack the cub. The cub's playful manner shows that it is unaware of the leopard and will be completely startled by the attack.

- Reinforce the idea that making predictions involves using details and clues provided in the text to anticipate what will happen later. Predictions can then be verified and evaluated.

Reading: Make Predictions

> A **prediction** is a logical assumption about what will happen next.

Skills and Strategies You Will Learn in Part 1

In Part 1, you will learn
- to **ask questions** and **make meaningful predictions** (p. 24)
- to **read ahead** to **verify,** and to **evaluate** and **revise predictions** (p. 46)
- to **use predictions** when you **read to perform a task** (p. 42)

Using the Skills and Strategies in Part 1

In Part 1, you will learn to **ask questions** that identify details that clarify your expectations and help you make predictions. You will also learn to check your predictions as you continue reading and to look back at clues you may have missed when your predictions need to be revised. **Making, verifying, and revising predictions** helps you recognize and understand the reasons for, and connections between, events and actions.

The chart models the skills and strategies you will learn in Part 1.

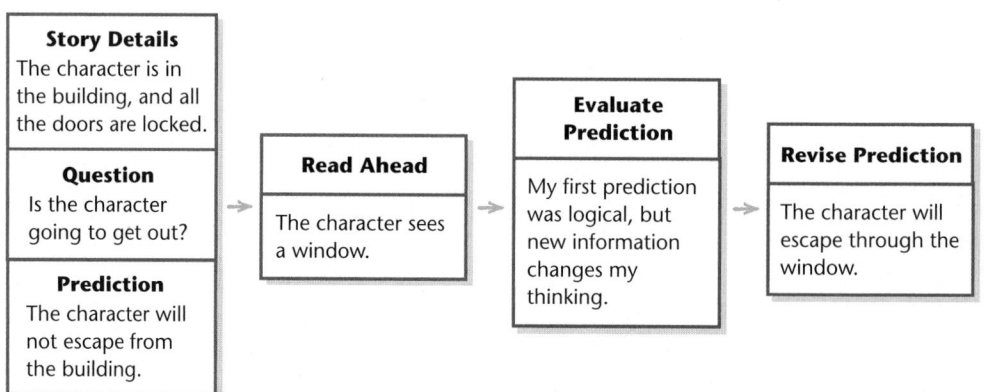

Story Details		Evaluate Prediction	
The character is in the building, and all the doors are locked.		My first prediction was logical, but new information changes my thinking.	
Question Is the character going to get out?	**Read Ahead** The character sees a window.		**Revise Prediction** The character will escape through the window.
Prediction The character will not escape from the building.			

22 ■ *Fiction and Nonfiction*

Professional Development

"Say Something" Bookmark

To help readers who are distracted while reading, you may want to try "Say Something" Bookmark (Blachowicz, 1996). This during-reading strategy breaks up selections into manageable chunks and demands that students write and respond to the text as they read. Before reading, ask students to take out a regular piece of notebook paper and fold it lengthwise. On one side, have them write their name, the selection title, and the heading *Vocabulary*. The flip side of the bookmark may be used to complete any number of "I" prompts, such as "I couldn't believe it when...," "I was surprised when...," "I wonder...," or "I was upset...."

To model this strategy, read a passage aloud, stopping every few paragraphs to give students time to jot down their reactions and/or list any unknown vocabulary words. This during-reading activity forces students to focus and evaluate what they are reading, while they are reading.

Academic Vocabulary: Words for Responding to Literature

The following words will help you write and talk about the selections in Part 1.

Word	Definition	Example Sentence
contemporary *adj.*	recent or current; living or happening at the same time	The setting is a *contemporary* American town.
involve *v.*	include; require	The author's recollections of childhood *involve* many humorous memories.
specific *adj.*	precise; definite	The details establish a *specific* setting.
participate *v.*	take part in; join	Several characters *participate* in the conflict over the farm.
contribute *v.*	give; add; provide	Details *contribute* to a story's mood.

Vocabulary Skill: Word Roots

▶ A **word root** is the basic unit of meaning in a word.

In Part 1, you will learn
- Latin root -*volve*- (p. 40)
- Latin root -*part*- (p. 40)
- Latin root -*tempor*- (p. 70)
- Latin root -*spec*- (p. 70)

Many English words are built upon **Latin or Greek roots.** Knowing roots can help you determine the meanings of words. Dictionaries provide information on the meaning and history of each word part.

The word is usually used as an adjective.   *The parts of the words are shown with their history.*

con•tem•po•rary (kən tem′ pə rer′ ē) *adj.* [< L *com*-, with + L *temporarium* < *tempus*, time: see **TEMPER**] 1. living or happening at the same period of time 2. of about the same age 3. of or in the same style of the present or recent times; modern. *n.-pl.* **rar•ies** 1. a person living in the same period as another . . .

The word can also be used as a noun. The entry shows the changes for the plural form of the noun.

Activity Arrange the words into three pairs according to the root they share: *involve, species, extemporaneous, revolve, inspect, contemporary.* Explain why you pair the words as you do.

Reading and Vocabulary Skills Preview ■ 23

Introduce Academic Vocabulary

- Introduce the academic vocabulary: words for responding to literature. Tell students that these are words that are useful for discussing and writing responses to literature.
- Review each word and have the students state the words aloud. Have students read aloud the words' definitions and the example sentences.
- Tell students to try to use these words as they discuss the selections in Part 1.

Introduce the Vocabulary Skill

- Introduce the vocabulary skill: word roots. Tell students that many words in English are derived from Latin or Greek. The Latin or Greek roots appear in English words. Recognizing these roots and their meanings is an effective way to learn new words and to build vocabulary.
- Have students look at the entry for *contemporary.* Lead students in a discussion about the word, pointing out each part of the entry.
- Point out the activity on this page. **Ask** students to pair the words, and then have student volunteers give their answers.
  Answers: in<u>volve</u> and re<u>volve</u>; <u>spec</u>ies and in<u>spec</u>t; ex<u>tempor</u>aneous and con<u>tempor</u>ary.
- Use these questions to give students practice with these roots:
  - What word describes something that lasts for a limited time?
    Answer: *temporary*
  - What word describes one who looks on or watches?
    Answer: *spectator*
  - When something rolls out or unfolds, it _____.
    Answer: *evolves*

Differentiated Instruction   Solutions for All Learners

Strategy for Less Proficient Learners
Encourage students to use vocabulary study cards for review and study. Have students write one of the words for responding to literature on one side of a 3x5 note card. On the back have them write the definition in their own words, along with an example. Have students practice their vocabulary using these cards. Students could also practice by using their cards with a partner.

Strategy for English Learners
Encourage students whose home language is a Romance language (derived from Latin) to use cognates to understand new English vocabulary. Encourage them to list words containing the root from their home language in a column alongside similar English words. Have students define the cognates and note the similarities and differences in the word meanings. Encourage them to use a dictionary if necessary.

Go Online For: Interactive
Vocabulary Crossword puzzles
    Visit: www.PHSchool.com
    Web Code: epj-5101
Give students this Web Code to access interactive crossword puzzles using Academic Vocabulary and Vocabulary Skill words from Part 1.

Planning Differentiated Instruction

Choosing Your Selection

You may use either selection to meet the lesson standards. The following guide will help you determine which of the two selections is more appropriate for your students.

Accessibility at a Glance

	The Washwoman	**New Directions**
Context	Setting: Jewish neighborhood in Poland, early 1900s, winter	Social: African American mother living in the South, early 1900s
Language	• Numerous long sentences with embedded clauses • Little dialogue	• Accessible vocabulary • Little dialogue
Concept Level	Challenging (determination to complete a difficult task)	Accessible (journey from adversity to success)
Literary Merit	Prize-winning author	Personal saga
Lexile	870L	1360L
Other		Inspirational/ motivational
Overall Rating	More challenging	More accessible

Because a number of factors help determine the relative accessibility of paired selections, the Lexile number of the more challenging selection may sometimes be lower than that of the more accessible selection.

Using the Other Selection You may use the other selection for homework or independent reading to reinforce the selection skills. If you use both selections, you can build a test for both using *ExamView® Test Bank* software.

Choosing Your Resources

[L1] Special Needs Students **[L4]** Advanced Students
[L2] Below-Level Students **[EL]** English Learners
[L3] All Students

FT Fast Track Instruction: To move the lesson more quickly, use the strategies and activities identified with **FT**.

Reading and Vocabulary Warm-ups provide support for below level students. **A** is for students reading two grades below level; **B** is for students reading one grade below level. For Selection Tests, **A** signifies "less challenging" and **B** "more challenging." For Graphic Organizer transparencies, **A** signifies "not filled in" and **B** "filled in."

Scaffolding for Less Proficient and Advanced Students

The leveled questions on Apply the Skills pages progress in the levels of thinking required to answer them. To address the needs of your different students, you may use the (a) level questions for your less proficient students, the (b) level with your on-level and advanced students. The occasional (c) level questions are appropriate for your advanced students.

Step-by-Step Teaching Guide	**Pacing Guide**	
PRETEACH		
• Administer Vocabulary and Reading Warm-Ups as necessary.		
• Introduce the Literary Analysis Skill: Narrative Essay. **FT**	10 min.	
• Introduce the Reading Skill: Making and Verifying Predictions. **FT**	10 min.	
• Prepare students to read by teaching the selection vocabulary. **FT**	10 min.	
• Build background and develop expressive vocabulary with Connecting to the Literature and Background.	10 min.	
• Engage students' interest with the motivation activity.	10 min.	
TEACH		
• Informally monitor comprehension while students read independently or in groups. **FT**	30 min.	
• Monitor students' comprehension with the Reading Check notes.	as students read	
• Reinforce vocabulary with Vocabulary Builder notes.	as students read	
• Develop students' understanding of narrative essays with the Literary Analysis annotations. **FT**	5 min.	
• Develop students' ability to make and verify predictions with the Reading Skill annotations. **FT**	10 min.	
ASSESS/EXTEND		
• Assess students' comprehension and mastery of the Reading Skill and Literary Analysis by having them answer the Apply the Skills questions. **FT**	35 min.	
• Have students complete the Vocabulary Builder activities. **FT**	5 min.	
• Apply students' ability to write an anecdote with the Writing activity. **FT**	30–45 min. or homework	
• Extend students' listening and speaking and research and technology skills with one or both of the Extend Your Learning activities.	15–30 min. or homework	
• Have students complete the Vocabulary Skill and Grammar Lesson.	5 min.	
• Monitor students' progress with the Assessment Practice.	20–40 min.	
• Administer **Selection Test A** or **Selection Test B**. **FT**	15 min.	

Go Online **For:** Information about Lexiles
Professional **Visit:** www.PHSchool.com
Development **Web Code:** eue-1111

Resources

Meeting Your Standards

Students will

1. **analyze and respond to literary elements.**
   - Literary Analysis: Narrative Essay

2. **read, comprehend, and analyze narrative essays.**
   - Reading Skill: Making and Verifying Predictions
   - Reading Strategy: Ask Questions to Make and Verify Predictions
   - Reading Check questions
   - Apply the Skills questions
   - Assessment Practice

3. **develop vocabulary.**
   - Vocabulary Builder
   - Word Roots

4. **apply grammar skills.**
   - Common Nouns and Proper Nouns

5. **develop writing proficiency.**
   - Work in Progress: Autobiographical Narrative
   - Anecdote

6. **extend learning.**
   - Listening and Speaking: Interview
   - Research and Technology: Oral Presentation

Block Scheduling: Use one 90-minute class period to preteach the skills and have students read the selection. Use a second 90-minute class period to assess students' mastery of skills, extend their learning, and monitor their progress.

Homework Suggestions

Following are possibilities for homework assignments.

- Support pages from *Unit 1 Resources*:
  Literary Analysis
  Reading Skill
  Build Vocabulary
  Enrichment

- An Extend Your Learning project and the Writing assignment for your chosen selection may be completed over several days.

PRENTICE HALL
TeacherEXPRESS Use this complete
Plan · Teach · Assess suite of powerful teaching tools to make lesson planning and testing quicker and easier.

PRENTICE HALL
StudentEXPRESS Use the
Learn · Study · Succeed Interactive Textbook (online and on CD-ROM) to make selections and activities come alive with audio and video support and interactive questions.

Build Skills *The Washwoman • New Directions*

Practice these skills with either "The Washwoman" (p. 26) or "New Directions" (p. 35).

❶ Literary Analysis
Narrative Essay

- Tell students that a *narrative essay*—nonfiction writing that tells about an actual person or event—has many of the same characteristics as fiction, such as characters, a conflict, a theme, and a resolution. As with fiction, authors of narrative essays include significant supporting details to help make or develop their point.

- Tell students that a narrative essay often uses a real-life experience to provide insight into life. For example, the stories of two women's struggles in "The Washwoman" and "New Directions" reveal universal truths about the strength of the human spirit.

- Tell students to look for the significant details in the selections they read and to think how these details help move the story forward and support the main idea.

❷ Reading Skill
Making and Verifying Predictions

- Tell students that making and verifying predictions will keep them actively involved in a story. Verifying predictions will also help students check their understanding of what they have read.

- Explain that to make logical predictions and verify them, students need to pay close attention to details as they read.

- Discuss the chart with students. Point out that the detail in the first box evokes a question that leads to a prediction. Remind students that to fill in the last box, they should read to find the answer to the question and then confirm or revise their original prediction.

- Give students a copy of **Reading Skill Graphic Organizer A** *(Graphic Organizer Transparencies,* p. 3). Have them fill in the graphic organizer to analyze the author's purpose as they read the assigned selection.

❶ Literary Analysis

A **narrative essay** is a short piece of nonfiction that tells a story about a real person or event. In a narrative essay, the author chooses to include **significant details** that help move the story forward or that help make his or her point about the subject. For example, if an author writing about a famous singer wants to stress that the singer comes from a musical family, the essay might mention that the singer's father plays guitar. The essay probably wouldn't mention that the singer's father collects stamps. As you read, notice how the author's choice of significant details influences your impressions of the people and events he or she describes.

❷ Reading Skill

A **prediction** is an informed idea about what might happen later in a narrative. Predictions are based on details in the text and your own experience. When you **verify predictions**, you read on to see if the prediction is correct.

Pause periodically while reading and **ask questions** about text details and events.

- Why does the author mention this detail?
- How might it become important later on?

Look for the answers as you read ahead. Use a chart like this to record your predictions and whether or not they are accurate.

Detail
". . . she could 'mix groceries well enough to scare hungry away.'"

↓

Question
Why does the author mention this detail?

↓

Prediction
The character might sell food to support her family.

↓

Verification?

Vocabulary Builder

The Washwoman

- **forebears** (fôr´ berz) *n.* ancestors (p. 27) *His* <u>forebears</u> *started the family business.*

- **rancor** (raŋ´kər) *n.* bitter hate (p. 28) *The rivals fumed with* <u>rancor</u> *for each other.*

- **atonement** (ə tōn´ mənt) *n.* act of making up for a wrongdoing or an injury (p. 28) *He volunteered at a nursing home as* <u>atonement</u> *for his misbehavior.*

- **obstinacy** (äb´ stə nə sē) *n.* stubbornness (p. 30) *The child refused to clean up, and she was punished for her* <u>obstinacy</u>.

New Directions

- **amicably** (am´ i kə blē) *adv.* in a friendly way (p. 35) *They settled their disagreements* <u>amicably</u>.

- **meticulously** (mə tik´ yōō ləs lē) *adv.* very carefully and precisely (p. 36) *She* <u>meticulously</u> *applied her makeup.*

- **ominous** (äm´ ə nəs) *adj.* threatening (p. 37) *The sound of the thunder seemed* <u>ominous</u>.

- **unpalatable** (un pal´ it ə bəl) *adj.* distasteful; unpleasant (p. 37) *She thought changing diapers was her most* <u>unpalatable</u> *chore.*

24 ■ Fiction and Nonfiction

Vocabulary Development

Vocabulary Knowledge Rating

Create a **Vocabulary Knowledge Rating Chart** for the selection you will teach from this set. Include the selection vocabulary from this page and the additional words students are asked to use at the end of Connecting to the Literature. These words will increase students' expressive vocabulary.

Give students a copy of the chart with the words on it. Introduce the words by reading them aloud and having students mark their rating in the Before Reading column. Urge them to be alert to these words as they read and discuss the selection because they will rate their knowledge of the words again after they finish.

If you wish, you may tally how many students know (or think they know) a word to gauge how much instruction you need to provide. As students read, point out the words and their context.

❸ Background

Jews in Poland "The Washwoman" takes place in the early twentieth century in what is now Poland. Centuries earlier, many Jewish people had settled there, drawn by the promise of religious tolerance. By Singer's time, Poland had been conquered by other countries. Yet, Poland's Jews held on to their traditions, continuing to speak Yiddish, a language blending German with Hebrew and other languages.

❹ Connecting to the Literature

Reading/Writing Connection In "The Washwoman," a woman struggles in the bitter cold to complete a chore. Write three or four reasons people might have for sticking to a difficult task. Use at least three of the following words: *accomplish, demonstrate, justify, confront.*

READ MORE

by Isaac Bashevis Singer
Gimpel the Fool and Other Stories
In My Father's Court

Meet the Author

Isaac Bashevis **Singer** (1904–1991)

Storytelling always had an important place in Isaac Bashevis Singer's life. He grew up in the city of Warsaw in what now is Poland. Singer's father was a rabbi, a teacher of the Jewish faith and laws. Advice-seekers streamed through the family home, telling their stories as the fascinated young Singer listened and observed.

"Life Itself Is a Story" Fleeing persecution against Jews, Singer left Poland for New York City in 1935. In New York, Singer began to make a name for himself as a writer. He set many of his tales in the world of European Jewry he had left. Ironically, as he wrote, World War II devastated that world. Villages like the one of his birth were wiped off the face of the earth even as Singer brought them to life on the page.

Fast Facts

▶ Singer wrote in Yiddish throughout his life, and he often translated his own work into English.

▶ In 1978, Singer won the Nobel Prize for Literature.

 Go Online
Author Link
For: More about the author
Visit: www.PHSchool.com
Web Code: epe-9102

The Washwoman ■ 25

❸ Background
Jews in Poland

It is not certain when the first Jewish people arrived in Poland, but many came during the 1300s when anti-Semitism was especially strong across much of Europe. Poland, in contrast, offered Jewish people sanctuary and legal rights that were unusual for the time period. By 1500, more than half of the world's Jewish population lived in Poland—a percentage that remained more or less constant until World War II. Although their legal rights and privileges varied over the centuries, Polish Jews often enjoyed security and freedom that was difficult to find in other countries.

❹ Connecting to the Literature

- Model use of the expressive vocabulary students are asked to use with these examples:

  1. Some people feel it is their responsibility to *accomplish* tasks they have undertaken.

  2. They want to *demonstrate* that they can overcome obstacles.

  3. Some people cannot *justify* giving up just because they are tired.

  4. They say it is satisfying to *confront* a difficult task and complete it.

- Help students further develop their expressive vocabulary by providing these words: *despite, endure, isolation,* and *labor.* Encourage students to use these words as they discuss the selection.

Go Online
Author Link For additional information about Isaac Bashevis Singer, have students type in the Web Code, then select *S* from the alphabet, and then select *Isaac Bashevis Singer.*

Differentiated Instruction   Solutions for All Learners

Support for Below-Level Students [L1, L2]	Support for English Learners [EL]
Unit 1 Resources	**Unit 1 Resources**
Vocabulary Warm-up Word Lists, p. 19	**Vocabulary Warm-up Word Lists**, p. 19
Vocabulary Warm-up Practice, p. 20	**Vocabulary Warm-up Practice**, p. 20
Reading Warm-up A, p. 21	**Reading Warm-up A**, p. 21
Selection Test A, pp. 29–31	**Listening to Literature Audio CD**
Graphic Organizer Transparencies	
Reading Skill Graphic Organizer, Transparency B, p. 4	

❶ Motivation

Prepare an **Anticipation Guide** (see *General Resources*, p. 10) with the following statements:

- The type of work a person does reveals his or her character.
- Working hard is its own reward.
- People contribute less to society as they age.
- A person can become wealthy if he or she works hard enough.

Give students a copy of the prepared Anticipation Guide and have students mark their responses in the Me column. Have students discuss the statements in pairs or groups and mark the Guides again in the Group column.

Concept Connector ➡

Students will return to the Anticipation Guide after completing *"The Washwoman."*

Learning Modalities
Musical/Rhythmic Learners

The washwoman in this essay says very little. As students read, have them "listen" to her silence. What effect does this silence have on them?

❷ About the Selection

In "The Washwoman," Singer recalls the woman who did his family's laundry when he was a child in Poland. Singer never forgets her courage and endurance.

❸ Humanities

The Oldest Inhabitant, 1876, by Julian Alden Weir

American painter Julian Alden Weir (1852–1919) was one of a family of artists and teachers. Weir studied art first with his father and later at the École des Beaux-Arts in Paris. Use this question for discussion:

- How would you describe the painter's attitude toward his subject?
  Possible response: The dignity of her pose and the soft lighting suggest that the painter respected and admired the woman.

The Washwoman ❶ ❷

Isaac Bashevis Singer

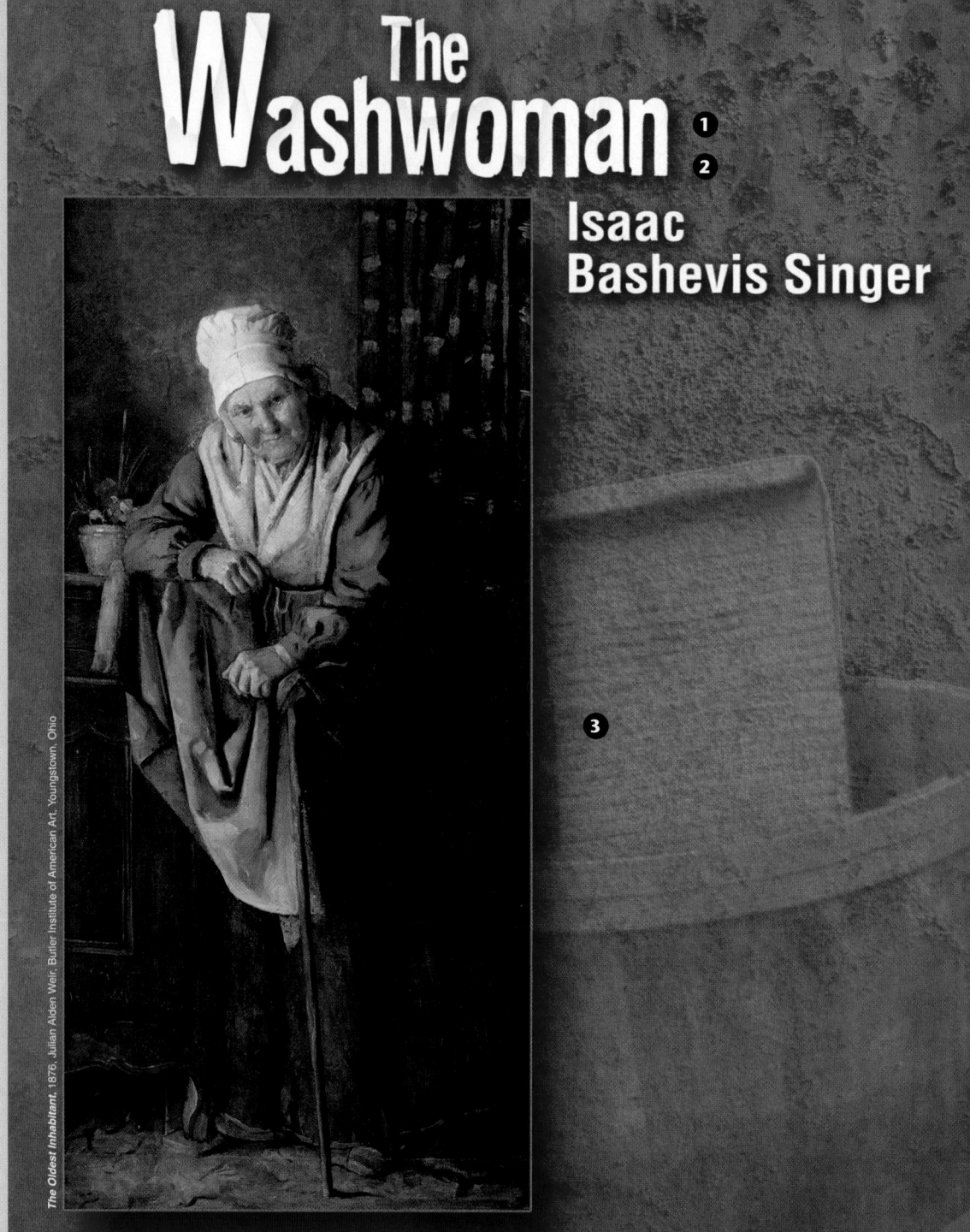

The Oldest Inhabitant, 1876, Julian Alden Weir, Butler Institute of American Art, Youngstown, Ohio

26 ■ *Fiction and Nonfiction*

❸

Vocabulary Development

Word Analysis

Call students' attention to the vocabulary word *forebears* in the third paragraph. Explain that the Anglo-Saxon prefix *fore-*, meaning "before," gives a clue to the word's meaning. Tell them that the Anglo-Saxon prefix *fore-* means "before." Students should readily see how the prefix contributes to the word's meaning: "those who came before" or "ancestors."

Ask students to think of other words containing *fore-*, and list the words on the board. Work as a class to write a brief definition of each word. Examples include *foretell:* "to say before, predict"; *forewarn:* "to warn before"; *forenoon:* "before noon"; *forecast:* "to estimate or plan ahead; predict."

O ur home had little contact with Gentiles.[1] The only Gentile in the building was the janitor. Fridays he would come for a tip, his "Friday money." He remained standing at the door, took off his hat, and my mother gave him six groschen.[2]

Besides the janitor there were also the Gentile washwomen who came to the house to fetch our laundry. My story is about one of these.

4 She was a small woman, old and wrinkled. When she started washing for us, she was already past seventy. Most Jewish women of her age were sickly, weak, broken in body. All the old women in our street had bent backs and leaned on sticks when they walked. But this washwoman, small and thin as she was, possessed a strength that came from generations of peasant <u>forebears</u>. Mother would count out to her a bundle of laundry that had accumulated over several weeks. She would lift the unwieldy pack, load it on her narrow shoulders, and carry it the long way home. She lived on Krochmalna Street too, but at the other end, near the Wola section. It must have been a walk of an hour and a half.

She would bring the laundry back about two weeks later. My mother had never been so pleased with any washwoman. Every piece of linen sparkled like polished silver. Every piece was neatly ironed. Yet she charged no more than the others. She was a real find. Mother always had her money ready, because it was too far for the old woman to come a second time.

Laundering was not easy in those days. The old woman had no faucet where she lived but had to bring in the water from a pump. For the linens to come out so clean, they had to be scrubbed thoroughly in a washtub, rinsed with washing soda, soaked, boiled in an enormous pot, starched, then ironed. Every piece was handled ten times or more. And the drying! It could not be done outside because thieves would steal the laundry. The wrung-out wash had to be carried up to the attic and hung on clotheslines. In the winter it would become as brittle as glass and almost break when touched. And there was always a to-do with other house-wives and washwomen who wanted the attic clothesline for their own use. Only God knows all the old woman had to endure each time she did a wash!

---

1. **Gentiles** any persons not Jewish; here, specifically Christians.
2. **groschen** (grō´ shən) Austrian cent or penny.

Literary Analysis
Narrative Essay
Which detail in this paragraph helps you identify this as a narrative essay?

Vocabulary Builder
forebears (fôr´ berz´)
n. ancestors

5 Reading Check
According to Singer, what is the washwoman's physical appearance?

The Washwoman ■ 27

4 Literary Analysis
Narrative Essay

- Have students consider the title of the essay and the main ideas in the bracketed passage. **Ask** students to identify the subject of the essay. **Answer:** The subject is the washwoman.

- **Ask:** Why does Singer begin the story with details about the janitor? **Answer:** The details help make the point that the narrator and his family had little contact with Gentiles, so readers know that the essay is about an unusual woman. This information creates interest and sets the plot in motion.

- Draw students' attention to the second paragraph. **Ask** them to respond to the Literary Analysis question: Which detail in this paragraph helps you identify this as a narrative essay? **Answer:** The author says that he is telling a story about a washwoman.

5 Reading Check

Possible response: The wash-woman is old and wrinkled, small and thin, but strong.

Differentiated
Instruction Solutions for All Learners

Strategy for Less Proficient Readers
Display **Reading Skill Graphic Organizer A** (*Graphic Organizer Transparencies,* p. 3), and review the process of making and verifying predictions. Fill in the first box of the organizer with the following sentence from p. 28: "The old woman did not want to become a burden, and so she bore her burden."

Guide students as they list questions that they might ask about the sentence. For example, will the old woman become a burden?

Why does she bear her burden? With students' input, choose a question for the second box of the organizer.

Next, tell students to think about what they have read and what they know about older people. Have students brainstorm for predictions and write them on sheets of paper. At the end of the selection, have students confirm or revise their predictions.

Literary Analysis

Narrative Essay

- Discuss the details that Singer includes about his mother. **Ask** students to respond to the Literary Analysis question: What point is the author making about his mother by including these significant details?

  Answer: She is a loving mother; she is superstitious and assumes nothing about the future, including the love and faithfulness of her children.

- Remind students that in a narrative essay an author includes only significant details. **Ask** students why these details are significant.

  Possible response: The details show the uncertainty of life. They suggest that the washwoman may have had a similar relationship with her son when he was young but that the future is unknown; the same fate could fall to any mother.

- Remind students that significant details often influence readers' impressions of characters and events. **Ask** students how the previous details affect their feelings about the narrator, his mother, and the washwoman. Do the characters seem more sympathetic? More understandable?

  Possible response: Students may agree that the details deepen their understanding and sympathy for the characters.

She could have begged at the church door or entered a home for the penniless and aged. But there was in her a certain pride and love of labor with which many Gentiles have been blessed. The old woman did not want to become a burden, and so she bore her burden.

My mother spoke a little Polish, and the old woman would talk with her about many things. She was especially fond of me and used to say I looked like Jesus. She repeated this every time she came, and Mother would frown and whisper to herself, her lips barely moving, "May her words be scattered in the wilderness."

The woman had a son who was rich. I no longer remember what sort of business he had. He was ashamed of his mother, the wash-woman, and never came to see her. Nor did he ever give her a groschen. The old woman told this without rancor. One day the son was married. It seemed that he had made a good match. The wedding took place in a church. The son had not invited the old mother to his wedding, but she went to the church and waited at the steps to see her son lead the "young lady" to the altar.

The story of the faithless son left a deep impression on my mother. She talked about it for weeks and months. It was an affront not only to the old woman but to the entire institution of mother-hood. Mother would argue, "Nu, does it pay to make sacrifices for children? The mother uses up her last strength, and he does not even know the meaning of loyalty."

And she would drop dark hints to the effect that she was not certain of her own children: Who knows what they would do some day? This, however, did not prevent her from dedicating her life to us. If there was any delicacy in the house, she would put it aside for the children and invent all sorts of excuses and reasons why she herself did not want to taste it. She knew charms that went back to ancient **6** times, and she used expressions she had inherited from generations of devoted mothers and grandmothers. If one of the children complained of a pain, she would say, "May I be your ransom and may you outlive my bones!" Or she would say, "May I be the atonement for the least of your fingernails." When we ate she used to say, "Health and marrow in your bones!" The day before the new moon she gave us a kind of candy that was said to prevent parasitic worms. If one of us had something in his eye, Mother would lick the eye clean with her tongue. She also fed us rock candy against coughs, and from time to time she would take us to be blessed against the evil eye. This did not prevent her from studying *The Duties of the Heart*, *The Book of the Covenant*, and other serious philosophic works.

Vocabulary Builder
rancor (raŋ´kər) *n.* bitter hate

Literary Analysis
Narrative Essay
What point is the author making about his mother by including these significant details?

Vocabulary Builder
atonement (ə tōn´mənt) *n.* act of making up for a wrongdoing or injury

Vocabulary Development

Expressive Vocabulary
Ask students to think about the washwoman and her work ethic. Why did she work so hard? Did she have any choices? How do you think she felt about the unending work in her life? As students discuss the washwoman and her work, encourage them to use the expressive vocabulary presented earlier. You might encourage them with sentence starters like these:

1. Every day the washwoman had to *confront* . . .
2. Although she is elderly, she could *accomplish* . . .
3. The washwoman's willingness to work *demonstrates* . . .
4. The washwoman finds a way to *justify* . . .

❼ ◀ Critical Viewing
How does this depiction of a neighborhood in Poland compare with Singer's description of his community? **[Compare]**

❽

But to return to the washwoman. That winter was a harsh one. The streets were in the grip of a bitter cold. No matter how much we heated our stove, the windows were covered with frostwork and decorated with icicles. The newspapers reported that people were dying of the cold. Coal became dear. The winter had become so severe that parents stopped sending children to cheder,[3] and even the Polish schools were closed.

❾

On one such day the washwoman, now nearly eighty years old, came to our house. A good deal of laundry had accumulated during the past weeks. Mother gave her a pot of tea to warm herself, as well as some bread. The old woman sat on a kitchen chair trembling and shaking, and warmed her hands against the teapot. Her fingers were gnarled from work, and perhaps from arthritis too. Her fingernails were strangely white. These hands spoke of the stubbornness of mankind, of the will to work not only as one's strength permits but beyond the limits of one's power. Mother counted and wrote down the list: men's undershirts, women's vests, long-legged drawers, bloomers, petticoats, shifts, featherbed covers, pillowcases, sheets, and the men's fringed garments. Yes, the Gentile woman washed these holy garments as well.

---

3. cheder (khā´ dər) *n.* religious school.

❿ ✓ Reading Check

Why does the washwoman do other people's laundry?

The Washwoman ■ 29

Differentiated Instruction   Solutions for All Learners

Strategy for Special Needs Students
Remind students that a narrative essay tells a story; therefore, its structure is much like that of a short story. Help students fill out a story map that identifies the essay's setting, characters, main events, and theme. Have students refer to the map as they read to help them comprehend the story that the essay tells.

Strategy for Advanced Readers
Have students consider which narrative element—plot, character, setting, or theme—is most important to this narrative essay. Have them write brief essays in which they identify the most important element, support their answers with evidence from the text, and explain how their answers are linked to Singer's purpose in writing the essay.

---

❼ Critical Viewing
Possible response: The neighborhoods seem similar. As in the washwoman's neighborhood, the picture shows that water comes from an outside well, people live in large apartment buildings, and women carry heavy loads.

❽ Humanities
In the Jewish Quarter Kazimierz in Cracow, artist unknown

For centuries, generations of Jewish families called the Kazimierz district in Cracow, Poland, home. The community was nearly destroyed during the Holocaust, but today it has become a monument to Jewish culture and history. Use these questions for discussion:

1. What does the painting suggest about the Jewish people who lived in such neighborhoods in Poland?
   Possible responses: They were hardworking but poor. They lived close together, so they knew their neighbors well.

2. How does the depiction of laundry in the picture compare to Singer's description of it in "The Washwoman"?
   Answer: In the picture, the laundry is hung outside to dry. Singer says this could not be done in his community because the laundry would be stolen.

❾ Critical Thinking
Compare and Contrast

- Read aloud the bracketed passage, and then have students reread the third paragraph on p. 27. **Ask** students how much time has passed between the two incidents. **Answer:** About ten years has passed between the two incidents.

- Have students compare and contrast how the washwoman is portrayed in the two passages. **Possible response:** The washwoman seems weaker in the second passage. She is still small and thin, but now her health is declining.

❿ Reading Check
Compare and Contrast
Answer: She does laundry to make a living.

Making and Verifying Predictions

- Point out that students should draw on their own knowledge and experience as they make and verify predictions. Have students discuss what they know about the dangers of severe winter weather.

- **Ask** students to answer the Reading Skill question: What prediction do you make based on these details about the cold and the washwoman's absence?
Possible response: Singer includes these details to impress upon the reader the harsh conditions that the washwoman has to endure. The washwoman's health will probably make it difficult for her to survive such extreme weather.

▶ **Monitor Progress:** Review students' graphic organizers to ensure that they are making and verifying predictions correctly.

▶ **Reteach:** If students have difficulty making accurate predictions, have them reread the essay and identify clues that would have led to a correct prediction.

The bundle was big, bigger than usual. When the woman placed it on her shoulders, it covered her completely. At first she swayed, as though she were about to fall under the load. But an inner <u>obstinacy</u> seemed to call out: No, you may not fall. A donkey may permit himself to fall under his burden, but not a human being, the crown of creation.

It was fearful to watch the old woman staggering out with the enormous pack, out into the frost, where the snow was dry as salt and the air was filled with dusty white whirlwinds, like goblins dancing in the cold. Would the old woman ever reach Wola?

She disappeared, and Mother sighed and prayed for her.

⓫ Usually the woman brought back the wash after two or, at the most, three weeks. But three weeks passed, then four and five, and nothing was heard of the old woman. We remained without linens. The cold had become even more intense. The telephone wires were now as thick as ropes. The branches of the trees looked like glass. So much snow had fallen that the streets had become uneven, and sleds were able to glide down many streets as on the slopes of a hill. Kindhearted people lit fires in the streets for vagrants[4] to warm themselves and roast potatoes in, if they had any to roast.

For us the washwoman's absence was a catastrophe. We needed the laundry. We did not even know the woman's address. It seemed certain that she had collapsed, died. Mother declared she had had a premonition, as the old woman left our house that last time, that we would never see our things again. She found some old torn shirts and washed and mended them. We mourned, both for the laundry and for the old, toil-worn woman who had grown close to us through the years she had served us so faithfully.

More than two months passed. The frost had subsided, and then a new frost had come, a new wave of cold. One evening, while Mother was sitting near the kerosene lamp mending a shirt, the door opened and a small puff of steam, followed by a gigantic bundle, entered. Under the bundle tottered the old woman, her face as white as a linen sheet. A few wisps of white hair straggled out from beneath her shawl. Mother uttered a half-choked cry. It was as though a corpse had entered the room. I ran toward the old woman and helped her unload her pack. She was even thinner now, more bent. Her face had become more gaunt, and her head shook from side to side as though she were saying no. She could not utter a clear word, but mumbled something with her sunken mouth and pale lips.

---

4. **vagrants** (vā′ grənts) *n.* people who wander from place to place, especially those without regular jobs.

30 ■ Fiction and Nonfiction

Vocabulary Builder
obstinacy (äb′ stə nə sē) *n.* stubbornness

Reading Skill
Making and Verifying Predictions What prediction do you make based on these details about the cold and the washwoman's absence?

Vocabulary Development

Vocabulary Knowledge Rating

When students have completed reading and discussing "The Washwoman," have them take out their **Vocabulary Knowledge Rating Chart** for this selection. Read the words aloud once more and have students rate their knowledge of the words again in the After Reading column. Clarify any words that are still problematic. Have students write their own definition and example or sentence in the appropriate column. Then have students complete the **Vocabulary Builder Practice** activities on p. 33. Encourage students to use the words in further discussion and written work about this selection. Remind them that they will be accountable for these words on the Selection Test.

After the old woman had recovered somewhat, she told us that she had been ill, very ill. Just what her illness was, I cannot remember. She had been so sick that someone had called a doctor, and the doctor had sent for a priest. Someone had informed the son, and he had contributed money for a coffin and for the funeral. But the Almighty had not yet wanted to take this pain-racked soul to Himself. She began to feel better, she became well, and as soon as she was able to stand on her feet once more, she resumed her washing. Not just ours, but the wash of several other families too.

"I could not rest easy in my bed because of the wash," the old woman explained. "The wash would not let me die."

"With the help of God you will live to be a hundred and twenty," said my mother, as a benediction.

"God forbid! What good would such a long life be? The work becomes harder and harder . . . my strength is leaving me . . . I do not want to be a burden on anyone!" The old woman muttered and crossed herself, and raised her eyes toward heaven.

Fortunately there was some money in the house and Mother counted out what she owed. I had a strange feeling: the coins in the old woman's washed-out hands seemed to become as worn and clean and pious as she herself was. She blew on the coins and tied them in a kerchief. Then she left, promising to return in a few weeks for a new load of wash.

But she never came back. The wash she had returned was her last effort on this earth. She had been driven by an indomitable will to return the property to its rightful owners, to fulfill the task she had undertaken.

And now at last her body, which had long been no more than a shard[5] supported only by the force of honesty and duty, had fallen. Her soul passed into those spheres where all holy souls meet, regardless of the roles they played on this earth, in whatever tongue, of whatever creed. I cannot imagine paradise without this Gentile washwoman. I cannot even conceive of a world where there is no recompense for such effort.

Reading Skill
Making and Verifying Predictions Was your earlier prediction about the old woman accurate? Why or why not?

13 ▲ Critical Viewing
What do you think it would be like to wash clothes using a washboard and tub like these? **[Speculate]**

---

5. **shard** (shärd) *n.* fragment or broken piece.

The Washwoman ■ 31

12 Reading Skill
Making and Verifying Predictions

• **Ask** students the Reading Skill question: Was your earlier prediction about the old woman accurate? Why or why not? **Possible response:** The prediction was not accurate; the old woman did not die.

• Have students share their experiences with making predictions about the essay. Encourage them to tell which predictions proved accurate and which did not.

• Discuss with students how making predictions affected their response to the narrative.

13 Critical Viewing

Possible response: This chore would be time-consuming and physically exhausting.

Concept Connector

Anticipation Guide
Have students return to their **Anticipation Guides** and respond to the statements again in the After Reading column. Then, lead a class discussion, probing for what students have learned that confirms or invalidates each statement.

Connecting to the Literature
Have students compare the sentences they wrote before reading with their thoughts about why people might stick to a difficult task. Ask them to explain whether their thoughts have changed and, if so, how.

Reading Skill Graphic Organizer
Have students review the graphic organizers they completed to make and verify predictions while reading. Show them **Reading Skill Graphic Organizer B** (*Graphic Organizer Transparencies,* p. 4) as an example. Then have students share the graphic organizers they did and the predictions they made about the essay.

Apply the Skills

The Washwoman

Thinking About the Selection

1. The washwoman believes in doing her duty and finds fulfillment in it.

2. (a) She does the laundry. (b) Singer cites the need to haul water and to compete for drying space in the attic.

3. (a) The washwoman is ill. (b) She is dedicated to her work, and it is important for her to finish what she starts.

4. (a) She is poor and has been abandoned by her son, who is ashamed of her and does not help her. She is not bitter toward him. (b) Singer says nothing about her family history or what she does in the present besides laundry. (c) Singer wanted the focus on the washwoman's working life. Including other details would not support this main idea.

5. (a) She faces poverty. She has to work under very difficult conditions to make a living. She suffers exhaustion and illness. (b) Despite the hardships of the weather and the heavy loads, she remains positive and without bitterness. She is determined to do her duty. (c) In spite of a difficult and unappreciated life, the old washwoman proves that people can endure, find satisfaction in their work, and remain positive about life.

6. (a) **Possible response: The Washwoman:** She is small, old, and wrinkled; she does her work conscientiously and charges no more than others; she is not bitter toward her son. **The Washwoman's Son:** He is wealthy; he is ashamed of his mother; he does not invite her to his wedding. Another sample answer can be found on **Literary Analysis Graphic Organizer B,** p. 7, in *Graphic Organizer Transparencies.*
(b) She is hardworking, honest, and determined; she still cares for her son. He is selfish and self-centered.

7. (a) An ordinary, humble, insignificant person can be a hero simply by refusing to give up. (b) Although old and growing weak, the washwoman

32

1. **Respond:** Why do you think the washwoman gives so much and asks so little in return?

2. (a) **Recall:** Which job does the washwoman perform for Singer's family? (b) **Connect:** Which laborious obstacles to doing the job well does Singer describe?

3. (a) **Recall:** What prevents the washwoman from returning to the family for several months? (b) **Draw Conclusions:** What does the washwoman's eventual return tell you about her character?

4. (a) **Recall:** What specific information about the washwoman's personal life does the author include? (b) **Speculate:** What other kinds of information about the washwoman might the author have chosen to include but left out? (c) **Assess:** Based on this essay, explain why an author might choose to include some details and omit others.

Literary Analysis

5. (a) In this **narrative essay,** what difficulties does the washwoman face? (b) How does she respond to those challenges? (c) What inspirational lesson does the author take away from the story of the washwoman's life?

6. (a) Use a chart like the one shown to record three **significant details** that Singer uses to describe the washwoman and her son.

The Washwoman	The Washwoman's Son

(b) What impression of each character does each detail create?

7. (a) What point does Isaac Bashevis Singer make in this narrative essay? (b) Which details in the essay best support this point?

Reading Skill

8. Write down three **predictions** that you made while reading "The Washwoman." Then, trade papers with a partner and discuss the accuracy of your predictions and the details you used to make them. Finally, explain how your method of making and verifying predictions has or has not changed as a result of your discussion.

returns the final load of laundry rather than giving in to her illness and failing to fulfill her obligation.

8. **Possible response:** The washwoman will survive her walk home in the severe weather. The family will not see the washwoman or their laundry again. The washwoman will ask her son to help her with her last load of laundry.

Essay at a Glance
The author finds meaning in the tale of a hardworking elderly woman who struggles against terrible hardships to keep her promises.

Go Online
Assessment
For: Self-test
Visit: www.PHSchool.com
Web Code: epa-6103

Narrative Essay: an essay that tells a story about real people or events

Significant Details: key pieces of information in a literary work

Prediction: an informed idea about what might happen later

Vocabulary Builder

Practice Use a word from the vocabulary list for "The Washwoman" on page 24 to replace each underlined word with its opposite.

1. The former enemies have put their old <u>friendship</u> behind them.
2. The actor's <u>flexibility</u> made him difficult to direct.
3. She inherited the family trade from her <u>children</u>.
4. Running extra laps was his <u>reward</u> for being late to practice.

Adding Words to Your Vocabulary A synonym is a word that has the same or a similar meaning as another word. Using a thesaurus, find a synonym for each word in the vocabulary list for "The Washwoman" on page 24. Use each synonym in a sentence that makes the meaning of the word clear. (For help with reference materials, see page R7.)

Writing

Using "The Washwoman" as a model, write an **anecdote**, a brief narrative, about a person whom you know and admire. For example, you might describe something admirable that the person did and what you learned from it.

- Before you draft, note what you admire about the person.
- Describe a specific event that illustrates the characteristics you admire in your subject.

For *Grammar, Vocabulary,* and *Assessment,* see **Build Language Skills,** pages 40–41.

Extend Your Learning

Listening and Speaking Conduct an **interview** with an older person whom you admire. Before you begin, list questions about the person's life. Speak with confidence and poise as you ask your questions, and listen carefully to the answers. Ask follow-up questions when appropriate. Record the person's answers, and share your findings with the class.

Research and Technology With classmates, use Internet and library resources to find information about Singer's native Poland, including its history of shifting borders. Share your findings with the class in an **oral presentation**.

- Divide the presentation so that each of you delivers part of it.
- Use visual aids in your presentation, including maps.

Assessment Resources

The following resources can be used to assess students' knowledge and skills.

Unit 1 Resources:
   Selection Test A, pp. 29–31
   Selection Test B, pp. 32–34

Go **Online**
—Assessment Students may use the **Self-test** to prepare for **Selection Test A** or **Selection Test B.**

Go **Online**
—Research **For:** An additional research activity
Visit: www.PHSchool.com
Web Code: epd-7101
For another research activity to extend students' learning, give students this Web Code.

Vocabulary Builder
Practice
1. rancor
2. obstinacy
3. forebears
4. atonement

Adding Words to Your Vocabulary
Sample answers:

1. forebears—ancestors; She found inspiration in the stories of her *ancestors.*
2. rancor—hatred; The *hatred* the brothers felt for one another made family get-togethers impossible.
3. atonement—penance; The boy washed the family cars as *penance* for breaking his curfew.
4. obstinacy—stubbornness; Her *stubbornness* prevented her from considering the opinions of others.

Writing

- To give students guidance for writing an anecdote, give them **Support for Writing** for "The Washwoman," p. 26 in *Unit 1 Resources.*
- To evaluate students' anecdotes, use the Descriptive Essay rubrics, pp. 55–56 in *General Resources.* In addition, you might evaluate for how well students use significant details in the structuring of their anecdotes.

Six Traits Focus

✔ Ideas	Word Choice
✔ Organization	Sentence Fluency
Voice	Conventions

ꟿ Writing and Grammar, Gold Level
Students will find guidance on narrative writing in Chapters 4 and 5.

Build Language Skills

Go to pages 40–41 for vocabulary and grammar lessons and assessment practice.

Extend Your Learning

The **Support for Extend Your Learning** page (*Unit 1 Resources,* p. 27) provides guided note-taking opportunities to help students complete the Extend Your Learning activities.

33

Teaching notes for Literary Analysis, Reading Skill, and Vocabulary Builder for this selection begin on p. 24.

❸ Background

Limited Options In the early 1900s, African Americans in the South faced extreme prejudice and hatred. During Reconstruction, federal soldiers protected the rights of the newly freed slaves. African Americans voted and served in government. When the troops withdrew, legal maneuvering, intimidation, and other tactics stripped African Americans of their rights and opportunities. At the turn of the twentieth century, opportunities for African Americans were at a low point. Many began migrating north in the hope of finding better living and working conditions. Those that stayed behind struggled to survive. In general, only the most menial tasks were open to them.

❹ Connecting to the Literature

• Model use of the expressive vocabulary students are asked to use with these examples:

1. To succeed in a new venture, people must be able to *analyze* their own abilities.

2. They need to *establish* a plan and then stick to it.

3. They cannot be afraid to *initiate* change.

4. Most importantly, they must be willing to *transform* themselves to meet the new circumstances.

• Help students further develop their expressive vocabulary by providing these words: *adapt, courageous, prospect,* and *transition.* Encourage them to use these words as they discuss the selection.

Go Online **Author Link** For additional information about Maya Angelou, have students type in the Web Code and then select *Maya Angelou.*

Build Understanding • *New Directions*

Narrative Essay

❸ Background

Limited Options In the early 1900s, job opportunities were unavailable to many Americans—particularly African Americans like Annie Johnson in "New Directions." At that time, the most common jobs available for African American women were cleaning, child care, and general household labor. For women who had families, caring for someone else's household was an extra burden.

❹ Connecting to the Literature

Reading/Writing Connection In "New Directions," an African American woman decides to make a major change in her life at a time when many choices are closed to her. List some of the character traits one might need to succeed in a new venture. Use at least three of these words: *analyze, establish, initiate, transform.*

Review

For **Literary Analysis, Reading Skill,** and **Vocabulary Builder,** see page 24.

READ MORE

by Maya Angelou *The Complete Collected Poems of Maya Angelou*

Meet the Author

Maya **Angelou** (b.1928)

Maya Angelou's life is a story of overcoming hardships and succeeding. She was raised in rural, segregated Arkansas. In 1940, she moved to San Francisco, where she worked as a waitress, cook, and dancer. In the 1950s, Angelou went to New York, where she discovered her talents as a writer.

"I am human, and nothing human can be alien to me." Angelou wrote these words, and she lives by them. She went on to become an author, a poet, a playwright, an editor, an actress, a director, and a teacher. Her many literary honors include a nomination for a Pulitzer Prize. She also read one of her poems at President Bill Clinton's inauguration in January 1993.

Fast Facts

▶ Angelou's first name is Marguerite. Her brother gave her the nickname *Maya* when she was a child.

▶ The feature film *Georgia, Georgia* was adapted from one of her stories.

 Go Online **Author Link** **For:** More about the author **Visit:** www.PHSchool.com **Web Code:** epe-9103

34 ■ Fiction and Nonfiction

Differentiated Instruction Solutions for All Learners

Support for Below-Level Students [L1, L2]	Support for English Learners [EL]
Unit 1 Resources	**Unit 1 Resources**
Vocabulary Warm-up Word Lists, p. 35	**Vocabulary Warm-up Word Lists,** p. 35
Vocabulary Warm-up Practice, p. 36	**Vocabulary Warm-up Practice,** p. 36
Reading Warm-up A, p. 37	**Reading Warm-up A,** p. 37
Selection Test A, pp. 47–49	**Reader's Notebook: English Learner's Version**
Graphic Organizer Transparencies	**Listening to Literature Audio CD**
Reading Skill Graphic Organizer Transparency B, p. 5	
Reader's Notebook: Adapted Version	
Adapted Reader's Notebook Audio CD	

NEW DIRECTIONS ① ②

MAYA ANGELOU

In 1903 the late Mrs. Annie Johnson of Arkansas found herself with two toddling sons, very little money, a slight ability to read and add simple numbers. To this picture add a disastrous marriage and the burdensome fact that Mrs. Johnson was a Negro.

When she told her husband, Mr. William Johnson, of her dissatisfaction with their marriage, he conceded that he too found it to be less than he expected, and had been secretly hoping to leave and study religion. He added that he thought God was calling him not only to preach but to do so in Enid, Oklahoma. He did not tell her that he knew a minister in Enid with whom he could study and who had a friendly, unmarried daughter. They parted <u>amicably</u>, Annie

Vocabulary Builder
amicably (am´ i kə blē) *adv.* in a friendly way

New Directions ■ 35

❶ Motivation

Prepare an **Anticipation Guide** (see *General Resources*, p. 10) with the following statements:

• Success depends upon being in the right place at the right time.

• If you think too much about making a change, you will lose your nerve and not do anything at all.

• All it takes to succeed in business is one good idea.

• Successful people stick to doing what they do best.

• Change is best made quickly and spontaneously.

Concept Connector ➡

Students will return to the Anticipation Guide after completing "New Directions."

Learning Modalities
Interpersonal Learners

Angelou does not tell us what Annie Johnson is feeling and rarely uses Annie's own words. Nevertheless, students should be able to intuit some of Annie's thoughts and feelings. As students read the essay, encourage them to put themselves in Annie's place. Have students list words and phrases that describe what Annie may be thinking and feeling at different points in the essay.

❷ About the Selection

"New Directions" is more than a biographical sketch of one woman's road from adversity to success; it is about choices. Annie Johnson is temporarily the victim of circumstances. She could give up, but she does not. Instead, she shows us that despite life's many obstacles success follows those who are courageous, creative, and flexible in their decisions. With hard work and initiative, it is possible to "cut a new path."

Differentiated
Instruction   Solutions for All Learners

Support for English Learners
Prepare students for reading by giving them a brief preview of the essay.

• Have students read aloud the essay title and then discuss its meaning.

• Ask students to describe the images, including what the images make them think of and how the images make them feel.

• Review the footnoted vocabulary words and other terms that may confuse students.

• Finally, make sure students understand the social conditions in which Annie lived.

Enrichment for Gifted/Talented Students
Have pairs of students role-play interviews with Annie Johnson. Have each pair prepare a list of questions to ask Annie about her new venture, using the essay for guidance. Then have pairs conduct their interviews in front of the class, with one student asking the questions in the role of a reporter and the other student answering the questions in the role of Annie Johnson.

❸ Reading Skill
Making and Verifying Predictions

- Have students **summarize** the dilemma that Annie faces.
  Answer: Annie's marriage is over, and she needs to find a way to support her children. She does not want to get a job that would require other people to raise her children, and the factories will not hire her.

- **Ask** students to respond to the Reading Skill question: What prediction do you make about Annie's plans? Why?
  Possible response: The author includes these details to show Annie's strength and determination in the face of such a dilemma. She is probably going to use her cooking skills to open a food stand or café for the factory workers.

- **Ask** students how they can verify their predictions.
  Answer: I need to keep reading the text to find out if my prediction is correct.

❹ Critical Viewing

Possible response: Because of their intense physical labor, lumber workers would be hungry after a few hours of work.

---

keeping the one-room house and William taking most of the cash to carry himself to Oklahoma.

Annie, over six feet tall, big-boned, decided that she would not go to work as a domestic and leave her "precious babes" to anyone else's care. There was no possibility of being hired at the town's cotton gin or lumber mill, but maybe there was a way to make the two factories work for her. In her words, "I looked up the road I was going and back the way I come, and since I wasn't satisfied, I decided to step off the road and cut me a new path." She told herself that she wasn't a fancy cook but that she could "mix groceries well ❸ enough to scare hungry away and from starving a man."

She made her plans meticulously and in secret. One early evening to see if she was ready, she placed stones in two five-gallon pails and carried them three miles to the cotton gin. She rested a little, and then, discarding some rocks, she walked in the darkness to the saw mill five miles farther along the dirt road. On her way back to her little house and her babies, she dumped the remaining rocks along the path.

That same night she worked into the early hours boiling chicken and frying ham. She made dough and filled the rolled-out pastry with meat. At last she went to sleep.

36 ■ *Fiction and Nonfiction*

Vocabulary Builder
meticulously (mə tik′ yōō ləs lē) *adv.* very carefully and precisely

Reading Skill
Making and Verifying Predictions What prediction do you make about Annie's plans? Why?

❹
◀ Critical Viewing Judging from this photograph, why do you think Annie Johnson felt that lumber workers would want to buy her pies? **[Draw Conclusions]**

Vocabulary Development

Vocabulary Knowledge Rating
When students have completed reading and discussing "New Directions," have them take out their **Vocabulary Knowledge Rating Chart** for this selection. Read the words aloud once more and have students rate their knowledge of the words again in the After Reading column. Clarify any words that are still problematic. Have students write their own definition and example or sentence in the appropriate column. Then have students complete the **Vocabulary Builder Practice** activities on p. 39. Encourage students to use the words in further discussion and written work about this selection. Remind them that they will be accountable for these words on the Selection Test.

The next morning she left her house carrying the meat pies, lard, an iron brazier, and coals for a fire. Just before lunch she appeared in an empty lot behind the cotton gin. As the dinner noon bell rang, she dropped the savors into boiling fat and the aroma rose and floated over to the workers who spilled out of the gin, covered with white lint, looking like specters.

Most workers had brought their lunches of pinto beans and biscuits or crackers, onions and cans of sardines, but they were tempted by the hot meat pies which Annie ladled out of the fat. She wrapped them in newspapers, which soaked up the grease, and offered them for sale at a nickel each. Although business was slow, those first days Annie was determined. She balanced her appearances between the two hours of activity.

So, on Monday if she offered hot fresh pies at the cotton gin and sold the remaining cooled-down pies at the lumber mill for three cents, then on Tuesday she went first to the lumber mill presenting fresh, just-cooked pies as the lumbermen covered in sawdust emerged from the mill.

For the next few years, on balmy spring days, blistering summer noons, and cold, wet, and wintry middays, Annie never disappointed her customers, who could count on seeing the tall, brown-skin woman bent over her brazier, carefully turning the meat pies. When she felt certain that the workers had become dependent on her, she built a stall between the two hives of industry and let the men run to her for their lunchtime provisions.

She had indeed stepped from the road which seemed to have been chosen for her and cut herself a brand-new path. In years that stall became a store where customers could buy cheese, meal, syrup, cookies, candy, writing tablets, pickles, canned goods, fresh fruit, soft drinks, coal, oil, and leather soles for worn-out shoes.

Each of us has the right and the responsibility to assess the roads which lie ahead, and those over which we have traveled, and if the future road looms <u>ominous</u> or unpromising, and the roads back uninviting, then we need to gather our resolve and, carrying only the necessary baggage, step off that road into another direction. If the new choice is also <u>unpalatable</u>, without embarrassment, we must be ready to change that as well.

Culture Connection

Iron Braziers Annie Johnson uses an iron brazier (brā´ zhər) to cook her meat pies. A brazier is a pan or bowl that holds burning coals or charcoal as a heat source for cooking. In some braziers, food is placed on a grill directly over the flames. Johnson uses hers to heat a pot of boiling fat so that she can deep-fry her pies.

An iron brazier would have been heavy and difficult to carry, especially along with the other supplies needed to cook the pies.

Johnson's process for cooking and selling her pies was laborious, but she made the best use of the means available to her.

Connect to the Literature

What does Johnson's willingness to endure the work involved in using an iron brazier suggest about her character?

Vocabulary Builder
ominous (äm´ ə nəs)
adj. threatening

unpalatable (un pal´ it ə bəl) *adj.* distasteful; unpleasant

New Directions ■ 37

❺ **Literature in Context**

Culture Connection The lowly, unsung lump of charcoal has been an essential factor in human progress for over six thousand years. Charcoal burning, begun in China, is regarded as one of the first industrial processes. Charcoal made possible the Bronze and Iron Ages and was a key ingredient in gunpowder.

Connect to the Literature Point out that the brazier, though heavy, gives Johnson a low-cost, portable stove. Then, **ask** the Connect to the Literature question: What does Johnson's willingness to endure the work involved in using an iron brazier suggest about her character?
Answer: Johnson shows determination and dedication in the face of hard work and obstacles.

Concept Connector

Anticipation Guide
Have students return to their **Anticipation Guides** and respond to the statements again in the After Reading column. Then, lead a class discussion, probing for what students have learned that confirms or invalidates each statement.

Connecting to the Literature
Have students compare the sentences they wrote before reading with their thoughts about why people might stick to a difficult task. Ask them to explain whether their thoughts have changed and, if so, how.

Reading Skill Graphic Organizer
Have students review the graphic organizers they completed to make and verify predictions while reading. Show them **Reading Skill Graphic Organizer B** (*Graphic Organizer Transparencies,* p. 5) as an example. Then have students share the graphic organizers they did and the predictions they made about the essay.

Apply the Skills

New Directions

Thinking About the Selection

1. **Respond:** What do you admire about Annie Johnson? Explain.
2. **(a) Recall:** Why does Annie Johnson have to find a source of income? **(b) Recall:** Why does she decide against a job as a domestic? **(c) Infer:** What does Annie Johnson's decision suggest about the kind of mother she is?
3. **(a) Recall:** What does Annie Johnson decide to do to earn a living? **(b) Evaluate:** How would you describe Annie Johnson's abilities as a businessperson? Explain.
4. **(a) Recall:** In what ways does Annie Johnson's business grow? **(b) Draw Conclusions:** What does her achievement suggest about the human spirit in general?
5. **Make a Judgment:** Do you think taking a "new direction" in life is worth the risk of failure? Explain.

Literary Analysis

6. **(a)** In this **narrative essay**, what problem sets the story in motion? **(b)** How is the problem overcome?
7. **(a)** Use a chart like the one shown to record three **significant details** that Angelou uses to describe Annie Johnson and her husband.

Annie Johnson	Annie Johnson's Husband

(b) What impression of each character does each of these details create?
8. **(a)** What point do you think Maya Angelou makes in this narrative essay? **(b)** Which details in the essay best support this point?

Reading Skill

9. Write down three **predictions** that you made while reading "New Directions." Then, trade papers with a partner and discuss the accuracy of your predictions and the details you used to make them. Finally, explain how your method of making and verifying predictions has or has not changed as a result of your discussion.

QuickReview

Essay at a Glance
The author finds inspiration in the tale of a young mother who starts a business to support her family.

Go Online
Assessment
For: Self-test
Visit: www.PHSchool.com
Web Code: epa-6104

Narrative Essay: an essay that tells a story about real people or events

Significant Details: key pieces of information in a literary work

Prediction: an informed idea about what might happen later

Answers (left column):

1. **Possible response:** Annie is a hard worker; she is willing to take chances; she cares very much about her children.

2. (a) Annie is a single mother, and her husband took most of their money when they divorced. (b) She does not want to leave her children in someone else's care. (c) Annie is a devoted mother.

3. (a) Annie sells her homemade meat pies to factory workers. (b) **Possible response:** Annie is a smart businessperson; she knows how to plan ahead and how to attract customers.

4. (a) Annie builds a stall between the two factories, and eventually the stall becomes a store. (b) It suggests that people can rise above circumstances and that as long as the spirit is unbroken, it will find a way to survive.

5. **Possible response:** Taking a new direction often can lead to a better life, so it is worth the risk of failure.

6. (a) Annie faces the problem of how to support herself and her children. (b) Annie starts a business selling meat pies to factory workers.

7. (a) **Possible response:** Annie Johnson: She will not leave her children; she is a good cook; she makes meticulous plans for her business. **Annie Johnson's Husband:** He wants to study religion and preach; he is interested in studying with a minister who has an unmarried daughter; he takes most of the family's money when he leaves.

   Another sample answer can be found on **Literary Analysis Graphic Organizer B,** p. 9, in *Graphic Organizer Transparencies.*

   (b) Annie is strong, determined, intelligent, and business savvy. Annie's husband is hypocritical, unfaithful, selfish, and irresponsible.

8. (a) **Possible response:** Angelou makes the point that people should have the courage to make changes and try new directions in their lives when necessary. (b) Annie takes a risk in trying to start her own business instead of taking a job as a domestic. She works hard in all kinds of weather. She builds a food stall, taking a chance that her customers will follow her. Then she expands and starts a store.

9. **Possible response:** She will make food and sell it to the factory workers. The factory workers will not be able to resist the smell of the fresh meat pies. Annie will build a successful business.

Vocabulary Builder

Practice Use a word from the "New Directions" vocabulary list on page 24 to replace each underlined word with its opposite.

1. When people act in a friendly manner, they behave <u>viciously</u>.
2. Some people think that spinach is <u>delicious</u>.
3. The rumble of a volcano is an <u>encouraging</u> sound.
4. You can avoid mistakes on tests by checking your work <u>carelessly</u>.

Adding Words to Your Vocabulary A **synonym** is a word that has the same or a similar meaning as another word. Using a thesaurus, find a synonym for each word in the vocabulary list for "New Directions" on page 24. Use each synonym in a sentence that makes the meaning of the word clear. (For help with reference materials, see page R7.)

Writing

Using "New Directions" as a model, write an **anecdote,** a brief narrative, about a person whom you know and admire. For example, you might describe something admirable that the person did and what you learned from it.

• Before you draft, note what you admire about the person.
• Describe a specific event that illustrates the characteristics you admire in your subject.

For *Grammar, Vocabulary,* and *Assessment,* see **Build Language Skills,** pages 40–41.

Extend Your Learning

Listening and Speaking With another student, role-play an **interview** between Annie Johnson and a potential employer. Listen carefully to what your partner says in the interview, and respond with appropriate questions or answers. Speak with confidence and poise. After the role play, give each other feedback on your work.

Research and Technology With classmates, follow Johnson's example and identify a business opportunity in your community. Deliver an **oral presentation** on your idea in class.

• Divide the presentation so that each of you delivers part of it.
• Incorporate maps and other visual aids into your presentation.

Apply the Skills ■ 39

Go Online **For:** An additional research activity
─Research **Visit:** www.PHSchool.com
         Web Code: epd-7102
For another research activity to extend students' learning, give students this Web Code.

Vocabulary Builder
Practice

1. amicably
2. unpalatable
3. ominous
4. meticulously

Adding Words to Your Vocabulary
Sample responses:

1. amicably—amiably; The couple *amiably* discussed their differences.
2. meticulously—carefully; The professor *carefully* reviewed the students' final exams.
3. ominous—threatening; The *threatening* clouds darkened the morning sky.
4. unpalatable—distasteful; She found her children's music to be *distasteful.*

Writing

• To give students guidance for writing an anecdote, give them **Support for Writing** for "New Directions," p. 42, in *Unit 1 Resources.*
• To evaluate students' anecdotes, use the Descriptive Essay rubrics, pp. 55–56 in *General Resources.* In addition, you might evaluate how well students use significant details in the structuring of their anecdotes.

Six Traits Focus

✔ Ideas		Word Choice
✔ Organization		Sentence Fluency
Voice		Conventions

WG **Writing and Grammar, Gold Level**
Students will find guidance on narrative writing in Chapters 4 and 5.

Build Language Skills

Go to pages 40–41 for vocabulary and grammar lessons and assessment practice.

Extend Your Learning

The **Support for Extend Your Learning** page (*Unit 1 Resources,* p. 43) provides guided note-taking opportunities to help students complete the Extend Your Learning activities.

Vocabulary Skill

- Introduce the word roots *-part-*, *-volute-*, and *-volve-*. Ask students to brainstorm for words that contain these roots.
  Possible Answers: *participle, partisan, particle, partial, partition, particular; convoluted, revolution; revolve, devolve.*

- Have students complete the Practice activity on this page.

Possible Answers

1. The root *-volve-* means "to roll," so *involve* means "to roll in" or "include" the characters.

2. The root *-part-* means "portion" or "part of," so *participation* means "becoming a part of" or "taking part in" the discussion.

3. *-Volut-* means "to roll," so *revolution* means that Earth "rolls around" the sun.

4. *-Part-* means "portion" or "part of," so *partition* means "something that divides" the room into two sides."

5. *-Volve-* means "to roll," so *revolve* means that the plot "rolls around" or "goes around" a conflict.

Grammar Lesson

- Tell students that three examples of common nouns are *war, city,* and *ocean.* **Ask** students to think of proper nouns that could take the place of these common nouns.
  Possible answers: *World War II, Paris, Atlantic Ocean.*

- Explain that proper nouns can be used as adjectives and that students should be able to recognize the difference.

Answers

1. Astronauts (c); moon (c); July (p); year (c); mother (c)

2. Millions (c); people (c); world (c); Neil Armstrong (p); person (c); moon (c)

3. Americans (p); pride (c)

4. president (c); crew(c); medals (c)

5. parade (c); New York City (p)

𝒲𝒢 **Writing and Grammar, Gold Level**
Students will find further instruction and practice on common and proper nouns in Chapter 16, Section 1.

Build Language Skills

The Washwoman • New Directions

Vocabulary Skill

Word Roots When you *participate* in an activity, you *involve* yourself in it. Both *participate* and *involve* have Latin roots. The word *participate* has the **Latin root *-part-*,** meaning "portion or part of." To *participate* is to "take part." Other cognates of *-part-* will be related to "portion, part."*Involve* has the **Latin root *-volve-*,** meaning "roll." *Involve* means "roll in," or "include." The root *-volve-* is closely related to the root *-volut-*, which also means "roll."

Practice Explain how one of the roots *-volve-*, *-volut-*, or *-part-* contributes to the meaning of the underlined word in each sentence. If necessary, use a dictionary for help. Then, write a new sentence using the underlined word.

1. Understanding the work <u>involves</u> studying the characters.

2. Your <u>participation</u> in the discussion is important.

3. Seasons are the result of Earth's <u>revolution</u> around the sun.

4. The <u>partition</u> divides the two sides of the room.

5. The plot <u>revolves</u> around a conflict.

Grammar Lesson

Common Nouns and Proper Nouns A **common noun** names any one of a class of people, places, or things. A **proper noun** names a specific person, place, or thing and begins with a capital letter.

Type	Common Noun	Proper Noun
person	student	Deana Johnson
place	city	Durham
thing	novel	*A Separate Peace*

Practice Copy each of the following sentences. Draw one line under each common noun and two lines under each proper noun.

1. Astronauts reached the moon in July of the year my mother was born.

2. Millions of people around the world watched Neil Armstrong become the first person to walk on the moon.

3. Americans were filled with pride.

4. The president awarded the crew medals.

5. They were honored with a parade in New York City.

𝒲𝒢 *Prentice Hall Writing and Grammar Connection: Chapter 16, Section 2*

40 ■ Fiction and Nonfiction

MorePractice

For more practice with common and proper nouns, see p. R39.

Teaching Resources

The following resources can be used to enrich or extend the instruction for Build Language Skills.

Unit 1 Resources
Build Language Skills: Vocabulary: The Latin roots *-part-*, *-volve-*, and *-volut-*, p. 45
Build Grammar Skills: Common Nouns and Proper Nouns: p. 46

Assessment Practice

Reading: Make Predictions

Directions: *Read the selection. Then, answer the questions.*

Lance pulled on his helmet and checked his skates one last time. He was a little nervous inside, but confident as well. He had been speed racing for three years and had won the finals the past two years. Now he felt he was ready to make it three years in a row.

Lance knew that even though he had won the past two years, he could not take anything for granted. He had trained every day for weeks, harder than in past years. Now he took his place in the line, waiting for the starting gun. He glanced at the racer next to him and saw fear in his eyes.

1. Which of the following would not help you make a prediction?
   A Lance had been racing for three years.
   B He had won the past two years.
   C He had trained harder than in past years.
   D The gun sounded, and the race was on.

2. Based on the details in the passage, what is a reasonable prediction about the race's end?
   A The boy next to Lance will win the race.
   B Lance will be disqualified for not wearing a helmet.
   C Lance will win the race.
   D Lance will become exhausted during the race and drop out.

3. Which of the following details makes that a logical prediction?
   A Lance glanced at the racer next to him.
   B Lance had to check his kneepads and skates.
   C Lance was nervous and seemed worried.
   D Lance had won before and had trained hard.

4. What detail in a future paragraph would make you revise your prediction?
   A Lance paces himself well.
   B The racer in front of Lance falls.
   C Lance feels that the training paid off.
   D Lance sets the pace at the beginning of the race.

Timed Writing: Narration [Critical Stance]

Write a brief narrative about a person who refused to give up and who eventually succeeded in spite of difficult odds. Base your story on actual events, and identify the challenges your subject faced. **(20 minutes)**

 Writing Workshop: *Work in Progress*

Autobiographical Narrative
Choose one item from the Memory List saved in your writing portfolio. Build the scene in your mind by adding other senses. Include what you heard, how warm or cold it was, and how it felt. Save your Memory List in your writing portfolio.

Build Language Skills ■ 41

Reading: Making and Verifying Predictions
1. D
2. C
3. D
4. B

Timed Writing
- Tell students that when writing their narration, they should include characters, a setting, a sequence of events, and a theme.
- Point out that they may save time if they quickly write a list of the sequence of events before they begin writing.
- Tell students that they should make the events and the theme clear to readers through the use of relevant supporting details.
- Assess students' essays on the clarity of the sequence of events and the theme. Evaluate their use of relevant supporting details to make the events and the theme clear.
- Suggest that students plan their time to give 5 minutes to planning, 10 minutes to writing, and 5 minutes to reviewing and revising.

Writing Workshop
Work in Progress

Autobiographical Narrative
- Have students go to their portfolios and take out the work they have completed so far on this assignment.
- Remind students that this work may be used in the autobiographical narrative they will write in the **Writing Workshop** at the end of Part 1.
- Have students close their eyes and visualize the scene that they are trying to describe. It may also be helpful if they draw the scene to try to remember what happened. Have students do the same exercise with the people in the scene.
- Remind students to clearly describe what is happening in the scene. Readers should be able to imagine the people and action from their descriptions.
- When students have finished this activity, have them keep it in their portfolios. They will use it as they continue this Work in Progress.

Meeting Your Standards

Students will

1. understand and explain the instructions found in recipes.
2. read a recipe.

See TeacherExpress™/Lesson View for a detailed lesson plan for Reading Informational Materials.

About Recipes

- Have students read "About Instructions: Recipes."

- Have students think about the first time they used recipes. Ask volunteers to share what they were preparing and if they needed help understanding the recipe instructions.

Reading Skill
Read to Perform a Task

- Remind students that it is important to follow the instructions exactly as given. Point out that recipes often provide instructions in steps, and this order can be instrumental in having a good outcome.

- Review the "Signal Words" chart. **Ask** volunteers to explain the meaning of each signal word and give an example of how failing to notice the signal word could cause a problem.

- **Possible responses:** *Gradually* means "not slow and not fast." Stirring too fast could cause splattering.

  Medium means "half-way between low and high." Cooking on high could result in burning the food.

  Lightly means "just a little." Flouring a surface heavily instead of lightly could result in a floury-bottomed cake.

  Spoonful is a subjective measurement that means "as much as a spoon can hold." Usually, the spoon size is specified and using less or more would affect the taste.

Instructions: Recipes

In Part 1, you are learning how to make predictions while reading literature. Predicting is also useful when you read instructions. Predictions allow you to anticipate when you will need certain materials and how you will use them. The instructions that follow are for a recipe. If you read "New Directions" by Maya Angelou, you will notice that Annie Johnson may have used a similar recipe to bake the meat pies she sold.

About Instructions: Recipes

Instructions provide a step-by-step guide to performing a specific task. A recipe is a form of instruction that tells you how to prepare something to eat. Recipes usually include the following elements:

- A list of all the <u>ingredients</u> you will need
- The exact <u>quantity</u> of each ingredient
- The <u>order</u> in which the ingredients should be combined
- The <u>methods</u> for combining the ingredients (such as mixing, blending, melting)
- The <u>time</u> required for cooking, baking, chilling, freezing, etc.
- The number of <u>servings</u> the recipe will make

Reading Skill

Like most instructions, recipes present a series of specific steps you must follow to complete a larger task. When **reading to perform a task,** pay attention to the order of the required steps. Check off each step as you complete it, or use a bookmark to keep your place on the page. Be sure to finish each step before going on to the next one, until your task is complete.

When you read a recipe, pay close attention to words that signal important details, especially words of quantity and adverbs that tell how to perform tasks. The chart shown here identifies signal words.

Recipe Instruction	Signal Word
Gradually add the broth and milk . . .	Gradually
Cook over *medium* heat . . .	medium
. . . on a *lightly* floured surface.	lightly
Put a *spoonful* of filling in center . . .	spoonful

Differentiated Instruction   Solutions for All Learners

Reading Support
Give students reading support with the appropriate version of the *Reader's Notebooks:*

Reader's Notebook, [L2]

Reader's Notebook: Adapted Version, [L1]

Reader's Notebook: English Learner's Version, [EL]

from **The Book Lover's Cookbook**
New Road Chicken Pies
by Shaunda Kennedy Wenger and Janet Kay Jensen

Oliver Twist's request for more gruel starts a riot, and Ma Joad agonizes over not being able to fill the bellies of hungry children who watch her family eat stew. When characters deal with food, whether they're eating, cooking, dreaming, manipulating, or suffering, they step off the page and connect with the reader.

Food scenes offer a universal platform that can foster connections between the reader and the character. Some food scenes bring

such strong feelings of nostalgia, the experience between the fiction of the story, the reality of the present, and the memories of the past blur to the point where we question, *Could I have known this author? Could I have known this character?*

This recipe links the real-life experience of preparing and eating delicious meat-pies to the characters and events in Maya Angelou's story "New Directions."

> The introduction describes the way in which a recipe can connect readers to literary characters.

New Road Chicken Pies (a.k.a. Turnovers)

FILLING:
1/2 cup potatoes, diced
1/4 cup carrots, diced
3 tablespoons celery, chopped
1 teaspoon onion, minced
1 tablespoon butter or margarine
3 tablespoons all-purpose flour
Salt and pepper to taste
1 cup chicken broth
1/3 cup milk
1 teaspoon fresh parsley, minced
1/4 cup frozen peas, thawed
1 1/2 cups chicken, cooked & diced

PASTRY DOUGH:
2/3 cup shortening or margarine
2 cups all-purpose flour
1/2 teaspoon salt
5 to 7 tablespoons water
1 egg white
1 teaspoon water

> The recipe begins with a complete list of every ingredient needed and the exact amounts required. Some items must be *diced, chopped, minced,* or *thawed* before the mixing of ingredients begins.

(continued)

Reading Recipes

- Point out that most cookbooks have many features in common. They typically have recipes organized into sections such as desserts, main dishes, and hors d'oeuvres. Tell students that they are going to read two pages from a cookbook that is a little different than most cookbooks. **Ask** them to read the title and tell what is different about this cookbook.
  Possible response: This cookbook has recipes that go along with works of literature.

- Have students read "New Road Chicken Pies."
  Ask a volunteer what literary work goes with the Chicken Pie recipe.
  Answer: The Chicken Pie recipe goes with "New Directions," the excerpt from Maya Angelou's memoir.

- Tell students that the cookbook writers named their recipes to go along with the literary works. **Ask** students for another name for New Road Chicken Pies.
  Possible responses: Turnovers, potpies, meat pies

- **Ask** a volunteer how we know that the cookbook authors prefer turnovers as the alternate name.
  Possible response: The title of the recipe is followed by "a.k.a. Turnovers," which means "also known as Turnovers."

- **Ask** students how much flour they would need to prepare this recipe.
  Answer: The recipe calls for 3 tablespoons of flour for the filling and 2 cups for the dough.

continued on p. 44

Differentiated Instruction — Solutions for All Learners

Enrichment for Less Proficient Readers
To emphasize the importance of precise instructions, have students make a secret sketch using circles, triangles, and squares. Then have students write step-by-step instructions for someone else to draw the same sketch. Have students switch instructions with partners and attempt to draw according to their partners' instructions. Have partners compare their drawings.

Enrichment for Advanced Readers
Challenge students to research the traditional recipes of a culture of their choosing. Encourage students to attempt the recipes at home. Have students bring two or three of these cultural recipes and describe them to the class. Ask them to make sure to comment on any unusual or hard-to-obtain ingredients, the relative ease or difficulty of preparation, and on any culturally-specific cooking methods.

Reading Recipes (cont.)

- Direct students to the instructions for making the filling (top of first card on p. 44). **Ask** a student to describe how the vegetables are prepared in this filling.
  Answer: The vegetables are first cooked then set aside. Then they are mixed into the sauce and heated.

- **Ask** a student to describe how the details of this recipe are organized
  Answer: The details are organized in step-by-step order.

- **Ask** students to calculate approximately how long it would take to make New Road Chicken Pies.
  Possible response: Assuming we use precooked and diced chicken, it would take approximately 70 or 75 minutes to prepare the dish: 15 minutes to clean and dice all vegetables, 10 minutes to gather and cook vegetables, 10 minutes to assemble and cook sauce until thickened, 10 minutes to prepare dough, 10 minutes flex time for moving from one step to the next, 15–20 minutes to cook the pies.

- Point out to students that, in the last paragraph of the instructions, a piece of information is given that the cook would want to know at the beginning. **Ask** a volunteer to identify the piece of information and tell why the cook needs to know it at the beginning.
  Answer: The cook needs to know that the pies are to bake at 375º so he or she can preheat the oven.

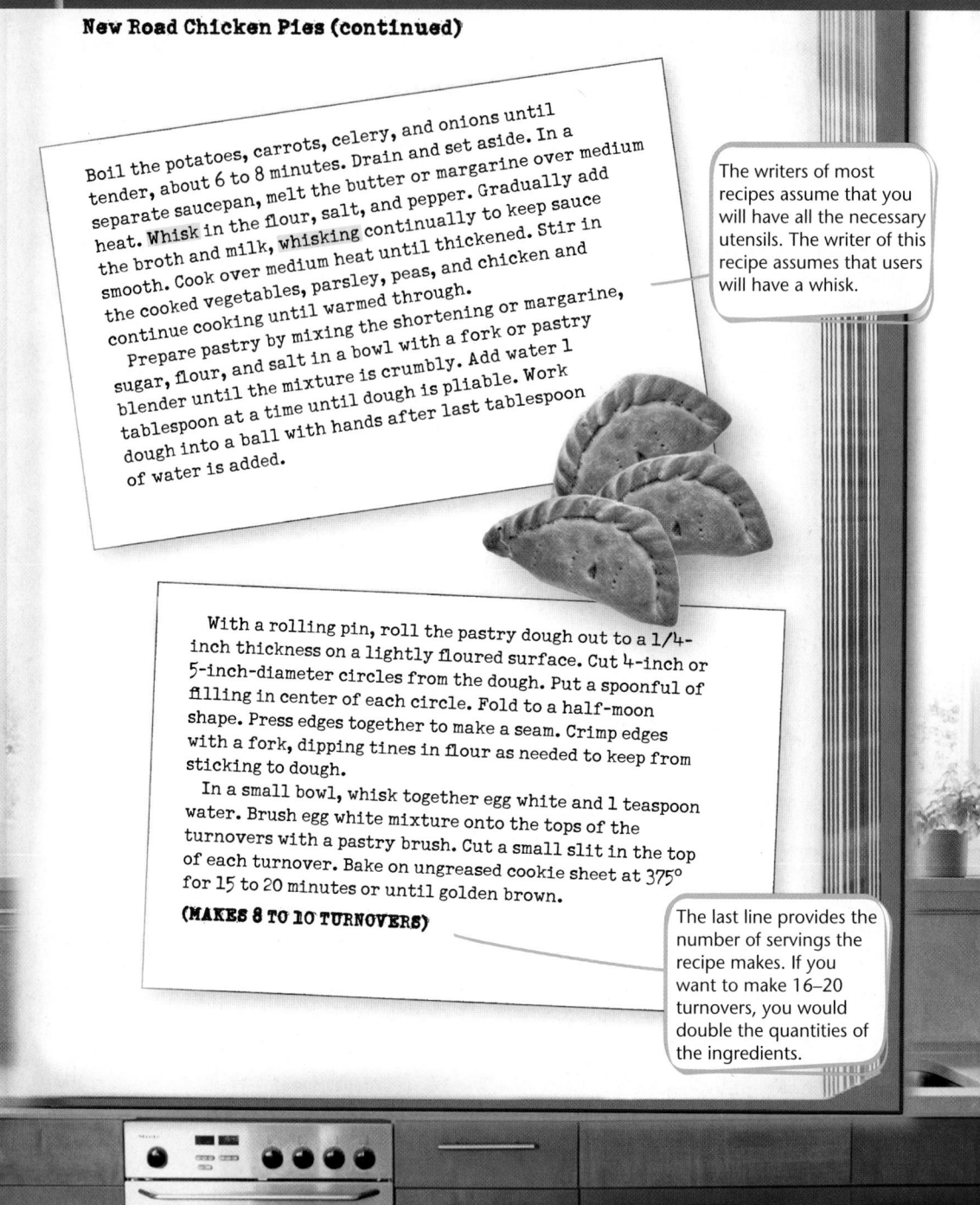

New Road Chicken Pies (continued)

Boil the potatoes, carrots, celery, and onions until tender, about 6 to 8 minutes. Drain and set aside. In a separate saucepan, melt the butter or margarine over medium heat. Whisk in the flour, salt, and pepper. Gradually add the broth and milk, whisking continually to keep sauce smooth. Cook over medium heat until thickened. Stir in the cooked vegetables, parsley, peas, and chicken and continue cooking until warmed through.

Prepare pastry by mixing the shortening or margarine, sugar, flour, and salt in a bowl with a fork or pastry blender until the mixture is crumbly. Add water 1 tablespoon at a time until dough is pliable. Work dough into a ball with hands after last tablespoon of water is added.

The writers of most recipes assume that you will have all the necessary utensils. The writer of this recipe assumes that users will have a whisk.

With a rolling pin, roll the pastry dough out to a 1/4-inch thickness on a lightly floured surface. Cut 4-inch or 5-inch-diameter circles from the dough. Put a spoonful of filling in center of each circle. Fold to a half-moon shape. Press edges together to make a seam. Crimp edges with a fork, dipping tines in flour as needed to keep from sticking to dough.

In a small bowl, whisk together egg white and 1 teaspoon water. Brush egg white mixture onto the tops of the turnovers with a pastry brush. Cut a small slit in the top of each turnover. Bake on ungreased cookie sheet at 375º for 15 to 20 minutes or until golden brown.

(MAKES 8 TO 10 TURNOVERS)

The last line provides the number of servings the recipe makes. If you want to make 16–20 turnovers, you would double the quantities of the ingredients.

Vocabulary Development

Vocabulary for Cookbooks and Recipes
Point out that cookbooks and recipes often use vocabulary that is specific to cooking. Add that the cutting-size directions in the "New Road Chicken Pies" recipe is a good example of this specialized vocabulary. Guide students to understand the meaning of the following words that are used in the recipe to clarify how small to cut different foods.

mince: to cut into very small pieces (smaller than a pea).

dice: to cut into small, even cubes (about the size of a large pea).

chop: to cut into pieces (about the size of a grape).

Reading: Read to Perform a Task

Directions: *Choose the letter of the best answer to each question.*

1. For eight to ten turnovers, how much celery do you use?
   A 1/4 cup
   B 3 teaspoons
   C 3 tablespoons
   D 5 to 7 stalks

2. When you add the broth and milk, how often should you whisk the sauce?
   A never
   B continually
   C three or four times
   D until the vegetables are cooked

3. Which of the following tasks do you perform just before baking?
   A slit the top of each turnover
   B dice the carrots
   C fold the dough into half-moon shapes
   D add the cooked vegetables to the sauce

Reading: Comprehension and Interpretation

Directions: *Write your answers on a separate piece of paper.*

4. What is the shape of the finished turnovers? **[Knowledge]**
5. Why might you need to dip the tines of the fork in flour when crimping the edges of the dough? **[Generating]**
6. Compare a section of the recipe that gives specific instructions or measurements to a part of the instructions that is more open-ended. Explain the possible reasons for the difference. **[Organizing]**

Timed Writing: Explanation [Cognitive]

Describe a process you know well, such as how to cook something, how to make something, or how to assemble something. Remember to identify all the ingredients, materials, or tools needed. Explain each step clearly and precisely, and be sure the steps follow a logical order. Include signal words that will help readers understand the steps in the process. **(20 minutes)**

Reading: Read to Perform a Task

1. C
2. B
3. A
4. A finished turnover is in the shape of a half moon.
5. You might need to dip the tines of the fork in flour when crimping the edges of the dough to keep the tines from sticking to the dough.
6. The recipe is very specific about the kind and amounts of ingredients. It is more open-ended about the diameter of the pastry circles, amount of filling (a spoonful), and cooking time (15 to 20 minutes).

Timed Writing

- Read the *Timed Writing* instructions together as a group. Remind students to include a list of ingredients, tools, or materials needed to complete the process. Also, make sure they plan to include several specific steps and have a clear beginning and end to the process.

- Suggest that students organize their time to give 5 minutes to planning, 10 minutes to writing, and 5 minutes to reviewing and revising.

Planning Differentiated Instruction

Choosing Your Selection

You may use either selection to meet the lesson standards. The following guide will help you determine which of the two selections is more appropriate for your students.

Accessibility at a Glance

	Sonata for Harp and Bicycle	The Cask of Amontillado
Context	Setting: haunted office building in London	Setting: gothic; set in the catacombs of eighteenth-century Europe
Language	• Accessible vocabulary • Conversational dialogue	• Numerous long sentences with embedded clauses • Difficult diction
Concept Level	Accessible (determination to solve a mystery and win another's love)	Challenging (ghastly quest for revenge)
Literary Merit	Contemporary	Classic
Lexile	960L	800L
Other	Suspenseful; surprise ending	Suspenseful
Overall Rating	More accessible	More challenging

Because a number of factors help determine the relative accessibility of paired selections, the Lexile number of the more challenging selection may sometimes be lower than that of the more accessible selection.

Using the Other Selection You may use the other selection for homework or independent reading to reinforce the selection skills. If you use both selections, you can build a test for both using *ExamView*® Test Bank software.

Choosing Your Resources

[L1] Special Needs Students [L4] Advanced Students
[L2] Below-Level Students [EL] English Learners
[L3] All Students

Reading and Vocabulary Warm-ups provide support for below level students. A is for students reading two grades below level; B is for students reading one grade below level. For Selection Tests, A signifies "less challenging" and B "more challenging." For Graphic Organizer transparencies, A signifies "not filled in" and B "filled in."

FT Fast Track Instruction: To move the lesson more quickly, use the strategies and activities identified with **FT**.

Scaffolding for Less Proficient and Advanced Students

The leveled questions on Apply the Skills pages progress in the levels of thinking required to answer them. To address the needs of your different students, you may use the (a) level questions for your less proficient students, the (b) level with your on-level and advanced students. The occasional (c) level questions are appropriate for your advanced students.

Step-by-Step Teaching Guide	Pacing Guide
PRETEACH	
• Administer Vocabulary and Reading Warm-ups as necessary.	
• Introduce the Literary Analysis Skill: Plot and Foreshadowing. **FT**	10 min.
• Introduce the Reading Skill: Making and Verifying Predictions. **FT**	10 min.
• Prepare students to read by teaching the selection vocabulary. **FT**	10 min.
• Build background and develop expressive vocabulary with Connecting to the Literature and Background.	10 min.
• Engage students' interest with the motivation activity.	10 min.
TEACH	
• Informally monitor comprehension while students read independently or in groups. **FT**	30 min.
• Monitor students' comprehension with the Reading Check notes.	as students read
• Reinforce vocabulary with Vocabulary Builder notes.	as students read
• Develop students' understanding of plot and foreshadowing with the Literary Analysis annotations. **FT**	5 min.
• Develop students' ability to make and verify predictions with the Reading Skill annotations. **FT**	10 min.
ASSESS/EXTEND	
• Assess students' comprehension and mastery of the Reading Skill and Literary Analysis by having them answer the Apply the Skills questions. **FT**	35 min.
• Have students complete the Vocabulary Builder activities. **FT**	5 min.
• Apply students' ability to write a critique with the Writing activity. **FT**	30–45 min. or homework
• Extend students' listening and speaking and research and technology skills with one or both of the Extend Your Learning activities.	15–30 min. or homework
• Have students complete the Vocabulary Skill and Grammar Lesson.	5 min.
• Monitor students' progress with the Assessment Practice.	20–40 min.
• Administer **Selection Test A** or **Selection Test B**. **FT**	15 min.

Go Online Professional Development **For:** Information about Lexiles
Visit: www.PHSchool.com
Web Code: eue-1111

Resources

Meeting Your Standards

Students will

1. **analyze and respond to literary elements.**
   - Literary Analysis: Plot and Foreshadowing

2. **read, comprehend, and analyze short stories.**
   - Reading Skill: Making and Verifying Predictions
   - Reading Strategy: Reading on to Verify Predictions
   - Reading Check questions
   - Apply the Skills questions
   - Assessment Practice

3. **develop vocabulary.**
   - Vocabulary Builder
   - Word Roots

4. **apply grammar skills.**
   - Abstract and Concrete Nouns

5. **develop writing proficiency.**
   - Work in Progress: Autobiographical Narrative
   - Critique

6. **extend learning.**
   - Listening and Speaking: Retelling
   - Research and Technology: Storyboard

Block Scheduling: Use one 90-minute class period to preteach the skills and have students read the selection. Use a second 90-minute class period to assess students' mastery of skills, extend their learning, and monitor their progress.

Homework Suggestions

Following are possibilities for homework assignments.

- Support pages from *Unit 1 Resources*:
  Literary Analysis
  Reading Skill
  Vocabulary Builder
  Enrichment

- An Extend Your Learning project and the Writing assignment for your chosen selection may be completed over several days.

PRENTICE HALL
TeacherEXPRESS™ Use this complete
Plan · Teach · Assess suite of powerful
teaching tools to make lesson planning and testing quicker and easier.

PRENTICE HALL
StudentEXPRESS™ Use the
Learn · Study · Succeed Interactive
Textbook (online and on CD-ROM) to make selections and activities come alive with audio and video support and interactive questions.

Practice these skills with either "Sonata for Harp and Bicycle" (p. 48) or "The Cask of Amontillado" (p. 61).

❶ Literary Analysis
Plot and Foreshadowing

- Tell students that in the selections they are about to read, each author creates suspense through a carefully structured *plot*—the sequence of events that catches readers' interest and takes them through the story.

- Have students help you outline the plot of a familiar story, such as "Goldilocks and the Three Bears." Point out that a climax rarely occurs halfway through a story; for example, in a suspenseful story, the climax often occurs near the end.

- Explain that foreshadowing often prepares readers for surprising or unlikely outcomes in a story. Encourage students to look for unusual story details that might foreshadow upcoming events.

- As students read, have them identify each part of the story's plot.

❷ Reading Skill
Making and Verifying Predictions

- Emphasize to students that a prediction is not a wild guess; it is based on clues in the story and students' own knowledge and experience.

- As they read, challenge students to pause at the end of every page or two and predict what will happen next.

- Give students a copy of **Reading Skill Graphic Organizer A** (*Graphic Organizer Transparencies*, p. 10). Have them use it to make and verify predictions as they read the assigned selection.

❶ Literary Analysis

Plot is the sequence of events in a narrative. It is structured around a **conflict**, or problem, and it can be divided into the following parts:

- **Rising Action:** central conflict is introduced
- **Climax:** high point of intensity in the conflict is reached
- **Falling Action:** conflict's intensity lessens
- **Resolution:** conflict concludes and loose ends are tied up

Writers use a variety of techniques to keep readers interested in the plot. One of these, **foreshadowing**, is the use of clues to hint at events that will happen later in a story. Authors use this technique to create **suspense**, a feeling of tension that keeps readers wondering what will happen next.

❷ Reading Skill

A **prediction** is an informed guess about what will happen later in a narrative. Notice details that may foreshadow future events. Make predictions based on those details, and then **read on to verify your predictions.** If a prediction turns out to be wrong, evaluate your reasoning.

- Did you misread details?
- Did the author purposely create false expectations in order to surprise you later in the story?

Revise, or change, your prediction based on your evaluation. Use a chart like the one shown to record your predictions and evaluate their accuracy. Analyze any inaccurate predictions to determine why they were incorrect.

Prediction
The butler will be exposed as the criminal.

↓

Outcome
The gardener is exposed as the criminal.

↓

Analysis of Prediction
The author created a surprise ending by misleading readers.

Vocabulary Builder

Sonata for Harp and Bicycle

- **tantalizingly** (tan′ tə līz′ iŋ lē) *adv.* in a teasing way (p. 50) *He held the ball tantalizingly out of reach.*

- **furtive** (fur′ tiv) *adj.* sneaky (p. 52) *With a furtive wink, he let his friend in on the joke.*

- **reciprocate** (ri sip′ rə kāt′) *v.* return (p. 54) *She refused to reciprocate his anger.*

46 ■ *Fiction and Nonfiction*

The Cask of Amontillado

- **precluded** (prē klood′ id) *v.* prevented (p. 61) *His injury precluded any hope of victory.*

- **retribution** (re′ trə byoo′shən) *n.* payback; punishment for a misdeed (p. 61) *He wanted retribution for the insult he had received.*

- **explicit** (eks plis′ it) *adj.* clearly stated (p. 63) *I could not ignore her explicit refusal.*

Vocabulary Development

Vocabulary Knowledge Rating

Create a **Vocabulary Knowledge Rating Chart** for the selection you will teach from this set. Include the selection vocabulary from this page and the additional words students are asked to use at the end of Connecting to the Literature. These words will increase students' expressive vocabulary.

Give students a copy of the chart with the words on it. Introduce the words by reading them aloud and having students mark their rating in the Before Reading column. Urge them to be alert to these words as they read and discuss the selection because they will rate their knowledge of the words again after they finish.

If you wish, you may tally how many students know (or think they know) a word to gauge how much instruction you need to provide. As students read, point out the words and their context.

Build Understanding • *Sonata for Harp and Bicycle*

❸ Background

Sonatas A sonata (sə nät′ ə) is a musical composition in several movements, or parts. Sonatas are often written for solo piano or for piano and another instrument. In titling her story "Sonata for Harp and Bicycle," Joan Aiken playfully suggests a musical structure that will, like a sequence of chords, be resolved harmoniously at the end.

❹ Connecting to the Literature

Reading/Writing Connection This story features a character who strives to solve a mystery. Many people, such as detectives and reporters, seek out the truth every day as part of their jobs. Write a few sentences describing the qualities a person would need for this type of work. Use at least three of these words: *anticipate, comprehend, confirm, eliminate, expose.*

READ MORE

by Joan Aiken
Midnight Is a Place
Night Fall

Meet the Author

Joan **Aiken** (1924–2004)

The daughter of an American poet, Conrad Aiken, and a Canadian mother, Jessie MacDonald, Joan Aiken was born and grew up in England. She lived with her family in an eerie old house, an experience that helped foster her fascination with mystery and the unexplained. Her mother's second husband was another writer, Martin Armstrong. Not surprisingly, Aiken knew when she was very young that she would become a writer someday.

The "Family Trade" Aiken began writing when she was five and published her first story at sixteen. After spending some time working in London for a magazine, an advertising agency, and the United Nations, she decided to pursue what she has called "the family trade." Her many literary works include novels, poems, plays, and stories for both children and adults.

Fast Facts

▶ Aiken did not attend a school until she was twelve. Before then, she was taught at home by her mother.

▶ Aiken once worked as an advertising copywriter, as does her main character in "Sonata for Harp and Bicycle."

For: More about the author
Visit: www.PHSchool.com
Author Link **Web Code:** epe-9104

Sonata for Harp and Bicycle ■ 47

❸ Background

Sonatas The musical structure of a sonata can be compared to a story's plot structure. It begins with an *exposition* (conflict introduced), which introduces a main and a secondary theme. Next comes the *development* (rising action), which freely plays with and spins out the two themes of the exposition until it reaches a climax. The next stage is the *recapitulation* (falling action), which repeats the exposition, often varying it somewhat. The sonata ends with the *coda* (resolution), which is a kind of comment on or summary of the previous stages. The coda is often much shorter than the other three sections.

❹ Connecting to the Literature

• To help students understand the meanings of the words they are asked to use, give them these sentences:

  1. Detectives must *anticipate* the actions of the people they investigate.
  2. They must fully *comprehend* the facts of a case.
  3. Evidence will *confirm* their predictions.
  4. Detectives *eliminate* any questions about a case.
  5. Their goal is to *expose* the truth.

• Help students further develop their expressive vocabulary by providing these words: *curiosity, ominous, stealthy,* and *undertake.* Encourage students to use these words as they discuss the selection.

Concept Connector ➡

Students will follow up on this activity after completing "Sonata for Harp and Bicycle."

Go Online For additional information about Joan Aiken, have students type in the Web Code and then select *Joan Aiken.*

Differentiated Instruction Solutions for All Learners

Support for Below-Level Students [L1, L2]	Support for English Learners [EL]
Unit 1 Resources	**Unit 1 Resources**
Vocabulary Warm-up Word Lists, p. 53	**Vocabulary Warm-up Word Lists**, p. 53
Vocabulary Warm-up Practice, p. 54	**Vocabulary Warm-up Practice**, p. 54
Reading Warm-up A, p. 55	**Reading Warm-up A**, p. 55
Selection Test A, pp. 63–65	**Reader's Notebook: English Learner's Version**
Graphic Organizer Transparencies	**Listening to Literature Audio CD**
Reading Skill Graphic Organizer, Transparency B, p. 11	
Reader's Notebook: Adapted Version	
Adapted Reader's Notebook Audio CD	

❶ Motivation

Tell students that Aiken's story is about an advertising copywriter who goes to work at a company that seems very ordinary, except for one thing: All employees are hurried out of the building each evening at five o'clock. The reason for this policy is a secret that employees do not learn until they have been with the company a long time. The copywriter is intrigued by this odd situation and sets out to unravel the mystery. Challenge students to predict what the secret might be.

Learning Modalities
Musical/Rhythmic Learners

Share the background information on sonatas on p. 47 of this teacher's edition. Have students read to see whether this story is in any sense written in sonata form. You might start them off by pointing out that the story is in three long sections followed by a final short paragraph. Have them compare this structure to a sonata's exposition, development, recapitulation, and coda. Remind students that *theme* is both a musical and a literary term.

❷ About the Selection

"Sonata for Harp and Bicycle" combines the elements of mystery, romance, and the supernatural—with a wink at Greek mythology included. A hero challenges the absurd rules of his office and the fears of his co-workers by entering the office building after dark—a forbidden act. He uses his problem-solving skills to rid the building of two ghosts and to ensure a triumph for love. Students will enjoy the skill with which Aiken uses visual and musical imagery to build suspense, as well as the touches of humor that lighten this modern-day ghost story.

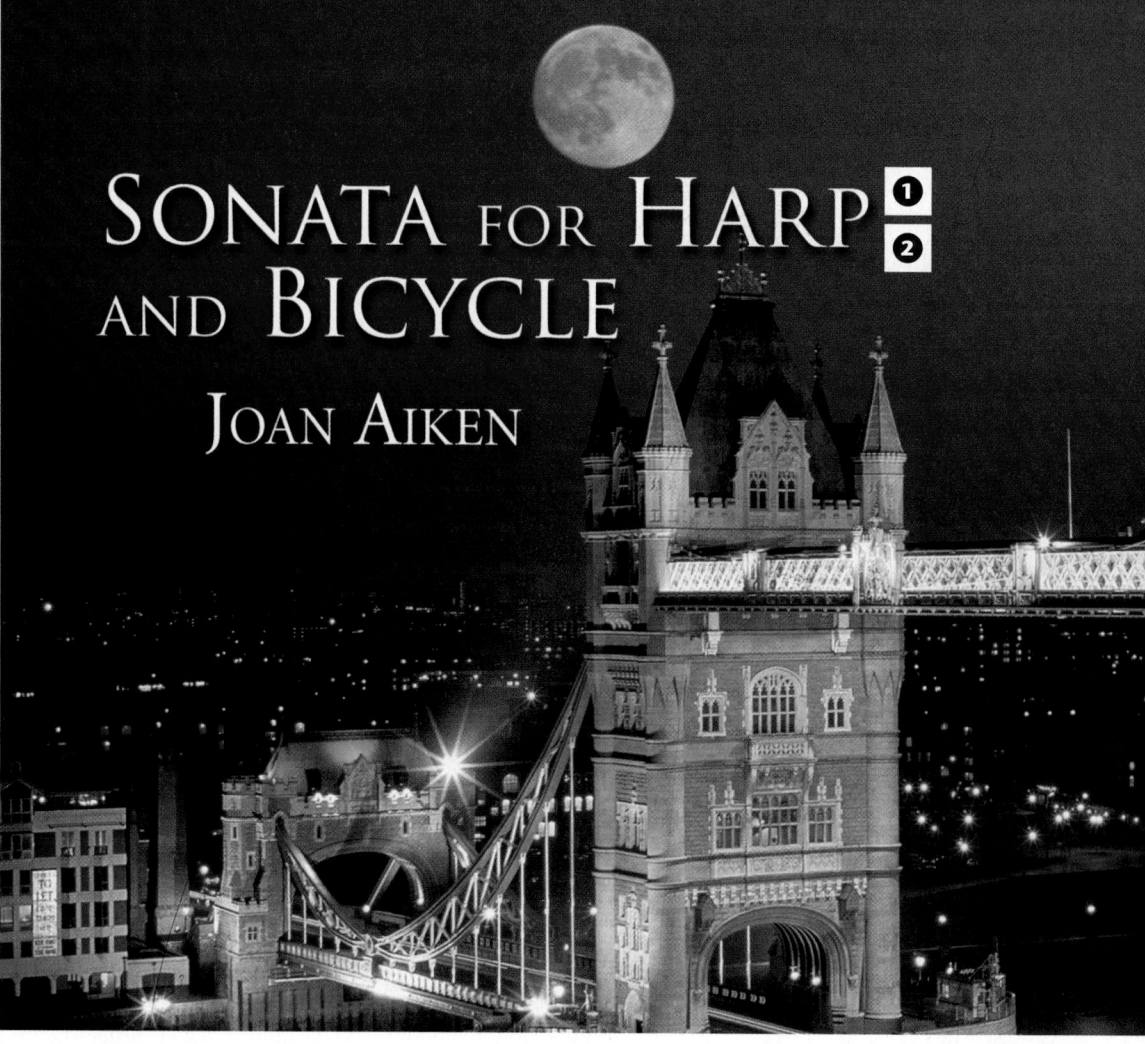

SONATA FOR HARP ❶❷
AND BICYCLE

JOAN AIKEN

❸ "**N**o one is allowed to remain in the building after five o'clock," Mr. Manaby told his new assistant, showing him into the little room that was like the inside of a parcel.

"Why not?"

"Directorial policy," said Mr. Manaby. But that was not the real reason.

Gaunt and sooty, Grimes Buildings lurched up the side of a hill toward Clerkenwell.[1] Every little office within its dim and crumbling exterior owned one tiny crumb of light—such was the proud

---

1. **Clerkenwell** district of London.

48 ■ Fiction and Nonfiction

Vocabulary Development

Think-Aloud: Context Clues

Direct students' attention to the word *infested* on p. 49. Using a think-aloud process, model how to use context to infer the meaning of an unknown word. Say to students:

> I'm going to think aloud to show you how I would figure out the meaning of *infested* based on its context.
>
> In this sentence, *infested* is used to describe how darkness comes into the building. The sentence before it describes how the lights are turned out, leaving an "uncontrollable mass of darkness." This mass comes in through the windows and doors. When the text says that the "darkness *infested* the building," it makes me think of an invasion. In the next sentence, Aiken compares the arrival of darkness to the flight of bats coming in to roost. So *infested* must mean an invasion or overrunning of a place by something unpleasant.

• Remind students that suspense is a feeling of tension that keeps readers wondering what will happen next. Point out that Aiken immediately creates suspense in the beginning of the story. **Ask** students to explain how the bracketed passage affects the reader.
Possible response: The passage immediately draws readers into the story by making them wonder why no one is allowed in the building after five o'clock. In addition, the description of darkness invading the building gives the reader a sense of suspense and foreboding.

• Ask students to identify this stage of the plot.
Answer: The passage is part of the rising action.

❹ **Reading Check**
Answer: The new assistant is told that no one is allowed to remain in the building after five o'clock.

❸ boast of the architect—but toward evening the crumbs were collected as by an immense vacuum cleaner, absorbed and demolished, yielding to an uncontrollable mass of dark that came tumbling in through windows and doors to take their place. Darkness infested the building like a flight of bats returning willingly to roost.

"Wash hands, please. Wash hands, please," the intercom began to bawl in the passages at a quarter to five. Without much need of prompting, the staff hustled like lemmings along the corridors to green- and blue-tiled washrooms that mocked with an illusion of cheerfulness the encroaching dusk.

❹ ✓ **Reading Check**

What is the new assistant told about being in the building after five o'clock?

Sonata for Harp and Bicycle ■ 49

Differentiated Instruction   Solutions for All Learners

Strategy for Advanced Readers
Call students' attention to the blend of humor, horror, and mystery that already pervades the story. For example, the mystery is established when the manager states that no one is allowed in the building after five o'clock. Horror is established as darkness infests the building. Humor is evident in the reference to the staff rushing out of the building "like lemmings." Ask students to analyze this mix of elements. Pose the following questions for students to discuss: Does Aiken combine these elements effectively, or is she trying to do too many things? Does the comedy negate the horror? Does the horror accentuate the comedy?

Tell students to look for these elements as they continue to read. Have them consider these questions: Does Aiken continue to include all three moods? Does she do so effectively? Provide opportunities for students to respond to these questions during class discussion.

- Remind students that the conflict is the central problem in a story.

- **Ask** students to respond to the Literary Analysis question: What problem for Jason is introduced in his conversation with Miss Golden? **Answer:** Jason wants to find out why no one is allowed in the building after five o'clock, but no one will tell him.

- Call students' attention to the description of Miss Golden's "terrified" eyes when she tells Jason to "Hush!" **Ask** students how these lines foreshadow events to come. **Answer:** They suggest that the answer to Jason's question is frightening.

- Discuss how the foreshadowing builds suspense. Remind students that the suspense will continue to build until the climax is reached.

"All papers into cases, please," the voice warned, five minutes later. "Look at your desks, ladies and gentlemen. Any documents left lying about? Kindly put them away. Desks must be left clear and tidy. Drawers must be shut."

A multitudinous shuffling, a rustling as of innumerable bluebottle flies might have been heard by the attentive ear after this injunction, as the employees of Moreton Wold and Company thrust their papers into cases, hurried letters and invoices into drawers, clipped statistical abstracts together and slammed them into filing cabinets, dropped discarded copy into wastepaper baskets. Two minutes later, and not a desk throughout Grimes Buildings bore more than its customary coating of dust.

"Hats and coats on, please. Hats and coats on, please. Did you bring an umbrella? Have you left any shopping on the floor?" At three minutes to five the homegoing throng was in the lifts[2] and on the stairs; a clattering, staccato-voiced flood darkened momentarily the great double doors of the building, and then as the first faint notes of St. Paul's[3] came echoing faintly on the frosty air, to be picked up near at hand by the louder chimes of St. Biddulph's-on-the-Wall, the entire premises of Moreton Wold stood empty.

"But why is it?" Jason Ashgrove, the new copywriter, asked his secretary one day. "Why are the staff herded out so fast? Not that I'm against it, mind you; I think it's an admirable idea in many ways, but there is the liberty of the individual to be considered, don't you think?"

"Hush!" Miss Golden, the secretary, gazed at him with large and terrified eyes. "You mustn't ask that sort of question. When you are ⑤ taken onto the Established Staff you'll be told. Not before."

"But I want to know now," Jason said in discontent. "Do you know?"

"Yes, I do," Miss Golden answered <u>tantalizingly</u>. "Come on, or we shan't have finished the Oat Crisp layout by a quarter to." And she stared firmly down at the copy in front of her, lips folded, candyfloss hair falling over her face, lashes hiding eyes like peridots,[4] a girl with a secret.

Jason was annoyed. He rapped out a couple of rude and witty rhymes which Miss Golden let pass in a withering silence.

"What do you want for your birthday, Miss Golden? Sherry? Fudge? Bubble bath?"

---

2. lifts *n.* British term for elevators.
3. St. Paul's famous church in London.
4. peridots (per´ i däts´) *n.* yellowish-green gems.

50 ■ *Fiction and Nonfiction*

Literary Analysis
Plot and Foreshadowing
What problem for Jason is introduced in his conversation with Miss Golden?

Vocabulary Builder
tantalizingly (tan´ tə līz´ iŋ lē) *adv.* in a teasing way

Vocabulary Development

Multiple Meanings
Point out the word *passages* on p. 51, and ask students to define the word as it is used in the text. (corridor) Tell students that *passage* has multiple meanings. Write these sentences on the board, and guide students in developing definitions for each use of the word *passage:*

1. Since *passage* of the law, lights have been required on every street corner.
2. The *passage* led visitors through the garden.
3. Have you read the *passage* in which Jason is given hints to the mystery?
4. Taking the job on Wall Street was a *passage* to a new way of life.
5. The older he got, the more he wanted to slow the *passage* of time.

   Ask students to write additional sentences showing the different meanings of the word *passage.*

Answers: 1. enactment of a law; 2. path; 3. excerpt from a piece of writing; 4. transition; 5. continuous flow or movement

6 "I want to go away with a clear conscience about Oat Crisps," Miss Golden retorted. It was not true; what she chiefly wanted was Mr. Jason Ashgrove, but he had not realized this yet.

"Come on, don't tease! I'm sure you haven't been on the Established Staff all that long," he coaxed her. "What happens when one is taken on, anyway? Does the Managing Director have us up for a confidential chat? Or are we given a little book called *The Awful Secret of Grimes Buildings*?"

Miss Golden wasn't telling. She opened her drawer and took out a white towel and a cake of rosy soap.

7 "Wash hands, please! Wash hands, please!"

Jason was frustrated. "You'll be sorry," he said. "I shall do something desperate."

"Oh no, you mustn't!" Her eyes were large with fright. She ran from the room and was back within a couple of moments, still drying her hands.

"If I took you out for a coffee, couldn't you give me just a tiny hint?"

Side by side Miss Golden and Mr. Ashgrove ran along the green-floored passages, battled down the white marble stairs among the hundred other employees from the tenth floor, the nine hundred from the floors below.

He saw her lips move as she said something, but in the clatter of two thousand feet the words were lost.

"—fire escape," he heard, as they came into the momentary hush of the carpeted entrance hall. And "—it's to do with a bicycle. A bicycle and a harp."

"I don't understand."

8 Now they were in the street, chilly with the winter dusk smells of celery on carts, of swept-up leaves heaped in faraway parks, and cold layers of dew sinking among the withered evening primroses in the bombed areas. London lay about them wreathed in twilit mystery and fading against the barred and smoky sky. Like a ninth wave the sound of traffic overtook and swallowed them.

"Please tell me!"

But, shaking her head, she stepped onto a scarlet homebound bus and was borne away from him.

Jason stood undecided on the pavement, with the crowds dividing around him as around the pier of a bridge. He scratched his head, looked about him for guidance.

An ambulance clanged, a taxi hooted, a drill stuttered, a siren wailed on the river, a door slammed, a brake squealed, and close beside his ear a bicycle bell tinkled its tiny warning.

A bicycle, she had said. A bicycle and a harp.

Sonata for Harp and Bicycle ■ 51

Reading Skill

Making and Verifying Predictions Which text clue leads you to predict that a romance will develop between Jason and Miss Golden? Explain.

 Reading Check

What question does Jason Ashgrove want answered by Miss Golden?

---

6 Reading Skill
Making and Verifying Predictions

- **Ask** students the Reading Skill question: Which text clue leads you to predict that a romance will develop between Jason and Miss Golden? Explain.
  Answer: The text clue is that Miss Golden "chiefly wanted" Jason, although Jason doesn't know it yet. The "yet" suggests that something more will develop between them.

- Point out how these text clues both foreshadow events and invite readers to make predictions.

7 Reading Skill
Making and Verifying Predictions

- **Ask** students what they predict Jason will do if Miss Golden doesn't tell him the secret of Grimes Buildings.
  Possible response: Jason will find a way to discover the answer by himself. Perhaps he will enter the building at night and solve the mystery.

- Have students record their predictions on copies of **Reading Skill Graphic Organizer A** (*Graphic Organizer Transparencies,* p. 10). Tell them to read on to verify the prediction and then to analyze its accuracy.

8 Critical Thinking
Cause and Effect

- Call students' attention to the bits of information that Jason hears about the fire escape, bicycle, and harp.

- **Ask** students what the effect would have been if Miss Golden had remained silent instead of giving these hints.
  Possible response: The hints are more intriguing than silence. They keep the reader interested in the story.

9 Reading Check

Answer: Jason wants to know why the staff is forced to leave the building so abruptly.

- Have students summarize the action in the bracketed passage.
- **Ask** students the Literary Analysis question: Why do Jason's actions increase the suspense of the narrative?
Answer: His actions increase the suspense because readers know something mysterious is going on in the building. At every footstep, they expect something terrifying to happen to Jason.
- **Ask** students how they can tell these events are still part of the rising action.
Answer: The tension and excitement keep increasing; the climax has not occurred yet.

⑪ Critical Viewing

Possible response: The tower looks ancient, a place with many stories, mysteries, and ghosts. It seems as if it would have many hidden nooks and corners where frightening things could hide.

Jason turned and stared at Grimes Buildings.

Somewhere, he knew, there was a back way in, a service entrance. He walked slowly past the main doors, with their tubs of snowy chrysanthemums, and up Glass Street. A tiny <u>furtive</u> wedge of darkness beckoned him, a snicket, a hacket, an alley carved into the thickness of the building. It was so narrow that at any moment, it seemed, the overtopping walls would come together and squeeze it out of existence.

Walking as softly as an Indian, Jason passed through it, slid by a file of dustbins,[5] and found the foot of the fire escape. Iron treads rose into the mist, like an illustration to a Gothic[6] fairy tale.

He began to climb.

⑩ When he had mounted to the ninth story he paused for breath. It was a lonely place. The lighting consisted of a dim bulb at the foot of every flight. A well of gloom sank beneath him. The cold fingers of the wind nagged and fluttered at the tails of his jacket, and he pulled the string of the fire door and edged inside.

Grimes Buildings were triangular, with the street forming the base of the triangle, and the fire escape the point. Jason could see two long passages coming toward him, meeting at an acute angle where he stood. He started down the left-hand one, tiptoeing in the cavelike silence. Nowhere was there any sound, except for the far-away drip of a tap. No night watchman would stay in the building; none was needed. Burglars gave the place a wide berth.

Jason opened a door at random; then another. Offices lay everywhere about him, empty and forbidding. Some held lipstick-stained tissues, spilled powder, and orange peels; others were still foggy with cigarette smoke. Here was a Director's suite of rooms—a desk like half an acre of frozen lake, inch-thick carpet, roses, and the smell of cigars. Here was a conference room with scattered squares of doodled blotting paper. All equally empty.

He was not sure when he first began to notice the bell. Telephone, he thought at first, and then he remembered that all the outside lines were disconnected at five. And this bell, anyway, had not the regularity of a telephone's double ring: there was a tinkle, and then silence; a long ring, and then silence; a whole volley of rings **⑫** together, and then silence.

Jason stood listening, and fear knocked against his ribs and shortened his breath. He knew that he must move or be paralyzed by it. He ran up a flight of stairs and found himself with two more endless green corridors beckoning him like a pair of dividers.

---

5. **dustbins** British term for garbage cans.
6. **Gothic** *adj.* mysterious.

Vocabulary Builder
furtive (fur´ tiv) *adj.*
sneaky

Literary Analysis
Plot and Suspense
How do Jason's actions increase the suspense of the narrative?

⑪ ▶ Critical Viewing
Based on this photo of Big Ben, a clock tower in London, England, why is an old London building at night an appropriate setting for a frightening story? **[Analyze]**

Vocabulary Development

Expressive Vocabulary
Ask students to list words and phrases that describe the character of Jason Grimes. Write their suggestions on the board. Then ask students to make up sentences about Jason and his nighttime adventure in Grimes Buildings. Encourage them to use the expressive words presented earlier. You might initiate the discussion with sentence starters such as the following:

1. Jason was able to *anticipate* . . .
2. Jason could not *comprehend* . . .
3. Jason asked Miss Golden to *confirm* . . .
4. Jason wanted to *eliminate* . . .
5. Jason hoped to *expose* . . .

Another sound now: a waft of ice-thin notes, riffling up an arpeggio[7] like a flurry of snowflakes. Far away down the passage it echoed. Jason ran in pursuit, but as he ran the music receded. He circled the building, but it always outdistanced him, and when he came back to the stairs he heard it fading away to the story below.

He hesitated, and as he did so heard again the bell; the bicycle bell. It was approaching him fast, bearing down on him, urgent, menacing. He could hear the pedals, almost see the shimmer of an invisible wheel. Absurdly, he was reminded of the insistent clamor of an ice-cream vendor, summoning children on a sultry Sunday afternoon.

There was a little fireman's alcove beside him, with buckets and pumps. He hurled himself into it. The bell stopped beside him, and then there was a moment while his heart tried to shake itself loose in his chest. He was looking into two eyes carved out of expressionless air; he was held by two hands knotted together out of the width of dark.

"Daisy, Daisy?" came the whisper. "Is that you, Daisy? Have you come to give me your answer?"

Jason tried to speak, but no words came.

"It's not Daisy! Who are you?" The sibilants[8] were full of threat. "You can't stay here. This is private property."

He was thrust along the corridor. It was like being pushed by a whirlwind—the fire door opened ahead of him without a touch, and he was on the openwork platform, clutching the slender railing. Still the hands would not let him go.

"How about it?" the whisper mocked him. "How about jumping? It's an easy death compared with some."

Jason looked down into the smoky void. The darkness nodded to him like a familiar.[9]

"You wouldn't be much loss, would you? What have you got to live for?"

Miss Golden, Jason thought. She would miss me. And the syllables Berenice Golden lingered in the air like a chime. Drawing on some unknown

---

7. **arpeggio** (är pej´ ō) *n.* notes of a chord played one after the other instead of together.
8. **sibilants** (sib´ əl entz) *n.* hissing sounds.
9. **a familiar** a spirit.

Sonata for Harp and Bicycle ■ 53

Literary Analysis
Plot and Foreshadowing What earlier details foreshadowed this mysterious ringing?

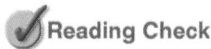 **Reading Check**

What makes the ringing sound that Jason hears inside the Grimes Buildings?

⓬ **Literary Analysis**
Plot and Foreshadowing

- Have students read the bracketed passage. **Ask** them to describe Jason's feelings at this point in the story.
  Possible response: Jason is becoming more and more frightened. He does not understand what is happening.

- **Ask** students to respond to the Literary Analysis question: What earlier details foreshadowed this mysterious ringing?
  Answer: First, Miss Golden said that the mystery involved a bicycle. Then, while Jason stood on the sidewalk after Miss Golden left, a bicycle bell tinkled nearby, giving Jason a "tiny warning."

- **Ask** students how the ringing bell contributes to the plot.
  Answer: The bell signals a new complication. The ringing is a new mystery for Jason—and the reader—to investigate.

⓭ **Reading Skill**
Making and Verifying Predictions

- Have students read about Jason's encounter with the ghost. **Ask** them to predict why the ghost haunts Grimes Buildings and to explain how they arrived at the prediction.
  Possible response: Daisy might be the ghost's lost love. Since the ghost is waiting for an answer from Daisy, Daisy must have failed to give this answer during the ghost's lifetime.

- Have students continue reading to verify their predictions.

⓮ **Reading Check**

Answer: A bicycle bell makes the ringing sound.

15 **Critical Viewing**

Possible response: It would make a soft, clear, rippling sound.

16 **Literary Analysis**
Plot and Suspense

- Review with students the events that have happened so far in the story. **Ask** them to compare the suspense in the bracketed passage with the suspense in the previous scene on the fire escape.
  Answer: The passage is very relaxed compared to the high suspense created when Jason and the ghost are on the fire escape.

- Remind students that the climax is the point of highest intensity and that it is followed by the falling action and resolution. **Ask** students whether they think they have now passed the climax of the story. Have them explain their answers.
  Possible response: No, the climax has not been reached. Jason has seen the ghost, but the mystery has not been solved yet. The tension is already starting to build again as Miss Golden tells Jason that he is doomed. Clearly, more is to come.

deposit of courage he shook himself loose from the holding hands and ran down the fire escape without looking back.

Next morning when Miss Golden, crisp, fragrant, and punctual, shut the door of Room 492 behind her, she stopped short of the hat-pegs with a horrified gasp.

"Mr. Ashgrove, your hair!"

"It makes me look more distinguished, don't you think?" he said.

It had indeed this effect, for his impeccable dark cut had turned to a stippled silver which might have been envied by many a diplomat.

"How did it happen? You've not—" her voice sank to a whisper—*"you've not been in Grimes Buildings after dark?"*

"Miss Golden—Berenice," he said earnestly. "Who was Daisy? Plainly you know. Tell me the story."

"Did you see him?" she asked faintly.

"Him?"

"William Heron—The Wailing Watchman. Oh," she exclaimed in terror, "I can see you did. Then you are doomed—doomed!"

"If I'm doomed," said Jason, "let's have coffee, and you tell me the story quickly."

"It all happened over fifty years ago," said Berenice, as she spooned out coffee powder with distracted extravagance. "Heron was the night watchman in this building, patrolling the corridors from dusk to dawn every night on his bicycle. He fell in love with a Miss Bell who taught the harp. She rented a room—this room—and gave lessons in it. She began to <u>reciprocate</u> his love, and they used to share a picnic supper every night at eleven, and she'd stay on a while to keep him company. It was an idyll,[10] among the fire buckets and the furnace pipes.

"On Halloween he had summoned up the courage to propose to her. The day before he had told her he was going to ask her a very important question, and he came to the Buildings with a huge bunch of roses and a bottle of wine. But Miss Bell never turned up.

"The explanation was simple. Miss Bell, of course, had been losing a lot of sleep through her nocturnal romance, and so she used to take a nap in her music room between seven and ten, to save going home. In order to make sure that she would wake up, she persuaded her father, a distant relative of Graham Bell,[11] to attach an alarm-waking fixture to her telephone which called her every night at ten. She was too modest and shy to let Heron know that

---

10. **idyll** (ī´dəl) *n.* romantic scene, usually in the country.
11. **Graham Bell** Alexander Graham Bell (1847–1922), the inventor of the telephone.

15 ▼ **Critical Viewing**
Describe the sound you think this harp would make.
[Speculate]

Vocabulary Builder
reciprocate (ri sip´ rə kāt´) *v.* return

she spent those hours in the building, and to give him the pleasure of waking her himself.

"Alas! On this important evening the line failed, and she never woke up. The telephone was in its infancy at that time, you must remember.

❼ "Heron waited and waited. At last, mad with grief and jealousy, having called her home and discovered that she was not there, he concluded that she had betrayed him; he ran to the fire escape, and cast himself off it, holding the roses and the bottle of wine.

"Daisy did not long survive him but pined away soon after. Since that day their ghosts have haunted Grimes Buildings, he vainly patrolling the corridors on his bicycle, she playing her harp in the room she rented. But they never meet. And anyone who meets the ghost of William Heron will himself, within five days, leap down from the same fatal fire escape."

She gazed at him with tragic eyes.

❽ "In that case we must lose no time," said Jason, and he enveloped her in an embrace as prompt as it was ardent. Looking down at the gossamer hair sprayed across his pin-stripe, he added, "Just the same it is a preposterous situation. Firstly, I have no intention of jumping off the fire escape—" here, however, he repressed a shudder as he remembered the cold, clutching hands of the evening before—"and secondly, I find it quite nonsensical that those two inefficient ghosts have spent fifty years in this building without coming across each other. We must remedy the matter, Berenice. We must not begrudge our new-found happiness to others."

He gave her another kiss so impassioned that the electric typewriter against which they were leaning began chattering to itself in a frenzy of enthusiasm.

"This very evening," he went on, looking at his watch, "we will put matters right for that unhappy couple and then, if I really have only five more days to live, which I don't for one moment believe, we will proceed to spend them together, my bewitching Berenice, in the most advantageous manner possible."

She nodded, spellbound.

"Can you work a switchboard?" he added. She nodded again. "My love, you are perfection itself. Meet me in the switchboard room then, at ten this evening. I would say, have dinner with me, but I shall need to make one or two purchases and see an old R.A.F.[12] friend. You will be safe from Heron's curse in the switchboard room if he always keeps to the corridors."

"I would rather meet him and die with you," she murmured.

---

12. **R.A.F.** Royal Air Force.

Literary Analysis
Plot and Foreshadowing How does this new information increase the suspense of the narrative?

Reading Skill
Making and Verifying Predictions What do you think Jason might do to "remedy the matter"?

 Reading Check

According to Berenice, what happens to anyone who meets the ghost of William Heron?

---

❼ Literary Analysis
Plot and Suspense

- Point out to students that the story of Heron and Daisy has its own plot. **Ask** students to identify the story's conflict, rising action, and climax.
  Answer: The conflict is Heron's wish to marry Daisy. The rising action includes the picnics, Daisy's use of the phone alarm to wake her, and Heron's plans for proposing. The climax occurs when Daisy fails to meet Heron and Heron jumps from the fire escape.

- Point out that although the story has elements of a plot, it is missing a resolution. Discuss how Jason's plan might lead to the resolution of Heron and Daisy's story—and also of his own.

- **Ask** students the Literary Analysis question: How does this new information increase the suspense of the narrative?
  Answer: The information makes Jason's situation much more serious; he must now to try survive a fatal curse.

❽ Reading Skill
Making and Verifying Predictions

- Have students share the predictions they have made so far. Talk about the predictions and the details and reasons students had for making them.

- **Ask** students to respond to the Reading Skill question: What do you think Jason might do to "remedy the matter"?
  Possible response: Since the central problem Jason faces is that the two ghosts have never met, he probably plans to arrange a meeting between them.

❾ Reading Check

Answer: The person is doomed to leap from the fire escape within five days.

Differentiated Instruction — Solutions for All Learners

Enrichment for Advanced Readers
Point out that by naming her protagonists "Jason" and "Miss Golden," Joan Aiken seems to be making a humorous reference to the Greek myth, "Jason and the Golden Fleece."

Have students learn more about the myth and then compare the quest, obstacles, and dangers that Jason faces in Grimes Buildings with those that challenged the Greek hero. As a group, have students discuss what effect this allusion has on the story. How does it add to their understanding of the plot and characters? How does it contribute to their understanding of the theme? Ask volunteers to present their findings and conclusions to the class.

55

- Have students identify what Jason carries into the building. Then **ask** them the Reading Skill question: What do you predict Jason will do with the two bunches of roses? Why?

Possible response: Jason will probably give one to Heron and Daisy and the other to Berenice.

▶ **Monitor Progress:** Ask students to explain how they made their predictions.

Possible response: Berenice said that Heron had brought a bottle of wine and a bunch of roses to give to Daisy when he proposed. So it is logical that one of the bunches of roses and one bottle of wine are for Heron and Daisy. Jason and Berenice are also in love, so it is possible that Jason brought the other roses and wine for Berenice.

▶ **Reteach:** If students have difficulty with this prediction, remind them of the romance between Jason and Berenice. Tell them to reread the story about Heron and Daisy on pp. 54–55 and look for references to the roses and wine. Then have students use the information to reevaluate their predictions. Follow up with students after they finish reading the story.

"My angel, I hope that won't be necessary. Now," he said, sighing, "I suppose we should get down to our day's work."

Strangely enough the copy they wrote that day, although engendered from such agitated minds, sold more packets of Oat Crisps than any other advertising matter before or since.

20 That evening when Jason entered Grimes Buildings he was carrying two bottles of wine, two bunches of red roses, and a large canvas-covered bundle. Miss Golden, who had concealed herself in the switchboard room before the offices closed for the night, eyed these things with surprise.

"Now," said Jason, after he had greeted her, "I want you first to ring our own extension."

"No one will reply, surely?"

"I think she will reply."

Sure enough, when Berenice rang Extension 170 a faint, sleepy voice, distant and yet clear, whispered, "Hullo?"

"Is that Miss Bell?"

"Yes."

Berenice went a little pale. Her eyes sought Jason's and, prompted by him, she said formally, "Switchboard here, Miss Bell. Your ten o'clock call."

"Thank you," the faint voice said. There was a click and the line went blank.

"Excellent," Jason remarked. He unfastened his package and slipped its straps over his shoulders. "Now plug into the intercom."

Berenice did so, and then said, loudly and clearly, "Attention. Night watchman on duty, please. Night watchman on duty. You have an urgent summons to Room 492. You have an urgent summons to Room 492." The intercom echoed and reverberated through the empty corridors, then coughed itself to silence.

"Now we must run. You take the roses, sweetheart, and I'll carry the bottles."

Together they raced up eight flights of stairs and along the passages to Room 492. As they neared the door a burst of music met them—harp music swelling out, sweet and triumphant. Jason took a bunch of roses from Berenice, opened the door a little way, and gently deposited them, with a bottle, inside the door. As he closed it again Berenice said breathlessly, "Did you see anyone?"

"No," he said. "The room was too full of music." She saw that his eyes were shining.

They stood hand in hand, reluctant to move away, waiting for they hardly knew what. Suddenly the door opened again. Neither

56 ■ *Fiction and Nonfiction*

Reading Skill
Making and Verifying Predictions What do you predict Jason will do with the two bunches of roses? Why?

Vocabulary Development

Vocabulary Knowledge Rating

When students have completed reading and discussing "Sonata for Harp and Bicycle," have them take out their **Vocabulary Knowledge Rating Chart** for this selection. Read the words aloud once more and have students rate their knowledge of the words again in the After Reading column. Clarify any words that are still problematic. Have students write their own definition and example or sentence in the appropriate column. Then have students complete the **Vocabulary Builder Practice** activities on p. 59. Encourage students to use the words in further discussion and written work about this selection. Remind them that they will be accountable for these words on the Selection Test.

Berenice nor Jason, afterward, would speak of what they saw but each was left with a memory, bright as the picture on a Salvador Dali[13] calendar, of a bicycle bearing on its saddle a harp, a bottle of wine, and a bouquet of red roses, sweeping improbably down the corridor and far, far away.

"We can go now," Jason said.

He led Berenice to the fire door, tucking the bottle of Médoc in his jacket pocket. A black wind from the north whistled beneath them as they stood on the openwork platform, looking down.

"We don't want our evening to be spoiled by the thought of a curse hanging over us," he said, "so this is the practical thing to do. Hang onto the roses." And holding his love firmly, Jason pulled the rip cord of his R.A.F. friend's parachute and leaped off the fire escape.

A bridal shower of rose petals adorned the descent of Miss Golden, who was possibly the only girl to be kissed in midair in the district of Clerkenwell at ten minutes to midnight on Halloween.

---

13. **Salvador Dali** (sal´ və dôr´ dä´ lē) modern artist (1904–1989) famous for his unusual pictures.

Reading Skill
Making and Verifying Predictions Do the events at the end of the story verify your predictions? Why or why not?

② Critical Viewing What advantages would patrolling corridors on bicycle offer as opposed to patrolling on foot? **[Evaluate]**

Sonata for Harp and Bicycle ■ 57

Apply the Skills

Sonata for Harp and Bicycle

Thinking About the Selection

1. **Respond:** If you were Jason, would you try to solve the mystery of the Grimes Buildings? Explain.
2. **(a) Recall:** What three important objects does Miss Golden mention to Jason as they leave the Grimes Buildings at five P.M.? **(b) Connect:** How does he use this information?
3. **(a) Recall:** What physical change has happened to Jason when he sees Miss Golden the next day? **(b) Analyze:** What evidence suggests that his encounter in the closed building has caused the change?
4. **(a) Recall:** What actions does Jason take to avoid the curse that awaits those who see Heron's ghost? **(b) Infer:** Who is more concerned about the curse—Jason or Miss Golden? Explain.
5. **Generalize:** What lesson do the circumstances of William Heron's death teach about the danger of making rash decisions?

Literary Analysis

6. Using a chart like the one shown, identify two key events in the **rising action,** one event in the **falling action,** and the event that marks the **climax.** Then, trade charts with a partner and discuss the reasons why you chose the events that you did. Finally, explain to your partner how your understanding of the story has or has not changed as a result of the discussion.

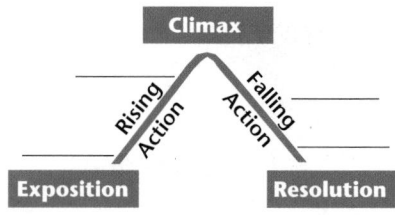

7. **(a)** Identify a statement or event that **foreshadows** Jason's decision to enter the Grimes Buildings after closing hours. **(b)** How does the use of foreshadowing increase the story's **suspense?** Explain.

Reading Skill

8. **(a)** What **prediction** did you make when Jason entered the Grimes Buildings after closing and heard a bicycle bell? **(b)** On what details did you base your prediction?
9. Was your prediction **verified** by later story events? Explain.

58 ■ *Fiction and Nonfiction*

QuickReview

Story at a Glance
Jason Ashgrove solves the mystery of the haunted Grimes Buildings.

Go Online
Assessment

For: Self-test
Visit: www.PHSchool.com
Web Code: epa-6105

Plot: the sequence of events in a narrative. Elements include *rising action, climax, falling action,* and *resolution.*

Foreshadowing: a hint or clue about events that will happen later in a story

Suspense: a feeling of tension caused by anticipation of what might happen later

Prediction: an informed idea about what might happen later

Answers (left column)

1. **Possible response:** Yes, because curiosity would overcome any hesitation over the risks. No, because it might be dangerous or a cause for being fired.

2. (a) Miss Golden drops hints about a fire escape, a bicycle, and a harp. (b) Jason finds the fire escape and uses it to get into the building.

3. (a) His hair has turned silvery. (b) The color change occurs immediately after his life-threatening encounter with a ghost. According to folklore, severe shock can cause hair to whiten overnight.

4. (a) He jumps off the fire escape but does so securely strapped in a parachute. (b) Miss Golden was more concerned because she assumed the curse could not be escaped and was not aware of Jason's plan.

5. If Heron had not killed himself, he would have seen Miss Bell the next day; she would have explained about the alarm, and they could have had a happy life together.

6. Possible response:

   Rising Action: Jason hears hints about the fire escape, bicycle, and harp; Jason enters the building and meets the ghost of Heron. **Falling Action:** Jason and Miss Golden leap from the fire escape. **Climax:** Jason places the bunch of roses and bottle of wine inside the room where the ghosts of Heron and Daisy are meeting.

   Another sample answer can be found on **Literary Analysis Graphic Organizer B,** p. 14, in *Graphic Organizer Transparencies.*

7. (a) **Possible response:** Jason's decision is foreshadowed by his vow to "do something desperate" when Miss Golden refused to explain the secret of Grimes Buildings. (b) It increases suspense by creating anticipation for a desperate action.

8. (a) **Possible response:** Students might have predicted that someone was haunting the building and riding a bike. (b) **Possible response:** Students might have

based the prediction on the way workers hurriedly left the building each night and the fact that Miss Golden said the mystery involved a bicycle.

9. **Possible response:** Students' predictions might have been verified when they discovered that the watchman's ghost rode his bicycle through the building each night.

Vocabulary Builder

Practice **Analogies** show the relationships between pairs of words. Use a word from the "Sonata for Harp and Bicycle" vocabulary list on page 46 to complete each analogy. For each case, your choice should create a word pair that matches the relationship between the first two words.

1. angry : shout :: _____ : whisper

2. steal : take :: _____ : give

3. hopelessly : far :: _____ : near

Adding Words to Your Vocabulary *Furtive* can be defined by its synonym *sneaky*. A **synonym** is a word that has the same or nearly the same definition as another word. Other synonyms for *furtive* include *stealthy*, *covert*, and *surreptitious*. These words are synonyms, but they do not mean exactly the same thing. Look up each word in a dictionary, and for each word, write a sentence that reflects its specific meaning. (For help with reference materials, see page R6.)

Writing

Joan Aiken has said, "A flat or unsatisfactory ending is the worst sin a writer can commit." Write a **critique** evaluating the ending of "Sonata for Harp and Bicycle," and state whether you find it satisfactory.

• Before writing, make a list of qualities that create satisfactory endings. Check off those qualities that appear in Aiken's story.

• Use the checklist as evidence in your critique.

For *Grammar, Vocabulary,* and *Assessment,* see **Build Language Skills,** pages 70–71.

Extend Your Learning

Listening and Speaking Present a **retelling** of "Sonata for Harp and Bicycle" from the ghosts' point of view. As you speak, use facial expressions and body movements to give personality to Heron and Miss Bell.

Research and Technology Work with classmates to create a **storyboard** for a movie version of "Sonata for Harp and Bicycle."

• Use Internet and library resources to find other storyboards that can serve as guides for your own.

• Decide as a group which story events to depict. Draw those scenes in comic book style, and write a brief description for each frame.

Apply the Skills ■ 59

Assessment Resources

The following resources can be used to assess students' knowledge and skills.

Unit 1 Resources:
    Selection Test A, pp. 63–65
    Selection Test B, pp. 66–68

Go Online
—Assessment— Students may use the **Self-test** to prepare for **Selection Test A** or **Selection Test B.**

Go Online **For:** An additional research activity
—Research— **Visit:** www.PHSchool.com
Web Code: epd-7103
For another research activity to extend students' learning, give students this Web Code.

Vocabulary Builder
Practice

1. furtive

2. reciprocate

3. tantalizingly

Adding Words to Your Vocabulary
Sample answers:

1. The *sneaky* child stole cookies from the plate.

2. The *stealthy* cat slipped through the grass toward the birdbath.

3. Only the FBI knew the mission of the *covert* group.

4. The thief made a *surreptitious* entry into the darkened house.

Writing

• To give students guidance for writing a critique, give them **Support for Writing** for "Sonata for Harp and Bicycle", p. 60 in *Unit 1 Resources.*

• To evaluate students' critiques, use the Response to Literature rubrics, pp. 57–58 in *General Resources.*

Six Traits Focus

✔	Ideas		Word Choice
	Organization		Sentence Fluency
✔	Voice		Conventions

Writing and Grammar, Gold Level
Students will find guidance on writing critiques in Chapter 13.

Build Language Skills

Go to pp. 70–71 for vocabulary and grammar lessons and assessment practice.

Extend Your Learning

The **Support for Extend Your Learning** page (*Unit 1 Resources,* p. 61) provides guided note-taking opportunities to help students complete the Extend Your Learning activities.

Teaching notes for Literary Analysis, Reading Skill, and Vocabulary Builder for this selection begin on p. 46.

❸ Background

Catacombs From before Roman times, people across the Mediterranean region built catacombs as places of burial. Greeks and Romans ordinarily used cremation, but Christians and Jewish people buried their dead. The catacombs were begun on a single level, with separate chambers or galleries laid out like a honeycomb. As the chambers filled, additional levels were dug deeper down and connected by stairs. Some catacombs had as many as five levels.

❹ Connecting to the Literature

- Model use of the expressive vocabulary students are asked to use with these examples:

  1. Readers enjoy trying to *interpret* the events described in scary stories.

  2. They like to *participate* in the experience by safely reading about it.

  3. Eerie characters *contribute* to the unsettling mood.

  4. A gloomy setting can *elevate* the sense of danger.

- Help students further develop their expressive vocabulary by providing these words: *devious, lure,* and *obsessive.* Encourage students to use these words as they discuss the selection.

Concept Connector ➡

Students will follow up on this activity after completing "The Cask of Amontillado."

Go **Online** For additional informa-
—Author Link tion about Edgar Allan Poe, have students type in the Web Code and then select *Edgar Allan Poe.*

Build Understanding • *The Cask of Amontillado*

Short Story

Background

Catacombs Much of the action in this story takes place in cata-combs—underground tunnels that house tombs. These long, often complex passageways stretch out like cities of the dead. In past centuries, some wealthy European families held funerals in catacombs beneath the family manor. The dead were laid to rest surrounded by the bones of their ancestors.

Connecting to the Literature

Reading/Writing Connection Write a short paragraph explaining why you think people enjoy reading stories set in scary places like catacombs. Use at least three of the following words: *interpret, participate, contribute, elevate.*

Review

For **Literary Analysis, Reading Skill,** and **Vocabulary Builder,** see page 46.

READ MORE

by
Edgar Allan Poe
"The Fall of the House of Usher"
"The Tell-Tale Heart"

Meet the Author

Edgar Allan **Poe** (1809–1849)

One of the first great American storytellers, Edgar Allan Poe made the most of a short, tragic life. Orphaned at the age of three, Poe was raised by foster parents, the Allans, from whom he took his middle name. The Allans were good to Poe and gave him an education, but he had to leave college when his foster father refused to pay Poe's gambling debts. Poe found some happiness when he married Virginia Clemm. Her death from tuberculosis in 1847 caused Poe to become increasingly antisocial. In 1849, he was discovered in a delirious condition on a Baltimore street, and three days later he was dead.

An Inspiration to Later Generations Like few others, Poe blazed trails for future writers. His work helped to define the short story, and his dark imagination helped establish the genre of horror literature now popularized by writers like Stephen King.

Fast Facts

▶ Poe invented the genre of the detective story with his tale "The Murders in the Rue Morgue."

▶ Poe's first book, *Tamerlane and Other Poems,* was a failure. Recently, an original copy sold for $150,000.

 Go **Online**
—Author Link

For: More about the author
Visit: www.PHSchool.com
Web Code: epe-9105

60 ■ Fiction and Nonfiction

Differentiated

Instruction Solutions for All Learners

Support for Below-Level Students [L1, L2]	Support for English Learners [EL]

Unit 1 Resources
  Vocabulary Warm-up Word Lists, p. 69
  Vocabulary Warm-up Practice, p. 70
  Reading Warm-up A, p. 71
  Selection Test A, pp. 81–83
Graphic Organizer Transparencies
  Reading Skill Graphic Organizer,
  Transparency B, p. 12
	Unit 1 Resources
	  Vocabulary Warm-up Word Lists, p. 69
	  Vocabulary Warm-up Practice, p. 70
	  Reading Warm-up A, p. 71
	
	Listening to Literature Audio CD

THE CASK OF AMONTILLADO[1]

EDGAR ALLAN POE

The thousand injuries of Fortunato I had borne as I best could, but when he ventured upon insult I vowed revenge. You, who so well know the nature of my soul, will not suppose, however, that I gave utterance to a threat. At *length* I would be avenged; this was a point definitely settled—but the very definitiveness with which it was resolved <u>precluded</u> the idea of risk. I must not only punish but punish with impunity.[2] A wrong is unredressed when <u>retribution</u> overtakes its redresser. It is equally unredressed when the avenger fails to make himself felt as such to him who has done the wrong.

It must be understood that neither by word nor deed had I given Fortunato cause to doubt my good will. I continued, as was my

---

1. **Amontillado** (ə män´ tə ya´ dō) *n.* a pale, dry sherry.
2. **impunity** (im pyoo´ nə tē´) *n.* freedom from consequences.

Vocabulary Builder
precluded (prē klood´ id) *v.* prevented

retribution (re´ trə byoo´ shən) *n.* payback; punishment for a misdeed

3 ✔ Reading Check

Why does the narrator vow revenge on Fortunato?

The Cask of Amontillado ■ 61

① Motivation
Students will discover that this horrifying tale of revenge is as gripping as any horror movie they've seen. Give them a verbal "trailer" of the story by reading aloud the following excerpts:

> "We . . . stood together upon the damp ground of the catacombs of the Montresors."

> "We had passed through long walls of piled skeletons, with casks and puncheons intermingling, into the inmost recesses. . . ."

Have students discuss these images. What do they think will happen in the catacombs?

Learning Modalities Musical/Rhythmic Learners
Have students note the many sound effects and sound-imitating words that Poe uses in his description of the events that take place in the catacombs. How does he use words to create sounds? How does he help readers hear the scene? What do the sound effects add to the story's mood? Which verbs and adjectives re-create sounds for the reader?

② About the Selection
"The Cask of Amontillado" illustrates how a person can become so obsessed with revenge that he or she can descend into madness and commit unspeakable acts. The main character, Montresor, has vowed to avenge the unnamed insults of Fortunato, an old acquaintance. With a mix of flattery and reverse psychology, Montresor lures and traps Fortunato in the catacombs below Montresor's house.

③ Reading Check
Answer: The narrator believes that Fortunato has injured and insulted him.

Differentiated Instruction Solutions for All Learners

Strategy for Special Needs Students
Read aloud the first two paragraphs of the story. Have students identify details that show the narrator's state of mind. List their suggestions on the board, and discuss their significance. As students read independently, they should continue to note actions and words that reveal the narrator's mental condition.

Enrichment for Gifted/Talented Students
Explain to students that this is a very visually detailed story. Both the costumes of the characters and the setting of the catacombs are vividly described. Suggest that students use these details from the story to draw, paint, or describe the costumes and props that they would use in a dramatized version of the story.

- Have students consider the relationship between predicting and foreshadowing. **Ask:** How can a writer's use of foreshadowing help readers make predictions are they read?
Answer: Foreshadowing is the writer's use of clues to hint at future events in a story. These hints can help readers make predictions about what may happen.

- Discuss what the bracketed passage foreshadows, and encourage students to base their predictions on such details.

- **Ask** students to respond to the Reading Skill question: What role do you predict Fortunato's "weak point" will play in the narrator's revenge?
Possible response: Fortunato has great pride in his knowledge of wine, so the narrator will probably use this arrogance to trap Fortunato and get revenge.

- Have students write their predictions on copies of **Reading Skill Graphic Organizer A** (*Graphic Organizer Transparencies,* p. 10). Tell them to read on to find out whether their predictions were accurate.

---

wont, to smile in his face, and he did not perceive that my smile *now* was at the thought of his immolation.[3]

④ He had a weak point—this Fortunato—although in other regards he was a man to be respected and even feared. He prided himself on his connoisseurship[4] in wine. Few Italians have the true virtuoso[5] spirit. For the most part their enthusiasm is adopted to suit the time and opportunity, to practice imposture upon the British and Austrian millionaires. In painting and gemmary, Fortunato, like his countrymen, was a quack, but in the matter of old wines he was sincere. In this respect I did not differ from him materially; I was skillful in the Italian vintages myself, and bought largely whenever I could.

It was about dusk, one evening during the supreme madness of the carnival season, that I encountered my friend. He accosted me with excessive warmth, for he had been drinking much. The man wore motley.[6] He had on a tight-fitting parti-striped dress, and his head was surmounted by the conical cap and bells. I was so pleased to see him that I thought I should never have done wringing his hand.

I said to him, "My dear Fortunato, you are luckily met. How remarkably well you are looking today. But I have received a pipe[7] of what passes for Amontillado, and I have my doubts."

"How?" said he. "Amontillado? A pipe? Impossible! And in the middle of the carnival!"

"I have my doubts," I replied: "and I was silly enough to pay the full Amontillado price without consulting you in the matter. You were not to be found, and I was fearful of losing a bargain."

"Amontillado!"

"I have my doubts."

"Amontillado!"

"And I must satisfy them."

"Amontillado!"

"As you are engaged, I am on my way to Luchesi. If any one has a critical turn it is he. He will tell me—"

"Luchesi cannot tell Amontillado from sherry."

"And yet some fools will have it that his taste is a match for your own."

"Come, let us go."

"Whither?"

"To your vaults."

---

3. **immolation** (im′ ə lā′ shən) *n.* destruction.
4. **connoisseurship** (kän′ ə sʉr′ ship) *n.* expert judgment.
5. **virtuoso** (vʉr′ choo ō′ sō) *adj.* masterly skill in a particular field.
6. **motley** (mät′ lē) *n.* a clown's multicolored costume.
7. **pipe** (pīp) *n.* large barrel, holding approximately 126 gallons.

62 ■ Fiction and Nonfiction

Vocabulary Development

Think-Aloud: Context
Call students' attention to the word *absconded* in the sixth paragraph on p. 63. Using a think-aloud process, model how to use context to infer the meaning of an unknown word. Say to students:

I'm going to think aloud to show you how I would figure out the meaning of *absconded* from its context.

The sentence in which *absconded* appears gives me two clues. First, I read that the attendants are not at home.

Then I learn that they went to "make merry," or enjoy themselves socially. So, I have a good idea already that *absconded* means "went off." However, the next couple of sentences also give clues. Montresor ordered the attendants not to leave, but they disappeared anyway. The attendants left, but they left secretly. I'm pretty sure that *absconded* means "left secretly."

"My friend, no; I will not impose upon your good nature. I perceive you have an engagement. Luchesi—"

"I have no engagement—come."

"My friend, no. It is not the engagement, but the severe cold with which I perceive you are afflicted. The vaults are insufferably damp. They are encrusted with niter."

"Let us go, nevertheless. The cold is merely nothing. Amontillado! You have been imposed upon. And as for Luchesi, he cannot distinguish sherry from Amontillado."

Thus speaking, Fortunato possessed himself of my arm; and putting on a mask of black silk and drawing a *roquelaure*[8] closely about my person, I suffered him to hurry me to my palazzo.

There were no attendants at home; they had absconded to make merry in honor of the time. I had told them that I should not return until the morning, and had given them explicit orders not to stir from the house. These orders were sufficient, I well knew, to insure their immediate disappearance, one and all, as soon as my back was turned.

I took from their sconces two flambeaux, and giving one to Fortunato, bowed him through several suites of rooms to the archway that led into the vaults. I passed down a long and winding staircase, requesting him to be cautious as he followed. We came at length to the foot of the descent, and stood together upon the damp ground of the catacombs of the Montresors.

The gait of my friend was unsteady, and the bells upon his cap jingled as he strode.

"The pipe," he said.

"It is farther on," said I; "but observe the white webwork which gleams from these cavern walls."

He turned towards me, and looked into my eyes with two filmy orbs that distilled the rheum of intoxication.

"Niter?" he asked, at length.

"Niter," I replied. "How long have you had that cough?"

---

8. **roquelaure** (räk´ ə lôr) *n.* knee-length cloak.

Keying Up—The Court Jester (detail), 1875, William Merritt Chase. Courtesy the Pennsylvania Academy of the Fine Arts, Philadelphia, Gift of the Chapellier Galleries

❺

❻ ▲ **Critical Viewing**
How does this costume compare with your image of Fortunato's costume? **[Compare and Contrast]**

Vocabulary Builder
explicit (eks plis´ it) *adj.* clearly stated

❼ ✓ **Reading Check**
What common interest does the narrator share with Fortunato?

The Cask of Amontillado ■ 63

❺ Humanities

Keying Up—The Court Jester (detail), 1875, by William Merritt Chase
American artist William Merritt Chase studied in New York with painter Joseph O. Eaton and at the National Academy of Design. *The Court Jester* won the Medal of Honor at the 1876 Centennial Exhibition in Philadelphia. Use these questions for discussion:

1. How does this painting help you understand the story?
   Answer: It shows how Fortunato was dressed. It adds details about the carnival.

2. Compare the man in the painting with the character of Fortunato.
   Possible response: The men are dressed similarly, and they both seem unaware of their surroundings and preoccupied.

❻ Critical Viewing

Answer: The costume in the painting matches the verbal description of Fortunato's costume.

❼ Reading Check

Both Montresor and Fortunato share an interest in wines.

Differentiated Instruction Solutions for All Learners

Strategy for Less Proficient Readers
To give students a context for the story and to model how to make and verify predictions, show them **Reading Skill Graphic Organizer B** (*Graphic Organizer Transparencies,* p. 12). The completed graphic organizer will give students insight into the process of predicting. They can use it as a model for making and verifying their own predictions about the story as they read.

Enrichment for Gifted/Talented Students
Have students create a soundtrack for "The Cask of Amontillado." Suggest that they first select music that reflects the moods of the story, from the carnival mood of the beginning to the eeriness of the crypt. Students may wish to add sound effects: the jingling of Fortunato's bells, the clank of chains, the scraping of trowel on stone. Invite students to play the soundtrack for the class.

- Point out to students how the suspense continues to increase as Fortunato and Montresor walk deeper into the catacombs.

- Call students' attention to the conversation in the bracketed passage, and **ask** them the Literary Analysis question: What fate does this conversation foreshadow for Fortunato?
  Answer: It foreshadows Fortunato's death by means other than an illness.

- Ask students how this conversation affects the story's plot.
  Answer: The rising action continues to build. The reader feels increasing fear and concern for Fortunato.

❾ **Critical Thinking**
Analyze

- Ask two volunteers to read aloud the dialogue in the bracketed passage. Have students give their impressions of the two characters.

- Point out that Montresor's words do not accurately reflect his thoughts and intentions. **Ask** how this affects students' impressions of Montresor's character.
  Possible response: It shows that he is very self-controlled. It shows that he finds it easy to lie and act a part. It shows that he is not impulsive; he does not speak without thinking.

"Ugh! ugh! ugh!—ugh! ugh! ugh!—ugh! ugh! ugh!—ugh! ugh! ugh!—ugh! ugh! ugh!"

My poor friend found it impossible to reply for many minutes.

"It is nothing," he said, at last.

"Come," I said, with decision, "we will go back; your health is precious. You are rich, respected, admired, beloved; you are happy, as once I was. You are a man to be missed. For me it is no matter. We will go back; you will be ill, and I cannot be responsible. Besides, there is Luchesi—"

"Enough," he said; "the cough is a mere nothing; it will not kill me. I shall not die of a cough."

❽ "True—true," I replied; "and, indeed, I had no intention of alarming you unnecessarily—but you should use all proper caution. A draft of this Médoc will defend us from the damps."

Here I knocked off the neck of a bottle which I drew from a long row of its fellows that lay upon the mold.

"Drink," I said, presenting him the wine.

He raised it to his lips with a leer. He paused and nodded to me ❾ familiarly, while his bells jingled.

"I drink," he said "to the buried that repose around us."

"And I to your long life."

He again took my arm, and we proceeded.

"These vaults," he said, "are extensive."

"The Montresors," I replied, "were a great and numerous family."

"I forget your arms."

"A huge human foot d'or, in a field azure; the foot crushes a serpent rampant whose fangs are imbedded in the heel."

"And the motto?"

"*Nemo me impune lacessit.*"[9]

"Good!" he said.

The wine sparkled in his eyes and the bells jingled. My own fancy grew warm with the Médoc. We had passed through long walls of piled skeletons, with casks and puncheons[10] intermingling, into the inmost recesses of the catacombs. I paused again, and this time I made bold to seize Fortunato by an arm above the elbow.

"The niter!" I said; "see, it increases. It hangs like moss upon the vaults. We are below the river's bed. The drops of moisture trickle among the bones. Come, we will go back ere it is too late. Your cough—"

"It is nothing," he said; "let us go on. But first, another draft of the Médoc."

---

9. ***Nemo me impune lacessit*** Latin for "No one attacks me with impunity."
10. **puncheons** (pun´ chənz) *n.* large barrels.

64 ■ Fiction and Nonfiction

Vocabulary Development

Expressive Vocabulary
Discuss how Poe's description of the catacombs evokes eerie, unsettling images. Ask students to list some of the words and phrases that Poe uses (for example, "piled skeletons," "recesses," "moss," "vaults," and "drops of moisture trickle among the bones.") As students discuss the setting, encourage them to use the expressive vocabulary presented earlier. You might encourage them with sentence starters like these:

1. The sound of Fortunato's cough *contributed* to . . .
2. Fortunato did not correctly *interpret* . . .
3. Montresor wanted Fortunato to *participate* . . .
4. Montresor's *devious* plan . . .
5. To *lure* Fortunato, Montresor had to . . .
6. Montresor was *obsessive* about . . .

I broke and reached him a flagon of De Grâve. He emptied it at a breath. His eyes flashed with a fierce light. He laughed and threw the bottle upwards with a gesticulation I did not understand.

I looked at him in surprise. He repeated the movement—a grotesque one.

"You do not comprehend?" he said.

"Not I," I replied.

"Then you are not of the brotherhood."

"How?"

"You are not of the masons."[11]

"Yes, yes," I said; "yes, yes."

"You? Impossible! A mason?"

"A mason," I replied.

"A sign," he said, "a sign."

"It is this," I answered, producing from beneath the folds of my *roquelaure* a trowel.

"You jest," he exclaimed, recoiling a few paces. "But let us proceed to the Amontillado."

"Be it so," I said, replacing the tool beneath the cloak and again offering him my arm. He leaned upon it heavily. We continued our route in search of the Amontillado. We passed through a range of low arches, descended, passed on, and descending again, arrived at a deep crypt, in which the foulness of the air caused our flambeaux rather to glow than flame.

At the most remote end of the crypt there appeared another less spacious. Its walls had been lined with human remains, piled to the vault overhead, in the fashion of the great catacombs of Paris. Three sides of this interior crypt were still ornamented in this manner. From the fourth side the bones had been thrown down, and lay promiscuously upon the earth, forming at one point a mound of some size. Within the wall thus exposed by the displacing of the bones, we perceived a still interior crypt or recess, in depth about four feet, in width three, in height six or seven. It seemed to have been constructed for no especial use within itself, but formed merely the

---

11. **masons** the Freemasons, an international secret society.

Literature in Context

Literature Connection

Poe and the Gothic Tradition The literary genre known as gothic fiction emerged in England in the late 1700s in works like *Castle of Otranto* (1765) by Horace Walpole and *The Mysteries of Udolpho* (1794) by Ann Radcliffe. The word *gothic* was originally used to describe a style of building that was common in the late Middle Ages. To writers in the eighteenth century, the cold chambers and secret passages of such buildings suggested mystery and dark tales of vengeance and passion.

Edgar Allan Poe translated the imagery and atmosphere of British gothic fiction to an American landscape, pioneering an American gothic tradition. Contemporary writers like Stephen King and Anne Rice, as well as countless filmmakers, carry on that tradition today.

Connect to the Literature

What qualities of gothic fiction do you find in "The Cask of Amontillado"? Explain.

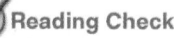

Reading Check

Where does Montresor bring Fortunato?

The Cask of Amontillado ■ 65

- Explain to students that the Masonic Order is a secret organization with exclusive membership. Point out that Fortunato cannot believe that Montresor is a mason, so once again he is insulting Montresor.

- Tell students that a trowel is a tool used for smoothing concrete and for applying mortar when laying bricks. It is also a symbol of the Masonic Order. **Ask** students what the trowel might foreshadow. **Possible response:** It foreshadows that Montresor will carry out a terrible act with the trowel. He might kill Fortunato and seal up his body in a crypt with bricks.

⑪ Literature in Context

Literature Connection Point out that originally, gothic literature was set in medieval castles and ancient structures such as the catacombs that Poe describes. Modern gothic literature is often placed in other settings, but the goal of the writing remains the same—to create a combined sense of unknown horror and empathy for the character involved in the situation. Gothic literature is not defined so much by setting, characterization, or plot but by its ability to create a mood and tone that evokes deep emotions in the reader.

Connect to the Literature Ask students to cite other contemporary writers and directors who carry on the gothic tradition. **Ask** the Connect to the Literature question: What qualities of gothic fiction do you find in "The Cask of Amontillado"?

Possible answer: Students may cite the dank, eerie setting of the vaults, the foul atmosphere, and Montresor's devious, demented revenge plot.

⑫ Reading Check

Answer: Montresor brings Fortunato to the deepest and farthest part of the catacombs, where some of the wine is stored.

- Have a volunteer read the passage aloud. Then **ask** students whether they think events have reached a climax. Have them explain their answers.
Answer: The climax has not yet been reached. Montresor's comment that he must "render [Fortunato] all the attentions in [his] power" suggests that something more is coming.

- **Ask** students what Montresor's comment might foreshadow and how this impacts the level of suspense.
Possible response: It foreshadows that Montresor plans to do more than leave Fortunato chained to the wall. This adds to readers' suspense as they wait to find out how far Montresor will go in his quest for revenge.

⓮ **Critical Viewing**

Answer: A mask can't change its expression, and it has no eyes, only holes for the wearer's eyes. Lack of expression can make any face seem sinister because the person's actions are hard to predict.

---

interval between two of the colossal supports of the roof of the catacombs, and was backed by one of their circumscribing walls of solid granite.

It was in vain that Fortunato, uplifting his dull torch, endeavored to pry into the depth of the recess. Its termination the feeble light did not enable us to see.

"Proceed," I said: "herein is the Amontillado. As for Luchesi—"

"He is an ignoramus," interrupted my friend, as he stepped unsteadily forward, while I followed immediately at his heels. In an instant he had reached the extremity of the niche, and finding his progress arrested by the rock, stood stupidly bewildered. A moment more and I had fettered him to the granite. In its surface were two iron staples, distant from each other about two feet, horizontally. From one of these depended a short chain, from the other a padlock. Throwing the links about his waist, it was but the work of a few seconds to secure it. He was too much astounded to resist. Withdrawing the key I stepped back from the recess.

"Pass your hand," I said, "over the wall; you cannot help feeling the niter. Indeed, it is very damp. Once more let me implore you to return. No? Then I must positively leave you. But I must first render you all the little attentions in my power."

"The Amontillado!" ejaculated my friend, not yet recovered from his astonishment.

"True," I replied; "the Amontillado."

As I said these words I busied myself among the pile of bones of which I have before spoken. Throwing them aside, I soon uncovered a quantity of building stone and mortar. With these materials and with the aid of my trowel, I began vigorously to wall up the entrance of the niche.

I had scarcely laid the first tier of the masonry when I discovered that the intoxication of Fortunato had in a great measure worn off. The earliest indication I had of this was a low moaning cry from the depth of the recess. It was not the cry of a drunken man. There was then a long and obstinate silence. I laid the second tier, and the third, and the fourth; and then I heard the furious vibrations of the chain. The noise lasted for several minutes, during which, that I might hearken to it with the more satisfaction, I ceased my labors and sat down upon the bones. When at last the clanking subsided, I resumed the trowel, and finished without

⓮ ▲ **Critical Viewing** Explain how the context of a story might make festive masks like these seem sinister. **[Interpret]**

Vocabulary Development

Vocabulary Knowledge Rating
When students have completed reading and discussing "The Cask of Amontillado," have them take out their **Vocabulary Knowledge Rating Chart** for this selection. Read the words aloud once more and have students rate their knowledge of the words again in the After Reading column. Clarify any words that are still problematic. Have students write their own definition and example or sentence in the appropriate column. Then have students complete the **Vocabulary Builder Practice** activities on p. 69. Encourage students to use the words in further discussion and written work about this selection. Remind them that they will be accountable for these words on the Selection Test.

interruption the fifth, the sixth, and the seventh tier. The wall was now nearly upon a level with my breast. I again paused, and holding the flambeaux over the masonwork, threw a few feeble rays upon the figure within.

A succession of loud and shrill screams, bursting suddenly from the throat of the chained form, seemed to thrust me violently back. For a brief moment I hesitated, I trembled. Unsheathing my rapier, I began to grope with it about the recess; but the thought of an instant reassured me. I placed my hand upon the solid fabric of the catacombs, and felt satisfied. I reapproached the wall; I replied to the yells of him who clamored. I reechoed, I aided, I surpassed them in volume and in strength. I did this, and the clamorer grew still.

It was now midnight, and my task was drawing to a close. I had completed the eighth, the ninth, and the tenth tier. I had finished a portion of the last and the eleventh; there remained but a single stone to be fitted and plastered in. I struggled with its weight; I placed it partially in its destined position. But now there came from out the niche a low laugh that erected the hairs upon my head. It was succeeded by a sad voice, which I had difficulty in recognizing as that of the noble Fortunato. The voice said—

"Ha! ha! ha!—he! he! he!—a very good joke, indeed—an excellent jest. We will have many a rich laugh about it at the palazzo—he! he! he!—over our wine—he! he! he!"

"The Amontillado!" I said.

"He! he! he!—he! he! he!—yes, the Amontillado. But is it not getting late? Will not they be awaiting us at the palazzo, the Lady Fortunato and the rest? Let us be gone."

"Yes," I said, "let us be gone."

"For the love of God, Montresor!"

"Yes," I said, "for the love of God!"

But to these words I hearkened in vain for a reply. I grew impatient. I called aloud—

"Fortunato!"

No answer. I called again—

"Fortunato!"

No answer still. I thrust a torch through the remaining aperture and let it fall within. There came forth in return only a jingling of the bells. My heart grew sick; it was the dampness of the catacombs that made it so. I hastened to make an end of my labor. I forced the last stone into its position; I plastered it up. Against the new masonry I reerected the old rampart of bones. For the half of a century no mortal has disturbed them. *In pace requiescat!*[12]

---

12. *In pace requiescat!* Latin for "May he rest in peace!"

Reading Skill

Making and Verifying Predictions Does this scene in which Montresor imprisons Fortunato verify your earlier predictions? Explain.

⑮ Reading Skill
Making and Verifying Predictions

- **Ask** students whether making predictions helps them concentrate on their reading. Have them explain their answers.
  Possible response: Most students will say that making predictions helps them concentrate because they are looking for clues and verification of their predictions.

- **Ask** the Reading Skill question on this page: Does this scene in which Montresor imprisons Fortunato verify your earlier predictions? Explain.
  Possible response: Students might have predicted this outcome based on clues such as Montresor's deep-seated desire for revenge, Fortunato's statement that the cough "will not kill me," and the fact that Montresor was carrying a trowel.

▶ **Monitor Progress:** Review students' graphic organizers to ensure that they have been effectively making and verifying predictions.

▶ **Reteach:** If students have difficulty making predictions, ask them to review the story and list clues that foreshadow Fortunato's final imprisonment. List the clues on the board, and discuss how they foreshadow the final scene.

Concept Connector

Connecting to the Literature
Have students compare the sentences they wrote before reading with their thoughts about why people enjoy reading stories set in scary places. Ask them to explain whether their thoughts have changed and, if so, how.

Reading Skill Graphic Organizer
Have students review the graphic organizers they prepared to make and verify predictions while reading. Show them **Reading Skill Graphic Organizer B** (*Graphic Organizer Transparencies,* p. 12) as an example. Then have students share the graphic organizers they did and the predictions they made about the story.

1. **Possible response:** He may be most disturbing when he kindly urges Fortunato to leave the cat-acombs.

2. (a) Montresor describes Fortunato as vain about his wine expertise and not perceptive enough to see that Montresor is his enemy. (b) Fortunato's pride in his wine expertise and his desire to be recognized for this make him receptive to Montresor's flattery.

3. (a) Montresor wears a mask and a cloak so that no one will recognize him. He makes sure his servants are out of the house. He remembers to bring a trowel. (b) He knows that the more he urges a return, the more a vain Fortunato will insist on proceeding.

4. (a) Fortunato has injured and insulted him. (b) Montresor feels that revenge counts for nothing unless the victim knows the avenger did it himself. (c) At the end, Montresor hesitates suggesting that he may have had some regret.

5. **Possible response:** No, because private revenge will ultimately damage society.

6. **Possible response: Rising Action:** Montresor invites Fortunato to the vaults to try his wine; Montresor chains Fortunato to the wall. **Falling Action:** Montresor replaces the bones to cover the crypt's entrance. **Climax:** Montresor thrusts his torch into the crypt and hears only the jingling of the bells on Fortunato's costume.

   Another sample answer can be found on **Literary Analysis Graphic Organizer B,** p. 16, in *Graphic Organizer Transparencies.*

7. (a) Montresor declares himself a "mason" and shows Fortunato a trowel that he has hidden under his cloak. (b) **Possible response:** Foreshadowing makes readers anxious about what Montresor is going to do. Clues suggest that he is planning something horrible, so readers anticipate it with uncertainty and dread.

68

The Cask of Amontillado

Thinking About the Selection

1. **Respond:** At what point in the story do you find Montresor most disturbing? Explain.
2. **(a) Recall:** How does Montresor describe Fortunato's strengths and weaknesses early in the story? **(b) Analyze:** Which character traits make Fortunato easy prey for Montresor?
3. **(a) Recall:** What specific steps does Montresor take to ensure that his plan works? **(b) Interpret:** Why does Montresor keep urging Fortunato to turn back?
4. **(a) Recall:** Why does Montresor hate Fortunato? **(b) Support:** Why does Montresor feel he has the right to punish Fortunato? **(c) Assess:** Does Montresor express any regret or ever question whether this punishment is just or rational?
5. **Evaluate:** Montresor acts as both judge and executioner in this story. Explain whether you think individuals are ever justified in taking justice into their own hands.

Literary Analysis

6. Using a chart like the one shown, identify two key events in the **rising action,** one event in the **falling action,** and the event that marks the **climax.** Then, trade charts with a partner and discuss the reasons why you chose the events that you did. Finally, explain to your partner how your understanding of the story has or has not changed as a result of the discussion.

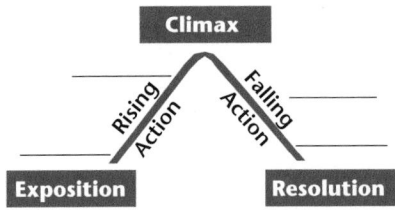

7. **(a)** Identify a statement or an event that **foreshadows** Fortunato's fate. **(b)** How does foreshadowing add to the **suspense?** Explain.

Reading Skill

8. **(a)** What **prediction** did you make after reading about Montresor's and Fortunato's shared interest in wine? **(b)** On what details did you base your prediction?
9. Was your prediction **verified** by later story events? Explain.

68 ■ Fiction and Nonfiction

QuickReview

Story at a Glance
Montresor lures Fortunato into the catacombs below his house to avenge an insult.

For: Self-test
Visit: www.PHSchool.com
Web Code: epa-6106

Plot: the sequence of events in a narrative. Elements include *rising action, climax, falling action,* and *resolution.*

Foreshadowing: a hint or clue about events that will happen later in a story

Suspense: a feeling of tension caused by anticipation of what might happen later

Prediction: an informed idea about what might happen later

8. (a) **Possible response:** Students might have predicted that Montresor would use Fortunato's interest in wine to exact his revenge. (b) **Possible response:** Yes, Fortunato went into the catacombs believing he was going to taste some wine.

9. **Possible response:** Clues include Montresor's stated desire for revenge and his comment that wine was Fortunato's weakness.

Vocabulary Builder

Practice **Analogies** show the relationships between pairs of words. Use a word from the vocabulary list for "The Cask of Amontillado" on page 46 to complete each analogy. For each case, your choice should create a word pair that matches the relationship between the first two words.

1. conversation: dialogue :: _____ : revenge
2. harmed : helped :: _____ : allowed
3. delicious : food :: _____ : instructions

Adding Words to Your Vocabulary *Precluded* can be defined by the synonym *prevented*. A **synonym** is a word that has the same or nearly the same definition as another word. Other synonyms for *precluded* include *hindered, deterred,* and *stopped.* These words are synonyms, but they do not mean exactly the same thing. Look up each word in a dictionary, and for each word, write a sentence that reflects its specific meaning. (For help with reference materials, see page R6.)

Writing

In writing "The Cask of Amontillado," Poe clearly intended to keep readers on the edge of their seats. Did he succeed? Write a **critique** in which you evaluate "The Cask of Amontillado" as a suspenseful story.

- Before writing, make a list of qualities a suspenseful story should have. Check off those qualities that appear in Poe's story.
- Consult your checklist as you write, and use it as evidence to support your argument.

For *Grammar, Vocabulary,* and *Assessment,* see **Build Language Skills,** pages 70–71.

Extend Your Learning

Listening and Speaking Present a **retelling** of Poe's story from Fortunato's point of view. As you speak, use facial expressions and body movements effectively to convey Fortunato's personality.

Research and Technology Work with classmates to create a **storyboard** for a movie version of "The Cask of Amontillado."

- Use Internet and library resources to find other storyboards that can serve as guides for your own.
- Decide as a group which events to depict. Draw those scenes in comic book style and write a brief description for each frame.

Apply the Skills ■ 69

Go Online **For:** An additional research activity
—Research **Visit:** www.PHSchool.com
Web Code: epd-7104
For another research activity to extend students' learning, give students this Web Code.

Vocabulary Development
Practice

1. retribution
2. precluded
3. explicit

Adding Words to Your Vocabulary
Sample responses:

1. A heavy downpour *prevented* the team from playing.
2. The deep snow *hindered* the rescue team's attempts to reach the stranded motorist.
3. He was determined to succeed and would not be *deterred* by one poor test result.
4. The car ran out of gas and *stopped* running.

Writing

- To give students guidance for writing a critique, give them **Support for Writing** for "The Cask of Amontillado", p. 76 in *Unit 1 Resources.*
- To evaluate students' critiques, use the Response to Literature rubrics, pp. 57–58 in *General Resources.* In addition, you might place emphasis on using evidence from the story to support students' ideas.

Six Traits Focus

✔	Ideas		Word Choice
	Organization		Sentence Fluency
✔	Voice		Conventions

 Writing and Grammar, Gold Level
Students will find guidance on writing a response to literature in Chapter 13.

Build Language Skills

Go to pp. 70–71 for vocabulary and grammar lessons and assessment practice.

Extend Your Learning

The **Support for Extend Your Learning** page (*Unit 1 Resources,* p. 77) provides guided note-taking opportunities to help students complete the Extend Your Learning activities.

Vocabulary Skill

- Introduce the word roots -tempor- and -spec-. Ask students to brainstorm for words that contain these roots.
  Possible Answers: *temporary, temporal, tempo, specify, spectacle, spectator, spectrum.*

- Have students complete the Practice activity on this page.

Possible Answers

1. impermanent
2. detail
3. spontaneous
4. pace
5. requirement

Grammar Lesson

- Tell students that concrete nouns exist physically. Tell students that abstract nouns do not exist physically. Tell students that abstract nouns require the reader to understand a concept. **Ask** students to give examples of concrete nouns and abstract nouns that are related to their school.
  Possible Answers: Concrete: desks, books. Abstract: education, intelligence

- Have students complete the Practice activity on this page.

Answers

1. Dreams (a), events (a), day (a)
2. psychologists (c), everything (a), brain (c)
3. thought (a), information (a), memory (a)
4. some (a), brain (c), fears (a), thoughts (a), hopes (a)
5. Daydreams (a), dreams (a)

Writing Application

To evaluate students' papers, make sure that the paragraphs include at least two concrete nouns and two abstract nouns.

Writing and Grammar, Gold Level

Students will find further instruction and practice on personal and reflexive pronouns in Chapter 16, Section 1.

Build Language Skills

Sonata for Harp and Bicycle • The Cask of Amontillado

Vocabulary Skill

Word Roots *Contemporary,* which means "of the current time," contains the **Latin root** *-tempor-,* which means "of time." *Specific* also contains a **Latin root:** *-spec-,* which means "see." When you make something *specific,* you make it able to be seen and known. Knowing these roots will help you understand and remember the meaning of words that contain them.

Practice Each of the following words is based on either *-tempor-* or *-spec-*. Explain how the meaning of the root can help you remember the meaning of the word. Then, write a synonym for each of the words.

1. temporary
2. specify
3. extemporaneous
4. tempo
5. specification

Grammar Lesson

Abstract and Concrete Nouns Nouns that name people, places, or things that can be seen or recognized through any of the five senses are called **concrete nouns.** Nouns that name ideas, actions, conditions, and qualities—things that cannot be recognized through the senses—are called **abstract nouns.**

Abstract Noun	Concrete Noun
Fortunato discovered Montresor's *intention,* but it was too late.	William Heron patrolled the halls on a *bicycle.*

Practice Copy the following sentences. Underline the concrete nouns once and the abstract nouns twice. Then, choose three concrete nouns and three abstract nouns and use them to write your own sentences.

1. Dreams are thought to be about events in your day.
2. Some psychologists believe that everything you do is recorded in your brain.
3. The thought of so much information being stored in your memory is amazing.
4. According to some, your brain sorts out your fears, thoughts, and hopes while you sleep.
5. Daydreams are different from the dreams you have when you sleep.

Prentice Hall Writing and Grammar Connection: Chapter 16, Section 1

MorePractice

For more practice with common and proper nouns, see Grammar Handbook, p. R39.

Teaching Resources

The following resources can be used to enrich or extend the instruction for Build Language Skills.

Unit 1 Resources
  Build Language Skills: Vocabulary: The Latin roots *-tempor-* and *-spec-*, p. 79
  Build Grammar Skills: Abstract and Concrete Nouns, p. 80

Assessment Practice

Reading: Make Predictions

Directions: *Read the selection. Then, answer the questions.*

And when finally they did meet up again, neither offered a clue to the other that he, or she, had been the object of obsessive thought for weeks. She spotted him as soon as she came into the store, but she kept her eyes strictly in front of her as she pulled out a cart and wheeled it toward the produce. And he, too, knew the instant she came through the door—though the orange bow was gone, replaced by a small but bright yellow flower instead—and he never once turned his head in her direction but watched her from the corner of his vision as he tried to swallow back the fear in his throat.

—from "Checkouts" by Cynthia Rylant

1. Which of the following details is least useful in making a prediction about what will happen?
   A He, or she, had been the object of obsessive thought for weeks.
   B She spotted him as soon as she came into the store.
   C He knew the instant she came through the door.
   D The orange bow was gone.

2. Which further detail is most relevant to a prediction made from the information in this passage?
   A The girl hated herself for not checking out at the boy's line.
   B This is often the way of children, when they truly want a thing.

   C And perhaps cats, who have been known to react in the same way . . .
   D the bag boy himself grew so bored with his job . . .

3. Which detail would verify a prediction that the boy and the girl will never reveal their feelings to each other?
   A The girl hated herself for not checking out at the boy's line.
   B This is often the way of children, when they truly want a thing.
   C And the bag boy let her leave the store, pretending to take no notice of her.
   D Strange, how attractive clumsiness can be.

Timed Writing: Explanation [Critical Stance]

Review "Sonato for Harp and Bicycle" or "The Cask of Amontillado." Write a brief explanation of how the author creates the mood of the story. **(20 minutes)**

 ## Writing Workshop: *Work in Progress*

Autobiographical Narrative

Use the scene description from the Memory List in your writing portfolio. Next to each person's description jot down how you reacted to what they were doing. Save this work in your writing portfolio.

Reading: Make Predictions

1. A
2. D
3. A
4 C

Timed Writing

- Tell students that when writing a critical stance, they should include a summary or description of the literary work under discussion.
- Make sure they understand that such summaries should be brief. The bulk of the essay should focus on the student's ideas.
- Suggest that students define key literary terms—for example, "mood"—that are stipulated in the assignment.
- Remind students that their opinions are not enough; they must support their ideas with details from the work.
- Assess students' critical stances by reviewing the clarity of their explanations and the thoroughness of their support.
- Suggest that students organize their time to give 5 minutes to reviewing the story and planning, 10 minutes to writing, and 5 minutes to revising and editing.

Writing Workshop
Work in Progress

Autobiographical Narrative

- Have students go to their portfolios and take out the work they have completed so far on this assignment.
- Remind students that this work may be used in the autobiographical narrative they will write in the **Writing Workshop** at the end of Part 1.
- Tell students to write down their mental, emotional, and physical reactions.
- Encourage students to use strong action verbs to relate their reactions.
- When students have completed this activity, have them keep it in their portfolios. They will use it as they continue the Work in Progress.

✔ Meeting Your Standards

Students will

1. analyze and respond to point of view in fiction.

2. compare the effect of point of view in two works of fiction.

3. write a comparison of point of view.

*See **TeacherExpress™/Lesson View** for a detailed lesson plan for Comparing Literary Works.*

Literary Analysis

❶ Point of View

- Read the instruction about point of view together.

- **Ask** students: Which point of view might make a narrative seem more personal and real? Explain.
  Possible response: First-person point of view might make a narrative seem more real because the reader seems to encounter an actual person.

- Point out that third-person limited point of view also reveals a single character's thoughts and feelings; the difference is that the narrator is not a character in the story.

- **Ask** students: Which point of view would allow readers to know the thoughts and feelings of all characters? Explain.
  Answer: Third-person omniscient reveals the thoughts and feelings of all characters; the narrator is all-knowing.

❷ Comparing Points of View

- Remind students that point of view affects what they know about the characters and plot of a story. Students will see these differences as they compare points of view in the two selections.

- **Ask** students which pronouns they might expect to see in each selection.
  Answer: "Checkouts" will probably use *he, she, him, her, they,* and *them.* "The Girl Who Can" will probably use *I, me,* and *my.*

❶ Point of View

Point of view is the perspective from which a story is narrated, or told.

- **First-person point of view:** The narrator is a character who participates in the action of the story and uses the first-person pronouns *I* and *me* to describe himself or herself.

- **Third-person point of view:** The narrator is not a character in the story but is a voice outside the action. The narrator uses the third-person pronouns *he, she, him, her, they,* and *them* to refer to all characters. There are two kinds of third-person point of view. In the **third-person omniscient point of view,** the narrator knows everything, including the thoughts and feelings of all the characters. In the **third-person limited point of view,** the narrator sees things through one character's eyes and reveals that character's feeling and thoughts. The narrator can describe what other characters do or say but not what they feel or think.

❷ Comparing Points of View

Point of view affects the type of information a reader receives.

- The first-person point of view in "The Girl Who Can" allows the reader to know all of the narrator's inner thoughts. Her sense of the world shapes the reader's experience of the story.

- By contrast, the omniscient point of view used in "Checkouts" lets the reader see opportunities the main characters do not even know they have.

Compare the effects of these two different points of view in these selections by using a Venn diagram like the one shown.

Vocabulary Builder

Checkouts

- **reverie** (rev´ ə rē) *n.* dreamy thought of pleasant things (p. 75) *Lost in reverie, she did not hear the bell.*

- **dishevelment** (di shev´ əl mənt) *n.* disorder; messiness (p. 76) *The wind left her hair in a state of dishevelment.*

- **perverse** (pər vʉrs´) *adj.* deviating from what is considered right or reasonable (p. 77) *He took perverse pleasure in arriving late.*

72 ■ Fiction and Nonfiction

The Girl Who Can

- **fertile** (fʉrt´ 'l) *adj.* able to make plants grow (p. 79) *They bought a farm with fertile soil.*

- **comprehension** (käm´ prē hen´ shən) *n.* understanding (p. 80) *The reason for his anger is beyond my comprehension.*

- **humble** (hum´ bəl) *adj.* modest; having humility (p. 81) *Although he won the race, he remained humble with his teammates.*

Vocabulary Development

Vocabulary Knowledge Rating
Create a **Vocabulary Knowledge Rating Chart** with the selection vocabulary and expressive vocabulary for both selections. Give students a copy. Introduce the words by reading them aloud and having students mark their rating in the Before Reading column. Urge them to be alert to these words as they read and discuss the selection because they will rate their knowledge of the words again after they finish.

If you wish, you may tally how many students know (or think they know) a word to gauge how much instruction you need to provide. As students read, point out the words and their context.

Build Understanding

❸ Reading/Writing Connection

The main characters in these stories have the chance to reach for opportunities, but they must balance goals against risk. Write a few sentences to explain how you might decide whether to take a chance at something you value. Use at least three of the following words in your response: *impact, display, reveal, emerge, signify.*

Meet the Authors

Cynthia **Rylant** (b. 1954)

Cynthia Rylant spent four years as a child living with her grandparents in a small town in West Virginia. With no public library and very little money to buy books, she started reading comic books. Once in college, she discovered great literature, but she did not consider becoming a writer until she took a job as a librarian and began reading children's books.

Writing About Her Life In her writing, Rylant draws upon her experiences as both a child and young adult. "The best writing," she says, "is that which is most personal, most revealing." She has written numerous award-winning stories, poems, and novels.

Ama Ata **Aidoo** (b. 1942)

Ama Ata Aidoo was born in Ghana, Africa, where her father was a village chief. He wanted his daughter to have a Western education and sent her to a university in Cape Coast, Ghana. Aidoo earned her bachelor's degree in English and later taught at universities in Ghana and the United States.

Works and Themes Aidoo has written plays, short stories, poetry, and novels. Her fiction, written in English, often explores the conflicts between Western and African cultures and the roles of women in modern society.

Go **Online**
Author Link
For: More about the authors
Visit: www.PHSchool.com
Web Code: epe-9106

Checkouts/The Girl Who Can ■ 73

❸ Connecting to the Literature

- Model use of the expressive vocabulary students are asked to use with these examples:
  1. I know that this decision will *impact* my future.
  2. I hope to *display* wisdom as I make this choice.
  3. If I carefully consider the situation, the right choice will *reveal* itself to me.
  4. When I *emerge* from this decision-making process, I will have learned more about myself.
  5. Whatever happens, I know my decision will *signify* growth and self-discovery.

- Help students further develop their expressive vocabularies by providing these words: *assess, consider, convey,* and *rely.*

Go **Online**
Author Link
For additional information about Cynthia Rylant and Ama Ata Aidoo, have students type in the Web Code, select *R* or *A* from the alphabet, and then select *Cynthia Rylant* or *Ama Ata Aidoo.*

Teaching Resources

The following resources can be used to enrich, extend, or differentiate the instruction for **Comparing Literary Works.**

Unit 1 Resources, pp. 87–93

Graphic Organizer Transparencies, pp. 17–20

Reader's Notebook

Reader's Notebook: Adapted Version

Reader's Notebook: English Learner's Version

Listening to Literature Audio CD

Checkouts

Cynthia Rylant

Food City, 1967, Richard Estes, Collection of the Akron Art Museum, Akron, Ohio, Museum Acquisition Fund, Photo by Richman Haire, © Richard Estes/Licensed by VAGA, New York, NY/Courtesy Marlborough Gallery, NY

Her parents had moved her to Cincinnati, to a large house with beveled glass[1] windows and several porches and the history her mother liked to emphasize. You'll love the house, they said. You'll be lonely at first, they admitted, but you're so nice you'll make friends fast. And as an impulse tore at her to lie on the floor, to hold to their ankles and tell them she felt she was dying, to offer anything, anything at all, so they might allow her to finish growing up in the town of her childhood, they firmed their mouths and spoke from their chests and they said, It's decided.

---

1. **beveled** (bev′ əld) **glass** *n.* glass having angled or slanted edges.

74 ■ *Fiction and Nonfiction*

❹ ▲ Critical Viewing
Which features of a supermarket might help people take their minds off their troubles? **[Analyze]**

Vocabulary Development

Vocabulary Builder Reinforcement
Students will benefit from additional examples and practice with the Vocabulary Builder words. Reinforce their comprehension with "show-you-know" sentences. The first part of the sentence uses the vocabulary word in an appropriate context. The second part of the sentence—the "show-you-know" part—clarifies the first. Model the strategy with this example for *reverie:*

The singer was lost in *reverie;* the daydream caused her to miss her cue.

Then give students these sentence prompts, and coach them in creating the clarification part:
1. The *dishevelment* of the fraternity house was appalling; _____.
   Possible response: the mess would take days to clean.
2. Most people found her love of snakes *perverse;* _____.
   Possible response: they consider the creatures to be revolting.

They moved her to Cincinnati, where for a month she spent the greater part of every day in a room full of beveled glass windows, sifting through photographs of the life she'd lived and left behind. But it is difficult work, suffering, and in its own way a kind of art, and finally she didn't have the energy for it anymore, so she emerged from the beautiful house and fell in love with a bag boy at the supermarket. Of course, this didn't happen all at once, just like that, but in the sequence of things that's exactly the way it happened.

She liked to grocery shop. She loved it in the way some people love to drive long country roads, because doing it she could think and relax and wander. Her parents wrote up the list and handed it to her and off she went without complaint to perform what they regarded as a great sacrifice of her time and a sign that she was indeed a very nice girl. She had never told them how much she loved grocery shopping, only that she was "willing" to do it. She had an intuition which told her that her parents were not safe for sharing such strong, important facts about herself. Let them think they knew her.

Once inside the supermarket, her hands firmly around the handle of the cart, she would lapse into a kind of <u>reverie</u> and wheel toward the produce. Like a Tibetan monk in solitary meditation, she calmed to a point of deep, deep happiness; this feeling came to her, reliably, if strangely, only in the supermarket.

Then one day the bag boy dropped her jar of mayonnaise and that is how she fell in love.

He was nervous—first day on the job—and along had come this fascinating girl, standing in the checkout line with the unfocused stare one often sees in young children, her face turned enough away that he might take several full looks at her as he packed sturdy bags full of food and the goods of modern life. She interested him because her hair was red and thick, and in it she had placed a huge orange bow, nearly the size of a small hat. That was enough to distract him, and when finally it was her groceries he was packing, she looked at him and smiled and he could respond only by busting her jar of mayonnaise on the floor, shards of glass and oozing cream decorating the area around his feet.

She loved him at exactly that moment, and if he'd known this perhaps he wouldn't have fallen into the brown depression he fell into, which lasted the rest of his shift. He believed he must have looked the fool in her eyes, and he envied the sureness of everyone around him: the cocky cashier at the register, the grim and harried store manager, the bland butcher, and the brazen bag boys who smoked in the warehouse on their breaks. He wanted a second chance. Another chance to be confident and say witty things to her

Literary Analysis
Point of View How does the use of pronouns in this paragraph show that this story is being told from the third-person point of view?

Vocabulary Builder
reverie (rev´ ə rē) *n.* dreamy thought of pleasant things

Literary Analysis
Point of View Whose thoughts and feelings are expressed in this paragraph?

✓ **Reading Check**
At first, why does the girl fascinate the boy?

Checkouts ■ 75

Differentiated
Instruction Solutions for All Learners

Reading Support
Have students complete the **Preview** and **Build Skills** pages for "Checkouts" in the appropriate versions of the **Reader's Notebooks.**
Reader's Notebook [L2]
Reader's Notebook: Adapted Version [L1]
Reader's Notebook: English Learner's Version [EL]

Accessibility at a Glance
Use this information to guide your teaching of "Checkouts."

Context	Contemporary: teenagers fall in love without ever meeting
Language	Informal: accessible sentence structure and vocabulary
Concept Level	More Accessible
Literary Merit	YA
Lexile	1350L

⑤ Literary Analysis
Point of View

- Remind students they should examine the pronouns used in a story to help identify the point of view.
- **Ask** the first Literary Analysis question: How does the use of pronouns in this paragraph show that this story is being told from the third-person point of view?
  Answer: The pronouns *her* and *she* indicate that the story is being told from the third-person point of view.
- **Ask** students which pronouns would indicate that a story is told from the first-person point of view.
  Answer: The first-person point of view would use pronouns such as *I, my,* and *me.*

⑥ Literary Analysis
Point of View

- Remind students that there are two types of third-person narrators: omniscient and limited. Have students **define** each type.
  Answer: In third-person omniscient, the narrator tells the thoughts and feelings of all the characters. In third-person limited, the narrator sees events through a single character's perspective.
- **Ask** students the second Literary Analysis question: Whose thoughts and feelings are expressed in this paragraph?
  Answer: The paragraph describes the thoughts and feelings of the bag boy.
- Have students **contrast** this passage with the first bracketed passage on the page.
  Answer: The first passage is told from the perspective of the girl, whereas this passage is told from the perspective of the bag boy.

⑦ Reading Check
Answer: The boy is fascinated by her thick, red hair with the huge orange bow. Also, she distracts him from his boring job.

8 **Literary Analysis**
Point of View

- Remind students that the narrator previously stated that the girl fell in love with the bag boy at the exact moment that he dropped the mayonnaise. Explain that this passage details the boy's thoughts and feelings about the same moment.

- **Ask** the Literary Analysis question: What does the narrator reveal about the boy's regrets?
Answer: The narrator reveals that the boy regrets not having made more of an effort to get to know the girl. He wishes he could have impressed her with confidence and clever conversation.

- Have students read the next several paragraphs. Then **ask:** How does the girl view the boy's clumsiness and awkwardness?
Answer: The girl finds these qualities attractive and begins to love the boy because of them, not in spite of them.

- Discuss with students how the author's choice of a third-person omniscient point of view allows readers access to the interior lives of both characters. **Ask** students how they think this adds to the story's meaning.
Possible response: Students might find that they can relate to the emotions of both characters, which enhances their response to the story.

9 **Literary Analysis**
Point of View

- After students read the bracketed passage, **ask** them how the characters react to finally seeing each other again.
Answer: The characters pretend not to notice each other and even make a point to avoid contact.

- **Ask** the Literary Analysis question: Which details here suggest the story is told from the omniscient point of view? Explain.
Answer: The paragraph discusses the thoughts and feelings of both the boy and the girl. The third-person omniscient point of view is all-knowing, so it can reveal the inner thoughts of multiple characters.

---

as he threw tin cans into her bags, persuading her to allow him to help her to her car so he might learn just a little about her, check out the floor of the car for signs of hobbies or fetishes and the bumpers for clues as to beliefs and loyalties.

But he busted her jar of mayonnaise and nothing else worked out for the rest of the day.

Strange, how attractive clumsiness can be. She left the supermarket with stars in her eyes, for she had loved the way his long nervous fingers moved from the conveyor belt to the bags, how deftly (until the mayonnaise) they had picked up her items and placed them in her bags. She had loved the way the hair kept falling into his eyes as he leaned over to grab a box or a tin. And the tattered brown shoes he wore with no socks. And the left side of his collar turned in rather than out.

The bag boy seemed a wonderful contrast to the perfectly beautiful house she had been forced to accept as her home, to the history she hated, to the loneliness she had become used to, and she couldn't wait to come back for more of his awkwardness and <u>dishevelment</u>.

Incredibly, it was another four weeks before they saw each other again. As fate would have it, her visits to the supermarket never coincided with his schedule to bag. Each time she went to the store, her eyes scanned the checkouts at once, her heart in her mouth. And each hour he worked, the bag boy kept one eye on the door, watching for the red-haired girl with the big orange bow.

Yet in their disappointment these weeks there was a kind of ecstasy. It is reason enough to be alive, the hope you may see again some face which has meant something to you. The anticipation of meeting the bag boy eased the girl's painful transition into her new and jarring life in Cincinnati. It provided for her an anchor amid all that was impersonal and unfamiliar, and she spent less time on thoughts of what she had left behind as she concentrated on what might lie ahead. And for the boy, the long and often tedious hours at the supermarket which provided no challenge other than that of showing up the following workday . . . these hours became possibilities of mystery and romance for him as he watched the electric doors for the girl in the orange bow.

And when finally they did meet up again, neither offered a clue to the other that he, or she, had been the object of obsessive thought for weeks. She spotted him as soon as she came into the store, but she kept her eyes strictly in front of her as she pulled out a cart and wheeled it toward the produce. And he, too, knew the instant she came through the door—though the orange bow was gone, replaced by a small but bright yellow flower instead—and he never once

76 ■ Fiction and Nonfiction

Literary Analysis
Point of View What does the narrator reveal about the boy's regrets?

Vocabulary Builder
dishevelment (di shev´ əl mənt) *n.* disorder; messiness

Literary Analysis
Point of View Which details here suggest the story is told from the omniscient point of view? Explain.

Vocabulary Development

Expressive Vocabulary
As students are discussing the relationship between the girl and the bag boy, encourage them to use the expressive vocabulary presented earlier. You might encourage them with sentence starters like these:

1. The *impact* of the bag boy dropping the mayonnaise…
2. Because the bag boy did not *display* confidence and wit, …

3. Both the girl and the bag boy refused to *reveal*…
4. The girl's feelings for the bag boy allowed her to *emerge*…
5. Their encounter at the movie theater might *signify*…

⑨ turned his head in her direction but watched her from the corner of his vision as he tried to swallow back the fear in his throat.

It is odd how we sometimes deny ourselves the very pleasure we have longed for and which is finally within our reach. For some <u>perverse</u> reason she would not have been able to articulate, the girl did not bring her cart up to the bag boy's checkout when her shopping was done. And the bag boy let her leave the store, pretending no notice of her.

This is often the way of children, when they truly want a thing, to pretend that they don't. And then they grow angry when no one tried harder to give them this thing they so casually rejected, and they soon find themselves in a rage simply because they cannot say yes when they mean yes. Humans are very complicated. (And perhaps cats, who have been known to react in the same way, though the resulting rage can only be guessed at.)

⑩ The girl hated herself for not checking out at the boy's line, and the boy hated himself for not catching her eye and saying hello, and they most sincerely hated each other without having ever exchanged even two minutes of conversation.

Eventually—in fact, within the week—a kind and intelligent boy who lived very near her beautiful house asked the girl to a movie and she gave up her fancy for the bag boy at the supermarket. And the bag boy himself grew so bored with his job that he made a desperate search for something better and ended up in a bookstore where scores of fascinating girls lingered like honeybees about a hive. Some months later the bag boy and the girl with the orange bow again crossed paths, standing in line with their dates at a movie theater, and, glancing toward the other, each smiled slightly, then looked away, as strangers on public buses often do, when one is moving off the bus and the other is moving on.

Vocabulary Builder
perverse (pər vʉrs´)
adj. deviating from what is considered right or reasonable

Literary Analysis
Point of View Which details in this paragraph might be omitted if the story were told from the third-person limited point of view? Explain.

Thinking About the Selection

1. **Respond:** Were you disappointed that the girl and boy did not get together? Explain.

2. **(a) Recall:** What do the boy and girl think about while they are apart? **(b) Speculate:** How do you think the two characters feel when they see each other at the movie theater?

3. **Draw Conclusions:** Does the experience described in the story seem like a missed opportunity or a necessary outcome? Explain.

4. **(a) Summarize:** Why do the boy and girl never act on their feelings? **(b) Make a Judgment:** Do you agree with the narrator that "humans are very complicated"? Explain.

Checkouts ■ 77

⑩ Literary Analysis

• Read aloud the bracketed passage. Point out that it describes the private emotions of both the girl and the boy.

• **Ask** the Literary Analysis question: Which details in this paragraph might be omitted if the story were told from the third-person limited point of view? Explain.
   Answer: If the story were told from the third-person limited point of view, one of the character's feelings would be omitted.

Concept Connector

Have students return to the Motivation activity on p. 74. Remind them that "Checkouts" describes one course that love at first sight can take. Ask students to discuss how the end of the story compares to their knowledge of love-at-first-sight stories in books or movies.

ASSESS

Answers

1. Many students will express disappointment that the two characters did not get together. Readers might say that they had been led to expect this kind of ending from a traditional story.

2. (a) They think about each other. (b) Each may feel that the other is much like a stranger one smiles at in passing.

3. Some students will say that it seems like a necessary outcome because if they had really wanted to meet, they would have made more of an effort. Others will say that it was a missed opportunity because it is hard to find someone similar in disposition.

4. (a) They are acting like children, pretending not to want what they most desire. (b) **Possible response:** Most students may recognize the behavior of the boy and girl and agree that humans are "complicated."

Differentiated Instruction   Solutions for All Learners

Vocabulary for Special Needs Students	**Strategy for Gifted/Talented Students**
Ask students to use the given definition and the context of the vocabulary word on this page to answer the following extension questions: What was *perverse* about the girl's decision to not go to the bag boy's checkout? What other types of decisions might be considered *perverse?* Why?	Suggest that students put themselves in the character of the red-haired girl or the bag boy when the boy drops the mayonnaise jar. Have each student compose a diary entry describing what happened as he or she lived through the experience. Students may describe their actions, thoughts, and feelings. They should conclude their diary entry by answering this question: What did this experience teach me about myself?

Women in Africa In rural African villages, the primary, traditional role for women has been to give birth and raise children. In recent years, however, many people have challenged this notion of women's role in society, advocating equality between men and women. Writers like Ama Ata Aidoo have been instrumental in promoting feminism within Africa and beyond.

⑫ Motivation

Tell students that it is common for parents and grandparents to have high expectations for young family members. Explain that in "The Girl Who Can," the narrator's grandmother hopes that the girl will one day be able to have children. Ask students to share some of the hopes and expectations that family members have for their children. Compare and contrast students' responses with those of the grandmother in the story.

Concept Connector ➡

Students will follow up on this activity after completing "The Girl Who Can."

⑬ About the Selection

In "The Girl Who Can," seven-year-old Adjoa challenges her grandmother's views about a woman's place in society. Convinced that Adjoa's legs are too thin for childbearing, the grandmother often worries about Adjoa's future. As Adjoa finds success as a runner, she gradually convinces her grandmother that there are other things she can accomplish in life besides motherhood. In this story, readers witness how traditional views and progressive notions about women can intersect across generations.

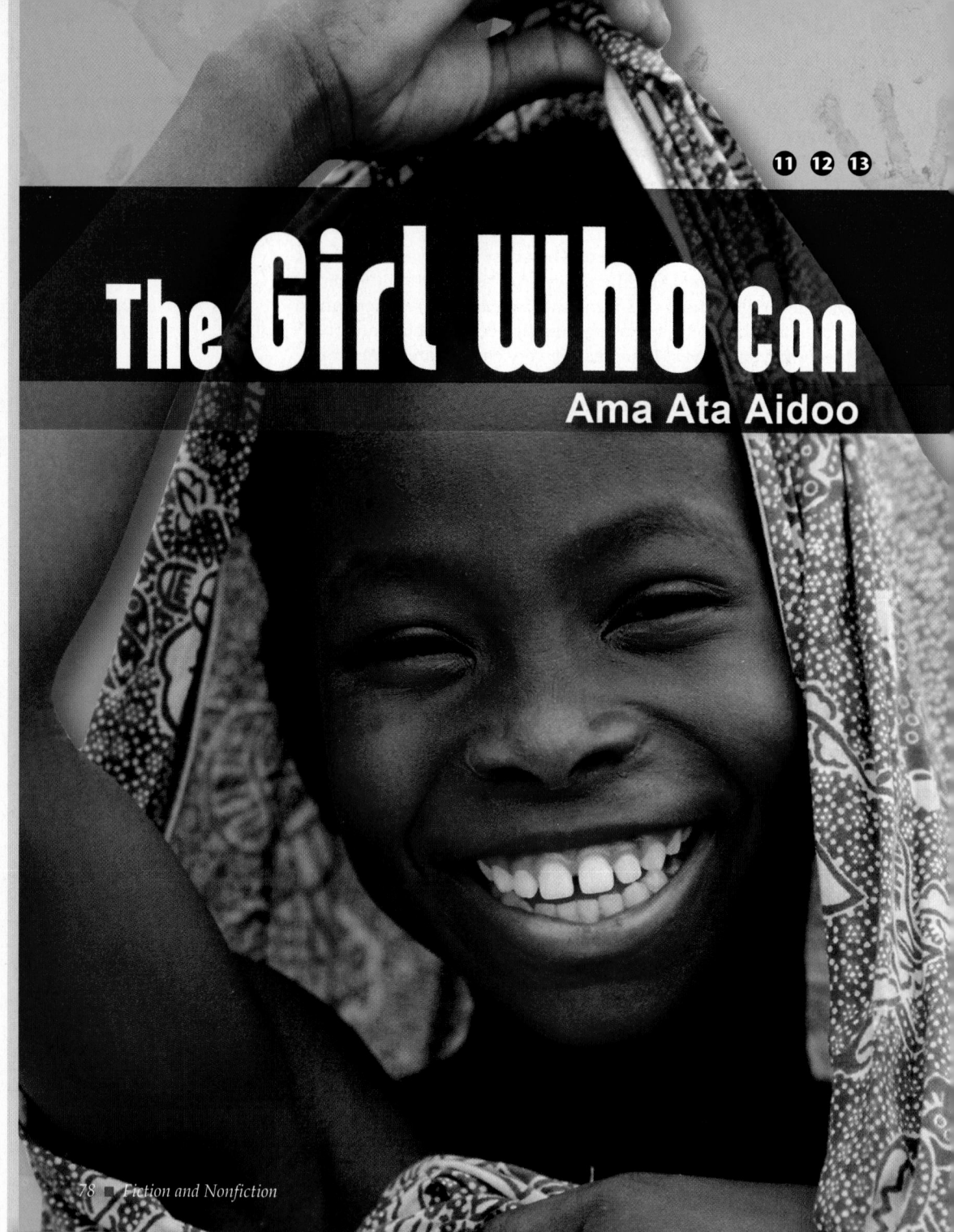

⑪ ⑫ ⑬

The Girl Who Can
Ama Ata Aidoo

78 ▪ Fiction and Nonfiction

Vocabulary Development

Word Forms
Expand students' vocabulary by helping them learn related forms of the Vocabulary Builder words. Two of the Vocabulary Builder words for "The Girl Who Can" have related forms. Give students a blank **Word Forms Chart** (*General Resources,* p. 16), with *comprehension* and *humble* in the correct columns. Work with the class, or have students work with a partner, to determine the related forms. The final chart should look like the one shown.

Noun	Verb	Adjective	Adverb
comprehension	comprehend	comprehensive	comprehensively
humbleness	humble	**humble**	humbly

They say that I was born in Hasodzi; and it is a very big village in the central region of our country, Ghana. They also say that when all of Africa is not choking under a drought, Hasodzi lies in a very <u>fertile</u> lowland in a district known for its good soil. Maybe that is why any time I don't finish eating my food, Nana says, "You Adjoa, you don't know what life is about . . . you don't know what problems there are in this life . . ."

As far as I could see, there was only one problem. And it had nothing to do with what I knew Nana considered as "problems," or what Maami thinks of as "the problem." Maami is my mother. Nana is my mother's mother. And they say I am seven years old. And my problem is that at this seven years of age, there are things I can think in my head, but which, maybe, I do not have the proper language to speak them out with. And that, I think, is a very serious problem because it is always difficult to decide whether to keep quiet and not say any of the things that come into my head, or say them and get laughed at. Not that it is easy to get any grown-up to listen to you, even when you decide to take the risk and say something serious to them.

Take Nana. First, I have to struggle to catch her attention. Then I tell her something I had taken a long time to figure out. And then you know what always happens? She would at once stop whatever she is doing and, mouth open, stare at me for a very long time. Then, bending and turning her head slightly, so that one ear comes down towards me, she'll say in that voice: "Adjoa, you say what?" After I have repeated whatever I had said, she would either, still in that voice, ask me "never, never, but NEVER to repeat THAT," or she would immediately burst out laughing. She would laugh and laugh and laugh, until tears run down her cheeks and she would stop whatever she is doing and wipe away the tears with the hanging edges of her cloth. And she would continue laughing until she is completely tired. But then, as soon as another person comes by, just to make sure she doesn't forget whatever it was I had said, she would repeat it to her. And then, of course, there would be two old people laughing and screaming with tears running down their faces. Sometimes this show continues until there are three, four or even more of such laughing and screaming tear-faced grownups. And all that performance for whatever I'd said? I find something quite confusing in all this. That is, no one ever explains to me why sometimes I shouldn't repeat some things I say; while at other times, some other things I say would not only be all right, but would be considered so funny they would be repeated so many times for so many people's enjoyment. You see how neither way of hearing me out can encourage me to express my thoughts too often?

14 ◀ **Critical Viewing**
Describe the feelings the girl in the photograph expresses. **[Interpret]**

Vocabulary Builder
fertile (fur′t′l) *adj.* able to make plants grow

Literary Analysis
Point of View Which pronouns in this paragraph show that this story is being told from the first-person point of view?

15

16 ☑ **Reading Check**
What does the narrator say is her problem?

The Girl Who Can ■ 79

14 Critical Viewing
Answer: The girl seems happy and energetic.

15 Literary Analysis
Point of View

• Remind students that identifying pronouns can help them determine the point of view of a story.

• **Ask** students to respond to the Literary Analysis question: Which pronouns in this paragraph show that this story is being told from the first-person point of view? **Answer:** The pronouns *I* and *me* indicate a first-person narrator.

• **Ask** students how the first-person point of view in this story differs from the third-person omniscient point of view in the previous story. **Answer:** In first-person point of view, the narrator participates in the story and tells the story from his or her viewpoint. In third-person omniscient point of view, the narrator does not participate in the story and is able to reveal the thoughts and feelings of multiple characters.

16 Reading Check
Answer: The narrator does not have the proper language to express her thoughts, and this makes it difficult for her to determine when to speak her mind and when to keep her thoughts to herself.

Differentiated
Instruction   Solutions for All Learners

Reading Support
Have students complete the **Preview** and **Build Skills** pages for "The Girl Who Can" in the appropriate versions of the **Reader's Notebooks.**

Reader's Notebook [L2]

Reader's Notebook: Adapted Version [L1]

Reader's Notebook: English Learner's Version [EL]

Accessibility at a Glance
Use this information to guide your teaching.

Context	Explores the traditional vs. modern view of the role of women
Language	Informal, conversational style; told by a young girl
Concept Level	More Accessible
Literary Merit	Cross-cultural experience
Lexile	870L

- Remind students that the story is told from Adjoa's point of view. Point out that she is seven years old, so her thoughts and words represent a child's perspective.

- **Ask** students what details about the narrator's reaction to older people reveal about her?
Answer: Adjoa's mystification about the behavior of adults suggests that she is very young and naïve.

- Point out that the reader can only gain insight into the mother's and grandmother's thoughts and feelings through what Adjoa reports.
Ask students what they think the advantages and disadvantages of first-person point of view are.
Possible response: The advantage is that the reader becomes very familiar with Adjoa and the way she thinks and feels. It makes the story more personal and real. The disadvantage is that the reader's knowledge of other characters is limited; the reader only learns about them through Adjoa's perspective, which is biased.

18 Critical Viewing

Possible response: Like Adjoa and her elders, the women and children in the photograph seem affectionate and close. The women probably want the best for their children, as Adjoa's elders want for her.

17 Like all this business to do with my legs. I have always wanted to tell them not to worry. I mean Nana and my mother. It did not have to be an issue for my two favorite people to fight over. I didn't want to be told not to repeat it or for it to be considered so funny that anyone would laugh at me until they cried. After all, they were my legs . . . When I think back on it now, those two, Nana and my mother must have been discussing my legs from the day I was born. What I am sure of is that when I came out of the land of sweet, soft silence into the world of noise and <u>comprehension</u>, the first topic I met was my legs.

That discussion was repeated very regularly.

Nana: "Ah, ah, you know, Kaya, I thank my God that your very first child is female. But Kaya, I am not sure about her legs. Hm . . . hm . . . hm . . ."

And Nana would shake her head.

Maami: "Mother, why are you always complaining about Adjoa's legs? If you ask me . . ."

Nana: "They are too thin. And I am not asking you!"

Nana has many voices. There is a special one she uses to shut everyone up.

"Some people have no legs at all," my mother would try again with all her small courage.

"But Adjoa has legs," Nana would insist; "except that they are too thin. And also too long for a woman. Kaya, listen. Once in a while, but only once in a very long while, somebody decides — nature, a child's spirit mother, an accident happens, and somebody gets born without arms, or legs, or both sets of limbs. And then let me touch wood; it is a sad business. And you know, such things are not for talking about every day. But if any female child decides to come into this world with legs, then they might as well be legs."

19 "What kind of legs?" And always at that point, I knew from her voice that my mother was weeping inside. Nana never heard such inside weeping.

Vocabulary Builder
comprehension (käm′ prē hen′ shen) *n.* understanding

18 ▼ Critical Viewing
Might these mothers and children have relationships similar to those between Adjoa and her elders? Explain. **[Connect]**

Vocabulary Development

Vocabulary Builder Reinforcement
To reinforce and assess students' comprehension of Vocabulary Builder words, give them sentences using the words in which the word may or may not be used correctly. Students must tell whether the use is correct and explain their answer. Use these sentences:

1. The *fertile* land produced excellent crops this year.
Answer: Yes, *fertile* is used correctly. It means "able to make plants grow."

2. Ryan felt that he had full *comprehension* of the case study, but he still didn't understand it.
Answer: No, *comprehension* is not used correctly. It means "understanding."

3. Despite his riches and fame, the prince was quite *humble*.
Answer: Yes, *humble* is used correctly. It means "modest."

Not that it would have stopped Nana even if she had heard it. Which always surprised me. Because, about almost everything else apart from my legs, Nana is such a good grown-up. In any case, what do I know about good grown-ups and bad grown-ups? How could Nana be a good grown-up when she carried on so about my legs? All I want to say is that I really liked Nana except for that.

Nana: "As I keep saying, if any woman decides to come into this world with her two legs, then she should select legs that have meat on them: with good calves. Because you are sure such legs would support solid hips. And a woman must have solid hips to be able to have children."

"Oh, Mother." That's how my mother would answer. Very, very quietly. And the discussion would end or they would move on to something else.

Sometimes, Nana would pull in something about my father:

How, "Looking at such a man, we have to be <u>humble</u> and admit that after all, God's children are many . . ."

How, "After one's only daughter had insisted on marrying a man like that, you still have to thank your God that the biggest problem you got later was having a granddaughter with spindly legs that are too long for a woman, and too thin to be of any use."

The way she always added that bit about my father under her breath, she probably thought I didn't hear it. But I always heard it. Plus, that is what always shut my mother up for good, so that even if I had not actually heard the words, once my mother looked like even her little courage was finished, I could always guess what Nana had added to the argument.

"Legs that have meat on them with good calves to support solid hips . . . to be able to have children."

So I wished that one day I would see, for myself, the legs of any woman who had had children. But in our village, that is not easy. The older women wear long wrap-arounds[1] all the time. Perhaps if they let me go bathe in the river in the evening, I could have checked. But I never had the chance. It took a lot of begging just to get my mother and Nana to let me go splash around in the shallow end of the river with my friends, who were other little girls like me. For proper baths, we used the small bathhouse behind our hut. Therefore, the only naked female legs I have ever really seen are those of other little girls like me, or older girls in the school. And those of my mother and Nana: two pairs of legs which must surely belong to the approved kind; because Nana gave birth to my mother and my mother gave birth to me. In my eyes, all my friends have got

---

1. **wrap-arounds** (rap´ ə roundz´) *n.* a type of garment that is open down the side and is wrapped around the body.

Literary Analysis
Point of View
What do we learn about the narrator's inner feelings from the words in this paragraph?

Vocabulary Builder
humble (hum´ bəl) *adj.* modest; having humility

Reading Check
According to the narrator, which topic makes the mother weep inside?

The Girl Who Can ■ 81

---

⑲ **Literary Analysis**
Point of View

- **Ask** students to respond to the Literary Analysis question: What do we learn about the narrator's inner feelings from the words in this paragraph?
  Answer: Readers learn that the narrator can tell when her mother is sad, an insight that her grandmother apparently does not possess. Readers also learn that Adjoa loves her grandmother but does not like how she harshly treats Adjoa's mother.

- **Ask** students how the revelation of these feelings influences their view of Adjoa's character.
  Possible response: Students might say that the feelings surprised them because they did not expect a seven-year-old to have such insight into her elders.

⑳ **Reading Check**

Answer: Adjoa's legs is the topic that upset her mother.

Differentiated Instruction
Solutions for All Learners

Strategy for English Learners
To give students a context for the story and to model how to compare points of view, show them **Comparing Points of View Graphic Organizer B** (*Graphic Organizer Transparencies*, p. 18). The completed graphic organizer will give students insight into the process of comparing points of view. They can use it as a model for making their own observations as they read.

Strategy for Advanced Readers
The selection describes three generations of women—Adjoa, her mother, and Nana—and their views regarding the role of women in society. Ask students to write a brief paper that compares and contrasts each character's viewpoint on this issue. Remind students to use evidence from the story to support their ideas.

- Remind students that first-person narrators can tell readers about their own thoughts and feelings, but they can only guess about other characters' interior lives by observing what the characters say and do.
- Read aloud the bracketed passage, and point out that Adjoa makes several observations about her grandmother's and mother's opinions regarding school. **Ask** students how Adjoa knows their opinions on this issue.
Answer: Adjoa has overheard their discussions.
- **Ask** what Adjoa's observations reveal about her mother's and grandmother's expectations for her.
Answer: Nana thinks school is a waste because Adjoa will grow up to be a mother and will have no use for an education. Adjoa's mother hopes that getting an education will allow Adjoa to become more than just a mother.

22 Critical Viewing

Possible responses: Students might say that the girls in the image match their image of Adjoa. Others might have pictured Adjoa in a different-looking school uniform.

legs that look like legs, but whether the legs have got meat on them to support the kind of hips that . . . that I don't know.

21 According to the older boys and girls, the distance between our little village and the small town is about five kilometers. I don't know what five kilometers mean. They always complain about how long it is to walk to school and back. But to me, we live in our village, and walking those kilometers didn't matter. School is nice. School is another thing Nana and my mother discussed often and appeared to have different ideas about. Nana thought it would be a waste of time. I never understood what she meant. My mother seemed to know—and disagreed. She kept telling Nana that she— that is, my mother—felt she was locked into some kind of darkness because she didn't go to school. So that if I, her daughter, could learn to write and read my own name and a little besides—perhaps be able to calculate some things on paper—that would be good. I could always marry later and maybe . . .

Nana would just laugh. "Ah, maybe with legs like hers, she might as well go to school."

Running with our classmates on our small sports field and winning first place each time never seemed to me to be anything about which to tell anyone at home. This time it was different. I don't know how the teachers decided to let me run for the junior section of our school in the district games. But they did.

When I went home to tell my mother and Nana, they had not believed it at first. So Nana had taken it upon herself to go and "ask into it properly." She came home to tell my mother that it was really true. I was one of my school's runners.

"Is that so?" exclaimed my mother. I know her. Her mouth moved as though she was going to tell Nana, that, after all, there was a secret about me she couldn't be expected to share with anyone. But then Nana herself looked so pleased, out of surprise, my mother shut her mouth up. In any case, since the first time they heard the news, I have often caught Nana staring at my legs with a strange look on her face, but still

82 ■ *Fiction and Nonfiction*

22 ▼ Critical Viewing
How does your view of the narrator compare to the girls in this image? **[Compare]**

Vocabulary Development

Expressive Vocabulary
As students are discussing Adjoa and her family, encourage them to use the expressive vocabulary presented earlier. You might encourage them with sentence starters like these:
1. Adjoa's education will *impact*...
2. Adjoa's grandmother is proud to *display*...
3. At first, Adjoa does not *reveal*...
4. Running allows Adjoa to *emerge*...
5. Her mother's views *signify*...

Country Profile: Ghana

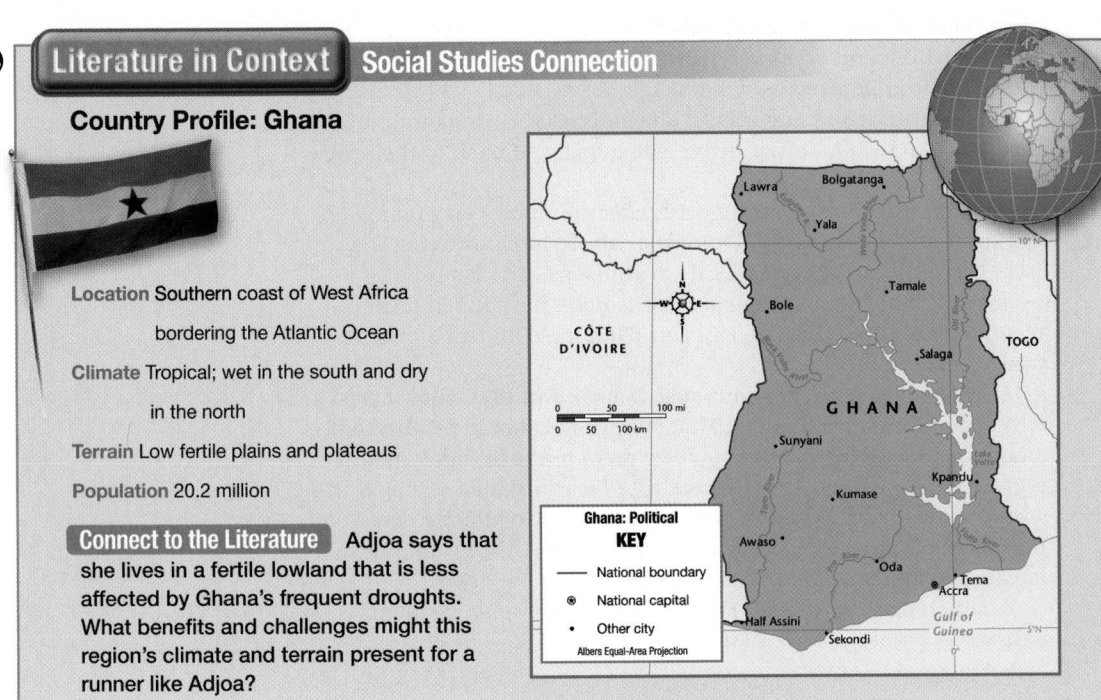

Location Southern coast of West Africa bordering the Atlantic Ocean

Climate Tropical; wet in the south and dry in the north

Terrain Low fertile plains and plateaus

Population 20.2 million

Connect to the Literature Adjoa says that she lives in a fertile lowland that is less affected by Ghana's frequent droughts. What benefits and challenges might this region's climate and terrain present for a runner like Adjoa?

---

pretending like she was not looking. All this week, she has been washing my school uniform herself. That is a big surprise. And she didn't stop at that, she even went to Mr. Mensah's house and borrowed his charcoal pressing iron. Each time she came back home with it and ironed and ironed and ironed the uniform, until, if I had been the uniform, I would have said aloud that I had had enough.

Wearing my school uniform this week has been very nice. At the parade, on the first afternoon, its sheen caught the rays of the sun and shone brighter than anybody else's uniform. I'm sure Nana saw that too, and must have liked it. Yes, she has been coming into town with us every afternoon of this district sports week. Each afternoon, she has pulled one set of fresh old cloth from the big brass bowl to wear. And those old clothes are always so stiffly starched, you can hear the cloth creak when she passes by. But she walks way behind us schoolchildren. As though she was on her own way to some place else.

Yes, I have won every race I ran for my school, and I have won the cup for the best all-round junior athlete. Yes, Nana said that she didn't care if such things are not done. She would do it. You know

Reading Check

After learning about her running talent, what does Nana do with the narrator's uniform?

The Girl Who Can ■ 83

---

❷❸ **Literature in Context**

Social Studies Connection Ghana has been an independent country since 1957, when it broke away from its colonizer, Great Britain. Since then, Ghana has not been able to harness its earning power as a player in the agriculture industry. While the fertile terrain ensures plentiful natural resources, the country remains relatively impoverished. Better technology might help Ghana to become more financially independent in the future.

Connect to the Literature Point out that Adjoa lives in a somewhat severe climate, but she does not often mention her physical surroundings.

Ask students the Connect to the Literature question: Adjoa says that she lives in a fertile lowland of central Ghana. What benefits and challenges might this region's climate and terrain present for a runner like Adjoa?

Answer: The hot climate might be difficult for a runner, who might become overheated. However, the flat, grassy land would provide an excellent surface for running.

❷❹ **Reading Check**

Answer: Nana repeatedly ironed the uniform.

83

Make Inferences

- Read aloud the bracketed passage. Explain that readers can infer the grandmother's thoughts and feelings through the narrator's description of her grandmother's behavior.

- **Ask** students to infer Nana's new thoughts and feelings about Adjoa's legs and to explain their reasoning.
Answer: Nana seems proud of Adjoa's accomplishment. She carries the trophy with care, and she admits that thin legs can be useful.

Concept Connector

Have students return to the Motivation activity on p. 78. Ask students to discuss how the grandmother's aspirations for Adjoa changed over the course of the story.

ASSESS

Answers

1. **Possible response:** Students may be surprised that Nana worried about Adjoa's childbearing potential.

2. (a) Nana worries that the narrator's legs are too thin. (b) Nana fears that Adjoa will not be able to bear children. (c) In Ghana women are expected to bear and raise children.

3. (a) Nana thinks that school is unnecessary. (b) The narrator's mother believes that school is valuable.

4. (a) Nana seems surprised that Adjoa's legs are good for something. (b) Nana is proud of Adjoa.

5. (a) Adjoa has acted out her belief that her legs are worth more than just supporting hips for childbearing. (b) Students may agree that it was better because Adjoa's actions provided irrefutable evidence of her belief; saying it aloud would have been the mere opinion of a child.

---

what she did? She carried the gleaming cup on her back. Like they do with babies, and other very precious things. And this time, not taking the trouble to walk by herself.

When we arrived in our village, she entered our compound to show the cup to my mother before going to give it back to the head-master.

25 Oh, grown-ups are so strange. Nana is right now carrying me on her knee, and crying softly. Muttering, muttering, muttering that: "saa, thin legs can also be useful . . . thin legs can also be useful . . ." that "even though some legs don't have much meat on them, to carry hips . . . they can run. Thin legs can run . . . then who knows? . . ."

I don't know too much about such things. But that's how I was feeling and thinking all along. That surely, one should be able to do other things with legs as well as have them because they can support hips that make babies. Except that I was afraid of saying that sort of thing aloud. Because someone would have told me never, never, but NEVER to repeat such words. Or else, they would have laughed so much at what I'd said, they would have cried.

It's much better this way. To have acted it out to show them, although I could not have planned it.

As for my mother, she has been speechless as usual.

Thinking About the Selection

1. **Respond:** What was the most surprising part of this story to you? Explain.

2. **(a) Recall:** What criticism does Nana make about the narrator's legs? **(b) Draw Conclusions:** In what ways does this criticism show that Nana fears for Adjoa's future? Explain. **(c) Make Generalizations:** Based on these details, what kinds of lives do you think many women in Ghana are expected to lead?

3. **(a) Recall:** What are Nana's feelings about the narrator going to school? **(b) Compare and Contrast:** How do the mother's feelings about school differ from Nana's?

4. **(a) Infer:** After Adjoa is chosen for the district games, why does Nana keep staring at her legs? **(b) Draw Conclusions:** Why does Nana iron Adjoa's school uniform so carefully?

5. **(a) Analyze:** At the end of the story, Adjoa says it was much better to "have acted it out to show them." What has she "acted out"? **(b) Evaluate:** Was it "better," as Adjoa says? Explain.

Vocabulary Development

Vocabulary Knowledge Rating

When students have completed reading and discussing "Checkouts" and "The Girl Who Can," have them take out their **Vocabulary Knowledge Rating Chart.** Read the words aloud once more and have students rate their knowledge of the words again in the After Reading column. Clarify any words that are still problematic. Have students write their own definition and example or sentence in the appropriate column. Then have students complete the **Vocabulary Builder Practice** activities on p. 85. Encourage students to use the words in further discussion and written work about the selections. Remind them that they will be accountable for these words on the Selection Test.

Apply the Skills

Checkouts • The Girl Who Can

Comparing Points of View

1. Use a chart like the one shown to note the actions, thoughts, and feelings of the listed characters in both stories.

Checkouts	Actions	Thoughts	Feelings
Girl			
Boy			

The Girl Who Can	Actions	Thoughts	Feelings
Nana			
Adjoa			

2. How does **point of view** affect what you know about the boy's feelings and thoughts compared to what you know about Nana's feelings and thoughts?

3. **(a)** Which details from your chart show that the **third-person omniscient point of view** in "Checkouts" gives readers insight into the inner lives of all the characters? Explain. **(b)** Which details show that the **first-person point of view** in "The Girl Who Can" lets the reader understand the narrator best of all? Explain.

Writing to Compare Literary Works

Compare and contrast the girl in "Checkouts" and the narrator in "The Girl Who Can." In an essay, explain how point of view affected your attitude toward the girls. Use these questions to get started:

- Who are the narrators in the two stories?
- How do you know what each girl is thinking?
- How do other characters react to each girl?

Vocabulary Builder

Practice For each item, write a new sentence that uses a word from the vocabulary list on page 72 and expresses a similar idea.

1. He laughed cruelly at himself.
2. She felt she did not deserve an award.
3. I finally grasp what you mean.
4. That soil is rich.
5. She became lost in thought.
6. He changed his untidy clothes.

QuickReview

Point of View: the perspective from which a story is told

First-Person Point of View: narration by a character who participates in the action

Third-Person Point of View: narration by an outside observer; *third-person omniscient point of view* is all-knowing; *third-person limited point of view* sees things through one character's eyes

Go Online
Assessment
For: Self-test
Visit: www.PHSchool.com
Web Code: epa-6107

Assessment Resources

The following resources can be used to assess students' knowledge and skills.

Unit 1 Resources:
Selection Test A, pp. 94–96
Selection Test B, pp. 97–99

Go Online Students may use the **Self-test** to
Assessment prepare for **Selection Test A** or
Selection Test B.

Comparing Points of View

1. **Sample response:** Character from "Checkouts": Boy. **Actions:** Dropping the mayonnaise. **Thoughts:** I look like a fool. **Feelings:** Depression and shame. Another sample can be found on **Comparing Points of View Graphic Organizer Transparency B,** p. 20 in *Graphic Organizer Transparencies.*

2. The third-person omniscient point of view in "Checkouts" lets the reader know exactly what the boy is thinking and feeling. Because Adjoa is the first-person narrator of "The Girl Who Can," readers know only what Adjoa guesses about Nana's thoughts and feelings.

3. (a) The thoughts and feelings of both the girl and the boy are listed. If the third-person limited or first-person points of view had been used, readers would know the thoughts and feelings of only one character. (b) The chart lists the thoughts and feelings of Adjoa, whereas Nana's thoughts and feelings can only be inferred.

Writing to Compare Literary Works

- Have students use the bulleted questions to develop their ideas.

- Encourage students to use the expressive vocabulary words: *impact, display, emerge, reveal,* and *signify.*

Six Traits Focus

✔	Ideas		Word Choice
✔	Organization		Sentence Fluency
	Voice		Conventions

Vocabulary Builder

1. He laughed *perversely* at his own mistake.

2. She *humbly* said she did not deserve any thanks.

3. I finally *comprehend* what you mean.

4. You can grow anything in that *fertile* soil.

5. She became lost in *reverie*.

6. He was irritated by all the complaints about his *dishevelment*.

In this Skills Review, students apply the skills taught in Part 1. The test format gives students practice in taking standardized tests. The result of this review test will help you check students' readiness for the **Benchmark Test** for Unit 1, Part 1.

Applying Reading Skills

Read the passage with the students. Guide them in identifying the clues to determine the logical prediction in item 1: she and her husband were planning to go to California. If necessary, have students review the instruction on p. 22. Then have them complete the remaining items on their own.

Applying Vocabulary Skills

Have students review the instruction on word roots on p. 23. Have students pay close attention to the definitions of the word roots.

Tips for
Test Taking

Because time is often a factor in many standardized tests, point out to students that they should answer the questions they know first and then go back and work on the remaining questions. This way they will receive credit for what they know and then can make educated guesses on the rest of the items.

ASSESS
Answers

1. B	9. A
2. B	10. A
3. C	11. A
4. C	12. A
5. D	13. C
6. B	14. D
7. D	15. A
8. A	

Reading: Make Predictions

Directions: *Questions 1–5 are based on the following selection.*

There are times when one decides to go in a different direction, not because it is better for oneself, but because it is obviously better for one's family. That is how my grandmother ended up "somewhere else."

She and her husband had been planning on going with the California gold rush crowd. They weren't going, like most of the rest, to pan for gold. My grandmother was smart, ambitious, and too practical to believe that riches just fell into your hands. But they figured there were enough fools who were going to follow gold fantasies that there would be plenty of business opportunities. And, though they worked hard, in the little town in which they lived there were all too few business opportunities.

1. What prior knowledge would help you make predictions based on this passage?
   A the history of working women
   B political history of the West
   C history of California
   D economic history of the South

2. According to the passage, the grandmother
   A will become a farmer in California.
   B will start a business in California.
   C will go to college in California.
   D will pan for gold in California.

3. What can you predict about the grandmother's success based on the details given about her character?
   A She is going to be easily fooled and led astray.
   B She will be unsuccessful and return to the South.
   C She will be a practical and successful businesswoman.
   D She will let her husband do all the work.

4. If this is the introduction to a written work, you can predict that the rest of the story will focus on
   A the family and the South.
   B the history of the family.
   C the narrator's grandmother.
   D the grandmother's ancestors.

5. What kind of details in the rest of the story would verify a prediction that Grandmother was successful in her new life?
   A Grandmother refuses to talk about her years in California.
   B Grandmother writes sad letters home to her friends in the South.
   C Grandmother sells her family's belongings to raise funds.
   D Grandmother buys a large house in California.

Assessment Practice

Directions: *Choose the definition that best fits the underlined word as it is used in the sentence.*

6. The <u>specific</u> requirements for this project are posted on the school's Web site.
   A expanded
   B exact
   C design
   D general

7. Isn't it strange that the same two people were <u>involved</u> in both accidents?
   A required
   B elaborated
   C cited
   D included

8. He looks so old and tired; it is difficult to believe that he is my <u>contemporary</u>.
   A about the same age
   B living in the same time
   C part of the modern world
   D antebellum

9. I understand that he is a major <u>contributor</u> to the Red Cross and will be honored for his generosity.
   A one who gives to
   B one who works with
   C one who writes for
   D one who is responsible for

10. We wrote a letter to the members of the Olympic track team asking them to <u>participate</u> in our fund-raiser.
    A take part
    B share
    C acknowledge
    D refer

11. The coach will <u>inspect</u> the field before we play.
    A pass or fail
    B decide on authenticity
    C look carefully at
    D maintain vigilance

12. The demolition of the building was quite a <u>spectacle</u>.
    A unusual sight
    B revolving activity
    C disappointment
    D concern

13. Some leaves have <u>revolute</u> edges.
    A moving in an upward direction
    B changing governments
    C rolled backward or downward
    D starting a change

14. The <u>revolving</u> Ferris wheel made me dizzy.
    A changing, or improving, considerably
    B dividing in several parts
    C starting, or beginning, several times
    D turning, or rolling, over

15. That is a <u>temporal</u> concern.
    A lasting only for a time
    B something that is of government
    C without a known end
    D something that is imposed

Reading and Vocabulary Skills Review ■ *87*

If students answer any of these questions incorrectly, have them review the instruction on the following pages in Part 1 before taking the **Benchmark Test**.

Question	Pages Where Instruction Is Located:
1	24, 46
2	24, 46
3	24, 46
4	24, 46
5	24, 46
6	23
7	23
8	23
9	23
10	23
11	70
12	70
13	70
14	40
15	40

Benchmark

Administer the **Benchmark Test** for Unit 1, Part 1. If the Benchmark Test reveals that some students need further work, use the Interpretation Guide to determine the appropriate reteaching page in the **Reading Kit**. You will also find the same instruction and practice available in the Success Tracker.

Go Online
Vocabulary
For: Interactive Crossword puzzles
Visit: www.PHSchool.com
Web Code: epj-5101
Give students this Web Code to access interactive crossword puzzles using Academic Vocabulary and Vocabulary Skill words from Part 1.

Meeting Your Standards

Students will

1. write an autobiographical narrative.

2. use writing strategies to generate ideas and to plan, organize, evaluate, and revise an autobiographical narrative.

3. apply grammar skills.

Writing Genres

Using the Form Point out to students that autobiographical narration is often incorporated into other types of writing. For example, speeches frequently include autobiographical segments.

Writing Workshop

Work in Progress

If students have done the Work-in-Progress assignments throughout Part 1, suggest that they examine their recorded ideas as they begin prewriting.

OES **Online Essay Scorer**

A writing prompt for this mode of writing can be found on the *PH Online Essay Scorer* at PHSuccessNet.com.

Prewriting

• Tell students that **choosing a topic** may come easier if they obtain another person's perspective by partnering up to discuss their blueprints.

• Tell students that creating a timeline will help them **gather details** and organize thoughts.

Six Traits Focus

✔	Ideas		Word Choice
✔	Organization		Sentence Fluency
	Voice		Conventions

WG **Writing and Grammar, Gold Level**

Students will find additional instruction on prewriting for an autobiographical narrative in Chapter 4, Section 2.

Narration: Autobiographical Narrative

Some of the best stories you may read are not imaginary—they describe real events in the writer's life and share the lessons or wisdom the writer gained from the experiences. Such stories are called **autobiographical narratives.** Follow the steps outlined in this workshop to write your own autobiographical narrative.

Assignment Write an autobiographical narrative about an event that taught you a valuable lesson.

What to Include Your autobiographical narrative should feature:
• A sequence of events involving you, the writer
• A problem, or conflict, and a lesson you learned from it
• Details that locate scenes and incidents in specific places
• Your personal thoughts, feelings, or views about the events
• Error-free grammar, including correct use of possessive nouns

To preview the criteria on which your autobiographical narrative may be judged, see the rubric on page 92.

Prewriting

Choosing Your Topic

Write your narrative about a topic that matters to you.

Blueprinting First, sketch a blueprint, or map, of a place you know well. Label each room or area. Then, jot down words or phrases you associate with each area. Choose one of these ideas as your topic.

Gathering Details

Structure the sequence. Create a detailed record of events by making a timeline. Write down the first incident related to your subject and record subsequent incidents in the order in which they occurred.

 Timeline

Event 2: Dad took off training wheels.

Event 4: Improved riding. Tried other activities.

Event 1: Dreamed of riding bike with no training wheels.

Event 3: Rode two-wheeled bike and fell.

88 ■ Fiction and Nonfiction

Using the Form

You may use elements of this form in these types of writing:
• letters and journals
• reflective essays
• persuasive essays

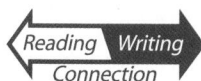 *Reading Writing Connection*

To get a feel for autobiographical narratives, read "My English" by Julia Alvarez on page 107.

Work in Progress
Review the work you did on pages 13, 19, 41 and 71.

Teaching Resources

The following resources can be used to enrich or extend the instruction for the Writing Workshop.

Unit 1 Resources
Writing Workshop: Narration: Autobiographical Narrative, p. 100
Writing Workshop: Integrating Grammar Skills: Revising to Correct Use of Possessive Nouns, p. 101

General Resources
Rubrics for Narration: Autobiographical Narrative, pp. 43–44

Graphic Organizer Transparencies
Graphic Organizer: Timeline, p. 242

Drafting

Shaping Your Writing

Identify your main point. As you draft, think about why this story matters to you. To do so, clearly state the main problem you experienced and what you learned from it. Organize your details to highlight the importance of that main point.

Pace the action. Details and description add substance to your essay, but too much can slow the pace, or flow, of the story. To maintain interest, use details to accomplish these goals:
- Emphasize the central conflict that sets the story in motion.
- Reveal some details up front, but delay others.

Providing Elaboration

Choose vivid details. As you write, do not just list events. Instead, use details to show readers what happened and how it felt. Add life to your story with precise descriptions of places, people, and events. The chart shown here provides some tips to help you elaborate further on an idea.

Story Element	Elaboration Tip
Experience	Explain its main effect on you.
Time and Place	Describe impressions using sensory details.
Suspense	Add details that raise the tension and heighten the story's problem.
Main Events of Story	Include thoughts or feelings that occurred to you at the time of the events.
Story Outcome	Consider other possible outcomes of events.

Revising

Revising Your Sentences

Vary your sentence beginnings. Even though your narrative is about an event that happened to you, avoid beginning every sentence with *I.* Look closely at the sentences in your draft, and vary sentence beginnings to make your story more interesting.

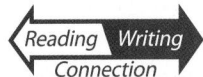

Reading Writing Connection

To read the complete student model, see page 91.

Student Model: Revising to Vary Sentence Beginnings

My sister and I were
~~I was~~ packing for an upcoming trip to youth camp one
late Thursday night in July. ~~I was with my sister.~~ I had
~~never attended~~ the camp, but it would be my older sister
Phoebe's third experience.

This was my first time attending

> A variety of sentence beginnings makes the essay more interesting.

Drafting

- Have students review the information in their timelines and delete any details that do not reinforce their main points.
- For each event listed on their timelines, encourage students to write a sentence or two about how they personally felt about it.

Six Traits Focus

✔	Ideas	✔	Word Choice
✔	Organization		Sentence Fluency
	Voice		Conventions

WG Writing and Grammar, Gold Level

Students will find additional instruction on drafting an autobiographical narrative in Chapter 4, Section 3.

Revising

- Have students highlight the first two or three words in every sentence in their drafts to better evaluate their sentence beginnings.
- Invite volunteers to come to the board and show how they rewrote their repetitive *I* sentences.

Six Traits Focus

	Ideas	✔	Word Choice
✔	Organization	✔	Sentence Fluency
	Voice		Conventions

WG Writing and Grammar, Gold Level

Students will find additional instruction on revising an autobiographical narrative in Chapter 4, Section 4.

Writing and Grammar Interactive Textbook CD-ROM

Students can use the following tools as they complete their autobiographical narratives:
- Timeline
- Self-Interview
- Language Variety

Tips for Using Rubrics

- Before students begin work on this assignment, have them preview the Rubric for Self-Assessment on p. 92 to know what is expected.
- Review the Assessment criteria in class. Before students use the Rubrics for Self-Assessment, work with them to rate the student model by applying one or two criteria to it.

- If you wish to assess students' autobiographical narratives with a 4-point, 5-point, or 6-point scoring rubric, see *General Resources,* pp. 43–44.

Integrating Grammar Skills

- Tell students to be careful not to confuse the plural, the singular possessive, and the plural possessive forms of a noun. Give them the following examples:

  Two girls waited to play the game. (plural)

  The older girl's father gave her a quarter. (singular possessive)

  Both girls' pockets were full of the tickets that they had won. (plural possessive)

- Write the following paragraph on the board. Call on students to correct the possessive forms of words.

  Sasha Walker dog barked at a cat that bolted across the yard. The dogs continuous barking alerted all of the neighbors dogs, and they started barking too. All of the dogs noise woke the neighbors. Peoples heads poked out of windows. My neighbors wife, Sara Jones, knocked on our door. Her familys dog had run away. Now the Joneses children were worried about their dog.

  Answer: *Sasha Walker's dog barked at a cat that bolted across the yard. The dog's continuous barking alerted all of the neighbors' dogs, and they started barking too. All of the dogs' noise woke the neighbors. People's heads poked out of windows. My neighbor's wife, Sara Jones, knocked on our door. Her family's dog had run away. Now the Joneses' children were worried about their dog.*

- Remind students that, as they go through their drafts, they should look for nouns that need to be put into the possessive form, as well as nouns that are already in the possessive form.

Writing and Grammar, Gold Level

Students will find additional instruction on possessive nouns in Chapter 29, Section 6.

Integrating Grammar Skills

Revising to Correct Use of Possessive Nouns

Possessive nouns show to whom places or things belong. A possessive noun is most often formed by adding an apostrophe or an apostrophe and an *s* to a noun.

Noun	Possessive Noun
the homework of the *student*	the *student's* homework

Because they modify other nouns, possessive nouns function in sentences as adjectives.

Forming Possessive Nouns Correctly

Singular Nouns

- Add an apostrophe and an *s* to show the possessive case of most singular nouns.

  the radiator of the car ⟶ the car's radiator

- When a singular noun ends in *s,* you may still be able to add an apostrophe and *s.* However, if the apostrophe and *s* make the word difficult to pronounce, the apostrophe may be used alone.

  the sleeve of the dress ⟶ the dress's sleeve

  the poetry of Burns ⟶ Burns' poetry

Plural Nouns

- Add an apostrophe to show the possessive case of plural nouns ending in *s* or *es:* the *representatives'* decision.
- Add an apostrophe and *s* to show the possessive case of plural nouns that do not end in *s* or *es:* the *men's* books.

Compound Nouns

- Add an apostrophe and *s* to the last word of a compound noun: the Prime Minister's visit.
- Add only an apostrophe if the last word of a compound noun ends in *s:* the Organization of Countess' work.

Apply It to Your Editing

Review the draft of your autobiographical narrative, highlighting all the possessive nouns. Check that you have used a singular possessive when you meant singular, and a plural possessive when you meant plural. Correct any errors you find.

Prentice Hall Writing and Grammar Connection: Chapter 29, Section 6

Differentiated Instruction   Solutions for All Learners

Support for English Learners

Point out to students that possession can also be shown using the preposition *of,* as in this example:

The trees of the forest were tall and thick.

Trees is a noun and *forest* is the object of the preposition, but together this construction shows possession. An apostrophe is not used.

Emphasize that this construction is primarily used with things, but almost never with people. Therefore, students might use this sentence: *Brian's house is white.* Students would probably *not* use this sentence: *The house of Brian is white.*

Have students go through their drafts to make sure that they have not used any "of constructions," with people as objects of their prepositions.

Student Model: Jonathan Chan
Royersford, PA

True Friend

Late one Thursday night in July, my sister and I were packing for our upcoming trip to youth camp. This was my first time attending the camp, but it would be my older sister Phoebe's third experience. Everything was running smoothly until my mother called from downstairs, "Don't forget to grab a sleeping bag from my closet!" Our mother never dreamed such a simple statement would start a desperate dash by both of us to seize the most coveted sleeping bag in our household.

The night-sky blue, extra long, brand new, one hundred percent fleece sleeping bag with a built-in pillow was one-of-a-kind. By comparison, the old sleeping bag, with a broken zipper and a small hole forming at the bottom, looked even worse. Phoebe and I reached for the beautiful new bag at the exact same moment. Insulting remarks sailed from our lips as we each grabbed it. Our stomps and yells attracted our parents to the fight scene. I began to argue that I had reached the bag first, when my sister simply let go, returned to her room, and slammed the door. She was so thoroughly angry, we did not speak again that night.

As the weekend progressed, our relationship did not improve. Even worse, she had shared the story with her friends. Phoebe's words were so moving, they convinced her friends to embark on a personal voyage to "get me." As a result, I spent the getaway with a target on my back.

As the skinny new kid at the camp, terror struck my heart when I heard a rumor about the plot against me. By Sunday morning, the plan, "Operation Little Brother," was all set. My sister's friends were on a mission.

I was shooting hoops in the gym that morning when my sister's friends appeared. I looked frantically for an escape but was quickly surrounded. The assailants closed to within inches of me when a familiar voice echoed through the emptiness of the open gymnasium. My sister walked calmly between her friends and me and said, "Do not bother him or you will feel the wrath of Phoebe." I was in awe. With this statement, "Operation Little Brother" came to an abrupt end. The sister I was feuding with had just saved me. Her friends never bothered me again.

On the trip home I asked her to explain her unlikely action. She simply replied, "I still don't like you, but I would dislike myself even more if I ever abandoned a friend in trouble." Since then, I have often modeled my actions to emulate my sister's behavior that day. I have learned that even when I am angry, I must stand up for my friends. My sister has taught me many things, but the most important lesson is how to be a true friend.

The author's use of dialogue helps to make this opening scene more real and vivid.

The detailed description of the sleeping bag helps to establish the conflict.

Here, the conflict intensifies.

The author uses specific details to paint a picture of the problem he faces.

The use of dialogue and description help to convey the drama of the moment and make it seem real.

The author concludes by drawing an important lesson from his experience.

Student Model

- Explain that the student model is a sample and that narratives may be longer.
- Write the following sentences on the board:

  Fiona waited for her brother at the top of the basement stairs. She peered down into the musty darkness, took a few steps back, and then yelled for her brother to hurry.

  Ask students to use dialogue to make this passage more real and vivid. Have volunteers write responses on the board.
  Possible response:
  Fiona waited for her brother at the top of the basement stairs. She peered down into the musty darkness, took a few steps back, and then yelled, "Jeremiah, this is ridiculous! Hurry up! "

- **Ask** students how the description of the sleeping bag helps establish the conflict.
  Answer: The details reveal the sleeping bag's appeal, showing readers why the siblings were fighting over it.

- **Ask** students what details the writer gives to show that the conflict had intensified.
  Answer: Their fight was lasting into the weekend, and she brought others into the fight.

- Remind students that an autobiographical narrative provides a personal insight gained from the experience described. **Ask** students what lesson Jonathan learned.
  Answer: He learned that, even when angry, he shouldn't abandon his friends.

Writing Genres

Autobiographical Writing on Applications Emphasize that autobiographical writing is not limited to school assignments. Explain to students that they will be asked to write about their experiences in other situations. For example, college and job applications frequently request short autobiographical essays to evaluate possible students or employees.

Editing and Proofreading

- Encourage students to use high-lighters to identify dates and facts in their narratives before checking the accuracy of the information.
- Have students circle all of their possessive nouns and exchange papers with partners. Have students go through the exchanged papers and check for correct use of possessive nouns.

Six Traits Focus

Ideas		Word Choice	
Organization		Sentence Fluency	
Voice		Conventions	✓

ASSESS

Publishing and Presenting

- As students practice their oral narratives, tell them to think about how they can use tone, pacing, gestures, and facial expressions to emphasize their marked passages.
- Encourage students to supplement their bulletin board displays with photographs or objects that relate to their narratives.

Reflecting on Your Writing

- Have students consider the significance of the events they described in their autobiographical narratives. Ask students the following questions: *Has writing an autobiographical narrative changed your opinion of the event? What did you learn about the significance of the event?*
- Have students reflect on the personal nature of an autobiographical narrative. Ask students whether they enjoyed writing a narrative focused on themselves.

Writing and Grammar, Gold Level

Students will find additional instruction on editing and proofreading, publishing and presenting, and reflecting on an autobiographical narrative in Chapter 4, Sections 5 and 6.

Writing Workshop

Editing and Proofreading

Check your draft for errors in grammar, spelling, and punctuation.
Focus on Dates and Facts: Review your manuscript and make sure you have provided accurate factual information. Capitalize the proper names of people or places and use correct punctuation when including dates.

Publishing and Presenting

Consider one of the following ways to share your writing:
Present an oral narrative. Mark up a copy of your autobiographical narrative, underlining any thoughts or conversations that you believe your audience would enjoy. As you present to your classmates, emphasize those passages. When you are done, gracefully accept your classmates' applause and praise.
Post your essay. Create a bulletin board display of the narratives written by you and your classmates. Have each writer supply a short comment about the event or idea that inspired his or her writing.

Reflecting on Your Writing

Writer's Journal Jot down your thoughts on writing an autobiographical narrative. Begin by answering these questions:
- How does the use of details help to make a narrative clearer and more vivid?
- What did you learn about yourself as you wrote?

Rubric for Self-Assessment

To assess your autobiographical narrative, use the following rubric.

Criteria	Rating Scale				
	Not very				*Very*
Focus: How central are you to the action of the story?	1	2	3	4	5
Organization: How clearly organized is the sequence of events?	1	2	3	4	5
Support/Elaboration: How powerfully are sensory details used to locate scenes in specific places?	1	2	3	4	5
Style: How clearly do you convey your insights, thoughts, and feelings?	1	2	3	4	5
Conventions: How correct is your grammar, especially your use of possessive nouns?	1	2	3	4	5

Prentice Hall Writing
and Grammar
Connection:
Chapter 29, Section 6

Tips for Test Taking

When students are taking a test that requires them to respond to a narrative writing prompt, they should devote the majority of their time to the drafting stage of the writing process. Tell students that the key to effective writing (and to making the most of the allotted time) is to organize their thoughts in the drafting stage. Students should pay careful attention to the main points of their essays and provide adequate support for these points. They should also remember that their time, and probably their space, is limited. Therefore, it is vital for them to include important ideas and eliminate unnecessary details. If students follow these suggestions during drafting, revision will be a smoother, less time-consuming process.

Unit 1 Part 2
Author's Purpose

Author's Purpose ■ *93*

Differentiated Instruction   Solutions for All Learners

Resources for Monitoring Progress

Unit 1 Resources
   Unit 1, Part 2 Diagnostic Test,
   pp. 109–111
   Unit 1, Part 2 Benchmark Test,
   pp. 198–203

Reading Kit

Success Tracker

Skills Overview

Reading Skill: Author's Purpose
- Previewing to identify author's purpose
- Reflecting to determine author's purpose

Vocabulary Development
- Word Origins

Literary Analysis
- Author's Voice and Autobiographical Writing: word choice, attitude, sentence structure
- Character: round/flat character, dynamic/static character

Writing
- Problem and Solution Essay
- Work in Progress, pp. 117, 145

Monitoring Progress

Diagnose: Before you begin Part 2, administer the **Diagnostic Test** for Unit 1, Part 2. This test will identify students' level of readiness for the reading and vocabulary skills in Part 2. Use the **Interpretation Guide** for the Diagnostic Test to determine which students need help with prerequisite skills before beginning Part 2.

Preteach and Prepare: Use the information indicated in the **Interpretation Guide** to help students build prerequisite skills. In addition, prepare students by using the **Vocabulary Warm-up** activities and the **Reading Warm-up** activities as necessary for each selection set.

Teach: Use the instructional plan and resources provided to teach the skills and selections.

Assess: After students have completed Part 2, administer the **Benchmark Test** for Unit 1, Part 2. The test results will indicate which skills students have mastered and those on which they need more work.

Reteach: Use the Interpretation Guide to determine the appropriate reteaching pages from the **Reading Kit.**

Intervention: The prerequisite and reteaching pages are also available in the **Success Tracker.**

Introduce the Reading Skill

- Introduce the reading skill: identifying author's purpose. Draw students' attention to the four general purposes for writing. Point out that sometimes these purposes are used in combination. For example, the use of information can increase the impact of writing designed to persuade. Persuasive or informative writing can also be entertaining.

- Emphasize that the author's purpose for writing influences the details the author chooses to include as well as the tone and the voice of the work.

Model the Reading Strategy

- Model how previewing a work helps students to determine the author's purpose. Ask yourself the following questions aloud about the textbook feature on this page, and answer them for the class:

  What is the title of the piece?
  Answer: "Reading and Vocabulary Skills Preview"

  What does the title tell me about the author's general purpose?
  Answer: The author plans to inform the reader of the reading and vocabulary skills that will be covered in this section.

  How has the author organized this feature?
  Answer: The author has organized it with headings and examples to make it easier for the reader to grasp the information.

- Reinforce the concept that previewing the title and the organizational structure of a written work can give the reader an idea of the author's purpose. By previewing, students can identify the author's general purpose, but they must read carefully to reflect on the author's specific purpose.

Reading: Author's Purpose

> An **author's purpose** is his or her reason for writing. There are four general purposes for writing—to entertain, to inform, to describe, and to persuade.

Skills and Strategies You Will Learn in Part 2

In Part 2, you will learn
- to **preview** a work to **determine the author's general purpose** (p. 96)
- to **reflect** on a work to **determine the author's specific purpose** (p. 122)
- to **recognize organizational features of a text** and how organization is utilized to implement the **author's purpose** (p. 118)

Using the Skills and Strategies in Part 2

In Part 2, you will learn to focus your reading by **previewing** the work to identify the author's purpose. You will also learn to **reflect** on and refine your concept of purpose while you continue to read. **Previewing, identifying the author's purpose,** and then **reflecting on that purpose** while you read helps you read intelligently.

This chart shows how you can apply the skills and strategies you will learn in Part 2.

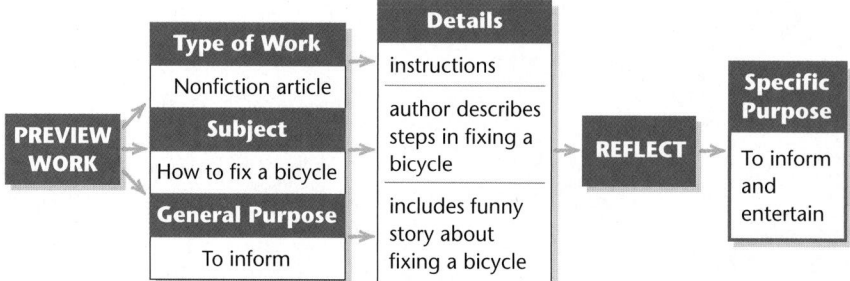

94 ■ *Fiction and Nonfiction*

Academic Vocabulary: Words for Evaluating Literature

The following words will help you write and talk about an author's purpose.

Word	Definition	Example Sentence
vital *adj.*	necessary	Sensory details are *vital* to a novel.
appreciate *v.*	recognize; understand and be grateful for	We seldom *appreciate* the precise use of language in a poem.
trivial *adj.*	of little or no importance	The story has too many *trivial* details.
display *v.*	exhibit; show	The character *displays* benevolent characteristics.
detect *v.*	discover	*Detecting* shifts of tone and mood in a work takes practice.

Vocabulary Skill: Word Origins

▶ The origin of a word is the language it came from.

In Part 2, you will learn
- Latin root *-via-* (p. 95)
- Latin combining form *-tri-* (p. 116)
- Latin root *-vit-* (p. 144)

The English language is made up of words that come from many different languages. Many words have the same root. The chart shows a dictionary entry and the changes this root has gone through.

via (vī′ə) [L. abl. sing. of *via*, a way < IE base *wei-*, to go strive toward> Gr *ienai,* to go, OE *wath*, a hunt, chase]
- tri**vial**
- **via**duct
- tri**via**

Activity Fill in the roots *via, tri,* or *vit* to complete the word that goes with each clue.
1. necessary to life   _____al
2. to change direction   de_____te
3. able to live   _____ble
4. a brief autobiography   _____ae
5. a three-pronged spear   _____dent

Tips for Test Taking

Point out to students that word roots often provide keys to understanding vocabulary on standardized tests. Remind students that the meanings of individual roots can often help them unlock the meanings of numerous words.

When taking a standardized test, students should look for word roots in unfamiliar vocabulary. Then, they should scan the answer choices for a word that incorporates the meaning of the root. If two answers are close in meaning, students should reread the question and answer choices to make sure they understand the question. Then, they should mark their answer selection.

Introduce Academic Vocabulary

- Introduce the academic vocabulary: words for evaluating literature. Tell students that these words are useful for discussing and writing responses to literature.
- Review each word, and have the students state the words aloud. Have students read aloud the words' definitions and the example sentences.
- Tell students to try to use these words as they discuss the selections in Part 2.

Introduce the Vocabulary Skill

- Introduce the vocabulary skill: word origins. Point out that English is a composite of many root words from other languages, and that many of these roots come from Latin. Remind students that recognizing these roots and their meanings will help them to build their vocabulary.
- Review the three roots on this page, their meanings, and the English words that contain these roots.
- Have students complete the activity. Have students discuss any answers that are unclear.
  Answers: 1. vital; 2. deviate; 3. viable; 4. vitae; 5. trident.
- Use these questions to give students practice with these roots:

  What word describes the capacity to live and develop?
  Answer: *vitality*

  What word describes a polygon having three sides?
  Answer: *triangle*

  What word describes a departure from accepted norms of behavior?
  Answer: *deviation*

Go Online **For:** Interactive **Vocabulary** crossword puzzle
Visit: www.PHSchool.com
Web Code: epj-5102
Give students this Web Code to access interactive crossword puzzles using Academic Vocabulary and Vocabulary Skill words from Part 2.

Planning Differentiated Instruction

Choosing Your Selection

You may use either selection to meet the lesson standards. The following guide will help you determine which of the two selections is more appropriate for your students.

Accessibility at a Glance

	from **A White House Diary**	**My English**
Context	Political: President Kennedy's assassination	Situation: Learning the English language
Language	• Accessible vocabulary • Formal language	• Difficult diction • Spanish words are footnoted.
Concept Level	Accessible (witnessing a tragedy; performing in a crisis)	Challenging (adapting to new situations; learning a new skill)
Literary Merit	Cross-generational	Cross-cultural experience
Lexile	820L	1070L
Overall Rating	More accessible	More challenging

Using the Other Selection You may use the other selection for homework or independent reading to reinforce the selection skills. If you use both selections, you can build a test for both using *ExamView*® **Test Bank** software.

Choosing Your Resources

[L1] Special Needs Students   [L4] Advanced Students

[L2] Below-Level Students   [EL] English Learners

[L3] All Students

Reading and Vocabulary Warm-ups provide support for below level students. **A** is for students reading two grades below level; **B** is for students reading one grade below level. For Selection Tests, **A** signifies "less challenging" and **B** "more challenging." For Graphic Organizer transparencies, **A** signifies "not filled in" and **B** "filled in."

FT Fast Track Instruction: To move the lesson more quickly, use the strategies and activities identified with **FT**.

Scaffolding for Less Proficient and Advanced Students

The leveled questions on Apply the Skills pages progress in the levels of thinking required to answer them. To address the needs of your different students, you may use the (a) level questions for your less proficient students, the (b) level with your on-level and advanced students. The occasional (c) level questions are appropriate for your advanced students.

Go Online **For:** Information about Lexiles
Professional   **Visit:** www.PHSchool.com
Development   **Web Code:** eue-1111

Step-by-Step Teaching Guide	Pacing Guide
PRETEACH	
• Administer Vocabulary and Reading Warm-ups as necessary.	
• Introduce the Literary Analysis Skill: Author's Voice and Autobiographical Writing. **FT**	10 min.
• Introduce the Reading Skill: Author's Purpose. **FT**	10 min.
• Prepare students to read by teaching the selection vocabulary. **FT**	10 min.
• Build background and develop expressive vocabulary with Connecting to the Literature and Background.	10 min.
• Engage students' interest with the motivation activity.	10 min.
TEACH	
• Informally monitor comprehension while students read independently or in groups. **FT**	30 min.
• Monitor students' comprehension with the Reading Check notes.	as students read
• Reinforce vocabulary with Vocabulary Builder notes.	as students read
• Develop students' understanding of author's voice and autobiographical writing with the Literary Analysis annotations. **FT**	5 min.
• Develop students' ability to understand the author's purpose with the Reading Skill annotations. **FT**	10 min.
ASSESS/EXTEND	
• Assess students' comprehension and mastery of the Reading Skill and Literary Analysis by having them answer the Apply the Skills questions. **FT**	35 min.
• Have students complete the Vocabulary Builder activities. **FT**	5 min.
• Apply students' ability to write a journal entry with the Writing activity. **FT**	30–45 min. or homework
• Extend students' listening and speaking and research and technology skills with one or both of the Extend Your Learning activities.	15–30 min. or homework
• Have students complete the Vocabulary Skill and Grammar Lesson.	5 min.
• Monitor students' progress with the Assessment Practice.	20–40 min.
• Administer **Selection Test A** or **Selection Test B**. **FT**	15 min.

Resources

Meeting Your Standards

Students will

1. **analyze and respond to literary elements.**
   - Literary Analysis: Author's Voice and Autobiographical Writing
2. **read, comprehend, and analyze autobiographies.**
   - Reading Skill: Author's Purpose
   - Reading Strategy: Previewing to identify an author's purpose
   - Reading Check questions
   - Apply the Skills questions
   - Assessment Practice
3. **develop vocabulary.**
   - Vocabulary Builder
   - The Latin roots *vit-*, *-via-*, and *tri-*
4. **apply grammar skills.**
   - **Personal and Reflexive Pronouns**
5. **develop writing proficiency.**
   - Work in Progress: **Problem-and-Solution Essay**
   - **Journal Entry**
6. **extend learning.**
   - Listening and Speaking: **Radio Broadcast**
   - Research and Technology: **Multimedia Presentation**

Block Scheduling: Use one 90-minute class period to preteach the skills and have students read the selection. Use a second 90-minute class period to assess students' mastery of skills, extend their learning, and monitor their progress.

Homework Suggestions

Following are possibilities for homework assignments.

- Support pages from *Unit 1 Resources:*
  Literary Analysis
  Reading Skill
  Vocabulary Builder
  Enrichment
- An Extend Your Learning project and the Writing assignment for your chosen selection may be completed over several days.

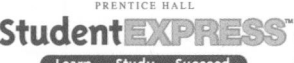

PRENTICE HALL
TeacherEXPRESS™ Use this complete
Plan · Teach · Assess   suite of powerful
teaching tools to make lesson planning and testing quicker and easier.

PRENTICE HALL
StudentEXPRESS™ Use the
Learn · Study · Succeed   interactive
textbook (online and on CD-ROM) to make selections and activities come alive with audio and video support and interactive questions.

❶ Literary Analysis
Voice

- Explain to students that *voice*—the way a writer sounds on the page—is hard to describe but unmistakable. Voice is partly defined by word choice and sentence structure. Explain that short words and sentences and a quick rhythm create one type of voice, while long words and sentences and a slow, rolling rhythm create another. Tell students that attitude and tone also contribute to voice.

- Point out that voice is especially relevant in autobiographical writing because it helps convey the writer's personality.

- As students read, encourage them to look for ways that word choice and sentence length and structure contribute to the writer's voice. Have students also note how the voice makes them feel about the narrative and about the writer.

❷ Reading Skill
Author's Purpose

- Emphasize that authors always write for both a general and a specific purpose. For example, a writer's general purpose may be to persuade people to come to a community theater production. The writer's specific purpose could be to show people that a particular community theater provides quality entertainment.

- Tell students that authors often have more than one general or specific purpose. For example, a writer's general purpose could be both to persuade and to entertain.

- Give students a copy of **Reading Skill Graphic Organizer A** (*Graphic Organizer Transparencies*, p. 22). Have them fill in the graphic organizer to analyze the author's purpose as they read the assigned selection.

Build Skills from *A White House Diary* • *My English*

Practice these skills with either the excerpt from *A White House Diary* (p. 98) or "My English" (p. 107).

❶ Literary Analysis

Voice is the way a writer sounds on the page. For example, the writer's voice in a work can be *smooth and sophisticated, choppy and blunt,* or *breathless and full of wonder.* Voice is a result of several elements:

- *Word Choice:* the kinds of words the writer uses
- *Attitude:* the way the writer feels about his or her subject
- *Sentence Structure:* the arrangement of words in sentences

In **autobiographical writing,** the author tells all or part of his or her own life's story. The kind of details that are included show what the writer notices, thinks, and feels about events. The voice of autobiographical writing usually reflects the writer's own personality and way of speaking.

❷ Reading Skill

An **author's purpose** is his or her main reason for writing. An author writes for a general purpose, such as to inform, to entertain, or to persuade. He or she also writes for a specific purpose, such as to expose a particular problem in society. Before you read, **preview to look for an author's purpose.**

- Notice information or ideas conveyed in the title.
- Look for any organizing features, like subheads.
- Identify the subject of photos, illustrations, or diagrams.

As you preview, use an organizer like the one shown to jot down ideas about the author's specific purpose. Later, as you read the full text, confirm whether your ideas are correct.

Text Feature	Insight About Purpose

Vocabulary Builder

from A White House Diary

- **tumultuous** (tōō mul′ chōō əs) *adj.* greatly disturbed; in an uproar (p. 101) *The year we moved cross-country was a* <u>*tumultuous*</u> *one.*

- **implications** (im′pli kā′ shənz) *n.* indirect results (p. 102) *He did not think about the* <u>*implications*</u> *of his decision to change jobs.*

- **poignant** (poin′ yənt) *adj.* emotionally touching (p. 103) *The moment of farewell is often very* <u>*poignant*</u>.

My English

- **bilingual** (bī lin′ gwəl) *adj.* using two languages (p. 107) *The* <u>*bilingual*</u> *student speaks both Japanese and English.*

- **countenance** (koun′ tə nəns) *n.* face (p. 109) *The child's overjoyed* <u>*countenance*</u> *showed her relief at being home.*

- **interminably** (in tʉr′ mi nə blē) *adv.* endlessly (p. 113) *To the tired, hungry audience, the speaker went on* <u>*interminably*</u>.

96 ■ *Fiction and Nonfiction*

Vocabulary Development

Vocabulary Knowledge Rating

Create a **Vocabulary Knowledge Rating Chart** for the selection you will teach from this set. Include the selection vocabulary from this page and the additional words students are asked to use at the end of Connecting to the Literature. These words will increase students' expressive vocabulary.

Give students a copy of the chart with the words on it. Introduce the words by reading them aloud and having students mark their rating in the Before Reading column. Urge them to be alert to these words as they read and discuss the selection because they will rate their knowledge of the words again after they finish.

If you wish, you may tally how many students know (or think they know) a word to gauge how much instruction you need to provide. As students read, point out the words and their context.

Autobiography

❸ Background

The Assassination of JFK President John F. Kennedy was a young, vibrant, and popular leader who had been elected in 1960. His assassination on November 22, 1963, was a stunning and unforgettable event. As the news media reported the tragedy, people wept openly in the streets. A mournful nation agreed with Lyndon B. Johnson, JFK's successor, when he said, "We have suffered a loss that cannot be weighed."

❹ Connecting to the Literature

Reading/Writing Connection For many Americans, the speeches of John F. Kennedy remain a source of inspiration and hope. Write a brief paragraph about a person whose actions or ideas you find inspiring. Use at least three of these words: *evoke, invoke, embody, motivate, illustrate.*

Meet the Author

Lady Bird **Johnson** (b. 1912)

Texas-born Claudia Alta Taylor received her nickname when a nurse said the two-year-old was "as pretty as a lady bird." A graduate of the University of Texas, Lady Bird met and married Lyndon Johnson, then a young Congressional aide, in 1934. Even though she was a shy woman, Lady Bird was a most valued advisor and effective campaigner for her husband, who said that voters "would happily have elected her over me."

Living History When President Kennedy was assassinated, Vice President Lyndon Johnson became president, and Lady Bird became First Lady of the United States. In this role, she made many contributions to her husband's agenda, including the launch of Head Start, a project that makes early childhood education available to all children.

Fast Facts

▶ In 1982, Lady Bird Johnson founded the National Wildflower Research Center in Austin, Texas.

▶ *A White House Diary* was published in 1970, shortly after the Johnsons returned to Texas, where Mrs. Johnson still lives.

For: More about the author
Visit: www.PHSchool.com
Web Code: epe-9108

from A White House Diary ■ 97

❸ Background
The Assassination of JFK

Shortly after President Kennedy's assassination, Lee Harvey Oswald, a supporter of Communist Cuba, was arrested for the crime. Two days later, during a transfer between jails, Oswald was fatally shot by a nightclub owner named Jack Ruby, who soon thereafter died of cancer. Neither man lived to stand trial.

Newly sworn-in President Johnson ordered the formation of a committee to investigate the assassination. The committee found no evidence of a conspiracy to assassinate John F. Kennedy, nor any evidence to connect Oswald to Ruby.

Despite the committee's findings, conspiracy theories still exist. However, no person has ever confessed to involvement in such a conspiracy, nor has any other hard evidence contradicted the committee's findings.

❹ Connecting to the Literature

• Model use of the expressive vocabulary students are asked to use with these examples:

1. For many people, memories of John F. Kennedy still *evoke* intense feelings.

2. People still *invoke* President Kennedy's name when they fight for civil rights.

3. The life and death of President Kennedy *embody* the best and worst of America.

4. He tried to *motivate* Americans to give their time to help the country.

5. The words and images in Lady Bird Johnson's narrative *illustrate* the feelings of the nation.

• Help students further develop their expressive vocabulary by providing these words: *horror, overwhelm, somber,* and *tragic.* Encourage students to use these words as they discuss the selection.

Go Online For additional information about Lady Bird Johnson, have students type in the Web Code, then select *J* from the alphabet, and then select *Lady Bird Johnson.*

Differentiated Instruction — Solutions for All Learners

Support for Below-Level Students [L1, L2]

Unit 1 Resources
Vocabulary Warm-up Word Lists, p. 112
Vocabulary Warm-up Practice, p. 113
Reading Warm-up A, p. 114
Selection Test A, pp. 122–124

Graphic Organizer Transparencies
Reading Skill Graphic Organizer, Transparency B, p. 23

Reader's Notebook: Adapted Version

Adapted Reader's Notebook Audio CD

Support for English Learners [EL]

Unit 1 Resources
Vocabulary Warm-up Word Lists, p. 112
Vocabulary Warm-up Practice, p. 113
Reading Warm-up A, p. 114

Reader's Notebook: English Learner's Version

Listening to Literature Audio CD

❶ Motivation

Prepare an **Anticipation Guide** (see *General Resources,* pp. 8–10) with the following statements:

• The greatest tragedies occur when they are least expected.

• If certain precautions are taken, tragedy can always be avoided.

• People can remain calm and objective in the worst of times.

• When life takes an unexpected turn, people should always step back and take a break.

Give students a copy of the prepared Anticipation Guide and have students mark their responses in the Me column. Have students discuss the statements in pairs or groups and mark the Guides again in the Group column.

Concept Connector ➡

Students will return to the Anticipation Guide after completing *A White House Diary.*

Learning Modalities
Interpersonal Learners

Lady Bird Johnson gives a very objective but also personal account of the day that President Kennedy was assassinated. She also gives glimpses into what other people were experiencing, thinking, and feeling that day. Urge students to pay attention to these often-subtle insights Lady Bird Johnson reveals while observing and interacting with other people.

❷ About the Selection

In this excerpt from *A White House Diary,* Lady Bird Johnson recalls the day President John F. Kennedy was shot in Dallas, Texas. Johnson, wife of the vice president, was in Kennedy's motorcade when the shots rang out. She describes the feelings of shock, horror, and helplessness at the event and recalls details of the somber plane flight back to Washington.

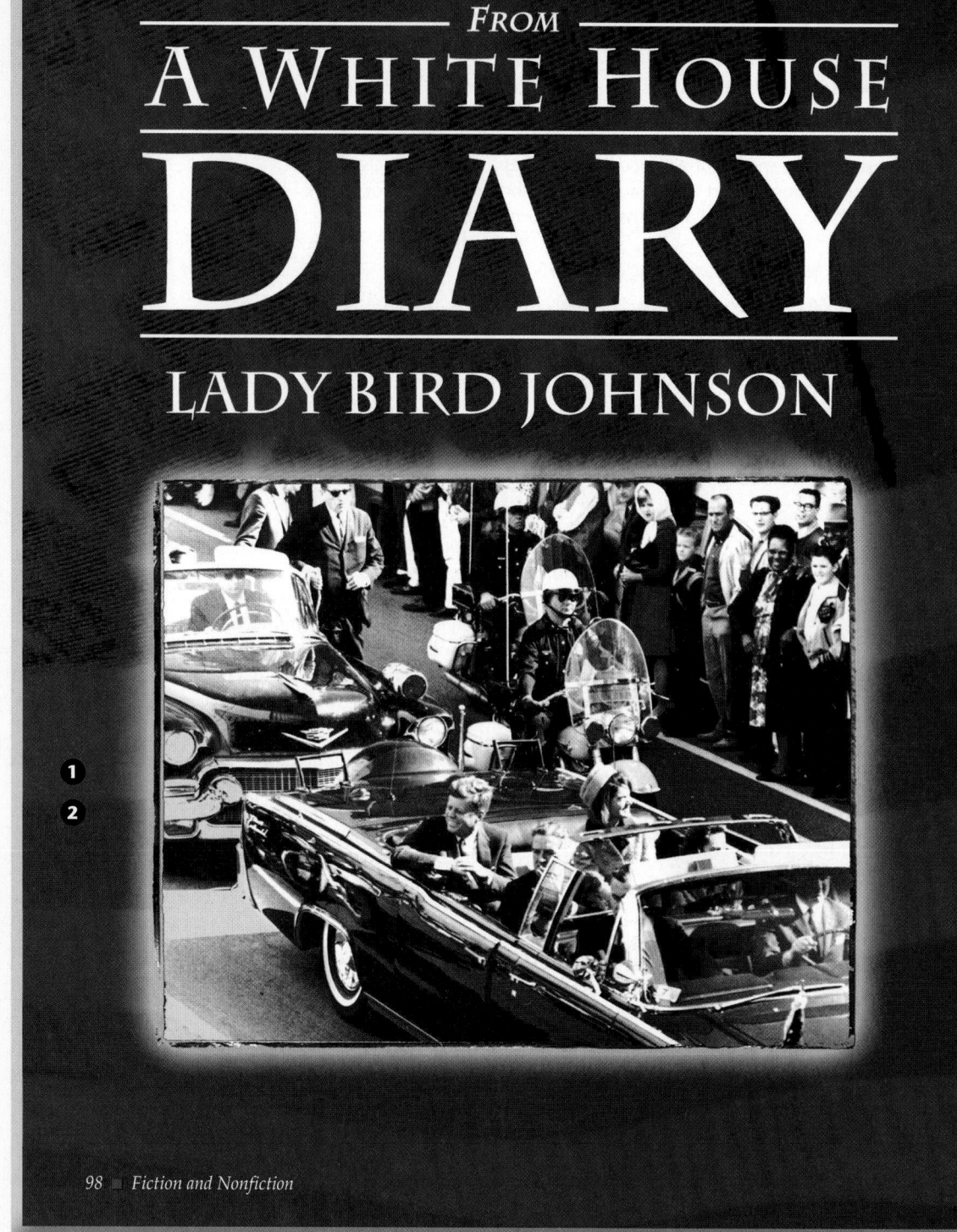

FROM
A WHITE HOUSE
DIARY
LADY BIRD JOHNSON

❶
❷

98 ■ *Fiction and Nonfiction*

Vocabulary Development

Multiple Meanings

Point out the word *report* in the third paragraph of p. 99, and ask students to define the word as it is used here. (a loud, explosive noise) Then explain that *report* is a word with multiple meanings. Write these sentences on the board, and ask student pairs to write definitions for each use of *report*.

1. The student read aloud her *report* on solar eclipses.
2. According to all *reports,* he may decide to run for office anyway.
3. I will *report* my findings on Tuesday.
4. The Army officer will *report* for duty.

Ask students to write more sentences showing the multiple meanings of *report*.

Answers: 1. a formal, organized account of some topic; 2. rumors or common talk; 3. give an account of; 4. show up, appear

DALLAS, FRIDAY, NOVEMBER 22, 1963

❸ It all began so beautifully. After a drizzle in the morning, the sun came out bright and clear. We were driving into Dallas. In the lead car were President and Mrs. Kennedy, John and Nellie Connally,[1] a Secret Service[2] car full of men, and then our car with Lyndon and me and Senator Ralph Yarborough.

The streets were lined with people—lots and lots of people—the children all smiling, placards, confetti, people waving from windows. One last happy moment I had was looking up and seeing Mary Griffith leaning out of a window waving at me. (Mary for many years had been in charge of altering the clothes which I purchased at Neiman-Marcus.)

Then, almost at the edge of town, on our way to the Trade Mart for the Presidential luncheon, we were rounding a curve, going down a hill, and suddenly there was a sharp, loud report. It sounded like a shot. The sound seemed to me to come from a building on the right above my shoulder. A moment passed, and **❹** then two more shots rang out in rapid succession. There had been such a gala air about the day that I thought the noise must come from firecrackers—part of the celebration. Then the Secret Service men were suddenly down in the lead car. Over the car radio system, I heard "Let's get out of here!" and our Secret Service man, Rufus Youngblood, vaulted over the front seat on top of Lyndon, threw him to the floor, and said, "Get down."

Senator Yarborough and I ducked our heads. The car accelerated terrifically—faster and faster. Then, suddenly, the brakes were put on so hard that I wondered if we were going to make it as we wheeled left and went around the corner. We pulled up to a building. I looked up and saw a sign, "HOSPITAL." Only then did I believe that this might be what it was. Senator Yarborough kept saying in an excited voice, "Have they shot the President? Have they shot the President?" I said something like, "No, it can't be."

As we ground to a halt—we were still the third car—Secret Service men began to pull, lead, guide, and hustle us out. I cast one last look over my shoulder and saw in the President's car a bundle of pink, just like a drift of blossoms, lying on the back seat. It was Mrs. Kennedy lying over the President's body.

---

1. John and Nellie Connally John Connally, then Governor of Texas, and his wife, Nellie.
2. Secret Service division of the U.S. Treasury Department, responsible for protecting the president.

❺ ◀ **Critical Viewing** What does this photograph reveal about the mood in the moments leading up to the assassination of President Kennedy? **[Infer]**

from *A White House Diary* ■ 99

Reading Skill
Author's Purpose
What would previewing this subhead suggest to you about the author's purpose in this part of her diary?

Literary Analysis
Voice and Autobiographical Writing What do the details about firecrackers tell you about the writer's attitude toward the events she describes?

❻ ✔ **Reading Check**

Where are the Johnsons taken after shots are fired?

Differentiated Instruction Solutions for All Learners

Strategy for Special Needs Students
After students read the first paragraph, create a chart on the board for students listing each of the people mentioned. As students continue reading, have them provide details that identify each person and his or her role in the event described. Have students make a copy of the chart for study and review.

Strategy for Less Proficient Readers
Help students better understand the author's purpose by showing them **Reading Skill Graphic Organizer B** (*Graphic Organizer Transparencies*, p. 23). Review the general purposes for writing and discuss the answers provided in the organizer. Encourage students to use these ideas to think about the author's purpose as they continue reading.

---

❸ Reading Skill
Author's Purpose

- Have students read the subhead that begins this page, and then **ask** them to respond to the Reading Skill question: What would previewing this subhead suggest to you about the author's purpose in this part of her diary?
  Answer: It suggests that she wants to report the events of one day.

- Read, or have a student read, the bracketed passage. **Ask** students what details Johnson gives in the passage and how these details contribute to the writer's purpose.
  Answer: The details set the scene by describing the weather, the people in the cars, and the people on the streets. These details help the author report the events of the day vividly.

❹ Literary Analysis
Voice and Autobiographical Writing

- **Ask** students to define autobiographical writing and to explain the details usually included in this type of work.
  Answer: Autobiographical writing is a work in which the author tells all or part of his or her own life story. The author usually includes details to show what he or she notices, thinks, and feels about events.

- Draw students' attention to the bracketed passage. **Ask** them to respond to the Literary Analysis question: What do the details about firecrackers tell you about the writer's attitude toward the events she describes?
  Answer: At the time she heard the sound, her attitude and mood were festive. She did not expect anything sinister to happen, and so interpreted the shots as firecrackers.

❺ Critical Viewing

Answer: The president and first lady are beaming at the crowd. Most people in the crowd are either attentive or smiling. The mood seems cheerful and happy.

❻ Reading Check

Answer: The Johnsons are rushed to the hospital.

Voice and Autobiographical Writing

- **Ask** students to describe Johnson's state of mind while she waits in the small hospital room.
  Possible response: She is uncertain about the extent of the tragedy and about where she and her husband will go.

- Discuss how Johnson tried to find out the President's condition by searching the faces of people. Point out to students that she got the most insight from the face of Kennedy's aide and friend, Kenny O'Donnell. Emphasize how autobiographical writing can humanize historic events by revealing personal details.

❽ Literature in Context

History Connection Along with introducing vital government programs, President Kennedy also proved that he could lead well in a crisis. In October 1962, the United States government found that the Soviet Union was building nuclear missile launchers in Cuba, which is only 90 miles away from Florida. The President had to decide if he should ignore the missiles or confront the Soviet Union, essentially risking nuclear war. President Kennedy chose an aggressive approach; he used the Navy to block Soviet ships from delivering military supplies to Cuba. After thirteen fearful, uneasy days, the Cuban Missile Crisis ended when the Soviet Union agreed to remove the missiles. In turn, President Kennedy publicly promised that the United States would not invade Cuba and secretly agreed to remove American missiles from Turkey. President Kennedy's decisions prevented Soviet missiles in Cuba, averted nuclear war, and paved the way for a slowing of the nuclear arms race.

Connect to the Literature Point out to students that President Kennedy built this legacy in less than one complete presidential term. **Ask** students the Connect to the Literature question: How does information about President Kennedy's ideas help explain the intense grief most Americans felt over his death?
Possible response: Americans mourned not only his death, but also the death of his influence on the future of America.

The Secret Service men rushed us to the right, then to the left, and then onward into a quiet room in the hospital—a very small room. It was lined with white sheets, I believe.

People came and went—Kenny O'Donnell, the President's top aide, Congressman Homer Thornberry, Congressman Jack Brooks. Always there was Rufe right there and other Secret Service agents—Emory Roberts, Jerry Kivett, Lem Johns, and Woody Taylor. People spoke of how widespread this might be. There was talk about where we would go—to the plane, to our house, back to Washington.

❼ Through it all Lyndon was remarkably calm and quiet. He suggested that the Presidential plane ought to be moved to another part of the field. He spoke of going back out to the plane in unmarked black cars. Every face that came in, you searched for the answer. I think the face I kept seeing the answer on was the face of Kenny O'Donnell, who loved President Kennedy so much.

It was Lyndon who spoke of it first, although I knew I would not leave without doing it. He said, "You had better try to see Jackie and Nellie." We didn't know what had happened to John.

I asked the Secret Service if I could be taken to them. They began to lead me up one corridor and down another. Suddenly I

---

❽ **Literature in Context** | **History Connection**

The Legacy of JFK

At the age of 43, John Fitzgerald Kennedy became the youngest president in American history. He brought to the White House a new energy, optimism, and hope for the future. The initiatives he sought changed America.

▲ Kennedy, shown here with astronaut John Glenn, committed the nation to space exploration.

Kennedy established the Peace Corps in 1961. To date, 178,000 volunteers have served in 137 countries.

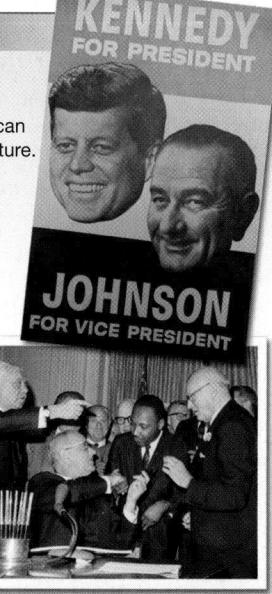

Kennedy ▶ initiated the Civil Rights Act. Johnson, with Dr. Martin Luther King, Jr., at his side, signed it into law in 1965.

Connect to the Literature How does information about President Kennedy's ideas help explain the intense grief most Americans felt over his death?

Vocabulary Development

Expressive Vocabulary
Create a cluster diagram on the board. In the center, write "The Assassination of President Kennedy." In the surrounding circle, have students identify people, events, and settings associated with the assassination. Then, ask students to provide sentences about these people, events, and settings, using the expressive vocabulary words introduced on p. 97: *evoke, invoke, embody, motivate, illustrate.* You might stimulate discussion by providing these sentence starters.

1. The sound of the gun shot *evoked* . . .
2. When President Kennedy was shot, they *invoked* . . .
3. Mrs. Kennedy *embodied* . . .
4. The sight of Mrs. Kennedy *motivated* . . .
5. The response of President Johnson *illustrates* . . .

9 ◀ **Critical Viewing**
What do these peoples' facial expressions reveal about their feelings following the assassination? **[Interpret]**

10 found myself face to face with Jackie in a small hallway. I believe it was right outside the operating room. You always think of someone like her as being insulated, protected. She was quite alone. I don't think I ever saw anyone so much alone in my life. I went up to her, put my arms around her, and said something to her. I'm sure it was something like "God, help us all," because my feelings for her were too <u>tumultuous</u> to put into words.

And then I went to see Nellie. There it was different, because Nellie and I have gone through so many things together since 1938. I hugged her tight and we both cried and I said, "Nellie, John's going to be all right." And Nellie said, "Yes, John's going to be all right." Among her many other fine qualities, she is also strong.

I turned and went back to the small white room where Lyndon was. Mac Kilduff, the President's press man on this trip, and Kenny O'Donnell were coming and going. I think it was from Kenny's face that I first knew the truth and from Kenny's voice that I first heard the words "The President is dead." Mr. Kilduff entered and said to Lyndon, "Mr. President."

It was decided that we would go immediately to the airport. Hurried plans were made about how we should get to the cars and who was to ride in which car. Our departure from the hospital and approach to the cars was one of the swiftest walks I have ever made.

We got in. Lyndon told the agents to stop the sirens. We drove along as fast as we could. I looked up at a building and there, already, was a flag at half-mast. I think that was when the enormity of what had happened first struck me.

Vocabulary Builder
tumultuous (tōō mul′ chōō əs) *adj.* greatly disturbed; in an uproar

11 ✔ Reading Check
How did Mrs. Johnson first know that the president was dead?

from A White House Diary ■ 101

9 **Critical Viewing**
Answer: President and Mrs. Johnson look solemn and serious. Mrs. Kennedy looks shocked, stunned, and on the verge of tears.

10 **Literary Analysis**
Voice and Autobiographical Writing
• Read aloud the bracketed passage, in which Johnson visits the two women who were in the motorcade with her when the shooting occurred. **Ask** students to give examples of how the author's voice is expressed in these two scenes.
Answer: When Johnson visits Mrs. Kennedy, her voice is heard when she comments that she has never seen anyone so alone and when she describes her inability to put her feelings into words. When Johnson visits Nellie Connally, her voice is heard when she describes how the situation was different because of her friendship with Nellie.

• **Ask** students what Johnson's attitude throughout the ordeal seems to be.
Possible response: Johnson seems distraught, tense, and sad, but she is also in control.

11 **Reading Check**
Answer: She learned the news from Kenny O'Donnell's facial expression, then his words.

Differentiated Instruction   Solutions for All Learners

Background for English Learners
Explain to students that President Kennedy was a young and vigorous president who challenged Americans with goals and ideals that gripped their imaginations. He stood up to the power of the Soviet Union in 1962 when that country placed missiles with nuclear warheads in Cuba. Later, he promoted the space program and set a goal of placing a man on the moon by 1969. He was active in civil rights legislation and enforcement. Kennedy's leadership inspired Americans, and his early and tragic death was devastating to the nation. The event immediately became a landmark in the lives of Americans living at the time. Even decades later, many Americans remember where they were and what they were doing at the exact moment they heard of the assassination of President Kennedy.

Author's Purpose

- Call attention to Johnson's description of the televised announcement that Lyndon Johnson was now president. Point out how Johnson does not draw conclusions or offer personal reactions to the scene. Her purpose is purely that of reporting what she saw and heard.

- Call students' attention to the description of the events on Air Force One leading to the swearing in of Lyndon Johnson as president. **Ask:** What are Johnson's purposes in describing this sequence of events in such detail?
Possible response: First, she wants to record specific details about an historic sequence of events. Second, she may want to show the speed and urgency with which events were happening.

▶ **Monitor Progress:** Ask students whether they accurately identified the author's purpose in writing this selection when they previewed the selection. Call on students to talk about the purposes they identified and the details that led them to this conclusion.

▶ **Reteach:** Show students **Reading Skill Graphic Organizer B** (*Graphic Organizer Transparencies,* p. 23). Have students look back over the selection to find the details given on the organizer that help readers determine the author's purpose.

⑬ **Critical Viewing**

Answer: Johnson may be concerned about the various problems he will now have to solve.

When we got to the field, we entered *Air Force One*[3] for the first time. There was a TV set on and the commentator was saying, "Lyndon B. Johnson, now President of the United States." The news commentator was saying the President had been shot with a 30-30 rifle. The police had a suspect. They were not sure he was the assassin.

⑫ On the plane, all the shades were lowered. We heard that we were going to wait for Mrs. Kennedy and the coffin. There was a telephone call to Washington—I believe to the Attorney General.[4]

It was decided that Lyndon should be sworn in here as quickly as possible, because of national and world <u>implications</u>, and because we did not know how widespread this was as to intended victims. Judge Sarah Hughes, a Federal Judge in Dallas—and I am glad it was she—was called and asked to come in a hurry to administer the oath.

Mrs. Kennedy had arrived by this time, as had the coffin. There, in the very narrow confines of the plane—with Jackie standing by Lyndon, her hair falling in her face but very composed, with me beside him, Judge Hughes in front of him, and a cluster of Secret Service people, staff, and Congressmen we had known for a long time around him—Lyndon took the oath of office.

---

3. Air Force One name of the airplane officially assigned to transport the president of the United States.
4. Attorney General chief law officer of the nation, head of the U.S. Department of Justice; at the time, the position was held by Robert Kennedy, the president's brother.

⑬ ▲ **Critical Viewing**
This photograph shows Lyndon Johnson assuming his duties as president. How do you think he felt at that moment? Why? **[Analyze]**

Vocabulary Builder
implications (im′ pli kā′ shənz) *n.* indirect results

Vocabulary Development

Vocabulary Knowledge Rating
When students have completed reading and discussing "The White House Diary," have them take out their **Vocabulary Knowledge Rating Chart** for this selection. Read the words aloud once more and have students rate their knowledge of the words again in the After Reading column. Clarify any words that are still problematic. Have students write their own defini-tion and example or sentence in the appropriate column. Then have students complete the **Vocabulary Builder Practice** activities on p. 105. Encourage students to use the words in further discussion and written work about this selection. Remind them that they will be accountable for these words on the Selection Test.

It's odd the little things that come to your mind at times of utmost stress, the flashes of deep compassion you feel for people who are really not at the center of the tragedy. I heard a Secret Service man say in the most desolate voice—and I hurt for him: "We never lost a President in the Service." Then, Police Chief Curry of Dallas came on the plane and said, "Mrs. Kennedy, believe me, we did everything we possibly could." That must have been an agonizing moment for him.

We all sat around the plane. The casket was in the corridor. I went in the small private room to see Mrs. Kennedy, and though it was a very hard thing to do, she made it as easy as possible. She said things like, "Oh, Lady Bird, we've liked you two so much. . . . Oh, what if I had not been there. I'm so glad I was there."

I looked at her. Mrs. Kennedy's dress was stained with blood. One leg was almost entirely covered with it and her right glove was caked, it was caked with blood—her husband's blood. Somehow that was one of the most poignant sights—that immaculate woman exquisitely dressed, and caked in blood.

I asked her if I couldn't get someone in to help her change and she said, "Oh, no. Perhaps later I'll ask Mary Gallagher but not right now." And then with almost an element of fierceness—if a person that gentle, that dignified, can be said to have such a quality—she said, "I want them to see what they have done to Jack."

I tried to express how we felt. I said, "Oh, Mrs. Kennedy, you know we never even wanted to be Vice President and now, dear God, it's come to this." I would have done anything to help her, but there was nothing I could do, so rather quickly I left and went back to the main part of the airplane where everyone was seated.

The flight to Washington was silent, each sitting with his own thoughts. One of mine was a recollection of what I had said about Lyndon a long time ago—he's a good man in a tight spot. I remembered one little thing he had said in that hospital room—"Tell the children to get a Secret Service man with them."

Finally we got to Washington, with a cluster of people waiting and many bright lights. The casket went off first, then Mrs. Kennedy, and then we followed. The family had come to join her. Lyndon made a very simple, very brief, and, I think, strong statement to the people there. Only about four sentences. We got in helicopters, dropped him off at the White House, and I came home in a car with Liz Carpenter.[5]

---

5. **Liz Carpenter** Mrs. Johnson's press secretary.

Vocabulary Builder
poignant (poin´ yənt) *adj.* emotionally touching

Literary Analysis
Voice and Autobiographical Writing What does this passage reveal about Mrs. Johnson's attitude toward Mrs. Kennedy?

from A White House Diary ■ 103

Concept Connector

Anticipation Guide
Have students return to their **Anticipation Guides** and respond to the statements again in the After Reading column. Then, lead a class discussion, probing for what students have learned that confirms or invalidates each statement.

Connecting to the Literature
Have students compare the sentences they wrote before reading with their thoughts about people whose actions or ideas inspire them. Ask them to explain whether their thoughts have changed and, if so, how.

Reading Skill Graphic Organizer
Ask students to review the graphic organizers they completed to identify the author's purpose while reading. Show them **Reading Skill Graphic Organizer B** (*Graphic Organizer Transparencies*, p. 23) as an example. Then have students share the graphic organizers they did and the author's purpose that they identified.

⓴ Reading Skill
Author's Purpose

- Point out that Johnson holds her emotions back during most of the story, telling only the facts. In recalling the Secret Service man and the police chief's apology, she allows herself to express sympathy.

- **Ask** students to respond to the Reading Skill question: What is the writer's purpose in including the comments of the Secret Service man?
  Possible response: Johnson may have wanted to show how this tragedy affected different people.

- Remind students that this is a diary entry. Point out, however, that the diaries of famous people are often written with an expectation that sooner or later their diaries will become public. Invite students to speculate on how this idea may or may not have influenced Johnson's purpose in writing her account of this event.
  Possible response: Johnson's diary is not a private document. As a public figure, she wrote it knowing that it would be published and be read by a wide audience. Her purposes in writing were most likely to share with other Americans an insider's look at a tragic historical incident and to go on record with accurate details about the events of that day.

⓯ Literary Analysis
Voice and Autobiographical Writing

- Discuss the uniqueness of this scene between Johnson and Kennedy, and stress that it would not exist in an outsider's account of the event. Lead students to recognize that only someone who was personally involved in the situation could provide this kind of insight, and that few people other than Lady Bird Johnson saw or spoke to Mrs. Kennedy in the hours immediately following her husband's death.

- **Ask** students the Literary Analysis question: What does this passage reveal about Mrs. Johnson's attitude toward Mrs. Kennedy?
  Answer: It shows that she was deeply moved by Mrs. Kennedy's loss and was concerned with how she was holding up.

Apply the Skills

from *A White House Diary*

Thinking About the Selection

1. **Respond:** What do you admire most about Mrs. Johnson? Explain.
2. **(a) Recall:** What does Mrs. Kennedy say when Mrs. Johnson offers to find someone to help her change her clothes? **(b) Interpret:** What does Mrs. Kennedy mean? **(c) Analyze:** Why do you think Mrs. Johnson reported this detail?
3. **(a) Recall:** What comment about her husband does Mrs. Johnson recall on the flight back to Washington? **(b) Interpret:** What character traits does this comment suggest President Johnson possessed? Explain. **(c) Support:** Which details from the selection show that Mrs. Johnson possesses similar character traits?
4. **Evaluate:** Do you think Mrs. Johnson effectively expresses what it felt like to live through this historic incident? Explain.

Literary Analysis

5. **(a)** Complete a chart like the one shown to find examples of Johnson's **word choice, attitude,** and **sentence structure.**

VOICE		
Word Choice	Attitude	Sentence Structure

   (b) Using examples from your chart, describe Johnson's **voice** in this work.
6. **(a)** What details about Lyndon Johnson are emphasized in Lady Bird Johnson's **autobiographical writing? (b)** Why would Lady Bird Johnson notice these details more than someone else might? **(c)** What are two other details about feelings and incidents that reflect Mrs. Johnson's unique perspective on events?

Reading Skill

7. Review the notes you made in your **preview** of the excerpt. Which of your ideas about the **author's purpose** were confirmed as you read the selection? Which were not? Explain.
8. **(a)** What general purpose do you think Mrs. Johnson had in writing this portion of *A White House Diary*? Explain. **(b)** What more specific purpose(s) do you think she had for writing? Support your answer with details from the diary.

104 ■ *Fiction and Nonfiction*

QuickReview

Diary at a Glance
Lady Bird Johnson, wife of President Lyndon Johnson, describes her experiences on the day John F. Kennedy was assassinated.

Go Online
Assessment
For: Self-test
Visit: www.PHSchool.com
Web Code: epa-6108

Autobiographical Writing: literary work in which an author tells all or part of his or her life's story

Voice: the way a writer "sounds" or "speaks" on the page

Author's Purpose: a writer's main reason for writing a literary work

Answers (column)

1. **Possible response:** Her great sympathy for other people's feelings is her best quality. She is aware of the grief of everyone around her and tries to help them all.

2. (a) She says, "I want them to see what they have done to Jack." (b) She wants the nation to see evidence of the brutality of the assassination. (c) It is a powerful comment that helps define Mrs. Kennedy's feelings.

3. (a) She remembers that she had said that "he's a good man in a tight spot." (b) This comment suggests that President Johnson reacts well under pressure. (c) **Possible response:** Mrs. Johnson's calmness, concern for others, and awareness of her public responsibilities in an extreme situation show that she is also a good person in a tight spot.

4. Yes, because she gives a vivid account that includes other people's feelings.

5. (a) **Sample response: Word Choice:** "that immaculate woman exquisitely dressed, and caked in blood" **Attitude:** "I went up to her, put my arms around her"; **Sentence Structure:** "We got in. Lyndon told the agents to stop the sirens. We drove along as fast as we could." (b) **Possible response:** Her voice is vivid and specific: "immaculate woman exquisitely dressed, and caked in blood"; simple: "We got in."; and compassionate and empathetic: "put my arms around her."

   Another sample answer can be found on **Literary Analysis Graphic Organizer B**, p. 26, in *Graphic Organizer Transparencies*.

6. (a) She says that he is calm and quiet, but also takes command and is considerate of others. (b) He is her husband. (c) **Possible response:** She notices the Secret Service man's anguish and Mrs. Kennedy's subtle anger.

7. **Possible response:** Students may have expected the purpose to be to describe the assassination. They may not have expected such a personal, emotional account.

8. (a) Her general purpose is to inform readers about the assassination. She gives details about events, the setting, and people's feelings. (b) She wants readers to understand the experiences of those at the scene. She tells about the sorrow on the faces of President Kennedy's advisers and about how Mrs. Kennedy reacted.

Vocabulary Builder

Practice **Analogies** show the relationships between pairs of words. To complete each analogy, use a word from the vocabulary list for the excerpt from *A White House Diary* on page 96. For each case, your choice should create a word pair that matches the relationship between the first two words given.

1. weak : strong :: calm : _____
2. rain : flood :: choice : _____
3. laughter : humorous :: sadness : _____

Adding Words to Your Vocabulary A word's **denotation** is its direct, literal meaning. A word's **connotations** are the ideas associated with it. For example, *stirring* and *poignant* share a similar denotative meaning. However, their connotative meanings are very different. Using a dictionary and a thesaurus, investigate the connotations of each word. Then, use each word in a sentence that illustrates its specific connotation. (For more on using a dictionary and a thesaurus, see pages R6–7.)

Writing

Using the excerpt from *A White House Diary* as inspiration, write a **journal entry** of your own in which you describe and react to an event of local, national, or global significance. As you prepare to write, consider the following questions:
- Who was affected by this event, and in what way?
- What specific words or images does this event call to mind?

For *Grammar, Vocabulary,* and *Assessment,* see **Build Language Skills,** pages 116–117.

Extend Your Learning

Listening and Speaking With three or four classmates, enact a **radio broadcast** of a news bulletin about the Kennedy assassination.
- As you work together to write a script, evaluate your word choices to make sure they suit your audience and purpose.
- Use appropriate vocal inflection to convey the gravity of the news.

Research and Technology Using presentation software, prepare a list of at least three main points and an **introduction for a multimedia presentation** about First Ladies in American history. Discuss how the role of the First Lady has changed over time.

Apply the Skills ■ 105

Assessment Resources

The following resources can be used to assess students' knowledge and skills.

Unit 1 Resources:
    Selection Test A, pp. 122–124
    Selection Test B, pp. 125–127

Go Online
Assessment Students may use the **Self-test** to prepare for **Selection Test A** or **Selection Test B**.

Go Online **For:** An additional research activity
Research **Visit:** www.PHSchool.com
Web Code: epd-7105
For another research activity to extend students' learning, give students this Web Code.

Vocabulary Builder
Practice
1. tumultuous
2. implications
3. poignant

Adding Words to Your Vocabulary
Sample answers:

1. He became frustrated and tore his room apart, leaving it in a *tumultuous* state.
2. She knows the work will be hard in honors classes, but she is aware of these *implications* and welcomes the challenge.
3. Cecelia's *poignant* eulogy brought everyone in the funeral home to tears.

Writing
- To give students guidance for writing a journal entry, give them **Support for Writing** for "A White House Diary," p. 119 in *Unit 1 Resources.*
- To evaluate students' journal entries, use the Narration: Autobiographical Rubrics, pp. 43–44 in *General Resources.* In addition, you might place emphasis on how students use specific words and images.

Six Traits Focus

✔ Ideas	✔ Word Choice
Organization	Sentence Fluency
✔ Voice	Conventions

Writing and Grammar, Gold Level
Students will find guidance on autobiographical writing in Chapter 4.

Build Language Skills
Go to pp. 116–117 for vocabulary and grammar lessons and assessment practice.

Extend Your Learning
The **Support for Extend Your Learning** page (*Unit 1 Resources,* p. 120) provides guided note-taking opportunities to help students complete the Extend Your Learning activities.

105

Teaching notes for *Literary Analysis, Reading Skill,* and *Vocabulary Builder* for this selection begin on p. 96.

❸ Background
Alvarez's Two Nationalities

Rafael Trujillo was a brutal dictator who came to power in the Dominican Republic in 1930. He repressed human rights and ran the country as if it were his personal estate. As a result, a small but active opposition arose, Alvarez's father among them. He and his family fled the country twice. In 1960, the family returned to New York City. Trujillo was assassinated in 1961, but Alvarez's family remained in New York. Alvarez grew up in a city in which many nationalities thrived, including large numbers of Hispanics. More than half a million Dominicans live in New York today.

❹ Connecting to the Literature

• Model use of the expressive vocabulary students are asked to use with these examples:

1. Under Trujillo, *debate* about democracy versus dictatorship was prohibited.

2. In a democracy, citizens can *demonstrate* against government policies.

3. A dictator can *deprive* you of fundamental rights.

4. Trujillo tried to *dictate* how people lived.

5. Alvarez's father and many others decided to *rebel* against the dictator.

• Help students further develop their expressive vocabulary by providing these words: *academic, aspiration, comprehend,* and *interact.* Encourage students to use these words as they discuss the selection.

Go Online For additional informa-
Author Link tion about Julia Alvarez, have students type in the Web Code, then select *A* from the alphabet, and then select *Julia Alvarez.*

106

Autobiographical Essay

Build Understanding • *My English*

❸ Background

Alvarez's Two Nationalities Julia Alvarez, the author of "My English," was born in New York but grew up in the Dominican Republic, a small Caribbean nation. An independent state since 1844, the Dominican Republic has often struggled with foreign conquest, political unrest, and dictatorship. Alvarez's family was forced to return to New York in 1960 because her father had participated in a movement against the brutal Dominican dictator Raphael Trujillo.

❹ Connecting to the Literature

Reading/Writing Connection Julia Alvarez has experienced both dictatorship and democracy. Write three statements contrasting these two forms of government. Use at least three of the following words: *debate, demonstrate, deprive, dictate, rebel.*

Review

For **Literary Analysis, Reading Skill,** and **Vocabulary Builder,** see page 96.

READ MORE

by Julia Alvarez
How the Garcia Girls Lost Their Accents

Meet the Author

Julia **Alvarez** (b. 1950)

When her family fled the Dominican Republic and returned to New York, Julia Alvarez was ten years old, and Spanish was her primary language. Painfully aware of not fitting in, Julia took refuge in reading and making up stories. She says, "I landed, not in the United States, but in the English language. That became my new home."

"I Write to Find Out Who I Am." Alvarez attended Middlebury College, where she won several poetry awards. She later earned a master's degree in creative writing from Syracuse University. Alvarez says that writing is "a way to understand yourself." Her writing has been praised for its humor, sensitivity, and insight.

Fast Facts

▶ Julia Alvarez has established a farm in the Dominican Republic called Alta Gracia. The farm includes a school and its own line of coffee.

▶ One of her books, *In the Time of the Butterflies,* was made into a film starring Salma Hayek.

Go Online
Author Link

For: More about the author
Visit: www.PHSchool.com
Web Code: epe-9109

106 ■ Fiction and Nonfiction

Differentiated Instruction Solutions for All Learners

Support for Below-Level Students [L1, L2]

Unit 1 Resources
 Vocabulary Warm-up Word Lists, p. 128
 Vocabulary Warm-up Practice, p. 129
 Reading Warm-up A, p. 130
 Selection Test A, pp. 140–142

Graphic Organizer Transparencies
 Reading Skill Graphic Organizer
 Transparency B, p. 24

Support for English Learners [EL]

Unit 1 Resources
 Vocabulary Warm-up Word Lists, p. 128
 Vocabulary Warm-up Practice, p. 129
 Reading Warm-up A, p. 130

Listening to Literature Audio CD

❶
❷

MY ENGLISH

Julia Alvarez

Mami and Papi used to speak it when they had a secret they wanted to keep from us children. We lived then in the Dominican Republic, and the family as a whole spoke only Spanish at home, until my sisters and I started attending the Carol Morgan School, and we became a <u>bilingual</u> family. Spanish had its many tongues as well. There was the castellano[1] of Padre[2] Joaquín from Spain, whose lisp we all loved to imitate. Then the educated español my parents' families spoke, aunts and uncles who were always correcting us children, for we spent most of the day with the maids and so had picked up their "bad Spanish." Campesinas,[3] they spoke a lilting,

❸

---

1. **castellano** (cä´ stä yä´ nō) Spanish for "Castilian," the most widely spoken dialect of the Spanish language.
2. **Padre** (pä´ drä) "Father" (Spanish), a form of address for a Roman Catholic priest.
3. **Campesinas** (cäm pä sē´ näs) "simple rural women; peasant women" (Spanish).

Vocabulary Builder
bilingual (bī liŋ´ gwəl) *adj.* using two languages

My English ■ 107

---

❸ Critical Thinking
Voice and Autobiographical Writing

- Read the passage in which Alvarez describes the many "tongues" of Spanish she spoke as a child. Point out that these are like the dialects of English. **Ask** students to describe different dialects that they know.
  Possible response: Students may cite the manner of speaking of a native Bostonian, a native Midwesterner, a Texan, or a Southerner.

- Point out that Alvarez compares some of these versions of Spanish to the educated Spanish her family wanted her to speak. Guide a discussion of standard English versus colloquial English.

❹ Literature in Context

Social Studies Connection The Dominican Republic, which is about twice the size of the state of New Hampshire, occupies two-thirds of the island of Hispaniola. The nation has a history of non-representative government. The last dictator lost power in 1966, but questionable election practices compromised representative government. Since 1996, however, regular, competitive elections have brought the Dominican Republic a more representative government. Since democracy took hold in 1996, the Dominican Republic has enjoyed one of the fastest growing economies in the Caribbean region.

Connect to the Literature Tell students that the United States has a large Dominican population, partly because of people who have immigrated for political reasons.
Ask the Connect to the Literature question: Based on the distance between the Dominican Republic and the United States, why do you think knowing both Spanish and English would be useful?
Answer: The close proximity of the Dominican Republic to the United States has allowed a high volume of travel between the two countries. Knowledge of both Spanish and English would make communication for tourism, business dealings, and friendship much easier.

---

animated campuno,[4] ss swallowed, endings chopped off, funny turns of phrases. This campuno was my true mother tongue, not the Spanish of Calderón de la Barca or Cervantes or even Neruda,[5] but of Chucha and Iluminada and Gladys and Ursulina from Juncalito and Licey and Boca de Yuma and San Juan de la Maguana.[6] Those women yakked as they cooked, they storytold, they gossiped, they sang—boleros, merengues, canciones, salves.[7] Theirs were the voices that belonged to the rain and the wind and the teeny, teeny stars even a small child could blot out with her thumb.

Besides all these versions of Spanish, every once in a while another strange tongue emerged from my papi's mouth or my mami's lips. What I first recognized was not a language, but a tone of voice, serious, urgent, something important and top secret being said, some uncle in trouble, someone divorcing, someone dead. *Say it in English so the children won't understand.* I would listen, straining to understand, thinking that this was not a different language but just another and harder version of Spanish. *Say it in English so the children won't understand.* From the beginning, English was the sound of worry and secrets, the sound of being left out.

I could make no sense of this "harder Spanish," and so I tried by other means to find out what was going on. I knew my mother's face by heart. When the little lines on the corners of her eyes crinkled, she was amused. When her nostrils flared and she bit her lips, she was trying hard not to laugh. She held her head down, eyes glancing up, when she thought I was lying. Whenever she spoke that gibberish English, I translated the general content by watching the Spanish expressions on her face.

Soon, I began to learn more English, at the Carol Morgan School. That is, when I had stopped gawking. The teacher and some of the American children had the strangest coloration: light hair, light eyes, light skin, as if Ursulina had soaked them in bleach too long,

---

4. **campuno** (cäm pōō′nō) Spanish dialect spoken in rural areas of the Dominican Republic.
5. **Calderón de la Barca** (cäl de rôn′ dä lä bär′ cä) . . . **Cervantes** (ser vän′ tes) . . . **Neruda** (nä rōō′ dä) important literary figures.
6. **Juncalito** (hōōn cä le′ tō) . . . **Licey** . . . **Boca de Yuma** (bō′ cä dä yōō′ mä) . . . **San Juan de la Maguana** (sän hwän′ dä lä mä gwä′ nä) small rural villages in the Dominican Republic.
7. **boleros** (bō ler′ ōs) . . . **merengues** (mə reŋ′ gäs) . . . **canciones** (cän sē ō′ nes) . . . **salves** (säl′ ves) Spanish and Latin American songs and dances.

108 ■ *Fiction and Nonfiction*

---

❹ Literature in Context

Social Studies Connection

The Dominican Republic The Dominican Republic occupies the eastern portion of the Caribbean island of Hispaniola, which it shares with the Republic of Haiti. Located about 600 miles southeast of Florida, this area was one of the landing points of Christopher Columbus's first voyage in 1492. The dominant language and culture are Spanish.

Connect to the Literature

Based on the distance between the Dominican Republic and the United States, why do you think knowing both Spanish and English would be useful?

Vocabulary Development

Expressive Vocabulary

As students discuss the Dominican Republic and information in the Literature in Context, encourage them to use the expressive vocabulary words introduced on p. 106. Use questions like the following to stimulate discussion. Tell students to use the expressive words in responding to each question.

1. Why might some Dominicans in the past have wanted to *rebel* against their government?

2. What would have been the subject of *debates* in the country during the early 1990s?

3. How did unfair election results *deprive* Dominicans of basic rights?

4. How could the government *dictate* economic policies?

5. How can you *demonstrate* that democracy is good for the Dominican Republic?

to' deteñio.[8] I did have some blond cousins, but they had deeply tanned skin, and as they grew older, their hair darkened, so their earlier paleness seemed a phase of their acquiring normal color. Just as strange was the little girl in my reader who had a *cat* and a *dog*, that looked just like un gatito y un perrito. Her mami was *Mother* and her papi *Father*. Why have a whole new language for school and for books with a teacher who could speak it teaching you double the amount of words you really needed?

Butter, butter, butter, butter. All day, one English word that had particularly struck me would go round and round in my mouth and weave through all the Spanish in my head until by the end of the day, the word did sound like just another Spanish word. And so I would say, "Mami, please pass la mantequilla." She would scowl and say in English, "I'm sorry, I don't understand. But would you be needing some butter on your bread?"

Why my parents didn't first educate us in our native language by enrolling us in a Dominican school, I don't know. Part of it was that Mami's family had a tradition of sending the boys to the States to boarding school and college, and she had been one of the first girls to be allowed to join her brothers. At Abbot Academy,[9] whose school song was our lullaby as babies ("Although Columbus and Cabot[10] never heard of Abbot, it's quite the place for you and me"), she had become quite Americanized. It was very important, she kept saying, that we learn our English. She always used the possessive pronoun: *your* English, an inheritance we had come into and must wisely use. Unfortunately, my English became all mixed up with our Spanish.

Mix-up, or what's now called Spanglish, was the language we spoke for several years. There wasn't a sentence that wasn't colonized by an English word. At school, a Spanish word would suddenly slide into my English like someone butting into line. Teacher, whose face I was learning to read as minutely as my mother's, would scowl but no smile played on her lips. Her pale skin made her strange <u>countenance</u> hard to read, so that I often misjudged how much I could get away with. Whenever I made a mistake, Teacher would shake her head slowly, "In English, YU-LEE-AH, there's no such word as *columpio.* Do you mean a *swing?*"

I would bow my head, humiliated by the smiles and snickers of the American children around me. I grew insecure about Spanish. My native tongue was not quite as good as English, as if words like

---

8. **to' deteñio** (tō dā tān yē' ō) "all washed out" or "completely colorless" (Spanish).
9. **Abbot Academy** boarding school for girls in Andover, Massachusetts; merged in 1973 with the neighboring boys' school, Phillips Academy.
10. **Cabot** (1450?–1498?) (kab' ət) John Cabot, Italian explorer who sailed in the service of England and discovered the coast of North America in 1497.

Literary Analysis
Voice and Autobiographical Writing Which words and phrases here convey the writer's uncertainty and unwillingness about learning English?

Vocabulary Builder
countenance (koun′t′n əns) *n.* face

❻ ✓ **Reading Check**

Which language did Alvarez learn to speak first—English or Spanish?

---

❺ **Literary Analysis**
Voice and Autobiographical Writing

• Remind students that voice is how the writer sounds and that it is created by word choice, attitude, and sentence length and structure.

• **Ask** students to respond to the Literary Analysis question: Which words and phrases in this paragraph convey the writer's attitude of uncertainty and unwillingness about learning English?
Answer: Alvarez uses words like *strangest* and *strange,* suggesting that she was not comfortable with the other students and her books. She also writes about "a whole new language" that is just "for school and for books," indicating that she did not see why she needed to learn English, especially when her teacher taught her "double the amount of words" she needed to know.

• Point out to students that Alvarez uses a wide range of sentence lengths and structures. Ask volunteers to give examples. Then **ask** what this variety indicates about voice.
Possible response: It indicates that Alvarez is confident and at ease with English.

❻ **Reading Check**

Answer: Alvarez learned to speak Spanish first.

Differentiated Instruction   Solutions for All Learners

Strategy for Special Needs Students
This selection can be especially challenging for some students due to the difficulty of the language in general and the intermingling of Spanish words and phrases. Even with footnoted translations, these terms can pose obstacles to understanding. You may want to preview difficult words prior to students reading each page. As students read, have them pause for sentences containing Spanish text or puzzling English words, and help them paraphrase the meaning.

Strategy for Advanced Readers
Explain to students that part of Alvarez's voice is displayed through humor. Have students go through the selection and identify specific passages where she uses humor to show her voice. Ask students how this reflects Alvarez's attitude toward her subject.

- Read aloud the bracketed passage. Have students translate the idioms and slang, and invite them to give other examples. Discuss how idioms, slang, and various colloquial expressions can pose an extra challenge to new speakers of English. Explain that most of these phrases make no sense if a reader or listener tries to decode them word by word. Also point out that most of them cannot be found in a standard dictionary.

- **Ask** students how an English learner could find out the meaning of these terms.
  Possible response: An English learner could ask an English-speaker to define the terms.

- **Ask** students to respond to the Literary Analysis question: How would you describe the author's voice based on her examples of idiomatic expressions?
  Possible response: Her voice is relaxed and playful.

8 Critical Viewing

Possible response: She would have felt overwhelmed and scared.

columpio were illegal immigrants trying to cross a border into another language. But Teacher's discerning grammar-and-vocabulary-patrol ears could tell and send them back.

Soon, I was talking up an English storm. "Did you eat English parrot?" my grandfather asked one Sunday. I had just enlisted yet one more patient servant to listen to my rendition of "Peter Piper picked a peck of pickled peppers" at breakneck pace. "Huh?" I asked impolitely in English, putting him in his place. *Cat got your tongue? No big deal! So there! Take that! Holy Toledo!* (Our teacher's favorite "curse word.") *Go jump in the lake! Really dumb. Golly. Gosh.* Slang, clichés, sayings, hotshot language that our teacher called, ponderously, idiomatic expressions. Riddles, jokes, puns, conundrums. *What is yellow and goes click-click? Why did the chicken cross the road? See you later, alligator.* How wonderful to call someone an alligator and not be scolded for being disrespectful. In fact, they were supposed to say back, *In a while, crocodile.*

There was also a neat little trick I wanted to try on an English-speaking adult at home. I had learned it from Elizabeth, my smart-alecky friend in fourth grade, whom I alternately worshiped and resented. I'd ask her a question that required an explanation, and she'd answer, "Because . . ." "Elizabeth, how come you didn't go to Isabel's birthday party?" "Because . . ." "Why didn't you put your name in your reader?" "Because . . ." I thought that such a cool way to get around having to come up with answers. So, I practiced saying it under my breath, planning for the day I could use it on an unsuspecting English-speaking adult.

One Sunday at our extended family dinner, my grandfather sat down at the children's table to chat with us. He was famous, in fact, for the way he could carry on adult conversations with his grandchildren. He often spoke to us in English so that we could practice speaking it outside the classroom. He was a Cornell[11] man, a United Nations representative from our country. He gave speeches in English. Perfect English, my mother's phrase. That Sunday, he asked me a question. I can't even remember what it was because I wasn't really listening but lying in wait for my chance. "Because . . .," I answered him. Papito waited a second for the rest of my sentence and then gave me a thumbnail grammar lesson, "*Because* has to be followed by a clause."

"Why's that?" I asked, nonplussed.[12]

"Because," he winked. "Just because."

---

11. **Cornell** Cornell University in Ithaca, New York.
12. **nonplussed** (nän plüst′) *v.* confused; baffled

8 ▶ Critical Viewing
How do you think Julia Alvarez would have felt encountering a bustling crowd like this one for the first time? **[Speculate]**

A beginning wordsmith, I had so much left to learn; sometimes it was disheartening. Once Tío[13] Gus, the family intellectual, put a speck of salt on my grandparents' big dining table during Sunday dinner. He said, "Imagine this whole table is the human brain. Then this teensy grain is all we ever use of our intelligence!" He enumerated geniuses who had perhaps used two grains, maybe three: Einstein, Michelangelo, da Vinci, Beethoven. We children believed him. It was the kind of impossible fact we thrived on, proving as it did that the world out there was not drastically different from the one we were making up in our heads.

Later, at home, Mami said that you had to take what her younger brother said "with a grain of salt." I thought she was still referring to Tío Gus's demonstration, and I tried to puzzle out what she was saying. Finally, I asked what she meant. "Taking what someone says with a grain of salt is an idiomatic expression in English," she explained. It was pure voodoo is what it was—what later I learned poetry could also do: a grain of salt could symbolize both the human brain and a condiment for human nonsense. And it could be itself, too: a grain of salt to flavor a bland plate of American food.

When we arrived in New York, I was shocked. A country where everyone spoke English! These people must be smarter, I thought. Maids, waiters, taxi drivers, doormen, bums on the street, all spoke this difficult language. It took some time before I understood that Americans were not necessarily a smarter, superior race. It was as

13. **Tío** (tē′ ō) "Uncle" (Spanish).

My English ■ 111

Reading Skill
Author's Purpose
Why do you think the writer includes these details about Mami's comments?

⑩ Reading Check

To what city does Alvarez's family relocate?

❾ Reading Skill
Author's Purpose

• Project **Reading Skill Graphic Organizer A,** (*Graphic Organizer Transparencies,* p. 22), and discuss the scene at the dinner table in which Tio Gus gives his demonstration with a grain of salt. Then read aloud the scene with Mami. Have students suggest details to add to the organizer. Then **ask** students the Reading Skill question: Why do you think the writer includes these details about Mami's comments? **Answer:** It illustrates Alvarez's learning process and her growing understanding of the power of words.

• Add students' comments on the significance of the details to the organizer. Then point out that this explains Alvarez's purpose in writing this scene—to show how learning English is a process that does not happen quickly.

⑩ Reading Check

Answer: The Alvarez family relocates to New York City.

Differentiated
Instruction   Solutions for All Learners

Enrichment for Gifted/Talented Students
There are several nicely constructed scenes with lively language on this page and in other portions of "My English" that lend themselves to a dramatic reading or dialogue. Examples include Alvarez's English storm at the top of p. 110, her "Because . . ." dialogue on the same page, and the "grain of salt" conversation on p. 111.

Invite students to work individually or in pairs and dramatize one of these scenes. Tell them to practice their scene thoroughly, using gestures and facial expressions to enliven the presentation. You might suggest they practice in teams so that students can critique each other's performance. Then have them perform their scenes for the class.

⓫ Critical Viewing

Possible response: The towering buildings that close in on all sides can be intimidating, causing a person to feel small and insignificant. Those same buildings and the welcoming Statue of Liberty also suggest limitless opportunities and new things to do and see.

⓬ Literary Analysis
Voice and Autobiographical Writing

• Read the first four sentences of the paragraph aloud. Call students' attention to Alvarez's comment that she began to hear English not as English "but as sense." Then **ask** students to compare this attitude with Alvarez's attitude when she first began to learn English.
Answer: At first she was insecure and intimidated. Now she has developed skill and confidence.

• **Ask** students in what situations she loses her confidence.
Answer: She loses her confidence when she hears a strong accent or when "the priest droned his sermon."

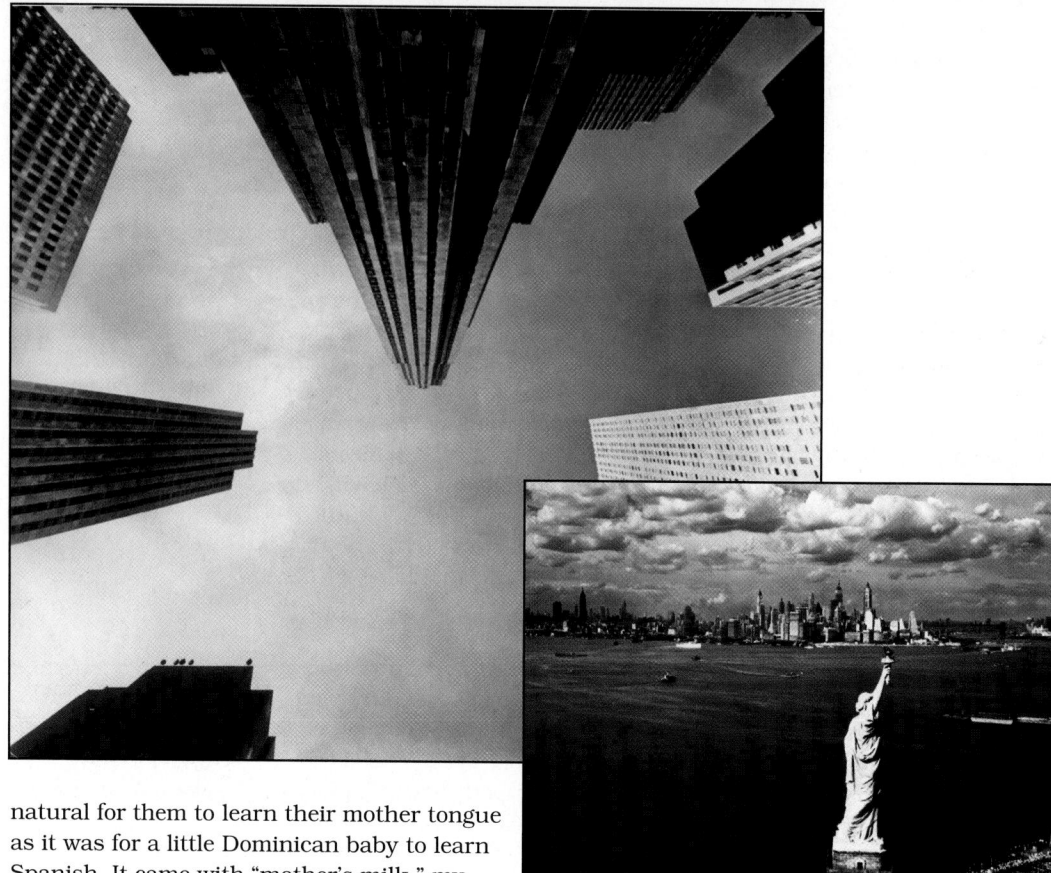

natural for them to learn their mother tongue as it was for a little Dominican baby to learn Spanish. It came with "mother's milk," my mother explained, and for a while I thought a mother tongue was a mother tongue because you got it from your mother's milk along with proteins and vitamins.

Soon it wasn't so strange that everyone was speaking in English instead of Spanish. I learned not to hear it as English, but as sense. I no longer strained to understand, I understood. I relaxed in this second language. Only when someone with a heavy southern or British accent spoke in a movie, or at church when the priest ⓬ droned his sermon—only then did I experience that little catch of anxiety. I worried that I would not be able to understand, that I wouldn't be able to "keep up" with the voice speaking in this acquired language. I would be like those people from the Bible we had studied in religion class, whom I imagined standing at the foot of an enormous tower[14] that looked just like the skyscrapers

---

14. enormous tower a reference to the Tower of Babel in Genesis 11:1–9. According to Genesis, early Babylonians tried to build a tower to heaven, but they were thwarted when God caused them to speak many languages rather than one.

112 ■ Fiction and Nonfiction

⓫ ▲ **Critical Viewing** Based on these photographs, why do you think Alvarez might have found New York to be both intimidating and exciting? **[Analyze]**

Vocabulary Development

Vocabulary Knowledge Rating
When students have completed reading and discussing "My English," have them take out their **Vocabulary Knowledge Rating Chart** for this selection. Read the words aloud once more and have students rate their knowledge of the words again in the After Reading column. Clarify any words that are still problematic. Have students write their own definition and example or sentence in the appropriate column. Then have students complete the **Vocabulary Builder Practice** activities on p. 115. Encourage students to use the words in further discussion and written work about this selection. Remind them that they will be accountable for these words on the Selection Test.

⑫ around me. They had been punished for their pride by being made to speak different languages so that they didn't understand what anyone was saying.

But at the foot of those towering New York skyscrapers, I began to understand more and more—not less and less—English. In sixth grade, I had one of the first in a lucky line of great English teachers who began to nurture in me a love of language, a love that had been there since my childhood of listening closely to words. Sister Maria Generosa did not make our class <u>interminably</u> diagram sentences from a workbook or learn a catechism[15] of grammar rules. Instead, she asked us to write little stories imagining we were snowflakes, birds, pianos, a stone in the pavement, a star in the sky. What would it feel like to be a flower with roots in the ground? If the clouds could talk, what would they say? She had an expressive, dreamy look that was accentuated by the wimple[16] that framed her face.

⑬ Supposing, just supposing . . . My mind would take off, soaring into possibilities, a flower with roots, a star in the sky, a cloud full of sad, sad tears, a piano crying out each time its back was tapped, music only to our ears.

Sister Maria stood at the chalkboard. Her chalk was always snapping in two because she wrote with such energy, her whole habit[17] shaking with the swing of her arm, her hand tap-tap-tapping on the board. "Here's a simple sentence: 'The snow fell.'" Sister pointed with her chalk, her eyebrows lifted, her wimple poked up. Sometimes I could see wisps of gray hair that strayed from under her headdress. "But watch what happens if we put an adverb at the beginning and a prepositional phrase at the end: 'Gently, the snow fell on the bare hills.'"

I thought about the snow. I saw how it might fall on the hills, tapping lightly on the bare branches of trees. Softly, it would fall on the cold, bare fields. On toys children had left out in the yard, and on cars and on little birds and on people out late walking on the streets. Sister Marie filled the chalkboard with snowy print, on and on, handling and shaping and moving the language, scribbling all over the board until English, those verbal gadgets, those tricks and turns of phrases, those little fixed units and counters, became a charged, fluid mass that carried me in its great fluent waves, rolling and moving onward, to deposit me on the shores of my new homeland. I was no longer a foreigner with no ground to stand on. I had landed in the English language.

---

15. **catechism** (kat′ə kiz′ əm) *n.* short book written in question-and-answer format.
16. **wimple** (wim′ pəl) *n.* cloth worn around the head, neck, and chin by some nuns.
17. **habit** (hab′ it) *n.* robe or dress worn by some nuns.

Vocabulary Builder
interminably (in tʉr′ mi nə blē) *adv.* endlessly

Literary Analysis
Voice and Autobiographical Writing Which words and phrases in this paragraph give the author's voice a poetic quality?

---

⑬ Literary Analysis
Voice and Autobiographical Writing

- Read aloud the bracketed passage. Then **ask** students to respond to the Literary Analysis question: Which words and phrases in this paragraph give the author's voice a poetic quality?
  Answer: Many of the words and phrases sound poetic, including "soaring into possibilities," "a flower with roots, a star in the sky, a cloud full of sad, sad tears, a piano crying," and "music only to our ears."

- Point out that Alvarez's change to a poetic voice has come near the end of her narrative. She began the narrative describing her early years as a poor and awkward speaker of English. Writing in a poetic voice would have conflicted with the situation she was describing. Now, as she is describing her grasp of the language, the poetic voice works to emphasize how she has become entranced in the language and is on her way to becoming a writer.

▶ **Monitor Progress:** Allow students to work in pairs. Ask each pair to look at an assigned paragraph somewhere in "My English" and to list several words or phrases to describe Alvarez's voice. As students present their responses, assess their understanding of voice.

▶ **Reteach:** Review the characteristics of voice. Then show students **Literary Analysis Graphic Organizer B** (*Graphic Organizer Transparencies,* p. 28) and discuss how the skill is applied. Then talk students through an analysis of voice in another paragraph of "My English."

Concept Connector

Anticipation Guide
Have students return to their **Anticipation Guides** and respond to the statements again in the After Reading column. Then, lead a class discussion, probing for what students have learned that confirms or invalidates each statement.

Connecting to the Literature
Have students compare the sentences they wrote before reading with their thoughts about democracies and dictatorships after reading "My English." Ask them to explain whether their thoughts have changed and, if so, how.

Reading Skill Graphic Organizer
Ask students to review the graphic organizers they completed to identify the author's purpose while reading. Show them **Reading Skill Graphic Organizer B** (*Graphic Organizer Transparencies,* p. 24) as an example. Then have students share the graphic organizers they did and the author's purposes that they identified.

Apply the Skills

My English

Thinking About the Selection

1. **Respond:** After reading her account of her early life, what question would you like to ask Julia Alvarez? Explain.
2. **(a) Recall:** When Alvarez was young, at what times did her parents speak English at home? **(b) Infer:** Why do you think Alvarez says that English was the "sound of being left out"?
3. **(a) Recall:** What method did Sister Maria Generosa use to teach English? **(b) Compare and Contrast:** How does this method differ from the way Alvarez was taught at the Carol Morgan School? **(c) Assess:** Which method does Alvarez prefer? Why?
4. **Evaluate:** How well do you think Alvarez succeeds in portraying the evolution of her relationship with the English language? Explain.

Literary Analysis

5. **(a)** Complete a chart like the one shown to find examples of Alvarez's **word choice**, **attitude**, and **sentence structure**.

VOICE		
Word Choice	Attitude	Sentence Structure

    (b) Using examples from your chart, describe Alvarez's **voice** in this work of nonfiction.
6. **(a)** What details about learning English are emphasized in Julia Alvarez's **autobiographical writing?** **(b)** Why would Alvarez notice these details more than someone else might? **(c)** What are two other details that reflect Alvarez's individual perspective on the English language?

Reading Skill

7. Review the notes you made in your **preview** of "My English." Which of your ideas about the **author's purpose** were confirmed as you read the selection? Which were not? Explain.
8. **(a)** What general purpose do you think Alvarez had in writing this essay? Explain. **(b)** What more specific purpose or purposes do you think she had for writing? Support your answer with details from the essay.

114 ■ *Fiction and Nonfiction*

QuickReview

Essay at a Glance
Julia Alvarez reflects on her changing relationship with the English language.

Go Online
Assessment
For: Self-test
Visit: www.PHSchool.com
Web Code: epa-6109

Autobiographical Writing: literary works in which an author tells all or part of his or her life's story

Voice: the way a writer "sounds" or "speaks" on the page

Author's Purpose: a writer's main reason for writing a literary work

---

Answers

1. **Possible response:** How did you become a successful writer? This question would fill the gap between her grasp of the English language and her success as a writer.

2. (a) Alvarez's parents used English when they were having discussions that were inappropriate for children to hear. (b) English kept her out of their conversation.

3. (a) Sister Generosa had students add colorful details to sentences and write creative stories. (b) The teacher at Carol Morgan School emphasized vocabulary and grammar. (c) Alvarez preferred Sister Generosa's method because it appealed to her creative side and inspired her.

4. **Possible response:** She does an excellent job because she shows her relationship with English in different periods of her life.

5. (a) **Sample response: Word Choice:** "a strange tongue emerged from my papi's mouth or my mami's lips"; **Attitude:** "Supposing, just supposing . . . My mind would take off, soaring into possibilities. . . ."; **Sentence Structure:** I thought about the snow. I saw how it might fall on the hills, tapping light only on the bare branches of trees."

   Another sample answer can be found on **Literary Analysis Graphic Organizer B,** p. 28 in *Graphic Organizer Transparencies.*

   (b) **Possible response:** Alvarez's voice is playful when she describes the "strange tongue" that came from my "papi's mouth." It is exultant, as when she describes her mind "soaring into possibilities." It is thoughtful, as when she describes thinking about the snow.

6. (a) Alvarez stresses that learning English is a process that grows into an automatic understanding of the language. (b) **Possible response:** She has a love for language that would make her focus on the small details in learning English and would also draw her to a writing career. (c) **Possible response:** She grew up in a bilingual household. Despite understanding the language, she

still had occasional fears of comprehension.

7. **Possible response:** Students may have expected Alvarez to describe or teach English.

8. (a) Her purpose is to entertain and to inform. (b) **Possible response:** She wants readers to learn compassion for those who do not yet know English well.

Vocabulary Builder

Practice **Analogies** show the relationships between pairs of words. To complete each analogy, use a word from the "My English" vocabulary list on page 96. For each case, your choice should create a word pair that matches the relationship between the first two words.

1. happily : sadly :: _____ : quickly

2. bipartisan : party :: _____ : language

3. frame : photograph :: _____ : expression

Adding Words to Your Vocabulary A word's **denotation** is its direct, literal meaning. A word's **connotations** are the ideas associated with it. For example, *eternally* and *interminably* share a similar denotative meaning. However, their connotative meanings are very different. Using a dictionary and a thesaurus, investigate the connotations of each word. Then, use each word in a sentence that illustrates its specific connotation. (For more on using a dictionary and a thesaurus, see pages R6–7.)

Writing

In "My English," Julia Alvarez writes about her experience with the English language—a subject of great importance to her. Using her work as inspiration, write a **journal entry** on a subject of importance to you. As you prepare to write, consider the following questions:

• Has this subject always been important to you? Why or why not?

• How does this subject influence your outlook on the world?

For *Grammar, Vocabulary,* and *Assessment,* see **Build Language Skills,** pages 116–117

Extend Your Learning

Listening and Speaking With three or four classmates, deliver a **radio broadcast** that advertises a foreign-language school. Use Alvarez's experience with English to guide your shaping of the school's message.

• As you work together to write a script, evaluate your word choices to make sure they suit your audience and purpose.

• Speak in an enthusiastic tone that generates interest in the school.

Research and Technology Prepare a list of at least three key points and the **introduction for a multimedia presentation** on immigration to the United States since 1800. Discuss the reasons people left their home countries and what they sought in America.

Assessment Resources

The following resources can be used to assess students' knowledge and skills.

Unit 1 Resources:
    Selection Test A, pp. 140–142
    Selection Test B, pp. 143–145

 Go Online
—Assessment— Students may use the **Self-test** to prepare for **Selection Test A** or **Selection Test B.**

Go Online
—Research—
For: An additional research activity
Visit: www.PHSchool.com
Web Code: epd-7106
For another research activity to extend students' learning, give students this Web Code.

Vocabulary Builder
Practice

1. interminably

2. bilingual

3. countenance

Adding Words to Your Vocabulary
Sample answers:

1. The awards show went on *interminably* and put half of the audience to sleep.

2. My mother rattled off her grocery list in English and then in Chinese, proving to my friends that she was *bilingual.*

3. Her *countenance* revealed her excitement over her upcoming vacation.

Writing

• To give students guidance for writing a journal entry, give them **Support for Writing** for "My English," p. 135, in *Unit 1 Resources.*

• To evaluate students' journal entries, use the Narration: Autobiographical Narrative rubrics, pp. 43–44 in *General Resources.* In addition, you might place emphasis on using only significant details.

Six Traits Focus

✔	Ideas	✔	Word Choice
	Organization		Sentence Fluency
✔	Voice		Conventions

WG Writing and Grammar, Gold Level
Students will find guidance on autobiographical writing in Chapter 4.

Build Language Skills
Go to pp. 116–117 for vocabulary and grammar lessons and assessment practice.

Extend Your Learning
The Support for Extend Your Learning page (*Unit 1 Resources,* p. 136) provides guided note-taking opportunities to help students complete the Extend Your Learning activities.

115

Vocabulary Skill

- Introduce the combining form *tri-*. Ask students to brainstorm for words that begin with *tri-* and mean "three."
  Possible Answers: *triple, triplets, triumvirate, triceps, triangle, triathlon.*

- Have students complete the Practice activity on this page.

Possible Answers

1. *Triplicate* comes from the Latin *triplicatus,* which means "to triple." Today it means "three identical versions of something."

2. *Trilogy* comes from the Greek *trilogia,* which means "a series of three related tragedies." Today it means "a group of three dramatic or literary works related in subject or theme."

3. *Triple* comes from the Latin *tri-,* which means "three." Today, *triple* means "consisting of three parts or three times as many."

4. *Via* comes from the Latin *via,* which means "road." Today, *via* means "by way of."

5. *Vital* comes from the Latin *vitalis,* meaning "of life," and from *vita,* meaning "life." Today, *vital* means "relating to a characteristic of life or necessary for life."

Grammar Lesson

- Point out that personal pronouns include *I, me, my, mine, we, us, our, ours, you, your, yours, he, she, him, her, his, hers, it, its, they, them, their,* and *theirs.*

- Point out that reflexive pronouns add *-self* or *-selves* to the following personal pronouns: *my, our, your, him, her, it, them.*

Answers

1. You (p), yourself (r)
2. They (p), themselves (r)
3. themselves (r)
4. We (p), ourselves(r)
5. He (p), himself (r)

Writing Application

Check students' papers to make sure that they contain at least two reflexive pronouns as well as personal pronouns.

Build Language Skills

from *A White House Diary* • *My English*

Vocabulary Skill

Word Origins The etymology of a word is both its origin and the history of how the word has changed. Words from other languages were adapted to fit the English-speaking culture, often by adding to the root as new inventions and ways of life demanded. For example, the Latin combining form *-tri-* meant "three" *or* "the crossroads or common place." Over the years, the word *trivial* has changed to mean "not important—common."

Practice Explain the origin of the underlined words.

1. Would you please submit that request in <u>triplicate</u>?
2. The plays were written as a <u>trilogy</u>.
3. The term <u>Triple</u> Alliance is used several times in history.
4. We are going to the West <u>via</u> Chicago.
5. We need to discuss a matter of <u>vital</u> importance.

Grammar Lesson

Personal and Reflexive Pronouns A **pronoun** is a word that stands for a noun or for a word that takes the place of a noun. A **personal pronoun** refers to the person speaking (first person), the person spoken to (second person), or the person or thing spoken about (third person). **Reflexive pronouns** end in *-self* or *-selves* and are used to indicate that someone or something performs an action to, for, or upon itself.

MorePractice

For more practice with personal and reflexive pronouns, see the Grammar Handbook, p. R39.

	First Person	Second Person	Third Person
Personal Pronouns	**Singular:** I, me, my, mine **Plural:** we, us, our, ours	**Singular:** you, your, yours **Plural:** you, your, yours	**Singular:** he, she, him, her, his, hers, it, its **Plural:** they, them, their, theirs
Reflexive Pronouns	**Singular:** myself **Plural:** ourselves	**Singular:** yourself **Plural:** yourselves	**Singular:** himself, herself, itself **Plural:** themselves

Practice Identify the pronouns in each of the following items, and indicate whether each pronoun is personal or reflexive. Recast the sentence without the reflexive pronoun.

1. You will have to learn the new system yourself.
2. They found themselves amused by the speaker's anecdotes.
3. Some fish feed themselves through a long tube.
4. We went to the library to study by ourselves.
5. He busied himself in the garden.

W̶G̶ Prentice Hall Writing and Grammar Connection: Chapter 16, Section 2

116 ■ *Fiction and Nonfiction*

Teaching Resources

The following resources can be used to enrich or extend the instruction for Build Language Skills.

Unit 1 Resources
   Build Language Skills: Vocabulary Skill: The Latin combining form *tri-*, p. 138
   Build Grammar Skills: Personal and Reflexive Pronouns, p. 139

Assessment Practice

Reading Skill: Author's Purpose

Directions: *Read about Lincoln. Then, answer the questions.*

Between the days in which he crawled as a baby on the dirt floor of a Kentucky cabin, and the time when he gave his final breath in Washington, he packed a rich life with work, thought, laughter, tears, hate, love.

With vast reservoirs of the comic and the droll, and notwithstanding a mastery of mirth and nonsense, he delivered a volume of addresses and letters of terrible and serious appeal, with import beyond his own day. . . .

Perhaps no human clay pot has held more laughter and tears.
—from *A Lincoln Preface* by Carl Sandburg

1. What is the purpose of the passage?
   A to persuade readers that Lincoln did not deserve his reputation
   B to make readers admire Lincoln's humor
   C to win favor with President Lincoln
   D to make readers see Lincoln as both human and remarkable

2. Sandburg's likely purpose for including the phrase "filled with laughter and tears" is to
   A make readers pity Lincoln.
   B comment on the tragedy of the Civil War.
   C emphasize Lincoln's outstanding qualities.
   D contrast Lincoln with other leaders.

3. What is a possible reason that Sandburg uses contrasting phrases?
   A to emphasize Lincoln's serious side
   B to show contrasts with the author's personality
   C to emphasize Lincoln's sense of humor
   D to reinforce the contrasts in Lincoln's life

4. The line containing "he delivered a volume . . ." serves to
   A remind the reader that Lincoln was an educated person.
   B remind the reader that Lincoln's ideas impacted the future.
   C reassure the reader that this is the Lincoln who gave the Gettysburg address.
   D assure the reader that the work is serious.

Timed Writing: Explanation [Critical Stance]

Review the excerpt from *A White House Diary* or "My English." Write an explanation of the values that the author reveals in her work. Use specifics from the text to support your points. **(20 minutes)**

Writing Workshop: *Work in Progress*

Problem-Solution Essay
Think of issues that concern people in your school or community. Jot down five problems you think can be solved. Choose one problem and write a statement of a possible solution. Put these notes in your writing folder.

Build Language Skills ■ *117*

Reading: Author's Purpose
1. D
2. C
3. D
4. B

Timed Writing

- Tell students that when writing a critical stance, they should include a summary or description of the literary work under discussion.

- Make sure students understand that these summaries should be brief, leaving the bulk of the essay for their own ideas.

- Remind students that their opinions must be supported with details from the work.

- Assess students' critical stances by reviewing the clarity of their explanations and the thoroughness of their support.

- Suggest that students organize their time to give 5 minutes to reviewing the essays and planning, 10 minutes to writing, and 5 minutes to revising and editing.

Writing Workshop
Work in Progress

Problem-Solution Essay

- Have students go to their portfolios and take out the work they have completed so far on this assignment.

- Remind students that this work may be used in the problem-solution essay they will write in the **Writing Workshop** at the end of Part 2.

- Have students reflect on the cause of the problem and brainstorm for possible solutions.

- Tell students to consider the consequences of their solution before deciding on it.

- When students have completed this activity, have them keep it in their portfolios. They will use it as they continue this Work in Progress.

Students will

1. understand and explain the use of Spanish/English dictionaries.
2. read entries in a Spanish/English dictionary.

See TeacherExpress™/Lesson View for a detailed lesson plan for Reading Informational Materials.

About Spanish/English Dictionaries

- Have students read "About Spanish/English Dictionaries."

- Discuss that a Spanish/English Dictionary is an example of a bilingual dictionary since it presents words and definitions in two languages.

- Have students share situations where they used, or could have used, a bilingual dictionary. Ask a volunteer who has used one to describe how the dictionary was helpful and whether or not it was simple to use.

Reading Skill
Recognizing Organizational Features of Printed Text

- Remind students that every type of text they read has special features that help readers understand. Point out that some common features include headings, tables of contents, and chapters.

- Review with students the "Questions to Ask About Organizational Features" chart. As a group, read the questions in the chart. Use this instructional page as an example text. After each question in the chart, ask a volunteer for an answer.

- Explain that Spanish/English dictionaries will include terminology specific to discussions about Spanish. Point out that even if some of the terminology is unfamiliar, students will still be able to use the dictionary for basic word meanings.

Spanish/English Dictionaries

In Part 2, you are learning how to determine the author's purpose while reading literature. This skill is also useful when reading informational texts, such as product user guides and dictionaries. In these types of texts, organizational features are designed for various purposes, such as calling attention to important text elements. If you read "My English" by Julia Alvarez, you may have wanted to use a Spanish/English dictionary.

About Spanish/English Dictionaries

Spanish/English dictionaries provide detailed information that can help you translate information from one language into the other. Like other bilingual dictionaries, Spanish/English dictionaries often include these features:

- Word definitions in both languages
- Parts of speech
- Gender forms
- Examples of how the word is used
- Examples of idioms, expressions like "hit the nail on the head," whose meanings differ from the meanings of the individual words
- Pronunciation key

Reading Skill

Before using a bilingual dictionary, you may want to review the user guide in the front of the book. The user guide will help you **recognize the organizational features of the text,** including headings, keywords, labels, and special notes to readers. Organizational features identify and emphasize specific pieces of information. The questions in the box shown can help you locate and understand labels and features of the user guide.

> ### Questions to Ask About Organizational Features
>
> ☐ What are the main headings on the page?
>
> ☐ How is certain information labeled or highlighted?
>
> ☐ What features have been pointed out? Why?
>
> ☐ What information is provided in the key?
>
> ☐ Are there special notes on the page?

Differentiated
Instruction   Solutions for All Learners

Reading Support
Give students reading support with the appropriate version of the *Reader's Notebooks:*

Reader's Notebook, [L2]

Reader's Notebook: Adapted Version, [L1]

Reader's Notebook: English Learner's Version, [EL]

Spanish-English Dictionary User Guide

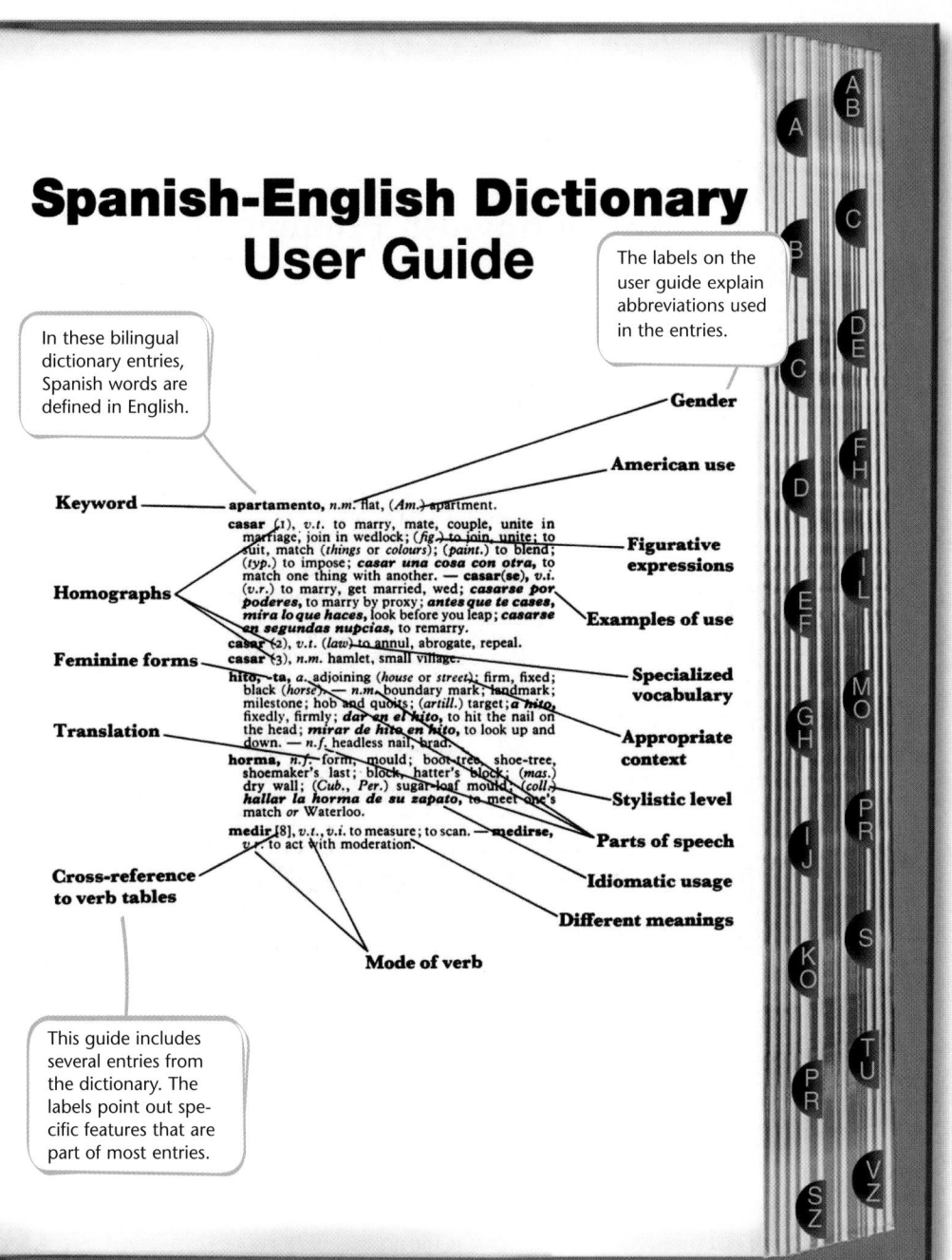

In these bilingual dictionary entries, Spanish words are defined in English.

The labels on the user guide explain abbreviations used in the entries.

This guide includes several entries from the dictionary. The labels point out specific features that are part of most entries.

Reading Spanish/English Dictionaries

- Remind students that they are familiar with the process of using a dictionary to learn the definition of an unfamiliar word. Point out that a Spanish/English dictionary is like other dictionaries except that you can look up a Spanish word to get the definition in English or an English word to get the definition in Spanish.

- Have students read "Spanish-English Dictionary."

- Direct students to look at the entry *medir*. **Ask** a volunteer to give the English meaning of the word. **Answer:** *Medir* means "to measure or scan" and "to act with moderation."

- Tell students that Spanish nouns have gender, which means they are identified as feminine or masculine. Have students look at the first dictionary entry. Ask a volunteer whether the Spanish word *apartamento* is masculine or feminine. **Answer:** *Apartamento* is a feminine noun.

continued on p. 120

Differentiated Instruction — Solutions for All Learners

Strategy for English Learners
Suggest that students who are English Learners bring a bilingual dictionary (English and their native language) to class on a regular basis. Encourage them to continually look up unfamiliar words they hear or read. Tell them that this extra effort may help them to learn English faster.

Enrichment for Advanced Readers
Ask students who are reading at an advanced level to bring a bilingual dictionary to class from home or to check one out of a library. Tell them to each use his or her dictionary to learn enough words in a foreign language to be able to describe a friend in three sentences. Allow time for students to demonstrate the new language.

119

Reading Spanish-English Dictionaries (cont.)

- **Ask** students why it is important to note in this dictionary the differences between pronunciations of Spanish words in Spain and in Latin America.

  Answer: A language that is used in more than one country, such as Spanish is used, is likely to have different dialects. Therefore, even though the language is essentially the same, many pronunciations might vary. In order for the dictionary to be useful to all people needing help with Spanish, the dictionary needs to highlight the differences between the main dialects.

- Tell students that in many languages words have a gender. When learning these languages, it is very important to learn the gender of nouns.

Key to Spanish Pronunciation

This guide explains how letters are pronounced in Spanish.

Vowels

i	seen
e	late
a	past (Northern English)
o	soldier
u	boot

Diphthongs

ie	*Yale*
ei	*paying*
eu	*pear,* July; *e-u* run together
ai, ay	*sky*
au	*cow*
oi, oy	*boy*
ue	*way*

Consonants

b, v (*initial*)	best
b, v (*intervocalic*)	like *b* without lips touching
c (*before a, o, u or consonant*), k, qu	*kind*
c (*before e or i*), z	*think*
ch	*choose*
d (*initial*)	*dear*
d (*intervocalic*)	*there*
f	*find*
g (*before a, o, u or consonant*)	*gain*

g (*before e or i*), j	loch (Scots)
h	*honour*
l	long
ll	million
m	mice
n	banner
ñ	onion
p	copper
r	large (Scots)
rr	round (Scots)
s	goose
t	tank
w	like Spanish b, v
x (*intervocalic*)	axe *or* pigskin *or* eggs
x (*before consonant*)	extreme *or* paste
y	yellow

American Spanish

The following are the main features which distinguish the pronunciation of American from that of Castilian Spanish; they also occur in Southern Spain

c (*before e or i*), z	goose
ll (*in many regions of Spain and of Spanish America*)	yellow
ll (*Argentina, Uruguay*)	pleasure
s (*at end of word or before a consonant; in parts of Southern Spain and America*)	

The pronunciation of Spanish spoken in Spain differs from the Spanish spoken in Latin America. These notes point out key distinctions.

Note on Spanish Gender

Most nouns in English do not have a gender. In Spanish, most nouns have either a masculine or feminine form. This note explains how the dictionary indicates the gender.

As a general rule, nouns ending in *-a, -ción, -gión, -sión, -tión, -xión, -dad, -tad, -tud, -ez* and *-umbre* are feminine; all other nouns are masculine. In the body of the text genders are given only where this rule does not apply or in order to clarify its application.

120 ■ *Fiction and Nonfiction*

Vocabulary Development

Vocabulary for Using Dictionaries

Tell students that dictionaries often use specialized terms to explain the use of words. These terms may be unfamiliar. Guide them to understand the meaning of the following words in "Spanish-English Dictionary User Guide."

- *homographs:* words that are spelled the same but have different meanings.
- *idiomatic usage:* A saying or expression that is characteristic of a group of people.
- *stylistic level:* level of speech. You typically speak standard English in a work or school setting, but often use slang when you are with your friends.
- *diphthong:* A one-syllable sound made of two vowel sounds. For example, *toy*.

Reading: Recognizing Organizational Features of Printed Text

Directions: *Choose the letter of the best answer to each question.*

1. Which feature would guide you to a specific entry in a dictionary?
   A keyword
   B feminine forms
   C homograph
   D mode of verb

2. Under which heading would you look to find the pronunciation of the *e* in the Spanish word *medir*?
   A Vowels
   B Diphthongs
   C Consonants
   D American Spanish

3. Where can you look to confirm whether a word ending in *-tad* is masculine or feminine?
   A in the Key to Spanish Pronunciation
   B in the entry for the word
   C in the Note on Spanish Gender
   D under the "Diphthongs" heading

Reading: Comprehension and Interpretation

Directions: *Write your answers on a separate sheet of paper.*

4. Based on the entry for *hito,* why would it be important to use the correct gender of a noun in Spanish? [**Applying**]

5. Explain how you would find the part of speech of a Spanish word. [**Analyzing**]

6. (a) What idiomatic usages are included for the word *casar*?
   (b) Why would someone wishing to speak another language find information on idioms useful? [**Generating**]

Timed Writing: Exposition [Critical Stance]

Write a brief expository essay to explain the purpose and usefulness of a bilingual dictionary. In your answer, explain who would benefit from such a dictionary, and identify two situations in which a bilingual dictionary would be helpful. **(20 minutes)**

Reading Informational Materials: Spanish/English Dictionaries ■ *121*

Reading: Recognizing Organizational Features

1. A
2. A
3. C
4. The masculine form of the noun means *boundary mark* or *landmark.* The feminine form means *headless nail* or *brad.* Therefore, using one for the other would completely change the meaning.
5. First, find the entry by looking up the keyword. Then read the entry to find the part of speech, which is the italicized initial immediately following the keyword.
6. (a) Idioms include *casarse por poderes,* to marry by proxy; *antes que te cases, mira lo que haces,* look before you leap; and *casarse en segundas nupcias,* to remarry. (b) Explanations of idioms would be useful because they clarify common usages that sometimes vary from literal meanings.

Timed Writing

- Read the *Timed Writing* instructions together as a group. Remind students to identify and explain two practical applications for a bilingual dictionary, such as writing to a Spanish pen pal or traveling in a Latin American country. Tell them to be specific about why it would be useful to use and understand Spanish in the situations they have chosen.

- Suggest that students plan their time to give 5 minutes to planning, 10 minutes to writing, and 5 minutes to reviewing and revising.

Extend the Lesson

Slang/Plain English Dictionary

To give students further practice with the concept of bilingual dictionaries, have them create entries for a Slang/Plain English dictionary. Tell them to each choose three slang terms and write plain English definitions. Then, have them write slang-ridden definitions for three plain English terms.

Planning Differentiated Instruction

Choosing Your Selection

You may use either selection to meet the lesson standards. The following guide will help you determine which of the two selections is more appropriate for your students.

Accessibility at a Glance

	The Secret Life of Walter Mitty	Uncle Marcos
Context	Situation: Alternate dream-world and real-world settings in a character's life	Setting: Latin America, before the advent of the airplane industry
Language	Use of nonsense words and real words in unrelated contexts	• Numerous long sentences with embedded clauses • Difficult diction
Concept Level	Challenging (desire to escape reality)	Challenging (character sketch of an eccentric relative)
Literary Merit	Prize-winning author	Internationally acclaimed author
Lexile	700L	1420L
Other	Character driven	Character driven
Overall Rating	More accessible	More challenging

Using the Other Selection You may use the other selection for homework or independent reading to reinforce the selection skills. If you use both selections, you can build a test for both using *ExamView® Test Bank* software.

Choosing Your Resources

[L1] Special Needs Students   [L4] Advanced Students

[L2] Below-Level Students   [EL] English Learners

[L3] All Students

Reading and Vocabulary Warm-ups provide support for below level students. **A** is for students reading two grades below level; **B** is for students reading one grade below level. For Selection Tests, **A** signifies "less challenging" and **B** "more challenging." For Graphic Organizer transparencies, **A** signifies "not filled in" and **B** "filled in."

FT Fast Track Instruction: To move the lesson more quickly, use the strategies and activities identified with **FT**.

Scaffolding for Less Proficient and Advanced Students

The leveled questions on Apply the Skills pages progress in the levels of thinking required to answer them. To address the needs of your different students, you may use the (a) level questions for your less proficient students, the (b) level with your on-level and advanced students. The occasional (c) level questions are appropriate for your advanced students.

Go Online For: Information about Lexiles
Professional Development   **Visit:** www.PHSchool.com
Web Code: eue-1111

Step-by-Step Teaching Guide	Pacing Guide
PRETEACH	
• Administer Vocabulary and Reading Warm-ups as necessary.	
• Introduce the Literary Analysis Skill: Character. **FT**	10 min.
• Introduce the Reading Skill: Author's Purpose. **FT**	10 min.
• Prepare students to read by teaching the selection vocabulary. **FT**	10 min.
• Build background and develop expressive vocabulary with Connecting to the Literature and Background.	10 min.
• Engage students' interest with the motivation activity.	10 min.
TEACH	
• Informally monitor comprehension while students read independently or in groups. **FT**	30 min.
• Monitor students' comprehension with the Reading Check notes.	as students read
• Reinforce vocabulary with Vocabulary Builder notes.	as students read
• Develop students' understanding of character with the Literary Analysis annotations. **FT**	5 min.
• Develop students' ability to recognize author's purpose with the Reading Skill annotations. **FT**	10 min.
ASSESS/EXTEND	
• Assess students' comprehension and mastery of the Reading Skill and Literary Analysis by having them answer the Apply the Skills questions. **FT**	35 min.
• Have students complete the Vocabulary Builder activities. **FT**	5 min.
• Apply students' ability to write a character profile with the Writing activity. **FT**	30–45 min. or homework
• Extend students' listening and speaking and research and technology skills with one or both of the Extend Your Learning activities.	15–30 min. or homework
• Have students complete the Vocabulary Skill and Grammar Lesson.	5 min.
• Monitor students' progress with the Assessment Practice.	20–40 min.
• Administer **Selection Test A** or **Selection Test B**. **FT**	15 min.

Resources

Meeting Your Standards

Students will

1. **analyze and respond to literary elements.**
   - Literary Analysis: Character

2. **read, comprehend, and analyze short stories.**
   - Reading Skill: Author's Purpose
   - Reading Strategy: Reflecting to Determine Author's Purpose
   - Reading Check questions
   - Apply the Skills questions
   - Assessment Practice

3. **develop vocabulary.**
   - Vocabulary Builder
   - The Latin roots *vita-*, *-via-*, and *tri-*

4. **apply grammar skills.**
   - **Pronouns: Relative, Interrogative, and Indefinite**

5. **develop writing proficiency.**
   - Work in Progress: **Problem-Solution Essay**
   - **Character profile**

6. **extend learning.**
   - Listening and Speaking: **Comic Scene**
   - Research and Technology: **Learning Log**

Block Scheduling: Use one 90-minute class period to preteach the skills and have students read the selection. Use a second 90-minute class period to assess students' mastery of skills, extend their learning, and monitor their progress.

Homework Suggestions

Following are possibilities for homework assignments.

- Support pages from *Unit 1 Resources:*
  Literary Analysis
  Reading Skill
  Vocabulary Builder
  Enrichment

- An Extend Your Learning project and the Writing assignment for your chosen selection may be completed over several days.

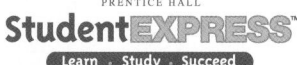

PRENTICE HALL
Teacher EXPRESS™ Use this complete
Plan · Teach · Assess suite of powerful teaching tools to make lesson planning and testing quicker and easier.

PRENTICE HALL
Student EXPRESS™ Use the
Learn · Study · Succeed interactive textbook (online and on CD-ROM) to make selections and activities come alive with audio and video support and interactive questions.

❶ Literary Analysis
Character

- Tell students that as they read the assigned selections, they will be looking for types of characters: round or flat and dynamic or static.

- Explain that to determine whether a character is round or flat, students should focus on details such as what a character says, does, and thinks. Tell students that flat characters often serve as functionaries to support the plot and reveal the round characters.

- Explain that to determine whether a character is dynamic or static, students should look for evidence that the character changes or grows at some point in the story.

- Have students identify one round and one flat character from a popular movie, such as *The Lord of the Rings.* Ask students to explain whether each character is dynamic or static.

- Encourage students to look for these character types as they read the selections.

❷ Reading Skill
Author's Purpose

- Explain that an author can have different purposes for writing, including the desire to persuade, inform, describe, or entertain. Tell students that pausing to reflect as they read will help them identify this purpose.

- Show students how they can use the graphic organizer to determine the author's purpose by recording and reflecting on story details.

- Give students a copy of **Reading Skill Graphic Organizer A** (*Graphic Organizer Transparencies*, p. 29). Have them fill in the graphic organizer as they reflect on the author's purpose in the assigned selection.

Build Skills *The Secret Life of Walter Mitty • Uncle Marcos*

Practice these skills with either "The Secret Life of Walter Mitty" (p. 124) or "Uncle Marcos" (p. 133).

❶ Literary Analysis

A **character** is a person or an animal who takes part in the action of a literary work.

- A **round character** is complex, showing many different qualities—revealing faults as well as virtues.
  A **flat character** is one-dimensional, showing a single trait

- A **dynamic character** develops, changes, and learns something during the course of a story—unlike a **static character,** who remains the same.

The main character of a story tends to be a round character and usually a dynamic one. The main character's development and growth are often central to a story's plot and theme. As you read, consider the traits that make characters seem round or flat, dynamic or static.

❷ Reading Skill

An **author's purpose** is his or her main reason for writing. In fiction, the specific purpose is often conveyed through the story's theme, message, or insight. Pause periodically while reading and **reflect** on the story's details and events to determine the author's purpose. Ask questions such as the following:

- *What significance might this event have?*

- *Why does the author include this detail?*

Based on your reflections, formulate ideas about what the author's purpose might be. Use a chart like the one shown to organize your thoughts.

Story Event or Detail

↓

Possible Significance

↓

Author's Purpose?

Vocabulary Builder

The Secret Life of Walter Mitty

- **distraught** (di strôt′) *adj.* troubled or confused (p. 126) *She was* distraught *over losing her wallet.*

- **insolent** (in′ sə lənt) *adj.* boldly disrespectful (p. 126) *Her* insolent *words offended the guests.*

- **inscrutable** (in skrōōt′ ə bəl) *adj.* baffling; mysterious (p. 129) *No one has ever solved the puzzle of his* inscrutable *personality.*

Uncle Marcos

- **pallid** (pal′ id) *adj.* pale (p. 133) *The flu gave him a weak and* pallid *appearance.*

- **disconsolately** (dis kän′ sə lit lē) *adv.* very unhappily (p. 138) *He gazed* disconsolately *as his friends drove to the game without him.*

- **unrequited** (un ri kwīt′ id) *adj.* not returned or repaid (p. 140) *Romance novels sometimes describe the sadness of* unrequited *love.*

122 ■ *Fiction and Nonfiction*

Vocabulary Development

Vocabulary Knowledge Rating

Create a **Vocabulary Knowledge Rating Chart** for the selection you will teach from this set. Include the selection vocabulary from this page and the additional words students are asked to use at the end of Connecting to the Literature. These words will increase students' expressive vocabulary.

Give students a copy of the chart with the words on it. Introduce the words by reading them aloud and having students mark their rating in the Before Reading column. Urge them to be alert to these words as they read and discuss the selection because they will rate their knowledge of the words again after they finish.

If you wish, you may tally how many students know (or think they know) a word to gauge how much instruction you need to provide. As students read, point out the words and their context.

Short Story

❸ Background

Reality and Imagination Psychologists say that a person's thoughts are often a series of seemingly unconnected reflections. An event in the real world can prompt unpredictable mental responses, such as memories, snippets of songs, or daydreams. In Thurber's story, random events cause Walter Mitty's thoughts to jump back and forth between his exciting "secret" life and his humdrum everyday existence.

❹ Connecting to the Literature

Reading/Writing Connection "The Secret Life of Walter Mitty" is about a man whose daydreams are more real and interesting to him than the workaday world that triggers them. Write down one ordinary event and one amazing daydream that it could prompt. Use at least three of these words: *derive, enhance, manifest, project.*

READ MORE

by James Thurber
*My World—
and Welcome to It*

Meet the Author

James **Thurber** (1894–1961)

James Thurber was a rare writer who expressed his comic genius in both words and pictures. He wrote stories, plays, essays, and poems, and he was also a great cartoonist. Born in Ohio, he joined the staff of *The New Yorker* magazine in 1927. "The Secret Life of Walter Mitty" was published in that magazine in 1939, becoming an instant success.

Humor and Anxiety Many of Thurber's stories and sketches grew directly out of his own life. As he put it, "Humor is a kind of emotional chaos told about calmly and quietly in retrospect." Thurber's characters try to stand up to the surprises of the modern world. Whether they succeed or fail, they always strike readers as authentic and very funny.

Fast Facts

▶ Thurber's cartoon characters included strangely shaped dogs who seemed to have human expressions.

▶ Thurber offered a Hollywood producer $10,000 *not* to make a movie about Walter Mitty. The movie was made anyway in 1947.

 Go Online
Author Link
For: More about the author
Visit: www.PHSchool.com
Web Code: epe-9110

❸ Background
Reality and Imagination

Most scientists say that daydreams fill much the same function as dreams. Daydreams relate to what is bothering us or to what we want to be doing. In the past, scientists believed that daydreams were unnecessary and counterproductive because they draw our attention away from the matter at hand; however, most scientists today suggest that daydreams are signs of a healthy psychological state.

❹ Connecting to the Literature

- Model use of the expressive vocabulary students are asked to use with these examples:

  1. A daydream might *derive* from a simple trip to the video store.
  2. Daydreams *enhance* life by allowing one's imagination to run free.
  3. A person's secret thoughts and wishes often *manifest* themselves in daydreams.
  4. Sometimes daydreams *project* the way a person would like to be seen by others.

- Help students further develop their expressive vocabulary by providing these words: *capacity, disconnect, enrich,* and *visualize.* Encourage students to use these words as they discuss the selection.

Concept Connector ➡

Students will follow up on this activity after completing "The Secret Life of Walter Mitty."

Go Online For additional informa-
Author Link tion about James Thurber, have students type in the Web Code and then select *James Thurber.*

Differentiated Instruction   Solutions for All Learners

Support for Below-Level Students [L1, L2]	Support for English Learners [EL]
Unit 1 Resources	**Unit 1 Resources**
Vocabulary Warm-up Word Lists, p. 146	**Vocabulary Warm-up Word Lists,** p. 146
Vocabulary Warm-up Practice, p. 147	**Vocabulary Warm-up Practice,** p. 147
Reading Warm-up A, p. 148	**Reading Warm-up A,** p. 148
Selection Test A, pp. 156–158	**Reader's Notebook: English Learner's Version**
Graphic Organizer Transparencies	**Listening to Literature Audio CD**
Reading Skill Graphic Organizer, Transparency B, p. 30	
Reader's Notebook: Adapted Version	
Adapted Reader's Notebook Audio CD	

❶ The Secret Life of
❷ Walter Mitty

James Thurber

The Man with Three Masks, John Rush, Courtesy of the artist

❹ ⚠ **Critical Viewing** Why might the man hold one mask up to his face and have other masks nearby? **[Analyze]**

124 ■ *Fiction and Nonfiction*

Vocabulary Development

⑤ "We're going through!" The Commander's voice was like thin ice breaking. He wore his full-dress uniform, with the heavily braided white cap pulled down rakishly over one cold gray eye. "We can't make it, sir. It's spoiling for a hurricane, if you ask me." "I'm not asking you, Lieutenant Berg," said the Commander. "Throw on the power lights! Rev her up to 8,500! We're going through!" The pounding of the cylinders increased: ta-pocketa-pocketa-pocketa-*pocketa-pocketa*. The Commander stared at the ice forming on the pilot window. He walked over and twisted a row of complicated dials. "Switch on No. 8 auxiliary!" he shouted. "Switch on No. 8 auxiliary!" repeated Lieutenant Berg. "Full strength in No. 3 turret!" shouted the Commander. "Full strength in No. 3 turret!" The crew, bending to their various tasks in the huge, hurtling eight-engined Navy hydroplane,[1] looked at each other and grinned. "The Old Man'll get us through," they said to one another. "The Old Man ain't afraid of Hell!" . . .

"Not so fast! You're driving too fast!" said Mrs. Mitty. "What are you driving so fast for?"

"Hmm?" said Walter Mitty. He looked at his wife, in the seat beside him, with shocked astonishment. She seemed grossly unfamiliar, like a strange woman who had yelled at him in a crowd. "You were up to fifty-five," she said. "You know I don't like to go more than forty. You were up to fifty-five." Walter Mitty drove on toward Waterbury in silence, the roaring of the SN202 through the worst storm in twenty years of Navy flying fading in the remote, intimate airways of his mind. "You're tensed up again," said Mrs. Mitty. "It's one of your days. I wish you'd let Dr. Renshaw look you over."

Walter Mitty stopped the car in front of the building where his wife went to have her hair done. "Remember to get those overshoes while I'm having my hair done," she said. "I don't need overshoes," said Mitty. She put her mirror back into her bag. "We've been all through that," she said, getting out of the car. "You're not a young man any longer." He raced the engine a little. "Why don't you wear your gloves? Have you lost your gloves?" Walter Mitty reached in a pocket and brought out the gloves. He put them on, but after she had turned and gone into the building and he had driven on to a red light, he took them off again. "Pick it up, brother!" snapped a cop as the light changed, and Mitty hastily pulled on his gloves and lurched ahead. He drove around the streets aimlessly for a time, and then he drove past the hospital on his way to the parking lot.

. . . "It's the millionaire banker, Wellington McMillan," said the pretty nurse. "Yes?" said Walter Mitty, removing his gloves slowly.

---

1. **hydroplane** (hīʹ drō plānʹ) *n.* seaplane.

Reading Skill
Author's Purpose
Pause to reflect. What does the phrase "intimate airways of his mind" suggest about the author's purpose in writing this story?

 ⑥ **Reading Check**

Why is Mrs. Mitty upset?

④ Critical Viewing

Possible response: The masks may represent different "faces" the man presents to other people. Each mask gives the man a different self.

⑤ Reading Skill
Author's Purpose

- Have students describe what is happening in the bracketed passage.
  Answer: Walter Mitty is daydreaming about himself as a military commander. His wife's words pull him back to reality, where he is driving a car.
- Remind students that reflecting on details in the story can help them determine an author's purpose. Show students how to use **Reading Skill Graphic Organizer A** (*Graphic Organizer Transparencies,* p. 29) to organize their thoughts.
- **Ask** students to respond to the Reading Skill question: Pause to reflect. What does the phrase "intimate airways of his mind" suggest about the author's purpose in writing this story?
  Answer: The phrase suggests that the author's purpose is to reveal the differences between the real world and the unseen, imaginary landscape of Mitty's mind.

⑥ Reading Check

Answer: Mrs. Mitty is upset because she thinks Mitty is driving too fast.

Differentiated Instruction Solutions for All Learners

Strategy for Less Proficient Readers
To give students a context for the story and to model how to determine an author's purpose, show them **Reading Skill Graphic Organizer B** (*Graphic Organizer Transparencies,* p. 30). The completed graphic organizer will give students insight into the process of reflecting to determine an author's purpose. They can use it as a model for organizing their thoughts about author's purpose as they read.

Enrichment for Gifted/Talented Students
Point out that "The Secret Life of Walter Mitty" can be an entertaining story to perform as a dramatic reading. Have three volunteers take the parts of Mitty's wife, the fantasy Mitty, and the real Mitty. Have them practice reading the first three paragraphs on p. 125, and then ask them to perform the reading for the class. Have other students prepare different passages in the story and then perform them for the class.

125

- **Ask** students to explain the difference between a round and a flat character.
Answer: A round character is complex and has many different qualities. A flat character is one-dimensional, usually identified to the reader through a single characteristic or trait.

- Have students read the bracketed passage and then identify where each paragraph takes place.
Answer: The first paragraph takes place in Mitty's fantasy life. The second paragraph takes place in Mitty's real life.

- **Ask** the Literary Analysis question: How does this shift in scenes show that Walter Mitty is a multidimensional character?
Answer: The shift reveals that Mitty is able to shift back and forth between his real-world personality and his daydream characters. This shows that he is a round character because he has more than one aspect to his personality.

- Remind students that characters can also be dynamic or static. **Ask** students whether Mitty shows signs of being dynamic or static. Have them give reasons for their opinions.
Possible response: So far, Mitty is a static character. Although he switches from daydreaming to reality, there is no evidence that his character is changing or growing in any way.

"Who has the case?" "Dr. Renshaw and Dr. Benbow, but there are two specialists here, Dr. Remington from New York and Mr. Pritchard-Mitford from London. He flew over." A door opened down a long, cool corridor and Dr. Renshaw came out. He looked <u>distraught</u> and haggard. "Hello, Mitty," he said. "We're having the devil's own time with McMillan, the millionaire banker and close personal friend of Roosevelt. Obstreosis of the ductal tract.[2] Tertiary. Wish you'd take a look at him." "Glad to," said Mitty.

In the operating room there were whispered introductions: "Dr. Remington, Dr. Mitty. Mr. Pritchard-Mitford, Dr. Mitty." "I've read your book on streptothricosis," said Pritchard-Mitford, shaking hands. "A brilliant performance, sir." "Thank you," said Walter Mitty. "Didn't know you were in the States, Mitty," grumbled Remington. "Coals to Newcastle,[3] bringing Mitford and me up here for tertiary." "You are very kind," said Mitty. A huge, complicated machine, connected to the operating table, with many tubes and wires, began at this moment to go pocketa-pocketa-pocketa. "The new anesthetizer is giving way!" shouted an intern. "There is no one in the East who knows how to fix it!" "Quiet, man!" said Mitty, in a low, cool voice. He sprang to the machine, which was now going pocketa-pocketa-queep-pocketa-queep. He began fingering delicately a row of glistening dials. "Give me a fountain pen!" he snapped. Someone handed him a fountain pen. He pulled a faulty piston out of the machine and inserted the pen in its place. "That will hold for ten minutes," he said. "Get on with the operation." A nurse hurried over and whispered to Renshaw, and Mitty saw the man turn pale. "Coreopsis has set in," said Renshaw nervously. "If you would take over, Mitty?" Mitty looked at him and at the craven figure of Benbow, who drank, and at the grave, uncertain faces of the two great specialists. "If you wish," he said. They slipped a white gown on him; he adjusted a mask and drew on thin gloves; nurses handed him shining . . .

"Back it up, Mac! Look out for that Buick!" Walter Mitty jammed on the brakes. "Wrong lane, Mac," said the parking-lot attendant, looking at Mitty closely. "Gee. Yeh," muttered Mitty. He began cautiously to back out of the lane marked "Exit Only." "Leave her sit there," said the attendant. "I'll put her away." Mitty got out of the car. "Hey, better leave the key." "Oh," said Mitty, handing the man the ignition key. The attendant vaulted into the car, backed it up with <u>insolent</u> skill, and put it where it belonged.

They're so cocky, thought Walter Mitty, walking along Main Street; they think they know everything. Once he had tried to take

---

2. obstreosis of the ductal tract Thurber has invented this and other medical terms.
3. coals to Newcastle The proverb "bringing coals to Newcastle" means bringing things to a place unnecessarily—Newcastle, England, was a coal center and so did not need coal brought to it.

Vocabulary Builder
distraught (di strôt′)
adj. troubled or confused

Literary Analysis
Character How does this shift in scenes show that Walter Mitty is a multidimensional character?

Vocabulary Builder
insolent (in′ sə lənt) *adj.* boldly disrespectful

Vocabulary Development

Expressive Vocabulary
As students are discussing Walter Mitty and his daydreams, encourage them to use the expressive vocabulary presented earlier. Stimulate discussion by having students use the words in their responses to the following questions:

1. Why do you think Mitty *derives* such pleasure from his daydreams?

2. Do you think the daydreams *enhance* the quality of his life? Why or why not?

3. What character traits *manifest* themselves in Mitty's daydreams?

4. What situations does Mitty *project* his fantasy characters into? What does this tell you about Mitty?

Challenge students to use these words as you continue to discuss the story.

his chains off, outside New Milford, and he had got them wound around the axles. A man had had to come out in a wrecking car and unwind them, a young, grinning garageman. Since then Mrs. Mitty always made him drive to a garage to have the chains taken off. The next time, he thought, I'll wear my right arm in a sling; they won't grin at me then. I'll have my right arm in a sling and they'll see I couldn't possibly take the chains off myself. He kicked at the slush on the sidewalk. "Overshoes," he said to himself, and he began looking for a shoe store.

When he came out into the street again, with the overshoes in a box under his arm, Walter Mitty began to wonder what the other thing was his wife had told him to get. She had told him, twice, before they set out from their house for Waterbury. In a way he hated these weekly trips to town—he was always getting something wrong. Kleenex, he thought, Squibb's, razor blades? No. Toothpaste, toothbrush, bicarbonate, carborundum, initiative and referendum?[4] He gave it up. But she would remember it. "Where's the what's-its-name?" she would ask. "Don't tell me you forgot the what's-its-name." A newsboy went by shouting something about the Water-bury trial.

. . . "Perhaps this will refresh your memory." The District Attorney suddenly thrust a heavy automatic at the quiet figure on the witness stand. "Have you ever seen this before?" Walter Mitty took the gun and examined it expertly. "This is my Webley-Vickers 50.80," he said calmly. An excited buzz ran around the courtroom. The Judge rapped for order. "You are a crack shot with any sort of firearms, I believe?" said the District Attorney, insinuatingly. "Objection!" shouted Mitty's attorney. "We have shown that the defendant could not have fired the shot. We have shown that he wore his right arm in a sling on the night of the fourteenth of July." Walter Mitty

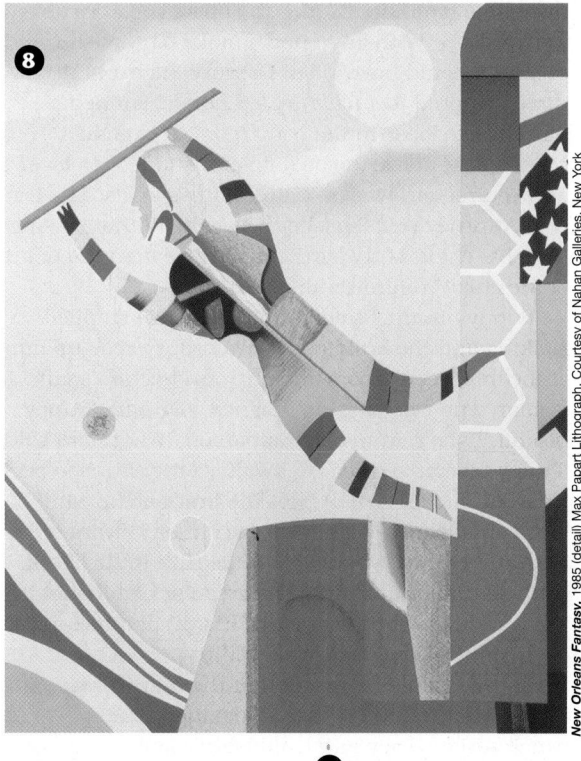

New Orleans Fantasy, 1985 (detail) Max Papart Lithograph, Courtesy of Nahan Galleries, New York

⑨ ▲ Critical Viewing
Describe a situation that might make Walter Mitty daydream about being a circus performer like the one shown. **[Hypothesize]**

⑩ ✓ Reading Check

Why does Mitty say that next time he will wear his arm in a sling?

---

4. **carborundum** (kär´ bə run´ dəm), **initiative** (i nish´ ē ə tiv) **and referendum** (ref´ ə ren´ dəm) Thurber is purposely making a nonsense list; *carborundum* is a hard substance used for scraping, *initiative* is the right of citizens to introduce ideas for laws, and *referendum* is the right of citizens to vote on laws.

The Secret Life of Walter Mitty ■ 127

⑧ Humanities

New Orleans Fantasy (detail), by Max Papart

In this lithograph, a colorfully dressed acrobat swings from a trapeze. While Walter Mitty never imagines himself as an acrobat in the story, the freedom and daring represented by the trapeze artist characterize Mitty's fantasies.

Max Papart (1911–1985) was a French lithographer whose fanciful style is represented in this painting. He studied art in Marseilles but traced his greatest influence to the works of surrealist painters he encountered at an exhibit in Paris in 1938. Use the following questions for discussion:

1. What character traits do you think Walter Mitty would associate with a trapeze artist such as the one shown in this painting?
   Possible response: Mitty might think the trapeze artist is daring, graceful, and breathtaking.

2. What introduction can you suggest for a Walter Mitty—like fantasy about being a trapeze artist?
   Possible response: Students may suggest a passage that describes the entrance of the famous artist Waltero Mitzini, or some variant.

⑨ Critical Viewing

Possible response: Walter Mitty's daydreams reflect a way to overcome any recent experience that embarrasses or humiliates him. A daydream about being a graceful trapeze artist might result after Mitty has done something clumsy or has been made to feel clumsy by others.

⑩ Reading Check

Answer: Mitty thinks that if he has his arm in a sling, the garageman will not expect him to be able to take off the car chains without help.

Differentiated Instruction   Solutions for All Learners

Background for English Learners
Students may benefit by knowing that many of the sound-effects terms, such as "pocketa-pocketa-pocketa," are nonsense words. Likewise, many of the technical words are either made up or used in ways that are different from their real meanings. *Coreopsis,* for example, is a flower, *obstreosis* is a nonsense word, and *streptothricosis* is a skin disease of animals such as cattle and horses.

Strategy for Advanced Readers
Ask students to make charts of all the characters that Mitty assumes in his daydreams. Have them describe the character traits that each character exhibits. Then have them discuss as a group what all of the characters have in common. Guide their discussion with this question: What void in Mitty's real personality do these fictitious characters fill?

Social Studies Connection With the introduction of airplanes for military purposes during World War I, fighter pilots quickly became international heroes. Germany's Baron von Richthofen—The Red Baron—was considered the best of them. He shot down 80 Allied planes before his death on April 21, 1918. An Australian anti-aircraft gun shot down Richthofen while he was chasing an inexperienced RAF pilot. The RAF buried Richthofen with full military honors.

In World War II, Germany sought to invade Great Britain, but they had to gain control of the air first. The RAF, although initially overmatched, put up a staunch defense and eventually took command of the air. They won the Battle of Britain, saving their country from invasion and ultimately giving the Allies the advantage to win World War II.

Connect to the Literature The RAF successes in World Wars I and II were keys to Britain's ultimate victory. The flying aces of the RAF were among the wars' most glamorous and popular heroes. **Ask** the Connect to the Literature question: What elements of life in the RAF would Mitty enjoy?

Answer: As a member of the RAF, Mitty would have enjoyed having the admiration of others and would have relished the thrills and dangers of that lifestyle.

raised his hand briefly and the bickering attorneys were stilled. "With any known make of gun," he said evenly, "I could have killed Gregory Fitzhurst at three hundred *feet with my left hand*." Pandemonium broke loose in the courtroom. A woman's scream rose above the bedlam and suddenly a lovely, dark-haired girl was in Walter Mitty's arms. The District Attorney struck at her savagely. Without rising from his chair, Mitty let the man have it on the point of the chin. "You miserable cur!" . . .

"Puppy biscuit," said Walter Mitty. He stopped walking and the buildings of Waterbury rose up out of the misty courtroom and surrounded him again. A woman who was passing laughed. "He said 'Puppy biscuit,'" she said to her companion. "That man said 'Puppy biscuit' to himself." Walter Mitty hurried on. He went into an A. & P., not the first one he came to but a smaller one farther up the street. "I want some biscuit for small, young dogs," he said to the clerk. "Any special brand, sir?" The greatest pistol shot in the world thought a moment. "It says 'Puppies Bark for It' on the box," said Walter Mitty.

His wife would be through at the hairdresser's in fifteen minutes, Mitty saw in looking at his watch, unless they had trouble drying it; sometimes they had trouble drying it. She didn't like to get to the hotel first; she would want him to be there waiting for her as usual. He found a big leather chair in the lobby, facing a window, and he put the overshoes and the puppy biscuit on the floor beside it. He picked up an old copy of *Liberty* and sank down into the chair. "Can Germany Conquer the World Through the Air?" Walter Mitty looked at the pictures of bombing planes and of ruined streets.

. . . "The cannonading has got the wind up in young Raleigh,[5] sir," said the sergeant. Captain Mitty looked up at him through tousled hair. "Get him to bed," he said wearily. "With the others. I'll fly alone." "But you can't, sir," said the sergeant anxiously. "It takes two men to handle that bomber and the Archies[6] are pounding hell

---

5. **has got the wind up in young Raleigh** has made young Raleigh nervous.
6. **Archies** slang term for antiaircraft guns.

⓫ **Literature in Context**

Social Studies Connection

The Royal Air Force Although he is American, Mitty fantasizes about being a brave and handsome English officer, a bomber pilot in the Royal Air Force (RAF). The RAF was officially formed in 1918 and distinguished itself in numerous air battles during World War I. RAF pilots would earn even greater distinction in the Battle of Britain during World War II. The reference to "Von Richtman's circus" recalls one of the RAF's finest moments—the shooting down in 1918 of Baron Manfred von Richtofen, also known as "The Red Baron," who was Germany's greatest fighter pilot.

Connect to the Literature

What elements of life in the RAF would Mitty enjoy?

Vocabulary Development

Vocabulary Knowledge Rating
When students have completed reading and discussing "The Secret Life of Walter Mitty," have them take out their **Vocabulary Knowledge Rating Chart** for this selection. Read the words aloud once more and have students rate their knowledge of the words again in the After Reading column. Clarify any words that are still problematic. Have students write their own definition and example or sentence in the appropriate column. Then have students complete the **Vocabulary Builder Practice** activities on p. 131. Encourage students to use the words in further discussion and written work about this selection. Remind them that they will be accountable for these words on the Selection Test.

out of the air. Von Richtman's circus[7] is between here and Saulier."
"Somebody's got to get that ammunition dump," said Mitty. "I'm
going over. Spot of brandy?" He poured a drink for the sergeant and
one for himself. War thundered and whined around the dugout and
battered at the door. There was a rending of wood and splinters flew
through the room. "A bit of a near thing," said Captain Mitty carelessly. "The box barrage is closing in," said the sergeant. "We only
live once, Sergeant," said Mitty, with his faint, fleeting smile. "Or do
we?" He poured another brandy and tossed it off. "I never see a man
could hold his brandy like you, sir," said the sergeant. "Begging
your pardon, sir." Captain Mitty stood up and strapped on his huge
Webley-Vickers automatic. "It's forty kilometers through hell, sir,"
said the sergeant. Mitty finished one last brandy. "After all," he said
softly, "what isn't?" The pounding of the cannon increased; there
was the rat-tat-tatting of machine guns, and from somewhere came
the menacing pocketa-pocketa-pocketa of the new flame-throwers.
Walter Mitty walked to the door of the dugout humming "Auprès de
Ma Blonde."[8] He turned and waved to the sergeant. "Cheerio!" he
said. . . .

Something struck his shoulder. "I've been looking all over this
hotel for you," said Mrs. Mitty. "Why do you have to hide in this old
chair? How did you expect me to find you?" "Things close in," said
Walter Mitty vaguely. "What?" Mrs. Mitty said. "Did you get the
what's-its-name? The puppy biscuit? What's in that box?" "Overshoes," said Mitty. "Couldn't you have put them on in the store?" "I
was thinking," said Walter Mitty. "Does it ever occur to you that I
am sometimes thinking?" She looked at him. "I'm going to take your
temperature when I get you home," she said.

They went out through the revolving doors that made a faintly
derisive whistling sound when you pushed them. It was two blocks
to the parking lot. At the drugstore on the corner she said, "Wait
here for me. I forgot something. I won't be a minute." She was more
than a minute. Walter Mitty lighted a cigarette. It began to rain, rain
with sleet in it. He stood up against the wall of the drugstore,
smoking. . . . He put his shoulders back and his heels together. "To
hell with the handkerchief," said Walter Mitty scornfully. He took
one last drag on his cigarette and snapped it away. Then, with that
faint, fleeting smile playing about his lips, he faced the firing squad;
erect and motionless, proud and disdainful, Walter Mitty the Unde-
feated, <u>inscrutable</u> to the last.

---

7. **Von Richtman's circus** German airplane squadron.
8. **"Auprès de Ma Blonde"** (ō prä′ də mä blôn′ də) "Next to My Blonde," a popular French song.

Literary Analysis
Character How do
Walter Mitty's
responses in this
paragraph indicate
that he is a complex
character?

Vocabulary Builder
inscrutable (in skrōōt′
ə bəl) *adj.* baffling;
mysterious

The Secret Life of Walter Mitty ■ 129

Apply the Skills

The Secret Life of Walter Mitty

Thinking About the Selection

1. **Respond:** Do you feel sorry for Walter Mitty? Why or why not?
2. **(a) Recall:** What distraction jars Mitty out of his first daydream? **(b) Compare and Contrast:** Explain how Mitty's behavior in this daydream differs from his behavior in real life.
3. **(a) Recall:** In the "real world," what tasks are Mitty and his wife carrying out? **(b) Infer:** What deeds is Mitty attempting to accomplish in his fantasy life? **(c) Compare and Contrast:** How do the tasks of his daily life compare to those of his fantasy life?
4. **(a) Infer:** Which aspects of Mitty's personality trigger his final daydream? **(b) Draw Conclusions:** In what ways is this daydream a comment on his fate in real life?
5. **(a) Evaluate:** Do Mitty's daydreams help him in any way or do they hurt him? Write down three details from the story that support your evaluation. **(b) Discuss:** Share your responses with a small group and discuss the differences and similarities among them. **(c) Reflect:** How has your evaluation grown or changed as a result of this discussion?

Literary Analysis

6. Mitty wants to be like the heroes in his daydreams. **(a)** Using a chart like the one shown, identify one detail from each of Mitty's daydreams and the quality that each detail reveals.

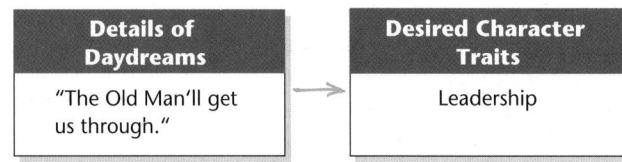

Details of Daydreams		Desired Character Traits
"The Old Man'll get us through."	→	Leadership

   (b) In a few sentences, summarize the **character** of the man Mitty wants to be.
7. Review the characters of Walter and Mrs. Mitty. **(a)** Determine whether each character is **round** or **flat**. Explain. **(b)** Determine whether each character is **static** or **dynamic**. Explain.

Reading Skill

8. **(a)** What specific **purpose** might James Thurber have had for creating the character of Walter Mitty? **(b)** Identify three details from the story and explain how **reflecting** on them helped you determine Thurber's purpose.

130 ■ *Fiction and Nonfiction*

QuickReview

Story at a Glance
A meek man daydreams to escape his humdrum life.

Go Online
Assessment
For: Self-test
Visit: www.PHSchool.com
Web Code: epa-6110

Character: a person or an animal who takes part in the action of a literary work. Characters can be *round* or *flat*, *dynamic* or *static*.

Author's Purpose: a writer's main reason for writing a literary work

ASSESS Answers

1. **Possible responses:** Some students may feel sorry for Mitty because he does not get respect.
2. (a) His wife tells him that he is driving too fast. (b) In his daydream, Mitty is a bold leader; in real life, he is meek.
3. (a) Mitty drops Mrs. Mitty at the hairdresser, buys overshoes, picks up dog food, and waits for his wife. (b) Mitty is landing a plane, doing surgery, testifying in court, fighting a war, and facing a firing squad. (c) The tasks of his daily life are boring and dull. The tasks of his fantasy life are exciting.
4. (a) Mitty's low self-esteem and his weariness at being patronized by his wife trigger his final daydream. (b) Mitty has stood up to his wife, and he may be anticipating what will happen to him when they get home.
5. (a) **Possible response:** His daydreams help him survive a humdrum life. (b) Students should compare and contrast their responses. (c) Students may have gained a more comprehensive picture of Mitty's character.
6. **Details of Daydreams—Desired Character Traits:** "Give me a fountain pen."—resourcefulness; Mitty let the man have it. . . . —gallantry; "We only live once, Sergeant."—fearlessness; He faced the firing squad. . . . —heroism.

   Another sample answer can be found on **Literary Analysis Graphic Organizer B**, p. 33 in *Graphic Organizer Transparencies*.

   (b) **Possible response:** Mitty wants to be a brilliant and heroic leader—a man who knows what to do and has the courage to do it.
7. (a) Mitty is a round character. He is capable of seeing himself in different roles, with different skills, responding to challenges. Mrs. Mitty is a flat character. She is revealed only as a controlling wife. (b) Both characters are static. Neither changes or learns anything in the story.
8. (a) **Possible response:** Thurber's purpose might have been to show the positive, self-affirming effects of imagination.
   (b) **Possible response:** When his wife makes him wear gloves, Mitty dreams of saving a life. When he does not park the car well, he dreams of being a star witness. When he speaks up to his wife, he imagines he is before a firing squad.

Vocabulary Builder

Practice Review the vocabulary list for "The Secret Life of Walter Mitty" on page 122. Then, decide whether each of the following statements below is true or false. Explain your answers.

1. Someone who is *distraught* is likely to behave in a calm manner.
2. Coaches encourage their players to be *insolent.*
3. *Inscrutable* handwriting is difficult to interpret.

Adding Words to Your Vocabulary Using a dictionary or a thesaurus, find an **antonym,** a word that has the opposite meaning, for each italicized word from the vocabulary list. Then, use each antonym correctly in a sentence. (For more on using a dictionary and a thesaurus, see pages R6–7.)

Writing

Write a **character profile** of one of the heroic personalities in Walter Mitty's daydreams.

- Begin by jotting down details that capture the character's appearance, personality, and achievements.
- Decide on a single impression to convey about the character.
- Organize and present details so that they all contribute to that one impression.

For *Grammar, Vocabulary,* and *Assessment,* see **Build Language Skills,** pages 144–145.

Extend Your Learning

Listening and Speaking Write and perform a comic **scene** based on one of Walter Mitty's daydreams.

- Choose the daydream you find most appealing.
- Write a script for the scene.
- Cast the scene, and briefly rehearse.

Perform the scene for the class.

Research and Technology Use a variety of sources, including the library and the Internet, to research scientific facts and theories about daydreams. Record your research in a **learning log,** a written record of information you discover about the topic. Analyze the information by discussing it with classmates and by comparing your findings to Thurber's story.

Apply the Skills ■ 131

Go Online
—Research **For:** An additional research activity
Visit: www.PHSchool.com
Web Code: epd-7107
For another research activity to extend students' learning, give students this Web Code.

Vocabulary Builder
Practice

1. False
2. False
3. True

Adding Words to Your Vocabulary
Possible response:

1. Mitty wished he could behave in a calm and confident manner.
2. Mrs. Mitty's friends thought Mitty was the most obedient husband they had ever met.
3. Was Mitty's true attitude obvious to everyone except his wife?

Writing

- To give students guidance for writing a character profile, give them **Support for Writing** for "The Secret Life of Walter Mitty," p. 153 in *Unit 1 Resources.*
- To evaluate students' character profiles, use the Descriptive Essay rubrics, pp. 55-56 in *General Resources.*

Six Traits Focus

✔	Ideas	✔	Word Choice
✔	Organization		Sentence Fluency
	Voice		Conventions

WG **Writing and Grammar,** Gold Level
Students will find guidance on descriptive writing in Chapter 6.

Build Language Skills

Go to pp. 144–145 for vocabulary and grammar lessons and assessment practice.

Extend Your Learning

The **Support for Extend Your Learning** page (*Unit 1 Resources,* p. 154) provides guided note-taking opportunities to help students complete the Extend Your Learning activities.

Teaching notes for Literary Analysis, Reading Skill, and Vocabulary Builder for this selection begin on p. 122.

❸ Background
Magical Realism

The name "magical realism" shows the contrast on which this literary style is based—it highlights and reveals magical occurrences in every-day life. Magic realism is a style most readers associate with modern and contemporary Latin American writers, but it is an international style. Magic realists include Salman Rushdie, Milan Kundera, and a number of other European and Eastern writers.

❹ Connecting to the Literature

- Model use of the expressive vocabulary students are asked to use with these examples:

  1. People might *enhance* the importance of an event through multiple retellings.

  2. Often a person must *alter* the truth of an event to make it more magical or mysterious.

  3. The facts of an event are easily *distorted* over time.

  4. What begins as an everyday occurrence might *evolve* into an event of great significance.

  5. These types of stories *generate* interest because they bring magic to everyday moments.

- Help students further develop their expressive vocabulary by providing these words: *appeal, defy, delight,* and *fantastic.* Encourage students to use these words as they discuss the selection.

Go Online
Author Link For additional information about Isabel Allende, have students type in the Web Code, then select *A* from the alphabet, and then select *Isabel Allende.*

Build Understanding • *Uncle Marcos*

Short Story

❸ Background

Magical Realism Imagine a world in which people float in the air and rain falls continuously for years. Such fantastic details fill stories and novels by a group of writers, including Isabel Allende, who are called magical realists. Works of magical realism blend fantastic details with realistic ones to stretch the boundaries of readers' imaginations.

❹ Connecting to the Literature

Reading/Writing Connection Some of the incidents in "Uncle Marcos" seem magical and mysterious. Write a brief description of an event that now seems magical or mysterious because it has been exaggerated over time with retelling. Use at least three of these words: *enhance, alter, distort, evolve, generate.*

Review

For **Literary Analysis, Reading Skill,** and **Vocabulary Builder,** see page 122.

READ MORE

by Isabel Allende
The Stories of Eva Luna
My Invented Country

Meet the Author

Isabel **Allende** (b. 1942)

The daughter of diplomats, Isabel Allende grew up in the South American country of Chile. Her uncle was the Chilean president Salvador Allende. When his government was overthrown in 1973, Isabel Allende fled to Venezuela. She lived there in exile until 1988, when she moved to California.

Family and Fiction "Uncle Marcos" is excerpted from Allende's first novel, *The House of the Spirits,* which was inspired by her own remarkable family. Allende's family stories, however, are usually told with large helpings of imagination. She delights in blending the real and the imaginary. Allende once summed up her profession by quoting her granddaughter. Asked what it means to have a great imagination, the child replied, "You can remember what never happened."

Fast Facts

▶ Allende's first novel, *The House of the Spirits,* began as a letter to her 100-year-old grandfather.
▶ Allende spends ten to twelve hours writing each day. She says the storytelling is the fun part but the writing "is a lot of work!"

For: More about the author
Visit: www.PHSchool.com
Web Code: epe-9111

132 ■ Fiction and Nonfiction

Differentiated Instruction Solutions for All Learners

Support for Below-Level Students [L1, L2]	Support for English Learners [EL]
Unit 1 Resources	**Unit 1 Resources**
Vocabulary Warm-up Word Lists, p. 162	**Vocabulary Warm-up Word Lists**, p. 162
Vocabulary Warm-up Practice, p. 163	**Vocabulary Warm-up Practice**, p. 163
Reading Warm-up A, p. 164	**Reading Warm-up A**, p. 164
Selection Test A, pp. 174–176	**Listening to Literature Audio CD**
Graphic Organizer Transparencies	
Reading Skill Graphic Organizer Transparency B, p. 31	

Uncle Marcos

from *The House of the Spirits*

Isabel Allende

. . . It had been two years since Clara had last seen her Uncle Marcos, but she remembered him very well. His was the only perfectly clear image she retained from her whole childhood, and in order to describe him she did not need to consult the daguerreotype[1] in the drawing room that showed him dressed as an explorer leaning on an old-fashioned double-barreled rifle with his right foot on the neck of a Malaysian tiger, the same triumphant position in which she had seen the Virgin standing between plaster clouds and <u>pallid</u> angels at the main altar, one foot on the vanquished devil. All Clara had to do to see her uncle was close her

Vocabulary Builder
pallid (pal´ id) *adj.*
pale

---

1. **daguerreotype** (də ger´ ō tīp´) *n.* early type of photograph.

❶ Motivation

Have students create a detailed character sketch based on the following rough description of the central character from "Uncle Marcos": an eccentric inventor and world adventurer whose relatives find him peculiar and at times embarrassing. Have students read the stories to see whether the character they've come up with is as interesting as the one Isabel Allende developed.

Concept Connector ➡

Students will follow up on this activity after completing "Uncle Marcos."

❷ About the Selection

In this excerpt from *The House of the Spirits,* Clara del Valle recalls her eccentric Uncle Marcos. Laughed at by some, but loved by many, Uncle Marcos impresses his community with his daring adventures in courtship, flight, rebirth, and clairvoyance. Through Clara's eyes, Uncle Marcos earns the renown he had gained only fitfully in his lifetime. The story conveys an important message about how individuals can be misjudged or underappreciated by some people but beloved by others.

Learning Modalities
Interpersonal Learners

As students read "Uncle Marcos," have them consider the point of view of Clara, the narrator. Ask students to think about how the story would be different if it were told from Uncle Marcos's point of view. Challenge students to write brief summaries of the story from Uncle Marcos's point of view.

Differentiated
Instruction   Solutions for All Learners

Strategy for Less Proficient Readers
The long paragraphs and sentences in "Uncle Marcos" may challenge some students. Preview the reading with them, page by page. Help them find the main idea in each paragraph, and then have them use this list to summarize Marcos's adventures. When students have finished reading, have them go back over the text and note how the details of each paragraph support and illuminate the main ideas.

Enrichment for English Learners
If any students are native speakers of Spanish, or are fluent in that language, encourage them to locate and read this excerpt in Spanish, the original language of *The House of the Spirits (La casa de los espíritus).* Challenge students to choose any two-paragraph section of the excerpt and translate it into English. Then have them compare and contrast their versions with the one in the textbook.

Infer

- Have students read the bracketed passage, and then **ask** what they can infer about Uncle Marcos's character. Have them identify details that support their answers. **Possible response:** The picture with the rifle and tiger suggests that Uncle Marcos is brave and adventurous. The pirate's mustache and sharklike smile create a rascally impression.

- **Ask:** What does the comparison between Marcos's photograph and the statue of the Virgin suggest? **Possible response:** It suggests that Marcos is somehow good in spirit, despite his adventurous nature, or that he has special powers.

❹ Critical Viewing

Answer: Such an inventor would be creative, imaginative, persistent, clever, and determined. He or she would persevere even if other people laughed or expressed doubts.

---

❸ eyes and there he was, weather-beaten and thin, with a pirate's mustache through which his strange, sharklike smile peered out at her. It seemed impossible that he could be inside that long black box that was lying in the middle of the courtyard.

Each time Uncle Marcos had visited his sister Nivea's home, he had stayed for several months, to the immense joy of his nieces and nephews, particularly Clara, causing a storm in which the sharp lines of domestic order blurred. The house became a clutter of trunks, of animals in jars of formaldehyde,[2] of Indian lances and sailor's bundles. In every part of the house people kept tripping over his equipment, and all sorts of unfamiliar animals appeared that had traveled from remote lands only to meet their death beneath Nana's irate broom in the farthest corners of the house. Uncle Marcos's manners were those of a cannibal, as Severo put it. He spent the whole night making incomprehensible movements in the drawing room; later they turned out to be exercises designed to perfect the mind's control over the body and to improve digestion. He performed alchemy[3] experiments in the kitchen, filling the house with fetid smoke and ruining pots and pans with solid substances that stuck to their bottoms and were impossible to remove. While the rest of the household tried to sleep, he dragged his suitcases up and down the halls, practiced making strange, high-pitched sounds on savage instruments, and taught Spanish to a parrot whose native language was an Amazonic dialect. During the day, he slept in a hammock that he had strung between two columns in the hall, wearing only a loincloth that put Severo in a terrible mood but that Nivea forgave because Marcos had convinced her that it was the same costume in which Jesus of Nazareth had preached. Clara remembered perfectly, even though she had been only a tiny child, the first time her Uncle Marcos came to the house after one of his voyages. He settled in as if he planned to stay forever. After a short time, bored with having to appear at ladies' gatherings where the mistress of the house played the piano, with playing cards, and with dodging all his relatives' pressures to pull himself together and take a job as a clerk in Severo del Valle's law practice, he bought a barrel organ and took **❺** to the streets with the hope of seducing his Cousin Antonieta and entertaining the public in the bargain. The machine was just a rusty box with wheels, but he painted it with seafaring designs and gave it

❹ ⯅ Critical Viewing In this story, a man builds a flying machine. Which character traits might you find in someone who would try to do this? **[Speculate]**

---

2. **formaldehyde** (for mal′ də hīd′) *n.* solution used as a preservative.
3. **alchemy** (al′ kə mē) *n.* early form of chemistry, with philosophic and magical associations.

134 ■ *Fiction and Nonfiction*

Vocabulary Development

Dictionary Use

Point out the word *depression* near the bottom of p. 135. Using a think-aloud process, model how to use context to infer the appropriate definition of the word. Say to students:

I'm going to think aloud to show you how I would figure out the correct dictionary definition of *depression* by using context clues. The dictionary says that depression can mean 1. a pushing down or depressing; 2. a low place or hollow in a surface; 3. sadness or low spirits;

4. a lowering of activity or amount; 5. a psychological term describing an emotional state characterized by a loss of hope.

In the paragraph, Marcos sinks into a "deep depression" after his beloved marries another man. I know he is sad about this, so I think definition 3 or 5 would fit. I think that definition 3 is best for this context.

a fake ship's smokestack. It ended up looking like a coal stove. The organ played either a military march or a waltz, and in between turns of the handle the parrot, who had managed to learn Spanish although he had not lost his foreign accent, would draw a crowd with his piercing shrieks. He also plucked slips of paper from a box with his beak, by way of selling fortunes to the curious. The little pink, green, and blue papers were so clever that they always divulged the exact secret wishes of the customers. Besides fortunes there were little balls of sawdust to amuse the children. The idea of the organ was a last desperate attempt to win the hand of Cousin Antonieta after more conventional means of courting her had failed. Marcos thought no woman in her right mind could remain impassive before a barrel-organ serenade. He stood beneath her window one evening and played his military march and his waltz just as she was taking tea with a group of female friends. Antonieta did not realize the music was meant for her until the parrot called her by her full name, at which point she appeared in the window. Her reaction was not what her suitor had hoped for. Her friends offered to spread the news to every salon[4] in the city, and the next day people thronged the downtown streets hoping to see Severo del Valle's brother-in-law playing the organ and selling little sawdust balls with a motheaten parrot, for the sheer pleasure of proving that even in the best of families there could be good reason for embarrassment. In the face of this stain to the family reputation, Marcos was forced to give up organ grinding and resort to less conspicuous ways of winning over his Cousin Antonieta, but he did not renounce his goal. In any case, he did not succeed, because from one day to the next the young lady married a diplomat who was twenty years her senior; he took her to live in a tropical country whose name no one could recall, except that it suggested negritude,[5] bananas, and palm trees, where she managed to recover from the memory of that suitor who had ruined her seventeenth year with his military march and his waltz. Marcos sank into a deep depression that lasted two or three days, at the end of which he announced that he would never marry and that he was embarking on a trip around the world. He sold his organ to a blind man and left the parrot to Clara, but Nana secretly poisoned it with an overdose of cod-liver oil, because no one could stand its lusty

---

4. **salon** (sə län') *n.* regular gathering of distinguished guests that meets in a private home.
5. **negritude** (neg' rə tood') *n.* blacks and their cultural heritage.

Literary Analysis
Character In what way does Uncle Marcos's behavior suggest that he is a multidimensional character?

 Reading Check

What does Uncle Marcos do with the barrel organ?

Uncle Marcos ■ 135

---

⑤ Literary Analysis
Character

• Remind students that characters can be round or flat and dynamic or static. Have students keep these aspects of character in mind as they read the bracketed passage.

• **Ask** students to respond to the Literary Analysis question: In what way does Uncle Marcos's behavior suggest that he is a multidimensional character?
Answer: His behavior suggests that there are many aspects to his personality. He is beloved by his nieces and nephews, a world traveler and adventurer, a collector of strange animals, a performer of unusual exercises, an alchemist, a musician, and a man who sleeps in a hammock and teaches a parrot to speak Spanish.

• **Ask** students whether, at this point in the story, they think Uncle Marcos is a static or dynamic character. Have them explain their answers.
Possible response: Uncle Marcos is dynamic because he changes, moving from one emotional state to another. Having failed in his courtship of Antonieta, he becomes depressed, then shakes himself out of his depression and embarks on a trip around the world.

⑥ Reading Check

Answer: He sells it to a blind man.

- Have students review the text on p. 135 about Marcos's experience as an organ grinder.
- Ask students to compare and contrast how the townspeople treated Marcos when he was an organ grinder with how they treat him in the bracketed passage.

Possible response: As an organ grinder, the townspeople laughed at Marcos and viewed him as a "stain" on his family's reputation. Now the townspeople view Marcos with interest and curiosity, especially after he announces his flight.

❽ Critical Viewing

Answer: Uncle Marcos would probably have liked and admired da Vinci. They are kindred spirits.

glance, its fleas, and its harsh, tuneless hawking of paper fortunes and sawdust balls.

That was Marcos's longest trip. He returned with a shipment of enormous boxes that were piled in the far courtyard, between the chicken coop and the woodshed, until the winter was over. At the first signs of spring he had them transferred to the parade grounds, a huge park where people would gather to watch the soldiers file by on Independence Day, with the goosestep they had learned from the Prussians. When the crates were opened, they were found to contain loose bits of wood, metal, and painted cloth. Marcos spent two weeks assembling the contents according to an instruction manual written in English, which he was able to decipher thanks to his invincible imagination and a small dictionary. When the job was finished, it turned out to be a bird of prehistoric dimensions, with the face of a furious eagle, wings that moved, and a propeller on its back. It caused an uproar. The families of the oligarchy[6] forgot all about the barrel organ, and Marcos became the star attraction of the season. People took Sunday outings to see the bird; souvenir vendors and strolling photographers made a fortune. Nonetheless, the public's interest quickly waned. But then Marcos announced that as soon as the weather cleared he planned to take off in his bird and cross the mountain range. The news spread, making this the most talked-about event of the year. The contraption lay with its stomach on terra firma,[7] heavy and sluggish and looking more like a wounded duck than like one of those newfangled airplanes they were starting to produce in the United States. There was nothing in its appearance to suggest that it could move, much less take flight across the snowy peaks. Journalists and the curious flocked to see it. Marcos smiled his immutable[8] smile before the avalanche of questions and posed for photographers without offering the least technical or scientific explanation of how he hoped to carry out his plan. People came from the provinces to see the sight. Forty years later his great-nephew Nicolás, whom Marcos did not live to see, unearthed the desire to fly that had always existed in the men of his lineage. Nicolás was interested in doing it for commercial reasons, in a gigantic hot-air sausage on which would be printed an advertisement for carbonated drinks. But when Marcos announced his plane trip, no one believed that his contraption could be put to any practical use. The appointed day dawned full of clouds, but so many people had turned out that Marcos did not want to

---

6. **oligarchy** (äl′ i gar′ kē) *n.* government ruled by a few.
7. **terra firma** (ter′ a fur′ ma) *n.* Latin term meaning "firm earth; solid ground."
8. **immutable** (im myōōt′ ə bəl) *adj.* never changing.

136 ■ Fiction and Nonfiction

Vocabulary Development

Word Analysis

Call students' attention to the words *invincible* near the top of p. 136 and *invisible* near the bottom of p. 137. Explain that each word begins with the prefix *in-*, which means "not."

Explain that *vincible* is an adjective that means "able to be defeated." So *invincible* means "not able to be defeated." Marcos's imagination could not be defeated. Explain in

the same way that *visible* means "able to be seen" and *invisible* means "not able to be seen."

Have students brainstorm for other words that use the prefix *in-*. Ask them to decode the words by combining the meaning of the base word with what they have learned about the prefix *in-*.

disappoint them. He showed up punctually at the appointed spot and did not once look up at the sky, which was growing darker and darker with thick gray clouds. The astonished crowd filled all the nearby streets, perching on rooftops and the balconies of the nearest houses and squeezing into the park. No political gathering managed to attract so many people until half a century later, when the first Marxist candidate attempted, through strictly democratic channels, to become President. Clara would remember this holiday as long as she lived. People dressed in their spring best, thereby getting a step ahead of the official opening of the season, the men in white linen suits and the ladies in the Italian straw hats that were all the rage that year. Groups of elementary-school children paraded with their teachers, clutching flowers for the hero. Marcos accepted their bouquets and joked that they might as well hold on to them and wait for him to crash, so they could take them directly to his funeral. The bishop himself, accompanied by two incense bearers, appeared to bless the bird without having been asked, and the police band played happy, unpretentious music that pleased everyone. The police, on horseback and carrying lances, had trouble keeping the crowds far enough away from the center of the park, where Marcos waited dressed in mechanic's overalls, with huge racer's goggles and an explorer's helmet. He was also equipped with a compass, a telescope, and several strange maps that he had traced himself based on various theories of Leonardo da Vinci and on the polar knowledge of the Incas.[9] Against all logic, on the second try the bird lifted off without mishap and with a certain elegance, accompanied by the creaking of its skeleton and the roar of its motor. It rose flapping its wings and disappeared into the clouds, to a send-off of applause, whistlings, handkerchiefs, drumrolls, and the sprinkling of holy water. All that remained on earth were the comments of the amazed crowd below and a multitude of experts, who attempted to provide a reasonable explanation of the miracle. Clara continued to stare at the sky long after her uncle had become invisible. She thought she saw him ten minutes later, but it was only a migrating sparrow. After three days the initial euphoria that had accompanied the first airplane flight in the country died down and no one gave the episode another thought, except for Clara, who continued to peer at the horizon.

After a week with no word from the flying uncle, people began to speculate that he had gone so high that he had disappeared into outer space, and the ignorant suggested he would reach the moon. With a mixture of sadness and relief, Severo decided that his

---

9. Leonardo da Vinci (lē′ ə när′ dō də vin′ chē) . . . **Incas** Leonardo da Vinci (1452–1519) was an Italian painter, sculptor, architect, and scientist. The Incas were Native Americans who dominated ancient Peru until the Spanish conquest.

Reading Skill
Author's Purpose
What does the statement "Clara would remember this holiday as long as she lived" suggest about the author's purpose in this story?

❿

Reading Check

Where does Uncle Marcos plan to fly in his flying machine?

Uncle Marcos ■ 137

---

❾ Reading Skill
Author's Purpose

- Ask students to define an author's purpose and to explain how readers can determine this.
  Answer: An author's purpose is his or her main reason for writing. Readers can determine an author's purpose by reflecting on story details and events.

- Write the following sentence on the board: "Clara would remember this holiday as long as she lived." Have students discuss what this event means to Clara.

- **Ask** students the Reading Skill Question: What does the statement "Clara would remember this holiday as long as she lived" suggest about the author's purpose in this story?
  Answer: The author wants to emphasize the affection and admiration Clara has for her uncle.

❿ Reading Check

Answer: He plans to cross the mountain range.

⓫ Reading Skill
Author's Purpose

- Have students summarize the bracketed passage.
  Answer: Uncle Marcos has returned from his flight. Even though the plane went down and he had to walk back, Uncle Marcos is in high spirits.

- **Ask** students the Reading Skill question: What do the narrator's observations about Marcos suggest about the author's purpose?
  Possible response: The author's purpose is to cast the situation in a humorous light and to help establish Marcos as an eternal optimist.

- Guide a discussion of how these details contribute to Allende's overall purpose, which is to entertain her readers.

▶ **Monitor Progress:** Review students' graphic organizers to make sure that they are correctly determining the author's purpose.

▶ **Reteach:** If students have trouble determining author's purpose, review the background information on p. 122. Then ask students to think of a writing assignment that they have done recently. Ask them why they wrote the piece. What did they want to achieve? What details did they include to achieve that purpose?

---

brother-in-law and his machine must have fallen into some hidden crevice of the cordillera,[10] where they would never be found. Nivea wept <u>disconsolately</u> and lit candles to San Antonio, patron of lost objects. Severo opposed the idea of having masses said, because he did not believe in them as a way of getting into heaven, much less of returning to earth, and he maintained that masses and religious vows, like the selling of indulgences, images, and scapulars,[11] were a dishonest business. Because of his attitude, Nivea and Nana had the children say the rosary,[12] behind their father's back for nine days. Meanwhile, groups of volunteer explorers and mountain climbers tirelessly searched peaks and passes, combing every accessible stretch of land until they finally returned in triumph to hand the family the mortal remains of the deceased in a sealed black coffin. The intrepid traveler was laid to rest in a grandiose funeral. His death made him a hero and his name was on the front page of all the papers for several days. The same multitude that had gathered to see him off the day he flew away in his bird paraded past his coffin. The entire family wept as befit the occasion, except for Clara, who continued to watch the sky with the patience of an astronomer. One week after he had been buried, Uncle Marcos, a bright smile playing behind his pirate's mustache, appeared in person in the doorway of Nivea and Severo del Valle's house. Thanks to

⓫ the surreptitious[13] prayers of the women and children, as he himself admitted, he was alive and well and in full possession of his faculties, including his sense of humor. Despite the noble lineage of his aerial maps, the flight had been a failure. He had lost his airplane and had to return on foot, but he had not broken any bones and his adventurous spirit was intact. This confirmed the family's eternal devotion to San Antonio, but was not taken as a warning by future generations, who also tried to fly, although by different means. Legally, however, Marcos was a corpse. Severo del Valle was obliged to use all his legal ingenuity to bring his brother-in-law back to life and the full rights of citizenship. When the coffin was pried open in the presence of the appropriate authorities, it was found to contain a bag of sand. This discovery ruined the reputation, up till then untarnished, of the volunteer explorers and mountain climbers, who from that day on were considered little better than a pack of bandits.

⓬ Marcos's heroic resurrection made everyone forget about his barrel-organ phase. Once again he was a sought-after guest in all

---

10. **cordillera** (kôr′ dil yer′ ə) *n.* system or chain of mountains.
11. **indulgences, images, and scapulars** (skap′ yə lərz) Indulgences are pardons for sins; images are pictures or sculptures of religious figures; and scapulars are garments worn by Roman Catholics as tokens of religious devotion.
12. **say the rosary** use a set of beads to say prayers.
13. **surreptitious** (sʉr′ əp tish′ əs) *adj.* secretive.

138 ■ *Fiction and Nonfiction*

Vocabulary Builder
disconsolately (dis kän′ sə lit lē) *adv.* very unhappily

Reading Skill
Author's Purpose
What do the narrator's observations about Marcos suggest about the author's purpose?

Vocabulary Development

Expressive Vocabulary
As students are discussing Uncle Marcos and his adventures, encourage them to use the expressive vocabulary presented earlier. Encourage them with sentence starters like these:
1. To *enhance* his life, Uncle Marcos . . .
2. Uncle Marcos *alters* . . .
3. The townspeople *distort* . . .
4. The relationship between Uncle Marcos and Clara *evolves* . . .
5. Uncle Marcos's exploits *generate* . . .
   Challenge students to use these words as you continue to discuss the story.

138

the city's salons and, at least for a while, his name was cleared. Marcos stayed in his sister's house for several months. One night he left without saying goodbye, leaving behind his trunks, his books, his weapons, his boots, and all his belongings. Severo, and even Nivea herself, breathed a sigh of relief. His visit had gone on too long. But Clara was so upset that she spent a week walking in her sleep and sucking her thumb. The little girl, who was only seven at the time, had learned to read from her uncle's storybooks and been closer to him than any other member of the family because of her prophesying powers. Marcos maintained that his niece's gift could be a source of income and a good opportunity for him to cultivate his own clairvoyance.[14] He believed that all human beings possessed this ability, particularly his own family, and that if it did not function well it was simply due to a lack of training. He bought a crystal ball in the Persian bazaar, insisting that it had magic powers and was from the East (although it was later found to be part of a buoy from a fishing boat), set it down on a background of black velvet, and announced that he could tell people's fortunes, cure the evil eye, and improve the quality of dreams, all for the modest sum of five centavos.[15] His first customers were the maids from around the neighborhood. One of them had been accused of stealing, because her employer had misplaced a valuable ring. The crystal ball revealed the exact location of the object in question: it had rolled beneath a wardrobe. The next day there was a line outside the front door of the house. There were coachmen, storekeepers, and milkmen; later a few municipal employees and distinguished ladies made a discreet appearance, slinking along the side walls of the house to keep from being recognized. The customers were received by Nana, who ushered them into the waiting room and collected their fees. This task kept her busy throughout the day and demanded so much of her time that the family began to complain that all there ever was for dinner was old string beans and jellied quince.[16] Marcos decorated the carriage house with some frayed curtains that had once belonged in the drawing room but that neglect and age had turned to dusty rags. There he and Clara received the customers. The two divines wore tunics "color of the men of light," as Marcos called the color yellow. Nana had dyed them with saffron powder, boiling them in pots usually reserved for rice and pasta. In addition to his tunic, Marcos wore a turban around his head and an Egyptian amulet around his neck. He had

⑬ ▲ Critical Viewing
What qualities of a crystal ball make it appear to have "magic powers"? **[Analyze]**

⑭ ✓ Reading Check
What power does Marcos believe Clara holds?

14. **clairvoyance** (kler voi′ əns) *n.* supposed ability to perceive unseen things.
15. **centavos** (sen tä′ vōs) *n.* coins equal to 1/100 of a cruzeiro, the basic monetary unit of Brazil.
16. **quince** (kwins) golden or greenish-yellow, hard, apple-shaped fruit.

Uncle Marcos ■ 139

---

⑫ Literary Analysis
Character

- Ask students what business Marco and Clara start together and why they decide to quit.
  Answer: Marcos and Clara tell people's fortunes. They quit the business because they realize that they have too much power over people. They are worried that someone might do something foolish as a result of one of their predictions.

- **Ask** students to respond to the Literary Analysis question: Which details in this passage indicate that Marcos has changed since the beginning of the story?
  Answer: At the beginning of the story, Marcos seemed indifferent to the people around him. Now he seems to genuinely care for others.

- Have students identify the aspects of character that this information reveals about Uncle Marcos.
  Answer: This information reveals that Uncle Marcos is a round, dynamic character.

⑬ Critical Viewing

Possible response: The crystal ball reflects light and magnifies images, making it appear to contain energy and light. It seems as if someone looking into it might see images from another dimension or time.

⑭ Reading Check

Answer: Marcos believes that Clara has the power to see the future.

Differentiated
Instruction — Solutions for All Learners

Enrichment for Advanced Readers
Review magical realism with students. Then have them meet in a group and discuss the elements of magic in "Uncle Marcos." Ask them to consider the following questions:
- Do the magical elements contribute to or detract from the story?
- How do the magical elements contribute to your understanding of Marcos and of Clara?
- How do the magical elements contribute to the theme?
- How does the magical realism of "Uncle Marcos" compare to that used in other magical realist stories that you have read?
  Have students present a summary of their ideas to the class.

139

- Ask students what they have learned about Clara's character throughout the story.
  Possible response: Clara has clairvoyant powers, and she loves and admires her uncle so much that she sleepwalks and sucks her thumb when he leaves.

- **Ask** the Literary Analysis question: Which details in this paragraph indicate that Clara, like Marcos, is a complex character?
  Answer: Details that indicate Clara is a complex character include her interest in Uncle Marcos's stories, how she memorized words from different Indian dialects, how she knew the exact way in which certain Indians pierced their lips and earlobes, and how she remembered the unpronounceable names of flora and fauna.

- Emphasize to students that just because a character is round does not mean the character is also dynamic. **Ask** students whether they think Clara is dynamic or static and to explain their reasoning.
  Answer: Clara is static. Although the reader learns about different aspects of Clara's character, there is no evidence that she changes or grows as a result of her experiences.

grown a beard and let his hair grow long and he was thinner than ever before. Marcos and Clara were utterly convincing, especially because the child had no need to look into the crystal ball to guess what her clients wanted to hear. She would whisper in her Uncle Marcos's ear, and he in turn would transmit the message to the client, along with any improvisations of his own that he thought pertinent. Thus their fame spread, because all those who arrived sad and bedraggled at the consulting room left filled with hope.

<u>Unrequited</u> lovers were told how to win over indifferent hearts, and the poor left with foolproof tips on how to place their money at the dog tracks. Business grew so prosperous that the waiting room was always packed with people, and Nana began to suffer dizzy spells from being on her feet so many hours a day. This time Severo had no need to intervene to put a stop to his brother-in-law's venture, for both Marcos and Clara, realizing that their unerring guesses could alter the fate of their clients, who always followed their advice to the letter, became frightened and decided that this was a job for swindlers. They abandoned their carriage-house oracle and split the profits, even though the only one who had cared about the material side of things had been Nana.

Of all the del Valle children, Clara was the one with the greatest interest in and stamina for her uncle's stories. She could repeat each and every one of them. She knew by heart words from several dialects of the Indians, was acquainted with their customs, and could describe the exact way in which they pierced their lips and earlobes with wooden shafts, their initiation rites, the names of the most poisonous snakes, and the appropriate antidotes for each. Her uncle was so eloquent that the child could feel in her own skin the burning sting of snakebites, see reptiles slide across the carpet between the legs of the jacaranda[17] room divider, and hear the shrieks of macaws behind the drawing-room drapes. She did not hesitate as she recalled Lope de Aguirre's search for El Dorado,[18] or the unpronounceable names of the flora and fauna her extraordinary uncle had seen; she knew about the lamas who take salt tea with yak lard and she could give detailed descriptions of the opulent women of Tahiti, the rice fields of China, or the white prairies of the North, where the eternal ice kills animals and men who lose their way, turning them to stone in seconds. Marcos had various travel journals in which he recorded his excursions and impressions, as well as a collection of maps and books of stories and fairy tales that he kept in the trunks he stored in the junk room at the far end of

---

17. jacaranda (jak′ ə ran′ də) type of tropical American tree.
18. Lope de Aguirre's (lō′ pā dā ä gēr′ rās) . . . **El Dorado** Lope de Aguirre was a Spanish adventurer (1510–1561) in colonial South America who searched for a legendary country called El Dorado, which was supposedly rich in gold.

140 ■ Fiction and Nonfiction

Vocabulary Builder
unrequited (un ri kwit′ id) *adj.* not returned or repaid

Literary Analysis
Character Which details in this paragraph indicate that Clara, like Marcos, is a complex character?

Vocabulary Development

Vocabulary Knowledge Rating
When students have completed reading and discussing "Uncle Marcos," have them take out their **Vocabulary Knowledge Rating Chart** for this selection. Read the words aloud once more and have students rate their knowledge of the words again in the After Reading column. Clarify any words that are still problematic. Have students write their own definition and example or sentence in the appropriate column. Then have students complete the **Vocabulary Builder Practice** activities on p. 143. Encourage students to use the words in further discussion and written work about this selection. Remind them that they will be accountable for these words on the Selection Test.

the third courtyard. From there they were hauled out to inhabit the dreams of his descendants, until they were mistakenly burned half a century later on an infamous pyre.

Now Marcos had returned from his last journey in a coffin. He had died of a mysterious African plague that had turned him as yellow and wrinkled as a piece of parchment. When he realized he was ill, he set out for home with the hope that his sister's ministrations and Dr. Cuevas's knowledge would restore his health and youth, but he was unable to withstand the sixty days on ship and died at the latitude of Guayaquil,[19] ravaged by fever and hallucinating about musky women and hidden treasure. The captain of the ship, an Englishman by the name of Longfellow, was about to throw him overboard wrapped in a flag, but Marcos, despite his savage appearance and his delirium, had made so many friends on board and seduced so many women that the passengers prevented him from doing so, and Longfellow was obliged to store the body side by side with the vegetables of the Chinese cook, to preserve it from the heat and mosquitoes of the tropics until the ship's carpenter had time to improvise a coffin. At El Callao[20] they obtained a more appropriate container, and several days later the captain, furious at all the troubles this passenger had caused the shipping company and himself personally, unloaded him without a backward glance, surprised that not a soul was there to receive the body or cover the expenses he had incurred. Later he learned that the post office in these latitudes was not as reliable as that of far-off England, and that all his telegrams had vaporized en route. Fortunately for Longfellow, a customs lawyer who was a friend of the del Valle family appeared and offered to take charge, placing Marcos and all his paraphernalia in a freight car, which he shipped to the capital to the only known address of the deceased: his sister's house. . . .

19. **Guayaquil** (gwī ä kēl´) seaport in western Ecuador.
20. **El Callao** (kə yä´ ō) seaport in western Peru.

⑯ Literature in Context

Humanities Connection

Magical Realists The literary movement known as Magical Realism is most closely associated with the wonder-filled novels and short stories of a group of twentieth-century Latin American authors. Isabel Allende is an important writer in this group. The great Argentinian writer Jorge Luis Borges is another. His style often combines realistic characters and events with details that seem to come out of dreams and myths. Gabriel García Márquez of Colombia is often considered the central figure of the movement. His works chronicle the lives of passionate and sympathetic characters who experience miraculous happenings and strange, unearthly events.

Connect to the Literature

What elements of "Uncle Marcos" confirm that it belongs to the literary movement known as Magical Realism?

Still Life Reviving, Remedios Varos, Collection of Beatriz Varo de Cano, Valencia, Spain.

Uncle Marcos ■ 141

⑯ Literature in Context

Humanities Connection Magical Realism, as represented by writers such as Allende and Marquez, challenges readers with a paradox by mixing mundane, everyday reality with magical events that are treated like common, everyday occurrences. Only the reader perceives that events have slipped into the supernatural. Although generally considered to have originated in South America, Magical Realism is also practiced by such diverse writers as Ben Okri of Nigeria, Toni Morrison of the United States, and Syl Cheney-Coker of Sierra Leone. The Nobel Prizes awarded to both Marquez and Morrison are evidence of Magical Realism's international acceptance and appreciation.

Connect to the Literature Point out the matter-of-fact language of "Uncle Marcos"; neither the narrator nor the characters seem surprised by the magical events that happen. **Ask** students the Connect to the Literature question: What elements of "Uncle Marcos" confirm that it belongs to the literary movement known as Magical Realism? **Answer:** The story intermingles the common occurrences of everyday life with magical, extraordinary events, such as Marcos's flight and Clara's clairvoyance. None of the characters seem to think these events are odd or miraculous.

Concept Connector

Connecting to the Literature
Ask students to review the character sketches they created for the Motivation activity. Have them share their ideas and talk about whether they anticipated the kind of character that they discovered Marcos to be.

Reading Skill Graphic Organizer
Have students review the graphic organizers they completed to determine the author's purpose while reading. Then show them **Reading Skill Graphic Organizer B** (*Graphic Organizers Transparencies,* p. 31) as an example. Have students share the graphic organizers they did and the details they identified that support their conclusions about the author's purpose.

Apply the Skills

Uncle Marcos

Thinking About the Selection

1. **Respond:** Which of Uncle Marcos's adventures would you most like to share with him? Why?
2. **(a) Recall:** What does Uncle Marcos do to try to win the hand of Cousin Antonieta? **(b) Connect:** Is her reaction what Uncle Marcos expects? Explain. **(c) Compare and Contrast:** How do the actions that each character takes after the courtship differ?
3. **(a) Recall:** What does Uncle Marcos make from the materials he brings back in "enormous boxes"? **(b) Infer:** What do you think motivates Uncle Marcos to undertake this project?
4. **(a) Compare and Contrast:** Compare and contrast Clara's reaction to her uncle's disappearance with those of the others. **(b) Interpret:** What does Clara's reaction show about her personality and her relationship to Uncle Marcos? Explain.
5. **(a) Draw Conclusions:** What life lessons can people learn from the character of Uncle Marcos? **(b) Discuss:** Share your responses with a small group and discuss the differences and similarities among them. **(c) Reflect:** How has your response grown or changed as a result of this discussion?

Literary Analysis

6. **(a)** Using a chart like the one shown, list at least three of Uncle Marcos's projects or adventures. Then, identify a quality that each project or adventure reveals.

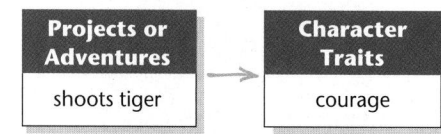

Projects or Adventures		Character Traits
shoots tiger	→	courage

 (b) Based on his projects and adventures, summarize the **character** of Uncle Marcos in a few sentences.
7. Review the characters of Clara and Uncle Marcos. **(a)** Determine whether each character is **round** or **flat**. Explain. **(b)** Determine whether each character is **static** or **dynamic**. Explain.

Reading Skill

8. **(a)** What specific **purpose** might Isabel Allende have had for creating the character of Uncle Marcos? **(b)** Identify three details from the story and explain how **reflecting** on them helped you determine Allende's purpose.

142 ■ *Fiction and Nonfiction*

QuickReview

Story at a Glance
An eccentric man makes a lasting impression on his niece.

Go Online
Assessment
For: Self-test
Visit: www.PHSchool.com
Web Code: epa-6111

Character: a person or an animal who takes part in the action of a literary work. Characters can be *round* or *flat*, *dynamic* or *static*.

Author's Purpose: a writer's main reason for writing a literary work

Answers (left and bottom columns)

1. **Possible response:** Students may cite the flight over the mountains because of the pleasure of flying.

2. (a) He serenades her with a barrel organ. (b) No, his efforts produce the opposite of what he intended. (c) Marcos swears he will never marry, and then goes on a trip around the world. Antonieta marries and leaves for a faraway place.

3. (a) He makes a flying machine. (b) Students may say that Marcos seeks risk and adventure in front of a huge audience.

4. (a) Clara never doubts that Marcos will return alive; Severo feels sad but relieved; Nivea feels sad. (b) Clara has faith that Uncle Marcos has not failed and is still alive, which indicates the strong bond she feels for him.

5. (a) **Possible response:** People should live their lives with good humor, confidence, and a sense of adventure. (b) Students should discuss the lessons that readers might learn from Marcos. (c) Students may find that they have seen new sides of Marcos as a result of the discussion.

6. (a) **Sample response: Projects or Adventures—Character Traits:** performs alchemy—curiosity; takes trip around world—adventurousness; builds flying machine—inventiveness

 Another sample answer can be found on **Literary Analysis Graphic Organizer B, p. 35** in *Graphic Organizer Transparencies.*

 (b) Marcos is an eccentric and adventurous man who takes chances. He is inventive and imaginative, and he has the courage to follow through with his dreams and ideas.

7. (a) Marcos and Clara are both round. Readers see different sides of their personalities. They learn, for example, that both characters have varied interests and feelings. (b) Marcos is a dynamic character, because he changes and develops during the story. For example, his emotions shift when he believes he can win Antonieta

and when she rejects him. Clara is a static character; readers do not see her change.

8. (a) Allende's purpose was to produce a memorable character whom readers will admire—or at least find intriguing—for his imagination, spirit, and energy. (b) The details of the wooing of Antonieta, the trip around the world, and the displays of clairvoyance make Marcos a vivid and unique presence for the reader.

Vocabulary Builder

Practice Review the vocabulary list for "Uncle Marcos" on page 122. Then, decide whether each of the following statements is true or false. Explain your answers.

1. Something that looks *pallid* is full of color.
2. Sighing *disconsolately* is a good way to express enthusiasm.
3. *Unrequited* love is symbolized by a wedding.

Adding Words to Your Vocabulary Using a dictionary or a thesaurus, find an **antonym**, a word that has the opposite meaning, for each italicized word from the vocabulary list. Then, use each antonym correctly in a sentence. (For more on using a dictionary and a thesaurus, see pages R6–7.)

Writing

Write a **character profile** of Uncle Marcos.
- Begin by jotting down details that capture the character's appearance, personality, and achievements.
- Decide on a single impression to convey about the character.
- Organize and present details so that they all contribute to that one impression.

For *Grammar, Vocabulary,* and *Assessment,* see **Build Language Skills,** pages 144–145.

Extend Your Learning

Listening and Speaking Write and perform a **scene** based on the passage in which Uncle Marcos makes his flight across the mountains.
- Write a script for the scene.
- Cast the scene, and briefly rehearse.

Perform the scene for the class.

Research and Technology Use a variety of sources, including the library and the Internet, to research the history of human flight. Record your research in a **learning log,** a written record of information you discover about the topic. Analyze the information by discussing it with classmates and by comparing your findings to Uncle Marcos's adventure with flight. In your discussions, decide if that aspect of the story is realistic or fantastic.

Apply the Skills ■ 143

Go Online **For:** An additional research activity
—Research **Visit:** www.PHSchool.com
   Web Code: epd-7108
For another research activity to extend students' learning, give students this Web Code.

Vocabulary Builder
Practice

1. False; *pallid* means "pale," which describes something that lacks color.
2. False; *disconsolately* means "unhappy." Sighing unhappily does not show enthusiasm.
3. False; *unrequited* means "not returned." Love that is not returned does not lead to marriage.

Adding Words to Your Vocabulary
Possible response:

pallid—colorful; The costume was colorful.

disconsolately—joyfully; Upon landing, Marcos laughed joyfully.

unrequited—returned; Antonieta returned her husband's love.

Writing

- To give students guidance for writing a character profile, give them **Support for Writing** for "Uncle Marcos", p. 169, in *Unit 1 Resources.*
- To evaluate students' character profiles, use the Descriptive Essay rubrics, pp. 55–56 in *General Resources.*

Six Traits Focus

✔ Ideas	✔ Word Choice
✔ Organization	Sentence Fluency
Voice	Conventions

Writing and Grammar, Gold Level
Students will find guidance on descriptive writing in Chapter 6.

Build Language Skills

Go to pp. 144–145 for vocabulary and grammar lessons and assessment practice.

Extend Your Learning

The Support for **Extend Your Learning** page (*Unit 1 Resources,* p. 170) provides guided note-taking opportunities to help students complete the Extend Your Learning activities.

Vocabulary Skill

- Introduce the word root *-vit-*. Ask students to brainstorm for words that include the root *-vit-*.
Possible responses: *vital, vitals, vitality, vita.* Explain how the meaning of "life" contributes to the meaning of each of these words.

- Have students complete the Practice activity on this page.

Answers

1. *-vita-*: The suffix *-able* was added to make the meaning "able to live."

2. *-volve-*: The prefix *re,* meaning "again," was added to make the meaning "to turn again."

3. *-vita-*: The suffix *-al* and the word *signs* were added to make the meaning "signs of life."

4. *-tri-; Athlon,* meaning "prize won in a contest," was added from the Greek, making the meaning "a three-part contest."

5. *-tri-; Triad,* from the Latin for "toward," was added, making the meaning "a union of three."

Grammar Lesson

- Point out that there are several other types of pronouns besides relative, interrogative, and indefinite.

- Have students complete the Practice activity on this page.

Answers

1. Some (indefinite)

2. Whose (interrogative)

3. who (relative)

4. whose (relative)

Writing Application

To evaluate students' papers, make sure that each of the three sentences contains a different type of the three pronouns.

$\mathcal{WG}$ **Writing and Grammar, Gold Level**

Students will find further instruction and practice on relative, interrogative, and indefinite pronouns in Chapter 16, Section 2.

Build Language Skills

The Secret Life of Walter Mitty • Uncle Marcos

Vocabulary Skill

Word Origins Words from Latin and Greek roots form the core of the English language. Numerous English words that have been invented, or coined, use a combination of roots from different languages. In 1913, C. Funk, a Polish biochemist, coined the word *vitamin* from the Latin *-vit-,* meaning "life," and the German word *amine,* from the mistaken idea that these substances contain amino acids. He believed that *vita-mins* were essential to life.

Practice Next to each word or compound word, write the root that it came from. Then, write down what has been added to the root as the word evolved.

1. viable
2. revolve
3. vital signs
4. triathlon
5. triad

Grammar Lesson

Pronouns: Relative, Interrogative, and Indefinite Pronouns are words that stand for nouns.

- A **relative pronoun** begins a subordinate clause and connects it to another idea in the sentence. The five relative pronouns are *that, which, who, whom,* and *whose.*

- An **interrogative pronoun** is used to begin a question. The five interrogative pronouns are *what, which, who, whom,* and *whose.*

- **Indefinite pronouns** refer to people, places, or things, often without specifying which ones.

MorePractice

For more practice with pronouns, see the Grammar Handbook, p. R39.

INDEFINITE PRONOUNS					
Singular				**Plural**	**Singular or Plural**
another	either	much	one	both	all most
anybody	everybody	neither	other	few	any none
anyone	everyone	nobody	somebody	many	more some
anything	everything	no one	someone	others	
each	little	nothing	something	several	

Practice Identify the pronouns in each sentence, and tell whether each one is relative, interrogative, or indefinite.

1. Some of the pies looked delicious.
2. Whose do you want to take?
3. Andrew is the sprinter who always wins.
4. We met Lori's dad, whose hair is red.

$\mathcal{WG}$ *Prentice Hall Writing and Grammar Connection: Chapter 16, Section 2*

144 ■ Fiction and Nonfiction

Teaching Resources

The following resources can be used to enrich or extend the instruction for Build Language Skills.

Unit 1 Resources
Build Language Skills: Vocabulary Skill: The Latin root *-vit-,* p. 172
Build Grammar Skills: Relative, Interrogative, and Indefinite Pronouns, p. 173

Assessment Practice

Reading Skill: Author's Purpose

Directions: *Read the selection. Then, answer the questions.*

   She had no proper wardrobe, no jewels, nothing. . . . She would have so loved to charm, to be envied, to be admired and sought after.

   She had a rich friend, a schoolmate from the convent she had attended, but she didn't like to visit her because it always made her so miserable when she got home again. She would weep for whole days at a time from sorrow, regret, despair, and distress. . . .

   She danced enraptured—carried away, intoxicated with pleasure, forgetting everything in this triumph of her beauty and the glory of her success, floating in a cloud of happiness. . . .

—from "The Necklace" by Guy de Maupassant

1. The emphasis on the character indicates that the author is highlighting
   A a trait of society.
   B a political insight.
   C a human trait.
   D a trend of the future.

2. From the passage, the reader can speculate that the author's purpose is
   A to impart a lesson about possessions.
   B to impart a lesson about quickly changing emotions.
   C to impart a lesson about music's power.
   D to demonstrate the joy of wealth.

3. What is the best description of the author's purpose?
   A to entertain
   B to inform
   C to describe
   D to persuade

4. What would previewing this work tell the reader?
   A This is a text to skim and scan.
   B This is a text to read normally.
   C Notes should be taken as you read.
   D Notes should be taken after you reflect on the text.

Timed Writing: Explanation

Review "The Secret Life of Walter Mitty" or "Uncle Marcos." Write an explanation of why, in your opinion, people long for adventure. Use specifics from the text to support your explanation. **(20 minutes)**

Writing Workshop: *Work in Progress*

Problem-Solution Essay

Build on the Problem/Solution Notes you created. List three specific examples of the problem. Then, list three examples of how your solution would work. Put these notes in your writing portfolio.

Build Language Skills ■ 145

Reading: Author's Purpose

1. C
2. B
3. C
4. B

Timed Writing

- Tell students that when they write an explanation, they should include the reasons for their opinions and examples to support those reasons.

- Remind students that to justify their explanation their examples and details must closely relate to their reasoning.

- Point out to students that they must have enough support for each reason to make it believable.

- Suggest that students organize their time to give 2 minutes to planning, 15 minutes to writing, and 3 minutes to reviewing and revising.

- Assess students' explanations based on the logic of their reasoning and on the strength of their examples and support for their reasoning.

Writing Workshop
Work in Progress

Problem-Solution Essay

- Have students go to their portfolios and take out the work they have completed so far on this assignment.

- Remind students that this work may be used in the problem-solution essay they will write in the **Writing Workshop** at the end of Part 2.

- Have students reflect on the problem-solution notes that they created earlier. After they have written the three specific examples of the problem, have them reflect on how their solution would work.

- Emphasize to students that they should be willing to change their solution if they are uncertain of its effectiveness.

- When students have completed this activity, have them keep it in their portfolios. They will use it as they continue the Work in Progress.

145

Comparing Literary Works • *Theme*

See TeacherExpress™/Lesson View for a detailed lesson plan for Comparing Literary Works.

Literary Analysis
❶ Theme

• Read the instruction about theme together. Tell students to think of theme as the message of the story. Explain that as they read, students should ask themselves what statement the writer is trying to make about life or the world.

• Tell students that sometimes the title will give a hint to a story's theme. **Ask** students what feelings or images the two selection titles suggest to them. **Possible response:** Students might say that the titles evoke feelings of sadness, emptiness, or fear.

❷ Comparing Themes

• Remind students that themes in works of fiction often reflect a larger meaning or universal truth.

• Give students a copy of **Comparing Theme Graphic Organizer A** (*Graphic Organizer Transparencies,* p. 36). Have them complete it as they read and compare the selections. Suggest that they include details like these:

• characters' thoughts or opinions

• setting

• story title

• word choice

❶ Theme

Theme is the central message or insight about life that is conveyed through a short story, an essay, or another literary work. Sometimes, the theme is stated directly. More often, it is suggested indirectly through the words and experiences of the characters or through the events of a story.

❷ Comparing Themes

The development of theme depends in part on the genre, or form, of the work.

• **Nonfiction:** In nonfiction literature, such as essays, the theme is usually stated directly as a main idea. Because the *structure,* or organization, of nonfiction writing varies, the theme may be stated in the beginning, the middle, or the end of a work. The writer supports, or proves, the idea with facts, details, and examples.

• **Fiction and poetry:** In most short stories, novels, poetry, and plays, the theme is implied, or suggested. Readers must figure out the theme by looking at the ideas expressed through story events, characters' statements and actions, or patterns of related images and ideas called *motifs.*

"If I Forget Thee, Oh Earth . . ."   Silent Spring

Deals with environmental issues.

Both of the following selections address the topics of the environment. However, the selections are different genres. "If I Forget Thee, Oh Earth . . ." is a short story, and the excerpt from *Silent Spring* is a work of nonfiction. As you read, use a Venn diagram like the one shown to compare the themes and the ways in which each author develops them.

Vocabulary Builder

"If I Forget Thee, Oh Earth . . ."

■ **purged** (pʉrjd) *v.* cleansed (p. 148) *The ointment purged the wound of infection.*

■ **perennial** (pə ren′ ē əl) *adj.* happening over and over; perpetual (p. 151) *The perennial floods wore down the rocks.*

from Silent Spring

■ **blight** (blīt) *n.* something that destroys or prevents growth (p. 154) *A terrible blight killed all their crops.*

■ **maladies** (mal′ ə dēz) *n.* diseases (p. 154) *They became sick from various maladies.*

■ **moribund** (môr′ i bund′) *adj.* dying (p. 155) *Due to the drought, my garden is moribund.*

146 ■ *Fiction and Nonfiction*

Vocabulary Development

Vocabulary Knowledge Rating
Create a **Vocabulary Knowledge Rating Chart** with the selection vocabulary and expressive vocabulary for both selections. Give students a copy. Introduce the words by reading them aloud and having students mark their rating in the Before Reading column. Urge them to be alert to these words as they read and discuss the selection because they will rate their knowledge of the words again after they finish.

If you wish, you may tally how many students know (or think they know) a word to gauge how much instruction you need to provide. As students read, point out the words and their context.

Build Understanding

❸ Connecting to the Literature

Reading/Writing Connection Both of these stories present a grim vision of the future that encourages readers to take action to protect Earth. Explain your vision of the future and what you think humans might do to preserve Earth. Use at least three of the following words in your response: *adapt, challenge, communicate, distribute, maximize.*

Meet the Authors

Arthur C. **Clarke** (b. 1917)

Born in England, Arthur C. Clarke is both a writer and a scientist. He wrote his first science-fiction stories during his teens, and he has since published more than fifty works of fiction and nonfiction.

A True Scientist Although best known for his science fiction, Clarke is a serious scientist as well. In 1945, he published a technical article called "Extra-Terrestrial Relays" in which he established the principles of the satellite communications system we have today.

Rachel **Carson** (1907–1964)

Even as a young girl, Rachel Carson thought of herself as a writer, and she entered college to pursue that goal. Once there, she renewed an interest in nature and switched her major to marine biology. She later earned a master's degree in zoology.

Environmental Activist Carson had long been worried about the overuse of pesticides. "Everything which meant most to me as a naturalist was being threatened," she said, and she felt that the most important thing she could do was publicize the facts. *Silent Spring* became one of the most influential environmental books ever written. Carson died of cancer before she witnessed the major impact of her book.

 For: More about the authors
Visit: www.PHSchool.com
Web Code: epe-9113

"If I Forget Thee, Oh Earth . . ." / from *Silent Spring* ■ 147

❸ Connecting to the Literature

- Model use of the expressive vocabulary students are asked to use with these examples:

  1. It has been a *challenge* for humans to balance their needs with the need to take care of Earth.

  2. We expect Earth to *adapt* to us, but in reality, it is we who should adapt to Earth.

  3. One way to start this process is to *communicate* the importance of taking care of natural resources.

  4. This will *maximize* humanity's chances of being able to enjoy Earth for centuries to come.

- Help students further develop their expressive vocabulary by providing these words: *efficient, conserve, optimistic, pessimistic.* Encourage students to use these words as they discuss the selections.

Go Online
Author Link For additional information about Arthur C. Clarke and Rachel Carson, have students type in the Web Code, select C from the alphabet, and then select *Arthur C. Clarke* or *Rachel Carson.*

Teaching Resources

The following resources can be used to enrich, extend, or differentiate the instruction for Comparing Literary Works.

Unit 1 Resources, pp. 180–186

Graphic Organizer Transparencies, pp. 36–39

Reader's Notebook

Reader's Notebook: Adapted Version

Reader's Notebook: English Learner's Version

Listening to Literature Audio CD

❶ Background

Environmentalism A major theme of these selections is that people must care for and defend the Earth, or suffer future consequences. People who work to protect and promote nature are called environmentalists. Collectively, environmentalists are known for spreading information about how humanity harms the planet and what action we can take to stop or reduce this damage.

❷ Motivation

Write the following quotation from "If I Forget Thee, Oh Earth..." on the board or read it aloud:

Never again would the supply ships come flaming down through the stars with gifts from home.... On the shadowed globe the lights of the cities had dimmed and died, and they were alone at last, as no man had ever been alone before.

Have students use the quotation to predict the answers to the following questions: Who is the speaker? Where is he? What is the shadowed globe? What has happened? Why are the people alone? Have students read the story to find out whether their inferences were correct.

Concept Connector ➡

Students will follow up on this activity after completing "If I Forget Thee, Oh Earth. . . ."

❸ About the Selection

The title of "If I Forget Thee, Oh Earth. . ." is a quotation from Psalm 137:

If I forget thee, O Jerusalem, let my right hand forget her cunning.

This vow expresses the emotion of Jews who were forced into exile in Babylon in 597 B.C. The exiles in Arthur C. Clarke's story are the sole survivors of a nuclear holocaust, now living on the moon.

The story provides an alarming warning that the human race might someday be forced into exile in space and be left with only memories of life on Earth.

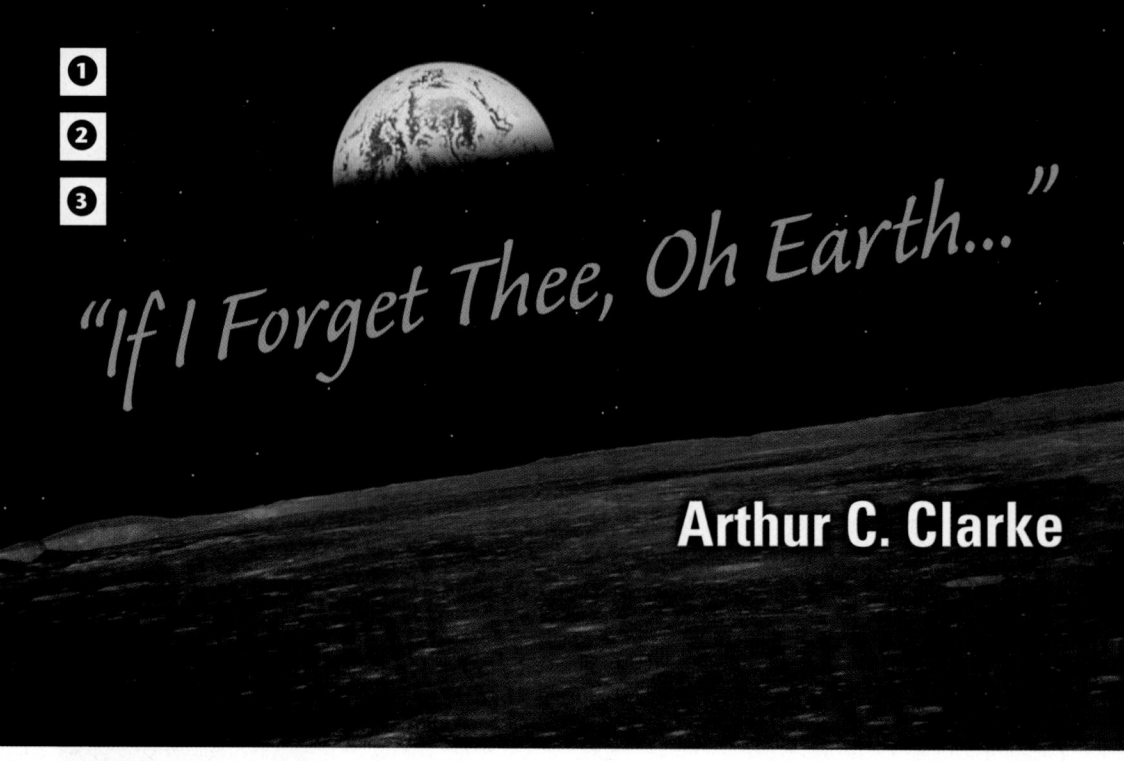

❶
❷
❸

"If I Forget Thee, Oh Earth..."

Arthur C. Clarke

❹ When Marvin was ten years old, his father took him through the long, echoing corridors that led up through Administration and Power, until at last they came to the uppermost levels of all and were among the swiftly growing vegetation of the Farmlands. Marvin liked it here: it was fun watching the great, slender plants creeping with almost visible eagerness toward the sunlight as it filtered down through the plastic domes to meet them. The smell of life was everywhere, awakening inexpressible longings in his heart: no longer was he breathing the dry, cool air of the residential levels, <u>purged</u> of all smells but the faint tang of ozone.[1] He wished he could stay here for a little while, but Father would not let him. They went onward until they had reached the entrance to the Observatory, which he had never visited: but they did not stop, and Marvin knew with a sense of rising excitement that there could be only one goal left. For the first time in his life, he was going Outside.

---

1. ozone (ō′ zōn′) *n.* form of oxygen with a sharp odor.

148 ■ Fiction and Nonfiction

Literary Analysis
Theme What information about Marvin's environment appears in this description of the Farmlands?

Vocabulary Builder
purged (pʉrjd) *v.* cleansed

There were a dozen of the surface vehicles, with their wide balloon tires and pressurized cabins, in the great servicing chamber.
His father must have been expected, for they were led at once to the
little scout car waiting by the huge circular door of the airlock.
Tense with expectancy, Marvin settled himself down in the cramped
cabin while his father started the motor and checked the controls.
The inner door of the lock slid open and then closed behind them:
he heard the roar of the great air pumps fade slowly away as the
pressure dropped to zero. Then the "Vacuum" sign flashed on, the
outer door parted, and before Marvin lay the land which he had
never yet entered.

He had seen it in photographs, of course: he had watched it
imaged on television screens a hundred times. But now it was lying
all around him, burning beneath the fierce sun that crawled so
slowly across the jet-black sky. He stared into the west, away from
the blinding splendor of the sun—and there were the stars, as he
had been told but had never quite believed. He gazed at them for a
long time, marveling that anything could be so bright and yet so
tiny. They were intense unscintillating points, and suddenly he
remembered a rhyme he had once read in one of his father's books:

> Twinkle, twinkle, little star,
> How I wonder what you are.

Well, he knew what the stars were. Whoever asked that question
must have been very stupid. And what did they mean by "twinkle"?
You could see at a glance that all the stars shone with the same
steady, unwavering light. He abandoned the puzzle and turned his
attention to the landscape around him.

They were racing across a level plain at almost a hundred miles
an hour, the great balloon tires sending up little spurts of dust
behind them. There was no sign of the Colony: in the few minutes
while he had been gazing at the stars, its domes and radio towers
had fallen below the horizon. Yet there were other indications of
man's presence, for about a mile ahead Marvin could see the curiously shaped structures clustering round the head of a mine. Now
and then a puff of vapor would emerge from a squat smokestack
and would instantly disperse.

They were past the mine in a moment: Father was driving with a
reckless and exhilarating skill as if—it was a strange thought to
come into a child's mind—he were trying to escape from something.
In a few minutes they had reached the edge of the plateau on which
the Colony had been built. The ground fell sharply away beneath
them in a dizzying slope whose lower stretches were lost in shadow.
Ahead, as far as the eye could reach, was a jumbled wasteland of

Literary Analysis
Theme What do the
words "burning
beneath the fierce
sun" suggest about
what Marvin is
observing?

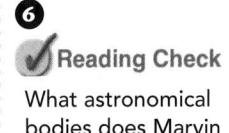

Reading Check

What astronomical
bodies does Marvin
see for the first time?

---

❹ Literary Analysis
Theme

• Remind students that the theme in
a work of fiction is often implied.
Ask students what details they can
look for to help determine a story's
theme.
Possible response: Details about
setting, characters, and plot may
help determine a story's theme.

• Discuss the setting described in the
bracketed passage on p. 148 and
Marvin's attitude toward it. Then
ask students the Literary Analysis
question: What information about
Marvin's environment appears in
this description of the Farmlands?
Possible response: Marvin is in a
building with many levels. The
Farmlands is in the top level, and it
seems to be a greenhouse area
with plants.

• Tell students that the importance
Marvin places on the Farmlands
suggests that it has something to
do with the story's theme.

❺ Literary Analysis
Theme

• Have students **contrast** the information about the Farmlands at the
beginning of the story with the
environment described in the
bracketed passage.
Answer: This environment is
harsher and less inviting than the
Farmlands, which seem fresh and
energizing.

• **Ask** the Literary Analysis question:
What do the words "burning
beneath the fierce sun" suggest
about what Marvin is observing?
Answer: The description suggests
a severe, unwelcoming environment.

❻ Reading Check

Answer: Marvin sees the sun and
the stars for the first time.

---

❼ Critical Thinking

Interpret

- Read aloud the bracketed passage. **Ask** students to identify details that describe the setting and to explain what effect these details have on the reader.
  Possible response: Details such as a "dizzying slope," a "jumbled wasteland," and mountain crests that "burn" in the setting sun have an ominous effect on the reader.

- **Ask** students whether they can deduce the Colony's location from the details given so far. If they have no idea, explain that Clarke has not invented this description; it is an accurate description of an actual place.
  Possible response: Students might associate the word "craters" with the moon.

❽ Literature in Context

Science Connection The International Space Station generates its own electric power through the use of giant solar panels. Still, the ISS is not entirely self-contained; it depends on the "home planet" for many supplies, including oxygen, food, fuel, and other consumables.

The astronauts stay connected to life on Earth in other important ways. The crew uses videophones and e-mail to stay in touch with their loved ones. Also, astronauts can watch DVDs and use other media tools to stay connected with current events and popular culture.

Connect to the Literature Point out that Marvin's space colony was entirely self-contained, with no connections to the uninhabited Earth. **Ask** students the Connect to the Literature question: How do you think the astronauts' feelings about living in outer space compare to Marvin's feelings?
Possible response: ISS astronauts are probably comforted by their connections with Earth, whereas Marvin is angered and saddened by Earth's destruction.

---

❼ craters, mountain ranges, and ravines. The crests of the mountains, catching the low sun, burned like islands of fire in a sea of darkness: and above them the stars still shone as steadfastly as ever.

There could be no way forward—yet there was. Marvin clenched his fists as the car edged over the slope and started the long descent. Then he saw the barely visible track leading down the mountainside, and relaxed a little. Other men, it seemed, had gone this way before.

Night fell with a shocking abruptness as they crossed the shadow line and the sun dropped below the crest of the plateau. The twin searchlights sprang into life, casting blue-white bands on the rocks ahead, so that there was scarcely need to check their speed. For hours they drove through valleys and past the foot of mountains whose peaks seemed to comb the stars, and sometimes they emerged for a moment into the sunlight as they climbed over higher ground.

And now on the right was a wrinkled, dusty plain, and on the left, its ramparts and terraces rising mile after mile into the sky, was a wall of mountains that marched into the distance until its peaks sank from sight below the rim of the world. There was no sign that men had ever explored this land, but once they passed the skeleton of a crashed rocket, and beside it a stone cairn[2] surmounted by a metal cross.

It seemed to Marvin that the mountains stretched on forever: but at last, many hours later, the range ended in a towering, precipitous headland[3] that rose steeply from a cluster of little hills. They drove down into a shallow valley that curved in a great arc toward the far side of the mountains: and as they did so, Marvin slowly realized that something very strange was happening in the land ahead.

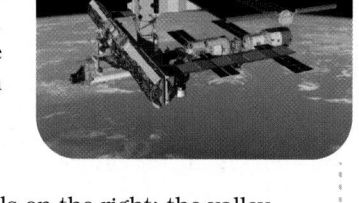

The sun was now low behind the hills on the right: the valley before them should be in total darkness. Yet it was awash with a cold white radiance that came spilling over the crags beneath which

---

2. **cairn** (kern) *n.* a cone-shaped pile of stones built as a monument.
3. **precipitous headland** (prē sip′ ə təs hed′ land′) *n.* steep cliff that juts out over water.

---

❽ Literature in Context

Science Connection

International Space Station In Arthur C. Clarke's story, a space colony is all that remains of the human species. If the idea of a space colony seems implausible, consider the fact that a small colony is being developed directly over your head in the form of an international space station. Sixteen nations are contributing scientific and technological resources to build the station, which has been under construction since 1998. The Space Station will be used for experiments and research, and it will also provide insight into the way humans can learn to live and work in outer space. The first astronaut crew arrived at the Station in November of 2000, and since then, people have lived and worked continuously at the station, more than 200 miles above Earth.

Connect to the Literature

How do you think the astronauts' feelings about living in outer space compare to Marvin's feelings?

Vocabulary Development

Vocabulary Builder Reinforcement
Students will benefit from additional examples and practice with the Vocabulary Builder words. Reinforce their comprehension with "show-you-know" sentences. The first part of the sentence uses the vocabulary word in an appropriate context. The second part of the sentence—the "show-you-know" part—clarifies the first. Model the strategy with this example for *distribute*:

She asked Paul to *distribute* the newspaper in his neighborhood; he gave each neighbor a copy later that day.

Then give students these sentence prompts, and coach them in creating the clarification part:

1. Sarah *purged* her closet of the clothes she didn't wear anymore; _____.
   Sample answer: when she was finished, she donated the clothes to charity.

2. Pizza was a *perennial* favorite in the school cafeteria; _____.
   Sample answer: students and staff requested it time and time again.

they were driving. Then, suddenly, they were out in the open plain, and the source of the light lay before them in all its glory.

It was very quiet in the little cabin now that the motors had stopped. The only sound was the faint whisper of the oxygen feed and an occasional metallic crepitation as the outer walls of the vehicle radiated away their heat. For no warmth at all came from the great silver crescent that floated low above the far horizon and flooded all this land with pearly light. It was so brilliant that minutes passed before Marvin could accept its challenge and look steadfastly into its glare, but at last he could discern the outlines of continents, the hazy border of the atmosphere, and the white islands of cloud. And even at this distance, he could see the glitter of sunlight on the polar ice.

It was beautiful, and it called to his heart across the abyss of space. There in that shining crescent were all the wonders that he had never known—the hues of sunset skies, the moaning of the sea on pebbled shores, the patter of falling rain, the unhurried benison of snow. These and a thousand others should have been his rightful heritage, but he knew them only from the books and ancient records, and the thought filled him with the anguish of exile.

Why could they not return? It seemed so peaceful beneath those lines of marching cloud. Then Marvin, his eyes no longer blinded by the glare, saw that the portion of the disk that should have been in darkness was gleaming faintly with an evil phosphorescence[4] and he remembered. He was looking upon the funeral pyre of a world— upon the radioactive aftermath of Armageddon[5]. Across a quarter of a million miles of space, the glow of dying atoms was still visible, a <u>perennial</u> reminder of the ruinous past. It would be centuries yet before that deadly glow died from the rocks and life could return again to fill that silent, empty world.

And now Father began to speak, telling Marvin the story which until this moment had meant no more to him than the fairy tales he had once been told. There were many things he could not understand: it was impossible for him to picture the glowing, multicolored pattern of life on the planet he had never seen. Nor could he comprehend the forces that had destroyed it in the end, leaving the Colony, preserved by its isolation, as the sole survivor. Yet he could share the agony of those final days, when the Colony had learned at last that never again would the supply ships come flaming down through the stars with gifts from home. One by one

---

4. **phosphorescence** (fäs′ fə res′ əns) *n.* emission of light resulting from exposure to radiation.
5. **Armageddon** (är′ mə ged′ ′n) *n.* in the Bible, the place where the final battle between good and evil is to be fought.

Literary Analysis
Theme Which details in these paragraphs provide an insight into what Marvin, and others in his colony, have lost?

Vocabulary Builder
perennial (pə ren′ ē əl) *adj.* happening over and over; perpetual

✓ **Reading Check**
What does Marvin notice in a portion of the disk?

❾ Literary Analysis
Theme

- Tell students to focus on adjectives in the first paragraph of the bracketed passage. Discuss how the words differ from the previous descriptions of Marvin's surroundings.

- **Ask** students to infer the identity of the "shining crescent."
Answer: It is Earth.

- **Ask** students what warning is implied in the description of Earth in the second paragraph of the bracketed passage.
Answer: The description implies a warning of the dangers of nuclear weapons. Clarke describes an Earth glowing with radiation and says it will be uninhabitable for centuries to come.

- **Ask** the Literary Analysis question: Which details in these paragraphs provide an insight into what Marvin, and others in his colony, have lost?
Answer: Details that describe the beauty and appeal of Earth—the sunsets, the sounds of rain and the ocean, the gentle fall of snow—provide a poignant reminder of everything the Colony members have lost.

❿ Reading Check
Answer: Marvin notices that a portion of the disk was glowing with radiation.

Differentiated
Instruction   Solutions for All Learners

Strategy for Special Needs Students
Have students create two-column charts, with one column labeled "Earth" and the other column labeled "Colony." Then, in each column, tell students to write adjectives from the story that describe the setting. After students finish their charts, have them write sentences summarizing each setting.

Strategy for English Learners
Tell students that certain words can be signals of a statement of opinion. In the story, words such as *beautiful, strange, fun, cramped, curiously, reckless,* and *exhilarating* express a person's feelings, not facts. Have students look for these and similar "signals of opinion" as they read. Discuss how the author's word choices impact the theme of the story.

151

⓫ Literary Analysis
Theme

- **Ask** students to respond to the Literary Analysis question: What message about the future is conveyed through the details in this paragraph?
  Answer: The message is that if Earth is destroyed by radiation, it will be uninhabitable for centuries to come; it is a warning against the use of nuclear weapons.

- **Ask** students how the writer communicated this theme throughout the story.
  Possible response: He communicated this theme through descriptions of the setting and through the actions and thoughts of Marvin and his father.

Concept Connector

Have students return to the Motivation activity on p. 148. Revisit the questions, and ask volunteers to share their original predictions. Have students revise their predictions based on the story.

ASSESS
Answers

1. Students may say that they would feel brave, hopeless, or angry in Marvin's situation.

2. (a) The dusty, cratered surface and an airless atmosphere suggest a lunar setting. (b) The accurate description of the moon's surface and it's nearness to earth make the story's plot seem more realistic.

3. (a) Marvin determines to take this trip one day with his own son. (b) Marvin's father wanted to pass on his own dream of making it possible for future generations to return to Earth.

4. (a) Earth was destroyed by nuclear war. (b) **Possible response:** Clarke might suggest that nuclear weapons be banned and that nations find peaceful ways to settle differences.

152

---

the radio stations had ceased to call: on the shadowed globe the lights of the cities had dimmed and died, and they were alone at last, as no men had ever been alone before, carrying in their hands the future of the race.

Then had followed the years of despair, and the long-drawn battle for survival in their fierce and hostile world. That battle had been won, though barely: this little oasis of life was safe against the worst that Nature could do. But unless there was a goal, a future toward which it could work, the Colony would lose the will to live, and neither machines nor skill nor science could save it then.

So, at last, Marvin understood the purpose of this pilgrimage. He would never walk beside the rivers of that lost and legendary world, or listen to the thunder raging above its softly rounded hills. Yet one day—how far ahead?—his children's children would return to claim their heritage. The winds and the rains would scour the poisons from the burning lands and carry them to the sea, and in the depths of the sea they would waste their venom until they could harm no living things. Then the great ships that were still waiting here on the silent, dusty plains could lift once more into space, along the road that led to home.

⓫

That was the dream: and one day, Marvin knew with a sudden flash of insight, he would pass it on to his own son, here at this same spot with the mountains behind him and the silver light from the sky streaming into his face.

He did not look back as they began the homeward journey. He could not bear to see the cold glory of the crescent Earth fade from the rocks around him, as he went to rejoin his people in their long exile.

Thinking About the Selection

1. **Respond:** How do you think you would handle Marvin's situation? Explain.

2. **(a) Recall:** At the end of the story, what does Marvin decide to do? **(b) Draw Conclusions:** What was the purpose of Marvin's trip with his father?

3. **(a) Infer:** What evidence indicates that the story is set on the moon? **(b) Analyze:** How does the choice of setting make the story more realistic?

4. **(a) Infer:** How did Earth come to be destroyed? **(b) Speculate:** What suggestions do you think Clarke would offer today to prevent a situation like the one in the story from occurring?

Literary Analysis
Theme What message about the future is conveyed through the details in this paragraph?

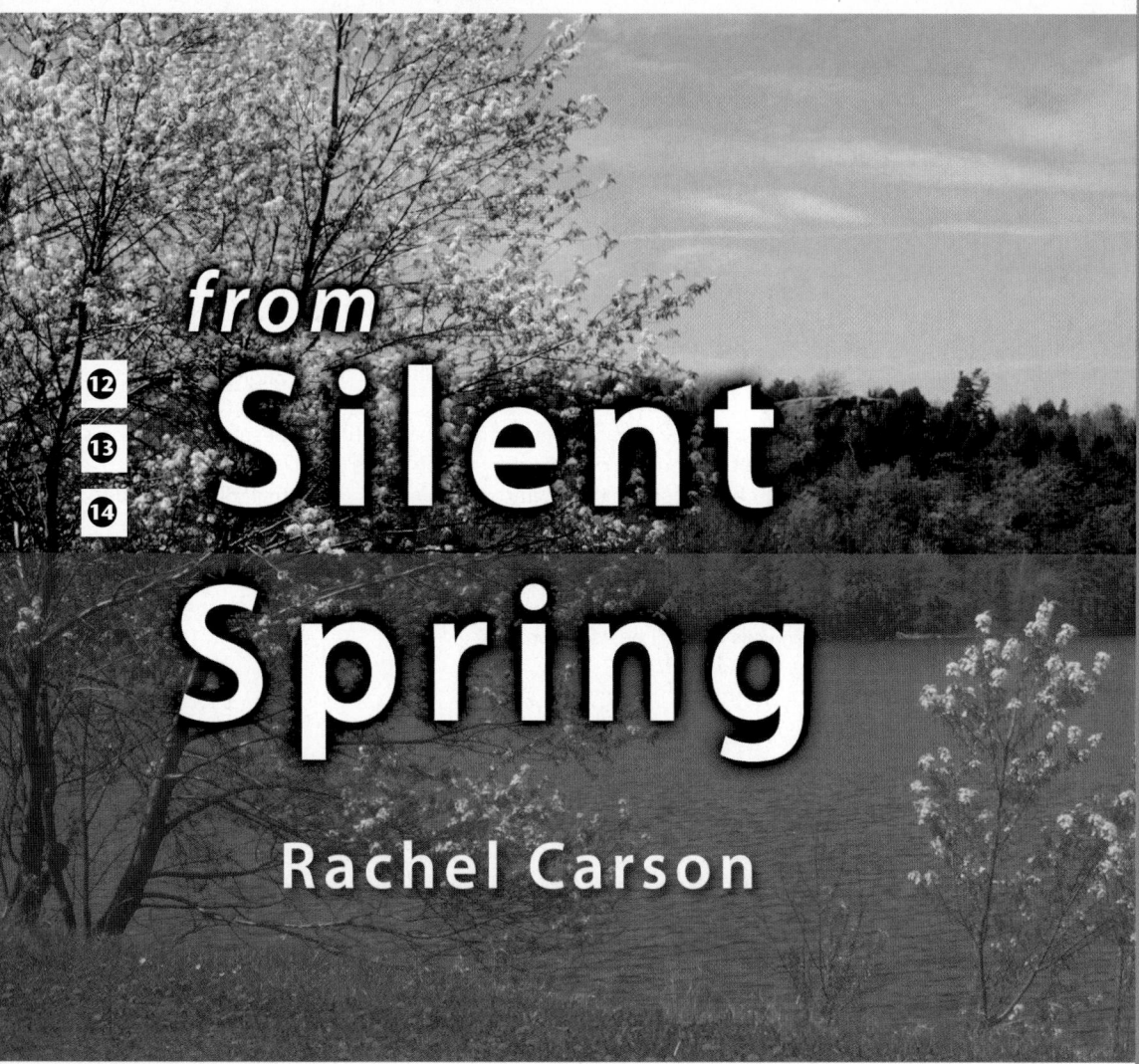

from Silent Spring

⑫
⑬
⑭

Rachel Carson

⑮ There was once a town in the heart of America where all life seemed to live in harmony with its surroundings. The town lay in the midst of a checkerboard of prosperous farms, with fields of grain and hillsides of orchards where, in spring, white clouds of bloom drifted above the green fields. In autumn, oak and maple and birch set up a blaze of color that flamed and flickered across a backdrop of pines. Then foxes barked in the hills and deer silently crossed the fields, half hidden in the mists of the fall mornings.

Literary Analysis
Theme Which details in this paragraph paint a picture of the beauty and energy of nature? Explain.

from *Silent Spring* ■ 153

Differentiated
Instruction   Solutions for All Learners

Accessibility at a Glance
Use this information to guide your teaching of *Silent Spring*.

Context	Written before people knew about the danger of pesticide use
Language	Conversational
Concept Level	More accessible
Literary Merit	Best-selling; landmark book
Lexile	1080L

153

- Read aloud the bracketed passage, and then **ask** students to identify the negative words that are being used to describe nature.
Answer: The negative words include "blight," "evil," "mysterious maladies," "shadow of death," "illness," and "death."

- **Ask** students how this passage compares with the previous positive description of the setting.
Answer: The setting was previously described as idyllic and nearly perfect. Now a "shadow of death" has been cast on the people and animals alike.

- **Ask** students how this comparison might contribute to the story's theme.
Possible response: The author is warning readers of the deadly threat of pesticides by showing them the destruction that pesticides can wreak.

Along the roads, laurel, viburnum and alder, great ferns and wildflowers delighted the traveler's eye through much of the year. Even in winter the roadsides were places of beauty, where countless birds came to feed on the berries and on the seed heads of the dried weeds rising above the snow. The countryside was, in fact, famous for the abundance and variety of its bird life, and when the flood of migrants was pouring through in spring and fall people traveled from great distances to observe them. Others came to fish the streams, which flowed clear and cold out of the hills and contained shady pools where trout lay. So it had been from the days many years ago when the first settlers raised their houses, sank their wells, and built their barns.

Then a strange <u>blight</u> crept over the area and everything began to change. Some evil spell had settled on the community: mysterious <u>maladies</u> swept the flocks of chickens; the cattle and sheep sickened and died. Everywhere was a shadow of death. The farmers

Vocabulary Builder
blight (blīt) *n.* something that destroys or prevents growth
maladies (mal′ ə dēz) *n.* diseases

⑰ ▼ **Critical Viewing** What might the author think about the aerial spraying of crops with chemicals that kill pests? **[Connect]**

Vocabulary Development

Expressive Vocabulary
As students discuss the theme of *Silent Spring,* encourage them to use the expressive vocabulary presented earlier. You might encourage them with sentence starters like these:
1. Carson presents a *challenge* to her readers by . . .

2. Through her description of nature, Carson *communicates* . . .
3. The story suggests that we can *maximize* . . .
4. Carson would say that we must *distribute* . . .
5. The animals in the story could not *adapt* . . .

spoke of much illness among their families. In the town the doctors had become more and more puzzled by new kinds of sickness appearing among their patients. There had been several sudden and unexplained deaths, not only among adults but even among children, who would be stricken suddenly while at play and die within a few hours.

There was a strange stillness. The birds, for example—where had they gone? Many people spoke of them, puzzled and disturbed. The feeding stations in the backyards were deserted. The few birds seen anywhere were <u>moribund</u>; they trembled violently and could not fly. It was a spring without voices. On the mornings that had once throbbed with the dawn chorus of robins, catbirds, doves, jays, wrens, and scores of other bird voices there was now no sound; only silence lay over the fields and woods and marsh.

On the farms the hens brooded, but no chicks hatched. The farmers complained that they were unable to raise any pigs—the

Vocabulary Builder
moribund (môr´ i bund´) *adj.* dying

 Reading Check **18**

What changes does the "strange blight" cause?

17 Critical Viewing
Answer: The author would disapprove of aerial spraying. Since the sprays kill insects, they are probably harmful to other living creatures.

18 Reading Check
Answer: Farm animals sicken and die. Farmers and their families fall ill; some die suddenly. Birds stop singing, creating a "strange stillness."

from *Silent Spring* ■ 155

Differentiated Instruction   Solutions for All Learners

Enrichment for Advanced Readers
Suggest that students read additional words by Rachel Carson. Provide students with **Authors In Depth**, Gold Level, which contains the following selections:
• from *The Sea Around Us* (p. 93)
• from *Always Rachel* (p. 97)
• "An Island I Remember" (p. 99)
• from *Under the Sea-Wind* (p. 104)

After students have read these or other works by Carson, have them form discussion groups in which they compare and contrast the selections. Suggest criteria for comparison, such as setting, theme, characters, and author's purpose. To extend the activity, have volunteers present to the class brief oral reports on their favorite Carson selections.

19 ## Literary Analysis
Theme

- **Ask** students the Literary Analysis question: How do you react to this description of a sudden change? What message is the author suggesting?
Possible response: The sudden change is disturbing. The author is trying to convey that humans are destroying the life of the planet.

20 ## Literary Analysis
Theme

Ask students to respond to the Literary Analysis question: Is the theme stated directly here or is it implied? Explain.
Answer: The theme is stated directly. Carson directly addresses her readers when she says that the use of pesticides can turn her imagined fable into reality.

Concept Connector

Have students return to the Motivation activity on p. 153. Discuss the effectiveness of the selection title.

ASSESS
Answers

1. Students may say that the suddenness of the change was most disturbing because the town seemed to be so healthy.

2. (a) Life is idyllic. The world is clean, beautiful, and fruitful. (b) The condition of life changes for the worse. Animals and people get sick and die.

3. (a) They sicken and die. (b) Carson's reference to "white chemical powder" indicates that the source of the problem is chemicals.

4. (a) The town does not exist. (b) **Possible response:** By using a fictional town, Carson creates a more vivid example.

5. (a) Carson blames people for causing the problem. (b) **Possible response:** People should respect the environment.

litters were small and the young survived only a few days. The apple trees were coming into bloom but no bees droned among the blossoms, so there was no pollination and there would be no fruit.

The roadsides, once so attractive, were now lined with browned and withered vegetation as though swept by fire. These, too, were silent, deserted by all living things. Even the streams were now life-less. Anglers[1] no longer visited them, for all the fish had died.

19 In the gutters under the eaves and between the shingles of the roofs, a white granular powder still showed a few patches; some weeks before it had fallen like snow upon the roofs and the lawns, the fields and streams.

No witchcraft, no enemy action had silenced the rebirth of new life in this stricken world. The people had done it themselves.

20 This town does not actually exist, but it might easily have a thousand counterparts in America or elsewhere in the world. I know of no community that has experienced all the misfortunes I describe. Yet every one of these disasters has actually happened somewhere, and many real communities have already suffered a substantial number of them. A grim specter has crept upon us almost unnoticed, and this imagined tragedy may easily become a stark reality we all shall know.

---

1. **anglers** (aŋ´ glərz) *n.* people who fish with a line and hook.

Literary Analysis
Theme How do you react to this description of a sudden change? What message is the author suggesting?

Literary Analysis
Theme Is the theme stated directly here or is it implied? Explain.

Thinking About the Selection

1. **Respond:** What do you find most troubling about the environmental problems described in this excerpt? Explain.

2. **(a) Recall:** What is the condition of life at the beginning of this excerpt? **(b) Compare and Contrast:** How does the condition of life change as the narrative continues?

3. **(a) Recall:** What happens to the farm animals and the vegetation? **(b) Infer:** What causes this sudden change?

4. **(a) Recall:** What information about the town does Carson reveal at the end of the excerpt? **(b) Speculate:** Would the narrative be more effective if the town was real? Why or why not?

5. **(a) Recall:** According to Carson, who caused the environmental problems? **(b) Speculate:** What suggestions do you think Carson would make to people today?

156 ■ Fiction and Nonfiction

Vocabulary Development

Vocabulary Knowledge Rating
When students have completed reading and discussing "If I Forget Thee, O Earth…" and *Silent Spring,* have them take out their **Vocabulary Rating Chart.** Read the words aloud once more and have students rate their knowledge of the words again in the After Reading column. Clarify any words that are still problematic. Have students write their own def- inition and example or sentence in the appropriate column. Then have students complete the **Vocabulary Builder Practice** activities on p. 157. Encourage students to use the words in further discussion and written work about the selections. Remind them that they will be accountable for these words on the Selection Test.

Apply the Skills

"If I Forget Thee, Oh Earth . . ." • from *Silent Spring*

Comparing Themes

1. Use a chart like the one shown to analyze the themes expressed in "If I Forget Thee, Oh Earth . . ." and the excerpt from *Silent Spring*. List important details from each selection, what you think the details mean, and the theme of the selection.

Details from "If I Forget Thee, Oh Earth . . ."	What They Mean	Theme
Details from *Silent Spring*	What They Mean	Theme

2. **(a)** Using details from the chart, explain how the themes in the two selections are similar. **(b)** How is the theme expressed differently in each one?

Writing to Compare Literary Works

Write an essay in which you compare your reactions to "If I Forget Thee, Oh Earth . . ." and the excerpt from *Silent Spring*. In your response, consider how the author's choice to write fiction or nonfiction affects your reading experience. Use the following questions to get started.

- Do you feel more affected by the experiences of the fictional character Marvin or by the words of Rachel Carson, the author of *Silent Spring*?
- Do you find fiction or nonfiction more effective in expressing a theme?
- Why do you think an author would choose one genre over another when conveying a theme?

Vocabulary Builder

Practice For each item, write a sentence in which you use the word pair correctly.

1. purged; weeds
2. perennial; campaign
3. blight; garden
4. maladies; doctor
5. moribund; sadness

QuickReview

Theme: the central message or insight about life that is conveyed through a literary work

Go Online
Assessment

For: Self-test
Visit: www.PHSchool.com
Web Code: epa-6112

Apply the Skills ■ 157

Comparing Themes

1. **Possible response:** Detail from "If I Forget Thee, Oh Earth . . .": "It would be centuries yet before that deadly glow died . . ." **Theme:** Humans have the ability to destroy themselves as well as the Earth. **Detail from Silent Spring:** "Then a strange blight crept over the area. . . .cattle and sheep sickened and died." **Theme:** People have polluted their environment, making it toxic to life.

Another sample can be found on **Comparing Themes Graphic Organizer Transparency B,** p. 39 in *Graphic Organizer Transparencies.*

2. (a) Both selections use imagined visions of the future to warn readers about the consequences of harming Earth. (b) Clarke's story belongs to the science-fiction genre. Rachel Carson grounds her piece in reality by describing a town that could exist anywhere in the world.

Writing to Compare Literary Works

- Have students refer to their completed charts comparing the themes in the two selections.
- Have students use the bulleted questions to develop their ideas.
- Encourage students to incorporate the expressive vocabulary words: *adapt, challenge, communicate, distribute, maximize.*

Six Traits Focus

✔	Ideas		Word Choice
✔	Organization		Sentence Fluency
	Voice		Conventions

Vocabulary Builder
Sample responses:

1. Mary *purged* the garden of *weeds.*
2. The church's *perennial campaign* for charity donations was sapping Sally's savings.
3. A *blight* killed most of the plants in my *garden.*
4. Simon's *maladies* were diagnosed by a *doctor.*
5. The *moribund* landscape filled her with overwhelming *sadness.*

In this Skills Review, students apply the skills taught in Part 2. The test format gives students practice in taking standardized tests. The result of this review test will help you check students' readiness for the **Benchmark Test** for Unit 1, Part 2.

Applying Reading Skills

Tell students to watch for clues to help them determine the author's purpose. Read the passage with the students and guide them in identifying clues to the author's purpose in item 3: The sentences have many descriptive words, such as *blackened, strangled, hurried,* and *malicious.* Then, have them complete the remaining items on their own.

Applying Vocabulary Skills

Remind students of the Latin roots/combining form *-vit-, -via-,* and *tri-.* Refer students to the definitions of these roots on p. 95. Point out that applying the meanings of these roots to the vocabulary questions can help them to answer the items.

Tips for
Test Taking

Tell students that if they are unsure about an answer for an item, they should eliminate any answers that are obviously incorrect. Then, they should reread the question and the answer choices to determine precisely what each is saying before they select an answer.

ASSESS

Answers

1. B
2. C
3. A
4. C
5. B

6. B
7. C
8. C
9. A
10. D

Reading: Author's Purpose

Directions: *Questions 1–5 are based on the following selections.*

Selection 1

The streets weren't always this clean in our little town, the trees weren't always as green, and the quiet peaceful cadence of crickets and birds did not always ring in the woods. The effort that it took to reclaim our town was tremendous, and we are in danger of losing what we fought so hard to achieve.

Selection 2

It was the town I grew up in, one of those small towns that seem to float peacefully on—no issues that aren't solved in town meetings, no crime that is not petty, no problems. Of course, the town did contain one Mrs. Funk. Mrs. Funk was eccentric in the way only old women who have lived someplace all of their lives can be eccentric. It wasn't her 15 cats, or her propensity to call everyone "sir," or even her purple shutters that resulted in this distinction. It was her immensely amusing schedule, one an army general would value.

1. The details in Selection 1 suggest which of the following?
   A The author is writing a scientific article.
   B The author is familiar with the place.
   C The author is writing an informative article.
   D The author has a specific opinion.

2. Details in Selection 1 show that the author's purpose is probably
   A to entertain.
   B to persuade.
   C to inform.
   D to describe.

3. Details in Selection 2 suggest that the author's purpose is
   A to entertain.
   B to persuade.
   C to inform.
   D to describe.

4. Which of the following would be most useful in evaluating the author's purpose for Selection 1?
   A a biography of the author
   B a review of the book
   C details of the entire selection
   D comments on the author's Web site

5. The third sentence in Passage 2 helps the reader
   A reevaluate the author's purpose.
   B confirm that this is written to entertain.
   C evaluate the position the author will take.
   D confirm that this is written to inform.

Assessment Practice

A. Directions: *Choose the word that best completes the sentence.*

6. Conditioning is considered _____ to becoming a competent athlete.
   - A unnecessary
   - B vital
   - C trivial
   - D likely

7. Following directions exactly is not _____; it is important in any experiment.
   - A possible
   - B vital
   - C trivial
   - D appreciated

8. We choose not to _____ graphic pictures of the war.
   - A appreciate
   - B detect
   - C display
   - D vitalize

9. Animals can _____ odors of which humans are unaware.
   - A detect
   - B trivialize
   - C capture
   - D appreciate

10. Those who are trying to concentrate rarely _____ hearing loud music.
    - A detect
    - B trivialize
    - C capture
    - D appreciate

11. Swimming, running, and bicycling are all part of a _____.
    - A viaticum
    - B vitality
    - C triathlon
    - D vitate

12. Ancient Romans called traveling expenses _____.
    - A viaticum
    - B vitality
    - C triathlon
    - D vitate

13. The power to go on living is also referred to as _____.
    - A viaticum
    - B vitality
    - C triathlon
    - D vitate

14. An accurate name for a combination of three herbal products is _____.
    - A vitamin
    - B triherbal
    - C viaherbal
    - D triamin

15. A curriculum vitae is a list of important accomplishments in _____.
    - A life
    - B the first third of one's career
    - C the last third of one's career
    - D a specific job

RETEACH

If students answer any of these questions incorrectly, have them review the instruction on the following pages in Part 2 before taking the **Benchmark Test.**

Question	Pages Where Instruction Is Located:
1	96, 122
2	96, 122
3	96, 122
4	96, 122
5	96, 122
6	95
7	95
8	95
9	95
10	95
11	144
12	116
13	144
14	116
15	116

Benchmark

Administer the **Benchmark Test** for Unit 1, Part 1. If the Benchmark Test reveals that some students need further work, use the Interpretation Guide to determine the appropriate reteaching page in the **Reading Kit.** You will also find the same instruction and practice available in the Success Tracker.

Go Online
Vocabulary **For:** Interactive crossword puzzle
Visit: www. PHSchool.com
Web Code: epj-5102
Give students this Web Code to access an interactive crossword puzzle using Academic Vocabulary and Vocabulary Skill words from Part 2.

159

Content Area Words

- Tell students that incorrectly spelling content area words is a common mistake in writing. Invite students to share content area words that they often misspell. **Possible responses:** Students might provide some of the following content area words:

  aluminum

  government

  argument

  physics

  independence

  geography

  Mississippi

  peninsula

- Have each student make a list of content words that he or she has difficulties with and exchange this list with a partner. Have partners test each other on the spellings of the content words.

- Tell students that because of the presence of silent letters, students should avoid relying on pronunciation to spell content words.

- Remind students that they should use dictionaries if they are unsure of the correct spelling of content area words.

WG Writing and Grammar, Gold Level
Students will find additional spelling instruction in Chapter 31, Section 4.

Spelling Workshop SPELLING

Content Area Words

Content area words are those that come from science, history, literature, and other subject areas that you may study.

An *Isthmus* or an *Island*? *Isthmus* and *island* are two examples of frequently misspelled content area words. While content area words are not necessarily difficult, they may have letters that are silent, like the *th* in *isthmus* or the *s* in *island,* or other challenging letter patterns. Focus on the words you may spell wrong and learn their correct spellings.

I hope this is an Isthmus and not an Island.

Practice Read the clues. Then, on a separate piece of paper, write the word from the word list that is indicated by the clue.

1. the opposite of comedy
2. fractions, algebra, geometry
3. very cold region
4. two lines that never come together
5. important body parts
6. comparison between two unlike things
7. study of the mind
8. the world all around us
9. leave one's country to live elsewhere
10. water and steam rising from the earth

Word List
environment
emigrate
muscles
geyser
arctic
tragedy
psychology
parallel
mathematics
metaphor

160 ■ *Fiction and Nonfiction*

Teaching Resources

The following resource can be used to enrich or extend the instruction for this Spelling Workshop.

Unit 1 Resources
   Spelling Workshop: Content Area
      Words, p. 195

Assessment Practice

A. Directions: *Choose the letter of the sentence in which the underlined word is spelled correctly.*

1. **A** Our class read a Greek <u>tradgedy</u>.
    B The main character had to <u>emigrate</u> from his homeland.
    C It seemed that every speech contained a <u>metephor</u>.
    D The play showed that people can overcome a bad <u>envirament</u>.

    C People would try to <u>emmigrate</u> to warmer areas.
    D They would look for a better <u>environment</u>.

2. **A** I have never been good at <u>mathamatics</u>.
    B I can't even draw <u>parralel</u> lines.
    C I get nervous and my <u>mussles</u> start to twitch.
    D Should I see a <u>psychology</u> specialist?

4. **A** The science-fiction story was set in a <u>parrellel</u> universe.
    B People sat and studied <u>mathematicks</u> all day.
    C Everyone's <u>muscles</u> got weak from not being used.
    D The story ended in <u>tradegy</u>.

3. **A** In an Ice Age, <u>artic</u> conditions would be widespread.
    B Every <u>giser</u> would freeze.

B. Directions: *Write the letter of the correct spelling of the word to fill in the blank.*

1. "The road was a ribbon" is a _____.
    A metephor
    B metaphor
    C metafore
    D metefor

4. Penguins do not live in the _____ region.
    A artic
    B arctic
    C arctick
    D artick

2. Old Faithful is a famous _____.
    A geiser
    B giser
    C geyser
    D gyser

5. This exercise will stretch your leg _____.
    A mussles
    B musels
    C musles
    D muscles

3. You can sometimes use _____ to train a pet.
    A sychology
    B sycholigy
    C phsychology
    D psychology

6. That factory pollutes the _____.
    A environment
    B enviroment
    C envirament
    D envirinment

Practice
1. tragedy
2. mathematics
3. arctic
4. parallel
5. muscles
6. metaphor
7. psychology
8. environment
9. emigrate
10. geyser
Assessment Practice
A.
1. B
2. D
3. D
4. C

B.
1. B
2. C
3. D
4. B
5. D
6. A

Meeting Your Standards

Students will

1. write a problem-and-solution essay.

2. use writing strategies to generate ideas and to plan, organize, evaluate, and revise the essay.

3. apply grammar skills.

 From the Author's Desk

Elizabeth McCracken

Show students Segment 3 on Elizabeth McCracken on *From the Author's Desk DVD*. Discuss the difference between writing a story, where characters dictate the direction of the tale, and writing a problem-and-solution essay, where the essay format is mapped out and concrete.

Writing Genres

Using the Form Point out to students that problem-and-solution essays are often incorporated into other types of writing.

- A letter to the editor might describe a problem and suggest ways to solve it.

- A proposal to a superior might outline strategies for solving a problem at work.

- A letter to a company might suggest a solution for fixing a flaw in one of their products.

Writing Workshop

Work in Progress

If students have done the Work-in-Progress assignments throughout Part 2, suggest that they examine their recorded ideas as they begin prewriting. They may have an idea in their portfolios that they wish to develop into a problem-and-solution essay.

 Online Essay Scorer

A writing prompt for this mode of writing can be found on the *PH Online Essay Scorer* at PHSuccessNet.com.

162

Exposition: Problem-and-Solution Essay

Some forms of expository writing engage us in the struggles and resolutions of our daily lives. In a **problem-and-solution essay,** an author identifies and explains a problem and then proposes a practical solution. Follow the steps in this workshop to write your own problem-and-solution essay.

Assignment Write a problem-and-solution essay about an issue that confronts your school or community.

What to Include Your problem-and-solution essay should feature the following elements:

- a statement of the problem and a suggested solution
- facts, statistics, and details that show the problem's scope and indicate how it can be solved
- language appropriate to the level of knowledge of your audience
- a logical organization
- error-free grammar, including correct use of pronouns

To preview the criteria on which your problem-and-solution essay may be assessed, see the rubric on page 169.

Writing Workshop: *Work in Progress*

If you have completed the Work-in-Progress assignments, you have several ideas in your portfolio that you might wish to pursue in your problem-and-solution essay. Continue to develop these ideas, or explore a new idea as you complete this Writing Workshop.

162 ■ *Fiction and Nonfiction*

Using the Form

You may use elements of this form in these types of writing:
- letters and memos
- proposals
- editorials

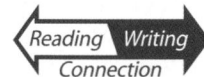 *Reading* / *Writing* / *Connection*

To get a feel for the use of problem-and-solution structure in a speech, read "First Inaugural Address" by Franklin Delano Roosevelt on page 503.

Teaching Resources

The following resources can be used to enrich or extend instruction for the Writing Workshop.

Unit 1 Resources
Writing Workshop: Exposition: Problem-and Solution Essay, p. 193
Writing Workshop: Integrating Grammar Skills: Revising Faulty Pronoun-Antecedent Agreement, p. 194

General Resources
Rubrics for Exposition: Problem-and Solution Essay, pp. 45–46

Graphic Organizer Transparencies
Graphic Organizer Transparency: Cause-and-Effect Flowchart, p. 233

From the Author's Desk DVD
Elizabeth McCracken, Segments 3 and 4

Prewriting

Choosing Your Topic

To select a topic for your problem-and-solution essay, use one of the following strategies:

- **Media Scan** Review local newspapers and television news programs for items about issues and problems in your community. List problems for which you can imagine practical solutions, and select one as your topic.

- **Sentence Starters** Complete the following sentence starters and jot down any associated ideas that come to mind. Then, choose one of the issues generated by the sentence starters as your topic.
    One thing that really annoys me is . . .
    The biggest problem people my age face is . . .
    Life would be better in my community if . . .
    The world would be a much better place if . . .

Narrowing Your Topic

Create a problem profile. Once you have chosen a topic, create a profile to help you focus your essay on a specific aspect of the problem. Answer the following questions about the problem:

- Who is affected by the problem?
- What causes the problem to occur?
- Is there more than one cause of the problem?
- What are some possible solutions to the problem?

Gathering Details

Consider your audience. Once you have clearly defined the problem, collect the details and information you will need to start your draft. Assess all possible solutions and weed out the less practical ones. Then, determine whom you want to reach with your essay and which aspects of the problem affect them most. For example, if you are trying to reach community leaders, you may shape your message differently than if you are trying to reach a peer group. As you narrow your focus, identify the ideas that will have the strongest impact on your target audience.

Work in Progress
Review the work you did on pages 117 and 145.

Problem Profile

Problem: Litter is creating an unsafe and unsightly environment.

Who is affected? Everyone on Earth

What causes the problem?
Lack of:
- responsibility
- environmental education
- sense of ownership

What are the possible solutions? Stiffer fines, more policing, more environmental education, volunteer trash pickup

Writing Workshop ■ 163

Prewriting

- Have students bring in local newspapers and newsletters to make a community collection that they can browse through in **choosing their topics.**

- Give students the example problem of a a deteriorating community playground, and have them **narrow the topic** by making a class problem profile.
  Possible response: Who is affected: *children and parents.* Causes of problem: *outdated playground equipment, lack of funds to improve or replace equipment.* Possible solutions: *implement new tax, have fund-raiser, lobby local businesses for funds and materials. Students could narrow the topic by focusing on the lack of funds to replace or improve equipment.*

- Have students **gather details** for the playground problem by identifying the target audience and the aspects of each solution that will have the strongest impact on this audience.
  Possible response: *The target audience is the whole community. Implementing the new tax could anger those who are not parents and make people feel that they are being forced to contribute. Having a fundraiser will give people the option to contribute. Lobbying local businesses could make the businesses feel pressured into donating or could give them an opportunity for positive publicity.*

Six Traits Focus

✔	Ideas		Word Choice
	Organization		Sentence Fluency
	Voice		Conventions

WG Writing and Grammar, Gold Level
Students will find additional instructions on prewriting for a problem-and-solution essay in Chapter 11, Section 2.

Writing and Grammar Interactive Textbook CD-ROM

Students can use the following tools as they complete their problem-and-solution essays:
- Audience Profile
- Sunburst Organizer
- Pronoun/Antecedent Checker

Tips for Using Rubrics

- Before students begin work on this assignment, have them preview the Rubric for Self-Assessment on p. 169 to know what is expected.

- Review the Assessment criteria in class. Before students use the Rubric for Self-Assessment, work with them to rate the student model by applying one or two criteria to it.

- If you wish to assess students' problem-and-solution essays with either a 4-point, a 5-point, or 6-point scoring rubric, see *General Resources*, pp. 45–46.

Drafting

- Take the class example of the community playground, and have volunteers think of ways to start the essay with a personal example, an anecdote, and a scenario.

  Possible responses: Personal example: *I took my younger brother to the playground, but we had to leave because the playground was unsafe.* Anecdote: *Most parents drive across town to another playground when their children want to play.* Scenario: *The outdated equipment could cause injuries, which increases the likelihood of lawsuits.*

- When displaying likely causes in their sunburst diagrams, have students create cause-and-effect chains. For instance: A chemical company convinces a farmer that he will produce more corn if he uses their fertilizer. The farmer spreads the fertilizer. Rain washes the fertilizer into rivers, streams, and lakes. Contamination of our water supply is a problem.

  Have students refer to the **Cause-and-Effect Flowchart** in *Graphic Organizer Transparencies,* p. 233.

- Give students these examples for providing elaboration on the community playground example: Statistics: *57% of community members have children;* Expert opinion: *a lawyer's appraisal of playground injury lawsuits;* Comparable situation: *a surrounding community's fundraiser for rebuilding its playground.*

- Give students these examples of skeptical questions for the playground example: *Would children use the new playground? Is it feasible to raise the necessary amount of money through fundraisers?*

Six Traits Focus

✔ Ideas	Word Choice
✔ Organization	Sentence Fluency
Voice	Conventions

WG Writing and Grammar, Gold Level

Students will find additional instruction on drafting a problem-and-solution essay in Chapter 11, Section 3.

Writing Workshop

Drafting

Shaping Your Writing

Engage your audience immediately. To make the problem real to your audience, consider one of these strategies for starting your essay:

- **Personal example:** Provide a detail from your own experience.

- **Anecdote:** Give a factual account of how the problem has already affected others.

- **Scenario:** Present a hypothetical but realistic picture of future consequences if the problem is not addressed.

Outline the problem clearly. Use a sunburst organizer to display aspects of the central problem, including likely causes. Then, select and develop only those details that will make the problem clear, significant, and urgent to your audience.

Providing Elaboration

Select convincing details. You cannot "prove" your solution in advance, but you can persuade the audience that your proposal is likely to work by using the following types of evidence:

- **Statistics:** Provide relevant numerical data.

- **Expert opinions:** Include the advice of those who have training or experience related to your topic problem.

- **Comparable situations:** Describe other real-life difficulties that were resolved by actions similar to the ones you propose.

Make sure that you establish clear connections among the various types of evidence you use.

Address readers' concerns. Include one or two skeptical questions. Then, provide well-supported answers that show why your solution is best.

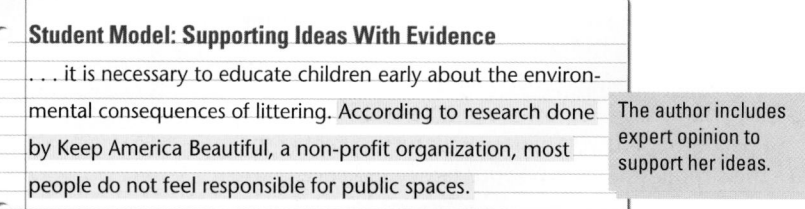

Student Model: Supporting Ideas With Evidence

. . . it is necessary to educate children early about the environmental consequences of littering. According to research done by Keep America Beautiful, a non-profit organization, most people do not feel responsible for public spaces.

The author includes expert opinion to support her ideas.

164 ■ *Fiction and Nonfiction*

Reading Writing Connection

To read the complete student model, see p. 168.

Tips for Test Taking

Point out that students may be asked to identify a problem and solution in a reading passage on a standardized test. Explain that students can ask themselves one question to identify the problem (What's wrong?) and another question to identify the solution (How does the writer propose to fix what's wrong?).

164

Elizabeth McCracken
On Word Choice

Elizabeth
McCracken

One of the best things about writing my novel *Niagara Falls All Over Again,* which tells the story of a comedy team, was that I could watch videotapes of old TV shows and movies, and claim that I was working. My favorites tapes were old episodes of a show that my beloved comic duo Abbott and Costello hosted once a month. This passage is basically just a description of what I saw when I was "working," watching *The Colgate Comedy Hour.*

"Write about your most beloved obsessions."
——Elizabeth McCracken

Professional Model:
from *Niagara Falls All Over Again*

We broke into television as the once-a-month hosts of a weekly hour-long live variety show. By 1951, our movie career was mostly over, and we were back where we'd begun, except famous, rich, and middle-aged: a thin man and a fat man on a stage, willing to do anything for a laugh. We were shameless. We insulted the band leader, we knocked down scenery on purpose, we tried to crack each other up. We broke props we'd need later, just so we could improvise first about the breakage, and then about the lack of props. Our old wheezing vaudeville jokes were new again, thanks to the postwar baby boom: the country was full of brand-new people with blissfully unsophisticated senses of humor. You could see Rocky search for the red light that told us which camera was paying attention, doing a slow burn and then saying, "Watch me, camera two," and tipping his hat. . . .

I have a weakness for repetition, both straight repeats (like all the We's) and slight variations, like *break, broke.*

Some writers say, Avoid adverbs. It's true that some people use adverbs to do the work that verbs and adjectives should do, but I use *blissfully* here as a joke—most people wouldn't see a lack of sophistication as *blissful.*

He's wearing a bowler hat. I draw my characters' clothing when I write (though I'm a very poor artist). I know them better if I know what they wear.

Writing Workshop ■ 165

Elizabeth McCracken

- Show students Segment 3 on Elizabeth McCracken on *From the Author's Desk DVD.* Discuss how McCracken uses word choice to add to the emotional effect of her writing.

- Point out to students McCracken's statement about adverbs. Write these two sentences on the board:

  After falling on the ice, Devon slowly walked to the car.

  After falling on the ice, Devon limped to the car.

  Point out to students that the first sentence has an adverb that does the work of the verb, which allows the writer to use a general, weak verb. Point out to students that the second sentence deletes the adverb and uses a more specific verb.

- Have students go through their essays and look for adverbs that do the work of the verbs or adjectives near them. Tell them to delete these adverbs and use more specific verbs or adjectives.

- Point out to students McCracken's comment about how she "draws (my) characters' clothing." Explain to students that this means she uses specific details to give readers a vivid mental picture of the clothing.

- Have students go through their essays and look for any descriptions or details that could be developed further to give a more vivid mental picture. Have students enhance their essays by adding more specific details to these parts.

165

Revising

- Write the following paragraph on the board:

    The community playground needs to be replaced. The playground is located down the street from me. The metal bars are covered in rust, and the wood is flaking and full of splinters. The slide is warped with age. The swing set wobbles dangerously when used. A new playground is desperately needed.

Have students revise the paragraph, putting a star next to the topic sentence and eliminating unnecessary sentences. Have a volunteer write the revised paragraph on the board.

Sample answer: *The community playground needs to be replaced. The metal bars are covered in rust, and the wood is flaking and full of splinters. The slide is warped with age. The swing set wobbles dangerously when used.*

- Write the following sentences on the board:

    Stray dogs roam the streets constantly.

    Stray dogs run around all of the time.

Tell students that one sentence has a general audience and the other sentence has a third-grade audience. Have a volunteer note which sentence applies to which audience, and explain why.

Answer: The first sentence is for a general audience; the second sentence is for a third-grade audience. The vocabulary in the first sentence is more advanced.

Six Traits Focus

	Ideas	✔	Word Choice
✔	Organization		Sentence Fluency
✔	Voice		Conventions

  Writing and Grammar, Gold Level

Students will find additional guidance for revising a problem-and-solution essay in Chapter 11, Section 4.

166

Writing Workshop

Revising

Revising Your Paragraphs

Support your generalizations. Look at each paragraph to be sure that the details support or explain the main idea of its topic sentence. Use the following strategy:

1. Highlight your topic sentence, the general statement in which you summarize the main idea of the paragraph.
2. Underline the supporting sentences that develop this idea.
3. Eliminate any sentences that do not support the main idea or that simply restate it.

Student Model: Revising to Support Generalizations

Litter is harmful for many reasons. For one, roadside litter is eventually washed into our waterways and oceans— water we use for drinking and recreation. Also, animals might entangle themselves or mistake trash for food and swallow it. ~~Air pollution is also a serious problem.~~

> Eliminating sentences that do not support the main idea makes the paragraph clearer and stronger.

Revising Your Word Choice

Evaluate your vocabulary. Review your draft as if you were a member of your target audience. Find specialized terms that need to be defined or vocabulary that seems too difficult or easy for your readers. Then, adjust your language accordingly.

General audience: Another way to fight fatigue is to exercise.

Target audience of experts: Another way to raise low levels of blood sugar is to get more exercise.

Peer Review: Exchange drafts with a partner. Review each other's work, circling words that are either too specialized and technical or too simple and basic for your target audiences. Then, revise your draft, replacing inappropriate terms with language that better suits your readers' experience and knowledge levels. Discuss your decisions with your partner.

Tips for Test Taking

Tell students that word choice is critical in any form of expository writing. To be successful, students must use clear and concise language. Remind students that a word is only effective when used in the proper context. Also point out that using fewer words often allows a clearer meaning to emerge.

Integrating Grammar Skills

Revising Faulty Pronoun-Antecedent Agreement

Pronouns are words that take the place of nouns. Antecedents are the nouns for which pronouns stand.

Prentice Hall Writing and Grammar Connection: Chapter 25, Section 2

Identifying Errors in Pronoun-Antecedent Agreement Pronouns "disagree" with their antecedents when they are mismatched in number, person, or gender. A pronoun should agree with its antecedent in number:

Incorrect: *Anne and Natasha* reminded *her* parents.
Correct: *Anne and Natasha* reminded *their* parents. (plural)
Incorrect: *Neither Carl nor Jeff* remember *their* ID number.
Correct: *Neither Carl nor Jeff* remembers *his* ID number. (singular)

A pronoun should agree with its antecedent in person:

Incorrect: When a *person* hurries, *you* often make mistakes.
Correct: When *a person* hurries, *he or she* often makes mistakes. (third-person singular)
Correct: When *people* hurry, *they* often make mistakes. (third-person plural)

Fixing Errors in Pronoun-Antecedent Agreement To correct pronoun-antecedent errors, first identify the antecedent of each pronoun. As you work through each paragraph of your draft, consider the following:

1. **For compound antecedents joined by *and,* use a plural personal pronoun.**
2. **For singular antecedents joined by *or* or *nor,* use a singular personal pronoun.**
3. **Check every occurrence of the pronoun *you* to make sure that you have not made a shift in person.**

Gender of Third-Person Singular Pronouns		
Masculine	**Feminine**	**Neuter**
he, him, his, himself	she, her, hers, herself	it, its, itself

Apply It to Your Editing

Review the first and last paragraphs in your draft. Underline each antecedent and circle each pronoun. Check the marked words for pronoun-antecedent agreement and fix any errors.

Writing Workshop ■ 167

Integrating Grammar Skills

- Read the following sentences aloud, and have students identify the pronouns and the antecedents:

  1. *Alicia lost her necklace.*
     Answer: pronoun: her; antecedent: Alicia

  2. *If Marcus would have run, he could have caught the bus.*
     Answer: pronoun: he; antecedent: Marcus

- Tell students that errors in pronoun-antecedent agreement often occur when the words in question are widely separated in a sentence.

- Write the following sentences on the board, and have students identify which sentences have pronoun-antecedent agreement:

  1. *Thomas lost his watch.*
  2. *Faith and Verona washed her dogs.*
  3. *If a child runs beside the pool, they could fall.*

  Answer: Sentence 1 has agreement.

- Write the following sentences on the board, and have volunteers correct pronoun-antecedent errors:

  1. *Jakeem or Roger is going to read their report today.*
     Answer: his report

  2. *When a student does well on a test, they should feel proud.*
     Answer: he or she should feel proud

  3. *Paige and Tabitha studied for her test.*
     Answer: their test

- When reviewing their drafts for pronoun-antecedent agreement, tell students to look for pronouns first and then find the appropriate antecedents.

𝒲𝒢 Writing and Grammar, Gold Level

Students will find additional instruction on pronoun-antecedent agreement in Chapter 25, Section 2.

167

Student Model

- Explain that the Student Model is a sample and that essays may be longer.
- Ask students to paraphrase the author's general statement of the problem.
  Possible response: Although they may not be aware of it, people who litter harm the environment and antagonize community appearance issues.
- Ask students to identify the paragraph in which the author gives more details about the problem.
  Answer: The author gives more details in the third paragraph.
- Have students identify the proposed solution to the problem.
  Answer: The proposed solution is to create a feeling of ownership of public spaces.
- Ask students to share their opinions on the effectiveness of the author's proposed solution.
  Answer: Students will probably agree that when people feel personally involved, they will be more concerned with the issue.

Writing Genres

Problem-and-Solution Essay Writing in the Workplace If students have concerns about problems in their own places of work, they can use the problem-and-solution essay to address concerns and to suggest solutions. Workplace suggestions are likely to be taken more seriously if a thorough analysis and a supported solution are submitted.

Student Model: Naomi Barrowclough
Maplewood, NJ

Environmental Un-Consciousness

During a recent Earth Day cleanup, I became disgusted by the amount of trash I picked up within a two-hour period. People had thrown little papers, bits of plastic, and candy wrappers until the mess formed a multicolored carpet over the green grass. Those who litter may not realize that litter creates serious environmental problems.

We've all been told not to litter, but it does not seem to sink in. One person may think his or her contribution is only a microscopic addition when viewed against the whole. But if every person shared this sense of irresponsibility, Earth would soon be overwhelmed by pollution.

Litter is harmful for many reasons. For one, roadside litter eventually washes into waterways and oceans—water we use for drinking and recreation. Also, animals might entangle themselves or mistake trash for food and swallow it. In our public spaces, children spend a great deal of time in areas where they could be physically harmed by the pollution caused by litter.

There is no simple solution to the problem of litter, only an array of possible solutions with one strategy in common: Create a feeling of ownership over public spaces. Some of the most popular sites for litter are beaches and parks because people feel no sense of ownership over these places. These same people would never litter in their own homes.

To create a feeling of ownership, it is necessary to educate children early about the environmental consequences of littering. According to research done by Keep America Beautiful, a non-profit organization, most people do not feel responsible for public spaces. They think "someone else" will clean up. To change this attitude, schools could lead field trips to local beaches or parks where students pick up trash and test water quality. If kids have to fish two shopping carts from the side of a stream, as I did, they might think twice about throwing something else on the ground. If they see that contaminated water is harmful to both humans and wildlife, they might stop someone they see littering.

There is no easy way to stop littering. Fines and policing alone will not do the trick because people will just look before they litter. Until people understand that littering is irresponsible and has devastating environmental consequences, they will continue to litter. The solution lies in education and creating a sense of ownership about our public spaces.

In the opening paragraph, Naomi provides a general statement of the problem.

Here, the author provides greater detail to explain the problem more fully.

Naomi introduces a general solution here.

In this paragraph, specific strategies for achieving the solution are introduced.

In the final paragraph, Naomi addresses a potential concern and then restates her solution.

Editing and Proofreading

Check your draft for errors in spelling, grammar, and punctuation.
Focus on Spelling: As you proofread, circle words that you are not sure how to spell, frequently misspell, or seldom use. Then, use reference resources to confirm the correct spelling of the circled words.

Publishing and Presenting

To make the best use of your problem-and-solution essay, share it with people who can help you make a difference.
Send a letter. Send your essay to the appropriate government official, agency, or organization. When you receive a response, share it with your classmates in a presentation. Save both the essay and response in your portfolio.
Make a speech. Deliver your essay as a speech to a group within your school or community that shares your concerns about the problem. Afterward, lead a question-and-answer session. Be sure to modify or restate your answers if the audience seems confused. Report any consequences of your speech to your classmates.

Reflecting on Your Writing

Writer's Journal Jot down your thoughts on writing a problem-and-solution essay. Begin by answering these questions:
- Which prewriting and drafting strategies were most useful to you?
- What new insights or techniques may help you analyze and respond to a problem in the future?

Rubric for Self-Assessment

To assess your problem-and-solution essay, use the following rubric.

Criteria	Rating Scale
	not very *very*
Focus: How adequately do you explore the problem in the essay?	1 2 3 4 5
Organization: How well do you organize the steps of the solution?	1 2 3 4 5
Support/Elaboration: How convincing are your facts, details, and reasons?	1 2 3 4 5
Style: How appropriate is the language for the audience's knowledge level?	1 2 3 4 5
Conventions: How correct is your grammar, especially your use of pronouns?	1 2 3 4 5

Writing Workshop ■ *169*

Editing and Proofreading

- Tell students to use dictionaries to confirm spellings.
- Have students write on the board any words they are not sure how to spell. As a class, go over the words and make corrections.

Six Traits Focus

	Ideas		Word Choice
✔	Organization		Sentence Fluency
	Voice	✔	Conventions

Publishing and Presenting

- If a student's existing essay seems inappropriate for submission to conventional outlets, brainstorm to generate a novel remedy. It may be a creative revision or discovery of an alternate organization.
- Discuss the additional information conveyed when a message is delivered as a speech or presentation. Tell students that body language can show how confident you are, vocal intonations can stress specific points, and eye contact can keep the audience engaged. Encourage students to be aware of these factors when speaking.

Reflecting on Your Writing

- Ask students whether it was difficult for them to find convincing details to show the merit of their solutions. Did students feel as if they acquired enough evidence to prove their solutions?
- Ask students how difficult it was to write for their target audience. How would their essays change if the audience were changed? Have students think of another audience that they could have written for, and reflect on how this change of audience would have altered the essay.

Writing and Grammar, Gold Level

Students will find additional guidance on editing and proofreading, publishing and presenting, and reflecting on a problem-and-solution essay in Chapter 11, Sections 5 and 6.

Tips for
Test Taking

Emphasize preparation and practice to lower test anxiety and raise achievement during a timed composition test. While many fear this task, few recognize the inherent advantages available. The steps in the writing process are known. The strategies and tactics to proficiently practice each step are available ahead of time. The opportunity even exists to produce a well-organized and polished essay in any writing mode before a test. Stress these advantages and the time and patience required to employ them.

Evaluating the Content

- Point out that many news broadcasts entertain as well as inform because they depend on viewers' ratings.

- Tell students that if they are unsure of the credibility of a fact, they should use another source to verify it. Suggest that they use library resources, encyclopedias, or Internet sources with addresses that end in *.gov, .edu, or .org.*

- Point out to students that when they identify and evaluate opinions, they should evaluate the credibility of the person speaking. Students must ask themselves: What are this person's credentials? Why should I believe what this person says?

Evaluating the Methods

- Tell students that they should not merely accept what media present at face value; students must watch or listen with a skeptical mind for the presence of bias.

- Tell students that as they are analyzing their media broadcasts, they should pay attention to their emotional states. As their emotions change—for example, if they experience anger, assurance, pride, or worry—they should look for charged language, charged images, and stereotypes that may have triggered those feelings.

Activity

To evaluate students' analysis, use the **Listening: Analyzing Media Messages** rubric, p. 80 in *General Resources.*

Analyzing Broadcast Media Presentations

While television, radio, the Internet, and other media sources can provide valuable information, you should analyze information critically and evaluate its reliability.

Determine Purpose

Media presentations may be intended to entertain, to inform, to persuade, or to achieve a combination of purposes. Knowing the purpose of a presentation will help you establish expectations and evaluate the presentation.

Evaluating the Content

Evaluate evidence and opinions included in the presentation. Determine whether what is presented meets the following criteria.

- **Relevance:** Statements should be related to the point being made. Watch for statements that are included for their shock value only.

- **Reliability:** Facts should come from reliable, verifiable sources. Opinions should come from experts, individuals, or groups who have experience and knowledge. Propaganda often uses "facts" that have no basis.

- **Consistency:** Statements should be consistent. Watch for statements that are inconsistent and geared to sway an audience.

Evaluating the Methods

Think about the methods used to present the information.

- **Charged Language** Listen for words and phrases that are meant to manipulate, or affect your emotions.

- **Charged Images** Images can also affect emotions. The use of an unflattering image of someone will usually make you think negatively about that person.

- **Use of Stereotypes** Stereotypes are simplified and often negative depictions of groups of people. They are a type of charged, or emotionally laden, content and should not be present in reliable broadcasts.

Activity **Prepare and Deliver a Speech** Analyze a television news program or talk show using the Feedback Form as a guide. Share your conclusions in a class discussion.

Media Presentation Feedback Form

Rating System
Poor 1 2 3 4 5 Excellent

Use of Facts
____ Relevant Facts
____ Reliable Support
____ Complete Support

Presentation
____ Sets
____ Graphics
____ Speaker's Tone
____ Speaker's Clarity

Does the presentation include charged language?

Does it include charged images?

Does it present stereotypes?

Conclusions
Was the presentation objective?

Was the presentation reliable?

A Pocketful of Rye

Agatha Christie
Signet, 2000

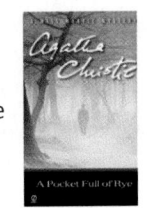

Mystery Elderly Miss Jane Marple may not look like a detective, but her keen mind and profound understanding of human nature help her unravel many mysteries that puzzle England's police. Here, she helps solve the murder of a rich businessman whose unpleasant family falls under suspicion for the crime.

Great Expectations

Charles Dickens
Pearson Prentice Hall, 2000

Novel This justly famous nineteenth-century novel follows the adventures of Pip, a poor young man who finds his life changed irrevocably when a mysterious benefactor bestows "great expectations" on him.

A Separate Peace

John Knowles
Bantam Books, 1959

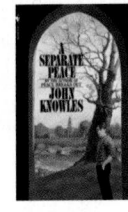

Novel Gene and Phineas share a room at Devon, an exclusive New England prep school, during the summer prior to World War II. The boys form a complex bond of friendship that draws out both their best and worst characteristics and ultimately leads to violence, a confession, and the betrayal of trust.

Rosa Parks: My Story

Rosa Parks with Jim Haskins
Puffin Books, 1992

Autobiography Rosa Parks describes her role in the civil rights movement. Her involvement began in 1955 on a bus in Montgomery, Alabama, and continued through the historic Supreme Court decision on segregation in 1956. This is a story of how one person's courage changed the course of the United States.

These titles are available in the Penguin/Prentice Hall Literature Library.
Consult your teacher before choosing one.

Planning Students' Further Reading

Discussions of literature can raise sensitive and often controversial issues. Before you recommend further reading to your students, consider the values and sensitivities of your community as well as the age, ability, and sophistication of your students. It is also good policy to preview literature before you recommend it to students. The notes below offer some guidance on specific titles.

[L4] *A Pocketful of Rye* While not graphically violent, the novel contains several murders. It also features an adulterous wife, romance and marriage for monetary gain, mental illness, religious zealotry, and crooked business deals. The murderer's identity may be especially disturbing because he is a charming man and loving husband, yet he is guilty of fratricide and the emotional abuse of a credulous female.

Reading level appropriate for high school students

[L3] *Great Expectations* This simplified version of the classic book includes ill treatment of Pip. Dickens writes from the standpoint of a child who endured this treatment and found it painful, but by the end of the novel, the child has risen above this abusive treatment and become a better person. There is reference to men beating women, as when Drummle is said to have ill-treated Estella. There is also mention of Pip's drinking alcohol.

Reading level appropriate for high school students

[L2] *A Separate Peace* The grimness of the war, Leper's insanity, Gene's psychological struggle, and Finny's death are potential sources of distress for students.

Lexile: 1110L

[L1, L2, EL] *Rosa Parks: My Story* This autobiography contains incidents of prejudice against African Americans in the southern United States during the twentieth century and uses occasional insensitive language. It mentions lynching and a charge of rape and includes a photograph of a Ku Klux Klan meeting.

Lexile: 970L

Professional Development

Response Journals

Students may respond to literature in a number of ways. Response journals are an opportunity for students to interact personally and independently with a piece of literature. Response Journals encourage students to make personal connections with the text, a valuable starting point for constructing their own understanding. You might wish to have them use response journals while reading any of these works or any other piece of literature.

Response journals can be set up in a number of ways and used for a variety of purposes. Initially, you may wish to guide students in their responses, with a Response Starters sheet, which provides a series of stems to be built into response statements. Later, students may work in a two-column response format, with prepared sheets or in their own notebooks.

See *General Resources*, pp. 17–20, for further guidance on using response journals.

Promote Independent Reading

Independent reading gives students an opportunity to practice the reading skills taught in this unit and to improve comprehension. When students read independently, they also increase their vocabulary and develop their own personal reading interests.

You may assign this selection to be read independently for homework, in class when students have completed other work, or for independent group work.

Develop Reading Preferences

After students have read this selection, ask them what they enjoyed about it. Build on their ideas to recommend further reading. Students who enjoy this selection might also enjoy other comics, as well as satire and arguments.

On Your Own
Readings in Media

Think About It Most people associate comics with superheroes, humorous animals, and amusing people who have exaggerated facial features. As you read this excerpt from *Understanding Comics,* consider how much the writer/illustrator changes your impressions and ideas about a typical comic strip.

excerpt from

Understanding Comics
Scott McCloud

172 ■ *Fiction and Nonfiction*

172

from *Understanding Comics* ■ 173

ON YOUR OWN

REINFORCE/RETEACH

Motivation

Ask for a show-of-hands to see how many students have read comics before. Call on volunteers to share examples of comics they like. Direct students to look at the images in this selection. Discuss differences between a page of comics and a page in a typical book. For example, comics have more pictures, comics have fewer words, comics have more white space, and comics look more inviting.

Reading Skill
Identifying an Author's Purpose

- Review author's purpose (p. 94)— the author's reason for writing what he or she wants to communicate to readers. Make sure students understand that authors write with a purpose, and, for readers, understanding the purpose makes it easier to understand the writing.

- Ask a student to read the first two frames of *Understanding Comics* on p. 172 and the last two frames on the bottom of p. 173. **Ask** a volunteer to explain McCloud's purpose in creating this comic.
Possible response: McCloud's purpose is to ask readers to critically analyze the world of comics in a serious way.

continued on p. 174

Differentiated Instruction   Solutions for All Learners

Background for Special Needs Students
Explain to students that the standard conventions for reading comics include starting at the top of the page and reading each row from left to right. Also, explain that, when the boxes are different sizes, you should read them in order based on the tops of the boxes. Point out that each box of the strip is called a frame. Have students look at the box layout on a page of McCloud's comic and note the different sizes of frames and how they are lined up. Direct students to draw ten boxes, or frames, on a piece of paper. Ask them to use two or three different-sized boxes. Then have students number each frame in the order they should be read. Finally, placing one word in each box and in the correct order, have them write this sentence in their frames: Comics only make sense when read in the correct order.

173

Reinforce/Reteach (cont.)

- Have students carefully look at all the characters on the globe on p. 174. **Ask** volunteers to name characters they recognize and share something they know about the characters. **Example:** Charlie Brown is a young boy who has everyday experiences with his school friends and generally finds the best in everyone.

- **Ask** why McCloud most likely placed the characters on a globe. **Possible response:** McCloud probably placed the many characters on a globe to show the great variety of characters and ideas represented in comics. Also the concept of a globe is usually used to show something that applies to everyone.

- **Ask** how the globe idea helps support McCloud's purpose for creating this comic. **Possible response:** The many characters on the globe show diversity in comics. Some of the characters are animals, some are people, some are superheroes, and some are monsters. Some of the characters are familiar and others are not. Also, the image of a globe represents ideas that are large and encompassing. These two concepts work together to show that comics is a broad field to be studied.

continued on p. 175

174 ■ *Fiction and Nonfiction*

Vocabulary Development

Vocabulary for Understanding Comic Books
This comic uses several specialized vocabulary words to help illustrate a point. Many of these words may be unfamiliar to students. Guide them to understand the meaning of the following words in "Understanding Comics."

sequential: following a sequence, order
neutral: not aligned with a particular group; independent
aesthetic: artistic
form: the shape and structure of something
content: meaning or significance

174

from *Understanding Comics* ■ 175

Reinforce/Reteach (cont.)

- **Ask** students to place one hand over the column of small double pictures. Then, ask a volunteer to describe what is happening in the first single small picture.
  Possible response: A man is holding his hat in place.

- Have students remove their hands. **Ask** a volunteer to tell what is happening in the side-by-side hat pictures.
  Possible response: The man is tipping his hat.

- **Ask** a volunteer to explain the main differences between looking at one or other of the pictures and looking at the two together.
  Possible response: The brain fills in what happens between the two pictures to create action.

- **Ask** students to describe McCloud's choice of words and tone in this comic.
  Answer: McCloud chose technical words and a serious tone in this comic.

- **Ask** students how his word choice and tone support his purpose as an author.
  Answer: Because his tone is serious and word choice technical, one infers that his purpose is to have readers take his ideas and comics seriously.

continued on p. 176

Differentiated Instruction   Solutions for All Learners

Strategy for Less Proficient Readers
Explain to students that knowing why an author is writing can make reading easier. Point out that McCloud is trying to convince us to believe comics deserve a serious study, and that one way to keep track of important ideas in this selection is to write notes about the reasons he thinks comics are important.

Background for English Learners
Students from other countries may not be familiar with American movie, television, and comic characters and, therefore, might not understand related references such as the different characters on the globe on p. 174 and "Batman" and "X-Men" on p. 179. Ask students to bring in related merchandise such as T-shirts, toys, and lunch boxes. Show a few minutes of different videos that show some of the characters in action.

- Draw students' attention to the fact that McCloud is using the pitcher, or vessel, as a way to align comics with other art forms. **Ask** students to identify some words that are related to other art forms.
  Possible response: Film, visual art, theatre, video, music, written word, writers, artists, trends, genres, styles, subject matter, themes.

- **Ask** students what McCloud most likely means when he writes that "the trick is to never mistake the message for the messenger."
  Possible response: McCloud is reminding readers that while comics may look like funny or silly images, the messages that they convey can be quite serious. It is important not to overlook the message of a comic just because the format may appear not to be serious.

continued on p. 177

176 ■ *Fiction and Nonfiction*

Vocabulary Development

Think-Aloud: Context

Direct students' attention to the word *juxtaposed* at the bottom of page 177. Using a think-aloud process, model how to use context to infer the meaning of an unknown word. Say to students:

I'm going to think aloud to show you how I would figure out the meaning of *juxtaposed* from its context.

From the conversation between McCloud and the audience, I know that the word *juxtaposed* somehow shows the difference between animation and comics. From McCloud's comment in the bottom left frame, I know that *juxtaposed* has something to do with spatial arrangements that are an issue in comics, but not an issue in animation. In the last frame, McCloud points out that comics are *juxtaposed* because, unlike in a movie, each frame of a comic must occupy different space. Putting these comments all together, I can guess that *juxtaposed* must mean to *place side-by-side*.

from *Understanding Comics* ■ 177

Reinforce/Reteach (cont.)

- Direct students' attention to the fact that the main character is on stage and being heckled, similar to a stand-up comic. **Ask** students how this setting for a serious discussion about comics contributes to McCloud's purpose.
  Possible response: It reinforces the idea that the message can be serious while the messenger can appear to be funny. It also gives comics credence as an art form by aligning with another art form: comedian/actor.

- **Ask** how debating the definition of comics supports McCloud's purpose.
  Possible response: McCloud wants readers to seriously analyze the world of comics. In order to do that, readers must take the time to think about what they are analyzing. This debate about definition forces readers to think about the nature of comics.

continued on p. 178

Instruction   Solutions for All Learners

Vocabulary for Less Proficient Readers
Explain to students that *onomatopoeia* is the use of words that imitate the sounds with which they are associated. Ask students to turn to p. 176 and note that, in several frames, the author uses onomatopoeia to help involve all senses in the experience. Point out that, when you read *Glug, Glug,* you can almost hear someone drinking something. As a group, ask students to say *Glug, Glug* a few times while they act as if they are drinking a large glass of water so they can experience onomatopoeia in action.

Enrichment for Gifted/Talented Students
Discuss that McCloud would like others to value comics as he does. Challenge students to each think of an activity or idea he or she believes is important but that others do not typically value. Have students create lists of at least three reasons why others should take a more serious look at their ideas or activities. Allow time for students to present their lists.

- Have students look at the strip of film on the left of p. 178. Tell them to imagine that it is film that is moving quickly. **Ask** a volunteer what on the film would appear to be moving.
  Answer: The man's hand.
  Explain that a typical comic version of the moving hand might show every fourth picture and then let your mind imagine the movement, whereas a film has to include more frames with smaller movements so your eye will think it is seeing movement.

- **Ask** students to compare McCloud's final definition of comics to his first attempt. Is it more accurate? Is it more complete?
  Possible response: McCloud's final definition is more complete because it includes what comics do as well as what they are. It also differentiates comics from animation.

continued on p. 179

178 ■ *Fiction and Nonfiction*

Extend the Lesson

Create a Definition
Tell students to think of a concept that they know a lot about, such as skateboarding, hanging out with friends, or cafeteria food. Then, as a group, follow the steps shown in "Understanding Comics" to develop a definition.

© and TM 1994 Scott McCloud

The complete *Understanding Comics* is 215 pages in 9 chapters and examines all aspects of comics. The above excerpt is from Chapter One.

Meet the Author

Scott McCloud started drawing comics at age twelve. After graduating from college, he began his career as a cartoonist. He has since published an award-winning comic book series called *Zot!* as well as *Destroy!*, a parody of superhero comics.

Readings in Media
Talk About It

Use these questions to guide a discussion of this selection.

1. Do you accept McCloud's final definition of comics?
2. McCloud compares comics to art forms such as film, music, and theater. Choose one of the following items to discuss with a group.
   - Do you think the same level of skill, imagination, and effort used to create other art forms is needed to create comics? Explain.
   - Government funding is sometimes given to support the arts. Do you think funding should be given to comics writers? Why or why not?

   Choose a point person to share your ideas with the class.

from *Understanding Comics* ■ 179

Reinforce/Reteach (cont.)

- Point out that, on pp. 177, 178, and part of 179, McCloud is within the comic on a stage talking to an audience. **Ask** students how McCloud's situation in the very last frame is different and how they can tell it is different.
  Possible response: It is different because McCloud is talking to the reader of this article. You can tell because he is no longer on stage and he is leaning out of the frame and "looking" at the reader.

Readings in Media
Talk About It

- Suggest that students work in groups to address these questions.
- To guide students' discussion, use the **Discussion Guide**, p. 39 in *General Resources*.

Differentiated Instruction   Solutions for All Learners

Support for English Learners
Slang presents a special challenge for English Language Learners.
Point out and discuss the meanings of these slang phrases from McCloud's comic:
Soon, I was hooked! (p. 172) (Interpretation: Soon, I enjoyed comics so much, I wanted to read them all the time!)
Sure, I realized that comic books were ....kiddie fare. (p. 173) (Interpretation: Sure, I realized that comic books were designed for young children.)

But to define comics, we must do a little aesthetic surgery.... (p. 175) (Interpretation: But to define comics, we must differentiate between the words and pictures and the messages they send.)
Beg pardon? (p. 177) (Interpretation: Could you repeat that please? I didn't understand what you said.)

Ask students to read the comics in a newspaper and look for uses of slang. Give students time to share the examples they find.

Introduce Unit 2

- Have small groups of students focus on different figures in the art on these pages. Have each group write a brief description of what is happening from that person's point of view. Discuss the descriptions as a class.

- Tell students that point of view is an essential element of all fiction, including the short stories they will read in this unit.

Instructional Resources

Unit 2 Resources support students in developing and mastering the unit skills and help you assess progress.

▶ **Progress Monitoring** These tests enable you to assess and monitor student progress in each part:

- **Diagnostic test**
- **Benchmark test**

▶ **Vocabulary Warm-ups**
Additional vocabulary support, based on Lexile scores of vocabulary words, is provided for each selection.

- **Word List A and Practice A** provide vocabulary-building activities for students reading two grades below level.

- **Word List B and Practice B** provide vocabulary-building activities for students reading one grade below level.

▶ **Reading Warm-ups** Two Reading Warm-ups for each selection provide a context for students to apply newly learned vocabulary. Each Reading Warm-up consists of a short reading passage loosely tied to a theme in the selection. Questions and activities guide students to focus on particular vocabulary items.

- **Reading Warm-up A**, for students reading two grades below level, focuses on the vocabulary items presented in Vocabulary Warm-up A.

- **Reading Warm-up B**, for students reading one grade below level, focuses on the vocabulary items presented in Vocabulary Warm-up B.

▶ **Selection Support** These practice pages are available for each selection:

- **Reading Skills**
- **Literary Analysis**
- **Vocabulary Builder**
- **Support for Writing**
- **Support for Extend Your Learning**
- **Enrichment**

PRENTICE HALL
TeacherEXPRESS™ You may also
Plan · Teach · Assess   access these
resources on TeacherExpress.

180

Unit
2

Short Stories

Assessment Resources

Program Assessment

Unit 2 Resources
   Selection Tests A and B

TeacherExpress™
   ExamView® Test Bank
   Software

Adequate Yearly Progress Monitoring Assessment

Unit 2 Resources
   Diagnostic Tests: Part 1,
   Part 2
   Benchmark Tests: Part 1,
   Part 2

Standardized Assessment

Standardized Test Preparation Workbook

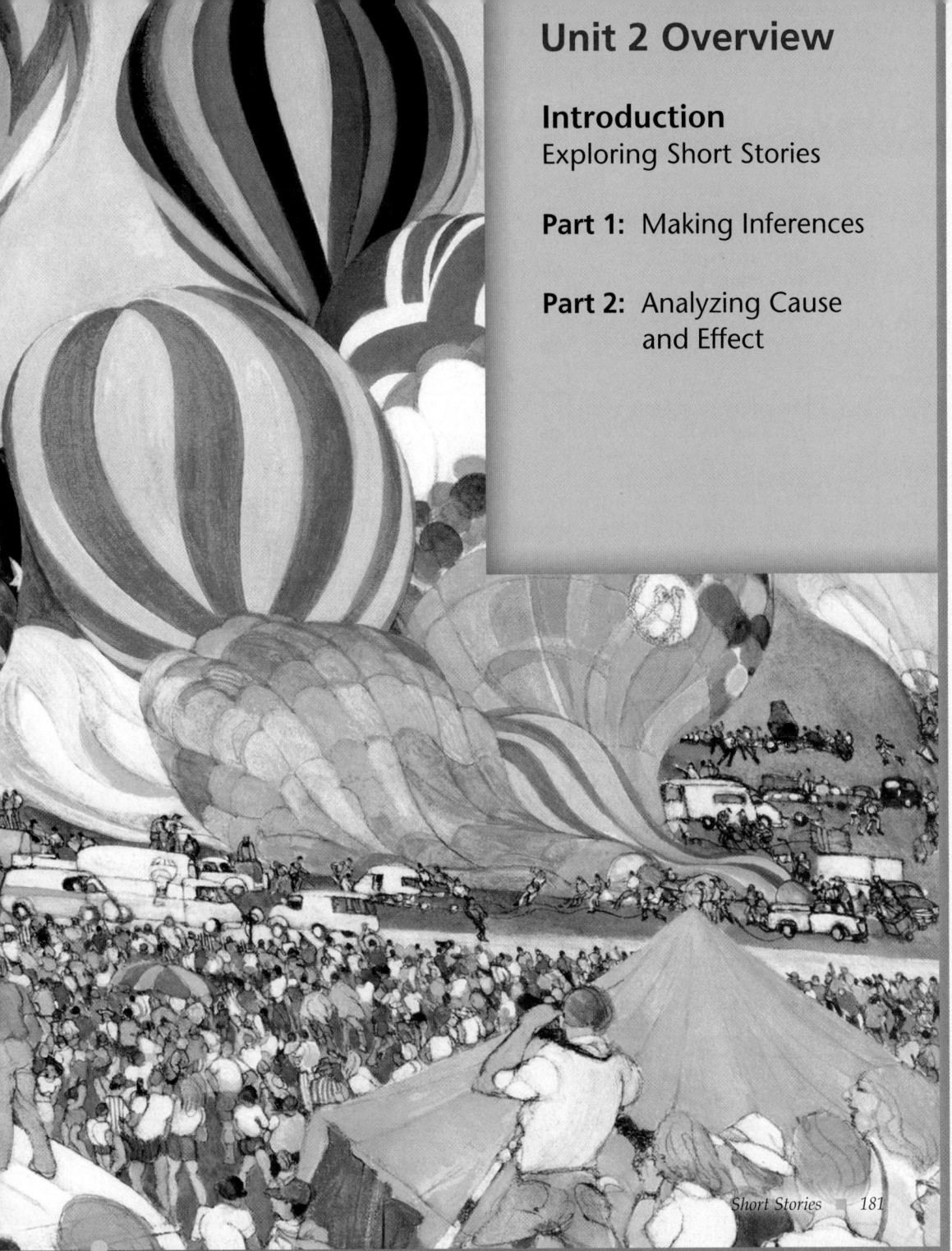

Unit 2 Overview

Introduction
Exploring Short Stories

Part 1: Making Inferences

Part 2: Analyzing Cause and Effect

Unit 2 Overview
Genre Focus
Author Wayson Choy introduces the literary genre, short story, with a model of it. Students read and analyze examples of short stories.

Using the Unit Selections
Teach Skills Instructional selections are presented in sets of two. To teach the skills and meet the objectives, you need to complete only one selection in each set.

Differentiate and Reinforce Choose the selection in a set that is best suited to your students. The selections are listed by accessibility in the Differentiated Instruction box below. You may use the other selection in the set to reinforce comprehension and skills or to provide enrichment.

Integrate Skills Each selection set gives students a reading strategy, literary analysis, and vocabulary development as well as opportunities for writing about the selection, research and technology, listening and speaking, grammar, and assessment practice.

See pages 197 and 289 for an overview of the skills in each part.

Using the Unit Features
These additional reading selections give you the opportunity to apply, reinforce, and extend the unit skills.

Reading Informational Materials Students learn to analyze and evaluate informational texts.

Comparing Literary Works Students read a pair of literary works to compare the treatment of a literary element.

On Your Own Students may read this selection independently, or you may teach it actively to reinforce a unit reading skill.

See the Unit 2 Overview and Pacing Plan on the following pages.

Differentiated Instruction   Solutions for All Learners

Accessibility for Ability Levels
This chart gives a general accessibility rating to help you decide which selection is more appropriate for your students. For additional guidance on factors that affect the accessibility of each selection, see the **Time and Resource Manager** for each selection set.

	Accessible	More Challenging
Part 1		
Set 1	The Most Dangerous Game	American History
Set 2	The Gift of the Magi	The Interlopers
Part 2		
Set 1	The Necklace	Rules of the Game
Set 2	Blues Ain't No Mockin Bird	The Invalid's Story

181

✓ Meeting Your Standards

Students will

1. recognize and appreciate short stories as a literary genre.
2. read and analyze a variety of short stories.
3. apply reading skills.
   - Making inferences
     - Asking questions to make inferences
     - Using your own prior knowledge and experience to make inferences
   - Analyzing cause and effect
     - Asking questions to analyze cause and effect
     - Visualizing the action to analyze cause and effect
4. analyze literary elements.
   - Conflict
   - Irony
   - Character and characterization
   - Dialogue
5. build vocabulary.
   - Word parts
   - Word roots
6. learn elements of grammar, usage, and style.
7. use a recursive writing process to write in a variety of forms.
   - Short story
   - Cause-and-effect essay
8. read informational materials.
   - Evaluating visual aids
   - Evaluating text format
9. compare literary works.
   - Setting
   - Symbolism
10. use technology to do research.
    - Photo essay
    - Plan for an illustrated report
    - Informative brochure
    - Photo collection
11. develop listening and speaking skills.
    - Speech
    - Debate
    - Monologue
    - Prepare and deliver a dialogue
12. develop spelling proficiency.

Unit Introduction and Part 1	Week 1					Week 2					Week 3				
	❶	❷	❸	❹	❺	❶	❷	❸	❹	❺	❶	❷	❸	❹	❺
Introduce the Unit author: Wayson Choy (p. 182).	●														
Introduce short stories (pp. 184–185).	●														
Teach the Model selection (pp. 187–194).	●	●													
Administer the Unit 2, Part 1 Diagnostic Test.			●												
Introduce the Reading and Vocabulary Skills for Part 1 (pp. 198–199).			●												
Teach one selection from Set 1 (pp. 202–235).		●	●	●	●										
Teach one selection from Set 2 (pp. 246–261).							●	●	●	●					
Teach Reading Informational Materials (pp. 240–242).											●				
Teach Comparing Literary Works (pp. 268–280).												●	●		
Complete the Reading and Vocabulary Review (pp. 282–283).														●	
Have students complete the Writing Workshop (pp. 284–288).											●	●	●	●	●
Administer the Unit 2, Part 1 Benchmark Test.															●

182a

Part 2	Week 1 ①	②	③	④	⑤	Week 2 ①	②	③	④	⑤	Week 3 ①	②	③	④	⑤
Administer the Unit 2, Part 2 Diagnostic Test.	●														
Introduce the Reading and Vocabulary Skills for Part 2 (pp. 290–291).	●														
Teach one selection from Set 1 (pp. 294–315).		●	●	●	●										
Teach one selection from Set 2 (pp. 322–339).						●	●	●	●						
Teach Reading Informational Materials (pp. 344–346).										●					
Teach Comparing Literary Works (pp. 350–366).											●	●			
Complete the Reading and Vocabulary Review (pp. 368–369).													●		
Have students complete the Writing Workshop (pp. 372–379).											●	●	●	●	●
Have students complete the Communications Workshop (p. 380).														●	
Have students complete the Spelling Workshop (pp. 370–371).														●	
Administer the Unit 2, Part 2 Benchmark Test.															●

Options for Block and Daily Scheduling

The assignments and activities in this unit planner are organized by week. You may adjust them to your daily or block schedule. The Time and Resource Managers for the selection sets give specific times to help your planning.

Options for Independent Reading

Use these independent reading options to differentiate, reinforce, and extend your instruction:

On Your Own

Students may read this selection on their own or you may use it to reteach and reinforce unit skills.

Billy Collins, "Candle Hat"

For Further Reading

Have students choose and read a full-length work while working on this unit.

[L1, L2, EL] Harper Lee, *To Kill a Mockingbird*

[L2] Sir Arthur Conan Doyle, *The Sherlock Holmes Mysteries*

[L3] Prentice Hall Anthology, *Literature of the Expanding Frontier*

[L4] Jack London, *The Sea-Wolf and Selected Stories*

[L4] Authors in Depth

Mark Twain, from *A Connecticut Yankee in King Arthur's Court*, "A Fable," from *Roughing It*

Ray Bradbury, "The Flying Machine," "The Pedestrian," "The Other Me," "January 1999: Rocket Summer" from *The Martian Chronicles*

[L1] Special Needs Students
[L2] Below-Level Students
[L3] All Students
[L4] Above-Level Students
[EL] English Learners

PRENTICE HALL
Teacher EXPRESS™
Plan · Teach · Assess
Use this complete suite of powerful teaching tools to make lesson planning and testing quicker and easier.

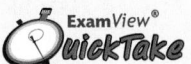
ExamView® QuickTake — Monitor student progress instantly.

Introduction:
The Short Story

Wayson Choy

✔ Meeting Your Standards

Students will

1. understand the characteristics of short stories.
2. read and analyze an example of a short story.
3. learn about author Wayson Choy.
4. build vocabulary.
5. begin the process of writing a problem/solution essay.

From the Author's Desk

❶ Introduce Wayson Choy

- Wayson Choy teaches English at Humber College in Toronto, Canada. His short story "The Jade Peony," which came from an exercise he did in a writing class, was anthologized so often that a publisher suggested that he develop it into a novel. He has since written *All That Matters,* a sequel to *The Jade Peony.* Ask students whether they have read or are familiar with any of his work.

- Use the *From the Author's Desk DVD* to introduce the author and the genre. Show Segments 1 and 2 to provide insights into how a combination of past and present infuses Wayson Choy's work and why his stories are character-based rather than plot-centered. After students have watched the segments, **ask:** How does being a second-generation Chinese Canadian influence Choy's fiction? **Possible response:** A sense of the past and his heritage permeates Choy's writing.

- Interested students might enjoy this work by Wayson Choy. (We suggest that you review materials before introducing them to students.)

- *Paper Shadows: A Chinatown Childhood,* a memoir

From the Author's Desk

Wayson Choy
❷ Talks About the Form

Your life, like mine, is surrounded by all kinds of stories. We collect them, and we tell them. Think how you are always hungry for stories that inspire or scare you, that make you thoughtful about important things, or remind you, in fresh ways, of your present or past.

In fact, everyone's life is an assemblage of short stories—like the kind that writers create to enhance our understanding of our own decisive moments and revelations.

▲ Wayson Choy draws on his own boyhood memories of Vancouver's Chinatown to re-create the experiences of Chinese Canadians who lived more than half a century ago.

Short Stories Deepen Our Awareness

More than just entertainment, a fine **short story** will always focus on a fragment of truth that matters to you. Such a story often relates a brief incident, to create a unity—a harmony of details—that will expose you to a deeper experience of life. The climax of a good short story can flash inside you like a bolt of lightning or gently glow like a candle. In fact, the light a fine story gives to you can linger for a lifetime.

For example, when I first read Shirley Jackson's "The Lottery," I came to realize that ordinary people—like you or me—can willfully take part in chilling.

❸ ▷ Critical Viewing Choy describes how important a short story can be for a reader. How does this illustration dramatize that importance? **[Interpret]**

182 ■ *Short Stories*

Teaching Resources

The following resources can be used to enrich, extend, or differentiate the instruction for the Unit Introduction and Model Selection.

Unit 2 Resources, pp. 1–13	**Reader's Notebook**
General Resources, p. 6	**Reader's Notebook: Adapted Version**
Graphic Organizer Transparencies, pp. 41–42	**Reader's Notebook: English Learner's Version**
From the Author's Desk DVD Wayson Choy, Segments 1 and 2	**Listening to Literature Audio CD**
	Adapted Reader's Notebook Audio CD

horrific events. And when I first read Truman Capote's "A Christmas Memory," his story made me think in new ways about a family member who loved me when I was very young, and who was now gone. Like me, you may discover that short stories can powerfully disturb and awaken you.

❹ The Best Stories Say, "*You Are Not Alone*"

But what makes a short story a good one? The passage here by the famous writer Somerset Maugham recalls Edgar Allan Poe's idea that a good story—like those collected in this unit—will "sparkle, excite or impress." Isn't that what your own favorite stories do for you?

The short story is a work of fiction created from the writer's imagination and personal vision. If you surrender to the writer's **narrative voice**—that enchanted moment when you begin to *hear* a storytelling voice—you will be transported into another world. And always, the best short stories will say to the deepest part of you . . . *You are not alone.*

It is not hard to state what Poe meant by a good short story: it is a piece of fiction, dealing with a single incident, material or spiritual, that can be read at a sitting; it is original, it must sparkle, excite or impress; and it must have a unity of effect or impression.
from "Credo of a Storyteller"
—W. Somerset Maugham

More About Wayson Choy

In his books, Wayson Choy (b. 1939) deals with a theme arising from the immigrant experience—the conflicts between generations and cultures. In *The Jade Peony*, he tells how members of the Chen family must balance their allegiance to the past and their dreams for the future in order to form their own identities. Choy published this novel, which he developed from his story "The Jade Peony," when he was in his late fifties. He taught for many years at Humber College, Toronto, Canada.

Fast Facts
► Late in life, Choy learned from a former babysitter that he had been adopted.
► Choy, who believes in luck, bought seven lottery tickets (he considers seven a lucky number) and won a large prize!

From the Author's Desk: Wayson Choy ■ 183

Go **Online** **For:** An online video
—Author Link **Visit:** www.PHSchool.com
Web Code: epe-8201
Give students this Web Code for a video clip of Wayson Choy.

❺ Elements of Short Stories

* Point out to students that the climax, or turning point, is the moment in the plot when something decisive happens to determine the future course of events and the eventual working out of the conflict.

* **Ask** students to discuss the differences between the direct method of characterization (the author's description of the character) and the indirect method (showing personality through words, behavior, and feelings or through other characters' observations about them).
Answer: In the direct method, the author tells readers what they should know about a character. In the indirect method, the author allows readers to draw their own conclusions.

continued on p. 185

Exploring Short Stories

❺ Elements of Short Stories

A **short story** is a brief work of fiction meant to be read in one sitting. Due to the length of a short story (usually between 500 and 10,000 words), it must be crafted in a concise, compact manner that accomplishes its purpose in relatively few words.

The following are some of the key elements of a short story.

Plot A short story's **plot** is its series of related events. Throughout the course of a story's plot, events unfold, build to a **climax** (or high point), and are then brought to a conclusion during the **resolution.**

Conflict The plot of a short story usually focuses on a **conflict,** or struggle. There are two main types of conflict in literature:

* An **external conflict** is a struggle between two characters, between an individual and a group, or between a character and a force of nature.
* An **internal conflict** is a struggle within the mind of one character.

Character The **characters** in a story are the personalities who participate in the action. Usually, characters are human beings, but they can also be animals or even objects. Writers use these methods of **characterization** to tell readers about characters:

* providing descriptions of what characters look like
* describing characters' words and actions
* showing characters interacting with one another
* sharing characters' thoughts and feelings

Setting The **setting** of a story is the time and place of the action.

- The time of a setting can be past, present, or future, and it may also include a specific year, season, or hour of day.
- Place can refer to the social, economic, or cultural environment as well as to a specific geographic location in a country, town, or community.

The setting provides a stage for the action of a story. It can also create a mood or an atmosphere or present a conflict for the characters to face.

Symbol A **symbol** is a person, place, or object that has a literal meaning and also stands for something larger, such as an idea or an emotion. Symbols may be particular to a specific literary work or universal.

Theme The **theme** of a short story is its central message or insight into life. This message may be stated or implied.

- A **stated theme** is expressed directly by the author.
- An **implied theme** is suggested indirectly through the experiences of the characters or through the events and the setting of the work.

Check Your Understanding

Choose the letter of the short story element that best matches each item.

1. A temple in India — **A** setting **B** character
2. A man struggles against the ocean waves **A** theme **B** conflict
3. A poor woman is unhappy with her life **A** character **B** plot
4. A girl begins to appreciate her culture **A** theme **B** setting
5. Two enemies become friends **A** setting **B** plot

Exploring Short Stories ■ 185

Elements of Short Stories (cont.)

- Point out to students that setting includes details about what the day is like, what time of year it is, and what the surroundings look like. This description not only creates a vivid backdrop for the action, it also creates atmosphere, or an emotional climate. Setting may figure prominently in the plot and conflict, it may reveal something about character, or it may contribute to the theme.
- Explain to students that few writers consciously decide on a theme and then write a story to reflect it. Instead, they attempt to write truthfully about life and their particular way of looking at it, which gives their fiction a central focus. The theme develops naturally as they write.
- **Ask** students to distinguish between the theme and the moral of a story.
  Possible response: A moral is a lesson the story teaches about how to conduct our lives. A theme is the author's observation about life and the way people live it.

ASSESS

Answers

1. A
2. B
3. A
4. A
5. B

From the Author's Desk

❶ Introduce the Selection

- Invite students to read Wayson Choy's introduction to his short story.

- Call students' attention to the terms used in discussing the story: *characters, themes,* and *symbol.* Ask students to identify these elements as they read "The Jade Peony."

❷ Background

Jade Peony A large, showy flower that blooms in spring and summer, the peony is a prized addition to temperate gardens around the world. In China it has long been a symbol of wealth and distinction.

Historically, jade has been the royal gemstone, the precious *yu.* The mineral most often occurs in various shades of green, but it also can be lavender, pink, white, and yellow. Jade is so hard that even a steel knife will not scratch it.

❸ Connecting to the Literature

- Have students brainstorm for a list of traditional good luck charms, such as the rabbit's foot and a four-leaf clover. Then, direct them to write a few sentences describing something they think would make a good amulet. To develop expressive vocabulary, tell students to use several of these words in their sentences: *signify, confirm, derive,* and *diminish.*

- To further develop students' expressive vocabulary, you may suggest that they also use three of these words: *stress, texture, temporary, abstract,* and *complex.*

- To help students understand the meanings of the words they are asked to use, give them these sentences:

  1. My amulet would *signify* that someone is watching over me.

  2. From carrying it I *derive* courage and the confidence to accomplish whatever I want.

  3. The charm I carry is a physical reminder of the *abstract* concept of wisdom.

Model Selection:
Short Story ❶

From the Author's Desk
Wayson Choy Introduces "The Jade Peony"

  ❷ ❸

During World War II, while my immigrant parents worked all hours, I was cared for by Chinatown's village elders in Vancouver, Canada. These elders told me such vivid myths involving ghosts, magic amulets, hissing dragons, and talking foxes, that I dreamed one day that I would tell my own tales.

Finding Inspiration
As a student, when I was assigned to write a story based on the color "pink"—I was stuck. My aunt recalled that rare jades were pink in tone, and that afternoon, another aunt mentioned how the peonies were flowering in her garden.

Suddenly, something magical happened: the two ideas came together. My imagination glimpsed a wrinkled hand passing a carved pink jade into a boy's small palm. After imagining these **characters**, the first words of "The Jade Peony" came to me: "When Grandmama died at 83 . . ."

Themes: Meanings and Questions That Haunt You
After some research and a dozen revisions, I realized that I had been focusing on life and dying, and the realities of love between generations. Years later, I understood that there were **themes**, meanings and questions —*hauntings*—that had attached themselves to my story. For example, how many kinds of love were there? Were spirits real? And was dying the end of everything? One theme came to possess me: *Love has no rules.* Therefore, I now write believing that I, and my readers, will continue to discover similar meanings.

Symbol: What Does the Jade Peony Mean?
But I wondered why I came up with the jade peony—what, as a **symbol**, did the amulet stand for? I realized it has many layers of meaning, related to love and memory. I thought of the jade left to me by my mother and father, just as you might think about some important legacy left to you by a friend or a family member. I also thought of the apron my mother last wore before she was rushed to the hospital. Whenever I think of that apron, I see my dead mother alive again, a vivid ghost standing over her stove to feed us all. Finally, I, as a writer created the symbol of the jade peony to make the people I love come alive again.

Vocabulary Development

Vocabulary Knowledge Rating Chart
Create a **Vocabulary Knowledge Rating Chart** with these words from the selection:

dissension   abomination   reprieve

Give students a copy of the chart. Introduce the words by reading them aloud and having students mark their rating in the Before Reading column. Urge them to be alert to these words as they read and discuss the selection because they will rate their knowledge of the words again after they finish.

If you wish, you may tally how many students know (or think they know) a word to gauge how much instruction you need to provide. As students read, point out the words and their context.

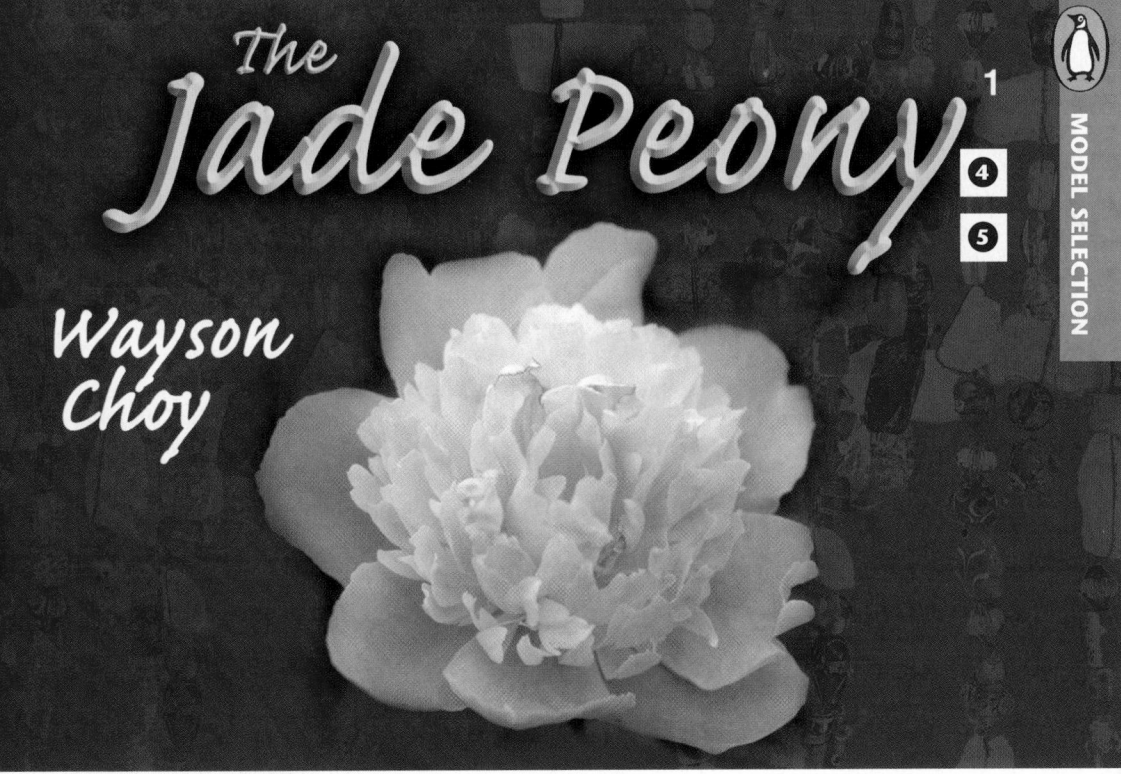

The Jade Peony

Wayson Choy

❻ When Grandmama died at 83 our whole household held its breath. She had promised us a sign of her leaving, final proof that her present life had ended well. My parents knew that without any clear sign, our own family fortunes could be altered, threatened. My stepmother looked endlessly into the small cluttered room the ancient lady had occupied. Nothing was touched; nothing changed. My father, thinking that a sign should appear in Grandmama's garden, looked at the frost-killed shoots and cringed: *no, that could not be it.*

My two older teenage brothers and my sister, Liang, age 14, were embarrassed by my parents' behavior. What would all the white people in Vancouver[2] think of us? We were Canadians now, *Chinese-Canadians*, a hyphenated reality that my parents could never accept. So it seemed, for different reasons, we all held our breath waiting for *something.*

---

1. Jade Peony (pē′ ə nē) jade is a hard, dense gemstone; a peony is a common garden flower, the Chinese variety of which produces large, single blossoms in early summer.
2. Vancouver (van kōō′ vər) large city in the province of British Columbia, Canada.

Wayson Choy
Author's Insight
With references to signs and threatened fortunes, I wanted to create a ghostly mystery about the grandmother's dying.

❼ **Reading Check**

What had Grandmama promised her family?

The Jade Peony ■ 187

Differentiated Instruction — Solutions for All Learners

Strategy for Special Needs Students
Have students read the adapted version of "The Jade Peony" in the *Reader's Notebook: Adapted Version.* They may also listen to the adapted version on the *Reader's Notebook: Adapted Version Audio CD.*

Support for Less Proficient Readers
Have students read "The Jade Peony" in the *Reader's Notebook.* After students finish the selection in the *Reader's Notebook,* have them complete the questions and activities in the Student Edition.

Support for English Learners
Have students read "The Jade Peony" in the *Reader's Notebook: English Learner's Version.* English learners may also read the selection as they listen to the recorded version on the **Listening to Literature Audio CD.**

TEACH

❹ Motivation
- Prepare an **Anticipation Guide** (See *General Resources,* pp. 8–10) with the following statements:
- Ghosts of the past often influence the present.
- Maintaining cultural traditions while learning new ones is challenging.
- Senior citizens should be respected for their wisdom.
- There is a thin line between memory and imagination.

Give students a copy of the prepared Anticipation Guide and have them mark their responses in the Me column. Have students discuss the statements in pairs or groups and mark the Guides again in the Group column.

Concept Connector ➡

Students will return to the Anticipation Guide after completing "The Jade Peony."

❺ About the Selection
In "The Jade Peony," a Chinese Canadian family engages in the delicate dance of retaining the old life while adjusting to the new. The bond between Sek-Lung, the youngest child and the narrator of the story, and the Grand Old One, his grandmother, helps to preserve the family history and soften the pain of loss.

❻ Author's Insight
- Have a volunteer read the bracketed passage aloud.
- Point out that Choy says he wanted to create a "ghostly mystery." Discuss with students what kind of mystery they think this story will be.
Possible response: It will probably not be an ordinary murder mystery. The word "ghostly" suggests that the mystery will be something supernatural.

❼ Reading Check
Answer: Grandmama promised the family a sign that her life ended well.

187

- Have a volunteer read the bracketed passage aloud.
- **Ask** students why Grandmama's refusal to go to the hospital is a conflict.
  Possible response: First, Grandmama's refusal to go to the hospital suggests that she wants to die or at least sees this as her time to die. Her family, on the other hand, does not want to lose her. The refusal may also represent the conflict between Eastern medical remedies and modern Western medicine, or the past and the present.
- Discuss with students whether the conflicts presented in the passage are internal or external.
  Possible responses: The conflict between Grandmama and the rest of the family is external. Grandmama's conflict with death is an example of an external conflict with fate or natural forces. Grandmama's conflict over using Western or Eastern medicine is an internal conflict.
- Tell students to watch for additional examples of these same conflicts as they continue reading the story.

❾ Critical Viewing

Possible response: Although these hands are probably fashioned out of metal, they look almost life-like. The viewer has a desire to touch them or to entwine fingers with them with the expectation that the hands are as plush and warm as Grandmama's palms. The hands are caught in a pose of being about to clasp, giving a magical sense of having someone close by, just within reach. The viewer can imagine that the hands had the same talents as Grandmama and the same ability to convey love.

---

❽ I was eight when she died. For days she had resisted going into the hospital . . . *a cold, just a cold* . . . and instead gave constant instruction to my stepmother and sister on the boiling of ginseng roots mixed with bitter extract.[3] At night, between wracking coughs and deadly silences, Grandmama had her back and chest rubbed with heated camphor[4] oil and sipped a bluish decoction[5] of an herb called Peacock's Tail. When all these failed to abate her fever, she began to arrange the details of her will. This she did with my father, confessing finally: "I am too stubborn. The only cure for old age is to die."

My father wept to hear this. I stood beside her bed; she turned to me. Her round face looked darker, and the gentleness of her eyes, the thin, arching eyebrows, seemed weary. I brushed the few strands of gray, brittle hair from her face; she managed to smile at me. Being the youngest, I had spent nearly all my time with her and could not imagine that we would ever be parted. Yet when she spoke, and her voice hesitated, cracked, the somber shadows of her room chilled me. Her wrinkled brow grew wet with fever, and her small body seemed even more diminutive.

"I—I am going to the hospital, Grandson." Her hand reached out for mine. "You know, Little Son, whatever happens I will never leave you." Her palm felt plush and warm, the slender, old fingers boney and firm, so magically strong was her grip that I could not imagine how she could ever part from me. Ever.

Her hands *were* magical. My most vivid memories are of her hands: long, elegant fingers, with impeccable nails, a skein[6] of fine, barely-seen veins, and wrinkled skin like light pine. Those hands were quick when she taught me, at six, simple tricks of juggling, learnt when she was a village girl in Southern Canton;[7] a troupe of actors had stayed on her father's farm. One of them, "tall and pale as the whiteness of petals," fell in love with her, promising to return. In her last years his image came back like a third being in our two lives. He had been magician, acrobat, juggler, and some of the things he taught her she had absorbed and passed on to me through her stories and games. But above all, without realizing it then, her hands conveyed to me the quality of their love.

Most marvelous for me was the quick-witted skill her hands revealed in making windchimes for our birthdays: windchimes in the likeness of her lost friend's only present to her, made of bits of

---

3. **ginseng** (jin´ seŋ) **roots . . . bitter extract** ginseng is a Chinese herb known for its healing properties; bitter extract is a liquid made from bitter plants or herbs.
4. **camphor** (kam´ fər) *n.* thick substance made from the bark and wood of the camphor tree.
5. **decoction** (dē käk´ shen) *n.* substance extracted by boiling.
6. **skein** (skān) *n.* something that resembles coiled yarn or thread.
7. **Canton** (kan tän´) major port city in southeastern China.

188 ■ *Short Stories*

---

❾ ▼ Critical Viewing
In what ways does this sculpture convey a sense of "magical" hands similar to Grandmama's? **[Connect]**

Vocabulary Development

Think-Aloud: Context
Direct students' attention to the word *abate* in the first paragraph on this page. Using a think-aloud process, model how to use context to infer the meaning of an unknown word. Say to students:

I'm going to think aloud to show you how I would figure out the meaning of *abate* from its context.

In this sentence, *abate* is used to describe how the herbal remedies failed to cure Grandmama. We know that she has resisted going to the hospital and that she has tried ginseng root, heated camphor oil, and Peacock's Tail. She still has the symptoms of her illness. She then decides to arrange the details of her will. She had hoped that the remedies would *abate* her fever. A sick person usually wants a fever to go down. I think *abate* must mean "to reduce or lessen."

string and scraps, in the center of which once hung a precious jade peony. This wondrous gift to her broke apart years ago, in China, but Grandmama kept the jade pendant[8] in a tiny red silk envelope, and kept it always in her pocket, until her death.

These were not ordinary, carelessly made chimes, such as those you now find in our Chinatown[9] stores, whose rattling noises drive you mad. But making her special ones caused <u>dissension</u> in our family, and some shame. Each one that she made was created from a treasure trove of glass fragments and castaway costume jewelry, in the same way that her first windchime had been made. The problem for the rest of the family was in the fact that Grandmama looked for these treasures wandering the back alleys of Keefer and Pender Streets,[10] peering into our neighbors' garbage cans, chasing away hungry, nervous cats and shouting curses at them.

"All our friends are laughing at us!" Older Brother Jung said at last to my father, when Grandmama was away having tea at Mrs. Lim's.

"We are not poor," Oldest Brother Kiam declared, "Yet she and Sek-Lung poke through those awful things as if—" he shoved me in frustration and I stumbled against my sister, "—they were beggars!"

"She will make Little Brother crazy!" Sister Liang said. Without warning, she punched me sharply in the back; I jumped. "You see, look how *nervous* he is!"

I lifted my foot slightly, enough to swing it back and kick Liang in the shin. She yelled and pulled back her fist to punch me again. Jung made a menacing move towards me.

"Stop this, all of you!" My father shook his head in exasperation. How could he dare tell the Grand Old One, his aging mother, that what was somehow appropriate in a poor village in China, was an <u>abomination</u> here. How could he prevent me, his youngest, from accompanying her? If she went walking into those alleyways alone she could well be attacked by hoodlums. "She is not a beggar looking for food. She is searching for—for. . . ."

My stepmother attempted to speak, then fell silent. She, too, seemed perplexed and somewhat ashamed. They all loved Grandmama, but she was *inconvenient*, unsettling.

As for our neighbors, most understood Grandmama to be harmlessly crazy, others that she did indeed make lovely toys but for what purpose? *Why?* they asked, and the stories she told me, of the juggler who smiled at her, flashed in my head.

---

8. **pendant** (pen´ dənt) *n.* hanging ornament, as on a necklace.
9. **Chinatown** (chī´ nə toun´) *n.* Chinese quarter of any city outside of China; in this case, of Vancouver.
10. **Keefer and Pender Streets** principal streets of Vancouver's Chinatown.

The Jade Peony ■ 189

Vocabulary Builder
dissension (di sen´ shən) *n.* difference of opinion; disagreement

Wayson Choy
Author's Insight
Here I wanted to show how the wind chimes were symbolically important to some family members but provoked a lot of conflict and inner turmoil among the others.

Vocabulary Builder
abomination (ə bäm´ ə nā´ shən) *n.* anything hateful and disgusting

 Reading Check
From whom did Grandmama learn juggling?

---

⑩ Author's Insight
- Ask volunteers to assume the roles of the narrator, his brothers, sister, and father and read the bracketed passage aloud.
- Then **ask** students what the wind chimes represent for the family. **Possible response:** On one level, the wind chimes are a precious gift that represent the family's past and Grandmama's love. However, they also represent how difficult it is to maintain cultural traditions in a new setting. The wind chimes depend on the collection of found materials, and that process makes Grandmama and Sek-Lung an embarrassment to the family.
- Discuss with students why Grandmama's behavior is seen as a disgrace to the family. **Possible response:** The family members are afraid that friends and neighbors will see Grandmama and Sek-Lung going through the trash and believe that they are poor, deranged, or mistreated. The family wants to appear prosperous and to fit in with their neighbors.
- Point out to students that these motivations can help explain the characters' actions now and later in the story.

⑪ Reading Check
Answer: Grandmama learned juggling from an actor who had stayed for a time on her father's farm.

Differentiated Instruction Solutions for All Learners

Strategy for Less Proficient Readers
Have students close their eyes and listen as another student reads the page aloud. Tell students to form mind pictures as they listen. What do the chimes look like? What do Grandmama and Sek-Lung look like when they are searching for materials? Then have students jot down what they saw in their mind pictures. Invite them to write a brief paragraph or draw a picture of the image that dominated the reading for them.

Enrichment for Advanced Readers
Have students do some library or Internet research about the history and uses of wind chimes, beginning with wind bells used in religious ceremonies. Some students may want to concentrate on the historical development, including the Japanese influence. Others may want to concentrate on the feng shui aspects of how wind chimes are believed to improve the quality of life.

⑫ Short Story
Character

- Have students read the page to themselves. Direct them to jot down a list of character traits for both Grandmama and Sek-Lung as they read.

- **Ask** students to describe the relationship that exists between Grandmama and Sek-Lung. Have them support their characterization with evidence from the passage.
Possible response: Grandmama and Sek-Lung are like co-conspirators, using a code name for their collection trips, sneaking the materials home and hiding them under the bed, and bringing them out only when no one else is home.

- **Ask** students what the relationship between grandmother and grandson reveals about their characters.
Possible response: Both are adventurous, appreciative of small, insignificant things, and detail-oriented. They share pleasure in pursuing the past in the present.

- **Ask** students what the narrator means when he calls his grandmother his spiritual playmate.
Possible response: He sees her as the companion of his soul. They both derive pleasure from the same things.

Finally, by their cutting remarks, the family did exert enough pressure so that Grandmama and I no longer openly announced our expeditions. Instead, she took me with her on "shopping trips," ostensibly for clothes or groceries, while in fact we spent most of our time exploring stranger and more distant neighborhoods, searching for splendid junk: jangling pieces of a vase, cranberry glass fragments embossed with leaves, discarded glass beads from Woolworth[11] necklaces. . . . We would sneak them all home in brown rice sacks, folded into small parcels, and put them under her bed. During the day when the family was away at school or work, we brought them out and washed every item in a large black pot of boiling lye[12] and water, dried them quickly, carefully, and returned them, sparkling, under her bed.

⑫ Our greatest excitement occurred when a fire gutted the large Chinese Presbyterian Church, three blocks from our house. Over the still-smoking ruins the next day, Grandmama and I rushed precariously over the blackened beams to pick out the stained glass that glittered in the sunlight. Small figure bent over, wrapped against the autumn cold in a dark blue quilted coat, happily gathering each piece like gold, she became my spiritual playmate: "There's a good one! *There!*"

Hours later, soot-covered and smelling of smoke, we came home with a carton full of delicate fragments, still early enough to steal them all into the house and put the small box under her bed. "These are special pieces," she said, giving the box a last push, "because they come from a sacred place." She slowly got up and I saw, for the first time, her hand begin to shake. But then, in her joy, she embraced me. Both of our hearts were racing, as if we were two dreamers. I buried my face in her blue quilt, and for a moment, the whole world seemed silent.

---

11. Woolworth a variety store belonging to the chain founded by Frank Woolworth in 1879.
12. lye (lī) *n.* substance derived from wood ashes, commonly used in making soap or for washing.

Short Story
Character Choy uses the search for windchime materials to establish a sense of the pact between the old woman and her grandson.

190 ■ *Short Stories*

"My juggler," she said, "he never came back to me from Honan[13] . . . perhaps the famine. . . ." Her voice began to quake. "But I shall have my sacred windchime . . . I shall have it again."

One evening, when the family was gathered in their usual places in the parlor, Grandmama gave me her secret nod: a slight wink of her eye and a flaring of her nostrils. There was *trouble* in the air. Supper had gone badly, school examinations were due, father had failed to meet an editorial deadline at the *Vancouver Chinese Times*. A huge sigh came from Sister Liang.

"But it is useless this Chinese they teach you!" she lamented, turning to Stepmother for support. Silence. Liang frowned, dejected, and went back to her Chinese book, bending the covers back.

⓭ "Father," Oldest Brother Kiam began, waving his bamboo brush in the air, "you must realize that this Mandarin only confuses us. We are Cantonese[14] speakers. . . ."

"And you do not complain about Latin, French or German in your English school?" Father rattled his newspaper, a signal that his patience was ending.

"But, Father, those languages are *scientific*," Kiam jabbed his brush in the air. "We are now in a scientific, logical world."

Father was silent. We could all hear Grandmama's rocker.

"What about Sek-Lung?" Older Brother Jung pointed angrily at me. "He was sick last year, but this year he should have at least started Chinese school, instead of picking over garbage cans!"

"He starts next year," Father said, in a hard tone that immediately warned everyone to be silent. Liang slammed her book.

Grandmama went on rocking quietly in her chair. She complimented my mother on her knitting, made a remark about the "strong beauty" of Kiam's brushstrokes which, in spite of himself, immensely pleased him. All this babbling noise was her family torn and confused in a strange land: everything here was so very foreign and scientific.

The truth was, I was sorry not to have started school the year before. In my innocence I had imagined going to school meant certain privileges worthy of all my brothers' and sister's complaints. The fact that my lung infection in my fifth and sixth years, mistakenly diagnosed as TB,[15] earned me some reprieve, only made me long for school the more. Each member of the family took turns on Sunday,

---

13. **Honan** (hō′ nän′) province in east central China.
14. **Mandarin** (man′ də rin) . . . **Cantonese** (kan′ tə nēz′) Mandarin is the most commonly spoken form of Chinese; Cantonese is a variety of Chinese spoken in some parts of China, including the cities of Canton and Hong Kong, and by most Chinese emigrants.
15. **TB** (tē′ bē′) *n.* abbreviation for tuberculosis, a contagious disease that begins in the lungs.

Vocabulary Builder
reprieve (ri prēv′) *n.* temporary relief; postponement of a penalty

⓮ ✔ **Reading Check**
What "treasures" do the old woman and her grandson find among the ruins of the church?

The Jade Peony ■ 191

⓭ **Short Story**
Conflict
- **Ask** students to summarize what is happening in the bracketed passage.
Possible response: The three older children are going to a separate school to learn Mandarin Chinese. Some of the children already speak Cantonese Chinese. The children complain about learning a language that will not serve them well in a scientific, logical world.
- **Ask** students to discuss how this incident contributes to the conflict set up earlier.
Possible response: This conflict continues the conflict between past and present, and between Eastern and Western ways of life. The children do not complain about learning Western languages like French, Latin, or German, which may serve them well in the present and future.

⓮ **Reading Check**
Answer: Grandmama and grandson gather broken pieces of the burned church's stained glass windows.

Enrichment for Less Proficient Readers
On this page Sek-Lung says that his real education comes from the countless hours he spends with his grandmother. Ask students to write about or discuss a person from whom they have learned something important. Suggest that students describe the person, tell about their time together, and explain how the interaction added to their education.

Enrichment for English Learners
Ask students to bring to class examples of cultural emblems like the wind chimes in the story. Have them tell about the history and meaning of the symbol, how it continues to be used in the present-day culture, and what memories they associate with the item.

teaching me or annoying me. But it was the countless hours I spent with Grandmama that were my real education. Tapping me on my head she would say, "Come, Sek-Lung, we have *our* work," and we would walk up the stairs to her small crowded room. There, in the midst of her antique shawls, the old ancestral calligraphy and multi-colored embroidered hangings, beneath the mysterious shelves of sweet herbs and bitter potions, we would continue doing what we had started that morning: the elaborate windchime for her death.

"I can't last forever," she declared, when she let me in on the secret of this one. "It will sing and dance and glitter," her long fingers stretched into the air, pantomiming the waving motion of her ghost chimes; "My spirit will hear its sounds and see its light and return to this house and say goodbye to you."

Deftly she reached into the carton she had placed on the chair beside me. She picked out a fish-shape amber piece, and with a long needle-like tool and a steel ruler, she scored[16] it. Pressing the blade of a cleaver against the line, with the fingers of her other hand, she lifted up the glass until it cleanly *snapped* into the exact shape she required. Her hand began to tremble, the tips of her fingers to shiver, like rippling water.

"You see that, Little One?" She held her hand up. "That is my body fighting with Death. He is in this room now."

My eyes darted in panic, but Grandmama remained calm, undisturbed, and went on with her work. Then I remembered the glue and uncorked the jar for her. Soon the graceful ritual movements of her hand returned to her, and I became lost in the magic of her task: she dabbed a cabalistic[17] mixture of glue on one end and skillfully dropped the braided end of a silk thread into it. This part always amazed me: the braiding would slowly, *very* slowly, *unknot*, fanning out like a prized fishtail. In a few seconds the clear, homemade glue began to harden as I blew lightly over it, welding to itself each separate silk strand.

Each jam-sized pot of glue was precious; each large cork had been wrapped with a fragment of pink silk. I remember this part vividly, because each cork was treated to a special rite. First we went shopping in the best silk stores in Chinatown for the perfect square of silk she required. It had to be a deep pink, a shade of color blushing toward red. And the tone had to match — as closely as

---

16. scored (skôr'd) *v.* put a notch or groove in.
17. cabalistic (kab'ə lis'tik) *adj.* relating to a secret or mystical belief or practice.

Vocabulary Development

192

possible — her precious jade carving, the small peony of white and light-red jade, her most lucky possession. In the center of this semi-translucent carving, no more than an inch wide, was a pool of pink light, its veins swirling out into the petals of the flower.

"This color is the color of my spirit," she said, holding it up to the window so I could see the delicate pastel against the broad strokes of sunlight. She dropped her voice, and I held my breath at the wonder of the color. "This was given to me by the young actor who taught me how to juggle. He had four of them, and each one had a center of this rare color, the color of Good Fortune." The pendant seemed to pulse as she turned it: "Oh, Sek-Lung! He had white hair and white skin *to his toes*! It's *true*, I saw him bathing." She laughed and blushed, her eyes softened at the memory. The silk had to match the pink heart of her pendant: the color was magical for her, to hold the unraveling strands of her memory. . . .

It was just six months before she died that we really began to work on her last windchime. Three thin bamboo sticks were steamed and bent into circlets; 30 exact lengths of silk thread, the strongest kind, were cut and braided at both ends and glued to stained glass. Her hands worked on their own command, each hand racing with a life of its own: cutting, snapping, braiding, knotting. . . . Sometimes she breathed heavily and her small body, growing thinner, sagged against me. *Death*, I thought, *He is in this room*, and I would work harder alongside her. For months Grandmama and I did this every other evening, a half dozen pieces each time. The shaking in her hand grew worse, but we said nothing. Finally, after discarding hundreds, she told me she had the necessary 30 pieces. But this time, because it was a sacred chime, I would not be permitted to help her tie it up or have the joy of raising it. "Once tied," she said, holding me against my disappointment, "not even I can raise it. Not a sound must it make until I have died."

"What will happen?"

"Your father will then take the center braided strand and raise it. He will hang it against my bedroom window so that my ghost may see it, and hear it, and return. I must say goodbye to this world properly or wander in this foreign land forever."

"You can take the streetcar!" I blurted, suddenly shocked that she actually meant to leave me. I thought I could hear the clear-chromatic chimes, see the shimmering colors on the wall: I fell against her and cried, and there in my crying I knew that she would die. I can still remember the touch of her hand on my head, and the smell of her thick woolen sweater pressed against my face. "I will always be with you, Little Sek-Lung, but in a different way . . . you'll see."

Short Story

Symbol In this passage, Choy connects the windchime with Grandmama's spirit, both in youth and old age.

Short Story

Plot With this discussion of the death, the author starts to bring the story full circle, back to the beginning discussion of "signs."

 Reading Check

What does Grandmama say is the color of her spirit?

The Jade Peony ■ 193

❼ Short Story
Symbol

- Have a volunteer read the two paragraphs aloud.
- Review with students what they already know about Grandmama and her wind chimes.
  Possible response: She makes them for people's birthdays; she spends many hours hunting for the materials that go into making them and hides them under the bed; most of her family is ashamed of the collection process and what it represents to outsiders; she goes through a number of rituals to make the wind chimes.
- Ask how the wind chimes are associated with Grandmama's spirit.
  Possible response: Grandmama's memory of the man who gave her the jade peony is vivid and spirited. Her hand "races with a life of its own."

❽ Short Story
Plot

- **Ask** students to explain why the wind chime is important in relation to Grandmama's death.
  Answer: The wind chime is a place for Grandmama's ghost to return to so that it does not have to wander.
- **Ask** students how the author connects the wind chime to the discussion of signs at the beginning of the story.
  Possible response: At the beginning of the story, the family is waiting for a sign that Grandmama's life has ended well. It turns out that Grandmama's wind chime will be the sign.

❾ Reading Check

Answer: Grandmama says that her spirit color is pink.

- Have a volunteer read aloud the bracketed passage.

- Based on previous details from the story, **ask** students to explain what the albino cat might symbolize. **Possible response:** It could be interpreted as a "visitor" from the spirit world coming to take Grandmama "home." The white cat could also represent Grandmama's actor friend who had such an important role in her life. He promised to come back for her and now he has.

- Then, **ask** students to comment on how Grandmama and Sek-Lung's father are similar and how they are different in the way they see the white cat. **Possible response:** Grandmama is very much a person of the past while her son plays a much more active role in the present (he works for a newspaper). However, the father does have a foot in the past because he works for a Chinese newspaper in Canada, and he wants his children to speak both Mandarin and Cantonese. Like his mother, he recognizes signs and believes in them.

Concept Connector ▬▬▬

Anticipation Guide Have students return to their Anticipation Guides and respond to the statements again in the After Reading column. They may do this individually or in their original pairs or groups. Then, lead a class discussion, probing for what students have learned that confirms or invalidates each statement. Encourage students to cite specific details, quotations, or other evidence from the text to support their responses to each statement.

◀──────

Months went by, and nothing happened. Then one late September evening, when I had just come home from Chinese School, Grandmama was preparing supper when she looked out our kitchen window and saw a cat—a long, lean white cat—jump into our garbage pail and knock it over. She ran out to chase it away, shouting curses at it. She did not have her thick sweater on and when she came back into the house, a chill gripped her. She leaned against the door: "That was not a cat," she said, and the odd tone of her voice caused my father to look with alarm at her. "I can not take back my curses. It is too late." She took hold of my father's arm: "It was all white and had pink eyes like sacred fire."

My father started at this, and they both looked pale. My brothers and sister, clearing the table, froze in their gestures.

"The fog has confused you," Stepmother said. "It was just a cat."

But Grandmama shook her head, for she knew it was a sign. "I will not live forever," she said. "I am prepared."

The next morning she was confined to her bed with a severe cold. Sitting by her, playing with some of my toys, I asked her about the cat: "Why did father jump at the cat with the pink eyes? He didn't see it, you did."

"But he and your mother know what it means."

"What?"

"My friend, the juggler, the magician, was as pale as white jade, and he had pink eyes." I thought she would begin to tell me one of her stories, a tale of enchantment or of a wondrous adventure, but she only paused to swallow; her eyes glittered, lost in memory. She took my hand, gently opening and closing her fingers over it. "Sek-Lung," she sighed, "*he* has come back to me."

Then Grandmama sank back into her pillow and the embroidered flowers lifted to frame her wrinkled face. I saw her hand over my own, and my own began to tremble. I fell fitfully asleep by her side. When I woke up it was dark and her bed was empty. She had been taken to the hospital and I was not permitted to visit.

A few days after that she died of the complications of pneumonia. Immediately after her death my father came home and said nothing to us, but walked up the stairs to her room, pulled aside the drawn lace curtains of her window and lifted the windchimes to the sky.

I began to cry and quickly put my hand in my pocket for a handkerchief. Instead, caught between my fingers, was the small, round firmness of the jade peony. In my mind's eye I saw Grandmama smile and heard, softly, the pink center beat like a beautiful, cramped heart.

194 ■ *Short Stories*

Vocabulary Development

Vocabulary Knowledge Rating
When students have completed reading and discussing "The Jade Peony," have them take out their **Vocabulary Rating Chart** for the short story. Read the words aloud once more and have students rate their knowledge of the words again in the After Reading column. Clarify any words that are still problematic.

Have students write their own definitions or examples in the appropriate column. Encourage students to use the words in further discussion and written work about this selection. Remind them that they will be accountable for these words on the Selection Test.

21 Q. Why did you tell this story in the first person?

A. I needed the reader to assume the world of the little boy—that is, to inhabit his world and to identify solely with his point of view. His "narrative voice" would tell his own truth as he experienced it with his beloved grandmother. The reader would then be locked into experiencing things that the more sensible family members could not understand. If the story works, you, the reader, might recall someone who loved or loves you as much.

23 Q. What is the meaning of the jade peony?

A. Chinese people believe that jade is very special, because the gemstone can inherit the good qualities, the spirit, of the person who owns it. Therefore, jade pieces, whether in the form of pendants, rings, or carved items, are often passed on from one beloved person to another.

Student Corner

24 Q. Why do you think the grandmother was able to develop such a close relationship with the narrator?
—Jacquelyn Simone, Endicott, New York

A. The grandmother and grandson were left at home alone together for a long period. During this time, she shared with him her life stories and her love of the old ways, and the young boy was hungry to know everything from someone who paid him so much attention. They both had a need to belong to each other, since the rest of the family did not have much time for them, nor did the family entirely approve of the two searching in the alleyways for material to make the windchimes. In the end, they found something deeply meaningful between themselves, more than the others ever understood.

Writing Workshop: *Work in Progress*

Short Story

Think of someone you have noticed in passing. Then, imagine that character's life by listing announcements about him or her that might have been printed in the newspaper. These could include birth, garduation, or marriage notices. Make a list of announcements and keep it in your writing portfolio.

From the Author's Desk: Wayson Choy ■ 195

Assessment Resources

The following resources can be used to assess students' knowledge and skills.

Unit 2 Resources:
    Selection Test A, pp. 8–10
    Selection Test B, pp. 11–13

Go Online Students may use the **Self-test** to
Assessment prepare for **Selection Test A** or
Selection Test B.

- Tell students that Wayson Choy is frequently asked questions like these about his work. His answers provide insight into decisions that a writer makes in order to create memorable short stories that will touch others.

21 After students read the first question and answer, **ask** them how the story would have been different if it had been told from the perspective of the father. Why is Sek-Lung the perfect narrator?
Possible response: The father, who shares the beliefs and traditions of his mother more directly than Sek-Lung does, would have told a more mature version of what happened. Sek-Lung is young and impressionable; his grandmother's ideas have a strong effect on him. Because he spends a lot of time with her, he has absorbed a sense of the past.

22 After students read the second question and answer, **ask** them what they think the jade peony represents, in addition to what Wayson Choy reveals.
Possible response: The jade peony may represent youth or love or hope for the grandmother.

23 After students read the final question and answer, **ask** students why the very young and very old are able to relate well.
Possible response: Young children respond to attention and have no stereotypes about old people.

Writing Workshop
Work in Progress

Short Story Students are asked to identify someone they have noticed in passing who could serve as the inspiration for a fictional character. Work with the class as a whole to help students brainstorm for scenes and situations they might mine for ideas. **Ask** students to suggest circumstances in which they have observed or noticed others. **Possible responses:** in an airport; at a train, bus, or subway station; at a convenience store; in a doctor's office; in an office-building elevator; at a mall; or on the main street of town.

After students have shared their ideas as a class, have them work privately to write down a list of possible characters and then to choose one to develop further.

1. Most students will probably appreciate the closeness Sek-Lung and Grandmama share.

2. (a) The albino acrobat who stayed at her father's farm when she was a young girl gave Grandmama her first wind chime. (b) Making wind chimes was a recreation of Grandmama's past. Not only was she maintaining tradition in creating the chimes, she was also using fragments from the past to make them.

3. (a) Sek-Lung supports and understands Grandmama's activities. The father understands what she is doing, but it bothers him that she is not more modern in her approach to things. The rest of the family is embarrassed by her behavior. (b) They represent different generations and ages and therefore different points of view about the immigrant experience and the importance of the past.

4. (a) The last wind chime has an important job to perform—capturing the grandmother's ghost so that she can rest in peace. (b) It will represent that she was satisfied with her life and that her rest is peaceful.

5. **Possible response:** The characters are the most important element. The setting could have been any Western city. The plot is only a framework in which the relationship between grandmother and grandson is built.

6. (a) **Possible response:** The past is important because it forms people's characters and a culture's shared understandings.
(b) **Sample response: What it says:** The family waits for a sign. **What it means:** Grandmama's rest is peaceful, and her family is safe. **Why it is important:** These signs or omens signify the attachment to and belief in the past.
(c) Students should support their opinions with evidence from the story.

Research the Author

Students may complete the research assignment for homework. Tell them that they can find information about Wayson Choy in a library or online.

196

Apply the Skills

Thinking About the Selection

1. **Respond:** What do you think of the relationship between Sek-Lung and his grandmother? Explain.

2. **(a) Recall:** Who gave the grandmother her first windchime? **(b) Infer:** Why do you think the making of windchimes became such a meaningful activity in the grandmother's later years?

3. **(a) Compare and Contrast:** How do Sek-Lung's reactions to his grandmother's activities differ from those of the other family members? **(b) Analyze:** How do you account for these differing attitudes within one family?

4. **(a) Infer:** What is different about the making of the grandmother's last windchime? **(b) Analyze:** What meaning will this windchime have for Sek-Lung and his family?

Short Story Review

5. Consider the setting, plot, and characters in "The Jade Peony." Which do you think is the most important element in this **short story**? Support your answer with details from the story.

6. **(a)** What is the underlying theme, or message, of this story? **(b)** Complete a chart like the one shown to examine details in the story. List events, actions, statements, or descriptions that you think are important to the story. Then, complete the rest of the chart. **(c)** Share your ideas with a partner. Finally, explain how your discussion did or did not change your interpretation of the story's theme.

What It Says	What It Means	Why It Is Important

Research the Author

Like Sek-Lung, Wayson Choy is both Chinese and Canadian. Using both Internet and print sources, create an **oral report** to discuss Choy's insights into his dual heritage. Follow these steps:

- Read biographical articles and interviews with Choy, and scan Choy's fictional works for comments that reflect his heritage.
- Select the most useful passages, and write a brief introduction. Then, write notes to connect and explain Choy's comments.
- Deliver your oral report to classmates. As you speak, include transitional words and phrases to clearly connect your ideas with passages from your research.

QuickReview

Story at a Glance
A young boy forges a special bond with his grandmother.

Go Online
Assessment
For: Self-test
Visit: www.PHSchool.com
Web Code: epa-6201

Short Story: a brief work of fiction

Characters: the personalities who participate in the action of a story

Theme: the central message or insight of a literary work

Go Online **For:** More about the author
Author Link Visit: www.PHSchool.com
Web Code: epe-8201
For additional information about Wayson Choy, give students this Web Code. After typing in the Web Code, students select *Wayson Choy.*

Unit 2
Part 1

Make Inferences

Skills You Will Learn

Literary Analysis: *Conflict and Resolution*
Reading Skill: *Identify Details to Make Inferences*

Reading Skill: *Evaluate Visual Aids*

Literary Analysis: *Irony and Surprise Ending*
Reading Skill: *Use Prior Knowledge to Make Inferences*

Literary Analysis: *Setting*

Literature You Will Read

Make Inferences ■ 197

Differentiated Instruction   Solutions for All Learners

Resources for Monitoring Progress

Unit 2 Resources
   Unit 2, Part 1 Diagnostic Test, pp. 15–17
   Unit 2, Part 1 Benchmark Test,
   pp. 101–106

Reading Kit

Success Tracker

Skills Overview
Reading Skill: Making Inferences
- Asking questions to make inferences
- Using your own prior knowledge and experience to make inferences

Vocabulary Development
- Word Parts

Literary Analysis
- Conflict: internal and external conflict, resolution and epiphany
- Irony: situational irony, surprise endings

Writing
- Short Story
- Work in Progress, pp. 195, 239, 265

Monitoring Progress

Diagnose: Before you begin Part 1, administer the **Diagnostic Test** for Unit 2, Part 1. This test will identify students' level of readiness for the reading and vocabulary skills in Part 1. Use the **Interpretation Guide** for the Diagnostic Test to determine which students need help with prerequisite skills before beginning Part 1.

Preteach and Prepare: Use the information indicated in the **Interpretation Guide** to help students build prerequisite skills. In addition, prepare students by using the **Vocabulary Warm-up** activities and the **Reading Warm-up** activities as necessary for each selection set.

Teach: Use the instructional plan and resources provided to teach the skills and selections.

Assess: After students have completed Part 1, administer the **Benchmark Test** for Unit 2, Part 1. The test results will indicate which skills students have mastered and those on which they need more work.

Reteach: Use the Interpretation Guide to determine the appropriate reteaching pages from the **Reading Kit.**

Intervention: The prerequisite and reteaching pages are also available in the **Success Tracker.**

Introduce the Reading Skill

- Introduce the reading skill: making inferences. Draw students' attention to the definition. Point out that writers do not state everything directly in the text. Often, writers suggest or imply ideas through information or details. When students identify these implied ideas, they are making inferences.

- Point out to students that asking questions can help them make inferences. For example, students might ask what a detail shows about a character's motivations or feelings. Students may also make inferences based on their prior knowledge. For example, if students know anything about the Mississippi River, they can make inferences about the difficulty of crossing it. Likewise, students can make inferences about a text based on details they gather from visual aids, such as maps. For example, if a map shows a large area with high elevations and no towns, students can make inferences about the challenges of living at extreme altitudes.

Model the Reading Strategies

- Have students look at the sample text on the page. Then ask these questions:

  Why did Joe tense? (The answer is an inference based on the details of a "low growl" and "dark shape" and on prior knowledge of what these things might mean.)

  Why was Joe relieved? (The answer is based on prior knowledge).

- Emphasize to students that inferences are logical assumptions about unstated information or ideas. Remind students that by combining their knowledge with what is stated, they can make logical inferences.

Reading: Make Inferences

> **Inferences** are logical assumptions about information or ideas that are not directly stated.

Skills and Strategies You Will Learn in Part 1

In Part 1, you will learn to
- **ask questions** to **make inferences** (p. 200)
- **use prior knowledge** and experiences to **make inferences** (p. 244)
- **use visual aids** as a basis for **inferences** (p. 240)

Using the Skills and Strategies in Part 1

In Part 1, you will learn to **pay attention to details** and visual aids that act as thinking clues. You will also learn to add your own knowledge and experience to these details in order to infer ideas that are not directly stated.

Identifying details and applying your knowledge help you infer important concepts in a work.

This example shows you how you will apply the skills and strategies you will learn in Part 1.

> **Example:** Joe tensed when he heard the low growl and saw a dark shape coming toward the cabin. He held the lantern higher, then breathed a sigh of relief. "Skip!" he called out. "Where have you been?"

Academic Vocabulary: Words for Understanding Literature

The following words will help you talk and write about your understanding of literature.

Word	Definition	Example Sentence
aspect *n.*	element or part	One important *aspect* of Poe's writing is his use of details.
motive *n.*	the reason a person acts in a certain way	The antagonist's *motive* was still not clear by the middle of the novel.
emotion *n.*	feeling	The work evokes strong *emotions*.
circumstance *n.*	fact or event	We analyzed the *circumstances* that contributed to the conflict.
categorize *v.*	classify; place within a group	We *categorized* the symbols by color.

Vocabulary Skill: Word Parts

A word **root** is the part of a word that contains its basic meaning. A **prefix** is a group of letters added to the beginning of a word to change its meaning.

In Part 1, you will learn:
- Latin root -*spec*- (p. 238)
- Latin prefix *circum*- (p. 238)
- Latin root -*mot*- (p. 264)

Knowing the meaning of common Latin word parts helps you understand and see connections in word meanings. The chart shows two words that share the root -*spec*-, which means "to see."

*spec*tator	*spec*tacle
one who sees or watches an event without taking part in it	something strange or remarkable to look at

Activity Use a dictionary to find a word that contains each word part: -*spec*-, *circum*-, and -*mot*-. Write a definition of each word, and explain how the word part relates to the definition.

Reading and Vocabulary Skills Preview ■ *199*

Instruction   Solutions for All Learners

Strategy for Less Proficient Readers
To complete the activity, pair students and provide them with a dictionary. Then suggest that they choose one of the three word roots and look up the word root in the dictionary. Have them find words that begin with the word root and use three of these words for the activity responses. Have students create vocabulary study cards for review and study. Have students write one root word and its meaning on one side of a 4" x 6" note card. On the other side, have students write English words and their meanings that are derived from the root word.

Strategy for English Learners
Encourage students whose home language is a Romance language (derived from Latin) to list any words with their definitions from their home language that contain these Latin roots. Then, have all the students list their words and definitions on a sheet of paper and make a copy of the sheet for each student to put in his or her notebook.

Introduce Academic Vocabulary

- Introduce the academic vocabulary: words for understanding literature. Tell students that these are words that are useful in reading and discussing literature.

- Review each word, and have the students state the words aloud. Have students read aloud the words' definitions and the example sentences.

- Suggest to students that when they are discussing literature, they can tell what *aspect* of the story they liked best, they can question a character's *motive* and describe his or her *emotion,* or they can explain the *circumstances* surrounding the conflict in a selection.

- Tell students to try to use these words as they discuss the selections in Part 1.

Introduce the Vocabulary Skill

- Introduce the vocabulary skill: word parts. Tell students that many words in English are derived from Latin. Latin word parts, including prefixes and word roots, appear in English words. Recognizing these word parts and their meanings is an effective way to build vocabulary.

- Use these questions to give students practice with word parts. Have students use a dictionary, if necessary:

  What word, containing the root -*grat*-, means thankfulness?
  Answer: *gratitude*

  What word, containing the prefix *ortho*-, meaning straight or true, and the root -*odon*-, meaning teeth, is the name for a doctor who straightens crooked teeth?
  Answer: *orthodontist*

Go **O**nline For: Interactive
Vocabulary Crossword Puzzles
Visit: www.PHSchool.com
Web Code: epj-5201
Give students this Web Code to access interactive crossword puzzles using Academic Vocabulary and Vocabulary Skill words from Part 1.

Planning Differentiated Instruction

Choosing Your Selection

You may use either selection to meet the lesson standards. The following guide will help you determine which of the two selections is more appropriate for your students.

Accessibility at a Glance

	American History	The Most Dangerous Game
Context	Setting: New Jersey tenement house, early 1960s, late autumn	Setting: Small jungle island in Caribbean
Language	• Accessible vocabulary • Spanish words are footnoted	• Difficult, formal vocabulary • Vocabulary is footnoted
Concept Level	Challenging (young girl sees firsthand the reality of prejudice)	Accessible (big game hunter finds himself the object of the hunt)
Literary Merit	Cross-cultural connection	Popular, award-winning story
Lexile	1010L	740L
Overall Rating	More challenging	More accessible

Using the Other Selection You may use the other selection for homework or independent reading to reinforce the selection skills. If you use both selections, you can build a test for both using *ExamView® Test Bank* software.

Choosing Your Resources

[L1] Special Needs Students   [L4] Advanced Students

[L2] Below-Level Students   [EL] English Learners

[L3] All Students

FT Fast Track Instruction: To move the lesson more quickly, use the strategies and activities identified with **FT**.

Reading and Vocabulary Warm-ups provide support for below level students. **A** is for students reading two grades below level; **B** is for students reading one grade below level. For Selection Tests, **A** signifies "less challenging" and **B** "more challenging." For Graphic Organizer transparencies, **A** signifies "not filled in" and **B** "filled in."

Scaffolding for Less Proficient and Advanced Students

The leveled questions on Apply the Skills pages progress in the levels of thinking required to answer them. To address the needs of your different students, you may use the (a) level questions for your less proficient students, the (b) level with your on-level and advanced students. The occasional (c) level questions are appropriate for your advanced students.

Go Online
Internet Activity
For: Information about Lexiles
Visit: www.PHSchool.com
Web Code: eue-1111

Step-by-Step Teaching Guide	Pacing Guide	
PRETEACH		
• Administer Vocabulary and Reading Warm-ups as necessary.		
• Introduce the Literary Analysis Skill: Conflict. **FT**	10 min.	
• Introduce the Reading Skill: Making Inferences. **FT**	10 min.	
• Prepare students to read by teaching the selection vocabulary. **FT**	10 min.	
• Build background and develop expressive vocabulary with Connecting to the Literature and Background.	10 min.	
• Engage students' interest with the motivation activity.	10 min.	
TEACH		
• Informally monitor comprehension while students read independently or in groups. **FT**	30 min.	
• Monitor students' comprehension with the Reading Check notes.	as students read	
• Reinforce vocabulary with Vocabulary Builder notes.	as students read	
• Develop students' understanding of conflict with the Literary Analysis annotations. **FT**	5 min.	
• Develop students' ability to make inferences with the Reading Skill annotations. **FT**	10 min.	
ASSESS/EXTEND		
• Assess students' comprehension and mastery of the Reading Skill and Literary Analysis by having them answer the Apply the Skills questions. **FT**	35 min.	
• Have students complete the Vocabulary Builder activities. **FT**	5 min.	
• Apply students' ability to write an alternate ending with the Writing activity. **FT**	30–45 min. or homework	
• Extend students' listening and speaking and research and technology skills with one or both of the Extend Your Learning activities.	15–30 min. or homework	
• Have students complete the Vocabulary Skill and Grammar Lesson.	5 min.	
• Monitor students' progress with the Assessment Practice.	20–40 min.	
• Administer **Selection Test A** or **Selection Test B. FT**	15 min.	

Resources

Meeting Your Standards

Students will

1. **analyze and respond to literary elements.**
   - Literary Analysis: Conflict

2. **read, comprehend, and analyze short stories.**
   - Reading Skill: Making Inferences
   - Reading Strategy: Asking Questions to Make Inferences
   - Reading Check questions
   - Apply the Skills questions
   - Assessment Practice

3. **develop vocabulary.**
   - Vocabulary Builder
   - The Latin roots *-spec-* and *-mot-* and the prefix *-circum-*

4. **apply grammar skills.**
   - Regular Verbs

5. **develop writing proficiency.**
   - Work in Progress: Short Story
   - Alternate ending

6. **extend learning.**
   - Listening and Speaking: Speech
   - Research and Technology: Photo essay

Block Scheduling: Use one 90-minute class period to preteach the skills and have students read the selection. Use a second 90-minute class period to assess students' mastery of skills, extend their learning, and monitor their progress.

Homework Suggestions

Following are possibilities for homework assignments.

- Support pages from *Unit 2 Resources*:
  - **Literary Analysis**
  - **Reading Skill**
  - **Build Vocabulary**
  - **Enrichment**

- An Extend Your Learning project and the Writing assignment for your chosen selection may be completed over several days.

PRENTICE HALL

Teacher EXPRESS™ Use this complete
[Plan · Teach · Assess]   suite of powerful
teaching tools to make lesson planning and testing quicker and easier.

PRENTICE HALL

Student EXPRESS™ Use the
[Learn · Study · Succeed]   Interactive
Textbook (online and on CD-ROM) to make selections and activities come alive with audio and video support and interactive questions.

❶ Literary Analysis

Conflict

- Tell students that *conflict* in a story—a struggle between opposing forces—grips readers and holds their attention.

- Explain to students that *external conflict* refers to what can usually be seen. For example, stories in which a person struggles to survive an earthquake or teams compete for a championship present external conflicts.

- Explain to students that *internal conflict* refers to a character's struggle with opposing thoughts, feelings, hopes, or desires.

Resolution

- Explain to students that the *resolution* [of a story] gives a sense of completeness because it releases the tension that the conflict creates.

- Suggest that students look for resolution in both stories as they read.

Epiphany

- Tell students that often *epiphanies* occur toward the end of a story, but this is not always the case.

- To explain the meaning of an epiphany, give students the example of a story about a single mother in a stressful financial situation. Toward the end of the story, the mother learns of a coworker's ill child. She has an epiphany, realizing that she should be thankful for a healthy, happy child. Tell students that the mother's conflict still exists, but her feelings about it have changed.

❷ Reading Skill

Making Inferences

- Point out to students that *inferences*—logical guesses based on details in a story—can be attained by asking questions. Provide a few examples, such as "Why is that character silent?" and "Why does the author say the sky looks dangerous?"

- Give students a copy of **Reading Skill Graphic Organizer A** (*Graphic Organizer Transparencies*, p. 43). Have them fill in the graphic organizer to make inferences as they read.

Build Skills   American History • The Most Dangerous Game

Practice these skills with either "American History" (p. 202) or "The Most Dangerous Game" (p. 215).

❶ Literary Analysis

Conflict is a struggle between opposing forces:

- With **external conflict,** a character struggles against an outside force, such as another character, society, or nature.

- With **internal conflict,** a character grapples with his or her own opposing feelings, beliefs, needs, or desires.

In narrative literature—works that tell stories—conflict and the search for a solution drive the plot. The solution usually occurs near the end of a story, during the **resolution.**

In some stories, however, the conflict is not truly solved. Instead, the character has an **epiphany,** or sudden flash of insight. The conflict remains, but the character's feelings about it change. As you read, notice conflicts characters face and decide whether they are truly resolved.

❷ Reading Skill

Inferences are logical assumptions based on details in a story. Making inferences about a text helps you understand information that is not stated directly. To make inferences as you read, **ask questions** such as these about characters' feelings and behavior:

- *What does this detail show about the reasons for a character's actions or words?*

- *What does this passage say about the character's unspoken feelings?*

Use a chart like the one shown to make inferences as you read.

Detail
The door was painted green, the color of hope.

↓

Question
Why might a writer describe a door as having the color of an emotion?

↓

Inference
The door stands for opportunity.

Vocabulary Builder

American History

- **tenement** (ten´ ə mənt) *n.* apartment house, often run-down (p. 203) *Many families lived in the large tenement.*

- **profound** (prō found´) *adj.* deep; intense (p. 203) *Mia felt profound sorrow when her dog died.*

- **vigilant** (vij´ ə lənt) *adj.* watchful (p. 206) *The guard kept a vigilant eye on the candidate.*

- **dilapidated** (də lap´ ə dāt´ id) *adj.* broken down (p. 210) *The old furniture was dilapidated.*

The Most Dangerous Game

- **palpable** (pal´ pə bəl) *adj.* able to be felt; easily perceived (p. 215) *The tension during the exam was palpable.*

- **indolently** (in´ də lənt lē) *adv.* lazily; idly (p. 217) *The sleepy cat yawned indolently.*

- **scruples** (scroo´ pəlz) *n.* misgivings about something one feels is wrong (p. 225) *Her scruples prevented her from lying.*

- **futile** (fyoot´ 'l) *adj.* useless; hopeless (p. 230) *My attempt to catch the mouse proved futile.*

200 ■ Short Stories

Vocabulary Development

Vocabulary Knowledge Rating

Create a **Vocabulary Knowledge Rating Chart** for the selection you will teach from this set. Include the selection vocabulary from this page and the additional words students are asked to use at the end of Connecting to the Literature. These words will increase students' expressive vocabulary.

Give students a copy of the chart with the words on it. Introduce the words by reading them aloud and having students mark their

rating in the Before Reading column. Urge them to be alert to these words as they read and discuss the selection because they will rate their knowledge of the words again after they finish.

If you wish, you may tally how many students know (or think they know) a word to gauge how much instruction you need to provide. As students read, point out the words and their context.

Build Understanding • *American History*

❸ Background

The Kennedy Assassination On November 22, 1963, President John F. Kennedy was shot and killed in Dallas, Texas, and the United States was plunged into mourning. Most people who lived through that time can still remember where they were when they heard the news. Kennedy's assassination and the nation's grief defined a generation. Key events in "American History" take place on that fateful day.

❹ Connecting to the Literature

Reading/Writing Connection Just as the Kennedy assassination serves as the backdrop for "American History," events occurring in the world today become the backdrop for our own stories. Describe two major world events that have taken place in your lifetime. Use at least three of the following words: *transform, emerge, define, precipitate.*

by Judith Ortiz Cofer
The Latin Deli:
Prose and Poetry
An Island Like You

Meet the Author

Judith Ortiz **Cofer** (b. 1952)

Judith Ortiz Cofer spent her childhood in two different cultures. Born in Puerto Rico, she moved with her parents to Paterson, New Jersey, when she was four years old. She grew up mostly in Paterson, but she also spent time in Puerto Rico with her *abuela* (grandmother).

The Art of Storytelling It was from her grandmother that Ortiz Cofer learned the art of storytelling. "When my *abuela* sat us down to tell a story," she says, "we learned something from it, even though we always laughed. That was her way of teaching." In her own work, Ortiz Cofer teaches readers about the richness and difficulty of coming of age in two cultures at once.

Fast Facts

▶ Ortiz Cofer's first novel, *The Line of the Sun,* was nominated for a Pulitzer Prize.
▶ Ortiz Cofer teaches for Operation Homecoming, a writing program for U.S. military personnel.

Go Online
Author Link
For: More about the author
Visit: www.PHSchool.com
Web Code: epe-9202

American History ■ 201

Differentiated Instruction   Solutions for All Learners

Support for Below-Level Students [L1, L2]

Unit 2 Resources
   Vocabulary Warm-up Word Lists, p. 18
   Vocabulary Warm-up Practice, p. 19
   Reading Warm-up A, p. 20
   Selection Test A, pp. 28–30

Graphic Organizer Transparencies
   Reading Skill Graphic Organizer,
   Transparency B, p. 44

Support for English Learners [EL]

Unit 2 Resources
   Vocabulary Warm-up Word Lists, p. 18
   Vocabulary Warm-up Practice, p. 19
   Reading Warm-up A, p. 20

Listening to Literature Audio CD

---

❸ Background
The Kennedy Assassination

The shock of the Kennedy assassination appeared in the faces and behavior of Americans from all walks of life—from bus drivers to Hollywood actors, from factory workers to university professors. Famous television news reporters cried on live television, and radio announcers found it difficult to speak. Schools and businesses were shut down, and the nation's daily routines were suspended. The Kennedy White House had been considered by many to be an American "Camelot," and Americans reacted as if an almost mythical leader such as King Arthur had been killed. This disturbing disruption of the ordered adult world is reflected in what the young narrator sees and hears in "American History."

❹ Connecting to the Literature

• To help students understand the meanings of the words they are asked to use, give them these sentences:

1. A natural disaster like a tsunami can *transform* people's lives.
2. Courage and generosity *emerge* in the face of such a crisis.
3. A tsunami can *define* a period in the lives of many people.
4. Such a disaster should *precipitate* an increase in scientific research on tsunamis.

• Help students further develop their expressive vocabulary by providing these words: *hostile, memorable,* and *significant.* Encourage students to use these words as they discuss the selection.

Go Online
Author Link For additional information about Judith Ortiz Cofer, have students type in the Web Code, then select C from the alphabet, and then select *Judith Ortiz Cofer.*

❶ Motivation

Prepare an Anticipation Guide (see *General Resources,* pp. 8–10) with the following statements:

- Major world events shape people's lives.
- Facing conflict is easy to do.
- Personal struggles are always less painful than societal struggles.
- Experiencing conflict is a necessary part of life.

Give students a copy of the prepared Anticipation Guide and have students mark their responses in the Me column. Have students discuss the statements in pairs or groups and mark the Guides again in the Group column.

Concept Connector ➡

Students will return to the Anticipation Guide after completing "American History."

Learning Modalities
Visual/Spatial Learners

Encourage students to pay attention to the descriptions of the buildings in "American History." The image of "El Building" with its fire escape and Eugene's house with its yard create an atmosphere and add to the characterizations of Elena, Eugene, and their parents. Have students visualize Elena's vantage point from her fire escape. How she can "keep [Eugene] company" and remain safely distant from him?

❷ About the Selection

In "American History," Elena, a Puerto Rican girl living in a tenement in New Jersey, becomes friends with a boy named Eugene from Georgia who lives in a house nearby. Elena struggles to control her feelings of elation in her friendship with Eugene, so different from the anguish of the nation on the day of the assassination of President John F. Kennedy. When the boy's mother harshly turns her away at their doorstep, Elena experiences a personal sorrow more intense than her feelings about the loss of the nation's leader.

American ❶ ❷ HISTORY

Judith Ortiz Cofer

202 ■ *Short Stories*

Vocabulary Development

Expressive Vocabulary
Ask students to discuss the historical events referred to in "American History." Encourage them to use the expressive vocabulary presented earlier. You might encourage them with sentence starters like these:
1. A national crisis can *transform* people by . . .
2. Challenges *emerge* when . . .
3. Significant events can *define* a . . .
4. Fear may *precipitate* reckless acts because . . .

I once read in a *Ripley's Believe It or Not* column that Paterson, New Jersey, is the place where the Straight and Narrow (streets) intersect. The Puerto Rican <u>tenement</u> known as El Building was one block up from Straight. It was, in fact, the corner of Straight and Market; not "at" the corner, but *the* corner. At almost any hour of the day, El Building was like a monstrous jukebox, blasting out *salsas*[1] from open windows as the residents, mostly new immigrants just up from the island, tried to drown out whatever they were currently enduring with loud music. But the day President Kennedy was shot there was a <u>profound</u> silence in El Building; even the abusive tongues of viragoes,[2] the cursing of the unemployed, and the screeching of small children had been somehow muted. President Kennedy was a saint to these people. In fact, soon his photograph would be hung alongside the Sacred Heart and over the spiritist altars that many women kept in their apartments. He would become part of the hierarchy of martyrs they prayed to for favors that only one who had died for a cause would understand.

On the day that President Kennedy was shot, my ninth grade class had been out in the fenced playground of Public School Number 13. We had been given "free" exercise time and had been ordered by our P.E. teacher, Mr. DePalma, to "keep moving." That meant that the girls should jump rope and the boys toss basketballs through a hoop at the far end of the yard. He in the meantime would "keep an eye" on us from just inside the building.

It was a cold gray day in Paterson. The kind that warns of early snow. I was miserable, since I had forgotten my gloves, and my knuckles were turning red and raw from the jump rope. I was also taking a lot of abuse from the black girls for not turning the rope hard and fast enough for them.

"Hey, Skinny Bones, pump it, girl. Ain't you got no energy today?" Gail, the biggest of the black girls had the other end of the rope, yelled, "Didn't you eat your rice and beans and pork chops for breakfast today?"

The other girls picked up the "pork chops" and made it into a refrain: "pork chop, pork chop, did you eat your pork chop?" They entered the double ropes in pairs and exited without tripping or missing a beat. I felt a burning on my cheeks and then my glasses fogged up so that I could not manage to coordinate the jump rope with Gail.

---

1. *salsas* (säl´ səs) songs written in a particular Latin American musical style.
2. *viragoes* (vi rä´ gōz) fierce, irritable women who often shout.

4 ◀ **Critical Viewing** Judging from this photograph of President Kennedy, why do you think people, like the adults in this story, felt so strongly about him? **[Interpret]**

Vocabulary Builder
tenement (ten´ ə mənt) *n.* apartment house, often run-down

profound (prō fŏund´) *adj.* deep; intense

Reading Check

On what memorable day in history does this story take place?

American History ■ 203

---

❸ Reading Skill
Making Inferences

- Remind students that asking questions about details is useful for making inferences at the beginning of a story. Discuss with students the environment described in the bracketed passage.

- **Ask** students what they can infer about the residents of El Building from the phrase, "whatever they were currently enduring." **Possible response:** The new immigrants' lives are difficult and likely filled with anxiety.

- **Ask** students what they can infer about the narrator from the mention early on of the assassination of President Kennedy. **Possible responses:** The historical event will have significance in the life of the main character in the story. Just as the people in El Building are affected emotionally by the shooting, the event will also mark an emotional moment in the narrator's life.

❹ Critical Viewing

Answer: The picture shows President Kennedy as a young, strong, commanding leader who inspires confidence and loyalty.

❺ Reading Check

Answer: The story takes place on November 22, 1963, the day President John F. Kennedy was assassinated.

Differentiated
Instruction   Solutions for All Learners

Strategy for Less Proficient Readers
To help students understand how to make inferences as they read, show them **Reading Skill Graphic Organizer B** (*Graphic Organizer Transparencies,* p. 44). The completed graphic organizer will give students insight into the process of asking and answering questions to make inferences. They can use the graphic organizer as a model for making their own inferences as they read.

Background for English Learners
Assist students by explaining the following cultural expressions and idioms:
- *Ripley's Believe It or Not*—a newspaper feature about amazing facts
- *Straight and Narrow*—description of the path that virtuous people follow in life
- *Keep an eye on*—watch over; supervise
    Then, ask students to share with the class any expressions or idioms with similar meaning in their home language.

6 ◀ Critical Viewing
How does the scene in this photograph compare to the view from the narrator's fire escape? **[Compare and Contrast]**

6 Critical Viewing

Answer: The scene is similar to the view from the narrator's fire escape because it shows a view of an urban neighborhood from a position above the housing. The scene is different because it shows an orderly row of attached houses, not the backyard of a single house in the shadow of a tenement building.

7 Reading Skill
Making Inferences

- **Ask** students to summarize how the narrator says she feels about going to school and living in the city in winter.
  Answer: She says that she hates the school, and she hates the city in winter.

- Have students speculate why the narrator might be especially in need of a friend.
  Possible responses: The narrator seems angry, lonely, and depressed. The school, the weather, and the other girls on the playground contribute to her distress and feelings of humiliation.

- **Ask** students the Reading Skill question: Which details in this passage lead you to infer that the narrator is fond of Eugene?
  Answer: The narrator, who is badly in need of a friend, considers Eugene a "source of beauty and light," and she looks forward to seeing him in school. She loves to read sitting on the fire escape looking down into his yard.

The chill was doing to me what it always did; entering my bones, making me cry, humiliating me. I hated the city, especially in winter. I hated Public School Number 13. I hated my skinny flat-chested body, and I envied the black girls who could jump rope so fast that their legs became a blur. They always seemed to be warm while I froze.

There was only one source of beauty and light for me that school year. The only thing I had anticipated at the start of the semester. That was seeing Eugene. In August, Eugene and his family had moved into the only house on the block that had a yard and trees. I could see his place from my window in El Building. In fact, if I sat on the fire escape I was literally suspended above Eugene's backyard. It was my favorite spot to read my library books in the summer. Until that August the house had been occupied by an old Jewish couple. Over the years I had become part of their family, without their knowing it, of course. I had a view of their kitchen and their backyard, and though I could not hear what they said, I knew when they were arguing, when one of them was sick, and many other things. I knew all this by watching them at mealtimes. I could see their kitchen table, the sink, and the stove. During good times, he sat at the table and read his newspapers while she fixed the meals. If they argued, he would leave and the old woman would sit and stare at nothing for a long time. When one of them was sick, the other would come and get things from the kitchen and carry them out on a tray. The old man had died in June. The last week of school I had not seen him at the table at all. Then one day I saw that there was a crowd in the kitchen. The old woman had finally emerged from the house on the arm of a stocky, middle-aged woman, whom I had seen there a few times before, maybe her daughter. Then a man had carried out suitcases. The house had stood empty for weeks. I had had to resist the temptation to climb down into the yard and water the flowers the old lady had taken such good care of.

204 ■ *Short Stories*

Reading Skill
Making Inferences
Which details in this passage lead you to infer that the narrator is fond of Eugene?

Vocabulary Development

Think-Aloud: Context
Direct students' attention to the word *linger* on p. 205. Using a think-aloud process, model how to use context to infer the meaning of an unknown word. Say to students:

I'm going to think aloud to show you how I would figure out the meaning of *linger* from its context.

In this sentence, *linger* is a verb that describes something Eugene does on the corner in front of El Building. Eugene and the narrator walk, then he lingers, and then, after "a few minutes," he continues walking. So *linger* involves pausing. The walk home from school seems to be slow and pleasant, and it seems that Eugene wants to stay with the narrator for a while before going home. So I think *linger* means to remain in one place for a brief period.

By the time Eugene's family moved in, the yard was a tangled mass of weeds. The father had spent several days mowing, and when he finished, from where I sat, I didn't see the red, yellow, and purple clusters that meant flowers to me. I didn't see this family sit down at the kitchen table together. It was just the mother, a red-headed tall woman who wore a white uniform—a nurse's, I guessed it was; the father was gone before I got up in the morning and was never there at dinner time. I only saw him on weekends when they sometimes sat on lawn chairs under the oak tree, each hidden behind a section of the newspaper; and there was Eugene. He was tall and blond, and he wore glasses. I liked him right away because he sat at the kitchen table and read books for hours. That summer, before we had even spoken one word to each other, I kept him company on my fire escape.

Once school started I looked for him in all my classes, but P.S. 13 was a huge, overpopulated place and it took me days and many discreet questions to discover that Eugene was in honors classes for all his subjects; classes that were not open to me because English was not my first language, though I was a straight A student. After much maneuvering, I managed "to run into him" in the hallway where his locker was—on the other side of the building from mine—and in study hall at the library where he first seemed to notice me, but did not speak; and finally, on the way home after school one day when I decided to approach him directly, though my stomach was doing somersaults.

I was ready for rejection, snobbery, the worst. But when I came up to him, practically panting in my nervousness, and blurted out: "You're Eugene. Right?" he smiled, pushed his glasses up on his nose, and nodded. I saw then that he was blushing deeply. Eugene liked me, but he was shy. I did most of the talking that day. He nodded and smiled a lot. In the weeks that followed, we walked home together. He would linger at the corner of El Building for a few minutes then walk down to his two-story house. It was not until Eugene moved into that house that I noticed that El Building blocked most of the sun, and that the only spot that got a little sunlight during the day was the tiny square of earth the old woman had planted with flowers.

I did not tell Eugene that I could see inside his kitchen from my bedroom. I felt dishonest, but I liked my secret sharing of his evenings, especially now that I knew what he was reading since we chose our books together at the school library.

One day my mother came into my room as I was sitting on the window-sill staring out. In her abrupt way she said: "Elena, you are

Literary Analysis
Conflict What internal conflict does the narrator experience as she prepares to approach Eugene?

Reading Check
Who is Eugene and how does the narrator meet him?

American History ■ 205

• Have students reread the bracketed passage, and **ask** them what the narrator wants to do.
Answer: She wants to meet Eugene.

• **Discuss** with students what the narrator says she is afraid will happen.
Answer: She is afraid that Eugene will reject her, act like a snob, or humiliate her in some way.

• **Ask** students the Literary Analysis question: What internal conflict does the narrator experience as she prepares to approach Eugene?
Answer: The narrator assumes that Eugene is different from her and will probably reject her. However, she also wants very much to meet him. Her fear and her desire are in conflict.

• Have students **identify** the visible signs of Elena's inner conflict.
Answer: Elena's visible nervousness and blurting out are outward signs of her internal conflict.

❾ **Reading Check**

Answer: Eugene is a boy whose family has recently moved into the house that the narrator can see from her apartment. She meets him by approaching him directly on the way home from school.

Point out to students that just as Elena experiences external and internal conflicts in "American History," so do her parents.

- Have students **describe** the sentiments that the narrator's mother reveals in the bracketed passage when she tells the narrator that she is acting "moony."
  Answer: Elena's mother is anxious about her daughter's physical and emotional development into a young woman, and she wants Elena to act mature and virtuous.

- **Ask** students what internal conflict in Elena's mother those feelings show.
  Possible response: The conflict in Elena's mother is between her natural love and concern for her daughter and her knowledge that her teenage daughter is growing up and becoming independent. She wants her daughter to become a responsible adult, and she also wants to continue to protect her.

- **Ask** students to infer the external conflict that Elena's parents reveal as they discuss their retirement.
  Answer: The external conflict the parents face is that, in order to fulfill their desire to buy a house on the beach and retire to Puerto Rico, they must struggle with the realities of working hard and saving money.

⑪ Critical Viewing

Answer: The snow in the photography resembles "the gray slush" that Elena describes.

---

acting 'moony.'" *Enamorada*³ was what she really said, that is—like a girl stupidly infatuated. Since I had turned fourteen . . . my mother had been more <u>vigilant</u> than ever. She acted as if I was going to go crazy or explode or something if she didn't watch me and nag me all the time about being a *señorita*⁴ now. She kept talking about virtue, morality, and other subjects that did not interest me in the least. My mother was unhappy in Paterson, but my father had a good job at the bluejeans factory in Passaic and soon, he kept assuring us, we would be moving to our own house there. Every Sunday we drove out to the suburbs of Paterson, Clifton, and Passaic, out to where people mowed grass on Sundays in the summer, and where children made snowmen in the winter from pure white snow, not like the gray slush of Paterson which seemed to fall from the sky in that hue. I had learned to listen to my parents' dreams, which were spoken in Spanish, as fairy tales, like the stories about life in the island paradise of Puerto Rico before I was born. I had been to the island once as a little girl, to grandmother's funeral, and all I remembered was wailing women in black, my mother becoming

---

3. *Enamorada* (ā nä´ mō rä´ dä) Spanish for "enamored; lovesick."
4. *señorita* (se´ nyô rē´ tä) *n.* Spanish for "young lady."

Vocabulary Builder
vigilant (vij´ ə lənt)
adj. watchful

⑪ ▼ Critical Viewing
Which description from the selection does this photograph suggest? **[Connect]**

206 ■ Short Stories

Vocabulary Development

Word Forms
Expand students' vocabulary by helping them learn related forms of the Vocabulary Builder words. Three of the Vocabulary Builder words for "American History" have related forms. Give students a blank **Word Form Chart** (*General*

Resources, p. 16) with *profound, discreet,* and *vigilant* in the correct columns. Work with the class, or have students work with a partner, to determine the related forms. The final chart should look like the one shown.

Noun	Verb	Adjective	Adverb
profundity		**profound**	profoundly
discretion		**discreet**	discreetly
vigilance		**vigilant**	vigilantly

10 hysterical and being given a pill that made her sleep two days, and me feeling lost in a crowd of strangers all claiming to be my aunts, uncles, and cousins. I had actually been glad to return to the city. We had not been back there since then, though my parents talked constantly about buying a house on the beach someday, retiring on the island—that was a common topic among the residents of El Building. As for me, I was going to go to college and become a teacher.

But after meeting Eugene I began to think of the present more than of the future. What I wanted now was to enter that house I had watched for so many years. I wanted to see the other rooms where the old people had lived, and where the boy spent his time. Most of all, I wanted to sit at the kitchen table with Eugene like two adults, like the old man and his wife had done, maybe drink some coffee and talk about books. I had started reading *Gone with the Wind*. I was enthralled by it, with the daring and the passion of the beautiful girl living in a mansion, and with her devoted parents and the slaves who did everything for them. I didn't believe such a world had ever really existed, and I wanted to ask Eugene some questions since he and his parents, he had told me, had come up from Georgia, the same place where the novel was set. His father worked for a company that had transferred him to Paterson. His mother was very unhappy, Eugene said, in his beautiful voice that rose and fell over words in a strange, lilting way. The kids at school called him "the **12** hick" and made fun of the way he talked. I knew I was his only friend so far, and I liked that, though I felt sad for him sometimes. "Skinny Bones" and the "Hick" was what they called us at school when we were seen together.

The day Mr. DePalma came out into the cold and asked us to line up in front of him was the day that President Kennedy was shot. Mr. DePalma, a short, muscular man with slicked-down black hair, was the science teacher, P.E. coach, and disciplinarian at P.S. 13. He was the teacher to whose homeroom you got assigned if you were a troublemaker, and the man called out to break up playground fights, and to escort violently angry teenagers to the office. And Mr. DePalma was the man who called your parents in for "a conference."

That day, he stood in front of two rows of mostly black and Puerto Rican kids, brittle from their efforts to "keep moving" on a November day that was turning bitter cold. Mr. DePalma, to our complete shock, was crying. Not just silent adult tears, but really sobbing. There were a few titters from the back of the line where I stood shivering.

"Listen," Mr. DePalma raised his arms over his head as if he were about to conduct an orchestra. His voice broke, and he covered his face with his hands. His barrel chest was heaving. Someone giggled behind me.

Literary Analysis
Conflict What external conflict does Eugene experience at school?

13 **Reading Check**

Why does the narrator want to discuss *Gone with the Wind* with Eugene?

American History ■ 207

- Remind students of the description of the noisy tenement building at the beginning of the story. Point out the contrast between the usual loud sounds of the building and the amazing quiet of the day President Kennedy is shot.

- Then have students read the bracketed passage, describing Elena's walk home.

- **Ask** students the Reading Skill question: Which details in Elena's description of her walk home let you infer the anguish people feel over the assassination of the president?
  Answer: Details include "an eerie feeling on the streets," only two men in the soda-bar talking in low voices, traffic moving slower than usual, no horns blasting, no men hanging out on the front stoop of El Building, no music from open doors, and Elena's mother crying in front of the television set.

⑮ Literary Analysis
Conflict

- Have students **consider** most citizens' typical reactions to the assassination of their president.
  Answer: Most citizens would feel grief and sadness, as well as shock and anger.

- Point out to students that an internal conflict does not have to be between a "right" feeling and a "wrong" feeling. Many internal conflicts are complex and between equally valid and authentic emotions.

- **Ask** students the Literary Analysis question: Which details in this passage reveal Elena's internal conflict over her reaction to the president's death?
  Answer: Elena describes her internal conflict clearly when she describes wanting to "feel the right thing" about the death of the president, but she "could not fight the feeling of elation" about seeing Eugene. Her unreasonable shame about her building blocking the sunlight also suggests her conflicting feelings.

"Listen," he repeated, "something awful has happened." A strange gurgling came from his throat, and he turned around and spat on the cement behind him.

"Gross," someone said, and there was a lot of laughter.

"The President is dead, you idiots. I should have known that wouldn't mean anything to a bunch of losers like you kids. Go home." He was shrieking now. No one moved for a minute or two, but then a big girl let out a "Yeah!" and ran to get her books piled up with the others against the brick wall of the school building. The others followed in a mad scramble to get to their things before somebody caught on. It was still an hour to the dismissal bell.

A little scared, I headed for El Building. There was an eerie feeling on the streets. I looked into Mario's drugstore, a favorite hangout for the high school crowd, but there were only a couple of old Jewish men at the soda-bar talking with the short order cook in tones that sounded almost angry, but they were keeping their voices low. Even the traffic on one of the busiest intersections in Paterson—Straight Street and Park Avenue—seemed to be moving slower. There were no horns blasting that day. At El Building, the usual little group of unemployed men were not hanging out on the front stoop making it difficult for women to enter the front door. No music spilled out from open doors in the hallway. When I walked into our apartment, I found my mother sitting in front of the grainy picture of the television set.

She looked up at me with a tear-streaked face and just said: "*Dios mio*,"[5] turning back to the set as if it were pulling at her eyes. I went into my room.

Though I wanted to feel the right thing about President Kennedy's death, I could not fight the feeling of elation that stirred in my chest. Today was the day I was to visit Eugene in his house. He had asked me to come over after school to study for an American history test with him. We had also planned to walk to the public library together. I looked down into his yard. The oak tree was bare of leaves and the ground looked gray with ice. The light through the large kitchen window of his house told me that El Building blocked the sun to such an extent that they had to turn lights on in the middle of the day. I felt ashamed about it. But the white kitchen table with the lamp hanging just above it looked cozy and inviting. I would soon sit there, across from Eugene, and I would tell him about my perch just above his house. Maybe I should.

In the next thirty minutes I changed clothes, put on a little pink lipstick, and got my books together. Then I went in to tell my mother

---

5. *Dios mio* (dē′ ōs mē′ ō) Spanish for "My God!"

208 ■ *Short Stories*

Reading Skill
Making Inferences
Which details in Elena's description of her walk home let you infer the anguish people feel over the assassination of the President?

Literary Analysis
Conflict Which details in this passage reveal Elena's internal conflict over her reaction to the President's death?

Vocabulary Development

Multiple Meanings
The word *resigned* has two meanings that students can learn to distinguish by paying attention to the different contexts in which they are used.

- When Elena's mother speaks "in a *resigned* tone" (p. 209), the word *resigned* is an adjective that means "uncomplaining, yielding, and accepting." A person who learns to accept the pain of a tragedy can become *resigned* to it. The use of the word *resigned* suggests that Elena's mother realizes and accepts that her daughter's feelings are going to be hurt.

- When an employee has quit a job, he or she has *resigned*. This use of the word *resigned* is as a verb in the past tense. It does not suggest any of the uncomplaining acceptance of the first meaning.

  Ask students to write a sentence for each meaning of the word *resigned*.

that I was going to a friend's house to study. I did not expect her reaction.

"You are going out *today?*" The way she said "today" sounded as if a storm warning had been issued. It was said in utter disbelief. Before I could answer, she came toward me and held my elbows as I clutched my books.

"*Hija,*[6] the President has been killed. We must show respect. He was a great man. Come to church with me tonight."

She tried to embrace me, but my books were in the way. My first impulse was to comfort her, she seemed so distraught, but I had to meet Eugene in fifteen minutes.

"I have a test to study for, Mama. I will be home by eight."

"You are forgetting who you are, *Niña.*[7] I have seen you staring down at that boy's house. You are heading for humiliation and pain." My mother said this in Spanish and in a resigned tone that surprised me, as if she had no intention of stopping me from "heading for humiliation and pain." I started for the door. She sat in front of the TV holding a white handkerchief to her face.

I walked out to the street and around the chainlink fence that separated El Building from Eugene's house. The yard was neatly edged around the little walk that led to the door. It always amazed me how Paterson, the inner core of the city, had no apparent logic to

6. *Hija* (ē′ hä) Spanish for "daughter."
7. *Niña* (nē′ nyä) Spanish for "child."

Literary Analysis
Conflict On the evening of the assassination, how do Elena's plans conflict with her mother's?

Reading Check

What plans had Elena made with Eugene?

American History ■ 209

16 Literary Analysis
Conflict

• **Ask** students what they think is important to Elena.
  Possible response: Elena's growing friendship and affection for Eugene is the most important aspect of her emotional life at this time.

• **Ask** students the Literary Analysis question: On the evening of the assassination, how do Elena's plans conflict with her mother's?
  Answer: Elena's mother thinks it is inappropriate for Elena to go out on the day of the president's death. Instead, she wants Elena to come to church with her.

• **Ask** students how Elena's reaction to her mother's embrace reveals the conflict.
  Answer: Elena does not move her books as her mother embraces her, suggesting a barrier between Elena's and her mother's views over the importance of the president's assassination; Elena's personal wishes overshadow the public significance of events that day.

17 Reading Check
Answer: Elena and Eugene had planned to go to Eugene's house after school to study for an American history test and to walk to the public library together.

- Point out to students that all the adults who are emotionally affected by the national tragedy of the president's assassination will likely reveal their emotions. Asking questions about why a character is acting in a particular manner helps the reader make inferences about how the characters' outward behavior reflects their inner pain and turmoil.

- **Ask** students the Reading Skill question: Based on the description of the woman's face, what do you think she was doing before Elena arrived?
Possible response: The woman was crying because of the Kennedy assassination.

▶ **Monitor Progress:** Monitor students' abilities to make inferences by evaluating their responses to this Reading Skill question.

▶ **Reteach:** If students have difficulty understanding how to make inferences, explain this alternative approach: Making an inference is like being a literary detective—looking at evidence, asking questions, and solving a mystery. When you read you notice details, and then you ask questions to try to figure out people's motives, thoughts, feelings, and even actions based on those details. Point out that when you make inferences you use a combination of logic, common sense, and everyday experience.

---

its architecture. Small, neat, single residences like this one could be found right next to huge, <u>dilapidated</u> apartment buildings like El Building. My guess was that the little houses had been there first, then the immigrants had come in droves, and the monstrosities had been raised for them—the Italians, the Irish, the Jews, and now us, the Puerto Ricans and the blacks. The door was painted a deep green: *verde*, the color of hope, I had heard my mother say it: *Verde-Esperanza.*[8]

18 I knocked softly. A few suspenseful moments later the door opened just a crack. The red, swollen face of a woman appeared. She had a halo of red hair floating over a delicate ivory face—the face of a doll—with freckles on the nose. Her smudged eye make-up made her look unreal to me, like a mannequin seen through a warped store window.

"What do you want?" Her voice was tiny and sweet-sounding, like a little girl's, but her tone was not friendly.

"I'm Eugene's friend. He asked me over. To study." I thrust out my books, a silly gesture that embarrassed me almost immediately.

"You live there?" She pointed up to El Building, which looked particularly ugly, like a gray prison with its many dirty windows and rusty fire escapes. The woman had stepped halfway out and I could see that she wore a white nurse's uniform with "St. Joseph's Hospital" on the name tag.

"Yes. I do."

She looked intently at me for a couple of heartbeats, then said as if to herself, "I don't know how you people do it." Then directly to me: "Listen. Honey. Eugene doesn't want to study with you. He is a smart boy. Doesn't need help. You understand me. I am truly sorry if he told you you could come over. He cannot study with you. It's nothing personal. You understand? We won't be in this place much longer, no need for him to get close to people—it'll just make it harder for him later. Run back home now."

I couldn't move. I just stood there in shock at hearing these things said to me in such a honey-drenched voice. I had never heard an accent like hers, except for Eugene's softer version. It was as if she were singing me a little song.

"What's wrong? Didn't you hear what I said?" She seemed very angry, and I finally snapped out of my trance. I turned away from the green door, and heard her close it gently.

Our apartment was empty when I got home. My mother was in someone else's kitchen, seeking the solace she needed. Father would come in from his late shift at midnight. I would hear them

---

8. *Verde-Esperanza* (ver´ dā es pä rän´ zä) Spanish for "green-hope."

210 ■ *Short Stories*

Vocabulary Development

Vocabulary Knowledge Rating
When students have completed reading and discussing "American History," have them take out their **Vocabulary Knowledge Rating Chart** for this selection. Read the words aloud once more and have students rate their knowledge of the words again in the After Reading column. Clarify any words that are still problematic. Have students write their own definition and example or sentence in the appropriate column. Then have students complete the Vocabulary Builder Practice activities on p. 213. Encourage students to use the words in further discussion and written work about this selection. Remind them that they will be accountable for these words on the Selection Test.

talking softly in the kitchen for hours that night. They would not discuss their dreams for the future, or life in Puerto Rico, as they often did; that night they would talk sadly about the young widow and her two children, as if they were family. For the next few days, we would observe *luto* [9] in our apartment; that is, we would practice restraint and silence—no loud music or laughter. Some of the women of El Building would wear black for weeks.

That night, I lay in my bed trying to feel the right thing for our dead President. But the tears that came up from a deep source inside me were strictly for me. When my mother came to the door, I pretended to be sleeping. Sometime during the night, I saw from my bed the streetlight come on. It had a pink halo around it. I went to my window and pressed my face to the cool glass. Looking up at the light I could see the white snow falling like a lace veil over its face. I did not look down to see it turning gray as it touched the ground below.

---

9. *luto* (lōō′ tō) Spanish for "mourning."

⑲ ▲ Critical Viewing
Do you think Elena would find this scene harsh or comforting? Explain. **[Speculate]**

Literary Analysis
Conflict and Epiphany What realization is the reason for Elena's tears?

Concept Connector

Anticipation Guide
Have students return to their **Anticipation Guides** and respond to the statements again in the After Reading column. They may do this individually or in their original pairs or groups. Then, lead a class discussion, probing for what students have learned that confirms or invalidates each statement. Encourage students to cite specific details, quotations, or other evidence from the text to support their responses to each statement.

Connecting to the Literature
Have students compare the sentences they wrote before reading with their thoughts about major world events. Ask them to explain whether their thoughts have changed and, if so, how.

Reading Skill Graphic Organizer
Have students review the graphic organizers they completed to make inferences while reading. Show them **Reading Skill Graphic Organizer B** (*Graphic Organizer Transparencies,* p. 44) as an example. Then have students share the graphic organizers they did and the inferences they made about the story and its characters.

Apply the Skills

American History

Thinking About the Selection

1. **Respond:** What would you like to say to Elena? Explain.
2. **(a) Recall:** In the first paragraph, what words does Elena use to describe her building? **(b) Recall:** How does she describe Eugene's house from her fire escape? **(c) Compare and Contrast:** Based on these descriptions, explain the contrast in Elena's feelings toward her own home and Eugene's house.
3. **(a) Recall:** What subject is Elena going to study with Eugene? **(b) Interpret:** What other reasons might Ortiz Cofer have for calling this story "American History"?
4. **(a) Analyze:** Where is Elena's mother and what is she doing when Elena returns from Eugene's house? **(b) Analyze:** In the last scene of the story, why does Elena say that her tears are just for herself?

Literary Analysis

5. **(a)** What is the main **conflict** in this story? Explain. **(b)** Is the main conflict primarily **internal** or **external**? Explain.
6. Use a chart like the one shown to provide specific details that reveal conflicts other than the main conflict.

Elena vs. another person	Elena vs. herself

7. Is there a **resolution** in this story or does Elena experience an **epiphany,** with no real end to the conflict? Support your answer with details from the story.

Reading Skill

8. **(a)** Identify three **inferences** you made while reading this story and the details you used to make them. **(b)** Did making inferences improve your understanding of the story? Explain.
9. **(a)** Write down two inferences you made about characters' responses to President Kennedy's assassination. Trade papers with a partner and compare the inferences you made. **(b)** Based on your inferences, discuss how the story would be different if Elena had tried to visit Eugene on a different day. **(c)** Pick one difference to share with the class.

QuickReview

Story at a Glance
A ninth-grade girl has a memorable experience on a day of national significance.

Go Online
Assessment
For: Self-test
Visit: www.PHSchool.com
Web Code: epa-6202

Conflict: a struggle between opposing forces

Resolution: the stage of the plot in which the conflict is solved

Epiphany: a character's sudden flash of insight

Inference: a logical assumption a reader makes based on details in the text

1. **Possible response:** Students may advise Elena to be strong in the face of her emotional pain.

2. (a) Elena describes her building as a "tenement" that is "like a monstrous jukebox." (b) She describes Eugene's house as small and neat. (c) Elena feels her home is large and noisy; Eugene's home is quiet and comfortable.

3. (a) They are going to study American history. (b) **Possible response:** The title suggests that Elena's experience of prejudice and rejection is a part of the national experience.

4. (a) She is seeking comfort in someone else's kitchen. (b) **Possible response:** Her tears are for herself because she feels her personal pain more intensely than she feels the pain of the national tragedy.

5. (a) **Possible response:** The main conflict is Elena's struggle to find happiness by becoming a part of Eugene's life. (b) The conflict is primarily internal because it focuses on Elena's feelings.

6. **Possible response:** Elena vs. another person: Elena's conflict with her mother's expectations of her occurs when Elena chooses to visit Eugene instead of attending church with her mother. Elena vs. herself: Elena is bothered by her inability to "feel the right thing" for the dead president.

   Another sample answer can be found on **Literary Analysis Graphic Organizer B,** p. 47 in *Graphic Organizer Transparencies.*

7. The story does not have a traditional resolution. Elena experiences an epiphany, which is that large social issues, such as prejudice, can crush private hopes and dreams.

8. (a) **Possible responses:** Inferences might include the love that people had for the president based on their anguish, Elena's respect for learning based on her interest in reading, and Eugene's mother's prejudice based on her treatment of Elena. (b) **Possible**

response: Making inferences gives readers a more in-depth look into characters and events.

9. (a) **Possible responses:** Mr. DePalma reacts with anguish and anger. Elena's mother reacts with quiet respect and sympathy. (b) **Possible response:** A different day might have been less dramatic, but Eugene's mother would have shown prejudice in any case. (c) Have each student share one difference.

Vocabulary Builder

Practice Use a word from the "American History" vocabulary list on page 200 to fill in the blank in each sentence. Then, explain the **context clues**, or key words and phrases, in each sentence that helped you.

1. During the blackout, the guard was more __?__ than usual.
2. The __?__ car had no wheels and was covered in rust.
3. She felt a __?__ sense of pride as she graduated with honors.
4. The serene garden contrasted with the bustling __?__.

Adding Words to Your Vocabulary Using a thesaurus, find an **antonym**, or word of opposite meaning, for each word in the vocabulary list for "American History" on page 200. Use each antonym in a sentence that makes the meaning of the word clear. (For more on using a thesaurus, see page R7.)

Writing

Write an **alternative ending** to "American History." Make sure your new ending meets these criteria:
- The ending flows logically out of earlier events.
- It is consistent with your understanding of the characters.
- It provides a satisfactory resolution to the conflict.

Use dialogue and details showing how characters feel and think.

For *Grammar, Vocabulary,* and *Assessment,*
see **Build Language Skills,** pages 238–239.

Extend Your Learning

Listening and Speaking Write and deliver a **speech** that eulogizes President Kennedy. As you write, imagine that your audience will be Elena and her classmates. Your language and tone should be appropriate for your audience and your purpose. While delivering your speech:
- Project your voice and maintain eye contact with your audience.
- Use vocal inflections and gestures that emphasize your message.

Research and Technology In a small group, create a **photo essay** about a day of national significance to the people of the United States. As a group, select a topic and conduct research to find photos. As you work, discuss the choice and arrangement of the photos and arrive at a consensus. Write suitable captions and display your photo essay.

Apply the Skills ■ 213

Extend Your Learning

The **Support for Extend Your Learning** page (*Unit 2 Resources,* p. 26) provides guided note-taking opportunities to help students complete the Extend Your Learning activities.

Go Online
—Research **For:** An additional research activity
Visit: www.PHSchool.com
Web Code: epd-7201
For another research activity to extend students' learning, give students this Web Code.

Vocabulary Builder
Practice

1. vigilant; A blackout would require special alertness for a guard.
2. dilapidated; Rust and lack of wheels indicate decay.
3. profound; Graduating with honors would provoke an intense feeling of pride.
4. tenement; A building with many people would be bustling.

Adding Words to Your Vocabulary
Sample answers:

1. tenement/mansion; One wealthy family lived in the twenty-room *mansion.*
2. profound/shallow; Her feelings are *shallow;* she does not care deeply about anyone.
3. vigilant/inattentive; The thieves escaped because the *inattentive* guards were daydreaming.
4. dilapidated/pristine; The furniture was brand new and in *pristine* condition.

Writing

- To give students guidance for writing an alternative ending, give them **Support for Writing** for "American History," p. 25 in *Unit 2 Resources.*
- To evaluate students' alternative endings, use the Narration rubrics, pp. 47–48 in *General Resources.*

Six Traits Focus

✔ Ideas		Word Choice
✔ Organization		Sentence Fluency
Voice		Conventions

Writing and Grammar, Gold Level
Students will find guidance on narration and short story writing in Chapter 5.

Build Language Skills

Go to pages 238–239 for vocabulary and grammar lessons and assessment practice.

❸ Background
Tests of Survival

One of the best-known of all big-game hunters was Theodore Roosevelt (1858–1919), president of the United States from 1901 to 1909. Though sickly as a child, Roosevelt became a vigorous outdoorsman. He traveled the world to hunt big game; on one year-long African safari, he shot nine lions, eight elephants, and thirteen rhinos. Today, governments carefully limit hunting to preserve animal populations and protect habitats. Roosevelt himself played a huge role in America's conservation movement. As president, he set aside 194 million acres in the United States as protected land, doubled the number of national parks, and founded 51 wildlife reserves.

❹ Connecting to the Literature

- To help students understand the meanings of the words they are asked to use, give them these sentences:

  1. I did not want to *contemplate* what would happen if I failed.
  2. Losing the game would *render* the other team champions for the year.
  3. Some of us tried to *simulate* the sounds of the animals.
  4. We knew we had to *utilize* every available resource.

- Help students further develop their expressive vocabulary by providing these words: *determination, endurance,* and *self-preservation.* Encourage students to use these words as they discuss the selection.

Go **Online**
Author Link
For additional information about Richard Connell, have students type in the Web Code and then select *Richard Connell.*

Build Understanding • *The Most Dangerous Game*

Short Story

❸ Background

Tests of Survival As civilizations advance, people no longer need to struggle for their basic survival. Nevertheless, some people still enjoy testing their bravery and physical skills in competitions. Today, computer games sometimes feature death-defying challenges. As this story shows, the sport of big-game hunting once served a similar purpose.

❹ Connecting to the Literature

Reading/Writing Connection Think about a game you have played or observed that you would never want to face in reality. Imagine that the game has become real. Write a paragraph describing what might happen. Use at least three of these words: *contemplate, render, simulate, utilize.*

Review

For **Literary Analysis, Reading Skill,** and **Vocabulary Builder,** see page 200.

READ MORE

For another adventure story, read "To Build a Fire" by Jack London

Meet the Author

Richard **Connell** (1893–1949)

Richard Connell seemed destined to become a writer: He was a sports reporter at the age of ten! At sixteen, he was editing his father's newspaper, the *Poughkeepsie News-Press,* in upstate New York. Connell attended Harvard University, where he worked on the *Daily Crimson* and the *Lampoon,* an early version of the humor magazine *National Lampoon.* During World War I, he edited his division's newspaper.

From Page to Screen In 1924, Connell published "The Most Dangerous Game." In 1936, he settled in Beverly Hills, California, where he started working as a screenwriter. Twice nominated for Academy Awards, he became one of the most successful screenwriters of his day.

Fast Facts

▶ "The Most Dangerous Game" won the prestigious O. Henry Memorial Award for short fiction when it was first published.

▶ The 1932 film version of "The Most Dangerous Game" is called *The Hounds of Zaroff.*

 Go **Online**
Author Link

For: More about the author
Visit: www.PHSchool.com
Web Code: epe-9203

214 ■ Short Stories

Differentiated
Instruction   Solutions for All Learners

Support for Below-Level Students [L1, L2]	Support for English Learners [EL]
Unit 2 Resources	**Unit 2 Resources**
Vocabulary Warm-up Word Lists, p. 34	Vocabulary Warm-up Word Lists, p. 34
Vocabulary Warm-up Practice, p. 35	Vocabulary Warm-up Practice, p. 35
Reading Warm-up A, p. 36	Reading Warm-up A, p. 36
Selection Test A, pp. 46–48	**Reader's Notebook: English Learner's Version**
Graphic Organizer Transparencies	**Listening to Literature Audio CD**
Reading Skill Graphic Organizer, Transparency B, p. 45	
Reader's Notebook: Adapted Version	
Adapted Reader's Notebook Audio CD	

214

THE MOST DANGEROUS GAME

RICHARD CONNELL

❶
❷

❸ ⚠ **Critical Viewing**
Based on the details in this image, what do you think this story will be about? **[Speculate]**

"Off there to the right—somewhere—is a large island," said Whitney. "It's rather a mystery—"

"What island is it?" Rainsford asked.

"The old charts call it 'Ship-Trap Island,'" Whitney replied. "A suggestive name, isn't it? Sailors have a curious dread of the place. I don't know why. Some superstition—"

"Can't see it," remarked Rainsford, trying to peer through the dank tropical night that was <u>palpable</u> as it pressed its thick warm blackness in upon the yacht.

"You've good eyes," said Whitney, with a laugh, "and I've seen you pick off a moose moving in the brown fall bush at four hundred yards, but even you can't see four miles or so through a moonless Caribbean[1] night."

---

1. **Caribbean** (kar´ ə bē´ ən) the Caribbean Sea, a part of the Atlantic Ocean, bounded by the north coast of South America, Central America, and the West Indies.

Vocabulary Builder
palpable (pal´ pə bəl) *adj.* able to be felt; easily perceived

The Most Dangerous Game ■ 215

TEACH

❶ Motivation
Prepare an Anticipation Guide (*General Resources,* pp. 8–10) with the following statements:
- Those who perform well under pressure tend to succeed.
- A person's character is revealed during intense competition.
- If faced with a seemingly impossible task, you should never try to accomplish it.
- The first impression you have of someone is always correct.

Give students a copy of the prepared Anticipation Guide and have students mark their responses in the Me column. Have students discuss the statements in pairs or groups and mark the Guides again in the Group column.

Concept Connector ➡
Students will return to the Anticipation Guide after completing "The Most Dangerous Game."

Learning Modalities
Bodily/Kinesthetic Learners

"The chase"—one person pursuing another—is the basis for many active games, from tag to hide-and-seek to paintball. Ask students whether it is more exciting to chase or be chased. After a group discussion, students can write brief journal entries about how they felt during games of pursuit. Have them apply this knowledge as they read the story of the "game" Zaroff forces Rainsford to play.

❷ About the Selection
In addition to keeping readers on the edge of their seats, "The Most Dangerous Game" asks an important question about human nature: Are human beings really civilized? The author contrasts Zaroff, whose style of living reflects highly cultured tastes but who hunts other human beings for sport, with Rainsford, who is horrified at the idea of taking a human life. However, when Rainsford is forced into the role of a "beast at bay," the primitive side of his nature emerges.

❸ Critical Viewing
Possible response: The story will be about an escaped prisoner or someone hiding in the jungle.

215

Conflict

- Have students consider what it means to be a hunter and what it means to be hunted. **Ask** students what Rainsford means when he says that Whitney is a hunter and not a philosopher.
Answer: Rainsford means that Whitney should simply enjoy what he does and not think about the consequences of hunting.

- **Ask** students if they agree with Whitney that animals can understand fear.
Possible response: Yes, animals are able to experience fear because it is linked to survival. Like humans, animals feel fear if their lives are threatened.

- **Ask** students the Literary Analysis question: How does Rainsford's attitude about hunting differ from Whitney's?
Answer: Whitney recognizes the feelings of his prey, but Rainsford has no sympathy for the animals he hunts.

❺ Critical Viewing

Answer: The image is different because it is not "as flat as a plate-glass window"; it is tumultuous. It is similar to the image in the story because it suggests a dark and dangerous rocky coast like the shore of Ship-Trap Island.

"Not four yards," admitted Rainsford. "Ugh! It's like moist black velvet."

"It will be light in Rio," promised Whitney. "We should make it in a few days. I hope the jaguar guns have come from Purdey's. We should have some good hunting up the Amazon. Great sport, hunting."

"The best sport in the world," agreed Rainsford.

"For the hunter," amended Whitney. "Not for the jaguar."

"Don't talk rot, Whitney," said Rainsford. "You're a big-game hunter, not a philosopher. Who cares how a jaguar feels?"

"Perhaps the jaguar does," observed Whitney.

"Bah! They've no understanding."

"Even so, I rather think they understand one thing—fear. The fear of pain and the fear of death."

"Nonsense," laughed Rainsford. "This hot weather is making you soft, Whitney. Be a realist. The world is made up of two classes—the hunters and the huntees. Luckily, you and I are the hunters. Do you think we've passed that island yet?"

"I can't tell in the dark. I hope so."

"Why?" asked Rainsford.

"The place has a reputation—a bad one."

"Cannibals?" suggested Rainsford.

"Hardly. Even cannibals wouldn't live in such a God-forsaken place. But it's gotten into sailor lore, somehow. Didn't you notice that the crew's nerves seemed a bit jumpy today?"

"They were a bit strange, now you mention it. Even Captain Nielsen—"

"Yes, even that tough-minded old Swede, who'd go up to the devil himself and ask him for a light. Those fishy blue eyes held a look I never saw there before. All I could get out of him was: 'This place has an evil name among sea-faring men, sir.' Then he said to me, very gravely: 'Don't you feel anything?'—as if the air about us

Literary Analysis
Conflict How does Rainsford's attitude about hunting differ from Whitney's?

❺ ▼ **Critical Viewing**
In what ways does this image differ from the Caribbean Sea as it is described in the story? In what ways is it similar? **[Compare and Contrast]**

Vocabulary Development

Expressive Vocabulary
Ask students to think about Rainsford, Whitney, and their passion for hunting. How do they prepare for a hunt? What means of travel do they use? What weapons do they use? What do they need to know about animals? As students discuss what the men do and how they do it, encourage them to use the expressive vocabulary presented earlier. You might encourage them with sentence starters like these:

1. Whitney would *contemplate* what an animal felt when . . .
2. To *render* an animal harmless, the hunters . . .
3. The color and pattern of their clothes would *simulate* . . .
4. As experienced hunters, they knew how to *utilize* . . .

was actually poisonous. Now, you mustn't laugh when I tell you this—I did feel something like a sudden chill.

"There was no breeze. The sea was as flat as a plate-glass window. We were drawing near the island then. What I felt was a—a mental chill; a sort of sudden dread."

"Pure imagination," said Rainsford. "One superstitious sailor can taint the whole ship's company with his fear."

"Maybe. But sometimes I think sailors have an extra sense that tells them when they are in danger. Sometimes I think evil is a tangible thing—with wave lengths, just as sound and light have. An evil place can, so to speak, broadcast vibrations of evil. Anyhow, I'm glad we're getting out of this zone. Well, I think I'll turn in now, Rainsford."

"I'm not sleepy," said Rainsford. "I'm going to smoke another pipe on the afterdeck."

"Good night, then, Rainsford. See you at breakfast."

"Right. Good night, Whitney."

There was no sound in the night as Rainsford sat there, but the muffled throb of the engine that drove the yacht swiftly through the darkness, and the swish and ripple of the wash of the propeller.

6 Rainsford, reclining in a steamer chair, <u>indolently</u> puffed on his favorite brier. The sensuous drowsiness of the night was on him. "It's so dark," he thought, "that I could sleep without closing my eyes; the night would be my eyelids—"

An abrupt sound startled him. Off to the right he heard it, and his ears, expert in such matters, could not be mistaken. Again he heard the sound, and again. Somewhere, off in the blackness, someone had fired a gun three times.

Rainsford sprang up and moved quickly to the rail, mystified. He strained his eyes in the direction from which the reports had come, but it was like trying to see through a blanket. He leaped upon the rail and balanced himself there, to get greater elevation; his pipe,

Vocabulary Builder
indolently (in´ də lənt lē) *adv.* lazily; idly

 Reading Check
What "two classes" does Rainsford believe make up the world?

217

217

❽ Literary Analysis
Conflict

- Remind students that a character can face an external conflict with another character, an animal, or nature itself.

- **Ask** students the Literary Analysis question: With what external conflict is Rainsford suddenly confronted?
  Answer: He is battling for his life against the sea.

- Discuss with students the fact that, just as in life, characters often do not choose their external conflicts. Conflicts may arise suddenly and force a character to marshal all possible resources in order to endure.

❾ Critical Viewing

Answer: He is surprised because the building is large and elaborate, a sign of European civilization on a wild and forbidding Caribbean island.

striking a rope, was knocked from his mouth. He lunged for it; a short, hoarse cry came from his lips as he realized he had reached too far and had lost his balance. The cry was pinched off short as the blood-warm waters of the Caribbean Sea closed over his head.

❽ He struggled up to the surface and tried to cry out, but the wash from the speeding yacht slapped him in the face and the salt water in his open mouth made him gag and strangle. Desperately he struck out with strong strokes after the receding lights of the yacht, but he stopped before he had swum fifty feet. A certain cool-headedness had come to him; it was not the first time he had been in a tight place. There was a chance that his cries could be heard by someone aboard the yacht, but that chance was slender, and grew more slender as the yacht raced on. He wrestled himself out of his clothes, and shouted with all his power. The lights of the yacht became faint and ever-vanishing fireflies; then they were blotted out entirely by the night.

Rainsford remembered the shots. They had come from the right, and doggedly he swam in that direction, swimming with slow, deliberate strokes, conserving his strength. For a seemingly endless time he fought the sea. He began to count his strokes; he could do possibly a hundred more and then—

Rainsford heard a sound. It came out of the darkness, a high screaming sound, the sound of an animal in an extremity of anguish and terror.

He did not recognize the animal that made the sound; he did not try to; with fresh vitality he swam toward the sound. He heard it again; then it was cut short by another noise, crisp, staccato.

"Pistol shot," muttered Rainsford, swimming on.

Ten minutes of determined effort brought another sound to his ears—the most welcome he had ever heard—the muttering and growling of the sea breaking on a rocky shore. He was almost on the rocks before he saw them; on a night less calm he would have been shattered against them. With his remaining strength he dragged himself from the swirling waters. Jagged crags appeared to jut into the opaqueness, he forced himself upward, hand over hand. Gasping, his hands raw, he reached a flat place at the top. Dense jungle came down to the very edge of the cliffs. What perils that tangle of trees and underbrush might hold for him did not concern Rainsford just then. All he knew was that he was safe from his enemy, the sea, and that utter weariness was on him. He flung himself down at the jungle edge and tumbled headlong into the deepest sleep of his life.

When he opened his eyes he knew from the position of the sun that it was late in the afternoon. Sleep had given him new vigor; a

Literary Analysis
Conflict With what external conflict is Rainsford suddenly confronted?

❾ ▶ **Critical Viewing** Why is Rainsford surprised to find a building, like the one shown here, on the remote island? **[Infer]**

Vocabulary Development

Think-Aloud: Context
Direct students' attention to the word *crags* on this page. Using a think-aloud process, model how to use context to infer the meaning of an unknown word. Say to students:

I'm going to think aloud to show you how I would figure out the meaning of *crags* from its context.

Crags is the subject of the sentence and, therefore, a noun. The paragraph says that the shoreline is rocky and that the rocks are dangerous. This suggests that the rocks are jagged. The story refers to *jagged crags;* therefore, *crags* must be referring to these dangerous rocks.

sharp hunger was picking at him. He looked about him, almost cheerfully.

"Where there are pistol shots, there are men. Where there are men, there is food," he thought. But what kind of men, he wondered, in so forbidding a place? An unbroken front of snarled and ragged jungle fringed the shore.

He saw no sign of a trail through the closely knit web of weeds and trees; it was easier to go along the shore, and Rainsford floundered along by the water. Not far from where he had landed, he stopped.

Some wounded thing, by the evidence a large animal, had thrashed about in the underbrush; the jungle weeds were crushed down and the moss was lacerated; one patch of weeds was stained crimson. A small, glittering object not far away caught Rainsford's eye and he picked it up. It was an empty cartridge.

"A twenty-two," he remarked. "That's odd. It must have been a fairly large animal too. The hunter had his nerve with him to tackle it with a light gun. It's clear that the brute put up a fight. I suppose the first three shots I heard was when the hunter flushed his quarry and wounded it. The last shot was when he trailed it here and finished it."

He examined the ground closely and found what he had hoped to find—the print of hunting boots. They pointed along the cliff in the direction he had been going. Eagerly he hurried along, now slipping on a rotten log or a loose stone, but making headway; night was beginning to settle down on the island.

Bleak darkness was blacking out the sea and jungle when Rainsford sighted the lights. He came upon them as he turned a crook in the coast line, and his first thought was that he had come upon a village, for there were many lights. But as he forged along he saw to his great astonishment that all the lights were in one enormous building—a lofty structure with pointed towers plunging upward into the gloom. His eyes made out the shadowy outlines of a palatial château;[2] it was set on a high bluff, and on three sides of it cliffs dived down to where the sea licked greedy lips in the shadows.

"Mirage," thought Rainsford. But it was no mirage, he found, when he opened the tall spiked iron gate. The stone steps were real enough; the massive

---

2. palatial (pə lā´ shəl) **château** (sha tō´) a mansion as luxurious as a palace.

The Most Dangerous Game ■ 219

⑫ **Reading Skill**
Making Inferences

- Tell students that when examining characters to make inferences they should pay attention to all relevant details. Tell students that they should examine a character's physical appearance, actions, dialogue, and thoughts.

- **Ask** students the Reading Skill question: Which details here lead you to infer that the two men Rainsford meets have a shared military past? Explain.
Answer: The giant man, who stands rigidly holding a gun, is dressed in a uniform, clearly indicating that he is or was part of a military unit. Then, as the slender man approaches, the giant makes a military salute and clicks his heels.

- Tell students that the giant man's salute references an old, formal European military style.

---

door with a leering gargoyle[3] for a knocker was real enough; yet about it all hung an air of unreality.

He lifted the knocker, and it creaked up stiffly, as if it had never before been used. He let it fall, and it startled him with its booming loudness. He thought he heard steps within; the door remained closed. Again Rainsford lifted the heavy knocker, and let it fall. The door opened then, opened as suddenly as if it were on a spring, and Rainsford stood blinking in the river of glaring gold light that poured out. The first thing Rainsford's eyes discerned was the largest man Rainsford had ever seen—a gigantic creature, solidly made and black-bearded to the waist. In his hand the man held a long-barreled revolver, and he was pointing it straight at Rainsford's heart.

Out of the snarl of beard two small eyes regarded Rainsford.

"Don't be alarmed," said Rainsford, with a smile which he hoped was disarming. "I'm no robber. I fell off a yacht. My name is Sanger Rainsford of New York City."

The menacing look in the eyes did not change. The revolver pointed as rigidly as if the giant were a statue. He gave no sign that he understood Rainsford's words, or that he had even heard them. He was dressed in uniform, a black uniform trimmed with gray astrakhan.[4]

⑫ "I'm Sanger Rainsford of New York," Rainsford began again. "I fell off a yacht. I am hungry."

The man's only answer was to raise with his thumb the hammer of his revolver. Then Rainsford saw the man's free hand go to his forehead in a military salute, and he saw him click his heels together and stand at attention. Another man was coming down the broad marble steps, an erect, slender man in evening clothes. He advanced to Rainsford and held out his hand.

In a cultivated voice marked by a slight accent that gave it added precision and deliberateness, he said: "It is a very great pleasure and honor to welcome Mr. Sanger Rainsford, the celebrated hunter, to my home."

Automatically Rainsford shook the man's hand.

"I've read your book about hunting snow leopards in Tibet, you see," explained the man. "I am General Zaroff."

Rainsford's first impression was that the man was singularly handsome; his second was that there was an original, almost bizarre quality about the general's face. He was a tall man past middle age, for his hair was a vivid white; but his thick eyebrows and pointed military mustache were as black as the night from

---

3. **gargoyle** (gär´ goıl´) *n.* strange and distorted animal form projecting from a building.
4. **astrakhan** (as´ trə kən) *n.* loosely curled fur made from the skins of very young lambs.

220 ■ *Short Stories*

Reading Skill
Making Inferences
Which details here lead you to infer that the two men Rainsford meets have a shared military past? Explain.

Vocabulary Development

Word Forms

Expand students' vocabulary by helping them learn related forms of the Vocabulary Builder words. Give students a blank **Word Form Chart** (*General Resources*, p. 16), with *palpable,* *indolently, scruples,* and *futile* in the correct columns. Work with the class, or have students work with a partner, to determine the related forms.

Noun	Verb	Adjective	Adverb
palpability		**palpable**	palpably
indolence		indolent	**indolently**
scruples	scruple	scrupulous	scrupulously
futility		**futile**	futilely

which Rainsford had come. His eyes, too, were black and very bright. He had high cheek bones, a sharp-cut nose, a spare, dark face, the face of a man used to giving orders, the face of an aristocrat. Turning to the giant in uniform, the general made a sign. The giant put away his pistol, saluted, withdrew.

"Ivan is an incredibly strong fellow," remarked the general, "but he has the misfortune to be deaf and dumb. A simple fellow, but, I'm afraid, like all his race, a bit of a savage."

"Is he Russian?"

"He is a Cossack," said the general, and his smile showed red lips and pointed teeth. "So am I."

"Come," he said, "we shouldn't be chatting here. We can talk later. Now you want clothes, food, rest. You shall have them. This is a most restful spot."

Ivan had reappeared, and the general spoke to him with lips that moved but gave forth no sound.

"Follow Ivan, if you please, Mr. Rainsford," said the general. "I was about to have my dinner when you came. I'll wait for you. You'll find that my clothes will fit you, I think."

It was to a huge, beam-ceilinged bedroom with a canopied bed big enough for six men that Rainsford followed the silent giant. Ivan laid out an evening suit, and Rainsford, as he put it on, noticed that it came from a London tailor who ordinarily cut and sewed for none below the rank of duke.

The dining room to which Ivan conducted him was in many ways remarkable. There was a medieval magnificence about it; it suggested a baronial hall of feudal times with its oaken panels, its high ceiling, its vast refectory table where twoscore men could sit down to eat. About the hall were the mounted heads of many animals—lions, tigers, elephants, moose, bears; larger or more perfect specimens Rainsford had never seen. At the great table the general was sitting, alone.

"You'll have a cocktail, Mr. Rainsford," he suggested. The cocktail was surpassingly good; and, Rainsford noted, the table appointments were of the finest—the linen, the crystal, the silver, the china.

They were eating *borsch*, the rich, red soup with whipped cream so dear to Russian palates. Half apologetically General Zaroff said: "We do our best to preserve the amenities of civilization here. Please

⓭ Literature in Context

History Connection

Cossacks Ivan and Zaroff are Cossacks, members of a people from southern Russia who also made up a special Russian military unit. As a people, Cossacks were famous for their fierceness, and the soldiers enjoyed a privileged status. Because of their elite position, these soldiers were also fiercely independent. When the czar—the ruler of Russia—was overthrown in the Russian Revolution of 1917, Cossacks like Zaroff were executed or forced into exile. As a Cossack, Zaroff is unwilling to acknowledge that the rules of ordinary people apply to him.

Connect to the Literature

What traits does Zaroff exhibit that might be due, in part, to his having been a Cossack?

◄ **Czar Nicholas II, overthrown in the Russian Revolution of 1917**

⓮ 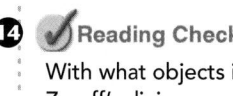 Reading Check

With what objects is Zaroff's dining room decorated?

The Most Dangerous Game ■ 221

⓭ Literature in Context: History Connection

History Connection *Cossack* comes from a Turkish word meaning "adventurer" or "free man." Early Cossacks included Tartar nomads and runaway serfs; they established several independent strongholds within Russia. Gradually, Cossacks allied themselves to the czar and joined Russian armies as elite cavalry units. Cossacks became famous for their skill as horsemen, for their loyalty to the czar, and for their ferocity in battle.

Connect to the Literature Tell students to compare the qualities of Cossacks to the qualities of Zaroff. **Ask** students the Connect to the Literature question: What traits does Zaroff exhibit that might be due, in part, to his having been a Cossack? **Answer:** Zaroff behaves toward Ivan as a strict military commander who is used to being obeyed instantly. He expects absolute loyalty from Ivan. He acts toward Rainsford like a man completely independent of outside authority and supremely confident of his skills.

⓮ Reading Check

Answer: His dining room is decorated with medieval-looking oaken panels, a huge table, and the mounted heads of many animals that Zaroff had killed.

Differentiated Instruction   Solutions for All Learners

Strategy for English Learners
Have students list the place names mentioned in the story, such as Rio and the Amazon on p. 216. Have students identify these places in their home languages, then find out where they are and learn one or two facts about them. Have students work together to make a set of flash cards that give clues to each place on the front and identify it on the back. Students can use the cards to learn the place names.

Enrichment for Gifted/Talented Students
Have students work together to make two classroom maps of Rainsford's adventures. The first map should be a long-distance view of the area where Rainsford falls overboard; the second, a close-up map of the island, showing Death Swamp (p. 229), Zaroff's chateau, and other important locations. Students can search the story for geographical clues and use an atlas to help them with the first map.

- Remind students that a character can face an external and an internal conflict at the same time.

- Point out that the external conflict and the internal conflict may arise from the same source.

- Point out the bracketed passage and **ask** students what questions might be running through Rainsford's mind during this conversation with Zaroff.
  Possible responses: Can I trust this man? Is this just a pleasant dinner, or am I in real danger?

- **Ask** students the Literary Analysis question: Explain how Rainsford's discomfort in this passage is both an internal and an external conflict.
  Answer: Rainsford's external conflict involves General Zaroff and the events that have landed Rainsford on the island. Rainsford's internal conflict is his struggle to understand Zaroff and decide whether or not to trust him.

---

forgive any lapses. We are well off the beaten track, you know. Do you think the champagne has suffered from its long ocean trip?"

"Not in the least," declared Rainsford. He was finding the general a most thoughtful and affable host, a true cosmopolite.[5] But there ⓯ was one small trait of the general's that made Rainsford uncomfortable. Whenever he looked up from his plate he found the general studying him, appraising him narrowly.

"Perhaps," said General Zaroff, "you were surprised that I recognized your name. You see, I read all books on hunting published in English, French, and Russian. I have but one passion in my life, Mr. Rainsford, and it is the hunt."

"You have some wonderful heads here," said Rainsford as he ate a particularly well cooked filet mignon. "That Cape buffalo is the largest I ever saw."

"Oh, that fellow. Yes, he was a monster."

"Did he charge you?"

"Hurled me against a tree," said the general. "Fractured my skull. But I got the brute."

"I've always thought," said Rainsford, "that the Cape buffalo is the most dangerous of all big game."

For a moment the general did not reply; he was smiling his curious red-lipped smile. Then he said slowly: "No. You are wrong, sir. The Cape buffalo is not the most dangerous big game." He sipped his wine. "Here in my preserve on this island," he said in the same slow tone, "I hunt more dangerous game."

Rainsford expressed his surprise. "Is there big game on this island?"

The general nodded. "The biggest."

"Really?"

"Oh, it isn't here naturally, of course. I have to stock the island."

"What have you imported, general?" Rainsford asked. "Tigers?"

The general smiled. "No," he said. "Hunting tigers ceased to interest me some years ago. I exhausted their possibilities, you see. No thrill left in tigers, no real danger. I live for danger, Mr. Rainsford."

The general took from his pocket a gold cigarette case and offered his guest a long black cigarette with a silver tip; it was perfumed and gave off a smell like incense.

"We will have some capital hunting, you and I," said the general. "I shall be most glad to have your society."

"But what game—" began Rainsford.

---

5. **cosmopolite** (käz mäp´ ə līt´) *n.* person at home in all parts of the world.

222 ■ *Short Stories*

Vocabulary Development

Think-Aloud: Context
Direct students' attention to the word *amenities* on page 221. Using a think-aloud process, model how to use context to infer the meaning of an unknown word. Say to students:

I'm going to think aloud to show you how I would figure out the meaning of *amenities* from its context.

Amenities is a plural noun in this sentence. The general says that *amenities* are part of civilization, therefore the term would refer to something unlike the jungle environment. The general also says that he does his "best to preserve the amenities." This statement tells me that *amenities* are likely very nice "things" that can be preserved. The two men are eating with china, crystal, and silver, and they are drinking champagne. Therefore, *amenities* must mean "pleasant or elegant things."

"I'll tell you," said the general. "You will be amused, I know. I think I may say, in all modesty, that I have done a rare thing. I have invented a new sensation. May I pour you another glass of port, Mr. Rainsford?"

"Thank you, general."

The general filled both glasses, and said: "God makes some men poets. Some He makes kings, some beggars. Me He made a hunter. My hand was made for the trigger, my father said. He was a very rich man with a quarter of a million acres in the Crimea,[6] and he was an ardent sportsman. When I was only five years old he gave me a little gun, specially made in Moscow for me, to shoot sparrows with. When I shot some of his prize turkeys with it, he did not punish me; he complimented me on my marksmanship. I killed my first bear in the Caucasus[7] when I was ten. My whole life has been one prolonged hunt. I went into the army—it was expected of noblemen's sons—and for a time commanded a division of Cossack cavalry, but my real interest was always the hunt. I have hunted every kind of game in every land. It would be impossible for me to tell you how many animals I have killed."

The general puffed at his cigarette.

"After the debacle[8] in Russia I left the country, for it was imprudent for an officer of the Czar to stay there. Many noble Russians lost everything. I, luckily, had invested heavily in American securities, so I shall never have to open a tea room in Monte Carlo or drive a taxi in Paris. Naturally, I continued to hunt—grizzlies in your Rockies, crocodiles in the Ganges, rhinoceroses in East Africa. It was in Africa that the Cape buffalo hit me and laid me up for six months. As soon as I recovered I started for the Amazon to hunt jaguars, for I had heard they were unusually cunning. They weren't." The Cossack sighed. "They were no match at all for a hunter with his wits about him, and a high-powered rifle. I was bitterly disappointed. I was lying in my tent with a splitting headache one night when a terrible thought pushed its way into my mind. Hunting was beginning to bore me! And hunting, remember, had been my life. I have heard that in America business men often go to pieces when they give up the business that has been their life."

"Yes, that's so," said Rainsford.

The general smiled. "I had no wish to go to pieces," he said. "I must do something. Now, mine is an analytical mind, Mr. Rainsford. Doubtless that is why I enjoy the problems of the chase."

"No doubt, General Zaroff."

---

6. **Crimea** (krī mē´ ə) region in southwestern Ukraine extending into the Black Sea.
7. **Caucasus** (kô´ kə səs) mountain range between the Black and Caspian seas.
8. **debacle** (di bä´ kəl) *n.* bad defeat (Zaroff is referring to the Russian Revolution of 1917, a defeat for upper-class Russians like himself).

The Most Dangerous Game ■ 223

Reading Skill
Making Inferences
How do the details about Zaroff's life support the inference that he feels neither guilt nor fear concerning hunting?

✓ Reading Check
Why does Zaroff recognize Rainsford's name?

16 Reading Skill
Making Inferences

- Remind students that most characters do not speak directly about their own qualities. Very few heroes, for example, say, "I am brave." Very few villains say, "I am evil." Their thoughts, actions, and conversations indirectly reveal their beliefs, likes, dislikes, hopes, and fears.

- Tell students that readers can also infer from a character's words the traits that he or she does *not* have.

- **Ask** students the Reading Skill question: How do the details about Zaroff's life support the inference that he feels neither guilt nor fear concerning hunting?
Answer: Zaroff says he speaks modestly, but he is actually proud of inventing a new hunting sensation. He brags about hunting during his childhood, killing a bear at ten, and hunting every kind of animal. His self-description betrays no guilt; in fact, he justifies himself by saying God created him to be a hunter. He is not afraid of any animal, even the fierce Cape buffalo and the jaguar.

17 Reading Check

Answer: Zaroff recognizes Rainsford's name because he has read Rainsford's book about hunting snow leopards in Tibet.

Differentiated Instruction   Solutions for All Learners

Background for Advanced Readers
On p. 223 Zaroff refers to "the debacle in Russia." He is speaking of the Bolshevik Revolution that ended the Russian monarchy and gave birth to the Soviet Union.

From the 1500s until 1917, Russia was ruled by monarchs called czars. The word *czar* is derived from Caesar, the first emperor of Rome. For most of the time, the Romanov family ruled the country. In 1905, a rebellion robbed the czar, Nicholas II, of much of his absolute power, making him a constitutional monarch. In March 1917, a moderate socialist

government came to power. The radical Bolsheviks, however, were not satisfied, and in October they seized power and established a communist government that would last until 1991. Zaroff's comment that "it was imprudent for an officer of the Czar to stay" in Russia was quite true; many Russian aristocrats became refugees.

Have students research the locations to which the Russian aristocrats fled. Why did they decide to settle in certain places? How were their lives changed by having to leave Russia?

- Briefly review Zaroff's career as a hunter. **Ask:** Why did Zaroff become bored with hunting? **Answer:** Hunting became too easy for Zaroff. Animal instinct is no match for human reason.

- **Ask** students the Literary Analysis question: How was the "tragic moment" Zaroff refers to the sign of an internal conflict? **Answer:** Zaroff was torn between two emotions: his passion for hunting and his growing boredom with it.

"So," continued the general, "I asked myself why the hunt no longer fascinated me. You are much younger than I am, Mr. Rainsford, and have not hunted as much, but you perhaps can guess the answer."

"What was it?"

"Simply this: hunting had ceased to be what you call 'a sporting proposition.' It had become too easy. I always got my quarry. Always. There is no greater bore than perfection."

The general lit a fresh cigarette.

18 "No animal had a chance with me any more. That is no boast; it is a mathematical certainty. The animal had nothing but his legs and his instinct. Instinct is no match for reason. When I thought of this it was a tragic moment for me, I can tell you."

Rainsford leaned across the table, absorbed in what his host was saying.

"It came to me as an inspiration what I must do," the general went on.

"And that was?"

The general smiled the quiet smile of one who has faced an obstacle and surmounted it with success. "I had to invent a new animal to hunt," he said.

"A new animal? You're joking."

"Not at all," said the general. "I never joke about hunting. I needed a new animal. I found one. So I bought this island, built this house, and here I do my hunting. The island is perfect for my purpose—there are jungles with a maze of trails in them, hills, swamps—"

"But the animal, General Zaroff?"

"Oh," said the general, "it supplies me with the most exciting hunting in the world. No other hunting compares with it for an instant. Every day I hunt, and I never grow bored now, for I have a quarry with which I can match my wits."

Rainsford's bewilderment showed in his face.

"I wanted the ideal animal to hunt," explained the general. "So I said: 'What are the attributes of an ideal quarry?' And the answer was, of course: 'It must have courage, cunning, and, above all, it must be able to reason.'"

"But no animal can reason," objected Rainsford.

"My dear fellow," said the general, "there is one that can."

"But you can't mean—" gasped Rainsford.

"And why not?"

"I can't believe you are serious, General Zaroff. This is a grisly joke."

19 "Why should I not be serious? I am speaking of hunting."

Vocabulary Development

Word Origin

- On p. 225 General Zaroff tells Rainsford that his "scruples are quite ill founded." Tell students that *scruple* is derived from the Latin for "pebble" and originally referred to a tiny unit of weight.

- **Ask** students to speculate with you how the meaning of *scruple* might have developed into its current sense of "moral concern or caution."

Possible response: A tiny unit of weight may be associated with preciseness and carefulness. Over time this meaning came to include a sense of moral carefulness, of carefully "weighing" the consequences of actions.

"Hunting? General Zaroff, what you speak of is murder."

The general laughed with entire good nature. He regarded Rainsford quizzically. "I refuse to believe that so modern and civilized a young man as you seem to be harbors romantic ideas about the value of human life. Surely your experiences in the war—"

"Did not make me condone cold-blooded murder," finished Rainsford stiffly.

Laughter shook the general. "How extraordinarily droll you are!" he said. "One does not expect nowadays to find a young man of the educated class, even in America, with such a naive, and, if I may say so, mid-Victorian point of view.[9] It's like finding a snuff-box in a limousine. Ah, well, doubtless you had Puritan ancestors. So many Americans appear to have had. I'll wager you'll forget your notions when you go hunting with me. You've a genuine new thrill in store for you, Mr. Rainsford."

"Thank you, I'm a hunter, not a murderer."

"Dear me," said the general, quite unruffled, "again that unpleasant word. But I think I can show you that your scruples are quite ill founded."

"Yes?"

"Life is for the strong, to be lived by the strong, and, if need be, taken by the strong. The weak of the world were put here to give the strong pleasure. I am strong. Why should I not use my gift? If I wish to hunt, why should I not? I hunt the scum of the earth—sailors from tramp ships—lascars,[10] blacks, Chinese, whites, mongrels—a thoroughbred horse or hound is worth more than a score of them."

"But they are men," said Rainsford hotly.

"Precisely," said the general. "That is why I use them. It gives me pleasure. They can reason, after a fashion. So they are dangerous."

"But where do you get them?"

The general's left eyelid fluttered down in a wink. "This island is called Ship-Trap," he answered. "Sometimes an angry god of the high seas sends them to me. Sometimes, when Providence is not so kind, I help Providence a bit. Come to the window with me."

Rainsford went to the window and looked out toward the sea.

"Watch! Out there!" exclaimed the general, pointing into the night. Rainsford's eyes saw only blackness, and then, as the general pressed a button, far out to sea Rainsford saw the flash of lights.

The general chuckled. "They indicate a channel," he said, "where there's none: giant rocks with razor edges crouch like a sea monster with wide-open jaws. They can crush a ship as easily as I crush this

---

9. **mid-Victorian point of view** a point of view emphasizing proper behavior and associated with the time of Queen Victoria of England (1819–1901).
10. **lascars** (las´ kərz) *n.* Indian or East Indian sailors, employed on European ships.

The Most Dangerous Game ■ 225

**Literary Analysis
Conflict and Epiphany** What does Rainsford suddenly understand about Zaroff?

**Vocabulary Builder
scruples** (skrōō´ pəlz) *n.* misgivings about something one feels is wrong

✓ **Reading Check**
What does Zaroff do to ease his boredom with hunting?

**⓳ Literary Analysis
Conflict and Epiphany**

- Remind students that an epiphany is a moment of sudden insight or revelation—a flash of understanding—that a character, and often the reader, experience.

- **Ask** students the Literary Analysis question: What does Rainsford suddenly understand about Zaroff? **Answer:** Rainsford suddenly understands that Zaroff hunts men; Zaroff is mentally unbalanced and a savage murderer.

⓴ Reading Check

Answer: Zaroff hunts human beings.

- Point out to students that Zaroff uses the example of the electric lights in the channel as a demonstration that he is civilized. He wants Rainsford to infer that he is a sophisticated, intelligent, modern man.

- **Ask** students the Reading Skill question: Based on this description, what can you infer about the method Zaroff uses to lure his quarry to the island?
Possible responses: Zaroff uses lights to lure ships onto the rocks, where the ships are destroyed and the men either drown or become stranded; Zaroff calculatingly destroys people and property for his own personal pleasure.

- Have students **discuss** Zaroff's comment that he is civilized because he uses electricity to lure the ships.
Possible responses: Zaroff has only a technological, material definition of civilization. Morally, he is a barbarian.

22 **Literary Analysis**
Conflict

- Tell students that just as Zaroff uses false lights to create the illusion of a channel and destroy ships, he also uses false reasoning to create the illusion that he is a fair and civilized man.

- **Ask** students to answer the Literary Analysis question: Is Zaroff's statement that his captives do not have to participate in the hunt true? Explain.
Answer: Captives do not have to participate, but the other option that they are given is even more undesirable. The captives can choose to have a faint chance of escape in the hunt or choose certain death at the hands of the brutal Ivan.

---

21 nut." He dropped a walnut on the hardwood floor and brought his heel grinding down on it. "Oh, yes," he said, casually, as if in answer to a question, "I have electricity. We try to be civilized here."

"Civilized? And you shoot down men?"

A trace of anger was in the general's black eyes, but it was there for but a second, and he said, in his most pleasant manner: "Dear me, what a righteous young man you are! I assure you I do not do the thing you suggest. That would be barbarous. I treat these visitors with every consideration. They get plenty of good food and exercise. They get into splendid physical condition. You shall see for yourself tomorrow."

"What do you mean?"

"We'll visit my training school," smiled the general. "It's in the cellar. I have about a dozen pupils down there now. They're from the Spanish bark San Lucar that had the bad luck to go on the rocks out there. A very inferior lot, I regret to say. Poor specimens and more accustomed to the deck than to the jungle."

He raised his hand, and Ivan, who served as waiter, brought thick Turkish coffee. Rainsford, with an effort, held his tongue in check.

"It's a game, you see," pursued the general blandly. "I suggest to one of them that we go hunting. I give him a supply of food and an excellent hunting knife. I give him three hours' start. I am to follow, armed only with a pistol of the smallest caliber and range. If my quarry eludes me for three whole days, he wins the game. If I find him"—the general smiled—"he loses."

"Suppose he refuses to be hunted?"

22 "Oh," said the general, "I give him his option, of course. He need not play the game if he doesn't wish to. If he does not wish to hunt, I turn him over to Ivan. Ivan once had the honor of serving as official knouter[11] to the Great White Czar, and he has his own ideas of sport. Invariably, Mr. Rainsford, invariably they choose the hunt."

"And if they win?"

The smile on the general's face widened. "To date I have not lost," he said.

Then he added, hastily: "I don't wish you to think me a braggart, Mr. Rainsford. Many of them afford only the most elementary sort of problem. Occasionally I strike a tartar.[12] One almost did win. I eventually had to use the dogs."

"The dogs?"

"This way, please. I'll show you."

---

11. knouter (nout′ ər) *n.* someone who beats criminals with a leather whip, or knout.
12. tartar (tärt′ ər) *n.* stubborn, violent person.

226 ■ *Short Stories*

Reading Skill
Making Inferences
Based on this description, what can you infer about the method Zaroff uses to lure his quarry to the island?

Literary Analysis
Conflict Is Zaroff's statement that his captives do not have to participate in the hunt true? Explain.

Vocabulary Development

Expressive Vocabulary
Ask students to continue the conversation between Rainsford and Zaroff, using the expressive vocabulary presented earlier. You might encourage students to respond either as Rainsford or as Zaroff to the following statements:

- Rainsford: "Zaroff, how can you even *contemplate* killing men?" (respond as Zaroff)
- Zaroff: "I *render* my prey fit and ready for the hunt." (respond as Rainsford)
- Rainsford: "You try to make a man *simulate* a jaguar or a buffalo." (respond as Zaroff)
- Zaroff: "Every animal has to *utilize* the tools it possesses by nature." (respond as Rainsford)

The general steered Rainsford to a window. The lights from the windows sent a flickering illumination that made grotesque patterns on the courtyard below, and Rainsford could see moving about there a dozen or so huge black shapes; as they turned toward him, their eyes glittered greenly.

"A rather good lot, I think," observed the general. "They are let out at seven every night. If anyone should try to get into my house—or out of it—something extremely regrettable would occur to him." He hummed a snatch of song from the Folies Bergère.[13]

24 "And now," said the general, "I want to show you my new collection of heads. Will you come with me to the library?"

"I hope," said Rainsford, "that you will excuse me tonight, General Zaroff. I'm really not feeling at all well."

"Ah, indeed?" the general inquired solicitously. "Well, I suppose that's only natural, after your long swim. You need a good, restful night's sleep. Tomorrow you'll feel like a new man, I'll wager. Then we'll hunt, eh? I've one rather promising prospect—"

Rainsford was hurrying from the room.

"Sorry you can't go with me tonight," called the general. "I expect rather fair sport—a big, strong black. He looks resourceful—Well good night, Mr. Rainsford; I hope you have a good night's rest."

The bed was good, and the pajamas of the softest silk, and he was tired in every fiber of his being, but nevertheless Rainsford could not quiet his brain with the opiate of sleep. He lay, eyes wide open. Once he thought he heard stealthy steps in the corridor outside his room. He sought to throw open the door; it would not open. He went to the window and looked out. His room was high up in one of the towers. The lights of the château were out now, and it was dark and silent, but there was a fragment of sallow moon, and by its wan light he could see, dimly, the courtyard; there, weaving in and out in the pattern of shadow, were black, noiseless forms; the hounds heard him at the window and looked up, expectantly, with their green eyes. Rainsford went back to the bed and lay down. By

13. **Folies** (fô′ lē) **Bergère** (ber zher′) musical theater in Paris.

23 ▲ **Critical Viewing**
Why might Zaroff have used dogs like these on his hunts? **[Connect]**

Reading Skill
Making Inferences
What kind of heads do you think Zaroff wants to show Rainsford? Explain.

25 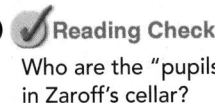 **Reading Check**
Who are the "pupils" in Zaroff's cellar?

The Most Dangerous Game ■ 227

23 Critical Viewing
Answer: The dogs' ferocity, size, and speed would intimidate Zaroff's victims, making them fear being tracked down and torn apart.

24 Reading Skill
Making Inferences
• **Ask** students to recall how Zaroff decorated his dining hall.
Answer: He decorated it with the heads of the animals he had killed.

• **Ask** students what Rainsford has learned about Zaroff's interest in hunting since their conversation began.
Answer: Rainsford has learned that Zaroff sees no difference between hunting animals and hunting humans.

• **Ask** students the Reading Skill question: What kind of heads do you think Zaroff wants to show Rainsford? Explain.
Answer: Zaroff wants to show Rainsford his collection of human heads in the library, mounted like the heads of the animals in the dining room. It is reasonable to infer that the heads are human because Zaroff refers to them as his "new collection."

25 Reading Check
Answer: The "pupils" are sailors from the Spanish bark San Lucar, which Zaroff had lured onto the rocks.

Differentiated
Instruction Solutions for All Learners

Strategy for Less Proficient Readers
To help students understand the horrific character of Zaroff, have them listen carefully to the conversation between Zaroff and Rainsford on the **Listening to Literature Audio CD.** Have them follow along with the text as they listen.

Point out that Zaroff speaks in a polite, sophisticated, and gentlemanly way about matters that are violent and cruel. Help students make a list of the expressions Zaroff uses that are much more depraved than they seem to

be. For example, when Zaroff says "training school," he really means prison. Other expressions include the following:
"some capital hunting" (p. 222)
"a new sensation" (p. 223)
"invent a new animal" (p. 224)
"that unpleasant word" (p. 225)
"play the game" (p. 226)
"something extremely regrettable" (p. 227)

26 Literary Analysis
Conflict

- Point out that the intensity of a conflict will change throughout a story. In addition, as a story develops, internal and external conflicts affect each other.

- **Ask** students to explain the common expression "a matter of life or death."
  Answer: A matter of life or death means an issue or event that can cause someone's death if it is not avoided or resolved.

- **Ask** students if they think that, in most cases, an external conflict that is "a matter of life or death" is more serious than an internal conflict.
  Possible response: Most students will agree that an external conflict that is a matter of life or death is more serious than any internal conflict.

- **Ask** students the Literary Analysis question: How does Rainsford's direct statement about wishing to leave make his internal conflict an external one?
  Answer: His statement shows that he is no longer struggling internally with the issue of whether or not to trust Zaroff. His feelings are now out in the open and will prompt Zaroff's response, most likely creating an external conflict.

27 Reading Skill
Making Inferences

- **Ask** students what choice Zaroff gives his captives.
  Answer: They can either be hunted by Zaroff or be tortured and killed by Ivan.

- **Ask** students the Reading Skill question: What inference can you make about the hunting trip Zaroff is suggesting?
  Answer: Rainsford is not going on the hunting trip as a companion for Zaroff; he is the prey.

---

many methods he tried to put himself to sleep. He had achieved a doze when, just as morning began to come, he heard, far off in the jungle, the faint report of a pistol.

General Zaroff did not appear until luncheon. He was dressed faultlessly in the tweeds of a country squire. He was solicitous about the state of Rainsford's health.

"As for me," sighed the general, "I do not feel so well. I am worried, Mr. Rainsford. Last night I detected traces of my old complaint."

To Rainsford's questioning glance the general said: "Ennui. Boredom."

Then, taking a second helping of crêpes suzette, the general explained: "The hunting was not good last night. The fellow lost his head. He made a straight trail that offered no problems at all. That's the trouble with these sailors; they have dull brains to begin with, and they do not know how to get about in the woods. They do excessively stupid and obvious things. It's most annoying. Will you have another glass of Chablis, Mr. Rainsford?"

26 "General," said Rainsford firmly, "I wish to leave this island at once."

The general raised his thickets of eyebrows; he seemed hurt. "But, my dear fellow," the general protested, "you've only just come. You've had no hunting—"

"I wish to go today," said Rainsford. He saw the dead black eyes of the general on him, studying him. General Zaroff's face suddenly brightened.

He filled Rainsford's glass with venerable Chablis from a dusty bottle.

"Tonight," said the general, "we will hunt—you and I."

Rainsford shook his head. "No, general," he said. "I will not hunt."

27 The general shrugged his shoulders and delicately ate a hothouse grape. "As you wish, my friend," he said. "The choice rests entirely with you. But may I not venture to suggest that you will find my idea of sport more diverting than Ivan's?"

He nodded toward the corner to where the giant stood, scowling, his thick arms crossed on his hogshead of chest.

"You don't mean—" cried Rainsford.

"My dear fellow," said the general, "have I not told you I always mean what I say about hunting? This is really an inspiration. I drink to a foeman worthy of my steel—at last."

The general raised his glass, but Rainsford sat staring at him.

28 "You'll find this game worth playing," the general said enthusiastically. "Your brain against mine. Your woodcraft against

228 ■ *Short Stories*

Literary Analysis
Conflict How does Rainsford's statement about wishing to leave make his internal conflict an external one?

Reading Skill
Making Inferences What inference can you make about the hunting trip Zaroff is suggesting?

Vocabulary Development

Think-Aloud: Context
Direct students' attention to the word *deplorable* on p. 229. Using a think-aloud process, model how to use context to infer the meaning of an unknown word. Say the following to students:

I'm going to think aloud to show you how I would figure out the meaning of *deplorable* from its context.

Deplorable is an adjective, describing the part of Zaroff's experience in which his favorite dog dies. Because Zaroff was obviously fond of this dog, *deplorable* must describe something "unfortunate" or "regrettable."

mine. Your strength and stamina against mine. Outdoor chess! And the stake is not without value, eh?"

"And if I win—" began Rainsford huskily.

"I'll cheerfully acknowledge myself defeated if I do not find you by midnight of the third day," said General Zaroff. "My sloop will place you on the mainland near a town."

The general read what Rainsford was thinking.

"Oh, you can trust me," said the Cossack. "I will give you my word as a gentleman and a sportsman. Of course you, in turn, must agree to say nothing of your visit here."

"I'll agree to nothing of the kind," said Rainsford.

"Oh," said the general, "in that case— But why discuss that now? Three days hence we can discuss it over a bottle of Veuve Cliquot, unless—"

The general sipped his wine.

Then a businesslike air animated him. "Ivan," he said to Rainsford, "will supply you with hunting clothes, food, a knife. I suggest you wear moccasins; they leave a poorer trail. I suggest too that you avoid the big swamp in the southeast corner of the island. We call it Death Swamp. There's quicksand there. One foolish fellow tried it. The deplorable part of it was that Lazarus followed him. You can imagine my feelings, Mr. Rainsford. I loved Lazarus; he was the finest hound in my pack. Well, I must beg you to excuse me now. I always take a siesta after lunch. You'll hardly have time for a nap, I fear. You'll want to start, no doubt. I shall not follow till dusk. Hunting at night is so much more exciting than by day, don't you think? Au revoir,[14] Mr. Rainsford, au revoir."

General Zaroff, with a deep, courtly bow, strolled from the room.

From another door came Ivan. Under one arm he carried khaki hunting clothes, a haversack of food, a leather sheath containing a long-bladed hunting knife; his right hand rested on a cocked revolver thrust in the crimson sash about his waist. . . .

Rainsford had fought his way through the bush for two hours. "I must keep my nerve. I must keep my nerve," he said through tight teeth.

He had not been entirely clear-headed when the château gates snapped shut behind him.

---

14. **Au** (ō´) **revoir** (rə vwär´) French for "until we meet again."

The Most Dangerous Game ■ 229

✓ Reading Check

What two suggestions does Zaroff give Rainsford before they begin the hunt?

28 Literary Analysis
Conflict

• **Ask** students to identify the "rules" of the deadly game that is the external conflict of the story.
Answer: Zaroff will give Rainsford clothes, food, and a hunting knife. Zaroff, on the other hand, will have a pistol. Rainsford will win his freedom if Zaroff does not find him by midnight of the third day.

• Have students who are familiar with chess describe the game to the class.

• **Ask** students how the hunt is, as Zaroff says, similar to "outdoor chess," and how it is different.
Answer: The hunt is like three-dimensional chess because it involves strategy, offensive and defensive maneuvering, and avoidance of capture. It is unlike chess because it is not played on a board, involves life and death, and gives one player, the hunter, a distinct advantage.

• **Ask** students what Rainsford says that reveals he still faces a continuing internal struggle?
Answer: Rainsford says, "I must keep my nerve. I must keep my nerve." This expression shows that Rainsford is struggling to overcome his fear and remain calm, logical, and in control.

29 Reading Check

Answer: Zaroff suggests that Rainsford wear moccasins and avoid Death Swamp.

Differentiated
Instruction   Solutions for All Learners

Strategy for Special Needs Students
As the hunt begins, be sure students understand what is going to happen. Help students fill in a spider map graphic organizer, with "the hunt for Rainsford" at the center. Have students supply the following information on the branches of the spider map:
• the "prize" Zaroff wants
• the "prize" Rainsford wants
• Zaroff's advantages
• Rainsford's disadvantages
• the time limit

Support for Less Proficient Readers
Point out that the writer provides three clues near the bottom of p. 229 to indicate the important passing of time:
• the use of an ellipsis after the words *about his waist*
• the space between the paragraphs
• the phrase *for two hours.*
    Be sure students understand that an ellipsis indicates that something has been omitted. In this case, the author has omitted a description of the first two hours of Rainsford's run through the bush.

229

His whole idea at first was to put distance between himself and General Zaroff, and, to this end, he had plunged along, spurred on by the sharp rowels of something very like panic. Now he had got a grip on himself, had stopped, and was taking stock of himself and the situation.

30 He saw that straight flight was <u>futile</u>; inevitably it would bring him face to face with the sea. He was in a picture with a frame of water, and his operations, clearly, must take place within that frame.

"I'll give him a trail to follow," muttered Rainsford, and he struck off from the rude paths he had been following into the trackless wilderness. He executed a series of intricate loops; he doubled on his trail again and again, recalling all the lore of the fox hunt, and all the dodges of the fox. Night found him leg-weary, with his hands and face lashed by the branches, on a thickly wooded ridge. He knew it would be insane to blunder on through the dark, even if he had the strength. His need for rest was imperative and he thought: "I have played the fox, now I must play the cat of the fable." A big tree with a thick trunk and outspread branches was nearby, and, taking care to **31** leave not the slightest mark, he climbed up into the crotch, and stretching out on one of the broad limbs, after a fashion, rested. Rest brought him new confidence and almost a feeling of security. Even so zealous a hunter as General Zaroff could not trace him there, he told himself; only the devil himself could follow that complicated trail through the jungle after dark. But, perhaps, the general was a devil—

An apprehensive night crawled slowly by like a wounded snake, and sleep did not visit Rainsford, although the silence of a dead world was on the jungle. Toward morning when a dingy gray was varnishing the sky, the cry of some startled bird focused Rainsford's attention in that direction. Something was coming through the bush, coming slowly, carefully, coming by the same winding way Rainsford had come. He flattened himself down on the limb, and through a screen of leaves almost

Vocabulary Builder
futile (fyōōt´ ´l) *adj.*
useless; hopeless

32 ▼ **Critical Viewing**
How does this picture support Rainsford's thought that straight flight through the jungle is futile?
[Integrate Vocabulary]

Vocabulary Development

Words That Build Conflict
Tell students that an author may use words that enhance the conflict in a story. Such words convey tension, the struggle of opposing forces, physical or mental strain, fear, doubt, and danger. Point out the following four words and explain how each word helps to build the conflict.

- *apprehensive* (p. 230) The "apprehensive night" is full of fear because Rainsford himself is fearful.

- *tensed* (p. 231) Rainsford's "every muscle tensed" because he is coiled to spring like an attacking animal.

- *quarry* (p. 231) Rainsford has become "quarry," a hunted animal.

- *precariously* (p. 231) The tree "leaned precariously," indicating a possible danger and adding to the tension of the situation.

as thick as tapestry, he watched. The thing that was approaching was a man.

It was General Zaroff. He made his way along with his eyes fixed in utmost concentration on the ground before him. He paused, almost beneath the tree, dropped to his knees and studied the ground. Rainsford's impulse was to hurl himself down like a panther, but he saw the general's right hand held something metallic—a small automatic pistol.

The hunter shook his head several times, as if he were puzzled. Then he straightened up and took from his case one of his black cigarettes; its pungent incense-like smoke floated up to Rainsford's nostrils.

Rainsford held his breath. The general's eyes had left the ground and were traveling inch by inch up the tree. Rainsford froze there, every muscle tensed for a spring. But the sharp eyes of the hunter stopped before they reached the limb where Rainsford lay; a smile spread over his brown face. Very deliberately he blew a smoke ring into the air; then he turned his back on the tree and walked carelessly away, back along the trail he had come. The swish of the underbrush against his hunting boots grew fainter and fainter.

The pent-up air burst hotly from Rainsford's lungs. His first thought made him feel sick and numb. The general could follow a trail through the woods at night; he could follow an extremely difficult trail; he must have uncanny powers; only by the merest chance had the Cossack failed to see his quarry.

Rainsford's second thought was even more terrible. It sent a shudder of cold horror through his whole being. Why had the general smiled? Why had he turned back?

Rainsford did not want to believe what his reason told him was true, but the truth was as evident as the sun that had by now pushed through the morning mists. The general was playing with him! The general was saving him for another day's sport! The Cossack was the cat; he was the mouse. Then it was that Rainsford knew the full meaning of terror.

"I will not lose my nerve. I will not."

He slid down from the tree, and struck off again into the woods. His face was set and he forced the machinery of his mind to function. Three hundred yards from his hiding place he stopped where a huge dead tree leaned precariously on a smaller, living one. Throwing off his sack of food, Rainsford took his knife from its sheath and began to work with all his energy.

The job was finished at last, and he threw himself down behind a fallen log a hundred feet away. He did not have to wait long. The cat was coming again to play with the mouse.

Reading Skill
Making Inferences
Which details in the description of Zaroff's searching the tree suggest that he knows Rainsford is there?

 Reading Check
On the first night of the hunt, where does Rainsford attempt to hide from Zaroff?

The Most Dangerous Game ■ 231

33 **Reading Skill**
Making Inferences
• **Ask** students what they can infer about Zaroff from the fact that he arrives at the tree in which Rainsford is hiding.
Answer: The inference is that Zaroff is a tremendously skilled hunter and tracker.
• **Ask** students the Reading Skill question: Which details in the description of Zaroff's searching the tree suggest that he knows Rainsford is there?
Answer: Zaroff's eyes stop before they reach the branch Rainsford is on. He smiles, blows a smoke ring very deliberately, turns his back, and walks away.
• **Ask** students what inference Rainsford makes from Zaroff's actions.
Answer: Rainsford knows that Zaroff knows where he is and that the hunter is just playing with his prey.

34 **Reading Check**
Answer: He tries to hide in a tree.

Differentiated
Instruction   Solutions for All Learners

Strategy for Less Proficient Readers
At the bottom of p. 231, the "job" Rainsford finishes is the building of a "Malay man-catcher." To help students visualize the Malay mancatcher, send a volunteer to the chalkboard to sketch a diagram based on details in the story, including the "trigger," a dead tree, and a cut living tree. You may wish to follow the same procedure for the two other traps Rainsford makes in the story. Interested students may wish to create models of these traps.

Enrichment for Advanced Readers
Point out Zaroff's emphasis on being civilized: He is always polite and well-dressed and has surrounded himself with luxuries. Have students consider what they think it means to be civilized. Ask whether, according to their definitions, animals are not more civilized than human beings (they do not kill for sport, they do not fight wars, they do not destroy the environment). Students can choose sides for a debate on the issue.

35 Literary Analysis
Conflict

- **Discuss** with students the letdown Rainsford must feel when his trap does not succeed. What must Rainsford think are his chances for survival?

  Possible response: Rainsford has put all his thought and effort into the trap, and it has failed to kill Zaroff. It is likely that he is demoralized and pessimistic about his chances of survival.

- **Ask** students the Literary Analysis question: Who seems to be winning the conflict at this point in the story? Explain.

  Answer: At this point, Zaroff seems to be winning. He has survived the trap and is confident that he will return and easily find Rainsford. Rainsford is now in a "desperate, hopeless flight."

- Have students **speculate** which man they think will win and why they think so.

  Possible responses: Students may say that Rainsford will win because he is clearly the hero, and the story has emphasized the skill, tenacity, and bravery with which he has faced a sadistic opponent. Other students may suggest that Rainsford may destroy Zaroff but he may have to give up his life to do so.

Following the trail with the sureness of a bloodhound, came General Zaroff. Nothing escaped those searching black eyes, no crushed blade of grass, no bent twig, no mark, no matter how faint, in the moss. So intent was the Cossack on his stalking that he was upon the thing Rainsford had made before he saw it. His foot touched the protruding bough that was the trigger. Even as he touched it, the general sensed his danger and leaped back with the agility of an ape. But he was not quite quick enough; the dead tree, delicately adjusted to rest on the cut living one, crashed down and struck the general a glancing blow on the shoulder as it fell; but for his alertness, he must have been smashed beneath it. He staggered, but he did not fall; nor did he drop his revolver. He stood there, rubbing his injured shoulder, and Rainsford, with fear again gripping his heart, heard the general's mocking laugh ring through the jungle.

"Rainsford," called the general, "if you are within the sound of my voice, as I suppose you are, let me congratulate you. Not many men know how to make a Malay mancatcher. Luckily, for me, I too have hunted in Malacca. You are proving interesting, Mr. Rainsford. I am going now to have my wound dressed; it's only a slight one. But I shall be back. I shall be back."

When the general, nursing his bruised shoulder, had gone, Rainsford took up his flight again. It was flight now, a desperate, hopeless flight, that carried him on for some hours. Dusk came, then darkness, and still he pressed on. The ground grew softer under his moccasins; the vegetation grew ranker, denser; insects bit him savagely. Then, as he stepped forward, his foot sank into the ooze. He tried to wrench it back, but the muck sucked viciously at his foot as if it were a giant leech. With a violent effort, he tore his foot loose. He knew where he was now. Death Swamp and its quicksand.

His hands were tight closed as if his nerve were something tangible that someone in the darkness was trying to tear from his grip. The softness of the earth had given him an idea. He stepped back from the quicksand a dozen feet or so, and, like some huge prehistoric beaver, he began to dig.

Rainsford had dug himself in in France when a second's delay meant death. That had been a placid pastime compared to his digging now. The pit grew deeper; when it was above his shoulders, he climbed out and from some hard saplings cut stakes and sharpened them to a fine point. These stakes he planted in the

35

Literary Analysis
Conflict Who seems to be winning the conflict at this point in the story? Explain.

Vocabulary Development

Vocabulary Builder Reinforcement
Students will benefit from additional examples and practice with the Vocabulary Builder words. Reinforce their comprehension with "show-you-know" sentences. The first part of the sentence uses the vocabulary word in an appropriate context. The second part of the sentence—the "show-you-know" part—clarifies the first. Model the strategy with this example for *palpable:*

The tension in the air was *palpable;* it felt as if the danger was a heavy hand on his shoulder.

Then give students this sentence prompt, and coach them in creating the clarification.

The boys stood around *indolently;*
_____.

Sample answer: They should have been doing something productive instead.

36

Literature in Context   History Connection

World War I Trenches

When Rainsford digs himself in, he is drawing on his experiences as a soldier. During World War I (1914–1918), European armies on both sides dug hundreds of miles of deep, narrow ditches. The soldiers lived in these trenches, from where they would charge the enemy's trenches.

Soldiers' equipment included masks to protect them from mustard gas and other chemical weapons.

A single pair of trench rats could produce as many as 880 offspring in one year.

LIFE IN THE TRENCHES

- Throughout the war, approximately seven thousand British soldiers were killed, wounded, or disabled every day while serving in the trenches.
- Soldiers living in trenches were plagued by lice, rats, beetles, and frogs.
- The trenches smelled terrible due to dead bodies, overflowing latrines, and unwashed men.

Connect to the Literature Rainsford says his time in the trenches was "placid" compared to his experience on the island. How does this information about trenches clarify his fear?

bottom of the pit with the points sticking up. With flying fingers he wove a rough carpet of weeds and branches and with it he covered the mouth of the pit. Then, wet with sweat and aching with tiredness, he crouched behind the stump of a lightning-charred tree.

He knew his pursuer was coming; he heard the padding sound of feet on the soft earth, and the night breeze brought him the perfume of the general's cigarette. It seemed to Rainsford that the general was coming with unusual swiftness; he was not feeling his way along, foot by foot. Rainsford, crouching there, could not see the general, nor could he see the pit. He lived a year in a minute. Then he felt an impulse to cry aloud with joy, for he heard the sharp crackle of the breaking branches as the cover of the pit gave way; he heard the sharp scream of pain as the pointed stakes found their mark. He leaped up from his place of concealment. Then he cowered back. Three feet from the pit a man was standing, with an electric torch in his hand.

"You've done well, Rainsford," the voice of the general called. "Your Burmese tiger pit has claimed one of my best dogs. Again you score. I think, Mr. Rainsford, I'll see what you can do against my whole pack. I'm going home for a rest now. Thank you for a most amusing evening."

37 ✓ **Reading Check**
What toll do Rainsford's two traps take on Zaroff?

The Most Dangerous Game ■ 233

---

36 ### Literature in Context

History Connection Modern artillery, machine guns, and barbed wire drastically changed the face of combat in World War I—but generals were slow to change their tactics. Massive assaults by hundreds of thousands of soldiers produced horrific casualties, but little or no gain on the battlefield. On the first day of the First Battle of the Somme, for example, nearly 60,000 British soldiers were killed or wounded. That Rainsford was able to survive trench warfare may help explain his abilities in his combat with Zaroff.

Connect to the Literature Tell students that some synonyms for "placid" are calm, peaceful, and serene. Then, **ask** the Connect to the Literature question: Rainsford says his time in the trenches was "placid" compared to his experience on the island. How does this information about trenches clarify his fear?
Answer: To call his experience in the horrific trenches "placid" in comparison to his island experience means that Rainsford is incredibly frightened.

37 ### Reading Check

Answer: The Malay mancatcher bruises Zaroff's shoulder. The Burmese tiger pit kills one of Zaroff's dogs.

Differentiated Instruction   Solutions for All Learners

Strategy for Less Proficient Readers

In 1932, RKO Studios in Hollywood began work on two films: *The Most Dangerous Game* and the more famous *King Kong.* Since the films were being shot at the same time, the studio saved money by using the same jungle sets and casting several of the same actors in both films. Have students gather for a screening of *The Most Dangerous Game.* Seeing the story brought to life on screen will help students follow the story's plot and themes. After seeing the film, have students compare and contrast it with the story. What are the obvious differences? Why do students think the filmmakers made these changes? Was the story or the film more exciting? more dramatic? more believable? Students can address these questions in a group discussion.

38 Literary Analysis
Conflict

- Point out that in many games and sports the conflict between opponents is made more intense when time limits are added. **Ask** students for examples of such games. **Possible answers:** football, basketball, soccer.

- **Ask** students the Literary Analysis question: What new internal conflict does the sound of the baying dogs create for Rainsford? **Answer:** Rainsford must now struggle to control his panic because he knows the dogs are drawing nearer and that he has a limited amount of time to think of a tactic.

- **Ask** students why they think poise and self-control—grace under pressure—are highly respected traits found in athletes, military leaders, and those in life-saving professions. **Possible response:** It is easy to give in to panic; maintaining calm shows the ability to control circumstances instead of being controlled by them. It is an ingredient of genuine heroism.

39 Critical Viewing

Answer: Cliffs lining the shore are like a prison wall, and the pounding waves of the sea make escape impossible.

At daybreak Rainsford, lying near the swamp, was awakened by a sound that made him know that he had new things to learn about fear. It was a distant sound, faint and wavering, but he knew it. It was the baying of a pack of hounds.

Rainsford knew he could do one of two things. He could stay where he was and wait. That was suicide. He could flee. That was postponing the inevitable. For a moment he stood there, thinking. An idea that held a wild chance came to him, and, tightening his belt, he headed away from the swamp.

The baying of the hounds drew nearer, then still nearer, nearer, ever nearer. On a ridge Rainsford climbed a tree. Down a watercourse, not a quarter of a mile away, he could see the bush moving. Straining his eyes, he saw the lean figure of General Zaroff; just ahead of him Rainsford made out another figure whose wide shoulders surged through the tall jungle weeds; it was the giant Ivan, and he seemed pulled forward by some unseen force; Rainsford knew that Ivan must be holding the pack in leash.

They would be on him any minute now. His mind worked frantically. He thought of a native trick he had learned in Uganda. He slid down the tree. He caught hold of a springy young sapling and to it he fastened his hunting knife, with the blade pointing down the trail; with a bit of wild grapevine he tied back the sapling. Then he ran for his life. The hounds raised their voices as they hit the fresh scent. Rainsford knew now how an animal at bay feels.

He had to stop to get his breath. The baying of the hounds stopped abruptly, and Rainsford's heart stopped too. They must have reached the knife.

He shinnied excitedly up a tree and looked back. His pursuers had stopped. But the hope that was in Rainsford's brain when he

Literary Analysis
Conflict What new internal conflict does the sound of the baying dogs create for Rainsford?

39 ▼ Critical Viewing How does this image clarify Rainsford's feeling that the island is a sort of prison, guarded by the surging sea? **[Connect]**

234   *Short Stories*

Vocabulary Development

Vocabulary Knowledge Rating
When students have completed reading and discussing "The Most Dangerous Game," have them take out their **Vocabulary Knowledge Rating Chart** for this selection. Read the words aloud once more and have students rate their knowledge of the words again in the After Reading column. Clarify any words that are still problematic. Have students write their own def-inition and example or sentence in the appropriate column. Then have students complete the **Vocabulary Builder Practice** activities on p. 237. Encourage students to use the words in further discussion and written work about this selection. Remind them that they will be accountable for these words on the Selection Test.

climbed died, for he saw in the shallow valley that General Zaroff was still on his feet. But Ivan was not. The knife, driven by the recoil of the springing tree, had not wholly failed.

"Nerve, nerve, nerve!" he panted, as he dashed along. A blue gap showed between the trees dead ahead. Ever nearer drew the hounds. Rainsford forced himself on toward that gap. He reached it. It was the shore of the sea. Across a cove he could see the gloomy gray stone of the château. Twenty feet below him the sea rumbled and hissed. Rainsford hesitated. He heard the hounds. Then he leaped far out into the sea. . . .

When the general and his pack reached the place by the sea, the Cossack stopped. For some minutes he stood regarding the blue-green expanse of water. He shrugged his shoulders. Then he sat down, took a drink of brandy from a silver flask, lit a perfumed cigarette, and hummed a bit from *Madame Butterfly*.[15]

General Zaroff had an exceedingly good dinner in his great paneled dining hall that evening. With it he had a bottle of Pol Roger and half a bottle of Chambertin. Two slight annoyances kept him from perfect enjoyment. One was the thought that it would be difficult to replace Ivan; the other was that his quarry had escaped him; of course the American hadn't played the game—so thought the general as he tasted his after-dinner liqueur. In his library he read, to soothe himself, from the works of Marcus Aurelius.[16] At ten he went up to his bedroom. He was deliciously tired, he said to himself, as he locked himself in. There was a little moonlight, so, before turning on his light, he went to the window and looked down at the courtyard. He could see the great hounds, and he called: "Better luck another time," to them. Then he switched on the light.

A man, who had been hiding in the curtain of the bed, was standing there.

"Rainsford!" screamed the general. "How in God's name did you get here?"

"Swam," said Rainsford. "I found it quicker than walking through the jungle."

The general sucked in his breath and smiled. "I congratulate you," he said. "You have won the game."

Rainsford did not smile. "I am still a beast at bay," he said, in a low, hoarse voice. "Get ready, General Zaroff."

The general made one of his deepest bows. "I see," he said. "Splendid! One of us is to furnish a repast for the hounds. The other will sleep in this very excellent bed. On guard, Rainsford. . . ."

He had never slept in a better bed, Rainsford decided.

---

15. *Madame Butterfly* an opera by Giacomo Puccini.
16. **Marcus Aurelius** (ô rē´ lē əs) Roman emperor and philosopher (A.D. 121–180).

Reading Skill
Making Inferences
When Rainsford leaps into the sea, what inference do you think the author wants you to make?

ⓐ Reading Skill
Making Inferences

- Remind students that the author has been emphasizing Rainsford's struggle for self-control and his fear of the ravenous dogs.

- **Ask** students the Reading Skill question: When Rainsford leaps into the sea, what inference do you think the author wants you to make?
  Answer: Rainsford's act suggests that he is willing to drown rather than be torn apart by the dogs.

- **Ask** students what important detail Rainsford sees before he leaps into the sea.
  Answer: He sees the chateau across the cove.

- **Ask** students what inference they can make based on that detail.
  Answer: Rainsford plans to swim across the cove to the chateau.

▶ **Monitor Progress:** Evaluate the reasonableness of students' inferences.

▶ **Reteach:** Remind students that an inference is based directly on a detail. Point out, for example, that the author deliberately mentions that Rainsford looks at the chateau before he jumps into the sea. It is reasonable to infer that he is going to try to swim to that location.

Concept Connector

Anticipation Guide
Have students return to their **Anticipation Guides** and respond to the statements again in the After Reading column. They may do this individually or in their original pairs or groups. Then, lead a class discussion, probing for what students have learned that confirms or invalidates each statement. Encourage students to cite specific details, quotations, or other evidence from the text to support their responses to each statement.

Connecting to the Literature
Have students compare the paragraphs they wrote before reading with their thoughts about what can happen if an undesired game becomes a reality. Ask them to explain whether their thoughts have changed and, if so, how.

Reading Skill Graphic Organizer
Ask students to review the graphic organizers they completed to make inferences. Show them **Reading Skill Graphic Organizer B** (*Graphic Organizer Transparencies*, p. 45) as an example. Then have students share the graphic organizers they did and the inferences they made.

1. **Possible responses:** Students will probably like Rainsford's courage, intelligence, and self-control under pressure. They may dislike his attitude about hunting.

2. (a) Zaroff believes that human beings are the most dangerous game. (b) Since he is a sadist and murderer, students probably will not find Zaroff civilized.

3. (a) Whitney believes that jaguars feel fear of pain and of death. (b) Rainsford believes that jaguars have no understanding and that it is useless to care about how they feel.

4. (a) Zaroff says, "You have won the game." (b) Rainsford fights with and kills Zaroff.

5. If Rainsford hunts, he will certainly think about his prey's experience.

6. (a) The main conflict is a life-or-death "game" between Rainsford and Zaroff. (b) The main conflict is external because it is between two characters.

7. Possible response: **Rainsford vs. Nature:** almost drowning at start of story; almost dying in jungle and swamp **Rainsford vs. Himself:** not panicking when thrown from boat; controlling his anxiety during hunt

   Another sample answer can be found on **Literary Analysis Graphic Organizer B,** p. 49 in *Graphic Organizer Transparencies.*

8. The main conflict has a resolution; Rainsford wins the hunt and kills Zaroff.

9. (a) **Possible responses:** Zaroff is barbaric because he hunts humans; Zaroff knows Rainsford is in the tree because he smiles and blows a smoke ring; Rainsford kills Zaroff because he sleeps in Zaroff's bed. (b) **Possible response:** Students may answer that inferences give them a better understanding of the characters and events.

10. (a) **Possible responses:** Whitney's desire to relate to the animals shows that he is a more sensitive man than Rainsford; Whitney has a vivid imagination,

Apply the Skills

The Most Dangerous Game

Thinking About the Selection

1. **Respond:** What do you like or dislike about Rainsford? Explain.
2. (a) **Recall:** According to Zaroff, what is the most dangerous game? (b) **Make a Judgment:** Based on this attitude, would you call Zaroff "civilized"? Why or why not?
3. (a) **Recall:** Early in the story, what fears does Whitney believe jaguars feel? (b) **Contrast:** How does Rainsford's attitude toward these animals differ from Whitney's?
4. (a) **Recall:** Near the end, with what words does Zaroff congratulate Rainsford? (b) **Infer:** What action does Rainsford then take?
5. **Speculate:** How might Rainsford's experience on the island change him? Use evidence from the text to support your answer.

Literary Analysis

6. (a) What is the main **conflict** in this story? Explain. (b) Is the main conflict primarily **internal** or **external**? Explain.
7. Use a chart like the one shown to provide specific details that reveal conflicts other than the main conflict.

Rainsford vs. nature	Rainsford vs. himself

8. Is there a **resolution** in this story or does Rainsford experience an **epiphany** with no real end to the conflict? Support your answer with details from the story.

Reading Skill

9. (a) Identify three **inferences** you made while reading this story and the details you used to make them. (b) Did making inferences improve your understanding of the story? Explain.
10. (a) Write down two inferences you made about Whitney. Trade papers with a partner and compare the inferences you made. (b) Based on your inferences, discuss how the story would be different if it had been Whitney on the island with Zaroff. (c) Pick one difference to share with the class.

236 ■ Short Stories

which becomes apparent when he says he feels a "mental chill" and believes in "vibrations of evil." (b) **Possible response:** If Whitney had been on the island, his sensitivity and active imagination would have added to his fear, making him easier prey for Zaroff.

QuickReview

Story at a Glance
A big-game hunter finds himself being hunted.

Go Online
Assessment
For: Self-test
Visit: www.PHSchool.com
Web Code: epa-6203

Conflict: a struggle between opposing forces

Resolution: the stage of the plot in which the conflict is solved

Epiphany: a character's sudden flash of insight

Inference: a logical assumption a reader makes based on details in the text

Vocabulary Builder

Practice Use a word from the vocabulary list for "The Most Dangerous Game" on page 200 to fill in each blank. Then, explain the **context clues,** or key words and phrases, that helped you.

1. His cheating at the game demonstrated a lack of __?__.
2. At the wedding, the joy in the air seemed __?__.
3. She tried to climb, but her high heels made her efforts __?__.
4. The lazy sloth hung __?__ from the tree branch.

Adding Words to Your Vocabulary Using a thesaurus, find an antonym for three words from the vocabulary list for "The Most Dangerous Game" on page 200. Use each antonym correctly in a sentence. (For more on using a thesaurus, see page R7.)

Writing

Write an **alternative ending** to "The Most Dangerous Game." Make sure your new ending meets these criteria:
* The ending flows logically out of earlier events.
* It is consistent with your understanding of the characters.
* It provides a satisfactory resolution to the conflict.

For *Grammar, Vocabulary,* and *Assessment,* see **Build Language Skills,** pp. 238–239.

Extend Your Learning

Listening and Speaking As Rainsford, write and deliver a **speech** to an audience of big-game hunters. In your speech, explain why your attitude toward big-game hunting has or has not changed as a result of story events. Your language and tone should be appropriate to your audience and purpose. As you deliver your speech in class:
* Project your voice and maintain eye contact with your audience.
* Use vocal inflections and gestures that emphasize your message.

Research and Technology In a small group, create a **photo essay** about two or three big-game species mentioned in the story. As you work, discuss the choice and arrangement of the photos as a group and arrive at a consensus. Write suitable captions and display your photo essay for the class.

Apply the Skills ■ 237

Assessment Resources

The following resources can be used to assess students' knowledge and skills.

Unit 2 Resources:
   Selection Test A, pp. 46–48
   Selection Test B, pp. 49–51

Go **O**nline
—Assessment
Students may use the **Self-test** to prepare for **Selection Test A** or **Selection Test B.**

Go **O**nline
—Research
For: An additional research activity
Visit: www.PHSchool.com
Web Code: epd-7202
For another research activity to extend students' learning, give students this Web Code.

ASSESS/EXTEND
Answers

Vocabulary Builder
Practice

1. scruples; "Cheating" reveals lack of conscience or moral concern.
2. palpable; "Joy in the air" indicates an untouchable thing made perceivable.
3. futile; The phrase "tried . . . but" shows a useless effort.
4. indolently; "Lazy" suggests "in an idle way."

Adding Words to Your Vocabulary
Sample answers:

palpable—intangible; Their ideals are influential although *intangible.*

indolently—industriously; The admired workers perform their jobs *industriously.*

futile—effective; Their efforts proved *effective* when the bridge was built.

Writing

* To give students guidance for writing an alternative ending, give them **Support for Writing** for "The Most Dangerous Game," p. 41, in *Unit 2 Resources.*
* To evaluate students' alternative endings, use the Narration: Short Story rubrics, pp. 47–48 in *General Resources.* In addition, you might evaluate how well students weave in dialogue and details in their endings.

Six Traits Focus

Ideas	✔	Word Choice	
Organization	✔	Sentence Fluency	
Voice		Conventions	

Writing and Grammar, Gold Level
Students will find guidance on narration and short story writing Chapter 5.

Build Language Skills
Go to pages 238–239 for vocabulary and grammar lessons and assessment practice.

Extend Your Learning
The **Support for Extend Your Learning** page (*Unit 2 Resources,* p. 42) provides guided note-taking opportunities to help students complete the Extend Your Learning activities.

237

Vocabulary Skill

- Introduce the root word -*spec-* and the prefix *circum-*. Ask students to brainstorm for words that contain these word parts.
  Possible responses: *spectator, spectacle, inspect, retrospect, introspection; circumspect, circumference,* and *circumstance*

- Explain how the meaning of "looking at" or "around" or "surrounding" contributes to the meaning of each word.

Answers

1. inspect: The root means "to look," and *inspect* means "to look at or examine carefully."

2. retrospect: The root means "to look," and *retrospect* means "a review of things in the past" or "to look back at the past."

3. circumvent: The prefix means "surrounding" or "around," and *circumvent* means "to go around so as to avoid something."

4. speculate: The root means "to look," and *speculate* means "to reflect or look at thoughtfully."

5. circumstance: The prefix means "surrounding" or "around," and *circumstance* means "something that has bearing on an event."

Grammar Lesson

- Tell students that regular verbs add -*d* or -*ed* to form the past participle, and they drop the final *e* and add -*ing* to form the present participle.

- Point out that most regular verbs are predictable and easy to spell.

Answers

1. look; is looking; looked; has looked

2. diverge; is diverging; diverged; has diverged

3. expect; is expecting; expected; has expected

4. observe; is observing; observed; has observed

5. walk; is walking; waked; has walked

Writing Application

Review students' papers to check whether they have used and identified each of the four principal parts.

238

Build Language Skills

American History • The Most Dangerous Game

Vocabulary Skill

Word Parts The Latin **root** -*spec-* means "look" or "see." This root appears in English words that have to do with "looking at," "looking upon," or "seeing" something. For example, when you discuss an *aspect* of a character, you look at a particular feature of the character.

The Latin **prefix** *circum-* means "around" or "surrounding" and is used as part of several English words.

Practice List these words on your paper. Then, next to each word, write a brief explanation of how the word part contributes to the word's meaning.

1. inspect **2.** retrospect **3.** circumvent **4.** speculate **5.** circumstance

Grammar Lesson

Regular Verbs A **verb** has four **principal parts:** the present, the present participle, the past, and the past participle. Most of the verbs in the English language, such as the verb *inspect,* are **regular verbs,** and you can form their principal parts following a predictable pattern. Notice that the final *e* may be dropped.

Present	Present Participle	Past	Past Participle
inspect	is inspecting	inspected	has inspected
race	is racing	raced	has raced

Practice Copy and complete the chart.

Present	Present Participle	Past	Past Participle
look			
diverge			
expect			
observe			
walk			

*W*_G *Prentice Hall Writing and Grammar Connection: Chapter 23, Section 1*

MorePractice

For more practice with verbs, see the Grammar Handbook, p. R39.

Teaching Resources

The following resources can be used to enrich or extend the instruction for Build Language Skills.

Unit 2 Resources
   Build Language Skills: Vocabulary: Word Parts, p. 44
   Build Grammar Skills: Regular Verbs, p. 45

Assessment Practice

Reading: Making Inferences

Directions: *Read the selection. Then, answer the questions.*

In sixth grade, I had one of the first in a lucky line of great English teachers who began to nurture in me a love of language, a love that had been there since my childhood of listening closely to words. Sister Maria Generosa did not make our class interminably diagram sentences from a workbook or learn a catechism of grammar rules. Instead, she asked us to write little stories imagining we were snowflakes, birds, pianos, a stone in the pavement, a star in the sky. What would it feel like to be a flower with roots in the ground? If the clouds could talk, what would they say? She had an expressive, dreamy look that was accentuated by the wimple that framed her face.

—from "My English," by Julia Alvarez

1. What can readers infer about the narrator?
   A She likes to write.
   B She doesn't like nature.
   C She has no imagination.
   D She thinks writers are dreamers.

2. What can readers infer about Sister Maria Generosa?
   A She doesn't understand grammar.
   B She also loves language.
   C She teaches religion.
   D She doesn't speak English.

3. What prior knowledge helps you make inferences about the narrator?
   A Sister Generosa also taught art.
   B Writing is part of the curriculum.
   C Teachers know grammar rules.
   D Writers generally love language.

4. Which detail is most helpful in making inferences about the narrator?
   A who began to nurture . . . of language,
   B did not make our class . . . of grammar rules.
   C write little stories . . . in the sky.
   D an expressive, dreamy look . . . her face.

Timed Writing: Interpretation [Critical Stance]

Review "The Most Dangerous Game" or "American History." Write a brief explanation of who the narrator is and how the narrator affects your impression of the story. Use examples from the story to illustrate your points. **(20 minutes)**

 ## Writing Workshop: *Work in Progress*

Short Story

Using the work from your writing portfolio as an outline, fill in the steps between announcements. Add important moments in your character's life. Put this paper in your writing portfolio.

Build Language Skills ■ 239

Timed Writing

- Tell students that in this timed writing they will review a story and explain how the narrator affects the story.
- Point out that they may save time if they first quickly jot down a list of the narrator's qualities and think about his or her impact on the story before they begin writing.
- Tell students that they need to write quickly, as time is short, but they also need to support their explanation with examples from the story.
- Assess students' essays on the clarity of their discussion of the narrator and his or her impact on the story. Evaluate their use of examples to support their ideas.
- Suggest that students organize their time to give five minutes to planning, ten minutes to writing, and five minutes to reviewing and revising.

Writing Workshop
Work in Progress

Short Story

- Have students go to their portfolios and take out the announcements they made in the **Work-in-Progress** assignment on p. 195.
- Remind students that this work may be used in the short story they will write in the **Writing Workshop** at the end of Part 1.
- Have students think about the announcements and the steps that take place between these announcements.
- Point out that students should include only moments that had an impact on their character's life.
- When students have finished this activity, have them save it in their portfolios. They will develop these ideas as they continue this Work in Progress.

239

Students will

1. understand and evaluate signs and instructions.
2. read signs and instructions for beach safety.

See TeacherExpress™/Lesson View for a detailed lesson plan for Reading Informational Materials.

About Signs and Instructions

- Have students read "About Signs and Instructions."

- Discuss with students occasions when they have encountered signs or brief instructions meant to ensure their safety. Have them describe where they saw the signs and how the signs were helpful.

- Explain to students that safety signs and instructions are often found when traveling. Point out that they appear on airplanes, ships, roadsides, and at popular tourist attractions. Add that safety signs and instructions also appear frequently on items for children.

Reading Skill
Evaluating Visual Aids

- Remind students that visual aids are images such as pictures, diagrams, arrows, and shapes that are used to help convey a message. Also, point out that along with the images, most visual aids also make use of vibrant colors and clear typeface.

- Review with students the "How to Evaluate Signs and Instructions" chart.

- Explain that visual aids are sometimes used to make sure that everyone gets the message. Also, point out that visual aids make it possible for people who cannot read the sign's language to understand the message. Point out that many signs convey the basic message in a picture, but the text provides more detail.

Signs and Instructions

In Part 1, you are learning how to make inferences while reading. Making inferences is also important in reading informational materials such as signs. Most signs depend on your ability to infer meaning from symbols and abbreviated statements. If you read "The Most Dangerous Game," you know that ocean waves and currents can be dangerous.

The signs and instructions here are posted to help swimmers and surfers avoid serious dangers.

About Signs and Instructions

Signs are a type of visual aid, or symbol, designed to communicate important messages quickly and effectively. Signs often include these elements:

- brief, clearly stated information
- large, easy-to-read lettering
- simple, bold pictures or symbols
- colors that help the words and pictures stand out

Instructions are not as concise as signs, but they provide direct statements and clear messages about how to handle particular situations.

Reading Skill

Like other visual aids, signs use pictures, color, and type to present information. An effective visual aid uses these elements to highlight different kinds of information on different parts of the message. When **evaluating visual aids**, look carefully at each element to see if it adds clarity and effectiveness to the message.

How to Evaluate Signs and Instructions

STOP
Does the sign grab your attention?

READ
Can you easily understand the message?

ASK
Are the elements used effectively to emphasize the most important information?

Differentiated Instruction — Solutions for All Learners

Reading Support
Give students reading support with the appropriate version of the *Reader's Notebooks:*

Reader's Notebook, **[L2]**

Reader's Notebook: Adapted Version, **[L1]**

Reader's Notebook: English Learner's Version, **[EL]**

BEACH SAFETY GUIDE: HIGH SURF SIGN

The word *warning* is the boldest element on the sign. The background for the word is orange—a color often used on warning signs and safety devices.

A simple picture illustrates the danger.

WARNING

HIGH SURF
CAN CAUSE SERIOUS
INJURIES OR DROWNING

IF IN DOUBT, DON'T GO OUT

WARNING LEVEL: *DANGEROUS* . . . a potential for *loss of life or limb* exists.

CONDITION: Large powerful waves are generated by winds and storms at sea sometimes thousands of miles from the Hawaiian Islands. Seasonal high surf occurs on all shores of O'ahu. Typically, shorelines facing North, East and West receive high surf during Winter months. Shores facing Southeast and Southwest receive high surf during Summer months. Surf on the North shore may reach heights of *twenty-five* feet plus,—on the West shore, *fifteen* feet plus!

INSTRUCTIONS: If you're uncertain of your abilities, don't go into the ocean during high surf, heed all posted high surf warnings! Your life could depend on it!

The uppercase, red letters in each head let readers know that they are reading important information.

241

Reading Signs and Instructions

- Tell students that they are likely to encounter signs and instructions when their safety could be at risk. Point out that these signs exist to help explain what dangers are present and how you should act to stay safe.

- Have students read "Beach Safety Guide: High Surf Sign" and the side notes.

- **Ask** students why this sign uses a simple picture.
  Possible response: This sign uses a simple picture to help communicate the message at a glance. It also communicates the basic message to people who cannot read the sign.

- Remind students that signs, like other visual aids, use images, color and typeface to clearly communicate an important message in a small space.

- **Ask** students to glance at the sign on p. 241 quickly and then look away. Ask a volunteer what words he or she could read in a glance.
  Possible response: High Surf Point out that, on signs with many words, the most important words/messages are given in the biggest letters.

- **Ask** students to note whether the words on the sign are in upper and lower case or all capital letters.
  Answer: The words on the sign are all upper case.

- Point out that not all signs warn of safety issues. Explain that signs such as "Rest Room" are for informational purposes. Also, explain that some signs, such as "Exit," can serve both informational and safety purposes, depending upon the situation. **Ask** volunteers to identify other informational signs they have seen.
  Possible responses: Dead End, Apple River Canyon State Park, Customer Service, Employees Only, Trash

continued on p. 242

Differentiated Instruction Solutions for All Learners

Strategy for Less Proficient Readers
Ask students to write a sentence telling what is happening in the picture on the *high surf* sign. Ask how many of their sentences included something about a person being tossed by a wave. Point out that carefully studying the pictures on signs can help you make sense of the words.

Enrichment for Gifted/Talented Students
Draw students' attention to some of the differences between the *High Surf* and *Strong Current* signs and the instructions below them. Point out that most signs have few words so that the whole sign can be read at a glance while the instructions are far more detailed. Also, explain that choosing the most meaningful and clear words for a sign can be challenging. Ask students to think of a sign that would be useful in your school. Have students work together to choose an image, color, and words for the sign. Ask them to use five or fewer words on the sign itself.

- Point out that, if one were spending time on a beach, it would be important to take the time to read the instructions that go with these signs. Point out that safety reminders are helpful to everyone, even people who have read or heard them before.

- **Ask** students what they should do if they are caught in a strong current.
  Answer: Try to remain calm. If possible, swim at a diagonal to the current rather than against it. If you are not able to swim out of the current, signal for help by waving one or both arms and calling for help.

- **Ask** students if they think the picture on the sign is effective enough to be able to determine the danger at a glance, or if they would need to read more to understand what the warning is about.
  Possible response: It is difficult to determine what the danger is solely from the picture, but the arrows give a sense of urgency and motion. The words make it clear that this is a warning for a dangerous situation.

BEACH SAFETY GUIDE: STRONG CURRENT SIGN

A specific warning message is stated briefly and clearly. The most important words are printed in the largest letters.

The information in the instructions is directly and simply stated.

WARNING LEVEL: *DANGEROUS* . . . a potential for *loss of life or limb* exists.

CONDITION: These are swift moving channels of water against which it is difficult to swim. Strong currents frequently accompany high surf and rapid tide changes and can be recognized as a turbulent channel of water between areas where waves are breaking.

INSTRUCTIONS: When caught in a strong current —Try to keep a level head, i.e., don't panic! Wave one or both hands in the air, and scream or call for help. Swim diagonally to the current, not against it.

OCEAN SAFETY TIPS:

- Swim in Lifeguarded Areas
- Never Swim Alone.
- Don't Dive Into Unknown Water or Into Shallow Breaking Waves.
- Ask a Lifeguard About <u>Beach and Surf Conditions</u> Before Swimming.
- If You Are Unable to Swim Out of a Strong Current, Signal for Help.
- Rely on Your Swimming Ability Rather Than a Flotation Device.
- Look For, Read and Obey All <u>Beach Safety Signs and Symbols</u>.
- If In Doubt, Just Stay Out!

242

Vocabulary Development

Vocabulary for Signs and Instructions
Point out that signs and instructions often use vocabulary that is specific to one particular setting, in this case a beach. Guide students to understand the meaning of the following words that are used in the signs and instructions:
generate: to be the cause of
current: flow in the water marked by force or strength
channel: a narrow path of water
turbulent: agitated or disturbed
flotation: act of floating

Reading: Evaluate Visual Aids

Directions: *Choose the letter of the best answer to each question.*

1. What specific danger does the first sign warn against?
   A deep water
   B sharp rocks
   C speedboats in the area
   D large, powerful waves

2. What is another way to describe "strong current"?
   A swift-moving channels of water
   B large waves along the shore
   C rocky area near a beach
   D deep water

3. If caught in a strong current, how should a person swim?
   A against the current
   B diagonally to the current
   C away from the current
   D sideways

Reading: Comprehension and Interpretation

Directions: *Write your answers on a separate piece of paper.*

4. **(a)** Describe the picture on the sign that warns about a strong current. **(b)** In what ways does the picture illustrate the instructions? **(c)** Would you recommend any changes to make the sign more effective? Explain. [Evaluating]

5. **(a)** In what ways might signs like these benefit those who do not read English? **(b)** Using these signs as examples, explain why signs are useful to society. [Applying]

6. **(a)** What other words could you use to express the message "If in doubt, don't go out"? **(b)** How does the use of rhyme add to the effectiveness of the message? **(c)** Are these words the most effective words to include at the bottom of each sign? Explain. [Evaluating]

Timed Writing: Persuasion [Connections]

Propose a safety sign to be posted in your school or neighborhood. Describe the sign and identify its purpose. Give reasons why the sign is needed. **(20 minutes)**

Reading Informational Materials: Signs and Instructions ■ 243

ASSESS

Answers

Reading: Evaluate Visual Aids

1. D
2. A
3. B
4. (a) A person is swimming, and two arrows are pointing in the opposite directions. (b) **Possible response:** The arrows try to demonstrate the swift moving channels of water found in a strong current. The picture also shows the person waving, or signaling for help. (c) **Possible response:** The picture could be revised to show more clearly that someone is having trouble in the water.
5. (a) The simple pictures suggest danger without need for words. (b) **Possible response:** Warning signs such as these can save lives.
6. (a) **Possible response:** If you are not sure that conditions are safe, do not go into the water. (b) **Possible response:** The rhyme makes it easier to remember. (c) **Possible response:** These words are an effective end to each sign because they cause the reader to think about the situation.

Timed Writing

- Read the *Timed Writing* instructions together as a group. Encourage students to first determine the purpose of the sign, then to develop the clearest method to communicate the main message.

- Since they only have ten minutes, advise students to use only one or two minutes for planning and save only one or two minutes for reviewing.

Extend the Lesson

Signs All Around Us

Ask students to watch for signs on their way home and to choose one to draw. Tell them to make sure to include the pictures and words and to either use the right colors or to label the colors. Have students bring their drawings to class. Discuss the different signs and whether or not they are helpful and easy to understand. Discuss issues that make a sign helpful and easy to understand. For example, graphics are easily interpreted, graphics relate well to the words, only a few words are used, words that are used are not super difficult words, color of sign makes sign show up well, words are big enough to easily see, words are in a color that shows up well against the background color, and sign does not have too much detail.

Planning Differentiated Instruction

Choosing Your Selection

You may use either selection to meet the lesson standards. The following guide will help you determine which of the two selections is more appropriate for your students.

Accessibility at a Glance

	The Gift of the Magi	The Interlopers
Context	Setting: New York City, early 1900s	Setting: Carpathian Mountains in central Europe, early 1900s
Language	• Time period specific vocabulary is footnoted • Short sentences	• Challenging diction • Long, complicated sentences
Concept Level	Accessible (material sacrifices for love)	Accessible (bitter family feud over land)
Literary Merit	Prize-winning author	Noted author
Lexile	910L	1230L
Other	Surprise ending	Surprise ending
Overall Rating	More accessible	More challenging

Using the Other Selection You may use the other selection for homework or independent reading to reinforce the selection skills. If you use both selections, you can build a test for both using *ExamView®* Test Bank software.

Choosing Your Resources

[L1] Special Needs Students   [L4] Advanced Students

[L2] Below-Level Students   [EL] English Learners

[L3] All Students

FT Fast Track Instruction: To move the lesson more quickly, use the strategies and activities identified with **FT**.

Reading and Vocabulary Warm-ups provide support for below level students. **A** is for students reading two grades below level; **B** is for students reading one grade below level. For Selection Tests, **A** signifies "less challenging" and **B** "more challenging." For Graphic Organizer transparencies, **A** signifies "not filled in" and **B** "filled in."

Scaffolding for Less Proficient and Advanced Students

The leveled questions on Apply the Skills pages progress in the levels of thinking required to answer them. To address the needs of your different students, you may use the (a) level questions for your less proficient students, the (b) level with your on-level and advanced students. The occasional (c) level questions are appropriate for your advanced students.

Go Online **For:** Information about Lexiles
Professional **Visit:** www.PHSchool.com
Development **Web Code:** eue-1111

Step-by-Step Teaching Guide	Pacing Guide	
PRETEACH		
• Administer Vocabulary and Reading Warm-ups as necessary.		
• Introduce the Literary Analysis Skill: Irony. **FT**	10 min.	
• Introduce the Reading Skill: Making Inferences. **FT**	10 min.	
• Prepare students to read by teaching the selection vocabulary. **FT**	10 min.	
• Build background and develop expressive vocabulary with Connecting to the Literature and Background.	10 min.	
• Engage students' interest with the motivation activity.	10 min.	
TEACH		
• Informally monitor comprehension while students read independently or in groups. **FT**	30 min.	
• Monitor students' comprehension with the Reading Check notes.	as students read	
• Reinforce vocabulary with Vocabulary Builder notes.	as students read	
• Develop students' understanding of irony with the Literary Analysis annotations. **FT**	5 min.	
• Develop students' ability to make inferences with the Reading Skill annotations. **FT**	10 min.	
ASSESS /EXTEND		
• Assess students' comprehension and mastery of the Reading Skill and Literary Analysis by having them answer the Apply the Skills questions. **FT**	35 min.	
• Have students complete the Vocabulary Builder activities. **FT**	5 min.	
• Apply students' ability to write a news story with the Writing activity. **FT**	30–45 min or homework	
• Extend students' listening and speaking and research and technology skills with one or both of the Extend Your Learning activities.	15–30 min. or homework	
• Have students complete the Vocabulary Skill and Grammar Lesson.	5 min.	
• Monitor students' progress with the Assessment Practice.	20–40 min.	
• Administer **Selection Test A** or **Selection Test B. FT**	15 min.	

Resources

PRINT

PRINT

Reader's Notebook [L2]

Reader's Notebook: Adapted Version [L1]

Reader's Notebook: English Learner's Version [EL]

TECHNOLOGY

Listening to Literature Audio CDs [L2, EL]

Reader's Notebook: Adapted Version Audio CD [L1, L2]

PRINT

TECHNOLOGY

Go Online: Research [L3]

Go Online: Self-test [L3]

ExamView® **Test Bank [L3]**

Meeting Your Standards

Students will

1. **analyze and respond to literary elements.**
   - Literary Analysis: Irony

2. **read, comprehend, and analyze short stories.**
   - Reading Skill: Making Inferences
   - Reading Strategy: Using your own prior knowledge and experience to make inferences
   - Reading Check questions
   - Apply the Skills questions
   - Assessment Practice

3. **develop vocabulary.**
   - Vocabulary Builder
   - The Latin roots -spec-, -mot-, and the prefix circum-

4. **apply grammar skills.**
   - Irregular Verbs

5. **develop writing proficiency.**
   - Work in Progress: Short Story
   - News Story

6. **extend learning.**
   - Listening and Speaking: Debate
   - Research and Technology: Plan for an illustrated report

Block Scheduling: Use one 90-minute class period to preteach the skills and have students read the selection. Use a second 90-minute class period to assess students' mastery of skills, extend their learning, and monitor their progress.

Homework Suggestions
Following are possibilities for homework assignments.

- Support pages from *Unit 2 Resources*:
  - **Literary Analysis**
  - **Reading Skill**
  - **Build Vocabulary**
  - **Enrichment**

- An Extend Your Learning project and the Writing assignment for your chosen selection may be completed over several days.

PRENTICE HALL
Teacher EXPRESS™
Plan · Teach · Assess Use this complete suite of powerful teaching tools to make lesson planning and testing quicker and easier.

PRENTICE HALL
Student EXPRESS™
Learn · Study · Succeed Use the Interactive Textbook (online and on CD-ROM) to make selections and activities come alive with audio and video support and interactive questions.

❶ Literary Analysis
Irony

- Discuss with students the following examples of ironic situations:
  —A great detective fails to see a clue that is right under his nose.
  —The weakest and most frightened person saves the day in a disaster movie.

- Explain that *situational irony* occurs when an outcome is the opposite of what a character or reader expects. For example, in "The Gift of the Magi," and "The Interlopers" the outcomes are not what the main characters think will happen.

- Tell students that a *surprise ending* is a literary device that creates irony suddenly. A good reader can remember (or return to the text and find) the clues that make the surprise ending believable.

❷ Reading Skill
Making Inferences

- Point out to students that inferences are based on details that an author provides and that the reader interprets based on his or her own knowledge and experiences. In other words, both the author and the reader contribute to the process. Making inferences is one of the most common ways in which readers participate in the stories they read.

- Explain to students how to use the graphic organizer on p. 244. Emphasize that an inference is always based on a detail—an action, a description, a thought, an omission, even a single word. Point out that the element of knowledge or experience that the reader contributes does not need to be complex, obscure, or excessively personal. It is usually common knowledge of ordinary life experiences.

- Give students a copy of **Reading Skill Graphic Organizer A** (*Graphic Organizer Transparencies,* p. 50). Have them fill in the graphic organizer to make inferences as they read the assigned selection.

Build Skills *The Gift of the Magi • The Interlopers*

Practice these skills with either "The Gift of the Magi" (p. 246) or "The Interlopers" (p. 255).

❶ Literary Analysis

Irony is a difference or a contradiction between appearance and reality or between what is expected and what actually happens.

- In **situational irony**, something happens in the story that contradicts the expectations of a character or a reader. For example, if a runner trains hard for a race, she should run well in it. However, if she trains so hard that she oversleeps and misses the race, that situation is ironic.

- A **surprise ending** often helps to create situational irony through a turn of events that takes a reader by surprise. To make a surprise ending believable, an author builds clues into the story that make the ending logical.

Irony and a surprise ending help convey the story's theme, or message.

❷ Reading Skill

An **inference** is a logical assumption that you make based on details in a text. In addition to what the author tells you, you can also **use your own prior knowledge and experience** to make inferences.

- As you read, watch movies and plays, and observe the world every day, you gather knowledge and experiences.

- When you read something new, look for ways in which the characters and situations resemble ones you have seen before.

- Then, apply that knowledge and experience to make inferences.

Use a chart like the one shown to record your inferences.

Detail
The king yawns when he is told that his people are starving.

↓

My Experience
The best leaders are those who show concern for their people.

↓

Inference
The author wants me to believe that the king is a bad leader.

Vocabulary Builder

The Gift of the Magi

- **instigates** (in´ stə gāts´) *v.* urges on; stirs up (p. 247) *When he is not watched carefully, he instigates trouble.*

- **depreciate** (dē prē´ shē āt´) *v.* reduce in value (p. 248) *Items that do not depreciate are good investments.*

- **discreet** (di skrēt´) *adj.* careful about what one says or does (p. 250) *Being discreet is a good way to avoid hurting people's feelings.*

The Interlopers

- **precipitous** (prē sip´ ə təs) *adj.* steep; sheer (p. 256) *At the edge of the cliff, you will face a precipitous drop.*

- **condolences** (kən dō´ lən səz) *n.* expressions of sympathy with another in grief (p. 258) *The mourners shared their condolences.*

- **languor** (laŋ´ gər) *n.* lack of vigor; weakness (p. 260) *After two days without rest, languor overcame them.*

244 ■ Short Stories

Vocabulary Development

Vocabulary Knowledge Rating
Create a **Vocabulary Knowledge Rating Chart** for the selection you will teach from this set. Include the selection vocabulary from this page and the additional words students are asked to use at the end of Connecting to the Literature. These words will increase students' expressive vocabulary.

Give students a copy of the chart with the words on it. Introduce the words by reading them aloud and having students mark their rating in the Before Reading column. Urge them to be alert to these words as they read and discuss the selection because they will rate their knowledge of the words again after they finish.

If you wish, you may tally how many students know (or think they know) a word to gauge how much instruction you need to provide. As students read, point out the words and their context.

Build Understanding •

❸

alue of Money In a story written years ago, prices may seem unrealistically low. The reason is inflation—the steady increase in the prices of most things over time. In this story, written around 1905, $32 is roughly one month's rent for Della and Jim. For most people today, $32 would not even cover one week's rent.

❹ Connecting to the Literature

Reading/Writing Connection Even with unexpected dollar amounts in "The Gift of the Magi," most readers can easily understand the issue at the heart of the story: How can you express love through a gift when funds are tight? Write a few sentences to suggest an answer. Use at least three of these words: *adjust, embody, assist, emphasize.*

READ MORE

by O. Henry
"The Last Leaf"
"The Princess and the Puma"

Meet the Author

O. **Henry** (1862–1910)

Born in North Carolina, William Sydney Porter, better known as O. Henry, dropped out of school at sixteen to work in his uncle's drugstore. In 1882, he left to seek his fortune in Texas. He worked on a ranch, then at a bank, and eventually started writing sketches. He became a reporter, columnist, and cartoonist for the *Houston Post.*

Writing Stories in Prison In 1896, Porter was jailed for his involvement in a bank scandal. While in prison, he began writing stories. When he was released, Porter changed his name to O. Henry, moved to New York City, and developed into one of America's most celebrated writers of short fiction.

Fast Facts

► O. Henry's gift for storytelling was nurtured by his sister Evelina, who developed a game in which she would start a story and her brother would finish it.

► Since 1919, the O. Henry Awards have been given to the best short stories written each year.

Go Online
Author Link

For: More about the author
Visit: www.PHSchool.com
Web Code: epe-9204

The Gift of the Magi ■ 245

❸ Background
The Value of Money

Explain to students that in order to convert the sums of money in this story to present-day prices, they will have to multiply them by anywhere from 10 to 100. The story is set in New York City in about 1905. In that time and place, a newspaper cost from 1¢ to 3¢, and a ride on the brand-new subway cost 5¢. In 2005, the daily *New York Times* cost $1, and the subway fare was $2. The monthly rent of many one-room Manhattan apartments was close to 50 times more than the $32 Jim and Della pay.

❹ Connecting to the Literature

• Model use of the expressive vocabulary students are asked to use with these examples:

1. You should *adjust* your expectations.

2. Search for gifts that *embody* all the love you feel.

3. Look for someone in the store to *assist* you.

4. Your gift should *emphasize* what is truly important to your loved one.

• Help students further develop their expressive vocabulary by providing these words: *intentions, self-sacrifice,* and *superficial.* Encourage students to use these words as they discuss the selection.

Go Online
Author Link For additional information about O. Henry, have students type in the Web Code and then select *O. Henry.*

Differentiated
Instruction **Solutions for All Learners**

Support for Below-Level Students [L1, L2]	Support for English Learners [EL]
Unit 2 Resources	**Unit 2 Resources**
Vocabulary Warm-up Word Lists, p. 52	**Vocabulary Warm-up Word Lists**, p. 52
Vocabulary Warm-up Practice, p. 53	**Vocabulary Warm-up Practice**, p. 53
Reading Warm-up A, p. 54	**Reading Warm-up A**, p. 54
Selection Test A, pp. 62–64	**Reader's Notebook: English Learner's Version**
Graphic Organizer Transparencies	**Listening to Literature Audio CD**
Reading Skill Graphic Organizer, Transparency B, p. 51	
Reader's Notebook: Adapted Version	
Adapted Reader's Notebook Audio CD	

❶ Motivation

Prepare an Anticipation Guide (*General Resources,* pp. 8–10) with the following statements:

- People who love each other won't make huge sacrifices.
- People with limited means can't buy anything to express their love.
- The love that inspires someone to buy a gift is more important than the gift itself.
- Modern society puts too much emphasis on giving expensive gifts.

Give students a copy of the prepared Anticipation Guide and have students mark their responses in the Me column. Have students discuss the statements in pairs or groups and mark the Guides again in the Group column.

Concept Connector ➡

Students will return to the Anticipation Guide after completing *"The Gift of the Magi."*

Learning Modalities
Visual/Spatial Learners

Use the photograph of the watch and fob chain on this page to help students grasp the function and value of these items. The watch chain or fob is not simply an attaching device but also a significant fashion accessory for a man of Jim's time. Ask students to think of present-day personal accessories that might be as cherished by a modern young man as the chain was prized by Jim.

❷ About the Selection

"The Gift of the Magi," is a story of self-sacrificing love—and its ironic consequences. On Christmas Eve, Della Young has only $1.87 to spend on a gift for her beloved husband Jim. Impulsively, Della decides to sell her beautiful knee-length brown hair. She buys Jim a platinum chain for his prized gold watch, curls and combs her short hair, and nervously waits for Jim to come home. When he sees her hair, he stops dead in the doorway, then slowly gives her his Christmas gift—a set of ornamental combs for her hair. When she gives him his watch chain, he confesses that he sold the watch to pay for the combs.

The title alludes to the wise men of Magi who brought gifts to the infant Jesus.

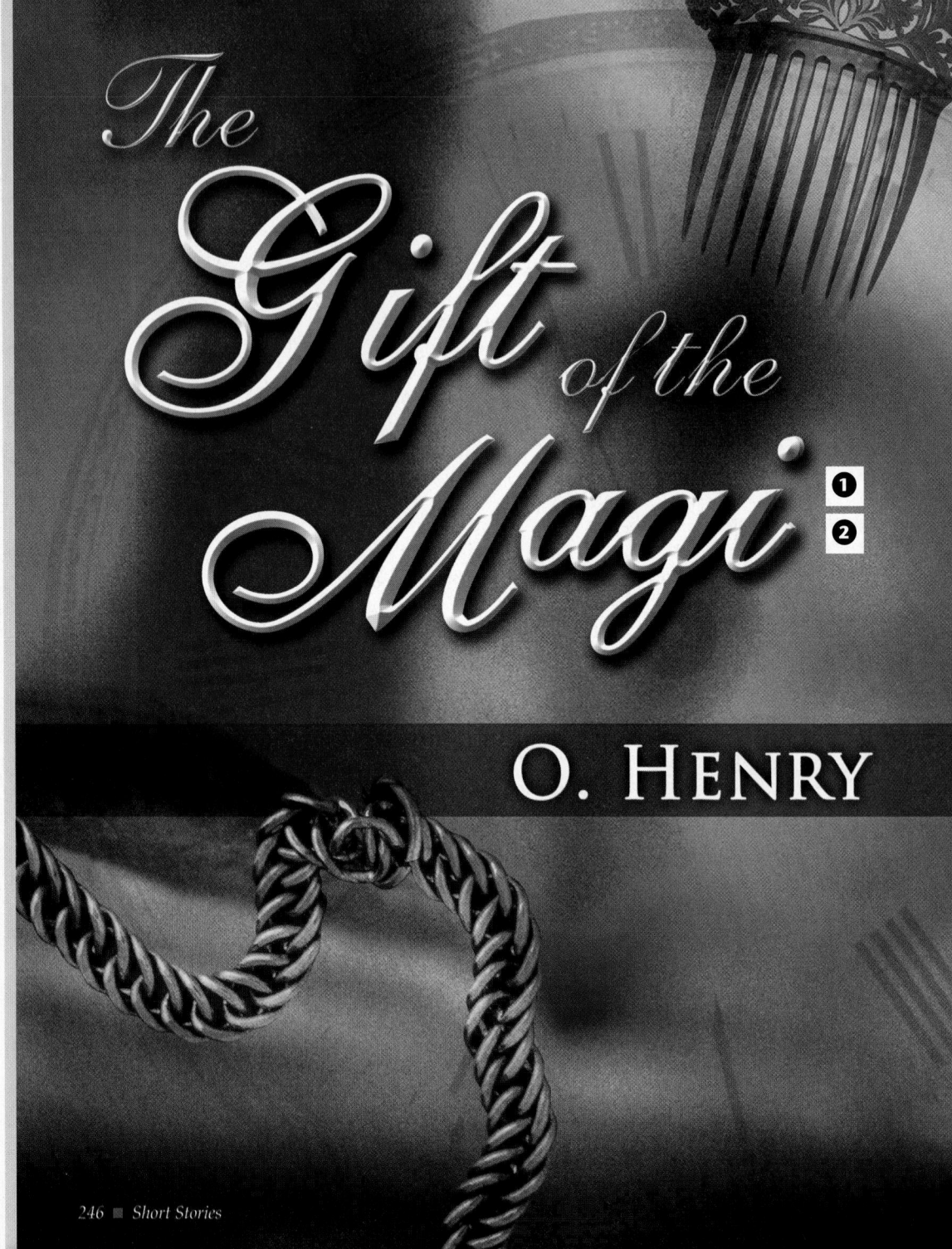

The Gift of the Magi ❶❷

O. HENRY

246 ■ Short Stories

Vocabulary Development

Expressive Vocabulary

Ask students to think about what city life in that time period was like for a couple like Jim and Della. What would their neighborhood have looked like? What would they have had in their apartment? What did they eat? What means of transportation did they use? What modern conveniences and appliances did they *not* have? As students discuss early twentieth-century life, encourage them to use the expressive vocabulary presented earlier. You might encourage them with sentence starters like these:

1. It would have been difficult to *adjust* to life in a crowded city because . . .
2. The worn carpet and sofa *embody* their financial situation because . . .
3. Modern appliances were not available to *assist* the couple in . . .
4. The cold and the snow *emphasize* the city's atmosphere of . . .

One dollar and eighty-seven cents. That was all. And sixty cents of it was in pennies. Pennies saved one and two at a time by bulldozing the grocer and the vegetable man and the butcher until one's cheeks burned with the silent imputation of parsimony[1] that such close dealing implied. Three times Della counted it. One dollar and eighty-seven cents. And the next day would be Christmas.

There was clearly nothing to do but flop down on the shabby little couch and howl. So Della did it. Which <u>instigates</u> the moral reflection that life is made up of sobs, sniffles, and smiles, with sniffles predominating.

While the mistress of the home is gradually subsiding from the first stage to the second, take a look at the home. A furnished flat at $8 per week. It did not exactly beggar description,[2] but it certainly had that word on the lookout for the mendicancy squad.[3]

In the vestibule below was a letter-box into which no letter would go, and an electric button from which no mortal finger could coax a ring. Also appertaining thereunto was a card bearing the name "Mr. James Dillingham Young."

The "Dillingham" had been flung to the breeze during a former period of prosperity when its possessor was being paid $30 per week. Now, when the income was shrunk to $20, the letters of "Dillingham" looked blurred, as though they were thinking seriously of contracting to a modest and unassuming D. But whenever Mr. James Dillingham Young came home and reached his flat above he was called "Jim" and greatly hugged by Mrs. James Dillingham Young, already introduced to you as Della. Which is all very good.

Della finished her cry and attended to her cheeks with the powder rag. She stood by the window and looked out dully at a gray cat walking a gray fence in a gray backyard. Tomorrow would be Christmas Day, and she had only $1.87 with which to buy Jim a present. She had been saving every penny she could for months, with this result. Twenty dollars a week doesn't go far. Expenses had been greater than she had calculated. They always are. Only $1.87 to buy a present for Jim. Her Jim. Many a happy hour she had spent planning for something nice for him. Something fine and rare and sterling—something just a little bit near to being worthy of the honor of being owned by Jim.

There was a pier glass between the windows of the room. Perhaps you have seen a pier glass in an $8 flat. A very thin and very agile person may, by observing his reflection in a rapid

---

1. **imputation** (im´ pyōō tā´ shən) **of parsimony** (pär´ sə mō´ nē) accusation of stinginess.
2. **beggar description** make description seem inadequate or useless.
3. **it certainly . . . mendicancy** (men´ di kən´ sē) **squad** it would have been noticed by the police who arrested beggars.

Vocabulary Builder
instigates (in´ stə gāts´) *v.* urges on; stirs up

Reading Skill
Inferences Based on this paragraph, what can you infer about Jim and the kind of person he would like to be?

4 ✓ Reading Check

How much money does Della have to buy a present for Jim?

---

3 Reading Skill
Inferences

- **Ask** students what they can infer about Della from her actions thus far in the story.
  Answer: Della is very frugal and deeply concerned about the little money she has. She is humiliated by the way she must deal with tradespeople, and she is worried about not having enough money to buy her husband a decent Christmas gift.

- **Ask** students what they think the detail of the mailbox card reveals about Jim.
  Answer: The name on the mailbox card sounds much more elegant than Jim's actual financial circumstances would confirm.

- **Ask** students the Reading Skill question: Based on this paragraph, what can you infer about Jim and the kind of person he would like to be?
  Answer: Jim has had high hopes for a career, but now he is facing reduced income and difficulties making ends meet. He would like to be much more financially successful. Nevertheless, he loves his wife and she him.

4 Reading Check
Answer: She has $1.87.

Differentiated
Instruction   Solutions for All Learners

Strategy for Less Proficient Readers
To give students a context for the story and to model how to use their own knowledge and experiences to make inferences, show them **Reading Skill Graphic Organizer B** (*Graphic Organizer Transparencies,* p. 51). The completed graphic organizer will give students insight into the process of inference. They can use it as a model for making inferences based on their own knowledge and experiences.

Strategy for Gifted/Talented Students
Ask students to recreate this story in a present-day setting. Challenge them to use the same characters involved in the same plot. The only difference is that students must substitute new alternatives for Della's cherished hair and Jim's treasured watch. Students might work in groups to think of possessions that might be treasured by a modern couple, and that might lead to the same ironic outcome as in O. Henry's story.

- Have students read the bracketed passage. **Ask** them to list the specific things Della does in this sequence.

   Answer: After looking at her reflection, Della turns pale and lets her long hair fall to its full length. She then ties her hair up again. She pauses a moment, cries briefly, then puts on a jacket and hat and leaves the apartment.

- Then, **ask** the Reading Skill question: Using your own prior knowledge and details from this passage, what can you infer about Della's thoughts and plans?

   Possible response: Della has thought of a way to pay for Jim's gift, an idea related in some way to her most cherished possession—her long cascade of hair. Della is distressed by the significance of her decision—she falters and cries—but she sets out to execute her plan.

▶ **Monitor Progress:** Assess students' understanding of making inferences by ensuring their answers provide insight into a character based on a specific detail.

▶ **Reteach:** If students have difficulty applying prior knowledge, start them off with the question, "Have you ever known someone who . . . ?" or "Have you ever heard of someone who . . . ?"

sequence of longitudinal strips, obtain a fairly accurate conception of his looks. Della, being slender, had mastered the art.

Suddenly she whirled from the window and stood before the glass. Her eyes were shining brilliantly, but her face had lost its color within twenty seconds. Rapidly she pulled down her hair and let it fall to its full length.

Now, there were two possessions of the James Dillingham Youngs in which they both took a mighty pride. One was Jim's gold watch that had been his father's and his grandfather's. The other was Della's hair. Had the Queen of Sheba lived in the flat across the airshaft, Della would have let her hair hang out the window some day to dry just to depreciate Her Majesty's jewels and gifts. Had King Solomon been the janitor, with all his treasures piled up in the basement, Jim would have pulled out his watch every time he passed, just to see him pluck at his beard from envy.

So now Della's beautiful hair fell about her rippling and shining like a cascade of brown waters. It reached below her knee and made itself almost a garment for her. And then she did it up again nervously and quickly. Once she faltered for a minute and stood still while a tear or two splashed on the worn red carpet.

On went her old brown jacket; on went her old brown hat. With a whirl of skirts and with the brilliant sparkle still in her eyes, she fluttered out the door and down the stairs to the street.

Where she stopped the sign read: "Mme. Sofronie. Hair Goods of All Kinds." One flight up Della ran, and collected herself, panting. Madame, large, too white, chilly, hardly looked the "Sofronie."

"Will you buy my hair?" asked Della.

"I buy hair," said Madame. "Take yer hat off and let's have a sight at the looks of it."

Down rippled the brown cascade.

"Twenty dollars," said Madame, lifting the mass with a practiced hand.

"Give it to me quick," said Della.

Oh, and the next two hours tripped by on rosy wings. Forget the hashed metaphor. She was ransacking the stores for Jim's present.

She found it at last. It surely had been made for Jim and no one else. There was no other like it in any of the stores, and she had turned all of them inside out. It was a platinum fob chain simple and chaste in design, properly proclaiming its value by substance alone and not by meretricious ornamentation—as all good things should do. It was even worthy of The Watch. As soon as she saw it she knew that it must be Jim's. It was like him. Quietness and value—the description applied to both. Twenty-one dollars they took from her for it, and she hurried home with the 87 cents. With that

Vocabulary Builder
depreciate (dē prē′ shē āt′) *v.* to reduce in value

Reading Skill
Inferences Using your own prior knowledge and details from this passage, what can you infer about Della's thoughts and plans?

Vocabulary Development

Word Analysis

- O. Henry makes a humorous exaggeration about Della's hair being able to depreciate a queen's jewels. Write the word *depreciate* on the board and point out that it is based on the Latin word for "price." The prefix *de-* here means "lower." *Depreciate* means "to lower or lessen price or value."

- Tell students that the prefix *de-* has other meanings: "away; off"; "remove"; "lower; down"; and "do the opposite of." Generally, the prefix has a "negative" effect, lowering or undoing the meaning of the root.

- **Ask** students to think of other words that have the *de-* prefix and write them on the board. Work as a class to provide brief definitions.

   Possible answers: *derail,* "to go off the track"; *depress,* "to press down"; *decentralize,* "to spread out"; *deflate,* "to remove the air from."

chain on his watch Jim might be properly anxious about the time in any company. Grand as the watch was he sometimes looked at it on the sly on account of the old leather strap that he used in place of a chain.

When Della reached home her intoxication gave way a little to prudence and reason. She got out her curling irons and lighted the gas and went to work repairing the ravages made by generosity added to love. Which is always a tremendous task, dear friends—a mammoth task.

Within forty minutes her head was covered with tiny, close-lying curls that made her look wonderfully like a truant schoolboy. She looked at her reflection in the mirror long, carefully, and critically.

"If Jim doesn't kill me," she said to herself, "before he takes a second look at me, he'll say I look like a Coney Island[4] chorus girl. But what could I do—oh! what could I do with a dollar and eighty-seven cents?"

At 7 o'clock the coffee was made and the frying-pan was on the back of the stove hot and ready to cook the chops.

Jim was never late. Della doubled the fob chain in her hand and sat on the corner of the table near the door that he always entered. Then she heard his step on the stair away down on the first flight, and she turned white for just a moment. She had a habit of saying little silent prayers about the simplest everyday things, and now she whispered: "Please God, make him think I am still pretty."

The door opened and Jim stepped in and closed it. He looked thin and very serious. Poor fellow, he was only twenty-two—and to be burdened with a family! He needed a new overcoat and he was without gloves.

Jim stopped inside the door, as immovable as a setter at the scent of quail. His eyes were fixed upon Della, and there was an

4. **Coney** (kō′ nē) **Island** beach and amusement park in Brooklyn, New York.

6 Literature in Context

Culture Connection

Watch Fob Chain A fob chain is central to the plot of "The Gift of the Magi." The word *fob* probably entered the English language from the German dialect word *fuppe,* meaning "pocket." During the nineteenth century, before the wristwatch became common, a man would carry a pocket watch that fit in a special vest pocket. To keep the watch from falling or becoming lost, it was fastened to the vest by means of a strap or chain (sometimes with an ornament, or a fob, at the end) that was attached to a pin with a locking clasp, making it secure. Sometimes, as pictured here, a chain's finely detailed metalwork elevated the piece to a work of art.

Connect to the Literature

In what ways does Della think the beautiful new fob chain will change Jim's behavior? Explain your answer.

7 ✔ Reading Check

What does Della sell for twenty dollars?

The Gift of the Magi ■ 249

249

Humanities

Hairdresser's Window, by John Sloan

John Sloan (1871–1951) was one of a group of young painters known as The Eight. Most had known one another during their student days in Paris and Philadelphia. While they worked toward fame and success, they supported themselves as magazine and newspaper illustrators. Eventually, they gravitated toward New York City.

Sloan and the rest of The Eight did not sentimentalize city life, but painted what they saw in all its liveliness, vividness, and warmth. Their frequent depictions of poor neighborhoods earned them the nickname "Ashcan School." Use these questions for discussion:

1. This painting shows New York City at the period of this story. How does it help you understand what Della's everyday life is like?
Possible response: The city is crowded. The colors are drab. There is little privacy. People stare at one another with curiosity rather than sympathy.

2. What details in the picture teach you something about the story's setting?
Possible response: The painting shows the hairstyles and styles of hats and clothing people wore, the prevalence of advertising signs, the mix of businesses in one block, and the atmosphere of a crowded city neighborhood.

9 Critical Viewing

Possible responses: Della may have felt afraid, nervous, confused, or self-conscious.

expression in them that she could not read, and it terrified her. It was not anger, nor surprise, nor disapproval, nor horror, nor any of the sentiments that she had been prepared for. He simply stared at her fixedly with that peculiar expression on his face.

Della wriggled off the table and went for him.

"Jim, darling," she cried, "don't look at me that way. I had my hair cut off and sold it because I couldn't have lived through Christmas without giving you a present. It'll grow out again—you won't mind, will you? I just had to do it. My hair grows awfully fast. Say 'Merry Christmas!' Jim, and let's be happy. You don't know what a nice—what a beautiful, nice gift I've got for you."

"You've cut off your hair?" asked Jim, laboriously, as if he had not arrived at that patent fact yet even after the hardest mental labor.

"Cut it off and sold it," said Della. "Don't you like me just as well, anyhow? I'm me without my hair, ain't I?"

Jim looked about the room curiously.

"You say your hair is gone?" he said, with an air almost of idiocy.

"You needn't look for it," said Della. "It's sold, I tell you—sold and gone, too. It's Christmas Eve, boy. Be good to me, for it went for you. Maybe the hairs of my head were numbered," she went on with a sudden serious sweetness, "but nobody could ever count my love for you. Shall I put the chops on, Jim?"

Out of his trance Jim seemed quickly to wake. He enfolded his Della. For ten seconds let us regard with <u>discreet</u> scrutiny some inconsequential object in the other direction. Eight dollars a week or a million a year—what is the difference? A mathematician or a wit would give you the wrong answer. The Magi brought valuable gifts, but that was not among them. This dark assertion will be illuminated later on.

Jim drew a package from his overcoat pocket and threw it upon the table.

9 ▼ Critical Viewing
How do you think Della felt in a street like this one as she approached Madame Sofronie's shop? **[Analyze]**

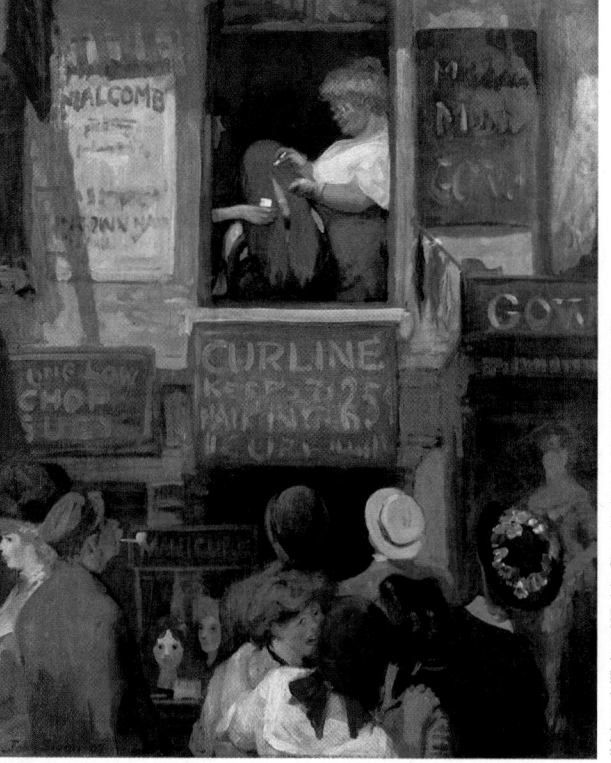

Hairdresser's Window, 1907, John Sloan, Wadsworth Atheneum, Hartford, CT

Vocabulary Builder
discreet (di skrēt´) *adj.* careful about what one says or does

Vocabulary Development

Vocabulary Knowledge Rating
When students have completed reading and discussing "The Gift of the Magi," have them take out their **Vocabulary Knowledge Rating Chart** for this selection. Read the words aloud once more and have students rate their knowledge of the words again in the After Reading column. Clarify any words that are still problematic. Have students write their own definition and example or sentence in the appropriate column. Then have students complete the **Vocabulary Builder Practice** activities on p. 253. Encourage students to use the words in further discussion and written work about this selection. Remind them that they will be accountable for these words on the Selection Test.

"Don't make any mistake, Dell," he said, "about me. I don't think there's anything in the way of a haircut or a shave or a shampoo that could make me like my girl any less. But if you'll unwrap that package you may see why you had me going a while at first."

White fingers and nimble tore at the string and paper. And then an ecstatic scream of joy; and then, alas! a quick feminine change to hysterical tears and wails, necessitating the immediate employment of all the comforting powers of the lord of the flat.

For there lay The Combs—the set of combs, side and back, that Della had worshipped for long in a Broadway window. Beautiful combs, pure tortoise shell, with jeweled rims—just the shade to wear in the beautiful vanished hair. They were expensive combs, she knew, and her heart had simply craved and yearned over them without the least hope of possession. And now, they were hers, but the tresses that should have adorned the coveted adornments were gone.

But she hugged them to her bosom, and at length she was able to look up with dim eyes and a smile and say: "My hair grows so fast, Jim!"

And then Della leaped up like a little singed cat and cried, "Oh, oh!"

Jim had not yet seen his beautiful present. She held it out to him eagerly upon her open palm. The dull precious metal seemed to flash with a reflection of her bright and ardent spirit.

"Isn't it a dandy, Jim? I hunted all over town to find it. You'll have to look at the time a hundred times a day now. Give me your watch. I want to see how it looks on it."

Instead of obeying, Jim tumbled down on the couch and put his hands under the back of his head and smiled.

"Dell," said he, "let's put our Christmas presents away and keep 'em a while. They're too nice to use just at present. I sold the watch to get the money to buy your combs. And now suppose you put the chops on."

The Magi, as you know, were wise men—wonderfully wise men—who brought gifts to the Babe in the manger. They invented the art of giving Christmas presents. Being wise, their gifts were no doubt wise ones, possibly bearing the privilege of exchange in case of duplication. And here I have lamely related to you the uneventful chronicle of two foolish children in a flat who most unwisely sacrificed for each other the greatest treasures of their house. But in a last word to the wise of these days let it be said that of all who give gifts these two were the wisest. Of all who give and receive gifts, such as they are wisest. Everywhere they are wisest. They are the magi.

Literary Analysis
Irony In what way does Jim's gift to Della create an ironic situation?

Literary Analysis
Surprise Ending Explain why the ending is a surprise to both the characters and the reader.

The Gift of the Magi ■ 251

Apply the Skills

The Gift of the Magi

Thinking About the Selection

1. **Respond:** If you were Jim or Della, how would you feel about the gift you received? Explain.
2. **(a) Recall:** What does Della do to get money for Jim's present? **(b) Infer:** What does her action suggest about her character?
3. **(a) Recall:** How does Jim react when he first sees that Della has cut her hair? **(b) Analyze:** Why does Della misunderstand Jim's reaction?
4. **Draw Conclusions:** O. Henry says of these "two foolish children" that they were "the wisest." How do you think he would define wisdom?
5. **(a) Take a Position:** Do you believe it is wise to give up your most treasured possession to buy something meaningful for a loved one? Why or why not? **(b) Discuss:** Share your ideas with a partner, and then explain how your answer has grown or changed.

Literary Analysis

6. **(a)** Identify **irony** in the story by using a chart like the one shown. In the first box, note the outcome that Jim and Della expect when they present their gifts to each other. In the second box, describe what actually happens.

7. **(a)** Which details in "The Gift of the Magi" make its **surprise ending** seem like a logical outcome of events? **(b)** Why do you think surprise endings are such a popular device in literature and in movies?

Reading Skill

8. **(a)** What **inferences** do you think O. Henry intended readers to make about the characters of Jim and Della? **(b)** Which details in the text support your inferences?
9. In what ways do your prior knowledge and experience of characters like Jim and Della help you make inferences about them? Explain.

252 ■ Short Stories

QuickReview

Story at a Glance
A young husband and wife with little money make great sacrifices to buy each other Christmas presents.

For: Self-test
Visit: www.PHSchool.com
Web Code: epa-6204

Irony: a difference or contradiction between appearance and reality

Situational irony: a story event that contradicts the expectations of a character or a reader

Surprise ending: a final plot twist that is logical but unexpected

Inference: a logical assumption a reader makes based on details in a text

Answers

1. **Possible responses:** Students would probably say they would feel deeply grateful but also perhaps a little guilty at the loss someone had suffered.
2. (a) Della sells her hair. (b) She is generous and self-sacrificing.
3. (a) Jim is stunned. (b) Della fears that Jim no longer finds her attractive.
4. **Possible response:** Wisdom is the understanding that some things, such as love, generosity, and kindness, are more important than money or coveted gifts.
5. (a) **Possible responses:** Students might say yes, because material possessions are much less important than love. (b) After discussion, some students may say that significant possessions may have more value than a possibly impermanent relationship.
6. (a) **What characters expect:** Their gifts will be perfect and much appreciated. **What actually happens:** Both of their gifts are useless. (b) This situational irony conveys the idea that life is not predictable and that gifts are not the most reliable means for expressing love. Another sample answer can be found on **Literary Analysis Graphic Organizer B, p. 54** in *Graphic Organizer Transparencies.*
7. (a) The emphasis on the appearance, the history, and the value of the watch sets up the surprise and makes Jim's selling of his watch just as believable as Della's selling of her hair. (b) **Possible responses:** Surprise endings are popular because people love surprises and because people admire clever manipulations of plot events.
8. (a) **Possible response:** O. Henry probably intended readers to infer that Jim and Della are both deeply in love, that they are willing to sacrifice greatly to express their love, and that their relationship is strong enough to survive hardships. (b) Details include the sacrifices of the watch and the hair, the concern each shows for the other's feel-

ings, and Jim's final gesture of putting his hands behind his head and smiling.

9. **Possible responses:** Students may be familiar with characters who were in love from books, televisions, or movies and understand how much these characters were willing to sacrifice for each other.

Vocabulary Builder

Practice Explain why each statement below is true or false.

1. One who *instigates* conflict might be called a "problem-solver."
2. After six years of hard use, a car will *depreciate* in value.
3. Only a *discreet* person should be trusted with a secret.

Adding Words to Your Vocabulary The word *discreet* is easy to confuse with the word *discrete,* which has a very different meaning. Use a dictionary to look up the meaning of *discrete.* Then, write three sentences that use the word correctly. (For more on using a dictionary, see p. R6.)

Writing

Write a brief **news story** about Jim and Della's experience. Your lead paragraph should introduce this human-interest story, present the basic facts, and make your reader want to read more.

- Focus on the questions *Who? What? When? Where? Why?* and *How?* Then, decide which facts you want to present in your lead.
- Read your lead paragraph to a classmate. Revise or eliminate any part that is not clear or that does not make your reader curious.
- Add a few more paragraphs to your report, including the details that tell the rest of the story.

For *Grammar, Vocabulary,* and *Assessment,* see **Build Language Skills,** pages 264–265.

Extend Your Learning

Listening and Speaking With a group of classmates, present a **debate** about the lesson of "The Gift of the Magi." Is the story's message that it is foolish to spend money on gifts instead of necessities or that sacrifice is the best expression of love?

- Listen to your opponents' arguments and respond appropriately.
- After each team speaks for the same amount of time, ask the audience to decide which group was more persuasive.

Research and Technology Prepare a **plan for an illustrated report** about life in New York or any other large American city around 1905, when "The Gift of the Magi" was written. Use library resources to find information and period illustrations. Look especially for pictures of clothing that appears different from today's styles.

Assessment Resources

The following resources can be used to assess students' knowledge and skills.

Unit 2 Resources:
    Selection Test A, pp. 62–64
    Selection Test B, pp. 65–67

Go Online
—Assessment Students may use the **Self-test** to prepare for **Selection Test A** or **Selection Test B.**

Go Online
—Research **For:** An additional research activity
Visit: www.PHSchool.com
Web Code: epd-7203
For another research activity to extend students' learning, give students this Web Code.

Vocabulary Builder
Practice

1. False, because starting a conflict is the opposite of problem solving.
2. True, because a car's value will decrease after six years.
3. True, because such a person will be careful about what he or she says.

Adding Words to Your Vocabulary

Sample responses: *Discrete* means separate and distinct, detached, disconnected, unrelated.

1. It would be wise to make a *discrete* file for that stack of personal letters.
2. Stay on the topic and ignore all those *discrete* issues.
3. Those molecules are *discrete* entities, unattached to other molecules.

Writing

- To give students guidance for writing a news story, give them **Support for Writing** for "The Gift of the Magi," p. 59, in *Unit 2 Resources.*
- To evaluate students' news stories, use the Narration: Short Story rubrics, pp. 47–48 in *General Resources.*

Six Traits Focus

✓ Ideas		Word Choice
✓ Organization		Sentence Fluency
Voice		Conventions

W/G Writing and Grammar, Gold Level
Students will find guidance on narrative writing in Chapters 4 and 5.

Build Language Skills

Go to pages 264–265 for vocabulary and grammar lessons and assessment practice.

Extend Your Learning

The **Support for Extend Your Learning** page (*Unit 2 Resources,* p. 60) provides guided note-taking opportunities to help students complete the Extend Your Learning activities.

Teaching notes for Literary Analysis, Reading Skill, and Vocabulary Builder for this selection begin on p. 244.

❸ Background
Family Feuds

The feud between the Hatfields, who lived on the West Virginia side of a stream that divides West Virginia and Kentucky, and the McCoys, who lived on the Kentucky side, has fascinated the public since the 1880s. It has passed into legend as the bloodiest disagreement among neighbors in American history.

Bad feelings had existed between the families since the Civil War, but it was a legal dispute over two hogs that led to the first shootings in 1878. Perhaps the climax of the feud came in 1888, when at least six people were killed, including one young McCoy woman and the Hatfield man convicted and executed for her murder. The two family patriarchs who began the feud lived to great old age.

❹ Connecting to the Literature

- Model use of the expressive vocabulary students are asked to use with these examples:

  1. In order to resolve a feud, it is important to first *analyze* its causes.

  2. People who are feuding need to *focus* on a peaceful solution, not on revenge.

  3. Everyone needs to *participate* in solving this long-standing problem.

  4. Each side needs to *verify* that the other side is sincere.

- Help students further develop their expressive vocabulary by providing these words: *antagonistic, continuous,* and *pacify.* Encourage students to use these words as they discuss the selection.

Go **Online**
Author Link For additional information about Saki, have students type in the Web Code, then select *S* from the alphabet, and then select *Saki.*

Short Story

Build Understanding • *The Interlopers*

❸ Background

Family Feuds A feud is a bitter, prolonged fight, typically between families or clans, that may continue for years or even generations. The brutality of a feud can make for gripping drama, as it does in "The Interlopers."

❹ Connecting to the Literature

Reading/Writing Connection All people argue from time to time, but most disagreements do not last for a lifetime, as they do in "The Interlopers." Make a list of the possible ways in which a long-standing feud can be resolved. Use at least three of the following words: *analyze, focus, participate, verify.*

Review

For **Literary Analysis, Reading Skill,** and **Vocabulary Builder,** see page 244.

READ MORE

by Saki
"The Open Window"
"Sredni Vashtar"

Meet the Author

Saki (1870–1916)

Saki is the pen name of the British writer H. H. Munro. Munro was born in Burma and sent at age two to live in England. As a young adult, he returned to Burma to serve in the police force. However, poor health forced him to return to England, where he began work as a journalist.

Talent and Tragedy In 1904, Munro published a collection of short stories entitled *Reginald.* He went on to write several more collections of stories and two novels. The abrupt ending of Saki's own life was as shocking as one of his plot twists: When World War I broke out, he enlisted in the British army and was killed fighting in France.

Fast Facts

▶ Munro's pen name is thought to be taken from a character in Persian poet Omar Khayyam's *The Rubaiyat.*
▶ To honor Saki, the king of England issued a scroll that reads, "Let those who come after see to it that his name is not forgotten."

For: More about the author
Visit: www.PHSchool.com
Web Code: epe-9205

254 ■ Short Stories

Differentiated Instruction Solutions for All Learners

Support for Below-Level Students [L1, L2]	Support for English Learners [EL]
Unit 2 Resources	**Unit 2 Resources**
Vocabulary Warm-up Word Lists, p. 68	Vocabulary Warm-up Word Lists, p. 68
Vocabulary Warm-up Practice, p. 69	Vocabulary Warm-up Practice, p. 69
Reading Warm-up A, p. 70	Reading Warm-up A, p. 70
Selection Test A, pp. 80–82	**Listening to Literature Audio CD**
Graphic Organizer Transparencies	
Reading Skill Graphic Organizer, Transparency B, p. 52	

THE INTERLOPERS

SAKI

1
2

In a forest of mixed growth somewhere on the eastern spurs of the Carpathians,[1] a man stood one winter night watching and listening, as though he waited for some beast of the woods to come within the range of his vision, and, later, of his rifle. But the game for whose presence he kept so keen an outlook was none that figured in the sportsman's calendar as lawful and proper for the chase: Ulrich von Gradwitz (ool' rik fôn gräd' vitz) patrolled the dark forest in quest of a human enemy.

3 ✓ **Reading Check**

Where does the story take place?

---

1. **Carpathians** (kär pā' thē ənz) mountains in central Europe.

The Interlopers ■ 255

Differentiated Instruction   Solutions for All Learners

Support for English Learners
As students read the story, have them choose several words they would like to make part of their spoken and written vocabularies. Have them practice saying the words. Then, ask them to make a flash card for each word by writing the word on one side of an index card and the meaning and a context sentence on the other.

Enrichment for Advanced Readers
As students read the story, have them consider how Saki's choice of words contributes to the mood and tone of "The Interlopers." Have them write a short paper on the topic of Saki's word choice in the "The Interlopers" in which they include examples of words and phrases from the story.

TEACH

❶ Motivation

Prepare an **Anticipation Guide** (*General Resources,* pp. 8–10) with the following statements:

- Serious arguments can begin over trivial matters.
- People who quarrel for a long time often forget why they started fighting in the first place.
- Arguments always weaken as time goes by.
- When arguing you should never give in or show weakness.

Give students a copy of the prepared Anticipation Guide and have students mark their responses in the Me column. Have students discuss the statements in pairs or groups and mark the Guides again in the Group column.

Concept Connector ➡

Students will return to the Anticipation Guide after completing "The Interlopers."

Learning Modalities
Interpersonal Learners

As students read "The Interlopers," have them identify points in the story at which the feuding families might have resolved their disagreement, as well as specific ways they might have gone about it. Ask students to invent the constructive dialogue Ulrich von Gradwitz and Georg Znaeym might have had that would have ended their feud.

❷ About the Selection

"The Interlopers" shows that a feud not only fuels feelings of hatred and bitterness, but it has the power to destroy feuding parties. The story begins at the climax of a generations-long feud, as two of the antagonists find themselves face to face in the forest. As they are about to destroy each other, a tree crashes down and traps them. During the time they are trapped, they agree to reconcile. As the story ends, however, it appears that their decision has come too late.

❸ Reading Check

Answer: The story takes place in a forest in the eastern Carpathian Mountains in central Europe.

255

• **Ask** students what the phrase "jealously guarded" suggests about Ulrich.
Answer: Ulrich is a possessive man who feels the need to ensure no one intrudes on his territory.

• **Ask** students what the words "embittered" and "detested" indicate about the two men's relationship.
Answer: The men hate each other intensely.

• **Ask** students the first Reading Skill question: What can you infer about the characters from their unwillingness to compromise?
Answer: Both men are extremely strong-willed and stubborn, each refusing to admit weakness or defeat.

❺ **Reading Skill**
Inferences

• Remind students that a feud can often be between two people as well as between two families.

• **Ask** students what the words "with none to witness" indicate about Ulrich's desire?
Answer: He hopes to be able to kill his enemy and not be publicly accused of murder or punished by the law.

• **Ask** students the second Reading Skill question: How does your knowledge of feuds help you infer the reason Ulrich hopes to meet Znaeym?
Answer: Because a family feud also generates such intense personal hatred, Ulrich hopes to kill Znaeym personally. He would thus gain the satisfaction of revenge, defend his family's honor, and hopefully avoid an involvement with the law.

The forest lands of Gradwitz were of wide extent and well stocked with game; the narrow strip of <u>precipitous</u> woodland that lay on its outskirt was not remarkable for the game it harbored or the shooting it afforded, but it was the most jealously guarded of all its owner's territorial possessions. A famous lawsuit, in the days of his grandfather, had wrested it from the illegal possession of a neighboring family of petty landowners; the dispossessed party had never acquiesced in the judgment of the Courts, and a long series of poaching affrays[2] and similar scandals had embittered the relationships between the families for three generations. The neighbor feud had grown into a personal one since Ulrich had come to be head of his family; if there was a man in the world whom he detested and wished ill to it was Georg Znaeym (gā´ ôrg znä´ im), the inheritor of the quarrel and the tireless game-snatcher and raider of the disputed border-forest. The feud might, perhaps, have died down or been compromised if the personal ill will of the two men had not stood in the way; as boys they had thirsted for one another's blood, as men each prayed that misfortune might fall on the other, and this wind-scourged winter night Ulrich had banded together his foresters to watch the dark forest, not in quest of four-footed quarry, but to keep a lookout for the prowling thieves whom he suspected of being afoot from across the land boundary. The roebuck which usually kept in the sheltered hollows during a storm wind, were running like driven things tonight, and there was movement and unrest among the creatures that were wont to sleep through the dark hours. Assuredly there was a disturbing element in the forest, and Ulrich could guess the quarter from whence it came.

He strayed away by himself from the watchers whom he had placed in ambush on the crest of the hill, and wandered far down the steep slopes amid the wild tangle of undergrowth, peering through the tree trunks and listening through the whistling and skirling of the wind and the restless beating of the branches for sight or sound of the marauders. If only on this wild night, in this dark, lone spot, he might come across Georg Znaeym, man to man, with none to witness—that was the wish that was uppermost in his thoughts. And as he stepped round the trunk of a huge beech he came face to face with the man he sought.

The two enemies stood glaring at one another for a long silent moment. Each had a rifle in his hand, each had hate in his heart and murder uppermost in his mind. The chance had come to give full play to the passions of a lifetime. But a man who has been brought up under the code of a restraining civilization cannot easily

---

2. **poaching** (pōch´ iŋ) **affrays** (ə frāz´) disputes about hunting on someone else's property.

Vocabulary Builder
precipitous (prē sip´ ə təs) *adj.* steep; sheer

Reading Skill
Inferences What can you infer about the characters from their unwillingness to compromise?

Reading Skill
Inferences How does your knowledge of feuds help you infer the reason Ulrich hopes to meet Znaeym?

Vocabulary Development

Expressive Vocabulary
Ask students to think about what nations experience when they endure centuries of conflict. What issues drive nations to try to destroy each other? Why do national conflicts endure? What kinds of solutions do peacemakers propose? As students discuss historical situations and current events, encourage them to use the expressive vocabulary presented earlier. You might encourage them with sentence starters like these:

1. When countries at odds with each other do not *analyze* their situation rationally, they become . . .
2. The national leaders need to *focus* on . . .
3. If both sides do not *participate* in the process of making peace, the result can be . . .
4. In tense peace negotiations, each side needs to *verify* that . . .

nerve himself to shoot down his neighbor in cold blood and without word spoken,
except for an offense against his hearth and
honor. And before the moment of hesitation had
given way to action a deed of Nature's own violence
overwhelmed them both. A fierce shriek of the storm
had been answered by a splitting crash over their heads,
and ere they could leap aside a mass of falling beech tree
had thundered down on them. Ulrich von Gradwitz found himself stretched on the ground, one arm numb beneath him and
the other held almost as helplessly in a tight tangle of forked
branches, while both legs were pinned beneath the fallen mass. His
heavy shooting-boots had saved his feet from being crushed to
pieces, but if his fractures were not as serious as they might have
been, at least it was evident that he could not move from his present
position till someone came to release him. The descending twigs had
slashed the skin of his face, and he had to wink away some drops of
blood from his eyelashes before he could take in a general view of
the disaster. At his side, so near that under ordinary circumstances
he could almost have touched him, lay Georg Znaeym, alive and
struggling, but obviously as helplessly pinioned down as himself. All
round them lay a thick-strewn wreckage of splintered branches and
broken twigs.

Relief at being alive and exasperation at his captive plight
brought a strange medley of pious thank-offerings and sharp curses
to Ulrich's lips. Georg, who was nearly blinded with the blood which
trickled across his eyes, stopped his struggling for a moment to listen, and then gave a short, snarling laugh.

"So you're not killed, as you ought to be, but you're caught, anyway," he cried; "caught fast. Ho, what a jest, Ulrich von Gradwitz
snared in his stolen forest. There's real justice for you!"

And he laughed again, mockingly and savagely.

"I'm caught in my own forest land," retorted Ulrich. "When my men
come to release us you will wish, perhaps, that you were in a better
plight than caught poaching on a neighbor's land, shame on you."

Georg was silent for a moment; then he answered quietly:

"Are you sure that your men will find much to release? I have
men, too, in the forest tonight, close behind me, and *they* will be
here first and do the releasing. When they drag me out from under

Literary Analysis
Irony Each character
wishes harm to the
other. What is the
irony in how the wish
is fulfilled?

 Reading Check

What happens to the
two men when the
tree falls?

The Interlopers ■ 257

- Remind students that, up to this point in their long feud, each man considers the other man to be an interloper on his land.

- **Ask** students the Literary Analysis question: How do Georg's words give a twist to the meaning of *interlopers*?
  Answer: At this point, the men consider "interlopers" anyone who would interfere with their feud, such as other neighbors or representatives of the law.

- **Ask** students how the men's new attitude toward "interlopers" indicates a change in their relationship with each other.
  Answer: Now that it is outsiders—those who might intrude upon their feud—who are the "interlopers," the men are united as they have never been before.

these branches it won't need much clumsiness on their part to roll this mass of trunk right over on the top of you. Your men will find you dead under a fallen beech tree. For form's sake I shall send my <u>condolences</u> to your family."

"It is a useful hint," said Ulrich fiercely. "My men had orders to follow in ten minutes' time, seven of which must have gone by already, and when they get me out—I will remember the hint. Only as you will have met your death poaching on my lands I don't think I can decently send any message of condolence to your family."

❽ "Good," snarled Georg, "good. We fight this quarrel out to the death, you and I and our foresters, with no cursed interlopers to come between us. Death and damnation to you, Ulrich von Gradwitz."

"The same to you, Georg Znaeym, forest-thief, game-snatcher."

Both men spoke with the bitterness of possible defeat before them, for each knew that it might be long before his men would

Vocabulary Builder
condolences (kən dō′ lən səz) *n.* expressions of sympathy with another in grief

Literary Analysis
Irony How do Georg's words give a twist to the meaning of *interlopers*?

Vocabulary Development

Word Analysis

- Ulrich remarks sneeringly that he cannot send a message of condolence to Georg's family. Write the word *condolence* on the board and point out that it is based on the Latin root *-dol-* which means "pain." The Latin word *dolere* means "to suffer."

- Ask students to think of other words with this root, and then work as a class to provide brief definitions.

Possible answers: *doldrums,* "period of stagnation or unhappy listlessness"; *doleful,* "full of sadness caused by pain"; *dolorous,* "marked by sorrow or pain."

- Have a volunteer look up in a dictionary the words that no one can define confidently.

seek him out or find him; it was a bare matter of chance which party would arrive first on the scene.

Both had now given up the useless struggle to free themselves from the mass of wood that held them down; Ulrich limited his endeavors to an effort to bring his one partially free arm near enough to his outer coat pocket to draw out his wine flask. Even when he had accomplished that operation it was long before he could manage the unscrewing of the stopper or get any of the liquid down his throat. But what a heaven-sent draft it seemed! It was an open winter, and little snow had fallen as yet, hence the captives suffered less from the cold than might have been the case at that season of the year; nevertheless, the wine was warming and reviving to the wounded man, and he looked across with something like a throb of pity to where his enemy lay, just keeping the groans of pain and weariness from crossing his lips.

10 ✓ Reading Check

What is each man's hope for rescue?

---

9 ▼ Critical Viewing What are some dangers the characters might face in a setting like this one? **[Analyze]**

The Interlopers ■ 259

9 **Critical Viewing**

Possible responses: Dangers include freezing to death, starving to death, being attacked by wild animals, and getting lost.

10 **Reading Check**

Answer: Each man hopes that his men—his foresters—will seek and find him before the other man's foresters arrive.

Differentiated
Instruction   Solutions for All Learners

Strategies for Less Proficient Readers
Display **Reading Skill Graphic Organizer A** (*Graphic Organizer Transparencies,* p. 50), and walk students through the process of applying prior knowledge and experience in order to make inferences.
• Have students identify details from the story, such as the crashing tree.
• Guide students as they apply prior knowledge or experience to each detail. For example, ask whether they have ever known someone who survived a near-fatal accident. How might such an experience change someone's

outlook on life? Have students ever read a news story in which people were drawn together by disaster? With students' input, choose an experience for the second box of the organizer.
• Tell students to form an inference based on the prior knowledge or experience. As students continue reading, tell them to look for other details that can yield useful inferences.

⑪ Reading Skill
Inferences

- **Ask** students what they can infer about someone who is silent during a time of stress or crisis.
  Possible response: Someone who is silent at such a time may be thinking about matters of great importance, reconsidering past decisions, or vowing to change.

- **Ask** students what they can infer about Ulrich from his statement beginning with "Neighbor."
  Possible response: Ulrich is experiencing a turning point in his life. His attitude toward himself and his enemy is changed from one of conflict to one of common humanity, and he realizes the foolishness of the longstanding quarrel.

- **Ask** students the Reading Skill question: What can you infer that Georg is considering during this long silence?
  Possible response: Georg may be considering that, since he is about to die, it may be a good idea to reconcile with his enemy. He may also be recognizing the time and energy wasted on the feud.

▶ **Monitor Progress:** Check that students try to use prior knowledge or experience to choose inferences founded on details in the story.

▶ **Reteach:** If necessary, remind students to ask themselves a question that begins, "Have I ever known or heard of someone who . . . ?"

⑫ Literary Analysis
Irony

- Remind students that the two men had just considered interlopers to be any outsiders who interfered in their feud.

- **Ask** students the Literary Analysis question: What is surprising about this new meaning of *interlopers*?
  Answer: Now the "interlopers" are those who might *prevent* the two men from reconciling.

- **Ask** students why this change is ironic.
  Answer: The change is ironic because it is the opposite of what the two men have always wanted and it is completely unexpected.

"Could you reach this flask if I threw it over to you?" asked Ulrich suddenly; "there is good wine in it, and one may as well be as comfortable as one can. Let us drink, even if tonight one of us dies."

"No, I can scarcely see anything; there is so much blood caked round my eyes," said Georg, "and in any case I don't drink wine with an enemy."

Ulrich was silent for a few minutes, and lay listening to the weary screeching of the wind. An idea was slowly forming and growing in his brain, an idea that gained strength every time that he looked across at the man who was fighting so grimly against pain and exhaustion. In the pain and <u>languor</u> that Ulrich himself was feeling the old fierce hatred seemed to be dying down.

⑪ "Neighbor," he said presently, "do as you please if your men come first. It was a fair compact. But as for me, I've changed my mind. If my men are the first to come you shall be the first to be helped, as though you were my guest. We have quarreled like devils all our lives over this stupid strip of forest, where the trees can't even stand upright in a breath of wind. Lying here tonight, thinking, I've come to think we've been rather fools; there are better things in life than getting the better of a boundary dispute. Neighbor, if you will help me to bury the old quarrel I—I will ask you to be my friend."

Georg Znaeym was silent for so long that Ulrich thought, perhaps, he had fainted with the pain of his injuries. Then he spoke slowly and in jerks.

"How the whole region would stare and gabble if we rode into the market square together. No one living can remember seeing a Znaeym and a von Gradwitz talking to one another in friendship. And what peace there would be among the forester folk if we ended our feud tonight. And if we choose to make peace among our people there is none other to interfere, no interlopers from outside . . . You would come and keep the Sylvester night beneath my roof, and I ⑫ would come and feast on some high day at your castle . . . I would never fire a shot on your land, save when you invited me as a guest; and you should come and shoot with me down in the marshes where the wildfowl are. In all the countryside there are none that could hinder if we willed to make peace. I never thought to have wanted to do other than hate you all my life, but I think I have changed my mind about things too, this last half-hour. And you offered me your wine flask . . . Ulrich von Gradwitz, I will be your friend."

⑬ For a space both men were silent, turning over in their minds the wonderful changes that this dramatic reconciliation would bring

260 ■ *Short Stories*

Vocabulary Builder
languor (laŋ´ gər) *n.* a lack of vigor; weakness

Reading Skill
Inferences What can you infer that Georg is considering during this long silence?

Literary Analysis
Irony What is surprising about this new meaning of *interlopers*?

Vocabulary Development

Vocabulary Knowledge Rating

When students have completed reading and discussing "The Interlopers," have them take out their **Vocabulary Knowledge Rating Chart** for this selection. Read the words aloud once more and have students rate their knowledge of the words again in the After Reading column. Clarify any words that are still problematic. Have students write their own definition and example or sentence in the appropriate column. Then have students complete the **Vocabulary Builder Practice** activities on p. 263. Encourage students to use the words in further discussion and written work about this selection. Remind them that they will be accountable for these words on the Selection Test.

260

about. In the cold, gloomy forest, with the wind tearing in fitful gusts through the naked branches and whistling round the tree trunks, they lay and waited for the help that would now bring release and succor to both parties. And each prayed a private prayer that his men might be the first to arrive, so that he might be the first to show honorable attention to the enemy that had become a friend.

Presently, as the wind dropped for a moment, Ulrich broke silence.

"Let's shout for help," he said; "in this lull our voices may carry a little way."

"They won't carry far through the trees and undergrowth," said Georg, "but we can try. Together, then."

The two raised their voices in a prolonged hunting call.

"Together again," said Ulrich a few minutes later, after listening in vain for an answering halloo.

"I heard something that time, I think," said Ulrich.

"I heard nothing but the pestilential wind," said Georg hoarsely.

There was silence again for some minutes, and then Ulrich gave a joyful cry.

"I can see figures coming through the wood. They are following in the way I came down the hillside."

Both men raised their voices in as loud a shout as they could muster.

"They hear us! They've stopped. Now they see us. They're running down the hill toward us," cried Ulrich.

"How many of them are there?" asked Georg.

"I can't see distinctly," said Ulrich; "nine or ten."

"Then they are yours," said Georg; "I had only seven out with me."

"They are making all the speed they can, brave lads," said Ulrich gladly.

"Are they your men?" asked Georg. "Are they your men?" he repeated impatiently as Ulrich did not answer.

"No," said Ulrich with a laugh, the idiotic chattering laugh of a man unstrung with hideous fear.

"Who are they?" asked Georg quickly, straining his eyes to see what the other would gladly not have seen.

"Wolves."

Literary Analysis
Irony In what way is the two men's cooperation an ironic situation?

Literary Analysis
Irony and Surprise Ending In what way does the story's surprise ending make the title ironic?

The Interlopers ■ 261

⑬ Literary Analysis
Irony

• Remind students that an ironic situation is one in which things are not what they seem to be or expectations are overturned or disappointed.

• **Ask** students what the two men are doing now that they have never done before.
Answer: The two men are each considering showing "honorable attention" to the other, cooperating, and sharing hope and joy.

• **Ask** students the first Literary Analysis question: In what way is the two men's cooperation an ironic situation?
Answer: Their cooperation is ironic because they had set out to kill each other. What they expected is the opposite of what is occurring.

⑭ Literary Analysis
Irony and Surprise Ending

• **Ask** students the second Literary Analysis question: In what way does the story's surprise ending make the title ironic?
Answer: The surprise ending conveys the irony that, even though they have reconciled with each other, unexpected interlopers—the wolves—will bring a lethal end to their plans. In a further ironic twist, it is the men's cries for help that summon their killers.

• Point out to students that part of irony is the tone, or attitude, it adds to a story.

• **Ask** students what final tone they think the author conveys with this ironic surprise ending.
Answer: The ironic ending adds a tone of sympathy for the men as well as a deep regret for all that they have lost by wasting a great deal of their lives in hatred and violence. It is now too late for them to enjoy their friendship.

Concept Connector

Anticipation Guide
Have students return to their **Anticipation Guides** and respond to the statements again in the After Reading column. They may do this individually or in their original pairs or groups. Then, lead a class discussion, probing for what students have learned that confirms or invalidates each statement. Encourage students to cite specific details, quotations, or other evidence from the text to support their responses to each statement.

Connecting to the Literature
Have students compare the lists they made before reading with their thoughts about resolving a feud. Ask them to explain whether their thoughts have changed and, if so, how.

Reading Skill Graphic Organizer
Ask students to review the graphic organizers they completed to make inferences. Show them **Reading Skill Graphic Organizer B** (*Graphic Organizer Transparencies,* p. 52) as an example. Then have students share the graphic organizers they did and the inferences they made.

Apply the Skills

The Interlopers

Thinking About the Selection

1. **Respond:** With whom did you sympathize: Ulrich, Georg, neither, or both? Why?
2. **(a) Recall:** Whose family won possession of the disputed land in the lawsuit? **(b) Interpret:** Why does Georg not consider himself a poacher?
3. **(a) Recall:** How long has the dispute between Ulrich and Georg been going on? **(b) Infer:** Which factors about the feud seem to contribute the most to Ulrich's anger at Georg?
4. **(a) Recall:** In what condition does the fallen tree leave each man? **(b) Draw Conclusions:** Why do the men decide to end their feud?
5. **(a) Evaluate:** Considering the cause of their predicament, do you think the two men deserved their fate? Why or why not? **(b) Discuss:** Share your ideas with a partner and then explain how your answer has grown or changed.

Literary Analysis

6. **(a)** Identify **irony** in the story by using a chart like the one shown. In the first box, note the outcome that Ulrich and Georg expect when they first confront each other in the forest. In the second box, describe what actually happens.

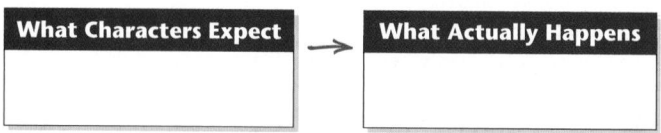

What Characters Expect		What Actually Happens

   (b) What theme or message about life does this **situational irony** convey?
7. **(a)** Which details in "The Interlopers" make its **surprise ending** seem like a logical outcome of events? **(b)** Why are surprise endings such a popular device in literature and in movies?

Reading Skill

8. **(a)** What **inferences** do you think Saki intended readers to make about the characters of Ulrich and Georg? **(b)** Which details in the text support your inferences?
9. In what ways do your prior knowledge and experience of characters like Ulrich and Georg help you to make inferences about them? Explain.

Story at a Glance
Two men in a bitter feud find themselves in a fatal struggle against nature.

Go **O**nline
—Assessment
For: Self-test
Visit: www.PHSchool.com
Web Code: epa-6205

Irony: a difference or contradiction between appearance and reality

Situational irony: a story event that contradicts the expectations of a character or a reader

Surprise ending: a final plot twist that is logical but unexpected

Inference: a logical assumption a reader makes based on details in a text

---

Answers (left column)

1. **Possible responses:** Students may sympathize with Ulrich because Georg was poaching on his land, with Georg because his family was dispossessed by the courts, with neither because they refused to compromise, or with both because of their fate.

2. (a) Ulrich's family won possession of the land. (b) Georg does not accept the court's decision.

3. (a) The feud extends back for two generations. (b) As head of his family, Ulrich deeply resents Georg as a "game-snatcher" and "raider" of his family's land.

4. (a) The tree pins and injures both men. (b) Their difficult circumstances help the men realize the futility of their dispute.

5. (a) **Possible responses:** Some students may believe that the men deserved their fate because of their stubborn hatred. (b) **Possible response:** Students may note that the story made them realize more intensely that people should resolve their differences.

6. (a) **What characters expect:** Each man expects that there will be a fight to the death and that he will be victorious. **What actually happens:** A tree falls and pins them down; they reconcile, but are discovered by wolves. (b) The situational irony conveys the idea that life isn't guaranteed and people should resolve issues with one another before it's too late. Another sample answer can be found on **Literary Analysis Graphic Organizer B,** p. 56 in *Graphic Organizer Transparencies.*

7. (a) Details include the wildness and danger of the forest and references to the "beast of the woods" and "four-footed quarry." (b) **Possible responses:** Surprise endings are popular because people love surprises.

8. (a) **Possible response:** Saki probably intended readers to infer that the men are proud and stubborn, and that their change at the end gives them a glimpse of the lives they could have led.

(b) Details include their insults, their intention to kill each other, and their vision of reconciliation.

9. **Possible responses:** Students may say that they have read stories and seen movies about people in conflict, thus understanding how fiercely people can hate each other.

Vocabulary Builder

Practice Explain why each statement below is true or false.

1. A drop of 2°F in a day is *precipitous*.
2. It is proper to express *condolences* to one who has suffered a loss.
3. A long drive can cause a feeling of *languor*.

Adding Words to Your Vocabulary The word *precipitous* is related to *precipitation*, which is often used as another term for *rain*. Use a dictionary to look up the meaning and origin of the word *precipitate*. Then, explain how the words *precipitous* and *precipitation* are related to each other. (For more on using a dictionary, see p. R6.)

Writing

Write a brief **news story** about Ulrich and Georg's experience. Your lead paragraph should make your reader want to read more.
- Focus on the questions *Who? What? When? Where? Why?* and *How?* Then, decide which of these facts to present in your lead.
- Read your lead paragraph to a classmate. Revise or eliminate any part that is not clear or that does not make your reader curious.
- Add a few more paragraphs to your report, including the details that tell the rest of the story.

For *Grammar, Vocabulary,* and *Assessment,* see **Build Language Skills,** pages 264–265.

Extend Your Learning

Listening and Speaking With a group of classmates, present a **debate** about the disputed land in "The Interlopers." Form groups to represent each man. Each group should then offer reasons to explain why its character is entitled to the land.
- Listen to your opponents' arguments and respond appropriately.
- After each team speaks for the same amount of time, ask the audience to decide which group was more persuasive.

Research and Technology The chilling ending of "The Interlopers" comes about because of the unexpected arrival of wolves. Prepare a **plan for an illustrated report** about wolves. Use library and Internet resources to find information, especially data about the interactions of wolves with people.

Apply the Skills ■ 263

Go Online **For:** An additional research activity
—Research— **Visit:** www.PHSchool.com
Web Code: epd-7204
For another research activity to extend students' learning, give students this Web Code.

Vocabulary Builder
Practice

1. False, because one degree is a very small amount.
2. True, because expressing sympathy for someone's loss is appropriate.
3. True, because a long drive can make one feel weak and listless.

Adding Words to Your Vocabulary

Sample responses: *Precipitate* means "to throw violently," "to fall as rain or snow," or "to come suddenly into some condition." Its origin is the Latin *praeceps,* which means "headlong" and is also the origin of *precipice. Precipitous* and *precipitation* are related because both are formed from the root *praeceps* and both refer to headlong falling. *Precipitous* often applies to cliffs and *precipitation* applies to rain.

Writing

- To give students guidance for writing a news story, give them **Support for Writing** for "The Interlopers," p. 75, in *Unit 2 Resources.*
- To evaluate students' news stories, use the Narration: Short Story rubrics, pp. 47–48 in *General Resources.*

Six Traits Focus

✔ Ideas		Word Choice
✔ Organization		Sentence Fluency
Voice		Conventions

WG **Writing and Grammar, Gold Level**
Students will find guidance on narrative writing in Chapters 4 and 5.

Build Language Skills

Go to pages 264–265 for vocabulary and grammar lessons and assessment practice.

Extend Your Learning

The **Support for Extend Your Learning** page (*Unit 2 Resources,* p. 76) provides guided note-taking opportunities to help students complete the Extend Your Learning activities.

Vocabulary Skill

• Introduce the word root -mot-. Ask students to brainstorm for words that contain this root. List their answers on the board.
Possible responses: *motivate, motion, motive, demote*

Answers

1. *motivation;* **meaning 1:** reason for doing something; **sentence 1:** Lee's motivation for making it to every game is to have a perfect attendance record. **relationship to root:** involves taking action; **meaning 2:** eagerness and willingness to do something; **sentence 2:** After acing her test, Elyse had even more motivation to succeed in class. **relationship to root:** involves one's attitude toward taking action

2. *motion;* **meaning 1:** the movement of a body from one place to another; **sentence 1:** The motion of the Earth makes the sun appear to rise and set. **relationship to root:** involves movement; **meaning 2:** a gesture; **sentence 2:** The baby learned the motion of waving goodbye. **relationship to root:** involves movement

3. *promote;* **meaning 1:** to raise in rank; **sentence 1:** Alice was happy to promote Andrea after her successful presentation. **relationship to root:** involves moving someone to a higher position; **meaning 2:** to make sure people know about a new product or event; **sentence 2:** Joy was excited to promote her book to a new audience. **relationship to root:** involves moving something into people's field of attention

Grammar Lesson

Point out to students that they need to learn the forms of irregular verbs by memorizing them.

Answers

1. beginning, began, have begun
2. hanging, hung, have hung
3. springing, sprang, have sprung
4. falling, fell, have fallen
5. driving, drove, have driven
6. singing, sang, have sung
7. standing, stood, have stood
8. swinging, swung, have swung
9. leading, led, have led
10. winning, won, have won

264

Build Language Skills

The Gift of the Magi • The Interlopers

Vocabulary Skill

Word Parts The **Latin root** -*mot*- means "move." The root is contained in the words *motivate,* which means "causing something to move or act," and *motive,* which means "the reason that something acts."

Practice Use a dictionary to find two meanings for each of the following words. On a chart like the one shown, write a sentence for both meanings of each word. Then, explain how each meaning is related to the idea of taking action.

motivation   motion   promote

	Meaning 1	Sentence 1	Meaning 2	Sentence 2
motor	Anything that produces motion	The car had a powerful motor.	To walk at a brisk pace	He motored around the corner.

Grammar Lesson

Irregular Verbs Unlike regular verbs, the past tense and past participle of **irregular verbs** are not formed by adding -*ed* to the present form. Instead, the past tense and past participle are formed in various ways. The past participle is always preceded by a helping verb. Look at the examples.

Present: run
Present Participle: running
Past: ran
Past Participle: (have) run

Practice Use a dictionary to help you identify present participle, past tense, and past participle for each verb. Write a sentence for each verb, using each principal part at least twice.

1. begin   4. fall   7. stand   10. won
2. hang   5. drive   8. swing
3. spring   6. sing   9. lead

 Prentice Hall Writing and Grammar Connection: Chapter 23, Section 1

264 ■ *Short Stories*

MorePractice

For more practice with verbs, see the Grammar Handbook, p. R39.

Teaching Resources

The following resources can be used to enrich or extend the instruction for Build Language Skills.

Unit 2 Resources
  Build Language Skills: Vocabulary Skill: Word Roots, p. 78
  Build Grammar Skills: Irregular Verbs: p. 79

Assessment Practice

Reading Skill: Make Inferences

Directions: *Read the selection, and then answer the questions.*

The thousand injuries of Fortunato I had borne as I best could, but when he ventured upon insult I vowed revenge. You, who so well know the nature of my soul, will not suppose, however, that I gave utterance to a threat. At *length* I would be avenged; this was a point definitely settled—but the very definitiveness with which it was resolved precluded the idea of risk. I must not only punish but punish with impunity. . . .

—from "The Cask of Amontillado," by Edgar Allan Poe

1. What can you infer about the narrator's relationship with Fortunato?
   A He has known Fortunato for a long time.
   B He has just met Fortunato.
   C He is related to Fortunato.
   D He admires Fortunato's skill as a wine-taster.

2. Based on details in the passage, which word would you use to describe the narrator?
   A forgiving
   B careless
   C patient
   D naive

3. What is a reasonable inference about Fortunato?
   A He always insults others.
   B He is aware of the narrator's dislike.
   C He knows the narrator.
   D He is afraid of the narrator and his friend.

4. What prior knowledge would be most helpful in making inferences about the speaker?
   A He lived in a time that allowed dueling.
   B His culture accepted revenge for dishonor.
   C The culture revered good will.
   D He and Fortunato were from different cultures.

Timed Writing: Explanation [Connections]

Review "The Gift of the Magi" or "The Interlopers." Explain the cause-effect chain of events in one of these works and how this sequence helps convey the theme. **(30 minutes)**

Writing Workshop: *Work in Progress*

Short Story

Using the work from your writing portfolio, write a letter from your character to a best friend explaining one event. In the letter, you should describe the event in detail and explain why it is important in the character's life.

Build Language Skills ■ 265

Reading Skill: Making Inferences

1. A
2. C
3. C
4. B

Timed Writing

- Tell students that when they write an explanation, they first need to organize the chain of events and identify how each step of the chain contributes to the outcome.

- Suggest that students first list the events and note each event's significance. This will save time as they write.

- Remind students that they need to use details to show how each event is related to the next event and to the story's outcome.

- Assess students' explanations of the accuracy of the sequence of events they describe and their understanding of how each event impacts on the next event. Also, evaluate how well students support their explanations.

- Suggest that students allow five minutes for planning, twenty minutes for writing, and five minutes for reviewing and revising.

Writing Workshop

Work in Progress

Short Story

- Have students go to their portfolios and take out the steps and significant moments from the previous **Work in Progress** on p. 239.

- Remind students that this work may be used in the short story that they will write in the **Writing Workshop** at the end of Part 1.

- Have students imagine that they are their character and have experienced one of the events significant to the character's life. Remind students to write their letter in first person.

- Point out to students that they should clearly explain the event and why it is important.

- When students have finished the activity, have them save the letters in their portfolios. They will use the letters as they continue this Work in Progress.

Comparing Literary Works · Setting

❶ Setting

The **setting** of a story is the time and place in which it occurs. The time may include not only the historical period but also a specific year, season, and hour of day. Place may involve not only geographical location, but also the social, economic, and cultural environment. Cultural aspects of a story's setting may be present in a variety of ways:

- the values and beliefs the characters hold
- the details of daily life, such as the work characters do, the foods they eat, and the clothing they wear
- the types of language, such as non-English words or slang, that characters use. To build setting, a writer may include *idioms*—phrases, such as "raining cats and dogs," whose meanings differ from those of the individual words.

❷ Comparing Setting

The importance of setting varies from story to story.

- Sometimes, the setting simply provides a backdrop for the action. In such a story, the setting could change, but characters' actions and events would remain the same.
- Alternatively, the setting may shape the characters and plot of a story. For example, in a story set within a Native American culture, characters may make specific decisions and choices based on the expectations of their culture.

The stories presented here are set in very different places, but a particular culture and belief system play an important role in each one. As you read, use a chart like the one shown to identify setting details that suggest the place, time, and culture shown in each story.

Setting Details

The Man to Send Rain Clouds	Old Man of the Temple
Place:	Place:
Time:	Time:
Culture:	Culture:

Vocabulary Builder

The Man to Send Rain Clouds

- **penetrated** (pen´ i trāt´ ed) *v.* broke through (p. 272) *I pressed until the thumbtack* <u>penetrated</u> *the wall.*

- **perverse** (pər vʉrs´) *adj.* deviating from what is considered right (p. 272) *It would be* <u>perverse</u> *to go swimming on such a cold day.*

Old Man of the Temple

- **awry** (ə rī´) *adj.* not straight (p. 276) *Some bricks were* <u>awry</u>, *sticking out from the flat edge of the wall.*

- **venture** (ven´ chər) *n.* an action involving risk (p. 280) *Stealing second base was a* <u>venture</u> *that paid off.*

Meeting Your Standards

Students will

1. analyze and respond to setting in fiction.
2. compare the effect of setting in two works of fiction.
3. write a comparison of settings.

*See **Teacher Express™/Lesson View** for a detailed lesson plan for Comparing Literary Works.*

Literary Analysis

❶ Setting

- Read aloud the instruction about *setting*—the time and place in which a story occurs.

- Point out that setting is sometimes specifically described at the beginning of a story. Other times, hints about setting are woven throughout a story.

- Have students preview the story images and predict details about the setting of each story.
  Possible response: Students might predict that "The Man to Send Rain Clouds" will be set in a Native American community in the southwestern United States. They might predict that "Old Man of the Temple" will be set in a religious community in the Far East.

❷ Comparing Setting

- Remind students that the importance of setting varies from story to story. In some stories, setting plays an important role in creating a story's meaning.

- Give students a copy of **Comparing Setting Graphic Organizer A** (*Graphic Organizer Transparencies,* p. 57) Have them complete it as they read and compare the selections.

Vocabulary Development

Vocabulary Knowledge Rating

Create a **Vocabulary Knowledge Rating Chart** with the selection vocabulary and expressive vocabulary for both selections. Give students a copy. Introduce the words by reading them aloud and having students mark their rating in the Before Reading column. Urge them to be alert to these words as they read and discuss the selection because they will rate their knowledge of the words again after they finish.

If you wish, you may tally how many students know (or think they know) a word to gauge how much instruction you need to provide. As students read, point out the words and their context.

❸ Connecting to the Literature

Reading/Writing Connection In both of these stories, the authors show the modern world combining with traditional ways. Write a few sentences in which you explain the benefits and drawbacks of maintaining traditions. Use at least three of the following words in your description: *challenge, display, emphasize, enrich.*

Meet the Authors

Leslie Marmon **Silko** (b. 1948)

Storytelling has always been an important part of Leslie Marmon Silko's life. Raised on the Laguna Pueblo reservation in New Mexico, she grew up listening to tribal stories told by her great-grandmother and great aunts. She has said that the oral tradition is "a collective memory and depends upon the whole community."

The Old and the New In her stories, novels, and poems, Silko explores what life is like for Native Americans in today's world. Many of her works capture the contrast between traditional values and beliefs and elements of modern life.

R. K. **Narayan** (1906–2001)

R. K. Narayan was born in the city of Madras in southern India. He was one of nine children in a middle-class family. After briefly working as a teacher, he became a writer. In 1960, his novel *The Guide* won India's highest literary honor.

Combining Themes Within a career that spanned nearly seventy years, Narayan wrote more than fifteen novels—as well as collections of short stories and essays. His works skillfully combine Western plots and themes with Indian subject matter.

Go Online
Author Link

For: More information about the authors
Visit: www.PHSchool.com
Web Code: epe-9207

❸ Connecting to the Literature

- Model use of the expressive vocabulary students are asked to use with these examples:
  1. Keeping tradition alive can be a *challenge* in today's world.
  2. Children often *display* an interest in their family's traditions.
  3. Yet to solely *emphasize* tradition can cause younger generations to feel that their contributions aren't important.
  4. Recognizing that some traditions must change can *enrich* the lives of all involved.

- Help students further develop their expressive vocabulary by providing these words: *ritual, benefit, examine, flexible.* Encourage students to use these words as they discuss the selections.

Go Online
Author Link For additional information about Leslie Marmon Silko and R. K. Narayan, have students type in the Web Code and then select *Leslie Marmon Silko* or *R. K. Narayan.*

Assessment Resources

The following resources can be used to enrich, extend, or differentiate the instruction for Comparing Literary Works.

Unit 2 Resources, pp. 86–92

Graphic Organizer Transparencies, pp. 57–60

❶ Background

History of the Pueblos "The Man to Send Rain Clouds" explores the traditions of the Pueblo people of the southwestern United States. The Pueblos have lived in the southwestern United States for nearly 2,000 years. They first came into contact with Europeans when the Spanish arrived in the 1500s. In modern times, the Pueblos have incorporated many aspects of the industrial world into their traditional lives. There are many Pueblo peoples, including the Hopi, Zuni, and Taos, who speak differing languages yet share a common heritage.

❷ Motivation

Ask students to name movies or television shows that depict death as honorable, humorous, frightening, sad, or mythical. List students' responses on the board, and then point out the ways in which death can provoke such different responses. Tell students that the selection they are about to read describes traditions and attitudes toward death with which students may not be familiar.

Concept Connector ➡

Students will follow up on this activity after completing "The Man to Send Rain Clouds."

❸ About the Selection

In "The Man to Send Rain Clouds," the death of an elderly Native American, Teofilo, serves as a backdrop to illuminate the actions, reactions, and interactions of the living. Although characters lead their lives according to centuries-old cultural rules and beliefs, these customs have been modified by outside influences. The funeral rites for Teofilo demonstrate how combining Native American and Christian traditions can create an enriching and redefining experience.

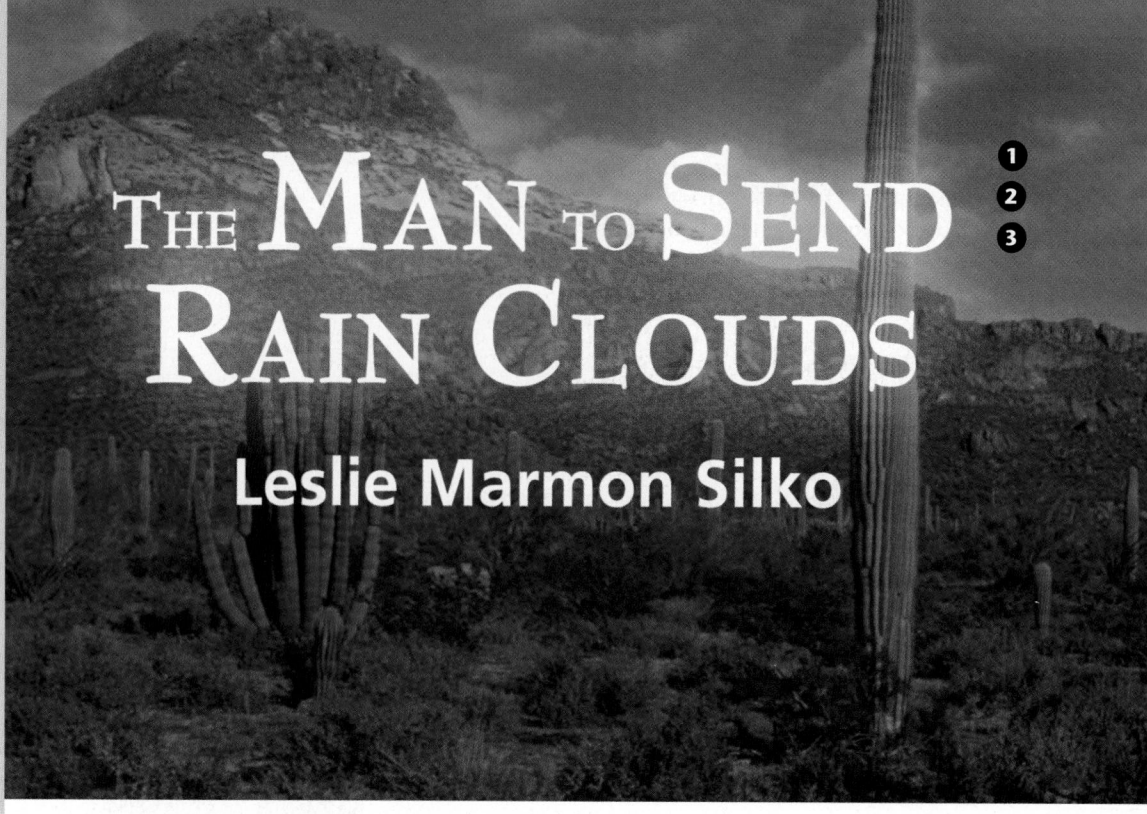

THE MAN TO SEND RAIN CLOUDS

Leslie Marmon Silko

❶
❷
❸

❹ They found him under a big cottonwood tree. His Levi jacket and pants were faded light blue so that he had been easy to find. The big cottonwood tree stood apart from a small grove of winterbare cottonwoods which grew in the wide, sandy arroyo.[1] He had been dead for a day or more, and the sheep had wandered and scattered up and down the arroyo. Leon and his brother-in-law, Ken, gathered the sheep and left them in the pen at the sheep camp before they returned to the cottonwood tree. Leon waited under the tree while Ken drove the truck through the deep sand to the edge of the arroyo. He squinted up at the sun and unzipped his jacket—it sure was hot for this time of year. But high and northwest the blue mountains were still in snow. Ken came sliding down the low, crumbling bank about fifty yards down, and he was bringing the red blanket.

❺ Before they wrapped the old man, Leon took a piece of string out of his pocket and tied a small gray feather in the old man's long

Literary Analysis
Setting What do the details about the trees, mountains, and sheep reveal about the characters' way of life?

---

1. **arroyo** (ə roī′ ō) *n.* a dry gully or hollow in the earth's surface.

268 ■ *Short Stories*

Vocabulary Development

Vocabulary Builder Reinforcement
Students will benefit from additional examples and practice with the Vocabulary Builder words. Reinforce their comprehension with "show-you-know" sentences. The first part of the sentence uses the vocabulary word in an appropriate context. The second part of the sentence—the "show-you-know" part—clarifies the first.

Give students these sentence prompts, and coach them in creating the clarification part:

1. The sharp point of the knitting needle *penetrated* the fabric of her skirt; _____.
   Sample answer: she doubted that the rip could ever be repaired.
2. Matt's obsession with snow skiing seemed *perverse* given that he lived in Hawaii; _____.
   Sample answer: water skiing would be a more appropriate interest.

white hair. Ken gave him the paint. Across the brown wrinkled forehead he drew a streak of white and along the high cheekbones he drew a strip of blue paint. He paused and watched Ken throw pinches of corn meal and pollen into the wind that fluttered the small gray feather. Then Leon painted with yellow under the old man's broad nose, and finally, when he had painted green across the chin, he smiled.

"Send us rain clouds, Grandfather." They laid the bundle in the back of the pickup and covered it with a heavy tarp before they started back to the pueblo.

They turned off the highway onto the sandy pueblo road. Not long after they passed the store and post office they saw Father Paul's car coming toward them. When he recognized their faces he slowed his car and waved for them to stop. The young priest rolled down the car window.

"Did you find old Teofilo?" he asked loudly.

Leon stopped the truck. "Good morning, Father. We were just out to the sheep camp. Everything is O.K. now."

6 ▲ **Critical Viewing**
Which physical features of the New Mexico landscape does this photograph reveal? **[Analyze]**

7 **Reading Check**
How do Leon and Ken prepare the old man's body before they move it?

The Man to Send Rain Clouds ■ 269

❹ Literary Analysis
Setting

• Remind students that the setting of a story includes where and when the action takes place. **Ask** them to identify words from the brack-eted passage that relate to setting.
Answer: Setting-related words include "cottonwood tree," "sandy arroyo," "sheep," "hot," "moun-tains," and "snow."

• **Ask** students to use these words to draw conclusions about the story's time and place.
Possible response: The place is somewhere in the Southwest or other desert environment. The time is probably late winter or early spring.

• **Ask** the students the Literary Analysis question on page 268: What do the details about the trees, mountains, and sheep reveal about the characters' way of life?
Answer: These details reveal that the characters live and work in a rural, desert environment and have important ties to nature.

❺ Critical Thinking
Make Inferences

• Read aloud the bracketed passage.

• Ask students to think about the actions that are taken when some-one in their family or community dies. Then, **ask** them why Leon and Ken might be performing these actions.
Answer: They are performing a funeral ritual of their culture.

❻ Critical Viewing

Possible response: The physical features include the dryness of the desert landscape and the desert plants, such as cacti.

❼ Reading Check

Answer: Leon and Ken tie a feather into Teofilo's hair and mark his face with streaks of paint.

❽ Literary Analysis
Setting

- Remind students that the setting might include the time of year or time of day. **Ask** them what time of day they can infer from the information in the passage.
  Answer: It is around noon (or lunchtime).

- Have students **infer** the time that Leon and Ken found Teofilo. Ask them to explain their reasoning.
  Answer: They found him early in the morning, because Louise and Teresa have lunch ready when the two men return with Teofilo's body.

❾ Literary Analysis
Setting

- Remind students that an important aspect of setting is the cultural environment in which a story takes place. Have them cite the two basic cultural elements they have been able to identify so far.
  Answer: The two cultural elements are Catholicism and the religion and culture of the Pueblo people.

- **Ask** the Literary Analysis question: Which detail here is a reminder of the Christian influence in the characters' lives?
  Answer: The church bells marking the noon hour are a reminder of the Christian influence.

- Ask students to predict how these cultural elements have affected the characters' way of life.
  Possible response: The characters' lives are probably a combination of Catholic and Pueblo beliefs and traditions.

"Thank God for that. Teofilo is a very old man. You really shouldn't allow him to stay at the sheep camp alone."

"No, he won't do that any more now."

"Well, I'm glad you understand. I hope I'll be seeing you at Mass[2] this week—we missed you last Sunday. See if you can get old Teofilo to come with you." The priest smiled and waved at them as they drove away.

❽ Louise and Teresa were waiting. The table was set for lunch, and the coffee was boiling on the black iron stove. Leon looked at Louise and then at Teresa.

"We found him under a cottonwood tree in the big arroyo near sheep camp. I guess he sat down to rest in the shade and never got up again." Leon walked toward the old man's bed. The red plaid shawl had been shaken and spread carefully over the bed, and a new brown flannel shirt and pair of stiff new Levi's were arranged neatly beside the pillow. Louise held the screen door open while Leon and Ken carried in the red blanket. He looked small and shriveled, and after they dressed him in the new shirt and pants he seemed more shrunken.

❾ It was noontime now because the church bells rang the Angelus.[3] They ate the beans with hot bread, and nobody said anything until after Teresa poured the coffee.

Ken stood up and put on his jacket. "I'll see about the gravediggers. Only the top layer of soil is frozen. I think it can be ready before dark."

Leon nodded his head and finished his coffee. After Ken had been gone for a while, the neighbors and clanspeople came quietly to embrace Teofilo's family and to leave food on the table because the gravediggers would come to eat when they were finished.

The sky in the west was full of pale yellow light. Louise stood outside with her hands in the pockets of Leon's green army jacket that was too big for her. The funeral was over, and the old men had taken their candles and medicine bags[4] and were gone. She waited until the body was laid into the pickup before she said anything to Leon. She touched his arm, and he noticed that her hands were still dusty from the corn meal that she had sprinkled around the old man. When she spoke, Leon could not hear her.

"What did you say? I didn't hear you."

"I said that I had been thinking about something."

"About what?"

---

2. **Mass** (mas) *n.* church service celebrated by Roman Catholics.
3. **Angelus** (an´ jə les) *n.* bell rung at morning, noon, and evening to announce a prayer.
4. **medicine bags** bags containing objects that were thought to have special powers.

270 ■ *Short Stories*

Literary Analysis
Setting Which detail here is a reminder of the Christian influence in the characters' lives?

Vocabulary Development

Vocabulary Builder Reinforcement
To reinforce and assess students' comprehension of Vocabulary Builder words, give them sentences using the words in which the word may or may not be used correctly. Students must tell whether the use is correct and explain their answer. Use these sentences:

1. He carefully screwed the lid onto the jar, making sure that it *penetrated*.
   Answer: No, *penetrated* is not used correctly. It means "found a way through." A lid only covers a jar; it doesn't go through it.

2. Amy's decision to spend her birthday touring cemeteries seemed *perverse*.
   Answer: Yes, *perverse* is used correctly. Most people would want to do something celebratory on their birthdays.

Henderson's painting illustrates the presence of Catholicism in a Native American community. The looming church evokes an air of mystery and secrecy. In contrast, the villagers are gathering for their feast day in a circle of warmth and light. Use the following questions for discussion:

1. How does the painting depict the relationship between the Catholic church and the community?
   Answer: The church has a strong presence in the village scene, but it is separated from the main square by trees and buildings.

2. How does this relationship compare to the church-community relationship described in the story?
   Possible response: As in the painting, a Catholic presence is evident, but not all of the people in the community seem to be strong followers of it.

⑪ Critical Viewing

Answer: Red rock formations, adobe homes, desert roads, and a Catholic church are all part of the New Mexico landscape that serves as the setting for the story.

⑫ Reading Check

Answer: The old men take their candles and medicine bags with them.

"About the priest sprinkling holy water for Grandpa. So he won't be thirsty."

Leon stared at the new moccasins that Teofilo had made for the ceremonial dances in the summer. They were nearly hidden by the red blanket. It was getting colder, and the wind pushed gray dust down the narrow pueblo road. The sun was approaching the long mesa where it disappeared during the winter. Louise stood there shivering and watching his face. Then he zipped up his jacket and opened the truck door. "I'll see if he's there."

Ken stopped the pickup at the church, and Leon got out: and then Ken drove down the hill to the graveyard where people were waiting. Leon knocked at the old carved door with its symbols of the Lamb.[5] While he waited he looked up at the twin bells from the king of Spain with the last sunlight pouring around them in their tower.

The priest opened the door and smiled when he saw who it was. "Come in! What brings you here this evening?"

⑪ ▲ **Critical Viewing**
How does the scene depicted in this painting compare to the images described in the story? **[Compare and Contrast]**

⑫ ✓ **Reading Check**

What do the old men take with them when the funeral is over?

5. **the Lamb** Jesus Christ, as the sacrificial Lamb of God.

The Man to Send Rain Clouds ■ 271

Differentiated
Instruction   Solutions for All Learners

Strategy for English Learners
Point out that the artwork can help students identify words in the story that are related to setting. Using the art on this page as a guide, have students list words from the story that relate to the image. Explain that these words help the reader use his or her imagination to picture where the story is taking place.

Strategy for Less Proficient Readers
Point out the text breaks in Silko's story, and explain that these indicate a change in time, place, or situation. Suggest that students work in pairs to identify how the setting changes at each of the text breaks. For example, the paragraph at the top of p. 270—before the first story break—takes place on the highway. Where are the characters on the other side of the story break? **Answer:** The characters are back at home.

- Have students **identify** the cultural and environmental elements of the setting as described in the bracketed passage.
Answer: The cultural setting explores the intersection of Catholic and Pueblo beliefs. The environmental setting is the dry New Mexico land.

- **Ask** the Literary Analysis question: What details of Leon's request to the priest combine Christian and Pueblo beliefs?
Answer: The priest believes that the Last Rites were necessary for Teofilo to have a Christian burial. Leon believes that all Teofilo needs from the priest is a sprinkling of holy water so that he will not be thirsty.

- **Ask** students, Which cultural element (Catholic or Pueblo) becomes dominant by the end of the passage Explain.
Possible response: The Native American beliefs become dominant, because Leon is willing to leave the priest rather than be persuaded that Teofilo should have a Catholic burial.

❹ **Literary Analysis**
Setting

- Point out to students that this story takes place over the course of a single day. **Ask** them what time of day the burial takes place and how they can infer this.
Answer: The burial takes place at dusk. The sun is falling as Leon and the priest leave the church. At the burial, the priest is "squinting at the last sunlight."

- Discuss the significance of the burial occurring as the sun sets. Explain how, in this instance, the setting might be interpreted as a metaphor for death.

The priest walked toward the kitchen, and Leon stood with his cap in his hand, playing with the earflaps and examining the living room—the brown sofa, the green armchair, and the brass lamp that hung down from the ceiling by links of chain. The priest dragged a chair out of the kitchen and offered it to Leon.

"No thank you, Father. I only came to ask you if you would bring your holy water to the graveyard."

The priest turned away from Leon and looked out the window at the patio full of shadows and the dining-room windows of the nuns' cloister[6] across the patio. The curtains were heavy, and the light from within faintly <u>penetrated</u>; it was impossible to see the nuns inside eating supper. "Why didn't you tell me he was dead? I could have brought the Last Rites[7] anyway."

Leon smiled. "It wasn't necessary, Father."

The priest stared down at his scuffed brown loafers and the worn hem of his cassock. "For a Christian burial it was necessary."

His voice was distant, and Leon thought that his blue eyes looked tired.

❸ "It's O.K. Father, we just want him to have plenty of water."

The priest sank down into the green chair and picked up a glossy missionary magazine. He turned the colored pages full of lepers and pagans[8] without looking at them.

"You know I can't do that, Leon. There should have been the Last Rites and a funeral Mass at the very least."

Leon put on his green cap and pulled the flaps down over his ears. "It's getting late, Father. I've got to go."

When Leon opened the door Father Paul stood up and said, "Wait." He left the room and came back wearing a long brown overcoat. He followed Leon out the door and across the dim churchyard to the adobe steps in front of the church. They both stooped to fit through the low adobe entrance. And when they started down the hill to the graveyard only half of the sun was visible above the mesa.

The priest approached the grave slowly, wondering how they had managed to dig into the frozen ground; and then he remembered that this was New Mexico, and saw the pile of cold loose sand beside the hole. The people stood close to each other with little clouds of steam puffing from their faces. The priest looked at them and saw a pile of jackets, gloves, and scarves in the yellow, dry tumbleweeds that grew in the graveyard. He looked at the red blanket, not sure ❹ that Teofilo was so small, wondering if it wasn't some <u>perverse</u> Indian trick—something they did in March to ensure a good harvest—wondering if maybe old Teofilo was actually at sheep camp

---

6. cloister (klɔis′ tər) *n.* place devoted to religious seclusion.
7. Last Rites religious ceremony for a dying person or for someone who has just died.
8. pagans (pā′ gənz) *n.* people who are not Christians, Muslims, or Jews.

272 ■ Short Stories

Literary Analysis
Setting What details of Leon's request to the priest combine Christian and Pueblo beliefs?

Vocabulary Builder
perverse (pər vʉrs′) *adj.* deviating from what is considered right

⑭ corraling the sheep for the night. But there he was, facing into a cold dry wind and squinting at the last sunlight, ready to bury a red wool blanket while the faces of his parishioners were in shadow with the last warmth of the sun on their backs.

His fingers were stiff, and it took him a long time to twist the lid off the holy water. Drops of water fell on the red blanket and soaked into dark icy spots. He sprinkled the grave and the water disappeared almost before it touched the dim, cold sand; it reminded him of something—he tried to remember what it was, because he thought if he could remember he might understand this. He sprinkled more water; he shook the container until it was empty, and the water fell through the light from sundown like August rain that fell while the sun was still shining, almost evaporating before it touched the wilted squash flowers.

The wind pulled at the priest's brown Franciscan robe[9] and swirled away the corn meal and pollen that had been sprinkled on the blanket. They lowered the bundle into the ground, and they didn't bother to untie the stiff pieces of new rope that were tied around the ends of the blanket. The sun was gone, and over on the **⑮** highway the eastbound lane was full of headlights. The priest walked away slowly. Leon watched him climb the hill, and when he had disappeared within the tall, thick walls, Leon turned to look up at the high blue mountains in the deep snow that reflected a faint red light from the west. He felt good because it was finished, and he was happy about the sprinkling of the holy water; now the old man could send them big thunderclouds for sure.

---

9. **Franciscan** (fran sis´ kən) **robe** robe worn by a member of the Franciscan religious order, founded in 1209 by Saint Francis of Assisi.

Literary Analysis
Setting Which details in the last paragraph reflect Native American practices and beliefs? Explain.

Thinking About the Selection

1. **Respond:** What did you find most interesting about this story?

2. **(a) Recall:** What do Leon and Ken find at the beginning of the story? **(b) Infer:** Why does Leon avoid telling Father Paul about Teofilo's death at first?

3. **(a) Infer:** Why is Father Paul upset about the burial ceremony? **(b) Infer:** What insight into the Pueblo people does Father Paul gain during the ceremony?

4. **(a) Interpret:** What feelings does Leon experience when the burial ceremony is over? **(b) Draw Conclusions:** What do Leon's thoughts after Teofilo's burial reveal about his views of death? **(c) Compare and Contrast:** What does the ending reveal about the contrasts between Pueblo and Christian beliefs?

The Man to Send Rain Clouds ■ 273

⑮ Literary Analysis
Setting

• **Ask** students to summarize the action occurring in the last paragraph of the story.
Answer: Teofilo is lowered into the ground; the priest walks away; Leon watches him climb into the hill; and Leon looks at the mountain and feels happy.

• **Ask** the Literary Analysis question: Which details in the last paragraph reflect Native American practices and beliefs? Explain.
Answer: Leon's emotions reflect the Native American attitude toward death; the natural setting reflects their closeness with the land; and Leon convincing the priest to use holy water reflects the belief that the dead man can deliver rain to the dry region.

Concept Connector

Have students return to the Motivation activity on p. 268. Discuss how the beliefs and practices surrounding death in the selection differ from those previously discussed.

ASSESS

Answers

1. Students might find the burial rituals most interesting.

2. (a) Leon and Ken find Teofilo's body. (b) Leon wants to give Teofilo a Native American burial.

3. (a) Father Paul is upset because the ceremony does not include the rites of the Catholic church. (b) He learns that the Pueblo people honor those who die and believe that the deceased can help the living.

4. (a) Leon feels glad that the funeral is over. He is also happy because he believes the use of the holy water will bring rain. (b) He believes that life continues after death. (c) **Possible response:** The story suggests that contrasting cultures do not have to clash.

273

⓰ Background

Universal Themes Most of Narayan's stories take place in the fictional town of Malgudi. While Malgudi is a distinctly southern Indian place, the tales that Narayan tells about it are universal. If the backdrop of any of Narayan's tales changed to a modern American town, the characters' struggles, plans, hopes, and dreams would still apply. It is his universal appeal to human experience that makes Narayan's writing so special.

⓱ Motivation

Point out to students that ideas about ghosts vary from culture to culture. In some cultures, ghosts are dead ancestors, angry because they have been excluded from paradise. Some are upset over unfinished work. Others return to contact relatives, friends, or enemies. Write the following passage from the selection on the board, or read it aloud:

> *"Dead! Dead!" he said. "Don't talk nonsense. How can I be dead when you see me before you now? If I am dead how can I be saying this and that?"*

Have students discuss what kind of ghost is speaking and whom he may be addressing.

Concept Connector ➡

Students will follow up on this activity after completing "Old Man of the Temple."

⓲ About the Selection

In "Old Man of the Temple," the Talkative Man describes a long-ago encounter with the ghost of an old man. The ghost has temporarily taken over the body of the Talkative Man's driver, Doss. The Talkative Man helps the ghost find its way to a permanent departure. The story explores a timeless theme: people's inability to let go of the past.

274 ■ Short Stories

Differentiated Instruction   Solutions for All Learners

Accessibility at a Glance

Context	Ghost story that alternates elements of reality and fantasy; set in India
Language	Heavy dialogue, use of historical and cultural terms
Concept Level	More challenging
Literary Merit	Noted author
Lexile	590L

Old Man of the Temple

R. K. Narayan

16
17
18

19

The Talkative Man said:

It was some years ago that this happened. I don't know if you can make anything of it. If you do, I shall be glad to hear what you have to say; but personally I don't understand it at all. It has always mystified me. Perhaps the driver was drunk; perhaps he wasn't.

I had engaged a taxi for going to Kumbum, which, as you may already know, is fifty miles from Malgudi.[1] I went there one morning and it was past nine in the evening when I finished my business and started back for the town. Doss [däs], the driver, was a young fellow of about twenty-five. He had often brought his car for me and I liked him. He was a well-behaved, obedient fellow, with a capacity to sit and wait at the wheel, which is really a rare quality in a taxi driver. He drove the car smoothly, seldom swore at passers-by, and exhibited perfect judgment, good

1. **Malgudi** (mäl gōō′ dē) fictional town about which Narayan often writes.

20 ▼ Critical Viewing
What mysterious events might occur in a temple like this? **[Speculate]**

19 Literary Analysis
Setting

- **Ask** students to identify the setting based on information in the bracketed passage.
  Answer: The setting is in the past ("some years ago"), during a taxi trip from Malgudi to Kumbum.

- Direct students' attention to the photograph on pp. 274–275. Tell them that in India, where the story is set, there are many temples similar to the one shown. Explain that Hinduism, the predominant religion of the region, provides the cultural setting of the story.

20 Critical Viewing

Possible response: Ghosts or demons might lurk inside the temple. The architecture is so exotic that almost anything might happen.

Differentiated Instruction   Solutions for All Learners

Strategy for Special Needs Students
Have a volunteer read aloud the story's opening. Point out that the phrase "some years ago" indicates that the story is set in the past. Ask students to identify and record other words that provide information about the setting. Ask students: Where does the narrator begin? What time is it? Where are the characters?

Strategy for Advanced Readers
Point out that the narrator, the Talkative Man, spends some time providing a detailed description of his driver, Doss. Ask: While the narrator does not choose to describe himself directly, does he reveal anything about himself in the first few paragraphs? What kind of person is the narrator? Ask students to make predictions about the narrator's characteristics based on context clues.

- Explain that writers often use details about setting to make their writing seem more realistic or life-like. Tell students to keep this in mind as they read the bracketed passage.

- **Ask** students the Literary Analysis question: Which details in this paragraph describe the place and the time in which the story occurs?
  Answer: It is eleven o'clock at night on a deserted village street in Koopal.

- **Ask** students to predict how the place and time will affect the events of the story.
  Possible response: Because it is dark and deserted, the story events will probably seem unsettling or frightening.

- Encourage students to think about how the mood of the story would be different if the setting were, for example, a sunny Monday afternoon on a busy city street. Tell students that writers often use setting to help set the mood of a story.

sense, and sobriety; and so I preferred him to any other driver whenever I had to go out on business.

It was about eleven when we passed the village Koopal [koo päl'], which is on the way down. It was the dark half of the month and the surrounding country was swallowed up in the night. The village **㉑** street was deserted. Everyone had gone to sleep; hardly any light was to be seen. The stars overhead sparkled brightly. Sitting in the back seat and listening to the continuous noise of the running wheels, I was half lulled into a drowse.

All of a sudden Doss swerved the car and shouted: "You old fool! Do you want to kill yourself ?"

I was shaken out of my drowse and asked: "What is the matter?"

Doss stopped the car and said, "You see that old fellow, sir. He is trying to kill himself. I can't understand what he is up to."

I looked in the direction he pointed and asked, "Which old man?"

"There, there. He is coming towards us again. As soon as I saw him open that temple door and come out I had a feeling, somehow, that I must keep an eye on him."

I took out my torch, got down, and walked about, but could see no one. There was an old temple on the roadside. It was utterly in ruins; most portions of it were mere mounds of old brick; the walls were <u>awry</u>; the doors were shut to the main doorway, and brambles and thickets grew over and covered them. It was difficult to guess with the aid of the torch alone what temple it was and to what period it belonged.

"The doors are shut and sealed and don't look as if they had been opened for centuries now," I cried.

"No, sir," Doss said coming nearer. "I saw the old man open the doors and come out. He is standing there; shall we ask him to open them again if you want to go in and see?"

I said to Doss, "Let us be going. We are wasting our time here."

We went back to the car. Doss sat in his seat, pressed the self-starter, and asked without turning his head, "Are you permitting this fellow to come with us, sir? He says he will get down at the next milestone."

"Which fellow?" I asked.

Doss indicated the space next to him.

"What is the matter with you, Doss? Have you had a drop of drink or something?"

"I have never tasted any drink in my life, sir," he said, and added, "Get down, old boy. Master says he can't take you."

"Are you talking to yourself?"

"After all, I think we needn't care for these unknown fellows on the road," he said.

276 ■ *Short Stories*

Literary Analysis
Setting Which details in this paragraph describe the place and the time in which the story occurs?

Vocabulary Builder
awry (ə rī') *adj.* not straight

Vocabulary Development

Expressive Vocabulary
As students are discussing the story's setting and characters, encourage them to use the expressive vocabulary presented earlier. Encourage them with sentence starters like these:

1. The ghost *challenges* . . .
2. The setting of the story *emphasizes* . . .

3. The ghost might *benefit* from . . .
4. The narrator approaches the temple to *examine* . . .

   Challenge students to use these words as you continue to discuss the story.

"Doss," I pleaded. "Do you feel confident you can drive? If you feel dizzy don't drive."

"Thank you, sir," said Doss. "I would rather not start the car now. I am feeling a little out of sorts." I looked at him anxiously. He closed his eyes, his breathing became heavy and noisy, and gradually his head sank.

"Doss, Doss," I cried desperately. I got down, walked to the front seat, opened the door, and shook him vigorously. He opened his eyes, assumed a hunched-up position, and rubbed his eyes with his hands, which trembled like an old man's.

"Do you feel better?" I asked.

"Better! Better! Hi! Hi!" he said in a thin, piping voice.

"What has happened to your voice? You sound like someone else," I said.

"Nothing. My voice is as good as it was. When a man is eighty he is bound to feel a few changes coming on."

"You aren't eighty, surely," I said.

"Not a day less," he said. "Is nobody going to move this vehicle? If not, there is no sense in sitting here all day. I will get down and go back to my temple."

"I don't know how to drive," I said. "And unless you do it, I don't see how it can move."

"Me!" exclaimed Doss. "These new chariots! God knows what they are drawn by, I never understand, though I could handle a pair of bullocks[2] in my time. May I ask a question?"

"Go on," I said.

"Where is everybody?"

"Who?"

"Lots of people I knew are not to be seen at all. All sorts of new fellows everywhere, and nobody seems to care. Not a soul comes near the temple. All sorts of people go about but not one who cares to stop and talk. Why doesn't the king ever come this way? He used to go this way at least once a year before."

"Which king?" I asked.

_____

2. **bullocks** (bool̄ əks) young bulls.

Critical Viewing
How does the man in this picture compare to your vision of the old man in the story? **[Compare and Contrast]**

Reading Check
How old does Doss say he is when he wakes up?

Old Man of the Temple ■ 277

Cultural Connection The word *Hinduism* comes from a term coined by ancient Greeks to describe the inhabitants of the Indus Valley. Indians did not use the word *Hindu* until the sixteenth century, and then only to identify their origin rather than their religion. Veda, or Vedic religion, are the Indian terms for what westerners call Hinduism. In modern times, however, Indians have accepted this term to designate their religion.

Hindus believe that everyone's view of the truth is affected by his or her time, place, origins, experiences, gender, age, and other factors. This view is conducive to a broad, all-embracing view of religious truth.

Connect to the Literature Point out that because of their respect for a variety of points of view, Hindus believe that the supreme religious virtue is tolerance. **Ask** students the Connect to the Literature question: Which aspects of Hinduism does Narayan include in his story?
Answer: The story suggests that death and life are intertwined through the dead man's possession of Doss. The narrator's patience with the old man and his fantastical stories reflects the Hindu belief in tolerance and reincarnation.

26 Critical Thinking
Evaluate

- Read aloud the bracketed passage, and point out to students how Krishna Battar describes the temple as an important, majestic creation.

- Read the narrator's statement that "People are becoming less godly nowadays," and explain that the narrator is comparing his cultural setting to that of Krishna Battar. The narrator claims that religion is no longer valued as it once was.

- **Ask** students to evaluate the validity of this statement based on details from the story.
Possible response: The temple of the narrator is now in ruins, which suggests that religion truly is less important than it was in Krishna Battar's time.

"Let me go, you idiot," said Doss, edging towards the door on which I was leaning. "You don't seem to know anything." He pushed me aside, and got down from the car. He stooped as if he had a big hump on his back, and hobbled along towards the temple. I followed him, hardly knowing what to do. He turned and snarled at me: "Go away, leave me alone. I have had enough of you."

"What has come over you, Doss?" I asked.

"Who is Doss, anyway? Doss, Doss, Doss. What an absurd name! Call me by my name or leave me alone. Don't follow me calling 'Doss, Doss.'"

"What is your name?" I asked.

"Krishna Battar [krish′ nə bə tar′], and if you mention my name people will know for a hundred miles around. I built a temple where there was only a cactus field before. I dug the earth, burnt every brick, and put them one upon another, all single-handed. And on the day the temple held up its tower over the surrounding country, what a crowd gathered! The king sent his chief minister . . ."

"Who was the king?"

"Where do you come from?" he asked.

"I belong to these parts certainly, but as far as I know there has been only a collector at the head of the district. I have never heard of any king."

"Hi! Hi! Hi!" he cackled, and his voice rang through the gloomy silent village. "Fancy never knowing the king! He will behead you if he hears it."

"What is his name?" I asked.

This tickled him so much that he sat down on the ground, literally unable to stand the joke any more. He laughed and coughed uncontrollably.

"I am sorry to admit," I said, "that my parents have brought me up in such utter ignorance of worldly affairs that I don't know even my king. But won't you enlighten me? What is his name?"

"Vishnu Varma [vish′ nōō vär′ mə], the emperor of emperors . . ."

I cast my mind up and down the range of my historical knowledge but there was no one by that name. Perhaps a local chief of pre-British days, I thought.

"What a king! He often visited my temple or sent his minister for the Annual Festival of the temple. But now nobody cares."

"People are becoming less godly nowadays," I said. There was silence for a moment. An idea occurred to me, I can't say why. "Listen to me," I said. "You ought not to be here any more."

278 ■ Short Stories

Culture Connection

Hinduism Hinduism is the religion of the majority of people in India, the setting for "Old Man of the Temple." Drawing from a set of beliefs that are thousands of years old, Hinduism teaches that death is a temporary stage in an endless cycle of reincarnation, or rebirths. The actions that someone performs in one life, good and bad, will determine the conditions of future rebirths.

Connect to the Literature

Which aspects of Hinduism does Narayan include in this story?

Vocabulary Development

Think-Aloud: Context
Direct students' attention to the word *snarled* at the top of this page. Using a think-aloud process, model how to use context to infer the meaning of an unknown word. Say to students:

I'm going to think aloud to show you how I would figure out the meaning of *snarled* from its context.

In this sentence, *snarled* is being used to describe the way that Doss/Krishna

Battar speaks to the narrator. We know from Doss's previous behavior that he is frustrated because he calls the narrator an idiot and pushes him. In the next few sentences, Doss seems to be enraged. He is clearly fed up with the narrator, so I think *snarled* means spoke angrily or harshly.

"What do you mean?" he asked, drawing himself up, proudly.

"Don't feel hurt; I say you shouldn't be here any more because you are dead."

"Dead! Dead!" he said. "Don't talk nonsense. How can I be dead when you see me before you now? If I am dead how can I be saying this and that?"

"I don't know all that," I said. I argued and pointed out that according to his own story he was more than five hundred years old, and didn't he know that man's longevity was only a hundred? He constantly interrupted me, but considered deeply what I said.

He said: "It is like this . . . I was coming through the jungle one night after visiting my sister in the next village. I had on me some money and gold ornaments. A gang of robbers set upon me. I gave them as good a fight as any man could, but they were too many for me. They beat me down and knifed me; they took away all that I had on me and left thinking they had killed me. But soon I got up and tried to follow them. They were gone. And I returned to the temple and have been here since . . ."

I told him, "Krishna Battar, you are dead, absolutely dead. You must try and go away from here."

"What is to happen to the temple?" he asked.

"Others will look after it."

"Where am I to go? Where am I to go?"

"Have you no one who cares for you?" I asked.

"None except my wife. I loved her very much."

"You can go to her."

"Oh, no. She died four years ago . . ."

Four years! It was very puzzling. "Do you say four years back from now?" I asked.

"Yes, four years ago from now." He was clearly without any sense of time.

So I asked, "Was she alive when you were attacked by thieves?"

"Certainly not. If she had been alive she would never have allowed me to go through the jungle after nightfall. She took very good care of me."

"See here," I said. "It is imperative you should go away from here. If she comes and calls you, will you go?"

"How can she when I tell you that she is dead?"

I thought for a moment. Presently I found myself saying, "Think of her, and only of her, for a while and see what happens. What was her name?"

"Seetha [sē′ thə], a wonderful girl . . ."

"Come on, think of her." He remained in deep thought for a while. He suddenly screamed, "Seetha is coming! Am I dreaming or what?

Literary Analysis
Setting What details of setting are revealed through the old man's story of the robbery?

Reading Check

Based on the old man's story, how old does the narrator think the old man is?

Old Man of the Temple ■ 279

㉗ Literary Analysis
Setting

• Have students look for details about Krishna Battar's setting in the bracketed passage. Point out that the descriptions of the dead man's surroundings make him seem more realistic and believable.

• **Ask** the Literary Analysis question: What details of setting are revealed through the old man's story of the robbery?
  Answer: The old man describes a jungle between two villages. Also, the robbery suggests that the social setting was dangerous and volatile.

㉘ Reading Check

Answer: The narrator calculates that the old man is more than five hundred years old.

Setting

Concept Connector

Have students return to the Motivation activity on p. 274. Ask volunteers to share their original thoughts about the ghost. Discuss what students have they learned about the ghost through the writer's use of setting.

ASSESS

Answers

1. Students may have been frightened or intrigued.

2. (a) Doss sees an old man. (b) The narrator can't see anyone.

3. (a) Doss falls heavily asleep and awakens as an old man. (b) The narrator is bewildered at first. (c) The narrator patiently asks questions and offers advice.

4. (a) The narrator suggests that the old man think about his wife. (b) The family explains the frequent knocking at the door, which shows that the narrator and Doss did not imagine the encounter with the old man. (c) Students might claim the information makes the story more effective because it adds credibility to the account.

5. Some students might try to explain what happened to the narrator. Others might simply rate the quality of his tall tale.

I will go with her . . ." He stood up, very erect; he appeared to have lost all the humps and twists he had on his body. He drew himself up, made a dash forward, and fell down in a heap.

Doss lay on the rough ground. The only sign of life in him was his faint breathing. I shook him and called him. He would not open his eyes. I walked across and knocked on the door of the first cottage. I banged on the door violently.

Someone moaned inside, "Ah, it is come!"

29 Someone else whispered, "You just cover your ears and sleep. It will knock for a while and go away." I banged on the door and shouted who I was and where I came from.

I walked back to the car and sounded the horn. Then the door opened, and a whole family crowded out with lamps. "We thought it was the usual knocking and we wouldn't have opened if you hadn't spoken."

"When was this knocking first heard?" I asked.

"We can't say," said one. "The first time I heard it was when my grandfather was living; he used to say he had even seen it once or twice. It doesn't harm anyone, as far as I know. The only thing it does is bother the bullock carts passing the temple and knock on the doors at night . . ."

I said as a <u>venture</u>, "It is unlikely you will be troubled any more."

It proved correct. When I passed that way again months later I was told that the bullocks passing the temple after dusk never shied now and no knocking on the doors was heard at nights. So I felt that the old fellow had really gone away with his good wife.

Literary Analysis
Setting What do the villagers' words reveal about the culture and belief system at work in the story?

Vocabulary Builder
venture (ven´ chər) *n.* an action involving risk

Thinking About the Selection

1. **Respond:** How would you have reacted if you were in the narrator's situation? Explain.

2. **(a) Recall:** Early in the story, what does Doss say he sees when the car swerves? **(b) Analyze:** Why does the narrator find Doss's words unbelievable?

3. **(a) Summarize:** Describe Doss's transformation. **(b) Analyze:** At first, how does the narrator react to the change? **(c) Extend:** In what ways does the narrator's reaction change?

4. **(a) Summarize:** How does the narrator finally get the ghost to go away? **(b) Connect:** What new information does the family at the end of the story provide? **(c) Support:** Do you think this information makes the story more or less effective? Explain.

5. **Evaluate:** How would you respond to the narrator's invitation to "hear what you have to say" about his story?

Vocabulary Development

Vocabulary Knowledge Rating

When students have completed reading and discussing "The Man to Send Rain Clouds" and "Old Man and the Temple," have them take out their **Vocabulary Knowledge Rating Chart.** Read the words aloud once more and have students rate their knowledge of the words again in the After Reading column. Clarify any words that are still problematic. Have students write their own definition and example or sentence in the appropriate column. Then have students complete the **Vocabulary Builder Practice** activities on p. 281. Encourage students to use the words in further discussion and written work about the selections. Remind them that they will be accountable for these words on the Selection Test.

Apply the Skills

The Man to Send Rain Clouds • Old Man of the Temple

Comparing Setting

1. **(a)** Describe the place, time, and culture of each story. **(b)** For each story, note at least two details that describe each aspect of the setting—the geographical location, the time, and the cultural environment.

2. If the setting changed, could either story take place without being totally different? Explain.

Writing to Compare Literary Works

In an essay, compare and contrast the way the setting in each story influences the characters and story events. Use the following questions and chart to get started:

- How do the characters in each story live?
- What cultural values and beliefs are present in each story?
- Does the setting itself cause or somehow affect the events that take place in each story?
- Do any of the characters in each story change their thinking or behavior because of the setting? Explain.

The Man to Send Rain Clouds	Old Man of the Temple
Effect of Setting on Characters:	Effect of Setting on Characters:

Role of Setting:	Role of Setting:

Vocabulary Builder

Practice Answer each question. Explain your answer.

1. Would you fix a group of wall hangings that are *awry*?
2. Would it be *perverse* to wear sunglasses at night?
3. Would you be certain about the outcome of a new business *venture*?
4. Would you be glad if a nail *penetrated* your bicycle tire?

QuickReview

Setting: the time and place in which a story occurs

Assessment
For: Self-test
Visit: www.PHSchool.com
Web Code: epa-6206

Assessment Resources

The following resources can be used to assess students' knowledge and skills.

Unit 2 Resources:
 Selection Test A, pp. 93–95
 Selection Test B, pp. 96–98

Go Online
Assessment Students may use the **Self-test** to prepare for **Selection Test A** or **Selection Test B.**

Comparing Setting

1. For "The Man to Send Rain Clouds," the place is New Mexico. The time is one day in early spring, from morning until dusk. The cultural setting includes both Pueblo and Catholic cultures. For "Old Man of the Temple," the place is Malgudi, a fictional town in India. The time is an unspecified day in the past, late at night. The cultural setting relates to Hinduism.

2. **Possible response:** In "The Man to Send Rain Clouds," the land and the culture of Native Americans contribute heavily to the meaning of the story. Changing the context would result in a very different story. In "Old Man of the Temple," setting is less important but still effective. The temple lends the story an air of mystery, and the Hindu culture helps explain the characters' reactions to the ghost.

Writing to Compare Literary Works

- Remind students that the two stories use setting in different ways. Have students refer to their completed graphic organizers comparing the settings in the selections.

- Have students use the bulleted questions to develop their ideas. Suggest that they also fill in the chart to help answer these questions.

Six Traits Focus

✔	Ideas		Word Choice
✔	Organization		Sentence Fluency
	Voice		Conventions

Vocabulary Builder
Sample answers:

1. Yes; crooked hangings need to be straightened.

2. Yes; most people wear them when they need to shield their eyes from the sun.

3. No; a venture involves risk, so the outcome is uncertain.

4. No; the nail would cause the tire to go flat.

281

In this Skills Review, students apply the skills taught in Part 1. The test format gives students practice in taking standardized tests. The result of this review test will help you check students' readiness for the **Benchmark Test** for Unit 2, Part 1.

Applying Reading Skills

Read the passage with the students. Guide them in identifying the clues to the answer for item 1: He confesses that he would not want his sister applying for the position. If necessary, have students review the instruction on p. 283. Then have them complete the remaining items on their own.

Applying Vocabulary Skills

Have students review the instruction on word roots on p. 199. Have students pay close attention to the meanings of the word roots.

Tips for
Test Taking

Very often students answer standardized test questions incorrectly because they do not take the time to make sure that they understand what a question is asking. Point out to students that although time is often a factor in many standardized tests, the extra seconds that they would spend carefully reading to understand what a question is asking will enable them to greatly improve their chances of selecting the correct answer.

Reading

"That is the letter which I have just received, Mr. Holmes, and my mind is made up that I will accept it. I thought, however, that before taking the final step I should like to submit the whole matter to your consideration."

"Well, Miss Hunter, if your mind is made up, that settles the question," said Holmes, smiling.

"But you would not advise me to refuse?"

"I confess that it is not the situation which I should like to see a sister of mine apply for."

—from *The Adventure of the Copper Beeches,* by Sir Arthur Conan Doyle

1. From Holmes's last reply, the reader can infer
   A that he is impolite and rude.
   B that he is politically conservative.
   C that he is polite and diplomatic.
   D that he does not approve of Miss Hunter.

2. From the conversation, the reader can infer
   A that Miss Hunter's mind is made up.
   B that Miss Hunter's mind is not really made up.
   C that Miss Hunter is asking Holmes's opinion out of habit.
   D that Miss Hunter doesn't care about Holmes's opinion.

3. The way the characters speak helps us infer that
   A the conversation is taking place in the future.
   B the conversation is taking place in the past.
   C the conversation is taking place in the present.
   D the conversation is taking place in the characters' minds.

4. Which would not be a reasonable inference based on the passage?
   A Holmes and Miss Hunter know each other fairly well.
   B Holmes and Miss Hunter have talked before.
   C Miss Hunter respects Holmes's opinion.
   D Holmes and Miss Hunter have just met.

5. From the tone of this conversation, which of the following would be a reasonable inference?
   A Miss Hunter will follow Holmes's advice.
   B Miss Hunter will not follow Holmes's advice.
   C Miss Hunter will attempt to convince Holmes to change his mind.
   D Miss Hunter will ignore Holmes's advice.

ASSESS

Answers

1. C	9. A
2. B	10. C
3. B	11. C
4. D	12. D
5. A	13. A
6. A	14. D
7. C	15. A
8. B	

Assessment Practice

Vocabulary

Directions: *Choose the word that best completes the sentence.*

6. Lisa wondered what Mary Ann's real _____ was in offering her a ride.
   A motive
   B attitude
   C opinion
   D topic

7. Examine each _____ of the story.
   A speculation
   B motivation
   C aspect
   D emotion

8. Although the candidate spoke with _____, no one believed he was sincere.
   A category
   B emotion
   C attitude
   D aspect

9. My biology homework is to study the _____ of Linnaeus's system of classification.
   A categories
   B emotions
   C attitudes
   D motives

10. The _____ that led to World War II are still debated by historians.
   A opinions
   B topics
   C circumstances
   D aspects

Directions: *Match each word with its definition.*

11. motionless
   A without direction
   B without looking ahead
   C without movement
   D without stopping

12. circulation
   A erratic motion
   B movement in a straight path
   C sporadic motion
   D movement around

13. motivity
   A the power of moving
   B the product of resting
   C the residual effect of stopping
   D the effect of being

14. spectacle
   A an interesting event
   B a moving object
   C a determined person
   D a remarkable sight

15. circumvent
   A to go around
   B to go through
   C to go back
   D to go inside

Reading and Vocabulary Skills Review ■ *283*

If students answer any of these questions incorrectly, have them review the instruction on the following pages in Part 1 before taking the **Benchmark Test**.

Question	Pages Where Instruction Is Located:
1	200, 244
2	200, 244
3	200, 244
4	200, 244
5	200, 244
6	199
7	199
8	199
9	199
10	199
11	264
12	238
13	264
14	238
15	238

Benchmark

Administer the **Benchmark Test** for Unit 2, Part 1. If the Benchmark Test reveals that some students need further work, use the Interpretation Guide to determine the appropriate reteaching page in the **Reading Kit**. You will also find the same instruction and practice available on **Success Tracker.**

Go Online
Vocabulary
For: Interactive Crossword Puzzles
Visit: www.PHSchool.com
Web Code: epj-5201
Give students this Web Code to access interactive crossword puzzles using Academic Vocabulary and Vocabulary Skill words from Part 1.

Writing Workshop

Narration: Short Story

Stories are one of the oldest and most familiar forms of literature. A traditional **short story** is a brief fictional narrative composed of plot, setting, and characters. Follow the steps outlined in this workshop to write your own short story.

Assignment Write a short story that presents characters in a specific setting engaged in a conflict that is resolved.

What to Include Your short story should feature the following elements:
- a main character who takes part in the action
- details that establish a particular time, place, and mood
- a conflict, or problem, that is introduced, developed, and resolved
- a central theme, or message about life
- error-free grammar, including correct use of verbs

To preview the criteria on which your short story may be assessed, see the rubric on page 288.

Prewriting

Choosing Your Topic
Use sentence starters. Complete the following sentence starters to search for a topic. Note any memories or ideas they inspire.
- The strangest place I ever visited is . . .
- I was shocked to discover that . . .
- One person whom I will never forget is . . .

Focus on the sentence that sparks your imagination, and jot down notes about a series of events that could form a plot.

Gathering Details
Develop characters. Use a chart like the one shown to note details that will help readers visualize your characters. Note how your characters speak, including any instances of dialect—regional speech—that will make them sound authentic.

Characters	Details
Giant	• Tall, shy • Follows, doesn't lead
Uno	• Nickname means "one" • Self-centered • Slick talker

284 ■ *Short Stories*

Writing Genres

Using the Form Point out to students that they may write short stories for a variety of purposes. For example:
- Short stories can be incorporated into speeches as anecdotes.
- A brief short story can illustrate a main point in an essay.

Writing Workshop
Work in Progress

If students have done the Work-in-Progress assignments throughout Part 1, suggest that they examine their recorded ideas as they begin prewriting.

Prewriting
- Have students work in small groups, completing the sentence starters aloud.
- Explain the four methods of characterization to students: what a narrator says, what a character says about him or herself, what a character does, and what other characters say about the character.

Six Traits Focus

✔	Ideas		Word Choice
✔	Organization		Sentence Fluency
	Voice		Conventions

Writing and Grammar, Gold Level
Students will find additional instruction on prewriting for a short story in Chapter 5, Section 2.

Writing and Grammar Interactive Textbook CD-ROM
Students can use the following tools:
- Story Map
- Character Trait Word Bin

Meeting Your Standards

Students will
1. write a short story.
2. use writing strategies to generate ideas and to plan, organize, evaluate, and revise a short story.
3. apply grammar skills.

Using the Form
You may use elements of this form in these types of writing:
- science fiction
- mysteries
- autobiographies

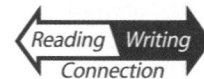
Reading → Writing Connection

To get a feel for short stories, read "The Gift of the Magi" by O. Henry on page 245.

Work in Progress
Review the work you did on pages 239 and 265.

Teaching Resources

The following resources can be used to enrich or extend the instruction for the Writing Workshop.

Unit 2 Resources
Writing Workshop: Narration: Short Story, p. 99
Writing Workshop: Integrating Grammar Skills: Revising Inconsistent Verb Tenses, p. 100

General Resources
Rubrics for Narration: Short Story, pp. 47–48
Graphic Organizer Transparencies: Plot Diagram, p. 238

Drafting

Shaping Your Writing

Plan the story line. Every paragraph in your story should help readers understand at least one of these elements:
- the **characters'** personalities, attitudes, and relationships
- the **setting** and its effect on events
- the **conflict** or struggles the characters face
- the **action** that occurs as a result of all of the above

Consider identifying one element, such as a place or an object, as a symbol that will help express the theme of your story.

Providing Elaboration

Show instead of tell. Use descriptions and dialogue to make events and characters vivid for your readers. Do not simply report that a street was noisy; give your readers details that let them hear the noise. Do not report that your characters had an argument; use dialogue to show it.

Revising

Revising Your Overall Structure

Maintain an effective sequence of events. Every detail in your story should deepen your portrayal of the characters or increase the tension of the conflict. Review your draft, noting any interruptions to the momentum of your plot. Consider modifying or deleting such interruptions.

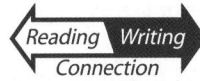
Reading | Writing
Connection

For the complete student model, see page 287.

Student Model: Revising to Clarify Sequence

Then, we noticed something strange. ~~For a second I~~ ~~thought about what it was like back up on the grass.~~ There were other, different words painted on the wall and what they said scared us all: "Your friend is here. Don't try to find him."

> The writer omits a detail that slows the story down.

Revising Your Word Choice

Use active language. To create dynamic sentences, choose the active voice instead of the passive voice. Make sure that the subjects in your sentences perform the action.

Passive Voice: The problem was solved by Curtis.
Active Voice: Curtis solved the problem.

Drafting

- Have students create four-column charts, labeling each *Characters, Setting, Conflict,* and *Action*. Ask students to categorize each of their story details under the appropriate heading. If a detail cannot be categorized, tell students to consider revising or deleting the detail.
- After students have written a portion of their first drafts, have them examine their writing and identify *telling* details. Ask volunteers to submit *telling* details; and, as a class, revise them into *showing* details through description and dialogue.

Six Traits Focus

	Ideas	✔	Word Choice
✔	Organization		Sentence Fluency
✔	Voice		Conventions

Writing and Grammar, Gold Level
Students will find additional instruction on drafting a short story in Chapter 5, Section 3.

Revising

- Have students record each of their story events in a plot diagram. Tell them to label each event *character* or *conflict*. If they are unable to label an event, they should consider revising or deleting it. Refer students to the Plot Diagram in **Graphic Organizer Transparencies,** p. 238.
- Have students review their stories, identifying instances of the passive voice. Ask volunteers to write such sentences on the board. As a class, revise these sentences using the active voice.

Six Traits Focus

✔	Ideas	✔	Word Choice
✔	Organization	✔	Sentence Fluency
✔	Voice		Conventions

Writing and Grammar, Gold Level
Students will find additional instruction on revising a short story in Chapter 5, Section 4.

Tips for Using Rubrics

- Before students begin work on this assignment, have them preview the Rubric for Self-Assessment on p. 288 to know what is expected.
- Review the Assessment criteria in class. Before students use the Rubric for Self-Assessment, work with them to rate the Student Model by applying one or two criteria to it.

- If you wish to assess students' short stories with a 4-point, 5-point, or a 6-point scoring rubric, see *General Resources*, pp. 47–48.

- Emphasize to students that not all shifts in tense are incorrect. For example, in this sentence, the shift in tense shows that the actions occurred at two different times.

  Babe Ruth set a home run record that we still admire.

- Tell students to choose a tense that makes sense and then to use it consistently throughout their stories, changing tenses only to show that one event comes before or after another event.

- Have students make the verb tenses in this paragraph consistent.

  I had trouble sleeping last night. The dog barked all night, which wakes me two or three times. My father had forgotten to shut the tool-shed door, and the wind keeps blowing it open. By the time the sun shines through my window, I give up on getting a good night's sleep.

  Answer: *I had trouble sleeping last night. The dog barked all night, which woke me two or three times. My father had forgotten to shut the tool-shed door, and the wind kept blowing it open. By the time the sun shone through my window, I had given up on getting a good night's sleep.*

W G Writing and Grammar, Gold Level

Students will find additional instruction on verb tenses in Chapter 23, Section 1.

Integrating Grammar Skills

Revising Inconsistent Verb Tenses

A tense is a form of a verb that expresses the time of an action. The six verb tenses are present, present perfect, past, past perfect, future, and future perfect. Inconsistent or unclear use of verb tenses can cause confusion in a story.

Identifying Inconsistent Verb Tenses Inconsistent verb tense occurs when a sentence begins in one tense and switches into another without explanation or logic.

> **Incorrect:** She *skied* every day we *go* to the mountains last winter.

> **Correct:** She *skied* every day we *went* to the mountains last winter.

Shifts in tense should always reflect a logical sequence.

> **Incorrect:** I *will be* on time today, but I *was* on time tomorrow.

> **Correct:** I *was* on time today, and I *will be* on time tomorrow.

Perfect tenses can clarify a sequence of actions.

> **Unclear:** By the time she *arrived,* we *started* the meeting.

> **Clear:** By the time she *arrived,* we *had started* the meeting.

Fixing Errors To maintain consistent use of verb tenses, scan your draft for shifts in tense.

1. **Identify the reason for each shift.** Correct any that are unnecessary.

2. **Determine which actions happened first.** When two actions occur at different times in the past, use the past perfect tense for the earlier action.

Uses of Past Perfect Tense	
Past action of condition completed before another	I had been to the museum before it was remodeled.
Continuing past action interrupted by another	I had been on the telephone when you rang the doorbell.

Apply It to Your Editing

Review a passage of your draft that includes both narrative and dialogue. Underline any shifts in tense that you find. Be sure that the shift represents a clear and logical time order. Fix any inconsistent tenses.

Prentice Hall Writing and Grammar Connection: Chapter 23, Section 1

Differentiated Instruction   Solutions for All Learners

Strategy for Less Proficient Readers
Have students select the three longest paragraphs in their drafts and circle all of the verbs. Next, have students identify the tense of each verb. Tell students to make sure that any change in tense is made for a logical reason.

Strategy for Advanced Readers
Review the use of perfect tenses with students, reminding students that these forms can precisely establish the time-order relationship of two or more events. Have students circle the verbs in their drafts, looking for ways to use present and past perfect tenses to clarify time sequence.

Student Model: Randy Hays
Clackamas, OR

The Oil Slick

The Oil Slick is a place where I play baseball with a bunch of friends. We call the field the "Oil Slick" because a boat carrying gallons of oil once sailed by. The boat sprang a leak, polluting the water around it. The Oil Slick also has a big hole in the outfield. . . .

> Randy starts the story with a detailed description of an interesting setting.

My nickname is Giant. It suits me because I am the tallest player on the team. . . . I only know the nicknames of the others on my team. They're called Ant, Dash, Rip, X-Ray, Target, Eye, Animal, Uno, and Cover. . . .

> The characters' quirky nicknames help the writer create a sense of what each one is like.

This morning, I headed out to the Oil Slick, ready to play. However, before we started, Uno held a meeting. "As you know," he said, "there is a hole in the outfield."

"Who can tell me why the hole is there?" There was silence until Uno spoke again. "That's what I thought," he said. "Some people say there's treasure buried on this field. Somebody probably tried to dig for it, and they left that hole behind. I thought maybe we should dig, too, but then I figured that'd be stupid. It's probably just a rumor. We wouldn't find anything, diggin' holes."

> Randy uses dialogue to introduce the mystery of the hole in the field—the source of the story's conflict.

Silence again until someone shouted. "Let's play already!" Everyone went to their positions and the game started. . . .

Rip hit the ball and it flew past the right-fielder, Eye. Concentrating on the ball, Eye ran toward the hole. He didn't know when to stop and he fell. . . .

We all ran and looked down the hole. Nobody had ever bothered to really look before, and it was deep, much deeper than we thought. Hoping to find Eye, we jumped in. . . .

When we saw what the hole truly was we forgot about Eye. We had expected dirt, rocks—the usual stuff you'd find in a hole. Instead, we saw smooth walls, stretching into the distance. All this time, without ever suspecting it, we had been playing above a maze of tunnels. . . .

We headed down the tunnel to our right. . . .These weren't ordinary tunnels. They had the names of famous baseball players carved right into the walls. Then, we noticed something strange. There were other, different words painted on the wall and what they said scared us all: "Your friend is here. Don't try to find him. Or else."

> The conflict intensifies here.

We continued through the tunnels until we emerged in a room which . . . had a sign that said, "You Found Him." Sure enough, there was Eye, leaning against a wall. He saw us and shouted, "Go! Now!"

But it was too late. A door slammed shut and we were trapped. Then, we heard a familiar voice. "You saw the warnings, but you didn't stop. Now you are trapped and the treasure is mine!". . .

Go Online
Read More
For: the complete student model
Visit: www.PHSchool.com
Web Code: epm-4201

Writing Workshop ■ 287

Student Model
- Explain that the Student Model is a sample and that short stories may be longer.
- Give students an example of a graveyard setting. Have students give a detailed description of the setting.
  Possible response: *We walked into the graveyard by the light of the moon, which highlighted the chipped and broken tombstones. Wind whipped and whistled through the long grass that surrounded the ancient tombstones.*
- Tell students to use distinct names for characters in their stories. Tell them that memorable, telling names will enhance their stories.
- Tell students that the use of dialogue helps place the reader in the story.
- Point out to students how the writing on the wall intensifies the conflict. Ask students to read on and identify what other details intensify the conflict further.
  Answer: The door slams shut and they find out that Uno wrote the threats and that he wants the treasure for himself.

Writing Genres
Short Story Writing in Letters
Explain to students that when writing letters or e-mails to friends or relatives, they often incorporate stories. A student may tell about a funny thing that happened to her in the grocery store or about a scary moment at softball practice. Point out that they can use the principles within this workshop to enhance their stories, giving their readers vividly portrayed and highly enjoyable stories to read.

Tips for
Test Taking

Encourage students to use the "Save As" feature on their computers to save different versions of their drafts in case they want to refer to earlier versions as they write. Students might find that they can use sentences or descriptions from earlier drafts, even if they cannot reuse entire paragraphs.

Editing and Proofreading

- Explain to students that when editing and proofreading dialogue, they should make sure that they begin a new paragraph each time they change speakers.

- Write the following passage on the board. Have volunteers revise the passage.

    'Where are the dogs"? Maria asked her brother.

    "They're outside." Jonah answered. "They're awfully quiet' Maria said, walking toward the kitchen window.

    Answer: *"Where are the dogs?" Maria asked her brother.*

    "They're outside," Jonah answered.

    "They're awfully quiet," Maria said, walking toward the kitchen window.

Six Traits Focus

Ideas		Word Choice	
Organization		Sentence Fluency	
Voice		Conventions	✔

ASSESS

Publishing and Presenting

- Tell students to think about places where they might change the pace of their readings or alter tone of voice to reflect actions, suspense, or mood in their stories.

- Students whose stories contain substantial dialogue might ask classmates to read the lines for particular characters.

Reflecting on Your Writing

- Ask students to respond to these additional questions as they reflect on their writing:

    1. *What did you find most difficult about writing a short story?*

    2. *What did you find most enjoyable or rewarding about writing a short story?*

    3. *What would you do differently the next time you write a short story?*

- Lead a discussion about the connection between reading short stories and writing them.

Writing Workshop

Editing and Proofreading

Check your draft for errors in spelling, grammar, and punctuation.
Focus on Punctuating Dialogue: Make sure that your characters' spoken words are properly indented and demonstrate correct use of commas and quotation marks. Follow this example:

> **Example:** "Don't forget to call us," Natalie reminded us as we left.
> Paul teased, "How *could* we forget?"

Prentice Hall Writing and Grammar Connection: Chapter 4

Publishing and Presenting

Consider one of the following ways to share your writing:
Deliver an oral presentation. Read your story aloud to your classmates. Get feedback from your classmates and make revisions based on their comments.
Create an anthology. Work with classmates to collect your stories in a single binder. Illustrate the stories with photographs or artwork and agree on a title for the collection. Contribute the anthology to the classroom or school library.

Reflecting on Your Writing

Writer's Journal Jot down your thoughts about writing a short story. Begin by answering these questions:
- Which prewriting and drafting strategies were most useful to you?
- How has the experience of writing a story affected the way you now read stories written by others?

Rubric for Self-Assessment

To assess your short story, use this rubric:

Criteria	Rating Scale *not very* *very*
Focus: How clear is the story's theme or message?	1 2 3 4 5
Organization: How clearly do you introduce, develop, and resolve the conflict?	1 2 3 4 5
Support/Elaboration: How well do you use details to establish time, place, and mood?	1 2 3 4 5
Style: How well do you describe the characters and setting?	1 2 3 4 5
Conventions: How correct is your grammar, especially your use of verb tenses?	1 2 3 4 5

288 ■ *Short Stories*

WG Writing and Grammar, Gold Level

Students will find additional guidance for editing and proofreading, publishing and presenting, and reflecting on a short story in Chapter 5, Sections 5 and 6.

Cause and Effect

Skills You Will Learn

Literary Analysis: *Character and Characterization*
Reading Skill: *Ask Questions to Analyze Cause and Effect*

Literary Analysis: *Dialogue and Dialect*
Reading Skill: *Visualize the Action*

Reading Skill: *Evaluate Text Format*

Literary Analysis: *Symbolism and Allegory*

Literature You Will Read

Cause and Effect ■ 289

Skills Overview
Reading Skill: Analyzing Cause and Effect
- Asking questions to analyze cause and effect
- Visualizing the action to analyze cause and effect

Vocabulary Development
- Word Roots

Literary Analysis
- Character and Characterizations: direct and indirect characterization
- Dialogue: dialect

Writing
- Cause and Effect Essay
- Work in Progress, pp. 319, 343

Monitoring Progress

Diagnose: Before you begin Part 2, administer the **Diagnostic Test** for Unit 2, Part 2. This test will identify students' level of readiness for the reading and vocabulary skills in Part 2. Use the **Interpretation Guide** for the Diagnostic Test to determine which students need help with pre-requisite skills before beginning Part 2.

Preteach and Prepare: Use the information indicated in the **Interpretation Guide** to help students build prerequisite skills. In addition, prepare students by using the **Vocabulary Warm**-up activities and the **Reading Warm**-up activities as necessary for each selection set.

Teach: Use the instructional plan and resources provided to teach the skills and selections.

Assess: After students have completed Part 2, administer the **Benchmark Test** for Unit 2, Part 2. The test results will indicate which skills students have mastered and those on which they need more work.

Reteach: Use the Interpretation Guide to determine the appropriate reteaching pages from the **Reading Kit.**

Intervention: The prerequisite and reteaching pages are also available in the **Success Tracker.**

Differentiated
Instruction   Solutions for All Learners

Resources for Monitoring Progress

Unit 2 Resources
> **Unit 2, Part 2 Diagnostic Test,**
> pp. 108–110
> **Unit 2, Part 2 Benchmark Test,**
> pp. 197–202

Reading Kit

Success Tracker

Introduce the Reading Skill

- Introduce the reading skill: analyzing cause and effect. Point out to students that when they try to determine what happened in a literary work, they are asking about *effect*. When students ask why something happened, they are asking about *cause*.

- Tell students that causes and effects are not always grouped together in a selection. Just as in real life, a cause may create an effect that does not appear until much later. For example, neglecting to change the oil in a car may not hurt the engine immediately, but eventually the dirty oil will seriously damage the engine and ruin the car. As they read, remind students to look for both immediate and long-range effects.

Model the Reading Strategies

- Model how asking questions can help students understand the causes and effects in a selection. Write the following sentence on the board:

   When heavy snow covered the roof, it collapsed.

   Then ask these questions:

   What happened?
   Answer: The weight of the snow collapsed the roof. (effect)

   Why did it happen?
   Answer: Details in the text may show a variety of answers. For example, the snowfall may have been so enormous it collapsed the roof; the roof itself may already have been weak. (causes)

- Reinforce the idea that determining the causes and effects in a selection will help students to understand the literature and will help them to see how the action progresses. Remind students that not all causes and effects are immediate. Sometimes students must read patiently to connect what happened with why it happened.

Reading: Cause and Effect

▶ A **cause** is the reason for an action or event. An **effect** is the result of an action or event.

Skills and Strategies You Will Learn in Part 2

In Part 2, you will learn
- to **ask questions** to **analyze cause** and **effect** (p. 292).
- to **visualize** the action to **analyze cause** and **effect** (p. 320).
- to **evaluate text format** and **analyze the effects** of format presentation (p. 344).

Using the Skills and Strategies in Part 2

In Part 2, you will learn to **ask questions** that help you recognize the relationships between events. You will practice **picturing the actions** and breaking down a chain of events to analyze causes and effects. Asking questions will help you define the cause-and-effect relationships in the text. Visualizing the action can also clarify these relationships.

The example shows you how you can apply some of the skills you will learn in Part 2.

Questions for analyzing causes and effects
- Why does the character miss the gas station?
- What is the result of missing the gas station?
- Why does the car run out of gas?
- What is the result of the car's running out of gas?

Professional Development
Think Aloud
The think-aloud strategy can be used to model any thinking process for students. In this process, you verbalize your thoughts as you read aloud a passage to students. This strategy works well to model the processes that good readers use to construct meaning and monitor comprehension. For example, if you have students who appear to be "reading" but are not really connecting or comprehending text, you may read a passage orally, interspersing your own thinking with the text. This allows the students to "see" inside your head as you apply a variety of comprehension strategies, such as making predictions, visualizing, rereading, making personal connections, and using context to understand vocabulary. Many of our students don't know how strategic readers work with and engage in text in meaningful ways. This process shows them how.

Academic Vocabulary: Words for Understanding Literature

The following words will help you write and talk about the literature in this unit.

Word	Definition	Example Sentence
sequence *n.*	series of connected things	The *sequence* of events is the basis of the plot.
topic *n.*	subject of a work or talk	The *topic* of that essay was interesting.
attitude *n.*	way of acting that shows a disposition or an opinion	The character's *attitude* was the cause of their disagreement.
verify *v.*	test whether something is true	*Verify* the cause-effect relationship.
imply *v.*	hint at or suggest	The author *implied* that the murderer was one of the principal characters.

Vocabulary Skills: Word Roots

▶ A word **root** can be used to infer the meaning of a word.

In Part 2, you will learn
- Latin root *-ver-* (p. 318)
- Latin root *-sequi-* (p. 342)

Knowing the meaning of word roots helps you understand and remember the meanings of words that contain them. Look at the following chart.

Activity Look up each example word in a dictionary. Then, write questions, using a different example word in each question. Trade questions with a partner and answer each other's questions.

Root	Meaning	Examples
-ver-	truth	verify, verdict
-sequi-	follow	sequence, sequel

Reading and Vocabulary Skills Preview ■ 291

Differentiated Instruction — Solutions for All Learners

Strategy for English Learners
To illustrate the idea of a causal chain, have students set up a short series of dominoes. Have one of the students push the first domino. Then ask students what caused the first domino to fall, then the second, then the third, and so forth. Explain that a causal chain is like dominoes falling; each effect becomes the next cause. Then, read aloud to students a short story that has a series of causes and effects. Afterwards, invite students to name as many causes and their effects as they can.

Strategy for Advanced Readers
Have students research a problem that has several causes and effects, such as world hunger or World War I. Allow students to conduct their research using the Internet or the school library. Encourage students to research thoroughly so that they find as many causes and effects as possible. Then, have students create a chart that lists the causes and effects and how they are related.

Introduce Academic Vocabulary

- Introduce the academic vocabulary: words for understanding literature. Tell students that these words are useful for analyzing causes and effects in a selection and for understanding how events progress in a literary work.
- Review each word, and have the students state the words aloud. Have students read aloud the words' definitions and the example sentences.
- Tell students to try to use these words as they discuss the selections in Part 2.

Introduce the Vocabulary Skill

- Introduce the vocabulary skill: word roots. Tell students that many words in English are derived from Latin, and Latin word roots appear in many English words. Recognizing these word roots and their meanings is an effective way to learn word meanings and to build vocabulary.
- Review the two word roots on this page, their meanings, and the English words that contain these roots.
- Have students complete the activity and discuss any answers that are unclear.
- Use these questions to give students practice with word roots.

  What word, containing the word root *-dict-*, describes a statement of what may happen in the future?
  Answer: *predict*

  What word, containing the word root *-ject-*, describes throwing out something or eliminating it from consideration?
  Answer: *reject*

  What word, containing the word root *-port-*, describes carrying something in from another country?
  Answer: *import*

Go Online **For:** Interactive Vocabulary Crossword Puzzles
Visit: www.PHSchool.com
Web Code: epj-5202
Give students this Web Code to access interactive crossword puzzles using Academic Vocabulary and Vocabulary Skill words from Part 2.

Planning Differentiated Instruction

Choosing Your Selection

You may use either selection to meet the lesson standards. The following guide will help you determine which of the two selections is more appropriate for your students.

Accessibility at a Glance

	The Necklace	Rules of the Game
Context	Historical; France, 1800s	Contemporary; San Francisco's Chinatown
Language	• Numerous long sentences with embedded modifying structures • Language from the period footnoted • Pronunciation provided for French words	• Accessible vocabulary • Relatively short sentences and clauses • Some dialogue in broken English
Concept Level	Accessible (desire for wealth and status; irony of outcome)	More complex (mother/daughter relationship; cross-cultural references)
Literary Merit	Traditional; well-noted author	Cross-cultural experience; noted author
Lexile	910L	1000L
Other	Surprise ending	
Overall Rating	More accessible	More challenging

Using the Other Selection You may use the other selection for homework or independent reading to reinforce the selection skills. If you use both selections, you can build a test for both using *ExamView®* **Test Bank** software.

Choosing Your Resources

[L1] Special Needs Students   **[L4]** Advanced Students

[L2] Below-Level Students   **[EL]** English Learners

[L3] All Students

Reading and Vocabulary Warm-ups provide support for below level students. **A** is for students reading two grades below level; **B** is for students reading one grade below level. For Selection Tests, **A** signifies "less challenging" and **B** "more challenging." For Graphic Organizer transparencies, **A** signifies "not filled in" and **B** "filled in."

FT Fast Track Instruction: To move the lesson more quickly, use the strategies and activities identified with **FT.**

Scaffolding for Less Proficient and Advanced Students

The leveled questions on Apply the Skills pages progress in the levels of thinking required to answer them. To address the needs of your different students, you may use the (a) level questions for your less proficient students, the (b) level with your on-level and advanced students. The occasional (c) level questions are appropriate for your advanced students.

Step-by-Step Teaching Guide	Pacing Guide	
PRETEACH		
• Administer Vocabulary and Reading Warm-ups as necessary.		
• Introduce the Literary Analysis Skill: Character and Characterization. **FT**	10 min.	
• Introduce the Reading Skill: Analyzing Cause and Effect. **FT**	10 min.	
• Prepare students to read by teaching the selection vocabulary. **FT**	10 min.	
• Build background and develop expressive vocabulary with Connecting to the Literature and Background.	10 min.	
• Engage students' interest with the motivation activity.	10 min.	
TEACH		
• Informally monitor comprehension while students read independently or in groups. **FT**	30 min.	
• Monitor students' comprehension with the Reading Check notes.	as students read	
• Reinforce vocabulary with Vocabulary Builder notes.	as students read	
• Develop students' understanding of character and characterization with the Literary Analysis annotations. **FT**	5 min.	
• Develop students' ability to analyze cause and effect with the Reading Skill annotations. **FT**	10 min.	
ASSESS/EXTEND		
• Assess students' comprehension and mastery of the Reading Skill and Literary Analysis by having them answer the Apply the Skills questions. **FT**	35 min.	
• Have students complete the Vocabulary Builder activities. **FT**	5 min.	
• Apply students' ability to write a presentation with the Writing activity. **FT**	30–45 min. or homework	
• Extend students' listening and speaking and research and technology skills with one or both of the Extend Your Learning activities.	15–30 min. or homework	
• Have students complete the Vocabulary Skill and Grammar Lesson.	5 min.	
• Monitor students' progress with the Assessment Practice.	20–40 min.	
• Administer **Selection Test A** or **Selection Test B. FT**	15 min.	

Go **O**nline
Professional
Development
For: Information about Lexiles
Visit: www.PHSchool.com
Web Code: eue-1111

Resources

 Meeting Your Standards

Students will

1. **analyze and respond to literary elements.**
   - Literary Analysis: Character and Characterization

2. **read, comprehend, and analyze short stories.**
   - Reading Skill: Analyzing Cause and Effect
   - Reading Strategy: Asking Questions to Analyze Cause and Effect
   - Reading Check questions
   - Apply the Skills questions
   - Assessment Practice

3. **develop vocabulary.**
   - Vocabulary Builder
   - The Latin roots *-ver-*, *-sequi-*

4. **apply grammar skills.**
   - Subject/Predicate

5. **develop writing proficiency.**
   - Work in Progress: Cause-and-Effect Essay
   - Written Presentation

6. **extend learning.**
   - Listening and Speaking: Monologue
   - Research and Technology: Informative brochure

Block Scheduling: Use one 90-minute class period to preteach the skills and have students read the selection. Use a second 90-minute class period to assess students' mastery of skills, extend their learning, and monitor their progress.

Homework Suggestions

Following are possibilities for homework assignments.

- Support pages from *Unit 2 Resources*:
  Literary Analysis
  Reading Skill
  Vocabulary Builder
  Enrichment

- An Extend Your Learning project and the Writing assignment for your chosen selection may be completed over several days.

PRENTICE HALL

Teacher EXPRESS™ Use this complete
Plan · Teach · Assess suite of powerful teaching tools to make lesson planning and testing quicker and easier.

PRENTICE HALL

Student EXPRESS™ Use the Interactive
Learn · Study · Succeed Textbook (online and on CD-ROM) to make selections and activities come alive with audio and video support and interactive questions.

292b

❶ Literary Analysis
Characterization

- Tell students that in *direct characterization,* the writer simply tells you what a character is like. In *indirect characterization,* writers suggest a character's personality through the character's appearance, words and actions, and the reactions of other characters.

- **Ask** students to identify the following statements from previous selections as examples of direct or indirect characterization.

  "Miss Golden, crisp, fragrant, and punctual, shut the door."— "Sonata for Harp and Bicycle" (direct)

  "Father was driving with a reckless and exhilarating skill." — "If I Forget Thee, Oh Earth..." (indirect)

  "[T]here he was, weather-beaten and thin, with a pirate's moustache through which his strange, sharklike smile peered out. . . ." — "Uncle Marcos" (indirect)

- Give students a copy of **Literary Analysis Graphic Organizer A** (*Graphic Organizer Transparencies,* p. 62). As they read the assigned selections, have students fill in the graphic organizer to show how story details reveal important information about characters.

❷ Reading Skill
Analyze Cause and Effect

- Tell students that analyzing causes and effects can help them understand the conflict in a story. For example, knowing the cause of resentment between two characters gives the reader insight into the conflict and how it might be resolved or how the characters might behave toward each other in the future.

- Encourage students to identify and analyze cause-and-effect relationships as they read the assigned selections.

Build Skills   *The Necklace • Rules of the Game*

Practice these skills with either "The Necklace" (p. 294) or "Rules of the Game" (p. 305).

❶ Literary Analysis

A **character** is a person, an animal, or even an object that participates in the action and experiences the events of a literary work. Writers communicate what characters are like through **characterization:**

- **Direct characterization:** The writer explains a character.
- **Indirect characterization:** The writer gives clues to a character by describing the character's behavior, words and thoughts, physical appearance, or how others react to the character.

Use a chart like this one to track characterization as you read.

Story Details	What They Show About the Character
Narrator's comments	
Character's thoughts and words	
Character's actions	
Character's appearance	
What others say or think about the character	

❷ Reading Skill

A **cause** is an event, an action, or a feeling that produces a result. An **effect** is the result produced. As you read, **ask questions to analyze cause and effect.**

- What happened?
- Why did it happen?
- What happens as a result?

A single cause may produce several effects. For example, a character who was once a poor student starts to do well in school. This gives her greater self-esteem. Effects may, in turn, become causes. For example, that same character's new confidence leads her to audition for a play.

Vocabulary Builder

The Necklace

- **rueful** (roo′ fəl) *adj.* feeling sorrow or regret (p. 294) *Her thoughtless comment soon made her rueful.*

- **resplendent** (ri splen′ dənt) *adj.* shining brightly (p. 297) *The winner's face was resplendent as he accepted the prize.*

- **disheveled** (di shev′ əld) *adj.* untidy (p. 300) *Val's disheveled hair showed he had overslept.*

- **profoundly** (prō found′ lē) *adv.* deeply (p. 301) *We were all profoundly moved by the long-lost brothers' reunion.*

292 ■ *Short Stories*

Rules of the Game

- **pungent** (pun′ jənt) *adj.* producing a sharp smell (p. 306) *The use of pungent spices promised a savory meal.*

- **benevolently** (bə nev′ ə lənt lē) *adv.* in a well-meaning way (p. 310) *The officer smiled benevolently at the children.*

- **retort** (ri tôrt′) *n.* sharp or clever reply (p. 310) *Her retort silenced her critic.*

- **malodorous** (mal ō′ dər əs) *adj.* having a bad smell (p. 313) *The malodorous bag was filled with garbage.*

Vocabulary Development

Vocabulary Knowledge Rating

Create a **Vocabulary Knowledge Rating Chart** for the selection you will teach from this set. Include the selection vocabulary from this page and the additional words students are asked to use at the end of Connecting to the Literature. These words will increase students' expressive vocabulary.

Give students a copy of the chart with the words on it. Introduce the words by reading them aloud and having students mark their rating in the Before Reading column. Urge them to be alert to these words as they read and discuss the selection because they will rate their knowledge of the words again after they finish.

If you wish, you may tally how many students know (or think they know) a word to gauge how much instruction you need to provide. As students read, point out the words and their context.

Build Understanding • *The Necklace*

❸ Background

European Society During the nineteenth century, the old social order in Europe changed. Previously, society was divided into two main classes: nobles, who owned land, and peasants, who farmed it. However, as industry spread, a new middle class emerged and people could rise—or sink—in social position. Some sought to own material goods as a mark of higher social standing.

❹ Connecting to the Literature

Reading/Writing Connection In "The Necklace," a character wishes she owned jewelry that is far more costly than she can afford. Write several reasons why a person might want to have expensive things. Use at least three of these words: *obtain, impress, exceed, identify.*

READ MORE

by Guy de Maupassant
A Day in the Country and Other Stories

Meet the Author

Guy de Maupassant (1850–1893)

Perhaps the best-known short-story writer in the world, Guy de Maupassant (gē də mō pä sän´) wrote tales that are realistic and pessimistic, and often offer surprise endings.

Friendship with Writers Following his army service, he settled in Paris, where he began to develop his skills as a writer, guided by the famous French author Gustave Flaubert. Maupassant also joined a circle of writers led by French novelist Emile Zola. With Zola's encouragement, Maupassant published his first short story, "Ball of Fat," in 1880. The story earned him immediate fame and freed him to write full time. "The Necklace" is perhaps his most widely read story.

Fast Facts
▶ Maupassant had a photographic memory.
▶ Maupassant wrote some 300 short stories, six novels, and other books.

 Go Online
Author Link

For: More about the author
Visit: www.PHSchool.com
Web Code: epe-9208

The Necklace ■ 293

❸ Background
European Society

The fictional Monsieur and Madame Loisel in "The Necklace" represent the bourgeoisie, or middle class—the social class between the working class and the very wealthy in nineteenth-century France. These characters are ordinary, middle-class people, with no inherited position or wealth. They live on M. Loisel's salary from his government job. The word *bourgeois* has come to mean conventional or ordinary, respectable but unimaginative, and, sometimes, selfishly materialistic.

❹ Connecting to the Literature

• Model use of the expressive vocabulary students are asked to use with these examples:

1. Some people may feel that expensive possessions help them *obtain* the respect and admiration of others.

2. Many people try to *impress* others with expensive things.

3. Certain types of people try to *exceed* their neighbors in acquiring expensive things.

4. Some people *identify* material possessions with success.

• Help students further develop their expressive vocabulary by providing these words: *asset, circumstance, intense,* and *prosper.* Encourage students to use these words as they discuss the selection.

Go Online
Author Link For additional information about Guy de Maupassant, have students type in the Web Code, then select *M* from the alphabet, and then select *Guy de Maupassant.*

The Necklace
Guy de Maupassant

She was one of those pretty, charming young women who are born, as if by an error of Fate, into a petty official's family. She had no dowry,[1] no hopes, not the slightest chance of being appreciated, understood, loved, and married by a rich and distinguished man; so she slipped into marriage with a minor civil servant at the Ministry of Education.

Unable to afford jewelry, she dressed simply: but she was as wretched as a déclassée, for women have neither caste nor breeding—in them beauty, grace, and charm replace pride of birth. Innate refinement, instinctive elegance, and suppleness of wit give them their place on the only scale that counts, and these qualities make humble girls the peers of the grandest ladies.

She suffered constantly, feeling that all the attributes of a gracious life, every luxury, should rightly have been hers. The poverty of her rooms—the shabby walls, the worn furniture, the ugly upholstery—caused her pain. All these things that another woman of her class would not even have noticed, tormented her and made her angry. The very sight of the little Breton girl who cleaned for her awoke <u>rueful</u> thoughts and the wildest dreams in her mind. She dreamt of thick-carpeted reception rooms with Oriental hangings, lighted by tall, bronze torches, and with two huge

---

1. **dowry** (dou´ rē) *n.* property that a woman brought to her husband at marriage.

Literary Analysis
Characterization
Using direct characterization, what does the author tell you about the young woman in the first two paragraphs?

Vocabulary Builder
rueful (roo´ fəl) *adj.* feeling sorrow or regret

footmen in knee breeches, made drowsy by the heat from the stove, asleep in the wide armchairs. She dreamt of great drawing rooms upholstered in old silks, with fragile little tables holding priceless knick-knacks, and of enchanting little sitting rooms redolent of perfume, designed for tea-time chats with intimate friends—famous, sought-after men whose attentions all women longed for.

4 When she sat down to dinner at her round table with its three-day-old cloth, and watched her husband opposite her lift the lid of the soup tureen and exclaim, delighted: "Ah, a good homemade beef stew! There's nothing better . . ." she would visualize elegant dinners with gleaming silver amid tapestried walls peopled by knights and ladies and exotic birds in a fairy forest; she would think of exquisite dishes served on gorgeous china, and of gallantries whispered and received with sphinx-like smiles while eating the pink flesh of trout or wings of grouse.

She had no proper wardrobe, no jewels, nothing. And those were the only things that she loved—she felt she was made for them. She would have so loved to charm, to be envied, to be admired and sought after.

5 She had a rich friend, a schoolmate from the convent she had attended, but she didn't like to visit her because it always made her so miserable when she got home again. She would weep for whole days at a time from sorrow, regret, despair, and distress.

Then one evening her husband arrived home looking triumphant and waving a large envelope.

"There," he said, "there's something for you."

She tore it open eagerly and took out a printed card which said:

"The Minister of Education and Madame Georges Ramponneau [ma dam' zhôrzh ram pə nō'] request the pleasure of the company of M. and Mme. Loisel [lwa zel'] at an evening reception at the Ministry on Monday, January 18th."

Instead of being delighted, as her husband had hoped, she tossed the invitation on the table and muttered, annoyed:

"What do you expect me to do with that?"

7 "Why, I thought you'd be pleased, dear. You never go out and this would be an occasion for you, a great one! I had a lot of trouble getting it. Everyone wants an invitation; they're in great demand and there are only a few reserved for the employees. All the officials will be there."

She looked at him, irritated, and said impatiently:

"I haven't a thing to wear. How could I go?"

It had never even occurred to him. He stammered:

"But what about the dress you wear to the theater? I think it's lovely. . . ."

Literary Analysis
Characterization
What does the husband's comment in this paragraph reveal indirectly about his character?

Reading Skill
Analyze Cause and Effect Why do visits to her rich friend always fill the young woman with despair?

6 Reading Check

Why does Madame Loisel suffer constantly?

The Necklace ■ 295

---

4 Literary Analysis
Characterization

- Draw students' attention to the bracketed passage. **Ask** students why they think the author mentions the "three-day-old cloth."
  Answer: The fact that a tablecloth has been in use for three days suggests that the couple does not have the money for fine linens to be changed daily. He is pointing out that the characters are not living luxuriously.

- **Ask:** Do you think the husband notices the "three-day-old cloth"? Why or why not?
  Answer: He probably does not notice it because he seems happy with the meal and his life in general.

- **Ask** students to respond to the Literary Analysis question: What does the husband's comment in this paragraph reveal indirectly about his character?
  Answer: It reveals that he is content and easily pleased; he is not interested in material possessions.

5 Reading Skill
Analyze Cause and Effect

- Have students read the bracketed passage and then **describe** how they think the woman's life is different from her friend's life.
  Answer: Madame Loisel lives in a shabby home with worn furniture; she dresses simply and has no expensive jewelry. Her friend is rich and able to afford the things Madame Loisel dreams of having, such as a large home with plush furnishings and expensive clothing and jewelry.

- **Ask** students the Reading Skill question: Why do visits to her rich friend always fill the young woman with despair?
  Answer: The woman sees elegance in her friend's life where there is poverty in her own; she sees all her friend's expensive possessions, which she believes she is entitled to as well.

6 Reading Check

Answer: She believes that she should be living a life of wealth and luxury.

Differentiated
Instruction   Solutions for All Learners

Vocabulary for Special Needs Students
The vocabulary in this selection may be daunting for some students. Help them look for context clues to understand some of the words. For example, the phrase "the poverty of her rooms" on p. 294 is followed by three examples that help readers see that *poverty* means "being poor" or "having little money."

A passage on p. 295 offers a series of synonyms such as *sorry, regret, despair,* and *distress,* which follow a description of Madame Loisel weeping for days at a time. Explain that this suggests that the four words are all different ways to say "unhappiness."

Point out that antonyms can also be context clues. For example, on p. 295, the phrase "instead of being delighted" is followed by the explanation that Madame Loisel "muttered, annoyed." Help students see that this suggests that *annoyed* is the opposite of *delighted.* Therefore, the word *delighted* must mean "pleased."

295

7 Reading Skill
Analyze Cause and Effect

- Have students read the bracketed passage, and then **ask** how they expected Madame Loisel to respond to the invitation.
  Answer: Students will probably say that they expected her to be ecstatic about the invitation.

- **Ask** students to describe her reaction to the invitation.
  Answer: She is annoyed and irritated.

- **Ask** students to respond to the Reading Skill question: Why is the husband surprised by his wife's reaction to the party invitation?
  Answer: He thought she would be happy because she is so interested in wealth and the upper class.

8 Critical Thinking
Infer

- **Ask** students to describe what M. Loisel probably thinks about his wife's reaction to the invitation.
  Answer: He is probably hurt and upset because he thought he was doing something nice for her.

- **Ask** what sacrifice he is willing to make so that his wife can have a new dress for the party.
  Answer: He is willing to give up buying a hunting gun for himself so she can buy a dress.

- **Ask** students what they can infer about M. Loisel's feelings for his wife.
  Answer: He loves his wife and wants to give her whatever she desires.

7 He fell silent, amazed and bewildered to see that his wife was crying. Two big tears escaped from the corners of her eyes and rolled slowly toward the corners of her mouth. He mumbled:

"What is it? What is it?"

But, with great effort, she had overcome her misery; and now she answered him calmly, wiping her tear-damp cheeks:

"It's nothing. It's just that I have no evening dress and so I can't go to the party. Give the invitation to one of your colleagues whose wife will be better dressed than I would be."

He was overcome. He said:

"Listen, Mathilde [ma tēld´], how much would an evening dress cost—a suitable one that you could wear again on other occasions, something very simple?"

She thought for several seconds, making her calculations and at the same time estimating how much she could ask for without eliciting an immediate refusal and an exclamation of horror from this economical government clerk.

At last, not too sure of herself, she said:

8 "It's hard to say exactly but I think I could manage with four hundred francs."

He went a little pale, for that was exactly the amount he had put aside to buy a rifle so that he could go hunting the following summer near Nanterre, with a few friends who went shooting larks around there on Sundays.

However, he said:

"Well, all right, then. I'll give you four hundred francs. But try to get something really nice."

As the day of the ball drew closer, Madame Loisel seemed depressed, disturbed, worried—despite the fact that her dress was ready. One evening her husband said:

"What's the matter? You've really been very strange these last few days."

And she answered:

"I hate not having a single jewel, not one stone, to wear. I shall look so dowdy.[2] I'd almost rather not go to the party."

He suggested:

9 "You can wear some fresh flowers. It's considered very chic[3] at this time of year. For ten francs you can get two or three beautiful roses."

That didn't satisfy her at all.

"No . . . there's nothing more humiliating than to look poverty-stricken among a lot of rich women."

---

2. dowdy (dou´dē) *adj.* shabby.
3. chic (shēk) *adj.* fashionable.

296 ■ Short Stories

Reading Skill
Analyze Cause and Effect Why is the husband surprised by his wife's reaction to the party invitation?

Vocabulary Development

Expressive Vocabulary
As students discuss Madame Loisel's attitude toward material possessions, encourage them to use the expressive vocabulary presented earlier. Have them consider why she was upset about the party invitation and her attitude toward her husband's offer to buy her a dress. You might encourage them with sentence starters like these:

1. M. Loisel thought his wife would be happy that he was able to *obtain* . . .
2. Madame Loisel was eager to *impress* . . .
3. The cost of a new dress would *exceed* . . .
4. As she searched through the box of jewelry, she tried to *identify* . . .

Then her husband exclaimed:

"Wait—you silly thing! Why don't you go and see Madame Forestier [fôr əs tyā´] and ask her to lend you some jewelry. You certainly know her well enough for that, don't you think?"

She let out a joyful cry.

"You're right. It never occurred to me."

The next day she went to see her friend and related her tale of woe.

Madame Forestier went to her mirrored wardrobe, took out a big jewel case, brought it to Madame Loisel, opened it, and said:

"Take your pick, my dear."

Her eyes wandered from some bracelets to a pearl necklace, then to a gold Venetian cross set with stones, of very fine workmanship. She tried on the jewelry before the mirror, hesitating, unable to bring herself to take them off, to give them back. And she kept asking:

"Do you have anything else, by chance?"

"Why yes. Here, look for yourself. I don't know which ones you'll like."

All at once, in a box lined with black satin, she came upon a superb diamond necklace, and her heart started beating with overwhelming desire. Her hands trembled as she picked it up. She fastened it around her neck over her high-necked dress and stood there gazing at herself ecstatically.

Hesitantly, filled with terrible anguish, she asked:

"Could you lend me this one—just this and nothing else?"

"Yes, of course."

She threw her arms around her friend's neck, kissed her ardently, and fled with her treasure.

The day of the party arrived. Madame Loisel was a great success. She was the prettiest woman there—<u>resplendent</u>, graceful, beaming, and deliriously happy. All the men looked at her, asked who she was, tried to get themselves introduced to her. All the minister's aides wanted to waltz with her. The minister himself noticed her.

She danced enraptured—carried away, intoxicated with pleasure, forgetting everything in this triumph of her beauty and the glory of her success, floating in a cloud of happiness formed by all this homage, all this admiration, all the desires she had stirred up—by this victory so complete and so sweet to the heart of a woman.

When she left the party, it was almost four in the morning. Her husband had been sleeping since midnight in a small, deserted sitting room, with three other gentlemen whose wives were having a wonderful time.

Literary Analysis
Characterization
What does Madame Loisel's comment reveal indirectly about her attitudes and values?

Vocabulary Builder
resplendent (ri splen´ dənt) *adj.* shining brightly

 Reading Check

Why does Madame Loisel visit Madame Forestier?

The Necklace ■ 297

9 Literary Analysis
Characterization

• **Ask** students why Madame Loisel is still dissatisfied even though she has a new dress.
  Answer: She does not have any jewels to wear.

• **Ask** students why she rejects her husband's suggestion to wear fresh flowers.
  Answer: She feels that she would still look poverty-stricken.

• **Ask** students the Literary Analysis question: What does Madame Loisel's comment reveal indirectly about her attitudes and values?
  Possible response: Her comment reveals that she believes she must have expensive things; she values appearances.

10 Critical Thinking
Analyze

• Read aloud the bracketed passage. **Ask** students to identify the kinds of jewels that Madame Loisel examines in this passage.
  Answer: She examines pearls, gold, and diamonds.

• **Ask** students to analyze what Madame Loisel wants as she looks at the jewelry.
  Possible response: She is only satisfied when she reaches the diamond necklace. She wants the life of comfort and beauty that diamonds represent.

11 Reading Check

Answer: She wants to borrow some jewelry.

Differentiated
Instruction   Solutions for All Learners

Strategy for Less Proficient Readers
To give students a context for the selection and help them understand how to identify and interpret details of characterization, show them **Literary Analysis Graphic Organizer B** (*Graphic Organizers,* p. 63). Review the completed organizer with them to make sure they see how the details lead to a logical interpretation of the character. Have students use the completed graphic organizer as a model for identifying other details of characterization as they continue to read the selection.

Analyze Cause and Effect

- Have students read the bracketed passage. Point out that Madame Loisel had been enjoying herself at the party, dancing and "floating in a cloud of happiness."

- **Ask** students what causes Madame Loisel's mood to change and why. **Answer:** Madame Loisel's mood changes when her husband brings their coats; she does not want the other women, who are wearing fur coats, to see her shabby wrap.

- Remind students that a single cause may produce several effects. **Ask:** What happens as a result of Madame Loisel's preoccupation with her wrap? **Answer:** The couple quickly leaves the party without stopping to call for a cab, and they end up having to walk in the cold.

13 Critical Viewing

Possible response: It could illustrate Madame Forestier giving Madame Loisel the necklace.

14 Humanities

The New Necklace, 1910, by William McGregor Paxton

William McGregor Paxton (1869–1941) was an American artist best known for his portraits of upper-class life. Use these questions for discussion.

1. If these women were Madame Loisel and Madame Forestier, which would you identify as Madame Loisel? **Answer:** The contrasting clothing and attitudes of the two women and the artist's use of light and shadow suggest that the figure standing on the right is Madame Loisel.

2. What does the painting suggest about the two women's attitudes toward the necklace? **Answer:** The seated woman seems to be holding the necklace carelessly, whereas the standing woman is reaching for it with great care. This suggests that the seated woman is accustomed to wealth, but the other woman is in awe of it.

He brought her wraps so that they could leave and put them around her shoulders—the plain wraps from her everyday life whose shabbiness jarred with the elegance of her evening dress. She felt this and wanted to escape quickly so that the other women, who were enveloping themselves in their rich furs, wouldn't see her.

Loisel held her back.

"Wait a minute. You'll catch cold out there. I'm going to call a **12** cab."

But she wouldn't listen to him and went hastily downstairs. Outside in the street, there was no cab to be found; they set out to look for one, calling to the drivers they saw passing in the distance.

They walked toward the Seine,[4] shivering and miserable. Finally, on the embankment, they found one of those ancient nocturnal broughams[5] which are only to be seen in Paris at night, as if they were ashamed to show their shabbiness in daylight.

It took them to their door in the Rue des Martyrs, and they went sadly upstairs to their apartment. For her, it was all over. And he was thinking that he had to be at the Ministry by ten.

She took off her wraps before the mirror so that she could see herself in all her glory once more. Then she cried out. The necklace was gone; there was nothing around her neck.

Her husband, already half undressed, asked:

"What's the matter?"

She turned toward him in a frenzy:

"The . . . the . . . necklace—it's gone."

He got up, thunderstruck.

"What did you say? . . . What! . . . Impossible!"

And they searched the folds of her dress, the folds of her wrap, the pockets, everywhere. They didn't find it.

He asked:

"Are you sure you still had it when we left the ball?"

"Yes. I remember touching it in the hallway of the Ministry."

"But if you had lost it in the street, we would have heard it fall. It must be in the cab."

"Yes, most likely. Do you remember the number?"

---

4. **Seine** (sān) river flowing through Paris.
5. **broughams** (brōōms) *n.* horse-drawn carriages.

298 ■ *Short Stories*

13 ▼ Critical Viewing
What important part of the story could this image illustrate? **[Connect]**

14

The New Necklace, 1910, William McGregor Paxton, Courtesy, Museum of Fine Arts, Boston

---

Vocabulary Development

Think Aloud: Context Clues
Tell students that sometimes story events and characters' reactions to events can be clues to the meaning of an unfamiliar word.

Direct students' attention to the word *dejection* at the top of p. 299. Using the think-aloud process, model how to use context to infer the meaning of an unknown word. Say to students:

I'm going to show you how I would figure out the meaning of *dejection*. In this sentence, *dejection* describes the state of mind of M. and Madame Loisel. I know that Madame Loisel has just discovered that she lost the diamond necklace. They have searched everywhere for it. All hope of finding it seems lost.

I know that if I had lost an expensive necklace that I had borrowed, and had little hope of finding it, I would feel depressed. So I think that *dejection* must mean depression or discouragement.

"No. What about you—did you notice it?"

"No."

They looked at each other in utter dejection. Finally Loisel got dressed again.

"I'm going to retrace the whole distance we covered on foot," he said, "and see if I can't find it."

And he left the house. She remained in her evening dress, too weak to go to bed, sitting crushed on a chair, lifeless and blank.

Her husband returned at about seven o'clock. He had found nothing.

He went to the police station, to the newspapers to offer a reward, to the offices of the cab companies—in a word, wherever there seemed to be the slightest hope of tracing it.

15 She spent the whole day waiting, in a state of utter hopelessness before such an appalling catastrophe.

Loisel returned in the evening, his face lined and pale; he had learned nothing.

"You must write to your friend," he said, "and tell her that you've broken the clasp of the necklace and that you're getting it mended. That'll give us time to decide what to do."

She wrote the letter at his dictation.

By the end of the week, they had lost all hope.

Loisel, who had aged five years, declared:

"We'll have to replace the necklace."

The next day they took the case in which it had been kept and went to the jeweler whose name appeared inside it. He looked through his ledgers:

"I didn't sell this necklace, madame. I only supplied the case."

Then they went from one jeweler to the next, trying to find a necklace like the other, racking their memories, both of them sick with worry and distress.

In a fashionable shop near the Palais Royal, they found a diamond necklace which they decided was exactly like the other. It was worth 40,000 francs. They could have it for 36,000 francs.

They asked the jeweler to hold it for them for three days, and they stipulated that he should take it back for 34,000 francs if the other necklace was found before the end of February.

Loisel possessed 18,000 francs left him by his father. He would borrow the rest.

He borrowed, asking a thousand francs from one man, five hundred from another, a hundred here, fifty there. He signed promissory notes,[6] borrowed at exorbitant rates, dealt with usurers and the entire race of moneylenders. He compromised his whole

---

6. **promissory** (präm´ i sôr´ē) **notes** written promises to pay back borrowed money.

Literary Analysis
Characterization
What do the Loisels' actions after the necklace is lost reveal about their individual characters?

16 ✓ **Reading Check**

What do the Loisels do to replace the necklace?

The Necklace ■ 299

15 **Literary Analysis**
Characterization

- Have students read the bracketed passage. Then, **ask** them what action M. Loisel takes to recover the missing necklace.
  Answer: He retraces the couple's steps, looking for the necklace. He goes to the police station and the cab company and offers a reward in the newspaper. He instructs his wife to write a letter to her friend in an attempt to buy time.

- **Ask:** What action does Madame Loisel take?
  Answer: She sits in a chair, waiting all day while her husband looks for the necklace. She writes the letter to her friend as he dictates it.

- Point out to students that it is M. Loisel who decides that the necklace must be replaced. Then, **ask** students the Literary Analysis question: What do the Loisels' actions after the necklace is lost reveal about their individual characters?
  Possible response: M. Loisel is a responsible person who attempts to make up for the loss. Madame Loisel is selfish and always feels that she has been wronged. In addition, she expects others to solve problems that she has created.

▶ **Monitor Progress:** Review students' graphic organizers to ensure that they are identifying and interpreting details of characterization.

▶ **Reteach:** If students have difficulty, help them identify details from p. 299 that support the characterization of M. Loisel as helpful and caring, and Madame Loisel as self-centered and helpless. Have students record the information on their graphic organizers.

16 **Reading Check**

Answer: They spend their savings and borrow money to buy a new necklace.

- Have students **summarize** Madame Forestier's attitude when Madame Loisel returns the necklace. **Ask** them how her attitude differs from when Madame Loisel borrowed the necklace.
Answer: She is irritated and impatient when Madame Loisel returns the necklace. When Madame Loisel first borrowed the necklace, Madame Forestier seemed friendly and generous.

- **Ask** students how Madame Forestier's attitude might have contributed to Madame Loisel's fear.
Possible response: Madame Loisel probably worried that Madame Forestier would carefully inspect the necklace because she was so irritated by its late return.

- **Ask** students the Reading Skill question: What fear prevents the Loisels from telling Madame Forestier the necklace was lost?
Possible response: They are afraid that they might be accused of stealing the necklace.

career, gave his signature even when he wasn't sure he would be able to honor it, and horrified by the anxieties with which his future would be filled, by the black misery about to descend upon him, by the prospect of physical privation and moral suffering, went to get the new necklace, placing on the jeweler's counter 36,000 francs.

When Madame Loisel went to return the necklace, Madame Forestier said in a faintly waspish tone:

"You could have brought it back a little sooner! I might have needed it."

She didn't open the case as her friend had feared she might. If she had noticed the substitution, what would she have thought? What would she have said? Mightn't she have taken Madame Loisel for a thief?

Madame Loisel came to know the awful life of the poverty-stricken. However, she resigned herself to it with unexpected fortitude. The crushing debt had to be paid. She would pay it. They dismissed the maid; they moved into an attic under the roof.

She came to know all the heavy household chores, the loathsome work of the kitchen. She washed the dishes, wearing down her pink nails on greasy casseroles and the bottoms of saucepans. She did the laundry, washing shirts and dishcloths which she hung on a line to dry; she took the garbage down to the street every morning, and carried water upstairs, stopping at every floor to get her breath. Dressed like a working-class woman, she went to the fruit store, the grocer, and the butcher with her basket on her arm, bargaining, outraged, contesting each sou[7] of her pitiful funds.

Every month some notes had to be honored and more time requested on others.

Her husband worked in the evenings, putting a shopkeeper's ledgers in order, and often at night as well, doing copying at twenty-five centimes a page.

And it went on like that for ten years.

After ten years, they had made good on everything, including the usurious rates and the compound interest.

Madame Loisel looked old now. She had become the sort of strong woman, hard and coarse, that one finds in poor families. Disheveled, her skirts askew, with reddened hands, she spoke in a loud voice, slopping water over the floors as she washed them. But sometimes, when her husband was at the office, she would sit down by the window and muse over that party long ago when she had been so beautiful, the belle of the ball.

---

7. **sou** (so͞o) *n.* former French coin, worth very little; the centime (sän′ tēm′), mentioned later, was also of little value.

Reading Skill
Analyze Cause and Effect What fear prevents the Loisels from telling Madame Forestier the necklace was lost?

Vocabulary Builder
disheveled (di shev′ əld) *adj.* untidy

Vocabulary Development

Vocabulary Knowledge Rating
When students have completed reading and discussing "The Necklace," have them take out their **Vocabulary Knowledge Rating Chart** for this selection. Read the words aloud once more and have students rate their knowledge of the words again in the After Reading column. Clarify any words that are still problematic. Have students write their own definition and example or sentence in the appropriate column. Then have students complete the **Vocabulary Builder Practice** activities on p. 303. Encourage students to use the words in further discussion and written work about this selection. Remind them that they will be accountable for these words on the Selection Test.

How would things have turned out if she hadn't lost that necklace? Who could tell? How strange and fickle life is! How little it takes to make or break you!

Then one Sunday when she was strolling along the Champs Elysées[8] to forget the week's chores for a while, she suddenly caught sight of a woman taking a child for a walk. It was Madame Forestier, still young, still beautiful, still charming.

Madame Loisel started to tremble. Should she speak to her? Yes, certainly she should. And now that she had paid everything back, why shouldn't she tell her the whole story?

She went up to her.

"Hello, Jeanne."

The other didn't recognize her and was surprised that this plainly dressed woman should speak to her so familiarly. She murmured:

"But . . . madame! . . . I'm sure . . . You must be mistaken."

"No, I'm not. I am Mathilde Loisel."

Her friend gave a little cry.

"Oh! Oh, my poor Mathilde, how you've changed!"

"Yes, I've been through some pretty hard times since I last saw you and I've had plenty of trouble—and all because of you!"

"Because of me? What do you mean?"

"You remember the diamond necklace you lent me to wear to the party at the Ministry?"

"Yes. What about it?"

"Well, I lost it."

"What are you talking about? You returned it to me."

"What I gave back to you was another one just like it. And it took us ten years to pay for it. You can imagine it wasn't easy for us, since we were quite poor. . . . Anyway, I'm glad it's over and done with."

Madame Forestier stopped short.

"You say you bought a diamond necklace to replace that other one?"

"Yes. You didn't even notice then? They really were exactly alike."

And she smiled, full of a proud, simple joy.

Madame Forestier, profoundly moved, took Mathilde's hands in her own.

"Oh, my poor, poor Mathilde! Mine was false. It was worth five hundred francs at the most!"

---

8. **Champs Elysées** (shän zā lē zā´) fashionable street in Paris.

Reading Skill
Analyze Cause and Effect What causes Madame Loisel to tremble at the sight of Madame Forestier?

Vocabulary Builder
profoundly (prō fɵund´ lē) *adv.* deeply

The Necklace ■ 301

⑱ Reading Skill
Analyze Cause and Effect

- **Ask** students to describe how Madame Loisel has changed since she began to repay the couple's debt.
  Answer: She has dismissed her maid and resigned herself to being poor. Her looks and manners have aged and roughened.

- Have students read the bracketed passage, and then **ask** them the Reading Skill question: What causes Madame Loisel to tremble at the sight of Madame Forestier?
  Possible response: Madame Forestier has kept her grace and beauty, while Madame Loisel has become old and coarse. Perhaps Madame Loisel is overwhelmed by painful memories awakened by the sight of her former friend.

- Point out to students that Madame Loisel wonders about how her life would have been different if it had not been for one event that set off a chain of causes and effects. Help students outline the causes and effects that have brought Madame Loisel to this point.

Concept Connector

Anticipation Guide
Have students return to their **Anticipation Guides** and respond to the statements again in the After Reading column. Then, lead a class discussion, probing for what students have learned that confirms or invalidates each statement.

Connecting to the Literature
Have students compare the sentences they wrote before reading with their thoughts about why people might emphasize expensive possessions. Ask them to explain any change.

Literary Skill Graphic Organizer
Have students review the graphic organizers they completed to identify and interpret details of characterization while reading. Show them **Literary Analysis Graphic Organizer B** (*Graphic Organizer Transparencies*, p. 63) as an example. Then have students share the graphic organizers they did and the details they identified about the characters.

Apply the Skills

The Necklace

Thinking About the Selection

1. **Respond:** Do you feel sorry for Madame Loisel at the end of the story? Why or why not?
2. **(a) Recall:** As the story begins, why is Madame Loisel unhappy with her life? **(b) Infer:** Do you think the author wants readers to sympathize with her unhappiness? Why or why not?
3. **(a) Recall:** How does her husband respond to Madame Loisel's disappointment over the invitation? **(b) Compare and Contrast:** How is M. Loisel different from his wife?
4. **(a) Interpret:** How does Madame Loisel change over the ten years as she works to pay off the cost of the necklace? **(b) Draw Conclusions:** What causes her to change?
5. **Analyze:** What message do you think the surprise ending about the necklace's actual value expresses? Explain.

Literary Analysis

6. Describe Madame Loisel's **character.** Support your answer with at least one example of each of the following methods of **indirect characterization** in the story: **(a)** Madame Loisel's actions and behavior; **(b)** her words and thoughts; and **(c)** the effect she has on other people.
7. **(a)** Is the conversation on the day of the ball in which the Loisels discuss Madame's attire an example of **indirect characterization** or **direct characterization**? Explain. **(b)** What do you learn about both Monsieur and Madame Loisel's characters from this exchange?

Reading Skill

8. Use a chart like the one shown to **analyze cause and effect** in this story. **(a)** Note two causes for Madame Loisel's decision to borrow the necklace from Madame Forestier. **(b)** List three effects of this decision.

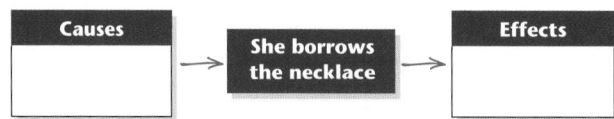

Causes		She borrows the necklace		Effects

9. Does Madame Loisel cause her own suffering? Explain your answer.

QuickReview

Who's Who in the Story
Mme. Loisel: a middle-class French woman who borrows a necklace

M. Loisel: her husband

Mme. Forestier: a wealthy friend who lends the necklace

Go **O**nline
—**Assessment**
For: Self-test
Visit: www.PHSchool.com
Web Code: epa-6207

Character: a person or an animal that partici-pates in the action of a literary work

Characterization: methods writers use to reveal characters' traits; writers may use *direct* or *indirect char-acterization*

Cause: an event, an action, or a feeling that produces a result

Effect: the result pro-duced by an event, an action, or a feeling

Answers (left column)

1. Some students may feel sorry for Madame Loisel because she loses so much and suffers needlessly. Others may feel that she brought on her own misfortunes.

2. (a) Beautiful and charming, she believes she is ill-suited for a lower-class life. (b) Some students may think that Maupassant wants readers to empathize with Mme. Loisel. However, others will think that she is a spoiled, self-centered woman.

3. (a) He tries to find a way for her to be happy. (b) He is much less selfish and much more loving than she is.

4. (a) She loses her charm and beauty and becomes old before her time. (b) Hard, rough work and hopelessness cause her to lose her beauty and become embittered.

5. Mme. Loisel has wasted her life chasing after material goods, which are worth less than love and strength of character.

6. Mme. Loisel is shallow, selfish, and self-centered. (a) **Actions:** She uses the money her husband has saved to buy a new dress for herself; (b) **Words and thoughts:** She dreams about all the beautiful luxuries she thinks she should have; she tells her husband that she is unhappy about the invitation to the party. (c) **Effect:** She makes her hus-band unhappy and finally causes him to incur a massive debt.

7. (a) It is an example of indirect characterization. The reader learns about the characters through their thoughts and what they say to each other. (b) M. Loisel loves his wife, tries to please her, and is willing to sacri-fice his own pleasure to make her happy. Madame Loisel is selfish and thoughtless; she complains about the invitation and about her clothing; she is willing to let her husband sacrifice his own pleasure for her.

8. **Possible response:** (a) **Causes:** She is invited to a party; she does not want to look like she is poor. (b) **Effects:** She looks beautiful at the party; she loses the necklace; she then lives in poverty. Another

sample answer can be found on **Reading Skill Graphic Organizer B,** p. 66 in *Graphic Organizer Transparencies.*

9. Some students will suggest that she causes her own suffering by being so discontented; others may say that she is a victim of fate.

Vocabulary Builder

Practice Tell whether each sentence below makes sense. Use the meaning of the italicized vocabulary word to explain your answer.

1. After the party, the hostess was *rueful* about her graceful hospitality.

2. The tired campers were *resplendent* as they hiked in the rain.

3. Alan went to the interview *disheveled* and wearing a new suit.

4. The class was *profoundly* moved by the story of the heroic dog.

Adding Words to Your Vocabulary Using a thesaurus, find a **synonym**, or word with a similar meaning, for each word in the vocabulary list for "The Necklace" on page 292. Then, use each synonym correctly in a sentence. (For more on using a thesaurus, see page R7.)

Writing

Think about a lesson that you could teach the Loisels to help them move on with their lives. Create a **written presentation** that details your suggestions to them.

• Jot down some of the issues they might face. For each, consider what you might teach them and how best to convey your ideas.

• Based on your audience, purpose, and point of view as an outsider, choose an appropriate text structure for your presentation. For example, you might write an essay, or you might tell a story with a moral. Include an introduction to briefly explain your choice.

For *Grammar, Vocabulary,* and *Assessment,* see **Build Language Skills,** pages 318–319.

Extend Your Learning

Listening and Speaking As Madame Loisel, write and deliver a **monologue** telling your husband the true value of the lost necklace.

• Consider the feelings and thoughts that Madame Loisel might want to share with her husband.

• Decide if Madame Loisel will defend herself or be apologetic.

• Use gestures and language appropriate to the character.

Research and Technology With classmates, use library and Internet resources to gather information about diamonds. Present your findings in an **informative brochure.** Take notes as you do your research, and decide which information would work best in a chart or drawing.

The Necklace ■ 303

Go Online **For:** An additional research activity
—Research **Visit:** www.PHSchool.com
Web Code: epd-7205
For another research activity to extend students' learning, give students this Web Code.

303

❸ Background

The Game of Chess The game of chess was originally known as *chaturanga,* a name that referred to the four divisions of the Indian army of the sixth century: elephants, horses, chariots, and foot soldiers. During the Middle Ages, games of chess became part of courtship rituals between knights and ladies.

❹ Connecting to the Literature

- To help students understand the meanings of the words they are asked to use, give them these sentences:

  1. Playing a game might *induce* a group of people to set aside their differences.

  2. Some kinds of games *evoke* pleasant memories of childhood.

  3. To *initiate* a game is to risk an emotional tug of war among players.

  4. Some games *generate* feelings of anger and hostility between teams.

- Help students further develop their expressive vocabulary by providing these words: *agitate, controversy, potential,* and *strategy.* Encourage them to use these words as they discuss the selection.

Go Online
Author Link For additional information about Amy Tan, have students type in the Web Code, then select *T* from the alphabet, and then select *Amy Tan.*

304

Build Understanding • *Rules of the Game*

Short Story

❸ Background

The Game of Chess A game of strategy, chess resembles a battle between two armies, each led by a figurehead king and a powerful queen. Chess may have started in India. After it spread to Persia (present-day Iran), Arab invaders introduced it to other lands. Today, it is played throughout the world.

❹ Connecting to the Literature

Reading/Writing Connection In "Rules of the Game," chess becomes both a bridge between individuals and cultures and the source of an emotional tug of war within a family. Write a brief account of how games can both unite and divide people. Use at least three of these words: *induce, evoke, initiate, generate.*

Review

For **Literary Analysis, Reading Skills,** and **Vocabulary Builder,** see page 292.

READ MORE

by Amy Tan
The Kitchen God's Wife
The Hundred Secret Senses

Meet the Author

Amy **Tan** (b. 1952)

As a child, Amy Tan did not imagine that she would become a successful novelist. Her parents, who had emigrated from China to the San Francisco Bay area, wanted her to become a doctor. Doubting her abilities in science, Tan instead majored in English in college. She went on to become a successful business writer.

Finding Herself in Fiction In her mid-thirties, Tan began writing stories. While she was surprised by the pleasure writing fiction gave her, she was even more surprised by the content of her work. Tan had tried to play down her ethnicity, but in her fiction, she found herself exploring the experiences of Chinese American women. In 1985, Tan wrote "Rules of the Game," which she later included in her best-selling first novel, *The Joy Luck Club.*

Fast Facts

▶ When she was eight, Tan's essay "What the Library Means to Me" won first prize in a local contest.

▶ *The Joy Luck Club* was made into a popular film in 1993.

For: More about the author
Visit: www.PHSchool.com
Web Code: epe-9209

304 ■ Short Stories

Differentiated Instruction   Solutions for All Learners

Support for Below-Level Students [L1, L2]	Support for English Learners [EL]

Unit 2 Resources
    Vocabulary Warm-up Word Lists, p. 127
    Vocabulary Warm-up Practice, p. 128
    Reading Warm-up A, p. 129
    Selection Test A, pp. 139–141
 	
Graphic Organizer Transparencies
    Literary Analysis Graphic Organizer,
    Transparency B, p. 64
	Unit 2 Resources
	    Vocabulary Warm-up Word Lists, p. 127
	    Vocabulary Warm-up Practice, p. 128
	    Reading Warm-up A, p. 129
	
	Listening to Literature Audio CD

① ② Rules of the Game

from The Joy Luck Club

Amy Tan

I was six when my mother taught me the art of invisible strength. It was a strategy for winning arguments, respect from others, and eventually, though neither of us knew it at the time, chess games.

"Bite back your tongue," scolded my mother when I cried loudly, yanking her hand toward the store that sold bags of salted plums. At home, she said, "Wise guy, he not go against wind. In Chinese we say, Come from South, blow with wind—poom!—North will follow. Strongest wind cannot be seen."

The next week I bit back my tongue as we entered the store with the forbidden candies. When my mother finished her shopping, she quietly plucked a small bag of plums from the rack and put it on the counter with the rest of the items.

My mother imparted her daily truths so she could help my older brothers and me rise above our circumstances. We lived in San Francisco's Chinatown. Like most of the other Chinese children who played in the back alleys of restaurants and curio shops, I didn't think we were poor. My bowl was always full, three five-course meals every day, beginning with a soup full of mysterious things I didn't want to know the names of.

We lived on Waverly Place, in a warm, clean, two-bedroom flat that sat above a small Chinese bakery specializing in steamed pastries and dim sum. In the early morning, when the alley was still

③ ✓ Reading Check

What "art" did the narrator learn from her mother?

Rules of the Game ■ 305

305

Analyze

- Have students read the bracketed passage. Then **ask** them what culture the narrator is describing.
  Answer: The narrator is describing Chinese culture.

- Have students **identify** which elements in this description are similar to American culture and which elements are associated more with Chinese culture.
  Possible response: The playground, its equipment, and feeding the pigeons are associated with American culture. The cooking smells, medicinal herb shop, and selling the turtles as food are associated with Chinese culture.

❺ Literary Analysis

Characterization

- Ask a volunteer to read aloud the bracketed passage, and then tell students that the sanddab is a fish commonly found in San Francisco Bay.

- **Ask** students why the sanddab reminds the narrator of her mother's story.
  Answer: The fish looks like it has been smashed flat, like the girl in the mother's story.

- Draw students' attention to the last sentence in the passage. **Ask** them to respond to the Literary Analysis question: What does this quotation reveal about the narrator's mother?
  Possible response: The quotation reveals that the mother does not speak English well and that her native language most likely is Chinese. She probably holds traditional Chinese cultural values as well.

---

quiet, I could smell fragrant red beans as they were cooked down to a pasty sweetness. By daybreak, our flat was heavy with the odor of fried sesame balls and sweet curried chicken crescents. From my bed, I would listen as my father got ready for work, then locked the door behind him, one-two-three clicks.

At the end of our two-block alley was a small sandlot playground with swings and slides well-shined down the middle with use. The play area was bordered by wood-slat benches where old-country people sat cracking roasted watermelon seeds with their golden teeth and scattering the husks to an impatient gathering of gurgling pigeons. The best playground, however, was the dark alley itself. It was crammed with daily mysteries and adventures. My brothers and I would peer into the medicinal herb shop, watching old Li dole out onto a stiff sheet of white paper the right amount of insect shells, saffron-colored seeds and <u>pungent</u> leaves for his ailing customers. It was said that he once cured a woman dying of an ancestral curse that had eluded the best of American doctors. Next to the pharmacy was a printer who specialized in gold-embossed wedding invitations and festive red banners.

Farther down the street was Ping Yuen Fish Market. The front window displayed a tank crowded with doomed fish and turtles struggling to gain footing on the slimy green-tiled sides. A handwritten sign informed tourists, "Within this store, is all for food, not for pet." Inside, the butchers with their bloodstained white smocks deftly gutted the fish while customers cried out their orders and shouted, "Give me your freshest," to which the butchers always protested, "All are freshest." On less crowded market days, we would inspect the crates of live frogs and crabs which we were warned not to poke, boxes of dried cuttlefish, and row upon row of iced prawns, squid, and slippery fish. The sanddabs made me shiver each time; their eyes lay on one flattened side and reminded me of my mother's story of a careless girl who ran into a crowded street and was crushed by a cab. "Was smash flat," reported my mother.

At the corner of the alley was Hong Sing's, a four-table cafe with a recessed stairwell in front that led to a door marked "Tradesmen." My brothers and I believed the bad people emerged from this door at night. Tourists never went to Hong Sing's, since the menu was printed only in Chinese. A Caucasian man with a big camera once posed me and my playmates in front of the restaurant. He had us move to the side of the picture window so the photo would capture

306 ■ *Short Stories*

Vocabulary Builder
pungent (pun´ jənt)
adj. producing a sharp smell

Literary Analysis
Characterization
What does this quotation reveal about the narrator's mother?

Vocabulary Development

Vocabulary Builder Reinforcement
Students will benefit from additional examples and practice with the Vocabulary Builder words. Reinforce their comprehension with "show-you-know" sentences. The first part of the sentence uses the vocabulary word in an appropriate context. The second part of the sentence—the "show-you-know" part—clarifies the first. Model the strategy with this example for *pungent*:

The *pungent* smell of fried chicken wafted from the restaurant; the strong aroma made me hungry.

Then, give students these sentence prompts, and coach them in creating the clarification part.
1. The meaning of her *retort* was unmistakable;

   Sample answer: its sharpness told me that she was very angry.
2. The old trench coat was *malodorous*;

   Sample answer: they could never get it to smell pleasant again.

the roasted duck with its head dangling from a juice-covered rope. After he took the picture, I told him he should go into Hong Sing's and eat dinner. When he smiled and asked me what they served, I shouted, "Guts and duck's feet and octopus gizzards!" Then I ran off with my friends, shrieking with laughter as we scampered across the alley and hid in the entryway grotto of the China Gem Company, my heart pounding with hope that he would chase us.

My mother named me after the street that we lived on: Waverly Place Jong, my official name for important American documents. But my family called me Meimei [mā´ mā´], "Little Sister," I was the youngest, the only daughter. Each morning before school, my mother would twist and yank on my thick black hair until she had formed two tightly wound pigtails. One day, as she struggled to weave a hard-toothed comb through my disobedient hair, I had a sly thought.

I asked her, "Ma, what is Chinese torture?" My mother shook her head. A bobby pin was wedged between her lips. She wetted her palm and smoothed the hair above my ear, then pushed the pin in so that it nicked sharply against my scalp.

"Who say this word?" she asked without a trace of knowing how wicked I was being. I shrugged my shoulders and said, "Some boy in my class said Chinese people do Chinese torture."

"Chinese people do many things," she said simply. "Chinese people do business, do medicine, do painting. Not lazy like American people. We do torture. Best torture."

My older brother Vincent was the one who actually got the chess set. We had gone to the annual Christmas party held at the First Chinese Baptist Church at the end of the alley. The missionary ladies had put together a Santa bag of gifts donated by members of another church. None of the gifts had names on them. There were separate sacks for boys and girls of different ages.

One of the Chinese parishioners had donned a Santa Claus costume and a stiff paper beard with cotton balls glued to it. I think the only children who thought he was the real thing were too young to know that Santa Claus was not Chinese. When my turn came up, the Santa man asked me how old I was. I thought it was a trick question; I was seven according to the American formula and eight by the Chinese calendar. I said I was born on March 17, 1951. That seemed to satisfy him. He then solemnly asked if I had been a very, very good girl this year and did I believe in Jesus Christ and obey my parents. I knew the only answer to that. I nodded back with equal solemnity.

Literary Analysis
Characterization
What does Mrs. Jong's response to the accusation that Chinese people do torture reveal about her personality?

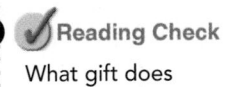

Reading Check

What gift does Vincent receive at the Christmas party?

❻ Literary Analysis
Characterization

- Have students read the bracketed passage. **Ask:** Why does Waverly ask her mother about Chinese torture, and what does the question reveal about Waverly's character? **Possible response:** She probably wants to give her mother a hard time. The question reveals that Waverly is mischievous and has a sense of humor.

- **Ask** students to respond to the Literary Analysis question: What does Mrs. Jong's response to the accusation that Chinese people do torture reveal about her personality? **Possible response:** Her response reveals that she is proud of her culture. It also reveals that she knows Waverly is baiting her and trying to make her defensive. Her response turns the tables on Waverly and demonstrates Mrs. Jong's sense of humor and intelligence.

❼ Reading Check

Answer: Vincent receives a used chess set.

❽ Literary Analysis
Characterization

- Refer students to the bracketed passage. **Ask:** What is Waverly attempting to do as she analyzes the size and shape of the gifts?
  Answer: She is trying to determine which package contains a nice gift.

- **Ask** students to respond to the Literary Analysis question: What does Waverly's thought process in this paragraph reveal indirectly about her character?
  Possible response: She is very careful and practical; she is analytical and calculating.

❾ Literary Analysis
Characterization

- Have a volunteer read aloud the bracketed passage. Discuss with students the different reactions of Mrs. Jong, Vincent, and Winston to the gift of the chess set.

- Then **ask** students what Mrs. Jong's statement and action suggest about her character.
  Answer: She is too proud to be comfortable accepting the incomplete, discarded set and tells Vincent to throw it out.

❿ Reading Skill
Analyze Cause and Effect

- **Ask** students why Waverly thinks the chessmen are so powerful.
  Answer: The patterns of the chessboard and the strategic puzzle of the chessmen's movements are loaded with meaning and mystery for Waverly. Her response suggests she has a strong affinity for the game.

- **Ask** students to respond to the Reading Skill question: What effect does the gift of the chess board have on Waverly?
  Possible response: She is fascinated by it and wants to learn its secrets.

- Ask students what Waverly's interest in the chess set causes her to do.
  Answer: It causes her to beg for her brother's permission to play.

Having watched the other children opening their gifts, I already knew that the big gifts were not necessarily the nicest ones. One girl my age got a large coloring book of biblical characters, while a less greedy girl who selected a small box received a glass vial of lavender toilet water. The sound of the box was also important. A ten-year-old boy had chosen a box that jangled when he shook it. It was a tin globe of the world with a slit for inserting money. He must have thought it was full of dimes and nickels, because when he saw that it had just ten pennies, his face fell with such undisguised disappointment that his mother slapped the side of his head and led him out of the church hall, apologizing to the crowd for her son who had such bad manners he couldn't appreciate such a fine gift.

As I peered into the sack, I quickly fingered the remaining presents, testing their weight, imagining what they contained. I chose a heavy, compact one that was wrapped in shiny silver foil and a red satin ribbon. It was a twelve-pack of Life Savers and I spent the rest of the party arranging and rearranging the candy tubes in the order of my favorites. My brother Winston chose wisely as well. His present turned out to be a box of intricate plastic parts; the instructions on the box proclaimed that when they were properly assembled he would have an authentic miniature replica of a World War II submarine.

Vincent got the chess set, which would have been a very decent present to get at a church Christmas party except it was obviously used and, as we discovered later, it was missing a black pawn and a white knight. My mother graciously thanked the unknown benefactor, saying, "Too good. Cost too much." At which point, an old lady with fine white, wispy hair nodded toward our family and said with a whistling whisper, "Merry, merry Christmas."

When we got home, my mother told Vincent to throw the chess set away. "She not want it. We not want it," she said, tossing her head stiffly to the side with a tight, proud smile. My brothers had deaf ears. They were already lining up the chess pieces and reading from the dog-eared instruction book.

I watched Vincent and Winston play during Christmas week. The chess board seemed to hold elaborate secrets waiting to be untangled. The chessmen were more powerful than Old Li's magic herbs that cured ancestral curses. And my brothers wore such serious faces that I was sure something was at stake that was greater than avoiding the tradesmen's door to Hong Sing's.

Literary Analysis
Characterization
What does Waverly's thought process in this paragraph reveal indirectly about her character?

Reading Skill
Cause and Effect
What effect does the gift of the chess board have on Waverly?

Vocabulary Development

Expressive Vocabulary
Ask students to think about what happened as Waverly's brothers began playing chess. How were relationships among the siblings affected? As students discuss the family's chess playing, encourage them to use the expressive vocabulary presented earlier. You might encourage them with sentence starters like these:

1. Waverly had a tough time trying to *induce* . . .
2. When one of the brothers lost a game of chess, it seemed to *evoke* . . .
3. Discussion of the rules of the game was sure to *initiate* . . .
4. Waverly found that the challenge of learning to play began to *generate* . . .

"Let me! Let me!" I begged between games when one brother or the other would sit back with a deep sigh of relief and victory, the other annoyed, unable to let go of the outcome. Vincent at first refused to let me play, but when I offered my Life Savers as replacements for the buttons that filled in for the missing pieces, he relented. He chose the flavors: wild cherry for the black pawn and peppermint for the white knight. Winner could eat both. As our mother sprinkled flour and rolled out small doughy circles for the steamed dumplings that would be our dinner that night, Vincent explained the rules, pointing to each piece. "You have sixteen pieces and so do I. One king and queen, two bishops, two knights, two castles, and eight pawns. The pawns can only move forward one step, except on the first move. Then they can move two. But they can only take men by moving crossways like this, except in the beginning, when you can move ahead and take another pawn."

"Why?" I asked as I moved my pawn. "Why can't they move more steps?"

"Because they're pawns," he said.

"But why do they go crossways to take other men? Why aren't there any women and children?"

"Why is the sky blue? Why must you always ask stupid questions?" asked Vincent. "This is a game. These are the rules. I didn't make them up. See. Here. In the book." He jabbed a page with a pawn in his hand. "Pawn. P-A-W-N. Pawn. Read it yourself."

My mother patted the flour off her hands. "Let me see book," she said quietly. She scanned the pages quickly, not reading the foreign English symbols, seeming to search deliberately for nothing in particular.

"This American rules," she concluded at last. "Every time people come out from foreign country, must know rules. You not know, judge say, Too bad, go back. They not telling you why so you can use their way go forward. They say, Don't know why, you find out yourself. But they knowing all the time. Better you take it, find out why yourself." She tossed her head back with a satisfied smile.

I found out about all the whys later. I read the rules and looked up all the big words in a dictionary. I borrowed books from the Chinatown library. I studied each chess piece, trying to absorb the power each contained.

I learned about opening moves and why it's important to control the center early on; the shortest distance between two points is straight down the middle. I learned about the middle game and why tactics between two adversaries are like clashing ideas; the one who plays better has the clearest plans for both attacking and getting

Literary Analysis
Characterization
What do you learn about Vincent based on this conversation?

Reading Check

How does Waverly convince Vincent to let her play chess?

Rules of the Game ■ 309

Cultural Connection In a typical endgame, both players have lost their queens and have limited resources. They attempt to checkmate each other's king, trapping the king in a position where no move is possible. Note to students that the terms *endgame* and *checkmate* are frequently applied beyond the game of chess—especially in military, political, and athletic contests.

Connect to the Literature Point out that chess masters develop their mastery over time and with discipline. **Ask** students the Connect to the Literature question: Why might it be difficult for a young beginning chess player like Waverly to master the endgame?

Answer: It is the most difficult part of the game, when mistakes can have more serious consequences. Waverly might not have the maturity or experience for this.

---

out of traps. I learned why it is essential in the endgame to have foresight, a mathematical understanding of all possible moves, and patience; all weaknesses and advantages become evident to a strong adversary and are obscured to a tiring opponent. I discovered that for the whole game one must gather invisible strengths and see the endgame before the game begins.

I also found out why I should never reveal "why" to others. A little knowledge withheld is a great advantage one should store for future use. That is the power of chess. It is a game of secrets in which one must show and never tell.

I loved the secrets I found within the sixty-four black and white squares. I carefully drew a handmade chessboard and pinned it to the wall next to my bed, where at night I would stare for hours at imaginary battles. Soon I no longer lost any games or Life Savers, but I lost my adversaries. Winston and Vincent decided they were more interested in roaming the streets after school in their Hopalong Cassidy cowboy hats.

On a cold spring afternoon, while walking home from school, I detoured through the playground at the end of our alley. I saw a group of old men, two seated across a folding table playing a game of chess, others smoking pipes, eating peanuts, and watching. I ran home and grabbed Vincent's chess set, which was bound in a cardboard box with rubber bands. I also carefully selected two prized rolls of Life Savers. I came back to the park and approached a man who was observing the game.

"Want to play?" I asked him. His face widened with surprise and he grinned as he looked at the box under my arm.

"Little sister, been a long time since I play with dolls," he said, smiling <u>benevolently</u>. I quickly put the box down next to him on the bench and displayed my <u>retort</u>.

Lau Po, as he allowed me to call him, turned out to be a much better player than my brothers. I lost many games and many Life Savers. But over the weeks, with each diminishing roll of candies, I added new secrets. Lau Po gave me the names. The Double Attack from the East and West Shores. Throwing Stones on the Drowning Man. The Sudden Meeting

310 ■ Short Stories

---

❸ Literature in Context

Cultural Connection

Endgame Endgame describes a tense period in a chess game when the end seems close at hand. With fewer pieces left, lines of attack and defense become clearer to both players. Mistakes are magnified in an endgame, when the margin between victory and defeat can be a single ill-considered move. In this story, Waverly develops a keen awareness of the strategies needed in the endgame to secure a victory.

Connect to the Literature

Why might it be difficult for a young beginning chess player like Waverly to master the endgame?

Vocabulary Builder
benevolently (bə nev´ ə lənt lē) *adv.* in a well-meaning way
retort (ri tôrt´) *n.* sharp or clever reply

Vocabulary Development

Think-Aloud: Context Clues
Direct students' attention to the word *etiquette* on p. 311. Using a think-aloud process, model how to use context to infer the meaning of an unknown word. Say to students:

I'm going to think aloud to show you how I would figure out the meaning of *etiquette* from its context.

In this sentence, *etiquette* is a noun and is being used in relation to a game of chess. At first it might seem that the word refers to a chess strategy, since the previous paragraph lists strategies. However, the following sentences list examples of etiquette—keep men in rows, never say "check" with vanity, do not throw pieces in the sandbox after losing a game. These are examples of what one should not do and are examples of poor behavior or poor manners. So, I think *etiquette* must refer to good manners.

of the Clan. The Surprise from the Sleeping Guard. The Humble Servant Who Kills the King. Sand in the Eyes of Advancing Forces. A Double Killing Without Blood.

There were also the fine points of chess etiquette. Keep captured men in neat rows, as well-tended prisoners. Never announce "Check" with vanity, lest someone with an unseen sword slit your throat. Never hurl pieces into the sandbox after you have lost a game, because then you must find them again, by yourself, after apologizing to all around you. By the end of the summer, Lau Po had taught me all he knew, and I had become a better chess player.

A small weekend crowd of Chinese people and tourists would gather as I played and defeated my opponents one by one. My mother would join the crowds during these outdoor exhibition games. She sat proudly on the bench, telling my admirers with proper Chinese humility, "Is luck."

⓮ A man who watched me play in the park suggested that my mother allow me to play in local chess tournaments. My mother smiled graciously, an answer that meant nothing. I desperately wanted to go, but I bit back my tongue. I knew she would not let me play among strangers. So as we walked home I said in a small voice that I didn't want to play in the local tournament. They would have American rules. If I lost, I would bring shame on my family.

"Is shame you fall down nobody push you," said my mother.

During my first tournament, my mother sat with me in the front row as I waited for my turn. I frequently bounced my legs to unstick them from the cold metal seat of the folding chair. When my name was called, I leapt up. My mother unwrapped something in her lap. It was her chang, a small tablet of red jade which held the sun's fire. "Is luck," she whispered, and tucked it into my dress pocket. I turned to my opponent, a fifteen-year-old boy from Oakland. He looked at me, wrinkling his nose.

As I began to play, the boy disappeared, the color ran out of the room, and I saw only my white pieces and his black ones waiting on the other side. A light wind began blowing past my ears. It whispered secrets only I could hear.

"Blow from the South," it murmured. "The wind leaves no trail." I saw a clear path, the traps to avoid. The crowd rustled. "Shhh! Shhh!" said the corners of the room. The wind blew stronger. "Throw sand from the East to distract him." The knight came forward ready for the sacrifice. The wind hissed, louder and louder. "Blow, blow, blow. He cannot see. He is blind now. Make him lean away from the wind so he is easier to knock down."

Reading Skill
Cause and Effect
What does Waverly anticipate would be the effect of her expressing her desire to play in local chess tournaments?

 Reading Check

How does Waverly's mother respond to Waverly's admirers in the park?

⓮ Reading Skill
Analyze Cause and Effect
- Have students read the bracketed paragraph. **Ask** them to describe how the suggestion that Waverly play in a tournament affects Mrs. Jong.
  Answer: Mrs. Jong smiles and says nothing.
- **Ask** students how Waverly interprets her mother's response.
  Answer: She thinks her mother does not want Waverly to play in tournaments.
- **Ask** students to respond to the Reading Skill question: What does Waverly anticipate would be the effect of her expressing her desire to play in local chess tournaments?
  Possible response: Waverly thinks that if she pleads to be allowed to play, her mother will almost certainly say no.
- **Ask** students how Waverly practices "invisible strength" with her mother and what the effect of that is.
  Answer: Waverly tells her mother that she does not want to play in a tournament because if she loses it will bring shame on her family. Her mother responds that Waverly should play.

⓯ Reading Check
Answer: She tells them that Waverly wins because of luck.

Differentiated Instruction   Solutions for All Learners

Enrichment for Gifted/Talented Students
Some students may be chess players themselves or be interested in learning to play chess. Encourage students to bring in a chess set and demonstrate to the class the basics of how the game is played. They might also create diagrams, charts, or other visuals to demonstrate chess moves or to explain chess terminology from the story.

Point out that some daily newspapers have board contests reproduced in the chess column. Suggest that interested students bring in the newspapers and work with other students to solve the contests.

16 Literary Analysis
Characterization

16 Literary Analysis
Characterization

- Have students read the bracketed passage, and then **identify** the conflict between Waverly and her mother.
  Answer: Her mother does not understand how the game of chess is played; Waverly gets exasperated with her for insisting that it is better to lose fewer pieces.

- **Ask** students to respond to the Literary Analysis question: What do Waverly's mother's comments here reveal indirectly about her ambitions for Waverly?
  Possible responses: She wants Waverly to continue to improve and win; she wants Waverly to be successful.

- ▶ **Monitor Progress:** Use students' answers to the previous question to gauge their understanding of characterization.

- ▶ **Reteach:** If students are having difficulty identifying and interpreting details of characterization, show them **Literary Analysis Graphic Organizer B** (*Graphic Organizer Transparencies*, p. 64). Point out how the details listed tell something about the character.

17 Reading Skill
Analyze Cause and Effect

- **Ask** students to respond to the Reading Skill question: Why is Waverly's picture in *Life* magazine?
  Answer: There has never been a female grandmaster in chess, and Waverly is seen as someone who might achieve this status.

- Refer students to the footnote describing Bobby Fischer. **Ask** them why Waverly's picture is placed next to Bobby Fischer's.
  Answer: Like Bobby Fischer, Waverly is a child prodigy at chess. She is near to disproving his statement that a girl could never be a grandmaster.

312

"Check," I said, as the wind roared with laughter. The wind died down to little puffs, my own breath.

My mother placed my first trophy next to a new plastic chess set that the neighborhood Tao society had given to me. As she wiped each piece with a soft cloth, she said, "Next time win more, lose less."

"Ma, it's not how many pieces you lose," I said. "Sometimes you need to lose pieces to get ahead."

"Better to lose less, see if you really need."

16 At the next tournament, I won again, but it was my mother who wore the triumphant grin.

"Lost eight piece this time. Last time was eleven. What I tell you? Better off lose less!" I was annoyed, but I couldn't say anything.

I attended more tournaments, each one farther away from home. I won all games, in all divisions. The Chinese bakery downstairs from our flat displayed my growing collection of trophies in its window, amidst the dust-covered cakes that were never picked up. The day after I won an important regional tournament, the window encased a fresh sheet cake with whipped-cream frosting and red script saying, "Congratulations, Waverly Jong, Chinatown Chess Champion." Soon after that, a flower shop, headstone engraver, and funeral parlor offered to sponsor me in national tournaments. That's when my mother decided I no longer had to do the dishes. Winston and Vincent had to do my chores.

"Why does she get to play and we do all the work," complained Vincent.

"Is new American rules," said my mother. "Meimei play, squeeze all her brains out for win chess. You play, worth squeeze towel."

17 By my ninth birthday, I was a national chess champion. I was still some 429 points away from grand-master status, but I was touted as the Great American Hope, a child prodigy and a girl to boot. They ran a photo of me in *Life* magazine next to a quote in which Bobby Fischer[1] said, "There will never be a woman grand master." "Your move, Bobby," said the caption.

The day they took the magazine picture I wore neatly plaited braids clipped with plastic barrettes trimmed with rhinestones. I was playing in a large high school auditorium that echoed with phlegmy coughs and the squeaky rubber knobs of chair legs sliding across freshly waxed wooden floors. Seated across from me was an American man, about the same age as Lau Po, maybe fifty. I

---

1. Bobby Fischer Born in 1943, this American chess prodigy attained the top rank of grandmaster in 1958.

Literary Analysis
Characterization
What do Waverly's mother's comments here reveal indirectly about her ambitions for Waverly?

Reading Skill
Cause and Effect
Why is Waverly's picture in *Life* magazine?

remember that his sweaty brow seemed to weep at my every move. He wore a dark, <u>malodorous</u> suit. One of his pockets was stuffed with a great white kerchief on which he wiped his palm before sweeping his hand over the chosen chess piece with great flourish.

In my crisp pink-and-white dress with scratchy lace at the neck, one of two my mother had sewn for these special occasions, I would clasp my hands under my chin, the delicate points of my elbows poised lightly on the table in the manner my mother had shown me for posing for the press. I would swing my patent leather shoes back and forth like an impatient child riding on a school bus. Then I would pause, suck in my lips, twirl my chosen piece in midair as if undecided, and then firmly plant it in its new threatening place, with a triumphant smile thrown back at my opponent for good measure.

I no longer played in the alley of Waverly Place. I never visited the playground where the pigeons and old men gathered. I went to school, then directly home to learn new chess secrets, cleverly concealed advantages, more escape routes.

But I found it difficult to concentrate at home. My mother had a habit of standing over me while I plotted out my games. I think she thought of herself as my protective ally. Her lips would be sealed tight, and after each move I made, a soft "Hmmmmph" would escape from her nose.

"Ma, I can't practice when you stand there like that," I said one day. She retreated to the kitchen and made loud noises with the pots and pans. When the crashing stopped, I could see out of the corner of my eye that she was standing in the doorway. "Hmmmmph!" Only this one came out of her tight throat.

⑲ ▲ Critical Viewing
Based on details in the painting, who do you think is winning this chess game? Explain. **[Analyze]**

Vocabulary Builder
malodorous (mal ō′ dər əs) *adj.* having a bad smell

⑳ ✓ Reading Check
What does Waverly achieve by her ninth birthday?

Rules of the Game ■ 313

- Have students read the bracketed passage. **Ask** what happens when Waverly complains about a noisy bedroom.
  Answer: Her brothers are forced to sleep in the living room.

- **Ask** students how they think Waverly's brothers felt about having to give up their bedroom.
  Answer: They were probably angry and resentful.

- **Ask** students how Waverly feels about her mother introducing her to strangers.
  Answer: She is embarrassed and resentful.

- **Ask** students to respond to the Reading Skill question: In what ways does Waverly's success at chess affect her family life? Explain.
  Possible response: On the positive side, Waverly is treated respectfully, allowed freedom, and given special privileges; her mother is very proud of her. On the negative side, her brothers' lives are disrupted, and they are probably resentful; Waverly is embarrassed and resentful at having her mother show her off.

My parents made many concessions to allow me to practice. One time I complained that the bedroom I shared was so noisy that I couldn't think. Thereafter, my brothers slept in a bed in the living room facing the street. I said I couldn't finish my rice; my head didn't work right when my stomach was too full. I left the table with half-finished bowls and nobody complained. But there was one duty I couldn't avoid. I had to accompany my mother on Saturday market days when I had no tournament to play. My mother would proudly walk with me, visiting many shops, buying very little. "This my daughter Wave-ly Jong," she said to whoever looked her way.

One day, after we left a shop I said under my breath, "I wish you wouldn't do that, telling everybody I'm your daughter." My mother stopped walking. Crowds of people with heavy bags pushed past us on the sidewalk, bumping into first one shoulder, then another.

㉑ "Aiii-ya. So shame be with mother?" She grasped my hand even tighter as she glared at me.

I looked down. "It's not that, it's just so obvious. It's just so embarrassing."

"Embarrass you be my daughter?" Her voice was cracking with anger.

"That's not what I meant. That's not what I said."

"What you say?"

I knew it was a mistake to say anything more, but I heard my voice speaking. "Why do you have to use me to show off? If you want to show off, then why don't you learn to play chess?" My mother's eyes turned into dangerous black slits. She had no words for me, just sharp silence.

I felt the wind rushing around my hot ears. I jerked my hand out of my mother's tight grasp and spun around, knocking into an old woman. Her bag of groceries spilled to the ground.

"Aii-ya! Stupid girl!" my mother and the woman cried. Oranges and tin cans careened down the sidewalk. As my mother stooped to help the old woman pick up the escaping food, I took off.

㉒ I raced down the street, dashing between people, not looking back as my mother screamed shrilly, "Meimei! Meimei!" I fled down an alley, past dark curtained shops and merchants washing the grime off their windows. I sped into the sunlight, into a large street crowded with tourists examining trinkets and souvenirs. I ducked into another dark alley, down another street, up another alley. I ran until it hurt and I realized I had nowhere to go, that I was not running from anything. The alleys contained no escape routes.

My breath came out like angry smoke. It was cold. I sat down on an upturned plastic pail next to a stack of empty boxes, cupping my

Vocabulary Development

Vocabulary Knowledge Rating
When students have completed reading and discussing "Rules of the Game," have them take out their **Vocabulary Knowledge Rating Chart** for this selection. Read the words aloud once more and have students rate their knowledge of the words again in the After Reading column. Clarify any words that are still problematic. Have students write their own definition and example or sentence in the appropriate column. Then have students complete the **Vocabulary Builder Practice** activities on p. 317. Encourage students to use the words in further discussion and written work about this selection. Remind them that they will be accountable for these words on the Selection Test.

chin with my hands, thinking hard. I imagined my mother, first walking briskly down one street or another looking for me, then giving up and returning home to await my arrival. After two hours, I stood up on creaking legs and slowly walked home.

The alley was quiet and I could see the yellow lights shining from our flat like two tiger's eyes in the night. I climbed the sixteen steps to the door, advancing quietly up each so as not to make any warning sounds. I turned the knob; the door was locked. I heard a chair moving, quick steps, the locks turning—click! click! click!—and then the door opened.

"About time you got home," said Vincent. "Boy, are you in trouble."

He slid back to the dinner table. On a platter were the remains of a large fish, its fleshy head still connected to bones swimming upstream in vain escape. Standing there waiting for my punishment, I heard my mother speak in a dry voice.

"We not concerning this girl. This girl not have concerning for us."

Nobody looked at me. Bone chopsticks clinked against the insides of bowls being emptied into hungry mouths.

I walked into my room, closed the door, and lay down on my bed. The room was dark, the ceiling filled with shadows from the dinner-time lights of neighboring flats.

In my head, I saw a chessboard with sixty-four black and white squares. Opposite me was my opponent, two angry black slits. She wore a triumphant smile. "Strongest wind cannot be seen," she said.

Her black men advanced across the plane, slowly marching to each successive level as a single unit. My white pieces screamed as they scurried and fell off the board one by one. As her men drew closer to my edge, I felt myself growing light. I rose up into the air and flew out the window. Higher and higher, above the alley, over the tops of tiled roofs, where I was gathered up by the wind and pushed up toward the night sky until everything below me disappeared and I was alone.

I closed my eyes and pondered my next move.

Reading Skill
Analyze Cause and Effect Why do you think Waverly and her mother stop speaking to each other?

---

② Reading Skill
Analyze Cause and Effect

- Have students read the bracketed passage and then **speculate** about why Waverly runs away.
  Possible responses: She is upset with her mother because she feels her mother embarrassed her; she may feel that her mother regards her as her own personal trophy; she is young and may feel too much pressure.

- **Ask** students to respond to the Reading Skill question: Why do you think Waverly and her mother stop speaking to each other?
  Possible response: Waverly's mother is angry because she feels Waverly is being disrespectful; Waverly feels that her mother is too controlling.

- **Ask:** As Waverly lies in her bed that night, how does she view her mother?
  Answer: She views her mother as her opponent.

- **Ask** students how Waverly's mother has demonstrated that "the strongest wind cannot be seen."
  Answer: Her mother has won a mental victory over Waverly by being silent.

Concept Connector

Anticipation Guide
Have students return to their **Anticipation Guides** and respond to the statements again in the After Reading column. Then, lead a class discussion, probing for what students have learned that confirms or invalidates each statement.

Connecting to the Literature
Have students compare the sentences they wrote before reading with their thoughts about ways in which games can both unite and divide people. Ask them to explain whether their thoughts have changed and, if so, how.

Literary Analysis Graphic Organizer
Have students review the graphic organizers they completed to identify and interpret details of characterization while reading. Show them **Literary Analysis Graphic Organizer B** (*Graphic Organizer Transparencies,* p. 64) as an example. Then have students share the graphic organizers they did and the details they identified in the selection.

1. Students may make a case for any of the characters being the most realistic.

2. (a) Waverly wants salted plums; her mother tells her to keep her needs secret. (b) Her mother buys the plums on a different occasion. (c) She learns how to hide her feelings in order to get what she wants.

3. (a) She gives the rules of behavior in the form of Chinese sayings. (b) She learns to give the appearance of one thing while actually doing another. She is able to hide the true meaning of her moves until it is too late for her opponent to launch a defense. (c) She manipulates her mother by pretending not to want things.

4. (a) Mrs. Jong gives Waverly privileges and shows her off in local stores. (b) She introduces Waverly to everyone who looks her way. (c) **Possible response:** The tug of war between mother and child is universal. The cultural factors are the strict rules of Chinese family life.

5. **Possible response:** Waverly will win the game of doing what she wants to do. She has learned from her mother.

6. Waverly is a strong-minded and intelligent girl. **Actions:** She quickly masters the game of chess. **Behavior:** She uses "invisible strength" to get her way; she is competitive at chess. **Words:** Waverly stands up to her mother when she tells her not to introduce her to anyone who looks her way; **Thoughts:** She uses life-savers to join the chess game with her brothers; **Effect:** Waverly's parents allow her many concessions, and her chess skills earn her wide respect.

7. (a) The discussion of Chinese torture is an example of indirect characterization. (b) Mrs. Jong is a strong, intelligent woman from a demanding culture.

8. **Causes:** Two causes for her success are her raw talent and her mother's teachings. **Effects:** Three effects of her success are increases in self-confidence, in

Apply the Skills

Rules of the Game

Thinking About the Selection

1. **Respond:** Which character did you find most realistic? Explain.
2. **(a) Recall:** Early in the story, what happens when Waverly asks for a bag of salted plums? **(b) Connect:** What happens when she stops asking? **(c) Apply:** How does Waverly later apply that strategy to her desire to play chess competitively?
3. **(a) Recall:** How does Mrs. Jong teach Waverly rules of behavior? **(b) Connect:** How does Waverly translate these rules into strategies for winning at chess? **(c) Extend:** How does she use these rules against her mother?
4. **(a) Describe:** What does Mrs. Jong do to show her pride in her daughter? **(b) Distinguish:** At the market, what does Mrs. Jong do that bothers Waverly? **(c) Assess:** Which aspects of the struggle between Waverly and Mrs. Jong are based on personal differences? Which are based on cultural differences? Explain.
5. **Speculate:** Who do you think will "win" the game between Waverly and her mother? Explain.

Literary Analysis

6. Describe the **character** of Waverly. Support your response with examples of her actions, behavior, words, and thoughts and with details about the effect she has on other people.
7. **(a)** Is the conversation in which Waverly and Mrs. Jong discuss Chinese torture an example of **direct characterization** or **indirect characterization?** Explain. **(b)** What do you learn about Mrs. Jong's character from this exchange?

Reading Skill

8. Use a chart like the one shown to **analyze cause and effect** in this story. **(a)** Note two causes for Waverly's success with chess. **(b)** List three effects of her success.

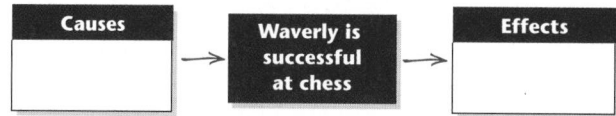

9. **(a)** Why does Mrs. Jong give Waverly special privileges? **(b)** How do these privileges affect Waverly and her relationship with her mother? Explain.

Story at a Glance
A young Chinese American girl tells how she learned to win at chess.

Assessment
For: Self-test
Visit: www.PHSchool.com
Web Code: epa-6208

Character: a person or an animal that participates in the action of a literary work

Characterization: methods writers use to reveal characters' traits; writers may use *direct* or *indirect characterization*

Cause: an event, an action, or a feeling that produces a result

Effect: the result produced by an event, action, or feeling

her status, and in her mother's pride. Another sample answer can be found on **Reading Skill Graphic Organizer B**, p. 68 in *Graphic Organizer Transparencies*.

9. (a) Mrs. Jong gives Waverly special privileges to encourage her to succeed. (b) Waverly becomes more independent and challenges her mother.

Vocabulary Builder

Practice Tell whether each sentence below makes sense. Use the meaning of the italicized vocabulary word to explain your answer.

1. The *pungent* scent of the baking pie drew the hungry crowd.
2. The girl was scared when the lady *benevolently* distributed cookies.
3. The audience was bored by the comedian's brilliant *retort*.
4. He gave his wife a bottle of expensive, *malodorous* perfume.

Adding Words to Your Vocabulary Using a thesaurus, find a **synonym**, or word with a similar meaning, for each word in the vocabulary list for "Rules of the Game" on page 292. Then, use each synonym correctly in a sentence. (For more on using a thesaurus, see page R7.)

Writing

Think about a lesson that you could teach Waverly and her mother to help them resolve their conflict. Create a **written presentation** that details your suggestions to them.

- Jot down some of the issues they face. For each, consider what you might teach them and how best to convey your ideas.
- Based on your audience, purpose, and point of view as an outsider, choose an appropriate text structure for your presentation. For example, you might write an essay, or you might tell a story with a moral. Include an introduction to briefly explain your choice.

For *Grammar, Vocabulary,* and *Assessment,* see **Build Language Skills,** pages 318–319.

Extend Your Learning

Listening and Speaking As Waverly, write and deliver a **monologue** explaining to a friend what you love about chess.

- Consider the feelings and thoughts Waverly might want to share.
- Decide which aspects of Waverly's relationship with her mother she will want to discuss.
- Use gestures and language appropriate to the character.

Research and Technology With classmates, create an **informative brochure** on chess. Use library and Internet resources to research the rules and strategies of the game. Take notes as you do research, and decide which information would work best in a chart or drawing.

Rules of the Game ■ 317

Assessment Resources

The following resources can be used to assess students' knowledge and skills.

Unit 2 Resources:
   Selection Test A, pp. 139–141
   Selection Test B, pp. 142–144

Go Online
—Assessment— Students may use the **Self-test** to prepare for **Selection Test A** or **Selection Test B.**

Go Online
—Research— **For:** An additional research activity
Visit: www.PHSchool.com
Web Code: epd-7206
For another research activity to extend students' learning, give students this Web Code.

Vocabulary Builder
Practice

1. Sensible, because *pungent* means "sharp smell," which would attract people.
2. Not sensible, because *benevolently* means "well-meaning."
3. Not sensible, because a brilliant *retort* means a brilliant "reply."
4. Not sensible, because *malodorous* refers to something that smells bad.

Adding Words to Your Vocabulary
Sample answers:

1. The *strong* scent of my father's cologne filled the bathroom.
2. Many people *kindly* contributed money to victims of the disaster.
3. His clever *reply* made everyone laugh.
4. The pile of dirty laundry was *smelly.*

Writing

- To give students guidance for writing their presentations, give them **Support for Writing** for "Rules of the Game," p. 134 in *Unit 2 Resources*.
- To evaluate students' presentations, use the Exposition: Cause-and-Effect Essay rubrics, pp. 49–50 in *General Resources*.

Six Traits Focus

✔ Ideas	✔ Word Choice
✔ Organization	Sentence Fluency
Voice	Conventions

WG Writing and Grammar, Gold Level

Students will find guidance on problem-and-solution writing in Chapter 11.

Build Language Skills

Go to pp. 318–319 for vocabulary and grammar lessons and assessment practice.

Extend Your Learning

The **Support for Extend Your Learning** page (*Unit 2 Resources,* p. 135) provides guided note-taking opportunities to help students complete the Extend Your Learning activities.

317

Vocabulary Skill

- Introduce the word roots *-ver-*, *-verd-*, and *-vert-*. Have them brainstorm for words that contain these roots.
  Possible responses: *verisimilitude, very; verdure; convert, divert, revert*

- Explain how the meaning of "truth," "green," or "turn" contributes to the meaning of each of these words.

- Have students complete the Practice activity on this page.

Answers

1. *verify;* root meaning: true; sentence: Can you verify that you were there?

2. *verdant;* root meaning: green; sentence: The verdant fields were covered with grazing sheep.

3. *versatile;* root meaning: turn; sentence: The worker was so versatile that we could use her anywhere in the business.

4. *verity;* root meaning: true; sentence: For many, the eternal verities are still love, honor, and family.

5. *verge;* root meaning: to turn, bend, be inclined; sentence: His defiant actions verged on treason.

Grammar Lesson

- Point out to students that the subject of a sentence always includes a noun or pronoun.

- Remind students that a sentence needs both a subject and a predicate to be a sentence.

  Possible responses:

  1. Hard work helped them succeed.

  2. The art museum contains work by Monet.

  3. We are buying candles to prepare for the hurricane.

  4. Rowena will decide on the colors for the room.

  5. The distressed plane landed in a desert area.

Writing Application

To assess students' papers, check for the presence of the required types of subjects and predicates.

318

Build Language Skills

The Necklace • Rules of the Game

Vocabulary Skill

Word Roots The **Latin root** *-ver-* comes from the Latin word for truth: *verus.* English words that contain this root, such as *verify* and *verdict,* have meanings related to "truth."

Not all words with the letters *v-e-r* indicate the Latin root *-ver-.* English words with the letters *ver* may also be related to the root *-verd-,* meaning "green," or *-vert-,* meaning "turn."

Practice Copy the following words. Explain whether each word is related to the root that means *truth, green,* or *turn.* Use a dictionary to check your work. Then, use each word in a sentence.

1. verify
2. verdant
3. versatile
4. verity
5. verge

Grammar Lesson

Subjects and Predicates There are two essential components of a sentence—the subject and the predicate. The **subject** is the word or group of words in a sentence that tells whom or what the sentence is about. The **predicate** is the verb or verb phrase that tells what the subject of the sentence does or is.

> **Example:** Remington painted scenes of the wild West.
>   (subject)   (predicate)
>   Remington was a famous American artist.
>   (subject)   (predicate)

Practice Write a sentence for each subject/predicate pair.

1. helped; work
2. museum; contains
3. are buying; we
4. Rowena; will decide
5. plane; landed

W̧G Prentice Hall Writing and Grammar Connection: Chapter 20, Section 1

MorePractice

For more practice with subjects and predicates, see the Grammar Handbook, p. R42.

Teaching Resources

The following resources can be used to enrich or extend the instruction for Build Language Skills.

Unit 2 Resources
  Build Language Skills: Vocabulary Skill: Word Roots, p. 137
  Build Grammar Skills: Subject/Predicate: p. 138

Reading Skill: Cause and Effect

Directions: *Read the selection. Then, answer the questions.*

For decades each of the states imposed a comparatively lengthy residence requirement for voting—typically, at least a year in the State, and 60 or 90 days in the county.

In the Voting Rights Act Amendments of 1970, Congress prohibited any requirement longer than 30 days for presidential elections. In *Dunn v. Blumstein,* 1972, the Supreme Court found Tennessee's residence requirement unconstitutional. The Supreme Court said that "30 days appears to be an ample period of time."

Nearly half the states now require voters to live in the state for 30 days and in some states, like New Hampshire, the period is even shorter. Arizona is the only state requiring more than 30 days' residency to vote.

1. Which of the following effects is correct?
   A The 90-day requirements were changed.
   B Residency requirements changed in the 70's.
   C In 1972, Congress passed a new voting law.
   D *Dunn v. Blumstein* changed Arizona law.

2. How many major reasons are given in the selection for the change in voting requirements?
   A four
   B three
   C two
   D one

3. Which is a direct cause of the current Tennessee residence requirement?
   A Voting Rights Act
   B *Dunn v. Blumstein,* 1972
   C the other states' regulations
   D the Amendments

4. According to the selection, which cause/effect relationship is correct?
   A Supreme Court decision/change in voting requirements
   B change in voting requirements/Supreme Court decision
   C change in law/change in state requirements
   D change in state requirements/change in law

Timed Writing: Interpretation [Critical Stance]

Review "Rules of the Game" or "The Necklace." Write a brief interpretation of the author's attitude toward one of the main characters. Use examples from the selection to support your interpretation. **(25 minutes)**

Writing Workshop: *Work in Progress*

Cause-and-Effect Essay

It is often easier to see effects than to understand causes; much of science is the attempt to find causes for known effects. List ten effects for which you do not know the cause. Put this work in your writing portfolio.

Build Language Skills ■ *319*

Reading: Making Inferences

1. A   3. B
2. C   4. C

Timed Writing

- Tell students that when they write an interpretation, they should explain the meaning of an element of a literary work.

- Point out that students may save time if they quickly jot down a list of indicators that show the author's attitude toward one of the main characters.

- Tell students that they need to write quickly, as time is short, but they need to support their interpretation with examples from the selection. Their support should be clear and convincing.

- Base your assessment of students' essays on their interpretation and the relevance and effectiveness of their supporting evidence.

- Suggest that students organize their time to allow five minutes for planning, ten minutes for writing, and ten minutes for reviewing and revising.

Writing Workshop
Work in Progress

Cause-and-Effect Essay

- Point out to students that this work may be used in the cause-and-effect essay they will write in the **Writing Workshop** at the end of Part 2.

- Suggest that students think of "why" questions that they have never had answered. For example, they might wonder why people become sick with certain illnesses, why earthquakes occur, or the reasons for a historical event, such as a war.

- If students are having difficulty writing their lists, suggest that they look at daily occurrences in their lives and determine whether they know the causes of the effects.

- When students have completed the activity, have them save the lists in their portfolios. They will use the lists as they continue this Work in Progress.

Planning Differentiated Instruction

Choosing Your Selection

You may use either selection to meet the lesson standards. The following guide will help you determine which of the two selections is more appropriate for your students.

Accessibility at a Glance

	Blues Ain't No Mockin Bird	The Invalid's Story
Context	Southern, rural United States	Nineteenth-century railway car
Language	• Accessible vocabulary • heavy use of dialect • dialogue	• Long sentences with embedded clauses • Language footnoted • use of dialect • dialogue
Concept Level	Accessible (family dignity and right to privacy)	Accessible (humor in difficult situation)
Literary Merit	Regional	Noted author
Lexile	950L	1020L
Other		Humorous
Overall Rating	More accessible	More challenging

Using the Other Selection You may use the other selection for homework or independent reading to reinforce the selection skills. If you use both selections, you can build a test for both using *ExamView*® **Test Bank** software.

Choosing Your Resources

[**L1**] Special Needs Students   [**L4**] Advanced Students

[**L2**] Below-Level Students   [**EL**] English Learners

[**L3**] All Students

Reading and Vocabulary Warm-ups provide support for below level students. **A** is for students reading two grades below level; **B** is for students reading one grade below level. For Selection Tests, **A** signifies "less challenging" and **B** "more challenging." For Graphic Organizer transparencies, **A** signifies "not filled in" and **B** "filled in."

FT Fast Track Instruction: To move the lesson more quickly, use the strategies and activities identified with **FT**.

Scaffolding for Less Proficient and Advanced Students

The leveled questions on Apply the Skills pages progress in the levels of thinking required to answer them. To address the needs of your different students, you may use the (a) level questions for your less proficient students, the (b) level with your on-level and advanced students. The occasional (c) level questions are appropriate for your advanced students.

Go **O**nline **For:** Information about Lexiles
Professional **Visit:** www.PHSchool.com
Development **Web Code:** eue-1111

Step-by-Step Teaching Guide	Pacing Guide
PRETEACH	
• Administer Vocabulary and Reading Warm-ups as necessary.	
• Introduce the Literary Analysis Skill: Dialogue. **FT**	10 min.
• Introduce the Reading Skill: Analyzing Cause and Effect. **FT**	10 min.
• Prepare students to read by teaching the selection vocabulary. **FT**	10 min.
• Build background and develop expressive vocabulary with Connecting to the Literature and Background.	10 min.
• Engage students' interest with the motivation activity.	10 min.
TEACH	
• Informally monitor comprehension while students read independently or in groups. **FT**	30 min.
• Monitor students' comprehension with the Reading Check notes.	as students read
• Reinforce vocabulary with Vocabulary Builder notes.	as students read
• Develop students' understanding of dialogue with the Literary Analysis annotations. **FT**	5 min.
• Develop students' ability to analyze cause and effect with the Reading Skill annotations. **FT**	10 min.
ASSESS/EXTEND	
• Assess students' comprehension and mastery of the Reading Skill and Literary Analysis by having them answer the Apply the Skills questions. **FT**	35 min.
• Have students complete the Vocabulary Builder activities. **FT**	5 min.
• Apply students' ability to write an informal letter with the Writing activity. **FT**	30–45 min. or homework
• Extend students' listening and speaking and research and technology skills with one or both of the Extend Your Learning activities.	15–30 min. or homework
• Have students complete the Vocabulary Skill and Grammar Lesson.	5 min.
• Monitor students' progress with the Assessment Practice.	20–40 min.
• Administer **Selection Test A** or **Selection Test B**. **FT**	15 min.

Resources

TECHNOLOGY
Go Online: Research [L3]
Go Online: Self-test [L3]
ExamView® **Test Bank [L3]**

Meeting Your Standards

Students will

1. analyze and respond to literary elements.
- Literary Analysis: Dialogue

2. read, comprehend, and analyze short stories.
- Reading Skill: Analyzing Cause and Effect
- Reading Strategy: Visualizing the Action to Analyze Cause and Effect
- Reading Check questions
- Apply the Skills questions
- Assessment Practice

3. develop vocabulary.
- Vocabulary Builder
- The Latin roots -ver-, -sequi-

4. apply grammar skills.
- Active and Passive Voice

5. develop writing proficiency.
- Work in Progress: Cause-and-Effect Essay
- Informal letter

6. extend learning.
- Listening and Speaking: Dialogue
- Research and Technology: Photo Collection

Block Scheduling: Use one 90-minute class period to preteach the skills and have students read the selection. Use a second 90-minute class period to assess students' mastery of skills, extend their learning, and monitor their progress.

Homework Suggestions
Following are possibilities for homework assignments.

- Support pages from *Unit 2 Resources*:
  Literary Analysis
  Reading Skill
  Vocabulary Builder
  Enrichment

- An Extend Your Learning project and the Writing assignment for your chosen selection may be completed over several days.

PRENTICE HALL
Teacher EXPRESS™ Use this complete
Plan · Teach · Assess suite of powerful
teaching tools to make lesson planning and testing quicker and easier.

PRENTICE HALL
Student EXPRESS™ Use the
Learn · Study · Succeed interactive
textbook (online and on CD-ROM) to make selections and activities come alive with audio and video support and interactive questions.

❶ Literary Analysis
Dialogue

- Tell students that *dialogue* is an important element of fiction. Although not all fiction includes dialogue, most authors use dialogue to help bring their characters to life.

- Explain that when writing dialogue, authors may use the character's *dialect* to help the reader "hear" what the character sounds like. By reflecting the way people actually speak, dialect enhances the realism of a literary work.

- Tell students that authors indicate how the dialect sounds by spelling words the way the character would pronounce them. For example, the author may indicate the character's pronunciation of *kind of* by spelling the phrase "kinda" or *nothing* by spelling the word "nuthin."

- Tell students that they can best understand dialect by saying it aloud. Encourage students to look for unusual spellings and then to say the word aloud as it is spelled.

❷ Reading Skill
Analyze Cause and Effect

- Tell students that "seeing" the action can help them understand its effect. For example, if they visualize the details of a character falling from a swing, they can better understand the effects on the character and on other characters who might be watching.

- Encourage students to use details to help them visualize events and understand the relationships between them as they read the assigned selection.

- Give students a copy of **Reading Skill Graphic Organizer A** (*Graphic Organizer Transparencies*, p. 69). Have them fill in the graphic organizer to identify the details of cause and effect as they read the assigned selection.

Practice these skills with either "Blues Ain't No Mockin Bird" (p. 322) or "The Invalid's Story" (p. 333).

❶ Literary Analysis

Dialogue is a conversation between or among characters in a literary work. In prose, dialogue is usually set off by quotation marks, and a new paragraph indicates a change in speaker. Writers use dialogue for these purposes:

- to reveal character traits and relationships
- to advance the action of the plot and develop the conflict
- to add variety, color, and realism to narratives

To make characters and settings more vivid, authors may write dialogue reflecting characters' dialect. **Dialect** is a way of speaking common to people of a region or group. A dialect's words, pronunciations, and grammar differ from those of the standard form of a language.

As you read, notice passages of dialogue and dialect, and determine what they show about the characters and the setting.

❷ Reading Skill

A **cause** is an event, an action, or a feeling that produces a result. An **effect** is the result produced. When reading a story, **visualize the action to analyze cause and effect.**

- Use text details to picture the setting, characters, and action.
- Use the details of your mental picture to help you identify the relationships between actions and events.

Organize your ideas in a chart like the one shown.

Cause
Steve turned on the sprinkler.

↓

Mental Picture
Matt on lawn Jaime on porch Sprinkler on lawn

↓

Effect
Matt got wet; Jaime just laughed.

Vocabulary Builder

Blues Ain't No Mockin Bird

- **formality** (fôr mal´ ə tē) *n.* attention to established rules or customs (p. 328) *His formality conveyed respect for his guests.*

- **reckless** (rek´ lis) *adj.* careless; rash (p. 328) *Reckless driving is a serious offense.*

The Invalid's Story

- **prodigious** (prō dij´ əs) *adj.* enormous (p. 334) *The Grand Canyon is a prodigious natural wonder.*

- **deleterious** (del´ ə tir´ ē əs) *adj.* harmful to health or well-being (p. 335) *Too much sun can be deleterious to one's skin.*

- **judicious** (jōō dish´ əs) *adj.* showing good judgment (p. 336) *Her decision to stay indoors during the storm was judicious.*

- **placidly** (plas´ id lē) *adv.* calmly; quietly (p. 336) *He smiled placidly, ignoring the noise.*

- **desultory** (des´ əl tôr´ ē) *adj.* random (p. 337) *They wandered through the park in a desultory way, with no clear destination.*

320 ■ *Short Stories*

Vocabulary Development

Vocabulary Knowledge Rating

Create a **Vocabulary Knowledge Rating Chart** for the selection you will teach from this set. Include the selection vocabulary from this page and the additional words students are asked to use at the end of Connecting to the Literature. These words will increase students' expressive vocabulary.

Give students a copy of the chart with the words on it. Introduce the words by reading them aloud and having students mark their rating in the Before Reading column. Urge them to be alert to these words as they read and discuss the selection because they will rate their knowledge of the words again after they finish.

If you wish, you may tally how many students know (or think they know) a word to gauge how much instruction you need to provide. As students read, point out the words and their context.

Short Story

❸ Background

Hawks Hawks are predators. They are fiercely territorial, and they often keep the same mate for life. Usually, hawks hunt rabbits, squirrels, and other birds. However, in rural areas they may kill and eat chickens. For a poor rural family like the one in this story, defending the family's flock of chickens from hawks is a matter of survival. Sometimes, when a farmer kills a hawk that has attacked his chickens, he displays it to frighten off other hawks.

❹ Connecting to the Literature

Reading/Writing Connection In "Blues Ain't No Mockin Bird," a man protects his family and livestock. Write a few sentences about what kinds of things you feel are worth protecting or defending. Use at least three of these words: *intervene, oblige, promote, prohibit.*

READ MORE

by Toni Cade Bambara
The Sea Birds Are Still Alive: Collected Stories

Meet the Author

Toni Cade **Bambara** (1939–1995)

Toni Cade Bambara was a social activist and a writer of short stories, a novel, plays, television scripts, and documentaries. She started writing when she was in kindergarten and had her first story published when she was a senior in college.

"I write because I must," Bambara said. "If there were no more presses, no more publishing houses, I'd still be writing." She was equally devoted to social change and worked to improve the condition of African Americans. Her writing echoes that concern. Her stories are often praised for their vivid portrayals of the daily lives of African Americans in the twentieth century.

Fast Facts

▶ Toni Cade Bambara was born Miltona Cade. She added Bambara to her name after finding it on a sketchbook belonging to her great-grandmother.

▶ Bambara is the name of an African tribe known for its textiles.

Go Online
Author Link

For: More about the author
Visit: www.PHSchool.com
Web Code: epe-9210

Blues Ain't No Mockin Bird ■ 321

❸ Background
Hawks

Even though most hawks are more useful to people than they are harmful, people are still sometimes intolerant of them. Hawks feed on rodents that can damage a farmer's crops. They usually find their prey while circling high above the ground. They swoop down, grab their prey with powerful talons, and kill it with their strong, pointed beaks.

❹ Connecting to the Literature

• Model use of the expressive vocabulary students are asked to use with these examples:

1. If I saw someone abusing an animal, I'm sure I would *intervene.*

2. Laws should *oblige* people to recycle plastic and paper to protect the environment.

3. I write letters to our senator to *promote* protection of our civil liberties.

4. Some organizations try to *prohibit* people from using animals in laboratory experiments.

• Help students further develop their expressive vocabulary by providing these words: *adolescent, earnest, outspoken,* and *emulate.* Encourage students to use these words as they discuss the selection.

Go Online
Author Link For additional information about Toni Cade Bambara, have students type in the Web Code, then select *B* from the alphabet, and then select *Toni Cade Bambara.*

Differentiated Instruction   Solutions for All Learners

Support for Below-Level Students [L1, L2]	Support for English Learners [EL]
Unit 2 Resources	**Unit 2 Resources**
Vocabulary Warm-up Word Lists, p. 145	Vocabulary Warm-up Word Lists, p. 145
Vocabulary Warm-up Practice, p. 146	Vocabulary Warm-up Practice, p. 146
Reading Warm-up A, p. 147	Reading Warm-up A, p. 147
Selection Test A, pp. 155–157	**Reader's Notebook: English Learner's Version**
Graphic Organizer Transparencies	**Listening to Literature Audio CD**
Reading Skill Graphic Organizer, Transparency B, p. 70	
Reader's Notebook: Adapted Version	
Adapted Reader's Notebook Audio CD	

❶ Motivation

Prepare an Anticipation Guide *General Resources,* pp. 8–10) with the following statements:

- Every person has the right to privacy.
- People place too high an importance on privacy.
- Public officials have the right to collect data on people to use as they wish.
- Government officials do not always treat people with the respect they deserve.

Give students a copy of the prepared Anticipation Guide and have students mark their responses in the Me column. Have students discuss the statements in pairs or groups and mark the Guides again in the Group column.

Concept Connector ➡

Students will return to the Anticipation Guide after completing "Blues Ain't No Mockin Bird."

Learning Modalities
Visual/Spatial Learners

Refer students to the painting on p. 322. As students read the story, have them create a similar portrait of Granddaddy. Have them try to reveal some elements of his character.

❷ About the Selection

Bambara's story explores the issues of family dignity and the right to privacy. When photographers come to gather footage for a documentary about the county food stamp campaign, the Cains take action.

❸ Humanities

Sharecropper, Elizabeth Catlett

Elizabeth Catlett (born 1919) grew up in Washington, D.C., during the era of segregation. She studied art with American artist Grant Wood. Many of her subjects are black women. Use this question for discussion:

- What predictions can you make about the story by looking at this illustration?

  Answer: An African American woman may play an important part in the story.

Blues Ain't No Mockin Bird

Toni Cade Bambara

❶
❷
❸

Sharecropper, Elizabeth Catlett, Courtesy The Estate of Thurlow E. Tibbs, Jr., © Elizabeth Catlett/Licensed by VAGA, New York, NY

322 ■ *Short Stories*

Vocabulary Development

Think Aloud: Context Clues

Direct students' attention to the words *wagon'd* in the fourth paragraph and *tire'd* in the fifth paragraph on p. 323. Using the think-aloud process, model how to use context to infer the meaning of unfamiliar words in dialect. Say to students:

> I'm going to show you how I would figure out the meaning of *wagon'd*. In

this sentence *wagon'd* is a type of contraction with *wagon* and another word. The sentence describes the men in the station wagon driving around all morning. This clue tells me that the second word in the contraction of *wagon'd* is *had*—the *wagon had* been roamin. . . .

The puddle had frozen over, and me and Cathy went stompin in it. The twins from next door, Tyrone and Terry, were swingin so high out of sight we forgot we were waitin our turn on the tire. Cathy jumped up and came down hard on her heels and started tap-dancin. And the frozen patch splinterin every which way underneath kinda spooky. "Looks like a plastic spider web," she said. "A sort of weird spider, I guess, with many mental problems." But really it looked like the crystal paperweight Granny kept in the parlor. She was on the back porch, Granny was, making the cakes drunk. The old ladle dripping rum into the Christmas tins, like it used to drip maple syrup into the pails when we lived in the Judson's woods, like it poured cider into the vats when we were on the Cooper place, like it used to scoop buttermilk and soft cheese when we lived at the dairy.

"Go tell that man we ain't a bunch of trees."

"Ma'am?"

"I said to tell that man to get away from here with that camera." Me and Cathy look over toward the meadow where the men with the station wagon'd been roamin around all mornin. The tall man with a huge camera lassoed to his shoulder was buzzin our way.

"They're makin movie pictures," yelled Tyrone, stiffenin his legs and twistin so the tire'd come down slow so they could see.

"They're makin movie pictures," sang out Terry.

"That boy don't never have anything original to say," say Cathy grown-up.

By the time the man with the camera had cut across our neighbor's yard, the twins were out of the trees swingin low and Granny was onto the steps, the screen door bammin soft and scratchy against her palms. "We thought we'd get a shot or two of the house and everything and then—"

"Good mornin," Granny cut him off. And smiled that smile.

"Good mornin," he said, head all down the way Bingo does when you yell at him about the bones on the kitchen floor. "Nice place you got here, aunty. We thought we'd take a—"

"Did you?" said Granny with her eyebrows. Cathy pulled up her socks and giggled.

"Nice things here," said the man, buzzin his camera over the yard. The pecan barrels, the sled, me and Cathy, the flowers, the printed stones along the driveway, the trees, the twins, the toolshed.

"I don't know about the thing, the it, and the stuff," said Granny, still talkin with her eyebrows. "Just people here is what I tend to consider."

◀ Critical Viewing As you read, compare Granny with the woman in the illustration. [**Compare and Contrast**]

Blues Ain't No Mockin Bird ■ 323

Literary Analysis
Dialogue and Dialect
Which features of the title and opening paragraph show that this story is written in dialect?

Reading Skill
Cause and Effect
Which details in the text help you to visualize the effect that the camera crew has on Granny?

Reading Check

What are the men doing on Granny's property?

---

❹ Literary Analysis
Dialogue and Dialect

- Have students read the title and the first paragraph of the story aloud. Encourage them to pronounce the words as they are spelled.

- **Ask** the Literary Analysis question: Which features of the title and opening paragraph show that this story is written in dialect? **Answer:** Features that show the story is written in dialect are the use of *ain't, no,* and the dropping of the final *g* in *mockin* in the title, as well as the dropping of the final *g* in several words in the first paragraph.

❺ Reading Skill
Cause and Effect

- Refer students to the bracketed passage. **Ask** them to describe what they think the author means when she says that Granny talks "with her eyebrows." **Answer:** She moves her eyebrows up and down, or squeezes them together to emphasize her feelings.

- **Ask** students the Reading Skill question: Which details in the text help you to visualize the effect that the camera crew has on Granny? **Possible response:** Students might say that the descriptions of Granny's smile, her eyebrows, and her way of saying "Good mornin" help them to visualize the camera crew's effect.

❻ Critical Viewing

Answer: They are both old; the woman in the picture has white hair. Granny's personality is forceful and hard; the woman's features in the picture are portrayed in strong, angular lines.

❼ Reading Check

Answer: They are filming the house and property.

Differentiated Instruction
Solutions for All Learners

Support for Special Needs Students
Help students understand the dialect in this story by providing them with **Readers Notebook: Adapted Version** and the **Adapted Reader's Notebook Audio CD**. After students have completed the story, discuss any questions they may have. You may help clarify the author's use of dialect by providing a Standard English version of some of the words and phrases.

Support for English Learners
To help students understand the dialect and visualize some of the unfamiliar imagery, have them use the **Reader's Notebook: English Learner's Version**. Then, as a group have them listen to the **Listening to Literature Audio CD**. Discuss some of the dialect with them, providing a Standard English version of a number of the words and phrases.

323

- Have students read the bracketed passage aloud. Then, **ask** students why Granny might be annoyed with the smiling man.
Answer: He walks on to her property without permission and begins filming.

- **Ask** students how the camera man addresses Granny. What does she mean by her response to him?
Answer: He calls her "aunty"; she tells him that she is not related to his mother, implying that he should not address her with such disrespectful familiarity.

- **Ask** students to respond to the Reading Skill question: What does the dialogue between Granny and the film crew show about their attitudes toward each other?
Answer: The film crew is condescending and assumes that they have the right to walk onto Granny's property and begin filming without asking. Granny is angry and insulted at the disrespectful way the film crew treats her, and she refuses to cooperate with them.

9 Critical Viewing

Possible response: A woman as proud and capable as Grannie would probably tend a neat and flourishing vegetable garden like the one in the photo.

Camera man stopped buzzin. Cathy giggled into her collar.

"Mornin, ladies," a new man said. He had come up behind us when we weren't lookin. "And gents," discoverin the twins givin him a nasty look. "We're filmin for the county," he said with a smile. "Mind if we shoot a bit around here?"

"I do indeed," said Granny with no smile. Smilin man was smiling up a storm. So was Cathy. But he didn't seem to have another word to say, so he and the camera man backed on out the yard, but you could hear the camera buzzin still. "Suppose you just shut that machine off," said Granny real low through her teeth, and took a step down off the porch and then another.

"Now, aunty," Camera said, pointin the thing straight at her.

"Your mama and I are not related."

Smilin man got his notebook out and a chewed-up pencil. "Listen," he said movin back into our yard, "we'd like to have a statement from you . . . for the film. We're filmin for the county, see. Part of the food stamp campaign. You know about the food stamps?"

Granny said nuthin.

"Maybe there's somethin you want to say for the film. I see you grow your own vegetables," he smiled real nice. "If more folks did that, see, there'd be no need—"

Granny wasn't sayin nuthin. So they backed on out, buzzin at our clothesline and the twins' bicycles, then back on down to the meadow. The twins were danglin in the tire, lookin at Granny. Me and Cathy were waitin, too, cause Granny always got somethin to say. She teaches steady with no let-up. "I was on this bridge one time," she started off. "Was a crowd cause this man was goin to jump, you understand. And a minister was there and the police and some other folks. His woman was there, too."

"What was they doin?" asked Tyrone.

"Tryin to talk him out of it was what they was doin. The minister talkin about how it was a mortal sin, suicide. His woman takin bites out of her own hand and not even knowin it, so nervous and cryin and talkin fast."

"So what happened?" asked Tyrone.

"So here comes . . . this person . . . with a camera, takin pictures of the man and the minister and the woman. Takin pictures of the man in his misery about to jump, cause life so bad and people been messin with him so bad. This person takin up the whole roll of film practically. But savin a few, of course."

"Of course," said Cathy, hatin the person. Me standin there wonderin how Cathy knew it was "of course" when I didn't and it was *my* grandmother.

Literary Analysis
Dialogue What does the dialogue between Granny and the film crew show about their attitudes toward each other?

9 ▶ Critical Viewing
Does this vegetable garden seem like one Granny would tend? Why or why not? **[Connect]**

Vocabulary Development

Expressive Vocabulary
Ask students to think about Granny's attitude toward the men who come to film. Then, encourage students to use the expressive vocabulary presented earlier as they discuss the selection. You might encourage them with sentence starters such as the following:

1. As the men began to film, Granny was quick to *intervene* . . .
2. She was unwilling to *oblige* . . .
3. The men wanted to *promote* . . .
4. Granny moved to *prohibit* . . .

After a while Tyrone say, "Did he jump?"

"Yeh, did he jump?" say Terry all eager. And Granny just stared at the twins till their faces swallow up the eager and they don't even care any more about the man jumpin. Then she goes back onto the porch and lets the screen door go for itself. I'm lookin to Cathy to finish the story cause she knows Granny's whole story before me even. Like she knew how come we move so much and Cathy ain't but a third cousin we picked up on the way last Thanksgivin visitin. But she knew it was on account of people drivin Granny crazy till she'd get up in the night and start packin. Mumblin and packin and wakin everybody up sayin, "Let's get on away from here before I kill me somebody." Like people wouldn't pay her for things like they said they would. Or Mr. Judson bringin us boxes of old clothes and raggedy magazines. Or Mrs. Cooper comin in our kitchen and touchin everything and sayin how clean it all was. Granny goin crazy, and Granddaddy Cain pullin her off the people, sayin, "Now,

---

Differentiated Instruction   Solutions for All Learners

Strategy for Less Proficient Readers

To give students a context for the story and help them see how visualizing actions can help them analyze cause and effect, show them the **Reading Skill Graphic Organizer B** (*Graphic Organizers*, p. 70). Review the completed organizer with them to make sure that they see how visualizing a cause can help them understand the effect.

Then have students gather in a small group and read the story aloud as though it were a play, with each reader taking one role. You may want to take the role of the narrator yourself. Pause two or three times during the reading to ask students to visualize an action and identify its effect. Allow students a chance to ask questions during the reading.

---

⑩ Critical Thinking

Infer

- Read aloud the bracketed passage. **Ask** students to summarize the story Granny tells in this passage. **Answer:** She sees a man about to commit suicide by jumping from a bridge; the man's wife and minister are trying to talk him out of it; meanwhile a photographer is taking photos of the event.

- Point out that Granny says the photographer uses almost the entire roll of film, but saves a few "of course." **Ask** students why they think the photographer saved a few pictures. Why did Granny say "of course"? **Possible response:** He saved the pictures to ensure he would get a photo of the man actually jumping from the bridge. Granny says "of course" because she knows the photographer was at the scene to snap a dramatic photo of someone jumping off the bridge.

- **Ask** students to explain Granny's attitude toward that photographer. **Answer:** She has contempt and disgust for him, because he is not interested in the welfare of the man who is suffering; he just wants to get a good picture, hoping that the man will actually jump.

⑪ Reading Check

Answer: She refuses to say anything.

⑪ ✓ Reading Check

How does Granny respond when "Smilin" asks her to make a statement?

Analyze

- **Ask** students to name the common fairy tale on which Cathy is basing her story.
  Answer: She is basing her story on "Goldilocks and the Three Bears."

- **Ask** students how Cathy's version differs from the fairy tale.
  Answer: In the fairy tale, Goldilocks is portrayed as a sweet little girl and not as someone who breaks into a house and steals and destroys things.

- **Ask** students why they think the author includes this story, as told by Cathy.
  Possible response: The author could be pointing out that the same story can be interpreted in more than one way, depending on the viewpoint of the storyteller. The author is also pointing out that the camera crew, like Goldilocks, has no respect for people's privacy or their homes and possessions. They feel free to walk onto the property without being invited.

⑬ **Literature in Context**

Science Connection Even though people typically consider *carnivores* to be four-legged animals such as lions and coyotes, hawks are also carnivores because they eat mammals and small birds. Canadian scientist Dr. Louis Lefebvre recently revealed a means of measuring avian intelligence based on their inventiveness in feeding habits. According to this scale, hawks are considered one of the most intelligent birds.

Connect to the Literature Point out to students that because some hawks mate for life, they are very protective of their mates. **Ask** students the Connect to the Literature question: What concerns prompt Granddaddy Cain's violence against the hawks?

Answer: Grandaddy Cain kills the first hawk to protect the family's chickens. He kills the second hawk because it flies at his family, trying to find a place to land.

now, Cora." But next day loadin up the truck, with rocks all in his jaw, madder than Granny in the first place.

⑫ "I read a story once," said Cathy soundin like Granny teacher. "About this lady Goldilocks who barged into a house that wasn't even hers. And not invited, you understand. Messed over the people's groceries and broke up the people's furniture. Had the nerve to sleep in the folks' bed."

"Then what happened?" asked Tyrone. "What they do, the folks, when they come in to all this mess?"

⑬ | Literature in Context | Science Connection

Hawks: Tales and Truths

A variety of hawk species, including the northern goshawk and the Cooper's hawk, are sometimes called *chickenhawks*, although no such species exists. This name comes from the belief that hawks prey on chickens. While hawks do sometimes eat chickens, in reality, raccoons pose greater threats to small barnyard animals.

◄ The average wingspan of the northern goshawk is forty-two inches.

- Most hawks prey on forest-dwelling rodents, rabbits, and birds.
- Some hawks mate for life.
- Female goshawks and Cooper's hawks are larger than the males.
- The eyesight of a hawk is eight times as powerful as a person's.
- Red-tailed hawks give a hoarse, two-to-three-second scream while soaring.

The wingspan of a ▷ Cooper's hawk like this one may be as wide as three feet.

Connect to the Literature What concerns prompt Granddaddy Cain's violence against the hawks?

"Did they make her pay for it?" asked Terry, makin a fist. "I'd've made her pay me."

I didn't even ask. I could see Cathy actress was very likely to just walk away and leave us in mystery about this story which I heard was about some bears.

"Did they throw her out?" asked Tyrone, like his father sounds when he's bein extra nasty-plus to the washin-machine man.

⓮ "Woulda," said Terry. "I woulda gone upside her head with my fist and—"

"You woulda done whatcha always do—go cry to Mama, you big baby," said Tyrone. So naturally Terry starts hittin on Tyrone, and next thing you know they tumblin out the tire and rollin on the ground. But Granny didn't say a thing or send the twins home or step out on the steps to tell us about how we can't afford to be fightin amongst ourselves. She didn't say nuthin. So I get into the tire to take my turn. And I could see her leanin up against the pantry table, staring at the cakes she was puttin up for the Christmas sale, mumblin real low and grumpy and holdin her forehead like it wanted to fall off and mess up the rum cakes.

Behind me I hear before I can see Granddaddy Cain comin through the woods in his field boots. Then I twist around to see the shiny black oilskin cuttin through what little left there was of yellows, reds, and oranges. His great white head not quite round cause of this bloody thing high on his shoulder, like he was wearin a cap on sideways. He takes the shortcut through the pecan grove, and the sound of twigs snapping overhead and underfoot travels clear and cold all the way up to us. And here comes Smilin and Camera up behind him like they was goin to do somethin. Folks like to go for him sometimes. Cathy say it's because he's so tall and quiet and like a king. And people just can't stand it. But Smilin and Camera don't hit him in the head or nuthin. They just buzz on him as he stalks by with the chicken hawk slung over his shoulder, squawkin, drippin red down the back of the oilskin. He passes the porch and stops a second for Granny to see he's caught the hawk at last, but she's just starin and mumblin, and not at the hawk. So he nails the bird to the toolshed door, the hammerin crackin through the eardrums. And the bird flappin himself to death and droolin down the door to paint the gravel in the driveway red, then brown, then black. And the two men movin up on tiptoe like they was invisible or we were blind, one.

"Get them persons out of my flower bed, Mister Cain," say Granny moanin real low like at a funeral.

"How come your grandmother calls her husband 'Mister Cain' all the time?" Tyrone whispers all loud and noisy and from the city and

---

Literary Analysis
Dialogue and Dialect
What does the idiom "gone upside her head" probably mean?

⓯ **Reading Check**

What does Granddaddy do with the hawk?

Blues Ain't No Mockin Bird ■ 327

⓮ Literary Analysis
Dialogue and Dialect

• Refer students to the bracketed passage. **Ask** students to describe Tyrone and Terry's attitude toward Goldilocks.
  Answer: They are upset that she barged into someone's house and broke their furniture.

• **Ask** students to respond to the Literary Analysis question: What does the idiom "gone upside her head" probably mean?
  Possible response: It means he would have slapped her on the side of the head.

• **Ask** students to identify the elements of dialect in this bracketed passage.
  Answer: Elements are the dropping of the final *g* in several words, and the use of *woulda* and *whatcha*.

• **Ask** students to read this sentence: "You woulda done whatcha always do—go cry to Mama, you big baby," said Tyrone. Then, have them rephrase the sentence in Standard English.
  Answer: The Standard English would read, "You would have done what you always do. . . . "

⓯ Reading Check

Answer: He nails the bird to the toolshed door.

- Have students read the bracketed passage. Then have them imagine the children falling to the ground. **Ask** why the children fall down on the ground when the flying hawk appears.
Answer: They are afraid the hawk will grab their hair or try to land on their head.

- **Ask** students what they think the children are probably doing with their hands as they lie on the gravel driveway.
Answer: They are probably holding their hands over their heads to protect themselves from the swooping hawk.

- **Ask** students the Reading Skill question: How does the arrival of the screaming hawk affect the film crew? How does it affect Granddaddy Cain?
Possible response: The film crew are scared, running around, ducking, and jiggling the camera. Granddaddy stands straight, watching the hawk, not appearing to be afraid.

▶ **Monitor Progress:** Remind students that there are two types of intruders from which Granddaddy Cain is trying to protect his family.

▶ **Reteach:** If students have difficulty identifying the similarities between the second hawk and the camera man and Smilin, have them reread the bracketed passage. Tell students that this passage includes details about how the scared hawk and men seem similarly frenzied, but that Granddaddy Cain is calm and focused as he protects his family.

---

don't know no better. Like his mama, Miss Myrtle, tell us never mind the <u>formality</u> as if we had no better breeding than to call her Myrtle, plain. And then this awful thing—a giant hawk—come wailin up over the meadow, flyin low and tilted and screamin, zigzaggin through the pecan grove, breakin branches and hollerin, snappin past the clothesline, flyin every which way, flyin into things <u>reckless</u> with crazy.

"He's come to claim his mate," say Cathy fast, and ducks down. We all fall quick and flat into the gravel driveway, stones scrapin my face. I squinch my eyes open again at the hawk on the door, tryin to fly up out of her death like it was just a sack flown into by mistake. Her body holdin her there on that nail, though. The mate beatin the air overhead and clutchin for hair, for heads, for landin space.

16 The camera man duckin and bendin and runnin and fallin, jigglin the camera and scared. And Smilin jumpin up and down swipin at the huge bird, tryin to bring the hawk down with just his raggedy ole cap. Granddaddy Cain straight up and silent, watchin the circles of the hawk, then aimin the hammer off his wrist. The giant bird fallin, silent and slow. Then here comes Camera and Smilin all big and bad now that the awful screechin thing is on its back and broken, here they come. And Granddaddy Cain looks up at them like it was the first time noticin, but not payin them too much mind cause he's listenin, we all listenin, to that low groanin music comin from the porch. And we figure any minute, somethin in my back tells me any minute now, Granny gonna bust through that screen with somethin in her hand and murder on her mind. So Granddaddy say above the buzzin, but quiet, "Good day, gentlemen." Just like that. Like he'd invited them in to play cards and they'd stayed too long and all the sandwiches were gone and Reverend Webb was droppin by and it was time to go.

They didn't know what to do. But like Cathy say, folks can't stand Granddaddy tall and silent and like a king. They can't neither. The smile the men smilin is pullin the mouth back and showin the teeth. Lookin like the wolf man, both of them. Then Granddaddy holds his hand out—this huge hand I used to sit in when I was a baby and he'd carry me through the house to my mother like I was a gift on a tray. Like he used to on the trains. They called the other men just waiters. But they spoke of Granddaddy separate and said, The Waiter. And said he had engines in his feet and motors in his hands and couldn't no train throw him off and couldn't nobody turn him round. They were big enough for motors, his hands were. He held that one hand out all still and it gettin to be not at all a hand but a person in itself.

"He wants you to hand him the camera," Smilin whispers to Camera, tiltin his head to talk secret like they was in the jungle or

---

Vocabulary Builder
formality (fôr mal´ ə tē)
n. attention to established rules or customs

reckless (rek´ lis) *adj.* careless; rash

Reading Skill
Cause and Effect
How does the arrival of the screaming hawk affect the film crew? How does it affect Granddaddy Cain?

Vocabulary Development

Vocabulary Knowledge Rating
When students have completed reading and discussing "Blues Ain't No Mockin Bird," have them take out their **Vocabulary Knowledge Rating Chart** for this selection. Read the words aloud once more and have students rate their knowledge of the words again in the After Reading column. Clarify any words that are still problematic. Have students write their own definition and example or sentence in the appropriate column. Then have students complete the **Vocabulary Builder Practice** activities on p. 331. Encourage students to use the words in further discussion and written work about this selection. Remind them that they will be accountable for these words on the Selection Test.

somethin and come upon a native that don't speak the language. The men start untyin the straps, and they put the camera into that great hand speckled with the hawk's blood all black and crackly now. And the hand don't even drop with the weight, just the fingers move, curl up around the machine. But Granddaddy lookin straight at the men. They lookin at each other and everywhere but at Granddaddy's face.

"We filmin for the county, see," say Smilin. "We puttin together a movie for the food stamp program . . . filmin all around these parts. Uhh, filmin for the county."

"Can I have my camera back?" say the tall man with no machine on his shoulder, but still keepin it high like the camera was still there or needed to be. "Please, sir."

Then Granddaddy's other hand flies up like a sudden and gentle bird, slaps down fast on top of the camera and lifts off half like it was a calabash[1] cut for sharing.

"Hey," Camera jumps forward. He gathers up the parts into his chest and everything unrollin and fallin all over. "Whatcha tryin to do? You'll ruin the film." He looks down into his chest of metal reels and things like he's protectin a kitten from the cold.

"You standin in the misses' flower bed," say Granddaddy. "This is our own place."

The two men look at him, then at each other, then back at the mess in the camera man's chest, and they just back off. One sayin over and over all the way down to the meadow, "Watch it, Bruno. Keep ya fingers off the film." Then Granddaddy picks up the hammer and jams it into the oilskin pocket, scrapes his boots, and goes into the house. And you can hear the squish of his boots headin through the house. And you can see the funny shadow he throws from the parlor window onto the ground by the string-bean patch. The hammer draggin the pocket of the oilskin out so Granddaddy looked even wider. Granny was hummin now—high not low and grumbly. And she was doin the cakes again, you could smell the molasses from the rum.

"There's this story I'm goin to write one day," say Cathy dreamer. "About the proper use of the hammer."

"Can I be in it?" Tyrone say with his hand up like it was a matter of first come, first served.

"Perhaps," say Cathy, climbin onto the tire to pump us up. "If you there and ready."

---

1. **calabash** (kal′ ə bash′) *n.* large gourd-like fruit.

Reading Skill
Cause and Effect
In what way does visualizing this scene help you understand the effects of Granddaddy's action?

Blues Ain't No Mockin Bird ■ 329

⑰ Reading Skill
Cause and Effect

• Refer students to the bracketed passage. **Ask** students what expression they visualize on Granddaddy's face. What is the tone of his voice?
Answer: He probably looks very stern and unsmiling; his voice probably sounds firm and unfriendly, maybe even threatening.

• **Ask** students what expression they visualize on the two men's faces.

• **Answer:** They probably look alarmed, maybe even frightened.

• **Ask** students the Reading Skill question: In what way does visualizing this scene help you understand the effects of Granddaddy's action?
Possible responses: Visualizing helps one understand that Granddaddy is probably threatening to the two men, and they are probably afraid of him.

Concept Connector

Anticipation Guide
Have students return to their **Anticipation Guides** and respond to the statements again in the After Reading column. Then, lead a class discussion, probing for what students have learned that confirms or invalidates each statement.

Connecting to the Literature
Have students compare the sentences they wrote before reading with their thoughts about the kinds of things that are worth protecting. Ask them to explain whether their thoughts have changed and, if so, how.

Reading Skill Graphic Organizer
Have students review the graphic organizers they completed to visualize the action to analyze cause and effect. Show them the **Reading Skill Graphic Organizer B** (*Graphic Organizer Transparencies*, p. 70) as an example. Then, have students share the graphic organizers they did and the details they visualized to help them determine cause and effect.

329

Apply the Skills

Blues Ain't No Mockin Bird

Thinking About the Selection

1. **Respond:** Which character would you most like to meet? Why?
2. **(a) Recall:** Why are the photographers filming in the area?
   (b) Infer: What message does Granny give the men through her speech and actions?
3. Make a chart like the one shown. **(a) Compare:** In the first column, write the ways that Camera and Smilin are like the hawks. **(b) Connect:** In the second column, write the ways that Granddaddy's actions are like the actions of the male hawk. **(c) Discuss:** Share your chart with a partner, and discuss your responses. Then, in the third column, explain whether you think the hawks represent Granddaddy and Granny, Smilin and Camera, or both pairs.

Hawks and Camera and Smilin	Hawks and Granddaddy	What the Hawks Represent

4. **Make a Judgment:** Is Granddaddy's treatment of the photographers justified? Support your view with story details.

Literary Analysis

5. Identify one example of **dialogue** that indicates the tension is increasing between Granny and the filmmakers.
6. Identify one example of dialogue that shows Granny is tough.
7. **(a)** Explain how the spelling and grammar used in the following passage indicate that it is an example of **dialect**. "Granny always got somethin to say. She teaches steady with no let-up."
   (b) Rewrite the passage in Standard English. **(c)** Explain how the use of dialect makes the characters and setting more vivid.

Reading Skill

8. **(a)** What is the **cause** of Granddaddy's decision to disassemble the men's camera? **(b)** What is the **effect** of Granddaddy's action on the cameramen? **(c)** What is the effect on Granny?
9. Which visual details in the story help you explain the causes and effects of Granddaddy's ruining the film?

330 ■ *Short Stories*

QuickReview

Story at a Glance
Granddaddy drives out two cameramen who have offended his wife.

For: Self-test
Visit: www.PHSchool.com
Web Code: epa-6209

Dialogue: a conversation between or among characters in a literary work

Dialect: the unique form of a language spoken by people of a region or group

Cause: an event, an action, or a feeling that produces a result

Effect: the result produced by a cause

Answers

1. **Possible response:** Students may select Granddaddy because he is imposing, or the narrator because she is perceptive.

2. **(a)** They are making a documentary about the food-stamp program. **(b)** She is asserting her dignity and personal rights; she is expressing anger at their trespassing.

3. **(a)** They swoop down on people; they are frightening or threatening; they stay together. **(b)** He is threatening when threatened; he tries to protect his mate and drive away enemies. **(c) Possible response:** The hawks represent Granny and Granddaddy, since the intruders have threatened Granny and Granddaddy, her mate, is trying to protect her.

4. **Possible responses:** Yes, because the photographers are rude, insensitive trespassers. No, because Granddaddy destroyed expensive film instead of simply telling them to go away.

5. **Possible response:** One example of dialogue is: "I don't know about the thing, the it, and the stuff. . . . Just people here is what I tend to consider."

6. **Possible response:** One example of dialogue is: "Your mama and I are not related."

7. **(a)** The grammar shows dialect by the phrase "always got," instead of "always has," and "teaches steady," instead of "teaches steadily." The spelling shows dialect with the *g* dropped from "somethin." **(b)** Granny always has something to say. She teaches steadily, with no pauses. **(c)** Dialect makes the characters seem more vivid because it represents a way that rural African Americans from the South might speak.

8. **Possible response: (a)** The men have taken motion pictures of his family. **(b)** They become intimidated and leave. **(c)** She begins humming and seems happy.

9. The details that help to visualize the causes are the man "buzzin his camera over the yard," the smilin man with his notebook and pencil, and the men looking at each other after Granddaddy takes the camera. The effects include the camera man clutching the film to his chest, and the men backing away.

Vocabulary Builder

Practice **Analogies** show the relationships between pairs of words. Use a word from the "Blues Ain't No Mockin Bird" vocabulary list on page 320 to complete each analogy. In each, your choice should create a word pair that matches the relationship between the first two words given. Explain the relationship that the pairs in each set share.

1. solution : intelligent :: accident : _____
2. sportsmanship : game :: _____ : ceremony

Adding Words to Your Vocabulary Using a thesaurus, find an **antonym**, or word of opposite meaning, for each word in the vocabulary list for "Blues Ain't No Mockin Bird" on page 320. Use each antonym in a sentence that makes the meaning of the word clear. (For more on using a thesaurus, see page R7.)

Writing

Write an **informal letter** from the point of view of a character in the story other than the narrator. Address the letter to a friend or relative and describe the events that the character observed.

- Before writing, list the personality traits of your character.
- Refer to your list as you write, making sure the details and language in your letter are consistent with the traits you listed.

For *Grammar, Vocabulary,* and *Assessment,* see **Build Language Skills,** pages 342–343.

Extend Your Learning

Listening and Speaking With a partner, role-play a **dialogue** between the cameraman and his boss. Follow these tips:
- Do not omit any important information, and do not exaggerate.
- Be polite, and use language appropriate to your situation.
- As the Boss, ask relevant questions and answers.
Read or perform the dialogue in class.

Research and Technology Work with a group of classmates to compile a **photo collection** of birds of prey like the hawks in "Blues Ain't No Mockin Bird." Consult library and Internet resources in your research of these birds, using keywords such as "hawks," "falcons," and "eagles." Print or copy the pictures and write an informative caption for each. Then, display your photo collection in class.

Blues Ain't No Mockin Bird ■ 331

Go Online
Research **For:** An additional research activity
Visit: www.PHSchool.com
Web Code: epd-7207
For another research activity to extend students' learning, give students this Web Code.

Vocabulary Builder
Practice

1. Reckless; A solution is achieved because someone is intelligent; an accident is caused because someone is reckless.
2. Formality; Sportsmanship is an important attitude in a game; formality is an important attitude in a ceremony.

Adding Words to Your Vocabulary

1. Because Andy was such a *careful* driver, he never had an accident or received a traffic violation.
2. The *informality* of the affair meant that everyone would dress casually.

Writing

- To give students guidance for writing their letter, give them **Support for Writing** for "Blues Ain't No Mockin Bird," p. 152 in *Unit 2 Resources.*
- To evaluate students' letters, use the Narration: Short Story rubrics, pp. 47–48 in *General Resources*. In addition, you might evaluate for the descriptive details.

Six Traits Focus

✔	Ideas	✔	Word Choice
	Organization		Sentence Fluency
✔	Voice		Conventions

Writing and Grammar, Gold Level
Students will find guidance on narrative letter writing in Chapter 5, sections 4 and 5.

Build Language Skills

Go to pp. 342–343 for vocabulary and grammar lessons and assessment practice.

Extend Your Learning

The **Support for Extend Your Learning** page (*Unit 2 Resources,* p. 153) provides guided note-taking opportunities to help students complete the Extend Your Learning activities.

❸ Background

Nineteenth-Century Train Travel
Mark Twain wrote this story in 1877, at a time when the American railroad was in its Golden Age and trains were the dominant form of transportation for both people and products. Twelve years earlier—on May 10, 1869—the Central Pacific and Union Pacific railroad lines had been connected in Promontory, Utah. The transcontinental railroad, which linked the railway network of the Northeast with California, was a monumental achievement of engineering. It involved the laying of 1,777 miles of track through forests and mountains and across rivers and deserts. Once completed, the railroad changed America. What had once been a six-month journey across the nation could now be completed in six days. Four other railroad lines were completed before the end of the nineteenth century.

❹ Connecting to the Literature

• Model use of the expressive vocabulary students are asked to use with these examples:

1. A gangster who attempts to *analyze* why he is a criminal is humorous.

2. Shifting the *focus* from the death of a man to the reaction of quarrelsome relatives arguing over his will created a comical situation.

3. Too many people attempted to *participate* in planning the funeral, causing some surprising results.

4. The amusing situation happened because the dog's owner did not *verify* that the animal was female.

• Help students further develop their expressive vocabulary by providing these words: *comprehend, defect, legitimate,* and *stimulate.* Encourage students to use these words as they discuss the selection.

Go Online
—Author Link For additional information about Mark Twain, have students type in the Web code and then select *Mark Twain.*

332

Short Story

Build Understanding • *The Invalid's Story*

❸ Background

Nineteenth-Century Train Travel In the late nineteenth century, when this story takes place, trains were the fastest way to travel and transport cargo. Nonetheless, train cars in which people with cargo had to travel were uncomfortable. The cars were poorly ventilated boxes on wheels, and had only small windows.

❹ Connecting to the Literature

Reading/Writing Connection In "The Invalid's Story," the author exaggerates the discomfort of two train travelers to create humor. Write a few sentences about why stories that create humor out of problems are funny. Use at least three of these words: *analyze, focus, participate, verify.*

Review

For **Literary Analysis, Reading Skill,** and **Vocabulary Builder,** see page 320.

READ MORE

by Mark Twain
Life on the Mississippi
The Adventures of Huckleberry Finn

Meet the Author

Mark **Twain** (1835–1910)

Born Samuel Clemens, Mark Twain grew up in the Mississippi River town of Hannibal, Missouri. He worked as a riverboat pilot, printer, prospector, reporter, and at many other jobs. Primarily, however, Clemens was a writer of comic stories, sketches, and novels. The most famous humorist of his day, he traveled the world entertaining people with his witty lectures.

"By the mark—twain" was a cry heard on the riverboats of Clemens's youth. It meant that the water was two fathoms deep—deep enough for a riverboat to pass unharmed. Harkening back to his youth working on those boats, Clemens took the name Mark Twain at age twenty-seven. Under that name, he wrote some of the most beloved fiction in American literature.

Fast Facts

▶ Mark Twain was the first writer to turn himself into a business. He even trademarked his name!

▶ Twain's first famous story was "The Celebrated Jumping Frog of Calaveras County."

 Go Online
—Author Link
For: More about the author
Visit: www.PHSchool.com
Web Code: epe-9211

332 ■ *Short Stories*

Differentiated Instruction Solutions for All Learners

Support for Below-Level Students [L1, L2]	**Support for English Learners [EL]**
Unit 2 Resources	**Unit 2 Resources**
Vocabulary Warm-up Word Lists, p. 161	Vocabulary Warm-up Word Lists, p. 161
Vocabulary Warm-up Practice, p. 162	Vocabulary Warm-up Practice, p. 162
Reading Warm-up A, p. 163	Reading Warm-up A, p. 163
Selection Test A, pp. 173–175	
Graphic Organizer Transparencies	**Listening to Literature Audio CD**
Reading Skill Graphic Organizer Transparency B, p. 71	

The Invalid's Story

Mark Twain

I seem sixty and married, but these effects are due to my condition and sufferings, for I am a bachelor, and only forty-one. It will be hard for you to believe that I, who am now but a shadow, was a hale, hearty man two short years ago—a man of iron, a very athlete!—yet such is the simple truth. But stranger still than this fact is the way in which I lost my health. I lost it through helping to take care of a box of guns on a two-hundred-mile railway journey one winter's night. It is the actual truth, and I will tell you about it.

I belong in Cleveland, Ohio. One winter's night, two years ago, I reached home just after dark, in a driving snowstorm, and the first thing I heard when I entered the house was that my dearest boyhood friend and schoolmate, John B. Hackett, had died the day before, and that his last utterance had been a desire that I would take his remains home to his poor old father and mother in Wisconsin. I was greatly shocked and grieved, but there was no time to waste in emotions; I must start at once. I took the card, marked "Deacon Levi Hackett, Bethlehem, Wisconsin," and hurried off through the whistling storm to the railway station. Arrived there I found the long white-pine box which had been described to me; I fastened the card to it with some tacks, saw it put safely aboard the express car, and then ran into the eating room to provide myself

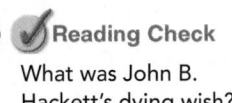

Reading Check

What was John B. Hackett's dying wish?

The Invalid's Story ■ 333

Differentiated Instruction   Solutions for All Learners

Enrichment for Advanced Readers
Suggest that students read additional works by Mark Twain. Provide students with **Authors In Depth**, Gold level, which contains the following selections:

- from *A Connecticut Yankee in King Arthur's Court*
- "A Fable"
- from *Roughing It*

After students have read these or other works by Twain, have them form discussion groups in which they compare and contrast the selections. Suggest criteria for comparison, such as setting, theme, characters, dialect, and humor.

333

➍ Critical Viewing

➍ Critical Viewing

Possible response: Students will probably say that getting from one place to another was very difficult in 1874. The painting shows that people had to rely on horse-drawn carriages to get to the train station. Moreover, people walking toward their train at the station had to avoid horses crossing their path. The trunk in the foreground clearly shows that most nineteenth-century luggage was not easy to handle.

➎ Humanities

Sacramento Railroad Station, 1874, by William Hahn

William Hahn's painting gives a dynamic and detailed glimpse of the rigors of transportation and the ordeal of travel in the late 1800s. Use the following for discussion:

1. How does the depiction of the station help to show how the boxes in the Twain story could have been switched?
   Possible response: Students may say that the confusion and disorganization depicted make it easy to see how the mix-up occurred.

2. What would this station scene be like in winter?
   Possible response: Have students list details that might be added to a winter scene, such as slush, snow, ice, and sleighs.

---

with a sandwich and some cigars. When I returned, presently, there was my coffin-box back again, apparently, and a young fellow examining around it, with a card in his hands, and some tacks and a hammer! I was astonished and puzzled. He began to nail on his card, and I rushed out to the express car, in a good deal of a state of mind, to ask for an explanation. But no—there was my box, all right, in the express car; it hadn't been disturbed. [The fact is that without my suspecting it a <u>prodigious</u> mistake had been made. I was carrying off a box of guns which that young fellow had come to the station to ship to a rifle company in Peoria, Illinois, and he had got my corpse.] Just then the conductor sang out "All aboard," and I jumped into the express car and got a comfortable seat on a bale of buckets. The expressman was there, hard at work—a plain man of fifty, with a simple, honest, good-natured face, and a breezy, practical heartiness in his general style. As the train moved off a stranger skipped into the car and set a package of peculiarly mature and capable Limburger cheese[1] on one end of my coffin-box—I mean my box of guns. That is to say, I know now that it was Limburger cheese, but at that time I never had heard of the article in my life, and of course was wholly ignorant of its character. Well, we sped through the wild night, the bitter storm raged on, a cheerless misery stole over me, my heart went down, down, down! The old expressman made a brisk remark or two about the tempest and the arctic weather, slammed his sliding doors to, and bolted them, closed his window down tight, and then went bustling around, here and there and yonder, setting things to rights, and all the time contentedly humming "Sweet By and By" in a low tone, and flatting a

---

1. **Limburger cheese** cheese with a strong odor.

Sacramento Railroad Station (detail), 1874, William Hahn, Fine Arts Museum of San Francisco

334 ■ *Short Stories*

➍ **Critical Viewing** Based on this 1874 painting of a railway station, what challenges did train travel pose at that time in history? **[Analyze]**

Vocabulary Development

Vocabulary Builder Reinforcement
Students will benefit from additional examples and practice with the Vocabulary Builder words. Reinforce their comprehension with "show-you-know" sentences. Model the strategy with this example for *deleterious:*

> The effects of the medication were *deleterious;* his condition grew worse.

1. He made a *judicious* selection when he chose his vice-presidential running mate; _____

Sample answer: they won the election by a landslide.

2. The waves *placidly* lapped the sandy shore; _____

Sample answer: it was a quiet and peaceful scene.

3. She made a *desultory* choice of an outfit to wear to the party; _____
Sample answer: she just grabbed the first thing she saw in her closet.

good deal. Presently I began to detect a most evil and searching odor stealing about on the frozen air. This depressed my spirits still more, because of course I attributed it to my poor departed friend. There was something infinitely saddening about his calling himself to my remembrance in this dumb, pathetic way, so it was hard to keep the tears back. Moreover, it distressed me on account of the old expressman, who, I was afraid, might notice it. However, he went humming tranquilly on, and gave no sign; and for this I was grateful. Grateful, yes, but still uneasy; and soon I began to feel more and more uneasy every minute, for every minute that went by that odor thickened up the more, and got to be more and more gamy and hard to stand. Presently, having got things arranged to his satisfaction, the expressman got some wood and made up a tremendous fire in his stove. This distressed me more than I can tell, for I could not but feel that it was a mistake. I was sure that the effect would be <u>deleterious</u> upon my poor departed friend. Thompson—the expressman's name was Thompson, as I found out in the course of the night—now went poking around his car, stopping up whatever stray cracks he could find, remarking that it didn't make any difference what kind of a night it was outside, he calculated to make us comfortable, anyway. I said nothing, but I believed he was not choosing the right way. Meantime he was humming to himself just as before; and meantime, too, the stove was getting hotter and hotter, and the place closer and closer. I felt myself growing pale and qualmish,[2] but grieved in silence and said nothing. Soon I noticed that the "Sweet By and By" was gradually fading out; next it ceased altogether, and there was an ominous stillness. After a few moments Thompson said—

"Pfew! I reckon it ain't no cinnamon't I've loaded up thish-year stove with!"

He gasped once or twice, then moved toward the cof—gun-box, stood over that Limburger cheese part of a moment, then came back and sat down near me, looking a good deal impressed. After a contemplative pause, he said, indicating the box with a gesture—

"Friend of yourn?"

"Yes," I said with a sigh.

"He's pretty ripe, ain't he!"

Nothing further was said for perhaps a couple of minutes, each being busy with his own thoughts; then Thompson said, in a low awed voice—

"Sometimes it's uncertain whether they're really gone or not—seem gone, you know—body warm, joints limber—and so, although

---

2. **qualmish** (kwäm′ ish) *adj.* suddenly sick.

Vocabulary Builder
deleterious (del′ ə tir′ ē əs) *adj.* harmful to health or well-being

Reading Skill
Cause and Effect
When you picture this scene, what details explain the cause of Thompson's gasp?

✓ **Reading Check**
What does the narrator say depressed his spirits?

The Invalid's Story ■ 335

- Have students read the bracketed passage. **Ask** why the narrator believes Thompson was not choosing the right way to make them comfortable.
  Answer: The narrator knows that the odor will get worse when the car is closed up.

- Tell students that the tune Thompson is humming, "Sweet By and By," is a church hymn that refers to the afterlife. **Ask** students how this detail adds to the humor of the scene.
  Possible response: Students may say that the tune, which is about the afterlife, relates to the corpse in the coffin. The title of the hymn contains the word "sweet," which is the opposite of the odor in the car.

- **Ask** students to respond to the Reading Skill question: When you picture this scene, what details explain the cause of Thompson's gasp?
  Possible response: The heat in the car makes the Limburger cheese smell worse; Thompson stops humming his tune; he makes the exclamation "pfew"; he comments that it does not smell like he has put cinnamon in the stove.

7 Reading Check
Answer: His spirits were depressed by the storm and later by the stench.

Differentiated
Instruction   Solutions for All Learners

Strategy for Special Needs Students
Students may be confused by the fact that readers know early on that the coffin has been replaced with a box of guns. They may wonder why the narrator and the expressman do not know it. Refer students to the opening paragraph that tells them that the narrator is telling the story long after it happened. Point out to students the passage in the middle of page 334 that begins "The fact is that without my suspecting it. . . ."

Analyze

- Refer students to the bracketed passage. **Ask** students what Thompson is talking about in this passage.
  Answer: He is talking about the inevitability of death.

- **Ask** students what the narrator means when he says that Thompson "stretched his nose out." Why did Thompson do this?
  Answer: He put his face out the window to get some fresh air. The odor in the car was unbearable.

- **Ask** students what the men believed was causing the odor. What was actually causing the odor? What was actually in the pine box?
  Answer: The men believed a decaying corpse in the box was causing the odor. Limburger cheese was actually causing the odor. The box contained a shipment of guns.

- **Ask** students to analyze the humor in the scene in which each of these two men alternately put their noses out the window for fresh air.
  Possible response: Students may respond that it is humorous that the men endure the odor because they believe it is the corpse, when in fact it is foul-smelling cheese. Additionally, the coffin's actual contents of guns—instead of a corpse—is oddly comical.

---

you think they're gone, you don't really know. I've had cases in my car. It's perfectly awful, becuz you don't know what minute they'll rise up and look at you!" Then, after a pause, and slightly lifting his elbow toward the box,—"But he ain't in no trance! No, sir, I go bail for him!"

We sat some time, in meditative silence, listening to the wind and the roar of the train; then Thompson said, with a good deal of feeling:

❽ "Well-a-well, we've all got to go, they ain't no getting around it. Man that is born of woman is of few days and far between, as Scriptur'[3] says. Yes, you look at it any way you want to, it's awful solemn and cur'us: they ain't nobody can get around it; all's got to go—just everybody, as you may say. One day you're hearty and strong"—here he scrambled to his feet and broke a pane and stretched his nose out at it a moment or two, then sat down again while I struggled up and thrust my nose out at the same place, and this we kept on doing every now and then—"and next day he's cut down like the grass, and the places which knowed him then knows him no more forever, as Scriptur' says. Yes'ndeedy, it's awful solemn and cur'us; but we've all got to go, one time or another; they ain't no getting around it."

There was another long pause; then—
"What did he die of?"
I said I didn't know.
"How long has he ben dead?"
It seemed <u>judicious</u> to enlarge the facts to fit the probabilities; so I said:
"Two or three days."

But it did no good: for Thompson received it with an injured look which plainly said. "Two or three years, you mean." Then he went right along, <u>placidly</u> ignoring my statement, and gave his views at considerable length upon the unwisdom of putting off burials too long. Then he lounged off toward the box, stood a moment, then came back on a sharp trot and visited the broken pane, observing:

"'Twould 'a' ben a durn sight better, all around, if they'd started him along last summer."

Thompson sat down and buried his face in his red silk handkerchief, and began to slowly sway and rock his body like one who is doing his best to endure the almost unendurable. By this time the fragrance—if you may call it fragrance—was just about suffocating, as near as you can come at it. Thompson's face was turning gray: I

---

3. Scriptur' scripture; the Bible.

Vocabulary Builder
judicious (jōō dish´ əs)
adj. showing good judgment

placidly (plas´ id lē)
adv. calmly; quietly

Vocabulary Development

Expressive Vocabulary
Ask students to think about the humor of the situation in which these two men find themselves. The men are suffering the effects of a foul odor without realizing its actual cause. Have students use the expressive vocabulary presented earlier to discuss the men's attempts to deal with the odor. You might encourage them with sentence starters like these:

1. The two men began to *analyze* . . .
2. They tried to *focus* . . .
3. They both began to *participate* in . . .
4. Neither of the men attempted to *verify* that . . .

knew mine hadn't any color left in it. By and by Thompson rested his forehead in his left hand, with his elbow on his knee, and sort of waved his red handkerchief toward the box with his other hand, and said:

9 "I've carried a many a one of 'em—some of 'em considerable overdue, too—but, lordy, he just lays over 'em all!—and does it easy. Cap, they was heliotrope[4] to him!"

This recognition of my poor friend gratified me, in spite of the sad circumstances, because it had so much the sound of a compliment.

Pretty soon it was plain that something had got to be done. I suggested cigars. Thompson thought it was a good idea. He said:

"Likely it'll modify him some."

We puffed gingerly along for a while, and tried hard to imagine that things were improved. But it wasn't any use. Before very long, and without any consultation, both cigars were quietly dropped from our nerveless fingers at the same moment. Thompson said, with a sigh:

"No, Cap, it don't modify him worth a cent. Fact is, it makes him worse, becuz it appears to stir up his ambition. What do you reckon we better do, now?"

I was not able to suggest anything: indeed, I had to be swallowing and swallowing all the time, and did not like to trust myself to speak. Thompson fell to maundering, in a <u>desultory</u> and low-spirited way, about the miserable experiences of this night: and he got to referring to my poor friend by various titles—sometimes military ones, sometimes civil ones; and I noticed that as fast as my poor friend's effectiveness grew, Thompson promoted him accordingly—gave him a bigger title. Finally he said:

"I've got an idea. Suppos'n' we buckle down to it and give the Colonel a bit of a shove toward t'other end of the car?—about ten foot, say. He wouldn't have so much influence, then, don't you reckon?"

I said it was a good scheme. So we took in a good fresh breath at the broken pane, calculating to hold it till we got through: then we went there and bent over that deadly cheese and took a grip on the box. Thompson nodded "All ready," and then we threw ourselves forward with all our might: but Thompson slipped, and slumped down with his nose on the cheese, and his breath got loose. He gagged and gasped, and floundered up and made a break for the door, pawing the air and saying hoarsely, "Don't hender me!—

---

4. **heliotrope** (hē′ lē ə trōp′) *n.* a sweet-smelling plant.

Literary Analysis
Dialogue and Dialect
Which features of Thompson's speech in this passage reflect a particular dialect?

Vocabulary Builder
desultory (des′ əl tôr′ ē) *adj.* random

10 ✓ Reading Check
How do the men use the window to lessen the effect of the odor?

The Invalid's Story ■ 337

---

9 Literary Analysis
Dialogue and Dialect

• Refer students to the bracketed passage. **Ask** students what Thompson is describing in this passage.
  Answer: He is describing the odor of what he thinks is the corpse.

• **Ask** students to respond to the Literary Analysis question: Which features of Thompson's speech in this passage reflect a particular dialect?
  Possible response: Examples of dialect include "a many a one of 'em" instead of the standard "many of them"; the abbreviated form "'em" instead of "them"; use of the word "considerable" when the standard adverb would be "considerably"; the exclamation "lordy"; the idiom "lays over 'em all!"; the term "Cap"; and the use of the singular verb "was" instead of the plural verb "were."

• **Ask** students to explain in their own words what Thompson is saying about the corpse.
  Answer: Thompson is saying that he has transported many corpses, some of which have been dead for quite awhile, but this one is by far the smelliest. The stink of this corpse makes the others smell like a fragrant plant.

10 Reading Check

Answer: They put their faces out the window periodically to breathe fresh air.

Cultural Connection The strong smell of Limburger cheese is said to "be able to fell trees." The name reminds many people of anything that smells potent enough to be detected for miles. One source cites a man named Limburger who had changed his name because people avoided him as if he were the cheese itself! Still, many people in various countries eat and enjoy Limburger.

Connect to the Literature

Ask students the Connect to the Literature question: Why do you think the narrator and Thompson are so confused about the source of the smell in the train car?

Possible response: Neither the narrator nor Thompson knows the cheese is there, nor do they know that the box contains guns instead of a body.

gimme the road! I'm a-dying; gimme the road!" Out on the cold platform I sat down and held his head awhile, and he revived. Presently he said:

"Do you reckon we started the Gen'rul any?"

I said no: we hadn't budged him.

"Well, then, that idea's up the flume. We got to think up something else. He's suited wher' he is, I reckon; and if that's the way he feels about it, and has made up his mind that he don't wish to be disturbed, you bet he's a-going to have his own way in the business. Yes, better leave him right wher' he is, long as he wants it so; becuz he holds all the trumps, don't you know, and so it stands to reason that the man that lays out to alter his plans for him is going to get left."

But we couldn't stay out there in that mad storm; we should have frozen to death. So we went in again and shut the door, and began to suffer once more and take turns at the break in the window. By and by, as we were starting away from a station where we had stopped a moment Thompson pranced in cheerily, and exclaimed:

"We're all right, now! I reckon we've got the Commodore this time. I judge I've got the stuff here that'll take the tuck out of him."

It was carbolic acid. He had a carboy of it. He sprinkled it all around everywhere; in fact he drenched everything with it, rifle-box, cheese and all. Then we sat down, feeling pretty hopeful. But it wasn't for long. You see the two perfumes began to mix, and then—well, pretty soon we made a break for the door; and out there Thompson swabbed his face with his bandanna and said in a kind of disheartened way:

"It ain't no use. We can't buck agin him.
He just utilizes everything we put up to modify him with, and gives it his own flavor and plays it back on us. Why, Cap, don't you know, it's as much as a hundred times worse in there now than it was when he first got a-going. I never did see one of 'em warm up to his work so, and take such a dumnation interest in it. No, sir, I never did, as long as I've ben on the road: and I've carried a many a one of 'em, as I was telling you."

Literature in Context

Cultural Connection

Limburger Cheese The foul stench that torments the narrator and Thompson comes from a package of Limburger cheese. This cheese was first made in Belgium and is now made in Germany and in the United States. It is notorious for its strong odor. The cheese is made from cow's milk and is "ripened" for about three months under specially controlled conditions. This ripening process gives Limburger cheese its distinctive smell and flavor. The cheese continues to ripen during shipping and its odor can become extremely intense.

Connect to the Literature

Why do you think the narrator and Thompson are so confused about the source of the smell in the train car?

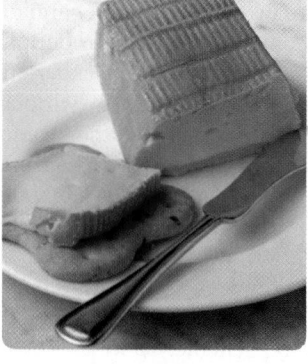

Vocabulary Development

Vocabulary Knowledge Rating

When students have completed reading and discussing "The Invalid's Story," have them take out their **Vocabulary Knowledge Rating Chart** for this selection. Read the words aloud once more and have students rate their knowledge of the words again in the After Reading column. Clarify any words that are still problematic. Have students write their own definition and example or sentence in the appropriate column. Then have students complete the **Vocabulary Builder Practice** activities. Encourage students to use the words in further discussion and written work about this selection. Remind them that they will be accountable for these words on the Selection Test.

We went in again after we were frozen pretty stiff; but my, we couldn't stay in, now. So we just waltzed back and forth, freezing, and thawing, and stifling, by turns. In about an hour we stopped at another station; and as we left it Thompson came in with a bag, and said—

"Cap, I'm a-going to chance him once more—just this once; and if we don't fetch him this time, the thing for us to do, is to just throw up the sponge and withdraw from the canvass. That's the way I put it up."

He had brought a lot of chicken feathers, and dried apples, and leaf tobacco, and rags, and old shoes, and sulphur, and asafetida, and one thing or another: and he piled them on a breadth of sheet iron in the middle of the floor, and set fire to them.

When they got well started. I couldn't see, myself, how even the corpse could stand it. All that went before was just simply poetry to that smell—but mind you, the original smell stood up out of it just as sublime as ever—fact is, these other smells just seemed to give it a better hold: and my, how rich it was! I didn't make these reflections there—there wasn't time—made them on the platform. And breaking for the platform, Thompson got suffocated and fell: and before I got him dragged out, which I did by the collar, I was mighty near gone myself. When we revived, Thompson said dejectedly:

"We got to stay out here, Cap. We got to do it. They ain't no other way. The Governor wants to travel alone, and he's fixed so he can outvote us."

And presently he added:

"And don't you know, we're pisoned. It's our last trip, you can make up your mind to it. Typhoid fever is what's going to come of this. I feel it a-coming right now. Yes, sir, we're elected, just as sure as you're born."

We were taken from the platform an hour later, frozen and insensible, at the next station, and I went straight off into a virulent fever, and never knew anything again for three weeks. I found out, then, that I had spent that awful night with a harmless box of rifles and a lot of innocent cheese; but the news was too late to save me; imagination had done its work, and my health was permanently shattered; neither Bermuda nor any other land can ever bring it back to me. This is my last trip; I am on my way home to die.

Reading Skill
Cause and Effect
What is the result of Thompson's final attempt to deal with the odor?

Reading Skill
Cause and Effect
What effect does the experience on the train have on the narrator's health?

The Invalid's Story ■ *339*

Concept Connector

Anticipation Guide
Have students return to their **Anticipation Guides** and respond to the statements again in the After Reading column. Then, lead a class discussion, probing for what students have learned that confirms or invalidates each statement.

Connecting to the Literature
Have students compare the sentences they wrote before reading with their thoughts about the role of humor in situations involving death. Ask them to explain whether their thoughts have changed and, if so, how.

Reading Skill Graphic Organizer
Have students review the graphic organizers they completed to identify details that helped them visualize effects while reading. Show them the **Reading Skill Graphic Organizer B** *(Graphic Organizer Transparencies,* p. 71) as an example. Then have students share the graphic organizers they did and the details they visualized to help them determine cause and effect.

⑫ Reading Skill
Cause and Effect

- Have students read the bracketed passage. **Ask** students to describe how Thompson tries to get rid of the odor.
  Answer: He piled things such as rags, chicken feathers, sulphur, in the middle of the floor and set fire to the pile.

- **Ask** students how the narrator describes the odor caused by the fire.
  Answer: He says that the odor they were trying to cover up was poetry compared to the odor caused by the fire.

- **Ask** students to respond to the first Reading Skill question: What is the result of Thompson's final attempt to deal with the odor?
  Answer: The odor of the fire is worse than the original odor; Thompson falls down suffocating, and the narrator drags him outside on the train platform.

▶ **Monitor Progress:** Using the **Reading Skill Graphic Organizer A** *(Graphic Organizer Transparencies,* p. 69), ask students to record the cause, mental image, and effect based on this question.

▶ **Reteach:** If students are having difficulty identifying details and visualizing an image, provide them with the **Reading Skill Graphic Organizer B** *(Graphic Organizer Transparencies,* p. 71). Review the graphic organizer with them, pointing out how the details of the mental picture help them understand the effects.

⑬ Reading Skill
Cause and Effect

- Have students read the last two paragraphs aloud. **Ask** them what Thompson thinks their exposure to the odor will cause.
  Answer: Thompson is convinced that they will get typhoid fever and die.

- **Ask** students to respond to the second Reading Skill question: What effect does the experience on the train have on the narrator's health?
  Answer: He claims that his health is ruined, and that he is going to die.

339

1. **Possible responses:** Many students may be entertained by the comical effects of a foul odor.

2. (a) The men believe a decaying corpse is causing the odor. (b) Limburger cheese is causing the smell. (c) The contrast between a serious and a harmless source of the odor is humorous.

3. (a) He says the corpse wants to travel alone because it is creating an offensive odor. (b) It adds to the humor because a corpse cannot deliberately do anything.

4. **Possible responses:** (a) Some sad details include the death of the narrator's friend, and the grieving parents. (b) Some humorous details include the fact that Limburger cheese is causing the smell, and that Thompson gasps over the box near the cheese. (c) Most students will say that the story is simply funny.

5. Dialogue that reveals the increasing smell is, "All that went before was just simply poetry to that smell . . ."

6. Dialogue that reveals the unfamiliarity between Thompson and the narrator is "Friend of yourn?" "Yes," I said with a sigh.

7. (a) Dialect in the following words and phrases: "Cap;" the use of "don't;" the phrase "modify him worth a cent"; the pronunciation of "becuz;" the idiom "stir up his ambition;" the use of "reckon"; and the phrase "we better do." (b) "No, sir, it does not change him at all. The fact is, it makes him worse, because it appears to make him release even more odor. What do you think we should do now?" (c) The use of dialect makes Thompson's character more specific because it provides him with a particular cultural background. His language is colorful and expressive, which makes the scene more vivid and comical.

8. (a) The cause of the smell is Limburger cheese. (b) The smell forces the men to flee the car.

9. Visual details include the coffin-like box, the passenger moving through who places the Limburger cheese on the box,

340

Apply the Skills

The Invalid's Story

Thinking About the Selection

1. **Respond:** Did you find this story entertaining? Explain.
2. (a) **Recall:** What do the men believe is creating the awful smell? (b) **Connect:** What is actually creating the smell? (c) **Compare and Contrast:** In what ways does the contrast between what they think is true and what is really true contribute to the humor?
3. (a) **Interpret:** Why does Thompson say the corpse "wants to travel alone"? (b) **Analyze:** How does Thompson's description of the corpse as deliberately trying to smell bad add to the story's humor?
4. Make a chart like the one shown. (a) **Compare:** In the first column, write a list of sad details in the story. (b) **Connect:** In the second column, write the details that add humor to the story. (c) **Discuss and Evaluate:** Share your chart with a partner and discuss your responses. Then, in the third column, explain whether you think the story is sad, funny, or both.

Sad Details	Humorous Details	Evaluation

Literary Analysis

5. Identify one example of **dialogue** in the story that indicates the smell is increasing. Explain your choice.
6. Identify an example of dialogue that shows that Thompson and the narrator do not know each other well. Explain your choice.
7. (a) In what way do the spelling, grammar, and words used in the following passage indicate that it is an example of **dialect?**
   No, Cap, it don't modify him worth a cent. Fact is, it makes him worse, becuz it appears to stir up his ambition. What do you reckon we better do, now?
   (b) Rewrite the passage in Standard English. (c) Explain how the use of dialect makes the characters and setting more vivid.

Reading Skill

8. (a) What is the **cause** of the smell in the express car? (b) What **effect** does the smell have on Thompson and the narrator?
9. Which visual details in the story help you to explain why the characters are mistaken about the true cause of the smell?

340 ■ Short Stories

and Thompson leaning over the box and gasping at the odor.

QuickReview

Story at a Glance
Two travelers on a train endure an odor they mistakenly think comes from a corpse.

Assessment
For: Self-test
Visit: www.PHSchool.com
Web Code: epa-6210

Dialogue: a conversation between or among characters in a literary work

Dialect: the unique form of a language spoken by people of a region or group

Cause: an event, an action, or a feeling that produces a result

Effect: the result produced by a cause

Vocabulary Builder

Practice **Analogies** show the relationships between pairs of words. Use a word from the vocabulary list for "The Invalid's Story" on page 320 to complete each analogy.

1. comedy : humorous :: measles : _____
2. graceful : clumsy :: _____ : foolish
3. tiny : small :: _____ : large
4. systematic : reliable :: _____ : unpredictable
5. violently : angry :: _____ : content

Adding Words to Your Vocabulary Using a thesaurus, find an **antonym**, or word of opposite meaning, for each word in the vocabulary list for "The Invalid's Story" on page 320. Use each antonym correctly in a sentence. (For more on using a thesaurus, see page R7.)

Writing

Write an **informal letter** from the point of view of Thompson. Address the letter to a friend or relative and describe what occurs in the story.
- Before you write, list Thompson's personality traits.
- Refer to your list as you write, making sure that the details and language in your letter fit the traits you listed.

For *Grammar, Vocabulary,* and *Assessment,* see **Build Language Skills,** pages 342–343.

Extend Your Learning

Listening and Speaking With a partner, assume the roles of the narrator and a doctor. Prepare and deliver a **dialogue** in which the narrator explains to the doctor why his health is "shattered."
- Do not omit any important information, and do not exaggerate.
- Be polite, and use language appropriate to your situation.
Read or perform the dialogue in class.

Research and Technology Mark Twain has one of America's most familiar faces. Work with a group to compile a **photo collection** that shows Twain at various ages. Consult library and Internet resources in your research. Print or copy the pictures and write an informative caption for each. Display your photo collection in class.

The Invalid's Story ■ 341

Assessment Resources

The following resources can be used to assess students' knowledge and skills.

Unit 2 Resources:
 Selection Test A, pp. 173–175
 Selection Test B, pp. 176–178

Go Online — **Assessment** Students may use the **Self-test** to prepare for **Selection Test A** or **Selection Test B.**

Go Online — **Research** **For:** An additional research activity
Visit: www.PHSchool.com
Web Code: epd-7208
For another research activity to extend students' learning, give students this Web Code.

Vocabulary Builder
Practice

1. deleterious; A comedy is humorous; measles are harmful.
2. judicious; The pairs of words are opposites.
3. prodigious; Tiny is the extreme of small, and prodigious, or enormous, is the extreme of large.
4. desultory; Reliable is a property of something that is systematic, and unpredictable is a property of something that is desultory, or random.
5. placidly; Both are adverbs that intensify the adjective.

Adding Words to Your Vocabulary
Sample answers:

1. A *healthy* diet will improve your athletic ability, because your body will function more efficiently.
2. A *foolish* choice can prevent you from getting into college.
3. The waves beat *furiously* on the shore, a sign that the hurricane was drawing near.
4. His *well-planned* design showed his care and thoughtfulness.

Writing

- To give students guidance for writing their letter, give them **Support for Writing** for "The Invalid's Story," p. 168 in *Unit 2 Resources.*
- To evaluate students' letters, use the Narration: Short Story rubrics, pp. 47–48 in *General Resources.*

Six Traits Focus

✔	Ideas	✔	Word Choice
	Organization		Sentence Fluency
✔	Voice		Conventions

Build Language Skills

Go to pp. 342–343 for vocabulary and grammar lessons and assessment practice.

Extend Your Learning

The **Support for Extend Your Learning** page (*Unit 2 Resources,* p. 169) provides guided note-taking opportunities to help students complete the Extend Your Learning activities.

341

Vocabulary Skill

- Introduce the word root *-sequi-*. Have students work in pairs using a dictionary to find other words that share this word root.
  Possible responses: *obsequious, sequel, sequential, sequacious*

- Have students complete the Practice activity on this page.

Possible responses:

1. *non sequitur;* a conclusion that does not follow from the evidence

2. *sequel:* a book, movie, play, etc., that continues the story of a previous one

3. *sequential:* happening in a sequence, or particular order

4. *subsequent:* coming after or following something else

Grammar Lesson

- Point out to students that the active voice is the voice that they should use for most of their writing.

- Have students complete the Practice activity on this page.

Answers

1. was ignored; passive voice; good choice because it places the emphasis on Matthew

2. was placed; passive voice; good choice because it stresses the story and shows its powerlessness

3. wrote; active; good choice because it stresses the author's activity

4. was helped; passive; not a good choice; searching for answers suggests an active pursuit

5. rescued; active; good choice because it is directly expresses what happened

Writing Application

To evaluate students' papers, make sure that two of the sentences use active voice and two use the passive voice.

Writing and Grammar, Gold Level

Students will find further instruction and practice on active and passive voice in Chapter 23, Section 2.

Build Language Skills

Blues Ain't No Mockin Bird • *The Invalid's Story*

Vocabulary Skill

Word Roots The **Latin root** *-sequi-* means "follow." A *sequence* is "a following of one thing after another."

➤ **Example:** The witness described the sequence of events.

Words with the root *-sequi-* will have meanings related to the idea of following.

Practice From your knowledge of the root, predict the meaning of these words. Check the dictionary definition. Explain how your predicted meaning compares to the dictionary definition.

1. non sequitur
2. sequel
3. sequential
4. subsequent

Grammar Lesson

Active and Passive Voice A verb in the **active voice** expresses an action done *by* its subject. A verb in the **passive voice** expresses an action done *to* its subject.

Active voice:
Mark Twain *wrote* "The Invalid's Story." (The subject, *Mark Twain,* performs the action of the verb *wrote.*)

Passive voice:
"The Invalid's Story" *was written* by Mark Twain. (The subject, *"The Invalid's Story,"* receives the action of the verb *was written.*)

Use the active voice for lively, direct writing. Use the passive voice when you want to minimize the performer of the action or when the performer of the action is unknown.

Practice Copy the following sentences and underline the verb or verbs in each one. **(a)** Identify the underlined verbs as active or passive voice. **(b)** Explain whether the active or passive voice is a good choice for the sentence.

1. Matthew was ignored by the reporter.
2. The story was placed on the last page.
3. She wrote a story about a mysterious disappearance.
4. In the search for answers, the reporter was helped by two eyewitnesses.
5. A neighbor rescued the trapped child.

Prentice Hall Writing and Grammar Connection: Chapter 5, Section 4

Teaching Resources

The following resources can be used to enrich or extend the instruction for Build Language Skills.

Unit 2 Resources
   Build Language Skills: Vocabulary Skill: Word Roots, p. 171
   Build Grammar Skills: Active and Passive Voice: p. 172

Reading: Cause and Effect

Directions: *Read the selection. Then answer the questions.*

A fierce storm had been beating down on the isolated house since sunrise. Now, as the wind shrieked, Andrew glanced out the window just in time to see the huge oak tree quiver and begin to fall straight toward him. He ducked away and ran toward the kitchen. As he did so, he stumbled and fell roughly to the floor beneath his desk. He rolled over just in time to see the oak splinter the window and crash down on him. Andrew gasped for breath as the wind howled through the shattered window. The oak lay propped on the solid desk, inches from his eyes. Except for a slight scrape on his knee, he had escaped without injury.

1. Why did Andrew end up under the desk?
   A A storm had blown a tree through his window.
   B He knew he could not get to the kitchen in time.
   C He dove under the desk to avoid being injured.
   D He stumbled while trying to run to safety.

2. Why was Andrew able to avoid serious injury?
   A The tree was blocked by the window.
   B The desk prevented the tree from hitting him.
   C He leaped aside into the kitchen.
   D He ran quickly.

3. What was the effect of the storm?
   A injury
   B damage
   C impairment
   D affliction

4. What would you have to picture in order to visualize the action?
   A an oak tree
   B the exterior of the house
   C the interior of the house
   D a solid desk

Timed Writing: Description [Cognition]

Review "Blues Ain't No Mockin Bird" or "The Invalid's Story." Write a brief description of the setting of the story. **(30 minutes)**

Writing Workshop: *Work in Progress*

Cause and Effect Essay

Highlight the one effect that you think is most interesting on your effect list. Write a list of questions that would help you define the cause for this effect. Put this paper in your writing portfolio.

Build Language Skills ■ *343*

Reading: Analyzing Cause and Effect

1. D   3. B
2. B   4. A

Timed Writing

- Tell students that when they write a description, they should use vivid language to describe all of the details that can be experienced through the senses.

- Suggest that students recall where the story took place, paying particular attention to those elements of setting that are important to the story's plot.

- Then, have students write their description. Encourage students to select details that are important to the story and that help the reader to picture the setting.

- Assess students' descriptions on the accuracy and importance of the details they choose.

- Suggest that students organize their time to allow five minutes for planning and reviewing the story, fifteen minutes for writing, and ten minutes for reviewing and revising.

Writing Workshop
Work in Progress

Cause-and-Effect Essay

- Have students go to their portfolios and take out the lists that they made in the **Work-in-Progress** assignment on p. 319.

- Remind students that this work may be used in the cause-and-effect essay they will write in the **Writing Workshop** at the end of Part 2.

- As students select their most interesting effect, have them remember that they should choose an effect that has a knowable cause. Selecting an effect that has no known cause will make their paper difficult to write.

- As students write their list of questions, have them think seriously about the possible cause. Their questions should reflect their attempts to determine the cause.

- When students have completed their lists of questions, have them save them in their portfolios. They will use them as they continue this Work in Progress.

See TeacherExpress™/Lesson View for a detailed lesson plan for Reading Informational Materials.

About Brochures

- Have students read "About Brochures."

- Ask volunteers to describe brochures they have seen for attractions such as zoos, theme parks, or state parks. Encourage them to note how the information is laid out, and how the brochure differs from a story or an article about a place. Ask students what they like and dislike about reading brochures.

Reading Skill
Evaluating Text Format

- Remind students that to evaluate text formats, they will analyze text and design features. Text features include headings, word choice, and placement. Design features include images, charts, graphs, color, and font choices.

- Review with students the Evaluating Text Format chart. Explain to students that writers and graphic designers work closely together to create brochures. The text and design features can be equally important in evaluating the overall format of the brochure.

- Divide the class into six groups, Assign each group one of the questions in the "Evaluate Text Format" chart. Ask the groups to look at the brochure front on p. 345 and figure out the answers to the questions. Then, have each group present its findings to the class.

Brochures

In Part 2, you are learning how to analyze causes and effects as you read literature. This skill is also useful when you read informational materials, such as brochures and advertisements. When writers and graphic designers create a brochure, they use specific design and organizational elements to produce the effects they want. If you read Mark Twain's "The Invalid's Story," you may have wanted to learn more about railways. The brochure that follows describes a museum that celebrates trains and railroads.

About Brochures

The **brochures** that organizations and businesses create can provide many types of information. They often include these features:

- Location map
- Contact information, including mailing address, e-mail address, and phone numbers
- Hours of operation and prices of admission
- Description of facilities, products, or services
- Photographs of products or services

Reading Skill

Brochures are designed so that words, colors, and images work together to present information in a logical and pleasing way. The **format** is the placement of text, including headings and captions, around design elements, such as pictures and maps. The format makes important information stand out. When you **evaluate text format,** you examine text and design features to determine the importance of the information presented. These features will help you distinguish between essential and nonessential information in printed materials.

Evaluating Text Format	
Heads	What is the largest head on the page? What information do the heads emphasize?
Images	Are photographs included? Are maps or graphics included? Where? How do the images support information in the text?
Organization	What information appears on the first page? Why? What information appears inside? Why?

344 ■ Short Stories

Differentiated Instruction   Solutions for All Learners

Reading Support
Give students reading support with the appropriate version of the *Reader's Notebooks:*

Reader's Notebook, [L2]

Reader's Notebook: Adapted Version, [L1]

Reader's Notebook: English Learner's Version, [EL]

North Carolina Transportation Museum

The subhead grabs your attention by challenging you to discover something new. It also makes readers consider what "moved"— trains, people, or maybe even ideas.

Discover the People and Machines That Have Moved North Carolina

North Carolina
HISTORIC SITES
Division of Archives and History
Department of Cultural Resources

The locator map is placed so readers see it immediately. It shows major roads and landmarks.

The museum's hours and cost of admission are located near the map. All the information needed to visit the museum is easy to find.

Hours:
Apr. 1–Oct. 31: Mon.–Sat. 9 A.M.–5 P.M.;
Sun. 1–5 P.M.
Nov. 1–Mar. 31: Tues.–Sat. 10 A.M.–4 P.M.
Sun. 1–4 P.M. Closed Mondays, New Year's Day, Veterans Day, Thanksgiving Day, and Christmas holidays.

Admission is free. Fee for train rides. Group rates available. Groups are requested to make advance reservations.

Reading Brochures

- Tell students they are likely to encounter brochures that encourage them to go somewhere, believe something, or to buy a product or service. Note that the creators of the brochures carefully choose the words and images to convey a specific message, and that it is important to read brochures carefully to fully understand what is being offered or promoted.

- Point out that this page shows only the front of the brochure for "North Carolina Transportation Museum" along with some side notes. As a group, make a list of the categories of information shown on the front of the brochure. Make sure to include the following: Name of attraction, Picture of attraction, Main point of attraction, Location map, Hours of business, and Admission information. Point out that these are typical features for the front of a brochure.

- Have students read the brochure.

- **Ask** a volunteer to identify the days the museum is closed. **Answer:** The museum is closed Mondays Nov. 1–Mar. 31, New Year's Day, Veterans Day, Thanksgiving Day, and Christmas holidays.

- **Ask** a volunteer to tell why the Transportation Museum probably decided to place hours and admission information on the front page and whether or not it was a good idea. **Possible response:** It is important to have location, hours, and admission information in an easy-to-find location.

continued on p. 346

Differentiated Instruction Solutions for All Learners

Strategy for Special Needs Students
Brochures present information in an unfamiliar format. Many readers struggle to process the text because they are overwhelmed by the visual content. Suggest students cover images while reading text so they are not distracted. Then when they view the images, students can think about how the images relate to the words they just read.

Enrichment for Gifted/Talented Students
Challenge students to sketch out a two-sided brochure promoting your school or an area attraction. Remind students that the purpose of the brochure is to entice others to want to visit, yet clearly communicate vital information. Allow time for students to present their brochures in class.

Reading Brochures (cont.)

- Have students look at the reverse side of the brochure on p. 346. **Ask** students which words their attention is drawn to and why.
  Possible response: My attention is drawn to "The Museum," "Barber Junction," "The Robert Julian Roundhouse," "Historic Spencer Shops," and "Learning Opportunities." I am drawn to these because they are in different typeface.

- Draw students' attention to the three subheads under the main head, "The Museum." **Ask** students how these subheads are organized.
  Answer: The subheads are about specific features or attractions at the museum.

- **Ask** students to evaluate this brochure by answering these questions: Do you feel you know what to expect if you were to visit the North Carolina Transportation Museum? Can you identify the highlights of this museum? Do you think the brochure is effective?
  Sample response: When visiting the museum, I can expect to find many restored locomotives from a variety of historic periods. I will learn about the repair facility, and be able to ride on a train. The highlights are the many historical artifacts. I think the brochure is effective because it tells what is available as well as when and where to see it.

- Have students find the Web site address at the bottom of the brochure. Point out that many organizations include Web sites on brochures. **Ask** a volunteer to predict something that might be found on the North Carolina Transportation Museum Web site that is not on the brochure.

- **Possible responses:** More pictures, more history of the museum, more information about things to see at the museum, an e-mail address, descriptions of special events, and written directions from main highways.

- Encourage students to visit the museum's Web site to see if those features are present.

The Museum

Barber Junction — This is the gateway to fun and excitement at the North Carolina Transportation Museum. Get your tickets here for train rides around the site, and pick up information about tours and exhibits.

The Robert Julian Roundhouse — View more than twenty-five restored locomotives and rail cars along with extensive exhibits tracing the history of railroads in the state. Videos and interactive exhibits, along with shop areas at which locomotives are still worked on today, are highlights of this unique historic building.

Historic Spencer Shops — The North Carolina Transportation Museum is located on the site of Southern Railway's steam locomotive repair facility in Spencer. While the museum is young—founded in 1977—the story of the Spencer Shops reaches back more than one hundred years.

Spencer Shops' mission was to repair steam locomotives that hauled Southern's passenger trains and freight trains filled with North Carolina furniture, textiles, tobacco, and produce.

Southern Railway was one of the first U.S. rail systems to experiment with diesel-electric locomotives, and by 1953 Southern had retired its last steam engine. Spencer Shops started on the road to decline, and employment dropped steadily through the 1950s and 1960s until it finally came to a halt in the late 1970s.

LEARNING OPPORTUNITIES — Education is a primary goal at the North Carolina Transportation Museum. A number of programs are offered to tour groups. In addition to 150,000 square feet of visual exhibits, hands-on activities are available, as are thirty-minute train rides around the site and rides on a restored turntable. Visitors who are here after the last train ride of the day can see the engine run onto the turntable and into the Roundhouse, where it remains for the night on cool evenings. A full-calendar of special events is offered, including temporary exhibits.

For more information, please contact:
North Carolina Transportation Museum
P.O. Box 165 Spencer, North Carolina 28159
(704) 636-2889
1-877-NCTMFUN
Fax (704) 639-1881
http://www.ah.dcr.state.nc.us/sections/hs/spencer/spencer.htm

Subheads call attention to activities and features of the museum.

The image of the man waving from the train shows the human connection to trains and presents them as much more than just equipment.

The brochure wraps up the presentation by inviting the reader to ask for more information. Contact information is clear and easy to find.

346 ■ Short Stories

Vocabulary Development

Vocabulary for Brochure Planning

Tell students that when discussing and planning brochures, there are some special terms that are used. Guide students to understand the meanings of the following words in this article:

Font: A set of type that is the same size and style

Head: A portion of the text that is often set larger and bolder and is positioned above the rest of the content

Subhead: A subordinate heading or title

Bold: A heavy, or dark, style of printing

Small Caps: When all letters are in capitals, but smaller than other capitalized letters of the same font and size

Tri-fold: A single piece of paper folded into thirds to create six sides

Assessment Practice

Reading: Evaluating Text Format

Directions: *Choose the letter of the best answer to each question about the brochure for the North Carolina Transportation Museum.*

1. Why does the designer place the map on the first page?
   - A The map is not related to the content of the second page.
   - B The map is more attractive than a photograph.
   - C This position makes the map more useful to the reader.
   - D There was no space on the second page.

2. What is the main subject of the information on the second page?
   - A where to get additional information
   - B sites and activities at the museum
   - C rates and fees at the museum
   - D volunteer opportunities

3. Under which head would someone look to find information about programs offered to tour groups at the museum?
   - A Hours
   - B Historic Spencer Shops
   - C Learning Opportunities
   - D For more information

Reading: Comprehension and Interpretation

Directions: *Write your answers on a separate piece of paper.*

4. Why do you think the writer chose to place information about learning opportunities near the end of the second page rather than before the description of the museum sites? **[Generating]**

5. **(a)** On what specific historic site is the North Carolina Transportation Museum located? **(b)** Why do you think this location was chosen for the museum? **(c)** In what ways does this location affect the activities and services the museum provides? **[Generating]**

Timed Writing: Persuasion [Critical Stance]

Use the brochure information to write a letter to an elected official in which you request financial support for the museum. Explain how trains have impacted people's lives and why the museum deserves public funding. **(20 minutes)**

Reading Informational Materials: Brochures ■ *347*

Reading: Evaluating Text Format

1. C
2. B
3. C
4. It is more logical to describe the museum and its facilities and then to inform the reader that learning opportunities are available. Placing learning opportunities earlier would leave the reader wondering what there was to learn about. Also, the museum might logically assume that, after reading the brochure, people would be interested in touring it, thus the end of the brochure is a logical place to put tour information.
5. (a) The museum is located in Spencer, North Carolina at the site of an historic locomotive repair shop. (b) This place is ideal for a transportation museum because it already has railroad track and authentic repair facilities from more than 100 years ago. (c) This location allows visitors to tour equipment and facilities in a real-world environment and to experience trains and turntables in actual use.

Timed Writing

- Read the *Timed Writing* instructions together as a group. Point out to students that their letters should include some key persuasive points, such as why the museum is important to the community, how trains affected the development of the United States, and why it is logical for the museum to receive government support. Also, make sure students realize that they must include an actual request for funds.

- Suggest that students plan their time to give 5 minutes to planning, 10 minutes to writing, and 5 minutes to reviewing and revising.

Extend the Lesson

Favorite Place

To give students further practice with brochures and text formats, have students create their own brochures, complete with formatted text. Tell them they can feature locations such as their kitchens, a friend's house, a vacation spot, or an imagined favorite place. Give them these parameters:

1. Describe at least three "attractions" in detail.
2. Include hours of operation.
3. Provide directions or a map.

4. Include at least two graphic images that are drawn, cut from a magazine, or printed from a computer.
5. Create a two-sided brochure, four-sided folded brochure, or six-sided tri-fold brochure.

Remind students to focus on the combination of graphic images and text to create persuasive brochures about their favorite places. Allow time for students to display brochures.

Comparing Literary Works · Symbolism and Allegory

Students will

1. analyze and respond to symbolism and allegory in fiction.

2. compare the effect of symbolism and allegory in two works of fiction.

3. write a comparison of symbolism and allegory.

See *TeacherExpress™/Lesson View* for a detailed lesson plan for Comparing Literary Works.

❶ Literary Analysis
Symbolism and Allegory

- Read the instruction about symbolism and allegory together. Give students some common concepts or feelings found in literature—such as hope and death—and have them list possible symbols for each.
Possible response: A flower or a sunrise might symbolize hope; nightfall or a skull might symbolize death.

- **Ask** students to brainstorm for allegorical books or short stories that they have read in the past. Have students **explain** what makes each work an allegory.
Possible response: Students might list such works as *Animal Farm, The Lord of the Flies,* or *Watership Down.*

- Explain that symbols can be used in any kind of story; each part of an allegory, on the other hand, combines to achieve an overall symbolic effect.

❷ Comparing Symbolism and Allegory

- Remind students that writers use symbols to enhance the meaning of a story. In an allegory, the story's meaning *depends* on symbols.

- Give students a copy of **Comparing Symbolism and Allegory Graphic Organizer A** (*Graphic Organizer Transparencies,* p. 76). Have them complete it as they read and compare the selections.

❶ Symbolism and Allegory

A **symbol** is a person, a place, a thing, or an event that represents both itself and a larger idea or feeling. **Symbolism** is the use of symbols in literature. For example, a writer might use a dove as a symbol for peace or a voyage as a symbol for the journey of life.

An **allegory** is a poem or story that has parallel literal and symbolic meanings. On the literal level, the story appears simply as it is told. On the symbolic level, every element in the story, including the characters, events, descriptions, and features of the setting, has a symbolic meaning. For example, an allegory in which a sailor crosses the ocean in a small boat might have these symbolic equivalents:

- The sailor represents a human being.
- Storms at sea represent the struggles of life.
- Wind and sails represent the help of friends.

While an allegory can be understood on the literal level, its full meaning is only clear on the symbolic level. Often, allegories may seem less realistic than non-allegorical works. Their characters may seem simple or one-dimensional, because their symbolic value is more important than a realistic depiction. Often, writers use allegories to comment on current events.

❷ Comparing Symbolism and Allegory

Symbols play an important role in both of the stories that follow. However, only one story is an allegory. As you read, use a chart like the one shown to interpret the symbols in each story. Then, determine which story uses symbols simply to enhance the meaning, and which is a full-blown, complete allegory.

Vocabulary Builder

The Scarlet Ibis

- **imminent** (im′ ə nənt) *adj.* likely to happen soon (p. 354) *Clouds gathered and rain was imminent.*

- **infallibility** (in fal′ ə bil′ ə tē) *n.* condition of not being likely to fail (p. 356) *After several victories, the team had a sense of infallibility.*

- **precariously** (pri ker′ ē əs lē) *adv.* insecurely (p. 358) *She clung precariously to the ledge, high above the surging river.*

The Golden Kite, the Silver Wind

- **vile** (vīl) *adj.* evil; wicked (p. 363) *Such a vile crime is hard to forgive.*

- **ravenous** (rav′ ə nəs) *adj.* greedily or wildly hungry (p. 363) *After his workout, John was ravenous.*

- **spurn** (spɜrn) *v.* reject with contempt or disdain (p. 364) *She will spurn the gift because it came from an enemy.*

The Scarlet Ibis	
Symbol: rotting brown petals	
Meaning: the end of summer	
The Golden Kite, the Silver Wind	
Symbol: city wall shaped like a club	
Meaning: a community's desire to protect itself	

348 ■ Short Stories

Vocabulary Development

Vocabulary Knowledge Rating

Create a **Vocabulary Knowledge Rating Chart** with the selection vocabulary and expressive vocabulary for both selections. Give students a copy. Introduce the words by reading them aloud and having students mark their rating in the Before Reading column. Urge them to be alert to these words as they read and discuss the selection because they will rate their knowledge of the words again after they finish.

If you wish, you may tally how many students know (or think they know) a word to gauge how much instruction you need to provide. As students read, point out the words and their context.

Build Understanding

❸ Connecting to the Literature

Reading/Writing Connection Both of the following stories deal with conflicts, or struggles, between individuals or entire communities. Describe some situations that you think could cause feelings of competitiveness or jealousy between people. Use at least three of the following words in your response: *conform, confront, displace, rebel, react.*

Meet the Authors

James **Hurst** (b. 1922)

James Hurst grew up along the coast of North Carolina, a place of quiet landscapes and violent storms. After studying chemical engineering and opera and serving in the army during World War II, Hurst took a job at a New York bank. For thirty-four years, he worked as a banker and spent his evenings writing stories.

Creating Symbolism The "Scarlet Ibis," published in 1960, is Hurst's best-known story. Hurst has said that he "wanted [the ibis] to represent [the character of Doodle]—not Doodle's physical self, but his spirit."

Ray **Bradbury** (b. 1920)

Born in Waukegan, Illinois, Ray Bradbury grew up in Arizona and California. He has been writing for more than sixty years and has published more than 500 stories. His work has earned him many honors, including the World Fantasy Award for lifetime achievement and the Grand Master Award from the Science Fiction Writers of America.

Writing to Entertain Bradbury is best known for his works of fantasy and science fiction. "I write for fun," Bradbury has said. "I don't see myself as a philosopher. That's awfully boring. . . . My goal is to entertain myself and others."

Go **Online**
Author Link
For: More information about the authors
Visit: www.PHSchool.com
Web Code: epe-9213

The Scarlet Ibis/The Golden Kite, the Silver Wind ■ 349

❸ Connecting to the Literature

- Model use of the expressive vocabulary students are asked to use with these examples:
  1. Sara refused to *conform* to the rules of the competition.
  2. After she was disqualified, she went to *confront* the judges.
  3. The judges said that another teammate would *displace* Sara as the winner.
  4. They refused to listen to Sara's reasoning, causing her to *rebel* and quit the team.
  5. She did not know how to *react* when the winner was announced.
- Help students further develop their expressive vocabulary by providing these words: *annoy, escalate, reject, resentful.* Encourage students to use these words as they discuss the selection.

Go **Online** For additional informa-
Author Link tion about James Hurst and Ray Bradbury, have students type in the Web Code and then select *James Hurst* or *Ray Bradbury.*

Teaching Resources

The following resources can be used to enrich, extend, or differentiate the instruction for Comparing Literary Works.

Unit 2 Resources, pp. 179–185

Graphic Organizer Transparencies, pp. 76–79

Listening to Literature Audio CD

❶ Background

The Ibis Altogether, there are about twenty species of ibis. This long-legged water bird is related to the heron, crane, and stork. Ibises eat plants, small shellfish, and mollusks. Ancient Egyptians worshipped the sacred ibis of Northern Africa, a relative of the scarlet ibis of this story.

❷ Motivation

Draw students into this compelling story by writing the following quotation on the board:

> At times I was mean to Doodle. One day I took him up to the barn loft and showed him his casket, telling him how we all believed he would die.

Explain that the narrator is Doodle's older brother and that Doodle is frail. Ask students to predict how the relationship between the brothers might affect the story.

Concept Connector ➡

Students will follow up on this activity after completing "The Scarlet Ibis."

❸ About the Selection

"The Scarlet Ibis" reveals that cruelty and selfishness can be entwined with love. The narrator begins by recounting his disappointment that his brother, Doodle, was born with severe physical disabilities. Motivated by pride and self-interest, the narrator helps his brother learn to walk. Not satisfied, the narrator pushes Doodle to learn to swim and run so that his brother will not be "different" when he starts school. It is only after abandoning Doodle in a storm and realizing the consequences of this action that the narrator realizes the depth of his feelings for his brother.

❹ Literary Analysis
Symbolism and Allegory

- Read aloud the bracketed passage, and **ask** students to identify and describe the symbol found in the first sentence.
  Answer: The bleeding tree is a symbol of death, and it suggests some type of violence.

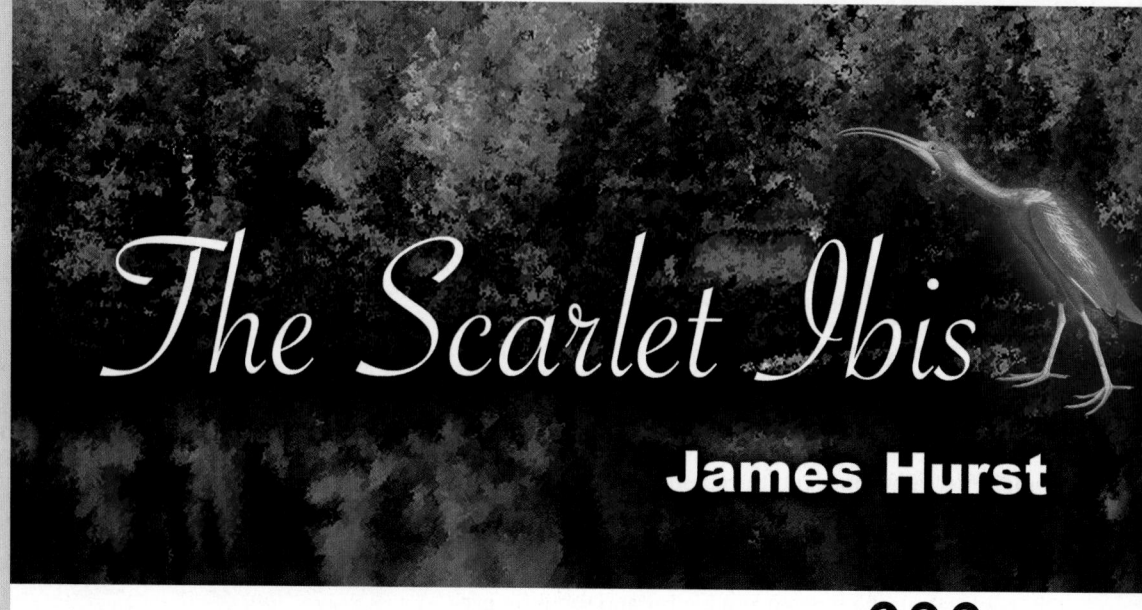

The Scarlet Ibis

James Hurst

❶ ❷ ❸

❹ It was in the clove of seasons, summer was dead but autumn had not yet been born, that the ibis lit in the bleeding tree. The flower garden was stained with rotting brown magnolia petals and ironweeds grew rank amid the purple phlox. The five o'clocks by the chimney still marked time, but the oriole nest in the elm was untenanted and rocked back and forth like an empty cradle. The last graveyard flowers were blooming, and their smell drifted across the cotton field and through every room of our house, speaking softly the names of our dead.

It's strange that all this is still so clear to me, now that the summer has long since fled and time has had its way. A grindstone stands where the bleeding tree stood, just outside the kitchen door, and now if an oriole sings in the elm, its song seems to die up in the leaves, a silvery dust. The flower garden is prim, the house a gleaming white, and the pale fence across the yard stands straight and spruce. But sometimes (like right now), as I sit in the cool, green-draped parlor, the grindstone begins to turn, and time with all its changes is ground away—and I remember Doodle.

❺ Doodle was just about the craziest brother a boy ever had. Of course, he wasn't a crazy crazy like old Miss Leedie, who was in love with President Wilson and wrote him a letter every day, but was a nice crazy, like someone you meet in your dreams. He was born when I was six and was, from the outset, a disappointment. He

350 ■ Short Stories

**Literary Analysis
Symbolism and
Allegory** What details about the flowers, weeds, and oriole nest symbolize death?

- **Ask** the Literary Analysis question: What details about the flowers, weeds, and oriole nest symbolize death?
  Answer: The magnolias are rotting, the weeds are "rank," the flowers—called "graveyard flowers"—seem to whisper the names of those who have died, and the oriole nest swings back and forth in the wind like an "empty cradle."

seemed all head, with a tiny body which was red and shriveled like an old man's. Everybody thought he was going to die—everybody except Aunt Nicey, who had delivered him. She said he would live because he was born in a caul[1] and cauls were made from Jesus' nightgown. Daddy had Mr. Heath, the carpenter, build a little mahogany coffin for him. But he didn't die, and when he was three months old Mama and Daddy decided they might as well name him. They named him William Armstrong, which was like tying a big tail on a small kite. Such a name sounds good only on a tombstone.

I thought myself pretty smart at many things, like holding my breath, running, jumping, or climbing the vines in Old Woman Swamp, and I wanted more than anything else someone to race to Horsehead Landing, someone to box with, and someone to perch with in the top fork of the great pine behind the barn, where across the fields and swamps you could see the sea. I wanted a brother. But Mama, crying, told me that even if William Armstrong lived, he would never do these things with me. He might not, she sobbed, even be "all there." He might, as long as he lived, lie on the rubber sheet in the center of the bed in the front bedroom where the white marquisette curtains billowed out in the afternoon sea breeze, rustling like palmetto fronds.[2]

It was bad enough having an invalid brother, but having one who possibly was not all there was unbearable, so I began to make plans to kill him by smothering him with a pillow. However, one afternoon as I watched him, my head poked between the iron posts of the foot of the bed, he looked straight at me and grinned. I skipped through the rooms, down the echoing halls, shouting, "Mama, he smiled. He's all there! He's all there!" and he was.

When he was two, if you laid him on his stomach, he began to try to move himself, straining terribly. The doctor said that with his weak heart this strain would probably kill him, but it didn't. Trembling, he'd push himself up, turning first red, then a soft purple, and finally collapse back onto the bed like an old worn-out doll. I can still see Mama watching him, her hand pressed tight across her mouth, her eyes wide and unblinking. But he learned to crawl (it was his third winter), and we brought him out of the front bedroom, putting him on the rug before the fireplace. For the first time he became one of us.

As long as he lay all the time in bed, we called him William Armstrong, even though it was formal and sounded as if we were referring to one of our ancestors, but with his creeping around on the

---

1. **caul** (kôl) *n.* membrane enclosing a baby at birth.
2. **palmetto** (pal met′ ō) **fronds** (frändz) *n.* palm leaves.

5 **Literary Analysis**
Symbolism and Allegory In what ways does the caul symbolize life and hope?

6 **Reading Check**

Who is Doodle?

---

5 **Literary Analysis**
Symbolism and Allegory

- Read aloud the bracketed passage, and have students **identify** details in the passage that symbolize death.
  Answer: The baby's head is described as being "shriveled like an old man's," and the narrator says that the baby's name is fit only for being on a tombstone. In addition, most of the family members believe that the baby will die and even go so far as to build a coffin for him.

- Tell students that the passage also contains symbols of hope and life, a pattern that readers will find throughout the story.

- **Ask** students to respond to the Literary Analysis question: In what ways does the caul symbolize life and hope?
  Answer: A caul is a traditional symbol of good luck. Furthermore, because Aunt Nicey says the caul is made from Jesus's nightgown, it seems to symbolize that the baby is blessed or special in some way.

6 **Reading Check**

Answer: Doodle is the narrator's younger brother.

Differentiated
Instruction Solutions for All Learners

Accessibility at a Glance

Context	Situational: Conflict between two young brothers
Language	Long sentences with embedded clauses; extensive description of setting
Concept Level	Accessible
Literary Merit	Widely anthologized
Lexile	1070L

❼ Literature in Context

Science Connection While known for its vibrant color, the scarlet ibis is not red when it is hatched. In fact, the young bird is brown and changes color as it grows. This interesting transformation is due to its diet, which contains a great deal of the pigment carotene. The scarlet ibis has been on the endangered species list for some time, but scientists are having limited success with breeding the birds in captivity.

Connect to the Literature Point out that in the story, the appearance of the scarlet ibis seems to surprise Doodle's family. **Ask** students the Connect to the Literature question: Why would the discovery of such a bird in coastal North Carolina, the setting of this story, be unexpected and dramatic?
Answer: The bird rarely appears north of Florida, and seeing a tropical bird in North Carolina would be quite unexpected.

❽ Literary Analysis
Symbolism and Allegory

- Read aloud the bracketed passage. Remind students that Doodle's original name, William Armstrong, was a symbol of his parents' aspirations for the fragile child. Explain that in the same way, renaming Doodle was another symbolic act.

- Discuss why the narrator thought his brother required a new name after he learned to crawl. **Ask** students why the narrator thought that "Doodle" was an appropriate name.
Answer: Doodle's backward crawl was reminiscent of that of a doodle-bug. Moreover, as the narrator points out, "nobody expects much from somebody called Doodle."

---

deerskin rug and beginning to talk, something had to be done about his name. It was I who renamed him. When he crawled, he crawled backwards, as if he were in reverse and couldn't change gears. If you called him, he'd turn around as if he were going in the other direction, then he'd back right up to you to be picked up. Crawling backward made him look like a doodle-bug, so I began to call him Doodle, and in time even Mama and Daddy thought it was a better name than William Armstrong. Only Aunt Nicey disagreed. She said caul babies should be treated with special respect since they might turn out to be saints. Renaming my brother was perhaps the kindest thing I ever did for him, because nobody expects much from someone called Doodle.

Although Doodle learned to crawl, he showed no signs of walking, but he wasn't idle. He talked so much that we all quit listening to what he said. It was about this time that Daddy built him a go-cart and I had to pull him around. At first I just paraded him up and down the piazza, but then he started crying to be taken out into the yard and it ended up by my having to lug him wherever I went. If I so much as picked up my cap, he'd start crying to go with me and Mama would call from wherever she was, "Take Doodle with you."

He was a burden in many ways. The doctor had said that he mustn't get too excited, too hot, too cold, or too tired and that he must always be treated gently. A long list of don'ts went with him, all of which I ignored once we got out of the house. To discourage his coming with me, I'd run with him across the ends of the cotton rows and careen him around corners on two wheels. Sometimes I accidentally turned him over, but he never told Mama. His skin was very sensitive, and he had to wear a big straw hat whenever he went out. When the going got rough and he had to cling to the sides of the go-cart, the hat slipped all the way down over his ears. He was a sight. Finally, I could see I was licked. Doodle was my brother and he was going to cling to me forever, no matter what I did, so I dragged him across the burning cotton field to share with him the only beauty I knew, Old Woman Swamp. I pulled the go-cart through the saw-tooth fern, down into the green dimness where the palmetto fronds whispered by the stream. I lifted him out and set him down in the soft rubber grass beside a tall pine. His eyes were round with wonder as he gazed

❼ Literature in Context

Science Connection

Scarlet Ibis Found mostly in the South American tropics, the strikingly beautiful scarlet ibis is a wading bird with long legs, a long, slender neck, black-tipped wings, and a wingspan of more than three feet. It seldom appears in the United States north of Florida.

Connect to the Literature

Why would the discovery of a scarlet ibis in coastal North Carolina, the setting of this story, be unexpected and dramatic?

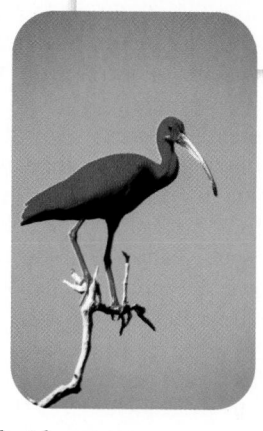

Vocabulary Development

Vocabulary Builder Reinforcement
To reinforce and assess students' comprehension of Vocabulary Builder words, give them sentences in which the word may or may not be used correctly. Students must tell whether the use is correct and explain their answer. Use these sentences:

1. The brightly shining sun suggested that the forecast for severe storms was *imminent*.
   Answer: No, *imminent* is not used correctly. The shining sun does not suggest an upcoming storm.

2. Superheroes usually possess a sense of *infallibility*.
   Answer: Yes, *infallibility* is used correctly. Superheroes typically are confident that their actions are always right.

3. The picture hung *precariously* from the wall; it was safely secured with nails.
   Answer: No, *precariously* is not used correctly. It means the opposite of secure.

352

about him, and his little hands began to stroke the rubber grass. Then he began to cry.

"For heaven's sake, what's the matter?" I asked, annoyed.

"It's so pretty," he said. "So pretty, pretty, pretty."

After that day Doodle and I often went down into Old Woman Swamp. I would gather wildflowers, wild violets, honeysuckle, yellow jasmine, snakeflowers, and water lilies, and with wire grass we'd weave them into necklaces and crowns. We'd bedeck ourselves with our handiwork and loll about thus beautified, beyond the touch of the everyday world. Then when the slanted rays of the sun burned orange in the tops of the pines, we'd drop our jewels into the stream and watch them float away toward the sea.

There is within me (and with sadness I have watched it in others) a knot of cruelty borne by the stream of love, much as our blood sometimes bears the seed of our destruction, and at times I was mean to Doodle. One day I took him up to the barn loft and showed him his casket, telling him how we all had believed he would die. It was covered with a film of Paris green[3] sprinkled to kill the rats, and screech owls had built a nest inside it.

Doodle studied the mahogany box for a long time, then said, "It's not mine."

"It is," I said. "And before I'll help you down from the loft, you're going to have to touch it."

"I won't touch it," he said sullenly.

"Then I'll leave you here by yourself," I threatened, and made as if I were going down.

Doodle was frightened of being left. "Don't go leave me, Brother," he cried, and he leaned toward the coffin. His hand, trembling, reached out, and when he touched the casket he screamed. A screech owl flapped out of the box into our faces, scaring us and covering us with Paris green. Doodle was paralyzed, so I put him on my shoulder and carried him down the ladder, and even when we were outside in the bright sunshine, he clung to me, crying, "Don't leave me. Don't leave me."

When Doodle was five years old, I was embarrassed at having a brother of that age who couldn't walk, so I set out to teach him. We were down in Old Woman Swamp and it was spring and the sick-sweet smell of bay flowers hung everywhere like a mournful song. "I'm going to teach you to walk, Doodle," I said.

He was sitting comfortably on the soft grass, leaning back against the pine. "Why?" he asked.

---

3. **Paris green** poisonous green powder used chiefly as an insecticide.

Literary Analysis
Symbolism and Allegory Which details in this paragraph symbolize life and beauty?

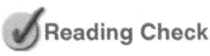 **Reading Check**

What does the narrator force Doodle to touch?

The Scarlet Ibis ■ 353

⑨ Literary Analysis
Symbolism and Allegory

- Read aloud the bracketed passage, and then have students **describe** the mood.
  Answer: The mood is positive. The boys seem to be happy and enjoying their time in the swamp.

- **Ask** the Literary Analysis question: Which details in this paragraph symbolize life and beauty?
  Answer: Symbols of life and beauty include the flowered necklaces and crowns and the image of the boys frolicking through the swamp wearing their "jewelry."

- **Ask** students to identify the symbolic value of the final image, where the boys drop their creations in the water and watch them float away.
  Possible response: The released necklaces and crowns in the setting sun might symbolize the end of the brothers' happy times.

⑩ Literary Analysis
Symbolism and Allegory

- Read aloud the bracketed passage, and remind students that symbols have a literal meaning and a figurative meaning.

- **Ask** students to explain the figurative meaning of the narrator forcing his brother to touch the coffin.
  Answer: In touching the coffin, Doodle is forced to recognize his mortality, or face the possibility of his own death.

- Have students **identify** a detail from the passage that might be an omen of death.
  Answer: The screech owl that flies at the boys might be an omen of death.

⑪ Reading Check

Answer: The narrator makes Doodle touch the coffin that was made for Doodle when he was born.

Differentiated
Instruction   Solutions for All Learners

Strategy for Less Proficient Readers
Long sentences like the one beginning "I thought myself pretty smart…" (p. 351) may prove a barrier to some students' enjoyment of the story. Have students break down long sentences like these by first identifying the main subject(s) and verb(s); in this case, the subject is *I* and the verbs are *thought* and *wanted*. The rest of the sentence's phrases and clauses give further details about this subject and verb. Once students have identified the sentence's main idea, they can look at the details.

Vocabulary for English Learners
With its references to many different plants, this story's setting provides students with an opportunity to extend their vocabularies. Have students list such words as *magnolia, bleeding tree, phlox, five o'clocks,* and so on and look them up in illustrated nature guides or encyclopedias.

⑫ Literary Analysis
Symbolism and Allegory

- Read aloud the bracketed passage, and call students' attention to the narrator's reference to pride.
- **Ask** the Literary Analysis question: How is pride like "a seed that bears two vines"?
  Answer: A single source of pride can cause both good and bad things to happen.
- **Ask** students what other images they associate with vines and how these images might apply to the story.
  Possible response: Students might think of vines as twisting and threatening. Similarly, they might predict that the narrator's pride will eventually overtake or harm Doodle.

⑬ Literary Analysis
Symbolism

- Guide students in identifying the key differences between the images presented in the bracketed passage: a "dark palmetto thicket" and a "cardinal in the lacy toothbrush tree."
- **Ask** students why the brothers' hope transformed from something hidden away in a thicket to a brilliantly visible cardinal.
  Answer: Doodle had learned to stand, which made the brothers' goal seem more attainable.

I hadn't expected such an answer. "So I won't have to haul you around all the time."

"I can't walk, Brother," he said.

"Who says so?" I demanded.

"Mama, the doctor—everybody."

"Oh, you can walk," I said, and I took him by the arms and stood him up. He collapsed onto the grass like a half-empty flour sack. It was as if he had no bones in his little legs.

"Don't hurt me, Brother," he warned.

"Shut up. I'm not going to hurt you. I'm going to teach you to walk." I heaved him up again, and again he collapsed.

This time he did not lift his face up out of the rubber grass. "I just can't do it. Let's make honeysuckle wreaths."

"Oh yes you can, Doodle," I said. "All you got to do is try. Now come on," and I hauled him up once more.

⑫ It seemed so hopeless from the beginning that it's a miracle I didn't give up. But all of us must have something or someone to be proud of, and Doodle had become mine. I did not know then that pride is a wonderful, terrible thing, a seed that bears two vines, life and death. Every day that summer we went to the pine beside the stream of Old Woman Swamp, and I put him on his feet at least a hundred times each afternoon. Occasionally I too became discouraged because it didn't seem as if he was trying, and I would say, "Doodle, don't you want to learn to walk?"

He'd nod his head, and I'd say, "Well, if you don't keep trying, you'll never learn." Then I'd paint for him a picture of us as old men, white-haired, him with a long white beard and me still pulling him around in the go-cart. This never failed to make him try again.

⑬ Finally one day, after many weeks of practicing, he stood alone for a few seconds. When he fell, I grabbed him in my arms and hugged him, our laughter pealing through the swamp like a ringing bell. Now we knew it could be done. Hope no longer hid in the dark palmetto thicket but perched like a cardinal in the lacy toothbrush tree, brilliantly visible. "Yes, yes," I cried, and he cried it too, and the grass beneath us was soft and the smell of the swamp was sweet.

With success so <u>imminent</u>, we decided not to tell anyone until he could actually walk. Each day, barring rain, we sneaked into Old Woman Swamp, and by cotton-picking time Doodle was ready to show what he could do. He still wasn't able to walk far, but we could wait no longer. Keeping a nice secret is very hard to do, like holding your breath. We chose to reveal all on October eighth, Doodle's sixth birthday, and for weeks ahead we mooned around the house, promising everybody a most spectacular surprise. Aunt Nicey said that,

Literary Analysis
Symbolism and Allegory How is pride like "a seed that bears two vines"?

Vocabulary Builder
imminent (im´ ə nənt) *adj.* likely to happen soon

Vocabulary Development

Expressive Vocabulary

As students discuss the relationship between the narrator and Doodle, encourage them to use the expressive vocabulary presented earlier. You might provide them with sentence starters like these:

1. The narrator wants Doodle to *conform*…
2. As the narrator remembers his brother, he must *confront*…
3. The narrator's shame of Doodle is *displaced* when…
4. Doodle does not *rebel* against his brother's demands because…
5. When the narrator tries to teach Doodle to walk, Doodle *reacts*…

after so much talk, if we produced anything less tremendous than the Resurrection,[4] she was going to be disappointed.

At breakfast on our chosen day, when Mama, Daddy, and Aunt Nicey were in the dining room, I brought Doodle to the door in the go-cart just as usual and had them turn their backs, making them cross their hearts and hope to die if they peeked. I helped Doodle up, and when he was standing alone I let them look. There wasn't a sound as Doodle walked slowly across the room and sat down at his place at the table. Then Mama began to cry and ran over to him, hugging him and kissing him. Daddy hugged him too, so I went to Aunt Nicey, who was thanks praying in the doorway, and began to waltz her around. We danced together quite well until she came down on my big toe with her brogans, hurting me so badly I thought I was crippled for life.

Doodle told them it was I who had taught him to walk, so everyone wanted to hug me, and I began to cry.

"What are you crying for?" asked Daddy, but I couldn't answer. They did not know that I did it for myself; that pride, whose slave I was, spoke to me louder than all their voices, and that Doodle walked only because I was ashamed of having a crippled brother.

Within a few months Doodle had learned to walk well and his go-cart was put up in the barn loft (it's still there) beside his little mahogany coffin. Now, when we roamed off together, resting often, we never turned back until our destination had been reached, and to help pass the time, we took up lying. From the beginning Doodle was a terrible liar and he got me in the habit. Had anyone stopped to listen to us, we would have been sent off to Dix Hill.

---

4. **the Resurrection** (rez′ ə rek′ shən) the rising of Jesus Christ from the dead after his death and burial.

Two Boys in a Punt, N.C. Wyeth, Collection of Dr. and Mrs. William A. Morton. Photography courtesy of th Brandywine River Museum.

▲ **Critical Viewing**
What can you tell about the brothers' relationship from the illustration and the details in the story? **[Interpret]**

✓ **Reading Check**
What surprise do the boys present?

The Scarlet Ibis ■ 355

Strategy for Gifted/Talented Students
Ask students to rewrite the scene with the narrator and Doodle in the barn loft in the first person from Doodle's point of view. Their versions should be no longer than one page and should reflect Doodle's feelings about his older brother, as well as his reactions to what happens in the loft. Have volunteers share their versions with the class.

Strategy for Advanced Readers
Have students discuss how they think Doodle feels about his brother. As they read, they should watch for clues about Doodle's feelings. They should also think about how they would feel if they were in Doodle's situation. Pose the following questions to students: Does Doodle admire his brother? Is he afraid of him? Does he love him? Make sure students support their answers with details from the story and from their own experiences.

---

⑭ **Humanities**

Two Boys in a Punt, by N. C. Wyeth
N. C. Wyeth studied for two years at the Howard Pyle School of Art in Wilmington, Delaware. Pyle, himself a well-known illustrator and graphic artist, emphasized realism and authenticity. Wyeth became one of the school's most successful and famous graduates. His best-known works are the brilliant oil paintings with which he illustrated *Treasure Island, Robin Hood, The Last of the Mohicans,* and others. Use the following question for discussion:

• Compare and contrast the boys in the painting with the brothers in "The Scarlet Ibis."
Answer: Both pairs spend time together in a rural setting. Neither boy in the painting appears dependent on the other; in the story, Doodle is dependent on the narrator.

⑮ **Critical Viewing**

Answer: The brothers in the story and in the painting share relaxed experiences in the outdoors.

⑯ **Literary Analysis**
Symbolism and Allegory

• Have students read the bracketed passage, and then remind them of the narrator's observation about pride on p. 354: "I did not know then that pride is a wonderful, terrible thing, a seed that bears two vines, life and death."

• **Ask** students to identify both results (the wonderful and the terrible) of the narrator's pride at this point in the story.
Answer: The wonderful result is Doodle's ability to walk; the terrible result is the narrator's guilt in knowing that his shame motivated the project.

⑰ **Reading Check**

Answer: The narrator has taught Doodle to walk by himself.

355

- Draw students' attention to the bracketed passage. Point out that the narrator claims that Doodle's stories were much more creative than his own. Explain that Doodle's interior life (or imagination) is more developed than his brother's—a characteristic that marks Doodle as special.

- **Ask** students to infer why all of the characters in Doodle's stories have wings.
Possible response: Doodle's winged characters might symbolize his wish for more physical freedom and ability.

- **Ask** students to respond to the Literary Analysis question: How might the peacock and the boy symbolize death?
Possible response: The peacock wraps up and buries the sleeping boy in its plumage. Death (the eternal sleep) is often symbolized by sleep.

My lies were scary, involved, and usually pointless, but Doodle's were twice as crazy. People in his stories all had wings and flew wherever they wanted to go. His favorite lie was about a boy named Peter who had a pet peacock with a ten-foot tail. Peter wore a golden robe that glittered so brightly that when he walked through the sunflowers they turned away from the sun to face him. When Peter was ready to go to sleep, the peacock spread his magnificent tail, enfolding the boy gently like a closing go-to-sleep flower, burying him in the gloriously iridescent, rustling vortex.[5] Yes, I must admit it. Doodle could beat me lying.

Doodle and I spent lots of time thinking about our future. We decided that when we were grown we'd live in Old Woman Swamp and pick dog-tongue for a living. Beside the stream, he planned, we'd build us a house of whispering leaves and the swamp birds would be our chickens. All day long (when we weren't gathering dog-tongue) we'd swing through the cypresses on the rope vines, and if it rained we'd huddle beneath an umbrella tree and play stickfrog. Mama and Daddy could come and live with us if they wanted to. He even came up with the idea that he could marry Mama and I could marry Daddy. Of course, I was old enough to know this wouldn't work out, but the picture he painted was so beautiful and serene that all I could do was whisper Yes, yes.

Once I had succeeded in teaching Doodle to walk, I began to believe in my own <u>infallibility</u> and I prepared a terrific development program for him, unknown to Mama and Daddy, of course. I would teach him to run, to swim, to climb trees, and to fight. He, too, now believed in my infallibility, so we set the deadline for these accomplishments less than a year away, when, it had been decided, Doodle could start to school.

That winter we didn't make much progress, for I was in school and Doodle suffered from one bad cold after another. But when spring came, rich and warm, we raised our sights again. Success lay at the end of summer like a pot of gold, and our campaign got off to a good start. On hot days, Doodle and I went down to Horsehead Landing and I gave him swimming lessons or showed him how to row a boat. Sometimes we descended into the cool greenness of Old Woman Swamp and climbed the rope vines or boxed scientifically beneath the pine where he had learned to walk. Promise hung about us like the leaves, and wherever we looked, ferns unfurled and birds broke into song.

19 That summer, the summer of 1918, was blighted. In May and June there was no rain and the crops withered, curled up, then died under the thirsty sun. One morning in July a hurricane came out of

5. **vortex** (vôr′ teks′) *n.* rushing whirl, drawing in all that surrounds it.

356 ■ *Short Stories*

Vocabulary Builder
infallibility (in fal′ ə bil′ ə tē) *n.* condition of not being likely to fail

Vocabulary Development

Word Analysis
Write the word *infallibility* on the board, and tell students that the prefix *in-* is a variant of *un-,* which usually means "not." *Infallibility* means "not having the quality of fallibility" or "not being able to be wrong."

Next, write the following words on the board: *secure, sufficient, elegant, direct,* and *accurate.* Ask students to add the prefix *in-* to

each word. They should also write a brief definition for each new word.

Answer: *insecure:* not safe; *insufficient:* not enough; *inelegant:* not elegant; crude; *indirect:* not direct or roundabout; *inaccurate:* not exact or containing mistakes.

the east, tipping over the oaks in the yard and splitting the limbs of the elm trees. That afternoon it roared back out of the west, blew the fallen oaks around, snapping their roots and tearing them out of the earth like a hawk at the entrails of a chicken. Cotton bolls were wrenched from the stalks and lay like green walnuts in the valleys between the rows, while the cornfield leaned over uniformly so that the tassels touched the ground. Doodle and I followed Daddy out into the cotton field, where he stood, shoulders sagging, surveying the ruin. When his chin sank down onto his chest, we were frightened, and Doodle slipped his hand into mine. Suddenly Daddy straightened his shoulders, raised a giant knuckly fist, and with a voice that seemed to rumble out of the earth itself began cursing heaven, hell, the weather, and the Republican Party. Doodle and I, prodding each other and giggling, went back to the house, knowing that everything would be all right.

And during that summer, strange names were heard through the house: Chateau-Thierry, Amiens, Soissons, and in her blessing at the supper table, Mama once said, "And bless the Pearsons, whose boy Joe was lost at Belleau Wood."[6]

So we came to that clove of seasons. School was only a few weeks away, and Doodle was far behind schedule. He could barely clear the ground when climbing up the rope vines and his swimming was certainly not passable. We decided to double our efforts, to make that last drive and reach our pot of gold. I made him swim until he turned blue and row until he couldn't lift an oar. Wherever we went, I purposely walked fast, and although he kept up, his face turned red and his eyes became glazed. Once, he could go no further, so he collapsed on the ground and began to cry.

"Aw, come on, Doodle," I urged. "You can do it. Do you want to be different from everybody else when you start school?"

"Does it make any difference?"

"It certainly does," I said. "Now, come on," and I helped him up.

As we slipped through dog days, Doodle began to look feverish, and Mama felt his forehead, asking him if he felt ill. At night he didn't sleep well, and sometimes he had nightmares, crying out until I touched him and said, "Wake up, Doodle. Wake up."

It was Saturday noon, just a few days before school was to start. I should have already admitted defeat, but my pride wouldn't let me. The excitement of our program had now been gone for weeks, but still we kept on with a tired doggedness. It was too late to turn back, for we had both wandered too far into a net of expectations and had left no crumbs behind.

---

6. **Chateau-Thierry** (shä´ tō´ tē er´ ē), **Amiens** (à myan´), **Soissons** (swä sôn´), . . . **Belleau** (be lō´) **Wood** places in France where battles were fought during World War I.

19 Literary Analysis
Symbolism and Allegory What might the "blighted" summer symbolize?

Reading Check

What plan does the narrator make for Doodle's future?

The Scarlet Ibis ■ 357

19 Literary Analysis
Symbolism and Allegory

- Point out details from the bracketed passage that have negative connotations, such as the withered, dead crops; the thirsty sun; the split trees; and the chicken entrails.

- Point out that this description of nature differs dramatically from the earlier, more serene description on p. 353.

- **Ask** the Literary Analysis question: What might the "blighted" summer symbolize?
  Answer: The blighted summer might symbolize sickness and death.

20 Literary Analysis
Symbolism and Allegory

- Remind students that symbols of death have appeared throughout the story. Explain that many of these symbols (such as the coffin) were related to Doodle and seem to be foreshadowing his death.

- **Ask** students to identify two symbols of death in the bracketed passage.
  Answer: Doodle's turning blue and his glazed eyes symbolize death.

- Have students consider the symbols used in the story to **predict** what might happen to Doodle.
  Possible response: Out of pride, the narrator might push Doodle too hard when teaching him to swim or climb vines. Doodle might collapse or die.

21 Reading Check

Answer: The narrator plans to teach Doodle to run, swim, climb trees, and fight before he starts school.

Differentiated Instruction   Solutions for All Learners

Enrichment for Gifted/Talented Students
The ibis, the screech owl, and an imaginary peacock play meaningful roles in this story. Ask students to create a poster, collage, or other artwork based on images of these birds. Challenge students to visually express the emotions and meanings these birds have for Doodle in the story.

Strategy for Advanced Readers
Have students write essays analyzing the symbolic importance of birds in this story, such as the screech owl (p. 353), the peacock (p. 356), and the ibis (pp. 358–359). Ask students to discuss the following questions: At what point in the plot does each bird appear? What actions does the bird take? How do the human characters react to the bird? Which bird seems to be given the most importance? Tell students to support their answers with details from the story.

Scarlet Ibis, by John James Audubon

John James Audubon (1785–1851) was born in Haiti and lived in France as a boy. He came to the United States in 1803. Audubon spent his life on the ambitious project of producing life-sized, accurate watercolor paintings of every bird in America. His two massive works, *The Birds of America* (1827–1838) and *Ornithological Biography* (1831–1839), are classics of science and art. Use these questions for discussion:

1. How does this illustration of the ibis help you appreciate the family's reaction to seeing it in their yard?
   Answer: The bird's brilliant color and distinctive appearance make the ibis seem rare and exotic.

2. Compare the ibis shown here to Doodle.
   Answer: Both are unusual, out of place, fragile; both possess a special beauty.

23 Critical Viewing

Possible responses: Students might be excited, intrigued, or awed.

Daddy, Mama, Doodle, and I were seated at the dining-room table having lunch. It was a hot day, with all the windows and doors open in case a breeze should come. In the kitchen Aunt Nicey was humming softly. After a long silence, Daddy spoke. "It's so calm, I wouldn't be surprised if we had a storm this afternoon."

"I haven't heard a rain frog," said Mama, who believed in signs, as she served the bread around the table.

"I did," declared Doodle. "Down in the swamp."

"He didn't," I said contrarily.

"You did, eh?" said Daddy, ignoring my denial.

"I certainly did," Doodle reiterated, scowling at me over the top of his iced-tea glass, and we were quiet again.

Suddenly, from out in the yard, came a strange croaking noise. Doodle stopped eating, with a piece of bread poised ready for his mouth, his eyes popped round like two blue buttons. "What's that?" he whispered.

I jumped up, knocking over my chair, and had reached the door when Mama called, "Pick up the chair, sit down again, and say excuse me."

By the time I had done this, Doodle had excused himself and had slipped out into the yard. He was looking up into the bleeding tree. "It's a great big red bird!" he called.

The bird croaked loudly again, and Mama and Daddy came out into the yard. We shaded our eyes with our hands against the hazy glare of the sun and peered up through the still leaves. On the top-most branch a bird the size of a chicken, with scarlet feathers and long legs, was perched precariously. Its wings hung down loosely, and as we watched, a feather dropped away and floated slowly down through the green leaves.

"It's not even frightened of us," Mama said.

"It looks tired," Daddy added. "Or maybe sick."

Doodle's hands were clasped at his throat, and I had never seen him stand still so long. "What is it?" he asked.

Daddy shook his head. "I don't know, maybe it's—"

24 At that moment the bird began to flutter, but the wings were uncoordinated, and amid much flapping and a spray of flying feathers, it tumbled down, bumping through the limbs of the bleeding tree and landing at our feet with a thud. Its long, graceful neck jerked twice into an S, then straightened out, and the bird was still. A white veil came over the eyes and the long white beak unhinged. Its legs were crossed and its clawlike feet were delicately

23 ▼ Critical Viewing
How would you react if this exotic bird—an ibis—showed up in your backyard? **[Relate]**

Vocabulary Builder
precariously (pri ker′ ē əs lē) *adv.* insecurely

Vocabulary Development

Word Forms

Expand students' vocabulary by helping them learn related forms of the Vocabulary Builder words. The three Vocabulary Builder words for "The Scarlet Ibis" have related forms. Give students a blank **Word Form Chart** (*General Resources*, p. 16), with *imminent, infallibility,* and *precariously* in the correct columns. Work with the class, or have students work with a partner, to determine the related forms. The final chart should look like the one shown.

Noun	Verb	Adjective	Adverb
imminence		**imminent**	imminently
infallibility		infallible	infallibly
precariousness		precarious	**precariously**

24 curved at rest. Even death did not mar its grace, for it lay on the earth like a broken vase of red flowers, and we stood around it, awed by its exotic beauty.

"It's dead," Mama said.

"What is it?" Doodle repeated.

"Go bring me the bird book," said Daddy.

I ran into the house and brought back the bird book. As we watched, Daddy thumbed through its pages. "It's a scarlet ibis," he said, pointing to a picture. "It lives in the tropics—South America to Florida. A storm must have brought it here."

Sadly, we all looked back at the bird. A scarlet ibis! How many miles it had traveled to die like this, in our yard, beneath the bleeding tree.

"Let's finish lunch," Mama said, nudging us back toward the dining room.

"I'm not hungry," said Doodle, and he knelt down beside the ibis.

"We've got peach cobbler for dessert," Mama tempted from the doorway.

Doodle remained kneeling. "I'm going to bury him."

"Don't you dare touch him," Mama warned. "There's no telling what disease he might have had."

"All right," said Doodle. "I won't."

Daddy, Mama, and I went back to the dining-room table, but we watched Doodle through the open door. He took out a piece of string from his pocket and, without touching the ibis, looped one end around its neck. Slowly, while singing softly "Shall We Gather at the River," he carried the bird around to the front yard and dug a hole in the flower garden, next to the petunia bed. Now we were watching him through the front window, but he didn't know it. His awkwardness at digging the hole with a shovel whose handle was twice as long as he was made us laugh, and we covered our mouths with our hands so he wouldn't hear.

When Doodle came into the dining room, he found us seriously eating our cobbler. He was pale and lingered just inside the screen door. "Did you get the scarlet ibis buried?" asked Daddy.

Doodle didn't speak but nodded his head.

Literary Analysis
Symbolism and Allegory In what ways are the bird's uncoordinated movements similar to Doodle's? Explain.

25

Reading Check
What does Doodle find in the bleeding tree?

The Scarlet Ibis ■ 359

---

24 Literary Analysis
Symbolism and Allegory

- Remind students of James Hurst's statement that the ibis is a symbol of Doodle's spirit. Explain that the bird and Doodle also share some physical similarities.

- **Ask** students the Literary Analysis question: In what ways are the bird's uncoordinated movements similar to Doodle's? Explain.
  Answer: The bird has trouble flying, just as Doodle has trouble walking.

- **Ask** students to predict how the story will end based on this paragraph.
  Possible response: Because the scarlet ibis is a symbol for Doodle, it seems likely that Doodle will also die.

25 Reading Check
Answer: Doodle finds a big red bird.

Differentiated Instruction   Solutions for All Learners

Strategy for Special Needs Students
Students may have trouble identifying why the ibis serves as a symbol for Doodle. Have students create two-column charts, one column labeled "Doodle" and the other labeled "ibis." Ask students to fill the chart with descriptions of Doodle and the bird's physical characteristics. Then have students draw lines to connect the similar traits. Finally, ask students to write a single sentence that summarizes these similarities.

Strategy for English Learners
To give students a context for the story and to model how to interpret elements of symbolism and allegory, show them **Comparing Symbolism and Allegory Graphic Organizer B**, located in *Graphic Organizer Transparencies*, p. 77. The completed graphic organizer will give students insight into symbolism and allegory. They can use it as a model for interpreting symbols as they read.

- Tell students that weather sometimes serves a symbolic purpose in literature. Explain that in the last paragraphs, a dramatic storm coincides with the story's climax.

- **Ask** the Literary Analysis question: What might "black clouds" symbolize? Explain.
Answer: Black clouds usually signal that a storm is about to come, so they might symbolize imminent trouble or danger.

- Discuss the symbolic value of the storm. Explain that storms are often associated with tragedy. Tell students that the presence of a storm at this point of the plot heightens the drama.

"Go wash your hands, and then you can have some peach cobbler," said Mama.

"I'm not hungry," he said.

"Dead birds is bad luck," said Aunt Nicey, poking her head from the kitchen door. "Specially red dead birds!"

As soon as I had finished eating, Doodle and I hurried off to Horsehead Landing. Time was short, and Doodle still had a long way to go if he was going to keep up with the other boys when he started school. The sun, gilded with the yellow cast of autumn, still burned fiercely, but the dark green woods through which we passed were shady and cool. When we reached the landing, Doodle said he was too tired to swim, so we got into a skiff and floated down the creek with the tide. Far off in the marsh a rail was scolding, and over on the beach locusts were singing in the myrtle trees. Doodle did not speak and kept his head turned away, letting one hand trail limply in the water.

After we had drifted a long way, I put the oars in place and made Doodle row back against the tide. Black clouds began to gather in the southwest, and he kept watching them, trying to pull the oars a little faster. When we reached Horsehead Landing, lightning was playing across half the sky and thunder roared out, hiding even the sound of the sea. The sun disappeared and darkness descended, almost like night. Flocks of marsh crows flew by, heading inland to their roosting trees, and two egrets, squawking, arose from the oyster-rock shallows and careened away.

Doodle was both tired and frightened, and when he stepped from the skiff he collapsed onto the mud, sending an armada of fiddler crabs rustling off into the marsh grass. I helped him up, and as he wiped the mud off his trousers, he smiled at me ashamedly. He had failed and we both knew it, so we started back home, racing the storm. We never spoke (What are the words that can solder cracked pride?), but I knew he was watching me, watching for a sign of mercy. The lightning was near now, and from fear he walked so close behind me he kept stepping on my heels. The faster I walked, the faster he walked, so I began to run. The rain was coming, roaring through the pines, and then, like a bursting Roman candle, a gum tree ahead of us was shattered by a bolt of lightning. When the deafening peal of thunder had died, and in the moment before the rain arrived, I heard Doodle, who had fallen behind, cry out, "Brother, Brother, don't leave me! Don't leave me!"

The knowledge that Doodle's and my plans had come to naught was bitter, and that streak of cruelty within me awakened. I ran as fast as I could, leaving him far behind with a wall of rain dividing us. The drops stung my face like nettles, and the wind flared the

Literary Analysis
Symbolism and Allegory What might "black clouds" symbolize? Explain.

Vocabulary Development

Vocabulary Builder Reinforcement
Students will benefit from additional examples and practice with the Vocabulary Builder words. Reinforce their comprehension with "show-you-know" sentences. The first part of each sentence uses the vocabulary word in an appropriate context. The second part of the sentence—the "show-you-know" part—clarifies the first part. Model this strategy with this example for *imminent:*

Her win was *imminent;* Sally could practically taste victory.

Then, give students these sentence prompts, and coach them in creating the clarification part:
1. Before he got lost, the guide had a sense of *infallibility;* _____.
   Possible response: afterward, he realized that he made mistakes like everyone else.
2. The glass was perched *precariously* on the end of the table; _____.
   Possible response: it seemed ready to fall at any moment.

wet glistening leaves of the bordering trees. Soon I could hear his voice no more.

I hadn't run too far before I became tired, and the flood of childish spite evanesced as well. I stopped and waited for Doodle. The sound of rain was everywhere, but the wind had died and it fell straight down in parallel paths like ropes hanging from the sky. As I waited, I peered through the downpour, but no one came. Finally I went back and found him huddled beneath a red nightshade bush beside the road. He was sitting on the ground, his face buried in his arms, which were resting on his drawn-up knees. "Let's go, Doodle," I said.

He didn't answer, so I placed my hand on his forehead and lifted his head. Limply, he fell backwards onto the earth. He had been bleeding from the mouth, and his neck and the front of his shirt were stained a brilliant red.

27

"Doodle! Doodle!" I cried, shaking him, but there was no answer but the ropy rain. He lay very awkwardly, with his head thrown far back, making his vermilion neck appear unusually long and slim. His little legs, bent sharply at the knees, had never before seemed so fragile, so thin.

I began to weep, and the tear-blurred vision in red before me looked very familiar. "Doodle!" I screamed above the pounding storm and threw my body to the earth above his. For a long long time, it seemed forever, I lay there crying, sheltering my fallen scarlet ibis from the heresy[7] of rain.

---

7. **heresy** (her´ ə sē) *n.* idea opposed to the beliefs of a religion or philosophy.

Literary Analysis
Symbolism and Allegory How are the details about the blood as well as Doodle's position beneath the bush similar to what happened to the scarlet ibis?

Thinking About the Selection

1. **Respond:** Do you blame the narrator for Doodle's death? Explain.

2. **(a) Recall:** Why does the narrator cry when everyone congratulates him for teaching Doodle to walk? **(b) Analyze:** What do the narrator's tears reveal about his conflicted, or mixed, feelings?

3. **(a) Recall:** What does Doodle do with the dead ibis?
   (b) Compare and Contrast: How does Doodle's reaction to the dead bird compare to those of his family members? **(c) Infer:** What do you think motivates Doodle to treat the ibis as he does?

4. **(a) Analyze:** Why do you think the narrator sets such demanding goals for Doodle? **(b) Draw Conclusions:** After Doodle's death, how do you think the narrator felt about his expectations of Doodle?

The Scarlet Ibis ■ *361*

27 Literary Analysis
Symbolism and Allegory

- Remind students that the story has established a strong connection between Doodle and the scarlet ibis.

- **Ask** the Literary Analysis question: How are the details about the blood as well as Doodle's position beneath the bush similar to what happened to the scarlet ibis? **Answer:** Doodle's blood recalls the color of the ibis and the bleeding tree. The description of Doodle's neck and legs mirrors that of the ibis on p. 359.

Concept Connector

Have students return to the Motivation activity on p. 350. Revisit your discussion about the brothers' relationship. Ask students if this story describes normal sibling rivalry, or is the narrator's meanness unnatural?

ASSESS

Answers

1. Students might blame the narrator because he pushed Doodle too far and then abandoned him in the storm. Alternatively, they might say that the narrator isn't responsible because Doodle's health was always fragile.

2. (a) The narrator cries because he knows that his reasons for teaching Doodle were selfish. (b) The narrator's tears reveal that he is ashamed of Doodle even though he loves him. His tears also reveal that he is ashamed of himself.

3. (a) Doodle buries the ibis. (b) Doodle experiences more grief about the dead bird than anyone else in his family. (c) Doodle is sensitive. He may have also identified with the bird's strangeness and weakness.

4. (a) **Possible response:** The narrator is encouraged by Doodle's success at walking. He also longs for Doodle to fit in at school. (b) The narrator clearly feels guilty about his expectations of Doodle. He describes himself as cruel and selfish.

㉘ Background

The Cold War The Cold War is called "cold" because no direct military combat was involved. The Cold War was a standoff between the United States and the Soviet Union, which were the only great powers in the world at the end of World War II.

㉙ Motivation

Initiate a discussion of rivalry. Include questions like these: How do rivals behave toward one another? How far will rivals go to outdo one another? What kinds of outcomes can result from a rivalry? Explain that students are about to read a story of the unexpected results of a rivalry.

Concept Connector ➡️

Students will follow up on this activity after completing "The Golden Kite, the Silver Wind."

㉚ About the Selection

"The Golden Kite, the Silver Wind" is a fable that highlights the negative consequences when competition is the only form of interaction. On a literal level, the story is about two rival towns that construct ever more complex walls to empower and protect themselves. On a symbolic level, it symbolizes the behaviors of nations or groups that, from fear or arrogance, build up their defenses rather than resolve their differences.

㉛ Critical Viewing

Answer: The mood of the leader in painting is serene, while the Mandarin's mood is agitated. Both are leaders of traditional Asian societies.

㉜ Humanities

The Nymph of the Lo River (detail), by Ku K'ai-Chih

To the ancient Chinese, the world was full of supernatural creatures. In this watercolor, the guardian of the Lo River has taken human form and is advising an official. Use this question for discussion:

• What setting can you infer from the details of this work of art?
  Answer: The details of the figures and their clothing suggest East Asia long ago.

The Golden Kite, the Silver Wind

RAY BRADBURY

Background "The Golden Kite, the Silver Wind" was written during the Cold War, a period of intense rivalry between the United States and the former Soviet Union that shaped world politics in the second half of the twentieth century. During this time, each action by one country—the creation of a weapon, the launching of a satellite—was countered by a reaction from the other country. As you read, think about the parallels between the story events and the conflicts of the Cold War.

"In the shape of a pig?" cried the Mandarin.[1]

"In the shape of a pig," said the messenger, and departed.

"Oh, what an evil day in an evil year," cried the Mandarin. "The town of Kwan-Si, beyond the hill, was very small in my childhood. Now it has grown so large that at last they are building a wall."

"But why should a wall two miles away make my good father sad and angry all within the hour?" asked his daughter quietly.

"They build their wall," said the Mandarin, "in the shape of a pig! Do you see? Our own city wall is built in the shape of an orange. That pig will devour us, greedily!"

"Ah."

They both sat thinking.

Life was full of symbols and omens. Demons lurked everywhere, Death swam in the wetness of an eye, the turn of a gull's wing meant rain, a fan held so, the tilt of a roof, and, yes, even a city wall was of immense importance. Travelers and tourists, caravans, musicians, artists, coming upon these two towns, equally judging the

㉛ ▼ Critical Viewing
How are the leader in this painting and the Mandarin in the story both similar and different? **[Compare and Contrast]**

The Nymph of the Lo River, section of a handscroll. (H. 9 1/2") Attributed to Ku K'ai-chih, Courtesy of the Freer Gallery of Art, Smithsonian Institution, Washington, D.C.

---

1. **Mandarin** (man´ də rin) *n.* a high official of China; here, the ruling leader.

362 ■ Short Stories

33 portents,[2] would say, "The city shaped like an orange? No! I will enter the city shaped like a pig and prosper, eating all, growing fat with good luck and prosperity!"

The Mandarin wept. "All is lost! These symbols and signs terrify. Our city will come on evil days."

"Then," said the daughter, "call in your stonemasons and temple builders. I will whisper from behind the silken screen and you will know the words."

The old man clapped his hands despairingly. "Ho, stonemasons!

"Ho, builders of towns and palaces!"

The men who knew marble and granite and onyx and quartz came quickly. The Mandarin faced them most uneasily, himself waiting for a whisper from the silken screen behind his throne. At last the whisper came.

"I have called you here," said the whisper.

"I have called you here," said the Mandarin aloud, "because our city is shaped like an orange, and the <u>vile</u> city of Kwan-Si has this day shaped theirs like a <u>ravenous</u> pig—"

Here the stonemasons groaned and wept. Death rattled his cane in the outer courtyard. Poverty made a sound like a wet cough in the shadows of the room.

"And so," said the whisper, said the Mandarin, "you raisers of walls must go bearing trowels and rocks and change the shape of our city!"

34 The architects and masons gasped. The Mandarin himself gasped at what he had said. The whisper whispered. The Mandarin went on: "And you will change our walls into a club which may beat the pig and drive it off!"

The stonemasons rose up, shouting. Even the Mandarin, delighted at the words from his mouth, applauded, stood down from his throne. "Quick!" he cried. "To work!"

When his men had gone, smiling and bustling, the Mandarin turned with great love to the silken screen. "Daughter," he whispered, "I will embrace you." There was no reply. He stepped around the screen, and she was gone.

Such modesty, he thought. She has slipped away and left me with a triumph, as if it were mine.

The news spread through the city; the Mandarin was acclaimed. Everyone carried stone to the walls. Fireworks were set off and the demons of death and poverty did not linger, as all worked together. At the end of the month the wall had been changed. It was now a mighty bludgeon with which to drive pigs, boars, even lions, far away. The Mandarin slept like a happy fox every night.

---

2. portents (pôr´ tentz´) *n.* things that are thought to be signs of events to come; omens.

The Golden Kite, the Silver Wind ■ 363

Literary Analysis
Symbolism and Allegory What qualities do the people believe the image of a pig symbolizes?

Vocabulary Builder
vile (vīl) *adj.* evil; wicked

ravenous (rav´ ə nəs) *adj.* greedily or wildly hungry

35 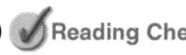Reading Check

Who whispers to the king from behind a silken screen?

---

33 **Literary Analysis**
Symbolism and Allegory

• Read aloud the bracketed paragraph. Point out how the Chinese people in the story place a strong value on symbols: "Life was full of symbols and omens."

• **Ask** the Literary Analysis question: What qualities do the people believe the image of a pig symbolizes?
Answer: The people believe that the pig symbolizes the other town's future luck and prosperity. A pig can eat, grow fat, and prosper.

34 **Literary Analysis**
Symbolism and Allegory

• Tell students that symbolism plays a key role in the rivalry between the towns described in the story. The leaders believe that the shape of the city walls symbolize each city's future.

• **Ask** students to explain why the city's walls must be changed into the shape of a club.
Answer: The walls must be changed so that the other town does not become more prosperous. A club can be used to beat down a pig.

• Have students **describe** the rivalry between the two towns.
Answer: The towns compete for tourists and travelers. Each leader wants his city to look more attractive and promising than the other.

35 **Reading Check**

Answer: The king's daughter is whispering from behind the screen.

Differentiated
Instruction Solutions for All Learners

Accessibility at a Glance

Context	Allegorical fable parallels events of the Cold War
Language	Some long sentences with embedded clauses
Concept Level	Challenging
Literary Merit	Prize-winning author
Lexile	1040L

Symbolism and Allegory

- **Ask** students to respond to the Literary Analysis question: In what ways does the "winter flower" describe the fleeting pleasure the Mandarin feels?
  Answer: The winter flower dies quickly. Similarly, the Mandarin's pleasure is short-lived.

- Tell students that this symbol appears in the form of a simile. Remind students that similes are comparisons that use the words *like* or *as*. Point out that both similes and metaphors are often used to develop symbols.

37 Critical Thinking

Predict

- Point out the consequences of the Mandarin's order to rebuild the walls in the shape of a club: The people have had to neglect their crops, and the whole city is impoverished.

- **Ask** students: What do you think the consequences of this latest action will be?
  Answer: Each city will rebuild its wall in a shape superior to the shape chosen by the other city.

- Point out to students how this chain of events was similar to the Cold War: Each action by the United States or the former Soviet Union was countered by a reaction from the other country.

"I would like to see the Mandarin of Kwan-Si when the news is learned. Such pandemonium and hysteria; he will likely throw himself from a mountain! A little more of that wine, oh Daughter-who-thinks-like-a-son."

36 But the pleasure was like a winter flower; it died swiftly. That very afternoon the messenger rushed into the courtroom. "Oh, Mandarin, disease, early sorrow, avalanches, grasshopper plagues, and poisoned well water!"

The Mandarin trembled.

"The town of Kwan-Si," said the messenger, "which was built like a pig and which animal we drove away by changing our walls to a mighty stick, has now turned triumph to winter ashes. They have built their city's walls like a great bonfire to burn our stick!"

The Mandarin's heart sickened within him, like an autumn fruit upon an ancient tree. "Oh, gods! Travelers will <u>spurn</u> us. Tradesmen, reading the symbols, will turn from the stick, so easily destroyed, to the fire, which conquers all!"

"No," said a whisper like a snowflake from behind the silken screen.

"No," said the startled Mandarin.

"Tell my stonemasons," said the whisper that was a falling drop of rain, "to build our walls in the shape of a shining lake."

The Mandarin said this aloud, his heart warmed.

"And with this lake of water," said the whisper and the old man, "we will quench the fire and put it out forever!"

37 The city turned out in joy to learn that once again they had been saved by the magnificent Emperor of ideas. They ran to the walls and built them nearer to this new vision, singing, not as loudly as before, of course, for they were tired, and not as quickly, for since it had taken a month to rebuild the wall the first time, they had had to neglect business and crops and therefore were somewhat weaker and poorer.

There then followed a succession of horrible and wonderful days, one in another like a nest of frightened boxes.

"Oh, Emperor," cried the messenger, "Kwan-Si has rebuilt their walls to resemble a mouth with which to drink all our lake!"

"Then," said the Emperor, standing very close to his silken screen, "build our walls like a needle to sew up that mouth!"

"Emperor!" screamed the messenger. "They make their walls like a sword to break your needle!"

The Emperor held, trembling, to the silken screen. "Then shift the stones to form a scabbard to sheathe that sword!"[3]

---

3. **scabbard** (skab′ ərd) **to sheathe** (shē*th*) **that sword!** case to hold the blade of the sword.

Literary Analysis
Symbolism and Allegory In what ways does the "winter flower" describe the fleeting pleasure the Mandarin feels?

Vocabulary Builder
spurn (spurn) *v.* reject with contempt or disdain

"Mercy," wept the messenger the following morn, "they have worked all night and shaped their walls like lightning which will explode and destroy that sheath!"

Sickness spread in the city like a pack of evil dogs. Shops closed. The population, working now steadily for endless months upon the changing of the walls, resembled Death himself, clattering his white bones like musical instruments in the wind. Funerals began to appear in the streets, though it was the middle of summer, a time when all should be tending and harvesting. The Mandarin fell so ill that he had his bed drawn up by the silken screen and there he lay, miserably giving his architectural orders. The voice behind the screen was weak now, too, and faint, like the wind in the eaves.

"Kwan-Si is an eagle. Then our walls must be a net for that eagle. They are a sun to burn our net. Then we build a moon to eclipse their sun!"

Like a rusted machine, the city ground to a halt.

At last the whisper behind the screen cried out:

"In the name of the gods, send for Kwan-Si!"

Upon the last day of summer the Mandarin Kwan-Si, very ill and withered away, was carried into our Mandarin's courtroom by four starving footmen. The two mandarins were propped up, facing each other. Their breaths fluttered like winter winds in their mouths. A voice said:

"Let us put an end to this."

The old men nodded.

"This cannot go on," said the faint voice. "Our people do nothing but rebuild our cities to a different shape every day, every hour. They have no time to hunt, to fish, to love, to be good to their ancestors and their ancestors' children."

"This I admit," said the mandarins of the towns of the Cage, the Moon, the Spear, the Fire, the Sword and this, that, and other things.

"Carry us into the sunlight," said the voice.

The old men were borne out under the sun and up a little hill. In the late summer breeze a few very thin children were flying dragon kites in all the colors of the sun, and frogs and grass, the color of the sea and the color of coins and wheat.

The first Mandarin's daughter stood by his bed.

"See," she said.

"Those are nothing but kites," said the two old men.

"But what is a kite on the ground?" she said. "It is nothing. What does it need to sustain it and make it beautiful and truly spiritual?"

"The wind, of course!" said the others.

"And what do the sky and the wind need to make them beautiful?"

39 ▲ Critical Viewing In what ways does a kite like the one shown here make the sky more beautiful? **[Assess]**

40 ✓ Reading Check

What kind of wall does the daughter suggest should be built to defeat Kwan-si's sun?

The Golden Kite, the Silver Wind ■ 365

38 Literary Analysis
Symbolism and Allegory

- Read aloud the bracketed paragraph, and then **ask** students what has happened to the town.
Answer: The town's population is sick and hungry. Many people are dying.

- Explain that sickness, hunger, and death are the same problems that the Mandarin had hoped to avoid by continually rebuilding the walls. Point out that his insistence on the symbolic value of the wall has been harmful to his people.

- **Ask** students what lesson here might be applied to the events of the Cold War.
Answer: The constant attempts by competing governments to best one another hurt the people.

39 Critical Viewing

Answer: The kite is colorful with an intricate design. It would be interesting and beautiful to see in the sky.

40 Reading Check

Answer: The daughter suggests that they build a moon to eclipse Kwan-si's sun.

Differentiated
Instruction   Solutions for All Learners

Enrichment for Advanced Readers
Suggest that students read additional works by Ray Bradbury. Provide students with **Authors In Depth**, Gold Level, which contains the following selections:
- *The Flying Machine* (p. 33)
- *The Pedestrian* (p. 37)
- "The Other Me" (p. 42)
- "January 1999: Rocket Summer" from *The Martian Chronicles* (p. 44)

After students have read these or other works by Bradbury, have them form discussion groups in which they compare and contrast the selections. Suggest criteria for comparison, such as setting, theme, characters, and author's purpose. To extend the activity, have volunteers present to the class brief oral reports on their favorite Bradbury selections.

④ Literary Analysis
Symbolism and Allegory

- Have students read the bracketed passage. Point out that the symbols of the kite and the wind embody the central theme of the story.

- **Ask** students to respond to the Literary Analysis question: What kind of relationship do the kite and the wind symbolize?
  Answer: They represent a cooperative relationship, in which each party benefits from the other.

- Tell students that in choosing harmonious shapes for their towns, the Mandarins have ended the problems of their people. Explain that the shapes of the kite and the wind represent the major theme of the story: Cooperation is preferable to competition.

Concept Connector

Have students return to the Motivation activity on p. 362. Revisit your discussion about rivalry. Pose the following question to students: Why can't rivalry always be resolved with a peaceful solution?

⬅

ASSESS

Answers

1. Students may say that the advice at the start of the story was not good because it led to so much destruction, but the advice at the end was good. Some students may think the advice at the beginning was necessary so that the two mandarins would learn a lesson.

2. (a) The townspeople seem happy to rebuild; they think they are better than the people of Kwan-Si. (b) The continued competition makes the people tired, hungry, and sick. (c) **Possible response:** They might have been wise to plead with the Mandarin to be allowed to tend their crops.

3. (a) The shapes of a kite and the wind complement one another. (b) The story suggests that if you try to be better than your neighbor, you won't have time for anything else. All rivalries are destructive; it is better to work together.

"A kite, of course—many kites, to break the monotony, the sameness of the sky. Colored kites, flying!"

"So," said the Mandarin's daughter. "You, Kwan-Si, will make a last rebuilding of your town to resemble nothing more nor less than the wind. And we shall build like a golden kite. The wind will beautify the kite and carry it to wondrous heights. And the kite will break the sameness of the wind's existence and give it purpose and meaning. One without the other is nothing. Together, all will be beauty and cooperation and a long and enduring life."

Whereupon the two mandarins were so overjoyed that they took their first nourishment in days, momentarily were given strength, embraced, and lavished praise upon each other, called the Mandarin's daughter a boy, a man, a stone pillar, a warrior, and a true and unforgettable son. Almost immediately they parted and hurried to their towns, calling out and singing, weakly but happily.

And so, in time, the towns became the Town of Golden Kite and the Town of the Silver Wind. And harvestings were harvested and business tended again, and the flesh returned, and disease ran off like a frightened jackal. And on every night of the year the inhabitants in the Town of the Kite could hear the good clear wind sustaining them. And those in the Town of the Wind could hear the kite singing, whispering, rising, and beautifying them.

"So be it," said the Mandarin in front of his silken screen.

Thinking About the Selection

1. **Respond:** Do you think the Mandarin's daughter gave her father good advice? Explain.

2. **(a) Interpret:** How do the townspeople react to the Mandarin's repeated instructions to rebuild the city?
   (b) Analyze Cause and Effect: How does the continued competition between the towns affect the people's health and well-being? Explain. **(c) Evaluate:** Should the people have continued to follow the Mandarin as a leader? Why or why not?

3. **(a) Evaluate:** Why are walls built as a kite and the wind more effective for a peaceful and harmonious relationship between the two towns? **(b) Draw Conclusions:** What lesson does this story teach for today's world?

366 ■ *Short Stories*

Literary Analysis
Symbolism and Allegory What kind of relationship do the kite and the wind symbolize?

Vocabulary Development

Vocabulary Knowledge Rating

When students have competed reading and discussing "The Scarlet Ibis" and "The Golden Kite, the Silver Wind" have them take out their **Vocabulary Knowledge Rating Chart**. Read the words aloud once more and have students rate their knowledge of the words again in the After Reading column. Clarify any words that are still problematic. Have students write their own definition and example or sentence in the appropriate column. Then, have students complete the **Vocabulary Builder Practice** on p. 367. Encourage students to use the words in further discussion and written work about these selections. Remind them that they will be accountable for these words on the Selection Test.

Apply the Skills

The Scarlet Ibis • The Golden Kite, the Silver Wind

Comparing Symbolism

1. Use a chart like the one shown to analyze how the characters, events, and setting in "The Golden Kite, the Silver Wind" could be **symbols** for leaders and world events during the Cold War.

Symbol	Qualities	Meaning
Mandarin	Leader of his town; worried about losing business and reputation	Leader of a nation who wants to stay on top
Mandarin's daughter		
Walls		

2. **(a)** In "The Scarlet Ibis," what does the ibis symbolize?
   (b) Which story details support your conclusion? Explain.

3. Based on your analysis of the **symbolism** in both stories, which is an **allegory**? Explain.

Writing to Compare Literary Works

Write an essay in which you compare the use of symbolism in "The Scarlet Ibis" and "The Golden Kite, the Silver Wind." Use these questions to help you get started:

- What message or lesson does the author of each story express?
- How does the author of each selection use symbols to develop the message?
- If the symbols were omitted from either story, would its message remain the same? Explain.

Vocabulary Builder

Practice Use the situation described in each of the following items to write a sentence in which you use a word from the vocabulary list on page 348.

1. telling a terrible lie
2. hearing a train whistle getting louder
3. turning down an invitation
4. achieving perfect exam scores
5. having a meal after a long hike
6. climbing a sheer cliff

QuickReview

Symbol: an object, a person, or a place that stands for a larger idea or feeling

Symbolism: the use of symbols in a literary work

Allegory: a literary work that has parallel literal and symbolic meanings

Go Online
Assessment

For: Self-test
Visit: www.PHSchool.com
Web Code: epa-6211

Apply the Skills ■ 367

Assessment Resources

The following resources can be used to assess students' knowledge and skills.

Unit 2 Resources:
   Selection Test A, pp. 186–188
   Selection Test B, pp. 189–191

Go Online
Assessment Students may use the **Self-test** to prepare for **Selection Test A** or **Selection Test B.**

367

Reading

Directions: *Questions 1–5 refer to the following selection.*

Increasing National Wealth: Mercantilists urged rulers to adopt policies to increase national wealth and government revenues. To boost production, governments exploited mineral and timber resources, built roads, and backed new industries. They imposed a single national currency and established standard weights and measures. Governments also sold monopolies to large producers in certain industries as well as to big overseas trading companies. Finally, governments imposed tariffs, or taxes on imported goods. Tariffs were designed to protect local industries from foreign competition by increasing the price of imported goods.

1. Standard weights and measures were an effect of which of the following?
   A a single national currency
   B productivity
   C mercantilism
   D monopolies

2. What was one effect of governments' attempt to boost production?
   A Governments backed new industry.
   B Governments backed foreign industry.
   C Governments started the mineral industry.
   D Governments took over certain industries.

3. Which of the following was not an effect of the effort to boost national wealth?
   A Tariffs were imposed.
   B Monopolies were sold.
   C Roads were built.
   D Mercantilism was mandated.

4. Which of the following was a cause of imposing tariffs?
   A aid to foreign governments
   B standardization of quality
   C isolation of the government
   D protection of local industries

5. Which cause-and-effect pair is correct?
   A Mercantilism caused an increase in the national debt.
   B Mercantilism caused a decrease in national wealth.
   C Mercantilism had no effect on economic policy.
   D Mercantilism affected governments' policies.

Assessment Practice

Vocabulary

Directions: *Choose the word that best completes the sentence.*

6. We repeated the experiment to _____ the results.
   A stress
   B verify
   C sequence
   D imply

7. The actor's tone _____ that his character is discouraged.
   A stresses
   B verifies
   C explains
   D implies

8. The _____ of events in the plot gives the reader insight into the theme.
   A implication
   B veracity
   C explained
   D sequence

9. When you determine the author's _____, you understand the work more fully.
   A attitude
   B stress
   C veracity
   D implication

10. The _____ of the talk is "Evaluating Media."
    A attitude
    B stress
    C topic
    D explanation

Directions: *Use the definition of the root to choose the correct definition of the word.*

11. sequela
    A a movie version of a novel
    B a result that follows a cause
    C a fake appearance
    D a circular argument

12. verisimilitude
    A the state of motion
    B the appearance of being true or real
    C the setting or place of an event
    D the object that follows another

13. sequential
    A progressing randomly
    B progressing in a linear way
    C progressing in a circular way
    D progressing sporadically

14. verily
    A green
    B angled
    C truly
    D finally

15. veritable
    A not reasonable
    B not connected
    C not reliable
    D not false

RETEACH

If students answer any of these questions incorrectly, have them review the instruction on the following pages in Part 2 before taking the **Benchmark Test.**

Question	Pages Where Instruction Is Located:
1	292, 320
2	292, 320
3	292, 320
4	292, 320
5	292, 320
6	291
7	291
8	291
9	291
10	291
11	342
12	318
13	342
14	318
15	318

Benchmark

Administer the **Benchmark Test** for Unit 2, Part 2. If the Benchmark Test reveals that some students need further work, use the Interpretation Guide to determine the appropriate reteaching page in the **Reading Kit.** You will also find the same instruction and practice available on **Success Tracker.**

Go **Online**
Vocabulary
For: Interactive Crossword Puzzles
Visit: www.PHSchool.com
Web Code: epj-5202

Give students this Web Code to access interactive crossword puzzles using Academic Vocabulary and Vocabulary Skill words from Part 2.

Students will

1. recognize unusual consonant groupings.
2. spell correctly words with unusual consonant groupings.

Unusual Consonant Groupings

- Point out that many unusual consonant groupings are silent or cannot be sounded out. Invite students to list words with consonant groupings that they find difficult to spell.

Possible responses: Students may provide some of the following words:

rhyme

rhinoceros

unknown

subtlety

chalet

rhinestone

scene

rhizome

- Allow time for students to review the word list. Then, group students into pairs, and have the first student read each word from the list to the second student. After each word is pronounced, have the second student try to spell the word correctly. After student pairs have finished, have them switch roles and repeat the exercise.

$\mathcal{WG}$ **Writing and Grammar, Gold Level**

Students will find additional spelling instruction in Chapter 31, Section 4.

Spelling Workshop SPELLING

Unusual Consonant Groupings

Certain words are difficult to spell because they contain unusual letter combinations. Some of these combinations involve consonants. Unexpected consonant groupings cause problems in many words.

Did You Use the Right Consonants? Certain consonant groupings, such as the *rh* in *rhythm,* don't occur in many words and can be difficult to remember. Other consonant groupings are hard to hear (e*x*hilarating) or contain a silent letter (sil*h*ouette). Read the words on the list and focus on the problem parts. Look at the consonant groupings, but note any problematic vowels as well. Make sure you can spell each word.

I like it, it's subtle.

Practice Unscramble the letters to correctly spell the words on the Word List.

1. cahalonnnt
2. yrmhht
3. hoisluetet
4. cipilidsne
5. urebchro

6. isincreem
7. ownreend
8. butles
9. ahiintlerxgat
10. tssiioonnccue

Word List
reminisce
discipline
brochure
rhythm
renowned
conscientious
silhouette
subtle
exhilarating
nonchalant

The following resource can be used to enrich or extend the instruction for this Spelling Workshop.

Unit 2 Resources
Spelling Workshop: Unusual Consonant Groupings, p. 194

Monitor Your Progress

Assessment Practice

Directions: *Write the letter of the sentence in which the underlined word is spelled correctly.*

1. **A** The students loved the <u>ryhthm</u> of the tango.
   B They found it entertaining and <u>exzilarating</u>.
   C They admired the <u>silhouette</u> made by the dancers.
   D Through <u>concientious</u> study, they learned much about Argentine culture.

2. **A** A <u>broshure</u> was handed out to each freshman.
   B It outlined <u>discipline</u> procedures in the school.
   C In the earlier version, the explanations were too <u>suttle</u>.
   D They let students be too <u>nonschalant</u> about following rules.

3. **A** The <u>renowned</u> scientist spoke to a large audience.
   B He began to <u>reminise</u> about his days in college.
   C He admitted that he was not a <u>conscienshious</u> student.
   D He did not learn <u>self-disipline</u> until years later.

4. **A** Ron excels at creating <u>subtle</u> designs.
   B Once he created the cover for an advertising <u>broachure</u>.
   C All of the figures on it were in <u>silhooette</u>.
   D It was a time-consuming but <u>exhiliarating</u> project.

Directions: *Write the letter of the correct spelling of the word to fill in the blank.*

1. When they questioned him, he acted _____.
   A nonshalantly
   B nonchalantly
   C nonchallantly
   D nonechalantly

2. Those divers are _____ for their daredevil stunts.
   A renownd
   B renowened
   C renowned
   D rinowned

3. The _____ of the waves put me to sleep.
   A rithem
   B rhythem
   C ryhthm
   D rhythm

4. Grandma likes to _____ about her childhood.
   A reminisce
   B remenisce
   C reminice
   D reminise

5. She is a _____ worker and deserves a raise.
   A conscienshious
   B conscientious
   C concientious
   D conscienshus

6. The roller coaster ride was _____.
   A exhilarating
   B exhiliarating
   C exzilarating
   D exilarating

Answers

Practice

1. nonchalant	6. reminisce
2. rhythm	7. renowned
3. silhouette	8. subtle
4. discipline	9. exhilarating
5. brochure	10. conscientious

Assessment Practice

1. C
2. B
3. A
4. A

1. B
2. C
3. D
4. A
5. B
6. A

Exposition: Cause-and-Effect Essay

Whether the subject is human nature, historical trends, or weather patterns, cause-and-effect reasoning explains why things happen. A **cause-and-effect essay** examines the relationship between or among two or more events, explaining how one causes another. In this workshop, you will write your own cause-and-effect essay.

Assignment: Write a cause-and-effect essay about an event or a condition in a subject area that interests you, such as business, the arts, technology, history, sports, or music.

What to Include: Your cause-and-effect essay should feature the following elements:

- a clear identification of a cause-and-effect relationship
- an analysis of specific aspects of the cause or causes that produce the effect
- facts, details, examples, and reasons that support your assertions and anticipate readers' questions
- a logical organization clarified by smooth transitions
- error-free grammar, including correct subject-verb agreement

To preview the criteria on which your cause-and-effect essay may be assessed, see the rubric on page 379.

 Writing Workshop: *Work in Progress*

If you have completed the Work-in-Progress assignments, you have in your portfolio several ideas to pursue in your cause-and-effect essay. You may continue to develop these ideas, or you might explore a new idea as you complete this Writing Workshop.

372 ■ *Short Stories*

Using the Form
You may use elements of this form in these types of writing:
- science reports
- history papers
- health articles

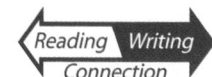
Reading ▶ **Writing**
Connection

To get a feel for cause-and-effect essays, read the excerpt from *Silent Spring* by Rachel Carson on page 153.

From the Author's Desk

Wayson Choy

Show students Segment 3 on Wayson Choy on *From the Author's Desk DVD.* Discuss what Choy says about the importance of knowing the rules of writing and being willing to break these rules in order to achieve desired results.

Writing Genres

Using the Form Explain that cause-and-effect exposition is often incorporated into other types of writing. Point out these examples:

- Science writing may require clear expositions of cause-and-effect relationships in biological, physical, and health sciences.
- A history research paper may require an explanation of the causes and the effects of a certain event.

 Writing Workshop
Work in Progress

If students have done the Work-in-Progress assignments throughout Part 2, suggest that they examine their portfolios for an idea to develop into a cause-and-effect essay.

 Online Essay Scorer

A writing prompt for this mode of writing can be found on the *PH Online Essay Scorer* at PHSuccessNet.com.

372

Teaching Resources

The following resources can be used to enrich or extend the instruction for the Writing Workshop.

Unit 2 Resources
Writing Workshop: Exposition: Cause-and-Effect Essay, p. 192
Writing Workshop: Integrating Grammar Skills: Revising Faulty Subject-Verb Agreement, p. 193

General Resources
Rubrics for Exposition: Cause-and-Effect Essay, pp. 49–50

Graphic Organizer Transparencies: Cause-and-Effect Flowchart, p. 233

From the Author's Desk DVD
Wayson Choy, Segment 3

Prewriting

Choosing Your Topic

To select a topic for your essay, use one of the following strategies:

- **Examine current events.** Scan newspapers or magazines for headlines that interest you. Use a three-column chart to examine possible causes and effects: In the middle column, write the event; in the left column, write possible causes; and in the right column, note possible effects. Review this chart for potential topics.

Causes	Event	Effect
• practice, focus • individual performance	Team Wins Championship	• increased fan interest • harder to buy tickets • revenue for city

- **List and freewrite.** Jot down any interesting events that come to mind from the worlds of business, science, technology, the arts, nature, politics, or sports. Then, circle the item that most intrigues you. Freewrite for three minutes about that topic. As you do, note any causes and effects that come to mind. Develop your topic from ideas you uncover in your freewriting.

Narrowing Your Topic

Categorize to narrow your topic. You may find that your topic is too big to manage in the scope of a single essay. Break your subject into smaller categories. For example, if your topic is about a record-breaking sports event, you might create categories such as "key player," "great coach," or "new equipment." Choose from your list of categories a more focused topic that interests you.

Gathering Details

Chart causes and effects. Using an index card or a self-sticking note, write the central event or circumstance that is your subject. Decide if you want to explore the causes that produced the event or the effects the event produced. In either case, write those factors on separate cards or notes. Write key details related to each cause or effect on the cards or notes. Then, arrange the cards or notes in a logical sequence.

Work in Progress
Review the work you did on pages 319 and 343.

Writing Workshop ■ 373

Prewriting

- To help students choose topics, provide them with current newspapers or magazines to scan, or schedule a visit to the library.

- Help students begin their free writing exercise by recording a class list of events on the board. To start the list, record recent important world and local happenings, including sports, politics, and current events.

- Show students how to narrow their topics by writing the topic *Volcanoes* on the board in the center of a web. In radiating circles, write *Volcanic Eruptions* and *Types of Volcanoes.* Then, start a new web for the topic *The Olympics* and invite volunteers to make suggestions to narrow the topic.
  Possible answers: *Gymnastic competition, famous Olympic athletes, and Olympic medals*

- Working with the topic *Volcanic Eruptions,* show students how to gather details by charting the effects of the topic. In radiating circles, add these effects to the web: *Shapes Land Formations, Changes Weather, Buries Cities,* and *Results in Deaths.* Students can continue to gather details for each effect by adding information to their charts. For example, with regard to *Shaping Land Formations,* the writer can add that volcanic eruptions *shape islands, mountains, and plains.*

Six Traits Focus

✔	Ideas		Word Choice
✔	Organization		Sentence Fluency
	Voice		Conventions

Writing and Grammar, Gold Level
Students will find additional instruction on prewriting for a cause-and-effect essay in Chapter 10, Section 2.

Writing and Grammar Interactive Textbook CD-ROM

Students can use the following tools as they complete their cause-and-effect essays:

- Topic Web

- Cause-and-Effect Organizer

- Unity and Coherence Revising Tool

Tips for Using Rubrics

- Before students begin work on this assignment, have them preview the Rubric for Self-Assessment on p. 379 to know what is expected.

- Review the Assessment criteria in class. Before students use the Rubric for Self-Assessment, work with them to rate the student model by applying one or two criteria to it.

- If you wish to assess students' cause-and-effect essays with either a 4-point, 5-point, or a 6-point scoring rubric, see *General Resources,* pp. 49–50.

Drafting

- Explain that chronological order can be shown in two ways. Students can begin with the first event and show how it led to subsequent events. Alternatively, they can begin with the final effect and trace it back to the first event that caused the chain of effects.

- Write the following statements on the board:

   Shawna did her chores for the week.

   Shawna's parents gave her an allowance for doing her chores.

   Shawna bought a new book with her money.

   Shawna enjoyed reading her new book.

   Use a cause-and-effect flowchart to demonstrate the two ways that students can show chronological order. Refer students to the Cause-and-Effect Flowchart in **Graphic Organizer Transparencies**, p. 233.

- Explain to students the differences among the types of illustrations: details come from observation and personal knowledge and experience; facts are based on research; examples can be fictional scenarios or real events in which the writer was not involved; and personal experiences are autobiographical.

- Using the topic *The Causes and Effects of Volcanic Eruptions in Hawaii,* suggest possible illustrations. Invite the students to suggest others.
   Possible responses: Detail: the appearance of dried lava on the landscape
   Fact: the recorded amount of people who have died as a result of volcanic eruptions in Hawaii
   Example: a specific volcanic eruption and the damage it did to a local village
   Personal Experience: the writer went on a helicopter ride above a location damaged by a volcanic

Six Traits Focus

✔ Ideas	✔ Word Choice
✔ Organization	Sentence Fluency
✔ Voice	Conventions

Writing and Grammar, Gold Level
Students will find additional instruction on drafting a cause-and-effect essay in Chapter 10, Section 3.

Drafting

Shaping Your Writing

Choose a structure. In your opening paragraph, introduce your topic and show why it is important. Here are two possibilities for organizing the body paragraphs of your essay:

- **Chronological order** is particularly valuable when tracing a chain, or sequence, of cause and effect. However, a time-order relationship is not in itself proof of cause and effect.

- **Order of importance** begins with the least important point and works toward the most important point. This pattern is especially effective when you are presenting a series of effects produced by a single event.

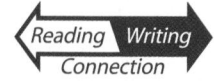
Reading Writing Connection

For the complete student model, see page 378.

Providing Elaboration

Use logical evidence. As you draft your essay, avoid opinions, unsupported assertions, and trivial details. Rely on facts, statistics, and examples to build a convincing web of support.

Student Model: Building Ideas With Facts

The oceans have been around since the beginning of time, yet we know relatively little about them. They are constantly moving and changing, turning up water that has been down in the depths for hundreds of years. One of these currents is the North Atlantic, also known as the Great Ocean Conveyor Belt.

In his opening paragraph, the writer establishes his topic and its importance with statements of fact.

Use the TRI method to develop paragraphs. Follow these steps:
1. **Topic:** Write a sentence stating your topic or key idea; label it (T).
2. **Restatement:** Write a sentence restating your topic; label it (R).
3. **Illustration:** Illustrate your point through details, facts, examples, or personal experience; label this section (I).

Once you feel comfortable with the TRI pattern, you can shift the sequence to suit the information you present.

▶ **Example:** Originally, the color purple was associated with royalty. (**T**) Only kings, queens, and members of the nobility wore purple-colored clothing. (**R**) In England, Queen Elizabeth I actually made a law prohibiting anyone except herself and her relatives from wearing purple. (**I**)

374 ■ Short Stories

Tips for Test Taking

Students will sometimes be required to write cause-and-effect essays in testing situations. Provide these tips for writing their essays:

- Make a list of your causes and effects before you begin writing your essay.

- Decide if you are going to present your causes and effects in chronological order or in order of importance.

- Make sure that all details given support either a cause or an effect. Avoid including unnecessary details to fill space.

Wayson Choy

On Showing Cause and Effect

An origami butterfly sits on my computer to remind me that just as a butterfly must first go through various stages, my first draft will be "re-created" many times before it can take flight. During that process, I keep in mind that a sense of cause and effect is as important in fiction as in nonfiction. So, I hone the action and dialogue "to show not tell about" the causes and effects in my characters' lives. The following draft from my novel *All That Matters* demonstrates how I do that.

Wayson Choy

I aim for "showing not telling."

——————Wayson Choy

Professional Model:

from *All That Matters*

I had given up a late afternoon soccer practice to do some serious studying ∧for Mr. Eades's first English test. There were plenty of others like us, books opened, eyes focused. Jenny pointed to the library seat ∧across from hers, and her eyes said, No fooling around! ~~Truth was, she took her English studies more seriously than she took me. It was frustrating. I just wanted to be with her. She was always in charge.~~

∧As she pushed my books across the table, I thought that she and I should have, two months ago, declared ourselves an official couple, especially after our fifth double date together. But Jenny didn't want that.

∧"Too showy," she had told me. "Maybe after we graduate. Next year."

∧She folded both our school sweaters together and neatly draped them over one of the empty chairs.

> I needed to expand this account with more details to show causes and effects in the relationship between the narrator and his girlfriend, Jenny.

> These two sentences tell that Jenny is an in-control girl who takes charge of the narrator. But I wanted to show it through dialogue and actions.

> The act of folding the sweaters symbolizes Jenny's shaping of the relationship.

From the Author's Desk: Wayson Choy ■ 375

From the Author's Desk
Wayson Choy

- Show students Segment 3 on Wayson Choy on *From the Author's Desk DVD.* Discuss how Choy uses writing as a way of discovering things about himself, his family, and his culture. Help students understand how writing helps him identify and think about the causes of events in his life and their lasting effects.

- Point out how the changes that Choy has made to his draft replace telling with showing. Ask students to explain how each change makes the passage more engaging.

- Call students' attention to Choy's comments about his changes. Ask what new causes and effects Choy introduces. Then, ask students how this new information changes what they know or think about the characters.

- Have students look closely at their own essays and try to identify ways in which they can show, rather than tell about, the cause-and-effect relationships.

Tips for Elaboration

Tell students that they can show, rather than tell, information in their writing through dialogue, sensory details, and character actions. Write the following sentence on the board: *It was hot in the house.*

Demonstrate for students how they can show, rather than tell, this information by writing the following statements on the board:

Dialogue: *"What I wouldn't do for an air-conditioner!" Juan exclaimed.*

Sensory Details: *A fan droned in the living room, nudging weak breezes through the stifling air.*

Character Actions: *Cara once again opened the freezer door and stood, letting the icy air chill the sweat on her face.*

Revising

- Write the following sentences on the board:

    Cause: *Devin carried the groceries into the house.*

    Effect: *The cat escaped out the door.*

  Ask students to provide details that will strengthen the connection between cause and effect.

  Possible response: *Devin forgot to watch for the cat when he opened the kitchen door.*

    Devin propped open the kitchen door when he went back to the car to get more groceries.

- Explain to students that a succession of short, choppy sentences can break up the rhythm of their essays, making them sound stilted. Explain that it is acceptable to use short sentences in combination with more complex sentences to give variety to their writing or to create emphasis.

- Remind students that when they combine two simple sentences by changing one into an introductory clause, the clause should end with a comma. Write the following sentences on the board and ask students to combine them in multiple ways. Identify each type of sentence and discuss its effect on readers.

    A dark funnel-cloud appeared just a few miles from town.

    Then, we huddled in the basement.

  Possible response: *When a dark funnel-cloud appeared just a few miles from town, we huddled in the basement.*

    This is a complex sentence, consisting of a dependent clause and an independent clause. The newly-combined sentence helps the reader see the causal relationship between the two events.

Six Traits Focus

✔	Ideas	✔	Word Choice
✔	Organization	✔	Sentence Fluency
		✔	Conventions

W͜G Writing and Grammar, Gold Level

Students will find additional instruction for revising a cause-and-effect essay in Chapter 10, Section 4.

Revising

Revising Your Overall Structure

Clarify cause-and-effect relationships. Review your entire draft, focusing on the causes and effects you have presented. With two highlighters, use one color to mark phrases that present causes and the other to mark those that discuss effects. You may need to add details to strengthen connections, insert transitional words to make links clear, or eliminate causes or effects that do not support your main point.

> **Student Model: Revising to Clarify Cause and Effect**
>
> The mechanisms by which the current works are very simple.
> As the water moves north, it ~~The water~~ cools down and the salinity rises. This occurs because the ~~The~~ arctic climate cools the water as it moves north.

This writer adds transitional words and phrases to clarify the cause-and-effect relationships.

Peer Review: Ask a partner to read your draft, and then conduct a conference about your work. Your reader should discuss the clarity of the cause-and-effect relationships you present throughout your essay. Consider modifying sentences, omitting or adding transitions, or reordering paragraphs to improve the logical flow of your ideas.

Revising Your Sentences

Combine short sentences. To evaluate the sentences in your writing, count the words in every sentence in your article, and record the numbers in the margin. If you find too many short sentences in your draft, look for places to combine them using the following strategies:

- Combine two sentences using subordinating clauses that start with conjunctions such as *after, although, despite, if,* and *whenever.*

- Use coordinating conjunctions such as *and, but, or, nor, for, so,* and *yet.*

▶ **Example: Short Sentences:**
  The team members lost hope. They found an unlikely inspiration to continue.
  Combined:
  The team members lost hope, but they found an unlikely inspiration to continue.

376 ■ *Short Stories*

Tips for
Improving Transitions

Emphasize that it is essential to make clear connections among ideas in a cause-and-effect essay. One way to do this is by using transitional words to indicate relationships. Explain that there are different types of transitional words that describe different relationships. Write these words on the board.

Transitions that show cause-and-effect:

because	since	in order to
consequently	as a result	besides
once	so	therefore

Transitions that show chronological or sequential order:

meanwhile	next	after
before	first	now
following	during	then

  Ask students to add additional transitional words to these lists.

Integrating Grammar Skills

Revising to Correct Faulty Subject-Verb Agreement

For a subject and verb to agree, they must agree in number.

Identifying Errors in Subject-Verb Agreement Errors in agreement often occur with compound subjects, with subjects joined by *or* or *nor*, and with indefinite pronouns serving as subjects. In the following example, subjects are underlined and verbs are set in italic type.

Compound Subject:

The <u>coach and the captain</u> *is going* *are going* to attend.

Subject Joined by *Or* or *Nor*:

<u>Either Jason or his brother</u> *are bringing* *is bringing* the snacks.

Indefinite Pronoun as Subject:

<u>Everybody</u> who supports our ideas *are helping* *is helping*.

If a plural subject is joined to a singular subject by *or* or *nor*, the verb should agree with the subject that is closer to it.

Correct: <u>Either the coach or the co-captains</u> *are going* to speak.

Correct: <u>Either the co-captains or the coach</u> *is going* to speak.

Fixing Errors To correct mismatched subjects and verbs, follow these steps:

1. **Identify whether the subject in a sentence is singular or plural.**
2. **Select the matching form of the verb:**
   - For compound subjects joined by *and,* use plural verb forms.
   - For singular subjects joined by *or* or *nor,* use singular verb forms.
   - When the subject is an indefinite pronoun, use the appropriate form of the verb. Use this chart for guidance.

Indefinite Pronouns	
Always Singular	anybody, anyone, anything, each, either, every, everybody, everyone, everything, neither, nobody, no one, nothing, somebody, someone, something
Always Plural	both, few, many, others, several
Singular or Plural	all, any, more, most, none, some

Apply It to Your Editing

Scan several paragraphs in your draft, underlining all compound subjects or indefinite pronouns. In each case, make sure that you have used the form of the verb that agrees with the subject.

Prentice Hall Writing and Grammar Connection: Chapter 25, Section 1

Writing Workshop ■ 377

Integrating Grammar Skills

- Write these sentences on the board.

  There are twenty questions on the test.

  There is twenty questions on the test.

  Point out to students that *questions* is the plural subject of each sentence. **Ask** students which sentence has subject-verb agreement. **Answer:** first sentence

- Write these sentences on the board. Have students identify the subjects and correct the verbs in each sentence:

  1. *Almost everyone in our class want to attend the performance.* **Answer:** everyone, wants

  2. *The cities of Richmond Heights and Clayton agrees to merge.* **Answer:** cities, agree

  3. *Julie, one of the Baxters' children, babysit regularly for Ms. Alvarez.* **Answer:** Julie, babysits

  4. *There is five children in our family.* **Answer:** children, are

  5. *Neither the chairperson nor the club members likes the results.* **Answer:** chairperson/members, like

- Give students additional examples of singular subjects, such as *runner, Ms. Andrews, student,* and *athlete.* Have them create sentences in which these nouns agree with the verbs *try, forget, anticipate,* and *start.*

- Have students work in pairs and exchange their drafts to identify errors in subject-verb agreement.

Writing and Grammar, Gold Level

Sttudents will find additional instruction on revising errors in subject-verb agreement in Chapter 25, Section 1.

Differentiated Instruction   Solutions for All Learners

Strategy for Less Proficient Students
Tell students that the key to subject-verb agreement is to correctly identify whether the subject of the sentence is singular or plural. Working with two paragraphs of their drafts, have students highlight or circle the subject of each sentence. Have them determine whether each subject is singular or plural, then check to see if the form of the verb matches.

Enrichment for Advanced Readers
Have students review their entire draft for sentences that use indefinite pronouns as subjects. Have them circle all the indefinite pronouns that can be singular or plural: *all, any, most, none, some.* Have them recheck agreement with verbs in these sentences and write a brief explanation of their choice of verb form.

Student Model

- Explain that the Student Model is a sample and that essays may be longer.

- Tell students that they need a factual foundation to make their essay convincing to readers.

- Give students the example of a cause-and-effect essay about how violent video games cause violent behavior. Have students think of differing opinions that could be acknowledged in the essay.

  Possible response: Violent video games do not cause violent behavior; they simply enhance violent tendencies that already exist.

- **Ask** students why the conjunction *consequently* is useful in a cause-and-effect essay.

  Answer: The word *consequently* means "as a result of," which means that it is used to link a cause and an effect.

- Tell students to gauge how unfamiliar their audience is going to be with the information in their essays and to write with this level of unfamiliarity in mind.

- Tell students that when describing a process, chronological order is a useful organizational structure.

  Ask students to think of a variety of processes that chronological order could be used to describe.

  Possible responses:
  Chronological order could be used to describe the process by which water evaporates, the process by which one attains their driver's license, or the process by which photographic film is developed.

Writing Genres

Cause-and-Effect Writing in Letters to the Editor Explain to students that if they feel strongly about changing situations in their communities, they can write letters to the editor of their local newspapers. They can organize their letters by utilizing cause-and-effect text structures to show how these issues are affecting their communities. For example, a community playground may be in need of repair. Using a cause-and-effect text structure, invite students to construct an outline for a letter to the editor on this topic.

Writing Workshop

Student Model: Glenn Milner
Charlotte, NC

Climate Effects of the North Atlantic Current

The oceans have been around since the beginning of time, yet we know relatively little about them. They are constantly moving and changing, turning up water that has been down in the depths for hundreds of years. One of these currents is the North Atlantic, also known as the Great Ocean Conveyor Belt.

Direct statements of fact form the basis of the essay.

The level of impact the current has on climate and the causes that change it are widely debated. The presumption held by most scientists is that we are currently experiencing global warming. Other theories state that global warming may influence the North Atlantic Current. This, consequently, may cause the exact opposite of warming— an ice age.

The writer builds interest by acknowledging that there are differing opinions on the topic.

Models have shown that any change in speed or location of the current may well cause a rapid climate shift of great magnitude (Burroughs 17). This shift would be caused by two key changes: a decrease in salinity and an increase in the temperature of water in the North Atlantic Current. These factors would, in turn, cause the current to slow down or shut down, sending the Northern Hemisphere into an ice age.

The coordinating conjunction consequently is particularly useful in a cause-and-effect essay.

The North Atlantic Current is a complicated system that runs for thousands of miles and combines water from all oceans. It moves heat from the tropics to the northern Atlantic. Robert Kunzig, the author of *The Restless Sea: Exploring the World Beneath the Waves . . .,* said that oceanographers call this the "global journey" of the Thermohaline Circulation, which is run by heat and salt (268). It is called a conveyor belt because warm water moves north on surface currents and then back south in deep cold-water currents, folding over itself like a conveyor belt. The heat has a drastic effect on the climate for the Northern Hemisphere. Without it, the average temperature would be much lower.

The writer takes the knowledge level of his audience into account and provides explanations of scientific concepts. He supports his ideas with research.

The mechanisms by which the current works are very simple. As the water moves north, it cools down. In addition, its salinity rises because winds that blow east to west across the equator transport moisture from the Atlantic to the Pacific, leaving the Atlantic more saline. The water that feeds the Atlantic from the Mediterranean is also salty because it is nearly landlocked and moisture evaporates from the Mediterranean, leaving it saltier (Mayewski 105). As the temperature decreases and salinity increases, the water becomes denser, causing it to sink. As it sinks, it spreads out deep in the ocean basin where it is pulled back toward the equator, thus creating the conveyor-like characteristics. . . .

The writer uses chronological order to explain the way the ocean currents work.

Go Online
Read More
For: the complete student model
Visit: www.PHSchool.com
Web Code: epm-4202

Editing and Proofreading

Check your draft for errors in spelling, grammar, and punctuation.
Focus on Sentence Clarity: Ensure that your sentences are clear by checking that the subjects agree with the verbs. In addition, be sure that every sentence expresses a complete thought.

Publishing and Presenting

Consider one of the following ways to share your work with others:
Present your essay. Use photographs, charts, and diagrams to help you explain the topic of your article. Include definitions of any challenging or specialized vocabulary your listeners will need to know in order to understand the information. Ask friends in the audience to provide feedback notes on your presentation.
Submit your essay for publication. If your essay focuses on a matter of local interest, send it to your school or community newspaper.

Prentice Hall Writing and Grammar Connection: Chapter 10

Reflecting on Your Writing

Writer's Journal Think about your experience of writing a cause-and-effect essay. Begin by answering these questions:
- What organizational strategy would you recommend to someone writing a cause-and-effect essay? Why?
- During the process of writing, what fresh information did you learn about the subject you chose?

Rubric for Self-Assessment

To assess your cause-and-effect essay, use the following rubric:

Criteria	Rating Scale				
	not very				*very*
Focus: How clearly do you identify and explore the cause-and-effect relationship?	1	2	3	4	5
Organization: How logical is your organization?	1	2	3	4	5
Support/Elaboration: How effective are your facts, details, and reasons?	1	2	3	4	5
Style: How well do you use transitional words and phrases?	1	2	3	4	5
Conventions: How correct is your grammar, especially your use of subject-verb agreement?	1	2	3	4	5

Writing Workshop ■ 379

Tips for Test Taking

Tell students that one of the last things they should do during the proofreading stage is to run the spell check on their computers. Emphasize, however, that the spell check does not catch all spelling errors. For example, the spell check will not recognize whether the word *your* is incorrectly used in place of the word *you're*. After using the spell check, it is essential for students to carefully proofread for additional spelling errors.

Editing and Proofreading

- Have students check for subject-verb agreement in their essays by circling each subject and each verb. Tell students to correct any errors they find.
- Also ask students to identify the subject and predicate in each sentence to help them identify incomplete sentences.

Six Traits Focus

Ideas		Word Choice	
Organization	✔	Sentence Fluency	
Voice		Conventions	✔

ASSESS

Publishing and Presenting

- Suggest that students consider adding flow charts to their essays to show the sequence of events. Have students refer to the Cause-and-Effect Flowchart in **Graphic Organizer Transparencies** on page 233.
- If students choose to submit their essays for publication in newspapers, advise them that they may need to restructure their essays into letters-to-the-editor. Tell students that they must state their topics early in the letters, and they must give their opinions about their topics.

Reflecting on Your Writing

- Engage the class in a discussion about the benefits of a cause-and-effect essay. Have students reflect on whether they believe that the cause-and-effect text structure leads to a thorough examination of a topic.
- Encourage students to reflect on how their attitudes toward their topics changed as a result of the writing process.

Writing and Grammar, Gold Level
Students will find additional guidance for editing and proofreading and publishing and presenting a cause-and-effect essay in Chapter 10, Sections 5 and 6.

Evaluate the Content

- Point out that understanding the author's purpose is as important in a speech as it is in any other form of communication.

- Tell students that evaluating arguments in a speech is important. **Ask:** Why is evaluating arguments so important when evaluating a speech?
Possible response: If the arguments are not well developed and well supported, the speech may misinform or encourage inappropriate action.

Evaluate the Delivery

- Encourage students to notice how a speaker uses his or her voice and body language. **Ask:** Why do the uses of voice and hand gestures or body language help deliver a speaker's message?
Possible response: They can hold the audience's attention and can help to emphasize a point the speaker makes.

- Encourage students to notice how a speaker uses his or her voice to hold an audience's attention.

Activity

Encourage students to support their evaluations with examples from the speech.

Assess the Activity

To evaluate students' analysis, use the **Listening: Evaluating a Persuasive Presentation** rubric, p. 79 in *General Resources*.

Evaluating a Speech

When you hear a formal speech or an informal talk, strive to be an active listener. Assess the credibility of the message and the effectiveness of the speaker's techniques. Learning how to evaluate a speech will give you a solid basis for improving your own oral presentations.

Evaluate Content

Create a context. Consider the following questions:

- What is the speaker's purpose?
- What knowledge, experience, or preparation equips the speaker to address the subject?
- What traditional, cultural, or historical influences shape the message?
- As a listener, what prior knowledge do you bring to the speaker's topic?

Evaluate the development of arguments. A good speaker presents arguments that are clearly stated, logically developed, and fully supported with evidence in the form of facts, statistics, anecdotes, and expert opinion. As an active listener, ask yourself whether the speaker's information is accurate, complete, and relevant. Assess whether the speaker's use of facts is fair and responsible or biased. Learn to anticipate weaknesses in certain types of arguments.

Evaluate Delivery

Note the speaker's choice of language. Listen for the speaker's use of words and phrases with positive or negative connotations, or associations. Note repetition of key words or stress given to certain phrases. Be alert to the fact that some speakers, as a substitute for good evidence or logical argument, may rely on emotionally "loaded" language.

Note the speaker's technique. A speech is more than words. Use the following questions to analyze nonverbal elements:

- Is the speaker's tone of voice, word choice, and rate of speaking appropriate for the audience, subject, and occasion?
- What is the effect of the speaker's nonverbal signals, such as eye contact, facial expressions, and gestures?
- When and why does the speaker pause, speak more loudly or softly, or speak more rapidly or slowly?

Type of Argument	Potential Flaw
Analogy: Compares one situation to another	Are the two situations really alike?
Authority: Cites the opinion of an expert	Is the expert knowledgeable and unbiased?
Emotion: Appeals to the audience's feelings	Is the full argument balanced between logic and emotion?
Causation: Shows a cause-and-effect relationship	Does the speaker oversimplify his or her arguments?

Activity **Analyze a Speech** With several classmates, view a political speech or a televised editorial. Using the evaluation tools from this workshop, assess the content and delivery of the speech, and generate a list of positive and negative points.

380 ■ Short Stories

Differentiated Instruction   Solutions for All Learners

Strategy for Advanced Readers
Explain that one way a speaker may support an argument is through the use of statistics. Explain that statistics provide information based on studies and may or may not be accurate. A listener must evaluate the source of the statistics and the validity of the statistic's use.

Point out that any statistics offered without a source or with a nonspecific source should not be trusted.

Write the following sentence on the board:

Three out of four doctors recommend brand X.

Ask: Is this statistic trustworthy? Why or why not?

Answer: The statistic is unreliable because the speaker provides no information about the study, such as, who conducted the study, how they conducted it, or who the doctors were.

Have students listen to a persuasive speech or a series of advertisements that use statistics. Then have them list the statistics and explain whether these statistics are reliable.

The Sea-Wolf and Selected Stories

Jack London
Signet Classic, 1964

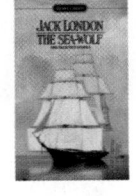

The Sea-Wolf is considered one of the greatest sea stories ever written, possibly because every reader finds his or her own connection with the character. *The Sea-Wolf* has been described as an adventure novel, a love story, a morality tale, and a novel of the sea. Set aboard a seal-hunting ship on the desolate Pacific Ocean, the plot centers around Wolf Larson's struggle for survival against the powerful forces of nature.

Literature of the Expanding Frontier

Prentice Hall Anthology
Prentice Hall, 1999

From the Leatherstocking Tales to John Steinbeck, this anthology conveys the wonder, excitement, and heartbreak of the western expansion in America. Pioneer stories, folk tales, and stories of immigrants and the prairie all are pieces of this view of a different time and place.

The Sherlock Holmes Mysteries

Sir Arthur Conan Doyle
Signet Classic, 1985

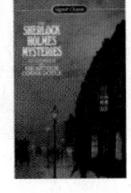

Sherlock Holmes is the 1800's equivalent of James Bond. He lives in London, uses logic and resourceful ploys to solve mysteries, and takes on cases that seem impossible to solve. These mysteries are part of the classic stories that started the genre of detective novels.

To Kill a Mockingbird

Harper Lee
Warner Books, 1982

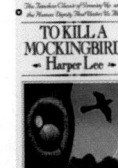

Set in the small Southern town of Maycomb, Alabama, during the Depression, *To Kill a Mockingbird* follows three years in the life of eight-year-old Scout Finch, her brother, Jem, and their father, Atticus—three years that encompass a mysterious neighbor, their father defending a young black man, and threats against Jem and Scout.

These titles are available in the Penguin/Prentice Hall Literature Library. Consult your teacher before choosing one.

Planning Students' Further Reading

Discussions of literature can raise sensitive and often controversial issues. Before you recommend further reading to your students, consider the values and sensitivities of your community as well as the age, ability, and sophistication of your students. It is also good policy to preview literature before you recommend it to students. The notes below offer some guidance on specific titles.

[L4] *The Sea-Wolf and Selected Stories* This volume includes scenes of violence and cruelty. Explain that these scenes provide an unsentimental look at the "darker" or "less civilized" side of human beings. Point out that London uses such scenes to provide insights about good and evil.

Lexile: 1020L

[L3] *Literature of the Expanding Frontier* Two sensitive topics raised in "Tennessee's Partner" are capital punishment and gender bias. The woman the hero marries has no real significance to him. The author makes her one dimensional and completely dispensable. In "Spirits of the Railway," issues of racism may disturb some students. In the excerpt from "The Life and Adventures of Nat Love," racial terms like "half-breed" and "colored" may prove controversial. In "Flight," name-calling leads to physical violence that some students may find disturbing.

Reading level appropriate for high school students

[L2] *The Sherlock Holmes Mysteries* The stories focus on murders and other crimes. Some feature drinking, drug use, infidelity and other betrayals, insensitive language, ethnic and sexual stereotypes, negative descriptions of immigrants, and insensitive descriptions of physical deformities.

Reading level appropriate for high school students

[L1, L2, EL] *To Kill a Mockingbird* Lee's novel contains some profanity and offensive racial terminology. The plot focuses on Tom Robinson, an African American accused of attempting to rape a white woman. This drama plays out in a setting in which African Americans have little chance of receiving justice.

Lexile: 870L

Professional Development

Literature Circles

Consider creating literature circles using the books on this page. Literature circles are an excellent way to foster independent reading and responding within a collaborative group environment. Students in literature circles not only collaborate to discover meaning; they develop responsibility and also have the pleasure of reading a good book and discussing it.

A literature circle is a temporary group formed to read and discuss books. The circle meets regularly, and each student takes on a specific role in the literature circle discussion. These discussions, based on students' own responses, involve a minimum of teacher intervention. While literature circles have a structure and specified roles, they can be modified to accommodate a variety of circumstances and needs.

See *General Resources*, pp. 21–23, for further guidance on setting up literature circles.

Using *On Your Own*

You may use this On Your Own feature in one of the following ways:

- For independent reading
- To reinforce/reteach one of the reading skills in this unit

Promote Independent Reading

Independent reading gives students an opportunity to practice the reading skills taught in this unit and to improve comprehension. When students read independently, they also increase their vocabulary and develop their own personal reading interests.

You may assign this selection to be read independently for homework, in class when students have completed other work, or for independent group work.

Develop Reading Preferences

After students have read this selection, ask them what they enjoyed about it. Build on their ideas to recommend further reading. Students who enjoy this selection might also enjoy reading about famous historical figures or the lives of artists.

Humanities

Self Portrait in the Studio,
c. 1794–95, by Francisco de Goya

Francisco de Goya (1746–1828) was a Spanish painter known for his realistic portrayal of life in the late eighteenth and early nineteenth centuries. He is considered a pioneer in the move to realistic vs. idealistic images in portraits. Use this question for discussion:

Since this painting is a self-portrait, this is how Goya saw himself. In what way does this self-portrait demonstrate realism rather than idealism?

Possible response: The portrait shows the artist with his foibles and flaws in his daily world. It also reveals his creative ingenuity, which prompted the invention of the lighted candle hat. An idealized image would probably not include such subject matter which, while clever, is also comical.

Think About It When you think of famous painters, you might imagine humorless people who work hard at producing serious "art." If that is the case, your imagination may be wrong! This poem by a contemporary American poet reveals the comic side of the great Spanish painter Francisco Goya (1746–1828). As you read this poem, think about why Goya would paint himself wearing this bizarre invention.

Candle Hat

Billy Collins

In most self-portraits it is the face that dominates:
Cézanne is a pair of eyes swimming in brushstrokes,
Van Gogh stares out of a halo of swirling darkness,
Rembrandt looks relieved, as if he were taking a breather
5 from painting *The Blinding of Samson.*

But in this one Goya stands well back from the mirror
and is seen posed in the clutter of his studio
addressing a canvas tilted back on a tall easel.

He appears to be smiling out at us as if he knew
10 we would be amused by the extraordinary hat on his head
which is fitted around the brim with candle holders,
a device that allowed him to work into the night.

You can only wonder what it would be like
to be wearing such a chandelier on your head
15 as if you were a walking dining room or concert hall.

But once you see this hat there is no need to read
any biography of Goya or to memorize his dates.

382 ■ *Short Stories*

Differentiated Instruction   Solutions for All Learners

Strategy for Less Proficient Readers
Poetry is a less familiar genre for many people. Comprehending the ideas in a poem can be difficult for inexperienced readers. Have students read one stanza at a time. Then, have them write the main idea for each stanza on a piece of paper. After they have read all the stanzas and figured out the main ideas, have students read the entire poem to appreciate the artistic, poetic elements.

Enrichment for Advanced Readers
Point out that, like many poems, "Candle Hat" does not rhyme. Explain that this poem is an example of free verse, or a poem that has no fixed meter or rhyme scheme. Challenge students to take a stanza and rewrite it using a pattern of rhyme and meter. Allow time for students to share their new versions.

To understand Goya you only have to imagine him
lighting the candles one by one, then placing
20 the hat on his head, ready for a night of work.

Imagine him surprising his wife with his new invention,
then laughing like a birthday cake when she saw the glow.

Imagine him flickering through the rooms of his house
with all the shadows flying across the walls.

25 Imagine a lost traveler knocking on his door
one dark night in the hill country of Spain.
"Come in," he would say, "I was just painting myself,"
as he stood in the doorway holding up the wand of a brush,
illuminated in the blaze of his famous candle hat.

Meet the Author

Billy Collins (b. 1941) served as the Poet Laureate of the United States from 2001 to 2003, and he has won many other awards and honors for his poetry. Collins often uses humor in his work, a quality that has helped endear him to readers and changed many people's notions about poetry.

Readings in Contemporary Poetry
Talk About It

Use these questions to guide a discussion of "Candle Hat."

1. **(a)** In what main way is Goya's self-portrait different from other self-portraits? **(b)** What information about himself was Goya able to show because of this difference?

2. **(a)** Explain what the poet means by this statement: "Once you see this hat there is no need to read / any biography of Goya." **(b)** Do you agree? Why or why not?

3. In a group, discuss the role that art and artists can play in society.
   • In what ways was Goya's candle hat a fresh solution to a problem?
   • Why do you think the poet uses the word "Imagine" to begin the first line of the last three stanzas of the poem?
   • Is imagination important to society? Explain.
   • Imagine you are the "lost traveler." What would you say about the artist when you returned home? Explain.

   Choose a point-person to share your group's ideas with the class.

On Your Own: Readings in Contemporary Poetry ■ 383

Extend the Lesson

Write a Poem

Point out that a person or pet with an interesting personality makes a good topic for a poem. Ask students to choose a person or pet to use as the subject of a poem. Remind students that a poem can have a pattern of rhythm and rhyme or can be written in free verse. Tell them to identify one or two character traits and then to show the traits through description and action, rather than telling readers about the trait (Show, don't tell!). Remind students that readers make inferences based on information that they read combined with experiences in their own lives. Allow time for students to share their poems.

Introduce Unit 3

- Tell students that all nonfiction is based on the premise that the concepts and evidence presented by the author are factual. An author may include anecdotes that are fictional, ideals that are personal, or language that is poetic, yet the assertion of all nonfiction—whether essays, articles, or speeches—is that it is true.
- Tell students that as they read the nonfiction in this unit, they will become more proficient in recognizing the techniques of narrative, reflective, and persuasive writing.

Instructional Resources

Unit 3 Resources support students in mastering the unit skills and help you assess students' progress.

▶ **Progress Monitoring** These tests enable you to assess and monitor student progress in each part:

- **Diagnostic test** • **Benchmark test**

▶ **Vocabulary Warm-ups** Additional vocabulary support, based on Lexile scores of vocabulary words, is provided for each selection.

- **Word List A and Practice A** provide activities for students reading two grades below level.
- **Word List B and Practice B** provide activities for students reading one grade below level.

▶ **Reading Warm-ups** Two Reading Warm-ups for each selection provide a context for students to apply newly learned vocabulary. Each Reading Warm-up consists of a short reading passage. Questions and activities guide students to focus on particular vocabulary items.

- **Reading Warm-up A**, for students reading two grades below level, focuses on the vocabulary items presented in Vocabulary Warm-up A.
- **Reading Warm-up B**, for students reading one grade below level, focuses on the vocabulary items presented in Vocabulary Warm-up B.

▶ **Selection Support** These practice pages are available for each selection:

- **Reading Skills**
- **Literary Analysis**
- **Vocabulary Builder**
- **Support for Writing**
- **Support for Extend Your Learning**
- **Enrichment**

PRENTICE HALL
TeacherEXPRESS™ You may also
Plan · Teach · Assess access these
resources on TeacherExpress.

384

Unit 3

Types of Nonfiction:
Essays, Articles, and Speeches

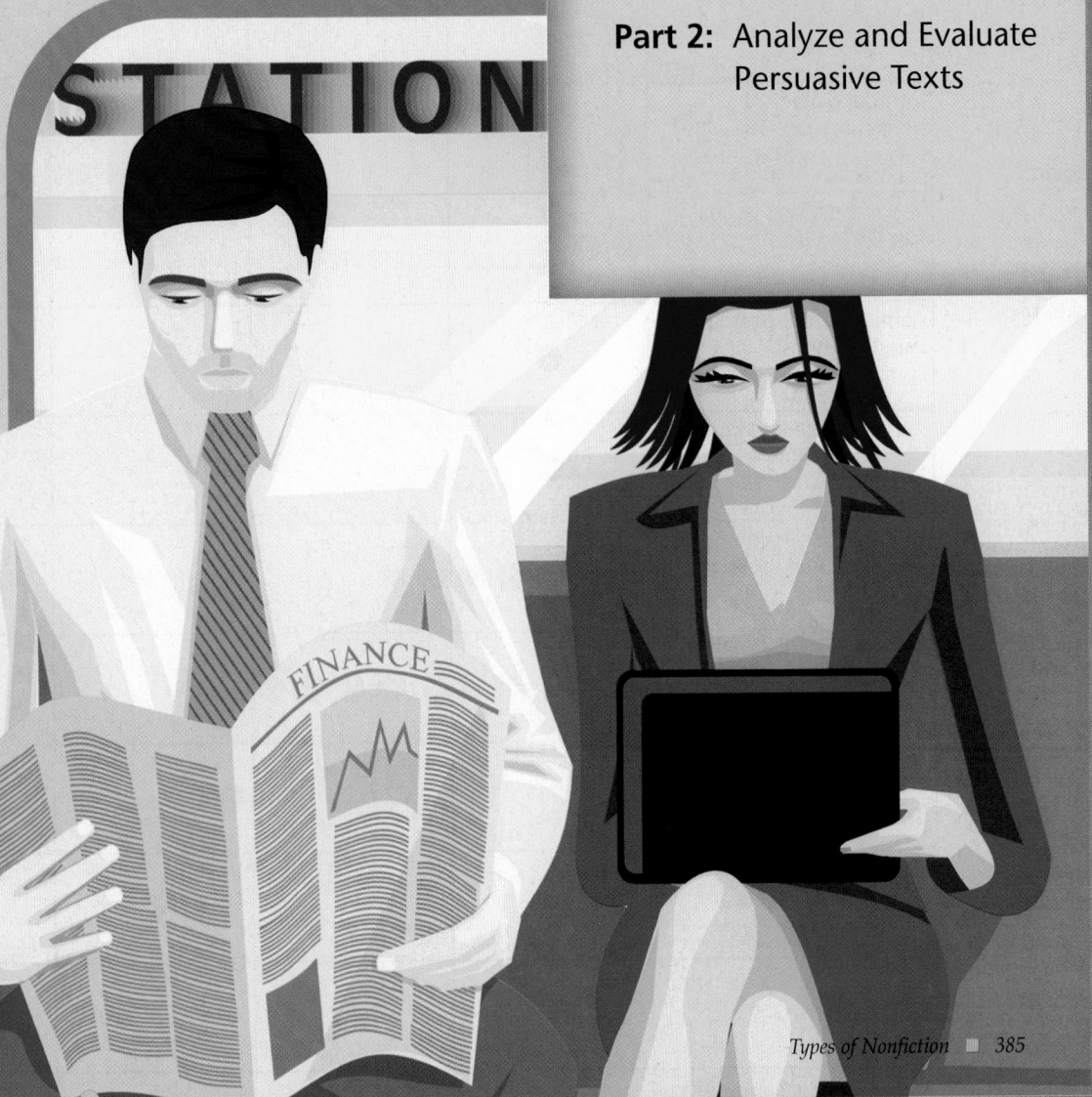

Unit 3 Overview

Introduction
Exploring Essays

Part 1: Identify Main Idea and Supporting Details

Part 2: Analyze and Evaluate Persuasive Texts

Types of Nonfiction ■ 385

Unit 3 Overview
Genre Focus

Author Rebecca Walker introduces the literary genre, nonfiction, with a model essay. Students read and analyze examples of essays, articles, and speeches.

Using the Unit Selections

Teach Skills Instructional selections are presented in sets of two. To teach the skills and meet the objectives, you need to complete only one selection in each set.

Differentiate and Reinforce Choose the selection in a set that is best suited to your students. The selections are listed by accessibility in the Differentiated Instruction box below. You may use the other selection in the set to reinforce comprehension and skills or to provide enrichment.

Integrate Skills Each selection set gives students a reading strategy, literary analysis, and vocabulary development as well as opportunities for writing about the selection, research and technology, listening and speaking, grammar, and assessment practice.

See pages 399 and 471 for an overview of the skills in each part.

Using the Unit Features

These additional reading selections give you the opportunity to apply, reinforce, and extend the unit skills.

Reading Informational Materials Students learn to analyze and evaluate informational texts.

Comparing Literary Works Students read a pair of literary works to compare the treatment of a literary element.

On Your Own Students may read this selection independently, or you may teach it actively to reinforce a unit reading skill.

See the Unit 3 Overview and Pacing Plan on the following pages.

Differentiated Instruction   Solutions for All Learners

Accessibility for Ability Levels
This chart gives a general accessibility rating to help you decide which selection is more appropriate for your students. For additional guidance on factors that affect the accessibility of each selection, see the **Time and Resource Manager** for each selection set.

	More Accessible	More Challenging
Part 1		
Set 1	A Celebration of Grandfathers	On Summer
Set 2	Single Room, Earth View	The News
Part 2		
Set 1	Carry Your Own Skis	Libraries Face Sad Chapter
Set 2	I Have a Dream	First Inaugural Address

Meeting Your Standards

Students will

1. **recognize and appreciate essays as a literary genre.**
2. **read and analyze a variety of essays.**
3. **apply reading skills.**
   - Identifying main idea and supporting details
     - Generate questions prior to reading
     - Rereading to identify the main idea and supporting details
   - Analyze and evaluate persuasive appeals
     - Rereading to analyze and evaluate persuasive appeals
     - Reading aloud
4. **analyze literary elements.**
   - Author's style
   - Expository essay
   - Persuasive essay
   - Persuasive speech
5. **build vocabulary.**
   - Prefixes
6. **learn elements of grammar, usage, and style.**
7. **use a recursive writing process to write in a variety of forms.**
   - Business letter
   - Editorial
8. **read informational materials.**
   - Reading for specific information
   - Distinguishing fact from opinion
9. **compare literary works.**
   - Biographical writing
   - Humorous essay
10. **use technology to do research.**
    - Annotated map
    - Journal entries
    - Comparative chart
    - Annotated source list
11. **develop listening and speaking skills.**
    - Panel discussion
    - Informal presentation
    - Persuasive speech
    - News report
12. **develop spelling proficiency.**

Unit Introduction and Part 1	Week 1					Week 2					Week 3				
	1	2	3	4	5	1	2	3	4	5	1	2	3	4	5
Introduce the Unit author: Rebecca Walker (pp. 386–387).	●														
Introduce types of nonfiction (pp. 388–389).	●														
Teach the Model selection (pp. 391–396).	●	●													
Administer the Unit 3, Part 1 Diagnostic Test.			●												
Introduce the Reading and Vocabulary Skills for Part 1 (pp. 400–401).			●												
Teach one selection from Set 1 (pp. 404–419).			●	●	●	●	●								
Teach one selection from Set 2 (pp. 426–441).							●	●	●	●					
Teach Reading Informational Materials (pp. 446–448).											●				
Teach Comparing Literary Works (pp. 452–462).												●	●		
Complete the Reading and Vocabulary Review (pp. 464–465).														●	
Have students complete the Writing Workshop (pp. 466–470).											●	●	●	●	●
Administer the Unit 3, Part 1 Benchmark Test.															●

Part 2	W1·1	W1·2	W1·3	W1·4	W1·5	W2·1	W2·2	W2·3	W2·4	W2·5	W3·1	W3·2	W3·3	W3·4	W3·5
Administer the Unit 3, Part 2 Diagnostic Test.	●														
Introduce the Reading and Vocabulary Skills for Part 2 (pp. 472–473).	●														
Teach one selection from Set 1 (pp. 476–487).		●	●	●	●										
Teach one selection from Set 2 (pp. 494–509).						●	●	●	●						
Teach Reading Informational Materials (pp. 514–518).										●					
Teach Comparing Literary Works (pp. 522–530).											●	●			
Complete the Reading and Vocabulary Review (pp. 532–533).													●		
Have students complete the Writing Workshop (pp. 536–543).											●	●	●	●	●
Have students complete the Communications Workshop (p. 544).														●	
Have students complete the Spelling Workshop (pp. 534–535).														●	
Administer the Unit 3, Part 2 Benchmark Test.															●

Options for Block and Daily Scheduling

The assignments and activities in this unit planner are organized by week. You may adjust them to your daily or block schedule. The Time and Resource Managers for the selection sets give specific times to help your planning.

Options for Independent Reading

Use these independent reading options to differentiate, reinforce, and extend your instruction:

On Your Own

Students may read this selection on their own or you may use it to reteach and reinforce unit skills.

"Cheerful Gift Becomes a Tradition"

For Further Reading

Have students choose and read a full-length work while working on this unit.

[L1, L2, EL] Erik Weihenmayer, *Touch the Top of the World*

[L2] Sojourner Truth, *Narrative of Sojourner Truth*

[L3] John Phillip Santos, *Places Left Unfinished at the Time of Creation*

[L4] Prentice Hall, *Biography and Autobiography Anthology*

[L4] Authors in Depth

Rudolfo Anaya, from *A New Mexico Christmas*, "At a Crossroads," from *A Chicano in China*

[L1] Special Needs Students
[L2] Below-Level Students
[L3] All Students
[L4] Above-Level Students
[EL] English Learners

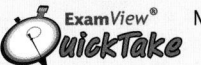

PRENTICE HALL
Teacher**EXPRESS**™
Plan · Teach · Assess
Use this complete suite of powerful teaching tools to make lesson planning and testing quicker and easier.

ExamView®
QuickTake
Monitor student progress instantly.

Students will

1. understand the characteristics, types, and purposes of essays, articles, and speeches.

2. learn about author Rebecca Walker.

3. read and analyze an example of an essay.

4. build vocabulary.

5. begin the process of writing a business letter.

🐧 **From the Author's Desk**

❶ **Introduce Rebecca Walker**

• Award-winning writer Rebecca Walker is the author of *To Be Real: Telling the Truth and Changing the Face of Feminism,* an anthology of feminist essays. Her articles about race, identity, and culture have appeared in major national magazines and anthologies.

• Use the *From the Author's Desk DVD* to introduce the author and the genre. Show Segment 2 to provide insight into Walker's opinion on what constitutes a good essay. **Ask:** According to Walker, what are the characteristics of a good essay?

Answer: Walker believes that a good essay will relay information, reinterpret ideas, and make the reader think about the subject in a different light.

• Interested students might enjoy these works by Rebecca Walker.

Black, White, and Jewish, Autobiography of a Shifting Self, an autobiography

Editor, *What Makes a Man: 22 Writers Imagine the Future,* a collection of essays about masculinity in America

❷ **Critical Viewing**

Possible responses: Some students may argue that the abstract quality of the image and the positioning of the text in the sky suggest the objectivity of articles. Others may assert that the interruption of the text by the little squares suggests the way in which personal emotions and thoughts "color" an essay.

Unit 3 Introduction: Types of Nonfiction

🐧 **From the Author's Desk**

Rebecca Walker
Talks About the Forms

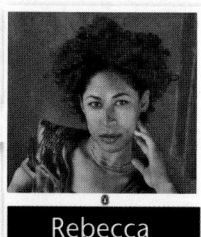

❶

Rebecca Walker is a writer and an activist whose works have been widely anthologized.

I have written both **articles,** brief nonfiction pieces often found in periodicals, and **essays,** nonfiction works of greater literary value in which authors express their emotions and thoughts. While I appreciate both forms, I am partial to the essay.

❸ **Comparing Articles and Essays**

The essay allows for the sharing of personal experience, the expression of emotion, and the subsequent creation of a subtle intimacy between author and reader. Some of the best essays are akin to life-changing conversations between parent and child, or teacher and student. Even after the author has died, her voice can reach through time to transform the reader.

While essays and articles both give accountings of real life, articles tend to be more objective in tone. They focus on the *what, when, where* and *why* of a particular situation, rather than on what the author feels about the answers to any of these questions.

Although the author undoubtedly has a point of view, he or she strives for an objective rendering of fact.

An essay draws the reader into the author's world, pointing, suggesting, persuading. An article observes and presents, and leaves the reader to make up her own mind.

❷ ◀ **Critical Viewing** Walker distinguishes between the objectivity of articles and the personal quality of essays. Which of these two forms does this image seem to represent? Why? **[Connect]**

386 ■ *Types of Nonfiction*

Teaching Resources

The following resources can be used to enrich, extend, or differentiate the instruction for the Unit Introduction and Model Selection.

Unit 3 Resources, pp. 1–13

General Resources, p. 6

Graphic Organizer Transparencies, pp. 81–82

From the Author's Desk DVD
   Rebecca Walker, Segments 1 and 2

Reader's Notebook

Reader's Notebook: Adapted Version

Reader's Notebook: English Learner's version

Listening to Literature Audio CD

Adapted Reader's Notebook Audio CD

❹ Essays That Engage and Challenge the Reader

I have always loved essays in which the author uses his personal experience to challenge the reader to think about the world in a different way. By sharing intimate details of his private life, the author invites the reader to empathize with him and, as a result, to support his conclusions.

Because I believe that most human beings change their feelings long before they change their minds, it seems undeniable that the creation of this emotional link is vital to one's impact as an author.

For example, in 1881 Frederick Douglass forwarded the abolitionist cause by sensitizing readers to the plight of enslaved African-Americans in his deeply personal essay "My Escape from Slavery." And in 1929 Virginia Woolf convinced readers that women deserved autonomy by sharing her own longing for a modest space and small income in *A Room of One's Own*.

> *Intellectual freedom depends upon material things. Poetry depends upon intellectual freedom. And women have always been poor, not for two hundred years merely, but from the beginning of time. Women have had less intellectual freedom than the sons of Athenian slaves. . . . That is why I have laid so much stress on money and a room of one's own.*
>
> **from *A Room of One's Own***
> —*Virginia Woolf*

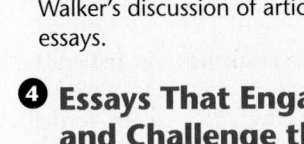

These are just two of the authors and essays that affected the consciousness of entire generations, prompting not just individual enlightenment, but larger political reform. I admire the way these authors used their own lives as the basis for the theories they espoused. In essence they ask the reader: Shouldn't society be constructed to ensure my happiness, too?

More About Rebecca Walker

When she was 25, Rebecca Walker (b. 1969) was named by *Time* magazine as one of fifty influential American leaders under the age of forty. Her essays and articles have appeared in many magazines and publications, and her books are taught in high schools and colleges in the United States and Canada. She has received awards for both her writing and her work as an advocate for young women. As Walker's essay "Before Hip-Hop Was Hip-Hop" shows, she has a lively interest in youth culture.

Fast Facts

▶ In 1992, Walker co-founded the Third Wave Foundation, dedicated to empowering women aged 15–30 through scholarship grants and project funding.
▶ In 1997, Walker appeared in the film *Primary Colors*.

From the Author's Desk: Rebecca Walker ■ 387

TEACH

❸ Rebecca Walker Talks About the Forms
Introduce Articles and Essays

- Explore students' knowledge of articles and essays by making connections to what they know. Invite students to give examples of articles and essays that they have read.

- **Ask:** Would a short nonfiction work on the subject of the death penalty be considered an essay or an article?

  Answer: It would be considered an essay if it provided the author's perspective on the death penalty. If it reported on how many people supported and opposed the death penalty, and listed their reasons, it would be an article.

- Have students read Rebecca Walker's discussion of articles and essays.

❹ Essays That Engage and Challenge the Reader

- Point out the heading and read aloud the first paragraph of this section. **Ask** students what it means for the writer of an essay to engage and challenge the reader.
  Possible response: To engage a reader means to catch the reader's attention. To challenge a reader means to present material that makes the reader think deeply or consider a new opinion.

- **"A Room of One's Own"** Virginia Woolf's 1929 essay, though written over 75 years ago, still speaks to women and writers everywhere.
  Ask: How does this quotation from "A Room of One's Own" "challenge the reader to think about the world in a different way"?
  Possible response: The quotation challenges readers to think about what women could achieve if they had both intellectual freedom and the material resources to take advantage of that freedom.

Go Online **For:** An online video
Author Link **Visit:** www.PHSchool.com
Web Code: epe-8301
Give students this Web Code for a video clip of Rebecca Walker.

387

❺ Characteristics of Essays, Articles, and Speeches

- Tell students that essays, articles, and speeches are often used to inform or persuade an audience. In general, articles present information more directly, while speeches and essays often blend information and opinion.

- Explain to students that essays can be short or long, formal and informal, and can cover a wide range of topics and purposes.

- Point out the discussion of style, tone, perspective, and purpose. Tell students that these four elements make up a writer's "voice," or personal way of communicating with the audience.

- **Ask** students how different audiences might react to the "voice" the writer uses in an essay or speech.
  Possible response: An audience of teachers or politicians might react positively to a serious, formal tone. An audience of young people might prefer a livelier or more dramatic style of presentation.

- As students read the selection, tell them to think about the style, tone, perspective, and purpose of the essay.

Exploring Types of Nonfiction

❺ Essays, Articles, and Speeches

Essays and articles are short works of nonfiction. Their authors are usually identified and are always real people. Speeches are nonfiction literary works that are delivered by a speaker to an audience.

- An **essay** examines and discusses a focused topic, often including the writer's personal viewpoints.

- An **article** provides information about a topic, person, or event.

- A **speech**—written to be read aloud—presents a topic and may persuade, inform, explain, or entertain.

The writer contributes more than information to nonfiction.

- **Style** is the particular way in which a writer uses language. Style reflects an author's personality. Factors that contribute to an author's style include level of formality, use of figurative language, diction or word choice, sentence patterns, and methods of organization.

- **Tone** is the author's attitude toward both the subject and readers or listeners. In conversations, you can hear a speaker's tone in the way words and phrases are spoken. When reading, you can "hear" tone in an author's choice of words and details. The tone of a literary work can often be described with a single word such as: *pompous, playful, serious, personal, sarcastic,* or *friendly.*

- **Perspective** is the viewpoint or opinion an author expresses about the subject, either directly or indirectly. **Bias** occurs when a writer makes a one-sided presentation (for example, by ignoring relevant facts or by using emotional language that unfairly sways readers' or listeners' feelings).

- **Purpose** is the author's reason for writing. Common purposes are to inform, to persuade, to honor, to entertain, to explain, and to warn.

❻ Types of Essays

Essays can be categorized by the author's purpose. These are common essay types:

- A **narrative essay** tells a story of actual events or an individual's life experiences.
- A **descriptive essay** creates an impression about a person, an object, or an experience by presenting physical details of sight, sound, smell, touch, or taste.
- An **expository essay** provides information, discusses ideas, or explains a process.
- A **persuasive essay** attempts to convince readers to take a specific course of action or adopt the writer's viewpoint.
- A **reflective essay** expresses the writer's thoughts and feelings in response to a personal experience or to an idea.

Check Your Understanding

Choose the letter of the answer that best matches each numbered item. Discuss your answers with a partner.

1. Formal, friendly, or casual   **a.** style   **b.** descriptive
2. Encouraging polite behavior   **a.** essay   **b.** bias
3. Retelling a historical event   **a.** persuasive   **b.** narrative
4. Explaining how Congress votes   **a.** expository   **b.** reflective
5. Comic, mysterious, or doubtful   **a.** tone   **b.** article

Exploring Types of Nonfiction 389

❻ Types of Essays

- Read through the list of essay types in the text. Tell students that they may also see the noun forms of the words: narration, description, exposition, persuasion, and reflection.

- Discuss how a writer might use more than one type of writing in a single essay.
  Possible response: A writer might include expository writing in a persuasive essay to explain the reasons he or she supports a viewpoint. A narrative essay might include descriptive passages to help readers picture an event the writer is discussing.

- If time permits, distribute copies of an essay from a news or current events magazine or your school newspaper. Invite students to discuss the author's purpose and the tone and style the writing displays.

- Tell students that as they read the selection on pp. 391–396, they should form opinions about the type of essay it is, and about the writer's style, tone, perspective, and purpose.

ASSESS

Answers

1. a
2. a
3. b
4. a
5. a

Differentiated Instruction   Solutions for All Learners

Support for Special Needs Students
Have students read the **Exploring Types of Nonfiction** pages in the *Reader's Notebook: Adapted Version*. This version provides a basic-level introduction to fiction and nonfiction.

Support for Less Proficient Readers
Have students read the **Exploring Types of Nonfiction** pages in the *Reader's Notebook*. This version provides a basic-level introduction to fiction and nonfiction.

Support for English Learners
Have students read the **Exploring Types of Nonfiction** pages in the *Reader's Notebook: English Learner's Version*. This version provides a basic-level introduction to fiction and nonfiction.

From the Author's Desk

❶ Introduce the Selection

- Invite students to read Rebecca Walker's introduction to the essay.

- Point out that Walker says a personal essay is "a revelation of the distinct imprint of her mind."

- **Ask:** Based on this comment, what kind of purpose and tone do you expect this essay will have?
Possible response: The essay's purpose will probably be to express a personal insight and the tone may be friendly to engage the reader.

❷ Background

Youth Culture The concept of "teenagers" arose only recently. Formerly, when children were old enough to work, they entered the world of adults. Now, adult rights and privileges come only when a person reaches the late teen years. Caught between childhood and adulthood, teens in each new generation develop their own vision of themselves.

❸ Connecting to the Literature

- Have students talk about the elements of youth culture in your area. Ask students to write a few sentences about how they define their own culture. To develop expressive vocabulary, tell students to use as least three of the following words: *assemble, commit, identify, persist, provoke,* and *transmit.*

- To further develop students' expressive vocabulary, suggest that they also use two of these words: *decade, dynamic, rhythm,* and *stereotype.*

- To help students understand the meanings of the words they are asked to use, give them these sentences:

  1. Music *provokes* strong feelings because it appeals to the mind and the senses.

  2. You should *commit* to values you believe in, such as peace and honesty.

  3. One *stereotype* about teens is that they take too many risks.

From the Author's Desk
Rebecca Walker Introduces "Before Hip-Hop Was Hip-Hop"

Writing is a lonely profession. A typical day for most writers does not include the lively banter enjoyed by those who work in brightly lit offices and interact in meeting rooms, elevators, and cafeterias.

A Portrait of the Writer at Work
We sit, usually completely alone, in our grand or modest workspaces, maybe with a cat or dog at our feet, a cup of tea or a bottle of water by the mousepad.

More often than not we work in silence, or maybe to the low hum of the television or the repetitive drone of a particularly evocative piece of music. We begin with a blank screen or piece of paper. If we are lucky, we have had some thought we find worthy, but more often we have not, and spend the next hours willing insight to dawn.

Purpose, Diction, Tone, and Level of Formality
Once we have a **purpose** and a direction, then the next bit of work begins: the arduous hunt for the **diction,** the words that can adequately express our still largely unborn revelation. Now we are looking for a feeling, a **tone** that will both track our thought and unlock its emotive power.

The choices we make in those moments—with what **level of formality** we will address the reader, what type of language we will employ, what **narrative structure** we will devise—all these and more create an experience. The result, like what you are reading right now, is a kind of literary transmission of the writer's soul, a revelation of the distinct imprint of her mind.

My Essay: A Different Perspective on Hip-Hop Culture
To face this hard and solitary work I must feel that I have something relevant to say. For instance, hip-hop culture is not often seen as a reflection of the deeply humanitarian impulses of urban youth. And yet I was there at its birth, I can testify to its noble roots. While writing the following essay I wondered, "If I don't tell this story, who will?"

Vocabulary Development

Vocabulary Knowledge Rating
Create a **Vocabulary Knowledge Rating Chart** with these words from the selection:

palpable	entrenched
bravado	lexicon

Give students a copy. Introduce the words by reading them aloud and having students mark their rating in the Before Reading column. Urge them to be alert to these words as they read and discuss the selection, because they will rate their knowledge of the words again after they finish.

If you wish, you may tally how many students know (or think they know) a word to gauge how much instruction you need to provide. As students read, point out the words and their context.

Before Hip-Hop Was Hip-Hop

Rebecca Walker

❻ If you ask most kids today about hip-hop, they'll spit out the names of recording artists they see on TV: Eminem, P. Diddy, J. Lo, Beyonce. They'll tell you about the songs they like and the clothes they want to buy. They'll tell you about the indisputable zones of hip-hop like "EO" (East Orange, New Jersey), the "ATL" (Atlanta, Georgia), and the "West Side" (Los Angeles, California), neighborhoods they feel they know because they've seen them in all the glossiest, "flossiest" music videos. Hip-hop is natural to these kids, like air or water, just there, a part of the digital landscape that streams through their lives.

I watch this cultural sea change with fascination. It astounds me that hip-hop has grown into a global industry, a force that dominates youth culture from Paris to Prague, Tokyo to Timbuktu. I can't

Rebecca Walker
Author's Insight
I chose to include slang to give the essay more flavor and authenticity. I wanted the reader to experience the language we created, not just read about it.

Before Hip-Hop Was Hip-Hop ■ 391

Differentiated Instruction Solutions for All Learners

Support for Special Needs Students
Have students read the adapted version of "Before Hip-Hop Was Hip-Hop" in the **Reader's Notebook: Adapted Version.** They may also listen to the adapted version on the **Reader's Notebook: Adapted Version Audio CD.**

Support for Less Proficient Readers
Have students read "Before Hip-Hop Was Hip-Hop" in the **Reader's Notebook.** After students finish the selection in the Reader's *Notebook,* have them complete the questions and activities in the Student Edition.

Support for English Learners
Have students read "Before Hip-Hop Was Hip-Hop" in the **Reader's Notebook: English Learner's Version.** English learners may also read the selection as they listen to the recorded version on the **Listening to Literature Audio CD.**

TEACH

❹ Motivation
- Invite students to share some of the statements they wrote about youth culture in your area.
- Then **ask:** Who creates youth culture: the bands that make the music and the designers who create the fashions, or the teens who buy the CDs and wear the styles?
  Possible response: Students may say that the bands and designers would not be successful without the support of the young people.

Concept Connector ➡
Students will follow up on this activity after completing the story.

❺ About the Selection
In "Before Hip-Hop Was Hip-Hop," Rebecca Walker addresses a topic that is seldom given serious attention: how young people created their own culture in the form of the hip-hop movement. Walker posits that, rather than a passing fad, hip-hop culture was a genuine expression of a new cosmopolitan sense of solidarity among urban American teens.

❻ Author's Insight
- Tell students that slang is a type of language that uses short-lived coinages and figures of speech in the place of standard terms.
- **Ask** students to point out examples of slang in the first paragraph.
  Answer: Students may mention the word "flossiest" and the abbreviations "EO" and "ATL."
- Then **ask** students why they think Walker says that slang adds "flavor and authenticity" to her essay.
  Possible response: Using slang is one method Walker employs to create a lively, engaging tone in her essay.

❼ Author's Insight

- Direct students' attention to Walker's comment. Point out the similarity between the West African word *hipi* and the English slang word *hippie*.

- Tell students that hippie culture of the 1960s and 1970s was one of the first youth cultures to develop in America.

- Have students **list** and **define** slang terms that were used during the hippie era.
  Possible responses: Students might list the words *groovy, far out, right on* (all signifying approval), *uptight* (tense, rigid), and *square* (old-fashioned).

- **Ask:** How does slang contribute to youth culture?
  Possible responses: Slang gives the youth community a shared language. Slang brings young people together and helps them communicate. Slang also marks youth culture as different from adult culture.

❽ Critical Viewing

Possible response: This image reflects a "cultural revolution" because the teenager is expressing himself through dance, and because people of different races, ages, and cultures are enjoying the performance.

---

believe that in small, all-white towns like Lincoln, Nebraska, high school boys wear their clothes in the latest "steelo": pants sagging off their waists, sports jerseys hanging to their knees, baseball hats cocked to one side. Even in the pueblos of Mexico, where mariachi bands and old school crooners still rule, it is hip-hop that sells cars, sodas, and children's toys on TV.

❼ The vast empire of hip-hop amazes me because I knew hip-hop before it was hip-hop. I was there when it all began.

Way back then, in what today's ninth graders might call the ancient eighties, there was no MTV or VH-1. We found out about music by listening to the radio, flipping through the stacks at the record store, or buying "mix tapes" from local deejays at two dollars apiece. Back then, we carried combs in our back pockets and clipped long strands of feathers to the belt loops of our designer jeans. We wore our names in cursive gold letters around our necks or in big brass letters on our belt buckles. We picked up words and inverted them, calling something that we thought was really cool, "hot," and something that had a whole lot of life, "def."

We didn't know a whole new language was rolling off our tongues as we flipped English upside down and pulled some Spanish and even a few words from Africa into our parlance. We didn't know that young people for years to come would recycle our fashions and sample the bass lines from our favorite tracks. We thought we were just being kids and expressing ourselves, showing the grown-ups we were different from them in a way that was safe and fun. In fact we were at the epicenter[1] of one of America's most significant cultural revolutions, making it happen. Who knew?

Not me.

❾ When I moved from Washington, D.C., to the Bronx the summer before seventh grade, I had one box of records, mostly albums I had ordered from the Columbia Record Club. In 1982, if you promised to buy a record a month for one whole year, the Club sent you eight records for a penny. I had Bruce Springsteen's "The River," REO Speedwagon's "The Letter,"

---

1. **epicenter** (ep´i sent´ ər) *n.* focal or central point.

392 ■ *Types of Nonfiction*

Rebecca Walker
Author's Insight
In college I learned that scholars believe the word "hip" comes from *hipi*, a word in the West African language Wolof. *Hipi* means "someone with his eyes open, aware of what is going on."

❽ ▼ Critical Viewing
How does this image suggest the author's belief that a "cultural revolution" was taking place? **[Infer]**

Vocabulary Development

Slang Terminology
Below is a list of some of the slang terms Walker has included in this essay. Students should define each of the following slang terms in their own words. Encourage students to use the context of the sentence to help them determine the meaning of each term.

flossiest	steelo
hot	def
flavor	sport
props	scratching

392

"Belladonna" by Stevie Nicks. I had "Stairway to Heaven," by Led Zeppelin and the soundtrack from the movie *Saturday Night Fever*, which I played so many times I thought my mother would go crazy from listening to me belt out the lyrics with those lanky, swanky Bee Gees.

9 Along with my albums I had loads of 45s, what today we would call singles, little records with just two songs on them, that I bought at the record store near my school for just a dollar a piece. I had Chaka Khan's "I'm Every Woman," and Luther Vandross' "Never Too Much," and Chuck Brown and Soul Searcher's big hit, "Bustin' Loose." I had Michael Jackson's "Rock with You" and even Aretha Franklin's cover of "You Make Me Feel Like a Natural Woman," which I sang along to in the mornings as I styled my hair.

If you had asked me then about rap music I would have shrugged my shoulders and looked at you like you were crazy. Rap music? What's that?

But then I started seventh grade and my whole world turned upside down. At Public School 141, I went to classes with kids from all over the Bronx. There were kids whose families came from Puerto Rico and the Dominican Republic, and kids whose families came from Russia and China. There were kids who were African-American and kids who were Irish-American, kids who were Italian-American and kids who were Greek-American. There were kids whose families were poor, kids whose families were well off, and kids whose families were somewhere in between. Some were Jewish, and others devout Catholics. Some were Muslim. Some of the Asian kids were even Buddhist.

The charge created by so many different elements coming together was <u>palpable</u>. The school crackled with energy, and as you can imagine, things weren't always smooth. There were some pretty <u>entrenched</u> cliques, and a few vicious fights in the schoolyard. But there was also so much "flavor." You could hear Spanish spoken with a thick "Nuyorican" accent to a kid wearing a "yamulke." A seemingly reserved Asian-American girl would get out of her parents' car, wait for them to drive off, and then unzip her coat to reveal a fire engine red Adidas sweatsuit. A guy in a preppy, button-down shirt would "sport" gold chains with pendants of every denomination: the Jewish Star of David, the Arabic lettering for Allah, and a shiny gold cross. He was everything, that was his "steelo," and everyone gave him "props" for it.

When I got to 141, I felt like a blank canvas. Nothing had prepared me for the dynamism, the screaming self-expression of the place and its students. For the first few weeks I secretly studied the habits of the seventh, eighth and ninth graders with whom I walked

Nonfiction Perspective Details of Walker's music preferences make it easier to understand how she sees her classmates and the world.

Vocabulary Builder
palpable (pal´ pə bəl) *adj.* able to be touched, felt, or handled; tangible
entrenched (en trenchd´) *adj.* securely established; unmovable

10 Reading Check

What changed in Walker's life the summer before seventh grade?

Before Hip-Hop Was Hip-Hop ■ 393

9 **Nonfiction**
Perspective

- **Ask** students what they notice about the list of bands, artists, and songs that Walker mentions in this passage.
  Answer: Students should recognize that Walker's musical taste was diverse. She mentions white and black artists; soul, disco, and heavy metal music; and music from earlier decades as well as the 1980s.
- Then, **ask** what these details reveal about Walker's perspective on music.
  Possible response: Walker's diverse musical taste reveals that she was open to many different kinds of music. Her likes were not restricted by categories such as race or musical style.

10 **Reading Check**
Answer: During the summer before seventh grade, Walker moved from Washington, D.C., to the Bronx.

Differentiated Instruction   Solutions for All Learners

Strategy for Special Needs Students
Use a globe or world map to demonstrate to students the diversity of the students who attended Walker's school in the Bronx. First, point out the locations of Puerto Rico and the Dominican Republic, which are close to the United States. Show students how to locate Africa, and then help them find the countries of Russia, China, Ireland, Italy, and Greece. Explain the scale of the map or globe, and help students calculate the distances from several of these countries to New York City.

Strategy for English Learners
Give students the opportunity to learn that slang occurs in all languages, not just in English. Invite English learners to teach the rest of the class some slang terms in their home languages. Ask them to explain the meaning of each term and the circumstances in which it would be used. Suggest that the whole class learn and use a slang or casual greeting from another language.

the halls and shared the cafeteria. I was transfixed by the way they infused their words with attitude and drama, moving their hands and heads as they spoke. I was captivated by the way many of them walked and ran and joked with each other with confidence and <u>bravado</u>. I noted what they wore and how they wore it: the razor sharp creases of their Jordache jeans, the spotless sneakers with the laces left loose and untied.

⓫ Slowly, I began to add some of what I saw into my "look." I convinced my grandmother to buy me a name chain to wear around my neck, and my stepmother to buy me dark dyed designer jeans. I bought my first pair of Nike sneakers, red, white and blue Air Cortez's, with money I saved from my allowance.

One by one, I started to make friends—Diane, Loida, James, Jesus, Maya. When James and Jesus weren't making fun of me for being so "square," they took me to parties on the Grand Concourse, the big boulevard lined with old apartment buildings and department stores that ran through the Bronx. The parties were incredible, filled with young people who didn't drink, smoke or fight, but who just wanted to dance and laugh and ooh and ahhh over the "scratching" sounds and funky beats the DJs coaxed out of their turntables.

⓭ A lot of the kids at the parties were "breakers" or "poppers and lockers," which meant they could breakdance, a style of movement that blends the Brazilian martial art of Capoeira with a dance called the Robot, and incorporates classical dance moves as well. The "breakers" moved in "crews" that competed against each other.

394 ■ *Types of Nonfiction*

Standing in a circle we watched as members of the different groups "moonwalked" into the center, and then hurled themselves to the floor, spinning on their heads, kicking their legs into the air, and making elaborate hand gestures, each more intricate and acrobatic than the last. Everyone at the party who wasn't "breaking" was a judge by default, and we registered our scores by clapping and yelling.

When Loida and Diane weren't "capping on" or making fun of my clothes, they were "hipping" me to Kiss 98.7 and WBLS, the radio stations that had started to slip some of the songs we liked into their rotation. Songs like "Planet Rock" by Soul Sonic Force and "Take Me Home" by Lisa Lisa and the Cult Jam. After school and on the weekends, they took me to the street vendors that sold the accessories we all coveted: the big knockoff Porsche sunglasses everybody wanted but not everybody could afford, and the heavy gold chains people collected around their necks like so many pieces of string. Loida and Diane also took me around the city on the bus, familiarizing me with the routes of the M1 and M3 and M7, showing me all the different neighborhoods like Little Italy and Chinatown, Bed-Stuy and Harlem.

I remember looking out the big sliding glass windows of the bus at the lines drawn in concrete and glass and thinking that while the world outside seemed so divided, inside, in my circle, among my friends, those lines didn't seem to exist. Loida was Dominican and Diane was Puerto Rican. Our friend Mary was Irish-American, and Lisa was Italian-American. Maya's family was from Haiti. Julius was Russian-American. We were different ages, with different likes and dislikes, but we were united in our love of hip-hop. We loved the "dope"[2] beats, the ever changing and ever expanding <u>lexicon</u>, the outrageous dance moves, the cocky swagger, the feeling that we were part of something dynamic and "fresh"[3] that was bigger than any one of us. That world, that other realm that we created on the streets and in our minds, that streamed from the radio in the privacy of our bedrooms and coursed between us as we talked on the phone, that was where we lived.

That was where we felt free.

Looking back on it now, I can see that hip-hop was born of the diversity I found at 141. Unlike the hip-hop of today, it didn't come pre-packaged from a marketing department with millions of dollars to spend. Our hip-hop was the product of a bunch of kids from a bunch of different places trying to talk to each other, trying to create a common language that could cut through the many languages peo-

2. **dope** (dōp) *adj.* slang term meaning "great; irresistible."
3. **fresh** (fresh) *adj.* slang term meaning "new."

Nonfiction
Purpose Walker's extensive descriptions here and throughout are meant to explain and inform.

Vocabulary Builder
lexicon (lek´si kän´) *n.* the special vocabulary of a particular subject

Reading Check

In what "world" do Walker and her friends feel free?

Before Hip-Hop Was Hip-Hop ■ 395

⓭ Nonfiction
Purpose
• Point out that the comment says the details in this passage are meant to "explain and inform." **Ask:** What kind of nonfiction writing does Walker use in this paragraph?
Answer: This passage is an example of expository writing that explains and informs about hip-hop culture.
• Then have students **explain** what other writing techniques this passage demonstrates.
Possible responses: Students may say that this passage is narrative, because it gives an account of events after school and on the weekends. Other students may say that it is descriptive writing because it presents physical details of a scene to make an impression on readers.
• **Ask** students whether they think this passage is essential to the essay or could be removed without weakening it.
Possible response: Students should realize that the essay would be much less interesting and much more abstract without passages that provide in-depth descriptions and exposition.

⓮ Reading Check
Answer: Walker and her friends felt most comfortable in the "world" of hip-hop they created "on the streets and in our minds."

Differentiated Instruction — Solutions for All Learners

Vocabulary for Less Proficient Readers
Tell students that writers often introduce words that readers may not know by using the new word and also a definition or synonym. Point out sentences in which Walker does this, as when she says her friends were "'capping on' or making fun of" her clothes. Point out the term "Bed-Stuy," for example, and ask students what other word in that sentence tells what Bed-Stuy is. (a neighborhood, Bedford-Stuyvesant)

Enrichment for Gifted/Talented Students
Challenge students to use the details in Walker's essay to create a presentation on hip-hop culture. Suggest that instead of a written report, they prepare a series of slides, storyboards, or posters that illustrate hip-hop fashions in an urban street scene, and create a "mix tape" (or CD) of hip-hop songs from the 1980s.

- Tell students that parts of the Bronx are famous—or infamous—as places of poverty and the related woes of crime and decay. Other parts are known as working-class areas where people strive to support their families. **Ask** how Walker's use of the phrase "Boogie Down Bronx" contradicts the usual impression of the Bronx.
  Answer: The name "Boogie Down Bronx" emphasizes fun and dancing and the amusements that teens made for themselves rather than the "grit and drive and hardness of the city."

- **Ask:** What conclusion about the Bronx might you draw from Walker's discussion of it?
  Possible response: Things are not always the way people think they are, or the way they first appear.

- **Ask:** How is this conclusion about the Bronx like the insight Walker is trying to convey about hip-hop culture?
  Possible response: The Bronx might seem tough and gritty, but those who lived there found fun and friendship. Hip-hop culture might at first seem frivolous, but it has a deeper meaning for those who participated in it.

⑯ Critical Viewing

Possible response: The moving hand and spinning turntable reflect the energy and motion of hip-hop dance and music.

Concept Connector

Invite students to revisit their remarks about youth culture and who creates it. Ask students to write about whether they agree with Walker that youth culture in general and the hip-hop movement in particular had larger significance for society.

---

ple spoke at home. Intuitively, kids were making a community where there was none; we were affirming our sameness in a world that seemed to only emphasize our difference. That desire to come together irrespective of superficial differences and sometimes in celebration of them, was what gave hip-hop authenticity, that was what kept it honest and as crucial to our well being as food. It's what kept it real.

⑮ I can't say much about hip-hop today, but I can say that old hip-hop, original hip-hop, changed my life forever. I only lived in the "Boogie Down Bronx" for a year, but those twelve months gave me so much. I learned that art could bring people together and make them forget their differences. I learned how good it could feel to move with a "posse," a group of friends who had my back no matter what. I learned that I could express myself and communicate with others through what I wore and how I walked and what music I liked. I learned that it doesn't take money or a special degree to transform the grit and drive and hardness of the city into something beautiful.

Loyalty. Community. Self-confidence. Creativity. Hip-hop taught me more about real life than anything I learned that year in class.

I hope when kids today look at shiny videos by their favorite hip-hop artists, they will see through the expensive cars and exotic locations, the women in skimpy outfits and the men trying to approximate a "gangsta" lean. I hope they will remember that hip-hop was born without a formula and without a lot of expensive props or violent undertones. I hope they will marvel at the fact that in the early days of hip-hop, young people were making it up as they went along, following their hearts, following what felt good. I hope they will think about what it takes to create culture that is unique and transcendent and honest, and I hope they begin to dream about creating a new world for themselves.

I hope hip-hop inspires them to make their own revolution.

Rebecca Walker
Author's Insight
I always liked this upbeat nickname for the Bronx, because it suggests dancing and having fun—not usually what this borough is known for.

⑯ ▼ **Critical Viewing** Which details in this image of a DJ suggest the energy of hip-hop? Explain. **[Interpret]**

Vocabulary Development

Vocabulary Knowledge Rating
When students have completed reading and discussing "Before Hip-Hop Was Hip-Hop," have them take out their **Vocabulary Rating Chart** for this selection. Read the words aloud once more and have students rate their knowledge of the words again in the After Reading column. Clarify any words that are still problematic. Have students write their own definitions or examples in the appropriate column. Encourage students to use the words in further discussion and written work about this selection. Remind them that they will be accountable for these words on the Selection Test.

17 Q. What kind of "revolution," if any, do you think young people are making now?

A. Young people today use technology to revolutionize the way people relate to each other across space, time, and culture. From instant text messaging to international Internet video gaming, young people are collapsing the distance between human beings, neutralizing physical and cultural divides through digital contact. This could become a powerful force for cross-cultural understanding and peace in the world.

18 Q. To what extent did you outline or plan your essay?

A. While I sometimes outline essays before I begin to write, I didn't outline this one. Instead, I allowed my memories to lead me through the piece, trusting they would reveal a story worth telling. Also, I knew I wanted the reader to come away from the essay feeling empowered, and with a fresh perspective on hip-hop. This intention was a powerful guide.

StudentCorner

19 Q. How did everyone at your school come up with a common language that you all understood?
—Ryan Tuggle, Littleton, Colorado

A. We certainly weren't conscious of coming up with a common language! It wasn't an intellectual pursuit like a school paper or a science project. The process was intuitive, a natural outgrowth of the dynamic circumstances we found ourselves in. What we were was open to the possibility of finding a common language. I think this simple, human openness was responsible for all that came after.

 ## Writing Workshop: *Work in Progress*

Business Letter
For a business letter you may write, list several consumer items that have not lived up to your expectations. Note what has been disappointing about each one. Put this Product List in your writing portfolio.

Assessment Resources

The following resources can be used to assess students' knowledge and skills.

Unit 3 Resources
Selection Test A, pp. 8–10
Selection Test B, pp. 11–13

Go **Online** Students may use the **Self-test** to
Assessment prepare for **Selection Test A** or
Selection Test B.

- Tell students that Rebecca Walker is frequently asked questions about her work. Her answers provide insight into the perspective she brings to her writing.

- In her comments Walker addresses her intention, or purpose, in writing this essay. Have students review this term on p. 388.

17 After students read the first question and answer, **ask** students to name ways that technology has affected their lives.
Possible responses: Technology, especially the Internet and instant messaging, has allowed them to interact with people all over the world, who may come from different cultures but share common interests.

18 The second question and answer relate to how a writer plans and organizes a piece of writing. Have students discuss the advantages and disadvantages of composing an essay in the way that Walker describes.
Possible response: Planning or outlining an essay usually makes it easier to write, but a spontaneous approach can create vivid, deeply felt description.

19 After students read the third question and answer, discuss with them why creating a common language is such a powerful concept.
Possible response: Any idea that improves human communication and understanding, such as creating a common language, can make the world a better place.

Writing Workshop
Work in Progress

Business Letter
In the **Work-in-Progress** assignments through Part 1, students will complete activities that prepare them for the **Writing Workshop** on business letters on p. 466. Work with students on this brief prewriting activity. Have them save their work in their portfolios for later use.

397

1. **Sample answer:** I enjoyed Walker's description of the music and dancing because they remind me of good times I have with my friends.

2. (a) PS 141 "crackled" with energy because the school included students from many different cultures. (b) Hip-hop bridged the gap between Walker and her friends because it gave them common interests. (c) Hip-hop allowed students a way to escape from the difficulties of their everyday lives.

3. (a) Walker believes that hip-hop of her day was born from youth and diversity, but that today it comes pre-packaged and is not created by teens. (b) **Possible response:** Walker's opinion is biased because she judges modern hip-hop only by what she hears on the radio.

4. (a) Walker felt that hip-hop culture belonged to her and her friends and defined them as a group with its own clear identity. New styles of dress, speech, dance, and music were hip-hop culture's badges of membership. (b) **Possible response:** Today, teenagers use similar elements of popular culture—clothing, music, and online journals—to help express themselves.

5. (a) Walker's tone is personal. (b) **Possible response:** Other adjectives to describe Walker's tone are *passionate* and *joyous*. (c) *Personal:* "I knew hip-hop before it was hip-hop. I was there when it all began." *Passionate:* "In fact, we were at the epicenter of one of America's most significant cultural revolutions, making it happen. Who knew?" *Joyous:* "The parties were incredible, filled with young people who didn't drink, smoke, or fight, but who just wanted to dance and laugh and ooh and ahhh over the 'scratching' sounds and funky beats the DJs coaxed out of their turntables."

6. (a) **Possible response: Level of Formality:** informal style, paragraphs 4, 15; **Word Choice:** use of slang, paragraphs 1, 13;

Apply the Skills

Types of Nonfiction

Thinking About the Selection

1. **Respond:** What did you enjoy most about Walker's descriptions of hip-hop culture during her youth? Explain.

2. **(a) Recall:** According to Walker, why did PS 141 "crackle" with energy? **(b) Analyze Cause and Effect:** In what specific ways did hip-hop help Walker and her friends bridge differences? **(c) Extend:** What other benefits did hip-hop provide to young people in that time and place? Explain.

3. **(a) Compare and Contrast:** What differences does Walker find between the music of her youth and today's hip-hop? **(b) Take a Position:** Do you think Walker's judgment is fair or biased? Explain your answer.

4. **(a) Interpret:** Why was it so important for Walker and her friends to define themselves through dress, special language, dance, and music? **(b) Generalize:** What strategies do teenagers use today to express themselves?

Types of Nonfiction Review

5. **(a)** Is the **tone** of Walker's **essay** personal or impersonal? **(b)** What other adjectives appropriately describe her tone? **(c)** Which details in the first three paragraphs support your answers?

6. **(a)** Use a chart like the one shown to analyze Walker's **style.** In each column, note passages that support your ideas. **(b)** In a small group, discuss the examples, and develop a one-sentence description of Walker's writing style.

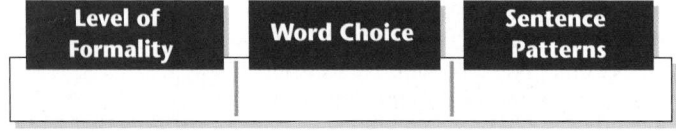

Level of Formality	Word Choice	Sentence Patterns

Research the Author

Using library and Internet resources, create a popular culture **timeline** of Rebecca Walker's life. Follow these steps:

- Identify key events in her life. List them in order.
- Add details about music, fashion, and dance at the time of each event. Use photographs and illustrations when possible.
- Present your timeline to the class.

398 ■ *Types of Nonfiction*

QuickReview

Essay at a Glance
This essay discusses the impact of hip-hop music and culture on the author's life.

Go Online
Assessment

For: Self-test
Visit: www.PHSchool.com
Web Code: epa-6301

Essay: a nonfiction work that explores a specific topic

Tone: the author's attitude toward both subject and audience, expressed in word choice and details

Style: the way in which an author uses language

Sentence Patterns: direct, short sentences: paragraphs 11, 20. **(b) Possible response:** Walker's writing style appeals to young people because it is direct, lively, and conversational.

Research the Author

Students may complete this research assignment for homework. Tell them that they can find information about Walker's work in the library or online.

Go Online
Author Link

For: More about the author
Visit: www.PHSchool.com
Web Code: epe-8301

For additional information about Rebecca Walker, give students this Web Code. After typing in the Web Code, students select *Rebecca Walker.*

Unit 3
Part 1

Main Idea and Supporting Details

Main Idea and Supporting Details   399

Differentiated
Instruction   Solutions for All Learners

Resources for Monitoring Progress

Unit 3 Resources
    Unit 3, Part 1 Diagnostic Test, pp. 15–17
    Unit 3, Part 1 Benchmark Test,
    pp. 101–106

Reading Kit

Success Tracker

Skills Overview
Reading Skill: Identifying Main Ideas and Supporting Details
- Generate questions prior to reading
- Rereading to identify main idea and supporting details

Vocabulary Development
- Prefixes

Literary Analysis
- Author's Style: diction, tone, syntax, using background, author bio, title
- Expository Essay: description, comparison and contrast, cause and effect

Writing
- Business Letter
- Work in Progress, pp. 397, 423, 445

Monitoring Progress

Diagnose: Before you begin Part 1, administer the **Diagnostic Test** for Unit 3, Part 1. This test will identify students' level of readiness for the reading and vocabulary skills in Part 1. Use the **Interpretation Guide** for the Diagnostic Test to determine which students need help with prerequisite skills before beginning Part 1.

Preteach and Prepare: Use the information indicated in the **Interpretation Guide** to help students build prerequisite skills. In addition, prepare students by using the **Vocabulary Warm-up** activities and the **Reading Warm-up** activities as necessary for each selection set.

Teach: Use the instructional plan and resources provided to teach the skills and selections.

Assess: After students have completed Part 1, administer the **Benchmark Test** for Unit 3, Part 1. The test results will indicate which skills students have mastered and those on which they need more work.

Reteach: Use the Interpretation Guide to determine the appropriate reteaching pages from the **Reading Kit.**

Intervention: The prerequisite and reteaching pages are also available in the **Success Tracker.**

Introduce the Reading Skill

- Introduce the reading skill: identify main idea and supporting details. Draw students' attention to the purposes of each. Tell students that they need to be able to identify the main idea of any text they read. Point out that they can determine the main idea by using the skills and strategies presented in Part 1.

- Tell students that sometimes the main idea of a piece of writing is not stated directly. Instead, the writer builds meaning through details, descriptions, examples, and other forms of evidence. The reader uses this information to identify the main idea. Explain that using the strategy of generating questions to determine the main idea means that students ask questions about the text to narrow the possibilities of what the main idea is.

Model the Reading Strategies

- Model how generating questions can help students to find the main idea. Write this sentence on the board.

  This article will discuss the emergence of universities in medieval Europe, and it will explain how this emergence was influenced by both church and state.

  Then, **ask** these questions:

  What part of this sentence shows what the main idea is?
  Answer: The words "This article will discuss" tell what the main idea is.

  Are there any supporting details?
  Answer: Yes. The words "this emergence was influenced by both church and state" support the main idea about the emergence of universities in medieval Europe.

- Reinforce the importance of identifying the main idea and supporting details for understanding a nonfiction work. By asking questions and rereading, students can identify main ideas and supporting details.

Reading: Identifying Main Idea and Supporting Details

> The **main idea** is the most important point in a literary work. **Supporting details** help identify the main idea.

Skills and Strategies You Will Learn in Part 1

In Part 1, you will learn
- to **generate questions** to **determine the main idea** and supporting details. (p. 402)
- to **reread** to **clarify the main idea.** (p. 424)
- to **apply** these skills when you **read technical documents** and other **forms of nonfiction.** (p. 446)

Using the Skills and Strategies in Part 1

In Part 1, you will learn to **ask questions** that help **identify the stated and implied main idea.** You will also learn to **clarify and confirm main ideas by rereading.** You will apply these skills as you read a variety of nonfiction texts.

The example shows how to use questions to find the main idea in nonfiction.

What is Mitosis?   When does Mitosis take place?

Mitosis is the process by which the cell nucleus is divided into two nuclei. Mitosis takes place in four phases: prophase, metaphase, anaphase, and telophase. The period between one mitosis and the next is called interphase. Chromosome replication occurs during interphase.

What is important about interphase?

Main Idea: The process of mitosis has four phases and an interphase.

Professional Development
The ReQuest Procedure

ReQuest, an acronym for Reciprocal Questioning, is an instructional strategy designed by A. V. Manzo (*Journal of Reading* 12:123–126, 1969) to help students develop an active, questioning approach as they read. You can use this strategy to help students learn to ask questions to make inferences.
- Model the process by reading a brief section of the text aloud. Ask and answer your own questions about the text, progressing from factual recall to questions that stimulate interpretive or applied thinking and lead to inferences.
- After modeling this question-and-response pattern, ask students to read the next segment of the text, and have them ask you questions about what they read. Answer the questions.
- Reinforce this questioning technique until students are comfortable applying it on their own.

For more on ReQuest, see *General Resources*, p. 27.

Academic Vocabulary: Words for Interpreting Literature

The following words will help you write and talk about the literature in this unit.

Word	Definition	Sample Sentence
equivalent *adj.*	equal in meaning	The author's description of the mountain seems the *equivalent* of a prose poem.
contemplate *v.*	consider or think about	The poem requires the reader to *contemplate* the meaning of love.
abstract *n.*	summary	After reading the *abstract,* the students decided it was worth reading the article.
hence *adv.*	as a result; therefore	The conflict in the story was never resolved; *hence,* the reader was left confused.
illuminate *v.*	make clear	Their actions *illuminated* the characters' motives.

Vocabulary Skills You Will Learn in Part 1

▶ A **prefix** is a word part that is added to the beginning of a word or another word part.

In Part 1, you will learn
- Latin prefix *con-/com-* (p. 422)   • Latin prefix *equi-* (p. 444)

Knowing the meaning of common prefixes helps you understand an unfamiliar word.

```
(prefix)    + (word root)    = word
com         + prehendere     = comprehend

(meaning)   + (meaning)      = new meaning
with        + catch hold of  = catch hold of with thought; understand
```

Activity Use a dictionary to find one word that contains the prefix *con-* and one word that contains the spelling variation *com-*. Define each word by relating it to the idea of "with" or "together."

Introduce Academic Vocabulary

- Introduce the academic vocabulary: words for interpreting literature. Tell students that these words are useful when discussing and interpreting literature.
- Review each word, and have the students state each one aloud. Have students read aloud the words' definitions and the example sentences.
- Tell students to try to use these words as they discuss the selections in Part 1.

Introduce the Vocabulary Skill

- Introduce the vocabulary skill: prefixes. Tell students that many words in English are formed using Latin prefixes. Recognizing these prefixes and understanding their meanings are effective ways to build vocabulary.
- Review the two prefixes on this page and their meanings.
- Use these questions to give students practice with Latin prefixes:

  What word, containing the prefix *ben-,* describes something that is good for you?
  Answer: *beneficial*

  What word, containing the prefix *dis-,* describes something that is broken or in bad condition?
  Answer: *disrepair*

Activity

Have students share their words and write the words and definitions on the board. Then, have students explain how their words relate to the idea of "with" or "together."

Go Online For: Interactive Vocabulary Crossword Puzzles
Visit: www.PHSchool.com
Web Code: epj-5301
Give students this Web Code to access interactive crossword puzzles using Academic Vocabulary and Vocabulary Skill words from Part 1.

Differentiated Instruction
Solutions for All Learners

Strategy for Less Proficient Readers
Students may have a difficult time finding the main idea of a passage. Point out that rereading is one effective strategy for helping students understand a passage.

Tell students that good readers often reread in order to understand what a sentence or a passage says. Write the following sentence on the board:

The conquest of ancient civilizations often led to their culture being destroyed.

Then, think aloud for students.

I don't understand what that sentence means. I need to read it again.

As I reread the sentence, I see that it discusses the conquest, or military defeat, of ancient civilizations. I see that it also discusses the destruction of cultures. Therefore, the sentence means that when ancient societies suffered military defeat, they also lost things that defined them as a culture.

Reinforce that rereading is one way to help understand the meaning of a work.

Planning Differentiated Instruction

Choosing Your Selection

You may use either selection to meet the lesson standards. The following guide will help you determine which of the two selections is more appropriate for your students.

Accessibility at a Glance

	A Celebration of Grandfathers	On Summer
Context	Setting: New Mexico in the 1940s	Setting: Various American cities and regions in the 1950s and 1960s
Language	• Spanish words are footnoted • Relatively short sentences and clauses	• Rich, figurative language • Diction more difficult
Concept Level	Accessible (praising the wisdom that comes with age)	Challenging (attitude that changes with age)
Literary Merit	Inspirational based on family memories	Series of anecdotal stories
Lexile	970L	1180L
Overall Rating	More accessible	More challenging

Using the Other Selection You may use the other selection for homework or independent reading to reinforce the selection skills. If you use both selections, you can build a test for both using *ExamView*® **Test Bank** software.

Choosing Your Resources

[L1] Special Needs Students [L4] Advanced Students
[L2] Below-Level Students [EL] English Learners
[L3] All Students

FT Fast Track Instruction: To move the lesson more quickly, use the strategies and activities identified with **FT**.

Reading and Vocabulary Warm-ups provide support for below level students. **A** is for students reading two grades below level; **B** is for students reading one grade below level. For Selection Tests, **A** signifies "less challenging" and **B** "more challenging." For Graphic Organizer transparencies, **A** signifies "not filled in" and **B** "filled in."

Scaffolding for Less Proficient and Advanced Students

The leveled questions on Apply the Skills pages progress in the levels of thinking required to answer them. To address the needs of your different students, you may use the (a) level questions for your less proficient students, the (b) level with your on-level and advanced students. The occasional (c) level questions are appropriate for your advanced students.

Go Online For: Information about Lexiles
Professional **Visit:** www.PHSchool.com
Development **Web Code:** eue-1111

Step-by-Step Teaching Guide	Pacing Guide	
PRETEACH		
• Administer Vocabulary and Reading Warm-ups as necessary.		
• Introduce the Literary Analysis Skill: Author's Style. **FT**	10 min.	
• Introduce the Reading Skill: Identify Main Idea and Supporting Details. **FT**	10 min.	
• Prepare students to read by teaching the selection vocabulary. **FT**	10 min.	
• Build background and develop expressive vocabulary with Connecting to the Literature and Background.	10 min.	
• Engage students' interest with the motivation activity.	10 min.	
TEACH		
• Informally monitor comprehension while students read independently or in groups. **FT**	30 min.	
• Monitor students' comprehension with the Reading Check notes.	as students read	
• Reinforce vocabulary with Vocabulary Builder notes.	as students read	
• Develop students' understanding of author's style with the Literary Analysis annotations. **FT**	5 min.	
• Develop students' ability to identify main idea and supporting details with the Reading Skill annotations. **FT**	10 min.	
ASSESS/EXTEND		
• Assess students' comprehension and mastery of the Reading Skill and Literary Analysis by having them answer the Apply the Skills questions. **FT**	35 min.	
• Have students complete the Vocabulary Builder activities. **FT**	5 min.	
• Apply students' ability to write a book jacket copy with the Writing activity. **FT**	30–45 min. or homework	
• Extend students' listening and speaking and research and technology skills with one or both of the Extend Your Learning activities.	15–30 min. or homework	
• Have students complete the Vocabulary Skill and Grammar Lesson.	5 min.	
• Monitor students' progress with the Assessment Practice.	20–40 min.	
• Administer **Selection Test A** or **Selection Test B**. **FT**	15 min.	

Resources

Meeting Your Standards

Students will

1. **analyze and respond to literary elements.**
   - Literary Analysis: Author's Style

2. **read, comprehend, and analyze short stories.**
   - Reading Skill: Identify Main Idea and Supporting Details
   - Reading Strategy: Generate Questions Prior to Reading
   - Reading Check questions
   - Apply the Skills questions
   - Assessment Practice

3. **develop vocabulary.**
   - Vocabulary Builder
   - The Latin prefixes con-/com-, equi-

4. **apply grammar skills.**
   - Direct and Indirect Objects

5. **develop writing proficiency.**
   - Work in Progress: Business Letter
   - Book jacket copy

6. **extend learning.**
   - Listening and Speaking: Panel Discussion
   - Research and Technology: Annotated Map

Block Scheduling: Use one 90-minute class period to preteach the skills and have students read the selection. Use a second 90-minute class period to assess students' mastery of skills, extend their learning, and monitor their progress.

Homework Suggestions

Following are possibilities for homework assignments.

- Support pages from *Unit 3 Resources*:
  Literary Analysis
  Reading Skill
  Build Vocabulary
  Enrichment

- An Extend Your Learning project and the Writing assignment for your chosen selection may be completed over several days.

PRENTICE HALL

Teacher EXPRESS Use this complete
Plan · Teach · Assess   suite of powerful
teaching tools to make lesson planning and testing quicker and easier.

PRENTICE HALL

Student EXPRESS Use the
Learn · Study · Succeed   Interactive
Textbook (online and on CD-ROM) to make selections and activities come alive with audio and video support and interactive questions.

❶ Literary Analysis
Style

- Tell students that as they read the assigned selection, they will notice the language the author uses (diction), the way the author arranges sentences (syntax), and the author's attitude toward the subject (tone). Tell students that these are some of the elements that make up a writer's style.

- Point out that word choice, or diction, signals the author's tone, or attitude, toward the subject. For example, "cold and aloof" indicates a negative attitude toward the subject, while "reserved and dignified" indicates a respectful attitude.

- Tell students that some authors use syntax to emphasize a point. Read this sentence as an example: "Quietly and smoothly, the small stream made its way through the valley." Explain that by placing the words *quietly* and *smoothly* at the beginning rather than in the middle of the sentence, the author emphasizes the idea of peacefulness.

❷ Reading Skill
Main Idea and Supporting Details

- Remind students that the main idea can appear at the beginning, middle, or end of a work and may be stated directly, or it may be implied. For example, in the first or second paragraph of an essay, an author may state, "Our family vacations were some of the best times of my childhood."

- Supporting details help convince the reader to accept or understand the author's main idea. For example, detailed descriptions of fun and adventure support the main idea that family vacations were good times. If the main idea is not stated directly, such details can lead the reader to identify it.

- Give students a copy of **Reading Skill Graphic Organizer A** (*Graphic Organizer Transparencies*, p. 83). Have them fill in the graphic organizer to identify the main idea and supporting details as they read the assigned selection.

402

Build Skills *A Celebration of Grandfathers • On Summer*

Practice these skills with either "A Celebration of Grandfathers" (p. 404) or "On Summer" (p. 415).

❶ Literary Analysis

An author's **style** is his or her unique way of using language. Some elements that contribute to an author's style are

- **Diction:** the words the author uses
- **Syntax:** the arrangement of words in sentences
- **Tone:** the author's attitude toward the audience or subject.

A writer's diction and syntax might be described as *formal* or *informal, technical* or *ordinary,* or *sophisticated* or *down-to-earth.* Tone might be described as *serious, playful, friendly,* or *harsh.*

❷ Reading Skill

The **main idea** is the central message, insight, or opinion in a work of nonfiction. **Supporting details** are the pieces of evidence that a writer uses to prove the main idea. These details can include facts, statistics, quotations, or anecdotes. To **identify the main idea and supporting details** in a work, **generate questions prior to reading.** Before you read, ask yourself questions such as

- *Why did the author choose this title?*
- *How might events in the author's life influence his or her attitude?*

As you read, look for details that answer those questions and point to the main idea. Use a chart like the one shown to help you.

Question
Why is it significant that the author, a famous musician, grew up in poverty?

↓

Detail/Answer
He could not afford music lessons.

↓

Main Idea?
The author supports free music programs.

Vocabulary Builder

A Celebration of Grandfathers

- **perplexes** (pər pleks′ iz) *v.* confuses or puzzles (p. 405) *His odd behavior* <u>perplexes</u> *them.*
- **absurdity** (ab sʉr′ də tē) *n.* something ridiculous or nonsensical (p. 405) *Our reasonable request was treated as an* <u>absurdity</u>*.*
- **permeate** (pʉr′ mē āt′) *v.* spread or flow throughout (p. 406) *It didn't take long for the odor to* <u>permeate</u> *the entire apartment.*
- **anguish** (aŋ′ gwish) *n.* great pain or suffering (p. 410) *The troubled expression on her face revealed the* <u>anguish</u> *she felt inside.*

On Summer

- **aloofness** (ə lo͞of′ nəs) *n.* quality of being distant or removed (p. 415) *His* <u>aloofness</u> *made him appear unfriendly.*
- **melancholy** (mel′ ən käl′ ē) *adj.* sad; gloomy (p. 415) *The rain set a* <u>melancholy</u> *mood.*
- **pretentious** (prē ten′ shəs) *adj.* grand in a showy way (p. 419) *His* <u>pretentious</u> *manner only impressed those who had just met him.*
- **apex** (ā′ peks′) *n.* highest point; peak (p. 419) *Playing in the World Series was the* <u>apex</u> *of his baseball career.*

Vocabulary Development

Vocabulary Knowledge Rating

Create a **Vocabulary Knowledge Rating Chart** for the selection you will teach from this set. Include the selection vocabulary from this page and the additional expressive vocabulary students are asked to use at the end of Connecting to the Literature. These words will increase students' expressive vocabulary.

Give students a copy of the chart with the words on it. Introduce the words by reading them aloud and having students mark their

rating in the Before Reading column. Urge them to be alert to these words as they read and discuss the selection because they will rate their knowledge of the words again after they finish.

If you wish, you may tally how many students know (or think they know) a word to gauge how much instruction you need to provide. As students read, point out the words and their context.

Build Understanding • *A Celebration of Grandfathers*

❸ Background

New Mexican Culture Native Americans occupied present-day New Mexico thousands of years before the Spanish arrived in the late 1500s. The area remained under Spanish and then Mexican rule until 1848, when the United States gained control. Since then, people from all over the world have settled in New Mexico. As a result, the region has become a kind of cultural crossroads.

❹ Connecting to the Literature

Reading/Writing Connection Growing up in New Mexico, Rudolfo Anaya learned respect for elders. Write five sentences explaining why our elders deserve respect. Use at least three of the following words: *appreciate, clarify, demonstrate, maximize.*

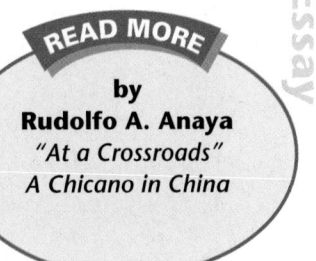

READ MORE

by
Rudolfo A. Anaya
"At a Crossroads"
A Chicano in China

Reflective Essay

Meet the Author

Rudolfo A. **Anaya** (b. 1937)

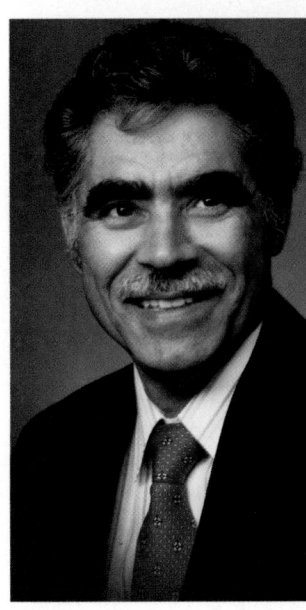

Born in New Mexico, Rudolfo A. Anaya is considered the founder of modern Chicano literature. His first novel, *Bless Me, Ultima,* was praised for its depiction of the culture and history of New Mexico. Today, it is considered a classic of American literature.

"I am an oral storyteller, but now I do it on the printed page." Anaya's storytelling reflects his interest in the folk tales of his native Hispanic culture, which combines Spanish, Mexican, and Central American influences. Anaya has won a number of awards, including the PEN Center West Award for his 1992 novel *Alburquerque.* He is currently a professor of English at the University of New Mexico.

Fast Facts

▶ The manuscript for *Bless Me, Ultima* was initially rejected by dozens of publishers, but the book has sold more than 360,000 copies.

▶ As a teenager, Anaya was paralyzed after he dove into an irrigation ditch and fractured two vertebrae in his neck. He recovered, but the ordeal forever changed his outlook on life.

 Go Online
Author Link

For: More about the author
Visit: www.PHSchool.com
Web Code: epe-9302

A Celebration of Grandfathers ■ 403

---

❸ Background
New Mexican Culture

Even though New Mexico is a cultural crossroad, the Pueblo Indians who have inhabited the region for centuries continue to follow many of their ancient traditions. Although the Pueblo people now use many modern conveniences, the basic social system remains. Their life centers on the village, and most of the people live in single story homes just as their ancestors did. Although some Pueblo people observe certain Catholic religious practices, most continue to practice their ancient religion.

❹ Connecting to the Literature

• Model use of the expressive vocabulary students are asked to use with these examples:

1. We should *appreciate* the wisdom that our elders have gained through experience.

2. Elders can help us *clarify* the life decisions that we have to make.

3. We can *demonstrate* our respect for elders by asking their advice.

4. We can *maximize* our chances for success if we ask the help and advice of our elders.

• Help students further develop their expressive vocabulary by providing these words: *complex, diminish, mutual,* and *technique.* Encourage students to use these words as they discuss the selection.

Go Online For additional information about Rudolfo Anaya, have students type in the Web Code and then select *Rudolfo Anaya.*

Differentiated Instruction   Solutions for All Learners

Support for Below-Level Students [L1, L2]	Support for English Learners [EL]
Unit 3 Resources 　**Vocabulary Warm-up Word Lists,** p. 18 　**Vocabulary Warm-up Practice,** p. 19 　**Reading Warm-up A,** p. 20 　**Selection Test A,** pp. 28–30	**Unit 3 Resources** 　**Vocabulary Warm-up Word Lists,** p. 18 　**Vocabulary Warm-up Practice,** p. 19 　**Reading Warm-up A,** p. 20
Graphic Organizer Transparencies 　**Reading Skill Graphic Organizer,** 　**Transparency B,** p. 84	**Reader's Notebook: English Learner's Version**
Reader's Notebook: Adapted Version	**Listening to Literature Audio CD**
Adapted Reader's Notebook Audio CD	

A Celebration of Grandfathers

❶
❷

Rudolfo A. Anaya

Don Nemesio, 1977, Esperanza Martinez, Courtesy of the artist

❹

B uenos días le de Dios, abuelo."[1] God give you a good day, grandfather. This is how I was taught as a child to greet my grandfather, or any grown person. It was a greeting of respect, a cultural value to be passed on from generation to generation, this respect for the old ones.

The old people I remember from my childhood were strong in their beliefs, and as we lived daily with them we learned a wise path of life to follow. They had something important to share with the young, and when they spoke the young listened. These old abuelos and abuelitas[2] had worked the earth all their lives, and so they

---

1. **Buenos días le de Dios, abuelo** (bwā′ nəs dē′ äs lā dā dē′ ōs ä bwā lō)
2. **abuelitas** (ä bwā lē′ täs) grandmothers.

404 ■ Types of Nonfiction

❸ ▲ Critical Viewing
As you read, consider which aspects of the man in this painting resemble the description of the elders in the essay. **[Compare and Contrast]**

Vocabulary Development

Think-Aloud: Context Clues
Direct students' attention to the word *authentic* on p. 405. Using a think-aloud process, model using context clues to infer the meaning of an unknown word. Say to the students:

I'm going to think aloud to show you how I would figure out the meaning of *authentic* from its context.

The author says, "Today we would say that the old *abuelitos* lived *authentic* lives." In the first four paragraphs on p. 405 the author has given a number of examples of how the old ones lived authentic lives. For example, he says that they "recognized the great design of creation," "knew the rhythms and cycles of time," "shared good times and hard times," and "worked with a deep faith."

From these examples, I think the author intends the word *authentic* to mean "genuine; truly connected to life; not artificial."

knew the value of nurturing, they knew the sensitivity of the earth. The daily struggle called for cooperation, and so every person contributed to the social fabric, and each person was respected for his contribution.

The old ones had looked deep into the web that connects all animate and inanimate forms of life, and they recognized the great design of the creation.

These *ancianos*[3] from the cultures of the Río Grande, living side by side, sharing, growing together, they knew the rhythms and cycles of time, from the preparation of the earth in the spring to the digging of the acequias[4] that brought the water to the dance of harvest in the fall. They shared good times and hard times. They helped each other through the epidemics and the personal tragedies, and they shared what little they had when the hot winds burned the land and no rain came. They learned that to survive one had to share in the process of life.

Hard workers all, they tilled the earth and farmed, ran the herds and spun wool, and carved their saints and their kachinas[5] from cottonwood late in the winter nights. All worked with a deep faith which <u>perplexes</u> the modern mind.

Their faith shone in their eyes; it was in the strength of their grip, in the creases time wove into their faces. When they spoke, they spoke plainly and with few words, and they meant what they said. When they prayed, they went straight to the source of life. When there were good times, they knew how to dance in celebration and how to prepare the foods of the fiestas.[6] All this they passed on to the young, so that a new generation would know what they had known, so the string of life would not be broken.

Today we would say that the old abuelitos lived authentic lives.

Newcomers to New Mexico often say that time seems to move slowly here. I think they mean they have come in contact with the inner strength of the people, a strength so solid it causes time itself to pause. Think of it. Think of the high, northern New Mexico villages, or the lonely ranches on the open llano.[7] Think of the Indian pueblo[8] which lies as solid as rock in the face of time. Remember the old people whose eyes seem like windows that peer into a distant past that makes <u>absurdity</u> of our contemporary world. That is what one feels when one encounters the old ones and their land, a pausing of time.

---

3. *ancianos* (än cē ä′ nōs) old people; ancestors.
4. *acequias* (ä sā kē′ əs) irrigation ditches.
5. *kachinas* (kə chē′ nəz) small wooden dolls, representing the spirit of an ancestor or a god.
6. *fiestas* (fē es′ təz) *n.* celebrations; feasts.
7. *llano* (yä′ nō) plain.
8. *pueblo* (pweb′ lō) *n.* village or town.

Literary Analysis
Style and Tone
Describe the author's tone as he discusses the "ancianos."

Vocabulary Builder
perplexes (pər pleks′ iz) *v.* confuses or puzzles
absurdity (ab sʉr′ də tē) *n.* something ridiculous or nonsensical

❻
✔Reading Check

What work did the ancianos do?

A Celebration of Grandfathers ■ 405

❹ **Humanities**

Don Nemesio, by Esperanza Martinez

An elderly man rests his hand on his elbow as he either looks intently at something out of the frame of the painting, or perhaps simply thinks to himself. Use these questions for discussion:

1. What can you tell about the man in the painting from the objects the artist chose to depict?
   Answer: He is Latino, probably of Mexican heritage, because he sits beside a stack of tortillas. The bowl on the table has a design that could be Mexican.

2. How does the man in the painting compare to your mental picture of Anaya's grandfather?
   Possible response: They are both old and thoughtful.

❺ **Literary Analysis**
Style and Tone

- Have students **note** the words and phrases that the author uses to describe the old ones and their actions.
  Possible responses: Students may suggest phrases such as "recognized the great design of creation," "knew the rhythms and cycles of time," "hard workers," "faith shone in their eyes."

- Remind students that the diction, or words an author uses, affects the tone of the work. Then **ask** students to respond to the Literary Analysis prompt: Describe the author's tone as he discusses the "ancianos."
  Possible response: Students may suggest that the author's tone is reverent or respectful.

❻ **Reading Check**

Possible response: They farmed and raised sheep for their wool.

Differentiated
Instruction   Solutions for All Learners

Enrichment for Advanced Readers
Suggest that students read additional works by Rudolfo Anaya. You may wish to use **Authors in Depth**, Gold Level, which contains the following selections:

- from "A New Mexico Christmas" (p. 135)
- "At a Crossroads" (p. 138)
- from *A Chicano in China* (two excerpts, pp. 146–148)

After students have read these or other works by Anaya, have them form discussion groups in which they compare and contrast the selections they have read. Suggest criteria for comparison, such as style, main ideas, and viewpoints. To extend the activity, have volunteers present to the class brief oral reports on their favorite Anaya selections.

Style

- Have students **identify** some of the Spanish words used by the author on this page and the previous pages.
  Answer: The author uses the words *abuelos, ancianos, acequitas,* and *curanderas.*

- Ask students to read the definition of these words from the footnotes. Point out that Anaya is writing in English, presumably for an English-speaking audience. Have students **discuss** why he might have chosen to use the Spanish words, rather than their English equivalents.
  Possible response: He is writing about his ancestors and their culture; it is natural that he would refer to their language. In addition, the nuances of word meanings in one language are often lost in translation to another language. Anaya's use of Spanish words emphasizes a very specific cultural outlook.

- **Ask** students how they think Anaya feels about the culture of the "old ones."
  Possible response: Students may suggest that Anaya admires the culture or feels part of it.

- **Ask** the Literary Analysis question: How does Anaya's use of Spanish words add to his message of being connected to his culture?
  Possible response: Students may suggest that Anaya's use of Spanish words shows that he is comfortable using Spanish and takes pride in his language and culture.

We have all felt time stand still. We have all been in the presence of power, the knowledge of the old ones, the majestic peace of a mountain stream or an aspen grove or red buttes rising into blue sky. We have all felt the light of dusk <u>permeate</u> the earth and cause time to pause in its flow.

❼ I felt this when first touched by the spirit of Ultima, the old *curandera*[9] who appears in my first novel, *Bless Me, Ultima.* This is how the young Antonio describes what he feels:

> When she came the beauty of the llano unfolded before my eyes, and the gurgling waters of the river sang to the hum of the turning earth. The magical time of childhood stood still, and the pulse of the living earth pressed its mystery into my living blood. She took my hand, and the silent, magic powers she possessed made beauty from the raw, sun-baked llano, the green river valley, and the blue bowl which was the white sun's home. My bare feet felt the throbbing earth, and my body trembled with excitement. Time stood still . . .

At other times, in other places, when I have been privileged to be with the old ones, to learn, I have felt this inner reserve of strength upon which they draw. I have been held motionless and speechless by the power of curanderas. I have felt the same power when I hunted with Cruz, high on the Taos [tä´ ōs] mountain, where it was more than the incredible beauty of the mountain bathed in morning light, more than the shining of the quivering aspen, but a connection with life, as if a shining strand of light connected the particular and the cosmic. That feeling is an epiphany of time, a standing still of time.

But not all of our old ones are curanderos or hunters on the mountain. My grandfather was a plain man, a farmer from Puerto de Luna[10] on the Pecos River. He was probably a descendent of those people who spilled over the mountain from Taos, following the Pecos River in search of farmland. There in that river valley he settled and raised a large family.

Bearded and walrus-mustached, he stood five feet tall, but to me as a child he was a giant. I remember him most for his silence. In the summers my parents sent me to live with him on his farm, for I was to learn the ways of a farmer. My uncles also lived in that valley, the valley called Puerto de Luna, there where only the flow of the river and the whispering of the wind marked time. For me it was a magical place.

---

9. ***curandera*** (kōō rän dä´ rä) medicine woman.
10. **Puerto de Luna** (pwer´ tō dä lōō´ ne) Port of the Moon, the name of a town.

406 ■ *Types of Nonfiction*

Vocabulary Builder
permeate (pʉr´ mē āt´)
v. spread or flow throughout

Literary Analysis
Style How does Anaya's use of Spanish words add to his message of being connected to his culture?

Vocabulary Development

Expressive Vocabulary

As students are discussing Anaya's use of Spanish words and his connection to his culture, encourage them to use the expressive vocabulary presented earlier. You might encourage them with sentence starters like these:

1. Using Spanish words shows that Anaya seems to *appreciate* . . .

2. Anaya uses a quotation from his novel to *demonstrate* . . .

3. To *clarify* the meaning of a Spanish word, Anaya . . .

4. Spanish words *maximize* Anaya's style by . . .

I remember once, while out hoeing the fields, I came upon an anthill, and before I knew it I was badly bitten. After he had covered my welts with the cool mud from the irrigation ditch, my grandfather calmly said: "Know where you stand." That is the way he spoke, in short phrases, to the point.

One very dry summer, the river dried to a trickle, there was no water for the fields. The young plants withered and died. In my sadness and with the impulses of youth I said, "I wish it would rain!" My grandfather touched me, looked up into the sky and whispered, "Pray for rain." In his language there was a difference. He felt connected to the cycles that brought the rain or kept it from us. His prayer was a meaningful action, because he was a participant with the forces that filled our world, he was not a bystander.

A young man died at the village one summer. A very tragic death. He was dragged by his horse. When he was found I cried, for the boy was my friend. I did not understand why death had come to one so young. My grandfather took me aside and said: "Think of the death of the trees and the fields in the fall. The leaves fall, and everything rests, as if dead. But they bloom again in the spring. Death is only this small transformation in life."

These are the things I remember, these fleeting images, few words.

I remember him driving his horse-drawn wagon into Santa Rosa in the fall when he brought his harvest produce to sell in the town. What a tower of strength seemed to come in that small man huddled on the seat of the giant wagon. One click of his tongue and the horses obeyed, stopped or turned as he wished. He never raised his whip. How unlike today when so much teaching is done with loud words and threatening hands.

I would run to greet the wagon, and the wagon would stop. "Buenos días le de Dios, abuelo," I would say. This was the

El Leñador, 1934, Tom Lea, Collection of the Museum of New Mexico, Museum of Fine Arts

❽

❾ ▲ Critical Viewing
How does the woodcutter in this painting compare with your image of the author's grandfather? **[Compare and Contrast]**

❿

✔️ **Reading Check**

Why did Anaya's parents send him to stay with his grandfather during summers?

A Celebration of Grandfathers ■ 407

❽ Humanities

El Leñador, by Tom Lea

A *leñador* is a woodcutter. This painting shows the woodcutter and his donkey with a load of wood. The woodcutter is probably using the stick to steer the animal on the uphill path. Use the following questions for discussion:

1. What can you infer about the life of the *leñador* in the painting?
   Answer: He probably works hard because he is alone and has chopped a lot of wood. He isn't rich, because he does manual labor and has only one donkey. His expression is tough and determined, suggesting that his tasks are difficult and strenuous.

2. What can you infer about the man's relationship with the donkey?
   Answer: They seem to be partners; the donkey wears no halter and is being directed only by a light stick. They apparently work well together and trust each other.

❾ Critical Viewing

Answer: The man in the painting looks strong and vigorous, not old. Some students may think his face is stern. Anaya's grandfather is also tough and determined; he probably appears older.

❿ Reading Check

Answer: He was sent to stay with his grandfather so that he could learn the ways of a farmer.

Differentiated

Instruction   Solutions for All Learners

Strategy for Special Needs Students
Provide students with the **Reading Strategy Graphic Organizer B,** p. 84, in *Graphic Organizer Transparencies.* Discuss the main idea and supporting details shown on the graphic organizer and how the graphic organizer relates to the text. Encourage students to use the graphic organizer as they continue to read the selection to help them identify main ideas and details.

Strategy for English Learners
If any students speak Spanish fluently, ask them to pronounce the Spanish words and phrases in this essay so that classmates can learn and appreciate them. Encourage students to amplify the translations of Spanish words in the footnotes, adding their specific denotations and connotations.

Main Idea

- Read aloud the paragraph beginning "We were all sons and daughters." **Ask** students why Anaya claims the old values are threatened.
  Answer: The sons and daughters are breaking with the past.

- Have students **explain** what Anaya claims is most threatened by the break with the past.
  Answer: The break threatens the relationships with old people.

- **Ask** what Anaya thinks is an important part of this relationship.
  Answer: It is important to understand the years of old people's final transformation.

- **Ask** the Reading Skill question: What main idea about the loss of values does Anaya state here?
  Answer: As the young people lose the old values, a part of their humanity will be lost.

⓬ **Critical Viewing**

Possible response: The landscape might be inspiring because the barren red rock mountains and remote valleys are ancient and grand—far more enduring than a single human life.

---

prescribed greeting of esteem and respect. Only after the greeting was given could we approach these venerable old people. "Buenos días te de Dios, mi hijo,"[11] he would answer and smile, and then I could jump up on the wagon and sit at his side. Then I, too, became a king as I rode next to the old man who smelled of earth and sweat and the other deep aromas from the orchards and fields of Puerto de Luna.

⓫ We were all sons and daughters to him. But today the sons and daughters are breaking with the past, putting aside los abuelitos. The old values are threatened, and threatened most where it comes to these relationships with the old people. If we don't take the time to watch and feel the years of their final transformation, a part of our humanity will be lessened.

I grew up speaking Spanish, and oh! how difficult it was to learn English. Sometimes I would give up and cry out that I couldn't learn. Then he would say, "Ten paciencia."[12] Have patience. *Paciencia*, a word with the strength of centuries, a word that said that someday we would overcome. *Paciencia*, how soothing a word

---

11. **mi hijo** (mē ē′ hō) my son.
12. **Ten paciencia** (ten pä sē en′ sē ä)

Reading Skill
Main Idea What main idea about the loss of values does Anaya state here?

⓬ ▼ **Critical Viewing** Why do you think a writer like Anaya might find this New Mexican landscape inspiring? **[Speculate]**

408 ■ *Types of Nonfiction*

Vocabulary Development

Dictionary Use

Refer students to the word *pungent* near the end of p. 409. Tell students that this word has several definitions. Using a think-aloud process, model how to use context to infer the appropriate definition of the word. Say to students:

I'm going to think aloud to show you how I would figure out the correct dictionary definition of *pungent* by using context clues.

The dictionary says that *pungent* can

mean **1.** producing a sharp sensation of smell or taste; **2.** piercing or painful; **3.** expressive or penetrating; **4.** clever or stimulating.

In the sentence, Anaya mentions the "smell of medications" and of urine. He uses *pungent* to describe the odor. Therefore, definition **1.** is the best definition for this context.

coming from this old man who could still sling hundred-pound bags over his shoulder, chop wood for hours on end, and hitch up his own horses and ride to town and back in one day.

"You have to learn the language of the Americanos,"[13] he said. "Me, I will live my last days in my valley. You will live in a new time, the time of the gringos."[14]

A new time did come, a new time is here. How will we form it so it is fruitful? We need to know where we stand. We need to speak softly and respect others, and to share what we have. We need to pray not for material gain, but for rain for the fields, for the sun to nurture growth, for nights in which we can sleep in peace, and for a harvest in which everyone can share. Simple lessons from a simple man. These lessons he learned from his past which was as deep and strong as the currents of the river of life, a life which could be stronger than death.

He was a man; he died. Not in his valley, but nevertheless cared for by his sons and daughters and flocks of grandchildren. At the end, I would enter his room which carried the smell of medications and Vicks, the faint pungent odor of urine, and cigarette smoke. Gone were the aroma of the fields, the strength of his young

---

13. **Americanos** (ä mer′ ē kä′ nōs) Americans.
14. **gringos** (grin′ gōs) *n.* foreigners; North Americans.

Literary Analysis
Style How does the author's repetition of the phrase "We need" add urgency to his message?

Reading Check
Why does Anaya's grandfather tell him that he must learn English?

A Celebration of Grandfathers ■ 409

⑬ Literary Analysis
Style
- Point out the repetition of "we" and "We need." Ask students to **identify** the tone of this paragraph.
  Answer: The tone is urgent.

- **Ask** the Literary Analysis question: How does the author's repetition of the phrase "We need" add urgency to his message?
  Answer: The repetition of "We need" includes readers and the author as one group. His use of the word "need" emphasizes his message that these elements of life are essential to health, happiness, and community. They are not frivolous luxuries.

▶ **Monitor Progress:** Ask students how tone and choice of words are related to an author's style. Students should be able to explain that the tone, diction, and syntax, or arrangement of words in a sentence, contribute to an author's style.

▶ **Reteach:** If students have difficulty identifying style, ask students to find details in the text that describe Anaya's grandfather. List the descriptive phrases on the board, and point out that such vivid language is part of Anaya's style.

⑭ Reading Check
Answer: He tells Anaya that he must learn English because he will live in a new time.

Differentiated
Instruction Solutions for All Learners

Support for Less Proficient Readers
Arrange for small groups of less proficient readers to listen to the **Listening to Literature Audio CD**. Encourage the group to read along with the recorded version. Then, have the group generate two or three questions that they have about the material. Discuss the questions with them and guide them to determining the answers.

Enrichment for Gifted/Talented Students
Have students draw sketches or prepare a photo collage showing grandparents or other older relatives they admire and respect. Under each sketch or photo, students should write captions that include the name and relationship of the person, and something about him or her that the student admires. Encourage students to display their sketches or collages in class.

Cultural Connection In *Bless Me, Ultima,* the character of Ultima who comes to live with Antonio's family is a folk healer who uses folk magic in the service of others. When Antonio struggles to understand the conflicting religious beliefs of his parents and struggles with questions of good and evil, Ultima teaches him lessons of moral independence. From her, Antonio learns to choose his own destiny.

Connect to the Literature Have students review Anaya's description of the land on p. 404. Have them note the words he uses to describe the land. Then **ask** the Connect to the Literature question: Based on what you know about Anaya's writing, how would you expect him to describe the bond between the people and the land? Explain your answer.

Possible responses: Students may suggest that Anaya feels that people should be connected to the land and respect it. In the excerpt from *Bless Me, Ultima,* Anaya describes the "pulse of the living earth" and how his bare feet "felt the throbbing earth."

---

manhood. Gone also was his patience in the face of crippling old age. Small things bothered him; he shouted or turned sour when his expectations were not met. It was because he could not care for himself, because he was returning to that state of childhood, and all those wishes and desires were now wrapped in a crumbling old body.

"Ten paciencia," I once said to him, and he smiled. "I didn't know I would grow this old," he said. "Now, I can't even roll my own cigarettes." I rolled a cigarette for him, placed it in his mouth and lit it. I asked him why he smoked, the doctor had said it was bad for him. "I like to see the smoke rise," he said. He would smoke and doze, and his quilt was spotted with little burns where the cigarettes dropped. One of us had to sit and watch to make sure a fire didn't start.

I would sit and look at him and remember what was said of him when he was a young man. He could mount a wild horse and break it, and he could ride as far as any man. He could dance all night at a dance, then work the acequia the following day. He helped neighbors, they helped him. He married, raised children. Small legends, the kind that make up everyman's life.

He was 94 when he died. Family, neighbors, and friends gathered; they all agreed he had led a rich life. I remembered the last years, the years he spent in bed. And as I remember now, I am reminded that it is too easy to romanticize old age. Sometimes we forget the pain of the transformation into old age, we forget the natural breaking down of the body. Not all go gentle into the last years, some go crying and cursing, forgetting the names of those they loved the most, withdrawing into an internal <u>anguish</u> few of us can know. May we be granted the patience and care to deal with our ancianos.

⓰ For some time we haven't looked at these changes and needs of the old ones. The American image created by the mass media is an image of youth, not of old age. It is the beautiful and the young who are praised in this society. If analyzed carefully, we see that same damaging thought has crept into the way society views the old. In response to the old, the mass media have just created old people

---

⓯ **Literature in Context**

Cultural Connection

Anaya's Best-Known Work In this essay, Anaya quotes from his novel *Bless Me, Ultima.* First published in 1972, the novel tells the story of a young boy, Antonio, who lives with his family in Guadalupe, New Mexico. Ultima, who is respected for her healing powers and her knowledge of the uses of plants, comes to live with Antonio's family. Ultima takes the boy under her wing and teaches him about the plants and trees of the area. She also teaches him some important lessons about life.

Connect to the Literature

Based on what you know about Anaya's writing, how would you expect him to describe the bond between people and the land? Explain your answer.

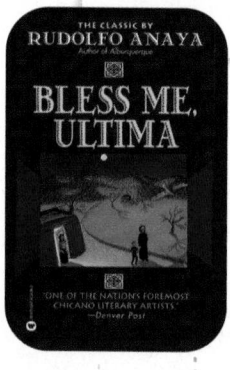

THE CLASSIC BY
RUDOLFO ANAYA
Author of Albuquerque

BLESS ME, ULTIMA

"ONE OF THE NATION'S FOREMOST CHICANO LITERARY ARTISTS"
—*Denver Post*

Vocabulary Builder
anguish (aŋ´ gwish) *n.* great pain or suffering

Vocabulary Development

Vocabulary Knowledge Rating
When students have completed reading and discussing "A Celebration of Grandfathers," have them take out their **Vocabulary Knowledge Rating Chart** for this selection. Read the words aloud once more and have students rate their knowledge of the words again in the After Reading column. Clarify any words that are still problematic. Have students write their own definition and example or sentence in the appropriate column. Then have students complete the **Vocabulary Builder Practice** activities on p. 413. Encourage students to use the words in further discussion and written work about this selection. Remind them that they will be accountable for these words on the Selection Test.

who act like the young. It is only the healthy, pink-cheeked, outgoing, older persons we are shown in the media. And they are always selling something, as if an entire generation of old people were salesmen in their lives. Commercials show very lively old men, who must always be in excellent health according to the new myth, selling insurance policies or real estate as they are out golfing; older women selling coffee or toilet paper to those just married. That image does not illustrate the real life of the old ones.

Real life takes into account the natural cycle of growth and change. My grandfather pointed to the leaves falling from the tree. So time brings with its transformation the often painful, wearing-down process. Vision blurs, health wanes; even the act of walking carries with it the painful reminder of the autumn of life. But this process is something to be faced, not something to be hidden away by false images. Yes, the old can be young at heart, but in their own way, with their own dignity. They do not have to copy the always-young image of the Hollywood star.

My grandfather wanted to return to his valley to die. But by then the families of the valley had left in search of a better future. It is only now that there seems to be a return to the valley, a revival. The new generation seeks its roots, that value of love for the land moves us to return to the place where our ancianos formed the culture.

I returned to Puerto de Luna last summer, to join the community in a celebration of the founding of the church. I drove by my grandfather's home, my uncles' ranches, the neglected adobe[15] washing down into the earth from whence it came. And I wondered, how might the values of my grandfather's generation live in our own? What can we retain to see us through these hard times? I was to become a farmer, and I became a writer. As I plow and plant my words, do I nurture as my grandfather did in his fields and orchards? The answers are not simple.

"They don't make men like that anymore," is a phrase we hear when one does honor to a man. I am glad I knew my grandfather. I am glad there are still times when I can see him in my dreams, hear him in my reverie. Sometimes I think I catch a whiff of that earthy aroma that was his smell, just as in lonely times sometimes I catch the fragrance of Ultima's herbs. Then I smile. How strong these people were to leave such a lasting impression.

So, as I would greet my abuelo long ago, it would help us all to greet the old ones we know with this kind and respectful greeting: "Buenos días le de Dios."

---

15. adobe (ə dō′ bē) *n.* sun-dried clay brick.

Reading Skill
Main Idea What main idea is supported by the detail of the neglected adobe homes?

A Celebration of Grandfathers ■ 411

16 Critical Thinking
Infer

- **Ask** students what the author thinks about how the media portrays the elderly.
  Answer: The media portrays the elderly as lively and youthful, which the author believes is a false image.

- **Ask** students why they think the author believes it is important to face the often painful process of aging.
  Possible response: The process of aging is part of the natural process of life. To pretend it is otherwise is to ignore the truth.

17 Reading Skill
Main Idea

- Have students read the paragraph aloud. Ask them to note some of the descriptive details the author uses in the paragraph.

- **Ask** students the Reading Skill question: What main idea is supported by the detail of the neglected condition of the adobe homes?
  Possible response: The main idea is the question of whether the values of the grandfather's generation will wash away like the adobe.

Concept Connector

Anticipation Guide
Have students return to their **Anticipation Guides** and respond to the statements again in the After Reading column. They may do this individually or in their original pairs or groups. Then, lead a class discussion, probing for what students have learned that confirms or invalidates each statement. Encourage students to cite specific details, quotations, or other evidence from the text to support their responses to each statement.

Connecting to the Literature
Have students compare the sentences they wrote before reading with their thoughts about older people after reading "A Celebration of Grandfathers." Ask them to explain whether their thoughts have changed and, if so, how.

Reading Skill Graphic Organizer
Ask students to review the graphic organizers they completed to identify the main idea and supporting details while reading. Show them **Reading Skill Graphic Organizer B** (*Graphic Organizer Transparencies,* p. 84) as an example.

1. Students may suggest that they found Anaya's description of his childhood memories of his grandfather most powerful, since he clearly conveys his grandfather's dignity, respect for nature, and wisdom.

2. (a) Anaya remembers their wisdom, knowledge, readiness to help one another, and generosity. (b) The old ones in the essay are self-sufficient, strong, wise, and independent. Modern mass media, according to Anaya, create misleading images of "youthful" old people—lively, healthy, and pink-cheeked.

3. (a) Anaya's grandfather refers to the present day, when time moves faster and does not allow for patience. He also understands that different kinds of knowledge, including the learning of English, will be important for his grandson's success. (b) Anaya implies that the new time will cause people to lose sight of the natural cycles of change, and that people must hold onto the old values and learn how to apply them to the new world.

4. (a) Old people should be treated with respect and care because they have wisdom and experience and because the transformations of age can be painful. (b) Most students will agree with Anaya. Many may have grandparents or other elderly relatives whom they love and honor and whom they have seen suffer from aging.

5. The use of repetition gives urgency to Anaya's message about the deep appreciation the elders had for the important things in life.

6. Students may say suggest the words *reverent* or *respectful*. Anaya describes the dignity and wisdom of the old ones.

7. **Possible response:** Diction: faith shone in their eyes; knew the rhythms and cycles of time; spoke plainly. **Style:** thoughtful; serious; urgent. **Tone:** so the string of life would not be broken; lived authentic lives; all sons and daughters to him. Another sample answer can be found on

Apply the Skills

A Celebration of Grandfathers

Thinking About the Selection

1. **Respond:** Which part of the essay is most powerful? Explain.
2. **(a) Recall:** What qualities of old people does Anaya remember from his childhood? **(b) Distinguish:** How are these qualities different from the images that Anaya says have been created by American mass media?
3. **(a) Recall:** What does Anaya's grandfather say is the "new time" in which Anaya will live? **(b) Infer:** What does the author imply about what this "new time" will bring for his people?
4. **(a) Draw Conclusions:** What opinion does Anaya offer on the way people should be treated as they grow old? **(b) Take a Position:** Do you agree with him? Explain. **(c) Discuss:** Discuss your answers with a partner. Then, explain how your answer has grown or changed as a result of the discussion.

Literary Analysis

5. At several points in his essay, Anaya strings together sentences that are structured in the same way, as in this example: "When they spoke, they spoke plainly and with few words, and they meant what they said. When they prayed, they went straight to the source of life. When there were good times, they knew how to dance in celebration. . . ." What effect does this aspect of the author's **syntax** create? Explain.
6. What one word might you use to describe the overall **tone** of "A Celebration of Grandfathers"? Explain.
7. Use a chart like the one shown to record examples of the **diction** and **tone** Anaya uses. Then, based on his diction and tone, write three adjectives in the center of the chart that describe Anaya's **style.**

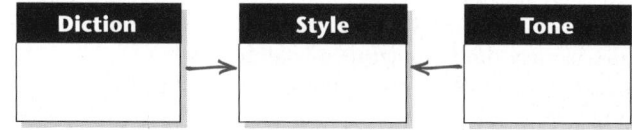

Reading Skill

8. State the **main idea** of Anaya's essay in your own words.
9. **(a)** List three **supporting details** that serve as evidence for the point that Anaya makes in his essay. **(b)** Do you think the author adequately supports his main idea with details? Why or why not?

QuickReview

Essay at a Glance
The author celebrates his native culture, in which older people are respected and honored.

Assessment
For: Self-test
Visit: www.PHSchool.com
Web Code: epa-6302

Author's Style: an author's way of writing; elements of style include *diction*, *syntax*, and *tone*

Main Idea: the central message, insight, or opinion in a work of nonfiction

Supporting Details: the pieces of evidence that a writer uses to prove a main idea

Literary Analysis Graphic Organizer B, p. 87, in *Graphic Organizer Transparencies.*

8. **Possible response:** Old people are strong, wise, and have something important to share.

9. (a) Supporting details might include, they were hard workers who tilled the earth and farmed, their faith "shone in their eyes," "they knew how to dance in celebration." (b) Yes. The author has used many details that show the strength and wisdom of the old ones, and how the author's grandfather passed on his wisdom.

Vocabulary Builder

Practice Determine whether each sentence below is true or false. Use the meaning of the underlined word to explain your reasoning.

1. A poor instruction manual is one that _perplexes_ its reader.
2. It is a compliment to have a business idea labeled "an _absurdity_."
3. To prevent a stain, allow ink to _permeate_ the fabric.
4. Comforting someone in _anguish_ is a kind action.

Adding Words to Your Vocabulary Using a thesaurus, find a **synonym**, or word of similar meaning, for each word italicized above. Use each synonym in a sentence that makes the meaning of the word clear. (For more on using a thesaurus, see page R7.)

Writing

Anaya's essay reflects his admiration for his elders. Think of an older person whom you admire. Write a few paragraphs of **book jacket copy** for a biography of that person. Book jackets often provide a brief introduction to a subject to entice people to read more.

- Include some highlights of the person's life.
- Choose details that will make the reader want to know more.

For *Grammar, Vocabulary,* and *Assessment,* see **Build Language Skills,** pp. 422–423.

Extend Your Learning

Listening and Speaking Anaya claims that "the American image created by the mass media is an image of youth, not old age." In a small group, hold a **panel discussion** about the validity of this claim. Consider these questions as you prepare:

- What is the age of most people in television shows and films?
- What messages do these images convey?

Each panelist should prepare notes to use during the discussion and should elaborate upon or illustrate each other's comments.

Research and Technology Use the Internet and an atlas to gather information about the geography and history of Puerta de Luna, a town Anaya discusses in his essay. Then, make an **annotated map** of New Mexico that shows the location of this town. Include a side column listing facts about the town.

Apply the Skills ■ 413

Extend Your Learning

The **Support for Extend Your Learning** page (*Unit 3 Resources,* p. 26) provides guided note-taking opportunities to help students complete the Extend Your Learning activities.

Go **Online**
——Research
For: An additional research activity
Visit: www.PHSchool.com
Web Code: epd-7301
For another research activity to extend students' learning, give students this Web Code.

Vocabulary Builder
Word Bank Practice

1. The sentence is true, because *perplexes* means it confuses its reader.

2. The sentence is false, because *absurdity* means something ridiculous.

3. The sentence is false. Allowing ink to spread through a fabric will not prevent a stain.

4. The sentence is true, because a person who is suffering should be comforted.

Adding Words to Your Vocabulary
Possible responses:

1. This instruction manual is so unclear that it just *confuses* me.

2. His idea for a new business was such *nonsense* that everyone just laughed.

3. Let the dye *saturate* the fabric so that the cloth is thoroughly colored.

4. Her *misery* at failing to make the team caused her grades to decline.

Writing

- To give students guidance for writing this book jacket copy, give them the **Support for Writing Lesson** for "A Celebration of Grandfathers," p. 25 in *Unit 3 Resources.*

- To evaluate students' book jacket copy, use the Biography rubrics, pp. 69–70, in *General Resources.* In addition, you might evaluate for how well students choose appropriate biographical highlights and interesting details of the person's life.

Six Traits Focus

Ideas		✔	Word Choice
Organization			Sentence Fluency
Voice			Conventions

WG **Writing and Grammar, Gold Level**
Students will find guidance on biographical writing in Chapter 4.

Build Language Skills

Go to pp. 422–423 for vocabulary and grammar lessons and assessment practice.

413

❸ Background
The Great Migration

Chicago was one of the most important destinations for African Americans migrating from the South. Between 1910 and 1920, Chicago's African American population grew from 44,000 to 110,000. An important link between Chicago and the rural African American communities of the South were the African American porters who worked on the Illinois Central Railroad. They carried the African American newspaper, the *Chicago Defender,* on their trips south. Southern African Americans were encouraged by reading the newspaper to migrate north.

❹ Connecting to the Literature

- Model use of the expressive vocabulary students are asked to use with these examples:

  1. My grandmother seemed to *embody* the work ethic passed down through our family.

  2. The old barn seemed to *signify* something important from the past.

  3. I did not expect that I would *react* so strongly to pictures of my father in military uniform.

  4. On visits to my grandparents' farm, talk of the past would always *dominate* the conversation.

- Help students further develop their expressive vocabulary by providing these words: *maternal, sentimental,* and *memorable.* Encourage students to use these words as they discuss the selection.

Go Online For additional informa-
—Author Link tion about Lorraine
Hansberry, have students type in the Web
Code, then select *H* from the alphabet,
and then select *Lorraine Hansberry.*

Reflective Essay

Build Understanding • *On Summer*

❸ Background

The Great Migration Beginning in the early 1900s, hundreds of thousands of African Americans left the rural South for northern cities. They fled discrimination and the floods and pests that threatened their livelihood as farmers. Many left relatives behind and, like Hansberry's Chicago family, journeyed south in summertime to visit.

❹ Connecting to the Literature

Reading/Writing Connection In "On Summer," the author's grandmother in Tennessee is a living link to her family's history. Write two or three sentences about a person, a place, or an object that reminds you of your connection with people of the past. Use at least three of these words: *embody, signify, dominate, react.*

Review

For **Literary Analysis, Reading Skill, and Vocabulary Builder,** see page 402

READ MORE
by
Lorraine Hansberry
To Be Young, Gifted, and Black
The Sign in Sidney Brustein's Window

Meet the Author

Lorraine **Hansberry** (1930–1965)

Lorraine Hansberry grew up on the South Side of Chicago, where her father prospered as a real-estate broker. At the time, many white people closed their neighborhoods, refusing to sell or rent property to African Americans. Hansberry's father fought this practice, taking his case all the way to the Supreme Court, where he won.

A Pioneering Playwright As her father fought to integrate Chicago's neighborhoods, Hansberry laid claim to territories of the imagination. With the 1959 production of her play *A Raisin in the Sun,* she became the first African American woman to have a drama produced on Broadway.

Fast Facts

▶ *A Raisin in the Sun* won a New York Drama Critics' Circle Award in 1959.

▶ A 1961 movie version of the play won recognition at the Cannes Film Festival.

Go Online
Author Link

For: More about the author
Visit: www.PHSchool.com
Web Code: epe-9303

On Summer

Lorraine Hansberry

❶ ❷

❸ It has taken me a good number of years to come to any measure of respect for summer. I was, being May-born, literally an "infant of the spring" and, during the later childhood years, tended, for some reason or other, to rather worship the cold aloofness of winter. The adolescence, admittedly lingering still, brought the traditional passionate commitment to melancholy autumn—and all that. For the longest kind of time I simply thought that *summer* was a mistake.

In fact, my earliest memory of anything at all is of waking up in a darkened room where I had been put to bed for a nap on a summer's afternoon, and feeling very, very hot. I acutely disliked

Vocabulary Builder
aloofness (ə lo͞of′ nəs)
n. quality of being distant or removed
melancholy (mel′ ən kä′ ē) *adj.* sad; gloomy

On Summer ■ 415

❶ Motivation
Prepare an **Anticipation Guide** (*General Resources,* pp. 8–10) with the following statements:

• Adults should pass on their childhood memories to future generations.

• Childhood memories provide a living link to a family's past.

• Memories that adults pass on to young people can give a clearer picture of history than books and movies.

Give students a copy of the prepared Anticipation Guide and have students mark their responses in the Me column. Have students discuss the statements in pairs or groups and mark the Guides again in the Group column.

Concept Connector ➡
Students will return to the Anticipation Guide after completing "On Summer."

Learning Modalities
Visual/Spatial Learners
Ask students to create posters or collages that visually suggest characteristics of their favorite season of the year. You may wish to have students form groups based on the seasons they prefer. Suggest that students create images or collect photographs from magazines that express both pleasant and unpleasant aspects of the season that they enjoy most. Exhibit the posters in the classroom.

❷ About the Selection
In "On Summer," Hansberry recalls her childhood dislike of summers. She remembers playing games with friends in the streets of Chicago and sleeping in the park when the nights were too hot to sleep in the house. During her eighth summer, she visits her grandmother in Tennessee. On a summer trip to Maine as an adult, she meets an elderly woman dying of cancer. Through conversations with this woman, Hansberry learns to respect and value summer as "the noblest of the seasons."

415

- Read the first two paragraphs of the essay aloud with the class. Then ask students to identify some of the words and phrases that the author uses to describe her feelings about summer.
  Answer: Some words and phrases include "very, very hot," "too-grainy texture of sand," "icky-perspiry feeling," "shadows too pronounced," "light too blinding."

- Remind students that the author's tone or attitude toward a subject is expressed in diction, or word choice.

- Ask the Literary Analysis question: How would you describe Hansberry's tone as she explains her childhood feelings about summer?
  Possible response: Students may suggest that the tone is one of dislike, disdain, or disgust.

❹ Literary Analysis
Style

- Refer students to the sentence containing the phrase *artsily-craftsily*. Ask students to explain what they think of when they hear the phrase *artsy-craftsy*.
  Possible response: Students may suggest that they think of something that is overdone or too elaborate, or something that is artificial or tries too hard to be artful.

- Ask the Literary Analysis question: In what way does the made-up word *artsily-craftsily* add to the sense of Hansberry's disdain for summer?
  Answer: The word adds to the author's idea that summer is overdone and too elaborate.

❸ the feeling then and retained the bias for years. It had originally been a matter of the heat but, over the years, I came actively to associate displeasure with most of the usually celebrated natural features and social by-products of the season: the too-grainy texture of sand; the too-cold coldness of the various waters we constantly try to escape into, and the icky-perspiry feeling of bathing caps.

It also seemed to me, esthetically[1] speaking, that nature had got inexcusably carried away on the summer question and let the whole thing get to be rather much. By duration alone, for instance, a summer's day seemed maddeningly excessive; an utter overstatement. Except for those few hours at either end of it, objects always appeared in too sharp a relief against backgrounds; shadows too pronounced and light too blinding. It always gave me the feeling of walking around in a motion picture which had been ❹ too artsily-craftsily exposed. Sound also had a way of coming to the ear without that muting influence, marvelously common to winter, across patios or beaches or through the woods. I suppose I found it too stark and yet too intimate a season.

My childhood Southside summers were the ordinary city kind, full of the street games which other rememberers have turned into fine ballets these days and rhymes that anticipated what some people insist on calling modern poetry:

> *Oh, Mary Mack, Mack, Mack*
> *All dressed in black, black, black*
> *With the silver buttons, buttons, buttons*
> *All down her back, back, back*
> *She asked her mother, mother, mother*
> *For fifteen cents, cents, cents*
> *To see the elephant, elephant, elephant*
> *Jump the fence, fence, fence*
> *Well, he jumped so high, high, high*
> *'Til he touched the sky, sky, sky*
> *And he didn't come back, back, back*
> *'Til the Fourth of Ju-ly, ly, ly!*

❺ Evenings were spent mainly on the back porches where screen doors slammed in the darkness with those really very special summertime sounds. And, sometimes, when Chicago nights got too steamy, the whole family got into the car and went to the park and slept out in the open on blankets. Those were, of course, the best times of all because the grownups were invariably reminded of

---

1. **esthetically** (es thet′ ik lē) *adv.* artistically.

416 ■ *Types of Nonfiction*

Vocabulary Development

Expressive Vocabulary
As students are discussing Hansberry's attitude toward summer, encourage them to use the expressive vocabulary presented earlier. You might encourage them with sentence starters like these:

1. When she was a child, summer seemed to *embody* . . .
2. I can understand how Hansberry could *react* . . .
3. Over the years, summer came to *signify* . . .
4. Her dislike for summer came to *dominate* . . .

having been children in rural parts of the country and told the best stories then. And it was also cool and sweet to be on the grass and there was usually the scent of freshly cut lemons or melons in the air. And Daddy would lie on his back, as fathers must, and explain about how men thought the stars above us came to be and how far away they were. I never did learn to believe that anything could be as far away as *that*. Especially the stars.

My mother first took us south to visit her Tennessee birthplace one summer when I was seven or eight, I think. I woke up on the back seat of the car while we were still driving through some place called Kentucky and my mother was pointing out to the beautiful hills on both sides of the highway and telling my brothers and my sister about how her father had run away and hidden from his master in those very hills when he was a little boy. She said that his mother had wandered among the wooded slopes in the moonlight and left food for him in secret places. They were very beautiful hills and I looked out at them for miles and miles after that wondering who and what a *master* might be.

I remember being startled when I first saw my grandmother rocking away on her porch. All my life I had heard that she was a great beauty and no one had ever remarked that they meant a half century before. The woman that I met was as wrinkled as a prune and could hardly hear and barely see and always seemed to be thinking of other times. But she could still rock and talk and even make wonderful cupcakes which were like cornbread, only sweet. She was captivated by automobiles and, even though it was well into the Thirties,[2] I don't think she had ever been in one before we came down and took her driving. She was a little afraid of them and could not seem to negotiate the windows, but she loved driving. She died the next summer and that is all that I remember about her, except that she was born in slavery and had memories of it and they didn't sound anything like *Gone With the Wind*.[3]

Like everyone else, I have spent whole or bits of summers in many different kinds of places since then: camps and resorts in the Middle West and New York State; on an island; in a tiny Mexican village; Cape Cod, perched atop the Truro bluffs at Longnook Beach that Millay wrote about; or simply strolling the streets of Provincetown[4] before the hours when the parties begin.

And, lastly, I do not think that I will forget days spent, a few summers ago, at a beautiful lodge built right into the rocky cliffs of a bay on the Maine coast. We met a woman there who had lived a

---

2. **Thirties** the 1930s.
3. **Gone With the Wind** novel set in the South during the Civil War period.
4. **Provincetown** resort town at the northern tip of Cape Cod, Massachusetts.

On Summer ■ 417

Literary Analysis
Style How does Hansberry's repetition of the word *And* to begin sentences emphasize the flow and abundance of her memories?

Reading Skill
Main Idea What information do these anecdotes about her trips to Tennessee add to your understanding of the author's childhood summers?

 Reading Check

Whom does Hansberry visit in Tennessee?

---

❽ Critical Viewing

Answer: Students will say that this photograph illustrates the area that Hansberry describes and that it helps them understand why the old woman was determined to live long enough to see another summer.

purposeful and courageous life and who was then dying of cancer. She had, characteristically, just written a book and taken up painting. She had also been of radical viewpoint all her life; one of those people who energetically believe that the world *can* be changed for the better and spend their lives trying to do just that. And that was the way she thought of cancer; she absolutely refused to award it the stature of tragedy, a devastating instance of the brooding doom and inexplicability[5] of the absurdity of human destiny, etc., etc. The kind of characterization given, lately, as we all know, to far less formidable foes in life than cancer.

❾ But for this remarkable woman it was a matter of nature in imperfection, implying, as always, work for man to do. It was an *enemy,* but a palpable one with shape and effect and source; and if it existed, it could be destroyed. She saluted it accordingly, without

---

5. **inexplicability** (in eks′ pli kə bil′ ə tē) *n.* condition of being unexplainable.

❽ ▼ Critical Viewing
How does this photograph of the Maine coast add to the description in the essay? **[Connect]**

Vocabulary Development

Vocabulary Knowledge Rating
When students have completed reading and discussing "On Summer," have them take out their **Vocabulary Knowledge Rating Chart** for this selection. Read the words aloud once more and have students rate their knowledge of the words again in the After Reading column. Clarify any words that are still problematic. Have students write their own definition and example or sentence in the appropriate column. Then have students complete the **Vocabulary Builder Practice** activities on p. 421. Encourage students to use the words in further discussion and written work about this selection. Remind them that they will be accountable for these words on the Selection Test.

despondency, but with a lively, beautiful and delightfully ribald anger. There was one thing, she felt, which would prove equal to its relentless ravages and that was the genius of man. Not his mysticism, but man with tubes and slides and the stubborn human notion that the stars are very much within our reach.

The last time I saw her she was sitting surrounded by her paintings with her manuscript laid out for me to read, because, she said, she wanted to know what a *young person* would think of her thinking; one must always keep up with what *young people* thought about things because, after all, they were *change*.

Every now and then her jaw set in anger as we spoke of things people should be angry about. And then, for relief, she would look out at the lovely bay at a mellow sunset settling on the water. Her face softened with love of all that beauty and, watching her, I wished with all my power what I knew that she was wishing: that she might live to see at least one more *summer*. Through her eyes I finally gained the sense of what it might mean; more than the coming autumn with its <u>pretentious</u> melancholy; more than an austere and silent winter which must shut dying people in for precious months; more even than the frivolous spring, too full of too many false promises, would be the gift of another summer with its stark and intimate assertion of neither birth nor death but life at the <u>apex</u>; with the gentlest nights and, above all, the longest days.

I heard later that she did live to see another summer. And I have retained my respect for the noblest of the seasons.

On Summer ■ 419

Literary Analysis
Style Which words convey Hansberry's feelings about the woman in Maine?

Vocabulary Builder
pretentious (prē ten′ shəs) *adj.* grand in a showy way
apex (ā′ peks′) *n.* highest point; peak

---

❾ Literary Analysis
Style

- Ask students to begin at the last paragraph on p. 418 and read to the end of the selection.

- Ask students how they would describe Hansberry's feelings about the woman in Maine.
  Answer: Students may suggest that Hansberry feels admiration for the woman's courage; she respects the woman for her strength in continuing to be productive in the face of her illness.

- Then **ask** the Literary Analysis question: Which words here convey Hansberry's feelings about the woman in Maine?
  Possible response: Students may suggest the phrases "lively, beautiful and delightfully ribald" and "her face softened with love."

Concept Connector

Anticipation Guide
Have students return to their **Anticipation Guides** and respond to the statements again in the After Reading column. They may do this individually or in their original pairs or groups. Then, lead a class discussion, probing for what students have learned that confirms or invalidates each statement.

Connecting to the Literature
Have students compare the sentences they wrote before reading with their thoughts about a connection to history and people of the past after reading "On Summer." Ask them to explain whether their thoughts have changed and, if so, how.

Reading Skill Graphic Organizer
Ask students to review the graphic organizers they completed to identify the main idea and supporting details while reading. Show them **Reading Skill Graphic Organizer B** (*Graphic Organizer Transparencies*, p. 85) as an example. Then have students share the graphic organizers they did and the main ideas and supporting details they identified.

Apply the Skills

On Summer

Thinking About the Selection

1. **Respond:** How do Hansberry's ideas about summer compare with your own? Make a list of some of the reasons why you like and dislike summer. Trade lists with a partner and discuss your answers. Then, explain how your answer has grown or changed as a result of the discussion.
2. **(a) Recall:** When does Hansberry first visit her grandmother? **(b) Infer:** Why do you think she includes the section about her grandmother in her essay?
3. **(a) Recall:** When does Hansberry's attitude toward summer change? **(b) Interpret:** At the end, she calls summer "the noblest of seasons." What do you think she means by this phrase?
4. **Evaluate:** How clearly do you think Hansberry explains the way her feelings about summer have changed? Explain your answer.

Literary Analysis

5. Hansberry begins many sentences in "On Summer" with the word *and*. What effect does this aspect of the author's **syntax** create? Explain.
6. What one word might you use to describe the overall **tone** of "On Summer"? Explain.
7. Review the last two paragraphs of "On Summer." Use a chart like the one shown to record examples of the **diction** and **tone** Hansberry uses in describing her associations with summer. Then, based on her diction and tone in these paragraphs, write three adjectives in the center of the chart to describe Hansberry's **style**.

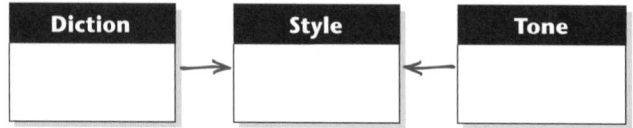

Reading Skill

8. State the **main idea** of "On Summer" in your own words.
9. **(a)** List three **supporting details** that serve as evidence for the point that Hansberry makes in the essay. **(b)** Do you think that the author adequately supports her main idea with details? Why or why not?

420 ■ Types of Nonfiction

QuickReview

Essay at a Glance
The author describes how and why her feelings about summer have changed.

For: Self-test
Visit: www.PHSchool.com
Web Code: epa-6303

Author's Style: an author's way of writing; elements of style include *diction*, *syntax*, and *tone*

Main Idea: the central message, insight, or opinion in a work of nonfiction

Supporting Details: the pieces of evidence that a writer uses to prove a main idea

---

Answers (left and bottom columns)

1. Students probably enjoy summer. They may mention they like summer because of freedom from school, vacations, and outdoor activities. They may dislike it because of the heat and because they get bored. After discussing with a partner, students may suggest that they have found more reasons to like or dislike summer.

2. (a) Hansberry is eight at her first visit. (b) It is a memory of a specific summer; it provides a contrast to her description of the woman in Maine.

3. (a) Hansberry's attitude changes during her time in Maine with the old woman. (b) She considers summer noble because it represents life "at the apex," in its most complete form.

4. Students may suggest that she explains her change in attitude clearly, since she states her attitude about summer early in the essay, and then describes how the woman in Maine affected her.

5. Students may suggest that the repeated use of the word *And* to begin sentences results in an innocent, almost childlike tone that reflects her memories of growing up.

6. Students may suggest the words *insightful* or *affectionate*. In the essay, she carefully examines her past memories, which she fondly describes, and she understands how her attitudes toward summer have changed.

7. **Possible response:** Diction: life at the apex, gentlest nights, longest days, noblest of the seasons; **Style:** thoughtful, solemn, formal; **Tone:** respectful, admiring, affectionate.

   Another sample answer can be found on **Literary Analysis Graphic Organizer B,** p. 89, in *Graphic Organizer Transparencies.*

8. **Possible response:** The main idea is that the author disliked summer as a young person, but learned to appreciate it as an adult.

9. (a) Supporting details might include, as a child, waking up from a summer nap and being very hot; as an adult, walking the streets of Provincetown and seeing a sunset over the water. (b) Students may suggest that she does not adequately support her main idea, since she includes many details that show that as a child she enjoyed summer rather than disliked it.

Vocabulary Builder

Practice Determine whether each sentence below is true or false. Use the meaning of the underlined word to explain your reasoning.

1. Greeting someone with *aloofness* shows respect for him or her.
2. Cheerful songs might change someone's *melancholy* mood.
3. A *pretentious* politician is likely to be unpopular with many voters.
4. One must climb a mountain to reach its *apex*.

Adding Words to Your Vocabulary Using a thesaurus, find a **synonym**, or word of similar meaning, for each italicized word above. Use each synonym in a sentence that makes the meaning of the word clear. (For more on using a thesaurus, see page R7.)

Writing

"On Summer" reflects Lorraine Hansberry's admiration for her elders. Think of an older person whom you admire. Write a few paragraphs of **book jacket copy** for a biography of that person. Book jackets often provide a brief introduction to a subject to entice people to read more.
- Include some highlights of the person's life.
- Choose details that will make the reader want to know more.

For *Grammar, Vocabulary,* and *Assessment,* see **Build Language Skills,** pp. 422–423.

Extend Your Learning

Listening and Speaking In a small group, hold a **panel discussion** on the pros and cons of each season of the year. Each panel member should speak in support of a favorite season. Consider these questions as you prepare:
- What in particular do you like about your favorite season?
- What are features of the season that others might dislike?

Each panelist should prepare notes to use during the discussion and should elaborate upon or illustrate each other's comments.

Research and Technology In her essay, Hansberry discusses the climate of Chicago, Illinois. Use the Internet and an atlas to gather data about Chicago's climate. Then, make an **annotated map** that shows Chicago in relation to the rest of the United States. Include a side column with facts about the city's climate.

Apply the Skills ■ 421

Extend Your Learning

The **Support for Extend Your Learning** page (*Unit 3 Resources,* p. 42) provides guided note-taking opportunities to help students complete the Extend Your Learning activities.

Go **Online**
Research
For: An additional research activity
Visit: www.PHSchool.com
Web Code: epd-7302
For another research activity to extend students' learning, give students this Web Code.

Vocabulary Builder
Word Bank Practice

1. The sentence is false, because *aloofness* means being distant or unfriendly.
2. The sentence is true, because *melancholy* means sadness.
3. The sentence is true, because *pretentious* people are viewed as pompous and phony.
4. The sentence is true, because the highest point of a mountain is its *apex.*

Adding Words to Your Vocabulary
Possible responses:

1. His coolness and *distance* made people reluctant to begin a conversation with him.
2. The sorrowful song about lost dreams filled the listeners with *sadness.*
3. His *showy* display of his wealth offended many people who were struggling to make a living.
4. The flag was planted on the *summit* of the hill where it could be seen for miles.

Writing

- To give students guidance for writing this book jacket copy, give them the **Support for Writing Lesson** for "On Summer," p. 41 in **Unit 3 Resources.**
- To evaluate students' book jacket copy, use the Biography rubrics, pp. 69–70, in *General Resources.* In addition, you might evaluate for how well students choose appropriate biographical highlights and interesting details.

Six Traits Focus

Ideas	✔ Word Choice
Organization	Sentence Fluency
Voice	Conventions

W₲ Writing and Grammar, Gold Level
Students will find guidance on biographical writing in Chapter 4.

Build Language Skills

Go to pp. 422–423 for vocabulary and grammar lessons and assessment practice.

Build Language Skills

A Celebration of Grandfathers • On Summer

Vocabulary Skill

- Introduce the prefix *con-* or *com-*. Ask students to brainstorm for words that contain these prefixes. **Possible responses:** *combine, combat, consist, consider, congress, contribution, conversation, convulsion, contain, contact, constitution*

- Explain how "with" or "together" contributes to the meaning of these words.

- Have students complete the Practice activity on this page.

Answers

1. base word: compel; compel is a verb; compulsion is a noun; *com-* + the root *-pel-* (drive), creates the meaning of being motivated with drive or force to do something

2. base word: conjoin; conjoin is a verb; conjunction is a noun; *com-* + the root *-junct-* (join) creates the meaning of joining together

3. base word: commit; commit is a verb; commitment is a noun; *com-* + the root *-mit-* (send) creates the meaning of pledging to a particular place or action

4. base word: confide; confide is a verb; confidence is a noun; *con-* + the root *-fid-* (trust) creates the meaning of doing something with trust

5. base word: compare; compare is a verb; comparison is a noun; *com-* + the root *-par-* (equal) creates the meaning of measuring the equality of two or more things

Grammar Lesson

- Tell students that they can substitute *to* or *for* in the sentence before an indirect object and have it make sense. For example, *I gave John the ball* can be restated *I gave the ball to John*. A direct object cannot be logically restated with *to* or *for*.

- Point out that pronouns functioning as indirect or direct objects use the objective case. Suggest that when using a compound object that includes a pronoun, students should read the sentence twice, once with each object to check for the proper case.

Answers

1. The ball hit the fans nearest to first base.

Vocabulary Skill

Prefixes The prefix *con-* or *com-* means "with" or "together." This prefix appears in English words that relate to the ideas of joining or coming together. For example, the word *concurrent* means "happening *along with* something else."

▶ **Example:** The two classes I wanted to take were *concurrent,* so I could attend only one.

Con- at the beginning of a word is not always a prefix meaning *with* or *together.* Sometimes, *con-* adds emphasis to the base word, as in *confirm.*

Practice Look up each word in a dictionary. Use the entry to help you locate the base word. Tell the part of speech for both words. Then, explain how the prefix contributes to the meaning.

▶ **Example:** Conjunction (n) a joining *together*; conjoin (v) join *together*.

1. compulsion
2. conjunction
3. commitment

4. confidence
5. comparison

Grammar Lesson

Direct and Indirect Objects A **direct object** is a noun or pronoun that *receives* the action of an action verb. An **indirect object** appears with a direct object and names the person or thing that something is *given to* or *done for.*

You can determine whether a word is a direct object by asking *Whom?* or *What?* after an action verb. You can tell whether a word is an indirect object by asking *To or for whom?* or *To or for what?*

> The family bought *an old house.* (Direct object—answers the question **what?**)

> The rain pelted *the campers.* (Direct object—answers the question **whom?**)

> I wrote my brother (indirect object) letters. (direct object)

Practice For each item, write a sentence in which you use the word or phrase as directed in the parenthetical information.

1. fans (as a direct object)
2. muffins, toast, and bagels (as a direct object in a question)
3. dancers and singers (as a direct object in a statement)

4. Maria and Joe (as an indirect object in a question)
5. me (as an indirect object in a statement)

*W*G *Prentice Hall Writing and Grammar Connection: Chapter 20, Section 3*

422 ■ Types of Nonfiction

MorePractice

For more practice with direct and indirect objects, see the Grammar Handbook, p. R42.

2. Did you buy muffins, toast, and bagels at the restaurant?

3. The theater hired twenty dancers and singers for the musical production.

4. Did you give Maria and Joe their tickets to the game?

5. When Jeremy gave me the house key, I put it in my pocket.

*W*G **Writing and Grammar, Gold Level**
Students will find further instruction and practice on direct and indirect objects in Chapter 20, Section 3.

Teaching Resources

The following resources can be used to enrich or extend the instruction for Build Language Skills.

Unit Resources
   Build Language Skills: Vocabulary: Prefixes, p. 44
   Build Grammar Skills: Direct and Indirect Objects, p. 45

Reading: Main Idea and Supporting Details

Directions: *Read the selection. Then, answer the questions.*

Today, New Mexico is the home of over 50,000 Pueblo people, descendants of Indians who inhabited the area for nearly 2,000 years. The ancient Pueblo Indians are known for their villages of adobe "apartment buildings." These building were up to four stories tall. These apartments could have as many as 1,000 rooms. Ladders connected the lower floors to the upper floors. A family's section was arranged in a row of rooms from the center of the apartment complex, with rooms connected by doorways. The ground-floor rooms were used for storage of grain and other goods.

1. A question to guide further reading to subsequent passages might be
   A What crops did the Pueblo people grow?
   B What architect designed these dwellings?
   C Would this be a good tourist attraction?
   D How did they build these dwellings?

2. The main idea of this paragraph is that
   A Pueblo people survived for nearly 2,000 years.
   B Ancient Pueblo Indians built adobe "apartment buildings."
   C Pueblos had as many as 1,000 rooms.
   D New Mexico is home to over 50,000 Pueblo people.

3. A key detail that would help define the main idea is
   A "Today, . . . Pueblo people. . . ."
   B "The ancient Pueblo Indians . . . buildings.'"
   C "Ladders connected . . . upper floors."
   D "The ground-floor . . . other goods."

4. Which is not a supporting detail?
   A "Today, . . . Pueblo people. . ."
   B "Ladders connected . . . upper floors."
   C "A family's section was . . . connected by doorways."
   D "These buildings were up to four stories tall."

Timed Writing: Evaluation [Critical Stance]

Review "On Summer" or "A Celebration of Grandfathers." Evaluate how well the author achieves his or her purpose. In your evaluation, cite details from the text to illustrate your points. **(20 minutes)**

Writing Workshop: *Work in Progress*

Business Letter
Choose one consumer item from your product list. Consider the types of information a company representative would need to know. Jot down three questions that would have to be answered for the reader to understand your complaint. Save these questions in your portfolio.

Reading: Main Idea and Supporting Details
1. D   3. C
2. B   4. A

Timed Writing

- Tell students that evaluations are most convincing when they are grounded in evidence from the text. Personal interpretation is important, but opinions alone are not sufficient. The critic must use textual evidence that will be convincing to the reader.

- Make sure students understand the criterion of this evaluation—how well does the author fulfill his or her purpose? This means that students must be clear about what the author's purpose is. Suggest that students begin by identifying the purpose of the essay they are evaluating.

- Assess students' essays on their clarity, organization, and use of textual details to support their ideas.

- Suggest that students organize their time to give five minutes to planning, ten minutes to writing, and five minutes to reviewing and revising.

Writing Workshop
Work in Progress

Business Letter

- Have students go to their portfolios and take out the product list that they made in the **Work-in-Progress** assignment on p. 397.

- Remind students that this work may be used in the business letter that they will write in the **Writing Workshop** at the end of Part 1.

- Have students imagine that they are a company's customer service representative. Then, have them think about what information they would need to authorize a refund of a customer's money.

- Remind students that these questions must be ones that the consumer can logically answer if the complaint is valid.

- When students have completed their questions, have them save them in their portfolios. They will use these questions as they continue this **Work in Progress.**

Planning Differentiated Instruction

Choosing Your Selection

You may use either selection to meet the lesson standards. The following guide will help you determine which of the two selections is more appropriate for your students.

Accessibility at a Glance

	The News	Single Room, Earth View
Context	Commentary on contemporary television newscasts	Personal reflections on viewing Earth from space
Language	Diction and concepts more difficult Complex sentence structure	Accessible vocabulary Relatively short sentences
Concept Level	Challenging (weighing the merits of broadcast journalism)	Accessible (commentary on the beauty of Earth as seen from space)
Literary Merit	Critique	Cross-curricular connection
Lexile	1170L	1320L
Overall Rating	More challenging	More accessible

Because a number of factors help determine the relative accessibility of paired selections, the Lexile number of the more challenging selection may sometimes be lower than that of the more accessible selection.

Using the Other Selection You may use the other selection for homework or independent reading to reinforce the selection skills. If you use both selections, you can build a test for both using *ExamView®* Test Bank software.

Choosing Your Resources

[L1] Special Needs Students   [L4] Advanced Students

[L2] Below-Level Students   [EL] English Learners

[L3] All Students

FT Fast Track Instruction: To move the lesson more quickly, use the strategies and activities identified with **FT**.

Reading and Vocabulary Warm-ups provide support for below level students. **A** is for students reading two grades below level; **B** is for students reading one grade below level. For Selection Tests, **A** signifies "less challenging" and **B** "more challenging." For Graphic Organizer transparencies, **A** signifies "not filled in" and **B** "filled in."

Scaffolding for Less Proficient and Advanced Students

The leveled questions on Apply the Skills pages progress in the levels of thinking required to answer them. To address the needs of your different students, you may use the (a) level questions for your less proficient students, the (b) level with your on-level and advanced students. The occasional (c) level questions are appropriate for your advanced students.

Step-by-Step Teaching Guide	Pacing Guide	
PRETEACH		
• Administer Vocabulary and Reading Warm-ups as necessary.		
• Introduce the Literary Analysis Skill: Expository Essay. **FT**	10 min.	
• Introduce the Reading Skill: Identify Main Idea and Supporting Details. **FT**	10 min.	
• Prepare students to read by teaching the selection vocabulary. **FT**	10 min.	
• Build background and develop expressive vocabulary with Connecting to the Literature and Background.	10 min.	
• Engage students' interest with the motivation activity.	10 min.	
TEACH		
• Informally monitor comprehension while students read independently or in groups. **FT**	30 min.	
• Monitor students' comprehension with the Reading Check notes.	as students read	
• Reinforce vocabulary with Vocabulary Builder notes.	as students read	
• Develop students' understanding of expository essays with the Literary Analysis annotations. **FT**	5 min.	
• Develop students' ability to identify main idea and supporting details with the Reading Skill annotations. **FT**	10 min.	
ASSESS/EXTEND		
• Assess students' comprehension and mastery of the Reading Skill and Literary Analysis by having them answer the Apply the Skills questions. **FT**	35 min.	
• Have students complete the Vocabulary Builder activities. **FT**	5 min.	
• Apply students' ability to write a script with the Writing activity. **FT**	30–45 min. or homework	
• Extend students' listening and speaking and research and technology skills with one or both of the Extend Your Learning activities.	15–30 min. or homework	
• Have students complete the Vocabulary Skill and Grammar Lesson.	5 min.	
• Monitor students' progress with the Assessment Practice.	20–40 min.	
• Administer **Selection Test A** or **Selection Test B. FT**	15 min.	

 Go Online
Professional Development
For: Information about Lexiles
Visit: www.PHSchool.com
Web Code: eue-1111

Resources

Meeting Your Standards

Students will

1. **analyze and respond to literary elements.**
   - Literary Analysis: Expository Essay

2. **read, comprehend, and analyze expository essays.**
   - Reading Skill: Identify Main Idea and Supporting Details
   - Reading Strategy: Rereading to Identify the Main Idea and Supporting Details
   - Reading Check questions
   - Apply the Skills questions
   - Assessment Practice

3. **develop vocabulary.**
   - Vocabulary Builder
   - Latin prefixes *con-/com-, equi-*

4. **apply grammar skills.**
   - Predicate Nominatives and Predicate Adjectives

5. **develop writing proficiency.**
   - Work in Progress: Business letter
   - Script

6. **extend learning.**
   - Listening and Speaking: Informal Presentation
   - Research and Technology: Journal Entries

Block Scheduling: Use one 90-minute class period to preteach the skills and have students read the selection. Use a second 90-minute class period to assess students' mastery of skills, extend their learning, and monitor their progress.

Homework Suggestions

Following are possibilities for homework assignments.

- Support pages from *Unit 3 Resources*:
  Literary Analysis
  Reading Skill
  Build Vocabulary
  Enrichment

- An Extend Your Learning project and the Writing assignment for your chosen selection may be completed over several days.

PRENTICE HALL

Teacher EXPRESS™
Plan · Teach · Assess Use this complete suite of powerful teaching tools to make lesson planning and testing quicker and easier.

PRENTICE HALL

Student EXPRESS™
Learn · Study · Succeed Use the Interactive Textbook (online and on CD-ROM) to make selections and activities come alive with audio and video support and interactive questions.

① Literary Analysis
Expository Essay

- Tell students that an *expository essay* attempts to give the reader new information or a new perspective or understanding about something. Then, ask the class to read the discussion of expository essay on this page.

- Tell students that most essays use some type of description. Description appeals to one or more of the senses. For example, if the essay is about a process, the writer might include vivid descriptions to help readers "see" the steps involved. As they read the assigned essay, have students notice to what senses descriptive passages in the essay appeal.

- Writers often compare or contrast the subject of their essays with something else to help clarify their ideas. For example, a writer might compare or contrast the view from an airplane with the view from a train. Encourage students to notice whether the writer uses comparison and contrast effectively.

- Remind students that a cause is the reason for an action or event. An effect is the result of an action or event. Writers often use cause and effect to help readers understand a process or an event. Have students watch for causes and effects in the assigned essay.

② Reading Skill
Rereading to Identify Main Idea and Supporting Details

- Tell students that the main idea is the most important concept in an essay. The main idea may not be stated directly. It may be implied. The reader must then look at the supporting details to determine the main idea.

- If students cannot identify supporting details easily, suggest that they reread passages. By pausing and rereading the text, the main idea and supporting details often become clearer.

- To help students identify the main idea of the assigned selection, give them a copy of the **Reading Skill Graphic Organizer A** (*Graphic Organizer Transparencies,* p. 90) to fill in as they read.

424

Build Skills *The News • Single Room, Earth View*

Practice these skills with either "The News" (p. 426) or "Single Room, Earth View" (p. 437).

① Literary Analysis

An **expository essay** is a short piece of nonfiction that presents information, discusses ideas, or explains a process. The writer may use a variety of techniques to provide support, depth, and context:

- **Description:** including language that appeals to the senses
- **Comparison and contrast:** showing similarities and differences between two or among more than two items
- **Cause and effect:** explaining the relationship between events, actions, or situations by showing how one can result in another

② Reading Skill

The **main idea** is the central message, insight, or opinion in a work of nonfiction. The **supporting details** are the pieces of evidence that a writer uses to prove his or her point. **Reread** to help you **identify the main idea and supporting details** in a work.

- Note key details to decide what the main idea might be.
- If a detail does not seem to support that main idea, reread the passage to be sure that you have not misinterpreted it.
- If necessary, revise your assumptions about the main idea.

Use a chart like the one shown to record the details of a work and the main idea they might support.

Vocabulary Builder

The News

- **compensation** (käm′ pən sā′ shən) *n.* anything that makes up for a loss, damage, or debt (p. 426) *When they ran out of prizes, they gave free tickets as compensation.*

- **temporal** (tem′ pə rəl) *adj.* having to do with time (p. 426) *His persistent lateness suggests that he has no temporal sense.*

- **revered** (ri vird′) *adj.* regarded with great respect and awe (p. 431) *Many students came to the retirement party for the revered teacher.*

- **daunting** (dônt′ iŋ) *adj.* intimidating (p. 432) *Climbing Mount Everest is a daunting task.*

Single Room, Earth View

- **articulate** (är tik′ yōō lit) *adj.* expressing oneself clearly and easily (p. 437) *The candidate is an articulate public speaker.*

- **novice** (näv′ is) *adj.* new to an activity; inexperienced (p. 438) *For a novice chess player, she shows great patience and maturity.*

- **diffused** (di fyōōzd′) *v.* spread out (p. 441) *The wind diffused the confetti over the field.*

- **extrapolating** (ek strap′ ə lāt′ iŋ) *v.* arriving at a conclusion by inferring from known facts (p. 441) *I decided I would like the whole CD by extrapolating from the first song.*

424 ■ Types of Nonfiction

Vocabulary Development

Vocabulary Knowledge Rating

Create a **Vocabulary Knowledge Rating Chart** for the selection you will teach from this set. Include the selection vocabulary from this page and the additional expressive vocabulary students are asked to use at the end of Connecting to the Literature. These words will increase students' expressive vocabulary.

Give students a copy of the chart with the words on it. Introduce the words by reading them aloud and having students mark their rating in the Before Reading column. Urge them to be alert to these words as they read and discuss the selection because they will rate their knowledge of the words again after they finish.

If you wish, you may tally how many students know (or think they know) a word to gauge how much instruction you need to provide. As students read, point out the words and their context.

Essay

❸ Background

Television News In 1948, only 400,000 American homes had a television. By 1960, more than 46 million American homes had a television, and TV began to take over as the news medium of choice. Today, television news is one of the most influential institutions in American culture.

❹ Connecting to the Literature

Reading/Writing Connection In "The News," Neil Postman analyzes the pros and cons of television news. Write a short paragraph telling how you learn about newsworthy events and explaining which medium you prefer. Use at least three of these words: *analyze, rely, clarify, indicate.*

READ MORE
by
Neil Postman
Technopoly: The Surrender of Culture to Technology
The End of Education

Meet the Author

Neil **Postman** (1931–2003)

Neil Postman was a media critic and a revered professor of communications at New York University, where he taught for more than forty years. He called his field "media ecology," and his great concern was the effect of television on Americans.

Teachings on Television Born in New York, Postman received a doctorate in education from Columbia University. He also wrote twenty books and hundreds of articles. One of his most intense arguments is set forth in *The Disappearance of Childhood* (1982), in which he asserts that television exposes children to adult concerns far too early.

Fast Facts

▶ Postman once said, "You have to understand, what Americans do is watch television. I am not saying that's who they are. But that is what they *do*. Americans . . . watch . . . television."

▶ In 1986, Postman won the George Orwell Award from the National Council of Teachers of English.

Go **Online**
Author Link

For: More about the author
Visit: www.PHSchool.com
Web Code: epe-9304

The News ■ 425

❸ Background
Television News

In 1980, Ted Turner, founder of Turner Broadcasting, created a 24-hour news station. The Cable News Network, or CNN, became the most important innovation in cable broadcasting, offering live news coverage from around the world, 24 hours a day. CNN news bureaus were opened in cities throughout the world. Today, several cable news operations compete for viewers, not only on television, but also on the Internet.

❹ Connecting to the Literature

- To help students understand the meanings of the words they are asked to use, give them these sentences:
  1. Television newscasts cannot thoroughly *analyze* world events.
  2. I often *rely* on television news alone for information on current events.
  3. Newspapers help me *clarify* an issue better than television newscasts can.
  4. Television newscasts do not always *indicate* the source for their stories.

- Help students further develop their expressive vocabulary by providing these words: *informative, intense, priority,* and *supplement.* Encourage students to use these words as they discuss the selection.

Go **Online** For additional information about Neil Postman,
Author Link
have students type in the Web Code and then select *Neil Postman.*

Ask students to work in small groups. Give them a copy of a **KWL Chart** (see *General Resources,* p. 12) with the topic identified as "Television News Broadcasts."

Ask students to work together to complete the first two columns. In the Know column, they can write what they know or what they learned doing the Connecting to the Literature activity. In the Want to Know column, they should write questions they have about television news broadcasts.

Concept Connector ➡

Students will assess what they have learned after completing "The News."

Learning Modalities
Verbal/Linguistic Learners

Have students compare television and newspaper coverage of a news event by having them watch a local or national newscast and making notes on the details reported about the event. Then have students find an account of the same event by reading their local newspaper or an online version of a newspaper. Have students list the ideas or insights given in the print or electronic newspaper that were not given in the televised story. Encourage students to share their findings with the class.

❷ About the Selection

In "The News," Neil Postman explains the limitations of television news coverage. He explains how television's reliance on visual images determines what stories are covered. Because little time can be devoted to analysis or explanation of a story, television news has become a kind of entertainment, with the news anchor as the host of the show.

The News

Neil Postman

❶ ❷

T he whole problem with news on television comes down to this: all the words uttered in an hour of news coverage could be printed on one page of a newspaper. And the world cannot be understood in one page. Of course, there is a compensation: television offers pictures, and the pictures move. It is often said that moving pictures are a kind of language in themselves, and there is a good deal of truth in this. But the language of pictures differs radically from oral and written language, and the differences are crucial for understanding television news.

To begin with, the grammar of pictures is weak in communicating past-ness and present-ness. When terrorists want to prove to the world that their kidnap victims are still alive, they photograph them holding a copy of a recent newspaper. The dateline on the newspaper provides the proof that the photograph was taken on or after that date. Without the help of the written word, film and videotape cannot portray temporal dimensions with any precision. Consider a film clip showing an aircraft carrier at sea. One might be able to identify the ship as Soviet[1] or American, but there would be no way of telling where in the world the carrier was, where it was headed, or when the pictures were taken. It is

Vocabulary Builder
compensation (käm´ pən sā´ shən) *n.* anything that makes up for a loss, damage, or debt

temporal (tem´ pə rəl) *adj.* having to do with time

---

1. **Soviet** (sō´ vē et´) belonging to the Soviet Union, the formerly socialist nation known today as Russia.

426 ■ *Types of Nonfiction*

Vocabulary Development

Multiple Meanings
Tell students that the vocabulary word *compensation* can be used in several ways. Refer them to the word as it is used in the first paragraph of this selection and to the definition shown on this page. Point out that in this case *compensation* refers to the advantage that television pictures offer.

Explain that the word *compensation* is often used to refer to salary or payment for work done. For example, "John was very happy with the *compensation* that he received on his new job."

Compensation can also be used to refer to a physical change brought on by a lack in another part of the body. For example, "Andy worked hard to build up the muscles in his right arm as *compensation* for the injury and loss of strength in his left arm."

Encourage students to write one or two sentences using *compensation* in different ways. Have them share their sentences with the class.

only through language—words spoken over the pictures or reproduced in them—that the image of the aircraft carrier takes on meaning as a portrayal of a specific event.

Still, it is possible to enjoy the image of the carrier for its own sake. One might find the hugeness of the vessel interesting; it signifies military power on the move. There is a certain drama in watching the planes come in at high speeds and skid to a stop on the deck. Suppose the ship were burning: that would be even more interesting. This leads to a second point about the language of pictures. The grammar of moving pictures favors images that change. That is why violence and destruction find their way onto television so often. When something is destroyed violently its constitution is altered in a highly visible way: hence the entrancing power of fire. Fire gives visual form to the ideas of consumption, disappearance, death—the thing which is burned is actually taken away by fire. It is at this very basic level that fires make a good subject for television news. Something was here, now it's gone, and the change is recorded on film.

Earthquakes and typhoons have the same power: before the viewer's eyes the world is taken apart. If a television viewer has relatives in Mexico City and an earthquake occurs there, then she may take an interest in the images of destruction as a report from a specific place and time. That is, she may look to television news for information about an important event. But film of an earthquake can still be interesting if the viewer cares nothing about the event itself. Which is only to say that there is another way of participating in the news—as a spectator who desires to be entertained. Actually to see buildings topple is exciting, no matter where the buildings are. The world turns to dust before our eyes.

Those who produce television news in America know that their medium favors images that move. That is why they despise "talking heads," people who simply appear in front of a camera and speak. When talking heads appear on television, there is nothing to record or document, no change in process. In the cinema the situation is somewhat different. On a movie screen, close-ups of a good actor speaking dramatically can sometimes be interesting to watch. When Clint Eastwood narrows his eyes and challenges his rival to shoot first, the spectator sees the cool rage of the Eastwood character take visual form, and the narrowing of the eyes is dramatic. But much of the effect of this small movement depends on the size of the movie screen and the darkness of the theater, which make Eastwood and his every action "larger than life."

The television screen is smaller than life. It occupies about 15 percent of the viewer's visual field (compared to about 70 percent for the movie screen). It is not set in a darkened theater closed off

---

❸ ◀ Critical Viewing
How does this backstage view of a news show compare with the news programs you may have seen on television? **[Use Prior Knowledge]**

Literary Analysis
Expository Essay
How do details about airplanes and fire support Postman's point that television favors change?

❺ ✓ Reading Check
Why do television producers despise "talking heads"?

The News ■ 427

---

❸ Critical Viewing
This backstage view shows a studio that is messier and less formal than the stage set the TV audience sees. The multiple monitors, pens and papers on the desks, and concentrated postures of the workers suggest the intensity of this environment. The photo also shows that the anchorperson, whom TV viewers usually see as the one in charge, is not necessarily calling the shots—these people behind the scenes play a critical role in the production.

❹ Literary Analysis
Expository Essay
- After reading the paragraph aloud, ask students to identify the images the author is describing here.
  Answer: The author is describing an aircraft carrier on fire with planes landing on it.
- **Ask** the Literary Analysis question: How do details about airplanes and fire support Postman's point that television favors change?
  Answer: This image is one of airplanes skidding to a stop on the deck of the ship, while fire roars, which is a dramatic scene that engages the viewer, who watches to see what will happen next.

❺ Reading Check
Answer: Television producers despise talking heads because television news needs images that move.

- Have students read the bracketed passage.
- **Ask** the Literary Analysis question: What topic will Postman analyze more closely in this expository essay?
  Answer: The essay will analyze the structure of a typical newscast.
- Have students **identify** the technique Postman uses to support his idea.
  Answer: Postman uses description to support his idea.

⑦ Critical Viewing

Answer: Postman would say that the image of the wind blowing the tree, the rough ocean, and the people trying to stand against the wind are typical of the turbulent, moving images in a television newscast.

from the world but in the viewer's ordinary living space. This means that visual changes must be more extreme and more dramatic to be interesting on television. A narrowing of the eyes will not do. A car crash, an earthquake, a burning factory are much better.

⑥   With these principles in mind, let us examine more closely the structure of a typical newscast. In America, almost all news shows begin with music, the tone of which suggests important events about to unfold. (Beethoven's Fifth Symphony would be entirely appropriate.) The music is very important, for it equates the news with various forms of drama and ritual—the opera, for example, or a wedding procession—in which musical themes underscore the meaning of the event. Music takes us immediately into the realm of the symbolic, a world that is not to be taken literally. After all, when events unfold in the real world, they do so without musical accompaniment. More symbolism follows. The sound of teletype machines can be heard in the studio, not because it is impossible to screen this noise out, but because the sound is a kind of music in itself. It tells us that data are pouring in from all corners of the globe, a sensation reinforced by the world map in the background (or clocks noting the time on different continents).

⑦ ▾ Critical Viewing
Which aspects of this picture would Postman say are typical of images in a television newscast?
[Connect]

428 ■ *Types of Nonfiction*

Vocabulary Development

Expressive Vocabulary
As students discuss Postman's analysis of a typical newscast, encourage them to use the expressive vocabulary presented earlier. You might offer them sentence starters like these:

1. Postman *analyzes* the role of . . .
2. He explains why television news must *rely* on . . .
3. To *clarify* the part that music plays in newscasts, Postman . . .
4. Newscasts use music to *indicate* . . .

8 Already, then, before a single news item is introduced, a great deal has been communicated. We know that we are in the presence of a symbolic event, a form of theater in which the day's events are to be dramatized. This theater takes the entire globe as its subject, although it may look at the world from the perspective of a single nation. A certain tension is present, like the atmosphere in a theater just before the curtain goes up. The tension is represented by the music, the staccato beat of the teletype machines, and the sight of newsworkers scurrying around typing reports and answering phones. As a technical matter, it would be no problem to build a set in which the newsroom staff remained off camera, invisible to the viewer, but an important theatrical effect would be lost. By being busy on camera, the workers help communicate urgency about the events at hand, which it is suggested are changing so rapidly that constant revision of the news is necessary.

The staff in the background also helps signal the importance of the person in the center, the anchorman (or -woman) "in command" of both the staff and the news. The anchorman plays the role of host. He welcomes us to the newscast and welcomes us back from the different locations we visit during filmed reports. His voice, appearance, and manner establish the mood of the broadcast. It would be unthinkable for the anchor to be ugly, or a nervous sort who could not complete a sentence. Viewers must be able to believe in the anchor as a person of authority and skill, a person who would not panic in a crisis—someone to trust.

This belief is based not on knowledge of the anchorman's character or achievements as a journalist, but on his presentation of self while on the air. Does he look the part of a trusted man? Does he speak firmly and clearly? Does he have a warm smile? Does he project confidence without seeming arrogant? The value the anchor must communicate above all else is control. He must be in control of himself, his voice, his emotions. He must know what is coming next in the broadcast, and he must move smoothly and confidently from segment to segment. Again, it would be unthinkable for the anchor to break down and weep over a story, or laugh uncontrollably on camera, no matter how "human" these responses may be.

Reading Skill
Main Idea How does each of these details support Postman's idea that a newscast is a form of theater?

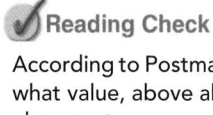

9 **Reading Check**

According to Postman, what value, above all else, must a news anchorperson convey?

The News ■ 429

---

8 **Reading Skill**
Main Idea

- Have students use the blank Reading Skills Organizer A (*Graphic Organizer Transparencies,* p. 90). As you read aloud from the top of p. 429 to the end of the paragraph, have students record details that support the idea of a newscast as a piece of theater.

- **Ask** students the Reading Skill question: How do each of these details support Postman's idea that a newscast is a form of theater? **Possible responses:** These details show how a newscast is like a form of theater by describing the subject of the production, the tension at the opening, and the sounds and sights that heighten the tension.

9 **Reading Check**

Answer: The anchorperson must convey the impression of control.

Differentiated
Instruction   Solutions for All Learners

Enrichment for Advanced Readers
Have students work in pairs to analyze a news broadcast using Postman's criteria. Have students view or videotape all or part of an evening broadcast news program, then write a report on a story from the news show. They should describe and analyze the introductory music and other introductory material, the moving images in the story, and the behavior of the anchor person. Then, have them explain whether their analysis supports Postman's claim that the news broadcast is a form of theater.

If time permits, have students present their report to the class. If possible, have them show the video recording of the news story.

⑩ Critical Thinking

Interpret

- Read aloud the passage beginning "While the form of a news broadcast. . ." Then, **ask** students to describe the main criteria producers use to choose stories for a news broadcast.
  Answer: The main criterion is the quality of the images for the story.

- Ask students to explain why, according to Postman, the most important news stories often do not get the most coverage on the news broadcasts.
  Answer: Sometimes the important news stories have very little action or moving images or require lengthy explanations.

- Ask students to explain whether they think Postman feels the public is well served by broadcast news.
  Possible responses: Students may suggest that Postman does not feel the public is well served, because important news stories are often not reported or they are not reported in detail. Thus, the public is not well informed.

⑪ Critical Viewing

Answer: In this image Jennings appears confident, trustworthy, firm, and in control—all traits that are expected in news anchors.

Many other features of the newscast help the anchor to establish the impression of control. These are usually equated with professionalism in broadcasting. They include such things as graphics that tell the viewer what is being shown, or maps and charts that suddenly appear on the screen and disappear on cue, or the orderly progression from story to story, starting with the most important events first. They also include the absence of gaps or "deadtime" during the broadcast, even the simple fact that the news starts and ends at a certain hour. These common features are thought of as purely technical matters, which a professional crew handles as a matter of course. But they are also symbols of a dominant theme of television news: the imposition of an orderly world—called "the news"—upon the disorderly flow of events.

⑩ While the form of a news broadcast emphasizes tidiness and control, its content can best be described as chaotic. Because time is so precious on television, because the nature of the medium favors dynamic visual images, and because the pressures of a commercial structure require the news to hold its audience above all else, there is rarely any attempt to explain issues in depth or place events in their proper context. The news moves nervously from a warehouse fire to a court decision, from a guerrilla war to a World Cup match, the quality of the film often determining the length of the story. Certain stories show up only because they offer dramatic pictures. Bleachers collapse in South America: hundreds of people are crushed—a perfect television news story, for the cameras can record the face of disaster in all its anguish. Back in Washington, a new budget is approved by Congress. Here there is nothing to photograph because a budget is not a physical event; it is a document full of language and numbers. So the producers of the news will show a photo of the document itself, focusing on the cover where it says: "Budget of the United States of America." Or sometimes they will send a camera crew to the government printing plant where copies of the budget are produced. That evening, while the contents of the budget are summarized by a voice-over, the viewer sees stacks of documents being loaded into boxes at the government printing plant. Then a few of the budget's more important provisions will be flashed on the screen in written form, but this is such a time-consuming process—using television as a printed page—that the producers keep it to a minimum. In short, the budget is not televisable, and for that reason its time on the news must be brief. The bleacher collapse will get more minutes that evening.

With priorities of this sort, it is almost impossible for the news to offer an adequate account of important

430 ■ *Types of Nonfiction*

⑪ ▼ Critical Viewing

How does this image of ABC News anchorman Peter Jennings compare with Postman's description of a typical anchorperson? **[Compare and Contrast]**

Vocabulary Development

Word Forms

Expand students' vocabulary by helping them learn related forms of the Vocabulary Builder words. Give students a blank **Word Form Chart** (*General Resources*, p. 16), with *compensation* and *revered* in the correct columns. Work with the class, or have students work with a partner, to determine the related forms. The final chart should look like the one shown.

Noun	Verb	Adjective	Adverb
compensation	compensate	compensational	compensationally
reverence	revere	**revered**/ reverent	reverently

events. Indeed, it is the trivial event that is often best suited for television coverage. This is such a commonplace that no one even bothers to challenge it. Walter Cronkite, a <u>revered</u> figure in television and anchorman of the CBS Evening News for many years, has acknowledged several times that television cannot be relied on to inform the citizens of a democratic nation. Unless they also read newspapers and magazines, television viewers are helpless to understand their world, Cronkite has said. No one at CBS has ever disagreed with his conclusion, other than to say, "We do the best we can."

Of course, it is a tendency of journalism in general to concentrate on the surface of events rather than underlying conditions; this is as true for the newspaper as it is for the newscast. But several features of television undermine whatever efforts journalists may make to give sense to the world. One is that a television broadcast is a series of events that occur in sequence, and the sequence is the same for all viewers. This is not true for a newspaper page, which displays many items simultaneously, allowing readers to choose the order in which they read them. If a newspaper reader wants only a summary of the latest tax bill, he can read the headline and the first paragraph of an article, and if he wants more, he can keep reading. In a sense, then, everyone reads a different newspaper, for no two readers will read (or ignore) the same items.

12

But all television viewers see the same broadcast. They have no choices. A report is either in the broadcast or out, which means that anything which is of narrow interest is unlikely to be included. As NBC News executive Reuven Frank once explained:

> A newspaper, for example, can easily afford to print an item of conceivable interest to only a fraction of its readers. A television news program must be put together with the assumption that each item will be of some interest to everyone that watches. Every time a newspaper includes a feature which will attract a specialized group it can assume it is adding at least a little bit to its circulation. To the degree a television news program includes an item of this sort . . . it must assume that its audience will diminish.

The need to "include everyone," an identifying feature of commercial television in all its forms, prevents journalists from offering lengthy or complex explanations, or from tracing the sequence of events leading up to today's headlines. One of the ironies of political life in modern democracies is that many problems which concern the "general welfare" are of interest only to

The News ■ 431

Vocabulary Builder
revered (ri vird′) *adj.*
regarded with great respect and awe

Literary Analysis
Expository Essay
According to Postman, how are newspaper and television journalism both similar and different?

13 **Reading Check**

What does Walter Cronkite say about television news viewers who do not also read print media?

---

12 Literary Analysis
Expository Essay

- Direct students' attention to the first two complete paragraphs on p. 431. Ask students to explain the technique that the author uses to support and develop his point. **Answer:** He is using comparison and contrast.

- Have students identify what is being compared and contrasted in these paragraphs. **Answer:** The author is comparing and contrasting how television and newspapers present the news.

- **Ask** the Literary Analysis question: According to Postman, how are newspaper and television journalism both similar and different? **Answer:** Both television and newspapers concentrate on the surface of events. Television presents news as a series of events, which is the same for all viewers. Unlike television news, a newspaper can be read in any order and to the depth of detail the reader chooses.

▶ **Monitor Progress:** Ask students what techniques the author has used so far in supporting and explaining his point. Students should be able to explain that the author has used description and comparison and contrast in the essay.

▶ **Reteach:** If students have difficulty identifying the techniques, ask them to reread the passage and use a Venn diagram to chart the similarities and differences. Then, ask students whether they agree with Postman's views on television journalism.

13 Reading Check

Answer: Cronkite says that people who do not also read newspapers cannot understand their world.

Differentiated Instruction   Solutions for All Learners

Strategy for English Learners
Arrange for English Learners to listen to the **Listening to Literature Audio CD.** Encourage students to read along with the recorded version. After students hear the CD, discuss the selection with students, eliciting and responding to questions. Point out any difficult vocabulary. Ask students to watch a news broadcast, or watch a videotape of a news broadcast together. Have them critique the program and offer suggestions on how they would improve it.

Enrichment for Gifted/Talented Students
Have students work in pairs to write a script for a television news story. Students may invent a news story or choose a current event. The script should include directions for introductory music and a description of the images to be used, as well as a script to be read by the anchor person. Tell students that the story must be limited to no more than three minutes.

• Refer students to the two paragraphs on this page. Ask them to
explain the advantages that newspapers have over television news
reports.
Answer: Because not every item in
a newspaper must appeal to most
readers, newspapers can include
items that might be of interest to
only a few readers. The content of
newspapers is not limited by time.

• Point out to students that even
though newspapers have many
advantages over television news,
millions of people rely solely on television for their news. Ask students
why they think this is so.
Possible responses: Students
may suggest that people prefer to
see moving images, or be entertained; some may suggest that
people do not want to take the
time to read newspapers.

⓯ **Critical Viewing**

Answer: He can begin reading on
whatever page he wishes; he can
read part of a story or skip stories
that do not interest him; he has a
wide variety of stories from which to
choose; the stories that he reads
present more details.

specialized groups. Arms control, for example, is an issue that literally concerns everyone in the world, and yet the language of arms control and the complexity of the subject are so <u>daunting</u> that only a minority of people can actually follow the issue from week to week and month to month. If it wants to act responsibly, a newspaper can at least make available more information about arms control than most people want. But commercial television cannot afford to do so.

This illustrates an important point in the psychology of television's appeal. Many of the items in newspapers and magazines are not, in a strict sense, demanded by a majority of readers. They are there because some readers *might* be interested or because the editors think their readers *should* be interested. On commercial television, "might" and "should" are not the relevant words. The pro-ducers attempt to make sure that "each item will be of some interest to everyone that watches," as Reuven Frank put it. What this means is that a newspaper or magazine can challenge its audience in a way that television cannot. Print media have the luxury of suggesting or inviting interest, whereas television must always concern itself with conforming to existing interests. In a way, television is more strictly

⓮ responsive to the demands of its huge audience. But there is one demand it cannot meet: the desire to be challenged, to be told "this is worth attending to," to be surprised by what one thought would not be of interest.

Another severe limitation on television is time. There is simply not enough of it. The evening news programs at CBS, NBC, and ABC all run for thirty minutes, eight of which are taken up by com-mercials. No one believes that twenty-two minutes for the day's news is adequate. For years news executives at ABC, NBC, and CBS have suggested that the news be expanded to one hour. But by tra-dition the half-hour after the national evening news is given over to the hundreds of local affiliate stations around the country to use as they see fit. They have found it a very profitable time to broadcast game shows or half-hour situation comedies, and they are reluctant to give up the income they derive from these programs.

⓯ ▲ **Critical Viewing**
How might this man's experience of reading a newspaper differ from his experience of watching television news? **[Connect]**

Vocabulary Builder
daunting (dônt´ iŋ) *adj.*
intimidating

Vocabulary Development

Vocabulary Knowledge Rating
When students have completed reading and discussing "The News," have them take out their **Vocabulary Knowledge Rating Chart** for this selection. Read the words aloud once more and have students rate their knowledge of the words again in the After Reading column. Clarify any words that are still problematic. Have students write their own definition and example or sentence in the appropriate col-umn. Then, have students complete the **Vocabulary Builder Practice** activities on p. 435. Encourage students to use the words in further discussion and written work about this selection. Remind them that they will be accountable for these words on the Selection Test.

The evening news produced by the three networks is profitable for both the networks and the local stations. The local stations are paid a fee by the network to broadcast the network news, and they profit from this fee since the news—produced by the network—costs them nothing. It is likely that they would also make money from a one-hour newscast, but not as much, they judge, as they do from the game shows and comedies they now schedule.

16 The result is that the evening news must try to do what cannot reasonably be done: give a decent account of the day's events in twenty-two minutes. What the viewer gets instead is a series of impressions, many of them purely visual, most of them unconnected to each other or to any sense of a history unfolding. Taken together, they suggest a world that is fundamentally ungovernable, where events do not arise out of historical conditions but rather explode from the heavens in a series of disasters that suggest a permanent state of crisis. It is this crisis—highly visual, ahistorical, and unsolvable—which the evening news presents as theater every evening.

17 The audience for this theater is offered a contradictory pair of responses. On the one hand, it is reassured by the smooth presentation of the news itself, especially the firm voice and steady gaze of the trusty anchorman. Newscasts frequently end with a "human-interest story," often with a sentimental or comic touch. Example: a little girl in Chicago writes Gorbachev a letter, and he answers her, saying that he and President Reagan are trying to work out their differences. This item reassures viewers that all is well, leaders are in command, we can still communicate with each other, and so on. But—and now we come to the other hand—the rest of the broadcast has told a different story. It has shown the audience a world that is out of control and incomprehensible, full of violence, disaster, and suffering. Whatever authority the anchorman may project through his steady manner is undermined by the terror inspired by the news itself.

This is where television news is at its most radical—not in giving publicity to radical causes, but in producing the impression of an ungovernable world. And it produces this impression not because the people who work in television are leftists or anarchists.[2] The anarchy in television news is a direct result of the commercial structure of broadcasting, which introduces into news judgments a single-mindedness more powerful than any ideology: the overwhelming need to keep people watching.

---

2. **leftists . . . anarchists** (an´ ər kists´) leftists desire to change the existing political order in the name of greater freedom for all; anarchists oppose any political authority.

Literary Analysis
Expository Essay
What sense of the world does television news cause?

Reading Skill
Main Idea What main idea does the anecdote about the little girl support?

16 **Literary Analysis**
Expository Essay

• Refer students to the bracketed passage. Ask students to identify the strategy the author uses to make the point in this paragraph. **Answer:** The author uses cause and effect.

• **Ask** the Literary Analysis question: What sense of the world does television news cause? **Answer:** The limitations of television news cause a sense of a world that is chaotic and ungovernable.

17 **Reading Skill**
Main Idea

• Have students read the passage. Tell them that Mikhail Gorbachev was president of the Soviet Union during the same time Ronald Reagan was the president of the United States. At the time, the two countries were still engaged in the Cold War.

• Have students explain why producers might include human interest stories, even though they are not important pieces of news. **Answer:** They include human interest stories to hold the audience's attention and to reassure the audience.

• **Ask** the Reading Skill question: What main idea does the anecdote about the little girl support? **Possible response:** The anecdote supports the idea that television attempts to convey the sense that no matter how chaotic the news reports seemed, leaders are in control and all is well.

Concept Connector

KWL Chart
Have students complete the last column of their **KWL Charts**. Ask them to evaluate what they learned in relation to the questions they had before reading.

Connecting to the Literature
Have students compare the sentences they wrote before reading "The News" with their thoughts about how they learn about news after reading the selection. Ask them to explain whether their thoughts have changed and, if so, how.

Reading Skill Graphic Organizer
Ask students to review the graphic organizers they completed to identify the main idea and supporting details while reading. Show them **Reading Skill Graphic Organizer B** (*Graphic Organizer Transparencies*, p. 91) as an example. Then, have students share the graphic organizers they did and the main ideas and supporting details they identified.

Apply the Skills

The News

Thinking About the Selection

1. **Respond:** Do you agree with Postman about the limitations of television? Why or why not?
2. **(a) Recall:** According to Postman, what elements make a news broadcast like a form of theater? **(b) Interpret:** What problem does Postman see in the similarity between television news and theater?
3. **(a) Recall:** What value does Postman say the news anchor must project above all others? **(b) Connect:** How does the impression created by the anchor relate to the "radical" nature of television?
4. **(a) Recall:** How long does an evening news broadcast usually have to present all the news? **(b) Cause and Effect:** What effects do time limits have on television news?
5. **Take a Position:** Do you think that changes should be made in television news broadcasts to make them more intellectually challenging? Give reasons and examples to support your position.

Literary Analysis

6. What is the topic of Neil Postman's **expository essay?**
7. What quotations does Postman use to make information clear to readers?
8. **(a)** Using a chart like the one shown, identify passages in which Postman uses **description, comparison and contrast,** or **cause and effect.** Find one example of each technique. **(b)** Explain how each example adds depth and context to the information Postman presents in that passage.

	Example	Effect
Description		
Comparison/Contrast		
Cause and Effect		

Reading Skill

9. State the **main idea** of "The News" in your own words.
10. **(a)** List three **supporting details** that serve as evidence for the points that Neil Postman makes in his essay. **(b)** Do you think the author adequately supports his main idea with details? Why or why not?

434 ■ Types of Nonfiction

QuickReview

Essay at a Glance
Neil Postman evaluates television as a news source.

Go Online
Assessment
For: Self-test
Visit: www.PHSchool.com
Web Code: epa-6304

Expository Essay: a short piece of nonfiction that presents information, discusses ideas, or explains a process. Writers may use *description, comparison and contrast,* and *cause and effect* to support ideas.

Main Idea: the central message, insight, or opinion in a work of nonfiction

Supporting Details: the pieces of evidence that a writer uses to prove a main idea

---

1. Some students may agree that television news provides only basic information. Others may disagree, noting that television today can provide direct and immediate coverage of events.

2. (a) The music in a news broadcast equates news with drama; computer monitors, maps, clocks, and workers scurrying about suggest urgency. (b) The comparison reveals that the news broadcast is an artificial order.

3. (a) The news anchor must project control. (b) The impression of control contradicts the impression of an ungovernable, chaotic world.

4. (a) An evening news broadcast lasts twenty-two minutes. (b) Time limits mean that the viewer gets only a series of impressions.

5. **Possible responses:** Students may say that catering to the lowest common denominator distorts the truth about the world. Others may say that most people cannot understand complex explanations.

6. The topic is television news broadcasts.

7. He uses quotations from Walter Cronkite and Reuven Frank to clarify information for readers.

8. (a) **Possible responses: Description:** description of burning aircraft carrier with planes landing; **Comparison/Contrast:** comparison of the size of television screen to size of movie theater screen; **Cause and Effect:** the need for television news stories to keep viewers watching results in brief stories. (b) The **description** example illustrates how moving images affect the audience. The **comparison and contrast** illustrates why moving images are more important on television. The **cause and effect** example shows why television news is inadequate.

Another sample answer can be found on **Literary Analysis Graphic Organizer B,** p. 94, in *Graphic Organizer Transparencies.*

9. **Possible response:** Because television news stories must appeal to everyone, they are shallow and give a false impression of the world.

10. (a) Supporting details include the length of newscasts; the Reuven Frank quote; the description of the news broadcast as a series of visual images. (b) Students may agree that Postman provides ample support.

Vocabulary Builder

Practice Review the vocabulary list for "The News" on page 424. Then, identify the word in each group that does not belong. Explain.

1. compensation, repayment, donation
2. temporal, necklace, clock
3. revered, scorn, ridicule
4. daunting, challenge, temptation

Adding Words to Your Vocabulary Using a thesaurus, find an **antonym**, or word of opposite meaning, for each vocabulary word. Use each antonym in a sentence that makes the meaning of the word clear. (For more on using a thesaurus, see page R7.)

Writing

Write the **script** for a public service announcement that encourages people to use a variety of news sources.
- Based on the Neil Postman essay, jot down details that might encourage people to use a variety of news sources.
- Describe visual elements that would create a persuasive message.
- In your script, include one direct quotation from Postman's essay, and describe the visual that would go with it.

For *Grammar, Vocabulary,* and *Assessment,* see **Build Language Skills,** pp. 444–445.

Extend Your Learning

Listening and Speaking In a group, videotape and watch several news broadcasts, paying special attention to the images presented. Then, give an **informal presentation** to discuss Postman's view that television news is dominated by the "need to keep people watching."
- Discuss the intellectual and emotional effects of the pictures.
- Point out what the pictures show about the broadcasters' intentions.

As you present, pause occasionally to summarize and evaluate your conclusions.

Research and Technology Use library and Internet resources to research the preparations that television journalists go through as they prepare a news story. Based on this information, write two **journal entries** that a reporter might write while preparing a story.

Apply the Skills ■ 435

Extend Your Learning

The **Support for Extend Your Learning** page (*Unit 3 Resources,* p. 60) provides guided note-taking opportunities to help students complete the Extend Your Learning activities.

Go Online
Research **For:** An additional research activity
Visit: www.PHSchool.com
Web Code: epd-7303
For another research activity to extend students' learning, give students this Web Code.

Vocabulary Builder
Word Bank Practice

1. *Donation* does not belong, since a donation is not earned.
2. *Necklace* does not belong, since it is not related to time.
3. *Revered* does not belong, since it refers to respect while the other two words signal disrespect.
4. *Temptation* does not belong, since *daunting* and *challenge* relate to something that is intimidating.

Adding Words to Your Vocabulary
Possible responses:

1. Instead of being happy with my salary, I'm really unhappy about the *cost* of getting to work.
2. Spiritual life has nothing to do with time, but with the *eternal.*
3. The Roman emperor Caligula is a *scorned* figure in history, condemned by historians for his cruelty.
4. The steep slope of the mountain was a *welcome* sight to the climbers, who had long looked forward to the challenge.

Writing

- To give students guidance for writing the script for a persuasive commercial, give them the **Support for Writing Lesson** for "The News," p. 59 in *Unit 3 Resources.*
- To evaluate students' script, use the rubrics for Persuasion: Persuasive Essays, pp. 53–54, in *General Resources.* In addition, you might evaluate how well students choose and describe appropriate persuasive visual images.

Six Traits Focus

✔ Ideas	✔ Word Choice	
Organization	Sentence Fluency	
Voice	Conventions	

Writing and Grammar, Gold Level
Students will find guidance on using persuasion in Chapters 7 and 8.

Build Language Skills

Go to pp. 444–445 for vocabulary and grammar lessons and assessment practice.

❸ Background
First American Woman in Space

Sally Ride's first mission in space aboard the *Challenger* lasted six days. During that time she helped deploy several space satellites. She embarked on another space mission in October 1984. During that mission her assignment was to make scientific observations of Earth.

❹ Connecting to the Literature

- Model use of the expressive vocabulary students are asked to use with these examples:

  1. After looking through the microscope, I had to *alter* my opinion of germs.

  2. The photograph seemed to *contradict* my childhood memories about the old farm.

  3. Seeing things from a distance can *emphasize* certain details not noticed up close.

  4. How you *perceive* situations often depends upon your past experiences.

- Help students further develop their expressive vocabulary by providing these words: *abstract, category, recur,* and *revise.* Encourage students to use these words as they discuss the selection.

Go Online
Author Link For additional information about Sally Ride, have students type in the Web Code, then select *R* from the alphabet, and then select *Sally Ride.*

Build Understanding • *Single Room, Earth View*

Essay

❸ Background

First American Woman in Space On June 18, 1983, when she worked as a flight engineer and mission specialist aboard the shuttle *Challenger,* Sally Ride became the first American woman in space. Her historic mission allowed her to experience what she recounts in "Single Room, Earth View."

❹ Connecting to the Literature

Reading/Writing Connection In this essay, Sally Ride describes what it is like to look at Earth from space. Write five sentences describing an experience you had of seeing something from a new perspective. Use at least three of the following words: *alter, contradict, emphasize, perceive.*

Review

For **Literary Analysis, Reading Skill,** and **Vocabulary Builder,** see page 424.

READ MORE
by
Sally Ride
To Space and Back
The Mystery of Mars
(with Tam O'Shaughnessy)

Meet the Author

Sally **Ride** (b. 1951)

Although best known as an astronaut, Sally Ride was also a talented athlete in her youth. She was a ranked player on the junior tennis circuit and considered turning professional before deciding to go to college instead.

The Right Stuff In 1978, Ride read a newspaper advertisement about NASA's search for astronauts. After extensive testing to be sure she had "the right stuff," NASA chose her as one of six women and twenty-five men accepted from among 8,000 applicants. Five years later, in 1983, she took her historic flight. Ride retired from NASA in 1987 and currently teaches physics at the University of California.

Fast Facts

▶ Sally Ride holds four degrees from Stanford University, including a Master's and a Doctorate.
▶ Ride played a key role in the investigations of both the *Challenger* and *Columbia* space shuttle disasters.

 Go Online
Author Link
For: More about the author
Visit: www.PHSchool.com
Web Code: epe-9305

Single Room, Earth View

Sally Ride

Everyone I've met has a glittering, if vague, mental image of space travel. And naturally enough, people want to hear about it from an astronaut: "How did it feel . . . ?" "What did it look like . . . ?" "Were you scared?" Sometimes, the questions come from reporters, their pens poised and their tape recorders silently reeling in the words; sometimes, it's wide-eyed, ten-year-old girls who want answers. I find a way to answer all of them, but it's not easy.

Imagine trying to describe an airplane ride to someone who has never flown. An <u>articulate</u> traveler could describe the sights but would find it much harder to explain the difference in perspective provided by the new view from a greater distance, along with the feelings, impressions, and insights that go with that new perspective. And the difference is enormous: Spaceflight moves the traveler another giant step farther away. Eight and one-half thunderous minutes after launch, an astronaut is orbiting high above the Earth, suddenly able to watch typhoons form, volcanoes smolder, and meteors streak through the atmosphere below.

❸ ▲ Critical Viewing
Based on this photograph, why might travel in the space shuttle defy description? **[Connect]**

Vocabulary Builder
articulate (är tik´ yōō lit) *adj.* expressing oneself clearly and easily

Single Room, Earth View ■ 437

437

- Have students read the first two paragraphs on this page.

- Ask students why Ride says that the view of the Hawaiian Islands from space is surreal.
  Answer: It looks just like a page from an atlas.

- Then **ask** the Reading Skill question: Which details support Ride's point about the difficulties of describing space travel?
  Answer: Details include the speed at which the shuttle orbits the Earth; if she turned away for a moment she could miss an entire land mass.

While flying over the Hawaiian Islands, several astronauts have marveled that the islands look just like they do on a map. When people first hear that, they wonder what should be so surprising about Hawaii looking the way it does in the atlas. Yet, to the astronauts it is an absolutely startling sensation: The islands really *do* look as if that part of the world has been carpeted with a big page torn out of Rand-McNally, and all we can do is try to convey the surreal quality of that scene.

④ In orbit, racing along at five miles per second, the space shuttle circles the Earth once every 90 minutes. I found that at this speed, unless I kept my nose pressed to the window, it was almost impossible to keep track of where we were at any given moment—the world below simply changes too fast. If I turned my concentration away for too long, even just to change film in a camera, I could miss an entire land mass. It's embarrassing to float up to a window, glance outside, and then have to ask a crewmate, "What continent is this?"

We could see smoke rising from fires that dotted the entire east coast of Africa, and in the same orbit only moments later, ice floes jostling for position in the Antarctic. We could see the Ganges River dumping its murky, sediment-laden water into the Indian Ocean and watch ominous hurricane clouds expanding and rising like biscuits in the oven of the Caribbean.

Mountain ranges, volcanoes, and river deltas appeared in salt-and-flour relief, all leading me to assume the role of a <u>novice</u> geologist. In such moments, it was easy to imagine the dynamic upheavals that created jutting mountain ranges and the internal wrenchings that created rifts and seas. I also became an instant believer in plate tectonics; India really *is* crashing into Asia, and Saudi Arabia and Egypt really *are* pulling apart, making the Red Sea wider. Even though their respective motion is really no more than mere inches a year, the view from overhead makes theory come alive.

Spectacular as the view is from 200 miles up, the Earth is not the awe-inspiring "blue marble" made famous by the photos from the moon. From space shuttle height, we can't see the entire globe at a glance, but we can look down the entire boot of Italy, or up the East Coast of the United States from Cape Hatteras to Cape Cod. The panoramic view inspires an appreciation for the scale of some of nature's phenomena. One day, as I scanned the sandy expanse of Northern Africa, I couldn't find any of the familiar landmarks—colorful outcroppings of rock in Chad, irrigated patches of the Sahara. Then I realized they were obscured by a huge dust storm, a

Reading Skill
Main Idea Which details support Ride's point about the difficulties of describing space travel?

Vocabulary Builder
novice (näv´ is) *adj.*
new to an activity; inexperienced

Vocabulary Development

Expressive Vocabulary
As students are discussing Ride's description of the things she saw on Earth from space, encourage them to use the expressive vocabulary presented earlier. You might encourage them with sentence starters like these:

1. Because the shuttle orbited Earth so quickly, Ride had to *emphasize* . . .
2. I can see how she would have to *alter* . . .
3. Her observations did not *contradict* . . .
4. An astronaut is able to *perceive* . . .

cloud of sand that enveloped the continent from Morocco to the Sudan.

Since the space shuttle flies fairly low (at least by orbital standards; it's more than 22,000 miles lower than a typical TV satellite), we can make out both natural and manmade features in surprising detail. Familiar geographical features like San Francisco Bay, Long Island, and Lake Michigan are easy to recognize, as are many cities, bridges, and airports. The Great Wall of China is not the only manmade object visible from space.

The signatures of civilization are usually seen in straight lines (bridges or runways) or sharp delineations (abrupt transitions from desert to irrigated land, as in California's Imperial Valley). A modern city like New York doesn't leap from the canvas of its surroundings, but its straight piers and concrete runways catch the eye—and around them, the city materializes. I found Salina, Kansas (and pleased my in-laws, who live there) by spotting its long runway amid the wheat fields near the city. Over Florida, I could see the launch pad where we had begun our trip, and the landing strip, where we would eventually land.

Some of civilization's more unfortunate effects on the environment are also evident from orbit. Oil slicks glisten on the surface of the Persian Gulf, patches of pollution-damaged trees dot the forests of central Europe. Some cities look out of focus, and their colors muted, when viewed through a pollutant haze. Not surprisingly, the effects are more noticeable now than they were a decade ago. An astronaut who has flown in both Skylab and the space shuttle reported that the horizon didn't seem quite as sharp, or the colors quite as bright, in 1983 as they had in 1973.

Of course, informal observations by individual astronauts are one thing, but more precise measurements are continually being made from space: The space shuttle has carried infrared film to document damage to citrus trees in Florida and in rain forests along the Amazon. It has carried even more sophisticated sensors in the payload bay. Here is one example: sensors used to measure atmospheric carbon monoxide levels, allowing scientists to study the environmental effects of city emissions and land-clearing fires.

Most of the Earth's surface is covered with water, and at first glance it all looks the same: blue. But with the right lighting conditions and a couple of orbits of practice, it's possible to make out the intricate patterns in the oceans—eddies and spirals become visible because of the subtle differences in water color or reflectivity.

Observations and photographs by astronauts have contributed significantly to the understanding of ocean dynamics, and some of

Literary Analysis
Expository Essay
What point about environmental change does Ride support with her descriptions in this paragraph?

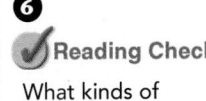

Reading Check

What kinds of structures reveal the "signatures of civilization" from space?

Single Room, Earth View ■ 439

❺ **Literary Analysis**
Expository Essay
• Have students read the bracketed passage. Ask them what Ride is describing in this paragraph.
  Answer: She is describing environmental damage on Earth that she sees from the space shuttle.
• Ask students to identify how Ride uses the strategy of compare and contrast to develop her point in these paragraphs.
  Answer: She compares the differences in how the Earth looked in 1973 and 1983.
• **Ask** the Literary Analysis question: What point about environmental change does Ride support with her descriptions in this paragraph?
  Answer: She makes the point that civilization has had damaging effects on the environment.
▶ **Monitor Progress:** Ask students to explain what the author is trying to do in this essay.
  Answer: She is presenting information.
  Ask students what techniques the author uses in this essay.
  Answer: She uses description, comparison and contrast, and cause and effect.
▶ **Reteach:** If students have difficulty identifying what the author is doing in this essay and the techniques she uses, ask students to reread the passage slowly and carefully. Have them use a graphic organizer—a Venn diagram, a main ideas and details web, or a cause/effect chart—to visualize the techniques.

❻ **Reading Check**
Answer: Bridges and runways reveal the "signatures of civilization" from space.

- Ask students what characteristics of the ocean Ride describes in this paragraph.
Answer: She describes circular and spiral eddies and standing waves.

- **Ask** students the Literary Analysis question: What relationship between space travel and ocean study does Ride identify here?
Answer: She explains how viewing the ocean from space reveals previously undiscovered characteristics that help scientists understand the energy balance in the oceans.

❽ **Literature in Context**

Science Connection A German meteorologist named Alfred Wegener proposed the theory of continental drift in 1912. He suggested that the shape and fit of the continents and the distribution of similar fossils and rock layers around the planet supported his theory. Based on his observations Wegener proposed that all of today's modern continents were once part of a supercontinent called Pangaea, or "All-earth." As Earth's rock plates moved millions of years ago, Pangaea broke apart, and the modern continents took shape.

Connect to the Literature Have students review Ride's description of mountain ranges, volcanoes, and river deltas on p. 438. Then, **ask** the Connect to the Literature question: The theories of plate tectonics and continental drift state that the Earth's crust is made of shifting "plates." What evidence for these theories might an astronaut see from space?
Possible responses: Students might suggest that the continents seem to fit together like a jigsaw puzzle. Students may note that Ride says that she could see that "India is crashing into Asia and Saudi Arabia and Egypt are pulling apart, making the Red Sea wider," which clarified for her the theory of plate tectonics.

---

❼ the more intriguing discoveries prompted the National Aeronautics and Space Administration to fly an oceanographic observer for the express purpose of studying the ocean from orbit. Scientists' understanding of the energy balance in the oceans has increased significantly as a result of the discoveries of circular and spiral eddies tens of kilometers in diameter, of standing waves hundreds of kilometers long, and of spiral eddies that sometimes trail into one another for thousands of kilometers. If a scientist wants to study features on this scale, it's much easier from an orbiting vehicle than from the vantage point of a boat.

Believe it or not, an astronaut can also see the wakes of large ships and the contrails of airplanes. The sun angle has to be just right, but when the lighting conditions are perfect, you can follow otherwise invisible oil tankers on the Persian Gulf and trace major shipping lanes through the Mediterranean Sea. Similarly, when atmospheric conditions allow contrail formation, the thousand-mile-long condensation trails let astronauts trace the major air routes across the northern Pacific Ocean.

Part of every orbit takes us to the dark side of the planet. In space, night is very, very black—but that doesn't mean there's

Literary Analysis
Expository Essay
What relationship between space travel and ocean study does Ride identify here?

❽
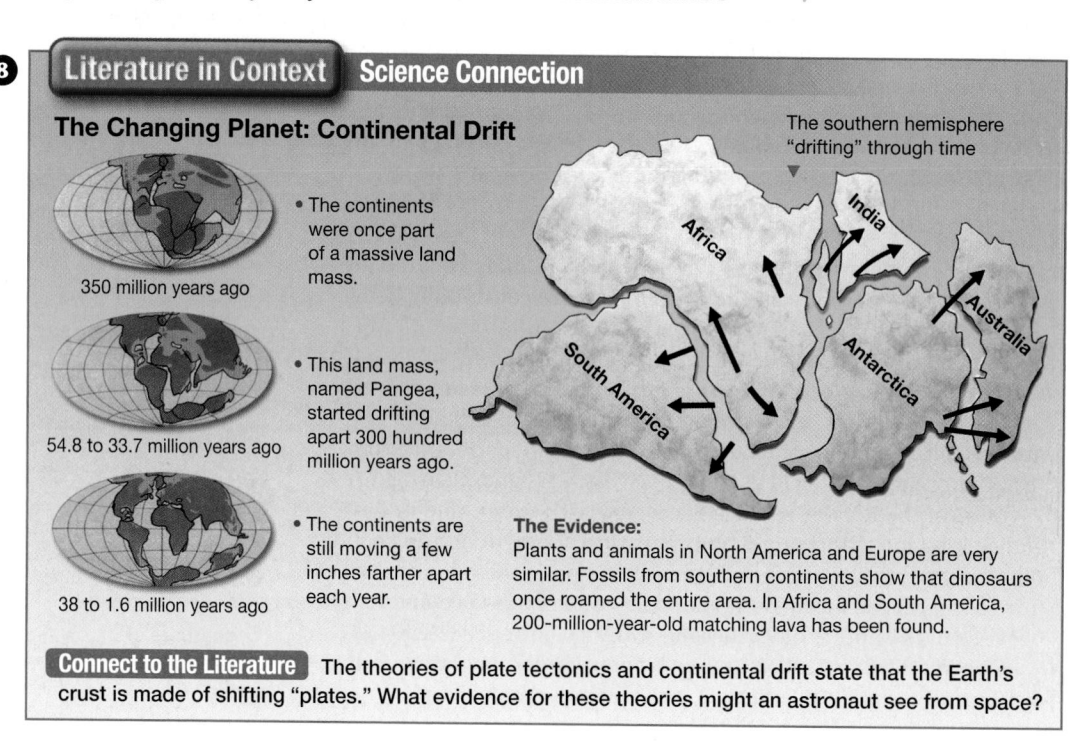

Literature in Context **Science Connection**

The Changing Planet: Continental Drift

350 million years ago

54.8 to 33.7 million years ago

38 to 1.6 million years ago

- The continents were once part of a massive land mass.

- This land mass, named Pangea, started drifting apart 300 hundred million years ago.

- The continents are still moving a few inches farther apart each year.

The southern hemisphere "drifting" through time

Africa   India   Australia
South America   Antarctica

The Evidence:
Plants and animals in North America and Europe are very similar. Fossils from southern continents show that dinosaurs once roamed the entire area. In Africa and South America, 200-million-year-old matching lava has been found.

Connect to the Literature The theories of plate tectonics and continental drift state that the Earth's crust is made of shifting "plates." What evidence for these theories might an astronaut see from space?

440 ■ *Types of Nonfiction*

Vocabulary Development

Vocabulary Knowledge Rating
When students have completed reading and discussing "Single Room, Earth View," have them take out their **Vocabulary Knowledge Rating Chart** for this selection. Read the words aloud once more and have students rate their knowledge of the words again in the After Reading column. Clarify any words that are still problematic. Have students write their own definition and example or sentence in the appropriate column. Then, have students complete the **Vocabulary Builder Practice** activities on p. 443. Encourage students to use the words in further discussion and written work about this selection. Remind them that they will be accountable for these words on the Selection Test.

nothing to look at. The lights of cities sparkle; on nights when there was no moon, it was difficult for me to tell the Earth from the sky—the twinkling lights could be stars or they could be small cities. On one nighttime pass from Cuba to Nova Scotia, the entire East Coast of the United States appeared in twinkling outline.

When the moon is full, it casts an eerie light on the Earth. In its light, we see ghostly clouds and bright reflections on the water. One night, the Mississippi River flashed into view, and because of our viewing angle and orbital path, the reflected moonlight seemed to flow downstream—as if Huck Finn had tied a candle to his raft.

Of all the sights from orbit, the most spectacular may be the magnificent displays of lightning that ignite the clouds at night. On Earth, we see lightning from below the clouds; in orbit, we see it from above. Bolts of lightning are <u>diffused</u> by the clouds into bursting balls of light. Sometimes, when a storm extends hundreds of miles, it looks like a transcontinental brigade is tossing fireworks from cloud to cloud.

Vocabulary Builder
diffused (di fyo͞ozd´) *v.*
spread out

As the shuttle races the sun around the Earth, we pass from day to night and back again during a single orbit—hurtling into darkness, then bursting into daylight. The sun's appearance unleashes spectacular blue and orange bands along the horizon, a clockwork miracle that astronauts witness every 90 minutes. But I really can't describe a sunrise in orbit. The drama set against the black backdrop of space and the magic of the materializing colors can't be captured in an astronomer's equations or an astronaut's photographs.

I once heard someone (not an astronaut) suggest that it's possible to imagine what spaceflight is like by simply <u>extrapolating</u> from the sensations you experience on an airplane. All you have to do, he said, is mentally raise the airplane 200 miles, mentally eliminate the air noise and the turbulence, and you get an accurate mental picture of a trip in the space shuttle.

extrapolating
(ek strap´ ə lāt´ iŋ) *v.*
arriving at a conclusion by inferring from known facts

Not true. And while it's natural to try to liken spaceflight to familiar experiences, it can't be brought "down to Earth"—not in the final sense. The environment is different, the perspective is different. Part of the fascination with space travel is the element of the unknown—the conviction that it's different from earthbound experiences. And it is.

Single Room, Earth View ■ 441

Concept Connector

KWL Chart
Have students complete the last column of their **KWL Charts**. Ask them to evaluate what they learned in relation to the questions they had before reading.

Connecting to the Literature
Have students compare the sentences they wrote before reading with their thoughts about their experience of seeing something from a new perspective after reading "Single Room, Earth View." Ask them to explain whether their thoughts have changed and, if so, how.

Reading Skill Graphic Organizer
Ask students to review the graphic organizers they completed to identify the main idea and supporting details while reading. Show them **Reading Skill Graphic Organizer B** (*Graphic Organizer Transparencies*, p. 96) as an example. Then have students share the graphic organizers they did and the main ideas and supporting details they identified.

⑨ Critical Thinking
Analyze

• Ask students to explain why it might seem logical to suggest that spaceflight is like riding in an airplane, only higher.
Answer: It seems logical because a plane flies, like a space shuttle, and is high above Earth; you can see a large geographic area from an airplane.

• Ask students what they think is different about the environment and the perspective in space flight.
Possible response: In spacecraft, there is weightlessness and lack of noise; the shuttle orbits Earth every 90 minutes, much faster than an airplane, so the astronauts go from day to night to day again within a few hours; from a space shuttle passengers can view whole continents at a time. From an airplane, the view would be much narrower.

1. Some students may say they would like to be an astronaut because they are interested in technology and space exploration. Others may say that it seems too dangerous a profession.

2. (a) Ride observed ice floes, continents, mountain ranges, volcanoes, river deltas, islands, and oceans. (b) Ride felt that she could almost see geological forces working the way the theories say they work.

3. (a) Ride saw damage to the environment and the haze that obscures most big cities. (b) The dimming of colors reflects an additional ten years of pollution.

4. Students may say that the essay has given them a new sense of the unity and fragility of the planet Earth.

5. The topic is space shuttle travel.

6. She discusses orbital path, the speed at which the shuttle travels, the theory of plate tectonics, the sensors she uses to measure carbon monoxide levels, and the patterns of water movement in the oceans.

7. **Possible responses:**
Description: the description of the view of the Hawaiian Islands from space; **Comparison/Contrast:** comparison of the appearance of Earth from space in 1973 with the view in 1983; **Cause and Effect:** the effects of pollution on Earth's environment. (b) The **description** example conveys the sense of awe that is experienced by viewing Earth from space. The **comparison and contrast** example emphasizes the changes that have taken place on Earth. The **cause and effect** example illustrates the various types of damage that has been done to the environment.

Another sample answer can be found on **Literary Analysis Graphic Organizer B**, p. 96, in *Graphic Organizer Transparencies.*

8. **Possible response:** The main idea is that space travel offers an amazing view of the world.

442

Apply the Skills

Single Room, Earth View

Thinking About the Selection

1. **Respond:** Based on Sally Ride's description of her experiences in space, would you like to be an astronaut? Why or why not?
2. **(a) Recall:** Which geological features did Ride observe from orbit? **(b) Interpret:** Why do you think Ride found it easier to imagine the workings of geological forces when she saw Earth from space?
3. **(a) Recall:** What "unfortunate effects" does Ride say she could see as she orbited Earth? **(b) Analyze:** Why would these effects make colors seen in 1983 seem not as bright as those seen ten years earlier?
4. **Assess:** Have Ride's descriptions of Earth changed the way you think about our planet? Explain your answer.

Literary Analysis

5. What is the topic of Sally Ride's **expository essay**?
6. What scientific data does Ride use to make information clear to her readers?
7. **(a)** Using a chart like the one shown, identify passages in which Ride uses **description, comparison and contrast,** or **cause and effect.** Find one example of each technique. **(b)** Explain how each example adds depth and context to the information Ride presents in that passage.

	Example	Effect
Description		
Comparison/Contrast		
Cause and Effect		

Reading Skill

8. State the **main idea** of the essay "Single Room, Earth View" in your own words.
9. **(a)** List three **supporting details** that serve as evidence for the points that Sally Ride makes in her essay. **(b)** Do you think the author adequately supports her main idea with details? Why or why not?

QuickReview

Essay at a Glance
The first American woman in space explains what can be seen and understood about Earth from the perspective of space.

Assessment
For: Self-test
Visit: www.PHSchool.com
Web Code: epa-6305

Expository Essay: a short piece of nonfiction that presents information, discusses ideas, or explains a process. Writers can use *description, comparison and contrast,* and *cause and effect* to support ideas.

Main Idea: the central message, insight, or opinion in a work of nonfiction

Supporting Details: the pieces of evidence that a writer uses to prove a main idea

9. (a) Supporting details might include, seeing the entire boot of Italy; the view of India crashing into Asia; and seeing the "signatures of civilization" such as the straight lines of bridges and roads. (b) Most students will say that she clearly supports her main idea, because she uses so many vivid details and descriptions.

Vocabulary Builder

Practice Review the vocabulary list for "Single Room, Earth View" on page 424. Then, identify the word in each group that does not belong with the others and explain your response.

1. articulate, eloquent, unclear
2. novice, seasoned, veteran
3. diffused, shared, withheld
4. extrapolating, rational, random

Adding Words to Your Vocabulary Using a thesaurus, find an **antonym**, or word of opposite meaning, for each vocabulary word. Use each antonym in a sentence that makes the meaning of the word clear. (For more on using a thesaurus, see page R7.)

Writing

Write the **script** for a commercial or public service announcement that NASA might use to attract candidates for astronaut training.
- Based on the Sally Ride essay, jot down details that might appeal to astronaut candidates.
- Describe visual elements that would attract candidates.
- In your script, include one direct quotation from Ride's essay, and describe the visual that would go with it.

For *Grammar, Vocabulary,* and *Assessment,* see **Build Language Skills,** pp. 444–445.

Extend Your Learning

Listening and Speaking In a group, study photographs of Earth taken from space and give an **informal presentation** to share the images with the rest of your class.
- Identify what natural features are shown in each photo.
- Point out "signatures of civilization" that the photos reveal.

As you present, pause occasionally to summarize and evaluate your conclusions.

Research and Technology Use library and Internet resources, including NASA's Web site, to research the training that astronauts undergo for space flight. Based on this information, write two **journal entries** that an astronaut might write while in training.

Apply the Skills ■ *443*

Assessment Resources

The following resources can be used to assess students' knowledge and skills.

Unit 3 Resources:
   Selection Test A, pp. 80–82
   Selection Test B, pp. 83–85

Go **Online**
Assessment
Students may use the **Self-test** to prepare for **Selection Test A** or **Selection Test B.**

Extend Your Learning

The **Support for Extend Your Learning** page (*Unit 3 Resources,* p. 76) provides guided note-taking opportunities to help students complete Extend Your Learning activities.

Go **Online**
Research
For: An additional research activity
Visit: www.PHSchool.com
Web Code: epd-7304
For another research activity to extend students' learning, give students this Web Code.

Vocabulary Builder
Word Bank Practice

1. *Unclear* does not belong, since the other two words refer to clear speech.
2. *Novice* does not belong, since it relates to *inexperience,* while the other two words indicate experience.
3. *Withheld* does not belong, since the other two words refer to being spread out.
4. *Random* does not belong, since the other two words relate to reasonable and purposeful thinking.

Adding Words to Your Vocabulary
Possible responses:

1. His speech was so *unclear* that people had trouble following it.
2. Harry is a *veteran* mountain climber, having led many climbing expeditions.
3. The poison gas remained *contained* in the canister and posed no danger to people.
4. While Sam arrived at an answer by extrapolating the data, Sue arrived at a more accurate answer by *calculating* it.

Writing

- To give students guidance for writing the script for a persuasive commercial, give them the **Support for Writing** for "Single Room, Earth View," p. 75 in **Unit 3 Resources.**
- To evaluate students' script, use the rubrics for Persuasion: Persuasive Essays, pp. 53–54, in **General Resources.**

Six Traits Focus

✔	Ideas	✔	Word Choice
	Organization		Sentence Fluency
	Voice		Conventions

Writing and Grammar, Gold Level
Students will find guidance on persuasion in Chapters 7 and 8.

Build Language Skills

Go to pp. 444–445 for vocabulary and grammar lessons and assessment practice.

443

Vocabulary Skill

- Introduce the prefix *equi-*. Point out that this prefix is easy to remember because it is very similar to the word *equal*. Ask students to brainstorm for words that contain this prefix.
  Possible responses: *equality, equalizer, equanimity, equation, equator, equilibrium, equinox*
- Have students complete the Practice activity on this page.

Answers

1. *equidistant;* equally distant; The diagonal is *equidistant* from both opposite angles.

2. *equitable;* fair; The grades Mrs. Brown gave were *equitable.*

3. *equilateral;* having all sides equal; The *equilateral* triangle has equal angles as well as equal sides.

4. *equivocal;* open to two or more interpretations; Because the directions were *equivocal,* Maria did not know what to do.

Grammar Lesson

- Point out to students that a predicate nominative can be interchanged with the subject of the sentence.
- Tell students that a predicate adjective can be placed beside the subject to modify it.
- Have students complete the Practice activity on this page.

Answers

1. good (pred. adj.); The class is good for learning writing.

2. physical exertion (pred. nom.); Rowing a rowboat is physical exertion for the arms and the back.

3. survival skill (pred. nom.); Today, knowing how to cook is a survival skill.

4. graceful (pred. adj.); The swan is graceful as it glides across the pond.

5. team (pred. nom.); The basketball championship team is our team.

Build Language Skills

The News • Single Room, Earth View

Vocabulary Skill

Prefixes The **prefix** *equi-* means "equal." The prefix is contained in the word *equivalent,* which means "equal in value." In the field of mathematics, the prefix **equi-** is used in the words *equilateral* and *equidistant* as a verbal reinforcement of a mathematical concept.

▶ **Example:** Her stony stare was the *equivalent* of a severe lecture on the importance of being punctual.

Practice All of the following words begin with the prefix *equi-*. Predict the meaning of each word. Check your definition in a dictionary. Then, use each word in an original sentence.

1. equidistant
2. equitable
3. equilateral
4. equivocal

Grammar Lesson

Predicate Nominatives and Predicate Adjectives A **predicate nominative** renames the subject of the sentence. The predicate nominative comes after a linking verb and renames, identifies, or explains the subject of the sentence. In a sentence with a predicate nominative, the linking verb acts as an equal sign between the subject and the predicate nominative.

▶ **Example:** The winner of the tournament is our **team**. *Team* renames *winner.*

A **predicate adjective** is an adjective that appears with a linking verb and *describes* the subject of the sentence.

▶ **Example:** The swimmer was *fast. Fast* describes *swimmer.*

Practice Circle and label the predicate nominative or predicate adjective in the following sentences. Then, use the predicate nominative or predicate adjective in a new sentence.

1. Swimming is good for strengthening muscles.
2. A sport is physical exertion for recreation or competition.
3. About 5,000 years ago, wrestling was essentially a survival skill.
4. The butterfly stroke appears graceful.
5. The winner of the tournament is our team.

W̶G̶ Prentice Hall Writing and Grammar Connection: Chapter 20, Section 3

MorePractice

For more practice with adjectives, see the Grammar Handbook, p. R40.

Teaching Resources

The following resources can be used to enrich or extend the instruction for Build Language Skills.

Unit 3 Resources
Build Language Skills: Vocabulary: Prefixes, p. 78
Build Grammar Skills: Predicate Nominatives and Predicate Adjectives, p. 79

Reading Skill: Main Idea and Supporting Details

Directions: *Read the selection. Then, answer the questions.*

In the 1960s, however, the FCC began to impose regulations. Responding to complaints from over-the-air broadcasters that cable stations were refusing to carry local stations, the FCC ruled that every cable system had to carry the programs of all local stations as well as those of their own.

By the 1970s, the FCC began to impose more regulations. The agency mandated that cable systems provide at least twenty channels and obtain public approval of changes in their rates. In the 1980s, the FCC ruled that rates for cable services would be deregulated.

1. A detail that is **not** necessary to support the main idea of the passage is
   A "The agency mandated that cable systems . . ."
   B ". . . the FCC ruled that every cable system. . . ."
   C "By the 1970s, the FCC began to impose more regulations."
   D "In the 1980s, the FCC ruled that rates for cable services would be deregulated."

2. Which detail's repetition signals that it should be part of the main idea?
   A the repetition of dates
   B the repetition of the word "channels"
   C the repetition of the word "ruled"
   D the repetition of the word "agency"

3. Which detail supports the main idea of the passage?
   A ". . . the FCC began to impose . . . ."
   B ". . . had to carry the programs. . . ."
   C ". . . cable systems provide. . . ."
   D ". . . complaints from . . ."

4. Which of the following is a main idea of the passage?
   A Cable systems need to be more accessible.
   B There has been a decrease in regulation of cable services.
   C The current cable industry seeks more control of the FCC.
   D The FCC has increasingly regulated the cable industry.

Timed Writing: Explanation

Review "Single Room, Earth View" or "The News." Explain how a different view can affect someone's attitude. State your thesis clearly, include examples, and explain how and why attitudes change. **(25 minutes)**

Writing Workshop: *Work in Progress*

Business Letter
From your writing portfolio, review the list of questions you generated. Answer each question using specific evidence: facts, dates, and examples. Formulate each answer to be clear and precise.

Build Language Skills ■ 445

Reading: Main Idea and Supporting Details

1. D
2. A
3. A
4. D

Timed Writing

- Tell students that when they write an explanation, they should include the reasons for their opinions and examples to support those reasons.

- Point out that a clear thesis and good examples are vital to this explanation.

- Suggest that students first brainstorm for some ideas about how attitudes change and examples of how they change.

- Then, have students state their thesis and write their explanations.

- Assess students' explanations on the validity of their examples and their explanations of how and why attitudes change.

- Suggest that students allow five minutes for prewriting, fifteen minutes for writing, and five minutes for reviewing and proofreading.

Writing Workshop
Work in Progress

Business Letter Have students go to their portfolios and take out the list they made in the **Work-in-Progress** assignment on p. 423.

- Remind students that this work may be used in the business letter that they will write in the **Writing Workshop** at the end of Part 1.

- After students have reviewed their list of questions, have them think about actual problems that they have had with the product. Remind them that they need specific information if they wish to have the company make an adjustment.

- Guide students to organize their information logically and to explain the answers completely.

- When students have completed their answers, have them save them in their portfolios. They will use the answers as they continue this Work in Progress.

Students will

1. understand and identify details in a technical document.

2. read a technical document about the space shuttle.

See TeacherExpress™/Lesson View for a detailed lesson plan for Reading Informational Materials.

About Technical Documents

- Have students read "About Technical Documents."

- Explain to students that technical documents contain detailed information about an item. Point out that information is often presented in text and may also be shown in a chart or graph.

- Invite students to share experiences they have had with technical documents. Ask them to tell why they needed to read the documents and whether the documents were easy to understand. Also, have students describe the look of the documents, including the use of charts, pictures, lists, and different font styles and sizes.

Reading Skill
Reading for Specific Information

- Tell students that the features of technical documents are included for specific reasons. Explain to students that, as readers of such documents, they will get the most meaning if they pay attention to all of the different features.

- Review with students the Type of Information chart.

- Remind students that technical documents include features such as charts, pictures, lists, and different font styles and sizes. Point out that using the chart is a good way to make sure the purposes of the different features are clear.

Technical Documents

In Part 1, you are learning how to identify the main idea and supporting details in literature. This skill is also useful when you read informational materials, such as journal articles or technical documents. Finding the main idea and supporting details helps you gather information more quickly and precisely. If you read Sally Ride's essay, "Single Room, Earth View," you may have wanted to know more about the space shuttle. The technical document that follows gives data and other information about this vehicle.

About Technical Documents

Technical documents provide detailed information on the use, construction, or design of items that are engineered or built. They often include these elements:

- descriptions of the item and its features
- explanations of what the item can do and how it performs under a range of conditions
- numeric data or specifications, such as size, weight, and measurements of performance
- descriptions of materials used to make the item
- diagrams and other graphics

Reading Skill

When you read technical documents, you are often **reading for specific information**. Diagrams, headings, labels, and a variety of visual features included in the document help lead you to the information you need. As you read, use a chart like the one shown to note the kinds of information you discover by using different features of the document.

Type of Information	Examples	Information Provided
Narrative text		
Diagrams	diagram of shuttle	parts of the shuttle launch configuration
Lists or Statistics		

Differentiated Instruction — Solutions for All Learners

Reading Support
Give students reading support with the appropriate version of the *Reader's Notebooks:*

Reader's Notebook [L2]

Reader's Notebook: Adapted Version, [L1]

Reader's Notebook: English Learner's Version, [EL]

These are the product specifications for the shuttle. The list format allows you to quickly scan the data for specific information.

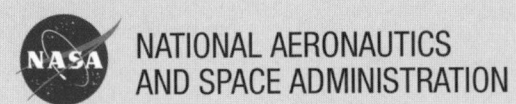

NATIONAL AERONAUTICS AND SPACE ADMINISTRATION

The introductory text gives the background and history of the shuttle.

Shuttle Statistics

Length
Space Shuttle:
56.14 meters (184.2 feet)
Orbiter:
37.23 meters (122.17 feet)

Height
Orbiter on runway:
17.27 meters (56.67 feet)

Wingspan
23.79 meters (78.06 feet)

Weight*
At liftoff: 2,041,166 kilograms
(4.5 million pounds)

End of mission: 104,326 kilograms
(230,000 pounds)

Maximum cargo to orbit
28,803 kilograms (63,500 pounds)

SRB Separation
Two minutes after launch

External Tank Separation
8.5 minutes after launch

Altitude: 109.26 kilometers
(59 nautical miles)

Velocity: 28,067 kph (17,440 mph)

Orbit
185 to 643 kilometers
(115 to 400 statute miles)

Velocity: 27,875 kph (17,321 mph)

*weight will vary depending on payloads and onboard consumables.

Space Shuttle Basics

The space shuttle is the world's first reusable spacecraft, and the first spacecraft in history that can carry large satellites both to and from orbit. The shuttle launches like a rocket, maneuvers in Earth orbit like a spacecraft and lands like an airplane. Each of the three space shuttle orbiters now in operation -- Discovery, Atlantis and Endeavour -- is designed to fly at least 100 missions. So far, altogether they have flown a combined total of less than one-fourth of that.

Columbia was the first space shuttle orbiter to be delivered to NASA's Kennedy Space Center, Fla., in March 1979. Columbia and the STS-107 crew were lost Feb. 1, 2003, during re-entry. The orbiter Challenger was delivered to KSC in July 1982 and was destroyed in an explosion during ascent in January 1986. Discovery was delivered in November 1983. Atlantis was delivered in April 1985. Endeavour was built as a replacement following the Challenger accident and was delivered to Florida in May 1991. An early space shuttle orbiter, the Enterprise, never flew in space but was used for approach and landing tests at the Dryden Flight Research Center and several launch pad studies in the late 1970s.

The space shuttle consists of three major components: the orbiter which houses the crew; a large external fuel tank that holds fuel for the main engines; and two solid rocket boosters which provide most of the shuttle's lift during the first two minutes of flight. All of the components are reused except for the external fuel tank, which burns up in the atmosphere after each launch.

These are the basic facts about the shuttle: the parts, main features, and what they do.

Reading Informational Materials: Technical Document ■ 447

Reading Technical Documents

- Tell students they are likely to encounter technical documents when researching certain topics, such as scientific or historical topics. Point out that these documents usually use lists, diagrams, and varied text to present information.

- Have students read "Space Shuttle Basics."

- **Ask** students what type of information they found in "Shuttle Statistics" and why a list is a good format for the information. **Possible response:** "Shuttle Statistics" provides numerical facts, such as measurements. This information works well in a list because there is no need for additional description, and the measurements add significant details to the document and are of interest to some readers.

- Have students review the first paragraph. **Ask** students to describe the type of information found in this paragraph and tell who would find this information most useful. **Possible responses:** The first paragraph provides general background information about the space shuttle. Someone who is just beginning to learn about the shuttle would be most interested in this information.

continued on p. 448

Differentiated Instruction
Solutions for All Learners

Strategy for Special Needs Students

Tell students that, unlike the pages of a novel, the pages in a technical document are not one block of flowing text. Point out that, when they turn to a page in a novel, they start reading at the top and read to the bottom, but when they turn to a page in a technical document, they have to make choices about where to start reading.

Advise them to begin by glancing over all the different headings and features, and then to read the main text. Tell them that, while they are reading the main text, they might come to a reference to a diagram, chart, or list, and if so, they should mark their place with a finger and look at the reference, and then go back to reading the main text. Point out that, unless they come to one of these references to diagrams or lists, they should read the whole main text before they look closely at the other features on the page.

Reading Technical Documents
(cont.)

- Direct students to the diagram of the shuttle. Tell them that technical documents often include diagrams to show complicated objects or processes that would be hard for readers to visualize and understand based only on a written description.

- Point out that the shuttle diagram presents some information that is also given in the text as well as some new information. **Ask** a volunteer to identify information the shuttle diagram provides that is not in the text.
Possible response: The diagram shows how the pieces fit together and how the shuttle looks during launch and in-flight.

- Point out that not all text details lend themselves to diagrams, charts, or lists. **Ask** a volunteer to scan the text and identify a detail or set of details, aside from the description of the space shuttle, that could be represented in a diagram, chart, or list.
Possible response: The information about NASA's improvements could be put into a chart.

The diagrams show you what the text has described. You can easily see the relative sizes of the parts and how they fit together.

External Tank

Solid Rocket Booster

Solid Rocket Booster

Orbiter

Space Shuttle
(launch configuration)

These paragraphs promote the shuttle and NASA's management of it.

orbiter flight configuration
(w/satellite in payload bay)

These lines state one of NASA's objectives. Its purpose is to reassure the public that safety is NASA's number one goal.

The longest the shuttle has stayed in orbit on any single mission is 17.5 days on mission STS-80 in November 1996. Normally, missions may be planned for anywhere from five to 16 days in duration. The smallest crew ever to fly on the shuttle numbered two people on the first few missions. The largest crew numbered eight people. Normally, crews may range in size from five to seven people. The shuttle is designed to reach orbits ranging from about 185 kilometers to 643 kilometers (115 statute miles to 400 statute miles) high.

The shuttle has the most reliable launch record of any rocket now in operation. Since 1981, it has boosted more than 1.36 million kilograms (3 million pounds) of cargo into orbit. More than 600 crew members have flown on its missions. Although it has been in operation for almost 20 years, the shuttle has continually evolved and is significantly different today than when it first was launched. NASA has made literally thousands of major and minor modifications to the original design that have made it safer, more reliable and more capable today than ever before.

Since 1992 alone, NASA has made engine and system improvements that are estimated to have tripled the safety of flying the space shuttle, and the number of problems experienced while a space shuttle is in flight has decreased by 70 percent. During the same period, the cost of operating the shuttle has decreased by one and a quarter billion dollars annually — a reduction of more than 40 percent. At the same time, because of weight reductions and other improvements, the cargo the shuttle can carry has increased by 7.3 metric tons (8 tons.)

NASA is prepared to continue flying the shuttle for at least the next decade and plans to continue to improve the shuttle during the next five years, with goals of increasing its safety by improving the highest-risk components. NASA will also be working with the Columbia Accident Investigation Board to correct any problems the board may find as it works to determine the cause of the Columbia accident.

In managing and operating the space shuttle, NASA holds the safety of the crew as its highest priority.

448 ■ *Types of Nonfiction*

Vocabulary Development

Vocabulary for Technical Documents
Point out that technical documents often use vocabulary that is specific to one particular setting, in this case the space shuttle. Guide students to understand the meaning of the following words that are used in *Space Shuttle Basics:*

orbit: a path of one object as it circles another.

atmosphere: the gaseous envelope around a planet.

modification: a limited change

maneuvers: a method of working that usually involves expert physical movements.

satellite: an object built to circle the earth, moon, or other planet.

Reading: Reading for Specific Information

Directions: *Choose the letter of the best answer to each question about "Space Shuttle Basics."*

1. Which space orbiters are now in use for space flights?
   A Discovery, Atlantis, and Endeavour
   B Columbia, Atlantis, and Enterprise
   C Challenger, Discovery, and Atlantis
   D Discovery, Atlantis, and Enterprise

2. What is the highest orbit the shuttle is designed to reach?
   A 185 kilometers
   B 185 statute miles
   C 400 kilometers
   D 400 statute miles

3. What is the shuttle's wingspan?
   A 56.24 meters
   B 37.23 meters
   C 17.27 meters
   D 23.79 meters

Reading: Comprehension and Interpretation

Directions: *Write your answers on a separate piece of paper.*

4. Why do you think the writer discusses the shuttle's launch record and design improvements? **[Generating]**
5. The writer of "Space Shuttle Basics" describes the external tank, the solid rocket boosters, and the orbiter. Why do you think the writer also provides a diagram of the shuttle showing these parts? **[Generating]**

Timed Writing: Exposition [Connections]

Review the "Shuttle Statistics" given in "Space Shuttle Basics." Then, explain the purpose and use of statistics or other numerical data in informational text. What is the benefit of providing this information numerically rather than as a running narrative? What is the benefit of providing numerical data in a list or chart form? Use details from "Space Shuttle Basics" in your answer. Make connections between the way the information is presented and the purposes for which it will probably be used. **(30 minutes)**

Reading Informational Materials: Technical Documents ■ 449

Answers

Reading: Reading for Specific Information

1. A
2. D
3. D
4. **Possible response:** The author probably discusses the shuttle's launch record because he or she previously mentioned accidents. The launch record shows that the space shuttle is largely a successful design. The author then mentions design improvements to show the progress being made to improve previous failings.
5. **Possible response:** The author probably included a diagram of the external tank, the solid rocket boosters, and the orbiter because in the description, he or she does not specify where they are located, just what their function is. The diagram shows where they are.

Timed Writing

- Read the Timed Writing instructions together as a group. Remind students to review the "Shuttle Statistics" list and think about the purposes these statistics have in this document and to readers of the document. Then, encourage them to transfer this understanding to technical documents in general.
- Suggest that students plan their time to give 10 minutes to planning, 15 minutes to writing, and 5 minutes to reviewing and revising.

Extend the Lesson

Technical Writing
To give students more practice with technical documents, choose a single page of a technical document and make copies for the students. Create a three-column chart on the board, and give it the same headings as used in the Type of Information chart on p. 446. As a group, fill in the chart based on the page from the technical document.

Meeting Your Standards

Students will

1. analyze and respond to biographical writing.
2. compare how two biographical writers present their subjects.
3. write a comparison of biographical writing.

See TeacherExpress™/Lesson View for a detailed lesson plan for Comparing Literary Works.

Literary Analysis

❶ Biographical Writing

• Read the instruction about biographical writing together. Tell students that, when reading biographies, they should evaluate the author's interpretation based on the facts presented. Explain that as they read, they should ask themselves if the author's interpretation is warranted.

• Explain that biographies are usually written about people of exceptional qualities or accomplishments. The author should convey the significance of his or her subject's life, and explain how it might apply to readers.

• Tell students that an author's interpretation makes a biography a more fulfilling and entertaining read.

❷ Comparing Biographical Writing

• Tell students that the more aspects of a subject's life that the writer addresses the more complete and balanced the biography will be.

• Give students a copy of **Comparing Biographical Writing Graphic Organizer A** (*Graphic Organizer Transparencies*, p. 97). Have them complete it as they read and compare the selections.

❶ Biographical Writing

Biographical writing is a form of nonfiction in which a writer tells the life story of another person. Biographies are often written about historical figures, but they are also written about modern-day people. The best biographies do not just list the facts, events, or accomplishments in the subject's life. Although factual information is important, the author of a good biography presents an interpretation of those pieces of information. The biographer shows why an understanding of the subject's life is meaningful to readers.

❷ Comparing Biographical Writing

In biographical writing, the details that an author chooses to describe help create our impression of the subject. Biographies often focus on one or all of the following aspects of a subject's life:

• personality
• relationships with family and others
• life events
• upbringing
• role in major social or historical events
• influence on others

Because biographies present the lives of real rather than fictional people, it is important that the biographer meet the highest standards of *ethics and truthfulness*. While he or she may interpret the facts and events of the subject's life, that interpretation must be reasonable and well supported. Using an organizer like the one shown, note details in these selections that describe specific aspects of each subject's life.

	Lincoln	Ashe
Personality		
Relationships		
Life events		
Upbringing		
Role in major events		
Influence on others		

Vocabulary Builder

from A Lincoln Preface

■ **despotic** (des pät′ ik) *adj.* like an absolute ruler or tyrant (p. 453) *In a* despotic *move, the leader of the country abolished civil rights.*

■ **censure** (sen′ shər) *n.* strong disapproval (p. 456) *The defeated candidate felt the* censure *of the voters.*

■ **droll** (drōl) *adj.* funny in an odd way (p. 458) *While he did not laugh, he found the movie* droll.

Arthur Ashe Remembered

■ **legacy** (leg′ ə sē) *n.* something handed down from an ancestor (p. 461) *The painter's* legacy *to her children was her love of art.*

■ **enigma** (i nig′ mə) *n.* mystery (p. 461) *The cloaked and masked figure remains an* enigma *to us.*

■ **lithe** (līth) *adj.* flexible (p. 462) *He has the* lithe *body of a swimmer.*

450 ■ *Types of Nonfiction*

Vocabulary Development

Vocabulary Knowledge Rating

Create a **Vocabulary Knowledge Rating Chart** with the selection vocabulary and expressive vocabulary for both selections. Give students a copy. Introduce the words by reading them aloud and having students mark their rating in the Before Reading column. Urge them to be alert to these words as they read and discuss the selection because they will rate their knowledge of the words again after they finish.

If you wish, you may tally how many students know (or think they know) a word to gauge how much instruction you need to provide. As students read, point out the words and their context.

Build Understanding

❸ Connecting to the Literature

Reading/Writing Connection The authors of these selections paint portraits of remarkable human beings. List some of the qualities that make a person special. Use at least three of the following words in your response: *commit, enrich, pursue, exceed, devote.*

Meet the Authors

Carl **Sandburg** (1878–1967)

Between the ages of thirteen and twenty, Carl Sandburg worked as a porter, scene changer, truck handler, dishwasher, and farm worker. Sandburg served briefly in Puerto Rico during the Spanish-American War, which brought on the strong antiwar feelings he would hold throughout his life.

Childhood Favorite Even as a child, Sandburg was fascinated by Abraham Lincoln. For thirty years, he collected material about Lincoln, and his single-mindeness paid off. Sandburg's six-volume work about Lincoln is considered the definitive biography of the former president.

John **McPhee** (b. 1931)

John McPhee's big break as a writer came in 1965, when *The New Yorker* magazine published his profile of Princeton basketball star Bill Bradley. That profile, which became the basis for McPhee's first book, combined two of the author's great loves: sports and his hometown of Princeton, New Jersey, where he still lives today.

Broader Interests McPhee continues to write about sports, but he has broadened his subject matter to include the natural world, with books on Alaska, whales, and the birch-bark canoe. In recognition of his extraordinary prose, McPhee has won many important honors, including a Pulitzer Prize.

 Go Online
Author Link

For: More about the authors
Visit: www.PHSchool.com
Web Code: epe-9307

from A Lincoln Preface / Arthur Ashe Remembered ■ 451

❸ Connecting to the Literature

• Model use of the expressive vocabulary students are asked to use with these examples:

1. Dedicated leaders must fully *commit* themselves to their cause.
2. They should *enrich* the lives of those around them.
3. They must *pursue* their goals in spite of hardships.
4. With luck and hard work, they will *exceed* the expectations of everyone.
5. Above all, leaders *devote* their lives to changing the world for the better.

• Help students further develop their expressive vocabulary by providing these words: *determine, engage, inspire,* and *resolve.* Encourage students to use these words as they discuss the selections.

Go Online
Author Link For additional information about Carl Sandburg and John McPhee, have students type in the Web Code and then select *Carl Sandburg* or *John McPhee.*

Teaching Resources

The following resources can be used to enrich or extend the instruction for Build Language Skills.

Unit 3 Resources
    Build Language Skills: Vocabulary: Prefixes, p. 78
    Build Grammar Skills: Predicate Nominatives and Predicate Adjectives, p. 79

451

❶ Background
Abraham Lincoln

Abraham Lincoln is remembered as one of our greatest presidents, yet at the time of his election, less than half the country supported him. One reason is that Lincoln was opposed to slavery—and many landowners in the South still kept slaves. After seven southern states left the Union, the Civil War broke out in April 1861. By June 1861, a total of eleven states had left the Union and joined the Confederacy.

❷ Motivation

Ask students to consider what makes a leader great. Is it wisdom, courage, luck, popularity, persuasiveness, personality, determination, success, creativity, adaptability, or something else? Work as a class to identify five key qualities of a great leader, then rank those qualities in order of importance.

Concept Connector ➡

Students will follow up on this activity after completing the excerpt from *A Lincoln Preface.*

❸ About the Selection

In this excerpt from *A Lincoln Preface*—Carl Sandburg's introduction to his monumental biography of Abraham Lincoln—the author strings together a series of anecdotes that show Lincoln's humor, determination, and political skills.

❹ Critical Viewing

Answer: This painting does portray Lincoln as a man of great power because it shows a man who appears to be burdened with serious, overwhelming concerns.

from A Lincoln Preface ❶ ❷ ❸
Carl Sandburg

❹ ▲ Critical Viewing Does this painting portray Lincoln as a man of great power? Explain. **[Make a Judgment]**

452 ■ *Types of Nonfiction*

Lincoln Proclaiming Thanksgiving, Dean Cornwell, The Lincoln Museum, Fort Wayne, Indiana

⑤

Background Ever since the birth of the United States in 1776, the issue of slavery had troubled the nation. Each time a new state entered the Union, Congress debated fiercely over whether it would be a slaveholding or free state. In 1860, when Abraham Lincoln was elected president, he refused to support any congressional proposal that would allow for new slave states. The southern slaveholding states resolved to fight to keep new states open to slavery. This conflict led to the outbreak of the Civil War in April 1861.

In the time of the April lilacs in the year 1865, a man in the City of Washington, D.C., trusted a guard to watch at a door, and the guard was careless, left the door, and the man was shot, lingered a night, passed away, was laid in a box, and carried north and west a thousand miles; bells sobbed; cities wore crepe;[1] people stood with hats off as the railroad burial car came past at midnight, dawn or noon.

During the four years of time before he gave up the ghost, this man was clothed with <u>despotic</u> power, commanding the most powerful armies till then assembled in modern warfare, enforcing drafts of soldiers, abolishing the right of habeas corpus,[2] directing politically and spiritually the wild, massive forces loosed in civil war.

Four billion dollars' worth of property was taken from those who had been legal owners of it, confiscated, wiped out as by fire, at his instigation and executive direction; a class of chattel[3] property recognized as lawful for two hundred years went to the scrap pile.

---

1. **crepe** (krāp) *n.* thin, black cloth worn to show mourning.
2. **habeas corpus** (hā′ bē əs kôr′ pəs) right of an imprisoned person to have a court hearing.
3. **chattel** (chat′ l) *n.* a movable item of personal property.

Vocabulary Builder
despotic (des pät′ ik) *adj.* like an absolute ruler or tyrant

⑥ ✔️ **Reading Check**

What violent event happened in April 1865?

from A Lincoln Preface ■ 453

454

---

❼ When the woman who wrote *Uncle Tom's Cabin*[4] came to see him in the White House, he greeted her, "So you're the little woman who wrote the book that made this great war," and as they seated themselves at a fireplace, "I do love an open fire: I always had one at home." As they were finishing their talk of the days of blood, he said, "I shan't last long after it's over."

An Illinois Congressman looked in on him as he had his face lathered for a shave in the White House and remarked, "If anybody had told me that in a great crisis like this the people were going out to a little one-horse town and pick out a one-horse lawyer for president, I wouldn't have believed it." The answer was, "Neither would I. But it was a time when a man with a policy would have been fatal to the country. I never had a policy. I have simply tried to do what seemed best each day, as each day came."

"I don't intend precisely to throw the Constitution overboard, but I will stick it in a hole if I can," he told a Cabinet officer. The enemy was violating the Constitution to destroy the Union, he argued, and therefore, "I will violate the Constitution, if necessary, to save the Union." He instructed a messenger to the Secretary of the Treasury, "Tell him not to bother himself about the Constitution. Say that I have that sacred instrument here at the White House, and I am guarding it with great care."

When he was renominated, it was by the device of seating delegates from Tennessee, which gave enough added votes to seat favorable delegates from Kentucky, Missouri, Louisiana, Arkansas, and from one county in Florida. Until late in that campaign of 1864, he expected to lose the November election; military victories brought the tide his way; the vote was 2,200,000 for him and 1,800,000 against him. Among those who bitterly fought him politically, and accused him of blunders or crimes, were Franklin Pierce, a former president of the United States; Horatio Seymour, the Governor of New York; Samuel F. B. Morse, inventor of the telegraph; Cyrus H. McCormick, inventor of the farm reaper; General George B. McClellan, a Democrat who had commanded the Army of the

---

4. **woman . . . Cabin** Harriet Beecher Stowe (1811–1896), whose novel stirred up opinion against slavery.

454 ■ *Types of Nonfiction*

❽

❾ ▲ **Critical Viewing**
What impression of Lincoln does this painting convey? **[Describe]**

Potomac; and the *Chicago Times*, a daily newspaper. In all its essential propositions the Southern Confederacy had the moral support of powerful, respectable elements throughout the North, probably more than a million votes believing in the justice of the cause of the South as compared with the North.

While propagandas raged, and the war winds howled, he sat in the White House, the Stubborn Man of History, writing that the Mississippi was one river and could not belong to two countries, that the plans for railroad connection from coast to coast must be pushed through and the Union Pacific[5] realized.

His life, mind and heart ran in contrasts. When his white kid gloves broke into tatters while shaking hands at a White House reception, he remarked, "This looks like a general bustification." When he talked with an Ohio friend one day during the 1864 campaign, he mentioned one public man, and murmured, "He's a thistle! I don't see why God lets him live." Of a devious Senator, he said, "He's too crooked to lie still!" And of a New York editor, "In early life in the West, we used to make our shoes last a great while with much mending, and sometimes, when far gone, we found the leather so rotten the stitches would not hold. Greeley is so rotten that nothing can be done with him. He is not truthful; the stitches all tear out." As he sat in the telegraph office of the War Department, reading cipher dispatches, and came to the words, Hosanna and Husband, he would chuckle, "Jeffy D.,"[6] and at the words, Hunter and Happy, "Bobby Lee."[7]

While the luck of war wavered and broke and came again, as generals failed and campaigns were lost, he held enough forces of the Union together to raise new armies and supply them, until generals were found who made war as victorious war has always been made, with terror, frightfulness, destruction, and valor and sacrifice past words of man to tell.

A slouching, gray-headed poet,[8] haunting the hospitals at Washington, characterized him as "the grandest figure on the crowded canvas of the drama of the nineteenth century—a Hoosier Michael Angelo."[9]

His own speeches, letters, telegrams and official messages during that war form the most significant and enduring document from any one man on why the war began, why it went on, and the dangers beyond its end. He mentioned "the politicians," over and again

---

5. **Union Pacific** railroad chartered by Congress in 1862 to form part of a transcontinental system.
6. **"Jeffy D."** Jefferson Davis (1808–1889), president of the Confederacy.
7. **"Bobby Lee"** Robert E. Lee (1807–1870), commander in chief of the Confederate army.
8. **slouching . . . poet** Walt Whitman (1819–1892).
9. **Michael Angelo** Michelangelo (mī´ kəl an´ jə lō´) (1475–1564) famous Italian artist.

Literary Analysis
Biographical Writing Which details present Lincoln as strong in the face of opposition? Explain.

⑪ Reading Check
Under what circumstances was Lincoln willing to violate the Constitution?

---

⑩ Literary Analysis
Biographical Writing

• Read aloud the bracketed paragraph. Explain that Sandburg uses details about Lincoln's role in an important event, the Civil War. Tell students that he describes Lincoln as steadfast and purposeful amid the distractions of a terrible war.

• **Ask** the Literary Analysis question: Which details present Lincoln as strong in the face of opposition? Explain.
Answer: Sandburg describes Lincoln as calm and self-assured in the face of great upheaval and opposition. The stubborn president continues to advocate unification, and he pushes for a transcontinental railroad even during wartime.

⑪ Reading Check
Answer: He was willing to violate the Constitution to save the Union.

---

⑫ Literary Analysis
Biographical Writing

- Read aloud the bracketed paragraph. Explain that it focuses on another of Lincoln's characteristics: his emotional sensitivity.

- **Ask** the Literary Analysis question: Which details in the passage show the emotional toll the war took on Lincoln?

Answer: Details such as Lincoln's silence, sleeplessness, and weeping indicate that the war was difficult for him emotionally.

"the politicians," with scorn and blame. As the platoons filed before him at a review of an army corps, he asked, "What is to become of these boys when the war is over?"

⑫ He was a chosen spokesman: yet there were times he was silent; nothing but silence could at those times have fitted a chosen spokesman; in the mixed shame and blame of the immense wrongs of two crashing civilizations, with nothing to say, he said nothing, slept not at all, and wept at those times in a way that made weeping appropriate, decent, majestic.

His hat was shot off as he rode alone one night in Washington; a son he loved died as he watched at the bed; his wife was accused of betraying information to the enemy, until denials from him were necessary; his best companion was a fine-hearted and brilliant son with a deformed palate and an impediment of speech; when a Pennsylvania Congressman told him the enemy had declared they would break into the city and hang him to a lamp-post, he said he had considered "the violent preliminaries" to such a scene; on his left thumb was a scar where an ax had nearly chopped the thumb off when he was a boy; over one eye was a scar where he had been hit with a club in the hands of a man trying to steal the cargo off a Mississippi River flatboat; he threw a cashiered[10] officer out of his room in the White House, crying, "I can bear <u>censure</u>, but not insult. I never wish to see your face again."

As he shook hands with the correspondent of the London *Times*, he drawled, "Well, I guess the London *Times* is about the greatest power on earth—unless perhaps it is the Mississippi River." He rebuked with anger a woman who got on her knees to thank him for a pardon that saved her son from being shot at sunrise; and when an Iowa woman said she had journeyed out of her way to Washington just for a look at him, he grinned, "Well, in the matter of looking at one another, I have altogether the advantage."

He asked his Cabinet to vote on the high military command, and after the vote, told them the appointment had already been made; one Cabinet officer, who had been governor of Ohio, came away personally baffled and frustrated from an interview, to exclaim, to a private secretary, "That man is the most cunning person I ever saw in my life"; an Illinois lawyer who had been sent on errands carrying his political secrets, said, "He is a trimmer[11] and such a trimmer as the world has never seen."

He manipulated the admission of Nevada as a state in the Union, when her votes were needed for the Emancipation Proclamation, saying, "It is easier to admit Nevada than to raise another million of

---

10. **cashiered** (ka shird´) *adj.* dishonorably discharged.
11. **trimmer** (trim´ er) *n.* person who changes his or her opinion to suit the circumstances.

Literary Analysis
Biographical Writing Which details in this passage show the emotional toll the war took on Lincoln?

Vocabulary Builder
censure (sen´ shər) *n.* strong disapproval

Vocabulary Development

Expressive Vocabulary
As students are discussing Lincoln, encourage them to use the expressive vocabulary presented earlier. You might encourage them with sentence starters like these:

1. During the Civil War, Lincoln decided to *commit* . . .
2. By reading about Lincoln, we can *enrich* . . .
3. Despite great obstacles, Lincoln continued to *pursue* . . .
4. Above all, he *exceeded* at . . .
5. As president, Lincoln had to *devote* . . .

soldiers." At the same time he went to the office of a former New York editor, who had become Assistant Secretary of War, and said the votes of three congressmen were wanted for the required three-quarters of votes in the House of Representatives, advising, "There are three that you can deal with better than anybody else. . . . Whatever promise you make to those men, I will perform it." And in the same week, he said to a Massachusetts politician that two votes were lacking, and, "Those two votes must be procured. I leave it to you to determine how it shall be done; but remember that I am President of the United States and clothed with immense power, and I expect you to procure those votes." And while he was thus employing every last resource and device of practical politics to constitutionally abolish slavery, the abolitionist[12] Henry Ward Beecher attacked him with javelins of scorn and detestation in a series of editorials that brought from him the single comment, "Is thy servant a dog?"

When the King of Siam sent him a costly sword of exquisite embellishment, and two elephant tusks, along with letters and a photograph of the King, he acknowledged the gifts in a manner as lavish as the Orientals. Addressing the King of Siam as "Great and Good Friend," he wrote thanks for each of the gifts, including "also two elephant's tusks of length and magnitude, such as indicate they could have belonged only to an animal which was a native of Siam." After further thanks for the tokens received, he closed the letter to the King of Siam with strange grace and humor, saying, "I appreciate most highly your Majesty's tender of good offices in forwarding to this Government a stock from which a supply of elephants might be raised on our soil. . . our political jurisdiction, however, does not reach a latitude so low as to favor the multiplication of the elephant, and steam on land as well as water has been our best agent of transportation . . . . Meantime, wishing for your Majesty a long and happy life, and, for the generous and emulous people of Siam, the highest possible prosperity, I commend both to the blessing of Almighty God."

He sent hundreds of telegrams, "Suspend death sentence" or "Suspend execution" of So-and-So, who was to be shot at sunrise.

12. **abolitionist** (ab′ ə lish′ ən ist) *n.* person in favor of doing away with slavery in the United States.

⓭ Literature in Context

History Connection

The Emancipation Proclamation
On January 1, 1863, Lincoln signed the Emancipation Proclamation, freeing the slaves in all Confederate states. The proclamation was largely a symbolic document because the federal government had no means to enforce it. Nevertheless, it gave Southern blacks cause to hope. Eventually, as Union armies advanced, freeing thousands of slaves, the promise of the Proclamation became a reality.

Connect to the Literature

How were Lincoln's efforts to admit Nevada into the Union related to the passage of the Emancipation Proclamation?

⓮ ✓ Reading Check

Who was Lincoln's best companion?

from *A Lincoln Preface* ■ 457

⓭ Literature in Context

History Connection Students may be surprised to learn what the Emancipation Proclamation actually says. On September 22, 1862, President Lincoln proclaimed that as of January 1, 1863, all slaves in states or territories in rebellion against the Union would be "thenceforward, and forever, free." The proclamation went on to say that states or territories would no longer be considered in rebellion against the Union if, on that date, they were represented in Congress. In other words, any Confederate state that rejoined the Union could keep its slaves. However, no state accepted this offer. On January 1, therefore, Lincoln issued a second proclamation that all slaves in these states were freed, that they would be welcomed into the Union army, and that the military and government of the United States would protect them.

Connect to the Literature Point out that Sandburg mentions the passage of the Emancipation Proclamation. **Ask** students the Connect to the Literature question: How were Lincoln's efforts to admit Nevada into the Union related to the passage of the Emancipation Proclamation?
Answer: Lincoln needed Nevada's votes in order to pass the Proclamation, so he made sure that the state was admitted to the Union.

⓮ Reading Check

Answer: His best companion was his son.

Differentiated Instruction   Solutions for All Learners

Strategy for Less Proficient Readers
Most of Sandburg's sentences are long and complex. Encourage students to break down lengthy sentences to help them determine meaning. As a class, work through the second paragraph on p. 456, which is one long sentence. Then, have students do the same with the next paragraph on p. 456. You may wish to divide students into groups to discuss what is being said.

Enrichment for Gifted/Talented Students
At the outbreak of World War II, American composer Aaron Copland (1900–1990) was commissioned to write *A Lincoln Portrait*. The piece blends original music with American folk tunes to accompany a script based on Lincoln's own words. Have students locate and listen to *A Lincoln Portrait*. Have them compare and contrast Copland's portrait of Lincoln to Sandburg's. Ask students to describe the similarities and differences of the two portrayals.

- Read aloud the bracketed passage. Explain that this detail reveals yet another element of Lincoln's personality.

- **Ask** the Literary Analysis question: What do you learn about Lincoln from the statement overheard by an Indiana man?
Answer: The statement demonstrates Lincoln's humor, gives a hint of his background, and reveals that he disliked violence.

The telegrams varied oddly at times, as in one, "If Thomas Samplogh, of the First Delaware Regiment, has been sentenced to death, and is not yet executed, suspend and report the case to me." And another, "Is it Lieut. Samuel B. Davis whose death sentence is commuted? If not done, let it be done."

While the war drums beat, he liked best of all the stories told of him, one of two Quakeresses[13] heard talking in a railway car. "I think that Jefferson will succeed." "Why does thee think so?" "Because Jefferson is a praying man." "And so is Abraham a praying man." "Yes, but the Lord will think Abraham is joking."

15 An Indiana man at the White House heard him say, "Voorhees, don't it seem strange to you that I, who could never so much as cut off the head of a chicken, should be elected, or selected, into the midst of all this blood?"

A party of American citizens, standing in the ruins of the Forum in Rome, Italy, heard there the news of the first assassination of the first American dictator, and took it as a sign of the growing up and the aging of the civilization on the North American continent. Far out in Coles County, Illinois, a beautiful, gaunt old woman in a log cabin said, "I knowed he'd never come back."

Of men taking too fat profits out of the war, he said, "Where the carcass is there will the eagles be gathered together."

An enemy general, Longstreet, after the war, declared him to have been "the one matchless man in forty millions of people," while one of his private secretaries, Hay, declared his life to have been the most perfect in its relationships and adjustments since that of Christ.

Between the days in which he crawled as a baby on the dirt floor of a Kentucky cabin, and the time when he gave his final breath in Washington, he packed a rich life with work, thought, laughter, tears, hate, love.

With vast reservoirs of the comic and the <u>droll</u>, and notwithstanding a mastery of mirth and nonsense, he delivered a volume of addresses and letters of terrible and serious appeal, with import beyond his own day, shot through here and there with far, thin ironics, with paragraphs having raillery[14] of the quality of the Book of Job,[15] and echoes as subtle as the whispers of wind in prairie grass.

Perhaps no human clay pot has held more laughter and tears.

16 The facts and myths of his life are to be an American possession, shared widely over the world, for thousands of years, as the

---

13. **Quakeresses** (kwā′ kər es əz) *n.* female members of the religious group known as the Society of Friends, or Quakers.
14. **raillery** (rā′ lər ē) *n.* good-natured teasing.
15. **Book of Job** (jōb) *n.* book of the Old Testament in which Job is tested by God.

458 ■ *Types of Nonfiction*

Literary Analysis
Biographical Writing What do you learn about Lincoln from the statement overheard by an Indiana man?

Vocabulary Builder
droll (drōl) *adj.* funny in an odd way

Vocabulary Development

Vocabulary Builder Reinforcement
Students will benefit from additional examples and practice with the Vocabulary Builder words. Reinforce their comprehension with "show-you-know" sentences. The first part of the sentence uses the vocabulary word in an appropriate context. The second part of the sentence—the "show-you-know" part—clarifies the first. Model the strategy with this example for *despotic*:

The *despotic* leader died at age 82; his people had suffered long under his rule.

1. She endured *censure* for forgetting to write the report; _____.
Sample answer: her professor was angry about her absent-mindedness.
2. While the play wasn't a comedy, it was quite *droll*; _____.
Sample answer: I caught myself laughing a few times.

tradition of Knute or Alfred, Lao-tse or Diogenes, Pericles or Caesar,[16] are kept. This because he was not only a genius in the science of neighborly human relationships and an artist in the personal handling of life from day to day, but a strange friend and a friendly stranger to all forms of life that he met.

He lived fifty-six years of which fifty-two were lived in the West— the prairie years.

16. **Knute** (knoot) **or Alfred, Lao-tse** (lou′ dzu′) **or Diogenes** (dī äj′ ə nēz′), **Pericles** (per′ ə klēz′) **or Caesar** (sē′ zər) well-known thinkers and leaders from different eras and places.

Literary Analysis
Biographical Writing According to Sandburg, what personal qualities make Lincoln a great historical figure?

Thinking About the Selection

1. **Respond:** Which story about Lincoln interested you the most? Why?

2. **(a) Recall:** To whom did Lincoln refer as "the little woman who wrote the book that made this great war"? **(b) Infer:** Why do you think Lincoln wanted to meet with this woman? **(c) Draw Conclusions:** What does Lincoln's interest in meeting this woman say about his character?

3. **(a) Recall:** How did Lincoln justify admitting Nevada to the Union? **(b) Connect:** What other examples of Lincoln's "practical" politics does the author note? **(c) Make a Judgment:** Does Sandburg seem to admire this aspect of Lincoln's character? Explain.

4. **(a) Recall:** According to Sandburg, what aspects of Lincoln's life will be "an American possession, shared widely over the world"? **(b) Interpret:** What does Sandburg mean by this comment?

5. **Evaluate:** Do you think Lincoln was justified in violating the Constitution to save the Union? Why or why not?

6. **Assess:** Sandburg says that Lincoln "packed a rich life with work, thought, laughter, tears, hate, and love." Do you think Sandburg provides examples of all of these qualities in this introduction to his biography of Lincoln?

16 Literary Analysis
Biographical Writing

Read aloud the last two paragraphs. Refer students to the footnote to clarify the references to historic figures.

- **Ask:** What is Sandburg saying about Lincoln by placing him in company with these figures?
- **Answer:** Sandburg is ranking Lincoln among the greatest civil and military leaders of all time.
- Then, **ask** the Literary Analysis question: According to Sandburg, what personal qualities make Lincoln a great historical figure?
- **Answer:** Sandburg believes Lincoln's greatness lay in his ability to understand and communicate with people of all backgrounds.

Concept Connector

Have students return to the Motivation activity on p. 452. Ask students to review their ideas. Having read about Lincoln, would they change their rankings of leadership qualities?

ASSESS

Answers

1. **Possible response:** The story of Lincoln's letter to the King of Siam interested me. It showed Lincoln's wit and political skill.

2. (a) Lincoln was referring to Harriet Beecher Stowe. (b) He had probably read her book and was impressed with her presentation of the evils of slavery. (c) He valued other people's accomplishments.

3. (a) He felt the war would be over sooner and he might save a million soldiers' lives. (b) Upon his request, Lincoln's Cabinet voted on a high military commander. After the vote Lincoln announced that he had already appointed someone. (c) Sandburg seems to approve of Lincoln's single-minded pursuit of a worthy goal.

4. (a) Sandburg was referring to the facts and myths of Lincoln's life. (b) He means that Lincoln is an enduring hero.

5. Students may agree that Lincoln's actions were a justifiable necessity to preserve the nation.

6. **Possible response:** Students will probably say that Sandberg does demonstrate all of these qualities in his introduction.

Differentiated Instruction   Solutions for All Learners

Enrichment for Advanced Readers
Encourage students who enjoyed this selection to dip into the work from which it is taken: Sandburg's classic two-volume biography of Lincoln, *The Prairie Years* and *The War Years*. Students can establish a purpose for reading before they begin. They should choose one period in Lincoln's life about which they would like to know more—for example, his boyhood, his law practice in Illinois, or the night of his assassination.

Students can look through the biography for their particular period of interest, reading a few chapters or pages here and there. When they are finished, they can give brief presentations on what they learned about Lincoln. Encourage them to read as much of the biography as they want to, but reassure them that there is no need to try to read it cover to cover.

He may have been best known as a tennis master, but Arthur Ashe (1943–1993) was also a dedicated advocate of many social causes. He spoke out angrily against South African apartheid after being denied a visa to that country because of his race. He was also a spokesman for underprivileged people who could not afford healthcare, and created the Arthur Ashe Institute for Urban Health just months before he died. This Institute is devoted to the national promotion of preventative care and health education.

18 **Motivation**

Engage students in a discussion about their favorite athletes. Ask them to identify the traits that they admire about each one and list their answers on the board. Tell students that Arthur Ashe was admired not only for his athleticism, but also for his devotion to important social causes.

Concept Connector ➡

Students will follow up on this activity after completing *Arthur Ashe Remembered*.

19 **About the Selection**

In "Arthur Ashe Remembered," John McPhee recalls American tennis champion Arthur Ashe as a cool, self-controlled player who always took risks on the court.

20 **Critical Viewing**

Answer: Ashe is probably excited, proud, and happy.

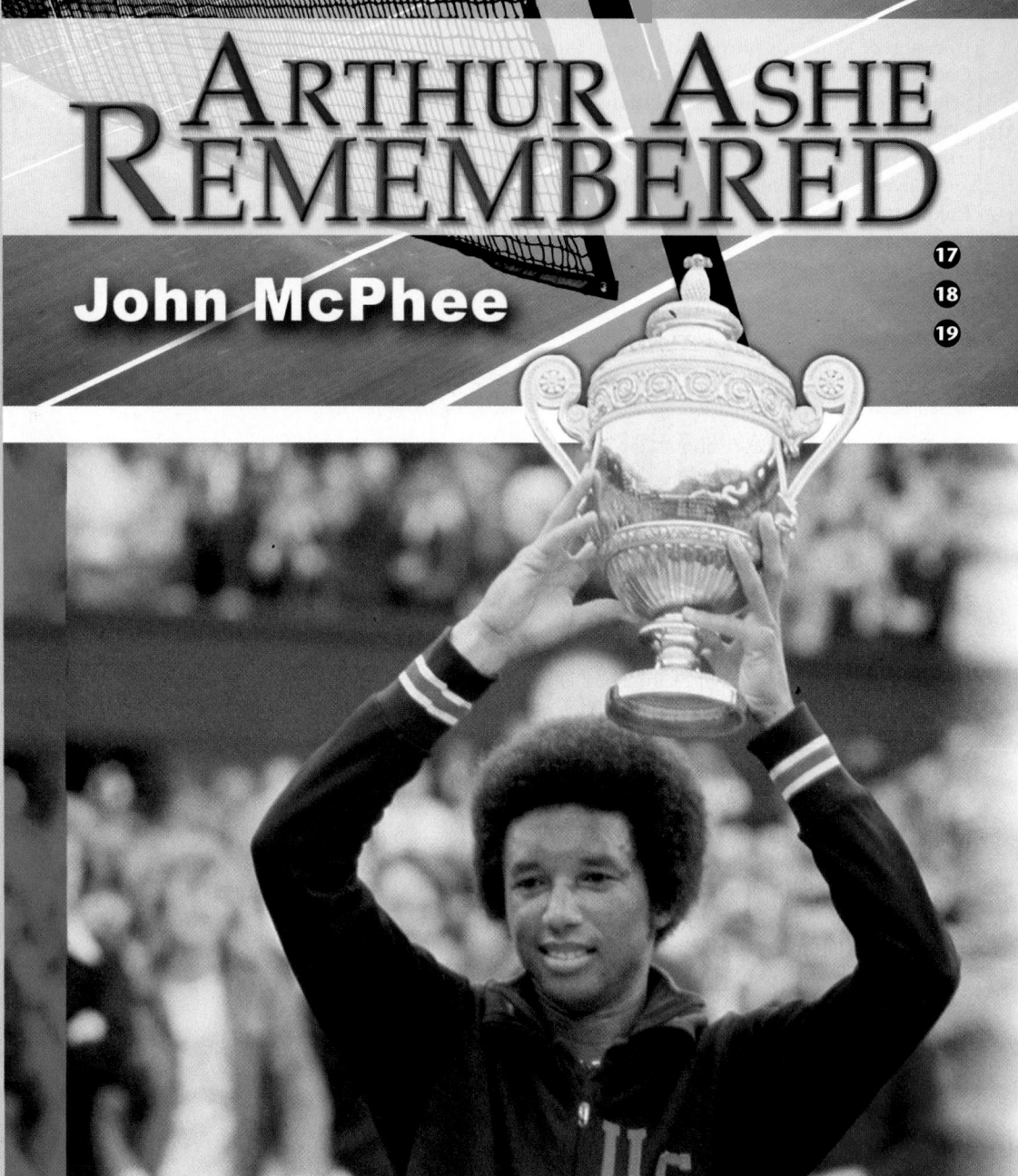

ARTHUR ASHE REMEMBERED

John McPhee

17
18
19

20 ▲ Critical Viewing Based on this photograph, what emotions did Ashe express when he won the Wimbledon Championship in 1975? **[Assess]**

Vocabulary Development

Vocabulary Builder Reinforcement
To reinforce and assess students' comprehension of Vocabulary Builder words, give them sentences using the words in which the word may or may not be used correctly. Students must tell whether the use is correct and explain their answer. Use these sentences:

1. Her new gown is a legacy.
   Answer: No, *legacy* is not used correctly. It means "something handed down from an ancestor," and a new gown is not from an ancestor.

2. I am faced with an *enigma:* I don't know whether to choose the red sofa or the white one.
   Answer: No, *enigma* is not used correctly. It means "a mystery," and a choice between two couches is not mysterious.

3. Yoga had made Ben's body *lithe*.
   Answer: Yes, *lithe* is used correctly. *Lithe* means "flexible," and yoga makes people more flexible.

Background Arthur Ashe was the first African American man to achieve greatness in tennis. When he was six years old, his mother died of heart disease. Ashe's father worked as a caretaker in a neighborhood park, where Ashe spent hours playing on the tennis courts. Ashe went on to win numerous honors in tennis, including the 1968 U.S. Open and the 1975 Wimbledon singles championship. Throughout his life, Ashe devoted himself to issues of human rights, education, and public health. After struggling with heart problems, he contracted AIDS from a transfusion during by-pass surgery. He founded the Arthur Ashe Foundation for the Defeat of AIDS before his death in 1993.

He once described his life as "a succession of fortunate circumstances." He was in his twenties then. More than half of his life was behind him. His memory of his mother was confined to a single image: in a blue corduroy bathrobe she stood in a doorway looking out on the courts and playing fields surrounding their house, which stood in the center of a Richmond playground. Weakened by illness, she was taken to a hospital that day, and died at the age of twenty-seven. He was six.

It was to be his tragedy, as the world knows, that he would leave his own child when she was six, that his life would be trapped in a medical irony as a result of early heart disease, and death would come to him prematurely, as it had to his mother.

His mother was tall, with long soft hair and a face that was gentle and thin. She read a lot. She read a lot to him. His father said of her, "She was just like Arthur Junior. She never argued. She was quiet, easygoing, kindhearted."

㉑ If by legacy her son never argued, he was also schooled, instructed, coached not to argue, and as he moved alone into alien country he fashioned not-arguing into an enigma and turned the enigma into a weapon. When things got tough (as I noted in these pages twenty-four years ago[1]), he had control. Even in very tight moments, other players thought he was toying with them. They rarely knew what he was thinking. They could not tell if he was angry. It was maddening, sometimes, to play against him. Never less than candid, he said that what he liked best about himself on a tennis court was his demeanor: "What it is is controlled cool, in a way. Always have the situation under control, even if losing. Never betray an inward sense of defeat."

---

1. twenty-four years ago McPhee refers to an article published in 1969.

Arthur Ashe Remembered ■ 461

㉑ Literary Analysis
Biographical Writing
- Read aloud the bracketed passage. Explain that John McPhee is describing Ashe as strong and self-controlled.
- **Ask** students to identify the details that McPhee uses to support this description.
  Answer: McPhee supports this description by saying that Ashe was brought up not to argue and that he had a maddening coolness on the tennis court.

㉒ Reading Check
Answer: They were both mild-mannered.

Vocabulary Builder
legacy (leg´ ə sē) *n.* something handed down from an ancestor
enigma (i nig´ mə) *n.* mystery

㉒

 Reading Check

What personality trait did Ashe share with his mother?

Differentiated Instruction Solutions for All Learners

Accessibility at a Glance
Use this information to guide your teaching of *Arthur Ashe Remembered.*

Context	Describes Arthur Ashe's hardships and personality
Language	Tennis vocabulary
Concept Level	More accessible
Literary Merit	Commemorative
Lexile	970L

㉒ Literary Analysis

Biographical Writing

- Read aloud the bracketed passage. Explain that McPhee uses details about Ashe's tennis game to make a statement about Ashe's personality.

- **Ask** the Literary Analysis question: How does this description of Ashe's tennis game portray his ability to remain calm and in control?
  Answer: In "indescribably bad" tennis moments, Ashe showed no emotion; he would simply push his glasses up on his nose. When the game became critical, Ashe would keep his composure and go for risky, challenging shots rather than conservative, cautious shots.

Concept Connector

Have students return to the Motivation activity on p. 460. Revisit the admirable traits that students listed about their favorite athletes. Based on the selection, ask volunteers to list Ashe's admirable traits.

ASSESS

Answers

1. **Possible response:** Students may find Arthur's signature tennis style interesting.

2. (a) Like his mother, Ashe was quiet, easygoing, and kind-hearted; he never argued.
   (b) Ashe likes the fact that he keeps control and never betrays "an inward sense of defeat."
   (c) Ashe was self-controlled, dignified, enigmatic, and unpredictable.

3. (a) Ashe called his life "a succession of fortunate circumstances."
   (b) No—Ashe's life began with the tragedy of his mother's death and ended with his own early death; also, the article focuses on Ashe's skill and talent, not on his luck.

4. (a) His demeanor was always controlled, but his shots were unpredictable and daring.
   (b) People should be daring in life and never give way to that "sense of defeat."

㉒   And of course he never did—not in the height of his athletic power, not in the statesmanship of the years that followed, and not in the endgame of his existence. If you wished to choose a single image, you would see him standing there in his twenties, his <u>lithe</u> body a braid of cables, his energy without apparent limit, in a court situation indescribably bad, and all he does is put his index finger on the bridge of his glasses and push them back up the bridge of his nose. In the shadow of disaster, he hits out. Faced with a choice between a conservative, percentage return or a one-in-ten flat-out blast, he chooses the blast. In a signature manner, he extends his left arm to point upward at lobs as they fall toward him. His overheads, in fire bursts, put them away. His backhand is, if anything, stronger than his forehand, and his shots from either side for the most part are explosions. In motions graceful and decisive, though, and with reactions as fast as the imagination, he is a master of drop shots, of cat-and-mouse, of miscellaneous dinks and chips and (riskiest of all) the crosscourt half-volley. Other tennis players might be wondering who in his right mind would attempt something like that, but that is how Ashe plays the game: at the tensest moment, he goes for the all but impossible. He is predictably unpredictable. He is unreadable. His ballistic serves move in odd patterns and come off the court in unexpected ways. Behind his impassive face—behind the enigmatic glasses, the lifted chin, the first-mate-on-the-bridge look—there seems to be, even from this distance, a smile.

Thinking About the Selection

1. **Respond:** What did you find most interesting about Arthur Ashe? Explain.

2. (a) **Recall:** According to his father, how was Ashe like his mother?
   (b) **Summarize:** What does Ashe say he likes best about himself on the court? (c) **Draw Conclusions:** Based on this article, how would you describe Ashe's character?

3. (a) **Recall:** How did Ashe once describe his life?
   (b) **Make a Judgment:** Does this description seem accurate based on the information in this biography?

4. (a) **Summarize:** Summarize Ashe's approach to tennis. (b) **Apply:** In what ways might Ashe's approach to tennis be seen as an approach to life?

Vocabulary Builder

lithe (līth) *adj.* flexible

Literary Analysis

Biographical Writing How does this description of Ashe's tennis game portray his ability to remain calm and in control?

Vocabulary Development

Vocabulary Knowledge Rating

When students have completed reading from *A Lincoln Preface* and *Arthur Ashe Remembered*, have them take out their **Vocabulary Rating Chart.** Read the words aloud once more and have students rate their knowledge of the words again in the After Reading column. Clarify any words that are still problematic. Have students write their own definition and example or sentence in the appropriate column. Then have students complete the **Vocabulary Builder Practice** activities on p. 463. Encourage students to use the words in further discussion and written work about the selections. Remind them that they will be accountable for these words on the Selection Test.

Apply the Skills

from *A Lincoln Preface* • *Arthur Ashe Remembered*

Comparing Biographical Writing

1. Identify at least three facts that each author includes about his subject. Then, explain what each fact shows about the subject.

2. (a) For each biography, note two statements the biographer makes that are interpretations of information about the subject. (b) What does each statement show about the biographer's feelings toward his subject? Explain.

Writing to Compare Literary Works

Write an essay in which you compare your reaction to the excerpt from *A Lincoln Preface* with "Arthur Ashe Remembered." In your response, explain how the writer's attitude toward his subject affects your reaction. Use these questions to get started:

- Does each writer clearly convey why his subject is important?
- Did you respond more to the description of Abraham Lincoln or the description of Arthur Ashe? Why?
- What main impression do you think each writer wants to convey?

Using a chart like the one shown, find details to support your response. You can use these notes to build your essay.

Author	Main Impression	Details
Sandburg		
McPhee		

Vocabulary Builder

Practice Rewrite each of the following sentences using a word from the vocabulary list on page 450. Explain which sentence is stronger.

1. The dictator's abuse of power frightened the citizens.
2. The movie was peculiar, yet amusing.
3. The members of Congress strongly disapprove of the president's decision.
4. The disappearance of various items caused everyone to wonder what could have happened.
5. The dancer could stretch and move in a flexible way.
6. The children felt fortunate to have several novels their mother had written when she was alive.

Apply the Skills ■ 463

QuickReview

Biographical Writing: nonfiction writing in which a writer tells the story of another person's life

Go Online
Assessment
For: Self-test
Visit: www.PHSchool.com
Web Code: epa-6306

463

In this Skills Review, students apply the skills taught in Part 1. The test format gives students practice in taking standardized tests. The result of this review test will help you check students' readiness for the **Benchmark Test** for Unit 3, Part 1.

Applying Reading Skills

Read the passage with the students. Guide them in identifying clues to determine the subject of the passage in item 1: the public library benefits those who cannot afford to buy books. If necessary, have students review the instruction on p. 400. Then have them complete the remaining items on their own.

Applying Vocabulary Skills

Have students review the instruction on prefixes on p. 401. Remind students to apply their knowledge about prefixes to the items on the test and to use the definition of the prefix to help to determine the meaning of the word.

Tips for Test Taking

When taking a standardized vocabulary test that asks you to fill in the blank, select the best answer, and then reread the sentence using that answer. You may find that the answer does not fit well when you insert it in the sentence, and you may need to reconsider your choice. Repeat this process with another possible answer.

Reading

Directions: *Questions 1–5 are based on the following selection.*

For those without money, the road to that treasure house of the imagination begins at the public library. When I was a boy, the rooms were crowded with immigrants and their children. That is, with people who came from places where there were no libraries for the poor. With their children, they built the New York in which we now live.

Today, the libraries of this city are still doing that work. The libraries of Brooklyn and Queens are jammed with the new immigrants and their astonishing children, the people who will build the New York of tomorrow. The older people want information about this new world, and how to get better jobs and green cards and citizenship. Their American children want to vanish into books their parents cannot afford, thus filling themselves with the endless possibilities of the future.

—from "Libraries Face Sad Chapter," by Pete Hamill

1. **What is the subject of the passage?**
   A immigrants
   B libraries
   C New York
   D Brooklyn and Queens

2. **A detail that contributes to the main idea is that libraries are most important to**
   A those with imagination.
   B the poor.
   C children.
   D American citizens.

3. **The author states that "libraries of Brooklyn and Queens are jammed with the new immigrants." Which of the following does this detail support?**
   A Brooklyn and Queens are important to immigrants.
   B There are many new immigrants.
   C Libraries are crowded places.
   D Many immigrants make use of libraries.

4. **Which of the following best reflects the author's main idea in this passage?**
   A Libraries are a vital resource for immigrants.
   B Libraries contain vital information.
   C Brooklyn and Queens have many libraries.
   D Libraries are what built New York.

5. **Which detail best supports the main idea of the passage?**
   A "Today, the libraries of this city are still doing that work."
   B "The road to that treasure house of the imagination begins at the public library."
   C "When I was a boy, the rooms were crowded with immigrants. . . ."
   D "The older people want information about this new world. . . ."

Assessment Practice

Vocabulary

Directions: *Choose the word that best completes the sentence.*

6. Anna's explanation served to _____ the situation.
   A assume
   B illuminate
   C contemplate
   D appreciate

7. Jason wanted to _____ the meaning of her words.
   A display
   B contemplate
   C assume
   D contribute

8. I have read through forty _____ and still cannot find the right article.
   A contemplations
   B abstracts
   C illuminates
   D aspects

9. He lied to her; _____, her anger flared.
   A displayed
   B hence
   C contributed
   D involved

10. Adam's mumbled response was the _____ of a confession.
    A circumstance
    B illumination
    C appreciation
    D equivalent

11. During the _____, the day and the night are the same length.
    A concurrent
    B composition
    C equinox
    D equivalent

12. Sally reread her _____ several times before submitting it.
    A concurrent
    B composition
    C equinox
    D equilateral

13. The nation comprised a(n) _____ of states.
    A concurrent
    B equilateral
    C equivalent
    D confederation

14. The programs were shown _____, so each could only capture half of the limited audience.
    A confederately
    B concurrently
    C equilaterally
    D equitably

15. The judge was an honorable person, and no one doubted the _____ of the decision.
    A equivalence
    B concurrent
    C equity
    D composition

If students answer any of these questions incorrectly, have them review the instruction on the following pages in Part 1 before taking the **Benchmark Test.**

Question	Pages Where Instruction Is Located:
1	402, 424
2	402, 424
3	402, 424
4	402, 424
5	402, 424
6	401
7	401
8	401
9	401
10	401
11	444
12	422
13	422
14	422
15	444

Benchmark

Administer the **Benchmark Test** for Unit 3, Part 1. If the Benchmark Test reveals that some students need further work, use the Interpretation Guide to determine the appropriate reteaching page in the **Reading Kit.** You will also find the same instruction and practice available on **Success Tracker.**

Go Online **For:** Interactive
Vocabulary Crossword Puzzles
Visit: www.PHSchool.com
Web Code: epj-5301
Give students this Web Code to access interactive crossword puzzles using Academic Vocabulary and Vocabulary Skill words from Part 1.

465

Writing Workshop

Meeting Your Standards

Students will

1. write a business letter.
2. use writing strategies to generate ideas and to plan, organize, evaluate, and revise the letter.
3. apply grammar skills.

Writing Genres

Using the Form Explain that business letters are useful in the following situation:

- Job applications and resumes often require cover letters.

 ## Writing Workshop

Work in Progress

If students have done the Work-in-Progress assignments throughout Part 1, suggest that they examine their recorded ideas as they begin prewriting.

OES Online Essay Scorer

A writing prompt for this mode of writing can be found on the *PH Online Essay Scorer* at PHSuccessNet.com.

Prewriting

- Tell students that as they **gather details** they can add information to their charts or revise existing information.

Six Traits Focus

✔	Ideas		Word Choice
	Organization		Sentence Fluency
	Voice		Conventions

Writing and Grammar Interactive Textbook CD-ROM

Students can use the following tools as they complete their business letters:

- Topic Bank
- Business Letter Shell

Workplace Writing: Business Letter

A **business letter** is a piece of correspondence that you write in the course of conducting business or professional matters. Effective business letters are clear, direct, courteous, and carefully formatted. Follow the steps outlined in this workshop to write your own business letter.

Assignment Write a business letter to a company in which you ask for information about a product or service you are interested in using.

What to Include Your letter should feature these elements:

- A heading, inside address, greeting, body, closing, and signature
- Formal, polite language, a clear purpose, and relevant background information
- Standard formatting with consistent spacing and indentation
- Error-free grammar, including correct use of compound subjects, objects, and complements

To preview the criteria on which your business letter may be assessed, see the rubric on page 470.

Prewriting

Choosing Your Topic

Brainstorm and Itemize Jot down a list of products or services that you currently use or are interested in using. For each, itemize by noting why this product or service interests you. Then, decide which details of performance, features, price, or reliability matter most to you. Review your work to choose a topic.

Products	Interest	Services	Interest
Bicycle repair kit	Which is the best?	Homework help	How much is too much?
Cell phone	Cheapest and best service?	Library research service	Help with the Internet?

Gathering Details

Conduct research. Use the Internet or your local phone book to locate the address of the company that provides the product or service you are investigating. Consider browsing stores that carry the products to learn more before you write.

466 ■ Types of Nonfiction

Using the Form

You may use elements of this form in these types of writing:

- requests for information, appointments, or interviews
- formal complaints or commendations
- proposals

Work in Progress
Review the work you did on pages 397, 423, and 445.

Teaching Resources

The following resources can be used to enrich or extend the instruction for the Writing Workshop.

Unit 3 Resources
Writing Workshop: Business Communications: Business Letter, p. 99
Writing Workshop: Integrating Grammar Skills: Sentence Combining to Revise Choppy Sentences, p. 100

General Resources
Rubrics for Business Letter, pp. 51–52
Graphic Organizer Transparencies: Three-column chart, p. 240

Drafting

Shaping Your Writing

Select a format. Choose a standard business letter format, using a consistent font and spacing. You may use block format, in which each part of the letter begins at the left margin. Alternatively, you may use modified block format, in which the heading, closing, and signature are indented to the center of the page. Use the checklist shown here to verify that your draft includes all six elements of a business letter.

Providing Elaboration

Consider your audience. You are addressing a busy professional, so include only essential information. State information clearly and use formal vocabulary, style, and tone.

Business Letter Elements

☐ **Heading**—the writer's address and organization (if any) and the date

☐ **Inside Address**—where the letter will be sent

☐ **Greeting**—a salutation always punctuated by a colon

☐ **Body**—a presentation of the writer's purpose

☐ **Closing**—an appropriate farewell

☐ **Signature**—a signed name

Revising

Revising Your Sentences

Highlight the active voice. A verb in the active voice expresses an action done *by* its subject. A verb in the passive voice expresses an action done *to* its subject.

> **Passive Voice:** The vacuum cleaner *was broken* by the salesman.
>
> **Active Voice:** The salesman *broke* the vacuum cleaner.

The active voice is preferable because it produces more direct and forceful sentences. Review your draft, highlighting verbs written in the passive voice; then, rewrite the sentences in the active voice where you can.

Revising Your Word Choice

Check your tone. To maintain a formal tone, avoid slang, contractions, and personal references. Review your draft, replacing casual language with more formal expressions.

Student Model: Revising to Create a Formal Tone

am in the market for a high-end,   I would like to obtain more
I ~~want a good,~~ reliable server. ~~Can you get me some straight
information about your line of servers.
info on your products without a lot of runaround?~~

> The revision is more formal and polite.

Writing Workshop ■ 467

Tips for Using Rubrics

- Before students begin work on this assignment, have them preview the Rubric for Self-Assessment on page 470 to know what is expected.

- Review the Assessment criteria in class. Before students use the Rubric for Self-Assessment, work with them to rate the student model by applying one or two criteria to it.

- If you wish to assess students' business letters with a 4-point, 5-point, or a 6-point scoring rubric, see *General Resources*, pages 51–52.

Drafting

- Provide students with models of business letters structured in block and modified block formats.

- Suggest that students revise the business letter elements checklist into an outline for their letters.

Six Traits Focus

	Ideas	✔	Word Choice
✔	Organization		Sentence Fluency
✔	Voice		Conventions

WG Writing and Grammar, Gold Level

Students will find additional instruction on drafting a business letter in Chapter 15, Section 1.

Revising

- Explain that the passive voice is acceptable when the person or thing being acted upon is the desired focus of the sentence. Give students this example:

  My father gave my mother a beautiful red rose for her birthday. My mother's treasured rose was illuminated by the morning sun.

  Have students **explain** why the passive voice is acceptable in the second sentence.

  Answer: Although the rose is acted upon by the morning sun, the treasured rose is the desired focus of the sentence.

- Write the following sentences on the board:

  I'd like to know about your new tennis shoes, because I've heard that they're not lousy.

  I would like some information on your new line of tennis shoes.

  Point out to students that *I'd, I've,* and *lousy* make the first sentence informal.

Six Traits Focus

	Ideas	✔	Word Choice
	Organization		Sentence Fluency
✔	Voice		Conventions

WG Writing and Grammar, Gold Level

Students will find additional instruction for revising a business letter in Chapter 15, Section 1.

Integrating Grammar Skills

- Point out to students that choppy sentences sometimes occur when writers are overly focused on clarity or when writers fail to write with the same fluidity they use with spoken language.

- Write the following sentences on the board and have students combine them. For enrichment, have students combine each sentence in more than one way and discuss the effects of each.

    1. *Jevon sat at the table. He ate his lunch.*
    2. *Fiona ordered steak. She ordered rice as well.*
    3. *Taylor is a dedicated student. She is also a talented athlete.*
    4. *His report is organized. It is also concise.*

Possible responses:

1. *Jevon sat at the table and ate his lunch.*
2. *Fiona ordered steak and rice.*
3. *Taylor is a dedicated student and a talented athlete.*
4. *His report is organized and concise.*

- As students review their drafts, have them use highlighters to identify sentences that share common elements.

- Ask volunteers to write examples of sentence combining from their letters on the board.

W G Writing and Grammar, Gold Level

Students will find additional instruction on combining sentences in Chapter 3, Section 1, and Chapter 22, Section 2.

Integrating Grammar Skills

Revising to Combine Choppy Sentences

Avoid choppy, disconnected sentences by combining two or more related ideas in a single sentence.

Methods of Sentence Combining Compound verbs—more than one verb linked to a single subject—can be used to combine two short sentences:

Choppy: I *disconnected* my phone. I *brought* it in for service.
Compound Verb: I *disconnected* my phone and *brought* it in for service.

Compound objects—more than one object linked to a single verb—can help combine sentences.

Choppy: I purchased *a scanner*. I purchased *a fax machine*.
Compound Object: I purchased *a scanner and a fax machine*.

A third option is the use of **compound predicate nominatives** or **predicate adjectives**.

Predicate Nominative	Predicate Adjective
a noun or pronoun that appears with a linking verb and renames, identifies, or explains the subject Example: Juice is a <u>beverage</u>.	an adjective that appears with a linking verb and describes the subject Example: Juice is <u>expensive</u>.

Choppy: My newest device *is a printer*. It is also *a scanner*. It is also *a fax machine*.
Compound Predicative Nominative: My newest device *is a printer, scanner, and fax machine*.
Choppy: The fax is *automated*. It is *fast*.
Compound Predicative Adjective: The fax is *automated and fast*.

Fixing Choppy Sentences Scan your draft for sentence variety.

1. **Read your draft aloud.** Listen for overuse of short sentences.
2. **Identify sentences that can be combined.** Look for sentences that share a common subject or a common predicate element.
3. **Use a variety of sentence combining techniques.** Use compound verbs, compound direct objects, or compound predicate nominatives or predicate adjectives to create a wider variety of flowing sentences.

Apply It to Your Editing

Review the body paragraphs in your letter, looking for opportunities to express related ideas or information in a single sentence. Combine these elements using one of the methods presented here.

468 ■ *Types of Nonfiction*

Prentice Hall Writing and Grammar Connection: Chapter 3, Section 1

Differentiated Instruction   Solutions for All Learners

Support for Advanced Readers

Point out to students that there is often more than one way to combine sentences. Also explain that some short sentences are acceptable; they add variety and interest when combined with longer sentences. Write these sentences on the board.

Jevon walked to school. Then he entered the classroom. He was early. He was also full of confidence.

Add these possible combinations to the board.

Jevon walked to school and entered the classroom. He was early and full of confidence.

Jevon walked to school. He entered the classroom early and full of confidence.

Point out that the second example demonstrates variety in writing by pairing a short sentence with a longer sentence. Have students review their drafts for a variety of sentence lengths.

Student Model: Robin Weber
St. Petersburg, FL

Intelligent Productions
220 Any Street, Suite 112
Any Town, NY 10000
December 13, 2006

The author uses modified block format.

G-2000 Computers
310 Infinite Loop
Any City, CA 94000

Dear Sir or Madam:

My business is currently in the market for several high-end, reliable server computers. I would like to obtain more information about your line of server products.

The author states his purpose clearly and concisely.

The computers we use are operating twenty-four hours a day, seven days a week, as servers hosting a high-traffic Internet Web site. Therefore, it would be unacceptable for my company to purchase computers that require periods of inactivity in order to remain in working condition. We are also concerned about technical support issues and costs.

In this paragraph, Robin provides important background information.

I would appreciate if you could send me the exact specifications on catalog items number 1444 and 2314. In addition, there is no information on warranties in your product descriptions. Any information you can provide in this regard would be very helpful in making my purchasing decision. Also, would it be possible to obtain a high volume discount? How would such an order affect delivery time?

The letter includes specific questions that Robin would like answered.

Please send me any information you have on these matters. I look foward to hearing from you.

In his conclusion, Robin summarizes the request using polite language.

Sincerely,

Robin Weber

Robin Weber

Writing Workshop ■ 469

Student Model

- Explain that the Student Model is a sample and that their own business letters may be longer.
- Explain that Robin assumes the proper voice by using formal language. **Ask** students to identify instances in the letter where formal language is used.
  Possible response: Students may note *Sir or Madam, I would appreciate,* or *we are also concerned* as examples of formal language.
- **Ask** students why the author states his purpose early in the letter and how he makes his purpose clear and concise.
  Possible response: He states the purpose early to let the reader know his intentions immediately. He makes his purpose clear and concise by avoiding chatty and unnecessary language.
- Point out that the background information helps the reader understand why the letter has been written.
- **Ask** students how the writer would modify this letter to use a block format.
  Answer: The writer could modify the letter by beginning each part at the left margin.
- Write these sentences on the board:

  I am excited to learn more about your product. Thank you for your time.

  Tell students that this is another example of a polite conclusion. Ask students to review their letters and to determine whether they have incorporated polite endings.

Writing Genres

Business Letters Explain to students that writing a business letter may seem like a skill that they will not need for a long time, but this is not true. Point out that job applications often require cover letters. Tell students that they may need to write to a company to voice a complaint or a compliment about a product or service. Also tell students that they may be asked to write to a local official, a business owner, or another organization on behalf of a club or organization to which they belong.

469

Editing and Proofreading

Editing and Proofreading

- Make sure that students go beyond the heading when looking for mistakes in the names and addresses. Tell them that they should review the entire letter.
- After they have checked names and addresses, have students exchange letters with partners. Ask partners to verify that the information is correct. Explain to students that when editing, it can be helpful to have someone else take another look for mistakes.

Six Traits Focus

Ideas		Word Choice	
Organization		Sentence Fluency	
Voice		✓	Conventions

ASSESS

Publishing and Presenting

- If students choose to mail their letters, review the proper format for addressing an envelope. Tell students who expect replies to enclose self-addressed, stamped envelopes as well.
- If students choose to present their letters orally, encourage them to practice reading their letters aloud beforehand. Have students make notes on their letters that will help convey a friendly, professional tone.

Reflecting on Your Writing

- Have a class discussion regarding using a business-like tone in letters. Ask students if and how they found the tone that they used different than the tone that they have used for other writing assignments.
- Have students compare writing a business letter to writing a letter to a friend.

WG Writing and Grammar, Gold Level

Students will find additional guidance for editing and proofreading, publishing and presenting, and reflecting on a business letter in Chapter 15, Section 1.

Check your draft for errors in format, grammar, and punctuation.

Focus on Accuracy: Make certain that the names of individuals and companies are spelled correctly and that the address is complete.

Publishing and Presenting

Consider one of the following ways to share your writing:

Send your letter. If your letter is written to an existing business, mail it. When you get a response, share it with classmates.

Conduct a discussion. Use your letter to begin a class discussion about the role of communication skills in everyday life. Improve the productivity of the discussion by being open to the variety of ideas your classmates suggest. Make notes on their comments, and add your letter and notes to your writing portfolio.

Reflecting on Your Writing

Writer's Journal Jot down your thoughts on the experience of writing a business letter. Begin by answering these questions.

- Which did you find easier, following the business letter format or maintaining a business-like tone? Explain.
- How will this experience change the way you write business letters in the future?

> *Prentice Hall Writing and Grammar Connection: Chapter 15*

Rubric for Self-Assessment

To assess your business letter, use the following rubric:

Criteria	Rating Scale
	not very very
Focus: How clearly do you state your purpose?	1 2 3 4 5
Organization: How thoroughly do you incorporate all the elements of a business letter?	1 2 3 4 5
Support/Elaboration: How effectively do you provide background information?	1 2 3 4 5
Style: How formal and polite is your use of language?	1 2 3 4 5
Conventions: How correct is your grammar, especially your use of compound subjects, objects, and complements?	1 2 3 4 5

Tips for Test Taking

Tell students that when they take a test that requires them to evaluate the components of a business letter, they may have difficulty remembering all six elements (heading, inside address, greeting, body, closing, and signature). Encourage students to combine their past experiences in writing business letters with common sense and then review the letter to check whether anything appears to be missing.

Persuasive Texts

Skills You Will Learn

Literary Analysis: *Persuasive Essay*
Reading Skill: *Rereading*

Literary Analysis: *Persuasive Speeches and Rhetorical Devices*
Reading Skill: *Reading Aloud*

Reading Skill: *Distinguishing Fact From Opinion*

Literary Analysis: *Humorous Essay*

Literature You Will Read

Persuasive Texts 471

Skills Overview

Reading Skill: Analyze and Evaluate Persuasive Appeals
- Rereading to analyze and evaluate persuasive appeals
- Read aloud

Vocabulary Development
- Prefixes

Literary Analysis
- Persuasive Essay: appeals to reason and emotion, author's motive
- Persuasive Speech: rhetorical devices, parallelism, restatement, repetition

Writing
- Editorial
- Work in Progress, pp. 491, 513

Monitoring Progress

Diagnose: Before you begin Part 2, administer the **Diagnostic Test** for Unit 3, Part 2. This test will identify students' level of readiness for the reading and vocabulary skills in Part 2. Use the **Interpretation Guide** for the Diagnostic Test to determine which students need help with prerequisite skills before beginning Part 2.

Preteach and Prepare: Use the information indicated in the **Interpretation Guide** to help students build prerequisite skills. In addition, prepare students by using the **Vocabulary Warm-up** activities and the **Reading Warm-up** activities as necessary for each selection set.

Teach: Use the instructional plan and resources provided to teach the skills and selections.

Assess: After students have completed Part 2, administer the **Benchmark Test** for Unit 3, Part 2. The test results will indicate which skills students have mastered and those on which they need more work.

Reteach: Use the Interpretation Guide to determine the appropriate reteaching pages from the **Reading Kit.**

Intervention: The prerequisite and reteaching pages are also available in the **Success Tracker.**

Differentiated Instruction
Solutions for All Learners

Resources for Monitoring Progress

Unit 3 Resources
 Unit 3, Part 2 Diagnostic Test, pp. 108–110
 Unit 3, Part 2 Benchmark Test, pp. 197–202

Reading Kit

Success Tracker

Reading and Vocabulary Skills Preview

Introduce the Reading Skill

- Introduce the reading skill: analyzing persuasive appeals. Draw students' attention to the definition. Tell students that writers use persuasive appeals in argumentative, or persuasive, essays or speeches. Point out that readers and listeners must be able to analyze persuasive appeals in order to evaluate them and understand their effects.

- Emphasize that the purpose of persuasive appeals is to motivate the reader or listener to action. Point out that unless students read and listen carefully to these appeals, they may be moved to action without even realizing how their feelings, thoughts, and decisions have been shaped.

Model the Reading Strategies

- Model how rereading the text and reading the text aloud can help students analyze persuasive appeals. Write the following sentence on the board:

    We will never give up, we will never retreat, we will never fail to defend our land.

    Then, **ask** these questions:

    What does the author use to gain the reader's attention?
    Answer: The author uses repetition to bring attention to this passage.

    When you read the passage aloud, how does it affect the listener?
    Answer: The repetition creates a rhythm and a sense of urgency and passion in the message.

- Tell students that rereading and reading a persuasive text aloud help the reader to analyze the types and effects of the appeals the author uses.

Reading: Analyzing Persuasive Appeals

> **Persuasive appeals** use logic or emotion to bring about a positive response to the writer's argument.

Skills and Strategies You Will Learn in Part 2

In Part 2, you will learn

- to **reread** the text to **analyze and evaluate persuasive appeals.** (p. 474)
- to **read the text aloud** to **analyze and evaluate persuasive appeals.** (p. 492)
- to **distinguish fact from opinion** in order to **analyze persuasive nonfiction texts.** (p. 514)

Using the Skills and Strategies in Part 2

In Part 2, you will learn to **recognize persuasive appeals.** You will also learn to **reread** to recognize the kinds of appeals an author uses and to determine whether the appeal is valid and effective. **Reading aloud** will help you appreciate and analyze devices such as repetition that contribute to persuasive appeals. In Part 2, you will apply the skills and strategies you learn to a variety of nonfiction texts.

The model shows you how you can apply these skills and strategies.

reread—repetition reinforces the concept that this is one person's fault.

read aloud—negative connotation   read aloud—negative connotation

He *has refused* his Assent to Laws, the most wholesome and necessary for the public good. He *has forbidden* his Governors to pass Laws of immediate and pressing importance, unless suspended in their operation till his Assent should be obtained. . . .

Declaration of Independence 1776

reread text—use of pronoun rather than name is negative

Academic Vocabulary: Words for Analyzing Literature

The following words will help you write and talk about interpretations of the literature in this unit.

Word	Definition	Example Sentence
anticipate *v.*	expect	Clues help the reader *anticipate* the story's climax.
internal *adj.*	on the inside	The plot centered on the main character's *internal* conflict.
derive *v.*	get from a source	I was able to *derive* some clues from the description of the characters.
texture *n.*	look and feel of something	The author's description of the material's *texture* was a clue.
signify *v.*	be a sign of something	The author used dreams to *signify* the character's internal conflict.

Vocabulary Skill: Prefixes

▶ A **prefix** is a word part that is added to the beginning of a word or another word part.

In Part 2, you will learn

- Latin prefix *ante-*   (p. 490)
- Latin prefix *inter-*   (p. 512)

Knowing the meaning of prefixes expands your vocabulary. Adding the definition of a prefix to a base word you are familiar with gives you a strategy for determining the meaning of new words.

▶ **Example:**

Unfamiliar Word:	*antedate*
Prefix:	*ante* = **before**
Word Root:	*date* = **specific time**
Definition:	*antedate:* **before a specific time**

Reading and Vocabulary Skills Preview ■ 473

Introduce Academic Vocabulary

- Introduce the academic vocabulary: words for analyzing literature. Tell students that these words are useful when reading and writing about literature.
- Review each word, and have students read aloud the words' definitions. Then, show students how these words can be used in analyzing literature. For example: The *internal* conflict of a character is vital to the plot. I *anticipate* what will happen early in the story. The symbol *signifies* the conflict that the character feels.
- Tell students to try to use these words as they discuss the selections in Part 2.

Introduce the Vocabulary Skill

- Introduce the vocabulary skill: prefixes. Tell students that prefixes are combined with other words or word parts to create many words in English. Latin is the source for many of these prefixes.
- Review the two prefixes on this page and their meanings.

Go Online
Vocabulary **For:** Interactive Crossword puzzles
Visit: www.PHSchool.com
Web Code: epj-5302
Give students this Web Code to access interactive crossword puzzles using Academic Vocabulary and Vocabulary Skill words from Part 2.

Differentiated Instruction   Solutions for All Learners

Strategy for Less Proficient Readers
To help students understand persuasive appeals, have them look at samples of advertising. Write these slogans on the board:

Brand X—for those who think young.

All winners wear brand Y shoes.

Ask students what phrases in these sentences try to convince the reader or listener to take some action.
Answer: Students should identify the phrases "think young" and "All winners."

Then, **ask** students why they think the advertisers used those words and what they hope to gain by doing so.
Possible responses: They are hoping to increase sales by associating brand X shoes with youth and brand Y shoes with winning.

Provide students with print ads from magazines or newspapers or have them listen to radio advertisements or watch television ads. Have students identify the persuasive appeals.

Planning Differentiated Instruction

Choosing Your Selection

You may use either selection to meet the lesson standards. The following guide will help you determine which of the two selections is more appropriate for your students.

Accessibility at a Glance

	Carry Your Own Skis	Libraries Face Sad Chapter
Context	Developing a sense of personal responsibility	Protecting America's public libraries
Language	• Mentions familiar situations • Simple sentences with vivid descriptions	• Diction more difficult • Allusions to great works of literature
Concept Level	Accessible; childhood memories of skiing led to developing responsibility	Accessible; childhood memories of using the public libraries and a call to protect them
Literary Merit	Cross-generational	Cross-generational
Lexile	980L	1070L
Overall Rating	More accessible	More challenging

Using the Other Selection You may use the other selection for homework or independent reading to reinforce the selection skills. If you use both selections, you can build a test for both using *ExamView®* **Test Bank** software.

Choosing Your Resources

[**L1**] Special Needs Students   [**L4**] Advanced Students
[**L2**] Below-Level Students   [**EL**] English Learners
[**L3**] All Students

FT Fast Track Instruction: To move the lesson more quickly, use the strategies and activities identified with **FT**.

Reading and Vocabulary Warm-ups provide support for below level students. **A** is for students reading two grades below level; **B** is for students reading one grade below level. For Selection Tests, **A** signifies "less challenging" and **B** "more challenging." For Graphic Organizer transparencies, **A** signifies "not filled in" and **B** "filled in."

Scaffolding for Less Proficient and Advanced Students

The leveled questions on Apply the Skills pages progress in the levels of thinking required to answer them. To address the needs of your different students, you may use the (a) level questions for your less proficient students, the (b) level with your on-level and advanced students. The occasional (c) level questions are appropriate for your advanced students.

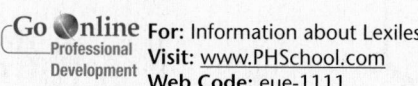
Go Online
Professional Development
For: Information about Lexiles
Visit: www.PHSchool.com
Web Code: eue-1111

Step-by-Step Teaching Guide	Pacing Guide	
PRETEACH		
• Administer Vocabulary and Reading Warm-ups as necessary.		
• Introduce the Literary Analysis Skill: Persuasive Essay. **FT**	10 min.	
• Introduce the Reading Skill: Analyze and Evaluate Persuasive Appeals. **FT**	10 min.	
• Prepare students to read by teaching the selection vocabulary. **FT**	10 min.	
• Build background and develop expressive vocabulary with Connecting to the Literature and Background.	10 min.	
• Engage students' interest with the motivation activity.	10 min.	
TEACH		
• Informally monitor comprehension while students read independently or in groups. **FT**	30 min.	
• Monitor students' comprehension with the Reading Check notes.	as students read	
• Reinforce vocabulary with Vocabulary Builder notes.	as students read	
• Develop students' understanding of persuasive essays with the Literary Analysis annotations. **FT**	5 min.	
• Develop students' ability to analyze and evaluate persuasive appeals with the Reading Skill annotations. **FT**	10 min.	
ASSESS/EXTEND		
• Assess students' comprehension and mastery of the Reading Skill and Literary Analysis by having them answer the Apply the Skills questions. **FT**	35 min.	
• Have students complete the Vocabulary Builder activities. **FT**	5 min.	
• Apply students' ability to write an abstract with the Writing activity. **FT**	30–45 min. or homework	
• Extend students' listening and speaking and research and technology skills with one or both of the Extend Your Learning activities.	15–30 min. or homework	
• Have students complete the Vocabulary Skill and Grammar Lesson.	5 min.	
• Monitor students' progress with the Assessment Practice.	20–40 min.	
• Administer **Selection Test A** or **Selection Test B**. **FT**	15 min.	

Resources

Meeting Your Standards

Students will

1. **analyze and respond to literary elements.**
   - Literary Analysis: Persuasive Essay

2. **read, comprehend, and analyze short stories.**
   - Reading Skill: Analyze and Evaluate Persuasive Appeals
   - Reading Strategy: Rereading to Analyze and Evaluate Persuasive Appeals
   - Reading Check questions
   - Apply the Skills questions
   - Assessment Practice

3. **develop vocabulary.**
   - Vocabulary Builder
   - Latin prefixes *ante-, inter-*

4. **apply grammar skills.**
   - Adjectives

5. **develop writing proficiency.**
   - Work in Progress: Editorial
   - Abstract

6. **extend learning.**
   - Listening and Speaking: Persuasive Speech
   - Research and Technology: Comparative Chart

Block Scheduling: Use one 90-minute class period to preteach the skills and have students read the selection. Use a second 90-minute class period to assess students' mastery of skills, extend their learning, and monitor their progress.

Homework Suggestions

Following are possibilities for homework assignments.

- Support pages from *Unit 3 Resources*:
  Literary Analysis
  Reading Skill
  Vocabulary Builder
  Enrichment

- An Extend Your Learning project and the Writing assignment for your chosen selection may be completed over several days.

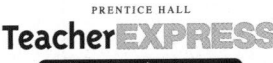

PRENTICE HALL
Teacher EXPRESS™ Use this complete
Plan · Teach · Assess suite of powerful
teaching tools to make lesson planning and testing quicker and easier.

PRENTICE HALL
Student EXPRESS™ Use the
Learn · Study · Succeed Interactive
Textbook (online and on CD-ROM) to make selections and activities come alive with audio and video support and interactive questions.

❶ Literary Analysis
Persuasive Essay

- Remind students that in a *persuasive essay,* the author attempts to persuade readers to form an opinion or to take an action.

- Ask the class to read the discussion of Literary Analysis on this page. Then, give students an example of how an author might appeal to reason. For example, an author attempting to persuade readers to take up bike riding as an alternative transportation might give statistics about how many people ride bikes to school and work, or quote statistics from experts about the health benefits of bike riding.

- Point out that authors also appeal to emotion. An author might talk about the feeling of freedom that comes when riding a bike at full speed, or how much fun it can be to ride bikes together with friends.

- Tell students that authors always have a motive or reason for attempting to persuade the reader. For example, an author encouraging bike riding may want to diminish air pollution, or the author may want to encourage physical fitness.

- Suggest that as students read the selection, they notice the author's use of reason and emotion to appeal to readers, and that they try to identify the author's motive in writing the essay.

❷ Reading Skill
Persuasive Appeals

- Tell students that authors may use logic, emotion, or a combination of both to sway the reader. Readers should evaluate whether the author's appeal is valid or convincing.

- Encourage students to examine the evidence and reasons the author uses to support his or her claim. For example, if an author uses a fact or statistic, you might question the source of the information. Does it sound convincing? Is it from a reliable or expert source?

- Give students a copy of the **Reading Skill Graphic Organizer A** (p. 102, *Graphic Organizer Transparencies*). Have them fill in the graphic organizer to identify the persuasive appeals used by the author.

Build Skills *Carry Your Own Skis • Libraries Face Sad Chapter*

Practice these skills with either "Carry Your Own Skis" (p. 476) or "Libraries Face Sad Chapter" (p. 483).

❶ Literary Analysis

A **persuasive essay** is a short nonfiction work that tries to convince a reader to think or act in a particular way. Persuasive essays usually include one or both of the following:

- **Appeals to reason:** logical arguments based on verifiable evidence, such as facts, statistics, or expert testimony
- **Appeals to emotion:** statements intended to affect listeners' feelings about a subject. These statements often include charged language—words with strong positive or negative associations.

An **author's motive** in a persuasive essay is his or her reason for, or interest in, persuading readers to accept his or her position.

❷ Reading Skill

Persuasive appeals are the arguments the author makes. To **analyze and evaluate persuasive appeals**, identify passages in which the author makes an argument in support of his or her position. Then, **reread** those passages to test the author's logic and reasoning. Ask yourself the following questions.

- Is the author's argument supported by evidence, or is it based on faulty assumptions?
- Does the author link ideas clearly or make leaps in logic?
- Is the argument consistent or is it contradictory?

Use a chart like the one shown to record your analysis of the author's arguments. Then, decide whether the author has made a convincing persuasive appeal.

Claim	Logical?

↓

Evaluation

Vocabulary Builder

Carry Your Own Skis

- **inevitability** (in ev´ i tə bil´ ə tē) *n.* quality of being certain to happen (p. 477) *The inevitability of losing did not keep the team from playing hard.*

- **potential** (pō ten´ shəl) *n.* possibility (p. 478) *She has the potential to be a great player, but she still needs a lot of practice.*

- **riddled** (rid´´ld) *adj.* affected throughout (p. 479) *The old tree was riddled with wormholes.*

Libraries Face Sad Chapter

- **curtailed** (kər tāld´) *v.* cut short; reduced (p. 485) *The game was curtailed by darkness.*

- **medium** (mē´ dē əm) *n.* means of communication (p. 485) *Television is today's most popular medium.*

- **duration** (doo rā´ shən) *n.* length of time something lasts (p. 487) *Attendees remained standing for the duration of the ceremony.*

474 ■ *Types of Nonfiction*

Vocabulary Development

Vocabulary Knowledge Rating

Create a **Vocabulary Knowledge Rating Chart** for the selection you will teach from this set. Include the selection vocabulary from this page and the additional expressive vocabulary students are asked to use at the end of Connecting to the Literature. These words will increase students' expressive vocabulary.

Give students a copy of the chart with the words on it. Introduce the words by reading them aloud and having students mark their rating in the Before Reading column. Urge them to be alert to these words as they read and discuss the selection because they will rate their knowledge of the words again after they finish.

If you wish, you may tally how many students know (or think they know) a word to gauge how much instruction you need to provide. As students read, point out the words and their context.

Build Understanding • *Carry Your Own Skis*

❸ Background

Cold-Weather Clothing Before the development of synthetic, lightweight, waterproof fabrics that "breathe" and keep the wearer dry, keeping warm on the ski slopes meant wearing heavy wool and cotton clothing. Garments made from these fabrics would become wet and cold in the snow, and they would stay wet and cold until removed.

❹ Connecting to the Literature

Reading/Writing Connection In "Carry Your Own Skis," Lian Dolan describes skiing in the mid-1960s: The absence of today's comfortable clothing and conveniences made skiing then seem like work. Yet Dolan's mother and aunt enjoyed the sport. Write five sentences explaining why some people enjoy activities that involve a degree of hardship. Use at least three of these words: *attain, challenge, concentrate, display, frustrate.*

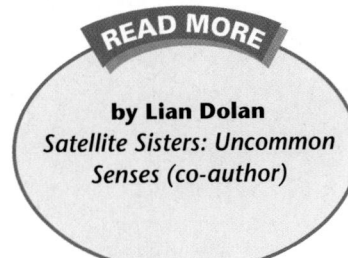

READ MORE

by Lian Dolan
Satellite Sisters: Uncommon Senses (co-author)

Meet the Author

Lian **Dolan** (b. 1966)

Lian Dolan is one of the "Satellite Sisters," a group of five sisters who host a weekly radio show. Before helping launch the show, Dolan tried everything from working as a waitress to producing films. She also writes the column "The Chaos Chronicles" for *Working Mother* magazine.

"The Sassiest" Lian is known as the sassiest of the sisters, and she is not afraid to express her opinions on any topic. Even though Lian is the youngest of the five sisters, she directs all of their writing projects. She enjoys being the "Head Sister," giving orders to her older siblings.

Fast Facts

▶ Dolan's writing has appeared in national magazines such as *Good Housekeeping* and *O, The Oprah Magazine.*

▶ The Satellite Sisters live in four different cities on two continents. They link via satellite for their weekly radio show.

For: More about the author
Visit: www.PHSchool.com
Web Code: epe-9308

Carry Your Own Skis ■ 475

❸ Background
Cold Weather Clothing

Because of modern technical advances, skiers today enjoy much more comfort than did Lian Dolan and her sisters. Experienced skiers today dress in layers, and do not use natural fibers such as cotton and wool. New fabrics such as microfleece keep heat in, but allow moisture to escape. One of the most recent developments in ski clothing is a "temperature control" fabric that has been used by astronauts. It keeps skiers warm, but does not overheat them.

❹ Connecting to the Literature

• To help students understand the meanings of the words they are asked to use, give them these sentences:

1. Some people think it is important to *attain* top honors in every sport they practice.

2. Even though running a marathon is a *challenge* to body and mind, thousands of people participate in these races each year.

3. Olympic gymnasts have to *concentrate* on what they are doing if they want to win medals.

4. Many athletes *display* their medals and trophies to remind themselves of the effort it took to win.

5. True champions do not let defeat *frustrate* them.

• Help students further develop their expressive vocabulary by providing these words: *aspect, drastic, dominate, potential,* and *velocity.* Encourage students to use these words as they discuss the selection.

Go Online For additional information about Lian Dolan, Author Link have students type in the Web Code and then select *Lian Dolan.*

Differentiated Instruction   Solutions for All Learners

Support for Below-Level Students [L1, L2]

Unit 3 Resources
    Vocabulary Warm-up Word Lists, p. 111
    Vocabulary Warm-up Practice, p. 112
    Reading Warm-up A, p. 113
    Selection Test A, pp. 121–123

Graphic Organizer Transparencies
    Reading Skill Graphic Organizer, Transparency B, p. 103

Reader's Notebook: Adapted Version

Adapted Reader's Notebook Audio CD

Support for English Learners [EL]

Unit 3 Resources
    Vocabulary Warm-up Word Lists, p. 111
    Vocabulary Warm-up Practice, p. 112
    Reading Warm-up A, p. 113

Reader's Notebook: English Learner's Version

Listening to Literature Audio CD

❶ Motivation

Prepare an **Anticipation Guide** (*General Resources,* pp. 8–10) with the following statements:

- Skiing today is not as challenging an activity as it was in past decades.
- Parents should insist that their children learn a challenging sport.
- Participating in sports helps children grow up to be responsible.
- A person does not have to enjoy a sport to benefit from practicing it.

Give students a copy of the prepared Anticipation Guide and have students mark their responses in the Me column. Have students discuss the statements in pairs or groups and mark the Guides again in the Group column.

Concept Connector ⟶

Students will return to the Anticipation Guide after completing "Carry Your Own Skis."

Learning Modalities
Bodily/Kinesthetic Learners

To help students appreciate Lian Dolan's struggles, suggest that they act out Dolan carrying her gear from the lodge to the car. They can simulate her burden by carrying something heavy in one arm, such as a book bag full of books, and a pair of long poles, such as two brooms or mops, in the other hand. Then, have students discuss how difficult this was for her as a child, and ask them to discuss why they think she did it.

❷ About the Selection

In "Carry Your Own Skis," Lian Dolan remembers her childhood struggles to keep up with her sisters on the ski slopes. During the family ski outings, at the end of the day Dolan was required to carry her skis from the lodge to the car, no matter how cold, wet, and tired she was. Learning to "carry your own skis" became an important lesson in personal responsibility that she still practices in all areas of her adult life.

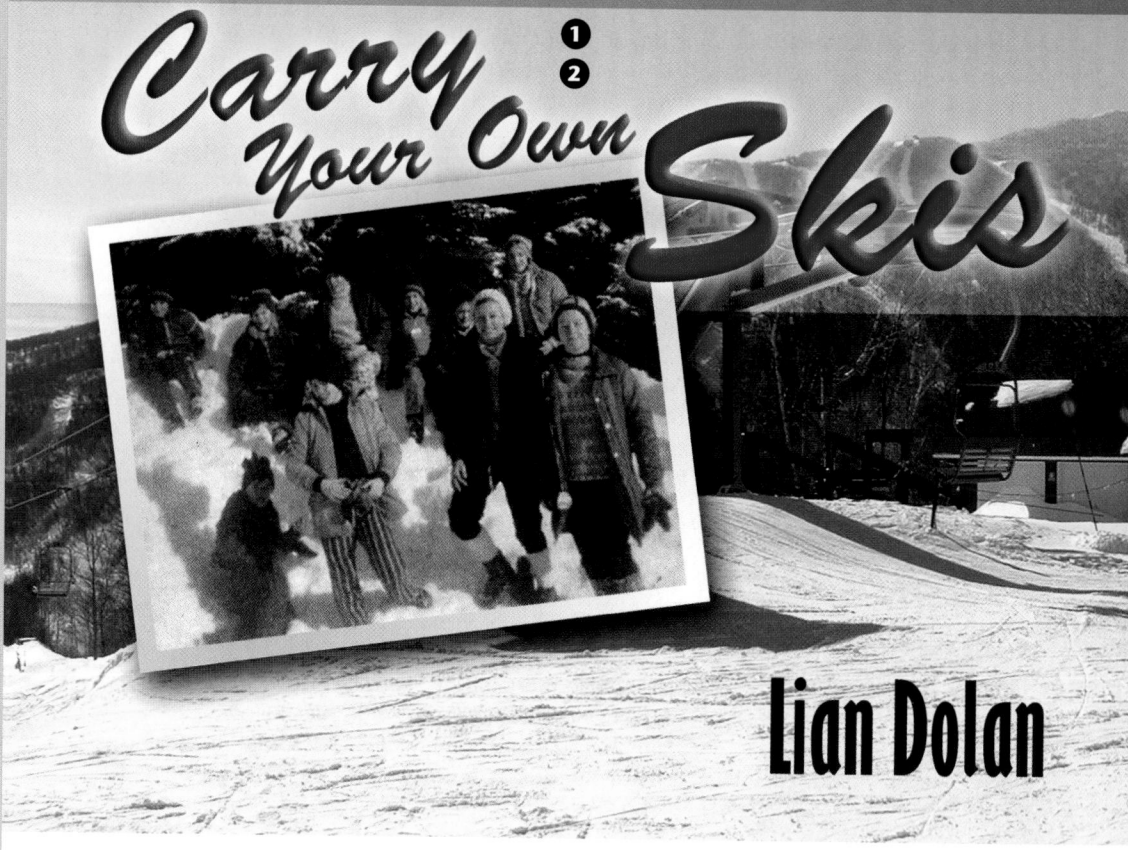

Carry Your Own Skis

Lian Dolan

W hen my mother was forty, she took up skiing. Or, more correctly, she and her twin sister took up skiing. They got on a bus, went to ski camp for a week, and learned to ski. After that, they'd get in the car and head up to Ladies Day at Powder Hill as often as they could to practice their stem christies.[1] Don't let the name fool you, Powder Hill (which later became the more Everest-like "Powder Ridge") was no pushover bunny slope.[2]

❸ This was in the mid-sixties, when skiing was work—decades before valet parking, fondue lunches, and gear that actually keeps you dry, warm, and safe. My mother and my aunt took up the kind

Reading Skill
Persuasive Appeals
How do the details about ski lodges of the 1960s support the author's position that skiing used to be a less luxurious sport?

---

1. **stem christies** turns made by angling one ski and then bringing the other into alignment.
2. **bunny slope** gently sloping hill used for practice by beginning skiers.

476 ■ *Types of Nonfiction*

Vocabulary Development

Think-Aloud: Expressive Vocabulary
Tell students that expressive vocabulary helps the student think about and write about literature. Using a think-aloud process, model how to use expressive vocabulary in discussing the selection. Say to students:

I'm going to think aloud to show you how I would use some expressive words to discuss these two pages of the selection:

When talking about Dolan's mother and her aunt learning to ski, I might use

a sentence such as, "Dolan's mother and aunt *display* an enormous determination in learning to ski and taking their children skiing."

To talk about Dolan's determination to ski along with the others, I might say, "Even though it was a terrific *challenge* for Dolan to keep up with her siblings, she did not allow the discomforts and hardships to *frustrate* her attempts to join in the fun."

of skiing that entailed wooden skis, tie boots, and rope tows[3] that could jerk your arm out of its socket. This was the kind of skiing where skiers, not the Sno-Cats, groomed the hill[4] in the morning. Ticket buyers were expected to sidestep up and down slopes and herringbone the lift lines.[5] The typical A-frame lodge had a big fireplace, a couple of bathrooms, rows of picnic tables, and maybe some hot chocolate for sale. At the end of the day, there were no hot toddies by a roaring fire in furry boots or drinks in the hot tub of a slopeside condo. Instead, my mother and her sister faced the inevitability of a station wagon with a dead battery and the long, dark drive back home in wet clothes.

Why did they learn to ski? It wasn't to spend some quality time outdoors together away from their responsibilities at home. They learned to ski so that they could take their collective children skiing, all seventeen of us. My mother's eight children and my aunt's nine. And learn to ski we did, eagerly. There was, however, one rule my mother had about skiing: Carry your own skis.

My mother didn't teach us to ski until we could carry our own skis from the car to the lodge in the morning and—this is key—from the lodge back to the car at the end of the day. Even cold, wet, and tired, we had to get our skis, poles, and boots back to that station wagon on our own. No falling behind. No dragging. And no whining. My mother had the responsibility for her gear, the giant lunch, the car, and the occasional trip to the ER for broken legs. We were in charge of our own gear and meeting at the end of the day. These were the conditions to be allowed to accompany siblings and cousins to the slopes. Carry your own skis or sit in the lodge all day.

No one wanted to get left in the lodge. A cold, wet day on the ice-blue slopes of New England, freezing in leather boots and the generation of ski clothes before microfibers was far preferable to being left out of all that fun. Miss the lunches of soggy tuna fish sandwiches and mini chocolate bars? No way! Sit in the lodge instead of side-slipping your way down a sheet of ice disguised as a trail or tramping through three feet of snow to get the pole you dropped under the chair lift? Not me! Forgo that last run of the day in near darkness, cold and alone and crying because your siblings have skied on ahead without you? Who'd want to miss all that fun? Sitting in the lodge all day just wasn't an option once we reached ski age. We were expected to participate. We learned to carry our own skis.

---

3. rope tows moving ropes that skiers hold to be pulled to the top of the hill.
4. groomed the hill packed and smoothed the snow.
5. herringbone the lift lines walk uphill to chair lift by stepping with skis pointed outward to avoid sliding back down the hill. The skis leave a "herringbone" pattern—a line of connected v-shapes—on the snow.

---

❹ ◀ Critical Viewing
What details in these photographs suggest they are from an earlier time? **[Infer]**

Vocabulary Builder
inevitability (in ev´ i tə bil′ ə tē) *n.* quality of being certain to happen

Literary Analysis
Persuasive Essay
Which details in this paragraph appeal to the emotions? Explain.

❻ ✓ Reading Check
Why did Dolan's mother and aunt learn to ski?

---

❸ Reading Skill
Persuasive Appeals
- **Ask** students to describe how the details about modern-day skiing in this description make life easier for skiers.
  Answer: People do not have to walk to a parking lot, or bring their own lunches, and their clothing does not get wet and cold.
- **Ask** students the Reading Skill question: How do the details about the ski lodges of the 1960s support the author's position that skiing used to be a less luxurious sport?
  Answer: In the 1960s, ski lodges did not provide luxuries for their guests, and skiers did not have special clothing to keep them comfortable.

❹ Critical Viewing
Answer: Clothing and equipment suggest an earlier time.

❺ Literary Analysis
Persuasive Essay
- **Ask** students to think about a time when they were left out of a game, perhaps because they were sick or because they were unable to do what everyone else was doing. Then, ask them what emotions they felt at the time.
  Answer: Students may suggest that they felt emotions such as disappointment, sadness, or anger.
- **Ask** students the Literary Analysis question: Which details in this paragraph appeal to the emotions? Explain.
  Answer: Students may suggest the description of the fear of being left out and of being alone and crying.

❻ Reading Check
Answer: They learned to ski so that they could take their children skiing.

Differentiated
Instruction   Solutions for All Learners

Background for English Learners
Although skiing was used as a means of transportation in Europe for thousands of years, skiing became popular as a sport in the 20th century. At first, skiers had to climb the mountainside to ski down. Today, chairlifts carry skiers and their equipment up the hills.

In the past, skis were made of wood. Today, they are made of much lighter and sturdier combinations of wood, lightweight metals, fiberglass, and carbon fiber. Skiers also must wear heavy boots that attach firmly to the skis. They carry a metal pole in each hand that helps them maintain their balance.

There are many popular ski resorts in the northeastern United States and in the Rocky Mountain region, where there are plentiful mountain slopes and winter snows. Resorts use snow-making machines to provide snow if the weather has failed.

4

Persuasive Appeals

- Ask students to describe some of the behavior that the author noticed in other children.
  Answer: Some girls never signed up to pack in or out for a camping trip or for clean-up duties.

- Ask students how the author's behavior differed from that of other children.
  Answer: She signed up to make sandwiches and to clean up; she loaded canoes and put up the tent.

- **Ask** students the Literary Analysis question: How does the author support her claim that some kids operate by different rules?
  Answer: The author supports her claim with the details of how other kids did not show the same level of responsibility and concern for community that she did.

❽ Critical Viewing

Answer: Students may say that the photograph suggests that skiing looks as much like work as it does recreation.

The lesson was simple, really. Be responsible for yourself and your stuff or you miss out. No one wanted to miss out. Getting across the icy parking lot and back seemed a small price to pay for the <u>potential</u> of great fun. And even if you dropped your poles or the bindings cut into your hands or you fell on your rear end, that was part of the experience. The "carry your own skis" mentality filtered into almost every area of our life as we were growing up. Doing homework, getting to practice, applying to college—be responsible for yourself and your stuff or you miss out.

❼ I began to notice the people who hadn't learned to carry their own skis when I was as young as eleven. I didn't have a name for this concept yet, but I had the notion that maybe other kids operated by a different set of rules. They thought that somewhere, somebody was going to take care of things for them. I remember the girls at summer camp who never signed up to pack out or pack in for a camping trip, expecting that someone else would provide food or do all the cleanup for them. But me? I would sign up to make the PB&Js and to clean up the mess. I'd load the canoes onto the truck and take 'em off again. And the tent? I'd put it up and I'd take it down. I didn't know any different. As a result, I was invited to go on a lot of camping trips. The lodge and back, baby—that was my attitude.

In high school, the kids who didn't carry their own skis called their parents to bring in assignments they'd forgotten or to ask for a

Vocabulary Builder
potential (pō ten´ shəl)
n. possibility

Reading Skill
Persuasive Appeals
How does the author support her claim that some kids operate by different rules?

❽ **▼ Critical Viewing**
Based on this photograph, does skiing look like work or recreation?
[Analyze]

478

Vocabulary Development

Vocabulary Knowledge Rating
When students have completed reading and discussing "Carry Your Own Skis," have them take out their **Vocabulary Knowledge Rating Chart** for this selection. Read the words aloud once more and have students rate their knowledge of the words again in the After Reading column. Clarify any words that are still problematic. Have students write their own defini-

tion and example or sentence in the appropriate column. Then, have students complete the **Vocabulary Builder Practice** activities on p. 481. Encourage students to use the words in further discussion and written work about this selection. Remind them that they will be accountable for these words on the Selection Test.

ride home instead of walking or taking the late bus. In college, the no-ski carriers all had pink T-shirts—a sure sign that they had never done laundry before—and they complained about how much work they had. Isn't that what college was about—doing your own laundry and finishing your work? Then you could get to the fun stuff.

The real world is <u>riddled</u> with people who have never learned to carry their own skis—the blame-shifters, the no-RSVPers, the coworkers who never participate in those painful group birthdays except if it's their own. I admit it: I don't really get these people.

9 I like the folks who clear the dishes, even when they're the guests. Or the committee members who show up on time, assignment completed and ready to pitch in on the next event. Or the neighbor who drives the carpool even though her kids are sick. I get these people. These people have learned to carry their own skis.

In early adulthood, carrying my own skis meant getting a job, paying off my student loans, and working hard for the company that was providing my paycheck. If I did those things, then I could enjoy the other areas of my life. Dull, yes, but freeing, too. When I wasn't responsible for myself or my stuff, I felt lousy. Sometimes I could get to the lodge, but I just couldn't get back to the station wagon at the end of the day. It was an unfamiliar feeling to let someone down by missing a deadline at work or not showing up for an early-morning run. . . . On days like that, the parking lot seemed bigger and icier than I had anticipated.

Now I have a life that includes a husband, two children, a dog, a house, friends, schools, and a radio show that involves lots of other people, including four sisters. The "stuff" of my life may seem much heavier than two skis, two boots, and two poles, but it isn't really—just a little bit trickier to carry. I have to do more balancing and let go of the commitments that I'd probably drop anyway. If I commit to more than I can handle, I miss out. That's when I think of Powder Hill.

10 The funny thing is, some of the worst moments of my childhood were spent on skis or in pursuit of skiing. The truth is, I didn't really like skiing as a kid. And I wasn't a very good skier. Most days, skiing for me was about freezing rain and constantly trying to catch up to my older, faster, more talented siblings. The hard falls on the hard ice. I can still feel the damp long underwear and the wet wool during the endless ride home. But whether I liked to ski or not didn't really matter. I was expected to learn to ski, and I did. And I also learned that in life you need to be responsible for yourself and your stuff or you miss out. The lodge and back, baby.

Carry Your Own Skis ■ 479

Vocabulary Builder
riddled (rid´ ld) *adj.*
affected throughout

Literary Analysis
Persuasive Essay
What does the paragraph beginning "I like . . . " suggest the author's motive for writing might be?

Reading Skill
Persuasive Appeals
Does the author clearly connect lessons learned from skiing with ideas about life? Explain.

Apply the Skills

Carry Your Own Skis

Thinking About the Selection

1. **Respond:** What more would you like to know about Dolan's child-hood? Explain your answer.
2. **(a) Recall:** What is the one rule that Dolan's mother had about skiing? **(b) Make a Judgment:** Do you think Dolan's mother's expectations of her children were reasonable? Why or why not?
3. **(a) Recall:** What lesson does Dolan say she learned from carrying her own skis? **(b) Connect:** In what other aspects of life does the author say this lesson has guided her behavior?
4. **(a) Take a Position:** Do you agree or disagree with Dolan's claim that people who do not take responsibility miss out on things? Explain. **(b) Discuss:** Share your response with a partner, and then explain how the discussion has or has not changed your response to the question.

Literary Analysis

5. **(a)** In this **persuasive essay,** what is the author trying to persuade readers to think or do? **(b)** What evidence does she use to support her position?
6. **(a)** Using a chart like the one shown, identify three passages in which Dolan argues for "the 'carry your own skis' mentality." In the right column, indicate whether each passage is an appeal to reason or to emotion. Explain.

Passage	Reason or Emotion

   (b) Which kind of appeals does the author seem to favor—**appeals to reason** or **appeals to emotion?**
7. What do you think is the **author's motive** for trying to persuade readers to agree with her?

Reading Skill

8. When you **analyze and evaluate** the **persuasive appeal** in "Carry Your Own Skis," do you find the author's arguments to be well-reasoned and logical? Explain your answer.
9. **(a)** Did the author convince you to accept her position? Why or why not? **(b)** Which passages are especially convincing? Explain.

QuickReview

Essay at a Glance
The author describes how she learned personal responsibility by carrying her own skis as a child.

Go Online
Assessment
For: Self-test
Visit: www.PHSchool.com
Web Code: epa-6307

Persuasive Essay: a short nonfiction work that tries to convince a reader to think or act in a particular way

Author's Motive: the author's reason for persuading readers to accept his or her position

Analyze and Evaluate Persuasive Appeals: test the logic and reasoning of the arguments an author makes

---

Answers

1. **Possible response:** Students may suggest that they would like to know more about Dolan's other activities.

2. (a) Her mother insists that they learn to carry their own skis to and from the lodge. (b) Most students will agree that her mother's expectations are reasonable, since she was unable to carry the children's skis for them.

3. (a) The lesson she learned was to fully participate in life, one has to take personal responsibility and carry one's own weight. (b) As an adult, this lesson guides her behavior at work and at home.

4. (a) Some students may agree that taking personal responsibility leads to a fuller life because a considerate and responsible person will be welcome in most situations. (b) Some students may state that they became convinced that being responsible is important to leading a happy life.

5. (a) The author is trying to persuade readers to believe that personal responsibility is a key ingredient for a happy, successful life. (b) As a child, she would have missed out on the fun if she had not carried her own skis; as a young girl, she was invited on many camping trips because she was willing to carry her share of the load.

6. (a) **Sample response: Passage:** Paragraph beginning "The lesson was simple." **Appeal:** reason; she explains in a logical way why it was important to "carry your own skis."

   Passage: Paragraph beginning "I like the folks who clear the dishes . . . ." **Appeal:** emotion; she explains that she has pleasant feelings about people who take responsibility.

   (b) The author seems to favor appeals to emotion. Another sample answer can be found on **Literary Analysis Graphic Organizer B,** p. 106, in *Graphic Organizer Transparencies.*

7. **Possible response:** The author may want others to enjoy life more; or she may want people to take responsibility for themselves.

8. **Possible response:** The author's arguments are well-reasoned; she gives specific examples of how taking responsibility has enriched her life.

9. (a) **Possible response:** The essay was convincing because the author gave specific examples of people who do accept responsibility.
   (b) **Possible response:** The most convincing passage is the one in which the author describes what would happen to her as a child if she did not carry her own skis.

Vocabulary Builder

Practice **Analogies** show the relationships between pairs of words. Use a word from the "Carry Your Own Skis" vocabulary list on page 474 to complete each analogy. In each, your choice should create a word pair that matches the relationship between the first two words given.

1. conflict : agreement :: uncertainty : _____
2. idea : reality :: _____ : actual
3. soaked : water :: _____ : dents

Adding Words to Your Vocabulary *Riddle,* the present-tense form of *riddled,* has a meaning different from the one used in the essay. Use a dictionary to discover this meaning. Then use *riddle* in three sentences reflecting this meaning. (For more on using a dictionary, see page R6.)

Writing

An **abstract** of a work is a type of summary. Readers check abstracts to see if an essay or article interests them or is relevant to their research. Write an abstract of "Carry Your Own Skis."
- Include the main point and briefly convey supporting details.
- Be sure your abstract will help those who have not read the essay.

For *Grammar, Vocabulary,* and *Assessment,* see **Build Language Skills,** pages 490–491.

Extend Your Learning

Listening and Speaking In "Carry Your Own Skis," Dolan describes the life lesson she learned while skiing. Choose a favorite activity, and give a **persuasive speech** that urges people to participate in it. Consider the following questions:
- What in particular do you enjoy about the activity?
- What life lessons could someone learn from it?

Practice in front of a mirror before giving your speech to the class.

Research and Technology With a group of classmates, research today's popular winter sports. Create and present a **comparative chart** that graphically shows which sports have the most active participants and the largest audience. Include a statement summarizing the information that the chart details.

Apply the Skills ■ 481

Go **Online**
—Research   **For:** An additional research activity
Visit: www.PHSchool.com
Web Code: epd-7305
For another research activity to extend students' learning, give students this Web Code.

Vocabulary Builder
Analogies Practice

1. *inevitability;* the two pairs of words are opposites.
2. *potential;* the two pairs of words are opposites.
3. *riddled;* soaked is the result of water and *riddled* is the result of dents.

Adding Words to Your Vocabulary
Possible responses:

1. There was only one *riddle* in the book that I could not solve.
2. Finding the person who committed this crime is a *riddle* that will take a long time to solve.
3. Check the key to find the answer to the *riddle* on page 22.

Writing

- To give students guidance for writing this abstract, give them the **Support for Writing Lesson** for "Carry Your Own Skis," p. 118 in *Unit 3 Resources.*
- To evaluate students' abstracts, use the Summary rubrics, pp. 63–64, in *General Resources.* In addition, you might evaluate for how useful the abstract might be to those who have not read the selection.

Six Traits Focus

✔	Ideas		Word Choice
✔	Organization		Sentence Fluency
	Voice		Conventions

Writing and Grammar, Gold Level
Students will find guidance on how to use effective sentences in their abstract in Chapter 22, sections 2, 3 and 4.

Build Language Skills

Go to pp. 490–491 for vocabulary and grammar lessons and assessment practice.

Extend Your Learning

The **Support for Extend Your Learning** page (*Unit 3 Resources,* p. 119) provides guided note-taking opportunities to help students complete the Extend Your Learning activities.

Teaching notes for *Literary Analysis, Reading Skill,* and *Vocabulary Builder* for this selection begin on p. 474.

❸ Background
Public Libraries

During the 1800s, large numbers of immigrants came to the United States. Public libraries played a vital role in the lives of these new immigrants. There they studied American history and government in preparation for citizenship. At the library, their children nourished their imaginations with the world's wonderful stories.

❹ Connecting to the Literature

- Model use of the expressive vocabulary students are asked to use with these examples:

  1. The wonderful pictures in the books helped me *perceive* the world in a new way.
  2. The books I found in the library began to *reveal* a magical world.
  3. I was eager to *respond* to every suggestion made by the librarian.
  4. I decided to *dedicate* myself to reading every book on the shelves.
  5. The librarian was careful not to *distribute* too many books to me at one time.

- Help students further develop their expressive vocabulary by providing these words: *engage, illuminate,* and *impact.* Encourage students to use these words as they discuss the selection.

Go **Online** For additional informa-
Author Link tion about Pete Hamill, have students type in the Web Code, then select *H* from the alphabet, and then select *Pete Hamill.*

Build Understanding • *Libraries Face Sad Chapter*

Essay

❸ Background

Public Libraries Although the first American library was established in 1638, it was not until the 1800s that public libraries became common in the United States. Since then, Americans have come to rely on public libraries as a free source of education, entertainment, and community.

❹ Connecting to the Literature

Reading/Writing Connection In "Libraries Face Sad Chapter," Pete Hamill describes his visits to a public library as a young child. Think of one of the first times that you visited a library, and write to describe the experience. Use at least three of these words: *perceive, reveal, respond, dedicate, distribute.*

Review

For **Literary Analysis, Reading Skill,** and **Vocabulary Builder,** see page 474.

READ MORE

by
Pete Hamill
*Snow in August
Forever*

Meet the Author

Pete **Hamill** (b. 1935)

Pete Hamill has had two novels on *The New York Times* Bestseller List, but he is first and foremost a journalist. After quitting school at sixteen to work in the Brooklyn Navy Yard, Hamill joined the U.S. Navy. He completed his high school education while in the navy.

"The work was everything." In 1960, Hamill went to work as a reporter for the *New York Post* newspaper. Although he would write for several other newspapers in his career, Hamill loved his job at the *Post.* He wrote, "Nothing before (or since) could compare with walking into the *New York Post* at midnight, being sent into the dark scary city on assignment and coming back to write a story."

Fast Facts

▶ Hamill has served as editor-in-chief of both the *New York Post* and the *New York Daily News.*
▶ During Hamill's long career as a reporter, he covered wars in a number of countries.

Go **Online**
Author Link

For: More about the author
Visit: www.PHSchool.com
Web Code: epe-9309

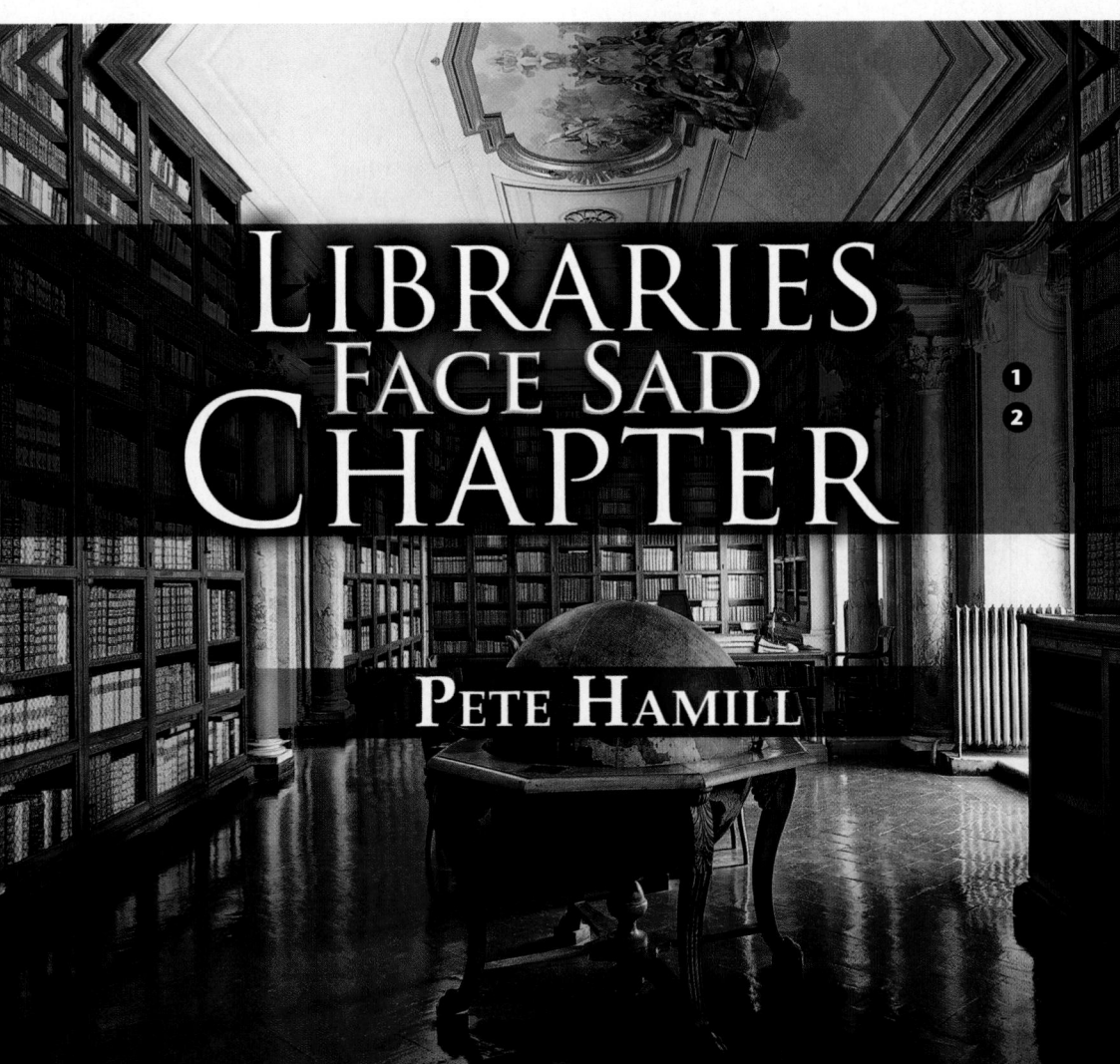

LIBRARIES FACE SAD CHAPTER

PETE HAMILL

The library was four blocks from where we lived, on the corner of Ninth St. and Sixth Ave., and it was one of the treasure houses of our Brooklyn lives.

This was in the years before television, when we saw movies once a week at the Minerva or the Avon or the RKO Prospect, and fed our imaginations through radio and books. That is, it was in a time when *The Count of Monte Cristo* was as vivid in our minds, and talk, and dreams, as Jack Roosevelt Robinson. Dumas told the

Libraries Face Sad Chapter ■ 483

Differentiated
Instruction   Solutions for All Learners

Support for Below-Level Students [L1, L2]

Unit 3 Resources
  Vocabulary Warm-up Word Lists, p. 127
  Vocabulary Warm-up Practice, p. 128
  Reading Warm-up A, p. 129
  Selection Test A, pp. 140–142

Graphic Organizer Transparencies
  Reading Skill Graphic Organizer,
  Transparency B, p. 104

Support for English Learners [EL]

Unit 3 Resources
  Vocabulary Warm-up Word Lists, p. 127
  Vocabulary Warm-up Practice, p. 128
  Reading Warm-up A, p. 129

Listening to Literature Audio CD

❶ Motivation

Prepare an **Anticipation Guide** (*General Resources,* pp. 8–10) with the following statements:

- Public libraries enrich the lives of children.
- Public libraries are an essential part of any community.
- Human beings need the stories and the information that only books can furnish.
- Members of a community should contribute to the support of a public library.

Give students a copy of the prepared Anticipation Guide and have students mark their responses in the Me column. Have students discuss the statements in pairs or groups and mark the Guides again in the Group column.

Concept Connector ➡

Students will return to the Anticipation Guide after completing "Libraries Face Sad Chapter."

Learning Modalities
Visual/Spatial Learners

Industrialist Andrew Carnegie contributed to the building of public libraries across the United States. The buildings themselves were built on classical designs, with columns and domes. Have students work as a group to collect photos of Carnegie libraries from various cities in the Untied States and arrange the photos in a collage. Then have them discuss the architecture, what messages the architecture seems to imply, and how the architecture might affect visitors to the library.

❷ About the Selection

In "Libraries Face Sad Chapter," Pete Hamill describes his memories of using the public library as a child. He explains the importance of the public libraries to generations of new immigrants to New York, as well as to all members of the community. At the time Hamill wrote this essay, New York faced serious financial crises and forced cutbacks in service. Hamill argues that despite these problems, libraries must be protected.

③ Literary Analysis
Persuasive Essay and Appeals to Emotion

• Read the passage aloud. Then ask students what the author is describing here.
Answer: He is describing his visits to the library and the books he read as a child.

• Ask students to describe how they think the author feels about his visits to the library.
Answer: He has pleasant memories and positive feelings.

• **Ask** the Literary Analysis question: Which words here suggest that the author appeals to positive feelings about childhood and imagination?
Answer: Words and phrases include "majestic aura," "astonishment," wonderful Babar books," "rich, golden, mysterious illustrations."

► **Monitor Progress:** Provide students with **Literary Analysis Graphic Organizer A**, p. 107, in *Graphic Organizer Transparencies* to complete as they read the essay.

► **Reteach:** If students have difficulty identifying persuasive appeals, remind them that a persuasive appeal aims to convince the reader to think or act in a certain way. Tell students that certain words can be signals of an opinion. On the board, brainstorm a list of these words from the story.

④ Critical Viewing

Possible response: Students may suggest that he would regard them with awe, or anticipation and excitement at what they might hold.

---

story of the count as vividly as Red Barber[1] recited the unfolding tale of No. 42.

③ We passed into that library between two mock-Corinthian columns that gave the building a majestic aura. For me, every visit was an astonishment. There was a children's room, first seen when I was 8, where I first read the wonderful Babar books, and then moved on to Howard Pyle's *Book of Pirates,* and all of Robert Louis Stevenson, with those rich, golden, mysterious illustrations by N.C. Wyeth.

There were bound volumes of a children's magazine called *St. Nicholas,* full of spidery drawings of animals that talked, and villains who didn't. There were picture books bursting with images of lost cities or the solar system. In that room, I learned that the world was larger than our neighborhood.

And then, at 10 or 11, I found my way into the adult stacks, to borrow books about the daily life of the Romans, the flight of Richard Hannay across Scotland, the conquests of Mexico and Peru, the cases of Sherlock Holmes. On a high shelf, presumed to be safe from the curious eyes of children, was a lavish (in memory) edition of *The Thousand and One Nights.*[2]

No teacher sent us to those leathery cliffs of books. Reading wasn't an assignment; it was a pleasure. We read for the combined thrills of villainy and heroism, along with knowledge of the vast world beyond the parish. Living in those other worlds, we could become other people: Jim Hawkins, or Edmund Dantes, or (most thrillingly) d'Artagnan, with his three musketeers.

---

1. ***The Count of Monte Cristo . . . Red Barber*** *The Count of Monte Cristo* is a nineteenth-century novel by Alexandre Dumas. Jackie Robinson was the first African American major league baseball player. He joined the Brooklyn Dodgers in 1947 and wore number 42. Dodgers games were broadcast on the radio, and the action was described by announcer Red Barber.
2. ***The Thousand and One Nights*** collection of ancient tales also known as the *Arabian Nights.* Although many of the tales, including "Aladdin," are now retold as children's stories, the original tellings are full of violence, bloodshed, poisonings, and betrayals.

Literary Analysis
Persuasive Essay
Which words here suggest that the author appeals to positive feelings about childhood and imagination?

④ ▼ **Critical Viewing**
How might the young Pete Hamill have regarded these books? **[Speculate]**

484 ■ *Types of Nonfiction*

Vocabulary Development

Expressive Vocabulary
As students are discussing Hamill's explanation of the dangers faced by libraries today, encourage them to use the expressive vocabulary presented earlier. You might encourage them with sentence starters like these:

1. A major threat to libraries that we *perceive* is . . .
2. Information contained in the libraries can *reveal* . . .
3. All human beings *respond* to . . .
4. If every citizen agrees to *dedicate* . . .
5. City government should be encouraged to *distribute* . . .

We could live in the South Seas, or Paris, or the Rome of Caligula. It never occurred to us that we were inheriting our little share of civilization. But that's what was happening.

Built by Carnegie

The library of my childhood is still there, since 1975 known as the Park Slope Branch of the Brooklyn Public Library. It was built with grant money from my favorite capitalist, Andrew Carnegie, in 1906. But once again, as happened in 1992, the teeming imaginative life of libraries is in danger of being <u>curtailed</u>. Services might be cut. Hours trimmed. Staff reduced. The reason is the same: money, or the lack of it.

Such reductions are absolutely understandable. As we all know, Mayor Bloomberg has more than a $4 billion shortfall that must be made up. Unlike the spend-more tax-less leaders of the federal government, the government of New York City can't print money to keep things going. In this season of post-September 11 austerities,[3] something must give. I hope it isn't the libraries.

The reason is simple: In hard times, libraries are more important than ever. Human beings need what books give them better than any other <u>medium</u>. Since those ancient nights around prehistoric campfires, we have needed myth. And heroes. And moral tales. And information about the world beyond the nearest mountains or oceans.

Today, with books and movies more expensive than ever, and television entertainment in free fall to the lowest levels of stupidity, freely circulating books are an absolute necessity. They are quite simply another kind of food. We imagine, and then we live.

Hard times are also an opportunity. Parents and teachers all moan about the refusal of the young to read. Here is the chance to revive the power of the printed page. The Harry Potter books show

---

3. **austerities** (ô sterʹ ə tēz) *n.* acts of self-discipline and self-denial.

Vocabulary Builder
curtailed (kər tāldʹ)
v. cut short; reduced
medium (mēʹ dē əm)
n. means of communication

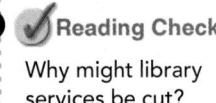

Reading Check
Why might library services be cut?

Libraries Face Sad Chapter ■ 485

that the audience for young readers is potentially immense. A child who starts with Harry Potter can find his or her way to Dumas and Arthur Conan Doyle, to Mark Twain and Walt Whitman, and, yes, to Tolstoy and Joyce and Proust.

Immigrants' Appreciation

For those without money, the road to that treasure house of the imagination begins at the public library. When I was a boy, the rooms were crowded with immigrants and their children. That is, with people who came from places where there were no libraries for

❼ ▲ Critical Viewing
How does this photograph support Hamill's idea that a library is a "treasure house of the imagination"? **[Connect]**

Vocabulary Development

Vocabulary Knowledge Rating
When students have completed reading and discussing "Libraries Face Sad Chapter," have them take out their **Vocabulary Knowledge Rating Chart** for this selection. Read the words aloud once more and have students rate their knowledge of the words again in the After Reading column. Clarify any words that are still problematic. Have students write their own definition and example or sentence in the appropriate column. Then have students complete the **Vocabulary Builder Practice** activities on p. 489. Encourage students to use the words in further discussion and written work about this selection. Remind them that they will be accountable for these words on the Selection Test.

the poor. With their children, they built the New York in which we now live.

Today, the libraries of this city are still doing that work. The libraries of Brooklyn and Queens are jammed with the new immigrants and their astonishing children, the people who will build the New York of tomorrow. The older people want information about this new world, and how to get better jobs and green cards and citizenship. Their American children want to vanish into books their parents cannot afford, thus filling themselves with the endless possibilities of the future.

They are no different from the Irish, the Jews and the Italians of my childhood. My father only went to the eighth grade in Belfast. I remember my mother drilling him at our kitchen table for his citizenship test, and I know that he first read the Constitution in a book borrowed from the Prospect Branch of the Brooklyn Public Library. Lying in a darkened bed off that kitchen, I first heard the language of the Bill of Rights.

That process must go on in all the places where the poor now live. If it's impossible for the city to do it, then we must do it ourselves. Bloomberg can give us the hard numbers, explain the shortfall in the library budget and explain how much we need. Then we should try to make it up with the establishment of a private fund to maintain the libraries at full strength for the <u>duration</u> of the crisis.

All of us whose lives have been affected by the treasures of public libraries could contribute. The rich could emulate Carnegie, who used his wealth to create more than 1,600 public libraries, including 65 in New York. But the middle class could also send in small amounts from $10 to $50.

This would be a kind of voluntary tax. On one level, it would be a powerful pledge to maintain the life of the mind among all classes in this city. That is obviously in our own interest. But above all, it would be a means of honoring the labor of those men and women who got us here, and who paid taxes to buy books for all New Yorkers, and first took us by the hand and walked us into the treasure houses. We who dreamed of Ebbets Field and the Chateau d'If on the same American nights owe debts to New York that we can never pay. This is one that must be honored.

❽ Literature in Context

History Connection

Andrew Carnegie (1835–1919) was a Scottish immigrant who became enormously wealthy in the steel business. In 1889, Carnegie published an essay entitled "The Gospel of Wealth." In it, he argued that the rich should use their money for the public good. Under his plan, "the surplus wealth of the few will become, in the best sense, the property of the many." Unlike many other wealthy men of his time, Carnegie acted on his belief. His many charitable acts included the building of more than 2,800 public libraries throughout the English-speaking world.

Connect to the Literature

How do you think Andrew Carnegie would react to the idea of cuts in library funding? Explain.

Vocabulary Builder
duration (dʊ rā′ shən) *n.* length of time something lasts

Libraries Face Sad Chapter ■ 487

❽ Literature in Context

History Connection Andrew Carnegie wrote that, "The man who dies rich dies disgraced." He lived by his words. An exceptional philanthropist, he gave away $350 million, which amounted to nearly 90% of his great fortune. In addition to the many libraries that he built, Carnegie contributed to the building of 7,000 church organs, and funded the Carnegie Foundation for the Advancement of Teaching, and the Carnegie Endowment for Peace.

Connect to the Literature After discussing Carnegie's contributions, **ask** the Connect to Literature question: How do you think Andrew Carnegie would react to the idea of cuts in library funding? Explain.

Possible response: Andrew Carnegie would probably oppose cuts in library funding, since he placed great importance on public libraries. He may well have offered to help fund the libraries himself.

Concept Connector

Anticipation Guide
Have students return to their **Anticipation Guides** and respond to the statements again in the After Reading column. They may do this individually or in their original pairs or groups. Then, lead a class discussion, probing for what students have learned that confirms or invalidates each statement. Encourage students to cite specific details, quotations, or other evidence from the text to support their responses to each statement.

Connecting to the Literature
Have students compare the sentences they wrote before reading with their thoughts about their first visit to the library after reading "Libraries Face Sad Chapter." Ask them to explain whether their thoughts have changed and, if so, how.

Reading Skill Graphic Organizer
Ask students to review the graphic organizers they completed to identify the persuasive appeals while reading. Show them **Reading Skill Graphic Organizer B** (*Graphic Organizer Transparencies*, p. 104) as an example.

1. Some students may say they share Hamill's feelings, since they had many happy experiences in a library as a child.

2. (a) He remembers *The Count of Monte Cristo,* the Babar books, the *Book of Pirates,* the Sherlock Holmes mysteries, and *St. Nicholas* magazine. (b) These memories suggest that Hamill loved the library as a child because it gave him access to books of adventure and imagination.

3. (a) He means that books nourish the mind and the imagination. (b) The comparison suggests that Hamill considers books a necessity of life.

4. (a) Some students may agree with Hamill that public libraries are essential; others may disagree, saying that the Internet and bookstores make public libraries unnecessary. (b) Some students may say that they have changed their mind, noting the cost to taxpayers of maintaining the libraries.

5. (a) He is trying to persuade people to support public libraries. (b) He cites his own experiences and the importance of the library to new immigrants.

6. **Sample response: Passage:** Paragraph beginning "We passed into that library . . ." **Appeal:** He appeals to emotion by recalling how important libraries were to him as a child.

   Passage: Paragraph beginning "This would be a kind of . . ."

   Appeal: He appeals to reason by explaining that the entire community benefits when libraries are viable. Another sample answer can be found on **Literary Analysis Graphic Organizer B,** p. 108, in *Graphic Organizer Transparencies.*

7. The author's motive is to persuade people how important libraries are so that they will help support them financially.

8. Most students will state that the author's arguments are well reasoned and logical; he gives facts and details to support his points.

Apply the Skills

Libraries Face Sad Chapter

Thinking About the Selection

1. **Respond:** Do you share Hamill's feelings about public libraries? Why or why not?

2. (a) **Recall:** What books and magazines does Hamill remember from early visits to the library? (b) **Infer:** What do these memories suggest about how Hamill felt about the library as a child?

3. (a) **Interpret:** What does Hamill mean by calling books "another kind of food"? (b) **Draw Conclusions:** What does this comparison suggest about the value he places on books?

4. (a) **Take a Position:** Do you agree or disagree with Hamill's claims about the importance of free public libraries? Explain.
   (b) **Discuss:** Share your response with a partner, and then explain how the discussion has or has not changed your response to the question.

Literary Analysis

5. (a) In this **persuasive essay,** what is the author trying to persuade readers to think or do? (b) What evidence does he use to support his position?

6. (a) Using a chart like the one shown, identify three passages in which Hamill asserts his position on public libraries. In the right column, indicate whether each passage is an appeal to reason or to emotion. Explain.

Passage	Reason or Emotion

   (b) Which kind of appeals does the author seem to favor— **appeals to reason** or **appeals to emotion?**

7. What do you think is the **author's motive** for trying to persuade readers to agree with him?

Reading Skill

8. When you **analyze and evaluate** the **persuasive appeal** in "Libraries Face Sad Chapter," do you find the author's arguments to be well-reasoned and logical? Explain your answer.

9. (a) Did the author convince you to accept his position? Why or why not? (b) Which passages are especially convincing? Explain.

488 ■ Types of Nonfiction

9. Most students will say that the author was convincing because his appeals to emotion were powerful, especially his description of his childhood experiences.

QuickReview

Essay at a Glance
The author asserts the importance of public libraries and the need to support them in hard times.

Go Online
Assessment
For: Self-test
Visit: www.PHSchool.com
Web Code: epa-6308

Persuasive Essay: a short nonfiction work that tries to convince a reader to think or act in a particular way

Author's Motive: the author's reason for persuading readers to accept his or her position

Analyze and Evaluate Persuasive Appeals: test the logic and reasoning of the arguments an author makes

Vocabulary Builder

Practice **Analogies** show the relationships between pairs of words. Use a word from the "Libraries Face Sad Chapter" vocabulary list on page 474 to complete each analogy. In each, your choice should create a word pair that matches the relationship between the first two words.

1. sugar : sweetness :: time : _____

2. bucket : water :: _____ : information

3. arrived : departed :: continued : _____

Adding Words to Your Vocabulary *Media,* the term used to refer collectively to newspapers, television, and other sources of information, is the plural form of the word *medium.* Use a dictionary to look up the plural forms of *datum, curriculum,* and *millennium.* Then, use each singular and plural form correctly in a sentence that illustrates its meaning. (For more on using a dictionary, see page R6.)

Writing

An **abstract** of a work is a type of summary. Readers check abstracts to see if an essay or article interests them or is relevant to their research. Write an abstract of "Libraries Face Sad Chapter."
- Include the main point and briefly convey supporting details.
- Be sure your abstract will help those who have not read the essay.

For *Grammar, Vocabulary,* and *Assessment,* see **Build Language Skills,** pages 490–491.

Extend Your Learning

Listening and Speaking In his essay, Hamill argues to preserve libraries. Choose a favorite place and give a **persuasive speech** urging people to preserve it. Consider these questions:
- What in particular do you enjoy about the place?
- In what ways does it benefit the community?

Practice in front of a mirror before giving your speech to the class.

Research and Technology Hamill discusses his use of the library as a young person. Research the services offered today by libraries. Create and present a **comparative chart** that shows the variety of services and the average numbers of people using them. Include a statement summarizing the information in the chart.

Apply the Skills ■ 489

Extend Your Learning

The **Support for Extend Your Learning** page (*Unit 3 Resources,* p. 135) provides guided note-taking opportunities to help students complete the Extend Your Learning activities.

Go Online
Research **For:** An additional research activity
Visit: www.PHSchool.com
Web Code: epd-7306
For another research activity to extend students' learning, give students this Web Code.

Vocabulary Builder
Analogies Practice

1. *duration; sweetness* is a characteristic of sugar; *duration* is a characteristic of time.

2. *medium;* a *bucket* carries water; a *medium* carries information.

3. *curtailed;* these pairs of words are opposites.

Adding Words to Your Vocabulary
Possible responses:

1. This *datum* is just one piece of information. We must collect all the *data* before we can reach a conclusion.

2. The *curriculum* for this class is an important part of the entire *curricula* for the program.

3. People celebrated the beginning of a new *millennium* in the year 2000. Two *millennia* have passed since the beginning of the Common Era.

Writing

- To give students guidance for writing this abstract, give them the **Support for Writing Lesson** for "Libraries Face Sad Chapter," p. 134 in *Unit 3 Resources.*

- To evaluate students' abstracts, use the Summary rubrics, pp. 63–64, in *General Resources.* In addition, you might evaluate for how useful the abstract might be to those who have not read the selection.

Six Traits Focus

✔	Ideas		Word Choice
✔	Organization		Sentence Fluency
	Voice		Conventions

WG Writing and Grammar, Gold Level
Students will find guidance on how to use effective sentences in their abstract in Chapter 22, sections 2, 3, and 4.

Build Language Skills

Go to pp. 490–491 for vocabulary and grammar lessons and assessment practice.

Vocabulary Skill

- Introduce the Latin prefix *ante-*. Point out to students not to confuse *ante-* or *anti-* with *anti-*, a prefix meaning *opposed to* or *against*.

- Have students complete the Practice activity on this page.

Answers

1. d; Look for the *antecedent* for the pronoun in the sentence.

2. e; *Ante meridiem* classes may be too early for those who like to sleep late.

3. b; Please wait in the *anteroom* until they announce your speech.

4. a; The *anterior* of the building is visible from the road.

5. c; An *antebellum* house was converted to a museum.

Grammar Lesson

- Point out that adjectives can precede or follow the nouns they modify.

- Explain to students that although adjectives can modify nouns and pronouns, adjectives cannot modify one other.

Answers

1. *crisp; clear;* The damp air was a *warning* sign that a storm was coming.

2. *early; unmistakable; wild;* In the *late* morning, I heard the *familiar* sound of *noisy* geese calling as they flew above.

3. *first; pungent; fallen;* It was the *last* day of autumn and the air was filled with the *earthy* odor of *rotten* leaves.

4. *red; brown; Maple* and *aspen* leaves danced in the air as they fell.

5. *few; thick;* In *six* months, the ground will be covered with a *fine* blanket of snow.

Build Language Skills

Carry Your Own Skis • Libraries Face Sad Chapter

Vocabulary Skill

Prefixes The **Latin prefix *ante-*** means "before" or "prior to." This prefix appears in words that relate to things that precede other things. The prefix of *anticipate* is **anti-** (a variant of the prefix ***ante-***), which also means "before" or "prior to."

Practice Match the following words with the correct definition. Use a dictionary if necessary. Then, write a sentence using each word.

1. antecedent	a. to the front of something
2. ante meridiem	b. a place through which one enters a room
3. anteroom	c. before a war
4. anterior	d. a happening or thing that comes before
5. antebellum	e. before noon

Grammar Lesson

Adjectives An **adjective** is a word used to give a noun or pronoun a more specific meaning. Adjectives modify nouns and pronouns by telling *what kind, which one, how many,* or *how much.*

Noun/ Pronoun	Question	Adjective and Noun/Pronoun
school	What kind?	martial arts school
student	Which one?	involved student
cars	How many?/How much?	three cars

Practice Identify each adjective. Then, write a new sentence replacing each adjective with a different adjective.

1. The crisp air was a clear sign that fall had arrived.

2. In the early morning, I heard the unmistakable sound of wild geese calling as they flew overhead.

3. It was the first day of autumn, and the air was filled with the pungent odor of fallen leaves.

4. Red and brown leaves crackled underfoot.

5. In a few months, the ground will be covered with a thick blanket of snow.

W_G *Prentice Hall Writing and Grammar Connection: Chapter 18, Section 1*

490 ■ *Types of Nonfiction*

MorePractice

For more practice with adjectives, see the Grammar Handbook, p. R40.

Teaching Resources

The following resources can be used to enrich or extend the instruction for Build Language Skills.

Unit 3 Resources
 Build Language Skills: Vocabulary: Latin Prefixes, p. 137
 Build Grammar Skills: Adjectives, p. 138

Assessment Practice

Reading: Analyzing Persuasive Appeals

Directions: *Read the selection. Then, answer the questions.*

Perhaps the greatest environmental tragedy of our time is the destruction of the Amazon rain forest. The rain forest has more species than any other area on Earth. Over 2,000 species of the plants are known to have value as medicines, but only about 10% of these have been studied. These species may disappear before scientists have a chance to study them and understand their value to human beings. Scientists agree that the disappearance of the rain forest will have a global impact. Some organizations recommend that nations buy and preserve rain forest land and educate local people about living in the rain forest without destroying it. These are small first steps in saving the rain forest, but they are worthy of our support.

1. The primary persuasive appeal that the author uses is
   A an appeal to emotion.
   B an appeal to ethics.
   C an appeal to belief.
   D an appeal to law.

2. A detail that does NOT persuade is
   A the destruction of the rain forest is a tragedy.
   B over 2,000 rain forest plants have value.
   C the rain forest has many species.
   D the disappearance of the rain forest may destroy the Earth.

3. The last sentence of the paragraph
   A summarizes the author's point of view.
   B provides a call to action.
   C provides a transition to the next idea.
   D explains the main idea.

4. Which of the following is an emotionally charged phrase?
   A "greatest environmental tragedy . . ."
   B "Some organizations recommend . . ."
   C "10% of these have been studied. . . ."
   D "[It] will have a global impact. . . ."

Timed Writing: Persuasion [Connection]

Choose an issue that is important to you, and write a letter to the editor of your local newspaper persuading people to accept your viewpoint. Use persuasive appeals and support your points. **(20 minutes)**

 ## Writing Workshop: *Work in Progress*

Editorial
Identify and list at least three specific elements of music, fashion, books, or movies that currently influence you and your friends. Put this list in your writing portfolio.

Build Language Skills ■ *491*

Reading: Analyzing Persuasive Appeals
1. B
2. C
3. B
4. A

Timed Writing

- Tell students that they will often be asked to write persuasive essays and will have opportunities to write letters to the editors of their local newspapers or magazines.

- Have students brainstorm for a list of topics that they find important. Then, have students select a topic and brainstorm for persuasive appeals and support.

- Once they have listed their appeals, have students begin writing, as time is short. They may wish to quickly outline the order of their appeals to help them write more easily.

- Assess students' letters on the validity of their appeals and the quality of their support as well as their organization and clarity.

- Suggest that students plan their time to allow six minutes for prewriting, ten minutes for writing, and four minutes for reviewing and revising.

Writing Workshop
Work in Progress

Editorial

- Have students select one of these topics: music, fashion, books, or movies.

- Remind students that this work may be used in the editorial in the **Writing Workshop** at the end of Part 2.

- You may wish to suggest that students brainstorm for specific elements and then limit their list to three. Point out that they should have some knowledge about the three elements they choose.

- When students have completed their lists, have them save them in their portfolios. They will use the lists as they continue this **Work in Progress.**

491

Planning Differentiated Instruction

Choosing Your Selection

You may use either selection to meet the lesson standards. The following guide will help you determine which of the two selections is more appropriate for your students.

Accessibility at a Glance

	I Have a Dream	**First Inaugural Address**
Context	Historical; America in the 1960s	Historical; America in the 1930s
Language	• Use of repetition reinforces concepts and makes them easier to understand • Uses biblical and political references • Simple sentence structure	• Complicated, complex sentences • Concepts more difficult
Concept Level	Accessible (a vision of America free of oppression, racism, and injustice)	Challenging (a plea to change Americans' attitudes of panic and fear)
Literary Merit	Dynamic civil rights leader	Inspiring political figure
Lexile	1140L	1190L
Other	Timeless	Powerful historical statement
Overall Rating	More accessible	More challenging

Using the Other Selection You may use the other selection for homework or independent reading to reinforce the selection skills. If you use both selections, you can build a test for both using *ExamView*® Test Bank software.

Choosing Your Resources

[L1] Special Needs Students   **[L4]** Advanced Students

[L2] Below-Level Students   **[EL]** English Learners

[L3] All Students

FT Fast Track Instruction: To move the lesson more quickly, use the strategies and activities identified with **FT**.

Reading and Vocabulary Warm-ups provide support for below level students. **A** is for students reading two grades below level; **B** is for students reading one grade below level. For Selection Tests, **A** signifies "less challenging" and **B** "more challenging." For Graphic Organizer transparencies, **A** signifies "not filled in" and **B** "filled in."

Scaffolding for Less Proficient and Advanced Students

The leveled questions on Apply the Skills pages progress in the levels of thinking required to answer them. To address the needs of your different students, you may use the (a) level questions for your less proficient students, the (b) level with your on-level and advanced students. The occasional (c) level questions are appropriate for your advanced students.

Step-by-Step Teaching Guide	**Pacing Guide**
PRETEACH	
• Administer Vocabulary and Reading Warm-ups as necessary.	
• Introduce the Literary Analysis Skill: Persuasive Speech. **FT**	10 min.
• Introduce the Reading Skill: Analyzing and Evaluating Persuasive Appeals. **FT**	10 min.
• Prepare students to read by teaching the selection vocabulary. **FT**	10 min.
• Build background and develop expressive vocabulary with Connecting to the Literature and Background.	10 min.
• Engage students' interest with the motivation activity.	10 min.
TEACH	
• Informally monitor comprehension while students read independently or in groups. **FT**	30 min.
• Monitor students' comprehension with the Reading Check notes.	as students read
• Reinforce vocabulary with Vocabulary Builder notes.	as students read
• Develop students' understanding of persuasive essays with the Literary Analysis annotations. **FT**	5 min.
• Develop students' ability to analyze and evaluate persuasive appeals with the Reading Skill annotations. **FT**	10 min.
ASSESS/EXTEND	
• Assess students' comprehension and mastery of the Reading Skill and Literary Analysis by having them answer the Apply the Skills questions. **FT**	35 min.
• Have students complete the Vocabulary Builder activities. **FT**	5 min.
• Apply students' ability to write a proposal with the Writing activity. **FT**	30–45 min. or homework
• Extend students' listening and speaking and research and technology skills with one or both of the Extend Your Learning activities.	15–30 min. or homework
• Have students complete the Vocabulary Skill and Grammar Lesson.	5 min.
• Monitor students' progress with the Assessment Practice.	20–40 min.
• Administer **Selection Test A** or **Selection Test B**. **FT**	15 min.

Go **Online** **For:** Information about Lexiles
Professional **Visit:** www.PHSchool.com
Development **Web Code:** eue-1111

Resources

 Meeting Your Standards

Students will

1. **analyze and respond to literary elements.**
   - Literary Analysis: Persuasive Speech

2. **read, comprehend, and analyze persuasive speeches.**
   - Reading Skill: Analyzing and Evaluating Persuasive Appeals
   - Reading Strategy: Reading Aloud
   - Reading Check questions
   - Apply the Skills questions
   - Assessment Practice

3. **develop vocabulary.**
   - Vocabulary Builder
   - Latin prefixes *ante-, inter-*

4. **apply grammar skills.**
   - Adverbs

5. **develop writing proficiency.**
   - Work in Progress: Editorial
   - Proposal

6. **extend learning.**
   - Listening and Speaking: Radio News Report
   - Research and Technology: Annotated Source List

Block Scheduling: Use one 90-minute class period to preteach the skills and have students read the selection. Use a second 90-minute class period to assess students' mastery of skills, extend their learning, and monitor their progress.

Homework Suggestions
Following are possibilities for homework assignments.

- Support pages from *Unit 3 Resources*:
  Literary Analysis
  Reading Skill
  Build Vocabulary
  Enrichment

- An Extend Your Learning project and the Writing assignment for your chosen selection may be completed over several days.

PRENTICE HALL
Teacher EXPRESS™
Plan · Teach · Assess
Use this complete suite of powerful teaching tools to make lesson planning and testing quicker and easier.

PRENTICE HALL
Student EXPRESS™
Learn · Study · Succeed
Use the Interactive Textbook (online and on CD-ROM) to make selections and activities come alive with audio and video support and interactive questions.

Build Skills *"I Have a Dream"* • *First Inaugural Address*

❶ Literary Analysis
Persuasive Speech

- Tell students that because speeches rely on the spoken rather than the written word, speakers often use special devices to emphasize their ideas and to help listeners remember the important points.

- Ask the class to read the discussion of Literary Analysis on this page. Then, give students some examples of rhetorical devices.

- For example, this sentence demonstrates both parallelism and repetition: "We will never give up; we will never surrender; we will never be defeated." The grammatical structure of the phrase "we will never" is an example of parallelism. "Never give up," "never surrender," "never be defeated" is an example of restatement.

- Point out that a speaker might use different images to express the same idea. For example, "This is a new dawn for our nation." "Beginning now, we have a blank page on which to write a new history."

- Point out that rhetorical devices are also used to arouse an emotional response in an audience.

- Suggest that as students read the selection, they notice the author's use of rhetorical devices and the effect they have on the listener.

❷ Reading Skill
Persuasive Techniques

- After students have read the Reading Skill section on this page, point out that speakers often use many of the same devices that writers do to persuade their audience. However, people who are listening to a speech cannot remember or check facts and statistics as readily as people who are reading a text.

- Remind students that a speech is intended primarily to be heard, not read, and the speaker relies on the sounds of words to help convey persuasive appeal.

- Give students a copy of the **Reading Skill Graphic Organizer A** (p. 109, *Graphic Organizer Transparencies*). Have them fill in the graphic organizer to identify the persuasive techniques used by the author.

Practice these skills with either "I Have a Dream" (p. 494) or "First Inaugural Address" (p. 503).

❶ Literary Analysis

A **persuasive speech** is a speech that tries to convince listeners to think or act in a certain way. Persuasive speeches may appeal to reason or emotion or both. In order to engage the audience, speakers often include **rhetorical devices**, patterns of words and ideas that create emphasis and stir emotion in the audience. Common rhetorical devices include the following:

- **Parallelism:** repeating a grammatical structure or an arrangement of words to create a sense of rhythm and momentum
- **Restatement:** expressing the same idea in different words to clarify and stress key points
- **Repetition:** expressing different ideas using the same words or images in order to reinforce concepts and unify the speech
- **Analogy:** drawing a comparison that shows a similarity between unlike things

Technique:	
Purpose	**Effect**

Technique:	
Purpose	**Effect**

❷ Reading Skill

Persuasive techniques are devices used to influence the audience in favor of the author's argument. In addition to presenting evidence in a persuasive speech, a speaker may also use emotionally charged language and rhetorical devices, such as those listed above.

To analyze and evaluate persuasive techniques, **read aloud** to hear the effect. Notice the emotional impact of certain words and the rhythm and momentum created by specific word patterns. Consider both the purpose and effect of these persuasive techniques. Use a chart like the one shown to organize your analysis.

Vocabulary Builder

"I Have a Dream"

- **hallowed** (hal´ ōd) *adj.* sacred (p. 496) *The battlefield is considered by many to be hallowed ground.*

- **degenerate** (dē jen´ ər āt´) *v.* grow worse (p. 497) *Don't let this discussion degenerate into a shouting match.*

- **creed** (krēd) *n.* statement of belief (p. 498) *The creed of brotherhood is preached by many who do not practice it.*

First Inaugural Address

- **abdicated** (ab´ di kāt´ id) *v.* gave up formally (p. 505) *The king abdicated his throne and left the country.*

- **evanescent** (ev´ ə nes´ ənt) *adj.* temporary; tending to disappear (p. 506) *The band's evanescent popularity was gone in a week.*

- **arduous** (är´ jōō əs) *adj.* difficult; laborious (p. 509) *Rebuilding the house by ourselves was an arduous task.*

492 ■ *Types of Nonfiction*

Vocabulary Development

Vocabulary Knowledge Rating
Create a **Vocabulary Knowledge Rating Chart** for the selection you will teach from this set. Include the selection vocabulary from this page and the additional expressive vocabulary students are asked to use at the end of Connecting to the Literature. These words will increase students' expressive vocabulary.

Give students a copy of the chart with the words on it. Introduce the words by reading them aloud and having students mark their rating in the Before Reading column. Urge them to be alert to these words as they read and discuss the selection because they will rate their knowledge of the words again after they finish.

If you wish, you may tally how many students know (or think they know) a word to gauge how much instruction you need to provide. As students read, point out the words and their context.

Build Understanding • *I Have a Dream*

Speech

❸ Background

The Civil Rights Movement The U.S. Constitution guarantees certain rights to all Americans. The struggle of African Americans to have their rights recognized is known as the civil rights movement. Marked by demonstrations and legal challenges, this movement began in the 1950s and was led by figures like Martin Luther King, Jr.

❹ Connecting to the Literature

Reading/Writing Connection In "I Have a Dream," Martin Luther King, Jr., challenges Americans to live up to national ideals of equality and justice. Write a short paragraph in which you describe some other ideals that you consider to be characteristically American. Use at least three of these words: *embody, comprise, define, invoke.*

READ MORE

by
Martin Luther King, Jr.
"Letter from Birmingham Jail"

Meet the Author

Dr. Martin Luther King, Jr. (1929–1968)

Born in Atlanta, Georgia, Dr. Martin Luther King, Jr., was the most charismatic leader of the civil rights movement. During the 1950s and 1960s, King organized nonviolent protests to bring about equal rights for all Americans.

A Voice for the Oppressed King first came to national attention in 1956 in Montgomery, Alabama, when he organized a 382-day boycott by African Americans of the city's segregated buses. He went on to lead other protests and to speak out eloquently against poverty and social injustice. He was assassinated on April 4, 1968. His birthday, January 15, has since become a national holiday.

Fast Facts

▶ At thirty-five, King became the youngest man and only the third black man to be awarded a Nobel Peace Prize.
▶ The song "Pride (in the Name of Love)" by the famous rock band U2 is a tribute to Martin Luther King, Jr.

 Go Online
Author Link

For: more about the author
Visit: www.PHSchool.com
Web Code: epe-9310

I Have a Dream ■ 493

❸ Background
The Civil Rights Movement

Rosa Parks and Dr. Martin Luther King became famous at about the same time. When Rosa Parks was arrested for refusing to give up her seat to a white person on the bus in Montgomery, Alabama, Dr. King became leader of the newly-formed Montgomery Improvement Association (MIA). Dr. King led the struggle against the city's policy of segregation on the public bus system.

❹ Connecting to the Literature

• Model use of the expressive vocabulary students are asked to use with these examples:
  1. Americans should *embody* the spirit of freedom.
  2. The rights outlined in our Constitution *comprise* the greatest ideals of the American people.
  3. Americans *define* their ideals in the laws of this country.
  4. American presidents often *invoke* dedication to freedom as the reason for their policies.

• Help students further develop their expressive vocabulary by providing these words: *enlighten, formulate, liberate, proclaim,* and *tolerate.* Encourage students to use these words as they discuss the selection.

Go Online
Author Link For additional information about Martin Luther King, Jr., have students type in the Web Code, then select *K* from the alphabet, and then select *Martin Luther King, Jr.*

Differentiated Instruction Solutions for All Learners

Support for Below-Level Students [L1, L2]	Support for English Learners [EL]
Unit 3 Resources	**Unit 3 Resources**
Vocabulary Warm-up Word Lists, p. 145	Vocabulary Warm-up Word Lists, p. 145
Vocabulary Warm-up Practice, p. 146	Vocabulary Warm-up Practice, p. 146
Reading Warm-up A, p. 147	Reading Warm-up A, p. 147
Selection Test A, pp. 155–157	**Reader's Notebook: English Learner's Version**
Graphic Organizer Transparencies	**Listening to Literature Audio CD**
Reading Skill Graphic Organizer, Transparency B, p. 110	
Reader's Notebook: Adapted Version	
Adapted Reader's Notebook Audio CD	

❶ Motivation

Prepare an **Anticipation Guide** (*General Resources,* pp. 8–10) with the following statements:

- A person can change the world by the force of his or her beliefs.
- People of all backgrounds will support a cause they believe is just.
- A strong moral code is an important motivation for fighting for justice.
- A powerful leader is necessary to make significant changes in the world.

Give students a copy of the prepared Anticipation Guide and have students mark their responses in the Me column. Have students discuss the statements in pairs or groups and mark the Guides again in the Group column.

Concept Connector ➡

Students will return to the Anticipation Guide after completing "I Have a Dream."

Learning Modalities
Verbal/Linguistic Learners

"I Have a Dream" makes a tremendous impression on everyone who hears King. If possible, show students the television broadcast of this speech. If this is not possible, have students listen to the **Listening to Literature Audio CD** that accompanies this selection. Point out the impact of hearing the speech delivered, rather than simply reading the words on a page.

❷ About the Selection

In "I Have a Dream," King blended simple words and images with biblical and political references to urge his audience to eliminate oppression, prejudice, segregation, and injustice.

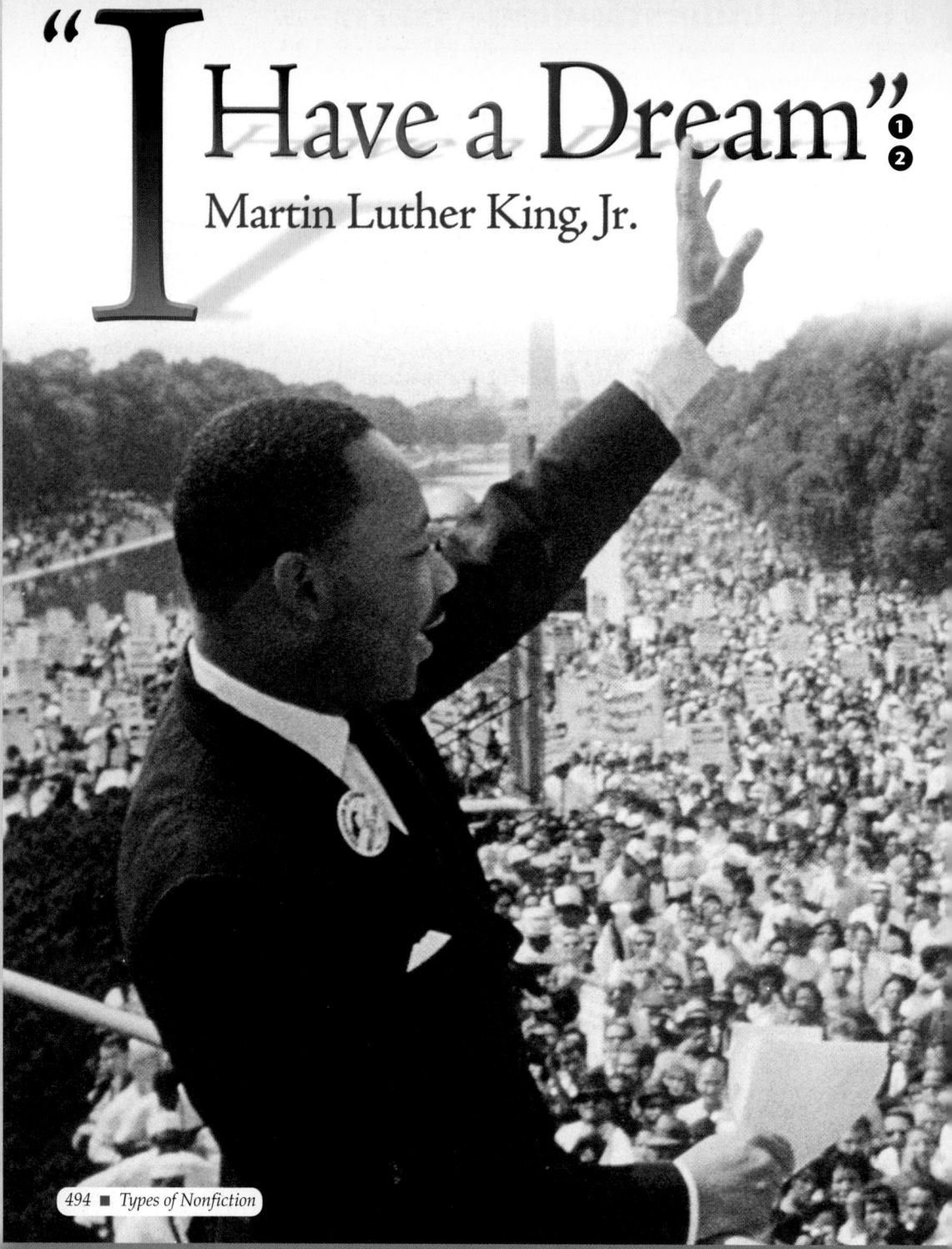

"I Have a Dream" ❶❷
Martin Luther King, Jr.

494 ■ *Types of Nonfiction*

Vocabulary Development

Expressive Vocabulary
As students are discussing the speech, encourage them to use the expressive vocabulary presented earlier. You might encourage them with sentence starters like these:

1. Dr. King's words *embody* . . .
2. Dr. King explains how the struggle for freedom and justice *comprise* . . .
3. He uses a number of examples to help *define* . . .
4. Dr. King uses language from the Bible to *invoke* . . .

Background Because speeches are written to be spoken aloud, they are a more fluid form of literature than most other nonfiction. A strong speaker will react to unspoken signals from his or her listeners and adjust a speech accordingly. He or she might change words or add whole phrases. This is the case with Dr. Martin Luther King, Jr., one of the greatest speakers of the modern age. The text that appears here represents the speech exactly as it was delivered by Dr. King on the steps of the Lincoln Memorial.

Five score years ago, a great American, in whose symbolic shadow we stand today, signed the Emancipation Proclamation. This momentous decree came as a great beacon light of hope to millions of Negro slaves who had been seared in the flames of withering injustice. It came as a joyous daybreak to end the long night of their captivity.

But one hundred years later, the Negro still is not free. One hundred years later, the life of the Negro is still sadly crippled by the manacles of segregation and the chains of discrimination. One hundred years later, the Negro lives on a lonely island of poverty in the midst of a vast ocean of material prosperity. One hundred years later, the Negro is still languished in the corners of American society and finds himself an exile in his own land. So we've come here today to dramatize a shameful condition.

In a sense we've come to our nation's Capital to cash a check. When the architects of our republic wrote the magnificent words of the Constitution and the Declaration of Independence, they were signing a promissory note[1] to which every American was to fall heir. This note was a promise that all men, yes, black men as well as white men, would be guaranteed the unalienable rights of life, liberty, and the pursuit of happiness.

It is obvious today that America has defaulted on this promissory note insofar as her citizens of color are concerned. Instead of honoring this sacred obligation, America has given the Negro people a bad check; a check which has come back marked "insufficient funds." But we refuse to believe that the bank of justice is bankrupt. We refuse to believe that there are insufficient funds in the great vaults of opportunity of this nation. And so we've come to cash this check—a check that will give us upon demand the riches of freedom

---

1. **promissory** (präm′ i sôr′ ē) **note** written promise to pay a specific amount.

---

5 ◄ **Critical Viewing** Which details in this photograph demonstrate the importance of the event at which King gave his speech? **[Analyze]**

Literary Analysis
Persuasive Speech
What idea does King's repetition of the phrase "One hundred years later" help to emphasize?

Literary Analysis
Persuasive Speech
Explain the analogy King makes between a financial transaction and the idea of justice.

6 ✓ **Reading Check**

What injustices are King and his listeners protesting?

I Have a Dream ■ 495

3 Literary Analysis
Persuasive Speech

• **Ask** students to read the paragraph aloud. Then, **ask** them to explain what rhetorical devices are used in the paragraph.
Answer: Parallelism and repetition are used with the phrase "one hundred years later."

• Have students state in their own words the injustices that King is outlining in the sentences beginning "one hundred years later."
Answer: He is stating that African Americans suffered segregation and discrimination, lived in poverty, and were not treated as full citizens.

• Then, **ask** students the Literary Analysis question: What idea does King's repetition of the phrase "one hundred years later" help to emphasize?
Answer: The phrase emphasizes a century of injustice for African Americans and implies a criticism that so little has been done in so long a time.

4 Literary Analysis
Persuasive Speech

• Read the bracketed paragraph and related footnote aloud.

• **Ask** students to identify the financial documents King mentions and to explain how they are usually used.

• **Answer:** King mentions a check, and a promissory note. People write checks instead of paying by cash. The check draws funds from the payer's bank account. The recipient can then go to a bank and convert the check into cash. A person gives someone else a promissory note as a pledge to pay at some future time.

• Then, **ask** students the Literary Analysis question: Explain the analogy King makes between a financial transaction and the idea of justice.

• **Answer:** King is saying that the promise of freedom and justice for African Americans is like the cash payment they are owed but have not yet received.

5 Critical Viewing

Answer: The size of the crowd and the location in the nation's capital suggest the importance of the event.

6 Reading Check

Answer: They are protesting segregation and discrimination.

495

⑦ Critical Viewing

Possible response: Students may describe King's expression as solemn, intense, or determined.

and the security of justice. We have also come to this <u>hallowed</u> spot to remind America of the fierce urgency of *now*. This is no time to engage in the luxury of cooling off or to take the tranquilizing drug of gradualism.

Now is the time to make real the promises of Democracy.

Now is the time to rise from the dark and desolate valley of segregation to the sunlit path of racial justice.

Now is the time to lift our nation from the quicksands of racial injustice to the solid rock of brotherhood.

Now is the time to make justice a reality for all of God's children.

It would be fatal for the nation to overlook the urgency of the moment. This sweltering summer of the Negro's legitimate discontent will not pass until there is an invigorating autumn of freedom and equality. Nineteen sixty-three is not an end, but a beginning. Those who hope that the Negro needed to blow off steam and will now be content will have a rude awakening if the nation returns to business as usual. There will be neither rest nor tranquillity in America until the Negro is granted his citizenship rights. The whirl-winds of revolt will continue to shake the foundations of our nation until the bright day of justice emerges.

Vocabulary Builder
hallowed (hal′ ōd) *adj.*
sacred

⑦ ▼ Critical Viewing
How would you describe King's expression as he delivers his speech? **[Analyze]**

496 ■ *Types of Nonfiction*

Vocabulary Development

Vocabulary Builder Reinforcement
Students will benefit from additional examples and practice with the Vocabulary Builder words. Reinforce their comprehension with "show-you-know" sentences. The first part of the sentence uses the vocabulary word in an appropriate context. The second part of the sentence—the "show-you-know" part—clarifies the first. Model the strategy with this example:

The orphans often wore *rueful* expressions; their loneliness showed through their big, sad eyes.

Then, give students these sentence prompts:

1. This building is a *hallowed* part of the university; _____
   Sample answer: some of history's greatest scholars have studied and taught here.

2. Her health is beginning to *degenerate*;_____
   Sample answer: soon she will have to be hospitalized.

But there is something that I must say to my people who stand on the warm threshold which leads into the palace of justice. In the process of gaining our rightful place we must not be guilty of wrongful deeds. Let us not seek to satisfy our thirst for freedom by drinking from the cup of bitterness and hatred. We must forever conduct our struggle on the high plane of dignity and discipline. We must not allow our creative protest to <u>degenerate</u> into physical violence. Again and again we must rise to the majestic heights of meeting physical force with soul force. The marvelous new militancy which has engulfed the Negro community must not lead us to a distrust of all white people, for many of our white brothers, as evidenced by their presence here today, have come to realize that their destiny is tied up with our destiny. And they have come to realize that their freedom is inextricably bound to our freedom. We cannot walk alone.

And as we walk, we must make the pledge that we shall always march ahead. We cannot turn back. There are those who are asking the devotees of civil rights, "When will you be satisfied?" We can never be satisfied as long as the Negro is the victim of the unspeakable horrors of police brutality. We can never be satisfied as long as our bodies, heavy with the fatigue of travel, cannot gain lodging in the motels of the highways and the hotels of the cities. We cannot be satisfied as long as the Negro's basic mobility is from a smaller ghetto to a larger one. We cannot be satisfied as long as a Negro in Mississippi cannot vote and a Negro in New York believes he has nothing for which to vote. No, no, we are not satisfied, and we will not be satisfied until justice rolls down like waters and righteousness like a mighty stream.

I am not unmindful that some of you have come here out of great trials and tribulations. Some of you have come fresh from narrow jail cells. Some of you have come from areas where your quest for freedom left you battered by the storms of persecution and staggered by the winds of police brutality. You have been the veterans of creative suffering. Continue to work with the faith that unearned suffering is redemptive.

Go back to Mississippi, go back to Alabama, go back to South Carolina, go back to Georgia, go back to Louisiana, go back to the slums and ghettos of our northern cities, knowing that somehow this situation can and will be changed. Let us not wallow in the valley of despair.

I say to you today, my friends, so even though we face the difficulties of today and tomorrow, I still have a dream. It is a dream deeply rooted in the American dream.

Vocabulary Builder
degenerate (dē jen´ ər āt´) v. grow worse

Literary Analysis
Persuasive Speech
What key idea does King restate when he says, "We cannot walk alone"?

❾ **Reading Check**

According to King, how should his people react to physical force?

I Have a Dream ■ 497

❽ **Literary Analysis**
Persuasive Speech

- Read the paragraph aloud. Ask students to describe what King is cautioning against in this paragraph.
  Answer: He is cautioning against bitterness, hatred, violence, and distrust of all white people.

- Have students explain how King describes the relationship between whites and African Americans.
  Answer: He says that the freedom of whites is tied to the freedom of African Americans.

- **Ask** students the Literary Analysis question: What key idea does King restate when he says, "We cannot walk alone"?
  Answer: He restates the idea that the destinies of white people and African Americans are tied together.

❾ **Reading Check**

Possible response: They should meet physical force with soul force (nonviolently).

Differentiated
Instruction   Solutions for All Learners

Enrichment for English Learners
King's speech refers to several states, such as Mississippi and Alabama, and several geographical features, such as the Alleghenies and the Colorado Rockies. Provide students with a map of the United States. Have them work in pairs to locate all the places mentioned by King on the map and to practice spelling the names of the places.

Enrichment for Gifted/Talented Students
Have students research the life of Mahatma Gandhi, another advocate of nonviolence and social justice. Ask students to draw parallels between the lives of the two men, including how they battled injustice and inequality. Have them locate one of Gandhi's speeches and compare it to King's "I Have a Dream" speech.

⑩ Literary Analysis
Persuasive Speech

- Ask students to read the passage aloud several times. Have them listen for a rhythm or repetition of sound.

- **Ask** students the Literary Analysis question: Identify the parallel clauses in this passage and explain how they emphasize King's ideas.
  Answer: The parallel clauses are variations of "I have a dream," which King uses to link his visions of justice, equality, and unity in America. By repeating "dream," King evokes "the American dream" while making clear that his inspirational ideas are yet to be fulfilled in reality.

▶ **Monitor Progress:** Ask students to pick out other examples of rhetorical devices on this page. Students should be able to identify the parallelism of "sons of former slaves . . . sons of former slaveowners" and "little black boys and girls . . . little white boys and girls."

▶ **Reteach:** If students have difficulty identifying rhetorical devices, have them reread this page and the previous page aloud. Point out examples of repetition. Tell students that such repetition reinforces King's message.

⑪ Reading Skill
Persuasive Techniques

- Ask students to read the paragraph aloud. Have them identify the repetition in the paragraph.
  Answer: The phrase "With this faith we will be able . . . " is repeated.

- **Ask** students the Reading Skill question: What idea does King reinforce using the rhythm of repetition?
  Answer: King reinforces the idea that African Americans will be able to achieve equality "with this faith."

I have a dream that one day this nation will rise up and live out the true meaning of its <u>creed</u>: "We hold these truths to be self-evident; that all men are created equal."

I have a dream that one day on the red hills of Georgia the sons of former slaves and the sons of former slaveowners will be able to sit down together at the table of brotherhood.

I have a dream that one day even the state of Mississippi, a state sweltering with the heat of injustice, sweltering with the heat of oppression, will be transformed into an oasis of freedom and justice.

⑩ I have a dream that my four little children will one day live in a nation where they will not be judged by the color of their skin but by the content of their character.

I have a dream today.

I have a dream that one day down in Alabama, with its vicious racists, with its governor still having his lips dripping with the words of interposition and nullification,[2] one day right down in Alabama little black boys and black girls will be able to join hands with little white boys and white girls as sisters and brothers.

I have a dream today.

I have a dream that one day every valley shall be exalted, every hill and mountain shall be made low, the rough places will be made plains, and the crooked places will be made straight, and the glory of the Lord shall be revealed, and all flesh shall see it together.[3]

⑪ This is our hope. This is the faith that I go back to the South with. With this faith we will be able to hew out of the mountain of despair a stone of hope. With this faith we will be able to transform the jangling discords of our nation into a beautiful symphony of brotherhood. With this faith we will be able to work together, to pray together, to struggle together, to go to jail together, to stand up for freedom together, knowing that we will be free one day.

This will be the day when all of God's children will be able to sing with new meaning

> My country, 'tis of thee,
> Sweet land of liberty,
>   Of thee I sing:
> Land where my fathers died,
> Land of the pilgrims' pride,
> From every mountainside
>   Let freedom ring.

---

2. interposition (in′ tər pə zish′ ən) **and nullification** (nul′ ə fi kā′ shən) disputed doctrine that a state can reject federal laws considered to be violations of its rights. Governor George C. Wallace used this doctrine to reject federal civil rights legislation.
3. every valley . . . all flesh shall see it together reference to a biblical passage (Isaiah 40:4–5). King is likening the struggle of African Americans to the struggle of the Israelites.

498 ■ *Types of Nonfiction*

Vocabulary Builder
creed (krēd) *n.* statement of belief

Literary Analysis
Persuasive Speech
Identify the parallel clauses in this passage and explain how they emphasize King's ideas.

Reading Skill
Persuasive Techniques
What idea does King reinforce using the rhythm of repetition?

Vocabulary Development

Vocabulary Knowledge Rating
When students have completed reading and discussing "I Have a Dream," have them take out their **Vocabulary Knowledge Rating Chart** for this selection. Read the words aloud once more and have students rate their knowledge of the words again in the After Reading column. Clarify any words that are still problematic. Have students write their own definition and example or sentence in the appropriate column. Then, have students complete the **Vocabulary Builder Practice** activities on p. 501. Encourage students to use the words in further discussion and written work about this selection. Remind them that they will be accountable for these words on the Selection Test.

And if America is to be a great nation this must become true. So let freedom ring from the prodigious hilltops of New Hampshire. Let freedom ring from the mighty mountains of New York. Let freedom ring from the heightening Alleghenies of Pennsylvania!

Let freedom ring from the snowcapped Rockies of Colorado!

Let freedom ring from the curvacious slopes of California!

But not only that; let freedom ring from Stone Mountain of Georgia!

Let freedom ring from Lookout Mountain of Tennessee!

Let freedom ring from every hill and molehill of Mississippi. From every mountainside, let freedom ring.

And when this happens, when we allow freedom to ring, when we let it ring from every village and every hamlet, from every state and every city, we will be able to speed up that day when all of God's children, black men and white men, Jews and Gentiles, Protestants and Catholics, will be able to join hands and sing in the words of the old Negro spiritual, "Free at last! free at last! thank God almighty, we are free at last!"

⑫ ▼ **Critical Viewing**
Which part of the speech do you think King is delivering in this photograph?
[Connect]

I Have a Dream ■ 499

Concept Connector

Anticipation Guide
Have students return to their **Anticipation Guides** and respond to the statements again in the After Reading column. They may do this individually or in their original pairs or groups. Then, lead a class discussion, probing for what students have learned that confirms or invalidates each statement. Encourage students to cite specific details, quotations, or other evidence from the text to support their responses to each statement.

Connecting to the Literature
Have students compare the sentences they wrote before reading with their thoughts about American ideals after reading "I Have a Dream." Ask them to explain whether their thoughts have changed and, if so, how.

Reading Skill Graphic Organizer
Ask students to review the graphic organizers they completed to identify the persuasive appeals while reading. Show them **Reading Skill Graphic Organizer B** (*Graphic Organizer Transparencies,* p. 110) as an example. Then have students share their graphic organizers.

Apply the Skills

I Have a Dream

Thinking About the Selection

1. **Respond:** What feelings does Dr. King's "I Have a Dream" speech stir in you? Explain.
2. **(a) Recall:** Which words does King quote from "My Country 'Tis of Thee"? **(b) Interpret:** What message does he send to his audience by quoting these lines?
3. **(a) Recall:** Which different parts of the United States does King mention in his speech? **(b) Connect:** How does the mention of all of these places tie in with the overall message of his speech?
4. **(a) Hypothesize:** Why do you think "I Have a Dream" has lived on as one of the best-known speeches in modern history? **(b) Make a Judgment:** Do you think it deserves this standing? Explain.

Literary Analysis

5. In this **persuasive speech,** what is Martin Luther King, Jr., trying to persuade his audience to think or do?
6. **(a)** In what ways does King appeal to emotion in this speech? Explain. **(b)** In what ways does he appeal to reason? Explain.
7. **(a)** Using a chart like the one shown, identify examples in King's speech of the **rhetorical devices** listed. (You may not be able to find an example of every device.) **(b)** Describe the effect of each example you cite.

	Example	Effect
Restatement		
Repetition		
Parallelism		
Analogy		

Reading Skill

8. **(a)** Identify a passage in which King uses emotionally charged language as a **persuasive technique. (b)** What specific purpose do you think King had in using such language? Explain. **(c)** Describe the emotional effect of the words King uses in the passage.
9. Do you think that King uses emotionally charged language and rhetorical devices effectively and convincingly in this speech? Explain your answer.

QuickReview

Speech at a Glance
Martin Luther King, Jr., shares his dream of racial equality in America.

For: Self-test
Visit: www.PHSchool.com
Web Code: epa-6309

Persuasive Speech: a speech that tries to convince listeners to think or act in a certain way

Rhetorical Devices: patterns of words and ideas that speakers use to create emphasis and stir emotion. These devices include *parallelism, restatement, repetition,* and *analogy.*

Persuasive Techniques: devices used to influence the audience in favor of the author's argument

---

Answers (left column)

1. **Possible responses:** Students may suggest the feelings of pride, elation, hope, enthusiasm for freedom, and friendship.

2. (a) King quotes the first stanza. (b) He reminds everyone that the country was founded on a promise of liberty.

3. (a) He mentions states in the South, the states of New York, New Hampshire, and Pennsylvania, the Rocky Mountains, and California. (b) The mention of these places ties in with his message of equality for everyone across the nation.

4. (a) **Possible response:** The speech dramatically expressed American values at a critical point in history. (b) **Possible response:** Yes, because it articulates American values with a purity and passion that still moves listeners.

5. The author is trying to persuade the audience to continue their fight for justice and equality.

6. (a) King appeals to emotion by describing a future America in which all people participate equally in the country's promise and prosperity. (b) He appeals to reason by explaining that America has not met its promises for all citizens.

7. (a) **Sample response:** Parallelism: **Example:** "sweltering summer of the Negro's legitimate discontent/invigorating autumn of freedom and equality" (b) **Effect:** Parallelism emphasizes the contrast between how African Americans are treated and how they should be treated.

Another sample answer can be found on **Literary Analysis Graphic Organizer B,** p. 113, in *Graphic Organizer Transparencies.*

8. **Possible response:** (a) paragraph beginning "This is our hope. This is the faith. . . ." uses emotionally charged language such as "faith," "hope," "mountain of despair," "beautiful symphony of brotherhood." (b) By using the language of religion, King may have wanted to imply that the struggle for civil rights is a religious crusade. (c) King's words make the audience see themselves as part of a great and holy movement.

9. **Possible response:** Most students will say that King is effective because the rhetorical devices and emotionally-charged language emphasize his ideas.

Vocabulary Builder

Practice **Analogies** show the relationships between pairs of words. Use a word from the "I Have a Dream" vocabulary list on page 492 to complete each analogy.

1. stumble : rise :: _____ : improve

2. oath : office :: _____ : religion

3. barren : desert :: _____ : church

Adding Words to Your Vocabulary Using a thesaurus, find a **synonym**, or word with a similar meaning, for each word in the "I Have a Dream" vocabulary list. Then, use each synonym correctly in a sentence. (For more on using a thesaurus, see page R7.)

Writing

Write a **proposal** to persuade your principal to invite a great speaker like Dr. King to address a school assembly.
- List some issues that concern students at your school.
- List possible speakers and the issues that each could discuss.
- Choose one speaker, and write a proposal supporting your choice.
End with an appeal to your principal to act on the proposal.

For *Grammar, Vocabulary,* and *Assessment,* see **Build Language Skills,** pages 512–513.

Extend Your Learning

Listening and Speaking Compose a **radio news report** that provides on-the-spot coverage of King's speech. Include the following:
- background information about the civil rights movement
- excerpts from King's speech
- a description of the speech's effect on the crowd

Broadcast your report to the class and record it for later evaluation.

Research and Technology In a group, create an **annotated source list** for a multimedia presentation about one aspect of the civil rights movement such as laws, marches, or leaders. Find sources of photographs and video and audio recordings of events. List each source following MLA format. (For more on MLA format, see page R33.) Briefly explain the information found in each source.

Apply the Skills ■ 501

Vocabulary Builder
Analogies Practice

1. *degenerate;* the two pairs of words are antonyms.

2. *creed;* you must observe an *oath* when you hold *office;* you must observe a *creed* when you follow a *religion.*

3. *hallowed; barren* is a characteristic of a *desert; hallowed* is a characteristic of a *church.*

Adding Words to Your Vocabulary
Possible responses:

1. This wood is beginning to *deteriorate* and fall apart.

2. These burial grounds are *sacred* to Native Americans.

3. The *doctrine* of the church has not changed for centuries.

Writing

- To give students guidance for writing the proposal, give them the **Support for Writing Lesson** for "I Have a Dream," p. 152 in *Unit 3 Resources.*

- To evaluate students' proposal, use the Persuasive Essay rubrics, pp. 53–54, in *General Resources.* In addition, you might evaluate the appropriateness of issues and possible speakers chosen by the students.

Six Traits Focus

Ideas		✔ Word Choice
Organization		Sentence Fluency
Voice		Conventions

WG **Writing and Grammar, Gold Level**
Students will find guidance on revising their persuasive proposal in Chapter 7, section 4.

Build Language Skills

Go to pp. 512–513 for vocabulary and grammar lessons and assessment practice.

Extend Your Learning

The **Support for Extend Your Learning** page (*Unit 3 Resources,* p. 153) provides guided note-taking opportunities to help students complete the Extend Your Learning activities.

501

Teaching notes for Literary Analysis, Reading Skill, and Vocabulary Builder for this selection begin on p. 492.

❸ Background
The Great Depression

Throughout his presidency, Franklin Roosevelt addressed the American people directly in speeches via the radio. Families gathered around their radios to hear Roosevelt talk on a variety of topics. These talks kept the American people informed of Roosevelt's plans and offered encouragement to Americans in times of crisis. This series of speeches given by Roosevelt became known as the "Fireside Chats."

❹ Connecting to the Literature

- Model use of the expressive vocabulary students are asked to use with these examples.

  1. My mother is always able to *evoke* a sense of optimism in me when I am down.

  2. When I was scared, my brother managed to *project* a sense of confidence.

  3. His words were able to *render* my fears powerless.

  4. The minister's sermon helped to *stimulate* me to help the disadvantaged.

  5. The coach's speech managed to *transform* everyone's attitude about the game.

- Help students further develop their expressive vocabulary by providing these words: *administer, drastic, implement,* and *initiate.* Encourage students to use these words as they discuss the selection.

Go **Online**
Author Link For additional information about Franklin D. Roosevelt have students type in the Web Code, then select *R* from the alphabet, and then select *Franklin D. Roosevelt.*

502

Build Understanding • *First Inaugural Address*

Speech

❸ Background

The Great Depression On March 4, 1933, newly elected President Franklin Delano Roosevelt delivered his inaugural address to a nation close to despair. The Great Depression had weighed down American life for over three years. Americans sat by their radios to hear the new president's address, a speech he had written himself. In this speech, Roosevelt gave Americans hope.

❹ Connecting to the Literature

Reading/Writing Connection The right words at the right time can inspire hope. Write a short paragraph describing a time when someone else's words inspired you. Use at least three of these words: *evoke, project, render, stimulate, transform.*

Review
For **Literary Analysis, Reading Skill,** and **Vocabulary Builder,** see page 492.

READ MORE

by
**Franklin D. Roosevelt
Second Inaugural Address**

Meet the Author

Franklin Delano
Roosevelt (1882–1945)

Franklin Delano Roosevelt had a relatively easy life until he was stricken with polio at age 39. Ironically, Roosevelt realized his potential as a leader only after falling victim to this illness. He was twice elected governor of New York; then, in 1932, he defeated President Herbert Hoover to become the nation's thirty-second president. Roosevelt won an unprecedented four terms as president.

A Leader in Dark Times Franklin Roosevelt led the nation through two great challenges: the Great Depression and World War II. The war was almost over when the president died of a cerebral hemorrhage in 1945.

Fast Facts
▶ Roosevelt helped found the March of Dimes, originally established to raise money to combat polio. His image was later put on the dime to honor his efforts.
▶ Roosevelt's wife, Eleanor, became one of the most active and widely admired first ladies in American history.

Go **Online**
Author Link

For: More about the author
Visit: www.PHSchool.com
Web Code: epe-9311

FIRST INAUGURAL ADDRESS ❶ ❷

Franklin Delano Roosevelt

President Hoover, Mr Chief Justice, my friends:

This is a day of national consecration,[1] and I am certain that my fellow-Americans expect that on my induction into the Presidency I will address them with a candor and a decision which the present situation of our nation impels.

This is pre-eminently the time to speak the truth, the whole truth, frankly and boldly. Nor need we shrink from honestly facing conditions in our country today. This great nation will endure as it has endured, will revive and will prosper.

❹ So first of all let me assert my firm belief that the only thing we have to fear is fear itself—nameless, unreasoning, unjustified terror which paralyzes needed efforts to convert retreat into advance.

❸ ✓ **Reading Check**

With what qualities does Roosevelt promise to address his audience?

---

1. **consecration** (kän´ si krā´ shən) *n.* dedication to something sacred.

First Inaugural Address ■ 503

Differentiated Instruction Solutions for All Learners

Support for Below-Level Students [L1, L2]

Unit 3 Resources
- Vocabulary Warm-up Word Lists, p. 161
- Vocabulary Warm-up Practice, p. 162
- Reading Warm-up A, p. 163
- Selection Test A, pp. 173–175

Graphic Organizer Transparencies
- Reading Skill Graphic Organizer, Transparency B, p. 111

Support for English Learners [EL]

Unit 3 Resources
- Vocabulary Warm-up Word Lists, p. 161
- Vocabulary Warm-up Practice, p. 162
- Reading Warm-up A, p. 163

Listening to Literature Audio CD

TEACH

❶ Motivation

Prepare an **Anticipation Guide** (*General Resources*, pp. 8–10) with the following statements:

- The best way for a president to gain the support of the people is to be absolutely truthful.
- Material wealth is not a sign of success.
- The people of a nation need to have a vision to inspire them.
- Citizens must be willing to sacrifice for the common good.
- In times of crisis, the president should be granted extra powers.

Give students a copy of the prepared Anticipation Guide and have students mark their responses in the Me column. Have students discuss the statements in pairs or groups and mark the Guides again in the Group column.

Concept Connector ➤

Students will return to the Anticipation Guide after completing "First Inaugural Address."

Learning Modalities
Interpersonal Learners

In this speech, Franklin Roosevelt outlines the crisis in which the nation finds itself, and he promises to resolve the nation's problems. Have students work in small groups to find some of the programs that Roosevelt instituted. Have them discuss how these programs helped the country. Encourage students to share their findings with the class.

❷ About the Selection

In "First Inaugural Address," newly elected President Roosevelt outlines the problems facing the American people. He encourages them with the now-famous phrase, "the only thing we have to fear is fear itself." Roosevelt calls on the people to support his efforts as he works for the greater good, and he promises to work for the benefit of the nation with courage and devotion.

❸ Reading Check

Answer: He promises to address his audience with candor and decision.

503

❹ Reading Skill
Persuasive Techniques

- Ask students to read the paragraphs, and then ask them what Roosevelt thinks the people might fear.
  Answer: They might fear that the country will never recover its prosperity, and that they and their children are doomed to live in poverty for the rest of their lives.

- Ask students to list what words or phrases they consider emotionally charged.
  Possible response: Students may suggest the phrases "nameless, unreasoning, unjustified terror," and "dark hour."

- **Ask** the Reading Skill question: How do you think Roosevelt wanted listeners to respond to the emotionally charged language here?
  Answer: He wanted them to realize that he understood the gravity of their problems and intensity of their concerns. He wanted them to know that he saw the truth of the situation and was not attempting to pretend that things were better than they seemed.

❺ Critical Viewing

Possible response: People would be fearful seeing so many out of work and unable to feed themselves. People might be afraid that they, too, would end up in a bread line.

---

❹ In every dark hour of our national life a leadership of frankness and vigor has met with that understanding and support of the people themselves which is essential to victory. I am convinced that you will again give that support to leadership in these critical days.

In such a spirit on my part and on yours we face our common difficulties. They concern, thank God, only material things. Values have shrunken to fantastic levels; taxes have risen; our ability to pay has fallen, government of all kinds is faced by serious curtailment of income; the means of exchange are frozen in the currents of trade; the withered leaves of industrial enterprise lie on every side; farmers find no markets for their produce; the savings of many years in thousands of families are gone.

More important, a host of unemployed citizens face the grim problem of existence, and an equally great number toil with little return. Only a foolish optimist can deny the dark realities of the moment.

❻ Yet our distress comes from no failure of substance. We are stricken by no plague of locusts.[2] Compared with the perils which our forefathers conquered because they believed and were not

---

2. **plague of locusts** according to Exodus 10:3–20, the plague of locusts was one of ten plagues inflicted by God on the Egyptians as punishment for enslaving the Israelites.

Reading Skill
Persuasive Techniques
How do you think Roosevelt wanted listeners to respond to the emotionally charged language here?

❺ ▼ **Critical Viewing**
This is a photograph of a bread line during the Great Depression. Why do you think conditions like this might make Americans fearful? **[Infer]**

504 ■ *Types of Nonfiction*

Vocabulary Development

Expressive Vocabulary
As students read and discuss Roosevelt's speech on these two pages, encourage them to use the expressive vocabulary presented earlier. You might encourage them with sentence starters like these:

1. Seeing people standing in bread lines might *evoke* . . .
2. Roosevelt seems to *project* . . .
3. He intends to *render* the money changers . . .
4. He hopes his words will *stimulate* . . .
5. Roosevelt tells the people that they need to *transform* . . .

afraid, we have still much to be thankful for. Nature still offers her bounty and human efforts have multiplied it. Plenty is at our doorstep, but a generous use of it languishes in the very sight of the supply.

Primarily, this is because the rulers of the exchange of mankind's goods have failed through their own stubbornness and their own incompetence, have admitted that failure and <u>abdicated</u>. Practices of the unscrupulous money changers stand indicted in the court of public opinion, rejected by the hearts and minds of men.

True, they have tried, but their efforts have been cast in the pattern of an outworn tradition. Faced by failure of credit, they have proposed only the lending of more money.

Stripped of the lure of profit by which to induce our people to follow their false leadership, they have resorted to exhortations, pleading tearfully for restored confidence. They know only the rules of a generation of self-seekers.

They have no vision, and when there is no vision the people perish.

The money changers have fled from their high seats in the temple[3] of our civilization. We may now restore that temple to the ancient truths.

The measure of the restoration lies in the extent to which we apply social values more noble than mere monetary profit.

---

3. money changers . . . temple allusion to Matthew 21:12–13, in which Jesus overturns the money changers' tables at the temple in Jerusalem. FDR is comparing those ancient money changers to modern bankers who took high risks with depositors' money and who charged excessive interest rates for loans.

Literary Analysis
Persuasive Speech
How might this description of national problems have changed people's minds about their troubles?

Vocabulary Builder
abdicated (ab´ di kāt´ id) *v.* gave up formally

⑦ ✓ **Reading Check**
On whom does Roosevelt place the largest blame for the Great Depression?

First Inaugural Address ■ 505

⑥ Literary Analysis
Persuasive Speech

• Have students read the paragraph. Ask what positive things Roosevelt describes in this paragraph.
Answer: He describes the plentiful natural resources that the nation has available.

• Then, **ask** the Literary Analysis question: How might this description of national problems have changed people's minds about their troubles?
Answer: Roosevelt said that the problems the nation faced did not come from God or nature. Instead, human beings created the problems, which means that human beings have the power to solve them. This statement would have emboldened Roosevelt's listeners and made them turn from despair to hope.

▶ **Monitor Progress:** Provide students with **Literary Analysis Graphic Organizer A**, p. 114 in *Graphic Organizer Transparencies*, to complete as they read the speech.

▶ **Reteach:** If students have difficulty identifying persuasive appeals, point out that words with a negative connotation reinforce a persuasive appeal. Brainstorm with students for a list of words with a negative connotation that appear on p. 505, including *failed, stubbornness, money changers, lure,* and *self-seekers.* Tell students to look for ways that Roosevelt uses words with positive connotations in the remainder of the speech.

⑦ Reading Check
Answer: He blames the "rulers of the exchange" or "money changers."

Differentiated Instruction Solutions for All Learners

Vocabulary for Special Needs Students
Much of the vocabulary in this selection will be unfamiliar to students. Have students work in pairs to read the selection, listing all of the words and phrases they do not understand. Then, have pairs work in small groups and have students compare their lists. Review the lists with the group and discuss the words in context, helping them identify context clues. You may also want to provide students with the **Vocabulary Warm-up Word Lists** and **Vocabulary Warm-up Practice**, pp. 161–162 in *Unit 3 Resources.*

Background for English Learners
Provide students with background on the Great Depression. Draw a timeline of events beginning with October 29, 1929 (Black Tuesday) to the date of Roosevelt's first inaugural address (March 4, 1933). Explain terms such as *soup kitchen, Hoovervilles, the Dust Bowl,* and the *New Deal.* Ask students to make a collage of the effects of the Great Depression using headlines, photos, and illustrations from magazines or Web sites.

- Ask students to read the two paragraphs aloud. Then ask what they think Roosevelt means by the "American spirit of the pioneer."
Possible response: Students may suggest that he means the strength and the willingness to work hard and persevere that pioneers possessed.

- **Ask** the Literary Analysis question: Identify the parallelism in the paragraph beginning "It is the way . . ." and explain what it emphasizes.
Answer: The parallel phrases are "It is the. . . ." They emphasize the idea that the pioneer spirit is what will insure that the nation will recover.

Happiness lies not in the mere possession of money; it lies in the joy of achievement, in the thrill of creative effort.

The joy and moral stimulation of work no longer must be forgotten in the mad chase of <u>evanescent</u> profits. These dark days will be worth all they cost us if they teach us that our true destiny is not to be ministered unto but to minister to ourselves and to our fellowmen.

Recognition of the falsity of material wealth as the standard of success goes hand in hand with the abandonment of the false belief that public office and high political position are to be valued only by the standards of pride of place and personal profit; and there must be an end to a conduct in banking and in business which too often has given to a sacred trust the likeness of callous and selfish wrongdoing.

Small wonder that confidence languishes, for it thrives only on honesty, on honor, on the sacredness of obligations, on faithful protection, on unselfish performance. Without them it cannot live.

Restoration calls, however, not for changes in ethics alone. This nation asks for action, and action now.

Our greatest primary task is to put people to work. This is no unsolvable problem if we face it wisely and courageously. . . .

I favor as a practical policy the putting of first things first. I shall spare no effort to restore world trade by international economic readjustment, but the emergency at home cannot wait on that accomplishment.

The basic thought that guides these specific means of national recovery is not narrowly nationalistic.

❽ It is the insistence, as a first consideration, upon the interdependence of the various elements in, and parts of, the United States—a recognition of the old and permanently important manifestation of the American spirit of the pioneer.

It is the way to recovery. It is the immediate way. It is the strongest assurance that the recovery will endure.

In the field of world policy I would dedicate this nation to the policy of the good neighbor—the neighbor who resolutely respects himself and, because he does so, respects the rights of others—the neighbor who respects his obligations and respects the sanctity of his agreements in and with a world of neighbors.

If I read the temper of our people correctly, we now realize as we have never before, our interdependence on each other; that we cannot merely take, but we must give as well; that if we are to go forward we must move as a trained and loyal army willing to sacrifice for the good of a common discipline, because, without such discipline, no progress is made, no leadership becomes effective.

Vocabulary Builder
evanescent (evˊ ə nesˊ ənt) *adj.* temporary; tending to disappear

Literary Analysis
Persuasive Speech
Identify the parallelism in the paragraph beginning "It is the way . . ." and explain what it emphasizes.

Vocabulary Development

Think-Aloud: Context
Direct students' attention to the word *languishes* on p. 506. Using a think-aloud process, model how to use context to infer the meaning of an unknown word. Say to students:

I'm going to think aloud to show you how I would figure out the meaning of *languishes* from its context.

In this sentence, *languishes* is used to describe what happens to confidence. In the previous sentence, Roosevelt says that people in banking and business have engaged in selfish wrongdoing. Then, he says that confidence "thrives only on honesty."

So, I think *languish* must mean "not thriving" or not exhibiting strength and vitality.

We are, I know, ready and willing to submit our lives and property to such discipline because it makes possible a leadership which aims at a larger good.

This I propose to offer, pledging that the larger purposes will bind upon us all as a sacred obligation with a unity of duty hitherto evoked only in time of armed strife.

With this pledge taken, I assume unhesitatingly the leadership of this great army of our people, dedicated to a disciplined attack upon our common problems.

❾ ✔ **Reading Check**

What does Roosevelt say is the "greatest primary task" facing the nation?

❿ Literature in Context — **Social Studies Connection**

Getting Back to Work: FDR and the WPA

In 1935, President Roosevelt established the Works Progress Administration (WPA) to aid struggling Americans. At the height of its activity, the WPA provided jobs to one third of the unemployed, ranging from artists to construction workers.

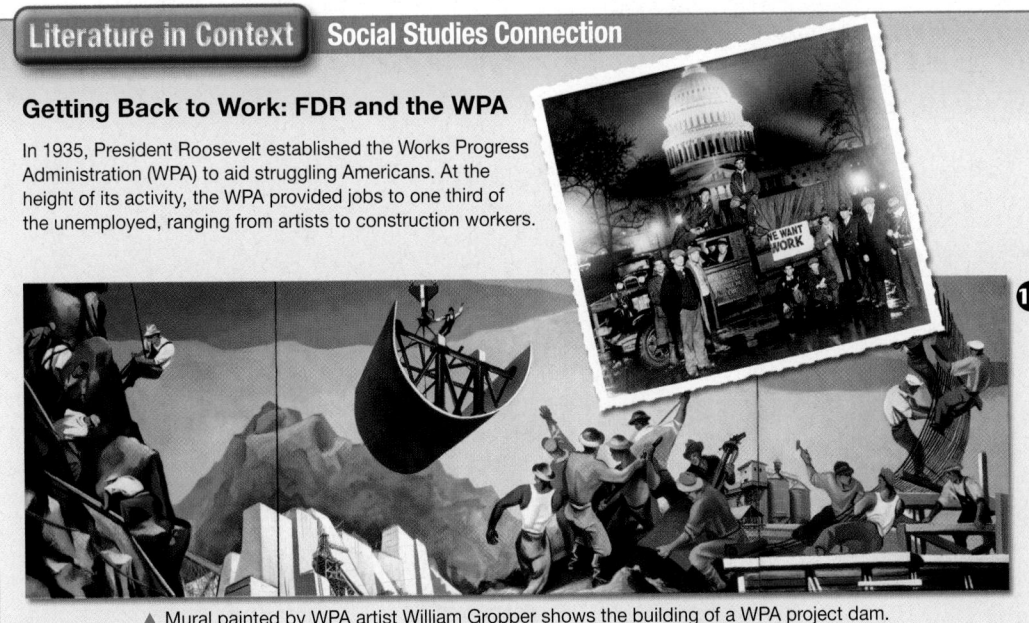

▲ Mural painted by WPA artist William Gropper shows the building of a WPA project dam. **⑪**

Americans Unemployed During the Great Depression

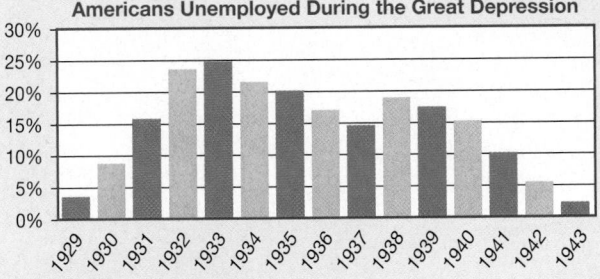

The WPA Projects

WPA workers produced:		
	650,000	miles of roads
	125,000	public buildings
	75,000	bridges
	8,000	parks
	800	airports

WPA artists created:		
	2,566	murals
	100,000	paintings
	17,700	sculptures
	300,000	fine prints

Connect to the Literature President Roosevelt gave his First Inaugural Address in March of 1933. Basing your answer on the chart of unemployment, explain why this was a particularly hard time in American life.

First Inaugural Address ■ 507

---

❾ Reading Check

Answer: He says the "greatest primary task" is to put people to work.

❿ Literature in Context

Social Studies Connection In 1935, Congress awarded the WPA (Work Progress Administration) $5 billion to underwrite public projects. President Roosevelt believed that simply giving money to people would lead to a "spiritual and moral disintegration." He thought people should work for the funds they received. The WPA decreased the national unemployment by putting about 8.5 million people back to work. The government hired painters, writers, musicians, sculptors, teachers, and film and theater artists, as well as construction workers and engineers. Roads, dams, public buildings, bridges, parks, and airports were built, and thousands of murals and paintings were created.

Connect to the Literature Point out the persuasive statements of President Roosevelt's Inaugural Address. **Ask** students the Connect to the Literature question: President Roosevelt gave his First Inaugural Address in March of 1933. Basing your answer on the chart of unemployment, explain why this was a particularly hard time in American life.

Answer: In 1933, unemployment reached a new height—almost 25% of Americans were out of work. The unemployment of at least 13 million people had a profoundly negative effect on the economy.

⑪ Humanities

Construction of a Dam by William Gropper, mural, Department of Interior Museum, Washington, D.C., Gropper painted this mural in 1939, working with oil paint on canvas. Gropper's inspiration for this mural was the construction of the Grand Coulee Dam on the Columbia River and the Davis Dam on the Colorado River. Use the following question for discussion:

• What message do you think the artist is trying to portray?
  Possible answer: The artist portrays the dignity of labor and the value of teamwork.

- Remind students that the American people were the audience for Roosevelt's speech. People all over the country tuned in their radios to hear his address.

- Have students read the bracketed passage on p. 509. Ask students why they think Roosevelt makes a point to mention the Constitution of the United States.
  Answer: He may have wanted to reassure listeners that, despite the economic crisis, the political structure of the country was sound. He may also have wanted to make clear that even as he took emergency measures to deal with the economic catastrophe, he would be guided by the laws of the country.

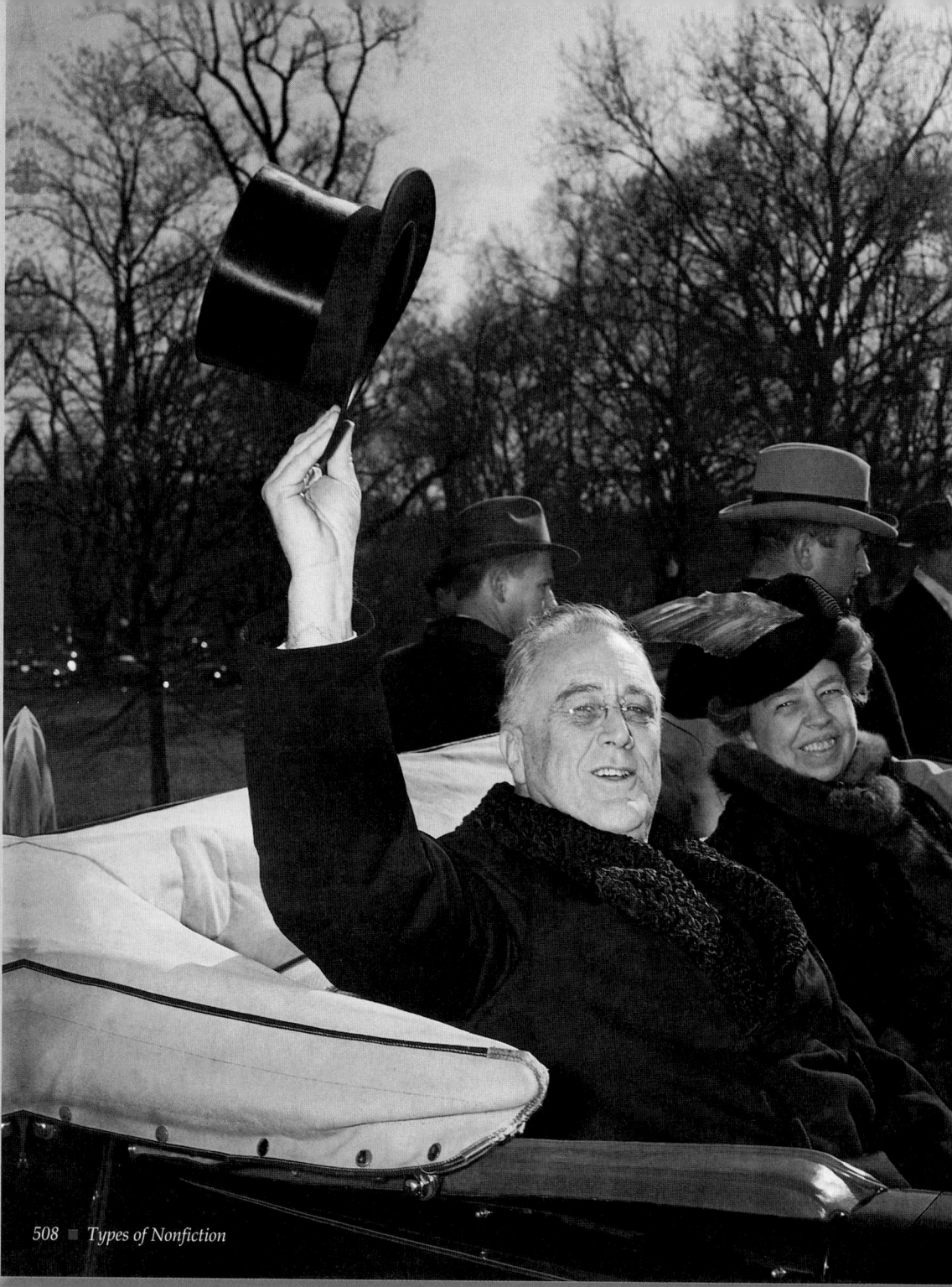

508 ■ *Types of Nonfiction*

Vocabulary Development

Vocabulary Knowledge Rating
When students have completed reading and discussing "First Inaugural Address," have them take out their **Vocabulary Knowledge Rating Chart** for this selection. Read the words aloud once more and have students rate their knowledge of the words again in the After Reading column. Clarify any words that are still problematic. Have students write their own definition and example or sentence in the appropriate column. Then, have students complete the **Vocabulary Builder Practice** activities on p. 511. Encourage students to use the words in further discussion and written work about this selection. Remind them that they will be accountable for these words on the Selection Test.

Action in this image and to this end is feasible under the forms of government which we have inherited from our ancestors.

Our Constitution is so simple and practical that it is possible always to meet extraordinary needs by changes in emphasis and arrangement without loss of essential form.

12 That is why our constitutional system has proved itself the most superbly enduring political mechanism the modern world has produced. It has met every stress of vast expansion of territory, of foreign wars, of bitter internal strife, of world relations. . . .

I am prepared under my constitutional duty to recommend the measures that a stricken nation in the midst of a stricken world may require.

These measures, or such other measures as the Congress may build out of its experience and wisdom, I shall seek, within my constitutional authority, to bring to speedy adoption.

But in the event that the Congress shall fail to take one of these two courses, and in the event that the national emergency is still critical, I shall not evade the clear course of duty that will then con-
13 front me.

I shall ask the Congress for the one remaining instrument to meet the crisis—broad executive power to wage a war against the emergency as great as the power that would be given me if we were in fact invaded by a foreign foe.

For the trust reposed in me I will return the courage and the devotion that befit the time. I can do no less.

We face the arduous days that lie before us in the warm courage of national unity; with the clear consciousness of seeking old and precious moral values; with the clean satisfaction that comes from the stern performance of duty by old and young alike.

We aim at the assurance of a rounded and permanent national life.

We do not distrust the future of essential democracy. The people of the United States have not failed. In their need they have registered a mandate that they want direct, vigorous action.

They have asked for discipline and direction under leadership. They have made me the present instrument of their wishes. In the spirit of the gift I take it.

In this dedication of a nation we humbly ask the blessing of God. May He protect each and every one of us. May He guide me in the days to come.

14 ◀ **Critical Viewing** This photograph of President Roosevelt was taken on the day of his first inauguration. Do you think he projects an image of confidence? Explain. [**Analyze**]

Literary Analysis
Persuasive Speech
What call to action does Roosevelt issue to Congress in this passage?

Vocabulary Builder
arduous (är′ jōō əs)
adj. difficult; laborious

---

13 Literary Analysis
Persuasive Speech

- Have students read the passage. Then, ask what Roosevelt is proposing.
  Answer: He is proposing to introduce measures necessary to solve the problems of the nation.

- **Ask** the Literary Analysis question: What call to action does Roosevelt issue to Congress in this passage?
  Answer: He calls on Congress to adopt his measures, or to grant him broad executive powers so that he can act on his own.

- Ask students whether they think Roosevelt was wise in suggesting that he might ask Congress for additional powers to "wage war" against the problems.
  Possible response: Some students may say that Roosevelt was wise in demonstrating that he would do everything possible to solve the problems; others may say that he may have given the impression of seeking to grasp too much power.

14 Critical Viewing

Answer: Most students will say that he projects an image of confidence, as he waves his hat and smiles.

Concept Connector

Anticipation Guide
Have students return to their **Anticipation Guides** and respond to the statements again in the After Reading column. They may do this individually or in their original pairs or groups. Then, lead a class discussion, probing for what students have learned that confirms or invalidates each statement. Encourage students to cite specific details, quotations, or other evidence from the text to support their responses to each statement.

Connecting to the Literature
Have students compare the sentences they wrote before reading with their thoughts about how someone's words inspired them after reading "First Inaugural Address." Ask them to explain whether their thoughts have changed.

Reading Skill Graphic Organizer
Ask students to review the graphic organizers they completed to identify the persuasive appeals while reading. Show them **Reading Skill Graphic Organizer B** (*Graphic Organizer Transparencies*, p. 111) as an example. Then have students share their graphic organizers.

Apply the Skills

First Inaugural Address

Thinking About the Selection

1. **Respond:** What feelings does Roosevelt's speech stir in you? Why?
2. **(a) Recall:** What words does Roosevelt use to describe the financial leaders who had caused the country's financial problems? **(b) Interpret:** What message does he send to the American people by describing financial leaders in these terms?
3. **(a) Recall:** What does Roosevelt say about Americans from earlier periods in history? **(b) Speculate:** How do you think his listeners felt on hearing about earlier Americans?
4. **Make a Judgment:** Roosevelt's speech was made over seventy years ago to a country in economic ruin. Which parts of the speech do you think would be most appealing to Americans today? Which parts might be less appealing? Explain.

Literary Analysis

5. In this **persuasive speech**, what is President Roosevelt trying to persuade his audience to think or do?
6. **(a)** In what ways does Roosevelt appeal to emotion in his speech? Explain. **(b)** In what ways does he appeal to reason? Explain.
7. **(a)** Using a chart like the one shown, identify examples in Roosevelt's speech of the **rhetorical devices** listed. (You may not be able to find an example of every device.) **(b)** Describe the effect of each example you cite.

	Example	Effect
Restatement		
Repetition		
Parallelism		
Analogy		

Reading Skill

8. **(a)** Identify a passage in which Roosevelt uses emotionally charged language as a **persuasive technique.** **(b)** What specific purpose do you think he had in using such language in the passage? Explain. **(c)** Describe the emotional effect of the passage.
9. Does Roosevelt use emotionally charged language and rhetorical devices effectively in this speech? Explain your answer.

QuickReview

Speech at a Glance
In his first inaugural address, FDR tells Americans how they will overcome the Great Depression.

Go Online
Assessment
For: Self-test
Visit: www.PHSchool.com
Web Code: epa-6310

Persuasive Speech: a speech that tries to convince listeners to think or act in a certain way

Rhetorical Devices: patterns of words and ideas that speakers use to create emphasis and stir emotion. These devices include *parallelism*, *restatement*, *repetition*, and *analogy*.

Persuasive Techniques: devices used to influence the audience in favor of the author's argument

---

Answers (left column)

1. Some students may say they have feelings of pride in their country and admiration for the achievements of generations past.

2. (a) He calls them unscrupulous money changers, false leaders, and self-seekers who have no vision. (b) He sends the message that the actions of these people and others like them will no longer be tolerated in America.

3. (a) He says they conquered perils because they were not afraid. (b) The recognition that earlier Americans had overcome adversity was probably encouraging.

4. **Possible response:** People today may approve of FDR's ideas about putting people to work and following the Constitution; references to sacrifice, discipline, and the performance of duty may be less appealing.

5. He is trying to persuade people to have hope, to support his proposals, and to trust him to lead the nation out of its difficulties.

6. (a) Roosevelt appeals to emotion by alluding to fear, to "money changers," and to our forefathers. (b) He appeals to reason when discussing the "common difficulties" that the people face and the plans he has for solving them.

7. **Sample answers:**
(a) **Parallelism:** "on honesty, on honor, on the sacredness of obligations, on faithful protection, on unselfish performance"
(b) **Effect:** This parallel listing of virtues creates a sense of momentum and urgency.

(a) **Restatement:** "Nature still offers her bounty. . . . Plenty is at our doorstep. . . ."
(b) **Effect:** The restatement emphasizes optimism and hope.

Another sample answer can be found on **Literary Analysis Graphic Organizer B,** page 115, in *Graphic Organizer Transparencies.*

8. (a) "We are stricken by no plague of locusts. . . ." (b) He wanted to emphasize that the problems the

nation faced were not insurmountable. Unlike the Biblical plague of locusts, America's economic woes did not come from God. (c) The emotional effect is to change depression and despair to determination and hope.

9. Some students may suggest that he made very little use of rhetorical devices, but relied primarily on emotionally-charged language. Most students will agree that Roosevelt uses emotionally-charged words effectively.

Vocabulary Builder

Practice **Analogies** show the relationships between pairs of words. Use a word from the "First Inaugural Address" vocabulary list on page 492 to complete each analogy.

1. coach : resigned :: ruler : _____
2. ongoing : rain :: _____ : lightning
3. vacation : relaxing :: labor : _____

Adding Words to Your Vocabulary Using a thesaurus, find a **synonym**, or word with a similar meaning, for each word in the "First Inaugural Address" vocabulary list. Then, use each synonym correctly in a sentence. (For more on using a thesaurus, see page R7.)

Writing

Write a **proposal** to persuade your principal to invite a great speaker like President Roosevelt to address a school assembly:
- List some issues that concern students at your school.
- List possible speakers and the issues that each could discuss.
- Choose a speaker, and write a proposal supporting your choice.
End with an appeal to your principal to act on the proposal.

For *Grammar, Vocabulary,* and *Assessment,* see **Build Language Skills,** pages 512–513.

Extend Your Learning

Listening and Speaking Compose a **radio news report** that provides on-the-spot coverage of Roosevelt's speech. Include the following in your report:
- background information about the Great Depression
- excerpts from Roosevelt's speech
- a description of the speech's effect on the crowd
Broadcast your report to the class, and record it for later evaluation.

Research and Technology In a group, create an **annotated source list** for a multimedia presentation about one aspect of the Great Depression, such as its causes, its effects, or the government's attempts to deal with it. Find sources of photographs and video and audio recordings from that time. Then, list those sources following MLA format. (For more on MLA format, see page R33.) Briefly explain the information found in each source.

Apply the Skills ■ 511

Go Online
—Research **For:** An additional research activity
Visit: www.PHSchool.com
Web Code: epd-7308
For another research activity to extend students' learning, give students this Web Code.

Vocabulary Builder
Analogies Practice

1. *abdicated;* both pairs of words indicate leaving a position.
2. *evanescent;* both pairs of words indicate a duration of an event.
3. *arduous;* both pairs of words indicate a condition of an activity.

Adding Words to Your Vocabulary
Possible responses:

1. He decided to *retire* and enjoy the last years of his life.
2. Their fame was just *temporary,* and they were soon forgotten by the public.
3. Moving furniture can be an extremely *difficult* job.

Writing

- To give students guidance for writing the proposal, give them the **Support for Writing Lesson** for "First Inaugural Address," p. 168 in *Unit 3 Resources.*
- To evaluate students' proposal, use the Persuasive Essay rubrics, pp. 53–54, in *General Resources.* In addition, you might evaluate the appropriateness of issues and possible speakers chosen by the students.

Six Traits Focus

✔	Ideas		Word Choice
	Organization		Sentence Fluency
	Voice		Conventions

Writing and Grammar, Gold Level
Students will find guidance on revising their persuasive proposal in Chapter 7, section 4.

Build Language Skills

Go to pp. 512–513 for vocabulary and grammar lessons and assessment practice.

Extend Your Learning

The **Support for Extend Your Learning** page (*Unit 3 Resources,* p. 169) provides guided note-taking opportunities to help students complete the Extend Your Learning activities.

511

Vocabulary Skill

- Introduce the prefix *inter-*. Ask students to brainstorm for words that begin with this prefix.
  Possible responses: *intervene, intersperse, intercept, interactive*

- Have students complete the Practice activity on this page.

Answers

1. *interject;* to insert between other elements; between; The student *interjected* his comments before he was called on.

2. *intermediate;* in a middle position or state; between; The *intermediate* school prepares students for high school.

3. *interior;* inner; within; The *interior* of the ear is essential to hearing.

4. *intermission;* a pause between the acts of a performance; between; During the *intermission*, we stretched our legs.

5. *interval;* a space between two objects, points, or units; between; We saw several *intervals* of highway that were not completed.

Grammar Lesson

- Point out that adverbs are very versatile. They even can join with adjectives to form compound words.

- Have students complete the Practice activity on this page.

Answers

1. *certainly;* modifies *felt,* verb; He definitely felt that he was successful.

2. *very;* modifies *good;* adjective; Grandmother took tremendously good care of this house.

3. *so;* modifies *terribly;* adverb; *terribly;* modifies *sang;* verb. Lester sang very beautifully.

4. *excitedly;* modifies *ran;* verb; Keri ran breathlessly into the dining room.

5. *away;* modifies *hid;* verb; The children hid quietly in the attic.

Build Language Skills

I Have a Dream • *First Inaugural Address*

Vocabulary Skill

Prefixes The **Latin prefix** *inter-* means "between, among, or within" and is contained in words that express a variety of ideas about "within" or "between." For example, *internal* expresses the idea of "within" something. Other words containing *inter-* relate to something "between," such as *interfere*, which means "to come in between for some purpose."

▶ **Example:** Sally did not want to *interfere* in the argument between two of her good friends.

Practice All of the following words contain the prefix *inter-*. Write a definition of each word, explaining whether the word expresses the idea of *between, among,* or *within*. Then, use each word in a sentence.

1. interject
2. intermediate
3. interior
4. intermission
5. interval

Grammar Lesson

Adverbs *Adverbs* are words that modify verbs, adjectives, and other adverbs. They answer the questions *Where? When? In what way?* and *To what extent?* about the words they modify.

Modifying a verb:	Modifying an adjective:
Dave drove the car <u>smoothly</u>. (The adverb *smoothly* modifies the verb *drove*.)	He drove an <u>extremely</u> large car. (The adverb *extremely* modifies the adjective *large*.)

Modifying another adverb:
He drove the car <u>very</u> smoothly.
(The adverb *very* modifies the adverb *smoothly*.)

MorePractice

For more practice with adverbs, see the Grammar Handbook, p. R41.

Practice Circle each of the adverbs, and underline the word or words it modifies. Indicate whether the modified word is a verb, an adjective, or an adverb. Rewrite each sentence, replacing the adverb with a new one.

1. He certainly felt that he was successful.
2. Grandmother took very good care of this house.
3. Lester sang so terribly.
4. Keri ran excitedly into the dining room.
5. The children hid away in the attic.

$W\!_G$ *Prentice Hall Writing and Grammar Connection: Chapter 18, Section 2*

Teaching Resources

The following resources can be used to enrich or extend the instruction for Build Language Skills.

Unit 3 Resources
  Build Language Skills: Vocabulary: Prefixes, p. 171
  Build Grammar Skills: Adverbs, p. 172

Reading Skill: Analyzing Persuasive Appeals

Directions: *Read the selection. Then, answer the questions.*

. . . as the first President of a united, democratic, nonracial, and nonsexist South Africa, to lead our country out of the valley of darkness. . . .

We know it well that none of us acting alone can achieve success. We must therefore act together as a united people. . . .

Let there be justice for all. . . .

<u>Never, never, and never again</u> shall it be that this beautiful land will again experience the oppression of one by another and suffer the indignity of being the skunk of the world.

The sun shall never set on so glorious a human achievement!

Let freedom reign. God bless Africa!

—from *Glory and Hope,* by Nelson Mandela

1. The emotional terms "valley of darkness" and "skunk of the world" are meant to persuade Mandela's listeners that
   A South Africa did not deserve negative world opinion.
   B South Africa's recent history was a time of suffering and shame.
   C his government will solve most of the people's problems.
   D South Africans are in danger of forgetting the lessons of their past.

2. What is the effect of the underlined phrase?
   A It comforts listeners with familiar words.
   B It surprises listeners with a new idea.
   C It rouses listeners with its repetition and rhythm.
   D It makes listeners ashamed.

3. The use of the statements beginning with "Let . . ." convey a tone of
   A happiness.
   B devotion.
   C confidence.
   D desperation.

Timed Writing: Evaluation [Critical Stance]

Review "I Have a Dream" by Dr. Martin Luther King, Jr., or President Franklin Roosevelt's First Inaugural Address. Write an evaluation of the persuasive techniques used in one of these selections. Include specific references from the text to support your ideas. **(30 minutes)**

 ## Writing Workshop: *Work in Progress*

Editorial

Review the portfolio list of Cultural Influences. Identify one cultural factor that you feel has the greatest effect on you and your friends. In a two-column chart, jot down three positive and three negative aspects of this influence. Save this chart in your writing portfolio.

Build Language Skills ■ 513

Answers

Reading: Persuasive Appeals
1. B
2. C
3. C

Timed Writing
- Tell students that when they write an evaluation, they should include clear statements of their views and examples to support them.
- Suggest that students make a list of persuasive techniques. As they review the speeches, write down the line numbers in which they find each technique.
- Once students begin writing, suggest that they cite the line numbers from which the support came.
- Assess students' evaluations based on their analysis of the persuasive techniques and the support they provide for that analysis.
- Suggest that students allow ten minutes for prewriting and planning, fifteen minutes for writing, and five minutes for reviewing and revising.

Writing Workshop
Work in Progress

Editorial
- Have students go to their portfolios and take out their list of cultural influences that they made in the **Work-in-Progress** assignment on p. 491.
- Remind students that this work may be used in the editorial they will write in the **Writing Workshop** at the end of Part 2.
- Have students reflect on the cultural factor they select. If they cannot list three positive and three negative aspects of this influence, have them select a different cultural factor or have them partner with another student who has selected a different factor. Then, each can contribute to the other's chart.
- Point out to students that these aspects can be as simple as a style change or as complex as something that has affected society's values.
- When students have completed their charts, have them save them in their portfolios. They will use the charts as they continue this **Work in Progress.**

See TeacherExpress™/Lesson View for a detailed lesson plan for Reading Informational Materials.

About Historical Studies

- Have students read "About Historical Research Studies."

- Explain to students that authors often write about historical events, speeches, or documents because they reflect the attitudes of the time and influence future events. Point out to students that they are likely to encounter historical research studies when reading or studying about history.

- Discuss with students any experiences they have had with historical research studies. Point out that they have probably read explanations and opinions regarding speeches such as Lincoln's Emancipation Proclamation and documents such as the U.S. Constitution.

- **Ask** a volunteer to share a memory about a speech or document that was critiqued or explained in a social studies textbook.

Reading Skill
Distinguishing Fact from Opinion

- Remind students that a fact can be proved. An opinion is a statement of belief that cannot be proved. Make sure students understand that, if they are unable to verify a statement it is an opinion, even if they agree with it.

- Explain that historical research studies will include both facts and opinions. Point out that careful review of statements while reading will help clarify which are facts and which are opinions.

514

Historical Research Study

In Part 2, you learned how to analyze and evaluate persuasive texts. You will also find this skill useful when reading informational materials, such as advertisements, editorials, and historical studies. If you read President Roosevelt's "First Inaugural Address," you will see how the author of the following historical study analyzes his speech.

About Historical Research Studies

In a **historical research study,** the writer evaluates and interprets a speech, a document, or an event in history. When a writer studies a speech, he or she analyzes the words to understand both their meaning for people at the time and the meaning they may hold for people today. The writer also shows how the speech connects to other ideas and other historical events. A historical study typically includes these features:

- an introduction stating the author's thesis, or main idea
- a summary of all or part of the historical document
- facts and opinions
- quotations, examples, or statistics
- explanations and interpretations
- transitions to link ideas
- a conclusion restating the thesis and main points

Reading Skill

When reading a historical study, **distinguish fact from opinion.** A **fact** can be proved true. In contrast, an **opinion** is what someone thinks. It may be valid, but it cannot be proved. A valid opinion is supported by facts.

Statements using absolute words such as *always, everybody,* and *never* indicate **overgeneralizations.** Overgeneralizations are statements that may look factual, but they are usually too broad to be proven true and should be distinguished from facts. As you read, record the facts and opinions you find in a chart like the one shown.

Statement	Provable?	Fact or Opinion
In 1921, Roosevelt contracted polio.	Yes. Check a biography or an encyclopedia entry about Roosevelt.	Fact
Fear is a fog; it obscures the truth.	No	Opinion

514 ■ *Essays*

from Nothing To Fear:
Lessons in Leadership from FDR

by Alan Axelrod

> The study begins with a quotation from FDR's speech. It reminds the reader of the speech and its famous line: "The only thing we have to fear is fear itself."

"This great nation will endure as it has endured, will revive and will prosper. So, first of all, let me assert my firm belief that the only thing we have to fear is fear itself—nameless, unreasoning, unjustified terror which paralyzes needed efforts to convert retreat into advance."

—First inaugural address, March 4, 1933

In *Defending Your Life,* a charmingly provocative 1991 movie written and directed by its star, Albert Brooks, we discover that the only truly unforgivable sin in life is fear. Killed in a head-on crash with a bus, yuppie Brooks finds himself transported to Judgment City, where he must "defend his life" before a pair of judges who will decide whether he is to be returned to Earth for another crack at life or be permitted to progress to the next plane of existence. His attorney (for the benevolent managers of the universe provide defense assistance) explains to him the nature of fear, which is, he says, a "fog" that obscures everything and that makes intelligent, productive action impossible.

> Axelrod uses this description of a popular movie as an engaging introduction.

It is a stimulating thought—that fear is not so much the sensation accompanying the realization of danger, but a fog, an obscurer of truth, an interference with how we may productively engage reality. Certainly this is the way FDR saw it. In 1921 polio threatened first to kill him and then paralyzed him, subjected him to a life of relentless pain, and nearly ended his career in public service. He could then and there have given in to the fog of fear, but he chose not to. He chose instead to understand polio, to see clearly the extent of his disability, and then to assess—also clearly—his options for overcoming that disability. He did not blink at the odds. He looked at them, contemplated them, assessed them, and then acted on them.

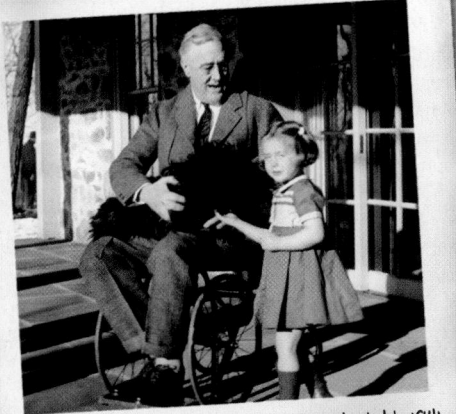

Franklin D. Roosevelt with a local child, 1941.

Reading Informational Materials: Historical Research Study ■ 515

515

Reading Historical Studies
(cont.)

- Ask students to read p. 516 and to pay attention to facts and opinions.

- Direct students to the second paragraph of p. 516. **Ask** a volunteer to identify the opinion in the paragraph and to tell whose opinion it is.
Answer: The opinion is that FDR lifted the fog of fear. It is Axelrod's opinion.

- **Ask** students how the quotation that begins "Values have shrunken to fantastic levels;" helps support the author's thesis.
Possible response: The author's thesis is that FDR believes fear clouds judgment and impedes action. The quotation shows that FDR would not allow fear to cloud his vision of the county's problems. Instead, he focuses his attention on the problems and their solutions.

- **Ask** students to find the two short phrases of FDR's that Axelrod uses as support for his opinion that the audience could "see it in a new light."
Answer: Axelrod uses these two phrases from FDR 's speech: "our common difficulties" and "concern, thank God, only material things."

- Point out that Axelrod assumes that, true to human nature, the people at the time of the Great Depression were comforted knowing that they were not alone with their problems and that the losses they were experiencing were not unbearable because they were only material things.

continued on p. 517

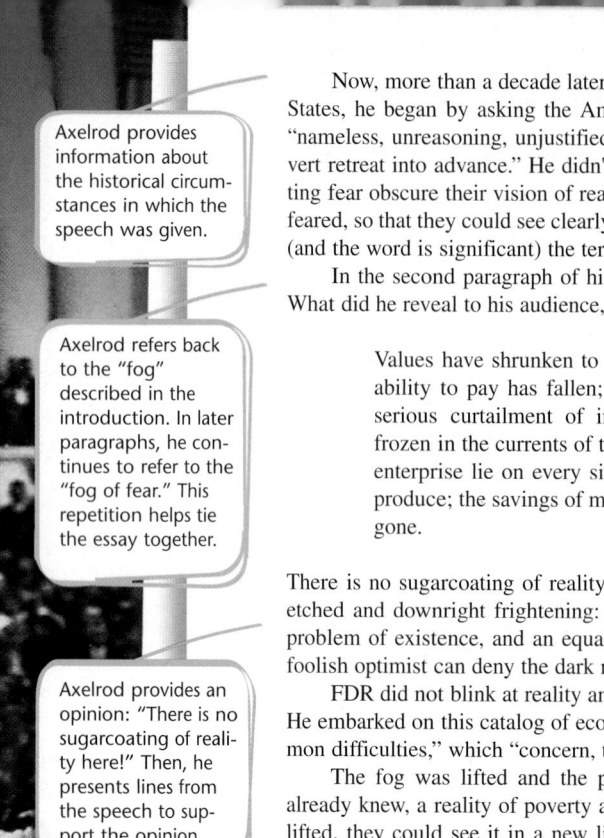

Axelrod provides information about the historical circumstances in which the speech was given.

Axelrod refers back to the "fog" described in the introduction. In later paragraphs, he continues to refer to the "fog of fear." This repetition helps tie the essay together.

Axelrod provides an opinion: "There is no sugarcoating of reality here!" Then, he presents lines from the speech to support the opinion.

Now, more than a decade later, assuming the office of president of the United States, he began by asking the American people to sweep aside the fog of fear, "nameless, unreasoning, unjustified terror which paralyzes needed efforts to convert retreat into advance." He didn't ask them to stop being afraid, but to stop letting fear obscure their vision of reality. He asked the people to confront what they feared, so that they could see clearly what needed to be done and thereby overcome (and the word is significant) the terror that *paralyzes*.

In the second paragraph of his inaugural speech, FDR lifted the fog of fear. What did he reveal to his audience, the American people?

> Values have shrunken to fantastic levels; taxes have risen; our ability to pay has fallen; government of all kinds is faced by serious curtailment of income; the means of exchange are frozen in the currents of trade; the withered leaves of industrial enterprise lie on every side; farmers find no markets for their produce; the savings of many years in thousands of families are gone.

There is no sugarcoating of reality here! The fog has lifted, the scene is sharply etched and downright frightening: "a host of unemployed citizens face the grim problem of existence, and an equally great number toil with little return. Only a foolish optimist can deny the dark realities of the moment."

FDR did not blink at reality and he did not allow his audience to do so either. He embarked on this catalog of economic disasters by defining them as "our common difficulties," which "concern, thank God, only material things."

The fog was lifted and the president's listeners could see the reality they already knew, a reality of poverty and despair, to be sure; yet with the fog of fear lifted, they could see it in a new light: Our common difficulties "concern, thank God, only material things."

Not one to blink at disaster, FDR also saw a way out of it:

> Yet our distress comes from no failure of substance. We are stricken by no plague of locusts. Compared with the perils which our forefathers conquered because they believed and were not afraid, we have still much to be thankful for. Nature still offers her bounty and human efforts have multiplied it. Plenty is at our doorstep. . .

Lift the fog of fear and you could see that the Great Depression was not of natural, supernatural, or inevitable origin. It was not a plague of biblical proportion. Our kind has conquered worse in the past. Nature has not failed us.

516 ■ *Types of Nonfiction*

Vocabulary Development

Vocabulary for Historical Research Studies
Point out that historical research studies often use vocabulary that is more common to one particular setting, in this case a speech given in 1933. Guide students to understand the meaning of the following words that are used in "From Nothing to Fear: Lessons in Leadership from FDR":

material: relating to physical objects.
sugarcoating: making superficially agreeable.
inaugural: marking a beginning.
indicted: charged with an offense.
evanescent: tending to vanish like vapor.

What, then, was the problem?

Plenty is at our doorstep, but a generous use of it languishes in the very sight of the supply. Primarily this is because rulers of the exchange of mankind's good have failed through their own stubbornness and their own incompetence, have admitted their failure, and have abdicated. Practices of unscrupulous money changers stand indicted in the court of public opinion, rejected by the hearts and minds of men.

> Axelrod provides a summary of the problems stated in the excerpt below.

The failure was a failure of particular human beings and the particular policies they pursued. "True," Roosevelt continued, these particular people "have tried, but their efforts have been cast in the pattern of an outworn tradition."

Faced by failure of credit they have proposed only the lending of more money. Stripped of the lure of profit by which to induce our people to follow their false leadership, they have resorted to exhortation, pleading tearfully for restored confidence. They know only the rules of a generation of self-seekers. They have no vision, and when there is no vision the people perish.

> The word "always" is an absolute. It signals a statement that looks like a fact, but is probably not a fact.

As a leader FDR always navigated between the radically new and unprecedented, on the one hand, and the age-old and unchanging, on the other. Early in the speech he evoked the Old Testament image of a plague of locusts. He used another biblical image, this one from the New Testament, in referring to the "unscrupulous money changers." Then he went on to speak of the Depression as a problem created by old ways of thinking. It was, he said, a problem that could not be solved by "efforts . . . cast in the pattern of outworn tradition," the pattern of a "generation of self-seekers."

Franklin D. Roosevelt addressing Congress, 1941.

The implication was unmistakable: Conquering the Depression would require new thinking. And yet FDR once again linked this need for fresh imagination and bold, new action with the timeless wisdom of Judeo-Christian tradition. In Proverbs 29:18 we are told, "Where there is no vision, the people perish," and FDR tells us that the Depression was created and is perpetuated by leaders who "have no vision, and when there is no vision the people perish." He continued with his echo of the Gospels:

> Axelrod uses transitions such as "yet FDR once again linked" and "He continued" to tie ideas together and explain his arguments.

Reading Historical Studies (cont.)

- Have students read p. 517. Direct students to the biblical quotations FDR uses to link ideas in his speech. Note that the author mentions these quotations to link together his own ideas as well.

- **Ask** students to explain how the quotation "The implication was unmistakable: Conquering the Depression would require new thinking" helps support the author's thesis that FDR believes fear clouds judgment and impedes action.
  Possible response: This statement supports the author's thesis that FDR felt fear clouded judgment because it shows that the author believes that, because FDR was able to set fear aside, he developed a vision and was not afraid to try something new.

- **Ask** students to identify a fact from p. 517.
  Possible response: It is a fact that Proverbs 29:18 says "Where there is no vision, the people perish." The accuracy of the quotation can be verified by looking it up in the Bible.

- Remind students that clue words, such as *always, never,* or *only* indicate a statement is an overgeneralization, rather than a fact. Ask volunteers to point out examples of generalizations on p. 517.
  Possible responses: Axelrod makes a generalization in the statement, "As a leader FDR always navigated between the radically new and unprecedented. . . ."

continued on p. 518

Differentiated Instruction
Solutions for All Learners

Background for English Learners
Provide background about the historical context of FDR's address. Make sure students realize that when FDR took office in 1933, the United States was in the depths of the Great Depression, and that many people lost everything they had. Point out that unemployment was very high, as was inflation, which resulted in most people having great difficulty buying even basic necessities. Discuss that FDR's speech was focused on solving these problems.

Enrichment for Advanced Readers
Challenge students to find a historical study of FDR's speech that is written by a different author. Have them compare the two studies. Allow time for students to share their findings.

517

- Point out to students that the end of this historical study is a summary of the author's main points in proving his thesis.

- Have students read the sentence beginning "Here then, in the space of the first few minutes . . ." **Ask** whether this sentence is a fact or opinion.
  Answer: This is an opinion because it cannot be proved.

- **Ask** students to evaluate how well the author supported his thesis.
  Possible responses: The author did a good job of supporting his thesis with examples. He included many quotations from the speech itself and tied those quotations to events of the time.

- Point out that the article ends with three quotes from FDR's speech. **Ask** volunteers to tell whether each of the quotes is a fact or an opinion.
  Answers: The quote "happiness lies not in the mere possession of money," is an opinion. When FDR said that morals and ethics must not be sacrificed in "the mad chase of evanescent profits," he is stating an opinion. And, when he says that "true destiny is not to be ministered unto but to minister to ourselves and our fellow men," he is also stating an opinion.

- Tell students to think about different times they have studied FDR in history class. **Ask** volunteers to share facts they remember that indicate whether FDR's speech was successful with the American people of the time.
  Possible response: History shows that FDR's speech was successful with the American people because he continued to be a popular president, the people supported the many job-producing projects he started, people began to have hope, and the American people followed his lead.

The money changers have fled from their high seats in the temple of our civilization. We may now restore that temple to the ancient truths. The measure of the restoration lies in the extent to which we apply social values more noble than mere monetary profit.

An inauguration is a beginning, as Roosevelt was well aware, and in his acceptance speech to the Democratic National Convention, he had already pledged to the American people a "New Deal." Americans would soon discover, during the dazzling first hundred days of the Roosevelt presidency, just how new a deal it would be, as program after innovative program was ushered into being. Yet all of this innovation was aimed at restoring the "temple of our civilization . . . to the ancient truths," the age-old redemption of the temple of the spirit from the grasp of the materialistic money changers.

Happiness lies not in the mere possession of money; it lies in the joy of achievement, in the thrill of creative effort. The joy and moral stimulation of work no longer must be forgotten in the mad chase of evanescent profits. These dark days will be worth all they cost us if they teach us that our true destiny is not to be ministered unto but to minister to ourselves and our fellow men.

Here then, in the space of the first few minutes of his first speech as leader of the American people, is what Franklin Roosevelt made visible in the absence of the fog of fear: that the economic disaster is serious, urgent, even life-threatening, *yet* it is an *economic* disaster, one concerning "thank God, only material things." Roosevelt's speech does not allow his listeners to turn away from the disaster. His words invite them to see beyond it, both to its cause in human errors, in the shortsighted pursuit of immediate material profit, and in the absence of greater vision, to its eventual resolution.

Franklin D. Roosevelt delivering a radio address, 1938.

That resolution is the subject of the rest of the speech, which broadly outlines innovative goals, policies, and programs aimed at ending the Great Depression. Yet the proposed means of resolution, radical as they may be, rest on restoring the "temple of our civilization . . . to the ancient truths." Paramount among these truths is a realization that "happiness lies not in the mere possession of money," that morals and ethics must not be sacrificed in "the mad chase of evanescent profits," and that our "true destiny is not to be ministered unto but to minister to ourselves and our fellow men."

> In the final paragraphs, the author summarizes the main ideas discussed in the study.

Vocabulary Development

Multiple Meanings
Discuss that many words have multiple meanings, and that readers have to figure out the relevant meanings to make sense of what they are reading. Point out the given multiple meanings of these three words, and discuss which meanings are used in the article.

fog: condensed water vapor, new growth of grass, a blur on a picture, a hazy sense of reality.
Answer: In the article, *fog* means "a hazy sense of reality."

assess: to determine value of property, to make a judgment, to test students.
Answer: In the article, *assess* means to make a judgment.

paralyze: to make powerless to make wise choices, to cause to physically not be able to move.
Answer: In the article, both meanings of *paralyze* are used.

Assessment Practice

Reading: Distinguishing Fact From Opinion

Directions: *Choose the letter of the best answer to each question about the historical research study.*

1. Which statement from the text is an opinion?
   - A "An inauguration is a beginning. . . ."
   - B "Our kind has conquered worse in the past."
   - C "In 1921 polio threatened first to kill him."
   - D "He evoked the . . . image of a plague of locusts."

2. Which statement from the text is a fact?
   - A "He began by asking the American people to sweep aside the 'nameless, unreasoning, unjustified terror.'"
   - B "Only a foolish optimist can deny the dark realities."
   - C "Roosevelt was 'not one to blink at disaster.'"
   - D "The only thing we have to fear is fear itself."

3. Which statement from the text is an overgeneralization?
   - A "Taxes have risen; our ability to pay has fallen."
   - B "They know only the rules of a generation of self-seekers."
   - C "Happiness is not in the mere possession of money."
   - D "This great nation will endure as it has endured."

Reading: Comprehension and Interpretation

Directions: *Write your answers on a separate piece of paper.*

4. What does Axelrod mean when he says that fear is a fog, "an obscurer of truth"? **[Generating]**

5. How does Axelrod support his belief that Roosevelt "navigated between the radically new . . . and the age-old and unchanging"? **[Analyzing]**

6. **(a)** Note two points at which Axelrod summarizes a section of the speech. **(b)** How effectively does each summary express the main idea of the original? Support your answer with details. **[Evaluating]**

Timed Writing: Analysis [Critical Stance]

Write an **analytical essay** discussing Axelrod's attitude toward President Roosevelt's views of the Great Depression. Address these questions: Does Axelrod approve of Roosevelt's words and outlook? Does he seem convinced by his arguments? Use details to support your conclusions. **(30 minutes)**

Reading Informational Materials: Historical Research Study ■ 519

Reading: Distinguishing Fact from Opinion

1. B
2. A
3. B
4. **Possible response:** Axelrod means that focusing on fear rather than on the problem at hand can cause one to think less clearly about potential solutions.
5. **Possible response:** Roosevelt shows his radically new ideas with the plans that make up the "New Deal." He shows his age-old and unchanging attitudes through his use of biblical allusions.
6. (a) Two points of summary: The paragraph beginning "Lift the fog of fear . . ." and the paragraph beginning "The failure was a failure of . . ."
   (b) **Possible response:** Each summary does an adequate job of expressing the main idea of the original. For example, in the first summary, Axelrod summarizes FDR's biblical metaphor by saying, "The Great Depression was not of . . . supernatural, or inevitable origin."

Timed Writing

- Read the Timed Writing instructions together as a group. Remind students that their essays should answer whether Axelrod approved of Roosevelt's words and outlook and whether he is convinced by Roosevelt's speech. Make sure they plan to support each part with examples from the historical research study.

- Suggest that students plan their time to give 10 minutes to planning, 15 minutes to writing, and 5 minutes to reviewing and revising.

Extend the Lesson

Historical Research Study
To give students more practice with historical research studies, have them choose an event, a speech, or a document from the past. Have them develop theses about the importance of their chosen events, speeches, or documents and support the theses with examples and facts. Allow time for students to share their historical research studies.

Students will

1. analyze and respond to humorous essays.

2. compare the effect of humor in two essays.

3. write a comparison of humorous essays.

*See **TeacherExpress™/Lesson View** for a detailed lesson plan for Comparing Literary Works.*

Literary Analysis
❶ Humorous Essay

• Read aloud the instruction about humorous essays.

• **Ask** students why humor might be an effective technique to use in writing an essay.
Possible response: Everyone likes to laugh, and a lighthearted essay might be less intimidating to read than one that uses a more serious tone.

• Point out the figures of speech often included in humorous essays: hyperbole and understatement.
Ask students for examples of each of these terms.
Sample answers: Hyperbole: Her feet were as long as skis. Understatement: After staying up for 48 hours straight, he was a little tired.

❷ Comparing Humorous Essays

• Point out that humorous essays can explore serious topics and issues in a lighthearted way. As students compare the two selections, they will see how humor can be used to convey serious messages.

• Give students a copy of **Comparing Humorous Essays Graphic Organizer A** (*Graphic Organizer Transparencies,* p. 116). Have them complete it as they read and compare the selections.

❶ Humorous Essay

A **humorous essay** is a form of nonfiction writing intended to make the reader laugh. In some forms of humorous writing, often described as harsh or biting, authors ridicule their subjects. In other forms of humorous writing, often described as gentle, authors treat their subjects with affection even as they make fun of them.

Humorous writing can include one or more of the following figures of speech:

• **hyperbole:** intentional (and sometimes outrageous) overstatement, or exaggeration—for example, describing a small patch of ice as a "vast, frozen wasteland."

• **understatement:** the presentation of an idea, a person, or an event in a way that makes it seem less than it is—for example, describing a huge loss as a "minor" setback.

In addition to these techniques, the writer's comic **diction,** or word choice, may include funny names, slang, or other examples of verbal humor.

❷ Comparing Humorous Essays

Although humorous writing is meant to entertain, it can have other purposes as well. For example, humor can be used to convey a serious message.

Use an organizer like the one shown to identify the serious issues or ideas addressed in "The Talk" and "Go Deep to the Sewer." Then, think about the reasons the authors may have chosen to use humor to explore these issues.

Vocabulary Builder

The Talk

■ **renegade** (ren′ ə gād′) *adj.* disloyal; traitorous (p. 523) *The renegade ballplayer signed up with the rival team.*

■ **feisty** (fīs′ tē) *adj.* full of spirit; energetic (p. 523) *The feisty monkey took the banana from the visitor.*

Go Deep to the Sewer

■ **lateral** (lat′ ər əl) *adj.* sideways (p. 526) *The rock climber moved up and then scaled in a lateral direction.*

■ **interpretation** (in tur′ prə tā shən) *n.* a subjective explanation (p. 529) *His interpretation helped me understand the complicated play.*

"Go Deep to the Sewer"

Detail
"I spent many happy years . . . hoping that a football would hit me before a Chevrolet did."

↓

Issue
Cosby lacked open space in which to play.

Vocabulary Development

Vocabulary Knowledge Rating
Create a **Vocabulary Knowledge Rating Chart** with the selection vocabulary and expressive vocabulary for both selections. Give students a copy. Introduce the words by reading them aloud and having students mark their rating in the Before Reading column. Urge them to be alert to these words as they read and discuss the selection because they will rate their knowledge of the words again after they finish.

If you wish, you may tally how many students know (or think they know) a word to gauge how much instruction you need to provide. As students read, point out the words and their context.

Build Understanding

❸ Connecting to the Literature

Reading/Writing Connection As these essays demonstrate, the experiences of childhood can provide great material for humorists. Briefly describe a childhood event that you might find funny later in life. Use at least three of the following words: *derive, imply, react, anticipate, provoke.*

Meet the Authors

Gary **Soto** (b. 1952)

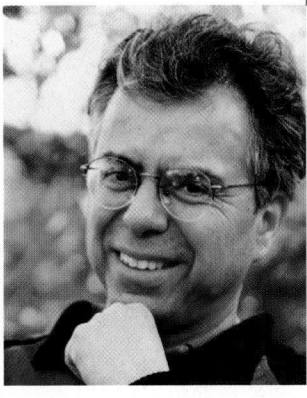

Gary Soto grew up in a Mexican American section of Fresno, California. As a child, he wanted to be either a priest or a scientist who studies fossils and bones. Then, in high school, he discovered great writers, including John Steinbeck and Robert Frost. In college, Soto started writing poetry.

Favorite Pastime Soto's favorite pastime is reading. He has said, "It appears these days I don't have much of a life because my nose is often stuck in a book. But I discovered that reading builds a life inside the mind." Soto has written several award-winning novels, short stories, and books of poetry.

Bill **Cosby** (b. 1937)

Bill Cosby grew up in the housing projects of Philadelphia, Pennsylvania. Although he left high school to join the navy, he earned a diploma through a correspondence course.

Finding Humor During the 1960s, Cosby began performing stand-up comedy. He based many of the characters in his early comedy routines, including Fat Albert and Junior Barnes, on school friends. Cosby has won numerous awards for his television shows and for his books. He has also earned a doctoral degree in education and several honorary degrees.

Go Online
Author Link

For: More information about the authors
Visit: www.PHSchool.com
Web Code: epe-9313

The Talk / Go Deep to the Sewer ■ 521

---

❸ Connecting to the Literature

- Model the expressive vocabulary students are asked to use with these examples:

  1. I can now *derive* pleasure from this memory, but it was embarrassing at the time.

  2. In first grade, I brought my snake, Seymour, to show-and-tell; I did not mean to *imply* that he was friendly.

  3. Seymour couldn't bite, but he would *react* aggressively when he felt threatened or annoyed.

  4. Maria did not *anticipate* Seymour's anger when she poked him to make sure he was real.

  5. After Seymour spit on her, the rest of the class knew not to *provoke* him.

- Help students further develop their expressive vocabulary by providing these words: *insisting, observe, regret, remarkable.* Encourage students to use these words as they discuss the selections.

Go Online
Author Link For additional information about Gary Soto and Bill Cosby, have students type in the Web Code and then select *Gary Soto* or *Bill Cosby.*

Teaching Resources

The following resources can be used to enrich, extend, or differentiate the instruction for Comparing Literary Works.

Unit 3 Resources, pp. 179–185

Graphic Organizer Transparencies,
pp. 116–119

Listening to Literature Audio CD (Includes "The Talk" only.)

521

Gary Soto Gary Soto often draws upon the memories of his childhood in Fresno, California, to provide inspiration for his writing. Unlike many writers from working-class backgrounds, however, Soto does not just write about the people he grew up with; he also writes *for* them, using language that is common and accessible. His insistence on making his work available to a broad audience, along with his ability to write from personal experience, has made him a popular writer with many kinds of readers.

2 Motivation

Ask students to list concerns or fears that adolescents commonly have about growing up. Write their ideas on the board, and then ask students to consider whether such concerns are realistic, comical, or misguided. Tell them that the selection they are about to read focuses on two boys who are worried that their appearances will prevent them from being happy in the future.

Concept Connector ➡

Students will follow up on this activity after completing "The Talk."

3 About the Selection

In "The Talk," Gary Soto recalls a poignant conversation as he and a friend wait for a beautiful girl to appear at her window. Although they are only twelve, the two boys have planned their adult lives in detail. As they share their dreams for the future, they discuss what they see as their biggest obstacle to happiness: their appearances. While maintaining a light tone, Soto describes the feelings of being young, poor, and insecure.

4 Critical Viewing

Possible response: Based on the title, students might guess that the essay will involve a serious conversation. The picture suggests that the conversation is somehow related to life in a small town among people who are neither extremely wealthy nor extremely poor.

THE TALK
Gary Soto
1
2
3

Ｍy best friend and I knew that we were going to grow up to be ugly. On a backyard lawn—the summer light failing west of the mulberry tree where the house of the most beautiful girl on the street stood—we talked about what we could do: shake the second-base dirt from our hair, wash our hands of frog smells and canal water, and learn to smile without showing our crooked teeth. We had to stop spitting when girls were looking and learn not to pile food onto a fork and into a fat cheek already churning hot grub.

We were twelve, with lean bodies that were beginning to grow in weird ways. First, our heads got large, but our necks wavered, frail as crisp tulips. The eyes stayed small as well, receding into pencil dots on each side of an unshapely nose that cast remarkable shadows when we turned sideways. It seemed that Scott's legs sprouted

4 ▲ Critical Viewing
Based on this image and title, what topics do you think the author of this essay might discuss? Explain. **[Predict]**

522 ■ Types of Nonfiction

Vocabulary Development

Vocabulary Builder Reinforcement
Students will benefit from additional examples and practice with the Vocabulary Builder words. Reinforce their comprehension with "show-you-know" sentences. The first part of the sentence uses the vocabulary word in an appropriate context. The second part of the sentence—the "show-you-know" part—clarifies the first. Model this strategy with this example:

The *renegade* soldier was caught leaking information; she will probably go to jail for her disloyalty.

Then, give students these sentence prompts, and coach them in creating the clarification part:
1. The *renegade* writer was bored with words; _____.
   Possible response: she decided to try painting instead
2. The *feisty* puppy ran around in circles; _____.
   Possible response: it needed to release some of its energy

muscle and <u>renegade</u> veins, but his arms, blue with ink markings, stayed short and hung just below his waist. My gangly arms nearly touched my kneecaps. In this way, I was built for picking up grounders and doing cartwheels, my arms swaying just inches from the summery grass.

We sat on the lawn, with the porch light off, waiting for the beautiful girl to turn on her bedroom light and read on her stomach with one leg stirring the air. This stirred us, and our dream was a clean dream of holding hands and airing out our loneliness by walking up and down the block.

When Scott asked whom I was going to marry, I said a brown girl from the valley. He said that he was going to marry a strawberry blonde who would enjoy Millerton Lake, dirty as it was. I said mine would like cats and the sea and would think nothing of getting up at night from a warm, restless bed and sitting in the yard under the icy stars. Scott said his wife would work for the first year or so, because he would go to trade school[1] in refrigeration. Since our town was made with what was left over after God made hell, there was money in air conditioning, he reasoned.

⑤ I said that while my wife would clean the house and stir pots of nice grub, I would drive a truck to my job as a carpenter, which would allow me to use my long arms. I would need only a stepladder to hand a fellow worker on the roof a pinch of nails. I could hammer, saw, lift beams into place, and see the work I got done at the end of the day. Of course, she might like to work, and that would be okay, because then we could buy two cars and wave at each other if we should see the other drive by. In the evenings, we would drink Kool-Aid and throw a slipper at our <u>feisty</u> dog at least a hundred times before we went inside for a Pop-Tart and hot chocolate.

Scott said he would work hard too, but now and then he would find money on the street and the two of them could buy extra things like a second TV for the bedroom and a Doughboy swimming pool for his three kids. He planned on having three kids and a ranch house on the river, where he could dip a hand in the water, drink, and say, "Ahh, tastes good."

But that would be years later. Now we had to do something about our looks. We plucked at the grass and flung it into each other's faces.

"Rotten luck," Scott said. "My arms are too short. Look at 'em."

"Maybe we can lift weights. This would make up for our looks," I said.

---

1. trade school school that specializes in teaching the skills needed to work in a particular job.

The Talk ■ 523

Vocabulary Builder
renegade (ren´ ə gād´) *adj.* disloyal; traitorous

Literary Analysis
Humorous Essay
Which details of the boys' youthful dreams might seem funny later in life?

Vocabulary Builder
feisty (fīs´ tē) *adj.* full of spirit; energetic

 ⑥ **Reading Check**

What are the boys worried they will be like when they grow up?

---

⑤ Literary Analysis
Humorous Essay

• Read aloud the bracketed passage, and point out that it describes the boys' dreams of the work they will do and the women they will marry. **Ask** students to summarize the boys' current situation.
Answer: The boys are at a particularly awkward phase of adolescence, yearning for a girl beyond their reach.

• **Ask** the Literary Analysis question: Which details of the boys' youthful dreams might seem funny later in life?
Possible response: Adults would probably find it funny that the boys expect to drink Kool-Aid and eat Pop Tarts when they are adults.

• Remind students that humorous essays often deal with serious topics. Have students **identify** the serious issue raised in the last bracketed paragraph.
Answer: The boys are worried about their looks.

⑥ Reading Check

Answer: The boys are worried that they will be ugly.

523

Humorous Essay

- Read the bracketed passage. Point out that Scott's statement is humorous and disturbing at the same time.

- **Ask** the Literary Analysis question: What serious issue does Scott's statement raise? Explain.
  Answer: The statement raises the issue that nice-looking people are often treated better or given more opportunities in society; people are often judged by their physical appearance alone.

❽ **Critical Thinking**
Speculate

- Read aloud the bracketed passage, and then remind students that Soto comments on a serious problem using elements of humorous writing.

- **Ask** students how the essay might have been different had Soto used a serious tone and no humor.
  Possible response: The essay would have seemed more sad and bleak. Readers might have pitied the boys instead of identifying with them.

Concept Connector

Have students return to the Motivation activity on p. 522. Ask students to compare the boys' fears with those they listed previously. Discuss how the boys might eventually overcome their concerns.

ASSESS

Answers

1. Students might say that they identify with the boys' insecurity.

2. (a) Scott wants to repair air conditioners. The narrator wants to be a carpenter. (b) **Possible response:** The boys seem prepared to work hard at physical trades and to be good providers for their families. They probably draw their strong work ethics and vocational plans from observation of the men in their community.

3. (a) No, it seems like the boys have watched her before. They are familiar with her routine of reading on the bed. (b) The girl seems to represent beauty and

524

---

❼ "I don't think so," Scott said, depressed. "People like people with nice faces."

He was probably right. I turned onto my stomach, a stalk of grass in my mouth. "Even if I'm ugly, my wife's going to be good-looking," I said. "She'll have a lot of dresses and I'll have more shirts than I have now. Do you know how much carpenters make?"

Then I saw the bedroom light come on and the beautiful girl walk into the room drying her hair with a towel. I nudged Scott's short arm and he saw what I saw. We flicked the stalks of grass, stood up, and walked over to the fence to look at her scrub her hair dry. She plopped onto the bed and began to comb it, slowly at first because it was tangled. With a rubber band, she tied it back, and picked up a book that was thick as a good-sized sandwich.

Scott and I watched her read a book, now both legs in the air and twined together, her painted toenails like red petals. She turned the pages slowly, very carefully, and now and then lowered her face into the pillow. She looked sad but beautiful, and we didn't know what to do except nudge each other in the heart and creep away to the front yard.

"I can't stand it anymore. We have to talk about this," Scott said.

"If I try, I think I can make myself better looking," I said. "I read an article about a girl whitening her teeth with water and flour."

❽ So we walked up the street, depressed. For every step I took, Scott took two, his short arms pumping to keep up. For every time Scott said, "I think we're ugly," I said two times, "Yeah, yeah, we're in big trouble."

Thinking About the Selection

1. **Respond:** What were your feelings for the boys as you read this essay? Explain.

2. **(a) Recall:** What jobs do the boys hope to have when they get older? **(b) Infer:** What do the boys' choice of future jobs suggest about their characters? Explain.

3. **(a) Infer:** Do you think this is the first time the boys have watched the beautiful girl? Why or why not? **(b) Draw Conclusions:** What does the girl in the window seem to represent for the two young boys?

4. **Speculate:** What advice do you think an adult might give the two boys to help them feel better about themselves?

Literary Analysis
Humorous Essay
What serious issue does Scott's statement raise? Explain.

---

the kind of life that is just out of the boys' reach. Merely looking at her causes the boys to think about their futures.

4. **Possible responses:** Everyone feels awkward when they are young and changing. They will almost certainly outgrow their current awkwardness.

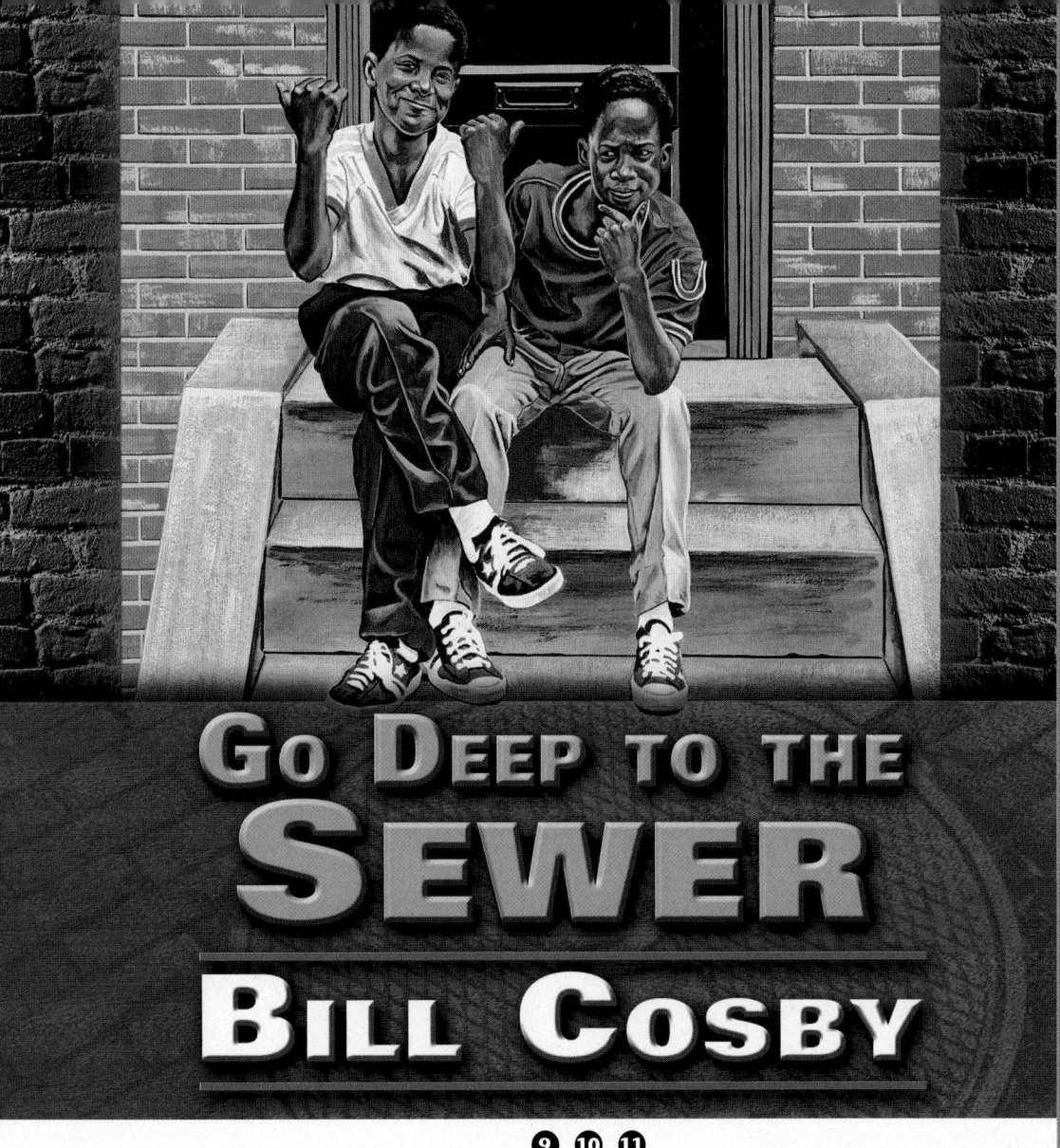

GO DEEP TO THE SEWER
BILL COSBY

9 10 11

The essence of childhood, of course, is play, which my friends and I did endlessly on streets that we reluctantly shared with traffic. As a daring receiver in touch football, I spent many happy years running up and down those asphalt fields, hoping that a football would hit me before a Chevrolet did.

12 ▲ Critical Viewing
Based on this picture and the title, what do you anticipate about the topic of this essay? **[Predict]**

Go Deep to the Sewer ■ 525

⓭ **Critical Viewing**

Answer: Manhole covers like the one shown were among the few stationary objects on the street where Cosby played games. Because of this, they were useful for marking the field of play.

My mother was often a nervous fan who watched me from her window.

"Bill, don't get run over!" she would cry in a moving concern for me.

"Do you see me getting run over?" I would cleverly reply.

And if I ever had been run over, my mother had a seat for it that a scalper[1] would have prized.

Because the narrow fields of those football games allowed almost no <u>lateral</u> movement, an end run was possible only if a car pulled out and blocked for you. And so I worked on my pass-catching, for I knew I had little chance of ever living my dream: taking a handoff and sweeping to glory along the curb, dancing over the dog dung like Red Grange.

The quarterback held this position not because he was the best passer but because he knew how to drop to one knee in the huddle and diagram plays with trash.

⓮ "Okay, Shorty," Junior Barnes would say, "this is you: the orange peel."

"I don' wanna be the orange peel," Shorty replied. "The orange peel is Albert. I'm the gum."

---

1. **scalper** (skalp´ er) *n.* person who buys tickets and sells them later at higher than regular prices.

Vocabulary Builder
lateral (lat´ ər əl) *adj.* sideways

⓭ ▼ **Critical Viewing**
Why were manhole covers, like the one shown, useful for defining the field of play in the ballgames Cosby played as a child? **[Connect]**

526 *Types of Nonfiction*

Vocabulary Development

Vocabulary Builder Reinforcement
To reinforce and assess students' comprehension of the Vocabulary Builder words, give them sentences in which the word may or may not be used correctly. Students must tell whether the use is correct and explain their answer. Use these sentences:

1. The *lateral* ski lift went straight up the mountain.
   Answer: No, *lateral* is not used correctly. It means sideways, not straight up.

2. My *interpretation* of the symbolism in the novel was different from my classmate's.
   Answer: Yes, *interpretation* is used correctly. Because they are personal explanations, interpretations can differ from person to person.

"But let's make 'em think he's the orange peel," I said, "an' let 'em think Albert's the manhole."

"Okay, Shorty," said Junior, "you go out ten steps an' then cut left behind the black Oldsmobile."

"I'll sorta go in it first to shake my man," said Shorty, "an' then, when he don' know where I am, you can hit me at the fender."

14

"Cool. An' Arnie, you go down to the corner of Locust an' fake takin' the bus. An' Cos, you do a zig out to the bakery. See if you can shake your man before you hit the rolls."

"Suppose I start a fly pattern to the bakery an' then do a zig out to the trash can," I said.

"No, they'll be expecting that."

I spent most of my boyhood trying to catch passes with the easy grace of my heroes at Temple;[2] but easy grace was too hard for me. Because I was short and thin, my hands were too small to catch a football with arms extended on the run. Instead, I had to stagger backwards and smother the ball in my chest. How I yearned to grab the ball in my hands while striding smoothly ahead, rather than receiving it like someone who was catching a load of wet wash. Often, after a pass had bounced off my hands, I returned to the quarterback and glumly said, "Jeeze, Junior, I don' know what happened." He, of course, knew what had happened: he had thrown the ball to someone who should have been catching it with a butterfly net.

15

Each of these street games began with a quick review of the rules: two-hand touch, either three or four downs, always goal-to-go, forward passing from anywhere, and no touchdowns called back because of traffic in motion. If a receiver caught a ball near an oncoming car while the defender was running for his life, the receiver had guts, and possibly a long excuse from school.

I will never forget one particular play from those days when I was trying so hard to prove my manhood between the manholes. In the huddle, as Junior, our permanent quarterback, dropped to one knee to arrange the garbage offensively, I said, "Hey, Junior, make me a decoy on this one."

Pretending to catch the ball was what I did best.

"What's a decoy?" he said.

"Well, it's—"

"I ain't got time to learn. Okay, Eddie, you're the Dr Pepper cap an' you go deep toward New Jersey."

"An' I'll fool around short," I said.

"No, Cos, you fake goin' deep an' then buttonhook at the DeSoto. An' Harold, you do a zig out between 'em. Somebody get free."

---

2. Temple Temple University in Philadelphia, Pennsylvania.

Go Deep to the Sewer ■ 527

Literary Analysis
Humorous Essay
What is funny about these plays?

Literary Analysis
Humorous Essay
What serious issues about playing in the street do the rules reveal?

 Reading Check

What do the boys use to "diagram" their plays?

527

⑰ Literary Analysis

- Have a volunteer read the bracketed passage.
- **Ask** the first Literary Analysis question: Which details about playing at night are exaggerated?
Answer: The darkness of evening play is exaggerated, as is the staggering around of the players in the dark. Cosby's claim that the football could have been seen "only on radar screens" is also exaggerated.

⑱ Literary Analysis
Humorous Essay

- Point out to students that when they are trying to entertain their friends with a personal story, they often exaggerate for humorous effect. **Ask** students which figure of speech involves exaggeration.
Answer: Exaggerating for humorous effect is hyperbole.

- **Ask** the second Literary Analysis question: Which statements about Spaldeens are examples of hyperbole? Explain.
Answer: Students may cite assertions about a Spaldeen's bounciness and the possibilities of hitting one into orbit or into another neighborhood as examples of hyperbole. Cosby is stretching a characteristic into an impossibility.

Moments later, the ball was snapped to him and I started sprinting down the field with my defender, Jody, who was matching me stride for stride. Wondering if I would be able to get free for a pass sometime within the next hour, I stopped at the corner and began sprinting back to Junior, whose arm had been cocked for about fifteen seconds, as if he'd been posing for a trophy. Since Eddie and Harold also were covered, and since running from scrimmage was impossible on that narrow field, I felt that this might be touch football's first eternal play: Junior still standing there long after Eddie, Harold, and I had dropped to the ground, his arm still cocked as he tried to find some way to pass to himself.

But unlimited time was what we had and it was almost enough for us. Often we played in the street until the light began to fade and the ball became a blur in the dusk. If there is one memory of my childhood that will never disappear, it is a bunch of boys straining to find a flying football in the growing darkness of a summer night.

There were, of course, a couple of streetlamps on our field, but they were useful only if your pattern took you right up to one of them to make your catch. The rest of the field was lost in the night; and what an adventure it was to refuse to surrender to that night, to hear the quarterback cry "Ball!" and then stagger around in a ⑰ kind of gridiron blindman's buff.

"Hey, you guys, dontcha think we should call the game?" said Harold one summer evening.

"Why do a stupid thing like that?" Junior replied.

"'Cause I can't see the ball."

"Harold, that don't make you special. Nobody can see the ball. But y' know it's up there."

And we continued to stagger around as night fell on Philadelphia and we kept looking for a football that could have been seen only on radar screens.

One day last year in a gym, I heard a boy say to his father, "Dad, what's a Spaldeen?"

This shocking question left me depressed, for it is one thing not to know the location of the White House or the country that gave its name to Swiss cheese, but when a boy doesn't know what a Spaldeen is, our educational system has failed. For those of you ⑱ ignorant of basic American history, a Spaldeen was a pink rubber ball with more bounce than can be imagined today. Baseball fans talk about the lively ball, but a lively baseball is a sinking stone compared to a Spaldeen, which could be dropped from your eye level and bounce back there again, if you wanted to do something boring with it. And when you connected with a Spaldeen in stickball, you put a pink rocket in orbit, perhaps even over the

528 ■ *Types of Nonfiction*

Literary Analysis
Humorous Essay
Which details about playing at night are exaggerated?

Literary Analysis
Humorous Essay
Which statements about Spaldeens are examples of hyperbole? Explain.

Vocabulary Development

Expressive Vocabulary
As students are discussing Cosby and his friends, encourage them to use the expressive vocabulary presented earlier. You might encourage them with sentence starters like these:

1. From their games, Cosby and his friends *derive* . . .
2. Their use of improvised equipment might *imply* . . .
3. If a car moved during play, they would *react* . . .
4. Cosby did not *anticipate* . . .
5. The sight of their street play might *provoke* . . .

18 house at the corner and into another neighborhood, where it might gently bop somebody's mother sitting on a stoop.

I love to remember all the street games that we could play with a Spaldeen. First, of course, was stickball, an organized version of which is also popular and known as baseball. The playing field was the same rectangle that we used for football: it was the first rectangular diamond. And for this game, we had outfield walls in which people happened to live and we had bases that lacked a certain uniformity: home and second were manhole covers, and first and third were the fenders of parked cars.

One summer morning, this offbeat infield caused a memorable <u>interpretation</u> of the official stickball rules. Junior hit a two-sewer **19** shot and was running toward what should have been third when third suddenly drove away in first. While the bewildered Junior tried to arrive safely in what had become a twilight zone, Eddie took my throw from center field and tagged him out.

"I'm not out!" cried Junior in outrage. "I'm right here on third!"

Vocabulary Builder
interpretation (in tur′ prə tā′ shən) *n.* a subjective explanation

20 ✓ Reading Check

What is a Spaldeen?

21 ◀ **Critical Viewing**
How do you think this stickball player compares to the boys in Cosby's essay? **[Compare]**

19 **Literary Analysis**
Humorous Essay

- **Ask** students to summarize the action in the bracketed passage.
Answer: Junior is running toward third base, which is a car. The car drives away, and Junior is tagged out.

- **Ask** students what is humorous about the story that Cosby presents here.
Answer: The thought of parts of the children's playing field driving away adds to the humor of the essay. The image of cars as bases is amusing.

20 **Reading Check**

Answer: A Spaldeen is a pink rubber ball that bounces easily.

21 **Critical Viewing**

Possible response: Like the children in the essay, this player seems to be involved in an informal game. He has no uniform and the bat seems to be improvised.

529

- Have a volunteer read aloud the bracketed passage. Then, **ask** students to respond to the Literary Analysis question: How do the details about "mobile" first base and the postman add to the humor here?
Answer: When a car that is serving as first base drives away, it heightens the hilarity of Fat Albert's slowness. The ball hitting the postman is another amusing image.

- **Ask** students to identify the figure of speech that Cosby uses most often for humorous effect.
Answer: Cosby often uses hyperbole.

Concept Connector

Have students return to the Motivation activity on p. 525. Ask volunteers to compare Cosby's description of childhood games with the experiences that students previously shared.

ASSESS

Answers

1. Some students might appreciate the adventure of playing these sports under difficult circumstances; others might prefer a more orderly setup.

2. (a) He describes himself as short and thin. (b) He could not catch passes easily. (c) **Possible response:** Cosby seems to remember these games fondly, so it does not seem that his size affected his enjoyment.

3. (a) They used cars and manholes as bases. (b) Cosby's description of the playing space suggests that the people in his neighborhood were poor but made the most of what they had.

4. (a) Children need more than anything else to play and to imagine. (b) Most students will agree that children need opportunities to play.

---

19 And he did have a point, but so did Eddie, who replied, not without a certain logic of his own, "But third ain't there anymore."

22 In those games, our first base was as mobile as our third; and it was a floating first that set off another lively division of opinion on the day that Fat Albert hit a drive over the spot from which first base had just driven away, leaving us without a good part of the right field foul line. The hit would have been at least a double for anyone with movable legs, but Albert's destination was first, where the play might have been close had the right fielder hit the cutoff man instead of a postman.

"Foul ball!" cried Junior, taking a guess that happened to be in his favor.

"You're out of your mind, Junior!" cried Albert, an observation that often was true, no matter what Junior was doing. "It went right over the fender!"

"What fender?"

"If that car comes back, you'll see it's got a fender," said Albert, our automotive authority.

However, no matter how many pieces of our field drove away, nothing could ever take away the sweetness of having your stick connect with a Spaldeen in a magnificent whoppp and drive it so high and far that it bounced off a window with a view of New Jersey and then caromed back to the street, where Eddie would have fielded it like Carl Furillo[3] had he not backed into a coal chute.

---

3. **Carl Furillo** baseball player for the Brooklyn Dodgers in the 1950s.

Thinking About the Selection

1. **Respond:** Would you enjoy playing stickball or football by the rules Bill Cosby describes? Explain.

2. **(a) Recall:** How does Cosby describe his physical size as a child? **(b) Analyze Cause and Effect:** How did Cosby's physical limitations affect his skill at football? **(c) Make a Judgment:** Do you think Cosby's physical size affected his enjoyment of the games? Explain.

3. **(a) Interpret:** What neighborhood features were part of the "diamond" on which Cosby and his friends played stickball? **(b) Analyze:** What does Cosby's description of the playing space show about the people who live in his neighborhood?

4. **(a) Speculate:** What does Cosby mean when he says, "The essence of childhood . . . is play"? **(b) Evaluate:** Do you agree with this idea? Explain.

530 ■ Types of Nonfiction

Vocabulary Development

Vocabulary Knowledge Rating
When students have completed reading and discussing "The Talk" and "Go Deep to the Sewer," have them take out their **Vocabulary Knowledge Rating Chart.** Read the words aloud once more and have students rate their knowledge of the words again in the After Reading column. Clarify any words that are still problematic. Have students write their own definition and example or sentence in the appropriate column. Then, have students complete the **Vocabulary Builder Practice** activities on p. 531. Encourage students to use the words in further discussion and written work about these selections. Remind them that they will be accountable for these words on the Selection Test.

Apply the Skills

The Talk • Go Deep to the Sewer

Comparing Humorous Essays

1. **(a)** Use a chart like the one shown to identify at least one example of **hyperbole,** one example of **understatement,** and one example of comic **diction** in each **humorous essay.**

Type	The Talk	Go Deep to the Sewer
Hyperbole		
Understatement		
Comic Diction		

(b) Explain how each example adds to the humor of the essay.

2. **(a)** In which story does the author use unusual or funny names as a humorous technique? **(b)** How do these names help paint a comic portrait of the people they indicate?

3. Would you describe the humor of these essays as harsh or gentle? Explain your answer using details from the texts.

Writing to Compare Literary Works

In an essay, discuss and compare the serious ideas expressed in each of these essays. Consider why the authors chose to present these issues through humor. Use these questions to get started:
- What challenges do the children in both essays face?
- What challenges do they face in their futures?
- What circumstances do you think may have added to those challenges? Note specific details from each essay that support your ideas.
- How does the use of humor help suggest that these challenges can be overcome?

Vocabulary Builder

Practice Review the vocabulary list on page 520. Then, answer each question. Explain your answer.

1. If you needed an employee who followed the rules, would you hire a *renegade* worker?
2. Would a tired animal be *feisty*?
3. Is someone's *interpretation* of an event the absolute truth?
4. Would someone climbing a ladder move in a *lateral* direction?

QuickReview

Humorous Essay: nonfiction writing intended to make the reader laugh

Assessment
For: Self-test
Visit: www.PHSchool.com
Web Code: epa-6311

In this Skills Review, students apply the skills taught in Part 2. The test format gives students practice in taking standardized tests. The result of this review test will help you check students' readiness for the **Benchmark Test** for Unit 3, Part 2.

Applying Reading Skill

Read the passage with students. Guide students in identifying the clues to the meaning of the subject in item 1: the passage implies that there is competition to be dominant in space exploration. If necessary, have students review the instruction on p. 472. Then have them complete the remaining items on their own.

Applying Vocabulary Skills

Remind students of the Latin prefixes *ante-* and *inter-*. Refer students to the definitions of these prefixes on p. 473. Point out that applying the meanings of these prefixes to the vocabulary questions can help them to answer the items.

Tips for
Test Taking

When taking a timed test, tell students to read through the questions quickly, answering those which they definitely know. Once they have answered those questions, they should go back and answer the rest of the questions. Remind them that if time is running out, it is usually better to make an educated guess than to leave a question blank.

Reading

Directions: *Questions 1–5 are based on the following passage.*

Those who came before us made certain that this country rode the first waves of the industrial revolution, the first waves of modern invention, and the first wave of nuclear power, and this generation does not intend to founder in the backwash of the coming age of space. We mean to be a part of it—we mean to lead it. For the eyes of the world now look into space, to the moon and to the planets beyond, and we have vowed that we shall not see it governed by a hostile flag of conquest, but by a banner of freedom and peace. We have vowed that we shall not see space filled with weapons of mass destruction, but with instruments of knowledge and understanding. . . .

We set sail on this new sea because there is new knowledge to be gained, and new rights to be won, and they must be won and used for the progress of all people. . . .

—from "Speech at Rice University, Houston, Texas, 1962"
by President John F. Kennedy

1. **What is the subject of the passage?**
   A nuclear power
   B the space race
   C America's past achievements
   D important sea voyages

2. **What idea is the author trying to persuade his audience to accept?**
   A The industrial revolution was important.
   B Exploration is important.
   C Space travel is important.
   D America must be the most powerful nation.

3. **To what emotion in the audience does the first sentence appeal?**
   A to pride
   B to anger
   C to fear
   D to despair

4. **The second paragraph opens with which type of appeal?**
   A appeal to emotion
   B appeal to reason
   C appeal to authority
   D appeal to statistics

5. **How does the speaker use sound to add to the persuasive appeal in the phrase "new knowledge to be gained, and new rights to be won"?**
   A It has an internal rhyme.
   B It uses parallel structure.
   C It adds new ideas.
   D It is a musical phrase.

532 ■ Types of Nonfiction

ASSESS

Answers

1. B	9. C
2. C	10. A
3. A	11. D
4. A	12. B
5. B	13. C
6. D	14. A
7. B	15. B
8. A	

Assessment Practice

Vocabulary

Directions: *Choose the word that best completes the sentence.*

6. No one knew what he intended to _____ by his absence.
   A anticipate
   B derive
   C texture
   D signify

7. What information can you _____ from this report?
   A participate
   B derive
   C display
   D contribute

8. I _____ the plot twist at the end of O'Henry's story.
   A anticipate
   B derive
   C participate
   D signify

9. We were glad to hear that she had no _____ injuries from the accident.
   A structural
   B textural
   C internal
   D trivial

10. The sweater had a very rough _____.
    A texture
    B illumination
    C anticipation
    D equivalence

Directions: *Complete each sentence with the correct word.*

11. Her _____ in other people's business was annoying.
    A antecede
    B antebellum
    C intersection
    D interference

12. This _____ mansion was built just before the Civil War began.
    A antecede
    B antebellum
    C intersection
    D interference

13. Many auto accidents have occurred at this _____.
    A antecede
    B antebellum
    C intersection
    D interference

14. The highest-ranking officer should _____ the others.
    A antecede
    B intercept
    C intersection
    D interference

15. They were able to _____ his message and learn of his plot.
    A antecede
    B intercept
    C antedate
    D interference

Reading and Vocabulary Skills Review ■ *533*

If students answer any of these questions incorrectly, have them review the instruction on the following pages in Part 2 before taking the **Benchmark Test.**

Question	Pages Where Instruction Is Located:
1	474, 492
2	474, 492
3	474, 492
4	474, 492
5	474, 492
6	473
7	473
8	473
9	473
10	473
11	512
12	490
13	512
14	490
15	512

Benchmark

Administer the **Benchmark Test** for Unit 3, Part 2. If the Benchmark Test reveals that some students need further work, use the Interpretation Guide to determine the appropriate reteaching page in the **Reading Kit.** You will also find the same instruction and practice available on **Success Tracker.**

Go Online
Vocabulary
For: Interactive Crossword Puzzle
Visit: www. PHSchool.com
Web Code: epj-5302
Give students this Web Code to access an interactive crossword puzzle using Academic Vocabulary and Vocabulary Skill words from Part 2.

Students will

1. learn about the strengths and weaknesses of spell-checker programs.
2. learn how to check for correct spellings using the dictionary.

Tools for Checking Spelling

- Emphasize to students that good writers always check their spelling before submitting their work. Students should become familiar with the various reference tools to help them spell correctly.

- Explain that spell-checker programs can only do what they have been programmed to do: identify mis-spelled words that have been listed in the program. They cannot rec-ognize words that are spelled cor-rectly but used incorrectly.

Dictionaries

- Point out to students that if a word is not in common use, they may need to go to a more complete dictionary or an unabridged dic-tionary to find the spelling.

- Tell students that if they cannot find the word in the dictionary, they might try looking up a syn-onym of the word to see whether the word is listed in the definition or in the list of synonyms.

- Explain to students that if they need to find the spellings of newer terms, they must consult an up-to-date dictionary.

𝒲𝒢 Writing and Grammar, Gold Level

Students will find additional spelling instruction in Chapter 31, Section 4.

Spelling Workshop

Tools for Checking Spelling

Sometimes it is hard to be sure that you have spelled certain words correctly. Fortunately, there are reference tools that can help you.

Computer Spell-checkers Most word-processing programs contain a feature that signals when you have typed a word incorrectly and suggests a replacement. Remember that computer programs can only check the words in their database. Here are some cautions about spell-checking programs:

- The program cannot tell you if you used the wrong homonym.
- It cannot tell if you have typed a title or proper name incorrectly.
- It cannot tell if you used the wrong word. The difference between "I bruised my knee" and "I braised my knee" is significant.
- The program may not always know the correct spelling for a word, especially if you are using a word that is not commonplace.

The e-mail was supposed to say "Take the boat around," not "aground."

Dictionaries Follow these steps to find spellings in a dictionary:

- **Check the first letters of a word.** Think of homophones for that sound.
- **Check the other letters.** Once you spell the first sound correctly, try sounding out the rest of the word. Look for likely spellings in the dictionary. If you don't find your word, look for more unusual spellings of the sound.

Practice Write one paragraph that contains errors a spell-checker would not find. Include at least four words from the list. Exchange paragraphs with a partner. Circle the errors and write the corrections.

534 ■ Types of Nonfiction

Word List

waste

waist

eliminate

once

ounce

illuminate

colleagues

February

literally

metaphorically

Teaching Resources

The following resource can be used to enrich or extend the instruction for this Spelling Workshop.

Unit 3 Resources
Spelling Workshop: Tools for Checking Spelling, p.194

Monitor Your Progress

Assessment Practice

Directions: There are errors in the following sentences. Some are misspellings. Others are problems with homonyms or other words used by mistake. Write the number of each sentence and the corrections it needs. If a sentence has no errors, write "none."

1. A small new mall has opened up in our busy city neighborhood.

2. Through not all the stores are filled yet, the ones I have seen so far look interesting.

3. The first store to open was a women's butique.

4. Its window is filled with stilish cloathes that girls my age would love to wear.

5. My friends and I can hardly wait to go inside.

6. There is also a small office supply store.

7. This should be useful for buying paper, ink cartriges, and other computer needs.

8. One really wired store looks like a haunted house from the outside.

9. In the window are groteskque masks and small carved gnomes.

10. Crazy black streamers hang for the ceiling.

11. The rumor is that a physic will be working part time there.

12. That place will be very useful the next time we play charades or have a costume party!

13. The director was literally beside himself with frustration.

14. Foreshadowing is when an author gives you clues to what is going to happen.

15. The sea goddess that loved Odysseus was Calypso.

16. James Thurber characterized Mitty as sort of absentminded.

17. We asked our parents to leave us go to the play.

18. I like football more then tennis.

19. He might of given us another chance; we didn't do anything horrible!

20. It is further to her house than we thought.

Answers

Practice

1. none
2. Though
3. boutique
4. stylish, clothes
5. none
6. supply
7. cartridges
8. weird
9. grotesque
10. from
11. psychic
12. none
13. delete "literally"
14. change "to" to "about"
15. change "that" to "who"
16. delete "sort of"
17. change "leave" to "let"
18. change "then" to "than"
19. change "of" to "have"
20. change "further" to "farther"

Tips for Improving Spelling

Tell students that one way to find spelling errors is to start at the bottom of their papers and read backward, focusing on the words one at a time. In this way, they will focus on each word, not on the meaning of the text, and they may find those errors that they would tend to miss as they become involved in the meaning of the words.

Students will

1. write an editorial.
2. use writing strategies to generate ideas, organize, evaluate, and revise the editorial.
3. apply grammar skills.

From the Author's Desk

Show students Segment 3 on Rebecca Walker on *From the Author's Desk DVD.* Discuss how when writing editorials, students should research information and use Rebecca Walker's technique of combining factual information with their own opinions.

Writing Genres

Using the Form Point out to students that editorial writing is often included in other types of writing. Mention these examples:

- Letters to the editors of newspapers and magazines are usually editorials in letter form.

- Speeches often include editorial elements.

- Position papers, which state a person or company's beliefs, may include editorial writing.

Writing Workshop
Work in Progress

If students have done the **Work-in-Progress** assignments throughout Part 2, suggest that they examine their recorded ideas as they begin prewriting. They may have an idea in their portfolios that they wish to develop into an editorial.

 Online Essay Scorer

A writing prompt for this mode of writing can be found on the *PH Online Essay Scorer* at PHSuccessNet.com.

536

Persuasion: Editorial

One decisive and public way to take a stand on an issue is to write an **editorial**. An editorial is a brief persuasive essay that presents and defends an opinion. In this workshop, you will write an editorial on a subject of your choice.

Assignment Write an editorial about an issue that confronts your school or community.

What to Include Your editorial should feature the following elements:
- A clear thesis statement—a statement of your position on an issue
- Evidence that supports your position and anticipates your readers' counterarguments
- Effective organization
- Persuasive language that emphasizes your arguments
- Error-free grammar, including correct use of parallel structures

To preview the criteria on which your editorial may be assessed, see the rubric on page 543.

Writing Workshop: *Work in Progress*

If you have completed the Work-In-Progress assignments, you have in your portfolio several ideas you might wish to pursue in your editorial. You may continue to develop these ideas, or you might choose to explore a new idea as you complete this Writing Workshop.

536 ■ *Types of Nonfiction*

Using the Form
You may use elements of this form in these types of writing:
- letters to the editor
- position papers
- speeches

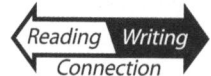
Reading **Writing** *Connection*

To get a feel for editorials, read "Libraries Face Sad Chapter" by Pete Hamill on page 483.

Teaching Resources

The following resources can be used to enrich or extend the instruction for the Writing Workshop.

Unit 3 Resources
 Writing Workshop: Persuasion: Editorial, p. 192
 Writing Workshop: Integrating Grammar Skills: Revising to Create Parallelism, p. 193

General Resources
 Rubrics for Persuasion: Persuasive Essay, pp. 53–54

From the Author's Desk DVD
 Rebecca Walker, Segments 3 and 4

Prewriting

Choosing Your Topic

To select a topic for your editorial, use one of the following strategies:

- **Scan newspapers.** As you page through a newspaper, look for stories that matter to you on a personal level. Notice articles that describe situations that strike you as unfair, foolish, or harmful. Use one of these news stories as a topic for your editorial.

- **Work with a partner.** Pair up with a classmate, and brainstorm for topics that are important to each of you, noting those that cause the most disagreement. Select an issue that has compelling arguments on both sides. Then, choose a position to support.

Narrowing Your Topic

Write a thesis statement. After reviewing the information you have in hand, decide which part of the issue to address. Write your opinion about the topic in one sentence. That sentence is your thesis statement, an expression of your position that you must now prepare to defend.

Gathering Details

Consider all sides of an issue. Gather evidence from a wide variety of sources. In a chart like the one shown, record evidence on both sides of an issue. Do not ignore information that contradicts or opposes your position. Your editorial will be more persuasive if you acknowledge and overcome opposing viewpoints. Plan to include summaries of opposing positions in order to refute them.

Support for school uniforms	Opposition to school uniforms
Reduce violence and discrimination	Take choice away from students
Create positive school image	Cause resentment among students

Appeal to logic and emotion. Effective persuasion speaks to both thought and feeling.

- *Logic:* Make a list of ideas, facts, and details that will make people think and analyze rather than feel.
- *Emotion:* Brainstorm for relevant anecdotes, or brief stories, descriptions, and personal examples that will affect readers' emotions. Quickly jot these down. As you work, experiment with language that carries strong emotional connotations:

Neutral connotation: Megan continues to work.
Strong connotation: Megan soldiers on.

Work in Progress
Review the work you did on pages 491 and 513.

Writing Workshop ■ 537

Prewriting

- Make a list of news stories on the board. Lead students in a discussion about the stories, giving students a chance to voice and develop their opinions about the issues. Help students **choose topics** about which they have strong opinions.

- To help students **narrow their topics** by developing thesis statements, tell them to answer this question: What is my position on this topic?

- Tell students to **gather details** in support of their thesis statements by collecting quotations and facts. Tell students to keep track of any ideas and phrases that are not their own so that they will remember to give appropriate credit.

Six Traits Focus

✔ Ideas	Word Choice
Organization	Sentence Fluency
Voice	Conventions

WG **Writing and Grammar, Gold Level**
Students will find additional instruction on prewriting for an editorial in Chapter 7, Section 2.

Writing and Grammar Interactive Textbook CD-ROM

Students can use the following tools as they complete their editorials:

- Pros and Cons Chart
- Transition Word Bin
- Editing Tool

Tips for
Using Rubrics

- Before students begin work on this assignment, have them preview the Rubric for Self-Assessment on p. 543 to know what is expected.

- Review the Assessment criteria in class. Before students use the Rubric for Self-Assessment, work with them to rate the student model by applying one or two criteria to it.

- If you wish to assess students' essays with a 4-point, a 5-point, or a 6-point scoring rubric, see *General Resources,* pp. 53–54.

Drafting

- As students rank their points, tell them to ask themselves this question: Which point will be most important to their intended audience?

- Write this example on the board and have students rank the points according to their persuasiveness:

  Thesis: Citizens should pay extra taxes to have the residential streets repaved.

  Intended Audience: Homeowners who move frequently

  Point 1: Repaving the streets would make driving smoother.

  Point 2: Repaving the streets would raise property value.

  Point 3: Repaving the streets would make the community more presentable.

  Have students state the reasoning behind their rankings.
  Possible Answer: Ranked from the most important—Point 2, Point 3, Point 1. Financial concerns would be most important to the audience. Resale values would also be affected by the physical appearance of the community.

- As students collect supporting evidence, have them mark each piece of evidence with a +, indicating a fact, or a –, indicating an opinion. Have students make sure that their facts outweigh their opinions.

- Have students review their supporting evidence and determine effectiveness by writing an *S* above statistical evidence, an *E* above expert opinions, a *P* above personal observations, and a *T* above testimonials.

Six Traits Focus

✔	Ideas	Word Choice
✔	Organization	Sentence Fluency
	Voice	Conventions

W G **Writing and Grammar, Gold Level**
Students will find additional instruction on drafting an editorial in Chapter 7, Section 3.

Writing Workshop

Drafting

Shaping Your Writing

Create a structure for your draft. Plan a strategy for presenting your ideas.

- **Evaluate your arguments.** Review all the points that support your thesis, and consider their impact on your intended audience. Then, rank them according to their persuasiveness.

- **Use an outline.** Use your ranking to write an outline showing order-of-importance organization. Start with your least important point and build toward your most persuasive point. In addition, be sure to indicate where you will address counterarguments. The chart shown demonstrates order-of-importance organization for an editorial.

Providing Elaboration

Distinguish between fact and opinion. Your thesis and arguments are statements of opinion that must be validated or supported with evidence. Facts—information that can be proved true—are the strongest evidence. Weak arguments pile opinions on top of opinions; strong arguments back opinions with relevant facts.

Provide evidence. For each point you make, produce convincing support. Types of effective evidence include the following:

- **Statistics:** numbers that show the impact of an issue or a proposal

- **Expert opinions:** the viewpoints or advice of those who have relevant training and experience

- **Personal observations:** your own experiences with the topic

- **Testimonials:** statements from observers that reinforce an argument

Organizing Your Arguments

↓

Present thesis statement.

↓

Present arguments to support thesis.

↓

Address counterarguments.

↓

Provide strongest argument in support of thesis.

↓

Conclude by restating thesis and presenting a memorable final thought or quotation.

To read the complete student model, see page 542.

Student Model: Supporting Opinion With Fact

While students' safety is often cited as a leading justification for requiring uniforms, safety hits the bottom of the list in a press release from the National Association of Elementary School Principals.

The writer supports his opinion with a meaningful fact—one that references the expert opinions of school principals.

Tips for Using Technology in Writing

Tell students that they should always question facts obtained from Internet sources. Point out that some commercial sites—those with addresses ending in .com—feature propaganda and can be unreliable. Tell them that reputable commercial sites, such as the *New York Times*, exist as well.

Tell students that educational and government sites—those with addresses ending in .edu and .gov—are usually reliable. Point out that even these sites, however, should be critically assessed.

Encourage students to ask these questions when using information from any Web site:

- Who is the author? Why is the author qualified to write on this subject?

- Why is the author writing on this subject? Does the author have a bias?

- Who sponsors the Web site? Does this sponsor have a bias on the topic?

- How does the information compare to information from other sources?

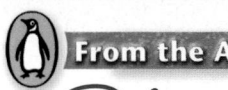

From the Author's Desk

Rebecca Walker

On Choosing the Right Details

Rebecca
Walker

This excerpt is from the introductory essay to a book I edited about new perspectives on masculinity. I think about what I am going to write for a long time, maybe months, before committing my thoughts to the page. Long before I sat down to write, I knew I would prompt readers to think about masculinity in new ways by using this personal exchange between my son and me. What I didn't know was how I would finish the piece.

"Taking one's initial impulse to completion, that's the challenge . . ."
———Rebecca Walker

Professional Model:
from *What Makes a Man:*

After a big bowl of his favorite pasta, he sat on a sofa in my study and read his science textbook as I wrote at my desk. . . . As we worked under the soft glow of paper lanterns, . . . I could feel a shift as he began to remember, deep in his body, that he was home, that he was safe, that he didn't have to brace to protect himself from the expectations of the outside world.

I wanted to convey a sense of peace and relaxation, so I added this detail to draw the reader into the tranquility of the "scene."

An hour or so passed like this before he announced that he had a question. . . . "I've been thinking that maybe I should play sports at school."

. . . I cocked my head to one side. "What brought this on?"

"I don't know," he said. "Maybe girls will like me if I play sports."

Excuse me?

I used italics here to suggest my surprise and outrage, and to reinforce a direct and intimate connection with the reader.

My boy is intuitive, smart, and creative. . . . At the time he loved animals, Japanese anime, . . . and everything having to do with snowboarding. He liked to help both of his grandmothers in the garden. He liked to read science fiction . . . and was beginning what I thought would be a lifelong love affair with chess.

I included actual things my son enjoyed to add authenticity and texture, and to provide a strong counterpoint to sports.

Maybe girls would like him if he played sports?

From the Author's Desk: Rebecca Walker ■ 539

 From the Author's Desk

Rebecca Walker

- Show students Segment 3 on Rebecca Walker on *From the Author's Desk DVD.* Discuss how Walker uses details to reinforce the goal that she has for the writing.

- Tell students that details can be used to convey the "feeling" of a setting. Give students the example of a deteriorated abandoned house as a setting. **Ask** students for a detail that could be put in the story to convey the scary "feeling" of the house.
  Possible response: The writer could use the detail of cold, biting air blowing through the broken jagged glass of the windows.

- **Ask** students how Walker's *"Excuse me?"* expression reinforces a connection with the reader.
  Possible response: The expression gives the reader a glance into the thought process of the narrator, showing the reader the narrator's true feelings about her son's request.

- Write the following two sentences on the board:
  1. *We walked through the unkept yard.*
  2. *We stepped over the mounds of trash and waded through the yard's knee-high tall grass.*

  Ask students which sentence gives more authenticity and texture. Have students explain their answers.
  Answer: Sentence 2 uses very specific details to make the description of the yard vivid and believable.

Revising

- Have students share their drafts in small groups. Have them write down questions and counterarguments that come to mind during the discussion. Tell students to address these issues as they make their revisions.

- Suggest that students write the opposing arguments they will address on self-sticking removable notes. Tell them to scan their drafts and stick the notes on the paragraphs where they can logically address these opposing views. After students have applied all of their notes, have them write their arguments and incorporate them into their essays.

- As students revise, have them focus on opportunities to replace weak verbs with strong verbs and overused and non-specific nouns and adjectives with vigorous, specific nouns and adjectives. Provide these additional examples. Have students choose the stronger, more exact verbs, nouns, and adjectives.

   1. *The mayor needs to show* (courageous, good) *leadership.*

   2. *We* (demand, want) *action on the proposal.*

   3. *The park's board of directors should* (grasp, take) *this opportunity.*

   4. *The* (leaders, city council) *has/have a responsibility to maintain our parks.*

Answers: *1. courageous, 2. demand, 3. grasp, 4. city council*

Six Traits Focus

✔	Ideas	✔	Word Choice
✔	Organization		Sentence Fluency
	Voice		Conventions

𝒲𝒢 Writing and Grammar, Gold Level

Students will find additional instruction for revising an editorial in Chapter 7, Section 4.

Revising

Revising Your Overall Structure

Revise to address readers' concerns. Not all of your readers will agree with your position. Show them that you are aware of their questions and understand their concerns.

- Review your draft and highlight controversial claims that a critic of your position would oppose.
- To make sure you understand each opposing argument, write a summary that captures its main idea and line of reasoning.
- For each claim, develop strong counterarguments that you can back up with explanations and evidence.
- Find a point in your editorial where you can include this information smoothly.

To read the complete student model, see page 542.

Student Model: Revising to Address the Opposition

Dress codes make the difference where it counts. ˄*They keep students safe while forcing them* ~~Students need~~ to do nothing other than make sure their clothes meet acceptable standards.

> Those who promote uniforms over dress codes are often concerned with safety, so the author revises to address that issue.

Revising Your Word Choice

Choose powerful words. To be persuasive, your essay should include words that convey meaning and emotion. Look at these examples:

Ordinary: Some adults *dislike* today's student fashions.
Powerful: Some adults *deplore* today's student fashions.

Ordinary: Joanna *did not want* to wear a uniform.
Powerful: Joanna *refused* to wear a uniform.

Review your earlier experiments with words that carry strong connotations. Determine whether to use those word choices.

Peer Review: Exchange drafts with a partner. Review each other's work, highlighting weak words that could be replaced by stronger ones. Then, revise your draft, replacing ordinary language with words that will make your readers feel and think. After you have made your revisions, exchange drafts with your partner again. Discuss whether the new word choices are effective.

Tips for Test Taking

Encourage students to use online dictionaries and thesauruses to replace weak nouns, verbs, and adjectives with more vivid, precise words. Tell students that when they use online thesauruses they should check the definitions of synonyms to make sure that the words fit the context of their writing.

Integrating Grammar Skills

Revising to Create Parallelism

Parallelism is the use of similar grammatical forms or patterns to express similar ideas. Effective use of parallelism adds rhythm and balance to your writing and strengthens connections among your ideas.

Sample Parallel Forms	
Nouns	sharp eyes, strong hands, deft fingers
Verbs	to ask, to learn, to share
Phrases	treating people fairly, being honest
Adverb clauses	when I am happy, when I am peaceful
Adjective clauses	those who read with care, those who act with concern

Identifying Nonparallel Constructions Parallel constructions place equal ideas in words, phrases, or clauses of similar types. Nonparallel constructions present equal ideas in an unnecessary mix of grammatical forms, producing awkward, distracting shifts for readers.

Nonparallel: Dress codes are less restrictive, less costly, and are not a controversial system.

Parallel: Dress codes are less restrictive, less costly, and less controversial.

Fixing Nonparallel Constructions To revise faulty parallelism, follow these steps:

1. **Identify similar or equal ideas within a sentence.**
2. **Determine whether the ideas are expressed in the same form**—for example, all nouns or all prepositional phrases.
3. **Rewrite the sentence so that all the elements match the stronger pattern.** Choose forms that produce the smoothest rhythm or require the fewest words.

Apply It to Your Editing

Review several paragraphs in your editorial, highlighting any sentences in which you present a series of ideas. In each case, make sure the constructions are parallel. If they are not, revise them.

Integrating Grammar Skills

- Read aloud the examples of nonparallel and parallel sentences.
- Guide students in an evaluation of each of the two sentences by asking these questions: Which is more rhythmic? Which is more memorable? Which is more effective? Lead students to understand that parallelism is more rhythmic, which makes it more memorable and effective.
- Provide students with these additional examples of sentences without parallelism and have them work individually to revise the statements for parallelism. **Ask** volunteers to share their revisions with the class.

  1. *I like riding my bike along the lake even more than I like to swim in it.*

  Answer: *I like riding my bike along the lake even more than I like swimming in it.*

  2. *The helicopter hovered above the treetops and then began swooping down toward the valley.*

  Answer: *The helicopter hovered above the treetops and then swooped down toward the valley.*

  3. *The audience was more ecstatic, more responsive, and it appreciated the performance more.*

  Answer: *The audience was more ecstatic, more responsive, and more appreciative of the performance.*

- After students revise their editorials for parallel construction, have them read their revised sentences aloud, evaluating the rhythm.

Differentiated Instruction   Solutions for All Learners

Strategies for English Learners
Tell students that understanding the connotations of words is important when revising word choices. Explain that a word's connotation is the feeling and mood that the word evokes. For example, *relaxed* and *lazy* have similar meanings but different connotations. Explain that *relaxed* has a more positive connotation. Tell students that it suggests a casual, at-ease attitude, whereas the connotation of *lazy* reflects an unwillingness to make an effort or a refusal to work.

Tell students that dictionaries will help them understand the connotations of words. Explain that sometimes dictionaries explain the differences, but usually they must look up a word, study the example sentences, and infer the connotation.

541

Student Model

- Explain that the Student Model is a sample and that their own editorials may be longer.

- Point out that the thesis statement is in the first paragraph, but it is not the first sentence. Tell students that the writer explains the situation first and places the thesis at the end, where it has greater impact.

- Explain that including information from a published press release adds credibility to Braden's arguments.

- **Ask** students to explain whether they think that Braden's evidence is convincing.
  Possible response: His evidence is convincing because it is factual and detailed.

- **Ask** students to identify the additional insight the writer offers in the concluding paragraph.
  Answer: The writer suggests that dress codes will help with violence and discrimination in schools.

Writing Genres

Persuasive Writing and Speaking Point out to students that they will use the techniques of persuasive writing in everyday situations. For example, persuasion could be used to try and convince a friend to go hiking instead of swimming. Students could also use persuasion when writing a note requesting a teacher's permission to attend a special event instead of class. Point out to students that as they grow older, they may choose careers, such as law, sales, or business management, in which persuasion plays an important role.

Student Model: Braden Danbury
Cumming, Georgia

Dress Codes May Succeed
Where School Uniforms Have Failed

School uniforms are becoming increasingly popular as a way to combat school violence and discrimination. Uniforms, while they may help somewhat, cause problems of their own. Students argue that it is their right to wear what they choose and uniforms violate that right. A less strict code is the answer to both of these problems, keeping appropriate attire in the school while allowing individuals to choose what they wear.

> The author offers a clear thesis statement in the form of a proposal that addresses a key problem.

Uniforms require students to wear specific shirts and pants or skirts, thus eliminating the element of choice. School uniforms may cause friction between students and school officials, which can have negative consequences. Dress codes, on the other hand, are less restrictive than school uniforms and cause less resentment among students. Students enjoy choosing what to wear to school each day, coordinating what they wear with how they feel.

While students' safety is often cited as a leading justification for requiring uniforms, safety hits the bottom of the list in a press release from the National Association of Elementary School Principals. In fact, safety ranks below such trivial things as school image. This calls into question why uniforms are touted as the answer to school safety issues.

> Braden finds a way to deal with counterarguments based on safety concerns.

Dress codes make the difference where it counts. They keep students safe while forcing them to do nothing other than make sure their clothes meet acceptable standards. An added benefit of dress codes is that schools with uniform policies pay much more than schools with dress codes. Schools with uniforms have to design, order, sell, and distribute the uniforms they wish to have for their school. In addition, school officials spend time and resources making sure they receive payment for uniforms. These expenses may be hidden, but they are real. Dress codes are much less expensive to implement and follow.

> Braden offers evidence that supports his position.

With the rise in school violence, students and their dress often come under suspicion and scrutiny. In addition, the wide variety of clothing in our high schools may lead students to make prejudicial judgments about each other. Dress codes address the problems of violence without causing resentment among students. They are less strict, giving the students more freedom in how they dress, while allowing school officials to set general guidelines. The amount of money it would take to implement a dress code is a fraction of the cost of school uniforms. Dress codes are not the only answer, but they are a step toward combating violence and discrimination in the schools.

> The author restates his thesis and summarizes his evidence. He also offers an additional insight.

542 ■ *Types of Nonfiction*

Tips for
Test Taking

Remind students that when they take written tests, it is important to read the writing prompt carefully. A good strategy is to look for key words in the prompt. For example, if they see words such as *persuasive, opinion,* or *think* in the prompt, students should recognize them as clues about what to expect in the rest of the prompt and to determine how to respond.

Editing and Proofreading

Check your draft for errors in format, grammar, and punctuation.

Focus on Spelling: An editorial that includes spelling errors loses its authority to convince. Check the spelling of each word. Look for words that you frequently misspell and make sure they are correct.

Publishing and Presenting

Consider one of the following ways to share your writing.

Deliver an oral presentation. Use your editorial as the basis for an oral presentation about your topic. As you speak, be sensitive to your audience. If they seem confused or doubtful, modify your word choice to clarify your ideas. After you finish, take a poll to determine whether or not you convinced your audience of your position.

Submit your editorial to a newspaper. Send your work to the school or community newspaper, or condense it into a letter to the editor.

Reflecting on Your Writing

Writer's Journal Think about the experience of writing an editorial. Begin by answering these questions:
- What new information have you learned about your topic?
- What did you learn about the process of writing persuasively? Do these insights apply to other types of writing?

Prentice Hall Writing and Grammar Connection: Chapter 7

Rubric for Self-Assessment

To assess your editorial, use the following rubric:

Criteria	Rating Scale
	not very very
Focus: How clearly does your thesis statement express an opinion?	1 2 3 4 5
Organization: How effectively do you organize your arguments?	1 2 3 4 5
Support/Elaboration: How well do you use evidence to support your position?	1 2 3 4 5
Style: How powerful is your use of persuasive language?	1 2 3 4 5
Conventions: How correct is your grammar, especially your use of parallel structures?	1 2 3 4 5

Differentiated Instruction — Solutions for All Learners

Strategies for Special Needs Students
Some students might be effective oral communicators, while others may communicate more effectively in writing. Help them choose methods of publishing their work that complement their strengths and promote confidence.

Strategies for English Learners
Students who are not yet proficient in English may need additional help with proofreading. You might work with each student to create a proofreading checklist that meets his or her specific needs. The list may include such items as verb tense, subject-verb agreement, pronoun-antecedent agreement, and homophones.

Editing and Proofreading

- Invite students to suggest words that they find themselves frequently misspelling, such as *canceled, harass,* or *nickel.*
- Begin a class word bank of frequently misspelled words and have students add to it throughout the year.

Six Traits Focus

Ideas	Word Choice
Organization	Sentence Fluency
Voice	✔ Conventions

ASSESS

Publishing and Presenting

- Encourage students to take, along with ending polls, preliminary polls to understand how students feel about the issues before they hear the editorials.

- Have listeners respond to the oral presentations with constructive criticism. Give students the following questions to formulate their feedback: Which point was most convincing? Were counterarguments addressed effectively? What additional arguments could be given to support the speaker's position?

- If students' editorials or letters are published, have them create a classroom display focusing on the theme of "Being Heard."

Reflecting on Your Writing

- Lead students in a discussion of the reflecting questions. Then ask students to respond to these additional questions: Do you feel that your argument is convincing? How comfortable are you with the persuasive writing process?

- Have students focus on parts of the assignment that gave them the greatest difficulty. Ask them to brainstorm future solutions to these problems.

WG Writing and Grammar, Gold Level

Students will find additional instruction on editing, proofreading, publishing, and presenting a persuasive essay in Chapter 7, Sections 5 and 6.

543

Meeting Your Standards

Students will

1. organize the content and learn as much as possible about the audience for a persuasive speech.

2. deliver a persuasive speech using appropriate eye contact, hand gestures, and volume and tone of voice.

Organizing Content

- Point out to students that gathering evidence is a crucial part of creating a persuasive speech; it is difficult for listeners to refute a speech that is backed by solid evidence. Tell students that their evidence must come from reliable sources and be verifiable. **Ask:** What types of sources provide reliable information? **Possible answers:** Students may cite experts in the field that the speech will address; *.gov, .edu,* and some *.org* websites; reputable journals and magazines; encyclopedias; reputable newspapers.

- Tell students that learning about their audience will reveal how much background information they need to include in their speech. For example, if a speaker knows beforehand that listeners' are likely to oppose the speech, the speaker can include types of information that are little known or that show flaws in the opposing position but buttress the speaker's position.

Giving the Speech

- Remind students that enunciating their words is vital for the success of the speech. If the speaker mumbles or cannot be heard clearly, the audience will be bored, no matter how persuasively the speaker has constructed the speech.

Assess the Activity

To evaluate students' delivery, use the Listening: Evaluating a Persuasive Presentation rubric, p. 79 in *General Resources.*

Delivering a Persuasive Speech

Persuasion is not merely a knack of public speaking; it is a valuable life skill that enables you to successfully present ideas and proposals. These speaking strategies can help you refine your persuasive speaking skills.

Organizing Content

Once you have determined your position on an issue, gather and arrange your evidence. You may want to use an order-of-importance organization, beginning with less-important points and leading up to your strongest argument. The Rating Evidence chart can help you assess the relative value of various types of evidence.

Know your audience. Understanding your audience offers a triple advantage. It allows you to:

- adjust word choice and evidence to the interests, cultural background, and knowledge levels of your listeners.

- anticipate questions and counterarguments. You can often disarm skeptical listeners by discussing and refuting their ideas.

- respond to the listeners' self-interests by showing how they are affected by the issue and might benefit from your proposals.

Rating Evidence

1. **Facts:** Provable statements about reality
2. **Statistics:** Numerical information about reality
3. **Expert opinions:** Informed viewpoints based on specialized training and observation
4. **General opinions:** Interesting but not necessarily reliable viewpoints
5. **Your opinion:** What needs to be proved by facts, statistics, and expert opinions

Giving the Speech

Effective persuasion begins in assurance. Demonstrate confidence in your ideas by your posture, bearing, and facial expression.

- Make eye contact with all your listeners, not just one or two people.
- Vary the volume and tone and pacing of your voice to emphasize key points and to keep your audience engaged.
- Edit your speech for Standard English grammar, syntax, and diction. Use slang only if it is appropriate for your audience and purpose.
- Include rhetorical devices, such as repetition or parallelism, to emphasize key ideas.
- Use hand gestures to support what you are saying.

Activity ▶ *Prepare and Deliver a Persuasive Speech* ▶ Choose a position on a current local or national issue about which you have strong feelings. Develop a persuasive speech in which you take a stand on this issue, and deliver it before your class. Then, poll your classmates to see if your speech has altered their perspective on the issue.

544 ■ Types of Nonfiction

Differentiated Instruction   Solutions for All Learners

Strategy for English Learners

Suggest that these students choose a topic with which they are familiar and for which they can find non-technical or local oral sources. If students are using oral sources, point out that they need to interview people who know the issue well and are considered experts.

Suggest that students take along a tape recorder when they interview their sources. Remind them that they should not record their sources unless they have received the interviewee's permission. Also, suggest that before they begin the interview, they record the interviewee's name, the date, and the time of the interview. Point out that during the interview they can also ask the interviewee to clarify any unclear ideas or technical vocabulary.

Once students have recorded the interview, they can listen to the recording and write words they do not understand and look these up in a dictionary.

Biography and Autobiography

Prentice Hall, 2000

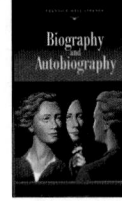

Anthology This collection of excerpts from twenty-two biographies and autobiographies presents glimpses into the compelling lives of fascinating and accomplished individuals.

Places Left Unfinished at the Time of Creation

John Philip Santos
Penguin Books, 1999

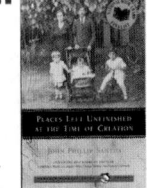

Memoir In this memoir, John Philip Santos weaves together dream fragments, family remembrances, and Chicano mythology, reaching back in time and place to blend the story of one Mexican family with the soul of an entire people. The story unfolds through unforgettable family figures: from Madrina, who was touched with epilepsy and prophecy ever since, as a girl, she saw a dying soul leave its body, to Teofilo, who was kidnapped as an infant and raised by the Kikapu Indians of Northern Mexico. At the heart of the book is Santos's search for the meaning of his grandfather's suicide in San Antonio, Texas, in 1939.

Narrative of Sojourner Truth

Sojourner Truth
Penguin Books, 1998

Autobiography Sojourner Truth was a woman transformed by the experience of slavery and the exhilaration of liberation. Born Isabella, she was emancipated when New York State outlawed slavery in 1827. Isabella cast aside her slave name and took the name Sojourner Truth, which more fully expressed her new mission in life. Truth embarked on a career as a prominent abolitionist and fiery orator, demanding the end of slavery in the United States. *Narrative of Sojourner Truth,* which describes her early life as a slave, was dictated by Truth to a neighbor and first published in 1850.

Touch the Top of the World

Erik Weihenmayer
Plume, 2002

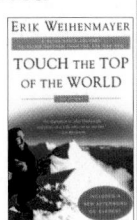

Nonfiction Adventure When Erik Weihenmayer realized he had an eye disorder that would leave him sightless by the age of thirteen, he lost hope that he could ever live a full life. This book tells the story of his phenomenal road back from the brink of despair. Helped by his family and his own driving will to succeed, Weihenmayer disregards all of society's assumptions about the limitations of blindness, becoming a teacher and a world-class mountaineer.

These titles are available in the Penguin/Prentice Hall Literature Library.
Consult your teacher before choosing one.

For Further Reading ■ 545

Planning Students' Further Reading

Discussions of literature can raise sensitive and often controversial issues. Before you recommend further reading to your students, consider the values and sensitivities of your community as well as the age, ability, and sophistication of your students. It is also good policy to preview literature before you recommend it to students. The notes below offer some guidance on specific titles.

[L4] *Biography and Autobiography Anthology* Sensitive issues include the racist attitudes of the 1940s and the actions of the Ku Klux Klan in "Separate But Equal?" "At Last I Kill a Buffalo" includes details of killing and skinning a buffalo. Other sensitive issues include world upheavals discussed in "Pen Pals"; gender discrimination in "Because You're a Girl"; social pressure on women to marry and settle down rather than be adventurous in "First Wings"; the challenges facing disabled individuals in "My Experience with ALS"; and the issue of South African apartheid in "Long Walk to Freedom."
Reading level appropriate for high school students

[L3] *Places Left Unfinished at the Time of Creation* Some students may be sensitive to the central idea of the memoir, which is the apparent suicide of the author's grandfather, an act kept secret by the family. Some students may find the graphic description of killing a deer to be upsetting.
Reading level appropriate for high school students

[L2] *Narrative of Sojourner Truth* Some students may feel angry and frustrated by the injustice of slavery and the many cruel acts that went unpunished. This autobiography contains disturbing references to slaves being brutally beaten and whipped, families being torn apart, and the use of racial epithets.
Reading level appropriate for high school students

[L1, L2, EL] *Touch the Top of the World* This book includes strong language and brief descriptions of gambling and spousal abuse. Some students may be upset by the sudden death of a parent and by the descriptions of the author's experience with the onset of blindness.
Reading level appropriate for high school students

Professional Development

Save the Last Word for Me

Save the Last Word for Me is an excellent strategy for developing active and reflective readers by eliciting responses to specific quotations or passages from literature.

As students read, have them copy down quotations that catch their attention. Then, have them paraphrase each quotation and react to each one. Students can begin by first writing one sentence stating their reaction and then two or three sentences explaining or justifying the reaction.

Students then gather in groups of three or four. The first student reads one of his or her quotations aloud along with the paraphrase, but not the reaction. The other group members respond to and discuss the quotation. When the others have responded, the original student then reads his or her reaction, thus having the "last word" on the quotation. The procedure continues until each person in the group has shared a statement and had the "last word" on it.

See *General Resources,* pp. 24–26, for further information on this strategy.

Using *On Your Own*

You may use this On Your Own feature in one of the following ways:

- For independent reading
- To reinforce/reteach one of the reading skills in this unit

Promote Independent Reading

Independent reading gives students an opportunity to practice the reading skills taught in this unit and to improve comprehension. When students read independently, they also increase their vocabulary and develop their own personal reading interests.

You may assign this selection to be read independently for homework, in class when students have completed other work, or for independent group work.

Develop Reading Preferences

After students have read this selection, ask them what they enjoyed about it. Build on their ideas to recommend further reading. Students who enjoy this selection might also enjoy news articles featuring unusual ideas of everyday people.

Think About It In this newspaper story, a Connecticut woman gives a whole new meaning to the expression "thinking outside the box." Her experiment of sending pumpkins through the mail caught on with postal workers and friends far and wide. Come to think of it, what packaging would be better protection from shipping damage than a tough pumpkin shell?

from **The Hartford Courant**

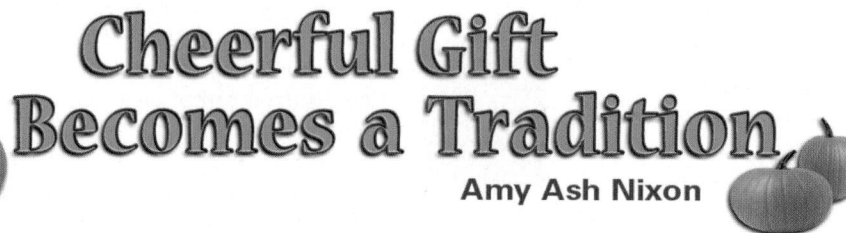

Cheerful Gift Becomes a Tradition
Amy Ash Nixon

Armed with a hand-painted pumpkin, an index card with her grandfather's Florida address and a handful of push pins, Amy Hillebrecht walked into a Plainville post office 10 years ago to see if she could mail a pumpkin without packaging it.

"He didn't have the four seasons there, and my grandmother had died a few years earlier, and I thought it would cheer him up," said Hillebrecht, who has made the pumpkin mailing an autumn ritual.

On Friday, Hillebrecht, of Southington, waited in line to send off this year's batch of five decorated pumpkins to friends as near as Southington and as far away as Colorado.

"They're pumpkins, little sugar pumpkins, but when people receive them, they say it just makes their day, and how cool is that?" asked Hillebrecht.

A special education teacher at McGee Middle School in Berlin, Hillebrecht is not sure where the notion came from, but she recalled hearing someone wondering if they could mail a peanut butter and jelly sandwich in only a plastic bag with an address label.

Hillebrecht decided to conduct her own test and came up with pumpkins. She wondered whether a pumpkin would make it to Florida unscathed.

Not only did the pumpkin reach her grandfather, but it got there with tender loving care, she said.

"The man from the post office drove it to my grandfather's condo in the front seat of his car so it didn't get damaged, and it made both their days," she said.

546 ■ *Types of Nonfiction*

Differentiated Instruction — Solutions for All Learners

Enrichment for Special Needs Students
Students with special needs often benefit from hands-on expression related to information they are learning. Have students use markers to decorate pumpkins. If real pumpkins are not available, have students create their designs on paper. Allow time for students to share their pumpkin designs.

Background for English Learners
For the benefit of students who are unfamiliar with American customs, point out that pumpkins are a common decoration and dessert item associated with fall in the United States. Ask volunteers to share ways that they decorate with pumpkins. Also, have them describe pumpkin-based food items their families enjoy.

The pumpkins are sent with nothing more than an address label taped to them and a priority mail sticker affixed to the stems.

Roy "Rocky" Roccapriore, a clerk at the Plainville Post Office, is an important part in Hillebrecht's annual mailing ritual. He's the person who helped Hillebrecht when she mailed her first pumpkin. She now goes to him each year.

On Friday morning, Roccapriore grinned a welcome and helped Hillebrecht tape the address labels on with stronger, waterproof tape.

"OK, this is the 2004 batch?" Roccapriore said. "OK. Four out of state, one in state."

Postage was about $5 to $6 apiece.

Customers waiting in line smiled at the oddity of the "packages" being weighed on the scale: fairly petite pumpkins with black hand-drawn eyes, noses and smiles with missing teeth.

Roccapriore said that Hillebrecht's pumpkin mailing is about his favorite experience as a mailman.

"You can't really put a price on doing something like this," he said. "They may only be pumpkins, but everyone smiles when they see them coming in, and I'm sure it's like that the whole way to where they're going."

One of the pumpkins mailed Friday was bound for Colorado, headed to Hillebrecht's friend, Hope Shenkman Kligerman.

Contacted shortly after her pumpkin began its journey, and unaware she was receiving one this year, Kligerman said, "Oh, oh, I'm getting one!"

"It's always so much fun to receive them," Kligerman said.

Meet the Author

Amy Ash Nixon is a general assignment reporter for *The Hartford Courant,* based in Hartford, the capital of Connecticut. The *Courant,* founded in 1764, is one of the oldest continuously published newspapers in the country.

Readings in Contemporary Culture
Talk About It

Use these questions to guide a discussion of the article.

1. (a) How did the postal workers react to Hillebrecht's first mailing?
   (b) Explain what postal worker Roccapriore meant when he said, "You can't really put a price on doing something like this."
2. In a group, consider why people give and receive gifts.
   • What factors make a gift especially valuable?
   • Whom does a gift most benefit—the giver or the receiver? Explain.

   Choose a point-person to share your group's ideas with the class.

Cheerful Gift Becomes a Tradition ■ 547

Extend the Lesson

Community Article
To give students more practice with news articles about everyday people, have them think about people they know who make a difference by doing small things. Then, have them write an article about the impact these small actions have on others. Allow time for students to share their articles.

REINFORCE/RETEACH

Motivation
Have students look at the photograph in this selection. Then, have them read the Think About It text. Ask students what they think the author will discuss in her article. Encourage them to read to learn more about the Connecticut woman's experiment.

Reading Skill
Identify Main Idea and Supporting Details

• Review the instruction on identifying the main idea and supporting details (p. 400). Remind students that they should recognize the main idea or message in a selection and then note the details that provide more information about it.

• Have students read "Cheerful Gift Becomes a Tradition."

• **Ask** students what this article is mostly about. Point out that asking them "what an article is mostly about" is the same as asking them to identify the main idea.
Possible response: A woman brings joy to many people by mailing pumpkins once a year.

• **Ask** students to identify some supporting details that provide more information about this main idea.
Possible response: The first time she mailed a pumpkin, the postal carrier kept it on the front seat of his truck and it made his day. People throughout the postal system get joy out of seeing the pumpkins. The woman's friend in Colorado says it is always fun to receive a pumpkin. The woman has mailed them once a year for the past ten years.

Readings in Contemporary Culture
Talk About It

• Suggest that students work in groups to address these questions.

• To guide student discussion, use the **Discussion Guide,** p. 39 in *General Resources.*

ON YOUR OWN

Introduce Unit 4

- Ask students to study the painting on these two pages, then to think of three words that express the color, the motion, and the feeling that they experience from the art.
- As volunteers share their three words, write them on the board as lines. Work as a class to shape these lines into a rough poetic form.
- Tell students that they may not have written a poem, but they have suggested the power of poetry to capture the emotion of an experience.

Instructional Resources

Unit 4 Resources support students in developing and mastering the unit skills and help you assess progress.

▶ **Progress Monitoring** These tests enable you to assess and monitor student progress in each part:
- **Diagnostic test**
- **Benchmark test**

▶ **Vocabulary Warm-ups** Additional vocabulary support, based on Lexile scores of vocabulary words, is provided for each selection.
- **Word List A and Practice A** provide vocabulary-building activities for students reading two grades below level.
- **Word List B and Practice B** provide vocabulary-building activities for students reading one grade below level.

▶ **Reading Warm-ups** Two Reading Warm-ups for each selection provide a context for students to apply newly learned vocabulary. Each Reading Warm-up consists of a short reading passage loosely tied to a theme in the selection. Questions and activities guide students to focus on particular vocabulary items.
- **Reading Warm-up A**, for students reading two grades below level, focuses on the vocabulary items presented in Vocabulary Warm-up A.
- **Reading Warm-up B**, for students reading one grade below level, focuses on the vocabulary items presented in Vocabulary Warm-up B.

▶ **Selection Support** These practice pages are available for each selection:
- **Reading Skills**
- **Literary Analysis**
- **Vocabulary Builder**
- **Support for Writing**
- **Support for Extend Your Learning**
- **Enrichment**

PRENTICE HALL
TeacherEXPRESS™ You may also
Plan · Teach · Assess access these
resources on TeacherExpress.

Unit 4
Poetry

Assessment Resources

Program Assessment

Unit 4 Resources
   Selection Tests A and B

TeacherExpress™
   ExamView® Test Bank
   Software

Adequate Yearly Progress Monitoring Assessment

Unit 4 Resources
   Diagnostic Tests: Part 1, Part 2
   Benchmark Tests: Part 1, Part 2

Standardized Assessment

Standardized Test Preparation Workbook

Unit 4 Overview

Introduction
Exploring Poetry

Part 1: Read Fluently

Part 2: Paraphrase

Poetry ■ *549*

Unit 4 Overview

Genre Focus
Author Pat Mora introduces the literary genre, poetry, with two poems. Students read and analyze examples of poetry.

Using the Unit Selections
Teach Skills Instructional selections are presented in sets of collections. To teach the skills and meet the objectives, you need to complete only one collection in each set.

Differentiate and Reinforce Choose the selection in a set that is best suited to your students. The selections are listed by accessibility in the Differentiated Instruction box below. You may use the other selection in the set to reinforce comprehension and skills or to provide enrichment.

Integrate Skills Each selection set gives students a reading strategy, literary analysis, and vocabulary development as well as opportunities for writing about the selection, research and technology, listening and speaking, grammar, and assessment practice.

See pages 561 and 625 for an overview of the skills in each part.

Using the Unit Features
These additional reading selections give you the opportunity to apply, reinforce, and extend the unit skills.

Reading Informational Materials Students learn to analyze and evaluate informational texts.

Comparing Literary Works Students read a pair of literary works to compare the treatment of a literary element.

On Your Own Students may read this selection independently, or you may teach it actively to reinforce a unit reading skill.

See the Unit 4 Overview and Pacing Plan on the following pages.

Differentiated
Instruction   Solutions for All Learners

Accessibility for Ability Levels
This chart gives a general accessibility rating to help you decide which selection is more appropriate for your students. For additional guidance on factors that affect the accessibility of each selection, see the **Time and Resource Manager** for each selection set.

	Accessible	**More Challenging**
Part 1		
Set 1	Collection 1	Collection 2
Set 2	Collection 1	Collection 2
Part 2		
Set 1	Collection 1	Collection 2
Set 2	Collection 1	Collection 2

549

Unit 4

OVERVIEW AND PACING PLAN — Poetry

Meeting Your Standards

Students will

1. recognize and appreciate poetry as a literary genre.
2. read and analyze a variety of poems.
3. apply reading skills.
   - Reading fluently
     - Reading in sentences
     - Using your sense
   - Paraphrasing
     - Picturing the action
     - Breaking down long sentences
4. **analyze literary elements.**
   - Figurative language
   - Sound devices
   - Narrative poetry
   - Rhyme
5. **build vocabulary.**
   - Suffixes
6. **learn elements of grammar, usage, and style.**
7. **use a recursive writing process to write in a variety of forms.**
   - Descriptive essay
   - Response to literature
8. **read informational materials.**
   - Making generalizations
   - Evaluating Web sources
9. **compare literary works.**
   - Imagery
   - Lyric poetry
10. **use technology to do research.**
    - Soundtrack
    - Illustrated version
    - Fact sheet
    - Annotated electronic database
11. **develop listening and speaking skills.**
    - Impromptu speech
    - Dramatic reading
    - Dialogue
    - Panel discussion
12. **develop spelling proficiency.**

Unit Introduction and Part 1	Week 1					Week 2					Week 3				
	1	2	3	4	5	1	2	3	4	5	1	2	3	4	5
Introduce the Unit author: Pat Mora (p. 550).	●														
Introduce poetry (pp. 552–553).	●														
Teach the Model selections (pp. 555–558).	●	●	●												
Administer the Unit 4, Part 1 Diagnostic Test.			●												
Introduce the Reading and Vocabulary Skills for Part 1 (pp. 562–563).			●												
Teach one collection from Set 1 (pp. 566–581).			●	●	●	●	●								
Teach one collection from Set 2 (pp. 592–607).							●	●	●	●					
Teach Reading Informational Materials (pp. 587–588).											●				
Teach Comparing Literary Works (pp. 614–616).												●	●		
Complete the Reading and Vocabulary Review (pp. 618–619).														●	
Have students complete the Writing Workshop (pp. 620–624).											●	●	●	●	●
Administer the Unit 4, Part 1 Benchmark Test.															●

Part 2	Week 1 ❶	❷	❸	❹	❺	Week 2 ❶	❷	❸	❹	❺	Week 3 ❶	❷	❸	❹	❺
Administer the Unit 4, Part 2 Diagnostic Test.	●														
Introduce the Reading and Vocabulary Skills for Part 2 (pp. 626–627).	●														
Teach one collection from Set 1 (pp. 630–647).		●	●	●	●										
Teach one collection from Set 2 (pp. 659–671).						●	●	●	●						
Teach Reading Informational Materials (pp. 653–654).										●					
Teach Comparing Literary Works (pp. 678–682).											●	●			
Complete the Reading and Vocabulary Review (pp. 684–685).													●		
Have students complete the Writing Workshop (pp. 688–695).										●	●	●	●	●	
Have students complete the Communications Workshop (p. 696).													●		
Have students complete the Spelling Workshop (pp. 686–687).													●		
Administer the Unit 4, Part 2 Benchmark Test.														●	

Options for Block and Daily Scheduling

The assignments and activities in this unit planner are organized by week. You may adjust them to your daily or block schedule. The Time and Resource Managers for the collection sets give specific times to help your planning.

Options for Independent Reading

Use these independent reading options to differentiate, reinforce, and extend your instruction:

On Your Own

Students may read this selection on their own or you may use it to reteach and reinforce unit skills.

Judith Ortiz Cofer, "The Serenade in Nine Innings"

For Further Reading

Have students choose and read a full-length work while working on this unit.

[L1, L2, EL] Edgar Allan Poe, *The Complete Poetry of Edgar Allan Poe*

[L2] Lewis Carroll, *Alice's Adventures in Wonderland*

[L3] Robert Frost, *Poems by Robert Frost: A Boy's Will and North of Boston*

[L4] Geoffrey Chaucer, *The Canterbury Tales*

[L4] Authors in Depth

Emily Dickinson, "A narrow Fellow in the Grass," "'Nature' is what we see," "Most she touched me by her muteness," "A fuzzy fellow, without feet," "How many Flowers fail in Wood," "It sifts from Leaden Sieves," "How happy is the little Stone," "Exhilaration is the Breeze," "Hope is a strange invention," "Opinion is a flitting thing," "The Bustle in a House," "A word is dead," "This is my letter to the World," "There is no Frigate like a Book," "Letter to Austin Dickinson"

[L1] Special Needs Students
[L2] Below-Level Students
[L3] All Students
[L4] Above-Level Students
[EL] English Learners

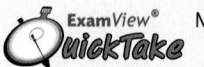

PRENTICE HALL
Teacher EXPRESS
Plan · Teach · Assess
Use this complete suite of powerful teaching tools to make lesson planning and testing quicker and easier.

ExamView® QuickTake Monitor student progress instantly.

Meeting Your Standards

✔ **Meeting Your Standards**

Students will

1. understand the characteristics, types, and purposes of poetry.

2. read and analyze two poems.

3. learn about poet Pat Mora.

4. build vocabulary.

5. begin the process of writing a descriptive essay.

🐧 **From the Author's Desk**

❶ Introduce Pat Mora

• Pat Mora is an award-winning author of poetry, nonfiction, and children's books. Drawing on the colorful traditions of the American Southwest and her Hispanic heritage, Mora explores issues of identity, culture, and society. Ask students if they have read or are familiar with any of her work.

• Use the *From the Author's Desk DVD* to introduce the author and the genre. Show Segment 2 to examine Mora's ideas about word choices in poetry. **Ask:** Why does Mora believe that every word matters when she writes poetry? **Answer:** Mora believes that poets must listen to each word, how it sounds on its own, and how it sounds with the words that surround it.

• Interested students might enjoy these works by Pat Mora.

• *The Big Sky,* poems that describe the Southwest

• *My Own True Name: New and Selected Poems for Young Adults,* a collection of more than sixty poems

❷ Critical Viewing

Possible response: Each reader is touched by the "river of poetry" in a different way. Despite these individual effects, poetry can bring people together.

550

Unit **4**

Introduction:
Poetry

❶

❸ 🐧 **From the Author's Desk**

Pat Mora
Talks About the Form

I've lived near two rivers: the Rio Grande that separates my native state of Texas from Mexico and the Ohio River that separates Ohio from Kentucky. When I watch a river flowing by, I think about the journey it has made and where it's going. Rivers democratically gather branches and leaves as they move along. The sun and moon both travel on the ripples. Though water slips through our fingers, rivers carve canyons.

Poetry's River Includes You

As one of my favorite poets, Mary Oliver, says in the quotation on the next page, "Poetry is a river." You and I can be part of it. No one will compose the poem about popcorn or tennis shoes that you will. When you sit and bring all of yourself to the page, all you've seen, heard, read, and felt, and when you begin to play with words, you can eventually write a unique poem. You will choose your own **form; images,** words that appeal to the senses; and **speaker,** the person who says the words of the poem.

Paintings and music are unique in the same way. Many artists and musicians could see a teenager sitting alone at a party. Each artist would paint the scene differently; each musician would create different sounds to capture the scene, the mood.

▲ **Pat Mora**
has received numerous awards for works that depict the beauty and varied cultures of the American Southwest.

❷ ▼ **Critical Viewing**
Pat Mora compares poetry to a river. What does this illustration suggest about the way the "river of poetry" affects its readers? **[Interpret]**

550 ■ *Poetry*

Teaching Resources

The following resources can be used to enrich, extend, or differentiate the instruction for the Unit Introduction and Model Selections.

Unit 4 Resources, pp. 1–13

General Resources, p. 6

Graphic Organizer Transparencies, pp. 121–122

From the Author's Desk DVD
    Pat Mora, Segments 1 and 2

Reader's Notebook

Reader's Notebook: Adapted Version

Reader's Notebook: English Learner's Version

Listening to Literature Audio CD

Adapted Reader's Notebook Audio CD

❹ A Poem Is Like a River in a Room

I like the spareness of poetry. It demands that I remove the unnecessary. For example, I could have a grand time filling a room with objects I like—flowers, folk art, books, family photos. Suppose, though, that I decided to focus my attention. What if I allowed myself less space and chose each detail carefully because I wanted to create surprises for visitors, to have you not just see the room but experience it. Suppose that I put one small river flowing through the middle of the room.

You walk in and stare and wonder, as readers sometimes wonder about poems, What's going on here? What's she trying to do? You listen to the river as I hope you listen to poems, and you hear something your neighbor or friend might miss. You connect with that river or that poem because you're you, and you're willing to risk releasing your imagination.

When I begin a poem, I sit with paper and pen. I try not to pressure myself to write a perfect first line. I write to get going, knowing I can discard whatever I write. The page is my landscape, and I'm like that river traveling along, exploring.

> *Poetry is a river; many voices travel in it; poem after poem moves along in the exciting crests and falls of the river waves.*
>
> **from A Poetry Handbook**
> —Mary Oliver

More About Pat Mora

In her works, Pat Mora (b. 1942) has explored the experience of being "American but hyphenated"; that is, a bilingual and bicultural Mexican American. She stresses the importance of family and cultural heritage, often using Spanish words and phrases in her writing. She has also published some works in bilingual editions.

Her poetry is spare, yet rich in imagery and feeling. Mora encourages her readers to write their own poems and to "enjoy the word-play."

Fast Facts

► Mora has hosted a radio show called *Voices: The Mexican American in Perspective.*
► In addition to being a writer and teacher, Mora has worked as a museum director and a college administrator.

From the Author's Desk: Pat Mora ■ 551

---

❸ Pat Mora Talks About the Form
Exploring Poetry

• Explore students' prior knowledge of poetry by making connections to what they know. Ask students to recall specific poems they have read. Do all poems have certain elements in common? If so, what are they?
Possible responses: Students may mention rhyme, rhythm, figurative language, and line arrangement.

• Tell students that poetry is found not only in textbooks, but all around them. **Ask** students where they might encounter poetry in everyday life.
Possible responses: Students should recognize that song lyrics share certain qualities with poetry. Students may also mention that some popular movies incorporate poetry into their scripts.

• Have students read Pat Mora's discussion of the form.

❹ A Poem Is Like a River in a Room
Discuss the Genre

• Point out that poets choose words carefully for the images and emotions they suggest.

• *A Poetry Handbook* Direct students' attention to the quotation from Mary Oliver, a Pulitzer-Prize winner and author of books of poetry, essays, and criticism. **Ask:** How does Oliver use language to enrich her comparison of poetry and a river?

• **Possible response:** Oliver begins with a simple metaphor: "Poetry is a river." Her word choices suggest both the motion of a river (*crests, falls, waves*) and the quality of poetry (*voices*).

Go Online For: An online video
Author Link Visit: www.PHSchool.com
Web Code: epe-8401
Give students this Web Code for a video clip of Pat Mora.

551

- Point out the many ways that poets have to convey meaning. Tell students that the techniques described here are a poet's toolkit for building layers of meaning and constructing vivid images.

- Review the definitions of *simile* and *metaphor* with students. Explain that these techniques are figures of speech or *figurative language,* expressions that are not meant to be taken literally.

- **Ask** students to think of examples of figures of speech. These may be ones they have heard or original ones.
  Possible responses: *Simile:* She sings like a lark. *Metaphor:* Poetry is a river.

- Point out the definition of free verse. Tell students that free verse may include rhyming words and strong rhythms, but in a less structured way than formal verse.

- Tell students that they will be reading two examples of free verse poetry. Suggest that they look for examples of the techniques mentioned on this page as they read.

Exploring Poetry

❺ Elements of Poetry

Poetry is a literary form that combines the precise meanings of words with their emotional associations, sounds, and rhythms. Many poems are structured in **stanzas,** or groupings of lines. Specific stanza types include **couplets,** which have two lines, and **quatrains,** which have four lines.

Poets use **figurative language,** such as metaphor, simile, personification, and onomatopoeia, to express ideas or feelings in a fresh way.

- Poets use **metaphors** to compare two apparently unlike things without using the words *like, as, than,* or *resembles,* as in "The sky is a patchwork quilt." Poets use **similes** to make such comparisons using connecting words, as in "The sky is like a patchwork quilt."

- **Personification** is language that attributes human qualities to non-human things.

- **Onomatopoeia** is the use of a word whose sound imitates its meaning. Examples of such words are *buzz, hiss, thud,* and *sizzle.*

- **Imagery** is descriptive language poets use to create word pictures, or **images.** Images are enhanced by **sensory language,** which provides details related to the senses.

Poets use a number of **sound devices** to achieve a musical quality.

- **Rhythm** is the pattern created by the stressed and unstressed syllables of words in sequence. A controlled pattern of rhythm is called **meter.**

- **Rhyme** is the repetition of identical or similar sounds in stressed syllables. A pattern of end rhymes is called a **rhyme scheme. Free verse** has no set meter or rhyme scheme.

- **Alliteration** is the repetition of the initial consonant sounds of words, as in the phrase "*dark days.*" **Assonance** is the repetition of vowel sounds in nearby words, as in the phrase "*child of silence.*" **Consonance** is the repetition of consonants within nearby words in which the separating vowels differ, as in the phrase "*live and love.*"

- **Repetition** is the use of any language element more than once.

❻ Types of Poetry

There are three main types of poetry.

- In a **narrative** poem, the writer tells a story in verse. Narratives can take many forms. For example, an **epic** is a long narrative poem about gods or heroes. In contrast, a **ballad** is a songlike narrative about an adventure or a romance.

- In a **dramatic** poem, the writer tells a story using a character's own thoughts or statements.

- A **lyric** is a brief poem in which the author expresses the feelings of a single speaker, creating a single effect on the reader. Lyrics are notable for their musical qualities, achieved through rhyme and rhythm.

❼ Forms of Poetry

Other poems can be categorized by form—their particular patterns of rhyme, rhythm, line structure, stanza format, or another element.

- A **haiku** is a poem containing three unrhymed lines of five, seven, and five syllables. This Japanese poetic form uses imagery to convey a single vivid emotion.

- A **sonnet** is a fourteen-line lyric poem with formal patterns of rhyme, rhythm, and line structure.

Check Your Understanding

Choose the letter of the answer that best matches each numbered item.

1. descriptive sensory language   A rhythm   B imagery
2. tale of a legendary hero   A sonnet   B epic
3. words used in unusual ways   A figurative language   B couplet
4. organization of lines   A rhyme   B stanza
5. pattern of stressed sounds   A haiku   B meter

❽ ▼ **Critical Viewing**
What simile could you write to describe this tornado? Explain. **[Synthesize]**

Exploring Poetry ■ 553

---

❻ Types of Poetry

Point out to students that both narrative and dramatic poems deal with characters, much like works of fiction. Lyrical poetry focuses on feelings and the uses of language.

❼ Forms of Poetry

- Tell students that the form of a poem is a way to describe its physical structure—the arrangement of lines and stanzas on a page.

- **Ask** students to name forms of poetry they might know.
  Possible response: Students may mention haiku, sonnets, limericks, cinquains, and concrete poems.

- Then, **ask** students whether they think that the forms of poetry that have been discussed could also be free verse poems.
  Possible response: Free verse poems cannot be sonnets, because sonnets have a specific pattern of rhyme and rhythm. Haiku follows a specific syllabic pattern and is not free verse. Limericks rely on rhythm and end rhyme to be effective, so they cannot be free verse. Cinquains have a definite formal structure, but no pattern of rhyme or meter, so they could fall into the free verse category. Concrete poems could be examples of free verse.

❽ Critical Viewing

Possible response: Students may liken the tornado to a pillar, a funnel, or a snake.

ASSESS

Answers

1. B
2. B
3. A
4. B
5. B

From the Author's Desk

❶ Introduce the Selections

- Have students read Pat Mora's introduction to her poems.

- Call students' attention to the terms used in discussing poetry: *theme, figurative language,* and *personification.*

- Ask students to identify these elements as they read "A Voice" and "Uncoiling."

❷ Background

Cultural Heritage Until recently, the popular metaphor for American society was the melting pot: Immigrants were expected to assimilate into the dominant culture and mingle their identity in the American mainstream. Now other metaphors are being explored, among them America as a tossed salad. In this perspective, each new culture adds its own special color and flavor, standing out rather than blending in.

❸ Connecting to the Literature

- Ask students to write a few sentences about the importance of cultural heritage. To develop expressive vocabulary, encourage students to use at least three of the following words: *enrich, immigrate, incorporate, maintain, perceive, transform.*

- To further develop students' expressive vocabulary, you may suggest that they also use two of these words: *controversy, domestic, significant, superior.*

- To help students understand the meanings of the words they are asked to use, given them these sentences:

  1. Customs from many cultures *enrich* American life.

  2. A memory of a loved one can *transform* a simple object into a valuable possession.

  3. The *controversy* over whether immigrants should learn English will not be settled soon.

From the Author's Desk
Pat Mora Introduces "A Voice" and "Uncoiling"

I am a writer because I'm a reader, and because I love words in English and Spanish, their pleasure and power. I'm also a writer because of my mother. Mom, a reader who knew both Spanish and English, was my first editor and gave me good advice on my writing assignments and speeches.

"A Voice": Mom's Power Is a Key to the Theme

When I became interested in spending more time writing, I interviewed my family. Have you done that? Every family has good stories to tell. I listened and wrote about the way Mom and Mexicans or people of Mexican descent felt. I wrote about her in the children's book *The Rainbow Tulip;* in my family memoir, *House of Houses;* and in poems such as "A Voice."

When I was a teacher, my students and I would sometimes discuss the **theme** of a poem. What was the poem really about? What did it mean? Sometimes people avoid poetry because they think it's a puzzle. I don't write poetry to confuse you or to preach. I'm exploring with words. Writing poetry is taking a word journey.

I wanted to tell the story of Mom, a high school student, attending a speech contest. She felt frightened at feeling different. We all know that feeling. I also wanted to explore Mom's power in the life of our family.

"Uncoiling": Figurative Language Helps You See

If I use **figurative language** effectively, a phrase like "spunky as a peacock" or "lace lullabies" in the poem "Uncoiling" helps you see what I'm seeing or hearing. Poets spend time choosing words, sounds; poets play with possibilities. The desert is, like my mother, a powerful woman in my life. In "Uncoiling," I chose **personification** to create her on the page for you.

Poetry is a word journey. If I succeed, it's a word journey for you too. I discover and you discover as you read. Poetry asks us to use our imagination, to fill in the silences, to leap.

554 ■ *Poetry*

Vocabulary Development

Vocabulary Knowledge Rating
Create a Vocabulary Knowledge Rating Chart with this word from the selection:

spunky

Give students a copy. Introduce the word by reading it aloud and having students mark their rating in the Before Reading column. Urge them to be alert to this word as they read and discuss the selection, because they will rate their knowledge of the word again after they finish.

If you wish, you may tally how many students know (or think they know) the word to gauge how much instruction you need to provide. As students read, point out the word and its context.

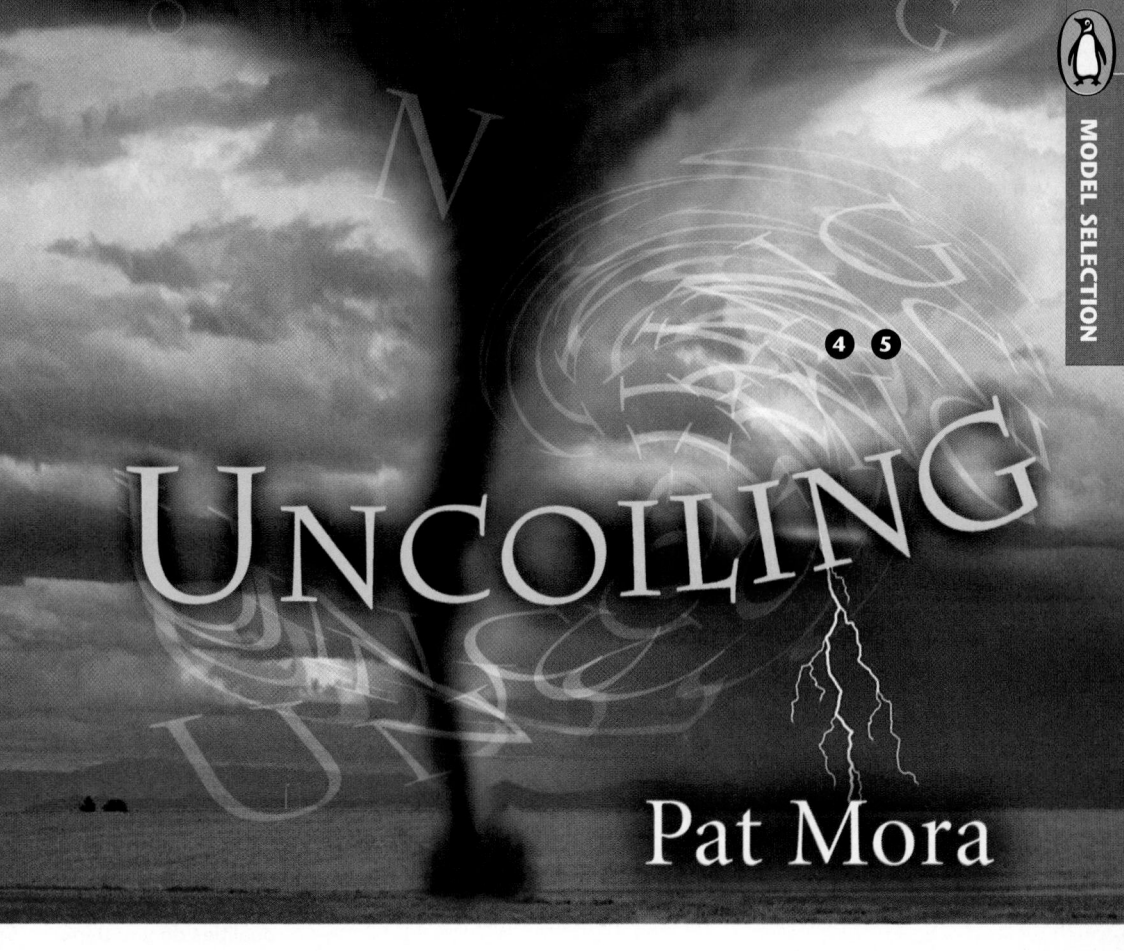

UNCOILING

Pat Mora

4 **5**

With thorns, she scratches
    on my window, tosses her hair dark with rain,
      snares lightning, cholla,[1] hawks, butterfly
        swarms in the tangles.

6 5 She sighs clouds,
    head thrown back, eyes closed, roars
                  and rivers leap,

boulders retreat like crabs
into themselves.

---

1. **cholla** (chōl´ yä) *n.* spiny cactus found in the southwestern United States and Mexico.

7 *Pat Mora*
Author's Insight
The desert, nature, is
no wimp. It survives
through strength. I
chose verbs like
"roars" to convey the
desert's energy and
power.

Uncoiling ■ 555

TEACH

4 **Motivation**
- **Ask** students to share with a partner one observation they wrote in the **Connecting to the Literature** activity and one way that cultural heritage is important to families.
Possible responses: Family traditions can help pass on important values to younger generations. Knowing about cultural heritage can help young people be proud of themselves.

- Urge students to keep in mind their ideas about cultural heritage and evaluate how Mora's poems discuss issues of culture and identity as they read these poems.

Concept Connector ➤
Students will follow up on this activity after completing the story.

---

5 **About the Selections**
In both "Uncoiling" and "A Voice," the land and people of the Southwest are dominant themes. Whether she is describing a natural phenomenon or recalling a family memory, Mora's writing is infused with a sense of place, depth of character, and vibrant, evocative language.

6 **Author's Insight**
- Tell students that vivid, active verbs help a writer convey strong emotions and paint memorable scenes for readers.

- **Ask** students what verbs, in addition to "roars," Mora uses to describe the storm.
Answer: Mora uses the verbs *scratches, tosses, snares,* and *sighs.*

- Discuss what images these verbs bring to mind.
Possible responses: The verbs *scratches, tosses,* and *snares* suggest a wild beast. The word *sighs* may bring to mind a human being.

Differentiated
Instruction   Solutions for All Learners

Support for
Special Needs Students
Have students read the adapted version of these selections in the *Reader's Notebook: Adapted Version.* They may also listen to the adapted version on the **Reader's Notebook: Adapted Version Audio CD.**

Support for
Less Proficient Readers
Have students read these selections in the *Reader's Notebook.* After students finish the selection in the *Reader's Notebook,* have them complete the questions and activities in the Student Edition.

Support for
English Learners
Have students read these selections in the *Reader's Notebook: English Learner's Version.* English learners may also read the selection as they listen to the recorded version on the **Listening to Literature Audio CD.**

- **Ask** students to find examples of the poetic techniques of alliteration and sensory language in these lines.
  Possible responses: Mora uses alliteration in the words "skirt starts its spin" and "lace lullabies." She uses sensory language with the words "howling" and "stinging."

- Then, **ask** how the women's reactions add to the description of the storm.
  Possible responses: The storm "spooks" the women, which makes it seem like a supernatural force. The women "scurry" to take precautions, which suggests the storm's speed.

- Discuss how the images in lines 20–23 present an altered impression of the storm and its effects.
  Possible responses: The softer images of the storm becoming "sound" rather than force and of spinning "herself / to sleep" suggest that the storm is lessening. The words "raw skin" remind the reader of the storm's power, but the mention of stars at the end may suggest a clearing sky.

8 Critical Viewing

Possible responses: Students may say that a storm like this might exhibit human qualities such as anger, passion, and violence.

```
10    She spews gusts and thunder,
          spooks pale women who scurry to
              lock doors, windows
                  when her tumbleweed skirt starts its spin.

      They sing lace lullabies
15        so their children won't hear
              her uncoiling
                  through her lips, howling
                      leaves off trees, flesh
                          off bones, until she becomes

20    sound, spins herself
          to sleep, sand stinging her ankles,
              whirring into her raw skin like stars.
```

Poetry

Imagery Mora's vivid images express both the appearance and the power of the storm.

8 ◄ Critical Viewing
What humanlike qualities do you think a tornado like the one shown here exhibits? **[Interpret]**

Vocabulary Development

Dictionary Use
Use a think-aloud process to show students how to use a dictionary to look up unfamiliar terms. Point out the word *tumbleweed* in line 13. Say:

I will use a dictionary to look up the term *tumbleweed* since the context of the stanza ("her tumbleweed skirt starts its spin") is not giving me enough information to understand the term's meaning.

I recognize the individual words *tumble* and *weed* and guess that the word refers to some sort of plant, but I need to know more to understand the image. I check the definition in the dictionary and learn that tumbleweed is a plant that grows in the Southwest and is blown along by the wind. The storm has a "tumbleweed skirt" because this image shows the effects of the wind.

A Voice

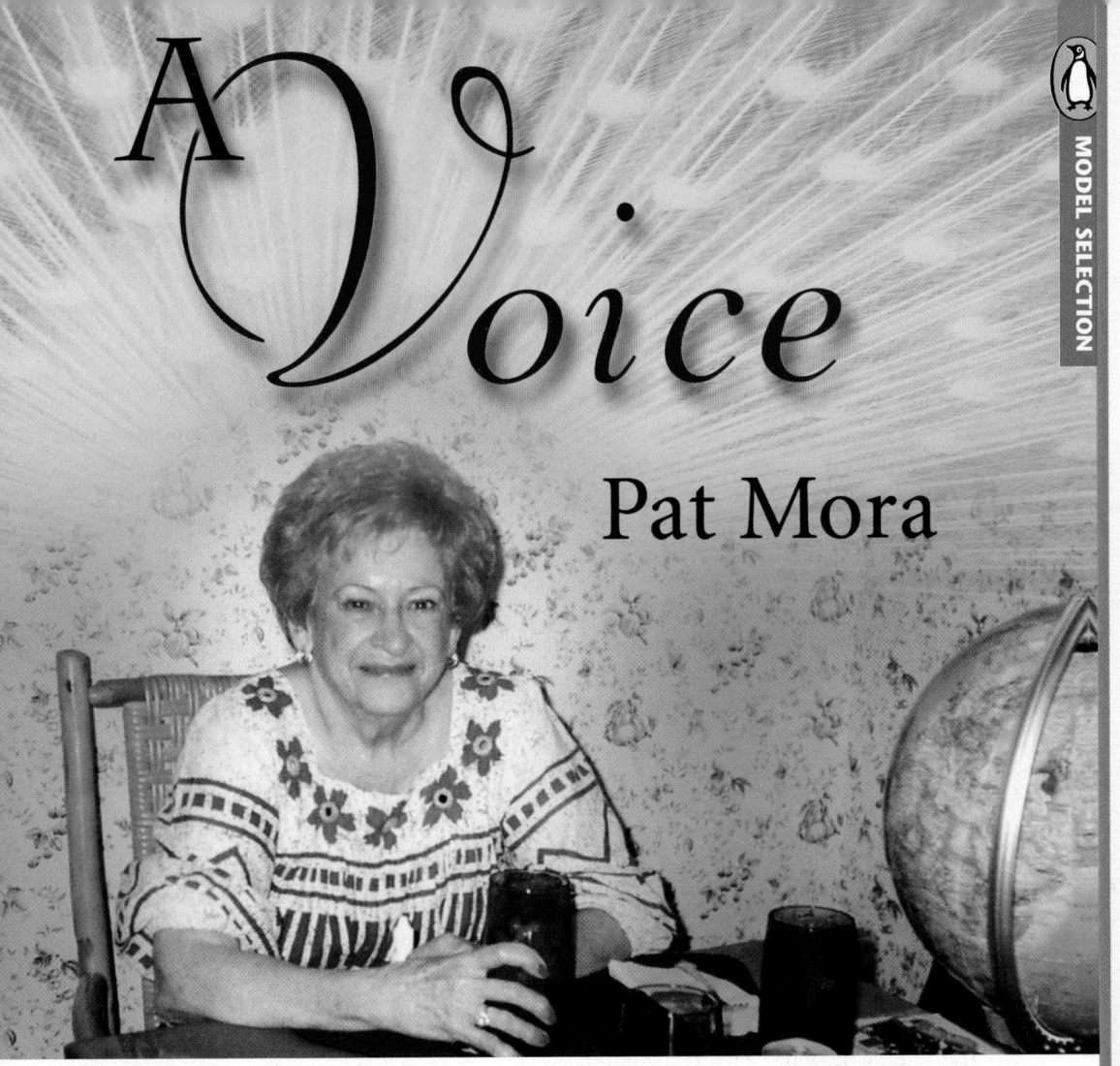

Pat Mora

Even the lights on the stage unrelenting
as the desert sun couldn't hide the other
students, their eyes also unrelenting,
students who spoke English every night

5   as they ate their meat, potatoes, gravy.
Not you. In your house that smelled like
rose powder, you spoke Spanish formal
as your father, the judge without a courtroom

❾ Author's Insight

- Discuss with students how foods are often associated with a particular culture. Point out that nearly all cultures have some form of bread. **Ask** what cultures students think of when they hear the words *tortilla, pita, panini, nan,* or *bagel.* Invite students to name other kinds of bread associated with different places or cultures.
  Possible responses: Tortilla, pita, panini, nan, and bagel suggest Hispanic, Middle Eastern, Italian, East Indian, and Jewish cultures. Other bread associations are soda bread/Ireland, crumpets/England, baguette/France, cornbread/Southern United States.

- **Ask:** What is implied by the use of the words "meat, potatoes, gravy"? Why do you think Mora does not use more specific terms such as pot roast or baked chicken, baked potatoes or mashed potatoes?
  Possible response: Mora is describing a "typical English-speaking" American household. The description is general rather than specific because she is talking about Americans in general, not about one particular American family.

❾ Pat Mora
Author's Insight
Food creates connections in our minds and gives us cultural clues. What if I'd said, "beans, tortillas, chile" instead?

A Voice ■ 557

Differentiated Instruction   Solutions for All Learners

Strategy for Less Proficient Readers
Have students reread "A Voice" in pairs. One student should read aloud a line or phrase, and the other should rewrite it using his or her own words. When they reach the end of the poem, have the partners switch roles. Then, have students compare their paraphrases of the poem. Discuss how their rewritten poems differ from the original and from their partner's interpretation.

Strategy for English Learners
Invite students to share ideas of how their home culture differs from mainstream American culture and any experiences they have had reconciling the two. Ask them to find lines in the poem that express similar feelings or experiences. Point out that the woman in the poem finds aspects of American culture that she enjoys, such as winning with words. Ask them to summarize the theme of the poem in one or two sentences. Then, ask them whether they agree with what the poem says about fitting into a new place.

- **Ask:** Why do you think Mora says that the father's walk is "slow/as a hot river"?
Possible response: The image suggests the heat of Mexico and a slower tempo of life. The image of a river also connects to the earlier lines about the father floating to a new country in the dark.

- Then, discuss other images that Mora uses in the poem and what they suggest to the reader.
Possible responses: Mora compares the father to a judge without a courtroom. This image suggests that he is wise and solemn, but out of place. She compares the aunt's voice to that of a spunky peacock, suggesting someone loud, vibrant, and eager to be seen.

⑪ Poetry
Repetition

- Tell students that writers often use repetition to signal to readers what is important in a piece of writing.

- **Ask:** What important point does Mora signal with the repetition of "you liked"?
Possible response: Mora emphasizes that her mother's strong motivations to speak overcame her fears.

- Point out the comment, which discusses the rhythmic effect of repetition. Remind students that free verse poetry does not have a fixed or formal rhythm or meter, but that the poet can still use rhythm when they choose.

- Then, **ask:** Why might using a rhythmic phrase be an important technique in free verse poetry?
Possible response: Because the whole poem does not conform to a rhythmic pattern, the use of a rhythmic phrase may add dramatic emphasis to certain words.

Concept Connector

Have students review the comments they made about cultural heritage before reading these poems. Then, ask students to discuss what one thing from their culture they would like to pass on to future generations. Tell students that what they name can be anything—a food, a story, an object, an attitude. Ask them to tell what their legacy might mean to a family member in the future.

---

⑩ 10   in the country he floated to in the dark
            on a flatbed truck. He walked slow
            as a hot river down the narrow hall
            of your house. You never dared to race past him

            to say, "Please move," in the language
            you learned effortlessly, as you learned to run,
      15   the language forbidden at home, though your mother
            said you learned it to fight with the neighbors.

⑪   You like winning with words. You liked
            writing speeches about patriotism and democracy.
            You liked all the faces looking at you, all those eyes.
      20   "How did I do it?" you ask me now. "How did I do it

            when my parents didn't understand?"
            The family story says your voice is the voice
            of an aunt in Mexico, <u>spunky</u> as a peacock.
            Family stories sing of what lives in the blood.

      25   You told me only once about the time you went
            to the state capitol, your family proud as if
            you'd been named governor. But when you looked
            around, the only Mexican in the auditorium,

            you wanted to hide from those strange faces.
      30   Their eyes were pinpricks, and you faked
            hoarseness. You, who are never at a loss
            for words, felt your breath stick in your throat

            like an ice cube. "I can't," you whispered.
            "I can't." Yet you did. Not that day but years later.
      35   You taught the four of us to speak up.
            This is America, Mom. The undoable is done

            in the next generation. Your breath moves
            through the family like the wind
            moves through the trees.

Poetry
Figurative Language
By comparing the father's walk to a "hot river," Mora suggests more than simply his rate of movement.

Poetry
Repetition Mora uses repetition in this stanza to create a rhythmic effect.

Vocabulary Builder
spunky (spun′ kē) *adj.* courageous; spirited

Vocabulary Development

Vocabulary Knowledge Rating
When students have completed reading and discussing "Uncoiling" and "A Voice," have them take out their **Vocabulary Knowledge Rating Chart** for this selection. Read the word aloud once more and have students rate their knowledge of the word again in the After Reading column. Clarify the words if it is still problematic. Have students write their own definitions or examples in the appropriate column. Encourage students to use the word in further discussion and written work about this selection. Remind them that they will be accountable for this word on the Selection Test.

From the Author's Desk
Pat Mora's Insights Into "A Voice" and "Uncoiling"

⓮ Q. Why did you use the title "A Voice" instead of the name of the person it is about?

A. Titles, like first and last lines, matter. The title is my first chance to snag your interest. I wanted to make you curious. Whose voice? Also, there's something powerful about a voice. Our voice, invisible as the wind, becomes part of the world. Mom's voice was hers (and how I loved it!), but it was—and is—also a force moving through us.

⓯ Q. How did you decide to give "Uncoiling" its shape on the page?

A. Most people don't like a wild desert storm. I do, probably because I always felt safe in my home. I liked watching and hearing the desert's power, but I never felt in danger. I wanted the poem's shape to convey a storm's disorder and lack of predictability. The lines aren't orderly. There's a bit of chaos right there on the page to help you experience the desert's mood.

StudentCorner

⓰ Q. Do you add some of your own emotions when writing about a tornado?

—Brandon Bishop, Grove City, Ohio

A. I'd never heard a tornado warning until I moved to the Midwest as an adult. The storm in the poem isn't a tornado but a grand desert dust storm with tumbleweeds flying. In El Paso, we could see the dust storm coming, and soon there was so much sand in the air that the mountain in the middle of town disappeared.

Writing Workshop: *Work in Progress*

Descriptive Essay

For a descriptive essay you may write, make a list of three places. For each place, write 10 words that describe how the place looks. Put this Sight List in your writing portfolio.

From the Author's Desk: Pat Mora ■ 559

Assessment Resources

The following resources can be used to assess students' knowledge and skills.

Unit 4 Resources
    Selection Test A, pp. 8–10
    Selection Test B, pp. 11–13

Go Online —Assessment Students may use the **Self-test** to prepare for **Selection Test A** or **Selection Test B.**

From the Author's Desk

Pat Mora's Insights

- Tell students that Pat Mora is frequently asked questions like these about her poetry. Her answers provide insight into decisions that a poet makes in order to create a memorable poem.

- Mora's comments address issues of character, speaker or narrator, and form. Have students review these concepts on pp. 550 and 553.

⓮ After students read the first question and answer, **ask** them whether they think Mora's strategy to capture the readers' attention with the title is effective. Does the strategy also work for the poem "Uncoiling"?
Possible responses: Some students may say that the titles did make them want to learn more by reading the poems. Other students may say that they wish the titles had given them more information about the topic or theme of the poem.

⓯ After students read the second question and answer, **ask** them how the shape of "A Voice" differs from "Uncoiling" and what the shape may mean.
Possible responses: "A Voice" is presented in regular stanzas of four lines each, except the final stanza, which has three lines. Mora may have wanted readers to focus on the words, rather than the shape of this poem.

⓰ After students read the last question and answer, suggest that they write poems about the kind of storms that occur in their area of the country and the sights, sounds, and feelings these storms evoke.

Writing Workshop
Work in Progress

In the **Work-in-Progress** assignments through Part 1, students will complete activities that prepare them for the **Writing Workshop** on descriptive essays on p. 620. Work with students on this brief prewriting activity. Have them save their work in their portfolios for later use.

559

1. **Possible responses:** Some students may find "Uncoiling" more powerful because of its vivid images. Other students may find "A Voice" more powerful because of its message.

2. (a) The speaker is describing a desert storm. (b) The storm knocks against the window, brings clouds, and spews gusts and thunder. (c) The actions gradually intensify from knocking to clouding over to causing violent winds.

3. (a) Pat Mora's mother is the subject of "A Voice." (b) The poem celebrates the occasion when Mora's mother gave a speech in the state capitol.

4. (a) Mora's mother feels fear at speaking in front of a large group of strange faces and cannot speak. (b) That day's failure taught Mora's mother that it was important to teach her children to use their voices.

5. (a) Mora gives the storm human qualities such as tossing her hair, throwing back her head, and closing her eyes. (b) The storm is wild, powerful, and destructive. The women are frightened and timid, but also protective.

6. (a) **Sample answer: What It Says:** The storm sighs; the mother's breath sticks in her throat. **What It Means:** The storm produces wind and clouds; the mother cannot make herself speak. **Effect:** The image describes the motion of the storm; the image conveys a feeling of fright and helplessness. (b) Students should support their opinions with evidence from the poems.

560

Apply the Skills

Poetry

Thinking About the Selections

1. **Respond:** Which poem did you find more powerful? Why?

2. **(a) Infer:** In "Uncoiling," what kind of storm does the speaker describe? **(b) Interpret:** Identify three actions the storm takes in the first five stanzas. **(c) Analyze:** How do these actions show the storm's increasing violence?

3. **(a) Recall:** Who is the subject of "A Voice"? **(b) Interpret:** Which of this person's childhood accomplishments does the poet celebrate?

4. **(a) Summarize:** What happens to the person at the state capitol? **(b) Analyze:** According to the speaker, how is the failure of that day transformed later in the subject's life?

Poetry Review

5. In "Uncoiling," Mora uses **personification** to give human attributes to the storm. **(a)** What human qualities does the storm possess? **(b)** How does the storm's behavior compare with the actions of the women in the poem?

6. **(a)** In the first column of a chart like the one shown, list **images** of breathing, speaking, or vocalizing from each poem. In the second column, note the literal meaning of the image. In the third column, describe the effect of the image—the word picture it conveys or feeling it expresses. **(b)** In a small group, discuss your findings to make sure you have included all possible images. Agree on the single most effective image and share your conclusion with the class.

What it says	What it means	Effect

Research the Author

Prepare a **report** in which you describe Pat Mora's views about her dual-language heritage and literary career. Follow these steps:
- Using the Internet and your library, find biographical sources with comments about Mora's writing in both Spanish and English.
- Refer to at least five poems in which Mora mentions her dual-language heritage.
- Share your report with your class.

QuickReview

Poems at a Glance

Uncoiling portrays the violent power of a storm.

A Voice celebrates a mother's inspirational influence on her family.

Go **Online**
—**Assessment**
For: Self-test
Visit: www.PHSchool.com
Web Code: epa-6401

Personification: a form of figurative language in which a nonhuman subject is given human traits

Imagery: descriptive language with which an author creates vivid word pictures

Skills Overview
Reading Skill: Reading Fluently
- Reading in sentences
- Using your senses

Vocabulary Development
- Suffixes

Literary Analysis
- Figurative Language: simile, metaphor, personification, paradox
- Sound Devices: alliteration, consonance, assonance, onomatopoeia

Writing
- Descriptive Essay
- Work in Progress, pp. 559, 585, 611

Skills You Will Learn

Literary Analysis: *Figurative Language*
Reading Skill: *Reading in Sentences*

Reading Skill: *Making Generalizations*

Literary Analysis: *Sound Devices*
Reading Skill: *Using Your Senses*

Literary Analysis: *Imagery*

Literature You Will Read

Monitoring Progress

Diagnose: Before you begin Part 1, administer the **Diagnostic Test** for Unit 4, Part 1. This test will identify students' level of readiness for the reading and vocabulary skills in Part 1. Use the **Interpretation Guide** for the Diagnostic Test to determine which students need help with prerequisite skills before beginning Part 1.

Preteach and Prepare: Use the information indicated in the **Interpretation Guide** to help students build prerequisite skills. In addition, prepare students by using the **Vocabulary Warm-up** activities and the **Reading Warm-up** activities as necessary for each selection set.

Teach: Use the instructional plan and resources provided to teach the skills and selections.

Assess: After students have completed Part 1, administer the **Benchmark Test** for Unit 4, Part 1. The test results will indicate which skills students have mastered and those on which they need more work.

Reteach: Use the Interpretation Guide to determine the appropriate reteaching pages from the **Reading Kit**.

Intervention: The prerequisite and reteaching pages are also available in the **Success Tracker.**

Read Fluently ■ *561*

Differentiated Instruction Solutions for All Learners

Resources for Monitoring Progress

Unit 4 Resources
　　Unit 4, Part 1 Diagnostic Test, pp. 15–17
　　Unit 4, Part 1 Benchmark Test, pp. 101–106

Reading Kit

Success Tracker

Introduce the Reading Skill

- Introduce the reading skill: reading fluently. Draw students' attention to the definition. Tell students that reading fluently is vital to understanding much of what they read. Point out that if readers do not read fluently—using punctuation as a guide—sentences will not make sense.

- Point out to students that reading fluently, guided by punctuation, is especially important when reading poetry. Poetry is often broken into lines that do not follow the punctuation. Readers should use the punctuation to help make sense of the meaning.

Model the Reading Strategies

- Model how using punctuation can help students read fluently. Point out the sample poem on this page. Have students read the poem without paying attention to the punctuation. Then, explain the instructions given with the poem, and ask students to read the poem according to the instructions.

- Have students tell the differences between reading the poem without punctuation and reading it with proper punctuation. **Ask** students why punctuation is important for understanding a poem. **Possible response:** Students may say that punctuation shows them how to group words so that they make sense.

- Reinforce the idea that fluent readers use punctuation to guide them in their reading of poetry and other writing.

Reading: Read Fluently

Reading fluently means having the skills to read easily, smoothly, and expressively.

Skills and Strategies You Will Learn in Part 1

In Part 1, you will learn
- to read **in sentences using punctuation** to help you **read fluently** (p. 564).
- to **use your senses** to help you **experience the images** described by a poet or an author (p. 590).
- to **make generalizations** about the meaning and imagery in poetry (p. 586).

Using the Skills and Strategies in Part 1

In Part 1, you will learn to **read fluently**—to read words smoothly in groups according to their meaning. You will practice **using punctuation to group words**. You will also practice relating words to your own knowledge through sensory details.

This example shows how you will apply the skills and strategies you will learn in Part 1.

Think about a time when you saw a single white puffy cloud in the sky.

I wandered[lonely as a cloud — There is no punctuation here, so continue reading.

That floats on high]o'er vales and hills,

When all at once I saw[a crowd, — The commas here indicate a pause.

A host, of golden daffodils.]

Think about what a yellow daffodil looks like, and then imagine seeing a whole field of them.

562 ■ *Poetry*

Professional Development
Most Important Word

This strategy works well with short pieces of poetry. After reading or hearing a poem, students select what they believe to be the most important word in the poem. Students write the word they have chosen and the reasons for their choice on a piece of paper. In small discussion groups, each student shares the word he or she chose and the reasons for choosing it.

After each group member has shared, groups vote on the "best" most important word. The group then formulates additional reasons for the group's choice.

Each group presents its choice for the most important word to the rest of the class, and the class votes on the one they feel is best.
Source: Camille Blachowicz, 1966.

Academic Vocabulary: Words for Analyzing Literature

The following words will help you as you read and analyze the literature in Part 1.

Word	Definition	Sample Sentence
considerable *adj.*	much or large; worth noting	His *considerable* talent was finally recognized.
deliberation *n.*	act of carefully thinking about an issue	Their *deliberations* about the validity of the theory lasted for two days.
transition *n.*	passing from one to another	There are *transitions* between ideas.
impact *n.*	force of a collision; shock	Imagery gave the poem great *impact*.
concept *n.*	idea	The poem was about the *concept* of life.

Vocabulary Skills: Suffixes

▶ A **suffix** is a letter, syllable, or group of syllables added to a word to alter its meaning or function.

In Part 1 you will learn
- the Latin suffix *-able* (p. 584)
- the Latin suffix *-tion* (p. 610)

Knowing the meaning of common suffixes helps you to determine a word's meaning.

▶ **Example:**
deliberate (carefully thinking through an issue)
+
tion (the act of)
_____

deliberation
(the act of carefully thinking through an issue)

Activity Add either *-able* or *-tion* to the following words. Use a dictionary to check your spelling. Then, give an example for each word.

drink   like   attend   attract   transit

Introduce Academic Vocabulary

- Introduce the academic vocabulary: words for analyzing literature. Tell students that these words are useful in analyzing literature.
- Review each word, and have students state the word aloud. Have students read aloud the words' definitions and the example sentences on the chart on this page. Clarify any words that students may not understand.
- Tell students to try to use these words as they discuss the selections in Part 1.

Introduce the Vocabulary Skill

- Introduce the vocabulary skill: suffixes. Tell students that many suffixes have Latin and Greek origins. Recognizing these suffixes and their meanings is an effective way to learn word meanings and to build vocabulary.
- Review the suffixes on this page and their meanings.
- Use these questions to give students practice with the suffixes:

  Which suffix, when added to *read*, means "capable of being read"?
  Answer: *-able*

  What is the new word that is formed from adding the suffix *-tion* to *graduate* and what is its definition?
  Answer: word: graduation; definition: *the act of graduating; finishing school and accepting an academic degree*

Activity

1. *drinkable:* capable of being drunk
2. *likable:* capable of being liked
3. *attention:* the act of attending
4. *attraction:* the state of being attracted
5. *transition:* the act of moving from one thing to another

Go **Online** **For:** Interactive
Vocabulary Crossword Puzzles
Visit: www.PHSchool.com
Web Code: epj-5401
Give students this Web code to access interactive crossword puzzles using Academic Vocabulary and Vocabulary Skill words from Part 1.

Differentiated Instruction   Solutions for All Learners

Strategy for Less Proficient Learners
When reading poetry, students may have a particularly difficult time reading fluently. Review with students the types of punctuation, such as the comma, semicolon, dash, period, and apostrophe, and what each type of punctuation indicates. Then, direct students' attention to a poem no longer than twenty lines.

Provide each student with a copy of the poem. Then, **ask:** Where are the punctuation marks, and what does each mark indicate?

Possible responses: Students will find the punctuation marks and tell what each one indicates. Point out any that students overlook.

Have students write in the pauses and stops on their copies. Then, have students recopy the poem in prose form. Have students compare the two versions, and point out that the two versions are the same words, just arranged differently on the page.

Planning Differentiated Instruction

Choosing Your Poetry Collection

You may use either collection of poems to meet the lesson standards. The following guide will help you determine which of the two collections is more appropriate for your students.

Accessibility at a Glance

	Collection 1	Collection 2
Context	Collection focuses on emotions.	Collection touches on societal issues (technology, ecology, conformity).
Language	Varied difficulties of vocabulary and sentence structure	Difficult vocabulary and sentence structure
Concept Level	Accessible	Challenging
Literary Merit	Noted poets	Noted poets
Lexile	NP	NP
Overall Rating	More accessible	More challenging

Using the Other Collection You may use the other collection of poems for homework or independent reading to reinforce the selection skills. If you use both collections, you can build a test for both using *ExamView®* Test Bank software.

Choosing Your Resources

[L1] Special Needs Students   [L4] Advanced Students
[L2] Below-Level Students   [EL] English Learners
[L3] All Students

FT Fast Track Instruction: To move the lesson more quickly, use the strategies and activities identified with **FT**.

Reading and Vocabulary Warm-ups provide support for below level students. **A** is for students reading two grades below level; **B** is for students reading one grade below level. For Selection Tests, **A** signifies "less challenging" and **B** "more challenging." For Graphic Organizer transparencies, **A** signifies "not filled in" and **B** "filled in."

Scaffolding for Less Proficient and Advanced Students

The leveled questions on Apply the Skills pages progress in the levels of thinking required to answer them. To address the needs of your different students, you may use the (a) level questions for your less proficient students, the (b) level with your on-level and advanced students. The occasional (c) level questions are appropriate for your advanced students.

Go Online **For:** Information about Lexiles
Professional **Visit:** www.PHSchool.com
Development **Web Code:** eue-1111

Step-by-Step Teaching Guide	Pacing Guide
PRETEACH	
• Administer Vocabulary and Reading Warm-ups as necessary.	
• Introduce the Literary Analysis Skill: Figurative Language. **FT**	10 min.
• Introduce the Reading Skill: Reading Fluently. **FT**	10 min.
• Prepare students to read by teaching the selection vocabulary. **FT**	10 min.
• Build background and develop expressive vocabulary with Connecting to the Literature and Background.	10 min.
• Engage students' interest with the motivation activity.	10 min.
TEACH	
• Informally monitor comprehension while students read independently or in groups. **FT**	30 min.
• Monitor students' comprehension with the Reading Check notes.	as students read
• Reinforce vocabulary with Vocabulary Builder notes.	as students read
• Develop students' understanding of figurative language with the Literary Analysis annotations. **FT**	5 min.
• Develop students' ability to read fluently with the Reading Skill annotations. **FT**	10 min.
ASSESS/EXTEND	
• Assess students' comprehension and mastery of the Reading Skill and Literary Analysis by having them answer the Apply the Skills questions. **FT**	35 min.
• Have students complete the Vocabulary Builder activities. **FT**	5 min.
• Apply students' ability to write a description of a scene with the Writing activity. **FT**	30–45 min. or homework
• Extend students' listening and speaking and research and technology skills with one or both of the Extend Your Learning activities.	15–30 min. or homework
• Have students complete the Vocabulary Skill and Grammar Lesson.	5 min.
• Monitor students' progress with the Assessment Practice.	20–40 min.
• Administer **Selection Test A** or **Selection Test B. FT**	15 min.

Resources

PRINT

Unit 4 Resources   Collection 1   Collection 2

TRANSPARENCY

Graphic Organizer Transparencies

PRINT

Reader's Notebook [L2]

Reader's Notebook: Adapted Version [L1]

Reader's Notebook: English Learner's Version [EL]

Unit 4 Resources

TECHNOLOGY

Listening to Literature Audio CDs [L2, EL]

Reader's Notebook: Adapted Version Audio CD [L1, L2]

PRINT

Unit 4 Resources

Build Language Skills: Vocabulary:
Latin suffixes *-able, -tion*, p. 44 **[L3]**
Build Language Skills: Grammar:
Preposition and Object of the Preposition, p. 45 **[L3]**

General Resources
Rubrics for Descriptive Essay, pp. 55–56 **[L3]**

TECHNOLOGY

Go Online: Research [L3]

Go Online: Self-test [L3]

ExamView® Test Bank [L3]

Meeting Your Standards

Students will

1. **analyze and respond to literary elements.**
   - Literary Analysis: Figurative Language

2. **read, comprehend, and analyze poems.**
   - Reading Skill: Reading Fluently
   - Reading Strategy: Reading in sentences
   - Reading Check questions
   - Apply the Skills questions
   - Assessment Practice

3. **develop vocabulary.**
   - Vocabulary Builder
   - Latin suffixes *-able* and *-tion*

4. **apply grammar skills.**
   - Preposition and Object of the Preposition

5. **develop writing proficiency.**
   - Work in Progress: Descriptive Essay
   - Description of a Scene

6. **extend learning.**
   - Listening and Speaking: Impromptu Speech
   - Research and Technology: Soundtrack

Block Scheduling: Use one 90-minute class period to preteach the skills and have students read the poetry collection. Use a second 90-minute class period to assess students' mastery of skills, extend their learning, and monitor their progress.

Homework Suggestions

The following are possibilities for homework assignments.

- Support pages from *Unit 4 Resources:*
  Literary Analysis
  Reading Skill
  Vocabulary Builder
  Enrichment

- An Extend Your Learning project and the Writing assignment for your chosen selection may be completed over several days.

PRENTICE HALL
TeacherEXPRESS™ Use this complete
Plan · Teach · Assess suite of powerful
teaching tools to make lesson planning and testing quicker and easier.

PRENTICE HALL
StudentEXPRESS™ Use the Interactive
Learn · Study · Succeed Textbook (online
and on CD-ROM) to make selections and activities come alive with audio and video support and interactive questions.

Build Skills *Poetry Collection 1 • Poetry Collection 2*

❶ Literary Analysis
Figurative Language

- Encourage students to pay close attention to *figurative language*—expressive language enriched by imagery and figures of speech—as they read the poems. Stress that understanding figurative language will help them to better understand and appreciate poetry.

- Review the instruction on *simile, metaphor, personification,* and *paradox.* Make sure students understand the differences in the figurative language presented by each example.

- Write the following sentence on the board:

  I turned the corner and the wind slapped me in the face.

  Ask students to identify the type of figurative language that is used and the meaning or effect that it conveys.
  Answer: The wind is personified through its "slap." This wording colorfully shows that the wind is strong.

- Give students a copy of **Literary Analysis Graphic Organizer A** (*Graphic Organizer Transparencies,* p. 123). Have them fill in the graphic organizer to record examples of figurative language as they read the assigned selections.

❷ Reading Skill
Reading Fluently

- Point out to students that when they read poetry fluently, they should read at a natural, rhythmic pace. Emphasize that unless a punctuation mark falls at the end of a line, there should be no hesitation as they read from one line to the next.

- Read a few lines from "Dream Deferred" to students to illustrate fluent reading. Invite volunteers to read after you.

You can apply the instruction on this page to these poems.

Poetry Collection 1	**Poetry Collection 2**
Dream Deferred, page 566	*All Watched Over by Machines of Loving Grace,* page 577
Dreams, page 567	
I Wandered Lonely as a Cloud, page 568	*"Hope" is the thing with feathers—,* page 578
Meciendo, page 570	*Much Madness is divinest Sense—,* page 579
Sonnets on Love XIII, page 573	*The War Against the Trees,* page 580

❶ Literary Analysis

Figurative language is language that is used imaginatively rather than literally. Figurative language includes one or more **figures of speech**, literary devices that make unexpected comparisons or change the usual meaning of words. The following are specific types of figures of speech:

- **Simile:** a comparison of two apparently unlike things using *like, as, than,* or *resembles*: "The sky is <u>like</u> a patchwork quilt."

- **Metaphor:** a description of one thing as if it were another: "The sky <u>is</u> a patchwork quilt."

- **Personification:** giving human characteristics to a nonhuman subject: "The <u>sea</u> was <u>angry</u> that day, my friends."

- **Paradox:** a statement, an idea, or a situation that seems contradictory but actually expresses a truth: "The more things change, the more they stay the same."

As you read, use a chart like the one shown to record examples of each type of figurative language you find.

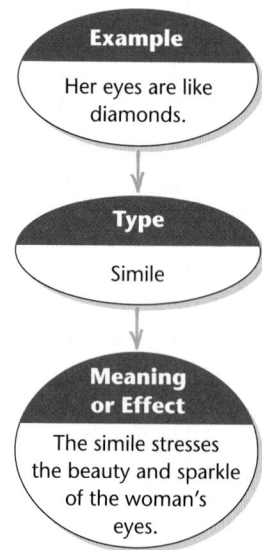

Example

Her eyes are like diamonds.

Type

Simile

Meaning or Effect

The simile stresses the beauty and sparkle of the woman's eyes.

❷ Reading Skill

Reading fluently is reading smoothly and continuously while also comprehending the text and appreciating the writer's artistry. To improve your fluency when reading poetry, **read in sentences.** Use punctuation rather than the ends of lines to determine where to pause or stop reading.

Vocabulary Builder

Poetry Collection 1

- **deferred** (dē fʉrd´) *v.* put off until a future time (p. 566) *Jackie <u>deferred</u> her trip to Italy until she had more money.*

- **pensive** (pen´ siv) *adj.* deeply or seriously thoughtful (p. 569) *Everyone remembered the professor as a quiet and <u>pensive</u> man.*

Poetry Collection 2

- **discerning** (di sʉrn´ iŋ) *adj.* having good judgment or understanding (p. 579) *The <u>discerning</u> viewer will realize what a bad movie this is.*

- **preliminaries** (prē lim´ ə ner´ ēz) *n.* steps or events before the main one (p. 581) *The pre-*

Vocabulary Development

Vocabulary Knowledge Rating
Create a **Vocabulary Knowledge Rating Chart** for the collection you will teach from this set. Include the vocabulary from this page and the additional words students are asked to use at the end of Connecting to the Literature. These words will increase students' expressive vocabulary.

Give students a copy of the chart with the words on it. Introduce the words by reading them aloud and having students mark their rating in the Before Reading column. Urge them to be alert to these words as they read and discuss the poems because they will rate their knowledge of the words again after they finish.

If you wish, you may tally how many students know (or think they know a word) to gauge how much instruction you need to provide. As students read, point out the words and their context.

Build Understanding • *Poetry Collection 1*

❸ Connecting to the Literature

Reading/Writing Connection In "Dreams," Langston Hughes advises readers to "hold fast" to dreams. Write a short paragraph explaining why you think dreams are so important to so many people. Use at least three of these words: *achieve, benefit, focus, maintain.*

Meet the Authors

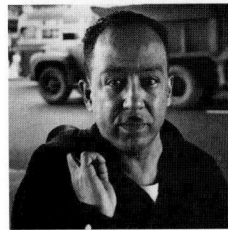

Langston **Hughes** (1902–1967)
Dream Deferred (page 566), Dreams (page 567)
Born in Joplin, Missouri, Langston Hughes was the first African American to earn a living by writing literary works. As a young man, he held a variety of jobs—teacher, ranch hand, and farmer, among others. He drew on all of these experiences, but primarily on his perspective as an African American, to create his great body of work.

William **Wordsworth** (1770–1850)
I Wandered Lonely as a Cloud (page 568)
William Wordsworth was born in England's rural Lake District. In 1798, he and fellow poet Samuel Taylor Coleridge published *Lyrical Ballads*—poems that use simple language to exalt everyday life. Emphasizing nature and the imagination, Wordsworth ushered in the age of Romanticism.

Gabriela **Mistral** (1889–1957)
Meciendo/Rocking (page 570)
Born in Chile as Lucila Godoy y Alcayaga, this writer formed her pen name from the names of her two favorite poets, the Italian Gabriele D'Annunzio and the French Frederic Mistral. Gabriela Mistral wrote many moving poems about children and motherhood. She was awarded the Nobel Prize in Literature in 1945.

Jean **de Sponde** (1557–1595)
Sonnets on Love XIII (page 573)
The French poet Jean de Sponde was a true Renaissance man who served in the court of King Henry IV, dabbled in chemistry, and published scholarly editions of ancient Greek texts. "Sonnets on Love XIII" is part of his finest work, *Sonnets of Love and Death*.

Go Online
Author Link
For: More about the authors
Visit: www.PHSchool.com
Web Code: epe-9402

Poetry Collection 1 ■ 565

---

❸ Connecting to the Literature

- Provide these sample sentences to demonstrate use of the expressive words:
  1. When dreams are realized, people can *achieve* wonderful things.
  2. Dreams *benefit* people by giving them hope for the future.
  3. Dreams help people *focus* on what matters the most.
  4. People must *maintain* their vision until they achieve their dreams.

- Help students further develop their expressive vocabulary by providing these words: *outcome, motivate, perspective,* and *undertake.* Encourage students to use these words as they discuss the poems.

Concept Connector ➡

Students will follow up on this activity after reading the poems in Poetry Collection 1.

Go Online For additional informa-
Author Link tion about the authors in Collection 1, have students type in the Web Code, select the first letter of the poet's last name, and then select the poet.

---

❶ Motivation

Ask students to talk about dreams. Prompt them with these questions: Why do people dream about things they would like to do? How do dreams make people feel? Are they important? Why? What happens to people when their dreams are postponed or deferred?

**Learning Modalities
Musical/Rhythmic Learners**

Have students read the poems aloud to themselves as smoothly and rhythmically as they can. If they like, they can "sing" the poems. They should tap on their desks lightly with a finger or pencil to indicate stressed words.

❷ About the Selections

"Dream Deferred" by Langston Hughes uses powerful images to depict the despair of shattered dreams. In "Dreams," Hughes uses two vivid metaphors to describe the importance of a dream to a person's life. In "I Wandered Lonely as a Cloud," Wordsworth looks back on a moment when he was inspired by the beauty of nature. In "Rocking," Mistral uses images of the sea, the wind, and the stars to express a mother's love. Sponde's "Sonnet on Love XIII" compares an ancient remark to the love the speaker feels for a beloved.

❸ Critical Viewing

Answer: Students may cite "like a heavy load" because it fits the figure's weary posture.

**❹ Reading Skill
Reading Fluently**

• Talk to students about ignoring line breaks and pausing for punctuation when reading poetry. Point out the bracketed passage and **ask** students how they would read this stanza.
Answer: A hesitation should occur after line 11.

• Read the poem aloud, demonstrating how to read through the end of lines. Then have students read it aloud.

Bernard's daddy, Raymond Lark, Collection of Mary Moran, New Jersey, Photo courtesy of Edward Smith and Comp...

❶
❷

Dream Deferred
Langston Hughes

Harlem

What happens to a dream <u>deferred</u>?

    Does it dry up
    like a raisin in the sun?
5   Or fester like a sore—
    And then run?
    Does it stink like rotten meat?
    Or crust and sugar over—
    like a syrupy sweet?

10 Maybe it just sags

❹ like a heavy load.
    Or does it explode?

566 ■ Poetry

❸ ▲ **Critical Viewing**
Which line of "Dream Deferred" might you use as a caption for this image? Explain. **[Connect]**

Vocabulary Builder
deferred (dē furd´) *adj.* put off until a future time

Vocabulary Development

Expressive Vocabulary
Ask students to think about the imagery Langston Hughes uses in "Dream Deferred" and "Dreams." Use the following questions to start a discussion: Which is the most powerful image? How do the images make you feel? Do the images capture the feeling of deferred dreams? Do the images reflect the importance of dreams? Encourage students to use the expressive vocabulary words presented earlier as they discuss these questions. You might prompt them with sentence starters like these:

1. The most powerful image the poems *focus* on is . . .
2. Through his images, Hughes *achieves* . . .
3. The *benefits* of dreams are shown through . . .
4. The images show that we must *maintain* our dreams or . . .

Dreams
Langston Hughes

⑤

Hold fast to dreams
For if dreams die
Life is a broken-winged bird
That cannot fly.

5   Hold fast to dreams
For when dreams go
Life is a barren field
Frozen with snow.

Reading Skill
Reading Fluently
How many sentences are in the first stanza?

Dreams ■ 567

⑤ Reading Skill
Reading Fluently

- Read the poem aloud in a smooth rhythm, pausing as you would in natural speech. Point out that some pauses occur even though there are no punctuation marks. For example, a slight pause might be given at the end of the first line before continuing on to line two. Emphasize that the pause occurs not because the line ends but because there is a slight break in the ideas. "Hold fast to dreams" is a complete thought. "For if dreams die," is a dependent clause that signals a shift in ideas.

- **Ask** students the Reading Skill question: How many sentences are in the first stanza?
Answer: There is one sentence in the first stanza.

Differentiated Instruction   Solutions for All Learners

Strategy for Less Proficient Readers
Copy both poems on the board. Circle the questions and statements in the poems, and discuss each one. Note the indentation in "Dream Deferred" and explain that the possible answers to this question form the topic of the poem. In "Dreams," make sure that students notice that the first and second stanzas begin with the same line. The three other lines in each stanza describe in metaphors what happens when people's dreams are frustrated.

Strategy for Gifted/Talented Students
Ask students to choose a simile from "Dream Deferred" or a metaphor from "Dreams" and illustrate it using art materials of their choice. Encourage them to use techniques and colors that express what the figurative language brings to their minds and how the figurative language affects them emotionally.

- Bring students' attention to the first line of the poem. **Ask** students to identify the figurative language that is used in this line.
  Answer: A simile compares the speaker's loneliness to that of a cloud. The speaker also uses personification when suggesting that the cloud feels lonely.

- **Ask** students the Literary Analysis question: To what does the speaker compare the daffodils in the simile in lines 7–8?
  Answer: The speaker compares the daffodils to stars in the Milky Way.

- **Ask** students to explain why the speaker's daffodil comparison is a simile and not a metaphor.
  Answer: The comparison is a simile because *as* is used in "Continuous *as* the stars."

- Point out to students that in the final lines of stanza two, the speaker describes the ten thousand daffodils as "Tossing their heads in a sprightly dance." **Ask** students to identify this figure of speech. Then, ask what characteristic helps them identify it.
  Answer: This figure of speech is personification. Students should recognize it because the speaker gives the daffodils the human characteristics of tossing their heads and dancing.

- Have students add the information to **Literary Analysis Graphic Organizer A** (p. 123 in *Graphic Organizer Transparencies*). Tell them to continue collecting figures of speech from the rest of the poems in the selection.

I WANDERED LONELY AS A CLOUD

WILLIAM WORDSWORTH

I wandered lonely as a cloud
That floats on high o'er vales[1] and hills,
When all at once I saw a crowd,
A host, of golden daffodils;
5   Beside the lake, beneath the trees,
Fluttering and dancing in the breeze.

⑥ Continuous as the stars that shine
And twinkle on the milky way,
They stretched in never-ending line
10   Along the margin of a bay:
Ten thousand saw I at a glance,
Tossing their heads in sprightly dance.

1. **o'er vales** over valleys.

Literary Analysis
Figurative Language
To what does the speaker compare the daffodils in the simile in lines 7–8?

Vocabulary Development

Think-Aloud: Context Clues
Direct students' attention to the word *bliss* in the second stanza on p. 569. Using a think-aloud process, model how to use context to infer the meaning of an unknown word. Say to students:

> I'm going to think aloud to show you how I would figure out the meaning of *bliss* from its context.
>
> In the line "they flash upon that inward eye" *they* refers to the daffodils and "inward eye" refers to the speaker's mind. Using this information, I can interpret that when the daffodils cross his mind his "heart with pleasure fills."
>
> The "inward eye" is referred to as "the bliss of solitude." Therefore, because the speaker's mind is filled with the joy of the daffodils, he must enjoy this solitude. This leads me to believe that *bliss* is a word that refers to something pleasant. It must mean "happiness" or "pleasure."

The waves beside them danced; but they
Outdid the sparkling waves in glee;

15 A poet could not but be gay,
In such a jocund² company;
I gazed—and gazed—but little thought

❼ What wealth the show to me had brought:

For oft, when on my couch I lie
20 In vacant or in <u>pensive</u> mood,
They flash upon that inward eye
Which is the bliss of solitude;
And then my heart with pleasure fills,
And dances with the daffodils.

---

2. **jocund** (jak′ ənd) *adj.* cheerful.

Vocabulary Builder
pensive (pen′ siv) *adj.*
deeply or seriously
thoughtful

569

• Refer students to line 18. **Ask** students this question: What "wealth" do memories of the scene give the speaker?
Answer: The "wealth" is a store of happy emotions that the speaker can call upon in later times of need.

• **Ask** students if they think the poet's choice of the word "wealth" is well suited. Have them explain their answers.
Possible response: "Wealth" is well suited because it compares the memory to an excessive amount of money or material possessions, and this relays how much the speaker treasures the memory.

Differentiated
Instruction   Solutions for All Learners

Strategy for Special Needs Students
Help students better understand figurative language by showing them **Literary Analysis Graphic Organizer B** (*Graphic Organizer Transparencies* p. 124). Review the types of figurative language: simile, metaphor, personification, and paradox. Ask them to look through the poems and locate the examples listed in the organizer. Use these examples to explain the characteristics of each figure of speech. Then encourage students to watch for other examples as they continue reading.

Support for English Learners
Write the words *cloud, hills, crowd, daffodils, trees,* and *breeze* on the board. Pronounce the words aloud with students, and then ask them to identify the words that rhyme. Now read the first stanza of "I Wandered Lonely as a Cloud." Help them identify the rhyme scheme. Then work through the remaining stanzas, helping them appreciate the regularity of the rhyme.

Meciendo

Gabriela Mistral

El mar sus millares de olas
mece, divino.
Oyendo a los mares amantes,
mezo a mi niño.

5 El viento errabundo en la noche
mece a los trigos.
Oyendo a los vientos amantes,
mezo a mi niño.

Dios Padre sus miles de mundos
10 mece sin ruido.
Sintiendo su mano en la sombra,
mezo a mi niño.

8 ▲ Critical Viewing
How well does this photograph illustrate the "loving sea" described in the poem? Explain. **[Evaluate]**

Rocking (Meciendo)
Gabriela Mistral
translated by Doris Dana

The sea rocks her thousands of waves.
The sea is divine.
Hearing the loving sea,
I rock my son.

5   The wind wandering by night
❾ rocks the wheat.
Hearing the loving wind,
I rock my son.

God, the Father, soundlessly rocks
10 His thousands of worlds.
Feeling His hand in the shadow,
I rock my son.

Literary Analysis
Figurative Language
What human traits
does the wind show in
the second stanza?

Meciendo / Rocking ■ 571

❾ **Literary Analysis**
Figurative Language

- **Ask** students the Literary Analysis question: What human traits does the wind show in the second stanza?
  Answer: The wind is "wandering" and "loving"; it "rocks the wheat."

- Discuss the effect of the personification in this poem. Then **ask** how the personification of the sea in the first stanza and of the wind in the second stanza affects the mood of the poem.
  Answer: It makes nature seem loving and humane.

- Point out that the human qualities of nature in the first two stanzas lead to the third stanza where the image of God replaces that of nature. Help students see the connection: that God is a gentle, human force that cares for people.

Differentiated Instruction   Solutions for All Learners

Strategy for English Learners
Encourage students fluent in Spanish to find other poems by Gabriela Mistral that are available in both Spanish and English. Have students work in small groups to prepare and perform readings of the works in both languages for the entire class. Tell them to be prepared to discuss how the two versions of each work differ in terms of rhyme scheme and other factors.

Strategy for Advanced Readers
Explain to students that they can learn something about a poem just by looking at it in its original language—even if they don't know that language. Have students look over both poems and compare the uses of rhyme and repetition to see if they notice any differences.

❿ Humanities

A Learned Man by Domenico Feti

Italian painter Domenico Feti (1588/89–1623?) was one of the early baroque painters. Feti's work is characterized by his use of light and shadow and by his portrayal of ordinary people with heroic qualities. Use these questions to stimulate discussion.

1. What does the painting suggest the man is doing? Explain why you think so.
   Answer: He is trying to solve a problem involving geography. He is looking at a map, holding his hand on a globe, and has several instruments used for geometry and geography. He appears to be deep in thought as though trying to solve a problem.

2. How does this painting reflect the image of Archimedes that is described in "Sonnet on Love XIII"?
   Answer: It shows an intelligent, studious man pondering a problem, as Archimedes might have done while thinking about how he could "move the world."

⓫ Critical Viewing

Possible response: Students might say that Archimedes would find the idea romantic. Some might say he would consider it nonsense for that reason. Others might say he would agree that love is a powerful human emotion that is capable of standing firm in a world of change.

❿

⓫ ⋀ Critical Viewing   Based on this depiction of Archimedes, how do you think he would have responded to de Sponde's poem? **[Speculate]**

572 ■ *Poetry*

Vocabulary Development

Vocabulary Knowledge Rating

When students have completed reading and discussing this group of poems, have them take out their **Vocabulary Knowledge Rating Chart** for Poetry Collection 1. Read the words aloud once more and have students rate their knowledge of the words again in the After Reading column. Clarify any words that are still problematic. Have students write their own definition and example or sentence in the appropriate column. Then, have students complete the **Vocabulary Builder Practice** activities on p. 575. Encourage students to use the words in further discussion and written work about these poems. Remind them that they will be accountable for these words on the Selection Test.

Sonnets on Love XIII

Jean de Sponde

translated by
David R. Slavitt

⑫ **Background**   Archimedes (är′ kə mē′ dēz′) (287?–212 B.C.) has been called the founder of theoretical mechanics. He was a brilliant Greek mathematician and inventor who once boasted that, given a place to stand in space and a long enough lever, he could move the Earth itself. Legend has it that when he made a great discovery, he jumped up and shouted "Eureka!" ("I have found it!").

"Give me a place to stand," Archimedes said,
"and I can move the world." Paradoxical, clever,
his remark which first explained the use of the lever
was an academic joke. But if that dead

5 sage could return to life, he would find a clear
demonstration of his idea, which is not
pure theory after all. That putative[1] spot
⑬ exists in the love I feel for you, my dear.

What could be more immovable or stronger?
10 What becomes more and more secure, the longer
it is battered by inconstancy and the stress

we find in our lives? Here is that fine fixed point
from which to move a world that is out of joint,
as he could have done, had he known a love like this.

---

1. **putative** (pyo͞ot′ ə tiv) *adj.* supposed; known by reputation.

Reading Skill
Reading Fluently
In what line does the sentence that starts in line 4 end?

---

⑫ Background

Archimedes Archimedes was a great friend of King Hiero of Syracuse. According to one story, Hiero heard Archimedes make his claim that he could move the world if he had a place to stand. Hiero challenged him to prove it. In the harbor lay a ship that the strength of many men could not launch. Archimedes built a system of pulleys and levers and launched the ship by himself, proving his claim.

According to another story, King Hiero had provided a goldsmith with exactly enough pure gold to make a crown. When he got the crown back, he suspected the goldsmith had diluted it with silver, keeping some of the pure gold. Hiero asked Archimedes to find out if it was possible to prove it. One day as Archimedes got into his bath, he realized that the water that overflowed the tub was exactly proportional to his body mass. He used this clue to solve the problem. Excited by his discovery, he jumped up and ran naked through the city yelling, "Eureka!" ("I have found it!")

⑬ Reading Skill
Reading Fluently

- Remind students that when they read poetry they should read in sentences. **Ask** students the Reading Skill question: In what line does the sentence that starts in line 4 end?
  Answer: It ends in the middle of line 7.

- Ask a volunteer to read the sentence aloud. If necessary, coach the student in reading it fluently without pausing at the end of each line.

▶ **Monitor Progress:** Assign portions of the sonnet to different students to read. Tell them to read fluently, pausing only for natural breaks and for punctuation.

▶ **Reteach:** If students continue to have difficulty reading fluently, have them guide you in rewriting the poem in paragraph form on the board. Then have students read it as prose. Discuss how fluent reading keeps related ideas together, making the meaning clearer, and keeps the rhythm natural.

Concept Connector

Connecting to the Literature
Have students compare the sentences they wrote before reading about why they think dreams are so important to people. Ask them to explain whether their thoughts have changed and, if so, how.

Literary Analysis Graphic Organizer
Ask students to review the graphic organizers they completed to identify figurative language in the poems. Show them **Literary Analysis Graphic Organizer B** (*Graphic Organizer Transparencies,* p. 124) as an example. Then have them share the graphic organizers they did and the figurative language they identified.

Apply the Skills

Poetry Collection 1

Thinking About the Selections

1. **Respond:** Which of these poems affected you the most? Why?
2. **(a) Recall:** To what two things does the speaker in "Dreams" compare life? **(b) Interpret:** Restate in your own words the advice that "Dreams" offers.
3. **(a) Recall:** How many questions does "Dream Deferred" ask? **(b) Contrast:** How is the last question different from the others?
4. **(a) Recall:** In "I Wandered Lonely as a Cloud," what natural sight does the speaker describe? **(b) Recall:** In "Meciendo/Rocking," what natural sights and sounds does the speaker describe? **(c) Compare and Contrast:** Explain how the natural sights and sounds affect both of the speakers.
5. **(a) Interpret:** In "Sonnets on Love XIII," to what does the speaker compare his love? **(b) Draw Conclusions:** What does this comparison suggest about the speaker's feelings? Explain.

Literary Analysis

6. **(a)** Identify one **simile** in "Dream Deferred" and one **metaphor** in "Dreams." **(b)** Explain what each **figure of speech** contributes to the overall meaning of the poem in which it appears.
7. **(a)** Identify one example of **personification** in Poetry Collection 1. **(b)** Explain how this use of **figurative language** contributes to the overall effect of the poem in which it appears.
8. **(a)** Identify the **paradox** in "Sonnets on Love XIII." **(b)** Explain how it seems contradictory but actually makes sense.

Reading Skill

9. **(a)** Using a graphic organizer like the one shown, rewrite one stanza in Poetry Collection 1 as a prose paragraph.

Stanza	Paragraph
God, the Father, soundlessly rocks His thousands of worlds. Feeling His hand in the shadow, I rock my son.	God, the Father, soundlessly rocks His thousands of worlds. Feeling His hand in the shadow, I rock my son.

(b) Read both the stanza and paragraph aloud. How does following the punctuation rather than the line breaks help you to **read fluently**?

574 ■ Poetry

QuickReview

Poems at a Glance
"Dream Deferred" explores the power of unfulfilled dreams.

"Dreams" advises readers to hold on to dreams.

"I Wandered Lonely as a Cloud" celebrates nature's beauty.

"Meciendo" finds comfort in nature's divine rhythms.

"Sonnets on Love XIII" addresses love's power and stability.

For: Self-test
Visit: www.PHSchool.com
Web Code: epa-6402

Figurative Language: language that is used imaginatively rather than literally, *including simile, metaphor, personification,* or *paradox*
Reading Fluently: reading smoothly and continuously with comprehension

---

1. **Sample response:** "Dreams" had the strongest effect on me because of the importance of the theme and because of the two superb metaphors.

2. (a) The speaker compares life to an injured bird and to a barren, frozen field. (b) **Possible response:** Cherish your dreams, for without them, life is meaningless and sterile.

3. (a) "Dream Deferred" asks six questions. (b) The last question is in italics, is separated from the other questions, and comes after a statement. This treatment makes the last question the one with the most impact.

4. (a) The poem describes a field of daffodils blowing in the breeze. (b) The speaker describes the sight and sound of waves and of the wind blowing wheat. (c) The sights and sounds fill the speakers with delight and comfort.

5. (a) The speaker compares his love to the spot in space on which he would stand to move the planet. (b) The comparison suggests that the speaker's love is powerful and immovable, just as Archimedes' comment suggests that his thoughts and ideas were so powerful that he could change the world.

6. (a) **Simile:** "Does it dry up like a raisin in the sun?"; **Metaphor:** "life is a broken-winged bird. . . ." (b) The simile in "Dream Deferred" makes the reader wonder if a deferred dream just wastes away. The metaphor in "Dreams" tells the reader that if dreams die we cannot live life to its fullest extent.

7. (a) **Possible response:** One example is in "I Wandered Lonely as a Cloud": "A host, of golden daffodils . . . Fluttering and dancing . . ." (b) It makes the daffodils appear alive and playful, which adds to the joy of the poem. Another sample answer can be found on **Literary Analysis Graphic Organizer B,** p. 124, in *Graphic Organizer Transparencies.*

8. (a) The paradox is between Archimedes' place to stand and the speaker's love for his beloved.

(b) The reader realizes that the scientific impossibility reveals an emotional truth.

9. (a) **Possible response:** "The wind wandering by night rocks the wheat. Hearing the loving wind, I rock my son." (b) When following the punctuation, similar ideas are kept together through sentence structure, making reading more fluent.

Vocabulary Builder

Practice **Analogies** show the relationships between pairs of words. Use a word from the Collection 1 list on page 564 to complete each analogy. Your choice should create a word pair that matches the relationship between the first two words given. Explain the relationship.

1. rushed : hurried :: _____ : delayed
2. active : exercise :: _____ : ponder

Adding Words to Your Vocabulary Using a thesaurus, find a **synonym**, or word with a similar meaning, for *deferred* and *pensive*. Use each synonym in a sentence that makes the meaning of the word clear. (For more on using a thesaurus, see page R7.)

Writing

Using the scenes described by Wordsworth or Mistral as a model, write a **description of a scene** in nature. Create your own descriptive word picture in a few paragraphs or a poem.
- Choose a scene that you know firsthand or from photographs.
- List details in the scene that appeal to one or more of the senses.
- Refer to your list of details as you draft your description, and work to convey a unified impression.

For *Grammar, Vocabulary,* and *Assessment,* see **Build Language Skills,** pages 584–585.

Extend Your Learning

Listening and Speaking Use the poems in Poetry Collection 1 as the basis for an **impromptu speech** about dreams, nature, or love.
- Do not write a script or an outline; instead, consider the central point you want to convey.
- Work to use a variety of sentence structures.
- Use body language and eye contact to convey sincerity.
Invite your audience to give you feedback about your performance.

Research and Technology In a group, discuss and agree upon a **soundtrack** of appropriate music to accompany each poem in Poetry Collection 1. Research the music of the period in which each poem was written, and choose music that fits each poem's mood and ideas. Invite classmates to read the poems while the music is playing.

Apply the Skills ■ 575

Assessment Resources

The following resources can be used to assess students' knowledge and skills.

Unit 4 Resources
  Selection Test A, p. 28–30
  Selection Test B, p. 31–33

Go **O**nline Students may use the **Self-test** to
—Assessment prepare for **Selection Test A** or
Selection Test B.

Go **O**nline **For:** An additional research activity
—Research **Visit:** www.PHSchool.com
Web Code: epd-7401
For another research activity to extend students' learning, give students this Web Code.

Vocabulary Builder
Practice
1. deferred
2. pensive

Adding Words to Your Vocabulary
Possible responses:

1. Deferred—postponed; The game was <u>postponed</u> because of rain.

2. Pensive—reflective; The rainy day put Juan in a <u>reflective</u> mood; he began to think about how proud he was of his brother.

Writing
- To give students guidance for writing a description of a scene, give them **Support for Writing** for Poetry Collection 1, p. 25, in *Unit 4 Resources.*

- To evaluate students' descriptions, use the Descriptive Essay rubrics, pp. 55–56 in *General Resources.*

Six Traits Focus

✔	Ideas	✔	Word Choice
✔	Organization		Sentence Fluency
	Voice		Conventions

W/G **Writing and Grammar, Gold Level**
Students will find guidance on descriptive writing in Chapter 6.

Build Language Skills
Go to pages 584–585 for vocabulary and grammar lessons and assessment practice.

Extend Your Learning
The **Support for Extend Your Learning** page (*Unit 4 Resources,* p. 26) provides guided note-taking opportunities to help students complete the Extend Your Learning activities.

Teaching notes for Literary Analysis, Reading Skill, and Vocabulary Builder for these selections begin on p. 564.

❸ Connecting to the Literature

- Provide these sample sentences to demonstrate use of the expressive words:

  1. Computers allow us to *maximize* our time and abilities.

  2. Computers enable us to *interact* with people all over the world without leaving home.

  3. Computers *minimize* the time we spend doing research.

  4. They *accelerate* the speed with which personal and social skills are declining.

  5. People who *deny* the impact of computers are out of touch with today's technology.

- Help students further develop their expressive vocabulary by providing these words: *anticipate, detriment, revolution,* and *serene.* Encourage students to use these words as they discuss the selections.

Concept Connector ➡

Students will follow up on this activity after reading the poems in Poetry Collection 2.

Go **Online** For additional informa-
Author Link tion about the authors in
Collection 2, have students type in the Web Code and then select the poet.

Poetry

❸ Connecting to the Literature

Reading/Writing Connection In "All Watched Over by Machines of Loving Grace," Richard Brautigan imagines a world in which human beings and computers live in perfect harmony. Write two sentences about the positive role of computers in our lives, and write another two about the negative side of the computer age. Use at least three of these words: *maximize, minimize, accelerate, deny, interact.*

Review
For **Literary Analysis, Reading Skill,** and **Vocabulary Builder,** see page 564.

Meet the Authors

Richard **Brautigan** (1935–1984)

"All Watched Over by Machines of Loving Grace" (page 577)
With his 1967 novel *Trout Fishing in America,* Richard Brautigan became a spokesperson of the hippie generation. Ironically, he was at least fifteen years older than the hippies and a product of the Beat generation that preceded them. Nevertheless, his writing demonstrates his free spirit. His books present sketches of a counterculture that resists dependence on machines, industry, and business.

Emily **Dickinson** (1830–1886)

"Hope" is the thing with feathers— (page 578);
Much Madness is divinest Sense— (page 579)
Despite her quiet exterior, Emily Dickinson's inner life overflowed with energy. She produced at least 1,775 poems. Dickinson looked deeply into simple subjects—a fly buzzing, a bird on a walk, the changing seasons. She also made profound explorations of love, death, and the relationship between the human and the divine. She remains unquestionably one of America's finest poets.

Stanley **Kunitz** (b. 1905)

The War Against the Trees (page 580)
Stanley Kunitz was born in Worcester, Massachusetts, and published his first book of poems in 1930. Kunitz has worked as an editor on many small magazines and has taught countless young poets. He was named the United States Poet Laureate in 2000.

Go **Online**
Author Link

For: More about the authors
Visit: www.PHSchool.com
Web Code: epe-9403

Differentiated Instruction   Solutions for All Learners

Support for Below-Level Students [L1, L2]	Support for English Learners [EL]
Unit 4 Resources 　**Vocabulary Warm-up Word Lists,** p. 34 　**Vocabulary Warm-up Practice,** p. 35 　**Reading Warm-up A,** p. 36 　**Selection Test A,** pp. 46–48 **Graphic Organizer Transparencies** 　**Literary Analysis Graphic Organizer, Transparency B,** p. 125	**Unit 4 Resources** 　**Vocabulary Warm-up Word Lists,** p. 34 　**Vocabulary Warm-up Practice,** p. 35 　**Reading Warm-up A,** p. 36 **Reader's Notebook: English Learner's Version** **Listening to Literature Audio CD**

All Watched Over by Machines of Loving Grace

Richard Brautigan

❶ ❷

I like to think (and
the sooner the better!)
of a cybernetic meadow
❸ where mammals and computers
5 live together in mutually
programming harmony
like pure water
touching clear sky.

I like to think
(right now, please!)
10 of a cybernetic forest
filled with pines and electronics
where deer stroll peacefully
past computers
as if they were flowers
15 with spinning blossoms.

I like to think
(it has to be!)
of a cybernetic ecology
where we are free of our labors
20 and joined back to nature,
returned to our mammal
brothers and sisters,
and all watched over
by machines of loving grace.

**Literary Analysis
Figurative Language**
What simile does the
speaker use in lines
4–8 to describe the
cybernetic meadow?

All Watched Over by Machines of Loving Grace ■ 577

- Discuss with students Dickinson's use of dashes. Point out that Dickinson did not always rely so heavily on dashes. She did so during her most prolific period, which was when this poem was written. Explain that the dash calls for a strong pause, although not quite as strong as that of a period. It suggests a certain indefiniteness, as though an idea is not totally ended, but is firmly interrupted. In some ways, the dash suggests more spontaneity than periods, hinting that the writer is spinning off ideas as she thinks of them. A fluent reading of Dickinson's poem should suggest this process.

- Demonstrate to students the skill of reading with fluency by reading the second stanza aloud slowly. Then, **ask** the Reading Skill question: Where in the second stanza could you replace a dash with a period to signify the end of a sentence?
Answer: The final dash in the stanza could be replaced with a period.

▶ **Monitor Progress:** Have different students read stanzas from the poem. Tell them to read fluently, pausing only for natural breaks and for punctuation.

▶ **Reteach:** If students continue to have difficulty reading fluently, have them guide you in rewriting the poem in paragraph form. Replace dashes, when possible, with more familiar punctuation. Then, have students read the poem as prose. Discuss how fluent reading keeps related ideas together, thus clarifying the meaning and maintaining a natural rhythm.

❺ **Critical Viewing**

Possible response: Birds sing so vivaciously they seem filled with optimism and hope. Their song is especially noticeable after storms pass or in the spring, making people think of better times to come.

"Hope" is the thing with feathers—
EMILY DICKINSON

"Hope" is the thing with feathers—
That perches in the soul—
And sings the tune without the words—
And never stops—at all—

5   And sweetest—in the Gale[1]—is heard—
❹   And sore must be the storm—
That could abash the little Bird
That kept so many warm—

I've heard it in the chillest land—
10 And on the strangest Sea—
Yet, never, in Extremity,
It asked a crumb—of Me.

---

1. **Gale** (gāl) *n.* strong wind.

Reading Skill
Reading Fluently
Where in the second stanza could you replace a dash with a period to signify the end of a sentence?

❺ ◀ **Critical Viewing**
Why might someone associate birds with hope? **[Speculate]**

578 ■ *Poetry*

Vocabulary Development

Expressive Vocabulary
After students read the two Dickinson poems, write the expressive vocabulary words introduced on p. 576 on the board: *maximize, minimize, accelerate, deny,* and *interact.* Have students use the expressive words when responding to questions about the main ideas of the poems. Ask questions such as:

1. Why do you think hope sometimes *accelerates* when times are at their worst?

2. Would Dickinson *deny* the importance of hope?

3. How does hope *interact* with our daily lives?

4. How can madness *maximize* sense, or logic and reason?

5. Do the ideas of the majority sometimes force people to *minimize* the expression of ideas? How?

Much Madness is divinest Sense—

EMILY DICKINSON

Much Madness is divinest Sense—
To a <u>discerning</u> Eye—
Much Sense—the starkest Madness—
6 'Tis the Majority
5 In this, as All, prevail—
Assent[1]—and you are sane—
Demur[2]—you're straightway dangerous—
And handled with a Chain—

---

1. Assent (ə sent´) v. agree.
2. Demur (dē mʉr´) v. hesitate because of doubts or objections.

Vocabulary Builder
discerning (di sʉrn´ iŋ)
adj. having good
judgment or
understanding

❻ Reading Skill
Reading Fluently
- Ask a student to read the poem aloud, using what he or she has learned about reading fluently.
- When the student has completed reading, discuss Dickinson's punctuation and explain how her poetry can be especially difficult because the dashes must be interpreted.

Much Madness is divinest Sense— ■ 579

Differentiated
Instruction   Solutions for All Learners

Enrichment for Advanced Readers
Suggest that students read additional poems by Emily Dickinson. Provide students with **Authors In Depth,** Gold Level, which contains the following poems:
"A narrow Fellow in the Grass" (p. 179)
" 'Nature' is what we see" (p. 180)
"Most she touched me by her muteness" (p. 181)
"A fuzzy fellow, without feet" (p. 182)
"How many Flowers fail in Wood" (p. 183)
"It sifts from Leaden Sieves" (p. 184)

"How happy is the little Stone" (p. 185)
"Exhilaration is the Breeze" (p. 186)
"Hope is a strange invention" (p. 187)
"Opinion is a flitting thing" (p. 188)
"The Bustle in a House" (p. 189)
"A word is dead" (p. 190)
"This is my letter to the World" (p. 191)
"There is no Frigate like a Book" (p. 192)
"Letter to Austin Dickinson" (p. 193)
    After students have read these or other poems by Dickinson, have them form discussion groups in which they compare and contrast the poems.

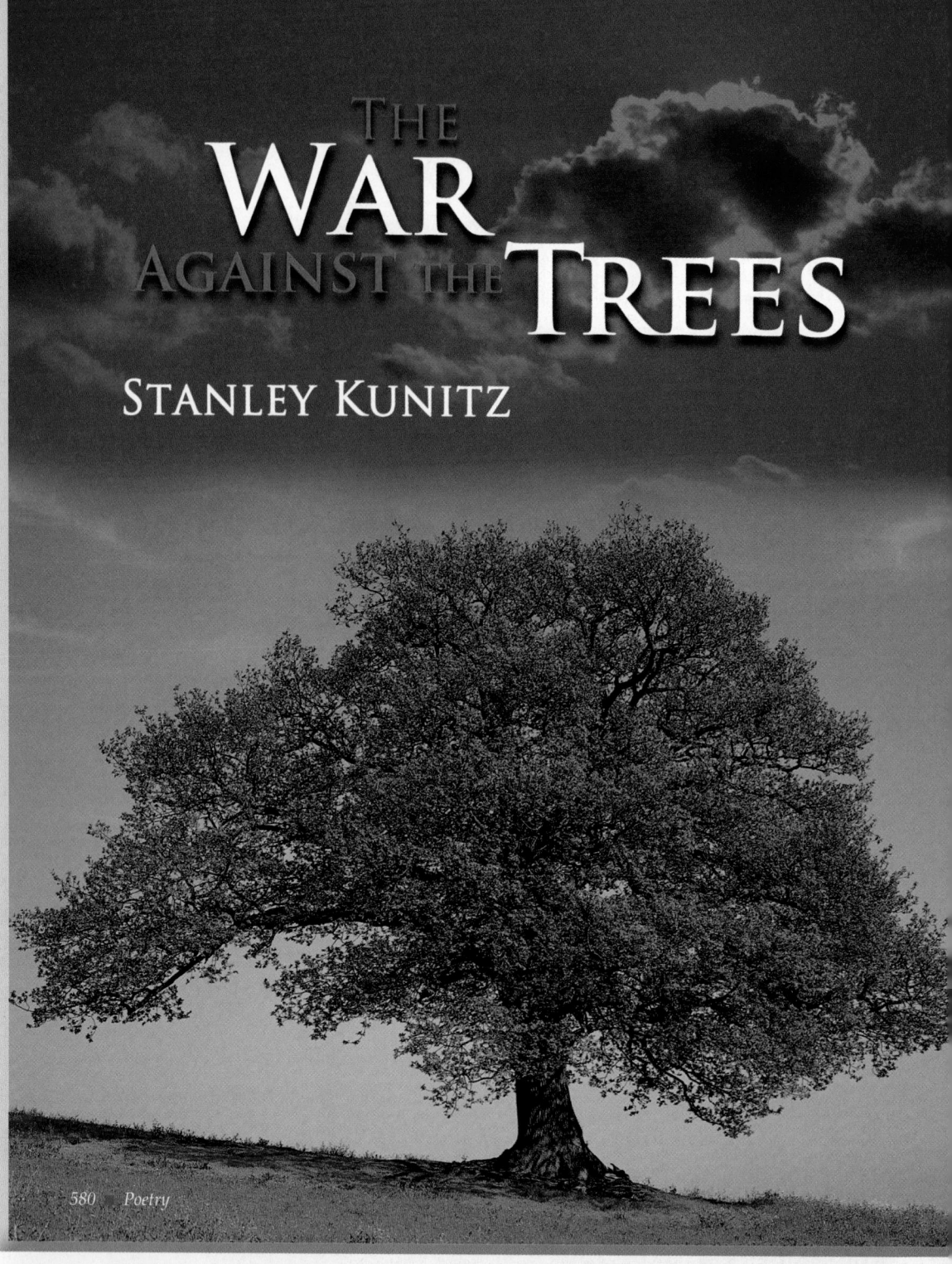

THE WAR AGAINST THE TREES

STANLEY KUNITZ

580   *Poetry*

Vocabulary Development

Vocabulary Knowledge Rating

When students have completed reading and discussing Poetry Collection 2, have them take out their **Vocabulary Knowledge Rating Chart** for these poems. Read the words aloud once more and have students rate their knowledge of the words again in the After Reading column. Clarify any words that are still problematic. Have students write their own definition and example or sentence in the appropriate column. Then have students complete the **Vocabulary Builder Practice** activities on p. 583. Encourage students to use the words in further discussion and written work about these poems. Remind them that they will be accountable for these words on the Selection Test.

The man who sold his lawn to standard oil
Joked with his neighbors come to watch the show
While the bulldozers, drunk with gasoline,
Tested the virtue of the soil
5   Under the branchy sky
By overthrowing first the privet-row.

Forsythia-forays and hydrangea-raids
Were but <u>preliminaries</u> to a war
❽   Against the great-grandfathers of the town,
10   So freshly lopped and maimed.
They struck and struck again,
And with each elm a century went down.

All day the hireling engines charged the trees,
Subverting them by hacking underground
15   In grub-dominions, where dark summer's mole
Rampages through his halls,
Till a northern seizure shook
Those crowns, forcing the giants to their knees.

I saw the ghosts of children at their games
20   Racing beyond their childhood in the shade,
And while the green world turned its death-foxed page
And a red wagon wheeled,
I watched them disappear
Into the suburbs of their grievous age.

25   Ripped from the craters much too big for hearts
The club-roots bared their amputated coils,
Raw gorgons matted blind, whose pocks and scars
Cried Moon! on a corner lot
One witness-moment, caught
30   In the rear-view mirrors of the passing cars.

Vocabulary Builder
preliminaries (prē lim′ ə ner′ ēz) *n.* steps or events before the main one

Literary Analysis
Figurative Language
What are the "giants" that are personified in line 18?

❼ ◄ **Critical Viewing** What does a tree like the one shown represent to the speaker of the poem? **[Connect]**

The War Against the Trees ■ 581

❽ **Literary Analysis**
Figurative Language

• Read the poem aloud for students, pausing after line 10. **Ask** students what these words mean: "war / Against the great-grandfathers."
Answer: It refers to the destruction of the old trees in the yard.

• Continue reading and pause again at the end of stanza three. **Ask** students the Literary Analysis question: What are the "giants" that are personified in line 18?
Answer: The giants are the large trees.

• Continue reading to the end of the poem.

• **Ask** students to identify the metaphor used in line 21.
Answer: "The green world turned its death-foxed page. . . ."

• Explain to students that the term "fox" is specific to books; it means a stained page.

• **Ask:** Now that you know the meaning of the term "foxed," explain the meaning of the metaphor.
Answer: The trauma of the trees is likened to the turning of a "death-foxed" page by the "green world" of nature. The metaphor suggests that death is the source of the stain on the book of nature.

Concept Connector

Connecting to the Literature
Have students compare the sentences they wrote before reading about the role of computers in our lives. Ask them to explain whether their thoughts have changed and, if so, how.

Literary Analysis Graphic Organizer
Ask students to review the graphic organizers they completed to identify figurative language in the poems. Show them **Literary Analysis Graphic Organizer B** (*Graphic Organizer Transparencies,* p. 125) as an example. Then, have students share the graphic organizers they did and the figurative language they identified.

Apply the Skills

Poetry Collection 2

1. **Sample answer:** "The War Against the Trees" made the strongest impression on me because of the ecological message and the powerful personification of the trees.

2. (a) The speaker compares computers with elements in nature. (b) **Possible response:** The comparison suggests that the speaker feels comfortable and safe with computers.

3. (a) Hope sings "sweetest" in times of extremity—in storm, "chillest land," or on "the strangest Sea." (b) Hope is most needed at the worst moments of people's lives.

4. (a) People who are involved with industry and development are at war with the trees. (b) The image of war victimizes the trees, showing that the speaker is concerned about their welfare.

5. (a) Any behavior that is different from that of the majority is considered insane. (b) Students will probably agree with the speaker, arguing that different ideas and opinions often are seen unfavorably.

6. (a) **Possible responses: Simile:** Mammals and computers that are "like pure water/touching clear sky" (from "All Watched Over"); **Metaphor:** "Hope is the thing with feathers" (from "Hope") (b) The simile in "All Watched Over" evokes feelings of peace and harmony. The metaphor in "Hope" identifies hope with a bird, conveying both its fragility and its forcefulness in the face of great odds.

7. (a) The trees in "The War Against the Trees" are described as "great-grandfathers." (b) This personification humanizes the trees and gives them stature, which helps the reader sympathize with their destruction.

8. (a) The paradox is between madness and wisdom. (b) The truth of this paradox is that society can pull people into false beliefs, and individuals who look beyond the beliefs—the wisest among us—may be seen as crazy or as fools.

9. (a) **Possible response:** I've heard it in the chillest land and

Thinking About the Selections

1. **Respond:** Which of these poems affected you the most? Why?
2. **(a) Recall:** To what does the speaker compare computers in the imaginary world of "All Watched Over by Machines of Loving Grace"? **(b) Interpret:** What does this comparison suggest about the speaker's feelings about computers in the real world?
3. **(a) Recall:** In "'Hope' is the thing with feathers—," when does hope sing the sweetest? **(b) Interpret:** Why does hope sing so well at these times?
4. **(a) Interpret:** In "The War Against the Trees," who or what is at war with the trees? **(b) Draw Conclusions:** What does the image of war suggest about the speaker's feelings toward the trees and what is happening to them? Explain.
5. **(a) Interpret:** In "Much Madness is divinest Sense—," what kind of behavior is considered insane? **(b) Evaluate:** Do you agree with the speaker's ideas? Why or why not?

Literary Analysis

6. **(a)** Identify a **simile** and a **metaphor** in Poetry Collection 2. **(b)** Explain what each **figure of speech** contributes to the overall meaning or effect of the poem in which it appears.
7. **(a)** Identify one example of **personification** in Collection 2. **(b)** Explain how this use of **figurative language** contributes to the overall meaning or effect of the poem in which it appears.
8. **(a)** Identify the **paradox** in "Much Madness is divinest Sense—." **(b)** Explain why it is a paradox.

Reading Skill

9. **(a)** Using a graphic organizer like the one shown, rewrite one stanza in Poetry Collection 2 as a prose paragraph.

Stanza	Paragraph
I've heard it in the chillest land— And on the strangest Sea— Yet, never, in Extremity, It asked a crumb—of Me.	I've heard it in the chillest land and on the strangest Sea, yet never, in Extremity, it asked a crumb of me.

(b) Read both the stanza and paragraph aloud. How does following the punctuation rather than the line breaks help you to **read fluently**?

QuickReview

Poems at a Glance
"All Watched Over by Machines of Loving Grace" presents a futuristic vision of a world run by computers.

"'Hope' is the thing with feathers—" discusses the power and constancy of hope.

"The War Against the Trees" explores the battle between "progress" and nature.

"Much Madness is divinest Sense—" explores the idea of sanity.

Assessment

For: Self-test
Visit: www.PHSchool.com
Web Code: epa-6403

Figurative Language: language that is used imaginatively rather than literally, including *simile, metaphor, personification,* or *paradox*

Reading Fluently: reading smoothly and continuously with comprehension

on the strangest Sea, yet, never, in Extremity, it asked a crumb of me (from "'Hope' is the thing with feathers—"). (b) **Sample answer:** Following the punctuation allows me to see the flow of the sentence and better grasp its meaning.

Another sample answer can be found on **Literary Analysis Graphic Organizer B,** p. 125, in *Graphic Organizer Transparencies.*

Vocabulary Builder

Practice **Analogies** show the relationships between pairs of words. Use a word from the Collection 2 list on page 564 to complete each analogy. Your choice should create a word pair that matches the relationship between the first two words given. Explain the relationship.

1. forgiving : fan :: _____ : expert

2. rehearsal : performance :: _____ : championship

Adding Words to Your Vocabulary Using a thesaurus, find a **synonym**, or word with a similar meaning, for *preliminaries* and *discerning*. Use each synonym in a sentence that makes the meaning of the word clear. (For more on using a thesaurus, see page R7.)

Writing

Using the scene described in "The War Against the Trees" as a model, write a **description of a scene** in nature. Create your own descriptive word picture in a few paragraphs or a poem.

- Choose a scene that you know firsthand or from photographs.
- List details in the scene that appeal to one or more of the senses.
- Refer to your list of details as you draft your description, and work to convey a unified impression.

For *Grammar, Vocabulary,* and *Assessment,* see **Build Language Skills,** pages 584–585.

Extend Your Learning

Listening and Speaking Use the poems in Poetry Collection 2 as the basis for an **impromptu speech** about dreams, nature, or love.

- Do not write a script or an outline; instead, consider the central point to convey.
- Work to use a variety of sentence structures.
- Use body language and eye contact to convey sincerity.

Invite your audience to give you feedback about your performance.

Research and Technology In a group, discuss and agree upon a **soundtrack** of appropriate music to accompany each poem in Poetry Collection 2. Research the music of the period in which each poem was written, and choose music that fits each poem's mood and ideas. Invite classmates to read the poems while the music is playing.

Apply the Skills ■ 583

Assessment Resources

The following resources can be used to assess students' knowledge and skills.

Unit 4 Resources
Selection Test A, pp. 46–48
Selection Test B, pp. 49–51

 Go Online
Assessment Students may use the **Self-test** to prepare for **Selection Test A** or **Selection Test B.**

Go Online **For:** An additional research activity
Research **Visit:** www.PHSchool.com
Web Code: epd-7402
For another research activity to extend students' learning, give students this Web Code.

Vocabulary Builder
Practice

1. discerning
2. preliminaries

Adding Words to Your Vocabulary
Possible responses:

discerning—perceptive; The *perceptive* judge made the right decision.

preliminaries—preparatories; The *preparatories* were held a week before the main contest.

Writing

- To give students guidance for writing a description of a scene, give them **Support for Writing** for Poetry Collection 2, p. 41, in *Unit 4 Resources.*
- To evaluate students' descriptions, use the Descriptive Essay rubrics, pp. 55–56 in *General Resources.*

Six Traits Focus

✔	Ideas	✔	Word Choice
✔	Organization		Sentence Fluency
	Voice		Conventions

WG **Writing and Grammar,** Gold Level
Students will find guidance on descriptive writing in Chapter 6.

Build Language Skills

Go to pages 584–585 for vocabulary and grammar lessons and assessment practice.

Extend Your Learning

The **Support for Extend Your Learning** page (*Unit 4 Resources,* p. 42) provides guided note-taking opportunities to help students complete the Extend Your Learning activities.

Build Language Skills

Poetry Collection 1 • Poetry Collection 2

Vocabulary Skill

- Introduce the suffix *-able*. Ask students to brainstorm for words that contain this suffix.
  Possible responses: *doable, livable, drivable, bendable, sinkable, acceptable, unthinkable, correctable, playable, moldable*

- Explain how "capable of being" or "having the quality of" contributes to the meaning of these words.

- Have students complete the Practice activity on this page.

Answers

1. able to be used; The shovel was so bent it was no longer *usable*.

2. able to be loved; Many people in the audience thought the young actress was *lovable*.

3. able to be retracted, or withdrawn; The tripod with the *retractable* legs is easier to carry.

4. free from stress or anxiety; able to be comforting; I like the soft couch better because it is more *comfortable*.

5. able to be washed; Alice will only buy clothes that are *washable* in a machine.

Grammar Lesson

- Tell students that prepositions usually relate to nouns, verbs, or adjectives.

- Point out that a pronoun that is the object of a preposition takes the objective case or form (for example, *me, him, her, them,* and *us*).

Answers

1. The cat ran up the tree. Instead of avoiding the tree, the cat ran up the tree.

2. Put the book beneath the desk. The book that is beneath the desk—not on the desk—cannot be used.

3. The space probe traveled beyond Mars. Instead of stopping at Mars, the probe went farther.

4. He ran from school. The child has changed directions.

5. Evelyn turned off the light. Instead of being in the light, Evelyn is now in the dark.

Vocabulary Skill

Suffixes The **Latin suffix** *-able* means "capable of being" or "having the quality of." Adding the suffix *-able* changes a base word to an adjective. For example, the word *considerable* means "worthy, or capable of, being considered." The addition of the suffix changes the verb "consider" to the adjective "considerable."

Practice Each of the following words contains the suffix *-able*. Write a definition of each word, and use it in a sentence.

1. usable
2. lovable
3. retractable
4. comfortable
5. washable

Grammar Lesson

Preposition and Object of the Preposition A **preposition** is a word that relates a noun or pronoun to another word in the sentence. Although most prepositions, such as *at, by, in,* and *with*, are single words, some prepositions, such as *because of* and *in addition to,* are **compound**. The **object of the preposition** is the noun or pronoun at the end of a prepositional phrase.

Common Prepositions: about, above, across, below, beyond, by, down, except, for, from, in, of, on, over, past, through, to, under, until, up, with

Common Compound Prepositions: according to, along with, in front of, instead of, next to

Object of a Preposition: Mr. Johnson ate at a good restaurant. (*restaurant* is the object of the preposition *at*)

Practice Rewrite the following sentences, substituting a different preposition for the italicized one. Then, write a brief explanation of how the new preposition changes the meaning of the sentence.

1. The cat ran *around* the tree.
2. Put the book *on* the desk.
3. The space probe traveled *to* Mars.
4. He ran *to* school.
5. Evelyn turned *on* the light.

W/G *Prentice Hall Writing and Grammar Connection: Chapter 19, Section 1.*

MorePractice

For more practice with prepositions and objects of the preposition, see the Grammar Handbook, pp. R41 and R43.

Teaching Resources

The following resources can be used to enrich or extend the instruction for Build Language Skills.

Unit 4 Resources

Build Language Skills: Vocabulary: Latin Suffixes, p. 44

Build Grammar Skills: Preposition and Object of the Preposition, p. 45

Assessment Practice

Reading Skill: Read Fluently

Directions: *Read the poem. Then, answer the questions.*

> I love to go out in late September
> among the fat, overripe, icy, black blackberries
> to eat blackberries for breakfast,
> the stalks very prickly, a penalty
> 5 they earn for knowing the black art
> of blackberry-making; and as I stand among them
> lifting the stalks to my mouth, the ripest berries
> fall almost unbidden to my tongue,
> as words sometimes do, certain peculiar words
> 10 like *strengths* or *squinched,*
> many-lettered, one-syllabled lumps,
> which I squeeze, squinch open, and splurge well
> in the silent, startled, icy, black language
> of blackberry-eating in late September.
> —"Blackberry Eating" by Galway Kinnell

1. Which line tells what the speaker loves to do?
 A line 3
 B line 6
 C line 10
 D line 13

2. Which of the following lines ends with a subject separated from its verb in the next line?
 A line 1
 B line 4
 C line 7
 D line 12

3. What does the punctuation in line 9, signal?
 A the end of an extended metaphor
 B a new analogy
 C the beginning of a series of similes
 D the start of the thematic explanation

4. How should lines 12–13 be read?
 A Pause briefly at the end of line 12.
 B Stop completely at the end of line 12.
 C Continue to the end of line 13.
 D Continue to the comma in line 13.

Timed Writing: Analysis [Critical Stance]

Review the poetry in *Poetry Collection 1* or *Poetry Collection 2*. Select a poem in which symbolism significantly contributes to the theme of the work. Explain how the symbols help convey the message of the poem. **(60 minutes)**

 ## Writing Workshop: *Work in Progress*

Descriptive Essay

Using your Sight List, choose one place that is most interesting. Add a list of adjectives that describe other characteristics of the place, such as smells or sounds. Save this Sensory Words list in your portfolio.

Answers

Reading: Reading Fluently
1. A
2. C
3. D
4. D

Timed Writing

- Tell students that when they write an analysis of a poem, they should pay attention to the poem's theme, structure, symbolism, and meaning.
- Have students review the poems and select one that meets the criteria of the assignment.
- Tell students to reread the poem and take notes on the symbolism and how it contributes to the theme. Remind students to record the line numbers of their references.
- When students have completed taking notes, suggest that they organize their notes and begin writing. Remind them to cite lines.
- Suggest that students plan their time to give twenty minutes to reviewing the poem, thirty minutes to writing, and ten minutes to reviewing and revising.
- Assess students' essays on their explanation of the symbolism, analysis of how it contributes to the theme, and effectiveness of their supporting evidence.

Writing Workshop
Work in Progress

Descriptive Essay

- Have students go to their portfolios and take out the Sight List they made in the **Work-in-Progress** assignment on p. 559.
- Remind students that this work may be used in the descriptive essay that they will write in the **Writing Workshop** at the end of Part 1.
- Once students have selected the place that they find most interesting, suggest they take a moment to visualize it and remember their experience of being there. Have them jot down any descriptive words about the place that occur to them.
- Have students review their list of words and circle any that are related to the senses of smell, sound, hearing, or taste. Then, have them add these words to their Sight List to create a Sensory Words list.
- When students have finished this activity, have them save their work in their portfolios. They will use it as they continue this **Work in Progress.**

Students will

1. understand and analyze case studies.

2. read a case study about careers in robotics.

See TeacherExpress™/Lesson View for a detailed lesson plan for Reading Informational Materials.

About Case Studies

- **Ask** a volunteer to define the term "case study."
  Possible response: A case study is a detailed analysis that tells who, what, where, when, and/or why about a specific person, group, project, or situation for the purpose of presenting a real-life example that can serve as a model.

- Have students read "About Case Studies."

- Explain to students that people often read case studies to learn about a situation or problem that is similar to something they face. Point out that case studies offer an example of how someone else has approached a situation. Tell students that, by reading case studies, they can see if they could or would want to do something similar.

Reading Skill
Making Generalizations

- Remind students that readers regularly make generalizations. Point out that it is helpful to take information from one setting and apply it to another.

- Review with students the Making Generalizations chart.

- Explain that case studies usually include an introduction, an analysis, details, and a conclusion. Tell students that, as readers, they will make generalizations based on what they learn from the analysis and details presented in case studies.

Reading Informational Materials

Case Studies

In Part 1, you are learning how to read fluently while reading literature. Reading fluently helps you to group words into meaningful chunks. This skill will help you connect ideas when reading informational materials such as a case study. If you read about the field of computers in Richard Brautigan's "All Watched Over by Machines of Loving Grace," you might enjoy this case study about careers in robotics.

About Case Studies

A **case study** is a detailed analysis of a person, group, project, or situation. It provides a real-life example of what happens in specific situations and can serve as a model for similar initiatives. A case study usually has these elements:

- An introduction explaining what is being studied and why
- Facts, examples, and quotations
- Instances of *inductive reasoning*—reasoning from specific examples to a general concept
- Instances of *deductive reasoning*—applying a general principle to a specific case
- A conclusion and recommendation summarizing the information and providing ideas for how to apply it

Reading Skill

A case study presents specific details and examples to illustrate the subject. A reader uses these details to make generalizations. **Generalizations** are broad statements that are true when applied to a variety of circumstances. Making generalizations helps us make decisions, and it helps us apply our reading to our lives. As you read the case study "Careers in Robotics," use a chart like the one shown to make meaningful generalizations based on the details in the text.

Details	Generalization
• While in college, Matt and Gil had many different career goals. • After college, they both became successful engineers.	Even if you are unsure about your goals while in school, you can still find a good career.

Differentiated Instruction Solutions for All Learners

Reading Support
Give students reading support with the appropriate version of the *Reader's Notebooks:*

Reader's Notebook, [L2]

Reader's Notebook: Adapted Version, [L1]

Reader's Notebook: English Learner's Version, [EL]

NASA Robotics Education Project

Careers in Robotics: A Case Study

Think you'll never use high school math? Think again . . .

> In the introduction, the author tells who the subjects of the study are, explains what they do, and points out that there is "no single path" to becoming a robotics engineer.

Gil Jones and Matt Zucker may seem like regular guys just out of college—but they have one of the coolest jobs around! They are both software engineers for a company that makes underwater robots, otherwise known as autonomous underwater vehicles (AUVs). AUVs are small, unmanned submarines that use on-board artificial intelligence to complete survey tasks with little or no human supervision.

Although Matt and Gil do the same job now, the difference in how they got there shows there really is no single path to robotics.

Getting There

> Quotations show that the information comes directly from the people being studied.

"I was a classic underachiever in high school," says Matt. "I got into college by the skin of my teeth. Once I got into college, though, I realized I wanted to focus on my interests. Studying something I liked really made it all worthwhile." In college at Vassar, Matt took his interests in biology and computers even further. He took classes in psychology, philosophy, anthropology, human brain and behavior, and artificial intelligence to work his way to a degree in cognitive science. His main interest? Helping robots and computers learn complex behaviors.

> The writer analyzes some of the steps Gil took that prepared him for a career in robotics.

Gil, on the other hand, was a good student in high school, but didn't start out in robotics either—he was more interested in political science. At Swarthmore College, he was inspired by computer science. "I wanted to focus on artificial intelligence. I took an artificial intelligence class where we started playing with toy robots, using Handyboards and sensors." Gil really got interested in robotics through AAAI robotics competitions (imagine creating a robot that can serve hors d'oeuvres!), and when he graduated with a degree in computer science, a lot of his experience was with robots.

587

continued on p.588

Reading Case Studies

- Remind students that case studies can help clarify situations. Point out to students that reading about how others have handled a difficult situation can give them some good ideas. Explain that case studies can serve as shortcuts to understanding situations without having to personally experience them.

- Have students read "Careers in Robotics: A Case Study" and the side notes.

- Explain that introductions to case studies typically explain what is being studied and why. **Ask** students to identify these two details in this case study.
  Possible response: This case study examines careers in robotics to show that there are different paths for getting involved in the field.

- **Ask** students what detail from Matt's college experience supports the generalization that young people can become successful college students even if they were not strong high school students.
  Possible response: Matt barely got into college, but he did well in college by taking courses that interested him.

- **Ask** students what detail from Gil's experiences supports the generalization that, as college students gain more experiences, they refine their interests.
  Possible response: Gil started out studying political science in college, but he was inspired by computer science and then became interested in robotics.

Differentiated Instruction   Solutions for All Learners

Support for Special Needs Students
One way to help students understand a concept is to relate it directly to them. Help students understand the relationship between details and generalizations using these two methods:

1. State details about them and ask students to make generalizations.
2. State generalizations about them and ask students to identify two details that support each generalization.

Enrichment for Gifted/Talented Students
Challenge students to learn more about the field of robotics. Encourage them to research applications for robots besides AUVs and to report their findings to the class.

- Remind students that case studies provide details and an analysis of a situation to help readers get a clear picture of the situation being studied. Point out that readers can use these details to form generalizations.

- **Ask** students which details support the generalization that real, hands-on experience is often the best way to get a job in a chosen career.
Possible response: Both Gil and Matt had internships. Gil also recommended doing internships for free to get in the door.

- Direct students to the conclusion of the case study. **Ask** them what generalizations they can make about a career in robotics. Tell them to base their responses on the details given about the field of robotics and Matt and Gil's interest in it.
Possible response: Robotics is a large, constantly changing field with many different possibilities.

- **Ask** students to choose other details in the case study and create generalizations from them.
Possible response: Some other generalizations one could make from the story include that a job in robotics is not boring; students unskilled in math might have difficulties in the field of robotics; and even when they like their jobs, many people explore career changes after they are out of college and working.

The statement that you do not have to attend engineering school to work in robotics is supported by the details about Matt and Gil. This is an example of inductive reasoning.

The writer offers specific strategies for duplicating Gil's and Matt's success. Quotations provide extra force and authenticity.

The writer helps readers arrive at the idea that to succeed they should pay attention in math class. This is an example of deductive reasoning.

In the last paragraph, the author offers encouraging words about the field of robotics.

The bottom line, both Gil and Matt agree, is that you don't have to go to an engineering school. Liberal arts universities and colleges will also give you the skills you need to do robotics. If you're interested in a lot of things—physics, math, science, engineering, communications, and others—you'll do well.

Landing the Job

Both Gil and Matt did summer internships during college that provided them with work experience and an idea of how to get a job in robotics. During one summer, Gil worked for the Naval Research Laboratory doing software artificial intelligence research and then, after graduating, spent the summer preparing for another AAAI competition. When one of his friends got a job at a robotics company, Gil learned about the company and then applied to be a software engineer. Matt got an internship at the same company during the summer between his junior and senior years and was then offered a job following graduation. What's their best advice for getting internships and jobs? Perseverance! "Just find someone who works in robotics and ask them for advice," says Matt. Gil adds, "Sometimes it's difficult to get in, but keep trying. Think about doing an internship for free. Often internships are the first step through the door."

Research, Programming, and . . . Cruising(?)

One of the great things about this job is the variety. Sometimes they spend all day reading up on robotics research, sometimes they spend all day in front of a computer . . . and sometimes they spend all day hanging out on a boat testing the robot in the ocean! "You're making something that has a purpose, something that's part of a bigger project," says Gil. "You get to see if what you did worked. Of course, that means you're entirely responsible." Another perk, according to Matt, is that "you usually get to learn something big and new every few weeks." One warning: Pay attention in high school math classes. "You'll use trigonometry like crazy!"

Next Steps

Both Matt and Gil plan on going back to school sometime to do graduate work. Matt wants to study computer science, focusing on computer graphics and computer-human interfaces. Eventually, he wants to be a professor. Gil plans to go back to school specifically in robotics. He finds underwater robotics exciting because it requires autonomy, but there are a lot of other cool areas of robotics he'd like to explore.

The draw for both of them is that robotics is a quickly changing and very open field. As they point out, "You can do new stuff in any of the related areas and that's exciting!"

Vocabulary Development

Vocabulary for Case Studies

Point out that case studies often use vocabulary that is specific to one particular setting, in this case the field of robotics. Guide students to understand the meaning of the following words that are used in "Careers in Robotics."

autonomous: done without outside control
artificial intelligence: the capability of machines to imitate intelligent human behavior

cognitive science: an interdisciplinary course of study to develop theories about human thought, learning, and perception
handyboard: a controller chip used to operate robots

Assessment Practice

Reading: Making Generalizations

Directions: *Choose the letter of the best answer to each question.*

1. Which detail from the study supports the generalization that it is wise to explore different subjects before choosing a career?

   A "I got into college by the skin of my teeth."

   B Matt took classes in psychology, philosophy, and anthropology.

   C Gil and Matt did summer internships to get experience.

   D You do not have to go to an engineering school.

2. An underachiever in high school, Matt pursued his interests in college and did well. What generalization can you make from Matt's experience?

   A Employers hire people who are interested in the field.

   B You have to like computer science to be good at robotics.

   C Hard work will result in good grades.

   D People learn better when they are interested in the subject.

3. Which detail from the study supports the generalization that one continues to study and learn after graduating from college?

   A Sometimes they spend all day reading up on robotics.

   B "You get to see if what you did worked."

   C Sometimes they spend all day on a boat testing robots.

   D One of the great things about the job is the variety.

Reading: Comprehension and Interpretation

Directions: *Write your answers on a separate piece of paper.*

4. What are the differences between Matt's path to a career in robotics and Gil's path? **[Organizing]**

5. Is this case study useful for students who are not interested in a career in robotics? Explain. **[Applying]**

Timed Writing: Exposition [Connections]

"Success is the sum of small efforts, repeated day in and day out."
—*Robert Collier*

   Use inductive reasoning to support or refute the quotation. Cite details from the article in your response. **(25 minutes)**

Reading Informational Materials: Case Studies ■ 589

Reading: Making Generalizations

1. B
2. D
3. A

4. **Possible response:** Matt was not a strong student in high school, but in college he did well because he took classes that interested him and worked his way to a degree in cognitive science. His main interest was in finding ways for robots and computers to learn. Gil was a strong student in high school and was interested in political science. In college, he became inspired by computer science, which led to his learning about and becoming interested in robotics.

5. **Possible response:** Yes, this case study is useful to students who are not interested in robotics because it shows how they can find rewarding careers by taking different classes, getting involved in various activities, and doing internships.

Timed Writing

- Read the Timed Writing instructions together as a group. Remind students that they should include details from the article that highlight how Matt and Gil felt about the variety in their experiences.

- Suggest that students plan their time to give 5 minutes to planning, 15 minutes to writing, and 5 minutes to reviewing and revising.

Extend the Lesson

Case Studies

To give students more practice with case studies, have them write one of their own. Tell them to choose topics about which they have knowledge, such as healthy relationships between members of a sports team or types of meals that are good choices for school cafeterias. Remind students to provide background information and examples that will promote meaningful generalizations. Tell them to structure their case studies by including an introduction, an analysis, details, and a conclusion.

Planning Differentiated Instruction

Choosing Your Poetry Collection

You may use either collection of poems to meet the lesson standards. The following guide will help you determine which of the two collections is more appropriate for your students.

Accessibility at a Glance

	Collection 1	Collection 2
Context	Outdoor activities and themes	Description of types of bells; admiration of basketball; description of a fictional character
Language	Accessible vocabulary; short sentences	Difficult diction; challenging vocabulary footnoted; "Jabberwocky" has invented words—students must infer meanings
Concept Level	Accessible	Challenging
Literary Merit	Noted poets	Noted poets
Lexile	NP	NP
Overall Rating	More accessible	More challenging

Using the Other Collection You may use the other collection of poems for homework or independent reading to reinforce the selection skills. If you use both collections, you can build a test for both using *ExamView*® **Test Bank** software.

Choosing Your Resources

[L1] Special Needs Students   **[L4]** Advanced Students

[L2] Below-Level Students   **[EL]** English Learners

[L3] All Students

FT Fast Track Instruction: To move the lesson more quickly, use the strategies and activities identified with **FT**.

Reading and Vocabulary Warm-ups provide support for below level students. **A** is for students reading two grades below level; **B** is for students reading one grade below level. For Selection Tests, **A** signifies "less challenging" and **B** "more challenging." For Graphic Organizer transparencies, **A** signifies "not filled in" and **B** "filled in."

Scaffolding for Less Proficient and Advanced Students

The leveled questions on Apply the Skills pages progress in the levels of thinking required to answer them. To address the needs of your different students, you may use the (a) level questions for your less proficient students, the (b) level with your on-level and advanced students. The occasional (c) level questions are appropriate for your advanced students.

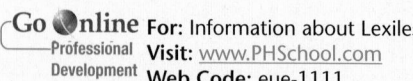

Go Online **For:** Information about Lexiles
Professional **Visit:** www.PHSchool.com
Development **Web Code:** eue-1111

Step-by-Step Teaching Guide	Pacing Guide
PRETEACH	
• Administer Vocabulary and Reading Warm-ups as necessary.	
• Introduce the Literary Analysis Skill: Sound Devices. **FT**	10 min.
• Introduce the Reading Skill: Reading Fluently. **FT**	10 min.
• Prepare students to read by teaching the selection vocabulary. **FT**	10 min.
• Build background and develop expressive vocabulary with Connecting to the Literature and Background.	10 min.
• Engage students' interest with the motivation activity.	10 min.
TEACH	
• Informally monitor comprehension while students read independently or in groups. **FT**	30 min.
• Monitor students' comprehension with the Reading Check notes.	as students read
• Reinforce vocabulary with Vocabulary Builder notes.	as students read
• Develop students' understanding of sound devices with the Literary Analysis annotations. **FT**	5 min.
• Develop students' ability to read fluently with the Reading Skill annotations. **FT**	10 min.
ASSESS/EXTEND	
• Assess students' comprehension and mastery of the Reading Skill and Literary Analysis by having them answer the Apply the Skills questions. **FT**	35 min.
• Have students complete the Vocabulary Builder activities. **FT**	5 min.
• Apply students' ability to write an editorial with the Writing activity. **FT**	30–45 min. or homework
• Extend students' listening and speaking and research and technology skills with one or both of the Extend Your Learning activities.	15–30 min. or homework
• Have students complete the Vocabulary Skill and Grammar Lesson.	5 min.
• Monitor students' progress with the Assessment Practice.	20–40 min.
• Administer **Selection Test A** or **Selection Test B**. **FT**	15 min.

Resources

PRINT

	Collection 1	Collection 2
Unit 4 Resources		
Vocabulary Warm-Up—Word Lists [L1, L2, EL]	p. 52	p. 68
Vocabulary Warm-Up—Practice [L1, L2, EL]	p. 53	p. 69
Reading Warm-Up A [L1, L2, EL]	p. 54	p. 70
Reading Warm-Up B [L1, L2, L3]	p. 55	p. 71
General Resources		
Vocabulary Knowledge Rating Chart, p. 6 [L3]		
Anticipation Guide, pp. 8–10 [L3]		

TRANSPARENCY

Graphic Organizer Transparencies		
Reading Skill Graphic Organizer A [L3]	p. 130	p. 130
Reading Skill Graphic Organizer B [L1, L2, EL]	p. 131	p. 132
Literary Analysis Graphic Organizer A [L3]	p. 133	p. 135
Literary Analysis Graphic Organizer B [L1, L2, EL]	p. 134	p. 136

PRINT

Reader's Notebook [L2]

Reader's Notebook: Adapted Version [L1]

Reader's Notebook: English Learner's Version [EL]

Unit 4 Resources		
Literary Analysis [L3]	p. 56	p. 72
Reading Skill [L3]	p. 57	p. 73
Vocabulary Builder [L3]	p. 58	p. 74

TECHNOLOGY

Listening to Literature Audio CDs [L2, EL]

Reader's Notebook: Adapted Version Audio CD [L1, L2]

PRINT

Unit 4 Resources		
Support for Writing [L3]	p. 59	p. 75
Support for Extend Your Learning [L3]	p. 60	p. 76
Enrichment [L4]	p. 61	p. 77
Selection Test A [L1, L2, EL]	pp. 62–64	pp. 80–82
Selection Test B [L3, L4]	pp. 65–67	pp. 83–85
Build Language Skills: Vocabulary: Latin suffixes -*able* and -*tion*, p. 78 [L3]		
Build Language Skills: Grammar: Prepositional Phrases, p. 79 [L3]		
General Resources		
Rubrics for Persuasive Writing, pp. 53–54 [L3]		

TECHNOLOGY

Go Online: Research [L3]

Go Online: Self-test [L3]

ExamView® **Test Bank [L3]**

Meeting Your Standards

Students will

1. **analyze and respond to literary elements.**
   - Literary Analysis: Sound Devices

2. **read, comprehend, and analyze poems.**
   - Reading Skill: Reading Fluently
   - Reading Strategy: Using Your Senses
   - Reading Check questions
   - Apply the Skills questions
   - Assessment Practice

3. **develop vocabulary.**
   - Vocabulary Builder
   - The Latin suffixes -*able* and -*tion*

4. **apply grammar skills.**
   - Prepositional Phrases

5. **develop writing proficiency.**
   - Work in Progress: Descriptive Essay
   - Editorial

6. **extend learning.**
   - Listening and Speaking: Dramatic Reading
   - Research and Technology: Illustrated Version

Block Scheduling: Use one 90-minute class period to preteach the skills and have students read the poetry collection. Use a second 90-minute class period to assess students' mastery of skills, extend their learning, and monitor their progress.

Homework Suggestions

Following are possibilities for homework assignments.

- Support pages from *Unit 4 Resources*:
  Literary Analysis
  Reading Skill
  Build Vocabulary
  Enrichment

- An Extend Your Learning project and the Writing assignment for your chosen selection may be completed over several days.

PRENTICE HALL

TeacherEXPRESS™ Use this complete
Plan · Teach · Assess suite of powerful
teaching tools to make lesson planning and testing quicker and easier.

PRENTICE HALL

StudentEXPRESS™ Use the
Learn · Study · Succeed Interactive
Textbook (online and on CD-ROM) to make selections and activities come alive with audio and video support and interactive questions.

❶ Literary Analysis
Sound Devices

- Emphasize that *alliteration* occurs at the beginning of words or in stressed syllables. Give students the following example of alliteration:

  Joel joked about John's gestures.

  Tell students that even though "g" is a different letter, it is still a part of the alliteration scheme because it has the same sound.

- Explain that *consonance* occurs when the same consonant sound follows different vowels. *So bit* and *sat* have consonance, but *bit* and *sit* do not because they share the same vowel sound; therefore, they rhyme.

- Emphasize that *assonance* is the repetition of similar but not necessarily identical vowel sounds. Explain that words that exhibit *assonance* end with different consonant sounds. Give students the example of *moat* and *lobe*.

- Tell students that onomatopoeia is when the sound of a word imitates its meaning. Give students the examples of *clang* and *buzz*.

- Have students brainstorm for examples of the sound devices. Write their examples on the board.

- Tell students to look for sound devices in the poetry selections.

❷ Reading Skill
Reading Fluently

- Emphasize that reading fluently means reading smoothly, pausing for punctuation instead of pausing at the ends of lines, and also means appreciating the meaning and artistry of the writing.

- Tell students that sensory language helps readers identify with and understand a setting or character by drawing on their own sensory memories.

- Give students a copy of **Reading Skill Graphic Organizer A** (p. 130 in *Graphic Organizer Transparencies*). Have them fill in the graphic organizer with sensory words and phrases from Poetry Collection 1.

Build Skills   *Poetry Collection 1 • Poetry Collection 2*

You can apply the instruction on this page to these poems.

Poetry Collection 1
Summer, page 592
The Eagle, page 593
Analysis of Baseball, page 594

Poetry Collection 2
The Bells, page 599
Slam, Dunk, & Hook,
page 604
Jabberwocky, page 606

❶ Literary Analysis

Poets use **sound devices** to emphasize the sound relationships among words. These devices include the following:

- **Alliteration:** the repetition of initial consonant sounds in stressed syllables: *"The fair breeze blew, the white foam flew . . ."*
- **Consonance:** the repetition of final consonant sounds in stressed syllables with different vowel sounds, as in *sit* and *cat*
- **Assonance:** the repetition of similar vowel sounds in stressed syllables that end with different consonants, as in *seal* and *meet*
- **Onomatopoeia:** the use of a word whose sound imitates its meaning, such as *pop* or *hiss*

All of these sound devices work to engage the reader's senses and create musical and emotional effects.

❷ Reading Skill

Reading fluently is reading smoothly and continuously while also comprehending the text and appreciating the writer's artistry. To avoid being tripped up by the meaning as you read, **use your senses.** To do so, notice language that appeals to the five senses. Record examples of sensory language in a chart like the one shown.

Senses	Words that appeal to the senses
Sight	
Hearing	
Smell	
Taste	
Touch	

Vocabulary Builder

Poetry Collection 1

- **clasps** (klasps) *v.* grips (p. 593) *The driver clasps the wheel tightly to steer.*

- **azure** (azh′ ər) *adj.* sky blue (p. 593) *She painted the ceiling azure so it would look like the sky.*

Poetry Collection 2

- **voluminously** (və lōō′ mə nəs lē) *adv.* fully; in great volume (p. 600) *Her coach praised her voluminously at the awards banquet.*

- **palpitating** (pal′ pə tāt′ iŋ) *adj.* beating rapidly; throbbing (p. 601) *The palpitating drums of the pep band excited the fans.*

- **metaphysical** (met′ ə fiz′ i kəl) *adj.* spiritual; beyond the physical (p. 605) *She says that songwriting is metaphysical— the songs come to her in dreams.*

- **jibed** (jībd) *v.* changed direction (p. 605) *As the wind shifted, the crew jibed to keep the sails full.*

590 ■ *Poetry*

Vocabulary Development

Vocabulary Knowledge Rating

Create a **Vocabulary Knowledge Rating Chart** for the collection you will teach from this set. Include the vocabulary from this page and the additional words students are asked to use at the end of Connecting to the Literature. These words will increase students' expressive vocabulary.

Give students a copy of the chart with the words on it. Introduce the words by reading them aloud and having students mark their rating in the Before Reading column. Urge them to be alert to these words as they read and discuss the poems because they will rate their knowledge of the words again after they finish.

If you wish, you may tally how many students know (or think they know) a word to gauge how much instruction you need to provide. As students read, point out the words and their context.

Build Understanding • *Poetry Collection 1*

❸ Connecting to the Literature

Reading/Writing Connection The poem "Summer" is a celebration of the year's hottest season. Write a short paragraph describing your favorite season and what you love about it. Use at least three of these words: *anticipate, coincide, display, participate.*

Meet the Authors

Walter Dean **Myers** (b. 1937)
Summer (page 592)
Growing up poor in West Virginia and New York City, Walter Dean Myers never imagined himself becoming a writer. Although he was writing poems and stories by his early teens, he believed that his dream of a literary career would never be realized. Myers's dream was fulfilled, however, when he won a writing contest sponsored by the Council on Interracial Books for Children for his book *Where Does a Day Go?*

Alfred, **Lord Tennyson** (1809–1892)
The Eagle (page 593)
The most popular British poet during his lifetime, Alfred, Lord Tennyson rose from humble beginnings to the position of poet laureate of England. Although he was enthralled by the technological advances of the Victorian Era, Tennyson remained a poet of nature, bringing both imagination and feeling to descriptions of the landscape and its inhabitants.

May **Swenson** (1919–1989)
Analysis of Baseball (page 594)
May Swenson has been called "one of the surest poets, clear-eyed and absolute." She was born in Logan, Utah, and attended Utah State University. After working for a while as a newspaper reporter, she moved to New York City, where she worked as an editor and as a college lecturer. Her poems were published in such magazines as *The New Yorker, Harper's,* and *The Nation.* Swenson also served as a Chancellor of The Academy of American Poets from 1980 to 1989.

For: More about the authors
Visit: www.PHSchool.com
Web Code: epe-9404

❸ Connecting to the Literature

- Provide these sample sentences to demonstrate use of the expressive vocabulary words:
  1. Through the long, cold winter and the damp spring, we *anticipate* the wonderful days of summer.
  2. For students, the hot days of summer *coincide* with their vacation from school.
  3. The summer *displays* its power on the hottest days under blue, cloudless skies.
  4. Summer is a good time to *participate* in swimming classes.
- Help students further develop their expressive vocabulary by providing these words: *atmosphere, considerable, proclaim,* and *tropical.* Encourage them to use these words as they discuss the poems.

Concept Connector ➤

Students will follow up on this activity after completing Poetry Collection 1.

Go Online For additional informa-
Author Link tion about the authors in Collection 1, have students type in the Web Code and then select the poet.

❶ Motivation

Write *summer* on the board, and ask students to brainstorm words to describe it. Tell them to think about the senses: sight, sound, touch, taste, and smell. Then have them preview the selections by looking at the titles and pictures. Invite students to add new words to the list.

Learning Modalities
Musical/Rhythmic Learners

Have students prepare dramatic readings of one or more of the three poems accompanied by prerecorded music or music they perform live. Before they prepare their readings and choose the music, students should spend some time discussing the feeling that each work expresses. What is the message of each? How do the sound devices in each poem contribute to the message?

❷ About the Selections

In "Summer," internal and terminal rhymes and a strong, irregular rhythm are as important as the literal meaning of the poet's words in creating a picture of summer. "The Eagle" is a brief, almost staccato, description of an eagle that captures the essence of the bird with its spare form, directness, and dramatic surge at the end. "Analysis of Baseball" presents the game, strategy, and poetry of the sport.

❸ Critical Viewing

Possible response: The poem focuses on wallowing in the heat, while the photograph shows an escape from the heat.

SUMMER ❶ ❷

Walter Dean Myers

I like hot days, hot days
Sweat is what you got days
Bugs buzzin from cousin to cousin
Juices dripping
5 Running and ripping
Catch the one you love days

Birds peeping
Old men sleeping
Lazy days, daisies lay
10 Beaming and dreaming
Of hot days, hot days,
Sweat is what you got days

❸ ▼ Critical Viewing
How well does this photograph illustrate the speaker's feelings about summer? Explain. [Evaluate]

592 ■ *Poetry*

Vocabulary Development

Expressive Vocabulary
Ask students to think about Tennyson's description of the eagle. Ask students to study the poem and then to describe the image that is created and their response to it. Tell them to use the expressive vocabulary words presented earlier. You might prompt them with sentence starters like these:

1. The first line, "He clasps the crag . . ." makes you *anticipate* . . .
2. Tennyson *displays* the eagle as . . .
3. The "lonely lands" *coincide* with . . .
4. This poem implies that eagles will not *participate* in . . .

The Eagle

Alfred, Lord Tennyson

He <u>clasps</u> the crag[1] with crooked hands;
Close to the sun in lonely lands,
Ring'd with the <u>azure</u> world, he stands.

4

The wrinkled sea beneath him crawls;
5 He watches from his mountain walls,
And like a thunderbolt he falls.

---

1. crag (krag) *n.* steep, rugged rock that rises above others or projects from a rock mass.

Vocabulary Builder
clasps (klasps) *v.* grips
azure (azhʹ ər) *adj.* sky blue

The Eagle ■ 593

❹ Literary Analysis
Sound Devices

- Read the first stanza aloud to students, and **ask** them to identify examples of alliteration.
  Answer: Alliteration is found in the words *clasps, crag, crooked,* and *close* and in the words *lonely* and *lands.*

- Reread the stanza and guide a discussion of the musical effects created by the alliteration and other sound devices. Point out that the repetition of sounds and cadence produces a regular rhythm that makes poetry memorable and affects how people hear and respond to the ideas.

- Read the first stanza aloud, and then **ask** students the Literary Analysis question: What final consonant sound is repeated frequently in the first ten lines of the poem?
  Answer: The final consonant sound "t" is repeated frequently.

- Point out that this poem uses onomatopoeia to help evoke the sounds of baseball. Have students **list** some examples.
  Answer: Examples include *thud, dud, thwack,* and *pow.*

▶ **Monitor Progress: Ask** students to find an example of assonance in lines 11–16.
  Answer: Assonance is found in *bounces* and *ground.*

▶ **Reteach:** Review the sound devices described on p. 590. Have students review the entire poem and give examples of each device.
  Possible response: Examples include the following: **alliteration:** *bat, bounce,* and *ball;* **consonance:** *bat* and *mitt;* **assonance:** *take* and *bait;* **onomatopoeia:** *dud* and *thwack.*

⑥ Critical Viewing

Possible response: Students may cite the word *pow.*

Analysis Of Baseball

May Swenson

It's about
the ball,
the bat,
and the mitt.
5 Ball hits
bat, or it
hits mitt.
⑤ Bat doesn't
hit ball, bat
10 meets it.
Ball bounces
off bat, flies
air, or thuds
ground (dud)
15 or it
fits mitt.

Bat waits
for ball
to mate.
20 Ball hates
to take bat's
bait. Ball
flirts, bat's
late, don't
25 keep the date.
Ball goes in
(thwack) to mitt,
and goes out
(thwack) back
30 to mitt.

Ball fits
mitt, but
not all

594 ■ *Poetry*

Literary Analysis
Sound Devices What final consonant sound is repeated frequently in the first ten lines of the poem?

⑥ ▶ **Critical Viewing** Which words in the poem might describe the action in this photograph? **[Connect]**

Vocabulary Development

Vocabulary Knowledge Rating
When students have completed reading and discussing Poetry Collection 1, have them take out their **Vocabulary Knowledge Rating Chart** for these poems. Read the words aloud once more and have students rate their knowledge of the words again in the After Reading column. Clarify any words that are still problematic. Have students write their own definition and example or sentence in the appropriate column. Then have students complete the **Vocabulary Builder Practice** activities on p. 597. Encourage students to use the words in further discussion and written work about these poems. Remind them that they will be accountable for these words on the Selection Test.

the time.
35 Sometimes
ball gets hit
(pow) when bat
meets it,
and sails
40 to a place
where mitt
has to quit
in disgrace.
That's about
45 the bases
❼ loaded,
about 40,000
fans exploded.

It's about
50 the ball,
the bat,
the mitt,
the bases
and the fans.
55 It's done
on a diamond,
and for fun.
It's about
home, and it's
60 about run.

Reading Skill
Reading Fluently To what senses do the words "40,000 fans exploded" appeal? Explain.

Analysis of Baseball ■ 595

❼ **Reading Skill**
Reading Fluently

- Assign a stanza to different students and ask them to read them aloud. Remind them to use their senses as they read. Coach them in reading the lines fluently.

- **Ask** students the Reading Skill question: To what senses do the words "40,000 fans exploded" appeal? Explain.
  Answer: The words appeal to sight ("40,000 fans") and to sound ("exploded").

- Have students **identify** some of the other memorable or powerful sensory images in the poem.
  Possible response: Students might mention "Ball bounces / off bat, flies / air, or thuds / ground (dud)," "Ball goes in / (thwack)," and "ball gets hit / (pow) . . . and sails."

Concept Connector

Connecting to the Literature
Have students compare the sentences they wrote before reading with their thoughts about their favorite season. Ask them to explain whether their thoughts have changed and, if so, how.

Reading Skill Graphic Organizer
Ask students to review the graphic organizers they completed to identify sensory language while reading. Show them **Reading Skill Graphic Organizer B** (*Graphic Organizer Transparencies,* p. 131) as an example. Then have students share the graphic organizers they did and the sensory language they identified.

Apply the Skills

Poetry Collection 1

Thinking About the Selections

1. **Respond:** How does each of these poems make you feel about its subject? Explain.
2. **(a) Recall:** In lines 1–2 of "Summer," how does the speaker describe summer? **(b) Interpret:** What kind of juices might be dripping in line 4? **(c) Connect:** In what way is the image in line 4 a continuation of the one in line 2? Explain.
3. **(a) Infer:** What is the eagle watching for in line 5 of "The Eagle"? **(b) Interpret:** What is the eagle doing when he "falls" in line 6?
4. **Make a Judgment:** Do you think the poem "Analysis of Baseball" can be appreciated by someone who is unfamiliar with the rules of baseball? Why or why not?

Literary Analysis

5. **(a)** For each poem in Poetry Collection 1, use a chart like the one shown to identify one example of each **sound device** listed.
   (b) In what way does each example add to the musical feeling of each poem?

	Example	**Effect**
Alliteration		
Consonance		
Assonance		

6. **(a)** Identify an example of **onomatopoeia** in "Analysis of Baseball." **(b)** What sound does the word imitate? **(c)** How well does the word imitate the sound? Explain your answer.
7. **(a)** Which of these poems do you think makes the most effective use of sound devices? Explain your choice. **(b)** Discuss your choice with a small group, and together decide on a single response to explain to the class.

Reading Skill

8. In what way does **reading fluently** help you to appreciate a poem's sound devices?
9. **(a)** Which of your senses, other than your sense of hearing, were most engaged by each of these poems? **(b)** Which specific words appealed to those senses?

Poems at a Glance
"**Summer**" celebrates the season.

"**The Eagle**" describes this awesome bird of prey.

"**Analysis of Baseball**" shares impressions of the game.

Go Online
Assessment
For: Self-test
Visit: www.PHSchool.com
Web Code: epa-6404

Sound Devices: language that emphasizes the sound relationships among words; sound devices include *alliteration, consonance, assonance,* and *onomatopoeia*

Reading Fluently: reading smoothly and continuously while comprehending the text and appreciating the writer's artistry

---

1. "Summer" may make students feel nostalgic about summers. "The Eagle" may evoke thoughts of heroism or individualism. "Analysis of Baseball" might make students eager to play or watch a game.

2. (a) Myers describes summer as so hot that people sweat. (b) Perspiration and nectar may be dripping. (c) Line 4 explains or elaborates line 2.

3. (a) The eagle is probably watching for something to eat. (b) The eagle is diving after its prey.

4. Yes, if the reader knows what a bat and a mitt are. The speaker clearly tells what is going on and how the ball, the bat, and the mitt interact.

5. (a) **Sample responses:** "Summer"—alliteration: "bugs buzzin"; consonance: "sweat . . . what"; assonance: "daisies lay"; onomatopoeia: "buzzin." "The Eagle"—alliteration: "clasps . . . crag"; consonance: "Ring'd . . . world"; assonance: "clasps . . . crag." "Analysis of Baseball"—alliteration: "ball . . . bat"; consonance: "mitt . . . bat"; assonance: "take . . . bait"; onomatopoeia: "dud." (b) These devices make the words of each poem sound like they fit together. Poems, like musical compositions, may have slow and fast, gentle or harsh, or loud and soft passages. Sound devices help to create these musical colors and textures.

Another sample answer can be found on **Literary Analysis Graphic Organizer B**, p. 134 in *Graphic Organizer Transparencies.*

6. (a) Students may say "thwack." (b) The word imitates the sound of a baseball landing in a mitt. (c) When a ball lands in a mitt "thwack" is a good representation of the sound heard.

7. (a) Students may choose "Analysis of Baseball" because of its obvious use of onomatopoeia. (b) Students should agree on their choices and have examples to support their views.

8. **Possible response:** Fluent reading helps readers hear and appreciate the musical qualities that sound devices instill in the poems.

9. (a) **Possible response:** Sight was the most commonly used sense in all of the poems. (b) **Possible response:** The following words appealed to the sense of sight: "Summer": "running and ripping," "old men sleeping," "daisies lay / beaming"; "The Eagle": "clasps the crag with crooked hands," "like a thunderbolt he falls"; "Analysis of Baseball": "Ball hits bat," "Ball bounces / off bat, flies / air."

Vocabulary Builder

Practice Identify the word in each group that does not belong with the others. Explain your response.

1. clasps, hands, blanket   2. azure, bread, green

Adding Words to Your Vocabulary *Azure* describes a certain shade of blue: deep sky-blue. The words *scarlet, indigo,* and *emerald* also describe specific shades of colors. Use a dictionary to discover what these colors are. Then, write a sentence for each word that reflects the color's specific shade. (For more on using a dictionary, see page R6.)

Writing

Write an **editorial**—a brief piece of writing that presents one side of an issue—related to one of the poems in this collection. For example, using Tennyson's "The Eagle" as inspiration, you might write an editorial about the need to preserve the North American bald eagle.
- State the issue clearly and express your opinion reasonably.
- Anticipate questions from those who might disagree with you.

Have several people respond to your editorial, including someone who disagrees with you. If you hear a point that you should have addressed, consider adding it.

For *Grammar, Vocabulary,* and *Assessment,* see **Build Language Skills,** pages 610–611.

Extend Your Learning

Listening and Speaking Prepare a **dramatic reading** that captures the musical qualities of one of the poems in the collection.
- Choose a poem and make notes about which words and sounds to emphasize and when to change your reading pace.
- Practice reading the poem aloud, recording yourself, if possible, so that you can hear and fix problem spots.

Present your dramatic reading in class.

Research and Technology In a group, create an **illustrated version** of one of the poems. Find photographs or original artwork. With the group, debate the merits of each choice and then reach an agreement about which images best capture the mood of the poem. Read the poem and share the art for classmates' enjoyment.

Apply the Skills ■ *597*

Go Online **For:** An additional research activity
Research **Visit:** www.PHSchool.com
Web Code: epd-7403
For another research activity to extend students' learning, give students this Web Code.

Vocabulary Builder
Practice

1. *Blanket* does not belong. *Clasps* is an action that *hands* perform.

2. *Bread* does not belong. *Azure* and *green* are colors.

Adding Words to Your Vocabulary
Possible responses:

1. scarlet: deep red; The scarlet bird was a cardinal.

2. indigo: deep violet blue; The boat was painted indigo and could barely be seen floating on the calm, blue lake.

3. emerald: deep green; The emerald necklace matched her green eyes.

Writing

- To give students guidance for writing an editorial, give them **Support for Writing** for Poetry Collection 1, p. 59, in *Unit 4 Resources.*

- To evaluate students' editorials, use the persuasion rubrics, pp. 53–54 in *General Resources.*

Six Traits Focus

✔	Ideas		Word Choice
✔	Organization		Sentence Fluency
	Voice		Conventions

WG **Writing and Grammar, Gold Level**
Students will find guidance on persuasive writing in Chapter 7.

Build Language Skills

Go to pages 610–611 for vocabulary and grammar lessons and assessment practice.

Extend Your Learning

The **Support for Extend Your Learning** page (*Unit 4 Resources,* p. 60) provides guided note-taking opportunities to help students complete the Extend Your Learning activities.

Teaching notes for Literary Analysis, Reading Skill, and Vocabulary Builder for this collection begin on p. 590.

❸ Connecting to the Literature

- Provide these sample sentences to demonstrate use of the expressive words:

  1. The sound of a school bell *signifies* the start of another school day.

  2. The bell *triggers* the memory of my homework assignment.

  3. I *appreciate* that the bell lets us know when school starts.

  4. As I *contemplate* the hours until the closing bell rings, I am confident.

  5. I wonder if everyone *interprets* the ring of a school bell in the same way.

- Help students further develop their expressive vocabulary by providing these words: *aware, circumstance, encounter,* and *impression.* Encourage students to use these words as they discuss the poems.

Concept Connector ➡️

Students will follow up on this activity after completing Poetry Collection 2.

──────────

Go Online For additional informa-
─ **Author Link** ─ tion about the authors in Collection 2, have students type in the Web Code and then select the poet.

Build Understanding • *Poetry Collection 2*

Poetry

❸ Connecting to the Literature

Reading/Writing Connection The speaker in "The Bells" describes a range of ideas associated with the sounds of different bells. Write a short paragraph describing the ideas that an everyday sound sparks for you. Use at least three of these words: *signify, trigger, appreciate, contemplate, interpret.*

Review

For **Literary Analysis, Reading Skill,** and **Vocabulary Builder,** see page 590.

Meet the Authors

Edgar Allan **Poe** (1809–1849)

The Bells (page 599)

As poems like "The Bells" illustrate, Edgar Allan Poe was a master at using rhythm and sound devices to powerful effect. Many scholars believe that the idea for "The Bells" was suggested to Poe by Marie Louise Shew, a woman with medical training who treated Poe when his health began to fail.

Yusef **Komunyakaa** (b. 1947)

Slam, Dunk, & Hook (page 604)

Yusef Komunyakaa grew up in Bogalusa, Louisiana. During the mid-1960s, he served in Vietnam as a reporter and an editor for the military newspaper *The Southern Cross.* Komunyakaa later turned his attention to poetry, winning a Pulitzer Prize for his book *Neon Vernacular: New and Selected Poems* (1993). Komunyakaa has said that he likes "connecting the abstract to the concrete."

Lewis **Carroll** (1832–1898)

Jabberwocky (page 606)

Charles Lutwidge Dodgson was a professor of mathematics and a talented early photographer. Today, he is best remembered for two children's books he wrote under the pen name Lewis Carroll: *Alice's Adventures in Wonderland* (1865) and its sequel, *Through the Looking Glass* (1871). Huge bestsellers almost from the moment they appeared, the "Alice" books have been the basis of numerous stage plays and films.

For: More about the authors
Visit: www.PHSchool.com
Author Link **Web Code:** epe-9405

Differentiated
Instruction   Solutions for All Learners

Support for Below-Level Students [L1, L2]	Support for English Learners [EL]
Unit 4 Resources	**Unit 4 Resources**
Vocabulary Warm-up Word Lists, p. 68	**Vocabulary Warm-up Word Lists,** p. 68
Vocabulary Warm-up Practice, p. 69	**Vocabulary Warm-up Practice,** p. 69
Reading Warm-up A, p. 70	**Reading Warm-up A,** p. 70
Selection Test A, pp. 80–82	**Reader's Notebook: English Learner's Version**
Graphic Organizer Transparencies	**Listening to Literature Audio CD**
Reading Skill Graphic Organizer, Transparency B, p. 132	

The Bells

Edgar Allan Poe

I

       Hear the sledges[1] with the bells—
           Silver bells!
What a world of merriment their melody foretells!
       How they tinkle, tinkle, tinkle,
5   In the icy air of night!
      While the stars, that oversprinkle
      All the heavens, seem to twinkle
        With a crystalline delight;
        Keeping time, time, time,
10   In a sort of Runic[2] rhyme,
To the tintinnabulation[3] that so musically wells
      From the bells, bells, bells, bells,
        Bells, bells, bells—
   From the jingling and the tinkling of the bells.

---

1. sledges (slej´ iz) *n.* sleighs.
2. Runic (ro͞o´ nik) *adj.* songlike; poetical.
3. tintinnabulation (tin´ ti na´ byo͞o la´ shən) *n.* ringing sound of bells.

> ✓ **Reading Check**
> What type of bells does section one describe?

The Bells ■ 599

❺ Literary Analysis
Sound Devices

- Explain that alliteration and rhymes are prominent in Poe's poem, but it is rich in other sound devices as well. **Ask** students to identify the assonance in lines 20 to 26.
  Answer: Assonance occurs in "molten golden-notes," "liquid ditty," and "out the sounding cells."

- Have students **identify** examples of onomatopoeia in lines 27 to 35.
  Answer: Words demonstrating onomatopoeia include *ringing, bells,* and *chiming.*

- **Ask** students the Literary Analysis question: What quality of alarm bells might the alliteration of the *t* sound in line 38 imitate?
  Possible response: The sharp consonant sounds of the *t's* (and *d's*) suggest the urgency and attack of warning or alarm bells.

II

15   Hear the mellow wedding bells,
Golden bells!
What a world of happiness their harmony foretells!
Through the balmy air of night
How they ring out their delight!
20   From the molten golden-notes,
And all in tune,
What a liquid ditty[4] floats
To the turtle-dove[5] that listens, while she gloats
On the moon!
25   Oh, from out the sounding cells,
What a gush of euphony[6] <u>voluminously</u> wells!
How it swells!
How it dwells
On the future! how it tells
30   Of the rapture that impels
To the swinging and the ringing
Of the bells, bells, bells,
Of the bells, bells, bells, bells
Bells, bells, bells—
35   To the rhyming and the chiming of the bells!

Vocabulary Builder
voluminously (və lo͞o′ mə nəs lē) *adv.* fully; in great volume

III

Hear the loud alarum[7] bells!
Brazen[8] bells!
What a tale of terror now their turbulency tells!
In the startled ear of night
40   How they scream out their affright!
Too much horrified to speak,
They can only shriek, shriek,
Out of tune,
In a clamorous appealing to the mercy of the fire,

Literary Analysis
Sound Devices What quality of alarm bells might the alliteration of the *t* sound in line 38 imitate?

---

4. ditty (dit′ ē) *n.* short, simple song.
5. turtle-dove (tʉrt′′l duv′) The turtle dove is traditionally associated with love.
6. euphony (yo͞o′ fə nē) *n.* pleasing sound.
7. alarum (ə ler′ əm) *adj.* sudden call to arms; alarm.
8. brazen (brā′ zən) *adj.* made of brass; having the ringing sound of brass.

600 ■ *Poetry*

Vocabulary Development

Expressive Vocabulary
Ask students to think about "The Bells" and the types of bells and situations described.

Ask students questions like the following to stimulate discussion. Use the expressive words listed on p. 598 in your questions, and ask students to respond using the words.

1. What does the ringing of the bells in section III *signify*?
2. What kind of response do the bells in section II *trigger*?
3. Which bells do people most *appreciate* hearing?
4. When you *contemplate* the bells in section IV, what thoughts and feelings come to mind?
5. How does the speaker want readers to *interpret* the meaning of "The Bells"?

45 In a mad expostulation[9] with the deaf and frantic fire
        Leaping higher, higher, higher,
            With a desperate desire,
            And a resolute endeavor
            Now—now to sit or never,
50   By the side of the pale-faced moon.
            Oh, the bells, bells, bells!
        What a tale their terror tells
                Of Despair!
        How they clang, and clash, and roar!
55   What a horror they outpour
        On the bosom of the <u>palpitating</u> air!
            Yet the ear it fully knows,
                By the twanging
                And the clanging,
60   How the danger ebbs and flows;
            Yet the ear distinctly tells,
                In the jangling,
                And the wrangling,
        How the danger sinks and swells,
65 By the sinking or the swelling in the anger of the bells—
            Of the bells—
        Of the bells, bells, bells, bells,
            Bells, bells, bells—
        In the clamor and the clangor of the bells!

IV

70   Hear the tolling of the bells—
                Iron bells!
    What a world of solemn thought their monody[10] compels!
            In the silence of the night,
            How we shiver with affright
75   At the melancholy menace of their tone!
            For every sound that floats
            From the rust within their throats
                Is a groan.
            And the people—ah, the people—

---

9. **expostulation** (ek späs′ chə lā′ shən) *n.* objection; complaint.
10. **monody** (mä′ nə dē) *n.* poem of mourning; a steady sound; music in which one instrument or voice is dominant.

Vocabulary Builder
palpitating (pal′ pə tāt′ iŋ) *v.* beating rapidly; throbbing

Literary Analysis
Sound Devices What is the effect of the repetition in lines 67–68?

⑦ ✓ Reading Check
What kind of story do the wedding bells tell?

⑥ Literary Analysis
Sound Devices

- Read lines 65–69 aloud to students. **Ask** students the Literary Analysis question: What is the effect of the repetition in lines 67–68?
  Answer: The repetition of the word *bells* creates a ringing effect almost like that of real bells ringing.

- Call students' attention to *clamor* and *clangor* in the final line of the passage, and **ask** them to analyze the sound devices represented by these two words.
  Answer: The sound effects of *clamor* and *clangor* are alliteration, onomatopoeia, and rhyme.

⑦ Reading Check
Answer: The wedding bells tell the story of future happiness and harmony.

The Bells ■ 601

Differentiated
Instruction   Solutions for All Learners

Strategy for Special Needs Students
Have students read sections II and III aloud several times. After the first reading, discuss the difference in tone between sections II and III. Focus on the first five lines of both verses. Make sure that students realize that both verses have exactly the same structure, but that the bells and their effects are completely different. Then, have the students reread the sections, using their tone of voice to express the difference in mood.

Strategy for English Learners
Make sure that students understand all potentially puzzling words in these verses in addition to those defined in the notes. Write some of the troublesome phrases on the board and preview them with students. For example, you might write "Harmony foretells" (line 17)—*sound predicts,* "liquid ditty" (line 22)—*smooth sound,* "monody compels" (line 72)—*song of mourning causes,* and so on. After students grasp the meaning of the verses, ask them to read the verses aloud together.

The Bells by Edmund Dulac

Edmund Dulac (1882–1953) was a French illustrator known for the color and imagination of his work. This painting, with its somber overall mood, illustrates Part IV of "The Bells." Use these questions for discussion:

1. Using this painting as an example, explain some of the advantages of illustrating a literary work with paintings rather than photographs.
   Possible response: One advantage is a painter's ability to stray from reality in order to create a certain impression or mood. Another is the ability to use light and composition as desired for emphasis or effect.

2. How could other sections of this poem be illustrated?
   Possible response: Students might suggest that paintings or photographs of sleighs, weddings, or fires might be used to illustrate the other parts of the poem.

The Bells, Edmund Dulac, New York Public Library

80　　　　　They that dwell up in the steeple,
　　　　　　　　　　All alone,
　　　　　And who tolling, tolling, tolling,
　　　　　　　In that muffled monotone,
　　　　　　　Feel a glory in so rolling
85　　　　　On the human heart a stone—
　　　　　They are neither man nor woman—
　　　　　They are neither brute nor human—
　　　　　　　They are Ghouls:[11]
　　　　　And their king it is who tolls;
　　　　　And he rolls, rolls, rolls,
90　　　　　　　　　Rolls
　　　　　　　A pæan from the bells!
　　　　　And his merry bosom swells
　　　　　With the pæan of the bells!
　　　　　And he dances and he yells;
95　　　　　Keeping time, time, time,
　　　　　In a sort of Runic rhyme,
　　　　　To the pæan of the bells—
　　　　　　　Of the bells:
　　　　　Keeping time, time, time,
100　　　　In a sort of Runic rhyme,
　　　　　To the throbbing of the bells—
　　　　　Of the bells, bells, bells—
　　　　　To the sobbing of the bells;
　　　　　Keeping time, time, time,
105　　　　As he knells, knells, knells,
　　　　　In a happy Runic rhyme,
　　　　　To the rolling of the bells—
　　　　　Of the bells, bells, bells—
　　　　　To the tolling of the bells,
110　　　　Of the bells, bells, bells, bells,
　　　　　　Bells, bells, bells—
　　　　　To the moaning and the groaning of the bells.

---

11. Ghouls (go͞olz) *n.* evil spirits that rob graves.

⑪ ◀ Critical Viewing Which kind of bells do you think this painting best illustrates? Why? **[Assess]**

The Bells ■ 603

Literary Analysis
Sound Devices What alliteration appears in lines 83–85?

Reading Skill
Reading Fluently
Which repeated words in this stanza might sound like the repetitive tolling of bells?

Night Games, Ernie Barnes

Ernie Barnes studied art history and painting before becoming a professional football player. As an artist, he puts all the "violence and power" he had felt on the field into his paintings. Ask students:

1. What can you infer about the players' lives?
   Possible response: The skyline indicates the players live in a city. Some are barefoot, and their basket is makeshift; this suggests a lack of resources.

2. How does the painting compare to details in the poem?
   Answer: In both poem and painting, players are poised in midair, lanky, and intense.

Night Games, Ernie Barnes, Courtesy of The Company of Art, Los Angeles

Slam, Dunk, & Hook

Yusef Komunyakaa

Fast breaks. Lay ups. With Mercury's[1]
Insignia[2] on our sneakers,
We outmaneuvered the footwork
Of bad angels. Nothing but a hot

---

1. Mercury's Mercury was the Roman god of travel, usually depicted with wings on his feet.
2. insignia (in sig´ nē ə) *n.* emblems or badges; logos.

Vocabulary Development

Relevant Topical Vocabulary
Tell students that this poem contains many terms that anyone unfamiliar with basketball may find puzzling. Write the following words on the board and discuss their meaning. Encourage students with basketball knowledge to elaborate and demonstrate.

fast break: a fast attempt to score before the defense can get in place
lay up: a shot made from near the basket—usually banked off the backboard

swish: the sound the ball makes when it drops smoothly through the netting of the hoop without touching the rim
dunk balls: a ball slammed through the basket from above by a leaping player
dribble: to move the ball by repeatedly bouncing it

Ask students to call out additional basketball terms from the poem. As a class, figure out the meanings.

5   Swish of strings like silk
       Ten feet out. In the roundhouse³
       Labyrinth⁴ our bodies
       Created, we could almost
       Last forever, poised in midair
10   Like storybook sea monsters.
       A high note hung there
       A long second. Off
       The rim. We'd corkscrew
       Up & dunk balls that exploded
15   The skullcap of hope & good
       Intention. Bug-eyed, lanky,
       All hands & feet . . . sprung rhythm.
       We were <u>metaphysical</u> when girls
       Cheered on the sidelines.
20   Tangled up in a falling,
       Muscles were a bright motor
       Double-flashing to the metal hoop
       Nailed to our oak.
       When Sonny Boy's mama died
25   He played nonstop all day, so hard
       Our backboard splintered.
       Glistening with sweat, we <u>jibed</u>
       & rolled the ball off our
       Fingertips. Trouble
30   Was there slapping a blackjack
       Against an open palm.
       Dribble, drive to the inside, feint,
       & glide like a sparrow hawk.
       Lay ups. Fast breaks.
35   We had moves we didn't know
       We had. Our bodies spun
       On swivels of bone & faith,
       Through a lyric slipknot
       Of joy, & we knew we were
40   Beautiful & dangerous.

---

3. roundhouse (round′ hous′) *n.* area on the court beneath the basket.
4. labyrinth (lab′ ə rinth′) *n.* maze.

⑬ ◀ Critical Viewing
Which details in this painting relate to lines in "Slam, Dunk, & Hook"? **[Connect]**

Vocabulary Builder
metaphysical (met′ ə fiz′ i kəl) *adj.* spiritual; beyond the physical
jibed (jībd) *v.* changed direction

Literary Analysis
Sound Devices
What sound does the poet emphasize with the use of assonance in lines 30 and 31?

Slam, Dunk, & Hook ■ 605

⑭ Literary Analysis
Sound Devices

- Have a volunteer read the bracketed passage. Tell students to listen for sound devices.

- **Ask** students the Literary Analysis question: What sound does the poet emphasize with the use of assonance in lines 30 and 31?
Answer: The poet emphasizes the /a/ sound in "slapping" and "blackjack."

▶ **Monitor Progress:** Read aloud lines 32 and 33 and ask students to identify the sound devices used.
Answer: Sound devices used: alliteration in "Dribble" and "drive"; assonance in "drive," "inside," "glide," and "like."

▶ **Reteach:** Review the definitions of the different sound devices. Have students brainstorm combinations of words that illustrate each type. Then slowly and clearly read a few lines from the poem. Guide students in identifying each type of sound device.

Differentiated Instruction — Solutions for All Learners

Strategy for Less Proficient Readers
Have students go through the poem, identifying all the vivid verbs they can find, such as *outmaneuvered, poised, corkscrew, dunk,* and *slapping.* Have students discuss the effect of these verbs. Why are these action verbs more effective than linking verbs? Challenge students to try writing a few sentences about basketball or another sport that they enjoy, using vivid verbs like those in this poem.

Strategy for English Learners
Suggest that students focus on their favorite sport (other than basketball). Have students work in teams to make a list of special terms used to describe the sport. Then have students write simple definitions of the terms to help newcomers to the sport.

15 Humanities

Illustration by Jane Breskin Zalben

Zalben illustrates and writes books for children. Her style is characterized by warm colors and friendly, gentle characters. Here, even her illustration of the Jabberwock depicts a monster that is not too threatening. Use these questions for discussion:

1. What makes the Jabberwock look threatening?
   Answer: The Jabberwock is very large compared to the knight who opposes him. Plus, the Jabberwock breathes fire.

2. If you were illustrating "Jabberwocky" for a new edition today, how would you make the pictures different from Zalben's?
   Answer: Students' answers will vary, but some may suggest a style of art that flows from modern-day science fiction and fantasy, and that uses computer graphics.

16 Critical Viewing

Answer: The fantastical aspects of "Jabberwocky" are conveyed with the burbling dragon, the egg blowing bubbles, and the calm, confident, strangely costumed child.

Jabberwocky
Lewis Carroll

'Twas brillig, and the slithy toves
    Did gyre and gimble in the wabe;
All mimsy were the borogoves,
    And the mome raths outgrabe.

5   "Beware the Jabberwock, my son!
    The jaws that bite, the claws that catch!
Beware the Jubjub bird, and shun
    The frumious Bandersnatch!"

He took his vorpal sword in hand:
10   Long time the manxome foe he sought—
So rested he by the Tumtum tree,
    And stood awhile in thought.

606

16 ▼ Critical Viewing Which aspects of this illustration convey the fantastical quality of "Jabberwocky"? **[Analyze]**

Vocabulary Development

Vocabulary Knowledge Rating

When students have completed reading and discussing Poetry Collection 2, have them take out their **Vocabulary Knowledge Rating Chart** for these poems. Read the words aloud once more and have students rate their knowledge of the words again in the After Reading column. Clarify any words that are still problematic. Have students write their own definition and example or sentence in the appropriate column. Then have students complete the **Vocabulary Builder Practice** activities on p. 609. Encourage students to use the words in further discussion and written work about these poems. Remind them that they will be accountable for these words on the Selection Test.

And as in uffish thought he stood,
        The Jabberwock, with eyes of flame,
15 Came whiffling through the tulgey wood,
        And burbled as it came!

    One, two! One, two! And through and through
        The vorpal blade went snicker-snack!
    He left it dead, and with its head
20   He went galumphing back.

    "And hast thou slain the Jabberwock?
        Come to my arms, my beamish boy!
    O frabjous day! Callooh! Callay!"
        He chortled in his joy.

25 'Twas brillig, and the slithy toves
        Did gyre and gimble in the wabe;
    All mimsy were the borogoves,
        And the mome raths outgrabe.

**Literary Analysis
Sound Devices** What sound or noise does the onomatopoeia *burbled* reflect?

Literature in Context

Language Connection

Carroll's Invented Language In the first chapter of *Through the Looking-Glass,* Alice encounters a creature called a Jabberwock. She cannot understand it, so Humpty Dumpty explains some of the words it uses, including these:

brillig: four o'clock in the afternoon, the time when you begin broiling things for dinner

toves: creatures that are something like badgers, something like lizards, and something like corkscrews

gyre: go round and round like a gyroscope

gimble: make holes like a gimlet (a hand tool that bores holes)

wabe: grass plot around a sundial

mome: having lost the way home

raths: something like green pigs

Connect to the Literature

What challenges do you think Carroll faced in writing a poem with invented language?

Jabberwocky ■ 607

⑰ Literary Analysis
Sound Devices

- Point out that Carroll's use of made-up language helped him play with sound devices. For example, in line 23, Carroll devised the words *callooh* and *callay* to achieve alliteration. Have students analyze other made-up words and decide how Carroll developed them as sound devices.

- **Ask** students the Literary Analysis question: What sound or noise does the onomatopoeia *burbled* reflect?
  Answer: It reflects the sound of water bubbling and gurgling.

⑱ Literature in Context

Language Connection Point out that many of Carroll's words are portmanteaus or blends. These are words made up of two different words. For example, Carroll forms *slithy* by combining *slimy* and *lithe. Brillig* might combine the word *brilliant* with *broiling.* The word *galumphing* was compiled from the words *galloping* and *triumphant.*

Connect to the Literature Explain to students that even though many of the words are nonsense words, they make sense because of the sound, their apparent part of speech, and their use in the context of the poem. **Ask** the Connect to the Literature question: What challenges do you think Carroll faced in writing a poem with invented language?
Possible response: Carroll's challenge was to make nonsense sound sensible. He accomplished this by placing his wildly inventive words within standard grammatical patterns.

Concept Connector

Connecting to the Literature
Have students compare the sentences they wrote before reading with their thoughts about the ideas evoked by everyday sounds. Ask them to explain whether their thoughts have changed and, if so, how.

Reading Skill Graphic Organizer
Have students review the graphic organizers they completed to identify sensory language. Show them **Reading Skill Graphic Organizer B** (*Graphic Organizer Transparencies*, p. 132) as an example. Then, have students share the graphic organizers they did and the sensory language they identified.

Apply the Skills

Poetry Collection 2

1. **Possible response:** "The Jabberwocky" was the most entertaining because of its creativity and silliness.

2. (a) The speaker describes the swish of the basketball net strings. (b) The sound is caused by the basketball dropping through the net.

3. (a) He slays the Jabberwock. (b) Students may agree that the poem makes fun of traditional heroic tales if not heroism itself.

4. Students may agree with Eliot, noting that the sounds and rhythms of "The Bells" are highly interesting in themselves.

5. (a) **Sample responses:** "The Bells"—alliteration: "What a tale of terror now their turbulency tells"; consonance: "human heart a stone"; assonance: "wrangling" and "danger"; onomatopoeia: "ringing." "Slam, Dunk & Hook"—alliteration: "Swish of strings like silk"; consonance: "but a hot"; assonance: "Up & dunk"; onomatopoeia: "swish." "Jabberwocky"—alliteration: "claws that catch"; consonance: "time the manxome"; assonance: "left it dead"; onomatopoeia: "snicker-snack." (b) These devices make the words of each poem sound like they fit together. Poems, like musical compositions, may have slow and fast, gentle or harsh, or loud and soft passages. Sound devices help to create these musical colors and textures.

   Another sample answer can be found on **Literary Analysis Graphic Organizer B**, p. 136 in *Graphic Organizer Transparencies.*

6. (a) One example is "jingling." (b) It imitates the sound of sleigh bells ringing. (c) The word captures the light, carefree ring of the sleigh bell.

7. (a) Students may choose "The Bells" because of its especially obvious use of alliteration and onomatopoeia. (b) Students should agree on their choices and have examples to support their opinions.

8. **Possible response:** Fluent reading helps readers hear and appre-

Thinking About the Selections

1. **Respond:** Which of these poems did you find most entertaining? Explain your choice.
2. (a) **Recall:** In lines 4–5 of "Slam, Dunk, & Hook," what sound does the speaker describe? (b) **Infer:** What action causes this sound?
3. (a) **Recall:** In "Jabberwocky," what does the hero do after being warned about the Jabberwock? (b) **Evaluate:** Do you think the poem pokes fun at heroism? Explain.
4. **Take a Position:** The poet T. S. Eliot once said that poetry can be enjoyed before it is understood. Could "The Bells" be used as evidence to support this idea? Explain.

Literary Analysis

5. (a) For each poem in Poetry Collection 2, use a chart like the one shown to identify one example of each **sound device** listed. (b) In what way does each example add to the musical feeling of each poem?

	Example	Effect
Alliteration		
Consonance		
Assonance		

6. (a) Identify an example of **onomatopoeia** in "The Bells." (b) What sound does the word imitate? (c) How well does the word imitate the sound? Explain your answer.
7. (a) Which of these poems do you think makes the most effective use of sound devices? Explain your choice. (b) Discuss your idea with a small group and together decide on a single response to explain to the class.

Reading Skill

8. In what way does **reading fluently** help you to appreciate a poem's sound devices?
9. (a) Which of your senses, other than your sense of hearing, were most engaged by each of these poems? (b) Which specific words appealed to those senses?

Poems at a Glance
"Slam, Dunk, & Hook" is a reminiscence of neighborhood basketball.

"Jabberwocky" is a poem about a fantastical creature.

"The Bells" describes the sounds of bells.

Go Online
Assessment

For: Self-test
Visit: www.PHSchool.com
Web Code: epa-6405

Sound Devices: language that emphasizes the sound relationships among words; sound devices include *alliteration, consonance, assonance,* and *onomatopoeia*

Reading Fluently: reading smoothly and continuously while comprehending the text and appreciating the writer's artistry

ciate the musical qualities of the poems.

9. (a) Students should recognize that other than sound, sight was the most commonly used sense in all of the poems. (b) **Possible response:** These words and phrases appealed to the sense of sight: "The Bells": "while the stars, that oversprinkle / All the heavens, seem to twinkle," "frantic fire / Leaping higher"; "Slam, Dunk, & Hook": "We outmaneuvered the footwork / of bad

angels" "Our backboard splintered"; "Jabberwocky": "Did gyre and gimble in the wabe," "with eyes of flame."

Vocabulary Builder

Practice Identify the word that does not belong and explain why.

1. metaphysical, concrete, bodily
2. jibed, turn, straight
3. voluminously, tiny, huge
4. palpitating, pulse, hum

Adding Words to Your Vocabulary *Jibe,* the present tense form of *jibed,* is a nautical term—a word related to sailing. *Tack, fathom,* and *headway* are other nautical terms used in conversation. Use a dictionary to learn the meanings of these words and how they relate to sailing. Then, write a sentence for each word that reflects its common usage. (For more on using a dictionary, see page R6.)

Writing

Write an **editorial**—a piece of writing that presents one side of an issue— related to one of the poems. Using "Slam, Dunk, & Hook" as inspiration, you could write about the need for more funding for neighborhood sports.

- State the issue clearly and express your opinion reasonably.
- Anticipate questions from those who might disagree with you.

Have several people respond to your editorial, including someone who disagrees with you. If you hear a point that you should have addressed, consider adding it.

For *Grammar, Vocabulary,* and *Assessment,* see **Build Language Skills,** pages 610–611.

Extend Your Learning

Listening and Speaking Prepare a **dramatic reading** that captures the musical qualities of one of the poems in the collection.

- Choose a poem and make notes about which words and sounds to emphasize and when to change your reading pace.
- Practice reading the poem aloud, recording yourself, if possible, so that you can hear and fix problem spots.

Present your dramatic reading in class.

Research and Technology In a group, create an **illustrated version** of one of the poems. Find photographs or original artwork. With the group, debate the merits of each choice and then reach an agreement about which images best capture the mood of the poem. Read the poem and share the art for classmates' enjoyment.

Assessment Resources

The following resources can be used to assess students' knowledge and skills.

Unit 4 Resources
Selection Test A, pp. 80–82
Selection Test B, pp. 83–85

Go **O**nline
—Assessment Students may use the **Self-test** to prepare for **Selection Test A** or **Selection Test B.**

Go **O**nline
—Research **For:** An additional research activity
Visit: www.PHSchool.com
Web Code: epd-7404
For another research activity to extend students' learning, give students this Web Code.

Vocabulary Builder
Practice

1. metaphysical; it has to do with spiritual things whereas *concrete* and *bodily* describe physical things.
2. straight; *jibed* and *turn* have similar meanings.
3. tiny; *voluminously* and *huge* describe large things.
4. hum; *hum* is a constant sound whereas *palpitating* and *pulse* refer to rhythmic beating.

Adding Words to Your Vocabulary

1. I used a *tack* to pin the schedule to the bulletin board.
2. Sophia couldn't *fathom* how her dog had escaped, so she continued to search the premises.
3. The new lawyer has lost only one case since she came *aboard.*
4. My mother told my brother to clean his room, but he has been too busy playing with his toys to make any *headway.*

Writing

- To give students guidance for writing an editorial, give them **Support for Writing** for Poetry Collection 2, p. 75 in *Unit 4 Resources.*
- To evaluate students' editorials, use the persuasion rubrics, pp. 53–54 in *General Resources.*

Six Traits Focus

✔ Ideas		Word Choice
✔ Organization		Sentence Fluency
	Voice	Conventions

Writing and Grammar, Gold Level
Students will find guidance on persuasive writing in Chapter 7.

Build Language Skills

Go to pages 610–611 for vocabulary and grammar lessons and assessment practice.

Extend Your Learning

The **Support for Extend Your Learning** page (*Unit 4 Resources,* p. 76) provides guided note-taking opportunities to help students complete the Extend Your Learning activities.

609

Build Language Skills

Poetry Collection 1 • Poetry Collection 2

Vocabulary Skill

- Introduce the suffix *-tion.* **Ask** students to brainstorm for words that contain this suffix.
  Possible responses: *concentration, mediation, remediation, fluoridation, ionization, perpetuation*
- Have students complete the Practice activity on this page.

Answers

1. *standardization;* The standardization of scores prevented any bias.

2. *instruction;* The computer programming instruction took several months.

3. *transition;* The transition from inches to meters is still not complete.

4. *substitution;* The substitution of players resulted in our team winning the game.

5. *termination;* The contract's termination took effect on Monday.

Grammar Lesson

- Prepositional phrases can precede or follow the words they modify, but they must be next to the words they modify to be clear.
- Have students complete the Practice activity on this page.

Answers

1. in the yard; adverb; The kids like to play kickball in the yard.

2. about the assignment; adverb; The students complained about the assignment.

3. of a bird; adjective; She has often been told that she has the appetite of a bird.

4. around the block; adverb; The grocery store is just around the block.

5. on the sidewalk; adverb; The ice-cream had fallen and was now melting on the sidewalk.

Vocabulary Skill

Suffixes The **Latin suffix** *-tion* means "the act of" or "the state of being." When a word contains *-tion* as a suffix, it is a noun. For example, the verb *deliberate* means "carefully think through an issue." When the suffix *-tion* is added, the word *deliberation* means "the act of carefully thinking about an issue."

Practice: Add the suffix *-tion* to the following verbs, and use each of the resulting nouns in a sentence.

1. standardize

2. instruct

3. transit

4. substitute

5. terminate

Grammar Lesson

Prepositional Phrases A **prepositional phrase** is a group of words beginning with a preposition and ending with a noun or pronoun. Prepositional phrases may function as adjectives or adverbs.

> Adjective phrase: The players on their team are more experienced.
> Adverb phrase: They played with more skill.

Practice Identify the prepositional phrase in each sentence. Tell whether it functions as an adjective or an adverb. Then, write a new sentence using the phrase.

1. We heard a noise in the yard.

2. Our teacher told us about the assignment.

3. Eddy made a picture of a bird.

4. We ran around the block.

5. He stood on the sidewalk.

$\mathcal{W}_G$ *Prentice Hall Writing and Grammar Connection: Chapter 21, Section 1*

MorePractice

For more practice with prepositional phrases, see the Grammar Handbook, p. R43.

Teaching Resources

The following resources can be used to enrich or extend the instruction for Build Language Skills.

Unit 4 Resources
  Build Language Skills: Vocabulary: Suffixes, p. 78
  Build Grammar Skills: Prepositional Phrases, p. 79

Assessment Practice

Reading Skill: Read Fluently

Directions: *Read the selection. Then, answer the questions.*

1 In Xanadu did Kubla Khan
2 A stately pleasure dome decree:
3 Where Alph, the sacred river, ran
4 Through caverns measureless to man
5   Down to a sunless sea.
6 So twice five miles of fertile ground
7 With walls and towers were girdled round
8 And there were gardens bright with sinuous rills,
9 Where blossomed many an incense-bearing tree;
10 And here were forests ancient as the hills,
11 Enfolding sunny spots of greenery.

—from *Kubla Khan* by Samuel Taylor Coleridge

1. Why does each line begin with a capital letter?
   A It is a poetic convention.
   B It is the start of a sentence.
   C It signals that the reader should pause.
   D It shows that the words are proper nouns.

2. Line 9 relies on which two senses?
   A taste and touch
   B sight and sound
   C sight and smell
   D sound and touch

3. Which sense is most evoked in this poem?
   A touch
   B sight
   C taste
   D smell

4. How many sentences are in this poem?
   A four sentences
   B eleven sentences
   C two sentences
   D one sentence

Timed Writing: Analysis [Critical Stance]

Review *Poetry Collection 1* or *Poetry Collection 2*. Explain the meaning of the figurative language in one of the poems and evaluate the effectiveness of the comparison. **(35 minutes)**

Writing Workshop: *Work in Progress*

Descriptive Essay

Using your Sensory Words list, write down three emotions that you associate with the place. Briefly jot down clue words about the reasons for those emotions; for example, meaningful events that happened there. Save this work in your writing portfolio.

Build Language Skills ■ *611*

Answers

Reading: Reading Fluently
1. A
2. C
3. B
4. C

Timed Writing

- Tell students that when they write an analysis of a poem, they should pay attention to the poem's theme, structure, figurative language, and meaning.

- Have students review the poems in the section. When students have selected their poems, have them include examples of the figurative language from the poem, cite the lines on which the examples appear, and note how that figurative language contributes to the poem.

- Assess students' analyses based on their explanations of how the figurative language adds to the poem and on their support for their analysis.

- Suggest that students allow ten minutes for selecting and reviewing the poem, twenty minutes for writing the analysis, and five minutes for reviewing and revising the analysis.

Writing Workshop
Work in Progress

Response to Literature

- Have students go to their portfolio and take out their Sensory Words list from the previous **Work in Progress** on p. 585.

- Remind students that this work may be used in the descriptive essay they will write in the **Writing Workshop** at the end of Part 1.

- As students write about the emotions they associate with their selected place, remind them that they should pay attention to the reasons for these feelings.

- When students have finished the activity, have them save the work in their portfolios. They will use it as they continue this **Work in Progress.**

Meeting Your Standards

Students will

1. analyze and respond to imagery in poetry.
2. compare the effect of imagery in three poems.
3. write a comparison of imagery.

See TeacherExpress™/Lesson View for a detailed lesson plan for Reading Informational Materials.

Literary Analysis

❶ Imagery

- Read the instruction about *imagery* aloud. Tell students to think of imagery as language that the writer uses to create word pictures for the reader.

- Imagery enables writers to convey a physical experience with great intensity and few words. For that reason, imagery is especially vital to poetry.

❷ Comparing Imagery

- Remind students that poets use imagery in many different ways. Students will see how different poets employ imagery as they read the three selections.

- Encourage students to read poetry as actively as possible, forming sensory images in their mind as they read. Tell them to picture the scene that the poet draws with words.

- Give students a copy of **Comparing Imagery Graphic Organizer A** (*Graphic Organizer Transparencies,* p. 137). Have them complete it as they read and compare the selections. Suggest that they include details like these:

    descriptive words and phrases that appeal to the senses

    what the descriptive words evoke

    what idea or message they could draw from the imagery

---

❶ Imagery

Imagery is language that appeals to one or more of the senses—sight, hearing, touch, taste, and smell. The use of imagery allows writers to express their ideas with vividness and immediacy. Images create mental pictures for readers and allow them to make connections between their own experiences and the worlds presented in poems.

❷ Comparing Imagery

Poets use imagery to give a sensuous basis to the experiences, thoughts, and feelings that they express in a poem. Through imagery, they convey to readers that the poem is a little world in itself, not just printed words on a page. These poetic worlds all relate to the one world we share, but each is unique. Two poets, for example, can use the same word to create different images, or they can describe similar images in different ways.

- In "Blackberry Eating," the word *black* stresses the rich color of blackberries. Combined with other details in the poem, this image appeals primarily to the senses of taste and sight.
- In "There Is No Word For Goodbye," the word *black* describes an elderly woman's eyes. The description appeals to the sense of sight and conveys an understanding of the woman's wisdom and depth.

Comparing imagery is an important step in analyzing the *aesthetic qualities* of a variety of poems. Poets, for example, often include patterns of images in their work. By making assertions about such image patterns, or *motifs*, you can better appreciate aesthetic differences and similarities among poems.

As you compare the imagery in these selections, start by noting that images appealing to the sense of touch play an important role. Then, you might note some differences among these image patterns.

As you read, compare the imagery in the poems. Use a chart like the one shown to identify images and note the senses they address.

Poem: "Blackberry Eating"	
Image: prickly stalks	
Sight	✔
Sound	
Taste	
Smell	
Touch	✔

Vocabulary Builder

Blackberry Eating

- **penalty** (pen´ əl tē) *n.* punishment (p. 615) *Mistakes are the <u>penalty</u> for working too quickly.*

- **unbidden** (un bid´ 'n) *adj.* without being asked; uninvited (p. 615) *The bee flew <u>unbidden</u> through the window.*

Daily

- **shriveled** (shriv´ əld) *adj.* shrunken and wrinkled (p. 616) *A raisin is a <u>shriveled</u> grape.*

- **scarred** (skärd) *adj.* marked or dented (p. 616) *The <u>scarred</u> road made bicycling a challenge.*

612 ■ *Poetry*

Vocabulary Development

Vocabulary Knowledge Rating

Create a **Vocabulary Knowledge Rating Chart** with the selection vocabulary and expressive vocabulary for the three selections. Give students a copy. Introduce the words by reading them aloud and having students mark their rating in the Before Reading Column. Urge them to be alert to these words as they read and discuss the selections because they will rate their knowledge of the words again after they finish.

If you wish, you may tally how many students know (or think they know) a word to gauge how much instruction you need to provide. As students read, point out the words and their context.

Build Understanding

❸ Connecting to the Literature

Reading/Writing Connection Each of the following poems uses language that appeals to the senses. Make a list of several common daily activities. Then, explain how each activity appeals to the senses of sight, sound, smell, taste, or touch. Use at least three of these words in your response: *emphasize, consume, appreciate, impact.*

Meet the Authors

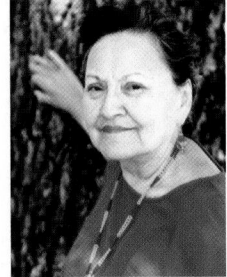

Mary **TallMountain** (1918–1994)

An Athabaskan Indian, Mary TallMountain was born in Nulato, Alaska, a small town on the Yukon River. The Athabaskans are a group of tribes that speak a variety of related languages and live in the American Southwest, parts of the Northwest, Alaska, and Canada. When TallMountain was six, her mother died, and she was adopted by a family who removed her from her people and culture. In "There Is No Word For Goodbye," TallMountain reconnects with her Native American roots.

Galway **Kinnell** (b. 1927)

Galway Kinnell was born in Providence, Rhode Island. In his poetry, he addresses the themes of mortality, selfhood, and the power of nature. In explaining why he is drawn toward writing about nature, Kinnell has said, "Part of poetry's usefulness in the world is that it pays some of our huge, unpaid tribute to the things and creatures that share the earth with us."

Naomi Shihab **Nye** (b. 1952)

Naomi Shihab Nye was born in St. Louis to a Palestinian father and an American mother. A successful poet, she has worked as a visiting writer at several colleges and universities. Of poems, she has said, "I liked the space around them, and the way they took you to a deeper, quieter place, almost immediately."

Go Online
Author Link

For: More about the authors
Visit: www.PHSchool.com
Web Code: epe-9407

There Is No Word For Goodbye / Blackberry Eating / Daily ■ 613

---

❸ Connecting to the Literature

- Model use of the expressive vocabulary students are asked to use with these examples:

  1. Sokoya wants to *emphasize* how she will live on, even after death.

  2. As you *consume* blackberries, your tongue and teeth turn purple.

  3. Galway Kinnell seems to *appreciate* the beauty in words.

  4. The word "blackberry" has an immediate *impact* on my sense of taste.

- Help students further develop their expressive vocabulary by providing these words: *admire, detest, examine, grasp.* Encourage students to use these words as they discuss the selections.

Go Online
Author Link For additional information about Mary TallMountain, Galway Kinnell, and Naomi Shihab Nye, have students type in the Web Code and then select the poet.

THERE IS NO WORD FOR GOODBYE **①②③**

MARY TALLMOUNTAIN

① Background

① Background

Death and the Afterlife A Shoshone legend tells of two caterpillar people who loved each other very much. When the caterpillar man died, the caterpillar woman pulled her sorrow around her like a shawl and mourned for a year. Then the Creator clapped his hands and the caterpillar woman burst forth as a butterfly.

② Motivation

Ask students to recall an experience from the past that is vivid in their memory. Ask them to identify the sights, sounds, tastes, textures, and smells linked to the experience.

Concept Connector ➡

Students will follow up on this activity after completing the three poems.

③ About the Poems

"There is No Word for Goodbye" describes a meaningful exchange about the finality of death between a young adult and an elderly aunt. "Blackberry Eating" compares the sensuous experience of eating ripe fruit with the process of writing. Finally, the busy speaker of "Daily" breathes new life into chores.

④ Literary Analysis

Imagery

• Remind students that imagery is descriptive language that appeals to the senses.

• **Ask** the first Literary Analysis question: Which word or words suggest that Sokoya is an elder?
Answer: The phrases "net of wrinkles" and "wise black pools" indicate that Sokoya is an elder.

⑤ Literary Analysis

Imagery

• Read aloud the bracketed stanza. **Ask** the second Literary Analysis question: Which image in lines 19–23 appeals to the sense of touch?

• **Possible response:** The image of the delicate bluebell flower helps convey the idea that Sokoya touched the speaker very gently.

④ Sokoya, I said, looking through
　　　　the net of wrinkles into
　　　　wise black pools
　　　　of her eyes.

5　What do you say in Athabaskan
　　　　when you leave each other?
　　　　What is the word
　　　　for goodbye?

　　A shade of feeling rippled
10　　　the wind-tanned skin.
　　　　Ah, nothing, she said,
　　　　watching the river flash.

　　She looked at me close.
　　　　We just say, Tlaa. That means,
15　　　See you.
　　　　We never leave each other.
　　　　When does your mouth
　　　　say goodbye to your heart?

　　She touched me light
20　　　as a bluebell.
⑤　　　You forget when you leave us,
　　　　You're so small then.
　　　　We don't use that word.

　　We always think you're coming back,
25　　　but if you don't,
　　　　we'll see you some place else.
　　　　You understand.
　　　　There is no word for goodbye.

　　　　Sokoya: Aunt (mother's sister)

614 ■ Poetry

Literary Analysis
Imagery Which words suggest that Sokoya is an elder?

Literary Analysis
Imagery Which image in lines 19–23 appeals to the sense of touch?

Vocabulary Development

Expressive Vocabulary
As students are discussing the poems, encourage them to use the expressive vocabulary presented earlier. You might encourage them with sentence starters like these:

1. Galway Kinnell uses imagery to *emphasize* . . .
2. The speaker of "Blackberry Eating" seems happy to *consume* . . .
3. The speaker of "Daily" appears to *appreciate* . . .
4. Sokoya's explanation of the word goodbye had such an *impact* on me that I . . .

BLACKBERRY EATING
GALWAY KINNELL

I love to go out in late September
among the fat, overripe, icy, black blackberries
to eat blackberries for breakfast,
the stalks very prickly, a <u>penalty</u>
5 they earn for knowing the black art
❻ of blackberry-making; and as I stand among them
lifting the stalks to my mouth, the ripest berries
fall almost <u>unbidden</u> to my tongue,
as words sometimes do, certain peculiar words
10 like *strengths* or *squinched*,
many-lettered, one-syllabled lumps,
which I squeeze, squinch open, and splurge well
in the silent, startled, icy, black language
of blackberry-eating in late September.

Vocabulary Builder
penalty (pen´ əl tē)
n. punishment
unbidden (un bid´
'n) *adj.* without being
asked; uninvited

Thinking About the Selections

1. **Respond:** Which description did you like the most in each poem? Explain.

2. **(a) Recall:** In "There Is No Word for Goodbye," who is Sokoya?
   (b) Infer: Why do you think the speaker wants to know the word for goodbye?

3. **(a) Connect:** What does Sokoya want the speaker to understand in the final stanza? **(b) Draw Conclusions:** Do you think Sokoya's words are comforting to the speaker? Explain.

4. **(a) Recall:** In "Blackberry Eating," identify two words that the speaker compares to blackberries. **(b) Compare and Contrast:** According to the speaker, what do these words have in common with blackberries?

5. **(a) Draw Conclusions:** Which aspect of writing does this poem capture in lines 9–13? Explain. **(b) Speculate:** Do you think the speaker of this poem enjoys writing poetry? Why or why not?

Blackberry Eating ■ 615

❻ **Literary Analysis**
Imagery
• Read the poem aloud. Tell students that the first three lines contain the central image of the poem.
• **Ask** students which words in the first three lines appeal to the sense of sight. Which appeal to the sense of touch?
  Answer: The words *fat, overripe,* and *black* all appeal to the sense of sight. The word "*icy*" appeals to the sense of touch.

ASSESS
Answers

1. **Possible responses:** Students may choose the description of the succulent blackberries as most appealing. The reader can almost taste the ripe berries. Students might also choose the description of Sokoya because of its rich, emotional texture.

2. (a) Sokoya is the speaker's aunt.
   (b) **Possible response:** Students may say that Sokoya will die soon and the speaker wants to say goodbye.

3. (a) Sokoya indicates that goodbyes are unnecessary because there is an afterlife where they will meet again. (b) Yes, the speaker is probably glad to hear that death is not the final goodbye.

4. (a) The speaker compares certain peculiar words such as *strengths* and *squinched* to blackberries.
   (b) The words come unbidden to his mind as berries come to the tongue.

5. (a) The poem captures the poet's love for the textures and colors of language. (b) The speaker clearly relishes writing as much as he enjoys eating blackberries.

- Read aloud the bracketed passage.
- **Ask** students what the narrator is doing in the first four lines of the poem.
- **Answer:** The narrator is telling about planting seeds.
- **Ask** the Literary Analysis question: Which senses does the imagery of the bed covers address?
  Answer: The rumpled covers appeal to the senses of sight and touch.

Concept Connector

Have students discuss how using their senses helped them recall the experiences they discussed in the Motivation activity. Ask them to describe how the sensory images in the poems make them seem more realistic or vivid.

ASSESS

Answers

1. Students may say that the description of the tortillas creates the clearest pictures. Other students may say the image of the bed covers is most vivid.

2. (a) The speaker recalls planting seeds, folding t-shirts, cooking, making a bed, addressing an envelope, typing, dusting, and washing clothes. (b) Yes, she seems to enjoy the tasks. From the last line, we can infer that the speaker feels that they are sacred.

3. (a) The last two lines do not describe daily tasks. (b) The speaker believes that there is holiness in even the most mundane daily tasks.

DAILY

NAOMI SHIHAB NYE

These <u>shriveled</u> seeds we plant,
corn kernel, dried bean,
poke into loosened soil,
cover over with measured fingertips

5   These T-shirts we fold into
❼   perfect white squares

These tortillas we slice and fry to crisp strips
This rich egg scrambled in a gray clay bowl

This bed whose covers I straighten
10   smoothing edges till blue quilt fits brown blanket
and nothing hangs out

This envelope I address
so the name balances like a cloud
in the center of the sky

15   This page I type and retype
This table I dust till the <u>scarred</u> wood shines
This bundle of clothes I wash and hang and wash again
like flags we share, a country so close
no one needs to name it

20   The days are nouns; touch them
The hands are churches that worship the world

Vocabulary Builder
shriveled (shriv´ əld)
adj. shrunken and wrinkled

Literary Analysis
Imagery Which senses does the imagery of the bed covers address?

Vocabulary Builder
scarred (skärd) *adj.* marked or dented

Thinking About the Selection

1. **Respond:** Which words create the clearest picture? Explain.

2. **(a) Recall:** Identify at least five tasks the speaker describes. **(b) Infer:** Does she seem to take pleasure in doing these tasks? Explain.

3. **(a) Analyze:** How do the final two lines differ from those that come before? **(b) Draw Conclusions:** What is the speaker's outlook on life?

Vocabulary Development

Vocabulary Knowledge Rating
When students have completed reading and discussing the three poems, have them take out their **Vocabulary Knowledge Rating Chart.** Read the words aloud once more and have students rate their knowledge of the words again in the After Reading column. Clarify any words that are still problematic. Have students write their own definition and example or sentences in the appropriate column. Then, have students complete the **Vocabulary Builder Practice** activities on p. 617. Encourage students to use the words in further discussion and written work about the selections. Remind them that they will be accountable for these words on the Selection Test.

Apply the Skills

Comparing Imagery

1. **(a)** For each poem, provide one example of **imagery** that appeals to the sense of touch. **(b)** Provide one example of imagery that appeals to the sense of sight.
2. **(a)** Which poems include imagery that appeals to the sense of taste? **(b)** Which poem includes imagery that appeals to the sense of smell? **(c)** Do any of the poems include imagery that appeals to the sense of sound? Explain your answers with specific examples from the poems.

Writing to Compare Literary Works

In an essay, compare and contrast how the poet's use of imagery adds to the meaning of each poem. Use the following questions to get started:

- In "Blackberry Eating," how do the images of blackberries help you understand the poet's ideas about words?
- In "Daily," how do the images help you understand the speaker's affection for ordinary things?
- In "There Is No Word For Goodbye," how do the images of Sokoya help you understand the speaker's feelings for her aunt?

Use a chart like the one shown to help you in your response.

Poem	Imagery	Message Conveyed
"There Is No Word For Goodbye"		
"Blackberry Eating"		
"Daily"		

Vocabulary Builder

Practice Answer each question. Explain your answer.

1. Would you eat an apple that is *shriveled*?
2. If someone arrived *unbidden* to a party, would he or she be greeted warmly?
3. Would a football team be excited about receiving a *penalty*?
4. Would a *scarred* piece of furniture look new?

Apply the Skills ■ 617

QuickReview

Imagery: an author's use of words and phrases that appeal to the senses

Go Online
Assessment
For: Self-test
Visit: www.PHSchool.com
Web Code: epa-6406

ASSESS

Answers

Comparing Imagery

1. (a) **Sample response: Example from "Blackberries" that appeals to the sense of touch:** "icy, black blackberries." (b) **Example from "Daily" that appeals to the sense of sight:** "These shriveled seeds we plant."

   Another sample can be found on **Comparing Imagery Graphic Organizer Transparency B,** p. 140 in *Graphic Organizer Transparencies.*

2. (a) "Blackberries" and "Daily" include imagery that appeals to the sense of taste. (b) The imagery in "Daily" appeals to the sense of smell. (c) "Daily" uses imagery— frying tortillas and typing—that appeals to the sense of sound.

Writing to Compare Literary Works

- Remind students that the three poems use imagery in different ways and for different effects. Have students refer to their completed chart comparing the imagery in the three selections.

- Have students use the bulleted questions to develop their ideas. Explain that they should organize their essays by addressing one question at a time.

- Encourage students to incorporate the expressive vocabulary words: *emphasize, consume, appreciate, impact.*

Six Traits Focus

✔	Ideas		Word Choice
✔	Organization		Sentence Fluency
	Voice		Conventions

Vocabulary Builder

1. No, you would not eat a shriveled apple, because it would not be fresh.

2. No, he would probably not be greeted warmly since he was not invited.

3. No, a football team would not appreciate a punishment.

4. No, a scarred piece of furniture would look used.

617

MONITORING PROGRESS

In this Skills Review, students apply the skills taught in Part 1. The test format gives students practice in taking standardized tests. The result of this review test will help you check students' readiness for the **Benchmark Test** for Unit 4, Part 1.

Applying Reading Skill

Read the passage with students. Guide them in identifying the clues to determine the correct number of sentences in the poem in item 1: Sentences do not end with semicolons or with the ends of lines. If necessary, have students review the instruction on p. 562. Then, have them complete the remaining items on their own.

Applying Vocabulary Skills

Have students review the instruction on suffixes on p. 563. Remind students to apply their knowledge about suffixes to the items on the test. Provide students with these words: *transition* and *capable.* Then, have students identify the suffixes and explain how the suffixes contribute to the words' meanings.

Tips for Test Taking

Remind students that just because a line ends with punctuation does not mean that the sentence has ended. For example, a comma does not signal the end of a sentence. Explain that sentences always end with periods, question marks, or exclamation points. If these marks are not in the text, the sentence has not ended.

Reading

Directions: *Questions 1–5 refer to the following poem.*

> There will come soft rains and the smell of the ground,
> And swallows circling with their shimmering sound;
>
> And frogs in the pools singing at night,
> 4   And wild plum trees in tremulous white;
>
> Robins will wear their feathery fire
> Whistling their whims on a low fence-wire;
>
> And not one will know of the war, not one
> 8   Will care at last when it is done.
>
> Not one would mind, neither bird nor tree
> If mankind perished utterly;
>
> And Spring herself, when she woke at dawn,
> 12   Would scarcely know that we were gone.
> —"There Will Come Soft Rains" by Sara Teasdale

1. How many sentences are there in this poem?
A four
B three
C two
D one

2. Where is the first pause in lines 7–8?
A at the end of line 7
B at the end of line 8
C after the word *war*
D after the word *last*

3. What senses does the poet appeal to in the first four lines?
A sight and smell
B touch, smell, hearing
C smell, sight, hearing
D touch and smell

4. What is the image described in lines 5–6?
A redbirds whistling in the wind
B robins that are on fire
C red-breasted robins sitting and singing on a fence
D birds with red feathers sitting on a fence wire

5. What point is the poet making in this poem?
A If human beings disappeared, nothing in nature would notice.
B Earth is most beautiful in the spring.
C Soft rains come in the spring to awaken the earth.
D Human beings are damaging the environment.

ASSESS

Answers

1. C	9. D
2. C	10. B
3. C	11. C
4. C	12. C
5. A	13. A
6. C	14. B
7. B	15. D
8. B	

Assessment Practice

Vocabulary

Directions: *Choose the letter of the word that best completes the sentence.*

6. The _____ from the meteor left an enormous hole.
   A deliberation
   B transition
   C impact
   D concept

7. I am having difficulty writing _____ between the introduction and the first body paragraph in this essay.
   A a deliberation
   B a transition
   C an impact
   D a concept

8. He had difficulty understanding the _____ of infinity.
   A transition
   B concept
   C impact
   D consideration

9. He left his _____ fortune to charity.
   A deliberate
   B impact
   C conceptual
   D considerable

10. The judge reached his decision after careful and _____ thought.
    A impact
    B deliberate
    C concept
    D diminish

11. We need a snack that is _____.
    A microwavate
    B microwave
    C microwaveable
    D microed

12. An _____ of the problem helped us resolve it.
    A articulacy
    B articulated
    C articulation
    D articulative

13. He is very friendly and _____.
    A amiable
    B amenable
    C animate
    D amiably

14. I do not agree with his _____ of that work as "fantasy."
    A categorized
    B categorization
    C categorizing
    D categoric

15. I wonder whether or not this law is _____.
    A enforceate
    B enforce
    C enforceably
    D enforceable

RETEACH

If students answer any of these questions incorrectly, have them review the instruction on the following pages in Part 1 before taking the **Benchmark Test**.

Question	Pages Where Instruction Is Located:
1	564, 590
2	564, 590
3	564, 590
4	564, 590
5	564, 590
6	563
7	563
8	563
9	563
10	563
11	584
12	610
13	584
14	610
15	584

Benchmark

Administer the **Benchmark Test** for Unit 4, Part 1. If the Benchmark Test reveals that some students need further work, use the Interpretation Guide to determine the appropriate reteaching page in the **Reading Kit**. You will also find the same instruction and practice available on **Success Tracker**.

Go Online
Vocabulary

For: Interactive Crossword Puzzle
Visit: www. PHSchool.com
Web Code: epj-5401
Give students this Web Code to access an interactive crossword puzzle using Academic Vocabulary and Vocabulary Skill words from Part 1.

Meeting Your Standards

Students will

1. write a descriptive essay.
2. use writing strategies to generate ideas, organize, evaluate, and revise the essay.
3. apply grammar skills.

Writing Genres

Using the Form Point out to students that descriptive writing is often incorporated into other types of writing. Point out these examples:

- Personal and business letters often describe places and events.
- Descriptive writing often appears in how-to articles.

Writing Workshop
Work in Progress

If students have done the **Work-in-Progress** assignments throughout Part 1, suggest that they examine their recorded ideas now.

OES Online Essay Scorer

A writing prompt for this mode of writing can be found on the *PH Online Essay Scorer* at PHSuccessNet.com.

Prewriting

- For each place students visit, suggest that they create five-column charts, labeling each column with one of the five senses. Tell students to record details that appeal to each of the five senses.

Six Traits Focus

✔	Ideas	✔	Word Choice
	Organization		Sentence Fluency
	Voice		Conventions

Writing and Grammar Interactive Textbook CD-ROM

Students can use the following tools as they complete their descriptions.

- List Graphic Organizer
- Sensory Word Bin

620

Description: Descriptive Essay

Descriptive writing begins not in your imagination, but in your senses—in your ability to notice physical details. While valuable on its own, description also helps you share an experience or portray a person. Use the steps outlined in this workshop to write a descriptive essay.

Assignment Write a description of a place that you enjoy or that is meaningful to you.

What to Include Your descriptive essay should feature

- sensory details that re-create sights, sounds, smells, tastes, and textures
- precise word choice that brings the subject into focus
- figurative language, such as metaphor and simile
- logical and consistent organization
- error-free grammar, especially your use of prepositional phrases

To preview the criteria on which your descriptive essay may be assessed, see the rubric on page 624.

Prewriting

Choosing Your Topic

Take notes. For a few days, be alert to the sights, sounds, smells, tastes, and textures you encounter in your daily routine. Jot down notes about the places you visit. Use the location that prompts the most entries as your topic.

Gathering Details

Plan to use figurative language. To create a vivid picture of your subject, use figurative language such as metaphors or similes. Compare an unfamiliar object or scene with something familiar to your readers.

Place	Basic Description	Figurative Language
school art room	Colorful paintbrushes sit in jars.	Paintbrushes, <u>their heads heavy with color</u>, sit in jars. (metaphor)
	This is a place where lots of things can happen.	<u>Like a garden</u>, this is a place of possibilities. (simile)

620 ■ *Poetry*

Using the Form

You may use elements of this form in these types of writing:

- autobiographical writing
- travel reports
- character sketches

To get a feel for descriptive essays, read the excerpt from *Silent Spring* on page 153.

Work in Progress

Review the work you did on pages 559, 585 and 611.

Teaching Resources

The following resources can be used to enrich or extend the instruction for the Writing Workshop.

Unit 4 Resources
Writing Workshop—Description: Descriptive Essay, p. 99
Writing Workshop—Integrating Grammar Skills, p. 100

General Resources
Rubrics for Description: Descriptive Essay, pp. 55–56

Drafting

Shaping Your Writing

Choose an effective organizational pattern. The following are two structures that work well with descriptive essays:

- **Spatial organization:** Describe your subject systematically from left to right, front to back, or top to bottom. Like a photographer, pan your "camera" over your subject, using transitional words and phrases like *above, below,* or *in the distance* that show spatial relationships.

- **Time-order organization:** Describe your subject as you first approach it and then as you move through or around it. In addition to words expressing spatial relationships, use words showing time-order relationships such as *initially, meanwhile,* or *finally.*

Providing Elaboration

Think about your audience. Consider your readers' knowledge of the place you are describing. If the place is unfamiliar, include more vivid details. If the place is familiar, draw your readers in by acknowledging shared experience.

Revising

Revising Your Overall Structure

Strengthen your main impression. A memorable descriptive essay conveys a single, strong impression of its subject. Review your work, adding details that support the main impression. Eliminate details that are irrelevant or distracting.

Reading — *Writing* — *Connection*

For the complete student model, see page 623.

Student Model: Revising to Strengthen the Main Impression

Inside I am met by a sound check of guitars vibrating through

speakers. I am surrounded by wood; wood floors, wood

ceiling, wood walls ∧ bounce around like mad.
; acoustic trampolines that make the music

> The writer adds detail to make the description more specific and vivid.

Revising Your Word Choice

Choose vivid words. Review your essay, circling vague or dull word choices. Consider replacements that paint a clear and colorful picture of your subject.

Dull: The air was *really* cold.

Vivid: The air was *piercingly* cold.

Writing Workshop ■ 621

Teach column

Drafting

- Tell students that *to the left, above,* and *nearby* are examples of spatial transitional words. Help students build a word bank of spatial transitional words.

Six Traits Focus

Ideas		✔ Word Choice
✔ Organization		Sentence Fluency
Voice		Conventions

WG Writing and Grammar, Gold Level
Students will find additional instruction on drafting a descriptive essay in Chapter 6, Section 3.

Revising

- Ask students to write down the overall impressions that they want to create. Tell students to have partners read their essays and to write down their overall impressions. Encourage partners to underline details in the essays that contribute to their impressions. After retrieving their essays, have students compare the two impressions and make revisions to close any gaps between them.

- Write the following sentences on the board:

   The tree provided shade.

   The towering pine sheltered the weary hikers from the scorching heat.

   Invite students to compare and contrast the two sentences, commenting on the word choice in each.

Six Traits Focus

Ideas		✔ Word Choice
Organization		Sentence Fluency
✔ Voice		Conventions

WG Writing and Grammar, Gold Level
Students will find additional instruction on revising a descriptive essay in Chapter 6, Section 4.

Tips for Using Rubrics

- Before students begin work on this assignment, have them preview the Rubric for Self-Assessment on page 624 to know what is expected.

- Review the Assessment criteria in class. Before students use the Rubric for Self-Assessment, work with them to rate the student model by applying one or two criteria to it.

- If you wish to assess students' descriptive essays with a 4-point, 5-point, or a 6-point scoring rubric, see *General Resources,* pp. 55–56.

621

Integrating Grammar Skills

- Write the following sample paragraph on the board. Read the paragraph aloud for students, and ask them to comment on the subject-verb pattern. Is the writing interesting? Is the pattern overused?

  The house stood far back from the road. A single light shown from one high window. The light revealed a man working at a desk. My mysterious neighbor paused on the road outside. She stared upward from the shadows.

- Ask students to work individually to revise the paragraph by moving some of the prepositional phrases to the beginning of the sentences to vary the pattern and to make the writing more engaging. Call on volunteers to read their revisions. Emphasize that there is more than one way to vary the sentence structures.

  Possible response: *The house stood far back from the road. From one high window, a single light shown. The light revealed a man working at a desk. On the road outside, my mysterious neighbor paused. She stared upward from the shadows.*

 Writing and Grammar, Gold Level
Students will find additional instruction on prepositional phrases in Chapter 21, Section 1.

Integrating Grammar Skills

Revising to Vary Sentence Patterns

Overuse of the basic subject-verb pattern can make your writing stiff. To add interest, begin some sentences with prepositional phrases.

Identifying Prepositional Phrases A preposition is a word that relates a noun or pronoun to another word in the sentence. The combination of preposition and accompanying noun or pronoun—the object of the preposition—is called a prepositional phrase.

Prentice Hall Writing and Grammar Connection: Chapter 21, Section 1

Preposition +	Noun/ Pronoun	=	Prepositional Phrase
over	moon		over the moon
under	porch		under the porch
behind	door		behind the red door

Many prepositions express spatial relationships. Appropriate use of such prepositions to begin sentences can clarify descriptive writing.

Varying Sentences With Prepositional Phrases In the following example, subjects are italicized, verbs are underlined, and prepositional phrases appear in parentheses.

> **Overuse of subject-verb pattern:** The *cave* was hidden (behind the trees). The *ground* was smooth (in front of it). *I* pulled away dead branches. *I* saw large paw prints (on the cave's dirt floor).

> **Revision:** The cave was hidden behind the trees. In front of it, the ground was smooth. I pulled away dead branches. On the cave's dirt floor, I saw large paw prints.

Follow these steps to vary your sentences in your writing.

1. **Read your draft aloud, listening for places where you overuse the subject-verb sentence pattern.**
2. **Rewrite some sentences to begin with a prepositional phrase.**
3. **If an introductory prepositional phrase contains four or more words, set it off with a comma.**

Apply It to Your Editing

Review the first and last paragraphs of your descriptive essay, looking for opportunities to vary a monotonous subject-verb sequence of sentences. Rewrite some sentences by beginning them with prepositional phrases.

Tips for Test Taking

Some standardized tests ask students to answer questions about sentence structure. Provide students with models to practice answering this type of question. Write the item below on the board. Ask a volunteer to select the correct response and to explain his or her reasoning.

> Revise the sentence so that it begins with a prepositional phrase.
>
> The saxophone is difficult to master for many young musicians.

A The saxophone, for many young musicians, is difficult to master.

B For many young musicians, the saxophone is difficult to master.

C Many young musicians find it difficult to master the saxophone.

D Mastering the saxophone is difficult for many young musicians.

Answer: B. *For many young musicians* is a prepositional phrase.

Student Model: Zachary DeBoer
Raleigh, NC

Ziggy's Coffeehouse

As I enter the gates of the fenced-in courtyard of the humble coffeehouse, smooth stones crunch beneath my shoes and strings of Christmas lights twinkle like the stars overhead. A stranger takes my five-dollar bill and makes a mark on my hand. The freezing winter air is perfectly still while I walk up the ramp and step into the mildly dilapidated structure. Inside I am met by a sound check of guitars vibrating through speakers. I am surrounded by wood; wood floors, wood ceiling, wood walls; acoustic trampolines that make the music bounce around like mad. The guys and girls in the band tonight are good friends of mine. As they run through their set list, there is a strong sense of camaraderie between them. They dream of record deals and radio play and 25-city tours. Perhaps they imagine that their venue is not a small café, but a mammoth, sold-out arena. They put on their best performance, playing just for us and singing: "We should be dancing. We need be dancing."

The place smells like aged wood and fresh coffee, but my lack of even a few dollar bills means I'll be drinking water tonight. There are three platforms in the cafe; the lowest has a set of double doors on the stage right side that have been swung open. The heat lamps radiate warmth as the frigid air rushes in from the doors, like a cold front passing through on a hot September day. On the second tier, those who prefer to act like adults sip their skinny decaf lattes. They seem mildly interested in the music, but most are there for the lack of something better to do. Are they swaying because of the music or because they have put a bit too much sugar in their coffees? Outside in the parking lot, kids talk cars and sports and who knows what else? I'm so captivated by the band that my ears can't tell. They laugh intermittently, oblivious to the music playing inside.

On the lowest level, immediately in front of the stage, the real fans are found. We push the tables back and dance around like no one is watching us and we sing along with the songs we know at the top of our lungs. This is where we artists are, the free spirits, the *real* cool kids. I don't know most of them but I feel a connection with all of them. We are friends now, brothers and sisters, united by the music. We jump up and down, careful not to bump into each other or the tables; we are captivated by the music but respectful of those around us. We have been liberated from the bonds of everyday life. We are transported to a state of bliss. We are not escaping reality; instead, we are experiencing true reality. As the soft lights from the stage shine onto the mellow brown of the all-wood venue, I realize: On this night, at this moment, there is nowhere else I'd rather be than this place.

Zachary uses sensory details to make this introduction vivid and interesting.

The writer does not limit himself to describing the setting; he imagines the thoughts and feelings of the people, as well.

Zachary uses details related to all the senses, including smell and taste.

The writer pays attention to all elements of the scene.

Zachary uses description to make a meaningful point.

Writing Workshop ■ 623

Differentiated
Instruction   Solutions for All Learners

Strategy for Less Proficient Readers
Work as a class to identify the sensory appeals of "Ziggy's Coffeehouse." Have students create five-column charts headed *Sight, Touch, Hearing, Taste,* and *Smell*. Have students work individually on the first paragraph, then discuss their findings as a class. After students complete their charts, ask them to describe the overall effect of Zach's sensory language.

Student Model

- Explain that the Student Model is a sample and that their own essays may be longer.
- **Ask** students to identify the physical senses Zach appeals to in his first three sentences.
  Answer: Zach appeals to touch (*smooth stones, freezing winter air*), hearing (*crunch*), and sight (*lights twinkle*).
  Ask: What simile does Zach use in the second paragraph to describe the temperature in the room?
  Answer: The combination of heat lamps and outdoor air is "like a cold front passing through on a hot September day."
- Review the final sentence with students. **Ask** them if Zach has provided sufficient details in this essay to support this conclusion.
  Possible response: Students may agree that Zach's abundance of detail enables the reader to fully understand his happiness at the end.
- Tell students that they should include all elements of a scene to give the reader a full picture of the environment.
- Tell students that readers can draw inspiration from powerful, meaningful statements that evolve from descriptions.

Writing Genres

Descriptive Writing on Science or Lab Reports Tell students that they may be asked to describe scientific observations in the form of reports. Point out that scientists must describe what they see, hear, taste, touch, and smell when conducting experiments. Although figurative language may not be appropriate in a scientific setting, language that appeals to the five senses is essential. A scientist uses the descriptions gathered during a process or experiment to draw conclusions and form hypotheses.

Editing and Proofreading

Editing and Proofreading

- Remind students that transitional words and phrases show connections between ideas. Often transitional words and phrases are set off with commas. Review the following examples with students.

    They had never been on vacation before. Indeed, they had never been far from home.

    It rained during their visit to the Grand Canyon; consequently, the visit was canceled.

Six Traits Focus

Ideas		Word Choice	
Organization		Sentence Fluency	
Voice		✔	Conventions

ASSESS

Publishing and Presenting

- Explain how visual aids can diversify and improve an oral presentation. Tell students that oral reading appeals to people who are auditory learners, but many people need a visual or the opportunity to touch something if they are to remember information. Visual aids help a speaker reach all learners.

- Provide copies of the visitor's guide to local libraries or the city chamber of commerce.

Reflecting on Your Writing

- Ask students to reflect on how successful they were in incorporating the five senses into their essays. Which senses were easy to address, and which were more difficult? Why?

- Ask students to reflect on the power of descriptive writing. Why do readers prefer novels and short stories with high levels of description?

Writing and Grammar, Gold Level

Students will find additional instruction on editing, proofreading, publishing, and presenting a descriptive essay in Chapter 6, Sections 6 and 7.

Check your draft for errors in spelling, grammar, and punctuation.

Focus on transitions: Make sure that you use transition words accurately and punctuate them correctly. If you begin a sentence with a transitional word or phrase, set it off with a comma.

Publishing and Presenting

Consider one of the following ways to share your writing.

Prepare an oral presentation. Descriptive writing is well suited to being read aloud. Gather photographs or illustrations, and select background music to enhance your reading.

Create a visitor's guide. With a group of classmates, assemble several essays that describe places of interest in your community, and create a guidebook for visitors. Encourage everyone in the group to participate, either by sharing his or her essays, drawing illustrations, designing layouts, or producing the guidebook. If possible, provide copies of the guidebook to your local library, town hall, or chamber of commerce for distribution to the public.

Reflecting on Your Writing

Writer's Journal Jot down your thoughts on the experience of writing a descriptive essay. Begin by answering these questions:
- In what ways, if any, did your view of your subject change as you wrote about it?
- What do you enjoy most about descriptive writing? Explain.

Prentice Hall Writing and Grammar Connection: Chapter 6

Rubric for Self-Assessment

To assess your descriptive essay, use the following rubric:

Criteria	Rating Scale				
	not very				*very*
Focus: How clearly do you describe your subject?	1	2	3	4	5
Organization: How logical and consistent is your organization?	1	2	3	4	5
Support/Elaboration: How well do you use sensory details?	1	2	3	4	5
Style: How effective is your use of figurative language?	1	2	3	4	5
Conventions: How correct is your grammar, especially your use of prepositional phrases?	1	2	3	4	5

624 ■ *Poetry*

Tips for
Using Technology in Writing

Whether students are giving oral presentations or preparing visitor's guides, computer programs and Internet resources provide ways to create multimedia products. The Internet provides access to photographic images that may complement oral presentations or visitor's guides. Students preparing oral presentations may also locate free music selections to incorporate into their presentations. Desk-top publishing software can help students design and organize their visitor's guides.

Unit 4
Part 2

Paraphrase

Skills You Will Learn

Literary Analysis: *Narrative Poetry and Mood*
Reading Skill: *Picturing the Action*

Reading Skill: *Evaluating Web Sources*

Literary Analysis: *Rhyme, Rhyme Scheme, and Meter*
Reading Skill: *Breaking Down Long Sentences*

Literary Analysis: *Lyric Forms: Sonnet, Haiku, and Free Verse*

Literature You Will Read

Paraphrase ■ 625

Skills Overview

Reading Skill: Paraphrasing
- Picturing the action
- Breaking down long sentences

Vocabulary Development
- Suffixes

Literary Analysis
- Narrative Poetry: mood, atmosphere, figurative language
- Rhyme: exact rhyme, slant rhyme, end rhyme, internal rhyme, rhyme scheme, meter

Writing
- Response to Literature
- Work in Progress, pp. 651, 675

Monitoring Progress

Diagnose: Before you begin Part 2, administer the **Diagnostic Test** for Unit 4, Part 2. This test will identify students' level of readiness for the reading and vocabulary skills in Part 2. Use the **Interpretation Guide** for the Diagnostic Test to determine which students need help with prerequisite skills before beginning Part 2.

Preteach and Prepare: Use the information indicated in the **Interpretation Guide** to help students build prerequisite skills. In addition, prepare students by using the **Vocabulary Warm-up** activities and the **Reading Warm-up** activities as necessary for each selection set.

Teach: Use the instructional plan and resources provided to teach the skills and selections.

Assess: After students have completed Part 2, administer the **Benchmark Test** for Unit 4, Part 2. The test results will indicate which skills students have mastered and those on which they need more work.

Reteach: Use the Interpretation Guide to determine the appropriate reaching pages from the **Reading Kit**.

Intervention: The prerequisite and reteaching pages are also available in the **Success Tracker**.

Differentiated Instruction   Solutions for All Learners

Resources for Monitoring Progress

Unit 4 Resources
 Unit 4, Part 2 Diagnostic Test,
 pp. 108–110
 Unit 4, Part 2 Benchmark Test,
 pp. 197–202

Reading Kit

Success Tracker

Introduce the Reading Skill

- Introduce the reading skill: paraphrasing. Point out that paraphrasing is not only helpful when trying to understand a text, but is also useful when taking notes for a research report or paper.

- Point out that paraphrases can be the same length or longer than the original. Paraphrasing does not mean summarizing, which is restating only the most important points in your own words; summaries are always much shorter than the original.

- Tell students that if they have properly paraphrased a passage, they should understand its meaning.

Model the Reading Strategies

- Model how picturing the action can help to paraphrase the action and understand a passage. Write this sentence from Shakespeare's *As You Like it* on the board:

  All the world's a stage,

  And all the men and women merely players:

  They have their exits and their entrances:

  And one man in his time plays many parts.

  Then, model thinking for students:

  Picture what typically happens during a play. What goes on?
  Answer: *Actors move onto the stage, speak their parts, and leave; they may change costumes and have an intermission for rest; sometimes they return to act new roles, and then leave the stage when finished.*

  Why is Shakespeare comparing the world to a stage?
  Answer: He wants to compare how people live their lives to the workings of a play.

  So, to paraphrase this text, what would I say?
  Answer: Life is like a play in which actors are people who come and go, playing many parts during their lifetimes.

- Emphasize that picturing the action will help students to paraphrase and better understand the text.

626

Reading: Paraphrase

> **Paraphrasing** is restating or explaining something in your own words.

Skills and Strategies You Will Learn in Part 2

In Part 2, you will learn
- **to picture the action** to help restate or **paraphrase** the action (p. 628).
- **to break down long sentences** so that they can be **paraphrased** (p. 657).
- **to evaluate Web sources** when researching articles on literature (p. 652).

Using the Skills and Strategies in Part 2

In Part 2, you will learn to **paraphrase**, or put something into your own words, to help you understand difficult or confusing text. You will learn to **analyze the sentences in a poem**, breaking them down into clauses and phrases. You will practice picturing action in order to restate the text in your own words.

The following example shows how you can apply these strategies.

1 If I could put the notion in his head:
2 "Why do they make good neighbors? Isn't it
3 Where there are cows? But here there are no cows.
4 Before I built a wall I'd ask to know
5 What I was walling in or walling out,
6 And to whom I was like to give offense.
7 Something there is that doesn't love a wall.
8 That wants it down."
      —from "Mending Wall" by Robert Frost

Break down the fourth sentence: Before I built a wall - I'd ask to know - what I was walling in or walling out - and to whom I was like to give offense.

Picture one person talking to another. The speaker is responding to something that the other has said.

Paraphrase: I would like him to think about why walls help neighbors get along. Walls are to keep cows in, and we don't have cows.

626 ■ *Poetry*

Professional Development
Developing Poetry Inquiry Skills

Introduce a poem to the class by first reading it aloud. Immediately ask students to write down three questions they have about the poem. The questions can be about a certain word ("What does this word mean?" "Why does the poet use this word here?"), a phrase, or a whole section.

After students have written their questions, form the students into small groups and have them generate answers to their questions. A recorder in each group then reports the results of these brief discussions.

The advantages of this strategy are that students are encouraged to ask their own questions. Students' discussion is a vehicle for learning, allowing students to try out emerging ideas on each other.

Source: Jeff Golub, 1994. *Activities for an Interactive Classroom.* Urbana, Illinois, NCTE.

Academic Vocabulary: Words for Analyzing Literature

The following words will help you as you read and analyze the literature in Part 2.

Word	Definition	Sample Sentence
usage *n.*	way of using something	The poet's *usage* of musical words adds to the beauty of the poem.
emphasize *v.*	to stress	Many poets *emphasize* rhythm.
mechanism *n.*	system or means of doing something; working parts of a machine	What *mechanism* does the author use to move the plot forward?
abstract *adj.*	not concrete; of thought	The author's use of *abstract* ideas made the work difficult to read.
distinct *adj.*	separate; well-defined	She has a *distinct* style.

Vocabulary Skill: Suffixes

A **suffix** is a word ending that forms a new word and may change a word's part of speech.

In Part 2, you will learn
- the suffix *-age* (p. 650)
- the suffix *-ism* (p. 674)
- the suffix *-ize* (p. 674)

-age Forms nouns related to conditions, results, costs, amounts, and places. (**marriage, postage, acreage, hermitage**)

-ism Forms nouns related to conditions, systems, or practices, or examples. (**mechanism, skepticism, modernism, Americanism**)

-ize Forms verbs related to making, becoming, combining, or doing what is indicated by the base word. (**Americanize, oxidize, theorize**)

Activity Add one of the suffixes to form the part of speech indicated. Check your spelling in a dictionary. Then, use the new word in a sentence.

1. active (noun) **2.** patriot (noun) **3.** computer (verb)
4. ton (noun) **5.** general (verb)

Reading and Vocabulary Skills Preview ■ 627

Differentiated Instruction   Solutions for All Learners

Strategy for Advanced Readers
If students have read "The Jabberwocky" on p. 606, ask them to paraphrase the poem. Point out that although some of the words are nonsensical, by looking at the parts of speech used and the definitions given, they can paraphrase the poem.

Next, point out to students that sound is also important in this poem to create a tone or atmosphere, and students should capture sound in their paraphrase. **Ask:** What tone do you pick up from the word usage?

Possible response: Some students might say that the tone seems sinister or dangerous. Some might say that this tone, combined with the imaginary words, creates a comic effect.

Then, have students paraphrase the poem. Finally, when students finish, have them compare their paraphrases with those of others in the class, noting similarities and differences in interpretation.

Introduce Academic Vocabulary
- Introduce the academic vocabulary: words for analyzing literature. Tell students that they may find these words useful as they analyze literature in Part 2.
- Review each word in the chart, and have the students state the words aloud. Have students read aloud the words' definitions and the example sentences.
- Tell students to try to use these words as they discuss the selections in Part 2.

Introduce the Vocabulary Skill
- Introduce the vocabulary skill: suffixes. Point out to students that Latin and Greek have provided many suffixes that are commonly found in English words.
- Review the three suffixes on this page, their meanings, and the English words that contain these suffixes.
- Have students complete the activity and discuss any unclear answers.

Activity
1. *activism;* The *activism* of the students improved the school.
2. *patriotism;* During World War II, many Americans showed their *patriotism.*
3. *computerize;* Can we *computerize* the business?
4. *tonnage;* The ship's *tonnage* was much greater than its appearance suggested.
5. *generalize;* The ability to *generalize* is an important study skill.

Go Online For: Interactive Vocabulary Crossword Puzzles
Visit: www.PHSchool.com
Web Code: epj-5402
Give students this Web Code to access interactive crossword puzzles using Academic Vocabulary and Vocabulary Skill words from Part 2.

627

Planning Differentiated Instruction

Choosing Your Poetry Collection

You may use either collection of poems to meet the lesson standards. The following guide will help you determine which of the two collections is more appropriate for your students.

Accessibility at a Glance

	Collection 1	**Collection 2**
Context	Narrative collection; each poem has an element of suspense	Narrative collection; each poem has a distinct atmosphere
Language	Straightforward vocabulary and sentence structure; some familiar experiences	Difficult vocabulary and sentence structure; each poem creates a mood
Concept Level	Accessible	Challenging
Literary Merit	Noted poets	Noted poets
Lexile	NP	NP
Overall Rating	More accessible	More challenging

Using the Other Collection You may use the other collection of poems for homework or independent reading to reinforce the selection skills. If you use both collections, you can build a test for both using *ExamView*® **Test Bank** software.

Choosing Your Resources

[**L1**] Special Needs Students   [**L4**] Advanced Students

[**L2**] Below-Level Students   [**EL**] English Learners

[**L3**] All Students

FT Fast Track Instruction: To move the lesson more quickly, use the strategies and activities identified with **FT**.

Reading and Vocabulary Warm-ups provide support for below level students. **A** is for students reading two grades below level; **B** is for students reading one grade below level. For Selection Tests, **A** signifies "less challenging" and **B** "more challenging." For Graphic Organizer transparencies, **A** signifies "not filled in" and **B** "filled in."

Scaffolding for Less Proficient and Advanced Students

The leveled questions on Apply the Skills pages progress in the levels of thinking required to answer them. To address the needs of your different students, you may use the (a) level questions for your less proficient students, the (b) level with your on-level and advanced students. The occasional (c) level questions are appropriate for your advanced students.

Go Online **For:** Information about Lexiles
Internet Activity **Visit:** www.PHSchool.com
Professional Development **Web Code:** eue-1111

Step-by-Step Teaching Guide	**Pacing Guide**
PRETEACH	
• Administer Vocabulary and Reading Warm-ups as necessary.	
• Introduce the Literary Analysis Skill: Narrative Poetry. **FT**	10 min.
• Introduce the Reading Skill: Paraphrasing. **FT**	10 min.
• Prepare students to read by teaching the selection vocabulary. **FT**	10 min.
• Build background and develop expressive vocabulary with Connecting to the Literature and Background.	10 min.
• Engage students' interest with the motivation activity.	10 min.
TEACH	
• Informally monitor comprehension while students read independently or in groups. **FT**	30 min.
• Monitor students' comprehension with the Reading Check notes.	as students read
• Reinforce vocabulary with Vocabulary Builder notes.	as students read
• Develop students' understanding of narrative poetry with the Literary Analysis annotations. **FT**	5 min.
• Develop students' ability to paraphrase with the Reading Skill annotations. **FT**	10 min.
ASSESS/EXTEND	
• Assess students' comprehension and mastery of the Reading Skill and Literary Analysis by having them answer the Apply the Skills questions. **FT**	35 min.
• Have students complete the Vocabulary Builder activities. **FT**	5 min.
• Apply students' ability to write a detailed description of a scene with the Writing activity. **FT**	30–45 min. or homework
• Extend students' listening and speaking and research and technology skills with one or both of the Extend Your Learning activities.	15–30 min. or homework
• Have students complete the Vocabulary Skill and Grammar Lesson.	5 min.
• Monitor students' progress with the Assessment Practice.	20–40 min.
• Administer **Selection Test A** or **Selection Test B. FT**	15 min.

Resources

PRINT

Unit 4 Resources

	Collection 1	Collection 2
Vocabulary Warm-Up—Word Lists [**L1, L2, EL**]	p. 111	p. 127
Vocabulary Warm-Up—Practice [**L1, L2, EL**]	p. 112	p. 128
Reading Warm-Up A [**L1, L2, EL**]	p. 113	p. 129
Reading Warm-Up B [**L1, L2, L3**]	p. 114	p. 130

General Resources

Vocabulary Knowledge Rating Chart, p. 6 [**L3**]

Anticipation Guide, pp. 8–10 [**L3**]

TRANSPARENCY

Graphic Organizer Transparencies

Reading Skill Graphic Organizer A [**L3**]	p. 142	p. 142
Reading Skill Graphic Organizer B [**L1, L2, EL**]	p. 143	p. 144
Literary Analysis Graphic Organizer A [**L3**]	p. 145	p. 147
Literary Analysis Graphic Organizer B [**L1, L2, EL**]	p. 146	p. 148

PRINT

Reader's Notebook [L2]

Reader's Notebook: Adapted Version [L1]

Reader's Notebook: English Learner's Version [EL]

Unit 4 Resources

Literary Analysis [**L3**]	p. 115	p. 131
Reading Skill [**L3**]	p. 116	p. 132
Vocabulary Builder [**L3**]	p. 117	p. 133

TECHNOLOGY

Listening to Literature Audio CDs [L2, EL]

Reader's Notebook: Adapted Version Audio CD [L1, L2]

PRINT

Unit 4 Resources

Support for Writing [**L3**]	p. 118	p. 134
Support for Extend Your Learning [**L3**]	p. 119	p. 135
Enrichment [**L4**]	p. 120	p. 136
Selection Test A [**L1, L2, EL**]	pp. 121–123	pp. 139–141
Selection Test B [**L3, L4**]	pp. 124–126	pp. 142–144

Build Language Skills: Vocabulary:
Latin suffixes *-age, -ism,* and *-ize,* p. 137 [**L3**]

Build Language Skills: Grammar:
Appositive Phrase, p. 138 [**L3**]

General Resources

Rubrics for Descriptive Essays, pp. 55–56 [**L3**]

TECHNOLOGY

Go Online: Research [L3]

Go Online: Self-test [L3]

ExamView® **Test Bank [L3]**

Meeting Your Standards

Students will

1. **analyze and respond to literary elements.**
   - Literary Analysis: Narrative Poetry

2. **read, comprehend, and analyze narrative poetry.**
   - Reading Skill: Paraphrasing
   - Reading Strategy: Picturing the Action
   - Reading Check questions
   - Apply the Skills questions
   - Assessment Practice

3. **develop vocabulary.**
   - Vocabulary Builder
   - Latin suffixes *-age, -ism, -ize*

4. **apply grammar skills.**
   - Appositive Phrase

5. **develop writing proficiency.**
   - Work in Progress: Response to Literature
   - Detailed description of a scene

6. **extend learning.**
   - Listening and Speaking: Dialogue
   - Research and Technology: Fact Sheet

Block Scheduling: Use one 90-minute class period to preteach the skills and have students read the collection. Use a second 90-minute class period to assess students' mastery of skills, extend their learning, and monitor their progress.

Homework Suggestions

Following are possibilities for homework assignments.

- Support pages from *Unit 4 Resources:*
  Literary Analysis
  Reading Skill
  Build Vocabulary
  Enrichment

- An Extend Your Learning project and the Writing assignment for your chosen collection may be completed over several days.

PRENTICE HALL

Teacher**EXPRESS™** Use this complete
Plan · Teach · Assess suite of powerful
teaching tools to make lesson planning and testing quicker and easier.

PRENTICE HALL

Student**EXPRESS™** Use the
Learn · Study · Succeed Interactive
Textbook (online and on CD-ROM) to make selections and activities come alive with audio and video support and interactive questions.

Build Skills   *Poetry Collection 1 • Poetry Collection 2*

Narrative Poetry

- Tell students that while *narrative poetry* has many of the same characteristics as narrative prose, narrative poetry is much more condensed. The poet usually does not give lengthy descriptions of setting or characters, but carefully chooses a few details to convey the information.

- Point out that just a few words can create an atmosphere. For example, the sentence, "Through the mist, silent, silver grey shadows drifted across the moon" creates an atmosphere of mystery.

- Tell students to look for the significant details in the selections they read and to think how these details help develop mood, atmosphere, or character.

❷ **Reading Skill**

Paraphrasing

- Tell students that paraphrasing lines of poetry helps them better understand the ideas and feelings that the poet is trying to convey.

- Explain that in addition to figurative language, poets often use unusual syntax, or arrangement of words in a sentence. Identifying the primary parts of the sentence—the subject and verb—will help students better understand the poem.

- Tell students that when they paraphrase poetry, they should look at complete sentences, rather than at each line. Write the following lines on the chalkboard:

  In the startled ear of night
  How they scream out their affright!
  Too much horrified to speak,
  They can only shriek, shriek,
  Out of tune.

  Guide students to identify the two complete sentences in these lines.

- Give students a copy of **Reading Skill Graphic Organizer A** (*Graphic Organizer Transparencies*, p. 142). Have them fill in the graphic organizer to paraphrase lines of poetry as they read the assigned poems.

You can apply the instruction on this page to these poems.

Poetry Collection 1	**Poetry Collection 2**
Casey at the Bat, page 631	*The Raven,* page 639
Fifteen, page 633	*The Horses,* page 644
Twister Hits Houston, page 634	*The Writer,* page 646

❶ **Literary Analysis**

Narrative poetry is verse that tells a story and includes the same literary elements as narrative prose: a plot, or sequence of events; specific settings; and characters who participate in the action.

Also like narrative prose, such as a short story, a narrative poem conveys a **mood**, or **atmosphere**—an overall feeling created by the setting, plot, words, and images. For example, a narrative poem's mood can be gloomy, joyous, or mysterious. Poetry's emphasis on precise words and images makes mood a powerful element in a narrative poem.

❷ **Reading Skill**

Paraphrasing is restating in your own words what someone else has written or said. A paraphrase retains the meaning but is simpler. Paraphrasing helps you read poetry because poems often contain **figurative language,** words that are used imaginatively rather than literally. To paraphrase a narrative poem, **picture the action.**

- Based on details in the poem, form a mental image of the setting, the characters, and the characters' actions.

- To be sure that your mental picture is accurate, pay attention to the way that the poet describes the scene.

- Then, use your own words to describe your mental image of the scene and the action taking place in it.

As you read, use a chart like this one to record your paraphrases.

Lines of Poetry
Blue were her eyes as the fairy-flax, / Her cheeks like the dawn of day /

↓

Details in Lines of Poetry
Her eyes were blue. Her cheeks were red.

↓

Paraphrase
She had blue eyes and red cheeks.

Vocabulary Builder

Poetry Collection 1

- **pallor** (pal´ ər) *n.* unnatural paleness (p. 631) *His pallor made us realize how ill he was.*

- **writhing** (riŧh´ iŋ) *v.* twisting; turning (p. 632) *He struggled to hold the writhing cat still.*

- **demure** (di myoor´) *adj.* modest (p. 633) *The movie star's demure behavior was refreshing in Hollywood.*

Poetry Collection 2

- **beguiling** (bē gīl´ iŋ) *v.* tricking; charming (p. 641) *The child's innocence was beguiling.*

- **respite** (res´ pit) *n.* rest; relief (p. 643) *The rain provided a respite from the long dry spell.*

- **archaic** (är kā´ ik) *adj.* from an earlier time; ancient (p. 645) *Some people say the old song is timeless; others say it is archaic.*

628 ■ *Poetry*

Vocabulary Development

Vocabulary Knowledge Rating
Create a **Vocabulary Knowledge Rating Chart** for the collection you will teach from this set. Include the vocabulary from this page and the additional words students are asked to use at the end of Connecting to the Literature. These words will increase students' expressive vocabulary.

Give students a copy of the chart with the words on it. Introduce the words by reading them aloud and having students mark their rat-ing in the Before Reading column. Urge them to be alert to these words as they read and discuss the poems because they will rate their knowledge of the words again after they finish.

If you wish, you may tally how many students know (or think they know) a word to gauge how much instruction you need to provide. As students read, point out the words and their context.

Build Understanding • *Poetry Collection 1*

❸ Connecting to the Literature

Reading/Writing Connection Each poem in this group has a unique mood or feeling. To get ready to appreciate the moods of these literary works, connect to details that influence your mood in everyday life, such as weather, events, or people's actions. Write several sentences about things that affect your mood. Use at least three of these words: *evoke, respond, reinforce, react, promote.*

Meet the Authors

Ernest Lawrence **Thayer** (1863–1940)
Casey at the Bat (p. 631)
It is not surprising that "Casey at the Bat" reads like a sports story in verse. The poet, Ernest Lawrence Thayer, worked for many years as a sports reporter on the staff of newspapers in New York and California. "Casey at the Bat" first appeared in the *San Francisco Examiner* in 1888. It became so popular that in 1953 it inspired an operetta called *The Mighty Casey.*

William **Stafford** (1914–1993)
Fifteen (p. 633)
Raised in Kansas, William Stafford did not publish his first book, *West of Your City,* until he was 46. However, he made up for lost time after that, publishing many collections, including *Traveling Through the Dark.* Fellow poet Robert Bly has said that Stafford's poems are "spoken like a friend over coffee."

Sandra **Cisneros** (b. 1954)
Twister Hits Houston (p. 634)
Sandra Cisneros was born in Chicago, but her family moved frequently between Chicago and Mexico City. She began her first novel, *The House on Mango Street,* while still a college student. Cisneros has worked with high-school students, serving as poet-in-residence in several schools. She has received many awards for her writing.

Author Link

For: More about these authors
Visit: www.PHSchool.com
Web Code: epe-9409

❸ Connecting to the Literature

- Model use of the expressive vocabulary students are asked to use with these examples:

  1. The smell of popcorn can usually *evoke* for me the memory of last summer's baseball game.

  2. The fans *respond* with cheers at the double play.

  3. The team's loss will surely *reinforce* my bad mood.

  4. The townspeople *react* quickly to the news of the tornado.

  5. The weather service is trying to *promote* a new early warning device.

- Help students further develop their expressive vocabulary by providing these words: *alter, depress, diminish,* and *significant.* Encourage students to use these words as they discuss the poems.

Concept Connector ➤

Students will reconsider their ideas after completing these poems.

Go **Online** For additional informa-
Author Link tion about Ernest Lawrence Thayer, William Stafford, and Sandra Cisneros, have students type in the Web Code and then select the poet.

Differentiated Instruction *Solutions for All Learners*

Support for Below-Level Students [L1, L2]
Unit 4 Resources
  Vocabulary Warm-up Word Lists, p. 111
  Vocabulary Warm-up Practice, p. 112
  Reading Warm-up A, p. 113
  Selection Test A, pp. 121–123
Graphic Organizer Transparencies
  Reading Skill Graphic Organizer, Transparency B
Reader's Notebook: Adapted Version
Adapted Reader's Notebook Audio CD

Support for English Learners [EL]
Unit 4 Resources
  Vocabulary Warm-up Word Lists, p. 111
  Vocabulary Warm-up Practice, p. 112
  Reading Warm-up A, p. 113
Reader's Notebook: English Learner's Version
Listening to Literature Audio CD

❶ Motivation

Ask student volunteers to share a thrilling or intense moment in their lives. It might be an exciting moment at a baseball or football game, or a frightening moment in a storm. Ask them to describe details of the setting in which the event occurred. Ask students whether they think the event could be the subject of a poem. Tell students they will be reading poems about intense moments people experience in these three poems.

Learning Modalities
Musical/Rhythmic Learners

The strong rhythm and regular rhyme scheme of "Casey at the Bat" have made it a favorite read-aloud for over a century. Have a group of interested students collaborate on a recitation of the poem. One student can read the narration, others can take the roles of Casey and the umpire, and the rest can be the fans, cheering and booing where the poem indicates. Work with students to help them decide on sound effects. After planning and rehearsing, students can perform for the class.

❷ About the Selections

"Casey at the Bat" uses vivid words and dramatic details to create suspense. It is the ninth inning, and Mudville is down by two runs. With two men on base, the mighty Casey strides to the plate. In "Fifteen," a fifteen-year-old boy's discovery of a motorcycle leads him to an important discovery about himself. He fantasizes about the adventures he might have with the motorcycle, but in the end the mature side of his character prevails. "Twister Hits Houston" retells the family story of what Papa and Mama were doing and what happened when a tornado struck their home.

❸ Critical Viewing

Answer: The batter in the painting seems poised and relaxed. Casey in the poem is haughty and scornful, then enraged.

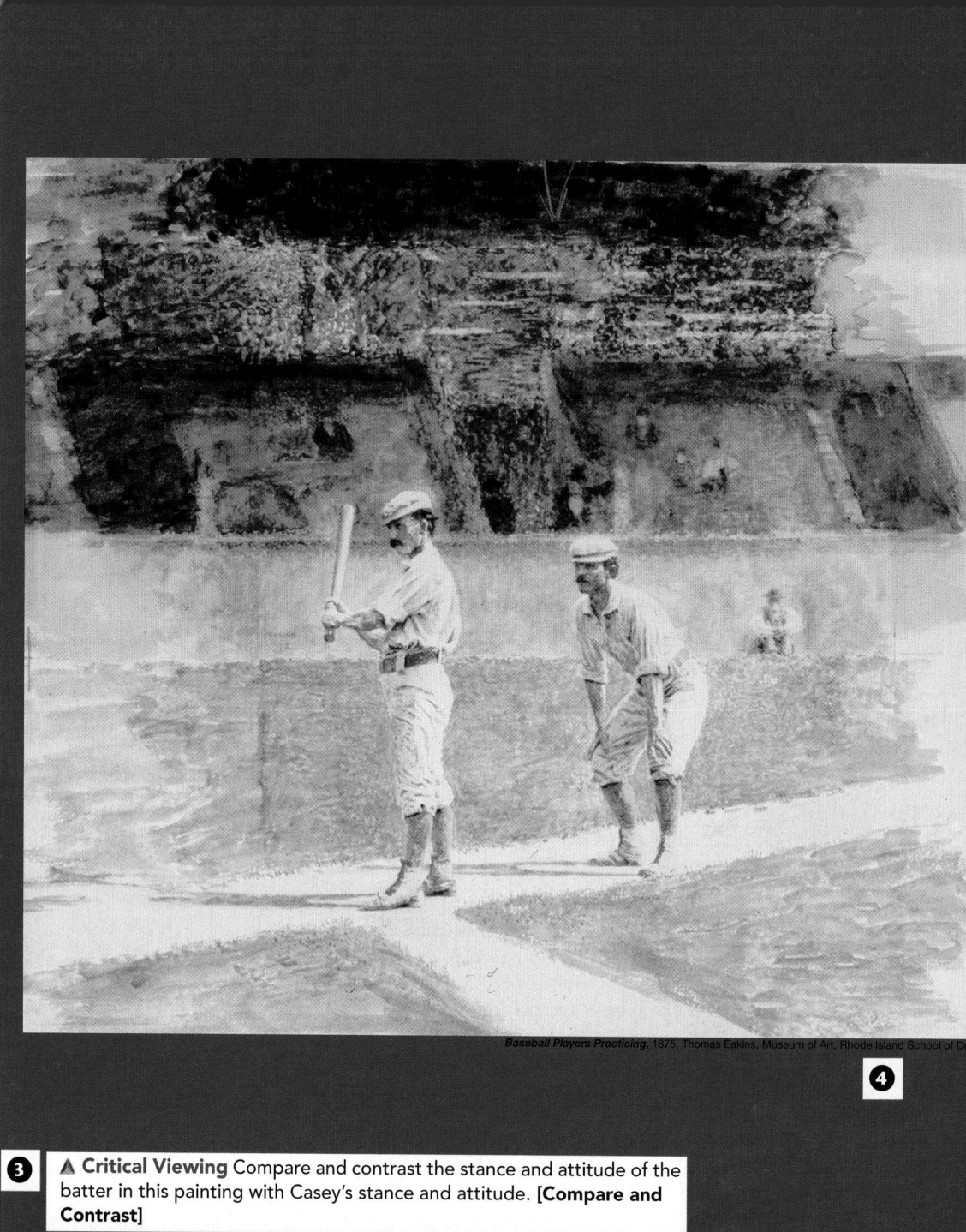

Baseball Players Practicing, 1875, Thomas Eakins, Museum of Art, Rhode Island School of De

❹

❸ ▲ **Critical Viewing** Compare and contrast the stance and attitude of the batter in this painting with Casey's stance and attitude. **[Compare and Contrast]**

630 ▫ *Poetry*

Vocabulary Development

Expressive Vocabulary

As students read the poems in this collection, ask them to think about the various moods expressed by the characters in the poems. Then encourage students to use the expressive vocabulary presented earlier as they discuss the poems. You might encourage them with sentence starters like these:

1. The umpire was able to *evoke* . . .
2. When Casey walked up to bat, the fans *responded* by . . .
3. The sight of the shiny motorcycle *reinforced* his feelings of . . .
4. Papa *reacted* to the tornado by . . .
5. The sight of the coming tornado *promoted* feelings of . . .

CASEY AT THE BAT

ERNEST LAWRENCE THAYER

❶
❷

It looked extremely rocky for the Mudville nine that day;
The score stood two to four, with but an inning left to play.
So, when Cooney died at second, and Burrows did the same,
A <u>pallor</u> wreathed the features of the patrons of the game.

5 A straggling few got up to go, leaving there the rest,
❺ With that hope which springs eternal within the human breast.
For they thought: "If only Casey would get a whack at that,"
They'd put even money now, with Casey at the bat.

But Flynn preceded Casey, and likewise so did Blake,
10 And the former was a pudd'n, and the latter was a fake.
So on that stricken multitude a deathlike silence sat;
For there seemed but little chance of Casey's getting to the bat.

But Flynn let drive a "single," to the wonderment of all.
And the much-despised Blakey "tore the cover off the ball."
15 And when the dust had lifted, and they saw what had occurred,
There was Blakey safe at second, and Flynn a-huggin' third.

Then from the gladdened multitude went up a joyous yell—
It rumbled in the mountaintops, it rattled in the dell;
It struck upon the hillside and rebounded on the flat;
20 For Casey, mighty Casey, was advancing to the bat.

There was ease in Casey's manner as he stepped into his place,
There was pride in Casey's bearing and a smile on Casey's face;
And when responding to the cheers he lightly doffed his hat,
No stranger in the crowd could doubt 'twas Casey at the bat.

Vocabulary Builder
pallor (pal´ ər) *n.*
unnatural paleness

Literary Analysis
Narrative Poetry
What is the setting of this narrative poem?

❻ **Reading Check**

Where are Blakey and Flynn when Casey comes to bat?

Casey at the Bat ■ 631

❹ Humanities
Baseball Players Practicing, by Thomas Eakins

The painting on p. 630 is by Philadelphia native Thomas Eakins (1844–1916), who is considered one of the two greatest American realist painters of the nineteenth century. (Winslow Homer is the other.) Eakins was also a great teacher of painting. Use the following questions for discussion:

1. How does this painting help you appreciate the poem?
   Answer: It illustrates the way players dressed and looked at the time the poem was written.

2. What does the painting show about the continuity of baseball?
   Answer: Baseball has not changed much, though batters and catchers now wear protective equipment.

❺ Literary Analysis
Narrative Poetry

• Have students **consider** the title of the poem and the image on p. 630. **Ask** them to identify the subject of the poem.
Answer: The subject is a baseball game.

• **Ask:** Based on the title, who will be the main character in this narrative?
Answer: Casey is the main character.

• Draw students' attention to the bracketed passage. **Ask** them to respond to the Literary Analysis question: What is the setting of this narrative poem?
Answer: The setting is a ballpark, in which a ballgame is being played.

❻ Reading Check

Answer: Blakey is on second base and Flynn is on third base.

- **Ask** students what they can infer from the fans' reaction to the umpire's call of strike.
Answer: The fans are intensely involved in the game and believe the umpire erred in his call.

- **Ask** students if they find the fans' reaction realistic.
Answer: Students may agree that today's fans get just as upset when calls go against their team, and that they care just as much about their team's success.

❽ **Literary Analysis**
Narrative Poetry and Mood

- Have students review lines 21 through 44. **Ask:** How does Casey's attitude change while he is at bat?
Answer: When he first comes up to the plate, he is confident and at ease. After two strikes, he becomes tense and fierce.

- Refer students to the bracketed passage. **Ask** students to respond to the Literary Analysis question: In what way does the poem's mood change in this stanza?
Possible response: The mood of the poem parallels Casey's attitude. With two strikes against him, Casey becomes intense—as does the poem.

---

25   Ten thousand eyes were on him as he rubbed his hands with dirt,
     Five thousand tongues applauded when he wiped them on his shirt;
     Then when the <u>writhing</u> pitcher ground the ball into his hip,
     Defiance glanced in Casey's eye, a sneer curled Casey's lip.

     And now the leather-covered sphere came hurtling through the air,
30   And Casey stood a-watching it in haughty grandeur there.
     Close by the sturdy batsman the ball unheeded sped;
     "That ain't my style," said Casey. "Strike one," the umpire said.

❼   From the benches, black with people, there went up a muffled roar,
     Like the beating of the storm waves on the stern and distant shore.
35   "Kill him! kill the umpire!" shouted someone on the stand;
     And it's likely they'd have killed him had not Casey raised his hand.

     With a smile of Christian charity great Casey's visage shone;
     He stilled the rising tumult, he made the game go on;
     He signaled to the pitcher, and once more the spheroid flew;
40   But Casey still ignored it, and the umpire said, "Strike two."

     "Fraud!" cried the maddened thousands, and the echo answered "Fraud!"
     But one scornful look from Casey and the audience was awed;
     They saw his face grow stern and cold, they saw his muscles strain,
     And they knew that Casey wouldn't let the ball go by again.

45   The sneer is gone from Casey's lips, his teeth are clenched in hate.
❽   He pounds with cruel vengeance his bat upon the plate:
     And now the pitcher holds the ball, and now he lets it go,
     And now the air is shattered by the force of Casey's blow.

     Oh, somewhere in this favored land the sun is shining bright,
50   The band is playing somewhere, and somewhere hearts are light:
     And somewhere men are laughing, and somewhere children shout,
     But there is no joy in Mudville: Mighty Casey has struck out.

Vocabulary Builder
writhing (rīth in) v.
twisting; turning

Literary Analysis
Narrative Poetry and Mood In what way does the poem's mood change in this stanza?

Vocabulary Development

Think Aloud: Context Clues
Direct students' attention to the word *haughty* in line 30. Using a think-aloud process, model how to use context to infer the meaning of an unknown word. Say to students:

I'm going to think aloud to show you how I would figure out the meaning of *haughty* from its context.

In this line *haughty* is being used to describe Casey's attitude as he comes to bat and takes the first pitch. From the previous lines, we know that Casey came to bat with an attitude of pride and confidence. In line 28 he is described as being defiant and having a sneer. In line 32, Casey says "That ain't my style," as he takes the first pitch.

From these clues, I think that *haughty* means having great pride and holding contempt for others.

Fifteen

William Stafford

South of the bridge on Seventeenth
I found back of the willows one summer
day a motorcycle with engine running
as it lay on its side, ticking over
5 slowly in the high grass. I was fifteen.

I admired all that pulsing gleam, the
shiny flanks, the <u>demure</u> headlights
fringed where it lay; I led it gently
to the road and stood with that
10 companion, ready and friendly. I was fifteen.

❾ We could find the end of a road, meet
the sky on out Seventeenth. I thought about
hills, and patting the handle got back a
confident opinion. On the bridge we indulged
15 a forward feeling, a tremble. I was fifteen.

Thinking, back farther in the grass I found
the owner, just coming to, where he had flipped
over the rail. He had blood on his hand, was pale—
I helped him walk to his machine. He ran his hand
20 over it, called me a good man, roared away.

I stood there, fifteen.

Vocabulary Builder
demure (di myoor´) *adj.*
modest

Reading Skill
Paraphrase Picture
the action in lines 11
and 12, and then
restate the phrase
"meet the sky" in your
own words.

Fifteen ■ 633

Analyze

- Have students read the poem on p. 635 aloud. **Ask** students who they think is the speaker, or the person telling this story. Have them explain their answer.
  Answer: The speaker is the son or daughter of the people in the poem, since the speaker calls them "Mama" and "Papa."

- **Ask** students who in the poem actually saw the tornado? Who repeats the story?
  Answer: Papa actually saw the tornado. Mama and the speaker are repeating the story.

- **Ask** students why they think the same details about the tree and the green sedan are repeated.
  Possible response: One version was what Papa said he saw; the other version was what Mama said Papa saw.

- **Ask** students whether they think this story will be handed down to following generations of this family. Why or why not?
  Possible response: The story will probably be handed down, because the story is about an intense and unusual moment. It has already been repeated by Mama and by the speaker, and it will probably continue to be repeated.

TWISTER *HITS* HOUSTON

Sandra Cisneros

634 ▪ Poetry

Vocabulary Development

Vocabulary Knowledge Rating
When students have completed reading and discussing this poetry collection, have them take out their **Vocabulary Knowledge Rating Chart** for this collection. Read the words aloud once more and have students rate their knowledge of the words again in the After Reading column. Clarify any words that are still problematic. Have students write their own def- inition and example or sentence in the appro- priate column. Then have students complete the **Vocabulary Builder Practice** activities on p. 637. Encourage students to use the words in further discussion and written work about these poems. Remind them that they will be account- able for these words on the Selection Test.

⑩
Papa was on the front porch.
Mama was in the kitchen.
Mama was trying
to screw a lightbulb into a fixture.
5   Papa was watching the rain.
Mama, it's a cyclone for sure,
he shouted to his wife in the kitchen.
Papa who was sitting on his front porch
when the storm hit
10   said the twister ripped
the big black oak to splinter,
tossed a green sedan into his garden,
⑪ and banged the back door
like a mad cat wanting in.
15   Mama who was in the kitchen
said Papa saw everything,
the big oak ripped to kindling,
the green sedan land out back,
the back door slam and slam.
20   I missed it.
Mama was in the kitchen Papa explained.
Papa was sitting on the front porch.
The light bulb is still sitting
where I left it. Don't matter now.
25   Got no electricity anyway.

> **Reading Skill**
> **Paraphrase** Restate the description in line 14 of the twister banging the back door.

⑫ ◄ **Critical Viewing** How does the power of the tornado in this photograph add to your understanding of the poem? **[Connect]**

Twister Hits Houston ■ 635

⑪ Reading Skill
Paraphrase

- Remind students that poets often use figurative language, such as metaphors and similes, to add color and impact to their poetry. Tell students that in line 14, "like a mad cat wanting in" is a simile the poet uses to describe the sound of the back door banging.

- Discuss with students what this banging might sound like.

- **Ask** students to respond to the Reading Skill prompt: Restate the description in line 14 of the twister banging the back door.
  Possible response: Students may suggest phrases such as "the back door banged loudly and continuously," or "the back door kept banging, banging, banging in the storm."

⑫ Critical Viewing

Possible response: The image shows the power of the storm and makes the image of a storm ripping up a tree and lifting a car more believable and vivid.

Concept Connector

Connecting to the Literature
Have students compare the sentences they wrote before reading with their thoughts about what details in their everyday lives influence their mood. Ask them to explain whether their thoughts have changed and, if so, how.

Reading Skill Graphic Organizer
Have students review the graphic organizers they completed to paraphrase lines of poetry. Show them **Reading Skill Graphic Organizer B** (*Graphic Organizer Transparencies,* p. 143) as an example. Then have students share the graphic organizers they did and the paraphrasing they completed.

1. **Sample response:** "Casey at the Bat" is the most exciting and interesting. It has more vivid details and an element of suspense that builds.

2. (a) The speaker uses details such as Casey's apparent pride, his defiant glance, a sneer on his lips, his clenched teeth.
   (b) Students may suggest that Casey is strong, confident or even arrogant, and a fierce competitor. (c) He may have been overly confident in letting two pitches go by without swinging, believing that he could get a hit whenever he wanted.

3. (a) He imagines riding it out on the open road, up and down hills.
   (b) **Possible response:** The motorcycle represents freedom, independence, and adventure.

4. (a) He sits on the front porch.
   (b) No, his behavior is not appropriate, since a tornado is very dangerous. A logical response would be to take cover, not sit calmly on the porch.

5. (a) **Sample answer:** "Casey at the Bat": **Setting**—the ballpark with a ballgame in the ninth inning; **Characters**—Cooney, Burrows, Flynn, Blakey, Casey, the umpire, the pitcher; **Plot**—The ballgame is in the ninth inning, with the opposing team leading by two runs. Casey comes to bat with two men on base, and proceeds to strike out.
   (b) The poet uses rhythm and rhyme to emphasize the excitement and suspense of a brief moment.

   Another sample answer can be found on **Literary Analysis Graphic Organizer B**, p. 146 in *Graphic Organizer Transparencies.*

6. **Possible response:** Three phrases include "I admired all that pulsing gleam"; "we could find the end of a road," "we indulged a forward feeling." These three phrases suggest both admiration for the power and beauty of the machine and a longing to travel.

7. (a) **Possible response:** The poem is effective in telling a brief story, since it captures the main

636

Apply the Skills

Poetry Collection 1

Thinking About the Selections

1. **Recall:** Which of the poems in this collection do you think has the most exciting or interesting plot? Explain your answer.
2. **(a) Recall:** In "Casey at the Bat," what details does the speaker use to describe Casey? **(b) Infer:** What does the description suggest about Casey's personality? **(c) Draw Conclusions:** How might his personality have affected the game's outcome?
3. **(a) Recall:** In the third stanza of "Fifteen," what does the speaker imagine doing with the motorcycle? **(b) Interpret:** What does the motorcycle represent to him? Explain.
4. **(a) Recall:** What does the speaker's father do throughout the storm in "Twister Hits Houston"? **(b) Make a Judgment:** Is his behavior appropriate for the situation? Explain your answer.

Literary Analysis

5. **(a)** Using a chart like the one shown, identify and briefly describe the story elements in each **narrative poem** in Poetry Collection 1.

	Setting	Characters	Plot
"Casey at the Bat"			
"Fifteen"			
"Twister Hits Houston"			

   (b) Explain why you think each writer chose to bring these elements to life through poetry rather than prose.
6. Identify three lines or phrases in "Fifteen" that contribute to the poem's **mood**, or **atmosphere**, of longing. Explain each choice.
7. **(a)** Do you think a poem is an effective way in which to tell a story? Why or why not? **(b)** Share your response with a partner, and then explain how someone else's response did or did not change your own.

Reading Skill

8. **(a) Paraphrase** lines 29 through 32 of "Casey at the Bat."
   (b) Does the strategy of picturing the action make it easier to restate these lines in your own words? Explain.

Poems at a Glance
In "**Casey at the Bat,**" a baseball team's star player tries to win the game.

In "**Fifteen,**" a motor-cycle at the side of a road sparks the speaker's imagination.

In "**Twister Hits Houston,**" the speaker witnesses a tornado's destructiveness.

Go Online
Assessment

For: Self-test
Visit: www.PHSchool.com
Web Code: epa-6407

Narrative Poetry: poetry that tells a story

Mood: *atmosphere,* or feeling, created in a literary work

Paraphrasing: restating in your own words what someone else has written or said

details vividly and concisely.
(b) Students may report that someone else's response changed their ideas.

8. (a) **Possible response:** The baseball came flying, but Casey ignored it, saying it wasn't his style. The umpire called strike one. (b) Picturing the action makes it easier to paraphrase because it allows me to simply write down what I see in my mind's eye.

636

Vocabulary Builder

Practice **Analogies** show the relationships between pairs of words. Use a word from the Poetry Collection 1 vocabulary list on page 628 to complete each analogy. In each, your choice should create a word pair that matches the relationship between the first two words given.

1. flapping : bird :: _____ : snake

2. blush : red :: _____ : white

3. boastful : proud :: _____ : humble

Adding Words to Your Vocabulary Using a thesaurus, find a **synonym** for each word in the Poetry Collection 1 vocabulary list on page 628. Use each synonym in a sentence that makes the meaning of the word clear. (For more on using a thesaurus, see page R7.)

Writing

Imagine that you are making a film based on "Casey at the Bat." Write a **description of the scene** that could be used to develop a script.
- Jot down details about the characters, setting, and action.
- Explain the mood you want to set and note how details about characters, setting, and action can evoke this mood.
- Suggest camerawork, lighting, and other elements.

Ask a classmate to decide if your writing conveys the poem's mood.

For *Grammar, Vocabulary,* and *Assessment,* see **Build Language Skills,** pages 650–651.

Extend Your Learning

Listening and Speaking With a partner, role-play a **dialogue** between the speaker of "Fifteen" and the motorcyclist.
- Review the poem to find relevant details.
- Decide on each person's main concerns.
- Use conversational styles, including humor, expressions, slang, or more formal words, appropriate to each character.

Listen carefully, and respond as your own character.

Research and Technology Use library and Internet resources to gather statistics for a **fact sheet** about tornadoes in the United States. Find out where, when, how often, and how severely tornadoes strike. Be sure to include statistics for tornadoes in Houston, Texas.

Apply the Skills ■ *637*

Go Online **For:** An additional research activity
—Research— **Visit:** www.PHSchool.com
Web Code: epd-7405
For another research activity to extend students' learning, give students this Web Code.

Vocabulary Builder
Practice

1. *writhing;* both pairs describe the action of a creature.

2. *pallor;* both pairs describe the color of a condition of the skin.

3. *demure;* both pairs are synonyms.

Adding Words to Your Vocabulary
Sample answers:

1. The *paleness* of his face made him appear very ill.

2. The dog was *twisting,* desperately attempting to escape its leash.

3. He was *modest* about how much he contributed to the team, insisting that he was just doing his job.

Writing

- To give students guidance for writing a scene for a movie, give them **Support for Writing** for Poetry Collection 1, p. 118 in *Unit 4 Resources.*

- To evaluate students' scenes, use the Descriptive Essay rubrics, pp. 55–56 in *General Resources.* In addition, you might evaluate for how well students use significant details in structuring their scenes.

Six Traits Focus

✔ Ideas	✔ Word Choice
✔ Organization	Sentence Fluency
Voice	Conventions

*W*G **Writing and Grammar, Gold Level**
Students will find guidance on descriptive writing in Chapters 4 and 5.

Build Language Skills

Go to pp. 650–651 for vocabulary and grammar lessons and assessment practice.

Extend Your Learning

The **Support for Extend Your Learning** page (*Unit 4 Resources,* p. 119) provides guided note-taking opportunities to help students complete Extend Your Learning activities.

❸ Connecting to the Literature

- To help students understand the meanings of the words they are asked to use, give them these sentences:

  1. The sight of a raven can *evoke* haunting memories.
  2. I *respond* to those memories with fear and loathing.
  3. Meter and rhyme can *reinforce* a poem's mood.
  4. We *react* to the thundering hooves and the sight of the charging herd.
  5. A parent tries to *promote* a child's happiness, wishing her a lucky passage in the journey of life.

- Help students further develop their expressive vocabulary by providing these words: *alter, depress, diminish,* and *significant.* Encourage students to use these words as they discuss the selection.

Concept Connector ➡️

Students will reconsider their ideas after completing these poems.

Go Online
——Author Link tion about Edgar Allan Poe, Edwin Muir, and Richard Wilbur, have students type in the Web Code and then select the poet.

Build Understanding • *Poetry Collection 2*

Poetry

❸ Connecting to the Literature

Reading/Writing Connection Each poem in this group has a unique mood or feeling. To get ready to appreciate the moods of these literary works, connect to details that influence your mood in everyday life—such as weather, events, or people's actions. Write several sentences about things that affect your mood. Use at least three of these words: *evoke, respond, reinforce, react, promote.*

Review

For **Literary Analysis, Reading Skill,** and **Vocabulary Builder,** see page 628.

Meet the Authors

Edgar Allan **Poe** (1809–1849)
The Raven (p. 639)
One of the first great American storytellers, Edgar Allan Poe often explored dark and bizarre events in his stories and poems. His inspiration may have come from his own life, which was often filled with sadness. He found some happiness in his marriage to Virginia Clemm, but after her death, Poe became depressed and antisocial. Many of his poems and stories focus on an ideal love that is lost.

Edwin **Muir** (1887–1959)
The Horses (p. 644)
An author of numerous books of poetry as well as several novels, Edwin Muir had visions of the future that were rooted in his past. He spent his early years on a farm in the Orkney Islands, north of Scotland. Much of the imagery in his poetry comes from these islands.

Richard **Wilbur** (b. 1921)
The Writer (p. 646)
As a young man, Richard Wilbur planned to be a cartoonist. Instead, he became an award-winning poet. By the time he was thirty, Wilbur had published two collections of poetry and established himself as an important young writer. In 1987, Wilbur was appointed Poet Laureate of the United States.

Go Online
——Author Link

For: More about these authors
Visit: www.PHSchool.com
Web Code: epe-9410

The Raven

EDGAR ALLAN POE

❶ ❷

Once upon a midnight dreary, while I pondered, weak and weary,
   Over many a quaint and curious volume of forgotten lore,
   While I nodded, nearly napping, suddenly there came a tapping,
   As of someone gently rapping, rapping at my chamber door.
5   "'Tis some visitor," I muttered, "tapping at my chamber door—
      Only this, and nothing more."

❸

   Ah, distinctly I remember it was in the bleak December,
   And each separate dying ember wrought its ghost upon the floor.
   Eagerly I wished the morrow—vainly I had tried to borrow
10 From my books surcease[1] of sorrow—sorrow for the lost Lenore—
   For the rare and radiant maiden whom the angels name Lenore—
      Nameless here for evermore.

---

1. **surcease** (sᴜr sēs´) *n.* end.

Literary Analysis
Narrative Poetry
Which details provide information about the setting and main character?

❹

✔ Reading Check

What sorrow is the speaker hoping to ease by reading?

The Raven ■ 639

❺ Reading Skill
Paraphrase

- Have students read the bracketed stanza. **Ask** students what the speaker is feeling, and what is causing his feeling.
  Answer: He is feeling terror; he has heard the tapping at the door, and now he hears the rustling of curtains.

- **Ask** students to respond to the Reading Skill prompt: Picture the action the speaker describes and paraphrase this stanza.
  Possible response: The rustling sound of the curtains terrifies me. To slow down my rapidly beating heart, I stand and keep telling myself that it is just some visitor knocking at the door.

❻ Literary Analysis
Narrative Poetry

- Have students review the first stanza of the poem. **Ask** them to describe the speaker's emotional state in this stanza.
  Answer: The speaker is sad and weary, thinking about his lost love.

- **Ask** students to respond to the Literary Analysis question: How has the speaker's emotional state changed since the first stanza?
  Possible response: The speaker, who was sad in the first stanza, is now both terrified and hopeful at the sound of tapping. He hopes it is the spirit of his lost love trying to contact him.

❼ Literature in Context

Cultural Connection Athena was the daughter and favorite child of the great god Zeus. According to Greek mythology, she sprang fully grown out of her father's head, wearing a robe and helmet. The ancient Greek city of Athens came to be named for this goddess when she gave the gift of the olive tree to the people of the city.

Connect to the Literature
Remind students what the speaker is reading in the opening lines of the poem. Then, **ask** the Connect to the Literature question: Do you think the speaker keeps a bust of Pallas because he values her as a symbol of warfare, as a symbol of wisdom, or neither? Explain.

Possible response: The speaker probably values Pallas as a symbol of wisdom or of classical learning because he seeks solace in books and seems to value the written word.

640

And the silken, sad, uncertain rustling of each purple curtain
Thrilled me—filled me with fantastic terrors never felt before;
15 So that now, to still the beating of my heart, I stood repeating
❺ "Tis some visitor entreating entrance at my chamber door—
Some late visitor entreating entrance at my chamber door—
    This it is and nothing more."

Presently my soul grew stronger; hesitating then no longer,
20 "Sir," said I, "or Madam, truly your forgiveness I implore;
But the fact is I was napping, and so gently you came rapping,
And so faintly you came tapping, tapping at my chamber door,
That I scarce was sure I heard you"—here I opened wide the door—
    Darkness there, and nothing more.

25 Deep into that darkness peering, long I stood there wondering, fearing,
Doubting, dreaming dreams no mortal ever dared to dream before;
But the silence was unbroken, and the darkness gave no token,
And the only word there spoken was the whispered word, "Lenore!"
This *I* whispered, and an echo murmured back the word, "Lenore!"
30   Merely this, and nothing more.

Then into the chamber turning, all my soul within me burning,
Soon I heard again a tapping somewhat louder than before.
❻ "Surely," said I, "surely that is something at my window lattice;
Let me see, then, what thereat[2] is, and this mystery explore—
35 Let my heart be still a moment and this mystery explore—
    'Tis the wind, and nothing more!"

---

2. thereat (*ther* at') *adv.* there.

❼ **Literature in Context**

Culture Connection

Pallas When the speaker says "a bust of Pallas" in line 41, he refers to a sculpture of the head and shoulders of the ancient Greek goddess Pallas Athena. Athena was the goddess of wisdom, skills, and warfare. She was also the patron goddess of Athens, the cultural center of ancient Greece. She was considered the guardian of the city.

Connect to the Literature

Do you think the speaker keeps a bust of Pallas because he values her as a symbol of warfare, as a symbol of wisdom, or neither? Explain.

640 ■ *Poetry*

Reading Skill
Paraphrase Picture the action the speaker describes and paraphrase this stanza.

Literary Analysis
Narrative Poetry
How has the speaker's emotional state changed since the first stanza?

Open here I flung the shutter, when, with many a flirt[3] and flutter,
In there stepped a stately raven of the saintly days of yore;
Not the least obeisance[4] made he; not an instant stopped or
    stayed he;

40 But, with mien[5] of lord or lady, perched above my chamber door—
Perched upon a bust of Pallas just above my chamber door—
    Perched, and sat, and nothing more.

Then this ebony bird beguiling my sad fancy[6] into smiling,
By the grave and stern decorum of the countenance[7] it wore,
45 "Though thy crest be shorn and shaven, thou," I said, "art sure
    no craven,[8]
Ghastly grim and ancient raven wandering from the Nightly
    shore—
Tell me what thy lordly name is on the Night's Plutonian[9] shore!"
    Quoth[10] the raven, "Nevermore."

Much I marveled this ungainly fowl to hear discourse so plainly,
50 Though its answer little meaning—little relevancy bore;
For we cannot help agreeing that no sublunary[11] being
Ever yet was blessed with seeing bird above his chamber door—
Bird or beast upon the sculptured bust above his chamber door,
    With such name as "Nevermore."

55 But the raven, sitting lonely on the placid bust, spoke only
That one word, as if his soul in that one word he did outpour.
Nothing farther then he uttered—not a feather then he fluttered—
Till I scarcely more than muttered, "Other friends have flown
    before—
On the morrow *he* will leave me, as my hopes have flown before."
60   Quoth the raven, "Nevermore."

Wondering at the stillness broken by reply so aptly spoken,
"Doubtless," said I, "what it utters is its only stock and store,
Caught from some unhappy master whom unmerciful Disaster
Followed fast and followed faster—so, when Hope he would
    adjure,[12]

---

3. **flirt** (flʉrt) *n.* quick, uneven movement.
4. **obeisance** (ō bā´ səns) *n.* bow or another sign of respect.
5. **mien** (mēn) *n.* manner.
6. **fancy** (fan´ sē) *n.* imagination.
7. **countenance** (kouunt´´n əns) *n.* facial appearance.
8. **craven** (krā´ vən) *n.* coward (usually an adjective).
9. **Plutonian** (ploō tō´ nē ən) *adj.* like the underworld, ruled over by the ancient Roman god Pluto.
10. **quoth** (kwōth) *v.* said.
11. **sublunary** (sub loōn´ ər ē) *adj.* earthly.
12. **adjure** (ə joor´) *v.* appeal to; ask earnestly.

The Raven ■ 641

Reading Skill
Paraphrase In your own words, describe how the raven behaved as it entered the chamber.

Vocabulary Builder
beguiling (bē gīl´ iŋ) *v.* tricking; charming

9
Reading Check
What one word does the raven repeat?

❽ Reading Skill
Paraphrase

• Have students read the bracketed stanza. Review the difficult vocabulary in this stanza found in the footnotes. **Ask** students to suggest what a "stately raven" might mean.
Possible response: It might mean an elegant or dignified black bird.

• Refer students to the phrase "saintly days of yore" in line 38. **Ask** students to define *yore*. If necessary, have them use a dictionary.
Answer: The word *yore* means "long ago."

• Have students **speculate** about why the speaker refers to the days of long ago as "saintly."
Possible response: He may have considered the past a better or unspoiled time; he may have been thinking of ancient times when classical learning was highly valued.

• **Ask** students to respond to the Reading Skill prompt: In your own words, describe how the raven behaved as it entered the chamber.
Answer: The raven stepped into the room, fluttering its feathers. It did not pay any attention to the speaker, but perched itself upon the bust of Athena as if it were nobility.

❾ Reading Check
Answer: The raven repeats the word *nevermore*.

Differentiated Instruction
Solutions for All Learners

Support for English Learners
Help guide these students through this set of poems by reviewing the vocabulary builder words and the footnotes with them. Then, play the **Listening to Literature Audio CD.** Give students an opportunity to explain their feelings about each poem.

Strategy for Less Proficient Readers
To give students a model for paraphrasing, show them the **Reading Skill Graphic Organizer B** (*Graphic Organizer Transparencies,* p. 144). The completed graphic organizer will give students insight into the process of paraphrasing. They can use it as a model for writing their own paraphrases as they read.

- Have students review the events in the poem up to this point. **Ask** what the speaker was concerned about when the poem opens. **Answer:** He was mourning his lost love Lenore and trying to forget his pain in books.

- **Ask** students how the speaker responded when the raven began knocking on the door. **Answer:** The speaker responded with terror when he heard the raven tapping at the door.

- **Ask** students to respond to the Literary Analysis question: What two conflicts or problems does the narrator face in this stanza? **Answer:** The speaker is trying to figure out what the raven means by repeating the word *nevermore*. He also is still feeling deep sadness over the loss of Lenore.

⑪ Critical Viewing

Answer: The raven is pure black, with piercing eyes and a long, sharply pointed beak. Other birds may seem cheerful because of their bright coloration or ordinary because of their subtle coloration. Ravens may seem more mysterious because they are black and, thus, associated with night, graveyards, and gloom.

65   Stern Despair returned, instead of the sweet Hope he dared
         adjure—
             That sad answer, 'Nevermore.'"

But the raven still beguiling all my sad soul into smiling,
Straight I wheeled a cushioned seat in front of bird, and bust, and
         door;
Then upon the velvet sinking, I betook myself to linking
70   Fancy unto fancy, thinking what this ominous bird of yore—
What this grim, ungainly, ghastly, gaunt, and ominous bird of yore
             Meant in croaking "Nevermore."

This I sat engaged in guessing, but no syllable expressing
To the fowl whose fiery eyes now burned into my bosom's core;
75   This and more I sat divining,¹³ with my head at ease reclining
⑩   On the cushion's velvet lining that the lamplight gloated o'er,
But whose velvet violet lining with the lamplight gloating o'er,
             She shall press, ah, nevermore!

---

13. divining (də vīn´ iŋ) *v.* guessing.

Literary Analysis
Narrative Poetry
What two conflicts or problems does the narrator face in this stanza?

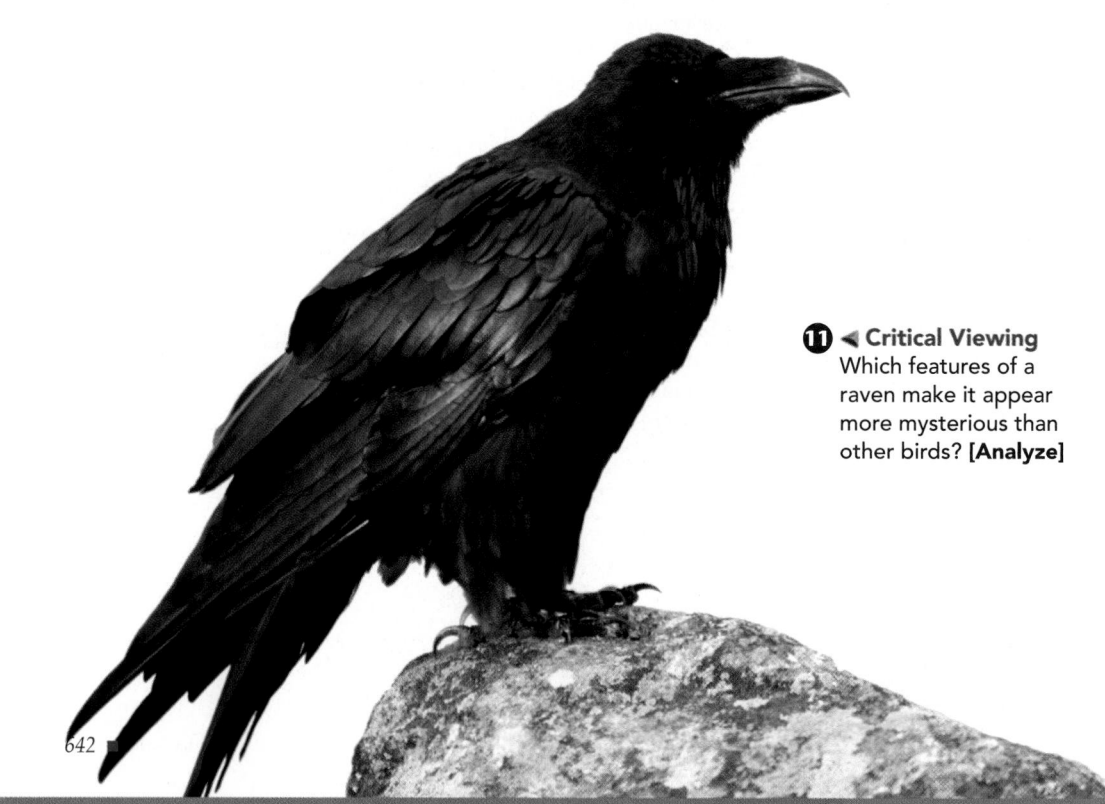

⑪ ◄ Critical Viewing
Which features of a raven make it appear more mysterious than other birds? **[Analyze]**

642

Vocabulary Development

Dictionary Use
Direct students' attention to the word *divining* in line 75. Using a think-aloud process, model how to use context clues to choose the correct dictionary definition of a word. Say to students:

   I'm going to look at the dictionary definition of the word *divining*. I see that the word *divine* can be an adjective, a noun, or a verb. Line 75 includes the phrase "I sat divining." The syntax indicates the word is a verb.

   The dictionary has three possible definitions for the verb *divine:* "to tell the future," "to guess," and "to use intuition to find out something."

   In line 73, the speaker says that he is "engaged in guessing." Therefore, I think that the dictionary meaning "to guess" is the correct meaning for this word in this context.

Then, methought, the air grew denser, perfumed from an unseen censer[14]

80 Swung by angels whose faint footfalls tinkled on the tufted floor.
"Wretch," I cried, "thy God hath lent thee—by these angels he hath sent thee
<u>Respite</u>—respite and Nepenthe[15] from thy memories of Lenore!
Let me quaff this kind Nepenthe and forget this lost Lenore!"
      Quoth the raven, "Nevermore."

85 "Prophet!" said I, "thing of evil!—prophet still, if bird or devil!—
Whether Tempter sent, or whether tempest tossed thee here ashore,
Desolate, yet all undaunted, on this desert land enchanted—
On this home by Horror haunted—tell me truly, I implore—
Is there—is there balm in Gilead?[16]—tell me—tell me, I implore!"
90   Quoth the raven, "Nevermore."

"Prophet!" said I, "thing of evil!—prophet still, if bird or devil!
By that Heaven that bends above us—by that God we both adore—
Tell this soul with sorrow laden if, within the distant Aidenn,[17]
It shall clasp a sainted maiden whom the angels name Lenore—
95 Clasp a rare and radiant maiden whom the angels name Lenore."
      Quoth the raven, "Nevermore."

"Be that word our sign of parting, bird or fiend!" I shrieked, upstarting—
"Get thee back into the tempest and the Night's Plutonian shore!
Leave no black plume as a token of that lie thy soul hath spoken!
100 Leave my loneliness unbroken!—quit the bust above my door!
Take thy beak from out my heart, and take thy form from off my door!"
      Quoth the raven, "Nevermore."

And the raven, never flitting, still is sitting, still is sitting
On the pallid bust of Pallas just above my chamber door;
105 And his eyes have all the seeming of a demon that is dreaming,
⓬ And the lamplight o'er him streaming throws his shadow on the floor;
And my soul from out that shadow that lies floating on the floor
      Shall be lifted—nevermore!

---

14. **censer** (sen´ sər) *n.* container for burning incense.
15. **Nepenthe** (nē pen´ *th*ē) *n.* drug believed by the ancient Greeks to cause forgetfulness of sorrow.
16. **balm** (bäm) **in Gilead** (gil´ ē əd) cure for suffering; the Bible refers to a medicinal ointment, or balm, made in a region called Gilead.
17. **Aidenn** name meant to suggest Eden or paradise.

The Raven ■ 643

Literary Analysis
Narrative Poetry and Mood How does the mood here compare with the mood at the beginning of the poem? Explain.

⓬ Literary Analysis
Narrative Poetry and Mood

• Read the last stanza aloud. Remind students that a narrative poem has all the elements a story, including the plot's resolution or ending. **Ask** students how this story ends.
Answer: The raven is still sitting on the statue and will never leave. The speaker will always mourn his lost love.

• Have students review the first two stanzas of the poem. **Ask** them to describe the mood in these two stanzas.
Answer: Students may suggest that the mood is one of gloom and sadness or melancholy.

• **Ask** students to respond to the Literary Analysis question: How does the mood here compare with the mood at the beginning of the poem? Explain.
Answer: The mood at the beginning of the poem is sad and melancholy. The speaker sits reading, trying to forget about the loss of his beloved Lenore. The mood at the end of the poem is one of gloomy despair, because the speaker sees that things will not change. The raven sits on the bust and will never leave, the speaker will never forget Lenore, and he will never stop mourning for her.

Differentiated Instruction   Solutions for All Learners

Enrichment for Gifted/Talented Students
Have students imagine events that might have led up to this moment described in the poem, and then ask them to write a brief sketch describing the events.
      Students might begin by addressing these questions:
      • Who was Lenore? What was her relationship to the speaker?
      • What kind of character was Lenore? What did she look like?

      • How did Lenore die?
      • Was Lenore a "real" person in the speaker's life, or just the product of his deranged mind?
Suggest that students write the sketch of Lenore and the speaker in prose or poetry form. Encourage them to share their sketches with the class.

- Remind students that this is a narrative poem, and that it is telling a story.

- Have students read the first stanza aloud. Then, **ask** them to describe in their own words the events that occurred up to this point.
Answer: A seven-day war destroyed most of the world. The survivors saw dead bodies piled on a passing warship and a plane plunging into the sea. Then, they heard nothing more. All the radios were silent.

- **Ask** students to respond to the Literary Analysis question: Which details in the first stanza reveal that the poem takes place in the future?
Answer: Details include the mention of "the seven days war that put the world to sleep," the silent radios, the sight of dead bodies on the deck of a warship, the description of the "old bad world" that destroyed its people all at once, and the phrase "the nations lying asleep."

14 Critical Viewing

Possible response: The colt might appear shy, like the ones in the poem. The adult horse seems lively and eager.

THE HORSES

EDWIN MUIR

Barely a twelvemonth after
The seven days war that put the world to sleep,
Late in the evening the strange horses came.
By then we had made our covenant with silence,
5   But in the first few days it was so still
We listened to our breathing and were afraid.
On the second day
The radios failed; we turned the knobs; no answer.
On the third day a warship passed us, heading north,
10 Dead bodies piled on the deck. On the sixth day
A plane plunged over us into the sea. Thereafter
13 Nothing. The radios dumb;
And still they stand in corners of our kitchens,
And stand, perhaps, turned on, in a million rooms
15 All over the world. But now if they should speak,
If on a sudden they should speak again,
If on the stroke of noon a voice should speak,
We would not listen, we would not let it bring
That old bad world that swallowed its children quick
20 At one great gulp. We would not have it again.
Sometimes we think of the nations lying asleep,
Curled blindly in impenetrable sorrow,
And then the thought confounds us with its strangeness.

15   The tractors lie about our fields; at evening
25 They look like dank sea-monsters couched and waiting.
We leave them where they are and let them rust:

Literary Analysis
Narrative Poetry
Which details in the first stanza reveal that the poem takes place in the future?

14 ▶ **Critical Viewing**
Do these horses appear "stubborn and shy" like the ones described in the poem? **[Compare and Contrast]**

Vocabulary Development

Expressive Vocabulary
As students read and discuss the settings, characters, and plots in these poems, encourage them to use the expressive vocabulary presented earlier. You might encourage them with sentence starters like these:

1. The opening lines of "The Raven" *evoke* feelings of . . .
2. Readers might *respond* to the knocking at the door with . . .
3. The description of destruction in "The Horses" *reinforces* . . .
4. The people in "The Horses" *react* . . .
5. The story of a trapped bird in "The Writer" might *promote* . . .

'They'll moulder away and be like other loam'.[1]
We make our oxen drag our rusty ploughs,
15 Long laid aside. We have gone back
30 Far past our fathers' land.
                        And then, that evening
Late in the summer the strange horses came.
We heard a distant tapping on the road,
A deepening drumming; it stopped, went on again
35 And at the corner changed to hollow thunder.
We saw the heads
Like a wild wave charging and were afraid.
We had sold our horses in our fathers' time
To buy new tractors. Now they were strange to us
40 As fabulous steeds set on an ancient shield
Or illustrations in a book of knights.
We did not dare go near them. Yet they waited,
Stubborn and shy, as if they had been sent
By an old command to find our whereabouts
45 And that long-lost <u>archaic</u> companionship.
In the first moment we had never a thought
That they were creatures to be owned and used.
Among them were some half-a-dozen colts
Dropped in some wilderness of the broken world,
50 Yet new as if they had come from their own Eden.[2]
Since then they have pulled our ploughs and borne our loads,
But that free servitude still can pierce our hearts.
Our life is changed; their coming our beginning.

---

1. **loam** (lōm) *n.* dark, rich soil.
2. **Eden** in the Bible, the garden where life began with Adam and Eve; paradise.

Reading Skill
Paraphrase Picture the scene here and paraphrase lines 31–32.

Vocabulary Builder
archaic (är kā´ ik) *adj.* from an earlier time; ancient

The Horses ■ 645

15 Reading Skill
Paraphrase

- Have students read the bracketed passage that begins on p. 644, line 24. Ask students to focus on lines 24–27.

- **Ask** students why they think people do not use the tractors. **Answer:** They may not want to use things from the "old bad world," or they may not have the gasoline or spare parts to keep the tractors running.

- **Ask** students what they picture when they read lines 24–27. **Answer:** Tractors sit around the fields, unused. The tractors will eventually rust and decay and become part of the soil.

- **Ask** students to respond to the Reading Skill prompt: Picture the scene here and paraphrase lines 31–32. **Answer:** Late one summer evening, the horses appeared.

▶ **Monitor Progress:** Review students' graphic organizers to ensure that they are able to accurately paraphrase.

▶ **Reteach:** If students have difficulty paraphrasing, have them reread lines 33–37. Help students to paraphrase these lines, for example: "The sound of the herd grew louder, and they were afraid of the wave of horses charging toward them."

Differentiated Instruction Solutions for All Learners

Strategy for Advanced Readers
Have each student choose one of the three poems in this collection and write a detailed analysis and interpretation of its meaning.

Students may paraphrase lines and stanzas in their search for what the poems mean. Encourage them to notice sound devices that poets use, including rhyme and alliteration.

Have them think about use of symbols in the poems.

Suggest that students do some background reading about the poets and examine other works by them as they work to interpret these poems.

- Have students read the first stanza. **Ask** students to respond to the Literary Analysis question: What details about the characters and setting are introduced in the first stanza?
Answer: Details include a room at the front of a house facing the east, with a window looking out over a linden tree. The characters are a daughter and the speaker, her parent.

- **Ask:** What image is suggested by the speaker's use of "prow," "light breaks," and "windows tossed with linden"?
Answer: Students may suggest that the image is that of a boat sailing into morning and being tossed by winds and waves.

- Have students read the poem through line 15. **Ask** what the image of a boat described above might suggest about the daughter.
Possible response: Students may say that the image of a boat being tossed by winds and waves might suggest that the daughter is at the beginning of a journey in which she might be tossed about. However, the journey may also be rewarding, since she is sailing into sun at the beginning of day.

The Writer
RICHARD WILBUR

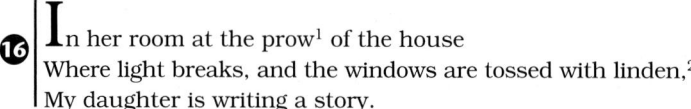

16 I n her room at the prow[1] of the house
Where light breaks, and the windows are tossed with linden,[2]
My daughter is writing a story.

I pause in the stairwell, hearing
5   From her shut door a commotion of typewriter-keys
Like a chain hauled over a gunwale.[3]

Young as she is, the stuff
Of her life is a great cargo, and some of it heavy:
I wish her a lucky passage.

10   But now it is she who pauses,
As if to reject my thought and its easy figure.
A stillness greatens, in which

The whole house seems to be thinking,
And then she is at it again with a bunched clamor
15   Of strokes, and again is silent.

---

1. **prow** (prou) *n.* front part of a ship or boat.
2. **linden** (lin´ dən) *n.* type of tree.
3. **gunwale** (gun´ əl) *n.* upper edge of the side of a ship or boat.

646 ■ *Poetry*

Literary Analysis
Narrative Poetry
What details about the characters and setting are introduced in the first stanza?

Vocabulary Development

Vocabulary Knowledge Rating
When students have completed reading and discussing this poetry collection, have them take out their **Vocabulary Knowledge Rating Chart.** Read the words aloud once more and have students rate their knowledge of the words again in the After Reading column. Clarify any words that are still problematic. Have students write their own definition and example or sentence in the appropriate column. Then, have students complete the **Vocabulary Builder Practice** activities on p. 649. Encourage students to use the words in further discussion and written work about these poems. Remind them that they will be accountable for these words on the Selection Test.

I remember the dazed starling[4]
Which was trapped in that very room, two years ago;
How we stole in, lifted a sash

17
20 And retreated, not to affright it;
And how for a helpless hour, through the crack of the door,
We watched the sleek, wild, dark

And iridescent creature
Batter against the brilliance, drop like a glove
To the hard floor, or the desk-top,

25 And wait then, humped and bloody,
For the wits to try it again; and how our spirits
Rose when, suddenly sure,

It lifted off from a chair-back,
Beating a smooth course for the right window
30 And clearing the sill of the world.

It is always a matter, my darling,
Of life or death, as I had forgotten. I wish
What I wished you before, but harder.

---

4. **starling** (stär´ lin) *n.* bird with black feathers that shine in a greenish or purplish way.

Reading Skill
Paraphrase Picture the action here and paraphrase lines 16–23.

18 ▼ Critical Viewing
Do you think a typewriter like this would allow a writer more or less creativity than a computer? **[Speculate]**

The Writer ■ 647

17 Reading Skill
Paraphrase

- Have students read the bracketed passage aloud. **Ask** what was trapped in the room and what the speaker tried to do about it.
  Answer: A bird was trapped in the room. The speaker opened a window and hoped that the bird would fly out.

- Encourage student volunteers to describe a time when some creature, such as a bird or squirrel, became trapped in their house. Have them explain how the creature behaved and what they did to help it escape.

- **Ask** students to respond to the Reading Skill prompt: Picture the action here and paraphrase lines 16–23.
  Answer: I remember when a confused bird became trapped in that room. We sneaked in and opened a window and then left the room, trying not to scare it. We watched the shiny, wild bird through a crack in the door as it tried to escape. It kept flying against the window glass, then falling to the floor.

18 Critical Viewing

Possible response: Some students may say that a typewriter would allow less creativity than a computer because it is very time-consuming to revise ideas once typed on paper. Other students may find no difference, asserting that creativity lies in the writer, not in the machine.

Concept Connector

Connecting to the Literature
Have students compare the sentences they wrote before reading with their thoughts about what details in their everyday lives influence their mood. Ask them to explain whether their thoughts have changed and, if so, how.

Reading Skill Graphic Organizer
Have students review the graphic organizers they completed to paraphrase lines of poetry. Show them **Reading Skill Graphic Organizer B** (*Graphic Organizer Transparencies*, p. 144) as an example. Then, have students share the graphic organizers they did and the paraphrasing they completed.

1. **Possible response:** "The Raven" is the most exciting and interesting. It has more vivid details and an element of horror.

2. (a) The speaker uses the adjectives *weak* and *weary*. (b) **Possible response:** The words *despairing* and *horrified* would describe the speaker's state of mind. (c) The raven's message and the speaker's interpretation of it as a statement of hopelessness change the speaker.

3. (a) The tractors have rusted in the fields. (b) **Possible response:** The tractors represent the "old bad world" while the horses represent the hope of a new world.

4. The sound of the starling beating against the window, then falling, then trying again, reminds the speaker of his daughter's typing, trying to set her imagination free.

5. (a) **Sample answer:** "The Raven": **Setting**—the speaker's room on a midnight in December; **Characters**—the speaker, a man mourning for his lost love, and the raven; **Plot**—The speaker, prompted by a strange tapping, opens the window to a raven that struts into his room and sits on top of a bust of Pallas. When the speaker questions the raven, it speaks only the word *nevermore*. Another sample answer can be found on **Literary Analysis Graphic Organizer B,** p. 148 in *Graphic Organizer Transparencies.* (b) Poetry allows the author to focus on the most meaningful details and to emphasize them through poetic devices, such as imagery and figurative language. The combination lets the poet tell a story with power, brevity, and great intensity of feeling.

6. **Possible response:** Three phrases include "by then we had made our covenant with silence"; "nations lying asleep, curled blindly in impenetrable sorrow"; "look like dank sea-monsters couched and waiting." These three phrases describe the strangeness and other-worldliness of the situation.

7. (a) **Possible response:** A poem is an effective way to tell a brief story because it captures the

---

Apply the Skills

Poetry Collection 2

Thinking About the Selections

1. **Recall:** Which of the poems in this collection do you think has the most exciting or interesting plot? Explain your answer.

2. (a) **Recall:** In the first line of "The Raven," which two adjectives does the speaker use to describe his state of mind? (b) **Draw Conclusions:** What words would you use to describe the speaker's state of mind at the end of the poem? (c) **Analyze Cause and Effect:** What has caused the speaker to change?

3. (a) **Recall:** What has happened to the tractors in "The Horses"? (b) **Interpret:** Why does the poet place the tractors and the horses side by side?

4. **Analyze:** Why does the speaker of "The Writer" recall the incident of the trapped starling? Explain your answer.

Literary Analysis

5. (a) Using a chart like the one shown, identify and briefly describe the story elements in each **narrative poem** in Poetry Collection 2.

	Setting	Characters	Plot
"The Raven"			
"The Horses"			
"The Writer"			

(b) Explain why you think each writer chose to bring these elements to life through poetry rather than prose.

6. Identify three lines or phrases in "The Horses" that contribute to the poem's mysterious and dreamlike **mood,** or **atmosphere.** Explain your choices.

7. (a) Do you think a poem is an effective way in which to tell a story? Why or why not? (b) Share your response with a partner, and then explain how someone else's response did or did not change your own.

Reading Skill

8. (a) **Paraphrase** lines 37 through 39 of "The Raven." (b) Does the strategy of picturing the action make it easier to restate these lines in your own words? Explain.

648 ■ Poetry

QuickReview

Poems at a Glance
In "**The Raven,**" the speaker is haunted by a mysterious bird.

In "**The Horses,**" the speaker describes a strange vision of the future.

In "**The Writer,**" the speaker is moved by the sound of his daughter typing a story.

Go Online
Assessment
For: Self-test
Visit: www.PHSchool.com
Web Code: epa-6408

Narrative Poetry:
poetry that tells a story

Mood: *atmosphere* or feeling created in a literary work

Paraphrasing: restating in your own words what someone else has written or said

---

main details vividly and concisely. (b) Students may report that someone else's response changed their ideas.

8. (a) **Possible response:** When I opened the window, a raven stepped in without stopping to notice me. (b) Picturing the action makes it easier to restate because it allows me to simply describe what I see in my imagination.

Vocabulary Builder

Practice **Analogies** show the relationships between pairs of words. Use a word from the Poetry Collection 2 vocabulary list on page 628 to complete each analogy. In each, your choice should create a word pair that matches the relationship between the first two words given.

1. stale : fresh :: _____ : modern

2. exercise : tiredness :: _____ : rest

3. teaching : professor :: _____ : trickster

Adding Words to Your Vocabulary Using a thesaurus, find a **synonym** for each word in the Poetry Collection 2 vocabulary list on page 628. Use each synonym in a sentence that makes the meaning of the word clear. (For more on using a thesaurus, see page R7.)

Writing

Imagine that you have been hired by a movie studio to make a short film based on "The Raven." Write a **description of the scene** that could be used to develop a script.

- Jot down details about the characters, setting, and action.
- Explain the mood you want to set and note how details about characters, setting, and action can evoke this mood.
- Suggest camerawork, lighting, and other elements.

Ask a classmate to decide if your writing conveys the poem's mood.

For *Grammar, Vocabulary,* and *Assessment,* see **Build Language Skills,** pages 650–651.

Extend Your Learning

Listening and Speaking With a partner, role-play a **dialogue** between the father and daughter in "The Writer."

- Review the poem to find relevant details.
- Decide on each person's main concerns.
- Use conversational styles, including humor, expressions, slang, or more formal words, appropriate to each character.

Listen carefully, and respond as your own character.

Research and Technology Use library and Internet resources to gather information for a **fact sheet** about ravens: what these birds look like, where they are found, and other key facts. Compare the details in your fact sheet with those in the poem.

Assessment Resources

The following resources can be used to assess students' knowledge and skills.

Unit 4 Resources
Selection Test A, pp. 139–141
Selection Test B, pp. 142–144

 Go Online
Assessment Students may use the **Self-test** to prepare for **Selection Test A** or **Selection Test B.**

Go Online **For:** An additional research activity
Research **Visit:** www.PHSchool.com
Web Code: epd-7406
For another research activity to extend students' learning, give students this Web Code.

Vocabulary Builder
Practice

1. *archaic*; both pairs are antonyms.

2. *respite*; exercise leads to tiredness, respite or pause leads to rest.

3. *beguiling*; in both pairs, the verb is an activity of the noun.

Adding Words to Your Vocabulary
Sample answers:

1. The *old-fashioned* bicycle reminded me of my grandfather, who rode one just like it when he was young.

2. The *pause* was a refreshing break from the hard work of the morning.

3. He was so *charming* that people never questioned him, and many bought his useless remedy for baldness.

Writing

- To give students guidance for writing a scene for a movie, give them **Support for Writing** for Poetry Collection 2, p. 134 in *Unit 4 Resources.*

- To evaluate students' scenes, use the Descriptive Essay rubrics, pp. 55–56 in *General Resources.* In addition, you might evaluate for how well students use significant details in structuring their scenes.

Six Traits Focus

✔	Ideas	✔	Word Choice
✔	Organization		Sentence Fluency
	Voice		Conventions

WG **Writing and Grammar,**
Gold Level
Students will find guidance on narrative writing in Chapters 4 and 5.

Build Language Skills

Go to pp. 650–651 for vocabulary and grammar lessons and assessment practice.

Extend Your Learning

The **Support for Extend Your Learning** page (*Unit 4 Resources,* p. 135) provides guided note-taking opportunities to help students complete the Extend Your Learning activities.

649

Build Language Skills

Poetry Collection 1 • Poetry Collection 2

Vocabulary Skill

* Introduce the suffix *-age*. After students have read the instructional material, have them brainstorm for words that contain this suffix. **Possible responses:** *baggage, coinage, parentage, breakage*

* Have students complete the Practice activity on this page.

Answers

1. We were *short* three bushels of apples. The *shortage* of apples will prevent us from making apple-sauce.

2. The storm sewer *drain* is plugged. When it rains, the *drainage* in our neighborhood is poor.

3. Jon went to the *post* office. I hope he has enough *postage* to send the package.

4. Soon Joanna's cousin will *marry*. I hope that she is ready for *marriage*.

5. I hope to plant an *acre* of trees. If I had more *acreage,* I would plant many more trees.

Grammar Lesson

* Point out that an appositive phrase usually follows the noun or pronoun that it identifies or explains.

* Tell students that an appositive phrase provides another name or noun for the noun it is set beside.

Answers

1. The *Iliad* begins when Paris, a Prince of Troy, runs off with Queen Helen.

2. Achilles, a powerful Greek warrior, eventually kills Hector.

3. Hector, Paris' brother, is the greatest fighter in Troy.

4. The Trojan War, a war between the Greeks and Trojans, is the backdrop of the *Iliad.*

5. Queen Helen, the wife of King Menelaus, was known for her beauty.

Vocabulary Skill

Suffixes The **Latin suffix** *-age* means "that which relates to the act of or the condition of." This suffix creates nouns—often from other nouns.

▶ **Example:** "He is descended from a *line* of kings. His *lineage* means he will inherit the throne."

Practice As in the example that has been given, write sentence pairs for each of the following. Use the base word in the first sentence and the base + *-age* word in the second sentence.

1. short　　**2.** drain　　**3.** post　　**4.** marry　　**5.** acre

Grammar Skill

Appositive Phrase An **appositive phrase** is a noun or pronoun with modifiers that adds information to the noun or pronoun it is placed next to. Appositive phrases that contain modifiers are set off with commas. Using appositives is a good way to make your writing more concise.

> **Less concise:**
> The *Iliad* relates the events of the Trojan war. The Trojan war was a legendary struggle between Greece and Troy.

Look at the more concise revision, in which the sentences are combined with an appositive phrase (underlined):

> **Appositive:**
> The *Iliad* relates the events of the Trojan war, <u>a legendary struggle between Greece and Troy.</u>

Practice Combine the sentences using appositive phrases.

1. The *Iliad* begins when Paris runs off with Queen Helen. Paris was a Prince of Troy.

2. Achilles eventually kills Hector. Achilles is a powerful Greek warrior.

3. Hector is the greatest fighter in Troy. Hector is Paris' brother.

4. The Trojan war is the backdrop of the *Iliad.* The Trojan war was between the Greeks and Trojans.

5. Queen Helen was known for her beauty. Queen Helen was the wife of King Menelaus.

W̸G *Prentice Hall Writing and Grammar Connection: Chapter 10, Section 4*

650 ■ *Poetry*

MorePractice

For more practice with appositive phrases, see the Grammar Handbook, p. R43.

Teaching Resources

The following resources can be used to enrich or extend the instruction for Build Language Skills.

Unit 4 Resources
　Build Language Skills: Vocabulary: Suffixes, p. 137
　Build Grammar Skills: Appositive Phrases, p. 138

Assessment Practice

Reading Skill: Paraphrase

Directions: *Read the poem. Then, answer the questions.*

> I wandered lonely as a cloud
> That floats on high o'er vales and hills
> When all at once I saw a crowd,
> A host of golden daffodils;
> 5 Beside the lake, beneath the trees,
> Fluttering and dancing in the breeze.
>
> Continuous as the stars that shine
> And twinkle on the milky way,
> They stretched in never-ending line
> 10 Along the margin of a bay:
> Ten thousand saw I at a glance,
> Tossing their heads in sprightly dance.
>   —from "I Wandered Lonely as a Cloud" by William Wordsworth

1. Which is the best paraphrase of line 6?
   A moving in the water
   B moving in the wind
   C dancing by the lake
   D dancing in the crowd

2. Which is a reasonable paraphrase of lines 4–7?
   A The stars keep on going.
   B You see numerous stars.
   C There were many daffodils.
   D The line of trees seemed endless.

3. Which of the following statements represents the best paraphrase of the first stanza?
   A Clouds and daffodils are part of nature, unlike human beings.
   B Walking by myself, I was amazed to see a huge field of daffodils.
   C I was by myself, but there were many daffodils, and I felt lonely.
   D It was a windy day, but I did not mind because of the beauty of the daffodils.

Timed Writing: Analysis [Connections]

Review the poems in **Poetry Collection 1** and **Poetry Collection 2**. Choose one poem in which the poet describes a universal human trait. Write an explanation of how the poet transmits a sense of this characteristic. Use specifics from the work as support. **(40 minutes)**

Writing Workshop: *Work in Progress*

Response to Literature

Review your notes about strong characters in "Uncoiling" and "A Voice." Identify the character that makes the strongest impression on you. Jot down details from the poem that help create that impression. Put your annotations in your writing portfolio.

Build Language Skills ■ *651*

Timed Writing

- Tell students that when they write an analysis of a poem, they should consider the poem's theme, rhyme scheme, use of figurative language, and expression of feelings.

- Have students review the poetry and select a poem that conveys a universal human characteristic.

- Suggest that students first take notes on how the poem transmits a sense of the characteristic. Remind students to jot down line numbers that they wish to reference in their writing.

- As students begin to write, point out that they need to support their explanation with examples from the poem.

- Assess students' analyses based on their choice of poems and characteristics and how they support their choices.

- Suggest that students plan their time to give ten minutes to reviewing the poem, twenty-five minutes to writing, and five minutes to reviewing and revising.

Writing Workshop
Work in Progress

Response to Literature

- Have students go to their portfolios and take out the work they have completed so far on this assignment. Remind them that this work may be used in the **Writing Workshop** on Response to Literature on p. 688.

- Guide students in completing the **Work-in-Progress** assignment on this page. When students have completed this activity, have them keep it in their portfolios. They will use is as they continue the **Work in Progress.**

See TeacherExpress™/Lesson View for a detailed lesson plan for Reading Informational Materials.

About Web Sites

- Have students read "About Web Sites."

- Discuss with students any experiences they have had using the Internet to search for information. Ask them to describe their searches. Also ask students to describe what was easy and what was difficult about using Web sites for research.

- Explain to students that they can use the Internet to find information on almost any topic. Make sure they realize that some Web sites provide reliable information and others do not.

Reading Skill
Evaluating Web Sources

- Review with students the "Common URL Endings" chart.

- Explain that, since anyone can create a Web site and add information to it, some Web sites provide biased information. **Ask** volunteers to identify some types of biased information that is available on Web sites.
  Possible response: Biased Web sites might include opinions, promotions, and misinformation.

- Tell students that many Web sites provide reliable facts and reasonable opinions. **Ask** volunteers to identify types of sites that probably offer reliable information.
  Possible response: Reliable information can typically be found on government sites, education sites, corporate sites, and major news sites.

Web Sites

In Part 2, you are learning how to paraphrase while reading literature. Paraphrasing is also useful when reading informational materials, such as newspaper articles and Web sites. Paraphrasing allows you to state the information in your own words to better understand the material. If you read Sandra Cisneros's "Twister Hits Houston," you could use this Web site to find facts about twisters.

About Web Sites

A **Web site** is a collection of information at a specific address on the World Wide Web. Software known as a **browser** enables you to access Web sites with your computer and the Internet. To connect to a site, type a Web address, or URL (Uniform Resource Locator), or click on a word or picture that links to it. Usually, you will be connected to a **home page**, which is like a table of contents. Web sites often have these features:

- A **keyword** or pull-down search function. In a keyword search, you type in a word, and the browser searches the site. A pull-down search provides choices of topics.
- A **bulletin board**, which lists relevant news or questions
- An **e-mail address** of someone at the site

Reading Skill

All Web sites do not present equally reliable information, so **evaluating Web sources** is essential. First, identify the sponsor of the site and assess the sponsor's credentials and expertise. Then, determine whether the sponsor is biased or favors a particular point of view. Bias can be revealed through opinions or through information that is either stressed or omitted. Finally, consider whether the information on the Web site is current. The URL ending indicates the general type of sponsor:

URL Ending	Description	Usual Intent
.edu or .gov	Site is maintained by an educational institution or government agency.	to provide reliable information
.org	Site is probably maintained by a nonprofit organization.	to provide information about an issue or a cause
.com	Site is maintained commercially or personally.	to sell or promote something
.net	Site is maintained by a network.	varies

652 ■ *Poetry*

The emblem indicates that this is a U.S. government site.

The "Search" button leads to a page where you can search by keyword.

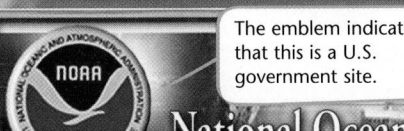 National Oceanic and Atmospheric Administration

| Home | Contacts | Media | Disclaimer | Search | People Locator |

Home Page Menu

Weather Page

Fujita Tornado Damage Scale

Category F0: Light Damage (<73 mph); Some damage to chimneys and sign boards, branches broken off trees, shallow-rooted trees pushed over.

Category F1: Moderate Damage (73-112 mph); Peels surface off roofs; mobile homes pushed off foundations or overturned; moving autos blown off road.

Category F2: Considerable Damage (113-157 mph); Roofs torn off frame houses; mobile homes demolished; boxcars overturned; large trees snapped or uprooted; light-object missiles generated; cars lifted off ground.

Category F3: Severe Damage (158-206 mph); Roofs and some walls torn off well-constructed houses, trains overturned; most trees in forest uprooted; heavy cars lifted off ground and thrown.

Category F4: Devastating Damage (207-260 mph); Well-constructed houses leveled; structure with weak foundations blown off some distance; cars thrown and large missiles generated.

Category F5: Incredible Damage (261-318 mph); Strong frame houses lifted off foundations and swept away; automobile sized missiles fly through the air in excess of 100 meters (109 yards); trees debarked.

Tornadoes

Tornadoes are one of nature's most violent storms. In an average year, about 1,000 tornadoes are reported across the United States, resulting in 80 deaths and over 1,500 injuries. A tornado is a violently rotating column of air extending from a thunderstorm to the ground. The most violent tornadoes are capable of tremendous destruction with wind speeds of 250 mph or more. Damage paths can be in excess of one mile wide and 50 miles long.

Tornadoes come in all shapes and sizes and can occur anywhere in the U.S. at any time of the year. In the southern states, peak tornado season is March through May, while peak months in the northern states are during the summer.

Preparedness Guides

- Are you prepared for Nature's Most Violent Storms? A preparedness guide including safety information for schools prepared by the National Weather Service, FEMA and the American Red Cross.

- Thunderstorms and Camping Safety

- Weather Safety for Kids - Owlie Skywarn's Weather Book about Tornadoes

More Info . . .

- Weather Glossary for Storm Spotters

These links connect to pages with more information. For example, clicking on "Weather Safety for Kids" takes you to the Web page shown on page 654.

- Storm Reports - includes monthly tornado statistics, deadly tornadoes, current severe weather reports and more from the National Weather Service's Storm Prediction Center.

- Tornadoes of the 20th Century - a list of the more notable tornado outbreaks that occurred in the U.S. during the 20th century.

Reading Informational Materials: Web Sites ■ 653

Reading Web Sites

- **Ask** volunteers to identify topics that they could research on the World Wide Web. After they share their ideas, make sure they know that information about almost any topic is available on Web sites.

- Explain to students that Web sites often are organized like books, with broad topics that contain more detailed information in subtopics. Point out that the underlined text is often a link to a different page with more information about the topic. Note that some information hunts are difficult and require the researcher to read many different pages before finding the information he or she wants.

- Have students read "Tornadoes."

- **Ask** students to identify the source of information for this Web site.
  Answer: The government agency, National Oceanic and Atmospheric Administration (NOAA).

- **Ask** students why this information is probably reliable.
  Answer: This information comes from a government agency that specializes in the research of weather-related events.

- Remind students that it is important to review both the source of information and the content to determine whether the Web site is reliable. Tell students that, if they are unsure about the reliability of information, it is a good idea to check another source for verification.

continued on page 654

Differentiated Instruction   Solutions for All Learners

Strategy for Special Needs Students
Before students visit a Web site, suggest that they take sheets of paper and write down exactly what they are looking for on the Web site. Tell them to refer to these notes before changing Web pages or clicking on links. This will help them remember what they are looking for as they move around the Web site.

Strategy for Advanced Readers
Remind students that you can't automatically believe everything you read on the Internet. Challenge students to find an example of a reliable Web site and an unreliable Web site about the same topic. For each Web site, ask students to determine the source of the information and to explain why they believe the Web site is reliable or not. Provide time for students to present their findings.

Reading Web Sites (cont.)

- Tell students that this page is the "Weather Safety for Kids" link from the main "Tornadoes" page. Make sure all students find the link right above "More Info . . ." on p. 653.

- Explain that links such as this page provide more detailed or simply different information than the main page of the Web site.

- Tell students to look at the bottom of the linked page and note the contact information. **Ask** a volunteer to tell how to get in contact with someone to ask for more information.

- **Answer:** Send an e-mail to noaa-outreach@noaa.gov.

- Remind students that one way to check on the reliability of information on a Web site is to note the date when the information was last updated. Point out that old information is less likely to be reliable.

- **Ask** a student to tell when this Web site was last updated.

- **Answer:** June 22, 20__

- **Ask** a volunteer what part of the Web address gives a clue that the information on the Web site is reliable.
  Answer: The ending *.gov* tells that the site is created and managed by the government, and the government is a reliable source of information.

- Tell students that Web-page links often have further links. **Ask** students how they can tell whether or not this linked page has additional links.
  Answer: The six underlined phrases that follow "What to do if . . ." are all links to additional pages. You can tell because they are in color and underlined.

Click on these links to find additional information about the topics listed.

This line identifies the date when the web page was updated.

This page provides an e-mail address so users can contact someone at the web site with comments or questions.

http://www.crh.noaa.gov/mkx/owlie/tornadoe1.htm

NOAA.GOV for Kids
FEMA.GOV for Kids

National Weather Service
Owlie Skywarn's Weather Book
Watch Out...Storms Ahead!

Owlie's Front Page

View My Safety Tips About...
Tornadoes
  Watches
  Warnings
Lightning
Flash Floods
Hurricanes
Winter Weather
Carbon Monoxide

TORNADO!

If you ever see a big black cloud with a funnel-like extension beneath it, watch out. It could be a tornado.

A tornado looks like a funnel with the fat part at the top. Inside it winds may be swirling around at 300 miles an hour. If it goes through a town, the tornado could flatten houses and buildings, lift up cars and trucks, shatter mobile homes into splinters. Sometimes the path is narrow but everything in the path gets wrecked. But you don't always see the funnel. It may be raining too hard. Or the tornado may come at night. Listen for the tornado's roar. Some people say it sounds like a thousand trains.

What to do if...

| You are in your house | You are downtown or in a shopping mall | You are outside |
| You are in school | You are in a mobile home | In Conclusion... |

Last updated June 22, 20__
URL: http://www.crh.noaa.gov/mkx/owlie/tornado1.htm

Educators and students should send their questions to the NOAA outreach team at noaa-outreach@noaa.gov.

Vocabulary Development

Vocabulary for Web Sites
Tell students that discussion of Web sites often involves using specialized terms that may be unfamiliar. Guide them to understand the meaning of the following words on the "Tornadoes" Web site.

navigation bar: A collection of links grouped together to help readers find information within a Web site.

Web site: A group of Web pages generally hyperlinked together.

Web page: An electronic document posted online.

hyperlink: An electronic link providing direct access from one location in a document to another document or another location within the same document.

Assessment Practice

Reading: Evaluating Web Sources

Directions: *Choose the letter of the best answer to each question about the NOAA Web site on "Tornadoes."*

1. For which of the following topics would this site provide valid information?
   A climate changes due to global warming
   B tide tables for the coming season
   C average temperatures and rainfall in your state
   D tornadoes during the 1980s and 1990s

2. Which link would you use to find reliable data on current storms in your area?
   A Storm Reports
   B Nature's Most Violent Storms?
   C Safety Tips about "Tornadoes"
   D Weather Glossary for Storm Spotters

3. How do you know the information on this site is reliable?
   A This is a government-sponsored weather Web site.
   B The site has pages for kids.
   C The site looks scientific.
   D Only experts would have access to this information.

Reading: Comprehension and Interpretation

Directions: *Write your answers on a separate piece of paper.*

4. Which link or links on the home page lead to information about measures schools can take to ensure the safety of students and teachers? **[Knowledge]**

5. Paraphrase the descriptions of Category F0 and Category F5 on the Fujita Tornado Damage Scale. **[Organizing]**

Timed Writing: Evaluation [Connections]

Write an evaluation of the Web site that answers these questions: What are its most helpful features? Who would find it the most useful? Is there anything that should be added to the site to make it better? Would you recommend this site to someone researching severe weather? **(35 minutes)**

Answers

Reading: Evaluating Web Sources

1. D
2. A
3. A
4. The link "Nature's Most Violent Storms" provides information about measures schools can take to ensure the safety of students and teachers. The "You are in school" link on the "Weather Safety for Kids" page may also provide safety measures for schools.
5. Category F0 tornadoes have wind speeds less than 73 mph and cause minor damage, such as broken tree branches and damage to chimneys. Category F5 tornadoes have wind speeds greater than 260 mph and cause tremendous damage, such as houses lifted from their foundation and objects as large as cars thrown over 100 meters.

Timed Writing

- Read the Timed Writing instructions together as a group. Remind students to address each of the four questions in the timed writing directions.

- Suggest that students plan their time to give 10 minutes to planning, 20 minutes to writing, and 5 minutes to reviewing and revising.

Extend the Lesson

Web Page Text
Discuss that Web sites begin with someone deciding what information to include. Ask each student to choose a topic that would make a meaningful Web site. Have them plan the information for an opening page of a Web site. Tell them to make sure they use only reliable information. Also, have them create a realistic-looking Web site and include at three least planned links. Allow time for students to share entries.

Planning Differentiated Instruction

Choosing Your Poetry Collection

You may use either collection to meet the lesson standards. The following guide will help you determine which of the two collections is more appropriate for your students.

Accessibility at a Glance

	Collection 1	Collection 2
Context	Collection features aspects of self-discovery (with the exception of the light-hearted "Macavity: The Mystery Cat")	Collection emphasizes the journeys in life
Language	Difficult sentence structure but familiar situations	Difficult vocabulary and sentence structure
Concept Level	More accessible	More challenging
Literary Merit	Noted poets	Noted poets
Lexile	NP	NP
Overall Rating	More accessible	More challenging

Using the Other Collection You may use the other collections of poems for homework or independent reading to reinforce the selection skills. If you use both collections, you can build a test for both using *ExamView® Test Bank* software.

Choosing Your Resources

[L1] Special Needs Students   **[L4]** Advanced Students

[L2] Below-Level Students   **[EL]** English Learners

[L3] All Students

FT Fast Track Instruction: To move the lesson more quickly, use the strategies and activities identified with **FT**.

Reading and Vocabulary Warm-ups provide support for below level students. **A** is for students reading two grades below level; **B** is for students reading one grade below level. For Selection Tests, **A** signifies "less challenging" and **B** "more challenging." For Graphic Organizer transparencies, **A** signifies "not filled in" and **B** "filled in."

Scaffolding for Less Proficient and Advanced Students

The leveled questions on Apply the Skills pages progress in the levels of thinking required to answer them. To address the needs of your different students, you may use the (a) level questions for your less proficient students, the (b) level with your on-level and advanced students. The occasional (c) level questions are appropriate for your advanced students.

Go Online **For:** Information about Lexiles
Internet Professional Development **Visit:** www.PHSchool.com
Web Code: eue-1111

Step-by-Step Teaching Guide	Pacing Guide
PRETEACH	
• Administer Vocabulary and Reading Warm-ups as necessary.	
• Introduce the Literary Analysis Skill: Rhyme. **FT**	10 min.
• Introduce the Reading Skill: Paraphrasing. **FT**	10 min.
• Prepare students to read by teaching the selection vocabulary. **FT**	10 min.
• Build background and develop expressive vocabulary with Connecting to the Literature and Background.	10 min.
• Engage students' interest with the motivation activity.	10 min.
TEACH	
• Informally monitor comprehension while students read independently or in groups. **FT**	30 min.
• Monitor students' comprehension with the Reading Check notes.	as students read
• Reinforce vocabulary with Vocabulary Builder notes.	as students read
• Develop students' understanding of rhyme with the Literary Analysis annotations. **FT**	5 min.
• Develop students' ability to paraphrase with the Reading Skill annotations. **FT**	10 min.
ASSESS/EXTEND	
• Assess students' comprehension and mastery of the Reading Skill and Literary Analysis by having them answer the Apply the Skills questions. **FT**	35 min.
• Have students complete the Vocabulary Builder activities. **FT**	5 min.
• Apply students' ability to write a poem with the Writing activity. **FT**	30–45 min. or homework
• Extend students' listening and speaking and research and technology skills with one or both of the Extend Your Learning activities.	15–30 min. or homework
• Have students complete the Vocabulary Skill and Grammar Lesson.	5 min.
• Monitor students' progress with the Assessment Practice.	20–40 min.
• Administer **Selection Test A** or **Selection Test B**. **FT**	15 min.

Resources

PRINT

	Collection 1	Collection 2
Unit 4 Resources		
Vocabulary Warm-Up—Word Lists [L1, L2, EL]	p. 145	p. 161
Vocabulary Warm-Up—Practice [L1, L2, EL]	p. 146	p. 162
Reading Warm-Up A [L1, L2, EL]	p. 147	p. 163
Reading Warm-Up B [L1, L2, L3]	p. 148	p. 164

General Resources
Vocabulary Knowledge Rating Chart, p. 6 [L3]
Anticipation Guide, pp. 8–10 [L3]

TRANSPARENCY

Graphic Organizer Transparencies

	Collection 1	Collection 2
Reading Skill Graphic Organizers A [L3]	p. 149	p. 149
Reading Skill Graphic Organizers B [L1, L2, EL]	p. 150	p. 151
Literary Analysis Graphic Organizer A [L3]	p. 152	p. 154
Literary Analysis Graphic Organizer B [L1, L2, EL]	p. 153	p. 155

PRINT

Reader's Notebook [L2]
Reader's Notebook: Adapted Version [L1]
Reader's Notebook: English Learner's Version [EL]
Unit 4 Resources

	Collection 1	Collection 2
Literary Analysis [L3]	p. 149	p. 165
Reading Skill [L3]	p. 150	p. 166
Vocabulary Builder [L3]	p. 151	p. 167

TECHNOLOGY

Listening to Literature Audio CDs [L2, EL]
Reader's Notebook: Adapted Version Audio CD [L1, L2]

PRINT

Unit 4 Resources

	Collection 1	Collection 2
Support for Writing [L3]	p. 152	p. 168
Support for Extend Your Learning [L3]	p. 153	p. 169
Enrichment [L4]	p. 154	p. 170
Selection Test A [L1, L2, EL]	pp. 155–157	pp. 173–175
Selection Test B [L3, L4]	pp. 158–160	pp. 176–178

Build Language Skills: Vocabulary:
Latin suffixes -age, -ism, and -ize, p. 171 [L3]
Build Language Skills: Grammar:
Infinitives and Infinitive Phrases, p. 172 [L3]

General Resources
Rubrics for Poems (Rhyming), pp. 65–66 [L3]

TECHNOLOGY

Go Online: Research [L3]
Go Online: Self-test [L3]
ExamView® Test Bank [L3]

Meeting Your Standards

Students will

1. **analyze and respond to literary elements.**
   - Literary Analysis: Rhyme

2. **read, comprehend, and analyze poems.**
   - Reading Skill: Paraphrasing
   - Reading Strategy: Breaking Down Long Sentences
   - Reading Check questions
   - Apply the Skills questions
   - Assessment Practice

3. **develop vocabulary.**
   - Vocabulary Builder
   - Latin suffixes -age, -ism, -ize

4. **apply grammar skills.**
   - Infinitives and Infinitive Phrases

5. **develop writing proficiency.**
   - Work in Progress: Response to Literature
   - Poem

6. **extend learning.**
   - Listening and Speaking: Panel Discussion
   - Research and Technology: Electronic Database

Block Scheduling: Use one 90-minute class period to preteach the skills and have students read the collection. Use a second 90-minute class period to assess students' mastery of skills, extend their learning, and monitor their progress.

Homework Suggestions

Following are possibilities for homework assignments.

- Support pages from *Unit 4 Resources*:
  Literary Analysis
  Reading Skill
  Build Vocabulary
  Enrichment

- An Extend Your Learning project and the Writing assignment for your chosen collection may be completed over several days.

PRENTICE HALL
Teacher EXPRESS™ Use this complete
Plan · Teach · Assess suite of powerful
teaching tools to make lesson planning and testing quicker and easier.

PRENTICE HALL
Student EXPRESS™ Use the
Learn · Study · Succeed Interactive
Textbook (online and on CD-ROM) to make selections and activities come alive with audio and video support and interactive questions.

❶ Literary Analysis

Rhyme

- Tell students that one thing that distinguishes poetry from prose is the use of *rhyme*. While not all poets use rhyme, it is one of the most common sound devices in poetry.

- Point out that most people think of rhyme in poetry as meaning the exact rhyme of words at the end of lines. However, exact rhyme may not always be possible, or even desirable. In some cases, exact rhyme can become monotonous, and the reader loses interest. Poets often choose to use a precise word that has a slant rhyme over a less precise word that has an exact rhyme.

- Tell students that sometimes poets emphasize a rhythm by using internal rhyme, or two or more words that rhyme within one line.

Rhyme Scheme

- Tell students that a set pattern of rhyme contributes to the rhythm of a poem.

- Point out that there are many different rhyme schemes. Some formally structured poems specify a certain rhyme scheme. For example a sonnet has a rhyme scheme of *abab, cdcd, efef, gg*.

- Tell students that some poems do not use rhyme at all or have an irregular pattern of rhyming.

Meter

- Tell students that meter gives emphasis to ideas in a poem and adds beauty or interest to the sound of the poem.

- Point out that some formally structured poems have a specified meter. For example, a sonnet has a certain pattern of stressed and unstressed syllables. All of Shakespeare's plays are written in a certain meter.

- Tell students that even in formally structured poems, poets may vary the meter slightly in some lines. Point out that an unvarying meter in a long poem can become monotonous and "sing-song."

- Encourage students to listen for these sound devices as they read these poems aloud.

Build Skills   *Poetry Collection 1 • Poetry Collection 2*

You can apply the instruction on this page to these poems.

Poetry Collection 1
We never know how high we are, page 659
The Road Not Taken, page 661
Macavity: The Mystery Cat, page 662

Poetry Collection 2
Fire and Ice, page 667
maggie and milly and molly and may, page 668
The Seven Ages of Man, page 671

❶ Literary Analysis

Rhyme is the repetition of sounds at the ends of words. There are several types of rhyme:

- **Exact rhyme:** the repetition of words that end with the same vowel and consonant sounds, as in *love* and *dove*

- **Slant rhyme:** the repetition of words that end with similar sounds but do not rhyme perfectly, as in *prove* and *glove*

- **End rhyme:** the rhyming of words at the ends of lines

- **Internal rhyme:** the rhyming of words within a line

A **rhyme scheme** is a regular pattern of end rhymes in a poem or stanza. A rhyme scheme is described by assigning one letter of the alphabet to each rhyming sound. For example, in "Ring Out, Wild Bells," Alfred, Lord Tennyson uses the rhyme scheme *abba*:

Ring out, wild bells, to the wild <u>sky</u>,	*a*
The flying cloud, the frosty <u>light</u>:	*b*
The year is dying in the <u>night</u>;	*b*
Ring out, wild bells, and let him <u>die</u>.	*a*

Meter is the rhythmical pattern in a line of poetry. It results from the arrangement of stressed (´) and unstressed (ˇ) syllables. When you read aloud a line with a regular meter, you can hear the steady rhythmic pulse of the stressed syllables:

The flýing clóud, the frósty líght

Hálf å leáğue, hálf å leáğue, / Hálf å leáğue onẃård

Not all poems include rhyme, a rhyme scheme, or a regular meter. However, poets often use one or more of these techniques to create musical effects and achieve a sense of unity in their poems.

As you read the poetry in this collection, notice rhyme and meter.

- Look for examples of different types of rhyme.
- Determine if the lines follow a rhyme scheme.
- Notice whether or not the lines follow a regular meter.

Vocabulary Development

Vocabulary Knowledge Rating
Create a **Vocabulary Knowledge Rating Chart** for the poems you will teach from this collection. Include the vocabulary from this page and the additional words students are asked to use at the end of Connecting to the Literature. These words will increase students' expressive vocabulary.

Give students a copy of the chart with the words on it. Introduce the words by reading them aloud and having students mark their rating in the Before Reading column. Urge them to be alert to these words as they read and discuss these poems because they will rate their knowledge of the words again after they finish.

If you wish, you may tally how many students know (or think they know) a word to gauge how much instruction you need to provide. As students read, point out the words and their context.

Resources

PRINT

	Collection 1	Collection 2
Unit 4 Resources		
Vocabulary Warm-Up—Word Lists [**L1, L2, EL**]	p. 145	p. 161
Vocabulary Warm-Up—Practice [**L1, L2, EL**]	p. 146	p. 162
Reading Warm-Up A [**L1, L2, EL**]	p. 147	p. 163
Reading Warm-Up B [**L1, L2, L3**]	p. 148	p. 164
General Resources		
Vocabulary Knowledge Rating Chart, p. 6 [**L3**]		
Anticipation Guide, pp. 8–10 [**L3**]		

TRANSPARENCY

Graphic Organizer Transparencies		
Reading Skill Graphic Organizers A [**L3**]	p. 149	p. 149
Reading Skill Graphic Organizers B [**L1, L2, EL**]	p. 150	p. 151
Literary Analysis Graphic Organizer A [**L3**]	p. 152	p. 154
Literary Analysis Graphic Organizer B [**L1, L2, EL**]	p. 153	p. 155

PRINT

Reader's Notebook [L2]

Reader's Notebook: Adapted Version [L1]

Reader's Notebook: English Learner's Version [EL]

Unit 4 Resources		
Literary Analysis [**L3**]	p. 149	p. 165
Reading Skill [**L3**]	p. 150	p. 166
Vocabulary Builder [**L3**]	p. 151	p. 167

TECHNOLOGY

Listening to Literature Audio CDs [L2, EL]

Reader's Notebook: Adapted Version Audio CD [L1, L2]

PRINT

Unit 4 Resources		
Support for Writing [**L3**]	p. 152	p. 168
Support for Extend Your Learning [**L3**]	p. 153	p. 169
Enrichment [**L4**]	p. 154	p. 170
Selection Test A [**L1, L2, EL**]	pp. 155–157	pp. 173–175
Selection Test B [**L3, L4**]	pp. 158–160	pp. 176–178
Build Language Skills: Vocabulary: Latin suffixes *-age, -ism,* and *-ize*, p. 171 [**L3**]		
Build Language Skills: Grammar: Infinitives and Infinitive Phrases, p. 172 [**L3**]		
General Resources		
Rubrics for Poems (Rhyming), pp. 65–66 [**L3**]		

TECHNOLOGY

Go Online: Research [L3]

Go Online: Self-test [L3]

ExamView® **Test Bank [L3]**

Meeting Your Standards

Students will

1. analyze and respond to literary elements.
- Literary Analysis: Rhyme

2. read, comprehend, and analyze poems.
- Reading Skill: Paraphrasing
- Reading Strategy: Breaking Down Long Sentences
- Reading Check questions
- Apply the Skills questions
- Assessment Practice

3. develop vocabulary.
- Vocabulary Builder
- Latin suffixes *-age, -ism, -ize*

4. apply grammar skills.
- Infinitives and Infinitive Phrases

5. develop writing proficiency.
- Work in Progress: Response to Literature
- Poem

6. extend learning.
- Listening and Speaking: Panel Discussion
- Research and Technology: Electronic Database

Block Scheduling: Use one 90-minute class period to preteach the skills and have students read the collection. Use a second 90-minute class period to assess students' mastery of skills, extend their learning, and monitor their progress.

Homework Suggestions

Following are possibilities for homework assignments.

- Support pages from *Unit 4 Resources*:
  Literary Analysis
  Reading Skill
  Build Vocabulary
  Enrichment

- An Extend Your Learning project and the Writing assignment for your chosen collection may be completed over several days.

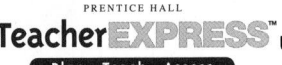

PRENTICE HALL

TeacherEXPRESS Use this complete
Plan · Teach · Assess suite of powerful
teaching tools to make lesson planning and testing
quicker and easier.

PRENTICE HALL

StudentEXPRESS Use the
Learn · Study · Succeed Interactive
Textbook (online and on CD-ROM) to make selections and activities come alive with audio and video support and interactive questions.

❶ Literary Analysis

Rhyme

- Tell students that one thing that distinguishes poetry from prose is the use of *rhyme*. While not all poets use rhyme, it is one of the most common sound devices in poetry.

- Point out that most people think of rhyme in poetry as meaning the exact rhyme of words at the end of lines. However, exact rhyme may not always be possible, or even desirable. In some cases, exact rhyme can become monotonous, and the reader loses interest. Poets often choose to use a precise word that has a slant rhyme over a less precise word that has an exact rhyme.

- Tell students that sometimes poets emphasize a rhythm by using internal rhyme, or two or more words that rhyme within one line.

Rhyme Scheme

- Tell students that a set pattern of rhyme contributes to the rhythm of a poem.

- Point out that there are many different rhyme schemes. Some formally structured poems specify a certain rhyme scheme. For example a sonnet has a rhyme scheme of *abab, cdcd, efef, gg.*

- Tell students that some poems do not use rhyme at all or have an irregular pattern of rhyming.

Meter

- Tell students that meter gives emphasis to ideas in a poem and adds beauty or interest to the sound of the poem.

- Point out that some formally structured poems have a specified meter. For example, a sonnet has a certain pattern of stressed and unstressed syllables. All of Shakespeare's plays are written in a certain meter.

- Tell students that even in formally structured poems, poets may vary the meter slightly in some lines. Point out that an unvarying meter in a long poem can become monotonous and "sing-song."

- Encourage students to listen for these sound devices as they read these poems aloud.

Build Skills   *Poetry Collection 1 • Poetry Collection 2*

You can apply the instruction on this page to these poems.

Poetry Collection 1	**Poetry Collection 2**
We never know how high we are, page 659	*Fire and Ice,* page 667
The Road Not Taken, page 661	*maggie and milly and molly and may,* page 668
Macavity: The Mystery Cat, page 662	*The Seven Ages of Man,* page 671

❶ Literary Analysis

Rhyme is the repetition of sounds at the ends of words. There are several types of rhyme:

- **Exact rhyme:** the repetition of words that end with the same vowel and consonant sounds, as in *love* and *dove*

- **Slant rhyme:** the repetition of words that end with similar sounds but do not rhyme perfectly, as in *prove* and *glove*

- **End rhyme:** the rhyming of words at the ends of lines

- **Internal rhyme:** the rhyming of words within a line

A **rhyme scheme** is a regular pattern of end rhymes in a poem or stanza. A rhyme scheme is described by assigning one letter of the alphabet to each rhyming sound. For example, in "Ring Out, Wild Bells," Alfred, Lord Tennyson uses the rhyme scheme *abba:*

Ring out, wild bells, to the wild <u>sky</u>,	*a*
The flying cloud, the frosty <u>light</u>:	*b*
The year is dying in the <u>night</u>;	*b*
Ring out, wild bells, and let him <u>die</u>.	*a*

Meter is the rhythmical pattern in a line of poetry. It results from the arrangement of stressed (´) and unstressed (^) syllables. When you read aloud a line with a regular meter, you can hear the steady rhythmic pulse of the stressed syllables:

The flýing clóud, the frósty líght

Hálf a leáǵue, hálf a leáǵue, / Hálf a leáǵue ońwàrd

Not all poems include rhyme, a rhyme scheme, or a regular meter. However, poets often use one or more of these techniques to create musical effects and achieve a sense of unity in their poems.

As you read the poetry in this collection, notice rhyme and meter.

- Look for examples of different types of rhyme.

- Determine if the lines follow a rhyme scheme.

- Notice whether or not the lines follow a regular meter.

Vocabulary Development

Vocabulary Knowledge Rating

Create a **Vocabulary Knowledge Rating Chart** for the poems you will teach from this collection. Include the vocabulary from this page and the additional words students are asked to use at the end of Connecting to the Literature. These words will increase students' expressive vocabulary.

Give students a copy of the chart with the words on it. Introduce the words by reading them aloud and having students mark their rating in the Before Reading column. Urge them to be alert to these words as they read and discuss these poems because they will rate their knowledge of the words again after they finish.

If you wish, you may tally how many students know (or think they know) a word to gauge how much instruction you need to provide. As students read, point out the words and their context.

Build Skills (Continued)

❷ Reading Skill

Paraphrasing is restating in your own words what someone else has written or said. A paraphrase should retain the essential meaning and ideas of the original but should be simpler to read. One way to simplify the text that you are paraphrasing is to **break down long sentences.** Divide long sentences into parts and paraphrase those parts.

- If a sentence contains multiple subjects or verbs, see if it can be separated into smaller sentences that each contain one subject and one verb.
- If a sentence contains colons, semicolons, or dashes, create separate sentences by treating those punctuation marks as periods.
- If a sentence contains long phrases or long passages in parentheses, turn each phrase or parenthetical passage into a separate sentence.

Poets often write sentences that span several lines to give their poems fluidity. By breaking down long sentences and paraphrasing them, you can enjoy a poem's fluid quality without missing its meaning.

As you read poetry and break down long sentences to paraphrase lines, use a chart like the one shown to record your work.

Original Lines	Lines in Smaller Sentences	Paraphrase
I celebrate myself and sing myself, / And what I assume you shall assume, / For every atom belonging to me as good belongs to you.	I celebrate myself. I sing myself. What I assume you shall assume. Every atom belonging to me as good belongs to you.	I celebrate myself and share my joy with you. What is mine is also yours.

Vocabulary Builder

Poetry Collection 1

- **warp** (wôrp) *v.* twist; distort (p. 659) *Skilled artists can warp wood into different shapes.*
- **diverged** (dī vʉrjd´) *v.* branched out in different directions (p. 661) *When the highway diverged, we were not sure which way to go.*
- **bafflement** (baf´ əl mənt) *n.* puzzlement; bewilderment (p. 662) *To the bafflement of many, the jet pilot was afraid of heights.*
- **depravity** (dē prav´ ə tē) *n.* crookedness; corruption (p. 663) *The criminal's depravity was well-known, and his arrest was cheered.*

Poetry Collection 2

- **suffice** (sə fīs´) *v.* be enough (p. 667) *Five tables will suffice for a party of this size.*
- **languid** (laŋ´ gwid) *adj.* drooping; weak (p. 668) *The heat of the summer afternoon made us all feel languid.*
- **woeful** (wō´ fəl) *adj.* full of sorrow (p. 671) *His woeful story brought us to tears.*
- **treble** (treb´ əl) *n.* high-pitched voice or sound (p. 671) *The harsh treble of her alarm clock woke everyone in the house.*

Poetry ■ 657

- Tell students that paraphrasing lines of poetry helps them better understand the ideas and feelings that the poet is trying to convey.
- Explain that poets often use long, complex sentences that might run for several lines of poetry. When paraphrasing poetry, students should look at complete sentences, rather than at each line.
- Tell students that they should find the beginning and the end of each complete sentence. They can write out each complete sentence, and then look for the breaks in clauses and phrases.
- Point out that one of the most important points in paraphrasing is to keep the original meaning of the lines being paraphrased. Students should check their paraphrase against the original carefully to make sure they have included the important ideas and not changed the meaning. Students should also check the surrounding context of the poem to make sure that their paraphrase fits the context of the entire poem and that they have not misinterpreted the lines.
- Give students a copy of **Reading Skill Graphic Organizer A** (*Graphic Organizer Transparencies,* p. 149). Have them fill in the graphic organizer to paraphrase lines of poetry as they read the assigned poems.

❸ Connecting to the Literature

- Model use of the expressive vocabulary students are asked to use with these examples:

  1. Many people do difficult things such as climb mountains just for the *challenge*.

  2. Some people's consciences *compel* them to do the right thing, even when it is unpopular.

  3. Some people do unpopular things to show that they will not *conform* to what others want.

  4. People often do difficult or unpopular things to *distinguish* themselves from the rest of the crowd.

- Help students further develop their expressive vocabulary by providing these words: *dominate, evaluate, induce,* and *internal*. Encourage students to use these words as they discuss the poems.

Concept Connector ➡

Students will reconsider their ideas after reading these poems.

Go **Online** For additional informa-
— **Author Link** tion about Robert Frost,
Emily Dickinson, and T. S. Eliot, have students type in the Web Code, select the first letter of the poet's last name, and then select the poet.

Build Understanding • *Poetry Collection 1*

Poetry

❸ Connecting to the Literature

Reading/Writing Connection In "The Road Not Taken," Robert Frost writes about making a difficult choice—a choice that is different from what most people would choose. Think about why people sometimes choose to do things that are difficult, challenging, or even unpopular. Use at least three of these words: *challenge, compel, conform, distinguish*.

Meet the Authors

Emily **Dickinson** (1830–1886)
We never know how high we are (p. 659)
Emily Dickinson's life in Amherst, Massachusetts, seemed to be quiet and uneventful. Yet the emotional power of her poems shows the wide range of her energy and imagination. She found profound meanings in simple subjects, and her poems still delight readers.

Robert **Frost** (1874–1963)
The Road Not Taken (p. 661)
In January 1961, when John F. Kennedy became president of the United States, he called on fellow New Englander Robert Frost to recite two poems at the inauguration. At the time, Frost was America's most famous living poet. He became famous when *A Boy's Will* (1913) and *North of Boston* (1914) won praise in both England and America.

T. S. **Eliot** (1888–1965)
Macavity: The Mystery Cat (p. 662)
A whimsical poem like "Macavity: The Mystery Cat" was a rarity in the writing of Thomas Sterns Eliot. He was better known for serious, philosophical poems. Born in the United States, Eliot settled in England. He became a highly influential poet and won the Nobel Prize in 1948.

For: More about these authors
Visit: www.PHSchool.com
Web Code: epe-9411

We never know how high we are

Emily Dickinson

Bubbles, Watercolor, 39" × 29" · Courtesy of Scott Burdick

We never know how high we are
Till we are asked to rise
And then if we are true to plan
Our statures touch the skies—
The Heroism we recite
Would be a normal thing
Did not ourselves the Cubits[1] <u>warp</u>
For fear to be a King—

---

1. Cubits (kyōō´ bitz) *n.* ancient measure using the length of the arm from the end of the middle finger to the elbow (about 18–22 inches).

We never know how high we are ■ 659

Vocabulary Builder
warp (wôrp) *v.* twist; distort

---

❶ Motivation

Prepare an **Anticipation Guide** (*General Resources*, pp. 8–10) with the following statements:

- Most people do not do all that they are capable of doing.
- People avoid trying to be all that they can for fear of failure.
- Few people take the most challenging course of action.
- Once you choose your path in life, you can never go back.

Give students a copy of the prepared Anticipation Guide and have students mark their responses in the Me column. Have students discuss the statements in pairs or groups and mark the Guides again in the Group column.

Concept Connector ⟶

Students will return to the Anticipation Guide after completing this poetry collection.

Learning Modalities
Interpersonal Learners

The infectious fun of "Macavity: The Mystery Cat" provides an opportunity for group reading and spontaneous discussion. Interpersonal learners will welcome this activity. Involve them in choral reading and discussion of the humor.

❷ About the Selections

In "We never know how high we are," Emily Dickinson speaks of the human fear of achieving greatness. According to the speaker, we impose limitations on ourselves because life seems safer in a cage than outside.

"The Road Not Taken" is about much more than a walk in the woods. The speaker must decide whether to pursue a more conventional direction or resist conformity by following his individual desires. He chooses the less conventional path, and as he reflects back years later, he feels he made the right decision.

"Macavity: The Mystery Cat" describes the mischievousness of a cat as if the characteristic were evidence of a super-criminal mind. Throughout, however, the lively verse of T.S. Eliot enlivens the poem with humor.

Differentiated Instruction   Solutions for All Learners

Support for Below-Level Students [L1, L2]	Support for English Learners [EL]
Unit 4 Resources	**Unit 4 Resources**
Vocabulary Warm-up Word Lists, p. 145	Vocabulary Warm-up Word Lists, p. 145
Vocabulary Warm-up Practice, p. 146	Vocabulary Warm-up Practice, p. 146
Reading Warm-up A, p. 147	Reading Warm-up A, p. 147
Selection Test A, pp. 155–157	**Reader's Notebook: English Learner's Version**
Graphic Organizer Transparencies	**Listening to Literature Audio CD** (Includes "The Road Not Taken" and "We never know how high we are" only.)
Reading Skill Graphic Organizer, Transparency B, p. 151	
Reader's Notebook: Adapted Version	
Adapted Reader's Notebook Audio CD	

❸ Critical Thinking
Analyze

- Have students read the poem on p. 661. Then have them examine the image on p. 660.

- **Ask** students to explain how this photograph relates to the poem.
  Answer: The photograph has a misty, dreamlike quality, which seems to hint at the look back in time that ends the poem. The well-traveled road looks like an easier choice, but the path covered in leaves looks more interesting. The poet speaks of a yellow wood and grassy paths, which seem more spring-like and brighter than the photographic image.

- Tell students that this poem is a metaphor—a figure of speech in which one thing is spoken of as though it were something else.
  Ask students what they think the poet means by the two roads diverging.
  Answer: The speaker has to choose between two options.

- The speaker emphasizes that the two roads are "really about the same." What does this suggest about the metaphor of the whole poem?
  Answer: Life does not offer just one clear choice to anyone; there are many equally tempting and attractive options that a person can choose.

660 ■ *Poetry*

❸

Vocabulary Development

Expressive Vocabulary
As students read the poems in this collection, discuss the ideas expressed in the poems. Encourage students to use the expressive vocabulary presented earlier as they discuss the poems. You might encourage them with sentence starters like these:

1. In "We never know how high we are," the poet says it is a *challenge* . . .
2. The speaker in "The Road Not Taken" feels *compelled* to . . .
3. In "The Road Not Taken," the speaker does not *conform* . . .
4. Macavity appears to want to *distinguish* himself from . . .

The Road Not Taken
Robert Frost

Two roads <u>diverged</u> in a yellow wood,
And sorry I could not travel both
And be one traveler, long I stood
And looked down one as far as I could
5 To where it bent in the undergrowth;

❹

Then took the other, as just as fair,
And having perhaps the better claim,
Because it was grassy and wanted wear;
Though as for that, the passing there
10 Had worn them really about the same,

And both that morning equally lay
In leaves no step had trodden black.
Oh, I kept the first for another day!
Yet knowing how way leads on to way,
15 I doubted if I should ever come back.

❺

I shall be telling this with a sigh
Somewhere ages and ages hence:
Two roads diverged in a wood, and I—
I took the one less traveled by,
20 And that has made all the difference.

❻ ◀ **Critical Viewing** Based on this image, explain why the idea of a fork in a road is an effective symbol for a life choice. **[Support]**

The Road Not Taken ■ 661

Vocabulary Builder
diverged (dī vʉrjd′) v. branched out in different directions

Reading Skill
Paraphrase In your own words, restate the decision the speaker makes in lines 6–8.

Literary Analysis
Rhyme and Rhyme Scheme What is the rhyme scheme of stanza four?

661

- Read the first two stanzas aloud for students. **Ask** students what fact is established about Macavity in these lines, and what is humorous about this.
Answer: Macavity is a cat, and the speaker describes him as a master criminal, even giving him the nickname of "the Hidden Paw," who defies the law and always successfully eludes law enforcement officials.

- Refer students to the second stanza of the poem. **Ask** students the Literary Analysis question: What type of rhyme does this stanza contain?
Answer: The stanza contains exact end rhyme.

- Have students read these two stanzas aloud, listening for the rhyme and the meter. **Ask** students to explain how the rhyme and meter of these stanzas contribute to the humor.
Possible response: The almost sing-song, fast-moving rhythm of the lines and the repetition of the "air" sound of the end rhyme give the lines an upbeat, humorous sound.

Macavity:
The Mystery Cat

T.S. Eliot

Macavity's a Mystery Cat: he's called the Hidden Paw—
For he's the master criminal who can defy the Law.
He's the <u>bafflement</u> of Scotland Yard,[1] the Flying Squad's[2]
    despair:
5 For when they reach the scene of crime—*Macavity's not
    there!*

❼ Macavity, Macavity, there's no one like Macavity,
He's broken every human law, he breaks the law of gravity.
His powers of levitation would make a fakir[3] stare,
10 And when you reach the scene of crime—*Macavity's not there!*
You may seek him in the basement, you may look up in the
    air—
But I tell you once and once again, *Macavity's not there!*

Macavity's a ginger cat, he's very tall and thin;
15 You would know him if you saw him, for his eyes are sunken in.

---

1. **Scotland Yard** London police.
2. **Flying Squad** criminal-investigation department.
3. **fakir** (fə kir′) *n.* Muslim or Hindu beggar who claims to perform miracles.

662 ■ *Poetry*

Vocabulary Builder
bafflement (baf′ əl mənt) *n.* puzzlement; bewilderment

Literary Analysis
Rhyme What type of rhyme does this stanza contain?

Vocabulary Development

Vocabulary Knowledge Rating
When students have completed reading and discussing this poetry collection, have them take out their **Vocabulary Knowledge Rating Chart** for these poems. Read the words aloud once more and have students rate their knowledge of the words again in the After Reading column. Clarify any words that are still problematic. Have students write their own definition and example or sentence in the appropriate column. Then have students complete the **Vocabulary Builder Practice** activities on p. 665. Encourage students to use the words in further discussion and written work about these poems. Remind them that they will be accountable for these words on the Selection Test.

His brow is deeply lined with thought, his head is highly
    domed;
His coat is dusty from neglect, his whiskers are uncombed.
He sways his head from side to side, with movements like a
    snake;
20 And when you think he's half asleep, he's always wide awake.

Macavity, Macavity, there's no one like Macavity,
For he's a fiend in feline shape, a monster of <u>depravity</u>.
You may meet him in a by-street, you may see him in the
    square—
25 But when a crime's discovered, then *Macavity's not there!*

He's outwardly respectable. (They say he cheats at cards.)
And his footprints are not found in any file of Scotland Yard's.
And when the larder's looted, or the jewel-case is rifled,
30 Or when the milk is missing, or another Peke's⁴ been stifled,
Or the greenhouse glass is broken, and the trellis past repair—
Ay, there's the wonder of the thing! *Macavity's not there!*

And when the Foreign Office find a Treaty's gone astray,
Or the Admiralty lose some plans and drawings by the way,
35 There may be a scrap of paper in the hall or on the stair—
But it's useless to investigate—*Macavity's not there!*
And when the loss has been disclosed, the Secret Service say:
'It *must* have been Macavity!'—but he's a mile away.
You'll be sure to find him resting, or a-licking of his thumbs,
40 Or engaged in doing complicated long division sums.

Macavity, Macavity, there's no one like Macavity,
There never was a Cat of such deceitfulness and suavity.
He always has an alibi, and one or two to spare:
❽ At whatever time the deed took place—MACAVITY WASN'T
45   THERE!
And they say that all the Cats whose wicked deeds are widely
    known
(I might mention Mungojerrie, I might mention Griddlebone)
Are nothing more than agents for the Cat who all the time
50 Just controls their operations: the Napoleon of Crime!⁵

---

4. **Peke** short for Pekingese, a small dog with long, silky hair and a pug nose.
5. **the Napoleon of Crime** criminal mastermind; emperor of crime—just as Napoleon Bonaparte (1769–1821) was a masterful military strategist who had himself crowned emperor.

Macavity: The Mystery Cat ■ 663

Vocabulary Builder
depravity (dē prav´ ə tē) *n.* crookedness; corruption

Reading Skill
Paraphrase Break down the sentence in lines 43–44 into three smaller sentences. Restate each sentence in your own words.

❽ Reading Skill
Paraphrase

- Have students read the balance of the poem, beginning with the third stanza on p. 662. **Ask** students to describe the character of Macavity in their own words.
  Possible response: Macavity is a ginger-colored cat that is not well kept. He's a clever criminal who gets into the food, breaks things, and destroys papers. Despite his crimes, no one can catch him. When the crimes are discovered, he is always long gone from the scene.

- **Ask** students to identify the three sentences in the sixth stanza, lines 33 through 40.
  Answer: "And when the Foreign Office . . . *Macavity's not there.*" "And when the loss . . . he's a mile away." "You'll be sure to find him . . . long division sums."

- Refer students to lines 43–44. **Ask** students to respond to the Reading Skill prompt: Break down the sentence in lines 43–44 into three smaller sentences. Restate each sentence in your own words.
  Answer: He always has an alibi. He has one or two to spare. At whatever time the deed took place, Macavity wasn't there! Macavity always has more than one alibi. He is never around when the crime is discovered.

▶ **Monitor Progress:** Review students' graphic organizers to ensure that they are able to paraphrase accurately.

▶ **Reteach:** If students have difficulty paraphrasing, have them retell a fairy tale or fable such as "Hansel and Gretel" or "The Three Little Pigs" in their own words. Paraphrasing a familiar story will provide them with practice.

Concept Connector

Anticipation Guide
Have students return to their **Anticipation Guides** and respond to the statements again in the After Reading column. They may do this individually or in their original pairs or groups. Then, lead a class discussion, probing for what students have learned that confirms or invalidates each statement. Encourage students to cite specific details, quotations, or other evidence from the poems to support their responses to each statement.

Connecting to the Literature
Have students compare the sentences they wrote before reading with their thoughts about why people might choose to do difficult things. Ask them to explain whether their thoughts have changed and, if so, how.

Reading Skill Graphic Organizer
Have students review the graphic organizers they completed to make and verify predictions while reading. Show them **Reading Skill Graphic Organizer B** (*Graphic Organizer Transparencies,* p. 150) as an example. Then have students share their graphic organizers.

1. **Sample response:** "Macavity: The Mystery Cat" sounds the best when read aloud. It has an upbeat meter and is humorous.

2. (a) If people are true to themselves, they rise to the occasion and "touch the skies." (b) People limit themselves through fear. The hero is the rare person who does not do this.

3. (a) The speaker must decide which road to take. (b) This choice might represent a choice of colleges to attend or a career to follow. (c) **Sample answer:** People my age have to face important choices as well, such as whether or not to play sports; whether to take or continue in music lessons; what friends to choose.

   Another sample answer can be found on **Literary Analysis Graphic Organizer B**, p. 153 in *Graphic Organizer Transparencies.*

4. Cats are mischievous and curious. They get into things, and they can move silently and quickly disappear.

5. Lines 1–3 ("Two roads diverged in a yellow wood, /And sorry I could not travel both/And be one traveler, long I stood") have both exact rhyme and end rhyme. The words *wood* and *stood* come at the end of the lines, and they are exact rhymes.

6. The words *glass* and *past* are examples of both internal rhyme and slant rhyme.

7. (a) The rhyme scheme is *abcb, abcb.* (b) **Possible response:** The change in rhymes indicates the shift of the discussion from the possibilities for human achievement to a reason why people fail to realize their full potential.

8. (a) "We never know how high we are" has a more regular meter. Every other line has the same meter, without any variance. (b) **Possible response:** The poem with the more regular meter is more enjoyable to read because it has a predictable flowing cadence.

Apply the Skills

Poetry Collection 1

Thinking About the Selections

1. **Respond:** Which poem sounds best when read aloud? Why?
2. (a) **Recall:** According to "We never know how high we are," what happens when people are asked to rise to an occasion? (b) **Interpret:** According to the speaker of the poem, why is heroism not "a normal thing"?
3. Fill out a three-column chart like the one shown. (a) **Recall:** In the first column, identify the decision faced by the speaker of "The Road Not Taken." (b) **Interpret:** In the second column, tell what other kinds of decisions this choice might represent. (c) **Discuss:** Share your chart with a partner. In the third column, explain how the message of the poem applies to people your age.

What Does It Say?	What Does It Mean?	Why Is It Important?

4. **Speculate:** Which qualities of cats might have caused T. S. Eliot to associate them with criminal activities in "Macavity: The Mystery Cat"? Explain.

Literary Analysis

5. Identify two lines in "The Road Not Taken" that illustrate both **exact rhyme** and **end rhyme.** Explain your choices.
6. Which two words in line 31 of "Macavity: The Mystery Cat" illustrate both **slant rhyme** and **internal rhyme?**
7. (a) Use letters to identify the **rhyme scheme** in "We never know how high we are." (b) In what way does the shift in rhyme scheme midway through the poem help to signal a turning point in the poem's message?
8. (a) Which poem has lines with a more regular **meter**—"The Road Not Taken" or "We never know how high we are"? Explain. (b) Which do you find more enjoyable to read—lines with a regular meter or lines with an irregular meter? Explain.

Reading Skill

9. (a) **Paraphrase** the first stanza of "The Road Not Taken" by re-writing it as a series of sentences. (b) In what way does **breaking down long sentences** make this poem's meaning more clear?

664 ■ *Poetry*

QuickReview

Poems at a Glance
"We never know how high we are" explores the nature of heroism.
"The Road Not Taken" explains a crucial decision.
"Macavity: The Mystery Cat" describes a feline criminal mastermind.

Assessment
For: Self-test
Visit: www.PHSchool.com
Web Code: epa-6409

Rhyme: repetition of sounds at the ends of words; types include *exact rhyme, slant rhyme, end rhyme,* and *internal rhyme*
Rhyme Scheme: a regular pattern of end rhymes
Meter: the rhythmical pattern in a line of poetry
Paraphrasing: restating in your own words what someone else has written or said

9. (a) **Sample response:** Two roads diverged in a yellow wood. I was sorry I could not travel both and be one traveler. Long I stood and looked down one as far as I could. I saw where it bent in the undergrowth. (b) Breaking down long sentences clarifies the meaning because the new, shorter sentences each contain one idea, which makes them easier to follow.

Vocabulary Builder

Practice Decide if each statement is true or false. Then, explain.

1. Two people whose opinions *diverged* would be in disagreement.
2. Reporters are taught to *warp* the facts of events they cover.
3. *Bafflement* is a likely reaction to a bizarre event.
4. Laws are written to encourage *depravity* in society.

Adding Words to Your Vocabulary Using a thesaurus, find a synonym for the italicized words in the Practice. Use each synonym correctly in a sentence. (For more on using a thesaurus, see page R7.)

Writing

Write a **poem** using the same rhyme scheme as a poem in Collection 1.

- Choose a poem and identify its rhyme scheme.
- Decide on a topic, an event, an experience, or an emotion that you would like to be the subject of your poem.
- Brainstorm for a list of images, details, phrases, or words.
- Draft your lines, making them rhyme only after you have expressed your ideas and feelings.

Ask a classmate to identify your poem's rhyme scheme.

For *Grammar, Vocabulary,* and *Assessment,*
see **Build Language Skills,** pages 674–675.

Extend Your Learning

Listening and Speaking With classmates, hold a **panel discussion** about possible interpretations of a poem in Poetry Collection 1.

- Before you begin, state the purpose of the discussion.
- During the discussion, demonstrate effective listening by paraphrasing the others' comments. Then, express your own ideas clearly.
- Analyze and reflect on ideas while also paying close attention.

Reach a consensus—one acceptable to most people panelists. Present a position statement of this interpretation.

Research and Technology Assemble an **annotated electronic database** of texts by and about Robert Frost. Conduct research to make a list of biographies and criticism about Frost. Identify books Frost wrote and listen to recordings of his work. For each source, write a statement noting the kind and quality of information it offers.

Apply the Skills ■ 665

Vocabulary Builder
Practice

1. True; *diverged* means separated.
2. False; *warp* means to distort.
3. True; *bafflement* means puzzlement.
4. False; *depravity* means corruption.

Adding Words to Your Vocabulary
Sample answers:

1. The old highway *separated* from the new one just past Main Street.
2. The stories he told thoroughly *distort* the truth.
3. His *confusion* about the situation was clear.
4. Police try to prevent *corruption* in society.

Writing

- To give students guidance for writing a poem, give them **Support for Writing** for Poetry Collection 2, p. 152 in *Unit 4 Resources.*
- To evaluate students' poems, use the Poem rubrics, pp. 65–66 in *General Resources.* In addition, you might evaluate for how well students develop original ideas and imagery.

Six Traits Focus

✔	Ideas	✔	Word Choice
	Organization		Sentence Fluency
	Voice		Conventions

Build Language Skills

Go to pp. 674–675 for vocabulary and grammar lessons and assessment practice.

Extend Your Learning

The **Support for Extend Your Learning** page (*Unit 4 Resources,* p. 153) provides guided note-taking opportunities to help students complete the Extend Your Learning activities.

Assessment Resources

The following resources can be used to assess students' knowledge and skills.

Unit 4 Resources
  Selection Test A, pp. 155–157
  Selection Test B, pp. 158–160

Go Online
Assessment Students may use the **Self-test** to prepare for **Selection Test A** or
Selection Test B.

Go Online
Research **For:** An additional research activity
Visit: www.PHSchool.com
Web Code: epd-7407
For another research activity to extend students' learning, give students this Web Code.

665

Teaching notes for Literary Analysis, Reading Skill, and Vocabulary Builder for this selection begin on p. 656.

❸ Connecting to the Literature

- Model use of the expressive vocabulary students are asked to use with these examples:

  1. An important period in life is when children begin to *acquire* language.

  2. An important period is in adolescence, when the body begins to *alter* in appearance.

  3. The next most important period is when young adults *cease* being dependent upon parents.

  4. Independence from parents will often *coincide* with choosing a career, one of the most important periods.

  5. Early middle age is an important period, when people *embody* the wisdom and experience of their earlier years.

- Help students further develop their expressive vocabulary by providing these words: *aspect, circumstance, comprehend, heredity,* and *reluctant.* Encourage students to use these words as they discuss the poetry collection.

Concept Connector ➡

Students will reconsider their ideas after reading these poems.

Go Online For additional information
——Author Link—— about Robert Frost, E. E. Cummings, and William Shakespeare, have students type in the Web Code, select the first letter of the poet's last name, and then select the poet.

Poetry

Build Understanding • *Poetry Collection 2*

❸ Connecting to the Literature

Reading/Writing Connection In "The Seven Ages of Man," one of Shakespeare's characters says that people play many different roles during their lives—taking on different identities, attitudes, relationships, and responsibilities at different ages. Make a list of what you think are the seven most important periods or ages in a person's life and give a reason for each. Use at least three of these words: *acquire, alter, cease, coincide, embody.*

Review
For **Literary Analysis, Reading Skill,** and **Vocabulary Builder,** see pages 656–657.

Meet the Authors

Robert **Frost** (1874–1963)

Fire and Ice (p. 667)
Like the title of his poem "Fire and Ice," Robert Frost seemed warm to some people, cold to other people. All agreed, however, that poetry came first in his life. Frost produced a large body of work and became the most popular American poet of his time, winning four Pulitzer Prizes.

E. E. **Cummings** (1894–1962)

maggie and milly and molly and may (p. 668)
Born in Cambridge, Massachusetts, Edward Estlin Cummings graduated from Harvard University. Both as poet and playwright, Cummings became notorious for his unconventional style, which reflected his individualistic outlook. Much of his work is playful and lyrical, and he often disregarded rules of grammar, spelling, and punctuation.

William **Shakespeare** (1564–1616)

The Seven Ages of Man (p. 671)
Shakespeare forged a perfect blend of high drama and exalted language. He wrote more than three dozen plays, and because of the timelessness of his themes and the beauty of his language, lines from his plays are quoted more often than those of any other writer. "The Seven Ages of Man" is considered one of his best speeches. (For more on William Shakespeare, see page 726.)

Go Online
——Author Link——
For: More about these authors
Visit: www.PHSchool.com
Web Code: epe-9412

666 ■ *Poetry*

666

FIRE AND ICE

❶
❷

Robert Frost

Some say the world will end in fire,
Some say in ice.
From what I've tasted of desire
I hold with those who favor fire.
5 But if it had to perish twice,
❸ I think I know enough of hate
To say that for destruction ice
Is also great
And would <u>suffice</u>.

Vocabulary Builder
suffice (sə fīs´) v. be
enough

Fire and Ice ■ 667

❶ Motivation

Prepare an Anticipation Guide (*General Resources,* pp. 8–10) with the following statements:

• Scientists are able to predict how the world will end.

• Desire is a stronger emotion than hate.

• The kinds of playthings you choose are clues to what kind of person you are.

• All human beings go through pre-determined stages of life.

Give students a copy of the prepared Anticipation Guide and have students mark their responses in the Me column. Have students discuss the statements in pairs or groups and mark the Guides again in the Group column.

Concept Connector ➡

Students will return to the Anticipation Guide after completing this poetry collection.

Learning Modalities
Visual/Spatial Learners

Have students preview the visuals that accompany the poems before reading. Encourage them to make predictions about each poem based on the accompanying artwork.

❷ About the Selections

The speaker in "Fire and Ice" considers two possible ends to the world. In "maggie and milly and molly and may," each character makes a self-discovery. In "The Seven Ages of Man," from the play *As You Like It,* the speaker traces the journey of all people from the cradle to the grave.

❸ Critical Thinking
Interpret

• Have students reread lines 3–4 and 6–8.

• **Ask** students what the speaker is suggesting by linking desire and hate to fire and ice.
Possible response: The world will die from either too much warm feeling—passion or desire—or too much cold feeling—hate or indifference.

Differentiated
Instruction Solutions for All Learners

Support for Below-Level Students [L1, L2]

Unit 4 Resources
  Vocabulary Warm-up Word Lists, p. 161
  Vocabulary Warm-up Practice, p. 162
  Reading Warm-up A, p. 163
  Selection Test A, pp. 173–175

Graphic Organizer Transparencies
  Reading Skill Graphic Organizer Transparency B, p. 151

Reader's Notebook

Reader's Notebook: Adapted Version

Support for English Learners [EL]

Unit 4 Resources
  Vocabulary Warm-up Word Lists, p. 161
  Vocabulary Warm-up Practice, p. 162
  Reading Warm-up A, p. 163

Reader's Notebook: English Learner's Version

Listening to Literature Audio CD

667

❹ Literary Analysis
Rhyme

• Read the poem to students. Ask students to identify some pairs of rhyming words in the poem.
Answer: Some rhyming words are *may/day, stone/alone, me/sea.*

• **Ask** students which two lines in the poem contain a slant rhyme.
Answer: The two lines are 5–6, with the words *star/were.*

• **Ask** students to respond to the Literary Analysis question: What type of rhyme does Cummings use in the first and last stanzas?
Answer: Cummings uses exact end rhyme in the first and last stanzas.

maggie and milly and molly and may

E. E. Cummings

maggie and milly and molly and may
went down to the beach (to play one day)

and maggie discovered a shell that sang
so sweetly she couldn't remember her troubles, and

5 milly befriended a stranded star
❹ whose rays five <u>languid</u> fingers were;

and molly was chased by a horrible thing
which raced sideways while blowing bubbles: and

may came home with a smooth round stone
10 as small as a world and as large as alone.

❺ For whatever we lose (like a you or a me)
it's always ourselves we find in the sea

Vocabulary Builder
languid (lan´ gwid)
adj. drooping; weak

Literary Analysis
Rhyme What type of rhyme does Cummings use in the first and last stanzas?

❻ ▶ **Critical Viewing** How well does this photograph illustrate the "stranded star" in the poem? **[Evaluate]** *maggie and milly and molly and may* 669

- **Ask** students whether they have held a shell to their ear to hear a rushing sound. Was that sound actually the crashing of the sea? Could the sound be described as the singing of the shell?

- Have students review the poem. **Ask:** What does the poet mean by "a shell that sang"? **Possible response:** The poet probably intends both a literal and metaphoric meaning. Maggie is so transported by her experience of the shell that she forgets her day-to-day preoccupations.

- Have students read lines 11–12. **Ask** them how it is possible for people to both lose themselves and find themselves. Then, have volunteers interpret the meaning of the passage. **Possible response:** Losing "a you or a me" means putting aside one's ordinary preoccupations; finding "ourselves" indicates finding one's true or larger self through communing with nature.

❻ Critical Viewing

Possible response: This is a good illustration of the "stranded star" since it is lying on a beach out of the water, and it has extended its "five languid fingers."

Differentiated
Instruction   Solutions for All Learners

Support for English Learners
Help guide these students through this set of poems by reviewing the vocabulary builder words and the footnotes with them. Focus particular attention on "The Seven Ages of Man," which may be especially difficult for students. Then play the **Listening to Literature Audio CD.** Give students an opportunity to explain their feelings and ideas about each poem.

Strategy for Less Proficient Readers
To give students a model for paraphrasing, show them the **Reading Skill Graphic Organizer B** (*Graphic Organizer Transparencies,* p. 151). Have students pay special attention to "The Seven Ages of Man." The completed graphic organizer will give students insight into the process of paraphrasing. They can use it as a model for writing their own paraphrases as they read.

669

❼ Humanities

The Seven Ages of Man, stained-glass window, Folger Shakespeare Library, Washington, D.C.

Stained glass is a term used for windows or other display pieces composed of small pieces of dyed and painted glass joined with seams of lead and mounted in a metal framework. The art achieved its greatest expression in the Gothic cathedrals of the twelfth through the fourteenth centuries. Use these questions for discussion.

1. The window represents the seven ages of man described by Shakespeare. Why do you think the panels are arranged as they are?

   Answer: They were meant to rise to the fourth age, which was considered the age when a man is "in his prime," and then fall to the seventh age when a man is back on the same level with the first.

2. Do you agree that the fourth age (the soldier) is man's prime? If not, which would you place in that position?

   Sample response: I agree that the fourth age is man's prime. People are at a peak physically as well as mentally.

670 ■ Poetry

❼

The Seven Ages of Man, Folger Shakespeare Library, Washington, D.C.

Vocabulary Development

Vocabulary Knowledge Rating

When students have completed reading and discussing this poetry collection, have them take out their **Vocabulary Knowledge Rating Chart** for these poems. Read the words aloud once more and have students rate their knowledge of the words again in the After Reading column. Clarify any words that are still problematic. Have students write their own definition and example or sentence in the appropriate column. Then have students complete the **Vocabulary Builder Practice** activities on p. 673. Encourage students to use the words in further discussion and written work about these poems. Remind them that they will be accountable for these words on the Selection Test.

The Seven Ages of Man
William Shakespeare

(8)
All the world's a stage,
And all the men and women merely players:[1]
They have their exits and their entrances;
And one man in his time plays many parts,

5   His acts being seven ages. At first the infant,
Mewling[2] and puking in the nurse's arms.
And then the whining schoolboy, with his satchel,
And shining morning face, creeping like snail
Unwillingly to school. And then the lover,

10   Sighing like furnace, with a <u>woeful</u> ballad
Made to his mistress' eyebrow. Then a soldier,
Full of strange oaths, and bearded like the pard,[3]
Jealous in honor,[4] sudden and quick in quarrel,
Seeking the bubble reputation

15   Even in the cannon's mouth. And then the justice,[5]
In fair round belly with good capon[6] lined,
With eyes severe and beard of formal cut,
Full of wise saws and modern instances;[7]
And so he plays his part. The sixth age shifts

20   Into the lean and slippered pantaloon,[8]
With spectacles on nose and pouch on side,
His youthful hose[9] well saved, a world too wide
For his shrunk shank;[10] and his big manly voice,
Turning again toward childish <u>treble</u>, pipes

25   And whistles in his sound. Last scene of all,
That ends this strange eventful history,
Is second childishness, and mere oblivion,
Sans[11] teeth, sans eyes, sans taste, sans everything.

---

1. players actors.
2. mewling (myōōl´ in) v. whimpering; crying weakly.
3. pard (pärd) n. leopard or panther.
4. Jealous in honor very concerned about his honor.
5. justice judge.
6. capon (kā´ pän´) n. roasted chicken.
7. wise saws and modern instances sayings and examples that show the truth of the sayings.
8. pantaloon (pan´ tə lōōn´) n. thin, foolish old man who was a character in old comedies.
9. hose (hōz) n. stockings.
10. shank (shaŋk) n. leg.
11. sans (sanz) prep. without; lacking.

The Seven Ages of Man ■ 671

Literary Analysis
Meter What is the pattern of stressed and unstressed syllables in lines 2–4?

Vocabulary Builder
woeful (wō´ fəl) adj. full of sorrow
treble (treb´ əl) n. high-pitched voice or sound

(9) ◄ Critical Viewing
How do the images in this stained-glass window add to your understanding of the poem? [Relate]

---

(8) Literary Analysis
Meter
- Tell students that "The Seven Ages of Man" is actually a speech delivered by a character in a play.
- Have students review the footnotes, discussing each one. Then, tell students to pay close attention to the meter as you read the poem aloud. You may wish to exaggerate the stressed syllables as you read to help students hear the meter.
- **Ask** students how many stressed syllables they hear in each line. **Answer:** There are five stressed syllables in each line.
- Review with students the discussion of meter on p. 656. Then, write line 17 on the chalkboard, and guide students to scan it, as follows:

  ^   /   ^   /   ^   /
  With eyes / se vere / and beard
  ^   /   ^   /
  / of form / al cut

- Tell students that line 17 is the way most lines in the passage are scanned. However, to keep the meter from becoming monotonous, some lines begin with a stressed syllable, and some lines have extra unstressed syllables.
- **Ask** students to respond to the Literary Analysis question: What is the pattern of stressed and unstressed syllables in lines 2–4? **Answer:** Line 2 has five sets of unstressed/stressed syllables, with the line ending in an unstressed syllable. Line 3 has five sets of unstressed/stressed syllables. Line 4 has five sets of unstressed/stressed syllables, with the exception of the second set or foot, which is a stressed/unstressed set.

▶ **Monitor Progress:** Ask students to identify the pattern of stressed and unstressed syllables in lines 21 and 22.

▶ **Reteach:** If students have difficulty identifying the pattern, have them read the poem aloud and clap when they hear a stressed syllable.

(9) Critical Viewing
Possible response: The images illustrate the stages of life discussed in the poem—infancy, childhood, youth, full manhood, middle age, old age, and extreme old age. The window helps me visualize the ideas the poem describes.

Concept Connector

Anticipation Guide
Have students return to their **Anticipation Guides** and respond to the statements again in the After Reading column. They may do this individually or in their original pairs or groups. Then, lead a class discussion, probing for what students have learned that confirms or invalidates each statement. Encourage students to cite specific details, quotations, or other evidence from the poems to support their responses to each statement.

Connecting to the Literature
Have students compare the sentences they wrote before reading with their thoughts about the most important periods in a person's life. Ask them to explain whether their thoughts have changed and, if so, how.

Reading Skill Graphic Organizer
Have students review the graphic organizers they completed to make and verify prediction while reading. Show them **Reading Skill Graphic Organizer B** (*Graphic Organizer Transparencies*, p. 151) as an example. Then have students share their graphic organizers.

671

1. **Possible response:** "maggie and milly and molly and may" sounds the best when read aloud. It has a lilting meter that makes it fun to read aloud.

2. (a) The speaker associates fire with passion or desire and ice with hatred. (b) Fire is a fitting metaphor for desire because desire "burns." Ice is a fitting metaphor for hate because hate is a "cold" emotion. (c) **Possible response:** People my age often have to deal with desires and with hatreds.

   Another sample answer can be found on **Literary Analysis Graphic Organizer B,** p. 155 in *Graphic Organizer Transparencies.*

3. (a) Maggie discovers a sweetly singing sea shell; Milly finds a stranded starfish; Molly is chased by a crab; May finds a smooth round stone. (b) Each character is drawn to something that reflects her inner wishes or fears.

4. **Possible responses:** Some students may suggest that their perspective is changed, since the stages seem to make sense; others may say that the stages seem to be artificial.

5. Lines 9–10 represent exact rhyme and end rhyme. The words *stone* and *alone* come at the end of the lines, and they are exact rhymes.

6. The words *severe* and *beard* represent internal rhyme and slant rhyme.

7. (a) The rhyme scheme is *abaabcbcb.* (b) In the first four lines, the speaker states how he thinks the world will end; in the last five lines, he presents an alternative ending.

8. (a) "Fire and Ice" has a more regular meter, since it follows the pattern of unstressed/stressed syllables throughout. (b) **Possible response:** The poem with the more regular meter is more enjoyable to read because it has a predictable rhythm.

9. (a) Maggie, Milly, Molly, and May went down to the beach to play one day. Maggie discovered a shell that sang so sweetly she couldn't remember her troubles.

Apply the Skills

Poetry Collection 2

Thinking About the Selections

1. **Respond:** Which poem sounds best when read aloud? Why?

2. Fill out a three-column chart like the one shown. **(a) Recall:** In the first column, identify which emotions the speaker in "Fire and Ice" associates with fire and ice. **(b) Interpret:** In the second column, explain why fire and ice are fitting metaphors for these emotions. **(c) Discuss:** Share your chart with a partner. Then, in the third column, explain how the poem's message applies to teenagers.

What Does It Say?	What Does It Mean?	Why Is It Important?

3. **(a) Recall:** In "maggie and milly and molly and may," what experience does each character have? **(b) Connect:** How does each character's experience support the conclusion in the poem's final line?

4. **Assess:** Does "The Seven Ages of Man" in any way change your perspective about the stages of life? Why or why not?

Literary Analysis

5. Identify two lines in "maggie and milly and molly and may" that illustrate both **exact rhyme** and **end rhyme.** Explain your choices.

6. Which two words in line 17 of "The Seven Ages of Man" illustrate both **slant rhyme** and **internal rhyme?**

7. **(a)** Use letters to identify the **rhyme scheme** in "Fire and Ice." **(b)** In what way does the shift in rhyme scheme midway through the poem help signal a turning point in the poem's message?

8. **(a)** Which poem has lines with a more regular **meter**—"Fire and Ice" or "The Seven Ages of Man"? Explain. **(b)** Which do you find more enjoyable to read—lines with a regular meter or lines with an irregular meter? Explain.

Reading Skill

9. **(a) Paraphrase** the first ten lines of "maggie and milly and molly and may" by rewriting them as a series of sentences. **(b)** In what way does **breaking down long sentences** make this poem's meaning more clear?

QuickReview

Poems at a Glance
"Fire and Ice" examines the destructive power of desire and hate.
"maggie and milly and molly and may" explores the significance of a trip to the sea.
"The Seven Ages of Man" presents a human life as having seven stages.

Go Online
Assessment

For: Self-test
Visit: www.PHSchool.com
Web Code: epa-6410

Rhyme: repetition of sounds at the ends of words; types include *exact rhyme, slant rhyme, end rhyme,* and *internal rhyme*

Rhyme Scheme: a regular pattern of end rhymes
Meter: the rhythmical pattern in a line of poetry
Paraphrasing: restating in your own words what someone else has written or said

Milly befriended a stranded star. Its rays were five languid fingers. Molly was chased by a horrible thing. It raced sideways while blowing bubbles. May came home with a smooth round stone. It was as small as a world and as large as alone. (b) Breaking down long sentences clarifies the meaning because the new, shorter sentences each contain one idea, which makes them easier to follow.

Vocabulary Builder

Practice Decide if each statement is true or false. Then, explain.

1. If something will *suffice*, it will be satisfactory.
2. Coaches hope their players will be *languid* during a game.
3. A *woeful* sight is likely to inspire pity.
4. A *treble* is a deep sound like a foghorn.

Adding Words to Your Vocabulary Using a thesaurus, find a synonym for the italicized words in the Practice. Use each synonym correctly in a sentence. (For more on using a thesaurus, see page R7.)

Writing

Write a **poem** using the same rhyme scheme as a poem in Poetry Collection 2.
- Choose a poem and identify its rhyme scheme.
- Decide on a topic, an event, an experience, or an emotion that you would like to be the subject of your poem.
- Brainstorm for a list of images, details, phrases, or words.
- Draft your lines, making them rhyme only after you have expressed your ideas and feelings.

Ask a classmate to identify your poem's rhyme scheme.

For *Grammar, Vocabulary,* and *Assessment,*
see **Build Language Skills,** pages 674–675.

Extend Your Learning

Listening and Speaking With classmates, hold a **panel discussion** about possible interpretations of a poem in Poetry Collection 2.
- Before you begin, state the purpose of the discussion.
- During the discussion, demonstrate effective listening by paraphrasing the others' comments. Then express your own ideas clearly.
- Analyze and reflect on ideas while following the discussion.

Reach a consensus, one acceptable to most panelists. Present a position statement of this interpretation.

Research and Technology Assemble an **annotated electronic database** of texts by and about Robert Frost. Conduct research to make a list of biographies and criticism about Frost. Identify books Frost wrote and listen to recordings of his work. For each source, write a statement noting the kind and quality of information it offers.

Apply the Skills ■ 673

Go Online
—Research **For:** An additional research activity
Visit: www.PHSchool.com
Web Code: epd-7408
For another research activity to extend students' learning, give students this Web Code.

Vocabulary Builder
Practice

1. True; *suffice* means that it is enough.
2. False; *languid* means weak or droopy.
3. True; *woeful* means sad.
4. False; *treble* means a high-pitched sound.

Adding Words to Your Vocabulary
Sample answers:

1. A light breakfast will *satisfy* me since I'm not feeling well today.
2. I feel unusually *droopy,* as if I did not get enough sleep.
3. Her *sad* expression tells me she is not feeling well either.
4. The *high-pitched* sound of a fire engine is ear-splitting.

Writing

- To give students guidance for writing a poem, give them **Support for Writing** for Poetry Collection 2, p. 168 in *Unit 4 Resources.*
- To evaluate students' poems, use the Poem rubrics, pp. 65–66 in *General Resources.* In addition, you might evaluate for how well students develop original ideas and imagery.

Six Traits Focus

✔	Ideas	✔	Word Choice
	Organization		Sentence Fluency
	Voice		Conventions

Build Language Skills

Go to pages 674–675 for vocabulary and grammar lessons and assessment practice.

Extend Your Learning

The **Support for Extend Your Learning** page (*Unit 4 Resources,* p. 169) provides guided note-taking opportunities to help students complete the Extend Your Learning activities.

Vocabulary Skill

- Introduce the suffixes *-ism* and *-ize*. After students have read the instructional material, have them brainstorm for words that contain these suffixes.
  Possible responses: *materialism, communism, imperialism, colonialism, capitalism; materialize, specialize, motorize, socialize*

- Have students use the dictionary to explain how the meaning of "a condition of being" or "the result of" or "to engage in" or "to cause to be" contributes to the meanings of each of these words.

- Have students complete the Practice activity on this page.

Answers

1. noun; liberalism
2. verb; revolutionize
3. verb; symbolize
4. noun; heroism
5. noun; symbolism

Grammar Lesson

- Point out to students that infinitives require the present tense of the verb; infinitives and infinitive phrases cannot be formed with other verb tenses.

- Have students complete the Practice activity on this page.

Answers

1. to get a statement; The police wanted to see the signed confession from the thief.

2. to chase; Soon there would be no more rabbits to raise.

3. to throw the debris overboard; They wanted to head the boat toward the open sea.

4. to soar over the mountains; The airplane was designed to carry 800 passengers.

5. to pass the test; Asking for help was her last hope to finish the task on time.

W_G **Writing and Grammar, Gold Level**
Students will find further instruction and practice on infinitives and infinitive phrases in Chapter 21, Section 1.

Build Language Skills

Poetry Collection 1 • Poetry Collection 2

Vocabulary Skill

Suffixes The word *witticism* contains the **suffix *-ism*,** which means "a condition of being" or "the result of" and forms nouns. *Witticism* is a noun that means "a clever or witty remark" and is based on *wit* or *witty*.

The **suffix *-ize*,** meaning "to engage in" or "to cause to be," forms verbs. For example, the word *stabilize* is the verb form of the adjective *stable* and means "make stable."

Practice: In the following sentences, decide what part of speech is needed to complete the sentence. Supply a word ending in *-ism* or *-ize*. You may choose a word from the list or supply one of your own. Explain your choices.

heroism   revolutionize   symbolize   symbolism

1. Many people believed his _____ cost him the election.
2. This idea will _____ the system.
3. What do you think we can use to _____ this idea?
4. Her _____ in the face of such great danger made everyone admire her.
5. He liked the _____ in the story.

Grammar Lesson

An **infinitive** is a verb form preceded by the word *to* that acts as a noun, an adjective, or an adverb. An infinitive phrase is an infinitive with its modifiers or complements. Like infinitives, infinitive phrases can function as nouns, adjectives, or adverbs.

> **Infinitive:**
> To play requires patience and practice. (infinitive acting as a noun)
>
> **Infinitive Phrase:**
> Jeanne was not afraid to speak her mind. (infinitive acting as an adverb by modifying *afraid*)

Practice Identify the infinitive or infinitive phrase. Then, rewrite the sentence using a different infinitive or infinitive phrase.

1. The police wanted to get a statement from the owner.
2. Soon there were no more rabbits to chase.
3. They wanted to throw the debris overboard.
4. The airplane was designed to soar over the mountains.
5. Asking for help was her last hope to pass the test.

W_G *Prentice Hall Writing and Grammar Connection: Chapter 21, Section 1*

MorePractice

For more practice with infinitives and infinitive phrases, see the Grammar Handbook, p. R44.

Teaching Resources

The following resources can be used to enrich or extend the instruction for Build Language Skills.

Unit 4 Resources
   Build Language Skills: Vocabulary: Suffixes, p. 171
   Build Grammar Skills: Infinitives and Infinitive Phrases, p. 172

Monitor Your Progress

Assessment Practice

Reading Skill: Paraphrase

Directions: *Read the passage. Then, answer the questions.*

(1) No wonder that Alexander carried the *Iliad* with him on his expeditions in a precious casket. (2) A written word is the choicest of relics. (3) It is something at once more intimate with us and more universal than any other work of art. (4) It is the work of art nearest to life itself. (5) It may be translated into every language, and not only be read but actually breathed from all human lips;—not be represented on canvas or in marble only, but be carved out of the breath of life itself. (6) The symbol of an ancient man's thought becomes a modern man's speech. (7) Two thousand summers have imparted to the monuments of Grecian literature, as to her marbles, only a maturer golden and autumnal tint, for they have carried their own serene and celestial atmosphere into all lands to protect them against the corrosion of time. (8) Books are the treasured wealth of the world and the fit inheritance of generations and nations.

—from *Walden* by Henry David Thoreau

1. The words "maturer golden and autumnal tint" can be paraphrased as
   - **A** ancient and yellowed.
   - **B** better and aged.
   - **C** old and irrelevant.
   - **D** important and overlooked.

2. The word "it" in sentence 4 refers to
   - **A** Alexander.
   - **B** a precious casket.
   - **C** the written word.
   - **D** a relic.

3. Sentence 7 can be briefly paraphrased as
   - **A** time makes books better.
   - **B** Grecian literature is important.
   - **C** the corrosion of time applies to literature.
   - **D** Grecian marble and Grecian literature are comparable.

4. Which of the following best states the main idea of the passage?
   - **A** Sentence 1
   - **B** Sentence 4
   - **C** Sentence 7
   - **D** Sentence 8

Timed Writing: Interpretation [Critical Stance]

Interpret Robert Frost's "The Road Not Taken" or "Fire and Ice." Identify the theme, and support your interpretation with evidence from the text. **(40 minutes)**

Writing Workshop: *Work in Progress*

Response to Literature

Review your notes, and write a one-sentence conclusion about that character. Use that sentence as the thesis for your response to literature.

Build Language Skills ■ 675

Answers

Reading Skill: Paraphrasing
1. B
2. C
3. A
4. D

Timed Writing

- Tell students that when they write an interpretation of poetry, they should consider the poem's theme and the role that figurative language plays. They must support their interpretation with examples from the poem.

- Have students review the two poems and identify the major theme in each one. Then, have students select the poem that they wish to use.

- Have students note the reasons for their choice of theme and list the lines from the text that provide support.

- Then, have students write their interpretations, supporting their ideas with sufficient evidence from the poem.

- Suggest that students allow ten minutes for selecting and reviewing the poem, twenty-five minutes for writing the interpretation, and five minutes for reviewing and revising.

- Assess students' interpretations based on the accuracy of their discussion of the theme, the reasons for their choices, and their textual support.

Writing Workshop
Work in Progress

Response to Literature

- Have students go to their portfolios and take out the work they have completed so far on this assignment. Remind them that this work may be used in the **Writing Workshop** on Response to Literature on p. 688.

- Guide students in completing the **Work-in-Progress** assignment on this page. When students have completed this activity, have them keep it in their portfolios. They will use is as they continue the **Work in Progress**.

675

Comparing Literary Works • Forms of Lyric Poetry

Meeting Your Standards

Students will

1. analyze and respond to lyric poetry.

2. compare the effects of different forms of lyric poetry.

3. write a comparison of lyric poems.

See TeacherExpress™/Lesson View for a detailed lesson plan for Comparing Literary Works.

Literary Analysis

❶ Lyric Poetry

- Remind students that there are three main types of poetry: lyric, narrative, and dramatic. Lyric poetry focuses on the emotions and observations of a single speaker.

- Tell students that lyric poetry is musical. Explain that the word *lyric* is derived from *lyre,* an instrument used in ancient Greece.

- Tell students that lyric poetry often uses imagery, which is language that appeals to the five senses.

❷ Comparing Lyric Forms: Sonnet, Haiku, and Free Verse

- Explain that there are many different lyric forms. The selections that students will read include one sonnet, three haikus, and two free verse poems.

- Explain that different lyric forms yield different effects. Sonnets are highly formal and are often written as love poems. Haiku, which are also highly formal, usually use imagery from nature to describe an emotion. Free verse poems are less formal, and so include a wider range of subjects.

- Give students a copy of **Comparing Lyric Poems Graphic Organizer A** (*Graphic Organizer Transparencies,* p. 156). Have them complete it as they read and compare the selections.

676

❶ Lyric Poetry

Lyric poetry is poetry with a musical quality in which the author expresses the thoughts and feelings of a single speaker. Unlike the author of a narrative poem, the author of a lyric poem does not try to tell a complete story. Instead, the poet describes an emotion or a mood, often by using vivid imagery, or language that appeals to the senses. A lyric poem is relatively short and in it, the poet usually achieves a single, unified effect.

❷ Comparing Forms of Lyric Poetry: Sonnet, Haiku, and Free Verse

There are a variety of lyric forms that can create different effects:

- A **sonnet** is a fourteen-line poem that is usually written in iambic pentameter and usually rhymes. Two common sonnet types are the Italian, or Petrarchan, and the English, or Shakespearean. The chart shown describes an English, or Shakespearean, sonnet.

- A **haiku** is an unrhymed Japanese verse form arranged into three lines of five, seven, and five syllables. The author of a haiku often uses a striking image from nature to convey a strong emotion.

- A **free verse** poem does not follow a regular pattern of rhythm or rhyme. The author of free verse employs sound and rhythmic devices, such as alliteration and repetition, and may even use rhyme—but not in a regular pattern.

As you read, think about ways in which the form of the poem helps shape or emphasize the poet's meaning.

Shakespearean Sonnet

formatting: usually presented with no spaces between the stanzas, which are unified by their distinct ideas and rhyme schemes

three quatrains (four-line stanzas): each explores a different aspect of the poem's theme

final couplet: the two lines at the end of a sonnet present a concluding comment

rhyme scheme: the lines in each quatrain follow a regular pattern of *abab cdcd efef gg*

Vocabulary Builder

Women

- **stout** (stout) *adj.* sturdy (p. 678) *The wrestler was strong and had a __stout__ build.*

I Hear America Singing

- **intermission** (in′ tər mish′ən) *n.* any kind of break; more specifically, a break during a performance (p. 681) *Although I was thirsty, I waited until __intermission__ to get a drink.*

Sonnet 30

- **woes** (wōz) *n.* great sorrows (p. 682) *Her troubles and __woes__ are a real burden.*

- **wail** (wāl) *n.* lament; cry of deep sorrow (p. 682) *When the child saw her broken doll, she let out a prolonged __wail__.*

Vocabulary Development

Vocabulary Knowledge Rating
Create a **Vocabulary Knowledge Rating Chart** with the selection vocabulary and expressive vocabulary for each poem. Give students a copy. Introduce the words by reading them aloud and having students mark their rating in the Before Reading column. Urge them to be alert to these words as they read and discuss the poems because they will rate their knowledge of the words again after they finish.

If you wish, you may tally how many students know (or think they know) a word to gauge how much instruction you need to provide. As students read, point out the words and their context.

Build Understanding

❸ Connecting to the Literature

Reading/Writing Connection These poems address a wide range of topics. List subjects that you think are suited to poetry. For each, write one sentence explaining why. Use three of these words: *signify, elaborate, emerge, stress, embrace.*

Meet the Authors

Alice **Walker** (b. 1944)

Alice Walker was born in Eatonton, Georgia. From the age of eight, she kept a journal and wrote poems. Today, Walker is an acclaimed novelist, short story writer, essayist, and poet. Her many works include the novel *The Color Purple,* which was made into a popular film.

Bashō (1644–1694) and **Chiyojo** (1703–1775)

One of the greatest Japanese poets, Bashō raised the haiku from a comic form to a high art. When he was young, he lived in luxury as the companion to the son of a lord. Later, he lived alone and devoted himself to haiku. Chiyojo was the wife of a samurai's servant. When her husband died, she became a nun and began studying poetry.

Walt **Whitman** (1819–1892)

American poet Walt Whitman celebrated the freedom of the individual and sang the praises of democracy. He published his first book of poetry, *Leaves of Grass,* at his own expense. Although it was a commercial failure, today *Leaves of Grass* is considered one of the most influential volumes in the history of American literature.

William **Shakespeare** (1564–1616)

English poet and playwright William Shakespeare is one of the most famous and beloved writers of all time. Experts believe Shakespeare possessed the largest vocabulary of any writer in history. His nearly forty plays, including *Romeo and Juliet, Hamlet,* and *Othello,* are still performed around the world, almost 400 years after his death.

Go **Online**
Author Link

For: More about the authors
Visit: www.PHSchool.com
Web Code: epe-9413

Women / Three Haiku / I Hear America Singing / Sonnet 30 ■ 677

---

❸ Connecting to the Literature

- Model use of the expressive vocabulary students are asked to use with these examples:

  1. Poets use interesting metaphors to *signify* death.
  2. Only poetic language can *elaborate* the emotions associated with marriage.
  3. Over centuries, we have seen poetry *emerge* as the preferred medium for discussing love.
  4. Poetry can adequately *stress* the drama involved in everyday life.
  5. Poetry can *embrace* the conflicting emotions involved in a serious illness.

- Help students further develop their expressive vocabulary by providing these words: *beautify, represent, reveal,* and *value.* Encourage students to use these words as they discuss the selections.

Go **Online**
Author Link For additional information about Alice Walker, Bashō, Chiyojo, Walt Whitman, and William Shakespeare, have students type in the Web Code and then select the poet.

Teaching Resources

The following resources can be used to enrich, extend, or differentiate the instruction for Comparing Literary Works.

Unit 4 Resources, pp. 179–185

Graphic Organizer Transparencies, pp. 156–159

Listening to Literature Audio CD

❶ Background

Desegregation In 1954, when the Supreme Court ruled against segregation, there were 17 states in which segregation was mandated. Three years later, only nine states had even started the process of desegregation. Segregation remained a problem in the South well into the 1960s.

❷ Motivation

Provide students with the following template, which represents the syllables of a haiku:

— — — — —

— — — — — — —

— — — — —

Remind students that haiku uses imagery from nature to convey emotion. Ask students to think of aspects of nature that bring them feelings of joy, surprise, or wonder. Have students write haiku about one of these topics.

Concept Connector ➡

Students will follow up on this activity after completing the poems.

❸ About the Selections

In "Women," the speaker recognizes that her way has been paved by African American women of previous generations. The haiku by Bashō and Chiyojo create dominant impressions in the reader's mind with one or two striking images from nature. "I Hear America Singing" celebrates the common working men and women of America. In "Sonnet 30," Shakespeare describes the world of memories and friendship.

❹ Literary Analysis
Lyric Poetry

• Have a volunteer read the bracketed passage. **Ask** students to identify the underlying meaning of the phrase "battered down doors." **Possible response:** The underlying meaning refers to the efforts these women made to fight limitations on African Americans' civil rights and educational and other opportunities.

• **Ask** the Literary Analysis question: Which words and images convey the women's determination to help their children? Explain.

The Quiltmakers, Paul Goodnight, Color Circle Art Publishing Inc.

Women
ALICE WALKER

❶
❷
❸

Background In "Women," the speaker praises African American women who fought for public school desegregation in the American South. Until the 1950s, African American and white students attended different schools in the South. In 1954, the U.S. Supreme Court ruled that segregated public schooling was unconstitutional.

They were women then
My mama's generation
Husky of voice—<u>Stout</u> of
Step
5 With fists as well as
Hands
How they battered down
Doors
And ironed
10 Starched white
Shirts
How they led
Armies
❹ Headragged Generals
15 Across mined
Fields
Booby-trapped
Ditches
To discover books
20 Desks
A place for us
How they knew what we
Must know
Without knowing a page
25 Of it
Themselves.

❺ ▲ Critical Viewing
Is the artist's attitude toward these women similar to the one expressed by the poet? **[Compare]**

Vocabulary Builder
stout (stout) *adj.* sturdy

Literary Analysis
Lyric Poetry Which words and images convey the women's determination to help their children? Explain.

Answer: The speaker describes the women as having husky voices, stout steps, and strong fists. This military imagery shows that the women were willing to fight for their children.

❺ Critical Viewing

Answer: The artist appears to honor and respect the women; this parallels the poet's attitude in "Women."

678

THREE HAIKU

Daniel C. Buchanan, translator

Temple bells die out.
The fragrant blossoms remain.
A perfect evening!
                    —Bashō

Dragonfly catcher,
How far have you gone today
In your wandering?
                    —Chiyojo

Bearing no flowers,
I am free to toss madly
Like the willow tree.
                    —Chiyojo

Thinking About the Selections

1. **Respond:** Which of these poems do you like best? Why?

2. **(a) Recall:** In "Women," what do the women want to "discover" and for whom? **(b) Interpret:** In lines 22–26, why is the women's knowledge so remarkable?

3. **(a) Recall:** In Bashō's haiku, what dies out and what remains? **(b) Interpret:** To which senses does Bashō's haiku appeal? **(c) Analyze:** Why are these senses most appropriate in a poem about evening?

4. **Assess:** Would the first Chiyojo haiku be as effective if it were written as a statement rather than as a question? Explain.

5. **Explain:** In the second Chiyojo haiku, what impression does the speaker convey by comparing herself to a willow tree?

Three Haiku ■ 679

❻ Background

Haiku The haiku form has endured across many centuries. It was first used by Buddhist monks in the 1400s. Over the next several centuries, haiku became wildly popular. More recently, haiku has influenced Western literary movements such as Imagism, a group of early twentieth-century poets led by Ezra Pound.

❼ Literary Analysis
Lyric Poetry

• Read aloud the bracketed haiku. Remind students that haiku uses imagery from nature.

• Ask students to identify the central images in this poem.
  Answer: The ringing of the bells and the fragrant blossoms are the central images.

ASSESS

Answers

1. **Possible response:** Some students might like the powerful message in "Women" and agree that education is the key to success. Other students might prefer the images of nature in the haiku.

2. (a) The women want to discover books—that is, education—for their children. (b) It is remarkable that the women knew that education was the key to their children's success even though they lacked it themselves.

3. (a) The bells die out and the fragrant blossoms remain. (b) The bells appeal to the sense of hearing and the blossoms appeal to the sense of smell. (c) Since you can not see at night, it is more appropriate to appeal to the senses of hearing and smell.

4. The question form is more effective. Its open ending seems an appropriate way to discuss a wanderer.

5. The poet may want to give the impression that she has no responsibilities or burdens.

Differentiated Instruction   Solutions for All Learners

Accessibility at a Glance
Use this information to guide your teaching of "Women" and "Three Haiku."

Context	"Women" reflects the struggles of African Americans in twentieth century America. The topics of the haiku are timeless.
Language	Conversational
Concept Level	More accessible
Literary Merit	Contemporary author and poet; noted Japanese poets

Leaves of Grass Although it was first published in 1855, it seems likely that Whitman had been working on *Leaves of Grass,* from which this poem comes, since the late 1840s. When it was first published, the collection was widely criticized because, among other things, it was written in free verse. Ironically, Whitman's work went on to inspire countless poets who eventually popularized free verse.

680 ■ Poetry

Vocabulary Development

Expressive Vocabulary
As students are discussing the selections, encourage them to use the expressive vocabulary presented earlier. You might encourage them with sentence starters like these:

1. In haiku, imagery from nature is used to *signify* . . .
2. The theme that Whitman seems to *elaborate* . . .
3. In "Women," the mothers think that education will help their children *emerge* . . .
4. Through the repetition of the word *singing,* the speaker of "I Hear American Singing" seems to *stress* . . .
5. In the second haiku by Chiyojo, the speaker seems to *embrace* . . .

I Hear America Singing ❽

Walt Whitman

❾
I hear America singing, the varied carols I hear,
Those of mechanics, each one singing his as it should be
    blithe and strong,
The carpenter singing his as he measures his plank or beam,
The mason singing his as he makes ready for work, or leaves
    off work,
5 The boatman singing what belongs to him in his boat, the
    deckhand singing on the steamboat deck,
The shoemaker singing as he sits on his bench, the hatter
    singing as he stands,
The wood-cutter's song, the ploughboy's on his way in the
    morning, or at noon <u>intermission</u> or at sundown,
The delicious singing of the mother, or of the young wife at
    work, or of the girl sewing or washing,
Each singing what belongs to him or her and to none else,
10 The day what belongs to the day—at night the party of young
    fellows, robust, friendly,
Singing with open mouths their strong melodious songs.

Literary Analysis
Lyric Poetry Which word in the opening line helps identify this as a lyric poem?

Vocabulary Builder
intermission (in′tər mish′ən) *n.* any kind of break; more specifically, a break during a performance

Thinking About the Selection

1. **Respond:** Which of the "songs" speaks to you the most? Explain.
2. **(a) Recall:** Identify three singers Whitman names. **(b) Interpret:** What does Whitman mean when he says he hears their songs?
3. **(a) Recall:** When does the mason sing? The ploughboy? **(b) Distinguish:** Why do you think Whitman pictures the American worker in various situations and times of day?
4. **(a) Generalize:** What kind of nation does Whitman depict? **(b) Speculate:** Do you think modern-day America is similar to the world Whitman presents? Why or why not?

I Hear America Singing ■ 681

❾ Literary Analysis
Lyric Poetry

- Read aloud the bracketed passage. Remind students that lyric poetry has identifiable characteristics.

- **Ask** the Literary Analysis question: Which word in the opening lines helps identify this as a lyric poem? **Answer:** The use of the personal pronoun "I" suggests that this poem will express the feelings and thoughts of a single speaker. The concept of "singing" further relates the poem to lyric poetry.

- Remind students that the poem is free verse because it does not follow any recognizable meter or rhyme scheme.

ASSESS

Answers

1. Students' responses will vary depending on interests. Explanations will probably connect "songs" with hobbies, acquaintances, or goals.

2. (a) "Singers" include mechanics, carpenter, mason, boatman, deckhand, shoemaker, hatter, wood-cutter, ploughboy, mother, wife, girl, and party of young fellows. (b) He means that he is aware of the pleasure they take in being alive, being busy, and having work that they like.

3. (a) The mason sings in the morning or evening. The ploughboy sings in the morning, at noon, or at sundown. (b) Whitman understands the rhythm and flow of life. It is these daily changes that create the rhythm of the "songs."

4. (a) Whitman depicts a strong, happy, hard-working nation. He also shows that this is a land of opportunities, that all work is honorable, and that everyone contributes to making the country strong. (b) All the jobs that Whitman lists still exist, but not so many people today work with their hands. Students may debate whether modern workers share the same eagerness and enjoyment in their tasks that Whitman depicts in his poem.

The Sonnets Altogether, Shakespeare wrote 154 sonnets. While scholars have not been able to pinpoint exactly when they were written, most people agree that they were all produced in the 1590s. Interestingly, more than 120 of his sonnets (including "Sonnet 30") are addressed to an unidentified man.

⑪ **Critical Thinking**
Evaluate

- Ask students to read the entire sonnet. Ask them what the last two lines in this poem are called.
  Answer: They are a rhymed couplet.

- Then, ask students how the meaning of this rhymed couplet differs from the first twelve lines.
  Answer: In the first twelve lines, the speaker laments all the losses and sorrows in his past; in the last two lines, the speaker celebrates friendship.

Concept Connector

Allow students to revisit the haiku they wrote. Tell them that their haiku, like the selections, should include references to both nature and emotion. After allowing time for revision, ask volunteers to share their poems with the class.

ASSESS

Answers

1. Students should support their answers with their ideas about friendship.

2. (a) He refers to his memories as "old woes." (b) It means "to cry." (c) Thinking of sad times in the past causes the speaker to cry.

3. (a) The speaker is reviewing the "costs" of past woes. (b) Reviewing the past is part of the grieving process.

4. Students should share their opinions on the ability of friendship to compensate for sorrows and losses.

SONNET 30 ⑩

WILLIAM SHAKESPEARE

When to the sessions of sweet silent thought
I summon up remembrance of things past,
I sigh the lack of many a thing I sought,
And with old <u>woes</u> new <u>wail</u> my dear times waste:[1]
5 Then can I drown an eye, unused to flow,
For precious friends hid in death's dateless[2] night,
⑪ And weep afresh love's long since cancelled woe,
And moan the expense[3] of many a vanished sight:
Then can I grieve at grievances foregone,[4]
10 And heavily from woe to woe tell o'er[5]
The sad account of fore-bemoanèd moan,[6]
Which I new pay as if not paid before.
But if the while I think on thee, dear friend,
All losses are restored and sorrows end.

---

1. **And . . . waste** and by grieving anew for past sorrows, ruin the precious present.
2. **dateless** endless.
3. **expense** loss.
4. **foregone** past and done with.
5. **tell o'er** count up.
6. **fore-bemoanèd moan** sorrows suffered in the past.

Vocabulary Builder
woes (wōz) *n.* great sorrows
wail (wāl) *n.* lament; cry of deep sorrow

Thinking About the Selection

1. **Respond:** Would you want the speaker as a friend? Explain.

2. **(a) Recall:** In line 4, how does the speaker refer to his memories?
   (b) Infer: In line 5, what does "drown an eye" mean?
   (c) Analyze Cause and Effect: What causes the speaker to "drown an eye"? Why?

3. **(a) Clarify:** What is the speaker describing in lines 10–12?
   (b) Relate: Why might someone spend time doing this?

4. **Evaluate:** Do you agree with the idea of friendship expressed at the end of the poem? Why or why not?

682 ■ *Poetry*

Vocabulary Development

Vocabulary Knowledge Rating
When students have completed reading and discussing the selections, have them take out their **Vocabulary Rating Chart.** Read the words aloud once more and have students rate their knowledge of the words again in the After Reading column. Clarify any words that are still problematic. Have students write their own definition and example or sentence in the appropriate column. Then, have students complete the **Vocabulary Builder Practice** activities on p. 683. Encourage students to use the words in further discussion and written work about the poems. Remind them that they will be accountable for these words on the selection test.

Apply the Skills

Women • Three Haiku • I Hear America Singing • Sonnet 30

Comparing Forms of Lyric Poetry

1. In his **sonnet**, Shakespeare presents an idea or a question in the first quatrain (four lines), explores the idea in the next two quatrains, and reaches a conclusion in the final couplet. Use a chart like the one shown to analyze the content of "Sonnet 30."

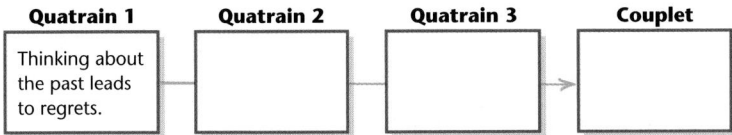

Quatrain 1	Quatrain 2	Quatrain 3	Couplet
Thinking about the past leads to regrets.			

2. Explain how "Three Haiku" fit the definition of the **haiku** form.

3. Both "I Hear America Singing" and "Women" are **free verse**, with a form imposed by the poet. **(a)** What is similar about the emotions conveyed in these poems? **(b)** Which poem follows more of a pattern? Explain.

Writing to Compare Literary Works

In an essay, compare the ways the different lyric forms affect the meanings of these poems. Choose two poems and structures to discuss. Use these questions to get started:

- How would the meaning of "Sonnet 30" be different without the final two lines?
- How does the strict form of the haiku help to capture the feeling of a brief moment in time?
- If "Women" were written with a strict form instead of in free verse, would the message be as strong?
- How does the loose, free feeling of Whitman's verse help him to express his vision of America?

Vocabulary Builder

Practice Based on each situation described below, write a sentence using a word from the vocabulary list on page 676.

1. waiting to make a phone call
2. mourning a friend's move across the country
3. sharing one's worries with a teacher
4. watching weight lifters

Women / Three Haiku / I Hear America Singing / Sonnet 30 ■ 683

QuickReview

Lyric Poetry: poetry which presents imagery and musical language to express the thoughts and feelings of a single speaker

Sonnet: a fourteen-line poem written in rhyming iambic pentameter; the *Shakespearean sonnet* is one type

Haiku: unrhymed Japanese verse form that consists of five, seven, and five syllables

Free Verse: poetry that does not follow a regular pattern of meter or rhyme

Go Online
Assessment
For: Self-test
Visit: www.PHSchool.com
Web Code: epa-6411

Comparing Lyric Poems

1. **Quatrain 2:** Thinking about the past can cause tears. **Quatrain 3:** The sadness of things that have happened in the past does not necessarily fade with time. **Couplet:** Friendship can help overcome sadness.

2. A haiku has three unrhymed lines. The first and last lines have five syllables; the middle line has seven. "Three Haiku" follow these formal requirements.

3. (a) Both poems sing the praises of people who believe in America and the idea of success. (b) "I Hear America Singing" follows more of a pattern because of its extensive use of repetition.

Writing to Compare Literary Works

- Remind students that while all of the selections are lyric poems, their different forms have different effects on the reader.

- Have students use the bulleted questions to develop their ideas. Tell them to organize their essays by addressing one question at a time.

- Encourage students to incorporate the expressive vocabulary words: *signify, elaborate, emerge, stress, embrace.*

Six Traits Focus

✔	Ideas	✔	Word Choice
✔	Organization		Sentence Fluency
	Voice		Conventions

Vocabulary Builder
Possible responses:

1. I waited until the *intermission* to call Mary.
2. The child *wailed* and stamped her feet to indicate her displeasure.
3. I called Jay late last night to share my *woes.*
4. I watched as the *stout* weightlifter picked up an enormous barbell.

Assessment Resources

The following resources can be used to assess students' knowledge and skills.

Unit 4 Resources
Selection Test A, pp. 186–188
Selection Test B, pp. 189–191

Go Online
Assessment Students may use the **Self-test** to prepare for **Selection Test A** or **Selection Test B.**

Reading and Vocabulary Skills Review

Applying Reading Skill

Read the passage with students. Remind students that paraphrasing rewrites the information in their own or other words. Guide students in finding the correct answer for item 1. Then have them complete the remaining items on their own. If necessary, have students reread the instruction on p. 626 before having them complete the remaining items on their own.

Applying Vocabulary Skills

Review the suffixes -age, -ism, and -ize. Then have students answer the vocabulary questions. If they have trouble, review the instruction on p. 627.

Tips for Test Taking

Students are often intimidated when asked to read a long passage or a passage with difficult vocabulary on a standardized test. Explain that a good strategy for addressing a long or difficult passage is to paraphrase it. Writing the main ideas of the passage in students' own words will help them overcome the obstacle of a passage being "too hard" and help students focus on the main ideas. Though some of the vocabulary may be unfamiliar to them, students can make inferences based on what they do understand to achieve a basic understanding of the text.

Reading

Directions: *Read the selection. Then, answer the questions.*

> The poetry of earth is never dead:
> When all the birds are faint with the hot sun,
> And hide in cooling trees, a voice will run
> 4 From hedge to hedge about the new-mown mead;
> That is the Grasshopper's—he takes the lead
> In summer luxury,—he has never done
> With his delights; for when tired out with fun
> 8 He rests at ease beneath some pleasant weed.

—from *On the Grasshopper and the Cricket* by John Keats

1. What is taking place in lines 2–5?
  A While birds sit in cool trees, the Grasshopper sings.
  B Birds are fainting in the sun and you can hear someone mowing the field.
  C Birds are fainting, and the Grasshopper takes the lead.
  D A Grasshopper is hiding from the heat.

2. Line 8 can be paraphrased as
  A the Grasshopper hides from the birds.
  B the birds rest in the weeds.
  C the Grasshopper rests in the weeds.
  D the weeds are a good hiding place.

Directions: *Read the passage, and then answer the questions.*

(1) John Keats was born in London, England, on October 31, 1795. (2) His parents died when he was young, and Keats was brought up by relatives. (3) Leigh Hunt, an editor of the *Examiner,* published the first sonnets by Keats and introduced him to an influential circle of poets.

3. Sentence 2 could be rephrased as
  A Keats was brought up by family members after his parents died.
  B Keats's parents died young and then he was raised by his aunt.
  C Keats died young after being raised by relatives.
  D Keats's relatives took care of his parents after his death.

4. The words "influential circle" mean
  A a group of friends who wrote poetry.
  B the same religious group.
  C important people with a common bond.
  D people with connections.

5. When paraphrasing sentence 3,
  A the sentence should be broken down into three parts.
  B the appositive is necessary.
  C the appositive is not necessary.
  D the sentence should be combined with sentence 2.

ASSESS

Answers

1. A	9. C
2. C	10. C
3. A	11. A
4. C	12. C
5. A	13. A
6. C	14. B
7. C	15. D
8. C	

Assessment Practice

Vocabulary

Directions: *Choose the word that best completes the sentence.*

6. He used imagery to _____ the point of the poem.
   - A trivialize
   - B derive
   - C emphasize
   - D mechanize

7. The poem was so _____ that no one could understand it.
   - A distinct
   - B emphasized
   - C abstract
   - D mechanized

8. The poet's unusual _____ of familiar words was striking.
   - A abstraction
   - B distinction
   - C usage
   - D mechanism

9. The character's boasting was his defense _____.
   - A distinction
   - B emphasis
   - C mechanism
   - D usage

10. The poem contains two _____ images.
    - A trivia
    - B derived
    - C distinct
    - D mechanized

Directions: *Use the definition of the suffix to choose the correct definition for the numbered word.*

11. sterilize
    - A to make something sterile
    - B the result of being sterile
    - C the result of being destroyed
    - D the condition of being sterile

12. criticism
    - A to offer suggestions
    - B related to literary writers
    - C the act of making judgments
    - D to disapprove

13. acreage
    - A related to the size of a piece of land
    - B to divide a piece of land
    - C related to farming
    - D farmland

14. mechanize
    - A a part of a machine
    - B to cause something to be done by machine
    - C to make machines
    - D a machine

15. coverage
    - A to cause to be covered
    - B to allow to be covered
    - C the result of being covered
    - D the condition of being covered

If students answer any of these questions incorrectly, have them review the instruction on the following pages in Part 2 before taking the **Benchmark Test.**

Question	Pages Where Instruction Is Located:
1	628, 656
2	628, 656
3	628, 656
4	628, 656
5	628, 656
6	627
7	627
8	627
9	627
10	627
11	678
12	678
13	650
14	678
15	650

Benchmark

Administer the **Benchmark Test** for Unit 4, Part 2. If the Benchmark Test reveals that some students need further work, use the Interpretation Guide to determine the appropriate reteaching page in the **Reading Kit.** You will also find the same instruction and practice available on **Success Tracker.**

Go Online
Vocabulary
For: Interactive Crossword Puzzles
Visit: www.PHSchool.com
Web Code: epj-5402
Give students this Web Code to access interactive crossword puzzles using Academic Vocabulary and Vocabulary Skill words from Part 2.

Meeting Your Standards

Students will

1. understand the use of affixes.
2. make the correct spelling changes when adding suffixes to a word.

Words with Affixes

• Tell students that whenever they add a suffix, they must be careful to see whether it necessitates changing the spelling of the word. Invite students to share words that require spelling changes when suffixes are added and to give the correct spelling of each word. **Possible answers:** Students might provide some of the following word pairs:

argue: argument

intense: intensity

curious: curiosity

compete: competitive

embody: embodiment

hesitate: hesitation

• Point out to students that they must proofread carefully when using words with suffixes. Using a spell-checking program can help to catch errors, but when students are in doubt about the correct spelling of a word, they should consult a dictionary.

Writing and Grammar, Gold Level
Students will find additional spelling instruction in Chapter 31, Section 3.

Spelling Workshop

Words with Affixes

Affixes Prefixes and suffixes, called affixes, are part of many English words. The base word does not change when you add a prefix. Suffixes may cause a spelling change to the end of the base word as well as within the base word.

Suffixes and Spelling Changes Suffixes can be added to base words in a number of different ways. Often, they cause no spelling change to the base word. Sometimes, though, final *e*'s are dropped or final *y*'s change to *i*. The final consonant in a word may change as well, as in *suspend-suspension.* The trickiest changes occur when the internal spelling of the base word changes. Many of the words in this list fall into this final category, so make particular note of the spelling of those words.

Practice On your paper, write the word from the Word List that is related to each word below. Underline any places where a spelling change occurs when a suffix is added. Explain the changes.

1. generous
2. ecstasy
3. proclaim
4. maintain
5. accompany
6. pretend
7. pronounce
8. spontaneous
9. repeat
10. consume

686 ■ Poetry

Word List
accompaniment
proclamation
pronounceable
consumption
repetition
maintenance
generosity
ecstatic
spontaneity
pretentious

Teaching Resources

The following resource can be used to enrich or extend the instruction for this Spelling Workshop.

Unit 4 Resources
Spelling Workshop: Words with Affixes, p. 194

Monitor Your Progress

Assessment Practice

A. Directions: *Write the letter of the sentence in which the underlined word is spelled correctly.*

1. **A** To achieve <u>spontaniety</u> in your piano playing, you must first practice.
   B <u>Repitition</u> of scales and simple pieces can help you improve.
   C <u>Accompaniement</u> from other instruments should not distract you.
   D One day, you will be <u>ecstatic</u> at your improvement.

2. **A** The mayor issued a new <u>proclaimation.</u>
   B It honored the <u>generosity</u> of volunteer helpers.
   C It praised the improvements made by <u>maintenence</u> workers.
   D It urged the <u>consumeption</u> of locally grown produce.

3. **A** Ida May often seems very <u>pretendsious.</u>
   B Her <u>pronounciation</u> of words like "to-mah-to" is laughable.
   C Her constant <u>repeatition</u> of "Really?" gets everyone irritated.
   D There is very little <u>spontaneity</u> in her speech or her ideas.

4. **A** My dad is on a <u>maintenance</u> diet to keep his weight down.
   B When he lost 40 pounds, he was <u>ecstastic.</u>
   C He still needs to watch his <u>consumpsion</u> of salty snacks.
   D Potato chips are his constant <u>accompanyment</u> when watching sports.

B. Directions: *Write the letter of the correct spelling of the word to fill in the blank.*

1. The governor's _____ established a new holiday.
   A proclaimation
   B proclamasion
   C proclaimasion
   D proclamation

2. The head of the student council made a very _____ speech.
   A pretentious
   B pretendious
   C pretendsious
   D pretentous

3. My pet bird's _____ of food is amazing.
   A consumtion
   B consumeption
   C consumption
   D consumetion

4. The scientific term was not _____.
   A prononcable
   B pronounceable
   C pronunceable
   D pronownceable

5. A new language can be learned by constant _____.
   A repetition
   B repeatition
   C repitition
   D repetision

6. She often sings with no _____.
   A accompaniement
   B accompanyment
   C accompanement
   D accompaniment

Spelling Workshop ■ 687

Answers

Practice
1. gen<u>ero</u>sity
2. ecsta<u>tic</u>
3. procl<u>ama</u>tion
4. main<u>tena</u>nce
5. accompan<u>i</u>ment
6. preten<u>tio</u>us
7. pronounceable
8. spontane<u>it</u>y
9. repetition
10. consum<u>p</u>tion

Assessment Practice
A.
1. D
2. B
3. D
4. A

B.
1. D
2. A
3. C
4. B
5. A
6. D

687

Meeting Your Standards

Students will

1. write a response to literature.

2. use writing strategies to generate ideas, organize, evaluate, and revise the response.

3. apply grammar skills.

 From the Author's Desk

Pat Mora

Show students Segment 3 on Pat Mora on *From the Author's Desk DVD*. Discuss how Mora creates a mood for writing and how she finds ideas. Ask students to respond to Mora's methods of revising to find just the right words and rhythms. Does this information make students think differently about Mora's work?

Writing Genres

Using the Form Point out to students that a response to a literary work is often incorporated into other types of writing. Point out these examples:

- Personal letters and emails may sometimes include responses to literature or film.

- Responses to literary works form the core of book reviews.

Writing Workshop
Work in Progress

If students have done the **Work-in-Progress** assignments throughout Part 2, suggest that they examine their recorded ideas as they begin prewriting. They may have an idea in their portfolios that they wish to develop into a response to literature.

OES Online Essay Scorer

A writing prompt for this mode of writing can be found on the *PH Online Essay Scorer* at **PHSuccessNet.com**.

688

Response to Literature

Often, our first reactions to creative works—poems, stories, songs, or films—are superficial: *I loved it! I hated it! I didn't get it!* By contrast, a formal **response to literature** gives you an opportunity to explore and explain the effects of a specific work. In doing so, you deepen your understanding of the work and also gain a greater appreciation of literary technique in general. Follow the steps in this workshop to write an essay in response to a literary selection of your choice.

Assignment Write a response to a work of literature that engages you as a reader.

What to Include Your response to literature should feature the following elements:

- an analysis of the work's content, its related ideas, and its effect on you
- a thesis statement that characterizes your response
- a focus on a single aspect or an overall view of the work
- evidence from the literary work or other texts to support the opinions you present
- error-free grammar, including correct usage when making comparisions

To preview the criteria on which your response to literature may be assessed, see the rubric on page 695.

 ## Writing Workshop: *Work in Progress*

If you have completed the Work-in-Progress assignments, you have several ideas in your portfolio that you might pursue in your response to literature. You may continue to develop these ideas, or you might explore a new idea as you complete this Writing Workshop.

688 ■ Poetry

Using the Form

You may use elements of this form in these types of writing:

- journals
- critical reviews
- literary analyses
- annotated bibliographies

Reading Writing Connection

To get a feel for responses to literature, read the excerpt from *Nothing to Fear: Lessons in Leadership from FDR* by Alan Axelrod on page 515.

Teaching Resources

The following resources can be used to enrich or extend the instruction for the Writing Workshop.

Unit 4 Resources
Writing Workshop—Response to Literature, p. 192
Writing Workshop—Integrating Grammar Skills, p. 193

General Resources
Rubrics for Response to Literature, pp. 57–58

From the Author's Desk DVD
Pat Mora, Segment 3

Prewriting

Choosing Your Topic

Make a top-ten list. Think of stories, poems, or other works of literature that you found memorable. Create a top-ten list of these titles and authors. Next to each entry, briefly note your initial reactions to the work and any ideas you might want to share about it. Review your list and choose one work as your topic.

Narrowing Your Topic

Clarify your purpose. Determine the specific purpose, or goal, of your essay. For example, you may want to share your enthusiasm for a new writer, find fresh insights into a well-known poem, or analyze the meaning of a short story. Write a statement of purpose for your essay. Use both the title and the author's name in your statement:

> **Example statement of purpose:** *In this essay, I will analyze the character of General Zaroff in Richard Connell's short story "The Most Dangerous Game."*

Identify types of details you will need. The purpose or goal of your essay determines the kinds of details you need to include. Consider these tips:

- **To praise,** include concrete details about what you liked.
- **To analyze,** back up your ideas with evidence from the selection.
- **To explain a personal response,** show how the work connects to your own experiences and ideas.

Gathering Details

Find supporting evidence. Return to the work of literature you have selected to find examples, excerpts, and direct quotations that relate to your topic. Prepare a series of index cards, with one card for every idea that you want to prove. Write your main point or idea across the top of the card. Underneath, write your notes on the details you gathered from the text to support that point or idea.

By breaking down the details and referring them back to your purpose, you will be able to present complex ideas in a sustained and compelling manner.

Work in Progress
Review the work you did on pages 651 and 675.

Identifying Supporting Evidence

What I want to prove:

General Zaroff's civilized exterior conceals a ruthless, heartless murderer.

How I can prove it:

His elegant castle is also a prison.

Prewriting

- Use this opportunity to encourage media literacy by allowing students to include films in their top-ten lists.
- If students have difficulty choosing topics, tell them that they can review the selections in *Prentice Hall Literature: Penguin Edition* and choose one that they especially enjoyed reading.
- Tell students that they can narrow their topics and identify their purposes by beginning with a question, such as *Why is General Zaroff an important character in Richard Connell's short story "The Most Dangerous Game"?*
- To help students gather details for a literary response such as this one on General Zaroff, ask them to list three to five character traits for General Zaroff. Tell them to write each trait at the top of a note card before gathering supporting examples and quotations. Guide students in listing main points for topics other than characters.

Six Traits Focus

✔	Ideas		Word Choice
✔	Organization		Sentence Fluency
	Voice		Conventions

W **Writing and Grammar, Gold Level**

Students will find additional instruction on prewriting for response to literature in Chapter 13, Section 2.

Writing and Grammar Interactive Textbook CD-ROM

Students can use the following tools as they complete their response to literature:

- Note Cards Organizer
- Comparatives Tool
- Sticky Notes

Tips for
Using Rubrics

- Before students begin work on this assignment, have them preview the Rubric for Self-Assessment on p. 695 to know what is expected.
- Review the Assessment criteria in class. Before students use the Rubric for Self-Assessment, work with them to rate the student model by applying one or two criteria to it.

- If you wish to assess students' essays with either a 4-point or a 6-point scoring rubric, see *General Resources*, pp. 57–58.

Drafting

- If students use questions to help them identify their purposes, suggest that they use the details they gathered to answer their questions in single sentences, such as *General Zaroff is an important character in Richard Connell's short story "The Most Dangerous Game" because he represents the triumph of animal instinct over human reason and compassion.* These single sentence answers may serve as the students' thesis statements. Emphasize that while students should formulate thesis statements before they begin writing, they are free to modify them as they continue the writing process.

- In creating their organizational charts, tell students to eliminate any details on their note cards that do not relate directly to their thesis statements. Now that they have working thesis statements, encourage students to go back to the stories and locate additional supporting details.

- With students, determine the audience for these responses and help students understand the difference between summarizing a literary work and providing supporting evidence for a thesis statement.

- Review how to punctuate quotations, and clarify the difference between summarizing and paraphrasing.

- *For more on elaboration, see Pat Mora's comments on p. 691.*

Six Traits Focus

✔ Ideas	Word Choice
✔ Organization	Sentence Fluency
Voice	✔ Conventions

Writing and Grammar, Gold Level

Students will find additional instruction on drafting a response to literature in Chapter 13, Section 3.

Writing Workshop

Drafting
Shaping Your Writing

Identify your thesis. Your draft should have a clear thesis statement that you will develop and support throughout your essay. Review your notes to draft a single sentence that combines the statement of purpose you wrote earlier with the ideas and evidence you have accumulated. Use this thesis statement to direct the writing of your essay.

> **Example thesis statement:** *In Richard Connell's short story "The Most Dangerous Game," the character of General Zaroff reveals the murderous mind lurking behind an illusion of refinement.*

Organize your ideas. Create an organizational chart like the one shown to present your ideas in a logical way. Be sure that your introduction includes your thesis and that every paragraph supports it.

Providing Elaboration

Consider your audience. The nature of your audience—who they are and what they know—influences the amount and kind of information you include in your response to literature. For example, if your audience already knows the work, limit the background information and proceed to your core ideas. If your audience is unfamiliar with the work, give more context and explanation.

Provide supporting details. Include evidence from the literary work for every claim you make in your essay. Consider these suggestions:

- **Quotations** can illustrate a character's attitude, a writer's word choice, or an essayist's opinion. Be sure that quotations are exact and enclosed in quotation marks.

- **Examples** of a character's actions or of a specific literary element can enhance your analysis.

- **Paraphrases**, or restatements in your own words, can help you explain a writer's theme, discuss the conflict, analyze a character, or clarify key ideas. Paraphrases must accurately reflect the original text.

Avoid padding your draft with irrelevant passages or unnecessary summaries of the plot.

690 ■ Poetry

Organize Your Ideas

Introduction
- Grab attention
- Identify author and title
- Offer brief summary
- State thesis

↓

Body
- Present supporting ideas
- Introduce each new idea in a new paragraph
- Use details to support each idea

↓

Conclusion
- Restate thesis
- Make a final point or present a final question or insight

Tips for
Using Technology in Writing

Encourage students to compose their drafts on computers. As students write, they will find that they may need to clarify or reword their thesis statements. They may also need to delete or add supporting details as they flesh out their thesis statements. Computers facilitate the process of adding and deleting material.

Also encourage students to save multiple drafts of their responses. Writers often find the need to go back to previous versions of a draft as they revise. By saving multiple drafts, students provide themselves with this option.

In some cases, students may find that they need to change the order in which they present their main points and supporting details to make their arguments more logical. The cut-and-paste feature in most word processing programs enables students to reorder ideas and entire paragraphs as they revise and refine their drafts.

Pat Mora

From the Author's Desk

Pat Mora

On Responding to Literature

Many of my best teachers are authors I will never meet. In the essay "Unseen Teachers," I explore how authors help me experience the world more intensely. Literature and all forms of art can make us more human.

This passage from the essay was inspired by a quotation from Southwest artist Georgia O'Keeffe saying that she was trying to prompt the viewer to notice. As I tried to show, writers who see their work as part of a group's struggle for justice do the same.

"I love words and their interweavings."

—————————Pat Mora

Professional Model:
from "Unseen Teachers," from *Nepantla*

I still smile at her [Georgia O'Keeffe's] laughing confession that by painting huge flowers, she forced us to notice. . . .

We too seek to force a society to notice the bitter and the sweet. Often we both participate in our communities and are solitary writers, a tension. The mere cover of Denise Levertov's *The Poet in the World* reminds me of her firm conviction: "Both life and poetry fade, wilt, shrink when they are divorced." Lorna Dee Cervantes, Sandra Cisneros, Alice Walker, Lucille Clifton, Amy Tan, Joy Harjo, and Linda Hogan are thick in the struggle of their people, and their writing is part of that struggle. Though the daily realities—high dropout rates, low per capita income, high unemployment— continue, these women teach me that the arrangement and rearrangement of work on the page is neither elitist nor irrelevant. It is the appropriate task of the person who weaves words for people's use.

I love art and often get ideas in museums. Many readers know O'Keeffe's paintings of flowers. Here, they make my thesis colorful and concrete.

I debated what names to include and what realities to list. These authors support the diversity that's a theme for the book.

Braids or weaves I wondered? Both, like writing, are hand activities. I chose weaves because weavers create both basic items of clothing and beautiful art pieces.

From the Author's Desk: Pat Mora ■ 691

🐧 **From the Author's Desk**

Pat Mora

• Show students Segment 3 on Pat Mora on *From the Author's Desk DVD.* Discuss how Pablo Neruda is another unseen teacher for Pat Mora and how he fits into Mora's group of writers who "are thick in the struggle of their people." Ask students to volunteer examples of unseen teachers in their own lives.

• Point out how Pat Mora uses the image of O'Keeffe's flower paintings to further her thesis. Have students brainstorm for images they can use to further ideas in their literary responses. Ask volunteers to share ideas for imagery with the class.

• **Ask** students how Mora's citing of names and daily realities helps further her thesis.
Possible answer: The names give readers examples of writers who are using their writing for good causes, and the daily realities show readers the importance of these writers' works.

• Explain to students how, like Pat Mora, they must be careful with their word choice. Ask students to review their drafts to identify words that are used incorrectly.

Differentiated Instruction   Solutions for All Learners

Enrichment for Advanced Readers
Pat Mora says that writers who see their work as part of a group's struggle for social justice prompt viewers to notice. Lead students in a discussion about what she means by this statement. Who are the groups who struggle for social justice? How can art and literature serve as a voice for the people who belong to these groups? Who is the intended audience for these artistic works? What does Mora hope that the audience will notice?

Revising

- If students have difficulty working with whole drafts, suggest that they print copies of their drafts to cut apart. Tell them to cut out their thesis statements, main points, and supporting details. Using a desktop or table to arrange their paper strips, students can examine each main point and detail for its relevance.

- Have students work with partners to eliminate unnecessary information.

- Provide students with more examples of dull and vague words to replace with more colorful and precise words.

  The character was happy.
  The character was ecstatic.

  Darkness fell fast.
  Darkness fell abruptly.

  Tomas came into the room slowly.
  Tomas entered the room cautiously.

- Help students identify words that convey approval or criticism. Compare *Her honest portrayal of her life captures the reader's attention* with *Her inaccurate portrayal of her life leaves the reader confused.* Encourage students to create a word bank for each type of word to use as reference tools.

Six Traits Focus

Ideas		✔	Word Choice
✔	Organization	✔	Sentence Fluency
	Voice		Conventions

Writing and Grammar, Gold Level
Students will find additional instruction on revising a response to literature in Chapter 13, Section 4.

Revising

Revising Your Overall Structure

Revise to eliminate unnecessary information. Review your draft to identify instances in which the information you provide may distract from your main idea.

- Underline your thesis and the main ideas of each paragraph.
- Highlight sentences that do not support your thesis.
- Consider revising details to make a tighter connection to your main idea.
- Eliminate any paragraphs or details that do not clearly contribute to your analysis.

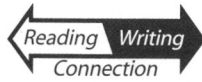

To read the complete student model, see page 694.

> **Student Model: Revising to Cut Unnecessary Details**
>
> When we first encounter General Zaroff, our initial reaction is one of delight and admiration for his wealth and charm. Zaroff lives in a massive castle, feasts on the finest delicacies, and wears expensive clothes. ~~He had previously been in the army and his strong personality has a frightening quality.~~

The writer eliminates a sentence because it does not support his main point.

Revising Your Word Choice

Check words of praise or criticism. Review your response to literature, making sure your word choices are precise and that they accurately reflect both your purpose and your attitude toward the literary work.

Vague: This *factual* account of the author's life is *interesting* to read.

Precise: This *honest* account of the author's life *captures* the reader's attention.

In addition, pay close attention to the degree, or form, of the adjectives you use, especially when making comparisons. Use the degree that accurately reflects your meaning.

Comparative degree: Zaroff is a *more disagreeable* character than Rainsford. *(Compares two items)*

Superlative degree: Zaroff is the *most disagreeable* character in the story. *(Compares more than two items)*

Peer Review: Exchange drafts with a partner. Review each other's work, circling words that convey approval or criticism or express degrees of comparison. Determine whether you have used these words correctly and whether they are precise or vague. Then, revise your draft, replacing vague, dull, or incorrect language with choices that pinpoint your meaning.

692 ■ Poetry

Tips for
Using Precise Words

Tell students that a question-and-answer strategy can help them identify vague words and choose more precise ones. Write this example on the board, and use the following questions to demonstrate.

In this mystery story, a newspaper reported an <u>incident</u> in which a <u>man</u> broke into a <u>house</u>. A neighbor heard a <u>big noise</u> and called the <u>authorities</u>, who found the man in the <u>house</u> cooking a meal.

Question nouns: *What is the incident?* (A *robbery* rather than an *incident*)

Question people: *Who are the man and the authorities?* (A *robber* rather than a *man*; *police* rather than *authorities*)

Question adjectives: *What kind of noise?* (A *crashing* noise rather than a *big* noise)

Question location: *Whose house? What part of the house?* (The *Myers'* house rather than *house*; *in the kitchen* rather than *in the house*)

Integrating Grammar Skills

Revising to Correct Common Usage Problems

Many students frequently misuse certain words and expressions.

Usage Problems With *Among* and *Between* *Among* and *between* are not interchangeable. *Among* always implies three or more elements. *Between* is generally used only with two elements. *Between* should be followed either by a plural (between trips; between friends) or by two expressions joined by *and*—not by *or* or *to*.

Prentice Hall Writing and Grammar Connection: Chapter 27, Section 2

> **Among:** Panic swept *among* the crew of Rainsford's yacht.
> **Between:** Rainsford had to choose *between* fleeing and dying.

Usage Problems With *Like, As, As If,* and *As Though* *Like* is a preposition meaning "similar to" or "such as." It should not be used in place of *as, as if,* or *as though,* which are conjunctions that introduce clauses.

> **As:** Rainsford fled, just *as* Zaroff had planned.
> **As if:** It looks *as if* it might rain.

Like is properly used as a preposition in phrases of comparison.

> **Like:** In his basic nature, Zaroff is *like* a predator. *Like* Rainsford, I too came to despise Zaroff.

Fixing Errors To fix usage problems, follow these steps:

1. **Revising usage problems with *among* and *between*:**
   - Identify the number of elements involved.
   - Use *between* with phrases involving two elements.
   - Use *among* with phrases involving three or more elements.

2. **Revising usage problems with *like, as, as if,* or *as though*:**
   - Determine how you are using the word.
   - If *like* is used to make a comparison, the usage is correct.
   - If you have used *like* to introduce a clause, replace it with the conjunction *as, as if,* or *as though.*

Apply It to Your Editing

Review the first page of your essay, and highlight any uses of *between, among, like, as, as if,* and *as though.* Use the methods described to revise any incorrect usage.

Integrating Grammar Skills

- On the chalkboard, provide students with these examples. Have students identify the correct and incorrect sentences and correct any errors in usage.

  1. *There was collaboration among the players and the coach.*
     Answer: Correct as is
  2. *Laughter swelled between the players on the soccer team.*
     Answer: among
  3. *There was no disagreement between our friends, family, and co-workers.*
     Answer: among
  4. *Among you and me, I don't think Juan and Sara will get along for five minutes.*
     Answer: Between

- Have students identify correct and incorrect uses of *like.* If the usage is incorrect, have them correct the sentence.

  1. *Jason is more like an acrobat than a football player.*
     Answer: Correct as is
  2. *In spite of the rain, we decided to go to the game like we had planned.*
     Answer: as
  3. *Elena treats her boyfriend like his feelings don't matter.*
     Answer: as if
  4. *Moya whispered her answer like no one wanted to hear it.*
     Answer: as though

Writing and Grammar, Gold Level

Students will find additional instruction in revising common usage problems in Chapter 27, Section 2.

Differentiated Instruction — Solutions for All Learners

Strategy for Special Needs Students
If students are having difficulty understanding the correct usage of *like, as, as if,* and *as though,* you may want to review these adverbs with them. For each use of these words in their papers, suggest that students read the sentence with each construction to identify the correct usage: *Rainsford fled, just like Zaroff planned. Rainsford fled, just as Zaroff planned. Rainsford fled, just as if Zaroff planned.* Tell students that when *as* or *as if* make sense in a sentence in place of *like,* they should substitute *as* or *as if.*

Enrichment for Gifted/Talented Students
Challenge students to write humorous paragraphs or poems about the use of troublesome words such as *between* and *among* and *like, as, as if,* and *as though.* Have them use as many of these words as possible in their writing. Invite them to share their compositions with the class.

693

Student Model

- Explain that the Student Model is a sample and that their own response to literature essays may be longer.

- Ask students to make sure that their titles convey an accurate impression of what is to come in their essays.

- **Ask** students to give examples of the strong language that the writer uses in his thesis statement. **Possible answers:** *civilized, murderous, illusion, charming, charismatic*

- Ask students whether they have used quotations in their responses to support their thesis statements. If not, have students review their literary selections to identify quotations that will help them to support their thesis statements.

- **Ask** students why the writer's conclusion leaves a lasting impression on the reader. **Possible Answer:** The writer relates his thesis to a universal and vivid image.

Writing Genres

Response to Art Discuss some of the situations in real life in which students will be challenged to present a solid, convincing explanation of their response to a work of art. For example, students may be called on by friends to tell why they liked a movie or theatrical performance. They may feel compelled to write a letter to the editor challenging a reviewer's comments about a favorite musician.

Student Model: Jeff Rutherford
Broken Arrow, OK

Characterization of General Zaroff

What lies at the heart of a refined man? In Richard Connell's short story "The Most Dangerous Game," the deranged, yet cunning and elegant, General Zaroff shares his taste for hunting with an unsuspecting visitor. Although he is civilized in his dress and habits, Zaroff's beliefs reveal a murderous mind behind the illusion of a charming, charismatic man.

When we first encounter General Zaroff, our initial reaction is one of delight and admiration for his wealth and charm. Zaroff lives in a massive castle, feasts on the finest delicacies, and wears expensive clothes. His luxurious surroundings and lifestyle reflect a highly civilized, eloquent, and proper gentleman. As readers soon learn, however, there is more to Zaroff than food and elegance.

Beneath Zaroff's fine qualities lies an overwhelming attitude of arrogance. This attitude comes from his firm belief that his way of thinking is superior to that of the average person. Zaroff also fancies himself a phenomenal hunter: "My hand was made for the trigger," he claims. It is this deadly mixture of arrogance, superior hunting skills, and belief that it is natural for the strong to prevail over the weak that makes him disregard the value of human life.

Zaroff's extreme beliefs lead him to conclude that only the intelligent mind of a human being can provide him with the dangerous game he desires. Rationalizing that "the weak were created to please the strong," he chooses to hunt humans instead of animals. Unfortunately, Rainsford steps into this situation. The major conflicts in "The Most Dangerous Game" demonstrate what happens during such an inhumane hunt.

However, the general's arrogance and disregard for human life blind him to the fear and desperation of his prey. His attitude leads to his own demise at the hands of Rainsford, his prey. The characterization of Zaroff as a murderer hiding behind a mask of civility shows that beneath even the most beautiful rose can lie a sharp and deadly thorn.

The title indicates that the essay will focus on a single character.

Jeff uses strong language to state his thesis clearly.

Direct quotations provide evidence for this understanding of Zaroff.

Jeff concludes his response with an analogy that neatly summarizes his analysis.

Tips for Test Taking

On many tests, students may be asked to respond to literature. Explain that this is an opportunity for students to draw on their prior knowledge and personal experience. For instance, students can use events out of their own lives, stories they have already read, and even family anecdotes as resources to connect personal responses to almost any literary work.

Students also need to remember how to structure responses to literature. Tell them to memorize these features of a literary response:

- an analysis of a work's content, its ideas, or its effect on the reader
- a focused thesis statement
- evidence to support the thesis statement

Editing and Proofreading

Check your draft for errors in format, grammar, and punctuation.
Focus on Direct Quotations: Make sure that the direct quotations that you have taken from the work of literature are accurate and enclosed by quotation marks. Use an indented block style—without quotation marks—when quoting a passage of more than ten lines.

Publishing and Presenting

Consider one of the following ways to share your writing.
Deliver an oral presentation. Read your response to literature aloud. Have a copy of the literary work on hand in the event that your classmates wish to read or review it.
Publish a collection of responses to literature. Gather the essays of several of your classmates. Organize them in a binder and make the collection available in the school library.

Reflecting on Your Writing

Writer's Journal Think about the experience of writing a response to literature. Begin by answering these questions:
- What fresh insights about the work did you discover as you prepared your response? Explain.
- If you could begin this writing process again, what might you do differently? Why?
- After writing your response, what questions about the literary work do you still have? How might you answer these questions?

> *Prentice Hall Writing and Grammar Connection: Chapter 13*

Rubric for Self-Assessment

To assess your response to literature, use the following rubric:

Criteria	Rating Scale
	not very very
Focus: How clear is your thesis statement?	1 2 3 4 5
Organization: How thoroughly do you analyze the work's content, ideas, or effect on the reader?	1 2 3 4 5
Support/Elaboration: How effectively do you include evidence from the literary work?	1 2 3 4 5
Style: How clearly do you use words of praise or criticism?	1 2 3 4 5
Conventions: How correct is your grammar, especially your use of *among* and *between,* and *like* and *as?*	1 2 3 4 5

Writing Workshop ■ *695*

Editing and Proofreading

- Remind students to place periods and commas inside quotation marks and to place semicolons and colons outside the quotation marks. Question marks and exclamation points go outside quotation marks unless they are part of the quotation.
- In addition to reviewing the proper punctuation for quotations, talk with students about how to imbed quotations into their own writing using colons and commas.

Six Traits Focus

Ideas		Word Choice	
Organization	✔	Sentence Fluency	
Voice		Conventions	✔

ASSESS

Publishing and Presenting

- Suggest that students complement the oral presentations of their papers with oral interpretations of excerpts from the literary works that they are analyzing.
- Have students talk with the librarian in advance about placing their collection in the library. They might also volunteer to create a display in the library that includes copies of the literature they have reviewed.

Reflecting on Your Writing

- Invite students to compare their experiences writing responses to literature to other types of writing they have done. Did they learn anything from the other writing that helped them with their responses to literature? Was this essay easier or more difficult than other kinds of writing? How? Which did they find more satisfying? Why?
- Ask students to relate the experience of responding to literature to the experience of responding to a film or CD.

🖊 Writing and Grammar, Gold Level

Students will find additional instruction on editing, proofreading, publishing, and presenting a response to literature in Chapter 13, Sections 5 and 6.

Differentiated Instruction   Solutions for All Learners

Strategy for Special Needs Students
Organize students into small groups to practice reading their presentations aloud. Urge them to practice looking up and making eye contact with classmates rather than staring fixedly at their essays while reading. Instruct listeners to provide constructive criticism.

Enrichment for Gifted/Talented Students
Encourage students to use appropriate performance techniques as they deliver their oral presentations. For instance, remind them to look around the room as they speak, making eye contact with various classmates. Suggest that they use facial expressions, body language, and voice intonation to give emphasis to their readings. If students include quotations, urge them to deliver these passages with suitable drama and emotion.

Students will

1. prepare an oral interpretation by understanding the literary selection, rehearsing the interpretation, and considering the audience.

2. give an oral interpretation using appropriate eye contact, a natural speaking pace, and appropriate voice intonation and body language.

Preparing the Interpretation

- Point out to students that before they can prepare their interpretation, they must be sure that they understand the selection.

- Suggest that students tape record or videotape their presentation as they practice. This will allow them to analyze their interpretation for pronunciation, emphasis, and tone of voice.

- Point out that the purpose of providing a brief introduction is to give the audience a context so that they have some sense of what to expect and can more easily understand a literary work that is unfamiliar, long, or abstract.

Giving the Interpretation

- Have students review the tips in the chart, discussing how each will improve their performance.

- If students are struggling with a poem's punctuation, suggest that they write the poem in prose format to eliminate the distraction of the line breaks.

Assess the Activity

To evaluate students' delivery, use the Speaking: Narrative Account rubric, p. 84 in *General Resources*.

Oral Interpretation of Literature

As you prepare your interpretation, you will deepen your understanding of a literary work. In presenting the interpretation, you will share your appreciation with others. The following strategies can help you prepare and deliver your oral interpretation.

Preparing the Interpretation

Understand the literature. Your interpretation should be based on an accurate understanding of the literary work's content and meaning. Make sure you are thoroughly familiar with your selection.

Rehearse the interpretation. Make a copy of the literary work on which to write performance notes. Plan and practice appropriate gestures, facial expressions, intonations, and timing until they feel natural. If certain words or phrases become stumbling points, memorize them to assure confidence and poise. Always practice aloud. Use the checklist shown here to help you prepare.

Consider your audience. Provide context to help your audience better understand the literary work you are presenting. Write an introduction to help your readers visualize the situation and characters. You may also include information about the author and the circumstances in which he or she wrote the selection.

Giving the Interpretation

Your familiarity with the selection should give you the freedom to maintain eye contact with your audience as you read.

Reading poetry Use the poem's punctuation, not the ends of lines, as cues to pause when reading. Avoid lapsing into sing-song rhythms; instead, maintain a flow that sounds like natural speech. Vary your volume and pace to create emphasis.

Reading stories and plays When expressing a character's quoted words, use a change in intonation to distinguish speech from narration. Modulate your vocal inflections, facial expressions, and posture to indicate whether a speaker is male or female, adult or child.

> **Oral Interpretation Tips**
>
> - Read the text multiple times.
> - Mark performance notes and cues on your reading copy.
> - Choose appropriate gestures, costumes, and props to suggest characters or situations.
> - Vary your pace and tone of voice to create emphasis.

Activity ▶ **Prepare and Deliver an Oral Interpretation** ▶ Choose a favorite poem, story, or play, and prepare an oral interpretation using the strategies outlined above. After presenting the interpretation to your class, ask your classmates to evaluate how well the presentation reflected the content and meaning of the work of literature.

Differentiated Instruction — Solutions for All Learners

Strategy for English Learners

In order for students to feel comfortable and to present an oral interpretation successfully, they need to select a literary work that has accessible language.

Help students choose a short selection that is not too complex. Then, have students go through the selection, underlining any vocabulary that they do not understand. Have them use a dictionary to define the words, and clarify for them any words that they still do not understand.

Once students understand their selection, **ask:** What feeling is the speaker showing, and how can you display this feeling in your presentation?

Possible responses: Students will indicate a variety of responses based on their selection. Guide them to use appropriate gestures and intonation based on their responses.

To help students with punctuation, tape record the problem words or the entire selection so that students can hear the words. You may also wish to provide additional instruction on the use of punctuation to guide reading.

For Further Reading

The Canterbury Tales

Geoffrey Chaucer

Globe Fearon, 1995

Book of Tales The classic collection of tales told by fictional pilgrims from all walks of life is translated here into modern English. The stories range from the funny to the bitter, giving an expansive view of life in Chaucer's day.

Poems by Robert Frost: A Boy's Will and North of Boston

Robert Frost

Signet, 2001

Collection These first two collections of poetry by one of America's most beloved poets bring the people and the landscape of rural New England to life. Frost introduces characteristic themes—the value of manual labor, the beauty of nature, the individual versus the community—and experiments with narrative poetry and blank verse.

Alice's Adventures in Wonderland

Lewis Carroll

Signet, 2000

Novel Alice falls into a strange world that has some odd parallels to our own. The rabbit, who is always late, the queen, who is always yelling, and Alice's own confusion will strike a familiar chord in many students.

The Complete Poetry of Edgar Allan Poe

Edgar Allan Poe

Signet, 1996

Collection The poems that have delighted and frightened generations of readers are collected in this anthology. Included are the poems famous for their psychological impact, such as "The Raven" and "The Bells."

These titles are available in the Penguin/Prentice Hall Literature Library. Consult your teacher before choosing one.

Planning Students' Further Reading

Discussions of literature can raise sensitive and often controversial issues. Before you recommend further reading to your students, consider the values and sensitivities of your community as well as the age, ability, and sophistication of your students. It is also good policy to preview literature before you recommend it to students. The notes below offer some guidance on specific titles.

[L4] *The Canterbury Tales* These tales contain murder and other violence, a knight who forces himself upon a maiden, sexual innuendo, crude humor, family betrayals, and clergy who break their vows. You may wish to remind students that Chaucer is satirizing the society of his time.

Reading level appropriate for high school students

[L3] *Poems by Robert Frost: A Boy's Will and North of Boston* The following poems in *A Boy's Will* contain overtly religious references to God: "A Prayer in Spring" (p. 32), "Revelation" (p. 43), "The Trial by Existence" (p. 44), "In Equal Sacrifice" (p. 47). Several poems in *North of Boston* deal with the subject of death, including "The Death of the Hired Man" (p. 69) and "Home Burial" (p. 86). "The Housekeeper" (p. 117) is about the problems of a man and a woman who have lived together for fifteen years but never married. "The Fear" (p. 125) is about the guilt a woman feels after she deserted her husband to be with another man.

Reading level appropriate for high school students

[L2] *Alice's Adventures in Wonderland* The book contains a character smoking a hookah, a mother who nurses and then shakes a baby, offhand and somewhat gruesome violence, and passing mention of wine and ethnic stereotyping. Also, the Introduction notes Carroll's deep interest in children and other idiosyncrasies.

Lexile: 890

[L1, L2, EL] *The Complete Poetry of Edgar Allan Poe* Poe's poems often touch on the supernatural and on death, including the eerie and haunting deaths of young women. Some details of Poe's biography may also be problematic for some.

Reading level appropriate for high school students

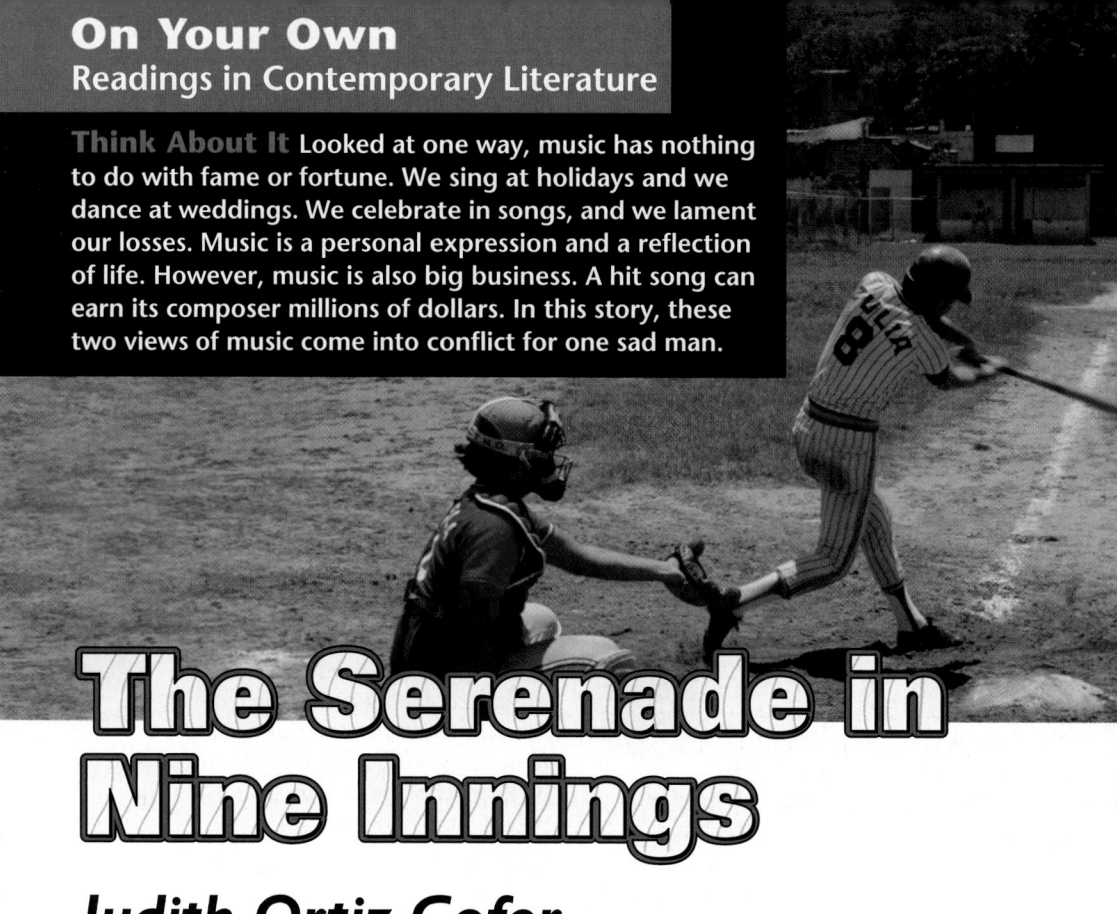

On Your Own
Readings in Contemporary Literature

Think About It Looked at one way, music has nothing to do with fame or fortune. We sing at holidays and we dance at weddings. We celebrate in songs, and we lament our losses. Music is a personal expression and a reflection of life. However, music is also big business. A hit song can earn its composer millions of dollars. In this story, these two views of music come into conflict for one sad man.

The Serenade in Nine Innings

Judith Ortiz Cofer

It seems that my father had a dream as a young man—of having a song he wrote recorded. It was not a love song or a song about love betrayed, which is the prime topic of Puerto Rican popular music; it was instead a lyrical piece about the only activity that gave him pure joy: baseball. He had been, at eighteen, a star pitcher for his high-school team, but then he broke his ankle in a collision with another player. The song was a dirge, a mournful hymn to his moment of glory, too soon gone; a melody sent into space like a time capsule to preserve a moment. My father played a few chords on an old guitar and sang it to his compañeros at Chavo's cafeteria one afternoon while he rested his swollen foot on a shoeshine stool. It was fiesta week in the pueblo, so there were also many strangers present—itinerant musicians, who made the circuit of festivals around the island. Some of these men congratulated my father on his fine composition; in fact, it was their compliments that planted the seed of hope in his heart. For weeks, as he recuperated and courted my mother, he perfected the lyrics and set them to a simpler melody, one that reflected the

698 ■ *Poetry*

feelings of yearning he had after meeting her. And she traded her heart for his song.

It was the week when they announced their engagement that he heard it—his song—played on the radio. Of course it had a different title—not "Serenade in Nine Innings," later to be referred to by him simply as "La Serenata," a title he had finally settled on after much thought. The rhythm had been speeded up so now it sounded more like a mambo rather than the bolero he had intended it to be. He had his friends listen to it, and they all agreed it was "Serenade" and it had been stolen! My father took a bus to the radio station in Ponce, pushed and harangued his way to the manager, who laughed in his face when he heard the story, dismissing him with "Go home and write another hit tune, son, and I'll believe you."

No one outside the pueblo ever believed him, of course. And he never tried writing another song, as far as I know. But for years, he noted how many times he heard the song played, computing in a series of ledgers how much money it had made for the thieves. In due time the story of his near brush with fame and fortune, the lost dream, became his cuento for life.

Meet the Author
Judith Ortiz Cofer (b. 1952) spent her childhood shuttling back and forth between her birthplace of Puerto Rico and her home in Paterson, New Jersey. The two cultures of her childhood would later have a profound impact on Ortiz Cofer's writing, which includes poetry, essays, novels, short stories, and creative nonfiction.

Readings in Contemporary Literature
Talk About It

Use these questions to guide a discussion of this story.

1. **(a)** What did the father do after he broke his ankle and was unable to play baseball? **(b)** What "seed of hope" did the musicians' compliments plant in his heart?

2. **(a)** How did the radio station manager respond to the father's protest? **(b)** What did the father never do again? **(c)** In addition to the song, what else was taken from him?

3. In a group, discuss the role that hope and striving can play in one's life.
   - What became the father's *cuento* for life?
   - How else might the father have reacted to this setback?
   - Have you ever done something for which you did not receive credit? Were you able to feel proud anyway? Explain.

   Choose a point-person to share your group's ideas with the class.

The Serenade in Nine Innings ■ 699

Extend the Lesson

Dream Story
To give students more practice with stories about people's dreams, have them write their own stories of dreams. Tell them that they can paraphrase dreams fulfilled, dreams lost, or even dreams they are still striving toward. Encourage students to add details that make readers feel they are with the narrator during the action.

Motivation
Have students look at the photograph in this selection. Then have them read the first line. Ask what they think will happen to the narrator and her father. Encourage them to read to find out if her father's dream is fulfilled.

Reading Skill
Paraphrase
- Review paraphrasing (p. 626): restating an author's ideas in your own words.
- Have a volunteer read the first paragraph of this story.
- **Ask** students to paraphrase the development of the narrator's father's song.
  Possible response: The narrator's father wrote a mournful song about his lost baseball career. Encouraged by local musicians, he reworked the lyrics and music into a love song.
- Have students read the rest of the "The Serenade in Nine Innings."
- **Ask** students to paraphrase what the song "Serenade" meant to the narrator's father while he was working to perfect it.
  Possible response: The song was his seed of hope following the end of his baseball career.
- **Ask** students to paraphrase how the narrator's father felt about the song "Serenade" after he heard it on the radio.
  Possible response: The narrator's father felt the song had been stolen from him. He continued to believe it throughout his life.
- **Ask** students to paraphrase the narrator's father's support for believing "Serenade" had been stolen.
  Possible response: The narrator's father felt "Serenade" was stolen because it had a familiar rhythm, and his friends agreed it was his song.

Readings in Contemporary Literature
Talk About It
- Suggest that students work in groups to address these questions.
- To guide students' discussion, use the **Discussion Guide**, p. 39 in *General Resources*.

Introduce Unit 5

- Explain to students that dramas are often broadly characterized as comedies or tragedies. Ask volunteers to offer brief definitions of a comedy and a tragedy.
  Possible response: Students may say that comedies offer humorous plots that end happily. Tragedies have serious plots that end in disaster for the main characters.
- Tell students that they will read an example of each of these dramatic forms in this unit.

Instructional Resources

Unit 5 Resources support students in developing and mastering the unit skills and help you assess students' progress.

▶ **Progress Monitoring** These tests enable you to assess and monitor student progress in each part:
- Diagnostic test
- Benchmark test

▶ **Vocabulary Warm-ups**
Additional vocabulary support, based on Lexile scores of vocabulary words, is provided for each selection.
- **Word List A and Practice A** provide vocabulary-building activities for students reading two grades below level.
- **Word List B and Practice B** provide vocabulary-building activities for students reading one grade below level.

▶ **Reading Warm-ups** Two Reading Warm-ups for each selection provide a context for students to apply newly learned vocabulary. Each Reading Warm-up consists of a short reading passage loosely tied to a theme in the selection. Questions and activities guide students to focus on particular vocabulary items.
- **Reading Warm-up A,** for students reading two grades below level, focuses on the vocabulary items presented in Vocabulary Warm-up A.
- **Reading Warm-up B,** for students reading one grade below level, focuses on the vocabulary items presented in Vocabulary Warm-up B.

▶ **Selection Support** These practice pages are available for each selection:
- Reading Skills
- Literary Analysis
- Vocabulary Builder
- Support for Writing
- Support for Extend Your Learning
- Enrichment

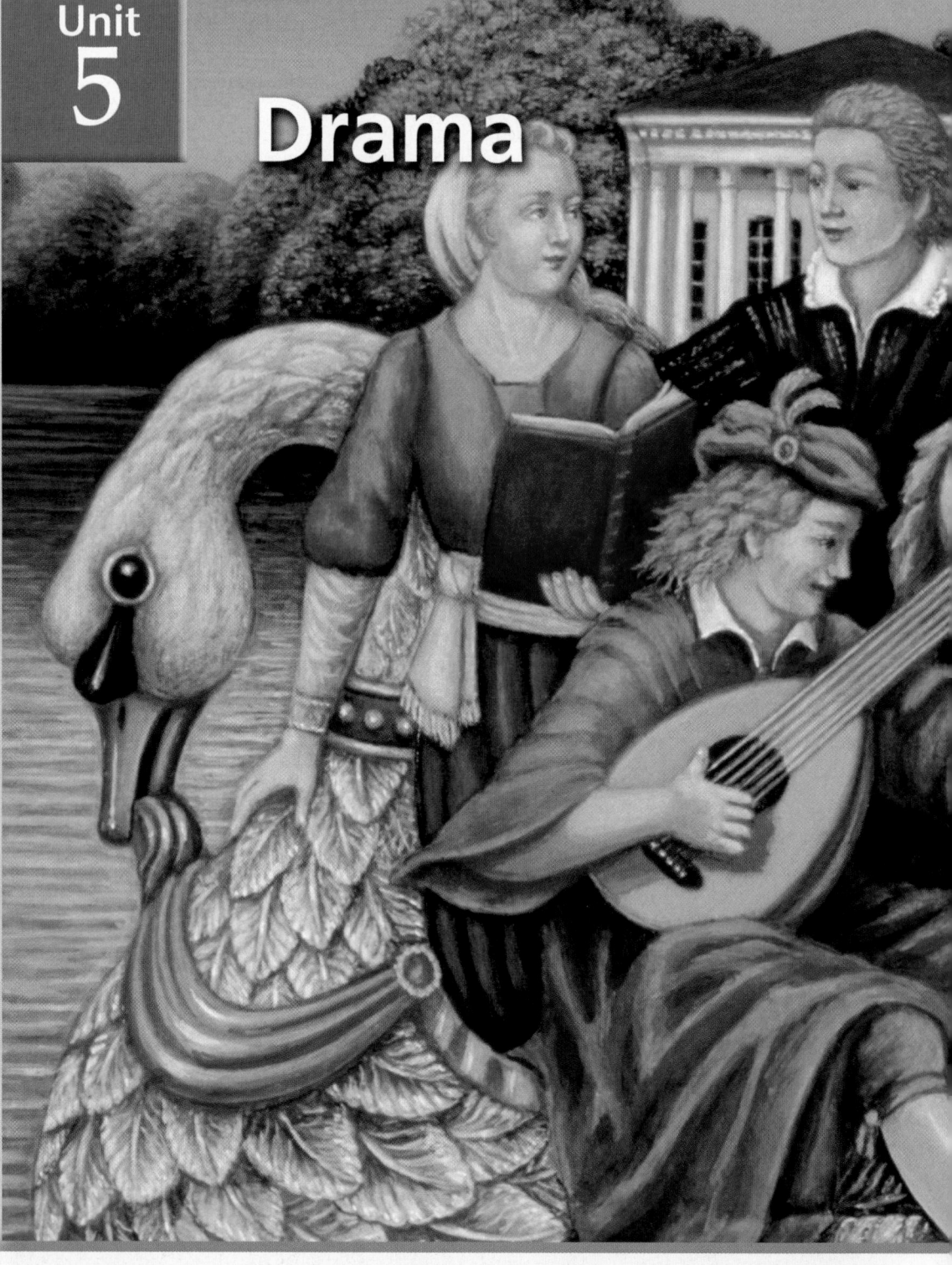

Unit 5
Drama

Assessment Resources

Program Assessment

Unit 5 Resources
  Selection Tests A and B

TeacherExpress™
  ExamView® Test Bank
  Software

Adequate Yearly Progress Monitoring Assessment

Unit 5 Resources
  Diagnostic Tests: Part 1, Part 2
  Benchmark Tests: Part 1, Part 2

Standardized Assessment

Standardized Test
  Preparation Workbook

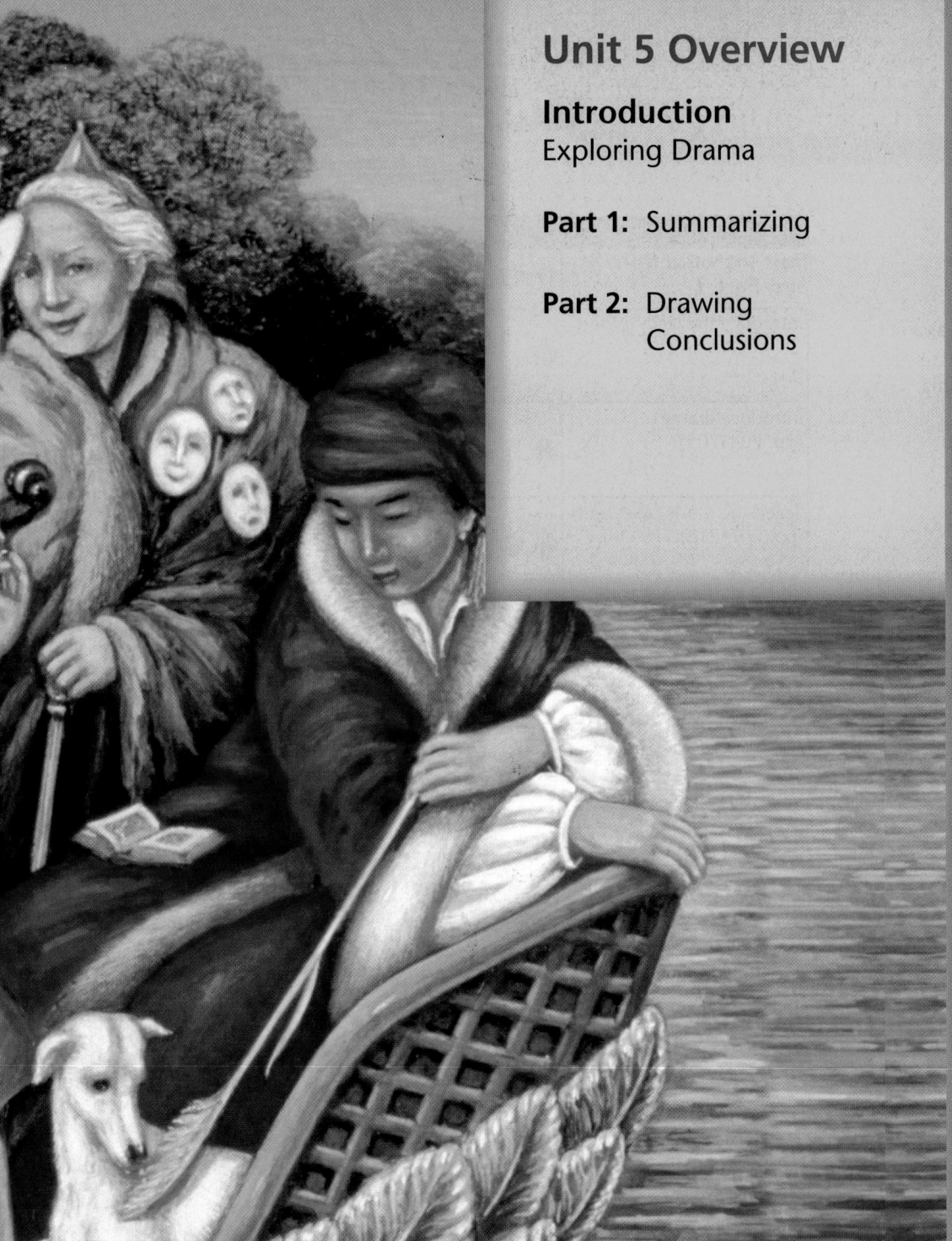

Unit 5 Overview

Introduction
Exploring Drama

Part 1: Summarizing

Part 2: Drawing Conclusions

Drama ■ *701*

Unit 5 Overview

Genre Focus

Author Gary L. Blackwood introduces the literary genre, drama, with scenes from *The Shakespeare Stealer*. Students read and analyze an example of drama.

Using the Unit Selections

Teach Skills Reading, literary analysis, and vocabulary skills to meet the standards are part of the instruction with each selection.

Differentiate and Reinforce Use the accessibility information in the Differentiated Instruction box to guide your teaching of the selections.

Integrate Skills Each selection set gives students a reading strategy, literary analysis, and vocabulary development as well as opportunities for writing about the selection, research and technology, listening and speaking, grammar, and assessment practice.

See pages 721 and 879 for an overview of the skills in each part.

Using the Unit Features

These additional reading selections give you the opportunity to apply, reinforce, and extend the unit skills.

Reading Informational Materials Students learn to analyze and evaluate informational texts.

Comparing Literary Works Students read a pair of literary works to compare the treatment of a literary element.

On Your Own Students may read this selection independently, or you may teach it actively to reinforce a unit reading skill.

See the Unit 5 Overview and Pacing Plan on the following pages.

Differentiated Instruction   Solutions for All Learners

Accessibility for Ability Levels
This chart gives general accessibility information to guide your instruction. For additional guidance on factors that affect the accessibility of each selection, see the **Time and Resource Manager** for each selection.

	More Accessible	More Challenging
Part 1		
		Romeo and Juliet
Part 2		
	The Inspector-General	

701

Unit 5

OVERVIEW AND PACING PLAN — Drama

Meeting Your Standards

Students will

1. recognize and appreciate drama as a literary genre.
2. read and analyze a variety of drama.
3. apply reading skills.
   - Summarizing
     - Using text aids
     - Reading in sentences
     - Paraphrasing
     - Breaking down long sentences
     - Identifying causes and effects
   - Summarizing
     - Drawing conclusions from dialogue and stage directions
4. analyze literary elements.
   - Dialogue
   - Blank verse
   - Dramatic speeches
   - Dramatic irony
   - Tragedy
   - Comedy
   - Dialogue
5. build vocabulary.
   - Word roots
6. learn elements of grammar, usage, and style.
7. use a recursive writing process to write in a variety of forms.
   - How-to Essay
   - Research report
8. read informational materials.
   - Skimming and scanning
   - Evaluate credibility of an author
9. compare literary works.
   - Archetypal theme
   - Satire
10. use technology to do research.
    - Annotated flowchart
    - Film review
    - Multimedia presentation
    - Informational chart
11. develop listening and speaking skills.
    - Mock trial
    - Readers theatre presentation
12. develop spelling proficiency.

Unit Introduction and Part 1	Week 1					Week 2					Week 3					
	1	2	3	4	5	1	2	3	4	5	1	2	3	4	5	
Introduce the Unit author: Gary L. Blackwood (pp. 702–703).	●															
Introduce drama (pp. 704–705).	●															
Teach the Model selection (pp. 707–718).	●	●	●													
Administer the Unit 5, Part 1 Diagnostic Test.			●													
Introduce the Reading and Vocabulary Skills for Part 1 (pp. 722–723).			●													
Teach The Tragedy of Romeo and Juliet (pp. 730–847).				●	●	●	●	●	●	●	●	●	●			
Teach Reading Informational Materials (pp. 852–854).														●		
Teach Comparing Literary Works (pp. 858–870).																
Complete the Reading and Vocabulary Review (pp. 872–873).																
Have students complete the Writing Workshop (pp. 874–878).																
Administer the Unit 5, Part 1 Benchmark Test.																

Week 4					Part 2	Week 1					Week 2				
❶	❷	❸	❹	❺		❶	❷	❸	❹	❺	❶	❷	❸	❹	❺
					Administer the Unit 5, Part 2 Diagnostic Test.	●									
					Introduce the Reading and Vocabulary Skills for Part 2 (pp. 880–881).	●									
					Teach *The Inspector General* (pp. 884–887).	●	●	●	●						
					Teach Reading Informational Materials (pp. 893–894).					●					
					Teach Comparing Literary Works (pp. 898–910).						●	●			
					Complete the Reading and Vocabulary Review (pp. 912–913).								●		
					Have students complete the Writing Workshop (pp. 916–927).						●	●	●	●	●
●	●				Have students complete the Communications Workshop (p. 928).									●	
		●			Have students complete the Spelling Workshop (pp. 914–915).									●	
●	●	●	●	●	Administer the Unit 5, Part 2 Benchmark Test.										●
			●												

Options for Block and Daily Scheduling

The assignments and activities in this unit planner are organized by week. You may adjust them to your daily or block schedule. The Time and Resource Managers for the selection sets give specific times to help your planning.

Options for Independent Reading

Use these independent reading options to differentiate, reinforce, and extend your instruction:

On Your Own

Students may read this selection on their own or you may use it to reteach and reinforce unit skills.

Victor Hernandez Cruz, "Problems with Hurricanes"

For Further Reading

Have students choose and read a full-length work while working on this unit.

[L1, L2, EL] Luigi Pirandello, *Six Characters in Search of an Author*

[L2] *Twentieth-Century American Drama*

[L3] Tennessee Williams, *Four Plays*

[L4] William Shakespeare, *Julius Caesar*

[L4] Authors in Depth

William Shakespeare, from *The Tragedy of King Lear,* from *A Midsummer Night's Dream,* "Sonnet 23," "Sonnet 27," "Sonnet 60," "Sonnet 98"

[L1] Special Needs Students
[L2] Below-Level Students
[L3] All Students
[L4] Above-Level Students
[EL] English Learners

PRENTICE HALL
 TeacherEXPRESS™
Plan · Teach · Assess Use this complete suite of powerful teaching tools to make lesson planning and testing quicker and easier.

ExamView®
QuickTake   Monitor student progress instantly.

From the Author's Desk

❶ Introduce Gary Blackwood

Gary Blackwood got the idea for *The Shakespeare Stealer* from a late 1960s newspaper article about the history of shorthand. In 1998 the book received a Best Book for Young Adults citation from the American Library Association. Ask students whether they have read or are familiar with his work.

• Use the *From the Author's Desk DVD* to introduce the author and the genre. Show Segments 1 and 2 to provide insights into what prompted Gary Blackwood to become a novelist and a playwright. **Ask:** How does Blackwood differentiate writing novels from writing plays?
Possible response: In plays, dialogue becomes extremely important because it has to carry the plot.

• Interested students might enjoy these works by Gary Blackwood.

The Dying Sun, a pioneer survival story set in 2050

Shakespeare's Scribe, a sequel to *The Shakespeare Stealer*

Shakespeare's Spy, a third tale in the Shakespeare series

❷ Critical Viewing

Possible response: The small figures holding books or looking at the large open book might be actors learning or reciting their parts. These figures show that the words on the page come to life when they are read.

702

Unit 5

Introduction
Drama

Gary L. Blackwood

❶

 From the Author's Desk

Gary L. Blackwood
Talks About the Form

❸

I consider myself, in all modesty, fairly successful as a playwright. Yet, even in a good year, only about ten percent of the money I make comes from productions of my plays; the other ninety percent is from my novels and nonfiction books.

So why, you may ask—as my wife often does—do I bother writing **drama** at all? Why not just devote all my time and effort to books?

When the House Lights Go Down

The short answer is, "Because I love the theater." During high school and college, and for several years afterward, I was mainly interested in **acting.** But when my first play was produced, I discovered that performing in someone else's play wasn't nearly as much fun as watching other people perform my play. (Actually, I ended up acting in my own play when the lead got sick, but that's another story.)

It's a great feeling, of course, to see a new book in print for the first time or to get a glowing review or an enthusiastic fan letter. But it doesn't compare to the feeling you get when the house lights go down and the stage lights come up and **actors** start saying **dialogue** that you created and the **audience** responds with laughter or, better yet, with rapt silence.

702 ■ *Drama*

▲ **Gary L. Blackwood** has written more than twenty novels and nonfiction books for young readers, in addition to several plays.

❷◄ Critical Viewing Blackwood describes the excitement of hearing his words spoken by actors. How does this illustration suggest the way actors bring a text to life? **[Connect]**

Drama: Actual People Doing Actual Things

I experience that same sort of excitement even when the drama or comedy I'm watching isn't mine. As indispensable as books and movies are, the theater offers something they don't: No matter how skimpy the **set** is, no matter how much the dialogue differs from everyday speech, you still get the sensation that what's taking place onstage is real. And it is. It's not just images projected on a screen or letters printed on a page. It's actual people doing actual things and actually speaking, with no quotation marks, no description, no exposition, no soundtrack.

After you experience any work of art, you have that moment of asking yourself, "From this I've learned . . . what?" . . . That's the bottom line question, and I believe that artists have a responsibility to address that—of course, not giving an answer, but at least giving an audience comfort with the realization that we're all wrestling with the same questions.

from an interview in *The Dramatist*
—*Israel Horovitz*

❹ Never the Same

Because it's live, not printed or recorded, you can never see the same play twice. Each **performance** is different. And a large part of what makes it different is the audience. Our reaction to the play actually contributes to it, influences it.

Another reason I love the theater is that it tends to challenge its audience more than books and movies do. I think most playwrights—including Israel Horovitz, who is quoted here—are less interested in offering an escape from real life than they are in reflecting real life and commenting on it.

More About Gary L. Blackwood

Before Gary L. Blackwood (b. 1945) adapted his popular novel *The Shakespeare Stealer* for the stage, he had written some notable plays: *Dark Horse*, a prizewinning courtroom drama, and *The Count of One*, a drama about the use of hypnotism. One of his books of historical fiction, *The Year of the Hangman*, is set in Colonial America. *Beyond the Door*, one of his science-fiction and fantasy novels, deals with an alternate world beyond a door in the library.

Fast Facts

▶ Blackwood attended a one-room schoolhouse where the library consisted of a single small bookcase.
▶ He sold his first story when he was nineteen.

From the Author's Desk: Gary L. Blackwood ■ *703*

---

❸ Gary Blackwood Talks About the Form
Exploring Drama

• Explore students' prior knowledge of drama. **Ask** students: How is drama similar to a short story or novel?
Possible response: Students should recognize that dramas, novels, and short stories are all narrative forms that share certain elements, including plot, characters, dialogue, setting, and theme.

• Then, **ask** students how drama differs from a novel or a short story.
Possible responses: When a play is performed live, the audience sees and hears rather than reads and imagines the action and dialogue. In a play, the dialogue must carry background information, reveal character, present conflict and resolution, and suggest the theme.

❹ Never the Same Play Twice

• **Ask** students whether they think that each reading of a novel or a short story can, like seeing a play, be brand new.
Possible response: Some students will say no, because the words are static on the page. Some students may say yes, because with each rereading, people bring new attitudes or experiences to the work.

• *The Dramatist* Explain to students that Israel Horovitz (b. 1939) is an award-winning actor and the author of more than fifty plays. Direct students' attention to the quotation from Horovitz. **Ask** students whether they agree with Horovitz's comment that artists have a responsibility to teach us something new or different in their works.
Possible response: Some students will agree that literature should present a theme to make it worthwhile. Other students will make a case for the benefits of pure entertainment.

Go **Online** **For:** An online video
Author Link **Visit:** www.PHSchool.com
Web Code: epe-8501
Give students this Web Code for a video clip of Gary Blackwood.

Exploring Drama

5 Elements of Drama

A drama, or play, is a story written to be performed by actors. It features **characters** facing a **conflict,** or struggle, that propels the sequence of events called the **plot.** The conflict reaches a **climax,** the point of greatest tension, and is then resolved. The **dialogue,** or speeches of the characters, tells the story, and not, as in fiction, the voice of a narrator.

These elements are specific to drama:

- **Acts** and **scenes** are the basic units of drama. A drama may consist of one or more acts, each of which may contain any number of scenes.

- The author of a play, called the **playwright,** provides the **script,** or text, of a play. The script contains both dialogue and stage directions.

Drama coach.

- **Stage directions** tell how the work is to be performed, or staged. Providing details about sets, lighting, sound effects, props, costumes, and acting, directions are often printed in italics and set off in brackets. Some playwrights use abbreviations to provide additional direction about where on-or offstage a speech may be delivered. These include O.S. for offstage; D.S. for downstage, or close to the audience; and U.S. for upstage, or far from the audience.

- **Sets** are the constructions indicating where the drama takes place. A set may include painted backdrops, wooden frames, and other elements.

- **Props** are movable objects, like swords or pens, that actors use onstage.

All the elements of drama combine in performance to produce the vivid illusion of reality known as **dramatic effect.** Through this effect, the dramatist explores a **theme,** or insight into life.

❻ Types of Drama and Dramatic Speech

The ancient Greeks, who developed drama, created two types of plays:

- A **tragedy** shows the downfall or death of the **tragic hero,** or main character. In ancient Greek drama, the hero was an outstanding person brought low by a **tragic flaw,** a mistaken action or defect in character. In modern tragedy, the hero can be an ordinary person destroyed by an evil force in society. Greek tragedy included a **chorus,** a group of performers who commented on the action. William Shakespeare sometimes used a single actor to perform the role of the chorus.

- A **comedy** has a happy ending, usually after an amusing series of predicaments. While tragedy emphasizes human greatness, comedy stresses the weaknesses of ordinary people or of society itself.

For both kinds of drama, you sometimes need to understand the **historical context,** the background of the era in which the play is set or written. In addition to dialogue involving conversations between two or more characters, dramatists use these types of **dramatic speech:**

- A **monologue** is a long, uninterrupted speech delivered by a character to other characters who are onstage but remain silent.

- A **soliloquy** is a speech in which a character alone on stage reveals private thoughts and feelings that the audience is allowed to overhear.

- An **aside** is a brief remark in which a character expresses private thoughts to the audience rather than to other characters.

❼ ▼ Critical Viewing
In what ways do you think viewing a live dramatic performance like this one differs from seeing a movie? Explain. **[Compare and Contrast]**

Check Your Understanding

Choose the letter of the answer that best completes each numbered item.

1. The sequence of events in a play is the   **a.** tragedy.   **b.** plot.
2. A flawed, noble character is vital to a   **a.** theme.   **b.** tragedy.
3. Unlike tragedy, comedy has a   **a.** happy ending.   **b.** dialogue.
4. Costume details are found in   **a.** monologues.   **b.** stage directions.
5. A brief remark made to the audience is   **a.** an aside.   **b.** a soliloquy.

Exploring Drama ■ 705

---

❻ Types of Drama and Dramatic Speech

- **Ask** students to define the word *tragedy.*
  Possible responses: Students may say that a tragedy is an unfortunate or disastrous occurrence, such as the death of a child or an earthquake that kills thousands of people.

- Point out the definition of tragedy given in the text. **Ask** students to explain how the ordinary definition of tragedy differs from the use of the word in relation to drama.
  Answer: The incidents mentioned earlier are not tragedies in the dramatic sense because they are random events and do not focus on the downfall of a tragic hero.

- Point out the definitions of monologue, soliloquy, and aside. Tell students that a monologue is like a speech and that the characters on the stage are its intended audience, as well as the viewers of the play. A soliloquy, also called an internal monologue, has no audience except the viewers of the play. An aside is like a miniature soliloquy and the viewers assume that the other characters on stage did not hear it.

❼ Critical Viewing

Possible response: A live dramatic performance might have fewer special effects, and the scenery for outdoor scenes might be less realistic than the sets in an average movie. In a live dramatic performance, the actors might alter the delivery of their lines from show to show, so the performance might be more charged and dynamic. The audience for a live performance would probably behave more formally than one for a movie because they would not want to disrupt the concentration of the actors on stage.

ASSESS

Answers

1. B
2. B
3. A
4. B
5. A

From the Author's Desk

❶ Introduce the Selection

- Invite students to read Gary Blackwood's introduction to his play.

- Call students' attention to the terms used in discussing the play: *characters, scenes, act, set, historical context, stage directions, script,* and *props.* Ask students to identify these elements as they read *The Shakespeare Stealer.*

❷ Background

Elizabethan Theater Queen Elizabeth I loved the theater. She especially enjoyed the plays of William Shakespeare, whose career she helped promote. The queen lent her financial support and prestige to major acting companies, which led to a flowering of English theater.

   Theater was popular entertainment for all classes of society. This is one of the reasons why Shakespeare's plays were so popular; they offered something for everyone.

❸ Connecting to the Literature

- Ask students to list some of the titles of their favorite books that have been turned into movies or plays. Have students write several sentences that explain the reasons for their preferences. To develop expressive vocabulary, tell students to use these words in their sentences: *revise, clarify, illuminate, compensate, supplement,* and *confirm.*

- To further develop students' expressive vocabulary, you may suggest that they also use two of these words: *aspect, category, dimension, episode,* and *perspective.*

- To help students understand the meanings of the words they are asked to use, give them these sentences:

  1. When an author *revises* a book to make it a screenplay, many scenes are cut.

  2. A good movie can *supplement* what you know about a character's personality.

  3. A film director's *perspective* on a work of fiction can be different from the author's.

Model Selection:
Drama ❶

 From the Author's Desk
Gary L. Blackwood Introduces *The Shakespeare Stealer*

❷ ❸

Adapting my young-adult novel *The Shakespeare Stealer* for the stage was a whole new experience for me. I'd written plenty of original plays, and even turned novels by other authors into plays, but I'd never tried to dramatize one of my own books.

From the Page to the Stage
It's not an easy thing to do. When you're the author of the book, your tendency is to try to put as much of it as possible into the play. My first draft was over two hours long and had roughly twenty **characters**. The problem was, the theater that initially produced it wanted a one-hour play that could be performed by nine actors.

   So I set to work cutting cherished **scenes** (including the sword battle with the thieves, which appears in the first **act** of the play), giving the boot to beloved characters, and doubling—having each actor play several roles. I kept on cutting right up until opening night.

No Horses or Rivers on the Set!
The second theater to produce it wanted a full-length play. Back went most of the deleted scenes, plus some new ones. Naturally, even in a longer version, I couldn't keep everything from the novel. I couldn't very well have the actors on horseback, for example, or practically drowning in the Thames River, as they do in the book.

   To simplify matters and make the play move quickly, I kept the number of scene changes to a minimum and let a single **set**—called a unit set—represent several different locations.

Historical Context: Re-creating Another Time Period
Despite all this, the play is very demanding technically. The **historical context** is just as important as it is in the book. In the book, however, I could get away with an occasional brief description of the clothing, the Globe Theatre, the sword-fighting moves, etc. On the stage, all that has to actually be re-created from brief **stage directions** included in the **script**. So the actors have to cope with early seventeenth-century costumes and **props**, learn Elizabethan sword-fighting techniques, and approximate London and Yorkshire accents.

706 ■ *Drama*

Vocabulary Development

Vocabulary Knowledge Rating Chart
Create a **Vocabulary Knowledge Rating Chart** with these words from the selection:

feckless	*spectral*
parsimonious	*rustic*

Give students a copy of the chart. Introduce the words by reading them aloud and having students mark their rating in the Before Reading column. Urge them to be alert to these words as they read and discuss the selection because they will rate their knowledge of the words again after they finish.

   If you wish, you may tally how many students know (or think they know) a word to gauge how much instruction you need to provide. As students read, point out the words and their context.

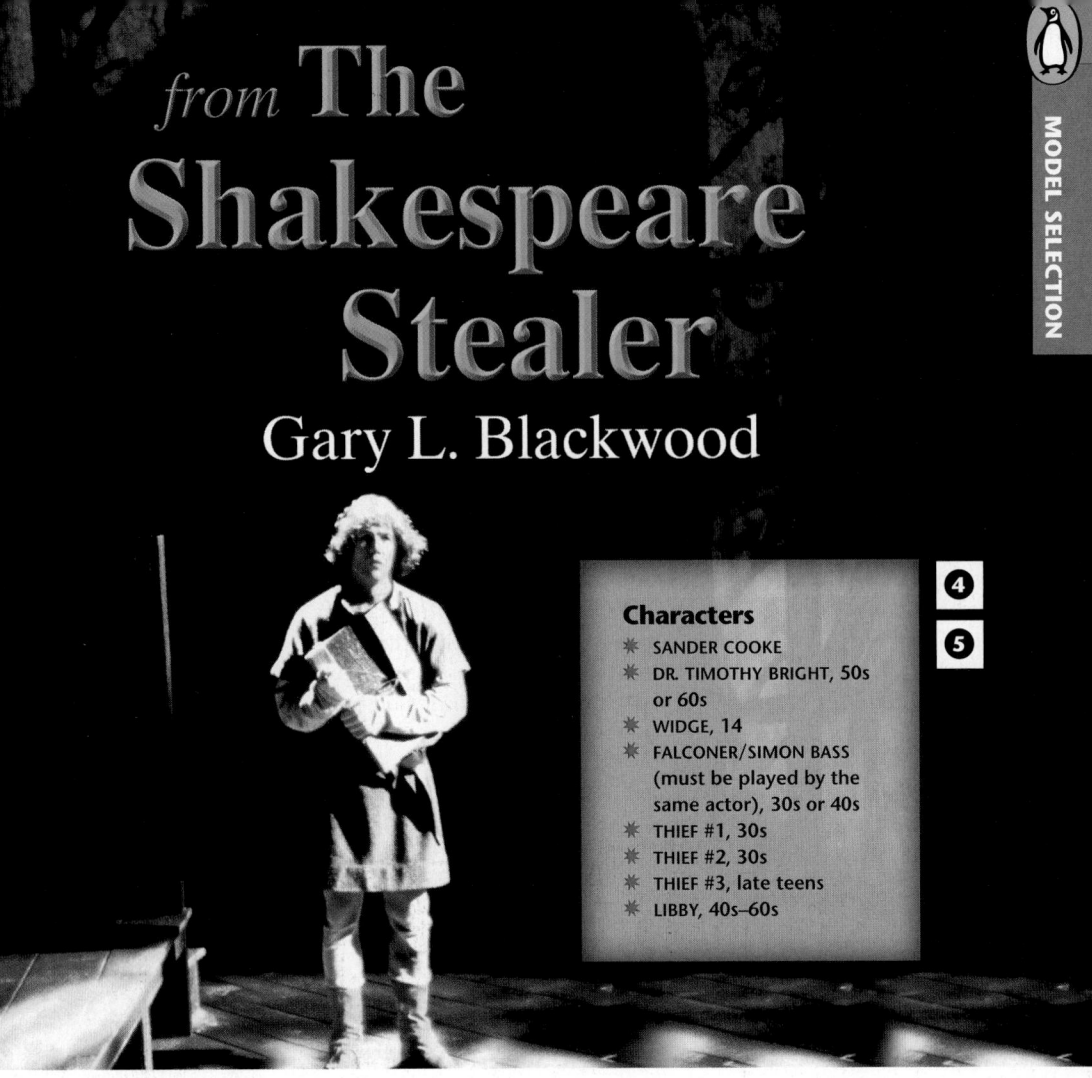

from **The Shakespeare Stealer**

Gary L. Blackwood

Characters

* SANDER COOKE
* DR. TIMOTHY BRIGHT, 50s or 60s
* WIDGE, 14
* FALCONER/SIMON BASS (must be played by the same actor), 30s or 40s
* THIEF #1, 30s
* THIEF #2, 30s
* THIEF #3, late teens
* LIBBY, 40s–60s

❹
❺

Prologue

❻

SANDER: I bid you welcome. For an hour or so
I ask you to imagine, if you will,
That this poor stage is not a stage at all
But England, some four hundred years ago.
That the actors who—I hope—will soon appear
Are something more than they appear to be,
That they are not mere shadows on a stage
But men and women of another age.

❼ ▲ **Critical Viewing**
What does the actor's expression suggest about Widge's feelings at this moment? **[Interpret]**

from *The Shakespeare Stealer* ■ 707

Differentiated Instruction   Solutions for All Learners

Support for Special Needs Students
Have students read the adapted version of *The Shakespeare Stealer* in the *Reader's Notebook: Adapted Version*. They may also listen to the adapted version on the *Reader's Notebook: Adapted Version Audio CD*.

Support for Less Proficient Readers
Have students read *The Shakespeare Stealer* in the *Reader's Notebook*. After students finish the selection in the *Reader's Notebook*, have them complete the questions and activities in the Student Edition.

Support for English Learners
Have students read the adapted version of *The Shakespeare Stealer* in the *Reader's Notebook: English Learner's Version*. English learners may also read the selection as they listen to the recorded version on the *Listening to Literature Audio CD*.

TEACH

❹ Motivation
Use the Vocab-o-Gram strategy (*General Resources*, p. 14) to introduce students to selection terminology and to make predictions about selection elements. Put the following words on the board or overhead:

feckless	parsimonious
spectral	rustic
prologue	apothecary
apprentice	prospects
master	farthing

Then give students the Vocab-o-Gram chart and have them work with a partner or group to place the words in appropriate categories and make predictions about the play. Have students discuss or explain their word placement, their reasons, and their predictions.

Concept Connector ➡

Students will re-examine their ideas after reading the play.

---

❺ About the Selection
Widge is the apprentice of Dr. Timothy Bright, a rector who is also the inventor of a swift-writing, or shorthand, technique. Under Bright's orders, Widge attends churches around town and copies the sermons using swift-writing; Bright uses Widge to steal the sermons so he does not have to write his own. In the first act of the play, Bright is angry that Widge was caught copying a sermon, which has left Bright open to accusations of theft. A mysterious traveler offers to buy Widge, and Bright agrees. Widge's next master is a businessman who wants to use the swift-writing techniques Widge has mastered to steal *Hamlet*, one of Shakespeare's great tragedies.

❻ Drama
Prologue

• A prologue is an introduction to a literary work, often one that sets the scene and introduces the conflict or the main characters.

• **Ask** students to summarize the purpose of the prologue here.
Possible response: It sets the time period and establishes that viewers and readers should think of the actors and their situation as real.

❼ Critical Viewing

Possible response: He looks earnest and purposeful but also anxious and unsure of himself.

- Have a volunteer read the stage directions.

- **Ask** students which props and stage directions in particular help the audience understand that the action takes place in the early seventeenth century.
Possible response: The setting is called an apothecary, there is a pot of burning pitch, and Widge uses a primitive pencil called a plumbago.

- Point out the paragraph that describes the entrance of Dr. Bright. **Ask** students what information the stage directions contain about this character.
Answer: The stage directions describe his age, weight, complexion, physical disabilities, and voice.

- Discuss with students how the description in the stage directions helps someone who is staging the play. **Ask:** How does it help someone who is reading the play?
Possible responses: This description tells someone who is staging the play what kind of actor should play the part and how he should look and sound. The description helps a reader of the play imagine what Dr. Bright looks like and conveys the information that he is somewhat comical.

Act I

At the rear of the playing area is a shallow, two-story set with a narrow flight of steps leading to the upper story. In the center of the upper story is a single wide doorway draped with a curtain. The lower story has two smaller openings, one at Left and one at Right, also covered by curtains. At various times, this set will represent DR. TIMOTHY BRIGHT'S *apothecary, with* WIDGE'S *living quarters upstairs;* SIMON BASS'S *house; and the backstage area at the Globe Theatre.*

❽ *At Lights Up, it is* DR. BRIGHT'S *apothecary in Berwick-in-Elmet, Yorkshire, c. 1601. A table at Center contains glass and earthenware jars and beakers. One of the containers bubbles over a pot filled with burning pitch.* WIDGE *sits on a stool at the table, copying something from a small bound notebook onto loose sheets of paper, using a plumbago pencil—a stick of graphite wrapped in paper, similar to a grease pencil or charcoal pencil.* WIDGE *is a slight boy of fourteen with a "pudding basin," or bowl, haircut. He wears a working-class tunic.*

All is quiet and peaceful for a long moment. Then the audience is startled by the entrance of DR. TIMOTHY BRIGHT, *a florid, overweight man in his forties or fifties, who is slightly deaf. He strides on brandishing a walking stick, and roaring—but he is nearly as comical as he is menacing.*

BRIGHT: You! . . . clod-pated drivel! (WIDGE *reacts, knocking a beaker to the floor, where it shatters, enraging* BRIGHT *even more*) You . . . halfwitted hoddypeak! Do you know what you've done?!

WIDGE: (*Puts the table between himself and* BRIGHT) I—I didn't mean to! I'll clean it up at once!

BRIGHT: Not *that,* you simpleton! This! (*He waves a paper about*) It's from the bishop's secretary. I've been accused of stealing sermons from my fellow rectors! How in heaven's name did the bishop get wind of this? Have you let a hint drop to anyone of what you were up to? Anyone at all?

WIDGE: Nay, I never! So help me God and halidom!

BRIGHT: Has anyone shown any signs of suspecting you?

WIDGE: Nay, no one.

BRIGHT: You're lying. No, don't bother to deny it. I've the proof here. The rector at Leeds caught you red-handed. Isn't that so? Isn't that so?

WIDGE: (*murmurs*) Aye.

BRIGHT: What's that? Speak up, boy!

WIDGE: Aye! It was a fortnight ago. 'A spotted me scribbling away, and afore I could make me escape, 'a collared me and snatched away me table-book!

BRIGHT: Why did you not tell me this sooner?

WIDGE: I was afeared. I kenned you'd be angry.

BRIGHT: You were right. But . . . if he took away your transcription of his sermon, then . . . then whose sermon was it that I . . . (*he doesn't want to say "stole"*) . . . used as my model last Sunday?

WIDGE: Well . . . I—I wrote it all out as best I could remember . . .

BRIGHT: *You?* I delivered a sermon composed by my idle-headed apprentice? You deceitful little whelp! When will you learn not to lie to me? Well, by St. Pintle, I'll teach you right from wrong! Come here! (WIDGE *dodges the man's grasp, circling the table, but then he slips on the contents of the broken beaker, and is caught.* BRIGHT *raises the stick as if to strike;* WIDGE *cowers and flinches. But then* BRIGHT *tosses him aside and, puffing with the exertion, plops down on the stool*) Ahh, what's the use of it? If I haven't beaten some sense into you by now, I never will. (*shakes his head*) When I think of all I've done for you, all the years I've invested in you. When I took you in five years ago—

WIDGE: Seven.

BRIGHT: Eh? What's that?

WIDGE: It's been seven years, sir.

BRIGHT: That's beside the point. When I took you in, you were a <u>feckless</u>, illiterate orphan with no prospects whatever in the world. I taught you to read and cipher, taught you about medicine, even taught you my system of swift writing, and this is what I get in return? (*waves the paper*) If someone were to offer it, I'd sell your services for a farthing; it's far more than you're worth. Yes, and I expect you'd jump at the chance to change masters, wouldn't you? Eh? (*The way* WIDGE *hangs his head makes it clear that he would*) Well, all I can say is, be careful what you wish for, boy. There are far worse places than this, believe me, and far worse masters than me.

WIDGE: (*aside*) Aye, the Devil, for one.

BRIGHT: What's that?

10 ◀ **Critical Viewing**   How do Widge's posture and attitude reflect his feelings about Dr. Bright? **[Connect]**

from *The Shakespeare Stealer* ■ 709

Gary L. Blackwood
Author's Insight Unless you use a narrator, everything in a play has to be conveyed through dialogue. In the book, the information in this scene is revealed through exposition, an explanation of background material.

Vocabulary Builder
feckless (fek´ lis) *adj.* careless; irresponsible

 Reading Check

11 What has Bright been accused of stealing?

---

9 **Author's Insight**

- Have two students read the parts of Bright and Widge on p. 709.
- Then, **ask** students to summarize the background information that Blackwood provides through the dialogue.
  Answer: Dr. Bright took in Widge, an orphan, when the boy was seven years old. Bright has taught Widge a number of skills, including swift writing, that the boy uses to copy other rectors' sermons so that Bright can use them. Widge was caught, and Bright has received a letter from the bishop's secretary. He becomes increasingly angry when he learns that Widge did not copy the sermon directly.
- **Ask** what this background information implies about Widge.
  Possible response: Widge must be intelligent to have learned the swift writing system. He may also be a good writer, because the sermon that he did not copy directly did not arouse Bright's suspicions.

10 **Critical Viewing**

Answer: Widge looks frightened and defensive. He looks as if he is frightened about the possibility of being yelled at or beaten.

11 **Reading Check**

Answer: Bright has been accused of stealing other rectors' sermons.

Differentiated
Instruction   Solutions for All Learners

Vocabulary for Special Needs Students
Students may need additional help with vocabulary from the play. Help them skim or scan the play, looking for words whose meanings are unclear to them, such as *apothecary, florid, brandishing, menacing, simpleton, fortnight, cower,* and *flinch.* Encourage students to work with a partner to look up the words in a dictionary and to write an original sentence using each word correctly.

Enrichment for Advanced Readers
Blackwood uses many archaic words or word forms to enhance the setting and atmosphere of his play. Have students collect these words, such as *nay, afore, cipher, farthing, afeared, kenned,* and *halidom,* find definitions, and create a classroom Elizabethan dictionary.

• Read aloud the bracketed passage of stage directions.

• **Ask** students what they learn about Falconer and what impressions this description of him creates.
Possible response: Falconer could be a symbolic death figure with his hooded cloak, grim facial expression, scarred face, dark beard, and hooked nose. He seems to foreshadow something terrible or dangerous to come.

• Point out to students that the actor who plays Falconer also portrays another character, Simon Bass. **Ask** students how this information could be important to the plays' costumer and director.
Possible response: Knowing that one actor plays both roles, the costumer and director might prefer to cast a clean-shaven actor who could be fitted with a false beard, hooked nose, and scar. This would allow the actor to change his appearance easily and perform both roles.

⑬ **Author's Insight**

• Ask two volunteers to read the roles of Bright and Falconer in the bracketed section.

• Then, **ask** students what they learn about the two men from their dialogue.
Possible response: Bright seems like the quintessential salesperson— willing to hedge the truth in order to put the best possible light on his product. Falconer seems straightforward but skeptical.

WIDGE: Nothing. (*He sets about cleaning up the broken beaker, while* BRIGHT *checks his boiling potion. The silence is broken by the sound of an iron door knocker pounding O.S. Right*)

BRIGHT: Yes, yes, coming. Bloody patients. Why can't they be sick in the daytime? (*He crosses to Left, reaches O.S to open a door, then backs up as* FALCONER *enters, a tall figure in a hooded cloak, looking* ⑫ *as grim as Death. Beneath the cloak he carries a rapier. We seldom see his face, but when he does reveal a glimpse of it, we see that he has a bushy, dark beard and a hooked nose. A nasty scar disfigures one side of his face*) G-good evening, sir. How may I serve you?

FALCONER: (*seems to reach for his rapier, but instead takes a leather-bound book from beneath his cloak. In a deep, almost* _spectral_ *voice*) This is yours, is it not?

BRIGHT: (*moves hesitantly closer to the man*) Why, yes. Yes, it is. It's a copy of my book on charactery.

FALCONER: Does it *work*?

BRIGHT: I beg your pardon?

FALCONER: Your system of charactery. Does it work?

BRIGHT: Of course it works. Using my system of swift writing, one may without effort transcribe the written or the spoken word—

FALCONER: How long does it take?

⑬ **BRIGHT:** As I was about to say, one may set down speech as rapidly as it is spoken—

FALCONER: (*impatient*) Yes, yes, but how long to learn it?

BRIGHT: Well, that depends upon the aptitude of the—

FALCONER: How *long*?

BRIGHT: (*nervously, stretching the truth*) Oh, two months, perhaps three. Well, let's say four. Five, at the outside.

FALCONER: (*tosses the book rather contemptuously onto the table*) To how many have you taught this system of yours?

BRIGHT: Let me see . . . There's my apprentice, here, and then . . .

FALCONER: How *many*?

BRIGHT: Well . . . one, actually.

FALCONER: And how proficient is he?

710 ■ *Drama*

Drama
Staging Detailed description of Falconer provides valuable information for both costumers and actors when staging the play.

Vocabulary Builder
spectral (spek′ trəl) *adj.* like a phantom or ghost

Gary L. Blackwood
Author's Insight Since dialogue comes more easily to me than narrative and description, there are long passages of it in my novels. Scenes like this one are taken almost directly from the book.

Vocabulary Development

Think-Aloud: Context Clues
Direct students' attention to the word *contemptuously* in the sixth line from the bottom of page 710. Using a think-aloud process, model how to use context to infer the meaning of an unknown word. Say to students:

I'm going to think aloud to show you how I would figure out the meaning of *contemptuously* from its context.

In this sentence, *contemptuously* is being used to describe the way Falconer throws down Bright's book on character.

I can tell he is impatient with Dr. Bright, particularly when his questions are not answered directly. I do not think Falconer has a high opinion of Dr. Bright even though he is obviously interested in the doctor's book. Because of this attitude, I conclude that Falconer is scornful of Dr. Bright and therefore acts as if the book is not worth his while. I think *contemptuously* means "feeling or showing that a thing is low or worthless."

Literature in Context | Culture Connection

Shorthand and Swiftwriting

Dr. Timothie Bright was a real person who developed a "swift-writing" system in 1588. Efforts to create a fast way of recording speech go back more than 2,000 years.

- In 63 B.C., Marcus Tiro invented a system of abbreviations to transcribe speeches. His ampersand (&) is still used today.
- Nineteenth-century writer Charles Dickens used Gurney's system, developed in 1707.
- Both the Pitman and Gregg systems, invented during the 1800s, are still in use.

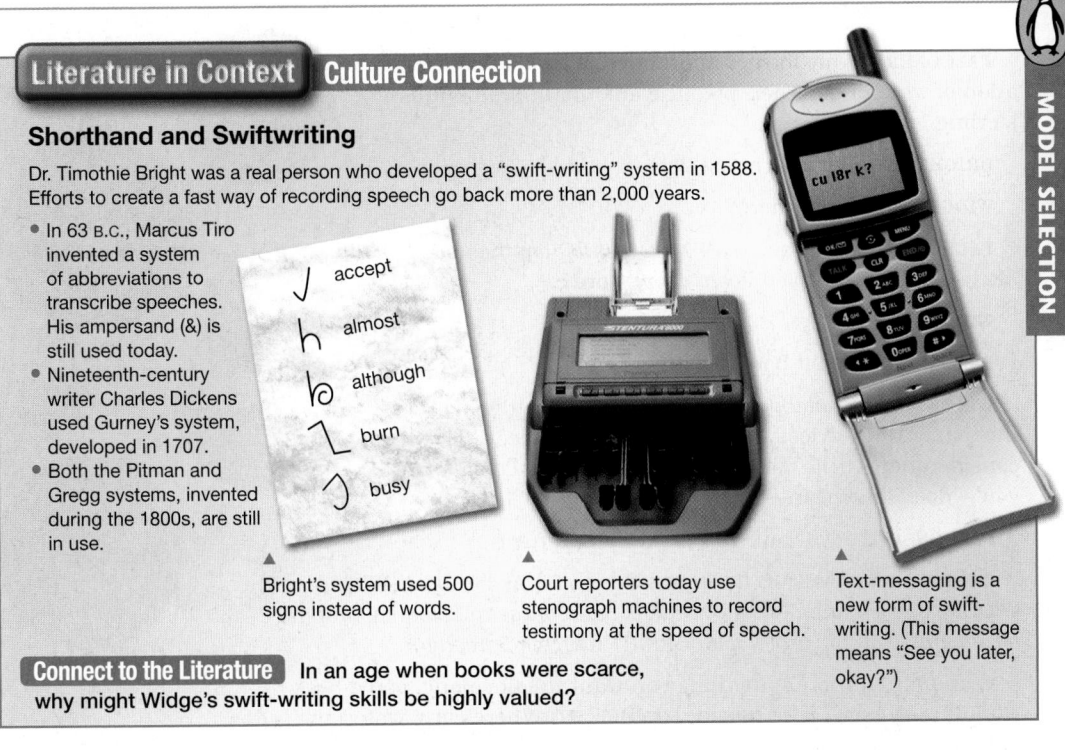

▲ Bright's system used 500 signs instead of words.

▲ Court reporters today use stenograph machines to record testimony at the speed of speech.

▲ Text-messaging is a new form of swift-writing. (This message means "See you later, okay?")

Connect to the Literature In an age when books were scarce, why might Widge's swift-writing skills be highly valued?

---

⑮ BRIGHT: Oh, quite proficient. Extremely. (WIDGE *is surprised to hear this*)

FALCONER: Show me.

BRIGHT: (*to* WIDGE) Are you deaf, boy? The gentleman wishes a demonstration of your skill.

WIDGE: (*picks up notebook and pencil*) What must I write?

FALCONER: Write this: "I hereby convey to the bearer of this paper the services of my former apprentice—"

WIDGE: Go on. I've kept up wi' you.

FALCONER: Your name.

WIDGE: Pardon?

FALCONER: What is your *name*?

BRIGHT: Widge. It's Widge. (*laughs as if to show that he realizes how odd it sounds*)

Drama
Dramatic Effect The author's instruction to actors about how to react to specific events or dialogue adds to the play's illusion of reality.

⑯ **Reading Check**

What kind of system has Dr. Bright invented?

from The Shakespeare Stealer ■ 711

- Explain to students that the word Transition is used in this play to indicate a break between scenes or settings.

- Discuss how directors make transitions between scenes in plays and movies. **Ask:** What are some different kinds of ways to mark a transition on stage and on screen? **Possible responses:** Transitions on stage are often made by lowering the curtain or dimming the stage lights. Film directors use blackouts too, as well as other visual effects such as a quick cut, a fade-out, or a wipe from side to side.

- **Ask** students to put themselves in the role of director and devise a way to handle the transition in this scene. **Possible response:** Students might suggest that the actors walk to the front of the stage as the curtain closes behind them. The curtain rises to reveal a backdrop of woods.

FALCONER: "—my former apprentice, Widge, in consideration of which I have accepted the amount of ten pounds sterling."

BRIGHT: (*staggered*) Ten p—?!

WIDGE: Is that all, then?

FALCONER: Let me see it. (WIDGE *hands him the notebook. Skeptical*) You've copied down every word?

WIDGE: Aye.

FALCONER: Read it back.

WIDGE: (*takes notebook*) "I hereby convey to the bearer of this paper the services of my former apprentice, Widge, in consideration— (*the meaning of the words finally sinks in*) Do you— does this mean—?

FALCONER: Copy it out, now, in a normal hand.

BRIGHT: (*when* WIDGE *hesitates*) Go on. Do as he says! (*While* WIDGE *copies it out,* FALCONER *takes out a purse and counts out ten sovereigns onto the table, with* BRIGHT *watching greedily*)

FALCONER: If there's anything you want to take along, you'd best fetch it now, boy. I'll be outside. (*to* BRIGHT) Where can I water my horse?

BRIGHT: On the north side of the house, there's a trough. (*to* WIDGE) Go on, lad. (*through the following* WIDGE *goes upstairs, collects his meager belongings, including a leather wallet on a strap. To* FALCONER) I hope you'll keep a close eye on the boy. (*The concern this implies is belied by* BRIGHT'S *next line*) He can be sluggish if you don't stir him from time to time with a stick. (FALCONER *exits*) Move your bones, boy, before he changes his mind. (WIDGE *descends the stairs reluctantly*)

WIDGE: Must I go with him, then?

BRIGHT: (*busy fondling the sovereigns*) Eh? Of course you must. He's paid for you, and far more handsomely than I would have dreamed.

WIDGE: Will you not bid me farewell, at least, sir?

BRIGHT: (*perfunctorily*) Of course, of course. Fair 'chieve you, boy, ⑰ fair 'chieve you.

Transition

Drama
Stage Directions
By simply indicating "Transition," Blackwood lets the director devise the best way to show a change of scene.

(FALCONER *enters at Down Right, looking about warily, trailed by* WIDGE, *who is rubbing his backside*)

WIDGE: Gog's blood, I'm glad to be off that horse.

FALCONER: It won't be for long. Here. (*Hands* WIDGE *a journey cake, nibbles at one himself, still looking about alertly. They pass a flask of something back and forth*)

WIDGE: When will we be at our destination?

FALCONER: When we get there.

WIDGE: These woods are much more . . . wild than around Berwick, and more dense. It feels almost as though they're closing in on us. (*shivers*)

FALCONER: Stop your wagging tongue. You'll have every cutpurse within a league down upon us.

WIDGE: Cutpurse? (*looks about even more fearfully*) You mean . . . there are thieves in these woods? (*realizes he's still talking*) Sorry.

(*Horse whinnies O.S. Right.* FALCONER *reacts, abruptly puts away the flask and loosens his rapier in its sheath, looking about and listening intently.* THREE THIEVES *enter at Left, one armed with a pistol, two with swords*)

THIEF #1: Don't move, if you value your life.

FALCONER: (*unexpectedly amiable*) God rest you, gentlemen.

THIEF #1: God, is it? Don't tell me you're a parson.

FALCONER: No, no. Far from it.

THIEF #1: Good. I don't like doing business with parsons. They're too <u>parsimonious</u>. (*Laughs*) All right, let's have it, then.

FALCONER: Have what?

THIEF #1: (*Laughs again*) Have what, 'a says! Have what? Why, have a pot of ale wi' us, of course. (*More soberly*) Come now, enough pleasantries. Let's have your purse, man.

FALCONER: (*Pulls out his hefty purse. Still amiable*) Ah. Forgive me for not taking your meaning.

THIEF #1: Oh, aye, an you forgive *me* for taking your purse.

(FALCONER *steps to the man, who holds out a hand for the purse. Instead of handing it over,* FALCONER *swings it swiftly upward, catching Thief #1 alongside the head. The man cries out, crumples to*

Gary L. Blackwood
Author's Insight
Shakespeare was very fond of *puns*—humorous plays on words that sound alike—so I made liberal use of them, too. Since they depend on words sounding alike, they work even better in a play than in a book.

Vocabulary Builder
parsimonious (pär´ sə mō´nē əs) *adj.* miserly; stingy

Reading Check
Why does Widge leave Bright to go with Falconer?

from *The Shakespeare Stealer* ■ 713

⓲ Author's Insight
- Have a volunteer read aloud the bracketed sentence.
- **Ask** students to explain the pun. **Answer:** Someone who is parsimonious is frugal to the point of being cheap, miserly, or stingy. The pun in this instance has more to do with the similarities in sound between the words *parson* and *parsimonious*; it also implies that all parsons are stingy. It is not a very clever pun, and its use by the Thief suggests that he is not very intelligent or shrewd.
- **Ask** students why a playwright—or any author—might use puns. **Possible responses:** Puns are funny and can provide a light moment in a serious scene. Puns may appeal to different audiences; some puns may be intellectual and arcane and others are common or vulgar.
- Then, **ask** students what purpose the pun in this scene serves. **Possible response:** The thief hopes that by making a joke, he can get Falconer to hand over his money without a fight or catch him off guard.

⓳ Reading Check
Answer: Widge did not have much choice. Bright sold him to Falconer.

Differentiated Instruction   Solutions for All Learners

Strategy for Special Needs Students
To help students keep track of the action in the play, have them create timelines of the events in the order they occur. Tell them to mark the entrance of a new character by using a second color and to mark a change of setting with a third color. Have them add to their timelines as they continue to read.

Strategy for English Learners
Students may need some help understanding puns in English. Explain that a pun is a joke or humorous remark that relies on two or more meanings of a multiple-meaning word, or the meanings of words that sound similar. Give a simple example, such as "There was a fight at the fish restaurant last night. It seems that the filets were battered." Explain that this pun uses two different meanings of the word *battered* to create humor.

Dialogue

- Introduce the term *comic relief*. Explain to students that it means the introduction of a comic element into a tense, dramatic, or suspenseful scene. Comic relief can be accomplished with a character, a line of dialogue, or even a facial expression.

- Tell students that Shakespeare often juxtaposed the serious and the silly, the tragic and the comic. Modern moviemakers also introduce comic elements into action sequences or serious scenes. **Ask** students what the effect of such juxtaposition might be. **Possible response:** By making the audience laugh in the middle of a serious scene, the playwright or director relieves the building tension for a moment. Or, as in this play, a joke or pun can restore a previously light-hearted mood.

21 Critical Viewing

Possible response: Widge looks much happier here than he has in previous photographs, and Libby had been described as sympathetic in the stage directions. Widge will probably find more happiness in his new life than he did with Dr. Bright.

---

the ground; his pistol goes off wildly. The other thieves spring forward. FALCONER *draws his rapier, parries an ineffectual blow, kicks the man in the groin.* WIDGE *picks up a rock, but has no chance to use it.* FALCONER *grasps the third man's blade in his cloak-wrapped hand, yanks it away, and slices the man's ribs with his own sword. With the thieves lying about groaning,* FALCONER *lifts his purse with the point of his sword, flips it in the air, catches it, then shakes a single coin from it and throws it at the men's feet)*

20 FALCONER: If this is a toll road, you might simply have *tolled* me.

THIEF #1: *(laughs, then groans in pain)* Would that you had been a parson after all.

FALCONER: *(to* WIDGE*)* Come. *(starts Off Right)*

WIDGE: What you did back there—I've never seen the like of it.

FALCONER: Yes, well, you haven't seen much, have you?

Transition

(A bed has been brought on upstairs, and a writing desk and two chairs downstairs. FALCONER *and* WIDGE *enter at Right.* WIDGE *is walking stiffly, wincing)*

WIDGE: Are we in London, then?

FALCONER: *(scoffing)* Hardly. This is Leicester.

*(*LIBBY, *a sympathetic, plain woman in a maid's garb, emerges from one of the downstairs doorways)*

LIBBY: Welcome back, sir.

FALCONER: The boy will be staying the night. Show him to the garret. *(Exits upstage)*

LIBBY: Yes, sir. *(looking Widge over)* Where you from, then?

WIDGE: Berwick-in-Elmet.

LIBBY: Where's *that?*

WIDGE: Up Yorkshire way. Near Leeds.

LIBBY: I see. Well, come. We'd best get you to your room. *(Leads him up the steps)* I'll bring you some food up in a bit. Here you are. It's not much.

WIDGE: More than I'm used to. Mind you, it could be a pit of snakes for all I care, I'm that exhausted. *(sinks down on the bed)* You didn't seem surprised at all, that 'a came back wi' *me* in tow.

LIBBY: Nothing the master does surprises me. Have a good rest.

Drama

Dialogue Falconer's awful pun on the word *told* restores a humorous tone to the scene after a violent struggle.

21 ▶ **Critical Viewing** Based on this photograph of Widge with Libby, do you think his new life will be better than his old one? **[Predict]**

Vocabulary Development

Expressive Vocabulary

As students are discussing the play, encourage them to use the expressive vocabulary presented earlier. You might encourage them with sentence starters like these:

1. The scene between Widge and Libby *illuminates* Widge's character by . . .
2. My opinion of Falconer's motivation was *confirmed* when he . . .
3. The *episode* in which Bright sells Widge made me think . . .
4. One *aspect* of drama that I notice in this play is . . .

Transition

(WIDGE *wakes up, rubs eyes, looks around at the unfamiliar surroundings then hobbles downstairs.* LIBBY *is at the bottom of the steps*)

LIBBY: I was just coming to wake you. The master said to bring you to him as soon as you were up. I don't think he expected you to sleep so late. (*They cross to where* SIMON BASS *sits at the writing desk. He is played by the same actor who plays* FALCONER, *minus the hooded cloak, the curly black wig, the hooked nose, the swarthy skin, the beard, the scar, and the high boots that make him several inches taller.* BASS *is much more approachable and genial, but a prickliness lurks beneath the surface*)

WIDGE: Will 'a be cross wi' me, do you wis?

LIBBY: I can't say. He's a queer one, the master is. (*sotto voce*) Not to tell him I said so, now. (*Leaning into desk area*) I've brought the boy, sir.

BASS: (*without turning; we still assume it's* FALCONER *sitting there*) Come in, Widge. (WIDGE *enters the "room," clearly awed by the furnishings*) Sit down.

WIDGE: Eh? Oh. (*sits*) Sorry. It's just that I've never seen such a grand room, with so many books, not even at Squire Cheyney's.

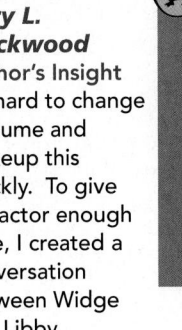

Gary L. Blackwood
Author's Insight
It's hard to change costume and makeup this quickly. To give the actor enough time, I created a conversation between Widge and Libby.

Reading Check

Where does Falconer bring Widge?

from *The Shakespeare Stealer* 715

22 Author's Insight

- Have students read the bracketed passage to themselves.
- Refer students to Falconer's entrance earlier in the play and your discussion of his appearance. Point out that Blackwood's comment refers to the fact that Falconer and Bass are played by the same actor.
- Then **ask** students to speculate about why Falconer and Simon Bass are played by the same actor. If necessary, refer students to Blackwood's introduction to this selection.
  Possible response: Blackwood said that he had to rewrite the play so it could be performed by the fewest actors possible.
- **Ask** students whether they think that the plot might require Falconer and Bass to be played by the same actor.
  Possible response: It is possible that Falconer and Bass are the same person—that Bass uses the alias Falconer so that he can conduct his business in secret.
- **Ask:** What evidence in the text supports this hypothesis?
  Possible response: Widge is bewildered by Bass's appearance and at first mistakes Bass for Falconer.

23 Reading Check

Answer: Falconer brings Widge to Leicester, to Simon Bass's house.

Dialogue

- Have a volunteer read the bracketed passage on p. 717. Then,
ask students why Bass might have
been concerned about Widge's
language.

  Possible responses: Bass might
  want Widge to represent himself as
  someone from the upper class
  rather than from the peasantry in
  order to do his job. Bass might feel
  that it reflects poorly on a master
  to have a rustic apprentice.

- Discuss with students whether the
  way a person speaks reveals anything about that person's intelligence or character.

  Possible responses: Some
  students may say that the way a
  person speaks reveals only where
  that person was raised. Other
  students may say that educated
  people speak more correctly than
  other people and sound more
  intelligent.

716 Drama

BASS: Wait until you see the houses in London. (*He turns, rises. We and* WIDGE *get our first good look at him. Widge is obviously bewildered*)

WIDGE: Who—who are you?

BASS: My name is Simon Bass. I'm your new master.

WIDGE: But—but I thought—

BASS: You thought the one who brought you here was to be your master.

WIDGE: Aye.

BASS: (*shrugs*) Falconer is not the most communicative of men, I warrant, nor the most genial. But he is reliable and effective. I could not go to Yorkshire myself . . . for various reasons. He got you here safe and sound, it appears.

WIDGE: (*squirming on his sore rear end*) Well, *safe*, at any rate.

㉔ BASS: Let's get down to business. You'll want to know what's expected of you.

WIDGE: Aye.

BASS: Very well. The first thing I expect is for you to say "yes," rather than *"aye."* I'd just as soon you did not sound like a complete <u>rustic</u>. Understood?

WIDGE: Aye—I mean, yes.

BASS: Excellent. Now, when you go to London—

WIDGE: London?

BASS: Yes. It's a large city to the south.

WIDGE: I ken that, but—

㉕ BASS: Let me finish, then ask questions. You will be attending a play called *The Tragedy of Hamlet, Prince of Denmark.* You will copy down the play, every word of it, in Dr. Bright's charactery, and then you will deliver it to me. (WIDGE *looks uncomfortable*) Do you have some objection to that?

WIDGE: Nay, not especially. It's only words, after all. It's just that— Well, when a wight back home caught me copying his sermons, 'a got very upset wi' me.

㉖ ◄ Critical Viewing Which details in this photograph show that Bass, at left, is more sophisticated than Widge? [**Compare and Contrast**]

from The Shakespeare Stealer ■ *717*

Drama
Dialogue Here and throughout the play, Blackwood uses words like *aye* and *rustic* to reinforce the setting in time and place.

Vocabulary Builder
rustic (rus´tik) *n.* unsophisticated person

㉗ **Reading Check**
What does Bass want Widge to do in London?

㉕ Background
Hamlet Tell students that *Hamlet* is one of Shakespeare's best-known tragedies. Invite students who are familiar with the play to describe or summarize it for the class. Students may know the play from the film version directed by and starring Mel Gibson.

㉖ Critical Viewing
Possible responses: Bass has on a suit that seems much fancier than Widge's simple tunic. His hairstyle is more sophisticated than Widge's "pudding-bowl" cut. His posture and demeanor are more upright and confident than Widge's. Bass is standing over Widge, ready to give him orders, and Widge looks subservient and timid.

㉗ Reading Check
Answer: Widge is expected to attend Shakespeare's play *Hamlet* and copy every word of it in Dr. Bright's charactery.

Differentiated
Instruction   Solutions for All Learners

Enrichment for Gifted/Talented Students Suggest that students write and perform what they imagine the next scene of *The Shakespeare Stealer* will be. You may wish to have two different groups of students write possible endings for the play and compare the two versions.	**Enrichment for Advanced Readers** If students are intrigued by this excerpt from *The Shakespeare Stealer,* suggest that they read the whole play or the young adult novel that the play is based on. Have students who read the play write a review of it as if they were theater or movie critics. Students who read the novel might report to the class on differences between the excerpt presented here and the beginning of the novel.

- Have two students read the brack-eted parts for Widge and Bass.

- **Ask** students what conflict Widge is plunged into with these lines.
Answer: Widge is being asked to steal Shakespeare's work.

- Discuss with students how Bass's motivation for stealing Shakespeare's works differs from Dr. Bright's copying of other rectors' sermons.
Possible response: Dr. Bright used copied sermons because he was lazy. Bass admits that his motivation is to make money.

- After pointing out that Widge's conflict is what sets the plot or action of the rest of the play in motion, **ask** students to speculate on how the plot will continue in the rest of the play.
Possible responses: Some stu-dents may say that Widge will be successful in copying Shakespeare's play. Other students may say that Widge will be caught. Students may speculate that Bass and Falconer will suffer a downfall but that Widge will prosper.

Concept Connector

Have students return to the Vocab-o-Gram they completed before read-ing the play. Review the vocabulary and clarify any words by returning to the selection or using a dictionary. Have students refine their predictions about the play.

BASS: Then you'll have to make certain you don't get caught, won't you? You will use a small tablebook, easily concealed . . . (*rummages through his desk*) You see how easily it's concealed? Even I can't find it. Ah, here it is. (*hands it to* WIDGE) Keep it in your wallet. You have a plumbago pencil?

WIDGE: Ay—Yes. An I might ask—for what purpose am I to do this?

BASS: Does it matter?

WIDGE: Nay; I was only curious. The only plays I've ever seen are the ones the church does at Easter and Yuletide, and those cer-tainly didn't seem worth stealing.

BASS: (*being prickly now*) I would prefer it if you did not use that term. I am not a thief. I am a man of business, and one of my more profitable ventures is a company of players. They are not so success-ful as the Lord Chamberlain's Men or the Admiral's Men, of course, but they draw a sizable audience here in the Midlands. If we could stage a current work, by a well-known poet, we could double our **28** profits. Now, sooner or later someone will pry this *Tragedy of Hamlet* from the grasp of its author, Mr. Shakespeare, just as they have his earlier plays. I would like that someone to be me. If I wait for others to do it, they will do a botched job, cobbled together from various sources, none of them very reliable. Mr. Shakespeare deserves bet-ter. He is a poet of quality, perhaps of genius, and if his work is to be borrowed, it should be done properly. That is your mission. If you fulfill it satisfactorily, the reward will be considerable.

WIDGE: And . . . what an I do not?

BASS: Falconer will make certain that you do.

WIDGE: Oh. I didn't ken that 'a would go wi' me.

BASS: Did you suppose I would send you off to London on your own? I might as well send you to Guiana. Go and rest now, or soak your haunches, or whatever you will. You'll be leaving for London early in the morning. (*He exits.* WIDGE *shuffles downstage as* LIBBY *enters at Left*)

Drama
Conflict With this speech, Blackwood lays out the central elements of his plot. Readers can link the title of the play with Bass's information to predict how the play will develop.

Vocabulary Development

Vocabulary Knowledge Rating
When students have completed reading and discussing *The Shakespeare Stealer,* have them take out their **Vocabulary Knowledge Rating Chart** for this play. Read the words aloud once more and have students rate their knowledge of the words again in the After Reading column. Clarify any words that are still problematic.

Have students write their own definitions or examples in the appropriate column. Encourage students to use the words in further discussion and written work about this selection. Remind them that they will be accountable for these words on the Selection Test.

From the Author's Desk
Gary L. Blackwood's Insights Into *The Shakespeare Stealer*

㉙ Q. Where did you get the idea for *The Shakespeare Stealer*?

A. I'd studied Elizabethan theater in college, and learned about how acting companies stole plays from one another. But it wasn't until I stumbled across a brief mention of Dr. Timothie Bright and his system of swift-writing that I came up with the notion of having someone steal *Hamlet* by copying it down in shorthand. In my first version of the story, that someone was Dr. Bright, not Widge.

㉚ Q. What was it like to play the lead role in your own play?

A. As an actor, I approached it much the same as I would any other play. I didn't know the lines by heart, so I still had to learn them, and I still had to listen to the director. As a playwright, I would have preferred to see what someone else would bring to the role.

㉛ Q. When the director and actors are rehearsing your play, do they ask your advice?

A. The director serves as liaison between the actors and the playwright, so I seldom give advice directly to the actors. Generally, directors just do things the way they think best and assume that, if I have a problem with it, I'll let them know.

StudentCorner

㉜ Q. How much of *The Shakespeare Stealer* is fact, and how much is fiction?

—Jessica Meyer, Crawfordsville, Indiana

A. As far as I know, everything relating to Elizabethan theater and plays is accurate. I couldn't hope to re-create sixteenth-century speech, but I did include lots of authentic words and phrases ("clod-pated drivel," "wight"). With the exception of Widge, Simon Bass, and Julian, all the major characters are based on real people.

Writing Workshop: *Work in Progress*

How-to Essay

For a how-to essay you may write, record five tasks that you do well. Choose one of those tasks, and make a list of steps necessary to accomplish it. Put this Task List in your writing portfolio.

From the Author's Desk: Gary L. Blackwood ■ 719

---

by thinking of five tasks, then selecting one of them and listing the steps needed to accomplish it. Point out to students that in this type of expository writing, they must anticipate an uninformed reader's confusion and must make their writing as clear, direct, and interesting as possible. Suggest that in listing the steps of the task, they put themselves in the reader's position and ask themselves what the reader needs to know to complete the process.

Apply the Skills

Drama

Thinking About the Selection

1. **Respond:** Do you think Bass's assignment to Widge is unethical or wrong? Why or why not?

2. **(a) Recall:** What special skill has Widge been taught by Dr. Bright? **(b) Summarize:** What happened when the rector at Leeds caught Widge transcribing a sermon? **(c) Infer:** What does this episode show about Widge's talent as a writer?

3. **(a) Infer:** How did Falconer learn about Dr. Bright's swift-writing system? Explain. **(b) Speculate:** Why does Falconer test Widge?

4. **(a) Recall:** How does Bass plan to profit from Widge's skill? **(b) Take a Position:** Do you see any similarities between Bass's plan and modern-day practices involving music or movies? Explain.

Drama Review

5. **(a)** Note three details in the **stage directions** that establish the setting of the **drama** in Shakespearean England. **(b)** Note three examples of **dialogue** that reinforce that setting.

6. **(a)** Use a chart like the one shown to explore how characters use **props** to reveal their personalities. **(a)** In the first column, list props that are used by Dr. Bright, Widge, and Falconer. In the second column, record how the characters use each prop. In the third column, describe what their actions show about their personalities. **(b)** In a small group, discuss your findings and share them with the class.

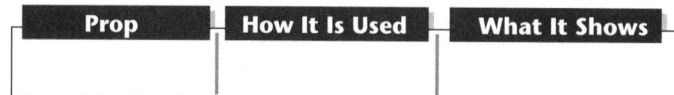

Prop	How It Is Used	What It Shows

Research the Author

Gary Blackwood has written several books that continue Widge's adventures. Write the **foreword,** or introductory material, to a collection of these works. Include summaries and statements by critics. Write to interest your peers in reading these works.

- Use the Internet and your library to locate Blackwood works that feature Widge and Shakespeare.
- Gather enough information to summarize the plots.
- Read the reviews, and identify key passages to use in your writing.
- Write your foreword and share it with the class.

Answers (left column)

1. Some students will say that it is wrong because it is stealing. Other students may say that it is similar to copying a video or audio tape, CD, or DVD and that they see nothing wrong with it—even though it is illegal.

2. (a) Dr. Bright has taught Widge swiftwriting. (b) The rector took away Widge's table-book and reported him and Dr. Bright to the bishop. (c) Widge was able to recall the sermon and produce a version good enough to convince Dr. Bright that it was authentic. Widge has a good memory and possibly a talent for writing.

3. (a) Falconer knows about swiftwriting from having read Dr. Bright's book. (b) He wants to see if the technique really works.

4. (a) Bass wants to steal *Hamlet* so that his theater company can stage a current work by a well-known poet and therefore double its profits. (b) There are similarities between Bass's plan and modern-day practices such as software piracy and bootleg editions of albums or movies.

5. (a) The first scene takes place in an apothecary. Widge uses an old-fashioned pencil. Falconer carries a rapier. (b) "So help me God and halidom." "You. . . halfwitted hoddypeak." "Fair 'chieve you."

6. (a) **Sample response: Prop:** Dr. Bright—walking stick. **How It Is Used:** He uses it to intimidate Widge. **What It Shows:** He likes to be in control of others, but his "bark" may be worse than his "bite." (b) Students should support their opinions with evidence from the text.

Research the Author

Students may complete this research assignment for homework. Tell them that they can find information about Gary L. Blackwood's other plays and novels in a library or online.

QuickReview

Selection at a Glance
The special talents of a young man lead him to adventure in Shakespearean England.

Go Online
Assessment

For: Self-test
Visit: www.PHSchool.com
Web Code: epa-6501

Drama: a narrative written to be performed by actors

Dialogue: conversation between or among characters; the words actors speak

Stage Directions: instructions about how a drama is to be performed

Props: objects that actors use onstage

Go Online
Author Link
For: More about the author
Visit: www.PHSchool.com
Web Code: epe-9501
For additional information about Gary L. Blackwood, give students this Web Code. After typing the Web Code, students select *Gary L. Blackwood.*

Skills You Will Learn

Literary Analysis: *Dialogue and Stage Directions*
Reading Skill: *Using Text Aids*

Literary Analysis: *Blank Verse*
Reading Skill: *Reading in Sentences*

Literary Analysis: *Soliloquy, Aside, and Monologue; Allusion*
Reading Skill: *Paraphrasing*

Literary Analysis: *Dramatic Irony; Comic Relief and Puns*
Reading Skill: *Breaking Down Long Sentences*

Literary Analysis: *Tragedy; Character's Motive*
Reading Skill: *Cause and Effect*

Reading Skill: *Skimming and Scanning*

Literary Analysis: *Archetypal Theme*

Literature You Will Read

Summarize 721

Skills Overview
Reading Skill: Summarizing
- Using text aids
- Reading in sentences
- Paraphrasing
- Breaking down long sentences
- Identifying causes and effects

Vocabulary Development
- Word Roots

Literary Analysis
- Dialogue: stage directions
- Blank Verse: iambic pentameter
- Dramatic Speeches: allusion, aside, soliloquy, monologue
- Dramatic Irony: comic relief, puns
- Tragedy: character's motive and resulting behavior

Writing
- How to Essay
- Work in Progress, pp. 723

Monitoring Progress

Diagnose: Before you begin Part 1, administer the **Diagnostic Test** for Unit 5, Part 1. This test will identify students' level of readiness for the reading and vocabulary skills in Part 1. Use the **Interpretation Guide** for the Diagnostic Test to determine which students need help with prerequisite skills before beginning Part 1.

Preteach and Prepare: Use the information indicated in the **Interpretation Guide** to help students build prerequisite skills. In addition, prepare students by using the **Vocabulary Warm-up** activities and the **Reading Warm-up** activities as necessary for each selection set.

Teach: Use the instructional plan and resources provided to teach the skills and selections.

Assess: After students have completed Part 1, administer the **Benchmark Test** for Unit 5, Part 1. The test results will indicate which skills students have mastered and those on which they need more work.

Reteach: Use the Interpretation Guide to determine the appropriate reteaching pages from the **Reading Kit**.

Intervention: The prerequisite and reteaching pages are also available in the **Success Tracker**.

Differentiated Instruction   Solutions for All Learners

Resources for Monitoring Progress

Unit 5 Resources
Unit 5, Part 1 Diagnostic Test, pp. 15–17
Unit 5, Part 1 Benchmark Test, pp. 117–122

Reading Kit

Success Tracker

Introduce the Reading Skill

- Introduce the reading skill: summarizing. Draw students' attention to the definition. Point out that summarizing is an excellent note-taking technique as it covers the main points of a text.

- Tell students that because summarizing requires them to put details from the text into their own words, it will increase their comprehension of the material and enhance their ability to remember what they've read. Furthermore, by focusing on the main points, students can quickly grasp and remember the most important ideas in a text.

- Point out that there are a number of strategies for summarizing. Tell students that they must select those techniques which most effectively fit the purpose of their reading and their individual needs.

Model the Reading Strategies

- To model these strategies, direct students to the graphic organizer on this page, and have them read the paragraph.

- **Ask** students which sentences they find confusing.
  Possible answers: Students may find sentence three or four difficult to understand.

- Have students look at the third sentence and point out how the comma helps to make the meaning of the sentence more accessible. Direct students to **note a** at the bottom of the paragraph.

- Tell students to break down sentence 4 into three parts, grouping ideas to understand what it says. Direct them to **note b**.

- Direct students to **note c. Ask:** What is the cause of the play's popularity?
  Answer: The play's timeless theme accounts for its popularity.

- Then, model for students how they might summarize the text. For example:

  The Tragedy of Romeo and Juliet, a famous love story by William Shakespeare, has remained popular for more than 500 years because it touches on a timeless theme.

Reading: Summarize

> To **summarize** is to briefly state the most important points of a text in your own words.

When you summarize, you retell the events and ideas in the original work in your own words. Because a summary includes only the most important points, it is significantly shorter than the original work.

Skills and Strategies You Will Learn in Part 1

In Part 1, you will learn
- to use **text aids** to determine important points to **summarize.** (p. 728)
- to **read according to punctuation** to **group ideas.** (p. 756)
- to **paraphrase,** or restate something in your own words. (p. 782)
- to **break down long sentences** and **paraphrase** them. (p. 814)
- to **identify cause-and-effect** relationships that you would include in a **summary.** (p. 832)
- to **skim and scan** to identify the most important points in a piece of writing. (p. 852)

Using the Skills and Strategies in Part 1

In Part 1, you will learn strategies that help you break down a text to identify the most important ideas and the relationships among them. You will also practice restating ideas in your own words and organizing them in a summary.

The Tragedy of Romeo and Juliet is one of the most famous love stories of all time. However, this play is much more than a simple love story. Written by William Shakespeare in the fifteenth century, [a] the play continues to be enjoyed by audiences more than 500 years later. [b] The reason *Romeo and Juliet,* like the rest of Shakespeare's work, enjoys an enduring popularity is that it touches on a timeless theme. [c]

[a] The comma helps you group the words in this long sentence into two ideas about the play.

[b] If you break down the sentence, you can paraphrase the main part.

[c] The cause of the play's popularity is one of the main points in the text and would be included in a summary.

---

722 ■ *Drama*

Professional Development

"That's a Quote"

Academic inquiry insists that students prove what they assert. This activity engages students in important research behavior necessary to prove their point.

Often understanding a character, the conflict or the theme is a matter of paying close attention to what the narrator or characters say. After completing a play or reading significant portions of it, have students find the quotation(s) or lines that they think best illustrate or describe any or all of the following:

- the theme
- the protagonist and antagonist
- the central tension or conflict

Have students share the quotations they have chosen and explain the reasons for their choices. Students' choices provide the opportunity for important discussion.

Academic Vocabulary: Words for Connecting Themes in Literature

The following words will help you write and talk about themes in the literature in this unit.

Word	Definition	Example Sentence
condense *v.*	shorten or make concise	The summary *condenses* the action.
relevant *adj.*	related to	The theme is as *relevant* today as it was in Shakespeare's time.
ambiguous *adj.*	having numerous possible meanings	We discussed the *ambiguous* ending.
elaborate *v.; adj.*	work out in detail; extremely detailed	The author *elaborates* on her ideas. There were *elaborate* descriptions of the island.
illuminate *v.*	make clear; provide insight	The speech will *illuminate* his motives.

Vocabulary Skill: Word Roots

▸ A **word root** is the basic meaning of a word.

In Part 1, you will learn
- Latin word root *-labor-* (p. 812)
- Latin word root *-lum-* (p. 850)

The word root *-labor-,* meaning "work," is found in words such as *elaborate.* The word root *-lum-* is found in words with meanings related to "light."

Activity Write what you think each word means, using the word's root as a clue. Paraphrase, or restate in your own words, the dictionary definition. Then, explain why your predicted definition is, or is not, accurate.

	luminous	belabor	laboratory	luminary
Predicted Definition				
Actual Definition				
Explanation				

Reading and Vocabulary Skills Preview ■ 723

Differentiated Instruction — Solutions for All Learners

Strategy for English Learners

The academic vocabulary in this section may be difficult for students to understand. Helping students relate these words to similar ones in their home language may allow them to use the words when discussing literature. Encourage students whose home language is derived from Latin, like Spanish or Italian, to use cognates to recognize new English words. They might find that many of the words in their home language also contain the same Latin roots that form the basis of English words. Suggest that students make a list of words from their home language that contain some of the Latin roots that appear in English words. Have them compare and contrast the spellings of these words. Ask students to also compare and contrast the meanings and context of these words. Then, have students present their findings to the class.

Introduce Academic Vocabulary

- Introduce the academic vocabulary: words for connecting themes in literature. Tell students that these words are useful when they talk and write about literature.
- Review each word and ask students to read each definition aloud. Read the example sentences and discuss how each word is used.
- Tell students to try to use these words as they discuss the selections in Part 1.

Introduce the Vocabulary Skill

- Introduce the vocabulary skill: word roots. Tell students that many words in English are derived from Latin. The Latin roots *-labor-* and *-lum-* are used in many English words. Recognizing these roots can help students define unfamiliar vocabulary words.
- Tell students that they can find word origin information, or word *etymology,* in dictionaries. Word origin information appears before a word's definition and in double brackets.
- Discuss how the words on the chart (*luminous, belabor, laboratory,* and *luminary*) relate to the meanings of their roots. If students have trouble identifying the relationships, they should consult their dictionaries.

Activity

Predicted definitions may vary, as will the explanations for the differences.

1. *Luminous* can be defined as "bright or full of light."
2. *Belabor* can be defined as "beat or discuss repeatedly or at length."
3. *Laboratory* can be defined as "a room or building equipped for scientific research."
4. *Luminary* can be defined as "an object that gives light or a person who inspires others."

Go Online For: Interactive
Vocabulary Crossword Puzzles
Visit: www.PHSchool.com
Web Code: epj-5501
Give students this Web Code to access interactive crossword puzzles using Academic Vocabulary and Vocabulary Skill words from Part 1.

723

Planning Differentiated Instruction

Accessibility at a Glance

	The Tragedy of Romeo and Juliet, Act I
Context	Historical; Verona, Italy
Language	Dialogue, prose, verse, soliloquies; Elizabethan terms and challenging vocabulary
Concept Level	Accessible; classic tale of star-crossed lovers
Literary Merit	Classic; noted poet and playwright
Lexile	NP
Overall Rating	More challenging

Choosing Your Resources

[L1] Special Needs Students   **[L4]** Advanced Students

[L2] Below-Level Students   **[EL]** English Learners

[L3] All Students

FT Fast Track Instruction: To move the lesson more quickly, use the strategies and activities identified with **FT.**

Reading and Vocabulary Warm-ups provide support for below level students. **A** is for students reading two grades below level; **B** is for students reading one grade below level. For Selection Tests, **A** signifies "less challenging" and **B** "more challenging." For Graphic Organizer transparencies, **A** signifies "not filled in" and **B** "filled in."

Scaffolding for Less Proficient and Advanced Students

The leveled questions on Apply the Skills pages progress in the levels of thinking required to answer them. To address the needs of your different students, you may use the (a) level questions for your less proficient students, the (b) level with your on-level and advanced students. The occasional (c) level questions are appropriate for your advanced students.

Go Online
Professional Development   **For:** Information about Lexiles
Visit: www.PHSchool.com
Web Code: eue-1111

Step-by-Step Teaching Guide	Pacing Guide	
PRETEACH		
• Administer Vocabulary and Reading Warm-ups as necessary.		
• Introduce the Literary Analysis Skills: Dialogue. **FT**	10 min.	
• Introduce the Reading Skill: Summarizing. **FT**	10 min.	
• Prepare students to read by teaching the selection vocabulary. **FT**	10 min.	
• Build background and develop expressive vocabulary with Connecting to the Literature and Background.	10 min.	
• Engage students' interest with the motivation activity.	10 min.	
TEACH		
• Informally monitor comprehension while students read independently or in groups. **FT**	30 min.	
• Monitor students' comprehension with the Reading Check notes.	as students read	
• Reinforce vocabulary with Vocabulary Builder notes.	as students read	
• Develop students' understanding of dialogue with the Literary Analysis annotations. **FT**	5 min.	
• Develop students' ability to summarize with the Reading Skill annotations. **FT**	10 min.	
ASSESS/EXTEND		
• Assess students' comprehension and mastery of the Reading Skill and Literary Analysis by having them answer the Apply the Skills questions. **FT**	35 min.	
• Have students complete the Vocabulary Builder activities. **FT**	5 min.	
• Apply students' ability to write a letter to an advice columnist with the Writing activity. **FT**	30–45 min. or homework	
• Extend students' listening and speaking skills with the Extend Your Learning activity.	15–30 min. or homework	
• Have students complete the Vocabulary Skill and Grammar Lesson.	5 min.	
• Monitor students' progress with the Assessment Practice.	20–40 min.	
• Administer **Selection Test A** or **Selection Test B. FT**	15 min.	

Resources

 Meeting Your Standards

Students will

1. **analyze and respond to literary elements.**
   - Literary Analysis: Dialogue

2. **read, comprehend, and analyze plays.**
   - Reading Skill: Summarizing
   - Reading Strategy: Using Text Aids
   - Reading Check questions
   - Apply the Skills questions
   - Assessment Practice

3. **develop vocabulary.**
   - Vocabulary Builder
   - Word Root *-labor-*

4. **apply grammar skills.**
   - Participle and Participle Phrases

5. **develop writing proficiency.**
   - Work in Progress: How-to Essay
   - Letter to an advice columnist

6. **extend learning.**
   - Listening and Speaking: Staged Performance

Block Scheduling: Use one 90-minute class period to preteach the skills and have students read Act 1. Use a second 90-minute class period to assess students' mastery of skills, extend their learning, and monitor their progress.

Homework Suggestions

Following are possibilities for homework assignments.

- Support pages from *Unit 5 Resources:*
   Literary Analysis
   Reading Skill
   Vocabulary Builder
   Enrichment

- An Extend Your Learning project and the Writing assignment for Act 1 may be completed over several days.

PRENTICE HALL

Teacher EXPRESS™ Use this complete

Plan · Teach · Assess   suite of powerful

teaching tools to make lesson planning and testing quicker and easier.

PRENTICE HALL

Student EXPRESS™ Use the

Learn · Study · Succeed   Interactive

Textbook (online and on CD-ROM) to make Act 1 and activities come alive with audio and video support and interactive questions.

❶ Background
Romeo and Juliet

The ideas that are the basis of *Romeo and Juliet* were borrowed from many sources. The theme appears as early as the fourth century in a Greek tale, and stories of ill-fated lovers were popular among Italian writers in the fifteenth and sixteenth centuries. Shakespeare's most direct source was a long English narrative poem written in 1562 by Arthur Brooke called the *Tragicall Historye of Romeus and Juliet.* Shakespeare borrowed freely from Brooke's story, cutting certain events and expanding others. Although Shakespeare used the characters in Brooke's poem, he developed them in greater depth and detail.

❷ Background
The Theater in Shakespeare's Day

Theaters of Shakespeare's day were not as sophisticated as those of today, but they were the stage for many of the greatest dramas in the English language. This fact alone suggests how advanced the theater arts were when Shakespeare was writing.

After 1599, most of Shakespeare's plays were first performed at the Globe theater, which was built by two brothers, Richard and Cuthbert Burbage. Richard was a leading member of the Lord Chamberlain's Men, the acting group that included Shakespeare and that performed his plays. The Burbages eventually dismantled the old theater and moved it to Bankside, a district of London's Southwark on the south bank of the River Thames.

In 1613, a cannon fired during a performance of Shakespeare's *Henry VIII* ignited the Globe's thatched roof, and the theater burned to the ground. It was rebuilt by the following June, this time with a tiled gallery roof and a circular shape. In 1642, the Puritans closed all theaters, and the Globe fell silent. Two years later, the Puritans demolished the theater and replaced it with tenements.

❸ Critical Viewing

Possible response: Many students may say the tall, octagonal shape of the theater is its most dominant attribute. Others might notice the almost rural setting next to the river with the city on the other side.

724

❶ Romeo and Juliet

Of all the love stories ever written, that of Romeo and Juliet is the most famous. To many people, Shakespeare's tragic lovers represent the essence of romantic love. When Shakespeare wrote *The Tragedy of Romeo and Juliet,* he was a young man, and the play is a young man's play about young love.

❷ The Theater in Shakespeare's Day

Romeo and Juliet, like most of Shakespeare's plays, was produced in a public theater. Public theaters were built around roofless courtyards without artificial light. Performances, therefore, were given only during daylight hours. Surrounding the courtyard were three levels of galleries with benches on which wealthier playgoers sat. Less wealthy spectators, called groundlings, stood and watched a play from the courtyard, which was called the pit.

Most of Shakespeare's plays were performed in the Globe theater. No one is certain exactly what the Globe looked like, though Shakespeare tells us it was round or octagonal. We know that it was open to the sky and held between 2,500 and 3,000 people. Scholars disagree about its actual dimensions and size. The discovery of its foundation in 1989 was exciting because the excavation has revealed clues about the plays, the actors, and the audience. The tiny part of the foundation initially uncovered yielded a great number of hazelnut shells. Hazelnuts were Elizabethan popcorn; people munched on them all during the performance.

The stage was a platform that extended into the pit. Actors entered and left the stage from doors located behind the platform. The portion of the galleries behind and above the stage was used primarily as dressing and

724 ◆ Drama

❸ ▼ Critical Viewing
Which attribute of the Globe is emphasized in this painting? **[Analyze]**

The Globe Theatre, London

Vocabulary Development

Dictionary Use
Read aloud the sentence containing the word *essence* in the first paragraph, and explain that this word has multiple meanings. Read the definitions in a dictionary and model how to figure out which meaning applies. Say to students:

I'm going to think aloud to show you how to determine which meaning for the word *essence* applies.

The first definition of *essence* means "entity, something that is or exists." I think this is close to the meaning in the

text, but if I substitute *entity* for *essence* it doesn't quite fit. The "entity of romantic love" doesn't make sense. I'll try the next definition: "a substance that has the flavor or fragrance of a plant or food." This doesn't make any sense. The next definition says "the fundamental nature or the most important characteristic of something." This makes sense. Shakespeare's tragic lovers could represent the fundamental nature of romantic love.

storage rooms. The second-level gallery right above the stage, however, was used as an upper stage. It would have been here that the famous balcony scene in *Romeo and Juliet* was enacted.

There was no scenery in the theaters of Shakespeare's day. Settings were indicated by references in the dialogue. As a result, one scene could follow another in rapid succession. The actors wore elaborate clothing. It was, in fact, typical Elizabethan clothing, not costuming. Thus, the plays produced in Shakespeare's day were fast-paced, colorful productions. Usually, a play lasted two hours.

One other difference between Shakespeare's theater and today's is that acting companies in the sixteenth century were made up only of men and boys. Women did not perform on the stage. This was not considered proper for a woman. As a general rule, boys of eleven, twelve, or thirteen—before their voices changed—performed the female roles.

The Globe Today

Building a replica of Shakespeare's Globe was the dream of American actor Sam Wanamaker. After long years of fund-raising and construction, the theater opened in London to its first full season on June 8, 1997, with a production of *Henry V*. Like the earlier Globe, this one is made of wood, with a thatched roof and lime plaster covering the walls. The stage and the galleries are covered, but the "bear pit," where the modern-day groundlings stand, is open to the skies, exposing the spectators to the weather.

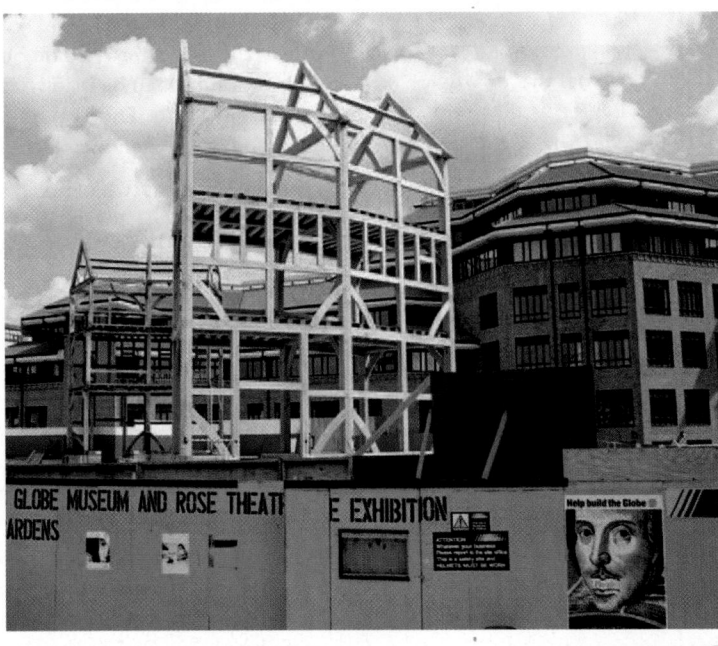

▲ Critical Viewing ❹
Which part of the replica of the Globe theater do you think is being built in this picture? **[Analyze]**

❺ Background
Sam Wanamaker

American actor Sam Wanamaker was first inspired to recreate the Globe in 1949 when he tried to find evidence of the original Globe and found nothing but a plaque on the wall of a brewery. This seemed to Wanamaker an inadequate memorial for such a landmark. Finally, in 1970, Wanamaker founded the Shakespeare Globe Playhouse Trust to work toward rebuilding the Globe. Work began seventeen years later in 1987. Construction proceeded slowly, and unfortunately, Sam Wanamaker died in 1993 without ever seeing his dream fulfilled. The Globe was finally completed in 1997.

❻ Background
The Globe Today

London's new Globe theater is considered a remarkable replica of Shakespeare's original. Located on the Thames, a short distance from the site of the original, it retains the characteristics of the first theater, including its circular shape, open center, and thatched roof. Since few details of the original theater are known, the builders relied on the building contracts, which are extant, for the rival theaters, the Rose and the Fortune, which were built by the same master carpenter who built the Globe.

The new Globe has seating for about 900 people in the galleries. Because the seats curve around the stage, everyone has a different view of the action. For some, the view is sometimes blocked by pillars, but no one is more than fifty feet from the stage. The yard, or pit, has room for about 700 groundlings, some of whom rest their arms on the edge of the stage. As in Elizabethan times, the players sometimes interact with the audience.

Plays are performed largely as they would have been in Shakespeare's time, with little or no scenery and people moving around in the yard.

725

Background
Spelling Shakespeare

The writer whose name is on thousands of volumes of plays and other works never signed his name *Shakespeare*. There were no spelling standards in Elizabethan times and people spelled their own names however they wished, changing them from day to day if it pleased them. Shakespeare's name has been spelled in over eighty different ways, including *Shakspere, Shagspeare, Shaxpere,* and *Shakestaffe.* Six documents are extant with the playwright's signature, and his name is spelled differently in each one. Writers and historians over time have agreed on the current spelling of *Shakespeare.*

Background
Shakespeare on Stage

Shakespeare was an important actor as well as a major playwright of the period. However, in his own plays, he seems to have played minor roles, often those of older men. For example, it is believed he played the role of the ghost in *Hamlet,* King Duncan in *Macbeth,* and King Henry in *Henry IV.*

His company, the Lord Chamberlain's Men, which later became known as the King's Men, was the most successful acting company of the period. During the reigns of both Elizabeth I and James I, the company performed frequently in the royal court. When James I became king, Shakespeare's theatrical company was named officers of the royal household.

Drama

Meet the Author

William **Shakespeare** (1564–1616)

Go Online
Author Link

For: More information about the author
Visit: www.PHSchool.com
Web Code: epe-9502

Almost 400 years after William Shakespeare's death, his thirty-seven plays continue to be read widely and produced frequently throughout the world. They have as powerful an impact on audiences today as when they were first staged.

Starting in Stratford Not much is known about Shakespeare's early life. One reason for this lack of information is that playwrights during Shakespeare's time were not considered very important people socially. Therefore, no biographies were written about him until many years after his death. Church and town records in his hometown of Stratford-on-Avon—a busy market town about seventy-five miles northwest of London—provide some clues about Shakespeare's beginnings, however. His mother, whose maiden name was Mary Arden, was the daughter of his father's landlord. His father, John, was a prosperous merchant in Stratford and even served a term as the town's mayor. John Shakespeare's social standing made it possible for William to attend Stratford Grammar School free of charge until the age of fourteen. There, he studied Latin and Greek, as well as British and world history. Shakespeare would later put all of these lessons to use in his plays about historical figures such as Julius Caesar, Pericles, Macbeth, Richard III, and Henry IV.

Building a Love of Theater Because Stratford was a commercial center, traveling companies of professional actors visited several times a year. Young William probably attended many of these performances, inspiring his interest in the stage. In 1582, at the age of eighteen, Shakespeare married and was soon the father of three children. It is uncertain how Shakespeare spent the next few years, but he did not settle down in Stratford. His heart was set on London and the theater, so he followed his heart there sometime before 1592, leaving his patient family behind. Stratford nevertheless remained an important part of Shakespeare's life, and he visited often. Once he had achieved success in London, Shakespeare purchased one of Stratford's nicest homes for his family, and he retired there after his playwriting career ended.

Stage Celebrity By 1594, William Shakespeare, now a Londoner, had developed a reputation as an actor, had written several plays, and had become the principal playwright of the Lord Chamberlain's

Men, a successful London theater company. He was also a part owner of the company, which meant that he earned money in three ways—from fees for his plays, from his acting salary, and from his share of the profits of the company. In 1599, the company built the famous Globe theater, where most of Shakespeare's plays were performed. When James I became king in 1603, Shakespeare and his partners renamed the company The King's Men. Shakespeare stayed with the company until 1610, when he retired to Stratford-on-Avon.

When Were They Written? Because Shakespeare wrote his plays to be performed, not published, no one knows exactly when each play was written. However, scholars have charted several distinct periods in Shakespeare's development as a playwright. During his early years, he wrote a number of comedies, several histories, and two tragedies. *Romeo and Juliet*—inspiration for the musical *West Side Story* as well as ballets, songs, stories, and movies—was written around 1595. Between that date and the turn of the seventeenth century, Shakespeare wrote several of his finest romantic comedies (*As You Like It, Twelfth Night,* and *Much Ado About Nothing*). During the first decade of the seventeenth century, Shakespeare created his greatest tragedies (*Hamlet, Othello, King Lear, Macbeth, Antony and Cleopatra,* and *Coriolanus*). Finally, toward the end of his career, Shakespeare wrote several plays referred to as romances or tragicomedies. Shakespeare's plays were finally published in a one-volume edition in 1623, seven years after his death. More than 1,000 copies of the first printing were sold for the considerable sum of one pound each—more than $50 per copy in today's currency.

Shakespeare's Impact on English

In addition to introducing many new words into the language, Shakespeare penned hundreds of memorable lines that are familiar to millions of people throughout the world—even to those who have never read one of his plays. The following are just a few of his most famous lines.

From *Hamlet*:

To be, or not to be: that is the question: / Whether 'tis nobler in the mind to suffer / The slings and arrows of outrageous fortune, / Or take arms against a sea of troubles. . . .

From *Romeo and Juliet*:

Parting is such sweet sorrow. . . .

From *Julius Caesar*:

Friends, Romans, countrymen, lend me your ears; / I come to bury Caesar, not to praise him.

Romeo and Juliet ◆ 727

Background
Shakespeare's Impact on English

Shakespeare's plays have not only had a powerful impact on audiences over the centuries, but they have also affected contemporary English in a major way. Dozens of familiar words and phrases were invented by Shakespeare. Individual words of his creation include *leapfrog, majestic, hint, lonely, excellent,* and *gloomy.* Phrases include "catch cold," "laugh it off," "fair play," "disgraceful conduct," and "foregone conclusion," to name just a few. As critic Christopher Morley has written, "Everyone is a Shakespeare scholar unconsciously. You yourself have probably quoted him today. . . ."

Differentiated Instruction   Solutions for All Learners

Background for English Learners
Students may have difficulty with some of the Elizabethan language of *Romeo and Juliet.* Some of these words occur frequently. Prepare students for reading by listing and explaining these words and their meanings:

against: for; in preparation for
alack alas (an exclamation of sorrow)
an, and if
anon soon
aye yes
but only; except
e'en even

e'er ever
haply perhaps
happy fortunate
hence away; from here
hie hurry
hither here
marry indeed
whence where
wilt will
withal in addition; notwithstanding
would wish

727

Build Skills *The Tragedy of Romeo and Juliet, Act I*

❶ Literary Analysis
Dialogue

- Tell students that in a play there is usually no narrator to tell the reader what the characters are like or what is happening. The reader or audience learns about the characters and the story from *dialogue* and *stage directions*.

- Through dialogue, or conversations with one another, characters reveal their relationships (do they like or dislike one another?), their attitudes (are they angry or sorrowful?), and their plans (what are they thinking of doing next?). Tell students that just as in real life, characters often reveal themselves in a way they did not intend through the words they speak.

- Encourage students to be alert to clues about characters and their relationships as they read the dialogue.

Stage Directions

- Tell students that just as dialogue reveals something about the characters, *stage directions* tell about the action.

- These notes, or stage directions, tell what characters are doing (entering or exiting a room, whispering to another or to themselves, drawing a sword) or what they are carrying in their hands. They also tell something about the setting. (Is it raining? Is the sun shining? Are they on the street or in a house?)

❷ Reading Skill
Summarizing

- Remind students that Shakespeare's plays were written 400 years ago. Since then, the English language has changed in many ways. Common words that we use today might have had a different meaning in the past. For example, *dignity* meant "high social rank" in Shakespeare's time.

- Tell students that as they read and *summarize* scenes, they should always check the *text aids* or notes that explain any confusing passages or unusual vocabulary.

- Give students a copy of **Reading Skill Graphic Organizer A** (*Graphic Organizer Transparencies,* p. 163). Have them fill in the graphic organizer as they summarize the scenes.

❶ Literary Analysis

Dialogue is conversation between characters. In prose, dialogue is usually set off with quotation marks. In drama, it generally follows the name of the speaker, as in this example:

> **BENVOLIO.** My noble uncle, do you know the cause?
> **MONTAGUE.** I neither know it nor can learn of him.

Dialogue reveals the personalities and relationships of the characters and advances the action of the play.

Stage directions are notes in the text of a play that describe how the work should be performed, or staged. These instructions are usually printed in italics and are sometimes set in brackets or parentheses. They describe scenes, lighting, and sound effects, as well as the appearance and physical actions of characters, as in this example:

> *Scene iii.* FRIAR LAWRENCE's *cell.*
> [*Enter* FRIAR LAWRENCE *alone, with a basket.*]

As you read, notice how the dialogue and stage directions work together to help you "see" and "hear" the play in your mind.

❷ Reading Skill

Summarizing is briefly stating the main points in a piece of writing. Pausing to summarize what you have read helps you check your comprehension before you read further. To be sure that you understand Shakespeare's language before you summarize, **use text aids**—the numbered explanations that appear with the text.

- If you are confused by a passage, check to see if there is a footnote or side note and read the corresponding explanation.

- Reread the passage, using the information from the note to be sure you grasp the meaning of the passage.

As you read Act I, use a chart like the one shown to record a summary of each scene.

ACT I	
Scene	Summary of Action

Vocabulary Builder

- **pernicious** (pər nish′ əs) *adj.* causing great injury or ruin (p. 735) *The spy's activities had a pernicious effect on the top-secret project.*

- **augmenting** (ôg ment′ iŋ) *v.* increasing; enlarging (p. 736) *With small deposits each week, our family is augmenting its savings.*

- **grievance** (grēv′ əns) *n.* injustice; complaint (p. 736) *The board investigated the worker's grievance against his supervisor.*

- **transgression** (trans gresh′ ən) *n.* wrongdoing; sin (p. 737) *Stealing from the poor is a transgression against humanity.*

728 ■ *Drama*

Vocabulary Development

Vocabulary Knowledge Rating

Create a **Vocabulary Knowledge Rating Chart** with these words from Act I:

pernicious   augmenting
grievance   transgression

Give students a copy. Introduce the words by reading them aloud and having students mark their rating in the Before Reading column. Urge them to be alert to these words as they read and discuss the selection, because they will rate their knowledge of the words again after they finish.

If you wish, you may tally how many students know (or think they know) a word to gauge how much instruction you need to provide. As students read, point out the words and their context.

Build Understanding • The Tragedy of Romeo and Juliet, Act I

❸ Background

Shakespeare's Source Shakespeare based his play about star-crossed lovers from feuding Italian families on a poem published in 1562 by Arthur Brooke. Brooke's 3,000-line poem has a highly moral tone: Disobedience, as well as fate, leads to the deaths of the two lovers. Shakespeare portrayed the young lovers more sympathetically. He also elevated these everyday characters by presenting their tale in a tragedy—a serious type of drama that traditionally involved kings, emperors, or other characters of great importance.

❹ Connecting to the Literature

Reading/Writing Connection *The Tragedy of Romeo and Juliet* was inspired by tales of ill-fated love that came before it. In turn, the play has inspired countless other interpretations. In a few sentences, explain why a romantic tragedy is an inspiring subject for writers, painters, and composers alike. Use at least three of these words: *illustrate, contrast, emphasize, reinforce, adapt.*

Elizabethan Language

As you read *Romeo and Juliet,* most of the unfamiliar words from Elizabethan English will be explained in footnotes. However, the following words appear so frequently that learning them now will make your reading of the play easier.

against for; in preparation for

alack alas (an exclamation of sorrow)

anon soon

aye yes

but only; except

e'en even

e'er ever

haply perhaps

happy fortunate

hence away; from here

hie hurry

hither here

marry indeed

whence where

wherefore why

wilt will

withal in addition; notwithstanding

would wish

The Tragedy of Romeo and Juliet, Act I ■ 729

❸ Background

The Tragedy of Romeo and Juliet has been made into a film many times, but teenagers do not often play the two young lovers. Franco Zeffirelli's 1968 film version, which starred Olivia Hussey and Leonard Whiting—fifteen and seventeen years old respectively—is said by critics to come closest to the characters as Shakespeare envisioned them.

❹ Connecting to the Literature

- To help students understand the meanings of the words they are asked to use, give them these sentences that describe people's emotions.

  1. The emotions of tragic lovers are so intense that painters might be inspired to *illustrate* the lovers together.

  2. The *contrast* between what is and what could have been between two tragic lovers might inspire authors.

  3. Tragic love *emphasizes* intense emotions, which may inspire authors or composers.

  4. Tragic love *reinforces* the importance of true love, which inspires artists.

  5. The theme of tragic love is so universal that artists can *adapt* it to music, literature, or visual art.

- Help students further develop their expressive vocabulary by providing these words: *anticipate, circumstance, impact, inevitable,* and *reluctant.* Encourage students to use these words as they discuss the selection.

Concept Connector ➤

Students will follow up on this activity after completing *The Tragedy of Romeo and Juliet,* Act I.

Go **Online** For additional informa-
—Author Link tion about William Shakespeare, have students type in the Web Code and then select *William Shakespeare.*

Differentiated Instruction Solutions for All Learners

Support for Below-Level Students [L1, L2]	Support for English Learners [EL]

Unit 5 Resources
  Vocabulary Warm-up Word Lists, p. 18
  Vocabulary Warm-up Practice, p. 19
  Reading Warm-up A, p. 20
  Selection Test A, pp. 28–30
Graphic Organizer Transparencies
  Reading Skill Graphic Organizer, Transparency B, p. 164
Reader's Notebook: Adapted Version
Adapted Reader's Notebook Audio CD
	Unit 5 Resources
	  Vocabulary Warm-up Word Lists, p. 18
	  Vocabulary Warm-up Practice, p. 19
	  Reading Warm-up A, p. 20
	Reader's Notebook: English Learner's Version
	Listening to Literature Audio CD

729

❶ Motivation

The Tragedy of Romeo and Juliet is probably Shakespeare's most famous play, and possibly the most famous play in all of English literature. Build students' interest in reading the play by inviting them to share what they know—or think they know—about Romeo and Juliet. After they have read Act I, they can ask themselves: In what ways does the play match my expectations? In what ways does it surprise me?

Learning Modalities
Interpersonal Learners

Have students work in pairs to analyze the prologue and the conflict that it describes. Then, have them work together to write a news broadcast about the conflict. Have each pair work as "co-anchors" for the broadcast.

❷ About the Selection

In *Romeo and Juliet* "A pair of star-crossed lovers . . . Doth with their death bury their parents' strife." The Prologue that opens the play tells briefly of the terrible events that mark a tender but tragic love, while the five scenes that follow set these events in motion. We first meet Romeo just after a bitter and long-standing feud between members of his family, the Montagues, and their foes the Capulets, has erupted into a street brawl. Romeo's kinsman, Benvolio, suggests that they secretly attend a feast being given that night by the Capulets. There, Romeo and Juliet meet for the first time.

❸ Background
Film

The photos that illustrate this play are stills from Franco Zeffirelli's film *Romeo and Juliet,* which was released in 1968. Zeffirelli has filmed several other works of Shakespeare, including *The Taming of the Shrew* and *Hamlet,* with Mel Gibson in the title role. Zeffirelli's films capture the zest and vitality of the Age of Shakespeare.

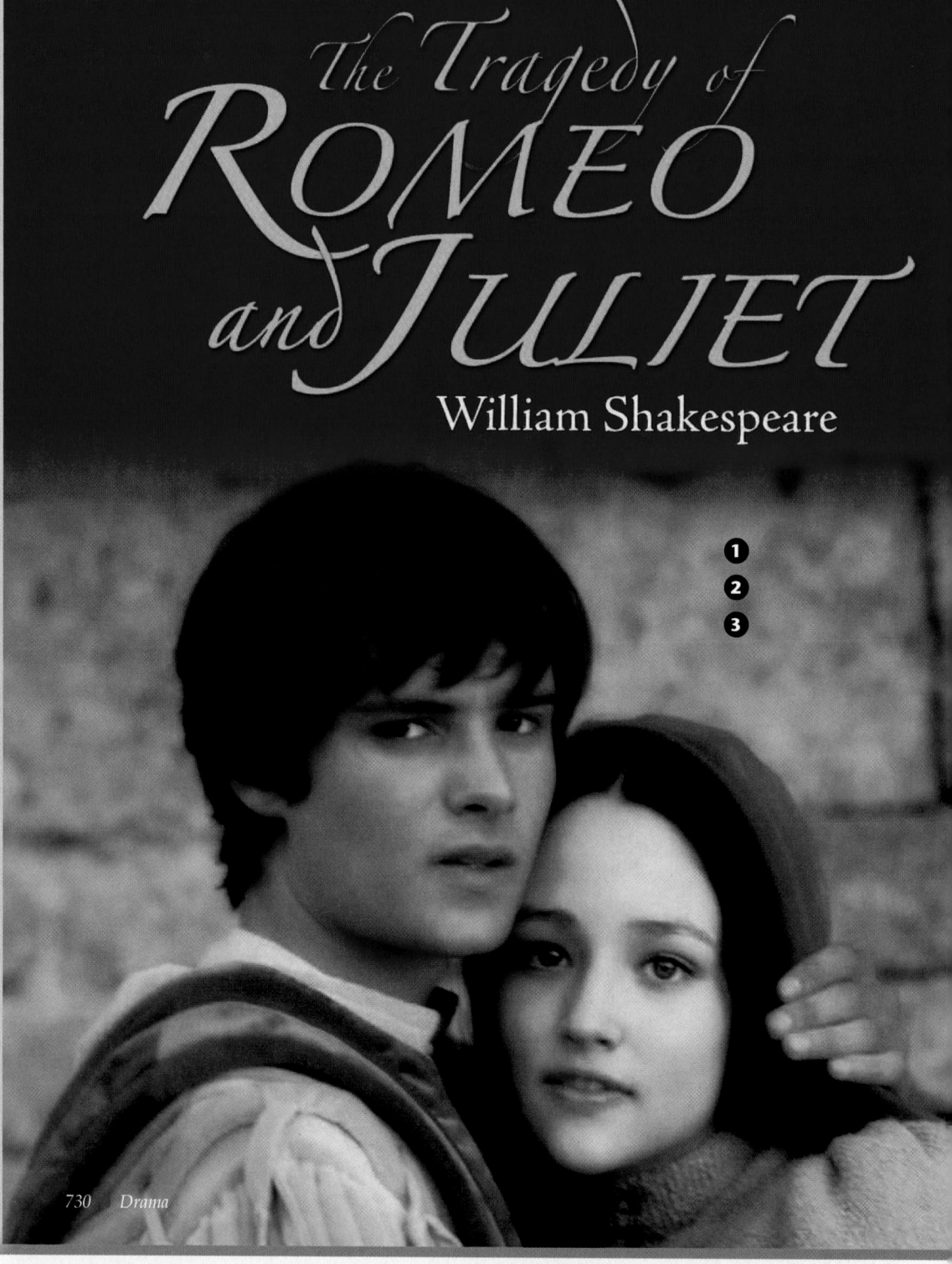

The Tragedy of ROMEO and JULIET

William Shakespeare

❶
❷
❸

730   *Drama*

Vocabulary Development

Think-Aloud: Dictionary Use

Direct students' attention to the word *naught* in line 11. Using a think-aloud process, model how to choose an appropriate definition from a dictionary entry.

The dictionary defines *naught* as "nothing" or "zero." It also gives an archaic or obsolete definition of "useless" or "evil." Since the context is a Shakespearean play, the archaic or obsolete definition may apply.

However, the lines 10 and 11 mention the rage of Romeo and Juliet's parents, which "naught" could remove but the end of Romeo and Juliet. *Evil* does not fit here. So I think that the definition for this context is "nothing."

I can test the definition by using it in the sentence: "Nothing could remove their parents' rage but their children's end."

CHARACTERS

CHORUS
ESCALUS, Prince of Verona
PARIS, a young count, kinsman to the Prince
MONTAGUE
CAPULET
AN OLD MAN, of the Capulet family
ROMEO, son to Montague
MERCUTIO, kinsman to the Prince and friend to Romeo
BENVOLIO, nephew to Montague and friend to Romeo
TYBALT, nephew to Lady Capulet
FRIAR LAWRENCE, Franciscan
FRIAR JOHN, Franciscan
BALTHASAR, servant to Romeo

SAMPSON, servant to Capulet
GREGORY, servant to Capulet
PETER, servant to Juliet's nurse
ABRAM, servant to Montague
AN APOTHECARY
THREE MUSICIANS
AN OFFICER
LADY MONTAGUE, wife to Montague
LADY CAPULET, wife to Capulet
JULIET, daughter to Capulet
NURSE TO JULIET
CITIZENS OF VERONA, Gentlemen and Gentlewomen of both houses, Maskers, Torchbearers, Pages, Guards, Watchmen, Servants, and Attendants

Scene: Verona; Mantua

[*Enter* CHORUS.]

CHORUS. Two households, both alike in dignity.[1]
In fair Verona, where we lay our scene,
From ancient grudge break to new mutiny.[2]
Where civil blood makes civil hands unclean.[3]
5 From forth the fatal loins of these two foes
A pair of star-crossed[4] lovers take their life;
Whose misadventured piteous overthrows[5]
Doth with their death bury their parents' strife.
The fearful passage of their death-marked love,
10 And the continuance of their parents' rage,
Which, but[6] their children's end, naught could remove,
Is now the two hours' traffic[7] of our stage;
The which if you with patient ears attend,
What here shall miss, our toil shall strive to mend.[8]

[*Exit.*]

PROLOGUE

❹ Background
Greek Chorus

The use of a *chorus*—a figure or group of figures who comment on a play's action—goes back to ancient Greek and Roman drama. In Shakespeare's time, it was common for a chorus to deliver a *prologue*—an opening speech that introduces the play's main characters, plot, and setting.

Differentiated Instruction   Solutions for All Learners

Strategy for Less Proficient Readers
Advise students to use the Character list on p. 731. They may check it whenever they are unsure of a character's identity. As an example, ask them to use the list to find Sampson, Gregory, Juliet, and Capulet. Discuss with students how Gregory and Sampson are connected to Juliet. Point out that Juliet is Capulet's daughter, and the two men are servants who work for Capulet.

Strategy for Special Needs Students
To give students a context for the play and to model how to summarize, show them **Reading Skill Graphic Organizer B** (*Graphic Organizer Transparencies,* p. 164). The completed graphic organizer will give students insight into the process of summarizing. They can use it as a model for summarizing scenes as they read.

⑤ Critical Thinking
Analyze

- Have students use the notes at the side to look up the meanings of footnoted terms.

- Ask students what two meanings of the phrase "to carry coals" are used in the exchange between Sampson and Gregory. As a hint, tell them that one usage is literal and one is idiomatic, or figurative. **Answer:** Literally, the phrase "carry coals" means "to sell coal," while figuratively the phrase means "to endure insults."

- **Ask** students what effect this wordplay has on the scene. **Answer:** Students may describe the effect as playful and humorous.

⑥ Literary Analysis
Dialogue

- Remind students that Sampson and Gregory are servants of the Capulets. Have them **describe** what they learn about Sampson and Gregory in this scene. **Possible response:** Sampson and Gregory are boastful, flippant, insulting, and apparently eager to do battle with Montague's men.

- **Ask** students to respond to the Literary Analysis question on p. 732: What does this conversation among servants reveal about the Montagues? **Answer:** The conversation reveals that there is great hostility between the Capulets and the Montagues and that both households are large, with numerous servants.

Scene i. Verona. A public place.

[*Enter* SAMPSON *and* GREGORY, *with swords and bucklers,*[1] *of the house of Capulet.*]

SAMPSON. Gregory, on my word, we'll not carry coals.[2]

❺ **GREGORY.** No, for then we should be colliers.[3]

SAMPSON. I mean, an we be in choler, we'll draw.[4]

GREGORY. Ay, while you live, draw your neck out of collar.[5]

5 **SAMPSON.** I strike quickly, being moved.

GREGORY. But thou art not quickly moved to strike.

SAMPSON. A dog of the house of Montague moves me.

GREGORY. To move is to stir, and to be valiant is to stand. Therefore, if thou art moved, thou run'st away.

10 **SAMPSON.** A dog of that house shall move me to stand. I will take the wall[6] of any man or maid of Montague's.

❻ **GREGORY.** That shows thee a weak slave; for the weakest goes to the wall.

SAMPSON. 'Tis true; and therefore women, being the weaker
15 vessels, are ever thrust to the wall. Therefore I will push Montague's men from the wall and thrust his maids to the wall.

GREGORY. The quarrel is between our masters and us their men.

20 **SAMPSON.** 'Tis all one. I will show myself a tyrant. When I have fought with the men, I will be civil with the maids—I will cut off their heads.

GREGORY. The heads of the maids?

SAMPSON. Ay, the heads of the maids or their maidenheads.
25 Take it in what sense thou wilt.

GREGORY. They must take it in sense that feel it.

SAMPSON. Me they shall feel while I am able to stand; and 'tis known I am a pretty piece of flesh.

GREGORY. 'Tis well thou art not fish; if thou hadst, thou hadst
30 been Poor John. Draw thy tool![7] Here comes two of the house of Montagues.

[*Enter two other Servingmen,* ABRAM *and* BALTHASAR.]

❼ **SAMPSON.** My naked weapon is out. Quarrel! I will back thee.

732 ■ *Drama*

---

1. **bucklers** small shields.
2. **carry coals** endure insults.
3. **colliers** sellers of coal.
4. **an . . . draw** If we are angered, we'll draw our swords.
5. **collar** hangman's noose.

6. **take the wall** assert superiority by walking nearer the houses and therefore farther from the gutter.

Literary Analysis
Dialogue What does this conversation among servants reveal about the Montagues?

7. **tool** weapon.

Vocabulary Development

Expressive Vocabulary
After students read through line 65 (p. 733), ask them to think what they have learned about the Capulets and Montagues so far. As students discuss these lines, encourage them to use the expressive vocabulary presented earlier. You might encourage them with sentence starters like these:

1. The deliberate attempt of Sampson and Gregory to start a fight with the Montagues *illustrates* . . .

2. The main *contrast* between Sampson and Gregory and Abram and Balthasar is . . .

3. The fight between Sampson and Gregory and Abram and Balthasar *emphasizes* . . .

4. The entrance of Benvolio *reinforces* . . .

5. Benvolio would like to *adapt* . . .

Challenge students to use these words as you continue to discuss the play.

GREGORY. How? Turn thy back and run?

SAMPSON. Fear me not.

7
35 GREGORY. No, marry. I fear thee!

SAMPSON. Let us take the law of our sides;[8] let them begin.

GREGORY. I will frown as I pass by, and let them take it as they list.[9]

SAMPSON. Nay, as they dare. I will bite my thumb[10] at them,
40   which is disgrace to them if they bear it.

ABRAM. Do you bite your thumb at us, sir?

SAMPSON. I do bite my thumb, sir.

ABRAM. Do you bite your thumb at us, sir?

8
SAMPSON. [*Aside to* GREGORY] Is the law of our side if I say ay?

45 GREGORY. [*Aside to* SAMPSON] No.

SAMPSON. No, sir, I do not bite my thumb at you, sir; but I bite my thumb, sir.

GREGORY. Do you quarrel, sir?

ABRAM. Quarrel, sir? No, sir.

50 SAMPSON. But if you do, sir, I am for you. I serve as good a man as you.

ABRAM. No better.

SAMPSON. Well, sir.

[*Enter* BENVOLIO.]

55 GREGORY. [*Aside to* SAMPSON.] Say "better." Here comes one of my master's kinsmen.

SAMPSON. Yes, better, sir.

ABRAM. You lie.

SAMPSON. Draw, if you be men. Gregory, remember thy
swashing[11] blow.   [*They fight.*]

60 BENVOLIO. Part, fools!
    Put up your swords. You know not what you do.

[*Enter* TYBALT.]

TYBALT. What art thou drawn among these heartless hinds?[12]
    Turn thee, Benvolio; look upon thy death.

BENVOLIO. I do but keep the peace. Put up thy sword,
65   Or manage it to part these men with me.

Romeo and Juliet, Act I ■ 733

Reading Skill
Summarizing How does footnote 8 help you understand Sampson's logic in line 36?

8. **take . . . sides** make sure the law is on our side.
9. **list** please.
10. **bite . . . thumb** make an insulting gesture.

Literary Analysis
Stage Directions
Which words in the stage directions in line 44 clarify that Sampson is not speaking to Abram?

11. **swashing** hard downward swordstroke.

12. **heartless hinds** cowardly servants. *Hind* also means "a female deer."

9 ✓ **Reading Check**

With which family are the quarreling servants affiliated?

---

❼ Reading Skill
Summarizing

- **Ask** students to identify the play on words used in the first two lines of the bracketed passage.
  Possible response: *Back* is used to mean "back you up," or "support you," as well as the back of a person who is running away in cowardice.

- Remind students to check the side of the page to see whether there is any footnote information to help them understand the language of the play.

- **Ask** students to respond to the Reading Skill question on p. 732: How does footnote 8 help you understand Sampson's logic in line 39?
  Answer: The footnote says that the phrase "take the law of our sides" means "make sure the law is on our side." Sampson's logic is to let the other side begin the fight because that will keep the law on Sampson and Gregory's side. When officials come to break up the fight, they will be harsher on those who actually started it.

❽ Literary Analysis
Stage Directions

- Have students **review** lines 32 through 43. **Ask** who is present on the stage at line 43.
  Answer: Abram and Balthasar and Sampson and Gregory are present.

- Invite or assign three students to read the bracketed passage aloud, each taking a part.

- **Ask** students to review the stage directions and then explain who is fighting in these lines.
  Answer: Sampson and Gregory fight Abram and Balthasar.

- **Ask** students to respond to the Literary Analysis question: Which words in the stage directions in line 44 clarify that Sampson is not speaking to Abram?
  Answer: The words "Aside to Gregory" clarify that Sampson is not speaking to Abram.

❾ Reading Check

Answer: The servants are from the Montague and Capulet families.

Strategy for English Learners
Students may have difficulty identifying the various factions in this scene.

    Students might better understand this scene as they read by making a chart to show the different affiliations as the stage fills up with characters. Column 1 of the chart should be labeled *Capulet,* Column 2 labeled *Montague,*

and Column 3, *Other.* As each character enters the stage, have students write the name in the correct column. If students have trouble identifying the affiliation of a character, have them refer to the Characters list on p. 731.

    Make sure students understand the function or role of each character.

- Choose four students to take each of the five parts in the bracketed passage. Have them read the lines aloud.

- **Ask:** What does Lady Capulet tell her husband he needs?
Answer: She tells him he needs a crutch, not a sword.

- **Ask** students to describe what seems to be the attitude of the two wives.
Possible response: They do not want their husbands to fight.

- **Ask** students what the two men's attitude says about the feud between their two families.
Answer: They must have carried the hostility for a long time; they still want to fight, even though they are too old to engage in sword fighting. Their enmity is very strong.

⑪ Reading Skill
Summarizing

- Read aloud lines 85 through 91. Have students read side notes 19 and 20. Then, **ask** students what the Prince accuses the families of doing to the citizens of Verona in these lines.
Possible response: Students may say that the Prince accuses the families of having three public brawls that have forced the citizens of the city to take up arms to stop the violence.

- Read aloud lines 92 through 99. **Ask** students to respond to the Reading Skill prompt: Summarize the warning that the Prince issues to the Montagues and Capulets in this speech.
Answer: The Prince tells them that if they ever disturb the peace again, they will pay for it with their lives.

734

TYBALT. What, drawn, and talk of peace? I hate the word
As I hate hell, all Montagues, and thee.
Have at thee, coward! [*They fight.*]

[*Enter an* OFFICER, *and three or four* CITIZENS *with clubs or partisans.*[13]]

OFFICER. Clubs, bills,[14] and partisans! Strike! Beat them down!
70   Down with the Capulets! Down with the Montagues!

[*Enter old* CAPULET *in his gown, and his* WIFE.]

CAPULET. What noise is this? Give me my long sword, ho!

⑩ **LADY CAPULET.** A crutch, a crutch! Why call you for a sword?

CAPULET. My sword, I say! Old Montague is come
And flourishes his blade in spite[15] of me.

[*Enter old* MONTAGUE *and his* WIFE.]

75   **MONTAGUE.** Thou villain Capulet!—Hold me not; let me go.

LADY MONTAGUE. Thou shalt not stir one foot to seek a foe.

[*Enter* PRINCE ESCALUS, *with his Train.*[16]]

PRINCE. Rebellious subjects, enemies to peace,
Profaners[17] of this neighbor-stainèd steel—
Will they not hear? What, ho! You men, you beasts,

13. **partisans** spearlike weapons with broad blades.
14. **bills** weapons consisting of hook-shaped blades with long handles.

15. **spite** defiance.

16. **Train** attendants.

17. **Profaners** those who show disrespect or contempt.

Literature in Context

History Connection

Prince of Verona When Prince Escalus intervenes in the fight between the Capulets and the Montagues, he does so under his authority as the *podesta,* or "chief magistrate," of Verona. The powers and duties of the podesta combined those of a modern mayor, chief of police, and head of the local militia. Scholars believe that Shakespeare based the character of Prince Escalus on Bartolomeo della Scala, who ruled the northern Italian city of Verona during the late-thirteenth and early-fourteenth centuries.

Connect to the Literature

Which part of his authority is Prince Escalus exercising in this scene—mayor, police chief, or head of the army? Explain.

734 ■ *Drama*

Professional Development
Translating Shakespeare

Shakespeare's language can be a challenge for many students. Struggling with the language prevents many students from enjoying and appreciating the plays. Here is a strategy that helps students work out the meaning of key passages.

Have students work in pairs to "translate" key sections of the play that are important to their overall understanding of the plot or characters. Start by reading aloud the segment on the **Listening to Literature CD.** Explain what each line means after students have heard it aloud. Then, have students work in pairs to rewrite the segment in their own words. Students then form groups of four and share their "translations," combining them to come up with one good translation to present to the class.

The Prince's speech on pages 734 and 735 provides an excellent opportunity to introduce the translation strategy. Be sure to allow time for groups to share their versions.

80　That quench the fire of your <u>pernicious</u> rage
　　With purple fountains issuing from your veins!
　　On pain of torture, from those bloody hands
　　Throw your mistempered[18] weapons to the ground
　　And hear the sentence of your moved prince.
85　Three civil brawls, bred of an airy word
　　By thee, old Capulet, and Montague,
　　Have thrice disturbed the quiet of our streets
　　And made Verona's ancient citizens
　　Cast by their grave beseeming ornaments[19]
90　To wield old partisans, in hands as old,
　　Cank'red with peace, to part your cank'red hate.[20]
⓫ If ever you disturb our streets again,
　　Your lives shall pay the forfeit of the peace.
　　For this time all the rest depart away.
95　You, Capulet, shall go along with me;
　　And, Montague, come you this afternoon,
　　To know our farther pleasure in this case,
　　To old Freetown, our common judgment place.
　　Once more, on pain of death, all men depart.

[Exit all but MONTAGUE, *his* WIFE, *and* BENVOLIO.]

100　**MONTAGUE.** Who set this ancient quarrel new abroach?[21]
　　Speak, nephew, were you by when it began?

　　BENVOLIO. Here were the servants of your adversary
　　And yours, close fighting ere I did approach.
　　I drew to part them. In the instant came
105　The fiery Tybalt, with his sword prepared;
　　Which, as he breathed defiance to my ears,
　　He swung about his head and cut the winds,
　　Who, nothing hurt withal, hissed him in scorn.
　　While we were interchanging thrusts and blows,
110　Came more and more, and fought on part and part,[22]
　　Till the Prince came, who parted either part.

　　LADY MONTAGUE. O, where is Romeo? Saw you him today?
　　Right glad I am he was not at this fray.

　　BENVOLIO. Madam, an hour before the worshiped sun
115　Peered forth the golden window of the East,
⓬　A troubled mind drave me to walk abroad:
　　Where, underneath the grove of sycamore
　　That westward rooteth from this city side,
　　So early walking did I see your son.

Vocabulary Builder
pernicious (pər nish′ əs) *adj.* causing great injury or ruin

18. **mistempered** hardened for a wrong purpose; bad-tempered.

19. **Cast . . . ornaments** put aside their dignified and appropriate clothing.
20. **Cank'red . . . hate** rusted from lack of use, to put an end to your malignant feuding.

Reading Skill
Summarizing Summarize the warning that the Prince issues to the Montagues and Capulets in this speech.

21. **Who . . . abroach?** Who reopened this old fight?

22. **on . . . part** on one side and the other.

⓭ Reading Check
Who stops the brawl between the Montagues and the Capulets?

Romeo and Juliet, Act I ■ 735

⓬ Critical Thinking
Infer

• Have students read the bracketed passage. **Ask** students what information is exchanged between Benvolio and Montague in these lines.
Answer: Montague tells Benvolio that Romeo is often out in the sycamore grove in the night, and as soon as dawn comes, he locks himself in his room and covers the windows to keep out the sunlight.

• Ask students what they can **infer** about Benvolio based on his interaction with Montague.
Answer: Benvolio is polite; he addresses Montague as "my noble uncle." He is concerned about Romeo's welfare.

⓭ Reading Check
Answer: Prince Escalus stops the brawl.

Differentiated Instruction　Solutions for All Learners

Strategy for English Learners
Point out to students that Shakespearean language often inverts the subject and the verb, or puts the object before the subject and verb. Point out examples in lines 82–83 ("from those bloody hands/Throw your mistempered weapons to the ground"); line 96 ("And, Montague, come you this afternoon"); lines 104–105 ("In the instant came/The fiery Tybalt"); line 112 ("O, where is Romeo? Saw you him today?"); and line 113 ("Right glad I am he was not at this fray.")
Review these lines with students. Demonstrate the customary syntax for the first of these lines. Then, guide students to restate each of these lines in more ordinary syntax. Encourage students to watch for inverted syntax and to restate the lines, which will help them understand the meaning and summarize passages.

- Read lines 156 through 166 aloud. **Ask** students what generalization both characters make in their conversation here about the effect of sadness on one's life.
Answer: They both suggest that when one is sad time moves very slowly.

- Remind students that even a few words spoken by a character can reveal his or her personality.

- **Ask** students what Benvolio's concern for Romeo reveals about Benvolio's personality.
Possible response: Students may say that Benvolio is a sensitive and loving cousin because he asks Romeo what is wrong, listens to the answer, and then sympathizes with Romeo's distress.

---

120 Towards him I made, but he was ware²³ of me
     And stole into the covert²⁴ of the wood.
     I, measuring his affections²⁵ by my own,
     Which then most sought where most might not be found,²⁶
     Being one too many by my weary self,
125 Pursued my humor not pursuing his,²⁷
     And gladly shunned who gladly fled from me.

⓬
MONTAGUE. Many a morning hath he there been seen,
     With tears augmenting the fresh morning's dew,
     Adding to clouds more clouds with his deep sighs;
130 But all so soon as the all-cheering sun
     Should in the farthest East begin to draw
     The shady curtains from Aurora's bed,
     Away from light steals home my heavy²⁸ son
     And private in his chamber pens himself,
135 Shuts up his windows, locks fair daylight out,
     And makes himself an artificial night.
     Black and portentous²⁹ must this humor prove
     Unless good counsel may the cause remove.

BENVOLIO. My noble uncle, do you know the cause?

140 **MONTAGUE.** I neither know it nor can learn of him.

BENVOLIO. Have you importuned³⁰ him by any means?

MONTAGUE. Both by myself and many other friends;
     But he, his own affections' counselor,
     Is to himself—I will not say how true—
145 But to himself so secret and so close,
     So far from sounding³¹ and discovery,
     As is the bud bit with an envious worm
     Ere he can spread his sweet leaves to the air
     Or dedicate his beauty to the sun.
150 Could we but learn from whence his sorrows grow,
     We would as willingly give cure as know.

[*Enter* ROMEO.]

BENVOLIO. See, where he comes. So please you step aside;
     I'll know his grievance, or be much denied.

MONTAGUE. I would thou wert so happy by thy stay
155 To hear true shrift.³² Come, madam, let's away.

[*Exit* MONTAGUE *and* WIFE.]

⓮
BENVOLIO. Good morrow, cousin.
ROMEO.   Is the day so young?

736 ■ *Drama*

---

23. ware aware; wary.

24. covert hidden place.

25. measuring . . . affections judging his feelings.

26. Which . . . found which wanted to be where there was no one else.

27. Pursued . . . his followed my own mind by not following after Romeo.

Vocabulary Builder
augmenting (ôg ment´ iŋ) *v.* increasing; enlarging

28. heavy sad, moody.

29. portentous promising bad fortune.

30. importuned questioned deeply.

31. sounding understanding.

Vocabulary Builder
grievance (grēv´ əns) *n.* injustice; complaint

32. I . . . shrift I hope you are lucky enough to hear him confess the truth.

Vocabulary Development

Word Analysis

Call students' attention to the word *transgression* on p. 737. Tell students that the prefix *trans-* means "across, beyond, or through."

Reinforce their understanding of the prefix *trans-* by having them write the second part of a sentence to clarify the meaning of the first. Give them this example using the word *transmit:*

I plan to *transmit* the message today; be prepared to receive it when I send it.

Then, give students these sentence prompts. Encourage them to use a dictionary if necessary.

1. The cloth was perfectly *transparent;* _____.

   Sample answer: I could see through it clearly.

2. I will *transplant* these seedlings in a few weeks; _____.

   Sample answer: they will grow quickly when moved to the rich soil of the garden.

BENVOLIO. But new struck nine.

ROMEO.   Ay me! Sad hours seem long.
Was that my father that went hence so fast?

BENVOLIO. It was. What sadness lengthens Romeo's hours?

160 **ROMEO.** Not having that which having makes them short.

⓮ BENVOLIO. In love?

ROMEO. Out—

BENVOLIO. Of love?

ROMEO. Out of her favor where I am in love.

165 **BENVOLIO.** Alas that love, so gentle in his view,[33]
Should be so tyrannous and rough in proof![34]

ROMEO. Alas that love, whose view is muffled still,[35]
Should without eyes see pathways to his will!
Where shall we dine? O me! What fray was here?
170 Yet tell me not, for I have heard it all.
Here's much to do with hate, but more with love.[36]
Why then, O brawling love, O loving hate,
O anything, of nothing first created!
O heavy lightness, serious vanity,
175 Misshapen chaos of well-seeming forms,
Feather of lead, bright smoke, cold fire, sick health,
Still-waking sleep, that is not what it is!
This love feel I, that feel no love in this.
Dost thou not laugh?

⓯ BENVOLIO.   No, coz,[37] I rather weep.

ROMEO. Good heart, at what?

180 **BENVOLIO.**   At thy good heart's oppression.

ROMEO. Why, such is love's <u>transgression</u>.
Griefs of mine own lie heavy in my breast,
Which thou wilt propagate, to have it prest
With more of thine.[38] This love that thou hast shown
185 Doth add more grief to too much of mine own.
Love is a smoke made with the fume of sighs;
Being purged, a fire sparkling in lovers' eyes;
Being vexed, a sea nourished with loving tears.
What is it else? A madness most discreet,[39]

Literary Analysis
Dialogue What does this conversation reveal about Romeo's state of mind?

33. view appearance.

34. in proof when experienced.

35. whose . . . still Cupid is traditionally represented as blindfolded.

36. but . . . love loyalty to family and love of fighting. In the following lines, Romeo speaks of love as a series of contradictions—a union of opposites.

37. coz cousin.

38. Which . . . thine which griefs you will increase by adding your own sorrow to them.

39. discreet intelligently sensitive.

Vocabulary Builder
transgression (trans gresh′ ən) *n.* wrongdoing; sin

Reading Check

What reason for his sadness does Romeo give to Benvolio?

Romeo and Juliet, Act I ■ 737

⓯ Literary Analysis
Dialogue

- Refer students to lines 167–179. Ask them what Romeo's words reveal about his personality.
Answer: Romeo's words show him to be a sensitive person with emotions that are very close to the surface.

- **Ask** students to respond to the Literary Analysis question on p. 737: What does this conversation reveal about Romeo's state of mind? Have students explain their answer.
Answer: The speech shows that Romeo is in a state of confusion. He makes many statements that contain opposites, such as "O brawling love ," O loving hate," "O heavy lightness," to show that he is in terrible conflict about his feelings.

⓰ Reading Check

Answer: Romeo tells Benvolio that he is sad because he is in love but is not loved in return.

- Based on footnotes 43–45, ask students to **describe** the kind of person Romeo loves.
Answer: She is chaste and has the good sense to avoid love. She is not charmed by the spell of love, and she does not put up with words and looks of love.

- Based on footnotes 46–47, what does Romeo claim will be her fate?
Answer: If she dies chaste, her beauty will die with her, since she will have no children.

▶ **Monitor Progress:** Review students' graphic organizers to ensure that they are accurately summarizing passages.

▶ **Reteach:** If students are having difficulty summarizing, have them reread the play to this point, reviewing the footnotes.

18 **Background**

Danae and Zeus

Line 210, "Nor ope her lap to saint-seducing gold," is an allusion to Danae and Zeus, characters from Greek mythology. Danae was the daughter of King Acrisius. When Acrisius received a prophecy that Danae's son would kill him, Acrisius wanted to make sure Danae had no children, so he locked her in a tower of bronze. But the god Zeus came to Danae in the form of a shower of gold. Soon after, Danae's son Perseus was born, and Perseus eventually fulfilled the prophecy and killed the king.

19 **Critical Viewing**

Possible response: Both characters appear to be depressed or out of sorts—Romeo because he is in love and Benvolio because he is concerned about Romeo.

---

190 A choking gall,[40] and a preserving sweet.
15 Farewell, my coz.

BENVOLIO.   Soft![41] I will go along.
And if you leave me so, you do me wrong.

ROMEO. Tut! I have lost myself; I am not here;
This is not Romeo, he's some other where.

195 **BENVOLIO.** Tell me in sadness,[42] who is that you love?

ROMEO. What, shall I groan and tell thee?

BENVOLIO.   Groan? Why, no;
But sadly tell me who.

ROMEO. Bid a sick man in sadness make his will.
Ah, word ill urged to one that is so ill!
200 In sadness, cousin, I do love a woman.

BENVOLIO. I aimed so near when I supposed you loved.

ROMEO. A right good markman. And she's fair I love.

BENVOLIO. A right fair mark, fair coz, is soonest hit.

ROMEO. Well, in that hit you miss. She'll not be hit
205 With Cupid's arrow. She hath Dian's wit,[43]
17 And, in strong proof[44] of chastity well armed,
From Love's weak childish bow she lives uncharmed.
She will not stay[45] the siege of loving terms,
Nor bide th' encounter of assailing eyes,
18 210 Nor ope her lap to saint-seducing gold.
O, she is rich in beauty; only poor
That, when she dies, with beauty dies her store.[46]

BENVOLIO. Then she hath sworn that she will still live chaste?

40. gall a bitter liquid.

41. Soft! Hold on a minute.

42. in sadness seriously.

43. Dian's wit the mind of Diana, goddess of chastity.
44. proof armor.
45. stay endure; put up with.

46. That . . . store in that her beauty will die with her if she does not marry and have children.

738 Drama

ROMEO. She hath, and in that sparing make huge waste;
215   For beauty, starved with her severity,
17   Cuts beauty off from all posterity.[47]
    She is too fair, too wise, wisely too fair
    To merit bliss by making me despair.[48]
    She hath forsworn to[49] love, and in that vow
220   Do I live dead that live to tell it now.

BENVOLIO. Be ruled by me; forget to think of her.

ROMEO. O, teach me how I should forget to think!

BENVOLIO. By giving liberty unto thine eyes.
    Examine other beauties.

ROMEO.   'Tis the way
225   To call hers, exquisite, in question more.[50]
20   These happy masks that kiss fair ladies' brows,
    Being black puts us in mind they hide the fair.
    He that is strucken blind cannot forget
    The precious treasure of his eyesight lost.
230   Show me a mistress that is passing fair:
    What doth her beauty serve but as a note
    Where I may read who passed that passing fair?[51]
    Farewell. Thou canst not teach me to forget.

BENVOLIO. I'll pay that doctrine, or else die in debt.[52]   [*Exit all.*]

Scene ii. *A street.*

[*Enter* CAPULET, COUNTY PARIS, *and the* CLOWN, *his servant.*]

CAPULET. But Montague is bound as well as I,
    In penalty alike; and 'tis not hard, I think,
    For men so old as we to keep the peace.

PARIS. Of honorable reckoning[1] are you both,
5   And pity 'tis you lived at odds so long.
    But now, my lord, what say you to my suit?

21 **CAPULET.** But saying o'er what I have said before:
    My child is yet a stranger in the world,
    She hath not seen the change of fourteen years;
10   Let two more summers wither in their pride
    Ere we may think her ripe to be a bride.

PARIS. Younger than she are happy mothers made.

CAPULET. And too soon marred are those so early made.

---

47. in . . . posterity By denying herself love and marriage, she wastes her beauty, which will not live on in future generations.

48. She . . . despair She is being too good—she will earn happiness in heaven by dooming me to live without her love.

49. forsworn to sworn not to.

50. 'Tis . . . more That way will only make her beauty more strongly present in my mind.

51. who . . . fair who surpassed in beauty that very beautiful woman.

52. I'll . . . debt I will teach you to forget, or else die trying.

1. reckoning reputation.

◀ **Critical Viewing**
What does this photograph reveal about the feelings of Romeo and Benvolio? **[Analyze]**

 Reading Check
What advice does Benvolio give to Romeo about the woman he loves?

Romeo and Juliet, Act I ■ *739*

- Have students read lines 221 through 234. **Ask** what Benvolio is urging Romeo to do.
  Answer: He is urging Romeo to forget about his love and look around for other girls.

- **Ask:** How does Romeo respond to Benvolio's suggestion?
  Answer: Romeo says he cannot forget his love. Looking at other beautiful girls will just remind him of her.

- **Ask** students what contrasting attitudes are revealed in this exchange between Romeo and Benvolio.
  Possible response: Benvolio is more realistic and believes that if one loves someone who does not reciprocate, one should find someone else. Romeo believes the opposite: once having committed to love, he can see no alternative.

21 Critical Thinking
Interpret

- Ask students to **review** lines 1–11 on p. 739. **Ask** them what Paris is requesting, and how Capulet answers him.
  Answer: Paris is asking to marry Capulet's daughter, and Capulet is telling him that the girl is just fourteen, and it will be two more years before she is ready to be a bride.

- Have students read lines 16–33 on page 740, referring to footnotes 4–6. Ask students to recall Romeo's response to Benvolio's suggestion that Romeo look at other beautiful women. Have students **compare** Capulet's advice to Paris with Benvolio's advice to Romeo.
  Answer: Capulet suggests that Paris come to his feast, meet many of the eligible women, and see that Juliet is only one of many possible wives.

22 Reading Check
Answer: He advises Romeo to forget her.

Differentiated Instruction   Solutions for All Learners

Enrichment for Gifted/Talented Students
Tell students that the situation in which Romeo and Benvolio find themselves is a common human condition. Young men fall in love with girls who do not love them in return, and the young men's friends urge them to find somebody else.

    Have students review the conversation between Benvolio and Romeo in lines 156–234. Then, have them rewrite the dialogue in modern language. Urge students to think about the language that they and their friends use every day to convey the same ideas. What words would a young man say to his lovelorn friend? Tell students they should not paraphrase each line, but simply condense the ideas into modern language.

    After they have produced a script, have them present the scene to the class.

- **Ask** students what the servant has been requested to do in lines 34–37.
Answer: He has been requested to find the people on the list that Lord Capulet hands him and to invite those people to Lord Capulet's home for a feast.

- **Ask** students to respond to the Reading Skill prompt: Use footnote 8 to help you summarize the servant's remarks in lines here.
Possible response: The servant wonders why he is asked to find the people who are on the list. He thinks people should stick with what they know, and he can't read. He has to find someone who can read the list for him.

24 **Literary Analysis**
Stage Directions

- **Ask** students why the servant approaches Romeo and Benvolio.
Answer: The servant cannot read the list of people who are being invited to Capulet's feast. When the servant sees Romeo and Benvolio, he knows by their bearing that they are able to read.

- **Ask** students to respond to the Literary Analysis question: What important information in the stage directions clarifies Romeo's speech here?
Answer: The stage directions state that he is reading the letter.

- **Ask** students what is in the letter that Romeo is reading.
Answer: He is reading the list of people who are to be invited to Capulet's feast.

Earth hath swallowed all my hopes[2] but she;
15   She is the hopeful lady of my earth.[3]
But woo her, gentle Paris, get her heart;
My will to her consent is but a part.
An she agree, within her scope of choice
Lies my consent and fair according voice,[4]
20   This night I hold an old accustomed feast,
Whereto I have invited many a guest,
Such as I love; and you among the store,
One more, most welcome, makes my number more.
21 At my poor house look to behold this night
25   Earth-treading stars[5] that make dark heaven light.
Such comfort as do lusty young men feel
When well-appareled April on the heel
Of limping Winter treads, even such delight
Among fresh fennel buds shall you this night
30   Inherit at my house. Hear all, all see,
And like her most whose merit most shall be;
Which, on more view of many, mine, being one,
May stand in number, though in reck'ning none.[6]
Come, go with me. [*To* SERVANT, *giving him a paper*]
     Go, sirrah, trudge about
35   Through fair Verona; find those persons out
Whose names are written there, and to them say
My house and welcome on their pleasure stay.[7]

[*Exit with* PARIS.]

SERVANT. Find them out whose names are written here? It is written that the shoemaker should meddle with his yard and
40   the tailor with his last, the fisher with his pencil and the painter with his nets;[8] but I am sent to find those persons
23 whose names are here writ, and can never find what names the writing person hath here writ. I must to the learned. In good time![9]

[*Enter* BENVOLIO *and* ROMEO.]

45   **BENVOLIO.** Tut, man, one fire burns out another's burning;
     One pain is less'ned by another's anguish;
Turn giddy, and be holp by backward turning;[10]
     One desperate grief cures with another's languish.
Take thou some new infection to thy eye,
50   And the rank poison of the old will die.

---

2. hopes children.

3. She . . . earth My hopes for the future rest in her; she will inherit all that is mine.

4. and . . . voice If she agrees, I will consent to and agree with her choice.

5. Earth-treading stars young ladies.

6. Which . . . none If you look at all the young girls, you may see her as merely one among many, and not worth special admiration.

7. stay await.

Reading Skill
Summarizing Use footnote 8 to help you summarize the servant's remarks here.
8. shoemaker . . . nets The servant is confusing workers and their tools. He intends to say that people should stick with what they know.

9. In good time! Just in time! The servant has seen Benvolio and Romeo, who can read.

10. Turn . . . turning If you are dizzy from turning one way, turn the other way.

ROMEO. Your plantain leaf[11] is excellent for that.

BENVOLIO. For what, I pray thee?

ROMEO. For your broken shin.

BENVOLIO. Why, Romeo, art thou mad?

ROMEO. Not mad, but bound more than a madman is;
55 Shut up in prison, kept without my food,
    Whipped and tormented and—God-den,[12] good fellow.

SERVANT. God gi' go-den. I pray, sir, can you read?

ROMEO. Ay, mine own fortune in my misery.

SERVANT. Perhaps you have learned it without book.
60 But, I pray, can you read anything you see?

ROMEO. Ay, if I know the letters and the language.

SERVANT. Ye say honestly. Rest you merry.[13]

ROMEO. Stay, fellow; I can read. [*He reads the letter.*]
    "Signior Martino and his wife and daughters;
65 County Anselm and his beauteous sisters;
    The lady widow of Vitruvio;
    Signior Placentio and his lovely nieces;
    Mercutio and his brother Valentine;
    Mine uncle Capulet, his wife and daughters;
70 My fair niece Rosaline; Livia;
    Signior Valentio and his cousin Tybalt;
    Lucio and the lively Helena."
    A fair assembly. Whither should they come?

SERVANT. Up.

75 **ROMEO.** Whither? To supper?

SERVANT. To our house.

ROMEO. Whose house?

SERVANT. My master's.

ROMEO. Indeed I should have asked you that before.

80 **SERVANT.** Now I'll tell you without asking. My master is the
    great rich Capulet; and if you be not of the house of
    Montagues, I pray come and crush a cup of wine. Rest you
    merry.   [*Exit.*]

BENVOLIO. At this same ancient[14] feast of Capulet's
85 Sups the fair Rosaline whom thou so loves;
    With all the admirèd beauties of Verona.
    Go thither, and with unattainted[15] eye

---

11. plantain leaf leaf used to stop bleeding.

12. God-den good afternoon; good evening.

13. Rest you merry May God keep you happy—a way of saying farewell.

Literary Analysis
Stage Directions
What important information in the stage directions clarifies Romeo's speech here?

14. ancient long-established; traditional.
15. unattainted unprejudiced.

26 ✓ **Reading Check**

Why does Capulet's servant talk to Romeo and Benvolio?

Romeo and Juliet, Act I ■ 741

---

25 **Critical Thinking**
Infer

- Have students read lines 84–89. **Ask** students what Benvolio is suggesting in these lines.
  Answer: He is suggesting that he and Romeo attend Capulet's feast.

- **Ask** students why this suggestion might seem foolish or even dangerous.
  Answer: Romeo is a Montague. His family are sworn enemies of the Capulets. The Montagues and the Capulets had been in a brawl the previous day, and they had been threatened with death if they fought again.

26 **Reading Check**

Answer: The servant wants them to read the letter.

Differentiated
Instruction — Solutions for All Learners

Strategy for Special Needs Students
Since there is little action in Scene ii, students may well struggle with its difficult language. Hearing the language spoken aloud may help them better understand the conversations. Encourage them to reread the scene, reading aloud along with them or providing them with the **Listening to Literature Audio CD** and having them read along with it.

Before having them reread and listen to the CD, review all the footnotes in the scene. Ask them to place sticky notes next to the difficult passages that are causing them trouble as they read along with the CD. After students hear scene ii, review and respond to any questions they have.

Analyze

• Have students read lines 90–101.

Ask: What does Romeo imply his love for Rosaline is like? What will happen if he withdraws his love for her?

Answer: He implies his love is like a religious devotion, and he will be a heretic if he turns from her.

• **Ask:** Under what condition does Romeo agree to go to the feast?

Answer: He agrees to go with the understanding that he is not going to look at other beauties, but to enjoy the beauty of his own love, Rosaline.

28 **Critical Viewing**

Answer: Students may infer that the women share a close relationship. Lady Capulet is kind but firm; the Nurse is a humorous character; and Juliet is an obedient daughter.

---

25 Compare her face with some that I shall show,
And I will make thee think thy swan a crow.

90 **ROMEO.** When the devout religion of mine eye
      Maintains such falsehood, then turn tears to fires:
  And these, who, often drowned, could never die,
      Transparent heretics, be burnt for liars!16
  One fairer than my love? The all-seeing sun
95 Ne'er saw her match since first the world begun.

27 **BENVOLIO.** Tut! you saw her fair, none else being by,
  Herself poised with herself in either eye;17
  But in that crystal scales18 let there be weighed
  Your lady's love against some other maid
100 That I will show you shining at this feast,
  And she shall scant show well that now seems best.

ROMEO. I'll go along, no such sight to be shown,
  But to rejoice in splendor of mine own.19   [*Exit all.*]

16. **When . . . liars!** When I see Rosaline as just a plain-looking girl, may my tears turn to fire and burn my eyes out!

17. **Herself . . . eye** Rosaline compared with no one else.
18. **crystal scales** your eyes.

19. **mine own** my own love, Rosaline.

Scene iii. A room in CAPULET'S *house.*
[*Enter* CAPULET'S WIFE, *and* NURSE.]

  LADY CAPULET. Nurse, where's my daughter? Call her forth to
    me.

  NURSE. Now, by my maidenhead at twelve year old,
    I bade her come. What, lamb! What, ladybird!
    God forbid, where's this girl? What, Juliet!
[*Enter* JULIET.]

28 ▼ Critical Viewing What do this picture and the conversation among Juliet, Lady Capulet, and the Nurse tell you about their relationship? [**Infer**]

742 ■ Drama

Vocabulary Development

Expressive Vocabulary
As students read and discuss Scene iii, have them consider the relationship among the three women—Juliet, the nurse, and Lady Capulet. How does Juliet treat the nurse? Her mother? What is Lady Capulet's attitude toward her daughter? Encourage students to use the expressive vocabulary presented earlier. You might encourage them with sentence starters like these:

1. The dialogue between Juliet and her nurse *illustrates* . . .

2. There is a great *contrast* between . . .
3. The nurse's talkativeness *emphasizes* . . .
4. The discussion of Juliet's coming birthday *reinforces* . . .
5. Juliet seems willing to *adapt* . . .

Challenge students to use these words as you continue to discuss the play.

5 **JULIET.** How now? Who calls?

NURSE.   Your mother.

JULIET.   Madam, I am here.
What is your will?

LADY CAPULET. This is the matter—Nurse, give leave[1] awhile;
We must talk in secret. Nurse, come back again.
I have rememb'red me; thou's hear our counsel.[2]
10   Thou knowest my daughter's of a pretty age.

NURSE. Faith, I can tell her age unto an hour.

LADY CAPULET. She's not fourteen.

NURSE.   I'll lay fourteen of my teeth—
And yet, to my teen[3] be it spoken, I have but four—
She's not fourteen. How long is it now
To Lammastide?[4]

15 **LADY CAPULET.**   A fortnight and odd days.[5]

NURSE. Even or odd, of all days in the year,
Come Lammas Eve at night shall she be fourteen.
Susan and she (God rest all Christian souls!)
Were of an age.[6] Well, Susan is with God;
20   She was too good for me. But, as I said,
On Lammas Eve at night shall she be fourteen;
That shall she, marry; I remember it well.
'Tis since the earthquake now eleven years.
And she was weaned (I never shall forget it),
25   Of all the days of the year, upon that day;
For I had then laid wormwood to my dug,
Sitting in the sun under the dovehouse wall.
My lord and you were then at Mantua.
Nay, I do bear a brain. But, as I said,
30   When it did taste the wormwood on the nipple
Of my dug and felt it bitter, pretty fool,
To see it tetchy and fall out with the dug!
Shake, quoth the dovehouse! 'Twas no need, I trow,
To bid me trudge.
35   And since that time it is eleven years,
For then she could stand high-lone; nay, by th' rood,
She could have run and waddled all about;
For even the day before, she broke her brow;
And then my husband (God be with his soul!
40   'A was a merry man) took up the child.
"Yea," quoth he, "dost thou fall upon thy face?

1. **give leave** Leave us alone.
2. **thou's . . . counsel** You shall hear our conference.

3. **teen** sorrow.
4. **Lammastide** August 1, a holiday celebrating the summer harvest.
5. **A fortnight and odd days** two weeks plus a few days.
6. **Susan . . . age** Susan, the Nurse's child, and Juliet were the same age.

Literary Analysis
Dialogue What do the Nurse's words here reveal about her devotion to Juliet?

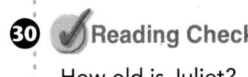
Reading Check
How old is Juliet?

Romeo and Juliet, Act I ■ 743

㉙ Literary Analysis
Dialogue

• Have students read the Nurse's speech, lines 16–48. Have them **speculate** on who Susan is.
Answer: Susan was the Nurse's daughter.

• **Ask:** What does the Nurse mean when she says that Susan and Juliet "were of an age"?
Answer: She means that Susan and Juliet were the same age.

• **Ask** students to respond to the Literary Analysis question: What do the Nurse's words here reveal about her devotion to Juliet?
Answer: Because Susan and Juliet were the same age, the Nurse became even more devoted to Juliet after Susan died.

• **Ask** students in which ways the Nurse's character, as revealed in her dialogue, contrasts with the characters of Lady Capulet and Juliet.
Answer: The Nurse talks at great length and repeats herself. Juliet and Lady Capulet speak little in this scene and when they do, they stay on the subject. These differences suggest that the Nurse is less reserved than either Lady Capulet or Juliet and that her relationships with others are less formal and more open than theirs are.

㉚ Reading Check
Answer: Juliet is fourteen.

Differentiated Instruction   Solutions for All Learners

Strategy for Less Proficient Readers
As Scene iii introduces a new set of characters, after students read through p. 743 you may wish to help students summarize the characters and action of the play to this point.
    Review the Prologue, p. 731. Point out that the story is about two lovers. Ask students what they have learned so far about the situation of the two. Lead students to recognize that Romeo belongs to the house of Montagues, bitter enemies of the Capulets. He is presently mourning over his love for Rosaline and swears he will never love another. Juliet is the daughter of Capulet. Her father has been approached by Paris, requesting her hand in marriage. Juliet is young, not yet fourteen. Juliet's father, Capulet, plans a feast that Paris will attend and that Romeo and Benvolio also plan to attend. Ask students to make one prediction about what might happen at the feast.
Answer: Students may suggest that Romeo and Juliet will meet.

- Have students read lines 50–62. **Ask** what the Nurse is discussing here. What is "it" to which she refers? **Answer:** The Nurse is telling a story about when Juliet was little and fell and bumped her head. *It* refers to Juliet.

- Tell students that the word *stinted* in line 57 means "ceased," meaning in this case that the child ceased crying. **Ask** students what Juliet means by her response to the Nurse in line 58. **Answer:** She is asking the Nurse to stop talking about when she was small.

- **Ask:** What does the Nurse's telling of this story reveal about her relationship to Juliet? **Answer:** She has cared for Juliet since she was very small; she is very fond of her.

- **Ask** students to respond to the Literary Analysis question: What does the conversation here reveal about the Nurse's personality? **Answer:** The Nurse can be talkative to the point of being annoying; however, she is genuinely devoted to Juliet and has her best interests at heart.

32 Reading Skill
Summarizing

- Have students read lines 75–78. **Ask** who is the subject of this discussion and what opinion the Nurse and Lady Capulet seem to have of this person. **Answer:** They are discussing Paris, and both the Nurse and Lady Capulet seem to have a high opinion of him.

- **Ask** students to respond to the Reading Skill prompt: Use the information in footnote 8 and the dialogue to help you summarize the Nurse's opinion of Paris. **Possible response:** The Nurse believes there is not an equal to Paris in all the world; he is the very model of a man.

33 Literary Analysis
Dialogue

- Have students recall Lord Capulet's dialogue with Paris on p. 739, and **compare** his views of Juliet and marriage with Lady Capulet's views. **Answer:** Lord Capulet thinks Juliet is too young to be married. Lady Capulet, who was already married

744

    Thou wilt fall backward when thou hast more wit;
    Wilt thou not, Jule?" and, by my holidam,
    The pretty wretch left crying and said, "Ay."
45 To see now how a jest shall come about!
    I warrant, and I should live a thousand years,
    I never should forget it. "Wilt thou not, Jule?" quoth he,
    And, pretty fool, it stinted and said, "Ay."

LADY CAPULET. Enough of this. I pray thee hold thy peace.

50 **NURSE.** Yes, madam. Yet I cannot choose but laugh
    To think it should leave crying and say, "Ay."
    And yet, I warrant, it had upon it brow
    A bump as big as a young cock'rel's stone;
    A perilous knock; and it cried bitterly.
55 "Yea," quoth my husband, "fall'st upon thy face?
    Thou wilt fall backward when thou comest to age,
    Wilt thou not, Jule?" It stinted and said, "Ay."

JULIET. And stint thou too, I pray thee, nurse, say I.

NURSE. Peace, I have done. God mark thee to His grace!
60 Thou wast the prettiest babe that e'er I nursed.
    And I might live to see thee married once,
    I have my wish.

LADY CAPULET. Marry, that "marry" is the very theme
    I came to talk of. Tell me, daughter Juliet,
65 How stands your dispositions to be married?

JULIET. It is an honor that I dream not of.

NURSE. An honor? Were not I thine only nurse,
    I would say thou hadst sucked wisdom from thy teat.

LADY CAPULET. Well, think of marriage now. Younger than you,
70 Here in Verona, ladies of esteem,
    Are made already mothers. By my count,
    I was your mother much upon these years
    That you are now a maid.[7] Thus then in brief;
    The valiant Paris seeks you for his love.

75 **NURSE.** A man, young lady! Lady, such a man
    As all the world—Why, he's a man of wax.[8]

LADY CAPULET. Verona's summer hath not such a flower.

NURSE. Nay, he's a flower, in faith—a very flower.

LADY CAPULET. What say you? Can you love the gentleman?
80 This night you shall behold him at our feast.

744 ■ *Drama*

---

7. **I . . . maid** I was your mother when I was as old as you are now.

8. **he's . . . wax** He's a model of a man.

---

and a mother when she was fourteen, apparently does not think Juliet is too young.

- **Ask** students to respond to the Literary Analysis question: What does the dialogue here reveal about Juliet's attitude toward marriage and Paris? **Possible response:** Juliet has not really thought about it, but she seems hesitant. She is willing to meet Paris and see whether she can like him, but only so far as her mother approves.

Read o'er the volume of young Paris' face,
And find delight writ there with beauty's pen;
Examine every married lineament,
And see how one another lends content;⁹
85 And what obscured in this fair volume lies
Find written in the margent¹⁰ of his eyes.
This precious book of love, this unbound lover,
To beautify him only lacks a cover.¹¹
The fish lives in the sea, and 'tis much pride
90 For fair without the fair within to hide.
③③ That book in many's eyes doth share the glory,
That in gold clasps locks in the golden story;
So shall you share all that he doth possess,
By having him making yourself no less.

95 **NURSE.** No less? Nay, bigger! Women grow by men.

LADY CAPULET. Speak briefly, can you like of Paris' love?

JULIET. I'll look to like, if looking liking move;¹²
But no more deep will I endart mine eye
Than your consent gives strength to make it fly.¹³

[Enter SERVINGMAN.]

100 **SERVINGMAN.** Madam, the guests are come, supper served up,
you called, my young lady asked for, the nurse cursed in the
pantry, and everything in extremity. I must hence to wait. I
beseech you follow straight.   *[Exit.]*

LADY CAPULET. We follow thee. Juliet, the County stays.¹⁴

105 **NURSE.** Go, girl, seek happy nights to happy days.   *[Exit all.]*

Scene iv. A street.

[Enter ROMEO, MERCUTIO, BENVOLIO, *with five or six other*
MASKERS; TORCHBEARERS.]

ROMEO. What, shall this speech¹ be spoke for our excuse?
Or shall we on without apology?

BENVOLIO. The date is out of such prolixity.²
We'll have no Cupid hoodwinked with a scarf,
5 Bearing a Tartar's painted bow of lath,
③④ Scaring the ladies like a crowkeeper,
Nor no without-book prologue, faintly spoke
After the prompter, for our entrance;
But, let them measure us by what they will,
10 We'll measure them a measure and be gone.

---

9. Examine . . . content
Examine every harmonious
feature of his face, and see
how each one enhances every
other. Throughout this
speech, Lady Capulet com-
pares Paris to a book.
10. margent margin. Paris's
eyes are compared to the margin of a book, where whatever
is not clear in the text (the rest
of his face) can be explained
by notes.
11. cover metaphor for wife.

Literary Analysis
Dialogue What does
the dialogue here
reveal about Juliet's
attitude toward
marriage and Paris?

12. I'll . . . move If looking
favorably at someone leads to
liking him, I will look at Paris in
a way that will lead to liking
him.
13. But . . . fly But I will not
look harder than you want me
to.
14. the County stays The
Count, Paris, is waiting.

1. this speech Romeo asks
whether he and his companions, being uninvited guests,
should follow custom by
announcing their arrival in a
speech.
2. The . . . prolixity Such
wordiness is outdated. In the
following lines, Benvolio says,
in sum, "Let us forget about
announcing our entrance with
a show. The other guests can
look over as they see fit. We
will dance a while, then leave."

③⑤ **Reading Check**

Why has Lady
Capulet come to talk
to Juliet?

Romeo and Juliet, Act I ■ 745

---

③④ Critical Thinking
Interpret

• Have students read lines 1–26.
Have them refer to the stage directions, the Characters list on p. 731,
and the image on page 746. Then
ask students to **interpret** what is
going on here. For example, who is
Mercutio, what do they think
Maskers are, and why are there
torchbearers in the scene?
Answer: Mercutio belongs to the
Prince's family and is also Romeo's
friend. Maskers are people dressed
in costumes and masks, and torchbearers are necessary because it is
after dark.

• Ask students to **infer** where the
group is as Scene iv opens.
Answer: The group is in the vicinity of the Montague home.

• Ask students to **explain** in their
own words what Romeo is asking
Benvolio in lines 1 and 2.
Possible response: "Should we
tell people who we are when we
get there, or should we go in without explaining ourselves?"

③⑤ Reading Check

Answer: She wants to discuss
whether Juliet would be interested in
marrying Paris.

ROMEO. Give me a torch. I am not for this ambling.
Being but heavy,³ I will bear the light.

MERCUTIO. Nay, gentle Romeo, we must have you dance.

ROMEO. Not I, believe me. You have dancing shoes
15   With nimble soles; I have a soul of lead
So stakes me to the ground I cannot move.

34 **MERCUTIO.** You are a lover. Borrow Cupid's wings
And soar with them above a common bound.

ROMEO. I am too sore enpiercèd with his shaft
20   To soar with his light feathers; and so bound
I cannot bound a pitch above dull woe.
Under love's heavy burden do I sink.

MERCUTIO. And, to sink in it, should you burden love—
Too great oppression for a tender thing.

25 **ROMEO.** Is love a tender thing? It is too rough,
Too rude, too boist'rous, and it pricks like thorn.

MERCUTIO. If love be rough with you, be rough with love.
Prick love for pricking, and you beat love down.
Give me a case to put my visage⁴ in.
30   A visor for a visor!⁵ What care I

3. heavy weighed down with sadness.

36 ▼ **Critical Viewing**
Which details in this photograph show how Romeo and his friends prepare to attend the feast? **[Analyze]**

4. visage mask.
5. A visor ... visor! A mask for a mask—which is what my real face is like!

746   *Drama*

Vocabulary Development

Vocabulary Builder Reinforcement
To reinforce and assess students' comprehension of Vocabulary Builder words, give them sentences using the words in which the word may or may not be used correctly. Students must tell whether the use is correct and explain their answer. Use these sentences:

1. The *pernicious* rumor that he was a thief ruined his entire career.
   Answer: Yes, *pernicious* is used correctly here, because it means "causing great injury," and the destruction of a career is a great injury.

2. His *transgression* made his parents very proud.
   Answer: No, *transgression* is not used correctly. A *transgression* is a wrongdoing, and parents would probably not be very proud if their son committed a wrongdoing.

What curious eye doth quote deformities?[6]
Here are the beetle brows shall blush for me.

BENVOLIO. Come, knock and enter; and no sooner in
But every man betake him to his legs.[7]

35 **ROMEO.** A torch for me! Let wantons light of heart
Tickle the senseless rushes[8] with their heels;
For I am proverbed with a grandsire phrase,[9]
I'll be a candleholder and look on;
The game was ne'er so fair, and I am done.[10]

40 **MERCUTIO.** Tut! Dun's the mouse, the constable's own word![11]
If thou art Dun,[12] we'll draw thee from the mire
Of this sir-reverence love, wherein thou stickest
Up to the ears. Come, we burn daylight, ho!

ROMEO. Nay, that's not so.

MERCUTIO.   I mean, sir, in delay
45 We waste our lights in vain, like lights by day.
Take our good meaning, for our judgment sits
Five times in that ere once in our five wits.[13]

37 ROMEO. And we mean well in going to this masque,
But 'tis no wit to go.

MERCUTIO.   Why, may one ask?

ROMEO. I dreamt a dream tonight.

50 **MERCUTIO.**   And so did I.

ROMEO. Well, what was yours?

MERCUTIO.   That dreamers often lie.

ROMEO. In bed asleep, while they do dream things true.

MERCUTIO. O, then I see Queen Mab[14] hath been with you.
She is the fairies' midwife, and she comes
55 In shape no bigger than an agate stone
On the forefinger of an alderman,
Drawn with a team of little atomies[15]
Over men's noses as they lie asleep;
39 Her wagon spokes made of long spinners'[16] legs,
60 The cover, of the wings of grasshoppers;
Her traces, of the smallest spider web;
Her collars, of the moonshine's wat'ry beams;
Her whip, of cricket's bone; the lash, of film;[17]
Her wagoner, a small gray-coated gnat,

6. quote deformities notice my ugly features.
7. betake . . . legs start dancing.
8. Let . . . rushes Let fun-loving people dance on the floor coverings.
9. proverbed . . . phrase directed by an old saying.
10. The game . . . done No matter how much enjoyment may be had, I will not have any.
11. Dun's . . . word! Lie low like a mouse—that is what a constable waiting to make an arrest might say.
12. Dun proverbial name for a horse.

Literary Analysis

Dialogue What contrast between Mercutio and Romeo does the dialogue reveal?

13. Take . . . wits Understand my intended meaning. That shows more intelligence than merely following what your senses perceive.
14. Queen Mab the queen of fairyland.

15. atomies creatures.
16. spinners spiders.
17. film spider's thread.

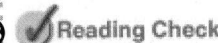

Reading Check

How does Romeo feel about going to the Capulets' feast?

Romeo and Juliet, Act I ■ 747

37 Literary Analysis
Dialogue

- Have students review footnotes 4 through 13.
- **Ask** students to respond to the Literary Analysis question: What contrast in their personalities does the dialogue between Romeo and Mercutio reveal?
  Answer: Mercutio is fun-loving, good-natured, and outgoing. He is able to enjoy life and poke fun at himself and others, in contrast to Romeo, who is moody and too-serious.

38 Reading Check

Answer: Romeo does not want to go to the feast. He is too sad and heavy-hearted about his love to enjoy himself.

747

- Ask students why Mercutio talks about Queen Mab in these lines. **Possible response:** Romeo has said he doesn't want to go to the dance because he had a dream. Mercutio says Romeo has been visited by Queen Mab, who brings dreams to sleeping humans.

- **Ask** students to respond to the Reading Skill prompt: Review Mercutio's speech and summarize his ideas about Queen Mab. **Possible response:** Queen Mab is a tiny fairy who rides a coach made of a hazelnut shell drawn by tiny little creatures whose harnesses are made of a spider web. Her whip is a cricket's bone with a spider's thread for a lash. She gallops every night through people's brains, bringing dreams to people according to their position in life. To lovers she brings dreams of love; to lawyers, she brings dreams of fees; to soldiers she brings dreams of war, and so on.

40 Literary Analysis
Dialogue

- **Ask** what Romeo might mean when he says to Mercutio "Thou talk'st of nothing." **Possible response:** Romeo thinks Mercutio is talking nonsense; or, Romeo means that by talking about dreams, which are not real, Mercutio is literally talking about nothing.

- Have students read lines 97–103. **Ask** students to respond to the Literary Analysis question on p. 748: What do Mercutio's comments about dreams reveal about his character? **Possible response:** Mercutio likes to indulge his sense of poetry, as he did in his speech about Queen Mab, and he likes to hear the sound of his own voice.

- **Ask** students how this contrasts with Romeo's character. **Answer:** Romeo is more down-to-earth and practical. He wants to proceed with whatever they are going to do.

---

65 Not half so big as a round little worm
Pricked from the lazy finger of a maid;
Her chariot is an empty hazelnut,
Made by the joiner squirrel or old grub,[18]
Time out o' mind the fairies' coachmakers.
70 And in this state she gallops night by night
Through lovers' brains, and then they dream of love;
On courtiers' knees, that dream on curtsies straight;
O'er lawyers' fingers, who straight dream on fees;
O'er ladies' lips, who straight on kisses dream,
75 Which oft the angry Mab with blisters plagues,
Because their breath with sweetmeats[19] tainted are.
Sometimes she gallops o'er a courtier's nose,
And then dreams he of smelling out a suit;[20]
And sometime comes she with a tithe pig's[21] tail
80 Tickling a parson's nose as 'a lies asleep,
39 Then he dreams of another benefice.[22]
Sometime she driveth o'er a soldier's neck,
And then dream he of cutting foreign throats,
Of breaches, ambuscadoes,[23] Spanish blades,
85 Of healths[24] five fathom deep; and then anon
Drums in his ear, at which he starts and wakes,
And being thus frighted, swears a prayer or two
And sleeps again. This is that very Mab
That plats[25] the manes of horses in the night
90 And bakes the elflocks[26] in foul sluttish hairs,
Which once untangled much misfortune bodes.
This is the hag, when maids lie on their backs,
That presses them and learns them first to bear,
Making them women of good carriage.[27]
This is she—

95 **ROMEO.**   Peace, peace, Mercutio, peace!
Thou talk'st of nothing.

MERCUTIO.   True, I talk of dreams;
Which are the children of an idle brain,
40 Begot of nothing but vain fantasy;
Which is as thin of substance as the air,
100 And more inconstant than the wind, who woos
Even now the frozen bosom of the North
And, being angered, puffs away from thence,
Turning his side to the dew-dropping South.

41 **BENVOLIO.** This wind you talk of blows us from ourselves.
105 Supper is done, and we shall come too late.

748 ■ *Drama*

18. old grub insect that bores holes in nuts.

19. sweetmeats candy.

20. smelling . . . suit finding someone who has a petition (suit) for the king and who will pay the courtier to gain the king's favor for the petition.
21. tithe pig pig donated to a parson.
22. benefice church appointment that included a guaranteed income.
23. ambuscadoes ambushes.
24. healths toasts ("To your health!").
25. plats tangles.
26. elflocks tangled hair.

27. carriage posture.

Reading Skill
Summarizing Review Mercutio's speech and summarize his ideas about Queen Mab.

Literary Analysis
Dialogue What do Mercutio's comments about dreams reveal about his character?

Vocabulary Development

Think-Aloud: Expressive Vocabulary
As students read and discuss the conversation between Mercutio and Romeo about dreams and Queen Mab, encourage them to use the expressive vocabulary presented earlier. Using a think-aloud process, model how to use the expressive vocabulary in discussing these lines. Say to students:

I'm going to think aloud to show you how I would use the expressive vocabulary.

If I were discussing the Queen Mab speech, I might say: *Mercutio's Queen Mab speech and Romeo's response to it helps to* **contrast** *the traits of these two characters.*

If I were discussing Mercutio's character, I might say: *Mercutio's long and detailed description of Queen Mab* **illustrates** *his fanciful imagination and his love of poetic language.*

ROMEO. I fear, too early; for my mind misgives
  Some consequence yet hanging in the stars
  Shall bitterly begin his fearful date
110 With this night's revels and expire the term
  Of a despisèd life, closed in my breast,
  By some vile forfeit of untimely death.²⁸
  But he that hath the steerage of my course
  Direct my sail! On, lusty gentlemen!

BENVOLIO. Strike, drum.
    [*They march about the stage, and retire to one side.*]

Scene v. A hall in CAPULET'S *house.*
[SERVINGMEN *come forth with napkins.*]

FIRST SERVINGMAN. Where's Potpan, that he helps not to
  take away? He shift a trencher!¹ He scrape a trencher!

SECOND SERVINGMAN. When good manners shall lie all in one
  or two men's hands, and they unwashed too, 'tis a foul thing.

5 **FIRST SERVINGMAN.** Away with the joint-stools, remove the
  court cupboard, look to the plate. Good thou, save me a
  piece of marchpane,² and, as thou loves me, let the porter
  let in Susan Grindstone and Nell. Anthony and Potpan!

SECOND SERVINGMAN. Ay, boy, ready.

10 **FIRST SERVINGMAN.** You are looked for and called for,
  asked for and sought for, in the great chamber.

THIRD SERVINGMAN. We cannot be here and there too.
  Cheerly, boys! Be brisk awhile, and the longest liver
  take all.   [*Exit.*]

[*Enter* CAPULET, *his* WIFE, JULIET, TYBALT, NURSE, *and all the* GUESTS
and GENTLEWOMEN *to the* MASKERS.]

15 **CAPULET.** Welcome, gentlemen! Ladies that have their toes
  Unplagued with corns will walk a bout³ with you.
  Ah, my mistresses, which of you all
  Will now deny to dance? She that makes dainty,⁴
  She I'll swear hath corns. Am I come near ye now?
20 Welcome, gentlemen! I have seen the day
  That I have worn a visor and could tell
  A whispering tale in a fair lady's ear,
  Such as would please. 'Tis gone, 'tis gone, 'tis gone.

Reading Skill
Summarizing Use footnote 28 to help you summarize Romeo's response to Benvolio.

28. my mind . . . death My mind is fearful that some future event, fated by the stars, shall start to run its course tonight and cut my life short.

1. trencher wooden platter.

2. marchpane marzipan, a confection made of sugar and almonds.

3. walk a bout dance a turn.
4. makes dainty hesitates; acts shy.

✓**Reading Check**
What does Romeo fear might happen in the near future?

Romeo and Juliet, Act I ■ 749

---

❹❶ Reading Skill
Summarizing

- Have students read lines 104–113. **Ask** what Benvolio means in line 105.
  Answer: Benvolio worries that everyone has finished eating by now and that they will all arrive late.
  Ask students the Reading Skill question: Use footnote 28 to help you summarize Romeo's response to Benvolio.
  Possible response: Romeo says that he is afraid that something he can't control will begin tonight, and the result will be his early death. But, he says, they should go on.

❹❷ Critical Thinking
Interpret

- Tell students that Shakespeare often uses humor based on characters from London's lower social classes of the time to break or interrupt the tension. Point out that the exchange between the servants is meant to be funny.

- **Ask** students what is meant to be humorous about the words of the second servingman in lines 3–4.
  Possible response: Griping about Potpan, the servingman says it's a foul thing when everything is left to those whose hands are dirty. The play on words is "'tis a foul thing," meaning both "it's too bad" and that dirty hands are foul.

- **Ask** students how minor characters like the servingmen add to the play.
  Answer: They add humor and help set up new scenes.

❹❸ Reading Check
Answer: Romeo fears he will die young.

Differentiated
Instruction   Solutions for All Learners

Enrichment for Gifted/Talented Students
Mercutio's Queen Mab speech is one of the finest and most famous passages of poetry in Shakespeare's early works. Artistically talented students may enjoy creating an illustration of the speech. Based on the descriptions in lines 53–94, have them draw an illustration of Queen Mab, who is "no bigger than an agate stone . . . " and pulled by a team of small creatures across men's noses at night, and so on.

Encourage students to write lines from the play as captions or call-outs next to elements in the illustration. For example, they might use the line "Her wagon spokes made of long spinners' legs" next to the spokes of the wagon. Have students display their work in the classroom.

Possible response: Some students may say that Romeo is romantic; others may say that Romeo is compulsive and naive.

45 Literary Analysis
Stage Directions

• Have students read lines 41–52. **Ask** what Romeo is describing in these lines.
Answer: He is describing a beautiful woman he has just seen.
Ask students to respond to the Literary Analysis question on p. 750: What do the stage direction in line 40 and the dialogue that follows reveal about Romeo?
Possible response: The stage direction reveals that Romeo has seen a beautiful woman whom he does not know, and he asks the servingman who she is. The dialogue that follows reveals that Romeo has fallen in love at first sight.

46 Critical Thinking
Infer

• Ask students to identify Romeo's meaning in lines 51–52.
Answer: Romeo's rhetorical question suggests that only now is he experiencing true love and true beauty.

• **Ask** students why they think Romeo seems to have so quickly and easily forgotten Rosaline.
Possible response: Students may suggest that Romeo was only infatuated with Rosaline and did not truly love her.

You are welcome, gentlemen! Come, musicians, play.

[*Music plays, and they dance.*]

25 A hall,[5] a hall! Give room! And foot it, girls.
More light, you knaves, and turn the tables up,
And quench the fire; the room is grown too hot.
Ah, sirrah, this unlooked-for sport comes well.
Nay, sit; nay, sit, good cousin Capulet;
30 For you and I are past our dancing days.
How long is't now since last yourself and I
Were in a mask?

SECOND CAPULET. By'r Lady, thirty years.

CAPULET. What, man? 'Tis not so much, 'tis not so much;
'Tis since the nuptial of Lucentio,
35 Come Pentecost as quickly as it will,
Some five-and-twenty years, and then we masked.

SECOND CAPULET. 'Tis more, 'tis more. His son is elder, sir;
His son is thirty.

CAPULET.   Will you tell me that?
His son was but a ward[6] two years ago.

40 **ROMEO.** [*To a* SERVINGMAN] What lady's that which doth enrich the hand
Of yonder knight?

SERVINGMAN. I know not, sir.

ROMEO. O, she doth teach the torches to burn bright!
It seems she hangs upon the cheek of night
45 As a rich jewel in an Ethiop's ear—
Beauty too rich for use, for earth too dear!
So shows a snowy dove trooping with crows
As yonder lady o'er her fellows shows.
The measure done, I'll watch her place of stand
50 And, touching hers, make blessèd my rude hand.
Did my heart love till now? Forswear[7] it, sight!
For I ne'er saw true beauty till this night.

TYBALT. This, by his voice, should be a Montague.
Fetch me my rapier, boy. What! Dares the slave
55 Come hither, covered with an antic face,[8]
To fleer[9] and scorn at our solemnity?

750 ■ *Drama*

---

44 ▲ Critical Viewing What can you tell about Romeo's personality from the fact that he has taken off his mask? **[Draw Conclusions]**

5. A hall clear the floor, make room for dancing.
6. ward minor.

Literary Analysis
Stage Directions What do the stage direction in line 40 and the dialogue that follows reveal about Romeo?

7. Forswear deny.
8. antic face strange, fantastic mask.
9. fleer mock.

Vocabulary Development

Vocabulary Builder Reinforcement
Students will benefit from additional examples and practice with the Vocabulary Builder words. Reinforce their comprehension with "show-you-know" sentences. The first part of the sentence uses the vocabulary word in an appropriate context. The second part of the sentence—the "show-you-know" part—clarifies the first. Model the strategy with this example for *pernicious:*

The effects of the medication were *pernicious;* she nearly died from the side-effects.

Then, give students these sentence prompts, and coach them in creating the clarification part:

1. The company had received a *grievance* about one of its products; _____.
Sample answer: they were investigating the basis for the complaint.

2. He is planning on *augmenting* his income; _____.
Sample answer: he is currently looking for a part-time job in the evening.

Now, by the stock and honor of my kin,
To strike him dead I hold it not a sin.

CAPULET. Why, how now, kinsman? Wherefore storm you so?

60 **TYBALT.** Uncle, this is a Montague, our foe,
A villain, that is hither come in spite
To scorn at our solemnity this night.

CAPULET. Young Romeo is it?

TYBALT.   'Tis he, that villain Romeo.

CAPULET. Content thee, gentle coz,[10] let him alone.
65 'A bears him like a portly gentleman,[11]
And, to say truth, Verona brags of him
To be a virtuous and well-governed youth.
I would not for the wealth of all this town
Here in my house do him disparagement.[12]
70 Therefore be patient; take no note of him.
It is my will, the which if thou respect,
Show a fair presence and put off these frowns,
An ill-beseeming semblance[13] for a feast.

TYBALT. It fits when such a villain is a guest.
I'll not endure him.

75 **CAPULET.**   He shall be endured.
What, goodman[14] boy! I say he shall. Go to![15]
Am I the master here, or you? Go to!
You'll not endure him, God shall mend my soul![16]
You'll make a mutiny among my guests!
80 You will set cock-a-hoop.[17] You'll be the man!

TYBALT. Why, uncle, 'tis a shame.

CAPULET.   Go to, go to!
You are a saucy boy. Is't so, indeed?
This trick may chance to scathe you.[18] I know what.
You must contrary me! Marry, 'tis time—
85 Well said, my hearts!—You are a princox[19]—go!
Be quiet, or—more light, more light!—For shame!
I'll make you quiet. What!—Cheerly, my hearts!

TYBALT. Patience perforce with willful choler meeting[20]
Makes my flesh tremble in their different greeting.
90 I will withdraw; but this intrusion shall,
Now seeming sweet, convert to bitt'rest gall.   [*Exit.*]

ROMEO. If I profane with my unworthiest hand

---

10. coz Here, "coz" is used as a term of address for a relative.
11. 'A . . . gentleman He behaves like a dignified gentleman.
12. disparagement insult.
13. ill-beseeming semblance inappropriate appearance.
14. goodman term of address for someone below the rank of gentleman.
15. Go to! expression of angry impatience.
16. God . . . soul! expression of impatience, equivalent to "God save me!"
17. You will set cock-a-hoop You want to swagger like a barnyard rooster.

Literary Analysis
Dialogue What does the dialogue between Capulet and Tybalt show about their relationship?

---

18. This . . . you This trait of yours may turn out to hurt you.
19. princox rude youngster; wise guy.
20. Patience . . . meeting enforced self-control mixing with strong anger.

 Reading Check

How does Capulet respond when Tybalt says he will not tolerate Romeo's presence at the party?

Romeo and Juliet, Act I ■ 751

---

47 Literary Analysis
Dialogue

- Have students read lines 53–87. Have students recall Tybalt's first appearance in the play (p. 733) and compare it with the dialogue in lines 53–58. Are the two scenes similar or different?
  Answer: Tybalt here, as earlier, is instantly ready to fight and kill anyone he sees as a threat to the Capulets. He is hotheaded and dangerous.

- **Ask** students what Tybalt means by his first line of dialogue.
  Answer: He means that he can tell who Romeo is by his voice. Since Romeo and his friends have put on masks, they cannot be recognized by their appearances.

- **Ask** what Tybalt means by saying that Romeo has come with an "antic face, / To fleer and scorn at our solemnity"?
  Answer: He means that Romeo has come wearing a mask to mock the Capulets in their important celebration.

- **Ask** how Capulet responds in lines 64–73 when he learns that Romeo is at his feast.
  Answer: He does not seem disturbed by Romeo's presence. He says that Romeo is behaving like a gentleman, and besides he has heard good things about Romeo. He does not want Romeo to be insulted in his house, so he advises Tybalt to ignore his presence.

- Have students review lines 60–87. Then, **ask** the Literary Analysis question: What does the dialogue between Capulet and Tybalt show about their relationship?
  Possible response: The dialogue shows that Capulet has authority over Tybalt, and that he thinks Tybalt is rude, arrogant, and a trouble-maker.

48 Reading Check

Answer: Capulet rebukes Tybalt's contrariness and tells him to leave Romeo alone.

Differentiated Instruction Solutions for All Learners

Strategy for Less Proficient Readers
Help students visualize the action in this scene by displaying the **Series-of-Events Chain Graphic Organizer** (*Graphic Organizer Transparencies*, p. 239). Begin with line 15, when Capulet welcomes his guests, urges them to dance, and then engages in a conversation with a relative. Meanwhile, Romeo sees a beautiful woman and asks a servant her name. Tybalt overhears him, recognizes his voice, and calls for his weapon.

Point out to students that at this point, Romeo has not exchanged words with Capulet or with Tybalt. Romeo hasn't even noticed Tybalt.

In the next event, Tybalt approaches his uncle, who tells Tybalt to just ignore Romeo, since he's not causing any trouble. When Tybalt continues his ranting, Capulet becomes angry. Remind students that meanwhile Romeo, unaware of the exchange between Tybalt and Capulet, is making his way toward the beautiful girl.

751

49 ## Literary Analysis
Dialogue and Stage Directions

- Have students read lines 92 through 109. **Ask** students why Romeo apologizes in lines 92–93. **Answer:** He has taken Juliet's hand in his.

- **Ask** students what Romeo means when he asks Juliet if saints have lips. What is Juliet's answer? **Answer:** Romeo suggests that saints, if they have lips, can kiss with lips rather than touch hands. Juliet deftly responds that saints' lips are used for prayer.

- **Ask** students to respond to the Literary Analysis question: What do the dialogue and stage directions in this passage reveal about Romeo and Juliet's feelings? **Answer:** They speak to each other about holding hands and kissing. The stage directions indicate that they kiss twice. The dialogue and stage directions reveal that Romeo and Juliet are strongly attracted to each other.

- **Ask** what character traits Romeo and Juliet reveal in their words to each other. **Answer:** Romeo and Juliet are both clever and playful; they also show a mixture of modesty and frankness.

50 ## Background
Sonnet

Point out that lines 92–105 form a Shakespearean sonnet. The original form of the sonnet, known as the Italian or Petrarchan sonnet, was created by the Italian poet Petrarch in the fourteenth century and consists of two stanzas—an octave with the rhyme scheme *abba abba* and a sestet with the rhyme scheme *cdecde* or *cdcdcd*. Shakespeare adapted a variant, which consists of three quatrains and a terminal couplet, and has the rhyme scheme *abab cdcd efef gg*.

Shakespeare, the acknowledged master of the sonnet, demonstrated his talent by working sonnets into *The Tragedy of Romeo and Juliet.*

51 ## Critical Viewing

Answer: Details such as pressing hands together and looking into each other's eyes suggest Romeo and Juliet's affection for each other.

---

49 This holy shrine,[21] the gentle sin is this:
My lips, two blushing pilgrims, ready stand
95   To smooth that rough touch with a tender kiss.

JULIET. Good pilgrim, you do wrong your hand too much,
    Which mannerly devotion shows in this;
For saints have hands that pilgrims' hands do touch
    And palm to palm is holy palmers'[22] kiss.

100 **ROMEO.** Have not saints lips, and holy palmers too?

JULIET. Ay, pilgrim, lips that they must use in prayer.

50 **ROMEO.** O, then, dear saint, let lips do what hands do!
    They pray; grant thou, lest faith turn to despair.

JULIET. Saints do not move,[23] though grant for prayers' sake.

105 **ROMEO.** Then move not while my prayer's effect I take.
    Thus from my lips, by thine my sin is purged.   [*Kisses her.*]

JULIET. Then have my lips the sin that they have took.

ROMEO. Sin from my lips? O trespass sweetly urged![24]
    Give me my sin again.   [*Kisses her.*]

JULIET.   You kiss by th' book.[25]

110 **NURSE.** Madam, your mother craves a word with you.

ROMEO. What is her mother?

NURSE.   Marry, bachelor,
Her mother is the lady of the house,
And a good lady, and a wise and virtuous.

21. **shrine** Juliet's hand.

22. **palmers** pilgrims who at one time carried palm branches from the Holy Land.
23. **move** initiate involvement in earthly affairs.

Literary Analysis
Dialogue and Stage Directions What do the dialogue and stage directions in this passage reveal about Romeo's and Juliet's feelings?

24. **O . . . urged!** Romeo is saying, in substance, that he is happy. Juliet calls his kiss a sin, for now he can take it back—by another kiss.
25. **by th' book** as if you were following a manual of courtly love.

51 ◄ **Critical Viewing** Which details in this photograph show Romeo's and Juliet's affection for each other? **[Draw Conclusions]**

752 ■ *Drama*

Vocabulary Development

Vocabulary Knowledge Rating
When students have completed reading and discussing Act I of *The Tragedy of Romeo and Juliet,* have them take out their **Vocabulary Knowledge Rating Chart** for this selection. Read the words aloud once more and have students rate their knowledge of the words again in the After Reading column. Clarify any words that are still problematic. Have students write their own definition and example or sentence in the appropriate column. Then have students complete the **Vocabulary Builder Practice** activities on p. 755. Encourage students to use the words in further discussion and written work about this selection. Remind them that they will be accountable for these words on the Selection Test.

I nursed her daughter that you talked withal.
115   I tell you, he that can lay hold of her
    Shall have the chinks.²⁶

ROMEO.   Is she a Capulet?
    O dear account! My life is my foe's debt.²⁷

BENVOLIO. Away, be gone; the sport is at the best.

ROMEO. Ay, so I fear; the more is my unrest.

120 **CAPULET.** Nay, gentlemen, prepare not to be gone;
    We have a trifling foolish banquet towards.²⁸
    Is it e'en so?²⁹ Why then, I thank you all.
    I thank you, honest gentlemen. Good night.
    More torches here! Come on then; let's to bed.
125   Ah, sirrah, by my fay,³⁰ it waxes late;
    I'll to my rest.   [*Exit all but* JULIET *and* NURSE.]

JULIET. Come hither, nurse. What is yond gentleman?

🔵52 NURSE. The son and heir of old Tiberio.

JULIET. What's he that now is going out of door?

130 **NURSE.** Marry, that, I think, be young Petruchio.

JULIET. What's he that follows here, that would not dance?

NURSE. I know not.

JULIET. Go ask his name—If he is married,
    My grave is like to be my wedding bed.

135 **NURSE.** His name is Romeo, and a Montague,
    The only son of your great enemy.

JULIET. My only love, sprung from my only hate!
    Too early seen unknown, and known too late!
    Prodigious³¹ birth of love it is to me
140   That I must love a loathèd enemy.

NURSE. What's this? What's this?

JULIET.   A rhyme I learnt even now.
    Of one I danced withal.   [*One calls within,* "Juliet."]

NURSE.   Anon, anon!
    Come, let's away; the strangers all are gone.   [*Exit all.*]

Romeo and Juliet, Act I ■ 753

---

26. chinks cash.
27. My life . . . debt Since Juliet is a Capulet, Romeo's life is at the mercy of the enemies of his family.

28. towards being prepared.
29. Is . . . so? Is it the case that you really must leave?
30. fay faith.

Literary Analysis
Dialogue and Stage Directions How can you tell that the dialogue that follows line 126 is a private conversation?

31. Prodigious monstrous; foretelling misfortune.

🔵52 Literary Analysis
Dialogue and Stage Directions

• **Ask** students what is happening in lines 117–126.
Answer: When Romeo realizes Juliet is a Capulet, he starts to leave. Capulet, seeing Romeo and his friends leaving, urges them to stay and have some food, but they rush out.

• Refer students to lines 125–126. **Ask** students to respond to the Literary Analysis question: How can you tell that the dialogue that follows line 126 is a private conversation?
Answer: The stage directions indicate that everyone but Juliet and her Nurse leave.

• **Ask** students what Juliet wants to know about Romeo after he leaves the feast.
Answer: Juliet asks the Nurse who Romeo is and whether he is married.

• After students have read Juliet's dialogue in lines 137–140, **ask** them in what ways are Juliet's thoughts shown to be similar to Romeo's thoughts?
Answer: Juliet is also appalled that she has fallen in love with the enemy of her family.

Concept Connector

Connecting to the Literature
Have students compare the sentences they wrote before reading with their thoughts about why a romantic tragedy is an inspiring subject for writers, painters, and composers. Ask them to explain whether their thoughts have changed and, if so, how.

Reading Skill Graphic Organizer
Have students review the graphic organizers they completed to summarize scenes. Show them **Reading Skill Graphic Organizer B** (*Graphic Organizer Transparencies,* p. 164) as an example. Then, have students share the graphic organizers they did and the summaries they completed.

Apply the Skills

The Tragedy of Romeo and Juliet, Act I

Thinking About the Selection

1. **Respond:** If you were Romeo or Juliet, would you pursue a relationship with the other? Explain.
2. **(a) Recall:** Based on Act I, what do you know about Romeo's and Juliet's lives? **(b) Compare and Contrast:** How are their personalities similar and different?
3. **(a) Recall:** What information about the two households is presented in the Prologue? **(b) Connect:** In what way does Juliet's comment in Act I, Scene v, lines 137–138, echo the Prologue?
4. **Analyze:** How do the comments of Mercutio and Benvolio add to your understanding of Romeo's character?
5. **(a) Analyze:** What threats to Romeo and Juliet's love already exist in Act I? **(b) Speculate:** How do you think Romeo and Juliet will react to these threats?
6. **Evaluate:** Based on Romeo's behavior in Act I, do you think Shakespeare accurately portrays a teenager in love? Explain.

Literary Analysis

7. Using a chart like the one shown, explain what the **dialogue** involving the Nurse, Juliet, and Lady Capulet in Act I, Scene iii, reveals about each character.

Character	Dialogue	→	Reveals

8. Most of the **stage directions** in Act I mark the characters' entrances and exits. **(a)** Identify three examples of stage directions that do more than simply dictate characters' movements on and off stage. **(b)** Explain what each of these directions tells us about the characters and the action.

Reading Skill

9. **Use text aids** to restate Capulet's scolding of Tybalt in Act I, Scene v, lines 77–87, in your own words.
10. **(a)** Using text aids to clarify her meaning, explain the play on words in Juliet's speech in Act I, Scene v, lines 96–99. **(b) Summarize** her speech in a few sentences.

QuickReview

Act I at a Glance
Romeo and Juliet meet at a ball given by Juliet's family. They fall immediately in love, only to discover that their families are enemies.

Go Online
Assessment
For: Self-test
Visit: www.PHSchool.com
Web Code: epa-6502

Dialogue: conversation between characters

Stage Directions: notes in the text of a play that describe how the work should be performed or staged

Summarizing: briefly stating the main points in a piece of writing

Answers

1. Some students may say they would follow their hearts.
2. (a) Both Romeo and Juliet are children of privilege with authoritative parents. (b) Romeo is moody, impulsive, and romantic. Juliet, by contrast, is a dutiful young girl who, before meeting Romeo, does not seem to have given much thought to love. When they meet, they are so in tune with each other that their words create a sonnet.
3. (a) Both families are of high social rank in Verona, and carry an ancient grudge. (b) Juliet realizes that she is in love with a family enemy.
4. The practical Benvolio and the joking Mercutio create a contrast to the moody and romantic Romeo.
5. (a) The families are feuding, and Juliet's parents are considering marrying her to Paris. (b) **Possible response:** Romeo and Juliet may attempt to meet in secret.
6. Romeo's brief passion for Rosaline and his instant love for Juliet show a teen's intense emotions.
7. **Character:** Nurse; **Dialogue:** lines 59–62. **Reveals:** She is very talkative; she is very fond of Juliet. **Character:** Juliet; **Dialogue:** lines 97–99. **Reveals:** Juliet is hesitant but willing to obey her mother. **Character:** Lady Capulet; **Dialogue:** lines 69–74. **Reveals:** Lady Capulet believes Juliet is not too young to marry. Another sample answer can be found on **Literary Analysis Graphic Organizer B**, p. 166 in *Graphic Organizer Transparencies.*
8. In Scene i, "Aside to Gregory" tells the reader that Sampson is whispering to Gregory so that Abram does not hear; In Scene i, "They fight" indicates that Gregory and Sampson are fighting Abram and Balthasar. In Scene v, "Music plays" indicates that guests at Capulet's feast begin to dance.
9. **Sample response:** "Leave him alone. Who's in charge here, me or you? If you don't leave him alone, my guests will riot. But

you want to act macho. That's going to hurt you."
10. (a) Juliet is playing on the words *palm* and *palmer*, implying that she and Romeo have kissed by touching hands. (b) **Sample response:** "Don't be concerned about your hand touching mine. Pilgrims placed their palms against a saint's palms, which is the same as a kiss."

Vocabulary Builder

Practice An **oxymoron** is a phrase combining contradictory or opposing ideas, often used as a figure of speech for poetic effect. Review the vocabulary list on page 728. Then, explain the meaning of each phrase and tell why each one is an oxymoron.

1. pernicious blessing
2. augmenting scarcity
3. flattering grievance
4. honorable transgression

Adding Words to Your Vocabulary *Diminishing* and *abridging* are both antonyms for the word *augmenting*. Use a dictionary to find the precise meaning of each word. For each word, write a sentence using it correctly. Then, share your sentences with classmates and discuss their differences and similarities. (For more on using a dictionary, see page R6.)

Writing

As either Romeo or Juliet, write a **letter to an advice columnist** requesting help with the problem of falling in love with someone whom you are not supposed to love.
- First, list the reasons your love may be doomed.
- Next, write a letter that explains your list and asks for advice.

After you have written your letter as Romeo or Juliet, write a response as the advice columnist. Suggest to Romeo or Juliet how he or she might handle this difficult situation. Share your letters with the class and discuss the power of writing using more than one voice.

For *Grammar*, *Vocabulary*, and *Assessment*, see **Build Language Skills,** pages 812–813.

Extend Your Learning

Listening and Speaking Select a scene from Act I and plan a **staged performance** with classmates. Choose a scene with at least three characters. Then, plan and rehearse the scene.
- Decide who will play each role.
- As you rehearse take turns critiquing the group's work.

Take care to express your thoughts clearly with attention to others, and convey criticism in a respectful way. Perform the scene for the class, and invite comments from the audience.

Apply the Skills ■ 755

Extend Your Learning

The **Support for Extend Your Learning** page (*Unit 5 Resources,* p. 26) provides guided note-taking opportunities to help students complete the Extend Your Learning activities.

 Go Online **For:** An additional research activity
Research **Visit:** www.PHSchool.com
        Web Code: epd-7501
For another research activity to extend students' learning, give students this Web Code.

Vocabulary Builder
Practice Analogies

1. A *pernicious blessing* is an apparent good fortune that is actually harmful.
2. *Augmenting scarcity* means increasing a shortage, making things worse.
3. A *flattering grievance* is a complaint that is actually an unintended compliment.
4. An *honorable transgression* is an action that is technically wrong but morally right.

Adding Words to Your Vocabulary
Sample answers:

Diminishing means "to make smaller in size or importance." His strength is *diminishing* as he grows older. *Abridging* means "to shorten." His job is *abridging* some of the lengthy essays in the collection.

Writing

- To give students guidance for writing a letter to an advice columnist and the response from an advice columnist, give them **Support for Writing** for Act I of *The Tragedy of Romeo and Juliet,* p. 25 in *Unit 5 Resources.*
- To evaluate students' letters, use the Exposition: Problem-Solution rubrics, pp. 45–46 in *General Resources.* In addition, you might evaluate for how well students use significant details in explaining their dilemma and the practicality of their responses to the problem.

Six Traits Focus

✔ Ideas	Word Choice
✔ Organization	Sentence Fluency
✔ Voice	Conventions

Writing and Grammar, Gold Level
Students will find guidance on problem-and-solution analysis in Chapter 11.

Build Language Skills

Go to pp. 812–813 for vocabulary and grammar lessons and assessment practice.

Planning Differentiated Instruction

Accessibility at a Glance

The Tragedy of Romeo and Juliet, Act II	
Context	Historical; Verona, Italy
Language	Dialogue, prose, verse, soliloquies, Elizabethan terms, and challenging vocabulary
Concept Level	Accessible; classic tale of star-crossed lovers
Literary Merit	Classic; noted poet and playwright
Lexile	NP
Overall Rating	More challenging

Choosing Your Resources

[L1] Special Needs Students   [L4] Advanced Students

[L2] Below-Level Students   [EL] English Learners

[L3] All Students

FT Fast Track Instruction: To move the lesson more quickly, use the strategies and activities identified with **FT.**

Reading and Vocabulary Warm-ups provide support for below level students. **A** is for students reading two grades below level; **B** is for students reading one grade below level. For Selection Tests, **A** signifies "less challenging" and **B** "more challenging." For Graphic Organizer transparencies, **A** signifies "not filled in" and **B** "filled in."

Scaffolding for Less Proficient and Advanced Students

The leveled questions on Apply the Skills pages progress in the levels of thinking required to answer them. To address the needs of your different students, you may use the (a) level questions for your less proficient students, the (b) level with your on-level and advanced students. The occasional (c) level questions are appropriate for your advanced students.

 Go Online For: Information about Lexiles
Professional **Visit:** www.PHSchool.com
Development **Web Code:** eue-1111

Step-by-Step Teaching Guide | Pacing Guide

PRETEACH

• Administer Vocabulary and Reading Warm-ups as necessary.	
• Introduce the Literary Analysis Skills: Blank Verse. **FT**	10 min.
• Introduce the Reading Skill: Summarizing **FT**	10 min.
• Prepare students to read by teaching the selection vocabulary. **FT**	10 min.
• Build background and develop expressive vocabulary with Connecting to the Literature and Background.	10 min.
• Engage students' interest with the motivation activity.	10 min.

TEACH

• Informally monitor comprehension while students read independently or in groups. **FT**	30 min.
• Monitor students' comprehension with the Reading Check notes.	as students read
• Reinforce vocabulary with Vocabulary Builder notes.	as students read
• Develop students' understanding of blank verse with the Literary Analysis annotations. **FT**	5 min.
• Develop students' ability to read in sentences with the Reading Skill annotations. **FT**	10 min.

ASSESS/EXTEND

• Assess students' comprehension and mastery of the Reading Skill and Literary Analysis by having them answer the Apply the Skills questions. **FT**	35 min.
• Have students complete the Vocabulary Builder activities. **FT**	5 min.
• Apply students' ability to write a parody with the Writing activity. **FT**	30–45 min. or homework
• Extend students' research and technology skills with the Extend Your Learning activity.	15–30 min. or homework
• Have students complete the Vocabulary Skill and Grammar Lesson.	5 min.
• Monitor students' progress with the Assessment Practice.	20–40 min.
• Administer **Selection Test A** or **Selection Test B. FT**	15 min.

Resources

Meeting Your Standards

Students will

1. **analyze and respond to literary elements.**
   - Literary Analysis: Blank verse

2. **read, comprehend, and analyze plays.**
   - Reading Skill: Summarizing
   - Reading Strategy: Reading in sentences
   - Reading Check questions
   - Apply the Skills questions
   - Assessment Practice

3. **develop vocabulary.**
   - Vocabulary Builder
   - Word Root *-labor-*

4. **apply grammar skills.**
   - Participle and Participle Phrases

5. **develop writing proficiency.**
   - Work in Progress: How-to Essay
   - Parody

6. **extend learning.**
   - Research and Technology: Annotated Flowchart

Block Scheduling: Use one 90-minute class period to preteach the skills and have students read Act II. Use a second 90-minute class period to assess students' mastery of skills, extend their learning, and monitor their progress.

Homework Suggestions

Following are possibilities for homework assignments.

- Support pages from *Unit 5 Resources*:
   Literary Analysis
   Reading Skill
   Build Vocabulary
   Enrichment

- An Extend Your Learning project and the Writing assignment for your chosen selection may be completed over several days.

PRENTICE HALL

Teacher EXPRESS™ Use this complete
Plan · Teach · Assess   suite of powerful
teaching tools to make lesson planning and testing
quicker and easier.

PRENTICE HALL

Student EXPRESS™ Use the
Learn · Study · Succeed   Interactive
Textbook (online and on CD-ROM) to make Act II
and activities come alive with audio and video support and interactive questions.

❶ Literary Analysis
Blank Verse

- Tell students that if every line of verse contained all iambic feet, the effect would become sing-song and monotonous. Some lines of blank verse include a foot with one stressed syllable followed by an unstressed syllable, or some other type of foot.

- Give students a copy **Literary Analysis Graphic Organizer A** (*Graphic Organizer Transparencies,* p. 167). Have them fill in the graphic organizer as they identify the characters' rank based on their understanding of blank verse.

❷ Reading Skill
Summarizing

- Remind students that in blank verse, thoughts or phrases often run past the end of a line. They should note where the punctuation in a line falls.

- Explain that Shakespeare often uses syntax not usual in modern English, such as inverting the subject.

Connecting to the Literature

Romeo and Juliet face a situation in which their personal feelings for each other conflict with family loyalties. Have students write a few sentences about other situations in which personal feelings might conflict with family loyalty. Have students use at least three of the following words: *anticipate, obstacle, reluctant,* and *mutual.*

- Provide these sample sentences to demonstrate their use:

  1. *Anticipate* resistance from the family if you want to go away to school instead of staying home.

  2. Family loyalty can be an *obstacle* in choosing a career.

  3. Some parents are *reluctant* to let their teenagers drive.

  4. Establishing a *mutual* agreement between parents and teens on curfew time can be difficult.

Encourage students to use these words as they discuss the selection.

756

Build Skills   *The Tragedy of Romeo and Juliet, Act II*

❶ Literary Analysis

Blank verse is unrhymed poetry written in a meter called iambic pentameter. A line written in iambic pentameter includes five stressed syllables, each preceded by an unstressed syllable, as in the following example:

> Bŭt sóft! Whăt líght thrŏugh yónděr wíndŏw bréaks?
> Ĭt ís thĕ éast, ănd Júliĕt ís thĕ sún!

Much of *The Tragedy of Romeo and Juliet* is written in blank verse. Shakespeare uses its formal meter to reinforce character rank. Important or aristocratic characters typically speak in blank verse. Minor or comic characters often do not speak in verse.

Based on your understanding of blank verse, use a chart like the one shown to identify characters' rank in this play.

❷ Reading Skill

Summarizing is briefly stating the main points in a piece of writing. Stopping periodically to summarize what you have read helps you to check your comprehension before you read further.

Summarizing is especially useful when reading a play that has long passages of blank verse. When you encounter one of these passages, **read in sentences**—just as if you were reading a poem. Pause according to punctuation instead of at the end of each line. As you become more accustomed to the form, you will be able to increase your speed.

Once you have grasped the meanings of individual sentences in blank verse, you can more easily and more accurately summarize long passages.

Vocabulary Builder

- **procure** (prō kyoor´) *v.* get; obtain (p. 763) *The hungry man tried to procure food.*

- **predominant** (prē däm´ ə nənt) *adj.* having dominating influence over others (p. 766) *Despite some disagreement, the predominant tone of the meeting was one of unity.*

- **intercession** (in´ tər sesh´ ən) *n.* act of pleading on another's behalf (p. 767) *Thanks to the intercession by Andy and Paula, Jim was allowed into the concert without a ticket.*

- **sallow** (sal´ ō) *adj.* of a sickly, pale-yellowish hue (p. 767) *When her sickness passed, her face no longer looked sallow.*

- **lamentable** (lam´ ən tə bəl) *adj.* distressing; sad (p. 769) *His lack of concern about his health is lamentable.*

- **unwieldy** (un wēl´ dē) *adj.* awkward; clumsy (p. 775) *Joe's sprained ankle made him unwieldy on the dance floor.*

756 ■ *Drama*

Vocabulary Development

Vocabulary Knowledge Rating

Create a **Vocabulary Knowledge Rating Chart** with these words from the selection:

| procure | predominant | intercession |
| sallow | lamentable | unwieldy |

Give students a copy. Introduce the words by reading them aloud and having students mark their rating in the Before Reading column. Urge them to be alert to these words as they read and discuss the selection, because they will rate their knowledge of the words again after they finish.

If you wish, you may tally how many students know (or think they know) a word to gauge how much instruction you need to provide. As students read, point out the words and their context.

ACT II

Review and Anticipate

Act I reveals a bitter, long-standing feud between the Montagues and the Capulets. It also introduces the play's title characters, who meet at a feast and immediately fall in love, only to discover that they come from opposing sides of the feud.

Based on what you have learned about the personalities of Romeo and Juliet, how do you expect them to respond to their love for each other and to the problems it poses? How do you think their families will react?

PROLOGUE

[*Enter* CHORUS.]

CHORUS. Now old desire[1] doth in his deathbed lie,
  And young affection gapes to be his heir;[2]
That fair[3] for which love groaned for and would die,

1. old desire Romeo's love for Rosaline.

2. young . . . heir Romeo's new love for Juliet is eager to replace his love for Rosaline.

3. fair beautiful woman (Rosaline).

Romeo and Juliet, Act II ■ 757

TEACH

❶ Motivation

Read aloud the paragraphs under **Review and Anticipate** on p. 757.

Lead a discussion on the two questions posed in these paragraphs: How will Romeo and Juliet respond to their love and its problems? How will their families react?

Write the two questions on the chalkboard. Then have the students offer responses to these questions. Instruct students to record their responses in their notebooks. They will return to these after reading Act II.

Learning Modalities
Intrapersonal Learners

Tell students that some critics say that Juliet is more mature than Romeo and teaches him the meaning of true love. Invite students to compare the two as they read this act and the rest of the play to see whether they agree or disagree with this assessment. Encourage them to identify specific evidence for their viewpoint.

❷ About the Selection

You may wish to have students summarize the main plot points of Act I before they begin to read Act II. The main action of *The Tragedy of Romeo and Juliet,* Act II, is the young couple's betrothal, which occurs the night they meet, and their marriage, which occurs the day after. The act invites the audience to speculate about Romeo and Juliet's love for each other. On the one hand, they are the archetypal teenage lovers— reckless, impulsive, passionate, and head over heels in love. On the other hand, they are growing toward an adult version of love—marriage, devotion, and a willingness to make sacrifices and take risks. As the play progresses, their love will continue to be tested.

Tell students that lines in iambic pentameter can also be rhymed. The rhyming of two successive lines creates a rhymed couplet. This form gives extra emphasis to the words a character speaks and creates a sense of completeness or finality. The exits of major characters and the ends of scenes are often marked by a rhymed couplet. Have students compare the rhyme scheme in the first twelve lines of the Chorus, beginning on p. 757, with the rhyme scheme in the final two lines.

❹ **Literary Analysis**
Blank Verse

• Refer students to Mercutio's speech, lines 7–21. Have students read lines 15–16 aloud, listening to the meter. **Ask** students to identify the meter in these two lines.
Answer: These two lines are in the blank verse pattern of iambic pentameter.

Ask students to respond to the Literary Analysis question: Based on the overall meter of his speech, how can you tell that Mercutio is an aristocrat?
Answer: The overall meter of the speech is iambic pentameter. This is the meter used for blank verse, and blank verse indicates an important or aristocratic character is speaking.

❺ **Critical Thinking**
Infer

• Refer students to Mercutio's speech, lines 7–21. **Ask** students how Mercutio makes fun of Romeo in this speech.
Answer: Mercutio calls Romeo "Madman" and "Lover" and suggests that Romeo is acting lovesick and sighing over his love.

• **Ask** students why Mercutio is describing the beauties of Rosaline in these lines.
Answer: Mercutio assumes that Romeo is still lovesick over Rosaline. He does not know that Romeo has fallen in love with Juliet.

758

      With tender Juliet matched, is now not fair.
5   Now Romeo is beloved and loves again,
      Alike bewitchèd[4] by the charm of looks;
   But to his foe supposed he must complain,[5]
      And she steal love's sweet bait from fearful hooks.
   Being held a foe, he may not have access
10   To breathe such vows as lovers use to swear,
   And she as much in love, her means much less
      To meet her new belovèd anywhere;
❸   But passion lends them power, time means to meet,
   Temp'ring extremities with extreme sweet.[6]
   [*Exit.*]

4. Alike bewitchèd Both Romeo and Juliet are enchanted.

5. complain address his words of love.

6. Temp'ring . . . sweet easing their difficulties with great delights.

Scene i. *Near* CAPULET'S *orchard.*

[*Enter* ROMEO *alone.*]

   ROMEO. Can I go forward when my heart is here?
     Turn back, dull earth,[1] and find thy center[2] out.

[*Enter* BENVOLIO *with* MERCUTIO. ROMEO *retires.*]

   BENVOLIO. Romeo! My cousin Romeo! Romeo!

   MERCUTIO.   He is wise.
     And, on my life, hath stol'n him home to bed.

5   **BENVOLIO.** He ran this way and leapt this orchard wall.
     Call, good Mercutio.

   MERCUTIO.   Nay, I'll conjure[3] too.
     Romeo! Humors! Madman! Passion! Lover!
     Appear thou in the likeness of a sigh;
     Speak but one rhyme, and I am satisfied!
10   Cry but "Ay me!" Pronounce but "love" and "dove";
❹   Speak to my gossip[4] Venus one fair word,
     One nickname for her purblind son and heir,
     Young Abraham Cupid, he that shot so true
     When King Cophetua loved the beggar maid!
15   He heareth not, he stirreth not, he moveth not;
     The ape is dead,[5] and I must conjure him.
❺   I conjure thee by Rosaline's bright eyes,
     By her high forehead and her scarlet lip,
     By her fine foot, straight leg, and quivering thigh,
20   And the demesnes that there adjacent lie,
     That in thy likeness thou appear to us!

   BENVOLIO. And if he hear thee, thou wilt anger him.

1. dull earth lifeless body.

2. center heart, or possibly soul (Juliet).

3. conjure recite a spell to make Romeo appear.

4. gossip merry old lady.

5. The ape is dead Romeo, like a trained monkey, seems to be playing.

Literary Analysis
Blank Verse Based on the overall meter of his speech, how can you tell that Mercutio is an aristocrat?

758 ■ *Drama*

Vocabulary Development

Word Forms
Two of the Vocabulary Builder words for Act II have related forms. Give students a blank **Word Form Chart** (*General Resource,* p. 16), with *predominant* and *lamentable* in the correct columns. Work with the class, or have students work with a partner, to determine the related forms. The final chart should look like the one shown.

Hold students accountable for integrating the related forms of the words into their speaking and writing.

Noun	Verb	Adjective	Adverb
predominance	predominate	**predominant**	predominantly
lament	lament	**lamentable**	lamentably

MERCUTIO. This cannot anger him. 'Twould anger him
To raise a spirit in his mistress' circle

25 Of some strange nature, letting it there stand
Till she had laid it and conjured it down.
That were some spite; my invocation
Is fair and honest; in his mistress' name,
I conjure only but to raise up him.

30 **BENVOLIO.** Come, he hath hid himself among these trees
To be consorted[6] with the humorous[7] night.
Blind is his love and best befits the dark.

MERCUTIO. If love be blind, love cannot hit the mark.
Now will he sit under a medlar[8] tree

35 And wish his mistress were that kind of fruit
As maids call medlars when they laugh alone.
O, Romeo, that she were, O that she were
An open *et cetera*, thou a pop'rin pear!
Romeo, good night. I'll to my truckle bed;[9]

40 This field bed is too cold for me to sleep.
Come, shall we go?

BENVOLIO.   Go then, for 'tis in vain
To seek him here that means not to be found.

[*Exit with others.*]

Scene ii. CAPULET'S *orchard.*

❻ **ROMEO.** [*Coming forward*] He jests at scars that never felt a
wound.

[*Enter* JULIET *at a window.*]

But soft! What light through yonder window breaks?
It is the East, and Juliet is the sun!
Arise, fair sun, and kill the envious moon,

5 Who is already sick and pale with grief
That thou her maid art far more fair than she.
Be not her maid, since she is envious.
Her vestal livery[1] is but sick and green,
❼ And none but fools do wear it. Cast it off.

10 It is my lady! O, it is my love!
❽ O, that she knew she were!
She speaks, yet she says nothing. What of that?
Her eye discourses; I will answer it.
I am too bold; 'tis not to me she speaks.

15 Two of the fairest stars in all the heaven,
Having some business, do entreat her eyes

6. consorted associated.

7. humorous humid; moody, like a lover.

8. medlar applelike fruit.

9. truckle bed trundlebed, placed under a larger bed when not in use.

Literary Analysis
Blank Verse Which line in Romeo's speech breaks the pattern of five stressed syllables per line?

1. livery clothing or costume worn by a servant.

❾ ✓ **Reading Check**

Whom does Romeo see at the window?

Romeo and Juliet, Act II ■ *759*

❻ **Background**

This is the beginning of the famous "balcony scene" in *The Tragedy of Romeo and Juliet*—one of the most famous scenes in all of Shakespeare's plays. In these lines Romeo is making an extended comparison here that reveals his strong feelings for Juliet. First, he says that Juliet's beauty is so great that she lights up the world, as the sun does when it rises. Then, he says that even the moon is envious of her, the way the moon might be envious of the brighter, "more fair" sun.

❼ **Critical Thinking**
Interpret

• Read Romeo's speech aloud, lines 2–25. Have students visualize the metaphors Shakespeare uses in this speech. To what objects does Romeo compare Juliet?
Answer: Romeo compares Juliet to the sun and her eyes to the stars.

• Have students **describe** how Romeo imagines he might touch Juliet's cheek, since he is too far away to do it himself.
Answer: He wishes he were a glove upon Juliet's hand, so that when she touched her cheek with her hand, he would be touching her, too.

❽ **Literary Analysis**
Blank Verse

• Read lines 2–19 aloud again as students follow along in their text. Have students listen closely to the meter.

• **Ask** students to respond to the Literary Analysis question: Which line in Romeo's speech breaks the pattern of five stressed syllables per line?
Answer: Line 11 breaks the pattern of five stressed syllables per line. It has only three stressed syllables.

❾ **Reading Check**

Answer: Romeo sees Juliet at the window.

❿ Reading Skill
Summarizing

- Have students read Juliet's speech about Romeo's name, lines 38–49. Ask students to **describe** the setting of this scene. To whom is Juliet speaking?

  Answer: The setting is the garden at Juliet's home. Juliet is standing on the balcony overlooking the garden. She is speaking to herself. She doesn't know that Romeo is watching and listening to her from the garden below.

- **Ask** students what Juliet is wishing for in this speech.

  Answer: She is wishing that Romeo had another name—that he was not a Montague, her family's enemy.

- **Ask** students where the sentence ends that begins in the middle of line 40. Have them read aloud or write out the complete sentence.

  Answer: The sentence ends in the middle of line 42. It reads "It is nor hand, nor foot, nor arm, nor face, nor any other part belonging to a man."

- Have students read aloud or write out the complete sentence that begins at line 45. Then, have them repeat it in modern English.

  Answer: "So Romeo would, were he not Romeo called, retain that dear perfection which he owes without that title." In modern English the sentence might read, "Romeo would still be as perfect if his name were not Romeo."

- **Ask** students to respond to the Reading Skill prompt: Briefly summarize Juliet's speech about Romeo's name.

  Answer: Juliet says that it is Romeo's name that is the enemy. Why is a name important anyway? It doesn't have anything to do with the person himself. If he had a different name, he would still be the same person. So Romeo should get rid of his name, which is not really part of him, and then he could have Juliet.

To twinkle in their spheres[2] till they return.
What if her eyes were there, they in her head?
The brightness of her cheek would shame those stars
20 As daylight doth a lamp; her eyes in heaven
❼ Would through the airy region stream so bright
That birds would sing and think it were not night.
See how she leans her cheek upon that hand,
O, that I were a glove upon that hand,
That I might touch that cheek!

JULIET.   Ay me!

25 **ROMEO.**   She speaks.
O, speak again, bright angel, for thou art
As glorious to this night, being o'er my head,
As is a wingèd messenger of heaven
Unto the white-upturnèd wond'ring eyes
30 Of mortals that fall back to gaze on him
When he bestrides the lazy puffing clouds
And sails upon the bosom of the air.

JULIET. O Romeo, Romeo! Wherefore art thou Romeo?[3]
Deny thy father and refuse thy name;
35 Or, if thou wilt not, be but sworn my love,
And I'll no longer be a Capulet.

ROMEO. [*Aside*] Shall I hear more, or shall I speak at this?

JULIET. 'Tis but thy name that is my enemy.
Thou art thyself, though not[4] a Montague.
40 What's Montague? It is nor hand, nor foot,
Nor arm, nor face, nor any other part
Belonging to a man. O, be some other name!
What's in a name? That which we call a rose
❿ By any other name would smell as sweet.
45 So Romeo would, were he not Romeo called,
Retain that dear perfection which he owes[5]
Without that title. Romeo, doff[6] thy name;
And for thy name, which is no part of thee,
Take all myself.

ROMEO.   I take thee at thy word.
50 Call me but love, and I'll be new baptized;
Henceforth I never will be Romeo.

⓫ **JULIET.** What man art thou, thus bescreened in night,
So stumblest on my counsel?[7]

ROMEO.   By a name
I know not how to tell thee who I am.

760 ■ Drama

2. **spheres** orbits.

3. **Wherefore . . . Romeo?** Why are you Romeo—a Montague?

4. **though not** even if you were not.

Reading Skill
Summarizing Briefly summarize Juliet's speech about Romeo's name.

5. **owes** owns; possesses.
6. **doff** remove.

7. **counsel** secret thoughts.

Vocabulary Development

Expressive Vocabulary

As students discuss this scene between Romeo and Juliet, encourage them to use the expressive vocabulary presented earlier. You might encourage them with sentence starters like these:

1. Romeo could not *anticipate* . . .
2. The two lovers' *circumstance* . . .
3. Juliet was *reluctant* to . . .
4. Romeo and Juliet shared a *mutual* . . .

Challenge students to use these words as you continue to discuss the play.

55 My name, dear saint, is hateful to myself
Because it is an enemy to thee.
Had I it written, I would tear the word.

JULIET. My ears have yet not drunk a hundred words
Of thy tongue's uttering, yet I know the sound.
60 Art thou not Romeo, and a Montague?

ROMEO. Neither, fair maid, if either thee dislike.

JULIET. How camest thou hither, tell me, and wherefore?
The orchard walls are high and hard to climb,
And the place death, considering who thou art,
65 If any of my kinsmen find thee here.

ROMEO. With love's light wings did I o'erperch[8] these walls;
For stony limits cannot hold love out,
And what love can do, that dares love attempt.
Therefore thy kinsmen are no stop to me.

70 JULIET. If they do see thee, they will murder thee.

ROMEO. Alack, there lies more peril in thine eye
Than twenty of their swords! Look thou but sweet,
And I am proof[9] against their enmity.

JULIET. I would not for the world they saw thee here.

75 ROMEO. I have night's cloak to hide me from their eyes;
And but[10] thou love me, let them find me here.
My life were better ended by their hate
Than death prorogued,[11] wanting of thy love.

JULIET. By whose direction found'st thou out this place?

80 ROMEO. By love, that first did prompt me to inquire.
He lent me counsel, and I lent him eyes.
I am no pilot; yet, wert thou as far
As that vast shore washed with the farthest sea,
I should adventure[12] for such merchandise.

85 JULIET. Thou knowest the mask of night is on my face;
Else would a maiden blush bepaint my cheek
For that which thou hast heard me speak tonight.
Fain would I dwell on form[13]—fain, fain deny
What I have spoke; but farewell compliment![14]
90 Dost thou love me? I know thou wilt say "Ay";
And I will take thy word. Yet, if thou swear'st,
Thou mayst prove false. At lovers' perjuries,
They say Jove laughs. O gentle Romeo,
If thou dost love, pronounce it faithfully.
95 Or if thou thinkest I am too quickly won,

**Literary Analysis
Blank Verse** In
line 57, how do the
stressed syllables
reinforce Romeo's
meaning?

8. **o'erperch** fly over.

9. **proof** protected, as by armor.

10. **And but** unless.

11. **prorogued** postponed.

12. **adventure** risk a long journey, like a sea adventurer.

13. **Fain . . . form** eagerly would I follow convention (by acting reserved).

14. **compliment** conventional behavior.

 Reading Check

Why does Romeo say
his name is hateful to
him?

Romeo and Juliet, Act II ■ 761

⑪ Literary Analysis
Blank Verse

- Have students read lines 49–57.
  Ask students who speaks line 49.
  Answer: Juliet speaks the first part of the line and Romeo speaks the second part.

- Ask students to **scan** line 49 to see how many beats each character speaks.
  Answer: Juliet speaks two beats of text, and Romeo speaks the remaining three beats.

- **Ask** students what strong feeling Romeo is expressing in lines 53–57.
  Answer: He is saying that he hates his name because his name is Juliet's enemy.

- **Ask** students to respond to the Literary Analysis question: In line 57, how do the stressed syllables reinforce Romeo's meaning?
  Answer: The stressed syllables, "I," "writ," "I," "tear," "word," reinforce Romeo's intense feeling about how hateful his name is to him.

⑫ Reading Check

Answer: Romeo's name is hateful to him because it is an enemy to Juliet, whose family is feuding with Romeo's family.

Differentiated
Instruction   Solutions for All Learners

Strategy for English Learners
Have students use the *Reader's Notebook: English Learner's Version* for Scene ii of this act. After students have completed the exercises, have them work in pairs to listen to the **Listening to Literature Audio CD,** and read along in the Student Edition.

Enrichment for Gifted/Talented Students
Have students look for sections of dialogue between Romeo and Juliet that they would use as the basis for a song in a musical version of the play. Have students establish criteria and then explain how their choices meet the criteria.

The picture on p. 762 shows the actress Olivia Hussey, who was fifteen when she played Juliet. Use the following questions for discussion.

1. Based on this image, how do you think the director envisioned Juliet?
   Answer: The director seemed to see Juliet as young, naive, passionate, and intense.

2. In this particular still photo, the actress playing Juliet stares out of the screen directly into the eyes of the audience. What is the effect of that stare?
   Answer: Having Juliet make direct eye contact with the audience draws them in, makes them sympathize with her, and puts them on her side.

⓮ **Critical Viewing**

Answer: The picture shows a serious character, maybe even cautious. Juliet exhibits both of these characteristics.

I'll frown and be perverse[15] and say thee nay,
So thou wilt woo; but else, not for the world.
In truth, fair Montague, I am too fond,[16]
And therefore thou mayst think my havior light;[17]
100   But trust me, gentleman, I'll prove more true
Than those that have more cunning to be strange.[18]
I should have been more strange, I must confess,
But that thou overheard'st, ere I was ware,
My truelove passion. Therefore pardon me,
105   And not impute this yielding to light love,
Which the dark night hath so discoverèd.[19]

ROMEO. Lady, by yonder blessèd moon I vow,
That tips with silver all these fruit-tree tops—

JULIET. O, swear not by the moon, th' inconstant moon,
110   That monthly changes in her circle orb,
Lest that thy love prove likewise variable.

⓯▼ROMEO. What shall I swear by?   ⓭

15. **be perverse** act contrary to my true feelings.

16. **fond** affectionate.

17. **my havior light** my behavior immodest or unserious.

18. **strange** distant and cold.

19. **discoverèd** revealed.

762 ■ *Drama*

⓮ ◄ **Critical Viewing**
How does Juliet's expression in this picture compare with the feelings she has conveyed in the play so far? **[Connect]**

Vocabulary Development

Vocabulary Builder Reinforcement
Students will benefit from additional examples and practice with the Vocabulary Builder words. Reinforce their comprehension with "show-you-know" sentences. The first part of the sentence uses the vocabulary word in an appropriate context. The second part of the sentence—the "show-you-know" part—clarifies the first. Model the strategy with *procure:*

We need to *procure* art supplies; we're almost out and need to get more to finish the project.

Then give students these sentence prompts, and coach them in creating the clarification part.

1. We need to identify the *predominant* problem; _____
   Sample answer: we should solve that before we address lesser problems.

2. The coach's *intercession* on behalf of the team was successful; _____
   Sample answer: they were able to get new uniforms.

JULIET.   Do not swear at all;
Or if thou wilt, swear by thy gracious self,
Which is the god of my idolatry,
And I'll believe thee.

115 **ROMEO.** If my heart's dear love—

   JULIET. Well, do not swear. Although I joy in thee,
I have no joy of this contract[20] tonight.
It is too rash, too unadvised, too sudden;
Too like the lightning, which doth cease to be

120 Ere one can say it lightens. Sweet, good night!
This bud of love, by summer's ripening breath,
May prove a beauteous flow'r when next we meet.
Good night, good night! As sweet repose and rest
Come to thy heart as that within my breast!

125 **ROMEO.** O, wilt thou leave me so unsatisfied?

   JULIET. What satisfaction canst thou have tonight?

   ROMEO. Th'exchange of thy love's faithful vow for mine.

   JULIET. I gave thee mine before thou didst request it;
And yet I would it were to give again.

130 **ROMEO.** Wouldst thou withdraw it? For what purpose, love?

   JULIET. But to be frank[21] and give it thee again.
And yet I wish but for the thing I have.
My bounty[22] is as boundless as the sea,
My love as deep; the more I give to thee,

135 The more I have, for both are infinite,
I hear some noise within. Dear love, adieu!

[NURSE *calls within.*]

   Anon, good nurse! Sweet Montague, be true.
Stay but a little, I will come again.   [*Exit.*]

   ROMEO. O blessèd, blessèd night! I am afeard,

140 Being in night, all this is but a dream,
Too flattering-sweet to be substantial.[23]

[*Enter* JULIET *again.*]

   JULIET. Three words, dear Romeo, and good night indeed.
If that thy bent[24] of love be honorable,
Thy purpose marriage, send me word tomorrow,

145 By one that I'll procure to come to thee,
Where and what time thou wilt perform the rite;
And all my fortunes at thy foot I'll lay
And follow thee my lord throughout the world.

Literary Analysis
Blank Verse The five stressed syllables of lines 112 and 115 are split between the two speakers. What does this weaving together of dialogue suggest about the speakers' relationship?

20. contract betrothal.

21. frank generous.

22. bounty what I have to give.

23. substantial real.
24. bent purpose; intention.

Vocabulary Builder
procure (prō kyoor´)
v. get; obtain

Reading Check

Why does Juliet tell Romeo not to swear his love by the moon?

Romeo and Juliet, Act II ■ 763

⓯ **Literary Analysis**
Blank Verse

• Remind students that although blank verse has five feet per line, a line can be split between two speakers.

• Ask students to **speculate** about why a poet might split a blank verse line between two speakers. **Answer:** Students may suggest that a poet might want to indicate fast-moving dialogue; the poet might also want to show a connection between two characters.

• **Ask** students to respond to the Literary Analysis question: The five stressed syllables of lines 112 and 115 are split between the two speakers. What does this weaving together of dialogue suggest about the speakers' relationship? **Possible response:** Students may suggest that two lovers who were talking would likely be finishing each other's sentences. They also may say that people in love "speak with one voice."

⓰ **Critical Thinking**
Interpret

• **Ask** students what Juliet says to Romeo in lines 142–148. **Answer:** Juliet tells Romeo that if he really wants to marry her, he should send her word the next day. She will meet him for the marriage and give up everything to follow him.

• **Ask** how Juliet's attitude in lines 142–148 has changed from the one she expressed in lines 116–122. **Answer:** In lines 116–122 Juliet expresses caution, saying that their rush to betrothal is "too rash, too unadvised, too sudden." By lines 142–148 she is ready to marry Romeo and give up everything for him.

⓱ **Reading Check**

Answer: The moon changes throughout the month, and if he swears by the moon his love might also prove to be changeable.

Differentiated Instruction   Solutions for All Learners

Enrichment for Gifted/Talented Students
Tell students that the timeless story of *The Tragedy of Romeo and Juliet* has been set to film and stage using many different settings, from the classical setting of the 1968 Zeffirelli film to a 1996 film starring Leonardo DiCaprio. That film is set in modern-day California in the fictional city of Verona Beach. This scene (Act II, Scene ii) is the most well known in the play and perhaps the most famous scene in all of Shakespeare's plays.

Have students listen to the scene in the **Listening to Literature Audio CD** as they read along. Then, have them sketch this "balcony scene," Scene ii. Encourage them to think about whether they want the sketch to reflect the classical medieval setting, a modern-day setting, or some other time and place. Remind them that the costumes and architecture should reflect the setting.

Have students display their sketches in the classroom.

Culture Connection Falconers begin training birds by placing a soft leather hood over their heads and attaching leather thongs to their legs. The falconer wears a heavy glove to protect his hand from the bird's sharp claws as he carries the bird on his fist for several hours a day. The bird then is taught to feed by flying after and catching a lure. The lure is a padded weight attached to a long cord. The wings of a pigeon or other bird are attached to the lure, along with a piece of meat. The falconer twirls the lure while the bird flies after it and catches it, feeding on the meat attached to the lure. Eventually the bird learns to kill for itself and return to the fist of the falconer.

Connect to the Literature Have students reread lines 158–159. Remind them that Juliet has been called away by her Nurse and has just returned to the balcony. Then **ask** the Connect to Literature question on p. 764: Why do you think Juliet wishes Romeo would respond to her voice as a falcon does to the falconer's commands?

Answer: Juliet wishes she could call softly, like a falconer to its bird, and Romeo would come back to her as willingly.

NURSE. [*Within*] Madam!

150 **JULIET.** I come anon.—But if thou meanest not well,
I do beseech thee—

❶❾ **NURSE.** [*Within*] Madam!

JULIET. By and by[25] I come.—
To cease thy strife[26] and leave me to my grief.
Tomorrow will I send.

ROMEO. So thrive my soul—

JULIET. A thousand times good night! [*Exit.*]

**Literary Analysis
Blank Verse** Three speakers share the rhythm of line 151. Does the Nurse's interruption complete or break the blank verse?

25. By and by at once.
26. strife efforts.

---

❶❽ **Literature in Context** | **Culture Connection**

Falconry

When Juliet longs for "a falc'ners voice," she is referring to someone who practices falconry, the sport of hunting with falcons. Falcon are swift, hawk-like birds of prey. The falconer trains the bird to respond to a combination of physical and vocal commands.

◄ Falconry began as a way to obtain food but gradually evolved into the "sport of kings."

During Shakespeare's time one's rank in society determined the kind of bird one could own:

Rank	Type of Bird
King	Gyr falcon
Prince	Peregrine falcon (male)
Knight	Saker falcon
Squire	Lanner falcon
Lady	Merlin (female)
Yeoman (landowner)	Goshawk
Servants, children	Kestrel

Thick leather ► gloves protected the falconer from the bird's talons.

Connect to the Literature Why do you think Juliet wishes Romeo would respond to her voice as a falcon does to the falconer's commands?

155   **ROMEO.** A thousand times the worse, to want thy light!
     Love goes toward love as schoolboys from their books;
     But love from love, toward school with heavy looks.

[*Enter* JULIET *again.*]

    JULIET. Hist! Romeo, hist! O for a falc'ner's voice
      To lure this tassel gentle[27] back again!
160   Bondage is hoarse[28] and may not speak aloud,
      Else would I tear the cave where Echo[29] lies
      And make her airy tongue more hoarse than mine
      With repetition of "My Romeo!"

    ROMEO. It is my soul that calls upon my name.
165   How silver-sweet sound lovers' tongues by night,
      Like softest music to attending ears!

    JULIET. Romeo!

    ROMEO.   My sweet?

    JULIET.   What o'clock tomorrow
      Shall I send to thee?

    ROMEO.   By the hour of nine.

    JULIET. I will not fail. 'Tis twenty year till then.
170   I have forgot why I did call thee back.

    ROMEO. Let me stand here till thou remember it.

    JULIET. I shall forget, to have thee still stand there,
      Rememb'ring how I love thy company.

    ROMEO. And I'll stay, to have thee still forget,
175   Forgetting any other home but this.

    JULIET. 'Tis almost morning. I would have thee gone—
      And yet no farther than a wanton's[30] bird,
      That lets it hop a little from his hand,
      Like a poor prisoner in his twisted gyves,[31]
180   And with a silken thread plucks it back again,
      So loving-jealous of his liberty.

    ROMEO. I would I were thy bird.

    JULIET.   Sweet, so would I.
      Yet I should kill thee with much cherishing.
      Good night, good night! Parting is such sweet sorrow
185   That I shall say good night till it be morrow.   [*Exit.*]

    ROMEO. Sleep dwell upon thine eyes, peace in thy breast!
      Would I were sleep and peace, so sweet to rest!

Literary Analysis
Blank Verse Based on the fact that Romeo and Juliet speak in blank verse, what can you conclude about their character rank?

27. **tassel gentle** male falcon.

28. **Bondage is hoarse** Being bound in by my family restricts my speech.

29. **Echo** In classical mythology, the nymph Echo, unable to win the love of Narcissus, wasted away in a cave until nothing was left of her but her voice.

30. **wanton's** spoiled, playful child's.

31. **gyves** (jivz) chains.

✓ **Reading Check**

What plan do Romeo and Juliet make for the following day?

Romeo and Juliet, Act II ■ 765

---

⑲ Literary Analysis
Blank Verse

- Have two volunteers read lines 150–151.

- **Ask** students to respond to the Literary Analysis question on p. 764: Three speakers share the rhythm of line 151. Does the Nurse's interruption complete or break the blank verse?
Answer: The Nurse's interruption breaks the blank verse. Her word "Madam," adds an extra foot. Juliet's line 151, when spoken without the interruption, is a blank verse line.

⑳ Background

When Romeo compares love with schoolboys leaving school and the absence of love with boys going to school in lines 156–157, he is expressing the common dislike of men of Shakespeare's time with their formal schooling. In Stratford, boys— and only boys—were expected to start school as soon as they could read and write. Most of their learning was in Latin.

㉑ Literary Analysis
Blank Verse

- **Ask** students what Romeo and Juliet are doing in lines 169–175.
Answer: The two are trying to find reasons to keep from having to say good night.

- **Ask** students to respond to the Literary Analysis question: Based on the fact that Romeo and Juliet speak in blank verse, what can you conclude about their character rank?
Answer: In Shakespeare's plays, characters who speak in blank verse are important or aristocratic. Romeo and Juliet are both.

㉒ Reading Check

Answer: Romeo will send word to Juliet about where to meet him, and she will go to him so they may be married.

Differentiated Instruction   Solutions for All Learners

Enrichment for Less Proficient Readers
Students may gain a better understanding of how blank verse indicates characters' rank by reading the **Authors in Depth,** Gold Level, selection from Shakespeare's *A Midsummer Night's Dream,* Act III, Scene i. In this comic scene, the clowns Quince, Bottom, Flute, Snout, Snug, and Starveling (who are carpenter, weaver, bellows-mender, tinker, joiner, and tailor respectively) interact with Titania, Queen of the Fairies.

Lead a reading of this selection, and then have students form discussion groups in which they compare and contrast the prose dialogue of the comic characters with the blank verse used by Titania and other fairies in the scene. Have students take turns reading some prose passages and blank verse passages aloud to help them hear the differences. Encourage them also to note how lines of blank verse are split among several speakers and the effect that has on the dialogue.

- Have students read lines 1–30 in Scene iii. Have them note the stage directions as the scene opens.

- **Ask** students to use the footnotes and context clues to determine what the Friar is doing in lines 7 and 8.
Answer: The Friar is collecting plants of different kinds, both poisonous and beneficial.

- **Ask** students to read lines 15–22 to learn what the Friar believes about the natural world.
Possible response: The Friar believes that things found in the natural world can be used for either good or evil.

- **Ask** students to respond to the Reading Skill prompt: Briefly state the main points of the Friar's speech in lines 1–30.
Answer: The sun is rising. I must gather herbs, both poisonous and beneficial. Even the most poisonous herbs have some virtue, and even the most beneficial herbs, if overused, are harmful. Some plants contain both good and ill. It is the same in man; and if the worse is predominant, then it eats up the soul.

Hence will I to my ghostly friar's[32] close cell,[33]
His help to crave and my dear hap[34] to tell.   [*Exit.*]

**Scene iii. Friar Lawrence's *cell.*

[*Enter* FRIAR LAWRENCE *alone, with a basket.*]

FRIAR. The gray-eyed morn smiles on the frowning night,
Check'ring the eastern clouds with streaks of light;
And fleckèd[1] darkness like a drunkard reels
From forth day's path and Titan's burning wheels.[2]

5   Now, ere the sun advance his burning eye
The day to cheer and night's dank dew to dry,
I must upfill this osier cage[3] of ours
With baleful[4] weeds and precious-juicèd flowers.
The earth that's nature's mother is her tomb.

10   What is her burying grave, that is her womb;
And from her womb children of divers kind[5]
We sucking on her natural bosom find,
Many for many virtues excellent,
None but for some, and yet all different.

15   O, mickle[6] is the powerful grace[7] that lies
23   In plants, herbs, stones, and their true qualities;
For naught so vile that on the earth doth live
But to the earth some special good doth give;
Nor aught so good but, strained[8] from that fair use,

20   Revolts from true birth,[9] stumbling on abuse.
Virtue itself turns vice, being misapplied,
And vice sometime by action dignified.

[*Enter* ROMEO.]

Within the infant rind[10] of this weak flower
Poison hath residence and medicine power;[11]

25   For this, being smelt, with that part cheers each part;[12]
Being tasted, stays all senses with the heart.[13]
Two such opposèd kings encamp them still[14]
In man as well as herbs—grace and rude will;
And where the worser is <u>predominant</u>,

30   Full soon the canker[15] death eats up that plant.

ROMEO. Good morrow, father.

FRIAR.   *Benedicite!*[16]
What early tongue so sweet saluteth me?
Young son, it argues a distemperèd head[17]
So soon to bid good morrow to thy bed.

766 ■ *Drama*

Reading Skill
Summarizing Briefly state the main points of the Friar's speech in lines 1–30.

1. **fleckèd** spotted.

2. **Titan's burning wheels** wheels of the sun god's chariot.

3. **osier cage** willow basket.

4. **baleful** poisonous.

5. **divers kind** different kinds.

6. **mickle** great.

7. **grace** divine power.

8. **strained** turned away.

9. **Revolts . . . birth** conflicts with its real purpose.

10. **infant rind** tender skin.

11. **and medicine power** and medicinal quality has power.

12. **with . . . part** with that quality—odor—revives each part of the body.

13. **stays . . . heart** kills (stops the working of the five senses along with the heart).

14. **still** always.

15. **canker** destructive caterpillar.

Vocabulary Builder
predominant (prē dām´ ə nənt) *adj.* having dominating influence over others

16. *Benedicite!* God bless you!

17. **distemperèd head** troubled mind.

Vocabulary Development

Word Analysis

Call students' attention to the word *intercession* in line 54 on p. 767. Have students note the word's definition in the side note. Tell students that the prefix *inter-* means "between or among." The root word is based on the Latin word for "go."

Tell students that based on the prefix, another way to define *intercession* is the "act of going between two people or groups in an effort to resolve a dispute or obtain a favor."

Ask students to suggest other words with the prefix *inter-*. Students may suggest words such as *interact, intercept, interchange,* and *international.*

35   Care keeps his watch in every old man's eye,
      And where care lodges, sleep will never lie;
      But where unbruisèd youth with unstuffed[18] brain
      Doth couch his limbs, there golden sleep doth reign,
      Therefore thy earliness doth me assure
40   Thou art uproused with some distemp'rature;[19]
      Or if not so, then here I hit it right—
      Our Romeo hath not been in bed tonight.

ROMEO. That last is true. The sweeter rest was mine.

FRIAR. God pardon sin! Wast thou with Rosaline?

45 **ROMEO.** With Rosaline, my ghostly father? No.
      I have forgot that name and that name's woe.

FRIAR. That's my good son! But where hast thou been then?

ROMEO. I'll tell thee ere thou ask it me again.
      I have been feasting with mine enemy,
50   Where on a sudden one hath wounded me
      That's by me wounded. Both our remedies
      Within thy help and holy physic[20] lies.
      I bear no hatred, blessèd man, for, lo,
      My <u>intercession</u> likewise steads my foe.[21]

55 **FRIAR.** Be plain, good son, and homely in thy drift.[22]
      Riddling confession finds but riddling shrift.[23]

ROMEO. Then plainly know my heart's dear love is set
      On the fair daughter of rich Capulet;
      As mine on hers, so hers is set on mine,
60   And all combined, save[24] what thou must combine
      By holy marriage. When and where and how
      We met, we wooed, and made exchange of vow,
      I'll tell thee as we pass; but this I pray,
      That thou consent to marry us today.

65 **FRIAR.** Holy Saint Francis! What a change is here!
      Is Rosaline, that thou didst love so dear,
      So soon forsaken? Young men's love then lies
      Not truly in their hearts, but in their eyes.
      Jesu Maria! What a deal of brine[25]
70   Hath washed thy <u>sallow</u> cheeks for Rosaline!
      How much salt water thrown away in waste
      To season love, that of it doth not taste!
      The sun not yet thy sighs from heaven clears,
      Thy old groans ring yet in mine ancient ears.
75   Lo, here upon thy cheek the stain doth sit
      Of an old tear that is not washed off yet.

Literary Analysis
Blank Verse What sets the Friar's lines apart from normal blank verse?

18. unstuffed not filled with cares.

19. distemp'rature illness.

Vocabulary Builde
intercession (in´ tər sesh´ ən) *n.* the act of pleading on another's behalf

20. physic (fiz´ ik) medicine.

21. My . . . foe my plea also helps my enemy (Juliet, a Capulet).

22. and . . . drift and simple in your speech.

23. Riddling . . . shrift A confusing confession will get you uncertain forgiveness. The Friar means that unless Romeo speaks clearly, he will not get clear and direct advice.

24. And . . . save and we are united in every way, except for (save).

25. brine salt water (tears).

Vocabulary Builde
sallow (sal´ ō) *adj.* of a sickly, pale-yellowish hue

 Reading Check

What does Romeo ask the Friar to do?

Romeo and Juliet, Act II ■ 767

Literary Analysis
Blank Verse

- Have students read all of Scene iii, pp. 766–768.
- Then, **ask** students to respond to the Literary Analysis question: What sets the Friar's lines apart from normal blank verse?
  Answer: Normal blank verse is unrhymed.
- Tell students that all of Scene iii is written in rhymed couplets. However, Friar Lawrence does not speak in rhymed couplets in other scenes. **Ask** students why they think Shakespeare chose to write this scene in rhyme.
  Possible response: Students may suggest that the rhymed lines set the Friar apart as a holy person, one who apparently has special powers to deal with the good and bad herbs, as well as to join two people in marriage.

Critical Thinking
Analyze

- **Ask** students to describe Romeo's relationship with Friar Lawrence based on what they have read so far.
  Answer: Romeo apparently has a close relationship with the Friar. The Friar knows about Rosaline and Romeo's feelings for her. Romeo is willing to tell the Friar about his change of heart from loving Rosaline to loving Juliet and to ask the Friar to marry them.
- Ask students what they can tell about the meaning of the Friar's speech in lines 65–68, based on emphasized words and/or syllables.
  Answer: The stressed words in lines 65–68 give readers the sense that Friar Lawrence is concerned about the *change* in Romeo's feelings, about *Rosaline,* whom Romeo apparently did *love* so *dear,* and who is now *forsaken.*

Reading Check
Answer: Romeo asks Friar Lawrence to marry him and Juliet.

Friar, which comes from the Latin word for *brother*, is a general term for a member of a religious order. Friars had no worldly possessions or fixed place to live, which allowed them to devote themselves exclusively to preaching, missionary work, or other charitable undertakings. Friars wore robes or *habits* that were gray, black, or white.

Students should understand the difference between a friar, such as Friar Lawrence, and a monk. A monk is a man who has taken religious vows of poverty, chastity, and obedience, and has retired from worldly life to live with other monks, studying the Scriptures, praying, and meditating. A friar lives among ordinary people and helps them, as Friar Lawrence tries, unsuccessfully, to help the two star-crossed lovers.

If e'er thou wast thyself, and these woes thine,
Thou and these woes were all for Rosaline.
And art thou changed? Pronounce this sentence then:
80 Women may fall[26] when there's no strength[27] in men.

ROMEO. Thou chidst me oft for loving Rosaline.

FRIAR. For doting,[28] not for loving, pupil mine.

ROMEO. And badst[29] me bury love.

FRIAR.   Not in a grave
To lay one in, another out to have.

85 **ROMEO.** I pray thee chide me not. Her I love now
Doth grace[30] for grace and love for love allow.[31]
The other did not so.

FRIAR.   O, she knew well
Thy love did read by rote, that could not spell.[32]
But come, young waverer, come go with me.
90 In one respect I'll thy assistant be;
For this alliance may so happy prove
To turn your households' rancor[33] to pure love.

ROMEO. O, let us hence! I stand on[34] sudden haste.

FRIAR. Wisely and slow. They stumble that run fast.   [*Exit all.*]

Scene iv. A street.

[*Enter* BENVOLIO *and* MERCUTIO.]

MERCUTIO. Where the devil should this Romeo be? Came he not home tonight?

BENVOLIO. Not to his father's. I spoke with his man.

MERCUTIO. Why, that same pale hardhearted wench, that Rosaline,
5 Torments him so that he will sure run mad.

BENVOLIO. Tybalt, the kinsman to old Capulet,
Hath sent a letter to his father's house.

MERCUTIO. A challenge, on my life.

10 **BENVOLIO.** Romeo will answer it.

MERCUTIO. Any man that can write may answer a letter.

BENVOLIO. Nay, he will answer the letter's master, how he dares, being dared.

26. **fall** be weak or inconstant.
27. **strength** constancy; stability.
28. **doting** being infatuated.
29. **badst** urged.
30. **grace** favor.
31. **allow** give.
32. **Thy . . . spell** your love recited words from memory with no understanding of them.
33. **rancor** hatred.
34. **stand on** insist on.

Literary Analysis
Blank Verse In what way is Mercutio's and Benvolio's speech in this scene different from what it was earlier in Act II?

Vocabulary Development

Vocabulary Builder Reinforcement
To reinforce and assess students' comprehension of Vocabulary Builder words, give them sentences using the words in which the word may or may not be used correctly. Students must tell whether the use is correct and explain their answer. Use these sentences.

1. The model had a lovely, *sallow* complexion.
   Answer: No, *sallow* is not used correctly. *Sallow* means "sickly and pale-yellowish," which would not make someone "lovely."

2. This backpack is so *unwieldy* I can barely get it under my desk.
   Answer: Yes, *unwieldy* is used correctly, since it means "awkward" or "not easy to handle."

MERCUTIO. Alas, poor Romeo, he is already dead: stabbed
15   with a white wench's black eye; run through the ear
    with a love song; the very pin of his heart cleft with the
    blind bow-boy's butt-shaft;[1] and is he a man to encounter
    Tybalt?

BENVOLIO. Why, what is Tybalt?

20 **MERCUTIO.** More than Prince of Cats.[2] O, he's the courageous
    captain of compliments.[3] He fights as you sing
    pricksong[4]—keeps time, distance, and proportion; he
    rests his minim rests,[5] one, two, and the third in your
    bosom! The very butcher of a silk button,[6] a duelist, a
25   duelist! A gentleman of the very first house,[7] of the first
    and second cause.[8] Ah, the immortal *passado*! The
    punto reverso! The hay![9]

BENVOLIO. The what?

MERCUTIO. The pox of such antic, lisping, affecting
30   fantasticoes—these new tuners of accent![10] "By Jesu, a very
    good blade! A very tall man! A very good whore!" Why,
    is not this a <u>lamentable</u> thing, grandsir, that we
    should be thus afflicted with these strange flies, these
    fashionmongers, these pardon-me's,[11] who stand so
35   much on the new form that they cannot sit at ease on
    the old bench? O, their bones, their bones!

[*Enter* ROMEO.]

BENVOLIO. Here comes Romeo! Here comes Romeo!

MERCUTIO. Without his roe, like a dried herring.[12] O flesh,
    flesh, how art thou fishified! Now is he for the numbers[13]
40   that Petrarch flowed in. Laura, to his lady, was
    a kitchen wench (marry, she had a better love to berhyme
    her), Dido a dowdy, Cleopatra a gypsy, Helen
    and Hero hildings and harlots, Thisbe a gray eye or so,
    but not to the purpose. Signior Romeo, *bonjour*!
45   There's a French salutation to your French slop. You
    gave us the counterfeit fairly last night.

ROMEO. Good morrow to you both. What counterfeit did I
    give you?

MERCUTIO. The slip,[14] sir, the slip. Can you not conceive?

50 **ROMEO.** Pardon, good Mercutio. My business was great,
    and in such a case as mine a man may strain courtesy.

---

1. blind bow-boy's butt-shaft Cupid's blunt arrow.

2. Prince of Cats Tybalt, or a variation of it, is the name of the cat in medieval stories of Reynard the Fox.

3. captain of compliments master of formal behavior.

4. as you sing pricksong with attention to precision.

5. rests . . . rests observes all formalities.

6. button exact spot on his opponent's shirt.

7. first house finest school of fencing.

8. the first and second cause reasons that would cause a gentleman to challenge another to a duel.

9. *passado*! . . . *punto reverso*! . . . hay! lunge . . . backhanded stroke . . . home thrust.

10. The pox . . . accent May the plague strike these absurd characters with their phony manners.

Vocabulary Builder

lamentable (lam´ ən tə bəl) *adj.* distressing; sad

11. these pardon-me's these men who are always saying "Pardon me."

12. Without . . . herring worn out.

13. numbers verses of love poems.

14. slip escape. *Slip* is also a term for a counterfeit coin.

29 ✓ Reading Check

What does the Friar think Romeo and Juliet's love will do for the Capulets and Montagues?

Romeo and Juliet, Act II ■ 769

---

28 Literary Analysis
Blank Verse

- Have students read lines 1–34. **Ask** students what they learn in this exchange between Benvolio and Mercutio.
 Answer: Benvolio says that Tybalt has sent a letter to Romeo at the Montague's house, and Mercutio says it probably challenges Romeo to a duel.

- **Ask** students how Mercutio seems to feel about the challenge.
 Answer: Mercutio seems to think that Tybalt is an accomplished swordsman, and Romeo in his lovelorn condition will be no match for him.

- **Ask** students to respond to the Literary Analysis question on p. 768: In what way is Mercutio's and Benvolio's speech in this scene different from what it was earlier in Act II?
 Answer: Their speech is not in blank verse, as it is in earlier scenes.

- Then, **ask** how they can tell that Mercutio's speech is not in blank verse.
 Answer: It does not have five stressed syllables per line.

29 Reading Check

Answer: He thinks Romeo and Juliet's love will end the feud between the two families.

Shakespeare would have been very familiar with Petrarch and Laura. Petrarch developed the Italian or Petrarchan sonnets to a high form, writing more than 300 sonnets to his beloved Laura over a period of twenty years.

Traditionally, Laura was believed to be Laura de Noves of Avignon, which is now in France. Supposedly, Petrarch saw Laura for the first time in St. Claire Church in Avignon on April 6, 1327. He fell in love with her and loved her the rest of his life, even though she was a married woman and a mother. Laura died during the terrible pandemic, the Black Death, which killed as much as a third of Europe's population. Even after her death, however, Petrarch continued writing sonnets expressing his love for her.

Petrarch's sonnets, inspired by Laura, were the inspiration for English poets, among them William Shakespeare, who developed the Elizabethan or Shakespearean sonnet to a splendid form, writing some of the most beautiful sonnets in the English language.

Connect to the Literature

Remind students how Romeo behaved in Act I over his unrequited love for Rosaline. Then, **ask** the Connect to the Literature question on p. 770: Why is Mercutio's use of grand references and exaggerated language a fitting way to tease Romeo?

Answer: Mercutio's teasing is fitting because Romeo had so exaggerated his sadness and pain over Rosaline, who did not return his love.

MERCUTIO. That's as much as to say, such a case as yours constrains a man to bow in the hams.[15]

ROMEO. Meaning, to curtsy.

55 **MERCUTIO.** Thou hast most kindly hit it.

ROMEO. A most courteous exposition.

MERCUTIO. Nay, I am the very pink of courtesy.

ROMEO. Pink for flower.

MERCUTIO. Right.

60 **ROMEO.** Why, then is my pump[16] well-flowered.

MERCUTIO. Sure wit, follow me this jest now till thou hast worn out thy pump, that, when the single sole of it is worn, the jest may remain, after the wearing, solely singular.[17]

65 **ROMEO.** O single-soled jest, solely singular for the singleness![18]

MERCUTIO. Come between us, good Benvolio! My wits faints.

ROMEO. Swits and spurs, swits and spurs; or I'll cry a match.[19]

15. hams hips.

16. pump shoe.

17. when . . . singular the jest will outwear the shoe and will then be all alone.

18. O . . . singleness! O thin joke, unique for only one thing—weakness!

19. Swits . . . match Drive your wit harder to beat me or else I will claim victory in this match of word play.

 Literature in Context

History Connection

Mercutio's Allusions The women Mercutio names as he taunts Romeo are famous figures in European literature and history. Laura was the name of a woman to whom the Italian poet Petrarch addressed much of his love poetry. Dido, according to Roman mythology, was the queen of Carthage and love interest of Aeneas, the founder of Rome. Cleopatra was the famed Egyptian queen with whom Julius Caesar and later Mark Antony fell in love. Helen, Hero, and Thisbe are all legendary beauties in Greek mythology. Mercutio mocks Romeo by saying that Romeo thinks none of them compare with Rosaline.

Connect to the Literature

Why is Mercutio's use of grand references and exaggerated language a fitting way to tease Romeo?

770 ■ *Drama*

MERCUTIO. Nay, if our wits run the wild-goose chase, I
    am done; for thou hast more of the wild goose in one of
70   thy wits than, I am sure, I have in my whole five. Was I
    with you there for the goose?

ROMEO. Thou wast never with me for anything when thou
    wast not there for the goose.

MERCUTIO. I will bite thee by the ear for that jest.

75 **ROMEO.** Nay, good goose, bite not!

MERCUTIO. Thy wit is a very bitter sweeting;[20] it is a most sharp
    sauce.

ROMEO. And is it not, then, well served in to a sweet goose?

MERCUTIO. O, here's a wit of cheveril,[21] that stretches from an
80   inch narrow to an ell broad!

ROMEO. I stretch it out for that word "broad," which added
    to the goose, proves thee far and wide a broad goose.

MERCUTIO. Why, is not this better now than groaning for
    love? Now art thou sociable, now art thou Romeo; now
85   art thou what thou art, by art as well as by nature. For
    this driveling love is like a great natural[22] that runs
    lolling[23] up and down to hide his bauble[24] in a hole.

BENVOLIO. Stop there, stop there!

MERCUTIO. Thou desirest me to stop in my tale against the
    hair.[25]

90 **BENVOLIO.** Thou wouldst else have made thy tale large.

MERCUTIO. O, thou art deceived! I would have made it
    short; for I was come to the whole depth of my tale,
    and meant indeed to occupy the argument[26] no longer.

ROMEO. Here's goodly gear![27]

[*Enter* NURSE *and her Man,* PETER.]

95   A sail, a sail!

MERCUTIO. Two, two! A shirt and a smock.[28]

NURSE. Peter!

PETER. Anon.

NURSE. My fan, Peter.

100 **MERCUTIO.** Good Peter, to hide her face; for her fan's the
    fairer face.

NURSE. God ye good morrow, gentlemen.

MERCUTIO. God ye good-den, fair gentlewoman.

Literary Analysis
Blank Verse Why do you think Romeo does not speak in blank verse in this conversation with his friends?

20. **sweeting** kind of apple.

21. **cheveril** easily stretched kid leather.

22. **natural** idiot.

23. **lolling** with tongue hanging out.

24. **bauble** toy.

25. **the hair** natural inclination.

26. **occupy the argument** talk about the matter.

27. **goodly gear** good stuff for joking (Romeo sees Nurse approaching).

28. **A shirt and a smock** a man and a woman.

 Reading Check

According to Mercutio, how—and why—has Romeo's attitude improved?

Romeo and Juliet, Act II ■ 771

---

31 Literary Analysis
Blank Verse

- Have students read these two pages, lines 37–90. **Ask** students why Romeo's friends are teasing him. Where do they believe Romeo spent the night?
  Answer: They believe he spent the night with Rosaline, and they are teasing him about her.

- **Ask** students how Romeo's verbal exchanges with Mercutio are different in this scene from what they were in Scenes i–iv in Act I.
  Answer: Romeo exchanges lively jokes with his friend. In Act I, Romeo was sad and mournful and did not appear to be having much fun.

- Tell students that this conversation between Romeo and Mercutio is one long battle of wits, in which each man is making puns out of the other man's words. Understanding the exact logic of the puns is less important than understanding the spirit of the game, which you might compare to ways that teenage boys today playfully trade insults.

- **Ask** students to respond to the Literary Analysis question: Why do you think Romeo does not speak in blank verse in this conversation with his friends?
  Possible response: Students may say that Shakespeare chose prose for this conversation because he wanted to capture the kinds of rude remarks and jokes that teenage boys might use to mock a lovesick friend.

32 Reading Check

Answer: Mercutio believes Romeo is back to his old self—joking and boisterous—because he is no longer pining for Rosaline.

Blank Verse

- Have students read lines 100–115. **Ask** students what kind of language they would expect Mercutio and Romeo to use, given that they are members of the upper class. **Possible response:** Mercutio and Romeo might be expected to speak in blank verse, the language of the upper class.

- **Ask** students to respond to the Literary Analysis question on p. 772: How does Shakespeare reveal Romeo and Mercutio's intelligence even when they are not speaking in blank verse? **Answer:** Shakespeare reveals their intelligence through their quick and imaginative wit.

▶ **Monitor Progress:** Ask students whether the characters on this page are speaking in blank verse. **Answer:** The characters are not speaking in blank verse.

- **Ask** students which characters on this page might normally be expected to speak in blank verse. Why? **Answer:** Mercutio, Romeo, and Benvolio would normally be expected to speak in blank verse, because they are members of the upper class.

▶ **Reteach:** If students have problems answering these questions, review the discussion of blank verse on p. 756. Guide students in scanning some lines of blank verse in this act.

③④ Critical Viewing

Answer: Romeo is behaving in a boisterous manner with his friends, having fun and trading insults. With Juliet, Romeo behaves in a quiet, gentlemanly manner and does not use the coarse language he uses among his friends.

NURSE. Is it good-den?

105 **MERCUTIO.** 'Tis no less, I tell ye; for the bawdy hand of the dial is now upon the prick of noon.

NURSE. Out upon you! What a man are you!

ROMEO. One, gentlewoman, that God hath made, himself to mar.

③③ **NURSE.** By my troth, it is well said. "For himself to mar," 110 quoth 'a? Gentlemen, can any of you tell me where I may find the young Romeo?

ROMEO. I can tell you; but young Romeo will be older when you have found him than he was when you sought him. I am the youngest of that name, for fault²⁹ of a 115 worse.

NURSE. You say well.

MERCUTIO. Yea, is the worst well? Very well took,³⁰ i' faith! Wisely, wisely.

NURSE. If you be he, sir, I desire some confidence³¹ with you.

120 **BENVOLIO.** She will endite him to some supper.

MERCUTIO. A bawd, a bawd, a bawd! So ho!

ROMEO. What hast thou found?

MERCUTIO. No hare, sir; unless a hare, sir, in a lenten pie, that is something stale and hoar ere it be spent.

[He walks by them and sings.]

125   An old hare hoar,
          And an old hare hoar,
             Is very good meat in Lent;
          But a hare that is hoar
          Is too much for a score
130   When it hoars ere it be spent.

Romeo, will you come to your father's? We'll to dinner thither.

ROMEO. I will follow you.

MERCUTIO. Farewell, ancient lady. Farewell, [*singing*] "Lady, lady, lady."³²   [*Exit* MERCUTIO, BENVOLIO.]

135 **NURSE.** I pray you, sir, what saucy merchant was this that was so full of his ropery?³³

Blank Verse How does Shakespeare reveal Romeo and Mercutio's intelligence even when they are not speaking in blank verse?

29. **fault** lack.

30. **took** understood.

31. **confidence** Nurse means "conference."

32. **"Lady . . . lady"** line from an old ballad, "Chaste Susanna."

33. **ropery** Nurse means "roguery," the talk and conduct of a rascal.

③④ ▶ **Critical Viewing** How does Romeo's behavior with the other young Montagues contrast with his behavior with Juliet? **[Compare and Contrast]**

Vocabulary Development

Think-Aloud: Expressive Vocabulary

As students are discussing the humor in Scene iv, encourage them to use the expressive vocabulary presented earlier. Using a think-aloud process, model how to use the expressive vocabulary. Say to students:

I'm going to think aloud to show you how I would use the expressive vocabulary in discussing this Scene.

If I were going to discuss the jokes and puns exchanged by Romeo and Mercutio, I might say, *Romeo and Mercutio seemed to* **anticipate** *what the other would say, and each one was ready with an immediate response.*

If I were talking about the Nurse, I might say, *The Nurse was* **reluctant** *to give her message to Romeo until his friends had left.*

Encourage students to use these and other expressive words as they discuss the rest of act.

ROMEO. A gentleman, nurse, that loves to hear himself talk and will speak more in a minute than he will stand to in a month.

140 **NURSE.** And 'a[34] speak anything against me, I'll take him down, and 'a were lustier than he is, and twenty such Jacks; and if I cannot, I'll find those that shall. Scurvy knave! I am none of his flirt-gills;[35] I am none of his skainsmates.[36] And thou must stand by too, and suffer
145 every knave to use me at his pleasure!

PETER. I saw no man use you at his pleasure. If I had, my weapon should quickly have been out, I warrant you. I dare draw as soon as another man, if I see occasion in a good quarrel, and the law on my side.

150 **NURSE.** Now, afore God, I am so vexed that every part about me quivers. Scurvy knave! Pray you, sir, a word; and, as I told you, my young lady bid me inquire you out. What she bid me say, I will keep to myself; but first let me tell ye, if ye should lead her in a fool's paradise, as
155 they say, it were a very gross kind of behavior, as they say; for the gentlewoman is young; and therefore, if you should deal double with her, truly it were an ill thing to be off'red to any gentlewoman, and very weak[37] dealing.

34. **'a** he.

35. **flirt-gills** common girls.
36. **skainsmates** criminals; cutthroats.

37. **weak** unmanly.

36 ✓**Reading Check**

What cautionary advice does the Nurse give Romeo?

35

Romeo and Juliet, Act II ■ 773

35 **Humanities**
Film

This picture from the movie *The Tragedy of Romeo and Juliet,* directed by Franco Zeffirelli, shows a crowd scene. Use the following for discussion:

1. Based on this image from the movie, what idea about this crowd do you think the director is trying to communicate?
   Answer: The director shows this crowd as joking, arrogant, and contemptuous. He uses facial expressions and body language to communicate these ideas.

2. What elements of this image help you better understand the events of the play?
   Answer: From the mocking faces of the boys, it is easy to see how crowds could get into fights and feuds. The boys in the crowd also look like close friends, so it is easy to imagine them taking revenge if someone were to attack one of them.

36 **Reading Check**

Answer: The Nurse tells Romeo not to mislead "my young lady," Juliet.

Differentiated
Instruction   Solutions for All Learners

Enrichment for Advanced Readers
Recommend that students watch the video of the musical *West Side Story,* which has a similar theme as *The Tragedy of Romeo and Juliet.*

Tell students the story is set in New York City in the late 1950s and concerns Tony, a founding member of a street gang, and Maria, the sister of the leader of a rival gang.

Encourage students to make a comparison/contrast chart as they watch, noting similarities and differences in the two works. Students should compare setting, characters, pivotal scenes (such as the first meeting of the lovers, the "balcony scene," the marriage), and the ending.

Have students share their charts with the class.

• Ask two volunteers to read aloud lines 164–181.

• **Ask** students to respond to the Reading Skill prompt: Read in sentences to summarize Romeo's instructions to the Nurse (lines 175–181).

Answer: Stay behind the abbey wall. Within the hour my servant will bring you a rope ladder. This will be my means of reaching the peak of happiness at night. Be reliable and I'll reward you. Greet your mistress for me.

38 Critical Thinking

Analyze

• Review with students the Nurse's role in the play thus far.

• Ask students to **describe** how the Nurse and Friar Lawrence have similar roles in the play, given what students know about the two characters so far.

Answer: The Nurse and Friar Lawrence are both willing—perhaps too willing—to help Romeo and Juliet be together.

---

160 **ROMEO.** Nurse, commend[38] me to thy lady and mistress. I protest unto thee—

NURSE. Good heart, and i' faith I will tell her as much. Lord, Lord, she will be a joyful woman.

ROMEO. What wilt thou tell her, nurse? Thou dost not
165 mark me.

NURSE. I will tell her, sir, that you do protest, which, as I take it, is a gentlemanlike offer.

ROMEO. Bid her devise
Some means to come to shrift[39] this afternoon;
170 And there she shall at Friar Lawrence' cell
Be shrived and married. Here is for thy pains.

NURSE. No, truly, sir; not a penny.

ROMEO. Go to! I say you shall.

NURSE. This afternoon, sir? Well, she shall be there.

175 **ROMEO.** And stay, good nurse, behind the abbey wall.
Within this hour my man shall be with thee
And bring thee cords made like a tackled stair.[40]
37 Which to the high topgallant[41] of my joy
Must be my convoy[42] in the secret night.
180 Farewell. Be trusty, and I'll quit[43] thy pains.
Farewell. Commend me to thy mistress.

NURSE. Now God in heaven bless thee! Hark you, sir.

ROMEO. What say'st thou, my dear nurse?

NURSE. Is your man secret? Did you ne'er hear say,
185 Two may keep counsel, putting one away?[44]

ROMEO. Warrant thee my man's as true as steel.

NURSE. Well, sir, my mistress is the sweetest lady. Lord,
Lord! When 'twas a little prating[45] thing—O, there is a
nobleman in town, one Paris, that would fain lay knife
190 aboard;[46] but she, good soul, had as lieve[47] see a toad,
38 a very toad, as see him. I anger her sometimes, and tell
her that Paris is the properer man; but I'll warrant
you, when I say so, she looks as pale as any clout[48]
in the versal world.[49] Doth not rosemary and Romeo
195 begin both with a letter?

ROMEO. Ay, nurse; what of that? Both with an R.

NURSE. Ah, mocker! That's the dog's name.[50] R is for the—
No; I know it begins with some other letter; and she
hath the prettiest sententious[51] of it, of you and rosemary,
200 that it would do you good to hear it.

774 ■ *Drama*

---

38. commend convey my respect and best wishes.

39. shrift confession.

Reading Skill
Summarizing Read in sentences to summarize Romeo's instructions to the Nurse (lines 175–181).

40. tackled stair rope ladder.

41. topgallant summit.

42. convoy conveyance.

43. quit reward; pay you back for.

44. Two . . . away Two can keep a secret if one is ignorant, or out of the way.

45. prating babbling.

46. fain . . . aboard eagerly seize Juliet for himself.

47. had as lieve would as willingly.

48. clout cloth.

49. versal world universe.

50. dog's name *R* sounds like a growl.

51. sententious Nurse means "sentences"—clever, wise sayings.

ROMEO. Commend me to thy lady.

NURSE. Ay, a thousand times. [*Exit* ROMEO.] Peter!

PETER. Anon.

NURSE. Before, and apace.[52]   [*Exit, after* PETER.]

Scene v. CAPULET'S orchard.

[*Enter* JULIET.]

JULIET. The clock struck nine when I did send the nurse;
    In half an hour she promised to return.
    Perchance she cannot meet him. That's not so.
    O, she is lame! Love's heralds should be thoughts,
5   Which ten times faster glides than the sun's beams
    Driving back shadows over low'ring[1] hills.
    Therefore do nimble-pinioned doves draw Love,[2]
    And therefore hath the wind-swift Cupid wings.
    Now is the sun upon the highmost hill
10 Of this day's journey, and from nine till twelve
    Is three long hours; yet she is not come.
    Had she affections and warm youthful blood,
    She would be as swift in motion as a ball;
    My words would bandy her[3] to my sweet love,
15 And his to me.
    But old folks, many feign[4] as they were dead—
    Unwieldy, slow, heavy and pale as lead.

[*Enter* NURSE *and* PETER.]

    O God, she comes! O honey nurse, what news?
    Hast thou met with him? Send thy man away.

20 **NURSE.** Peter, stay at the gate.   [*Exit* PETER.]

JULIET. Now, good sweet nurse—O Lord, why lookest thou sad?
    Though news be sad, yet tell them merrily;
    If good, thou shamest the music of sweet news
    By playing it to me with so sour a face.

25 **NURSE.** I am aweary, give me leave[5] awhile.
    Fie, how my bones ache! What a jaunce[6] have I!

JULIET. I would thou hadst my bones, and I thy news.
    Nay, come, I pray thee speak. Good, good nurse, speak.

NURSE. Jesu, what haste? Can you not stay a while?
30 Do you not see that I am out of breath?

JULIET. How art thou out of breath when thou hast breath
    To say to me that thou art out of breath?

Literary Analysis
Blank Verse What is
the effect of hearing
Romeo's blank verse
after long passages of
prose?

52. Before, and apace Go
ahead of me, and quickly.

1. low'ring darkening.

2. Therefore . . . Love
therefore, doves with quick
wings pull the chariot of
Venus, goddess of love.

3. bandy her send her rapidly.

4. feign act.

Vocabulary Builder
unwieldy (un wēl′ dē)
adj. awkward; clumsy

5. give me leave excuse me;
give me a moment's rest.

6. jaunce rough trip.

Reading Check

What does Romeo ask
the Nurse to tell
Juliet?

Romeo and Juliet, Act II ■ 775

---

39 Literary Analysis
Blank Verse

- Have students review Romeo's lines starting with line 161. **Ask** students if they notice any change in his speech.
 Answer: Romeo is now speaking in blank verse.

- **Ask** students to respond to the Literary Analysis question: What is the effect of hearing Romeo's blank verse after long passages of prose? **Answer:** Students may suggest that the change in the means of expression emphasizes the change in emotional state. After the boyish and boisterous exchange with his friends, he is now turning to serious concerns, and this is reflected in his speech.

40 Critical Thinking
Analyze

- **Ask** students what problem Juliet is having with her Nurse.
 Answer: Juliet is complaining that her Nurse is late.

- **Ask** students why Juliet is so impatient.
 Answer: Juliet knows the Nurse will have word of Romeo and his plans for their marriage.

41 Reading Check

Answer: Romeo asks the Nurse to tell Juliet to meet him at Friar Lawrence's that afternoon, after saying to her family that she is going to confession.

Differentiated
Instruction   **Solutions for All Learners**

Strategy for Special Needs Students
Help students understand the flavor of this scene between Juliet and her Nurse by having them listen to the **Listening to Literature Audio CD.**

Discuss with students how Juliet might feel as she waits for the Nurse to arrive. Have students describe what she is doing while waiting.
Answer: Students may suggest that she is pacing back and forth in her room.

Have students describe what emotion they hear in Juliet's voice as she attempts to get the Nurse to tell her what Romeo said.

Answer: Students may suggest that they hear Juliet getting more and more frustrated.

Encourage students to speculate about why the Nurse takes so long in telling Juliet what happened.
Possible response: Students may suggest that she does not realize how anxious Juliet is; she is absentminded and thoughtless; she may deliberately want to keep Juliet in suspense.

775

42 **Critical Viewing**

Answer: Romeo and Juliet are holding each other, showing their affection. They are also looking upward, as if they were listening to someone such as the Friar.

43 **Critical Thinking**
Analyze

• Refer students to the bracketed passage. Have students **describe** what Juliet finally does to get an answer from the Nurse.
Answer: Juliet asks the Nurse to tell her simply whether the news is good or bad; she can get the details later.

• **Ask** students how the Nurse takes Juliet's request for good or bad news.
Answer: She takes it to mean that Juliet is asking whether her choice of a man is good or bad, and then she goes on to give her opinion of Romeo.

44 **Literary Analysis**
Blank Verse

• Ask students to read lines 46–57 aloud. How would they identify the form of writing?
Possible answer: Students may say that some of the lines are blank verse and some are not.

• **Ask** students to respond to the Literary Analysis question: What might Shakespeare be indicating about the Nurse's character by having her switch between prose and blank verse?
Answer: Shakespeare might be indicating the Nurse is trying to match Juliet's mood and method of speech in this emotionally charged scene, but because it is not her normal way of speaking, she does not quite carry it off. It also suggests that she is both an honorable character with deep feelings and serious intentions and something of a busybody.

45 **Reading Check**

Answer: He is handsome and gentle but does not have good manners.

> The excuse that thou dost make in this delay
> Is longer than the tale thou dost excuse.
35   Is thy news good or bad? Answer to that.
> Say either, and I'll stay the circumstance.[7]
> Let me be satisfied, is't good or bad?

43   **NURSE.** Well, you have made a simple[8] choice; you know
40   not how to choose a man. Romeo? No, not he. Though
> his face be better than any man's, yet his leg excels all
> men's; and for a hand and a foot, and a body, though
> they be not to be talked on, yet they are past compare.
> He is not the flower of courtesy, but, I'll warrant him,
> as gentle as a lamb. Go thy ways, wench; serve God.
45   What, have you dined at home?

> **JULIET.** No, no. But all this I did know before.
> What says he of our marriage? What of that?

> **NURSE.** Lord, how my head aches! What a head have I!
> It beats as it would fall in twenty pieces.
50   My back a[9] t'other side—ah, my back, my back!
44   Beshrew[10] your heart for sending me about
> To catch my death with jauncing up and down!

> **JULIET.** I' faith, I am sorry that thou art not well.
> Sweet, sweet, sweet nurse, tell me, what says my love?

55 **NURSE.** Your love says, like an honest gentleman, and a
> courteous, and a kind, and a handsome, and, I warrant,
> a virtuous—Where is your mother?

> **JULIET.** Where is my mother? Why, she is within.
> Where should she be? How oddly thou repliest!
60   "Your love says, like an honest gentleman,
> 'Where is your mother?'"

> **NURSE.**   O God's Lady dear!
> Are you so hot?[11] Marry come up, I trow.[12]
> Is this the poultice[13] for my aching bones?
> Henceforward do your messages yourself.

65 **JULIET.** Here's such a coil![14] Come, what says Romeo?

> **NURSE.** Have you got leave to go to shrift today?

> **JULIET.** I have.

> **NURSE.** Then hie you hence to Friar Lawrence' cell;
> There stays a husband to make you a wife.
70   Now comes the wanton[15] blood up in your cheeks:
> They'll be in scarlet straight at any news.
> Hie you to church: I must another way,

776 ■ *Drama*

---

42 ▶ **Critical Viewing**
Which details in this picture reflect the feelings Romeo and Juliet have for each other? [**Interpret**]

7. stay the circumstance wait for the details.

8. simple foolish; simpleminded.

9. a on.

10. Beshrew shame on.

Literary Analysis
Blank Verse What might Shakespeare be indicating about the Nurse's character by having her switch between prose and blank verse?

11. hot impatient; hottempered.

12. Marry . . . trow Indeed, cool down, I say.

13. poultice remedy.

14. coil disturbance.

15. wanton excited.

45 **Reading Check**

How does the Nurse describe Romeo?

Vocabulary Development

Word Analysis
Draw student's attention to the word *unwieldy* in line 17 on p. 775. Point out that this word contains the prefix *un-*, meaning "not." Tell students that *non-* is another prefix that generally means "not," and that these two prefixes can be used with the same word, with each prefix giving a slightly different meaning.

The prefix *un-* is used to indicate the opposite of something, as in *unwieldy*, or "not able to be wielded." The prefix *non-* is used to give a negative meaning to something.

These two prefixes can be attached to the same word to convey slightly different meanings. For example, a *non-American* is a person who is not an American citizen. To be *un-American* is to act in a way opposite to American values.

Have students brainstorm for other words that can be used with either *un-* or *non-* to give different meanings. **Answer:** Students might suggest words such as *conventional* and *responsive*.

Romeo and Juliet, Act II ■ 777

46 Background
Period Clothing

46 Background
Period Clothing

The costumes in this photograph and in the photograph on p. 773 reflect fashions that were popular during the Italian Renaissance. Men wore a shirt beneath a short, close-fitting jacket called a doublet. They also wore fitted tights, or hose, that reached from waist to toe. Sleeves were fastened to the body of the garment with laces tipped with metal aglets.

Women wore a nightgown-like chemise beneath a high-waisted gown with a tight-fitting bodice. The gown of a noble lady was made of rich fabrics such as velvet, satin, cloth-of-gold, or brocade, and was usually elaborately embroidered. Throughout the Renaissance, pearls were extremely popular gems and were used in embellishing clothing. In the photograph on p. 833, Juliet's gown and cap are studded with pearls.

Differentiated Instruction   Solutions for All Learners

Background for Gifted/Talented Students

Tell students that various actresses who have played Juliet have brought their own interpretation of the character to the role. One famous actress was Sarah Siddons (1755–1831), who critics claimed was the greatest Shakespearean actress of her time. One theater-goer wrote this of her performance in Act II, Scene v: "The pouting scene with the old Nurse was the cleverest thing I ever saw—so pretty, so babyish, so charming. . . ."

Have students work in groups of three or four to perform dramatic interpretations of Scene v. Students should take turns playing Juliet and the Nurse. Encourage students to use their own imagination in interpreting how Juliet might speak and behave. Point out that as long as they have a basic understanding of the scene and of Juliet's character, there is no "right" way to deliver the lines. Encourage students to perform their scene for the class.

- Ask students to **interpret** the phrase "hie you to the cell" in line 77.
  Possible response: Students should see that the phrase means something like, "Get yourself to the cell," or "Go to the cell."

- **Ask** students to respond to the Literary Analysis question: What effect is created by making Juliet's last line rhyme with the Nurse's last line?
  Answer: The lines create a rhyming couplet, which Shakespeare often uses to close a scene. It also shows that the Nurse and Juliet are in agreement about Juliet's wedding plans.

    To fetch a ladder, by the which your love
    Must climb a bird's nest soon when it is dark.
75 I am the drudge, and toil in your delight:
    But you shall bear the burden soon at night.
    Go; I'll to dinner; hie you to the cell.

47 **JULIET.** Hie to high fortune! Honest nurse, farewell.

                                      [Exit all.]

Scene vi. Friar Lawrence's cell.

[*Enter* FRIAR LAWRENCE *and* ROMEO.]

    FRIAR. So smile the heavens upon this holy act
    That afterhours with sorrow chide us not![1]

    ROMEO. Amen, amen! But come what sorrow can,
48   It cannot countervail[2] the exchange of joy
5   That one short minute gives me in her sight.
    Do thou but close our hands with holy words,
    Then love-devouring death do what he dare—
    It is enough I may but call her mine.

    FRIAR. These violent delights have violent ends
10 And in their triumph die, like fire and powder,[3]
    Which, as they kiss, consume. The sweetest honey
    Is loathsome in his own deliciousness
    And in the taste confounds[4] the appetite.
    Therefore love moderately: long love doth so;
15 Too swift arrives as tardy as too slow.

[*Enter* JULIET.]

    Here comes the lady. O, so light a foot
    Will ne'er wear out the everlasting flint.[5]
    A lover may bestride the gossamers[6]
    That idles in the wanton summer air,
20 And yet not fall; so light is vanity.[7]

    JULIET. Good even to my ghostly confessor.

    FRIAR. Romeo shall thank thee, daughter, for us both.

    JULIET. As much to him,[8] else is his thanks too much.

    ROMEO. Ah, Juliet, if the measure of thy joy
25 Be heaped like mine, and that thy skill be more
    To blazon it,[9] then sweeten with thy breath
    This neighbor air, and let rich music's tongue
    Unfold the imagined happiness that both
    Receive in either by this dear encounter.

Literary Analysis
Blank Verse What effect is created by making Juliet's last line rhyme with the Nurse's last line?

1. That . . . not! that the future does not punish us with sorrow.

2. countervail equal.

3. powder gunpowder.

4. confounds destroys.

5. flint stone.

6. gossamers spider webs.

7. vanity foolish things that cannot last.

8. As . . . him the same greeting to him.

9. and . . . it and if you are better able to proclaim it.

Vocabulary Development

Vocabulary Knowledge Rating
When students have completed reading and discussing Act II of *The Tragedy of Romeo and Juliet,* have them take out their **Vocabulary Knowledge Rating Chart** for this selection. Read the words aloud once more and have students rate their knowledge of the words again in the After Reading column. Clarify any words that are still problematic. Have students write their own definition and example or sentence in the appropriate column. Then, have students complete the **Vocabulary Builder Practice** activities on p. 781. Encourage students to use the words in further discussion and written work about this selection. Remind them that they will be accountable for these words on the Selection Test.

30 **JULIET.** Conceit, more rich in matter than in words,
    Brags of his substance, not of ornament.[10]
    They are but beggars that can count their worth;
    But my true love is grown to such excess
    I cannot sum up sum of half my wealth.

35 **FRIAR.** Come, come with me, and we will make short work;
    For, by your leaves, you shall not stay alone
    Till Holy Church incorporate two in one.

    [*Exit all.*]

10. Conceit . . . ornament
Understanding does not need
to be dressed up in words.

49 ▲ **Critical Viewing** How does this image of fifteenth-century Verona reflect scenery and intrigues in Romeo and Juliet's lives? **[Synthesize]**

48 Literary Analysis
Blank Verse

- Have students read lines 3–8 on p. 778 aloud. Ask students to identify how many stressed syllables are in each line.
  Answer: There are five stressed syllables in each line.

- **Ask** students how an actor should pronounce *the exchange* to keep the meter of blank verse.
  Possible response: Students may suggest that the word *the* should run together with the *ex-* in *exchange* to create one syllable instead of two, so that it would be pronounced something like *theex change.*

▶ **Monitor Progress:** Use students' responses to assess their understanding of blank verse.

▶ **Reteach:** If students have difficulty identifying the meter, have them work in pairs to scan lines 3–8 in Scene vi.

42 Critical Viewing

Possible response: The forbidding walls, the densely packed buildings, and the winding paths all suggest the secrecy of Verona.

Concept Connector

Connecting to the Literature
Have students compare the sentences they wrote about conflict over family loyalties. Ask them to explain whether their thoughts have changed, and, if so, how.

Literary Analysis Graphic Organizer
Have students review the graphic organizers

they completed while reading to identify characters' rank based on their understanding of blank verse. Show them **Literary Analysis Graphic Organizer B** (*Graphic Organizer Transparencies,* p. 168) as an example. Then have students share the graphic organizers they did and how they identified characters' rank.

1. **Possible responses:** Some students may say that Friar Lawrence is wise because Romeo and Juliet seem to be in love and their marriage would unify the warring families. Others may characterize the Friar as well-intentioned but unwise.

2. (a) Romeo and Juliet declare their love for each other in the balcony scene. (b) The darkness conceals Romeo from Juliet's relatives. It also provides an illusion of privacy so that Juliet feels she can speak her thoughts aloud.

3. (a) The Friar says that Romeo is fickle. Romeo argues that Rosaline did not return his love and Juliet does. (b) The Friar wants to end the feud between the families, while the couple wants to be together because they are in love.

4. (a) Juliet awaits the Nurse. (b) Juliet is highly impatient and her exasperation increases as she tries to extract news from the breathless Nurse.

5. **Possible response:** Students may say that the romantic words and images, the danger of discovery, the vivid descriptions, and the expressions of devotion are extremely powerful.

6. Use an overhead projector to mark the unaccented and accented syllables in these passages as a class.

7. **Blank Verse Pattern:**

   ⌣ / , ⌣ / , ⌣ / , ⌣ / , ⌣ /

   Romeo: Can I go forward when my heart is here?

   ⌣ / , ⌣ / , ⌣ / , ⌣ / , ⌣ /

   Juliet: But my true love is grown to such excess.

   Key Words: *I, forward, heart, here, my, love, grown, such, excess*

   Significance: The words help communicate key ideas.

   (Another sample answer can be found on **Literary Analysis Graphic Organizer B,** p. 168 in *Graphic Organizer Transparencies.*)

8. (a) The Capulets and the Montagues, their friends, the Prince, and the Friar speak in blank verse. The servants and the Nurse are common people

---

Apply the Skills

The Tragedy of Romeo and Juliet, Act II

Thinking About the Selection

1. (a) **Respond:** Is Friar Lawrence wise to agree to marry Romeo and Juliet? Explain. (b) **Discuss:** In a small group, share your responses. As a group, choose one idea to share with the class.
2. (a) **Recall:** Where do Romeo and Juliet first mutually declare their love? (b) **Interpret:** What role does darkness play in the scene?
3. (a) **Recall:** What weakness in Romeo does the Friar point out before agreeing to help? (b) **Compare and Contrast:** How do the Friar's motives differ from the couple's own motives?
4. (a) **Recall:** For whom does Juliet wait in Act II, Scene v? (b) **Analyze:** What are her feelings as she waits?
5. **Evaluate:** Why do you think the love scene in Capulet's garden is one of the most famous dramatic scenes in all literature?

Literary Analysis

6. Copy the following passages of **blank verse.** Then, indicate the pattern of accented (´) and unaccented (⌣) syllables in each line.
   (a) Act II, Scene ii, lines 43–51
   (b) Act II, Scene vi, lines 3–8
7. Using a chart like the one shown, rewrite the following two lines, marking stressed and unstressed syllables. Then, identify the key words stressed in each line, and explain what meaning is conveyed by the emphasis on those words.
   (a) **ROMEO.** Can I go forward when my heart is here?
   (b) **JULIET.** But my true love is grown to such excess.

Blank Verse Pattern	Key Words	Significance

8. (a) Identify the aristocratic and common people in Acts I and II based on whether or not they speak in blank verse. (b) Why do you think Shakespeare chose to have aristocratic characters speak in blank verse instead of ordinary prose?

Reading Skill

9. (a) How many sentences are in lines 1–8 of Act II, Scene v? (b) Write a **summary** of these lines.

780 ■ *Drama*

QuickReview

Act II at a Glance
Romeo and Juliet pledge their love to each other. With the aid of Juliet's Nurse and Friar Lawrence, they arrange to be married in secret by the Friar.

Go Online
Assessment
For: Self-test
Visit: www.PHSchool.com
Web Code: epa-6503

Blank Verse: unrhymed poetry written in iambic pentameter, a meter consisting of five stressed syllables, each preceded by an unstressed syllable

Summarizing: briefly stating the main points in a piece of writing

and, for the most part, speak in prose. (b) Blank verse signals seriousness and status. Shifts from verse to prose emphasize changes in mood and tone.

9. (a) There are six sentences in these lines. (b) It was nine o'clock when Juliet sent the Nurse, who promised to return in half an hour. Juliet worries that perhaps the Nurse cannot meet Romeo and frets that she is so slow.

Vocabulary Builder

Practice Answer each question. Then, explain your answer.

1. Where would you go to *procure* groceries?
2. What is the *predominant* feeling at a celebration?
3. How many people are needed for an *intercession* to occur?
4. Is a *sallow* complexion a sign of good health?
5. If a situation is *lamentable*, are people likely to be happy about it?
6. Is an *unwieldy* package something you would want to carry far?

Adding Words to Your Vocabulary The word *intercession* might easily be confused with *interception*. Use a dictionary to find out the meaning of the word *interception*, and then write a few sentences explaining how an intercession is different from an interception. (For more on using a dictionary, see page R6.)

Writing

A **parody** is a humorous piece of writing that mocks the characteristics of another work. A parody may be gentle or scathing, and it may distort the plot, characters, themes, or language of its target. Write a parody of the famous balcony scene in *Romeo and Juliet*. In your writing, make light of Romeo and Juliet's exaggerated professions of love.

- Reread the scene, and take notes about any elements of it that could be funny.
- Choose a focus. For example, you might decide that no one would speak the way Shakespeare's lovers do.
- Write your parody as a script for an original play, including dialogue and stage directions.

For *Grammar, Vocabulary,* and *Assessment,* see **Build Language Skills,** pages 812–813.

Extend Your Learning

Research and Technology Conduct research to create an **annotated flowchart** that displays and explains the structure of the nobility in sixteenth-century Verona. Your flowchart should show the relative positions of the Prince, Count Paris, the Montagues, and the Capulets. Organize text and images logically, and use correct grammar. Remember to document sources for both ideas and images. (For more on citing sources, see page R33.) Include the flowchart in your multimedia portfolio.

Apply the Skills ■ 781

Extend Your Learning

The **Support for Extend Your Learning** page (*Unit 5 Resources,* p. 42) provides guided note-taking opportunities to help students complete Extend Your Learning activities.

Go Online
Research **For:** An additional research activity
Visit: www.PHSchool.com
Web Code: epd-7502
For another research activity to extend students' learning, give this Web Code.

Vocabulary Builder
Practice

1. You would go to a supermarket, since *procure* means "to get."
2. The *predominant,* or most important feeling, is happiness.
3. At least two people are needed, since one person *intercedes* on behalf of another person.
4. A *sallow,* or sickly yellowish, complexion is a sign of poor health.
5. People will not be happy about a *lamentable,* or sad, situation.
6. No, since something *unwieldy* is awkward.

Adding Words to Your Vocabulary
Sample response:

Interception means "the act of stopping or interrupting something before the arrival at a particular place." *Intercession* means "the act of pleading on someone's behalf." If someone were in trouble and about to be punished, then an *intercession* by another person could prevent it. If a football is being thrown, a member of the opposing team could score an *interception* by catching the ball before it reaches the intended receiver.

Writing

- To give students guidance for writing a parody, give them **Support for Writing** for Act II, *The Tragedy of Romeo and Juliet,* p. 41, in *Unit 5 Resources.*
- To evaluate students' parodies, use the Generic [Holistic] Writing rubrics, pp. 77–78 in *General Resources.* In addition, you might evaluate how well students use imagery and/or humor in their parodies.

Six Traits Focus

✓	Ideas	✓	Word Choice
	Organization		Sentence Fluency
✓	Voice		Conventions

Build Language Skills

Go to pp. 812–813 for vocabulary and grammar lessons and assessment practice.

Planning Differentiated Instruction

Accessibility at a Glance

	The Tragedy of Romeo and Juliet, Act III
Context	Historical; Verona, Italy
Language	Dialogue, prose, verse, soliloquies, Elizabethan terms, and challenging vocabulary
Concept Level	Accessible; classic tale of star-crossed lovers
Literary Merit	Classic; noted poet and playwright
Lexile	NP
Overall Rating	More challenging

Choosing Your Resources

[**L1**] Special Needs Students   [**L4**] Advanced Students

[**L2**] Below-Level Students   [**EL**] English Learners

[**L3**] All Students

FT Fast Track Instruction: To move the lesson more quickly, use the strategies and activities identified with **FT**.

Reading and Vocabulary Warm-ups provide support for below level students. **A** is for students reading two grades below level; **B** is for students reading one grade below level. For Selection Tests, **A** signifies "less challenging" and **B** "more challenging." For Graphic Organizer transparencies, **A** signifies "not filled in" and **B** "filled in."

Scaffolding for Less Proficient and Advanced Students

The leveled questions on Apply the Skills pages progress in the levels of thinking required to answer them. To address the needs of your different students, you may use the (a) level questions for your less proficient students, the (b) level with your on-level and advanced students. The occasional (c) level questions are appropriate for your advanced students.

Go **Online**
Professional
Development
For: Information about Lexiles
Visit: www.PHSchool.com
Web Code: eue-1111

Step-by-Step Teaching Guide	Pacing Guide
PRETEACH	
• Administer Vocabulary and Reading Warm-ups as necessary.	
• Introduce the Literary Analysis Skills: Dramatic Speeches. **FT**	10 min.
• Introduce the Reading Skill: Summarizing **FT**	10 min.
• Prepare students to read by teaching the selection vocabulary. **FT**	10 min.
• Build background and develop expressive vocabulary with Connecting to the Literature and Background.	10 min.
• Engage students' interest with the motivation activity.	10 min.
TEACH	
• Informally monitor comprehension while students read independently or in groups. **FT**	30 min.
• Monitor students' comprehension with the Reading Check notes.	as students read
• Reinforce vocabulary with Vocabulary Builder notes.	as students read
• Develop students' understanding of dramatic speeches with the Literary Analysis annotations. **FT**	5 min.
• Develop students' ability to summarize and paraphrase with the Reading Skill annotations. **FT**	10 min.
ASSESS/EXTEND	
• Assess students' comprehension and mastery of the Reading Skill and Literary Analysis by having them answer the Apply the Skills questions. **FT**	35 min.
• Have students complete the Vocabulary Builder activities. **FT**	5 min.
• Apply students' ability to write an editorial with the Writing activity. **FT**	30–45 min. or homework
• Extend students' listening and speaking and research and technology skills with one or both of the Extend Your Learning activities.	15–30 min. or homework
• Have students complete the Vocabulary Skill and Grammar Lesson.	5 min.
• Monitor students' progress with the Assessment Practice.	20–40 min.
• Administer **Selection Test A** or **Selection Test B**. **FT**	15 min.

Resources

Meeting Your Standards

Students will

1. **analyze and respond to literary elements.**
   - Literary Analysis: Dramatic Speeches

2. **read, comprehend, and analyze plays.**
   - Reading Skill: Summarizing
   - Reading Strategy: Paraphrasing
   - Reading Check questions
   - Apply the Skills questions
   - Assessment Practice

3. **develop vocabulary.**
   - Vocabulary Builder
   - Word Roots *-labor-*

4. **apply grammar skills.**
   - Participle and Participle Phrases

5. **develop writing proficiency.**
   - Work in Progress: How-to Essay
   - Editorial

6. **extend learning.**
   - Research and Technology: Film Review

Block Scheduling: Use one 90-minute class period to preteach the skills and have students read Act III. Use a second 90-minute class period to assess students' mastery of skills, extend their learning, and monitor their progress.

Homework Suggestions

The following are possibilities for homework assignments.

- Support pages from *Unit 5 Resources:*
  Literary Analysis
  Reading Skill
  Build Vocabulary
  Enrichment

- An Extend Your Learning project and the Writing assignment for Act III may be completed over several days.

PRENTICE HALL
TeacherEXPRESS™ Use this complete
Plan · Teach · Assess   suite of powerful
teaching tools to make lesson planning and testing quicker and easier.

PRENTICE HALL
StudentEXPRESS™ Use the
Learn · Study · Succeed   Interactive
Textbook (online and on CD-ROM) to make Act III and activities come alive with audio and video support and interactive questions.

Build Skills The Tragedy of Romeo and Juliet, Act III

❶ Literary Analysis
Dramatic Speeches

- Define the three kinds of *dramatic speeches* and give these examples: **Soliloquy**—Act II, Scene v, lines 1–18; **Aside**—Act II, Scene ii, line 37; **Monologue**—Act I, Scene iv, lines 52–95.

- Tell students that *allusions* rely on the knowledge of the reader or audience. Most of Shakespeare's allusions were well-known to Shakespeare's audience.

- Give students a copy of **Literary Analysis Graphic Organizer A** (*Graphic Organizer Transparencies,* p. 171). Have them fill in the graphic organizer to identify allusions and to record the effect they have.

❷ Reading Skill
Summarizing

- Tell students that they have paraphrased passages in the play as they have read the first two acts.

- Point out that the difference between summarizing and paraphrasing is that when paraphrasing, they include all the ideas in a passage, restated in their own words. When summarizing, they include only the main ideas of a passage, but not all the details.

Connecting to the Literature

- Romeo and Juliet are about to be married in secret. Write several sentences about why young people might want to engage in secretive behavior. Have students use at least three of these words: *comply, drastic, eloquent,* and *tolerate.*

- Provide these sample sentences to demonstrate their use:

  1. Children do not always *comply* with the wishes of their parents.

  2. Young lovers sometimes take *drastic* steps to be together.

  3. Young people in love are often *eloquent* when speaking of the object of their affection.

  4. Parents often will not *tolerate* their children's friends.

Encourage students to use these words as they discuss the selection.

Literary Analysis

Plays often include these types of **dramatic speeches:**

- **Soliloquy:** a lengthy speech in which a character—usually alone on stage—expresses his or her true thoughts or feelings. Soliloquies are unheard by other characters.
- **Aside:** a character revealing his or her true thoughts or feelings in a remark that is unheard by other characters
- **Monologue:** a lengthy speech by one person. Unlike a soliloquy, a monologue is addressed to other characters.

Dramatic speeches often include **allusions**—references to well-known people, places, or events from mythology or literature. For example, in Act II, Mercutio insultingly calls Tybalt "Prince of Cats," alluding to a cat named Tybalt in French fables.

As you read, consider what each type of speech reveals about the speaker and his or her relationships with other characters. Use a chart like the one shown to note the effect of any allusions you find.

Reading Skill

Summarizing is briefly stating the main points in a piece of writing. Before you summarize a long passage of a play by Shakespeare, you should **paraphrase** it, or restate the lines in your own words. For example, compare these two versions of a speech by Romeo:

Shakespeare's version: "This gentleman, the Prince's near ally, / My very friend, hath got his mortal hurt / In my behalf. . . ."
Paraphrase: My good friend, a close relative of the prince, has been fatally wounded in defending me.

Once you have paraphrased small portions of text, you can more easily and accurately summarize an entire passage.

Allusion
Tybalt, Prince of Cats

Refers to
Cat in French fables

Purpose
Insults Tybalt by making fun of his name

Vocabulary Builder

- **gallant** (gal´ ənt) *adj.* brave and noble (p. 787) *We called the firefighters gallant, but they said they were just doing their job.*
- **fray** (frā) *n.* noisy fight (p. 788) *The crew argued, but the captain stayed above the fray.*
- **martial** (mär´ shəl) *adj.* military (p. 789) *The band played martial music to honor the soldiers.*
- **exile** (ek´ sīl´) *v.* banish (p. 790) *Years ago, rulers would exile criminals to faraway places.*
- **eloquence** (el´ ə kwəns) *n.* speech or writing that is graceful and persuasive (p. 791) *The eloquence of her speech moved the audience.*
- **fickle** (fik´ əl) *adj.* changeable (p. 802) *His fickle sense of style made buying clothes hard.*

Vocabulary Development

Vocabulary Knowledge Rating
Create a **Vocabulary Knowledge Rating Chart** with these words from the selection:

gallant	fray	martial
exile	eloquence	fickle

Give students a copy. Introduce the words by reading them aloud and having students mark their rating in the Before Reading column. Urge them to be alert to these words as they read and discuss the selection, because they will rate their knowledge of the words again after they finish.

If you wish, you may tally how many students know (or think they know) a word to gauge how much instruction you need to provide. As students read, point out the words and their context.

ACT III

Review and Anticipate

In Act II, Romeo and Juliet express their mutual love and enlist the aid of Juliet's nurse and Friar Lawrence to arrange a secret marriage ceremony. As the act closes, the young couple is about to be married. Before performing the ceremony, the Friar warns, "These violent delights have violent ends. . . ." How might this statement hint at events that will occur in Act III or later in the play?

Scene i. A public place.

[*Enter* MERCUTIO, BENVOLIO, *and* MEN.]

BENVOLIO. I pray thee, good Mercutio, let's retire.
The day is hot, the Capulets abroad,
And, if we meet, we shall not 'scape a brawl,
For now, these hot days, is the mad blood stirring.

5 **MERCUTIO.** Thou art like one of these fellows that, when he
enters the confines of a tavern, claps me his sword upon the
table and says, "God send me no need of thee!" and by the
operation of the second cup draws him on the drawer,[1] when
indeed there is no need.

10 **BENVOLIO.** Am I like such a fellow?

MERCUTIO. Come, come, thou art as hot a Jack in thy mood as
any in Italy; and as soon moved to be moody, and as soon
moody to be moved.[2]

1. and . . . drawer and by the effect of the second drink, draws his sword against the waiter.

2. and . . . moved and as quickly stirred to anger as you are eager to be so stirred.

✓ Reading Check

Why does Benvolio want to get off the street?

Romeo and Juliet, Act III ■ 783

783

④ Literary Analysis
Dramatic Speeches

- Have students recall from earlier acts the kind of character Benvolio exhibits. **Ask** whether they agree with Mercutio's description of Benvolio. **Answer:** Students should recall that it was Benvolio who attempted to break up a fight in Act I. He is not hotheaded and always ready for a fight.

- Remind students that a *soliloquy* is delivered to the audience by a character who is alone on stage, while a *monologue* is a long speech delivered to other characters in a scene.
  Ask students the Literary Analysis question: Which details of Mercutio's speech indicate that it is a monologue and not a soliloquy?
  Answer: Mercutio is not alone when he gives the speech. He speaks directly to Benvolio, and other characters are listening.

⑤ Reading Skill
Summarizing

- Ask students what they expect to happen when Tybalt comes on stage.
  Possible response: Students may say that because Tybalt and Mercutio are hotheaded, they will probably fight.

- **Ask** students to respond to the Reading Skill question: How would you paraphrase the exchange between Tybalt and Mercutio?
  Possible response: TYBALT: Hello, gentlemen. I'd like a word with one of you. MERCUTIO: Just a word? You can do better than that. Make it a word and a punch. TYBALT: I might just do that if you give me a reason. MERCUTIO: Can't you find a reason of your own? TYBALT: Mercutio, you consort with Romeo. MERCUTIO: Consort? What do you think we are—musicians? If you're going to call us musicians, you'll be hearing some sour notes. Here's my sword—this will make you dance. Consort, my foot!

784

BENVOLIO. And what to?

15 **MERCUTIO.** Nay, and there were two such, we should have none shortly, for one would kill the other. Thou! Why, thou wilt quarrel with a man that hath a hair more or a hair less in his beard than thou hast. Thou wilt quarrel with a man for cracking nuts, having no other reason but because thou
20 hast hazel eyes. What eye but such an eye would spy out such a quarrel? Thy head is as full of quarrels as an egg is full of meat; and yet thy head hath been beaten as addle[3] as an egg for quarreling. Thou hast quarreled with a man for coughing in the street, because he hath wakened thy dog
25 that hath lain asleep in the sun. Didst thou not fall out with a tailor for wearing his new doublet[4] before Easter? With another for tying his new shoes with old riband?[5] And yet thou wilt tutor me from quarreling![6]

BENVOLIO. And I were so apt to quarrel as thou art, any man
30 should buy the fee simple[7] of my life for an hour and a quarter.[8]

MERCUTIO. The fee simple? O simple![9]

[*Enter* TYBALT, PETRUCHIO, *and* OTHERS.]

BENVOLIO. By my head, here comes the Capulets.

MERCUTIO. By my heel, I care not.

35 **TYBALT.** Follow me close, for I will speak to them.
Gentlemen, good-den. A word with one of you.

MERCUTIO. And but one word with one of us? Couple it with something; make it a word and a blow.

⑤ **TYBALT.** You shall find me apt enough to that, sir, and you will
40 give me occasion.[10]

MERCUTIO. Could you not take some occasion without giving?

TYBALT. Mercutio, thou consortest[11] with Romeo.

MERCUTIO. Consort?[12] What, dost thou make us minstrels? And thou make minstrels of us, look to hear nothing but
45 discords.[13] Here's my fiddlestick; here's that shall make you dance. Zounds,[14] consort!

BENVOLIO. We talk here in the public haunt of men.
Either withdraw unto some private place,
Or reason coldly of your grievances,
50 Or else depart. Here all eyes gaze on us.

784 ■ *Drama*

Literary Analysis
Dramatic Speeches
Which details of Mercutio's speech indicate that it is a monologue and not a soliloquy?

3. **addle** scrambled; crazy.

4. **doublet** jacket.

5. **riband** ribbon.

6. **tutor . . . quarreling** instruct me not to quarrel.

7. **fee simple** complete possession.

8. **an hour and a quarter** length of time that a man with Mercutio's fondness for quarreling may be expected to live.

9. **O simple!** O stupid!

Reading Skill
Summarizing How would you paraphrase the exchange between Tybalt and Mercutio?

10. **occasion** cause; reason.

11. **consortest** associate with.

12. **Consort** associate with; "consort" also meant a group of musicians.

13. **discords** harsh sounds.

14. **Zounds** exclamation of surprise or anger ("By God's wounds").

Vocabulary Development

Vocabulary Builder Reinforcement
Students will benefit from additional examples and practice with the Vocabulary Builder words. Reinforce their comprehension with "show-you-know" sentences. The first part of the sentence uses the vocabulary word in an appropriate context. The second part of the sentence—the "show-you-know" part—clarifies the first. Model the strategy with this example for *gallant:*

He was a *gallant* soldier; he risked his life to save his buddy.

Then, give students these sentence prompts and coach them in creating the clarification part:
  1. Jimmy was always in the *fray;*

  Sample response: he was constantly fighting with his brothers.
  2. He was a master of *martial* arts;

  Sample response: he could defeat anyone in hand-to-hand combat.

MERCUTIO. Men's eyes were made to look, and let them gaze.
    I will not budge for no man's pleasure, I.

[*Enter* ROMEO.]

TYBALT. Well, peace be with you, sir. Here comes my man.[15]

MERCUTIO. But I'll be hanged, sir, if he wear your livery.[16]
55   Marry, go before to field,[17] he'll be your follower!
    Your worship in that sense may call him man.

TYBALT. Romeo, the love I bear thee can afford
    No better term than this: thou art a villain.[18]

ROMEO. Tybalt, the reason that I have to love thee
    Doth much excuse the appertaining[19] rage
    To such a greeting. Villain am I none.
    Therefore farewell. I see thou knowest me not.

TYBALT. Boy, this shall not excuse the injuries
    That thou hast done me; therefore turn and draw.

65 **ROMEO.** I do protest I never injured thee,
    But love thee better than thou canst devise[20]
    Till thou shalt know the reason of my love;
    And so, good Capulet, which name I tender[21]
    As dearly as mine own, be satisfied.

70 **MERCUTIO.** O calm, dishonorable, vile submission!
    Alla stoccata[22] carries it away.   [*Draws.*]
    Tybalt, you ratcatcher, will you walk?

TYBALT. What wouldst thou have with me?

MERCUTIO. Good King of Cats, nothing but one of your
75   nine lives. That I mean to make bold withal,[23] and, as
    you shall use me here-after, dry-beat[24] the rest of the
    eight. Will you pluck your sword out of his pilcher[25]
    by the ears? Make haste, lest mine be about your
    ears ere it be out.

80 **TYBALT.** I am for you.   [*Draws.*]

ROMEO. Gentle Mercutio, put thy rapier up.

MERCUTIO. Come, sir, your *passado*!   [*They fight.*]

ROMEO. Draw, Benvolio; beat down their weapons.
    Gentlemen, for shame! Forbear this outrage!
85   Tybalt, Mercutio, the Prince expressly hath
    Forbid this bandying in Verona streets.

15. **man** man I am looking for; "man" also meant "manservant."

16. **livery** servant's uniform.

17. **field** dueling place.

18. **villain** low, vulgar person.

19. **appertaining** appropriate.

20. **devise** understand; imagine.

21. **tender** value.

22. ***Alla stoccata*** at the thrust—an Italian fencing term that Mercutio uses as a nickname for Tybalt.

23. **make bold withal** make bold with; take.

24. **dry-beat** thrash.

25. **pilcher** scabbard.

❼ ✓ Reading Check

From whom is Mercutio protecting Romeo when he draws his sword?

Romeo and Juliet, Act III ■ *785*

❻ Critical Thinking
Infer Cause and Effect

• Point out to students that the confrontation involving Tybalt, Romeo, and Mercutio is made worse because all three characters are acting on incomplete knowledge and false assumptions. **Ask** students what Tybalt thinks Romeo's motive was for coming to the Capulet's party, and what Romeo's real motive was.
    Answer: Tybalt thinks Romeo came to the party to mock the Capulets, but Romeo came only to see Rosaline.

• Point out to students that both Tybalt and Mercutio believe that Romeo is a foe of the Capulets. **Ask** students whether this is still true.
    Answer: Romeo is now married to Juliet; Tybalt is his wife's cousin. Romeo wants no more quarreling with the Capulets.

❼ Reading Check

Answer: Mercutio is protecting Romeo from Tybalt.

Answer: A number of other young men are standing around watching Mercutio and Tybalt fight. Several of them together could easily have stopped the fight.

9 Background
Fencing

When Tybalt, Mercutio, and Romeo fence, they fight to kill. Fencing became a sport only in the late 1700s; today fencers compete at the Olympic Games.

The object of fencing is to touch the opponent with a sword and to avoid being touched. Three different weapons may be used: the *foil,* the *epee,* and the *saber.* These differ in size, weight, and appearance, but all include devices to blunt their points for safety. Fencers wear a strong wire-mesh mask and protective clothing to avoid injury. They must develop precision, speed, timing, and tactical judgment. Many professional actors study and practice fencing for use on the stage.

Have students discuss what a dueling scene adds to a performance. Have them compare and contrast the dueling scenes in *The Tragedy of Romeo and Juliet* with action scenes in contemporary movies, including car chases, shoot-outs, and martial arts sequences.

Hold, Tybalt! Good Mercutio!

[TYBALT *under* ROMEO'S *arm thrusts* MERCUTIO *in, and flies.*]

9 MERCUTIO.   I am hurt.
A plague a[26] both houses! I am sped.[27]
Is he gone and hath nothing?

BENVOLIO.   What, art thou hurt?

90 **MERCUTIO.** Ay, ay, a scratch, a scratch. Marry, 'tis enough.
Where is my page? Go, villain, fetch a surgeon. [*Exit* PAGE.]

ROMEO. Courage, man. The hurt cannot be much.

10 MERCUTIO. No, 'tis not so deep as a well, nor so wide as
a church door; but 'tis enough, 'twill serve. Ask for
95 me tomorrow, and you shall find me a grave man. I
am peppered,[28] I warrant, for this world. A plague o'

8 ▲ Critical Viewing
Which details in this photograph suggest that the duel between Mercutio and Tybalt could have been stopped? [**Analyze**]

26. **a** on.

27. **sped** wounded; done for.

28. **peppered** finished off.

Vocabulary Development

Expressive Vocabulary
As students discuss this scene in which Mercutio and Tybalt are killed, have students use the expressive vocabulary presented earlier. You might encourage them with sentence starters like these:

1. Despite the threat of death, neither Mercutio nor Tybalt would *comply* . . .
2. Romeo's *eloquent* words failed . . .
3. Romeo wanted to avoid the *drastic* . . .
4. Mercutio could not *tolerate* . . .
   Challenge students to use these words as you continue to discuss the play.

both your houses! Zounds, a dog, a rat, a mouse, a
100 cat, to scratch a man to death! A braggart, a rogue,
a villain, that fights by the book of arithmetic![29] Why
the devil came you between us? I was hurt under
your arm.

ROMEO. I thought all for the best.

MERCUTIO. Help me into some house, Benvolio,
Or I shall faint. A plague a both your houses!
105 They have made worms' meat of me. I have it,[30]
And soundly too. Your houses! [*Exit* MERCUTIO *and* BENVOLIO.]

ROMEO. This gentleman, the Prince's near ally,[31]
My very friend, hath got his mortal hurt
In my behalf—my reputation stained
110 With Tybalt's slander—Tybalt, that an hour
Hath been my cousin. O sweet Juliet,
Thy beauty hath made me effeminate
And in my temper soft'ned valor's steel!

[*Enter* BENVOLIO.]

BENVOLIO. O Romeo, Romeo, brave Mercutio is dead!
115 That <u>gallant</u> spirit hath aspired[32] the clouds,
Which too untimely here did scorn the earth.

ROMEO. This day's black fate on moe[33] days doth depend;[34]
This but begins the woe others must end.

[*Enter* TYBALT.]

BENVOLIO. Here comes the furious Tybalt back again.

120 **ROMEO.** Alive in triumph, and Mercutio slain?
Away to heaven respective lenity,[35]
And fire-eyed fury be my conduct[36] now!
Now, Tybalt, take the "villain" back again
That late thou gavest me; for Mercutio's soul
125 Is but a little way above our heads,
Staying for thine to keep him company.
Either thou or I, or both, must go with him.

TYBALT. Thou, wretched boy, that didst consort him here,
Shalt with him hence.

ROMEO.   This shall determine that.
[*They fight.* TYBALT *falls.*]

BENVOLIO. Romeo, away, be gone!

---

29. by . . . arithmetic by formal rules.

Reading Skill
Summarizing Paraphrase Mercutio's line "A plague a both your houses!" and summarize his reasons for uttering this curse.

30. I have it I have got my deathblow.

31. ally relative.

32. aspired climbed to.

Vocabulary Builder
gallant (gal´ ənt) *adj.* brave and noble

33. moe more.

34. depend hang over.

35. respective lenity thoughtful mercy.

36. conduct guide.

11 ✓ **Reading Check**
What is the outcome of the duel between Tybalt and Mercutio?

Romeo and Juliet, Act III ■ 787

---

10 **Reading Skill**
Summarizing

• **Ask** students to read lines 86 through 104. Have them summarize what has happened since Tybalt injured Mercutio.
Answer: Tybalt flees; Mercutio says he is dying and blames Romeo for coming between him and Tybalt; Romeo says he was just trying to help; Mercutio curses the Montagues and Capulets several times; Benvolio carries Mercutio offstage.

• Have students read line 104. **Ask** students to respond to the Reading Skill prompt: Paraphrase Mercutio's line "A plague a both your houses!" and summarize his reasons for uttering this curse.
Possible answer: "Curse the Capulets and the Montagues both." Mercutio is cursing both families, because their feuding has led to his death.

11 **Reading Check**
Answer: When Romeo attempts to come between Tybalt and Mercutio, Tybalt strikes Mercutio under Romeo's arm and kills Mercutio.

Differentiated
Instruction   Solutions for All Learners

Strategy for English Learners
To help students through this long and intense act, lead a quick "selection tour" before they read. Focus their attention on the pictures, the questions in the side margins, and reading check questions. Pay special attention to the footnotes, making sure that they understand the explanations.

Reassure students that it is not necessary to understand every word or every line to under-

stand and appreciate the play. Advise them that if they get stuck on a line or a passage they can't understand even with the footnotes, they should flag it with a sticky note, and then keep reading. After they complete reading the act, review the questions they have marked with the sticky notes.

⓬ Critical Thinking

Interpret

- Have students read lines 130–134. **Ask** students what urgent warning Benvolio is giving to Romeo in these lines.
  Answer: Benvolio is telling Romeo to stop standing around staring. He wants Romeo to flee.

- Have students explain why Benvolio is so concerned.
  Answer: If Romeo is present when the Prince arrives, Romeo will be condemned to death for fighting, according to the Prince's order earlier.

⓭ Critical Viewing

Answer: The bystanders seem shocked and horrified at Tybalt's slaying.

The citizens are up, and Tybalt slain.
Stand not amazed. The Prince will doom thee death
If thou art taken. Hence, be gone, away!

⓬ **ROMEO.** O, I am fortune's fool!³⁷

BENVOLIO.   Why dost thou stay?
                                        [*Exit* ROMEO.]

[*Enter* CITIZENS.]

135 **CITIZEN.** Which way ran he that killed Mercutio?
Tybalt, that murderer, which way ran he?

BENVOLIO. There lies that Tybalt.

CITIZEN.   Up, sir, go with me.
I charge thee in the Prince's name obey.

[*Enter* PRINCE, OLD MONTAGUE, CAPULET, *their* WIVES, *and all.*]

PRINCE. Where are the vile beginners of this <u>fray</u>?

140 **BENVOLIO.** O noble Prince, I can discover³⁸ all
The unlucky manage³⁹ of this fatal brawl.

37. **fool** plaything.

Vocabulary Builder
fray (frā) *n.* noisy fight

38. **discover** reveal.

39. **manage** course.

⓭ ▼ **Critical Viewing**
Based on this photograph, how would you describe bystanders' reactions to Romeo's slaying of Tybalt? **[Infer]**

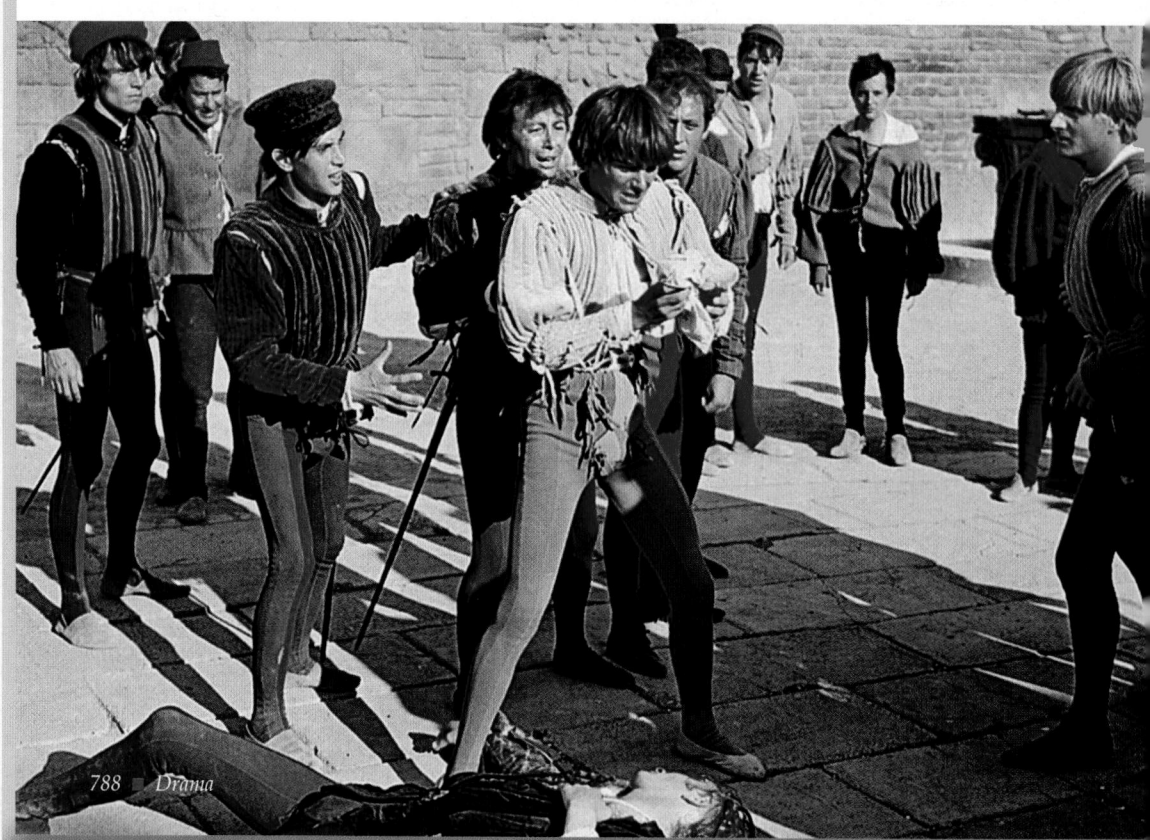

788 ■ *Drama*

There lies the man, slain by young Romeo,
That slew thy kinsman, brave Mercutio.

LADY CAPULET. Tybalt, my cousin! O my brother's child!
145   O Prince! O cousin! Husband! O, the blood is spilled
Of my dear kinsman! Prince, as thou art true,
For blood of ours shed blood of Montague.
O cousin, cousin!

PRINCE. Benvolio, who began this bloody fray?

150 **BENVOLIO.** Tybalt, here slain, whom Romeo's hand did slay.
Romeo, that spoke him fair, bid him bethink
How nice[40] the quarrel was, and urged withal
Your high displeasure. All this—utterèd
With gentle breath, calm look, knees humbly bowed—
155   Could not take truce with the unruly spleen[41]
Of Tybalt deaf to peace, but that he tilts[42]
With piercing steel at bold Mercutio's breast;
Who, all as hot, turns deadly point to point,
And, with a <u>martial</u> scorn, with one hand beats
160   Cold death aside and with the other sends
14 It back to Tybalt, whose dexterity
Retorts it. Romeo he cries aloud,
"Hold, friends! Friends, part!" and swifter than his tongue,
His agile arm beats down their fatal points,
165   And 'twixt them rushes; underneath whose arm
An envious[43] thrust from Tybalt hit the life
Of stout Mercutio, and then Tybalt fled;
But by and by comes back to Romeo,
Who had but newly entertained[44] revenge,
170   And to't they go like lightning; for, ere I
Could draw to part them, was stout Tybalt slain;
And, as he fell, did Romeo turn and fly.
This is the truth, or let Benvolio die.

LADY CAPULET. He is a kinsman to the Montague;
175   Affection makes him false, he speaks not true.
Some twenty of them fought in this black strife,
And all those twenty could but kill one life.
I beg for justice, which thou, Prince, must give.
Romeo slew Tybalt; Romeo must not live.

180 **PRINCE.** Romeo slew him; he slew Mercutio.
Who now the price of his dear blood doth owe?

16 **MONTAGUE.** Not Romeo, Prince; he was Mercutio's friend;

---

40. **nice** trivial.

41. **spleen** angry nature.
42. **tilts** thrusts.

Vocabulary Builder
martial (mär′ shəl) *adj.*
military

Literary Analysis
Dramatic Speeches
Which details of
Benvolio's speech
suggest that he is
trying to portray
Romeo favorably?

43. **envious** full of hatred.

44. **entertained** considered.

✓ **Reading Check**
What makes Lady
Capulet distrust
Benvolio's account of
the brawl?

Romeo and Juliet, Act III ■ *789*

---

14 **Literary Analysis**
Dramatic Speeches

- **Ask** students whether Benvolio's speech on p. 789 is a soliloquy or a monologue. Why?
  Answer: Benvolio's speech is a monologue. He delivers it to the Prince, and other characters listen.

- **Ask** students whether Benvolio's monologue describing the fight is factual or biased. How do you know?
  Answer: His description is basically factual, though his adjectives slyly favor Mercutio, the Prince's relative.

- **Ask** students to respond to the Literary Analysis question: Which details of Benvolio's speech suggest that he is trying to portray Romeo favorably?
  Possible response: Benvolio says that Romeo was reasonable and tried to avoid the fight. When Tybalt and Mercutio began to fight, Romeo attempted to stop it, placing himself between the two. After Tybalt killed Mercutio he fled, but came back to fight Romeo, who was by then angry at his friend's death.

15 **Reading Check**
Answer: Lady Montague distrusts Benvolio's account because he is Romeo's kinsman.

Differentiated Instruction   Solutions for All Learners

Enrichment for Advanced Readers
Tell students that some critics have argued that Shakespeare kills off Mercutio so early in the play because the lively, exuberant character of Mercutio makes Romeo pale in comparison.

Another critic argues that Mercutio becomes irrelevant once Juliet and Romeo fall profoundly in love. Mercutio has no place in the play once it becomes dominated by the love between Romeo and Juliet.

Have students form small groups to discuss these questions: Was Mercutio killed off because he was more interesting than Romeo? If Shakespeare had not killed him off early in the drama, what role might he have continued to play? If Mercutio had not been killed by Tybalt, would Romeo have killed Tybalt?

By discussing these questions, students may more clearly appreciate the genius of Shakespeare in destroying one of the most interesting and vibrant characters in the play.

Interpret

- Have students read lines 180–195. Remind students what the Prince had decreed earlier about street fighting. **Ask** students what "the price of his dear blood" might be. **Answer:** The price would be Romeo's life.

- **Ask** why Montague pleads for Romeo's life. **Answer:** Montague is Romeo's father.

- **Ask** what sentence the Prince pronounces for Romeo and what warning he gives Montague. **Answer:** He exiles Romeo and warns Montague that no pleading will make him change his mind; if Romeo is found in the city he will pay with his life.

17 **Literary Analysis**

Dramatic Speeches

- **Ask** students what information the stage directions provide for Scene ii. **Answer:** Scene ii is set in Capulet's orchard. Juliet enters alone.

- **Ask** students to respond to the Literary Analysis question: How can you tell that Juliet's speech is a soliloquy? **Answer:** The speech is a soliloquy because Juliet is alone on stage and expresses her thoughts in a lengthy speech to the audience. Moreover, even though an aside is also spoken directly to the audience, it is very short.

- **Ask** students what the audience learns from this soliloquy about what Juliet wants to happen and about her feelings. **Answer:** The audience learns that Juliet is impatient for the night to come, so that she can be with her husband on their wedding night. The audience learns that Juliet is both passionate and modest.

His fault concludes but what the law should end,
The life of Tybalt.[45]

185 **PRINCE.** And for that offense
Immediately we do <u>exile</u> him hence.
I have an interest in your hate's proceeding.
My blood[46] for your rude brawls doth lie a-bleeding;
But I'll amerce[47] you with so strong a fine
190 That you shall all repent the loss of mine.
I will be deaf to pleading and excuses;
Nor tears nor prayers shall purchase out abuses.
Therefore use none. Let Romeo hence in haste,
Else, when he is found, that hour is his last.
195 Bear hence this body and attend our will.[48]
Mercy but murders, pardoning those that kill.

[*Exit with others.*]

Scene ii. CAPULET'S *orchard.*

[*Enter* JULIET *alone.*]

JULIET. Gallop apace, you fiery-footed steeds,[1]
Towards Phoebus' lodging![2] Such a wagoner
As Phaëton[3] would whip you to the west
And bring in cloudy night immediately.
5 Spread thy close curtain, love-performing night,
That runaways' eyes may wink,[4] and Romeo
Leap to these arms untalked of and unseen.
Lovers can see to do their amorous rites,
And by their own beauties; or, if love be blind,
10 It best agrees with night. Come, civil night,
Thou sober-suited matron all in black,
And learn me how to lose a winning match,
Played for a pair of stainless maidenhoods.
Hood my unmanned blood, bating in my cheeks,[5]
15 With thy black mantle till strange[6] love grow bold,
Think true love acted simple modesty,
Come, night; come, Romeo; come, thou day in night;
For thou wilt lie upon the wings of night
Whiter than new snow upon a raven's back.
20 Come, gentle night; come, loving, black-browed night;
Give me my Romeo; and when I shall die,
Take him and cut him out in little stars,
And he will make the face of heaven so fine
That all the world will be in love with night
25 And pay no worship to the garish sun.

790 ■ *Drama*

---

45. His fault . . . Tybalt by killing Tybalt, he did what the law would have done.

Vocabulary Builder
exile (ek´ sīl´) *v.* banish

46. My blood Mercutio was related to the Prince.
47. amerce punish.

48. attend our will await my decision.

1. fiery-footed steeds horses of the sun god, Phoebus.

2. Phoebus' lodging below the horizon.

Literary Analysis
Dramatic Speeches
How can you tell that Juliet's speech is a soliloquy?

3. Phaëton Phoebus' son, who tried to drive his father's horses but was unable to control them.

4. That runaways' eyes may wink so that the eyes of busybodies may not see.

5. Hood . . . cheeks hide the untamed blood that makes me blush.

6. strange unfamiliar.

Vocabulary Development

Multiple Meanings

Refer students to the word *civil* in Scene ii, line 10. Tell students that in this line the word *civil* is used in its obsolete sense of "somber; not gaudy or showy," a definition that was usually applied to clothing. Today, one use of the word *civil* reflects a related older meaning: "refraining from being rude," as in "keep a civil tongue."

Tell students that today, however, the most common use of the word *civil* is in its meanings related to citizens, cities, law, and government, and it is used in many common phrases. Write the following phrases on the chalkboard:

civil rights, civil servant; civil engineer, civil war, civil defense, civil disobedience, civil marriage

Ask students to choose two of these phrases and use the dictionary to find their definitions. Then explain what meaning of the word *civil* is reflected in each phrase.

Mythology Connection

Cockatrice In a play on words, Juliet links "Ay" with the dangerous "eye" of a cockatrice (Act III, scene ii, line 47). The cockatrice is a serpent that, according to myth, could kill with a look or transform people into stone. The creature resembles a snake with the head and yellow feathers of a rooster. It feared the song of the rooster and its own reflection in a mirror.

Connect to the Literature

How does Juliet's allusion to a cockatrice reinforce the nature of her conversation with the Nurse?

> O, I have bought the mansion of a love,
> But not possessed it; and though I am sold,
> Not yet enjoyed. So tedious is this day
> As is the night before some festival
> 30 To an impatient child that hath new robes
> And may not wear them. O, here comes my nurse,
>
> [*Enter* NURSE, *with cords.*]
>
> And she brings news; and every tongue that speaks
> But Romeo's name speaks heavenly <u>eloquence</u>.
> Now, nurse, what news? What hast thou there, the cords
> That Romeo bid thee fetch?
>
> 35 **NURSE.**   Ay, ay, the cords.
>
> **JULIET.** Ay me! What news? Why dost thou wring thy hands?
>
> **NURSE.** Ah, weraday![7] He's dead, he's dead, he's dead!
> We are undone, lady, we are undone!
> Alack the day! He's gone, he's killed, he's dead!
>
> **JULIET.** Can heaven be so envious?
>
> 40 **NURSE.**   Romeo can,
> Though heaven cannot. O Romeo, Romeo!
> Who ever would have thought it? Romeo!
>
> **JULIET.** What devil art thou that dost torment me thus?
> This torture should be roared in dismal hell.
> 45 Hath Romeo slain himself? Say thou but "Ay,"
> And that bare vowel "I" shall poison more
> Than the death-darting eye of cockatrice.

Vocabulary Builder
eloquence (el´ ə kwəns) *n.* speech that is graceful and persuasive

7. **Ah, weraday!** alas!

Reading Check
❶⓮ What punishment does the Prince order for Romeo?

Romeo and Juliet, Act III ■ 791

⓭ Literature in Context

Mythology Connection According to legend, the cockatrice is hatched from the egg of a rooster brooded by a toad or a serpent. A similar creature is the basilisk, which also possessed a lethal glance—and therefore also had a deadly fear of mirrors. Both creatures appear as literary allusions in Shakespeare's plays and other classic literature.

Connect to the Literature
Remind students that Juliet is beside herself with anguish. The Nurse has said only Romeo's name, and has not mentioned Tybalt.

Ask the students the Connect to the Literature question on p. 791: How does Juliet's allusion to a cockatrice reinforce the tone of her conversation with the Nurse?
Answer: Juliet's reference to the deadly creature intensifies the frantic grief that she is expressing.

⓮ Reading Check

Answer: The Prince orders exile as a punishment for Romeo.

Enrichment for Gifted/Talented Students
Help students appreciate the beauty of Shakespeare's poetry by referring them to Scene ii, lines 17–25. Have them write out the lines on a separate sheet, and read the lines aloud. Ask them to explain the metaphor in lines 17–19.
Answer: Romeo is the brightness in the night; the night is black as a raven, and Romeo is the brightness in it, as white as snow against the black of night.

Have students notice the repetition of the word *night*. Ask them to point out other words

with the *i* sound in this passage and explain the effect of these *i* sounds.
Answer: Other *i* words include *lie, whiter, I, die, fine.* These words help create a smooth, flowing sound.

Point out the jarring effect line 25 has on the ear after the previous smooth, flowing lines. Ask students how this jarring sound is in keeping with the sense or meaning of the line.
Answer: The jarring sound reflects the unfavorable comparison of the "garish sun" to the "loving" night.

- Have students read lines 73–84. **Ask** how Juliet's attitude changes abruptly in line 73.
  Answer: She goes from being in anguish, believing that Romeo is dead, to being angry and even hateful toward Romeo when she learns that he has killed her dear cousin Tybalt.

- Have students **identify** some of the opposites Juliet uses to demonstrate her conflicted feelings about Romeo.
  Possible response: Opposites include: "Beautiful tyrant!" "Fiend angelical!" "Dove-feathered raven!" "Wolvish-ravening lamb."

- **Ask** students to respond to the Reading Skill prompt: Briefly summarize Juliet's remarks about Romeo in lines 73–85.
  Answer: Juliet says that Romeo is the opposite of what he appears. He seems to be beautiful, kind, and honorable, but he is truly hateful and deceitful.

I am not I, if there be such an "Ay,"[8]
Or those eyes' shot[9] that makes thee answer "Ay."
50 If he be slain, say "Ay"; or if not, "No."
Brief sounds determine of my weal or woe.

NURSE. I saw the wound, I saw it with mine eyes,
(God save the mark![10]) here on his manly breast.
A piteous corse,[11] a bloody piteous corse;
55 Pale, pale as ashes, all bedaubed in blood,
All in gore-blood. I sounded[12] at the sight.

JULIET. O, break, my heart! Poor bankrout,[13] break at once!
To prison, eyes; ne'er look on liberty!
Vile earth, to earth resign;[14] end motion here,
60 And thou and Romeo press one heavy bier![15]

NURSE. O Tybalt, Tybalt, the best friend I had!
O courteous Tybalt! Honest gentleman!
That ever I should live to see thee dead!

JULIET. What storm is this that blows so contrary?[16]
65 Is Romeo slaught'red, and is Tybalt dead?
My dearest cousin, and my dearer lord?
Then, dreadful trumpet, sound the general doom![17]
For who is living, if those two are gone?

NURSE. Tybalt is gone, and Romeo banishèd;
70 Romeo that killed him, he is banishèd.

JULIET. O God! Did Romeo's hand shed Tybalt's blood?

NURSE. It did, it did! Alas the day, it did!

JULIET. O serpent heart, hid with a flow'ring face!
Did ever dragon keep so fair a cave?
75 Beautiful tyrant! Fiend angelical!
Dove-feathered raven! Wolvish-ravening lamb!
Despisèd substance of divinest show!
Just opposite to what thou justly seem'st—
⑳ A damnèd saint, an honorable villain!
80 O nature, what hadst thou to do in hell
When thou didst bower the spirit of a fiend
In mortal paradise of such sweet flesh?
Was ever book containing such vile matter
So fairly bound? O, that deceit should dwell
In such a gorgeous palace!

85 **NURSE.**   There's no trust,
No faith, no honesty in men; all perjured,

---

8. **"Ay"** yes.

9. **eyes' shot** the Nurse's glance.

10. **God save the mark!** May God save us from evil!

11. **corse** corpse.

12. **sounded** swooned; fainted.

13. **bankrout** bankrupt.

14. **Vile . . . resign** let my body return to the earth.

15. **bier** platform on which a corpse is displayed before burial.

16. **contrary** in opposite directions.

17. **dreadful . . . doom** let the trumpet that announces doomsday be sounded.

Reading Skill
Summarizing Briefly summarize Juliet's remarks about Romeo in lines 73–85.

Vocabulary Development

Vocabulary Builder Reinforcement
To reinforce and assess students' comprehension of Vocabulary Builder words, give them sentences using the words in which the word may or may not be used correctly. Students must tell whether the use is correct and explain their answer. Use these sentences:

1. He was hoping that the judge would *exile* him so he would not have to leave.
   Answer: No. To be *exiled* means a person is banished from a place and must leave it.

2. Her *eloquence* was so remarkable that the audience got up and left.
   Answer: No. *Eloquence* is graceful and persuasive speech, which would hold an audience's interest.

3. Her *fickle* behavior toward her friends made everyone love her.
   Answer: No. If a person is fickle, she is changeable, which would make it difficult for her to keep friends.

All forsworn,[18] all naught, all dissemblers.[19]
Ah, where's my man? Give me some aqua vitae.[20]
These griefs, these woes, these sorrows make me old.
Shame come to Romeo!

90 **JULIET.** Blistered be thy tongue
For such a wish! He was not born to shame.
Upon his brow shame is ashamed to sit;
For 'tis a throne where honor may be crowned
Sole monarch of the universal earth.
95 O, what a beast was I to chide at him!

NURSE. Will you speak well of him that killed your cousin?

JULIET. Shall I speak ill of him that is my husband?
Ah, poor my lord, what tongue shall smooth thy name
When I, thy three-hours wife, have mangled it?
100 But wherefore, villain, didst thou kill my cousin?
That villain cousin would have killed my husband.
Back, foolish tears, back to your native spring!
Your tributary[21] drops belong to woe,
Which you, mistaking, offer up to joy.
105 My husband lives, that Tybalt would have slain;
And Tybalt's dead, that would have slain my husband.
All this is comfort; wherefore weep I then?
Some word there was, worser than Tybalt's death,
That murd'red me. I would forget it fain;
110 But O, it presses to my memory
Like damnèd guilty deeds to sinners' minds!
"Tybalt is dead, and Romeo—banishèd."
That "banishèd," that one word "banishèd,"
Hath slain ten thousand Tybalts. Tybalt's death
115 Was woe enough, if it had ended there;
Or, if sour woe delights in fellowship
And needly will be ranked with[22] other griefs,
Why followed not, when she said "Tybalt's dead,"
Thy father, or thy mother, nay, or both,
120 Which modern[23] lamentation might have moved?
But with a rearward[24] following Tybalt's death,
"Romeo is banishèd"—to speak that word
Is father, mother, Tybalt, Romeo, Juliet,
All slain, all dead. "Romeo is banishèd"—
125 There is no end, no limit, measure, bound,
In that word's death; no words can that woe sound.
Where is my father and my mother, nurse?

18. **forsworn** are liars.

19. **dissemblers** hypocrites.

20. **aqua vitae** brandy.

21. **tributary** in tribute.

Literary Analysis
Dramatic Speeches
What makes this
speech a monologue
but not a soliloquy?

22. **needly . . . with** must be accompanied by.

23. **modern** ordinary.

24. **rearward** follow up; literally, a rear guard.

 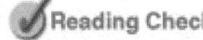 **Reading Check**

What is Juliet's initial
reaction to Romeo's
involvement in Tybalt's
death?

Romeo and Juliet, Act III ■ 793

㉑ Literary Analysis
Dramatic Speeches

• **Ask** students why they think Juliet first condemns Romeo for killing Tybalt and then changes her mind. **Possible response:** Juliet responds to the news first in terms of thinking about her family. Tybalt is her cousin and she condemns Romeo for killing him. Then, she realizes that she is Romeo's family now, and that Tybalt would have killed Romeo if he had had the chance.

• **Ask** students to respond to the Literary Analysis question: What makes this speech a monologue but not a soliloquy? **Answer:** Juliet's speech is not a soliloquy because she is not alone and does not deliver her words to the audience, but to her Nurse.

• Point out that although Juliet is delivering her words to her Nurse, she is really addressing someone else. **Ask** students whom she is addressing. How can they tell? **Answer:** Beginning in line 98 Juliet is addressing Romeo. She refers to "thy name," and "thy three-hours wife," and "thou kill my cousin." She is also addressing herself. In line 102 she speaks to her tears, "Back, foolish tears." In line 118, Juliet refers to the Nurse as "she"— "when she said"—indicating that she is addressing someone other than the Nurse, that is, herself.

▶ **Monitor Progress:** Use students' responses to these questions to monitor their understanding of dramatic speeches.

▶ **Reteach:** If students have difficulty identifying dramatic speeches, review the discussion on Build Skills p. 782. In addition, have them read aloud Juliet's speech, beginning at line 90. By hearing the speech, they may be better able to understand with whom Juliet is speaking.

㉒ Reading Check

Answer: Juliet is angry and reviles Romeo for killing Tybalt, calling Romeo a beautiful deceiver.

Differentiated
Instruction Solutions for All Learners

Strategy for Special Needs Students.
Tell students that in this act there has been one important soliloquy on p. 790 and an important monologue on p. 793.

Tell students that a key to identifying a dramatic speech is to look for a long block of text with only one speaker. Once they have identified that a passage is a dramatic speech, they should look at the surrounding stage directions to tell whether or not the character is alone on stage. Remind students that in a soliloquy, the speaker *is* alone. In a monologue, other characters are present.

Point out on p. 790 the lines in the text where Juliet enters the stage "alone," indicating that the following long block of text is a soliloquy. Point out on p. 791 the stage direction indicating the Nurse enters. This signals the end of the soliloquy. Refer them to p. 793, line 97, where Juliet begins to speak. Have students note that in line 96, Nurse addresses a question to Juliet, a sign that Juliet is not alone and that the following long speech is a monologue.

793

NURSE. Weeping and wailing over Tybalt's corse.
Will you go to them? I will bring you thither.

130 **JULIET.** Wash they his wounds with tears? Mine shall be spent,
When theirs are dry, for Romeo's banishment.
Take up those cords. Poor ropes, you are beguiled,
Both you and I, for Romeo is exiled.
He made you for a highway to my bed;
135 But I, a maid, die maiden-widowèd.
Come, cords; come, nurse. I'll to my wedding bed;
And death, not Romeo, take my maidenhead!

NURSE. Hie to your chamber. I'll find Romeo
To comfort you. I wot[25] well where he is.
140 Hark ye, your Romeo will be here at night.
I'll to him; he is hid at Lawrence' cell.

JULIET. O, find him! Give this ring to my true knight
And bid him come to take his last farewell. [*Exit* with NURSE]

Scene iii. Friar Lawrence's cell.

[*Enter* FRIAR LAWRENCE.]

FRIAR. Romeo, come forth; come forth, thou fearful man.
Affliction is enamored of thy parts,[1]
And thou art wedded to calamity.

23 ▲ Critical Viewing
How does Romeo's expression in this picture compare to your impression of him as you read?
[Compare and Contrast]

25. **wot** know.

1. **Affliction . . . parts** misery is in love with your attractive qualities.

[*Enter* ROMEO.]

ROMEO. Father, what news? What is the Prince's doom?[2]

5 What sorrow craves acquaintance at my hand
That I yet know not?

FRIAR.   Too familiar
Is my dear son with such sour company.
I bring thee tidings of the Prince's doom.

ROMEO. What less than doomsday[3] is the Prince's doom?

10 **FRIAR.** A gentler judgment vanished[4] from his lips—
Not body's death, but body's banishment.

ROMEO. Ha, banishment? Be merciful, say "death";
For exile hath more terror in his look,
Much more than death. Do not say "banishment."

15 **FRIAR.** Here from Verona art thou banishèd.
Be patient, for the world is broad and wide.

ROMEO. There is no world without[5] Verona walls,
But purgatory, torture, hell itself.
Hence banishèd is banished from the world,
20 And world's exile is death. Then "banishèd"
Is death mistermed. Calling death "banishèd,"
Thou cut'st my head off with a golden ax
And smilest upon the stroke that murders me.

FRIAR. O deadly sin! O rude unthankfulness!
25 Thy fault our law calls death;[6] but the kind Prince,
Taking thy part, hath rushed[7] aside the law,
And turned that black word "death" to "banishment."
This is dear mercy, and thou seest it not.

ROMEO. 'Tis torture, and not mercy. Heaven is here,
30 Where Juliet lives; and every cat and dog
And little mouse, every unworthy thing,
Live here in heaven and may look on her;
But Romeo may not. More validity,[8]
More honorable state, more courtship lives
35 In carrion flies than Romeo. They may seize
On the white wonder of dear Juliet's hand
And steal immortal blessing from her lips,
Who, even in pure and vestal modesty,
Still blush, as thinking their own kisses sin;
40 But Romeo may not, he is banishèd.
Flies may do this but I from this must fly;
They are freemen, but I am banishèd.

25

2. **doom** final decision.

3. **doomsday** my death.

4. **vanished** escaped; came forth.

5. **without** outside.

6. **Thy fault . . . death** for what you did our law demands the death penalty.

7. **rushed** pushed.

Reading Skill
Summarizing
Paraphrase Romeo's complaint in lines 29–33, and then summarize his reaction to his banishment.

8. **validity** value.

 26 **Reading Check**

What punishment does the Friar say Romeo could have received for his crime?

Romeo and Juliet, Act III ■ 795

㉕ Reading Skill
Summarizing

- Ask students how Romeo describes banishment to the Friar.
  Answer: Romeo compares banishment to death.

- Have students explain how the Friar attempts in lines 10–11, 15–16, and 27–28, to comfort Romeo in the face of his banishment.
  Possible response: The Friar tells Romeo that he is not being put to death but only banished from Verona. He tells Romeo that the Prince has shown mercy, though Romeo cannot see this.

- **Ask** students to respond to the Reading Skill item on p. 795: Paraphrase Romeo's complaint in lines 29–33, and then summarize his reaction to his banishment.
  Answer: "It is not merciful to send me away. My only heaven is here with Juliet. Here everything that lives and moves can be in Juliet's presence, whether it is worthy or not. But I cannot see her."
  Summary: Banishment is not merciful, because I cannot be with Juliet.

㉖ Reading Check

Answer: The Friar reminds Romeo that the Prince could have put Romeo to death.

Differentiated Instruction
Solutions for All Learners

Strategy for Less Proficient Readers
Help students understand Romeo's behavior in this scene by having them use the *Reader's Notebook: Adapted Version* and listening to **Adapted Reader's Notebook Audio CD.** Ask students to describe how Romeo sounds in this scene. **Answer:** Students may suggest that Romeo sounds distraught and in despair.

Point out that Romeo has thrown himself on the ground. (See line 83 on p. 797 in which the Friar tells the Nurse that Romeo is on the ground "with his own tears made drunk." The Nurse then tells him to "Stand up, stand up!"

and "Stand, and you be a man.") Remind students that Romeo attempts to kill himself in front of the Friar and the Nurse, and the Friar chides him for being womanish and beastly.

Then lead a discussion group addressing these questions:

- Is Romeo overreacting or reacting appropriately to his situation?
- Do you agree with the Friar that Romeo is acting "womanish"?

795

Remind students of earlier passages in the play in which readers are given suggestions as to what will ultimately happen—for example, Romeo and Juliet mutually sense that something will doom their love. Then, point out the foreshadowing in Romeo's monologue beginning on p. 795 in which he asks the Friar to give him some way to kill himself rather than leave Juliet.

Ask students to keep this scene in mind as they complete the play. The references to *poison* and to *knife* in line 44 are significant.

㉘ Reading Skill
Summarizing

• **Ask** students what the Friar suggests to Romeo as a possible comfort to the young man.
Answer: The Friar suggests that an armor for Romeo to use against the hated idea of banishment is philosophy.

• **Ask** students to respond to the Reading Skill prompt: Summarize Romeo's ideas in lines 57–60. What do they suggest about his state of mind?
Answer: Romeo says that philosophy is useless unless it can make a Juliet, move a town, and reverse a Prince's order. It is no help, and he doesn't want to hear any more about it. These words suggest that Romeo is overcome by emotion and cannot listen to reason.

㉗
And sayest thou yet that exile is not death?
Hadst thou no poison mixed, no sharp-ground knife,
45 No sudden mean[9] of death, though ne'er so mean,[10]
But "banishèd" to kill me—"banishèd"?
㉕ O friar, the damnèd use that word in hell;
Howling attends it! How hast thou the heart,
Being a divine, a ghostly confessor,
50 A sin-absolver, and my friend professed,
To mangle me with that word "banishèd"?

FRIAR. Thou fond mad man, hear me a little speak.

ROMEO. O, thou wilt speak again of banishment.

FRIAR. I'll give thee armor to keep off that word;
55 Adversity's sweet milk, philosophy,
To comfort thee, though thou art banishèd.

ROMEO. Yet "banishèd"? Hang up philosophy!
㉘ Unless philosophy can make a Juliet,
Displant a town, reverse a prince's doom,
60 It helps not, it prevails not. Talk no more.

FRIAR. O, then I see that madmen have no ears.

ROMEO. How should they, when that wise men have no eyes?

FRIAR. Let me dispute[11] with thee of thy estate.[12]

ROMEO. Thou canst not speak of that thou dost not feel.
65 Wert thou as young as I, Juliet thy love,
An hour but married, Tybalt murderèd,
Doting like me, and like me banishèd,
Then mightst thou speak, then mightst thou tear thy hair,
And fall upon the ground, as I do now,
70 Taking the measure of an unmade grave.

[*Knock.*]

FRIAR. Arise, one knocks. Good Romeo, hide thyself.

ROMEO. Not I; unless the breath of heartsick groans
Mistlike infold me from the search of eyes. [*Knock.*]

FRIAR. Hark, how they knock! Who's there? Romeo, arise;
75 Thou wilt be taken.—Stay awhile!—Stand up; [*Knock.*]
Run to my study.—By and by![13]—God's will,
What simpleness[14] is this.—I come, I come! [*Knock.*]
Who knocks so hard? Whence come you? What's your will?

[*Enter* NURSE.]

NURSE. Let me come in, and you shall know my errand.

9. mean method.

10. mean humiliating.

Reading Skill
Summarizing
Summarize Romeo's ideas in lines 57–60. What do they suggest about his state of mind?

11. dispute discuss.

12. estate condition; situation.

13. By and by! In a minute! (said to the person knocking).

14. simpleness silly behavior (Romeo does not move).

Vocabulary Development

Expressive Vocabulary
To reinforce students' use of the expressive vocabulary, have them use words in sentences about the scene between Romeo and the Friar. Use these sentence starters:
1. Although he hates the thought, Romeo will be forced to *comply* . . .
2. Romeo suggests a *drastic* plan to . . .
3. Romeo makes an *eloquent* . . .
4. Romeo cannot *tolerate* . . .

I come from Lady Juliet.

80 **FRIAR.** Welcome then.

NURSE. O holy friar, O, tell me, holy friar,
  Where is my lady's lord, where's Romeo?

FRIAR. There on the ground, with his own tears made drunk.

NURSE. O, he is even in my mistress' case,
85   Just in her case! O woeful sympathy!
  Piteous predicament! Even so lies she,
  Blubb'ring and weeping, weeping and blubb'ring.
  Stand up, stand up! Stand, and you be a man.
  For Juliet's sake, for her sake, rise and stand!
90   Why should you fall into so deep an O?[15]

ROMEO. [*Rises.*] Nurse—

NURSE. Ah sir, ah sir! Death's the end of all.

ROMEO. Spakest thou of Juliet? How is it with her?
  Doth not she think me an old murderer,
95   Now I have stained the childhood of our joy
  With blood removed but little from her own?
  Where is she? And how doth she? And what says
  My concealed lady[16] to our canceled love?

NURSE. O, she says nothing, sir, but weeps and weeps;
100   And now falls on her bed, and then starts up,
  And Tybalt calls; and then on Romeo cries,
  And then down falls again.

ROMEO. As if that name,
  Shot from the deadly level[17] of a gun,
  Did murder her; as that name's cursèd hand
105   Murdered her kinsman. O, tell me, friar, tell me,
  In what vile part of this anatomy
  Doth my name lodge? Tell me, that I may sack[18]
  The hateful mansion.

[*He offers to stab himself, and* NURSE *snatches the dagger away.*]

FRIAR. Hold thy desperate hand.
  Art thou a man? Thy form cries out thou art;
110   Thy tears are womanish, thy wild acts denote
  The unreasonable fury of a beast.
  Unseemly[19] woman in a seeming man!
  And ill-beseeming beast in seeming both![20]
  Thou hast amazed me. By my holy order,
115   I thought thy disposition better tempered.

Literary Analysis
Dramatic Speeches
What does this brief speech by the Nurse reveal about her relationship with Romeo?

15. O cry of grief.

16. concealed lady secret bride.

17. level aim.

18. sack plunder.

19. Unseemly inappropriate (because unnatural).

20. And . . . both! Romeo has inappropriately lost his human nature because he seems like a man and woman combined.

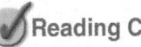 **Reading Check**

What does Romeo nearly do before the Nurse stops him?

Romeo and Juliet, Act III ■ *797*

Literary Analysis
Dramatic Speeches
• Have students read lines 84–90. **Ask** students what the Nurse is scolding Romeo about. **Answer:** She is scolding him for weeping and crying, saying he should stand up like a man for Juliet's sake.
• **Ask** students to respond to the Literary Analysis question: What does this brief speech by the Nurse reveal about her relationship with Romeo?
Possible response: It reveals that she thinks of him as a child, just as she does Juliet, and she feels sympathy for him, even though she scolds him.

Reading Check
Answer: Romeo nearly stabs himself.

- Have students read the Friar's monologue beginning at line 108 on p. 797. **Ask** students why the Friar scolds Romeo in lines 108–114. What does he accuse Romeo of being?
Answer: He scolds Romeo for attempting to kill himself. He calls him womanish and a beast.

- **Ask** students to what the Friar compares Romeo's mind in lines 130–134.
Answer: He compares Romeo's mind to a flask of gunpowder in an untrained soldier's hand, which is ignited through the soldier's own ignorance and blows him up.

- **Ask** students what reasons the Friar gives Romeo for being happy in his situation.
Answer: He tells Romeo that he should be happy because Juliet is alive, Tybalt would have killed him if he had not killed Tybalt first, and he received a sentence of exile instead of death.

- **Ask** students what plan the Friar puts forward in lines 146–154 to resolve Romeo's unhappiness.
Answer: He tells Romeo to go to Juliet, but to leave her before dawn so that he can leave the city without being seen. He is to go to the city of Mantua, where he should stay until the Friar informs his family of the marriage and gains a pardon from the Prince, at which time he will return to Verona with joy much greater than was his sorrow at leaving.

- **Ask** students to respond to the Reading Skill prompt: Briefly state the main points of the Friar's speech to Romeo.
Answer: The Friar says that Romeo is acting womanish and like a beast in trying to kill himself. He is being irrational, and he should pull himself together and think of the things he has to be thankful for. He should go to Juliet for the night, and then leave for Mantua, and meanwhile the Friar will announce their wedding and reconcile his family and the Prince, and he can then return to Verona.

Hast thou slain Tybalt? Wilt thou slay thyself?
And slay thy lady that in thy life lives,
By doing damnèd hate upon thyself?
Why railest thou on thy birth, the heaven, and earth?
120 Since birth and heaven and earth, all three do meet
In thee at once; which thou at once wouldst lose.
Fie, fie, thou shamest thy shape, thy love, thy wit,[21]
Which, like a usurer,[22] abound'st in all,
And usest none in that true use indeed
125 Which should bedeck[23] thy shape, thy love, thy wit.
Thy noble shape is but a form of wax,
Digressing from the valor of a man;
Thy dear love sworn but hollow perjury,
Killing that love which thou hast vowed to cherish;
130 Thy wit, that ornament to shape and love,
Misshapen in the conduct[24] of them both,
Like powder in a skilless soldier's flask,[25]
Is set afire by thine own ignorance,
And thou dismemb'red with thine own defense.[26]
135 What, rouse thee, man! Thy Juliet is alive,
For whose dear sake thou wast but lately dead.[27]
㉛ There art thou happy.[28] Tybalt would kill thee,
But thou slewest Tybalt. There art thou happy.
The law, that threat'ned death, becomes thy friend
140 And turns it to exile. There art thou happy.
A pack of blessings light upon thy back;
Happiness courts thee in her best array;
But, like a misbehaved and sullen wench,[29]
Thou puts up[30] thy fortune and thy love.
145 Take heed, take heed, for such die miserable.
Go get thee to thy love, as was decreed,
Ascend her chamber, hence and comfort her.
But look thou stay not till the watch be set,[31]
For then thou canst not pass to Mantua,
150 Where thou shalt live till we can find a time
To blaze[32] your marriage, reconcile your friends,
Beg pardon of the Prince, and call thee back
With twenty hundred thousand times more joy
Than thou went'st forth in lamentation.
155 Go before, nurse. Commend me to thy lady,
And bid her hasten all the house to bed,
Which heavy sorrow makes them apt unto.[33]
Romeo is coming.

21. wit mind; intellect.

22. Which, like a usurer who, like a rich money-lender.

23. bedeck do honor to.

24. conduct management.

25. flask powder flask.

26. And thou . . . defense the friar is saying that Romeo's mind, which is now irrational, is destroying rather than aiding him.

27. but lately dead only recently declaring yourself dead.

28. happy fortunate.

29. wench low, common girl.

30. puts up pouts over.

31. watch be set watchmen go on duty.

32. blaze announce publicly.

33. apt unto likely to do.

Reading Skill
Summarizing Briefly state the main points of the Friar's speech to Romeo.

Vocabulary Development

Word Analysis

Draw student's attention to the word *misbehaved* in line 143 on p. 798. Point out that this word contains the prefix *mis-*, which can mean "wrong" or can mean "bad."

Have students explain whether the prefix *mis-* in each sentence means "wrong" or whether it means "bad."

1. The Mayor has been accused of *misgoverning* this city for the past four years.
Answer: *Mis-* means "bad"; *misgoverning* means "governing badly."

2. He often *mispronounces* my last name.
Answer: *Mis-* means "wrong." To *mispronounce* a word is to pronounce it wrongly.

3. She has had a series of *misfortunes*.
Answer: *Mis-* means "bad"; *misfortune* means bad luck.

4. He was frantically looking for the keys he had *misplaced*.
Answer: *Mis-* means "wrong." To misplace something is to put it in the wrong place.

NURSE. O Lord, I could have stayed here all the night
160   To hear good counsel. O, what learning is!
      My lord, I'll tell my lady you will come.

ROMEO. Do so, and bid my sweet prepare to chide.[34]
                    [NURSE *offers to go in and turns again.*]

NURSE. Here, sir, a ring she bid me give you, sir.
      Hie you, make haste, for it grows very late.   [*Exit.*]

165   **ROMEO.** How well my comfort is revived by this!

      FRIAR. Go hence; good night; and here stands all your state:[35]
      Either be gone before the watch be set,
      Or by the break of day disguised from hence.
      Sojourn[36] in Mantua. I'll find out your man,
170   And he shall signify[37] from time to time
      Every good hap to you that chances here.
      Give me thy hand. 'Tis late. Farewell; good night.

      ROMEO. But that a joy past joy calls out on me,
      It were a grief so brief to part with thee.
175   Farewell.   [*Exit all.*]

Scene iv. A room in CAPULET'S house.

[*Enter old* CAPULET, *his* WIFE, *and* PARIS.]

      CAPULET. Things have fall'n out, sir, so unluckily
      That we have had no time to move[1] our daughter.
      Look you, she loved her kinsman Tybalt dearly,
      And so did I. Well, we were born to die.
5   'Tis very late; she'll not come down tonight.
      I promise you, but for your company,
      I would have been abed an hour ago.

      PARIS. These times of woe afford no times to woo.
      Madam, good night. Commend me to your daughter.

10   **LADY.** I will, and know her mind early tomorrow;
      Tonight she's mewed up to her heaviness.[2]

      CAPULET. Sir, Paris, I will make a desperate tender[3]
      Of my child's love. I think she will be ruled
      In all respects by me; nay more, I doubt it not.
15   Wife, go you to her ere you go to bed;
      Acquaint her here of my son[4] Paris' love
      And bid her (mark you me?) on Wednesday next—
      But soft! What day is this?

---

34. chide rebuke me (for slaying Tybalt).

35. here . . . state this is your situation.

36. Sojourn remain.

37. signify let you know.

1. move discuss your proposal with.

Literary Analysis
Dramatic Speeches
Is Paris's brief remark in line 8 an aside? Explain.

2. mewed . . . heaviness locked up with her sorrow.

3. desperate tender risky offer.

4. son son-in-law.

 Reading Check

What reason do the Capulets give Paris to explain why Juliet cannot see him?

Romeo and Juliet, Act III ■ *799*

- Have students read lines 19–36.
Ask: What is ironic about this scene involving Lord and Lady Capulet and Paris? What do readers and the audience know that the Capulets and Paris do not know?
Answer: It's ironic that the three are discussing the marriage of Juliet to Paris; the reader knows that Juliet is already married to Romeo.

- Have students contrast Capulet's words in this scene with his previous talk with Paris, in which he said that Juliet's consent to marriage was important to him.
Answer: In this scene, Capulet thinks Juliet will do as he asks.

- **Ask** students to respond to the Reading Skill prompt: Summarize Lord Capulet's remarks about the timing of Juliet's marriage to Paris.
Answer: Capulet says at first that the wedding should be the following Wednesday, and then, realizing that it is Monday, says Wednesday is too soon and it should be set for Thursday.

---

32 | **PARIS.**   Monday, my lord.

CAPULET. Monday! Ha, ha! Well, Wednesday is too soon.
20   A⁵ Thursday let it be—a Thursday, tell her,
     She shall be married to this noble earl.
     Will you be ready? Do you like this haste?
34 We'll keep no great ado⁶—a friend or two;
     For hark you, Tybalt being slain so late,
25   It may be thought we held him carelessly,⁷
     Being our kinsman, if we revel much.
     Therefore we'll have some half a dozen friends,
     And there an end. But what say you to Thursday?

PARIS. My lord, I would that Thursday were tomorrow.

30 **CAPULET.** Well, get you gone. A Thursday be it then.
     Go you to Juliet ere you go to bed;
     Prepare her, wife, against⁸ this wedding day.
     Farewell, my lord.—Light to my chamber, ho!
     Afore me,⁹ it is so very late
35   That we may call it early by and by.
     Good night.   [*Exit all.*]

Scene v. CAPULET'S orchard.

[*Enter* ROMEO *and* JULIET *aloft.*]

   JULIET. Wilt thou be gone? It is not yet near day.
     It was the nightingale, and not the lark,
     That pierced the fearful hollow of thine ear.
     Nightly she sings on yond pomegranate tree.
5   Believe me, love, it was the nightingale.

   ROMEO. It was the lark, the herald of the morn;
     No nightingale. Look, love, what envious streaks
     Do lace the severing¹ clouds in yonder East.
     Night's candles² are burnt out, and jocund day
10   Stands tiptoe on the misty mountaintops.
     I must be gone and live, or stay and die.

   JULIET. Yond light is not daylight; I know it, I.
     It is some meteor that the sun exhales³
     To be to thee this night a torchbearer
15   And light thee on thy way to Mantua.
     Therefore stay yet; thou need'st not to be gone.

36 ▼ **ROMEO.** Let me be ta'en, let me be put to death.
     I am content, so thou wilt have it so.

800 ■ *Drama*

---

5. **A** on.

6. **We'll . . . ado** We will not make a great fuss.

7. **held him carelessly** did not respect him enough.

Reading Skill
Summarizing
Summarize Lord Capulet's remarks about the timing of Juliet's marriage to Paris.

8. **against** for.

9. **Afore me** indeed (a mild oath).

1. **severing** parting.

2. **Night's candles** stars.

3. **exhales** sends out.

Vocabulary Development

Think-Aloud: Context Clues
Direct students' attention to the word *revel* in line 26 on p. 800. Using a think-aloud process, model how to use context to infer the meaning of an unknown word. Say to students:

I'm going to think aloud to show you how I would figure out the meaning of *revel* from its context.

In this sentence, *revel* is used as a verb. The speaker, Lord Capulet, is talking about the upcoming marriage of Juliet and Paris. Capulet says that people may think that they are not concerned about Tybalt's death if they *revel* too much. Apparently, one would not want to *revel* during a sad time.

Capulet goes on to say that they will only have a half a dozen friends at the wedding. This means that the celebration is being limited, so I think that *revel* refers to celebrating with a large gathering at a feast or a party, or, in this case, a wedding.

Literature Connection

The Nightingale and the Lark The nightingale and the lark are two birds that appear frequently in literature, particularly in poetry. Both birds are admired and adored for their beautiful singing, and they also have symbolic associations. The nightingale and its song are traditionally associated with night; the lark and its song with dawn. Shakespeare draws on these associations in this exchange between Romeo and Juliet.

Connect to the Literature

Why do Romeo and Juliet have negative associations with the lark at this point in the play?

I'll say yon gray is not the morning's eye,
20 'Tis but the pale reflex of Cynthia's brow;⁴
36 Nor that is not the lark whose notes do beat
The vaulty heaven so high above our heads.
I have more care to stay than will to go.
Come, death, and welcome! Juliet wills it so.
25 How is't, my soul? Let's talk; it is not day.

JULIET. It is, it is! Hie hence, be gone, away!
It is the lark that sings so out of tune,
Straining harsh discords and unpleasing sharps.⁵
Some say the lark makes sweet division;⁶
30 This doth not so, for she divideth us.
Some say the lark and loathèd toad change eyes;⁷
O, now I would they had changed voices too,
Since arm from arm that voice doth us affray,⁸
Hunting thee hence with hunt's-up⁹ to the day.
35 O, now be gone! More light and light it grows.

ROMEO. More light and light—more dark and dark our woes.

[*Enter* NURSE.]

NURSE. Madam!

JULIET. Nurse?

---

4. reflex . . . brow reflection of the moon (Cynthia was a name for the moon goddess).

Literary Analysis
Dramatic Speeches
What meaning does the allusion in line 20 add to Romeo's speech?

5. sharps shrill high notes.

6. division melody.

7. change eyes exchange eyes (because the lark has a beautiful body with ugly eyes and the toad has an ugly body with beautiful eyes).

8. affray frighten.

9. hunt's-up morning song for hunters.

37 **Reading Check**

What do the Capulets plan for Juliet on Thursday?

Romeo and Juliet, Act III ■ *801*

Literature Connection More than fifty different species of birds appear in Shakespeare's plays. Students may recall Benvolio, earlier in the play, telling Romeo that there are more attractive women than Rosaline:

> "Compare her face with some that I shall show,/And I will make thee think thy swan a crow."

Shakespeare was particularly fond of the skylark and used it in fifteen of his plays, including *Richard III*, *Love's Labor's Lost*, *A Midsummer Night's Dream*, *Titus Andronicus*, *Cymbeline*, and *King Lear*, as well as in two poems. But the most famous of the lark imagery occurs in *The Tragedy of Romeo and Juliet* in Act III, Scene v.

Connect to the Literature Point out that Romeo and Juliet both dread their parting. Then **ask** the Connect to the Literature question: Why do Romeo and Juliet have negative associations with the lark at this point in the play?
Answer: The lark signals morning, and Romeo must leave Juliet in the morning.

36 Literary Analysis
Dramatic Speeches

- **Ask** students what the two references to birds mean in this exchange between Romeo and Juliet.
  Answer: The two lovers argue about whether they hear the lark or the nightingale. Juliet says it was the nightingale, which means it is still night and Romeo can stay awhile. Romeo says it was the lark, which means it is daybreak and he must leave.

- **Ask** students to respond to the Literary Analysis question on p. 801: What meaning does the allusion in line 20 add to this speech?
  Answer: The allusion shows that Romeo accepts Juliet's judgment about whether it is daybreak or night. Romeo says that what he thought was the light of morning is just a reflection of Cynthia's brow, meaning the moon. He is willing to take Juliet's word for the time of day if it means he can stay with her.

37 Reading Check

Answer: The Capulets plan Juliet's wedding to Paris on Thursday.

Strategy Special Needs Students
To model how to show the effects of allusions, show students the **Literary Analysis Graphic Organizer B** (*Graphic Organizer Transparencies*, p. 172). The completed graphic organizer will give students insight into recording allusions and analyzing the effects they have. They can use it as a model for recording allusions as they read

Strategy for Less Proficient Readers
Show students the **Literary Analysis Graphic Organizer B** (*Graphic Organizer Transparencies*, p. 172). The completed graphic organizer will give students insight into recording allusions and understanding the effects on the text. Point out how they would use the organizer to record the allusion to Cynthia on p. 801. Students can use the organizer as a model for recording allusions as they read.

- Ask students how Juliet uses figurative language to show Romeo how she will age while he is absent.
  Answer: Juliet says that when Romeo is away from her, every minute will appear to be many days long so that she will be much older when she sees him again.

- Have students **translate** Romeo and Juliet's conversation in lines 48–53 into modern English.
  Possible response: ROMEO: Good-bye! I won't miss any chance to be in touch with you, Juliet. JULIET: Do you think we'll ever see each other again? ROMEO: I'm sure of it. And later on we'll laugh about all of the problems we're having right now.

- Have students identify the explanation Romeo gives for why he and Juliet both look so pale.
  Answer: He says that they are both sad, and that sadness drains their blood.

- **Ask** students to respond to the Reading Skill prompt: Identify the key points of the farewell dialogue between Romeo and Juliet.
  Answer: Juliet tells Romeo that every minute he is gone will seem like an age to her. Romeo tells her that he will be in touch at every opportunity. When Juliet asks if he thinks they will meet again, Romeo tells her that they will laugh about these troubles some day. They both note that they look pale, and Romeo says it is the sadness that makes them look so pale.

NURSE. Your lady mother is coming to your chamber.
40   The day is broke; be wary, look about.   [*Exit.*]

JULIET. Then, window, let day in, and let life out.

ROMEO. Farewell, farewell! One kiss, and I'll descend.
                     [*He goeth down.*]

JULIET. Art thou gone so, love-lord, ay husband-friend?
   I must hear from thee every day in the hour,
45   For in a minute there are many days.
   O, by this count I shall be much in years[10]
   Ere I again behold my Romeo!

ROMEO. Farewell!
   I will omit no opportunity
50   That may convey my greetings, love, to thee.

JULIET. O, think'st thou we shall ever meet again?

ROMEO. I doubt it not; and all these woes shall serve
   For sweet discourses[11] in our times to come.

JULIET. O God, I have an ill-divining[12] soul!
55   Methinks I see thee, now thou art so low,
   As one dead in the bottom of a tomb.
   Either my eyesight fails, or thou lookest pale.

ROMEO. And trust me, love, in my eye so do you.
   Dry sorrow drinks our blood.[13] Adieu, adieu!   [*Exit.*]

60 **JULIET.** O Fortune, Fortune! All men call thee <u>fickle</u>.
   If thou art fickle, what dost thou[14] with him
   That is renowned for faith? Be fickle, Fortune,
   For then I hope thou wilt not keep him long
   But send him back.

[*Enter* MOTHER.]

65 **LADY CAPULET.** Ho, daughter! Are you up?

JULIET. Who is't that calls? It is my lady mother.
   Is she not down so late,[15] or up so early?
   What unaccustomed cause procures her hither?[16]

LADY CAPULET. Why, how now, Juliet?

JULIET.   Madam, I am not well.

70 **LADY CAPULET.** Evermore weeping for your cousin's death?
   What, wilt thou wash him from his grave with tears?
   And if thou couldst, thou couldst not make him live.
   Therefore have done. Some grief shows much of love;
   But much of grief shows still some want of wit.

802 ■ Drama

Reading Skill
Summarizing Identify the key points of the farewell conversation between Romeo and Juliet.

10. much in years much older.

11. discourses conversations.

12. ill-divining predicting evil.

13. Dry sorrow . . . blood It was once believed that sorrow drained away the blood.

14. dost thou do you have to do.

Vocabulary Builder
fickle (fik´ əl) *adj.* changeable

15. Is she . . . late Has she stayed up so late?

16. What . . . hither? What unusual reason brings her here?

Vocabulary Development

Multiple Meanings

Refer students to the word *Fortune* in Scene v, line 60. Tell students that the word *Fortune* in this line refers to the Greek goddess of chance. In medieval and Renaissance times, Fortune was used as a personification of fate and was considered a force or power that would bring good or bad luck.

Today, people use the word *fortune* to mean luck, as in, "He had the good *fortune* to get the job, even though he was not the most qualified." In this case, the idea of fate is usually not associated with the word.

Fortune is also used to refer to what is going to happen to someone in the future, such as in the phrase *fortune teller*, meaning "someone who predicts what will happen to another in the future."

Finally, *fortune* can mean "great wealth," such as "He inherited his *fortune* from his father."

Ask students to write a sentence for each of these meanings of the word *fortune*.

75 **JULIET.** Yet let me weep for such a feeling[17] loss.

LADY CAPULET. So shall you feel the loss, but not the friend
   Which you weep for.

JULIET.   Feeling so the loss,
   I cannot choose but ever weep the friend.

LADY CAPULET. Well, girl, thou weep'st not so much for his death
80   As that the villain lives which slaughtered him.

JULIET. What villain, madam?

39 LADY CAPULET.   That same villain Romeo.

JULIET. [*Aside*] Villain and he be many miles asunder.[18]—
   God pardon him! I do, with all my heart;
   And yet no man like he doth grieve my heart.

85 **LADY CAPULET.** That is because the traitor murderer lives.

JULIET. Ay, madam, from the reach of these my hands.
   Would none but I might venge my cousin's death!

LADY CAPULET. We will have vengeance for it, fear thou not.
   Then weep no more. I'll send to one in Mantua,
90   Where that same banished runagate[19] doth live,
   Shall give him such an unaccustomed dram[20]
   That he shall soon keep Tybalt company;
   And then I hope thou wilt be satisfied.

JULIET. Indeed I never shall be satisfied
95   With Romeo till I behold him—dead[21]—
   Is my poor heart so for a kinsman vexed.
   Madam, if you could find out but a man
   To bear a poison, I would temper[22] it;
   That Romeo should, upon receipt thereof,
100   Soon sleep in quiet. O, how my heart abhors
   To hear him named and cannot come to him,
   To wreak[23] the love I bore my cousin
   Upon his body that hath slaughtered him!

LADY CAPULET. Find thou the means, and I'll find such a man.
105   But now I'll tell thee joyful tidings, girl.

JULIET. And joy comes well in such a needy time.
   What are they, I beseech your ladyship?

LADY CAPULET. Well, well, thou hast a careful[24] father, child;
   One who, to put thee from thy heaviness,
110   Hath sorted out[25] a sudden day of joy
   That thou expects not nor I looked not for.

17. **feeling** deeply felt.

Literary Analysis
Dramatic Speeches
What qualities of an aside do you find in lines 82–84?

18. **asunder** apart.

19. **runagate** renegade; runaway.

20. **unaccustomed dram** unexpected dose of poison.

21. **dead** Juliet is deliberately ambiguous here. Her mother thinks *dead* refers to Romeo. But Juliet is using the word with the following line, in reference to her heart.

22. **temper** mix; weaken.

23. **wreak** (rēk) avenge; express.

24. **careful** considerate.
25. **sorted out** selected.

40 ✓ **Reading Check**
What are Lady Capulet's plans for Romeo?

Romeo and Juliet, Act III ■ *803*

39 Literary Analysis
Dramatic Speeches

- **Ask** students what is ironic about Lady Capulet's words to Juliet in lines 70–74.
  Answer: Lady Capulet thinks Juliet is mourning Tybalt's death, but Juliet is sad because of Romeo's absence and their situation in general.

- **Ask** students to answer the Literary Analysis question on p. 803: What qualities of an aside do you find in lines 82–84?
  Answer: Juliet speaks her words about Romeo to the audience because she does not want her mother to hear them.

- **Ask** students to state the meaning of lines 82–84 in their own words.
  Possible response: He is not at all like a villain. I hope God forgives him! I do, and yet he makes me very sad.

- **Ask** students to explain the double meanings in line 84—the one that Juliet's mother understands and the one Juliet really means.
  Answer: Juliet's mother understands her to mean that Romeo has grieved her because he has taken Tybalt's life; Juliet really means that she grieves for Romeo because she has to be parted from him.

40 Reading Check

Answer: Lady Capulet plans to have Romeo poisoned.

Differentiated
Instruction   Solutions for All Learners

Background for Gifted/Talented Students
Point out that on p. 803 Lady Capulet mentions murdering Romeo with poison. Tell students that during the late 1400s, poisoning was a common method of homicide, especially in Italy. The art of poison reached its height under the powerful Borgia family, whose most notable member was Pope Alexander VI. The Borgias poisoned their political enemies with such frequency that the phrase "tasting the cup of the Borgias" became a euphemism for

death. The Borgias developed a potent poison known as *cantarelle*.

Apothecaries and so-called sorcerers of the time were adept at mixing deadly poisons for use by anyone who would pay.

Ask students to think about the Friar's special knowledge about poison herbs. Have them be alert as they read for the role that poison will play in the next acts.

41

41 Background
Film

Many filmmakers have tried their hands at Shakespeare's timeless romance. In 1916, Gordon Edwards and Maxwell Karger directed a silent version with the text in subtitles. Twenty years later, George Cukor directed a talking version starring Leslie Howard and Norma Shearer in the title roles, with John Barrymore and Basil Rathbone as Mercutio and Tybalt.

In 1968, Zeffirelli's version was released. Filmed in Italy, the movie featured exquisite period costumes and settings—as can be seen in the stills accompanying the play in this text.

In 1996, Baz Luhrmann directed a movie version of *The Tragedy of Romeo and Juliet* with an abridged text, filmed in Italy. The movie has a contemporary setting with Latin and punk-rock music on the soundtrack. Use the following for discussion:

1. If you were filming *The Tragedy of Romeo and Juliet,* which time period would you choose for a setting? Why?
   Answer: Answers should include details about the period that would support the plot of the play.

2. Why do some directors change the period and setting of Shakespeare's play?
   Answer: Students may say that the directors want to show the audience that the play is timeless and has universal meaning.

42 Critical Viewing

Answer: Students may say that the picture conveys Juliet's desperation as she pleads to her mother not to make her go through with a marriage to Paris.

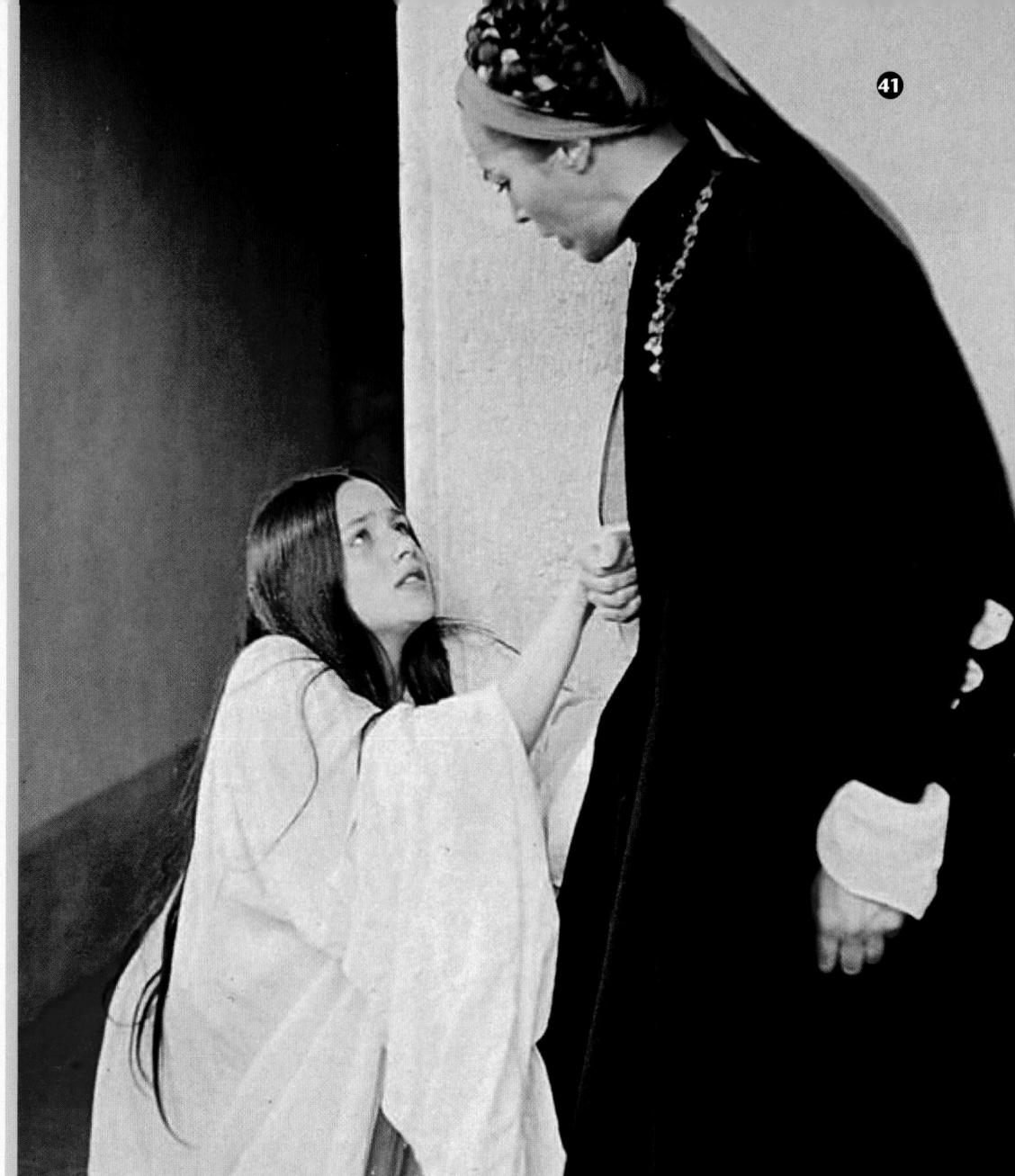

42 ▲ **Critical Viewing** Do you think these actors accurately convey Juliet's response to her parents' plan for her marriage? **[Evaluate]**

804 ■ *Drama*

Vocabulary Development

Expressive Vocabulary
As students discuss the rest of this scene in which Lord and Lady Capulet confront Juliet about marrying Paris, have them use the expressive vocabulary presented earlier. Give them these sentence starters:
1. Juliet does not want to *comply* . . .
2. Capulet threatens *drastic* . . .
3. Juliet makes an *eloquent* plea to . . .
4. Capulet refuses to *tolerate.* . .

JULIET. Madam, in happy time!²⁶ What day is that?

LADY CAPULET. Marry, my child, early next Thursday morn
    The gallant, young, and noble gentleman,
115   The County Paris, at Saint Peter's Church,
    Shall happily make thee there a joyful bride.

JULIET. Now by Saint Peter's Church, and Peter too,
    He shall not make me there a joyful bride!
    I wonder at this haste, that I must wed
120   Ere he that should be husband comes to woo.
    I pray you tell my lord and father, madam,
    I will not marry yet; and when I do, I swear
    It shall be Romeo, whom you know I hate,
    Rather than Paris. These are news indeed!

125 **LADY CAPULET.** Here comes your father. Tell him so yourself,
    And see how he will take it at your hands.

[*Enter* CAPULET *and* NURSE.]

CAPULET. When the sun sets the earth doth drizzle dew,
    But for the sunset of my brother's son
    It rains downright.
130   How now? A conduit,²⁷ girl? What, still in tears?
    Evermore show'ring? In one little body
    Thou counterfeits a bark,²⁸ a sea, a wind:
    For still thy eyes, which I may call the sea,
    Do ebb and flow with tears; the bark thy body is,
135   Sailing in this salt flood; the winds, thy sighs,
    Who, raging with thy tears and they with them,
    Without a sudden calm will overset
    Thy tempest-tossèd body. How now, wife?
    Have you delivered to her our decree?

140 **LADY CAPULET.** Ay, sir; but she will none, she gives you
       thanks.²⁹
    I would the fool were married to her grave!

CAPULET. Soft! Take me with you,³⁰ take me with you, wife.
    How? Will she none? Doth she not give us thanks?
    Is she not proud?³¹ Doth she not count her blest,
145   Unworthy as she is, that we have wrought³²
    So worthy a gentleman to be her bride?

JULIET. Not proud you have, but thankful that you have.
    Proud can I never be of what I hate,
    But thankful even for hate that is meant love.

150 **CAPULET.** How, how, how, how, chopped-logic?³³ What is this?

---

26. in happy time just in time.

27. conduit water pipe.

28. bark boat.

Reading Skill
Summarizing
Summarize the comparison Lord Capulet makes in lines 130–138.

29. she will none . . . thanks she will have nothing to do with it, thank you.

30. Soft! Take . . . you Wait a minute. Let me understand you.

31. proud pleased.

32. wrought arranged.

33. chopped-logic contradictory, unsound thought and speech.

 Reading Check
Rather than Paris, whom does Juliet threaten to marry?

Romeo and Juliet, Act III ■ 805

㊸ Reading Skill
Summarizing

• Have students **determine** whether Lady Capulet's words about telling Juliet joyful tidings are ironic. Why or why not?
Sample response: Her words are ironic because readers and audience members know that her news will be a dreadful shock to Juliet.

• **Ask** students to respond to the Reading Skill item on p. 805: Summarize the comparison Lord Capulet makes in lines 130–138.
Possible response: Lord Capulet compares Juliet's body to a little boat tossed on a sea of her tears, with her sighs as the wind.

㊹ Reading Check
Answer: Juliet threatens to marry Romeo.

Differentiated Instruction   **Solutions for All Learners**

Strategy for Less Proficient Readers
Help students understand Juliet's surprise at her mother's announcement that she is to marry Paris on Thursday. Point out that Paris has never approached Juliet to court her; in fact, Juliet may not even know Paris. Up to this point she had no idea that her parents were planning her marriage.

Strategy for Advanced Readers
Point out the word *marry,* the first word in line 113 of Lady Capulet's speech on p. 805. Ask students whether the word is a pun as it is used here and suggest that they use the glossary of Elizabethan words on p. 729 for assistance.
Answer: The word is used to mean "indeed," as in "Indeed, my child, early next Thursday morn." It is also used in the conventional way, meaning "to wed," in which case Lady Capulet's words mean, "You will be married, my child, early next Thursday morn."

- **Ask** students what Capulet means in lines 150–154.
  Answer: He means that he thinks Juliet is talking in circles and making no sense.

- **Ask** students why they think Capulet is so angry.
  Answer: He is angry because he thinks he has made a good match for Juliet, and she is resisting marrying Paris; he thinks she is being ungrateful.

- Have students read lines 161–169. Then **ask** students to respond to the Literary Analysis question: What feelings and personality traits does Capulet reveal in this brief speech?
  Answer: Capulet reveals intense anger and disgust at Juliet; he reveals a bad temper and an unkind nature.

"Proud"—and "I thank you"—and "I thank you not"—
And yet "not proud"? Mistress minion[34] you,
Thank me no thankings, nor proud me no prouds,
But fettle[35] your fine joints 'gainst Thursday next
155   To go with Paris to Saint Peter's Church,
Or I will drag thee on a hurdle[36] thither.
Out, you greensickness carrion![37] Out, you baggage![38]
You tallow-face![39]

LADY CAPULET.   Fie, fie! What, are you mad?

45 JULIET. Good father, I beseech you on my knees,
160   Hear me with patience but to speak a word.

CAPULET. Hang thee, young baggage! Disobedient wretch!
I tell thee what—get thee to church a Thursday
Or never after look me in the face.
Speak not, reply not, do not answer me!
165   My fingers itch. Wife, we scarce thought us blest
That God had lent us but this only child;
But now I see this one is one too much,
And that we have a curse in having her.
Out on her, hilding![40]

NURSE.   God in heaven bless her!
170   You are to blame, my lord, to rate[41] her so.

CAPULET. And why, my Lady Wisdom? Hold your tongue,
Good Prudence. Smatter with your gossips, go![42]

NURSE. I speak no treason.

CAPULET.   O, God-i-god-en!

NURSE. May not one speak?

CAPULET.   Peace, you mumbling fool!
175   Utter your gravity[43] o'er a gossip's bowl,
For here we need it not.

LADY CAPULET.   You are too hot.

CAPULET. God's bread![44] It makes me mad.
Day, night; hour, tide, time; work, play;
Alone, in company; still my care hath been
180   To have her matched; and having now provided
46 A gentleman of noble parentage,
Of fair demesnes,[45] youthful, and nobly trained,
Stuffed, as they say, with honorable parts,[46]
Proportioned as one's thought would wish a man—
185   And then to have a wretched puling[47] fool,

---

34. Mistress minion Miss Uppity.

35. fettle prepare.

36. hurdle sled on which prisoners were taken to their execution.

37. greensickness carrion anemic lump of flesh.

38. baggage naughty girl.

39. tallow-face wax-pale face.

Literary Analysis
Dramatic Speeches
What feelings and personality traits does Lord Capulet reveal in this brief speech?

40. hilding worthless person.

41. rate scold; berate.

42. Smatter . . . go! Go chatter with the other old women.

43. gravity wisdom.

44. God's bread! By the holy Eucharist!

45. demesnes property.

46. parts qualities.

47. puling whining.

A whining mammet,[48] in her fortune's tender,[49]
To answer "I'll not wed, I cannot love;
I am too young, I pray you pardon me"!
But, and you will not wed, I'll pardon you!
190 Graze where you will, you shall not house with me.
Look to't, think on't; I do not use to jest.
46 Thursday is near; lay hand on heart, advise:[50]
And you be mine, I'll give you to my friend;
And you be not, hang, beg, starve, die in the streets,
195 For, by my soul, I'll ne'er acknowledge thee,
Nor what is mine shall never do thee good.
Trust to't. Bethink you. I'll not be forsworn.[51]   [*Exit.*]

JULIET. Is there no pity sitting in the clouds
That sees into the bottom of my grief?
200 O sweet my mother, cast me not away!
Delay this marriage for a month, a week;
Or if you do not, make the bridal bed
In that dim monument where Tybalt lies.

LADY CAPULET. Talk not to me, for I'll not speak a word.
205 Do as thou wilt, for I have done with thee.   [*Exit.*]

48. mammet doll.

49. in . . . tender when good fortune is offered her.

50. advise consider.

Reading Skill
Summarizing Summarize the threat that Lord Capulet makes to Juliet in this monologue.

51. forsworn made to violate my promise.

47 ✓ Reading Check

How do the Capulets respond to the Nurse's attempts to defend Juliet?

48 ◄ **Critical Viewing** How has Juliet's life changed since the moment pictured here, when she first saw Romeo? **[Analyze Cause and Effect]**

Romeo and Juliet, Act III ■ 807

46 **Reading Skill**
Summarizing

- **Ask** students what Capulet's main criticism of Juliet seems to be in lines 177–197.
  Answer: Capulet says in different ways that Juliet is ungrateful for the wonderful marriage contract he has arranged for her.

- Have students read lines 182–197. Then, **ask** students to respond to the Reading Skill prompt: Summarize the threat that Lord Capulet makes to Juliet in this monologue.
  Answer: Capulet tells Juliet that if she does not marry Paris, he will disown her and throw her out of his house.

- **Ask** students what Juliet does when she cannot convince her father to change his mind.
  Answer: Juliet turns her attention to her mother.

- Have students read lines 200–204. Then, **ask** what options Juliet offers her mother.
  Answer: Juliet asks her mother not to turn her back on her, but to delay the marriage for a month, or even a week. Juliet says that if her mother won't help her, Juliet will end up dead, like Tybalt.

▶ **Monitor Progress:** Use students' responses to assess their understanding of summarizing.

▶ **Reteach:** If students have difficulty identifying the main ideas in a passage, have them work in pairs to summarize lines 214–219.

47 **Reading Check**

Answer: The Capulets tell the Nurse to be quiet.

48 **Critical Viewing**

Juliet's expression is both intense and innocent, suggesting that she has a forceful personality but lacks experience.

Differentiated
Instruction   Solutions for All Learners

Strategy for Less Proficient Readers
After students have read p. 808, help them summarize Act III by using the **Series-of-Events Chain Graphic Organizer** in *Graphic Organizer Transparencies,* p. 239. Have students recall that in Scene i: Mercutio and Tybalt fight, Romeo attempts to stop them, and Mercutio is killed. Then, Romeo kills Tybalt, and the Prince exiles Romeo. Scene ii: Nurse tells Juliet the news of Tybalt's death and Romeo's exile. Scene iii: the Friar comforts Romeo, plans his return Verona, and sends him to Juliet.

Scene iv: Capulet agrees that Paris and Juliet should marry on Thursday. Scene v opens with Romeo leaving Juliet's room after their wedding night, and then Lady Capulet telling Juliet of the wedding, Juliet telling her father she will not marry Paris, her father threatening to disown her, and finally, the Nurse advising her to forget Romeo and marry Paris.

After completing the organizer with students, have them discuss the details of each scene.

- **Ask** students what advice the Nurse gives Juliet.
  Answer: The Nurse tells Juliet to forget that she is married to Romeo. He is banished, and he will never dare to come back; he may as well be dead. She should marry Paris. Paris is a better man, anyway.

- Have students read lines 237–244. Then, **ask** students to respond to the Literary Analysis question on p. 808: What feelings toward her Nurse does Juliet reveal in this soliloquy?
  Answer: Juliet feels anger and disgust toward her Nurse. She feels that she has been betrayed by the "wicked fiend" who has advised her to forget her husband.

JULIET. O God!—O nurse, how shall this be prevented?
My husband is on earth, my faith in heaven.[52]
How shall that faith return again to earth
Unless that husband send it me from heaven
210 By leaving earth?[53] Comfort me, counsel me.
Alack, alack, that heaven should practice stratagems[54]
Upon so soft a subject as myself!
What say'st thou? Hast thou not a word of joy?
Some comfort, nurse.

215 **NURSE.**   Faith, here it is.
Romeo is banished; and all the world to nothing[55]
That he dares ne'er come back to challenge[56] you;
Or if he do, it needs must be by stealth.
Then, since the case so stands as now it doth,
I think it best you married with the County.
220 O, he's a lovely gentleman!
Romeo's a dishclout to him.[57] An eagle, madam,
Hath not so green, so quick, so fair an eye
As Paris hath. Beshrew my very heart,
I think you are happy in this second match,
225 For it excels your first; or if it did not,
Your first is dead—or 'twere as good he were
As living here and you no use of him.

JULIET. Speak'st thou from thy heart?

NURSE. And from my soul too; else beshrew them both.

230 **JULIET.** Amen!

NURSE. What?

JULIET. Well, thou hast comforted me marvelous much.
Go in; and tell my lady I am gone,
Having displeased my father, to Lawrence' cell,
235 To make confession and to be absolved.[58]

NURSE. Marry, I will; and this is wisely done.   [*Exit.*]

JULIET. Ancient damnation![59] O most wicked fiend!
Is it more sin to wish me thus forsworn,
Or to dispraise my lord with that same tongue
240 Which she hath praised him with above compare
So many thousand times? Go, counselor!
Thou and my bosom henceforth shall be twain.[60]
I'll to the friar to know his remedy.
If all else fail, myself have power to die.   [*Exit.*]

52. **my faith in heaven** my marriage vow is recorded in heaven.

53. **leaving earth** dying.
54. **stratagems** tricks; plots.

55. **all . . . nothing** the odds are overwhelming.
56. **challenge** claim.

57. **a dishclout to him** a dishcloth compared with him.

58. **be absolved** receive forgiveness for my sins.
59. **Ancient damnation!** Old devil!
60. **Thou . . . twain** You will from now on be separated from my trust.

Literary Analysis
Dramatic Speeches
What feelings toward her Nurse does Juliet reveal in this soliloquy?

50 ▶ **Critical Viewing**
Why is a balcony well suited for a soliloquy?
[Assess]

Vocabulary Development

Vocabulary Knowledge Rating
When students have completed reading and discussing Act III of *The Tragedy of Romeo and Juliet,* have them take out their **Vocabulary Knowledge Rating Chart** for this selection. Read the words aloud once more and have students rate their knowledge of the words again in the After Reading column. Clarify any words that are still problematic. Have students write their own definition and example or sentence in the appropriate column. Then have students complete the **Vocabulary Builder Practice** activities on p. 811. Encourage students to use the words in further discussion and written work about this selection. Remind them that they will be accountable for these words on the Selection Test.

50 Critical Viewing

Possible response: A balcony would isolate and emphasize Juliet and allow her to more easily address the audience with her soliloquy.

Romeo and Juliet, Act III 809

Concept Connector

Connecting to the Literature
Have students compare the sentences they wrote about why young people might want to engage in secretive behavior. Ask them to explain whether their thoughts have changed, and, if so, how.

Literary Analysis Graphic Organizer
Have students review the graphic organizers they completed while reading to identify allusions and note their effect. Show them **Literary Analysis Graphic Organizer B** (*Graphic Organizer Transparencies,* p. 172) as an example. Then have students share the graphic organizers they did and how they identified characters' rank.

Apply the Skills

The Tragedy of Romeo and Juliet, Act III

Thinking About the Selection

1. **Respond:** What would you do if you were in Romeo's or Juliet's situation? Explain.
2. **(a) Recall:** Make a three-column chart. In the first column, write the remark regarding the Montagues and Capulets that Mercutio makes three times as he is dying. **(b) Infer:** In the second column, explain what Mercutio means by this exclamation.
   (c) Interpret: In the third column, explain how his remark reinforces ideas set forth in the play's Prologue.

Mercutio's Dying Remark

What Does It Say?	What Does It Mean?	Why Is It Important?

3. **(a) Recall:** How and why does Romeo kill Tybalt?
   (b) Interpret: What does Romeo mean when he says, after killing Tybalt, "I am fortune's fool"?
4. **(a) Analyze:** Describe the clashing emotions Juliet feels when the Nurse reports Tybalt's death and Romeo's punishment.
   (b) Compare and Contrast: In what ways are Romeo's and Juliet's reactions to Romeo's banishment similar and different? Explain.
5. **Resolve:** How might Tybalt's death have been avoided?

Literary Analysis

6. **(a)** What thoughts and feelings does Juliet express in the **soliloquy** that opens Scene ii of Act III? **(b)** When Juliet makes an **allusion** to Phoebus and Phaëton, what is she hoping will happen soon?
7. What criticisms of Romeo does the Friar address in his Scene iii **monologue** beginning, "Hold thy desperate hand"?
8. **(a)** In Act III, Scene v, when her mother refers to Romeo as a villain, Juliet utters the **aside,** "Villain and he be many miles asunder." What does Juliet mean? **(b)** Why is it important that the audience, but not Lady Capulet, hears Juliet's remark?

Reading Skill

9. **(a) Paraphrase** lines 29–51 in Act III, Scene iii. **(b)** Based on your paraphrase, write a few sentences that **summarize** what Romeo says to the Friar in these lines.

QuickReview

Act III at a Glance
After Juliet's cousin Tybalt kills Mercutio, Romeo kills Tybalt and is banished from Verona. The newly-weds have one night together before Romeo flees. Juliet's parents plan to marry her to Count Paris.

Go Online
Assessment
For: Self-test
Visit: www.PHSchool.com
Web Code: epa-6504

Dramatic Speeches: words spoken by a single character to comment on the action. Common types include *soliloquy, monologue,* and *aside.*

Summarizing: briefly stating the main points in a piece of writing

---

1. **Possible responses:** Students may say that they would reveal their marriage to their parents.

2. (a) "A plague on both your houses." (b) Mercutio means the statement as a curse, blaming both sides for the quarrel. (c) The lines echo the Prologue because the Prologue briefly explains the terrible events that happen to the two "star-crossed lovers" who are from the rival households.

3. (a) Romeo kills Tybalt in a sword fight to avenge Mercutio's death. (b) Romeo feels he is a victim of fate.

4. (a) Juliet's vacillation between rage and love is expressed in a series of oxymorons ("Fiend angelical"). Her tumultuous emotions subside into grief at Romeo's banishment. (b) Both Romeo and Juliet react drastically to his banishment. Juliet alludes to suicide in Scene ii, and Romeo asserts that separation from Juliet will be far worse than death.

5. **Possible response:** Students may say that Romeo could have held his temper or revealed his secret marriage.

6. (a) Juliet is impatient for the night to arrive so she can be with her new husband. (b) She is hoping the sun will set quickly, so that Romeo will come.

7. The Friar calls Romeo "woman-ish" and "beastly" for attempting to kill himself, and claims that Romeo will kill Juliet by killing himself.

8. (a) Juliet means that there is a vast distance between Romeo and a villain; in other words, Romeo is not a villain at all. (b) It is important that Lady Capulet not hear how Juliet feels, but also that the audience knows Juliet's true feelings.

9. (a) Banishment is torture, not mercy, for heaven is where Juliet lives. While every little creature may look upon Juliet, I cannot. I must go. Even flies have it better than I, for they can hear Juliet speak. But I cannot hear Juliet's voice because I am banished. You say that exile is not death, but it is. The damned howl the word

banished in hell. How can you torture me with the word *ban-ished?* (b) **Possible response:** Banishment is not mercy, because I am separated from Juliet. Every other living creature can see her, but not me, and that is torture.

Vocabulary Builder

Practice Identify which two words in each group are synonyms and which one is an antonym of the other two. Explain your response.

1. gallant, courageous, cowardly
2. fray, truce, brawl
3. exile, banishment, welcome
4. martial, peaceful, warlike
5. eloquence, expressiveness, awkwardness
6. fickle, unpredictable, constant

Adding Words to Your Vocabulary The word *martial* literally means "of Mars." Mars is the ancient Roman god of war, and so *martial* describes anything related to war. The words *jovial* and *mercurial* also owe their meanings to associations with certain Roman gods. Use a dictionary to find out the meaning of each word and how it relates to a particular Roman god. Then, write a few sentences explaining how the origin of each word is reflected in its everyday usage. (For more on using a dictionary, see page R6.)

Writing

Imagine that you are the editor of a newspaper in Verona at the time of the play. Write an **editorial** addressing the Prince's response to the deaths of Tybalt and Mercutio.

- Reread the Prince's dialogue in the scene.
- Decide whether Romeo's sentence was appropriate, and explain.
- Write the editorial, supporting your ideas with details from Acts I–III.

Share your editorial with classmates, and encourage them to write letters to the editor in support of or in opposition to your editorial.

For *Grammar, Vocabulary,* and *Assessment,* see **Build Language Skills,** pages 812–813.

Extend Your Learning

Research and Technology In a small group, view a film of the ballet *Romeo and Juliet* by Russian composer Sergei Prokofiev. Take notes on how the dance, the music, and the camerawork communicate the play's ideas. Locate a review of the film and compare it to your own opinion. Then, use your notes to present a **film review** for the rest of the class.

Apply the Skills ■ 811

Assessment Resources

The following resources can be used to assess students' knowledge and skills.

Unit 5 Resources
    Selection Test A, pp. 62–64
    Selection Test B, pp. 65–67

Go Online
Assessment Students may use the **Self-test** to prepare for **Selection Test A** or **Selection Test B.**

Extend Your Learning

The **Support for Extend Your Learning** page (*Unit 5 Resources,* p. 58) provides guided note-taking opportunities to help students complete the Extend Your Learning activities.

Go Online
Research Activity **For:** An additional research activity **Visit:** www.PHSchool.com **Web Code:** epd-7503
For another research activity to extend students' learning, give students this Web Code.

Vocabulary Builder
Practice

1. *Cowardly;* it is an antonym of *gallant* and *courageous.*
2. *Truce;* it is an antonym of *fray* and *brawl.*
3. *Welcome;* it is an antonym of *exile* and *banishment.*
4. *Peaceful;* it is an antonym of *martial* and *warlike.*
5. *Awkwardness;* it is an antonym of *expressiveness,* which describes *eloquence.*
6. *Constant;* it is an antonym of *fickle* and *unpredictable.*

Adding Words to Your Vocabulary
Sample response:

1. *Jovial* means "genial and full of hearty good humor." Jove refers to the god Jupiter. In astrology, people born under the planet Jupiter's influence are good-humored.
2. *Mercurial* means to be "eloquent, shrewd, and clever." These qualities are associated with the god Mercury, the messenger of the gods. Mercury was noted for his eloquence and cleverness.

Writing

- To give students guidance for writing an editorial, give them **Support for Writing** for *The Tragedy of Romeo and Juliet,* Act III, p. 57, in **Unit 5 Resources.**
- To evaluate students' editorials, use the Persuasion: Persuasive Essay rubrics, pp. 53–54 in **General Resources.**

Six Traits Focus

✔ Ideas		Word Choice
✔ Organization	✔	Sentence Fluency
	Voice	✔ Conventions

W G **Writing and Grammar, Gold Level**
Students will find guidance on persuasive writing in Chapter 7.

Build Language Skills

Go to pp. 812–813 for vocabulary and grammar lessons and assessment practice.

811

Vocabulary Skill

- Introduce the word root -labor-. English words that contain the -labor- root will generally relate to the concept of work.

- Have students complete the Practice activity on this page.

Possible Answers

1. (a) *Elaboration* of your main points is important when you are writing about a literary selection. (b) The house was *elaborately* decorated for the celebration. (c) He *elaborated* on his theory for an hour.

2. (a) Remodeling the house will require hours of *labor*. (b) She *laboriously* copied the text using calligraphy. (c) As the students were *laboring,* the bell rang.

Grammar Lesson

- Tell students that regular verbs are predictable because they follow certain rules, but irregular verbs are unpredictable, and students may need to check the form in their dictionaries.

Answers

1. *Petroleum reserves discovered in the northwest corner of the state helped to boost the economy of New Mexico.* The emphasis shifts from the where the petroleum was discovered to how it helped New Mexico.

2. *Looking for a sparsely populated area, the federal government went to New Mexico twenty years later.* The emphasis shifts from time to purpose.

3. *Initiated by the United States, several treaties try to limit nuclear weapons.* The emphasis shifts from *treaties* to United States involvement.

4. *These treaties, depending on mutual self-interest, hold countries accountable for their weapons.* The emphasis shifts from *self-interest* to the *treaties* and their function.

Build Language Skills

Romeo and Juliet, Acts I–III

Vocabulary Skill

Word Roots The **Latin word root** *-labor-* means "work." Words that contain this word root have meanings related to work. For example, the verb *elaborate* means "work out in great detail." You can help yourself remember the "detail" part of the definition by remembering that to add details, or to elaborate, is more work than skipping the details.

Practice Use each form of *elaborate* and *labor* in a sentence. Look at the meaning of each word and the examples of its use in a dictionary. Revise your sentences as needed.

1. (a) elaboration   (b) elaborately   (c) elaborated
2. (a) labor   (b) laboriously   (c) laboring

Grammar Skill

Participle and Participle Phrases A **participle** is a verb form that is used as an adjective. **Present participles** end in *-ing*. The **past participles** of regular verbs end in *-ed*.

A **participle phrase** is a group of words that functions as an adjective in the sentence and contains a participle.

Present Participle	*growing* child
Past Participle	*troubled* child
Participle Phrase	*Focusing* intently, the driver managed to avoid an accident.

Practice Change the sentence pattern in each of the following so the participle is in a different place in the sentence. Explain how this changes the emphasis on the subject.

1. Discovered in the northwest corner of the state, petroleum reserves helped boost the economy of New Mexico.

2. Twenty years later, the federal government, looking for a sparsely populated area, went to New Mexico.

3. There have been several treaties, initiated by the United States, that try to limit nuclear weapons.

4. Depending on mutual self-interest, these treaties hold countries accountable for their weapons.

MorePractice

For more practice with participles and participle phrases, see the Grammar Handbook, pp. R43–44.

W_G *Prentice Hall Writing and Grammar Connection: Chapter 21, Section 11*

Teaching Resources

The following resources can be used to enrich or extend the instruction for Build Language Skills.

Unit 5 Resources
Build Language Skills: Vocabulary: Word Roots, p. 460
Build Grammar Skills: Participle and Participle Phrases, p. 461

Reading Skill: Summarize

Directions: *Read the selection. Then, answer the questions.*

> Full of vexation come I, with complaint
> Against my child, my daughter Hermia.—
> Stand forth, Demetrius.—My noble lord,
> 25 This man hath my consent to marry her.—
> Stand forth, Lysander. And, my gracious duke,
> This man hath bewitched the bosom of my child. . . .
> 41 I beg the ancient privilege of Athens:
> As she is mine, I may dispose of her,
> Which shall be either to this gentleman
> Or to her death, according to our law. . . .
>   from *A Midsummer Night's Dream* by William Shakespeare

1. What happens in line 24?
   A Demetrius steps forward.
   B Demetrius marries Hermia.
   C Demetrius consents to marry Hermia.
   D Demetrius leaves.

2. Which statement accurately paraphrases the ideas in lines 22–23?
   A I come here very angry, to compliment my daughter Hermia.
   B I am full of complaints, and my daughter Hermia is against me.

   C I am angry, and my daughter Hermia knows it.
   D I am here to complain about my daughter Hermia, who has made me very angry.

3. The most important point in lines 33–36 is that
   A Hermia lives in Athens.
   B Hermia is the daughter of the speaker.
   C Hermia will either marry or be killed.
   D Hermia's father knows the law.

Timed Writing: Interpretation [Connections]

> "What's in a name?
> That which we call a rose
> by any other name would smell as sweet."
>   from *Romeo and Juliet* by William Shakespeare

Interpret this quotation from the play. Paraphrase the idea expressed in the lines, and explain its significance. **(30 minutes)**

 ## Writing Workshop: *Work in Progress*

How-to Essay

Review the Step List from your writing portfolio. Visualize performing each step, and mark if you have forgotten a step. After you have finished visualizing the task, go back and fill in the missing steps. Put this work in your writing portfolio.

Answers

Reading: Summarizing
1. A
2. D
3. C

Timed Writing

- Tell students that they will have 30 minutes to write an interpretation of a quotation from *Romeo and Juliet*.

- Suggest that students first make sure that they understand the quotation. If necessary, hint at the reference to *a name*.

- Point out to students that they should find references in the play to support their interpretation and use those references in their writing.

- Assess students' interpretations on the accuracy of their explanation of the quote and their explanation of why the concept is important to the play. Also, look at the support they provided for their interpretation. Be sure that students have answered and explained all parts of the assignment.

- Suggest that students plan their time to give 7 minutes to reviewing the quotation, 18 minutes to writing, and 5 minutes to reviewing and revising.

Writing Workshop
Work in Progress

How-to Essay

- Have students go to their portfolio and take out their list of steps.

- Remind students that this work may be used in the how-to essay they will write in the **Writing Workshop** at the end of Part 1.

- Have students physically go through the motions of following the steps to help them remember what the process requires.

- When students have completed their revised steps, have them save them in their portfolios. They will use them as they continue this **Work in Progress.**

Planning Differentiated Instruction

Accessibility at a Glance

	The Tragedy of Romeo and Juliet, Act IV
Context	Historical; Verona, Italy
Language	Dialogue, prose, verse, soliloquies, Elizabethan language, and challenging vocabulary
Concept Level	Accessible; classic tale of star-crossed lovers
Literary Merit	Classic; noted poet and playwright
Lexile	NP
Overall Rating	More challenging

Choosing Your Resources

[L1] Special Needs Students   [L4] Advanced Students
[L2] Below-Level Students   [EL] English Learners
[L3] All Students

FT Fast Track Instruction: To move the lesson more quickly, use the strategies and activities identified with **FT**.

Reading and Vocabulary Warm-ups provide support for below level students. **A** is for students reading two grades below level; **B** is for students reading one grade below level. For Selection Tests, **A** signifies "less challenging" and **B** "more challenging." For Graphic Organizer transparencies, **A** signifies "not filled in" and **B** "filled in."

Scaffolding for Less Proficient and Advanced Students

The leveled questions on Apply the Skills pages progress in the levels of thinking required to answer them. To address the needs of your different students, you may use the (a) level questions for your less proficient students, the (b) level with your on-level and advanced students. The occasional (c) level questions are appropriate for your advanced students.

Go Online
Professional Development
For: Information about Lexiles
Visit: www.PHSchool.com
Web Code: eue-1111

Step-by-Step Teaching Guide	Pacing Guide	
PRETEACH		
• Administer Vocabulary and Reading Warm-ups as necessary.		
• Introduce the Literary Analysis Skills: Dramatic Irony. **FT**	10 min.	
• Introduce the Reading Skill: Breaking Down Long Sentences. **FT**	10 min.	
• Prepare students to read by teaching the selection vocabulary. **FT**	10 min.	
• Build background and develop expressive vocabulary with Connecting to the Literature and Background.	10 min.	
• Engage students' interest with the motivation activity.	10 min.	
TEACH		
• Informally monitor comprehension while students read independently or in groups. **FT**	30 min.	
• Monitor students' comprehension with the Reading Check notes.	as students read	
• Reinforce vocabulary with Vocabulary Builder notes.	as students read	
• Develop students' understanding of dramatic irony with the Literary Analysis annotations. **FT**	5 min.	
• Develop students' ability to break down long sentences with the Reading Skill annotations. **FT**	10 min.	
ASSESS/EXTEND		
• Assess students' comprehension and mastery of the Reading Skill and Literary Analysis by having them answer the Apply the Skills questions. **FT**	35 min.	
• Have students complete the Vocabulary Builder activities. **FT**	5 min.	
• Apply students' ability to write an abstract with the Writing activity. **FT**	30–45 min. or homework	
• Extend students' research and technology skills with the Extend Your Learning activity.	15–30 min. or homework	
• Have students complete the Vocabulary Skill and Grammar Lesson.	5 min.	
• Monitor students' progress with the Assessment Practice.	20–40 min.	
• Administer **Selection Test A** or **Selection Test B**. **FT**	15 min.	

Resources

Meeting Your Standards

Students will

1. **analyze and respond to literary elements.**
   - Literary Analysis: Dramatic Irony

2. **read, comprehend, and analyze plays.**
   - Reading Skill: Summarizing
   - Reading Strategy: Breaking Down Long Sentences
   - Reading Check questions
   - Apply the Skills questions
   - Assessment Practice

3. **develop vocabulary.**
   - Vocabulary Builder
   - Word Root -lum-

4. **apply grammar skills.**
   - Gerund and Gerund Phrases

5. **develop writing proficiency.**
   - Work in Progress: How-to Essay
   - Abstract

6. **extend learning.**
   - Research and Technology: Multimedia Presentation

Block Scheduling: Use one 90-minute class period to preteach the skills and have students read Act IV. Use a second 90-minute class period to assess students' mastery of skills, extend their learning, and monitor their progress.

Homework Suggestions

Following are possibilities for homework assignments.

- Support pages from *Unit 5 Resources:*
   Literary Analysis
   Reading Skill
   Vocabulary Builder
   Enrichment

- An Extend Your Learning project and the Writing assignment for Act IV may be completed over several days.

PRENTICE HALL

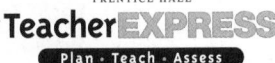 Use this complete
suite of powerful
teaching tools to make lesson planning and testing quicker and easier.

PRENTICE HALL

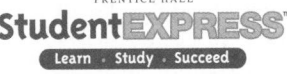 Use the
Interactive
Textbook (online and on CD-ROM) to make Act IV and activities come alive with audio and video support and interactive questions.

PRETEACH

❶ Literary Analysis
Dramatic Irony

- Remind students that they have experienced *dramatic irony* in earlier scenes in which the characters do not know as much as they, the readers, do.

- Tell students that *comic relief* often involves characters introduced for the sole purpose of adding humor.

- Point out that some of Shakespeare's *puns* involve obsolete language. Encourage them to read the footnotes to make sure they understand the language and the puns.

❷ Reading Skill
Summarizing

- Encourage students to be alert for sentences with inverted subject and verb as they summarize passages.

- Give students a copy of **Reading Skill Graphic Organizer A** (*Graphic Organizer Transparencies,* p. 175). Have them fill in the graphic organizer as they summarize the scenes.

Connecting to the Literature

- Remind students that Romeo has risked his life to be with Juliet. Have students use at least three of these expressive words in sentences in which they give some reasons why people might want to risk their lives: *intense, liberate, potential,* and *sacrifice.*

- Provide these sample sentences to demonstrate use of the expressive words:

  1. Someone may deliberately risk his life to experience *intense* excitement.

  2. People may risk their lives to *liberate* other people.

  3. Seeing a *potential* danger to a child may cause people to risk their lives.

  4. Someone may *sacrifice* his life to save a friend.

- Encourage students to use these words as they discuss Act IV.

814

Build Skills *The Tragedy of Romeo and Juliet, Act IV*

❶ Literary Analysis

Dramatic irony is a contradiction between what a character thinks and says and what the audience or reader knows is true. For example, in Act III, Capulet plans Juliet's wedding to Paris. He does not know what you know: that Juliet is already married to Romeo. Dramatic irony involves the audience emotionally in the story.

Shakespeare knew his audience could become *too* involved in the intense emotion of *Romeo and Juliet.* Therefore, he made sure to include the following elements to lighten the play's mood:

- **Comic relief:** a technique used to interrupt a serious scene by introducing a humorous character or situation

- **Puns:** plays on words involving a word with multiple meanings or two words that sound alike but have different meanings. For example, the dying Mercutio makes a pun involving two meanings of the word *grave:* "Ask for me tomorrow, and you shall find me a grave man."

As you read, notice how Shakespeare uses dramatic irony, comic relief, and puns to balance emotional suspense with laughter and wit.

❷ Reading Skill

Summarizing is briefly stating the main points in a piece of writing. Stopping periodically to summarize what you have read helps you to check your comprehension before you read further.

Before you summarize a long passage of Shakespearean dialogue, you should **break down long sentences.**

- If a sentence contains multiple subjects or verbs, separate it into smaller sentences with one subject and one verb.

- If a sentence contains colons, semicolons, or dashes, treat them as periods in order to make smaller sentences.

Use a chart like this to help you break down long sentences.

Vocabulary Builder

- **pensive** (pen' siv) *adj.* deeply thoughtful (p. 816) *She listened intently, looking <u>pensive</u>.*

- **enjoined** (en joind') *v.* ordered (p. 820) *The jurors were <u>enjoined</u> not to discuss the case.*

- **wayward** (wā' wərd) *adj.* headstrong (p. 821) *The <u>wayward</u> boy did not listen to anyone and insisted on working alone.*

- **dismal** (diz' məl) *adj.* causing gloom or misery (p. 821) *The <u>dismal</u> sight of his abandoned house made the old man sad.*

- **loathsome** (lōth' səm) *adj.* disgusting; detestable (p. 823) *The <u>loathsome</u> smell of rotten eggs filled the laboratory.*

814 ■ *Drama*

Line of Dialogue

Immoderately she weeps for Tybalt's death,/ And therefore have I little talked of love;/ For Venus smiles not in a house of tears.

⬇

Line in Smaller Sentences

1. Immoderately she weeps for Tybalt's death.
2. Therefore have I little talked of love.
3. Venus smiles not in a house of tears.

⬇

Summary of Line

Paris has not talked of love with Juliet because she is crying over Tybalt's death.

Vocabulary Development

Vocabulary Knowledge Rating

Create a **Vocabulary Knowledge Rating Chart** with these words from Act IV:

pensive	dismal
enjoined	loathsome
wayward	

Give students a copy. Introduce the words by reading them aloud and having students mark their rating in the Before Reading column. Urge them to be alert to these words as they read and discuss the Act IV of *The Tragedy of Romeo and Juliet,* because they will rate their knowledge of the words again after they finish.

If you wish, you may tally how many students know (or think they know) a word to gauge how much instruction you need to provide. As students read, point out the words and their context.

ACT IV

❶
❷

Review and Anticipate

Romeo and Juliet are married for only a few hours when disaster strikes. In Act III, Juliet's cousin Tybalt kills Mercutio, and then Romeo kills Tybalt. This leads to Romeo's banishment from Verona. To make matters worse, Juliet's parents are determined to marry her to Paris. Will Romeo and Juliet ever be able to live together as husband and wife? What, if anything, can the lovers now do to preserve their relationship?

Scene i. FRIAR LAWRENCE'S cell.

[*Enter* FRIAR LAWRENCE *and* COUNTY PARIS.]

    FRIAR. On Thursday, sir? The time is very short.

    PARIS. My father[1] Capulet will have it so,
        And I am nothing slow to slack his haste.[2]

    FRIAR. You say you do not know the lady's mind.
5   Uneven is the course;[3] I like it not.

❹   **PARIS.** Immoderately she weeps for Tybalt's death,
        And therefore have I little talked of love;
        For Venus smiles not in a house of tears.

---

1. father future father-in-law.

2. I . . . haste I will not slow him down by being slow myself.

3. Uneven . . . course irregular is the plan.

❸ Reading Check

What is the Friar's complaint to Paris about the impending wedding?

Romeo and Juliet, Act IV ■ *815*

TEACH

❶ Motivation

As this act opens, plans for Juliet's marriage to Paris are moving ahead. Romeo is exiled in Mantua, and Juliet alone must decide what to do about marrying Paris.

Have students imagine themselves in Juliet's place. Remind them that only the Nurse and the Friar know of her marriage to Romeo. The Nurse has already betrayed her, advising her to forget Romeo, pretend she never married him, and go ahead and marry Paris.

Have students brainstorm for solutions to Juliet's problem. Write the possible solutions on the chalkboard. Then, next to each, have students write the possible consequences of the solution.

Finally, have students read Act IV to see how Juliet addresses her problem.

Learning Modalities
Verbal/Linguistic
Tell students that this act alternates scenes of high emotion with scenes of humor. As students read this act, have them note how the act is structured—which scenes are emotionally charged and which scenes provide the comic relief. Then, have students discuss how the comic scenes and their placement in the story affect the act. Ask what would happen if the comic scenes were left out. How do the comic scenes further the action of the play?

❷ About the Selection

Act IV belongs to Juliet as she interacts with the Friar, Paris, her parents, and the Nurse. Using witty wordplay and misleading statements, Juliet avoids suspicion about her true intent. Her unwillingness to confront her parents, along with her trust in the Friar, leads her further along the road to tragedy. Act IV illustrates a paradox at work within Juliet: She is brave enough to follow the Friar's risky plan, but she is at the same time afraid to tell her parents the truth.

❸ Reading Check

Answer: The Friar complains about the hastiness of the planned wedding.

❹ Literary Analysis
Dramatic Irony

Ask students what Paris is trying to explain to the Friar in his speech here.

Answer: Paris is explaining why his marriage to Juliet must occur as quickly as possible.

- Remind students that *dramatic irony* is a contradiction between what a character thinks is true and what the reader or audience knows is true.

- **Ask** students what the reader and the audience knows about why Juliet is crying.
  Answer: Juliet is crying because her parents are trying to marry her to Paris when she and Romeo are already married.

- **Ask** students to respond to the Literary Analysis question: In what way does Paris's comment show that he does not understand the real reason that Juliet is crying?
  Answer: Paris says that Juliet is crying over Tybalt's death.

❺ Critical Thinking
Predicting

- **Ask** students whether Juliet actually lies to Paris at any time in this exchange. What does she do?
  Answer: Juliet does not lie to Paris, but she keeps him off balance with her clever wordplay.

- Have students **interpret** the exchange in lines 35–36.
  Answer: Paris says that Juliet's face belongs to him. Juliet seems to agree with him, but readers know that Juliet means that her face belongs to Romeo.

- **Ask** students whether Juliet will consider Paris an ally based on this dialogue. Why or why not?
  Answer: Juliet will not consider Paris an ally because he wants to marry her. Also, she plays word games with him instead of answering him truthfully.

---

10 Now, sir, her father counts it dangerous
That she do give her sorrow so much sway,
And in his wisdom hastes our marriage
❹ To stop the inundation⁴ of her tears,
Which, too much minded⁵ by herself alone,
May be put from her by society.
15 Now do you know the reason of this haste.

FRIAR. [*Aside*] I would I knew not why it should be slowed.—
Look, sir, here comes the lady toward my cell.

[*Enter* JULIET.]

PARIS. Happily met, my lady and my wife!

JULIET. That may be, sir, when I may be a wife.

20 PARIS. That "may be" must be, love, on Thursday next.

JULIET. What must be shall be.

FRIAR.   That's a certain text.⁶

PARIS. Come you to make confession to this father?

JULIET. To answer that, I should confess to you.

PARIS. Do not deny to him that you love me.

25 JULIET. I will confess to you that I love him.

❺ PARIS. So will ye, I am sure, that you love me.

JULIET. If I do so, it will be of more price,⁷
Being spoke behind your back, than to your face.

PARIS. Poor soul, thy face is much abused with tears.

30 JULIET. The tears have got small victory by that,
For it was bad enough before their spite.⁸

PARIS. Thou wrong'st it more than tears with that report.

JULIET. That is no slander, sir, which is a truth;
And what I spake, I spake it to my face.

35 PARIS. Thy face is mine, and thou hast sland'red it.

JULIET. It may be so, for it is not mine own.
Are you at leisure, holy father, now,
Or shall I come to you at evening mass?

FRIAR. My leisure serves me, pensive daughter, now.
40 My lord, we must entreat the time alone.⁹

PARIS. God shield¹⁰ I should disturb devotion!

816 ■ Drama

4. **inundation** flood.
5. **minded** thought about.

Literary Analysis
Dramatic Irony In what way does Paris' comment show that he does not understand the real reason that Juliet is crying?

6. **That's . . . text** That is a certain truth.

7. **price** value.

8. **before their spite** before the harm that the tears did.

Vocabulary Builder
pensive (pen´ siv) *adj.*
deeply thoughtful

9. **entreat . . . alone** ask to have this time to ourselves.

10. **shield** forbid.

Vocabulary Development

Vocabulary Building Reinforcement

Reinforce student's comprehension with "show-you-know" sentences. The first part of the sentence uses the vocabulary word in an appropriate context. The second part of the sentence—the "show-you-know" part—clarifies the first. Model the strategy with this example for *pensive*:

She seemed to be in a *pensive* mood; she was quiet, staring off into the distance as if she were deep in thought.

Then, give students these sentence prompts, and coach them in creating the clarification part:

1. He had always been a *wayward* child;_____
   Sample answer: his parents could never get him to do as they wished.

2. It was a *dismal* day; _____
   Sample answer: it was damp and cold, and the rain began in the late afternoon.

Juliet, on Thursday early will I rouse ye.
Till then, adieu, and keep this holy kiss.   [*Exit.*]

JULIET. O, shut the door, and when thou hast done so,
45   Come weep with me—past hope, past care, past help!

FRIAR. O Juliet, I already know thy grief;
It strains me past the compass of my wits.[11]
I hear thou must, and nothing may prorogue[12] it,
On Thursday next be married to this County.

50   **JULIET.** Tell me not, friar, that thou hearest of this,
Unless thou tell me how I may prevent it.
If in thy wisdom thou canst give no help,
Do thou but call my resolution wise
And with this knife I'll help it presently.[13]
55   God joined my heart and Romeo's, thou our hands;
6   And ere this hand, by thee to Romeo's sealed,
Shall be the label to another deed,[14]
Or my true heart with treacherous revolt
Turn to another, this shall slay them both.
60   Therefore, out of thy long-experienced time,
Give me some present counsel; or, behold,
'Twixt my extremes and me[15] this bloody knife
Shall play the umpire, arbitrating[16] that
Which the commission of thy years and art
65   Could to no issue of true honor bring.[17]
Be not so long to speak. I long to die
If what thou speak'st speak not of remedy.

FRIAR. Hold, daughter. I do spy a kind of hope,
Which craves[18] as desperate an execution
70   As that is desperate which we would prevent.
If, rather than to marry County Paris,
7   Thou hast the strength of will to slay thyself,
Then is it likely thou wilt undertake
A thing like death to chide away this shame,
75   That cop'st with death himself to scape from it;[19]
And, if thou darest, I'll give thee remedy.

JULIET. O, bid me leap, rather than marry Paris,
From off the battlements of any tower,
Or walk in thievish ways,[20] or bid me lurk
80   Where serpents are; chain me with roaring bears,
Or hide me nightly in a charnel house,[21]
O'ercovered quite with dead men's rattling bones,

---

11. **past . . . wits** beyond the ability of my mind to find a remedy.

12. **prorogue** delay.

13. **presently** at once.

14. **Shall . . . deed** shall give the seal of approval to another marriage contract.

15. **'Twixt . . me** between my misfortunes and me.

16. **arbitrating** deciding.

17. **Which . . . bring** which the authority that derives from your age and ability could not solve honorably.

Literary Analysis
Puns Which two meanings of the word "long" does Juliet use to make a pun in line 66?

18. **craves** requires.

19. **That cop'st . . . it** that bargains with death itself to escape from it.

20. **thievish ways** roads where criminals lurk.

21. **charnel house** vault for bones removed from graves to be reused.

8 ✓ **Reading Check**

What does Juliet threaten to do to avoid marrying Paris?

Romeo and Juliet, Act IV ■ *817*

---

6 Literary Analysis
Puns

- Have students read lines 46–49. Ask them to **identify** the Friar's message to Juliet in these lines.
  Answer: The Friar has no more ideas about what to do for the two lovers. He says that nothing will delay the marriage and Juliet should accept the inevitable.

- Have students read lines 50–67. **Ask** how Juliet responds to the Friar's suggestion.
  Answer: Juliet tells him not to speak of the wedding unless he can tell her how to prevent it. Otherwise she will die.

- **Ask** students in which two ways Juliet uses the word *speak* in line 67.
  Answer: She uses *speak'st* to mean "say," and she uses *speak* to mean "inform."

- **Ask** students to respond to the Literary Analysis question: Which two meanings of the word *long* does Juliet use to make a pun in line 66?
  Answer: In the first sentence, she uses *long* to mean "do not take a long time." In the second sentence she uses it to mean "I wish."

7 Critical Thinking
Analyze

- Have students think about how the Friar has involved himself with Romeo and Juliet. Then ask students whether they think the Friar has acted responsibly so far. Why or why not?
  Possible response: Students may suggest that the Friar has helped Romeo and Juliet deceive their parents, and now he is going to suggest a dangerous solution to Juliet's problems, rather than advising her to tell the truth to her parents. He does not seem to be acting responsibly.

8 Reading Check

Answer: Juliet threatens to kill herself with a knife rather than marry Paris.

- Have students read lines 90–102.
Ask what the Friar tells Juliet to do.
Answer: He tells her to go home, be cheerful, and tell her parents that she will marry Paris.

- **Ask** students to predict what the Friar's complete plan will turn out to be.
Possible response: The Friar plans to put Juliet into a deep sleep so that she appears to be dead, thereby avoiding marriage to Paris.

❿ Background
Medicine

In this scene, the Friar gives Juliet a potion that will make her appear dead when she drinks it. It may be difficult to believe that someone could be thought dead when he or she was not. However, the technology for determining death was very primitive in the times in which these events took place. Medieval doctors did not use a stethoscope, which was invented in 1816. Doctors at this time determined death by putting their ear next to the patient's body to hear the sounds of the body's organs.

⓫ Critical Viewing

Answer: The vial contains a liquid that creates a state of simulated death.

---

85   With reeky[22] shanks and yellow chapless[23] skulls;
Or bid me go into a new-made grave
And hide me with a dead man in his shroud—
Things that, to hear them told, have made me tremble—
And I will do it without fear or doubt,
To live an unstained wife to my sweet love.

FRIAR. Hold, then. Go home, be merry, give consent
90   To marry Paris. Wednesday is tomorrow.
❾   Tomorrow night look that thou lie alone;
Let not the nurse lie with thee in thy chamber.
❿   Take thou this vial, being then in bed,
And this distilling liquor drink thou off;
95   When presently through all thy veins shall run
A cold and drowsy humor;[24] for no pulse
Shall keep his native[25] progress, but surcease;[26]
No warmth, no breath, shall testify thou livest;
The roses in thy lips and cheeks shall fade
100 To wanny ashes,[27] thy eyes' windows[28] fall
Like death when he shuts up the day of life;
Each part, deprived of supple government,[29]

22. **reeky** foul-smelling.

23. **chapless** jawless.

24. **humor** fluid; liquid.

25. **native** natural.

26. **surcease** stop.

27. **wanny ashes** to the color of pale ashes.

28. **eyes' windows** eyelids.

29. **supple government** ability for maintaining motion.

⓫ ▼ **Critical Viewing**
According to the play, what power does the vial hold? **[Connect]**

818 ■ *Drama*

Vocabulary Development

Expressive Vocabulary
As students read through Scene i, have them think about Juliet's predicament, and the remedy that Friar Lawrence suggests. As students discuss these lines, encourage them to use the expressive vocabulary presented earlier. You might encourage them with sentence starters like these:

1. Juliet's *intense* sorrow . . .
2. The potion Friar Lawrence offered has the *potential* . . .
3. Juliet hopes to *liberate* . . .
4. She is willing to make any *sacrifice* to . . .
5. The Friar did not *assess* . . .

Challenge students to use these words as you continue to discuss the play.

Shall, stiff and stark and cold, appear like death;
And in this borrowed likeness of shrunk death

105 Thou shalt continue two-and-forty hours,
And then awake as from a pleasant sleep.
Now, when the bridegroom in the morning comes
To rouse thee from thy bed, there art thou dead.
Then, as the manner of our country is,

110 In thy best robes uncovered on the bier[30]
Thou shalt be borne to that same ancient vault
Where all the kindred of the Capulets lie.
In the meantime, against[31] thou shalt awake,
Shall Romeo by my letters know our drift;[32]

115 And hither shall he come; and he and I
Will watch thy waking, and that very night
Shall Romeo bear thee hence to Mantua.
And this shall free thee from this present shame,
If no inconstant toy[33] nor womanish fear

120 Abate thy valor[34] in the acting it.

JULIET. Give me, give me! O, tell not me of fear!

FRIAR. Hold! Get you gone, be strong and prosperous
In this resolve. I'll send a friar with speed
To Mantua, with my letters to thy lord.

125 **JULIET.** Love give me strength, and strength shall help afford.
Farewell, dear father.   [*Exit with* FRIAR.]

Scene ii. Hall in CAPULET'S *house.*

[*Enter* FATHER CAPULET, MOTHER, NURSE, *and* SERVINGMEN, *two or three.*]

   CAPULET. So many guests invite as here are writ.
                                 [*Exit a* SERVINGMAN.]
   Sirrah, go hire me twenty cunning[1] cooks.

   SERVINGMAN. You shall have none ill, sir; for I'll try[2] if they can
   lick their fingers.

5   **CAPULET.** How canst thou try them so?

   SERVINGMAN. Marry, sir, 'tis an ill cook that cannot lick his own
   fingers.[3] Therefore he that cannot lick his fingers goes not
   with me.

   CAPULET. Go, begone.
                     [*Exit* SERVINGMAN.]

---

30. uncovered on the bier displayed on the funeral platform.

31. against before.

32. drift purpose; plan.

33. inconstant toy passing whim.

34. Abate thy valor Lessen your courage.

**Literary Analysis
Dramatic Irony** What information does Juliet now have that Romeo does not?

1. cunning skillful.

2. try test.

3. 'tis . . . fingers It is a bad cook who will not taste his own cooking.

 Reading Check

According to the Friar, how will Romeo learn of Juliet's plan to meet him?

Romeo and Juliet, Act IV ▪ 819

**⓬ Critical Thinking
Predicting**

• Have students read lines 106–113. **Ask** them to compare modern burial arrangements with those of the Capulets.
Answer: In Juliet's time, people were wrapped in robes and put into a large vault, or tomb. Modern funeral practices include embalming and burial; cremation is a common alternative. These practices would preclude using the Friar's plan in the present day.

• **Ask** students to predict what the Friar plans to have happen next. Then, ask students to read the rest of his monologue to check their predictions.
Possible response: The Friar will make arrangements to find Romeo and reunite him with Juliet when she awakens from her sleep in the tomb.

**⓭ Literary Analysis
Dramatic Irony**

• Ask students what Juliet says to the Friar when he says that the plan will only work if she has courage.
Answer: She says she does not want to hear from him about fear and that her love gives her strength.

• **Ask** students to respond to the Literary Analysis question: What information does Juliet now have that Romeo does not?
Answer: Juliet now has a plan for escaping marriage to Paris by feigning death. Romeo's lack of knowledge about this plan will have fateful consequences.

⓮ Reading Check

Answer: Friar Lawrence will send another friar to Mantua with letters to Romeo explaining the plan.

⓯ Background

Names

Students may find the word *County* a strange one as a title for Paris. The word was an English form for the Italian *conte,* meaning "count," or "earl."

⓰ Literary Analysis

Dramatic Irony

- Have students read lines 24–31. **Ask** students to explain what Juliet tells her father in lines 24–26 and what he takes it to mean.
Answer: She tells her father that she has met Paris and has professed as much love as she modestly could. He takes it to mean that she is now happy to be marrying Paris.

- **Ask** students what change in schedule is revealed in this conversation.
Answer: Lord Capulet says they will not wait until Thursday; the wedding will occur "tomorrow morning."

- **Ask** students how this change of the wedding date might affect the outcome of the Friar's plan.
Answer: The Friar has less time to notify Romeo, so Romeo might not be at the tomb when Juliet awakens.

- **Ask** students to respond to the Literary Analysis question: What is ironic about Lord Capulet's relief in this scene?
Answer: Capulet is relieved because he believes Juliet and Paris will be married tomorrow according to his wishes. In fact, the change of the date and haste of the marriage will bring tragedy to his family.

We shall be much unfurnished⁴ for this time.

10   What, is my daughter gone to Friar Lawrence?

NURSE. Ay, forsooth.⁵

CAPULET. Well, he may chance to do some good on her.
A peevish self-willed harlotry it is.⁶

[*Enter* JULIET.]

NURSE. See where she comes from shrift with merry look.

15 **CAPULET.** How now, my headstrong? Where have you been
gadding?

JULIET. Where I have learnt me to repent the sin
Of disobedient opposition
To you and your behests,⁷ and am <u>enjoined</u>
By holy Lawrence to fall prostrate⁸ here
20   To beg your pardon. Pardon, I beseech you!
Henceforward I am ever ruled by you.

⓯ **CAPULET.** Send for the County. Go tell him of this.
I'll have this knot knit up tomorrow morning.

JULIET. I met the youthful lord at Lawrence' cell
25   And gave him what becomèd⁹ love I might,
Not stepping o'er the bounds of modesty.

⓰ **CAPULET.** Why, I am glad on't. This is well. Stand up.
This is as't should be. Let me see the County.
Ay, marry, go, I say, and fetch him hither.
30   Now, afore God, this reverend holy friar,
All our whole city is much bound¹⁰ to him.

JULIET. Nurse, will you go with me into my closet¹¹
To help me sort such needful ornaments¹²
As you think fit to furnish me tomorrow?

35 **LADY CAPULET.** No, not till Thursday. There is time enough.

CAPULET. Go, nurse, go with her. We'll to church tomorrow.
[*Exit* JULIET *and* NURSE.]

LADY CAPULET. We shall be short in our provision.¹³
'Tis now near night.

CAPULET.   Tush, I will stir about,
And all things shall be well, I warrant thee, wife.
40   Go thou to Juliet, help to deck up her.¹⁴
I'll not to bed tonight; let me alone.
I'll play the housewife for this once. What, ho!¹⁵

820 ■ *Drama*

---

4. **unfurnished** unprepared.
5. **forsooth** in truth.
6. **A peevish . . . it is** It is the ill-tempered, selfish behavior of a woman without good breeding.

Vocabulary Builder
enjoined (en joind´)
v. ordered

7. **behests** requests.
8. **fall prostrate** lie face down in humble submission.

9. **becomèd** suitable; proper.

Literary Analysis
Dramatic Irony What is ironic about Lord Capulet's relief in this scene?

10. **bound** indebted.
11. **closet** private room.
12. **ornaments** clothes.

13. **short . . . provision** lacking time for preparation.

14. **deck up her** dress her; get her ready.
15. **What, ho!** Capulet is calling for his servants.

Vocabulary Development

Word Analysis

Refer students to the Vocabulary Builder word *wayward* on p. 821, line 46. Tell students that the suffix *-ward* means "in a direction." This suffix appears in the word *wayward,* which means "headstrong," or "insistent upon going in one's own direction."

Write the following words on the chalkboard: *forward, skyward,* and *outward.*

Ask students to use the meaning of the suffix *-ward*—"in a direction"—to define each of these words.
Answer: *Forward* means "in the direction of the front or head." *Skyward* means "in the direction of the sky." *Outward* means "to or toward the outside."

They are all forth; well, I will walk myself
To County Paris, to prepare up him
45 Against tomorrow. My heart is wondrous light,
Since this same <u>wayward</u> girl is so reclaimed.

[*Exit with* MOTHER.]

Scene iii. JULIET'S chamber.

[*Enter* JULIET *and* NURSE.]

JULIET. Ay, those attires are best; but, gentle nurse,
I pray thee leave me to myself tonight;
For I have need of many orisons[1]
To move the heavens to smile upon my state,[2]
5 Which, well thou knowest, is cross[3] and full of sin.

[*Enter* MOTHER.]

LADY CAPULET. What, are you busy, ho? Need you my help?

JULIET. No, madam; we have culled[4] such necessaries
As are behoveful[5] for our state tomorrow.
So please you, let me now be left alone,
10 And let the nurse this night sit up with you:
For I am sure you have your hands full all
In this so sudden business.

LADY CAPULET.   Good night.
Get thee to bed, and rest: for thou hast need.

[*Exit* MOTHER *and* NURSE.]

JULIET. Farewell! God knows when we shall meet again.
15 I have a faint cold fear thrills through my veins
That almost freezes up the heat of life.
I'll call them back again to comfort me.
Nurse!—What should she do here?
My <u>dismal</u> scene I needs must act alone.
20 Come, vial.
What if this mixture do not work at all?
Shall I be married then tomorrow morning?
No, no! This shall forbid it. Lie thou there.

[*Lays down a dagger.*]

What if it be a poison which the friar
25 Subtly hath minist'red[6] to have me dead,
Lest in this marriage he should be dishonored
Because he married me before to Romeo?

Vocabulary Builder
wayward (wā´ wərd)
adj. headstrong

1. **orisons** prayers.
2. **state** condition.
3. **cross** selfish; disobedient.

Reading Skill
Summarizing Briefly
state the reasons
Juliet gives her Nurse
and Lady Capulet for
why she should be
alone.

4. **culled** chosen.
5. **behoveful** desirable;
appropriate.

Vocabulary Builder
dismal (diz´ məl)
adj. causing gloom or
misery

6. **minist'red** given me.

✓ **Reading Check**

How does Juliet
regain her parents'
favor?

Romeo and Juliet, Act IV ■ *821*

---

⑰ Reading Skill
Summarizing

- Have students read lines 1–12.
  Then, **ask** students to identify the
  setting of this scene and which
  characters are present.
  Answer: The scene is Juliet's bedroom. She and the Nurse are present as the scene opens, and her
  mother enters.

- **Ask** why Lady Capulet and Nurse
  come to Juliet's room.
  Answer: They want to help her
  get ready for the wedding the next
  day.

- **Ask** students to respond to the
  Reading Skill prompt: Briefly state
  the reasons Juliet gives her Nurse
  and Lady Capulet for why she
  should be alone.
  Answer: She says she has many
  prayers to say; she and the Nurse
  have chosen all her things for the
  next day.

⑱ Critical Thinking
Interpret

- Have students read lines 24–27.
  Ask students why Juliet might
  wonder whether the Friar has given
  her a drink that really will kill her.
  Answer: Juliet recognizes that the
  Friar has put himself in a difficult
  position. He has married Romeo
  and Juliet secretly, and he has
  encouraged Juliet to go along with
  the plans for marriage to Paris. If
  the marriage takes place, the Friar
  has made Juliet a bigamist.
  However, if Juliet really dies, his
  scheme will not be revealed. Other
  students might argue that Friar
  Lawrence is, after all, a member of
  the Church, and would not know-
  ingly kill a person.

⑲ Reading Check

Answer: She tells her father that she
has seen Paris and has pledged as
much love to him as she modestly
could.

Strategy for Less Proficient Readers
Point out to students that Juliet's soliloquy in
Act IV, scene iii, lines 14–59 is one of the high
points of the play.

    Help students appreciate this soliloquy by
first reviewing the footnotes with students,
making sure they understand all the terms.

    Then, explain the scene to students: Juliet
is contemplating what she is facing, and she is
frightened. She wonders what will happen if
the potion doesn't work. What will happen if it

is too strong and kills her? What if she wakes
before Romeo arrives, and she must lie there in
the tomb among the dead bodies? Tybalt lies
there, his body decaying. What if the spirits of
the dead rise up? What if she goes mad?

    After students have visualized Juliet's anxi-
eties, have them listen to this soliloquy on the
Listening to Literature Audio CD as they read
along.

821

Film

Juliet kneels as she drinks the fateful potion in this scene from Zeffirelli's *Romeo and Juliet.* Juliet's closed eyes and supplicating posture suggest an attitude of prayer. Use the following questions for discussion:

1. Look at Juliet's expression. What emotion or emotions is she experiencing?
   Answer: Students may say that Juliet's expression reflects her desperation or fear, her love for Romeo, or her determination to act.

2. What elements of the setting help to reinforce these emotions?
   Answer: Students may say the dimly lit background emphasizes the impending tragedy, and that Juliet's white robes emphasize her youth and purity.

822 ▪ *Drama*

Vocabulary Development

Multiple Meanings

Call students' attention to the word *spit* on p. 823, line 56. Tell students that the word has two different sets of meanings, with two different origins.

The first set of meanings of *spit* comes from a Middle English word meaning "a point." Here the word can mean: 1. (noun) "a thin pointed rod on which meat is placed to be roasted; 2. (noun) "a point of land that extends into the water"; 3. (verb) "to thrust a pointed rod through."

The second set of meanings is related to the Latin word *sputum.* In this sense, *spit* can mean 1. (verb) "to eject saliva from the mouth"; 2. (verb) "to rain or snow slightly"; 3. (noun) "saliva."

After reading these two sets of definitions to students, ask students to read lines 55–57 and explain which definition of *spit* they think applies in this context
Answer: Juliet means "to thrust a pointed rod through," from the first set of meanings.

I fear it is; and yet methinks it should not,
For he hath still been tried⁷ a holy man.

30 How if, when I am laid into the tomb,
I wake before the time that Romeo
㉑ Come to redeem me? There's a fearful point!
Shall I not then be stifled in the vault,
To whose foul mouth no healthsome air breathes in,
35 And there die strangled ere my Romeo comes?
Or, if I live, is it not very like
The horrible conceit⁸ of death and night,
Together with the terror of the place—
As in a vault, an ancient receptacle
40 Where for this many hundred years the bones
Of all my buried ancestors are packed;
Where bloody Tybalt, yet but green in earth,⁹
Lies fest'ring in his shroud; where, as they say,
At some hours in the night spirits resort—
45 Alack, alack, is it not like¹⁰ that I,
So early waking—what with <u>loathsome</u> smells,
And shrieks like mandrakes¹¹ torn out of the earth,
㉒ That living mortals, hearing them, run mad—
O, if I wake, shall I not be distraught,¹²
50 Environèd¹³ with all these hideous fears,
And madly play with my forefathers' joints,
And pluck the mangled Tybalt from his shroud,
And, in this rage, with some great kinsman's bone
As with a club dash out my desp'rate brains?
55 O, look! Methinks I see my cousin's ghost
Seeking out Romeo, that did spit his body
Upon a rapier's point. Stay, Tybalt, stay!
Romeo, Romeo, Romeo, I drink to thee.
              [*She falls upon her bed within the curtains.*]

Scene iv. *Hall in* CAPULET'S *house.*

[*Enter* LADY OF THE HOUSE *and* NURSE.]

     LADY CAPULET. Hold, take these keys and fetch more spices,
          nurse.

㉓ ◀ Critical Viewing Do you think Juliet's decision to take the potion is
courageous? Why or why not? **[Evaluate]**

---

7. tried proved.

8. conceit idea; thought.

9. green in earth newly
entombed.
10. like likely.

Vocabulary Builder
loathsome (lōth′ səm)
adj. disgusting;
detestable

11. mandrakes plants with
forked roots that resemble
human legs. The mandrake
was believed to shriek when
uprooted and cause the hearer
to go mad.
12. distraught insane.
13. Environèd surrounded.

Reading Skill
Summarizing Sum-
marize the fears that
Juliet expresses in this
soliloquy.

㉔ ✓Reading Check

What does Juliet do
after her mother and
the Nurse leave her
chambers?

Romeo and Juliet, Act IV ■ 823

㉑ Background
Juliet's fears of being buried alive in
the tomb, or of dying from the
potion, were well founded. During
the period in which the play is set,
people's fear of being buried alive
was legitimate, as comas and other
physiological states could mimic
death for a time. Although the play
never says what the Friar's potion is,
it is likely to have been a very strong
tranquilizer made from a local plant.
Taking such a drug would be an
enormous risk, and Juliet is right to
be fearful.

㉒ Reading Skill
Summarizing
• Have students review Juliet's entire
soliloquy, beginning on p. 821,
line 14.
• **Ask** students to respond to the
Reading Skill prompt: Summarize
the fears that Juliet expresses in this
soliloquy.
Answer: She wonders what will
happen if the potion doesn't work,
and then she will have to go
through with the wedding. What
will happen if the Friar has deliberately made the potion strong
enough to kill her and save himself? What if she wakes before
Romeo arrives? That would be the
worst. She would have to lie there
in the tomb among the dead bodies. Tybalt lies there, his body still
decaying. What if the spirits of the
dead rise up, or she goes mad in
the hideous place?

㉓ Critical Viewing
Possible response: Some students
may say Juliet's decision is courageous because she believes that this
is her only chance for happiness with
Romeo. Others may say that her
decision is foolish because she is not
certain that the Friar is trustworthy,
and there are too many ways the
plan can go wrong.

㉔ Reading Check
Answer: Juliet faces her anxieties
about taking the potion, and then
she drinks it.

25 Critical Thinking
Interpret

- Ask students what kinds of activities are taking place in this scene. What is the general mood?
  Answer: The Capulets are making food preparations for the wedding; servants who have been on watch are now ordered to bed; Lord and Lady Capulet are insulting each other; Capulet calls to the Nurse to wake Juliet. The general mood is one of excitement and good cheer.

- **Ask** students to predict how the activities and mood in this household will change shortly.
  Answer: When the Capulets find Juliet and believe she is dead, the preparations will begin for a funeral rather than a wedding, and the mood will change from excitement and joy to grief and sorrow.

26 Literary Analysis
Puns

- Have students read lines 16–21. **Ask** what the fellows who enter here are carrying.
  Answer: They are carrying spits and logs for the fire, and baskets.

- **Ask** students what Capulet asks them to fetch. Why does Capulet tell them to ask Peter for help?
  Answer: He asks them to fetch drier logs. He tells them to ask Peter because he does not think they can figure out where to find drier logs.

- **Ask** what pun Capulet makes with the word *loggerhead* in line 25.
  Answer: The second fellow says that he has a head—that is the intelligence—to find the logs. Capulet replies that he is a "logger-head," meaning a blockhead.

- **Ask** students to respond to the Literary Analysis question on p. 824: In what way does Capulet's pun in line 21 contribute to the mood of scene iv ?
  Possible response: Students may say that the pun adds to the general mood of good humor as the household prepares for the coming wedding feast.

NURSE. They call for dates and quinces[1] in the pastry.[2]

[*Enter old* CAPULET.]

    CAPULET. Come, stir, stir, stir! The second cock hath crowed,
      The curfew bell hath rung, 'tis three o'clock.
5   Look to the baked meats, good Angelica;[3]
      Spare not for cost.

    NURSE.   Go, you cotquean,[4] go,
      Get you to bed! Faith, you'll be sick tomorrow
      For this night's watching.[5]

    CAPULET. No, not a whit. What, I have watched ere now
10   All night for lesser cause, and ne'er been sick.

    LADY CAPULET. Ay, you have been a mouse hunt[6] in your time;
      But I will watch you from such watching now.

                      [*Exit* LADY *and* NURSE.]

    CAPULET. A jealous hood,[7] a jealous hood!
[*Enter three or four* FELLOWS *with spits and logs and baskets.*]
                      Now, fellow,
      What is there?

15 **FIRST FELLOW.** Things for the cook, sir; but I know not what.

    CAPULET. Make haste, make haste. [*Exit* FIRST FELLOW.] Sirrah,
      fetch drier logs.
      Call Peter; he will show thee where they are.

    SECOND FELLOW. I have a head, sir, that will find out logs
      And never trouble Peter for the matter.

20 **CAPULET.** Mass,[8] and well said; a merry whoreson, ha!
      Thou shalt be loggerhead.[9]

               [*Exit* SECOND FELLOW, *with the others.*]
           Good faith, 'tis day.
      The County will be here with music straight,
      For so he said he would.   [*Play music.*]
            I hear him near.
      Nurse! Wife! What, ho! What, nurse, I say!

[*Enter* NURSE.]
25   Go waken Juliet; go and trim her up.
      I'll go and chat with Paris. Hie, make haste,
      Make haste! The bridegroom he is come already:
      Make haste, I say.   [*Exit.*]

1. **quinces** golden, apple-shaped fruits.
2. **pastry** baking room.
3. **Angelica** This is probably the Nurse's name.
4. **cotquean** (kät´ kwēn´) man who does housework.
5. **watching** staying awake.

6. **mouse hunt** woman chaser.

7. **jealous hood** jealousy.

8. **Mass** by the Mass (an oath).
9. **loggerhead** blockhead.

Literary Analysis
Puns In what way does Capulet's pun in line 21 contribute to the mood of Scene iv?

Scene v. JULIET'S chamber.

NURSE. Mistress! What, mistress! Juliet! Fast,[1] I warrant her,
    she.
Why, lamb! Why, lady! Fie, you slugabed.[2]
Why, love, I say! Madam; Sweetheart! Why, bride!
What, not a word? You take your pennyworths now;
5 Sleep for a week; for the next night, I warrant,
The County Paris hath set up his rest
That you shall rest but little. God forgive me!
Marry, and amen. How sound is she asleep!
I needs must wake her. Madam, madam, madam!
10 Ay, let the County take you in your bed;
He'll fright you up, i' faith. Will it not be?
                [Draws aside the curtains.]
What, dressed, and in your clothes, and down again?[3]
I must needs wake you. Lady! Lady! Lady!
Alas, alas! Help, help! My lady's dead!
15 O weraday that ever I was born!
Some aqua vitae, ho! My lord! My lady!

[Enter MOTHER.]

LADY CAPULET. What noise is here?

NURSE.   O lamentable day!

LADY CAPULET. What is the matter?

NURSE.   Look, look! O heavy day!

LADY CAPULET. O me, O me! My child, my only life!
20 Revive, look up, or I will die with thee!
Help, help! Call help.

[Enter FATHER.]

CAPULET. For shame, bring Juliet forth; her lord is come.

NURSE. She's dead, deceased; she's dead, alack the day!

LADY CAPULET. Alack the day, she's dead, she's dead, she's
    dead!

25 CAPULET. Ha! Let me see her. Out alas! She's cold,
Her blood is settled, and her joints are stiff;
Life and these lips have long been separated.
Death lies on her like an untimely frost
Upon the sweetest flower of all the field.

---

1. **Fast** fast asleep.
2. **slugabed** sleepyhead.

Literary Analysis
Dramatic Irony In what way does the Nurse's carefree chatter add to the irony of the scene?

3. **down again** back in bed.

 Reading Check

What does the Nurse find when she draws aside the curtains in Juliet's chamber?

Romeo and Juliet, Act IV ■ 825

Differentiated Instruction   Solutions for All Learners

Strategy for Less Proficient Readers
Have students refer to the silly conversation between Capulet and the Fellows on p. 824. Point out that this is an example of *comic relief.* Have students note that this scene follows Juliet's intense soliloquy in Scene iii, and precedes the discovery of Juliet's apparently lifeless body in Scene v. Point out that this scene gives the audience or the reader time to recover from the heightened emotions of the previous scene. It also creates an air of suspense about what will happen when Juliet is discovered.

Strategy for English Learners
Students may be confused by the Nurse's repeated use of the word *why* in the opening of this scene. Point out that the repetition of the word *why* emphasizes the number of times the Nurse struggles to wake Juliet. Read Scene v, lines 1–10 aloud for students, modeling how the Nurse uses the word. Point out that the word itself suggests the meaning, "Why won't you wake up, girl!" or words to that effect.

825

Literary Analysis
Dramatic Irony

- Refer students to the bracketed passage. **Ask** students why the Friar has come to the Capulets' home.
  Answer: He has come to marry Juliet and Paris.

- Have students read line 38.
  Ask students to respond to the first Literary Analysis question: In what way does the Friar's question add to the dramatic irony of the scene?
  Possible response: The Friar knows that everyone will believe that Juliet is dead, and he will be escorting her to the church for burial, not for a wedding.

- Ask students to what Lord Capulet compares death in lines 36–39.
  Answer: Capulet compares Death to Juliet's bridegroom, Capulet's son-in-law, and Capulet's heir. He says that Death will be left with everything when Capulet dies.

- **Ask** students how Paris's words in lines 41–42 contribute to the dramatic irony.
  Answer: Paris has come to the Capulets looking forward to seeing Juliet on their wedding day. Now he sees her dead, or so he thinks.

30 **Literary Analysis**
Puns

- Point out to students that in the first and second lines of each of the speeches by Lady Capulet, Paris, and Capulet in this passage, the character uses a long series of adjectives to describe the day or the event. Nurse also uses a series of laments, although her vocabulary is more limited than the other three characters.

- **Ask** students how these series of adjectives affect the reader or audience.
  Answer: The adjectives reinforce the sense of lamenting and the grief that the characters have for Juliet.

- **Ask** students to respond to the second Literary Analysis question: How is the effect of the pun in lines 46–47 different from the effect of the comic puns earlier in Act IV?
  Possible response: The previous puns added to the humor of the scene. These lines emphasize the grief that Lady Capulet feels.

826

NURSE. O lamentable day!

30 **LADY CAPULET.**   O woeful time!

CAPULET. Death, that hath ta'en her hence to make me wail,
29 Ties up my tongue and will not let me speak.

[Enter FRIAR LAWRENCE and the COUNTY PARIS, with MUSICIANS.]

FRIAR. Come, is the bride ready to go to church?

CAPULET. Ready to go, but never to return.
35 O son, the night before thy wedding day
Hath Death lain with thy wife. There she lies,
Flower as she was, deflowerèd by him.
Death is my son-in-law, Death is my heir;
My daughter he hath wedded. I will die
40 And leave him all. Life, living, all is Death's.

PARIS. Have I thought, love, to see this morning's face,
And doth it give me such a sight as this?

LADY CAPULET. Accursed, unhappy, wretched, hateful day!
Most miserable hour that e'er time saw
45 In lasting labor of his pilgrimage!
But one, poor one, one poor and loving child,
But one thing to rejoice and solace⁴ in,
And cruel Death hath catched it from my sight.

NURSE. O woe! O woeful, woeful, woeful day!
50 Most lamentable day, most woeful day
That ever ever I did yet behold!
O day, O day, O day! O hateful day!
Never was seen so black a day as this.
O woeful day! O woeful day!

55 **PARIS.** Beguiled,⁵ divorcèd, wrongèd, spited, slain!
Most detestable Death, by thee beguiled,
By cruel, cruel thee quite overthrown.
O love! O life!—not life, but love in death!

31 **CAPULET.** Despised, distressèd, hated, martyred, killed!
60 Uncomfortable⁶ time, why cam'st thou now
To murder, murder our solemnity?⁷
O child, O child! My soul, and not my child!
Dead art thou—alack, my child is dead,
And with my child my joys are buried!

826 ■ *Drama*

Literary Analysis
Dramatic Irony In what way does the Friar's question add to the dramatic irony of the scene?

Literary Analysis
Dramatic Irony
How is the effect of the pun in lines 46–47 different from the effect of the comic puns earlier in Act IV?

4. **solace** find comfort.
5. **Beguiled** cheated.

6. **Uncomfortable** painful, upsetting.
7. **solemnity** solemn rites.

Vocabulary Development

Synonyms

Refer students to lines 49–64 on p. 826. Point out the many adjectives that the characters use to describe their grief at what they believe is Juliet's death.

Have students use a dictionary or thesaurus to find a synonym for three of these adjectives. Then, have them imagine they are one of the characters in this passage and use these synonyms in three sentences describing their grief for Juliet.

Help students get started by giving them this example:

A synonym for *woeful* is *sorrowful*.
This is the most *sorrowful* day of my life; my dear child is dead.

32

Literature in Context

Culture Connection

Rosemary When the Capulets discover Juliet apparently dead, the Friar advises, "Dry up your tears and stick your rosemary / On this fair corse." Rosemary is an evergreen herb that traditionally signifies remembrance, loyalty, and love. Shakespeare often included references to herbs in his plays for symbolic purposes, and rosemary is one herb that turned up often in his works. *Hamlet, King Lear, The Winter's Tale,* and *Pericles* all include references to rosemary as a symbol of remembrance.

Connect to the Literature

Why do you think the Friar tells the Capulets to lay a sprig of rosemary on Juliet's body?

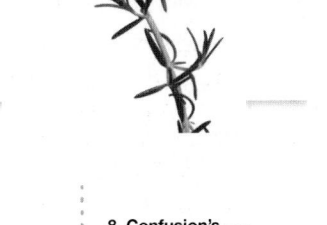

65 **FRIAR.** Peace, ho, for shame! Confusion's cure lives not
      In these confusions.[8] Heaven and yourself
      Had part in this fair maid—now heaven hath all,
      And all the better is it for the maid.
      Your part in her you could not keep from death,
70   But heaven keeps his part in eternal life.
      The most you sought was her promotion,
      For 'twas your heaven she should be advanced;
      And weep ye now, seeing she is advanced
      Above the clouds, as high as heaven itself?
75   O, in this love, you love your child so ill
      That you run mad, seeing that she is well.[9]
      She's not well married that lives married long,
      But she's best married that dies married young.
      Dry up your tears and stick your rosemary[10]
80   On this fair corse, and, as the custom is,
      And in her best array bear her to church:
      For though fond nature[11] bids us all lament,
      Yet nature's tears are reason's merriment.[12]

      CAPULET. All things that we ordainèd festival[13]
85   Turn from their office to black funeral—
      Our instruments to melancholy bells,
      Our wedding cheer to a sad burial feast;
      Our solemn hymns to sullen dirges[14] change;
      Our bridal flowers serve for a buried corse;
90   And all things change them to the contrary.

8. Confusion's . . . confusions The remedy for this calamity is not to be found in these outcries.

9. well blessed in heaven.

10. rosemary evergreen herb signifying love and remembrance.

11. fond nature mistake-prone human nature.

12. Yet . . . merriment While human nature causes us to weep for Juliet, reason should cause us to be happy (since she is in heaven).

13. ordainèd festival planned to be part of a celebration.

14. dirges funeral hymns.

 Reading Check

33

What does the Friar recommend that the Capulets do when they discover Juliet and believe she is dead?

Romeo and Juliet, Act IV ■ *827*

Differentiated Instruction   Solutions for All Learners

Strategy for Advanced Readers

Discuss with students Friar Lawrence's role in *The Tragedy of Romeo and Juliet.* Point out that literary critics see Friar Lawrence in basically two opposing ways. In one view, the Friar is a surrogate father figure to Romeo, aiding and counseling the young man. In the other view, the Friar is a well-meaning but incompetent counselor who leads Romeo and Juliet to their deaths.

  Have students work in small groups to discuss these characterizations of Friar Lawrence:

- a busybody who knows nothing about life or love
- a well-meaning but incompetent counselor
- a wise and sage counselor, whose plans go awry because of circumstances beyond his control

Have students report the result of their discussion to the class.

---

31 Critical Thinking
Predicting

• Have students read lines 55–58. **Ask** students how Paris reacts to Juliet's death. Is it similar to or different from the responses of the Capulets?
Possible response: Rather than feeling sorrow, Paris feels he has been cheated. All three characters focus on their own loss rather than on the fact that Juliet has been deprived of her life at a very young age.

• **Ask** students what Capulet's remarks in lines 59–64 might foreshadow about the future.
Answer: Capulet's words foreshadow Juliet's real death.

32 Literature in Context
Rosemary

Rosemary is popular today for its many uses. It is still considered an emblem of remembrance. Its fragrant stems are used in floral arrangements. Dried branches of rosemary are made into fragrant wreaths at Christmas time. The oil of the plant is used in toiletries and in aromatherapy products.

  Rosemary is also a popular herb in cooking. The leaves—dried or fresh—are used in soups, stews, tomatoes and tomato sauces, and in a variety of recipes for meats and vegetables.

Connect to the Literature
Remind students of rosemary's significance as an emblem of remembrance and love. Remind them also of rosemary's fragrance. Then, **ask** the Connect to the Literature question on p. 827: Why do you think the Friar tells the Capulets to lay a sprig of rosemary on Juliet's body?
Answer: The Friar suggests rosemary as an emblem of remembrance and love for Juliet. The Friar may also be thinking of the fragrant properties of rosemary, which would be comforting to Juliet when she awoke in the damp, dark tomb.

33 Reading Check

Answer: He tells them to dry their tears, place rosemary on her body, and carry her to church.

827

Dramatic Irony

• Have students read lines 91–95.
Ask what the Friar is telling Lord and Lady Capulet and Paris.
Answer: He is telling them to prepare to follow the body of Juliet to her burial.

• Have students read the footnote. Then **ask** what the Friar means by lines 94–95.
Answer: He implies that the forces of fate are angry with them for some reason, and he urges them to do the proper thing and not anger the heavens further.

• **Ask** students to respond to the Literary Analysis question: In what way does the dramatic irony of the Friar's words heighten the play's suspense?
Possible response: The Friar wants to hurry them to the burial while Juliet is still in her coma-like state, but he claims he does not want them to cross the fates again. This heightens the suspense, as the audience sees that the plan has worked so far and wonders how everything will work once Juliet awakes.

▶ **Monitor Progress:** Use the students' answers to these questions to assess their understanding of dramatic irony.

▶ **Reteach:** If students are having difficulty with the concept of dramatic irony, review p. 814. Remind students that irony occurs when the audience knows something contradictory to what the characters believe. In this scene, everyone but the Friar believes Juliet is dead. Only the reader and the Friar know the true cause of her death-like state.

35 **Critical Thinking**
Make Judgments

• **Ask** students which characters are left on stage when the Capulets, the Friar, Paris, and the Nurse exit.
Answer: The musicians remain and Peter enters immediately.

• **Ask** students why they think Shakespeare chose to end Scene v with the bantering of the musicians.
Possible responses: The banter of the musicians provides comic relief from the high drama of Juliet's actions and her family's grief.

828

34
FRIAR. Sir, go you in; and, madam, go with him;
And go, Sir Paris. Everyone prepare
To follow this fair corse unto her grave.
The heavens do low'r[15] upon you for some ill;
95 Move them no more by crossing their high will.

[Exit, casting rosemary on her and shutting the curtains. The NURSE and MUSICIANS remain.]

FIRST MUSICIAN. Faith, we may put up our pipes and be gone.

35
NURSE. Honest good fellows, ah, put up, put up!
For well you know this is a pitiful case.[16]   *[Exit.]*

FIRST MUSICIAN. Ay, by my troth, the case may be amended.

[Enter PETER.]

100 **PETER.** Musicians, O, musicians, "Heart's ease," "Heart's ease"!
O, and you will have me live, play "Heart's ease."

FIRST MUSICIAN. Why "Heart's ease"?

PETER. O, musicians, because my heart itself plays "My heart is full."
O, play me some merry dump[17] to comfort me.

105 **FIRST MUSICIAN.** Not a dump we! 'Tis no time to play now.

PETER. You will not then?

FIRST MUSICIAN. No.

PETER. I will then give it you soundly.

35
FIRST MUSICIAN. What will you give us?

110 **PETER.** No money, on my faith, but the gleek.[18] I will give you[19] the minstrel.[20]

FIRST MUSICIAN. Then will I give you the serving-creature.

PETER. Then will I lay the serving-creature's dagger on your pate.
I will carry no crotchets.[21] I'll *re* you, I'll *fa* you. Do you note me?

115 **FIRST MUSICIAN.** And you *re* us and *fa* us, you note us.

SECOND MUSICIAN. Pray you put up your dagger, and put out your wit.
Then have at you with my wit!

Literary Analysis
Dramatic Irony In what way does the dramatic irony of the Friar's words heighten the play's suspense?

15. **low'r** frown.

16. **case** situation; instrument case.

17. **dump** sad tune.

18. **gleek** scornful speech.
19. **give you** call you.
20. **minstrel** a contemptuous term (as opposed to "musician").
21. **crotchets** whims; quarter notes.

Vocabulary Development

Vocabulary Knowledge Rating
When students have completed reading and discussing Act IV of *The Tragedy of Romeo and Juliet,* have them take out their **Vocabulary Knowledge Rating Chart** for this act. Read the words aloud once more and have students rate their knowledge of the words again in the After Reading column. Clarify any words that are still problematic. Have students write their own definition and example or sentence in the appropriate column. Then, have students complete the **Vocabulary Builder Practice** activities on p. 831. Encourage students to use the words in further discussion and written work about this selection. Remind them that they will be accountable for these words on the Selection Test.

PETER. I will dry-beat you with an iron wit, and put up my iron
dagger. Answer me like men.
120 "When griping grief the heart doth wound,
        And doleful dumps the mind oppress,
     Then music with her silver sound"—
     Why "silver sound"? Why "music with her silver sound"?
     What say you, Simon Catling?

125 **FIRST MUSICIAN.** Marry, sir, because silver hath a sweet sound.

PETER. Pretty! What say you, Hugh Rebeck?

SECOND MUSICIAN. I say "silver sound" because musicians
   sound for silver.

PETER. Pretty too! What say you, James Soundpost?

130 **THIRD MUSICIAN.** Faith, I know not what to say.

PETER. O, I cry you mercy,[22] you are the singer. I will say for
   you. It is "music with her silver sound" because musicians
   have no gold for sounding.
        "Then music with her silver sound
135   With speedy help doth lend redress."   [*Exit.*]

FIRST MUSICIAN. What a pestilent knave is this same!

SECOND MUSICIAN. Hang him, Jack! Come, we'll in here, tarry
   for the mourners, and stay dinner.   [*Exit with others.*]

Literary Analysis
Puns What kind of
mood does the pun
in line 127 help to
create in this scene?

22. cry you mercy beg your
pardon.

Romeo and Juliet, Act IV ■ 829

---

36 Background
Names
Shakespeare is having fun with the
names of the musicians. The three
musicians' names are based on musical terms. A *catling* is a lute string. A
rebeck is a kind of violin. A *soundpost*
is part of a violin.

37 Literary Analysis
Puns

- Have students read lines 118–129.
  Ask students why three lines are
  set off with quotation marks.
  Answer: These lines are the lyrics
  of a song.
- **Ask** students what the phrase *silver
  sound* refers to in these lines.
  Answer: The phrase refers to the
  beautiful sound that music makes.
- **Ask** students to explain the pun in
  the phrase "musicians sound for
  silver."
  Answer: The pun is that music
  makes a silver sound. Musicians
  also sound—or play—for silver, or
  money.
- **Ask** students to respond to the
  Literary Analysis question: What
  kind of mood does the pun in lines
  127–128 help to create in this
  scene?
  Answer: The pun helps to create a
  lighthearted mood, in contrast to
  the somber mood earlier in the
  scene.

Concept Connector

Connecting to the Literature
Have students compare the sentences they
wrote before reading with their thoughts about
why people might want to risk their lives. Ask
them to explain whether their thoughts have
changed and, if so, how.

Reading Skill Graphic Organizer
Have students review the graphic organizers
they completed to summarize lines of dialogue.
Show them **Reading Skill Graphic Organizer B**
(*Graphic Organizer Transparencies,* p. 176) as
an example. Then, have students share the
graphic organizers they did and the summaries
they completed.

Apply the Skills

The Tragedy of Romeo and Juliet, Act IV

Thinking About the Selection

1. **(a) Respond:** Should Romeo and Juliet have followed Friar Lawrence's advice? Why or why not? **(b) Discuss:** Share your response with a partner, and then discuss how hearing someone else's response did or did not change your own.
2. **(a) Recall:** What is Friar Lawrence's plan for Juliet? **(b) Analyze:** Why do you think Juliet trusts the Friar?
3. **(a) Recall:** What three fears does Juliet reveal in her Act IV, Scene iii, soliloquy? **(b) Interpret:** What does the soliloquy reveal about her personality?
4. **(a) Evaluate:** Do you think drinking the potion is a brave act or a foolish act? Explain. **(b) Draw Conclusions:** How has Juliet changed in the course of the play?

Literary Analysis

5. In what way is Juliet's encounter with Paris in Friar Lawrence's cell an instance of **dramatic irony?**
6. Complete a chart like the one shown to demonstrate why Capulet's statement in Act IV, Scene iv, line 25, is an example of dramatic irony.

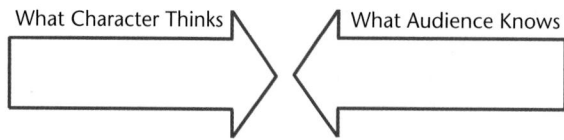

What Character Thinks   What Audience Knows

7. Explain how Capulet's encounter with the fellows in Act IV, Scene iv, represents an example of **comic relief.**
8. **(a)** Explain the **pun** in the Nurse's exchange with the First Musician in Act IV, Scene v, lines 97–98. **(b)** In what way is the conversation that follows among the musicians and Peter an example of comic relief?

Reading Skill

9. **(a) Summarize** lines 50–59 of Juliet's monologue to Friar Lawrence in Act IV, Scene i. **(b)** In what way does breaking down this long sentence into smaller ones make the meaning of Juliet's speech clearer?

830 ■ Drama

QuickReview

Act IV at a Glance
Juliet promises to marry Paris and then avoids the wedding by drinking a potion that puts her in a deathlike sleep. Her family grieves to find Juliet apparently lifeless on her wedding day.

Go Online
Assessment

For: Self-test
Visit: www.PHSchool.com
Web Code: epa-6505

Dramatic Irony: a contradiction between what a character thinks and says and what the audience or reader knows is true

Comic Relief: a humorous character or situation that lightens the mood of a serious scene

Pun: a play on words

Summarizing: briefly stating the main points in a piece of writing

---

Answers

1. (a) Many students may find the advice risky and deceitful. (b) After discussion, some students may note that the couple had no other choices.

2. (a) Friar Lawrence will give Juliet a potion to make her comatose. She will be placed in the tomb. Friar Lawrence will bring Romeo to the tomb, and they will be there when Juliet wakes. Romeo will then take Juliet to Mantua. (b) **Sample response:** Juliet trusts the Friar because he is older and a clergyman.

3. (a) The potion may not work; it may kill her; she may wake up before Romeo comes. (b) The soliloquy reveals that Juliet is fully aware of the grave risks she is undertaking, yet she will proceed.

4. (a) **Sample response:** It is a courageous act because it is her only way to be with Romeo again. It is a foolish act because she is relying on an unknown potion and the actions of others to save her. (b) Juliet has developed; she is no longer a girl, but a woman willing to risk danger for her love.

5. She leads him to believe that she is looking forward to their wedding. She and the audience know that she is already married and has no intention of marrying him.

6. **What the character thinks:** Capulet thinks that Juliet is in her bed asleep.
   What the audience knows: The audience knows that Juliet is in a comatose state and cannot be awakened. Another sample answer can be found on **Literary Analysis Graphic Organizer B**, p. 178 in *Graphic Organizer Transparencies.*

7. The humorous scene breaks the intensity of the act because it follows Juliet's intense soliloquy and precedes the discovery of her body.

8. (a) The pun is on the word *case*, in which the Nurse tells the musician that this is a pitiful case, meaning a sad situation, and it also refers to the musician's instrument case. (b) The scene relieves the intensity of the previ-

ous scene in which Juliet is believed dead, and it sets up the suspense for Act V.

9. (a) Juliet tells the Friar that if he cannot help her then she will kill herself. Therefore, he must tell her something immediately or she will die. (b) Breaking down the sentence into smaller ones makes the meaning clear, since each sentence has one main idea.

Vocabulary Builder

Practice Indicate whether each of the following statements is *True* or *False*. Revise the sentences that are false to make them true.

1. Clowns make children laugh by appearing *pensive*.
2. If you have been *enjoined* to attend an event, you should not go.
3. A *wayward* person would probably dislike orders.
4. If you were in a *dismal* mood, you would be good company.
5. A *loathsome* meal is not likely to be eaten quickly.

Adding Words to Your Vocabulary Using a thesaurus, find a **synonym**, or word with a similar meaning, for each italicized word in the Practice items. Then, use each synonym correctly in a sentence. (For more on using a thesaurus, see page R7.)

Writing

Write an **abstract**, or summary, of what has happened so far in *Romeo and Juliet*. Imagine that you are writing for an audience member who has missed everything up to the beginning of Act V.

- Review Acts I–IV and list of the major events in the play so far.
- Describe the main characters, noting relationships among them.
- Note the most memorable scenes in Acts I–IV and the overall mood.
- Use the information you compile to write a one-paragraph summary of the play's action.

Read your abstract to someone who has not read *Romeo and Juliet*. Clarify any information that your reader finds confusing.

For *Grammar, Vocabulary,* and *Assessment,* see **Build Language Skills,** pages 850–851.

Extend Your Learning

Research and Technology With a partner, create a **multimedia presentation** on Renaissance music. Use library or Internet resources to collect examples of music that would have been played by musicians in Act IV, Scene v. Find pictures of instruments from the period as well. Present your findings in class and lead a discussion about the cultural values the music expresses.

Assessment Resources

The following resources can be used to assess students' knowledge and skills.

Unit 5 Resources
Selection Test A, pp. 78–80
Selection Test B, pp. 81–83

Go **O**nline
—Assessment Students may use the **Self-test** to prepare for **Selection Test A** or **Selection Test B**.

Go **O**nline **For:** An additional research activity
—Research **Visit:** www.PHSchool.com
Web Code: epd-7504
For another research activity to extend students' learning, give students this Web Code.

Vocabulary Builder
Practice

1. False. Clowns make children laugh by being *boisterous*.
2. False. If you have been *enjoined* to attend an event, you are *required* to go.
3. True.
4. False. If you were in a *cheerful* mood, you would be good company.
5. True.

Adding Words to Your Vocabulary

1. She was in a *thoughtful* mood.
2. He did not always do as he was *ordered*.
3. She was a *headstrong* child.
4. The weather has been *gloomy* for a week.
5. The movie's blood and gore was truly *disgusting*.

Writing

- To give students guidance for writing an abstract, give them **Support for Writing** for Act IV of *The Tragedy of Romeo and Juliet*, p. 75 in *Unit 5 Resources.*
- To evaluate students' abstracts, use the Summary rubrics, pp. 63–64 in *General Resources.* In addition, you might evaluate for how well students use significant details and organize their summary.

Six Traits Focus

	Ideas		Word Choice
✔	Organization	✔	Sentence Fluency
	Voice		Conventions

 Writing and Grammar, Gold Level
Students will find guidance on narrative writing in Chapter 11.

Build Language Skills

Go to pp. 850–851 for vocabulary and grammar lessons and assessment practice.

Extend Your Learning

The **Support for Extend Your Learning** page (*Unit 5 Resources,* p. 76) provides guided note-taking opportunities to help students complete the Extend Your Learning activity.

Planning Differentiated Instruction

Accessibility at a Glance

	The Tragedy of Romeo and Juliet, Act V
Context	Historical; Verona, Italy
Language	Dialogue, prose, verse, soliloquies, Elizabethan terms, and challenging vocabulary
Concept Level	Accessible; classic tale of star-crossed lovers
Literary Merit	Classic; noted poet and playwright
Lexile	NP
Overall Rating	More challenging

Choosing Your Resources

[L1] Special Needs Students   [L4] Advanced Students

[L2] Below-Level Students   [EL] English Learners

[L3] All Students

FT Fast Track Instruction: To move the lesson more quickly, use the strategies and activities identified with **FT**.

Reading and Vocabulary Warm-ups provide support for below level students. **A** is for students reading two grades below level; **B** is for students reading one grade below level. For Selection Tests, **A** signifies "less challenging" and **B** "more challenging." For Graphic Organizer transparencies, **A** signifies "not filled in" and **B** "filled in."

Scaffolding for Less Proficient and Advanced Students

The leveled questions on Apply the Skills pages progress in the levels of thinking required to answer them. To address the needs of your different students, you may use the (a) level questions for your less proficient students, the (b) level with your on-level and advanced students. The occasional (c) level questions are appropriate for your advanced students.

Go Online
Professional Development
For: Information about Lexiles
Visit: www.PHSchool.com
Web Code: eue-1111

Step-by-Step Teaching Guide	Pacing Guide
PRETEACH	
• Administer Vocabulary and Reading Warm-ups as necessary.	
• Introduce the Literary Analysis Skills: Tragedy. **FT**	10 min.
• Introduce the Reading Skill: Summarizing. **FT**	10 min.
• Prepare students to read by teaching the selection vocabulary. **FT**	10 min.
• Build background and develop expressive vocabulary with Connecting to the Literature and Background.	10 min.
• Engage students' interest with the motivation activity.	10 min.
TEACH	
• Informally monitor comprehension while students read independently or in groups. **FT**	30 min.
• Monitor students' comprehension with the Reading Check notes.	as students read
• Reinforce vocabulary with Vocabulary Builder notes.	as students read
• Develop students' understanding of tragedy with the Literary Analysis annotations. **FT**	5 min.
• Develop students' ability to identify causes and effects with the Reading Skill annotations. **FT**	10 min.
ASSESS/EXTEND	
• Assess students' comprehension and mastery of the Reading Skill and Literary Analysis by having them answer the Apply the Skills questions. **FT**	35 min.
• Have students complete the Vocabulary Builder activities. **FT**	5 min.
• Apply students' ability to write a persuasive letter with the Writing activity. **FT**	30–45 min. or homework
• Extend students' listening and speaking skills with the Extend Your Learning activity.	15–30 min. or homework
• Have students complete the Vocabulary Skill and Grammar Lesson.	5 min.
• Monitor students' progress with the Assessment Practice.	20–40 min.
• Administer **Selection Test A** or **Selection Test B. FT**	15 min.

Resources

Meeting Your Standards

Students will

1. **analyze and respond to literary elements.**
   - Literary Analysis: Tragedy

2. **read, comprehend, and analyze plays.**
   - Reading Skill: Summarizing
   - Reading Strategy: Identifying Causes and Effects
   - Reading Check questions
   - Apply the Skills questions
   - Assessment Practice

3. **develop vocabulary.**
   - Vocabulary Builder
   - Word Root *-lum-*

4. **apply grammar skills.**
   - Gerund and Gerund Phrases

5. **develop writing proficiency.**
   - Work in Progress: How-to Essay
   - Persuasive letter

6. **extend learning.**
   - Listening and Speaking: Mock Trial

Block Scheduling: Use one 90-minute class period to preteach the skills and have students read Act V. Use a second 90-minute class period to assess students' mastery of skills, extend their learning, and monitor their progress.

Homework Suggestions
Following are possibilities for homework assignments.

- Support pages from *Unit 5 Resources:*
  Literary Analysis
  Reading Skill
  Vocabulary Builder
  Enrichment

- An Extend Your Learning project and the Writing assignment for Act V may be completed over several days.

PRENTICE HALL
TeacherEXPRESS™ Use this complete
Plan · Teach · Assess   suite of powerful
teaching tools to make lesson planning and testing quicker and easier.

PRENTICE HALL
StudentEXPRESS™ Use the
Learn · Study · Succeed   Interactive
Textbook (online and on CD-ROM) to make Act V and activities come alive with audio and video support and interactive questions.

Build Skills
The Tragedy of Romeo and Juliet, Act V

❶ Literary Analysis
Tragedy

• Tell students that most of Shakespeare's tragic heroes are complex characters, often riddled with internal conflict, who often do bad things. Romeo and Juliet are two of the "purest" of the tragic characters. Their primary *motives* are simple and straightforward—they love each other and want to be together.

• As students read, have them be alert for what moves these tragic characters to act.

❷ Reading Skill
Summarizing

• Remind students that *causes* and *effects* are not individual events, but form a chain of events. For example, a cause leads to an effect, which may in turn become a cause for another event.

• Give students a copy **Reading Skill Graphic Organizer A** (*Graphic Organizer Transparencies,* p. 179). Have them fill in the graphic organizer to record the chain of causes and effects.

Connecting to the Literature

• In *The Tragedy of Romeo and Juliet,* tragedy leads to some positive effects for other characters. Have students write several sentences explaining how tragedies can have positive effects. Have them use at least three of the following words: *assess, circumstance, react,* and *significant.*

• Provide these sample sentences to demonstrate their use:

   1. Authorities may *assess* the laws that resulted in a tragedy.

   2. People may change the *circumstance* that led to the tragedy.

   3. People may learn to *react* differently when their loved ones are in trouble.

   4. A tragedy can cause *significant* changes in other's attitudes about what is important in life.

• Encourage students to use these words as they discuss Act V.

❶ Literary Analysis

A **tragedy** is a drama in which the central character, who is of noble stature, meets with disaster or great misfortune. The tragic hero's downfall is usually the result of one of the following:

   • *fate*, or the idea of a pre-planned destiny

   • a serious character flaw

   • some combination of both

Motive is an important element of a tragic hero's character. A character's motive is the reason for his or her thoughts or actions. In many of Shakespeare's tragedies, the hero's motives are basically good but misguided. As a result, the hero suffers a tragic fate that may seem undeserved.

Although tragedies are sad, they can also be uplifting. They show the greatness and nobility of the human spirit when faced with grave challenges. As you read the conclusion of *Romeo and Juliet,* consider what positive message might be conveyed by the play's tragic events.

❷ Reading Skill

Summarizing is briefly stating the main points in a piece of writing. In summarizing the action, it is useful to first **identify causes and effects.**

   • A *cause* is an event, action, or emotion that produces a result.

   • An *effect* is the result produced by the cause.

Tragedies often involve a chain of events that advance the plot and lead to the final tragic outcome. Understanding the sequence of causes and effects will help you summarize complicated plots like the one in *Romeo and Juliet.* As you read Act V, use a chart like this to record causes and effects.

Cause
Juliet takes the potion.

↓

Effect/Cause
Everyone thinks she is dead.

↓

Effect

Vocabulary Builder

■ **remnants** (rem´ nənts) *n.* what is left over; remainders (p. 834) *The remnants of the house still stood after the fire.*

■ **penury** (pen´ yōō rē) *n.* extreme poverty (p. 834) *His choice was either to find work or to live in penury.*

■ **haughty** (hôt´ ē) *adj.* arrogant (p. 838) *He acts haughty onstage but humble offstage.*

■ **ambiguities** (am´ bə gyōō´ ə tēz) *n.* statements or events whose meanings are unclear (p. 845) *Voters were confused by the ambiguities in the candidate's speech.*

■ **scourge** (skʉrj) *n.* instrument for inflicting punishment (p. 847) *Longer practices were the scourge that the coach used to punish the players for their laziness.*

832 ■ *Drama*

Vocabulary Development

Vocabulary Knowledge Rating

Create a **Vocabulary Knowledge Rating Chart** with these words from Act V:

remnants	ambiguities
penury	scourge
haughty	

Give students a copy. Introduce the words by reading them aloud and having students mark their rating in the Before Reading column. Urge them to be alert to these words as they read and discuss Act V, because they will rate their knowledge of the words again after they finish.

   If you wish, you may tally how many students know (or think they know) a word to gauge how much instruction you need to provide. As students read, point out the words and their context.

ACT V

❶
❷

Review and Anticipate

To prevent her marriage to Paris, Juliet has taken the Friar's potion and, as Act V begins, is in a temporary deathlike sleep. Her unsuspecting family plans her funeral. Meanwhile, the Friar has sent a messenger to Mantua to tell Romeo of the ruse, so that he may return and rescue Juliet from her family tomb. What do you think might go wrong with the Friar's plan?

Scene i. MANTUA. A STREET.

[*Enter* ROMEO.]

    ROMEO. If I may trust the flattering truth of sleep,[1]
    My dreams presage[2] some joyful news at hand.
    My bosom's lord[3] sits lightly in his throne,
    And all this day an unaccustomed spirit
5   Lifts me above the ground with cheerful thoughts.
    I dreamt my lady came and found me dead
    (Strange dream that gives a dead man leave to think!)
    And breathed such life with kisses in my lips
    That I revived and was an emperor.
10   Ah me! How sweet is love itself possessed,
    When but love's shadows[4] are so rich in joy!

[*Enter* ROMEO'S MAN, BALTHASAR, *booted.*]

❹ | News from Verona! How now, Balthasar?

1. flattering . . . sleep
pleasing illusions of dreams.

2. presage foretell.

3. bosom's lord heart.

4. shadows dreams; unreal images.

 **Reading Check**

Why is Romeo in a good mood?

Romeo and Juliet, Act V ■ 833

834

❹ Literary Analysis
Motive

- Have students read lines 12–16.
- Have students determine the reason for Romeo's second question to Balthasar.
  Answer: Romeo has been expecting to hear from the Friar and wonders why Balthasar does not have letters for him.
- **Ask:** Which person is Romeo most concerned about in his questions to Balthasar?
  Answer: Romeo asks about Juliet three times and his father once.
- **Ask** the first Literary Analysis question: What motivates Romeo's questions?
  Answer: Romeo has been away from Juliet, not by choice, and is eager to know how she is.

❺ Literary Analysis
Tragedy

- Have students speculate on Balthasar's meaning in line 17.
  Answer: Balthasar means that although she is dead, Juliet is well because she is in heaven.
- **Ask** students the second Literary Analysis question: In what way does Romeo's remark in line 24 reinforce fate's role in the tragedy?
  Answer: When Romeo says "Then I defy you, stars!" he means that the stars (representing fate) have been responsible for Juliet's death, and Romeo is now their enemy. He will now defy fate, setting in motion a series of events that will culminate in tragedy.

---

❹ Dost thou not bring me letters from the friar?
How doth my lady? Is my father well?
15 How fares my Juliet? That I ask again,
For nothing can be ill if she be well.

MAN. Then she is well, and nothing can be ill.
Her body sleeps in Capels' monument,[5]
And her immortal part with angels lives.
20 I saw her laid low in her kindred's vault
And presently took post[6] to tell it you.

❺ O, pardon me for bringing these ill news,
Since you did leave it for my office,[7] sir.

ROMEO. Is it e'en so? Then I defy you, stars!
25 Thou knowest my lodging. Get me ink and paper
And hire post horses. I will hence tonight.

MAN. I do beseech you, sir, have patience.
Your looks are pale and wild and do import
Some misadventure.[8]

ROMEO.   Tush, thou art deceived.
30 Leave me and do the thing I bid thee do.
Hast thou no letters to me from the friar?

MAN. No, my good lord.

ROMEO.   No matter. Get thee gone.
And hire those horses. I'll be with thee straight.

[*Exit* BALTHASAR.]

Well, Juliet, I will lie with thee tonight.
35 Let's see for means. O mischief, thou art swift
To enter in the thoughts of desperate men!
I do remember an apothecary,[9]
And hereabouts 'a dwells, which late I noted
In tatt'red weeds, with overwhelming brows,
40 Culling of simples.[10] Meager were his looks,
Sharp misery had worn him to the bones;

❻ And in his needy shop a tortoise hung,
An alligator stuffed, and other skins
Of ill-shaped fishes; and about his shelves
45 A beggarly account[11] of empty boxes,
Green earthen pots, bladders, and musty seeds,
Remnants of packthread, and old cakes of roses[12]
Were thinly scatterèd, to make up a show.
Noting this penury, to myself I said,
50 "And if a man did need a poison now
Whose sale is present death in Mantua,

834 ■ *Drama*

Literary Analysis
Motive What motivates Romeo's questions?

5. **Capels' monument** the Capulets' burial vault.

6. **presently took post** immediately set out on horseback.

7. **office** duty.

Literary Analysis
Tragedy In what way does Romeo's remark in line 24 reinforce fate's role in the tragedy?

8. **import / Some misadventure** suggest some misfortune.

9. **apothecary** one who prepares and sells drugs and medicines.

10. **In tatt'red . . . simples** in torn clothing, with overhanging eyebrows, sorting out herbs.

11. **beggarly account** small number.

12. **cakes of roses** pressed rose petals (used for perfume).

Vocabulary Builder
remnants (rem´ nənts)
n. what is left over; remainders

penury (pen´ yōō rē)
n. extreme poverty

Vocabulary Development

Think-Aloud: Expressive Vocabulary
As students discuss this scene, encourage them to use the expressive vocabulary presented earlier. Using a think-aloud process, model how to use the expressive vocabulary. Say the following to students:

I'm going to think aloud to show you how I would use the expressive vocabulary in discussing this scene.

If I were going to discuss Romeo's response to the news about Juliet, I

might say, *Romeo did not take time to* **assess** *the truth of the news he heard.*

If I were talking about the apothecary Romeo consulted, I might say, *The apothecary blames his* **circumstance**, *not his desire, for giving Romeo the poison.*

Encourage students to use these and other expressive words as they discuss the rest of Act V.

Here lives a caitiff[13] wretch would sell it him."
O, this same thought did but forerun my need,
And this same needy man must sell it me.

❻

55 As I remember, this should be the house.
Being holiday, the beggar's shop is shut.
What, ho! Apothecary!

[*Enter* APOTHECARY.]

APOTHECARY.   Who calls so loud?

ROMEO. Come hither, man. I see that thou art poor.
    Hold, there is forty ducats.[14] Let me have
60 A dram of poison, such soon-speeding gear[15]
    As will disperse itself through all the veins
    That the life-weary taker may fall dead,
    And that the trunk[16] may be discharged of breath
    As violently as hasty powder fired
65 Doth hurry from the fatal cannon's womb.

APOTHECARY. Such mortal drugs I have; but Mantua's law
    Is death to any he that utters[17] them.

ROMEO. Art thou so bare and full of wretchedness
    And fearest to die? Famine is in thy cheeks,
70 Need and oppression starveth in thy eyes,
    Contempt and beggary hangs upon thy back:
    The world is not thy friend, nor the world's law;
    The world affords no law to make thee rich;
    Then be not poor, but break it and take this.

❼

75 **APOTHECARY.** My poverty but not my will consents.

ROMEO. I pay thy poverty and not thy will.

APOTHECARY. Put this in any liquid thing you will
    And drink it off, and if you had the strength
    Of twenty men, it would dispatch you straight.

80 **ROMEO.** There is thy gold—worse poison to men's souls,
    Doing more murder in this loathsome world,
    Than these poor compounds[18] that thou mayst not sell.
    I sell thee poison; thou hast sold me none.
    Farewell. Buy food and get thyself in flesh.
85 Come, cordial[19] and not poison, go with me
    To Juliet's grave; for there must I use thee.   [*Exit all.*]

---

13. **caitiff** miserable.

14. **ducats** (duk′ əts) gold coins.

15. **soon-speeding gear** fast-working stuff.

16. **trunk** body.

17. **utters** sells.

Literary Analysis
Motive What is the apothecary's motive for selling Romeo the poison?

18. **compounds** mixtures.

19. **cordial** health-giving drink.

❽ ✓ **Reading Check**

What does Romeo learn from Balthasar?

Romeo and Juliet, Act V ■ 835

❻ Critical Thinking
Infer

• Ask students to read Romeo's soliloquy beginning on p. 834, line 34. Ask them to **infer** what kind of reputation an apothecary had in these times.
Possible response: The apothecary was not a highly respected person, judging from Romeo's descriptions of him and his shop.

• **Ask** students what causes Romeo to buy poison from an apothecary.
Answer: Romeo intends to kill himself because he believes Juliet is dead.

❼ Literary Analysis
Motive

• Remind students that in a tragedy, the main character is partially brought down by a character flaw. **Ask** them what character flaw motivates Romeo to act so quickly.
Answer: Romeo acts without thinking. He does not pause to verify Balthasar's news or to consider waiting until he can speak with the Friar.

• **Ask** students what Romeo says about the law when the apothecary tells him that it is illegal to sell poison.
Answer: Romeo says that the law of the world is not the apothecary's friend because there is no law that will make the apothecary rich.

• **Ask** students to respond to the Literary Analysis question: What is the apothecary's motive for selling Romeo the poison?
Answer: The apothecary is poor and starving; his situation will cause him to sell Romeo the poison, even though the law forbids it.

❽ Reading Check

Answer: Romeo learns that Juliet is believed dead.

Differentiated
Instruction   Solutions for All Learners

Strategy for Special Needs Students
This act moves quickly through a series of events to its tragic conclusion. To give students a context for this act and to model how to identify cause and effect, show them **Reading Skill Graphic Organizer B** (*Graphic Organizer Transparencies* p. 180). The completed graphic organizer will give students insight into the process of summarizing by identifying causes and effects.

Strategy for Less Proficient Readers
Have students use the *Reader's Notebook: Adapted Version* along with the **Adapted Reader's Notebook Audio CD.** Suggest that students read along as they listen to the CD. Encourage students to use the *Reader's Notebook: Adapted Version* as an introduction to the act. Challenge them to read the act in the standard text after they hear the adapted version.

835

- **Ask** students to explain the reason that Friar John could not deliver his news to Romeo.
Possible response: Friar John went to look for another friar to go with him. He found the friar helping townspeople who were sick with the plague. The health officials would not let either friar leave the area, for fear they would spread the infection, so Friar John was not able to go to Mantua.

- **Ask** students what they predict will be the effect of Friar John's failure to deliver the letter to Romeo.
Answer: Without knowing that Juliet is actually alive, Romeo will kill himself.

❿ Literature in Context
Plague Searchers

Italy—the setting for *The Tragedy of Romeo and Juliet*—was especially hard hit by the Black Death. Italian merchants were the first to bring the Black Death to Europe. In 1347 a fleet of their ships arrived in a port town on Sicily, an island just off the tip of the Italian mainland. Other Italian merchant ships carrying the plague docked in the major port cities of Genoa and Venice—not far from Verona—as well as other ports along Italy's Mediterranean coast. Within several months, all of Italy was overwhelmed with the plague. By the time the Black Death had run its course, between 40 and 50 percent of Italy's total population had died.

Connect to the Literature
Remind students of why Friar John was unable to deliver Friar Lawrence's letter. Then, **ask** the Connect to Literature question: What does the Black Death add to the tragedy in *Romeo and Juliet*?
Answer: Because of the Black Death, Friar John was quarantined and unable to deliver Friar Lawrence's letter. Romeo received news that Juliet was dead, but never received the letter from Friar Lawrence explaining that she was merely drugged.

Scene ii. FRIAR LAWRENCE's *cell.*

[*Enter* FRIAR JOHN, *calling* FRIAR LAWRENCE.]

    JOHN. Holy Franciscan friar, brother, ho!

[*Enter* FRIAR LAWRENCE.]

    LAWRENCE. This same should be the voice of Friar John.
      Welcome from Mantua. What says Romeo?
      Or, if his mind be writ, give me his letter.

5   **JOHN.** Going to find a barefoot brother out,
      One of our order, to associate[1] me
      Here in this city visiting the sick,
      And finding him, the searchers of the town,
      Suspecting that we both were in a house
10   Where the infectious pestilence did reign,
      Sealed up the doors, and would not let us forth,
      So that my speed to Mantua there was stayed.

    LAWRENCE. Who bare my letter, then, to Romeo?

    JOHN. I could not send it—here it is again—
15   Nor get a messenger to bring it thee,
      So fearful were they of infection.

1. associate accompany.

Reading Skill
Summarizing Briefly state the causes and effects of Friar John's failure to deliver Friar Lawrence's letter.

---

❿ Literature in Context

History Connection

Plague Searchers The Black Plague, or Black Death, was a disease that swept through Europe, Asia, and the Middle East during the 1300s, with outbreaks continuing until 1400. It is thought that as much as a third of Europe's population died of the disease between 1347 and 1351. During an outbreak of plague, officials would appoint plague searchers to quarantine people infected with the disease and dispose of victims' remains. In *Romeo and Juliet,* Friar John is quarantined by plague searchers who fear he has been infected. As a result, he is unable to deliver Friar Lawrence's letter to Romeo.

Connect to the Literature
What does the Black Death add to the tragedy in *Romeo and Juliet*?

LAWRENCE. Unhappy fortune! By my brotherhood,
The letter was not nice,[2] but full of charge,
Of dear import;[3] and the neglecting it
May do much danger. Friar John, go hence,
Get me an iron crow and bring it straight
Unto my cell.

JOHN. Brother, I'll go and bring it thee. [*Exit.*]

LAWRENCE. Now must I to the monument alone.
Within this three hours will fair Juliet wake.
She will beshrew[4] me much that Romeo
Hath had no notice of these accidents;[5]
But I will write again to Mantua,
And keep her at my cell till Romeo come—
Poor living corse, closed in a dead man's tomb! [*Exit.*]

Scene iii. A churchyard; in it a monument belonging to the
CAPULETS.

[*Enter* PARIS *and his* PAGE *with flowers and sweet water.*]

PARIS. Give me thy torch, boy. Hence, and stand aloof.[1]
Yet put it out, for I would not be seen.
Under yond yew trees lay thee all along,[2]
Holding thy ear close to the hollow ground.
So shall no foot upon the churchyard tread
(Being loose, unfirm, with digging up of graves)
But thou shalt hear it. Whistle then to me,
As signal that thou hearest something approach.
Give me those flowers. Do as I bid thee, go.

PAGE. [*Aside*] I am almost afraid to stand alone
Here in the churchyard; yet I will adventure.[3] [*Retires.*]

PARIS. Sweet flower, with flowers thy bridal bed I strew
  (O woe! thy canopy is dust and stones)
Which with sweet[4] water nightly I will dew;
  Or, wanting that, with tears distilled by moans.
The obsequies[5] that I for thee will keep
Nightly shall be to strew thy grave and weep.[BOY *whistles.*]
The boy gives warning something doth approach.
What cursèd foot wanders this way tonight
To cross[6] my obsequies and true love's rite?
What, with a torch? Muffle me, night, awhile. [*Retires.*]

[*Enter* ROMEO, *and* BALTHASAR *with a torch, a mattock, and a crow of iron.*]

2. **nice** trivial.

3. **full of charge, / Of dear import** urgent and important.

4. **beshrew** blame.

5. **accidents** happenings.

Literary Analysis
Motive What motivates Friar Lawrence's decision to go to the monument?

1. **aloof** apart.

2. **lay . . . along** lie down flat.

3. **adventure** chance it.

4. **sweet** perfumed.

5. **obsequies** memorial ceremonies.

6. **cross** interrupt.

✓ Reading Check

Why was Friar John unable to deliver the letter to Romeo?

Romeo and Juliet, Act V ■ *837*

⑪ Reading Skill
Summarizing

- Have students explain how the letter fit into Friar Lawrence's plan for uniting Romeo and Juliet.
  Answer: Friar Lawrence had given Juliet the potion to make her appear dead and thus avoid marriage to Paris. She was to be buried in the family tomb. Meanwhile, Friar Lawrence would send a letter to Romeo explaining the plan. Romeo would be told to arrive at the tomb when Juliet awoke and then take her to Mantua.

- **Ask** students to respond to the Reading Skill prompt on p. 836: Briefly state the causes and effects of Friar John's failure to deliver Friar Lawrence's letter.
  Answer: Friar John cannot deliver the letter because he is quarantined by authorities who fear he may have been infected by the plague. Romeo hears from Balthasar that Juliet is dead, but he does not receive the letter from Friar Lawrence explaining the true situation. Romeo purchases poison and prepares to kill himself.

⑫ Literary Analysis
Motive

- **Ask** students why they think Friar Lawrence asks Friar John to get him a crow in lines 21–22.
  Answer: Students should infer that a crow is a crowbar and that Friar Lawrence will need the tool to force his way into the Capulet tomb where Juliet is lying.

- **Ask** students the Literary Analysis question: What motivates Friar Lawrence's decision to go to the monument?
  Answer: The Friar wants to be at the monument to ease Juliet's shock at awakening in a tomb and to explain why Romeo is not yet there.

⑬ Reading Check

Answer: He was detained and quarantined by authorities who thought he might be infected with the plague.

⓮ **Literary Analysis**
Motive

- Have students recall what Paris brought to the tomb, and **ask** what Romeo brings to the tomb. **Answer:** Paris brings flowers and perfume, and Romeo brings tools to help him get into the tomb.

- Have students note the stage direction in line 21. Tell them that "retire" means that Paris steps back out of sight to see who is approaching. He watches, unseen by Romeo and Balthasar.

- **Ask** students to respond to the Literary Analysis question: What different motives do Paris and Romeo have for visiting Juliet's tomb? **Answer:** Paris visits the tomb to bring Juliet flowers; Romeo visits the tomb to kill himself.

- **Ask** students what reason Romeo gives Balthasar for entering the tomb. What does Romeo say will happen if Balthasar tries to spy on him? **Answer:** Romeo tells Balthasar he is going to get a ring from Juliet's finger. He says that he will kill Balthasar if he does not obey him.

- **Ask** students whether Balthasar believes Romeo has come to get a ring. Ask whether students believe Romeo will really kill Balthasar. **Answer:** Balthasar says in an aside that he does not believe Romeo's story. Students may say that Romeo is exaggerating about killing Balthasar to show him how serious he is about not being disturbed.

ROMEO. Give me that mattock and the wrenching iron.
  Hold, take this letter. Early in the morning
  See thou deliver it to my lord and father.
25 Give me the light. Upon thy life I charge thee,
  Whate'er thou hearest or seest, stand all aloof
  And do not interrupt me in my course.
  Why I descend into this bed of death
  Is partly to behold my lady's face,
30 But chiefly to take thence from her dead finger
  A precious ring—a ring that I must use
  In dear employment.[7] Therefore hence, be gone.
⓮ But if thou, jealous,[8] dost return to pry
  In what I farther shall intend to do,
35 By heaven, I will tear thee joint by joint
  And strew this hungry churchyard with thy limbs.
  The time and my intents are savage-wild,
  More fierce and more inexorable[9] far
  Than empty[10] tigers or the roaring sea.

40 **BALTHASAR.** I will be gone, sir, and not trouble ye.

ROMEO. So shalt thou show me friendship. Take thou that.
  Live, and be prosperous; and farewell, good fellow.

BALTHASAR. [Aside] For all this same, I'll hide me hereabout.
  His looks I fear, and his intents I doubt.   [Retires.]

45 **ROMEO.** Thou detestable maw,[11] thou womb of death,
  Gorged with the dearest morsel of the earth,
  Thus I enforce thy rotten jaws to open,
  And in despite[12] I'll cram thee with more food.
              [ROMEO opens the tomb.]

PARIS. This is that banished haughty Montague
50 That murd'red my love's cousin—with which grief
  It is supposed the fair creature died—
  And here is come to do some villainous shame
  To the dead bodies. I will apprehend[13] him.
  Stop thy unhallowèd toil, vile Montague!
55 Can vengeance be pursued further than death?
  Condemnèd villain, I do apprehend thee.
  Obey, and go with me; for thou must die.

⓯ **ROMEO.** I must indeed; and therefore came I hither.
  Good gentle youth, tempt not a desp'rate man.
60 Fly hence and leave me. Think upon these gone;
  Let them affright thee. I beseech thee, youth,

Literary Analysis
Motive What different motives do Paris and Romeo have for visiting Juliet's tomb?

7. **dear employment** important business.

8. **jealous** curious.

9. **inexorable** uncontrollable.

10. **empty** hungry.

11. **maw** stomach.

12. **despite** scorn.

Vocabulary Builder
haughty (hôt′ ē) adj. arrogant

13. **apprehend** seize; arrest.

838 ■ Drama

Vocabulary Development

Vocabulary Builder Reinforcement
Reinforce students' comprehension with "show-you-know" sentences. The first part of the sentence uses the vocabulary word in an appropriate context. The second part of the sentence—the "show-you-know" part—clarifies the first. Model the strategy with this example:
Remnants of the party filled the room; used napkins, empty glasses and cans, and half-eaten plates of food were all that were left of the celebration.

Then give students these sentence prompts, and coach them in creating the clarification part.
1. He feared that he might soon be living in *penury;* _____
   Sample answer: he couldn't find a job, and all his savings were nearly gone.
2. He is known for his *haughty* attitude; _____
   Sample answer: his arrogance has cost him many friends.

Put not another sin upon my head
By urging me to fury. O, be gone!
By heaven, I love thee better than myself,
For I come hither armed against myself.
Stay not, be gone. Live, and hereafter say
A madman's mercy bid thee run away.

PARIS. I do defy thy conjurations.[14]
And apprehend thee for a felon[15] here.

ROMEO. Wilt thou provoke me? Then have at thee, boy!
[*They fight.*]

PAGE. O Lord, they fight! I will go call the watch.
[*Exit.* PARIS *falls.*]

PARIS. O, I am slain! If thou be merciful,
Open the tomb, lay me with Juliet.
[*Dies.*]

ROMEO. In faith, I will. Let me peruse[16] this face.
Mercutio's kinsman, noble County Paris!
What said my man when my betossèd[17] soul
Did not attend[18] him as we rode? I think

Reading Skill
Summarizing Summarize the causes that you think will produce a tragic effect in the confrontation between Romeo and Paris.

14. **conjurations** solemn appeals.

15. **felon** criminal.

16. **peruse** look over.

17. **betossèd** upset.

18. **attend** give attention to.

 Reading Check

What happens to Paris at Juliet's tomb?

 ◀ **Critical Viewing**
Do you think this image of Romeo accurately conveys his feelings as he enters the Capulets' tomb? Why or why not? **[Evaluate]**

---

⑮ Reading Skill
Summarizing

- Point out that other events in the play have resulted from the characters having inaccurate or incomplete information. **Ask** students what inaccurate information Paris has that makes him so angry with Romeo.
Answer: Paris knows nothing of the love and marriage of Romeo and Juliet. He thinks that Juliet has died because of her grief over Tybalt, making Romeo the ultimate cause of both deaths.

- **Ask** students to respond to the Reading Skill prompt: Summarize the causes that you think will produce a tragic effect in the confrontation between Romeo and Paris.
Possible response: Ignorance is the cause of the fatal confrontation. Paris is unaware that Romeo and Juliet are married; he blames Romeo for the deaths of both Tybalt and Juliet. Seeing Romeo trying to break into the Capulet family tomb is triply offensive to Paris. Romeo is unaware of Paris's love for Juliet. He is not even aware that it is Paris whom he is killing.

⑯ Reading Check

Answer: Paris is killed in a fight with Romeo.

⑰ Critical Viewing

Answer: Students may say that Romeo's upright stance and facial expression suggest that he is determined to follow through on his plan to die.

Differentiated
Instruction   Solutions for All Learners

Enrichment for Gifted/Talented Students

This final scene of the play is long and complicated, with many characters coming and going, and with limited stage directions, which may make the action difficult to follow.

Ask students to rewrite this last scene in prose, with a narrator filling in the action and summarizing much of the dialogue. For example, in lines 7–12, a prose version might read:

"Paris took the flowers from the page, telling him to leave. 'If you hear someone coming, whistle as a signal,' he told the page. The

page left, muttering to himself about being afraid to be alone in the churchyard."

Encourage students to visualize the scene as they write and to give a fuller description of the setting. Have students write what dialogue they think will add to the story, using Shakespeare's words where suitable, or recasting the language into modern English where necessary for brevity and clarity.

Have students share their completed scenes with a classmate.

- Have students read lines 74–87.
  Ask how Romeo feels about killing Paris. How can you tell?
  Answer: Romeo is sorry that he had to kill Paris. He speaks of him as a "slaught'red youth" and places him in the tomb by Juliet as Paris requested.

- Have students recall another important scene in the play in which someone wanted to fight Romeo and Romeo tried to keep from doing so.
  Answer: In Act III, Scene i, Romeo tried to avoid dueling with Tybalt.

- **Ask** students what Romeo believes he is seeing as he describes Juliet in lines 92–96.
  Answer: Romeo believes that Juliet is dead, but death has not been able to destroy her beauty.

- **Ask** students to respond to the Literary Analysis question: What tragic mistake does Romeo make regarding Juliet's appearance?
  Answer: Romeo believes that Juliet is dead despite the signs of life and health in her appearance.

19 **Critical Viewing**

Answer: Juliet does not look as if she has been dead for two days. According to lines 94–95, her lips and cheeks are rosy, rather than pale.

He told me Paris should have married Juliet.
Said he not so, or did I dream it so?
80 Or am I mad, hearing him talk of Juliet,
To think it was so? O, give me thy hand,
One writ with me in sour misfortune's book!
I'll bury thee in a triumphant grave.
A grave? O, no, a lanthorn,[19] slaught'red youth,
85 For here lies Juliet, and her beauty makes
This vault a feasting presence[20] full of light.
18 Death, lie thou there, by a dead man interred.
                              [*Lays him in the tomb.*]
How oft when men are at the point of death
Have they been merry! Which their keepers[21] call
90 A lightning before death. O, how may I
Call this a lightning? O my love, my wife!
Death, that hath sucked the honey of thy breath,
Hath had no power yet upon thy beauty.
Thou art not conquered. Beauty's ensign[22] yet
95 Is crimson in thy lips and in thy cheeks,
And death's pale flag is not advancèd there.

19. **lanthorn** windowed structure on top of a room to admit light; also, a lantern.

20. **feasting presence** chamber fit for a celebration.

21. **keepers** jailers.

22. **ensign** banner.

Literary Analysis
Tragedy What tragic mistake does Romeo make regarding Juliet's appearance?

19 ◄ **Critical Viewing** What clues about Juliet's appearance, as it is shown here, should have led Romeo to realize she was still alive? **[Support]**

840 ■ *Drama*

Vocabulary Development

Expressive Vocabulary
As students discuss this final scene of the play, encourage them to make full use of the expressive vocabulary presented earlier. You might encourage them with sentence starters like these:

1. Paris was quick to *react* when he saw Romeo at Juliet's tomb.
2. Juliet was horrified at the *circumstance* that greeted her when she awoke.
3. Friar Lawrence did not take the time to *assess* the possible tragic outcome of his plan.
4. Friar Lawrence did not recognize the *significant* risks to Romeo and Juliet.

Tybalt, liest thou there in thy bloody sheet?
O, what more favor can I do to thee
Than with that hand that cut thy youth in twain
100　To sunder²³ his that was thine enemy?
Forgive me, cousin! Ah, dear Juliet,
Why art thou yet so fair? Shall I believe
That unsubstantial Death is amorous,²⁴
And that the lean abhorrèd monster keeps
105　Thee here in dark to be his paramour?
For fear of that I still will stay with thee
And never from this pallet²⁵ of dim night
Depart again. Here, here will I remain
With worms that are thy chambermaids. O, here
110　Will I set up my everlasting rest
And shake the yoke of inauspicious²⁶ stars
From this world-wearied flesh. Eyes, look your last!
Arms, take your last embrace! And, lips, O you
The doors of breath, seal with a righteous kiss
115　A dateless²⁷ bargain to engrossing²⁸ death!
❷⓪　Come, bitter conduct;²⁹ come, unsavory guide!
Thou desperate pilot,³⁰ now at once run on
The dashing rocks thy seasick weary bark!
Here's to my love! [Drinks.] O true apothecary!
120　Thy drugs are quick. Thus with a kiss I die.　　　　[Falls.]

[Enter FRIAR LAWRENCE, with lanthorn, crow, and spade.]

FRIAR. Saint Francis be my speed!³¹ How oft tonight
Have my old feet stumbled³² at graves! Who's there?

BALTHASAR. Here's one, a friend, and one that knows you well.

FRIAR. Bliss be upon you! Tell me, good my friend,
125　What torch is yond that vainly lends his light
To grubs³³ and eyeless skulls? As I discern,
It burneth in the Capels' monument.

BALTHASAR. It doth so, holy sir; and there's my master,
One that you love.

FRIAR.　　　　　　Who is it?

❷①　BALTHASAR.　　　　　　　　　Romeo.

FRIAR. How long hath he been there?

130　BALTHASAR.　　　　　　　　　Full half an hour.

FRIAR. Go with me to the vault.

BALTHASAR.　　　　　　　I dare not, sir.

---

23. **sunder** cut off.

24. **amorous** full of love.

25. **pallet** bed.

26. **inauspicious** promising misfortune.

27. **dateless** eternal.

28. **engrossing** all-encompassing.

29. **conduct** guide (poison).

30. **pilot** captain (Romeo himself).

31. **speed** help.

32. **stumbled** stumbling was thought to be a bad omen.

Literary Analysis
Tragedy In what way is Friar Lawrence's late arrival another example of chance contributing to this tragedy?

33. **grubs** worms.

✓ **Reading Check**
Does Friar Lawrence arrive in time to save Romeo?

Romeo and Juliet, Act V ■ 841

841

23 Critical Viewing

Possible response: Juliet appears sorrowful, rather than fearful, as she stabs herself. It appears she longs to die to be reunited in death with her husband.

24 Critical Thinking
Predicting

• Ask students what is ironic about Balthasar's description of his dream.
Answer: The events in his "dream" actually took place.

• Ask students what Juliet's first thought might be as she awakens and sees the Friar.
Possible response: Students may predict that Juliet will remember why she is in a tomb and be relieved that the plan is working out.

• **Ask** students what they think will happen when Juliet discovers that Romeo is dead.
Answer: Juliet will kill herself, too.

25 Literary Analysis
Motive

• What explanation does the Friar give to Juliet for what has happened?
Answer: The Friar lays the blame for the events at the feet of a greater power, which might be the gods, chance, or fate.

• **Ask** students to respond to the Literary Analysis question: Why do you think Friar Lawrence wants to "dispose of Juliet" in a sisterhood of nuns?
Possible response: The Friar may feel that a convent would be the best place for Juliet to recover from her grief and live out her ruined life. A less charitable interpretation is that the Friar hopes to prevent Juliet from revealing the full scope of the tragedy, exposing his own culpability.

26 Reading Check

Answer: She uses Romeo's dagger to stab herself.

My master knows not but I am gone hence,
And fearfully did menace me with death
If I did stay to look on his intents.

135   **FRIAR.** Stay then; I'll go alone. Fear comes upon me.
24   O, much I fear some ill unthrifty³⁴ thing.

    BALTHASAR. As I did sleep under this yew tree here,
I dreamt my master and another fought,
And that my master slew him.

    FRIAR.   Romeo!
140   Alack, alack, what blood is this which stains
The stony entrance of this sepulcher?
What mean these masterless³⁵ and gory swords
To lie discolored by this place of peace? [*Enters the tomb.*]
Romeo! O, pale! Who else? What, Paris too?
145   And steeped in blood? Ah, what an unkind³⁶ hour
Is guilty of this lamentable chance!
The lady stirs.   [JULIET *rises.*]

    JULIET. O comfortable³⁷ friar! Where is my lord?
I do remember well where I should be,
150   And there I am. Where is my Romeo?

    FRIAR. I hear some noise. Lady, come from that nest
Of death, contagion, and unnatural sleep.
A greater power than we can contradict
25   Hath thwarted our intents. Come, come away.
155   Thy husband in thy bosom there lies dead;
And Paris too. Come, I'll dispose of thee
Among a sisterhood of holy nuns.
Stay not to question, for the watch is coming.
Come, go, good Juliet. I dare no longer stay.

160   **JULIET.** Go, get thee hence, for I will not away.   [*Exit* FRIAR.]
What's here? A cup, closed in my truelove's hand?
Poison, I see, hath been his timeless³⁸ end.
O churl!³⁹ Drunk all, and left no friendly drop
To help me after? I will kiss thy lips.
165   Haply some poison yet doth hang on them
To make me die with a restorative.⁴⁰   [*Kisses him.*]
Thy lips are warm!

    CHIEF WATCHMAN. [*Within*] Lead, boy. Which way?

    JULIET. Yea, noise? Then I'll be brief. O happy⁴¹ dagger!
                        [*Snatches* ROMEO'S *dagger.*]
170   This is thy sheath; there rust, and let me die.
                    [*She stabs herself and falls.*]

842 ■ Drama

---

23 Critical Viewing

Does Juliet appear more sorrowful or fearful in this picture? **[Analyze]**

34. unthrifty unlucky.

35. masterless discarded (without masters).

36. unkind unnatural.

37. comfortable comforting.

Literary Analysis

Motive Why do you think Friar Lawrence wants to "dispose of Juliet" in a sisterhood of nuns?

38. timeless untimely; too soon.

39. churl rude fellow.

40. restorative medicine.

41. happy convenient; opportune.

26 Reading Check

What does Juliet do when she finds Romeo dead?

842

Romeo and Juliet, Act V ■ *843*

This scene from Zeffirelli's *Romeo and Juliet* marks the culmination of the tragedy. Have students discuss the movie still, using the following questions:

1. What is so tragic about Juliet's death?
   Answer: Juliet is young and innocent; she had nothing to do with the blood feud between the two families. She wakes only minutes too late. Expecting her husband, she discovers his corpse.

2. Discuss the lighting for this still. What makes it effective?
   Answer: Students may say that the shadows surrounding Juliet suggest the tragic circumstances that have enveloped her, or that death is closing in on her. The lighting focuses attention on Juliet's face and also highlights a column that points to Romeo.

Differentiated Instruction   Solutions for All Learners

Enrichment for Advanced Readers

Tell students that *The Tragedy of King Lear* is considered by many critics to be Shakespeare's greatest tragedy.

Remind students that in a tragedy, the central character meets with great misfortune, often because of a serious character flaw. Remind students that in *The Tragedy of Romeo and Juliet*, Romeo's serious flaw is his impatience. If he had waited for a letter from the Friar, or if he had not been so hasty to kill himself, he and Juliet could have been united.

Suggest that students form a small group to read and discuss Act I, Scene i of *The Tragedy of King Lear* in **Authors in Depth,** Gold Level.

Encourage students to address the following questions in their discussion:
• Who is the tragic hero of the play?
• What will prove to be Lear's serious character flaw?
• Which of the three sisters will prove to be loyal, and which will prove to be treacherous?

Literary Analysis
Tragedy

- **Ask** students why the Chief Watchman is demanding that everyone in the vicinity be held, or arrested.
Answer: The Chief Watchman is acting as a modern police officer would; he is securing the scene of the crime and rounding up the suspects.

- **Ask** students to respond to the Literary Analysis question: How might the tragic ending have been averted if the characters had come to the churchyard in a different order?
Answer: If the Friar had arrived first, he could have explained the circumstances to Romeo; if Paris had arrived after Romeo, Romeo and Juliet might have already fled to Mantua, and so forth.

29 **Critical Thinking**
Analyze

- **Ask** students whether they think the Prince contributes to the tragedy in this play. If so, how?
Possible response: Students may suggest that the Prince could have intervened in the feuding sooner. Likewise, he could have found a punishment other than exile or death for Romeo.

- **Ask** students who, if anyone, should be punished for this tragedy.
Possible responses: Some students may suggest that Romeo, who killed Paris, is dead, and Romeo and Juliet killed themselves, so there is no one to punish. Others may suggest that the Friar, who orchestrated much of the tragedy through his foolishness should be punished. Others may say that the Capulet and Montague families should be punished, since they indirectly brought about the tragedy because of their feuding.

844

[*Enter* PARIS' BOY *and* WATCH.]

BOY. This is the place. There, where the torch doth burn.

CHIEF WATCHMAN. The ground is bloody. Search about the
churchyard.
Go, some of you; whoe'er you find attach.[42]

[*Exit some of the* WATCH.]

Pitiful sight! Here lies the County slain;

175 And Juliet bleeding, warm, and newly dead,
Who here hath lain this two days buried.
Go, tell the Prince; run to the Capulets;
Raise up the Montagues; some others search.

[*Exit others of the* WATCH.]

28 We see the ground whereon these woes do lie,
180 But the true ground[43] of all these piteous woes
We cannot without circumstance descry.[44]

[*Enter some of the* WATCH, *with* ROMEO'S MAN, BALTHASAR.]

SECOND WATCHMAN. Here's Romeo's man. We found him in the
churchyard.

CHIEF WATCHMAN. Hold him in safety till the Prince come
hither.

[*Enter* FRIAR LAWRENCE *and another* WATCHMAN.]

THIRD WATCHMAN. Here is a friar that trembles, sighs and weeps.
185 We took this mattock and this spade from him
As he was coming from this churchyard's side.

CHIEF WATCHMAN. A great suspicion! Stay the friar too.

[*Enter the* PRINCE *and* ATTENDANTS.]

29 **PRINCE.** What misadventure is so early up,
That calls our person from our morning rest?

[*Enter* CAPULET *and his* WIFE *with others*.]

190 **CAPULET.** What should it be, that is so shrieked abroad?

LADY CAPULET. O, the people in the street cry "Romeo,"
Some "Juliet," and some "Paris"; and all run
With open outcry toward our monument.

PRINCE. What fear is this which startles in your ears?

195 **CHIEF WATCHMAN.** Sovereign, here lies the County Paris slain;
And Romeo dead; and Juliet, dead before,
Warm and new killed.

PRINCE. Search, seek, and know how this foul murder comes.

CHIEF WATCHMAN. Here is a friar, and slaughtered Romeo's man,

844 ■ *Drama*

---

42. attach arrest.

43. ground cause.

44. without circumstance descry see clearly without details.

Literary Analysis
Tragedy How might the tragic ending have been averted if the characters had come to the churchyard in a different order?

Vocabulary Development

Vocabulary Builder Reinforcement
To reinforce and assess students' comprehension of Vocabulary Builder words, give them sentences using the words in which the word may or may not be used correctly. Students must tell whether the use is correct and explain their answer. Use these sentences.

1. There were many *ambiguities* in the situation; it was clear exactly what happened.
Answer: No, *ambiguities* is not used correctly. *Ambiguities* refers to things that are not clear.

2. During the Middle Ages, disease was the common *scourge* of human beings.
Answer: Yes, *scourge* is used correctly, since it refers to something that causes pain or inflicts punishment.

200 With instruments upon them fit to open
     These dead men's tombs.

    CAPULET. O heavens! O wife, look how our daughter bleeds!
     This dagger hath mista'en, for, lo, his house[45]
     Is empty on the back of Montague,
205 And it missheathèd in my daughter's bosom!

    LADY CAPULET. O me, this sight of death is as a bell
     That warns my old age to a sepulcher.

[*Enter* MONTAGUE *and others.*]

    PRINCE. Come, Montague; for thou art early up
     To see thy son and heir more early down.

210 **MONTAGUE.** Alas, my liege,[46] my wife is dead tonight!
     Grief of my son's exile hath stopped her breath.
     What further woe conspires against mine age?

    PRINCE. Look, and thou shalt see.

30 **MONTAGUE.** O thou untaught! What manners is in this,
215 To press before thy father to a grave?

    PRINCE. Seal up the mouth of outrage[47] for a while,
     Till we can clear these <u>ambiguities</u>
     And know their spring, their head, their true descent;
     And then will I be general of your woes[48]
220 And lead you even to death. Meantime forbear,
     And let mischance be slave to patience.[49]
     Bring forth the parties of suspicion.

    FRIAR. I am the greatest, able to do least,
     Yet most suspected, as the time and place
225 Doth make against me, of this direful[50] murder;
     And here I stand, both to impeach and purge[51]
     Myself condemnèd and myself excused.

    PRINCE. Then say at once what thou dost know in this.

    FRIAR. I will be brief, for my short date of breath[52]
230 Is not so long as is a tedious tale.
     Romeo, there dead, was husband to that Juliet;
     And she, there dead, that's Romeo's faithful wife.
32 I married them; and their stol'n marriage day
     Was Tybalt's doomsday, whose untimely death
235 Banished the new-made bridegroom from this city;
     For whom, and not for Tybalt, Juliet pined.
     You, to remove that siege of grief from her,
     Betrothed and would have married her perforce

---

45. house sheath.

46. liege (lēj) lord.

Reading Skill
Summarizing Summarize the losses that the families have experienced as a result of Romeo and Juliet's relationship.

Vocabulary Builde
ambiguities (am′ bə gyōō′ ə tēz) *n.* statements or events whose meanings are unclear

47. mouth of outrage violent cries.
48. general . . . woes leader in your sorrow.
49. let . . . patience Be patient in the face of misfortune.

50. direful terrible.

51. impeach and purge accuse and declare blameless.

52. date of breath term of life.

 31 **Reading Check**

What effect did Romeo's exile have on his mother?

Romeo and Juliet, Act V ■ *845*

---

30 **Reading Skill**
Summarizing

- Ask students what the Prince means by telling Montague that his son is "early down."
  Answer: The Prince means that Romeo has met an untimely death.

- Ask students to respond to the Reading Skill question: Summarize the losses that the families have experienced as a result of Romeo and Juliet's relationship.
  Answer: Mercutio and Tybalt died because of the feud between the two families. Those who died as a result of Romeo and Juliet's relationship are Paris, Romeo and Juliet, and Lady Montague.

▶ **Monitor Progress:** Review students' graphic organizers to ensure that they are able to identify causes and effects.

▶ **Reteach:** If students have difficulty identifying cause and effect, provide them with **Reading Skill Graphic Organizer, Transparency B,** (*Graphic Organizer Transparencies*, p. 180) as a model.

31 **Reading Check**

Answer: Romeo's mother died of grief at Romeo's exile.

Differentiated
Instruction   Solutions for All Learners

Strategy for Special Needs Students
Have students review this last act by providing them with the *Reader's Notebook: Adapted Version.* After they have completed the notebook, have form groups to listen to the act on the **Adapted Reader's Notebook Audio CD.**

Strategy for English Learners
For students who may be struggling with the play, provide them with the *Reader's Notebook: English Learner's Version* for Act V. Have them work in groups to complete the notebook activities, and then have the group review the act on the **Listening to Literature Audio CD.**

- **Ask** students to interpret the Friar's words in lines 231–235 on p. 845. **Possible response:** The Friar is admitting that his actions played a part in the deaths of Romeo, Juliet, and Paris, but that he did not actually kill anyone.

- **Ask** students to respond to the Literary Analysis question: What examples of fate or character flaws do you find in the tragic events that the Friar recounts? **Answer:** Examples of character flaws include: Romeo and Juliet's haste in falling in love and secretly marrying; Romeo's vengeful response to Mercutio's slaying in killing Tybalt; the Capulets' haste in arranging for a marriage that Juliet did not consent to; and Romeo's rash intention to die on learning of Juliet's supposed death. Examples of fate involve messages—the true message that Romeo never receives; the false report he does receive. Multiple instances of "bad timing" on the fatal night are also fateful.

33 **Critical Thinking**

Analyze

- **Ask** students to read lines 265–269. What punishment does the Friar suggest if he is deemed responsible? **Answer:** The Friar says that if the tragedy is his fault, by law he should be executed.

- **Ask** what the Friar could have done differently that might have prevented the tragedy from happening. **Answer:** Students may suggest that Friar Lawrence could have avoided the feigned death and instead, arranged for Juliet to run away to join Romeo in Mantua. He could have gotten word to Romeo by more reliable means; he could have gone more quickly to the tomb; he could have prevented Juliet's suicide by insisting that she leave with him, or by staying with her to face the watch.

---

240   To County Paris. Then comes she to me
     And with wild looks bid me devise some mean
     To rid her from this second marriage,
     Or in my cell there would she kill herself.
     Then gave I her (so tutored by my art)
245   A sleeping potion; which so took effect
     As I intended, for it wrought on her
     The form of death. Meantime I writ to Romeo
     That he should hither come as[53] this dire night
     To help to take her from her borrowed grave,
     Being the time the potion's force should cease,
250   But he which bore my letter, Friar John,
     Was stayed by accident, and yesternight
     Returned my letter back. Then all alone
32   At the prefixèd hour of her waking
     Came I to take her from her kindred's vault;
255   Meaning to keep her closely[54] at my cell
     Till I conveniently could send to Romeo.
     But when I came, some minute ere the time
     Of her awakening, here untimely lay
     The noble Paris and true Romeo dead.
260   She wakes; and I entreated her come forth
     And bear this work of heaven with patience;
     But then a noise did scare me from the tomb,
     And she, too desperate, would not go with me,
     But, as it seems, did violence on herself.
265   All this I know, and to the marriage
     Her nurse is privy;[55] and if aught in this
33   Miscarried by my fault, let my old life
     Be sacrificed some hour before his time
     Unto the rigor[56] of severest law.

270 **PRINCE.** We still have known thee for a holy man.
     Where's Romeo's man? What can he say to this?

     BALTHASAR. I brought my master news of Juliet's death;
     And then in post he came from Mantua
     To this same place, to this same monument.
275   This letter he early bid me give his father,
     And threat'ned me with death, going in the vault,
     If I departed not and left him there.

     PRINCE. Give me the letter. I will look on it.
     Where is the County's page that raised the watch?
280   Sirrah, what made your master[57] in this place?

846 ■ *Drama*

Literary Analysis

Tragedy What examples of fate or character flaws do you find in the tragic events that the Friar recounts?

53. as on.

54. closely hidden; secretly.

55. privy secretly informed about.

56. rigor strictness.

57. made your master was your master doing.

Vocabulary Development

Vocabulary Knowledge Rating

When students have completed reading and discussing Act V of *The Tragedy of Romeo and Juliet,* have them take out their **Vocabulary Knowledge Rating Chart** for Act V. Read the words aloud once more and have students rate their knowledge of the words again in the After Reading column. Clarify any words that are still problematic. Have students write their own definition and example or sentence in the appropriate column. Then have students complete the **Vocabulary Builder Practice** activities on p. 849. Encourage students to use the words in further discussion and written work about this selection. Remind them that they will be accountable for these words on the Selection Test.

BOY. He came with flowers to strew his lady's grave;
And bid me stand aloof, and so I did.
Anon comes one with light to ope the tomb;
And by and by my master drew on him;
285 And then I ran away to call the watch.

PRINCE. This letter doth make good the friar's words,
Their course of love, the tidings of her death;
And here he writes that he did buy a poison
Of a poor 'pothecary and therewithal
290 Came to this vault to die and lie with Juliet.
Where be these enemies? Capulet, Montague,
See what a <u>scourge</u> is laid upon your hate,
That heaven finds means to kill your joys with love.
And I, for winking at[58] your discords too,
295 Have lost a brace[59] of kinsmen. All are punished.

CAPULET. O brother Montague, give me thy hand.
This is my daughter's jointure,[60] for no more
Can I demand.

MONTAGUE.   But I can give thee more;
For I will raise her statue in pure gold,
300 That whiles Verona by that name is known,
There shall no figure at such rate[61] be set
As that of true and faithful Juliet.

CAPULET. As rich shall Romeo's by his lady's lie—
Poor sacrifices of our enmity![62]

305 **PRINCE.** A glooming[63] peace this morning with it brings.
The sun for sorrow will not show his head.
Go hence, to have more talk of these sad things;
Some shall be pardoned, and some punishèd;
For never was a story of more woe
310   Than this of Juliet and her Romeo.   [*Exit all.*]

Vocabulary Builder
scourge (skʉrj) *n.*
instrument for
inflicting punishment

58. **winking at** closing my
eyes to.

59. **brace** pair (Mercutio and
Paris).

60. **jointure** wedding gift;
marriage settlement.

61. **rate** value.

62. **enmity** hostility.

63. **glooming** cloudy;
gloomy.

Literary Analysis
Motive What might
be Lord Montague's
motive for the
promise he makes to
Lord Capulet?

㉞ Literary Analysis
Motive

- Have students read lines 296–304.
Ask how the relationship between Capulet and Montague has changed.
Answer: Capulet and Montague have resolved their feud.

- **Ask** students the Literary Analysis question: What might be Lord Montague's motive for the promise he makes to Capulet?
Answer: Montague may wish to honor Juliet's faithfulness to his son. He may also want to have a reminder of the cost of the feud between the Montagues and Capulets, so that the feud will never be renewed.

Concept Connector

Anticipation Guide
Have students return to their **Anticipation Guides** and respond to the statements again in the After Reading column. They may do this individually or in their original pairs or groups. Then, lead a class discussion, probing for what students have learned that confirms or invalidates each statement. Encourage students to cite specific details, quotations, or other evidence from the text to support their responses to each statement.

Connecting to the Literature
Have students compare the sentences they wrote before reading with their thoughts about how tragedies can have positive effects. Ask them to explain whether their thoughts have changed and, if so, how.

Reading Skill Graphic Organizer
Have students review the graphic organizers they completed to identify causes and effects while reading. Show them **Reading Skill Graphic Organizer B** (*Graphic Organizer Transparencies,* p. 180) as an example. Then have students share their graphic organizers.

Apply the Skills

The Tragedy of Romeo and Juliet, Act V

Thinking About the Selection

1. **Respond:** Were you surprised by the way in which this play ends? Why or why not?
2. **(a) Recall:** In Act V, Scene i, what causes Romeo to exclaim, "Then I defy you, stars"? **(b) Connect:** In what way are Romeo's words consistent with what you know of his character?
3. **(a) Recall:** Identify at least three events that cause the Friar's scheme to fail. **(b) Analyze:** Why is it not surprising that the scheme fails?
4. **(a) Recall:** How does the relationship between the feuding families change at the end of the play? **(b) Draw Conclusions:** Were Romeo and Juliet's deaths necessary for this change to occur? Explain. **(c) Make a Judgment:** Is the end of long-term violence between their families a fair exchange for the deaths of Romeo and Juliet? Explain.

Literary Analysis

5. **(a)** Use a chart like the one shown to identify details of the elements that contribute to the **tragedy** in the play.

Romeo's and Juliet's Personalities	Fate or Chance	Other Causes

   (b) Which element is most responsible for the tragic events? Explain.
6. **(a)** What is the Friar's **motive** for helping Romeo and Juliet? **(b)** To what extent is he responsible for their tragedy? Explain.
7. What theme or message does Shakespeare attempt to convey through the tragic events in the play?
8. What positive message about the human spirit, if any, does this tragic play offer? Explain.

Reading Skill

9. **(a)** What events cause Romeo and Paris to arrive at Juliet's tomb at the same time? **(b)** What is the effect of their arriving at the same time?
10. **(a)** Analyze the chain of causes and effects that leads to the tragic ending of the play. **(b) Summarize** the events that occur at the tomb.

QuickReview

Act V at a Glance
Hearing of Juliet's death, Romeo buys poison and goes to her tomb in Verona, where he kills Paris. He finds Juliet's body and poisons himself. Juliet wakes, sees Romeo, and stabs herself. The grieving families agree to end their feud.

Go Online
Assessment
For: Self-test
Visit: www.PHSchool.com
Web Code: epa-6506

Tragedy: a drama in which the central character meets with disaster or great misfortune

Motive: the reason behind a character's thoughts or actions

Summarizing: briefly stating the main points in a piece of writing

Answers (left column)

1. Students may be surprised that Romeo kills Paris, or that Lady Montague dies of grief.

2. (a) Romeo is challenging fate. (b) This is consistent with his rash, dramatic character.

3. (a) The Friar's message goes astray; the Capulets rush Juliet's wedding; Romeo arrives at the tomb before the Friar. (b) The Friar's plan relies too much on perfect timing.

4. (a) The fathers shake hands and promise to build monuments to the other's child. (b) Some students may say that the marriage by itself might have ended the feud. (c) Most will say that it is not a fair exchange.

5. (a) **Personalities:** Romeo: impulsive, hotheaded; Juliet: strong-willed, disobedient; **Fate:** the accidental meeting; Tybalt's misunderstanding of Romeo; the Friar's luckless plan. **Other Causes:** The feud between the Montagues and the Capulets. (b) Fate is most responsible for the tragic events, because it took a long series of mischances to produce the fatal outcome. Another sample answer can be found on **Literary Analysis Graphic Organizer B**, p. 182 in *Graphic Organizer Transparencies.*

6. (a) The Friar wants to end the feud between the families. (b) He is responsible to some extent, because his plan is too elaborate and time-sensitive.

7. Shakespeare appears to be saying that old anger can destroy new love.

8. Shakespeare affirms that love—even in death—can triumph over dissension and enmity.

9. (a) Paris comes to mourn Juliet. Romeo arrives to die beside her. (b) Paris believes Romeo is vandalizing the tomb and provokes him into a combat fatal to Paris.

10. (a) Romeo hears of Juliet's death, and hastens to her tomb to die, missing the Friar's letter, but meeting, and killing, Paris. Juliet awakens to find Romeo dead; she stabs herself. (b) Families, servants, lawmen, and the Prince gather at the tomb; the Friar explains everything. The Prince, Capulets, and Montague meet at the tomb, and the two families end their feud.

Vocabulary Builder

Practice Identify the word in each group that does not belong with the others. Explain your response.

1. remnants, future, past
2. penury, poor, wealthy
3. haughty, proud, insecure
4. ambiguities, absolute, uncertain
5. scourge, pleasure, happiness

Adding Words to Your Vocabulary The word *haughty* has many **synonyms,** or words with a similar meaning. One of those words is *supercilious,* a word with an interesting origin that has to do with eyebrows. Use a dictionary to find out the origin of the word *supercilious.* Then, write a few sentences explaining how the origin of this word relates to its everyday usage. (For more on using a dictionary, see page R6.)

Writing

As Friar Lawrence, write a **persuasive letter** to both Lord Capulet and Lord Montague. The letter should urge them to end their feud.
- Make a list of factual evidence and emotional pleas that might convince the families to end their feud.
- Begin your draft by explaining the marriage.

Ask a classmate to read your draft from the point of view of both families. Revise your letter if it appears to favor one side.

For *Grammar, Vocabulary,* and *Assessment,* see **Build Language Skills,** pages 850–851.

Extend Your Learning

Listening and Speaking As a class, conduct a **mock trial** to investigate the causes of the tragedy in *Romeo and Juliet.*
- Assign roles: the main characters of the play, the lawyers, and the judge. The rest of the class should serve as the jury.
- Take depositions, or statements in which each character tells the story from his or her perspective.
- Use language—formal, informal, slang, or jargon—that fits the social, cultural, regional, and professional status of each character.

Jury members listening to both witnesses and lawyers should work to distinguish between valid claims and *propaganda*—arguments that twist or ignore facts to present a biased and distorted picture of events.

Apply the Skills ■ *849*

Assessment Resources

The following resources can be used to assess students' knowledge and skills.

Unit 5 Resources
Selection Test A, pp. 96–98
Selection Test B, pp. 99–101

 Go Online
Assessment Students may use the **Self-test** to prepare for **Selection Test A** or **Selection Test B**

Go Online
Research **For:** An additional research activity
Visit: www.PHSchool.com
Web Code: epd-7505
For another research activity to extend students' learning, give students this Web Code.

Vocabulary Builder
Practice

1. remnants; *remnants* are leftovers, *future* and *past* are categories of time.
2. wealthy; it has the opposite sense of *penury* and *poor.*
3. insecure; it is an antonym of *haughty* and *proud.*
4. absolute; *ambiguities* and *uncertain* both indicate a lack of clarity.
5. scourge; it is an antonym of *pleasure* and *happiness.*

Adding Words to Your Vocabulary

Supercilious comes from the Latin *supercilium,* which means "eyebrow." A raised eyebrow gives a facial expression that appears haughty. Therefore, *supercilious* is a synonym for *haughty.*

Writing

- To give students guidance for writing a persuasive letter, give them **Support for Writing** for Act V of *The Tragedy of Romeo and Juliet,* p. 91 in **Unit 5 Resources.**
- To evaluate students' letters, use the Persuasion: Persuasive Essay rubrics, pp. 53–54 in **General Resources.** In addition, you might evaluate for how well students use significant details to support their argument.

Six Traits Focus

	Ideas	Word Choice ✔
✔	Organization ✔	Sentence Fluency ✔
	Voice	Conventions ✔

W/G **Writing and Grammar, Gold Level**
Students will find guidance on persuasive writing in Chapter 7.

Build Language Skills

Go to pp. 850–851 for vocabulary and grammar lessons and assessment practice.

Extend Your Learning

The **Support for Extend Your Learning** page (*Unit 5 Resources,* p. 92) provides guided note-taking opportunities to help students complete the Extend Your Learning activity.

Vocabulary Skill

- Stress that recognizing the Latin root *-lum-* will help students decode the meanings of new or unfamiliar words. English words that contain the *-lum-* root will generally relate to the concept of light, either in the literal or figurative sense.

- Have students complete the Practice activity on this page.

Possible Answers

1. (a) We need *illumination* if we wish to find out what is in the dark basement. (b) The street lamp was *illuminating* our front yard.

2. (a) The moon was *luminous* in the autumn sky. (b) The moon was shining *luminously* from behind the clouds.

3. (a) Some deep sea fish are *luminescent*, shining in the gloom. (b) These creatures can produce their own light source, or *luminescence*.

4. (a) The Nobel Prize-winner is a *luminary* in her field. (b) The gathering of *luminaries*, each more famous than the last, was a privilege to experience.

Grammar Lesson

- Direct students to the graphic organizer on this page. Point out to students the examples that show how gerunds and gerund phrases function in sentences.

- Have students complete the Practice activity on this page.

Answers

1. He suggests that *walking* to school would be good exercise.

2. *Screaming* is one of those sounds that mean danger.

3. The cat made a sound like *screeching*.

4. The soccer player ran with the defense chasing him.

5. *Studying* the environment is one thing that makes science fun for me.

𝒲𝒢 Writing and Grammar, Gold Level

Students will find further instruction and practice on gerunds and gerund phrases in Chapter 21, Section 1.

Build Language Skills

Romeo and Juliet, Acts IV–V

Vocabulary Skill

Word Roots The **word root** *-lum-* means "light." Words that contain the word root *-lum-* have meanings related to light. For example, *illuminate* means, literally, "brings light to." It is often used in the figurative sense: When a fact or an idea is brought to light, it is *illuminated*, or clarified.

▶ **Example:** Juliet's conversation with the nurse is *illuminating*.

Practice Write a sentence using each word that contains the root *-lum-*. Then, check the meaning and examples of usage of each word in a dictionary to revise your sentences, if necessary.

1. (a) illumination (b) illuminating
2. (a) luminous (b) luminously
3. (a) luminescent (b) luminescence
4. (a) luminary (b) luminaries

Grammar Skill

Gerund and Gerund Phrase A **gerund** is a form of a verb that acts as a noun. It can function as a subject, an object, a predicate noun, or the object of a preposition. A **gerund phrase** is a gerund and its modifiers. A gerund phrase also acts as a noun.

Subject	*Remodeling* the building's style was a good idea.
Direct Object	Michael enjoys *painting*.
Predicate Noun	His favorite sport is *fishing*.
Object of the Preposition	Lucille never gets tired of *singing*.
Gerund Phrase	The *loud, shrill howling* continued all morning.

Practice Change one of the verbs to a gerund and then use that gerund, or gerund phrase, to combine the two sentences.

1. He suggests that we walk to school. It would be good exercise.
2. There are sounds that mean danger. A scream is one of those sounds.
3. The cat made a strange sound. It was a screech.
4. The soccer player ran. The defense chased him.
5. Science is fun for me. I like to study the environment.

𝒲𝒢 *Prentice Hall Writing and Grammar Connection: Chapter 21, Section 1.*

850 ■ Drama

MorePractice

For more practice with gerunds, see the Grammar Handbook, p. R44.

Teaching Resources

The following resources can be used to enrich or extend the instruction for Build Language Skills.

Unit 5 Resources

Build Language Skills: Vocabulary: Word Roots, p. 94

Build Grammar Skills: Gerunds and Gerund Phrases, p. 95

Reading Skill: Summarize

Directions: *Read the selection. Then, answer the questions.*

Last Friday was opening night for the Drama Club's production of *Cats*. The performances and the music were terrific. The cast has been rehearsing for months, and it showed. There were a few blunders, but most of the audience did not notice. Jim missed his entrance on the opening dance number, but he was only a second late. It is surprising that there were not more mistakes. The stomach virus that caused so many class absences last week also led to about half the cast missing the last dress rehearsals. The audience gave the cast and crew a well-deserved standing ovation.

1. Which of the following is the most important idea to include in a summary?
   A Jim was a few seconds late.
   B A dance number had a mistake.
   C The Drama Club performed *Cats*.
   D There was a standing ovation.

2. What is the best paraphrase of the first three sentences of the selection?
   A The Drama Club had its first performance of *Cats* last Friday.
   B After months of rehearsal, the Drama Club gave an amazing opening night show of *Cats*.

   C On Friday, the performances were fantastic and the music was good.
   D Last Friday, the Drama Club produced a wonderful *Cats*. They had rehearsed for months.

3. What is the most important result of the stomach virus to include in a summary of this selection?
   A Students missed class.
   B Jim missed the performance.
   C Actors missed rehearsals.
   D Jim missed his entrance.

Timed Writing: Interpretation [Critical Stance]

In a tragedy, the tragic hero meets with disaster because of a character flaw or fate. Who is the tragic hero in *Romeo and Juliet*? Defend your choice, and argue whether fate or a character flaw contributed more to the disaster. Use specific details from the text to support your interpretation. **(40 minutes)**

 ## Writing Workshop: *Work in Progress*

How-to Essay

Review the Steps List from your writing portfolio. Use stick figures to make a "cartoon frame" for each step on your list. Then, in each dialogue bubble, write a sentence in which you explain the step. Save this work in your writing portfolio.

Build Language Skills ■ *851*

Reading: Summarizing
1. C
2. B
3. C

Timed Writing

- Tell students that they will have 40 minutes to write an interpretation. This paper focuses on one aspect of a play and an interpretation of that aspect.

- Have students read the assignment carefully and select their central character. Then, have students jot down notes and references from the play.

- As students write, remind them that they must cite the lines that they use to support their interpretation.

- Assess students' interpretations on the development of their ideas and the relevance and accuracy of their support.

- Suggest that students allow 10 minutes for selecting and reviewing the play, 25 minutes for writing the interpretation, and 5 minutes for reviewing and revising the interpretation.

Writing Workshop
Work in Progress

How-to Essay

- Have students go to their list of steps from the **Work in Progress** on p. 813.

- Remind students that this work may be used in the how-to essay they will write in the **Writing Workshop** at the end of Part 1.

- Have students review each step on the list to make sure that they have included all the steps of the process.

- Point out that their bubble must include information that will help those who are unfamiliar with the process. They must not assume that others already have knowledge of the process.

- When students have completed their "cartoon frame," have them save these in their portfolios. They will use them in the **Writing Workshop** on p. 874.

See TeacherExpress™/Lesson View for a detailed lesson plan for Reading Informational Materials.

About Atlases

- Have students read "About Atlases."

- Explain to students that they are likely to use an atlas when searching for information about a geographic location.

- Discuss with students any experiences they have had using an atlas for information. Ask what information they were looking for and how easy it was to find in an atlas.

Reading Skill
Skimming and Scanning

- Remind students that skimming and scanning are techniques to help you locate information more quickly.

- Review with students the questions to ask when skimming and scanning.

- Explain that atlases will present information through both text and graphics.

Atlases

In Part 1, you are learning how to summarize as you read. This skill is also useful when reading encyclopedia or atlas entries. When you read an atlas entry, summarizing helps you identify the main point and better understand what you have read. If you read *Romeo and Juliet*, you might be interested in the atlas entry about Italy, the setting of the play.

About Atlases

An **atlas** is a book of maps showing physical features of the world, such as cities, mountains, rivers, and roads. Some atlases include facts and statistics about the places presented. Many modern atlases provide brief articles on topics such as population, climate, government, transportation, and tourism.

A map in an atlas is usually accompanied by a legend, a key that explains the symbols and colors used in the map. For example, symbols might represent features such as national or state capitals. Color codes might be used to indicate land height or population densities. The legend may also indicate to what mileage the map is scaled.

Reading Skill

Atlases provide a broad range of information. To find the material you need, adjust your reading rate by **skimming and scanning.**

- By skimming, you get an idea of the organization and scope of the work before reading it closely. To skim, read quickly, taking in words in groups. Stop for headings and other text that is set off, such as bold text.

- By scanning, you can quickly locate specific information. Move your eyes rapidly over the page. Look for words related to the information you are seeking. Stop and read the paragraphs that contain these words.

Use the questions shown in the box to guide you as you skim and scan the atlas that follows.

Questions to Ask When Skimming and Scanning

- What information is provided in the legend of the map?
- In the atlas article, which text is set in large or bold print?
- What are the main subheads on the page?
- For each subhead, what is one key fact you can find quickly?

Differentiated
Instruction   Solutions for All Learners

Reading Support
Give students reading support with the appropriate version of the *Reader's Notebooks:*

Reader's Notebook, [L2]

Reader's Notebook: Adapted Version, [L1]

Reader's Notebook: English Learner's Version, [EL]

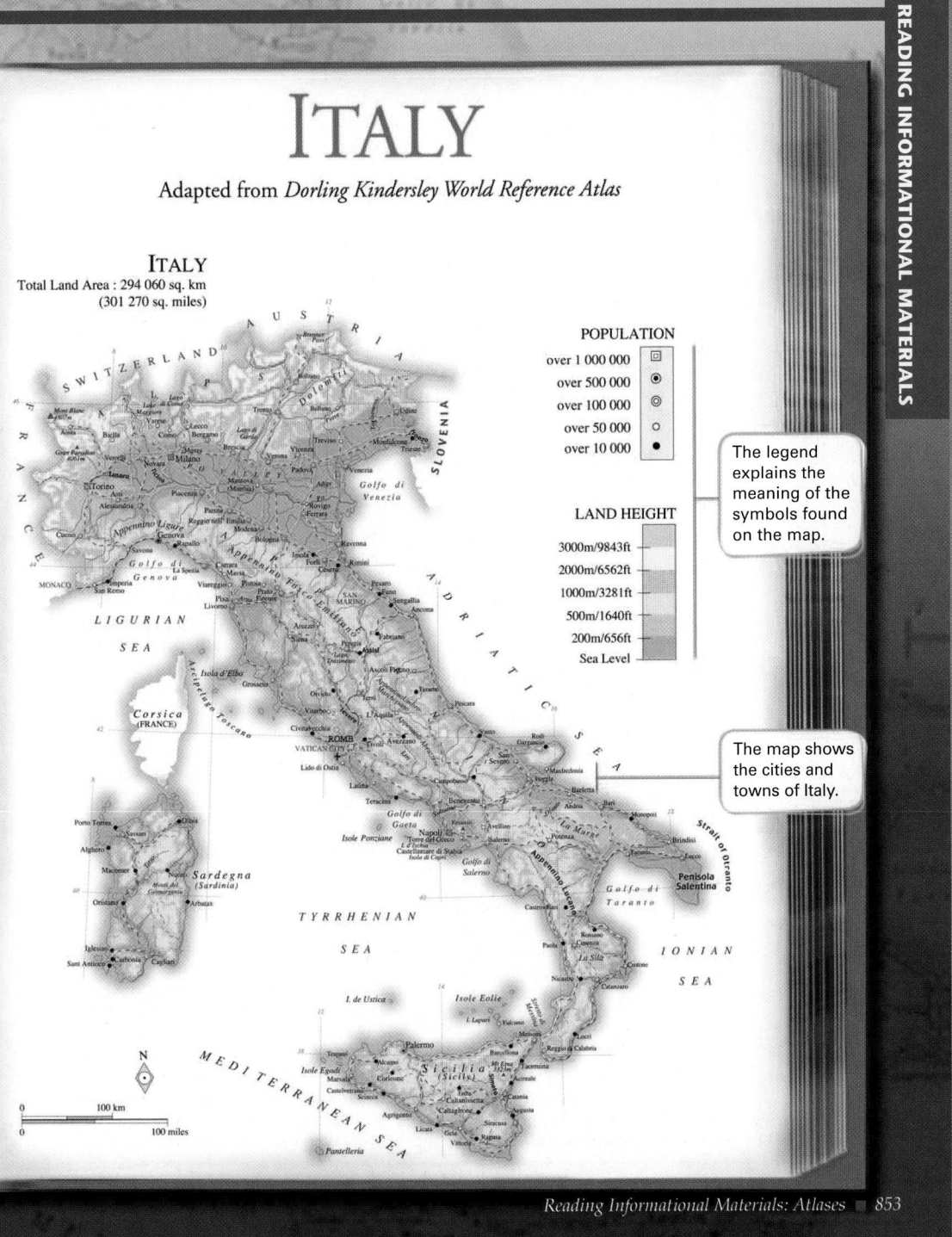

ITALY

Adapted from *Dorling Kindersley World Reference Atlas*

ITALY
Total Land Area : 294 060 sq. km
(301 270 sq. miles)

POPULATION
over 1 000 000
over 500 000
over 100 000
over 50 000
over 10 000

LAND HEIGHT
3000m/9843ft
2000m/6562ft
1000m/3281ft
500m/1640ft
200m/656ft
Sea Level

The legend explains the meaning of the symbols found on the map.

The map shows the cities and towns of Italy.

Reading Atlases

- Remind students that they should preview text that has special formatting, such as bold headings and legends or notes that accompany graphic images, to find out what information is in this entry.
- Have students read the atlas entry for "Italy."
- **Ask** students: Based on the legend for the map of Italy, what information do you expect to learn from this map?
  Possible response: I expect to learn about the population and topography of Italy because the legend shows which symbols represent certain population numbers and the height of land.
- Remind students that skimming and scanning the atlas entry will help them understand the organization of the entry before they begin reading for information.

continued on p. 854

Differentiated
Instruction   Solutions for All Learners

Support for Special Needs Students
Review with students the questions for skimming and scanning text. Then point out that the atlas entry includes graphics that provide hints about the content of each section.

Enrichment for Gifted/Talented Students
Challenge students to learn more about one of the Italian cities from the atlas. Allow time for students to share information and any photographs they find.

853

Reading Atlases (cont.)

- Remind students that atlases use bold headings and graphics to help you locate information quickly.

- **Ask** students what kind of information is found under the heading "Climate"?
  Possible response: Information about temperature and weather can be found under "Climate."

- **Ask** students under which section they would find information about the TAV (high speed train).
  Answer: Transportation.

Reading Informational Materials

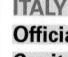

The atlas article begins with a list of basic information about the country depicted in the map.

ITALY

Official Name: *Italian Republic*
Capital: *Rome*
Population: *57.2 million*
Currency: *the euro*
Official Language: *Italian*

Lying in southern Europe, Italy comprises the famous boot-shaped peninsula stretching 500 miles into the Mediterranean and a number of islands—Sicily and Sardinia being the largest. The Alps form a natural boundary to the north, while the Apennine Mountains run the length of the peninsula. The south is an area of seismic activity, epitomized by the volcanoes of Mounts Etna and Vesuvius. United under ancient Roman rule, Italy subsequently developed into a series of competing kingdoms and states, not fully reunited until 1870. Italian politics was dominated by the Christian Democrats (CD) from 1945 to 1992 under a system of political patronage and a succession of short-lived governments. Investigations into corruption from 1992 on led to the demise of this system in the elections of 1994.

Subheads break the information into the same specific categories for each country.

CLIMATE

Southern Italy has a Mediterranean climate; the north is more temperate. Summers are hot and dry, especially in the south. Temperatures range from 75°F to over 81°F in Sardinia and Sicily. Southern winters are mild; northern ones are cooler and wetter. The mountains usually experience heavy snow. The Adriatic coast suffers from cold winds such as the bora.

Symbols highlight key information in each category.

TRANSPORTATION

 Leonardo da Vinci (Fiumicino), Rome 15.55m passengers   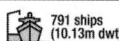 791 ships (10.13m dwt)

Many of Italy's key routes are congested. The trans-Apennine *autostrada* (expressway) from Bologna to Florence is being doubled in size. A high-speed train program (*treno ad alta velocità*—TAV) is planned to link Turin, Milan, Venice, Bologna, Florence and Naples to Rome. Most of Italy's exports travel by road, via Switzerland and Austria. Only 16% goes by sea.

TOURISM

 27.5m visitors   Up 4% in 1994

Italy has been a tourist destination since the 16th century and probably invented the concept. Roman Popes consciously aimed to make their city the most beautiful in the world to attract travelers. In the 18th century, Italy was the focus of any Grand Tour. Today, its many unspoilt centers of Renaissance culture continue to make Italy one of the world's major tourism destinations. The industry accounts for 3% of Italy's GDP, and hotels and restaurants employ one million out of a working population of 21 million.

Most visitors travel to the northern half of the country, to cities such as Rome, Florence, Venice and Padova. Many are increasingly traveling to the northern lakes. Beach resorts such as Rimini attract a large, youthful crowd in summer. Italy is also growing in popularity as a skiing destination.

PEOPLE

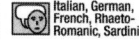 Italian, German, French, Rhaeto-Romanic, Sardinian   505 people per sq. mile

Italy is a remarkably homogeneous society. Most Italians are Roman Catholics, and Italy has far fewer ethnic minorities than its EU neighbors. Most are fairly recent immigrants from Ethiopia, the Philippines and Egypt. A sharp rise in illegal immigration in the 1980's and 1990's, from North and West Africa, Turkey and Albania, generated a right-wing backlash and tighter controls. It became a major election issue in 1993 and a factor in the rise of the federalist Northern League.

854 ■ Drama

Vocabulary Development

Vocabulary for Atlases
Point out that reference materials, such as atlases, often use vocabulary that is specific to one particular setting, in this case Italy. Guide students to understand the meaning of the following words that are used in the *Italy* atlas entry:

peninsula: a body of land jutting out from a larger body and surrounded by water on three sides

seismic: caused by or subject to earthquakes

patronage: support of an influential person

succession: a number of persons that follow each other in sequence

Assessment Practice

Reading: Skimming and Scanning

Directions: *Choose the letter of the best answer to each question about the atlas entry.*

1. What is the approximate population of Assisi?
    A over 1,000,000
    B over 100,000
    C over 50,000
    D over 10,000

2. If you were scanning the atlas article for information about the weather of southern Italy in the winter, under which subhead would you stop and read?
    A Climate
    B Transportation
    C Tourism
    D People

3. Under which subhead would you skim to find the religion of the majority of people in Italy?
    A Climate
    B Transportation
    C Tourism
    D People

Reading: Comprehension and Interpretation

Directions: *Write your answers on a separate piece of paper.*

4. Which five seas border Italy? [**Knowledge**]
5. Why is Rome printed in bold, capital letters on the map? [**Generating**]
6. What percentage of Italy's exports travel by sea? [**Integrating**]

Timed Writing: Exposition [Interpreting]

Summarize the information presented in this atlas entry about Italy. Using information from both the graphics and text, briefly describe the country's size and location, its land and climate, and its people. Then, note key facts that would help tourists make the most of a trip there.
(40 minutes)

Reading: Skimming and Scanning

1. D
2. A
3. D
4. **Answer:** The Ligurian, Tyrrhenian, Ionian, Mediterranean, and Adriatic Seas border Italy.
5. **Answer:** Rome is in bold capital letters because it is the capital of Italy.
6. **Answer:** Sixteen percent of Italy's exports travel by sea.

Timed Writing: Exposition

- Read the Timed Writing instructions together as a group.
- Students should allow 15 minutes to plan their summary, 20 minutes to write the summary, and 5 minutes to review their writing.
- Student summaries should include information about Italy's size, location, land, climate, and people. It should also include an overview of facts for tourists.

Extend the Lesson

Atlas Entry
To give students further practice with the organization and features of text in atlases, have students choose a topic they know well and divide it into three sub-topics. Use formatting to direct readers to find information about your topic.

Meeting Your Standards

Students will

1. analyze and respond to the archetypal theme of ill-fated love.

2. compare the archetypal theme of ill-fated love in two literary works.

3. write a comparison of the use of the archetypal theme of ill-fated love in two literary works.

See TeacherExpress™/Lesson View for a detailed lesson plan for Comparing Literary Works.

Literary Analysis

❶ Archetypal Theme: Ill-fated Love

• Read the instruction about archetypal theme together. Tell students that the word *archetype* comes from an ancient Greek word meaning "beginning or original type." Tell students to think of an archetype as the most basic, original, or fundamental form of a character, a plot, or an idea.

• Explain to students that, as they read, they should be alert to the most common experience or universal idea that the story is trying to convey.

❷ Comparing Presentations of an Archetypal Theme

• Remind students that the same archetypal themes may appear in works of different genres. The theme of ill-fated love, for example, may be treated in folktales, epics, novels, lyric poems, plays, and even nonfiction. Students will see how Ovid's retelling of a myth and Shakespeare's drama deal with the same archetypal theme when they compare these two selections.

• Give students a copy of **Comparing Presentations of an Archetypal Theme Graphic Organizer A** (*Graphic Organizer Transparencies*, p. 183). Have them complete it as they read and compare the selections.

❶ Archetypal Theme: Ill-fated Love

An **archetype** is a plot, character, image, or setting that appears in literature from around the world and throughout history. Archetypes represent truths about life and are said to mirror the working of the human mind. Common archetypes include the following:

• Characters: the hero; the outcast
• Plot types: the quest, or search; the task
• Symbol: water as a symbol of life; fire as a symbol of power

A **theme** is the central idea, message, or insight of a literary work. **Archetypal themes** are those that develop or explore fundamental, or archetypal, ideas. One example of an archetypal theme is ill-fated love, which appears in literature from all over the world.

❷ Comparing Presentations of an Archetypal Theme

Works of literature may differ in their presentations of the same archetypal theme for many reasons, including these:

• the values of the era in which the work was written
• the author's purpose for writing
• the author's culture and language, including any literary styles and expectations

As you read Ovid's "Pyramus and Thisbe," make comparisons to Shakespeare's treatment of a similar tale in *Romeo and Juliet.* Refer to the Prologue in Act I (lines 1–13), the balcony scene (Act II, Scene ii, lines 49–189), and the death scene (Act V, Scene iii, lines 22–170) in *Romeo and Juliet.* Then, consider Shakespeare's treatment of the same story in *A Midsummer Night's Dream.* Use a chart like the one shown to organize your observations.

Characters	
Similarities	Differences

Events	
Similarities	Differences

Vocabulary Builder

"Pyramus and Thisbe"

■ **lament** (lə ment´) *v.* express deep sorrow; mourn (p. 859) *Many friends showed up at the funeral to* lament *their loss.*

■ **inevitable** (in ev´ i tə bəl) *adj.* unavoidable,

856 ■ *Drama*

certain (p. 860) *After he missed his nap, the toddler's tantrum was* inevitable.

from *A Midsummer Night's Dream*

■ **enamored** (en am´ ərd) *v.* filled with love and desire; charmed (p. 867) *She was* enamored *of his personality, not his looks.*

■ **enthralled** (en thrôld) *v.* held as in a spell; captivated (p. 867) *The audience sat* enthralled *by the movie's special effects.*

Vocabulary Development

Vocabulary Knowledge Rating
Create a **Vocabulary Knowledge Rating Chart** with the selection vocabulary and expressive vocabulary for both selections. Give students a copy. Introduce the words by reading them aloud and having students mark their rating in the Before Reading column. Urge them to be alert to these words as they read and discuss the selection because they will rate their knowledge of the words again after they finish.

If you wish, you may tally how many students know (or think they know) a word to gauge how much instruction you need to provide. As students read, point out the words and their context.

Build Understanding

❸ Connecting to the Literature

Reading/Writing Connection *Romeo and Juliet,* "Pyramus and Thisbe," and *A Midsummer Night's Dream* all tell of young people in love who face serious obstacles. Write a paragraph in which you explain why people enjoy love stories, whether they end happily or sadly. Use at least three of the following words in your response: *enrich, sustain, console, transform, unify.*

Meet the Author

Ovid (43 B.C.–A.D. 17)

Educated in Rome, Ovid began his career writing poems about love and pleasure. However, the emperor Augustus wanted citizens to focus on morality and work toward an ideal Roman state. In response, Ovid decided to write about myths and traditional stories, such as "Pyramus and Thisbe."

Achievement and Exile After completing his masterpiece, *Metamorphoses,* in A.D. 8, Ovid was banished to a remote village on the Black Sea. The reasons for his banishment are not entirely clear, but the emperor might have felt that Ovid's work endangered public morals. Exile to a half-civilized place on the edge of the empire was a severe punishment for this worldly poet. Although he continued to write, he was never allowed to return to Rome.

William **Shakespeare** (1564–1616)

The greatest of all playwrights, William Shakespeare was born in the town of Stratford-on-Avon and gained his successes in the flourishing theatrical world of London. He worked as an actor, a playwright, and part owner of a theater company, earning enough to retire to Stratford in 1610.

Kings and Clowns, Lovers and Villains Shakespeare's 37 plays are populated with a wide range of characters who embody the depth and variety of human experience. No writer has played a more significant role in shaping the English language and English literature.

Go **O**nline
Author Link
For: More information about the authors
Visit: www.PHSchool.com
Web Code: epe-9503

Romeo and Juliet / Pyramus and Thisbe / from A Midsummer Night's Dream ■ 857

❸ Connecting to the Literature

- Model use of the expressive vocabulary students are asked to use with these examples:
  1. People enjoy love stories because they *enrich* our lives and touch our emotions.
  2. Tales of lovers overcoming difficulties *sustain* us during our own troubles.
  3. Love stories can sometimes *console* us when we experience sadness and loss.
  4. Readers and audiences also enjoy the spectacle of seeing love *transform* people's lives.
  5. In some stories, love has the power to *unify* people divided by fear, hate, and ignorance.

- Help students further develop their expressive vocabulary by providing these words: *parallel, harmonious,* and *amorous.*

Encourage students to use these words as they discuss the selections.

Go **O**nline
Author Link
For additional information about Ovid and William Shakespeare, have students type in the Web Code, and then select *Ovid* or *William Shakespeare.*

Teaching Resources

The following resources can be used to enrich, extend, or differentiate the instruction for Comparing Literary Works.

Unit 5 Resources, pp. 102–112

Graphic Organizer Transparencies, pp. 183–186

Listening to Literature Audio CD

857

❶ Background

Metamorphoses Tales of metamorphosis did not originate with Ovid. Stories of gods or people being transformed into plants, animals, or inanimate objects were popular even in the time of Homer, and almost certainly grew out of the folk tradition. Ovid's collection (a poem, not prose, as in Edith Hamilton's version) includes examples of characters being transformed into trees, reeds, flowers, streams, fountains, insects, snakes, birds, animals, stars, and a variety of monsters. Metamorphosis is itself an archetypal theme, just like ill-fated love.

❷ Motivation

Prepare an **Anticipation Guide** (*General Resources,* pp. 8–10) with the following statements:

- A crisis can make a person change shockingly fast.
- The most important changes are those that take place slowly.
- Love is the greatest cause of change in people's lives.
- Important changes are caused by the decisions people make.

Give students a copy of the prepared Anticipation Guide and have students mark their responses in the Me column. Have students discuss the statements in pairs or groups and mark the Guides again in the group column.

Concept Connector ➡

Students will return to the Anticipation Guide after completing the selections.

❸ About the Selection

Edith Hamilton's retelling of Ovid's "Pyramus and Thisbe" reads like a fairy tale, even beginning "Once upon a time." Pyramus and Thisbe, children of neighboring families in Babylon, love each other but are forbidden to marry. Through a chink in the wall that joins their houses, they express their love and plan their escape. They agree to run away and meet at a tomb under a mulberry tree, but their plans miscarry through a tragic misunderstanding.

PYRAMUS AND THISBE
OVID

Retold by **Edith Hamilton**

❶
❷
❸
❹

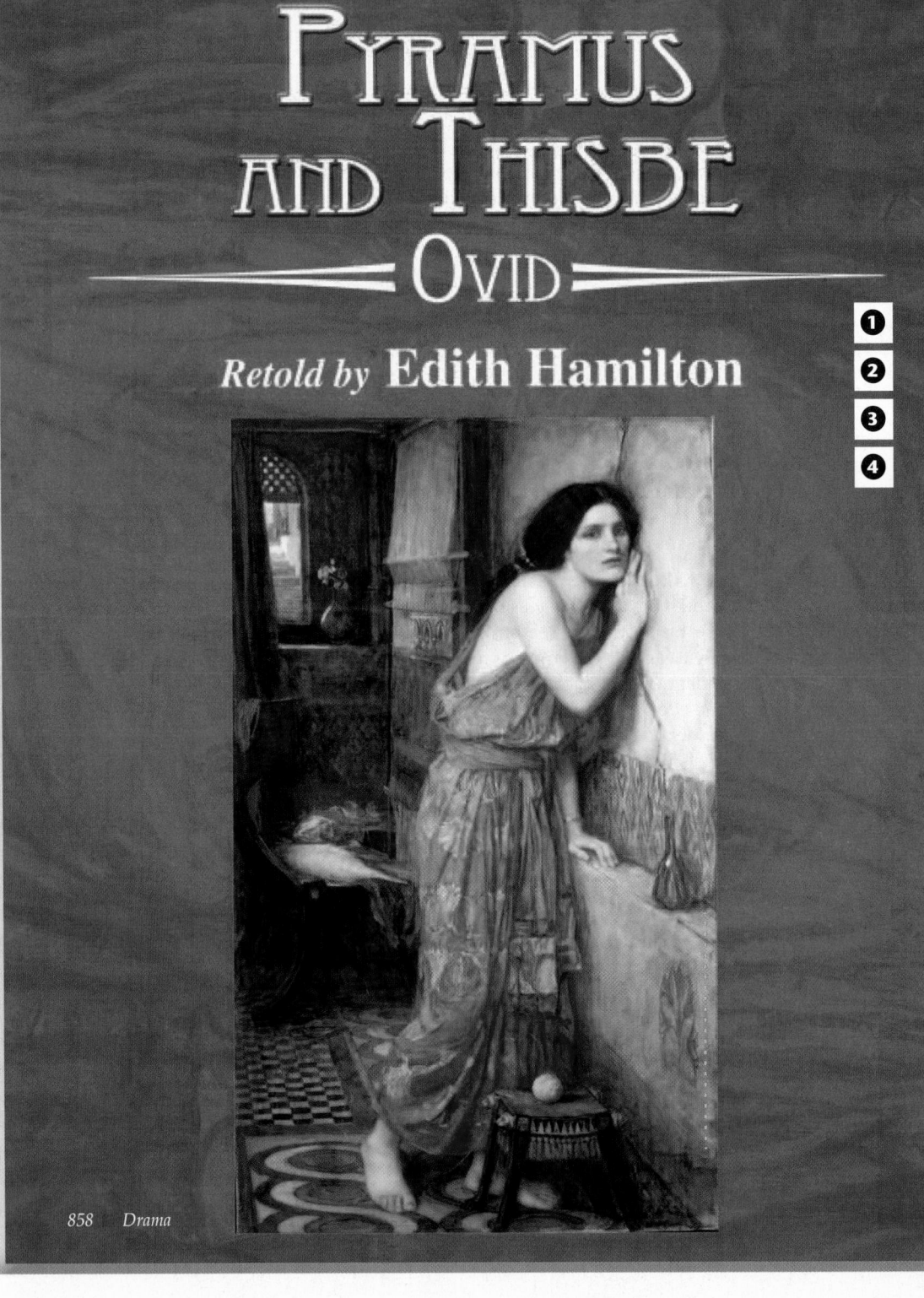

858 *Drama*

Background The tale of Pyramus and Thisbe appears in Book IV of *Metamorphoses*, Ovid's greatest achievement. A poem of nearly 12,000 lines, it tells a series of stories beginning with the creation of the world and ending with the death of Julius Caesar. In each story, someone or something undergoes a change. Divided into fifteen books, the stories are linked by clever transitions, so that the entire work reads as one long, uninterrupted tale.

Once upon a time the deep red berries of the mulberry tree[1] were white as snow. The change in color came about strangely and sadly. The death of two young lovers was the cause.

Pyramus and Thisbe, he the most beautiful youth and she the loveliest maiden of all the East, lived in Babylon, the city of Queen Semiramis, in houses so close together that one wall was common to both. Growing up thus side by side they learned to love each other. They longed to marry, but their parents forbade. Love, however, cannot be forbidden. The more that flame is covered up, the hotter it burns. Also love can always find a way. It was impossible that these two whose hearts were on fire should be kept apart.

In the wall both houses shared there was a little chink.[2] No one before had noticed it, but there is nothing a lover does not notice. Our two young people discovered it and through it they were able to whisper sweetly back and forth. Thisbe on one side, Pyramus on the other. The hateful wall that separated them had become their means of reaching each other. "But for you we could touch, kiss," they would say. "But at least you let us speak together. You give a passage for loving words to reach loving ears. We are not ungrateful." So they would talk, and as night came on and they must part, each would press on the wall kisses that could not go through to the lips on the other side.

Every morning when the dawn had put out the stars, and the sun's rays had dried the hoarfrost on the grass, they would steal to the crack and, standing there, now utter words of burning love and now <u>lament</u> their hard fate, but always in softest whispers. Finally a day came when they could endure no longer. They decided that that very night they would try to slip away and steal out through the city into the open country where at last they could be together in freedom. They agreed to meet at a well-known place, the Tomb of Ninus, under a tree there, a tall mulberry full of snow-white berries, near which a cool spring bubbled up. The plan pleased them and it seemed to them the day would never end.

---

1. **mulberry** (mul′ ber′ rē) **tree** *n.* tree with an edible, purplish red fruit.
2. **chink** (chiŋk) *n.* narrow opening; crack.

---

5 ◀ **Critical Viewing**
What do you think the girl is feeling as she listens through the crack in the wall? **[Speculate]**

Literary Analysis
Archetypal Theme
What is the main obstacle the lovers face?

Vocabulary Builder
lament (lə ment′)
v. express deep sorrow; mourn

7 ✓ **Reading Check**
How do Pyramus and Thisbe communicate with each other?

Pyramus and Thisbe ■ 859

---

4 Humanities
Thisbe, by John William Waterhouse

John William Waterhouse (1849–1917) was an English Pre-Raphaelite painter who loved Greek myth and classical history. He often painted strong or tragic female characters, such as Shakespeare's Ophelia and Homer's Penelope. Use the following question for discussion:

• **Ask** students why they think Waterhouse paints Thisbe in a red gown.
  Answer: The color of her gown suggests the mulberry that turns red in her memory.

5 Critical Viewing
Possible responses: The girl may be feeling love, longing, frustration, disappointment, fear, doubt, or resentment.

6 Literary Analysis
Archetypal Theme

• Remind students that an archetypal theme addresses a basic, common, or universal aspect of human experience. **Ask** students to identify some of the most common issues that teenagers have always faced.
  Possible responses: Teenagers must deal with restrictions placed on them by parents, the demands of society, peer pressure, and anxieties about their future.

• **Ask** students the Literary Analysis question: What is the main obstacle the lovers face?
  Answer: The lovers' main obstacle is the restriction placed on them by their parents.

• Have students **speculate** about a range of possible resolutions to the lovers' situation.
  Possible responses: The lovers may try to run away together. They might try to talk to their parents.

7 Reading Check
Answer: Pyramus and Thisbe whisper through a chink in the wall that joins their houses.

❽ Literary Analysis
Archetypal Theme

- **Ask** students what personality traits they think Thisbe probably has, based on her actions so far.
Possible responses: She is obedient to her parents, based on her endurance of their restrictions. She is sensitive and romantic, based on her whispering through the wall.

- Have students read the bracketed passage. Then, **ask** the Literary Analysis question: What does Thisbe's "bold" behavior suggest about the power of love?
Answer: Her behavior suggests that love can give people courage, make them forceful and practical, or even make them desperate and willing to break rules.

- Discuss with students the different kinds of metamorphoses that people can experience—including physical, intellectual, spiritual, and emotional. **Ask** students how they think love can affect all the different kinds of metamorphosis.
Possible responses: Love can cause people to try to make themselves more physically attractive and more intellectually and financially successful. Love can foster spiritual growth and lead to self-discipline, self-sacrifice, and emotional maturity.

❾ Critical Viewing

In the story, the lioness is bloody from a recent kill; this lioness is clean. Both lionesses are fierce and powerful hunters.

❽ At last the sun sank into the sea and night arose. In the darkness Thisbe crept out and made her way in all secrecy to the tomb. Pyramus had not come; still she waited for him, her love making her bold. But of a sudden she saw by the light of the moon a lioness. The fierce beast had made a kill; her jaws were bloody and she was coming to slake her thirst in the spring. She was still far enough away for Thisbe to escape, but as she fled she dropped her cloak. The lioness came upon it on her way back to her lair and she mouthed it and tore it before disappearing into the woods. That is what Pyramus saw when he appeared a few minutes later. Before him lay the bloodstained shreds of the cloak and clear in the dust were the tracks of the lioness. The conclusion was <u>inevitable</u>. He never doubted that he knew all. Thisbe was dead. He had let his love, a tender maiden, come alone to a place full of danger, and not been there first to protect her. "It is I who killed you," he said. He lifted up from the trampled dust what was left of the cloak and kissing it again and again carried it to the mulberry tree. "Now," he said, "you shall drink my blood too." He drew his sword and plunged it into his side. The blood spurted up over the berries and dyed them a dark red.

Literary Analysis
Archetypal Theme
What does Thisbe's "bold" behavior suggest about the power of love?

Vocabulary Builder
inevitable (in ev´ i tə bəl)
adj. unavoidable; certain

▼ **Critical Viewing ❾**
Explain the similarities and differences between this lioness and the one Thisbe sees? [**Compare and Contrast**]

860 ☐ *Drama*

Vocabulary Development

Vocabulary Builder Reinforcement
Students will benefit from additional examples and practice with the Vocabulary Builder words. Reinforce their comprehension with "show-you-know" sentences. The first part of the sentence uses the vocabulary word in an appropriate context. The second part of the sentence—the "show-you-know" part—clarifies the first. Model the strategy with this example:

When they announced the results, she began to *lament*; her cries and moans could be heard through the door.

Then, give students these sentence prompts, and coach them in creating the clarification part:

1. He wondered if he would *lament* his decision; _____.
Sample answer: he did not want to mourn and live with sorrow for the rest of his life.

2. The team knew their defeat was *inevitable*; _____.
Sample answer: they had not won a game all year and were certain to lose this one.

Thisbe, although terrified of the lioness, was still more afraid to fail her lover. She ventured to go back to the tree of the tryst, the mulberry with the shining white fruit. She could not find it. A tree was there, but not one gleam of white was on the branches. As she stared at it, something moved on the ground beneath. She started back shuddering. But in a moment, peering through the shadows, she saw what was there. It was Pyramus, bathed in blood and dying. She flew to him and threw her arms around him. She kissed his cold lips and begged him to look at her, to speak to her. "It is I, your Thisbe, your dearest," she cried to him. At the sound of her name he opened his heavy eyes for one look. Then death closed them.

She saw his sword fallen from his hand and beside it her cloak stained and torn. She understood all. "Your own hand killed you," she said, "and your love for me. I too can be brave. I too can love. Only death would have had the power to separate us. It shall not have that power now." She plunged into her heart the sword that was still wet with his life's blood.

The gods were pitiful at the end, and the lovers' parents too. The deep red fruit of the mulberry is the everlasting memorial of these true lovers, and one urn holds the ashes of the two whom not even death could part.

Literary Analysis
Archetypal Theme
In deciding to return to the tree, is Thisbe guided more by love or by reason? Explain.

Thinking About the Selection

1. **Respond:** What advice would you give to Pyramus and Thisbe as they whisper through the wall?

2. **(a) Recall:** How do the parents feel about the romance between Pyramus and Thisbe? **(b) Analyze Cause and Effect:** What actions do Pyramus and Thisbe take as a result of their parents' feelings? **(c) Make a Judgment:** Do you think Pyramus and Thisbe or their parents are more responsible for the tragic outcome?

3. **(a) Recall:** What does the chink in the wall enable the couple to do? **(b) Speculate:** How might the story be different if the chink did not exist?

4. **(a) Draw Conclusions:** What does the mulberry tree symbolize in this story? **(b) Analyze:** How does this symbol reinforce the story's theme?

5. **Speculate:** Do you think this story will continue to appeal to readers in the future? Why or why not?

Pyramus and Thisbe ■ *861*

❿ Literary Analysis
Archetypal Theme
- Have students read the final paragraphs of the story.
- **Ask** students the Literary Analysis question: In deciding to return to the tree, is Thisbe guided more by love than by reason? Explain. **Answer:** Thisbe is guided more by love than by reason; she did not want to fail her lover.

Concept Connector

Have students return to their **Anticipation Guides** and respond to the statements again in the After Reading column. They may do this individually or in their original pairs or groups. Then lead a discussion probing for what students have learned that confirms or invalidates each statement.

ASSESS

Answers

1. Students may advise the lovers to find a way to persuade their parents to let them marry.

2. (a) The parents forbid the romance. (b) They whisper through the wall, plan an escape, and run away. (c) Some students will blame the parents; others will blame the lovers.

3. (a) It enables the couple to whisper and express their feelings. (b) **Possible response:** The lovers would have had to find another way to communicate, or their love may have faded.

4. (a) The mulberry symbolizes the true love of Pyramus and Thisbe. (b) The fruit of the mulberry, dyed red by blood, represents the sacrifice the lovers make for each other.

5. **Possible response:** The story will endure as long as people experience frustration and encounter restrictions to their love.

Differentiated Instruction
Solutions for All Learners

Strategy for Less Proficient Readers
To help students grasp the sequence of events leading to the tragedy of Pyramus and Thisbe, have them create a storyboard of the plot. Tell students to review the story and list what happens. Then, have them put the events in order with a simple drawing to illustrate each event.

Enrichment for Advanced Readers
Have students read and report on another story from Ovid's *Metamorphoses.* They might consider the stories of Actaeon, Daphne, Arachne, Phaethon, or Narcissus. Ask students to tell how the story is like, or unlike, the tale of Pyramus and Thisbe.

Background

A Midsummer Night's Dream

Although Shakespeare derived plots from many sources, his own imagination seems to have been the main source for *A Midsummer Night's Dream.* He may, however, have read the story of Pyramus and Thisbe in an English translation of Ovid's *Metamorphoses* that appeared in England in 1565. He may also have discovered it in a work by Chaucer, the *Legend of Good Women.* Nevertheless, his way of using the story is wholly original: By using unprofessional "actors" to play out the tragic story with such exaggeration, he makes the main plot of the play more fully comic.

❶❷ Motivation

Prepare an **Anticipation Guide** (*General Resources,* pp. 8–10) with the following statements:

- Love at first sight is possible.
- People who fall in love quickly are doomed to regret it.
- Being in love is like being under a spell.

Give students a copy of the prepared Anticipation Guide and have students mark their responses in the Me column. Have students discuss the statements in pairs or groups and mark the Guides again in the group column.

Concept Connector ➡

Students will return to the Anticipation Guide after completing the selections.

❶❸ About the Selection

In the excerpt from *A Midsummer Night's Dream,* the playing out of the story of Pyramus and Thisbe provides a parody of the actions of the lovers in the main plot of the play. The Clowns—uneducated workers—rehearse and make special efforts to ensure that they will not scare anyone with the violence of the story. Bottom and Snug plan to tell the audience that they are not really Pyramus and a lion. When Robin turns Bottom into an ass, the audience knows that his metamorphosis is metaphorically true. Titania, who has been enchanted, loves Bottom as an ass, and Bottom delights in his enchantment.

862 *Drama*

from A Midsummer Night's Dream ⓫ ⓬ ⓭

William Shakespeare

Background In *A Midsummer Night's Dream*, Shakespeare creates comedy out of misunderstandings, magic transformations, and the interactions of characters from three different worlds: the noble class, the working class, and the realm of the fairy spirits. In this scene, several local craftsmen (the "Clowns") prepare to put on a play for the duke's wedding. Robin, the fairy king's jester, discovers the actors and decides to play a trick on one of them. All of this happens as Titania, the queen of the fairies, sleeps nearby. The actors do not know that Titania is under a spell that will cause her to fall in love with the first person she sees upon waking.

Act III, Scene i

With TITANIA *still asleep onstage, enter the* CLOWNS, BOTTOM, QUINCE, SNOUT, STARVELING, SNUG, *and* FLUTE.

BOTTOM. Are we all met?

⓮ **QUINCE.** Pat,[1] pat. And here's a marvels convenient place for our rehearsal. This green plot shall be our stage, this hawthorn brake[2] our tiring-house,[3] and we will do it in action as we will
5 do it before the Duke.

BOTTOM. Peter Quince?

QUINCE. What sayest thou, bully[4] Bottom?

BOTTOM. There are things in this comedy of Pyramus and Thisbe that will never please. First, Pyramus must draw a sword to kill
10 himself, which the ladies cannot abide. How answer you that?

SNOUT. By 'r lakin,[5] a parlous fear.

STARVELING. I believe we must leave the killing out, when all is done.[6]

⓰ ◀ **Critical Viewing** How would you describe Titania in the image shown here?

1. **pat** exactly; right on time.

2. **brake** thicket.

3. **tiring house** room used for dressing, or attiring.

4. **bully** jolly fellow.

5. **By 'r lakin** shortened version of "By your ladykin (little lady)."

6. **when all is done** after all.

⓯ **Reading Check**

Who is asleep onstage when the Clowns enter?

from A Midsummer Night's Dream ■ 863

---

❶❼ Literary Analysis
Archetypal Theme

- Have students read the bracketed passage. **Ask** them what Bottom and the other Clowns are afraid of doing when they present their play.
- **Answer:** They are afraid of frightening and offending the audience.
- **Ask** students the Literary Analysis question: How do the Clowns plan to soften their presentation of the lion?
  Possible response: Bottom instructs the actor to identify himself, peek out of the neck of the lion costume, and assure the ladies that he is not a real lion.
- **Ask** students why the concerns of the Clowns are comic.
  Answer: Their concerns are comic because the audience knows that the people who will be watching the play could not possibly think that the lion is real.

❶❽ Literature in Context

Almanacs The best known of American almanacs is the one published by Benjamin Franklin in Philadelphia during the years 1732–1757—*Poor Richard's Almanack.* Franklin followed English models, but he made his almanac more literary by having characters deliver comic comments and useful proverbs.

Connecting to the Literature
Point out that almanacs cannot predict whether or not the moon will be hidden by clouds on any given night. **Ask** students the Connect to the Literature question: Do you think the "Clowns" are wise to rely on the accuracy of the almanac with regard to moonlight? Why or why not?
Answer: The Clowns are foolish to rely on the accuracy of an almanac for moonlight; an almanac cannot predict a cloudless night.

BOTTOM. Not a whit! I have a device to make all well. Write me a
15 prologue, and let the prologue seem to say we will do no harm
with our swords, and that Pyramus is not killed indeed. And, for
the more better assurance, tell them that I, Pyramus, am not
Pyramus, but Bottom the weaver. This will put them out of fear.

QUINCE. Well, we will have such a prologue, and it shall be written
20 in eight and six.[7]

BOTTOM. No, make it two more. Let it be written in eight and
eight.

SNOUT. Will not the ladies be afeard of the lion?

STARVELING. I fear it, I promise you.

25 **BOTTOM.** Masters, you ought to consider with yourself, to bring
in God shield us! a lion among ladies is a most dreadful thing.
For there is not a more fearful wildfowl than your lion living,
and we ought to look to it.

❶❼ **SNOUT.** Therefore another prologue must tell he is not a lion.

30 **BOTTOM.** Nay, you must name his name, and half his face must
be seen through the lion's neck, and he himself must speak
through, saying thus, or to the same defect: "Ladies," or "Fair
ladies, I would wish you," or "I would request you," or "I would
entreat you not to fear, not to tremble! My life for yours. If you
35 think I come hither as a lion, it were pity of my life.[8] No, I am no
such thing. I am a man as other men are." And there indeed let
him name his name and tell them plainly he is Snug the joiner.

7. eight and six ballad meter containing alternating eight- and six-syllable lines.

Literary Analysis
Archetypal Theme
How do the Clowns plan to soften their presentation of the lion?

8. it were . . . my life risky for me.

---

❶❽ Literature in Context

Humanities Connection

Almanacs

When Bottom calls for an almanac, he is referring to a type of book that was very popular in Elizabethan times. The almanac was essentially a calendar, but it also provided lists of upcoming natural events, such as tides, full moons, and eclipses. The book was especially useful to farmers because it included gardening tips and weather predictions. Almanacs of various kinds are still published and consulted today.

Connect to the Literature

Do you think the "Clowns" are wise to rely on the accuracy of the almanac with regard to moonlight? Why or why not?

Vocabulary Development

Word Analysis
Bottom suggests adding a *prologue* to the play—a speech that would be given before, or ahead of, the rest of the play. The prefix *pro-* means "forward or ahead of." Bottom wants to speak *before* the events of the play begin so that the audience will not be frightened by the violent actions that will follow.

Have students identify the meaning of each of the following words with the prefix *pro-*, using a dictionary if necessary.

proceed – move forward
proclaim – announce or put forward
produce – bring out or bring forward
progress – move forward
project – throw forward
promote – move forward
propel – push or drive forward
protrude – thrust forward or stick out

QUINCE. Well, it shall be so. But there is two hard things: that is, to bring the moonlight into a chamber, for you know Pyramus
40 and Thisbe meet by moonlight.

SNOUT. Doth the moon shine that night we play our play?

BOTTOM. A calendar, a calendar! Look in the almanac. Find out moonshine, find out moonshine.

QUINCE *takes out a book.*

QUINCE. Yes, it doth shine that night.

45 **BOTTOM.** Why, then, may you leave a casement of the great chamber window, where we play, open, and the moon may shine in at the casement.

QUINCE. Ay, or else one must come in with a bush of thorns[9] and a lantern and say he comes to disfigure[10] or to present the
50 person of Moonshine. Then there is another thing: we must have a wall in the great chamber, for Pyramus and Thisbe, says the story, did talk through the chink of a wall.

SNOUT. You can never bring in a wall. What say you, Bottom?

BOTTOM. Some man or other must present Wall. And let
55 him have some plaster, or some loam, or some roughcast[11] about him to signify wall, or let him hold his fingers thus, and through that cranny shall Pyramus and Thisbe whisper.

⑲ QUINCE. If that may be, then all is well. Come, sit down, every mother's son, and rehearse your parts. Pyramus, you begin. When you have spoken your speech, enter into that brake, and so everyone according to his cue.

Enter ROBIN invisible to those onstage.

ROBIN. *(aside)*
What hempen homespuns[12] have we swaggring
    here
So near the cradle[13] of the Fairy Queen?
What, a play toward?[14] I'll be an auditor—
65 An actor too perhaps, if I see cause.

QUINCE. Speak, Pyramus.—Thisbe, stand forth.

BOTTOM. *(as Pyramus)*
Thisbe, the flowers of odious savors sweet—

QUINCE. Odors, odors!

BOTTOM. *(as Pyramus)*
                    . . . odors savors sweet.
So hath thy breath, my dearest Thisbe dear—

---

9. **a bush of thorns** according to legend, the man in the moon collected firewood on Sundays and was thus banished to the sky.

10. **disfigure** Quince means *figure*, as in "symbolize" or "stand for."

11. **plaster . . . roughcast** three different blended materials, each used for plastering walls.

12. **hempen homespuns** characters wearing clothing homemade from hemp, probably from the country.

13. **cradle** bower where Titania sleeps.

14. **toward** being rehearsed.

⑳ Reading Check

How do the Clowns plan to present the wall that separates Pyramus and Thisbe?

---

⑲ Critical Thinking
Evaluate

- Have students evaluate the planning and decision-making of the Clowns. First, **ask** students to list the criteria for a good rehearsal. **Possible responses:** A good rehearsal might be described as organized, practical, imaginative, creative, intelligent, and efficient.

- Then, **ask** students to identify the problems and issues that the actors face and how they decide to solve them. **Answer:** They will not scare the audience by including a prologue and having the lion talk. They will show moonshine by opening a window or having a man carry a lantern. They will represent a wall by having a man wear plaster and hold his fingers apart for the chink in the wall.

- Then, have students **apply** the rehearsal criteria to the Clowns' actions and decisions.

- Finally, have students **evaluate** the rehearsal as a whole. **Possible response:** Students might say that the rehearsal seems unorganized and inefficient but that the actors are imaginative and creative in their attempts to solve problems.

⑳ Reading Check

Answer: The Clowns plan to have a man dressed in plaster who will hold his fingers to represent the chink in the wall.

Differentiated Instruction   Solutions for All Learners

Strategy for Less Proficient Readers
List the names of all the Clowns on the board—Quince, Bottom, Snout, Starveling, Snug, and Flute. Have students listen to the rehearsal portion of the scene on the **Listening to Literature Audio CD.** As they listen, point to the name of each speaker so that students can recognize especially the characters and the characteristics of Bottom and Quince.

Strategy for Gifted/Talented Students
Suggest that students give a performance of the rehearsal portion of this scene from *A Midsummer Night's Dream* (the first 95 lines). Assign roles and encourage students to create their own costumes and props. Remind them that the Clowns are funny because they act so seriously. Have them rehearse their performance and present it to the class.

㉑ Critical Thinking
Make Inferences

- Point out that Shakespeare sometimes names his characters according to their personal qualities and that this adds to the comic effect.

- **Ask** students what they can infer about Flute from his name.
Answer: Flute, apparently the youngest of the group, has a very high voice, appropriate for playing Thisbe.

- **Ask** students what they can infer about Snout and Starveling from their names.
Answer: Snout's name suggests that he has a big or distinctive nose, and Starveling's name suggests that he is very thin and gaunt from having little to eat.

㉒ Critical Viewing

Answer: Bottom would probably be angry and insulted.

70   But hark, a voice! Stay thou but here awhile.
And by and by I will to thee appear. *(He exits.)*

ROBIN. *(aside)*
A stranger Pyramus than e'er played here.

(He exits.)

FLUTE. Must I speak now?

QUINCE. Ay, marry, must you, for you must
75   understand he goes but to see a noise that
he heard and is to come again.

㉑ **FLUTE.** *(as Thisbe)*
Most radiant Pyramus, most lily-white of hue,
Of color like the red rose on triumphant[15] brier,
Most brisky juvenal[16] and eke[17] most lovely Jew,[18]
80   As true as truest horse, that yet would never tire.
I'll meet thee, Pyramus, at Ninny's tomb.[19]

QUINCE. "Ninus tomb," man! Why, you must not
speak that yet. That you answer to Pyramus. You
speak all your part[20] at once, cues and all.—
85   Pyramus, enter. Your cue is past. It is "never tire."

FLUTE. O!
(As Thisbe) As true as truest horse, that yet would
never tire.

Enter ROBIN, *and* BOTTOM *as Pyramus with the
ass-head.*[21]

BOTTOM. *(as Pyramus)*
If I were fair, fair Thisbe, I were[22] only thine.

QUINCE. O monstrous! O strange! We are haunted.
90   Pray, masters, fly, masters! Help!

㉓   QUINCE, FLUTE, SNOUT, SNUG, *and* STARVELING *exit.*

ROBIN. I'll follow you. I'll lead you about a round,[23]
Through bog, through bush, through brake, through brier.
Sometime a horse I'll be, sometime a hound,
A hog, a headless bear, sometime a fire.[24]

㉒ ▲ Critical Viewing
How would Bottom feel if he knew how he looked to others? **[Speculate]**

15. triumphant splendid; magnificent.

16. juvenal juvenile; a young person.

17. eke also.

18. Jew shortening of "jewel" to complete the rhyme.

19. Ninny's tomb refers to Ninus, legendary founder of biblical city of Nineveh.

20. part script containing stage cues, which Flute is accused of missing or misreading.

21. with the ass-head wearing an ass-head.

22. were would be.

23. about a round in a roundabout, like a circle dance.

24. fire will-o'-the-wisp.

866 ■ Drama

Vocabulary Development

Malapropisms

Malapropisms are vocabulary mistakes, blunders in which people say words that do not mean what they think they do. Shakespeare uses malapropisms in the Clown scenes in *A Midsummer Night's Dream,* and these mistakes are funny because the word used often has a meaning wildly different from the one intended.

- Have students identify the malapropism in line 67 (*odious* instead of *odors*).
- Have them look up *odious* in a dictionary and state its meaning.
- Then, have them explain why this vocabulary mistake would be funny when it is spoken by a lover to his beloved.

95 And neigh, and bark, and grunt, and roar, and burn,
Like horse, hound, hog, bear, fire, at every turn.

He exits.

BOTTOM. Why do they run away? This is a knavery of them to make me afeard.

Enter SNOUT.

23 **SNOUT.** O Bottom, thou art changed! What do I see on thee?

100 **BOTTOM.** What do you see? You see an ass-head of your own, do you? *(SNOUT exits.)*

Enter QUINCE.

QUINCE. Bless thee, Bottom, bless thee! Thou art translated!²⁵ *(He exits.)*

BOTTOM. I see their knavery. This is to make an ass of me, to fright me, if they could. But I will not stir from this place, do what they can. I will walk up and down here, and I will sing,
105 that they shall hear I am not afraid.
(He sings.) The ouzel cock,²⁶ so black of hue,
With orange-tawny bill,
The throstle²⁷ with his note so true,
110 *The wren with little quill—*²⁸

TITANIA. *(waking up)*
What angel wakes me from my flow'ry bed?

BOTTOM. *(sings)*
The finch, the sparrow, and the lark,
The plainsong cuckoo²⁹ gray,
Whose note full many a man doth mark
115 *And dares not answer "nay"—*³⁰
for, indeed, who would set his wit to so foolish a bird? Who would give a bird the lie³¹ though he cry "cuckoo" never so?³²

TITANIA.
I pray thee, gentle mortal, sing again.
Mine ear is much enamored of thy note,
120 So is mine eye <u>enthralled</u> to thy shape,
And thy fair virtue's force perforce doth move me³³
On the first view to say, to swear, I love thee.

BOTTOM. Methinks, mistress, you should have little reason for that. And yet, to say the truth, reason and love keep little
125 company together nowadays. The more the pity that some

Literary Analysis
Archetypal Theme
How does Bottom's transformation make fun of the character of Pyramus?

25. translated changed; transformed.

26. ouzel cock male blackbird.

27. throstle thrush; a bird.

28. quill literally, a small reed pipe, but here meaning a tiny piping song.

29. plainsong cuckoo bird whose song is likened to church music called plainsong.

30. Whose . . . "nay" whose song married men listen to as a sign that their wives may be unfaithful, and who cannot deny that this may be so.

31. Who would . . . the lie who would use his intelligence to answer a foolish bird, yet who would dare to contradict the cuckoo's taunt?

32. never so over and over; ever so much.

33. thy . . . move me your beauty is so powerful it moves me whether I want it to or not.

Vocabulary Builder
enamored (en amˊ ərd) *v.* filled with love and desire; charmed
enthralled (en *th*rôldˊ) *v.* held as in a spell; captivated

24 **Reading Check**

What physical change happens to Bottom?

from A Midsummer Night's Dream ■ 867

---

23 **Literary Analysis**
Archetypal Theme
- **Ask** students how love determined the fate of Pyramus.
  Answer: Love drove Pyramus to run away with Thisbe and then to kill himself when he thought she was dead.
- **Ask** students in what sense Pyramus was "transformed" by his love.
  Answer: Love robbed Pyramus of his reason and he became completely ruled by passion.
- **Ask** students to answer the Literary Analysis question: How does Bottom's transformation make fun of the character of Pyramus?
  Possible responses: Because Bottom is a foolish fellow playing the role of a romantic hero with great exaggeration, his transformation into an ass mirrors Pyramus' transformation by love into a rash and foolish man. Bottom's transformation is a parody of Pyramus' loss of self-control. Both characters are enchanted, one tragically, one comically.

24 **Reading Check**
Answer: Bottom is transformed into an ass, or donkey.

Differentiated
Instruction Solutions for All Learners

Strategy for Special Needs Students
Help students connect with the concept of metamorphosis by drawing what they think Bottom looked like before and after his transformation. Ask students to name other characters that change into animals—for example, Spider-Man, Catwoman, and Wolverine. Discuss what these characters gain and lose by their metamorphoses.

Strategy for English Learners
Shakespearean English poses challenges for English Learners. Provide definitions of some common Elizabethan words:
- *Thee* and *thou* mean "you."
- *Thy* means "your."
- *Doth* means "does."
- *Art* means "are."
- *Methinks* means "I think."
- *E'er* means "ever."
- *Sayest* means "say." Many verbs add the -est ending.

25 **Critical Viewing**

Answer: Titania and Bottom seem to be madly in love and completely absorbed with each other.

honest neighbors will not make them friends. Nay, I can gleek[34] upon occasion.

TITANIA.
Thou art as wise as thou art beautiful.

BOTTOM. Not so neither; but if I had wit enough to get out of
130 this wood, I have enough to serve mine own turn.

TITANIA.
Out of this wood do not desire to go.
Thou shalt remain here whether thou wilt or no.
I am a spirit of no common rate.[35]
The summer still doth tend[36] upon my state,
135 And I do love thee. Therefore go with me.
I'll give thee fairies to attend on thee,
And they shall fetch thee jewels from the deep
And sing while thou on pressed flowers dost sleep.

868 ■ *Drama*

25 ▲ **Critical Viewing**
How do Titania and Bottom seem to feel about each other in this image? **[Describe]**

34. **gleek** jest; joke.

35. **rate** value; rank.

36. **still doth tend** still serves.

Vocabulary Development

Think-Aloud: Context
Direct students' attention to the word *gambol* in line 144 on p. 869. Using a think-aloud process, model how to use context to infer the meaning of an unknown word. Say the following to students:

I'm going to think aloud to show you how I would figure out the meaning of *gambol* from its context.

Titania tells the Fairies to "gambol" in Bottom's eyes. She has previously told them to be "kind and courteous," so "gambol" must be something positive. In the same line, she tells the Fairies to "hop in his walks," that is, dance around him wherever he goes. So *gambol* probably means "dance and skip around, to frolic."

And I will purge thy mortal grossness[37] so
140 That thou shalt like an airy spirit go.—
Peaseblossom, Cobweb, Mote,[38] and Mustardseed!

Enter four Fairies: PEASEBLOSSOM, COBWEB,
MOTE, *and* MUSTARDSEED.

PEASEBLOSSOM. Ready.

COBWEB.   And I.

MOTE.   And I.

MUSTARDSEED.   And I.

ALL.   Where shall we go?

TITANIA.
Be kind and courteous to this gentleman.
Hop in his walks and gambol in his eyes;
145 Feed him with apricocks and dewberries.[39]
With purple grapes, green figs, and mulberries;
The honey-bags steal from the humble-bees,
And for night-tapers crop their waxen thighs
And light them at the fiery glowworms' eyes
150 To have my love to bed and to arise;
And pluck the wings from painted butterflies
To fan the moonbeams from his sleeping eyes.
Nod to him, elves, and do him courtesies.

PEASEBLOSSOM. Hail, mortal!

155 **COBWEB.** Hail!

MOTE. Hail!

MUSTARDSEED. Hail!

BOTTOM. I cry your Worships mercy,[40] heartily.—
I beseech your Worship's name.

160 **COBWEB.** Cobweb.

BOTTOM. I shall desire you of more acquaintance, good Master
Cobweb. If I cut my finger, I shall make bold with you.[41]—Your
name, honest gentleman?

PEASEBLOSSOM. Peaseblossom.

165 **BOTTOM.** I pray you, commend me to Mistress Squash,[42] your
mother, and to Master Peascod,[43] your father. Good Master
Peaseblossom, I shall desire you of more acquaintance, too.—Your
name, I beseech you, sir?

MUSTARDSEED. Mustardseed.

from A Midsummer Night's Dream ■ *869*

---

37. mortal grossness the physical, mortal state of human beings.

38. Mote a speck, but also moth, as this word was pronounced similarly.

39. apricocks and dewberries apricots and blackberries.

Literary Analysis
Archetypal Theme
How do Titania's commands emphasize the absurdity of her feelings toward Bottom?

40. cry . . . mercy beg your pardon.

41. Master . . . you Cobwebs were used to stop bleeding.

42. squash an unripe pea pod.

43. peascod a ripe pea pod.

✓ **Reading Check**
How does Titania want the fairies to treat Bottom?

---

26 Literary Analysis
Archetypal Theme
- **Ask** students to summarize what Titania wants the fairies to do for Bottom.
  Answer: She wants them to dance around him, feed him fruits and honey, light his way to bed, and fan him when he is sleeping.
- **Ask** students to answer the Literary Analysis question: How do Titania's commands emphasize the absurdity of her feelings toward Bottom?
  Answer: Titania's commands are appropriate to give honor to a king, not a donkey. A donkey would not appreciate such courtesies or sleep in a bed.
- **Ask** students why Titania's love is ill-fated.
  Answer: She is made to love a donkey.
- Point out that the archetypal theme of ill-fated love can be treated tragically, as it is in the tale of Pyramus and Thisbe, or comically, as it is in *A Midsummer Night's Dream.*

27 Reading Check
Answer: Titania wants the fairies to treat Bottom with kindness and courtesy.

Differentiated Instruction   Solutions for All Learners

Strategy for English Learners
Shakespearean sentence structure can be problematic. Point out that Shakespeare and other poets of his time sometimes put the verb at the *end* of the sentence. This "inversion" was used to create rhymes and control the rhythm. For example, "Thou shalt like an airy spirit go" means "You shall go like an airy spirit."

Have students find other sentences in the scene that place the verb at the end. Have them reorder the words to sound like modern English sentences, such as the following:
- "Out of this wood do not desire to go."
- "By and by I will to thee appear."

869

Have students return to their **Anticipation Guides** and respond to the statements again in the After Reading column. They may do this individually or in their original pairs or groups. Then lead a discussion probing for what students have learned that confirms or invalidates each statement.

ASSESS

Answers

1. **Possible response:** Students might find the Clowns' rehearsal the funniest aspect

2. (a) The Clowns are preparing a play about Pyramus and Thisbe. (b) Bottom is magically transformed into an ass; the rehearsal ends with the actors fleeing in panic.

3. (a) Robin, a fairy, changes Bottom as a joke. (b) Bottom is unaware of the change; he cannot understand his friends' reactions. (c) Bottom's personality is unchanged; he retains his usual self-confidence.

4. (a) Titania is the fairy queen. (b) The match between a queen and a donkey-head mocks the idea that love unites opposites.

5. Bottom's transformation emphasizes the truth that he is an affable buffoon (or ass) who has an exaggerated idea of himself.

6. (a) The Clowns plan to explain that Pyramus is only an actor who will not actually die; they will change the lion costume to show the actor within. (b) Students may agree that the audience will find the Clowns' intended tragedy to be hilarious.

170 **BOTTOM.** Good Master Mustardseed, I know your patience[44] well. That same cowardly, giantlike ox-beef hath devoured many a gentleman of your house. I promise you, your kindred hath made my eyes water ere now. I desire you of more acquaintance, good Master Mustardseed.

175 **TITANIA.** Come, wait upon him. Lead him to my bower.
The moon, methinks, looks with a watery eye,
And when she weeps, weeps every little flower,
Lamenting some enforcèd chastity.[45]
Tie up my lover's tongue. Bring him silently.

They exit.

44. your patience your story; your experience.

45. enforcèd chastity violation; requirement.

Thinking About the Selection

1. **Respond:** Which aspect of this excerpt did you find funniest? Explain.

2. **(a) Recall:** What are the Clowns trying to accomplish in this scene? **(b) Analyze Cause and Effect:** What events prevent their success? Explain.

3. **(a) Recall:** How is Bottom transformed? **(b) Infer:** Is Bottom aware of his transformation? Explain. **(c) Analyze:** Does the transformation alter Bottom's personality as well as his appearance? Why or why not?

4. **(a) Recall:** Who is Titania? **(b) Analyze:** In what ways does the match between Titania and Bottom mock typical portrayals of romantic love?

5. **Analyze:** Does Bottom's transformation actually reveal a truth about his character? Explain.

6. **(a) Summarize:** What alterations to script and costumes do the Clowns plan in order to minimize the frightening aspects of their play? **(b) Speculate:** Do you think the Clowns' eventual audience will enjoy their production of "Pyramus and Thisbe"? Why or why not?

Vocabulary Development

Vocabulary Knowledge Rating
When students have completed reading and discussing "Pyramus and Thisbe" and the excerpt from *A Midsummer Night's Dream,* have them take out their **Vocabulary Knowledge Rating Chart.** Read the words aloud once more and have students rate their knowledge of the words again in the After Reading column. Clarify any words that are still problematic. Have students write their own definition and example or sentence in the appropriate column. Then, have students complete the **Vocabulary Builder Practice** activities on p. 871. Encourage students to use the words in further discussion and written work about the selections. Remind them that they will be accountable for these words on the Selection Test.

Apply the Skills

Romeo and Juliet • **Pyramus and Thisbe** •

from *A Midsummer Night's Dream*

Comparing Archetypal Themes

1. Use a chart like the one shown to identify the characters, obstacles, and main events in Shakespeare's *Romeo and Juliet* and Ovid's "Pyramus and Thisbe."

Selection	Characters	Obstacles	Main Events
Romeo and Juliet			
Pyramus and Thisbe			

2. **(a)** Using your chart, explain similarities in the way both *Romeo and Juliet* and "Pyramus and Thisbe" present the **archetypal theme of ill-fated love. (b)** What are the differences in the way the two selections present this theme?

3. **(a)** Why is Titania and Bottom's love ill-fated? **(b)** How do these reasons compare to the obstacles faced by Romeo and Juliet or Pyramus and Thisbe?

Writing to Compare Literary Works

In an essay, compare and contrast the way Shakespeare uses the characters and events from "Pyramus and Thisbe" in *Romeo and Juliet* with the way he uses them in *A Midsummer Night's Dream*. Discuss why you think Shakespeare would explore the same story in both a tragedy and a comedy. Use the following questions to help you write your essay.

- How do the different settings and characters in each of Shakespeare's plays affect the two presentations of the archetypal theme?
- How do you think Shakespeare wanted audiences to feel while watching the ill-fated love in *Romeo and Juliet*?
- How do you think he wanted audiences to feel while watching Titania and Bottom's ill-fated love?

Vocabulary Builder

Practice For each item, write a sentence correctly using the word pairs.

1. enamored; wonderful
2. inevitable; surprise
3. enthralled; view
4. lament; tragedy

Apply the Skills ■ 871

QuickReview

Theme: the central idea of a literary work

Archetype: a plot, character, setting, symbol, or image that recurs in the literature of many different cultures

Archetypal theme: the central message of a literary work that is based on an archetypal idea

Assessment
For: Self-test
Visit: www.PHSchool.com
Web Code: epa-6507

Comparing Archetypal Themes

1. **Sample responses:** *Romeo and Juliet*—**Characters:** Romeo, Juliet, Mercutio, Tybalt, Friar Lawrence; **Obstacles:** feud, ages of the lovers, arranged marriage; **Events:** lovers meeting, secret wedding, banishment, error by Romeo, deaths of lovers.

   "Pyramus and Thisbe"—**Characters:** Pyramus, Thisbe, lion; **Obstacles:** parents' restrictions, ages of the lovers, lion; **Events:** running away, lion, error by Pyramus, deaths of the lovers. Another sample can be found on **Graphic Organizer Transparency B,** p. 186 in *Graphic Organizer Transparencies.*

2. **(a)** In both plays, lovers are destroyed through chance and fatal misunderstanding. **(b)** *Romeo and Juliet* presents the theme with greater length, complexity, and realism. The characters are more emotionally involving. Pyramus and Thisbe meet their fate alone; the fate of Romeo and Juliet involves many people.

3. **(a)** Titania and Bottom belong to different worlds. **(b)** Titania and Bottom are entangled by magic. The humans face real-world obstacles.

Writing to Compare Literary Works

- Have students refer to their completed chart of similarities and differences.
- Have students use the bulleted questions to develop their ideas.

Six Traits Focus

✔	Ideas		Word Choice
✔	Organization		Sentence Fluency
	Voice		Conventions

Vocabulary Builder
Sample responses:

1. They were *enamored* of the *wonderful* music around them.
2. Disaster seemed *inevitable,* but the outcome was a joyful *surprise.*
3. The painter was *enthralled* by the *view* of the mountains.
4. As the *tragedy* became clear, the village began to *lament.*

Assessment Resources

The following resources can be used to assess students' knowledge and skills.

Unit 5 Resources
Selection Test A, pp. 109–111
Selection Test B, pp. 112–114

Go Online
Assessment Students may use the **Self-test** to prepare for **Selection Test A** or **Selection Test B.**

871

Applying Reading Skills

Read the passage with students. Guide students to paraphrase the next to the last sentence in the passage. Point out that although the sentence is lengthy, they should paraphrase it by section.

If necessary, have students reread the instruction on p. 722 before having them complete the remaining items on their own.

Applying Vocabulary Skills

Remind students that Latin word roots give readers clues to help them determine the meanings of unfamiliar words. Have students review the word roots -labor- and -lum- from Part 1. Ask students to define each Latin word root and name some vocabulary words that contain these roots.

If they have difficulty, review the instruction on p. 723. Then, have them complete the vocabulary items in this section.

Tips for
Test Taking

Students may have difficulty summarizing material on a standardized test. Explain that a good strategy for summarizing is to underline the main ideas in the passage. Remind students that when they look for the best answer choice for a summary, the summary should provide the same emphasis on ideas that the original text provided.

Reading: Summarize

Directions: *Questions 1–4 are based on the following selection.*

Many of Shakespeare's plays were performed in the Globe theater. It was a wooden structure with a thatched roof over the stage. The audience surrounded the stage on three sides. Those who wished to sit down in a covered gallery could do so for a price.

Because the audience surrounded the stage on three sides, Shakespeare often wrote a word for an actor to repeat three times. For example, in one play, a character says, "Tomorrow, and tomorrow, and tomorrow. . . ." This repetition allowed an actor to address all sides of the audience.

In 1613, a spark from a cannon fired during a performance of *Henry VIII* set fire to the thatched roof, and the Globe burned down. It was rebuilt, this time with a tile roof, and it stood until 1644, when it was destroyed again, this time by the Puritans.

1. **What is the best paraphrase of the sentence that begins, "It was rebuilt . . ."?**
   A The theater was rebuilt with a tile roof and lasted until the Puritans tore it down in 1644.
   B The theater that was torn down by the Puritans had a tile roof and it lasted until 1644.
   C In 1644, the Puritans tore down the theater that had been rebuilt with a tile roof.
   D The tile roof on the rebuilt theater lasted until 1644, when the Puritans tore the theater down.

2. **What is the most important idea in the second paragraph?**
   A The lines that were repeated were repeated three times.
   B In one play, a character says, "Tomorrow, and tomorrow, and tomorrow. . . ."
   C The audience surrounded the stage on three sides.
   D Shakespeare wrote some lines to be repeated so that an actor could turn to each section of the audience.

3. **Which pair of details is necessary to summarize the cause of the fire that destroyed the first Globe?**
   A *Henry VIII*; 1613
   B theater destroyed; tile roof
   C spark; thatched roof
   D no one hurt; theater rebuilt

4. **What is the most important effect of the cannon's being shot during *Henry VIII*?**
   A The new theater was built with a tile roof.
   B The original Globe was destroyed.
   C No one was badly hurt.
   D The rebuilt theater stood until 1644.

872 ■ *Drama*

ASSESS

Answers

1. A	8. B
2. C	9. C
3. C	10. A
4. B	11. A
5. C	12. A
6. B	13. C
7. B	14. B

Assessment Practice

Vocabulary

Directions: *Choose the letter of the word that is the best definition of the italicized word in the context of the sentence.*

5. **Even though the play is set in ancient times, it is *relevant* to today's readers.**
   A conforming
   B proper
   C pertinent
   D harmonious

6. **Ramon was hoping that a discussion would *illuminate* his understanding of the play.**
   A irradiate
   B clarify
   C interpret
   D lighten

7. **The writer needs to *condense* this story; we don't have that much space in the magazine.**
   A summarize
   B shorten
   C constrict
   D consolidate

8. **You must *elaborate* on the details of the incident to make it more interesting.**
   A garnish
   B expand
   C embellish
   D complicate

9. **Harry felt that the character's motives were *ambiguous* and not clearly developed.**
   A faint
   B inconspicuous
   C vague
   D intricate

Directions: *Choose the word or phrase that means the same as the italicized word.*

10. **a *laborious* task**
    A hard; difficult
    B made or done with ease
    C mentally challenging
    D painful

11. **an *elaborate* plan**
    A complicated and detailed
    B foolproof
    C risky and dangerous
    D difficult to perform

12. **the *illumination* of the room**
    A filling with light
    B understanding
    C entrance or doorway
    D explanation

13. **an *elaborately* decorated room**
    A done without effort
    B professionally designed
    C worked out in great detail
    D carefully put together

14. **how he *elaborates***
    A complicates with details
    B adds details
    C subtracts details
    D changes details

Reading and Vocabulary Skills Review ■ 873

If students answer any of these questions incorrectly, have them review the instruction on the following pages in Part 1 before taking the **Benchmark Test.**

Question	Pages Where Instruction Is Located:
1	782
2	728
3	832
4	832
5	723
6	850
7	723
8	723
9	723
10	812
11	812
12	850
13	812
14	812

Benchmark

Administer the **Benchmark Test** for Unit 5, Part 1. If the Benchmark Test reveals that some students need further work, use the Interpretation Guide to determine the appropriate reteaching page in the **Reading Kit.** You will also find the same instruction and practice available on **Success Tracker.**

Go **Online**
Vocabulary
For: Interactive Crossword Puzzles
Visit: www.PHSchool.com
Web Code: epj-5502
Give students this Web Code to access interactive crosswords puzzles using Academic Vocabulary and Vocabulary Skill words from Part 1.

Meeting Your Standards

Students will

1. write a how-to essay.

2. use writing strategies to generate ideas and to plan, organize, evaluate, and revise the essay.

3. apply grammar skills.

Writing Genres
Using the Form

Point out to students that elements of a how-to essay are often incorporated into other types of writing. Point out these examples:

- Scientific papers often explain how an experiment was done.

- Speeches and presentations in classes such as science and social studies often include an explanation of how a problem was solved.

Writing Workshop
Work in Progress

If students have done the Work-in-Progress assignments throughout Part 1, suggest that they examine their recorded ideas as they begin prewriting.

OES Online Essay Scorer

A writing prompt for this mode of writing can be found on the *PH Online Essay Scorer* at PHSuccessNet.com.

Prewriting

- Tell students to **choose a topic** with information in it that others may need.

- When **gathering details**, have students omit any details that are irrelevant and do not help clarify the explanation.

Six Traits Focus

✔	Ideas		Word Choice
✔	Organization		Sentence Fluency
	Voice		Conventions

874

Exposition: How-to Essay

A **how-to essay** provides step-by-step instructions that tell readers how to accomplish a specific task. The best how-to essays are enriched by a writer's practical experience, so that readers can avoid mistakes and follow the best path to a desired outcome. Use the steps outlined in this workshop to write a how-to essay.

Assignment Write a how-to essay about an activity or a process that you know well.

What to Include Your how-to essay should feature the following elements:
- specific factual information presented logically and accurately
- step-by-step directions for each stage in the process
- examples and definitions that demonstrate key concepts
- instructions that anticipate readers' questions
- error-free grammar, including your use of modifying phrases

To preview the criteria on which your how-to essay may be assessed, see the rubric on page 878.

Prewriting

Choosing Your Topic

Make a calendar. For each day of the week, write down your activities. Then, identify an activity from your calendar to describe in a how-to essay. Or, describe another activity with which you are familiar.

Gathering Details

List the materials. Write down all the materials, tools, and information your readers will need to accomplish the activity you plan to describe. First, make a list of items needed. Then, note all the steps involved—in the order in which they occur. Take time to identify basic rules of behavior—for example, about safety, care of equipment, or working with others.

Materials for Making Pizza Dough

1. Oven set at 450°
2. Pizza stone
3. 3/4 cup warm water
4. 2 cups flour
5. 1 teaspoon yeast

874 ■ *Drama*

Using the Form

You may use how-to elements in these types of writing:
- repair instructions
- travel directions
- recipes
- training manuals
- problem solving

Work in Progress

Review the work you did on pages 719, 813, and 851.

Teaching Resources

The following resources can be used to enrich or extend the instruction for the Writing Workshop.

Unit 5 Resources
Writing Workshop: Exposition: How-to Essay, p. 115
Writing Workshop: Integrating Grammar Skills: Revising to Combine Sentences with Phrases, p. 116

General Resources
Rubrics for Exposition: How-to Essay, pp. 59–60

Drafting

Shaping Your Writing

Organize information. After gathering all the information you want to include in your draft, select an organization that will make sense to your readers. Chronological, or step-by-step, order is usually best suited to this kind of writing. Use the chart shown to help you organize your information effectively.

Providing Elaboration

Use graphic devices and formatting. Locate or create graphics to reinforce your instructions, and place them at appropriate points in your essay. If you have access to a computer, use graphics features to create helpful diagrams and drawings. Use the automatic numbering or bulleting feature to indicate each step in the process you are describing.

Organizing Information

1. State the purpose of your how-to essay.
2. List the materials and conditions necessary to complete the activity.
3. Provide examples to demonstrate the activity.
4. List steps to complete in consecutive order.
5. Suggest solutions to common problems when performing the activity.

Revising

Revising Your Paragraphs

Revise for clarity. Look over your draft to identify instructions, steps, or information that may be unclear to your reader. Mark these sections, and then go back to them, rewriting or adding language that better explains your points. If the order in which you have explained steps is confusing, rearrange paragraphs to create a better flow of information.

Student Model: Revising for Clarity

Once you feel confident enough, begin to "run" --read
aloud--your lines . . . with another person. . . . This
prepares you for being onstage with other actors.

The writer defined a term that may be unfamiliar to readers and added information to explain the value of a strategy.

Revising Your Word Choice

Revise for transitions. Look for sections in your draft that need transitional language to connect the steps in your activity. In this example, the words *first* and *then* make the instruction easier to understand.

▶ **Example:** Wash the bowl and add the eggs.
    First, wash the bowl, and *then* add the eggs.

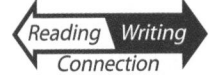
Reading Writing Connection

To read the complete student model, see page 877.

Writing Workshop ■ 875

Drafting

- Explain to students that a well-organized essay will more clearly communicate information to readers.
- Caution students against overusing visual aids; too many pictures will create clutter. Have students read through their drafts to determine the places that would benefit from visual explanations.

Six Traits Focus

Ideas	Word Choice
✔ Organization	Sentence Fluency
Voice	Conventions

WG Writing and Grammar, Gold Level
Students will find additional instruction on drafting a how-to essay in Chapter 30, Section 3.

Revising

- Tell students that when they revise for clarity, they should keep in mind their audience's knowledge of the topic. Tell students to explain or extract terminology or concepts with which the audience will be unfamiliar.
- Have students exchange drafts with a partner. After reading his or her partner's draft, have each student explain the process the essay describes. Tell students to note ways in which their partner's explanation differs from his or her intentions. Use these differences to clarify the explanation and revise the essay.
- Offer students language that can be used to make transitions and connect their steps such as, *after, as soon as, immediately, finally, second, third, next,* and *last.*

Six Traits Focus

Ideas	✔ Word Choice
✔ Organization	Sentence Fluency
✔ Voice	Conventions

WG Writing and Grammar, Gold Level
Students will find additional instruction on revising a how-to essay in Chapter 3, Section 3.

Tips for Using Rubrics

- Before students begin work on this assignment, have them preview the Rubric for Self-Assessment (p. 878) to know what is expected.
- Review the Assessment criteria in class. Before students use the Rubric for Self-Assessment, work with them to rate the Student Model by applying one or two criteria to it.

- If you wish to assess students' how-to essays with either a 4-point or a 6-point scoring rubric, see *General Resources,* pp. 59–60.

Integrating Grammar Skills

- Tell students that some shorter sentences give writing a variety, but an excessive amount of them makes writing stilted and unnatural.

- Have students combine these sentences by creating appositive phrases.

  1. *Reorganizing a closet forces its owner to make tough decisions. It is one of the most dreaded household chores.* **Answer:** Reorganizing a closet, one of the most dreaded household chores, forces its owner to make tough decisions.

  2. *Gerard enjoys eating fruit and granola. He is a strict vegetarian.* **Answer:** Gerard, a strict vegetarian, enjoys eating fruit and granola.

- Divide students into pairs. Give students the following sets of sentences. Have them work together to combine each set by converting one sentence into a verbal phrase. Have students identify the type of verbal phase they create.

  1. *Mya walked across the balance beam. She held her arms out to her side.* **Possible response:** *Holding her arms out to her side, Mya walked across the balance beam.* (participial)

  2. *It is fulfilling for me to volunteer at the women's shelter. It is also beneficial for the women.* **Possible response:** *Volunteering at the women's shelter is fulfilling for me and beneficial for the women.* (gerund)

  3. *Jose has a homework assignment. He must write two entries in his journal.* **Possible response:** *Jose's homework assignment is to write two entries in his journal.* (infinitive)

- Ask students which of the following two sentences has a misplaced modifier, and have students correct this sentence.

  1. *Drinking the bottle, Colette smiled at the baby.*

  2. *Closing his ears, Mikah scolded the screeching bird.* **Answer:** Sentence 1 has a misplaced modifier and should be rewritten as follows: *Colette smiled at the baby drinking the bottle.*

Integrating Grammar Skills

Revising to Combine Sentences With Phrases

To avoid a series of too many simple sentences, combine some sentences by converting the idea in one sentence into a modifying phrase in another sentence.

Identifying Modifying Phrases An **appositive phrase** is a group of words that clarifies the meaning of a noun or pronoun. The following sentences can be combined using an appositive phrase.

Prentice Hall Writing and Grammar Connection: Chapter 22, Section 4

Original: Sophia is a talented actress. She has appeared in over twenty productions.

Combined: Sophia, *a talented actress,* has appeared in over twenty productions. (appositive phrase)

Verbal phrases, which use verbs as nouns, adjectives, or adverbs, can also be used to combine sentences. Verbal phrases may be classified as participial, gerund, and infinitive, depending on their function.

When adding a modifying phrase to a sentence, place the phrase close to the word it modifies. A misplaced modifier can confuse readers.

Participial	*Finding himself alone onstage,* Aaron paced nervously.	Adjective modifies *Aaron*
Gerund	*Meeting with new people* is difficult for some people.	Noun acts as subject of sentence
Infinitive	The director's advice was *to focus first on learning the lines.*	Noun acts as complement of verb *was*

Misplaced: *Hanging from a silken thread,* Jeremy noticed a spider. (Participial phrase seems to modify *Jeremy*.)

Correct: Jeremy noticed a spider *hanging from a silken thread.*

Combining With Phrases Follow these steps to revise a series of short sentences by using phrases to combine them.

1. **Express the information from one sentence as an appositive or a verbal phrase.**

2. **Insert the phrase in a new sentence, locating it near the word or words being modified.**

3. **Make sure that the revised sentence is punctuated correctly.**

Apply It to Your Editing

Review the last four paragraphs of your draft, looking for short sentences that might be combined using appositive, participial, gerund, or infinitive phrases. Consider combining these sentences.

876 ■ *Drama*

Tips for
Using Technology in Writing

If students are using word processing software, suggest that they use the *cut, copy,* and *paste* features to combine sentences. After they have combined choppy sentences, advise students to check each new sentence they have created to make sure it reads properly and has appropriate punctuation, including additional commas as needed, and a period.

Student Model: Carmen Rose Viviano-Crafts
Syracuse, NY

Preparing for a Dramatic Role

One of the first challenges of a new dramatic role is the task of memorizing lines. Use the following guidelines to memorize lines more efficiently:

1. Read the entire play at least twice to familiarize yourself with the setting and situations. When performing, it is essential to know what is going on around you in order to provide the appropriate reactions.

2. Highlight or underline all your lines to identify when your character speaks.

3. Begin to concentrate solely on your parts. Look at the script scene by scene, memorizing one or two scenes a day, depending on how much time you have. Reading the lines out loud speeds up the process by making the lines more memorable.

4. Once you feel confident enough, begin to "run"—read aloud—your lines. Read them aloud, with another person reading the other characters' lines. This prepares you for being onstage with other actors.

5. When you begin rehearsing with fellow cast members, you will be able to try out different ways of saying things, and you'll start to develop your character. Here are the steps to use when developing a character:

   • If your role is based on a real person, research that person or observe someone in a similar situation. Try to find out as much information as you can so that you can play the part realistically.
   • If you are playing a fictional character, study the script closely. The character's words can tell you about his or her feelings, likes, and dislikes.
   • Once you have learned some aspects of your character, begin to delve into the mind and soul of the person. Make up an entire life story for your character. The more you know about the person, the easier it is to put yourself in his or her place. Think of a past experience to relate to something your character is going through. Bring the emotions you felt in that situation to your character's situation.
   • Finally, conduct general conversations with other cast members, with each of you speaking from your own character's point of view. Ask things like "How do you feel about me?" and "How do you think I feel about you?" This lets you know how you are perceived by the other actors/characters in the play and allows you to react more realistically.

6. After each rehearsal, consider what worked well and what felt wrong to you. Use your after-rehearsal notes as feedback to improve your next performance.

> The numbering system allows Carmen to present information logically.

> By offering time suggestions, the essay anticipates readers' questions and concerns.

> Advice about conducting research elaborates on the writer's earlier suggestions.

> These ideas explain the value of each strategy.

Writing Workshop ■ 877

Student Model

• Explain that the Student Model is a sample and that their own essays may be longer.

• **Ask** students why Carmen's numbering system is effective. **Answer:** It separates the steps, making it easier for the reader to follow the process. It also helps the reader to focus on the steps one at time, rather than all together.

• Give students the example of a student who is writing an essay about how to stay healthy. Write the following sentences on the chalkboard:

You should avoid certain foods. You should take vitamins every day.

Ask students what questions or concerns about these sentences the writer should address in his or her essay.
Possible response: *What kinds of foods should I avoid? What kind of vitamins should I take?*

• Draw students' attention to the way in which Carmen offers suggestions to help the reader better perform the process, as well as explanations to reinforce the importance of the information she has chosen to include in her essay.

Writing Genres
How-to Explanations in the Workplace and at Home
Explain to students that there are many instances in their lives in which they will have to explain the steps in a process. At work, for example, they might be required to provide information to coworkers about how to use a particular computer program. At home, they might have to explain to a parent how to use a VCR to record a favorite program.

Differentiated Instruction   Solutions for All Learners

Strategy for Less Proficient Readers
Organize students into small groups. Have students attach a blank piece of paper to their essays and share their papers among the group. Every student should have a chance to silently read each essay. Tell students to notice any places in the essays that are confusing. Have students write their feedback to other students' essays on the blank piece of paper. Students can then use the comments to revise their essays.

Strategy for Advanced Readers
Ask students to write the how-to essay without the numbers. They should rely on transition words to communicate the sequence of the steps. Challenge them to organize the steps into logical paragraphs. Have students work in pairs to see if the essay is clear and complete.

Editing and Proofreading

- Tell students that bullets or numbering will enhance a how-to essay if used properly, but if used improperly, these elements will prevent a clear portrayal of the process.
- Stress to students the importance of consistency in their lists. Tell students that if readers see inconsistencies they are liable to focus on these rather than on the information presented. Tell students that it is important not to have such distractions in their writing.

Six Traits Focus

Ideas		Word Choice
Organization	✔	Sentence Fluency
Voice	✔	Conventions

ASSESS

Publishing and Presenting

- For any processes that can be demonstrated in class, have students give the oral presentation while a partner demonstrates the steps.
- As students create a collection of how-to essays encourage them to organize them logically, perhaps by dividing the essays into categories.

Reflecting on Your Writing

- Ask students if it was difficult for them to analyze and explain a familiar process. Did they have trouble breaking down the process into steps?
- Ask if how-to writing seems more natural to them than other forms of writing. Ask if they would be comfortable writing such an essay in a test situation.

Writing Workshop

Editing and Proofreading

Check your draft for errors in spelling, grammar, and punctuation.

Focus on Lists: If you include bullets or numbered lists in your essay, be sure that you use these elements consistently in your final draft. Check that numbers are consecutive and that bullets are the same size and shape. In addition, check that spacing is consistent and appropriate.

Publishing and Presenting

Consider one of the following ways to share your writing:
Deliver an oral presentation. Share your essay with classmates and give an instructional presentation. If the process you describe can be done in a classroom, have a classmate demonstrate the steps as you describe them. Ask for feedback about the clarity of your presentation.
Prepare a how-to manual. With a group of classmates, collect several how-to essays into a booklet. Add step-by-step photographs or illustrations to your instructions. Make the collection available to the class.

Reflecting on Your Writing

Writer's Journal Jot down your thoughts about writing a how-to essay. Begin by answering these questions.
- What new insights have you acquired about the process that you have explained?
- In what ways is a how-to essay similar to and different from other types of writing?

Rubric for Self-Assessment

To evaluate your how-to essay, use the following rubric:

Criteria	Rating Scale				
	not very				very
Focus: How specific is your focus?	1	2	3	4	5
Organization: How logical is your organization of the process into steps?	1	2	3	4	5
Support/Elaboration: How effective are your examples in demonstrating key concepts?	1	2	3	4	5
Style: How well do your instructions anticipate readers' questions?	1	2	3	4	5
Conventions: How correct is your grammar, especially your use of modifying phrases?	1	2	3	4	5

878 ■ *Drama*

Tips for
Test Taking

When students are taking a test that requires them to explain the steps in a process, they should pay careful attention to the use of transitional words and phrases. Remind students that these words and phrases tell readers where they are in the process and explain how one step relates to the next.

Draw Conclusions

Skills Overview

Reading Skill: Summarizing
- Drawing conclusions from dialogue and stage directions

Vocabulary Development
- Word Roots

Literary Analysis
- Comedy: dramatic irony

Writing
- Research Report
- Work in Progress, p. 891

Skills You Will Learn

Literary Analysis: *Comedy and Dramatic Irony*
Reading Skill: *Drawing Conclusions From Dialogue and Stage Directions*

Reading Skill: *Evaluating the Author's Credibility*

Literary Analysis: *Satire*

Literature You Will Read

Monitoring Progress

Diagnose: Before you begin Part 2, administer the **Diagnostic Test** for Unit 5, Part 2. This test will identify students' level of readiness for the reading and vocabulary skills in Part 2. Use the **Interpretation Guide** for the Diagnostic Test to determine which students need help with prerequisite skills before beginning Part 2.

Preteach and Prepare: Use the information indicated in the **Interpretation Guide** to help students build prerequisite skills. In addition, prepare students by using the **Vocabulary Warm-up** activities and the **Reading Warm-up** activities as necessary for each selection set.

Teach: Use the instructional plan and resources provided to teach the skills and selections.

Assess: After students have completed Part 2, administer the **Benchmark Test** for Unit 5, Part 2. The test results will indicate which skills students have mastered and those on which they need more work.

Reteach: Use the Interpretation Guide to determine the appropriate reteaching pages from the **Reading Kit**.

Intervention: The prerequisite and reteaching pages are also available in the **Success Tracker**.

Draw Conclusions 879

Differentiated Instruction — Solutions for All Learners

Resources for Monitoring Progress

Unit 5 Resources
    Unit 5, Part 2 Diagnostic Test,
    pp. 124–126
    Unit 5, Part 2 Benchmark Test,
    pp. 163–168

Reading Kit

Success Tracker

Introduce the Reading Skill

- Introduce the reading skill: drawing conclusions. Draw students' attention to the definition. Tell students that readers can draw their own conclusions from the clues and details provided by the author in the text. Explain that in nonfiction, writers tend to state ideas more directly; however, in drama and fiction, writers tend to be much more subtle in expressing ideas. It is important that students learn how to draw conclusions from the clues and details provided in a text. Remind students that they must be able to support their conclusions with reasonable interpretations of the details in the literary work.

- Emphasize that conclusions are based on textual details. Two strategies that can guide students in drawing conclusions when reading dramatic literature are using dialogue and stage directions.

Model the Reading Strategies

- Model how to pull details together to draw conclusions about a text. Direct students' attention to the graphic organizer on this page. Have them look at the outer circles. Then lead them through each series of circles to the inner circle labeled "draw conclusions."

- **Ask** students: How does what the characters say and to whom they say it lead readers or an audience to draw conclusions about the play?
  Possible answer: What the characters say to each other gives the reader an idea of what is going on, what the conflicts are, and what types of people the characters are.

- Reinforce that using the clues provided by the author helps readers to draw conclusions.

Reading: Draw Conclusions

> A **conclusion** is a decision or an opinion reached by logically combining details.

Skills and Strategies You Will Learn in Part 2
In Part 2, you will learn
- to **draw conclusions** based on **dialogue** and **stage directions.** (p. 882)
- to **evaluate an author's credibility** before you **draw conclusions.** (p. 892)

Using the Skills and Strategies in Part 2
In Part 2, you will learn to pull details together to **draw conclusions.** You will practice identifying these details in dialogue and stage directions and learn strategies for using them to draw conclusions. In addition, you will learn how to **evaluate an author's credibility.**

880 ■ Drama

Academic Vocabulary: Words for Connecting Themes in Literature

The following words will help you write and talk about themes in the literature of this unit.

Word	Definition	Example Sentence
revise *v.*	read carefully to correct; change or amend	The new events led us to *revise* our interpretation of the theme.
convince *v.*	overcome doubts; persuade	The disastrous outcome *convinced* the character he had made poor choices.
implement *v.*	put into action; fulfill or accomplish	Writers *implement* a variety of techniques to develop characters.
strategy *n.*	science of managing or planning; plan	Fortunately, the villain's *strategy* failed.
compile *v.*	put together; compose by gathering materials	I will *compile* a list of characters in the play.

Vocabulary Skill: Word Roots

▶ A **word root** is the basic unit of meaning in a word.

In Part 2, you will learn
- Latin word root *-vis-* or *-vid-* (p. 890)
- Latin word root *-vinc-* or *-vict-* (p. 890)

As word roots pass through different languages over time, they sometimes develop more than one form. For example, words that have meanings related to *seeing* may contain either the word root *-vis-*, as in *visible,* or *-vid-*, as in *video.*

Activity Look up each example word on the chart. For each word, tell what meanings the word root or related roots had and how the word root contributes to the current meaning of the word.

Related Roots	-vis-, -vid-	-vinc-, -vict-
Meaning	see	conquer
Example Words	revise, vision, video	convince, victory, evict

Reading and Vocabulary Skills Preview ■ 881

Go Online For: Interactive
Vocabulary Crossword Puzzles
Visit: www.PHSchool.com
Web Code: epj-5502
Give students this Web Code to access interactive crossword puzzles using Academic Vocabulary and Vocabulary Skill words from Part 2.

Introduce Academic Vocabulary

- Introduce the academic vocabulary: words for connecting themes in literature. Tell students that these words are useful when discussing literature.
- Review each word, and ask volunteers to read each definition aloud. Read the example sentences and discuss how each word is used.
- Tell students to use these words as they discuss the selections in Part 2.

Introduce the Vocabulary Skill

- Introduce the vocabulary skill: word roots. Tell students that many words in English are derived from Latin. The Latin roots *-vid-, -vis-, -vinc-,* and *-vict-* are used in many English words. Recognizing these roots can help students define unfamiliar vocabulary words.
- Tell students that they can find word origin information, or word *etymology,* in dictionaries. Word origin information appears before a word's definition and in double brackets.

Activity

1. *Revise* comes from Middle French, *reviser,* which came from Latin, *revisere,* meaning *to look at again;* the root is similar to the English word.
2. *Vision* is derived from Middle English from Old French, from Latin, meaning *to see;* the root is similar to the definition for *sight.*
3. *Video* is derived from Latin, meaning *sight;* the root is similar to the current meaning *relating to televised images.*
4. *Convince* comes from the Latin, *convincere,* meaning *to prove wrong or to conquer in argument;* this is similar to the current meaning *persuade.*
5. *Victory* is derived from Middle English from Old French from Latin, meaning *victor;* the root is similar to the current meaning *defeat of an opponent.*
6. *Evict* is derived from Middle English from the Latin, meaning *to vanquish;* the root is similar to the current meaning for *expel.*

Planning Differentiated Instruction

Accessibility at a Glance

The Inspector-General	
Context	Setting: Rural, Czarist Russia
Language	• Accessible vocabulary • Dialogue • Idiomatic expressions footnoted
Concept Level	Accessible (peasant outsmarts government official)
Literary Merit	classic
Lexile	NP
Overall Rating	More accessible

Choosing Your Resources

[L1] Special Needs Students   **[L4]** Advanced Students

[L2] Below-Level Students   **[EL]** English Learners

[L3] All Students

FT Fast Track Instruction: To move the lesson more quickly, use the strategies and activities identified with **FT**.

Reading and Vocabulary Warm-ups provide support for below level students. **A** is for students reading two grades below level; **B** is for students reading one grade below level. For Selection Tests, **A** signifies "less challenging" and **B** "more challenging." For Graphic Organizer transparencies, **A** signifies "not filled in" and **B** "filled in."

Scaffolding for Less Proficient and Advanced Students

The leveled questions on Apply the Skills pages progress in the levels of thinking required to answer them. To address the needs of your different students, you may use the (a) level questions for your less proficient students, the (b) level with your on-level and advanced students. The occasional (c) level questions are appropriate for your advanced students.

Go **Online**
Professional **For:** Information about Lexiles
Development **Visit:** www.PHSchool.com
Web Code: eue-1111

Step-by-Step Teaching Guide

	Pacing Guide
PRETEACH	
• Administer Vocabulary and Reading Warm-ups as necessary.	
• Introduce the Literary Analysis Skill: Comedy. **FT**	10 min.
• Introduce the Reading Skill: Drawing Conclusions. **FT**	10 min.
• Prepare students to read by teaching the selection vocabulary. **FT**	10 min.
• Build background and develop expressive vocabulary with Connecting to the Literature and Background.	10 min.
• Engage students' interest with the motivation activity.	10 min.
TEACH	
• Informally monitor comprehension while students read independently or in groups. **FT**	30 min.
• Monitor students' comprehension with the Reading Check notes.	as students read
• Reinforce vocabulary with Vocabulary Builder notes.	as students read
• Develop students' understanding of comedy with the Literary Analysis annotations. **FT**	5 min.
• Develop students' ability to draw conclusions with the Reading Skill annotations. **FT**	10 min.
ASSESS/EXTEND	
• Assess students' comprehension and mastery of the Reading Skill and Literary Analysis by having them answer the Apply the Skills questions. **FT**	35 min.
• Have students complete the Vocabulary Builder activities. **FT**	5 min.
• Apply students' ability to write a short play with the Writing activity. **FT**	30–45 min. or homework
• Extend students' listening and speaking and research and technology skills with one or both of the Extend Your Learning activities.	15–30 min. or homework
• Have students complete the Vocabulary Skill and Grammar Lesson.	5 min.
• Monitor students' progress with the Assessment Practice.	20–40 min.
• Administer **Selection Test A** or **Selection Test B**. **FT**	15 min.

Resources

 Meeting Your Standards

Students will

1. **analyze and respond to literary elements.**
   - Literary Analysis: Comedy

2. **read, comprehend, and analyze plays.**
   - Reading Skill: Drawing Conclusions
   - Reading Strategy: Drawing Conclusions from Dialogue and Stage Directions
   - Reading Check questions
   - Apply the Skills questions
   - Assessment Practice

3. **develop vocabulary.**
   - Vocabulary Builder
   - The Latin roots *-vis-, -vid-, -vinc-*

4. **apply grammar skills.**
   - Main and Subordinate Clauses

5. **develop writing proficiency.**
   - Work in Progress: Research Report
   - Short play

6. **extend learning.**
   - Listening and Speaking: Readers Theatre Presentation
   - Research and Technology: Informational Chart

Block Scheduling: Use one 90-minute class period to preteach the skills and have students read the selection. Use a second 90-minute class period to assess students' mastery of skills, extend their learning, and monitor their progress.

Homework Suggestions

Following are possibilities for homework assignments.

- Support pages from *Unit 5 Resources:*
  Literary Analysis
  Reading Skill
  Build Vocabulary
  Enrichment

- An Extend Your Learning project and the Writing assignment for your chosen selection may be completed over several days.

PRENTICE HALL
TeacherEXPRESS™ Use this complete
Plan · Teach · Assess suite of powerful
teaching tools to make lesson planning and testing quicker and easier.

PRENTICE HALL
StudentEXPRESS™ Use the Interactive
Learn · Study · Succeed Textbook (online and on CD-ROM) to make selections and activities come alive with audio and video support and interactive questions.

❶ Literary Analysis
Comedy

- Tell students that *comedy* is a light form of drama. A comedy may not evoke outright laughter, but a comic play typically amuses the audience.

- Point out that authors often convey humor in a play through the dialogue.

- Tell students to look for clues in the dialogue of *The Inspector-General* that let the audience know the secret that escapes the inspector-general's notice until the very end.

Dramatic Irony

- Tell students that *dramatic irony* is a contradiction between what a character thinks and says and what the audience knows.

- Explain that the example of the driver and housekeeper illustrates dramatic irony: The audience and the driver know the situation, but only the inspector-general believes that nobody else knows his true identity. The boldness with which the driver speaks and his passenger's incapacity to object is ironic and humorous.

- Have students note examples of dramatic irony as they read the play.

❷ Reading Skill
Drawing Conclusions

- Point out to students that they reach conclusions about a play by connecting details from the dialogue and the actions. Most of the ideas conveyed in a play come not from what is directly stated but from putting details together and arriving at new information.

- Tell students they can draw conclusions about "The Inspector-General" by being alert to what characters say and do throughout the play and how their words affect events.

- Give students a copy of **Reading Skill Graphic Organizer A** (*Graphic Organizer Transparencies,* p. 188). Have them fill in the graphic organizer to draw conclusions as they read the assigned selection. In addition, have students use the graphic organizer on this page to help them draw conclusions based on details.

882

Build Skills *The Inspector-General*

❶ Literary Analysis

Comedy is a form of drama that is lighter in mood than tragedy, ends happily, and aims primarily to amuse. The humor in comic plays may arise from one or more of the following elements:

- funny names
- witty dialogue
- comic situations, such as deception by a character, misunderstandings, or mistaken identities

The humor of comic situations often relies on **dramatic irony**, which is a contradiction between what a character thinks and says and what the audience knows to be true. In comedies, the audience often knows the truth about a situation in the play while the characters remain unaware. As a result, the characters' statements and behavior may seem funny to the audience.

❷ Reading Skill

A **conclusion** is a decision or an opinion that you reach based on details in a text. In drawing conclusions, you consider both stated and implied information. To draw conclusions about characters in a play, **use both dialogue and stage directions** to find meaningful information.

- Consider what characters' words suggest about their personalities and circumstances.

- Read stage directions closely for details about the scene, characters' appearances, and characters' behavior. Take note of other information that could prove essential to the plot or ideas expressed in the play.

As you read, use a chart like the one shown to record conclusions you draw about characters.

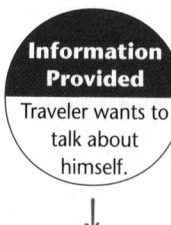

Information Provided
Traveler wants to talk about himself.

Conclusion
He thinks he is an important man.

Vocabulary Builder

- **anonymous** (ə nän´ ə məs) *adj.* without a known or acknowledged name (p. 884) *These poems were composed a long time ago by* <u>anonymous</u> *writers.*

- **trundle** (trun´ dəl) *v.* roll along (p. 884) *While we were chatting, the shopping cart began to* <u>trundle</u> *down the aisle.*

- **discreetly** (di skrēt´ lē) *adv.* without drawing attention (p. 886) *The candidate avoided embarrassment by* <u>discreetly</u> *straightening his crooked tie during the debate.*

- **cunning** (kun´ in) *adj.* skilled in deception (p. 886) *The small but* <u>cunning</u> *animal is usually able to outwit and escape its predators.*

882 ■ Drama

Vocabulary Development

Vocabulary Knowledge Rating

Create a **Vocabulary Knowledge Rating Chart** for this selection. Include the selection vocabulary from this page and the additional words students are asked to use at the end of Connecting to the Literature. These words will increase students' expressive vocabulary.

Give students a copy of the chart with the words on it. Introduce the words by reading them aloud and having students mark their rating in the Before Reading column. Urge them to be alert to these words as they read and discuss the selection because they will rate their knowledge of the words again after they finish.

If you wish, you may tally how many students know (or think they know) a word to gauge how much instruction you need to provide. As students read, point out the words and their context.

Build Understanding • *The Inspector-General*

❸ Background

Inspectors General "The Inspector-General" is set in imperial Russia, before the 1917 communist revolution, when the country was ruled by an emperor, or czar. To oversee the many officials in Russia's vast expanse, the czars employed inspectors-general. They observed how local schools, courts, and hospitals were functioning. Many resented the czar's authority, however, and inspectors-general were often unwelcome.

❹ Connecting to the Literature

Reading/Writing Connection In "The Inspector-General," an official in disguise finds out more than he wants to know. Imagine a scene in which someone—a public official, an athlete, a celebrity—secretly overhears people talking about him or her. Write a few sentences describing the person's reactions to such a conversation. Use at least three of these words: *distort, ignore, interpret, respond, injure.*

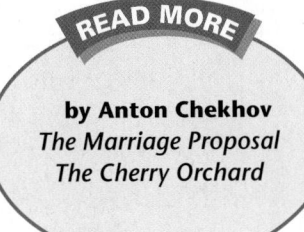

READ MORE

by Anton Chekhov
The Marriage Proposal
The Cherry Orchard

Meet the Author

Anton **Chekhov** (1860–1904)

The grandson of a former serf who had purchased his freedom, Anton Chekhov grew up in a small Russian coastal town. He later attended medical school in Moscow, where he began writing humorous stories. Writing soon became his major focus.

Passion and Compassion Chekhov wrote many short stories as well as several acclaimed plays, including *The Seagull* (1896), *Uncle Vanya* (1897), and *The Three Sisters* (1901). His characters range from old peasants to young society women, from those whom life has treated kindly, to those who are disappointed. Chekhov treats them all with respect and sympathy. His humor and ability to portray characters of great depth and authenticity have helped make Chekhov a beloved author.

Fast Facts

▶ In 1890, Chekhov journeyed across Siberia to write a report on conditions at the convict settlement of Sakhalin.
▶ Chekhov married a famous actress, Olga Knipper.

Go Online
Author Link
For: More about the author
Visit: www.PHSchool.com
Web Code: epe-9504

The Inspector-General ■ 883

❸ Background
Inspectors General

Although inspectors general were unpopular wherever they went, these officials of the Czarist government were intended to provide some stability and accountability in local governments. Because of the vast size of the empire in an era of slow transportation, local government officials sometimes set up their own fiefdoms, running the towns as they wished, often in highly corrupt ways. The job of the inspectors general was to reign in the corruption and make the local officials accountable to the czar.

❹ Connecting to the Literature

- Model use of the expressive vocabulary students are asked to use with these examples:

  1. He *distorts* everything I have ever said or done!
  2. I will pretend to *ignore* them, and maybe they will finally let the matter rest.
  3. It is entirely false to *interpret* my actions in that way.
  4. Please *respond* in a timely manner.
  5. Why do they want to *injure* my reputation like that?

- Help students further develop their expressive vocabulary by providing these words: *appropriate, circumstance, dispute, encounter,* and *impress.* Encourage students to use these words as they discuss the selection.

Go Online
Author Link For additional information about Anton Chekhov, have students type in the Web Code and then select *Anton Chekhov.*

❶ Motivation

Prepare an **Anticipation Guide** (see *General Resources*, pp. 8–10) with the following statements:

- Sometimes we can be so clever that we fool no one.
- People in small communities cannot outsmart the central government.
- No one likes to be made a fool of.
- If you want to know what the rich and powerful are up to, talk to their servants.

Give students a copy of the prepared Anticipation Guide and have students mark their responses in the Me column. Have students discuss the statements in pairs or groups and mark the Guides again in the Group column.

Concept Connector ➡

Students will return to the Anticipation Guide after completing "The Inspector-General."

Learning Modalities
Bodily/Kinesthetic Learners

The stage directions in "The Inspector-General" include gestures and facial expressions that help reveal the characters' feelings and motives. Students can help classmates appreciate this aspect of the comedy by performing a version that captures these important nonverbal details.

❷ About the Selection

Brimming with ironies, "The Inspector-General" shows what happens when the tables are turned on a self-satisfied fellow who is proud of his craftiness. Traveling "incognito on a secret inspection," Pyotr Pavlovich Posudin discovers that the joke is on him.

❸ Humanities

Valmondois Sous La Neige, by Maurice de Vlaminck

Maurice de Vlaminck was born in Paris in 1876. In the early 1900s, he belonged to a group of artists dubbed the Fauves—meaning "wild beasts"—because of their bold use of color. De Vlaminck later turned to painting evocative landscapes. Use the following question for discussion:

- What might life be like in a setting such as the one depicted?
  Answer: Students may say life would be dreary and uneventful.

The Inspector-General

Anton Chekhov

Adapted by Michael Frayn

❶
❷
❸

The curtain goes up to reveal falling snow and a cart facing away from us. Enter the STORYTELLER, who begins to read the story. Meanwhile, the TRAVELER enters. He is a middle-aged man of urban appearance, wearing dark glasses and a long overcoat with its collar turned up. He is carrying a small traveling bag. He climbs into the cart and sits facing us.

STORYTELLER. The Inspector-General. In deepest incognito,[1] first by express train, then along back roads, Pyotr Pavlovich Posudin[2] was hastening toward the little town of N, to which he had been summoned by an <u>anonymous</u> letter. "I'll take them by surprise," he thought to himself. "I'll come down on them like a thunderbolt out of the blue. I can just imagine their faces when they hear who I am . . ." [*Enter the DRIVER, a peasant, who climbs onto the cart, so that he is sitting with his back to us, and the cart begins to <u>trundle</u> slowly away from us.*] And when he'd thought to himself for long enough, he fell into conversation with the driver of the cart. What did he talk about? About himself, of course. [*Exit the STORYTELLER.*]

---

1. **incognito** (in´ kä g nē´ tō´) *n.* a disguised condition.
2. **Pyotr Pavlovich Posudin** (pyō´ tər päv lō´ vich pō syoo´ dən)

884 ■ *Drama*

Vocabulary Builder
anonymous (ə nän´ ə məs) *adj.* without a known or acknowledged name

trundle (trun´ dəl) *v.* roll along

Vocabulary Development

Expressive Vocabulary

Guide a discussion about the conversation between the traveler and the driver. Use the following questions to stimulate discussion.

As students discuss the traveler and the driver, encourage them to use the expressive vocabulary presented earlier. You might encourage them with sentence starters like these:

1. The traveler asks the driver about the new Inspector-General. How does the driver *respond*?

2. Does the traveler *interpret* the driver's remarks accurately?

3. Do you think the driver's comments *injure* the traveler in any way?

4. Will the traveler *ignore* the driver's insults about the inspector-general?

5. Does the driver *distort* the sneaky habits of the new inspector-general?

TRAVELER. I gather you've got a new Inspector-General in these parts.

DRIVER. True enough.

TRAVELER. Know anything about him? [*The driver turns and looks at the* TRAVELER, *who turns his coat collar up a little higher.*]

DRIVER. Know anything about him? Of course we do! We know everything about all of them up there! Every last little clerk—we know the color of his hair and the size of his boots! [*He turns back to the front, and the* TRAVELER *permits himself a slight smile.*]

TRAVELER. So, what do you reckon? Any good, is he? [*The* DRIVER *turns around.*]

DRIVER. Oh, yes, he's a good one, this one.

TRAVELER. Really?

DRIVER. Did one good thing straight off.

TRAVELER. What was that?

DRIVER. He got rid of the last one. Holy terror he was! Hear him coming five miles off! Say he's going to this little town. Somewhere like we're going, say. He'd let all the world know about it a month before. So now he's on his way, say, and it's like thunder and lightning coming down the road. And when he gets where he's going he has a good sleep, he has a good eat and drink—and then he starts. Stamps his feet, shouts his head off. Then he has another good sleep, and off he goes.

TRAVELER. But the new one's not like that?

DRIVER. Oh, no, the new one goes everywhere on the quiet, like. Creeps around like a cat. Don't want no one to see him, don't want no one to know who he is. Say he's going to this town down the road here. Someone there sent him a letter on the sly, let's say. "Things going on here you should know about." Something of that kind. Well, now, he creeps out of his office, so none of them up there see him go. He hops on a train just like anyone else, just like you or me. Then when he gets off he don't go jumping into a cab or nothing fancy. Oh, no. He wraps himself up from head to toe so you can't see his face, and he wheezes away like an old dog so no one can recognize his voice.

TRAVELER. Wheezes? That's not wheezing! That's the way he talks! So I gather.

◄ **Critical Viewing**
How might the people of a small town like this react to the arrival of an inspector? **[Speculate]**

Reading Skill
Drawing Conclusions
What conclusion about the Inspector-General can you draw from the stage direction that he "permits himself a slight smile"?

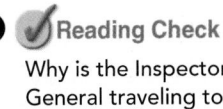
Reading Check
Why is the Inspector-General traveling to the town?

The Inspector-General ■ 885

❹ Reading Skill
Drawing Conclusions

- Have students take roles and read from the opening dialogue to the end of the bracketed passage.

- **Ask** students the Reading Skill question: What conclusion about the inspector-general can you draw from the stage direction that he "permits himself a slight smile"? **Answer:** Students may conclude that the inspector-general is confident that the villagers are exceptionally naïve and know nothing about him. The smile represents his desire to appear amused and at ease when he is really nothing of the sort.

- **Ask** students what clues led them to form their conclusion. **Possible response:** In the storyteller's comments, he says the inspector-general is pleased with himself and the deception he is executing. "I'll come down on them like a thunderbolt," he thinks to himself. His smile confirms that he is pleased and confident the townspeople know nothing.

❺ Reading Check

Answer: The inspector-general is traveling to the town to check on its management. He does so in response to an anonymous letter.

❻ Literary Analysis
Comedy

- Have two students perform this passage of dialogue for the class. Instruct students to ham it up and use facial expressions to enhance the meaning.

- When students finish acting, **ask** them the Literary Analysis question: How does your knowledge of the traveler's true identity make this dialogue humorous?
  Answer: The dialogue is humorous because the audience knows that the traveler is the inspector-general, exactly the person whom the driver is insulting. It is an example of dramatic irony: The audience knows something the character does not.

- **Ask** students if the driver is also in on the joke.
  Answer: Students should at least begin to realize that the driver knows exactly whom he is talking to.

▶ **Monitor Progress:** Ask students how the driver's awareness of who his passenger is contributes to the humor.
  Answer: The driver's knowledge that he is carrying the inspector-general means that he, too, is in on the joke. Only the inspector-general himself seems to remain in the dark.

▶ **Reteach:** Have students turn back to p. 882 and name the three elements that help make comedies humorous. Then ask them to explain dramatic irony. Finally, have students work in pairs and find examples of at least two of each of these elements in the play.

DRIVER. Oh, is it? But the tales they tell about him. You'd laugh till you burst your tripes![3]

TRAVELER. [*sourly*]. I'm sure I would.

DRIVER. He drinks, mind!

TRAVELER. [*startled*]. Drinks?

DRIVER. Oh, like a hole in the ground. Famous for it.

TRAVELER. He's never touched a drop! I mean, from what I've heard.

DRIVER. Oh, not in public, no. Goes to some great ball—"No thank you, not for me." Oh, no, he puts it away at home! Wakes up in the morning, rubs his eyes, and the first thing he does, he shouts, "Vodka!" So in runs his valet with a glass. Fixed himself up a tube behind his desk, he has. Leans down, takes a pull on it, no one the wiser.

TRAVELER. [*offended*]. How do you know all this, may I ask?

DRIVER. Can't hide it from the servants, can you? The valet and the coachman have got tongues in their heads. Then again, he's on the road, say, going about his business, and he keeps the bottle in his little bag. [*The* TRAVELER *discreetly pushes the traveling bag out of the* DRIVER'S *sight*.] And his housekeeper . . .

TRAVELER. What about her?

DRIVER. Runs circles around him, she does, like a fox round his tail. She's the one who wears the trousers.[4] The people aren't half so frightened of him as they are of her.

TRAVELER. But at least he's good at his job, you say?

DRIVER. Oh, he's a blessing from heaven, I'll grant him that.

TRAVELER. Very cunning—you were saying.

DRIVER. Oh, he creeps around all right.

TRAVELER. And then he pounces, yes? I should think some people must get the surprise of their life, mustn't they?

DRIVER. No, no—let's be fair, now. Give him his due. He don't make no trouble.

TRAVELER. No, I mean, if no one knows he's coming . . .

DRIVER. Oh, that's what he thinks, but we all know.

TRAVELER. You know?

---

3. **tripes** (trīps) *n.* parts of the stomach, usually of an ox or a sheep, when used as food.
4. **wears the trousers** has the greatest authority; is really in charge.

886 ■ *Drama*

Literary Analysis
Comedy How does your knowledge of the Traveler's true identity make this dialogue humorous?

Vocabulary Builder
discreetly (di skrēt´ lē) *adv.* without drawing attention

Vocabulary Builder
cunning (kun´ iŋ) *adj.* skilled in deception

Vocabulary Development

Vocabulary Knowledge Rating

When students have completed reading and discussing "The Inspector-General," have them take out their **Vocabulary Knowledge Rating Chart** for this selection. Read the words aloud once more and have students rate their knowledge of the words again in the After Reading column. Clarify any words that are still problematic. Have students write their own definition and example or sentence in the appropriate column. Then have students complete the **Vocabulary Builder Practice** activities on p. 889. Encourage students to use the words in further discussion and written work about this selection. Remind them that they will be accountable for these words on the Selection Test.

DRIVER. Oh, some gentleman gets off the train at the station back there with his greatcoat up to his eyebrows and says, "No, I don't want a cab, thank you, just an ordinary horse and cart for me." Well, we'd put two and two together, wouldn't we! Say it was you, now, creeping along down the road here. The lads would be down there in a cab by now! By the time you got there the whole town would be as regular as clockwork! And you'd think to yourself, "Oh, look at that! As clean as a whistle! And they didn't know I was coming!" No, that's why he's such a blessing after the other one. This one believes it!

TRAVELER. Oh, I see.

DRIVER. What, you thought we wouldn't know him? Why, we've got the electric telegraph these days! Take today, now. I'm going past the station back there this morning, and the fellow who runs the buffet comes out like a bolt of lightning. Arms full of baskets and bottles. "Where are you off to?" I say. "Doing drinks and refreshments for the Inspector-General!" he says, and he jumps into a carriage and goes flying off down the road here. So there's the old Inspector-General, all muffled up like a roll of carpet, going secretly along in a cart somewhere—and when he gets there, nothing to be seen but vodka and cold salmon!

TRAVELER. [*shouts*]. Right—turn around, then . . . !

DRIVER. [*to the horse*]. Whoa, boy! Whoa! [*To the* TRAVELER.] Oh, so what's this, then? Don't want to go running into the Inspector-General, is that it? [*The* TRAVELER *gestures impatiently for the* DRIVER *to turn the cart around.* DRIVER *to the horse.*] Back we go, then, boy. Home we go. [*He turns the cart around, and the* TRAVELER *takes a swig from his traveling bag.*] Though if I know the old devil, he's like as not turned around and gone home again himself. [*Blackout.*]

White Night, 1901, Edvard Munch. Photo: J. Lathion © Nasjonalgalleriet 1997, ©2003 The Munch Museum/The Munch-Ellingsen Group/Artists Rights Society/(ARS), NY

❼

❽ ⚠ Critical Viewing
How does the countryside depicted in this painting compare to the setting of the play? **[Compare and Contrast]**

**Reading Skill
Drawing Conclusions**
What conclusion can you draw based on the Traveler's sudden order to turn around?

The Inspector-General ■ 887

The Inspector-General

Thinking About the Selection

1. **(a) Questions:** Students may ask: Who sent the anonymous letter? Why? Will the inspector-general ever visit the town again?
   (b) Partner's Answers: Students should answer the questions as well as possible and should then explore the answers with their partners. **(c) Understanding of the Play:** Students should summarize how their knowledge of the play has changed after their discussions.

2. **(a)** The traveler pushes the bag containing his flask out of view of the driver. **(b)** The traveler is embarrassed by his drinking habits.

3. **(a)** The town gets everything in order so the inspector-general will find nothing wrong. **(b)** The traveler realizes he is wasting his time trying to find anything amiss, and he is embarrassed to realize that all his cleverness has been so transparent.

4. The cleverer man is the driver. He knows all about the traveler and has used his wit both to insult the inspector-general and to get him to leave town.

5. The play ends happily, or at least humorously, as the inspector-general leaves town with no harm done except to his pride; the driver's dialogue is witty as he cleverly insults the inspector-general who is forced to bear the barbs in silence in order to keep his identity secret; the situation of the inspector-general sneaking into town in disguise while everyone around him knows his identity is humorous; Chekhov amuses the audience by letting them in on all the secrets.

6. **(a)** The storyteller sets up the dramatic irony by letting the audience in on the secret, first by explaining that the traveler is incognito and then by explaining that the inspector-general thinks he will surprise the townspeople. **(b) Possible response:** The driver comments that "He drinks, mind!" to which the traveler responds "[startled] Drinks?" The driver then says, "Oh, like a hole in the ground. Famous for it."

1. **(a) Respond:** What questions do you still have after reading "The Inspector-General"? Write your questions in the first column of a three-column chart like the one shown. **(b) Discuss:** Trade lists with a partner. In the second column of the chart, try to answer your partner's questions. Then, discuss the questions and answers. **(c) Assess:** In the third column, explain how your understanding of the work has or has not changed based on the discussion.

Questions	Partner's Answers	Understanding of the Play

2. **(a) Recall:** What does the Traveler do when the Driver mentions that the Inspector-General keeps a flask of vodka? **(b) Infer:** What does this action tell you about the Traveler?

3. **(a) Recall:** According to the Driver, what preparations does the town make for the Inspector-General's arrival? **(b) Interpret:** Why does the Driver's account provoke the Traveler's demand to turn around?

4. **Evaluate:** Who do you think is the wiser and cleverer man—the Driver or the Traveler? Explain.

Literary Analysis

5. Note specific ways in which "The Inspector-General" does or does not meet these criteria for **comedy:** It ends happily; it uses witty dialogue; it presents a comic situation; it seeks to amuse.

6. **(a)** What information, conveyed by the Storyteller, sets up the **dramatic irony** in "The Inspector-General"? **(b)** Identify an exchange between the Driver and the Traveler that highlights the dramatic irony of the situation.

Reading Skill

7. What **conclusions** can you draw about the character of the Traveler based on the stage directions *sourly, startled,* and *offended* that precede three of his lines?

8. What conclusions can you draw about the character of the Driver based on his dialogue with the Traveler? Explain your answer.

888 ■ *Drama*

QuickReview

Play at a Glance
A smug inspector-general is outsmarted by a peasant.

Comedy: a form of drama that ends happily and aims primarily to amuse

Dramatic Irony: a contradiction between what a character thinks and says and what the audience knows to be true

Conclusion: decision or opinion based on details in a text

Assessment
For: Self-test
Visit: www.PHSchool.com
Web Code: epe-6508

7. **Possible response:** Students may conclude that the inspector-general is foolish, arrogant, and self-deluded.

8. The driver is clever and has a sense of humor. All of the dialogue supports this conclusion. Any example will suffice.

Vocabulary Builder

Practice Indicate whether each statement is *True* or *False*. Explain your answers. Then, revise false sentences to make them true.

1. Someone making an *anonymous* donation wants recognition.
2. A tricycle is something that might *trundle*.
3. The best way to send a message *discreetly* is to shout.
4. If a man is *cunning*, he may not always tell the truth.

Adding Words to Your Vocabulary Using a thesaurus, find one synonym and one antonym for each italicized word in the Practice section. Then, use each new word correctly in a sentence. (For more on using a thesaurus, see page R7.)

Writing

Write a brief **play** in which students outwit a bully. Use a realistic school setting, and be sure that dialogue sounds true-to-life.

Create *dramatic irony* by including scenes in which the audience knows something the bully does not know. Write to entertain and teach without being cruel, even to the character of the bully.

For *Grammar, Vocabulary,* and *Assessment,* see **Build Language Skills,** pages 890–891.

Extend Your Learning

Listening and Speaking With two other students, prepare a **Readers Theatre presentation** of "The Inspector-General." Do not provide props or staging; instead, focus on a well-prepared reading of the play. Remember that your purpose is to entertain your audience.
- Choose roles—the Traveler, the Driver, and a narrator.
- Experiment to find a suitable tone of voice and style of delivery. Perform the play in front of a small group or the entire class.

Research and Technology Use library and Internet resources to research what life was like in Russia during the rule of the czars, including the role of inspectors-general at that time. As you research, take careful notes and observe which research terms and processes help you locate the best information. Organize your findings in an **informational chart**, and present it to your class.

Apply the Skills ■ 889

Vocabulary Skill

- Stress that recognizing the Latin root -vis- and its variant -vid-, and the word root -vinc- and its variant -vict- will help students decode the meanings of new or unfamiliar words. English words that contain the -vis- or -vid- root will generally relate to the concept of "sight" or "seeing" in the figurative or literal sense. English words that contain the -vinc- or -vict- root will generally relate to the concept of "conquering" in the figurative or literal sense.

- Have students complete the Practice activity on this page.

Possible Answers

1. When you *revise,* you *look* for ideas, organizational strategies, or thesis statements that need to be clarified or strengthened.

2. Although *invisible* means "not able to be seen," *invincible* comes from a different word root and means "unconquerable."

3. One *victory* that makes me proud to be a *winner* is overcoming my fear of speaking in public.

Grammar Lesson

- Tell students that a main clause will make sense by itself or will state a complete thought. However, a subordinate or dependent clause will not express a complete thought.

- Have students complete the Practice activity on this page.

Answers

1. This is a subordinate clause. When the phone rang, I answered it.

2. This is a main clause.

3. This is a main clause.

4. This is a subordinate clause. Planning for the future is good, but decisions are difficult.

5. This is a main clause.

𝒲𝒢 Writing and Grammar, Gold Level

Students will find further instruction and practice on main and subordinate clauses in Chapter 21, Section 2.

Build Language Skills

The Inspector-General

Vocabulary Skill

Word Roots The **Latin word root** -vis- and its variant -vid- mean "see." Words that contain these word roots, such as *visible* and *video,* have meanings related to "seeing." The **word root** -vinc-, along with its variant -vict-, means "conquer." Words that contain these word roots have meanings that can be traced back to ideas about winning or being stronger. For example, to *convince* someone, you must have a stronger argument than the other person has.

Practice Check the meaning of each italicized word in a dictionary. Then, answer each question in a complete sentence that incorporates the italicized word and the underlined word.

▶ **Example: Q:** Does a person who cannot <u>see</u> the road signs have good enough *vision* to drive? Explain.

    A: A person who cannot see road signs does not have good enough vision to drive and might have accidents.

1. What do you <u>look</u> for when you *revise* something you have written?

2. If <u>invisible</u> means "not able to be seen," what do you think *invincible* means?

3. What is one *victory* that makes you proud to have been the <u>winner</u>?

Grammar Lesson

Main and Subordinate Clauses A **clause**, a group of words that contains a subject and a verb, can be a **main** (independent) **clause** or a **subordinate** (dependent) **clause**. If the group of words needs additional information to make sense, it is a subordinate clause. Subordinate clauses can function as noun, adjective, or adverbial clauses.

▶ **Example:** Main clause   The reporter shouted.
             Subordinate clause   but the reporter shouted

Practice Define each of the following as a main or subordinate clause. Then, add to each subordinate clause to make it a main clause.

1. when the phone rang
2. the phone rang
3. decisions are difficult at times
4. but decisions are difficult
5. the Dead Sea in Israel has a lower elevation

𝒲𝒢 *Prentice Hall Writing and Grammar Connection: Chapter 20, Section 3.*

890 ■ *Drama*

MorePractice

For more practice with main and subordinate clauses, see the Grammar Handbook, p. R44.

Teaching Resources

The following resources can be used to enrich or extend the instruction for Build Language Skills.

Unit 5 Resources
    Build Language Skills: Vocabulary: Word Roots, p. 137
    Build Grammar Skills: Main and Subordinate Clauses, p. 138

Reading Skill: Draw Conclusions

Directions: *Read the selection. Then, answer the questions.*

The social significance of Chekhov's dramatic art is a vast theme. . . . What did he intend in presenting these characters and these situations? Why did he believe it was necessary "to depict life as it is and people as they are . . ."?

Perhaps in his aversion from everything stilted, affected, and pretentious he just created out of the sincerity and directness of his—very Russian—character. Perhaps his natural tolerance, his saving sense of humour, and deep sympathy with human beings moved him to show that people—however misguided, silly, ineffectual—are still lovable.

from Introduction to *Anton Chekhov: Plays* by Elisaveta Fen

1. The phrase "natural tolerance" could best be replaced by
   A recognition and respect for people.
   B innate ability to depict situations.
   C response to the humorous.
   D development of background.

2. The language in the selection leads the reader to conclude that
   A the author dislikes Chekhov's writing.
   B the author admires Chekhov's writing.

   C the author is a sociologist evaluating Chekhov's writing.
   D the author makes excuses for Chekhov's work.

3. From descriptive details in the selection, the reader can conclude that
   A Chekhov wrote mainly fantasy.
   B Chekhov wrote mainly documentaries.
   C Chekhov wrote about high society.
   D Chekhov wrote about normal people.

Timed Writing: Interpretation [Critical Stance]

Symbolism plays a significant role in both *Romeo and Juliet* and *The Inspector-General.* Choose one of the plays, and explain how one set of symbols contributes to a major theme in the work. Support your views with specifics from the play. **(60 minutes)**

 ## Writing Workshop: *Work in Progress*

Research Report

For a research report you may be asked to write, discuss the details in *The Shakespeare Stealer* that seem drawn from historical research—for example, details about language, dress, writing, materials, or theatrical practices of the day. Keep these notes in your writing portfolio.

Build Language Skills ■ *891*

Reading: Drawing Conclusions
   1. A
   2. B
   3. D

Timed Writing: Interpretation

- Tell students that they will have 60 minutes to write an interpretation of one of the plays in this section. Their interpretations should include a thesis and support from the text to support that thesis.

- Have students identify a major theme in one of the plays they have read. Then, have them identify a set of symbols that contributes to that theme.

- Have students jot down references from the play that support how the symbols contribute to the theme. Then, have students begin their writing.

- Assess students' interpretations on the development of their interpretations and how well they support them with examples from the text.

- Suggest that students plan their time to 20 minutes to reviewing the play, 30 minutes to writing, and 10 minutes to reviewing and revising.

Writing Workshop

Work in Progress

Research Report

- Have students prepare to take notes and then lead them in a discussion of the scene from *The Shakespeare Stealer.*

- Remind students that this work may be used in the research report they will write in the **Writing Workshop** at the end of Part 2.

- Point out that students should record those parts of the discussion that are relevant for the research report they may write later. Remind them that until they have selected their topics, all of the discussion may be relevant, as well as the page references relating to the discussion.

- When students have completed their notes, have them save them in their portfolios. They will use them in the **Writing Workshop** on p. 916.

See TeacherExpress™/Lesson View for a detailed lesson plan for Reading Informational Materials.

About Reviews

- Have students read "About Reviews."

- As a group, brainstorm for a list of events that might be reviewed in the local paper. Make sure the list includes movies, plays, CDs, and books.

- Ask volunteers to describe reviews they have read. Have them share how the reviews made them feel about the works being reviewed. Then, ask students to explain whether the reviews influenced their decisions to see, read, or listen to the works being reviewed.

- Ask students who read reviews, and then saw or read the works, if they agreed with the reviews after having experienced the works for themselves.

Reading Skill
Evaluating Credibility of an Author

- Remind students that it is important to consider whether or not the author of a review is reliable before making any judgments or decisions based on the information he or she provides.

- Review with students the "Evaluating the Credibility of an Author" chart. Point out that details about the writer's expertise are given, but that the other three categories are blank.

- Explain that reviews represent the author's opinion about a work, and that authors should provide examples in support of their opinions.

892

Book Review

In Part 2, you learned how to draw conclusions when you read literature. Drawing conclusions is also important when reading informational material such as editorials and reviews because it helps you weigh the facts and details in a text and form your own opinions. If you read Anton Chekhov's "The Inspector General," you may be interested in this review of a translation of Chekhov's plays.

About Reviews

Reviews are essays that express the writer's opinion about a created work, such as a book, a film, a recording, or a performance. Reviews appear in newspapers, magazines, and on Web sites, and are sometimes collected in books. In addition to expressing the reviewer's opinion, many reviews provide background and history about both the work and its creator. Based on information in a review, readers may decide if they want to read the book, see the play, or watch the movie. Reviews often include these features:

- An introduction that states the main idea or thesis
- Opinions about the strengths and weaknesses of the subject
- Examples, quotations, facts, or other support for the opinion
- A conclusion that restates the opinion and gives a recommendation

Reading Skill

Before you accept the opinions of a reviewer, evaluate the author's credibility. When you **evaluate the author's credibility,** you judge whether he or she is knowledgeable and fair. An unfair reviewer may express **bias**, an opinion he or she formed prior to experiencing a work. Credible authors avoid bias and present a balanced view. Use a chart like the one shown to evaluate the credibility of the author of the review, "Chekhov in American."

Evaluating the Credibility of an Author	
Writer's expertise or level of knowledge	Familiar with Chekhov's plays. Knows facts and other details about Chekhov. Cites Tolstoy, Chekhov, and Schmidt.
Intent or reasons for writing	
Bias toward the subject	
Thorough support for opinions	

892 ■ Drama

Differentiated Instruction   Solutions for All Learners

Reading Support
Give students reading support with the appropriate version of the *Reader's Notebooks:*

Reader's Notebook, [L2]

Reader's Notebook: Adapted Version, [L1]

Reader's Notebook: English Learner's Version, [EL]

Chekhov in American

Adam Kirsch

A Review of a Translation of Chekhov's Plays

In the introduction, the reviewer states his general subject—Chekhov's plays. He also gives background on the plays and identifies a controversy.

In the English-speaking world Anton Chekhov is far better known for his plays than for his short stories. But during his lifetime Chekhov's stories made his reputation; his plays were given a more ambivalent reception, even by his fellow writers. Shortly after Chekhov's death, in 1904, Tolstoy voiced a common feeling that plays like *Uncle Vanya* and *Three Sisters* weren't quite dramas. "To evoke a mood," he said in an interview, "you want a lyrical poem. Dramatic forms serve, and ought to serve, quite different aims. In a dramatic work the author ought to deal with some problem that has yet to be solved and every character in the play ought to solve it according to the idiosyncrasies of his own character. . . . But you won't find anything of the kind in Chekhov."

In this criticism Tolstoy hit on exactly those features that have made Chekhov's plays the fundamental works of modern drama. Like lyric poems, they favor mood over plot; there is no overriding "problem," and when problems do appear, the playwright never seems to endorse any solutions. Chekhov's dramatic form allowed him to present things on the stage "just as complicated and just as simple as . . . in real life," as he famously wrote. "People are sitting at a table having dinner, that's all, but at the same time their happiness is being created, or their lives are being torn apart."

But Chekhov's emphasis on tone and mood, and his faithful re-creation of ordinary conversation with all its hesitations, references, and silences, make him an unusually difficult playwright to translate. Just as difficult to convey is the class dynamic that Chekhov treated again and again: there is no precise English, much less American, equivalent of his gentry, trying to live a city life on income from vast, ungovernable, debt-ridden estates. To an audience that doesn't share Chekhov's basic cultural knowledge, his plays can seem far more meandering, depressing, and vague than they were intended to be.

In his new translation of Chekhov's complete plays Paul Schmidt has these

Here, the reviewer introduces a specific focus—the challenges of translating Chekhov.

Reading Reviews

- Remind students that an author writes a review to express his or her opinion about the work. Point out that readers must carefully evaluate the information the author uses to support his or her opinion.
- Have students read "Chekhov in American" and the side notes.
- **Ask** students to identify the focus of Kirsch's review. **Possible response:** Kirsch focuses his review on the quality of the translation to American English.
- Direct students to Kirsch's development of ideas. Point out that he begins his review with a broad overview of the topic—Chekhov's plays. Ask students to read the first paragraph to see the overview.
- Point out that Kirsch then narrows his comments to elements unique to Chekhov—his focus on tone and mood, rather than on plot. **Ask** a volunteer to identify the paragraphs where Kirsch discusses these issues. **Answer:** Kirsch discusses Chekhov's tone and mood in paragraphs two and three.
- **Ask** a volunteer to summarize Chekhov's position on mood and plot. **Possible response:** Chekhov chose mood over plot in an effort to view the realities of life through ordinary conversation.

continued on p. 894

Differentiated Instruction   Solutions for All Learners

Strategy for English Learners
Students learning English might have a difficult time identifying how word choices impact tone. Discuss the idea that connotation is an important aspect of language learning, and that it is connotation issues that create the differences between English and American translations of Chekhov's works. Tell students that one helpful strategy is to translate something into English and then paraphrase the information. Point out that sometimes paraphrasing helps readers use more natural language.

Enrichment for Advanced Readers
Remind students that the comparison of Schmidt's translation and those of Constance Garnett and Elisaveta Fen highlight the importance of connotation in language. Challenge students to think of idioms or sayings in American English that could be confusing to someone learning English in America. Allow time for students to share their lists of idioms and sayings.

- Point out that Kirsch is specifying that his review will discuss how well Schmidt's translations convey the nuances of class and culture to modern American readers.

- Tell students that reliable reviewers will use examples to support their opinions. **Ask** students to identify examples that help support Kirsch's review.
  Possible response: He uses a quote from the author Schmidt. He also shows a comparison between the text he is reviewing and a previous translation.

- **Ask** students to identify the main point of Kirsch's review.
  Possible response: Kirsch's main point is that Schmidt's translations are, for American readers, superior to older, British versions because he uses language the way modern Americans do.

- **Ask** students to describe Kirsch's overall impression of Schmidt's translations.
  Possible response: Kirsch feels that Schmidt's translations are an improvement in the area of American English translations of Chekhov's plays.

---

problems very much in mind. Both an actor and a Russian scholar, Schmidt sets out to give us a Chekhov who makes sense. He writes in his introduction, "Above all, I hope these translations will provide actors and directors with a clear sense of how the plays are meant to work and how they should sound." His guiding stars are clarity and relevance — particularly relevance to an American audience. "I want to emphasize," he writes, "that this is an American translation, not simply another 'English' translation."

> The writer uses a quotation to further explain and support his opinion.

The result is a surprisingly lively Chekhov, colloquial and clear, which will come as a revelation to those who know the playwright through the widely read but rather stiff British translations of Constance Garnett and Elisaveta Fen. Everything about Schmidt's book, from the organization and footnotes to the language itself, is meant to clear away the obscurity and sentimentality with which Chekhov is often burdened. The plays that emerge are funnier and more muscular than one might have expected.

> This clearly stated evaluation is the main point of the review.

The most striking element in Schmidt's "American" translation is his attempt to put Chekhov's Russian into modern American idiom. There's no doubt that we sorely need such a translation; even the most casual dialogue can sound faintly absurd in the starchy British English of many popular editions of Chekhov. Take, for instance, this exchange from Act I of *Ivanov* in Elisaveta Fen's Penguin translation.

> Examples of two different translations vividly illustrate the reviewer's opinion.

ANNA PETROVNA: Who was it talking here just now? Was it you, Misha? Why are you stamping about like that?

BORKIN: Anyone who had to

---

deal with your cher Nicolàs would stamp about!

ANNA PETROVNA: I say, Misha, will you have some hay brought to the croquet lawn?

BORKIN: Leave me alone, please.

ANNA PETROVNA: Tut-tut, what a tone of voice!

Schmidt turns this passage into something American actors can plausibly say onstage.

ANNA: What's going on out there? Is that you, Misha? What are you marching around like that for?

BORKIN: Trying to talk sense into your friend Nicholas here. Voilà. Enough to make anybody start marching.

ANNA: Misha, I want some hay brought up to the croquet lawn; don't forget to tell them.

BORKIN: Oh, leave me alone, will you?

ANNA: How rude! Will you please not take that tone with me?

For a playwright as frequently misunderstood as Chekhov, this is perhaps the greatest service that any translator could have performed. A generation from now Schmidt's American English may sound as antiquated as Elisaveta Fen's British English, but until then Schmidt's Chekhov should be the first choice for any American reader.

> In the final paragraph, the writer restates his opinion about Schmidt's work.

Vocabulary Development

Vocabulary for Reviews

Tell students that this review of Paul Schmidt's translations uses specialized vocabulary to discuss how language use conveys meaning. Guide them to understand the meaning of the following words that are used in "Chekhov in American."

antiquated: old or no longer used

colloquial: style used in familiar, informal conversation

obscurity: quality of not being easily understood or clearly expressed

gentry: members of the upper class or aristocracy

Assessment Practice

Reading: Evaluating Credibility of an Author

Directions: *Choose the letter of the best answer to each question.*

1. In this review, Adam Kirsch clearly expresses this opinion:
   A Chekhov's plays are stronger in English than in Russian.
   B Chekhov's plays are important dramatic works.
   C Chekhov should have written poetry instead of drama.
   D Chekhov's plays are not interesting.

2. Kirsch thinks Schmidt's translations
   A can only be understood by American audiences.
   B should have been done by someone else.
   C do not accurately reproduce the mood of the original plays.
   D will become the standard translations for many generations.

3. Kirsch's main purpose in writing this review is to
   A express an opinion about Schmidt's translation.
   B describe what he likes about Chekhov's plays.
   C explain why Tolstoy's criticism of Chekhov's plays is incorrect.
   D explain the themes and plots in Chekhov's plays.

4. Which of the following details contributes to Kirsch's credibility?
   A He has read many works by and about Chekhov.
   B He likes Chekhov's work.
   C He does not like most English translations of Chekhov's work.
   D He is published in a newspaper.

Reading: Comprehension and Interpretation

Directions: *Write your answers on a separate piece of paper.*

5. Explain the main problem Kirsch has with most English translations of Chekhov. **[Knowledge]**
6. Describe the differences between the two versions of dialogue spoken by Anna and Borkin that Kirsch quotes. **[Organizing]**

Timed Writing: Exposition [Critical Stance]

Chekhov once said that dramas present things "just as complicated and just as simple as . . . in real life." Think about one play, television show, or movie that presents a realistic, or ordinary, depiction of life. Explain how the drama you choose illustrates Chekhov's words. **(40 minutes)**

Reading Informational Materials ■ 895

Reading: Evaluating Credibility of an Author

1. B
2. D
3. A
4. A
5. Kirsch feels that most English translations of Chekhov's plays do not adequately convey the tone and mood of the originals. He feels most English translations sound false and stiff.
6. The British translation does not sound like a conversation you would typically hear in America. It is difficult to understand exactly what is going on. The second translation—from Paul Schmidt's volume—sounds much more like a typical American conversation, and it is easier to understand the full meaning behind the words.

Timed Writing

- Read the Timed Writing instructions together as a group. Make sure students understand that they are to choose a play, television show, or movie that shows everyday life and events. Then, explain that they are to explore how the play, show, or movie depicts typical life as both complicated and simple.
- Suggest that students plan their time to give 10 minutes to planning, 20 minutes to writing, and 10 minutes to reviewing and revising.

Extend the Lesson

Writing Reviews
Give students further practice with reviews. Have them write reviews of literary works of their own choosing. Encourage them to select a narrow focus rather than try to address all aspects of the work. Tell them to make sure to clearly identify the work being reviewed, state the focus of the review, provide examples from the text as support, and offer a clearly expressed opinion about the work.

Comparing Literary Works • *Satire*

❶ Satire

Satire is writing that exposes and makes fun of the foolishness and faults of an individual, an institution, a society, or a situation. Although a satire often makes readers laugh, it may also aim to correct the flaws that it criticizes. Some satires address serious social problems, while others address less important issues and subjects.

❷ Comparing Satires

Satirical writings vary in style and **tone**, the writer's attitude toward the subject, the audience, or both.

- A satire may be gentle and sympathetic or angry and bitter in tone.
- A satire may use sarcasm or irony—language that means the opposite of what it says. For example, a satirist may mention the "overwhelming generosity" of someone who is a noted miser.
- A satire may exaggerate faults in order to make them both funny and obvious.

In addition, the **perspective**, or viewpoint, of the satirist plays a key role. Some satirists write as outside onlookers, while others include themselves as objects of the satire.

As you read the excerpts from *The Importance of Being Earnest* and *Big Kiss,* answer questions like those in the chart to better understand the satire. Then, compare and contrast the satirical elements of each selection.

Questions About Satire	
subject	• What or whom is ridiculed? • Is the topic serious or trivial? • Does the writer include him- or herself as an object of the satire?
tone	• Is the tone gentle or harsh? • Does the writer use sarcasm or irony?
purpose	• Is the satire funny? • Does the satirist want to correct the flaws he/she exposes?

Vocabulary Builder

from The Importance of Being Earnest

- **demonstrative** (di män′ strə tiv) *adj.* showing feelings openly (p. 899) *She was <u>demonstrative</u> in her affection for the child, hugging her often.*

- **ignorance** (ig′ nə rəns) *n.* lack of knowledge or education (p. 902) *The driver exhibited <u>ignorance</u>, so the police officer explained the law.*

from Big Kiss

- **allotment** (ə lät′ mənt) *n.* share; portion (p. 906) *When they divided the supplies, my <u>allotment</u> was small.*

- **assiduous** (ə sij′ ōō əs) *adj.* done with constant and careful attention; diligent (p. 910) *She is <u>assiduous</u> about studying.*

Students will

1. analyze and respond to satire.
2. compare satire in two literary works.
3. write a comparison of the use of satire in two literary works.

See *TeacherExpress™/Lesson View* for a detailed lesson plan for *Comparing Literary Works.*

Literary Analysis

❶ Satire

- Read the definition and explanation of satire together.

- Emphasize that although some satirists address trivial, superficial issues, such as how someone dresses or talks, they can still be "seriously funny." That is, it is possible to be funny and serious at the same time.

- Be sure students understand that satirists often seek to make an improvement in the world. Whether a satirist attacks one person or a large group, the goal is to make the world a better place by eliminating, or simply exposing error, folly, intellectual or moral weakness, corruption, or outright evil.

❷ Comparing Presentations of Satire

- Remind students that satire can take almost any literary form—fiction, poetry, drama, nonfiction, song lyrics, movie scripts. Here, students will be comparing a satiric play and a satiric essay.

- Give students a copy of **Comparing Satires Graphic Organizer A** (*Graphic Organizer Transparencies,* p. 192). Have them complete it as they read and compare the selections.

Vocabulary Development

Vocabulary Knowledge Rating

Create a **Vocabulary Knowledge Rating Chart** with the selection vocabulary and expressive vocabulary for both selections. Give students a copy. Introduce the words by reading them aloud and having students mark their rating in the Before Reading column. Urge them to be alert to these words as they read and discuss the selection because they will rate their knowledge of the words again after they finish.

If you wish, you may tally how many students know (or think they know) a word to gauge how much instruction you need to provide. As students read, point out the words and their context.

Build Understanding

❸ Connecting to the Literature

Reading/Writing Connection Both of these selections poke fun at an aspect of society or of people's behavior. List a few television shows, movies, or comedians that poke fun at politics, the entertainment industry, or another area of life. Then, briefly explain why you think satire can help people see subjects differently. Use at least three of the following words in your response: *assess, confront, contradict, minimize, construct.*

Meet the Authors

Oscar **Wilde** (1854–1900)

Oscar Wilde was educated in Dublin and at Oxford University, where he became notorious for his wit. While he wrote poems and celebrated works of fiction, it was in his plays that Wilde's genius found its voice.

The Importance of Being Funny In a series of brilliant comedies, including *A Woman of No Importance* and *An Ideal Husband,* Wilde targeted the straight-laced manners and hypocrisy of English society in the 1890s. His masterpiece is *The Importance of Being Earnest* (1895), a drama about Victorian values that still entertains audiences today.

Henry **Alford** (b. 1962)

Henry Alford calls himself an "investigative humorist," a comic journalist who unearths humor wherever it hides. Armed with dry wit and charm, he uncovers what makes popular culture funny, amazing, or outrageous.

Comic Escapades *Big Kiss: One Actor's Desperate Attempt to Claw His Way to the Middle* chronicles Alford's adventures as he tries to become an actor. He faces humiliation at the hands of acting teachers and directors, but he relishes his minor victory as an extra in *Godzilla.*

For: More information about the authors
Visit: www.PHSchool.com
Web Code: epe-9505

from *The Importance of Being Earnest* / from *Big Kiss* ■ 897

❸ Connecting to the Literature

• Model use of the expressive vocabulary students are asked to use with these examples:

1. Satirists help people *assess* the words and actions of public figures.
2. Satire is a powerful way to *confront* corruption.
3. When the facts *contradict* appearances, satire can help reveal the truth.
4. Politicians may try to *minimize* the damage caused by satirical writing.
5. In some satires, readers find out how to *construct* a better society.

• Help students further develop their expressive vocabulary by providing these words: *greed, arrogance,* and *caricature.* Encourage students to use these words as they discuss the selections.

Go Online For additional informa-
Author Link tion about Oscar Wilde and Henry Alford, have students type in the Web Code and then select *Oscar Wilde* or *Henry Alford.*

Teaching Resources

The following resources can be used to enrich, extend, or differentiate the instruction for Comparing Literary Works.

Unit 5 Resources, pp. 145–151

Graphic Organizer Transparencies, pp. 192–195

Listening to Literature Audio CD

❶ Background

The Importance of Being Earnest The subtitle of Wilde's 1895 play is "A Trivial Comedy for Serious People," stressing the vital link between the humorous and the serious. One of Wilde's techniques for achieving this link is to reverse common expressions. *Earnest* is full of lines that are not only funny but also cause us to think about how they might be true. Wilde believed that the purpose of art was a kind of useful lying: "Lying, the telling of beautiful untrue things, is the proper aim of art." Wilde's "lies" do satirize Victorian society, but their main purpose is to be purely delightful. As Wilde said, *Earnest* is "exquisitely trivial, a delicate bubble of fancy, and it has its philosophy. . . . That we should treat all the trivial things of life seriously, and all the serious things of life with sincere and studied triviality."

❷ Motivation

Have students share what they know about Victorian society, including class differences and social expectations. Allow students to preview the images in the selection for ideas. Ask students to predict which aspects of Victorian society would make good topics for satirical writing.

Concept Connector ➡

Students will return to this activity after completing the excerpt from *The Importance of Being Earnest.*

❸ About the Selection

In this excerpt from *The Importance of Being Earnest,* Jack finally gets a chance to propose to Gwendolen. Jack is astounded that Gwendolen loves him, thinking his name Ernest, and he begins his awkward proposal. Lady Bracknell interrupts, sends Gwendolen out, and interviews Jack to determine his suitability for marriage. Her questions satirize Victorian values, and Jack's answers do not satisfy her snobbish requirements. To Lady Bracknell, being found in a handbag does not constitute being of a good family, and she storms out.

from **The Importance of Being Earnest** ❶ ❷ ❸

Oscar Wilde

The following excerpt is from Act I of The Importance of Being Earnest. The play takes place in England in the 1890s, during the reign of Queen Victoria, a time when elegance, manners, and social status were of great importance. In this scene, John Worthing, nicknamed Jack, visits the London apartment of his friend Algernon. Jack loves Algernon's cousin, Gwendolen. In order to maintain his spotless reputation at his home in the country, Jack takes on a different identity when he is in the city. When he is out in the country, he pretends to have a brother named Ernest, and when he visits London, Jack pretends to be Ernest. Gwendolen knows nothing about Jack's real name or his double identity.

898 ■ Drama

CHARACTERS
John Worthing, JP
Lady Bracknell
Hon. Gwendolen Fairfax

Lady Bracknell and Algernon go into the music room, Gwendolen remains behind.

JACK. Charming day it has been, Miss Fairfax.

GWENDOLEN. Pray don't talk to me about the weather, Mr Worthing. Whenever people talk to me about the weather, I always feel quite certain that they mean something else. And that makes me so nervous.

JACK. I do mean something else.

GWENDOLEN. I thought so. In fact, I am never wrong.

JACK. And I would like to be allowed to take advantage of Lady Bracknell's temporary absence. . . .

GWENDOLEN. I would certainly advise you to do so. Mamma has a way of coming back suddenly into a room that I have often had to speak to her about.

❹

JACK. *(nervously)* Miss Fairfax, ever since I met you I have admired you more than any girl . . . I have ever met since . . . I met you.

GWENDOLEN. Yes, I am quite aware of the fact. And I often wish that in public, at any rate, you had been more <u>demonstrative</u>. For me you have always had an irresistible fascination. Even before I met you I was far from indifferent to you. *(Jack looks at her in amazement)* We live, as I hope you know, Mr Worthing, in an age of ideals. The fact is constantly mentioned in the more expensive monthly magazines, and has reached the provincial pulpits I am told; and my ideal has always been to love someone of the name of Ernest. There is something in that name that inspires absolute confidence. The moment Algernon first mentioned to me that he had a friend called Ernest, I knew I was destined to love you.

JACK. You really love me, Gwendolen?

GWENDOLEN. Passionately!

JACK. Darling! You don't know how happy you've made me.

❺ ◀ **Critical Viewing** Judging from the actor playing Jack in this photograph, what do you think Jack will be like? **[Predict]**

Literary Analysis
Satire Which words here make fun of Gwendolen's haughtiness?

Vocabulary Builder
demonstrative
(di mänˊ strə tiv) *adj.*
showing feelings openly

❻ ✅ Reading Check
What is Gwendolen's "ideal"?

from *The Importance of Being Earnest* ■ 899

- Have students read the bracketed passage. Then, **ask** them how Gwendolen manipulates the conversation with Jack from the start.
  Answer: Gwendolen tells Jack that she does not want to talk about the weather.

- **Ask** students the Literary Analysis question: Which words here make fun of Gwendolen's haughtiness?
  Answer: Gwendolen says, "I am never wrong," and she says that she is "quite aware of the fact" that Jack admires her. In fact, she *is* wrong about Jack's name. She also says that she has admonished her mother about barging into rooms, although that seems unlikely.

- **Ask** students in what sense both lovers might be called "enchanted."
  Answer: Jack is so in love with Gwendolen that he ignores her haughtiness and foolishness. Gwendolen, although in love with Jack, seems equally in love with her idea of herself, social forms, and her comical "ideal" to love someone named Ernest.

❺ **Critical Viewing**

Possible response: Some students may expect Jack to be serious; others may think he will be mischevous.

❻ **Reading Check**

Answer: Her "ideal" is to love a man named Ernest.

Differentiated
Instruction   **Solutions for All Learners**

Accessibility at a Glance
Use this information to guide your teaching of the excerpt from *The Importance of Being Earnest.*

Context	A comedy of manners set in Victorian England
Language	Elegant, upper-class speech; satiric quips; witty exchanges
Concept Level	More challenging
Literary Merit	Classic author

❼ Literary Analysis
Satire

- Remind students that, although the speaker indicator in the text says "JACK," Gwendolen believes that she is in love with a man named Ernest.

- **Ask** students the Literary Analysis question: What is ironic about Gwendolen's fascination with the name Ernest and her feelings for Jack?
  Answer: Gwendolen's fascination with Jack is ironic because it is based on a name that is not his. Her passion is founded on an illusion.

- **Ask** students why Gwendolen's fascination with the name Ernest is an example of satire.
  Possible responses: Wilde is making fun of a person who is so shallow that she will fall in love with a man and marry him merely because of his name.

- **Ask** students why Wilde's choice of the name Ernest adds to the satire.
  Answer: Wilde adds to the satire by making the name itself a homonym for *earnest,* a synonym for *sincere.*

❽ Critical Viewing

Possible responses: Jack's expression might be described as showing astonishment, uncertainty, or anxiety.

GWENDOLEN. My own Ernest!

JACK. But you don't really mean to say that you couldn't love me if my name wasn't Ernest?

GWENDOLEN. But your name is Ernest.

JACK. Yes, I know it is. But supposing it was something else? Do you mean to say you couldn't love me then?

❼ **GWENDOLEN.** *(glibly)* Ah! that is clearly a metaphysical speculation, and like most metaphysical speculations has very little reference at all to the actual facts of real life, as we know them.

JACK. Personally, darling, to speak quite candidly, I don't much care about the name Ernest. . . . I don't think the name suits me at all.

GWENDOLEN. It suits you perfectly. It is a divine name. It has music of its own. It produces vibrations.

JACK. Well, really, Gwendolen, I must say that I think there are lots of other much nicer names. I think Jack, for instance, a charming name.

GWENDOLEN. Jack? . . . No, there is very little music in the name Jack, if any at all, indeed. It does not thrill. It produces absolutely no vibrations. . . . I have known several Jacks, and they all, without exception, were more than usually plain. Besides, Jack is a notorious domesticity for John! And I pity any woman who is married to a man called John. She would probably never be allowed to know the entrancing pleasure of a single moment's solitude. The only really safe name is Ernest.

JACK. Gwendolen, I must get christened at once—I mean we must get married at once. There is no time to be lost.

GWENDOLEN. Married, Mr Worthing?

JACK. *(astounded)* Well . . . surely. You know that I love you, and you led me to believe, Miss Fairfax, that you were not absolutely indifferent to me.

GWENDOLEN. I adore you. But you haven't proposed to me yet. Nothing has been said at all about marriage. The subject has not even been touched on.

JACK. Well . . . may I propose to you now?

900 ■ Drama

Literary Analysis
Satire What is ironic about Gwendolen's fascination with the name Ernest and her feelings for Jack?

❽ ▲ **Critical Viewing**
How would you describe the expression on Jack's face in the image above? **[Describe]**

Vocabulary Development

Vocabulary Builder Reinforcement

Students will benefit from additional examples and practice with the Vocabulary Builder words. Reinforce their comprehension with "show-you-know" sentences. The first part of the sentence uses the vocabulary word in an appropriate context. The second part of the sentence—the "show-you-know" part—clarifies the first. Model the strategy with this example:

When he read the questions on the test, he realized his *ignorance;* there were so many facts he simply did not know.

Then give students these sentence prompts, and coach them in creating the clarification part:

1. She knew that a formal dinner was not a place to be *demonstrative;* _____.
   Sample answer: she would have to keep her feelings to herself.

2. The professor admitted his *ignorance;* _____.
   Sample answer: he planned to research the topic later.

GWENDOLEN. I think it would be an admirable opportunity. And to spare you any possible disappointment, Mr Worthing, I think it only fair to tell you quite frankly beforehand that I am fully determined to accept you.

JACK. Gwendolen!

GWENDOLEN. Yes, Mr Worthing, what have you got to say to me?

JACK. You know what I have got to say to you.

GWENDOLEN. Yes, but you don't say it.

JACK. Gwendolen, will you marry me? *(Goes on his knees)*

GWENDOLEN. Of course I will, darling. How long you have been about it! I am afraid you have had very little experience in how to propose.

JACK. My own one, I have never loved anyone in the world but you.

GWENDOLEN. Yes, but men often propose for practice. I know my brother Gerald does. All my girlfriends tell me so. What wonderfully blue eyes you have, Ernest! They are quite, quite blue. I hope you will always look at me just like that, especially when there are other people present.

(Enter Lady Bracknell)

⑨ **LADY BRACKNELL.** Mr Worthing! Rise, sir, from this semi-recumbent posture. It is most indecorous.

GWENDOLEN. Mamma! *(He tries to rise; she restrains him)* I must beg you to retire. This is no place for you. Besides, Mr Worthing has not quite finished yet.

LADY BRACKNELL. Finished what, may I ask?

GWENDOLEN. I am engaged to Mr Worthing, mamma.

(They rise together)

LADY BRACKNELL. Pardon me, you are not engaged to anyone. When you do become engaged to someone, I, or your father, should his health permit him, will inform you of the fact. An engagement should come on a young girl as a surprise, pleasant or unpleasant, as the case may be. It is hardly a matter that she could be allowed to arrange for herself. . . . And now I have a few questions to put to you, Mr Worthing. While I am making these inquiries, you, Gwendolen, will wait for me below in the carriage.

GWENDOLEN. *(reproachfully)* Mamma!

Literary Analysis
Satire What does Lady Bracknell's use of elaborate expressions suggest about her character?

⑩
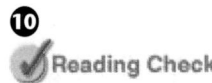Reading Check
What is Gwendolen's response to Jack's proposal?

from *The Importance of Being Earnest* ■ 901

---

⑨ Literary Analysis
Satire

- Tell students that *recumbent* means "lying-down." Remind them that Jack is proposing to Gwendolen, and **ask** what they think "semi-recumbent posture" means.
  Answer: The expression means "kneeling."

- **Ask** students to respond to the Literary Analysis question: What does Lady Bracknell's use of elaborate expressions suggest about her character?
  Answer: Lady Bracknell is devoted to the forms of society and its elegant speech, including euphemisms—words that are considered less offensive than clear and direct speech. Lady Bracknell is a slave to social conventions.

- **Ask** students to explain why Lady Bracknell's use of such expressions is an example of satire.
  Answer: Such expressions reveal that Lady Bracknell is both domineering and prudish. By exaggerating her speech with such expressions, Wilde enables us to laugh at her and recognize that she and the society she represents are overly restrictive, blinded by social convention, and hypocritical.

⑩ Reading Check
Answer: Gwendolen accepts Jack's proposal.

- **Ask** students what questions they think parents should ask a young man who wants to marry their daughter.
Possible response: The main questions should be "Do you love her?" and "Does she love you?" Other questions might involve where and how the young people plan to live.

- Have students read the bracketed passage, and then **ask** them the Literary Analysis question: Is Lady Bracknell truly "a really affectionate mother"? Explain.
Answer: Lady Bracknell is not "really affectionate" because she cares more about money and social position than about her daughter's emotional happiness.

- Have students **explain** why Lady Bracknell's description of herself as "really affectionate" is satirical.
Answer: Her description is satiric because she thinks that "affection" is shown by a concern for money and social position instead of kindness and understanding. Wilde is satirizing her triviality, her mercenary values, and her self-serving attitudes.

LADY BRACKNELL. In the carriage, Gwendolen!

Gwendolen goes to the door. She and Jack blow kisses to each other behind Lady Bracknell's back. Lady Bracknell looks vaguely about as if she could not understand what the noise was. Finally turns round

Gwendolen, the carriage!

GWENDOLEN. Yes, mamma.

Goes out, looking back at Jack

LADY BRACKNELL. *(sitting down)* You can take a seat, Mr Worthing. *(Looks in her pocket for note-book and pencil)*

JACK. Thank you, Lady Bracknell, I prefer standing.

LADY BRACKNELL. *(pencil and note-book in hand)* I feel bound to tell you that you are not down on my list of eligible young men, although I have the same list as the dear Duchess of Bolton has. We work together, in fact. However, I am quite ready to enter your name, should your answers be what a really affectionate mother requires. How old are you?

JACK. Twenty-nine.

LADY BRACKNELL. A very good age to be married at. I have always been of opinion that a man who desires to get married should know either everything or nothing. Which do you know?

JACK. *(after some hesitation)* I know nothing, Lady Bracknell.

LADY BRACKNELL. I am pleased to hear it. I do not approve of anything that tampers with natural <u>ignorance</u>. Ignorance is like a delicate exotic fruit; touch it and the bloom is gone. The whole theory of modern education is radically unsound. Fortunately in England, at any rate, education produces no effect whatsoever. If it did, it would prove a serious danger to the upper classes, and probably lead to acts of violence in Grosvenor Square. What is your income?

JACK. Between seven and eight thousand a year.

Literary Analysis
Satire Is Lady Bracknell truly "a really affectionate mother?" Explain.

Vocabulary Builder
ignorance (ig′ nə rəns) *n.* lack of knowledge or education

Vocabulary Development

Think Aloud: Context
Direct students' attention to the word *reproachfully* at the top of this page. Using a think-aloud process, model how to use context to infer the meaning of an unknown word. Say to students:

I'm going to think aloud to show you how I would figure out the meaning of *reproachfully* from its context.

The stage direction tells how Gwendolen says "Mamma!" Her expres-

sion is "full of reproach." Her mother is telling her to leave the room and wait in the carriage, which Gwendolen does not want to do. Gwendolen disapproves, but in the Victorian era, she would never dare show real anger toward her mother. So *reproachfully* must mean "expressing disapproval or blame."

LADY BRACKNELL. *(makes a note in her book)* In land, or in investments?

JACK. In investments, chiefly.

LADY BRACKNELL. That is satisfactory. What between the duties expected of one during one's lifetime, and the duties exacted from one after one's death, land has ceased to be either a profit or a pleasure. It gives one position, and prevents one from keeping it up. That's all that can be said about land.

JACK. I have a country house with some land, of course, attached to it, about fifteen hundred acres, I believe; but I don't depend on that for my real income. In fact, as far as I can make out, the poachers are the only people who make anything out of it.

LADY BRACKNELL. A country house! How many bedrooms? Well, that point can be cleared up afterwards. You have a town house, I hope? A girl with a simple, unspoiled nature, like Gwendolen, could hardly be expected to reside in the country.

JACK. Well, I own a house in Belgrave Square, but it is let by the year to Lady Bloxham. Of course, I can get it back whenever I like, at six months' notice.

LADY BRACKNELL. Lady Bloxham? I don't know her.

JACK. Oh, she goes about very little. She is a lady considerably advanced in years.

LADY BRACKNELL. Ah, nowadays that is no guarantee of respectability of character. What number in Belgrave Square?

JACK. 149.

LADY BRACKNELL. *(shaking her head)* The unfashionable side. I thought there was something. However, that could easily be altered.

JACK. Do you mean the fashion, or the side?

LADY BRACKNELL. *(sternly)* Both, if necessary, I presume. What are your politics?

JACK. Well, I am afraid I really have none. I am a Liberal Unionist.

LADY BRACKNELL. Oh, they count as Tories. They dine with us. Or come in the evening, at any rate. Now to minor matters. Are your parents living?

JACK. I have lost both my parents.

▲ Critical Viewing

12 How do these actresses' portrayals of Lady Bracknell and Gwendolen compare to your mental image of the characters? **[Compare and Contrast]**

Literary Analysis

Satire Does Gwendolen really have a "simple, unspoiled, nature"? Explain.

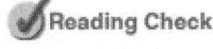

Reading Check

14 On what list of Lady Bracknell's does Jack's name not appear?

from *The Importance of Being Earnest* ■ 903

---

⑫ Critical Viewing
Possible response: She looks exactly as I thought—overdressed, bossy, and loud.

⑬ Literary Analysis
Satire

- Read aloud the bracketed passage, and point out that Lady Bracknell's comment about the country house is another of Wilde's humorous contradictions. Living in the country is usually associated with having a "simple, unspoiled nature."

- **Ask** students the Literary Analysis question: Does Gwendolen really have a "simple, unspoiled nature"? Explain.
  Answer: No, Gwendolen is a more manipulative and calculating person than she says she is. She is fairly wealthy, snobbish, and pampered, and she knows how to get Jack to do whatever she wants.

- **Ask** students why Lady Bracknell's comment about Gwendolen is satiric.
  Answer: Gwendolen is far from simple. Wilde is satirizing the values and attitudes of Gwendolen and her mother. As representatives of their class, both are superficial and manipulative.

⑭ Reading Check
Answer: Jack does not appear on Lady Bracknell's list of young men eligible to marry Gwendolen.

Differentiated Instruction   Solutions for All Learners

Strategy for Less Proficient Readers
Write the following questions on the board: *What does Jack try to do? What does Gwendolen expect Jack to do? Why is Lady Bracknell outraged?* Have students listen to the scene on the **Listening to Literature Audio CD.** Pause the CD several times to allow students to answer the questions aloud.

Strategy for Gifted/Talented Students
Have students perform the excerpt or part of the excerpt. Encourage them to convey the comedy of manners with precise pronunciation and articulation. Remind them that the satire is effective because the characters are serious: Money, marriage, respectability, and social position are vital to them.

903

- **Ask** students the first Literary Analysis question: How does Jack's explanation of being "found" make fun of the Victorian value of proper lineage and family ties?
Answer: Jack's "lineage" is unknown, and his very name is the result of chance, violating the established social order. Wilde reduces "lineage" to an absurd reliance on something ultimately arbitrary and irrelevant.

- **Ask** students why Lady Bracknell is so disturbed by the handbag story.
Answer: The appearance of social impropriety is what most disturbs Lady Bracknell.

- **Ask** students: What quality more important than lineage does Jack have?
Answer: He has a strong and self-less love for Gwendolen.

⑯ **Literary Analysis**
Satire

- **Ask** students what Lady Bracknell's mention of the French Revolution reveals about her values.
Answer: Lady Bracknell compares Jack's personal history to the over-throw of aristocratic values that accompanied the French Revolution. The exaggeration sati-rizes her lack of proportion in any-thing that has to do with manners and morals.

- **Ask** students to respond to the Literary Analysis prompt: Explain how Lady Bracknell's use of exag-geration adds to the satire.
Answer: Her exaggerated concern for "ordinary decencies" and her elaborate, socially acceptable ways of talking about unacceptable mat-ters satirize her society's fears and hypocrisies. Her words are as out of proportion as her values.

- **Ask** students what Lady Bracknell most fears.
Answer: She is terrified that soci-ety may think she is related in any way with a "social indiscretion."

LADY BRACKNELL. Both? . . . That seems like carelessness. Who was your father? He was evidently a man of some wealth. Was he born in what the Radical papers call the purple of commerce, or did he rise from the ranks of the aristocracy?

JACK. I am afraid I really don't know. The fact is, Lady Bracknell, I said I had lost my parents. It would be nearer the truth to say that my parents seem to have lost me. . . . I don't actually know who I am by birth. I was . . . well, I was found.

⑮ **LADY BRACKNELL.** Found!

JACK. The late Mr Thomas Cardew, an old gentleman of a very charitable and kindly disposition, found me, and gave me the name of Worthing, because he happened to have a first-class ticket for Worthing in his pocket at the time. Worthing is a place in Sussex. It is a seaside resort.

LADY BRACKNELL. Where did the charitable gentleman who had a first-class ticket for this seaside resort find you?

JACK. (gravely) In a hand-bag.

LADY BRACKNELL. A hand-bag?

JACK. (very seriously) Yes, Lady Bracknell. I was in a hand-bag—a somewhat large, black leather handbag, with handles to it—an ordinary hand-bag in fact.

LADY BRACKNELL. In what locality did this Mr James, or Thomas, Cardew come across this ordinary hand-bag?

JACK. In the cloak-room at Victoria Station. It was given to him in mistake for his own.

LADY BRACKNELL. The cloak-room at Victoria Station?

JACK. Yes. The Brighton line.

LADY BRACKNELL. The line is immaterial. Mr Worthing, I confess I feel somewhat bewildered by what you have just told me. To be born, or at any rate bred, in a hand-bag, whether it had handles or not, seems to me to display a contempt for the ordinary decencies of family life that reminds one of the worst excesses of the French ⑯ Revolution. And I presume you know what that unfortunate movement led to? As for the particular locality in which the hand-bag was found, a cloak-room at a railway station might serve to conceal a social indiscretion—has probably, indeed, been used for that purpose before now—but it could hardly be regarded as an assured basis for a recognized position in good society.

JACK. May I ask you then what you would advise me to do? I need

904 ■ Drama

Literary Analysis
Satire How does Jack's explanation of being "found" make fun of the Victorian value of proper lineage and family ties?

Literary Analysis
Satire Explain how Lady Bracknell's use of exaggeration adds to the satire.

Vocabulary Development

Word Forms
Expand students' vocabulary by helping them learn related forms of the Vocabulary Builder words. Give students a blank **Word Form Chart** (*General Resources*, p. 16), with *demonstrative* and *ignorance* in the correct columns. Work with the class, or have students work with a partner, to determine the related forms. The final chart should look like the one shown. Hold students accountable for integrating the related forms of the words into their speaking and writing.

Noun	Verb	Adjective	Adverb
demonstration	demonstrate	**demonstrative**	demonstratively
ignorance	ignore	ignorant	ignorantly

hardly say I would do anything in the world to ensure Gwendolen's happiness.

LADY BRACKNELL. I would strongly advise you, Mr Worthing, to try and acquire some relations as soon as possible, and to make a definite effort to produce at any rate one parent, of either sex, before the season is quite over.

JACK. Well, I don't see how I could possibly manage to do that. I can produce the hand-bag at any moment. It is in my dressing-room at home. I really think that should satisfy you, Lady Bracknell.

LADY BRACKNELL. Me, sir! What has it to do with me? You can hardly imagine that I and Lord Bracknell would dream of allowing our only daughter—a girl brought up with the utmost care—to marry into a cloak-room, and form an alliance with a parcel? Good morning, Mr Worthing!

Lady Bracknell sweeps out in majestic indignation

JACK. Good morning! (*Algernon, from the other room, strikes up the Wedding March. Jack looks perfectly furious, and goes to the door*) For goodness' sake don't play that ghastly tune, Algy! How idiotic you are!

Literary Analysis
Satire How does Lady Bracknell's final demand add to the satire?

Thinking About the Selection

1. **Respond:** Would you like to spend time with the characters in this play? Why or why not?

2. **(a) Recall:** How does Gwendolen respond to Jack's proposal? **(b) Infer:** How would you describe Gwendolen's feelings toward Jack?

3. **(a) Recall:** According to Lady Bracknell, how should a young girl learn she is engaged? **(b) Infer:** What do Lady Bracknell's remarks suggest about Victorian attitudes toward marriage and family?

4. **(a) Summarize:** Write a summary of the personal information that Lady Bracknell needs from Jack. **(b) Interpret:** In what ways does Lady Bracknell find Jack both acceptable and unacceptable as a possible husband? **(c) Assess:** Based on her judgment of Jack, describe Lady Bracknell's character.

5. **(a) Draw Conclusions:** What values does Lady Bracknell hold dear? Explain. **(b) Compare and Contrast:** How do you think Lady Bracknell's values compare to the values of most people today? Explain.

from *The Importance of Being Earnest* ■ 905

5. (a) She values money, property, propriety, appearances, and the judgments of society. (b) **Possible response:** In the modern world, social class has less significance than it did for the Victorians, but the influence of money is still great.

charge of arranging marriages, and obedience to parents is expected.

4. (a) She wants to know his age, whether he knows everything or nothing, his income, property, politics, and parents. (b) All of Jack's answers are acceptable, except the tale of his parentage. (c) Her rejection of Jack because of his lack of family shows how dependent she is on rules of propriety and the judgment of society.

⑰ Literary Analysis
Satire

- **Ask** students to identify Lady Bracknell's final demand.
  Answer: She tells Jack to acquire some relations and at least one parent before the social season is over.

- **Ask** students what Lady Bracknell's reference to the "season" means.
  Answer: The "season" refers to the fall and winter months in London, during which period members of the upper class attend balls, theatrical events, and other social engagements.

- **Ask** students to answer the Literary Analysis question: How does Lady Bracknell's final demand add to the satire?
  Answer: It is not possible to manufacture or discover relatives that do not exist. Lady Bracknell's demand emphasizes her belief that nothing is more important than appearances and the requirements of the social season. For all her arrogance, she is herself a slave to social convention.

Concept Connector

Have students return to the Motivation activity on p. 898. Ask them to revise or verify their predictions now that they have read the excerpt.

ASSESS

Answers

1. **Possible response:** No, the characters are so concerned with manners and society that they would be boring.

2. (a) Gwendolen accepts Jack even before he proposes. (b) Gwendolen does seem to like Jack, although her feelings are undoubtedly colored by her concern for proprieties and her odd infatuation with his false name. Jack seems able to give her the social and financial life she wants, but, like her mother, she would almost certainly reject Jack if he did not have money or wasn't pretending to be named Ernest.

3. (a) Her mother or father should inform her. (b) **Possible response:** The remarks indicate the fierce Victorian faith in marriage and family. Parents are in

from **BIG KISS**

ONE ACTOR'S DESPERATE ATTEMPT TO CLAW HIS WAY TO THE MIDDLE

Henry Alford

⑱ ⑲ ⑳

I n the acting profession, as in life, you must make the most of your tiny <u>allotment</u>. He who waits until he has been cast as Othello to pull out all the stops is setting himself up for disappointment—it will be Othello, not Desdemona,[1] who is strangled in this production. So when a classmate told me she was helping to cast extras for the remake of Godzilla, I quickly recommended myself for duty. I clearly had not slayed them at improv camp in Wisconsin; here was an opportunity to channel my feelings of disappointment into bravura acting. And perhaps, in so doing, to achieve every extra's dream: to be awarded a line of dialogue.

    My classmate called me two days later and said that the filming, **㉑** to be done that Sunday, would involve prodigious amounts of stage rain. I assured her that I was no stranger to adverse meteorological conditions, natural and man-made, and, as such, could "play wet."

1. **Othello. . . Desdemona** In Shakespeare's play, *Othello,* kills his wife, Desdemona, because he believes she had an affair. He later discovers she had been faithful and his grief causes him to kill himself.

906 ■ *Drama*

Vocabulary Builder
allotment (ə lät′ mənt)
n. share; portion

Literary Analysis
Satire Which details make Alford's role as an extra sound important?

21

The pay for non-Screen Actors Guild[2] talent was seventy-five dollars; I needed to be available all day and night. I was to wear a raincoat and carry a black umbrella.

The harbinger[3] of location shooting in a metropolitan area is a table on the sidewalk, heaped high with haggard bagels. When I arrived at the appointed location in the Financial District that Sunday morning at six-thirty, although the chaos I found there—Teamsters[4] bickering over sports scores, thick black cables veining the streets as if to depict the late stages of arteriosclerosis—had all the earmarks of filmmaking, I did not see the telltale breadstuffs and so was moved to ask the first walkie-talkie-wielding individual I saw, "Where are the bagels?"

"Are you SAG or non-SAG?" she asked.

"Non."

"You're in the tent."

She pointed to a huge, dun-colored tent around which loitered hundreds of men and women, many of whom were also wearing raincoats and carrying umbrellas. "My people," I exclaimed. I walked over to the tent and, seeing a line formed at one of the twenty or so tables thereunder, queued up. Four minutes later the casting people had checked my name off on a list and I had been given a voucher, the form by which I would be paid.

All was actor-clogged; I could barely find an empty seat at a table. I was glad I finally did—we proceeded to wait for two hours. During this time, small groups of us were presented to a young, unshaven man from Wardrobe who was, by turns, exhausted and sniffy. He looked at the camouflage cap that the fortysomething gentleman ahead of me in line was wearing and said, "I don't know anyone who would wear that cap." Then he scanned me—that is to say, my tan raincoat, my black umbrella, and my wingtips encased in black rubbers—and yawned, "You're fine."

22

Shortly thereafter we were herded down to the set in groups of thirty or forty. The set was Federal Hall, the majestic site of George Washington's inauguration, rich in Corinthian columns and impressive stairways, which dead-ends Broad Street in the manner of a lion's gaping jaws. Halfway up its main stairs was a podium, festooned with red, white, and blue bunting and a sign reading RE-ELECT MAYOR EBERT. I wondered aloud, "Where's the reptile?"

The self-appointed expert in my group explained, "They're gonna blue-screen[5] him in later."

---

2. **Screen Actors Guild (SAG)** labor union for performers.
3. **harbinger** (här´ bin jər) something that comes before to give an indication of what follows.
4. **Teamsters** (tēm´ stərz) members of a large labor union for truck drivers and other occupations.
5. **blue-screen** filming against a blue background, in order to apply special effects later.

Literary Analysis

Satire What does the word "herded" convey about the experience of extras?

Reading Check

What does Alford say is every extra's dream?

from *Big Kiss* ■ 907

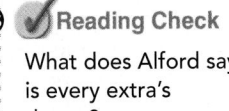

Differentiated Instruction Solutions for All Learners

Accessibility at a Glance
Use this information to guide your teaching of the excerpt from *Big Kiss*.

Context	First-person report of being a movie extra
Language	Contemporary; some comically pretentious vocabulary
Concept Level	More accessible
Literary Merit	Popular; journalistic
Lexile	1150L

cled man was handing out props. It looked like about a third of the extras were being given still cameras and two thirds were being given placards reading RE-ELECT EBERT.

"I hope I get a camera," the woman standing behind me in line said.

Eager to be filmed shooting at Godzilla, I responded, "I hope I get a Taser."

Moments later I was handed three props—a fake 35 millimeter camera, a fanny pack, and a press badge. I looked at the badge. The first thing I noticed was that the photo on it was of the man who had just handed it to me. Hovering over the photo was the name Sean Haworth and the call letters WAQR. These call letters sounded more like radio than TV to me; but then why was I carrying a still camera?

Rather than let this seeming contradiction bother me, I decided to base my character interpretation on it. What if Sean Haworth labored under the impression that if he took a good enough photograph it would be aired on the radio? Wouldn't this, character-wise, raise the stakes, and imbue him with the driven quality that makes for an interesting dramatic character? Poor Sean, you can almost hear the editorial staff at WAQR whispering over the water cooler. If only he understood that ours is an aural medium.

But five minutes later an assistant director who had assembled about a hundred of us in front of Federal Hall took away my camera.

❷❺ "I based my character interpretation on that!" I exclaimed, hoping that this would translate to him as "Serious actor. Could handle a line of dialogue."

"I need it for up front," he reported tersely, then walked to the front of the crowd.

One of my fellow colleagues—a vivacious English as a Second Language tutor and sometime actress in her early thirties with whom I had fallen into conversation back in the tent—witnessed my loss of camera and counseled, "You were probably overpropped anyway."

"Yes," I responded, "my work was getting proppy."

We proceeded to work for almost eleven hours, lunch break included, on variations of a single shot. In it, about four hundred of us New Yorkers are standing in the rain, listening to Mayor Ebert

❷❹ ▼ Critical Viewing How do the "extras" in this image from the movie *Godzilla* help increase the impact of the scene? **[Analyze]**

Literary Analysis
Satire Explain the satire in Alford's reaction when the assistant director takes his camera.

---

5. **blue-screen** filming against a blue background, in order to apply special effects later.

908 ■ *Drama*

Recipe for a Monster

He's big, he's green, he's mean, and his breath is radioactive. Godzilla—named "Gojira" in his native Japan—has been stomping on Tokyo since 1954 when he made his movie debut. A dinosaur transformed into a giant monster as the result of atomic testing, Godzilla's appearance was created by scientists and sculptors using the ingredients below.

Take 1 Tyrannosaurus skeleton + Add 1 Chinese dragon + Mix in a pinch of crocodile 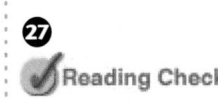 Raise the heat. Serve with a heaping portion of special effects.

Connect to the Literature How do you think Alford's performance might have changed if Godzilla had been played by an actor instead of being a special effect?

(Michael Lerner) give a speech. All of a sudden, we hear a thump. Some of the crowd—those born between January and April, to be precise—look behind them, down Broad Street, whence the sound originates. The mayor continues to netter on when thump! May through August now look down the street, too, expressing restlessness, a sense of discomfort, the vague possibility that this little piece of earth they call their own will soon be rent asunder. Then seconds later a third THUMP!: Godzilla appears, causing the crowd, regardless of natal season, to shriek with abandon, perhaps to drop umbrellas or placards, and to run off in a prescribed direction.

Since I was born in February, my prescribed direction was straight ahead, up the thirty or so stairs of Federal Hall. So, hearing my thump, I would look behind me down Broad Street in highly nuanced, ever-burgeoning panic; erupt into a despair-tinged, Edvard Munch-calibre scream[6] on hearing the third thump; run northward, negotiating my way through what was, by now, a very festival of bad acting; ascend the stairs two at a time; look behind me again while closing my umbrella (note the elegant adherence to decorum, even in the face of apocalypse); and then hurl my body against Federal Hall's massive stone doors in an attempt to gain entry.

6. Edvard Munch-calibre scream an outcry with the intensity of *The Scream*, a famous painting by Norwegian artist Edvard Munch [munk] (1863–1944), which shows a person screaming.

27

✓ **Reading Check**

How do the filmmakers divide the crowd of extras into two groups?

from *Big Kiss* ■ 909

---

26 Literature in Context

Media Connection In *Big Kiss*, Alford's task is to respond to an invisible monster and the filmmakers will "blue-screen him in later." However, blue-screen acting takes skill and practice, and film schools offer courses in how to do it. To improve their believability, acting students learn to focus their eyes and concentrate on simulated objects and actions. They learn to make their imagined perceptions more physically evident to the audience. With the recent growth in computer-generated imagery, some movies—such as *Sky Captain and the World of Tomorrow* (2004)—now combine actors and *entirely* computer-generated backgrounds. As a result, skilled blue-screen actors are more and more in demand.

Connect to the Literature
Discuss with students the pros and cons of having an actor in a costume play Godzilla versus using a special effect. **Ask** students the Connect to the Literature question: How do you think Alford's performance might have changed if Godzilla had been played by an actor instead of being a special effect?
Possible responses: Alford's performance might have been more realistic if he had been able to respond to a physically present monster. However, it may have been more difficult for him to portray genuine terror in the face of a man in a rubber suit.

27 Reading Check

Answer: The people in the crowd are divided according to when they were born.

Differentiated Instruction   Solutions for All Learners

Strategy for Special Needs Students
Have students act out the movements of the crowd of extras, according to Alford's description. Explain that they will react to the thumping sound according to when they were born. Then have them form a group and turn, look, exclaim, and run from the monster in different directions—according to when they were born.

Strategy for Less Proficient Readers
Students may have some difficulty picking up on the humorous tone and satiric intent of some of Alford's lines. Focus on the following lines to help them hear Alford's self-mocking tone and recognize the satire:
"My people," I exclaimed.
"I hope I get a Taser."
"My work was getting proppy."
"Zilla monster ate me baby!"

Satire

- **Ask** students to answer the Literary Analysis question: How do the extras' hopes to be noticed compare to their actual experiences? Explain.

  Answer: The extras hope they will be picked out of the crowd, but they are all reduced to anonymous figures in the rain.

Concept Connector

Ask students to revisit their answers to the questions posed in the Motivation activity. Discuss whether students' opinions about appearing in a movie have changed since reading the excerpt.

ASSESS

Answers

1. (a) Every extra's dream is to be awarded a line of dialogue. (b) **Possible response:** Alford seems to feel his experience was worthwhile because at least he worked in a movie and learned something about himself and the people who work as extras.

2. (a) Alford and the other extras are supposed to look around, shriek, and run away. (b) Many engage in "scenery chewing," some run directly at the camera, and one repeatedly drops and retrieves her prop. (c) They want to be noticed.

3. **Possible responses:** The pros may be the chance of being noticed, a paycheck, and the satisfaction of contributing to a movie. The cons may include anonymity, long hours of waiting, and physical strain.

I loved this work. I would be hard-pressed to recount any event from my personal or professional life that more accurately typified the phrase crazy fun. Yes, my colleagues and I encountered much wetness; the rain machines were <u>assiduous</u> in their ministrations. Moreover, no lines of dialogue were being doled out by the director or assistant directors. But the acting task at hand wedded blitz-krieg-strength drama with stuntman-strength athleticism and, as such, was wholly engaging. Screaming at full force in the canyons of Wall Street on a Sunday morning was particularly liberating. On the first few takes (by the end of the day we would do more than twenty) I would yell, "There he is!" By the eighth take I was screaming, "Here comes trouble!" By the late afternoon, punchy, I was shrieking, in an accent vaguely Caribbean, vaguely Cockney, "'Zilla monster ate me baby!" causing the self-appointed expert to glare at me and say, "Let's keep it real, huh?"

28 This statement might have chastened were it not for the other extras. Seldom have I seen such a preponderance of scenery-chewing; my colleagues' every utterance and movement seemed to offer ready proof that vaudeville[7] is not dead. Several of the extras, in an attempt to make themselves noticed, would run directly at the camera. Another one, a tall, fiftysomething woman who appeared to be a recent graduate of the Lucille Ball School of Clown Makeup, made such a spectacle of repeatedly dropping and then retrieving her umbrella that an assistant director was forced to take the umbrella away from her; the woman, divested of her gimmick, then devoted her energies to shrieking.

"That woman just screamed right in my eardrum," the ESL tutor told me between takes, motioning with her head toward the offender.

"Yes," I acknowledged, "her work is particularly broad."

---

7. **vaudeville** (vôd′ vil) old-fashioned stage shows of mixed specialty acts, including songs, dances, and comic skits.

Thinking About the Selection

1. **(a) Recall:** According to Alford's opening paragraph, what is every extra's dream? **(b) Analyze:** Even though his dream does not come true, does he still feel his experience was worthwhile? Explain.

2. **(a) Recall:** What are Alford and the other extras required to do during the scene? **(b) Generalize:** What do they actually do? **(c) Analyze:** Why do they do so much more than required?

3. **Evaluate:** Based on Alford's account, what do you think are the pros and cons of being an extra in a movie? Explain.

910 ■ *Drama*

Vocabulary Builder
assiduous (ə sij′ ōō əs) *adj.* done with constant and careful attention; diligent

Literary Analysis
Satire How do the extras' hopes to be noticed compare to their actual experiences? Explain.

Vocabulary Development

Vocabulary Knowledge Rating

When students have completed reading and discussing the excerpts from *The Importance of Being Earnest* and *Big Kiss,* have them take out their **Vocabulary Knowledge Rating Chart.** Read the words aloud once more and have students rate their knowledge of the words again in the After Reading column. Clarify any words that are still problematic. Have students write their own definition and example or sentence in the appropriate column. Then, have students complete the **Vocabulary Builder Practice** activities on p. 911. Encourage students to use the words in further discussion and written work about the selections. Remind them that they will be accountable for these words on the Selection Test.

Apply the Skills

from *The Importance of Being Earnest* • from *Big Kiss*

Comparing Satires

1. **(a)** Use a chart like the one shown to identify elements of **satire** in both *The Importance of Being Earnest* and *Big Kiss*.

Selection	Subject of the Satire	Foolishness or Faults Exposed	Author's Tone of Attitude
The Importance of Being Earnest			
Big Kiss			

   (b) Explain specific ways in which both selections use humor to expose people's foolishness or flaws.
2. **(a)** Which selection satirizes serious social issues and which satirizes trivial or light-hearted issues? **(b)** Which selection is harsher towards the people it satirizes? Explain.

Writing to Compare Literary Works

The **perspective**, or vantage point, of the writer helps to shape the satire. In *The Importance of Being Earnest,* Wilde is not part of the events he satirizes. In the excerpt from *Big Kiss,* Alford is a participant in the action, satirizing himself along with the other actors. In an essay, discuss how these different perspectives affect the satire. Use these questions to help organize your thoughts:

- What purpose do you think Wilde had in writing this play about Victorian society?
- Do you think Wilde likes his characters, or finds them funny?
- Does Alford's point of view make him more, or less, sympathetic to the other actors he satirizes?
- How do Alford's inner thoughts and feelings add to the humor of the satire?
- Which satire do you think is more successful? Why?

Vocabulary Builder

Practice Use each word pair below correctly in a sentence.

1. assiduous/energy
2. prodigious/tiny
3. allotment/unfair
4. ignorance/school
5. demonstrative/speaker

QuickReview

Satire: writing that exposes and makes fun of the foolishness and faults of an individual, institution, society, or situation

Go Online
Assessment

For: Self-test
Visit: www.PHSchool.com
Web Code: epa-6509

Apply the Skills ■ 911

911

In this Skills Review, students apply the skills taught in Part 2. The test format gives students practice in taking standardized tests. The results of this review test will help you check students' readiness for the **Benchmark Test** for Unit 5, Part 2.

Applying Reading Skill

Read the passage with students. Remind them to draw conclusions based on dialogue, stage directions, and the author's credibility. Guide them in identifying the details and dialogue that provide the answer to item 1.

If necessary, have students reread the instruction on p. 880 before having them complete the remaining items on their own.

Applying Vocabulary Skills

Remind students that Latin word roots give readers clues to help them infer the meanings of unfamiliar words. Ask students to provide definitions for the roots *-vid-*, *-vis-*, and *-vinc-*. If they have trouble, review the instructions on p. 881.

Point out that the word evident, as it appears in the reading selection, contains the root *-vid-*. Evident is used to describe Elizabeth's unhappy state of mind in the stage direction, and it means "easy to perceive, clear, or obvious." The playwright wants the reader to know that Elizabeth's unhappiness is obvious and that the actress playing her part must display this emotion.

Tips for
Test Taking

Drawing conclusions based on a passage is often difficult for students when they take standardized tests. Explain to students that the basis for any conclusions they draw must be in the passage itself. Suggest that when they select an answer for a question that requires them to draw a conclusion, that they check to see if the basis for that answer appears in the text. If it does not, then the conclusion is not valid.

Reading

Directions: *Questions 1–5 are based on the following selection.*

[*Scene: The lights are brought up on the [small-town] drugstore.* WAITRESS *is there.* INEZ STANLEY *comes into the drugstore. She stands for a moment thinking. The* WAITRESS *goes over to her.*]

WAITRESS. Can I help you?

INEZ. Yes, you can if I can think of what I came in here for. Just gone completely out of my mind. I've been running around all day. You see, I'm expecting some company tonight. My brother Horace. He's coming on a visit.

[ELIZABETH CREWS *and her daughter* EMILY *come into the drugstore.* EMILY *is about seventeen and very pretty. This afternoon, however, it is evident that she is unhappy.*]

ELIZABETH. We've just been by your house.

INEZ. You have? Hello, Emily.

EMILY. Hello.

ELIZABETH. We made some [candy] and took it over for Horace.

INEZ. Well, that's so sweet of you.

ELIZABETH. What time is he coming in?

INEZ. Six thirty.

1. **What is taking place in this scene?**
   A A woman and her daughter meet the woman's friend in a drugstore.
   B A woman is shopping for a dress for her daughter.
   C Two teenagers are discussing a dance.
   D Three women are meeting for lunch.

2. **What can you conclude about Inez?**
   A She is in an angry mood.
   B She is worried about her brother.
   C She is in a hurry.
   D She is distracted.

3. **What can you conclude about Emily?**
   A She does not like Inez.
   B She is anxious to see Horace.
   C She is not her usual self this day.
   D She is angry with her mother.

4. **Based on the dialogue, what might you conclude about Inez's husband, Herman?**
   A He is a very generous and loving husband.
   B He insists on having his meals on time.
   C He does not like Inez to go visiting.
   D He likes to help out around the house.

5. **What can you conclude about Elizabeth and Emily?**
   A Elizabeth and Emily are devoted to each other.
   B Elizabeth seems to be domineering.
   C Emily is a sullen and difficult daughter.
   D Emily treats her mother with disrespect.

912 ■ *Drama*

ASSESS
Answers

1. A	9. B
2. D	10. A
3. C	11. C
4. B	12. D
5. B	13. A
6. C	14. D
7. B	15. B
8. B	

Assessment Practice

Vocabulary

Directions: *Choose the word that best completes the sentence.*

6. Margaret was able to _____ her friend to go to the movies.
   A compile
   B revise
   C convince
   D implement

7. The committee decided to _____ the plan for a new school building.
   A convince
   B implement
   C compile
   D strategize

8. Virginia developed a _____ for studying for the exam.
   A compilation
   B strategy
   C mechanism
   D trial

9. She did not have time to _____ the draft of her essay.
   A compile
   B revise
   C convince
   D implement

10. The reporter had to _____ his list of sources for the article.
    A strategize
    B convince
    C revise
    D implement

Directions: *Choose the correct word for each definition or explanation.*

11. the state of having overcome a challenge
    A conviction
    B vision
    C victorious
    D convict

12. one who goes to see an exhibit
    A supervisor
    B convict
    C visionary
    D visitor

13. one who oversees and directs another's work
    A supervisor
    B visionary

C revisionist
D convict

14. one who has been found guilty and imprisoned
    A victim
    B visionary
    C supervisor
    D convict

15. an image of something beyond one's self
    A revision
    B vision
    C convict
    D visionary

If students answer any of these questions incorrectly, have them review the instruction on the following pages in Part 2 before taking the **Benchmark Test.**

Question	Pages Where Instruction Is Located:
1	880, 882
2	880, 882
3	880, 882
4	880, 882
5	881
6	881
7	881
8	881
9	881
10	881
11	890
12	890
13	890
14	890
15	890

Benchmark

Administer the **Benchmark Test** for Unit 5, Part 2. If the Benchmark Test reveals that some students need further work, use the Interpretation Guide to determine the appropriate reteaching page in the **Reading Kit.** You will also find the same instruction and practice available on **Success Tracker.**

Go Online
Vocabulary

For: Interactive Crossword Puzzles
Visit: www.PHSchool.com
Web Code: epj-5502
Give students this Web Code to access interactive crossword puzzles using Academic Vocabulary and Vocabulary Skill words from Part 2.

Meeting Your Standards

Students will

1. understand the reasons to end a word with a silent *e*.
2. know when to drop the silent *e* when adding suffixes.
3. know when to keep the silent *e* when adding suffixes.

Using Silent *e*

- Read the instruction aloud. Explain that there are a number of reasons to end a word with a silent *e*. Remind students that often the silent *e* affects the pronunciation of the word. In fact, some different words are spelled the same except for the silent *e*, such as *bit* and *bite*.

- Review the reasons to drop the *e* when adding a suffix. Remind students to drop the *e* when the added word ending begins with a vowel. For example, *convince* becomes *convinced*, not *convinceed*. **Ask** students to list some suffixes that would eliminate the silent *e*. **Possible answers:** Students may find the word endings *-ing, -ance, -ant, -ent, -ence, -ive, -able*, and *-ed*.

- Review the reason to keep the final *e*. Remind students to keep the silent *e* when the added word ending begins with a consonant. For example, *engage* becomes *engagement*, not *engagment*. **Ask** students to list suffixes that follow this rule. **Possible answers:** Students may find the word endings *-ment, -ly, -s*, and *-ful*.

- Remind students to proofread their writing to check for any errors with the use of the silent *e*.

✍ Writing and Grammar, Gold Level
Students will find additional spelling instruction in Chapter 30, Section 4.

Spelling Workshop

Using Silent *e*

In English, silent *e* performs a number of jobs. Knowing these jobs will help you determine when you should and should not add silent *e* to the end of a word.

In addition, there are rules for when to keep or drop the *e* at the end of a word when adding suffixes. Knowing these rules will help you spell different forms of a word correctly.

Reasons to end a word with silent *e*
- It makes the vowel in the preceding syllable say its name.
- English words usually do not end with a *v* or a *u*.
- It softens the final *c* or *g*.
- It avoids a syllable with no vowel. This usually applies to words that end with the *l* sound, like *bottle*.
- It helps avoid confusion. Words that end in a consonant followed by an *s* look like plurals. The *e* following the consonant *s* combination eliminates confusion.

Drop the *e*
- When the ending you are adding begins with a vowel: amaze, amazing

Keep the *e*
- When the ending you are adding begins with a consonant: amaze, amazement

Practice A Write each word from the word list. Identify the reason that helps you remember to use an *e* at the end of the word. Then, identify another word that illustrates the reason.

Practice B Use the rules for keeping or dropping the *e* to add the word endings indicated.

1. revise + ing
2. alternative + ly
3. involve + ing
4. involve + ment

914 ■ *Drama*

Word List
alternative
circumstance
revise
involve
resource
college
credible
rectangle
dense
engage

Teaching Resources

The following resource can be used to enrich or extend the instruction for this Spelling Workshop.

Unit 5 Resources
Spelling Workshop: Using Silent *e*, p. 160

Assessment Practice

Directions: *Choose the sentence in which all the words are spelled correctly.*

1. **A** We looked for an alternative solution to the problem.
   B The circumstances made it difficult to bring the task to completeion.
   C The expert we had hired was an excellent resours.
   D In the end, we had to revis the plan.

2. **A** Their involvment was very helpful.
   B The shrubs around the house grew densly.
   C I am almost finished completeing my college application.
   D We drew a rectangle around the word we needed to study.

3. **A** The author gave credibl reasons for accepting his ideas.
   B We hoped to find an alternativ way to get to the store.
   C His story is engaging because the characters are so interesting.
   D Alternatively, you could involv several other students.

4. **A** We consulted several credibel resources.
   B The dense foliage blocked the sun.
   C We wanted to go to the party, but we had another engagment.
   D My sister started collage this year.

5. **A** The painting was abstract, with several rectangals of different colors.
   B We spent a long time revising the paper.
   C The circumstanses were favorable for us to succeed.
   D This book is a good resourc for the information.

6. **A** We hoped more students would become involvd.
   B The dens fog made driving difficult.
   C Colege is a good place to meet new people.
   D He gave a credible reason for being late.

7. **A** Did you involve all the students by asking their opinons?
   B Consult several resoursis before making a decision.
   C We tried to engage the children in a conversation, but they were shy.
   D An alternativ game plan was needed.

8. **A** The zookeeper tried engageing the monkeys with new toys.
   B We need to revize the plan before we present it.
   C We identified the circumstance that was causing the problem.
   D This book is an alternativ to the one that you are reading.

9. **A** He told an incredibel story.
   B We needed to revise only a few words.
   C She announced her engagment on Saturday.
   D We will involve everyone in coming up with an alternateve plan.

10. **A** We wanted to announce the news yesterday, but the announcment did not come out until today.
    B Who will help you when you are revising your paper?
    C The roads were clogged with dens traffic.
    D That is an incredable idea.

Spelling Workshop ■ 915

Practice A

1. *Alternative:* English words do not end with a *v* or a *u*. Another word that follows this rule is *revolve*.

2. *Circumstance;* the silent *e* softens the final *c* or *g*. Another word that follows this rule is *sauce*.

3. *Revise;* the silent *e* helps avoid confusion so that it doesn't look like a plural. Another word that follows this rule is *confuse*.

4. *Involve;* English words do not end with a *v* or a *u*. Another word that follows this rule is *interrogative*.

5. *Resource;* the silent *e* softens the final *c* or *g*. Another word that follows this rule is *dance*.

6. *College;* the silent *e* softens the final *c* or *g*. Another word that follows this rule is *page*.

7. *Credible;* the silent *e* avoids a syllable with no vowel. Another word that follows this rule is *syllable*.

8. *Rectangle;* the silent *e* avoids a syllable with no vowel. Another word that follows this rule is *divisible*.

9. *Dense;* the silent *e* helps avoid confusion so that it doesn't look like a plural. Another word that follows this rule is *revise*.

10. *Engage;* the silent *e* softens the final *c* or *g*. Another word that follows this rule is *rage*.

Practice B

1. *revising*
2. *alternatively*
3. *involving*
4. *involvement*

Assessment Practice

A

1. A	6. D
2. D	7. C
3. C	8. C
4. B	9. B
5. B	10. B

From the Author's Desk

Gary L. Blackwood

Show students Segment 3 on Gary L. Blackwood on the *From the Author's Desk DVD.* Discuss the value of primary and secondary sources in research writing.

Writing Genres

Using the Form Point out to students that elements of research writing are often incorporated into other types of writing. Offer these examples:

- Original scientific research requires documentation and a coherently written report.

- Reporting on current events for newspapers or magazines relies on reliable research and accurate documentation.

- Biographical writing uses quotations and information from accurate sources that detail the subject's life.

Writing Workshop
Work in Progress

If students have done the Work-in-Progress assignments throughout Part 2, suggest that they examine their recorded ideas as they begin prewriting. They may have an idea in their portfolios that they wish to research.

Online Essay Scorer

A writing prompt for this mode of writing can be found on the *PH Online Essay Scorer* at PHSuccessNet.com.

916

Research Writing: Research Report

A **research report** presents and interprets information gathered through the extensive study of a subject. Use the steps outlined in this workshop to write a research report.

Assignment Write a research report on a subject that is both interesting and worth exploring in depth.

What to Include Your research report should feature the following characteristics of research writing:

- a thesis statement that is clearly expressed
- factual support from a variety of reliable, credited sources
- a clear organization that includes an introduction, a body, and a conclusion
- a bibliography or works-cited list that provides a complete listing of research sources formatted in an approved style
- error-free grammar, including the correct use of adverb clauses

To preview the criteria on which your research report may be assessed, see the rubric on page 927.

Writing Workshop: *Work in Progress*

If you have completed the Work-in-Progress assignment, you have several ideas in your portfolio that you might wish to pursue in your report. You may continue to develop these ideas, or you might explore a new idea as you complete this Writing Workshop.

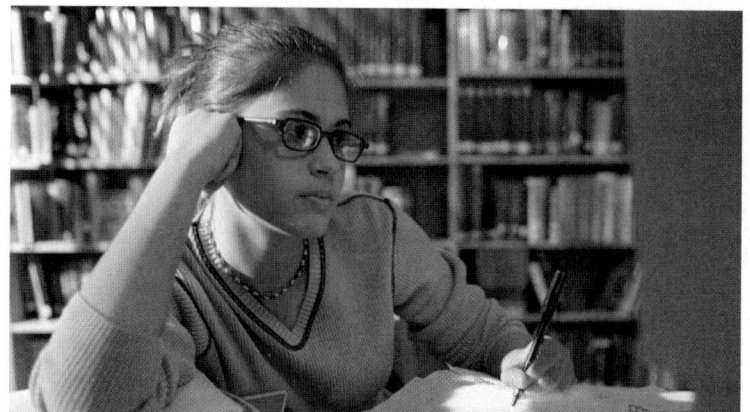

916 ■ Drama

Using the Form

You may use elements of research in these types of writing:

- lab reports
- documentaries
- annotated bibliographies
- histories
- persuasive essays

To get a feel for research writing, read the selection from *Nothing To Fear* by Alan Axelrod on page 515.

Prewriting

Choosing Your Topic

- **Brainstorm for Categories** Identify an area of general interest, and rapidly list more specific categories that come to mind. For example, from the general area of art, you might list the following: sculpture, drawing, painting, and ceramics. Repeat the process: from painting, you might list Impressionism, Cubism, and Pop Art. Continue listing categories until you find a topic that you would like to research.

- **Notebook Review** Flip through the notebooks you keep for each class in school to find subjects or ideas that spark your interest. Choose one of these as the topic of your research paper.

Narrowing Your Topic

Identify an open-ended research question. Before you begin, consider a question that you would like to answer about your topic. Review your notes, and jot down a question that expresses this interest clearly. The question will help you identify specific information and avoid gathering details and data that are too broad for your purpose. In fact, the answer to your question may become your thesis statement.

   Question: How did the school of painting called Impressionism begin?

Gathering Details Through Research

Use a variety of primary and secondary sources. As you study your topic, use both *primary sources* (firsthand or original accounts, such as interview transcripts and newspaper articles) and *secondary sources* (accounts that are not original, such as encyclopedia entries).

Find appropriate sources. Depending on your topic, you may find the information you need in specialized resources such as almanacs (for social, cultural, and natural statistics), government publications (for law, government programs, and information on subjects such as agriculture), information services, and microfiche (for back issues of periodicals). Consult your librarian to determine the best sources to use.

   You can find sources of specific information through a card catalog, an online search, or these more complex resources:

Databases: Access databases of information to find appropriate sources. For example, the Modern Language Association (MLA) database indexes articles on topics within the humanities.

Work in Progress
Review the work you did on page 891.

Writing Workshop ■ 917

Prewriting

- Help students **choose a topic** for their reports by suggesting they choose something from a list of things that interest them, such as people, careers, conflicts, historical events, and so on.

- Tell students to identify a research question to **narrow their topics** by filling out the first two columns of a KWL chart. In the first column, have them list topics that they know something about. In the second column, have them write several questions they have about the topics. For instance, if they are interested in NASCAR, one of their questions might be, "How and when did NASCAR get started?" Tell students to choose the question that they are most interested in. Students may wish to complete the KWL chart after they write.

continued on p. 918

Tips for
Using Rubrics

- Before students begin work on this assignment, have them preview the Rubric for Self-Assessment (p. 927) to know what is expected.

- Review the Assessment criteria in class. Before students use the Rubric for Self-Assessment, work with them to rate the student model by applying one or two criteria to it.

- If you wish to assess students' research report with either a 4-point or a 6-point scoring rubric, see *General Resources,* pp. 61–62.

Prewriting (cont.)

- As students are **gathering details** remind them that some Internet sites provide unreliable and undocumented information. Tell students that *.gov, .edu* and *.org* websites are generally more reliable than *.com* websites.

- Contact a librarian and arrange for students to go on a guided library tour. Have the librarian point out to students where and how they can find information, such as how to gain access to database indexes and where they can find periodicals. Make sure that the librarian shows students the type of information that each source presents. Encourage students to ask the librarian questions.

Six Traits Focus

✔ Ideas	Word Choice
Organization	Sentence Fluency
Voice	Conventions

⚜ Writing and Grammar, Gold Level

Students will find additional instruction on prewriting for a research report in Chapter 12, Section 2.

Writing and Grammar Interactive Textbook CD-ROM

Students can use the following tools as they complete their research report:

- KWL Chart
- Transitions Words
- Language Variety

Gathering Details Through Research, (continued)

Indexes: Locate magazine or newspaper articles by consulting the *Readers' Guide to Periodical Literature*.

SAMPLE *READERS' GUIDE* ENTRY

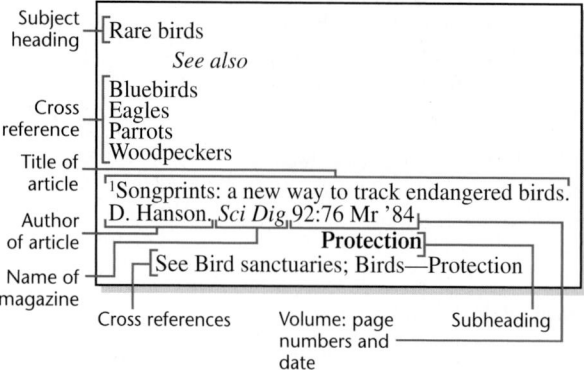

Question your sources. As you locate information, choose sources representing a variety of viewpoints. If you find information you do not trust, consult a second source to verity its validity.

Record and organize information. Take notes as you locate pertinent information, and keep a reference list of every source you use.

- **Source Cards:** Create a separate source card that identifies the author, title, publisher, city, date of publication, and page number of each source you consult. For Internet sources, record the name and Web address of the site, as well as the date you accessed the information.

- **Notecards:** For each item of information, create a separate notecard that includes both the fact or idea and its source.

Quote accurately. Responsible research begins with the first note you take. Be sure to quote and paraphrase your sources accurately so you can identify these sources later. In your notes, circle all quotes and paraphrases to distinguish them from your own comments. When photocopying from a source, include the copyright information. Be sure to include the Web addressess of printouts from online sources.

Source Card

[A]

Marsh, Peter, M.D. *Eye to Eye: How People Interact.* Topsfield, MA: Salem House Publishers, 1988. (p. 54)

Note Card

Gestures vary from culture to culture. The American "OK" symbol (thumb and forefinger) is considered insulting in Greece and Turkey.

Source Card: A

Drafting

Shaping Your Writing

Propose a thesis statement. Review your notes and take a position that can be supported by most of the information that you have gathered. Include this position in your draft in the form of a thesis statement.

> **Sample Thesis Statement:** Claude Monet's handling of light in his water lily paintings is typical of Impressionist techniques.

Choose a text structure. Use your thesis statement and your knowledge of your audience to choose an organizational structure. Consider these options:

- **Chronological order:** present events in the order in which they occur; ideal for reporting a subject's history

- **Order of importance:** present details in order of increasing or decreasing significance; ideal for building an argument

- **Comparison and contrast:** present similarities and differences; ideal for addressing two or more subjects

Write an outline. To make an outline, use headings to identify the main idea you will cover in each section of your report. Order these ideas so they flow logically. Use this outline to develop your draft.

Providing Elaboration

Make direct references to sources. Use one of these methods to incorporate the facts, examples, and quotations you have found:

- **Direct Quotation** Enclose a writer's exact words in quotation marks. Be sure any omission does not alter the intent of the passage. Indicate omitted words with **ellipses,** or three dots.

- **Paraphrase** Restate a writer's specific ideas in your own words, accurately reflecting the writer's meaning.

- **Summary** Condense an extended idea into a brief statement in your own words. Use a summary to introduce background information or to review the key ideas of your own report.

Credit your sources. To avoid **plagiarism**—presenting another's work as your own—you must include documentation every time you use another writer's ideas. Circle all ideas and words in your draft that are not your own. Note the author's last name and the page numbers of material used. Later, you can use these notes to create formal citations.

Writing Workshop ■ 919

Drafting

- Remind students that a thesis statement clearly communicates the main idea or purpose of an essay.

- Explain that drafting an essay is easier once an organizational system has been chosen. Discuss the merits of each type of organization described in the text. Ask for volunteers to share their topic and the type of organization that they are thinking of using.

- Give students a copy of the Outline in **Graphic Organizer Transparencies,** p. 237, and have them use it to outline their ideas.

- Show students how to paraphrase by writing the following example on the chalkboard:

  Direct Quotation: *"Eleanor of Aquitaine was a medieval woman who leaped over the barriers of proper behavior set for her sex."*

  Paraphrase: *Eleanor of Aquitaine did not conform to the expectations for women during the Middle Ages.*

- Give students the following examples of transition words and phrases: *as a result, consequently, also, despite, however,* and *for instance.*

  Encourage students to use these and other transition words and phrases as they integrate their references.

Six Traits Focus

✔	Ideas		Word Choice
✔	Organization		Sentence Fluency
	Voice		Conventions

WG Writing and Grammar, Gold Level

Students will find additional instruction on drafting a research report in Chapter 12, Section 3.

Differentiated Instruction   Solutions for All Learners

Strategy for Less Proficient Readers

Help students identify gaps in their research by analyzing their topics in terms of *who?, what?, when?, where?, why?,* and *how?* Have students create questions using these words, such as the following: Who was Jackie Robinson? What did he do to become a good ballplayer? When was he recognized for his achievements? Where did he play before he joined the major league? Why was he ostracized by fans? How did he overcome taunts and cruelties? Answers to these questions can help students identify areas that need further research and give students ideas for their outlines.

From the Author's Desk

Gary L. Blackwood

On Showing, Not Telling

Gary L. Blackwood

To me, research is as much fun as beachcombing: You never know what fascinating items you're going to find. Since books are generally more reliable than the Internet, I do most of my beachcombing in libraries. I know that some people consider nonfiction dull, but I find good nonfiction more compelling than a novel, because I know the events really happened. Who could invent a story as singular and mysterious as that of Kaspar Hauser, which I came upon while researching my four-volume work *Unsolved History*?

"It helps to read sentences aloud."
—Gary L. Blackwood

Professional Model:

from *Perplexing People,* a volume in the *Unsolved History* series published by Benchmark Books (Marshall Cavendish) Sept. 2005

~~Sometime in the afternoon of~~ ʌ*On* May 26, 1828, a peculiar boy of about sixteen appeared, seemingly from nowhere, on a street in the German city of Nuremberg. His clothing was shabby and ill-fitting and he walked with a ~~peculiar~~ʌ*strange* waddling gait, as though intoxicated. His face wore a vacant expression; he spoke and understood only a few words. Within a year he would become one of the ~~best known and most discussed~~ ʌ*most celebrated and controversial* people in Europe. . . .

The police questioned the boy, but his replies consisted of two phrases in ungrammatical German: "Don't know" and "I want to be a horseman as my father is." When they gave him paper and a pen ~~and asked to write his name and address,~~ he produced a series of scribbles, of which only two were intelligible: "cavalryman" and "Kaspar Hauser."

Writing can be factual without also being sleep-inducing. I try to liven things up by using vivid adjectives.

To add interest and a feeling of authenticity, I use a lot of quotes from primary sources—people who actually witnessed or participated in the events or chroniclers of the time.

Good prose—whether it's fiction or nonfiction—is clear and concise. I do a lot of cutting of superfluous words and phrases, and I may reword a sentence half a dozen times before I'm satisfied with it.

920 ■ *Drama*

Tips for
Improving Word Choice

Revising

Revising Your Overall Structure

Evaluate your sources. Underline any fact in your draft that may not have a trustworthy source. For example, you may have found information from a newspaper or a Web site known for sensationalizing or exaggerating events. Try to confirm this information through a more reliable source, such as an established encyclopedia, a scholarly Web site, or a reputable newspaper. If you cannot verify essential information, consider removing it from your draft.

Student Model: Evaluating Sources

A good way for people to convey a positive message is to avoid certain movements. ~~When people cross their arms it is always a sign of defensiveness.~~

> The writer found that this was a controversial claim that was supported by only one source. Since it was inessential to her basic argument, she chose to eliminate it.

Revising Your Word Choice

Revise to vary word choice. Except for specific terminology required by your topic, avoid overuse of words and expressions. Review your draft to identify words that you may have overused. For each, generate a list of possible synonyms, and substitute them as appropriate.

Example Synonym Banks

invention: innovation, development, contrivance, device
theory: belief, policy, system, position, idea, supposition

Peer Review: Exchange drafts with a partner. As you read each other's reports, circle or highlight words that recur over and over. Working together, identify replacements to improve word variety in the writing.

Revising Your Format

Revise to follow a consistent format. As you finalize your report, be sure that it meets your teacher's criteria for length, format, and documentation of sources. The Modern Language Association (MLA) requires parenthetical citations of sources and a works-cited list that includes only the sources used in the report.

To credit sources within a research paper, include direct documentation in the form of footnotes, endnotes, or parenthetical citations. At the end of your paper, provide a reference list giving complete bibliographic information. If possible, use the footnoting function in a word processing program to aid your efforts.

Tips for
Using Technology in Writing

If students who are using word processors decide to order their information differently, suggest that they use the cut-and-paste function to quickly move their sentences and paragraphs to different places in the report.

Remind students that they should save their document frequently during their revisions to prevent any loss of work.

Revising

- Students may have difficulty deciding if their sources are reliable. Have students work in pairs to evaluate each other's work and find additional sources to confirm information.

- Remind students of your criteria for length, format, and documentation of sources.

- Emphasize to students that when they document sources they must follow the standard format exactly. Tell students to pay attention to the order of the information, the punctuation marks used, and the use of italics. Tell students that even the smallest details of formatting are important.

- Tell students that when they replace overused words with synonyms, they should make sure that the new word fits into the context of the sentence. Give students the following example of two revisions and **ask** students which revision is a better choice. Have students explain their answers.
  Original sentence: *Olivia deduced a change in her friend. She couldn't decide if the change was mental or physical.*
  Revision #1: *Olivia inferred a change in her friend. She couldn't decide if the change was mental or physical.*
  Revision #2: *Olivia noticed a change in her friend. She couldn't decide if the mutation was mental or physical.*
  Answer: Revision #1 is a better choice because it fits the context of the sentence better. The use of *inferred* indicates a process of thought rather than the act of simple observation that *noticed* suggests. In addition, the word "mutation" in revision #2 is an inappropriate word choice for this context.

- Encourage students to use a thesaurus when revising to vary word choice.

Six Traits Focus

	Ideas	✔	Word Choice
✔	Organization		Sentence Fluency
	Voice		Conventions

Writing and Grammar, Gold Level
Students will find additional guidance for revising a research report in Chapter 12, Section 4.

Revising (cont.)

- Tell students that when they replace overused words with synonyms they should make sure that the new word fits into the context of the sentence. Give students the following example of two revisions and **ask** students which revision is a better choice. Have students explain their answers.
  Original sentence: *Olivia noticed a change in her friend. She couldn't decide if the change was mental or physical.*
  Revision #1: *Olivia noticed a change in her friend. She couldn't decide if the difference was mental or physical.*
  Revision #2: *Olivia noticed a change in her friend. She couldn't decide if the mutation was mental or physical.*
  Answer: Revision #1 is a better choice because it fits the context of the sentence better. The use of *mutation* implies a deeper, more scientific change and therefore, does not fit in the context of these sentences.
- Encourage students to use a thesaurus when revising to vary word choice.

Six Traits Focus

	Ideas	✔	Word Choice
✔	Organization		Sentence Fluency
	Voice		Conventions

WG **Writing and Grammar, Gold Level**

Students will find additional guidance for revising a research report in Chapter 12, Section 4.

Writing Workshop

Preparing a Reference List

Bibliographic Form Present your sources in a standardized format. Include authors' names, source titles, place of publication, publishers, and the dates of publication. For online references, indicate the date on which you accessed the site. The following examples are in MLA format:

For a book with one author:

Wolfe, Tom. *The Right Stuff.* New York: Bantam Books, 1979.

For an article:

Quittner, Joshua. "Digital Video Daze." *Time.* 2 Nov. 1998: 112.

For an online source:

"Half Past Autumn: Newshour Transcript" *Online Newshour.* 19 Oct. 1998. http://www.pbs.org/newshour/bb/ entertainment/jan–june98/gordon_1/

Footnotes and endnotes When using footnotes or endnotes to provide citation, include full details about the source and cite the page number. Indicate a citation by placing a number at the end of a passage. Place footnote documentation at the bottom of the page on which the number appears; place endnote documentation on a page preceding the reference list.

First footnote or endnote for a book:

1. Wolfe, Tom, *The Right Stuff* (New York: Bantam books, 1979), 61.

Subsequent footnotes or endnotes citing same source:

2. Wolfe 92.

Parenthetical citations To cite parenthetically, include source information in parentheses after the quoted material. This information, along with your reference list, directs readers to your source.

> In her analysis of heroic behavior, Lewis suggests, "If you look inside yourself, you might find a hero waiting" (Lewis 90).

For more information on citing sources, see page R33–34.

Integrating Grammar Skills

Revising to Combine Sentences Using Adverb Clauses

Adverb clauses can be used to combine information from two sentences into one sentence. Often, the revised sentence will make an intended meaning more obvious.

Prentice Hall Writing and Grammar Connection: Chapter 21, Section 2

Two sentences: I joined the panel. Jay is the leader.
Combined: I joined the panel because Jay is the leader.

Identifying Adverb Clauses A clause is any group of words with a subject and a verb. An *independent clause* can stand by itself as a complete sentence; a *subordinate clause* is not complete because it does not express a full idea. An *adverb clause* is a subordinate clause that modifies a noun in a sentence. It begins with a subordinating conjunction that tells *where, when, in what way, to what extent, under what condition,* or *why.*

When: *After I read the report,* I agreed with the mayor.
Condition: Don will ask for a refund *if you will go with him.*
In what way: The bulldog yawned *as if he were utterly bored.*
Why: I drew a map *so that they would not get lost.*

Combining Sentences When combining two short sentences using adverb clauses, follow these steps.

1. **Look for a relationship between the ideas of the two clauses.**

2. **Select the appropriate subordinate conjunction to show that relationship.** Place the adverb clause at the beginning or end of the combined sentence—wherever it conveys your intent more clearly.

3. **Use a comma to separate a subordinate clause only when it begins a sentence.**

Common Subordinate Conjunctions			
after	because	since	when
although	before	so that	whenever
as	even though	unless	whether
as soon as	if	until	while

Apply It to Your Editing

Review several paragraphs of your report and highlight any consecutive short sentences that you find. Look for a possible adverbial relationship (*where, when, in what way,* and so on) in two of the sentences. Following the steps outlined here, combine the sentences using an appropriate subordinating conjunction.

Integrating Grammar Skills

- Write the words *even if, in order that, once, although, before, while,* and *when* on the board and explain that these are additional subordinate conjunctions students might use to introduce an adverb clause in their reports.

- Ask students to practice identifying the adverb clauses in the following sentences. Then, have them **identify** the word that the clause modifies:

  1. NASCAR has become a part of the American landscape *because Americans are in love with their cars.*
     Answer: The clause modifies "has become."

  2. NASCAR drivers tend to play up their bad-boy reputations *when they are interviewed on television.*
     Answer: The clause modifies "play up."

  3. The weight of their reputations feels heavier *than it ever has.*
     Answer: The clause modifies "heavier."

Writing and Grammar, Gold Level

Students will find additional instruction on combining sentences using adverb clauses in Chapter 3, Section 1 and Chapter 22, Section 2.

Differentiated Instruction — Solutions for All Learners

Strategy for Special Needs Students

Review the major parts of speech with students using the following example sentences.

- The *fans* cheer. (noun subject)
- *Run* home! (verb)
- Robinson hits the *ball.* (direct object)
- The players run *fast.* (adverb)
- What a *noisy* crowd! (adjective)
- I want to go *to the game.* (prepositional phrase)

Write each sentence on the board and underline the italicized words. Ask students to identify the parts of speech. Provide help and additional examples if necessary.

Student Model

- Explain that the Student Model is a sample and that their own research reports may be longer.

- Tell students that it is important to grab the reader's attention immediately so that readers become engaged in your report and are interested in reading on.

- Point out to students that the second sentence immediately uses a paraphrase from a source to back up the first sentence. **Ask** students why that is an effective technique. **Possible responses:** By quoting an expert stating that 68% of human communication is nonverbal, Lyndsey immediately sets her point up as valid. The reader now is ready to accept the premise of the paper and the examples and details that follow.

- Write the following sample thesis statement on the board and model how to clarify it.

  Jackie Robinson joined the Major Leagues against the wishes of many white players even though he had an outstanding record.

  Revised: *Despite Jackie Robinson's outstanding record, many white players opposed his addition into the Major Leagues.*

Student Model: Lyndsey Regan
Canyon Country, CA

Body Language

When we speak to other people, they are not only listening to our actual words, but sensing our facial expression, tone of voice, gestures, level of eye contact, posture, and movements as well. Nonverbal communication, or body language, makes up approximately 65 percent of human communication (Aylesworth 3). Body language has a major impact on how others perceive what we say. It can also be a tool for miscommunication when the speaker and listener are from different cultures or are communicating through technology that deprives them of visual cues. In fact, we often realize the importance of body language only when we cannot interpret someone else's body language correctly.

In *Eye to Eye: How People Interact,* Dr. Peter Marsh explains that before we speak, our gestures, posture, and facial expressions are already broadcasting messages to those around us. While we are speaking, these gestures continue to communicate messages—usually clarifying what we are saying, but sometimes contradicting us in telltale ways (Marsh 116–119).

Often, body language is an unconscious act that triggers the most developed senses in other people—hearing and sight (Aylesworth 18). That is why body language is such a great way to emphasize words and ideas. Many people take advantage of this. Advertisers, for example, cast actors in their commercials who use body language that appeals to viewers.

Studies have shown that people's body language changes when they are not telling the truth (Vrij, Edward, Roberts, and Bull 239–263). If someone's body language is inconsistent with what he or she is saying, people tend to believe what the body is telling them. A good way for people to convey a positive message is to avoid certain movements, like fidgeting or letting your eyes wander. Instead, good communicators maintain steady eye contact, nod in agreement, and smile. You may notice that people on television, like hosts of infomercials and talk-shows, generally display this positive body language when speaking.

The opening line captures the reader's attention by presenting a surprising perspective.

The author expresses her thesis statement clearly and concisely.

Lyndsey smoothly introduces a research source and explains the ideas it provided.

924 ■ *Drama*

Differentiated Instruction   Solutions for All Learners

Strategy for English Learners
Have students work in pairs to read through the Student Model, noting any words or phrases they need to look up for better understanding. After students have looked up these words and phrases, have a class discussion in which each pair takes a turn identifying and describing a troublesome word or phrase. Keep going until students have touched on every troublesome word or phrase.

Body language is usually learned, but it can also be inherited. It is affected by age, gender, background, and situation. The meaning of body language can change depending on cultural context. According to Dr. Marsh, each culture has developed its own repertoire of symbolic gestures, many with original associations that have now long been forgotten (Marsh 53–54). This causes people to be alarmed by foreign visitors or nervous around people when they visit new countries.

In the United States, people have a wide variety of regional influences because the country is a melting pot of diverse cultures. A gesture that means the same thing throughout the United States is the "OK" sign made with the thumb and forefinger. This gesture is interpreted similarly in some European countries, but if you were to perform this sign in Greece or Turkey, it would be considered very insulting (Marsh 54).

There are other cultural differences in body language within Europe. In Germany, body language often reflects social status, and Germans often use body language for emphasis. Italian gestures are often passionate, emotional expressions communicated with the face, arms, and shoulders. Italians often use body language to clarify themselves or to express urgency. In France, people tend to use more formal gestures. They are generally not as expressive or insistent as Italians. The body language of the French is not nearly as casual as we are used to in America (Ruesch and Kees 23–25). As you can see by exploring a few examples from different cultures, there are many differences in body language. Therefore, when you communicate with people from other countries, take special care in your use of body language.

Technological advancements in our society affect the way we communicate. For example, when we speak on the telephone, we are unable to see the person on the other end of the line. The message that a person may be trying to convey may be misinterpreted without the additional visual information provided by his or her body language. With electronic mail, there is no visual or verbal communication whatsoever. As a result, people cannot completely understand the meaning of what is being communicated. Therefore, people using e-mail should be careful about what they write. To avoid miscommunication, communicating the old-fashioned way—in person—may be the best approach.

> Whenever Lyndsey presents a specific piece of evidence that is not her own idea or common knowledge, she cites it using the appropriate format.

> The author's organizational structure is logical and clear. First, she discusses how body language is used in a variety of cultures. Next, she gives examples of what happens when we do not have body language to guide us.

Writing Workshop ■ 925

Body Language

- Point out the internal citations Lyndsey uses in her report. Remind students to refer to their note cards when making citations in their reports.

- Explain to students that the parenthetical citation and the accompanying Works Cited page of this sample model are the most frequently used method of citing source information.

- Explain that Lyndsey addresses many different topics under the main subject of body language. **Ask** students to identify some of the specific topics she explores. **Answer:** Under the overall subject of body language, Lyndsey addresses cultural differences and the effects of technology.

continued on p. 926

925

Body Language (cont.)

- Point out how Lyndsey uses her conclusion to summarize and tie together all the topics she covered in her report.

- **Ask** students what other purposes a conclusion can serve.
  Possible response: A conclusion can end a paper with a memorable feature, like a quote, or it can provide a strong restatement of the paper's main ideas.

- Point out that the first two works on Lyndsay's Works-Cited List are both a book with one author. The third is a book with two authors, and the fourth is a journal article with four authors.

- Encourage students to use these as a model for their own Works-Cited Lists.

- Provide students with a Works Cited Style Sheet copied from a style manual, such as *The Chicago Manual of Style,* since many sources will not fit into the form of the citations shown here.

- Establish an acceptable format for Internet sources in your classroom. Clarify the format for students.

Writing Genres

Research Writing for College and Careers Explain that students will most likely be required to write research papers for many college classes. Also, tell students that many careers require research writing, including attorney, business manager, Web site writer, and graphic designer.

Writing Workshop

In conclusion, body language is a significant component of communication, even though we are often not aware of it. Body language, like facial expression and gestures, frequently enables people to clearly understand one another, but we must remember that people cannot always be read like a book. With cultural differences, body language can take on different meanings, and this allows for potential miscommunication. Changes in technology present a different kind of problem but with a similar result. When body language cannot be seen, people may misinterpret the meaning of the communicator, making them angry or confused. As you can see, the additional information we provide with our body language plays a major role in how we communicate our thoughts and ideas.

Works-Cited List

Aylesworth, Thomas G. *Understanding Body Talk.* New York: F. Watts, 1979.

Marsh, Peter, M.D. *Eye to Eye: How People Interact.* Topsfield, MA: Salem House Publishers, 1988.

Ruesch, Jurgen, and Weldon Kees. *Nonverbal Communication: Notes on the Visual Perception of Human Relations.* Berkeley, CA: University of California Press, 1969.

Vrij, Aldert, Katherine Edward, Kim P. Roberts, and Ray Bull. "Detecting Deceit via Analysis of Verbal and Nonverbal Behavior." *Journal of Nonverbal Behavior,* Winter 2000: 239–263.

After her conclusion, Lyndsey presents the complete information for the works cited in her report using MLA, a common style for citation.

926 ■ *Drama*

Tips for
Using Technology in Writing

Remind students that the Internet is a haven of inaccurate information, and that sites with *.gov, .edu,* and *.org* endings are generally the most reliable ones. Tell students that they can also use the Internet to obtain bibliographies containing the names and authors of books and articles on their topic. These bibliographies may help students rely less on Internet sources and focus more on traditionally reliable sources.

Editing and Proofreading

Check your draft to correct errors in format, grammar, and punctuation.

Focus on Format: Make sure that you have accurately followed the preferred system for crediting sources within your paper and for listing bibliographical information at the end. Double-check the punctuation and capitalization of these elements. (For more on formatting citations, see pages R33–34.)

Publishing and Presenting

Consider one of the following ways to share your writing:
Deliver an oral presentation. Read your research report aloud to your classmates. You may also consider re-creating the report as a multimedia presentation using presentation software. Add appropriate visual aids as needed. You may want to provide a copy of your bibliography or works-cited page to any students who wish to learn more.
Organize a panel discussion. If several of your classmates have written on a similar topic, plan a discussion to compare and contrast your findings. Speakers can summarize their research before opening the panel to questions from the class.

Reflecting on Your Writing

Writer's Journal Jot down your thoughts on the experience of writing a research report. Begin by answering these questions:
- How did writing a research report affect your appreciation, understanding, or opinion of your topic?
- What were the best and worst parts of this experience?

Prentice Hall Writing and Grammar Connection:
Chapter 12

Rubric for Self-Assessment

To assess your research report, use the following rubric:

Criteria	Rating Scale
	not very very
Focus: How clear is your thesis statement?	1 2 3 4 5
Organization: How logical and consistent is your organization?	1 2 3 4 5
Support/Elaboration: How effective and varied is your support?	1 2 3 4 5
Style: How well do you summarize background information?	1 2 3 4 5
Conventions: According to an accepted format, how complete and accurate are your citations?	1 2 3 4 5

Editing and Proofreading

- Tell students to go through their papers and make sure that they have credited every source that they used. Emphasize to students the serious nature of plagiarism and the importance of giving a writer credit for his or her work.
- After students have thoroughly examined their parenthetical and bibliographical information, have them exchange papers and examine each other's citations. Tell students that because of the precise formatting it can be easy to miss small errors. Tell students that their partners may catch errors that they have continuously looked over.

Six Traits Focus

Ideas	Word Choice
Organization	Sentence Fluency
Voice	✔ Conventions

ASSESS

Publishing and Presenting

- If students are preparing to deliver their reports as speeches, have them practice in pairs. Partners should offer suggestions about delivery and should ask questions about each other's topics, as an audience might.
- If several students have researched related topics, suggest that they combine their work into a compilation of chapters on a particular subject.

Reflecting on Your Writing

- To help students evaluate how the research changed their view of the topic, have them write three facts that they learned through the research. Have students add these facts to the last column of their KWL charts. Then, have them explain why each fact is important to the topic.
- As students identify the best and worst aspects of this experience, remind them of the steps at the beginning of the process that may be difficult to remember, such as choosing and narrowing the topic, or identifying reliable sources.

Tips for Test Taking

When students are taking a test that requires them to respond to an expository writing prompt, they should spend time organizing the order of the information in their responses. After students have brainstormed the details that they will use, encourage them to use an outline to organize that information. A few minutes spent organizing will make the drafting and revising stages much easier.

Writing and Grammar, Gold Level
Students will find additional guidelines for editing and proofreading and publishing and presenting a research report in Chapter 12, Sections 5 and 6.

Organizing Content

- Point out that students must consider what equipment is available when they plan their presentation.

- Remind students that planning their content and their media simultaneously makes more sense than planning each individually. Point out that this will help them shape their content and their presentation according to the media available.

- Point out to students that they must avoid overwhelming their audience and themselves with too much media. If the media becomes the focal point, the audience will miss the message of the presentation.

Preparing the Presentation

- Establish a certain length of time for their presentations.

- Remind students that their presentations should be smooth and continuous. If gaps exist in their presentations, they could lose their audience.

- When students rehearse their presentations, have them make sure they are comfortable with the technology they are using. If the technology has the possibility of failure, have them consider how they can work around that failure and still present their message.

Assess the Activity

To evaluate students' delivery, use the *Speaking: Delivering a Research Presentation* rubric, p. 87 in **General Resources**.

928

Multimedia Presentation of a Research Report

Modern classrooms offer students several ways to add sound and visuals to a verbal report. Students may choose from an array of equipment to make multimedia presentations. The following strategies will help you develop and deliver a multimedia presentation of a research report.

Organizing Content

Your choice of media depends on the equipment available to you, your topic, and your target audience. Use the following tips:

- Use a two-column format for your outline. Arrange the content of your report in the left column; plan media elements in the right column. Use this same pattern in your final script: Run your speaking text in the left column and your media cues in the right.

- Choose media appropriate to your content. Dry recitation of statistics can be replaced with colorful graphs and charts. If your report is historical, incorporate music from the time period. Photographs or video images may clarify complex procedures.

- Distribute media use evenly throughout your report. This will make it easier for you to manage the equipment and to maintain audience interest.

Preparing the Presentation

An effective multimedia presentation is the result of planning and practice. These tips may help you prepare:

- If possible, rehearse your presentation in the room where it will take place. Check sightlines to make sure that your visual materials will be seen by all of your audience. Do a sound check as well.

- Make sure that words on your slides are readable; do not put too much content on any one slide.

- Practice shifting from spoken content to media elements. Plan what you will do and say if any piece of equipment fails.

> **Feedback Form for Multimedia Presentations**
>
> **Rating System**
> + = Excellent   ✓ = Average   – = Weak
>
> **Content and Organization**
> Media appropriate to topic _____
> Media well distributed _____
> Media enhances key points _____
>
> **Delivery:**
> Equipment functioning _____
> Media visible and audible _____
> Smooth transitions _____

Activity ▸ *Presentation and Feedback* ▸ Use a research report from your portfolio as the basis of a multimedia presentation. Plan and practice your presentation using the guidelines above. After your presentation, use the Feedback Form to collect comments from your classmates.

928 ■ Drama

Julius Caesar

William Shakespeare

Globe Fearon, 1996

Drama Shakespeare's tale of power and betrayal is retold in modern English. The classic story invites the audience into a world of power and corruption where the lines of loyalty blur and it is sometimes difficult to decide who is a friend and who is a foe.

Four Plays by Tennessee Williams

Tennessee Williams

Signet Classic, 1976

Each of the four plays represents a masterpiece of American theater. The Williams plays deal poignantly with the drama of daily life. These are works in which ordinary people make decisions that dramatically change their lives and the lives of those closest to them.

Twentieth-Century American Drama

A Prentice Hall Anthology

Prentice Hall, 2000

Drama Collection This collection contains four of the most important plays of twentieth-century America. *The Crucible,* Arthur Miller's famous refutation of oppression and censorship, is set during the Salem witch trials. *The Glass Menagerie,* by Tennessee Williams, is set in the Midwest during the Great Depression. Thornton Wilder's *Our Town* and Arthur Miller's *Death of a Salesman* add to this look at America and American values.

Six Characters in Search of an Author

Luigi Pirandello

Signet Classic, 1998

Drama Pirandello's best-known play challenges audiences to decide which is more real: an actor or a character. During a rehearsal, the cast and crew of a play are visited by six characters who need to have their story told. This innovative drama breaks down theatrical barriers while questioning the reality of life itself.

These titles are available in the Penguin/Prentice Hall Literature Library. Consult your teacher before choosing one.

For Further Reading ■ *929*

ters in the play-within-a-play struggle to reconcile their feelings of guilt and responsibility for an incident in which the father visits a brothel where his stepdaughter, who had left with his wife years before, has been compelled to work.

Planning Students' Further Reading

Discussions of literature can raise sensitive and often controversial issues. Before you recommend further reading to your students, consider the values and sensitivities of your community as well as the age, ability, and sophistication of your students. It is also good policy to preview literature before you recommend it to students. The notes below offer some guidance on specific titles.

[L4] *Julius Caesar*

The play includes assassination, suicides, soothsayers and supernatural omens, and reference to harlots.

[L3] *Four Plays by Tennessee Williams*

All these plays involve at least some sexual discussion and situations, and there is usually graphic violence. In *Summer and Smoke,* a major character is involved with a "loose" woman (who is Mexican), and her father later shoots his father. There are discussions of the male character's sexual needs. In *Orpheus Descending,* two characters become involved in an adulterous affair. Later, one of these characters is shot on stage and the other, we are told, is tortured and killed with a blowtorch. In *Suddenly Last Summer,* the main story involves the death, by cannibalism, of a man who seduced young boys. In *Period of Adjustment,* characters' sexual problems are discussed.

[L2] *Twentieth-Century American Drama*

Our Town deals directly with death and includes references to one character's suicide. In *The Glass Menagerie,* Tom abuses alcohol. The play focuses on Laura's physical disabilities and Amanda's belief that the only appropriate goals for Laura are marriage and a family. Also, Jim uses a derogatory term for German Americans. *Death of a Salesman* includes scenes from Willy's adulterous affair. Biff and Happy steal things. Finally, the play concludes with Willy's suicide. *The Crucible* deals with people who believed in the literal existence of Satan and witchcraft. The play also includes references to adultery and John Proctor's use of the word *whore.*

[L1, L2, EL] *Six Characters in Search of an Author*

Issues of prostitution, incest, and suicide are central to the play's investigation of tragedy. The charac-

Using *On Your Own*

You may use this On Your Own feature in one of the following ways:

- For independent reading
- To reinforce/reteach one of the reading skills in this unit

Promote Independent Reading

Independent reading gives students an opportunity to practice the reading skills taught in this unit and to improve comprehension. When students read independently, they also increase their vocabulary and develop their own personal reading interests.

You may assign this selection to be read independently for homework, in class when students have completed other work, or for independent group work.

Develop Reading Preferences

After students have read this selection, ask them what they enjoyed about it. Build on their ideas to recommend further reading. Students who enjoy this selection might also enjoy other contemporary poems, stories set in Puerto Rico, or writings about storms.

Think About It Hurricanes are dangerous storms—sometimes hundreds of miles long. These enormous storms have two main parts: the eye and the wall of clouds that surround it. The eye of the storm is calm with very few clouds. However, the wall of clouds outside of the eye produces powerful winds and heavy rainfall. As you read, try to imagine these dangerous winds carrying the objects the speaker describes.

Problems With Hurricanes

Victor Hernández Cruz

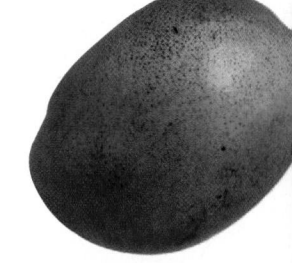

A campesino[1] looked at the air
And told me:
With hurricanes it's not the wind
or the noise or the water.
5   I'll tell you he said:
it's the mangoes, avocados
Green plantains[2] and bananas
flying into town like projectiles.

How would your family
10 feel if they had to tell
The generations that you
got killed by a flying
Banana.

---

1. campesino (käm´ pe sē´ nō) *n.* Spanish term for a simple farmer or another person who lives in a rural area.
2. plantains (plan´ tinz) *n.* starchy tropical fruits that resemble bananas.

930 ■ *Poetry*

Death by drowning has honor
15 If the wind picked you up
   and slammed you
   Against a mountain boulder
   This would not carry shame
   But
20 to suffer a mango smashing
   Your skull
   or a plantain hitting your
   Temple at 70 miles per hour
   is the ultimate disgrace.

25 The campesino takes off his hat—
   As a sign of respect
   toward the fury of the wind
   And says:
   Don't worry about the noise
30 Don't worry about the water
   Don't worry about the wind—
   If you are going out
   beware of mangoes
   And all such beautiful
35 sweet things.

Meet the Author
Victor Hernández Cruz (b. 1949) is one of the pioneering poets who created the Nuyorican style of poetry, a new form that combines the English of New York City, the Spanish of Puerto Rico, and street slang. Cruz has twice been crowned the World Heavyweight Poetry champion in Taos, New Mexico.

Readings in Contemporary Poetry
Talk About It
Use these questions to guide a discussion of this poem.

1. **(a)** According to the campesino, what is the biggest safety concern in a hurricane? **(b)** Is this statement funny, true, or both?

2. Cruz uses playful words to describe a serious subject. In a group, consider how his word choices affect the poem.
   - Which words would not belong in a more serious poem?
   - How are the final two lines of the poem different from the rest? Are "beautiful sweet things" only fruit? Do these final lines change the poem's meaning in any way?

   Choose a point-person to share your group's ideas with the class.

Problems with Hurricanes ■ *931*

Extend the Lesson

Summary
To give students more exposure to both contemporary poetry and summarizing, divide them into groups of four or five students, and challenge each group to find a contemporary poem. Allow time for the groups to share and summarize their poems.

Motivation
Have students look at the images in this selection and read the Think About it Text. Ask what they think the author will discuss in this poem. Encourage them to read to learn more about this author's feelings about hurricanes.

Reading Skill
Summarize
- Review summarizing (p. 724)—restating in your words an overview of the general ideas of a selection.

- Have students read "Problems with Hurricanes."

- **Ask** students to summarize the main ideas of the first stanza.
  Possible response: The narrator is told that the most dangerous aspect of hurricanes is the flying fruit.

- **Ask** students to state the central idea of the second and third stanzas.
  Possible response: In his conversation with the *campesino,* the narrator is asked to consider the impact a person's cause of death has on remaining family members.

- Remind students that when summarizing a text, they should include information that is implied as well as information that is directly stated.

- Explain to students that an *allegory* is a representation of an abstract idea by characters or events. **Ask** a volunteer to tell how the fruit in the poem is an allegory.
  Possible response: In his description of hurricanes, Cruz uses the fruit to point out that the wind and the water are main features of hurricanes, but much of the danger comes from common things that are turned into flying debris.

Readings in Contemporary Poetry
Talk About It
- Suggest that students work in groups to address these questions.
- To guide students' discussion, use the **Discussion Guide**, p. 39 in *General Resources.*

931

Introduce Unit 6

- Direct students' attention to the art on these two pages. **Ask** students what this painting is about—what theme is this painting expressing? **Possible response:** Students may say that the painting is about heroism, the struggle against nature, danger, the watchfulness of gods.

- Tell students that in this unit they will encounter literature that develops the same themes they have found in the painting.

Instructional Resources

Unit 6 Resources support students in developing and mastering the unit skills and help you assess progress.

▶ **Progress Monitoring** These tests enable you to assess and monitor student progress in each part:

- **Diagnostic test** • **Benchmark test**

▶ **Vocabulary Warm-ups**
Additional vocabulary support, based on Lexile scores of vocabulary words, is provided for each selection.

- **Word List A and Practice A** provide activities for students reading two grades below level.

- **Word List B and Practice B** provide activities for students reading one grade below level.

▶ **Reading Warm-ups** Two Reading Warm-ups for each selection provide a context for students to apply newly learned vocabulary. Each Reading Warm-up consists of a short reading passage. Questions and activities guide students to focus on particular vocabulary items.

- **Reading Warm-up A**, for students reading two grades below level, focuses on the vocabulary items presented in Vocabulary Warm-up A.

- **Reading Warm-up B**, for students reading one grade below level, focuses on the vocabulary items presented in Vocabulary Warm-up B.

▶ **Selection Support** These practice pages are available for each selection:

- **Reading Skills**
- **Literary Analysis**
- **Vocabulary Builder**
- **Support for Writing**
- **Support for Extend Your Learning**
- **Enrichment**

TeacherEXPRESS™ You may also
Plan · Teach · Assess access these
resources on TeacherExpress.

932

Unit 6
Themes in Literature
Heroism

Assessment Resources

Program Assessment

Unit 6 Resources
    Selection Tests A and B

TeacherExpress™
    ExamView® Test Bank
    Software

Adequate Yearly Progress Monitoring Assessment

Unit 6 Resources
    Diagnostic Tests: Part 1, Part 2
    Benchmark Tests: Part 1, Part 2

Standardized Assessment

Standardized Test Preparation Workbook

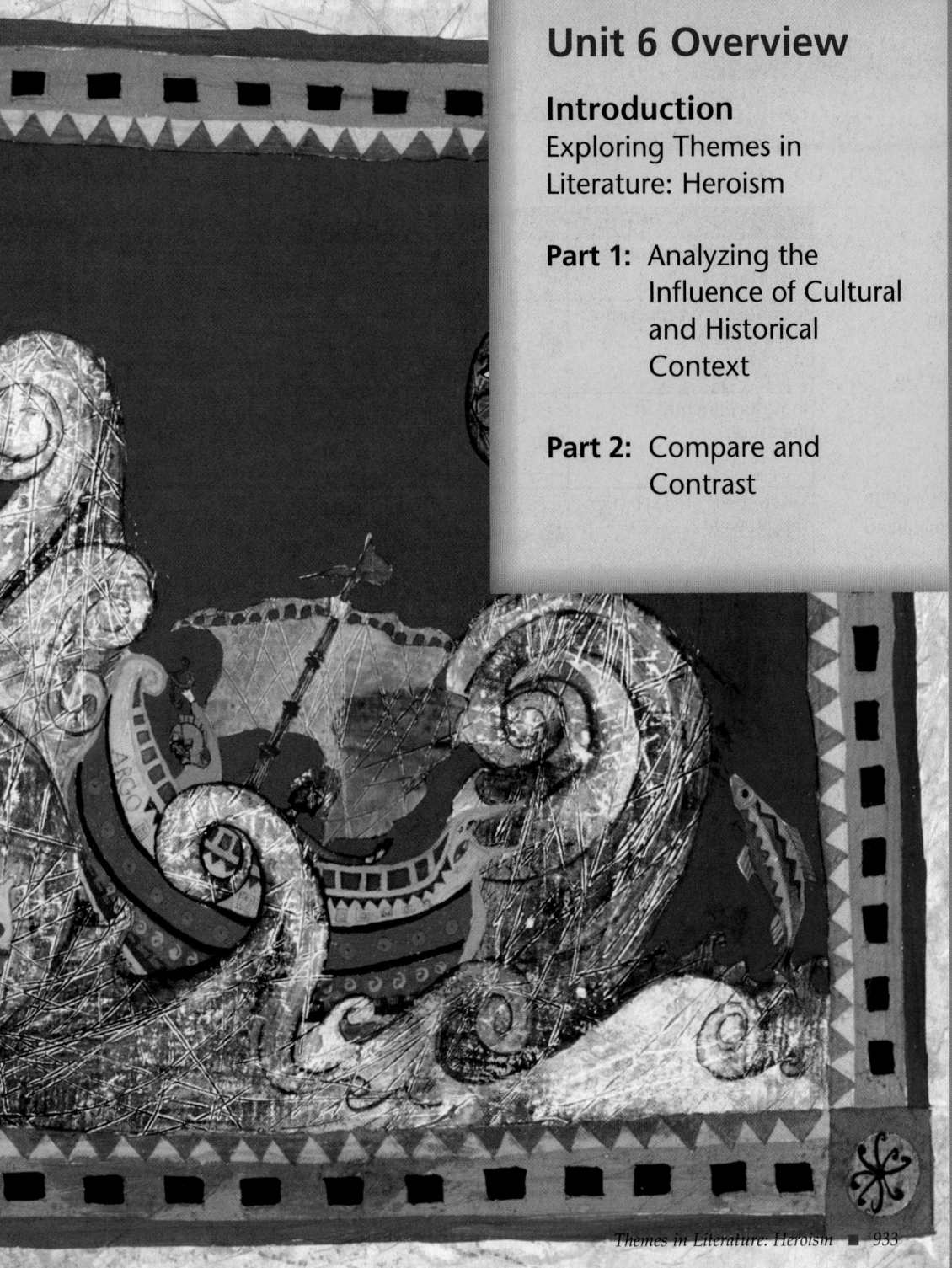

Unit 6 Overview

Introduction
Exploring Themes in
Literature: Heroism

Part 1: Analyzing the
Influence of Cultural
and Historical
Context

Part 2: Compare and
Contrast

Themes in Literature: Heroism ■ *933*

Unit 6 Overview
Genre Focus

Author Dean Smith introduces the
themes in literature with a model.
Students read and analyze examples
of themes in literature.

Using the Unit Selections

Teach Skills Instructional selections
are presented in sets of two. To teach
the skills and meet the objectives,
you need to complete only one selection in each set.

Differentiate and Reinforce Choose
the selection in a set that is best
suited to your students. The selections are listed by accessibility in the
Differentiated Instruction box below.
You may use the other selection in
the set to reinforce comprehension
and skills or to provide enrichment.

Integrate Skills Each selection set
gives students a reading strategy,
literary analysis, and vocabulary
development as well as opportunities
for writing about the selection,
research and technology, listening
and speaking, grammar, and assessment practice.

See pages 945 and 1045 for an
overview of the skills in each part.

Using the Unit Features

These additional reading selections
give you the opportunity to apply,
reinforce, and extend the unit skills.

Reading Informational Materials
Students learn to analyze and evaluate informational texts.

Comparing Literary Works
Students read a pair of literary works
to compare the treatment of a literary element.

On Your Own Students may read
this selection independently, or you
may teach it actively to reinforce a
unit reading skill.

*See the Unit 6 Overview and Pacing
Plan on the following pages.*

Differentiated Instruction   Solutions for All Learners

Accessibility for Ability Levels
This chart gives a general accessibility rating to
help you decide which selection is more appropriate for your students. For additional guidance
on factors that affect the accessibility of each
selection, see the **Time and Resource Manager**
for each selection set.

	Accessible	**More Challenging**
Part 1		
Set 1		*from* the Odyssey, Part 1
Set 2		*from* the Odyssey, Part 2
Part 2		
Set 1	Three Skeleton Key	The Red-headed League
Set 2	There is a Longing	Glory and Hope

Unit 6

OVERVIEW AND PACING PLAN

Themes in Literature

✓ Meeting Your Standards

Students will

1. **recognize and appreciate themes in literature.**
2. **read and analyze a variety of themes in literature.**
3. **apply reading skills.**
   - Historical and cultural context
     - Using background and prior knowledge
     - Identify influences on your own reading and responses
   - Comparing and contrasting
     - Generating questions after reading
     - Using self-monitoring
4. **analyze literary elements.**
   - Epic hero and Flashback
   - Epic simile
   - Protagonist and antagonist
   - Author's purpose and philosophical assumptions
5. **build vocabulary.**
   - Word roots
6. **learn elements of grammar, usage, and style.**
7. **use a recursive writing process to write in a variety of forms.**
   - Timed writing
   - Comparison-and-contrast essay
8. **read informational materials.**
   - Following directions
   - Setting a purpose for reading
9. **compare literary works.**
   - Contemporary interpretations
   - Tall tale and myth
10. **use technology to do research.**
    - Illustrated travelogue
    - "Director's Influences" chart
    - Oral report
    - Outline
11. **develop listening and speaking skills.**
    - Everyday conversation
    - Debate
    - Interview
    - Panel discussion
12. **develop spelling proficiency.**

Unit Introduction and Part 1	Week 1					Week 2					Week 3				
	❶	❷	❸	❹	❺	❶	❷	❸	❹	❺	❶	❷	❸	❹	❺
Introduce the Unit author: Dean Smith.	●														
Introduce themes in literature.	●														
Teach the Model selection (pp. 939–942).	●	●													
Administer the Unit 6, Part 1 Diagnostic Test.			●												
Introduce the Reading and Vocabulary Skills for Part 1.			●												
Teach selection (pp. 950–987).			●	●	●	●	●								
Teach selection (pp. 993–1017).							●	●	●	●					
Teach Reading Informational Materials (pp. 1023–1024).											●				
Teach Comparing Literary Works (pp. 1028–1036).												●	●		
Complete the Reading and Vocabulary Review.														●	
Have students complete the Writing Workshop.											●	●	●	●	●
Administer the Unit 6, Part 1 Benchmark Test.															●

Part 2	Week 1 ❶	❷	❸	❹	❺	Week 2 ❶	❷	❸	❹	❺	Week 3 ❶	❷	❸	❹	❺
Administer the Unit 6, Part 2 Diagnostic Test.	●														
Introduce the Reading and Vocabulary Skills for Part 2.	●														
Teach one selection from Set 1 (pp. 1050–1089).	●	●	●	●	●										
Teach one selection from Set 2 (pp. 1100–1107).						●	●	●	●						
Teach Reading Informational Materials (pp. 1095–1096).										●					
Teach Comparing Literary Works (pp. 1114–1128).											●	●			
Complete the Reading and Vocabulary Review.													●		
Have students complete the Writing Workshop.											●	●	●	●	●
Have students complete the Communications Workshop.														●	
Have students complete the Spelling Workshop.														●	
Administer the Unit 6, Part 2 Benchmark Test.															●

Options for Block and Daily Scheduling

The assignments and activities in this unit planner are organized by week. You may adjust them to your daily or block schedule. The Time and Resource Managers for the selection sets give specific times to help your planning.

Options for Independent Reading

Use these independent reading options to differentiate, reinforce, and extend your instruction:

On Your Own

Students may read this selection on their own or you may use it to reteach and reinforce unit skills.

Martin Espada, "Alabanza: In Praise of Local 100"

For Further Reading

Have students choose and read a full-length work while working on this unit.

[L1, L2, EL] Homer, *The Odyssey*

[L2] Robert Louis Stevenson, *The Strange Case of Dr. Jekyll & Mr. Hyde*

[L3] Ursula K. Le Guin, *The Left Hand of Darkness*

[L4] H.G. Wells, *War of the Worlds*

[L4] Authors in Depth

Sir Arthur Conan Doyle, "The Final Problem," from *The Hound of the Baskervilles*

[L1] Special Needs Students
[L2] Below-Level Students
[L3] All Students
[L4] Above-Level Students
[EL] English Learners

PRENTICE HALL

 Teacher**EXPRESS**™ Use this complete suite
Plan · Teach · Assess of powerful teaching
tools to make lesson planning and testing quicker and easier.

ExamView® QuickTake Monitor student progress instantly.

Students will

1. understand how the themes of leadership and heroism are developed in literature.

2. read and analyze an exposition on the subject of leadership.

3. learn about coach Dean Smith and sports writer John Kilgo.

4. build vocabulary.

5. prepare for general assessment writing.

 From the Author's Desk

❶ Introduce Dean Smith and John Kilgo

- Dean Smith, veteran basketball coach for the University of North Carolina, spent his career shaping successful teams and coaching future basketball superstars, including Michael Jordan. John Kilgo's experience as a sports journalist has helped Smith bring his philosophy to a wider audience.

- Use the *From the Author's Desk DVD* to introduce the authors and the literary themes. Show Segments 2 and 4 to introduce Smith's thoughts about leadership and how he encouraged his players' success both on and off the court. After students have viewed these segments, **ask** how Smith says skills learned in sports can be applied to other parts of a person's life.
Possible response: People can learn to maximize their strengths and work on weaknesses.

- Interested students might enjoy these works by Dean Smith and John Kilgo.

A Coach's Life, an account of Smith's career in college basketball

A Season of Dreams, an account of North Carolina's 1993 national championship season

❷ Critical Viewing

Possible response: This figure shows leadership by climbing two incomplete ladders, a difficult and dangerous feat. He leads by example, showing courage and resourcefulness.

934

Unit 6

Introduction
Themes in Literature: Heroism ❶

❸ **From the Author's Desk**

Coach Dean Smith with John Kilgo
Talk About Leadership and Heroism

Before I agreed to write a book on the **theme of leadership,** I had to be convinced that a college basketball coach qualified as a true leader. I wondered whether all leaders have something in common, from heroic political figures like Nelson Mandela to mythic heroes like Odysseus down to coaches of winning teams.

Does Coaching Qualify as Leadership?

Each season, as North Carolina's basketball coach, I led thirteen to fifteen dedicated, talented young men who loved playing the sport. I knew as I began my career in coaching that I had to motivate, teach, and discipline fairly, and to care deeply about those I led, just as all effective leaders do. Experts in leadership later proved to me that coaching is leadership.

If a coach is a leader and teacher, the game of basketball itself could teach our society some important lessons. The game reflects the ideals of our **culture.** In college basketball, we begin the game 0–0. There's no advantage for being rich, no disadvantage for being poor. Basketball teaches us that people of all races and nationalities, holding various political and religious beliefs, can excel when given a fair and equal chance.

934 ■ *Themes in Literature: Heroism*

▲ **Dean Smith,** the legendary basketball coach, has collaborated with John Kilgo on a book about coaching and leadership.

❷ ◄ **Critical Viewing**
How does the figure in this picture demonstrate qualities of leadership? **[Interpret]**

Teaching Resources

The following resources can be used to enrich, extend, or differentiate the instruction for the Unit Introduction and Model Selection.

Unit 6 Resources, pp. 1–13

General Resources, p. 5

Graphic Organizer Transparencies, pp. 197–198

From the Author's Desk DVD
  Dean Smith and John Kilgo, Segments 2 and 4

Reader's Notebook

Reader's Notebook: Adapted Version

Reader's Notebook: English Learner's Version

Listening to Literature Audio CD

Adapted Reader's Notebook Audio CD

❹ True Heroes Help Others

For me, the true heroes of basketball are not the players out for themselves, but those who help their team and their community. Before each practice at North Carolina, a Thought for the Day, which had nothing to do with basketball, was given to each player. He was expected to memorize it and be able to recite it if called upon.

One day's thought was: "Do something every day for someone who can't pay you back." We wanted our players to be involved with their community, take part in campus politics, make friends on campus with non-athletes, and experience the fulfillment one receives from helping someone in need, with no desire to be recognized publicly for the good works. I required this not for the sport, but to teach players about our culture and its values.

Grandpere, while you're over in that neighborhood, I noticed that Jim Abbot's ten year old boy is dragging his leg in a brace that didn't look right to me. . . . Why don't you hop into your car tomorrow and have Stephen drive you through the district? You'll be amazed what it does to you to make connections with people who need you. . . .

from *Magnificent Obsession*
—Lloyd C. Douglas

The inspiration for my belief in helping others came not only from the example set by my parents but also from literature, the novel *Magnificent Obsession,* which I quote from here.

This novel is the story of a wealthy doctor who gives away his fortune to people in need who cannot pay him back. This passage, in which a character encourages his wealthy grandfather to help the poor, shows that true leaders, true heroes, are givers, not takers.

More About Dean Smith and John Kilgo

Dean Smith (b. 1931), who spent thirty-six years as head coach of the University of North Carolina's Tar Heels, has been called the greatest college basketball coach who ever lived. He has the most wins for coaching in college basketball history: 879. **John Kilgo** (b. 1935), who has spent forty years writing about North Carolina sports, publishes a magazine called *Carolina Blue.* For fifteen years, he was a co-host of Smith's TV show.

Fast Facts

▶ Smith was inducted into the Naismith Basketball Hall of Fame in 1983.
▶ He was named Sportsman of the Year by *Sports Illustrated* in 1997.

From the Author's Desk: Dean Smith with John Kilgo ■ 935

- Tell students that oral stories may have been simplified to make the retelling easier or embroidered to make them more captivating to their audiences. **Ask** students to list as many kinds of oral stories as they can think of.
Possible responses: Students may mention folk tales, fairy tales, fables, tall tales, legends, myths, nursery rhymes, ballads, proverbs, parables, and riddles.

- **Ask** students to brainstorm for a list of universal themes.
Possible responses: Students may mention the pain of loss, conflict between generations, the search for self, rites of passage, and the need for acceptance.

- Explain to students that *archetypes* are motifs that recur throughout history and literature. Common archetypes include three wishes, the journey of discovery, the wise elder, and the magical transformation. Discuss with students how these archetypes are used in stories they know.
Possible responses: As an example, students may say that Obi-Wan Kenobi *(Star Wars)* and Albus Dumbledore *(Harry Potter)* are two examples of the wise elder archetype.

Exploring Themes in Literature

❺ Universal Themes in the Oral Tradition

Written literature grew out of the **oral tradition,** the passing of stories, poems, and sayings by word of mouth. Around campfires and at other gatherings, people told tales about love, ambition, and friendship. Expressing their human concerns in stories, they explored **universal themes,** insights into life that are true for many different times and cultures. The following are examples of common universal themes:

- the importance of heroism
- the strength of loyalty
- the power of love
- the dangers of greed

Storytellers explored such themes by means of **archetypes,** the situations, characters, images, and symbols that appear in the tales of various cultures. Here are some important archetypes:

Cornered by Mike Baldwin

- the **hero's quest,** in which a brave or clever person undergoes tests or trials while searching for something of great value

- the struggle between the **protagonist,** the main character, and the **antagonist,** a person or force that opposes the protagonist

- the **monster,** a nonhuman or semi-human creature that menaces human society and must be destroyed by the hero

- the **trickster,** a clever character who can fool others but often gets into trouble through curiosity

- the **circle** as a symbol of loyalty, completion, or protection

The **historical context** is the social and cultural background of a particular tale. This context influences the presentation of archetypes. Yet, even with cultural variations, one can recognize archetypes across time and culture.

6 Forms That Express Universal Themes

Anonymous storytellers developed various forms to express universal themes and archetypes. At first, these forms lived only in the memory, and a tale might vary with every telling. Later in history, stories were written down and individual authors emerged.

- **Myths** explain the actions of gods and the humans who interact with them. Myths also explain the causes of natural phenomena.
- **Folk tales** focus on human or animal heroes and, unlike myths, are not primarily concerned with gods or creation.
- **Legends** are folk tales that recount the adventures of a human hero and are based on a historical truth. A legend told in an exaggerated way is a **tall tale.**
- **Epics** are long narrative poems that describe the exploits of larger-than-life heros. The hero usually engages in a dangerous journey or quest that is important to the history of a group or culture.

All of these narrative forms express the **values,** ideals, and behaviors cherished by a society. **Shared values** are held in common by people across cultures. In contrast, **culturally distinct values** are specific to a group. In a literary work, **cultural details** are the beliefs, traditions, and customs that reflect a particular society. Modern literature, though written by individuals rather than fashioned by a group, can also express universal themes.

Check Your Understanding

Decide which lettered term or phrase best matches the numbered phrase.

1. example of a universal theme   **a.** the monster   **b.** the power of love
2. brave person on a quest   **a.** epic hero   **b.** antagonist
3. important archetype   **a.** trickster   **b.** culture
4. passing on of tales by word of mouth **a.** narrative form **b.** oral tradition
5. legend told in an exaggerated way **a.** tall tale   **b.** myth

6 Narrative Forms That Express Universal Themes

- Explain to students that myths were the first attempts at scientific explanations. Unable to explain phenomena in the natural world, early people ascribed them to a supernatural force, such as a god or goddess.
- Tell students that epics combine the features of myths and legends. The hero on the quest is helped or hindered by gods and other supernatural creatures. Because of their length, epics more than the other narrative forms provide a portrait of an entire culture, including its values, beliefs, laws, arts, and ways of life.

ASSESS
Answers

1. B
2. A
3. A
4. B
5. A

Differentiated Instruction   Solutions for All Learners

Support for Special Needs Students
Have students read the **Exploring Themes in Literature** pages for *The Carolina Way* in the *Reader's Notebook: Adapted Version.* This version provides a basic-level introduction to the selection.

Support for Less Proficient Readers
Have students read the **Exploring Themes in Literature** pages for *The Carolina Way* in the *Reader's Notebook.* This version provides a basic-level introduction to the selection.

Support for English Learners
Have students read the **Exploring Themes in Literature** pages for *The Carolina Way* in the *Reader's Notebook: English Learner's Version.* This version provides a basic-level introduction to the selection.

From the Author's Desk

❶ Introduce the Selection

• Invite students to read Dean Smith's introduction to *The Carolina Way.*

• Call students' attention to the terms used in discussing the selection: *purpose* and *audience.* Ask students to identify these elements as they read the selection.

❷ Background

Athletics The ancient Greeks valued athletics highly. Sports had varied purposes, including preparing hardy Spartan boys to become warriors and honoring the gods at competitions such as the Olympics. Modern American culture values athletics as well; few can deny that athletics have a pervasive influence on how our society defines itself.

❸ Connecting to the Literature

• Ask students to discuss the ways in which sports express cultural values. At the end of the discussion, suggest that they write several sentences that summarize the role that sports play in the culture of the United States. To develop expressive vocabulary, tell students to use at least three of these words in their sentences: *confirm, persist, illustrate, participate, dominate,* and *signify.*

• To further develop students' expressive vocabulary, you may suggest that they also use at least two of these words: *controversy, attitude, prestige,* and *individual.*

• To help students understand the meanings of the words they are asked to use, give them these sentences:

1. Sports programs *dominate* the airwaves on weekends.

2. Americans' interest in sports can *signify* that winning is important to us.

3. Some athletes do not deserve the wealth and *prestige* that come with professional sports success.

Model Selection:
Themes ❶

 From the Author's Desk
Dean Smith and John Kilgo Introduce *The Carolina Way*

 ❷ ❸

Both of my parents were schoolteachers in my hometown of Emporia, Kansas. I developed a passion for athletics at an early age, but my parents insisted that sports not interfere with my studies, and if they did, sports took a backseat.

My parents received much joy and fulfillment from helping students learn and develop into good citizens, and were the major influences that led me to a career of teaching and coaching.

Creating a Culture of Unselfishness
At the University of North Carolina, I wanted to build a program in which all the players on the team, regardless of their backgrounds, respected each other, and highly talented players saw the wisdom of putting team goals in front of individual awards.

The Brightest Statistic
While a winning basketball program is very important at UNC, we established from the start that academics came first. Thanks to our players, we won 879 games and many championships in my thirty-six years as UNC's coach, but the statistic that stands brightest is that 96.6 percent of our players graduated, and more than a third of those went on to professional and graduate school.

Success Means Building Character
The university administration supported our efforts to build a program that emphasized education first, and the fact that we won almost eighty percent of our games says much about the players we had in our program. Thanks to them, some now refer to our method as "The Carolina Way."

That is also the title of the book I wrote about my coaching experience and philosophy. My **purpose** in writing this book was to demonstrate the methods we used to promote unselfish play and dedication to scholarship. And I was writing for an **audience** that I hoped would include not only athletes and sports fans but anyone who plays or works with others. As you read this excerpt from the book, you may be surprised to learn that I rarely talked to my players about winning!

938 ■ *Themes in Literature: Heroism*

Vocabulary Development

Vocabulary Knowledge Rating Chart
Create a **Vocabulary Knowledge Rating Chart** with this word from the selection:

tenets

Give students a copy of the chart. Introduce the word by reading it aloud and having students mark their rating in the Before Reading column. Urge them to be alert to this word as they read and discuss the selection because they will rate their knowledge of the word again after they finish.

If you wish, you may tally how many students know (or think they know) the word to gauge how much instruction you need to provide. As students read, point out the word and its context.

Play **Hard;**
Play **Together;**
Play **Smart**

from **The Carolina Way**

Dean Smith *with* **John Kilgo**

④

⑤

I never went into a season as North Carolina's head coach thinking we'd just plug things into the previous year's plan and duplicate ourselves. As I said, we never had the same team return, and there were any number of other variables from one year to the next. We couldn't have had the long run of success that we enjoyed if we'd been too stubborn to change and come up with new ideas and different ways to play the game.

⑥ ▲ **Critical Viewing**
What does this photograph tell you about the way Coach Dean Smith (in the blue suit) works with his players? **[Analyze]**

from The Carolina Way ■ *939*

TEACH

❹ **Motivation**
Have students brainstorm for a list of sports metaphors—phrases and sayings that come from sports but have been generalized into other areas of life. Give them examples like these to get them started: *game plan, step up to the plate, drop the ball, par for the course, throw in the towel, slam dunk,* and *play hard ball.* Ask students to identify which sport the saying comes from, what it means in relationship to the sport, and what its generalized meaning is. Then discuss with students what these numerous sports metaphors reveal about the culture of the United States.

Concept Connector ▶
Students will re-examine their ideas after reading this excerpt from *The Carolina Way.*

❺ **About the Selection**
In this excerpt from *The Carolina Way,* coach Dean Smith, who describes himself as an "open-minded dictator," offers his simple program for building and maintaining a winning team, whether it be in sports, business, or any other area of life.

❻ **Critical Viewing**
Possible responses: The photo suggests that Coach Smith pays attention and listens well. His interactions with his players are very important to him.

Differentiated
Instruction Solutions for All Learners

Strategy for
Special Needs Students
Have students read the adapted version of *The Carolina Way* in the *Reader's Notebook: Adapted Version.* They may also listen to the adapted version on the *Reader's Notebook: Adapted Version Audio CD.*

Support for
Less Proficient Readers
Have students read *The Carolina Way* in the *Reader's Notebook.* After students finish the selection in the *Reader's Notebook,* have them complete the questions and activities in the Student Edition.

Support for
English Learners
Have students read the adapted version of *The Carolina Way* in the *Reader's Notebook: English Learner's Version.* English learners may also read the selection as they listen to the recorded version on the **Listening to Literature Audio CD.**

- Have a volunteer read the passage.
- **Ask** students to explain how Smith differentiates a philosophy from a system.

Possible response: According to Smith's definition, a system is an organized set of related principles or rules. A system would demand that each player adjust to rules. A philosophy, on the other hand, is much more loosely organized and accounts for change and individual differences.

❽ Themes in Literature
Leadership

- **Ask** students if Smith were a "life coach" instead of a basketball coach, which of his three tenets would be the same.

Possible responses: Students may point out that all of them have a general application: Living by the three tenets would probably ensure success at most tasks.

- Point out the irony of a coach who seldom talked about winning. Discuss with students how this action showed leadership.

Possible response: Students may recognize that Smith was exhibiting the behavior that he wanted his players to practice.

❾ Author's Insight

- Point out Smith's comment that his philosophy eliminates excuse-making.
- Discuss with students whether not making excuses results in a better basketball player, a better team member, or a better person.

Possible responses: Not making excuses can help people play better by ensuring that they try hard. It makes better team members by discouraging blaming. It improves people's character in general.

I will repeat this several times in this book: Don't fear change. Sometimes change can refresh a stale team; sometimes it's mandated by changing personnel; sometimes the rules of the game change. We adapted each year to hide our weaknesses and accentuate our strengths.

❼ Although we didn't have a system at North Carolina, we certainly had a philosophy. We believed in it strongly and didn't stray very far from it. It pretty much stayed the same from my first year as head coach. It was our mission statement; our strategic plan, our entire approach in a nutshell: Play hard; play smart; play together.

Hard meant with effort, determination, and courage; *together* meant unselfishly, trusting your teammates, and doing everything possible not to let them down; *smart* meant with good execution and poise, treating each possession as if it were the only one in the game.

❽ That was our philosophy; we believed that if we kept our focus on those <u>tenets</u>, success would follow. Our North Carolina players seldom heard me or my assistants talk about winning. Winning would be the by-product of the process. There could be no shortcuts.

Making winning the ultimate goal usually isn't good teaching. Tom Osborne, the great former football coach of the University of Nebraska, said that making winning the goal can actually get in the way of winning. I agree. So many things happened in games that were beyond our control: the talent and experience of the teams; bad calls by officials; injuries; bad luck.

❾ By sticking to our philosophy, we asked realistic things from our players. A player could play hard. He could play unselfishly and do things to help his teammates succeed. He could play intelligently if we did the job in practice as coaches. We measured our success by how we did in those areas.

When we put these elements together, the players had fun, one of my goals as their coach. I wanted our players to enjoy the experience of playing basketball for North Carolina. Each player on our team knew he was important. Each did a terrific job of sharing the ball, which also made the game enjoyable for more players. All won and lost as a team.

Of course it is easier to talk about playing hard, playing smart, and playing together than it is to do all three. It begins by the recruiting of unselfish players, who subscribe to the philosophy of team over individual. In a summer physical education class I once taught at the Air Force Academy there was one young man who shot every time he touched the ball. Exasperated from watching him, I pulled his four teammates off the court. He asked who would throw the ball inbounds to him. "You understand that it takes at least one more player," I said to him.

940 ■ Themes in Literature: Heroism

Dean Smith
Author's Insight
A system signifies being rigid and unwilling to accept change. Our philosophy welcomed new and better ways of doing things.

Vocabulary Builder
tenets (ten´ its) *n.* principles or beliefs

Dean Smith
Author's Insight
We asked our players to concentrate only on those things within their control. This philosophy also eliminates excuse-making.

Themes in Literature
Leadership Smith describes his ideas about successful coaching.

Vocabulary Development

Expressive Vocabulary
As students are discussing *The Carolina Way,* encourage them to use the expressive vocabulary presented earlier. You might encourage them with sentence starters like these:

1. Coach Smith's philosophy might cause some *controversy* because . . . .
2. Americans' *attitudes* about sports are . . . .
3. *Individual* sports differ from team sports . . . .
4. One stereotype about athletes that *persists* is . . . .

Playing Hard

Maybe a player wasn't the fastest, the tallest, or the most athletic person on the court. In the course of any given game that was out of his control. But each of them could control the effort with which he played. "Never let anyone play harder than you," I told them. "That is part of the game you can control." If another team played harder than we did, we had no excuse for it. None. We worked on it in every practice. If a player didn't give maximum effort, we dealt with it right then. We stopped practice and had the entire team run sprints for the offending player. We played a style of basketball that was physically exhausting and made it impossible for a player to go full throttle for forty minutes. When he got tired, he flashed the tired signal, a raised fist, and we substituted for him. He could put himself back in the game once he had rested. We didn't want tired players on the court because they usually tried to rest on defense. That wouldn't work in our plan. Therefore we watched closely in practice and in games to make sure players played hard. If they slacked off, it was important to catch them and get them out of the game, or if it occurred in practice, to have the entire team run.

Playing Together

One of the first things I did at the beginning of preseason practice was to spell out for our players the importance of team play. Basketball is a game that counts on togetherness. I pointed out that seldom, if ever, did the nation's leading scorer play on a ranked team. He certainly didn't play on a championship team. I made them understand that our plan would fall apart if they didn't take care of one another: set screens; play team defense; box out; pass to the open man. One man who failed to do his job unselfishly could undermine the efforts of the four other players on the court.

⑩ ▼ Critical Viewing
How does this photograph show that Coach Smith's players (in white) "play hard"?
[Connect]

Dean Smith
Author's Insight
Basketball is fun for the players when everyone on the team is treated equally and with respect. Players savor team accomplishments long after individual ones are forgotten.

⑬

Reading Check

According to Coach Smith, what can a player always control?

from The Carolina Way ■ 941

- Have a volunteer read the bracketed passage aloud.
- **Ask** students how these behaviors and values might be applied in a business or in the classroom.
  Possible response: Establishing good habits in employees and being sure that skills are practiced until perfected could ensure that everyone does his or her best. This, in turn, would benefit everyone in a business or classroom situation.

15 Critical Viewing

Possible response: Smith appears to be talking to all the players, not just one. He is not singling any individual out for special attention.

Concept Connector

Have students return to the list of sports metaphors they generated and the discussion they had about the role of sports in contemporary society. Have students compare and contrast their ideas now that they have completed *The Carolina Way.* To what extent have they revised or refined their ideas?

←

Playing Smart

14 We taught and drilled until we made the things we wanted to see become habits. The only way to have a smart team is to have one that is fundamentally sound. We didn't skimp on fundamentals. We worked on them hard in practice and repeated them until they were down cold. We didn't introduce something and then move away from it before we had nailed it. Our entire program was built around practice, which we will talk more about in a later chapter. Practice, competitive games, late-game situations, and my relationship with our players are what I've missed most since I retired from coaching. We expected our team to execute well and with precision. If we practiced well and learned, we could play smart. It was another thing we could control.

I stay in touch with many members of my extended family, former Carolina basketball players. These men have brought great happiness to my life. Ninety-six percent of them earned their college degrees, and one-third of those continued their studies at graduate and professional schools. It's the way a teacher's career should be judged. Our former players are doing great things for people in all walks of life.

The Carolina Way isn't the only way, that's for certain. But playing hard, playing smart, playing together certainly worked well for us.

Our trophy case is full, but far more important, our Museum of Good Memories runneth over.

Themes in Literature
Cultural Context
Details here show the values and behaviors that lead to success.

15 ▽ **Critical Viewing**
How does this photograph show that Coach Smith emphasizes the whole team, not just the "star" player? **[Analyze]**

Vocabulary Development

Vocabulary Knowledge Rating
When students have completed reading and discussing *The Carolina Way,* have them take out their **Vocabulary Rating Chart** for the selection. Read the word aloud once more and have students rate their knowledge of the word again in the After Reading column. Have students write their own definition or example in the appropriate column. Encourage students to use the word in further discussion and written work about this selection. Remind them that they will be accountable for the word on the Selection Test.

From the Author's Desk
Coach Dean Smith's and John Kilgo's Insights Into Their Book

16 Q. Did you develop your coaching "philosophy" over the years, or did you formulate it at the start of your career?

A. I learned basketball from my father, who was my high school coach, from my college coaches at the University of Kansas, Dr. Forrest (Phog) Allen and Dick Harp, and from Bob Spear and Frank McGuire, whom I assisted at the Air Force Academy and North Carolina, respectively. I had my own ideas, of course, which I updated annually to best suit our personnel and to adapt to rules changes. I also received valuable ideas from all of my assistant coaches at North Carolina.

17 Q. Do you remain in touch with your players after they have graduated?

A. Yes. I'm constantly in touch with our former players. Seldom does a week go by that I don't talk to at least a few of them. One of the best compliments given to me came from Phil Ford, who was National Player of the Year for us in 1978, when he said: "When I signed with Coach Smith and North Carolina, I knew I'd be getting a great coach for four years. I ended up with a great coach for four years and a friend for a lifetime."

StudentCorner

18 Q. How would kids who don't play a sport apply your methods?
—Lisa Avilez, Zion, Illinois

A. By concentrating on things within your control. Our players were taught to play hard, play smart, play together. Non-athletes can study and work hard, make intelligent life decisions, and be unselfish in their relationships with family and friends. You can also treat each individual honestly and with respect.

Writing Workshop: *Work in Progress*

Writing for Assessment

To prepare for general assessments, make a list of literary works or historical events you might use to discuss the theme of courage. Jot down your ideas about how each item illustrates courage. Save this Courage List in your portfolio.

From the Author's Desk: Dean Smith and John Kilgo ■ 943

Assessment Resources

The following resources can be used to assess students' knowledge and skills.

Unit 6 Resources
Selection Test A, pp. 8–10
Selection Test B, pp. 11–13

Go Online
Assessment Students may use the **Self-test** to prepare for **Selection Test A** or **Selection Test B.**

---

1. Some students may agree with Smith; others may contend that winning is more important. Students should give reasons in support of their opinions.

2. (a) Factors beyond the control of a coach or team include the talent and experience of the opposing team, bad calls by officials, injuries, and bad luck. (b) **Possible response:** If each player plays hard, plays smart, and plays together, they as a team should be able to counteract the unexpected. If they cannot counteract it, then at least they have given it their best shot.

3. (a) Smith believes a teacher's career should be judged by how his or her students succeed out in the world. (b) **Possible response:** As a coach, he is a teacher. There is no difference.

4. (a) **Sample answer: Values:** Play hard. **Specific Examples:** Give maximum effort, including in practice. Admit to being tired and take a break so you do not slack off. **Application to Life:** Be the best you can be. Do not be ashamed to ask for help if you need it. (b) and (c) After discussion, groups should present their ideas.

5. Students will probably agree that sports are an essential part of the cultural context in the United States. They should cite evidence from the text in explaining their answers.

Research the Author

Students may complete this research assignment for homework. Tell them that they can find information about Dean Smith and his players in a library or online.

Go Online **For:** More information Author Link about Dean Smith and John Kilgo, **Visit:** www.PHSchool.com **Web Code** epe-9601. For additional information about Dean Smith and John Kilgo, give students this Web Code. After typing the Web Code, students select *S* or *K* from the alphabet and then select *Dean Smith* or *John Kilgo*.

Apply the Skills

Themes in Literature: Heroism

Thinking About the Selection

1. **Respond:** Do you agree that playing a sport the right way is more important than winning? Explain.

2. **(a) Recall:** According to Smith, which factors in sports are beyond a team's control? **(b) Draw Conclusions:** How does Smith's philosophy provide a response to the unexpected in sports?

3. **(a) Recall:** According to Smith, how should a teacher's career be judged? **(b) Evaluate:** By his standards, is Smith's lifework meaningful because he was a teacher or because he was a coach? Explain.

Reviewing Themes in Literature

4. Using a three-column chart like the one shown, analyze the values that Smith emphasized as basketball coach for North Carolina. **(a)** In the first column, list the three **values** or goals that Smith taught. In the second column, give a specific example of how Smith promoted each value among his players. In the third column, suggest ways in which Smith's values can be applied to people in any walk of life. **(b)** Discuss your ideas in a small group, and add any new insights to your chart. **(c)** Share your ideas with the class.

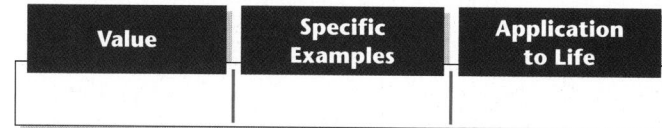

Value	Specific Examples	Application to Life

5. Do you think that sports are an essential part of the **cultural context** of the United States? Use details from Smith's essay to support your answer.

Research the Author

Many of Dean Smith's players have achieved great success in life. Use comments from Smith's former players to create a **testimonial poster** that shows the positive results of Smith's coaching beliefs.

• Using both Internet and library sources, identify famous athletes, coaches, or leaders who have played for Dean Smith.
• Collect comments about Smith made by these former players. Focus on statements relating to values that have aided their success.
• Present these comments on a poster. Include photographs of Smith and the people whom you quote.

944 ■ Themes in Literature: Heroism

QuickReview

Selection at a Glance Coach Dean Smith outlines the values that produced a culture of success in the University of North Carolina men's basketball program.

Go Online Assessment

For: Self-test
Visit: www.PHSchool.com
Web Code: epe-6601

Values: ideals or model behaviors admired and held by a group

Cultural Context: the beliefs, values, traditions, and practices of a group or a civilization

Cultural and Historical Context

Skills You Will Learn

Literary Analysis: *Epic Hero and Flashback*
Reading Skill: *Using Background and Prior Knowledge*

Literary Analysis: *Epic Simile*
Reading Skill: *Identifying Influences on Your Own Responses*

Reading Skill: *Following Directions*

Literary Analysis: *Contemporary Interpretations of Classic Works/Allusions*

Literature You Will Read

Cultural and Historical Context 945

Differentiated Instruction   Solutions for All Learners

Resources for Monitoring Progress

Unit 6 Resources
    Unit 6, Part 1 Diagnostic Test, pp. 15–17
    Unit 6, Part 1 Benchmark Test, pp. 69–74

Reading Kit

Success Tracker

Skills Overview

Reading Skill: Historical and Cultural Context
- Using background and prior knowledge
- Identify influences on your own reading and responses

Vocabulary Development
- Word roots

Literary Analysis
- Epic Hero and Flashback
- Epic Simile

Writing
- Timed Writing
- Work in Progress, pp. 943, 991, 1021

Monitoring Progress

Diagnose: Before you begin Part 1, administer the **Diagnostic Test** for Unit 6, Part 1. This test will identify students' level of readiness for the reading and vocabulary skills in Part 1. Use the **Interpretation Guide** for the Diagnostic Test to determine which students need help with prerequisite skills before beginning Part 1.

Preteach and Prepare: Use the information indicated in the **Interpretation Guide** to help students build prerequisite skills. In addition, prepare students by using the **Vocabulary Warm-up** activities and the **Reading Warm-up** activities as necessary for each selection set.

Teach: Use the instructional plan and resources provided to teach the skills and selections.

Assess: After students have completed Part 1, administer the **Benchmark Test** for Unit 6, Part 1. The test results will indicate which skills students have mastered and those on which they need more work.

Reteach: Use the Interpretation Guide to determine the appropriate reteaching pages from the **Reading Kit.**

Intervention: The prerequisite and reteaching pages are also available in the **Success Tracker.**

Introduce the Reading Skill

- Introduce the reading skill: analyzing the influence of cultural and historical context. Explain that the cultural and historical setting for a literary work has a great influence on the content of the piece, as it determines what the characters believe and how they react to events.

- After reviewing the three strategies, point out to students that people's cultural and historical formation influence how they experience and understand the world. By attempting to understand the cultural and historical context in which a text is written, students can better relate to the characters and the theme of the text.

Model the Reading Strategies

- Model how to analyze the influence of cultural and historical context by guiding students through the example. Write this passage on the board:

  I am frustrated because Mother will not let me go to school; Father says that education is wasted on girls. He says that girls just need to learn to take care of a house and children.

  Ask the following questions:

  What does the narrator have in common with readers? (She wants something she cannot have; she disagrees with parents sometimes.)

  What cultural clues are present in the passage? (The distinction between male and female roles indicates a past era, as does calling parents Mother and Father.)

- Reinforce that understanding cultural and historical contexts is important for students to understand a text.

Reading and Vocabulary Skills Preview

Reading: Analyzing Cultural and Historical Context

> The **cultural and historical context** is the social and cultural information, including the attitudes and customs, of the time and place in which a work is set.

Skills and Strategies You Will Learn in Part 1

- **to use background and prior knowledge** to **identify the influences** of **cultural and historical context** in you own reading (p. 948)
- **to relate to your own experiences** to help you understand the **influence of the cultural and historical context** (p. 992)
- **to follow directions** in order to help you **analyze cultural and historical contexts** (p. 1022)

Using the Skills and Strategies in Part 1

In Part 1, you will learn to recognize how the culture and time period in which a work of literature is set affects the work. You will also learn how your own experiences help you relate to a different culture and how to use directions in a text to add to your cultural understanding.

The following chart shows the key questions you can ask to analyze cultural and historical context.

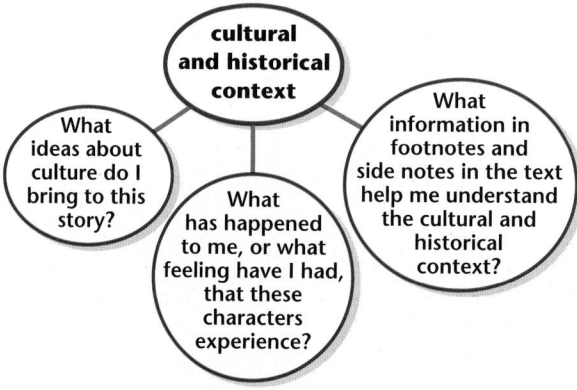

946 ■ *Themes in Literature: Heroism*

Professional Development

Question-Answer Relationships (QARs)

As students read the literature selections, they encounter a variety of questions on the pages. The Question-Answer Relationships strategy (Raphael, 1982; 1986) helps students recognize different types of questions and understand how to answer them.

Teach students that questions based solely on the text fall into two categories:

- **In the Book or Right There** questions involve recall or a literal response. The answers are "right there" in the text.
- **Think and Search** questions are also text related but require more analysis for an answer. Students will have to think about what they have read and search the text to find the answer.

Other types of questions require students to use their own knowledge and/or information from the text.

- **Author and You** questions ask students to synthesize what they know with information in the text. Students must put text information together with applicable prior knowledge.
- **On My Own** questions go beyond the text. Students can answer these questions by drawing on their own knowledge and experience.

When students can identify the source of answers to questions, they are able to answer the questions more effectively.

For more on QARs, see *General Resources*, page 28.

Academic Vocabulary: Words for Developing Concepts in Literature

These words will help you write and talk about concepts in literature.

Word	Definition	Example Sentence
controversy *n.*	discussion over opposing viewpoints; dispute	The **controversy** over who authored the poem continues.
technique *n.*	methods used to create an artistic work	Repetition of words and phrases is one **technique** used in epic poetry.
appraise *v.*	judge the quality or worth of something; set a value on something	Her article attempts to **appraise** the work of ancient Greek poets.
confirm *v.*	prove the truth or authenticity	Scholars can **confirm** that the manuscript was authentic.
complex *adj.*	complicated or intricate	The poem was filled with **complex** detail.

Vocabulary Skill: Word Roots

▶ A **word root** is the part of a word that contains its basic meaning.

In Part 1, you will learn

- Latin prefix *contra-* (p. 990)
- Greek word root *-techni-* (p. 1020)

Word parts help you determine the meaning of an unfamiliar word. Knowing that *contra-* means "against" helps you define words such as *contradict,* which means "speak against."

Activity Write the definition of each of the following words. Then, write the definition of the word with *contra-* added.

1. diction/contradiction
2. alto/contralto
3. distinguish/contradistinguish
4. position/contraposition

Reading and Vocabulary Skills Preview ■ 947

Introduce Academic Vocabulary

- Introduce the academic vocabulary: words for developing concepts in literature. Tell students that these words are useful for writing and discussing literature.
- Review each word, and have students state the word aloud. Have students read aloud the words' definitions and the example sentences on the chart on this page. Clarify any words that students may not understand.
- Tell students to try to use these words as they discuss the selections in Part 1.

Introduce the Vocabulary Skill

- Introduce the vocabulary skill: word roots. Tell students that many words in English are derived from Latin and Greek. The Latin prefix *contra-* and the Greek root *-techni-* are used in many English words. Recognizing these prefixes and roots can help students define unfamiliar vocabulary words.
- Review the prefix and root on this page and their meanings.
- Have students use a dictionary to find the meanings of words. Point out that the addition of the prefix *contra-* gives the words the meaning of "against" or "opposite."

1. diction: the choice and use of words and phrases to express meaning; contradiction: a difference between two statements, beliefs, or ideas about something that means they cannot both be true
2. alto: woman with a low singing voice; contralto: the lowest female singing voice, or a woman who has this voice
3. distinguish: to recognize or understand the difference between two similar things, people, and so on; contradistinguish: distinguish one thing from another by contrasting
4. position: the manner in which a person or thing is placed; contraposition: a placing opposite or over against

Go Online For: Interactive
Vocabulary Crossword Puzzles
Visit: www.PHSchool.com
Web Code: epj-5601
Give students this Web Code to access interactive crossword puzzles using Academic Vocabulary and Vocabulary Skill words from Part 1.

Planning Differentiated Instruction

Accessibility at a Glance

	from the Odyssey, Part 1
Context	Historical: Ancient Greece
Language	Narrative poem; formal language; allusions to Greek mythology
Concept Level	Challenging (journey of epic hero)
Literary Merit	Noted author; classic work
Lexile	NP
Overall Rating	More challenging

Choosing Your Resources

[L1] Special Needs Students   **[L4]** Advanced Students

[L2] Below-Level Students   **[EL]** English Learners

[L3] All Students

FT Fast Track Instruction: To move the lesson more quickly, use the strategies and activities identified with **FT**.

Scaffolding for
Less Proficient and Advanced Students

The leveled questions on Apply the Skills pages progress in the levels of thinking required to answer them. To address the needs of your different students, you may use the (a) level questions for your less proficient students, the (b) level with your on-level and advanced students. The occasional (c) level questions are appropriate for your advanced students.

Step-by-Step Teaching Guide	Pacing Guide	
PRETEACH		
• Administer Vocabulary and Reading Warm-ups as necessary.		
• Introduce the Literary Analysis Skill: Epic Hero. **FT**	10 min.	
• Introduce the Reading Skill: Analyzing the Influence of Cultural and Historical Context. **FT**	10 min.	
• Prepare students to read by teaching the selection vocabulary. **FT**	10 min.	
• Build background and develop expressive vocabulary with Connecting to the Literature and Background.	10 min.	
• Engage students' interest with the motivation activity.	10 min.	
TEACH		
• Informally monitor comprehension while students read independently or in groups. **FT**	30 min.	
• Monitor students' comprehension with the Reading Check notes.	as students read	
• Reinforce vocabulary with Vocabulary Builder notes.	as students read	
• Develop students' understanding of the epic hero with the Literary Analysis annotations. **FT**	5 min.	
• Develop students' ability to analyze the influence of historical and cultural context with the Reading Skill annotations. **FT**	10 min.	
ASSESS/EXTEND		
• Assess students' comprehension and mastery of the Reading Skill and Literary Analysis by having them answer the Apply the Skills questions. **FT**	35 min.	
• Have students complete the Vocabulary Builder activities. **FT**	5 min.	
• Apply students' ability to write an everyday epic with the Writing activity. **FT**	30–45 min. or homework	
• Extend students' research and technology skills with the Extend Your Learning activity.	15–30 min. or homework	
• Have students complete the Vocabulary Skill and Grammar Lesson.	5 min.	
• Monitor students' progress with the Assessment Practice.	20–40 min.	
• Administer **Selection Test A** or **Selection Test B**. **FT**	15 min.	

Resources

 Meeting Your Standards

Students will

1. **analyze and respond to literary elements.**
   - Literary Analysis: Epic Hero and Flashback

2. **read, comprehend, and analyze short stories.**
   - Reading Skill: Analyzing the Influence of Cultural and Historical Context
   - Reading Strategy: Using Background and Prior Knowledge
   - Reading Check questions
   - Apply the Skills questions
   - Assessment Practice

3. **develop vocabulary.**
   - Vocabulary Builder
   - Latin prefix *contra-*

4. **apply grammar skills.**
   - Simple and Compound Sentences

5. **develop writing proficiency.**
   - Work in Progress: Timed Writing
   - Everyday epic

6. **extend learning.**
   - Research and Technology: Illustrated Travelogue

Block Scheduling: Use one 90-minute class period to preteach the skills and have students read Part 1. Use a second 90-minute class period to assess students' mastery of skills, extend their learning, and monitor their progress.

Homework Suggestions

The following are possibilities for homework assignments.

- Support pages from *Unit 6 Resources:*
  Literary Analysis
  Reading Skill
  Vocabulary Builder
  Enrichment

- An Extend Your Learning project and the Writing assignment for Part 1 of the *Odyssey* may be completed over several days.

PRENTICE HALL
TeacherEXPRESS™ Use this complete
Plan · Teach · Assess suite of powerful
teaching tools to make lesson planning and testing quicker and easier.

PRENTICE HALL
StudentEXPRESS™ Use the Interactive
Learn · Study · Succeed Textbook (online
and on CD-ROM) to make selections and activities come alive with audio and video support and interactive questions.

Build Skills from the *Odyssey*, Part 1

Practice these skills with the excerpt from the *Odyssey*, Part 1.

❶ Literary Analysis

An **epic hero** is the larger-than-life central character in an **epic**—a long narrative poem about important events in the history or folklore of a nation or culture. Through adventurous deeds, the epic hero demonstrates traits that are valued by the society in which the epic originates. Here, Odysseus shows his courage and leadership:

> Now, by the gods, I drove my big hand spike
> deep in the embers, charring it again,
> and cheered my men along with battle talk
> to keep their courage up; no quitting now.

Many epics begin *in medias res* ("in the middle of things"), meaning that much of the important action in the story occurred before the point at which the poem begins. Therefore, the epic hero's adventures are often recounted in a **flashback,** a scene that interrupts the sequence of events in a narrative to relate earlier events.

❷ Reading Skill

The **historical and cultural context** of a work is the backdrop of details of the time and place in which the work is set or in which it was written. These details include specific events, beliefs, and customs. When you read a work from another time and culture, **use background and prior knowledge** to analyze the influence of the historical and cultural context.

- Read the author biography, footnotes, and other text aids.
- Note how characters' behavior and attitudes reflect the context.

As you read, use a chart like the one shown to note the influence of ancient Greek culture in Homer's *Odyssey*.

Vocabulary Builder

- **plundered** (plun´ dərd) *v.* took goods by force; looted (p. 951) *The fierce pirates captured the merchant ship and plundered it.*

- **dispatched** (di spacht´) *v.* finished quickly (p. 960) *Remarkably, she dispatched this assignment a full hour before anyone else did.*

- **mammoth** (mam´ əth) *adj.* enormous (p. 963) *The mammoth ship made all others in the harbor look tiny.*

- **assuage** (ə swāj´) *v.* calm; pacify (p. 971) *Gentle words may assuage their anger.*

- **bereft** (bē reft´) *adj.* deprived (p. 973) *Bereft of sleep, she struggled to stay awake in class.*

- **ardor** (är´ dər) *n.* passion; enthusiasm (p. 978) *The audience cheered with ardor.*

- **insidious** (in sid´ ē əs) *adj.* characterized by craftiness and betrayal (p. 981) *The traitor's insidious actions led to the city's downfall.*

948 ■ *Themes in Literature: Heroism*

Historical / Cultural Detail

"Now Zeus the lord of cloud roused in the north a storm against the ships. . . ."

Background

Zeus is king of the gods in Greek mythology.

Analysis

The *Odyssey* reflects a belief that the gods participate actively in the lives of mortals.

---

❶ Literary Analysis
Epic Hero

- Explain that the notion of hero and the traits associated with heroism can change across time and across cultures.

- Read the description of *epic* and *epic hero* with the class. Have students give examples of other epics they might have encountered, such as the King Arthur tales or the Gilgamesh stories.

- Alert students to Odysseus' reputation as a wily hero, and have them look for the significant details in the selection that show him demonstrating his resourcefulness to get out of the trouble he encounters.

Flashback

- Tell students that they may often encounter examples of flashback in movies and television programs, as characters remember events that happened long before.

- Read the description of flashback together. Tell students they will find examples of flashback in the story in places where Odysseus recounts his tale to other characters.

❷ Reading Skill
Historical and Cultural Context

- Explain that learning more about the historical and cultural context gives students more insight into a selection and its characters. For example, the *Odyssey* begins by addressing a Muse, or inspiring spirit. Knowing that many ancient Greek writings start in this fashion will help students understand that the *Odyssey* is part of a larger tradition of storytelling.

- Discuss the chart with students. Point out the reference to Zeus in the first box. Discuss how knowledge of Zeus' position in mythology adds to a reader's understanding of the passage.

- Give students a copy of **Reading Skill Graphic Organizer A** (*Graphic Organizer Transparencies,* p. 199). Have them fill in the graphic organizer to identify historical and cultural details as they read the assigned selection.

Vocabulary Development

Vocabulary Development

Create a **Vocabulary Knowledge Rating Chart** for Part 1 of the *Odyssey*. Include the vocabulary from this page and the additional words students are asked to use at the end of Connecting to the Literature. These words will increase students' expressive vocabulary.

Give students a copy of the chart with the words on it. Introduce the words by reading them aloud and having students mark their rating in the Before Reading column. Urge them to be alert to these words as they read and discuss Part 1 because they will rate their knowledge of the words again after they finish.

If you wish, you may tally how many students know (or think they know) a word to gauge how much instruction you need to provide. As students read, point out the words and their context.

Build Understanding • from the *Odyssey*

❸ Background

The Trojan War The *Odyssey* describes the experiences of the Greek hero Odysseus as he made his way home after the Trojan War. According to legend, the Trojan War was sparked when Paris ran off with Helen. A Greek force attacked Troy (in modern-day Turkey) to recapture her and was finally victorious after ten years of fighting.

❹ Connecting to the Literature

Reading/Writing Connection In the *Odyssey*, Homer describes a journey filled with amazing adventures. Write a paragraph that tells of a journey you have taken or imagined. Describe something challenging or amazing that occurred. Use at least three of these words: *coincide, eliminate, encounter, highlight, interact.*

READ MORE

by Homer
The *Iliad*

Meet the Author

Homer (ca. 800 B.C.)

Homer is the legendary poet credited with writing the *Iliad* and the *Odyssey*. Their length and scope, gripping stories, imagery, and style have captured readers' imaginations for almost 3,000 years.

Did Homer Exist? Scholars disagree about whether the *Iliad* and the *Odyssey* were really written by Homer. According to tradition, Homer was born in western Asia Minor and was blind. However, many scholars feel confident that the *Iliad* and the *Odyssey* are the result of generations of oral poetic composition, masterpieces to which numerous ancient singers contributed. If Homer existed, he may have been the greatest in a long line of Greek epic storytellers.

Fast Facts

▶ The adjective *Homeric* means "large-scale; massive; epic in scope."

▶ Homer's stories have been the basis for many Hollywood movies, including *Troy* in 2004.

Go Online
Author Link

For: More information about the author
Visit: www.PHSchool.com
Web Code: epe-9602

from the *Odyssey* ■ 949

❸ Background
The Trojan War

The siege of Troy finally ended when the Greeks pretended to depart, leaving a giant wooden horse behind. Thinking that they had won the war, the Trojans dragged the horse inside the walls of their city. That night, Greek warriors who had hidden within the hollow horse crept out and opened the city gates to their waiting comrades, who then conquered the city.

❹ Connecting to the Literature

• Model use of the expressive vocabulary students are asked to use with these examples:

1. During your studies, you may *encounter* many references to Odysseus.

2. Reading about Greek architecture was a *highlight* of our report.

3. Our reading of the *Odyssey* will *coincide* with a showing of a film about ancient Greece.

4. We would like to *eliminate* any confusion about the hero's actions.

5. Students will *interact* with one another by performing certain sections of the *Odyssey*.

• Help students further develop their expressive vocabulary by providing these words: *gale, nymph, trickster,* and *voyage.* Encourage students to use these words as they discuss the selection.

Go Online
Author Link For additional information about Homer, have students type in the Web Code, then select *H* from the alphabet, and then select *Homer.*

949

1 **Motivation**

Prepare an **Anticipation Guide** (see *General Resources,* pp. 8–10) with the following statements:

- The best travel is one that is well planned and has no surprises.
- Good leaders are people who can think on their feet.
- Fear is an excellent motivator.
- It is important to be able to adapt to changes.

Give students a copy of the prepared Anticipation Guide and have students mark their responses in the Me column. Have students discuss the statements in pairs or groups and mark the Guides again in the Group column.

Concept Connector ➡

Students will return to the Anticipation Guide after completing Part 1 of the *Odyssey.*

Learning Modalities
Visual/Spatial Learners

Encourage students to use the illustration on page 950 to get a sense of the challenges facing Odysseus and his men as they try to sail home to Greece.

2 **About the Selection**

The *Odyssey* is a classic adventure story. It combines realistic elements of historical events with wildly imagined scenes of fantastic places and creatures. The epic also includes skillful characterizations. Odysseus, for example, represents the model epic hero: A leader of courage, daring, and wit, he pursues his goal—to return home after many years of war—in the face of many setbacks. However, he is also overly curious, foolishly cocky, and clever to the point of being tricky.

3 **Critical Viewing**

Possible response: The variation of light and darkness creates a mood of otherwordliness, mystery, and danger. The sun is hopeful.

from the

Odyssey

Homer Translated by Robert Fitzgerald

Ulysses Deriding Polyphemus, 1819, J.M.W. Turner, The National Gallery, London

3 ▲ Critical Viewing Do the images in this painting evoke feelings of hope or doom? Explain. **[Analyze]**

950 ■ *Themes in Literature: Heroism*

Vocabulary Development

Word Analysis
Call students' attention to the vocabulary word *plundered* in line 4. Explain that it came from the Germanic word *plünderen,* meaning "to pillage" or "to rob of household goods," and that the word came into wide usage during the Thirty Years' War, around 1630. Explain that soldiers often took "spoils" or valuable possessions, from the cities they defeated. Troy, therefore, would have been plundered of its valuables by the victorious Greek army.

Tell students to look for other words that relate to wartime, such as *stronghold, valor, stormed, enslaved,* and *muster.*

PART 1
The Adventures of Odysseus

In the opening verses, Homer addresses the muse of epic poetry. He asks her help in telling the tale of Odysseus.

Sing in me, Muse,[1] and through me tell the story
of that man skilled in all ways of contending,
the wanderer, harried for years on end,
after he <u>plundered</u> the stronghold
5 on the proud height of Troy.[2]
                    He saw the townlands
and learned the minds of many distant men,
and weathered many bitter nights and days
in his deep heart at sea, while he fought only
to save his life, to bring his shipmates home.
10 But not by will nor valor could he save them,
for their own recklessness destroyed them all—
children and fools, they killed and feasted on
the cattle of Lord Helios,[3] the Sun,
and he who moves all day through heaven
15 took from their eyes the dawn of their return.
Of these adventures, Muse, daughter of Zeus,[4]
tell us in our time, lift the great song again.

> **Note:** In translating the *Odyssey*, Fitzgerald spelled Greek names to suggest the sound of the original Greek. In these excerpts, more familiar spellings have been used. For example, Fitzgerald's "Kirkê," "Kyklops," and "Seirênês" are spelled here as "Circe," "Cyclops," and "Sirens."

1. Muse (myo͞oz) any one of the nine goddesses of the arts, literature, and sciences; the spirit that is thought to inspire a poet or other artist.

2. Troy (trоi) city in northwest Asia Minor; site of the Trojan War.

Vocabulary Builder
plundered (plun´ dərd)
v. took goods by force; looted

3. Helios (hē′ lē äs′) sun god.

4. Zeus (zo͞os) king of the gods.

6 ✓ Reading Check

What city did Odysseus and his men plunder?

from the *Odyssey,* Part I ■ 951

4 Humanities

Ulysses Deriding Polyphemus,
before 1830, by J.M.W. Turner

Turner began as a watercolor painter, influenced by the baroque landscape paintings of the seventeenth century. *Ulysses Deriding Polyphemus* was exhibited at the Royal Academy in 1829. Use this question for discussion:

• How does this painting help you understand the story?
  Possible response: The painting shows the tension and energy in the Greeks' escape from Cyclops' Island.

5 Literary Analysis
The Epic Hero

• Remind students of other heroes they have encountered in their reading. Have the class discuss what makes characters appear especially "heroic." Then **ask** students what qualities of Odysseus mark him as a hero.
  Answer: Odysseus has a "deep heart" and he bravely fights to bring his shipmates home.

• Have students review the description of epic hero on p. 948. Discuss the phrase "skilled in all ways of contending" in line 2, which means, in essence, "versatile." Ask students to explain how being skilled in many ways can be a heroic quality.

6 Reading Check

Answer: Odysseus and his men plundered the city of Troy.

Differentiated Instruction   Solutions for All Learners

Support for Less Proficient Readers
Point out that this page describes events that will be recounted during the telling of the epic. Ask students to summarize the page, then tell what they can infer from it.

Enrichment for Advanced Readers
Point out to students that reading the legends, epics, myths, and folk literature of a culture will help them understand a culture. The *Odyssey* provides historical background as well as cultural insights. Discuss students' responses at the end of each day's reading.

❼ Literary Analysis
Epic Hero

- Discuss with students how Odysseus' speech on p. 953 serves to introduce him and to illustrate his character. Point out that gives details of his background and childhood in this opening speech.

- **Ask** students where his home was and why he holds it dear.
Possible response: His home is Ithaca, which has a view of other islands. He says that it was rocky, but good for a boy's training.

- **Ask** students to name qualities they associate with heroism.
Answer: Students may say that bravery or determination is a heroic quality.
Ask students the Literary Analysis question on page 953: For what quality does Odysseus say he is famous?
Possible response: Odysseus is famous for his guile, or cunning, which makes him effective in both war and peace.

CHARACTERS

Alcinous (al sin´ ō əs)—king of the Phaeacians, to whom Odysseus tells his story

Odysseus (ō dis´ ē əs)—king of Ithaca

Calypso (kə lip´ sō)—sea goddess who loved Odysseus

Circe (sur´ sē)—enchantress who helped Odysseus

Zeus (zōōs)—king of the gods

Apollo (ə päl´ ō)—god of music, poetry, prophecy, and medicine

Agamemnon (ag´ ə mem´ nän´)—king and leader of Greek forces

Poseidon (pō sī´ dən)—god of sea, earthquakes, horses, and storms at sea

Athena (ə thē´ nə)—goddess of wisdom, skills, and warfare

Polyphemus (päl´ i fē´ məs)—the Cyclops who imprisoned Odysseus

Laertes (lā ur´ tēz´)—Odysseus' father

Cronus (krō´ nəs)—Titan ruler of the universe; father of Zeus

Perimedes (per´ ə mē´ dēz)—member of Odysseus' crew

Eurylochus (yōō ril´ ə kəs)—another member of the crew

Tiresias (tī rē´ sē əs)—blind prophet who advised Odysseus

Persephone (pər sef´ ə nē)—wife of Hades

Telemachus (tə lem´ ə kəs)—Odysseus and Penelope's son

Sirens (sī´ rənz)—creatures whose songs lure sailors to their deaths

Scylla (sil´ ə)—sea monster of gray rock

Charybdis (kə rib´ dis)—enormous and dangerous whirlpool

Lampetia (lam pē´ shə)—nymph

Hermes (hur´ mēz´)—herald and messenger of the gods

Eumaeus (yōō me´ əs)—old swineherd and friend of Odysseus

Antinous (an tin´ ō əs)—leader among the suitors

Eurynome (yōō rin´ ə mē)—housekeeper for Penelope

Penelope (pə nel´ ə pē)—Odysseus' wife

Eurymachus (yōō ri´ mə kəs)—suitor

Amphinomus (am fin´ ə məs)—suitor

Vocabulary Development

Words from Greek Mythology
The names and actions of the characters listed may be more meaningful to students if they are familiar with examples that have entered English usage. Have students look up the words *odyssey* and *siren* and use these words in a sentence that shows their general meaning. Challenge students to find the derivation of other words from mythology, including *atlas, echo, mentor,* and *morphine.*

Sailing from Troy

Ten years after the Trojan War, Odysseus departs from the goddess Calypso's island. He arrives in Phaeacia, ruled by Alcinous. Alcinous offers a ship to Odysseus and asks him to tell of his adventures.

7 "I am Laertes'[5] son, Odysseus.
                              Men hold me
formidable for guile[6] in peace and war:
20 this fame has gone abroad to the sky's rim.

My home is on the peaked sea-mark of Ithaca[7]
under Mount Neion's wind-blown robe of leaves,
in sight of other islands—Dulichium,
Same, wooded Zacynthus—Ithaca
25 being most lofty in that coastal sea,
and northwest, while the rest lie east and south.
A rocky isle, but good for a boy's training;
I shall not see on earth a place more dear,
8 though I have been detained long by Calypso,[8]
30 loveliest among goddesses, who held me
in her smooth caves, to be her heart's delight,
as Circe of Aeaea,[9] the enchantress,
desired me, and detained me in her hall.
But in my heart I never gave consent.
35 Where shall a man find sweetness to surpass
his own home and his parents? In far lands
he shall not, though he find a house of gold.

What of my sailing, then, from Troy?
                              What of those years
of rough adventure, weathered under Zeus?
40 The wind that carried west from Ilium[10]
brought me to Ismarus, on the far shore,
a strongpoint on the coast of Cicones.[11]
I stormed that place and killed the men who fought.
Plunder we took, and we enslaved the women,
45 to make division, equal shares to all—
but on the spot I told them: 'Back, and quickly!
Out to sea again!' My men were mutinous,[12]

---

5. Laertes (lā ʉr′ tēz′)

6. guile (gīl) *n.* craftiness; cunning.

7. Ithaca (ith′ ə kə) island off the west coast of Greece.

Literary Analysis
Epic Hero For what quality does Odysseus say he is famous?

8. Calypso (kə lip′ sō) sea goddess who loved Odysseus.

9. Circe (sʉr′ sē) **of Aeaea** (ē′ ē ə)

10. Ilium (il ē əm) Troy.

11. Cicones (si kō′ nēz)

12. mutinous (my̅o̅o̅t′n əs) *adj.* rebellious.

9 Reading Check
Who has asked Odysseus to tell his tale?

---

from the *Odyssey*, Part I ▪ 953

8 **Critical Thinking**
Interpret

- Point out that the desire to return home drives all of the action in the *Odyssey*.

- Explain that Calypso and Circe are two enchantresses. Calypso is a sea nymph who holds Odysseus under her spell for seven years. Circe turns Odysseus' men into pigs.

- **Ask** students how Odysseus feels about his home on Ithaca. Why does he stay with Calypso and Circe when he is so eager to return to Ithaca? Draw students' attention to the second paragraph. **Answer:** Odysseus is eager to return to his home. He says that he "never gave consent" to stay with Calypso or Circe, indicating that he was under a spell and never in control of his own actions.

9 **Reading Check**

Answer: Alcinous, king of the Phaeacians, asks Odysseus to tell his story.

Differentiated
Instruction   Solutions for All Learners

Strategy for Less Proficient Readers
Display the **Series-of-Events Chain** *(Graphic Organizer Transparencies,* p. 239), and have students chart the story that Odysseus relates. Fill in the first box of the organizer with the following sentence from p. 953: "The wind that carried west from Ilium brought me to Ismarus."

Guide students as they list events that Odysseus describes, for example, his men's battles with the Cicones, his arrival on the island of the Lotus-Eaters, and his encounter with the Cyclops. You may suggest that students write the names of the islands or creatures in each box as they encounter them. On a second reading, they can go back and jot down what happened to Odysseus and his men at each place or with each creature.

Tell students that when they complete their Series-of-Events Chain, they will have a rough outline of the major events in Odysseus' tale.

953

- **Ask** students what mistakes Odysseus and his men made on Ismarus.
  Possible response: Odysseus' men were greedy and mutinous, drinking wine and feasting on sheep and cattle, but paying little attention to people who went inland. The crew's behavior exposed them to the Cicone army.

- Point out the ways in which Odysseus' description reveals the tactics of Greek warfare. For example, the Cicones fight on horseback, while the Greeks are armed with lances.

- **Ask** students what the empty benches in line 63 reveal about the outcome of the battle, as well as the type of ship Odysseus sailed in.
  Possible response: The "empty benches" show the number of men killed in battle. The benches also show how the sailors sat on the boat, possibly to row with oars.
  Ask students the Reading Skill question: What beliefs and values are reflected in lines 65–69?
  Possible response: The sailors' grief indicates how close they are to one another and how much they honor the men with whom they fight.

⑪ **Literary Analysis**
Epic Hero and Flashback

- Remind students that Odysseus is explaining to his listener why it has taken him so long to return home.
  Ask students to mark the words that show the passage of time in the first 10 lines of The Lotus Eaters.
  Answer: The words *now, two long days and nights, until,* and *then* show the passage of time.
  Ask students the Literary Analysis question: What words in line 82 remind you that this part is a flashback?
  Possible response: The phrase *that time* indicates that Odysseus is retelling one of the many incidents that happened on his journey.

---

fools, on stores of wine. Sheep after sheep
they butchered by the surf, and shambling cattle,
50   feasting,—while fugitives went inland, running
to call to arms the main force of Cicones.
This was an army, trained to fight on horseback
or, where the ground required, on foot. They came
with dawn over that terrain like the leaves
55   and blades of spring. So doom appeared to us,
dark word of Zeus for us, our evil days.
My men stood up and made a fight of it—
backed on the ships, with lances kept in play,
from bright morning through the blaze of noon
60   holding our beach, although so far outnumbered;
but when the sun passed toward unyoking time,
then the Achaeans,[13] one by one, gave way.
Six benches were left empty in every ship
that evening when we pulled away from death.
65 │ And this new grief we bore with us to sea:
    │ our precious lives we had, but not our friends.
⑩ │ No ship made sail next day until some shipmate
    │ had raised a cry, three times, for each poor ghost
    │ unfleshed by the Cicones on that field.

The Lotus-Eaters

70   Now Zeus the lord of cloud roused in the north
a storm against the ships, and driving veils
of squall moved down like night on land and sea.
The bows went plunging at the gust; sails
cracked and lashed out strips in the big wind.
75   We saw death in that fury, dropped the yards,
unshipped the oars, and pulled for the nearest lee:[14]
then two long days and nights we lay offshore
worn out and sick at heart, tasting our grief,
until a third Dawn came with ringlets shining.
80   Then we put up our masts, hauled sail, and rested,
letting the steersmen and the breeze take over.

    │ I might have made it safely home, that time,
⑪ │ but as I came round Malea the current
    │ took me out to sea, and from the north
85 │   a fresh gale drove me on, past Cythera.

954 ■ *Themes in Literature: Heroism*

---

13. Achaeans (ə kē′ ənz) *n.* Greeks; here, Odysseus' men.

Reading Skill
Historical and Cultural Context
What beliefs and values are reflected in lines 65–69?

14. lee (lē) *n.* area sheltered from the wind.

Literary Analysis
Epic Hero and Flashback What words in line 82 remind you that this part is a flashback?

Vocabulary Development

Expressive Vocabulary
Ask students to think about Odysseus' travels with his men. Were they more terrified by their battles with the seas, or by their encounters with monsters? Did they ever lose hope of returning home? Which of their delays are avoidable, and which are unavoidable? As students discuss the Greeks' voyage home, encourage them to use the expressive vocabulary presented earlier. You might encourage them with sentence starters like these:

1. The Greeks' *encounter* with the Cicones could have been avoided if . . .
2. The sailors *interact* with people who forget their memories when . . .
3. Odysseus takes the time to *highlight* his men's grief at the death of their comrades after . . .
4. Odysseus cannot *eliminate* his men's errors when . . .

Nine days I drifted on the teeming sea
before dangerous high winds. Upon the tenth
we came to the coastline of the Lotus-Eaters,
who live upon that flower. We landed there
90   to take on water. All ships' companies
mustered alongside for the mid-day meal.
Then I sent out two picked men and a runner
to learn what race of men that land sustained.
They fell in, soon enough, with Lotus-Eaters,
95   who showed no will to do us harm, only
offering the sweet Lotus to our friends—
but those who ate this honeyed plant, the Lotus,
never cared to report, nor to return:
they longed to stay forever, browsing on
100 that native bloom, forgetful of their homeland.
I drove them, all three wailing, to the ships,
tied them down under their rowing benches,
and called the rest: 'All hands aboard;
come, clear the beach and no one taste
105 the Lotus, or you lose your hope of home.'
Filing in to their places by the rowlocks
my oarsmen dipped their long oars in the surf,
and we moved out again on our sea faring.

Literary Analysis
Epic Hero Which characteristics of an epic hero does Odysseus show in this episode?

Thinking About the Selection

1. **Respond:** What is your first impression of Odysseus? Which of his qualities do you admire? Explain.

2. **(a) Recall:** While on Ismarus, in what ways do Odysseus' men disobey orders? **(b) Analyze Cause and Effect:** What is the result of this disobedience? **(c) Speculate:** What lesson might Odysseus take away from this experience?

3. **(a) Recall:** What happens to the men who eat the Lotus? **(b) Infer:** What does this episode suggest about the main problem that Odysseus has with his men? **(c) Evaluate:** Do you think Odysseus responds appropriately to the three men who long to stay with the Lotus-Eaters? Why or why not?

4. **(a) Recall:** Note two points at which Odysseus mentions a desire to return home. **(b) Infer:** What significant role might his longing for home play in Odysseus' epic journey?

⓬ **Literary Analysis**

- Read aloud lines 101–105, describing Odysseus' treatment of his men.

- **Ask** students the Literary Analysis question: Which characteristics of an epic hero does Odysseus show in this episode?
  Possible response: Odysseus displays wisdom when he sends out a scouting party, rather than putting all of his men at risk. When Odysseus realizes the danger of the Lotus, he acts decisively, ordering his ships to sail immediately. He also shows leadership in explaining to his men why they must leave.

ASSESS

Answers

1. **Possible response:** Students might say that they are impressed with Odysseus. They might admire the determination that he maintained over his long voyage home and the values that motivate him to return.

2. (a) The Greeks mutinied, drank wine, and refused to come back to the ship. (b) As a result of their disobedience, they are attacked by the Cicones and many Greeks are killed. (c) Odysseus might learn that he needs to exercise discipline over his men.

3. (a) The men who eat the Lotus are lulled into a state of calm forgetfulness and no longer want to return home. (b) Odysseus apparently has trouble instilling a sense of self-control and discipline into his men. (c) **Possible response:** Odysseus has no choice but to force the men back on the ship; their skills are needed on board to help everyone get home safely.

4. (a) He mentions a desire to return home as he describes being held by Circe (line 35) and when he describes his escape from the Lotus-Eaters (line 105). (b) **Possible response:** His longing for home might give Odysseus extra strength or drive to escape from difficulties.

- Point out to students that conflicts in the *Odyssey* are signaled before they actually occur. **Ask** students to point out some of the warnings of conflict in this passage.
  Answer: Odysseus finds fault with the Cyclopes' uncivilized ways. The Cyclopes do not farm, and they have no laws. They deal out rough justice to women and children.

- **Ask** students the Reading Skill question: Given Odysseus' criticism of the Cyclopes, what kind of society do you think the Greeks valued?
  Possible responses: The Greeks must have valued an ordered society that practiced agriculture and abided by rules of law.

⑭ Reading Skill
Historical and Cultural Context

- Read the passage together with students, pointing out the words *alone, remote, solitude* that describe how the Cyclops lived separate from others.

- **Ask** students why Odysseus holds those who eat wheaten bread in high esteem.
  Possible response: Wheat bread perhaps shows refinement and is an indication of civilization.

The Cyclops

In the next land we found were Cyclopes,[15]
110   giants, louts, without a law to bless them.
In ignorance leaving the fruitage of the earth in mystery
to the immortal gods, they neither plow
nor sow by hand, nor till the ground, though grain—
⑬   wild wheat and barley—grows untended, and
115   wine-grapes, in clusters, ripen in heaven's rains.
Cyclopes have no muster and no meeting,
no consultation or old tribal ways,
but each one dwells in his own mountain cave
dealing out rough justice to wife and child,
120   indifferent to what the others do. . . .

As we rowed on, and nearer to the mainland,
at one end of the bay, we saw a cavern
yawning above the water, screened with laurel,
and many rams and goats about the place
125   inside a sheepfold—made from slabs of stone
earthfast between tall trunks of pine and rugged
towering oak trees.
                                                  A prodigious[16] man
slept in this cave alone, and took his flocks
⑭   to graze afield—remote from all companions,
130   knowing none but savage ways, a brute
so huge, he seemed no man at all of those
who eat good wheaten bread; but he seemed rather
a shaggy mountain reared in solitude.
We beached there, and I told the crew
135   to stand by and keep watch over the ship:
as for myself I took my twelve best fighters
and went ahead. I had a goatskin full
of that sweet liquor that Euanthes' son,
Maron, had given me. He kept Apollo's[17]
140   holy grove at Ismarus; for kindness
we showed him there, and showed his wife and child,
he gave me seven shining golden talents[18]
perfectly formed, a solid silver winebowl,
and then this liquor—twelve two-handled jars
145   of brandy, pure and fiery. Not a slave
in Maron's household knew this drink; only
he, his wife and the storeroom mistress knew;

15. Cyclopes (sī klō′ pēz′) *n.* plural form of **Cyclops** (sī′ kläps′), race of giants with one eye in the middle of the fore-head.

Reading Skill
Historical and Cultural Context Based on Odysseus' criticism of the Cyclopes, what kind of society do you think the Greeks valued?

16. prodigious (prō dij′ əs) *adj.* enormous.

Reading Skill
Historical and Cultural Context What does this passage reveal about ancient Greek attitudes toward the importance of community?

17. Apollo (ə päl′ ō) god of music, poetry, prophecy, and medicine.

18. talents units of money in ancient Greece.

and they would put one cupful—ruby-colored,
honey-smooth—in twenty more of water,
150 but still the sweet scent hovered like a fume
over the winebowl. No man turned away
when cups of this came round.

A wineskin full

I brought along, and victuals[19] in a bag,
for in my bones I knew some towering brute
155 would be upon us soon—all outward power,
a wild man, ignorant of civility.

We climbed, then, briskly to the cave. But Cyclops
had gone afield, to pasture his fat sheep,
so we looked round at everything inside:
160 a drying rack that sagged with cheeses, pens
crowded with lambs and kids,[20] each in its class:
firstlings apart from middlings, and the 'dewdrops,'
or newborn lambkins, penned apart from both.
And vessels full of whey[21] were brimming there—
165 bowls of earthenware and pails for milking.
My men came pressing round me, pleading:

19. victuals (vit′ ə'lz) *n.* food or other provisions.

20. kids young goats.

21. whey (hwā) *n.* thin, watery part of milk separated from the thicker curds.

16 ✓ Reading Check
Where is Cyclops when Odysseus and his men enter the cave?

15 ◄ Critical Viewing
How does this image of Apollo compare with your impressions of the ancient Greek gods? **[Compare and Contrast]**

from the *Odyssey, Part I* ■ *957*

15 Critical Viewing
Answer: The calm dignity of this image of Apollo contrasts with the seductiveness of Calypso and the stormy wrath of Zeus, gods who have been mentioned earlier.

16 Reading Check
Answer: The Cyclops is in the field taking care of his sheep.

Differentiated Instruction Solutions for All Learners

Support for Less Proficient Readers
Point out that this page describes the food that the Greeks find in the Cyclops cave. Ask a volunteer to read lines 159–165. List the food on the board. Then ask students to draw the scene in the Cyclops' cave.

Support for English Language Learners
Reread lines 158–165. Point out the terms that describe the animals, such as firstlings, middlings, and dewdrops. Ask students why those animals would have to be separated. Finally, have students find other words to describe animal offspring such as *nestling, fawn, duckling, eaglet, cub, gosling, joey, piglet,* and *cygnet.* Have students identify the parent of each of these offspring.

- Point out that in this passage, Odysseus reveals one of the qualities that get him into trouble: he doesn't listen to his men.

- **Ask** students if they think that Odysseus should stay and get more information, or that he should leave and avoid trouble.
Possible response: Students may say that they think Odysseus should leave now unless he is sure he can find an escape route.

- **Ask** students the Literary Analysis question: What character flaw does Odysseus reveal by refusing to leave the cave?
Possible response: Odysseus' curiosity leads him to disregard good advice. He knows it would be wise to seize the food and leave, but he is too curious to see the "cave man."

18 **Literary Analysis**
Epic Hero

- Have students read aloud lines 204–215. Discuss what verbal inflection they might use in the phrases "We served under Agamemnon," "the whole world knows," and "have a care."

- **Ask** students what earlier events would give Odysseus reason to be proud of his men and his own behavior.
Possible response: The Greeks have defeated the Trojans at war; Odysseus and his men have sailed through many storms and have escaped the Cicones and the Lotus-Eaters.

'Why not
take these cheeses, get them stowed, come back,
throw open all the pens, and make a run for it?
We'll drive the kids and lambs aboard. We say
170   put out again on good salt water!'

Ah,
how sound that was! Yet I refused. I wished
17 to see the cave man, what he had to offer—
no pretty sight, it turned out, for my friends.
We lit a fire, burnt an offering,
175   and took some cheese to eat; then sat in silence
around the embers, waiting. When he came
he had a load of dry boughs[22] on his shoulder
to stoke his fire at suppertime. He dumped it
with a great crash into that hollow cave,
180   and we all scattered fast to the far wall.
Then over the broad cavern floor he ushered
the ewes he meant to milk. He left his rams
and he-goats in the yard outside, and swung
high overhead a slab of solid rock
185   to close the cave. Two dozen four-wheeled wagons,
with heaving wagon teams, could not have stirred
the tonnage of that rock from where he wedged it
over the doorsill. Next he took his seat
and milked his bleating ewes. A practiced job
190   he made of it, giving each ewe her suckling;
thickened his milk, then, into curds and whey,
sieved out the curds to drip in withy[23] baskets,
and poured the whey to stand in bowls
cooling until he drank it for his supper.
195   When all these chores were done, he poked the fire,
heaping on brushwood. In the glare he saw us.

'Strangers,' he said, 'who are you? And where from?
What brings you here by seaways—a fair traffic?
Or are you wandering rogues, who cast your lives
200   like dice, and ravage other folk by sea?'

We felt a pressure on our hearts, in dread
of that deep rumble and that mighty man.
18 But all the same I spoke up in reply:

Literary Analysis
Epic Hero What character flaw does the hero Odysseus reveal by refusing to leave the cave?

22. boughs (bouz) *n.* tree branches.

23. withy (wi*th*′ ē) *adj.* made from tough, flexible twigs.

Vocabulary Development

Think-Aloud: Context
Direct students' attention to the word *rogues* on this page, line 199. Using a think-aloud process, model how to use context to infer the meaning of an unknown word. Say to students:

    I'm going to think aloud to show you how I would figure out the meaning of *rogue* from its context.

    In this sentence, *rogue* is used by the Cyclops to describe people who "ravage other folk by sea." We know that earlier in the passage the Greeks have stolen into the Cyclops' cave, and, from his point of view, they could be robbers. The word *ravage,* or ruin, is a clue that a *rogue* is a person who does no good. Since the Greeks have broken into the Cyclops' cave, I think *rogue* refers to some kind of a scoundrel.

'We are from Troy, Achaeans, blown off course
205 by shifting gales on the Great South Sea;
homeward bound, but taking routes and ways
18 uncommon; so the will of Zeus would have it.
We served under Agamemnon,[24] son of Atreus—
the whole world knows what city
210 he laid waste, what armies he destroyed.
It was our luck to come here; here we stand,
19 beholden for your help, or any gifts
you give—as custom is to honor strangers.
We would entreat you, great Sir, have a care
215 for the gods' courtesy; Zeus will avenge
the unoffending guest.'

He answered this
from his brute chest, unmoved:

'You are a ninny,
or else you come from the other end of nowhere,
telling me, mind the gods! We Cyclopes
220 care not a whistle for your thundering Zeus
or all the gods in bliss; we have more force by far.
I would not let you go for fear of Zeus—
you or your friends—unless I had a whim[25] to.
Tell me, where was it, now, you left your ship—
225 around the point, or down the shore, I wonder?'

He thought he'd find out, but I saw through this,
and answered with a ready lie:

20 'My ship?
Poseidon[26] Lord, who sets the earth a-tremble,
broke it up on the rocks at your land's end.
230 A wind from seaward served him, drove us there.
We are survivors, these good men and I.'

Neither reply nor pity came from him,
but in one stride he clutched at my companions
and caught two in his hands like squirming puppies
235 to beat their brains out, spattering the floor.
Then he dismembered them and made his meal,
gaping and crunching like a mountain lion—
everything: innards, flesh, and marrow bones.
We cried aloud, lifting our hands to Zeus,
240 powerless, looking on at this, appalled;

---

24. Agamemnon (ag′ ə mem′ nän′) king who led the Greek army during the Trojan War.

Reading Skill
Historical and Cultural Context What ancient Greek beliefs regarding the gods, military might, and respect for strangers does Odysseus express in his words to the Cyclops?

25. whim (hwim) *n.* sudden thought or wish to do something.

26. Poseidon (pō sī′ dən) god of the sea, earthquakes, horses, and storms at sea.

Literary Analysis
Epic Hero In what way does Odysseus' response show that he is "formidable for guile"?

21 Reading Check
What does Odysseus tell the Cyclops happened to his ship?

from the Odyssey, Part I ■ 959

---

19 **Reading Skill**
Historical and Cultural Context

- Point out to students Odysseus' use of the word *courtesy* in line 215. Explain to students that *courtesy* meant more than just "politeness" in Greek society. Ancient Greek custom held that any guest must be offered hospitality in one's home. All guests were treated with courtesy, in part because the gods could assume human form and might appear at one's doorstep.

- Now **ask** students the Reading Skill question: What ancient Greek beliefs does Odysseus express in his words to Cyclops?
Possible response: Odysseus' answer shows that the Greek custom of hospitality is well established. The rules of hospitality are part of the Greeks' religious beliefs and are thought to be enforced by the gods.

20 **Literary Analysis**
Epic Hero

- **Ask** students why the Cyclops would want to know the location of the Greeks' ship.
Possible response: He might want to rob the ship of any goods, or he might want to kill any other sailors left on board.

- Point out to students that Odysseus' response is a "ready lie," meaning that he thought of the response quickly. **Ask** them what the ability to have a "ready lie" shows about Odysseus.
Possible response: Odysseus is quick thinking. He immediately sees the Cyclops' reason for asking about his ship and is able to formulate a plausible answer quickly.

- **Ask** students the Literary Analysis question: In what way does Odysseus' response show that he is "formidable for guile"?
Possible response: Odysseus is clever enough to see through his opponent's trickery and to outwit him in return.

21 **Reading Check**

Answer: Odysseus says that his ship has broken up on the rocks. He lies because he thinks that Cyclops may want to destroy the Greek ship.

- Point out that Odysseus is prepared to kill Cyclops by stabbing him in the liver. **Ask** students what factors complicate the Greeks' attempts at escaping.
  Possible response: The Cyclops has sealed the entrance to the cave with a huge stone, too big for humans to move. The Cyclops continues to eat Odysseus' men as long as they are trapped in the cave.

- Then **ask** the Literary Analysis question: How do lines 244–250 show Odysseus' ability to think ahead?
  Possible response: Odysseus realizes that, although he could successfully kill the Cyclops, he would doom himself to imprisonment in the cave. He knows his escape must involve the Cyclops removing the stone blocking the entry to the cave.

23 Critical Viewing

Answer: Athena's posture in this statue indicates action. Her arm is drawn back as if she is about to hurl a spear. She is wearing a helmet, which indicates that she is ready for battle. Overall, this statue indicates Athena's warlike powers and her skill in battle.

---

but Cyclops went on filling up his belly
with manflesh and great gulps of whey,
then lay down like a mast among his sheep.
My heart beat high now at the chance of action,
245   and drawing the sharp sword from my hip I went
along his flank to stab him where the midriff
22   holds the liver. I had touched the spot
when sudden fear stayed me: if I killed him
we perished there as well, for we could never
250   move his ponderous doorway slab aside.
So we were left to groan and wait for morning.

When the young Dawn with fingertips of rose
lit up the world, the Cyclops built a fire
and milked his handsome ewes, all in due order,
255   putting the sucklings to the mothers. Then,
his chores being all <u>dispatched</u>, he caught
another brace[27] of men to make his breakfast,
and whisked away his great door slab
to let his sheep go through—but he, behind,
260   reset the stone as one would cap a quiver.[28]
There was a din[29] of whistling as the Cyclops
rounded his flock to higher ground, then stillness.
And now I pondered how to hurt him worst,
if but Athena[30] granted what I prayed for.
265   Here are the means I thought would serve my turn:

a club, or staff, lay there along the fold—
an olive tree, felled green and left to season[31]
for Cyclops' hand. And it was like a mast
a lugger[32] of twenty oars, broad in the beam—
270   a deep-sea-going craft—might carry:
so long, so big around, it seemed. Now I
chopped out a six foot section of this pole
and set it down before my men, who scraped it;
and when they had it smooth, I hewed again
275   to make a stake with pointed end. I held this
24   in the fire's heart and turned it, toughening it,
then hid it, well back in the cavern, under
one of the dung piles in profusion there.
Now came the time to toss for it: who ventured
280   along with me? whose hand could bear to thrust
and grind that spike in Cyclops' eye, when mild

Epic Hero How do lines 244–250 show Odysseus' ability to think ahead?

Vocabulary Builder
dispatched (di spacht´) *v.* finished quickly

27. **brace** (brās) *n.* pair.

28. **cap a quiver** (kwiv´ ər) close a case holding arrows.

29. **din** (din) *n.* loud, continuous noise; uproar.

30. **Athena** (ə *thē´* nə) goddess of wisdom, skills, and warfare.

31. **felled green and left to season** chopped down and exposed to the weather to age the wood.

32. **lugger** (lug´ ər) *n.* small sailing vessel.

23 Critical Viewing
What traits does this statue of Athena illustrate? **[Interpret]**

Vocabulary Development

Multiple Meanings
Draw students' attention to the use of the word *dispatched* in line 256. Ask students whether they have encountered this word in other contexts and ask them to give examples of other usages. Then have students look up the word to see its alternative meanings. Ask students to write sentences showing *dispatch* used to indicate the following definitions: "to send a message"; "to finish quickly"; "to kill"; and "to ask to leave."

24 sleep had mastered him? As luck would have it,
the men I would have chosen won the toss—
four strong men, and I made five as captain.

285 At evening came the shepherd with his flock,
his woolly flock. The rams as well, this time,
entered the cave: by some sheepherding whim—
or a god's bidding—none were left outside.
He hefted his great boulder into place
290 and sat him down to milk the bleating ewes
in proper order, put the lambs to suck,
and swiftly ran through all his evening chores.
Then he caught two more men and feasted on them.
My moment was at hand, and I went forward
295 holding an ivy bowl of my dark drink,
looking up, saying:

                          'Cyclops, try some wine.
Here's liquor to wash down your scraps of men.
Taste it, and see the kind of drink we carried
25 under our planks. I meant it for an offering
300 if you would help us home. But you are mad,
unbearable, a bloody monster! After this,
will any other traveler come to see you?'

He seized and drained the bowl, and it went down
so fiery and smooth he called for more:

305 'Give me another, thank you kindly. Tell me,
how are you called? I'll make a gift will please you.
Even Cyclopes know the wine grapes grow
out of grassland and loam in heaven's rain,
but here's a bit of nectar and ambrosia!'[33]

310 Three bowls I brought him, and he poured them down.
I saw the fuddle and flush come over him,
then I sang out in cordial tones:

                          'Cyclops,
you ask my honorable name? Remember
the gift you promised me, and I shall tell you.
315 My name is Nohbdy: mother, father, and friends,
everyone calls me Nohbdy.'

Literary Analysis
Epic Hero What heroic qualities does Odysseus reveal as he plots against the Cyclops?

Literary Analysis
Epic Hero What plan do you think Odysseus has in mind by offering the Cyclops the wine?

33. nectar (nek´ tər) **and ambrosia** (am brō´ zhə) drink and food of the gods.

26 **Reading Check**

What does Odysseus plan to do with the stake that he and his men make?

from the *Odyssey, Part I* ■ *961*

---

24 **Literary Analysis**
Epic Hero

• Review with students the plans that Odysseus makes to attempt his escape. **Ask** students how long it took them to figure out what Odysseus was doing with the olive tree.
Possible response: Students may say they did not see Odysseus' intention until he declares that he will "grind that spike" into the Cyclops' eye.

• **Ask** students the Literary Analysis question: What heroic qualities does Odysseus reveal as he plots against the Cyclops?
Possible response: Odysseus shows the ability to construct a carefully detailed plan. He has the discipline to carry through each step of the plan, without rushing in a way that would tip off the Cyclops that he is about to be tricked.

• Point out how Odysseus combines the bravery and strength of an epic hero with intelligence and cunning. Have students give examples of more one-dimensional heroes and compare them with the depth of Odysseus' character.

25 **Literary Analysis**
Epic Hero

• Review with students Odysseus' earlier discussion of this wine and its potency. Remind students that humans enjoyed the drink when it was considerably diluted with water.

• **Ask** students the Literary Analysis question: What plan do you think Odysseus has in mind by offering the Cyclops wine?
Possible responses: Odysseus hopes to slow the Cyclops' reaction time or perhaps put him to sleep.

26 **Reading Check**

Answer: Odysseus plans to blind the Cyclops by ramming the stake into the creature's eye.

Historical and Cultural Context

- Have students review the text to find instances in which Odysseus evokes the gods. Remind them that Zeus was thought to "avenge" guests who were treated improperly.

- **Ask** students what impact Odysseus' reference to "the gods" might have on his audience. **Possible response:** The audience might see that, in contrast to the godless Cyclops, Odysseus was a god-fearing hero.

- **Ask** students the Reading Skill question: What cultural values are represented in Odysseus' reference to "the gods" in line 323? **Possible response:** Odysseus' response shows that he is a man who respects the authority of the gods. The reference to "the gods" shows that he asks for help from a greater power in his time of need.

And he said:

'Nohbdy's my meat, then, after I eat his friends.
Others come first. There's a noble gift, now.'

Even as he spoke, he reeled and tumbled backward,
320   his great head lolling to one side; and sleep
took him like any creature. Drunk, hiccuping,
he dribbled streams of liquor and bits of men.

㉗ Now, by the gods, I drove my big hand spike
deep in the embers, charring it again,
325   and cheered my men along with battle talk
to keep their courage up: no quitting now.
The pike of olive, green though it had been,
reddened and glowed as if about to catch.
I drew it from the coals and my four fellows
330   gave me a hand, lugging it near the Cyclops
as more than natural force nerved them; straight
forward they sprinted, lifted it, and rammed it
deep in his crater eye, and leaned on it
turning it as a shipwright turns a drill
335   in planking, having men below to swing
the two-handled strap that spins it in the groove.
So with our brand we bored[34] that great eye socket
while blood ran out around the red-hot bar.
Eyelid and lash were seared; the pierced ball
340   hissed broiling, and the roots popped.

In a smithy
one sees a white-hot axehead or an adze
plunged and wrung in a cold tub, screeching steam—
the way they make soft iron hale and hard—:
just so that eyeball hissed around the spike.
345   The Cyclops bellowed and the rock roared round him,
and we fell back in fear. Clawing his face
he tugged the bloody spike out of his eye,
threw it away, and his wild hands went groping;
then he set up a howl for Cyclopes
350   who lived in caves on windy peaks nearby.
Some heard him; and they came by divers[35] ways
to clump around outside and call:

'What ails you,
Polyphemus?[36] Why do you cry so sore
in the starry night? You will not let us sleep.

Reading Skill
Historical and Cultural Context What cultural values are represented in Odysseus' reference to "the gods" in line 323?

34. bored (bôrd) *v.* made a hole in.

35. divers (dī´ vərz) *adj.* several; various.

36. Polyphemus (päl´ i fē´ məs)

Vocabulary Development

Word Analysis
In line 353, Odysseus reveals that the Cyclops' name is *Polyphemus.* The name means "much or many" (*poly*) and "telling" (*phemus*). In other words, Polyphemus—"much telling"—is a braggart. Have students use the dictionary to find other words with the prefix *poly-* and use their knowledge of this Greek word part to help figure out the definition. Sample vocabulary words could include *polymath* (much learning), *polyglot* (many tongues), and *polychrome* (many colors).

355 Sure no man's driving off your flock? No man
    has tricked you, ruined you?'

                                    Out of the cave
    the <u>mammoth</u> Polyphemus roared in answer:

    'Nohbdy, Nohbdy's tricked me, Nohbdy's ruined me!'

    To this rough shout they made a sage[37] reply:

360 'Ah well, if nobody has played you foul
    there in your lonely bed, we are no use in pain
    given by great Zeus. Let it be your father,
    Poseidon Lord, to whom you pray.'

                                    So saying
    (28) they trailed away. And I was filled with laughter
365 to see how like a charm the name deceived them.
    Now Cyclops, wheezing as the pain came on him,
    fumbled to wrench away the great doorstone
    and squatted in the breach with arms thrown wide
    for any silly beast or man who bolted—
370 hoping somehow I might be such a fool.
    But I kept thinking how to win the game:
    death sat there huge; how could we slip away?
    I drew on all my wits, and ran through tactics,
    reasoning as a man will for dear life,
375 until a trick came—and it pleased me well.
    The Cyclops' rams were handsome, fat, with heavy
    fleeces, a dark violet.

                                    Three abreast
    I tied them silently together, twining
    cords of willow from the ogre's bed;
380 then slung a man under each middle one
    to ride there safely, shielded left and right.
    So three sheep could convey each man. I took
    the woolliest ram, the choicest of the flock,
    and hung myself under his kinky belly,
385 pulled up tight, with fingers twisted deep
    in sheepskin ringlets for an iron grip.
    So, breathing hard, we waited until morning.

    When Dawn spread out her fingertips of rose
    the rams began to stir, moving for pasture,

Vocabulary Builder
mammoth (mam´ əth)
adj. enormous

37. sage (sāj) *adj.* wise.

Literary Analysis
Epic Hero What does
Odysseus' gleeful
response to his
successful trick reveal
about his character?

 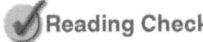

(29) ✓ **Reading Check**

What do the other
Cyclops think
Polyphemus is saying
when he says,
"Nohbdy's tricked
me"?

from the Odyssey, Part I ■ 963

---

(28) Literary Analysis
Epic Hero

- Remind students of the Greeks' dire circumstances. **Ask** students how many of Odysseus' men the Cyclops has eaten.
  Answer: The Cyclops has eaten six men.

- Have students describe Odysseus' wordplay, in which he claims that his name is "Nohbdy" or "Nobody." **Ask** students why his game turns out to be important to his survival.
  Possible response: Odysseus' claim that he is "Nohbdy" is important because it keeps the other Cyclopes from coming to Polyphemus' rescue.

- **Ask** students the Literary Analysis question: What does Odysseus' gleeful response to his successful trick reveal about his character?
  Possible response: Odysseus' laughter shows his great love of life. He takes enormous pleasure in his trick and is able to set aside the suffering he has endured to appreciate how thoroughly his wordplay fooled the Cyclopes.

- Have students discuss Odysseus' laughter and compare it with other heroes they have encountered in their reading. **Ask** them whether a hero with a sense of humor is ordinary or unusual.
  Possible response: Students may say that most heroes are more serious than Odysseus.

(29) Reading Check

Answer: The other Cyclopes think that Polyphemus is saying "I am in pain, but no one has tricked me." They believe that there is nothing they can do to help Polyphemus.

Differentiated
Instruction   Solutions for All Learners

Strategy for Special Needs Students
The Greeks' encounter with the Cyclops involves many plot turns and setbacks. Have students mark pages with different colored self-stick adhesive notes, using one color for instances in which the Cyclops overpowers the Greeks and another color for instances in which Odysseus outwits the Cyclops. Once students have found the instances and marked them, have them jot down the most important details of the encounter on the note.

Strategy for English Learners
Provide English learners with an oral synopsis of key content areas before they begin reading the Cyclops section of the *Odyssey*. A synopsis could note the following elements of the plot: The Greeks' landing on the Cyclops' island; the Greeks' discovery of the Cyclops' cave; their entrapment in the cave; Odysseus' daring plot to blind the Cyclops; and the Greeks' escape using the Cyclops' sheep. Also discuss the ways in which Odysseus' curiosity, cunning, and trickery play a role in the Greeks' capture and their escape.

- Have students describe the Cyclops and the type of life he leads. **Ask** them what the Cyclops' greatest assets or weapons are.
  Possible response: The Cyclops is a herder, but he lives in solitude. His greatest asset is his size and strength.

- Review with students the Cyclops' conversations with Odysseus. **Ask** what the conversations reveal about the Cyclops' personality.
  Possible response: The Cyclops is a creature of action and can be tricked, for example, when Odysseus claimed that his name was "Nohbdy."

- Remind students that the Cyclops must know that the Greeks are still in his cave, because the stone has blocked its entrance.
  Ask students the Literary Analysis question: What details of this speech show that Polyphemus is far less clever than Odysseus?
  Possible response: Polyphemus knows the ram is acting in an unusual manner. The change in the ram's behavior, however, does not make the Cyclops suspicious. He does not seem to expect that the Greeks might try to escape.

---

390   and peals of bleating echoed round the pens
       where dams with udders full called for a milking.
       Blinded, and sick with pain from his head wound,
       the master stroked each ram, then let it pass,
       but my men riding on the pectoral[38] fleece

395   the giant's blind hands blundering never found.
       Last of them all my ram, the leader, came,
       weighted by wool and me with my meditations.
       The Cyclops patted him, and then he said:

       'Sweet cousin ram, why lag behind the rest
400   in the night cave? You never linger so,
       but graze before them all, and go afar
       to crop sweet grass, and take your stately way
       leading along the streams, until at evening
       you run to be the first one in the fold.
405   Why, now, so far behind? Can you be grieving
       over your Master's eye? That carrion rogue[39]
       and his accurst companions burnt it out
       when he had conquered all my wits with wine.
       Nohbdy will not get out alive, I swear.
410   Oh, had you brain and voice to tell
       where he may be now, dodging all my fury!
       Bashed by this hand and bashed on this rock wall
       his brains would strew the floor, and I should have
       rest from the outrage Nohbdy worked upon me.'

415   He sent us into the open, then. Close by,
       I dropped and rolled clear of the ram's belly,
       going this way and that to untie the men.
       With many glances back, we rounded up
       his fat, stiff-legged sheep to take aboard,
420   and drove them down to where the good ship lay.
       We saw, as we came near, our fellows' faces
       shining; then we saw them turn to grief
       tallying those who had not fled from death.
       I hushed them, jerking head and eyebrows up,
425   and in a low voice told them: 'Load this herd;
       move fast, and put the ship's head toward the breakers.'
       They all pitched in at loading, then embarked
       and struck their oars into the sea. Far out,
       as far off shore as shouted words would carry,
430   I sent a few back to the adversary:

38. **pectoral** (pek´ tə rəl) *adj.* located in or on the chest.

39. **carrion** (kar´ ē ən) **rogue** (rōg) repulsive scoundrel.

Literary Analysis
Epic Hero What details of this speech show that Polyphemus is far less clever than Odysseus?

Vocabulary Development

Animal Terms
The description of the Greeks' escape includes a number of words relating to animals, especially sheep: *rams, dams, udders, pasture, milking, fleece, wool, graze, fold,* and *herd.* Ask students to indicate which words they can figure out by the context of the passage. Students may need to look up some multiple-meaning words in the dictionary, for example *fold* and *dams,* to learn the definition used in the selection. Ask students to show their understanding of the animal words by using them in sentences.

'O Cyclops! Would you feast on my companions?
Puny, am I, in a cave man's hands?
How do you like the beating that we gave you,
you damned cannibal? Eater of guests
435 under your roof! Zeus and the gods have paid you!'

The blind thing in his doubled fury broke
a hilltop in his hands and heaved it after us.
Ahead of our black prow it struck and sank
whelmed in a spuming geyser, a giant wave
440 that washed the ship stern foremost back to shore.
I got the longest boathook out and stood
fending us off, with furious nods to all
to put their backs into a racing stroke—
row, row, or perish. So the long oars bent
445 kicking the foam sternward, making head
until we drew away, and twice as far.
Now when I cupped my hands I heard the crew
in low voices protesting:

31

                    'Godsake, Captain!
Why bait the beast again? Let him alone!'

450 'That tidal wave he made on the first throw
all but beached us.'

                    'All but stove us in!'
'Give him our bearing with your trumpeting,
he'll get the range and lob a boulder.'

                    'Aye
He'll smash our timbers and our heads together!'
455 I would not heed them in my glorying spirit,
but let my anger flare and yelled:

                    'Cyclops,
if ever mortal man inquire
how you were put to shame and blinded, tell him
Odysseus, raider of cities, took your eye:
460 Laertes' son, whose home's on Ithaca!'

At this he gave a mighty sob and rumbled:
'Now comes the weird[40] upon me, spoken of old.
A wizard, grand and wondrous, lived here—Telemus,[41]
a son of Eurymus;[42] great length of days

Literary Analysis
Epic Hero Despite his heroism, what human weaknesses does Odysseus reveal as he sails away?

40. **weird** (wird) *n.* fate or destiny.

41. **Telemus** (tel e´ məs)

42. **Eurymus** (yōō rim´ əs)

32 ✓ Reading Check

How do the men escape from Cyclops' cave?

from the Odyssey, *Part I* ■ 965

---

31 Literary Analysis
Epic Hero

- Recall with students Odysseus' earlier behavior, in which he exulted in tricking the Cyclops. **Ask** students how this example is similar or different from the earlier one. **Possible response:** Earlier, Odysseus gloated silently over his victory. Here, he shouts his victory to the Cyclops.

- Point out to students the prudence of leaving the island silently. **Ask** them what the Greeks have to gain by taunting the Cyclops. **Possible response:** The Greeks have nothing to gain. They can only enrage their enemy.

- **Ask** the Literary Analysis question: Despite his heroism, what human weaknesses does Odysseus reveal as he sails away? **Possible response:** Odysseus allows his anger and arrogance to get the best of him. It would have been much wiser to be quiet. He is acting in a boastful and vindictive manner.

32 Reading Check

Answer: Odysseus smuggles his men out by tying the Cyclops' sheep together in sets of three and binding one man under the middle sheep of each set. The men escape when the Cyclops releases his sheep to graze.

Differentiated
Instruction   Solutions for All Learners

Strategy for Less Proficient Readers
As students read the Cyclops section of the *Odyssey,* have them note each time the Greeks find themselves in a different location. Their note paper would have different headings, such as "Arrive on the Beach," "Trapped in the Cyclops' Cave," and "Escaping in their Ships." Ask students to write two sentences for each location: one that explains how the Greeks got there, and one that explains how they left.

Strategy for Gifted/Talented Students
Odysseus' escape from the Cyclops shows the hero's flair for drama. Have students perform a dramatic interpretation of Odysseus' taunts to the Cyclops, his men's pleas for him to stop, and Polyphemus' sobbing prayer for revenge. Ask students to provide different interpretations: Can Polyphemus be portrayed as a sympathetic victim in this scene? Or can Odysseus, an epic hero, be interpreted as a bully? Ask students to explain the different readings that they provide.

965

㉝ Reading Skill
Historical and Cultural Context

- Refer students to their copies of **Reading Skill Graphic Organizer A** (p. 199 in *Graphic Organizer Transparencies*). Have students put relevant quotations in the Historical/Cultural Detail box. Quotations might include, "I'll treat you well, praying the god of earthquake to befriend you," or "The god of earthquake could not heal you there!"

- Have students review the passage to see what they can learn about the god Poseidon from the text. **Ask** what the passage reveals about the Cyclops' father. **Possible response:** Poseidon must be a god of the ocean, because he is "girdler of the islands." He also can cause earthquakes.

- **Ask** students the Reading Skill question: What do lines 472–493 suggest about ancient Greek beliefs about the gods' involvement in the mortal world? **Possible responses:** The Greeks believe that the gods have control over specific elements of human life and can be asked to intervene in human affairs.

▶ **Monitor Progress:** Review students' graphic organizers to ensure that they are making reasonable inferences.

▶ **Reteach:** Work with students to make a chart showing the Greek gods and goddesses who have been mentioned to this point: Zeus, Athena, Apollo, and Poseidon. Discuss with students the qualities of these deities and their connections with human beings and other creatures on Earth.

㉞ Reading Check

Answer: The Cyclops prays that Odysseus will lose all his men and, if he returns at all, that he may arrive home only after many "dark" years of hardship. The Cyclops' prayer amounts to an extremely precise prophecy.

---

465 he had in wizardry among the Cyclopes,
     and these things he foretold for time to come:
     my great eye lost, and at Odysseus' hands.
     Always I had in mind some giant, armed
     in giant force, would come against me here.
470 But this, but you—small, pitiful and twiggy—
     you put me down with wine, you blinded me.
     Come back, Odysseus, and I'll treat you well,
     praying the god of earthquake[43] to befriend you—
     his son I am, for he by his avowal
475 fathered me, and, if he will, he may
     heal me of this black wound—he and no other
㉝   of all the happy gods or mortal men.'

     Few words I shouted in reply to him:

     'If I could take your life I would and take
480 your time away, and hurl you down to hell!
     The god of earthquake could not heal you there!'

     At this he stretched his hands out in his darkness
     toward the sky of stars, and prayed Poseidon:

     'O hear me, lord, blue girdler of the islands,
485 if I am thine indeed, and thou art father:
     grant that Odysseus, raider of cities, never
     see his home: Laertes' son, I mean,
     who kept his hall on Ithaca. Should destiny
     intend that he shall see his roof again
490 among his family in his father land,
     far be that day, and dark the years between.
     Let him lose all companions, and return
     under strange sail to bitter days at home.'

966 ■ *Themes in Literature: Heroism*

43. god of earthquake Poseidon.

Reading Skill
Historical and Cultural Context What do lines 472–493 suggest about ancient Greek beliefs about the gods' involvement in the mortal world?

㉞ **Reading Check**

What does the Cyclops ask for in his prayer to Poseidon?

Vocabulary Development

Expressive Vocabulary
As students are discussing Odysseus' escape from the Cyclops, encourage them to use the expressive vocabulary presented earlier. You might encourage them with sentence starters like these:

1. The Greeks' escape from the Cyclops *coincides* with . . .
2. Odysseus could have avoided another *encounter* with the Cyclops if . . .
3. The Cyclops' prayer to his father *highlights* . . .
4. The Cyclops wanted to *eliminate* Odysseus' hope of . . .

Polyphemus, The Cyclops from Homer's *The Odyssey*, N. C. Wyeth

35 ▲ Critical Viewing Odysseus and his surviving men escape in their ship as the blinded Cyclops hurls boulders and curses. How does this illustration compare to your mental image of the scene? **[Analyze]**

35 **Critical Viewing**

Answer: The illustration depicts the moment after Odysseus taunts the Cyclops while his men sail furiously away from the island. In the image, the giant has broken off the top of a hill and is preparing to hurl it at Odysseus' ship. The artist has added some details not evident in the poem, including the swirling steam around the giant. Also, for emphasis, he adds a glow around the ship.

36 **Humanities**

Polyphemus, The Cyclops, by N.C. Wyeth

N.C. Wyeth (1882–1945) was an American artist whose enchanting illustrations of children's classics made him popular and successful. He illustrated several novels by Robert Louis Stevenson and James Fenimore Cooper.

Polyphemus was commissioned for a luxury edition of the *Odyssey* published in 1929. The illustration demonstrates the skill with which Wyeth was able to depict fantastic creatures. Use the following questions for discussion.

1. Which lines in the Odyssey match the moment portrayed by Wyeth in this painting?
   Answer: The picture illustrates the lines "The blind thing in his doubled fury broke/ a hilltop in his hands and heaved it after us," lines 436–437.

2. How does the mood of the illustration reflect that of the story?
   Possible response: The gloomy, stormy skies and seas suggest the danger and tension surrounding the event.

Differentiated

Instruction   Solutions for All Learners

Enrichment for Gifted/Talented Students
Have students draw a "before" and "after" portrait of the Cyclops and his island. Suggest that the portraits illustrate the Cyclops' animals, his daily labor, and his relationship with the other Cyclopes on his island. Challenge students to try to illustrate many of the changes brought by the Greeks, including the Cyclops' blindness and the binding together of the sheep.

Enrichment for Advanced Readers
Have students do research to find out the Cyclops' family tree. Have them learn more about Poseidon, his relationships to other Greek gods, and his other children, both mortal and immortal. Ask students to speculate about the positive and negative aspects of being so closely related to an immortal deity.

- Remind students that spoils, such as the sheep, often were divided among soldiers by rank. Odysseus could have taken the larger part for himself.

- **Ask** students why Odysseus might want to be generous with his men. **Possible response:** He might want to keep their loyalty. He might want to thank them for their good work in escaping from the Cyclops.

- Then **ask** the Literary Analysis question: What admirable quality does Odysseus show by dividing the sheep among his men? **Possible response:** Odysseus shows a sense of fairness by dividing the sheep equally among his men—"share and share alike."

    In these words he prayed, and the god heard him.

495   Now he laid hands upon a bigger stone
    and wheeled around, titanic for the cast,
    to let it fly in the black-prowed vessel's track.
    But it fell short, just aft the steering oar,
    and whelming seas rose giant above the stone

500   to bear us onward toward the island.

                       There
    as we ran in we saw the squadron waiting,
    the trim ships drawn up side by side, and all
    our troubled friends who waited, looking seaward.
    We beached her, grinding keel in the soft sand,

505   and waded in, ourselves, on the sandy beach.
    Then we unloaded all the Cyclops' flock

③⑦ to make division, share and share alike,
    only my fighters voted that my ram,
    the prize of all, should go to me. I slew him

510   by the seaside and burnt his long thighbones
    to Zeus beyond the stormcloud, Cronus'⁴⁴ son,
    who rules the world. But Zeus disdained my offering:
    destruction for my ships he had in store
    and death for those who sailed them, my companions.

515   Now all day long until the sun went down
    we made our feast on mutton and sweet wine,
    till after sunset in the gathering dark
    we went to sleep above the wash of ripples.

    When the young Dawn with fingertips of rose

520   touched the world, I roused the men, gave orders
    to man the ships, cast off the mooring lines;
    and filing in to sit beside the rowlocks
    oarsmen in line dipped oars in the gray sea.
    So we moved out, sad in the vast offing,⁴⁵

525   having our precious lives, but not our friends.

44. Cronus (krō´ nəs) Titan who was ruler of the universe until he was overthrown by his son Zeus.

Literary Analysis
Epic Hero What admirable quality does Odysseus show by dividing the sheep among his men?

45. offing (ôf´ iŋ) *n.* distant part of the sea visible from the shore.

Vocabulary Development

Think-Aloud: Context Clues
Direct students' attention to the word *disdained* on line 512 of this page. Using a think-aloud process, model how to use context to infer the meaning of an unknown word. Say to students:

    I'm going to think aloud to show you how I would figure out the meaning of *disdained* from its context.

    In this sentence, *disdained* describes Zeus' reaction to Odysseus' offering.

Odysseus says that he burned the ram's thighbones as an offering to the god. Zeus' response, though is "destruction for my ships" and "death for those who sailed them." The words *destruction* and *death* indicate Zeus's displeasure. I think *disdained* must mean that Zeus disliked the gift or else rejected it.

The Land of the Dead

Odysseus and his men sail to Aeolia, where Aeolus,[46] *king of the winds, sends Odysseus on his way with a gift: a sack containing all the winds except the favorable west wind. When they are near home, Odysseus' men open the sack, letting loose a storm that drives them back to Aeolia. Aeolus casts them out, having decided that they are detested by the gods. They sail for seven days and arrive in the land of the Laestrygonians,*[47] *a race of cannibals. These creatures destroy all of Odysseus' ships except the one he is sailing in. Odysseus and his reduced crew escape and reach Aeaea, the island ruled by the sorceress-goddess Circe. She transforms half of the men into swine. Protected by a magic herb, Odysseus demands that Circe change his men back into human form. Before Odysseus departs from the island a year later, Circe informs him that in order to reach home he must journey to the land of the dead, Hades, and consult the blind prophet Tiresias.*

We bore down on the ship at the sea's edge
and launched her on the salt immortal sea,
stepping our mast and spar in the black ship;
embarked the ram and ewe and went aboard

530   in tears, with bitter and sore dread upon us.
But now a breeze came up for us astern—
a canvas-bellying landbreeze, hale shipmate
sent by the singing nymph with sunbright hair;[48]
so we made fast the braces, took our thwarts,

535   and let the wind and steersman work the ship
with full sail spread all day above our coursing,
till the sun dipped, and all the ways grew dark
upon the fathomless unresting sea.
                                    By night

our ship ran onward toward the Ocean's bourne,

540   the realm and region of the Men of Winter,
hidden in mist and cloud. Never the flaming
eye of Helios lights on those men
at morning, when he climbs the sky of stars,
nor in descending earthward out of heaven;

545   ruinous night being rove over those wretches.
We made the land, put ram and ewe ashore,
and took our way along the Ocean stream
to find the place foretold for us by Circe.

46. **Aeolia** (ē ō′ lē ə) . . . **Aeolus** (ē′ ə ləs)

47. **Laestrygonians** (les tri gō′ nē ənz)

48. **singing nymph . . . hair** Circe.

Reading Skill
Historical and Cultural Context
What details here suggest that the source of wind was mysterious to ancient Greeks?

 Reading Check
What does Circe say that Odysseus must do in order to reach home?

from the Odyssey, *Part I* ■ *969*

38 Reading Skill
Historical and Cultural Context

- Remind students of the number of gods and goddesses in Odysseus' tale and their powers. For example, Poseidon can cause earthquakes. Zeus can send storms that can harm Odysseus' men.

- Have students **describe** the wind that controls the Greeks' ships. **Possible response:** It is a strong wind that comes from the land and fills their sails. The wind originates from a nymph.

- **Ask** the Reading Skill question: What details here suggest that the source of wind was mysterious to ancient Greeks? **Answer:** Odysseus claims that Circe, a nymph, creates the wind.

39 Reading Check

Answer: Circe says that Odysseus must go to Hades, the land of the dead, in order to reach home. In Hades, Odysseus must consult the blind prophet Tiresias.

Differentiated Instruction   Solutions for All Learners

Strategy for Special Needs Students
To help students begin the new section, direct them to the italicized summary and review with them the parts of the story that have been omitted. Help students make the transition to the new section and answer any questions they may have about Circe's role in Odysseus' next adventure.

Strategy for English Learners
Some of the vocabulary that relates to sailing and oceans may prove unfamiliar to students. Preview and teach the sea-faring jargon before students read the story: *mast* (tall pole that holds a sail), *spar* (another pole that holds a sail), *canvas-bellying landbreeze* (a wind that fills a sail), and *Ocean's bourne* (boundary of the ocean).

⑩ Humanities

Odysseus in the Land of the Dead,
by N. C. Wyeth

This painting was commissioned for a 1929 limited edition of the *Odyssey*. The 500 copies of this edition included sixteen full-color illustrations signed by N. C. Wyeth. Use these questions for discussion:

1. Which lines in Homer's *Odyssey* are illustrated by this picture?
   Answer: The painting illustrates lines 564–578.

2. Do you think the artist portrayed Odysseus as Homer pictured him at this moment?
   Answer: The artist has captured Homer's image of Odysseus crouching by the "bloody pit" with his drawn sword, sick with fear but determined to achieve his goal of consulting Tiresias.

3. Do you think that Wyeth has accurately portrayed the dead?
   Possible responses: Yes, because Homer says that the dead appear in "their bloody gear," or as they were when they died. No, because the dead look skeletal and long dead, rather than recently deceased.

Odysseus in the Land of the Dead, from Homer's The Odyssey, N. C. Wyeth, Brandywine River Museum

⑩

④ ▲ Critical Viewing What can you infer about ancient Greek beliefs concerning death and the afterlife from lines 555–577 and from this illustration? **[Infer]**

Vocabulary Development

Vocabulary Builder Reinforcement
To reinforce and assess students' comprehension of Vocabulary Builder words, give them sentences using the words in which the word may or may not be used correctly. Students must tell whether the use is correct.

1. The furious customers were *assuaged* by the store's refusal to take back the shoddy merchandise.
   Answer: No, *assuaged* is not used correctly. It means "to calm or pacify," but the customers are not calmed by the store's policy.

2. After the waiter apologized for his error and brought the correct dessert, the diners were *assuaged* and promised to return to the restaurant soon.
   Answer: Yes, *assuaged* is used correctly here. The diners are pleased and calmed after the waiter's apology.

There Perimedes and Eulylochus[49]
550 pinioned[50] the sacred beasts. With my drawn blade
I spaded up the votive[51] pit, and poured
libations[52] round it to the unnumbered dead:
sweet milk and honey, then sweet wine, and last
clear water; and I scattered barley down.
555 Then I addressed the blurred and breathless dead,
vowing to slaughter my best heifer for them
before she calved, at home in Ithaca,
and burn the choice bits on the altar fire;
as for Tiresias, I swore to sacrifice
560 a black lamb, handsomest of all our flock.
Thus to <u>assuage</u> the nations of the dead
I pledged these rites, then slashed the lamb and ewe,
letting their black blood stream into the wellpit.
Now the souls gathered, stirring out of Erebus,[53]
565 brides and young men, and men grown old in pain,
and tender girls whose hearts were new to grief;
many were there, too, torn by brazen lanceheads,
battle-slain, bearing still their bloody gear.
From every side they came and sought the pit
570 with rustling cries; and I grew sick with fear.
But presently I gave command to my officers
to flay those sheep the bronze cut down, and make
burnt offerings of flesh to the gods below—
to sovereign Death, to pale Persephone.[54]
575 Meanwhile I crouched with my drawn sword to keep
the surging phantoms from the bloody pit
till I should know the presence of Tiresias.[55]

One shade came first—Elpenor, of our company,
who lay unburied still on the wide earth
580 as we had left him—dead in Circe's hall,
untouched, unmourned, when other cares compelled us.
Now when I saw him there I wept for pity
and called out to him:

49. Perimedes (per′ ə mē′ dēz) **and Eurylochus** (yōō ril′ ə kəs)

50. pinioned (pin′ yənd) *v.* confined or shackled.

51. votive (vōt′ iv) *adj.* done to fulfill a vow or express thanks.

52. libations (lī bā′ shənz) *n.* wine or other liquids poured upon the ground as a sacrifice or offering.

Vocabulary Builder
assuage (ə swāj′) *v.* calm; pacify

53. Erebus (er′ ə bəs) dark region under the earth through which the dead pass before entering the realm of Hades.

54. Persephone (pər sef′ ə nē) wife of Hades.

55. Tiresias (tī rē′ sē əs)

42 ✓ Reading Check

Whom is Odysseus trying to summon by making sacrifices?

from the *Odyssey,* Part I ■ 971

41 **Critical Viewing**

Answer: From the illustration, we can infer that the Greeks believed that a person's spirit continued to exist after death. The spirit had to make a long journey to the underworld and could not complete its journey unless the proper rites were observed. The spirits that had not yet reached the underworld were frightening, restless, and hungry.

42 **Reading Check**

Answer: Odysseus is trying to summon the dead prophet Tiresias.

Differentiated
Instruction   Solutions for All Learners

Support for Special Needs Students
Many of the events of in this section are effects caused by earlier events. Help students trace these events by providing the **Cause and Effect Flowchart** (*Graphic Organizer Transparencies,* p. 233). Provide students with stems that indicate causes, such as "After Odysseus offers sacrifices . . ." or "Because the Greeks did not bury Elpenor . . .", and have students fill in the effects.

Enrichment for Advanced Readers
After students have read the description of the Greeks' offerings to the dead, ask them to research the customs surrounding death in a culture other than their own. Cite, for example, the funeral pyre of the Hindus, the Jewish custom of sitting shiva, and the Mandan Indian tradition of leaving the dead body on an elevated platform to decay naturally. Have students share their findings with the class.

'How is this, Elpenor,
how could you journey to the western gloom
585 swifter afoot than I in the black lugger?'
He sighed, and answered:

'Son of great Laertes,
Odysseus, master mariner and soldier,
bad luck shadowed me, and no kindly power;
ignoble death I drank with so much wine.
590 I slept on Circe's roof, then could not see
the long steep backward ladder, coming down,
and fell that height. My neckbone, buckled under,
snapped, and my spirit found this well of dark.
Now hear the grace I pray for, in the name
595 of those back in the world, not here—your wife
and father, he who gave you bread in childhood,
and your own child, your only son, Telemachus,[56]
long ago left at home.

When you make sail
and put these lodgings of dim Death behind,
600 you will moor ship, I know, upon Aeaea Island;
there, O my lord, remember me, I pray,
do not abandon me unwept, unburied,
to tempt the gods' wrath, while you sail for home;
but fire my corpse, and all the gear I had,
605 and build a cairn[57] for me above the breakers—
an unknown sailor's mark for men to come.
Heap up the mound there, and implant upon it
the oar I pulled in life with my companions.'

He ceased, and I replied:

'Unhappy spirit,
610 I promise you the barrow and the burial.'

So we conversed, and grimly, at a distance,
with my long sword between, guarding the blood,
while the faint image of the lad spoke on.
Now came the soul of Anticlea, dead,
615 my mother, daughter of Autolycus,[58]
dead now, though living still when I took ship
for holy Troy. Seeing this ghost I grieved,
but held her off, through pang on pang of tears,
till I should know the presence of Tiresias.

972 ■ *Themes in Literature: Heroism*

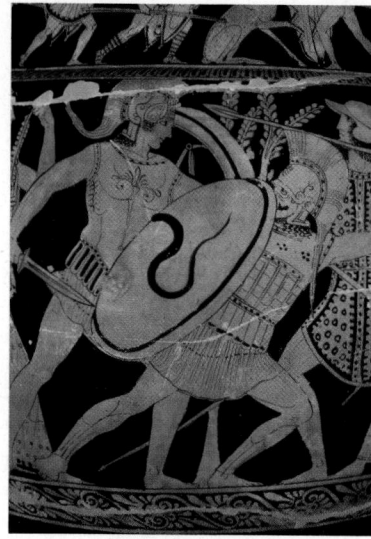

44

45 ▲ **Critical Viewing**
How do the characters on this vase compare with your image of the characters in the *Odyssey?* **[Compare and Contrast]**

56. Telemachus (tə lem′ ə kəs)

57. cairn (kern) *n.* conical heap of stones built as a monument.

58. Autolycus (ô täl′ i kəs)

Reading Skill
Historical and Cultural Context
What ancient Greek values and beliefs are suggested by Elpenor's requests?

972

620 Soon from the dark that prince of Thebes[59] came forward
bearing a golden staff; and he addressed me:

‘Son of Laertes and the gods of old,
Odysseus, master of landways and seaways,
why leave the blazing sun, O man of woe,
625 to see the cold dead and the joyless region?
Stand clear, put up your sword;
let me but taste of blood, I shall speak true.’

At this I stepped aside, and in the scabbard
let my long sword ring home to the pommel silver,
630 as he bent down to the somber blood. Then spoke
the prince of those with gift of speech:

                                    ‘Great captain,
a fair wind and the honey lights of home
are all you seek. But anguish lies ahead;
the god who thunders on the land prepares it,
635 not to be shaken from your track, implacable,
in rancor for the son whose eye you blinded.

46 One narrow strait may take you through his blows:
denial of yourself, restraint of shipmates.
When you make landfall on Thrinacia first
640 and quit the violet sea, dark on the land
you’ll find the grazing herds of Helios
by whom all things are seen, all speech is known.
Avoid those kine,[60] hold fast to your intent,
and hard seafaring brings you all to Ithaca.
645 But if you raid the beeves, I see destruction
for ship and crew. Though you survive alone,
<u>bereft</u> of all companions, lost for years,
under strange sail shall you come home, to find
your own house filled with trouble: insolent men
650 eating your livestock as they court your lady.
Aye, you shall make those men atone in blood!
But after you have dealt out death—in open
combat or by stealth—to all the suitors,
go overland on foot, and take an oar,
655 until one day you come where men have lived
with meat unsalted, never known the sea,
nor seen seagoing ships, with crimson bows
and oars that fledge light hulls for dipping flight.
The spot will soon be plain to you, and I

Reading Skill
Historical and Cultural Context
What ancient Greek value is reflected in the “narrow strait” that Tiresias describes (lines 637–638)?

60. kine (kīn) *n.* cattle.

Vocabulary Builder
bereft (bē reft´) *adj.*
deprived

47 ✓ Reading Check
According to Tiresias, what will Odysseus find when he returns home?

from the *Odyssey,* Part I ■ 973

46 **Reading Skill**
Historical and Cultural Context

- Have students recall some of the incidents that led to trouble in Odysseus’ voyage, for example, his men’s mutiny, or his refusal to leave the Cyclops’ cave when he could have escaped easily.

- **Ask** students if they see any patterns in the events that have caused Odysseus trouble.
Possible response: Odysseus’ men have not obeyed him, and Odysseus himself has not shown self-discipline.

- **Ask** the Reading Skill question: What ancient Greek value is reflected in the “narrow strait” that Tiresias describes?
Possible responses: Tiresias indicates that Odysseus can overcome Poseidon’s wrath if Odysseus focuses on his task and disciplines both himself and his crew. Odysseus will be able to return home only if he can practice self-restraint.

- Point out that the “narrow strait” also refer to a real place — the Straits of Gibraltar.

47 Reading Check

Answer: Tiresias predicts that Odysseus will find his home full of suitors eating his food and courting his wife.

Differentiated
Instruction Solutions for All Learners

Strategy for Less Proficient Readers
Have students prepare a two-column chart. In one column, they should write the events Tiresias foretells. As they read on, have them fill in the adventures to which the prophecies refer. Students will discover that line 637 refers to Scylla and Charybdis; line 638 refers to The Sirens; lines 639–646 refer to “ . . . Twenty years gone, and I am home again” [Part 2]; and line 651 refers to Odysseus’ Revenge [Part 2].)

Strategy for Gifted/Talented Students
Suggest that students draw or paint a scene from the *Odyssey* in the same style as that shown on p. 972. Encourage students to research other examples of Greek art to gather specific details they might include, such as the patterns and borders used to frame the images.

973

1. Students may say that Odysseus' plan was well thought out; for example, he did not act on his first impulse, to attack the Cyclops.

2. (a) From Maron, Odysseus received gold, a silver winebowl, and twelve jars of brandy. (b) **Possible response:** Hospitality is highly valued; hosts are judged by their courteousness and the richness of the gifts they presents to their guests.

3. (a) Odysseus and his men believe an appeal to the custom of honoring strangers will be respected. (b) **Possible response:** He violates the laws of hospitality, of honoring the gods—and the taboo against cannibalism.

4. (a) They attach themselves to the underside of the Cyclops' sheep. Thus camouflaged from the Cyclops' groping hands, they escape when Polyphemus lets his flocks out to graze. (b) Odysseus displays a stubborn curiosity that leads him into danger and a vindictive boastfulness. He also displays positive qualities, such as cleverness, leadership, and bravery.

5. (a) Odysseus weeps when he encounters Elpenor. He also weeps when he sees his mother, Anticlea, but he does not let her approach. When he sees Tiresius, he allows him to approach and listens to his prophecy. (b) Odysseus shows compassion for his mother and for Elpenor; he reveals determination to achieve his goal even when he is afraid.

6. (a) Tiresias predicts Odysseus will lose ship and crew, struggle alone for years, and arrive home only to find his house filled with trouble. (b) Odysseus may note that the grim fate can be averted by avoiding the cattle of Helias. Or, he may feel he has no other choices.

7. Based on the prophecies, Odysseus will need courage, resourcefulness, and strong leadership.

---

660   can tell you how: some passerby will say,
"What winnowing fan is that upon your shoulder?"
Halt, and implant your smooth oar in the turf
and make fair sacrifice to Lord Poseidon:
a ram, a bull, a great buck boar; turn back,
665   and carry out pure hecatombs[61] at home
to all wide heaven's lords, the undying gods,
to each in order. Then a seaborne death
soft as this hand of mist will come upon you
when you are wearied out with rich old age,
670   your country folk in blessed peace around you.
And all this shall be just as I foretell.'

61. hecatombs (hek´ ə tōmz´) *n.* large-scale sacrifices to the gods in ancient Greece; often, the slaughter of 100 cattle at one time.

Thinking About the Selection

1. **Respond:** What do you think of Odysseus' plan for escaping from Polyphemus? Explain.

2. (a) **Recall:** Before the meeting with the Cyclops, what had Odysseus received from Maron at Ismarus? (b) **Generalize:** What does the encounter with Maron reveal about ancient Greek attitudes regarding hospitality?

3. (a) **Recall:** How do Odysseus and his companions expect to be treated by the Cyclops? (b) **Infer:** What "laws" of behavior and attitude does Polyphemus violate?

4. (a) **Summarize:** How do Odysseus and his crew escape from the Cyclops? (b) **Evaluate:** What positive and negative character traits does Odysseus demonstrate in his adventure with the Cyclops?

5. (a) **Compare and Contrast:** Compare and Contrast Odysseus' reactions to the three ghosts he meets in the Land of the Dead—Elpenor, Anticlea, and Tiresias. (b) **Analyze:** What character trait does Odysseus display in the Land of the Dead that he did not reveal earlier?

6. (a) **Summarize:** What difficulty does Tiresias predict for the journey to come? (b) **Speculate:** Why would Odysseus continue, despite the grim prophecies?

7. (a) **Assess:** Judging from Tiresias' prediction, which heroic qualities will Odysseus need to rely upon as he continues his journey? Explain.

974 ■ *Themes in Literature: Heroism*

The Sirens

Odysseus returns to Circe's island. The goddess reveals his course to him and gives advice on how to avoid the dangers he will face: the Sirens, who lure sailors to their destruction; the Wandering Rocks, sea rocks that destroy even birds in flight; the perils of the sea monster Scylla and, nearby, the whirlpool Charybdis;[62] *and the cattle of the sun god, which Tiresias has warned Odysseus not to harm.*

62. Charybdis (kə rib′ dis)

As Circe spoke, Dawn mounted her golden throne,
and on the first rays Circe left me, taking
her way like a great goddess up the island.
675   I made straight for the ship, roused up the men
to get aboard and cast off at the stern.
They scrambled to their places by the rowlocks
and all in line dipped oars in the gray sea.
But soon an offshore breeze blew to our liking—
680   a canvas-bellying breeze, a lusty shipmate
sent by the singing nymph with sunbright hair.
So we made fast the braces, and we rested,
letting the wind and steersman work the ship.
The crew being now silent before me, I
685   addressed them, sore at heart:

                             'Dear friends,
more than one man, or two, should know those things
Circe foresaw for us and shared with me,
48 so let me tell her forecast: then we die
with our eyes open, if we are going to die,
690   or know what death we baffle if we can. Sirens
weaving a haunting song over the sea
we are to shun, she said, and their green shore
all sweet with clover; yet she urged that I
alone should listen to their song. Therefore
695   you are to tie me up, tight as a splint,
erect along the mast, lashed to the mast,
and if I shout and beg to be untied,
take more turns of the rope to muffle me.'

I rather dwelt on this part of the forecast,
700   while our good ship made time, bound outward down
the wind for the strange island of Sirens.

Literary Analysis
Epic Hero What does Odysseus reveal about his character by sharing information with his men?

 Reading Check
What instructions does Odysseus give his shipmates as they prepare to deal with the Sirens?

from the *Odyssey*, Part I ■ 975

---

48 **Literary Analysis**
Epic Hero

- Discuss with students how good leaders give responsibilities to their followers and trust them to do their work well.

- **Ask** students how Odysseus' men might respond if asked to do a task that has not been explained to them.
  Possible response: Odysseus' men have mutinied before. If asked to do something that did not make sense to them, they might refuse.

- **Ask** the Literary Analysis question: What does Odysseus reveal about his character by sharing information with his men?
  Possible response: Odysseus shows that he trusts his men to follow his orders. He also shows that he is a not a leader who must keep all knowledge and power to himself.

49 **Reading Check**
Answer: Odysseus has asked his men to tie him to the mast.

Circe Meanwhile Had Gone Her Ways . . . , (1924) by William Russell Flint

The Scottish painter and illustrator William Russell Flint (1880–1969) became interested in watercolor at a young age. For many years, this was his favorite medium, and his works were exhibited in Europe to much acclaim. Flint was elected to the Royal Academy in 1924 and was knighted in 1947. He added another dimension to his work when he began to create illustrations for various literary works. Use these questions for discussion.

1. What special abilities does Circe seem to have?
   Answer: She seems to command the attention and obedience of animals, such as the sheep.

2. What elements in the painting give a sense of the setting of the *Odyssey*?
   Possible response: The time and place are suggested in Circe's clothes and pose; the carved marble pedestal; the stylized spirals of the rams' horns and wool of the blue-and-purple decorations on the ship; and the form of the ship in the background.

51 **Critical Viewing**

Answer: Circe looks seductive, confident of her power, mysterious, and a bit mischievous.

50

Circe Meanwhile Had Gone Her Ways. . ., 1924, William Russell Flint Collection of the New York Public Library, Astor, Lenox, and Tilden Foundations

51 ▲ Critical Viewing The sorceress Circe both helps and hinders Odysseus on his journey home. What can you tell about Circe from this illustration? **[Deduce]**

Then all at once the wind fell, and a calm
came over all the sea, as though some power
lulled the swell.
                          The crew were on their feet
705 briskly, to furl the sail, and stow it; then,
     each in place, they poised the smooth oar blades
     and sent the white foam scudding by. I carved
     a massive cake of beeswax into bits
52 and rolled them in my hands until they softened—
710 no long task, for a burning heat came down
     from Helios, lord of high noon. Going forward
     I carried wax along the line, and laid it
     thick on their ears. They tied me up, then, plumb
     amidships, back to the mast, lashed to the mast,
715 and took themselves again to rowing. Soon,
     as we came smartly within hailing distance,
     the two Sirens, noting our fast ship
     off their point, made ready, and they sang:

          This way, oh turn your bows,
720   *Achaea's glory,*
          As all the world allows—
               Moor and be merry.

          Sweet coupled airs we sing.
               No lonely seafarer
725   *Holds clear of entering*
               Our green mirror.

          Pleased by each purling note
               Like honey twining

from the *Odyssey*, Part I ■ 977

Reading Skill
Historical and Cultural Context
What does Odysseus' mention of Helios reveal about ancient Greek beliefs regarding astronomical events?

53 **Reading Check**
How does Odysseus keep his shipmates from hearing the Sirens sing?

---

52 Reading Skill
Historical and Cultural Context

- Have students imagine how early peoples might have viewed the sun. **Ask** them what someone looking at the sun without modern instruments might think it was made of.
  Possible response: The sun might appear to be a ball of fire.

- Discuss with students what types of instruments or tools might be needed to study the sun and learn more about it. Have students think about how recently people have learned to study planets and stars and describe them accurately.

- **Ask** the Reading Skill question: What does Odysseus' mention of Helios reveal about ancient Greek beliefs regarding astronomical events?
  Possible response: Greeks believed that gods controlled the sun and the planets. They thought that the god Helios provided the light and heat of the sun.

▶ **Monitor Progress:** Review students' graphic organizers to ensure that they are making reasonable inferences.

▶ **Reteach:** Point out to students that the Greeks did not understand the science behind the rising and setting of the sun. The Greeks believed that a god drove a chariot across the sky as a way of explaining daylight. Ask students to use research tools to find other examples of the ways Greeks explained natural phenomena.

53 Reading Check

Answer: Odysseus puts wax in his men's ears so they cannot hear the Sirens.

Differentiated Instruction   Solutions for All Learners

Strategy for Gifted/Talented Students
Ask students to set the Sirens' song to music. They can select existing instrumental music or compose their own accompaniment. Students also may want to chant the words in a rap. Offer opportunities for students to perform the song for the class.

Strategy for Advanced Readers
Challenge students to update the Sirens' song for the present day. What new temptations or needs would they insert in the song? Suggest that they rewrite the song or compose a new version of their own.

- Point out the Sirens' strategy with students, explaining that they offer men the opportunity to escape from their homesickness and enjoy themselves. The men who are lured in by the Sirens then die at sea.
- Then **ask** students what types of flattery would be most effective with a ship of sailors.
Possible responses: Sailors might be flattered by people who praise their sailing skills or their bravery.
- **Ask** the Literary Analysis question: Which details in the Sirens' song are designed to flatter the epic hero?
Possible response: The description of the Greeks' victory over Troy is designed to flatter Odysseus.

730   *From her throat and my throat,*
           Who lies a-pining?

       Sea rovers here take joy
           Voyaging onward,
       As from our song of Troy
       Graybeard and rower-boy
735   *Goeth more learnèd.*

       All feats on that great field
           In the long warfare,
       Dark days the bright gods willed,
           Wounds you bore there,
740 **54** *Argos' old soldiery* [63]
           On Troy beach teeming,
       Charmed out of time we see.
       No life on earth can be
           Hid from our dreaming.

745   The lovely voices in <u>ardor</u> appealing over the water
       made me crave to listen, and I tried to say
       'Untie me!' to the crew, jerking my brows;
       but they bent steady to the oars. Then Perimedes
       got to his feet, he and Eurylochus,
750   and passed more line about, to hold me still.
       So all rowed on, until the Sirens
       dropped under the sea rim, and their singing
       dwindled away.
                                   My faithful company
       rested on their oars now, peeling off
755   the wax that I had laid thick on their ears;
       then set me free.

Scylla and Charybdis

                                   But scarcely had that island
       faded in blue air than I saw smoke
       and white water, with sound of waves in tumult—
       a sound the men heard, and it terrified them.
760   Oars flew from their hands; the blades went knocking
       wild alongside till the ship lost way,
       with no oar blades to drive her through the water.

Literary Analysis
Epic Hero Which details in the Sirens' song are designed to flatter the epic hero?

63. Argos' old soldiery soldiers from Argos, a city in ancient Greece.

Vocabulary Builder
ardor (är′ dər) *n.* passion; enthusiasm

Vocabulary Development

Word Analysis
Tell students that the root word of *ardor* comes from a Latin word meaning "to burn." It can be a literal burning, as in a flame, or a metaphorical burning, as in enthusiasm (*His ardor for soccer was intense*) or passion (*His ardor for his wife pushed him to impress her with his bravery*). Have students look at the context of the Sirens' song and describe the type of "burning" they convey in their song.

Well, I walked up and down from bow to stern,
trying to put heart into them, standing over
765   every oarsman, saying gently,

                          'Friends,
have we never been in danger before this?

55 More fearsome, is it now, than when the Cyclops
penned us in his cave? What power he had!
Did I not keep my nerve, and use my wits
770 to find a way out for us?

                         Now I say
by hook or crook this peril too shall be
something that we remember.

                      Heads up, lads!
We must obey the orders as I give them.
Get the oar shafts in your hands, and lay back
775 hard on your benches; hit these breaking seas.
Zeus help us pull away before we founder.
You at the tiller, listen, and take in
all that I say—the rudders are your duty;
keep her out of the combers and the smoke;[64]
780 steer for that headland; watch the drift, or we
fetch up in the smother, and you drown us.'

That was all, and it brought them round to action.
But as I sent them on toward Scylla,[65] I
told them nothing, as they could do nothing.
785 They would have dropped their oars again, in panic,
to roll for cover under the decking. Circe's
bidding against arms had slipped my mind,
so I tied on my cuirass[66] and took up
two heavy spears, then made my way along
790 to the foredeck—thinking to see her first from there,
the monster of the gray rock, harboring
torment for my friends. I strained my eyes
upon the cliffside veiled in cloud, but nowhere
could I catch sight of her.

                    And all this time,
795 in travail,[67] sobbing, gaining on the current,
we rowed into the strait—Scylla to port
and on our starboard beam Charybdis, dire

Literary Analysis
Epic Hero What parts of Odysseus' speech demonstrate his strength as a leader?

64. the combers (kōm′ ərs) **and the smoke** the large waves that break on the beach and the ocean spray.

65. Scylla (sil′ ə)

66. cuirass (kwi ras′) *n.* armor for the upper body.

67. travail (trə vāl′) *n.* very hard work.

56 **Reading Check**
What demand does Odysseus make of his men as they approach the rough waters?

from the *Odyssey,* Part I ■ 979

- Remind students that genuine feeling for the men he leads is one of the traits that marks Odysseus as hero.

- Have students to recall other instances in which men have been lost during the voyage. **Ask** how Odysseus and his men responded. **Answer:** When men were lost to the Cicones, the sailors wept. They also grieved to see how many men were lost to the Cyclops.

- **Ask** the Literary Analysis question: What quality of heroic leadership does Odysseus show in lines 823–825?
Possible response: As Odysseus witnesses the terrible death of his men, he suffers "deathly pity" and calls the sight "far the worst" he has ever suffered.

---

gorge[68] of the salt seatide. By heaven! when she
vomited, all the sea was like a cauldron
800   seething over intense fire, when the mixture
suddenly heaves and rises.

             The shot spume
soared to the landside heights, and fell like rain.
But when she swallowed the sea water down
we saw the funnel of the maelstrom,[69] heard
805   the rock bellowing all around, and dark
sand raged on the bottom far below.
My men all blanched against the gloom, our eyes
were fixed upon that yawning mouth in fear
of being devoured.

          Then Scylla made her strike,
810   whisking six of my best men from the ship.
I happened to glance aft at ship and oarsmen
and caught sight of their arms and legs, dangling
high overhead. Voices came down to me
in anguish, calling my name for the last time.

815   A man surfcasting on a point of rock
for bass or mackerel, whipping his long rod
to drop the sinker and the bait far out,
will hook a fish and rip it from the surface
to dangle wriggling through the air:

                 so these
820   were borne aloft in spasms toward the cliff.

She ate them as they shrieked there, in her den,
in the dire grapple, reaching still for me—
and deathly pity ran me through
57   at that sight—far the worst I ever suffered,
825   questing the passes of the strange sea.

              We rowed on.
The Rocks were now behind; Charybdis, too,
and Scylla dropped astern.

The Cattle of the Sun God

58   In the small hours of the third watch, when stars
that shone out in the first dusk of evening
830   had gone down to their setting, a giant wind

68. gorge (gôrj) *n.* throat or gullet.

69. maelstrom (māl′ strəm) *n.* large, violent whirlpool.

Literary Analysis
Epic Hero What quality of heroic leadership does Odysseus show in lines 823–825?

Vocabulary Development

Vocabulary Builder Reinforcement
To reinforce and assess students' comprehension of Vocabulary Builder words, give them sentences using the words in which the word may or may not be used correctly. Students must tell whether the use is correct and explain their answer use these sentences:

1. One of the disloyal men made an *insidious* argument that tempted others to make dangerous choices.
Answer: Yes, *insidious* is used correctly here. Insidious means "crafty," and the disloyal man tempts others.

2. The faithful servant made an *insidious* choice that proved to be safe and reasonable.
Answer: No, *insidious* is not used correctly. It means "crafty" or "disloyal," but the servant is loyal and makes a reasonable choice.

blew from heaven, and clouds driven by Zeus
shrouded land and sea in a night of storm;

58

so, just as Dawn with fingertips of rose
touched the windy world, we dragged our ship

835　to cover in a grotto, a sea cave
where nymphs had chairs of rock and sanded floors.
I mustered all the crew and said:

　　　　　　　　　　'Old shipmates,
our stores are in the ship's hold, food and drink;
the cattle here are not for our provision,

840　or we pay dearly for it.
　　　　　　　　　　　　Fierce the god is

59

who cherishes these heifers and these sheep:
Helios; and no man avoids his eye.'

To this my fighters nodded. Yes. But now
we had a month of onshore gales, blowing

845　day in, day out—south winds, or south by east.
As long as bread and good red wine remained
to keep the men up, and appease their craving,
they would not touch the cattle. But in the end,
when all the barley in the ship was gone,

850　hunger drove them to scour the wild shore
with angling hooks, for fishes and seafowl,
whatever fell into their hands; and lean days
wore their bellies thin.
　　　　　　　　　　The storms continued.
So one day I withdrew to the interior

855　to pray the gods in solitude, for hope
that one might show me some way of salvation.
Slipping away, I struck across the island
to a sheltered spot, out of the driving gale.
I washed my hands there, and made supplication

860　to the gods who own Olympus,70 all the gods—
but they, for answer, only closed my eyes
under slow drops of sleep.
　　　　　　　　　　Now on the shore Eurylochus
made his <u>insidious</u> plea:
　　　　　　　　　　　　'Comrades,' he said,
'You've gone through everything; listen to what I say.

865　All deaths are hateful to us, mortal wretches,
but famine is the most pitiful, the worst
end that a man can come to.

from the *Odyssey*, Part I　■　981

---

58 Reading Skill
Historical and Cultural Context
Which details here suggest that ancient Greeks believed the gods controlled the weather?

Reading Skill
Historical and Cultural Context
How does this passage show that ancient Greeks believed their gods had human-like emotions?

70. Olympus (ō lim′ pəs) Mount Olympus, home of the gods.

Vocabulary Builder
insidious (in sid′ ē əs) *adj.* characterized by craftiness and betrayal

60 ✓Reading Check
Who owns the heifers and sheep on the island?

---

58 **Reading Skill**
Historical and Cultural Context

- Review with students some of the specific gods that Odysseus has encountered and the elements that these gods controlled. Poseidon, for example, could cause earthquakes, while Helios controlled the sun.

- **Ask** students why the Greeks might have imagined that individual gods controlled different natural elements.
Possible response: The Greeks might have imagined gods controlling each element as a way to explain how their world worked.

- **Ask** the first Reading Skill question: Which details here suggest that ancient Greeks believed the gods controlled the weather?
Possible response: Odysseus claims that Zeus creates storms and can manipulate winds and clouds.

59 **Reading Skill**
Historical and Cultural Context

- Remind students of the times that Odysseus has sacrificed animals to the gods. Ask them what emotion he hoped to elicit from the gods with this sacrifice.
Possible response: Odysseus wanted to appease them and try to win their forgiveness for his wrongdoing.

- Then have students recall Odysseus' argument with Poseidon. **Ask** how Poseidon felt toward Odysseus.
Answer: Poseidon was angry with Odysseus because he had blinded Poseidon's son, the Cyclops.

- **Ask** the second Reading Skill question: How does this passage show that ancient Greeks believed their gods had human-like emotions?
Possible response: The passage shows that Helios loves his sheep and would be angry if they were hurt.

60 **Reading Check**
Answer: The sun god Helios owns the heifers and sheep on the island.

- Discuss with students Odysseus' response to the shortage of food. **Ask** them why they think Odysseus is able to resist the temptation of eating the cows he sees before him.
Possible response: Odysseus received Circe's warning and clearly knows that he and his men will suffer if the cows are harmed. Perhaps Odysseus has more self-discipline then his men have.

- Then **ask** why they think Eurylochus was able to convince the sailors successfully that they should eat the cattle.
Possible response: The sailors were all hungry, and Odysseus was not there to remind them of the punishment they would receive for harming the cattle.

- **Ask** the Literary Analysis question: How are the values of Eurylochus different from those of Odysseus?
Possible response: Eurylochus believes it is better to tempt the wrath of the gods and sacrifice the cattle than to risk starvation on the island. Odysseus believes that the warning to avoid eating the cattle must be observed at all costs.

                                        Will you fight it?
Come, we'll cut out the noblest of these cattle
for sacrifice to the gods who own the sky;
870   and once at home, in the old country of Ithaca,
if ever that day comes—
we'll build a costly temple and adorn it
61 with every beauty for the Lord of Noon.[71]
But if he flares up over his heifers lost,
875   wishing our ship destroyed, and if the gods
make cause with him, why, then I say: Better
open your lungs to a big sea once for all
than waste to skin and bones on a lonely island!'

Thus Eurylochus; and they murmured 'Aye!'
880   trooping away at once to round up heifers.
Now, that day tranquil cattle with broad brows
were gazing near, and soon the men drew up
around their chosen beasts in ceremony.
They plucked the leaves that shone on a tall oak—
885   having no barley meal—to strew the victims,
performed the prayers and ritual, knifed the kine
and flayed each carcass, cutting thighbones free
to wrap in double folds of fat. These offerings,
with strips of meat, were laid upon the fire.
890   Then, as they had no wine, they made libation
with clear spring water, broiling the entrails first;
and when the bones were burnt and tripes shared,
they spitted the carved meat.
                                        Just then my slumber
left me in a rush, my eyes opened,
895   and I went down the seaward path. No sooner
had I caught sight of our black hull, than savory
odors of burnt fat eddied around me;
grief took hold of me, and I cried aloud:

'O Father Zeus and gods in bliss forever,
900   you made me sleep away this day of mischief!
O cruel drowsing, in the evil hour!
Here they sat, and a great work they contrived.'[72]

Lampetia[73] in her long gown meanwhile
had borne swift word to the Overlord of Noon:

71. Lord of Noon Helios.

Literary Analysis
Epic Hero How are the values of Eurylochus different from those of Odysseus?

72. contrived (kən trīvd´) *v.* thought up; devised.

73. Lampetia (lam pē´ shə) a nymph.

32

Literature in Context Geography Connection

Real Places and Imaginary Events in the *Odyssey*

Odysseus' journey carries him to real places, including Troy, Sparta, and the Strait of Gibraltar. However, in the story, many of these real places are populated by imaginary creatures, such as the Cyclops and the Sirens. The combination of real places and fantastic events is part of the story's appeal.

ITALY
AEAEA (Circe)
CORSICA
Ismarus (Cicones)
SARDINIA
Mt. Olympus
Troy
TURKEY
Sirens' Island
Land of the Laestrygones
Scylla and Charybdis
Phaeacia
GREECE
ITHACA
Aeolus' Island
SICILY
Strait of Gibraltar
Land of the Dead
Sparta
Cape Malea
Cyclopes' Land
THRINACIA (Cattle of the Sun God)
CRETE
TUNISIA
CYTHERA
OGYGIA (Calypso)
Mediterranean Sea
Land of the Lotus Eaters
N
0   150   300 mi
0   150   300 km

Connect to the Literature Why does the inclusion of real places make the story's imaginary events more believable?

905 'They have killed your kine.'

And the Lord Helios
burst into angry speech amid the immortals:

'O Father Zeus and gods in bliss forever,
punish Odysseus' men! So overweening,
now they have killed my peaceful kine, my joy
910 at morning when I climbed the sky of stars,
and evening, when I bore westward from heaven.
Restitution or penalty they shall pay—
and pay in full—or I go down forever
to light the dead men in the underworld.'

915 Then Zeus who drives the stormcloud made reply:

63 ✓ Reading Check
What do Odysseus' shipmates do while he is sleeping?

from the *Odyssey*, Part I ■ 983

Literature in Context

62 Literature in Context

Geography Connection Odysseus sailed throughout the Mediterranean, leaving from Troy in modern day Turkey, past Crete, to several small islands off the coast of Sicily, Tunisia, Sardinia, Italy, and Corsica. Scholars speculate that the "narrow strait" mentioned in line 637 might be the Straits of Gibraltar.

Connect to the Literature You may wish to compare the places on the map on p. 983 with a modern-day map of the Mediterranean. Point out the location of Troy, Ithaca, and the Straits of Gibraltar. **Ask** students the Connect to the Literature question: Why does the inclusion of real places make the story's imaginary events more believable?
Answer: Real places lend credibility to Homer's tale. By mentioning them, he also helps the readers of his time connect to the story.

63 Reading Check

Answer: While Odysseus is sleeping, his men sacrifice some of the cattle belonging to Helios.

Differentiated

Instruction   Solutions for All Learners

Strategy for Gifted/Talented Students
Ask students to draw their own map tracing Odysseus' route. Encourage them to add photographs or illustrations to depict the Mediterranean setting and specific episodes and figures from the *Odyssey*.

Strategy for Advanced Readers
Most sea captains keep a log, a record of events and sailing data for each day of a voyage. Ask students to write three to five entries in a ship's log that Odysseus might have kept on his journey. Entries should be based on events from Part 1 of the *Odyssey*.

- Read aloud Helios' complaint to Zeus in lines 907–914. Then discuss with students Odysseus' unusual perspective. **Ask** students how Odysseus could have information about a conversation between two gods.

  Possible response: Odysseus was not present, so he must have been told the information by someone who was there.

- Discuss whether Odysseus could have known about Helios' conversation with Zeus at the time that it happened. **Ask** students whether Odysseus might have made different decisions if he had known about Zeus' promise to hit his ship with a "bolt."

  Possible response: Odysseus could not have known of the conversation until later. He shows no indication that he is threatened by Zeus when he tries to sail away.

- **Ask** the Literary Analysis question: What details in lines 920–932 clarify the flashback presented here?

  Answer: Odysseus indicates that he learned this information later from Calypso, who was told the story by the god Hermes.

'Peace, Helios: shine on among the gods,
shine over mortals in the fields of grain.
Let me throw down one white-hot bolt, and make
splinters of their ship in the winedark sea.'

920   —Calypso later told me of this exchange,
64   as she declared that Hermes[74] had told her.
Well, when I reached the sea cave and the ship,
I faced each man, and had it out; but where
could any remedy be found? There was none.
925   The silken beeves[75] of Helios were dead.
The gods, moreover, made queer signs appear:
cowhides began to crawl, and beef, both raw
and roasted, lowed like kine upon the spits.

Now six full days my gallant crew could feast
930   upon the prime beef they had marked for slaughter
from Helios' herd; and Zeus, the son of Cronus,
added one fine morning.
                                  All the gales
had ceased, blown out, and with an offshore breeze
we launched again, stepping the mast and sail,
935   to make for the open sea. Astern of us
the island coastline faded, and no land
showed anywhere, but only sea and heaven,
when Zeus Cronion piled a thunderhead
above the ship, while gloom spread on the ocean.
940   We held our course, but briefly. Then the squall
struck whining from the west, with gale force, breaking
both forestays, and the mast came toppling aft
along the ship's length, so the running rigging
showered into the bilge.
                                  On the afterdeck
945   the mast had hit the steersman a slant blow
bashing the skull in, knocking him overside,
as the brave soul fled the body, like a diver.
With crack on crack of thunder, Zeus let fly
a bolt against the ship, a direct hit,
950   so that she bucked, in reeking fumes of sulphur,
and all the men were flung into the sea.
They came up 'round the wreck, bobbing awhile
like petrels[76] on the waves.

74. Hermes (hur´ mēz´) *n.* god who serves as herald and messenger of the other gods.

75. beeves (bēvz) *n.* alternate plural form of "beef."

Literary Analysis
Epic Hero and Flashback
What details in lines 920–921 clarify the flashback presented here?

76. petrels (pe´ trəlz) *n.* small, dark sea birds.

984   ■ *Themes in Literature: Heroism*

Vocabulary Development

Ocean and Sailing Terms
You may wish to clarify with students the terms related to the ocean that are used in this section of the *Odyssey*. With a clearer sense of what these terms mean, students should get a better picture of this crucial scene in the story.

Gales: winds
Astern: behind a ship

Thunderhead: storm cloud
Squall: storm
Bilge: the bottommost, interior part of a ship
Stepping the mast and sail: setting up a mast and sail by securing it into the hull of a ship, usually on the ship's keel

No more seafaring
homeward for these, no sweet day of return;
955   the god had turned his face from them.

                                    I clambered
fore and aft my hulk until a comber
split her, keel from ribs, and the big timber
floated free; the mast, too, broke away.
A backstay floated dangling from it, stout
960   rawhide rope, and I used this for lashing
mast and keel together. These I straddled,
riding the frightful storm.

                                    Nor had I yet
seen the worst of it: for now the west wind
dropped, and a southeast gale came on—one more
965   twist of the knife—taking me north again,
straight for Charybdis. All that night I drifted,
and in the sunrise, sure enough, I lay
off Scylla mountain and Charybdis deep.
There, as the whirlpool drank the tide, a billow
970   tossed me, and I sprang for the great fig tree,
catching on like a bat under a bough.
Nowhere had I to stand, no way of climbing,
the root and bole[77] being far below, and far
above my head the branches and their leaves,
975   massed, overshadowing Charybdis pool.
But I clung grimly, thinking my mast and keel
would come back to the surface when she spouted.
And ah! how long, with what desire, I waited!
till, at the twilight hour, when one who hears
980   and judges pleas in the marketplace all day
between contentious men, goes home to supper,
the long poles at last reared from the sea.

Now I let go with hands and feet, plunging
straight into the foam beside the timbers,
985   pulled astride, and rowed hard with my hands
to pass by Scylla. Never could I have passed her
had not the Father of gods and men,[78] this time,
kept me from her eyes. Once through the strait,
nine days I drifted in the open sea
990   before I made shore, buoyed up by the gods,

Literary Analysis
Epic Hero Which of Odysseus' heroic qualities does he demonstrate in this passage?

77. **bole** (bōl) *n.* tree trunk.

78. **Father . . . men** Zeus.

 Reading Check
How is Odysseus' ship destroyed?

from the *Odyssey, Part I* ■ 985

65 Literary Analysis
Epic Hero

- Recount with students the calamity that has befallen Odysseus' men, discussing the destruction of their ship and the death of his crew. **Ask** students if there are any other survivors from the wreck.
  Answer: Odysseus does not mention any survivors.

- Read aloud lines 948–955. Then **ask** students what hope they see for Odysseus to return home.
  Possible response: Students may say that Odysseus has escaped from disasters before. Or they may say that he no longer has men to assist him, and that he has powerful gods angry at him, so his chances for survival do not look promising.

- **Ask** the Literary Analysis question: Which of Odysseus' heroic qualities does he demonstrate in this passage?
  Possible response: Odysseus is brave, resourceful, and skillful at seafaring. He also is determined. Even though it would seem that he is destined for certain death, he refuses to give up.

66 Reading Check

Answer: Zeus destroys the ship with a "bolt."

Concept Connector

Anticipation Guide
Have students return to their Anticipation Guides and respond to the statements again in the After Reading column. They may do this individually or in their original pairs or groups. Then, lead a class discussion, probing for what students have learned that confirms or invalidates each statement. Encourage students to cite specific details, quotations, or other evidence from the text to support their responses to each statement.

Connecting to the Literature
Have students compare the sentences they wrote before reading with their thoughts about journeys and adventures after reading the *Odyssey*. Ask them to explain whether their thoughts have changed and, if so, how.

Literary Analysis Graphic Organizer
Ask students to review the graphic organizers they completed to chart historical/cultural details. Show them **Literary Analysis Graphic Organizer B** (p. 202 in *Graphic Organizer Transparencies*) as an example. Then have students share their graphic organizers.

985

⑥⑦ Humanities

La Nef de Telemachus (The Ship of Telemachus)

This is an illustration for the *Odyssey*. It was inspired by statues, pottery, and frescoes from ancient Greece. The rich blue of the ocean, echoed in the duller blue of the cloudy sky, forms a striking frame for the massive black ship. Powered by sail and oar, this craft is the kind on which Odysseus and his men would have sailed to and from Troy. Use the following questions for discussion.

1. How do you think this ship compares in size with Columbus's vessels or with a modern ocean liner?
Answer: This ship is smaller than a fifteen-century wooden ship, and it is much smaller than a hotel-sized ocean liner.

2. How do you think this ship would fare in a storm?
Answer: As a relatively small ship, this craft would be buffeted by a storm and might be damaged or even sunk.

⑥⑧ Critical Viewing

Answer: Most ships today are powered by engines and propellers rather than by the wind and oars. Today's ships make use of highly advanced technology both to navigate and to communicate with other ships.

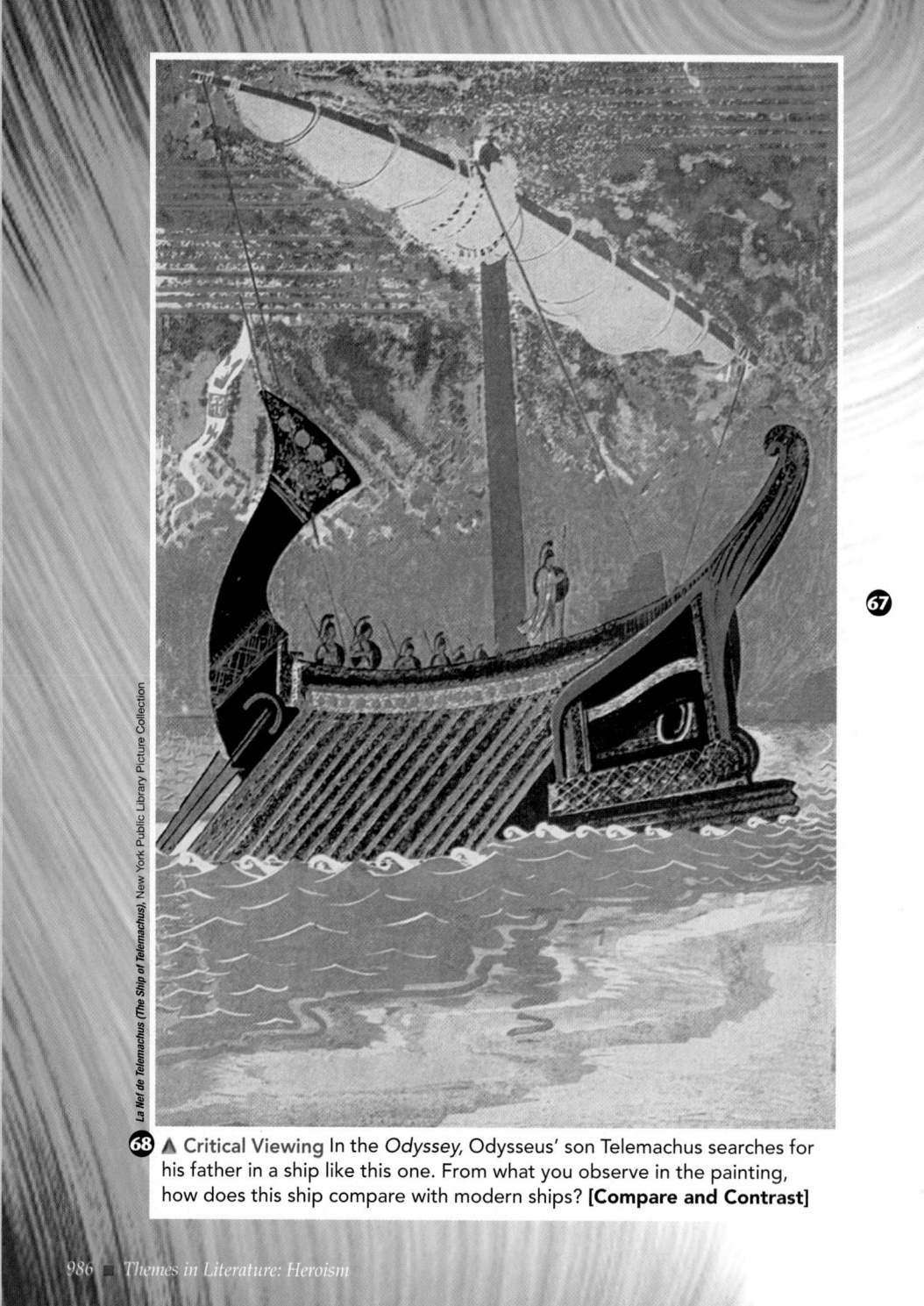

⑥⑦

La Nef de Telemachus (The Ship of Telemachus), New York Public Library Picture Collection

⑥⑧ ▲ Critical Viewing In the *Odyssey*, Odysseus' son Telemachus searches for his father in a ship like this one. From what you observe in the painting, how does this ship compare with modern ships? **[Compare and Contrast]**

986 ■ *Themes in Literature: Heroism*

Vocabulary Development

Vocabulary Knowledge Rating
When students have completed reading and discussing "The Odyssey, Part 1," have them take out their **Vocabulary Knowledge Rating Chart** for this selection. Read the words aloud once more and have students rate their knowledge of the words again in the After Reading column. Clarify any words that are still problematic. Have students write their own definition and example or sentence in the appropriate column. Then have students complete the **Vocabulary Builder Practice** activities on p. 989. Encourage students to use the words in further discussion and written work about this selection. Remind them that they will be accountable for these words on the Selection Test.

69 Literary Analysis
Epic Hero and Flashback

- Model for students the change in voice that occurs in line 993.
- **Ask** the Literary Analysis question: In what way do lines 994–997 remind you that Odysseus is telling his story to an audience?
Possible response: Odysseus breaks off his narrative and speaks directly to his host.

upon Ogygia[79] Isle. The dangerous nymph
Calypso lives and sings there, in her beauty,
and she received me, loved me.

995 |the same tale that I told last night in hall
 |to you and to your lady? Those adventures
 |made a long evening, and I do not hold
 |with tiresome repetition of a story."

But why tell

79. Ogygia (o jij′ ē ə)

Literary Analysis
Epic Hero and Flashback In what way do lines 994–997 remind you that Odysseus is telling his story to an audience?

Thinking About the Selection

1. **Respond:** In which adventure in this section do you think Odysseus acts most heroically? Explain.

2. **(a) Recall:** How do the Sirens lure travelers to their destruction? **(b) Compare and Contrast:** How does the danger posed by the Sirens compare to that posed by the Lotus-Eaters?

3. **(a) Make a Judgment:** Was Odysseus right not to tell his men about his decision to sail toward Scylla? **(b) Hypothesize:** What might have happened if Odysseus had told them everything?

4. **(a) Recall:** What does Eurylochus say to persuade the crew to kill the cattle of the sun god? **(b) Analyze:** After all the men have experienced, why do you think they still disobey Odysseus' command? **(c) Relate:** If you had been in their position, do you think you would have eaten the cattle? Why or why not?

5. **(a) Make a Judgment:** Do the members of the crew deserve the punishment they receive for killing the cattle? Explain.

from the *Odyssey, Part I* ■ *987*

ASSESS

Answers

1. Students might admire Odysseus' skill and bravery when faced with the lose-lose choice between Scylla and Charybdis.

2. (a)They sing an irresistible song that lures travelers to destruction. (b) Both involve the perils of giving in to temptation. The Sirens lure sailors by singing a seductive song. The Lotus-Eaters cause men to forget their homes and their journey by feeding them the Lotus. The Sirens seem to be aware that they are doing something wrong, whereas the Lotus-Eaters do not.

3. (a) Some students may reply that Odysseus was wise to keep the information from his men in order to minimize their panic. Others might think that the men have a right to know what danger lies in store for them. (b) Possible response: Had they know what awaited them, Odysseus' men might have panicked or refused to sail through the strait.

4. (a) Eurylochus claims that there is no fate worse than starvation. He also claims that Helios might be appeased later on. (b) Odysseus is not there to supervise his men when they have grown hungry. (c) Benefiting from hindsight, most students probably would have avoided the cattle.

5. Most students may agree that the sailors deserved to be punished, but in some measure short of death.

987

1. Odysseus can make mistakes, but he forms a powerful bond with his crew.

2. (a) He forces the men who ate the lotus back onto the ship. (b) Odysseus understands that their judgment is impaired by the lotus.

3. (a) The crew is hungry and Odysseus is not there. (b) Odysseus is alarmed, and he blames the gods for letting him sleep. (c) He believes that the gods are involved in everyday life.

4. (a) Students may say the story endures because of its pace, adventures, and remarkable characters. (b) Students might point out that the Odysseus' struggles help this tale endure.

5. (a) **Action:** Odysseus tricks the Cyclops to escape his cave; he taunts the Cyclops and receives Poseidon's wrath; he urges men not to lose heart in rough seas. (b) **Trait:** cleverness; pride or boldness; fellowship (c) The Greeks admired wit, cleverness, and boldness.

6. The Trojan War ends; the winds carry Odysseus to Ismarus where his men battle the Cicones; he escapes from the Lotus-Eaters, the land of forgetfulness; he is captured by and escapes from the Cyclops; he sails to Aeolia and to Laestrygonia and later reaches Aeaea, where he is held by the sorceress Circe; he visits the Land of the Dead to get information from Tiresius; he escapes from the Sirens by lashing himself to a mast; he loses men to the sea monster Scylla; his men anger the sun god Helios when they eat his cattle; and Zeus punishes the men by destroying Odysseus' ship.

7. Odysseus makes himself a sympathetic character and the focal point of the tale.

8. Greek religious beliefs are illustrated in the way the Greeks speak directly to the gods, offer them sacrifices, and suffer their anger.

9. Odysseus would have benefited from a navigation system and a communication system.

988

Apply the Skills

from the *Odyssey, Part 1*

Thinking About the Selection

1. **Respond:** If you were one of Odysseus' crew, how would you feel about having him as your leader? Explain your response.
2. **(a) Recall:** In the episode of the Lotus-Eaters, how does Odysseus handle the men who ate the lotus? **(b) Interpret:** What does Odysseus understand that his men do not?
3. **(a) Recall:** In the episode of the Cattle of the Sun God, why does the crew kill the cattle? **(b) Interpret:** How does Odysseus react to this action? **(c) Analyze:** What does Odysseus' reaction show about the importance of the gods to him?
4. **(a) Evaluate:** The *Odyssey* has entertained people for thousands of years. Why do you think it has remained such an enduring work of literature? **(b) Discuss:** In a small group, share your ideas. As a group, choose one response to share with the class.

Literary Analysis

5. **(a)** Using a chart like the one shown as a model, identify three other actions that the **epic hero** Odysseus performs. **(b)** For each action, identify the character trait that it reveals. **(c)** Based on your responses, explain which character traits the ancient Greeks admired most.

Action		Trait
Resists temptations of Calypso and Circe.	**Odysseus** →	Self-control

6. Odysseus recounts most of the action in Part 1 in the form of a **flashback.** List the events of Part 1 in chronological sequence, beginning with the end of the Trojan War.
7. The epic hero recounts his own adventures. In what way does this affect your reaction to the events he describes? Explain.

Reading Skill

8. Consider the **cultural and historical context** of Homer's *Odyssey.* What role do ancient Greek religious beliefs play in the epic? Explain your answer.
9. What abilities or features of modern technology could have helped Odysseus on his journey had they been available in ancient times? Explain your answer.

988 ■ Themes in Literature: Heroism

QuickReview

Part 1 at a Glance
The hero Odysseus enjoys amazing adventures and endures great hardships on his quest to return home.

Go Online
—Assessment
For: Self-test
Visit: www.PHSchool.com
Web Code: epa-6602

Epic Hero: the larger-than-life central character in an epic

Flashback: a scene that interrupts the sequence of events in a narrative to relate earlier events

Historical and Cultural Context: the events, beliefs, and customs that define the time and place in which a work is set or in which it was written

Vocabulary Builder

Practice Identify the word in each group that does not belong with the others. Explain your response.

1. plundered, robbed, donated
2. dispatched, hesitated, completed
3. mammoth, small, tiny
4. assuage, soothe, increase
5. bereft, after, without
6. ardor, spirited, careless
7. insidious, traitorous, friendly

Adding Words to Your Vocabulary The word *dispatched* is the past-tense form of the verb *dispatch,* which means "finish quickly." Use a dictionary to find the definition of the noun *dispatcher,* which has a very different meaning. Then, explain how the words are related. (For more on using a dictionary, see page R6.)

Writing

Write an **everyday epic.** Choose an everyday event, and write an account that makes it seem larger than life. Recite your work for the class.

- Outline the plot of your story, adding points for epic traits such as adventure, bravery, and extreme challenges. Plan appearances by gods and monsters.
- Use multiple points of view. Begin with the voice of a speaker outside the story, and then have one of the characters tell the tale.

For *Grammar, Vocabulary,* and *Assessment,* see **Build Language Skills,** pages 990–991.

Extend Your Learning

Listening and Speaking With two classmates, improvise an **everyday conversation** among ordinary Greeks discussing Odysseus' exploits. Each character's statements should reflect the ancient Greek values shown in the *Odyssey.*

Research and Technology Use library and Internet resources to research the complete story of the *Odyssey.* Then, create an **illustrated travelogue** that shows the sequence of Odysseus' wanderings. Include pictures of the places that Odysseus visited, and describe the events that took place in each location.

Apply the Skills ■ *989*

Extend Your Learning

The **Extend Your Learning** support page (*Unit 6 Resources,* p. 26) provides guided note-taking opportunities to help students complete the Extend Your Learning activities.

Go Online
Research **For:** An additional research activity
Visit: www.PHSchool.com
Web Code: epd-7601
For another research activity to extend students' learning, give students this Web Code.

Vocabulary Development
Practice

1. Donated; *Plundered* and *robbed* are synonyms.
2. Hesitated; *Dispatched* and *completed* are synonyms.
3. Mammoth; *Small* and *tiny* are synonyms.
4. Increase; *Assuage* and *soothe* are synonyms.
5. After; *Bereft* and *without* are synonyms.
6. Careless; *Ardor* and *spirited* are synonyms.
7. Friendly; *Insidious* and *traitorous* are synonyms.

Adding Words to Your Vocabulary
Sample answers:

The word *dispatch* also can mean "the sending of a letter or messenger." A *dispatcher* would be "a person who sends a letter or message."

Writing

- To give students guidance for writing an everyday epic, give them the Writing Support page for this selection, p. 25 in *Unit 6 Resources.*
- To evaluate students' epics, use the Autobiographical Narrative rubric, p. 43–44 in *General Resources.* In addition, you might evaluate narratives on basis of exaggeration—how well students can take an ordinary event and make it appear extraordinary.

Six Traits Focus

✔ Ideas	✔ Word Choice	
✔ Organization	Sentence Fluency	
✔ Voice	Conventions	

WG **Writing and Grammar, Gold Level**
Students will find guidance on epic writing in Chapter 5.

Build Language Skills

Go to pp. 990–991 for vocabulary and grammar lessons and assessment practice.

Vocabulary Skill

- Introduce the prefix *contra-*. Ask students to brainstorm for words that contain this prefix. **Possible responses:** *contra, contrast, contravene, contrary*
- Have students complete the Practice activity on this page.

Possible Answers

1. The merchandise illegally brought in was *contraband.* Knowing that the word *contra-* means "against" provides a clue to the meaning of *contraband:* "goods that are illegal or against the law."

2. Anne did not *contradict* her boss, even though she knew the boss was wrong. *Contra-* means "against," and *-dict* means "speak," so *contradict* means "to speak against."

3. The label on the medication *contraindicates* its use for your illness, so don't take it. *Contra-* means "against," so *contraindicate* means "against what is advisable."

4. The mayor took a stand in *contraposition* to the government policy. *Contra-* means "against," so *contraposition* is a position opposite to or against.

Grammar Lesson

- Explain that a comma and a coordinating conjunction can join two independent clauses.

- Semicolons can also combine two simple sentences into a compound sentence. The semicolon shows that the sentences are more closely related than two sentences that are separated by a period.

- Have students complete the Practice activity on this page.

Answers

1. simple sentence

2. Compound sentence; *but* is the coordinating conjunction.

3. simple sentence

4. Compound sentence; *so* is the coordinating conjunction.

5. simple sentence

Build Language Skills

from the *Odyssey*, Part 1

Vocabulary Skill

Word Roots Knowing that the **Latin prefix *contra-*** means "against" provides a clue to the meaning of the word *controversy,* which is "parties having opinions against each other."

▶ **Example:** There is a *controversy* over who actually wrote the Shakespearean plays.

Practice Use each of the following words in an original sentence. Then, explain how knowing the meaning of the prefix *contra-* provides a context clue for understanding the sentence.

1. contraband   **2.** contradict   **3.** contraindicate   **4.** contraposition

Grammar Lesson

Simple and Compound Sentences A **simple sentence** consists of a single independent clause. Although a simple sentence is just one independent clause with one subject and one verb, the subject, verb, or both may be compound.

A **compound sentence** consists of two or more independent clauses. The clauses can be joined by a comma and a coordinating conjunction or by a semicolon.

Simple sentence	He remembered an old story.
Simple sentence with compound subject	He and she remembered an old story.
Compound sentence	The stars shone, and they remembered an old story.

Practice Identify each of the following sentences as simple or compound. For compound sentences, identify the coordinating conjunction.

1. Marvin went outside.

2. He looked down the street, but he saw no one.

3. The weather was perfect after the rain.

4. He wanted to start a game, so he looked for his friends.

5. They played all afternoon and into the evening.

WG *Prentice Hall Writing and Grammar Connection: Chapter 21, Section 2*

990 ■ *Themes in Literature: Heroism*

MorePractice

For more practice with simple and compound sentences, see the Grammar Handbook, p. R42.

WG **Writing and Grammar, Gold Level**
Students will find further instruction and practice on simple and compound sentences in Chapter 21, Section 2.

Teaching Resources

The following resources can be used to enrich or extend the instruction for Build Language Skills.

Unit 6 Resources
Build Language Skills: Vocabulary: Word Roots, p. 28
Build Grammar Skills: Simple and Compound Sentences, p. 29

Assessment Practice

Reading Skill: Analyzing Cultural and Historical Context

Directions: *Read the selection. Then, answer the questions.*

King Acrisius of Argos had one child, a daughter, Danae. She was extremely beautiful, but this was no comfort to the King, who wished for a son. He journeyed to Delphi to ask the god if there was any hope that some day he would be the father of a boy. The priestess told him no, and added that his daughter would have a son who would kill him.

—"Perseus" retold by Edith Hamilton

1. From the cultural and historical context of this passage, what can a reader infer that the ancient Greeks valued?
   A beautiful children above all
   B boy and girl children equally
   C girls more highly than boys
   D boys more highly than girls

2. From the cultural and historical context of this passage, what can a reader infer that the ancient Greeks believed?
   A All kings must journey to Delphi.
   B Oracles can foretell the future.
   C Greek princesses were more beautiful than any others.
   D Every generation fears destruction by its own offspring.

3. What common human trait does the king demonstrate?
   A a desire to know the future
   B the wish to have a daughter
   C a lack of respect
   D the desire to travel

4. From the context of this passage, what can the reader infer?
   A The culture is similar to modern American culture.
   B The culture has several points in common with modern American culture.
   C The culture has little in common with modern American culture.
   D The culture is not indicated.

Timed Writing: Explanation [Critical Stance]

The *Odyssey* has always been considered an important work. Write an explanation of why Western culture has valued this epic. Use details from the text to support your assumptions. **(30 minutes)**

Writing Workshop: *Work in Progress*

Writing for Assessment

Using your Background List, add major characters and stages of the plot of the literary works. Then, add the major cause-effect sequence to each historical event. Save this work in your writing portfolio.

Build Language Skills ■ *991*

Reading: Analyzing Cultural and Historical Context

1. D
2. B
3. A
4. C

Timed Writing

- Tell students that in this timed writing they will write an explanation of a text and support their assumptions with specific examples from the text.

- Have students list the beliefs and values found in the *Odyssey*. You may wish to suggest that they use a Venn diagram to determine the similarities between the beliefs and values expressed in the *Odyssey* and Western cultural beliefs and values. Point out that students may wish to make specific references to characters and actions.

- Tell students that they need to support their explanations with specific examples from the epic as well as from Western culture.

- Suggest that students plan their time to give ten minutes to reviewing the epic, fifteen minutes to writing, and five minutes to reviewing and revising.

- Assess students' essays based on their explanations and support for these explanations from the text and from Western culture.

Writing Workshop
Work in Progress

Work in Progress

- Have students go to their portfolios and take out the work they have completed so far on this assignment. Remind them that this work may be used in the **Writing Workshop** on timed essays on p. 1040.

- Guide students in completing the **Work-in-Progress** assignment on this page. When students have completed this activity, have them keep it in their portfolios. They will use it as they continue the **Work in Progress**.

Planning Differentiated Instruction

Accessibility at a Glance

	from the Odyssey, Part 2
Context	Historical: Ancient Greece
Language	Narrative poem; formal language; allusions to Greek mythology
Concept Level	Challenging (journey of epic hero)
Literary Merit	Noted author; classic work
Lexile	NP
Overall Rating	More challenging

Choosing Your Resources

[**L1**] Special Needs Students   [**L4**] Advanced Students

[**L2**] Below-Level Students   [**EL**] English Learners

[**L3**] All Students

FT Fast Track Instruction: To move the lesson more quickly, use the strategies and activities identified with **FT**.

Scaffolding for Less Proficient and Advanced Students

The leveled questions on Apply the Skills pages progress in the levels of thinking required to answer them. To address the needs of your different students, you may use the (a) level questions for your less proficient students, the (b) level with your on-level and advanced students. The occasional (c) level questions are appropriate for your advanced students.

Step-by-Step Teaching Guide

	Pacing Guide
PRETEACH	
• Administer Vocabulary and Reading Warm-ups as necessary.	
• Introduce the Literary Analysis Skill: Epic Simile. **FT**	10 min.
• Introduce the Reading Skill: Analyzing the Influence of Cultural and Historical Context. **FT**	10 min.
• Prepare students to read by teaching the selection vocabulary. **FT**	10 min.
• Build background and develop expressive vocabulary with Connecting to the Literature and Background.	10 min.
• Engage students' interest with the motivation activity.	10 min.
TEACH	
• Informally monitor comprehension while students read independently or in groups. **FT**	30 min.
• Monitor students' comprehension with the Reading Check notes.	as students read
• Reinforce vocabulary with Vocabulary Builder notes.	as students read
• Develop students' understanding of epic simile with the Literary Analysis annotations. **FT**	5 min.
• Develop students' ability to identify influences on their reading and responses with the Reading Skill annotations. **FT**	10 min.
ASSESS/EXTEND	
• Assess students' comprehension and mastery of the Reading Skill and Literary Analysis by having them answer the Apply the Skills questions. **FT**	35 min.
• Have students complete the Vocabulary Builder activities. **FT**	5 min.
• Apply students' ability to write a biography of Odysseus with the Writing activity. **FT**	30–45 min. or homework
• Extend students' listening and speaking skills with the Extend Your Learning activity.	15–30 min. or homework
• Have students complete the Vocabulary Skill and Grammar Lesson.	5 min.
• Monitor students' progress with the Assessment Practice.	20–40 min.
• Administer **Selection Test A** or **Selection Test B**. **FT**	15 min.

Resources

Meeting Your Standards

Students will

1. **analyze and respond to literary elements.**
   - Literary Analysis: Epic Simile

2. **read, comprehend, and analyze short stories.**
   - Reading Skill: Analyzing the Influence of Cultural and Historical Context
   - Reading Strategy: Identifying Influences on Your Own Reading and Responses
   - Reading Check questions
   - Apply the Skills questions
   - Assessment Practice

3. **develop vocabulary.**
   - Vocabulary Builder
   - Greek root -*techni*-

4. **apply grammar skills.**
   - Complex and Compound-Complex Sentences

5. **develop writing proficiency.**
   - Work in Progress: Timed Writing
   - Biography of Odysseus

6. **extend learning.**
   - Listening and Speaking: Debate

Block Scheduling: Use one 90-minute class period to preteach the skills and have students read Part 2. Use a second 90-minute class period to assess students' mastery of skills, extend their learning, and monitor their progress.

Homework Suggestions

The following are possibilities for homework assignments.

- Support pages from *Unit 6 Resources:*
  Literary Analysis
  Reading Skill
  Vocabulary Builder
  Enrichment

- An Extend Your Learning project and the Writing assignment for the *Odyssey,* Part 2 may be completed over several days.

PRENTICE HALL

TeacherEXPRESS™
[Plan · Teach · Assess] Use this complete suite of powerful teaching tools to make lesson planning and testing quicker and easier.

PRENTICE HALL

StudentEXPRESS™
[Learn · Study · Succeed] Use the Interactive Textbook (online and on CD-ROM) to make selections and activities come alive with audio and video support and interactive questions.

❶ Literary Analysis
Epic Simile

- Tell students that an epic hero can seem larger than life. Similarly, an *epic simile* is more elaborate than the simple comparisons writers often make. Where a simple simile might compare a tall man to a tree, an epic simile could go on to describe his feet as roots, his hair as leaves, and his fingertips as branches reaching up into the sky.
- Give students copies of **Literary Analysis Graphic Organizer A** (*Graphic Organizer Transparencies*, p. 205). Have them fill in their graphic organizers, noting epic similes as they read the selection.

❷ Reading Skill
Historical and Cultural Context

- Have students read the description of historical and cultural context.
- Discuss the chart with students. Remind students that Homer's environment was very different from their own, and his text reflects the beliefs of his time.
- Give students a copy of **Reading Skill Graphic Organizer A** (*Graphic Organizer Transparencies*, p. 203). Have them fill in the graphic organizer to identify how historical details in the text can have different meanings for different cultures.

Connecting to the Literature

Model use of this expressive vocabulary with these examples:

1. The Sirens seemed to *magnetize* those who heard their song.
2. I *marvel* that Odysseus was able to make it back to Ithaca.
3. Odysseus and his crew had to *confront* many challenges.
4. Odysseus *interrogates* Penelope's suitors.

Help students further develop their expressive vocabulary by providing these words: *courtesy, deception,* and *furious.* Encourage students to use these words as they discuss the selection.

Build Skills from the *Odyssey*, Part 2

❶ Literary Analysis

An **epic simile** is an elaborate comparison that may extend for several lines. Epic similes may use the words *like, as, just as,* or *so* to make the comparison. Unlike a normal simile, which draws a comparison to a single, distinct image, an epic simile is longer and more involved. It might recall an entire place or story. In Part 1, lines 268–271, Odysseus uses an epic simile to stress the size of the fallen tree from which he creates a weapon.

> And it was like a mast / a lugger of twenty oars, broad in the beam— / a deep-sea-going craft—might carry: / so long, so big around, it seemed.

As you read, notice how Homer uses epic similes—sometimes called Homeric similes—to bring descriptions to life.

❷ Reading Skill

The **historical and cultural context** of a work is the backdrop of details of the time and place in which the work is set or in which it was written. These details include the events, beliefs, and customs of a specific culture and time. When you **identify influences on your own reading and responses,** the historical and cultural context reflected in a work becomes more apparent.

- As you read a work from another time and culture, keep your own beliefs and customs in mind.
- Notice the ways in which your reactions to ideas and situations in the work differ from the reactions of the characters.
- Consider whether your reactions reflect your cultural values.

Use a chart like the one shown to note the differences between your own influences and those reflected in the *Odyssey*.

Detail in Text

Odysseus says he and his crew plundered Ismarus.

Meaning for Characters

Winners can take valuables from the defeated.

Meaning in My Culture

Looting is shameful.

Vocabulary Builder

- **dissemble** (di sem´ bəl) *v.* conceal under a false appearance; disguise (p. 994) *The spy was able to dissemble and seem like a patriot.*

- **incredulity** (in´ krə dōō´ lə tē) *n.* unwillingness or inability to believe (p. 996) *During the eclipse, they were silent with incredulity.*

- **bemusing** (bē myōōz´ iŋ) *v.* stupefying or muddling (p. 999) *After bemusing the audience, the speaker received little applause.*

- **equity** (ek´ wit ē) *n.* fairness; justice (p. 1004) *Laws are meant to treat everyone with equity.*

- **maudlin** (môd´ lin) *adj.* tearfully and foolishly sentimental (p. 1004) *The soap opera evoked maudlin responses in the audience.*

- **contempt** (kən tempt´) *n.* disdain or scorn (p. 1011) *A good athlete shows respect, not contempt, for an opponent.*

Vocabulary Development

Vocabulary Knowledge Rating

Create a **Vocabulary Knowledge Rating Chart** for Part 2 of the *Odyssey*. Include the selection vocabulary from this page and the expressive vocabulary words. These words will increase students' expressive vocabulary.

Give students a copy of the chart with the words on it. Introduce the words by reading them aloud and having students mark their rating in the Before Reading column. Urge

them to be alert to these words as they read and discuss Part 2 because they will rate their knowledge of the words again after they finish.

If you wish, you may tally how many students know (or think they know) a word to gauge how much instruction you need to provide. As students read, point out the words and their context.

from the

Odyssey

Homer Translated by Robert Fitzgerald

PART 2
The Return of Odysseus

Review and Anticipate

In Part 1 of the Odyssey, *Odysseus and his companions face many perils on their voyage from Troy to Ithaca. At some moments, they are tempted to forsake their voyage; at others, their lives are endangered by powerful enemies. Ultimately, Odysseus' men bring about their own destruction at the hand of Zeus when they kill the cattle belonging to Helios.*

As Part 2 begins, Odysseus is alone when he reaches Ithaca after a twenty-year absence. What do you predict will happen when Odysseus arrives home?

from the *Odyssey,* Part 2 ■ *993*

❶ Motivation

Prepare an **Anticipation Guide** (*General Resources,* pp. 8–10) with the following statements:

- People anxiously await for their family members to return home.
- The important things in one's home will never change, no matter how long you stay away.
- You should never trust people to remain faithful to your memory if you have been gone for a long time.
- You can never go home again.

Give students copies of the prepared Anticipation Guide. Have students mark their responses in the Me column. Then have students discuss the statements in pairs or groups and mark the Guides again, this time in the Group column.

Concept Connector ➤

Students will return to the Anticipation Guide after completing the *Odyssey,* Part 2.

Learning Modalities Interpersonal Learners

Key scenes in the *Odyssey,* Part 2 focus on tests—Odysseus tests people to see whether they have remained faithful to him. Penelope tests Odysseus to see whether he is truly who he claims to be. Ask these students to consider the unstated rules that govern interactions between people, especially in relationships that require trust. Have students describe an encounter in which people have tested one another to find out what they know, who they are, or whether they should be trusted.

Of the two great epic poems attributed to Homer, the *Iliad* has been called a war poem, and the *Odyssey* has been called a postwar poem. The wanderings of Odysseus after his victory at Troy and the difficulties of readjusting to a civil society upon his eventual return home have helped make the themes of the *Odyssey* relevant to many generations of readers. The theme of the returning veteran, with the struggles to reestablish relationships with spouses and friends (and perhaps with a child for the first time) add a human poignancy to this epic adventure. Discuss with students the difficulties and emotions that Odysseus is likely to face after twenty years away.

❸ **Reading Check**

Answer: Athena tells Odysseus that there are many suitors at the palace trying to persuade Penelope that Odysseus is surely dead after all this time, and so she must marry again. Each wants to be her new husband. Athena tells Odysseus that it is time he put an end to all this.

❷ **"Twenty years gone, and I am back again . . ."**

Odysseus has finished telling his story to the Phaeacians. The next day, young Phaeacian noblemen conduct him home by ship. He arrives in Ithaca after an absence of twenty years. The goddess Athena appears and informs him of the situation at home. Numerous suitors, believing Odysseus to be dead, have been continually seeking the hand of his wife, Penelope, in marriage, while overrunning Odysseus' palace and enjoying themselves at Penelope's expense. Moreover, they are plotting to murder Odysseus' son, Telemachus, before he can inherit his father's lands. Telemachus, who, like Penelope, still hopes for his father's return, has journeyed to Pylos and Sparta to learn what he can about his father's fate. Athena disguises Odysseus as a beggar and directs him to the hut of Eumaeus,[1] his old and faithful swineherd. While Odysseus and Eumaeus are eating breakfast, Telemachus arrives. Athena then appears to Odysseus.

1. Eumaeus (yōō mē′ əs)

. . . From the air
she walked, taking the form of a tall woman,
handsome and clever at her craft, and stood
1000   beyond the gate in plain sight of Odysseus,
unseen, though, by Telemachus, unguessed,
for not to everyone will gods appear.
Odysseus noticed her; so did the dogs,
who cowered whimpering away from her. She only
1005   nodded, signing to him with her brows,
a sign he recognized. Crossing the yard,
he passed out through the gate in the stockade
to face the goddess. There she said to him:

"Son of Laertes and the gods of old,
1010   Odysseus, master of landways and seaways,
<u>dissemble</u> to your son no longer now.
The time has come: tell him how you together
will bring doom on the suitors in the town.
I shall not be far distant then, for I
1015   myself desire battle."

                Saying no more,
she tipped her golden wand upon the man,
making his cloak pure white, and the knit tunic
fresh around him. Lithe and young she made him,

Vocabulary Builder
dissemble (di sem′ bəl) *v.* conceal under a false appearance; disguise

❸ ✓ Reading Check

What does Athena reveal to Odysseus about the situation he will find at home?

Vocabulary Development

Think-Aloud: Context
Direct students' attention to the dogs' behavior at the appearance of Athena on this page: they *cowered* at the sight of the goddess. Using a think-aloud process, model how to use context to infer the meaning of an unknown word.

    The dogs *cowered* because they see Athena. In the same sentence, they also whimper, or cry, and seem to run away from her. Are there any more clues? Well, Athena is a goddess and very powerful. The dogs might be afraid and run away from a powerful person. I think that *to cower* means to show fear before a powerful person or thing.

Eumaeus, the Swineherd from Homer's *The Odyssey*, N.C. Wyeth, The Museum of Texas Tech University

⑤ ▲ Critical Viewing What can you tell about Eumaeus from this illustration? **[Infer]**

Eumaeus, the Swineherd, by N. C. Wyeth

This illustration, like many for this selection, was among the sixteen paintings N. C. Wyeth, America's foremost illustrator of children's books and classics, painted for a 1929 edition of the *Odyssey*. Use the following questions for discussion:

1. In the *Odyssey*, Eumaeus is characterized as being loyal and noble. How does Wyeth's painting convey these traits?
   Possible response: Eumaeus is pictured as tall, straight, and sturdy. He looks like a man who will not be easily moved. This firmness of his stance makes him look trustworthy.

2. Which dog in the illustration might be Argus?
   Possible response: Argus is described in lines 1163–1168 as "an old hound, lying near." Argus would be the dog on the left, lying down.

❺ Critical Viewing

Possible response: Eumaeus appears to be patient, loyal, and practical. The pigs in the sty behind him are a clue to his profession.

Differentiated Instruction   Solutions for All Learners

Strategy for Less Proficient Readers
Have partners paraphrase the opening passage that describes the entrance of Athena. A possible paraphrase might be: "The goddess Athena, looking like a beautiful, intelligent woman, appeared to Odysseus. Telemachus, however, could not see her."

Strategy for English Learners
Students may find the appearance of a goddess in this scene challenging. Explain that gods and goddesses often appear in human form in Greek literature. Tell them that readers would be familiar with this convention, as well as with Telemachus' inability to see the god, although his father sees her plainly. Ask students to identify details that emphasize Athena's godlike qualities—for example, her height and the dogs' fear of her—and the details that make her seem more like a human being.

- Tell students that the Greeks believed their gods often intervened in the affairs of human beings, taking an interest in their welfare and helping or hindering them. Remind them of the gods who have made Odysseus' journey back to Ithaca so difficult.

- **Ask** students the Reading Skill question: What do lines 1021–1029 suggest about the way ancient Greeks responded to the presence of a god?
Possible response: Taking the transformed Odysseus for a god, Telemachus shows awe, fear, and reverence. However, he also speaks freely to the "god," and makes requests. These lines suggest that Greeks responded to the gods as higher, but approachable, beings.

---

ruddy with sun, his jawline clean, the beard
1020 no longer gray upon his chin. And she
withdrew when she had done.
                              Then Lord Odysseus
reappeared—and his son was thunderstruck.
Fear in his eyes, he looked down and away
as though it were a god, and whispered:

❻   "Stranger,
1025 you are no longer what you were just now!
Your cloak is new; even your skin! You are
one of the gods who rule the sweep of heaven!
Be kind to us, we'll make you fair oblation[2]
and gifts of hammered gold. Have mercy on us!"

1030 The noble and enduring man replied:

"No god. Why take me for a god? No, no.
I am that father whom your boyhood lacked
and suffered pain for lack of. I am he."

Held back too long, the tears ran down his cheeks
1035 as he embraced his son.
                              Only Telemachus,
uncomprehending, wild
with incredulity, cried out:
                              "You cannot
be my father Odysseus! Meddling spirits
conceived this trick to twist the knife in me!
1040 No man of woman born could work these wonders
by his own craft, unless a god came into it
with ease to turn him young or old at will.
I swear you were in rags and old,
and here you stand like one of the immortals!"

1045 Odysseus brought his ranging mind to bear
and said:
                              "This is not princely, to be swept
away by wonder at your father's presence.
No other Odysseus will ever come,
for he and I are one, the same; his bitter
1050 fortune and his wanderings are mine.
Twenty years gone, and I am back again
on my own island.

What do lines 1021–1029 suggest about the way ancient Greeks responded to the presence of a god?

2. oblation (äb lā′ shən) *n.* offering to a god.

Vocabulary Builder
incredulity (in′ krə do͞o′ lə tē) *n.* unwillingness or inability to believe

---

Vocabulary Development

Word Forms

Two of the Vocabulary Builder words for the *Odyssey* can form other parts of speech by adding suffixes. Give students a blank **Word Form Chart** (*General Resources*, p. 16) with *dissemble* and *incredulity* in the correct columns. Work with the class, or have students work with a partner, to determine the related forms. The final chart should look like the one shown.

Hold students accountable for integrating the related forms of the words into their speaking and writing.

Noun	Verb	Adjective	Adverb
dissembler	dissemble	dissembling	dissemblingly
incredulity		incredulous	incredulously

As for my change of skin,
that is a charm Athena, Hope of Soldiers,
uses as she will; she has the knack
1055 to make me seem a beggar man sometimes
and sometimes young, with finer clothes about me.
It is no hard thing for the gods of heaven
to glorify a man or bring him low."

When he had spoken, down he sat.
                              Then, throwing
1060 his arms around this marvel of a father
Telemachus began to weep. Salt tears
rose from the wells of longing in both men,
and cries burst from both as keen and fluttering
as those of the great taloned hawk,
1065 whose nestlings farmers take before they fly.
So helplessly they cried, pouring out tears,
and might have gone on weeping so till sundown,
had not Telemachus said:

                    "Dear father! Tell me
what kind of vessel put you here ashore
1070 on Ithaca? Your sailors, who were they?
I doubt you made it, walking on the sea!"

Then said Odysseus, who had borne the barren sea:

"Only plain truth shall I tell you, child.
Great seafarers, the Phaeacians, gave me passage
1075 as they give other wanderers. By night
over the open ocean, while I slept,
they brought me in their cutter,[3] set me down
on Ithaca, with gifts of bronze and gold
and stores of woven things. By the gods' will
1080 these lie all hidden in a cave. I came
to this wild place, directed by Athena,
so that we might lay plans to kill our enemies.
Count up the suitors for me, let me know
what men at arms are there, how many men.
1085 I must put all my mind to it, to see
if we two by ourselves can take them on
or if we should look round for help."
                              Telemachus
replied:

Literary Analysis
Epic Simile To what are Odysseus' and Telemachus' cries compared in the epic simile in lines 1063-1065?

3. **cutter** (kut´ər) *n.* small, swift ship or boat carried aboard a large ship to transport personnel or supplies.

 Reading Check

Why is Telemachus initially doubtful that the man before him is Odysseus, his father?

❼ Literary Analysis
Epic Simile

• Remind students that an *epic simile* is a device to help describe what is happening in the *Odyssey*. Beyond that, however, an epic simile underscores the drama of the action and paints vivid images in the reader's mind.

• **Ask** students the Literary Analysis question: To what are Odysseus' and Telemachus' cries compared in this epic simile?
Answer: The cries of Odysseus and Telemachus are compared to those of a hawk that has lost its nestlings to a farmer.

❽ Reading Check

Answer: Telemachus is initially doubtful because of the change in Odysseus' appearance, which leads Telemachus to assume he is a god.

❾ Reading Skill
Historical and Cultural Context

- Remind students that Athena was the goddess of wisdom. Then **ask** students why she might be particularly interested in helping Odysseus.
Possible response: Odysseus is known for his wit and cleverness. Athena, the goddess of wisdom, may admire his intelligence.

- Then **ask** students the Reading Skill question: What does Odysseus' statement in lines 1109–1111 suggest about ancient Greek beliefs about the gods' interest in human affairs.
Possible response: Odysseus' response indicates that the Greeks believed they could depend on the gods to help them in very specific ways in time of need.

- Discuss with students how Homer's story shows the Greek gods responding to humans' material needs in very active ways. In this section, for example, Athena has disguised Odysseus and then restored him to his youthful appearance.

"O Father, all my life your fame
as a fighting man has echoed in my ears—
1090 your skill with weapons and the tricks of war—
but what you speak of is a staggering thing,
beyond imagining, for me. How can two men
do battle with a houseful in their prime?⁴
For I must tell you this is no affair
1095 of ten or even twice ten men, but scores,
throngs of them. You shall see, here and now.
The number from Dulichium alone
is fifty-two picked men, with armorers,
a half dozen; twenty-four came from Same,
1100 twenty from Zacynthus; our own island
accounts for twelve, high-ranked, and their retainers,
Medon the crier, and the Master Harper,
besides a pair of handymen at feasts.
If we go in against all these
1105 I fear we pay in salt blood for your vengeance.
You must think hard if you would conjure up
the fighting strength to take us through."

Odysseus
who had endured the long war and the sea
answered:

"I'll tell you now.
1110 Suppose Athena's arm is over us, and Zeus
her father's, must I rack my brains for more?"

Clearheaded Telemachus looked hard and said:

"Those two are great defenders, no one doubts it,
but throned in the serene clouds overhead;
1115 other affairs of men and gods they have
to rule over."

And the hero answered:
"Before long they will stand to right and left of us
in combat, in the shouting, when the test comes—
our nerve against the suitors' in my hall.
1120 Here is your part: at break of day tomorrow
home with you, go mingle with our princes.
The swineherd later on will take me down
the port-side trail—a beggar, by my looks,
hangdog and old. If they make fun of me
1125 in my own courtyard, let your ribs cage up

998 ■ Themes in Literature: Heroism

4. in their prime in the best or most vigorous stage of their lives.

Reading Skill
Historical and Cultural Context
What does Odysseus' statement in lines 1109–1111 suggest about ancient Greek beliefs about the gods' interest in human affairs?

Vocabulary Development

Vocabulary Builder Reinforcement
Students will benefit from additional examples and practice with the Vocabulary Builder words. Reinforce their comprehension with "show-you-know" sentences. The first part of the sentence uses the vocabulary word in an appropriate context. The second part of the sentence—the "show-you-know" part—clarifies the first. Model the strategy with the example for *bemusing*:
The *bemusing* air in the garden made us sleepy with its odor of sweet flowers.

Then give students these sentence prompts and coach them in creating the clarification part.
1. The *bemusing* singer drew us in with her amazing voice; _____
Sample answer: her songs lulled us into forgetting all our troubles.
2. We questioned the *equity* of the law; _____
Sample answer: it seemed to favor one group of people over another.

998

your springing heart, no matter what I suffer,
no matter if they pull me by the heels
or practice shots at me, to drive me out.
Look on, hold down your anger. You may even
1130 plead with them, by heaven! in gentle terms
to quit their horseplay—not that they will heed you,
rash as they are, facing their day of wrath.
Now fix the next step in your mind.

                       Athena,
counseling me, will give me word, and I
1135 shall signal to you, nodding: at that point
round up all armor, lances, gear of war
left in our hall, and stow the lot away
back in the vaulted storeroom. When the suitors
miss those arms and question you, be soft
1140 in what you say: answer:

                 'I thought I'd move them
out of the smoke. They seemed no longer those
bright arms Odysseus left us years ago
when he went off to Troy. Here where the fire's
hot breath came, they had grown black and drear.
1145 One better reason, too, I had from Zeus:
suppose a brawl starts up when you are drunk,
you might be crazed and bloody one another,
and that would stain your feast, your courtship. Tempered
iron can magnetize a man.'

                     Say that.
1150 But put aside two broadswords and two spears
for our own use, two oxhide shields nearby
when we go into action. Pallas Athena
and Zeus All-Provident will see you through,
<u>bemusing</u> our young friends.

                   Now one thing more.
1155 If son of mine you are and blood of mine,
let no one hear Odysseus is about.
Neither Laertes, nor the swineherd here,
nor any slave, nor even Penelope.
But you and I alone must learn how far
1160 the women are corrupted; we should know
how to locate good men among our hands,
the loyal and respectful, and the shirkers[5]
who take you lightly, as alone and young."

🔟 Literature in Context

Cultural Connection

Athena Athena was the goddess of wisdom, skills, and warfare. When she helps Odysseus in this epic, it is not the first time that she offers assistance to a Greek hero. In Homer's *Iliad,* Athena helps the Greek hero Achilles defeat the Trojan warrior Hector. Athena favored Achilles for his unmatched skill in battle, but Odysseus was her favorite among the Greeks. He displayed not only skill in warfare, but also ingenuity and cunning.

Connect to the Literature

Which of Odysseus' deeds in the *Odyssey* might have helped him to earn Athena's favor? Explain.

Vocabulary Builder
bemusing (bē myoōz´ iŋ) *v.* stupefying or muddling

5. **shirkers** (shʉrk´ ərz)
n. people who get out of doing what needs to be done.

🔟 Reading Check

How does Odysseus tell his son to respond if the suitors "practice shots" on Odysseus?

from the *Odyssey,* Part 2 ■ 999

🔟 Literature in Context

Cultural Connection The Greeks had more than one god whom they believed was assigned to war. The god Ares represented the spirit of battle—a grimmer, bloodier side of war than that associated with Athena. Her association was more with the intellectual and civilized side of war, which she combined with the values of justice and skill. Athena was associated with war, but she was also a keeper of civilization, as shown by her namesake city, Athens, the birthplace of democracy.

Connect to the Literature
Remind students of Odysseus' early claim that he is "formidable for guile in peace and war" (line 19). Then **ask** the Connect to Literature question: Which of Odysseus' deeds in the *Odyssey* might have helped him to earn Athena's favor? Explain.
Possible response: Athena may have been impressed by Odysseus' clever thinking as he escaped from the Cyclops. She may have appreciated how his escape required both intelligence and physical strength.

⓫ Reading Check

Answer: If the suitors "practice shots" on Odysseus, who is pretending to be a beggar, Telemachus is to hold his anger and refrain from acknowledging his father.

Differentiated
Instruction   Solutions for All Learners

Strategy for Special Needs Students
Students may need additional support and practice with the Reading Skill, Historical and Cultural Context. Explain that many details within the text offer insight into the way Greeks lived at the time of Homer. For example, Odysseus' instructions to hide weapons from the suitors (lines 1135–1138) reveals how much "gear of war" was stored in a house at any time.

To model how to analyze the historical and cultural context, show students **Reading Skill Graphic Organizer B** (*Graphic Organizer Transparencies,* p. 204). The completed chart will give students insight into the process of analyzing a story's context. They can use it as a model for their own analysis as they read.

999

⑫ Critical Viewing

Answer: Students may say that the Greeks incorporated worship of their gods into everyday events. The scenes on the pottery show the importance to the Greeks of honoring and commemorating significant events in Greek history and mythology.

⑬ Humanities

Greek vessel

This vessel is one of several being used to illustrate this edition of the *Odyssey*. The Greeks used such vessels to store or transport liquids such as oil or wine. Greek artists used several methods to decorate these vessels. In the "black figure" technique, color is applied to the figures, with the background taking the natural color of the clay. The vessel on p. 1000 is an example of this style. In the "red figure" technique, the process is reversed; the background is painted black. The *krater*, or bowl, on p. 972 is an example of the red figure process.

These artifacts have survived for thousands of years—a durable art form that is not only intrinsically beautiful, but that presents a detailed picture of the life and culture of ancient Greeks. Use the following question for discussion:

• In 1,000 years, what objects from our own culture might reveal our values to the people who find them?
Possible response: Our televisions, computers, and musical equipment might indicate our culture's interest in entertainment.

Argus

Odysseus heads for town with Eumaeus. Outside the palace, Odysseus' old dog, Argus, is lying at rest as his long-absent master approaches.

                                        While he spoke
    an old hound, lying near, pricked up his ears
1165 and lifted up his muzzle. This was Argus,
    trained as a puppy by Odysseus,
    but never taken on a hunt before
    his master sailed for Troy. The young men, afterward,
    hunted wild goats with him, and hare, and deer,
1170 but he had grown old in his master's absence.
    Treated as rubbish now, he lay at last
    upon a mass of dung before the gates—
    manure of mules and cows, piled there until
    fieldhands could spread it on the king's estate.
1175 Abandoned there, and half destroyed with flies,
    old Argus lay.
                        But when he knew he heard
    Odysseus' voice nearby, he did his best
    to wag his tail, nose down, with flattened ears,
    having no strength to move nearer his master.
1180 And the man looked away,
    wiping a salt tear from his cheek; but he
    hid this from Eumaeus. Then he said:

    "I marvel that they leave this hound to lie
    here on the dung pile;
1185 he would have been a fine dog, from the look of him,
    though I can't say as to his power and speed
    when he was young. You find the same good build
    in house dogs, table dogs landowners keep
    all for style."

                        And you replied, Eumaeus:

1190 "A hunter owned him—but the man is dead
    in some far place. If this old hound could show
    the form he had when Lord Odysseus left him,
    going to Troy, you'd see him swift and strong.
    He never shrank from any savage thing
1195 he'd brought to bay in the deep woods; on the scent

⑫ ▼ **Critical Viewing**
What can you infer about the ancient Greeks based on the fact that they depicted their gods on everyday objects like this urn? **[Infer]**

⑬

no other dog kept up with him. Now misery
has him in leash. His owner died abroad,
and here the women slaves will take no care of him.
You know how servants are: without a master
1200   they have no will to labor, or excel.
14 For Zeus who views the wide world takes away
half the manhood of a man, that day
he goes into captivity and slavery."

Eumaeus crossed the court and went straight forward
1205 into the megaron[6] among the suitors:
but death and darkness in that instant closed
the eyes of Argus, who had seen his master,
Odysseus, after twenty years.

The Suitors

*Still disguised as a beggar, Odysseus enters his home. He is
confronted by the haughty[7] suitor Antinous.[8]*

But here Antinous broke in, shouting:

                "God!
1210 What evil wind blew in this pest?

                  Get over,

stand in the passage! Nudge my table, will you?
Egyptian whips are sweet
to what you'll come to here, you nosing rat,
making your pitch to everyone!
1215 These men have bread to throw away on you
because it is not theirs. Who cares? Who spares
another's food, when he has more than plenty?"

With guile Odysseus drew away, then said:

"A pity that you have more looks than heart.
1220 You'd grudge a pinch of salt from your own larder
to your own handyman. You sit here, fat
16 on others' meat, and cannot bring yourself
to rummage out a crust of bread for me!"

Then anger made Antinous' heart beat hard,
1225 and, glowering under his brows, he answered:

Reading Skill
**Historical and
Cultural Context**
How do Eumaeus'
beliefs about
servitude and slavery
compare with those of
your own culture?

6. megaron (meg' ə rön)
n. great, central hall of the
house, usually containing a
center hearth.

7. haughty (hôt' ē) *adj.*
arrogant.

8. Antinous (an tin' ō əs)

 15 Reading Check

How does Antinous
react to Odysseus,
who is disguised as a
beggar?

from the *Odyssey, Part 2* ■ *1001*

---

14 **Reading Skill**
**Historical and Cultural
Context**

- Discuss with students how many
cultures have practiced slavery,
often enslaving people that were
captured in war. Slavery based on
race was practiced in American
colonies and in the United States
until the Civil War.

- Then **ask** the Reading Skill question: How do Eumaeus' beliefs
about servitude and slavery compare with those of your culture?
Sample responses: Eumaeus
believes that slaves will not do
good work if they are not super-
vised. My culture believes that
enslaving people is morally wrong
and that no one should be subjected to slavery, even if it is under
a "good" master such as Odysseus.

15 **Reading Check**

Answer: Antinous berates Odysseus
and throws a stool at him.

Differentiated
Instruction   Solutions for All Learners

Strategy for Gifted/Talented Students
Challenge students to draw a portrait of
Odysseus in his disguise as a beggar. Tell students that their portraits should reflect not only
Odysseus' humble appearance, but also should
suggest his hidden qualities as a hero. Students
may want to contrast his appearance with that
of the swineherd Eumaeus or with one of the
proud suitors, such as Antinous.

Strategy for Advanced Readers
Ask students why they think dogs are often
called "man's best friend" and discuss their
ideas. Point out that the bond between dogs
and people may go back as far as 25,000 years,
as shown in Paleolithic cave drawings of dogs.

   Have students find out more about how
dogs are viewed in different cultures. Assign
students to research the roles dogs have played
in diverse societies, such as the hunting dog,
the farm dog, the sled dog, and in ancient
Egypt, the dog god. Have students share their
findings with the class.

1001

- Remind students of Greek culture's emphasis on hospitality. Point out also that Antinous is an unwanted guest in another person's home, and that he has been treated with courtesy.

- **Ask** students how they think a polite guest would treat the entrance of a beggar.
Possible response: Students may say that a more polite guest could have offered food to the beggar and asked him to leave. An even more gracious guest would offer to share his meal and find the beggar a seat.

- **Ask** students the first Reading Skill question: What conflicting values does this exchange between Antinous and Odysseus reveal?
Possible response: Odysseus practices the values of the gods and treats strangers with courtesy. Antinous is not only rude, he also violates his culture's rules regarding hospitality.

17 **Reading Skill**
Historical and Cultural Context

- Review the exchange between Antinous and Odysseus, beginning with the suitor's insult of the disguised Odysseus.

- **Ask** students why Antinous becomes so angry with the beggar.
Answer: The disguised Odysseus points out Antinous' selfish and inappropriate behavior.

- **Ask** the second Reading Skill question: What values regarding the use of physical force are evident in this speech?
Possible response: Odysseus' speech indicates that physical force is appropriate when defending one's property. Antinous, however, used force for an inappropriate reason.

- Discuss with students the difference in power between Antinous (a suitor) and a beggar, who is Odysseus in disguise. Tell them that Antinous takes advantage of someone who is in a lower social and economic class, and who is not in a position to defend himself.

"Now!
You think you'll shuffle off and get away
after that impudence?[9] Oh, no you don't!"

The stool he let fly hit the man's right shoulder
on the packed muscle under the shoulder blade—
1230 like solid rock, for all the effect one saw.
Odysseus only shook his head, containing
thoughts of bloody work, as he walked on,
then sat, and dropped his loaded bag again
16 upon the door sill. Facing the whole crowd
1235 he said, and eyed them all:

"One word only,
my lords, and suitors of the famous queen.
One thing I have to say.
There is no pain, no burden for the heart
when blows come to a man, and he defending
1240 his own cattle—his own cows and lambs.
17 Here it was otherwise. Antinous
hit me for being driven on by hunger—
how many bitter seas men cross for hunger!
If beggars interest the gods, if there are Furies[10]
1245 pent in the dark to avenge a poor man's wrong, then may
Antinous meet his death before his wedding day!"

Then said Eupeithes' son, Antinous:

"Enough.
Eat and be quiet where you are, or shamble elsewhere,
unless you want these lads to stop your mouth
1250 pulling you by the heels, or hands and feet,
over the whole floor, till your back is peeled!"

But now the rest were mortified, and someone
spoke from the crowd of young bucks to rebuke him:

"A poor show, that—hitting this famished tramp—
1255 bad business, if he happened to be a god.
You know they go in foreign guise, the gods do,
18 looking like strangers, turning up
in towns and settlements to keep an eye
on manners, good or bad."

But at this notion

Reading Skill
Historical and Cultural Context
What conflicting values does this exchange between Antinous and Odysseus reveal?

9. **impudence** (im´ pyoo dəns) *n.* quality of being shamelessly bold; disrespectful.

Reading Skill
Historical and Cultural Context
What values regarding the use of physical force are evident in this speech?

10. **Furies** (fyoor´ ēz) *n.* three terrible female spirits who punish the doers of unavenged crimes.

Reading Skill
Historical and Cultural Context
What ancient Greek belief is conveyed in this suitor's speech?

Vocabulary Development

Expressive Vocabulary
As students are discussing Odysseus' encounter with the suitors, encourage them to use the expressive vocabulary presented earlier. You might encourage them with sentence starters like these.

1. Odysseus practiced *deception* when he . . .
2. The suitors' behavior made Odysseus *furious* because . . .
3. The Greek culture required that hosts extend *courtesy* to . . .

1260 Antinous only shrugged.

Telemachus,
after the blow his father bore, sat still
without a tear, though his heart felt the blow.
Slowly he shook his head from side to side,
containing murderous thoughts.

Penelope
1265 on the higher level of her room had heard
the blow, and knew who gave it. Now she murmured:

"Would god you could be hit yourself, Antinous—
hit by Apollo's bowshot!"

And Eurynome[11]

her housekeeper, put in:

"He and no other?
1270 If all we pray for came to pass, not one
would live till dawn!"

Her gentle mistress said:

"Oh, Nan, they are a bad lot; they intend
ruin for all of us; but Antinous
appears a blacker-hearted hound than any.
1275 Here is a poor man come, a wanderer,
driven by want to beg his bread, and everyone
in hall gave bits, to cram his bag—only
Antinous threw a stool, and banged his shoulder!"

So she described it, sitting in her chamber
1280 among her maids—while her true lord was eating.
Then she called in the forester and said:

"Go to that man on my behalf, Eumaeus,
and send him here, so I can greet and question him.
Abroad in the great world, he may have heard
1285 rumors about Odysseus—may have known him!"

Penelope

In the evening, Penelope interrogates the old beggar.

"Friend, let me ask you first of all:
who are you, where do you come from, of what nation

---

11. Eurynome (yōō rin′ əm ē)

19

✓ Reading Check

How does Penelope regard Antinous?

from the *Odyssey*, Part 2 ■ 1003

1003

- Read aloud lines 1290–1297 and tell students it is an example of an epic simile.

- Ask students to draw the Literary Analysis graphic organizer on p. 1018, or give them a copy of **Literary Analysis Graphic Organizer A** (*Graphic Organizer Transparencies,* p. 205). Have students write down the two items that are being compared in this epic simile, and the details that are included in the comparison.

- Discuss with students Odysseus' reasons for drawing this extended comparison and point out that he is avoiding Penelope's question about his homeland. Then **ask** what they think Odysseus' comparison reveals about his feelings toward his wife.
Possible response: The epic simile indicates that Odysseus believes that Penelope has been faithful to him.

- After students have discussed Odysseus' comparison, ask them to fill out the "Purpose" section of their graphic organizers.

▶ **Monitor Progress:** Review students' graphic organizers to ensure that they understand the items being compared in the epic simile and the purpose of the comparison.

▶ **Reteach:** Explain to students that Odysseus is comparing Penelope's name to the honor of a good king. In other words, he believes she has been faithful to him.

---

and parents were you born?"

And he replied:

"My lady, never a man in the wide world
1290 should have a fault to find with you. Your name
has gone out under heaven like the sweet
honor of some god-fearing king, who rules
20 in <u>equity</u> over the strong: his black lands bear
both wheat and barley, fruit trees laden bright,
1295 new lambs at lambing time—and the deep sea
gives great hauls of fish by his good strategy,
so that his folk fare well.

O my dear lady,
this being so, let it suffice to ask me
of other matters—not my blood, my homeland.
1300 Do not enforce me to recall my pain.
My heart is sore; but I must not be found
sitting in tears here, in another's house:
it is not well forever to be grieving.
One of the maids might say—or you might think—
1305 I had got <u>maudlin</u> over cups of wine."

And Penelope replied:

"Stranger, my looks,
my face, my carriage,[12] were soon lost or faded
when the Achaeans crossed the sea to Troy,
Odysseus my lord among the rest.
1310 If he returned, if he were here to care for me,
I might be happily renowned!
But grief instead heaven sent me—years of pain.
Sons of the noblest families on the islands,
Dulichium, Same, wooded Zacynthus,[13]
1315 with native Ithacans, are here to court me,
against my wish; and they consume this house.
Can I give proper heed to guest or suppliant
or herald on the realm's affairs?

How could I?
wasted with longing for Odysseus, while here
1320 they press for marriage.

Ruses[14] served my turn
to draw the time out—first a close-grained web
I had the happy thought to set up weaving
on my big loom in hall. I said, that day:

Vocabulary Builder
equity (ek´ wit ē)
n. fairness; justice

Vocabulary Builder
maudlin (môd´ lin)
adj. tearfully and
foolishly sentimental

12. carriage (kar´ ij)
n. posture.

13. Zacynthus (za sin´ *th*us)

14. ruses (rōōz´ iz) *n.* tricks.

Vocabulary Development

Word Analysis
Call students' attention to the word *equity* and its definition. Tell students that the Latin root *–equi–* means "same" or "equal." Ask students to think of other words that contain this root, and ask a volunteer to list them on the board. Possibilities include *equidistant, equilateral,* and *equivalent.*

Have students look up the listed words in a dictionary to clarify the definitions. Then have students use each word in a sentence that illustrates its meaning.

'Young men—my suitors, now my lord is dead,
1325   let me finish my weaving before I marry,
or else my thread will have been spun in vain.
It is a shroud I weave for Lord Laertes
when cold Death comes to lay him on his bier.
The country wives would hold me in dishonor
1330   if he, with all his fortune, lay unshrouded.'
I reached their hearts that way, and they agreed.
So every day I wove on the great loom,
but every night by torchlight I unwove it;
and so for three years I deceived the Achaeans.
1335   But when the seasons brought a fourth year on,
㉑ as long months waned, and the long days were spent,
through impudent folly in the slinking maids
they caught me—clamored up to me at night;
I had no choice then but to finish it.
1340   And now, as matters stand at last,
I have no strength left to evade a marriage,
cannot find any further way; my parents
urge it upon me, and my son
will not stand by while they eat up his property.
1345   He comprehends it, being a man full-grown,
able to oversee the kind of house
Zeus would endow with honor.

                                                            But you too
confide in me, tell me your ancestry.
You were not born of mythic oak or stone."

---

*Penelope again asks the beggar to tell about himself. He
makes up a tale in which Odysseus is mentioned and
declares that Penelope's husband will soon be home.*

1350   "You see, then, he is alive and well, and headed
homeward now, no more to be abroad
far from his island, his dear wife and son.
Here is my sworn word for it. Witness this,
god of the zenith, noblest of the gods,[15]
1355   and Lord Odysseus' hearthfire, now before me:
I swear these things shall turn out as I say.
Between this present dark and one day's ebb,
after the wane, before the crescent moon,
Odysseus will come."

from the *Odyssey*, Part 2 ■ 1005

Reading Skill
Historical and
Cultural Context
How do the ancient
Greek ideas in
Penelope's speech
about honoring the
dead compare to
modern ideas?

**15. god of the zenith, noblest
of the gods** Zeus.

Reading Check
How was Penelope
able to delay marriage
for three years?

㉑ Reading Skill
Historical and Cultural
Context

- Read aloud Penelope's description
of making her husband a shroud.
Then discuss with students how a
shroud would represent Penelope's
respect for her dead husband. **Ask**
how weaving a shroud could show
honor toward the person who had
died.
Possible response: Students may
say that weaving a shroud is an
established custom that has
evolved to show respect. They may
say that the Greeks may have
believed that they should clothe a
dead person in a fine garment
before they send them into the
underworld.

- **Ask** students why Penelope says
the "country wives" would disrespect her if she did not weave a
shroud.
Answer: Penelope would be violating a Greek custom by neglecting to clothe her dead husband's
body properly.

- Then discuss with the class ways
that people today try to honor
their dead. You may want to mention the custom of traffic stopping
to let a funeral procession pass, the
playing of taps at military funerals,
or holidays such as All Saints' Day
or Dia de los Muertos that remember loved ones who have passed
away. Have volunteers offer examples they have seen of people
showing respect for the dead.

- **Ask** students the Reading Skill
question: How do the ancient
Greek ideas in Penelope's speech
about honoring the dead compare
to modern ideas?
Possible response: Students may
say that both the Greeks and
people in modern times have
rituals that honor the dead. They
may observe that modern society
does not always follow a strict set
of burial customs as people did in
ancient Greece.

㉒ Reading Check

Answer: Penelope said that she
could not marry until she completed
weaving her dead husband's shroud.
She wove the shroud by day and
unraveled it each night.

Humanities

The Trial of the Bow, by
N. C. Wyeth

N. C. Wyeth studied with Howard
Pyle, an illustrator famous for his
work on children's classics such as
the tales of Robin Hood. Pyle encouraged Wyeth to make his paintings
dramatic and to paint from his own
experience.

In *The Trial of the Bow,* Penelope
promises that she will marry the man
who can string Odysseus' bow and
shoot an arrow through twelve ax
handle sockets. In this painting,
Odysseus, disguised as a beggar, has
succeeded in the first part of this
challenge. Use these questions for
discussion:

1. Why do you think Wyeth chose
   to illustrate this particular
   moment in the story?
   Answer: This is an especially
   dramatic moment because
   Odysseus is about to win the
   contest, reveal his true identity to
   the suitors, and then take his
   revenge.

2. Why didn't the artist illustrate the
   scene a few moments later, when
   the arrow goes through the ax
   handles?
   Answer: At that point, Odysseus
   would no longer be focusing on
   the target, but would be giving
   instructions to Telemachus. This
   moment shows Odysseus at his
   best—muscles flexed and his
   attention fixed on his target.

24 ## Critical Viewing

Answer: The emotional tension is
captured in the physical tension of
Odysseus' arm and leg muscles and
the taut bowstring. In addition,
everyone else is focused on the
targets. Additional suspense comes
from the point in time the picture
captures: The arrow has not been
released, and the viewers, like the
people in the painting, wait in
expectation.

The Trial of the Bow from Homer's *The Odyssey,* N.C. Wyeth, The Museum of Texas Tech University

23

24 ▲ Critical Viewing The winner of the archery contest will win Penelope's
hand in marriage. What details or artistic techniques capture the tension
in this scene? **[Interpret]**

1006   Themes in Literature: Heroism

The Challenge

*Pressed by the suitors to choose a husband from among them,
Penelope says she will marry the man who can string
Odysseus' bow and shoot an arrow through twelve axhandle
sockets. The suitors try and fail. Still in disguise, Odysseus
asks for a turn and gets it.*

               And Odysseus took his time,
1360   turning the bow, tapping it, every inch,
for borings that termites might have made
while the master of the weapon was abroad.
The suitors were now watching him, and some
jested among themselves:

              "A bow lover!"

1365   "Dealer in old bows!"

              "Maybe he has one like it
at home!"

         "Or has an itch to make one for himself."

"See how he handles it, the sly old buzzard!"

And one disdainful suitor added this:
"May his fortune grow an inch for every inch he bends it!"

1370   But the man skilled in all ways of contending,
satisfied by the great bow's look and heft,
like a musician, like a harper, when
with quiet hand upon his instrument
25 he draws between his thumb and forefinger
1375 a sweet new string upon a peg: so effortlessly
Odysseus in one motion strung the bow.
Then slid his right hand down the cord and plucked it,
so the taut gut vibrating hummed and sang
a swallow's note.

            In the hushed hall it smote the suitors
1380 and all their faces changed. Then Zeus thundered
overhead, one loud crack for a sign.
And Odysseus laughed within him that the son

Literary Analysis
Epic Simile Which
of Odysseus' qualities
is highlighted in the
epic simile in lines
1372–1379?

26 Reading Check

What means does
Penelope decide she
will use to choose a
husband?

---

from the Odyssey, Part 2 ■ 1007

㉕ Literary Analysis
Epic Simile

- **Ask** students to discuss why
Odysseus may give such special
attention to the bow.
  Possible response: Odysseus has
  not seen this cherished possession
  in twenty years; he is clearly savor-
  ing the experience of holding it
  again. He must also make sure the
  bow is fully reliable as a weapon.

- **Ask** students the Literary Analysis
question: Which of Odysseus'
qualities is highlighted in the epic
simile in lines 1372–1379.
  Possible response: The epic simile highlights Odysseus' skillfulness
  with the bow. The comparison with
  a musician shows the grace and
  ease he brings to archery.

- Draw students' attention to the
aptness of the simile, pointing out
the similarity of a taut bowstring to
the taut string of a harp.

㉖ Reading Check

Answer: Penelope says that she will
marry whoever can string Odysseus'
bow and shoot an arrow through
twelve ax handle sockets.

Instruction   Solutions for All Learners

Strategy for Special Needs Students
Students may need help to understand the
comparison made by the epic simile. Have
students use a **Venn Diagram** (*Graphic
Organizer Transparencies,* p. 244) to see the
major similarities and differences in the comparison between the bow and the harp. After
students have made these broad distinctions,
discuss with them how the long list of details in
the comparison makes up the literary form
called the epic simile.

Strategy for Less Proficient Readers
Students may have difficulty understanding
how the epic simile fits into the plot of the
Odyssey. For support, show them **Literary
Analysis Graphic Organizer B** (*Graphic
Organizer Transparencies,* p. 206) Use the
completed graphic organizer to demonstrate
how the simile reveals more about Odysseus'
character.

Answer: Students may find the hunter's posture on the pottery to be somewhat stylized and artificial in contrast to the easy grace that Odysseus displays.

ASSESS

Answers

1. Students may respond that even though Odysseus arrives disguised as a beggar, they would be more intrigued and curious than Telemachus and Penelope seem to be. The beggar seems to know more about their situation than most strangers would.

2. (a) Telemachus first thinks Odysseus is a beggar. Then, after Athena changes his appearance, Telemachus thinks he is a god. (b) Telemachus is at first confused and skeptical, then throws his arms around his father and begins to cry. Tears run down Odysseus' face as he reveals himself to his son.

3. (a) Antinous insults the apparent beggar and flings a stool at him. (b) Antinous may despise people he regards as his inferiors.

4. (a) Odysseus initially tells Penelope that he is a wanderer with a past too painful to reveal. (b) Students may suggest that Odysseus feels that he is not yet ready to trust that his wife has been loyal to him. Or, he may not want to reveal too much until he has executed his plan. (c) Some students may say that it is always wrong to deceive a loved one. Others may say he is acting in their mutual best interest—that to execute his planned revenge successfully, it is best not to involve his wife.

---

of crooked-minded Cronus had flung that omen down.
He picked one ready arrow from his table
1385 where it lay bare: the rest were waiting still
in the quiver for the young men's turn to come.
He nocked[16] it, let it rest across the handgrip,
and drew the string and grooved butt of the arrow,
aiming from where he sat upon the stool.

                                        Now flashed
1390 arrow from twanging bow clean as a whistle
through every socket ring, and grazed not one,
to thud with heavy brazen head beyond.

                                Then quietly
Odysseus said:

                        "Telemachus, the stranger
you welcomed in your hall has not disgraced you.
1395 I did not miss, neither did I take all day
stringing the bow. My hand and eye are sound,
not so contemptible as the young men say.
The hour has come to cook their lordships' mutton—
supper by daylight. Other amusements later,
1400 with song and harping that adorn a feast."

He dropped his eyes and nodded, and the prince
Telemachus, true son of King Odysseus,
belted his sword on, clapped hand to his spear,
and with a clink and glitter of keen bronze
1405 stood by his chair, in the forefront near his father.

16. nocked (näk′d) set an arrow into the bowstring.

27 ▲ **Critical Viewing** Does the hunter pictured here show the same grace as does Odysseus in lines 1370–1392? Explain. **[Compare and Contrast]**

Thinking About the Selection

1. **Respond:** If you were Telemachus or Penelope, how would you react to the stranger's arrival? Why?

2. **(a) Recall:** Who does Telemachus think Odysseus is when they first reunite? **(b) Compare and Contrast:** Compare Odysseus' emotions with those of Telemachus at their reunion.

3. **(a) Recall:** Describe Antinous' treatment of Odysseus. **(b) Analyze Cause and Effect:** Why do you think Antinous treats Odysseus as he does?

4. **(a) Recall:** What does Odysseus tell Penelope about himself? **(b) Infer:** Why do you think Odysseus chooses not to reveal his identity to his wife? **(c) Take a Position:** Is it wrong for Odysseus to deceive Penelope? Explain.

1008 ■ *Themes in Literature: Heroism*

Vocabulary Development

Archery Terms
Have students identify the words used to describe Odysseus' bow. Ask them to fill in a **Web** (*Graphic Organizer Transparencies*, p. 245) with the archery terms used in the selection. Students can write the words used to describe the bow, the arrow, or the act of shooting. Examples of this special vocabulary would include *arrow, quiver, nocked, handgrip, string,* and *twanging.* Have students use the web to show the relationships between the words and how they explain the act of shooting an arrow.

Odysseus' Revenge

Now shrugging off his rags the wiliest[17] fighter of the islands
leapt and stood on the broad doorsill, his own bow in his
    hand.
He poured out at his feet a rain of arrows from the quiver
and spoke to the crowd:

       "So much for that. Your clean-cut game is over.
1410 Now watch me hit a target that no man has hit before,
if I can make this shot. Help me, Apollo."

He drew to his fist the cruel head of an arrow for Antinous
just as the young man leaned to lift his beautiful drinking
    cup,
embossed, two-handled, golden: the cup was in his fingers:
1415 the wine was even at his lips: and did he dream of death?
How could he? In that revelry[18] amid his throng of friends
who would imagine a single foe—though a strong foe
    indeed—
28 could dare to bring death's pain on him and darkness on his
    eyes?
Odysseus' arrow hit him under the chin
1420 and punched up to the feathers through his throat.

Backward and down he went, letting the winecup fall
from his shocked hand. Like pipes his nostrils jetted
crimson runnels, a river of mortal red,
and one last kick upset his table
1425 knocking the bread and meat to soak in dusty blood.
Now as they craned to see their champion where he lay
the suitors jostled in uproar down the hall,
everyone on his feet. Wildly they turned and scanned
the walls in the long room for arms; but not a shield,
1430 not a good ashen spear was there for a man to take and
    throw.
All they could do was yell in outrage at Odysseus:

"Foul! to shoot at a man! That was your last shot!"
"Your own throat will be slit for this!"
         "Our finest lad is down!
You killed the best on Ithaca."
       "Buzzards will tear your eyes out!"
1435 For they imagined as they wished—that it was a wild shot,
an unintended killing—fools, not to comprehend

---

17. wiliest (wī′ ē əst) *adj.*
craftiest; slyest.

18. revelry (rev′ əl rē) *n.* noisy
festivity.

Reading Skill
Historical and Cultural Context
Does the manner in which Odysseus kills Antinous agree with your idea of a "fair fight"? Explain.

 Reading Check

Whom does Odysseus kill first?

from the Odyssey, *Part 2* ■ *1009*

---

28 Reading Skill
Historical and Cultural Context

- Remind students that Antinous was the most obnoxious suitor and the first to insult Odysseus. Penelope thought he was the worst of the lot.
- Tell students that there are different cultural responses to insults. **Ask** students to give examples of cultural responses to anger or insult that they have found in their reading.
Possible response: Students may say that in some cultures, people fight duels in response to insults. In other cultures, insults may be forgiven with apologies or gifts.
- **Ask** the Reading Skill question: Does the manner in which Odysseus kills Antinous agree with your idea of a "fair fight"?
Possible response: Students may say that the fight was not fair because Antinous did not get a chance to fight back. Other students may say that Odysseus acted fairly because Antinous had insulted him and taken advantage of his family and their hospitality.

29 Reading Check
Answer: Odysseus kills the suitor Antinous first.

Differentiated
Instruction   Solutions for All Learners

Strategy for English Learners
Students may need help reading and understanding Odysseus' battle with the suitors. Before addressing the Reading Skill question, preview the bracketed passage with **Listening to Literature Audio CDs.** Have students read along as they listen. They may need particular help understanding how the descriptions break into the action. For example, explain that lines 1415–1418 break to show that Antinous did not dream that he had a deadly enemy in Odysseus' house.

Enrichment for Advanced Readers
To enrich the Reading Skill exercise, encourage students to research rules of warfare. For example, students might find information about ancient Greek customs that were observed during wartime, the various customs that once applied to dueling, or the Geneva Convention guidelines that apply to the treatment of prisoners today. Have students share their research with the rest of the class.

1009

30 Humanities

The Slaughter of the Suitors,
by N.C. Wyeth

In this painting of Odysseus' revenge, Wyeth adds drama and animation to an already exciting story. His depiction includes several pieces of Greek armor; the fighters' helmets and armor would likely have been made of bronze. Use the following questions for discussion.

1. Which lines from the *Odyssey* does this painting illustrate?
   Answer: It illustrates lines 1521–1530.

2. Who are the four figures on the right side of the painting? How do you know?
   Answer: They are Odysseus, Telemachus, Eumaeus, and the cowherd. They are wearing armor, have weapons, and are obviously winning the battle.

3. What details make the painting exciting?
   Possible responses: The flung spear, the spears about to be thrown, the position of the men's bodies, or the dust of battle make the painting exciting. The giant columns in the background create a heroic mood for the scene.

31 Critical Viewing

Answer: Students may say that the suitors were sitting at tables. Others may say that Odysseus' bow and arrows should have been represented.

The Slaughter of the Suitors from Homer's *The Odyssey*, N.C. Wyeth

31 ▲ Critical Viewing Do you think this illustration presents the slaughter of the suitors accurately? Explain. **[Evaluate]**

they were already in the grip of death.
But glaring under his brows Odysseus answered:

"You yellow dogs, you thought I'd never make it
1440 home from the land of Troy. You took my house to
     plunder. . .
You dared bid for my wife while I was still alive.
Contempt was all you had for the gods who rule wide
     heaven,
contempt for what men say of you hereafter.
Your last hour has come. You die in blood."

1445 As they all took this in, sickly green fear
pulled at their entrails, and their eyes flickered
looking for some hatch or hideaway from death.
Eurymachus[19] alone could speak. He said:

"If you are Odysseus of Ithaca come back,
1450 all that you say these men have done is true.
Rash actions, many here, more in the countryside.
But here he lies, the man who caused them all.
Antinous was the ringleader, he whipped us on
to do these things. He cared less for a marriage
1455 than for the power Cronion has denied him
as king of Ithaca. For that
he tried to trap your son and would have killed him.
He is dead now and has his portion. Spare
your own people. As for ourselves, we'll make
1460 restitution of wine and meat consumed,
and add, each one, a tithe of twenty oxen
with gifts of bronze and gold to warm your heart.
Meanwhile we cannot blame you for your anger."

Odysseus glowered under his black brows
1465 and said:
        "Not for the whole treasure of your fathers,
all you enjoy, lands, flocks, or any gold
put up by others, would I hold my hand.
There will be killing till the score is paid.
You forced yourselves upon this house. Fight your way out,
1470 or run for it, if you think you'll escape death.
I doubt one man of you skins by."

They felt their knees fail, and their hearts—but heard
Eurymachus for the last time rallying them.

Vocabulary Builder
contempt (kən tempt′)
n. disdain or scorn

Reading Skill
Historical and Cultural Context
What cultural values are revealed by Odysseus' explanation for his anger in lines 1441–1444?

19. **Eurymachus** (yōō ri′ mə kəs)

Reading Check
What does Eurymachus offer Odysseus to try to calm his anger?

from the *Odyssey*, Part 2 ■ 1011

32 Reading Skill
Historical and Cultural Context

- Review with students the indignities that Odysseus has suffered at the hands of the suitors, reminding him that they have abused his home, his wife, his child, and his hospitality.
- **Ask** students to recall the Greeks' beliefs about the rules of hospitality and how the gods' figure into those beliefs.
  Answer: Strangers to one's home should be treated with courtesy. The Greeks believed that gods could visit homes in disguise and would punish humans who did not treat them well.
- **Ask** the Reading Skill question: What cultural values are revealed by Odysseus' explanation for his anger in lines 1441–1444?
  Possible responses: Odysseus is angry because the suitors have plundered his house and tried to claim his wife while he was gone. He also is angry because the suitors have dishonored the Greeks' religious laws regarding hospitality and the authority of the gods.

33 Reading Check

Answer: He offers to make restitution of all the meat and wine consumed, plus gifts of oxen, bronze, and gold.

1011

• Have students review the Literary Analysis section of the Build Skills page, p. 992. **Ask** them to compare a typical simile with an epic simile and to give an example of each.

Possible response: A typical simile makes a comparison to one thing, for example, "The arrow flew like a hawk." An epic simile is longer and more complex. A possible example is, "The arrow flew like a hawk. Its feathers glinted in the sun, and its point bit like a hawk's beak. It attacked its victim as a hawk clutches its prey."

• Stress to students that not all similes in the *Odyssey* are epic similes.

• Then **ask** students the Literary Analysis question: Why is the comparison of Eurymachus' sharp sword to a razor only a simile and not an epic simile?

• **Possible response:** This is a simile because it compares a sword to a razor. An epic simile, however, is an elaborate comparison that can run across several lines. Here, the comparison is mentioned once and is not sustained.

▶ **Monitor Progress:** Review students' graphic organizers to ensure that they understand the comparison and why it is not an epic simile.

▶ **Reteach:** Work with students to expand this simile into an epic simile. Brainstorm words that might be used to extend the simile, including *blade, slice, sever, slash,* and *cut.*

"Friends," he said, "the man is implacable.
1475 Now that he's got his hands on bow and quiver
he'll shoot from the big doorstone there
until he kills us to the last man.

Fight, I say,
let's remember the joy of it. Swords out!
Hold up your tables to deflect his arrows.
1480 After me, everyone: rush him where he stands.
If we can budge him from the door, if we can pass
into the town, we'll call out men to chase him.
This fellow with his bow will shoot no more."

③④ He drew his own sword as he spoke, a broadsword of fine bronze,
1485 honed like a razor on either edge. Then crying hoarse and loud
he hurled himself at Odysseus. But the kingly man let fly
an arrow at that instant, and the quivering feathered butt
sprang to the nipple of his breast as the barb stuck in his liver.
The bright broadsword clanged down. He lurched and fell aside,
1490 pitching across his table. His cup, his bread and meat,
were spilt and scattered far and wide, and his head slammed on the ground.
Revulsion, anguish in his heart, with both feet kicking out,
he downed his chair, while the shrouding wave of mist closed on his eyes.

Amphinomus now came running at Odysseus,
1495 broadsword naked in his hand. He thought to make
the great soldier give way at the door.
But with a spear throw from behind Telemachus hit him
between the shoulders, and the lancehead drove
clear through his chest. He left his feet and fell
1500 forward, thudding, forehead against the ground.
Telemachus swerved around him, leaving the long dark spear
planted in Amphinomus. If he paused to yank it out
someone might jump him from behind or cut him down with a sword
at the moment he bent over. So he ran—ran from the tables
1505 to his father's side and halted, panting, saying:

③⑤ ↓ "Father let me bring you a shield and spear,

1012 ■ *Themes in Literature: Heroism*

Literary Analysis
Epic Simile Why is the comparison of Eurymachus' sharp sword to a razor only a simile and not an epic simile?

a pair of spears, a helmet.
I can arm on the run myself; I'll give
outfits to Eumaeus and this cowherd.
1510 Better to have equipment."

                  Said Odysseus:
"Run then, while I hold them off with arrows
as long as the arrows last. When all are gone
if I'm alone they can dislodge me."

35   Quick
upon his father's word Telemachus
1515 ran to the room where spears and armor lay.
He caught up four light shields, four pairs of spears,
four helms of war high-plumed with flowing manes,
and ran back, loaded down, to his father's side.
He was the first to pull a helmet on
1520 and slide his bare arm in a buckler strap.
The servants armed themselves, and all three took their
    stand
beside the master of battle.

                While he had arrows
he aimed and shot, and every shot brought down
one of his huddling enemies.
1525 But when all barbs had flown from the bowman's fist,
he leaned his bow in the bright entryway
beside the door, and armed: a four-ply shield
hard on his shoulder, and a crested helm,
horsetailed, nodding stormy upon his head,
1530 then took his tough and bronze-shod spears. . . .

---

*Aided by Athena, Odysseus, Telemachus, Eumaeus, and
other faithful herdsmen kill all the suitors.*

And Odysseus looked around him, narrow-eyed,
for any others who had lain hidden
while death's black fury passed.
                In blood and dust
he saw that crowd all fallen, many and many slain.

1535 Think of a catch that fishermen haul in to a half-moon bay
in a fine-meshed net from the whitecaps of the sea:
36 how all are poured out on the sand, in throes for the salt sea,
twitching their cold lives away in Helios' fiery air:
so lay the suitors heaped on one another.

Reading Skill
Historical and Cultural Context
What cultural values are reflected in Telemachus' behavior toward his father?

Literary Analysis
Epic Simile Which aspects of the slain suitors' appearance does the epic simile in lines 1535–1539 emphasize?

37 ✓ **Reading Check**

Who helps Odysseus defeat the suitors?

from the *Odyssey*, Part 2 ■ 1013

35 Reading Skill
Historical and Cultural Context

- Discuss with students the ways that different cultures emphasize that children should honor their parents. You may want to cite the example of ancestor worship in Chinese culture or the biblical commandment to "honor thy father and mother."

- Have students **describe** how Telemachus responded to his father's return and what those actions reveal about him.
Possible response: Telemachus wept with joy when his father revealed himself, and he has obeyed his father's commands to prepare for battling the suitors. Telemachus' response shows his love and respect for his father.

- **Ask** the Reading Skill question: What cultural values are reflected in Telemachus' behavior toward his father?
Answer: Telemachus shows respect for his father as he fights beside him in battle and hurries to bring him the weapons that he needs for the fight.

36 Literary Analysis
Epic Simile

- **Ask** the Literary Analysis question: Which aspects of the slain suitors' appearance does the epic simile in lines 1535–1539 emphasize?
Possible responses: The image of the fish flopping on the deck of a ship emphasizes the suitors' struggling and writhing in their final moments.

- Point out to students that the comparison of the suitors to dying fish does not serve to make their deaths glorious. Homer does not try to immortalize the suitors.

37 Reading Check

Answer: Athena, Telemachus, Eumaeus, and a herdsman help Odysseus defeat the suitors.

1013

❸❽ Humanities

The Fall of Troy, by Romare Bearden

Born in North Carolina, African American artist Romare Bearden grew up in New York. His work is most remarkable for its sophisticated use of the idiom of Cubism to portray the everyday realities of African American life. *The Fall of Troy* is a collage from a series done by Bearden on the adventures of Odysseus. The large white horse to the right is the Trojan horse; the boats in the harbor are waiting to carry Odysseus and his men from Troy to numerous adventures. Use these questions for discussion:

• Which aspects of the collage recall what you have read from the *Odyssey*? Which aspects of the collage reflect a modern mind at work?

Answer: Students should recognize epic references such as the Trojan Horse, the burning towers of Troy, and the sea and ships. Modern references include the collage technique; the flat, childlike style of the cutouts; and the whimsical inclusion of dolphins and other sea creatures.

❸❾ Critical Viewing

Answer: Students should compare their impressions of such specific details as the Trojan Horse, the burning towers, and the waiting ships.

The Fall of Troy from *The Odysseus Suite*, 1979, Romare Bearden, serigraph 18 × 24 © Romare Bearden Foundation / Licensed VAGA, New York NY

❸❾ ▲ Critical Viewing How does your mental image of events in the *Odyssey* compare to this artist's interpretation of those events? **[Compare and Contrast]**

1014   *Themes in Literature: Heroism*

Vocabulary Development

"Deceptive" Terms
Odysseus' return is full of the idea of secrets and deception. Review with students the words that Penelope uses on p. 1015 here to describe this deception:

   frauds: means of deceiving people
   impostors: cheaters, people who assume false disguises
   underhanded: secret, not straight-forward

Penelope's Test

Penelope tests Odysseus to prove he really is her husband.

1540 Greathearted Odysseus, home at last,
      was being bathed now by Eurynome
      and rubbed with golden oil, and clothed again
      in a fresh tunic and a cloak. Athena
      lent him beauty, head to foot. She made him
1545 taller, and massive, too, with crisping hair
      in curls like petals of wild hyacinth
      but all red-golden. Think of gold infused
      on silver by a craftsman, whose fine art
      Hephaestus[20] taught him, or Athena: one
1550 whose work moves to delight: just so she lavished
      beauty over Odysseus' head and shoulders.
      He sat then in the same chair by the pillar,
      facing his silent wife, and said:

                    "Strange woman,
      the immortals of Olympus made you hard,
1555 harder than any. Who else in the world
      would keep aloof as you do from her husband
      if he returned to her from years of trouble,
      cast on his own land in the twentieth year?

      Nurse, make up a bed for me to sleep on.
1560 Her heart is iron in her breast."

                    Penelope
      spoke to Odysseus now. She said:

                    "Strange man,
      if man you are . . . This is no pride on my part
      nor scorn for you—not even wonder, merely.
      I know so well how you—how he—appeared
1565 boarding the ship for Troy. But all the same . . .

      Make up his bed for him, Eurycleia.
      Place it outside the bedchamber my lord
      built with his own hands. Pile the big bed
      with fleeces, rugs, and sheets of purest linen."

1570 With this she tried him to the breaking point,

Literary Analysis
Epic Simile

Epic Simile Which details in the epic simile in lines 1547–1551 compare Odysseus' hair to a work of art?

20. Hephaestus (hē fes´ təs) god of fire and metalworking.

Reading Check

How does Odysseus describe Penelope's attitude toward him?

---

40 Literary Analysis
Epic Simile

- Discuss the contrast between Odysseus' appearance and his earlier appearance as a beggar. Ask students why they think Homer emphasizes Odysseus' physical attractiveness as this point.

- **Possible response:** Homer is drawing a sharp contrast to Odysseus' previous guise as a beggar. Odysseus is being prepared almost as a new bridegroom, an appropriate comparison as he approaches Penelope to renew their marriage.

- Then **ask** students which parts of Odysseus' appearance are emphasized.
  Answer: His hair and his height are emphasized.

- **Ask** the Literary Analysis question: Which details in the epic simile in lines 1547–1551 compare Odysseus' hair to a work of art?
  Possible responses: The comparison to gold and silver, as well as the term *craftsman* and the references to Hephaestus and Athena all compare Odysseus' hair to artwork.

41 Reading Check

Answer: Odysseus describes Penelope as hard and aloof.

Concept Connector

Anticipation Guide
Have students return to their Anticipation Guides and respond to the statements again in the After Reading column. They may do this individually or in their original pairs or groups. Then, lead a class discussion, probing for what students have learned that confirms or invalidates each statement. Encourage students to cite specific details, quotations, or other evidence from the text to support their responses to each statement.

Connecting to the Literature
Have students write a paragraph about the conflict between Odysseus and Penelope. Challenge students to use at least five of the expressive vocabulary words provided earlier in their paragraphs.

Literary Analysis Graphic Organizer
Ask students to review the graphic organizers they completed to chart historical/cultural details. Show them **Literary Analysis Graphic Organizer B** (*Graphic Organizer Transparencies*, p. 206) as an example. Then have students share their graphic organizers.

- Read aloud the bracketed passage. Then **ask** students to identify the items that are being compared. **Answer:** The trunk of the olive tree is compared to a pillar.

- **Ask** students to list any supporting details about the appearance or other qualities of the pillar.

- **Answer:** No other details are included.

- **Ask** students to respond to the Literary Analysis prompt: Explain why the simile comparing the olive trunk to a pillar is not an epic simile.

  Answer: The text compares the two items but does not draw out the explanation by including other details. The comparison is mentioned only once and is not extended.

and he turned on her in a flash raging:

"Woman, by heaven you've stung me now!
Who dared to move my bed?
No builder had the skill for that—unless
1575   a god came down to turn the trick. No mortal
in his best days could budge it with a crowbar.
There is our pact and pledge, our secret sign,
built into that bed—my handiwork
and no one else's!

㊷   An old trunk of olive
1580   grew like a pillar on the building plot,
and I laid out our bedroom round that tree,
lined up the stone walls, built the walls and roof,
gave it a doorway and smooth-fitting doors.
Then I lopped off the silvery leaves and branches,
1585   hewed and shaped that stump from the roots up
into a bedpost, drilled it, let it serve
as model for the rest. I planed them all,
inlaid them all with silver, gold and ivory,
and stretched a bed between—a pliant web
1590   of oxhide thongs dyed crimson.
                There's our sign!
I know no more. Could someone else's hand
have sawn that trunk and dragged the frame away?"

Their secret! as she heard it told, her knees
grew tremulous and weak, her heart failed her.
1595   With eyes brimming tears she ran to him,
throwing her arms around his neck, and kissed him,
murmuring:
                "Do not rage at me, Odysseus!
No one ever matched your caution! Think
what difficulty the gods gave: they denied us
1600   life together in our prime and flowering years,
kept us from crossing into age together.
Forgive me, don't be angry. I could not
welcome you with love on sight! I armed myself
long ago against the frauds of men,
1605   impostors who might come—and all those many
whose underhanded ways bring evil on! . . .
But here and now, what sign could be so clear
as this of our own bed?
No other man has ever laid eyes on it—

Literary Analysis

Epic Simile Explain why the simile comparing the olive trunk to a pillar is not an epic simile.

Vocabulary Development

Vocabulary Knowledge Rating

When students have completed reading and discussing the *Odyssey*, Part 2, have them take out their **Vocabulary Knowledge Rating Chart** for this selection. Read the words aloud once more and have students rate their knowledge of the words again in the After Reading column. Clarify any words that are still problematic. Have students write their own definition and example or sentence in the appropriate column. Then have students complete the **Vocabulary Builder Practice** activities on p. 1019. Encourage students to use the words in further discussion and written work about the *Odyssey*. Remind them that they will be accountable for these words on the Selection Test.

1610 only my own slave, Actoris, that my father
sent with me as a gift—she kept our door.
You make my stiff heart know that I am yours."

Now from his breast into his eyes the ache
of longing mounted, and he wept at last,
1615 his dear wife, clear and faithful, in his arms,
longed for as the sunwarmed earth is longed for by a
    swimmer
43 spent in rough water where his ship went down
under Poseidon's blows, gale winds and tons of sea.
Few men can keep alive through a big surf
1620 to crawl, clotted with brine, on kindly beaches
in joy, in joy, knowing the abyss[21] behind:
and so she too rejoiced, her gaze upon her husband,
her white arms round him pressed as though forever.

The Ending

*Odysseus is reunited with his father. Athena commands that
peace prevail between Odysseus and the relatives of the slain
suitors. Odysseus has regained his family and his kingdom.*

Thinking About the Selection

1. **Respond:** Do you think Odysseus acts heroically in this section of
the *Odyssey*? Why or why not?

2. **(a) Recall:** How does Odysseus respond when Eurymachus offers to
repay Odysseus for what the suitors have taken from his house?
(b) Infer: What does Odysseus' response reveal about his character?

3. **(a) Recall:** How does the fight turn out? **(b) Analyze:** Why does
Odysseus take equal revenge on all the suitors?

4. **(a) Analyze:** What does Penelope's doubt about her husband's
return suggest about her character? **(b) Draw Conclusions:** Given
Odysseus' reputation for guile, in what way is Penelope an appropriate companion for Odysseus?

5. **(a) Summarize:** During Odysseus' long absence, how does Penelope
handle the problem of the suitors? **(b) Summarize:** How does
Odysseus handle the problem upon his return? **(c) Make a
Judgment:** Do you think their means of handling the problem is
appropriate? Why or why not?

from the Odyssey, Part 2 ■ *1017*

43 **Literary Analysis
Epic Simile**

- Review with students some of the
incidents in which Odysseus faced
storms or rough seas on his return
home.

- **Ask** the Literary Analysis question:
In what way does this epic simile
recall the dangers Odysseus faced
on his journey home?
Possible response: Odysseus
longs for his wife as a drowning
person longs for dry land. The
comparison to "rough water,"
"gale winds," and "tons of sea"
recall the many times that
Odysseus faced and that Odysseus
was nearly drowned before he
could return home.

ASSESS

Answers

1. Students may believe that some
sort of revenge is justified, but
that Odysseus overreacts. They
may say that he also could have
been heroic by showing forgiveness.

2. (a) Odysseus will not be satisfied
with treasure. He says the suitors
must fight their way out. (b)
Possible response: Odysseus
can be inflexible and unforgiving
when he thinks he has been
treated
disrespectfully.

3. (a) Caught by surprise, the suitors are quickly overcome by
Odysseus, his son, and his servants. (b) Odysseus regards all
the suitors as equally guilty of
invading his home.

4. (a) Penelope's doubt shows her
caution. It may show how she
has had to protect her feelings as
she waited for her husband's
return. (b) Penelope is an appropriate companion for Odysseus
because she, too, is clever.

5. (a) Penelope handles the problem by weaving a shroud, then
unraveling it each night.
(b) Odysseus disguises himself
and, after seeing the suitors'
disrespect, makes a plan to kill
them. (c) Students may say that
Odysseus should have forced the
suitors to leave, rather than kill
them. They may say that
Penelope should have been more
assertive in expelling the suitors.

1. Odysseus faced dangers, but Penelope endured years of uncertainty and waiting.

2. (a) Odysseus is helped by Athena, Eumaeus, Telemachus, and a cowherd. (b) Odysseus is comfortable with both goddesses and with swineherds.

3. (a) Odysseus asks Telemachus to move the armor so the suitors will not have access to it. (b) When the suitors begin to fight, they have no weapons.

4. (a) Penelope lets Odysseus think that she has moved his bed. Odysseus passes her test when he reveals that the bedpost was hewn from a live olive tree and could not be moved. (b) She has grown cautious and must be sure. (c) The happiness of the reunited couple is shadowed by the trials of the past.

5. (a) Odysseus' planning of his revenge is consistent with the cunning and guile he has shown elsewhere. His success in battle is not surprising. The harshness of his revenge recalls his treatment of Cyclops. (b) Students may say that the revenge is justified within the culture of his time.

6. (a) **Sample response: Items Being Compared:** Odysseus' longing for his wife compared to a swimmer's longing for the shore. **Details of Epic Simile:** "rough water," "Poseidon's blows," "gale winds and tons of sea," "big surf," "clotted with brine," "kindly beaches." **Purpose:** to show the intensity of Odysseus' feelings as he returns to Penelope. (b) The image indicates that being with Penelope is another life-saving rescue.

7. (a) His actions show that he values honor—his and Penelope's—above all; he will not accept apologies, but requires that the suitors battle to the death. (b) Greeks honored battle, especially to defend or uphold one's family, home, or honor. The Greeks did not appear to value negotiation or reparation for wrongs that had been done.

Apply the Skills

from the *Odyssey, Part 2*

Thinking About the Selection

1. **Respond:** Who do you think faced greater hardships—Odysseus or Penelope? Explain your response.
2. **(a) Recall:** When Odysseus returns to his home, who helps him? **(b) Interpret:** What does the varying social status of Odysseus' helpers suggest about his character?
3. **(a) Recall:** What planning does Odysseus do before he battles the suitors? **(b) Analyze:** How does his planning help him defeat his opponents?
4. **(a) Recall:** What is Penelope's test, and how does Odysseus pass it? **(b) Infer:** Why does Penelope feel the need to test Odysseus even though he has abandoned his disguise? **(c) Interpret:** Is the mood after the test altogether happy? Explain.
5. **(a) Connect:** Are Odysseus' actions in dealing with the suitors consistent with his actions in earlier episodes of the epic? Explain. **(b) Make a Judgment:** Do you think that Odysseus' revenge is justified? Why or why not?

Literary Analysis

6. **(a)** Using a chart like the one shown, analyze the **epic simile** in lines 1613–1624.

Items Being Compared	Details of Epic Simile	Purpose

(b) Why is this simile a powerful and fitting image for the conclusion of the *Odyssey*?

Reading Skill

7. **(a)** What attitudes and values are reflected in Odysseus' actions toward the suitors? **(b)** What do his actions suggest about the **cultural and historical context** of Homer's *Odyssey* and the attitudes and values of ancient Greeks? Explain your answer.
8. **(a)** Name one of Odysseus' cultural beliefs, attitudes, or practices that is similar to an idea or a tradition in your own culture. **(b)** Name one that is significantly different. **(c)** Do you think that Odysseus' values are unique to his culture, or are they universal? Explain.

1018 ■ Themes in Literature: Heroism

QuickReview

Part 2 at a Glance
Odysseus returns home, defeats the suitors, and reclaims his wife and kingdom.

Go Online
Assessment
For: Self-test
Visit: www.PHSchool.com
Web Code: epa-6603

Epic Simile: an elaborate comparison that may extend for several lines

Historical and Cultural Context: the events, beliefs, and customs that define the time and place in which a work is set or in which it was written

8. **Possible responses:**
(a) Odysseus believed in the practice of hospitality. (b) The practice of settling disputes through violence is not accepted today. (c) Many of Odysseus' values are universal, such as that of hospitality and his longing for home. His belief that the gods participate in human affairs may be unique to his culture.

Vocabulary Builder

Practice Indicate whether each statement is *True* or *False*. Explain your answers. Then, revise false sentences to make them true.

1. People sometimes *dissemble* in order to hide their true feelings.
2. An event that is common and predictable evokes *incredulity*.
3. If road signs are *bemusing* drivers, the signs are working well.
4. A good judge is one with a strong sense of *equity*.
5. A pep band should play *maudlin* songs if it wants to excite fans.
6. Successful salespeople always show *contempt* for customers.

Adding Words to Your Vocabulary Use a dictionary to find the adjective form of the noun *incredulity*. Use that adjective in a sentence. Then, explain the difference between that adjective and *incredible*. (For more on using a dictionary, see page R6.)

Writing

Write a short **biography of Odysseus** based on details in the *Odyssey*. Present the basic facts of his life and adventures, and hold the reader's attention by describing the dramatic situations with gripping detail.

- List events in the *Odyssey* that are suitable for your biography. Focus on events that reveal the character of Odysseus.
- As you draft, include quotations from the epic to add detail and depth.

For *Grammar, Vocabulary,* and *Assessment,* see **Build Language Skills,** pages 1020–1021.

Extend Your Learning

Listening and Speaking Conduct a **debate** on whether Odysseus should be prosecuted for the murders of Penelope's suitors.
- Divide into two opposing teams.
- With teammates, prepare an argument expressing your position. Be sure to support it with details from the *Odyssey*.

Present your argument before the class, and then switch sides so that each team debates the issue from both sides.

Research and Technology With the help of a teacher, select and view a movie based on the *Odyssey*. Take notes on which aspects of the film come from the epic and which show the director's modern influences or perspective. Record your ideas, including an assessment of the director's purpose in making the film, in a **"Director's Influences" chart.**

Apply the Skills ■ 1019

Go Online
Research — **For:** An additional research activity **Visit:** www.PHSchool.com **Web Code:** epd-7602
For another research activity to extend students' learning, give students this Web Code.

Vocabulary Development
Practice

1. True; Odysseus did not want his true feelings known as he tested others' loyalty.
2. False; a usual event does provoke attention. An event that is uncommon evokes *incredulity*.
3. False; bemused drivers will not drive well. If road signs are *bemusing*, they will distract drivers.
4. True; a judge with a sense of *equity* would treat people fairly.
5. False; maudlin songs would make people feel sad. A band should play *maudlin* songs if it wants a crowd to be depressed.
6. False; people who treat customers with contempt would not succeed. Salespeople who show *contempt* for customers will lose business.

Adding Words to Your Vocabulary

Incredulous is the adjective form of *incredulity*. I could tell my sister did not believe my excuse because she gave me an *incredulous* look. The word *incredulous* means "doubting" or "unable to believe." The word *incredible* means "unusual or not probable."

Writing

- To give students guidance for writing a biography, give them the Writing Support page for this selection, p. 43 in *Unit 6 Resources.*
- To evaluate students' biographies, use the Biography rubrics, pp. 69–70 in *General Resources.*

Six Traits Focus

✔ Ideas	✔ Word Choice
Organization	Sentence Fluency
✔ Voice	Conventions

Build Language Skills

Go to pp. 1020–1021 for vocabulary and grammar lessons and assessment practice.

Extend Your Learning

The **Extend Your Learning** support page (*Unit 6 Resources*, p. 44) provides guided note-taking opportunities to help students complete the Extend Your Learning activities.

1019

Vocabulary Skill

- Introduce the vocabulary skill: word roots. Have students look at the word root *-techni-*.

- Have students complete the Practice activity on this page.

Possible Answers

1. The *technician* quickly spotted the computer problem.

2. Due to *technical* difficulties, the station went off the air.

3. The legal case was dismissed on a *technicality*.

4. Our society will become a *technocracy* if we continue to rely so heavily on technology.

5. The use of *technography* enabled the people in the remote office to participate in the meeting.

Grammar Lesson

- Point out that by varying the four types of sentences students can add variety to their writing.

- Have students complete the Practice activity on this page.

Answers

1. complex; *The shield was made of oxhide* is an independent clause; *that the warrior carried* is a subordinate clause.

2. compound-complex; *We read the play* is an independent clause; *when our teacher assigned it* is a subordinate clause; *we did not see the movie* is an independent clause.

3. compound-complex; *She solved the mystery* is an independent clause; *She left for Uruguay* is an independent clause; *which is a country in South America* is a subordinate clause.

4. complex; *Arthur bought the magnificent painting* is an independent clause; *that he admired in the gallery* is a subordinate clause.

5. complex; *He was late for his appointment with the guidance counselor* is an independent clause; *because his alarm clock did not ring* is a subordinate clause.

Build Language Skills

from the *Odyssey*, Part 2

Vocabulary Skill

Word Roots Word roots can provide *context clues* to help you understand unfamiliar words. The **Greek word root** *-techni-* *(-techn-)* is used in words related to art, skill, or craft, such as the word *technique*.

▶ **Example:** Our society depends on *technology* to function.

Practice Use each of the following words in a sentence that would help someone understand what the word means.

1. technician   2. technical   3. technicality
4. technocracy   5. technography

Grammar Lesson

Complex and Compound-Complex Sentences A **complex sentence** consists of one independent clause, which can stand by itself as a sentence, and at least one subordinate clause, which cannot stand by itself as a sentence. A **compound-complex sentence** consists of two or more independent clauses and one or more subordinate clauses.

> **Complex sentence:** When the lights came on, he saw the audience.

> **Compound-complex sentence:** When the lights came on, he saw the audience, and he waved to his parents.

Practice Identify each sentence as complex or compound-complex. Identify the independent clauses and the subordinate clauses.

1. The shield that the warrior carried in the first battle was made of oxhide.

2. We read the play when our teacher assigned it, but we did not see the movie.

3. She solved the mystery, and then she left for Uruguay, which is a country in South America.

4. Arthur bought the magnificent painting that he admired in the gallery.

5. He was late for his appointment with the guidance counselor because his alarm clock did not ring.

 Prentice Hall Writing and Grammar Connection: Chapter 21, Section 2

MorePractice

For more practice with complex and compound-complex sentences, see the Grammar Handbook, p. R42.

Teaching Resources

The following resources can be used to enrich or extend the instruction for Build Language Skills.

Unit 6 Resources
Build Language Skills: Vocabulary: Greek root *-techni-*, p. 46
Build Grammar Skills: Complex and Compound-Complex Sentences, p. 47

Reading Skill: Analyzing Cultural and Historical Context

Directions: *Read the selection. Then, answer the questions.*

The King was convinced that the only way to save himself was to kill his daughter, Danae, before she could have a child. The oracle had foretold his death at the hands of her son. Yet, he was afraid of the gods who prohibited shedding the blood of kin. Acrisius was fearful of killing Danae so instead he had a house built of bronze. He had the house sunk underground with only part of the roof open so light and air could come through. He had Danae put in the house and guarded carefully. One day she was visited by Zeus disguised in a shower of gold. The myth tells us that Danae had a son whose father was Zeus.

1. From the context of this passage, what can a reader infer?
   A The ancient Greeks believed in fate but sometimes tried to alter it.
   B The ancient Greeks felt that a person's fate could never be changed.
   C The ancient Greeks believed that the gods would always make them happy.
   D The ancient Greeks had no way of knowing what the gods meant for them.

2. From the cultural and historical context of this passage, what can a reader infer about the ancient Greeks?
   A They lived in bronze houses sunk underground.
   B They believed that the clouds were really gold mines.

C They felt that daughters had the right to disobey their fathers.
   D They believed that the gods could appear in any shape or form.

3. What assumption can the reader make about Greek culture?
   A They believed the gods were not important.
   B They believed the gods could be swayed.
   C They believed the gods were myths.
   D They believed the gods were real.

4. Which concept does our society share with this myth?
   A Murder is not allowed.
   B Oracles are believed.
   C Kings are all powerful.
   D Power is not to be used harshly.

Timed Writing: Interpretation (Critical Stance)

Write an essay in which you interpret the character of Penelope based on the decisions she makes and the actions she performs. Cite specific events in the *Odyssey*, identify Penelope's decisions and actions, and interpret why she does what she does. **(45 minutes)**

 ## Writing Workshop: *Work in Progress*

Writing for Assessment
Use your background list to generate possible writing questions. What general question might you ask about one of the historical events or literary works on your list?

Build Language Skills ■ *1021*

Answers

Reading Skill: Analyzing Cultural and Historical Context
1. A   3. D
2. D   4. A

Timed Writing
- Tell students that they will be asked to write an interpretation of the character of Penelope.
- Have students jot down a list of Penelope's decisions and actions. Then have students identify what character traits influence these actions. Suggest that this information provides them with information for their interpretation.
- As students write, remind them that they must support their interpretations with examples from the *Odyssey*.
- Assess students' interpretations based on their use of examples of Penelope's actions, decisions, and personality traits to support their views.
- Suggest that students plan their time to give ten minutes to listing ideas about Penelope, twenty-five minutes to writing their interpretations, and ten minutes to reviewing and revising.

Writing Workshop
Work in Progress

- Have students go to their portfolios and take out the work they have completed so far on this assignment. Remind them that this work may be used in the **Writing Workshop** on timed essays on p. 1040.
- Guide students in completing the **Work-in-Progress** assignment on this page. When students have completed this activity, have them keep it in their portfolios. They will use is as they continue the **Work in Progress**.

See TeacherExpress™/Lesson View for a detailed lesson plan for Reading Informational Materials.

About Applications

- Have students read "About Applications."

- As a group, brainstorm for situations that typically require applications. Make sure to include ideas such as college admittance, scholarships, jobs, and loans from a bank.

- Ask volunteers to describe applications they have seen or filled out.

- Point out that *referees* (often referred to as references) are people who give *references* (written or verbal recommendations) about a person. Point out that having good references can often determine whether or not a person gets a job. **Ask** students to identify types of people that make good referees.

- **Possible responses:** Teachers, neighbors, employers, coaches, and clergy are all good people to ask for references because they have seen the applicant work with others and have a sense of the applicant's personality.

Reading Skill
Following Directions

- Remind students that following directions means completing steps exactly as they are stated, even if there are other ways to complete the task.

- Review with students the checklist for following directions.

- Point out that most applications do not include specific directions for all the blanks and boxes. Explain that many of the directions are implied.

Applications

In Part 1, you learned how to analyze the influence of cultural and historical context by reading the *Odyssey* by Homer. The application that follows relates to an opportunity to understand history and other cultures even more deeply through archaeological exploration.

About Applications

Applications are documents that companies, schools, and other organizations use to gather information and determine whether someone is qualified to serve in a job or to participate in a program. People also complete applications when they want to rent an apartment, take out a loan, get a driver's license, or achieve other such goals. A person may be asked for the following types of information on an application:

- personal information, such as name, address, and date of birth
- educational background
- specific experience that applies to the position
- references from people who know the applicant

Reading Skill

Following directions is a critical skill when completing any application. Often, the information on an application is the only data decision-makers have about an applicant. Therefore, the application must be complete and accurate. In addition, the ability to follow directions shows that you can read and think clearly. The following checklist will help guide you in completing an application.

Following Directions on an Application: A Checklist
Gather details about your education, work experience, and references before starting.
Read the application thoroughly before you begin.
Write neatly, using blue or black ink.
Respond specifically and accurately.
If you have questions, ask for help.
Before listing anyone as a personal reference, make sure he or she is willing to write a letter or speak for you.

Differentiated Instruction   Solutions for All Learners

Reading Support

Give students reading support with the appropriate version of the *Reader's Notebooks:*

Reader's Notebook, [L2]

Reader's Notebook: Adapted Version, [L1]

Reader's Notebook: English Learner's Version, [EL]

THE AMERICAN SCHOOL OF CLASSICAL STUDIES AT ATHENS

BULLETIN

EXCAVATIONS IN THE ATHENIAN AGORA VOLUNTEER PROGRAM
SUMMER 20_ _

The American School of Classical Studies at Athens announces a program for volunteer excavators wishing to participate in the archaeological excavations of the Athenian Agora during the summer of 20_ _. Approximately thirty-five volunteers are chosen on the basis of academic qualifications and interest in the archaeological field. All participants are expected to work the entire six-week season.

Work of the Volunteer Staff

The Volunteer Staff will participate in all aspects of the archaeological field-work under the supervision of a staff of field archaeologist and technical experts, all of whom have extensive field experience and advanced academic training in classical archaeology. Volunteers will be trained in the basic techniques of excavation: working with pick, trowel, shovel, and wheelbarrow; cleaning and investigating stratigraphy; delicate cleaning of artifacts in the ground; sifting of excavated earth and techniques of flotation; washing and basic conservation of pottery and other objects; clerical work involved in the keeping of excavation records. All tasks will be assigned in rotation, and volunteers are expected to participate in them all. Room and a modest allowance for board are provided for the time volunteers are working at the excavations. Travel arrangements to and from Greece are the responsibility of each volunteer.

The 20_ _ Season

The excavations of 20_ _ are planned for six weeks beginning early June and continuing until late July. Fieldwork is in progress five days a week, Monday through Friday, from 7 a.m. to 3 p.m. with a 30-minute break at midmorning. Volunteers are expected to be on the site during these hours and to work at the excavations for the full six weeks.

To request applications or additional information, please see the contact information on page 3.

POSTMARK DEADLINE: DECEMBER 15, 20 _ _.
Applicants can expect to receive notification after February 15, 20_ _.

Reading Informational Materials: Applications ■ 1023

This section gives general information about the available opportunities.

This section provides more specific information about the work and the responsibilities of volunteers.

The due date for the application is indicated in bold, underlined type so it stands out.

Reading Applications

- Explain to students that some applications provide additional information about the organization, so applicants fully understand the purpose of the application.
- Have students read the application to the American School of Classical Studies excavation program.
- Tell students that each section provides important information that could help when filling out the application. **Ask** students to describe the information in the section "Work of the Volunteer Staff." **Possible response:** This section describes the tasks involved with the position.
- **Ask** students why the "Work of the Volunteer Staff" information is important to applicants. **Possible response:** Knowing what is required allows applicants to decide for sure whether or not they want to apply for the job. Also, the section clarifies that applicants must pay their own transportation to Greece, which alerts students to the need to determine whether or not they can afford to take the position if it is offered to them.
- **Ask** students to identify a type of person who would be ideally suited for this program. **Possible responses:** Someone working on a degree in ancient Greece, archaeology, or excavation and who is available to volunteer for the summer would be ideally suited for this position.
- Tell students that application deadlines are often strictly enforced, so they should always make sure that they understand them. Point out that the application gives very specific directions about when to apply for the job and when applicants will learn if they are accepted. **Ask** students to find these timings. **Answer:** Applications must be postmarked no later than December 15, 20__. Applicants will learn if they have been selected sometime after February 15, 20__.

continued on p. 1024

Differentiated Instruction
Solutions for All Learners

Vocabulary for Special Needs Students
Since students might not understand some of the key terms and phrases in this application, they might be confused about the whole purpose of the application. Review the following terms and phrases with these students.

Athens: a city in the country of Greece
academic qualifications: grades and classes in archaeology

field experience: time spent digging in the ground to find items that were used many years ago
delicate cleaning of artifacts in the ground: carefully washing and dusting items that are uncovered
conservation of pottery: methods of safely digging up and keeping old clay items
clerical work: paper work

- Point out to students that the top part of the application form asks for typical specific information. **Ask** volunteers to identify personal details that are often requested on applications, but that are not requested on this one.
  Possible response: Many applications also ask for e-mail addresses, both cell phone and home phone numbers, job history, social security number, and citizenship status.

- **Ask** students what kind of information would likely go under the heading "Special qualifications and other relevant information."
  Possible response: Applicants could write information about clubs to which they belong or research they have conducted that is related to archaeology.

- Point out that the deadline for submitting the application is included on both pages of the application. **Ask** students whether they think this redundancy was a mistake or not and to explain their reasoning.
  Answer: The repetition is probably intended to ensure that applicants notice the deadline.

- Remind students that possible sources of references include neighbors, employers, coaches, and clergy. Ask students to each identify three people they could ask for a reference.

- Point out that, according to the directions, applicants must send something besides the one-page application form. **Ask** students what else applicants must send.
  Answer: Applicants must also send a one-page personal statement.

EXCAVATIONS IN THE ATHENIAN AGORA
APPLICATION FOR VOLUNTEER PROGRAM 20_ _

Full Name: _____

Address: _____

Telephone: _____ Date of Birth: _____

EDUCATION

High School _____

Dates Attended: _____ Date (or Expected Date) of graduation: _____

List courses (if any) taken in Archaeology, Classics, and related fields (continue on back if necessary): _____

_____

_____

_____

The first part of this section asks for archaeology-related experience. The second asks for any similar experience, such as membership in a history or science club.

List any ARCHAEOLOGICAL EXPERIENCE:

Give name of site, name of Director, dates: _____

_____

_____

Special qualifications and other relevant information: _____

_____

Dates Available: Full Season (6 weeks) _____

In addition to this brief form, the organization requires each applicant to write a short essay in which he or she explains his or her interest.

PERSONAL STATEMENT:

Please attach a personal statement explaining your interest in the Agora Excavations. Please discuss more fully your qualifications, career goals and interests, and any other relevant information. This essay should not exceed more than one side of one 8 1/2 x 11 page.

INTERVIEW:

I will telephone to arrange date for interview _____

I cannot be interviewed because of distance _____

REFEREES:

Referees are people with good credentials who can recommend the applicant for the position.

Give names and addresses of two persons whom you have asked to write in support of your application. They should be familiar with your academic studies and/or archaeological interest. _____

_____

Signature: _____ Date: _____

Completed applications and letters of recommendation should be sent to the appropriate address listed on page 3. All application materials should be postmarked no later than December 15, 20_ _.

Vocabulary Development

Vocabulary for Archaeological Digs

Point out that applications often use vocabulary that is specific to one particular setting, in this case an archaeological dig in Greece. Guide students to understand the meaning of the following words that are used in the application to the American School of Classical Studies:

excavation: the process of exposing to view by digging away a covering

archaeological: related to the scientific study of material remains of past human life and activities

stratigraphy: the arrangement of rocks in layers or strata; or the branch of geology that studies such layers of rock

Reading: Following Directions

Directions: *Choose the letter of the best answer to each question about the application.*

1. What is a responsibility of each volunteer?
   - **A** to pay all expenses during the course of the fieldwork
   - **B** to notify the program director of all travel arrangements
   - **C** to receive training in archaeology before the program starts
   - **D** to participate in all excavation tasks

2. What additional information should an applicant provide on the write-on lines under "Education"?
   - **A** high-school grade point average
   - **B** literature classes taken
   - **C** archaeology and classics courses taken
   - **D** hours completed for graduation

3. What specific directions are given regarding the personal essay that accompanies the application?
   - **A** The essay should be no longer than five pages.
   - **B** The essay should be stapled to the application.
   - **C** The essay should be no longer than a single 8 1/2 × 11 page.
   - **D** The essay should have a cover sheet.

Reading: Comprehension and Interpretation

Directions: *Write your answers on a separate sheet of paper.*

4. Explain the purpose of the personal essay. **[Applying]**
5. What kind of information might an organization learn from referees that is different from information the applicant provides? **[Organizing]**

Timed Writing: Persuasion [Connections]

Imagine that you are applying for the program represented on this application. Write the requested essay that would accompany the form. Describe your goals and ambitions clearly. Avoid clichés or jargon and use formal, polite language that shows respect toward your audience. **(45 minutes)**

Reading Informational Materials: Applications ■ 1025

Answers

Reading: Following Directions

1. D
2. C
3. C
4. The purpose of the essay is to explain one's interest in the Agora Excavations and to offer fuller details about qualifications, career goals, and relevant interests.
5. **Possible response:** Referees can provide a more objective idea of an applicant's attitudes and effort levels as well as how well the applicant works with other.

Timed Writing

- Read the *Timed Writing* instructions together as a group. Make sure students understand that they are to assume that they are interested in taking part in the Agora Excavations. Tell students that their essays should clearly describe their goals and ambitions. Remind them to use formal language.

- Suggest that students plan their time to give 15 minutes to planning, 20 minutes to writing, and 10 minutes to reviewing and revising.

Extend the Lesson

Ideal Positions

To give students further practice with applications, have them make lists of their skills and qualifications. Then have students think of positions for which they are ideally suited. Finally, have students write job descriptions for their ideal jobs.

Meeting Your Standards

Students will

1. analyze and respond to contemporary interpretations.
2. compare contemporary interpretations.
3. write a comparison of contemporary interpretations.

See TeacherExpress™/Lesson View for a detailed lesson plan for Comparing Literary Works.

Literary Analysis

❶ Contemporary Interpretations

- Read the instruction about contemporary interpretations together. Be sure that students understand the meaning of *contemporary*— "taking place in our time or in the very recent past."

- Tell students that although the four contemporary interpretations in this section are poems, contemporary interpretations may take any literary form. In addition, a contemporary interpretation does not have to have the same form as the original.

❷ Comparing Contemporary Interpretations

- Remind students that comparing contemporary interpretations usually reveals just as much about the contemporary writers as it does about the ancient writers.

- Give students a copy of **Comparing Contemporary Interpretations Graphic Organizer A** (*Graphic Organizer Transparencies,* p. 207). Have them complete it as they read and compare the selections. Suggest that they focus on details like these:

    historical backgrounds

    cultural attitudes

    authors' purposes

❶ Contemporary Interpretations

A **contemporary interpretation** of a literary work is a new piece of writing, such as a poem, story, or play, that a modern-day author bases on an ancient work. An **allusion** is a reference to a well-known person, place, event, literary work, or work of art. The characters and events of Homer's *Odyssey* are timeless and universal in their appeal and meaning and have inspired many contemporary interpretations. By reinventing Homer's tales, or by making allusions to them, modern-day writers shed new light on Homer's ancient words. The new literary work thus makes a powerful connection between the people of different countries, eras, and cultures. Contemporary interpretations may allude to any aspects of the original work, including plot, characters, settings, imagery, language, or theme.

❷ Comparing Contemporary Interpretations

Even when they are based on the same work, contemporary interpretations can differ widely in purpose and theme. The writers' cultural and historical backgrounds, attitudes, and beliefs profoundly affect their perceptions of the ancient work. These factors also influence their creation of the new literary work. As you read, use a chart like the one shown to note the allusion each poet makes to Homer's *Odyssey*. Then, think about the ways in which the allusion helps each poet express a new meaning.

Poem:
Allusion to the *Odyssey:*
Meaning:

Vocabulary Builder

An Ancient Gesture

- **authentic** (ô then′ tik) *adj.* genuine; true (p. 1029) *Lab tests prove that the document is* <u>authentic</u> *and not a forgery.*

Siren Song

- **picturesque** (pik′ chər esk′) *adj.* like or suggesting a picture (p. 1031) *The grand and* <u>picturesque</u> *desert landscape stretched out before us.*

Prologue and Epilogue from *The Odyssey: A Stage Version*

- **siege** (sēj) *n.* encirclement of a fortified place by an opposing armed force intending to take it (p. 1032) *The castle withstood the* <u>siege</u> *for two months.*

Ithaca

- **lofty** (lôf′ tē) *adj.* very high; noble (p. 1035) *With* <u>lofty</u> *goals, you can achieve great things.*

- **defrauded** (dē frôd′ id) *v.* cheated (p. 1036) *By charging too much, they* <u>defrauded</u> *the public.*

1026 ■ *Themes in Literature: Heroism*

Vocabulary Development

Vocabulary Knowledge Rating

Create a **Vocabulary Knowledge Rating Chart** with the selection vocabulary and expressive vocabulary for each poem. Give students a copy. Introduce the words by reading them aloud and having students mark their rating in the Before Reading column. Urge them to be alert to these words as they read and discuss the poems because they will rate their knowledge of the words again after they finish.

If you wish, you may tally how many students know (or think they know) a word to gauge how much instruction you need to provide. As students read, point out the words and their context.

Build Understanding

❸ Connecting to the Literature

Reading/Writing Connection Each poem in this section draws inspiration from Homer's *Odyssey*. This ancient poem features Odysseus as its central heroic figure. List Odysseus' heroic qualities, and then write a paragraph in which you explain the qualities that define a hero today. Use at least three of the following words in your response: *aspect, manifest, confront, enlighten, integrate.*

Meet the Author

Edna St. Vincent **Millay** (1892–1950)

Edna St. Vincent Millay is remembered for her artistic experimentation and her rebelliousness. Her poetry collection *The Harp Weaver and Other Poems* (1923) earned her a Pulitzer Prize.

Margaret **Atwood** (b. 1939)

Much of Margaret Atwood's writing is about what it means to be a woman in a period of social change. In "Siren Song," Atwood presents another of her themes—the role of mythology in people's lives.

Derek **Walcott** (b. 1930)

Born in St. Lucia, an island in the Caribbean Sea, Walcott writes poems that reflect his background. In 1992, he won the Nobel Prize in Literature. "Prologue" and "Epilogue" are from his stage version of the *Odyssey.*

Constantine **Cavafy** (1863–1933)

Constantine Cavafy was born to Greek parents in Alexandria, Egypt. "Ithaca" showcases his creative method: using Greek mythology to speak to the modern reader.

-Author Link

For: More about the authors
Visit: www.PHSchool.com
Web Code: epe-9603

Comparing Literary Works ■ 1027

❸ Connecting to the Literature

- Model use of the expressive vocabulary students are asked to use with these examples:

  1. Some of today's heroes *integrate* old-fashioned courage with modern technology.
  2. A modern hero may *manifest* a wide range of qualities.
  3. Heroism may be the willingness to *confront* a problem and risk everything to solve it.
  4. The brilliant actions of heroes *enlighten* the rest of us.

- Help students further develop their expressive vocabulary by providing these words: *chronicle, endurance, grieve,* and *timeless.* Encourage students to use these words as they discuss the selections.

Go Online
Author Link For additional information about Edna St. Vincent Millay, Margaret Atwood, Derek Walcott, and Constantine Cavafy, have students type in the Web Code and then select the author.

1027

❶ Background

Heroism Old and New Just as the heroic character of Odysseus can be revisited today to reveal the qualities that the ancient Greeks valued in a man, Penelope's character can reveal the qualities valued in a woman. Odysseus' courage, adventurous spirit, and guile are celebrated in the *Odyssey*, while Penelope is most notable for her loyalty and patience. She also shares some of her husband's gift for cleverness in holding off the suitors and testing Odysseus' identity. In "An Ancient Gesture," Millay uses Odysseus and Penelope to ask what both characters reveal about the heroism of suffering.

❷ Motivation

Draw a cluster diagram on the board and in the center write *hero*. Ask students what they associate with being a hero, based on prior knowledge and experience. Then ask how the meaning of *hero* has changed from ancient times to today. Tell students that the poems they are going to read look at the *Odyssey* with a fresh perspective and offer contemporary interpretations of what it means to be a hero.

Concept Connector ➡

Students will follow up on this activity after completing the poems.

❸ About the Selections

In "An Ancient Gesture," a gesture by Penelope is echoed by a modern woman, suggesting that enduring grief and loneliness is itself heroic. In "Siren Song," a Siren admits that her song is a cry for help that continues to lure and destroy men. "Prologue and Epilogue from the *Odyssey*" retells the opening and closing of Homer's poem in a modern idiom. "Ithaca" applies the image of the epic journey to everyone's life.

❹ Critical Viewing

Possible response: Penelope's posture and facial expression show complete indifference to the suitors

AN ANCIENT GESTURE

Edna St. Vincent Millay

❶
❷
❸

❹ ▲ Critical Viewing What is Penelope's attitude toward the suitors? How can you tell? **[Infer; Support]**

1028 ■ *Themes in Literature: Heroism*

Vocabulary Development

Word Analysis

In this poem, Millay describes an *antique* gesture. The Latin word *antiquus* means old or ancient, and its root, *antiqu-*, helps to form several useful English words. Write these related words on the board, and help students work out the definitions and use them in sentences.

antiques: old objects, such as furniture and silver, usually at least one hundred years old

antiquing: searching for antiques

antiquary: person who collects or studies antiques or ancient artworks

antiquarian: concerning antiques or ancient artifacts; another name for an antiquary

antiquity: ancient times; early history, before the Middle Ages

antiquated: out-of-date; no longer useful

I thought, as I wiped my eyes on the corner of my apron:
Penelope did this too.
And more than once: you can't keep weaving all day
And undoing it all through the night;
5 Your arms get tired, and the back of your neck gets tight;
❺ And along towards morning, when you think it will never
    be light,
And your husband has been gone, and you don't know
    where, for years,
Suddenly you burst into tears;
There is simply nothing else to do.

10 And I thought, as I wiped my eyes on the corner of my apron:
This is an ancient gesture, <u>authentic</u>, antique,
In the very best tradition, classic, Greek;
Ulysses[1] did this too.
But only as a gesture,—a gesture which implied
15 To the assembled throng that he was much too moved
    to speak.
He learned it from Penelope . . .
Penelope, who really cried.

---

1. Ulysses Latin name for Odysseus.

Thinking About the Selection

1. **Respond:** Does this poem make you feel more or less sympathetic to Penelope than the *Odyssey* did? Explain.

2. **(a) Recall:** What is the "ancient gesture"? **(b) Summarize:** According to the speaker, what caused Penelope to employ this gesture? **(c) Infer:** What might have caused the speaker to make a similar gesture?

3. **(a) Recall:** According to the speaker, who else made this ancient gesture? **(b) Compare and Contrast:** How did this gesture differ from Penelope's? **(c) Analyze:** What do the different qualities of their gestures show about these characters?

4. **(a) Assess:** What questions about the speaker are left unanswered? **(b) Analyze Cause and Effect:** What effect do these unanswered questions create?

5. **Speculate:** What advice do you think Penelope would give to the speaker of this poem? Explain.

An Ancient Gesture ■ 1029

Literary Analysis
Contemporary Interpretations What connection does the speaker make between herself and Penelope?

Vocabulary Builder
authentic (ô then´ tik) *adj.* genuine; true

❺ **Literary Analysis**
Contemporary Interpretations

- Read aloud the poem, and then **ask** students why the speaker is crying.
  Answer: The speaker is crying because her husband has been gone for years.

- **Ask** students the Literary Analysis question: What connection does the speaker make between herself and Penelope?
  Possible response: Both Penelope and the speaker know the great sadness of lost husbands, and they both cry and wipe their eyes on their aprons.

ASSESS

Answers

1. **Possible response:** Students may say that the poem makes them feel more sympathetic because it describes personal feelings in a way that feels more intimate.

2. (a) The ancient gesture is wiping crying eyes with an apron. (b) Her husband had been gone for years, and she thought he was probably dead. (c) Her husband has also been gone for years, and she does not know where he is.

3. (a) Ulysses also made this gesture. (b) His gesture was made to manipulate a crowd. (c) Penelope and the speaker know genuine grief. Ulysses learned to simulate grief by watching his wife.

4. (a) The reader does not know why her husband has gone, where he's gone, or whether he is still alive. (b) **Possible responses:** The unanswered questions create a sense of mystery and sadness; the lack of specific detail allows the reader to focus on emotions.

5. **Possible responses:** Penelope might tell the speaker to keep faith, because her husband might return.

1029

❻ Literary Analysis
Contemporary Interpretations

- Remind students that the Sirens are creatures—each half-bird and half-woman—whose song lures men to destruction.

- Have students read aloud the poem. Then **ask:** What do the men see on the beach?
  Answer: They see skulls.

- **Ask** students what the men should infer from the skulls.
  Answer: They should infer that they will meet death among the Sirens.

- **Ask** students the Literary Analysis question: What allusion do lines 4–9 make to the *Odyssey?*
  Answer: The lines allude to the episode in which Odysseus and his men row past the Sirens. Odysseus puts wax in his men's ears but has himself tied to the mast so that he can hear the song.

- Point out that the men meet their deaths because they go "overboard." **Ask** students what double meaning "go overboard" has for those who pursue the Sirens.
  Answer: The men leap out of their ship, but they also "go overboard" with passion. They abandon both their boat and their reason.

SIREN SONG

Margaret Atwood

This is the one song everyone
would like to learn: the song
that is irresistible:

the song that forces men
5 to leap overboard in squadrons
even though they see the beached skulls

❻

the song nobody knows
because anyone who has heard it
is dead, and the others can't remember.

10 Shall I tell you the secret
and if I do, will you get me
out of this bird suit?[1]

---

1. bird suit Sirens are usually represented as half bird and half woman.

1030 ■ *Themes in Literature: Heroism*

Literary Analysis
Contemporary Interpretations and Allusion What allusion do lines 4–9 make to the *Odyssey?*

Vocabulary Development

Word Analysis
Atwood's poem tells of a song that is *irresistible.* Point out to students that the prefix *ir-* means "not," and it is used before words beginning with *r*. List the following words on the board. Have students tell the meaning of each word, and use each word in a sentence that demonstrates its meaning.

irrational: lacking reason; absurd
irreconcilable: conflicting; that cannot be made to agree

irregular: not standard or ordinary
irrelevant: not relevant or pertinent
irreparable: that cannot be fixed
irresistible: that cannot be resisted
irresponsible: unreliable, careless
irreverent: disrespectful

I don't enjoy it here
squatting on this island
15 looking picturesque and mythical

with these two feathery maniacs,
I don't enjoy singing
this trio, fatal and valuable.

I will tell the secret to you,
20 to you, only to you.
Come closer. This song

❼

is a cry for help: Help me!
Only you, only you can,
you are unique

25 at last. Alas
it is a boring song
but it works every time.

Siren Song ■ 1031

Vocabulary Builder

picturesque (pik′ chər esk′) *adj.* like or suggesting a picture

Literary Analysis

Contemporary Interpretations What does the contemporary Siren say to flatter and lure the listener?

Thinking About the Selection

1. **Respond:** Do you like the speaker in this poem? Why or why not?

2. **(a) Recall:** In the first stanza, what song does the speaker say everyone wants to learn? **(b) Analyze Cause and Effect:** What does this song have the power to do?

3. **(a) Recall:** What does the speaker want in exchange for revealing the song's secret? **(b) Interpret:** Why does the speaker want to make this deal?

4. **(a) Analyze:** Why do you think the speaker's compliment in line 24 is so effective? **(b) Make Generalizations:** What might the speaker be saying about the relationships between men and women?

5. **(a) Summarize:** How does the speaker feel about her song and its secret? **(b) Support:** Which details in the poem support your answer?

---

❼ Literary Analysis
Contemporary Interpretations

- **Ask** students the Literary Analysis question: What does the contemporary Siren say to flatter and lure the listener?
  Answer: She says that she needs help and that only the listener can help her.

- **Ask** students what this contemporary interpretation suggests about the character of the men who give in to the Siren's song.
  Possible response: The men are weak, vain, or foolish.

- **Ask** students: In this contemporary interpretation, what seems to be the effect of the song on the Siren herself?
  Possible response: Because the Siren continues to sing the song that she knows to be boring and destructive, she remains, after all, a monster.

ASSESS
Answers

1. **Possible response:** Students may not like the speaker of the poem because she is bored by her own song, trapped by her role as a Siren, and casual about destroying men.

2. (a) Everyone wants to learn the song that is irresistible. (b) The song has the power to drive men crazy and destroy them.

3. (a) In exchange, the speaker says she wants the listener to get her out of her bird suit. (b) The speaker says that she wants to be freed from her role as a Siren.

4. (a) The compliment is effective because everyone wants to be unique, and the Siren plays on the man's vanity. (b) The speaker suggests that some relationships between men and women are based on a pretense of need.

5. (a) The speaker feels her song is boring but unfailingly effective. (b) In the final three lines, she sighs "Alas," admits the song is "boring," but notes that "it works every time."

Differentiated
Instruction   Solutions for All Learners

Strategy for Gifted/Talented Students
Suggest that students create a picture or a sculpture of a Siren. They may research a Siren's appearance in works of art or rely purely on their own imaginations. Challenge some students to create an image of Margaret Atwood's modern Siren. Some students may wish to accompany their images with music or sound effects that convey the Siren's song.

Strategy for Advanced Readers
Margaret Atwood uses an allusion from classic literature to create a contemporary interpretation of some relationships between men and women. Ask students to write brief essays in which they use another character from literature (Romeo or Juliet, for example) to make their own contemporary interpretation of some relationships between men and women.

- **Ask** students to respond to the Literary Analysis question: What actions in lines 6–8 reflect the *Odyssey*? Explain.
  Answer: The lines reflect the unending waves of the sea on which Odysseus travels, the tireless weaving of Penelope as she makes and unmakes the shroud, and the repeated rising of the sun at dawn after dawn, which Homer describes as "rosy-fingered."

- **Ask** students: What point about his story is the contemporary singer communicating with these lines?
  Possible response: The singer communicates the point that his song, his story, and his theme are universal and timeless.

Prologue and Epilogue from
The Odyssey: A Stage Version
DEREK WALCOTT

PROLOGUE

Sound of surf.

BILLY BLUE *(Sings)*

Gone sing 'bout that man because his stories please us,
Who saw trials and tempests for ten years after Troy.

I'm Blind Billy Blue, my main man's sea-smart Odysseus,
Who the God of the Sea drove crazy and tried to destroy.

5 Andra moi ennepe mousa polutropon hos mala polla . . .
The shuttle of the sea moves back and forth on this line,

8

All night, like the surf, she shuttles and doesn't fall
Asleep, then her rosy fingers at dawn unstitch the design.

When you hear this chord
(Chord)

                      Look for a swallow's wings,
10 A swallow arrowing seaward like a messenger

Passing smoke-blue islands, happy that the kings
Of Troy are going home and its ten years' <u>siege</u> is over.

So my blues drifts like smoke from the fire of that war,
Cause once Achilles was ashes, things sure fell apart.

15 Slow-striding Achilles, who put the hex on Hector
A swallow twitters in Troy. That's where we start.
(Exit.)

1032 ■ *Themes in Literature: Heroism*

Literary Analysis
Contemporary
Interpretations What actions in lines 6–8 reflect Homer's *Odyssey*? Explain.

Vocabulary Builder
siege (sēj) *n.* encirclement of a fortified place by an opposing armed force intending to take it

Vocabulary Development

Compound Adjectives

Like Homer, Walcott's singer uses compound adjectives to add a concrete vividness to his descriptions: *sea-smart* Odysseus, *smoke-blue* islands, *rock-steady* woman. Point out to students that each of these compound adjectives consists of a noun and a related adjective that, together, increase the descriptive power of the expression.

Have students tell in their own words what they think each of the following compound adjectives means: *rosy-fingered* dawn, *wine-dark* sea, *ivory-wristed* goddess. Then ask students to combine modern nouns and adjectives to create some contemporary compound adjectives of their own—for example, *computer-savvy* student or *fashion-conscious* model.

EPILOGUE

BILLY BLUE *(Sings)*

I sang of that man against whom the sea still rages,
Who escaped its terrors, that despair could not destroy,

9

Since that first blind singer, others will sing down the ages
20 Of the heart in its harbour, then long years after Troy,
after Troy.

And a house, happy for good, from a swallow's omen,
Let the trees clap their hands, and the surf whisper amen.

For a rock, a rock, a rock, a rock-steady woman
Let the waves clap their hands and the surf whisper amen.

25 For that peace which, in their mercy, the gods allow men.
(Fade. Sound of surf.)

Literary Analysis
**Contemporary
Interpretations** Which
words suggest that
the story of Homer's
Odyssey will always be
meaningful?

Thinking About the Selection

1. **Respond:** Do you think the speaker is someone whom you would like to know? Explain.
2. **(a) Recall:** In the Prologue, who is the speaker's "main man"?
   (b) Interpret: What is the speaker's attitude toward this "main man"?
3. **(a) Recall:** What is the speaker's name? **(b) Infer:** What type of music does the speaker sing? **(c) Analyze:** Considering the loneliness, death, and defeat that occur in Homer's *Odyssey,* why is the speaker's musical style appropriate?
4. **(a) Recall:** How is Penelope described in the Epilogue?
   (b) Infer: What seems to be the speaker's attitude toward Penelope?
5. **(a) Generalize:** Overall, which elements from Homer's *Odyssey* seem most interesting to Walcott? **(b) Evaluate:** Do you think the poet treats the original text with respect? Why or why not?

Prologue and Epilogue from *The Odyssey* ■ 1033

Differentiated
Instruction   Solutions for All Learners

Strategy for Less Proficient Readers
Students may need to hear Walcott's poem read aloud to grasp the connection between Homer and Blind Billy Blue. Remind them that Homer (or the long line of poet/performers he represents) was a blind singer and entertainer. Have students read along as they listen to the recording on the **Listening to Literature Audio CD.**

Strategy for Gifted/Talented Students
Billy Blue sings the blues in these passages. Suggest that students prepare a performance of the Prologue and Epilogue as a blues song. Ask students to find instrumental music or recordings to accompany the text. The performer might read or sing the passages to the blues rhythms.

9 Literary Analysis
**Contemporary
Interpretations**

- **Ask** students the Literary Analysis question: Which words suggest that the story of the *Odyssey* will always be meaningful?
  Answer: "Others will sing down the ages" suggests that the story will always be meaningful.

- **Ask** students: What do you think is the meaning of the story that will last so long?
  Possible responses: The meaning may be that one should never give up; that resourcefulness is the most valuable quality a hero can have; or that it is possible to be a hero in every age and culture.

ASSESS

Answers

1. **Possible response:** Students may say that they would like to know the speaker because he speaks in the idiom of popular culture.

2. (a) Odysseus is the speaker's "main man." (b) He admires Odysseus for his courage, intelligence, and resourcefulness.

3. (a) The speaker is Blind Billy Blue. (b) The speaker sings blues. (c) The blues often focus on loss, loneliness, and suffering.

4. (a) Penelope is described as "rock-steady." (b) The speaker admires Penelope for her endurance and steadfastness.

5. (a) Walcott seems most interested in the personal elements of the tale, the ability of Odysseus and Penelope to endure, and their relationship with each other. (b) **Possible response:** Walcott treats it with respect because he is true to the action and theme of the original.

⑩ Critical Viewing

Possible response: The journey of Odysseus is suggested by the picture's vast expanse of open sea and sky, its sense of loneliness and isolation, and its suggestion of adventure beyond the horizon.

⑩ ▲ **Critical Viewing** Which aspects of this image relate to Odysseus' journey? **[Connect]**

ITHACA

Constantine Cavafy

When you start on your journey to Ithaca,
then pray that the road is long,
full of adventure, full of knowledge.
⑪ Do not fear the Lestrygonians[1]
5 and the Cyclopes and the angry Poseidon.
You will never meet such as these on your path,
if your thoughts remain <u>lofty</u>, if a fine
emotion touches your body and your spirit.
You will never meet the Lestrygonians,
10 the Cyclopes and the fierce Poseidon,
if you do not carry them within your soul,
if your soul does not raise them up before you.

Then pray that the road is long.
That the summer mornings are many,
15 that you will enter ports seen for the first time
with such pleasure, with such joy!
Stop at Phoenician markets,
and purchase fine merchandise,
mother-of-pearl and corals, amber and ebony,

---

1. Lestrygonians (les tri gŏ′ nē ənz) cannibals who destroy all of Odysseus' ships except his own and kill the crews.

Vocabulary Builder
lofty (lôf′ tē) *adj.* very high; noble

⑫ Reading Check

What advice does the speaker give about meeting the Lestrygonians?

Ithaca ■ 1035

1035

Literary Analysis
Contemporary Interpretations

- **Ask** students the Literary Analysis question: How does Odysseus' desire for an end to his journey differ from the contemporary poet's attitude toward the journey?
  Answer: Odysseus faces life-threatening dangers and wants to reach home as soon as possible. The contemporary poet says not to hurry but to savor all the experiences along the way.

Concept Connector

Have students refer to the cluster diagrams they made before reading the poems. Ask them to describe any new insights they have gained about what it can mean to be a hero.

⬅️

ASSESS

Answers

1. **Possible response:** Many students may say that a journey of adventure appeals to them.

2. (a) People can avoid them by maintaining lofty thoughts and fine emotions, and by not carrying the Lestrygonians and the Cyclops within their souls.
   (b) **Possible response:** People often create their own opportunities or difficulties.

3. (a) People should pray for a long road, many summer mornings, and entrance into new ports.
   (b) Activities linked to these prayers are stopping at markets, buying fine things, and learning from those with knowledge.

4. (a) Ithaca marks the end of the journey. (b) Ithaca might be old age or death.

5. (a) **Possible response:** Even if the destination is disappointing, it is the experience gained that matters. (b) Most students may agree with the emphasis on the importance of the journey.

6. (a) **Possible response:** The speaker might have advised Odysseus to travel slowly and, if possible, to learn all he could from each encounter. (b) Students may agree and say that that is the best way to live life.

---

20 and pleasurable perfumes of all kinds,
buy as many pleasurable perfumes as you can;
visit hosts of Egyptian cities,
to learn and learn from those who have knowledge.

Always keep Ithaca fixed in your mind.
25 To arrive there is your ultimate goal.
But do not hurry the voyage at all.
🔞 It is better to let it last for long years;
and even to anchor at the isle when you are old,
rich with all that you have gained on the way,
30 not expecting that Ithaca will offer you riches.

Ithaca has given you the beautiful voyage.
Without her you would never have taken the road.
But she has nothing more to give you.

And if you find her poor, Ithaca has not <u>defrauded</u> you.
35 With the great wisdom you have gained, with so much experience,
You must surely have understood by then what Ithaca means.

Thinking About the Selection

1. **Respond:** Does the journey described in this poem appeal to you? Explain.

2. **(a) Recall:** According to the speaker, how can you avoid meeting the Lestrygonians, the Cyclopes, and Poseidon? **(b) Infer:** Why might a person carry such terrors as these in his or her own soul?

3. **(a) Recall:** What three things does the speaker say you should pray for on the journey to Ithaca? **(b) Connect:** What activities and pleasures are linked to these prayers?

4. **(a) Recall:** According to the speaker, why is Ithaca important? **(b) Interpret:** What might Ithaca symbolize for the poet?

5. **(a) Interpret:** What message is conveyed in the last three lines of the poem? **(b) Assess:** Do you agree with this message? Explain.

6. **(a) Speculate:** What advice might the speaker have given to Odysseus during his long journey? **(b) Take a Position:** Do you agree with this advice? Explain.

Literary Analysis
Contemporary Interpretations How does Odysseus' desire for an end to his journey differ from the contemporary poet's attitude toward the journey?

Vocabulary Builder
defrauded (dē frôd´ id) *v.* cheated

Vocabulary Development

Vocabulary Knowledge Rating
When students have completed reading and discussing "An Ancient Gesture," "Siren Song," "Prologue and Epilogue," and "Ithaca," have them take out their **Vocabulary Knowledge Rating Chart.** Read the words aloud once more and have students rate their knowledge of the words again in the After Reading column. Clarify any words that are still problematic.

Have students write their own definition and example or sentence in the appropriate column. Then have students complete the **Vocabulary Builder Practice** activities on p. 1037. Encourage students to use the words in further discussion and written work about the poems. Remind them that they will be accountable for these words on the Selection Test.

Apply the Skills

An Ancient Gesture • *Siren Song* • **Prologue and Epilogue from** *The Odyssey* • *Ithaca*

Comparing Contemporary Interpretations

1. The author of each **contemporary interpretation** in this section uses Homer's ideas as inspiration for new ideas. Use a chart like the one shown to explain how each poem is like and unlike Homer's *Odyssey.*

2. Select one poem in this section, and identify the comment the poet is making about modern life. Support your explanation with details from your completed chart.

3. **(a)** Identify an **allusion** in two of the poems. **(b)** Explain what the reference adds to the meaning of the poem. **(c)** Tell which allusion you think is more effective, and why.

Writing to Compare Literary Works

Each poet in this section finds something valuable in Homer's *Odyssey* to use in his or her literary work. In an essay, discuss specific ways in which Odysseus' journey provides worthwhile material for modern-day writers. Use the following questions to get started:

- What is each contemporary author's reason for writing?
- What conflicts or situations in Homer's *Odyssey* might be viewed very differently by modern-day writers?
- What modern-day conflict or situation does Homer help each poet address?
- Which poem did you enjoy most? Why?

Vocabulary Builder

Practice For each item, write a sentence in which you correctly use the given word pair.

1. authentic; genuine
2. picturesque; pleasing
3. siege; danger
4. lofty; challenge
5. defrauded; honest

Apply the Skills ■ 1037

QuickReview

Contemporary Interpretation: a present-day literary work that refers to an ancient work to convey contemporary ideas

Allusion: reference to a well-known person, place, event, literary work, or work of art

Go Online
Assessment
For: Self-test
Visit: www.PHSchool.com
Web Code: epa-6604

1. **Sample responses:** "An Ancient Gesture": reflects Penelope's sorrow and endurance, but portrays Odysseus as manipulative and less heroic. "Siren Song": uses mythological creature; but portrays Siren as a reluctant destroyer. "Prologue and Epilogue": tells the tale of heroic adventure; but uses modern popular idiom, puts greater emphasis on Penelope. "Ithaca": uses image of journey; but portrays journey as opportunity for discovery and self-development.

2. **Possible response:** In "An Ancient Gesture," the poet says that modern life is just as full of sorrow and loneliness as ancient life.

3. (a) In "Ithaca," the poet alludes to the Lestrygonians. In "Prologue and Epilogue," the poet alludes to Penelope as the "rock-steady woman." (b) The allusions bring in everything that the reader knows about them from reading the *Odyssey*. (c) **Possible response:** The allusion to the Lestrygonians in "Ithaca" is more effective because it relates a reference from an ancient tale to a modern viewpoint: People create their own monsters.

Writing to Compare Literary Works

- Have students use the bulleted questions to develop their ideas.

- Encourage students to incorporate the expressive vocabulary words: *integrate, manifest, confront,* and *enlighten.*

Six Traits Focus

✔	Ideas	✔	Word Choice
✔	Organization		Sentence Fluency
	Voice		Conventions

Vocabulary Builder
Sample responses:

1. Michael knew the painting was *authentic* when he saw the *genuine* signature.

2. The *picturesque* view would be *pleasing* to any artist.

3. The city was under *siege* and in *danger* of destruction.

4. His goals were *lofty*, but this time the *challenge* was too difficult.

5. They *defrauded* the *honest* investors who trusted them.

1037

Reading and Vocabulary Skills Review

In this Skills Review, students apply the skills taught in Part 1. The test format gives students practice in taking standardized tests. The result of this review test will help you check students' readiness for the **Benchmark Test** for Unit 6, Part 1.

Applying Reading Skill

Read the passage with students. Guide them in identifying the clues to determine Telemachus's emotions item 1: Tell students to notice the tone of disbelief in Telemachus's words. If necessary, have students reread the instruction on p. 946 before having them complete the remaining items on their own.

Applying Vocabulary Skills

Have students review the instruction on prefixes and word roots on p. 947. Remind students to apply their knowledge about prefixes and word roots to the items on the test. Provide students with these words: *contradict* and *technical*. Then have students identify the prefix *contra-* and the word root *-techni-*. Explain how the prefix and word root contribute to the words' meanings.

Tips for Test Taking

Students are often overwhelmed when taking a long, standardized test—especially when they encounter difficult questions. Remind students to pace themselves during the test. By continuing to work on questions, instead of spending excessive time on a single difficult question, students have a greater chance of answering more questions, and they may find that the next questions help to clarify what was really asked in a previous question that they had skipped.

Reading: Analyzing Cultural and Historical Context

Directions: *Questions 1–5 are based on the following selection.*

> [Telemachus speaks.] "You cannot
> be my father Odysseus! Meddling spirits
> conceived this trick to twist the knife in me!
> 1040 No man of woman born could work these wonders
> by his own craft, unless a god came into it
> with ease to turn him young or old at will.
> I swear you were in rags and old,
> and here you stand like one of the immortals!"
>
> 1045 Odysseus brought his ranging mind to bear and said:
> "This is not princely, to be swept
> away by wonder at your father's presence.
> No other Odysseus will ever come,
> for he and I are one, the same; his bitter
> 1050 fortune and his wanderings are mine.
> Twenty years gone, and I am back again
> on my own island.
> As for my change of skin,
> that is a charm [the goddess] Athena, Hope of Soldiers,
> uses as she will; . . .

—from the *Odyssey*

1. **Telemachus realizes his father has returned. What common human emotions does he express in the first three lines?**
   A anger and hatred
   B surprise and shock
   C fear
   D love

2. **What does Telemachus believe caused his father to appear to be an old man?**
   A his father's tricks
   B meddling spirits
   C trickery
   D time

3. **How is what Odysseus tells his son in lines 1048–1050 similar to what any father might tell a son?**
   A He scolds him for being easily tricked.
   B He tells him to behave appropriately.
   C He tells him to believe the gods.
   D He scolds him for not recognizing his own father.

4. **According to the passage, what did the Greeks believe about the gods?**
   A They were cruel and vengeful.
   B They did not care about human beings.
   C They could affect the lives of humans.
   D They were all-powerful.

1038 ■ *Themes in Literature: Heroism*

ASSESS

Answers

1. B	9. B
2. B	10. C
3. B	11. A
4. A	12. C
5. C	13. B
6. C	14. C
7. A	15. A
8. A	

Assessment Practice

Vocabulary

Directions: *Choose the letter of the word that best completes the sentence.*

5. Jerry's playing _____ was remarkable.
   A controversy
   B complex
   C technique
   D impact

6. The plot was so _____ that few could follow it.
   A complex
   B confirmed
   C controversial
   D deliberate

7. He found it difficult to _____ the value of the art.
   A contemplate
   B complicate

   C diminish
   D appraise

8. The story caused a great deal of _____.
   A complexity
   B controversy
   C technique
   D appraisal

9. The board met to _____ the appointment of the new president.
   A impact
   B diminish
   C confirm
   D complicate

Directions: *Using the definition of the word roots, choose the word that best fits the context of the sentence.*

10. Andy needed _____ assistance to fix the problem.
    A technical
    B contrary
    C contradictory
    D technocratic

11. The new _____ allowed them to communicate more easily.
    A technography
    B contravention
    C technology
    D technocrat

12. In _____ to the inexperience of his opponent, Julio had years of experience in the sport.
    A contravention

    B contradistinction
    C technography
    D technology

13. He attempted to _____ the law by using a false identification card.
    A contradict
    B technographic
    C contravene
    D technologically

14. The evidence was so _____ that the jury could not agree on a verdict.
    A contradictory
    B technographic
    C technological
    D contrapuntal

Reading and Vocabulary Skills Review ■ *1039*

If students answer any of these questions incorrectly, have them review the instruction on the following pages in Part 1 before taking the **Benchmark Test.**

Question	Page(s) Where Instruction Is Located:
1	948, 992
2	948, 992
3	948, 992
4	948, 999
5	947
6	947
7	947
8	947
9	947
10	947,1020
11	947,1020
12	947, 990
13	947, 990
14	947, 990

Benchmark

Administer the **Benchmark Test** for Unit 6, Part 1. If the Benchmark Test reveals that some students need further work, use the Interpretation Guide to determine the appropriate reteaching page in the **Reading Kit.** You will also find the same instruction and practice available on **Success Tracker.**

Go **Online**   **For:** Interactive
—Vocabulary   Crossword Puzzles
Visit: www.PHSchool.com
Web Code: epj-5601
Give students this Web Code to access interactive crossword puzzles using Academic Vocabulary and Vocabulary Skill words from Part 1.

Meeting Your Standards

Students will

1. write a timed essay.
2. use writing strategies to generate ideas and to plan, organize, evaluate, and revise a timed essay.
3. apply grammar skills.

Writing Genres

Using the Form Point out to students that timed essays are often incorporated into other types of writing. Many jobs require employees to write quick responses to questions.

Writing Workshop

Work in Progress

If students have done the **Work-in-Progress** assignments throughout Part 1, suggest that they look through their recorded ideas prior to the timed writing.

OES **Online Essay Scorer**

A writing prompt for this mode of writing can be found on the *PH Online Essay Scorer* at PHSuccessNet.com.

Prewriting

- Remind students that when **choosing a topic,** they should select topics that they can easily list three details about.

- When **gathering details,** students should relate their main ideas to the key words in the prompt.

Six Traits Focus

✔ Ideas	Word Choice	
✔ Organization	Sentence Fluency	
Voice	Conventions	

Writing and Grammar Interactive Textbook CD-ROM

Students can use the following tools as they complete their timed essays:

- Chart
- Transition Word Bin

Writing for Assessment: Timed Essay

Teachers often use **timed essays,** written responses to prompts or questions, to measure your mastery of essential skills. Usually, the essay must be completed within a specific—and brief—time period. Use the steps in this workshop to sharpen your skills in writing a timed essay.

Assignment Write a timed essay in response to this prompt, or ask your teacher to provide you with one.

- In an *essay,* identify and discuss a character from a literary work or a film who was brave in the face of danger.

What to Include: Your timed essay should feature these elements:

- a direct response to the test question or prompt
- a clear, well-supported thesis statement or main idea
- specific information about the topic drawn from your knowledge
- a clear organization
- on-time completion
- error-free grammar, including correct sentence formation

To preview the criteria on which your timed essay may be assessed, see the rubric on page 1044.

Prewriting

Spend about a quarter of your time prewriting.

Choosing Your Topic

Review the prompts. When you are given a choice among questions, choose the one that relates to the topic you know the best. Or, choose the question that engages your strongest skills.

Gathering Details

Clarify the question. Circle the verbs in the assignment that define what is expected. Use these key words to direct your response.

- **Analyze:** examine how various elements contribute to the whole.
- **Describe:** give main features and examples of each.
- **Compare and contrast:** stress how two works or other items are alike and different.
- **Discuss:** support a generalization with facts and examples.
- **Explain:** clarify by probing reasons, causes, results, and effects.
- **Defend:** support your position with examples from the text.

After reviewing the question, write a sentence to express the idea you will develop. Then, gather a few details to support this idea.

1040 ■ Themes in Literature: Heroism

Using the Form

You will use writing for assessment strategies in the following situations:

- end-of-year tests
- standardized tests
- college entrance exams, such as SAT and ACT

Work in Progress

Review the work you did on pages 943, 991, and 1021.

Teaching Resources

Unit 6 Resources
Writing Workshop: Timed Essay, p. 67
Writing Workshop: Integrating Grammar Skills: Revising Fragments and Run-on Sentences, p. 68

General Resources
Rubrics for Writing for Assessment, pp. 73–74

Graphic Organizer Transparencies:
Outline, p. 237

Drafting

Spend about half your time drafting.

Make a quick outline. Start with a sketch, or brief outline, of your essay. State your thesis in the *introduction*. In the *body* of the essay, present at least two main points that support your thesis. In the *conclusion*, restate the answer to the essay question and sum up your main points.

Fill in the details. Using your outline, draft your response, incorporating facts, examples and quotations that support your ideas. Do not include a detail unless you can connect it to your thesis.

Revising

Spend about a quarter of your time revising and editing.

Revising Your Overall Structure

Revise for Unity. You will not be able to do a complete revision of your draft. When you have finished writing, compare the first paragraph of your essay with the last:

- The first paragraph should contain a focus or thesis that clearly responds to the essay question.

- The final paragraph should restate your thesis and summarize your supporting evidence.

- If the main points of the first and final paragraphs do not connect, revise either paragraph to make the writing more coherent. Add transitions or more information in the body paragraphs.

Revising Word Choice

Revise for formal language. Neatly replace informal or vague words with more appropriate and formal language.

Informal: The railroad was the *thing* that most contributed to the
success of new businesses.

Formal: The railroad was the *factor* that most contributed to the
success of new businesses.

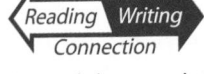

To read the complete student model, see page 1043.

Student Model: Revising a Conclusion

I think that Jackie Joyner-Kersee and Stevie Wonder are admirable for overcoming their disabilities. ∧Stevie Wonder overcame blindness to bring music to the world. Joyner-Kersee stunned us with her athleticism, despite her asthma. They teach me to never give up.

The writer summarizes his supporting arguments to give greater weight and clarity to his thesis.

Writing Workshop ■ 1041

Drafting

- Remind students that their outlines should not be formal or elaborate, but should reflect the key points within the introduction, body and conclusion.

- Advise students that, since they will not have time to make a clean final copy, they should, if possible, write their drafts on every other line of their papers. This will provide space to insert changes and corrections.

Refer students to the Outline in the Graphic Organizer Transparencies, p. 237.

Six Traits Focus

Ideas		Word Choice
✔ Organization		Sentence Fluency
Voice		Conventions

Writing and Grammar, Gold Level
Students will find additional instruction on drafting a timed essay in Chapter 14, Section 2.

Revising

- Tell students to make sure that all of the supporting evidence is restated in the final paragraph.

- Remind students that timed essays have an audience of well-educated adults. Explain that word choice should be appropriate for that audience unless otherwise indicated.

Six Traits Focus

Ideas	✔	Word Choice
✔ Organization		Sentence Fluency
✔ Voice	✔	Conventions

Writing and Grammar, Gold Level
Students will find additional instruction on revising a timed essay in Chapter 14, Section 3.

Tips for
Using Rubrics

- Before students begin work on this assignment, have them preview the Rubric for Self-Assessment on p. 1044 to know what is expected.

- Review the Assessment criteria in class. Before students use the Rubric for Self-Assessment, work with them to rate the student model by applying one or two criteria to it.

- If you wish to assess students' timed essays with either a 4-point or a 6-point scoring rubric, see *General Resources*, pp. 73–74.

Integrating Grammar Skills

- Write the following "sentences" on the board, and have students identify each as a fragment or a run-on:

  1. *Children love playing basketball they love playing baseball as well.*

  2. *Even though I tried.*

  Answers: 1. run-on 2. fragment

- Have students revise the sentence fragments in the following passage and note whether they corrected them by attachment or expansion:

  I have always enjoyed waterskiing. Because of its excitement. Skidding across the water. You feel like you could fly. Fantastic feeling!

  Possible response: *I have always enjoyed waterskiing because of its excitement.* (attachment) *Skidding across the water, you feel like you could fly.* (attachment) *It's a fantastic feeling!* (expansion)

- Have students revise the following run-on sentences, using the method that they think is most appropriate:

  1. *Misha won the first race she lost the second one.*

  2. *My brother's stomach ached, he had eaten too many cookies.*

  3. *The dog scraped at the back door, when I opened the door he shot out into the yard.*

  4. *Neil works at the record store he plays guitar at the coffee shop.*

  Possible response:

  1. *Misha won the first race, but she lost the second one.*

  2. *My brother's stomach ached; he had eaten too many cookies.*

  3. *The dog scraped at the back door. When I opened the door he shot out into the yard.*

  4. *Neil works at the record store, and he plays guitar at the coffee shop.*

- Tell students that when they are scanning their essays for fragments and run-ons, they should concentrate on each sentence in their essay individually.

Writing and Grammar, Gold Level

Students will find additional instruction on revising choppy sentences in Chapter 22, Section 4.

Integrating Grammar Skills

Revising to Correct Fragments and Run-ons

Sentence errors are common in writing that is done for assessment. A **fragment** is a group of words that does not express a complete thought but is punctuated as if it were a sentence. A **run-on** is two or more complete sentences that are not properly joined or separated.

Identifying and Correcting Fragments Fragments incomplete thoughts express. Often, they offer information that belongs to a nearby sentence. Correct fragments by attaching them to these sentences.

> **Fragment:** They waited at the bus stop. *Huddled under an umbrella.*
> **Revised:** They waited at the bus stop, huddled under an umbrella.

Other fragments can be corrected through expansion—adding the words needed to make complete sentence.

> **Fragment:** *As long as you agree to help.*
> **Expanded:** I will wash the car as long as you agree to help.

Identifying and Correcting Run-ons Run-ons include sentences that are fused without any punctuation at all or that are linked by only a comma.

> **Fused:** She speaks Spanish fluently she does not speak Italian at all.
> **Comma splice:** She speaks Spanish fluently, she does not speak Italian at all.

Three Ways to Correct a Run-on Sentence

Use an appropriate end mark to separate a run-on into two sentences. Begin the second sentence with a capital letter.	She speaks Spanish fluently. She does not speak Italian at all.
Use a comma and a coordinating conjunction, such as *and, but, or, for, and nor,* to combine two related independent clauses.	She speaks Spanish fluently, but she does not speak Italian at all.
Use a semicolon to connect two closely related ideas.	She speaks Spanish fluently; she does not speak Italian at all.

Apply It to Your Editing

Scan the body paragraphs of your timed essay for fragments and run-ons by looking for sentences that seem too short or too long. Neatly correct any sentence problems you find using the strategies that have been presented.

1042 ■ *Themes in Literature: Heroism*

Prentice Hall Writing and Grammar Connection: Chapter 22, Section 4

Tips for Test Taking

- **Read the question.** Tell students to read the prompt carefully and to circle key words. Remind them to make sure that the thesis and details relate to the prompt.

- **Deal with the time limitation.** Make sure that students can see a clock or a watch or that someone announces times during the writing process.

- **Practice.** Practice timed writing situations with students so that working within a time frame becomes less stressful. For example, have students quickly formulate a thesis for a prompt or write a paragraph in fifteen minutes.

Student Model: Eddie Harris
Chicago, IL

Question: *In an essay, discuss how someone you admire overcame an obstacle in order to succeed.*

The best way to overcome a disability is to face it head-on and not let it prevent you from achieving great things. This is the lesson I draw from the lives of two people whom I admire—the musician Stevie Wonder and the track-and-field star Jackie Joyner-Kersee. I respect them for their courage and strength in overcoming obstacles. Both are African Americans with disabilities who defied obstacles in order to be successful in their fields.

Stevie Wonder became blind after he was born prematurely and received too much oxygen. But that did not stop him from becoming one of the best musicians ever. He started out singing rock and roll songs outside a church in Detroit. Eventually, he found his way to Motown Studios at a time when Motown was one of the top recording studios in America. There his career skyrocketed. He became one of the best Motown singers even though he was only ten years old.

He has since been nominated for more Grammy awards than any other musician. His blindness is no disability for him. On the music charts, Stevie Wonder opened the gates for a new sound . . . not just for African Americans but for everyone else as well.

Another person that I admire for the way she overcame obstacles is Jackie Joyner-Kersee, a famous track-and-field star. She was born in East St. Louis, Illinois, and her family was very poor. Her parents thought that track and field was inappropriate for a girl. When she was nine, she entered her first track-and-field competition. Even though she lost, she didn't give up. Jackie entered another race. Her parents were shocked when she won.

In the late 1980s, she was diagnosed with asthma. This has not interfered with her performance as an athlete. Jackie is a world champion in both the long jump and heptathlon and has many Olympic medals to prove it.

Jackie Joyner-Kersee continues to be a role model for young people with disabilities like me. I think that Jackie Joyner-Kersee and Stevie Wonder are admirable for overcoming their disabilities. Stevie Wonder overcame blindness to bring music to the world. Joyner-Kersee stunned us with her athleticism, despite her asthma. They teach me to never give up, no matter how intimidating the obstacles I face in life.

Eddie uses a general statement to introduce his response to the essay question.

The writer presents a thesis statement that focuses his answer to the essay question.

In the body of the essay, Eddie supports his general statement with specific factual information.

He concludes by restating his thesis and reinforcing it with personal insight.

Writing Workshop ■ *1043*

Student Model

- Explain that the Student Model is a sample and that their own essays may be longer.
- **Ask** students how the thesis statement focuses on the essay question.
  Answer: The thesis statement defines who the paper will be focusing on (two famous African Americans), what they had to overcome (disabilities), and how their success is being defined (notoriety in their chosen fields).
- Have students identify details that develop the paragraphs on Stevie Wonder. **Ask** students to explain how those details relate to the thesis.
  Possible responses: blind (obstacle), singing outside a church (defied obstacle), Motown (success), one of best at ten (success), nominated for most Grammies (success), opened gates for new sound (success)
- **Ask** students to identify details that develop the paragraphs on Jack Joyner-Kersee and to explain how those details relate to the thesis.
  Possible responses: born into poor family (obstacle), parents' feelings about track and field (obstacle), lost event but didn't give up (defied obstacle), won race (success), asthma (obstacle), world champion, Olympic medals (success).
- **Ask** students to identify the personal insight in the conclusion.
  Possible response: *They teach me to never give up, no matter how intimidating the obstacles I face in life.*

Writing Genres

Occasions for Writing a Timed Essay Tell students that they will encounter situations where they will have to form a timed response for assessment. For example, in college students might use this skill on college admittance tests, on tests and reports, and during questioning after presentations. In the workforce, students could have to use this skill on job applications, in job interviews, during questioning after presentations, and in memos.

Editing and Proofreading

To give students practice in making clear, readable changes to their drafts, have them revise a paragraph of their writing and exchange it with a partner to check for legibility.

Six Traits Focus

Ideas		Word Choice	
Organization		Sentence Fluency	
Voice		Conventions	✔

ASSESS

Publishing and Presenting

- Review the rubric with the study groups, and suggest that the group members use the rubric as a guide for recommending essay improvements.
- Have students give examples of how their scorer's comments will help them improve future essays.

Reflecting on Your Writing

- Ask students if they followed the advise for time management given in the workshop?
- Ask students whether they feel more comfortable with timed essays after completing the workshop. Will they feel more comfortable with future timed essays?

WG **Writing and Grammar, Gold Level**
Students will find additional guidelines for editing and proofreading, publishing and presenting, and reflecting in Chapter 14, Sections 4 and 5.

Editing and Proofreading

Check your draft to correct errors in spelling, grammar, and punctuation.

Focus on Legibility: Because you will not have time to make a clean copy of your final draft, make sure your revisions and corrections are clear and readable. Draw a single line through words you wish to delete, and use a caret [^] or an arrow to show where you are adding words.

Publishing and Presenting

Consider one of the following ways to share your writing:
Organize a study group. Compare your timed essay with those of your classmates. Discuss with the group the ways you could improve your essay writing.
Prepare for future exams. Use your essay as a study tool. Review the grade you received and the scorer's comments to help you improve future performance.

Reflecting on Your Writing

Writer's Journal Jot down your thoughts about writing a timed essay. Begin by answering these questions.
- What strategy in this workshop might best help you complete your next essay test?
- What do you find most challenging about taking an essay test?

Prentice Hall Writing and Grammar Connection: Chapter 14

Rubric for Self-Assessment

To assess your timed essay, use the following rubric:

Criteria	Rating Scale
	not very very
Focus: How clear is your thesis statement or main idea?	1 2 3 4 5
Organization: How logical is your organization?	1 2 3 4 5
Support/Elaboration: How effectively do you include specific information drawn from your experience, your reading, or class discussion?	1 2 3 4 5
Style: How direct is your response to the question or prompt?	1 2 3 4 5
Conventions: How correct is your grammar, especially your avoidance of fragments and run-ons?	1 2 3 4 5

1044 ■ Themes in Literature: Heroism

Tips for
Using Technology in Writing

If students are allowed to use computers for their test, they could use styling features, such as boldface, to introduce subheads that emphasize the organizational plan of their essays. They also could highlight their thesis statements and topic sentences to ensure that they have supplied and placed them effectively. If test constraints allow, they could use the *Thesaurus, Dictionary,* and *Spelling and Grammar* functions, under *Tools* on their toolbar, to edit and revise their work.

Compare and Contrast

Skills You Will Learn

Literary Analysis: *Protagonist and Antagonist*
Reading Skill: *Generating Questions After Reading*

Reading Skill: *Setting a Purpose for Reading*

Literary Analysis: *Author's Purpose and Philosophical Assumptions*
Reading Skill: *Using Self-Monitoring*

Literary Analysis: *Heroes in Tall Tale and Myth*

Literature You Will Read

Differentiated Instruction
Solutions for All Learners

Resources for Monitoring Progress

Unit 6 Resources
    Unit 6, Part 2 Diagnostic Test, pp. 76–78
    Unit 6, Part 2 Benchmark Test,
    pp. 161–166

Reading Kit

Success Tracker

Skills Overview
Reading Skill: Drawing Conclusions
- Generating questions after reading
- Using self-monitoring

Vocabulary Development
- Context Clues

Literary Analysis
- Protagonist and Antagonist
- Author's Purpose and Philosophical Assumptions: audience

Writing
- Comparison and Contrast Essay
- Work in Progress, pp. 1091, 1109

Monitoring Progress

Diagnose: Before you begin Part 2, administer the **Diagnostic Test** for Unit 6, Part 2. This test will identify students' level of readiness for the reading and vocabulary skills in Part 2. Use the **Interpretation Guide** for the Diagnostic Test to determine which students need help with prerequisite skills before beginning Part 2.

Preteach and Prepare: Use the information indicated in the **Interpretation Guide** to help students build prerequisite skills. In addition, prepare students by using the **Vocabulary Warm-up** activities and the **Reading Warm-up** activities as necessary for each selection set.

Teach: Use the instructional plan and resources provided to teach the skills and selections.

Assess: After students have completed Part 2, administer the **Benchmark Test** for Unit 6, Part 2. The test results will indicate which skills students have mastered and those on which they need more work.

Reteach: Use the Interpretation Guide to determine the appropriate reteaching pages from the **Reading Kit.**

Intervention: The prerequisite and reteaching pages are also available in the **Success Tracker.**

Introduce the Reading Skill

- Introduce the reading skill: compare and contrast. Explain that comparison and contrast allows the reader to see similarities and differences and thereby understand the motivations and actions of characters in a piece of literature.

- After reviewing the three strategies, stress the importance of determining the antagonist and protagonist in a piece of literature. Failure to identify the protagonist and antagonist early in the story can lead to misreading and confusion on the part of the reader. The use of comparison and contrast provides evidence to help the reader identify the roles of the characters.

Model the Reading Strategies

- Model how comparing and contrasting characters can help students to identify the characters' strengths and weaknesses. Write the following sentence on the board:

  Seeing that John did not understand the assignment, Suzanne offered to explain the work to him, while James turned away in disgust.

  Then ask these questions:

  What qualities can you see in Suzanne? (She is helpful, kind, knowledgeable, and patient.)

  What qualities do you see in James? (James is knowledgeable but lacks patience and compassion for those who do not understand.)

- Tell students that if they were to read a story about similar characters, the author would be likely to be subjective in his descriptions of each character. By comparing and contrasting these descriptions, the reader could determine which character was the protagonist and which was the antagonist.

- Reinforce that comparing and contrasting means identifying similarities and differences between two or more things.

Reading: Compare and Contrast

A **comparison** tells how two or more things are alike. A **contrast** tells how two or more things are different. When you compare and contrast, you identify similarities and differences between two or among more than two things.

Skills and Strategies You Will Learn in Part 2

- **to compare and contrast characters** to help **determine the protagonist and antagonist** in a piece of literature (p. 1048)
- **to generate questions after reading** to clarify comparisons and contrasts (p. 1048)
- **to compare and contrast ideas** to **self-monitor your reading** (p. 1098)
- **to set a purpose for reading** to focus on **comparing and contrasting.** (p. 1094)

Using the Skills and Strategies in Part 2

In Part 2, you will learn that **comparing and contrasting** is a basic reasoning skill that will help you analyze similarities and differences of elements within a text. For example, comparing and contrasting characters in a piece of literature will help you identify their strengths and weaknesses. After you **set a purpose for reading,** comparing and contrasting ideas will help you **monitor your reading.**

The following chart shows how you can apply these strategies.

Purpose: To identify differences in characters and in ideas

John — wealthy, private school, loves mountain climbing

well educated, concerned about environment

George — from farmland, public school, loves mountain biking

Professional Development

PMI Technique

Responding to literature is often a mixed experience. Not only do individuals vary in their likes and dislikes, but individuals often find stories that provoke strong emotions. The PMI activity allows students to build on their visceral responses as the basis for exploration and discussion.

Have students divide a sheet of paper into three columns, labeled as follows:

PLUS (what I like)
MINUS (what I don't like)
INTERESTING (what I find interesting)

As students are reading an assigned selection, ask them to make notes in each column. There is no requirement to write in each column. After students have completed reading, they share and discuss (or debate) what they have written.

Source: Kay Burke, How to Assess Authentic Learning, 1999. SkyLight Professional Development.

Academic Vocabulary: Words for Evaluating Literature

These words will also help you as you write and talk about your evaluation of the literary techniques and themes.

Word	Definition	Example Sentence
cogent *adj.*	convincing; powerfully appealing	He expressed a **cogent** argument in his defense.
significant *adj.*	important; full of meaning	The character's loss of the gold ring was a **significant** event in the story.
defect *n.*	an imperfection	His pride was a fatal **defect**.
compelling *v.*	forcing or pressuring	The importance of the quest was **compelling** him to continue despite the danger.
coherent *adj.*	orderly or logical; sticking together	His paper was **coherent**.

Vocabulary Skill: Context Clues

▶ A **word root** is the part of the word that contains its basic meaning.

In Part 2, you will learn

- the Latin word root *-sign-* (p. 1092)
- the Latin word root *-her-* (p. 1110)

WORD ROOTS	
-her-: "cling or stick"	-sign-: "signal; meaning"
We will adhere to the rules.	*Distant thunder signifies a storm.*
"We will stick to the rules."	"Distant thunder means a storm is coming"

Activity Write a sentence for each word. Explain how knowing the meaning of a root helps you understand the meaning of the sentence.

1. signature   **2.** signify   **3.** inherent

Reading and Vocabulary Skills Preview ■ 1047

Go Online For: Interactive
Vocabulary Crossword Puzzle
Visit: www.PHSchool.com
Web Code: epj-5602
Give students this Web Code to access an interactive crossword puzzle using Academic Vocabulary and Vocabulary Skill words from Part 2.

Introduce Academic Vocabulary

- Introduce the academic vocabulary: words for evaluating literature. Tell students that these words are useful when they write or discuss their evaluation of literary techniques and themes.
- Tell students to use these words as they discuss the selections in Part 2.

Introduce the Vocabulary Skill

- Introduce the vocabulary skill: context clues. Students can determine the meaning of an unfamiliar word by examining the other words surrounding it in a sentence.
- Point out that the Latin roots *-sign-* and *-her-* are used in many English words. Recognizing these roots can also help students define unfamiliar vocabulary words.
- Review the two suffixes on this page, their meanings, and the English words that contain these suffixes.
- Have students complete the activity and discuss any unclear answers.

Possible Answers:

1. Please write your *signature* on the bottom line so that the contract is official. The root *-sign-* means "signal or meaning," so knowing this meaning might help the reader to know that a *signature,* which is written, is a sign that the person agrees with the contract.

2. Does your raised hand *signify* your agreement? Knowing that the root *-sign-* means "signal or meaning" shows that the raised hand signals agreement.

3. Long hair is *inherent* in that species of dog. Because *-her-* means "cling or stick," inherent means that it is natural part of the species.

Planning Differentiated Instruction

Choosing Your Selection

You may use either selection to meet the lesson standards. The following guide will help you determine which of the two selections is more appropriate for your students.

Accessibility at a Glance

	Three Skeleton Key	**The Red-headed League**
Context	Life and death struggle with a mob of rats	Sherlock Holmes mystery story
Language	Subject-specific vocabulary	Difficult vocabulary; extensive amount of dialogue
Concept Level	Accessible (struggle for survival)	Challenging (complex mystery)
Literary Merit	Suspenseful	Classic
Lexile	1200L	1120L
Overall Rating	More accessible	More challenging

Because a number of factors help determine the relative accessibility of paired selections, the Lexile number of the more challenging selection may sometimes be lower than that of the more accessible selection.

Using the Other Selection You may use the other selection for homework or independent reading to reinforce the selection skills. If you use both selections, you can build a test for both using *ExamView*® Test Bank software.

Choosing Your Resources

[L1] Special Needs Students   **[L4]** Advanced Students

[L2] Below-Level Students   **[EL]** English Learners

[L3] All Students

FT Fast Track Instruction: To move the lesson more quickly, use the strategies and activities identified with **FT**.

Reading and Vocabulary Warm-ups provide support for below level students. **A** is for students reading two grades below level; **B** is for students reading one grade below level. For Selection Tests, **A** signifies "less challenging" and **B** "more challenging." For Graphic Organizer transparencies, **A** signifies "not filled in" and **B** "filled in."

Scaffolding for Less Proficient and Advanced Students

The leveled questions on Apply the Skills pages progress in the levels of thinking required to answer them. To address the needs of your different students, you may use the (a) level questions for your less proficient students, the (b) level with your on-level and advanced students. The occasional (c) level questions are appropriate for your advanced students.

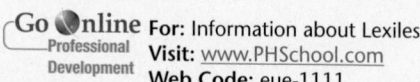

Go Online **For:** Information about Lexiles
Professional **Visit:** www.PHSchool.com
Development **Web Code:** eue-1111

Step-by-Step Teaching Guide	Pacing Guide
PRETEACH	
• Administer Vocabulary and Reading Warm-ups as necessary.	
• Introduce the Literary Analysis Skill: Protagonist and Antagonist. **FT**	10 min.
• Introduce the Reading Skill: Comparing and Contrasting. **FT**	10 min.
• Prepare students to read by teaching the selection vocabulary. **FT**	10 min.
• Build background and develop expressive vocabulary with Connecting to the Literature and Background.	10 min.
• Engage students' interest with the motivation activity.	10 min.
TEACH	
• Informally monitor comprehension while students read independently or in groups. **FT**	30 min.
• Monitor students' comprehension with the Reading Check notes.	as students read
• Reinforce vocabulary with Vocabulary Builder notes.	as students read
• Develop students' understanding of protagonist and antagonist with the Literary Analysis annotations. **FT**	5 min.
• Develop students' ability to compare and contrast with the Reading Skill annotations. **FT**	10 min.
ASSESS/EXTEND	
• Assess students' comprehension and mastery of the Reading Skill and Literary Analysis by having them answer the Apply the Skills questions. **FT**	35 min.
• Have students complete the Vocabulary Builder activities. **FT**	5 min.
• Apply students' ability to write journal entries with the Writing activity. **FT**	30-45 min. or homework
• Extend students' listening and speaking and research and technology skills with one or both of the Extend Your Learning activities.	15-30 min. or homework
• Have students complete the Vocabulary Skill and Grammar Lesson.	5 min.
• Monitor students' progress with the Assessment Practice.	20-40 min.
• Administer **Selection Test A** or **Selection Test B**. **FT**	15 min.

Resources

PRINT

	Three Skeleton Key	The Red-headed League
Unit 6 Resources		
Vocabulary Warm-up Word Lists [L1, L2, EL]	p. 79	p. 95
Vocabulary Warm-up Practice [L1, L2, EL]	p. 80	p. 96
Reading Warm-up A [L1, L2, EL]	p. 81	p. 97
Reading Warm-up B [L1, L2, L3]	p. 82	p. 98
General Resources		
Vocabulary Knowledge Rating Chart, p. 5 [L3]		
Anticipation Guide, p. 8–10 [L3]		

TRANSPARENCY

Graphic Organizer Transparencies		
Literary Analysis Graphic Organizer A [L3]	p. 212	p. 212
Literary Analysis Graphic Organizer B [L1, L2, EL]	p. 213	p. 214
Reading Skill Graphic Organizer A [L3]	p. 215	p. 217
Reading Skill Graphic Organizer B [L1, L2, EL]	p. 216	p. 218

PRINT

Reader's Notebook [L2]

Reader's Notebook: Adapted Version [L1]

Reader's Notebook: English Learner's Version [EL]

Unit 6 Resources		
Literary Analysis [L3]	p. 83	p. 99
Reading Skill [L3]	p. 84	p. 100
Vocabulary Builder [L3]	p. 85	p. 101

TECHNOLOGY

Listening to Literature Audio CDs [L2, EL]

Reader's Notebook: Adapted Version Audio CD [L1, L2]

PRINT

Unit 6 Resources		
Support for Writing [L3]	p. 86	p. 102
Support for Extend Your Learning [L3]	p. 87	p. 103
Enrichment [L4]	p. 88	p. 104
Selection Test A [L1, L2, EL]	pp. 89–91	pp. 107–109
Selection Test B [L3, L4]	pp. 92–94	pp. 110–112
Build Language Skills: Vocabulary: Latin root -sign-, p. 105 [L3]		
Build Language Skills: Grammar: Commas, p. 106 [L3]		

General Resources

Rubrics for Autobiographical Narrative, pp. 43–44 [L3]

TECHNOLOGY

Go Online: Research [L3]

Go Online: Self-test [L3]

ExamView® **Test Bank [L3]**

 Meeting Your Standards

Students will

1. **analyze and respond to literary elements.**
   - Literary Analysis: Protagonist and Antagonist

2. **read, comprehend, and analyze short stories.**
   - Reading Skill: Comparing and Contrasting
   - Reading Strategy: Generating Questions after Reading
   - Reading Check questions
   - Apply the Skills questions
   - Assessment Practice

3. **develop vocabulary.**
   - Vocabulary Builder
   - Latin root -sign-

4. **apply grammar skills.**
   - Commas

5. **develop writing proficiency.**
   - Work in Progress: Comparison-and-Contrast Essay
   - Journal entries

6. **extend learning.**
   - Listening and Speaking: Interview
   - Research and Technology: Oral Report

Block Scheduling: Use one 90-minute class period to preteach the skills and have students read the selection. Use a second 90-minute class period to assess students' mastery of skills, extend their learning, and monitor their progress.

Homework Suggestions

Following are possibilities for homework assignments.

- Support pages from *Unit 6 Resources*:
  Literary Analysis
  Reading Skill
  Vocabulary Builder
  Enrichment

- An Extend Your Learning project and the Writing assignment for your chosen selection may be completed over several days.

 Use this complete suite of powerful teaching tools to make lesson planning and testing quicker and easier.

 Use the Interactive Textbook (online and on CD-ROM) to make selections and activities come alive with audio and video support and interactive questions.

❶ Literary Analysis
Protagonist and Antagonist

- Tell students that in the selections, they will encounter *protagonists,* or main characters, whose choices and actions are of interest to the reader.

- Explain that an *antagonist* is a character or force that opposes the protagonist. Tell students that readers become interested in how the protagonist responds to the challenges presented by an antagonist. Point out that an antagonist may be external—another character or a force of nature]—or internal—the character's inner fears.

- Give students a copy of **Literary Analysis Graphic Organizer A** (*Graphic Organizer Transparencies,* p. 212). Have them use it to identify the protagonist and antagonist in a story as well as their goals, motives, and conflicts.

❷ Reading Skill
Comparing and Contrasting Characters

- Tell students that comparing and contrasting characters is identifying and contemplating their similarities and differences. Explain that characters in the stories they will read respond differently to a crisis or a mystery.

- Tell students that they can compare characters from within the same story, characters from different stories, or one character at different points in a story.

- Point out that when a character changes within the story, this change provides readers with an opportunity to compare and contrast the character at the beginning of a story, at interval points, and at the end.

- Lead students to understand that contrasts or differences between characters or within them help create a conflict.

- Have students return to the bulleted list of questions on p. 1048 as they read the story. Explain that these questions, in addition to their own questions, will help them track how, or if, a character changes over the course of a story.

Practice these skills with either "Three Skeleton Key" (p. 1050) or "The Red-headed League" (p. 1067).

❶ Literary Analysis

The **protagonist** is the chief character in a literary work. Some literary works also have an **antagonist**—a character or force that opposes the protagonist. The antagonist is often another character, but may also be an external force, such as nature.

Although the protagonist is not always an admirable or even a likeable character, readers are interested in what happens to him or her.

- The protagonist's motives may be universally understood feelings and goals, such as curiosity, or the search for love.
- The protagonist's conflict with the antagonist may represent a universal struggle, such as the conflict between good and evil.

As you read, fill in a chart like the one shown.

❷ Reading Skill

Comparing and contrasting characters is recognizing and thinking about their similarities and differences. You can compare different characters within a work, characters from different works, or a single character at different points. As you read, ask questions about each character whom you are comparing. Then, **generate questions after reading** that are specific to the story.

- What are the character's actions?
- What are the character's reasons for his or her actions?
- What qualities does the character demonstrate?

Use your questions and answers to think about the significance of the similarities and differences you discover.

Vocabulary Builder

Three Skeleton Key

- **lurched** (lʉrcht) *v.* moved awkwardly and suddenly (p. 1053) *The newborn calf lurched forward as he tried to stand.*
- **diminution** (dim′ ə nōō′ shən) *n.* lessening (p. 1058) *The players' diminution of enthusiasm caused them to play poorly.*
- **derisive** (di rī′ siv) *adj.* mocking (p. 1061) *The critic's derisive laugh offended the artist.*

The Red-headed League

- **introspective** (in′ trə spek′ tiv) *adj.* having to do with looking into one's own thoughts and feelings (p. 1080) *The touching movie put me in an introspective mood.*
- **vex** (veks) *v.* annoy (p. 1081) *My allergies continued to vex me throughout the spring.*
- **formidable** (fôr′ mə də bəl) *adj.* awe-inspiring (p. 1081) *Mt. Everest is a formidable sight.*

1048 ■ Themes in Literature: Heroism

Vocabulary Development

Vocabulary Knowledge Rating

Create a **Vocabulary Knowledge Rating Chart** for the selection you will teach from this set. Include the selection vocabulary from this page and the additional words students are asked to use at the end of Connecting to the Literature. These words will increase students' expressive vocabulary.

Give students a copy of the chart with the words on it. Introduce the words by reading them aloud and having students mark their rating in the Before Reading column. Urge them to be alert to these words as they read and discuss the selection because they will rate their knowledge of the words again after they finish.

If you wish, you may tally how many students know (or think they know) a word to gauge how much instruction you need to provide. As students read, point out the words and their context.

Build Understanding • *Three Skeleton Key*

❸ Background

Lighthouses A lighthouse, or "light," is a tower built on an island or other prominent point to warn ships away from treacherous areas near a coast. The tower is usually several stories high, with a large, bright, movable light at the top. Most lighthouses are now automated, but they used to be occupied by people who maintained and operated the light, moving the beam across the water when a ship approached. A lighthouse is often located on a key, which is a small island or a reef near a larger land mass.

❹ Connecting to the Literature

Reading/Writing Connection Lighthouse operators, like those in this story, often had little contact with the outside world during their shifts. Write a short paragraph describing the positive and negative aspects of such isolation. Use at least three of these words: *isolate, access, forgo, induce.*

READ MORE

George Toudouze
Histoire de la Marine

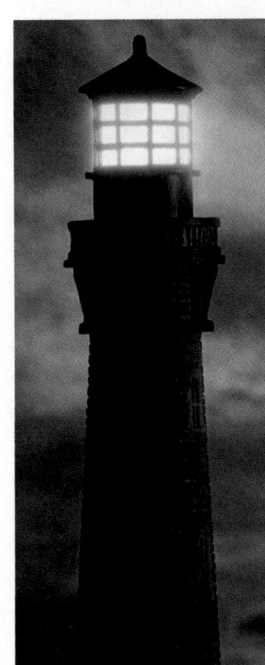

Meet the Author

George G. **Toudouze** (1877–1971)

The award-winning writer, editor, and scholar George Gustave Toudouze was born in Paris, France.

Writer of the Sea A maritime expert, Toudouze wrote nineteen books about the ocean and served as chief editor of *The French Maritime and Colonial League*. He also earned a doctorate of letters at the Sorbonne, one of the oldest and most distinguished universities in the world, and he went on to become a professor of history and dramatic literature at the Paris Conservatory. His claim to fame, however, rests entirely upon one story, "Three Skeleton Key," which was published in 1937 in *Esquire* magazine.

Fast Facts

▶ "Three Skeleton Key" is the only story of Toudouze's to appear in English.
▶ The story became the basis for a successful radio play, broadcast in 1949.

For: More information about the author
Visit: www.PHSchool.com
Web Code: epe-9607

Three Skeleton Key ■ 1049

---

❸ Background
Lighthouses

Lighthouses provide an unusual setting for short stories. A writer may select a lighthouse as the setting for a story in order to create a mood of loneliness or of contemplation. Traditionally, lighthouse operators were left alone for long periods of time. They tended to be independent souls who were reliable workers and content to spend time alone. When using this setting in a story, writers must be inventive to find a source of conflict to drive the story and help the characters develop.

❹ Connecting to the Literature

- Model use of the expressive vocabulary students are asked to use with these examples:
  1. Lighthouse operators agree to *isolate* themselves on an island for long periods of time.
  2. Today, lighthouse operators have plenty of *access* to the mainland via telephones and computers.
  3. Traditionally, lighthouse operators would *forgo* having active social lives while working their shifts.
  4. No one could *induce* a social butterfly to work in such isolation.
- Help students further develop their expressive vocabulary by providing these words: *anomaly, compel, drastic,* and *withdraw*. Encourage students to use these words as they discuss the selection.

Go Online For additional information about George G.
Author Link Toudouze, have students type in the Web Code and then select *George G. Toudouze*.

Differentiated Instruction — Solutions for All Learners

Support for Below-Level Students [L1, L2]

Unit 6 Resources
   Vocabulary Warm-up Word Lists, p. 79
   Vocabulary Warm-Up Practice, p. 80
   Reading Warm-up A, p. 81
   Selection Test A, pp. 89–91

Graphic Organizer Transparencies
   Literary Analysis Graphic Organizer Transparency B, p. 213

Reader's Notebook: Adapted Version

Adapted Reader's Notebook Audio CD

Support for English Learners [EL]

Unit 6 Resources
   Vocabulary Warm-up Lists, p. 79
   Vocabulary Warm-up Practice, p. 80
   Reading Warm-up A, p. 81

Reader's Notebook: English Learner's Version

Listening to Literature Audio CD

❶ Motivation

Prepare an **Anticipation Guide** (see *General Resources,* pp. 8–10) with the following statements:

- "Every man for himself" is a good strategy to follow during a crisis.
- Perseverance can lead to success.
- Dire situations can cause people to behave erratically.
- People always act similarly in a crisis.

Give students a copy of the prepared Anticipation Guide and have students mark their responses in the Me column. Have students discuss the statements in pairs or groups and mark the Guides again in the Group column.

Concept Connector ➡

Students will return to the Anticipation Guide after completing "Three Skeleton Key."

Learning Modalities
Visual/Spatial Learners

Have students compile a list of the words Toudouze uses on pp. 1054–1056 and later in the story to describe the rats. Have students use the details about the rats' appearance, sound, smell, and movement as the basis for a series of illustrations. Under their illustrations, have students write captions from the story that support their drawings.

❷ About the Selection

In "Three Skeleton Key," the narrator has just returned to the lighthouse on Three Skeleton Key after a short break from his duties. He is prepared for another monotonous period of service with his fellow lighthouse keepers, Le Gleo and Itchoua. Nine days after his return, however, Itchoua wakes the other two men in the middle of the night to watch the unusual movements of a large ship that is drifting toward the lighthouse. In daylight, the men realize, to their horror, that the ship has been overrun by a vicious swarm of rats that have killed the ship's crew. The ship runs aground at the lighthouse and the starving rats swarm over the lighthouse.

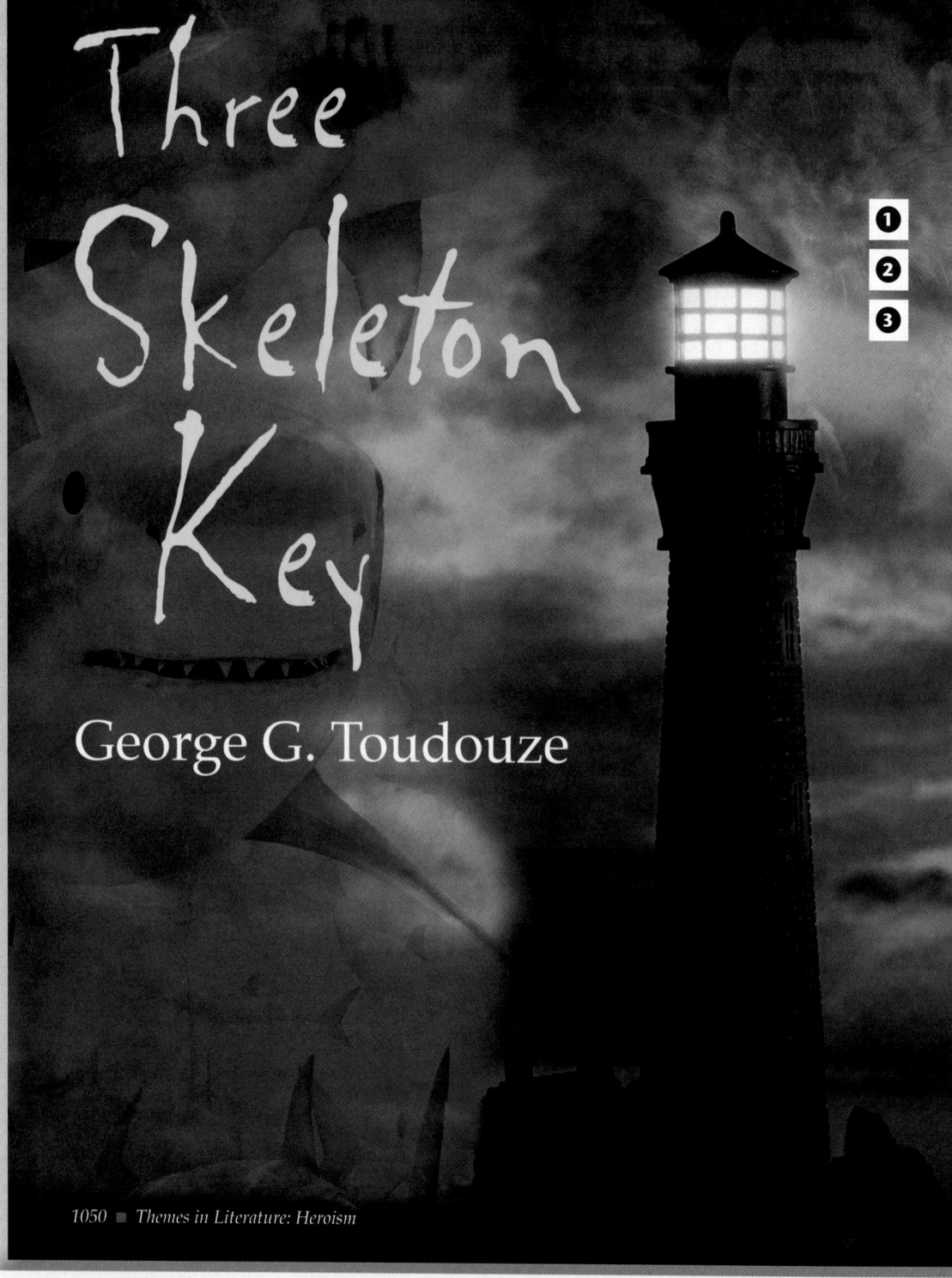

Three Skeleton Key

George G. Toudouze

❶
❷
❸

1050 ■ *Themes in Literature: Heroism*

Vocabulary Development

Multiple Meanings

Point out the word *key* on p. 1050. Tell students that *key* has multiple meanings. Write the following sentences on the board, and guide students in developing definitions for each use of the word *key.*

1. Use the *key* to unlock the door.
2. The computer will ask you to *key* in your password.
3. Getting plenty of rest is *key* to staying healthy.
4. The trip from the mainland to the *key* is a short one.

Review the meanings of the word and decide which definition best fits the use of the word *key* in the story's title.

Answers: 1. instrument for unlocking something; 2. to type data on a keyboard; 3. essential or important; 4. low-lying reef or island. Definition 4 best fits the story's title.

My most terrifying experience? Well, one does have a few in thirty-five years of service in the Lights, although it's mostly monotonous routine work—keeping the light in order, making out the reports.

When I was a young man, not very long in the service, there was an opening in a lighthouse newly built off the coast of Guiana,[1] on a small rock twenty miles or so from the mainland. The pay was high, so in order to reach the sum I had set out to save before I married, I volunteered for service in the new light.

Three Skeleton Key, the small rock on which the light stood, bore a bad reputation. It earned its name from the story of the three convicts who, escaping from Cayenne[2] in a stolen dugout canoe, were wrecked on the rock during the night, managed to escape the sea but eventually died of hunger and thirst. When they were discovered, nothing remained but three heaps of bones, picked clean by the birds. The story was that the three skeletons, gleaming with phosphorescent light,[3] danced over the small rock, screaming. . . .

But there are many such stories, and I did not give the warnings of the old-timers at the Isle de Sein[4] a second thought. I signed up, boarded ship, and in a month I was installed at the light.

Picture a gray, tapering cylinder, welded to the solid black rock by iron rods and concrete, rising from a small island twenty odd miles from land. It lay in the midst of the sea, this island, a small, bare piece of stone, about one hundred fifty feet long, perhaps forty wide. Small, barely large enough for a man to walk about and stretch his legs at low tide.

This is an advantage one doesn't find in all lights, however, for some of them rise sheer from the waves, with no room for one to move save within the light itself. Still, on our island, one must be careful, for the rocks were treacherously smooth. One misstep and down you would fall into the sea—not that the risk of drowning was so great, but the waters about our island swarmed with huge sharks who kept an eternal patrol around the base of the light.

Still, it was a nice life there. We had enough provisions to last for months, in the event that the sea should become too rough for the supply ship to reach us on schedule. During the day we would work about the light, cleaning the rooms, polishing the metalwork and the lens and reflector of the light itself, and at night we would sit on

---

1. **Guiana** (gē an´ə) region on the northern coast of South America.
2. **Cayenne** (kī en´) capital city of French Guiana.
3. **phosphorescent** (fäs´fə res´ənt) **light** a glowing light produced by certain natural chemical reactions.
4. **Isle de Sein** (ēl´ də sen´) island off the northwestern coast of France.

Literary Analysis
Protagonist and Antagonist Which details in the first four paragraphs suggest that the narrator is the central character in this story?

❺ ✓ Reading Check

What is especially dangerous about the waters surrounding Three Skeleton Key?

Three Skeleton Key ■ 1051

❸ **Critical Thinking**
Analyze

• Invite students to look at the illustration and the text on p. 1050 for clues to the story.

• **Ask** students to identify what clues the illustration provides and to make predictions based on them. **Possible response:** The illustration suggests that the story involves a lighthouse. The darkness of the illustration and the lettering of the title both suggest that the story will be scary or eerie.

• Have students return to their predictions as they read the story to confirm or update them.

❹ **Literary Analysis**
Protagonist and Antagonist

• Remind students that the protagonist of a story is its central and most compelling character.

• **Ask** students to respond to the Literary Analysis question: Which details in the first four paragraphs suggest that the narrator is the central character in this story? **Answer:** The narrator tells the story using the first person, so he is probably important to the story. Also, the narrator is focusing on details about his own life, rather than details about someone else's life.

• **Ask** students what they know about the narrator/ protagonist after reading the first four paragraphs. **Answer:** The narrator is no longer a young man. He became a lighthouse operator in Guiana in order to make money. The narrator was not frightened by scary stories about the island.

• Discuss with students whether they think the narrator is trustworthy and will tell a story that they can believe. Elicit from students that the narrator seems honest and not easily frightened or upset.

❺ **Reading Check**

Answer: Huge sharks swarm the waters around the lighthouse.

❻ Critical Viewing

Answer: Like the ship in the story, the ship in the photograph has several masts. It is a sailing ship, which establishes that the time period is in the past.

❼ Reading Skill
Comparing and Contrasting Characters

- **Ask** students the Reading Skill question: What difference in the characters' ages does the narrator point out.
  Answer: Itchoua is twelve or so years older than the other two men.

- **Ask** students what else they learn about the two characters, Le Gleo and Itchoua.
  Answer: Le Gleo is a Breton. Itchoua is a Basque.

- Point out that the narrator does not say much about the other two characters at this point. Tell students that the other two men will distinguish themselves as the story progresses. Have students pay attention to the differences in the three men's actions and reactions during the story.

the gallery and watch our light, a twenty thousand candle-power lantern, swinging its strong, white bar of light over the sea from the top of its hundred-twenty-foot tower. Some days, when the air would be very clear, we could see the land, a thread-like line to the west. To the east, north and south stretched the ocean. Landsmen, perhaps, would soon have tired of that kind of life, perched on a small island off the coast of South America for eighteen weeks, until one's turn for leave ashore came around. But we liked it there, my two fellow-tenders and myself—so much so that, for twenty-two months on end with the exception of shore leaves, I was greatly satisfied with the life on Three Skeleton Key.

❼ I had just returned from my leave at the end of June, that is to say mid-winter in that latitude, and had settled down to the routine with my two fellow-keepers, a Breton[5] by the name of Le Gleo and the head-keeper, Itchoua, a Basque[6] some dozen years or so older than either of us.

Eight days went by as usual, then on the ninth night after my return, Itchoua, who was on night duty, called Le Gleo and me, sleeping in our rooms in the middle of the tower, at two in the morning. We rose immediately and, climbing the thirty or so steps that led to the gallery, stood beside our chief.

Itchoua pointed, and following his finger, we saw a big three-master, with all sail set, heading straight for the light. A queer course, for the vessel must have seen us, our light lit her with the glare of day each time it passed over her.

Now, ships were a rare sight in our waters, for our light was a warning of treacherous reefs, barely hidden under the surface and running far out to sea. Consequently we were always given a wide berth, especially by sailing vessels, which cannot maneuver as readily as steamers.

No wonder that we were surprised at seeing this three-master heading dead for us in the gloom of early morning. I had immediately recognized her lines, for she stood out plainly, even at the distance of a mile, when our light shone on her.

She was a beautiful ship of some four thousand tons, a fast sailor that had carried cargoes to every part of the world, plowing the seas unceasingly. By her lines she was identified as Dutch-built, which was understandable as Paramaribo and Dutch Guiana are very close to Cayenne.

Watching her sailing dead for us, a white wave boiling under her bows, Le Gleo cried out:

---

5. **Breton** (bret´n) person born or living in Brittany, a region on the northwestern coast of France.
6. **Basque** (bask) member of a people who inhabit a region between Spain and France on the Bay of Biscay.

1052 ■ *Themes in Literature: Heroism*

❻ ▶ Critical Viewing How does this photograph of a Dutch sailing ship help establish the time period of the story? **[Connect]**

Reading Skill
Contrasting Characters What difference in the characters' ages does the narrator point out?

Vocabulary Development

Vocabulary Builder Reinforcement
Students will benefit from additional examples and practice with the Vocabulary Builder words. Reinforce their comprehension with "show-you-know" sentences. The first part of the sentence uses the vocabulary word in an appropriate context. The second part of the sentence—the "show-you-know" part—clarifies the first. Model the strategy with this example for *lurched:*
1. When she stepped on the wrong pedal, the car *lurched* forward; it moved suddenly out of the parking space.

Then give students these sentence prompts, and coach them in creating the clarification part:
1. The *diminution* of the rain meant that the team could go outside and practice; _____.
   Sample answer: the rain had slowed to a barely recognizable drizzle.
2. The audience's *derisive* laughter embarrassed the play's cast; _____.
   Sample answer: the play was a serious drama, but the audience was mocking it.

"What's wrong with her crew? Are they all drunk or insane? Can't they see us?"

Itchoua nodded soberly, looked at us sharply as he remarked: "See us? No doubt—if there is a crew aboard!"

"What do you mean, chief?" Le Gleo had started, turned to the Basque, "Are you saying that she's the Flying Dutchman?"[7]

His sudden fright had been so evident that the older man laughed:

"No, old man, that's not what I meant. If I say that no one's aboard, I mean she's a derelict."

Then we understood his queer behavior. Itchoua was right. For some reason, believing her doomed, her crew had abandoned her. Then she had righted herself and sailed on, wandering with the wind.

The three of us grew tense as the ship seemed about to crash on one of our numerous reefs, but she suddenly <u>lurched</u> with some change of the wind, the yards swung around, and the derelict came clumsily about and sailed dead away from us.

In the light of our lantern she seemed so sound, so strong, that Itchoua exclaimed impatiently:

"But why the devil was she abandoned? Nothing is smashed, no sign of fire—and she doesn't sail as if she were taking water."

Le Gleo waved to the departing ship:

"Bon voyage!"[8] he smiled at Itchoua and went on. "She's leaving us, chief, and now we'll never know what—"

"No she's not!" cried the Basque. "Look! She's turning!"

As if obeying his words, the derelict three-master stopped, came about and headed for us once more. And for the next four hours the vessel played around us—zigzagging, coming about,[9] stopping, then suddenly lurching forward. No doubt some freak of current and wind, of which our island was the center, kept her near us.

Then suddenly, the tropic dawn broke, the sun rose and it was day, and the ship was plainly visible as she sailed past us. Our light

Vocabulary Builder
lurched (lʉrcht) *v.*
moved awkwardly and suddenly

Reading Check

In the middle of the night, what surprising sight does Itchoua show his companions?

---

7. **Flying Dutchman** fabled ghost ship doomed to sail forever
8. **Bon voyage** (bän′ vои äzh′) French for "pleasant journey;" a farewell to a traveler.
9. **coming about** changing direction according to the direction of the wind.

Three Skeleton Key ■ 1053

- Have students reread the section in which the three characters watch the ship crash and sink.

- **Ask** students the Reading Skill question: In what ways are Le Gleo's and the narrator's reactions to the doomed ship similar and different?
  Answer: Le Gleo is excited to see the ship crash, while the narrator is unhappy to see the beautiful ship demolished. They are both having an emotional reaction; Le Gleo is shouting and excited, while the narrator is shedding tears.

- **Ask** students to compare their own reactions to those of the characters. Ask students if the sinking ship inspires any particular feelings.
  Possible response: Students may suggest that the image of a sinking ship fills them with dread or with interest.

⓫ **Critical Viewing**
Possible response: The fact that the rat can easily walk on ropes suggests that it would be well suited for life on a ship. The rat appears sleek and balanced, suggesting that the seawater and the motion of a rolling ship would not affect it.

---

extinguished, we returned to the gallery with our glasses and inspected her.

The three of us focused our glasses on her poop,[10] saw standing out sharply, black letters on the white background of a life-ring, the stenciled name:

"*Cornelius-de-Witt*, Rotterdam."

We had read her lines correctly, she was Dutch. Just then the wind rose and the *Cornelius-de-Witt* changed course, leaned to port and headed straight for us once more. But this time she was so close that we knew she would not turn in time.

⓾ "Thunder!" cried Le Gleo, his Breton soul aching to see a fine ship doomed to smash upon a reef, "She's going to pile up! She's gone!"

I shook my head:

"Yes, and a shame to see that beautiful ship wreck herself. And we're helpless."

There was nothing we could do but watch. A ship sailing with all sail spread, creaming the sea with her forefoot as she runs before the wind, is one of the most beautiful sights in the world—but this time I could feel the tears stinging my eyes as I saw this fine ship headed for her doom.

All this time our glasses were riveted on her, and we suddenly cried out together:

"The rats!"

Now we knew why this ship, in perfect condition, was sailing without her crew aboard. They had been driven out by the rats. Not those poor specimens of rats you see ashore, barely reaching the

---

10. **poop** (p$\overline{oo}$p) *n.* raised deck at the rear of a sailing ship.

Reading Skill
Contrasting Characters In what ways are Le Gleo's and the narrator's reactions to the doomed ship similar and different?

⓫ ▼ **Critical Viewing**
Based on this photograph, which of a rat's traits make it well-suited for life on a ship? [Analyze]

1054 ■ *Themes in Literature: Heroism*

Vocabulary Development

Words from an Earlier Time
The lighthouse operators in "Three Skeleton Key" lived in an earlier time. In the story, they use now-obscure language and unusual technical terms to describe the world they live in. You might wish to clarify with students terms related to nineteenth-century lighthouses, sailing, and the sea.

dugout canoe: a canoe made from a hollowed out log
candle-power: the intensity of a light source

landsmen: a person who has lived always on land, as opposed to sailors who live at sea
fellow-tenders: co-workers, or fellow lighthouse tenders
three-master: a ship with three main masts
derelict: a ship that has been abandoned on the open sea

length of one foot from their trembling noses to the tip of their skinny tails, wretched creatures that dodge and hide at the mere sound of a footfall.

No, these were ships' rats, huge, wise creatures, born on the sea, sailing all over the world on ships, transferring to other, larger ships as they multiply. There is as much difference between the rats of the land and these maritime rats as between a fishing smack and an armored cruiser.

The rats of the sea are fierce, bold animals. Large, strong and intelligent, clannish and seawise, able to put the best of mariners to shame with their knowledge of the sea, their uncanny ability to foretell the weather.

And they are brave, these rats, and vengeful. If you so much as harm one, his sharp cry will bring hordes of his fellows to swarm over you, tear you and not cease until your flesh has been stripped from the bones.

The ones on this ship, the rats of Holland, are the worst, superior to other rats of the sea as their brethren are to the land rats. There is a well-known tale about these animals.

A Dutch captain, thinking to protect his cargo, brought aboard his ship—not cats—but two terriers, dogs trained in the hunting, fighting and killing of vicious rats. By the time the ship, sailing from Rotterdam, had passed the Ostend light, the dogs were gone and never seen again. In twenty-four hours they had been overwhelmed, killed and eaten by the rats.

At times, when the cargo does not suffice, the rats attack the crew, either driving them from the ship or eating them alive. And

Reading Skill
Contrasting Characters In what way are the rats on the *Cornelius-de-Witt* different from other rats in the world?

Reading Check

What detail do the men notice that shows that the crew of the *Cornelius-de-Witt* did not abandon ship?

Three Skeleton Key ■ 1055

⑫ Reading Skill
Comparing and Contrasting Characters

- Remind students that animals may be characters in a story. Suggest that the swarm of rats is a character in the story, the way a force of nature, such as a snowstorm, might be in a Jack London story. Tell students that, as characters, the rats will shape the story in an important way.

- **Ask** students how the rats probably contributed to the state of the ship.
  Answer: The rats overpowered and killed the crew of the ship.

- **Ask** students the Reading Skill question: In what way are the rats on the *Cornelius-de-Witt* different from other rats in the world?
  Answer: Unlike other rats which are skinny, wretched, and meek, the rats on the ship are huge, wise, sea-faring creatures that are strong, brave, clannish, and quick to defend themselves. They are vicious rats.

⑬ Reading Check
Answer: The small boats are still on the ship, which tells the narrator that the crew did not abandon the ship.

1055

⓮ Literary Analysis
Protagonist and Antagonist

- Have students refer to **Literary Analysis Graphic Organizer A** (*Graphic Organizer Transparencies*, p. 212). Review what students know about the protagonist's goals and actions so far in the story. **Answer:** Students should remember that the protagonist has taken the job of lighthouse keeper in order to make money to get married.

- Point out that until this point in the story, the protagonist has not had any conflicts. **Ask** students to predict what conflict the protagonist may experience after the *Cornelius-de-Witt* sinks. **Possible response:** If the rats on the ship make it to the lighthouse, the narrator will have to fight for his life.

- **Ask** the Literary Analysis question: What details here might make readers sympathetic toward the narrator? Why? **Possible response:** The narrator explains that the ship is isolated and that the chances of the ship actually hitting the island were slight, but it happened anyway. Readers will feel sympathetic because of the narrator's dire situation and his bad luck.

- As students continue to read the story, have them fill in the rest of the **Literary Analysis Graphic Organizer A.**

⓯ Critical Viewing

Possible response: Its sharp claws and attack stance make it appear fearsome.

---

studying the *Cornelius-de-Witt*, I turned sick, for her small boats were all in place. She had not been abandoned.

Over her bridge, on her deck, in the rigging, on every visible spot, the ship was a writhing mass—a starving army coming towards us aboard a vessel gone mad!

⓮ Our island was a small spot in that immense stretch of sea. The ship could have grazed us, passed to port or starboard with its ravening cargo—but no, she came for us at full speed, as if she were leading the regatta at a race, and impaled herself on a sharp point of rock.

There was a dull shock as her bottom stove in, then a horrible crackling as the three masts went overboard at once, as if cut down with one blow of some gigantic sickle. A sighing groan came as the water rushed into the ship, then she split in two and sank like a stone.

But the rats did not drown. Not these fellows! As much at home in the sea as any fish, they formed ranks in the water, heads lifted, tails stretched out, paws paddling. And half of them, those from the forepart of the ship, sprang along the masts and onto the rocks in the instant before she sank. Before we had time even to move, nothing remained of the three-master save some pieces of wreckage floating on the surface and an army of rats covering the rocks left bare by the receding tide.

Thousands of heads rose, felt the wind and we were scented, seen! To them we were fresh meat, after possible weeks of starving. There came a scream, composed of innumerable screams, sharper than the howl of a saw attacking a bar of iron, and in the one motion, every rat leaped to attack the tower!

We barely had time to leap back, close the door leading onto the gallery, descend the stairs and shut every window tightly. Luckily the door at the base of the light, which we never could have reached in time, was of bronze set in granite and was tightly closed.

The horrible band, in no measurable time, had swarmed up and over the tower as if it had been a tree, piled on the embrasures of

1056 ■ *Themes in Literature: Heroism*

Literary Analysis
Protagonist and Antagonist What details here might make readers sympathetic toward the narrator? Why?

⓯ ▼ Critical Viewing
Which details in the photograph make this rat appear fearsome, like the ones in "Three Skeleton Key"? **[Analyze]**

Vocabulary Development

Expressive Vocabulary
Encourage students to use the expressive vocabulary presented earlier to discuss the unusual events in the story. Write their suggestions on the board. You might initiate the discussion with sentence starters like these:

1. To *isolate* themselves from the rats, the men . . .
2. The rats cannot gain *access* . . .
3. When the ship comes close, the men *forgo* . . .
4. The fear that something is not right with the ship *induces* the characters to . . .

the windows, scraped at the glass with thousands of claws, covered the lighthouse with a furry mantle and reached the top of the tower, filling the gallery and piling atop the lantern.

Their teeth grated as they pressed against the glass of the lantern-room, where they could plainly see us, though they could not reach us. A few millimeters of glass, luckily very strong, separated our faces from their gleaming, beady eyes, their sharp claws and teeth. Their odor filled the tower, poisoned our lungs and rasped our nostrils with a pestilential, nauseating smell. And there we were, sealed alive in our own light, prisoners of a horde of starving rats.

That first night, the tension was so great that we could not sleep. Every moment, we felt that some opening had been made, some window given away, and that our horrible besiegers were pouring through the breach. The rising tide, chasing those of the rats which had stayed on the bare rocks, increased the numbers clinging to the walls, piled on the balcony—so much so that clusters of rats clinging to one another hung from the lantern and the gallery.

With the coming of darkness we lit the light, and the turning beam completely maddened the beasts. As the light turned, it successively blinded thousands of rats crowded against the glass, while the dark side of the lantern-room gleamed with thousands of points of light, burning like the eyes of jungle beasts in the night.

All the while we could hear the enraged scraping of claws against the stone and glass, while the chorus of cries was so loud that we had to shout to hear one another. From time to time, some of the rats fought among themselves and a dark cluster would detach itself, falling into the sea like a ripe fruit from a tree. Then we would see phosphorescent streaks as triangular fins slashed the water—sharks, permanent guardians of our rock, feasting on our jailors.

The next day we were calmer, and amused ourselves by teasing the rats, placing our faces against the glass which separated us. They could not fathom the invisible barrier which separated them from us, and we laughed as we watched them leaping against the heavy glass.

But the day after that, we realized how serious our position was. The air was foul; even the heavy smell of oil within our stronghold could not dominate the fetid odor of the beasts massed around us, and there was no way of admitting fresh air without also admitting the rats.

The morning of the fourth day, at early dawn, I saw the wooden framework of my window, eaten away from the outside, sagging inwards. I called my comrades and the three of us fastened a sheet of tin in the opening, sealing it tightly. When we had completed the task, Itchoua turned to us and said dully:

Literary Analysis
Protagonist and Antagonist With what external force are the narrator, Le Gleo, and Itchoua now in conflict?

Reading Skill
Comparing Characters In what way do the sharks and the rats behave similarly?

Reading Check

What do the rats do almost immediately after landing on the island?

Three Skeleton Key ■ *1057*

⑯ Literary Analysis
Protagonist and Antagonist

- **Ask** the Literary Analysis question: With what external force are the narrator, Le Gleo, and Itchoua now in conflict?
Answer: The rats are the force with which the men are now in conflict.

- Review the definitions of protagonist and antagonist with students. **Ask** students to explain how the rats now fit the definition of antagonist.
Answer: The rats are a force that opposes the protagonist and his friends. The protagonist must struggle for survival against the rats.

- **Ask** students to identify the conflict between the men and the rats.
Answer: The rats want to attack and kill the men. The men want to survive the attack of the rats.

⑰ Reading Skill
Comparing and Contrasting Characters

- Remind students that, like the rats, the sharks are also characters in the story.

- **Ask** the Reading Skill question: In what way do the sharks and the rats behave similarly?
Answer: Like the rats, the sharks are wild animals that travel in swarms and attack their food fiercely.

⑱ Reading Check

Answer: Upon landing, the rats immediately swarm the lighthouse tower, covering it from top to bottom.

Differentiated Instruction   Solutions for All Learners

Strategy for Special Needs Students
Students may benefit from using a timeline to plot out the events in the story. Give students copies of the **Timeline Graphic Organizer Transparency** in *Graphic Organizer Transparencies,* p. 242. Have students work in pairs or small groups to review the story and identify when events happened. Tell students that the story takes place over the course of about ten days. Have students label the timeline with days that are mentioned in the story and the significant events that happened on these days.

Strategy for Advanced Readers
Students should understand that the characters' feelings about their predicament change over the course of the story. Have students write a daily journal entry for each of the men that covers the time the men are trapped in the lighthouse. Remind students to choose words that match the voice and feelings of each character. After students complete the story and complete their entries, ask them to sum up how each of the characters changed during the crisis.

Analyze and Predict

- Have students reread p. 1058, paying attention to how the men respond to the emergency.

- **Ask** students to identify the strategies the men use to pass the time and to stay calm while they are under siege from the rats.
  Answer: They entertain themselves by watching the rats fall, counting the rats, and studying the leader rats.

- **Ask** students what the men's activities say about them.
  Possible response: The men stay calm at first and try to make the best of their situation. The narrator and Itchoua seem to be people who are not prone to getting excited or upset.

- Remind students to think about what they already know about the characters. **Ask** students to predict how the men's situation might change and how the men will react.
  Possible response: The rats could find a way in, and the men will have to react quickly to save their lives. Le Gleo is easily frightened and therefore, will probably falter. Itchoua and the narrator will probably be stronger in the situation because of their calmer natures.

⑳ Critical Viewing

Answer: Sharks are much bigger than rats and have much sharper teeth. The rats can't swim away from a school of hungry sharks.

"Well—the supply boat came thirteen days ago, and she won't be back for twenty-nine." He pointed at the white metal plate sealing the opening through the granite—"If that gives way—" he shrugged—"they can change the name of this place to Six Skeletons Key."

⑲ The next six days and seven nights, our only distraction was watching the rats whose holds were insecure fall a hundred and twenty feet into the maws of the sharks—but they were so many that we could not see any <u>diminution</u> in their numbers.

Thinking to calm ourselves and pass the time, we attempted to count them, but we soon gave up. They moved incessantly, never still. Then we tried identifying them, naming them.

One of them, larger than the others, who seemed to lead them in their rushes against the glass separating us, we named "Nero";[11] and there were several others whom we had learned to distinguish through various peculiarities.

But the thought of our bones joining those of the convicts was always in the back of our minds. And the gloom of our prison fed these thoughts, for the interior of the light was almost completely dark, as we had to seal every

---

11. Nero (nir´ ō) (A.D. 37–68) Roman emperor who was notoriously cruel.

1058 ■ *Themes in Literature: Heroism*

Vocabulary Builder
diminution (dim´ ə noo͞´ shən) *n.* lessening

⑳ ▼ **Critical Viewing**
Why are even the fierce ship rats no match for a school of sharks like these? **[Assess]**

Vocabulary Development

Think-Aloud: Context

Direct students' attention to the word *maniacal* in the first full paragraph on p. 1059. Using a think-aloud process, model how to use context to infer the meaning of an unknown word. Say to students:

I'm going to think aloud to show you how I would figure out the meaning of *maniacal* from its context.

The paragraph in which *maniacal* appears gives me three clues. First, I read that Le Gleo has had nightmares.

The nightmares are full of crazy things like dancing skeletons. Then, I learn that Le Gleo's descriptions of these nightmares are not only *maniacal* but also *raving*. I know that you rave when you act crazy or insane. Finally, I recognize the word *maniac* in the word *maniacal*. A maniac is someone who acts crazy or insane. So my guess is that *maniacal* means "like a crazy or insane person."

window in the same fashion as mine, and the only space that still admitted daylight was the glassed-in lantern-room at the very top of the tower.

Then Le Gleo became morose and had nightmares in which he would see the three skeletons dancing around him, gleaming coldly, seeking to grasp him. His maniacal, raving descriptions were so vivid that Itchoua and I began seeing them also.

It was a living nightmare, the raging cries of the rats as they swarmed over the light, mad with hunger; the sickening, strangling odor of their bodies—

True, there is a way of signaling from light-houses. But to reach the mast on which to hang the signal we would have to go out on the gallery where the rats were.

21

Literary Analysis Protagonist and Antagonist In addition to the rats, what other problems do the men face?

22 ✓ **Reading Check**

What happens in Le Gleo's nightmares?

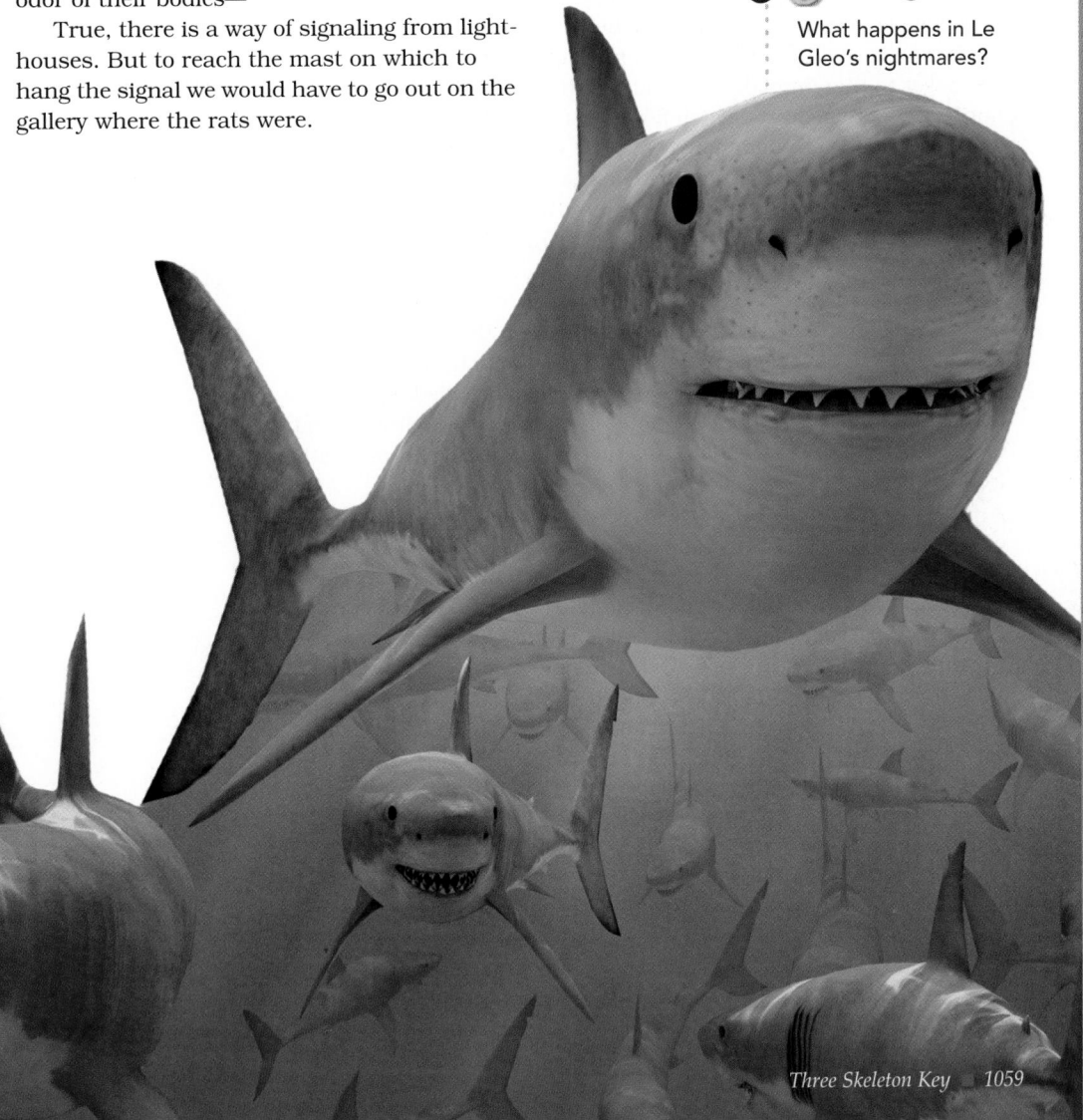

Three Skeleton Key 1059

21 **Literary Analysis Protagonist and Antagonist**

- Remind students that conflict is part of what makes a protagonist interesting to a reader. Readers want to know how the protagonist overcomes obstacles and resolves problems.

- Also, remind students that conflict may be external or internal. For example, the lighthouse keepers' struggle with the rats is an external conflict. An internal struggle is one that a character has within his or her own mind.

- Have students reread the first full paragraph on p. 1059. Then, **ask** students the Literary Analysis question: In addition to their struggle against the rats, what other problems do the men face?
Answer: The men struggle with their own fears.

- **Ask** students to identify these other conflicts as internal or external.
Answer: The men's struggle with their own fears is an internal struggle because it takes place in their minds.

22 **Reading Check**

Answer: Three skeletons dance around Le Gleo and try to grab him.

Enrichment for Gifted/Talented Students
Have students work in pairs or small groups to talk about how to turn the story into an effective movie script. Students should work together to identify key dialogue, images, and scenes from the story to incorporate into a script. Have students create a five-to-ten-page script and ask them to read their scripts aloud to the class. Ask the class to evaluate if the scripts are as suspenseful and interesting as the original story.

Strategy for Advanced Readers
Have students analyze the character of the narrator. What do they think of him? Is he heroic, or is he simply an ordinary man? Which aspects of his character help him through the ordeal of the rats? Will he survive the rats' siege? Have students write a brief character profile of the narrator. Encourage them to compare the narrator to heroes from other stories, or from movies or television shows.

- Make sure that students understand that a motive is a reason for taking action. For example, the rats' motive for attacking the lighthouse is to get food. The narrator's motive for taking the lighthouse job is to earn money so that he can get married.

- **Ask** students the Literary Analysis question: What do you think motivates the narrator and Le Gleo to risk their own lives to help Itchoua? **Possible response:** They want to save him because he is their friend and colleague. Also, they have a better chance of surviving if all three men stay together.

- Have students refer to their **Literary Analysis Graphic Organizer A.** Review students' comments and notes. Turn their attention to the box labeled *Universal Motives or Struggles.*

- Lead the class in a discussion of the motives and struggles that the men share in this story. Elicit from students that all three men have the same motive—to survive the invasion of the rats.

There was only one thing left to do. After debating all of the ninth day, we decided not to light the lantern that night. This is the greatest breach of our service, never committed as long as the tenders of the light are alive; for the light is something sacred, warning ships of danger in the night. Either the light gleams, a quarter hour after sundown, or no one is left alive to light it.

Well, that night, Three Skeleton Light was dark, and all the men were alive. At the risk of causing ships to crash on our reefs, we left it unlit, for we were worn out—going mad!

At two in the morning, while Itchoua was dozing in his room, the sheet of metal sealing his window gave way. The chief had just time enough to leap to his feet and cry for help the rats swarming over him.

 But Le Gleo and I, who had been watching from the lantern-room, got to him immediately, and the three of us battled with the horde of maddened rats which flowed through the gaping window. They bit, we struck them down with our knives—and retreated.

We locked the door of the room on them, but before we had time to bind our wounds, the door was eaten through and gave way, and we retreated up the stairs, fighting off the rats that leaped on us from the knee-deep swarm.

I do not remember, to this day, how we ever managed to escape. All I can remember is wading through them up the stairs, striking them off as they swarmed over us; and then we found ourselves, bleeding from innumerable bites, our clothes shredded, sprawled across the trapdoor in the floor of the lantern-room—without food or drink. Luckily, the trapdoor was metal set into the granite with iron bolts.

The rats occupied the entire light beneath us, and on the floor of our retreat lay some twenty of their fellows, who had gotten in with us before the trapdoor closed, and whom we had killed with our knives. Below us, in the tower, we could hear the screams of the rats as they devoured everything edible that they found. Those on the outside squealed in reply, and writhed in a horrible curtain as they stared at us through the glass of the lantern.

Itchoua sat up, stared silently at his blood trickling from the wounds on his limbs and body, and running in the streams on the floor around him. Le Gleo, who was in as bad a state (and so was I, for that matter) stared at the chief and me vacantly, started as his gaze swung to the multitude of rats against the glass, then suddenly began laughing horribly:

"Hee! Hee! The Three Skeletons! Hee! Hee! The Three Skeletons are now *six* skeletons! *Six* skeletons!"

He threw his head back and howled, his eyes glazed, a trickle of saliva running from the corners of his mouth and running the

Literary Analysis
Protagonist and Antagonist What do you think motivates the narrator and Le Gleo to risk their own lives to help Itchoua?

Vocabulary Development

Word Analysis
Point out the prefix *in-* in *innumerable*, on p. 1060. Tell student that the prefix *in-* means "not."

Then, direct students to the word *immediately* on the same page. The prefix *im-* means "not" as well.

Ask students to use their knowledge of prefixes and roots to figure out the literal meanings of the words *innumerable* and *immediately.*

Possible response: *Innumerable* has the root *-num-,* which is in *number* and *numeral. -Able* is a suffix meaning "able." *Innumerable* literally means "not countable, or too many to count."

In *immediately,* the suffix *-ly* makes the word an adverb. The root *-med-* is used in words like *medium* or *median,* which mean "in between." *Immediately* means "without having any interference, or quickly."

blood flowing over his chest. I shouted to him to shut up, but he did not hear me, so I did the only thing I could to quiet him—I swung the back of my hand across his face.

The howling stopped suddenly, his eyes swung around the room, then he bowed his head and began weeping softly, like a child.

Our darkened light had been noticed from the mainland, and as dawn was breaking, the patrol was there to investigate the failure of our light. Looking through my binoculars, I could see the horrified expression on the faces of the officers and crew when, the daylight strengthening, they saw the light completely covered by a seething mass of rats. They thought, as I afterwards found out, that we had been eaten alive.

But the rats had also seen the ship, or had scented the crew. As the ship drew nearer, a solid phalanx[12] left the light, plunged into the water and, swimming out, attempted to board her. They would have succeeded, as the ship was hove to, but the engineer connected his steam to a hose on the deck and scalded the head of the attacking column, which slowed them up long enough for the ship to get under way and leave the rats behind.

Then the sharks took part. Belly up, mouths gaping, they arrived in swarms and scooped up the rats, sweeping through them like a sickle through wheat. That was one day that sharks really served a useful purpose.

The remaining rats turned tail, swam to the shore, and emerged dripping. As they neared the light, their comrades greeted them with shrill cries, with what sounded like a derisive note predominating. They answered angrily and mingled with their fellows. From the several tussles that broke out, they resented being ridiculed for their failure to capture the ship.

But all this did nothing to get us out of our jail. The small ship could not approach, but steamed around the light at a safe distance, and the tower must have seemed fantastic, some weird, many-mouthed beast hurling defiance at them.

Finally, seeing the rats running in and out of the tower through the door and the windows, those on the ship decided that we had perished and were about to leave when Itchoua, regaining his senses, thought of using the light as a signal. He lit it and, using a plank placed and withdrawn before the beam to form the dots and dashes, quickly sent out our story to those on the vessel.

Our reply came quickly. When they understood our position— how we could not get rid of the rats, Le Gleo's mind going fast,

---

12. **phalanx** (fā′laŋks′) *n.* group of individuals advancing in a close, compact formation.

Reading Skill
Contrasting Characters What differences between the narrator and Le Gleo do their reactions make clear?

Vocabulary Builder
derisive (di rī′ siv)
adj. mocking

Reading Check

What do the men do that results in the arrival of a patrol ship?

Three Skeleton Key ■ 1061

---

24 Reading Skill
Comparing and Contrasting Characters

- Point out that although the men have a common enemy and conflict in the rats, their different reactions to their situation puts them in conflict with one another. Have students **summarize** how the men have reacted since the rats broke through the lighthouse wall.
  Answer: Le Gleo stares vacantly, laughs and shouts hysterically, and then cries after the narrator hits him. The narrator tries to stay calm but yells at Le Gleo and hits him. Then, he uses his binoculars to look for help. Itchoua sits and stares at his wounds before taking action.

- **Ask** students the Reading Skill question: What differences between the narrator and Le Gleo do their reactions make clear?
  Answer: Le Gleo's hysterical laughing, shouting, and crying show that he can not handle a crisis, while the narrator's handling of Le Gleo shows that he wants to get a grip on the situation and will not be distracted by Le Gleo's insanity. The narrator's reaction shows that he is able to function in a crisis.

25 Reading Skill
Comparing and Contrasting Characters

- Draw students' attention to the reaction of the rats to those that had failed to reach the ship and had returned to the lighthouse. Tell students that the rats on the lighthouse seemed to greet their failed "comrades" with derisive scorn.

- **Ask** students to compare the rats' reactions to their "comrades'" failures to the men's responses to each other.
  Possible response: The rats on the lighthouse taunt the rats that failed to reach the ship. The men are more supportive of each other. Even though the narrator hits Le Gleo, he does not deride him. The men stick together.

26 Reading Check

Answer: The men choose not to light the lighthouse. A boat patrols to find out why the light was not lit.

1061

27 Critical Viewing
Answer: The white foam in the photograph suggests that the shark is plowing through the water at great speed. The sharks' speed, along with their gaping mouths and sharp teeth, would make it easy for the sharks to sweep through the smaller, slower rats.

28 Reading Skill
Comparing and Contrasting Characters

• Ask a volunteer to read aloud the last sentence on p. 1062. "They were true rats of Holland, fearing no man, fighting for the right to live!"

• **Ask** students the Reading Skill question: What similarity between the rats and the men does the narrator's remark about the rats reveal?
Answer: Both the men and the rats have strong survival instincts.

• Challenge students to **make a generalization** about the difference between the way the rats and the men fight for survival.
Answer: The men stick together and every rat fights for itself.

Itchoua and myself covered with bites, cornered in the lantern-room without food or water—they had a signalman send us their reply.

His arms swinging like those of a windmill, he quickly spelled out: "Don't give up. Hang on a little longer! We'll get you out of this!"

Then she turned and steamed at top speed for the coast, leaving us little reassured.

She was back at noon, accompanied by the supply ship, two small coast guard boats, and the fire boat—a small squadron. At twelve-thirty the battle was on.

After a short reconnaissance,[13] the fire boat picked her way slowly through the reefs until she was close to us, then turned her powerful jet of water on the rats. The heavy stream tore the rats from their places, hurled them screaming into the water where the sharks gulped them down. But for every ten that were dislodged, seven swam ashore, and the stream could do nothing to the rats within the tower. Furthermore, some of them, instead of returning to the rocks, boarded the fire boat, and the men were forced to battle them hand to hand. They were true rats of Holland, fearing no man, fighting for the right to live!

---

13. **reconnaissance** (ri kän´ə səns) *n.* exploratory survey or examination.

1062 ■ *Themes in Literature: Heroism*

27 ▲ Critical Viewing Based on this photograph, how easily do you think the sharks could sweep through the rats? Explain. **[Evaluate]**

Reading Skill Comparing Characters What similarity between the rats and the men does the narrator's remark about the rats reveal?

Vocabulary Development

Vocabulary Knowledge Rating
When students have completed reading and discussing "Three Skeleton Key," have them take out their **Vocabulary Knowledge Rating Chart** for this selection. Read the words aloud once more and have students rate their knowledge of the words again in the After Reading column. Clarify any words that are still problematic. Have students write their own definition and example or sentence in the appropriate column. Then have students complete the **Vocabulary Builder Practice** activities on p. 1065. Encourage students to use the words in further discussion and written work about this selection. Remind them that they will be accountable for these words on the Selection Test.

Nightfall came, and it was as if nothing had been done, the rats were still in possession. One of the patrol boats stayed by the island; the rest of the flotilla[14] departed for the coast. We had to spend another night in our prison. Le Gleo was sitting on the floor, babbling about skeletons, and as I turned to Itchoua, he fell unconscious from his wounds. I was in no better shape and could feel my blood flaming with fever.

Somehow the night dragged by, and the next afternoon I saw a tug, accompanied by the fire boat, coming from the mainland with a huge barge in tow. Through my glasses, I saw that the barge was filled with meat.

Risking the treacherous reefs, the tug dragged the barge as close to the island as possible. To the last rat, our besiegers deserted the rock, swam out and boarded the barge reeking with the scent of freshly cut meat. The tug dragged the barge about a mile from shore, where the fire boat drenched the barge with gasoline. A well placed incendiary shell from the patrol boat set her on fire.

The barge was covered with flames immediately, and the rats took to the water in swarms, but the patrol boat bombarded them with shrapnel from a safe distance, and the sharks finished off the survivors.

A whaleboat from the patrol boat took us off the island and left three men to replace us. By nightfall we were in the hospital in Cayenne.

What became of my friends? Well, Le Gleo's mind had cracked and he was raving mad. They sent him back to France and locked him up in an asylum,[15] the poor devil; Itchoua died within a week; a rat's bite is dangerous in that hot, humid climate, and infection sets in rapidly.

As for me—when they fumigated[16] the light and repaired the damage done by the rats, I resumed my service there. Why not? No reason why such an incident should keep me from finishing out my service there, is there?

Besides—I told you I liked the place—to be truthful, I've never had a post as pleasant as that one, and when my time came to leave it forever, I tell you that I almost wept as Three Skeleton Key disappeared below the horizon.

Literary Analysis
Protagonist and Antagonist In what way does human intelligence ultimately overcome the rats' brutality?

Reading Skill
Contrasting Characters How is Le Gleo changed by the attack?

---

14. **flotilla** (flō til′ ə) *n.* small fleet.
15. **asylum** (ə sī′ ləm) *n.* institution for the care of the mentally ill.
16. **fumigated** (fyoo′ mə gāt′ id) *v.* disinfected with fumes.

Three Skeleton Key ■ 1063

---

29 Literary Analysis
Protagonist and Antagonist

- Make sure that students understand how well the men in the boats worked together to save the men in the lighthouse.
  Ask students the Literary Analysis question: In what way does human intelligence ultimately overcome the rats' brutality?
  Answer: The men on the boats work together to outwit the rats, luring them into a trap.

30 Reading Skill
Comparing and Contrasting Characters

- Remind students that it is important to compare and contrast the same character at different points in the story.

- **Ask** students the Reading Skill question: How is Le Gleo changed by the attack?
  Answer: He is now insane and living in an asylum.

▶ **Monitor Progress:** Ask students to define how each character was changed by the event.
  Possible response: Itchoua is dead. The narrator seems little changed. Le Gleo has gone insane.

▶ **Reteach:** If students have trouble comparing characters before and after the story, have them create a two-column chart labeled "At the Beginning" and "After the End." Have students review the story for details about each character and fill in the chart.

Concept Connector

Anticipation Guide
Have students return to their **Anticipation Guides** and respond to the statements again in the After Reading column. They may do this individually or in their original pairs or groups. Then, lead a class discussion, probing for what students have learned that confirms or invalidates each statement. Encourage students to cite specific details, quotations, or other evidence from the text to support their responses to each statement.

Connecting to the Literature
Have students compare the sentences they wrote before reading with their thoughts about the pros and cons of living in isolation. Ask them to explain whether their thoughts have changed and, if so, how.

Literary Analysis Graphic Organizer Ask students to review the graphic organizers they completed while reading. Show them **Literary Analysis Graphic Organizer B** (*Graphic Organizer Transparencies*, p. 213) as an example. Then have students share their graphic organizers.

1. Students may feel disgust at the thought of the invading rats.

2. (a) The rats arrive at the lighthouse when their ship sinks. (b) **Possible response:** The rats are dangerous and destructive. (c) The rescuers lure the rats to a barge of meat, set it on fire, and force the rats into shark-infested water.

3. (a) Itchoua says that if the window breaks "they can change the name of this place to Six Skeletons Key." (b) Itchoua means that the three would die. (c) The remark emphasizes how dire the situation is and adds new meaning to the title.

4. (a) Intelligent: The narrator calls the rats "wise"; they have knowledge of the sea, they are able to foretell the weather, and they work together. Vicious: The narrator details the rats' frenzied attacks; they fight amongst themselves. (b) **Possible response:** By mentioning their size, strength, and intelligence, the author makes the rats seem deadly.

5. (a) The narrator is the protagonist. (b) The protagonist's goal is to survive the rats. (c) Readers are invested in the character and want him to live.

6. (a) The rats are the antagonists. (b) The antagonists' goal is to devour the men.

7. (a) The conflict is interesting because each side's goal is very basic—survival. (b) The conflict represents the universal struggle to survive.

8. Possible questions include: Did the ordeal change the narrator? What enabled the narrator to keep his outlook?

9. (a) **Beginning:** The narrator is young and inexperienced. He enjoys life. He is not superstitious. **End:** The narrator has barely survived the attack, and he has lost two friends. He is wiser now. **Beginning and End:** He still enjoys the island and his work on it, and he still doesn't believe the superstitions. (b) The narrator is wiser but basically unchanged. Another sample answer can be found on **Reading**

1064

Apply the Skills

Three Skeleton Key

Thinking About the Selection

1. **Respond:** What feelings does this story stir in you, and why?
2. (a) **Recall:** How do the rats come to the lighthouse? (b) **Infer:** What impression of the rats does this method of arrival create? (c) **Summarize:** Explain how the rescuers defeat the rats.
3. (a) **Recall:** What does Itchoua say about the name of the island and what will happen if the window seal gives way? (b) **Infer:** What does he mean by this remark? (c) **Interpret:** How does this remark create suspense and add meaning to the story's title?
4. (a) **Categorize:** Which details portray the rats as intelligent and organized and which portray them as mindlessly vicious? (b) **Evaluate:** Does Toudouze make you believe that actual rats would be capable of the actions he describes? Explain.

Literary Analysis

5. (a) Identify the **protagonist** in the narrative. (b) What is the protagonist's goal? (c) Why are readers interested in whether the protagonist achieves his goal?
6. (a) Identify the **antagonist**. (b) What is the antagonist's goal?
7. (a) Why is the story's conflict interesting? (b) What universal struggle does this conflict represent?

Reading Strategy

8. What are two specific questions you can ask to help you **compare and contrast** the narrator's actions, reasoning, and outlook at the beginning of the attack and at the end?
9. (a) Complete a Venn diagram like the one shown to compare and contrast the narrator's outlook at the beginning of the story with his outlook at the end of the story. (b) Explain whether the narrator has or has not changed as a result of his experience.

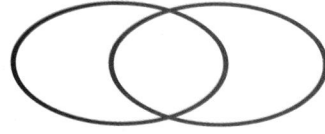

Beginning Only   End Only

Beginning and End

10. (a) In what ways do the narrator, Le Gleo, and Itchoua act differently from one another during the attack? (b) What is one reason the author may have for showing these three different reactions?

QuickReview

Story at a Glance
Three men are trapped in an island lighthouse besieged by bloodthirsty rats.

Go Online
Assessment
For: Self-test
Visit: www.PHSchool.com
Web Code: epa-6605

Protagonist: the character in a literary work whose fortunes are of greatest interest to readers

Antagonist: a character or force in conflict with the protagonist

Comparing and Contrasting: recognizing similarities and differences

Skill Graphic Organizer B, p. 216 in *Graphic Organizer Transparencies.*

10. (a) Itchoua is resourceful. Le Gleo loses his mind with fear. The narrator is calm and observant. (b) **Possible response:** The author may have wanted to show varying responses to stress.

Vocabulary Builder

Practice **Analogies** show the relationships between pairs of words. Use a word from the "Three Skeleton Key" vocabulary list on page 1048 to complete each analogy.

1. enlargement : increase :: _____ : decrease
2. glided : graceful :: _____ : clumsy
3. complimentary : praise :: _____ : ridicule

Adding Words to Your Vocabulary Using a dictionary and a thesaurus, find an antonym, for each vocabulary word in the story. Explain your choices. Then, use each antonym in a sentence. (For more on using a dictionary and a thesaurus, see pp. R6–7.)

Writing

Imagine that you are one of the characters in "Three Skeleton Key" other than the narrator. Write three **journal entries** describing the events in the story as they unfold.

- Review the story and create a timeline for the major events.
- Decide which days you will record in your journal.
- Write your thoughts about what happens each day.

As you write, stay in character, making sure that your journal reflects any changes that the character experiences in the story.

For *Grammar, Vocabulary,* and *Assessment,* see **Build Language Skills,** pages 1092–1093.

Extend Your Learning

Listening and Speaking With another student, role-play an **interview** between a television talk show host and the narrator of "Three Skeleton Key." Listen carefully to what your partner says in the interview, and respond with appropriate questions or answers. After the role play, give each other feedback on your work.

Research and Technology Research the topic of ship rats and prepare an **oral report** for the class. Find answers to these questions:
- How do these rats differ physically from other rats?
- Where do such rats live, and how long can they survive?

Refer to multiple sources, such as the Internet, encyclopedias, and science books. Compare what you learn to Toudouze's descriptions.

Apply the Skills ■ 1065

Go Online **Research** **For:** An additional research activity
Visit: www.PHSchool.com
Web Code: epd-7603
For another research activity to extend students' learning, give students this Web Code.

Vocabulary Development
Practice

1. diminution; the two words in each pairing are synonyms.
2. lurched; the second word describes the action of the first word.
3. derisive; the first word gives a quality of the second word.

Adding Words to Your Vocabulary
Sample answers:

1. An antonym of *diminution* is *increase.* When the economy improved, the bank saw an *increase* in investment.
2. An antonym of *lurched* is *slid.* The skaters *slid* across the ice.
3. An antonym of *derisive* is *supportive.* The audience rising to its feet was a *supportive* gesture directed toward the singer.

Writing
- To give students guidance for writing their journal entries, give them **Support for Writing** for "Three Skeleton Key," p. 86 in *Unit 6 Resources.*
- To evaluate students' journal entries, use the Autobiographical Narrative rubrics, pp. 43–44 in *General Resources.*

Six Traits Focus

✔ Ideas		Word Choice
	Organization	Sentence Fluency
✔ Voice		Conventions

Build Language Skills

Go to pages 1092–1093 for vocabulary and grammar lessons and assessment practice.

Extend Your Learning

The **Support for Extend Your Learning** page (*Unit 6 Resources,* p. 87) provides guided note-taking opportunities to help students complete the Extend Your Learning activities.

Teaching notes for Literary Analysis, Reading Skill, and Vocabulary Builder for this selection begin on p. 1048.

❸ Background
Sherlock Holmes

London's popular *Strand* magazine commissioned a series of six Sherlock Holmes stories from writer Arthur Conan Doyle in 1891. Readers went wild for Holmes after the first story appeared, and Doyle was able to nearly double his fee for another six stories. Doyle's final Holmes story appeared in 1927, but the detective is as popular today as he was when his creator was alive. Holmes has been the subject of scholarly biographies, fans have founded numerous societies and reading clubs, and writers such as Laurie King continue to publish new Holmes adventures. Doyle created one of the most beloved literary characters of all time in his keen-eyed, sharp-witted consulting detective.

❹ Connecting to the Literature

• Model use of the expressive vocabulary students are asked to use with these sentences:

1. The first thing people *perceive* about our house is its deep blue color.

2. When I *observe* the painting, I notice its vibrant colors and carefully constructed details.

3. The high back of the chair *differentiates* it from the other furniture in our living room.

4. A close examination of the curtains will *reveal* the dust that has collected on them.

• Help students further develop their expressive vocabulary by providing these words: *rational, speculate, tangible, urban,* and *visual.* Encourage students to use these words as they discuss the selection.

Go Online
Author Link For additional information about Sir Arthur Conan Doyle, have students type in the Web Code, then select *D* from the alphabet, and then select *Sir Arthur Conan Doyle.*

Build Understanding • *The Red-headed League*

Short Story

❸ Background

Sherlock Holmes This story is one of many tales about the exploits of the world's most famous fictional detective, Sherlock Holmes. Often depicted wearing a plaid cape and a deerstalker cap, Sherlock Holmes is recognized by people everywhere.

❹ Connecting to the Literature

Reading/Writing Connection Sherlock Holmes has remarkable powers of observation. Test your skill by describing a familiar object. Use at least three of these words: *perceive, observe, differentiate, reveal.*

Review

For **Literary Analysis, Reading Skill,** and **Vocabulary Builder,** see page 1048.

READ MORE

by Sir Arthur Conan Doyle
The Complete Sherlock Holmes
The Lost World

Meet the Author

Sir Arthur **Conan Doyle** (1859–1930)

Sir Arthur Conan Doyle began his career as a doctor. He also pursued a career in writing. In a few years, he sold his first novel, *A Study in Scarlet,* which introduced Sherlock Holmes to the world.

The World's Favorite Detective It is likely that Conan Doyle modeled Sherlock Holmes on Dr. Joseph Bell, a professor of his who could diagnose illnesses from clues that other physicians had missed. Conan Doyle made the narrator of the Holmes mysteries Dr. John Watson. Watson greatly admires Holmes but can never match his friend's powers of observation and reasoning.

Readers grew to love Sherlock Holmes. When Conan Doyle killed him off in a story in 1893, readers protested so strongly that the author was forced to bring back the beloved detective.

Fast Facts

▶ Although Holmes is often depicted in a plaid cape and deerstalker hat, the stories never mention such clothing.

▶ The famous catchphrase "Elementary, my dear Watson" was only used in films—never in Conan Doyle's stories.

Go Online
Author Link
For: More information about the author
Visit: www.PHSchool.com
Web Code: epe-9608

1066 ■ *Themes in Literature: Heroism*

Differentiated Instruction   *Solutions for All Learners*

Support for Below-Level Students [L1, L2]	Support for English Learners [EL]
Unit 6 Resources	**Unit 6 Resources**
Vocabulary Warm-up Word Lists, p. 95	Vocabulary Warm-up Word Lists, p. 95
Vocabulary Warm-Up Practice, p. 96	Vocabulary Warm-up Practice, p. 96
Reading Warm-up A, p. 97	Reading Warm-up A, p. 97
Selection Test A, pp. 107–109	
Graphic Organizer Transparencies	**Listening to Literature Audio CD**
Literary Analysis Graphic Organizer Transparency B, p. 214	

THE RED-HEADED LEAGUE ❶ ❷

SIR ARTHUR CONAN DOYLE

I had called upon my friend, Mr. Sherlock Holmes, one day in the autumn of last year and found him in deep conversation with a very stout, florid-faced, elderly gentleman with fiery red hair. With an apology for my intrusion, I was about to withdraw when Holmes pulled me abruptly into the room and closed the door behind me.

"You could not possibly have come at a better time, my dear Watson," he said cordially.

"I was afraid that you were engaged."

"So I am. Very much so."

The Red-headed League ■ 1067

❶ Motivation
Prepare an **Anticipation Guide** (see *General Resources,* pp. 8–10) with the following statements:

- It is important to pay attention to the small details in life.
- Being observant is a skill that is not very useful.
- When two people observe the same thing, they always interpret it the same way.
- You should be wary of things that are too good to be true.

Give students a copy of the prepared Anticipation Guide and have students mark their responses in the Me column. Have students discuss the statements in pairs or groups and mark the Guides again in the Group column.

Concept Connector ➡

Students will return to the Anticipation Guide after completing "The Red-headed League."

Learning Modalities
Visual/Spatial Learners
Students should enjoy the illustrations that accompany this selection. Share the information in the Humanities note on p. 1072. As students read the story, have them study the details of the illustrations and find the passage in the story that each one depicts.

❷ About the Selection
In "The Red-headed League," pawnbroker Jabez Wilson consults detective Sherlock Holmes about the mysterious "Red-headed League" that offered him employment for several weeks and then disappeared. Holmes soon discovers that master criminals invented the League to lure Wilson from his pawnshop so that they could dig a tunnel from his cellar into the vaults of a nearby bank.

❸ Reading Skill
Comparing Characters

- Explain to students that one of the roles Dr. Watson plays in Sherlock Holmes stories is to stand in for the reader. Like the reader, Watson always misses clues and is often confused. His job is to ask Holmes questions and make him explain his deductions.

- **Ask** students the Reading Skill question: According to Holmes, what do he and Watson have in common?
  Answer: Both Holmes and Watson have a love of bizarre events and mysteries.

❹ Literary Analysis
Protagonist and Antagonist

- Point out that in the first few paragraphs of the story, readers already know that this is a mystery story. It is clear, too, that Holmes solves problems for people, and that he is good at this work.

- Review the characteristics of a protagonist. Remind students that a protagonist is a character who may have flaws but who always interests the reader.

- **Ask** students the Literary Analysis question: What details in Holmes's speech here help present him as a protagonist?
  Answer: Holmes is clearly an interesting character who is in charge of what happens in the story.

- Have students write their ideas on copies of **Literary Analysis Graphic Organizer A** (*Graphic Organizer Transparencies,* p. 212). Remind students as they read to write down information about the protagonist's goals, actions, and conflicts.

"Then I can wait in the next room."

"Not at all. This gentleman, Mr. Wilson, has been my partner and helper in many of my most successful cases, and I have no doubt that he will be of the utmost use to me in yours also."

The stout gentleman half rose from his chair and gave a bob of greeting, with a quick little questioning glance from his small, fat-encircled eyes.

❸ "Try the settee,"[1] said Holmes, relapsing into his armchair and putting his finger tips together, as was his custom when in judicial moods. "I know, my dear Watson, that you share my love of all that is bizarre and outside the conventions and humdrum routine of everyday life. You have shown your relish for it by the enthusiasm which has prompted you to chronicle, and, if you will excuse my saying so, somewhat to embellish so many of my own little adventures."

"Your cases have indeed been of the greatest interest to me," I observed.

"You will remember that I remarked the other day, just before we went into the very simple problem presented by Miss Mary Sutherland, that for strange effects and extraordinary combinations we must go to life itself, which is always far more daring than any effort of the imagination."

"A proposition which I took the liberty of doubting."

"You did, Doctor, but none the less you must come round to my view, for otherwise I shall keep on piling fact upon fact on you until your reason breaks down under them and acknowledges me to be right. Now, Mr. Jabez Wilson here has been good enough to call upon me this morning, and to begin a narrative which promises to be one of the most singular which I have listened to for some time. ❹ You have heard me remark that the strangest and most unique things are very often connected not with the larger but with the smaller crimes, and occasionally, indeed, where there is room for doubt whether any positive crime has been committed. As far as I have heard it is impossible for me to say whether the present case is an instance of crime or not, but the course of events is certainly among the most singular that I have ever listened to. Perhaps, Mr. Wilson, you would have the great kindness to recommence your narrative. I ask you not merely because my friend Dr. Watson has not heard the opening part but also because the peculiar nature of the story makes me anxious to have every possible detail from your lips. As a rule, when I have heard some slight indication of the course of events, I am able to guide myself by the thousands of

---

1. settee (se tē´) *n.* small sofa.

1068 ■ *Themes in Literature: Heroism*

Reading Skill
Comparing Characters According to Holmes, what do he and Watson have in common?

Literary Analysis
Protagonist and Antagonist What details in Holmes's speech here help present him as a protagonist?

Vocabulary Development

Word Forms
Give students a blank **Word Form Chart** (*General Resources,* p. 16) with *introspective, vex,* and *formidable* in the correct columns. Work with the class, or have students work with a partner, to determine the related forms.

Hold students accountable for integrating the related forms of the words into their speaking and writing.

Noun	Verb	Adjective	Adverb
introspection	introspect	**introspective**	introspectively
vexation	**vex**	vexatious	vexatiously
formidability		**formidable**	formidably

other similar cases which occur to my memory. In the present instance I am forced to admit that the facts are, to the best of my belief, unique."

The portly client puffed out his chest with an appearance of some little pride and pulled a dirty and wrinkled newspaper from the inside pocket of his great coat. As he glanced down the advertisement column, with his head thrust forward and the paper flattened out upon his knee, I took a good look at the man and endeavored, after the fashion of my companion, to read the indications which might be presented by his dress or appearance.

5 I did not gain very much, however, by my inspection. Our visitor bore every mark of being an average commonplace British tradesman, obese, pompous, and slow. He wore rather baggy gray shepherd's check trousers, a not over-clean black frock coat, unbuttoned in the front, and a drab waistcoat with a heavy brassy Albert chain, and a square pierced bit of metal dangling down as an ornament. A frayed top hat and a faded brown overcoat with a wrinkled velvet collar lay upon a chair beside him. Altogether, look as I would, there was nothing remarkable about the man save his blazing red head, and the expression of extreme chagrin and discontent upon his features.

Sherlock Holmes's quick eye took in my occupation, and he shook his head with a smile as he noticed my questioning glances. "Beyond the obvious facts that he has at some time done manual labor, that he takes snuff,[2] that he is a Freemason,[3] that he has been in China, and that he has done a considerable amount of writing lately, I can deduce nothing else."

Mr. Jabez Wilson started up in his chair, with his forefinger upon the paper, but his eyes upon my companion.

"How, in the name of good fortune, did you know all that, Mr. Holmes?" he asked. "How did you know, for example, that I did manual labor? It's as true as gospel, for I began as a ship's carpenter."

"Your hands, my dear sir. Your right hand is quite a size larger than your left. You have worked with it, and the muscles are more developed."

"Well, the snuff, then, and the Freemasonry?"

"I won't insult your intelligence by telling you how I read that, especially as, rather against the strict rules of your order, you use an arc-and-compass breastpin."

"Ah, of course, I forgot that. But the writing?"

---

2. **snuff** (snuf) *n.* powdered tobacco.
3. **Freemason** member of a secret society.

Reading Skill
Contrasting Characters How are Watson and Holmes different in terms of their powers of observation?

6 Reading Check

What facts about Mr. Wilson does Holmes deduce based on Wilson's appearance?

The Red-headed League ■ 1069

Math Connection When this story was written, British money was divided into pounds, shillings, and pence. Twelve pence (pennies) made a shilling, and twenty shillings made a pound. Other coins included the crown (worth 5 shillings), the sovereign (worth one pound), the half-crown, the half sovereign, and the florin (worth 2 shillings). Late in the twentieth century, England shifted to a decimal monetary system in which 100 pence made one pound.

Connect to the Literature Before students answer the question, ask them to think of get-rich-quick schemes they have heard about or seen advertisements for in the media. Invite students to share their responses to such advertisements. Elicit from students that even though many schemes are suspect, some people are always interested. They may suggest that getting a lot of money for little work always sounds appealing. **Ask** students the Connect to the Literature question: Why might an offer of a large sum of money "for purely nominal services" be cause for suspicion?

Answer: The promise of receiving a lot of money for little work is almost always too good to be true.

"What else can be indicated by that right cuff so very shiny for five inches, and the left one with the smooth patch near the elbow where you rest it upon the desk?"

"Well, but China?"

"The fish that you have tattooed immediately above your right wrist could only have been done in China. I have made a small study of tattoo marks and have even contributed to the literature of the subject. That trick of staining the fishes' scales of a delicate pink is quite peculiar to China. When, in addition, I see a Chinese coin hanging from your watch-chain, the matter becomes even more simple."

Mr. Jabez Wilson laughed heavily. "Well, I never!" said he. "I thought at first that you had done something clever, but I see that there was nothing in it, after all."

"I begin to think, Watson," said Holmes, "that I make a mistake in explaining. '*Omne ignotum pro magnifico*,'[4] you know, and my poor little reputation, such as it is, will suffer shipwreck if I am so candid. Can you not find the advertisement, Mr. Wilson?"

"Yes, I have got it now," he answered with his thick red finger planted halfway down the column. "Here it is. This is what began it all. You just read it for yourself, sir."

I took the paper from him and read as follows:

To THE RED-HEADED LEAGUE:

On account of the bequest of the late Ezekiah Hopkins, of Lebanon, Pennsylvania, U. S. A., there is now another vacancy open which entitles a member of the League to a salary of £4 a week for purely nominal services. All red-headed men who are sound in body and mind, and above the age of twenty-one years, are eligible. Apply in person on Monday, at eleven o'clock, to Duncan Ross, at the offices of the League, 7 Pope's Court, Fleet Street.

"What on earth does this mean?" I ejaculated after I had twice read over the extraordinary announcement.

Holmes chuckled and wriggled in his chair, as was his habit when in high spirits. "It is a little off the beaten track, isn't it?" said

---

4. ***Omne ignotum pro magnifico*** (äm´ nā ig nō´ təm prō mag nē´ fē kō) Latin for "Whatever is unknown is magnified."

1070 ■ *Themes in Literature: Heroism*

7 Literature in Context

Math Connection

Pound Conversions The advertisement that concerns Mr. Wilson announces a salary of four pounds a week. The pound is the monetary unit of Great Britain. Its equivalency in American dollars fluctuates depending on current economic conditions. At the time Doyle wrote the story, one British pound equaled about $4.85, so four pounds would have equaled about $19.40. This was considered a large amount at the time in which the story is set, particularly for easy work.

Connect to the Literature

Why might an offer of a large sum of money "for purely nominal services" be cause for suspicion?

Vocabulary Development

Expressive Vocabulary
Encourage students to use the expressive vocabulary presented earlier to discuss the differences between Holmes and Watson. Write their suggestions on the board. You might initiate the discussion with sentence starters like these:

1. Holmes and Watson *perceive* . . .
2. Watson likes to *observe* . . .
3. The reader can *differentiate* Watson from Holmes by . . .
4. Holmes *reveals* to Watson . . .

Accept all of students' answers. Ask the class to determine if words are used properly in context. Point out to students sentences that use the words correctly.

he. "And now, Mr. Wilson, off you go at scratch and tell us all about yourself, your household, and the effect which this advertisement had upon your fortunes. You will first make a note, Doctor, of the paper and the date."

"It is *The Morning Chronicle* of April 27, 1890. Just two months ago."

"Very good. Now, Mr. Wilson?"

"Well, it is just as I have been telling you, Mr. Sherlock Holmes," said Jabez Wilson, mopping his forehead; "I have a small pawnbroker's business at Coburg Square, near the City. It's not a very large affair, and of late years it has not done more than just give me a living. I used to be able to keep two assistants, but now I only keep one; and I would have a job to pay him but that he is willing to come for half wages so as to learn the business."

"What is the name of this obliging youth?" asked Sherlock Holmes.

"His name is Vincent Spaulding, and he's not such a youth, either. It's hard to say his age. I should not wish a smarter assistant, Mr. Holmes; and I know very well that he could better himself and earn twice what I am able to give him. But, after all, if he is satisfied, why should I put ideas in his head?"

"Why, indeed? You seem most fortunate in having an employee who comes under the full market price. It is not a common experience among employers in this age. I don't know that your assistant is not as remarkable as your advertisement."

"Oh, he has his faults, too," said Mr. Wilson. "Never was such a fellow for photography. Snapping away with a camera when he ought to be improving his mind, and then diving down into the cellar like a rabbit into its hole to develop his pictures. That is his main fault, but on the whole he's a good worker. There's no vice in him."

"He is still with you, I presume?"

"Yes, sir. He and a girl of fourteen, who does a bit of simple cooking and keeps the place clean—that's all I have in the house, for I am a widower and never had any family. We live very quietly, sir, the three of us; and we keep a roof over our heads and pay our debts, if we do nothing more.

"The first thing that put us out was that advertisement. Spaulding, he came down into the office just this day eight weeks, with this very paper in his hand, and he says:

"'I wish to the Lord, Mr. Wilson, that I was a red-headed man.'

"'Why that?' I asks.

"'Why,' says he, 'here's another vacancy on the League of the Red-headed Men. It's worth quite a little fortune to any man who

---

Literary Analysis
Protagonist and Antagonist Which details in the description of Vincent Spaulding attract Holmes's notice?

 9 **Reading Check**

Who is eligible for the position posted in the advertisement?

The Red-headed League ■ 1071

---

8 **Literary Analysis**
Protagonist and Antagonist

- Remind students that the antagonist provides obstacles and conflicts to the protagonist. Tell students that, at this point in the story, the protagonist Holmes does not yet have an antagonist.

- Challenge students to predict who Holmes's antagonist will be. Have students **consider** the likely candidates based on the reading so far. **Answer:** Students may suggest that whoever set up Mr. Wilson will be Holmes's antagonist. Mr. Wilson himself is another candidate.

- **Ask** students the Literary Analysis question: Which details in the description of Vincent Spaulding attract Holmes's notice? **Answer:** The detail that catches Holmes's attention is that Spaulding works for half the wages he could get elsewhere.

9 **Reading Check**

Answer: Any red-headed man who is over the age of 21 and in good physical and mental health is eligible.

Differentiated
Instruction Solutions for All Learners

Strategy for Less Proficient Readers
As students read, they can fill out graphic organizers that identify details about the plot, characters, setting, and theme of the story. Afterwards, they can use their notes to briefly retell the story to a partner. Listeners should be sure students' retellings are accurate in detail.

Enrichment for Advanced Readers
Have students gather in a small group to debate which of the four short-story elements (plot, character, setting, theme) is most important to "The Red-headed League." In discussing each element, students should consider questions such as "Would the story have worked in a different setting or with different characters?" and "What is the message at the heart of the story?" Ask students to summarize their discussion for the class.

⑩ Reading Skill
Contrasting Characters

- **Ask** students to sum up what they know about Mr. Wilson and to make a generalization about him. **Answer:** Mr. Wilson works hard but does not make a lot of money. He is a pawnbroker who does not go out very much. He would like to make more money.

- **Ask** students the Reading Skill question: In what ways does Wilson's lack of awareness of the outside world present a contrast to Holmes and Watson? **Answer:** Holmes and Watson are the opposite; they are detectives who must have knowledge about the world around them.

- **Invite** students to think of labels for each of the characters they have met so far. For example, they might label Holmes "Mr. Know-It-All." Discuss students' labels and encourage them to think of new labels for characters as they meet them or as they learn more about characters they have already labeled.

⑪ Humanities

Illustrations for "The Red-headed League," by Sidney Paget

Englishman Sidney Paget (1860–1908) had a successful career as a painter and illustrator. He is best remembered for his original illustrations for the Holmes stories, which first appeared in the popular *Strand* magazine. Use the following question for discussion:

- How do Paget's illustrations help you appreciate the story? **Possible response:** They show the styles of hair and clothing worn at the time. They depict dramatic moments in the story.

---

gets it, and I understand that there are more vacancies than there are men, so that the trustees are at their wits' end what to do with the money. If my hair would only change color, here's a nice little crib all ready for me to step into.'

⑩ "'Why, what is it, then?' I asked. You see, Mr. Holmes, I am a very stay-at-home man, and as my business came to me instead of my having to go to it, I was often weeks on end without putting my foot over the doormat. In that way I didn't know much of what was going on outside, and I was always glad of a bit of news.

"'Have you never heard of the League of the Red-headed Men?' he asked with his eyes open.

"'Never.'

"'Why, I wonder at that, for you are eligible yourself for one of the vacancies.'

"'And what are they worth?' I asked.

"'Oh, merely a couple of hundred a year, but the work is slight, and it need not interfere very much with one's other occupations.'

"Well, you can easily think that that made me prick up my ears, for the business has not been over-good for some years, and an extra couple of hundred would have been very handy.

"'Tell me all about it,' said I.

"'Well,' said he, showing me the advertisement, 'you can see for yourself that the League has a vacancy, and there is the address where you should apply for particulars. As far as I can make out, the League was founded by an American millionaire, Ezekiah Hopkins, who was very peculiar in his ways. He was himself red-headed, and he had a great sympathy for all red-headed men; so when he died it was found that he had left his enormous fortune in the hands of trustees, with instructions to apply the

⑪

1072 ■ *Themes in Literature: Heroism*

Reading Skill
Contrasting Characters In what ways does Wilson's lack of awareness of the outside world present a contrast to Holmes and Watson?

Vocabulary Development

Multiple Meanings

Point out the word *vacancy* on p. 1072 and ask students to think about the word's meaning. Tell students that *vacancy* has several meanings. Write the following sentences on the board, and guide students in developing definitions for each use of the word *vacancy*.

1. The beach's *vacancy* during the winter makes me feel lonely.
2. The look on her face reflected the *vacancy* of her mind.
3. The post office has a *vacancy* in the sorting department.

Ask students to write additional sentences showing the different meanings of *vacancy*. Review the meanings of the word and decide which definition best fits the use of the word *vacancy* on this page. **Answers:** 1. emptiness or blankness; 2. the state of being free of thought; 3. an unfilled position or job. Definition 3 best fits the meaning of the word as it is used on p. 1072.

interest to the providing of easy berths to men whose hair is of that color. From all I hear it is splendid pay and very little to do.

"'But,' said I, 'there would be millions of red-headed men who would apply.'

"'Not so many as you might think,' he answered. 'You see it is really confined to Londoners, and to grown men. This American had started from London when he was young, and he wanted to do the old town a good turn. Then, again, I have heard it is no use your applying if your hair is light red, or dark red, or anything but real bright, blazing, fiery red. Now, if you cared to apply, Mr. Wilson, you would just walk in; but perhaps it would hardly be worth your while to put yourself out of the way for the sake of a few hundred pounds.'

"Now, it is a fact, gentlemen, as you may see for yourselves, that my hair is of a very full and rich tint, so that it seemed to me that if there was to be any competition in the matter I stood as good a chance as any man that I had ever met. Vincent Spaulding seemed to know so much about it that I thought he might prove useful so I just ordered him to put up the shutters for the day and to come right away with me. He was very willing to have a holiday,[5] so we shut the business up and started off for the address that was given us in the advertisement.

"I never hope to see such a sight as that again, Mr. Holmes. From north, south, east, and west every man who had a shade of red in his hair had tramped into the city to answer the advertisement. Fleet Street was choked with red-headed folk, and Pope's Court looked like a coster's orange barrow.[6] I should not have thought there were so many in the whole country as were brought together by that single advertisement. Every shade of color they were—straw, lemon, orange, brick, Irish-setter, liver, clay; but, as Spaulding said, there were not many who had the real vivid flame-colored tint. When I saw how many were waiting, I would have given it up in despair; but Spaulding would not hear of it. How he did it I could not imagine, but he pushed and pulled and butted until he got me through the crowd, and right up to the steps which led to the office. There was a double stream upon the stair, some going up in hope, and some coming back dejected; but we wedged in as well as we could and soon found ourselves in the office."

"Your experience has been a most entertaining one," remarked Holmes as his client paused and refreshed his memory with a huge pinch of snuff. "Pray continue your very interesting statement."

"There was nothing in the office but a couple of wooden chairs and a deal table, behind which sat a small man with a head that

---

5. **holiday** day off from work; vacation.
6. **coster's orange barrow** pushcart of a seller of oranges.

**⑫ Reading Skill
Contrasting Characters** Who seems more invested in Wilson's joining the Red-headed League— Wilson or Spaulding? Explain.

⑬ Reading Check

Who helps Wilson push through the crowd of men applying for the Red-headed League?

The Red-headed League ■ 1073

• Ask students to think about the conventions of murder mysteries or thrillers they have read or seen. For example, most television crime shows start with a murder or other serious crime and the police spend the rest of the show trying to solve it.

• **Ask** students how this story is different from these other mysteries. **Possible response:** In other mysteries, the crime takes place at the beginning of the story, and the detective has to figure out who has committed it. Here, it is not clear what the crime is, let alone who did it. Holmes has to figure out both things.

• Remind students that when reading a Sherlock Holmes mystery that they should be suspicious of every character they meet—except for Holmes and Watson, of course.

• **Ask** students the Reading Skill question: In what way is the man's behavior toward Mr. Wilson different from his behavior toward the other candidates? **Answer:** The man has been easily finding reasons to disqualify the other men, but he is immediately favorable to Mr. Wilson.

• **Ask** students if they are suspicious of the way that the position at the Red-headed League was filled. Have students explain their answers. **Answer:** Students may suggest that they are suspicious because the position seemed to be filled arbitrarily. Students may also be weary of how the interviewer warmed so easily to Mr. Wilson.

was even redder than mine. He said a few words to each candidate as he came up, and then he always managed to find some fault in them which would disqualify them. Getting a vacancy did not seem to be such a very easy matter, after all. However, when our turn came the little man was much more favorable to me than to any of the others, and he closed the door as we entered, so that he might have a private word with us.

"'This is Mr. Jabez Wilson,' said my assistant, 'and he is willing to fill a vacancy in the League.'

"'And he is admirably suited for it,' the other answered. 'He has every requirement. I cannot recall when I have seen anything so fine.' He took a step backward, cocked his head on one side, and gazed at my hair until I felt quite bashful. Then suddenly he plunged forward, wrung my hand, and congratulated me warmly on my success.

"'It would be injustice to hesitate, said he. 'You will, however, I am sure, excuse me for taking an obvious precaution.' With that he seized my hair in both his hands, and tugged until I yelled with the pain. 'There is water in your eyes,' said he as he released me. 'I perceive that all is as it should be. But we have to be careful, for we have twice been deceived by wigs and once by paint. I could tell you tales of cobbler's wax which would disgust you with human nature.' He stepped over to the window and shouted through it at the top of his voice that the vacancy was filled. A groan of disappointment came up from below, and the folk all trooped away in different directions until there was not a red head to be seen except my own and that of the manager.

"'My name,' said he, 'is Mr. Duncan Ross, and I am myself one of the pensioners upon the fund left by our noble benefactor. Are you a married man, Mr. Wilson? Have you a family?'

"I answered that I had not.

"His face fell immediately.

"'Dear me!' he said gravely, 'that is very serious indeed! I am sorry to hear you say that. The fund was, of course, for the propagation and spread of the red-heads as well as for their maintenance. It is exceedingly unfortunate that you should be a bachelor.'

"My face lengthened at this, Mr. Holmes, for I thought that I was not to have the vacancy after all; but after thinking it over for a few minutes he said that it would be all right.

"'In the case of another,' said he, 'the objection might be fatal, but we must stretch a point in favor of a man with such a head of hair as yours. When shall you be able to enter upon your new duties?'

"'Well, it is a little awkward, for I have a business already,' said I.

Vocabulary Development

Think-Aloud: Context
Direct students' attention to the word *benefactor* on this page. Using a think-aloud process, model how to use context to infer the meaning of an unknown word. Say to students:

I'm going to think aloud to show you how I would figure out the meaning of *benefactor* from its context.

In this sentence, Mr. Ross uses the word *benefactor* to refer to the man who left money for the Red-headed League.

The word *noble* suggests that *benefactor* has a positive connotation. Also, *benefactor* reminds me of *benefit* and *beneficial,* which also have positive connotations.

It is a positive thing to leave money to help out strangers, so I think that a benefactor refers to someone who gives money or who donates to charitable causes.

"'Oh, never mind about that, Mr. Wilson!' said Vincent Spaulding. 'I should be able to look after that for you.'

"'What would be the hours?' I asked.

"'Ten to two.'

"Now a pawnbroker's business is mostly done of an evening, Mr. Holmes, especially Thursday and Friday evening, which is just before pay-day; so it would suit me very well to earn a little in the mornings. Besides, I knew that my assistant was a good man, and that he would see to anything that turned up.

"'That would suit me very well,' said I. 'And the pay?'

"'Is £4 a week.'

"'And the work?'

"'Is purely nominal.'

"'What do you call purely nominal?'

"'Well, you have to be in the office, or at least in the building, the whole time. If you leave, you forfeit your whole position forever. The will is very clear upon that point. You don't comply with the conditions if you budge from the office during that time.'

"'It's only four hours a day, and I should not think of leaving,' said I.

15 "'No excuse will avail,' said Mr. Duncan Ross; 'neither sickness nor business nor anything else. There you must stay, or you lose your billet.'[7]

"'And the work?'

"'Is to copy out the Encyclopedia Britannica. There is the first volume of it in that press. You must find your own ink, pens, and blotting-paper, but we provide this table and chair. Will you be ready tomorrow?'

"'Certainly,' I answered.

"'Then, good-bye, Mr. Jabez Wilson, and let me congratulate you once more on the important position which you have been fortunate enough to gain.' He bowed me out of the room, and I went home with my assistant, hardly knowing what to say or do, I was so pleased at my own good fortune.

"Well, I thought over the matter all day, and by evening I was in low spirits again; for I had quite persuaded myself that the whole affair must be some great hoax or fraud, though what its object might be I could not imagine. It seemed altogether past belief that anyone could make such a will, or that they would pay such a sum for doing anything so simple as copying out the Encyclopedia Britannica. Vincent Spaulding did what he could to cheer me up, but by bedtime I had reasoned myself out of the whole thing. However,

---

7. **billet** (bil´ it) *n.* position; job.

Literary Analysis
Protagonist and Antagonist Which details in the description of Wilson's responsibilities make Ross seem like a suspicious character?

 Reading Check

16 Who offers to look after Wilson's pawnbroker business while he is at his other job?

The Red-headed League ■ 1075

15 **Literary Analysis**
Protagonist and Antagonist

- After students read about Mr. Wilson's duties at the Red-headed League, **ask** them the Reading Skill question: Which details in the description of Wilson's responsibilities make Ross seem like a suspicious character?
  Answer: Ross seems suspicious because of his insistence on staying in the room, the odd job of encyclopedia writing, and the lack of a supply of writing materials.

- **Ask** students to predict what Sherlock Holmes may think about this episode of Mr. Wilson's story.
  Answer: Students may suggest that Sherlock Holmes will know what Ross is up to and will identify the crime that Ross is probably committing.

16 **Reading Check**

Answer: Spaulding offers to look after Mr. Wilson's business while Wilson does his duties for the League.

Differentiated Instruction Solutions for All Learners

Strategy for Special Needs Students
Have students choose partners with whom to read the story. Each partner should read on his or her own, and then pause every one or two pages to summarize the story up to that point. Each partner should make sure that the other's summary is accurate. Students can try predicting what may happen in the next page or two.

Strategy for English Learners
After reading each page of the selection, have students list words they don't understand or recognize. Ask a student who is proficient in English to help each English learner figure out the problematic words. Have English learners keep a log of the words they have learned, their definitions, and additional sentences using the words.

- **Ask** students to summarize the routine that Mr. Wilson and Mr. Ross develop over the course of the eight weeks.
  Answer: Mr. Wilson goes to the office at 10 o'clock every morning, copies the encyclopedia, and leaves at 2 o'clock every afternoon. Mr. Ross meets Mr. Wilson at the door and checks on him periodically throughout the day. Over time, Mr. Ross checks in less frequently.

- **Ask** students to explain why Mr. Ross checks in less frequently.
  Answer: Mr. Ross probably realized that he could trust Mr. Wilson to stay in the office.

in the morning I determined to have a look at it anyhow, so I bought a penny bottle of ink, and with a quill-pen, and seven sheets of foolscap paper, I started off for Pope's Court.

"Well, to my surprise and delight, everything was as right as possible. The table was set out ready for me, and Mr. Duncan Ross was there to see that I got fairly to work. He started me off upon the letter A, and then he left me; but he would drop in from time to time to see that all was right with me. At two o'clock he bade me good-day, complimented me upon the amount that I had written, and locked the door of the office after me.

"This went on day after day, Mr. Holmes, and on Saturday the manager came in and planked down four golden sovereigns for my week's work. It was the same next week, and the same the week after. Every morning I was there at ten, and every afternoon I left at two. By degrees Mr. Duncan Ross took to coming in only once of a morning, and then, after a time, he did not come in at all. Still, of course, I never dared to ⑰ leave the room for an instant, for I was not sure when he might come, and the billet was such a good one, and suited me so well, that I would not risk the loss of it.

"Eight weeks passed away like this, and I had written about Abbots and Archery and Armor and Architecture and Attica, and hoped with diligence that I might get on to the B's before very long. It cost me something in foolscap, and I had pretty nearly filled a shelf with my writings. And then suddenly the whole business came to an end."

Vocabulary Development

Vocabulary Builder Reinforcement
Give students sentences using the words in which the word may or may not be used correctly. Students must tell whether the use is correct and explain their answer. Use these sentences:

1. Juan was feeling *introspective,* so he went to the festival and met new people.
   Answer: No, *introspective* is not used correctly. It means "having to do with looking into one's own thoughts." A social activity would prevent this.

2. The child was getting *vexed* by all of the gifts she was receiving at her birthday party.
   Answer: No, *vex* is not used correctly. It is not likely that gifts would annoy a child on her birthday.

3. Providing food for the massive wedding was a formidable task for the caterer.
   Answer: Yes, *formidable* is used correctly. *Formidable* means "overwhelming," and catering a large wedding would be overwhelming.

"To an end?"

"Yes, sir. And no later than this morning. I went to my work as usual at ten o'clock, but the door was shut and locked, with a little square of cardboard hammered on to the middle of the panel with a tack. Here it is, and you can read for yourself."

He held up a piece of white cardboard about the size of a sheet of notepaper. It read in this fashion:

THE RED-HEADED LEAGUE IS DISSOLVED.
October 9, 1890.

Sherlock Holmes and I surveyed this curt announcement and the rueful face behind it, until the comical side of the affair so completely overtopped every other consideration that we both burst out into a roar of laughter.

"I cannot see that there is anything very funny," cried our client, flushing up to the roots of his flaming head. "If you can do nothing better than laugh at me, I can go elsewhere."

"No, no," cried Holmes, shoving him back into the chair from which he had half risen. "I really wouldn't miss your case for the world. It is most refreshingly unusual. But there is, if you will excuse my saying so, something just a little funny about it. Pray what steps did you take when you found the card upon the door?"

"I was staggered, sir. I did not know what to do. Then I called at the offices round, but none of them seemed to know anything about it. Finally, I went to the landlord, who is an accountant living on the ground floor, and I asked him if he could tell me what had become of the Red-headed League. He said that he had never heard of any such body. Then I asked him who Mr. Duncan Ross was. He answered that the name was new to him.

"'Well,' said I, 'the gentleman at No. 4.'

"'What, the red-headed man?'

"'Yes.'

"'Oh,' said he, 'his name was William Morris. He was a solicitor[8] and was using my room as a temporary convenience until his new premises were ready. He moved out yesterday.'

"'Where could I find him?'

"'Oh, at his new offices. He did tell me the address. Yes, 17 King Edward Street, near St. Paul's.'

"I started off, Mr. Holmes, but when I got to that address it was a manufactory of artificial kneecaps, and no one in it had ever heard of either Mr. William Morris or Mr. Duncan Ross."

"And what did you do then?" asked Holmes.

---

8. **solicitor** (sə lis´ it ər) *n.* member of the legal profession.

Reading Skill Contrasting Characters How do the reactions of Watson and Holmes to the announcement compare with Mr. Wilson's? Explain.

Literary Analysis Protagonist and Antagonist What does William Morris's dishonesty about his identity suggest about his character?

 Reading Check

After eight weeks at his new job, what does Wilson find posted on the door?

The Red-headed League ■ 1077

- At this point in the story, have students make a list of characters who might be considered suspects. Students' lists should contain Spaulding and Ross/Morris.

- Then, have students identify reasons why these characters might be suspects. Elicit from students that the men have acted suspiciously—Spaulding has been enthusiastic about Wilson getting the position at the league. Ross has lied about his identity.

- **Ask** students the Literary Analysis question: What reason might Holmes have for being suspicious of Vincent Spaulding?
Answer: Spaulding's willingness to work at half wages interests Holmes, but the detail about the white mark on Spaulding's forehead seems to interest him more.

- Challenge students to **explain** Holmes's excitement after hearing the description of Spaulding.
Answer: Holmes probably knows about a criminal who has a white mark on his forehead.

"I went home to Saxe-Coburg Square, and I took the advice of my assistant. But he could not help me in any way. He could only say that if I waited I should hear by post. But that was not quite good enough, Mr. Holmes. I did not wish to lose such a place without a struggle, so, as I had heard that you were good enough to give advice to poor folk who were in need of it, I came right away to you."

"And you did very wisely," said Holmes. "Your case is an exceedingly remarkable one, and I shall be happy to look into it. From what you have told me I think that it is possible that graver issues hang from it than might at first sight appear."

"Grave enough!" said Mr. Jabez Wilson. "Why, I have lost four pound a week."

"As far as you are personally concerned," remarked Holmes, "I do not see that you have any grievance against this extraordinary league. On the contrary, you are, as I understand, richer by some £30, to say nothing of the minute knowledge which you have gained on every subject which comes under the letter A. You have lost nothing by them."

"No, sir. But I want to find out about them, and who they are, and what their object was in playing this prank—if it was a prank—upon me. It was a pretty expensive joke for them, for it cost them two and thirty pounds."

"We shall endeavor to clear up these points for you. And, first, one or two questions, Mr. Wilson. This assistant of yours who first called your attention to the advertisement—㉑ how long had he been with you?"

"About a month then."

"How did he come?"

"In answer to an advertisement."

"Was he the only applicant?"

"No, I had a dozen."

Literary Analysis
Protagonist and Antagonist What reason might Holmes have for being suspicious of Vincent Spaulding?

Vocabulary Development

Word Analysis
Read aloud the last paragraph on p. 1079. Point out the definition of the word *introspective* in the margin. Write the word on the board and break it up into its prefix, root, and suffix. Students should easily understand that *intro-* means "into, inside, inward." If you or any students in the class wear eyeglasses, point them out and tell the class that eyeglasses are also called *spectacles.* This clue will help students remember that *-spec-* has to do with looking or seeing.

Challenge students to put the pieces of the word together to understand that *introspective* means "able to look inward at one's own thoughts." Encourage students to think of other words based on the root *-spec-*.
Possible responses: *respect, prospect, aspect, inspect, spectator, spectacular, spectrum,* and other forms of these words.

"Why did you pick him?"

"Because he was handy and would come cheap."

"At half-wages, in fact."

"Yes."

"What is he like, this Vincent Spaulding?"

"Small, stout-built, very quick in his ways. No hair on his face, though he's not short of thirty. Has a white splash of acid upon his forehead."

Holmes sat up in his chair in considerable excitement. "I thought as much," said he. "Have you ever observed that his ears are pierced for earrings?"

"Yes, sir. He told me that a gypsy had done it for him when he was a lad."

"Hum!" said Holmes, sinking back in deep thought. "He is still with you?"

"Oh, yes, sir; I have only just left him."

"And has your business been attended to in your absence?"

"Nothing to complain of, sir. There's never very much to do of a morning."

"That will do, Mr. Wilson. I shall be happy to give you an opinion upon the subject in the course of a day or two. Today is Saturday, and I hope that by Monday we may come to a conclusion."

"Well, Watson," said Holmes when our visitor had left us, "what do you make of it all?"

"I make nothing of it," I answered frankly. "It is a most mysterious business."

"As a rule," said Holmes, "the more bizarre a thing is the less mysterious it proves to be. It is your commonplace, featureless crimes which are really puzzling, just as a commonplace face is the most difficult to identify. But I must be prompt over this matter."

"What are you going to do, then?" I asked.

"To smoke," he answered. "It is quite a three pipe problem, and I beg that you won't speak to me for fifty minutes." He curled himself up in his chair, with his thin knees drawn up to his hawk-like nose, and there he sat with his eyes closed and his black clay pipe thrusting out like the bill of some strange bird. I had come to the conclusion that he had dropped asleep, and indeed was nodding myself, when he suddenly sprang out of his chair with the gesture of a man who has made up his mind and put his pipe down upon the mantelpiece.

"Sarasate[9] plays at the St. James's Hall this afternoon," he remarked. "What do you think, Watson? Could your patients spare you for a few hours?"

---

9. **Sarasate** (sä rä sä′ tä) Spanish violinist and composer.

Literary Analysis
Protagonist and Antagonist What does Holmes's expectation of reaching a conclusion in two days reveal about his character?

Reading Check

What reasons does Mr. Wilson give for hiring Vincent Spaulding?

The Red-headed League ■ 1079

- **Ask** students to identify the actions taken by Holmes and the details that he has noticed during his visit to Mr. Wilson's shop.
Answer: Holmes has studied the houses on the street, met Spaulding and looked at the knees of his trousers, and tapped on the pavement.

- **Ask** students to use their own powers of deduction to guess at what Holmes has discovered.
Possible response: Holmes has discovered a secret passage under the house by tapping on the stones, and the passage leads to another building. Mr. Spaulding is a suspect because of the evidence on his trousers.

25 Reading Skill
Comparing Characters

- Point out that Holmes has started his search for answers in earnest at this point in the story. After students finish reading p. 1080, **ask** them to think of adjectives that describe Holmes during this part of the crime-solving process.
Possible response: Holmes is observant, focused, thorough, introspective, and unwilling to share information.

- **Ask** students the Reading Skill question: Based on Holmes's remark about Spaulding, what trait do the two men share? Explain.
Answer: Both men are very intelligent. Holmes is impressed by Spaulding's intelligence and by his daring nature.

"I have nothing to do today. My practice is never very absorbing."

"Then put on your hat and come. I am going through the City first, and we can have some lunch on the way. I observe that there is a good deal of German music on the program, which is rather more to my taste than Italian or French. It is <u>introspective</u>, and I want to introspect. Come along!"

We traveled by the Underground as far as Aldersgate; and a short walk took us to Saxe-Coburg Square, the scene of the singular story which we had listened to in the morning. It was a poky, little, shabby-genteel place, where four lines of dingy two-storied brick houses looked out into a small railed-in enclosure, where a lawn of weedy grass and a few clumps of faded laurel bushes made a hard fight against a smoke-laden and uncongenial atmosphere. Three gilt balls and a brown board with "JABEZ WILSON" in white letters, upon a corner house, announced the place where our red-headed client carried on his business. Sherlock Holmes stopped in front of it with his head on one side and looked it all over, with his eyes shining brightly between puckered lids. Then he walked slowly up the street, and then down again to the corner, still looking keenly at the houses. Finally he returned to the pawnbroker's, and, having thumped vigorously upon the pavement with his stick two or three times, he went up to the door and knocked. It was instantly opened by a bright-looking, clean-shaven young fellow, who asked him to step in.

"Thank you," said Holmes, "I only wished to ask you how you would go from here to the Strand."

"Third right, fourth left," answered the assistant promptly, closing the door.

"Smart fellow, that," observed Holmes as we walked away. "He is, in my judgment, the fourth smartest man in London, and for daring I am not sure that he has not a claim to be third. I have known something of him before."

"Evidently," said I, "Mr. Wilson's assistant counts for a good deal in this mystery of the Red-headed League. I am sure that you inquired your way merely in order that you might see him."

"Not him."

"What then?"

"The knees of his trousers."

"And what did you see?"

"What I expected to see."

"Why did you beat the pavement?"

"My dear doctor, this is a time for observation, not for talk. We are spies in an enemy's country. We know something of Saxe-Coburg Square. Let us now explore the parts which lie behind it."

1080 ■ *Themes in Literature: Heroism*

Vocabulary Builder
introspective (in′ trə spek′ tiv) *adj.* having to do with one's own thoughts and feelings

Reading Skill
Comparing Characters Based on Holmes's remark about Spaulding, what trait do the two men share? Explain.

Vocabulary Development

Expressive Vocabulary
Encourage students to use the expressive vocabulary presented earlier to discuss Mr. Wilson' character. You might initiate the discussion with sentence starters like these:

1. The requirements of the position at the Red-headed League might make a *rational* person suspicious because . . .

2. Mr. Wilson at first *speculates* that the Red-headed League might . . .

3. Mr. Wilson's fears about the league are lessened when he sees *tangible* evidence, such as . . .

4. Readers know that Mr. Wilson lives in an *urban* area because . . .

5. Mr. Wilson provided an interesting *visual* image when he described . . .

The road in which we found ourselves as we turned round the corner from the retired Saxe-Coburg Square presented as great a contrast to it as the front of a picture does to the back. It was one of the main arteries which conveyed the traffic of the City to the north and west. The roadway was blocked with the immense stream of commerce flowing in a double tide inward and outward, while the footpaths were black with the hurrying swarm of pedestrians. It was difficult to realize as we looked at the line of fine shops and stately business premises that they really abutted on the other side upon the faded and stagnant square which we had just quitted.

"Let me see," said Holmes, standing at the corner and glancing along the line, "I should like just to remember the order of the houses here. It is a hobby of mine to have an exact knowledge of London. There is Mortimer's, the tobacconist, the little newspaper shop, the Coburg branch of the City and Suburban Bank, the Vegetarian Restaurant, and McFarlane's carriage-building depot. That carries us right on to the other block. And now, Doctor, we've done our work, so it's time we had some play. A sandwich and a cup of coffee, and then off to violin land, where all is sweetness and delicacy and harmony, and there are no red-headed clients to <u>vex</u> us with their conundrums."

My friend was an enthusiastic musician, being himself not only a very capable performer but a composer of no ordinary merit. All the afternoon he sat in the stalls wrapped in the most perfect happiness, gently waving his long, thin fingers in time to the music, while his gently smiling face and his languid, dreamy eyes were as unlike those of Holmes, the sleuthhound, Holmes the relentless, keen-witted, ready-handed criminal agent, as it was possible to conceive. In his singular character the dual nature alternately asserted itself, and his extreme exactness and astuteness represented, as I have often thought, the reaction against the poetic and contemplative mood which occasionally predominated in him. The swing of his nature took him from extreme languor to devouring energy; and, as I knew well, he was never so truly <u>formidable</u> as when, for days on end, he had been lounging in his armchair amid his improvisations and his black-letter editions. Then it was that the lust of the chase would suddenly come upon him, and that his brilliant reasoning power would rise to the level of intuition, until those who were unacquainted with his methods would look askance at him as on a man whose knowledge was not that of other mortals. When I saw him that afternoon so enwrapped in the music at St. James's Hall I felt that an evil time might be coming upon those whom he had set himself to hunt down.

"You want to go home, no doubt, Doctor," he remarked as we emerged.

Vocabulary Builder
vex (veks) *v.* annoy

formidable (fôr´ mə də bəl) *adj.* awe-inspiring

Reading Check

Which aspect of Spaulding's appearance does Holmes want to observe?

The Red-headed League ■ 1081

26 Critical Thinking
Analyze

- Explain to students that one of the reasons Holmes is such a well-loved character is that he is unpredictable. Point out that, instead of charging out to find the criminal, Holmes goes to a concert to enjoy himself.

- Ask students to reread the longest paragraph on p. 1081 and to use the information in it to learn more about Holmes' character. **Ask** students to make a generalization about the two sides of Holmes's nature?
Answer: Holmes is either dreaming and contemplative or energetic and searching. He can swing from one personality to the other without warning.

- Have students return to **Literary Analysis Graphic Organizer A** (*Graphic Organizer Transparencies*, p. 212). Have students use the information on p. 1081 to provide insight into Holmes's actions and goals. Students should understand that one of Holmes's goals is to solve puzzles and thwart criminals. Another is to enjoy the simple pleasures of food and entertainment.

27 Reading Check

Answer: Holmes wants to look at the knees of Spaulding's trousers.

Differentiated
Instruction   Solutions for All Learners

Strategy for Special Needs Students
Have students think of questions that they asked while reading the story that they were not able to answer on their own. They can discuss their questions with a partner. Have students work together to look back at the story to try and find the answers. Remind them that not all questions readers have are answered in a story; sometimes readers have to answer questions for themselves. For example,

"The Red-headed League" does not explain how Holmes knew the criminal at the center of the story.

After this exercise, students can gather in groups, introduce their questions, and discuss their attempts to find answers. Have students share ideas about their answers to each other's questions. Remind students to support all answers with details from the story.

- Remind students that in a mystery, the conflict is between the detective, who wants to solve a crime and catch the criminal, and the criminal, who wants to break the law and get away with it.

- Point out that on p. 1082, the crime (or the conflict) is finally beginning to emerge.

- Challenge students to **explain** what they know about the crime at the center of the story.
  Answer: The crime has not yet happened. Holmes hopes to prevent it from happening. It is a serious crime—serious enough to require Watson's gun and a police officer.

- Then **ask** them to guess at the identity of the criminal, or the antagonist in the story.
  Possible response: Based on Holmes's inquiries, the criminal is probably Spaulding.

29 **Literature in Context**

Culture Connection Hansoms were not the only form of transportation in Holmes's London. The London Underground is one of the world's oldest subway systems; trains began running in 1863. The Metropolitan Line, the oldest in the system, was completed in 1884. By 1900, three separate companies had constructed individual train lines. On p. 1080, Holmes and Watson take a Metropolitan Line train from Baker Street station, which is across the street from Holmes's flat.

Connect to the Literature Have students study the illustration of the hansom cab on p. 1082 and think about the advantages and disadvantages of using a horse-powered vehicle rather than a motorized vehicle. **Ask** students the Connect to the Literature question: What problems would traveling by hansom pose for someone rushing to stop a crime?

Answer: A hansom would be slow and difficult to maneuver if a person was rushing to stop a crime.

"Yes, it would be as well."

"And I have some business to do which will take some hours. This business at Coburg Square is serious."

"Why serious?"

28 "A considerable crime is in contemplation. I have every reason to believe that we shall be in time to stop it. But today being Saturday rather complicates matters. I shall want your help tonight."

"At what time?"

"Ten will be early enough."

"I shall be at Baker Street at ten."

"Very well. And, I say, Doctor, there may be some little danger, so kindly put your army revolver in your pocket." He waved his hand, turned on his heel, and disappeared in an instant among the crowd.

I trust that I am not more dense than my neighbors, but I was always oppressed with a sense of my own stupidity in my dealings with Sherlock Holmes. Here I had heard what he had heard, I had seen what he had seen, and yet from his words it was evident that he saw clearly not only what had happened but what was about to happen, while to me the whole business was still confused and grotesque. As I drove home to my house in Kensington I thought over it all, from the extraordinary story of the red-headed copier of the Encyclopedia down to the visit to Saxe-Coburg Square, and the ominous words with which he had parted from me. What was this nocturnal expedition, and why should I go armed? Where were we going, and what were we to do? I had the hint from Holmes that this smooth-faced pawnbroker's assistant was a formidable man—a man who might play a deep game. I tried to puzzle it out, but gave it up in despair and set the matter aside until night should bring an explanation.

It was a quarter past nine when I started from home and made my way across the Park, and so through Oxford Street to Baker Street. Two hansoms were standing at the door, and as I entered the passage I heard the sound of voices from above. On entering his room I found Holmes in animated conversation with two men, one of whom I recognized as Peter Jones, the official police agent, while the other was a long, thin, sadfaced man, with a very shiny hat and oppressively respectable frock coat.

1082 ■ *Themes in Literature: Heroism*

---

29 **Literature in Context**

Culture Connection

Hansoms The hansom, also known as the hansom cab, is a two-wheeled covered carriage for two passengers that is pulled by one horse. The cab was named for its inventor, Joseph Hansom (1803–1882), a London architect. By the late 1850s, the hansom was popular in New York and Boston as well as in London. Customers could enjoy a scenic and romantic ride in private with an unobstructed view because the driver sat above and behind the passengers' cab. Today, updated hansom cabs are a popular tourist attraction in New York's Central Park. However, in this story, they are a common form of transportation.

Connect to the Literature

What problems would traveling by hansom pose for someone rushing to stop a crime?

Vocabulary Development

Think-Aloud: Context
Direct students' attention to the word *ominous* in the long paragraph on this page. Using a think-aloud process, model how to use context to infer the meaning of an unknown word. Say to students:

I'm going to think aloud to show you how I would figure out the meaning of *ominous* from its context.

The sentence in which *ominous* appears gives me a clue. Watson uses the word to describe Holmes's parting remark. I look back at the previous paragraph and reread Holmes's words: "And, I say, Doctor, there may be some little danger, so kindly put your army revolver in your pocket." To me, Holmes's words seem like a warning of danger. I look again at the word *ominous*. What does it sound or look like? It kind of reminds me of the word *omen*. An *omen* is also a kind of warning. My guess, then, is that *ominous* is used to describe something that "warns of future danger or threats."

"Ha! our party is complete," said Holmes, buttoning up his pea-jacket and taking his heavy hunting crop from the rack. "Watson, I think you know Mr. Jones, of Scotland Yard? Let me introduce you to Mr. Merryweather, who is to be our companion in tonight's adventure."

"We're hunting in couples again, Doctor, you see," said Jones in his consequential way. "Our friend here is a wonderful man for starting a chase. All he wants is an old dog to help him to do the running down."

"I hope a wild goose may not prove to be the end of our chase," observed Mr. Merryweather gloomily.

"You may place considerable confidence in Mr. Holmes, sir," said the police agent loftily. "He has his own little methods, which are, if he won't mind my saying so, just a little too theoretical and fantastic, but he has the makings of a detective in him. It is not too much to say that once or twice, as in that business of the Sholto murder and the Agra treasure, he has been more nearly correct than the official force."

"Oh, if you say so, Mr. Jones, it is all right," said the stranger with deference. "Still, I confess that I miss my rubber.[10] It is the first Saturday night for seven-and-twenty years that I have not had my rubber."

"I think you will find," said Sherlock Holmes, "that you will play for a higher stake tonight than you have ever done yet, and that the play will be more exciting. For you, Mr. Merryweather, the stake will be some £30,000; and for you, Jones, it will be the man upon whom you wish to lay your hands."

"John Clay, the murderer, thief, smasher, and forger. He's a young man, Mr. Merryweather, but he is at the head of his profession, and I would rather have my bracelets on him than on any criminal in London. He's a remarkable man, is young John Clay. His grandfather was a royal duke, and he himself has been to Eton[11] and Oxford.[12] His brain is as cunning as his fingers, and though we meet signs of him at every turn, we never know where to find the man himself. He'll crack a crib[13] in Scotland one week, and be raising money to build an orphanage in Cornwall the next. I've been on his track for years and have never set eyes on him yet."

"I hope that I may have the pleasure of introducing you tonight. I've had one or two little turns also with Mr. John Clay, and I agree with you that he is at the head of his profession. It is past ten,

---

10. **rubber** a term for a type of card game.
11. **Eton** famous British secondary school for boys.
12. **Oxford** oldest university in Great Britain.
13. **crack a crib** commit burglary.

Reading Skill
Comparing Characters Despite their differences, in what ways are Sherlock Holmes and John Clay similar?

 Reading Check

With whom is Holmes speaking when Watson arrives?

The Red-headed League ■ 1083

③⓪ Reading Skill
Comparing Characters

- **Explain** that one way writers build tension in a story is to give their protagonist and antagonist equal but opposite strengths. Give students the example of the cartoon characters Wiley E. Coyote and Roadrunner. Wiley is sly and grumpy, but Roadrunner is equally cheerful and quick. Challenge students to think of examples of other protagonists and antagonists whose qualities are well matched.

- **Ask** students the Reading Skill question: Despite their differences, in what ways are Sherlock Holmes and John Clay similar?
  Answer: Both Holmes and Clay are remarkable, intelligent, unpredictable, and cultured men.

- Then, **ask** how the two men are different.
  Answer: Holmes is a detective and Clay is a criminal. Holmes helps citizens, while Clay robs citizens.

③① Reading Check

Answer: Holmes was speaking to Peter Jones, a police officer, and Mr. Merryweather, a bank director.

Differentiated Instruction   Solutions for All Learners

Strategy for Special Needs Students
To help students understand the similarities and differences between Holmes and his opponent Clay, have students create a simple two-column chart, labeling one column *Holmes* and the other *Clay.* Students should jot down what they know about the two characters. Then have students circle the characteristics the two characters have in common. Allow students to work with a partner to write a generalization about the similarities and differences between the two men.

Strategy for Advanced Readers
Have students form groups and make lists of all of the clues in the story. Have students play detectives, analyzing the clues and comprising their own theories of what is behind the formation of the League. Have students present their theories to the class and involve the class in a debate about the possibility of their theories.

Infer

- Tell students that one way to make inferences about characters is to analyze their actions and dialogue.

- **Ask** students how Holmes reacts on p. 1085 when Mr. Merryweather makes an unnecessary noise.
Answer: Holmes becomes irritated with him.

- **Challenge** students to analyze Holmes's response to Mr. Merryweather and make an inference about Holmes's character based on his response.
Possible response: Holmes reprimands Mr. Merryweather severely and treats him like a child. This response shows that Holmes's biggest concern is solving the case; he is not concerned with hurting Mr. Merryweather's feelings. His response also shows that he has full faith in his theories, revealing that he is a very confident man.

however, and quite time that we started. If you two will take the first hansom, Watson and I will follow in the second."

Sherlock Holmes was not very communicative during the long drive and lay back in the cab humming the tunes which he had heard in the afternoon. We rattled through an endless labyrinth of gas-lit streets until we emerged into Farrington Street.

"We are close there now," my friend remarked. "This fellow Merryweather is a bank director, and personally interested in the matter. I thought it as well to have Jones with us also. He is not a bad fellow, though an absolute imbecile in his profession. He has one positive virtue. He is as brave as a bulldog and as tenacious as a lobster if he gets his claws upon anyone. Here we are, and they are waiting for us."

We had reached the same crowded thoroughfare in which we had found ourselves in the morning. Our cabs were dismissed, and, following the guidance of Mr. Merryweather, we passed down a narrow passage and through a side door, which he opened for us. Within there was a small corridor, which ended in a very massive iron gate. This also was opened, and led down a flight of winding stone steps, which terminated at another formidable gate. Mr. Merryweather stopped to light a lantern, and then conducted us down a dark, earth-smelling passage, and so, after opening a third door, into a huge vault or cellar, which was piled all round with crates and massive boxes.

"You are not very vulnerable from above," Holmes remarked as he held up the lantern and gazed about him.

Vocabulary Development

Dictionary Use
Using a think-aloud process, model how to use a dictionary to identify the meaning of *labyrinth*, which appears at the top of p. 1084. Say to students:

I'm going to think aloud to show you how I would find the correct meaning of *labyrinth* in the dictionary.

There are three definitions. The first definition is "a maze or network of twisting passages." That fits. The men have just traveled on winding streets.

The second definition is "a confusing arrangement or state of affairs." This definition is more abstract than the first.

The third definition is a medical one—"the inner ear." This definition is obviously incorrect.

Let's insert the first definition into the sentence. "We rattled through an endless maze or network of gas-lit streets until we emerged into Farrington Street." The first definition works best.

"Nor from below," said Mr. Merryweather, striking his stick upon the flags which lined the floor. "Why, dear me, it sounds quite hollow!" he remarked, looking up in surprise.

"I must really ask you to be a little more quiet!" said Holmes severely. "You have already imperiled the whole success of our expedition. Might I beg that you would have the goodness to sit down upon one of those boxes, and not to interfere?"

The solemn Mr. Merryweather perched himself upon a crate, with a very injured expression upon his face, while Holmes fell upon his knees upon the floor and, with the lantern and a magnifying lens, began to examine minutely the cracks between the stones. A few seconds sufficed to satisfy him, for he sprang to his feet again and put his glass in his pocket.

"We have at least an hour before us," he remarked, "for they can hardly take any steps until the good pawnbroker is safely in bed. Then they will not lose a minute, for the sooner they do their work the longer time they will have for their escape. We are at present, Doctor—as no doubt you have divined—in the cellar of the City branch of one of the principal London banks. Mr. Merryweather is the chairman of directors, and he will explain to you that there are reasons why the more daring criminals of London should take a considerable interest in this cellar at present."

"It is our French gold," whispered the director. "We have had several warnings that an attempt might be made upon it."

"Your French gold?"

"Yes. We had occasion some months ago to strengthen our resources and borrowed for that purpose 30,000 napoleons from the Bank of France. It has become known that we have never had occasion to unpack the money, and that it is still lying in our cellar. The crate upon which I sit contains 2,000 napoleons packed between layers of lead foil. Our reserve of bullion is much larger at present than is usually kept in a single branch office, and the directors have had misgivings upon the subject."

"Which were very well justified," observed Holmes.

"And now it is time that we arranged our little plans. I expect that within an hour matters will come to a head. In the meantime, Mr. Merryweather, we must put the screen over that dark lantern."

"And sit in the dark?"

"I am afraid so. I had brought a pack of cards in my pocket, and I thought that, as we were a *partie carrée*,[14] you might have your rubber after all. But I see that the enemy's preparations have gone so far that we cannot risk the presence of a light. And, first of all, we

---

14. *partie carrée* (pär tē´ cä rā´) French for "group of four."

Literary Analysis
Protagonist and Antagonist What kind of enemy does Holmes anticipate he and his companions will face?

Reading Check

Where does Mr. Merryweather lead Holmes and his companions?

The Red-headed League ■ 1085

33 Literary Analysis
Protagonist and Antagonist

- **Ask** students the Literary Analysis question: What kind of enemy does Holmes anticipate he and his companions will face?
  Answer: The criminals are smart enough to wait until the pawnbroker is safely in bed, yet daring enough to attempt to rob a major London bank.

- Point out that Holmes has created a picture of his antagonist as a daring, reckless man. **Ask** students how Holmes compares, particularly in the last paragraph on p. 1085 that begins, "I am afraid so. . ."
  Answer: Holmes is not reckless but calm. He calmly gives instructions. He shows his thoughtful and civilized side, too. He brings playing cards for Mr. Merryweather.

34 Reading Check

Answer: Mr. Merryweather leads the men to the cellar of his bank where French gold is being stored.

Differentiated
Instruction Solutions for All Learners

Strategy for English Learners
Students may be confused by the dialogue and the unfolding of events in the last part of the story. It may help them to listen to the last part of the story on **Listening to Literature Audio CD.** Ask students to read along as they listen. At the end of each page, stop the CD and ask students to summarize what has happened. If students are still confused, play the CD again and talk about the specific words or pieces of information that confuse them.

Strategy for Advanced Readers
Ask students to think of modern mysteries or thrillers they have read and to compare them to "The Red-headed League." Students should identify similarities and differences in the plots and characters, and in the authors' writing styles. Ask students to comment on which type of story—modern or traditional—they prefer and to explain why.

- Remind students that Watson's job is to stand in for the readers in the story. Like them, he observes Holmes in action and asks questions the reader probably has. His emotional state should reflect what the reader should be feeling.

- Have students reread the passage on p. 1086 where Watson describes how time has passed.

- **Ask** students the Literary Analysis question: What details of Watson's account build the suspense of the conflict?
  Answer: Watson tells of his watchfulness, tension, and fear. His comment about being afraid to move and feeling nervous should make readers feel the suspense. When Watson sees the gleam of light, the readers should be very curious about what is going to happen next.

36 **Reading Skill**
Comparing Characters

- Students should understand that the story is approaching its climax. Now they will begin to see the pieces of the story come together.

- **Ask** students the Reading Skill question: In what ways is the first burglar's appearance similar to that of Vincent Spaulding?
  Answer: Like Vincent Spaulding, the first burglar is quick, slender, and boyish looking.

- **Ask** students how the second burglar is similar in appearance to William Morris (Duncan Ross).
  Answer: Like Morris, the second burglar has red hair.

---

must choose our positions. These are daring men, and though we shall take them at a disadvantage, they may do us some harm unless we are careful. I shall stand behind this crate, and do you conceal yourselves behind those. Then, when I flash a light upon them, close in swiftly. If they fire, Watson, have no compunction about shooting them down."

I placed my revolver, cocked, upon the top of the wooden case behind which I crouched. Holmes shot the slide across the front of his lantern and left us in pitch darkness—such an absolute darkness as I have never before experienced. The smell of hot metal remained to assure us that the light was still there, ready to flash out at a moment's notice. To me, with my nerves worked up to a pitch of expectancy, there was something depressing and subduing in the sudden gloom, and in the cold dank air of the vault.

"They have but one retreat," whispered Holmes. "That is back through the house into Saxe-Coburg Square. I hope that you have done what I asked you, Jones?"

"I have an inspector and two officers waiting at the front door."

"Then we have stopped all the holes. And now we must be silent and wait."

35 What a time it seemed! From comparing notes afterwards it was but an hour and a quarter, yet it appeared to me that the night must have almost gone, and the dawn be breaking above us. My limbs were weary and stiff, for I feared to change my position; yet my nerves were worked up to the highest pitch of tension, and my hearing was so acute that I could not only hear the gentle breathing of my companions, but I could distinguish the deeper, heavier in-breath of the bulky Jones from the thin, sighing note of the bank director. From my position I could look over the case in the direction of the floor. Suddenly my eyes caught the glint of a light.

At first it was but a lurid spark upon the stone pavement. Then it lengthened out until it became a yellow line, and then, without any warning or sound, a gash seemed to open and a hand appeared; a white, almost womanly hand, which felt about in the center of the little area of light. For a minute or more the hand, with its writhing fingers, protruded out of the floor. Then it was withdrawn as suddenly as it appeared, and all was dark again save the single lurid spark which marked a chink between the stones.

36 Its disappearance, however, was but momentary. With a rending, tearing sound, one of the broad, white stones turned over upon its side and left a square, gaping hole, through which streamed the light of a lantern. Over the edge there peeped a clean-cut, boyish face, which looked keenly about it, and then, with a hand on either side of the aperture, drew itself shoulder-high and

Literary Analysis
Protagonist and Antagonist What details of Watson's account help build the suspense of the conflict?

Reading Skill
Comparing Characters In what ways is the first burglar's appearance similar to that of Vincent Spaulding?

Vocabulary Development

Word Analysis

Point out the word *expectancy* in the first paragraph on p. 1086. Write the word on the board and challenge students to define it. Students should understand that the word *expectancy* means "state of waiting or looking forward to a probable event."

Explain that *ex-* is a Latin prefix meaning "out" or "out of." When *ex-* is combined with the root *-spec-,* the *s* is dropped, because its sound is already made by the letter *x.* Knowing the prefix and the root should help students figure out that *ex + spec* means "looking out" or "looking forward."

Have students apply the same process to define the word *inspector.* Students should explain that because the prefix *in-* means "in" or "into," an inspector is a person who looks into, or investigates, things.

waist-high, until one knee rested upon the edge. In another instant he stood at the side of the hole and was hauling after him a companion, lithe and small like himself, with a pale face and a shock of very red hair.

"It's all clear," he whispered. "Have you the chisel and the bags? Great Scott! Jump, Archie, jump, and I'll swing for it."

Sherlock Holmes had sprung out and seized the intruder by the collar. The other dived down the hole, and I heard the sound of rending cloth as Jones clutched at his skirts. The light flashed upon the barrel of a revolver, but Holmes's hunting crop came down on the man's wrist, and the pistol clinked upon the stone floor.

"It's no use, John Clay," said Holmes blandly. "You have no chance at all."

"So I see," the other answered with the utmost coolness. "I fancy that my pal is all right, though I see you have got his coattails."

"There are three men waiting for him at the door," said Holmes.

"Oh, indeed! You seem to have done the thing very completely. I must compliment you."

"And I you," Holmes answered. "Your red-headed idea was very new and effective."

"You'll see your pal again presently," said Jones. "He's quicker at climbing down holes than I am. Just hold out while I fix the derbies."[15]

"I beg that you will not touch me with your filthy hands," remarked our prisoner as the handcuffs clattered upon his wrists. "You may not be aware that I have royal blood in my veins. Have the

---

15. **derbies** handcuffs.

Reading Check

What color is Clay's accomplice's hair?

The Red-headed League ■ 1087

Infer

• Students may think that John Clay is a new character. Point out that John Clay is the real name of a character they have met before.

• **Ask** students who they believe John Clay is. Tell them to use details from the story to comprise their answers.
Answer: Students should suggest that Vincent Spaulding is really John Clay because they know that Holmes has been concentrated on and suspicious of Spaulding.

• Ask students to continue reading to learn if their inference is correct.

38 Reading Check

Answer: Clay's accomplice has red hair.

Differentiated Instruction   Solutions for All Learners

Enrichment for Gifted/Talented Students
Have students plan and perform a dramatic version of "The Red-headed League." Seven students could play the roles of the detectives, the police officer, the banker, Mr. Wilson, and the criminals. Others in the group could direct rehearsals, collaborate on a script, decide on a type of presentation (dramatic reading, radio play, video, and so on). One team of students might work on developing sets. What props or sound would make an audience think of nineteenth-century London? Allow time for rehearsals, and then have students perform for the class. Afterwards, have the audience compare the performance with the story, comment on any differences, and discuss the effect on the overall impact of the piece.

Ask students the Reading Skill question: What difference between Holmes and Clay is revealed by Holmes's refusal to accept a reward?
Answer: Unlike Clay, Holmes uses his intellect to help others, not to make money.

▶ **Monitor Progress:** Ask students to summarize how Holmes and Clay are similar and different.
Answer: Both Holmes and Clay are daring, intelligent, and cultured. Unlike Holmes, Clay is a criminal.

▶ **Reteach:** If students have trouble identifying similarities and differences, give them a copy of **Reading Skill Transparency B** (*Graphic Organizer Transparencies,* p. 218). Show students the completed graphic organizer and point out the details that show similarities in the characters and the details that show differences in the characters.

goodness, also, when you address me always to say 'sir' and 'please.'"

"All right," said Jones with a stare and a snigger. "Well, would you please, sir, march upstairs, where we can get a cab to carry your Highness to the police station?"

"That is better," said John Clay serenely. He made a sweeping bow to the three of us and walked quietly off in the custody of the detective.

"Really, Mr. Holmes," said Mr. Merryweather as we followed them from the cellar, "I do not know how the bank can thank you or repay you. There is no doubt that you have detected and defeated in the most complete manner one of the most determined attempts at bank robbery that have ever come within my experience."

39 "I have had one or two little scores of my own to settle with Mr. John Clay," said Holmes. "I have been at some small expense over this matter, which I shall expect the bank to refund, but beyond that I am amply repaid by having had an experience which is in many ways unique, and by hearing the very remarkable narrative of the Red-headed League."

"You see, Watson," he explained in the early hours of the morning as we sat over a glass of whisky and soda in Baker Street, "it was perfectly obvious from the first that the only possible object of this rather fantastic business of the advertisement of the League, and the copying of the Encyclopedia, must be to get this not over-bright pawnbroker out of the way for a number of hours every day. It was a curious way of managing it, but, really, it would be difficult to suggest a better. The method was no doubt suggested to Clay's ingenious mind by the color of his accomplice's hair. The £4 a week was a lure which must draw him, and what was it to them, who were playing for thousands? They put in the advertisement, one rogue has the temporary office, the other rogue incites the man to apply for it, and together they manage to secure his absence every morning in the week. From the time that I heard of the assistant having come for half wages, it was obvious to me that he had some strong motive for securing the situation."

"But how could you guess what the motive was?"

40 "Had there been women in the house, I should have suspected a mere vulgar intrigue. That, however, was out of the question. The man's business was a small one, and there was nothing in his house which could account for such elaborate preparations, and such an expenditure as they were at. It must, then, be something out of the house. What could it be? I thought of the assistant's fondness for photography, and his trick of vanishing into the cellar. The cellar! There was the end of this tangled clue. Then I made

Reading Skill
Contrasting Characters What difference between Holmes and Clay is revealed by Holmes's refusal to accept a reward?

Vocabulary Development

Vocabulary Knowledge Rating
When students have completed reading and discussing "The Red-headed League," have them take out their **Vocabulary Knowledge Rating Chart** for this selection. Read the words aloud once more and have students rate their knowledge of the words again in the After Reading column. Clarify any words that are still problematic. Have students write their own definition and example or sentence in the appropriate column. Then have students complete the **Vocabulary Builder Practice** activities on p. 1091. Encourage students to use the words in further discussion and written work about this selection. Remind them that they will be accountable for these words on the Selection Test.

inquiries as to this mysterious assistant and found that I had to deal with one of the coolest and most daring criminals in London. He was doing something in the cellar—something which took many hours a day for months on end. What could it be, once more? I could think of nothing save that he was running a tunnel to some other building.

"So far I had got when we went to visit the scene of action. I surprised you by beating upon the pavement with my stick. I was ascertaining whether the cellar stretched out in front or behind. It was not in front. Then I rang the bell, and, as I hoped, the assistant answered it. We have had some skirmishes, but we had never set eyes upon each other before. I hardly looked at his face. His knees were what I wished to see. You must yourself have remarked how worn, wrinkled, and stained they were. They spoke of those hours of burrowing. The only remaining point was what they were burrowing for. I walked round the corner, saw that the City and Suburban Bank abutted on our friend's premises, and felt that I had solved my problem. When you drove home after the concert I called upon Scotland Yard and upon the chairman of the bank directors, with the result that you have seen."

"And how could you tell that they would make their attempt tonight?" I asked.

"Well, when they closed their League offices that was a sign that they cared no longer about Mr. Jabez Wilson's presence—in other words, that they had completed their tunnel. But it was essential that they should use it soon, as it might be discovered, or the bullion might be removed. Saturday would suit them better than any other day, as it would give them two days for their escape. For all these reasons I expected them to come tonight."

"You reasoned it out beautifully," I exclaimed in unfeigned admiration. "It is so long a chain, and yet every link rings true."

"It saved me from ennui,"[16] he answered, yawning. "Alas! I already feel it closing in upon me. My life is spent in one long effort to escape from the commonplaces of existence. These little problems help me to do so."

"And you are a benefactor of the race," said I.

He shrugged his shoulders. "Well, perhaps, after all, it is of some little use," he remarked. "'L'homme c'est rien—l'oeuvre c'est tout,'[17] as Gustave Flaubert wrote to George Sand."[18]

---

16. **ennui** (än' wē') *n.* boredom.
17. ***L'homme c'est rien—l'oeuvre c'est tout*** (lum se rē en' lœvr se tōō) French for "Man is nothing—the work is everything."
18. **Gustave Flaubert** (gōōs täv' flō ber') . . . **George Sand** notable French novelists of the nineteenth century.

The Red-headed League ■ 1089

Literary Analysis Protagonist and Antagonist What was Clay's (Spaulding's) motivation in arranging for Wilson to be out of the house?

Literary Analysis Protagonist and Antagonist What does Holmes claim is his reason for solving crimes?

40 Literary Analysis Protagonist and Antagonist

- Remind students that a character's motivation is his or her reason for doing something. For example, Watson's motivation for working with Holmes is his enjoyment in watching Holmes work or his desire to learn how to solve crimes.
- **Ask** students the first Literary Analysis question: What was Clay's (Spaulding's) motivation in arranging for Wilson to be out of the house?
  Answer: His motivation was to get Wilson out of the house while he and Duncan Ross dug a tunnel from the pawnshop cellar to the basement of a nearby bank.

41 Literary Analysis Protagonist and Antagonist

- Have students reread the last four paragraphs of the story. Make sure that they understand the meaning of the word *ennui*.
- **Ask** students the second Literary Analysis question: What does Holmes claim is his reason for solving crimes?
  Answer: Holmes suggests that solving crimes keeps him from getting bored. Crime solving lets him escape from the ordinariness of life.

Concept Connector

Anticipation Guide
Have students return to their **Anticipation Guides** and respond to the statements again in the After Reading column. They may do this individually or in their original pairs or groups. Then, lead a class discussion, probing for what students have learned that confirms or invalidates each statement. Encourage students to cite specific details, quotations, or other evidence from the text to support their responses to each statement.

Connecting to the Literature
Have students compare the sentences they wrote before reading with their thoughts about the powers of observation. Ask them to explain whether their thoughts have changed and, if so, how.

Literary Analysis Graphic Organizer
Ask students to review the graphic organizers they completed. Show them **Literary Analysis Graphic Organizer B** (*Graphic Organizer Transparencies,* p. 214) as an example. Then have students share their graphic organizers.

Apply the Skills

The Red-headed League

Thinking About the Selection

1. **(a) Respond:** What did you think of Holmes's solution to the mystery? **(b)** Did you find it a satisfying ending? Explain.
2. **(a) Recall:** Why does Jabez Wilson visit Sherlock Holmes? **(b) Infer:** Why does Holmes find Wilson's story interesting?
3. **(a) Recall:** What happens the night of the attempted burglary? **(b) Analyze Cause and Effect:** Which clues found at Saxe-Coburg Square lead to Holmes's solution of the mystery? **(c) Speculate:** What details could have been misinterpreted, leading to an incorrect conclusion?
4. **(a) Recall:** What remark does Holmes make about commonplace crimes? **(b) Infer:** What does Holmes mean? **(c) Interpret:** What does his remark suggest about the qualities that make a great detective?

Literary Analysis

5. **(a)** Identify the **protagonist** in the narrative. **(b)** What is the protagonist's goal? **(c)** Why are readers interested in whether the protagonist achieves his goal?
6. **(a)** Identify the **antagonist**. **(b)** What is the antagonist's goal?
7. **(a)** Why is the story's conflict interesting? **(b)** What universal struggle does this conflict represent?

Reading Strategy

8. What are two specific questions you can ask after reading to help you **compare and contrast** Holmes's actions, reasoning, and outlook at the beginning of the case and after it is solved?
9. **(a)** Use a Venn diagram to compare and contrast Holmes's character at the beginning and end of the story.

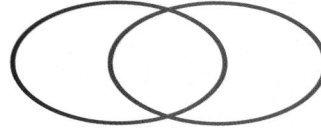

Beginning Only / End Only / Beginning and End

(b) Explain whether Holmes changes during the story.
10. **(a)** In what ways do Watson, Holmes, and Wilson act differently from one another during the case? **(b)** What is one reason the author may have for showing these three different reactions?

QuickReview

Story at a Glance
Sherlock Holmes uses his keen powers of observation to foil a bank robbery.

Go Online
Assessment
For: Self-test
Visit: www.PHSchool.com
Web Code: epa-6606

Protagonist: the character in a literary work whose fortunes are of greatest interest to readers

Antagonist: a character or force in conflict with the protagonist

Comparing and Contrasting: recognizing similarities and differences

Answers

1. (a) Students may find the solution clever. (b) They should find the ending satisfying; the guilty people were caught.

2. (a) Wilson wants to know about the Red-headed League. (b) Holmes enjoys it because it is unique.

3. (a) Holmes and his friends hide in the cellar and catch the criminals when they return to steal the gold. (b) Spaulding's trousers showed that he had been digging in the cellar. The bank's property bordered Wilson's shop. (c) **Possible response:** Spaulding's trousers might have gotten dirty because he was on the floor looking for something. The other details might have been coincidences.

4. (a) "It is your commonplace, featureless crimes which are really puzzling, just as a commonplace face is the most difficult to identify." (b) He means that adept criminals make their crimes unremarkable, making them difficult to solve. (c) The remark suggests that great detectives know that crimes are not as they seem.

5. (a) Holmes is the protagonist. (b) His goal is to understand the Red-headed League plot. (c) Readers too are curious about the odd league.

6. (a) John Clay and William Morris are the antagonists. (b) Their goal is to rob the bank.

7. (a) Readers want to know who will prevail. (b) The conflict represents the universal struggle between good and evil.

8. How has Holmes's view of the world changed after he solves the case? How has Holmes changed as a person by solving the case?

9. (a) **Beginning:** Holmes is intrigued by Wilson's story. **End:** Holmes can take pride in capturing a known criminal. **Beginning and End:** Holmes uses deduction to solve crimes. He solves crimes to escape boredom. He awaits the next new crime. (b) Holmes is basically unchanged. He is neither wiser nor richer after the story.

Another sample answer can be found on **Reading Skill Graphic Organizer B**, p. 218 in *Graphic Organizer Transparencies.*

10. (a) Watson notices details but does not make accurate deductions. Holmes notices details and makes accurate deductions based on them. He develops and tests theories. Wilson is not observant and does not draw conclusions. (b) By showing the three men in action, the writer shows Holmes as the superior detective.

Vocabulary Builder

Practice **Analogies** show the relationships between pairs of words. Use a word from the vocabulary list for "The Red-headed League" on page 1048 to complete each analogy.

1. kind : gentle :: _____ : fearsome
2. burn : candle :: _____ : problem
3. descending : downward :: _____ : inward

Adding Words to Your Vocabulary Using a dictionary and a thesaurus, find an antonym for each vocabulary word. Explain your choices. Then, use each correctly in a sentence. (For more on using a dictionary and a thesaurus, see pp. R6–7.)

Writing

Imagine that you are one of the characters in "The Red-headed League" other than Dr. Watson. Write three **journal entries** describing the events in the story as they unfold.

- Review the story and create a timeline for the major events.
- Decide which days you will record in your journal.
- Write your thoughts about what happens each day.

As you write, stay in character, making sure that your journal reflects any changes that the character experiences in the story.

For *Grammar, Vocabulary,* and *Assessment,* see **Build Language Skills,** pages 1092–1093.

Extend Your Learning

Listening and Speaking With another student, role-play an **interview** in which Officer Jones interrogates John Clay about his plan. Listen carefully to what your partner says in the interview, and respond with appropriate questions or answers. After the role play, give each other feedback on your work.

Research and Technology Research the science of detective work and prepare an **oral report** for the class. Find information on fingerprinting, lie detectors, and police sketches. Refer to multiple sources, such as the Internet, encyclopedias, and criminology books. Compare what you learn to Holmes's methods.

The Red-headed League ■ 1091

Assessment Resources

The following resources can be used to assess students' knowledge and skills.

Unit 6 Resources
  Selection Test A, p. 107–109
  Selection Test B, p. 110–112

Go Online
Assessment Students may use the **Self-test** to prepare for **Selection Test A** or **Selection Test B.**

Go Online
Research **For:** An additional research activity
Visit: www.PHSchool.com
Web Code: epd-7604
For another research activity to extend students' learning, give students this Web Code.

Vocabulary Builder
Practice

1. formidable; The two words in each pairing are synonyms.
2. vex; The first word is a possible verb of the second word.
3. introspective; The two words in each pairing are synonyms.

Adding Words to Your Vocabulary
Sample response:

1. A word with the opposite meaning of *formidable* is *easy.* I thought the test would be difficult, but it was *easy.*
2. A word with the opposite meaning of *vex* is *soothe.* The sound of water can *soothe* one's troubled mind.
3. A word with the opposite meaning of *introspective* is *outgoing.* The *outgoing* teenager loves social events.

Writing

- To give students guidance for writing journal entries, give them **Support for Writing** for "The Red-headed League," p. 102 in *Unit 6 Resources.*
- To evaluate students' journal entries, use the Autobiographical Narrative rubrics, pp. 43–44 in *General Resources.*

Six Traits Focus

✔	Ideas		Word Choice
	Organization		Sentence Fluency
✔	Voice		Conventions

Build Language Skills

Go to pages 1092–1093 for vocabulary and grammar lessons and assessment practice.

Extend Your Learning

The Support for Extend Your Learning page (*Unit 6 Resources,* p. 103) provides guided note-taking opportunities to help students complete the Extend Your Learning Activities.

1091

Vocabulary Skill

- Introduce the vocabulary skill: context clues. Stress that recognizing the Latin root *-sign-* will help students decode the meanings of new or unfamiliar words.

- Have students complete the Practice activity on this page.

Possible Answers

1. The traffic *signal* was flashing red.

2. The *ensign* flew from the mast of the ship.

3. Our teacher will *assign* the homework today.

4. I will *resign* from my job to accept the new position.

Grammar Lesson

- Point students' attention to the comma rules on this page. Clarify any rules that students may find confusing. Tell students that they must learn these rules to make sure that their comma use is correct.

Answers

1. "Please leave the building," (direct quotation) said the fire marshal.

2. Actually, (introductory word) my sister is older than my brother.

3. His voice is powerful, deep, (items in a series) and resonant, (compound sentence) and these qualities, which I envy, (both for nonessential elements) make him a fine speaker.

Build Language Skills

Three Skeleton Key • The Red-headed League

Vocabulary Skill

Context Clues and Word Roots The **Latin word root** *-sign-* means "sign or meaning." It can stand on its own, as in the word *sign,* or it can be the root of another word, such as *signify,* meaning "to mean something or to stand for something." This word root can be a **context clue** to help you figure out the meaning of a sentence.

Practice Use each of the following *-sign-* words in a sentence. Then, exchange papers with another student and write a sentence explaining how knowing the meaning of *-sign-* helps you understand the sentence.

1. signal
2. ensign
3. assign
4. resign

Grammar Lesson

Using Commas Correctly Use commas when you need to indicate a short pause in your writing. Two basic principles guide all comma usage.

MorePractice

For more practice with commas, see the Grammar Handbook, pp. R47–48.

USE COMMAS TO SEPARATE . . .	USE COMMAS TO SET OFF . . .
— **two independent clauses in a compound sentence** I turned the ignition key, but the car did not start. — **three or more words, phrases, or clauses in a series** He spoke with passion, with gravity, and with sorrow. — **parts of dates, places, or certain titles** We went to Sonoma, California, for the weekend.	— **an introductory word, phrase, or clause** Coincidentally, we all ended up at the same beach. — **parenthetical or nonessential expressions** The magazine, which I unfortunately misplaced, had some great articles. — **direct quotations** President Roosevelt declared, "The only thing we have to fear is fear itself."

Practice Copy each sentence, and add commas where they are necessary, indicating which rule(s) you are following.

1. "Please leave the building" said the fire marshal.

2. Actually my sister is older than my brother.

3. His voice is powerful deep and resonant and these qualities which I envy make him a fine speaker.

W/G Prentice Hall Writing and Grammar Connection: Chapter 29, Section 2

1092 ■ Themes in Literature: Heroism

Teaching Resources

The following resources can be used to enrich or extend the instruction for Build Language Skills.

Unit 6 Resources

Build Language Skills: Vocabulary: Word Root *-sign-*, p. 105

Build Grammar Skills: Commas, p. 106

Reading Skill: Compare and Contrast

Directions: *Read the selection. Then, answer the questions.*

He fell silent, amazed and bewildered to see that his wife was crying. . . . He mumbled:

"What is it? What is it?"

But, with great effort, she had overcome her misery; and now she answered him calmly, wiping her tear-damp cheeks:

"It's nothing. It's just that I have no evening dress and so I can't go to the party. Give the invitation to one of your colleagues whose wife will be better dressed than I would be."

He was overcome. He said:

"Listen, Mathilde, how much would an evening dress cost. . . ?"

She thought for several seconds, making her calculations and at the same time estimating how much she could ask for without eliciting an immediate refusal . . . from the economical government clerk.

—from "The Necklace" by Guy de Maupassant

1. Which of the following is not a fact that defines the wife's character?
   A She wants to go to the dance.
   B She wishes her husband paid more attention to her.
   C She calculates how much she can ask for.
   D She cries to gain sympathy.

2. Which question would be most helpful in *contrasting* the husband and wife?
   A Does she really want to go to the ball?
   B Why is he confused by her reaction?
   C How do their feelings about money differ?
   D Why does the wife cry?

Timed Writing: Explanation (Connections)

Review "Three Skeleton Key" or "The Red-headed League." For either story, explain the key details that provide clues to the mystery's solution and how the author presents these clues. **(40 minutes)**

 Writing Workshop: *Work in Progress*

Comparison and Contrast

For a comparison-and-contrast essay you may write, choose two places that you know well. For each, note the purpose, sound, and look of the place. Save this Comparison List in your writing portfolio.

Reading Skill: Compare and Contrast
1. B
2. C

Timed Writing: Explanation

- Tell students that when they write an explanation, they should use clear language and show how one idea logically flows into the next idea.
- Suggest that students first list clues to the mystery. Then, have them tell how the author reveals each clue.
- Assess students' essays on their organization and use of details as well as the clarity of their explanations.
- Suggest that students plan their time to give 10 minutes to reviewing the story, 20 minutes to writing, and 10 minutes to reviewing and revising.

Writing Workshop
Work in Progress

- Have students go to their portfolios and take out the work they have completed so far on this assignment. Remind them that this work may be used in the **Writing Workshop** on Comparison-and-Contrast essays on p. 1134.
- Guide students in completing the **Work-in-Progress** assignment on this page. When students have completed this activity, have them keep it in their portfolios. They will use it as they continue the **Work in Progress**.

Reading Informational Materials

Meeting Your Standards

Students will

1. understand and find information in an encyclopedia entry.
2. read an encyclopedia entry.

See TeacherExpress™/Lesson View for a detailed lesson plan for Reading Informational Materials.

About Encyclopedia Entries

- Have students read "About Encyclopedia Entries."

- Explain to students that they are likely to encounter encyclopedia entries when researching a topic for school or out of curiosity.

- Talk with students about encyclopedia entries they have used. Have them describe what was helpful about the style and organization of the encyclopedia entries.

- As a group, brainstorm for a list of topics that students might logically look up in an encyclopedia.

Reading Skill
Setting a Purpose for Reading

- Remind students that when they read, it is to satisfy a purpose. Point out that, for example, they might read for entertainment, for facts they need in a class, for details they need at work, or for general information. Make sure they realize that it is often helpful to think about the purpose for reading before students begin to read.

- Review with students the K-W-L chart.

Encyclopedia Entries

In Part 2, you learned how to compare and contrast when you read literature. This skill is also useful when reading informational materials such as biographies, magazine articles, and encyclopedia entries. Comparing and contrasting helps you understand ideas, data, and other information by exploring their similarities and differences. If you read "The Red-Headed League" by Sir Arthur Conan Doyle, you will appreciate this encyclopedia entry about detective stories.

About Encyclopedia Entries

Encyclopedias are reference works containing factual articles. There are many types of encyclopedias. General encyclopedias provide information in all subject areas. Specialized encyclopedias provide information on particular subjects, such as twentieth-century inventors or African American writers. Encyclopedias are published in both electronic format, such as CD-ROM, and in print, or book, form. Most print encyclopedias consist of many volumes, which are arranged alphabetically. Articles within each volume are usually arranged alphabetically by topic. Encyclopedia entries often have the following characteristics:

- an introduction in which the author identifies the topic and gives an overview
- subheads with which the author organizes information and helps readers locate specific facts
- sources for additional information

Reading Skill

Setting a purpose for reading can help you focus, save time, and get the most out of a work. For example, your purpose for reading might be to gain general knowledge about a topic, to find a specific piece of information, or to analyze an author's ideas. To set a purpose for reading, first decide what you want to learn about a topic. Preview the material to get a sense of its scope and organization. Then, use a K-W-L chart like the one shown to set a specific purpose for your reading.

What I Know	What I Want to Know	What I Learned
Arthur Conan Doyle wrote detective stories.	When were the first detective stories written?	Edgar Allen Poe wrote the first detective story in 1841.

1094 ■ *Themes in Literature: Heroism*

Detective Story

The first paragraph defines the detective story and gives an overview of the characters and plots used.

Bold subheads call attention to main ideas.

Detective story is a work of fiction about a puzzling crime, a number of clues, and a detective who solves the mystery. In most detective stories, the crime is murder and the clues lead to or away from the solution.

The pattern of most detective stories is the same, whether the tale is a novel, a novelette, or a short story. The author presents the crime, the detective, and several clues and suspects. The detective follows the clues and may even discover additional crimes. The climax of the story comes when the detective reveals the criminal and tells how the mystery was solved.

Certain conventions have developed from the detective story pattern. The author is expected to "play fair" with the reader. That is, the reader should be given exactly the same information that the detective uses to find the criminal. Readers can treat the story as a battle of wits between themselves and the detective.

The detective in most of these stories is not a professional police officer but a private consultant. For example, G. K. Chesterton's Father Brown is a priest, Rex Stout's Nero Wolfe is a gourmet and intellectual, and S. S. Van Dine's Philo Vance is a sophisticated socialite. Fictional professional detectives include Wilkie Collins's Sgt. Cuff, John Creasey's Inspector Gideon (written under the name of J. J. Marric), and Georges Simenon's Inspector Maigret. Romance or financial gain may be a factor in a detective story, but the main theme is the mystery and its solution.

History of the detective story began with Edgar Allan Poe's "The Murders in the Rue Morgue" (1841). With this story and "The Mystery of Marie Rogêt" and "The Purloined Letter," Poe created the literary tradition of detective fiction. His detective was C. Auguste Dupin, a brilliant amateur who uses logic to solve mysteries.

Charles Dickens tried the new form in *Bleak House* (1852–1853) and in his unfinished novel, *The Mystery of Edwin Drood*. Wilkie Collins's *The Moonstone* (1868) was one of the most important early detective novels. Sherlock Holmes and his comrade, Dr. John Watson, appeared in 1887 in Sir Arthur Conan Doyle's *A Study in Scarlet*. Holmes is the most famous character in detective fiction—and perhaps in all fiction.

The discussion of the history of the detective story is given in chronological, or time, order. The main writers in the development of the detective story are cited.

READING INFORMATIONAL MATERIALS

Reading Encyclopedia Entries

- Draw a K-W-L chart on the board. Point out to the students that they are going to read an encyclopedia article entitled *Detective Story*. **Ask** students to fill in the first two columns. Tell them they will fill in the last column after they read the article.
  Possible response: K column: The detective story is a favored genre for novels, television shows, and movies. W column: When was the first detective story written?

- Make sure students realize that the entry in the **W** column presents a purpose for reading. Challenge them to look for the detail(s) while reading the article.

- Have students read "Detective Story."

- **Ask** volunteers for ideas of things to write in the **L** column. Make sure the ideas include the answer to the query in the **W** column.
  Possible response: The first mystery story was written by Edgar Allan Poe in 1841.

- Have students review the headings in the *Detective Story* encyclopedia entry. **Ask** them how the headings can help readers set reading purposes. Encourage them to give examples.
  Possible responses: Headings can help someone locate a specific kind of information. For example, people reading this article to find out when the first detective story was written would skip over the "pattern" section and read the "history" section.

continued on p. 1096

Differentiated Instruction   Solutions for All Learners

Strategy for Less Proficient Readers

Remind students that subheadings offer readers a chance to set reading purposes for small sections of text. Use the following language to model creating a reading purpose with the subheading "the pattern" in the *Detective Story* article:

"The pattern" as it relates to detective stories. . . I wonder if this section tells about a typical sequence that mystery stories follow.

Point out that the questioning and purpose-setting takes only a few seconds, and that, as readers continue on, they look for the answer(s) to their question(s). In this case, it would be that the article does indicate that most detective stories follow the same pattern: crime, clues, suspects, detective finds additional clues and solves the crime.

Reading Encyclopedia Entries (cont.)

- **Ask** students why the entry includes the names of so many authors but few details about their works.
  Possible response: This entry is just an overview. Learning some names of authors might help a reader locate some detective stories to learn more.

- Remind students that the second page of this entry is a continuation of the "History" subtopic. **Ask** students how the history section is organized. **Answer:** The history section is organized chronologically.

- **Ask** students to glance over the list of related articles and draw a conclusion about the nature of most of the articles.
  Possible response: Since most of the articles are about mystery writers mentioned in the article, these related articles are probably bibliographical entries.

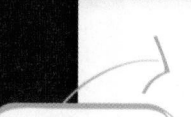

Detective Story

The entry gives specific details, including dates and principal writers, but it doesn't go into great depth about these writers.

The early 1900's were a period of excitement and originality in detective fiction. In *The Singing Bone* (1912), the English author R. Austin Freeman introduced the *inverted* detective story, in which the criminal is known from the beginning. The mystery is whether—and how—the criminal will be uncovered. The American writer Jacques Futrelle created a character called the Thinking Machine, and the Hungarian-born Baroness Orczy introduced the Old Man in the Corner. The period from 1925 to 1935 brought the publication of the first or major works by such masters as Margery Allingham, Nicholas Blake, John Dickson Carr, Dame Agatha Christie, Erle Stanley Gardner, Dashiell Hammett, Michael Innes, Msgr. Ronald Knox, Ngaio Marsh, Ellery Queen, Dorothy Sayers, Georges Simenon, Rex Stout, and S. S. Van Dine.

In the 1920's, *Black Mask* magazine introduced a distinctly American style of mystery, often called "private eye" or "hard-boiled" mysteries. These stories focused on a tough detective hero and featured action and violence and a colorful narrative style. Dashiell Hammett was the leader of this style in the 1920's,

followed a decade later by Raymond Chandler. The style continues to enjoy great popularity today.

During the mid- and late 1900's, a new generation of detective-story writers gained popularity. They included the American writers Sue Grafton, Tony Hillerman, Emma Lathen, Elmore Leonard, Ross Macdonald, John D. MacDonald, Ed McBain, Walter Mosley, Sara Paretsky, and Robert B. Parker; the English writers Dick Francis, P. D. James, James McClure, and Ruth Rendell; Jan-willem Van de Wetering of the Netherlands; and the Swedish team of Maj Sjöwall and Per Wahlöö.

David Geherin

The encyclopedia credits the author of the entry.

Related articles in *World Book* include:

Chandler, Raymond	Hillerman, Tony
Chesterton, G. K.	Holmes, Sherlock
Christie, Dame Agatha	James, P. D.
Collins, Wilkie	MacDonald, John D.
Cornwell, Patricia	Marsh, Dame Ngaio
Creasey, John	McBain, Ed
Doyle, Sir Arthur Conan	Orczy, Baroness
Francis, Dick	Parker, Robert B.
Gardner, Erle Stanley	Poe, Edgar Allan
Grafton, Sue	Queen, Ellery
Grimes, Martha	Rinehart, Mary R.
Hammett, Dashiell	Sayers, Dorothy L.
Heyer, Georgette	Simenon, Georges
	Stout, Rex
	Van Dine, S. S.

Additional resources

Henderson, Lesley, ed. *Twentieth-Century Crime and Mystery Writers,* 3rd ed. St. James Pr., 1991.
Symons, Julian. *Bloody Murder: From the Detective Story to the Crime Novel.* 3rd ed. Mysterious Pr., 1992.

"Related articles" refers the reader to other entries in the encyclopedia that give more information on detective stories. "Additional resources" directs a reader to sources of more in-depth information.

Vocabulary Development

Vocabulary for Detective Stories

Point out that encyclopedia entries often use vocabulary that is specific to one particular topic, in this case detective stories as a genre of fiction. Guide students to understand the meaning of the following words that are used in "Detective Stories":

novelette: a short novel
climax: the point of greatest intensity; the conclusion

conventions: an established technique, practice, or device
consultant: one who gives professional advice or services
inverted: a story told in reverse sequence

Reading: Setting a Purpose for Reading

Directions: *Choose the letter of the best answer to each question about reading the encyclopedia entry.*

1. Which is the most likely purpose for reading this entry?

   A   to learn about movies based on detective stories

   B   to learn about short stories

   C   to learn which writers are famous for detective stories

   D   to learn detailed information about one writer

2. Where in the entry would you find information about ways in which the character of the detective has changed over time?

   A   in the introduction

   B   in the section with the subhead "The pattern"

   C   in the section with the subhead "History"

   D   in the final paragraph

3. Which of the following details would you learn by reading the "Detective Story" entry?

   A   in-depth critical reactions to detective stories

   B   how Edgar Allan Poe came up with ideas for detective stories

   C   why detective story writers during the 1920s were so popular

   D   the names of popular detective story writers of the 1990s

Reading: Comprehension and Interpretation

Directions: *Write your answers on a separate piece of paper.*

4. What is the typical pattern of most detective stories? **[Organizing]**

5. What does it mean for an author of a detective story to "play fair" with the reader? **[Applying]**

6. Explain the "distinctly American style of mystery" that was introduced in the 1920s. **[Organizing]**

Timed Writing: Exposition [Connections]

Explain why detective stories belong in the larger category of narrative fiction by identifying the elements they share with short stories and novels. Then, explain what makes detective stories different from other forms of narrative fiction. In your answer, use details from the encyclopedia entry and from literature as support. **(45 minutes)**

Reading Informational Materials: Encyclopedia Entries ■ 1097

Reading: Setting a Purpose for Reading

1. C

2. C

3. D

4. The typical pattern of a detective story begins with an introduction of a crime, a detective, and several clues and suspects. The detective follows the clues, which leads to the climax of the story, which is when the detective reveals the criminal and how he or she solved the mystery.

5. **Possible response:** "Play fair" means that the author gives readers the same information acquired by the detective so that readers have a fair chance to solve the mystery while they are reading.

6. The American style of mystery focused on a tough detective as hero and featured action, violence, and a colorful narrative style.

Timed Writing

- Read the Timed Writing instructions as a class. Make sure students understand that their essays should clearly identify elements of detective stories that are similar to short stories and novels as well as elements that are different. Remind students that they are to use information from the article to support their points.

- Suggest that students plan their time to give 10 minutes to planning, 25 minutes to writing, and 10 minutes to reviewing and revising.

Extend the Lesson

Encyclopedia Articles Comparison

To give students further practice with encyclopedia articles, have them each choose a topic of interest. Tell them to each find at least four encyclopedia articles about the topic and write a report explaining how the encyclopedia articles are alike and how they are different. Provide time for students to share their reports.

Planning Differentiated Instruction

Choosing Your Selection

You may use either selection to meet the lesson standards. The following guide will help you determine which of the two selections is more appropriate for your students.

Accessibility at a Glance

	There Is a Longing	Glory and Hope
Context	Message of empowerment for Native Americans	President Nelson Mandela's inaugural address
Language	Accessible vocabulary	Long, complicated sentences
Concept Level	Accessible (hope for the future)	Accessible (hope for the future)
Literary Merit	Inspirational	Inspirational
Lexile	900L	1390L
Overall Rating	More accessible	More challenging

Using the Other Selection You may use the other selection for homework or independent reading to reinforce the selection skills. If you use both selections, you can build a test for both using *ExamView*® **Test Bank** software.

Choosing Your Resources

[L1] Special Needs Students **[L4]** Advanced Students

[L2] Below-Level Students **[EL]** English Learners

[L3] All Students

FT Fast Track Instruction: To move the lesson more quickly, use the strategies and activities identified with **FT**.

Reading and Vocabulary Warm-ups provide support for below level students. **A** is for students reading two grades below level; **B** is for students reading one grade below level. For Selection Tests, **A** signifies "less challenging" and **B** "more challenging." For Graphic Organizer transparencies, **A** signifies "not filled in" and **B** "filled in."

Scaffolding for
Less Proficient and Advanced Students

The leveled questions on Apply the Skills pages progress in the levels of thinking required to answer them. To address the needs of your different students, you may use the (a) level questions for your less proficient students, the (b) level with your on-level and advanced students. The occasional (c) level questions are appropriate for your advanced students.

Go **Online** **For:** Information about Lexiles
Professional **Visit:** www.PHSchool.com
Development **Web Code:** eue-1111

Step-by-Step Teaching Guide

Step-by-Step Teaching Guide	Pacing Guide
PRETEACH	
• Administer Vocabulary and Reading Warm-ups as necessary.	
• Introduce the Literary Analysis Skill: Author's purpose and philosophical assumptions. **FT**	10 min.
• Introduce the Reading Skill: Comparing and Contrasting. **FT**	10 min.
• Prepare students to read by teaching the selection vocabulary. **FT**	10 min.
• Build background and develop expressive vocabulary with Connecting to the Literature and Background.	10 min.
• Engage students' interest with the motivation activity.	10 min.
TEACH	
• Informally monitor comprehension while students read independently or in groups. **FT**	30 min.
• Monitor students' comprehension with the Reading Check notes.	as students read
• Reinforce vocabulary with Vocabulary Builder notes.	as students read
• Develop students' understanding of author's purpose and philosophical assumptions with the Literary Analysis annotations. **FT**	5 min.
• Develop students' ability to compare and contrast with the Reading Skill annotations. **FT**	10 min.
ASSESS/EXTEND	
• Assess students' comprehension and mastery of the Reading Skill and Literary Analysis by having them answer the Apply the Skills questions. **FT**	35 min.
• Have students complete the Vocabulary Builder activities. **FT**	5 min.
• Apply students' ability to write a letter with the Writing activity. **FT**	30–45 min. or homework
• Extend students' listening and speaking and research and technology skills with one or both of the Extend Your Learning activities.	30–45 min. or homework
• Have students complete the Vocabulary Skill and Grammar Lesson.	5 min.
• Monitor students' progress with the Assessment Practice.	20–40 min.
• Administer **Selection Test A** or **Selection Test B**. **FT**	15 min.

Resources

TECHNOLOGY

Go Online: Research [L3]
Go Online: Self-test [L3]
ExamView® **Test Bank [L3]**

 Meeting Your Standards

Students will

1. **analyze and respond to literary elements.**
   - Literary Analysis: Author's purpose and philosophical assumptions

2. **read, comprehend, and analyze speeches.**
   - Reading Skill: Comparing and Contrasting
   - Reading Strategy: Using self-monitoring
   - Reading Check questions
   - Apply the Skills questions
   - Assessment Practice

3. **develop vocabulary.**
   - Vocabulary Builder
   - Latin root -her-

4. **apply grammar skills.**
   - Colons , Semicolons, and Ellipsis Points

5. **develop writing proficiency.**
   - Work in Progress: Comparison-and-Contrast Essay
   - Letter

6. **extend learning.**
   - Listening and Speaking: Panel Discussion
   - Research and Technology: Outline

Block Scheduling: Use one 90-minute class period to preteach the skills and have students read the selection. Use a second 90-minute class period to assess students' mastery of skills, extend their learning, and monitor their progress.

Homework Suggestions

Following are possibilities for homework assignments.

- Support pages from *Unit 6 Resources*:
   Literary Analysis
   Reading Skill
   Vocabulary Builder
   Enrichment

- An Extend Your Learning project and the Writing assignment for your chosen selection may be completed over several days.

PRENTICE HALL
TeacherEXPRESS™ Use this complete
(Plan · Teach · Assess) suite of powerful teaching tools to make lesson planning and testing quicker and easier.

PRENTICE HALL
StudentEXPRESS™ Use the
(Learn · Study · Succeed) Interactive
Textbook (online and on CD-ROM) to make selections and activities come alive with audio and video support and interactive questions.

Build Skills *There Is a Longing • Glory and Hope*

Practice these skills with either "There Is a Longing" (p. 1100) or "Glory and Hope" (p. 1105).

- Tell students that authors always have a reason for writing. Sometimes they write to meet the readers' needs—if readers need information, the writer provides it. Authors may also write to entertain, to report, to express feelings or ideas, or to persuade.

- Point out that writers often draw on their own philosophical beliefs or assumptions in presenting a particular argument or idea.

- Tell students that effective readers will often try to pinpoint the philosophical assumptions that underlie a writer's words and ideas.

- Have students preview the selections in this set and jot down notes or ideas about the writers' purposes and their philosophical assumptions.

- Give students a copy of **Literary Analysis Graphic Organizer A** (*Graphic Organizer Transparencies,* p. 219). Have them use it to record their ideas about and evaluation of a writer's philosophical assumptions.

❷ Reading Skill
Comparing and Contrasting

- Explain that writers often use comparison-and-contrast as a strategy for making a point in their writing. Explain that both writers in this selection set compare the way things used to be with the way things are now. They also make predictions about the future.

- Remind students that it is their job as readers to identify the elements being compared and contrasted and to evaluate the writer's ideas. Students should ask themselves as they read "Is this comparison accurate? Is it fair? Is it clear?"

- Offer students the **Venn Diagram** on p. 244 of *Graphic Organizer Transparencies.* Remind students that a Venn diagram is helpful in determining similarities and differences. Encourage students to use the organizer as they read.

❶ Literary Analysis

An **author's purpose,** or goal, is shaped by his or her **philosophical assumptions,** or basic beliefs. These philosophical assumptions may be a political ideology, moral or ethical beliefs, or assumptions about human nature. In some cases, the author may use these basic beliefs as support for his or her argument. The response of the **audience,** or readers, to the author's work will depend on whether the audience shares the basic beliefs underlying the author's purpose.

To read critically, identify the basic beliefs and assumptions in the author's work. Determine whether you accept them and whether others in the intended audience would be likely to accept them. Then, evaluate whether these assumptions help the author achieve his or her purpose. Use a chart like the one shown to record your ideas as you read.

❷ Reading Skill

Comparing and contrasting is recognizing similarities and differences. In persuasive writing, authors often use a compare-and-contrast organization to show the similarities and differences between one point of view and another. As you read, **use self-monitoring techniques** like these to make sure you understand the comparisons:

- Identify the things or ideas being compared.
- Restate the similarities and differences in your own words.
- Explain the significance of the similarities and differences.

If you cannot identify, restate, or explain the author's points, reread to clarify or to find words or phrases that were unclear.

Philosophical Assumptions
The basic beliefs included in the author's work

Evaluation
How basic beliefs do or do not support author's purpose

Vocabulary Builder

There Is a Longing

- **determination** (dē tʉr´ mi nā´ shən) *n.* firm intention (p. 1100) *The runner's determination enabled him to win the race.*

- **endurance** (en dʊr´ əns) *n.* ability to withstand hardship (p. 1100) *Surviving the hurricane required courage and endurance.*

Glory and Hope

- **confer** (kən fʉr´) *v.* give (p. 1105) *The school will confer an honorary degree on the singer.*

- **pernicious** (pər nish´ əs) *adj.* destructive (p. 1106) *A pernicious insect destroyed the tree.*

- **covenant** (kuv´ ə nənt) *n.* agreement or contract, especially a sacred one (p. 1107) *They made a covenant to be friends forever.*

Vocabulary Development

Vocabulary Knowledge Rating
Create a **Vocabulary Knowledge Rating Chart** for the selection you will teach from this set. Include the selection vocabulary from this page and the additional words students are asked to use at the end of Connecting to the Literature. These words will increase students' expressive vocabulary.

Give students a copy of the chart with the words on it. Introduce the words by reading them aloud and having students mark their rating in the Before Reading column. Urge them to be alert to these words as they read and discuss the selection because they will rate their knowledge of the words again after they finish.

If you wish, you may tally how many students know (or think they know) a word to gauge how much instruction you need to provide. As students read, point out the words and their context.

❸ Background

The Struggle of Native Americans When Europeans settled in the Americas, they encountered tribal peoples who had lived on the land for thousands of years. The initial fear and prejudice led to violence and many native tribes were destroyed. Nevertheless, Native American culture survived. Today, Native Americans continue to discover ways to succeed in the twenty-first century while maintaining their own cultural identity.

❹ Connecting to the Literature

Reading/Writing Connection Chief Dan George recognizes the importance of cultural identity. Write a paragraph to explain why it is or is not important to connect to your heritage and history. Use at least three of these words: *reinforce, contemporary, domestic, spectrum.*

READ MORE

by the Author
My Heart Soars (1974)
My Spirit Soars (1982)

Meet the Author

Chief Dan **George** (1899–1981)

Chief Dan George had many careers, including actor and writer. Chief of a Salish Band of Native Americans in British Columbia, Canada, he was deeply concerned about improving the relationships between Native Americans and other North Americans.

Celebrity Activist Chief Dan George used the prominence he gained from his film and television roles to raise public awareness about the plight of Canada's native peoples. By the 1960s, he had become an unofficial spokesman for Native Americans and the environment. Throughout all of his endeavors against injustice, he always advocated peace over violence.

Fast Facts
▶ His Native American name is "Tes-wah-no."
▶ He was nominated for an Academy Award as Best Supporting Actor for his role in the movie *Little Big Man.*

Go **O**nline
Author Link
For: More information about the author
Visit: www.PHSchool.com
Web Code: epe-9609

There Is a Longing ■ 1099

---

❸ Background
The Struggle of Native Americans

Indian Nations are sovereign governments, which means they are have a different relationship with the United States federal government than the fifty states do. Provisions in the United States Constitution and centuries of treaties are the basis of the federal government's dealings with the Indian Nations. Despite this special relationship, interactions between the Indian Nations and the United States have often been troubled. After years of conflict and unresolved treaty issues, the National Congress of American Indians was founded in 1944. Its goal was to provide representation of the different American Indian tribes at the national level. Since then, the NCAI has helped federal lawmakers create legislation that recognizes the needs of the Indian Nations.

❹ Connecting to the Literature

• Model use of the expressive vocabulary students are asked to use with these examples:

1. Family reunions help people *reinforce* their connections to their family history.

2. Members of *contemporary* American families are often located across wide distances and keep in touch only by phone and e-mail.

3. Unlike in the 1950s, today there are many *domestic* situations in which both parents work.

4. In most American schools, the cultural make-up of the students is spread across a wide *spectrum.*

• Help students further develop their expressive vocabulary by providing these words: *civic, partisan, relevance,* and *subjective.* Encourage students to use these words as they discuss the selection.

Go **O**nline For additional informa-
Author Link tion about Chief Dan George, have students type in the Web Code, then select *G* from the alphabet, and then select *Chief Dan George.*

Differentiated

Instruction Solutions for All Learners

Support for Below-Level Students [L1, L2]	Support for English Learners [EL]
Unit 6 Resources	**Unit 6 Resources**
Vocabulary Warm-up Word Lists, p. 113	Vocabulary Warm-up Word Lists, p. 113
Vocabulary Warm-up Practice, p. 114	Vocabulary Warm-up Practice, p. 114
Reading Warm-up A, p. 115	Reading Warm-up A, p. 115
Selection Test A, pp. 123–124	**Reader's Notebook: English Learner's Version**
Graphic Organizer Transparencies	
Literary Analysis Graphic Organizer Transparency B, p. 220	**Listening to Literature Audio CD**
Reader's Notebook: Adapted Version	
Adapted Reader's Notebook Audio CD	

❶ Motivation

Initiate a discussion of civil rights. Include questions like these: How can a group demand its rights? What obstacles is that group likely to meet? Why is it important for a group to lobby for its rights? Students may answer these questions based on their knowledge of civil rights movements they have studied.

Concept Connector ➡

Students will follow up on this activity after completing "There Is a Longing."

Learning Modalities
Verbal/Linguistic Learners

Have students read aloud the poem and think about the speaker who is expressing such hopeful thoughts. After reading, ask students to participate in a discussion about the speaker. Challenge students to restate the speaker's goals and desires in their own words and to think of one or two words that sum up the speaker's tone or attitude toward his subject.

❷ About the Selection

In "There Is a Longing," Chief Dan George believes that Native Americans must ensure their survival and their standing in today's world by acknowledging their ancient heritage and pride in traditional values as they also work to embrace what is best of "the white man's success."

❸ Humanities

We the People, by Kathy Morrow

Artist Kathy Morrow grew up on Apache and Sioux reservations, where her father trained Native American police forces. Her title is taken from the preamble to the United States Constitution: "We, the people of the United States of America . . ." Use this question for discussion:

- How does this artwork convey a sense of longing and determination?
  Possible response: Students may observe that the outstretched hands convey a sense of reaching out. The movement of the eagle seems focused and follows the direction of the reaching.

THERE IS A

CHIEF DAN GEORGE

We the People, Kathy Morrow, Original scratchboard painting with hand-loomed beadwork. Courtesy of the artist.

There is a longing in the heart of my people
to reach out and grasp that which is needed
for our survival. There is a longing among
the young of my nation to secure for themselves
5 and their people the skills that will
provide them with a sense of worth and
purpose. They will be our new warriors.
Their training will be much longer and
more demanding than it was in olden days.
10 The long years of study will demand more
<u>determination</u>; separation from home and
family will demand <u>endurance</u>. But they
will emerge with their hand held forward,
not to receive welfare, but to grasp the
15 place in society that is rightly ours.

I am a chief, but my power to make war
is gone, and the only weapon left to me
is speech. It is only with tongue and speech
that I can fight my people's war.

Vocabulary Builder
determination (dē tur′ mi nā′ shən) *n.* firm intention
endurance (en door′ əns) *n.* ability to withstand hardship

1100 ■ Themes in Literature: Heroism

Vocabulary Development

Vocabulary Knowledge Rating

When students have completed reading and discussing "There Is a Longing," have them take out their **Vocabulary Knowledge Rating Chart** for this selection. Read the words aloud once more and have students rate their knowledge of the words again in the After Reading column. Clarify any words that are still problematic. Have students write their own definition and example or sentence in the appropriate column. Then have students complete the **Vocabulary Builder Practice** activities on p. 1103. Encourage students to use the words in further discussion and written work about this selection. Remind them that they will be accountable for these words on the Selection Test.

LONGING

❹ **Critical Viewing**

Answer: The painting illustrates the blending of old and new traditions. It illustrates the chief's wish that his people be "the proudest segment of your society... ruling and being ruled by the knowledge and freedoms of our great land."

❺ **Literary Analysis**
Philosophical Assumptions

• **Ask** students what Chief Dan George asks the Great Spirit to grant him.
Answer: He wants courage, and he wants to live in harmony with the environment. He also wants to accept the new culture in which he lives.

• **Ask** students the Literary Analysis question: What belief about the keys to success in the "new culture" does this passage reflect?
Answer: Chief Dan George believes that the keys to success—education and government—are good because they offer American Indians a chance to be proud and in charge of their societies.

▶ **Monitor Progress:** Ask students to articulate Chief Dan George's ideas about modern American culture.
Answer: Students should understand that Chief Dan George believes that modern culture has good things to offer his people, like education and leadership.

▶ **Reteach:** If students have trouble identifying the writer's philosophical assumptions, **ask** students a simpler question: What is important to Chief Dan George? Guide students through the selection looking for answers. Explain to students that these answers show Chief Dan George's basic beliefs. Tell students that these beliefs are his philosophical assumptions.
Answers: Chief Dan George believes the following things are important: his people, his heritage, his people's pride, harmony with the environment, and harmony with modern society.

20 Oh, Great Spirit![1] Give me back the courage
of the olden Chiefs. Let me wrestle with
my surroundings. Let me once again,
live in harmony with my environment.
Let me humbly accept this new culture

25 and through it rise up and go on. Like
the thunderbird[2] of old, I shall rise again
out of the sea; I shall grab the instruments
of the white man's success—his
education, his skills. With these new tools

30 I shall build my race into the proudest
segment of your society. I shall see our
young braves and our chiefs sitting in
the houses of law and government, ruling
and being ruled by the knowledge and

35 freedoms of our great land.

---

1. Great Spirit for many Native Americans, the greatest power or god.
2. thunderbird powerful supernatural creature that was thought to produce thunder by flapping its wings and to produce lightning by opening and closing its eyes. In the folklore of some Native American nations, the thunderbird is in constant warfare with the powers beneath the waters.

❹ ▲ **Critical Viewing**
Which images in this painting reflect ideas found in the speech? **[Analyze]**

Literary Analysis
Philosophical Assumptions What belief about the keys to success in the "new culture" does this passage reflect?

There Is a Longing ■ 1101

Concept Connector

Motivation
Have students reconsider their discussion of civil rights. Then, lead a class discussion, probing for what students have learned that confirms or invalidates their original ideas. Encourage students to cite specific details, quotations, or other evidence from the text to support their statements.

Connecting to the Literature
Have students compare the sentences they wrote before reading with their thoughts about connecting to one's heritage and past. Ask them to explain whether their thoughts have changed and, if so, how.

Literary Analysis Graphic Organizer Ask students to review the graphic organizers they completed. Show them **Literary Analysis Graphic Organizer B** (*Graphic Organizer Transparencies,* p. 220) as an example. Then have students share their graphic organizers.

There Is a Longing

1. (a) Students may say that they were most affected by the pride in the last sentence. (b) Students may say that hearing someone else's response made them see the poem in a new light.

2. (a) His people long to take their place in society. (b) He fears that he may not have the courage and wisdom of former chiefs.

3. (a) They will need many years of school. (b) He wants his people to be able to grasp opportunity.

4. (a) He can only fight with words. (b) He can make speeches and use logic as his weapon.

5. If his people follow his suggestions, their lives will be improved; they will be able to help their families and communities.

6. (a) His purpose is to empower Native Americans so that they can re-emerge as a proud and strong people. (b) He assumes that his people wish to survive and prosper, the greatness of the Native American people is in the future as well as the past, and the road will be difficult.

7. (a) The audience originally was Native American Indians. (b) The speaker refers to his people; he addresses the Great Spirit directly; he refers at the end of the poem to "our young braves and our chiefs." (c) Students should suggest that the audience shares his faith and his belief in the potential of Native Americans.

8. Though the speech was intended for Native Americans, it now has a broader appeal.

9. (a) **Past:** His people were once great. They fought war with weapons. Training was easier in the past. The olden Chiefs had great courage.

Present: The people are filled with longing. They are faced with hard work, isolation, and studying. The Chief has only the power to make speeches.

Future: The people can be great again. They can be leaders. They can be educated. They can be free. (b) By comparing the past, present, and future, the writer shows how the former

Apply the Skills

There Is a Longing

❸ Thinking About the Selection

1. (a) **Respond:** Which statements in "There Is a Longing" affected you the most? Explain. (b) **Discuss:** Share your response with a partner. Explain how hearing someone else's response did or did not change your own.

2. (a) **Recall:** What does Chief Dan George say is his community's longing? (b) **Infer:** What is his greatest fear?

3. (a) **Recall:** What training will the new warriors have to endure? (b) **Analyze:** Why does Chief Dan George believe that this training is necessary?

4. (a) **Infer:** In what way is Chief Dan George different from the "olden" chiefs? (b) **Interpret:** What does the chief mean when he refers to fighting a war "with tongue and speech"?

5. **Assess:** Do you think the chief's goal of achieving success through education and skills is the best means for improving his people's lives? Explain.

❹ Literary Analysis

6. (a) What is Chief Dan George's **purpose** in writing? (b) What are the **philosophical assumptions**, or basic beliefs, that help to shape his purpose?

7. (a) For what **audience** did Chief Dan George originally write? (b) What details in the text indicate his intended audience? (c) Do you think his intended audience shared his basic beliefs? Support your answer with details from the text.

8. Using Chief Dan George's speech as an example, explain how the audience for a speech can change over time.

Reading Skill

9. (a) Use a chart like the one shown to record the ideas Chief Dan George presents about the past, present, and future.

Past	Present	Future

(b) Explain the point Chief Dan George makes by **comparing and contrasting** the past, present, and future.

1102 ■ *Themes in Literature: Heroism*

QuickReview

Speech at a Glance
A Native American chief calls for changes to improve the lives of his people.

Go Online
Assessment
For: Self-test
Visit: www.PHSchool.com
Web Code: epa-6607

Purpose: what the author hopes to accomplish by communicating his or her message

Philosophical Assumptions: basic beliefs

Audience: the people who will read or hear the author's message

Comparing and Contrasting: recognizing similarities and differences

greatness of his people can be reestablished.

Another sample answer can be found on **Reading Skill Graphic Organizer B,** p. 223 in *Graphic Organizer Transparencies.*

Vocabulary Builder

Practice Indicate whether each statement is *True* or *False*. Explain your answers. Then, revise any sentences that are false to make them true.

1. Difficult tasks require *determination* to be completed.
2. Rock climbing requires less *endurance* than television watching.

Adding Words to Your Vocabulary Using a thesaurus, find a **synonym**, or word with a similar meaning, for each italicized word. Then, use each synonym correctly in a sentence. (For more on using a thesaurus, see page R7.)

Writing

In "There Is a Longing," Chief Dan George presents a vision for the future of his people. Write a **letter** to Chief Dan George expressing your feelings about the speech and identifying passages that you found most inspiring.

- List words that describe how the speech makes you feel. Next to each word, write the line or lines from the speech that evoke that emotion.
- Tell the author why you are writing and why you think "There Is a Longing" has a message for *all* readers.
- As you draft, use a friendly yet respectful tone.

For *Grammar, Vocabulary,* and *Assessment,*
see **Build Language Skills,** pages 1110–1111.

Extend Your Learning

Listening and Speaking In a group, hold a **panel discussion** on the kind of world you hope future generations will enjoy. Keep in mind the issues that Chief Dan George addresses. Consider these tips:

- Make note cards to use for extemporaneous, or unrehearsed, delivery of your ideas.
- Show respect for everyone's opinions and speak in turn.

Analyze the process to decide how to improve future discussions.

Research and Technology Use library and Internet resources to prepare an **outline** for a biographical report about Chief Dan George or another famous Native American. Include basic facts, major accomplishments, and beliefs and values.

Apply the Skills ■ 1103

Go Online
Research **For:** An additional research activity
Visit: www.PHSchool.com
Web Code: epd-7605
For another research activity to extend students' learning, give students this Web Code.

Vocabulary Builder
Practice

1. True; a difficult task requires that a person have a firm intention before starting.

2. False; rock climbing requires more ability to withstand hardship than watching television does. Rock climbing requires more *endurance* than television watching.

Adding Words to Your Vocabulary
Sample responses:

1. A synonym of *determination* is *resolve.* Studying a difficult language such as Chinese or Russian requires a student to have plenty of *resolve.*

2. A synonym of *endurance* is *stamina.* The runner needed great *stamina* to run the marathon.

Writing

- To give students guidance for writing their letters, give them **Support for Writing** for "There Is a Longing," p. 120 in *Unit 6 Resources.*

- To evaluate students' letters, check students' letter format against the one shown in the Business Letter rubrics, pp. 51–52 in *General Resources.* Make sure that students express their ideas in the letters while respecting the conventions of letter-writing.

Six Traits Focus

✔	Ideas		Word Choice
✔	Organization		Sentence Fluency
✔	Voice	✔	Conventions

Build Language Skills

Go to pages 1110–1111 for vocabulary and grammar lessons and assessment practice.

Extend Your Learning

The **Support for Extend Your Learning** page (*Unit 6 Resources,* p. 121) provides guided note-taking opportunities to help students complete the Extend Your Learning Activities.

1103

Teaching notes for Literary Analysis, Reading Skill, and Vocabulary Builder for this selection begin on p. 1098.

❸ Background
Apartheid

Apartheid laws categorized all South Africans as either white, black, Asian, or "colored" (meaning "of mixed ancestry"). These groups were to live apart in defined areas and have their own separate political institutions. Intermarriage between races was illegal. Black South Africans were the least privileged of the four groups.

The 1991 repeal of apartheid did not solve South Africa's problems overnight, and some painful legacies remain to be overcome.

❹ Connecting to the Literature

- Model use of the expressive vocabulary students are asked to use with these examples:
  1. A patriot will always *derive* feelings of pride for his or her country's achievements.
  2. Citizens *signify* their approval of a leader's ideas by voting for him or her.
  3. A leader like Nelson Mandela will *devote* his or her entire life to the cause of justice and equality.
  4. The sound of one's national anthem playing can *evoke* great feelings of pride.
- Help students further develop their expressive vocabulary by providing these words: *anticipate, aspiration, enlighten,* and *sanction.* Encourage students to use these words as they discuss the selection.

Go Online For additional informa-
Author Link tion about Nelson Mandela, have students type in the Web Code, then select *M* from the alphabet, and then select *Nelson Mandela.*

Build Understanding • *Glory and Hope*

Speech

❸ Background

Apartheid In Afrikaans, one of the languages of South Africa, *apartheid* means "apartness." Apartheid is the policy of segregation and discrimination that was once practiced against nonwhites by the South African government. When apartheid became law in 1948, it affected housing, education, and transportation. In order to help end apartheid, many nations reduced trade with South Africa. Apartheid was finally abolished in 1991.

❹ Connecting to the Literature

Reading/Writing Connection In "Glory and Hope," Nelson Mandela gives some of the reasons he feels love for his country and pride in its triumph. Write several sentences about reasons people might feel pride, love, or hope for their country. Use at least three of the following words: *derive, signify, devote, evoke.*

Meet the Author

Nelson **Mandela** (b. 1918)

Nelson Rolihlahla Mandela was born in South Africa, a nation whose white government maintained a strict policy of apartheid, or legal discrimination against blacks. In 1944, Mandela began protesting apartheid. Twenty years later, after several arrests, he was sentenced to life in prison for acts of protest.

Freedom for a Man and a Nation In 1990, after long years of imprisonment, Mandela was released. He continued to fight for equal rights for all South Africans. In 1991, apartheid was finally abolished and, in 1993, Mandela and South African president F. W. de Klerk shared the Nobel Prize for Peace. The next year, Mandela became the first black man to be elected president of South Africa. He retired from public life in 1999, and he currently lives in his birthplace, Qunu, Transkei.

Fast Facts

▶ Nelson Mandela once said, "The struggle is my life."
▶ Mandela's prison for so many years, Robben Island, has now been turned into a learning center.

Go Online
Author Link
For: More information about the author
Visit: www.PHSchool.com
Web Code: epe-9610

1104 ■ Themes in Literature: Heroism

Review

For **Literary Analysis, Reading Skill,** and **Vocabulary Builder,** see page 1098.

READ MORE

by the Author *Long Walk to Freedom: The Autobiography of Nelson Mandela*

GLORY AND HOPE

Nelson Mandela ❶ ❷

Your majesties, your royal highnesses, distinguished guests, comrades and friends: Today, all of us do, by our presence here, and by our celebrations in other parts of our country and the world, <u>confer</u> glory and hope to newborn liberty.

Out of the experience of an extraordinary human disaster that lasted too long must be born a society of which all humanity will be proud.

Our daily deeds as ordinary South Africans must produce an actual South African reality that will reinforce humanity's belief in justice, strengthen its confidence in the nobility of the human soul and sustain all our hopes for a glorious life for all.

All this we owe both to ourselves and to the peoples of the world who are so well represented here today.

To my compatriots, I have no hesitation in saying that each one of us is as intimately attached to the soil of this beautiful country as are the famous jacaranda trees of Pretoria and the mimosa trees of the bushveld.[1]

Each time one of us touches the soil of this land, we feel a sense of personal renewal. The national mood changes as the seasons change.

We are moved by a sense of joy and exhilaration when the grass turns green and the flowers bloom.

That spiritual and physical oneness we all share with this common homeland explains the depth of the pain we all carried in our

---

1. **bushveld** (bōōsh′ velt) *n.* South African grassland with abundant shrubs and thorny vegetation.

❸ ▲ **Critical Viewing**
What does this photograph of outgoing South African president F. W. de Klerk and Nelson Mandela suggest about the two men's vision for their country? **[Analyze]**

Vocabulary Builder
confer (kən fur′) *v.* give

❹ ☑ **Reading Check**
What does Mandela say must be born "out of the experience of an extraordinary human disaster"?

Glory and Hope ■ 1105

❺ Critical Thinking
Evaluate

- Have students **identify** the message Mandela conveys in the first four paragraphs on p. 1106.
  Answer: Mandela says that all South Africans suffered under apartheid and that he hopes that in the future they will treat one another as equals and work together to build a democratic society.

- Invite students to evaluate Mandela's message. **Ask** them if they think democracy is an achievable goal for South Africa.
  Possible response: Students may say that it is an obtainable goal because many other societies have started democracies from scratch, although it has taken several generations to reach a stable place.

❻ Literature in Context

Humanities Connection An organization known as ANSA, which was originally called Artists for a Free South Africa, was developed by artists to support the South African move toward freedom. Alfre Woodard, Danny Glover, Blair Underwood, Mary Steenburgen, Robert and Donna Brown Guillaume, and other artists created the organization in 1989. ANSA has had its hand in not only apartheid awareness campaigns, but also in the promotion and development of a new South Africa.

Connect to the Literature
Discuss with students how celebrities can use their fame to draw media attention to important issues. **Ask** students the Connect to the Literature question: How might the efforts of artists around the world have given Nelson Mandela and other South Africans hope for the future?
Possible response: South Africans probably felt that they were not alone in their struggle; there was a world community acknowledging and supporting their plight.

hearts as we saw our country tear itself apart in terrible conflict, and as we saw it spurned, outlawed and isolated by the peoples of the world, precisely because it has become the universal base of the <u>pernicious</u> ideology and practice of racism and racial oppression.

We, the people of South Africa, feel fulfilled that humanity has taken us back into its bosom, that we, who were outlaws not so long ago, have today been given the rare privilege to be host to the nations of the world on our own soil.

We thank all our distinguished international guests for having come to take possession with the people of our country of what is, after all, a common victory for justice, for peace, for human dignity.

We trust that you will continue to stand by us as we tackle the challenges of building peace, prosperity, nonsexism, nonracialism and democracy.

We deeply appreciate the role that the masses of our people and their democratic, religious, women, youth, business, traditional and other leaders have played to bring about this conclusion. Not least among them is my Second Deputy President, the Honorable F. W. de Klerk.

We would also like to pay tribute to our security forces, in all their ranks, for the distinguished role they have played in securing

Vocabulary Builder
pernicious (pər nish′ əs) *adj.* destructive

Literature in Context | Humanities Connection

Voices for Change

By raising worldwide awareness of the injustices suffered under South Africa's racially divided system, artists of all kinds played a vital role in helping the country become a more just society.

South African novelist **Nadine Gordimer** writes about the pain of racial divisions in her homeland.

Playwright **Athol Fugard** was one of the first white South African dramatists to collaborate with black actors.

On Broadway from 1988 to 1989, **Sarafina!** was a popular musical about protests that took place in South Africa in 1976.

The album "Sun City" raised more than $1 million dollars for South Africa's freedom fight. "Little Steven" Van Zandt (left) organized the project and Bono (right) participated.

Connect to the Literature How might the efforts of artists around the world have given Nelson Mandela and other South Africans hope for the future?

Vocabulary Development

Vocabulary Knowledge Rating
When students have completed reading and discussing "Glory and Hope," have them take out their **Vocabulary Knowledge Rating Chart** for this selection. Read the words aloud once more and have students rate their knowledge of the words again in the After Reading column. Clarify any words that are still problematic. Have students write their own definition and example or sentence in the appropriate column. Then have students complete the **Vocabulary Builder Practice** activities on p. 1109. Encourage students to use the words in further discussion and written work about this selection. Remind them that they will be accountable for these words on the Selection Test.

our first democratic elections and the transition to democracy, from bloodthirsty forces which still refuse to see the light.

The time for the healing of the wounds has come.

The moment to bridge the chasms that divide us has come.

The time to build is upon us.

We have, at last, achieved our political emancipation. We pledge ourselves to liberate all our people from the continuing bondage of poverty, deprivation, suffering, gender and other discrimination.

We succeeded to take our last steps to freedom in conditions of relative peace. We commit ourselves to the construction of a complete, just and lasting peace.

We have triumphed in the effort to implant hope in the breasts of the millions of our people. We enter into a <u>covenant</u> that we shall build the society in which all South Africans, both black and white, will be able to walk tall, without any fear in their hearts, assured of their inalienable right to human dignity—a rainbow nation at peace with itself and the world.

As a token of its commitment to the renewal of our country, the new Interim Government of National Unity will, as a matter of urgency, address the issue of amnesty for various categories of our people who are currently serving terms of imprisonment.

We dedicate this day to all the heroes and heroines in this country and the rest of the world who sacrificed in many ways and surrendered their lives so that we could be free.

Their dreams have become reality. Freedom is their reward.

We are both humbled and elevated by the honor and privilege that you, the people of South Africa, have bestowed on us, as the first President of a united, democratic, nonracial and nonsexist South Africa, to lead our country out of the valley of darkness.

We understand it still that there is no easy road to freedom.

We know it well that none of us acting alone can achieve success.

We must therefore act together as a united people, for national reconciliation, for nation building, for the birth of a new world.

❼ Let there be justice for all.

Let there be peace for all.

Let there be work, bread, water and salt for all.

Let each know that for each the body, the mind and the soul have been freed to fulfill themselves.

Never, never and never again shall it be that this beautiful land will again experience the oppression of one by another and suffer the indignity of being the skunk of the world.

The sun shall never set on so glorious a human achievement!

Let freedom reign. God bless Africa!

Glory and Hope ■ 1107

Vocabulary Builder
covenant (kuv´ə nənt) *n.* agreement or contract, especially a sacred one

Reading Skill
Comparing and Contrasting What important difference does Mandela point out about South Africa's future as compared to its past?

1. (a) Students may admire Mandela's idealism and eloquence. (b) Hearing someone else's response may not alter their response.

2. (a) Liberty is newborn. (b) "Newborn" creates a sense of excitement and freshness.

3. (a) The covenant is to create a "rainbow nation at peace with itself and the world." (b) Students may cite such ideas as equality, dignity, and peace.

4. (a) "Glory" is the triumph of actual results, while "hope" is optimism about future results. (b) Mandela feels that the present moment is glorious and that the future is hopeful.

5. **Possible response:** Perhaps Mandela's greatest challenge is overcoming racism.

6. (a) His purpose is to let people know that he is hopeful about South Africa's future. (b) He assumes that apartheid was wrong and that democracy is a good form of government. Also, Mandela believes that South Africa is a beautiful land with people who deserve freedom.

7. (a) Mandela's audience was the citizens of South Africa primarily, but also dignitaries from other countries. (b) Mandela begins by addressing "distinguished guests, comrades, and friends." (c) Most citizens share his beliefs because these beliefs target justice, peace, and work "for all."

8. Though the speech was intended for South Africans, it now speaks of justice and hope to an international audience.

9. (a) **Past:** South Africa was oppressed by the apartheid system."

Present: South Africa is experiencing "newborn liberty."

Future: South Africa faces many challenges to becoming a full-fledged democracy.

(b) Mandela shows that the country has already come a long way, and, it will find its way to peace. Another sample answer can be found on **Reading Skill Graphic Organizer B,** p. 225 in *Graphic Organizer Transparencies.*

Apply the Skills

Glory and Hope

Thinking About the Selection

1. (a) **Respond:** What do you admire most about the message in "Glory and Hope"? Explain. (b) **Discuss:** Share your response with a partner. Explain how hearing someone else's response did or did not change your own.

2. (a) **Recall:** What does Nelson Mandela say is "newborn" in his country? (b) **Interpret:** What emotion does the word "newborn" add to his remarks?

3. (a) **Recall:** Into what "covenant" does Mandela say the South African people are now entering? (b) **Generalize:** Which ideas in the speech are especially important for safeguarding the human rights of all people throughout today's world?

4. (a) **Interpret:** What do the words "glory" and "hope" mean? (b) **Connect:** How does the title of the speech connect with the ideas that Mandela conveys?

5. **Take a Position:** Basing your answer on Mandela's speech, what do you think was the new leader's greatest challenge? Explain.

Literary Analysis

6. (a) What is Nelson Mandela's **purpose** in his speech? (b) What are the **philosophical assumptions,** or basic beliefs, that help to shape his purpose?

7. (a) For what **audience** did Nelson Mandela originally speak? (b) What details in the text indicate his intended audience? (c) Do you think his intended audience shared his basic beliefs? Support your answer with details from the text.

8. (a) Using Nelson Mandela's speech as an example, explain how the audience for a speech can change over time.

Reading Skill

9. (a) Use a chart like the one shown to record the ideas Nelson Mandela presents about the past, present, and future.

Past	Present	Future

(b) Explain the point that Nelson Mandela makes by **comparing and contrasting** the past, present, and future.

1108 ■ Themes in Literature: Heroism

QuickReview

Speech at a Glance
At his presidential inauguration, Nelson Mandela celebrates South Africa's triumph over apartheid and envisions a future of freedom and peace.

Go Online
Assessment
For: Self-test
Visit: www.PHSchool.com
Web Code: epa-6608

Purpose: what the author hopes to accomplish by communicating his or her message

Philosophical Assumptions: basic beliefs

Audience: the people who will read or hear the author's message

Comparing and Contrasting: recognizing similarities and differences

Vocabulary Builder

Practice Indicate whether each statement is *True* or *False*. Explain your answers. Then, revise any sentences that are false to make them true.

1. A signature serves to *confer* authenticity to a document.
2. A *pernicious* idea is always welcome at a team meeting.
3. Each party in a *covenant* hopes that the other party will break it.

Adding Words to Your Vocabulary Using a thesaurus, find a **synonym**, or word with a similar meaning, for each italicized word in the Practice section. Then, use each synonym correctly in a sentence. (For more on using a thesaurus, see page R7.)

Writing

In "Glory and Hope," Nelson Mandela presents a vision for the future of his people. Write a **letter** to Nelson Mandela expressing your feelings about the speech and identifying inspiring passages.

- Make a list of words that describe how the speech makes you feel. Next to each word, write the sentence or sentences from the speech that evoke that emotion.
- Tell the author why you are writing and why you think "Glory and Hope" has a message for *all* readers.
- As you draft, use a friendly yet respectful tone.

For *Grammar, Vocabulary,* and *Assessment,* see **Build Language Skills,** pages 1110–1111.

Extend Your Learning

Listening and Speaking In a group, hold a **panel discussion** on the kind of world you hope future generations will enjoy. Keep in mind the issues that Mandela addresses. Consider these tips:

- Make note cards to use for extemporaneous, or unrehearsed, delivery of your ideas.
- Show respect for everyone's opinions and speak in turn.

Analyze the process to decide how to improve future discussions.

Research and Technology Use library and Internet resources to prepare an **outline** for a biographical report about Nelson Mandela. Be sure that your outline includes the basic facts of his life, his major accomplishments, and his beliefs.

Apply the Skills ■ *1109*

Extend Your Learning

The **Support for Extend Your Learning** page (*Unit 6 Resources,* p. 135) provides guided note-taking opportunities to help students complete the Extend Your Learning Activities.

Go Online
Research **For:** An additional research activity
Visit: www.PHSchool.com
Web Code: epd-7606
For another research activity to extend students' learning, give students this Web Code.

Vocabulary Builder
Practice

1. True; a signature gives a document authenticity.

2. False; a pernicious, or destructive, idea would not be welcome. A *pernicious* idea is never welcome at a team meeting.

3. False; the sacred nature of a covenant implies that the parties are committed to it. Each party in a *covenant* hopes that the other party will keep it.

Adding Words to Your Vocabulary
Sample responses:

1. A synonym of *confer* is *donate.* The lawyer agreed to *donate* free legal advice to the neighborhood association.

2. A synonym of *pernicious* is *hurtful.* Her *hurtful* words ended their friendship.

3. A synonym of *covenant* is *pact.* The children made a *pact* to always defend one another.

Writing

- To give students guidance for writing their letters, give them **Support for Writing** for "Glory and Hope," p. 134 in *Unit 6 Resources.*

- To evaluate students' letters, adapt the **Business Letter** rubrics, pp. 51–52 in *General Resources.* Make sure that students express their response to Mandela's message while respecting the conventions of a formal letter.

Six Traits Focus

✔	Ideas		Word Choice
✔	Organization		Sentence Fluency
✔	Voice	✔	Conventions

Build Language Skills

Go to pages 1110–1111 for vocabulary and grammar lessons and assessment practice.

Build Language Skills

There Is a Longing • Glory and Hope

Vocabulary Skill

∘ Introduce the vocabulary skill: context clues. Tell students that they can determine the meaning of an unfamiliar word by examining the other words surrounding it in a sentence. Stress that recognizing the Latin root -her- will also help students decode the meanings of new or unfamiliar words.

• Have students complete the Practice activity on this page.

Possible Answers

1. The root -her- means "to cling," and co- means "together," so *coherence* means "clinging together."

2. *Adherence* means sticking or clinging to, because -her- means "sticking" and ad- means "to."

3. *Incoherent* means lacking cohesion or not making things stick together. *In-* means not, and *coherent* means sticking together.

Grammar Lesson

• Point out to students that a semicolon does not require a coordinating conjunction to join two independent clauses; however, the semicolon does indicate that the two clauses are closely related.

• Have students complete the Practice activity on this page.

Answers

1. The astronauts looked out beyond the planets, beyond the stars, beyond. . . .

2. The sweatshirt fit perfectly; it completed the disguise.

3. She knew the best things to eat: whole grains, fruits, vegetables.

4. They came; they saw; they conquered.

5. I left the woods, and I would never be the same again.

Vocabulary Skill

Context Clues and Word Roots The **Latin word root** *-her-* means "to cling or stick to" and is the root for the word *inherent,* which means "something that is an inseparable quality of something else."

Practice: The underlined words in the following sentences contain the word root *-her-*. Explain how the meaning of the root provides a **context clue** to the meaning of the sentence.

1. The paper lacked <u>coherence</u>.
2. Dan's <u>adherence</u> to the policy is admirable.
3. The accident left him <u>incoherent</u>.

Grammar Lesson

Using Colons, Semicolons, and Ellipsis Points Correctly
Punctuation helps a writer clarify the meaning of a sentence. A **colon** is used mainly to list items following an independent clause. A **semicolon** is used to join independent clauses that are closely related. A semicolon is also used to separate independent clauses or items in a series that already contains several commas.

Ellipsis points (. . .) are punctuation marks that show that something has not been expressed. Ellipsis points usually indicate

• words that have been left out of a quotation.
• a series that continues beyond the items mentioned.
• time passing or action occurring in a narrative.

Colon The flowers seemed human: nodding, bending, dancing.
Semicolon The teacher lifted the desk herself; the sight greatly impressed the students.
Ellipsis Points He struck out . . . but the end of the game would surprise them all.

Practice Write these sentences on your paper, adding colons, semicolons, or ellipsis points wherever necessary.

1. The astronauts looked out beyond the planets, beyond the stars, beyond.
2. The sweatshirt fit perfectly it completed the disguise.
3. She knew the best things to eat whole grains, fruits, vegetables.
4. They came they saw they conquered.
5. I left the woods and I would never be the same again.

MorePractice

For more practice with punctuation, see the Grammar Handbook, pp. R47–50.

Teaching Resources

The following resources can be used to enrich or extend the instruction for Build Language Skills.

Unit 6 Resources
Build Language Skills: Vocabulary: Word Root *-her-*, p. 137
Build Grammar Skills: Colons, Semicolons, and Ellipsis Points, p. 138

Reading Skill: Comparing and Contrasting

Directions: *Read the passage, and then answer the questions that follow. Mark the letters of your answers on a bubble sheet if your teacher provides one; otherwise, write the letters of the correct answers on a separate piece of paper.*

I have a dream that one day this nation will rise up and live out the true meaning of its creed: "We hold these truths to be self-evident; that all men are created equal."

I have a dream that one day on the red hills of Georgia the sons of former slaves and the sons of former slaveowners will be able to sit down together at a table of brotherhood.

I have a dream that one day even the state of Mississippi, a desert state sweltering with the heat of injustice and oppression, will be transformed into an oasis of freedom and justice.

I have a dream that my four little children will one day live in a nation where they will not be judged by the color of their skin but by the content of their character.

—from "I Have a Dream" by Martin Luther King, Jr.

1. In this speech, the speaker compares
   A brothers to sisters.
   B slaves to slaveowners.
   C injustice and oppression to the heat of a desert.
   D truths that are self-evident to truths that are not self-evident.

2. In this speech, the speaker contrasts
   A freedom and justice.
   B his four little children.
   C Georgia and Mississippi.
   D the present and the future.

Timed Writing: Analysis

Review "There Is a Longing" or "Glory and Hope." Using quotations from the text, write an analysis of what the speaker wants for his people. **(60 minutes)**

Writing Workshop: *Work in Progress*

Comparison and Contrast

Add to the Comparison List in your writing portfolio. Think about the two places you have listed. Next, write down emotions you connect with each one. Then, use a Venn diagram to compare and contrast the two places. Save your work in your portfolio.

Build Language Skills ■ 1111

Reading Skill: Comparing and Contrasting

1. C
2. D

Timed Writing: Analysis

- Tell students that they will frequently be asked to write an analysis of something they have read. The analysis should include a thesis statement of what the speaker wants for his people and quotations from the speech supporting the thesis.

- Suggest that students use 15 minutes for planning, 35 minutes for writing, and 10 minutes for reviewing and revising.

Writing Workshop
Work in Progress

Comparison-and-Contrast Essay

- Have students go to their portfolios and take out the work they have completed so far on this assignment. Remind them that this work may be used in the **Writing Workshop** on Comparison-and-Contrast essays on p. 1134.

- Guide students in completing the **Work-in-Progress** assignment on this page. When students have completed this activity, have them keep it in their portfolios. They will use is as they continue the **Work in Progress**.

Comparing Literary Works · *Tall Tale and Myth*

See TeacherExpress™/Lesson View for a detailed lesson plan for Reading Informational Materials.

Literary Analysis

❶ Tall Tale and Myth

- Read the instruction about tall tale and myth together. Tell students that tall tales and myths reflect one of the strongest impulses of the imagination—the desire to tell stories.

- Explain to students that tall tales and myths are fictions that reflect the circumstances of time and place, and they often have specific purposes beyond mere entertainment.

❷ Comparing a Tall Tale and a Myth

- Remind students that the character of the hero is one feature that tall tales and myths often share. The great heroes are both universal and local. Students will see how the American Pecos Bill and the ancient Greek Perseus are alike and how they are different when they compare these two selections.

- Give students a copy of **Comparing Tall Tale and Myth Graphic Organizer A** (*Graphic Organizer Transparencies,* p. 226). Have them complete it as they read and compare the selections. Suggest that they focus on the hero's

  origins

  obstacles

  motivations

❶ Tall Tale and Myth

A **tall tale** is a type of folk tale that contains some or all of the following features:
- a larger-than-life central hero
- far-fetched situations and amazing feats
- humor
- *hyperbole,* or exaggeration

The exaggerated situations and descriptions in a tall tale, offered in vivid and often increasingly ridiculous detail, highlight how unbelievable the story really is.

Tall tales are a particularly American form of story. Many tall tales originated during the American frontier period and reflect the challenges and values of that place and time.

A **myth** is an anonymous story that explains the actions of gods or human heroes, the reasons for certain traditions, or the causes of natural features. Many cultures have their own *mythology,* or collection of myths, that expresses the central values of the people who made up these stories and passed them on by word of mouth.

Mythic heroes often share three characteristics:
- they have at least one divine parent,
- they gain special knowledge or weapons, and
- they face seemingly impossible tasks.

❷ Comparing Tall Tales and Myths

In general, tall tales describe how humans make things happen on their own, while myths tell how gods shape human life. Tall tales are often a type of *legend,* a traditional story about the past that is usually based on historical fact. Myths, in contrast, are religious in origin. However, both these forms developed in the *oral tradition*—they were passed on by word of mouth—and both express the values of the people who created them.

Use a chart like the one shown to compare and contrast these two selections.

Pecos	Perseus

↓ ↓

Hero is human or partly divine?

↓ ↓

Hero performs amazing feats?

↓ ↓

Hero works alone or receives divine aid?

↓ ↓

Story has humor and exaggeration or does not?

Vocabulary Builder

Pecos Bill: The Cyclone

- **usurped** (yo͞o sʉrpt´) *v.* took power or position without right (p. 1117) *The young knight imprisoned the king and <u>usurped</u> the throne.*

- **skeptics** (skep´ tiks) *n.* people who doubt and question generally accepted ideas (p. 1120) *He was one of the <u>skeptics</u> who did not believe the world was flat.*

Perseus

- **mortified** (môrt´ ə fīd´) *adj.* extremely embarrassed (p. 1123) *She blushed, <u>mortified</u> at her mistake.*

- **revelry** (rev´ əl rē) *n.* noisy merrymaking (p. 1125) *Parades filled the city with the spirit of <u>revelry</u>.*

1112 ■ *Themes in Literature: Heroism*

Vocabulary Development

Vocabulary Knowledge Rating
Create a **Vocabulary Knowledge Rating Chart** with the selection vocabulary and expressive vocabulary for both selections. Give students a copy. Introduce the words by reading them aloud and having students mark their rating in the Before Reading column. Urge them to be alert to these words as they read and discuss the selection because they will rate their knowledge of the words again after they finish.

If you wish, you may tally how many students know (or think they know) a word to gauge how much instruction you need to provide. As students read, point out the words and their context.

Build Understanding

3 Connecting to the Literature

Reading/Writing Connection Both Pecos Bill and Perseus are larger-than-life heroes who triumph over terrifying opponents. Write a paragraph about what you think it means to be larger than life. Use at least three of the following words in your response: *impact, negate, illuminate, exceed, undertake.*

Meet the Author

Harold W. **Felton** (1902–1991)

Harold William Felton practiced law and worked for the Internal Revenue Service, but over the years, he became increasingly interested in the legends and folklore of the United States.

Collector and Reteller Felton published collections of stories about folk heroes and the cowboys of the West. His book *Legends of Paul Bunyan* contains more than one hundred folk tales about the great logger.

Edith **Hamilton** (1867–1963)

Edith Hamilton was a groundbreaking educator who helped found the Bryn Mawr School in Baltimore, the first college preparatory school for women. She taught a generation of young women not to limit their goals simply because they were not men.

Modern Woman, Ancient Tales After leaving Bryn Mawr, Hamilton began writing articles about ancient Greece, which she later turned into a book entitled *The Greek Way* (1930). Her other books include *The Roman Way* (1932) and *Mythology* (1942), which are both beautifully crafted retellings of the Greek myths.

Go Online
Author Link
For: More about the authors
Visit: www.PHSchool.com
Web Code: epe-9611

Pecos Bill: The Cyclone / Perseus ■ 1113

---

3 Connecting to the Literature

- Model use of the expressive vocabulary students are asked to use with these examples:

  1. Larger-than-life heroes can have a tremendous *impact* on people's lives.
  2. The great feats of a hero often *negate* any bad qualities he or she may have.
  3. Tales of heroes *illuminate* a culture's values.
  4. The battles of heroes *exceed* what any mortal person could do.
  5. A hero has the courage to *undertake* a seemingly impossible task.

- Help students further develop their expressive vocabulary by providing these words: *accumulate, phenomenal, far-fetched, exceptional.* Encourage students to use these words as they discuss the selections.

Go Online
Author Link For additional information about Harold W. Felton and Edith Hamilton, have students type in the Web Code and then select *Harold W. Felton* or *Edith Hamilton.*

Teaching Resources

The following resources can be used to enrich, extend, or differentiate the instruction for Comparing Literary Works.

Unit 6 Resources, pp. 143–149

Graphic Organizer Transparencies, pp. 226–229

Listening to Literature Audio CD

❶ Background

Pecos Bill Pecos Bill is a fictional character invented in 1923 by Edward O'Reilly, a magazine writer. O'Reilly's stories describe Bill's life as a cowboy, train robber, and western fighter who traveled the southwest, particularly Texas and Arizona. Bill's horse, Widow Maker, was an equally important character. According to the tall tales, Bill raised the powerful and brave animal on nitroglycerine and dynamite.

❷ Motivation

Prepare an **Anticipation Guide** (*General Resources,* pp. 8–10) with the following statements:

- Mythological heroes are not at all like modern-day heroes.

- Women can be heroes just as surely as men can.

- Courage is the most important quality of a hero.

- No one invents tall tales any more.

Give students a copy of the prepared Anticipation Guide and have students mark their responses in the Me column. Have students discuss the statements in pairs or groups and mark the Guides again in the group column.

Concept Connector ➡

Students will return to the Anticipation Guide after completing "Pecos Bill: The Cyclone."

❸ About the Selection

"Pecos Bill: The Cyclone" is a tall tale that tells how the fictional cowboy Pecos Bill tames an angry cyclone that threatens to destroy an Independence Day celebration. The Independence Day setting emphasizes Bill's Americanness and his embodiment of the spirit of freedom. Bill rides the cyclone like a bucking bronco (using a common Western skill) until it loses its strength. Bill's encounter with the cyclone causes some of the West's natural wonders, such as the Grand Canyon and Death Valley.

PECOS BILL
THE CYCLONE

HAROLD W. FELTON

❶
❷
❸

1114   *Themes in Literature: Heroism*

One of Bill's greatest feats, if not the greatest feat of all time, occurred unexpectedly one Fourth of July. He had invented the Fourth of July some years before. It was a great day for the cowpunchers.[1] They had taken to it right off like the real Americans they were. But the celebration had always ended on a dismal note. Somehow it seemed to be spoiled by a cyclone.

Bill had never minded the cyclone much. The truth is he rather liked it. But the other celebrants ran into caves for safety. He invented cyclone cellars for them. He even named the cellars. He called them "'fraid holes." Pecos wouldn't even say the word "afraid." The cyclone was something like he was. It was big and strong too. He always stood by musing pleasantly as he watched it.

The cyclone caused Bill some trouble, though. Usually it would destroy a few hundred miles of fence by blowing the postholes away. But it wasn't much trouble for him to fix it. All he had to do was to go and get the postholes and then take them back and put the fence posts in them. The holes were rarely ever blown more than twenty or thirty miles.

In one respect Bill even welcomed the cyclone, for it blew so hard it blew the earth away from his wells. The first time this happened, he thought the wells would be a total loss. There they were, sticking up several hundred feet out of the ground. As wells they were useless. But he found he could cut them up into lengths and sell them for postholes to farmers in Iowa and Nebraska. It was very profitable, especially after he invented a special posthole saw to cut them with. He didn't use that type of posthole himself. He got the prairie dogs to dig his for him. He simply caught a few gross[2] of prairie dogs and set them down at proper intervals. The prairie dog would dig a hole. Then Bill would put a post in it. The prairie dog would get disgusted and go down the row ahead of the others and dig another hole. Bill fenced all of Texas and parts of New Mexico and Arizona in this manner. He took a few contracts and fenced most of the Southern Pacific right of way too. That's the reason it is so crooked. He had trouble getting the prairie dogs to run a straight fence.

As for his wells, the badgers dug them. The system was the same as with the prairie dogs. The labor was cheap so it didn't make much difference if the cyclone did spoil some of the wells. The

---

1. **cowpunchers** (kou′ pun′ chərz) *n.* cowboys.
2. **gross** (grōs) *n.* twelve dozen.

5 ◄ Critical Viewing   Does this cyclone seem capable of destroying a "few hundred miles of fence"? Explain. **[Assess]**

Literary Analysis
Tall Tale and Myth
Which description in the first paragraph contains hyperbole?

Reading Check
Where does Pecos Bill get the postholes he sells to farmers in Iowa and Nebraska?

---

4 **Literary Analysis**
Tall Tale and Myth

- Point out to students that wild exaggerations often signal that a story is a tall tale.

- **Ask** students to answer the Literary Analysis question: Which description in the first paragraph contains hyperbole?
  Answer: The exaggerations are the statements that Bill's feat was the "greatest" feat of all time, that Bill "invented" the Fourth of July, and that a cyclone "always" ended the celebration.

- **Ask** students to describe the tone of voice with which the narrator presents the exaggerations.
  Answer: The narrator's tone is objective, serious, and straightforward.

- Point out to students that this serious tone is usually used in tall tales and adds to the humor.

5 **Critical Viewing**

Answer: The cyclone seems more than capable of destroying miles of fence because it is large and is coming from an area of very dark clouds.

6 **Reading Check**

Answer: When the cyclone blew the earth away from his wells, Bill cut the wells into lengths and sold them as postholes.

Differentiated
Instruction   Solutions for All Learners

Accessibility at a Glance
Use this information to guide your teaching of "Pecos Bill: The Cyclone."

Context	Set in American West in frontier times
Language	Short sentences, American vernacular and idioms
Concept Level	Accessible
Literary Merit	Tall tale
Lexile	790L

- Have students read the first paragraph.

- **Ask** the first Literary Analysis question: Which realistic details in this paragraph add humor?
Possible response: Prarie dog holes didn't keep in storage, couldn't stand handling, and wore out quickly. Applying these practical consequences to inanimate holes is absurd and therefore amusing.

❽ **Literary Analysis**
Tall Tale and Myth

- Remind students that a story is given its flavor by specific, concrete details of time and place.

- **Ask** students the Literary Analysis question: Which details give this tall tale a particularly American flavor?
Answer: The culture of this tale is clearly American. It celebrates the Fourth of July; it features cowboys, cyclones, fences, and prairie dogs; and it specifically mentions several American states.

- **Ask** students why they think the writer decided to set the tale on the Fourth of July.
Possible response: The Fourth of July is the definitive American holiday, the day that most directly celebrates the American character.

---

badgers were digging all of the time anyway. They didn't seem to care whether they dug wells or just badger holes.

One year he tried shipping the prairie dog holes up north, too, for postholes. It was not successful. They didn't keep in storage and they couldn't stand the handling in shipping. After they were installed they seemed to wear out quickly. Bill always thought the difference in climate had something to do with it.

It should be said that in those days there was only one cyclone. It was the first and original cyclone, bigger and more terrible by far than the small cyclones of today. It usually stayed by itself up north around Kansas and Oklahoma and didn't bother anyone much. But it was attracted by the noise of the Fourth of July celebration and without fail managed to put in an appearance before the close of the day.

On this particular Fourth of July, the celebration had gone off fine. The speeches were loud and long. The contests and games were hard fought. The high point of the day was Bill's exhibition with Widow Maker, which came right after he showed off Scat and Rat.[3] People seemed never to tire of seeing them in action. The mountain lion was almost useless as a work animal after his accident, and the snake had grown old and somewhat infirm, and was troubled with rheumatism in his rattles. But they too enjoyed the Fourth of July and liked to make a public appearance. They relived the old days.

Widow Maker had put on a good show, bucking as no ordinary horse could ever buck. Then Bill undertook to show the gaits[4] he had taught the palomino.[5] Other mustangs at that time had only two gaits. Walking and running. Only Widow Maker could pace. But now Bill had developed and taught him other gaits. Twenty-seven in all. Twenty-three forward and three reverse. He was very proud of the achievement. He showed off the slow gaits and the crowd was eager for more.

He showed the walk, trot, canter, lope, jog, slow rack, fast rack, single foot, pace, stepping pace, fox trot, running walk and the others now known. Both men and horses confuse the various gaits nowadays. Some of the gaits are now thought to be the same, such as the rack and the single foot. But with Widow Maker and Pecos Bill, each one was different. Each was precise and to be distinguished from the others. No one had ever imagined such a thing.

---

3. **Widow Maker . . . Scat and Rat.** Widow Maker is a mustang, a type of wild horse. Scat is Bill's mountain lion, and Rat is Bill's pet rattlesnake.
4. **gaits** (gāts) *n.* foot movements of a horse.
5. **palomino** (pal′ ə mē′ nō) *n.* golden-tan or cream-colored horse that has a white, silver, or ivory tail and, often, white spots on the face and legs.

1116 ■ *Themes in Literature: Heroism*

Literary Analysis
Tall Tale and Myth
Which realistic details in this paragraph add humor?

Literary Analysis
Tall Tale and Myth
Which details give this tall tale a particularly American flavor?

Vocabulary Development

Vocabulary Builder Reinforcement
Students will benefit from additional examples and practice with the Vocabulary Builder words. Reinforce their comprehension with "show-you-know" sentences. The first part of the sentence uses the vocabulary word in an appropriate context. The second part of the sentence—the "show-you-know" part—clarifies the first. Model the strategy with this example for *usurped:*

The new leader clearly *usurped* his authority; he gave orders he had no right to give.
Then give students this sentence prompt, and coach them in creating the clarification part:

- The crowd was amazed but full of *skeptics*; _____ .
Sample answer: most of the people did not believe what they had just seen.

Then the cyclone came! All of the people except Bill ran into the 'fraid holes. Bill was annoyed. He stopped the performance. The remaining gaits were not shown. From that day to this horses have used no more than the gaits Widow Maker exhibited that day. It is unfortunate that the really fast gaits were not shown. If they were, horses might be much faster today than they are.

Bill glanced up at the cyclone and the quiet smile on his face faded into a frown. He saw the cyclone was angry. Very, very angry indeed.

The cyclone had always been the center of attention. Everywhere it went people would look up in wonder, fear and amazement. It had been the undisputed master of the country. It had observed Bill's rapid climb to fame and had seen the Fourth of July celebration grow. It had been keeping an eye on things all right.

In the beginning, the Fourth of July crowd had aroused its curiosity. It liked nothing more than to show its superiority and power by breaking the crowd up sometime during the day. But every year the crowd was larger. This preyed on the cyclone's mind. This year it did not come to watch. It deliberately came to spoil the celebration. Jealous of Bill and of his success, it resolved to do away with the whole institution of the Fourth of July once and for all. So much havoc and destruction would be wrought that there would never be another Independence Day Celebration. On that day, in future years, it would circle around the horizon leering and gloating. At least, so it thought.

The cyclone was resolved, also, to do away with this bold fellow who did not hold it in awe and run for the 'fraid hole at its approach. For untold years it had been the most powerful thing in the land. And now, here was a mere man who threatened its position. More! Who had <u>usurped</u> its position!

When Bill looked at the horizon and saw the cyclone coming, he recognized the anger and rage. While a cyclone does not often smile, Bill had felt from the beginning that it was just a grouchy fellow who never had a pleasant word for anyone. But now, instead of merely an unpleasant character, Bill saw all the viciousness of which an angry cyclone is capable. He had no way of knowing that the cyclone saw its kingship tottering and was determined to stop this man who threatened its supremacy.

But Bill understood the violence of the onslaught even as the monster came into view. He knew he must meet it. The center of the cyclone was larger than ever before. The fact is, the cyclone had been training for this fight all winter and spring. It was in best form and at top weight. It headed straight for Bill intent on his destruction. In an instant it was upon him. Bill had sat quietly and silently on the great pacing mustang. But his mind was working

Vocabulary Builder
usurped (yo͞o surpt')
v. took power or position without right

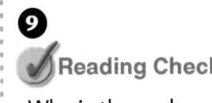
Reading Check

Why is the cyclone angry with Bill?

Pecos Bill: The Cyclone ■ 1117

❾ Reading Check

Answer: The cyclone is angry because Bill is not afraid of it and because Bill has taken over its position as the most powerful thing in the land.

Differentiated
Instruction   Solutions for All Learners

Strategy for Less Proficient Readers
Students may have difficulty imagining some of the wild, exaggerated events that take place in "Pecos Bill: The Cyclone." Suggest that each student work with a partner to read aloud the story. Each partner should read a section and then stop so that the listening partner can summarize what has happened. Then, partners should switch roles. Encourage students to draw or act out the events as well as describe them orally.

Strategy for English Learners
Students may have trouble with words that relate to the American Old West. As students read, have them list unfamiliar words and phrases. Students may identify words such as *posthole, prairie dog, mountain lion, mustang,* and *quirt.* Have each student use a dictionary and work with a partner who is proficient in English to determine the meanings of the words. Encourage the proficient speaker to use gestures and draw pictures that illustrate the terms.

Science Connection The word *cyclone* used to be applied only to a tornado, the funnel-shaped storm that is popularly called a "twister." In the movie *The Wizard of Oz,* for example, the tornado that lifts Dorothy's house and carries it away is called a "cyclone." Visualizing Pecos Bill's storm as a tornado probably does make it easier to imagine how he would be able to "ride" it, and at the bottom of p. 1118, Bill's cyclone is called a "tornado."

The term *cyclone,* however, actually includes all classes of storms, from local thunderstorms to devastating typhoons and hurricanes. The word *cyclone* itself comes from the Greek word *kyklon,* meaning a circle or the coil of a snake. Today, "cyclone" is usually applied only to the destructive tropical storms that are called hurricanes in the Atlantic Ocean and typhoons in the Western Pacific.

Connect to the Literature
Remind students of the destructive nature of cyclones. Then **ask** the Connect to the Literature question: Why might a literary character like Bill be especially beloved by people who lived in areas affected by cyclones?
Possible response: They might appreciate imagining a cyclone being rendered helpless by a person.

---

rapidly. In the split second between his first sight of the monster and the time for action he had made his plans. Pecos Bill was ready! Ready and waiting!

Green clouds were dripping from the cyclone's jaws. Lightning flashed from its eyes as it swept down upon him. Its plan was to envelop Bill in one mighty grasp. Just as it was upon him, Bill turned Widow Maker to its left. This was a clever move for the cyclone was right-handed, and while it had been training hard to get its left in shape, that was not its best side. Bill gave rein to his mount. Widow Maker wheeled and turned on a dime which Pecos had, with great foresight and accuracy, thrown to the ground to mark the exact spot for this maneuver. It was the first time that anyone had thought of turning on a dime. Then he urged the great horse forward. The cyclone, filled with surprise, lost its balance and rushed forward at an increased speed. It went so fast that it met itself coming back. This confused the cyclone, but it did not confuse Pecos Bill. He had expected that to happen. Widow Maker went into his twenty-first gait and edged up close to the whirlwind. Soon they were running neck and neck.

At the proper instant Bill grabbed the cyclone's ears, kicked himself free of the stirrups and pulled himself lightly on its back. Bill never used spurs on Widow Maker. Sometimes he wore them for show and because he liked the jingling sound they made. They made a nice accompaniment for his cowboy songs. But he had not been singing, so he had no spurs. He did not have his rattlesnake for a quirt.[6] Of course there was no bridle. It was man against monster! There he was! Pecos Bill astride a raging cyclone, slick heeled and without a saddle!

The cyclone was taken by surprise at this sudden turn of events. But it was undaunted. It was sure of itself. Months of training had given it a conviction that it was invincible. With a mighty heave, it twisted to its full height. Then it fell back suddenly, twisting and turning violently, so that before it came back to earth, it had turned around a thousand times. Surely no rider could ever withstand such an attack. No rider ever had. Little wonder. No one had ever ridden a cyclone before. But Pecos Bill did! He fanned the tornado's ears with his hat and dug his heels into the demon's flanks and yelled, "Yipee-ee!"

---

6. quirt (kwurt) *n.* riding whip with a braided lash and a short handle.

1118 ■ *Themes in Literature: Heroism*

---

⑩ **Literature in Context**

Science Connection

Cyclones A cyclone is an area o rapidly spinning winds that is associated with severe thunderstorms. The rotating wi can reach speeds of 250 miles p hour and are capable of lifting e very heavy objects into the colu of circulating air. Cyclones deve when warm and cold masses of collide, causing abrupt changes wind speed and direction. Cyclo that were over a mile wide and t have spread damage along a fif mile path have been recorded. Unlike Pecos Bill, most people a smart enough to take shelter underground when they see a cyclone coming.

Connect to the Literature

Why might a literary character li Bill be especially beloved by pe who live in areas affected by cyclones?

Vocabulary Development

Word Forms

Expand students' vocabulary by helping them learn related forms of the Vocabulary Builder words. Two of the Vocabulary Builder words for "Pecos Bill: The Cyclone" and "Perseus" have related forms. Give students a blank **Word Form Chart** (*General Resources,* p. 16), with *skeptics* and *mortified* in the correct columns. Work with the class, or have students work with a partner, to determine the related forms. The final chart should look like the one shown. Hold students accountable for integrating the related forms of the words into their speaking and writing.

Noun	Verb	Adjective	Adverb
skeptics		skeptical	skeptically
mortification	mortify	mortified	

The people who had run for shelter began to come out. The audience further enraged the cyclone. It was bad enough to be disgraced by having a man astride it. It was unbearable not to have thrown him. To have all the people see the failure was too much! It got down flat on the ground and rolled over and over. Bill retained his seat throughout this ruse. Evidence of this desperate but futile stratagem[7] remains today. The great Staked Plains, or as the Mexicans call it, Llano Estacado is the result. Its small, rugged mountains were covered with trees at the time. The rolling of the cyclone destroyed the mountains, the trees, and almost everything else in the area. The destruction was so complete, that part of the country is flat and treeless to this day. When the settlers came, there were no landmarks to guide them across the vast unmarked space, so they drove stakes in the ground to mark the trails. That is the reason it is called "Staked Plains." Here is an example of the proof of the events of history by careful and painstaking research. It is also an example of how seemingly inexplicable geographical facts can be explained.

It was far more dangerous for the rider when the cyclone shot straight up to the sky. Once there, the twister tried the same thing it had tried on the ground. It rolled on the sky. It was no use. Bill could not be unseated. He kept his place, and he didn't have a sky hook with him either.

As for Bill, he was having the time of his life, shouting at the top of his voice, kicking his opponent in the ribs and jabbing his thumb in its flanks. It responded and went on a wild bucking rampage over the entire West. It used all the bucking tricks known to the wildest broncos as well as those known only to cyclones. The wind howled furiously and beat against the fearless rider. The rain poured. The lightning flashed around his ears. The fight went on and on. Bill enjoyed himself immensely. In spite of the elements he easily kept his place. . . .

The raging cyclone saw this out of the corner of its eye. It knew then who the victor was. It was twisting far above the Rocky Mountains when the awful truth came to it. In a horrible heave it disintegrated! Small pieces of cyclone flew in all directions. Bill still kept his seat on the main central portion until that rained out from under him. Then he jumped to a nearby streak of lightning and slid down it toward earth. But it was raining so hard that the rain put out the lightning. When it fizzled out from under him, Bill dropped the rest of the way. He lit in what is now called Death Valley. He hit quite hard, as is apparent from the fact that he so compressed the

---

7. **futile** (fyo͞ot′'l) **stratagem** (strat′ ə jəm) useless or hopeless plan.

Literary Analysis
Tall Tale and Myth
In his encounter with the cyclone, which details show Bill's physical strength and lack of fear?

Reading Check

What does Bill do with the cyclone that had never been done before?

Pecos Bill: The Cyclone ■ 1119

⓫ **Literary Analysis**
Tall Tale and Myth

- **Ask** students to name some qualities that they think would have been valued by cowboys or frontiersmen.
  Possible responses: Cowboys and frontiersmen would have valued physical strength, endurance, fearlessness, and horsemanship.

- **Ask** students to answer the Literary Analysis question: In his encounter with the cyclone, which details show Bill's physical strength and lack of fear?
  Answer: Not only does Bill not run away, but he is able to ride the cyclone and not be thrown. In fact, Bill actually enjoys the ride, displaying his fearlessness.

- **Ask** students what Bill's way of dealing with the cyclone tells about the values of the culture of the American West.
  Answer: In this encounter, Bill is the hero who embodies the strength, fearlessness, and horsemanship that were prized by his culture.

⓬ **Reading Check**
Answer: Bill rides the cyclone.

Differentiated
Instruction   Solutions for All Learners

Strategy for Special Needs Students
Because the events in "Pecos Bill: The Cyclone" are episodic and not necessarily in chronological order, students may have some trouble following the tale. Suggest that students adapt the tale to a comic-strip format, using frames or boxes for each episode. Have students work in pairs to figure out how many episodes are in the story and then draw or sketch one scene in each frame. Assure students that their drawings do not have to be perfect or even realistic; they can use simple stick figures.

Strategy for Advanced Readers
Suggest that each student write an updated version of the Pecos Bill story that includes contemporary cultural references and explains at least one event that could take place in modern life. Students can update the character of Pecos Bill, changing his occupation from cowboy to any contemporary occupation. Challenge students to use exaggeration and understatement in their stories. Invite volunteers to read aloud their stories to the class.

⑬ Literary Analysis
Tall Tale and Myth

- Remind students that one purpose of tall tales and myths is to explain natural phenomena.

- **Ask** students the first Literary Analysis question: According to the tale, how does Bill create a natural phenomenon?
Answer: Bill lands with such force that he creates Death Valley, and the rain washes out the Grand Canyon that had been started by Paul Bunyan.

⑭ Literary Analysis
Tall Tale and Myth

- **Ask** students the second Literary Analysis question: Which details in this paragraph are examples of humorous exaggeration?
Answer: Bill's six-shooters were changed into a water pistol and a popgun, and his bowie knife became a penknife. These changes comically suggest the force of the impact.

Concept Connector ➡

Have students return to their **Anticipation Guides** and respond to the statements again in the After Reading column. Then lead a discussion probing for what students have learned that confirms or invalidates each statement.

ASSESS
Answers

1. **Possible responses:** Students may find Bill's riding of the cyclone the funniest because it is so wildly impossible.

2. (a) He calls them "'fraid holes." (b) It is clear that Bill does not experience fear at all.

3. (a) Bill will not say the word *afraid* aloud. (b) Bill's fearlessness is in part what makes him a folk hero.

4. (a) **Possible response:** The cyclone is jealous, angry, and threatened. (b) **Possible response:** Like Bill, the cyclone is bold, strong, and powerful.

---

place that it is still two hundred and seventy-six feet below sea level. The Grand Canyon was washed out by the rain, though it must be ⑬ understood that this happened after Paul Bunyan had given it a good start by carelessly dragging his ax behind him when he went west a short time before.

The cyclones and the hurricanes and the tornadoes nowadays are the small pieces that broke off of the big cyclone Pecos Bill rode. In fact, the rainstorms of the present day came into being in the same way. There are always <u>skeptics</u>, but even they will recognize the logic of the proof of this event. They will recall that even now it almost always rains on the Fourth of July. That is because the rainstorms of today still retain some of the characteristics of the giant cyclone that met its comeuppance at the hands of Pecos Bill.

Bill lay where he landed and looked up at the sky, but he could see no sign of the cyclone. Then he laughed softly as he felt the warm sand of Death Valley on his back. . . .

It was a rough ride though, and Bill had resisted unusual tensions and pressures. When he got on the cyclone he had a twenty-dollar gold piece and a bowie knife in his pocket. The ⑭ tremendous force of the cyclone was such that when he finished the ride he found that his pocket contained a plugged nickel[8] and a little pearl-handled penknife. His two giant six-shooters were compressed and transformed into a small water pistol and a popgun.

It is a strange circumstance that lesser men have monuments raised in their honor. Death Valley is Bill's monument. Sort of a monument in reverse. Sunk in his honor, you might say. Perhaps that is as it should be. After all, Bill was different. He made his own monument. He made it with his hips, as is evident from the great depth of the valley. That is the hard way.

---

8. plugged nickel fake nickel.

Thinking About the Selection

1. **Respond:** Which parts of the tale did you find funniest? Explain.

2. (a) **Recall:** What term does Bill use to refer to the cyclone cellars?
(b) **Interpret:** What do you learn about the character of Pecos Bill from his reaction to the cellars?

3. (a) **Recall:** What word is Bill unwilling to say aloud?
(b) **Draw Conclusions:** How does his resolve never to say this word explain, in part, why he is a folk hero?

4. (a) **Interpret:** What are three human characteristics of the cyclone?
(b) **Compare:** How does the cyclone resemble Pecos Bill himself?

1120 ■ *Themes in Literature: Heroism*

Literary Analysis
Tall Tale and Myth
According to the tale, how does Bill create a natural phenomenon?

Vocabulary Builder
skeptics (skep´ tiks) *n.* people who doubt and question generally accepted ideas

Literary Analysis
Tall Tale and Myth
Which details in this paragraph are examples of humorous exaggeration?

Vocabulary Development

The Prefix *trans-*
Bill's two six-shooters are *transformed* into a water pistol and popgun—that is, they *cross over* into other forms. Tell students that the prefix *trans-* means "across" or "over." Have students define each of the following words and explain how each word incorporates the idea of "across" or "over."

    transport—to carry across
    transatlantic—across the Atlantic Ocean

transfer—to carry or move over from one place to another
transgress—to cross over a line, to break a law
transition—crossing over from one stage or form to another
translate—to change over from one language to another

Perseus

Edith Hamilton

⑮ ⑯ ⑰

⑱ ▲ **Critical Viewing** The man with the sword is Perseus as an adult. Judging from this painting, how do you think others perceive him? **[Interpret]**

King Acrisius [a kris′ ē əs] of Argos had only one child, a daughter, Danaë [dan′ ā ē]. She was beautiful above all the other women of the land, but this was small comfort to the King for not having a son. He journeyed to Delphi to ask the god if there was any hope that some day he would be the father of a boy. The priestess told him no, and added what was far worse: that his daughter would have a son who would kill him.

The only sure way to escape that fate was for the King to have Danaë instantly put to death—taking no chances, but seeing to it himself. This Acrisius would not do. His fatherly affection was not strong, as events proved, but his fear of the gods was. They visited with terrible punishment those who shed the blood of kindred.

⑲ ✓ **Reading Check**

What does the priestess say Danae's son will do?

Perseus ■ 1121

---

⑮ **Background**
Greek Gods

Zeus, chief of all the Greek gods, rules over the earth. His two brothers, Poseidon and Hades, rule over the seas and the underworld. Athena is Zeus' daughter; she has no mother. She sprang full grown and armed from Zeus' head. Hermes, the son of Zeus and Maia, is a messenger of the gods. The medical insignia students can see on doctors' diplomas depicts the staff of Hermes.

⑯ **Motivation**

Engage students' interest by reading this passage from "Perseus":

He stood up before them all and did exactly what the King had hoped he would do, declared that he would give him a present better than any there. He would go off and kill Medusa and bring back her head as a gift. . . . No one in his senses would have made such a proposal. Medusa was one of the Gorgons.

Ask students to imagine what type of creature Medusa might be. What would make her so terrifying? Have each student write or draw a description of what Medusa might look like.

Concept Connector

Students will return to this activity after completing "Perseus."

⟵

⑰ **About the Selection**

In "Perseus," when the oracle prophesies that Acrisius will die by the hand of his grandson, Acrisius shuts his daughter Danaë away to prevent her from meeting men. However, Zeus transforms himself into a shower of gold and visits Danaë, and she conceives a son. Acrisius sets her and baby Perseus adrift in a wooden chest, but they are rescued. When he is grown, Perseus kills the Gorgon, kills a sea monster, sets the princess Andromeda free, and marries her.

⑱ **Critical Viewing**

Answer: Perseus is treated with respect, gratitude, and admiration.

⑲ **Reading Check**

Answer: Her son will kill Acrisius.

- Remind students of the common characteristics of a hero, including a semi-divine birth.

- **Ask** students to answer the Literary Analysis question: Which elements of Perseus' story so far suggest that he will be a mythic hero?
Answer: He is the subject of a prophecy, the result of a miraculous birth, and most importantly, the son of Zeus.

- **Ask** students to speculate on any superhuman powers that Perseus might have, based on his parentage.
Possible response: Perseus may have tremendous strength and fearlessness, and he can probably expect to be aided by various immortals.

Acrisius did not dare slay his daughter. Instead, he had a house built all of bronze and sunk underground, but with part of the roof open to the sky so that light and air could come through. Here he shut her up and guarded her.

> So Danaë endured, the beautiful,
> To change the glad daylight for brass-bound walls,
> And in that chamber secret as the grave
> She lived a prisoner. Yet to her came
> Zeus in the golden rain.

20 As she sat there through the long days and hours with nothing to do, nothing to see except the clouds moving by overhead, a mysterious thing happened, a shower of gold fell from the sky and filled her chamber. How it was revealed to her that it was Zeus who had visited her in this shape we are not told, but she knew that the child she bore was his son.

For a time she kept his birth secret from her father, but it became increasingly difficult to do so in the narrow limits of that bronze house and finally one day the little boy—his name was Perseus—was discovered by his grandfather. "Your child!" Acrisius cried in great anger. "Who is his father?" But when Danaë answered proudly, "Zeus," he would not believe her. One thing only he was sure of, that the boy's life was a terrible danger to his own. He was afraid to kill him for the same reason that had kept him from killing her, fear of Zeus and the Furies who pursue such murderers. But if he could not kill them outright, he could put them in the way of tolerably certain death. He had a great chest made, and the two placed in it. Then it was taken out to sea and cast into the water.

In that strange boat Danaë sat with her little son. The daylight faded and she was alone on the sea.

> When in the carven chest the winds and waves
> Struck fear into her heart she put her arms,
> Not without tears, round Perseus tenderly
> She said, "O son, what grief is mine.
> But you sleep softly, little child,
> Sunk deep in rest within your cheerless home,
> Only a box, brass-bound. The night, this darkness visible,
> The scudding waves so near to your soft curls,
> The shrill voice of the wind, you do not heed,
> Nestled in your red cloak, fair little face."

Through the night in the tossing chest she listened to the waters that seemed always about to wash over them. The dawn came, but with no comfort to her for she could not see it. Neither could she see that around them there were islands rising high above the sea, many islands. All she knew was that presently a wave seemed to lift

Literary Analysis
Tall Tale and Myth
Which elements of Perseus' story so far suggest that he will be a mythic hero?

Vocabulary Development

The Latin root -mort-
Point out to students that human beings are described as *mortals* and that gods are called *immortals*. The root -mort- is from the Latin word for death. Mortals are subject to death; immortals never die. The nouns derived from these words are *mortality* and *immortality*. Note also that when Perseus appears without a gift, he is keenly *mortified*. *Mortified* also shares this root. It may help students to think of mortified as being "embarrassed to death."

them and carry them swiftly on and then, retreating, leave them on something solid and motionless. They had made land; they were safe from the sea, but they were still in the chest with no way to get out.

Fate willed it—or perhaps Zeus, who up to now had done little for his love and his child—that they should be discovered by a good man, a fisherman named Dictys. He came upon the great box and broke it open and took the pitiful cargo home to his wife who was as kind as he. They had no children and they cared for Danaë and Perseus as if they were their own. The two lived there many years, Danaë content to let her son follow the fisherman's humble trade, out of harm's way. But in the end more trouble came. Polydectes [pol i dek´ tèz], the ruler of the little island, was the brother of Dictys, but he was a cruel and ruthless man. He seems to have taken no notice of the mother and son for a long time, but at last Danaë attracted his attention. She was still radiantly beautiful even though Perseus by now was full grown, and Polydectes fell in love with her. He wanted her, but he did not want her son, and he set himself to think out a way of getting rid of him.

There were some fearsome monsters called Gorgons who lived on an island and were known far and wide because of their deadly power. Polydectes evidently talked to Perseus about them; he probably told him that he would rather have the head of one of them than anything else in the world. This seems practically certain from the plan he devised for killing Perseus. He announced that he was about to be married and he called his friends together for a celebration, including Perseus in the invitation. Each guest, as was customary, brought a gift for the bride-to-be, except Perseus alone. He had nothing he could give. He was young and proud and keenly <u>mortified</u>. He stood up before them all and did exactly what the King had hoped he would do, declared that he would give him a present better than any there. He would go off and kill Medusa and bring back her head as his gift. Nothing could have suited the King better. No one in his senses would have made such a proposal. Medusa was one of the Gorgons,

> And they are three, the Gorgons, each with wings
> And snaky hair, most horrible to mortals.
> Whom no man shall behold and draw again
> The breath of life,

for the reason that whoever looked at them were turned instantly into stone. It seemed that Perseus had been led by his angry pride into making an empty boast. No man unaided could kill Medusa.

21 ⓐ **Critical Viewing**
Which scene in the story does this art illustrate? **[Connect]**

Vocabulary Builder
mortified (môrt´ ə fīd´) *adj.* extremely embarrassed

22 **Reading Check**
What does Perseus promise to give the king as a gift?

Perseus ■ 1123

21 **Critical Viewing**
Answer: The art illustrates the scene in which Dictys finds Danaë and her baby inside the chest. The man cannot be Acrisius setting them adrift, because he is not wearing a crown.

22 **Reading Check**
Answer: Perseus promises the head of Medusa as a gift.

Differentiated Instruction Solutions for All Learners

Strategy for Special Needs Students
The formal, academic style of Edith Hamilton's retelling of the myth of Perseus may prove a barrier to some students. You may want to read to them parts of "The Gorgon's Head" in Nathaniel Hawthorne's *A Wonder Book,* an American collection of the Greek myths written for children. "The Gorgon's Head" tells the same story as Hamilton's "Perseus" in a lighter, more entertaining, and more accessible style.

As students listen to the story (some may read it themselves), have them list the names and identifications of the characters and write the basic events of the plot. Afterward, students should be ready and able to more easily read Hamilton's "Perseus" and answer the Thinking About questions at the end.

- **Ask** students what act of "folly" Perseus has committed.
  Answer: He has promised to perform an impossible feat—killing the Medusa. No human could perform this task without supernatural aid.

- Point out to students that great heroes are sometimes propelled into crises by the same fearless recklessness that helps them perform the very feats that make them heroes. This is one of the factors that makes their characters interestingly human.

- **Ask** students to answer the Literary Analysis question: Which details in this paragraph show Perseus' special status as a mythic hero?
  Answer: Two gods watch over him and give him help, protection, and guidance.

- **Ask** students how they think a modern hero, facing a battle with a terrible monster, would differ from a mythological hero.
  Possible response: A modern hero would not receive supernatural help. He or she would have to find a natural way, perhaps with the help of technology, to win the battle.

24 **Critical Viewing**

Answer: Students should recognize the Gorgon Medusa from the snakes that wreathe her face.

But Perseus was saved from his folly. Two great gods were watching over him. He took ship as soon as he left the King's hall, not daring to see his mother first and tell her what he intended, and he sailed to Greece to learn where the three monsters were to be found. He went to Delphi, but all the priestess would say was to bid **23** him seek the land where men eat not Demeter's golden grain, but only acorns. So he went to Dodona, in the land of oak trees, where the talking oaks were which declared Zeus's will and where the Selli lived who made their bread from acorns. They could tell him, however, no more than this, that he was under the protection of the gods. They did not know where the Gorgons lived.

When and how Hermes and Athena came to his help is not told in any story, but he must have known despair before they did so. At last, however, as he wandered on, he met a strange and beautiful person. We know what he looked like from many a poem, a young man with the first down upon his cheek when youth is loveliest, carrying, as no other young man ever did, a wand of gold with wings at one end, wearing a winged hat, too, and winged sandals. At sight of him hope must have entered Perseus' heart, for he would know that this could be none other than Hermes, the guide and the giver of good.

This radiant personage told him that before he attacked Medusa he must first be properly equipped, and that what he needed was in the possession of the nymphs of the North. To find the nymphs' abode, they must go to the Gray Women who alone could tell them the way. These women dwelt in a land where all was dim and shrouded in twilight. No ray of sun looked ever on that country, nor the moon by night. In that gray place the three women lived, all gray themselves and withered as in extreme old age. They were strange creatures, indeed, most of all because they had but one eye for the three, which it was their custom to take turns with, each removing it from her forehead when she had had it for a time and handing it to another.

All this Hermes told Perseus and then he unfolded his plan. He would himself guide Perseus to them. Once there Perseus must keep hidden until he saw one of them take the eye out of her forehead to pass it on. At that moment, when none of the three could see, he must rush forward and seize the eye and refuse to give it back until they told him how to reach the nymphs of the North.

He himself, Hermes said, would give him a sword to attack Medusa with—which could not be bent or broken by the Gorgon's scales, no matter how hard they were. This was a wonderful gift, no doubt, and yet of what use was a sword when the creature to be struck by it could turn the swordsman into stone before he was

1124 ■ *Themes in Literature: Heroism*

Literary Analysis
Tall Tale and Myth
Which details in this paragraph show Perseus' special status as a mythic hero?

24
▲ **Critical Viewing**
Who is portrayed in this art? Explain how you know. **[Connect]**

Vocabulary Development

Expressive Vocabulary
As students discuss Perseus and the idea of the hero, encourage them to use the expressive vocabulary presented earlier. You might encourage them with sentence starters like these:

1. In ancient times, a prophecy had a tremendous *impact;* for Perseus, it meant . . .

2. The Medusa had a fatal gaze; Perseus had to find a way to *negate*. . .

3. At first, the hero's mind was shrouded in darkness; he needed the gods to *illuminate* . . .

4. With the help of the gods, the young hero's power would *exceed* . . .

5. Considering the obstacles, it was foolish to *undertake*. . .

within striking distance? But another great deity was at hand to help. Pallas Athena stood beside Perseus. She took off the shield of polished bronze which covered her breast and held it out to him. "Look into this when you attack the Gorgon," she said. "You will be able to see her in it as in a mirror, and so avoid her deadly power."

Now, indeed, Perseus had good reason to hope. The journey to the twilight land was long, over the stream of Ocean and on to the very border of the black country where the Cimmerians dwell, but Hermes was his guide and he could not go astray. They found the Gray Women at last, looking in the wavering light like gray birds, for they had the shape of swans. But their heads were human and beneath their wings they had arms and hands. Perseus did just as Hermes had said, he held back until he saw one of them take the eye out of her forehead. Then before she could give it to her sister, he snatched it out of her hand. It was a moment or two before the three realized they had lost it. Each thought one of the others had it. But Perseus spoke out and told them he had taken it and that it would be theirs again only when they showed him how to find the nymphs of the North. They gave him full directions at once; they would have done anything to get their eye back. He returned it to them and went on the way they had pointed out to him. He was bound, although he did not know it, to the blessed country of the Hyperboreans [hī per bō′ rē anz], at the back of the North Wind, of which it is said: "Neither by ship nor yet by land shall one find the wondrous road to the gathering place of the Hyperboreans." But Perseus had Hermes with him, so that the road lay open to him, and he reached that host of happy people who are always banqueting and holding joyful <u>revelry</u>. They showed him great kindness: they welcomed him to their feast, and the maidens dancing to the sound of flute and lyre paused to get for him the gifts he sought. These were three: winged sandals, a magic wallet which would always become the right size for whatever was to be carried in it, and, most important of all, a cap which made the wearer invisible. With these and Athena's shield and Hermes' sword Perseus was ready for the Gorgons. Hermes knew where they lived, and leaving the happy land the two flew back across Ocean and over the sea to the Terrible Sisters' island.

By great good fortune they were all asleep when Perseus found them. In the mirror of the bright shield he could see them clearly, creatures with great wings and bodies covered with golden scales and hair a mass of twisting snakes. Athena was beside him now as well as Hermes. They told him which one was Medusa and that was important, for she alone of the three could be killed; the other two were immortal. Perseus on his winged sandals hovered above them, looking, however, only at the shield. Then he aimed a stroke down

25

27

Literary Analysis
Tall Tale and Myth
What heroic qualities does Perseus reveal in his encounter with the Gray Women?

Vocabulary Builder
revelry (rev′ əl rē) *n.* noisy merrymaking

26

Reading Check

Who comes to Perseus' aid?

Perseus ■ 1125

Differentiated
Instruction   Solutions for All Learners

Strategy for Gifted/Talented Students
It is an ancient human custom to build monuments to honor heroes, often by erecting statues and plaques in public places. Ask students to design a monument for Perseus. Have students work in teams to decide which particular deed or deeds to emphasize and which physical details to include. Students can then draw plans for their monument or create an actual model.

Strategy for Advanced Readers
Challenge students to create a brief encyclopedia of mythology that informs readers about all the places and characters alluded to in the story of Perseus. Students can look in reference books or collections of myths to find out who the Seli are, where Dodona is, and so on. Each page of the encyclopedia can give an explanation and show an illustration of the place or the character.

• Remind students that mythological heroes possess more than brute strength. They are usually great in body, mind, and heart. Perseus has physical prowess, but the gods give him great knowledge, too.

• **Ask** students to answer the Literary Analysis question: What special knowledge helps Perseus kill Medusa?
Answer: Athena and Hermes tell Perseus which of the Gorgons is Medusa, the only one who can be killed.

• **Ask** students to speculate about what other kinds of special knowledge the gods might give a mythological hero.
Possible response: The gods might tell a hero the meaning of a mysterious oracle, where to go on a quest, or how to rescue a loved one. They might also reveal the secret of the hero's identity, parentage, or destiny.

---

❷⃝ at Medusa's throat and Athena guided his hand. With a single sweep of his sword he cut through her neck and, his eyes still fixed on the shield with never a glance at her, he swooped low enough to seize the head. He dropped it into the wallet which closed around it. He had nothing to fear from it now. But the two other Gorgons had awakened and, horrified at the sight of their sister slain, tried to pursue the slayer. Perseus was safe; he had on the cap of darkness and they could not find him.

> So over the sea rich-haired Danaë's son,
> Perseus, on his winged sandals sped,
> Flying swift as thought.
> In a wallet of silver,
> A wonder to behold,
> He bore the head of the monster,
> While Hermes, the son of Maia,
> The messenger of Zeus,
> Kept ever at his side.

On his way back he came to Ethiopia and alighted there. By this time Hermes had left him. Perseus found, as Hercules was later to find, that a lovely maiden had been given up to be devoured by a horrible sea serpent. Her name was Andromeda and she was the daughter of a silly vain woman,

> That starred Ethiop queen who strove
> To set her beauty's praise above
> The sea-nymphs, and their power offended.

She had boasted that she was more beautiful than the daughters of Nereus, the Sea-god. An absolutely certain way in those days to draw down on one a wretched fate was to claim superiority in anything over any deity[1]; nevertheless people were perpetually doing so. In this case the punishment for the arrogance the gods detested fell not on Queen Cassiopeia [kas′ ē ō pē′ ə], Andromeda's mother, but on her daughter. The Ethiopians were being devoured in numbers by the serpent; and, learning from the oracle that they could be freed from the pest only if Andromeda were offered up to it, they forced Cepheus [sē′ fəs], her father, to consent. When Perseus arrived the maiden was on a rocky ledge by the sea, chained there to wait for the coming of the monster. Perseus saw her and on the instant loved her. He waited beside her until the great snake came for its prey; then he cut its head off just as he had the Gorgon's. The headless body dropped back into the water; Perseus took Andromeda to her parents and asked for her hand, which they gladly gave him.

---

1. deity (dē′ ə tē) *n.* a god.

1126 ■ Themes in Literature: Heroism

Vocabulary Development

Think-Aloud: Context
Direct students' attention to the word *vain* near the middle of this page. Using a think-aloud process, model how to use context to infer the meaning of an unknown word. Say to students:

> I'm going to think aloud to show you how I would figure out the meaning of *vain* from its context.

Andromeda was the daughter of a "silly vain woman" who boasted that she was more beautiful than the daughters of the sea-god. So being *vain* has something to do with boasting. This woman also "claim[s] superiority" based on her beauty, and she is punished for her "arrogance." So being *vain* means being arrogant or boastful about a personal quality such as beauty.

28

28 Humanities

Perseus and Andromeda (detail), by Paolo Veronese

Paolo Veronese ("Paolo of Verona") (1528–1588), Tintoretto, and Titian are three great painters of the end of the Italian Renaissance. All are known for their brilliant colors and the epic sweep of their historical, religious, and mythological scenes. This detail from Veronese's painting shows Perseus in the act of slaying the sea monster. Use the following questions for discussion:

1. What details of Perseus' equipment does the artist include?
   Answer: Students should recognize the sword, magic cap, winged sandals, and magic wallet.

2. How does color contribute to the drama of the scene?
   Answer: The blood-red colors of Perseus' clothing flow toward the gaping red mouth of the monster. The vivid colors highlight the two combatants.

29 Critical Viewing

Answer: The hero's strong arm and his focus on the beast emphasize his strength and bravery. The winged sandals also indicate that he has received divine help.

30 Reading Check

Answer: Perseus rescues Andromeda, an Ethiopian princess.

29 ◀ **Critical Viewing**
In what ways does this painting emphasize Perseus' physical strength and bravery? **[Interpret]**

With her he sailed back to the island and his mother, but in the house where he had lived so long he found no one. The fisherman Dictys' wife was long since dead, and the two others, Danaë and the man who had been like a father to Perseus, had had to fly and hide themselves from Polydectes, who was furious at Danaë's refusal to marry him. They had taken refuge in a temple, Perseus was told. He learned also that the King was holding a banquet in the palace and all the men who favored him were gathered there. Perseus instantly

30 ✔ **Reading Check**
Who does Perseus rescue from the sea serpent?

Perseus ■ 1127

Differentiated
Instruction Solutions for All Learners

Strategy for Special Needs Students
Have students discuss their opinions of Perseus as a hero. Do they find him heroic? Why or why not? How does Perseus compare to students' personal heroes or to heroes they admire from movies, television, or other stories? Does Perseus seem more heroic as the story progresses, or does he seem heroic right from the beginning? Have students defend their opinions with specific details from the myth.

Strategy for Less Proficient Readers
Have students work together in pairs or in small groups to answer questions 3 and 4 under Comparing Tall Tales and Myths on p. 1129. For question 3, encourage them to suggest specific ways in which the heroes are similar and how they are different, discuss those ways, and then make a group list. Have them define what they mean by a hero before they begin to answer question 4.

- Have students **restate** the prophecy that caused Danaë to be imprisoned in the first place.
Answer: The oracle prophesied that Danaë's son would kill Acrisius.

- **Ask** students to answer the Literary Analysis question: How do the events at the end of the story relate to situations described at the beginning?
Answer: When Perseus accidentally kills Acrisius with a discus, he fulfills the prophecy made at the beginning of the story.

Concept Connector ━━━━━
Have students return to the Motivation activity and revise their descriptions of Medusa based on their reading of "Perseus."

◀━━━━━━━━━

ASSESS

Answers

1. **Possible response:** Students may choose the rescue of Andromeda, because acts alone to save a beautiful princess.

2. (a) He is embarrassed because he has no gift for the King and rashly promises to bring the best gift of all. (b) Like Athena and Hermes, Perseus is a child of Zeus.

3. (a) Perseus' weapons are a sword which cannot be bent or broken by the Gorgon's scales, a polished bronze shield, winged sandals, a magic wallet, and a cap of invisibility. He hovers with the sandals, looks only at the shield, cuts off Medusa's head with the sword, puts the head in the wallet, and escapes from the other Gorgons with the aid of the cap of invisibility. (b) He might never have found Medusa. He might have wandered forever. If he had found Medusa, she and her sisters would probably have killed him.

4. (a) First audience may have learned to respect their gods and to accept their fates.
(b) **Possible response:** Students may suggest that people still need to accept situations that are beyond their power to change.

---

saw his opportunity. He went straight to the palace and entered the hall. As he stood at the entrance, Athena's shining buckler on his breast, the silver wallet at his side, he drew the eyes of every man there. Then before any could look away he held up the Gorgon's head; and at the sight one and all, the cruel King and his servile courtiers, were turned into stone. There they sat, a row of statues, each, as it were, frozen stiff in the attitude he had struck when he first saw Perseus.

When the islanders knew themselves freed from the tyrant it was easy for Perseus to find Danaë and Dictys. He made Dictys king of the island, but he and his mother decided that they would go back with Andromeda to Greece and try to be reconciled to Acrisius, to see if the many years that had passed since he had put them in the chest had not softened him so that he would be glad to receive his daughter and grandson. When they reached Argos, however, they found that Acrisius had been driven away from the city, and where **③①** he was no one could say. It happened that soon after their arrival Perseus heard that the King of Larissa, in the North, was holding a great athletic contest, and he journeyed there to take part. In the discus-throwing when his turn came and he hurled the heavy missile, it swerved and fell among the spectators. Acrisius was there on a visit to the King, and the discus struck him. The blow was fatal and he died at once.

So Apollo's oracle was again proved true. If Perseus felt any grief, at least he knew that his grandfather had done his best to kill him and his mother. With his death their troubles came to an end. Perseus and Andromeda lived happily ever after. Their son, Electryon, was the grandfather of Hercules.

Medusa's head was given to Athena, who bore it always upon the aegis, Zeus's shield, which she carried for him.

Thinking About the Selection

1. **Respond:** Which of Perseus' adventures would make the best action-adventure movie? Why?

2. **(a) Recall:** Why does Perseus set out to kill Medusa? **(b) Infer:** What detail of Perseus' background might have led Athena and Hermes to help Perseus in his quest?

3. **(a) Summarize:** Explain the weapons Perseus uses and the actions he takes to kill Medusa. **(b) Hypothesize:** What might have happened to Perseus if he had not received help from the gods?

4. **(a) Interpret:** What lesson do you think this ancient myth taught its first audiences? **(b) Extend:** In what ways is this myth still relevant today? Explain.

1128 ■ *Themes in Literature: Heroism*

Vocabulary Development

Vocabulary Knowledge Rating
When students have completed reading and discussing "Pecos Bill: The Cyclone" and "Perseus," have them take out their **Vocabulary Rating Chart.** Read the words aloud once more and have students rate their knowledge of the words again in the After Reading column. Clarify any words that are still problematic. Have students write their own definition and example or sentence in the appropriate column. Then have students complete the **Vocabulary Builder Practice** activities on p. 1129. Encourage students to use the words in further discussion and written work about the selections. Remind them that they will be accountable for these words on the Selection Test.

Apply the Skills

Pecos Bill: The Cyclone • Perseus

Comparing Tall Tales and Myths

1. Use a chart like the one shown to identify the ways in which "Pecos Bill: The Cyclone" contains the elements of a **tall tale**.

Larger-than-life hero	Far-fetched situations	Amazing feats	Humor	Hyperbole

2. **(a)** What divine actions does the **myth** of Perseus describe? **(b)** In what ways is Perseus a typical **mythic hero?**

3. **(a)** What weapons, skills, and knowledge does Perseus use to defeat the Medusa? **(b)** What weapons, skills, and knowledge does Pecos Bill use to defeat the cyclone? **(c)** In what ways are Pecos Bill's and Perseus' achievements both similar and different?

4. **(a)** What makes Pecos Bill a hero? **(b)** What makes Perseus a hero?

Writing to Compare Literary Works

The heroes of tall tales and myths usually represent some aspects of the cultures that create them. At the same time, every hero embodies some universal qualities—traits that are valued in all cultures. In an essay, compare and contrast the values that Pecos Bill and Perseus represent. Use these questions to help organize your thoughts:

- Whom does each hero respect? What does each fear?
- What does each hero desire? What does each accomplish?
- Does the hero act primarily on his own behalf or on behalf of others?

Vocabulary Builder

Practice For each item, use a word from the vocabulary list on page 1112 in a sentence describing the situation.

1. trying to convince those with different ideas
2. celebrating a championship season
3. embarrassment at forgetting a gift
4. taking over a coach's job

QuickReview

Tall Tale: a folk tale that features humor, exaggeration, and a hero who performs amazing deeds

Myth: an anonymous tale that explains the actions of gods and heroes or the causes of natural phenomena

Go Online
Assessment

For: Self-test
Visit: www.PHSchool.com
Web Code: epa-6609

Vocabulary Builder

Sample responses:

1. The *skeptics* were difficult to convince.
2. After we won the championship, the *revelry* continued all night.
3. We were *mortified* at having forgotten the gift at home.
4. She was only an assistant, but she *usurped* the head coach's job.

---

1. **Sample responses: situations:** postholes blown away, resentful cyclone; **feats:** riding and taming cyclone; **humor:** prairie dogs digging postholes, badgers digging wells, six-shooters become popgun and water pistol; **hyperbole:** always raining on Fourth of July, horse learning 27 gaits, creating Death Valley.

Another sample can be found on **Comparing Literary Works Graphic Organizer Transparency B,** p. 229 in *Graphic Organizer Transparencies.*

2. **(a)** Divine actions include Zeus's visit to Danae as a shower of gold, and the gifts and guidance of Athena and Hermes. **(b)** Perseus is a typical mythic hero in having a divine parent, receiving help from the gods, defeating monsters, and fulfilling an oracle.

3. **(a)** Perseus uses a sword, shield, winged sandals, magic wallet, and cap of invisibility. He is skilled, resourceful, and listens to the gods. **(b)** Bill's "weapon" is his horse Widow Maker. His skills include strength, speed, endurance, and horsemanship. **(c)** Both men defeat inhuman monsters and rescue the defenseless. Perseus, though headstrong, is fulfilling the will of the gods, while Bill is following his own wild impulses.

4. **(a)** Bill is brave, tough, energetic, resourceful, and optimistic. **(b)** Perseus is the son of a god, slays a monster, and rescues a princess.

Writing to Compare Literary Works

- Have students use the bulleted questions to develop their ideas.
- Encourage students to incorporate the expressive vocabulary words: *impact, negate, illuminate, exceed, undertake.*

Six Traits Focus

✔	Ideas		Word Choice
✔	Organization		Sentence Fluency
	Voice		Conventions

MONITORING PROGRESS

In this Skills Review, students apply the skills taught in Part 2. The test format gives students practice in taking standardized tests. The results of this review test will help you check students' readiness for the **Benchmark Test** for Unit 6, Part 2.

Applying Reading Skill

Read the passage with students. Ask students to compare and contrast the two speakers in a sentence for each. Then have students identify the conflict. They should be able to determine where each character stands in the conflict. Although students may have difficulty with the Greek names, they should be able to understand the basis for the conflict.

If necessary, have students reread the instruction on p. 1046 before having them complete the remaining items on their own.

Applying Vocabulary Skills

Remind students that Latin word roots give readers clues to help them determine the meanings of unfamiliar words. Ask students to provide the meanings for the word roots -sign- and -her-. Also remind students that they can find context clues from the surrounding material in a sentence if they need to determine the meaning of an unfamiliar word. If they have trouble, review the instruction on p. 1047.

Tips for
Test Taking

Students may encounter unfamiliar vocabulary words when taking a standardized test. Remind students to look to a word's root to help them determine its meaning. If they need more clues to a word's meaning, they can also look to its context in a sentence for more information.

Reading and Vocabulary Skills Review

Reading: Compare and Contrast

Directions: *Questions 1–5 are based on the following selection.*

ANTIGONE. I thought so. And that is why I wanted you
   To come out here with me. There is something we must do.

ISMENE. Why do you speak so strangely?

ANTIGONE. Listen, Ismene:
   Creon buried our brother Eteocles
   With military honors, gave him a soldier's funeral,
   And it was right that he should; but Polyneices [Antigone's other brother],
   Who fought as bravely and died as miserably,—
   They say that Creon has sworn
   No one shall bury him, no one mourn for him,
   But his body must lie in the fields, a sweet treasure
   For carrion birds to find as they search for food.
   That is what they say, and our good Creon is coming here
   To announce it publicly; and the penalty—
   Stoning to death in the public square!
                                    There it is,
   And now you can prove what you are:
   A true sister, or a traitor to your family.

ISMENE. Antigone, you are mad! What could I possibly do?

ANTIGONE. Ismene, I am going to bury him. Will you come?

ISMENE. Bury him! You have just said the new law forbids it.
                                    —from *Antigone,* by Sophocles

1. What issue is the source of conflict in this passage?
   A   the war of the Argives
   B   the relationship between the sisters
   C   the burial of Polyneices
   D   the death of Eteocles

2. How are Antigone and Ismene similar?
   A   Both have suffered the same loss.
   B   Both are angry at Creon.
   C   Both are determined to avenge the death of their brother.
   D   Both believe Creon is a just king.

3. How are Antigone and Ismene different?
   A   Antigone loves her brothers; Ismene does not.
   B   Antigone is defiant; Ismene is obedient.
   C   Antigone believes in upholding the law; Ismene believes in following one's heart.
   D   Antigone mourns the loss of her brothers; Ismene is indifferent to their loss.

1130 ■ *Themes in Literature*

ASSESS

Answers

1. C	8. C
2. A	9. A
3. B	10. D
4. B	11. B
5. A	12. B
6. B	13. A
7. B	

Assessment Practice

Vocabulary

Directions: *Choose the best definition for each italicized word.*

4. **Both opponents in the debate present** *cogent* **evidence to support their position.**
   A   sticky
   B   forceful and to the point
   C   confusing and meaningless
   D   self-righteous

5. **The main character found his conscience was** *compelling* **him to tell the truth.**
   A   driving
   B   clarifying
   C   not allowing
   D   signaling

6. **The rules are clear and** *coherent.*
   A   strict
   B   logical
   C   transparent
   D   puzzling

7. **This work is a** *significant* **addition to the literary criticism of Greek poetry.**
   A   trivial
   B   meaningful
   C   exceptional
   D   useless

8. **The lack of strong characters is a major** *defect* **of the play.**
   A   perfection
   B   importance
   C   shortcoming
   D   addition

Directions: *Choose the correct definition of each word.*

9. **insignificant**
   A   trivial
   B   lacking a plan
   C   full of meaning
   D   being an obvious clue

10. **coherently**
   A   confusedly
   B   in a loud manner
   C   full of importance
   D   clearly

11. **design**
   A   to give a signal
   B   to mark out or make a plan
   C   to confuse
   D   to captivate

12. **reassign**
   A   to make meaningless
   B   to mark out for a purpose once again
   C   to make clear
   D   to hand over or give authority to

13. **inherently**
   A   inseparably within
   B   in a clear way
   C   unconditionally
   D   in a confused manner

If students answer any of these questions incorrectly, have them review the instruction on the following pages in Part 2 before taking the **Benchmark Test.**

Question	Pages Where Instruction Is Located:
1	1048, 1112
2	1048, 1112
3	1048, 1112
4	1047
5	1047
6	1047
7	1047
8	1047
9	1047, 1092
10	1047, 1110
11	1047, 1092
12	1047, 1092
13	1047, 1110

Benchmark

Administer the **Benchmark Test** for Unit 6, Part 2. If the Benchmark Test reveals that some students need further work, use the Interpretation Guide to determine the appropriate reteaching page in the **Reading Kit.** You will also find the same instruction and practice available on **Success Tracker.**

Go Online
Vocabulary
For: Interactive Crossword Puzzle
Visit: www.PHSchool.com
Web Code: epj-5602
Give students this Web Code to access an interactive crossword puzzle using Academic Vocabulary and Vocabulary Skill words from Part 2.

Spelling on College Entrance Exams

- Remind students that reading carefully is the key to finding many errors. Tell students that if they frequently do not catch misspelled words, they should start at the end of the sentence and read backwards, one word at a time. Invite students to share words that they commonly misspell.

  Possible responses: *a lot, argument, disappearance, embodiment, indefinitely, occurrence, rhythm, withdrawal*

- Have students make up a list of ten common words that they consistently misspell. Have them use the list for a bookmark and review the list at least twice each day. When they are comfortable knowing that they have mastered the words, have students create a new list of ten more words they have difficulty spelling.

Writing and Grammar, Gold Level

Students will find additional spelling instruction in Chapter 31, Section 4.

Spelling on College Entrance Exams

Spelling items come up on most college entrance exams. Doing well with them involves paying attention to small things, recalling a few basic rules, and knowing your own spelling weaknesses.

Spell It Right Spelling is not the most important part of college entrance exams. However, spelling items do occur in English usage sections of most tests. Use these recommendations to help you prepare.

- Look for homophone errors, easily confused words, or simple words that are spelled incorrectly. Remember, for instance, that *a lot* is two words and that *you're,* not *your,* is the contraction for "you are."
- Review word formation rules that people sometimes forget.
  — When adding endings to multisyllable words whose final letters are a consonant + y, double the final consonant if the accent is on the final syllable.
  — When adding prefixes to words, do not drop any letters.
  — When adding suffixes to words, remember that final consonant + *y* usually changes to *i*. Final *e*'s are usually dropped when the suffix begins with a vowel—but not when the base word ends in *ce* or *ge*.
- Know the words that give you trouble, and work out memory tricks to help with them.

Practice For each word on the word list, write a memory aid. Share the memory aid with a partner or the class.

Example: to **adapt** is **A** necessary survival skill.

Word List
adapt
adopt
preferred
misshapen
courageous
loneliness
acclaim
sophomore
parentheses
preceding

I could have adapted if they adopted a "no test" policy!

Teaching Resources

The following resource can be used to enrich or extend the instruction for this Spelling Workshop.

Unit 6 Resources
Spelling Workshop: Spelling on College Entrance Exams, p. 158

Assessment Practice

A. Directions: *Write the letter of the item that contains a spelling, punctuation, capitalization, or usage error. Choose E if there are no errors in the sentence.*

1. My sister is a sophomore at the
   (A)   (B)
University of Dayton in Ohio, so last year,
         (C)   (D)
she attended a community college. No error
                                      (E)

2. The preceeding day, the third
         (A)
Friday of the month, Travis
      (B)
had gone for his regular doctor's
   (C)   (D)
appointment. No error
         (E)

3. Some people, such as the volunteers
            (A)
at Price Hospital, are content to stay out
      (B)
of the limelight, others, though, must
         (C)
have constant acclaim. No error
               (D)   (E)

4. Writers who overuse parenthesees in
         (A)   (B)
their essays tend not only to confuse
   (C)
readers but also to annoy them. No error
         (D)   (E)

B. Directions: *Write the letter of the version of the underlined section that makes the item correct and appropriate. If you think the original version is best, choose "NO CHANGE."*

When my grandmother first planted the little tree, it was a sad, mishapen
                                                            1

stick. As summer passed, though, it adopted to its
                                           2

environment. It clearly preferred well-irrigated soil, so we watered
                              3

it constantly.

1. **A** NO CHANGE
   B tree it was a sad, mishapen
   C tree, it was a sad, misshapen
   D tree, it would be a sad, mishapen

2. **A** NO CHANGE
   B adapted to its
   C adopted to his
   D adapted to it's

3. **A** NO CHANGE
   B prefered well-irrigated soil, so
   C prefered well-irrigated soil so
   D preferred well-irrigated soil, but

Assessment Practice
A.
  1. D
  2. A
  3. C
  4. B
B.
  1. C
  2. B
  3. A

Spelling Workshop ■ *1133*

PRETEACH

☑ Meeting Your Standards

Students will

1. write a comparison-and-contrast essay.

2. use writing strategies to generate ideas and to plan, organize, evaluate, and revise the essay.

3. apply grammar skills.

 From the Author's Desk

Dean Smith and John Kilgo

Show students Segment 3 on Dean Smith and John Kilgo on *From the Author's Desk DVD.* Discuss using comparison-and-contrast skills to determine which events to include in a piece.

Writing Genres

Using the Form Point out to students that comparison-and-contrast essays are often incorporated into other types of writing. Point out these examples:

• Comparison-and-contrast skills are often needed to answer essay questions on tests.

• On college and scholarship applications, students might be asked to compare and contrast experiences.

• Comparison-and-contrast skills are used in persuasive writing and research writing.

♫ Writing Workshop
Work in Progress

If students have done the Work-in-Progress assignments throughout Part 2, suggest that they examine their recorded ideas as they begin prewriting. They may have an idea in their portfolios that they wish to develop into a comparison-and-contrast essay.

 Online Essay Scorer

A writing prompt for this mode of writing can be found on the *PH Online Essay Scorer* at PHSuccessNet.com.

1134

Writing Workshop

Exposition: Comparison-and-Contrast Essay

You make comparisons every day. Whether you are considering foods, ideas, actions, or careers, comparative thinking is an underlying factor of almost every choice you make. A **comparison-and-contrast essay** is a written exploration of the similarities and differences between two things or among more than two things. Use the steps outlined in this workshop to write a comparison-and-contrast essay.

Assignment Write a comparison-and-contrast essay about two events, ideas, or historical leaders.

What to Include Your comparison-and-contrast essay should have the following characteristics:

• an analysis and discussion of similarities and differences between two or among more than two things, people, places, or ideas

• accurate, factual details about each subject

• a purpose for comparing and contrasting

• a balanced presentation of each subject using either subject-by-subject or point-by-point organization

• error-free grammar, including varied sentence structure and length

To preview the criteria on which your comparison-and-contrast essay may be assessed, see the rubric on page 1141.

 Writing Workshop: *Work in Progress*

If you have completed the Work-in-Progress assignments, you have several ideas in your portfolio that you might wish to pursue in your essay. You may continue to develop these ideas, or you might choose to explore a new idea as you complete this Writing Workshop.

1134 ■ *Themes in Literature: Heroism*

Using the Form

You will use elements of comparison and contrast in these types of writing:

• essays on historical figures and events

• consumer reports

• essays on works of art, literature, or music

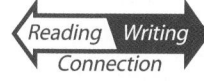
◄ Reading ► Writing
Connection

To get a feel for comparison-and-contrast writing, read "The News" by Neil Postman on page 426.

Teaching Resources

The following resources can be used to enrich or extend the instruction for the Writing Workshop.

Unit 6 Resources
Writing Workshop: Exposition: Comparison-and-Contrast Essay, p. 156
Writing Workshop: Integrating Grammar Skills: Revising to Vary Sentence Structure and Length, p. 157

General Resources
Rubrics for Exposition: Comparison-and-Contrast Essay, pp. 75–76

Graphic Organizer Transparencies
Venn Diagram, p. 244; Outline, p. 237

From the Author's Desk DVD
Dean Smith and John Kilgo, Segments 3 and 4

Prewriting

Choosing Your Topic

In your essay, compare things that are both closely related and significantly different. Use these strategies for choosing a topic.

- **Finding Related Pairs** Explore topics in terms of clear opposites, clear similarities, or close relationships. Start with names of people, places, objects, or ideas. Note related subjects that come to mind. Notice relationships that interest you, and choose one to develop.

- **Exploring Categories** Working with a group, make a list of categories, such as famous athletes, famous artists, vacation spots, or favorite foods. Then, choose one category, and discuss it in greater depth. Identify specific topics within the category that present clear similarities and differences.

Narrowing Your Topic

Specify your purpose. To identify a purpose for your essay, consider the following possibilities:

- **To persuade**—You want readers to accept your opinion that one subject is preferable to another.

- **To explain**—You want readers to understand something special about the subjects.

- **To describe**—You want readers to understand the basic similarities and differences between your subjects.

Gathering Details

Use a Venn diagram. Gather and organize details for your essay using a Venn diagram. Record similarities in the space where the circles overlap, and note differences in the outer sections of the circles.

Reading Literature
- requires concentration
- requires light
- silent
- private

(overlap)
- entertaining
- portable, can be enjoyed anywhere

Listening to Music
- allows listener to do other things
- requires equipment and electricity
- audible (but headphones?)
- public

Writing Workshop ■ *1135*

Work in Progress

Review the work you did on pages 1111 and 1093.

Brainstorming for Topic Pairs

Hockey vs. soccer
Middle school vs. high school
Love for my town vs. boredom with it
Music vs. literature
Video vs. DVD

Prewriting

- Help students **choose their topics** by writing the following general subject categories on the board: *sports, movies, music.* Invite students to suggest two other general topic areas, and add those to the list.

- Help students **narrow their topics** by giving the following examples of how to specify purpose when comparing and contrasting two American wars: *Will they want to* **persuade** *the reader that the Vietnam War was as divisive in the U.S. as the Civil War? Will they want to* **explain** *the similarities and differences of the letters written home by soldiers in the Union Army and soldiers in the Confederate Army? Will they want to* **describe** *the similarities and differences of the parades given for soldiers returning from WWII and soldiers returning from Vietnam?*

- When students are **gathering details** for their Venn Diagrams, encourage them to use their own knowledge as well as research. *Refer students to the* **Venn Diagram** *in* **Graphic Organizer Transparencies,** *p. 244.*

Six Traits Focus

✔	Ideas	Word Choice
✔	Organization	Sentence Fluency
	Voice	Conventions

Writing and Grammar, Gold Level

Students will find additional instruction on prewriting for a comparison-and-contrast essay in Chapter 9, Section 2.

Writing and Grammar Interactive Textbook CD-ROM

Students can use the following tools as they complete their comparison-and-contrast essays:

- Topic Bin
- Venn Diagram Organizer
- Sentence Length Revising Tool

Tips for Using Rubrics

- Before students begin work on this assignment, have them preview the Rubric for Self-Assessment on p. 1141 to know what is expected.

- Review the Assessment criteria in class. Before students use the Rubric for Self-Assessment, work with them to rate the student model by applying one or two criteria to it.

- If you wish to assess students' comparison-and-contrast essays with either a 4-point or 6-point scoring rubric, see *General Resources,* pp. 75–76.

Drafting

- Note that students might use point-by-point organization if their information is technical or very detailed. This structure will help the reader remember and keep track of numbers, complicated ideas, or numerous names.

- Tell students that they might use subject-by-subject organization if the information can be easily remembered and understood.

- Have students make an outline with their points as the topics and their details as the subtopics. Have students make sure that every topic has at least one subtopic.

  *Refer students to the **Outline** in **Graphic Organizer Transparencies**, p. 237.*

- As students write their essays, remind them that they can support their generalizations with quotations from people who know about the subject.

Six Traits Focus

Ideas	✔ Word Choice
✔ Organization	Sentence Fluency
✔ Voice	Conventions

Writing and Grammar, Gold Level

Students will find additional instruction on drafting a comparison-and-contrast essay in Chapter 9, Section 3.

Drafting

Shaping Your Writing

Choose an organization. Select an organization that suits your topic. Point-by-point and subject-by-subject plans are the most common types of organization used in comparison-and-contrast writing.

- **Point-by-Point Organization** Move between your subjects as you discuss points of comparison. First, compare one element of both subjects, and then address another element of both subjects. Continue this process until you have covered all the features. This method allows you to sharpen your points of similarity and difference.

- **Subject-by-Subject Organization** Compare your subjects as complete units. First, discuss all the features of one subject; then, discuss all the features of the other. While this format allows you to focus on one subject at a time, take care that you address the same features and devote equal time to each subject.

Point-by-Point Plan

Point 1
- Subject A
- Subject B

Point 2
- Subject A
- Subject B

Subject-by-Subject Plan

Subject A
- Point 1
- Point 2

Subject B
- Point 1
- Point 2

Reading ◄ Writing Connection

To read the complete student model, see page 1140.

Providing Elaboration

Support generalizations with specifics. Whether your purpose in comparing and contrasting two subjects is to describe, to persuade, or to explain, provide enough detail to fully develop your points. Support your statements about similarities and differences with facts, examples, and other forms of evidence.

> **Student Model: Providing Specific Details**
>
> I am fond of the size of Bernice and I detest it, too. I'm glad that only fifteen cars is a major traffic jam. But I hate that I have to drive sixteen miles to the nearest major store. I love and hate that my town is so small that I know everybody's first, middle, and last names. I like it because I have a "tab" at the grocery store . . . .

Lauren gives specific, balanced support for each "love" and "hate" statement.

Differentiated Instruction   Solutions for All Learners

Strategy for Less Proficient Readers

After students have chosen an organization for their topics, have them make outlines to map their essay layout. Have students mirror the outline offered in the Point-by-Point Plan Graphic or the Subject-by-Subject Plan Graphic. As students draft, have them check off the details as they include them in their essays. *Refer students to the **Outline** in **Graphic Organizer Transparencies**, p. 237.*

Strategy for Advanced Readers

Have students examine the strength of their supporting details by asking themselves the following questions: *How can I make my details more specific? Have I supported my points with enough details? Have I used varied forms of evidence? Do my details reinforce my purpose?* Answering the questions will help students shape their writing.

Coach Dean Smith and John Kilgo

On Word Choice

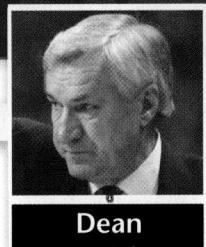

Dean Smith

"Good writing is hard work."
—Coach Dean Smith and John Kilgo

John Kilgo, my co-author, took notes of our conversations related to this book and put my ideas into written form. I have strong feelings about what I want my words to convey, which means we did extensive rewriting and revising. When we finally signed off on a chapter, it was always shorter, sharper in focus, and less repetitive than the original.

Professional Model:

from The Carolina Way

A steady focus on taking care of the little things, attending diligently to the many details involved with building a team, helped us produce a mind-set that enhanced our ability to handle the big things. . . . Here are some of the so-called little things that we integrated into our program:

Punctuality: Players knew I arrived early for meetings and practices, and I expected everyone to be there and ready to go. . . . Tardiness is the ~~definition~~ ʌheight of arrogance. In effect, you're saying, "My time is more important than yours." Being on time is being considerate of others. . . .

Swearing: We discouraged it in our program. When a player cursed in practice, the entire team ran for him. . . . This is not an easy subject to talk about because it can sound ~~sanctimonious~~ ʌpious. . . . However, I believe that anger can be expressed without using profanity.

Top priority: We checked on the class attendance of our players, as well as their grades and academic progress.

We used the phrase "produce a mind-set," because it's important for readers to know that our program had a strong philosophy concerning team-building techniques that we instilled in our players beginning with the first day they stepped on campus.

We first wrote that tardiness is the "definition" of arrogance, but changed it to "height of arrogance" on the rewrite. Using "height of arrogance" seemed to more strongly emphasize how unacceptable tardiness was in our program.

We first used "sanctimonious" in describing the difficulty in even discussing the subject of swearing, but changed it to "pious," which sounds less "preachy," or at least we thought so at the time. Also, words have a rhythm, and "pious" just seemed to fit better here.

From the Author's Desk ■ 1137

- Show students Segment 3 on Dean Smith and John Kilgo on *From the Author's Desk DVD*. Discuss their emphasis on the importance of revision.

- Ask students to define the word *mind-set* and to explain what this word conveys to the reader. **Possible response:** If your mind is set, you carry the attitude with you at all times. It becomes a part of you. This word conveys that the coach took his program very seriously.

- Explain to students that using precise words to convey meaning is critical to the reader's understanding. The word "sanctimonious" is an excellent word; it's just not the right word for the sentence.

- Have students go through their essays and highlight any words that do not fit into the context of their writing. Have students use a thesaurus to find more suitable wording.

Revising

- Supply each student with two different-colored pencils or highlighters, and have them follow the instructions in the text.

- Ask students for examples of transitional words or phrases. **Possible responses:** *conversely, similarly, on the contrary, instead, in contrast*

- When students review each other's essays, have them look for vague, weak verbs. Write on the board the following example:

  She went *into the room.*

  She stormed *into the room.*

  She floated *into the room.*

  She stomped *into the room.*

  Ask students to determine which is the vague verb and which are the vivid, precise verbs. Ask them what image the stronger verbs communicate.

  Answer: *Went* is a vague verb. *Stormed, floated,* and *stomped* are vivid, precise verbs. *Stormed and stomped* suggest anger, and *floated* suggests happiness or dreaminess.

- Have student pairs work together to identify stronger words and constructions to replace the circled items in each other's essays.

  For more on revising, see Coach Dean Smith and John Kilgo's comments on p. 1137.

Six Traits Focus

✔	Ideas	✔	Word Choice
✔	Organization	✔	Sentence Fluency
✔	Voice		Conventions

Writing and Grammar, Gold Level

Students will find additional instruction on revising a comparison-and-contrast essay in Chapter 9, Section 4.

Writing Workshop

Revising

Revising Your Paragraphs

Revise to make comparisons and contrasts clear. Using two different colors, mark your draft to distinguish between the two subjects you discuss. Whether you have used point-by-point or subject-by-subject organization, this color coding will clearly reveal whether or not you have made a balanced presentation of both subjects. If necessary, expand or reduce coverage of one of your subjects to achieve balance. Next, evaluate the places where the two colors—and subjects—meet. Add transitional words to make the shifts clear.

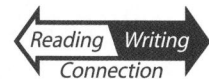

To read the complete student model, see page 1140.

> **Student Model: Revising for Clarity**
>
> I love and hate the security in my town for a number of reasons. I love it because I know that it is my dogs scratching at my door at 5:30 in the morning and not some dangerous stranger. In my town, a fifteen-car traffic jam is front-page news. On the other hand, I hate that it gets a little boring sometimes. I don't want criminals at my door, but a little excitement would be nice.

A topic sentence helps call out the point of comparison. The transition *on the other hand* shows readers the shift between subjects.

Revising Your Word Choice

Revise to add specifics. To help your readers understand the comparisons you make, add enough detail to explain the differences and similarities you see. Look for places where you can add information that strengthens your description or analysis.

Peer Review: Exchange drafts with a partner. As you read each other's essay, circle any vague language that you find. Consider choices that convey your meaning more precisely. Then, discuss with your reader specific details that would make your comparisions more vivid. Consider adding these details.

Vague: In contrast to literature, popular music forms a soundtrack for our lives.

Specific: In contrast to literature that we must read to enjoy, popular music, like the Top 40 tunes we hear on the radio, forms a soundtrack for our lives. We can enjoy it as we drive, shop, or even fall asleep at night.

1138 ■ *Themes in Literature: Heroism*

Tips for Using Technology in Writing

If students are using word-processing software to draft and revise their comparison-and-contrast essays, suggest that they use the *Find* feature of the software to locate conjunctions such as *and, but,* and *yet.* When they find a conjunction, have them examine the sentence to determine whether it is a compound sentence. If it is, have students be sure that they have a comma before the conjunction.

Students can also use features of the Writing and Grammar Interactive Textbook CD-ROM to draft or revise their essays.

Integrating Grammar Skills

Revising: Vary Sentence Structure and Length

A sequence of sentences of the same length and the same structural pattern can have a tedious effect on readers. By varying sentence length, introducing new sentence beginnings, and inverting subject-verb order, you can make your paragraphs more interesting and readable.

Vary sentence length. Once you have identified an unbroken series of long sentences, look for an opportunity to include a short sentence. Since the short sentence will draw the reader's attention, use it to emphasize an important detail or idea. Be sure that the short sentence is a complete thought and not a fragment.

> **Original:** Memories of long hours of practice, the brutal weather, the aches and bruises of an endless season were erased by the single shining fact that we had won the championship.
>
> **Revised:** Memories of long hours of practice, the brutal weather, the aches and bruises of an endless season were erased by a single shining fact. We had won the championship.

Vary sentence beginnings. If you have written a series of sentences beginning with a noun or pronoun, look for opportunities to start sentences with different parts of speech.

> **Adverb clause:** *Anywhere you go,* you will still find most people care about others.
>
> **Prepositional phrase:** *After a long Saturday of work,* Sarah did not feel like going out.
>
> **Complement:** *Most interesting to me* was an electronic display of the battlefield. (complement of the subject *an electronic display*)
>
> **Direct object:** *Our report* I gave to the editor; my opinion I kept to myself. (objects of the verb *gave*)

Vary subject-verb order. You can vary sentence beginnings by reversing the usual subject-verb order.

> **Original:** The mystery guest is here at last.
> **Inverted:** Here at last is the mystery guest.

Apply It to Your Editing

As you review the three longest paragraphs in your draft, place brackets around each sentence. Examine the length and pattern of each sentence to look for ways to improve the variety of your sentences. Change sentence lengths, alter sentence beginnings, and invert subject-verb order.

> *Prentice Hall Writing and Grammar Connection: Chapter 22, Section 3*

Integrating Grammar Skills

- Have students read aloud their essays to listen for sentence patterns.
- Write this example on the board to show students how to revise a series of long sentences:

  Original: When Elvis performed live, the fans screamed during the entire performance, urged him to sing their favorite songs, and begged for sweat-soaked scarves and kisses. When you speak to these same fans today, they talk about him in a reverent light, and they reminisce about what a force he was, proving that, in some ways, Elvis will always be alive.

  Revision: When Elvis performed live, the fans screamed during the entire performance, urged him to sing their favorite songs, and begged him for sweat-soaked scarves and kisses. When you speak to these same fans today, they talk about him in a reverent light, and they reminisce about what a force he was. In some ways, Elvis will always be alive.

- Write the following sentence on the board, and have students use alternate beginnings for it. Suggest that they use adverb clauses, participles, and prepositional phases.

  Elvis Presley was the King of Music.

  Possible response: *Adverb Clause: When my grandmother was a teenager, Elvis Presley was the King of Music. Participle: Looking back, I understand why Elvis Presley was called the King of Music. Prepositional Phrase: After all this time, Elvis Presley remains the King of Music.*

- Write on the board the following sample of varying subject-verb order:

  Original: The King of Music is here. Revised: Here is the King of Music.

- After students have revised their three paragraphs, have them exchange papers, look over the three paragraphs, and give each other suggestions for sentence improvement.

WG Writing and Grammar, Gold Level

Students will find additional instruction on revising sentence structure in Chapter 22, Section 3.

Student Model

- Explain that the Student Model is a sample, and comparison-and-contrast essays may be longer.

- Direct students' attention to the first sentence in the Student Model. **Ask** students how this thesis statement sets the tone of the essay.
  Possible response: The thesis statement sets up a playful tone by casually placing the words *love* and *hate* together and by comparing the town with Mayberry, a fictional town in a television comedy.

- **Ask** students to identify the second point that Lauren addresses.
  Answer: Her second point is the size of the town.

- **Ask** students to identify details that develop the paragraph on size. Which details reflect her love? Which details reflect her hate?
  Possible response: Love: fifteen cars is a traffic jam; has tab at the grocery and drug stores; knows everyone's first, middle, and last names; has made trustworthy friends. Hate: has to drive sixteen miles to the nearest major store; knows everyone's first, middle, and last names; everybody knows her dating history, height, weight, and age; paper reports visits to nursing homes.

- **Ask** students how Lauren's humor helps her reflect on her ideas.
  Possible response: Lauren's humor allows her to make light of her annoyances, showing that her pet peeves are trivial in comparison to what she loves about the town.

Writing Genres

Comparison-and-Contrast Essays in Careers Explain to students that the type of reasoning that goes into writing a comparison-and-contrast essay will be useful as they make decisions throughout their lives. In addition, comparison-and-contrast essays are often written by professionals such as scientists, researchers, and doctors. They answer questions such as the following: How is the newly discovered dinosaur alike or unlike those already unearthed? How is this new medical treatment different than previous forms of treatment? What are the similarities and differences among several recycling programs?

Student Model: Lauren De Loach
Bernice LA

Ambivalence

When I consider my conflicting feelings about my hometown, I see that there are things that I love and hate about living in Bernice, Louisiana, a nineties version of Mayberry. I love the security of a small town, and I hate it. I love the way that my town is not clouded by the smog of a city, and I hate it too. I love it and I hate that I love it.

I love and hate the security in my town for a number of reasons. I love it because I know that it is my dogs scratching at my door at 5:30 in the morning and not some dangerous stranger. In my town, a fifteen-car traffic jam is front-page news. On the other hand, I hate that it gets a little boring sometimes. I don't want criminals at my door, but a little excitement would be nice.

I am fond of the size of Bernice and I detest it, too. I'm glad that only fifteen cars is a major traffic jam. But I hate that I have to drive sixteen miles to the nearest major store. I love and hate that my town is so small that I know everybody's first, middle, and last names. I like it because I have a "tab" at the grocery store and the drug store, so that eliminates the necessity of money. I hate that everybody knows me because that means that everybody finds out about whom I'm dating, whom I once dated, my height, weight, and age. I also hate that we all know each other so well that the most entertaining news we can come up with to put in the *Bernice Banner* is that Peggy Jane and her brother JC visited their Aunt Goosey Lou in the nursing home. But by knowing everyone so well, I've made friends who are trustworthy because we know all of one another's deepest secrets.

Even though I say that I detest some things, home wouldn't be home without these silly quirks. I love that my parents and their friends are known as the "elite group" because they have traveled beyond Texas, Arkansas, and Mississippi. I love saying that I have read the *Iliad* to people who think I would not read such a book. I know that it sounds like I love the provincialism that small towns can impose, but the smells of fresh-cut grass and the gardenia bush outside my door are what make my home my home.

This is what I love and what I hate, but I don't really. The overall feeling I get from living in Bernice is ambivalence. I love it and I hate that I love such goofy things. But the parts of home that seem so trivial are the ones that make you who you are. That makes a place your home.

> Lauren's essay will compare two feelings: what she loves and what she hates about her hometown.

> Using a point-by-point organization, Lauren addresses the first contrast in her attitudes about her town: She feels ambivalence about its security.

> These facts support the writer's ideas and opinions.

> Lauren's comparison allows her to be funny, but it also helps her reflect on her ideas.

Editing and Proofreading

Check your draft to correct errors in spelling, grammar, and punctuation.

Focus on Compound Sentences: Comparison-and-contrast essays often contain compound sentences—those with two independent clauses joined by a semicolon or a coordinating conjunction, such as *or, and,* or *but.* Check that you have correctly punctuated these sentences.

> **Conjunction:** I liked the chili, but it was spicy.
>
> **Semicolon:** I rushed out; I was late for the bus.

Publishing and Presenting

Consider one of the following ways to share your writing:

Deliver an oral presentation. Read your comparison-and-contrast essay aloud to an audience of your classmates. If possible, include props or visuals to enhance the reading.

Make a poster. Present your comparison-and-contrast findings visually in a poster. Using a graphic organizer such as a Venn diagram, show the differences and similarities of your subjects. If possible, add photographs and illustrations to show the distinctive elements of your subjects.

Reflecting on Your Writing

Writer's Journal Jot down your thoughts on writing a comparison-and-contrast essay. Begin by answering these questions.

- Did your ideas change as you compared your subjects?
- Which strategy for prewriting, drafting, revising, or editing helped you the most with this assignment?

> *Prentice Hall Writing and Grammar Connection: Chapter 9*

Rubric for Self-Assessment

To assess your comparison-and-contrast essay, use the following rubric:

Criteria	Rating Scale
	not very *very*
Focus: How clear is your purpose for comparing and contrasting?	1 2 3 4 5
Organization: How balanced is your organization?	1 2 3 4 5
Support/Elaboration: How accurate and factual are the details you use to support your ideas?	1 2 3 4 5
Style: How effectively do you use transitions to clarify ideas?	1 2 3 4 5
Conventions: How correct is your grammar, especially related to your use of varied sentence structure and length?	1 2 3 4 5

Writing Workshop ■ 1141

Tips for Test Taking

Remind students of the distinction between *compare* (show the similarities) and *contrast* (show the differences). Point out that keeping these meanings in mind when a standardized test question focuses on comparison and contrast will help them select or organize their answers.

Editing and Proofreading

- Have students go through their essays and underline every compound sentence. Tell students to make sure that each sentence has two independent clauses and is punctuated by a comma and a coordinating conjunction or by a semicolon.
- Tell students to make sure that sentences with semicolons contain two independent clauses with related ideas.

Six Traits Focus

Ideas		Word Choice	
Organization		Sentence Fluency	
Voice		Conventions	✔

ASSESS

Publishing and Presenting

- If students are preparing to deliver oral presentations, have them practice in pairs. Partners should offer each other suggestions about delivery and should ask questions about each other's topics, as an audience might.
- Have students review class posters and then discuss what was helpful about the posters. Ask students what techniques they found the most creative and informational.

Reflecting on Your Writing

- Ask students whether the Venn diagram was helpful in gathering details.
- Suggest that students respond to the following questions in their journals: Do you believe that you achieved your purpose? Explain your answer. Were you satisfied with how you organized your essay?

WG Writing and Grammar, Gold Level

Students will find additional guidelines for editing and proofreading, publishing and presenting, and reflecting on a comparison-and-contrast essay in Chapter 9, Sections 5 and 6.

Meeting Your Standards

Students will

1. compare media coverage for clarity, tone, credibility, images, quotations, and balance.

2. present their findings in either whole-to-whole or part-to-part organizational patterns.

Comparing Coverage

- Explain that some news reporters aim for more sensationalism rather than clear coverage. If the headline tells much more than the story in either report, students should note that.

- Tell students to look at the images carefully. They should ask themselves these questions: Are the images representative of the situation? Do they show the individuals or the situation unfairly?

- Warn students that news reports may have a hidden agenda to have viewers see the report in a particular way. Watching for balance can help viewers determine the fairness of the report.

Presenting Your Findings

- Students may wish to do whole-to-whole comparisons on shorter news reports. Point out that this style also works well with reports that are similar.

- Explain to students that if they are comparing lengthy reports or reports with multiple differences, they may find part-to-part comparisons more useful.

Assess the Activity

To evaluate students' presentations, use the Listening: Evaluating a Media Presentation, p. 82 in **General Resources.**

Comparing Media Coverage

Modern news media have developed a broad array of techniques and technologies for conveying their messages. Use the following comparison strategies to assess the accuracy and objectivity of media coverage, and evaluate media impact on your life.

Comparing Coverage

With a team of classmates, record news reports from two different news programs. Try to select items that are reported on the same event or issue, that aired on the same day, and that are about the same length. As you view each news report several times, make inferences and ask questions. Consider the following:

- **Clarity** Does the on-air reporter clearly present the *who, what, how, when,* and *why* elements of the story? Is the "headline"—the main point—prominent in the newscast?
- **Tone** What is the reporter's tone? Does the reporter use language that is factual or emotional, objective or involved?
- **Credibility** What facts are used to build the story? Are informational sources reliable and objective? Are potential biases acknowledged?
- **Images** Are photographs and video clips used? Are these images relevant to the content of the story?
- **Quotations** Who is interviewed or quoted? What is the role of each speaker? Does the speaker have an inherent bias? Do the interviews contribute facts, insights, emotions, entertainment, or propaganda to the story?
- **Balance** Does the story include multiple perspectives or viewpoints about the event or issue? Does the story tilt toward a particular argument or viewpoint?

Presenting Your Findings

Consider one of the following patterns of organization.

- **Whole-to-whole** Present a complete analysis of one of the broadcasts; then, do the same for the other. Be sure to cover the same factors in each analysis. Summarize your conclusions about both newscasts.
- **Part-to-part** Organize your discussion according to specific categories. For example, discuss both stories in terms of credibility, use of images, tone, and so on.

> *Activity* › *Analysis and Presentation* ► Using the above guidelines, analyze two different news broadcasts of the same story. Present your findings to the class. If possible, illustrate your findings with clips from the broadcasts.

1142 ■ Themes in Literature

Differentiated Instruction   Solutions for All Learners

Strategy for English Learners
Students may have difficulty with the vocabulary in media broadcasts. As they listen to the media reports, have students write down any unfamiliar words in the broadcast. After they identify difficult words, have them look them up in a dictionary. Suggest that students also carefully observe the images shown and the body language and tone of voice of the reporters and those interviewed to help them in their comparisons.

Strategy for Advanced Learners
Suggest that students gather information from a news incident and create a video that presents the material from two different perspectives. Have students analyze how each perspective requires them to report. When they finish, have them share their work with the class and write a reflection of how each perspective affected their reporting.

The War of the Worlds

H.G. Wells
Globe Fearon, 1993

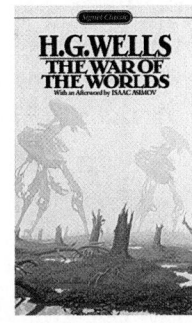

Novel In this realistically told science fiction tale, invaders from outer space attack the Earth. A radio adaptation of the story once convinced listeners that the invasion was real—they fled their homes.

The Left Hand of Darkness

Ursula Le Guin
Ace Books, 1969

Novel This is the journal of a Terran, sent as an envoy from the Council of Ekumen to form an alliance with the planet Getham. Getham is a unique planet—it is ruled by a king who distrusts technology, yet harbors a group of people whose psychological understanding is unparalleled in the universe.

Strange Case of Dr. Jekyll and Mr. Hyde

Robert Louis Stevenson
Prentice Hall, 2000

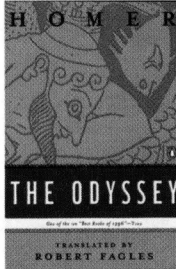

Novel This is the story of a mild-mannered doctor who explores his dark side—with terrifying results. Fascinated with the idea of evil, the story's main character, Dr. Jekyll, develops a potion that changes him into the violent Mr. Hyde. Before long, however, Jekyll finds himself transforming into Hyde without the aid of the potion, leaving him, along with terrified readers, to wonder which personality will finally win out.

The Odyssey

Homer translated by Robert Fagles
Penguin Books, 1996

Epic This is the story of Odysseus, a Greek hero of the Trojan War who offended Poseidon. The *Odyssey* chronicles Odysseus' ten year adventurous journey home as he and his crew wandered through uncharted oceans filled with mythical and human enemies. At home the situation is dismal. Presuming that Odysseus is dead, suitors for his wife's hand are draining the country's resources and plotting to kill his son. This epic has survived for 3000 years because it explores the passion and problems of powerful people.

These titles are available in the Penguin/Prentice Hall Literature Library.

The Lexile number is just one of several criteria used to determine the reading levels of books; therefore, in some cases, one book may be ranked higher than another even though it has a lower Lexile number.

Planning Students' Further Reading

Discussions of literature can raise sensitive and often controversial issues. Before you recommend further reading to your students, consider the values and sensitivities of your community as well as the age, ability, and sophistication of your students. It is also good policy to preview literature before you recommend it to students. The notes below offer some guidance on specific titles.

[L4] *The War of the Worlds*
Pacemaker: Some readers may be offended by Wells's unflattering portrait of a clergyman. The portrayal of superior beings from another planet may also offend some students' religious beliefs.

This novel contains some graphic descriptions of violence and warfare; weaponry suggestive of germ and chemical warfare; thoughts of suicide; and an unsympathetic depiction of a clergyman.

Lexile: 1170

[L3] *The Left Hand of Darkness*
The alien beings in this story change gender—each one is sometimes male, sometimes female.

Lexile: 970

[L2] *The Strange Case of Dr. Jekyll and Mr. Hyde*
The novel contains murder and suicide. It depicts use of a drug with unrealistic and powerful, though negative, effects and shows scientific or medical experimentation in a negative light. It also associates moral corruption with physical traits (although the novel's frequent use of the term *deformity* refers to inner corruption, not something physical). Women play a very minor role in the tale.

Lexile: 1040

[L1, L2, EL] *The Odyssey*
There are numerous scenes of explicit violence in *The Odyssey* of Homer, but the climatic sequence of Odysseus' blood vengeance on the suitors is especially explicit and gory. You might wish to emphasize to students the historical specificity of such a solution and elicit the idea that such personal forms of wreaking justice no longer conform to civilized standards of conduct.

Lexile: 1050

Using *On Your Own*

You may use this On Your Own feature in one of the following ways:

• For independent reading
• To reinforce/reteach one of the reading skills in this unit

Promote Independent Reading

Independent reading gives students an opportunity to practice the reading skills taught in this unit and to improve comprehension. When students read independently, they also increase their vocabulary and develop their own personal reading interests.

You may assign this selection to be read independently for homework, in class when students have completed other work, or for independent group work.

Develop Reading Preferences

After students have read this selection, ask them what they enjoyed about it. Build on their ideas to recommend further reading. Students who enjoy this selection might also enjoy other poems or stories about people affected by the September 11th attacks.

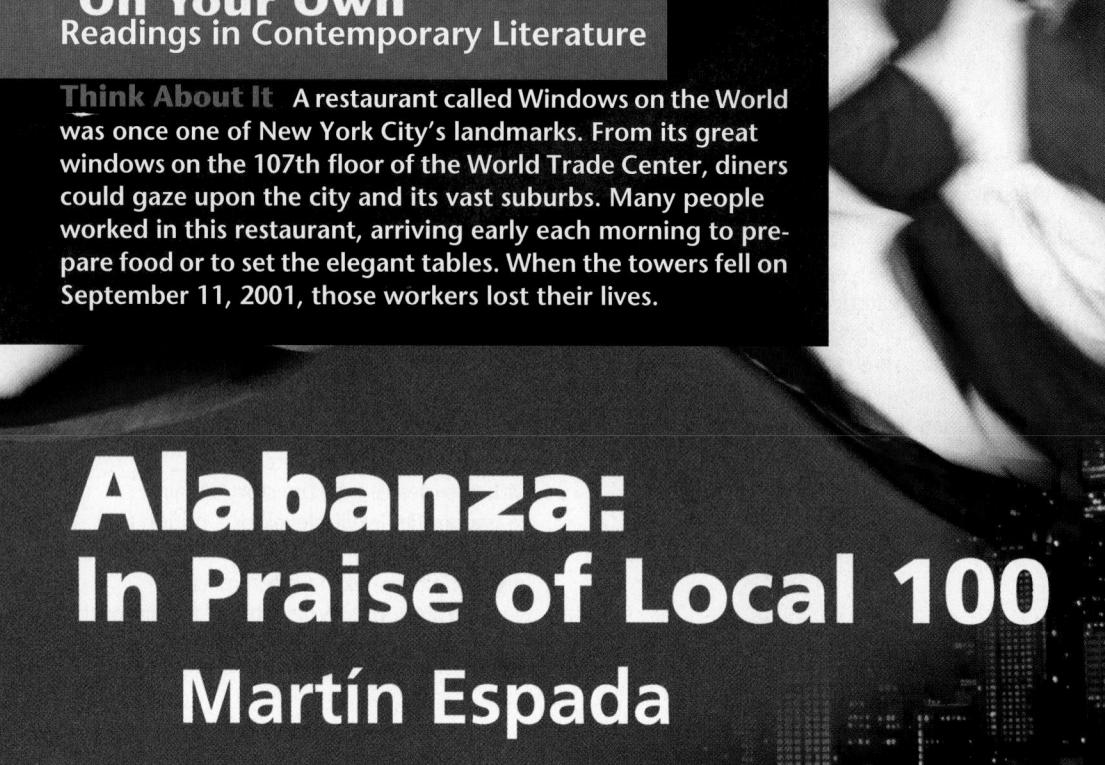

On Your Own
Readings in Contemporary Literature

Think About It A restaurant called Windows on the World was once one of New York City's landmarks. From its great windows on the 107th floor of the World Trade Center, diners could gaze upon the city and its vast suburbs. Many people worked in this restaurant, arriving early each morning to prepare food or to set the elegant tables. When the towers fell on September 11, 2001, those workers lost their lives.

Alabanza: In Praise of Local 100
Martín Espada

for the 43 members of Hotel Employees and Restaurant Employees Local 100, working at the Windows on the World restaurant who lost their lives in the attack on the World Trade Center

Alabanza[1] Praise the cook with the shaven head
and a tattoo on his shoulder that said *Oye,*
a blue-eyed Puerto Rican with people from Fajardo,
the harbor of pirates centuries ago.
5   Praise the lighthouse in Fajardo, candle
glimmering white to worship the dark saint of the sea.
Alabanza. Praise the cook's yellow Pirates cap
worn in the name of Roberto Clemente, his plane
that flamed into the ocean loaded with cans for Nicaragua,
10   for all the mouths chewing the ash of earthquakes.
Alabanza. Praise the kitchen radio, dial clicked
even before the dial on the oven, so that music and Spanish
rose before bread. Praise the bread. *Alabanza.*

---

1. Alabanza (äl'ə ban' za) Spanish for "praise."

1144 ■ *Themes in Literature: Heroism*

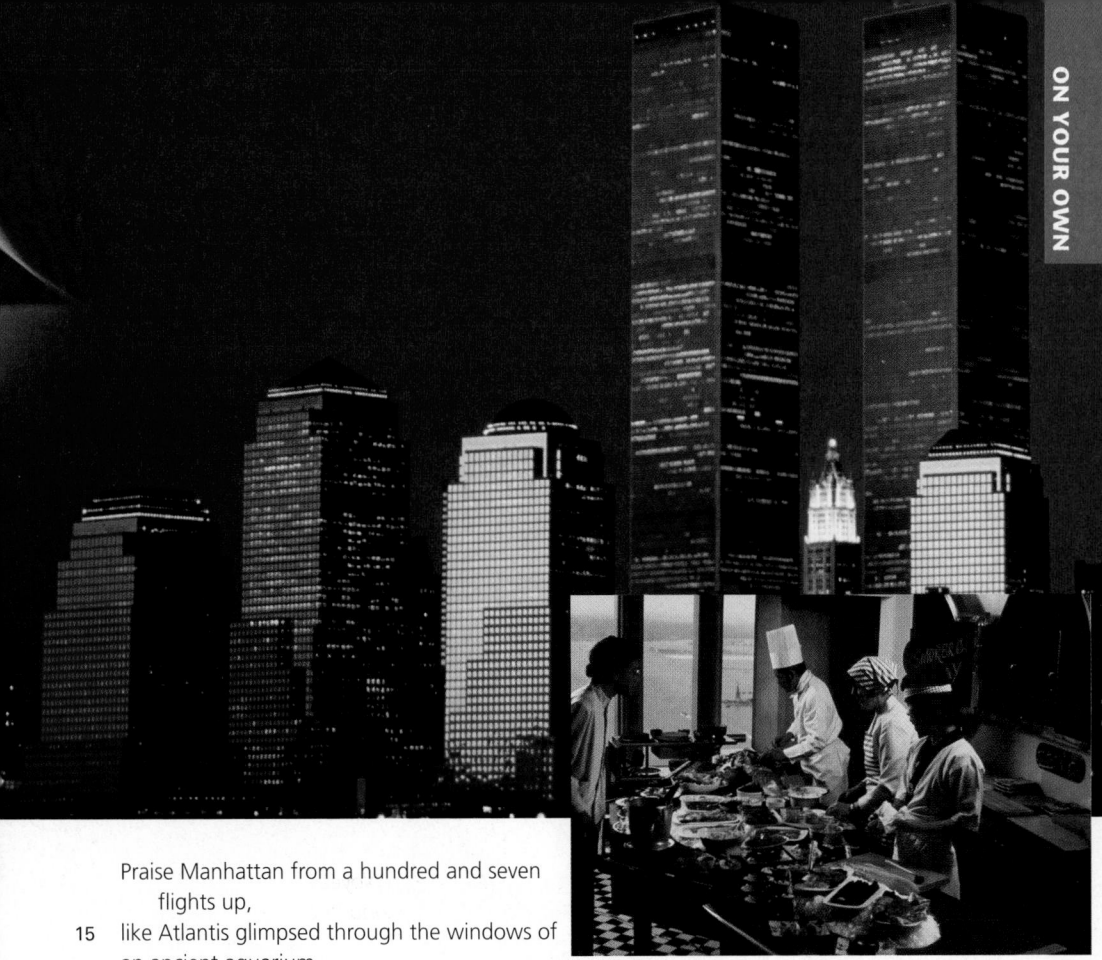

Praise Manhattan from a hundred and seven
   flights up,
15   like Atlantis glimpsed through the windows of
an ancient aquarium.
Praise the great windows where immigrants from the kitchen
could squint and almost see their world, hear the chant of nations:
Ecuador, México, Republica Dominicana,
20   *Haiti, Yemen, Ghana, Bangladesh.*
Alabanza. Praise the kitchen in the morning,
where the gas burned blue on every stove
and exhaust fans fired their diminutive propellers,
hands cracked eggs with quick thumbs
25   or sliced open cartons to build an altar of cans.
Alabanza. Praise the busboy's music, the chime-chime
of his dishes and silverware in the tub.
Alabanza. Praise the dish-dog, the dishwasher
who worked that morning because another dishwasher
30   could not stop coughing, or because he needed overtime
to pile the sacks of rice and beans for a family

Alabanza: In Praise of Local 100 ■ 1145

Differentiated
Instruction   Solutions for All Learners

Strategy for Special Needs Students
Students might struggle with getting meaning from poetry, because they have difficulties forming abstract images. Help them turn the abstract image of the cook into a concrete image by having them draw the cook. Guide them to study the first stanza to find needed details such as his shaved head, tattoo, blue eyes, dark hair, and Roberto Clemente hat.

Strategy for Less Proficient Readers
Remind students that, in some ways, poems are organized like other texts. Tell them, for example, that poems are divided into sections called stanzas and that stanzas are sort of like paragraphs. Point out that, like a paragraph, each stanza in "Alabanza" is about one idea. Guide them to understand that the first stanza is about the people: the workers; the second stanza is about the location: the kitchen; and the third stanza is about the event: the September 11th attacks.

Motivation
Have students look at the photographs in this selection. Ask them to predict the topic of this poem. Encourage them to read to understand the connection among the photographs.

Point out that every generation lives through significant historical events, which individuals remember and relate to throughout the rest of their lives. Ask students to talk about their memories of the September 11th attacks. Encourage them to share what they were doing when they first heard news of these events and how it made them feel.

Reading Skill
Comparing and Contrasting
- Have students read "Alabanza."
- **Ask** students to identify the people who are described in "Alabanza." **Possible response:** The poem describes the kitchen workers at the Windows on the World restaurant who died in the September 11th attacks.
- **Ask** students to identify a key way that the workers in "Alabanza" are similar. **Possible response:** The workers are all immigrants to America and many have family back in their home countries.
- **Ask** students to describe ways that the workers are different from each other. **Possible response:** The workers come from many different countries, and they have different jobs in the restaurant.
- Direct students' attention to the beginning of the second stanza. **Ask** a volunteer to interpret the reference to "Atlantis." **Possible response:** Espada is comparing pre-attack Manhattan to the legendary submerged city of Atlantis. People looking out on the city of Atlantis from the aquarium might not have realized what was going on that caused the city to sink nor that the great city would be lost. Likewise, the kitchen staff looking out of the restaurant windows did not realize what was about to happen.

continued on p. 1146

- **Ask** students to carefully study the picture on this page and share things they learn from it and ideas they get from it.
  Possible response: The picture might make people think about how hard the firemen worked to save people following the World Trade Center attacks, and how the task was so overwhelmingly huge.

- Point out to students the repetition of "Alabanza." **Ask** students to describe when the poet uses "Alabanza."
  Possible response: In the first two stanzas, Espada casually uses "Alabanza" paired with each use of the English word "praise" as well as at the end of the first two stanzas. In each case, the use precedes or follows a description of someone or something that was lost in the Sept. 11th attacks. In the third stanza, he uses "Alabanza" without using the English word "praise" and he uses it in a more formal, prayerful way.

- Tell students that poets can carefully choose their words so that readers can "hear sounds in their minds." Have students read the poem again and make a list of the sounds they "hear." **Ask** volunteers to name sounds they could "hear" and tell how the author helped them to "hear" the sounds.
  Possible response: Readers can "hear" a radio clicking on and a song sung in Spanish, a group of people talking all at once in different languages, exhaust fans whirring, egg shells cracking, the slitting of cardboard cartons, dishes and silverware clanging, a person coughing non-stop, the loud croaking of lots of frogs, a woman quietly singing along with a radio song, and explosive thunder. The poet helps readers "hear" the sounds by using action words that conjure up specific sounds.

continued on p. 1147

1146   *Themes in Literature: Heroism*

floating away on some Caribbean island plagued by frogs.
Alabanza. Praise the waitress who heard the radio in the kitchen
and sang to herself about a man gone. *Alabanza.*

35 After the thunder wilder than thunder,
after the booming ice storm of glass from the great windows,
after the radio stopped singing like a tree full of terrified frogs,
after night burst the dam of day and flooded the kitchen,
for a time the stoves glowed in darkness like the lighthouse in Fajardo,
40 like a cook's soul. Soul I say, even if the dead cannot tell us
about the bristles of God's beard because God has no face,
soul I say, to name the smoke-beings flung in constellations
across the night sky of this city and cities to come.
Alabanza I say, even if God has no face.

45 *Alabanza.* When the war began, from Manhattan to Kabul
two constellations of smoke rose and drifted to each other,
mingling in icy air, and one said with an Afghan tongue:
Teach me to dance. We have no music here.
And the other said with a Spanish tongue:
50 *I will teach you. Music is all we have.*

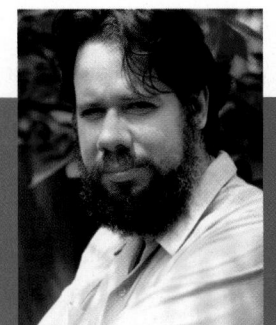

Meet the Author
Martín Espada (b. 1957) was born in Brooklyn, New York. His poems draw upon his Puerto Rican heritage as well as his early work experiences, which ranged from gas station attendant to lawyer. Espada is currently a professor of English at the University of Massachusetts in Amherst.

Readings in Contemporary Literature
Talk About It
Use these questions to guide a discussion of the poem.

1. (a) Why are the workers able to "hear the chant of nations"?
   (b) How does this "chant of nations" change in the last five lines?

2. In a group, discuss why the author may have chosen to write about this group of people rather than others who perished on that day.
   - Why do you think that the poet repeats the Spanish word for praise? What is he praising?
   - The poet imagines a meeting of the souls of those who died in the attacks and in the war that followed. What is he suggesting about the connections between these two groups?

Choose a point-person to share your group's ideas with the class.

Alabanza: In Praise of Local 100 ■ 1147

Reinforce/Reteach (cont.)

- **Ask** students to identify a comparison used in the descriptions in the last stanza.
  Possible response: The broken glass is compared to an ice storm.

- **Ask** what contrast is made between the Afghan and the Spanish speakers.
  Answer: The Afghan speaker says they have no music and cannot dance. The Spanish speaker says music is all they have.

- **Ask** a volunteer to explain what Espada means by the "two constellations of smoke that rose and drifted to each other."
  Possible response: He is using imagery of the two burning towers of the World Trade Centers to represent the human loss experienced both in Kabul and Manhattan.

- **Ask** a volunteer how readers can tell how the poet feels about the war against terrorism.
  Possible response: When the poet talks about the constellations meeting, readers can perceive that the poet recognizes that the ensuing war is ravaging two cultures. When he describes a Spanish voice offering to teach an Afghan speaker to dance, readers can infer that the poet believes that even in time of war, people of different cultures can reach out to each other.

Readings in Contemporary Literature
Talk About It

- Suggest that students work in groups to address these questions.

- To guide students' discussion, use the **Discussion Guide**, p. 39 in *General Resources*.

Extend the Lesson

Praise Poem
To give students further practice with poetry, have students think of a person or group who deserves praise. Ask students to write a poem in praise of this person or group of people. Allow time for students to share their poems.

RESOURCES

GLOSSARY

High-utility and Academic Vocabulary words appear in green.

A

abdicated (abʹ di kātʹ id) *v.* gave up formally

abomination (ə bämʹ ə nāʹ shən) *n.* anything hateful and disgusting

abstract (abʹ straktʹ) *adj.* not concrete; of thought

abstract (ab straktʹ) *n.; v.;* summary; summarize

absurdity (ab sʉrʹ də tē) *n.* something ridiculous or nonsensical

allotment (ə lätʹ mənt) *n.* share; portion

aloofness (ə lo͞ofʹ nəs) *n.* quality of being distant or removed

ambiguities (amʹ bə g yo͞oʹ ə tēz) *n.* statements or events whose meanings are unclear

ambiguous (am bigʹyo͞o əs) *adj.* having numerous possible meanings

amicably (amʹ i kə blē) *adv.* in a friendly way

anguish (aŋʹ gwish) *n.* great pain or suffering

anonymous (ə nänʹ ə məs) *adj.* without a known or acknowledged name

anticipate (an tisʹ ə pātʹ) *v.* expect

apex (āʹ peksʹ) *n.* highest point; peak

appraise (ə prāzʹ) *v.* judge the quality or worth of something; set a value on something

appreciate (ə prēʹ shē ātʹ) *v.* recognize; understand and be grateful for

archaic (är kāʹ ik) *adj.* from an earlier time; ancient

ardor (ärʹ dər) *n.* passion; enthusiasm

arduous (ärʹ jo͞o əs) *adj.* difficult; laborious

articulate (är tikʹ yo͞o lit) *adj.* expressing oneself clearly and easily

aspect (asʹ pektʹ) *n.* element or part

assiduous (ə sijʹ o͞o əs) *adj.* done with constant and careful attention; diligent

assuage (ə swājʹ) *v.* calm; pacify

atonement (ə tōnʹ mənt) *n.* act of making up for a wrongdoing or injury

attitude (atʹ ə to͞od) *n.* way of acting that shows a disposition or an opinion

augmenting (ôg mentʹ iŋ) *v.* increasing; enlarging

authentic (ô *th*enʹ tik) *adj.* genuine; true

awry (ə rīʹ) *adj.* not straight

azure (azhʹ ər) *adj.* sky blue

B

bafflement (bafʹ əl mənt) *n.* puzzlement; bewilderment

beguiling (bē gilʹ iŋ) *v.* tricking; charming

bemusing (bē myo͞ozʹ iŋ) *v.* stupefying or muddling

benevolently (bə nevʹ ə lənt lē) *adv.* in a well-meaning way

bereft (bē reftʹ) *adj.* deprived

bilingual (bī liŋʹ gwəl) *adj.* using two languages

blight (blīt) *n.* something that destroys or prevents growth

bravado (brə väʹ dō) *n.* pretended courage or defiant confidence

C

categorize (katʹ ə gə rīzʹ) *v.* classify, place within a group

censure (senʹ shər) *n.* strong disapproval

circumstance (sʉrʹ cəm stansʹ) *n.* fact or event

clasps (klasps) *v.* grips

cogent (kōʹ jənt) *adj.* convincing; powerfully appealing

coherent (kō herʹ ənt) *adj.* orderly or logical; sticking together

compelling (kəm pelʹ iŋ) *v.* forcing or pressuring

compensation (kämʹ pən sāʹ shən) *n.* anything that makes up for a loss, damage, or debt

compile (kəm pīlʹ) *v.* put together; compose by gathering materials

complex (käm pleksʹ) *adj.* complicated or intricate

comprehension (kämʹ prē henʹ shen) *n.* understanding

concept (känʹ septʹ) *n.* idea

condense (kən densʹ) *v.* shorten or make concise

condolences (kən dōʹ lən səz) *n.* expressions of sympathy with another in grief

confer (kən fʉrʹ) *v.* give

confirm (kən fʉrmʹ) *v.* prove the truth or authenticity

considerable (kən sidʹer ə bəl) *adj.* much or large; worth noting

contemplate (känʹ təm plātʹ) *v.* consider or think about

contemporary (kən temʹ pə rerʹ ē) *adj.* recent or current; living or happening at the same time

contempt (kən temptʹ) *n.* disdain or scorn

contribute (kən tribʹyo͞ot) *v.* give, add, provide

controversy (känʹ trə vūrʹsē) *n.* discussion over opposing viewpoints; dispute

convince (kən vinsʹ) *v.* overcome doubts; persuade

Glossary ■ *R-1*

GLOSSARY

countenance (kount´'n əns) n. face

covenant (kuv´ə nənt) n. agreement or contract, especially a sacred one

creed (krēd) n. statement of belief

cunning (kun´ iŋ) adj. skilled in deception

curtailed (kər tāld´) v. cut short; reduced

D

daunting (dônt´ iŋ) adj. intimidating

defect (dē´ fekt´) n. imperfection

deferred (dē furd´) adj. put off until a future time

defrauded (dē frôd´ id) v. cheated

degenerate (dē jen´ ər āt´) v. grow worse

deleterious (del´ ə tir´ ē əs) adj. harmful to health or well-being

deliberation (di lib´ər ā´shən) n. act of carefully thinking about an issue

demonstrative (di män´ strə tiv) adj. showing feelings openly

demure (di myo͞or´) adj. modest

depravity (dē prav´ ə tē) n. crookedness; corruption

depreciate (dē prē´ shē āt´) v. reduce in value

derisive (di rī´ siv) adj. mocking

derive (di rīv´) v. get from a source

despotic (des pät´ ik) adj. like an absolute ruler or tyrant

desultory (des´ əl tôr´ ē) adj. random

detect (dē tekt´) v. discover

determination (dē tur´ mi nā´ shən) n. firm intention

diffused (di fyo͞ozd´) v. spread out

dilapidated (də lap´ə dāt´ id) adj. broken down

diminution (dim´ ə no͞o´ shən) n. lessening

discerning (di surn´ iŋ) adj. having good judgment or understanding

disconsolately (dis kän´ sə lit lē) adv. very unhappily

discreet (di skrēt´) adj. careful about what one says or does

discreetly (di skrēt´ lē) adv. without drawing attention

disheveled (di shev´ əld) adj. untidy

dishevelment (di shev´ əl ment) n. disorder; messiness

dismal (diz´ məl) adj. causing gloom or misery

dispatched (di spacht´) v. finished quickly

display (di splā´) v. exhibit; show

dissemble (di sem´ bəl) v. conceal under a false appearance; disguise

dissension (di sen´ shən) n. difference of opinion; disagreement

distinct (di stiŋkt´) adj. from; separate; well-defined

distraught (di strôt´) adj. troubled or confused

diverged (dī vurjd´) v. branched out in different directions

droll (drōl) adj. funny in an odd way

duration (do͝o rā´ shən) n. length of time something lasts

E

elaborate (ē lab´ə rāt´) v.; adj. work out in detail; extremely detailed

eloquence (el´ ə kwəns) n. speech or writing that is graceful and persuasive

elusive (ē lo͞o´ siv) adj. hard to grasp or retain mentally

emotion (ē´ mō´shən) n. feeling

emphasize (em´fə sīz´) v. stress; give special importance to

enamored (en am´ ərd) v. filled with love and desire; charmed

endurance (en do͝or´ əns) n. ability to withstand hardship

enigma (i nig´ mə) n. mystery

enjoined (en joind´) v. ordered

enthralled (en thrôld´) v. held as in a spell; captivated

entrenched (en trenchd´) adj. securely established; unmovable

equity (ek´ wit ē) n. fairness; justice

equivalent (ē kwiv´ə lənt) adj. equal in meaning

evanescent (ev´ ə nes´ ənt) adj. temporary; tending to disappear

exile (ek´ sīl´) v. banish

explicit (eks plis´ it) adj. clearly stated

extrapolating (ek strap´ ə lāt´ iŋ) v. arriving at a conclusion by inferring from known facts

F

feckless (fek´ lis) adj. careless; irresponsible

feisty (fīs´ tē) adj. full of spirit; energetic

fertile (furt´'l) adj. able to make plants grow

fickle (fik´ əl) adj. changeable

forebears (fôr´ berz) n. ancestors

formality (fôr mal´ ə tē) n. attention to established rules or customs

formidable (fôr´ mə də bəl) adj. awe-inspiring

fray (frā) n. noisy fight

furtive (fur´ tiv) adj. sneaky

futile (fyo͞ot´ 'l) adj. useless; hopeless

G

gallant (gal´ ənt) *adj.* brave and noble

grievance (grēv´ əns) *n.* injustice; complaint

H

hallowed (hal´ ōd) *adj.* sacred

haughty (hôt´ ē) *adj.* arrogant

hence (hens) *adv.* as a result; therefore

humble (hum´ bəl) *adj.* modest; having humility

I

ignorance (ig´ nə rəns) *n.* lack of knowledge or education

illuminate (i lōō´mə nāt´) *v.* make clear; provide insight

imminent (im´ ə nənt) *adj.* likely to happen soon

impact (im´ pakt´) *n.* force of a collision; shock

implement (im´plə ment) *v.* put into action; fulfill or accomplish

implications (im´ pli kā´ shənz) *n.* indirect results

imply (im plī´) *v.* hint at or suggest

incredulity (in´ krə dōō´ lə tē) *n.* unwillingness or inability to believe

indolently (in´ də lənt lē) *adv.* lazily; idly

inevitability (in ev´ i tə bil´ ə tē) *n.* quality of being certain to happen

inevitable (in ev´ i tə bəl) *adj.* unavoidable, certain

infallibility (in fal´ ə bil´ ə tē) *n.* condition of not being likely to fail

inscrutable (in skrōōt´ ə bəl) *adj.* baffling; mysterious

insidious (in sid´ ē əs) *adj.* characterized by craftiness and betrayal

insolent (in´ sə lənt) *adj.* boldly disrespectful

instigates (in´ stə gāts´) *v.* urges on; stirs up

intercession (in´ tər sesh´ ən) *n.* the act of pleading on another's behalf

interminably (in tur´ mi nə blē) *adv.* endlessly

intermission (in´ tər mish´ən) *n.* any kind of break; more specifically, a break during a performance

internal (in tur´nəl) *adj.* on the inside

interpretation (in tur´ prə tā´ shən) *n.* a subjective, or personal, explanation

introspective (in´ trə spek´ tiv) *adj.* having to do with looking into one's own thoughts and feelings

involve (in välv´) *v.* include; require

J

jibed (jībd) *v.* changed direction

judicious (jōō dish´ əs) *adj.* showing good judgment

L

lament (lə ment´) *v.* express deep sorrow; mourn

lamentable (lam´ ən tə bəl) *adj.* distressing; sad

languid (laŋ´ gwid) *adj.* drooping; weak

languor (laŋ´ gər) *n.* lack of vigor; weakness

lateral (lat´ ər əl) *adj.* sideways

legacy (leg´ ə sē) *n.* something handed down from an ancestor

lexicon (lek´si kän´) *n.* the special vocabulary of a particular subject

lithe (līth) *adj.* flexible

loathsome (lōth´ səm) *adj.* disgusting; detestable

lofty (lôf´ tē) *adj.* very high; noble

lurched (lurcht) *v.* moved awkwardly and suddenly

M

maladies (mal´ ə dēz) *n.* diseases

malodorous (mal ō´ dər əs) *adj.* having a bad smell

mammoth (mam´ əth) *adj.* enormous

martial (mär´ shəl) *adj.* military

maudlin (môd´ lin) *adj.* tearfully and foolishly sentimental

mechanism (mek´ə niz´əm) *n.* system or means of doing something; working parts of a machine

medium (mē´ dē əm) *n.* means of communication

melancholy (mel´ ən käl´ ē) *adj.* sad; gloomy

metaphysical (met´ ə fiz´ i kəl) *adj.* spiritual; beyond the physical

meticulously (mə tik´ yōō ləs lē) *adv.* very carefully and precisely

moribund (môr´ i bund´) *adj.* dying

mortified (môrt´ ə fīd´) *adj.* extremely embarrassed

motive (mōt´iv) *n.* the reason a person acts in a certain way.

N

naive (nä ēv´) *adj.* unsophisticated

novice (näv´ is) *adj.* new to an activity; inexperienced

O

obstinacy (äb´ stə nə sē) *n.* stubbornness

ominous (äm´ ə nəs) *adj.* threatening

P

pallid (pal´ id) *adj.* pale

pallor (pal´ ər) *n.* unnatural paleness

palpable (pal´ pə bəl) *adj.* able to be felt; easily perceived

palpitating (pal´ pə tāt´ iŋ) *v.* beating rapidly; throbbing

parsimonious (pär′ sə mō′ nē əs) *adj.* miserly; stingy

participate (pär tis′ ə pāt′) *v.* take part in; join

penalty (pen′ əl tē) *n.* punishment

penetrated (pen′ i trāt′ ed) *v.* broke through

pensive (pen′ siv) *adj.* deeply or seriously thoughtful

penury (pen′ yoo rē) *n.* extreme poverty

perennial (pə ren′ ē əl) *adj.* happening over and over; perpetual

permeate (pur′ mē āt′) *v.* spread or flow throughout

pernicious (pər nish′ əs) *adj.* causing great injury or ruin; destructive

perplexes (pər pleks′ iz) *v.* confuses or puzzles

pertinent (purt′n ənt) *adj.* relevant; having a connection to the matter at hand

perverse (pər vurs′) *adj.* deviating from what is considered right or reasonable

picturesque (pik′ chər esk′) *adj.* like or suggesting a picture

placidly (plas′ id lē) *adv.* calmly; quietly

plundered (plun′ dərd) *v.* took goods by force; looted

poignant (poin′ yənt) *adj.* emotionally touching

potential (pō ten′ shl) *n.* possibility

precariously (pri ker′ ē əs lē) *adv.* insecurely

precipitous (prē sip′ ə təs) *adj.* steep; sheer

precluded (prē klood′ id) *v.* prevented

predominant (prē däm′ ə nənt) *adj.* having dominating influence over others

preliminaries (prē lim′ ə ner′ ēz) *n.* steps or events before the main one

pretentious (prē ten′ shəs) *adj.* grand in a showy way

procure (prō kyoor′) *v.* get; obtain

prodigious (prō dij′ əs) *adj.* enormous

profound (prō found′) *adj.* deep; intense

profoundly (prō found′ lē) *adv.* deeply

pungent (pun′ jənt) *adj.* producing a sharp smell

purged (purjd) *v.* cleansed

R

rancor (raŋ′ kər) *n.* bitter hate

ravenous (rav′ ə nəs) *adj.* greedily or wildly hungry

reciprocate (ri sip′ rə kāt′) *v.* return

reckless (rek′ lis) *adj.* careless; rash

relevant (rel′ə vənt) *adj.* related to

remnants (rem′ nənts) *n.* what is left over; remainders

renegade (ren′ ə gād′) *adj.* disloyal; traitorous

reprieve (ri prēv′) *n.* temporary relief; postponement of a penalty

respite (res′ pit) *n.* rest; relief

resplendent (ri splen′ dənt) *adj.* shining brightly

retort (ri tôrt′) *n.* sharp or clever reply

retribution (re′ trə byoo′ shən) *n.* payback; punishment for a misdeed

revelry (rev′ əl rē) *n.* noisy merry-making

revered (ri vird′) *adj.* regarded with great respect and awe

reverie (rev′ ə rē) *n.* dreamy thought of pleasant things

revise (ri vīz′) *v.* read carefully to correct; change or amend

riddled (rid′ ′ld) *adj.* affected throughout

rueful (roo′ fəl) *adj.* feeling sorrow or regret

rustic (rus′ tik) *n.* simple, unsophisticated person

S

sallow (sal′ ō) *adj.* of a sickly, pale-yellowish hue

scarred (skärd) *adj.* marked or dented

scourge (skurj) *n.* instrument for inflicting punishment

scruples (skroo′ pəlz) *n.* misgivings about something one feels is wrong

sequence (sē′ kwəns) *n.* series of connected things

shriveled (shriv′ əld) *adj.* shrunken and wrinkled

siege (sēj) *n.* encirclement of a fortified place by an opposing armed force intending to take it

significant (sig nif′ə kənt) *adj.* important; full of meaning

signify (sig′nə fī′) *v.* be a sign of something

skeptics (skep′ tiks) *n.* people who doubt and question generally accepted ideas

specific (spə sif′ik) *adj.* precise, or definite

spectral (spek′ trəl) *adj.* like a phantom or ghost

spunky (spuŋ′ kē) *adj.* courageous; spirited

spurn (spurn) *v.* reject with contempt or disdain

stout (stout) *adj.* sturdy

strategy (strat′ə jē) *n.* science of managing or planning; plan of action

suffice (sə fīs′) *v.* be enough

T

tantalizingly (tan′ tə līz′ iŋ lē) *adv.* in a teasing way

technique (tek nēk′) *n.* methods used to create an artistic work

temporal (tem′ pə rəl) *adj.* having to do with time

tenement (ten´ ə mənt) *n.* apartment house, often run-down

tenets (ten´ itz) *n.* principles or beliefs

texture (teks´chər) *n.* the look and feel of something

topic (täp´ ik) *n.* subject of a work or talk

transgression (trans gresh´ ən) *n.* wrongdoing; sin

transition (tran zish´ ən) *n.* passing from one to another

treble (treb´ əl) *n.* high-pitched voice

trivial (triv´ ē əl) *adj.* of little or no importance

trundle (trun´ dəl) *v.* roll along

tumultuous (to͞o mul´ cho͞o əs) *adj.* greatly disturbed; in an uproar

U

unbidden (un bid´ 'n) *adj.* without being asked; uninvited

unpalatable (un pal´ it ə bəl) *adj.* distasteful; unpleasant

unrequited (un ri kwīt´ id) *adj.* not returned or repaid

unwieldy (un wēl´ dē) *adj.* awkward; clumsy

usage (yo͞o´sij) *n.* way of using something

usurped (yo͞o sʉrpt´) *v.* took power or position without right

V

venture (ven´ chər) *n.* an action involving risk

verify (ver´ ə fī´) *v.* test whether something is true

vex (veks) *v.* annoy

vigilant (vij´ ə lənt) *adj.* watchful

vile (vīl) *adj.* evil; wicked

vindictive (vin dik´tiv) *adj.* revengeful; inclined to seek vengeance

vital (vīt´'l) *adj.* necessary or essential

voluminously (və lo͞o´ mə nəs lē) *adv.* fully; of great volume

W

wail (wāl) *n.* lament; cry of deep sorrow

warp (wôrp) *v.* twist; distort

wayward (wā´ wərd) *adj.* headstrong

woeful (wō´ fəl) *adj.* full of sorrow

woes (wōz) *n.* great sorrows

writhing (rīth´ iŋ) *v.* twisting; turning

USING A DICTIONARY

A **dictionary** is a reference book containing an alphabetical list of words along with their pronunciations, definitions, and other information about them. Dictionaries are helpful when you need to find the meaning, the pronunciation, or the part of speech of a word. You may also consult a dictionary to trace a word's *etymology*, or its origins. Etymology explains how words change, how they are borrowed from other languages, and how new words are invented, or "coined."

A Sample Dictionary Entry

Here is an entry from a dictionary. Notice what it tells about the word *anthology*.

> **anthology** (an thäl′ə jē) *n., pl.* –**gies** [Gr. *anthologia*, a garland, collection of short poems < *anthologos*, gathering flowers < *anthos*, flower + *legein*, to gather] a collection of poems, stories, songs, excerpts, etc., chosen by the compiler

Dictionaries provide the *denotation* of each word, or its objective meaning. The symbol < means "comes from" or "is derived from." In this case, the Greek words for "flower" and "gather" combined to form a Greek word that meant a garland, and then that word became an English word that means a collection of literary flowers—a collection of literature like the one you are reading now.

Idiomatic Expressions

Dictionaries also provide information about idiomatic expressions. An idiomatic expression is a phrase that means something different from the combined meanings of its individual words. For example, "lay eyes on" is an idiomatic expression meaning "to see." Another common idiomatic expression is "raining cats and dogs," which means "it is raining very hard." In a dictionary, idiomatic expressions are usually included in the entry for the keyword in the phrase.

Activities:

1. Look up the word *obscure* in a dictionary. (a) What is its etymology? (b) Explain what its etymology reveals about the development of English.

2. Look up the word *boot* in a dictionary. (a) Identify at least two idiomatic expressions associated with the word.
   (b) Explain what each idiomatic expression means.

USING A THESAURUS

A **thesaurus** is a book of synonyms, or words that have similar meanings. Words in a thesaurus are often arranged by concept, such as "wisdom" or "wealth." Use a thesaurus to increase your vocabulary or to find alternative words to express your meaning.

- Do not choose a word just because it sounds interesting or smart. Choose the word that expresses exactly the meaning you intend.
- When choosing a word, note both its *denotative* and *connotative* meanings. A word's connotations are the emotional associations that it calls to mind. The connotation may not reflect your intentions, even if the denotation does so.
- To avoid errors, look up the word in a dictionary to check its precise meaning and to make sure you are using it properly.

A Sample Thesaurus Entry

Here is an entry from a thesaurus. Notice what it tells about the word *book*.

book *noun*

A printed and bound work: tome, volume. *See* WORDS.

book *verb* 1. To register in or as if in a book: catalog, enroll, inscribe, list, set down, write down. *See* REMEMBER. 2. To cause to be set aside, as for one's use, in advance: bespeak, engage, reserve. *See* GET.

If the word can be used as different parts of speech, as *book* can, the thesaurus entry provides synonyms for the word as each part of speech. A thesaurus entry also gives specific synonyms for each connotation of the word.

Activity:

Look up the word *pacify* in a thesaurus. (a) What are three synonyms for this word? (b) Explain how the connotations of the synonyms differ.

THE HISTORY OF THE ENGLISH LANGUAGE

A Merging of Cultures

Old English English began about the year 500 when Germanic tribes from the middle of Europe traveled west and settled in Britain. These peoples—the Angles, Saxons, and Jutes—spoke a Germanic language that combined with Danish and Norse when Vikings attacked Britain and added some Latin elements when Christian missionaries arrived. The result was Old English, which looked like this:

> Hwaet! We Gar-Dena   in gear-dagum,
>
> peod-cyninga,   prym gefrunon,
>
> hu da aepelingas   ellen fremedon!

These words are the opening lines of the Old English epic poem *Beowulf*, probably composed in the eighth century. In modern English, they mean: "Listen! We know the ancient glory of the Spear-Danes, and the heroic deeds of those noble kings!"

Middle English The biggest change in English took place after the Norman Conquest of Britain in 1066. The Normans spoke a dialect of Old French, and Old English changed dramatically when the Normans became the new aristocracy. From about 1100 to 1500, the people of Britain spoke what we now call Middle English.

> A Knyght ther was, and that a worthy man,
>
> That fro the tyme that he first bigan
>
> To riden out, he loved chivalrie,
>
> Trouthe and honour, fredom and curtesie.

These lines from the opening section of Geoffrey Chaucer's *Canterbury Tales* (c. 1400) are much easier for us to understand than the lines from *Beowulf*. They mean: "There was a knight, a worthy man who, from the time he began to ride, loved chivalry, truth, honor, freedom, and courtesy."

Modern English During the Renaissance, with its emphasis on reviving classical culture, Greek and Latin languages exerted a strong influence on the English language. In addition, Shakespeare added about two thousand words to the language. Grammar, spelling, and pronunciation continued to change. Modern English was born.

> But soft! What light through yonder window breaks?
>
> It is the East, and Juliet is the sun!

These lines from Shakespeare's *Romeo and Juliet* (c. 1600) need no translation, although it is helpful to know that "soft" means "speak softly." Since Shakespeare's day, conventions of usage and grammar have continued to change. For example, the *th* at the ends of many verbs has become *s*. In Shakespeare's time, it was correct to say "Romeo *hath* fallen in love." In our time, it is right to say "he *has* fallen in love." However, the changes of the past five hundred years are not nearly as drastic as the changes from Old English to Middle English, or from Middle English to Modern English. We still speak Modern English.

Old Words, New Words

Modern English has a larger vocabulary than any other language in the world. The *Oxford English Dictionary* contains about a half million words, and it is estimated that another half million scientific and technical terms do not appear in the dictionary. Here are the main ways that new words enter the language:

- **War**—Conquerors introduce new terms and ideas—and new vocabulary. Example: *anger*, from Old Norse.
- **Immigration**—When large groups of people move from one country to another, they bring their languages with them. Example: *boycott*, from Ireland.
- **Travel and Trade**—Those who travel to foreign lands and those who do business in faraway places bring new words back with them. Example: *shampoo,* from Hindi.
- **Science and Technology**—In our time, the amazing growth of science and technology adds multitudes of new words to English. Example: *Internet.*

English is also filled with **borrowings**, words taken directly from other languages. Sometimes, borrowed words maintain the same meanings they have in their original languages: *pajamas* (Hindi), *sauna* (Finnish), *camouflage* (French), *plaza* (Spanish). Sometimes borrowed words take on new meanings. *Sleuth*, for example, an Old Norse word for *trail*, now means the person who follows a trail—a detective.

Mythology contributed to our language too. Some of the days of the week are named after Norse gods—Wednesday was Woden's Day, Thursday was Thor's Day. Greek and Roman myths have given us many words, such as *jovial* (from Jove), *martial* (from Mars), *mercurial* (from Mercury), and *herculean* (from Hercules).

Americanisms are words, phrases, or usages that originated in American English or that are unique to the way Americans speak. They are expressions of our national character in all its variety: *easy as pie, prairie dog, bamboozle, panhandle, halftime, fringe benefit, bookmobile, jackhammer, southpaw, lickety split.*

Activity:
Look up the following words in a dictionary. Describe the most probable ways in which these words entered American English.

bloom   bandana   souvenir   volcano   pixel

The Influence of English
There are about three hundred million native English speakers, and about the same number who speak English as a second language. Although more people speak Mandarin Chinese, English is the dominant language of trade, tourism, international diplomacy, science, and technology.

Language is a vehicle of both communication and culture, and the cultural influence of English in the twenty-first century is unprecedented in the history of the world's languages. Beyond business and science, English spreads through sports, pop music, Hollywood movies, television, and journalism. A book that is translated into English reaches many more people than it would in its native language alone. Perhaps most significantly, English dominates the Internet. The next time you log on, notice how many Web sites from around the world also have an English version. The global use of English is the closest the world has ever come to speaking an international language.

Activity:
Choose one area of culture—such as sports, fashion, the arts, or technology—and identify three new words that English has recently added to the *world's* vocabulary. (a) In what ways does a shared language benefit the world? (b) In what ways might a global language be a detriment to the world?

The History of the English Language ■ R-9

LITERARY TERMS

ACT *See* Drama.

ALLEGORY An *allegory* is a story or tale with two or more levels of meaning—a literal level and one or more symbolic levels. The events, setting, and characters in an allegory are symbols for ideas and qualities.

ALLITERATION *Alliteration* is the repetition of initial consonant sounds. Writers use alliteration to give emphasis to words, to imitate sounds, and to create musical effects. In the following line from Edgar Allan Poe's "The Raven" (p. 639), there is alliteration of the *w* sound:

> Once upon a midnight dreary, *w*hile I pondered *w*eak and *w*eary, . . .

ALLUSION An *allusion* is a reference to a well-known person, place, event, literary work, or work of art. In O. Henry's "The Gift of the Magi" (p. 246), the title and details of the story refer to the biblical account of the Magi, wise men who brought gifts to the baby Jesus.

ANALOGY An *analogy* makes a comparison between two or more things that are similar in some ways but otherwise unalike.

ANECDOTE An *anecdote* is a brief story about an interesting, amusing, or strange event told to entertain or to make a point. In the excerpt from "A Lincoln Preface" (p. 452), Carl Sandburg tells anecdotes about Abraham Lincoln.

See also Narrative.

ANTAGONIST An *antagonist* is a character or force in conflict with a main character, or protagonist.

ANTICLIMAX Like a climax, an *anticlimax* is a turning point in a story. However, an anticlimax is always a letdown. It's the point at which you learn that the story will not turn out the way you had expected. In Thayer's "Casey at the Bat" (p. 631), the anticlimax occurs when Casey strikes out instead of hitting a game-winning run, as everyone had expected.

ARCHETYPE An *archetype* is a type of character, detail, image, or situation that appears in literature from around the world and throughout history. Some critics believe that archetypes reveal deep truths about human experience.

ASIDE An *aside* is a short speech delivered by a character in a play in order to express his or her true thoughts and feelings. Traditionally, the aside is directed to the audience and is presumed to be inaudible to the other actors.

ASSONANCE *Assonance* is the repetition of vowel sounds followed by different consonants in two or more stressed syllables. Assonance is found in the phrase "weak and weary" in Edgar Allan Poe's "The Raven" (p. 639).

ATMOSPHERE *See* Mood.

AUTOBIOGRAPHY An *autobiography* is a form of nonfiction in which a writer tells his or her own life story. An autobiography may tell about the person's whole life or only a part of it. An example of an autobiography is the excerpt from *A White House Diary* (p. 98).

See also Biography *and* Nonfiction.

BALLAD A *ballad* is a songlike poem that tells a story, often one dealing with adventure and romance. Most ballads are written in four- to six-line stanzas and have regular rhythms and rhyme schemes. A ballad often features a refrain—a regularly repeated line or group of lines.

See also Oral Tradition.

BIOGRAPHY A *biography* is a form of nonfiction in which a writer tells the life story of another person. Biographies have been written about many famous people, historical and contemporary, but they can also be written about "ordinary" people. An example of a biography is the excerpt from *Arthur Ashe Remembered* (p. 460).

See also Autobiography *and* Nonfiction.

BLANK VERSE *Blank verse* is poetry written in unrhymed iambic pentameter lines. This verse form was widely used by William Shakespeare.

See also Meter.

CHARACTER A *character* is a person or an animal that takes part in the action of a literary work. The main character, or protagonist, is the most important character in a story. This character often changes in some important way as a result of the story's events. In Richard Connell's "The Most Dangerous Game" (p. 215), Rainsford is the main character and General Zaroff is the antagonist, or character who opposes the main character.

Characters are sometimes classified as round or flat, dynamic or static. A *round character* shows many different traits—faults as well as virtues. A *flat character* shows only one trait. A *dynamic character* develops and grows during the course of the story; a *static character* does not change.

See also Characterization and Motivation.

CHARACTERIZATION *Characterization* is the act of creating and developing a character. In *direct characterization*, the author directly states a character's traits. For example, at the beginning of "The Necklace" (p. 294), Maupassant directly characterizes Madame Loisel: "She was one of those pretty, charming young women. . . ."

In *indirect characterization*, an author provides clues about a character by describing what a character looks like, does, and says, as well as how other characters react to him or her. It is up to the reader to draw conclusions about the character based on this indirect information.

The most effective indirect characterizations usually result from showing characters acting or speaking.

See also Character.

CLIMAX The *climax* of a story, novel, or play is the high point of interest or suspense. The events that make up the rising action lead up to the climax. The events that make up the falling action follow the climax.

See also Conflict, Plot, *and* Anticlimax.

COMEDY A *comedy* is a literary work, especially a play, that has a happy ending. Comedies often show ordinary characters in conflict with society. These conflicts are resolved through misunderstandings, deceptions, and concealed identities, which result in the correction of moral faults or social wrongs. Types of comedy include *romantic comedy*, which involves problems among lovers, and the *comedy of manners*, which satirically challenges the social customs of a sophisticated society. Comedy is often contrasted with tragedy, in which the protagonist meets an unfortunate end.

COMIC RELIEF *Comic relief* is a technique that is used to interrupt a serious part of a literary work by introducing a humorous character or situation.

CONFLICT A *conflict* is a struggle between opposing forces. Characters in conflict form the basis of stories, novels, and plays.

There are two kinds of conflict: external and internal. In an *external conflict,* the main character struggles against an outside force. This force may be another character, as in Richard Connell's "The Most Dangerous Game" (p. 215), in which Rainsford struggles with General Zaroff. The outside force could also be the standards or expectations of a group, such as the family prejudices that Romeo and Juliet struggle against. Their story (p. 730) shows them in conflict with society. The outside force may be nature itself, a person-against-nature conflict. The two men who are trapped by a fallen tree in Saki's "The Interlopers" (p. 255) face such a conflict.

An *internal conflict* involves a character in conflict with himself or herself. In "Checkouts" (p. 74), two young people who meet by chance in a supermarket agonize over whether they should speak to each other.

See also Plot.

CONNOTATION The *connotation* of a word is the set of ideas associated with it in addition to its explicit meaning.

See also Denotation.

CONSONANCE *Consonance* is the repetition of final consonant sounds in stressed syllables with different vowel sounds, as in *hat* and *sit.*

CONTEMPORARY INTERPRETATION A *contemporary interpretation* is a literary work of today that responds to and sheds new light on a well-known, earlier work of literature. Such an interpretation may refer to any aspect of the older work, including plot, characters, settings, imagery, language, and theme. Edna St. Vincent Millay's poem "An Ancient Gesture" (p. 1028), for example, provides a modern perspective on the characters Penelope and Odysseus in the *Odyssey.*

COUPLET A *couplet* is a pair of rhyming lines, usually of the same length and meter. In the following couplet from a poem by William Shakespeare, the speaker comforts himself with the thought of his love:

> For thy sweet love remember'd such wealth brings
>
> That then I scorn to change my state with kings.

See also Stanza.

DENOTATION The *denotation* of a word is its dictionary meaning, independent of other associations that the word may have. The denotation of the word *lake,* for example, is an inland body of water. "Vacation spot" and "place where the fishing is good" are connotations of the word *lake.*

See also Connotation.

DENOUEMENT *See* Plot.

DESCRIPTION A *description* is a portrait in words of a person, a place, or an object. Descriptive writing uses sensory details, those that appeal to the senses: sight, hearing, taste, smell, and touch. Description can be found in all types of writing. Rudolfo Anaya's essay "A Celebration of Grandfathers" (p. 404) contains descriptive passages.

DEVELOPMENT *See* Plot.

DIALECT *Dialect*, the form of language spoken by people in a particular region or group, may involve changes to the pronunciation, vocabulary, and sentence structure of standard English. An example from Mark Twain's "The Invalid's Story" (p. 333) is a character's use of the term *yourn* for *yours*.

DIALOGUE A *dialogue* is a conversation between characters that may reveal their traits and advance the action of a narrative. In fiction or nonfiction, quotation marks indicate a speaker's exact words, and a new paragraph usually indicates a change of speaker. Following is an exchange between the narrator and his frail younger brother, Doodle, in "The Scarlet Ibis" (p. 350):

> "Aw, come on Doodle," I urged. "You can do it. Do you want to be different from everybody else when you start school?"
>
> "Does it make any difference?"

Quotation marks are not used in a *script*, the printed copy of a play. Instead, the dialogue follows the name of the speaker, as in this example from Chekhov's *The Inspector General* (p. 884):

> **DRIVER.** Oh, yes, he's a good one, this one.

DICTION *Diction* refers to an author's choice of words, especially with regard to range of vocabulary, use of slang and colloquial language, and level of formality. These lines from Ernest Lawrence Thayer's poem "Casey at the Bat" (p. 631) are an example of colloquial, informal diction: "It looked extremely rocky for the Mudville nine that day; / The score stood two to four; with but an inning left to play."

See also Connotation *and* Denotation.

DIRECT CHARACTERIZATION *See* Characterization.

DRAMA A *drama* is a story written to be performed by actors. The script of a drama is made up of *dialogue*—the words the actors say—and *stage directions*, which are comments on how and where action happens.

The drama's *setting* is the time and place in which the action occurs. It is indicated by one or more sets, including furniture and backdrops, that suggest interior or exterior scenes. *Props* are objects, such as a sword or a cup of tea, that are used onstage.

At the beginning of most plays, a brief *exposition* gives the audience some background information about the characters and the situation. Just as in a story or novel, the plot of a drama is built around characters in conflict.

Dramas are divided into large units called *acts,* which are divided into smaller units called *scenes.* A long play may include many sets that change with the scenes, or it may indicate a change of scene with lighting.

See also Dialogue, Genre, Stage Directions, *and* Tragedy. *Romeo and Juliet* (p. 730) is a long play in five acts.

DRAMATIC IRONY *See* Irony.

DRAMATIC MONOLOGUE A *dramatic monologue* is a poem in which a character reveals himself or herself by speaking to a silent listener.

DRAMATIC POETRY *Dramatic poetry* is poetry that utilizes the techniques of drama. The dialogue used in Edgar Allan Poe's "The Raven" (p. 639) makes it dramatic dialogue. A *dramatic monologue* is a poem spoken by one person, addressing a silent listener.

END RHYME *See* Rhyme.

EPIC An *epic* is a long narrative poem about the deeds of gods or heroes. Homer's *Odyssey* (p. 950) is an example of epic poetry. It tells the story of the Greek hero Odysseus, the king of Ithaca.

An epic is elevated in style and usually follows certain patterns. The poet begins by announcing the subject and asking a Muse—one of the nine goddesses of the arts, literature, and sciences—to help. An *epic hero* is the larger-than-life central character in an epic. Through behavior and deeds, the epic hero displays qualities that are valued by the society in which the epic originated.

See also Epic Simile *and* Narrative Poem.

EPIC SIMILE An *epic simile*, also called *Homeric simile*, is an elaborate comparison of unlike subjects. In this example from the *Odyssey* (p. 950), Homer compares the bodies of men killed by Odysseus to a fisherman's catch heaped up on the shore:

> Think of a catch that fishermen haul in to a
>   half-moon bay
>
> in a fine-meshed net from the whitecaps of the sea:
> how all are poured out on the sand, in throes
>   for the salt sea,
>
> twitching their cold lives away in Helios' fiery air:
>   so lay the suitors heaped on one another.

See also Figurative Language *and* Simile.

EPIPHANY An *epiphany* is a character's sudden flash of insight into a conflict or situation. At the end of Judith Ortiz Cofer's story "American History" (p. 202), for example, the central character experiences an epiphany.

ESSAY An *essay* is a short nonfiction work about a particular subject. While classification is difficult, five types of essays are sometimes identified.

A *descriptive essay* seeks to convey an impression about a person, place, or object. In "A Celebration of Grandfathers" (p. 404), Rudolfo Anaya describes the cultural values that his grandfather and other "old ones" from his childhood passed down.

A *narrative essay* tells a true story. In "The Washwoman" (p. 26), Isaac Bashevis Singer tells of his childhood in Poland.

An *expository essay* gives information, discusses ideas, or explains a process. In "Single Room, Earth View" (p. 437), Sally Ride explains what it is like to be in outer space.

A *persuasive essay* tries to convince readers to do something or to accept the writer's point of view. Pete Hamill's "Libraries Face Sad Chapter" (p. 483) is a persuasive essay.

A *visual essay* is an exploration of a topic that conveys its ideas through visual elements as well as language. Like a standard essay, a visual essay presents an author's views of a single topic. Unlike other essays, however, much of the meaning in a visual essay is conveyed through illustrations or photographs.

See also Description, Exposition, Genre, Narration, Nonfiction, *and* Persuasion.

EXPOSITION *Exposition* is writing or speech that explains a process or presents information. In the plot of a story or drama, the exposition is the part of the work that introduces the characters, the setting, and the basic situation.

EXTENDED METAPHOR In an *extended metaphor*, as in regular metaphor, a writer speaks or writes of a subject as though it were something else. An extended metaphor sustains the comparison for several lines or for an entire poem.

See also Figurative Language *and* Metaphor.

EXTERNAL CONFLICT *See* Conflict.

FALLING ACTION *See* Plot.

FANTASY A *fantasy* is highly imaginative writing that contains elements not found in real life. Examples of fantasy include stories that involve supernatural elements, stories that resemble fairy tales, and stories that deal with imaginary places and creatures.

See also Science Fiction.

FICTION *Fiction* is prose writing that tells about imaginary characters and events. The term is usually used for novels and short stories, but it also applies to dramas and narrative poetry. Some writers rely on their imaginations alone to create their works of fiction. Others base their fiction on actual events and people, to which they add invented characters, dialogue, and plot situations.

See also Genre, Narrative, *and* Nonfiction.

FIGURATIVE LANGUAGE *Figurative language* is writing or speech not meant to be interpreted literally. It is often used to create vivid impressions by setting up comparisons between dissimilar things.

Some frequently used figures of speech are *metaphors, similes,* and *personifications.*

See also Literal Language.

FLASHBACK A *flashback* is a means by which authors present material that occurred earlier than the present tense of the narrative. Authors may include this material in a character's memories, dreams, or accounts of past events.

FOIL A *foil* is a character who provides a contrast to another character. In *Romeo and Juliet* (p. 730), the fiery temper of Tybalt serves as a foil to the good nature of Benvolio.

FOOT *See* Meter.

FORESHADOWING *Foreshadowing* is the use in a literary work of clues that suggest events that have yet to occur. This technique helps create suspense, keeping readers wondering about what will happen next.

See also Suspense.

FREE VERSE *Free verse* is poetry not written in a regular pattern of meter or rhyme. Like Whitman's "I Hear America Singing" (p. 680), however, it may use parallelism and various sound devices.

GENRE A *genre* is a category or type of literature. Literature is commonly divided into three major genres: poetry, prose, and drama. Each major genre is in turn divided into smaller genres, as follows:

1. Poetry: Lyric Poetry, Concrete Poetry, Dramatic Poetry, Narrative Poetry, and Epic Poetry

2. Prose: Fiction (Novels and Short Stories) and Nonfiction (Biography, Autobiography, Letters, Essays, and Reports)

3. Drama: Serious Drama and Tragedy, Comic Drama, Melodrama, and Farce

See also Drama, Poetry, *and* Prose.

HAIKU The *haiku* is a three-line verse form. The first and third lines of a haiku each have five syllables. The second line has seven syllables. A haiku seeks to convey a single vivid emotion by means of images from nature.

HOMERIC SIMILE *See* Epic Simile.

HYPERBOLE A *hyperbole* is a deliberate exaggeration or overstatement. In Mark Twain's "The Notorious Jumping Frog of Calaveras County," the claim that Jim Smiley would follow a bug as far as Mexico to win a bet is a hyperbole. As this example shows, hyperboles are often used for comic effect.

IAMB *See* Meter.

IDIOM An *idiom* is an expression that is characteristic of a language, region, community, or class of people. *Idiomatic expressions* often arise from figures of speech and therefore cannot be understood literally. In "The Invalid's Story" (p. 333), for example, a character uses the idiom *throw up the sponge*, meaning "surrender."

See *also* Dialect.

IMAGE An *image* is a word or phrase that appeals to one or more of the five senses—sight, hearing, touch, taste, or smell. Writers use images to re-create sensory experiences in words.

See also Description.

IMAGERY *Imagery* is the descriptive or figurative language used in literature to create word pictures for the reader. These pictures, or images, are created by details of sight, sound, taste, touch, smell, or movement.

INDIRECT CHARACTERIZATION *See* Characterization.

INTERNAL *See* Conflict.

INTERNAL RHYME *See* Rhyme.

IRONY *Irony* is the general term for literary techniques that portray differences between appearance and reality, or expectation and result. In *verbal irony*, words are used to suggest the opposite of what is meant. In *dramatic irony*, there is a contradiction between what a character thinks and what the reader or audience knows to be true. In *irony of situation*, an event occurs that directly contradicts the expectations of the characters, the reader, or the audience.

LEGEND *See* Oral Tradition.

LITERAL LANGUAGE *Literal language* uses words in their ordinary senses. It is the opposite of *figurative language*. If you tell someone standing on a diving board to jump in, you speak literally. If you tell someone on the street to jump in a lake, you are speaking figuratively.

See also Figurative Language.

LYRIC POEM A *lyric poem* is a highly musical verse that expresses the thoughts, observations, and feelings of a single speaker.

MAIN CHARACTER *See* Character.

METAPHOR A *metaphor* is a figure of speech in which one thing is spoken of as though it were something else. Unlike a simile, which compares two things using *like* or *as*, a metaphor implies a comparison between them. In "Dreams" (p. 567), Langston Hughes uses a metaphor to show what happens to a life without dreams:

> . . . if dreams die
>
> Life is a broken-winged bird
>
> That cannot fly.

See also Extended Metaphor *and* Figurative Language.

METER The *meter* of a poem is its rhythmical pattern. This pattern is determined by the number and types of stresses, or beats, in each line. To describe the meter of a poem, you must scan its lines. Scanning involves marking the stressed and unstressed syllables, as shown with the following two lines from "I Wandered Lonely as a Cloud" by William Wordsworth (p. 568):

> Ĭ wán|dĕřed lońe|lў ás| ă clóud
>
> Thăt floáts | ŏn hígh| o' ĕr váles| ănd hílls.

As you can see, each strong stress is marked with a slanted line (´) and each unstressed syllable with a horseshoe symbol (˘). The stressed and unstressed syllables are then divided by vertical lines (|) into groups called *feet*. The following types of feet are common in English poetry:

1. *Iamb:* a foot with one unstressed syllable followed by a stressed syllable, as in the word "again"

2. *Trochee:* a foot with one stressed syllable followed by an unstressed syllable, as in the word "wonder"

3. *Anapest:* a foot with two unstressed syllables followed by one strong stress, as in the phrase "on the beach"

4. *Dactyl:* a foot with one strong stress followed by two unstressed syllables, as in the word "wonderful"

5. *Spondee:* a foot with two strong stresses, as in the word "spacewalk"

Depending on the type of foot that is most common in them, lines of poetry are described as *iambic, trochaic, anapestic*, and so forth.

Lines are also described in terms of the number of feet that occur in them, as follows:

1. *Monometer:* verse written in one-foot lines
   All things
   Must pass
   Away.

2. *Dimeter:* verse written in two-foot lines
   Thomas | Jefferson
   What do | you say
   Under the | gravestone
   Hidden | away?
   —Rosemary and Stephen Vincent Benét,
   "Thomas Jefferson, 1743–1826"

3. *Trimeter:* verse written in three-foot lines
   I know | not whom | I meet
   I know | not where | I go.

4. *Tetrameter:* verse written in four-foot lines

5. *Pentameter:* verse written in five-foot lines

6. *Hexameter:* verse written in six-foot lines

7. *Heptameter:* verse written in seven-foot lines

Blank verse, used by Shakespeare in *Romeo and Juliet* (p. 730), is poetry written in unrhymed iambic pentameter.

Free verse, used by Walt Whitman in "I Hear America Singing" (p. 680), is poetry that does not follow a regular pattern of meter and rhyme.

MONOLOGUE A *monologue* in a play is a speech by one character that, unlike a *soliloquy*, is addressed to another character or characters. An example from Shakespeare's *Romeo and Juliet* (p. 730) is the speech by the Prince of Verona in Act 1, Scene i, lines 72–94.

See also Soliloquy.

MONOMETER *See* Meter.

MOOD *Mood*, or *atmosphere*, is the feeling created in the reader by a literary work or passage. The mood is often suggested by descriptive details. Often the mood can be described in a single word, such as lighthearted, frightening, or despairing. Notice how this passage from Edgar Allan Poe's "The Cask of Amontillado" (p. 61) contributes to an eerie, fearful mood:

> "The niter!" I said; "see, it increases. It hangs like moss upon the vaults. We are below the river's bed. The drops of moisture trickle among the bones. Come, we will go back ere it is too late."

See also Tone.

MORAL A *moral* is a lesson taught by a literary work, especially a fable—many fables, for example, have a stated moral at the end. It is customary, however, to discuss contemporary works in terms of the themes they explore, rather than a moral that they teach.

MOTIVATION *Motivation* is a reason that explains or partially explains why a character thinks, feels, acts, or behaves in a certain way. Motivation results from a combination of the character's personality and the situation he or she must deal with. In "Checkouts" (p. 74), the main character is motivated by conflicting feelings.

See also Character *and* Characterization.

MYTH A myth is a *fictional* tale that describes the actions of gods and heroes or explains the causes of natural phenomena. Unlike legends, myths emphasize supernatural rather than historical elements. Many cultures have collections of myths, and the most familiar in the Western world are those of the ancient Greeks and Romans. "Perseus" (p. 1121) is a retelling of a famous ancient Greek myth.

See also Oral Tradition.

NARRATION *Narration* is writing that tells a story. The act of telling a story in speech is also called narration. Novels and short stories are fictional narratives. Nonfiction works—such as news stories, biographies, and autobiographies—are also narratives. A narrative poem tells a story in verse.

See also Anecdote, Essay, Narrative Poem, Nonfiction, Novel, *and* Short Story.

NARRATIVE A *narrative* is a story told in fiction, nonfiction, poetry, or drama.

See also Narration.

NARRATIVE POEM A *narrative poem* is one that tells a story. "Casey at the Bat" (p. 630) is a humorous narrative poem about the last inning of a baseball game. Edgar Allan Poe's "The Raven" (p. 639) is a serious narrative poem about a man's grief over the loss of a loved one.

See also Dramatic Poetry, Epic, *and* Narration.

NARRATOR A *narrator* is a speaker or character who tells a story. The writer's choice of narrator determines the story's *point of view*, which directs the type and amount of information the writer reveals.

When a character in the story tells the story, that character is a *first-person narrator*. This narrator may be a major character, a minor character, or just a witness. Readers see only what this character sees, hear only what he or she hears, and so on. The first-person narrator may or may not be reliable. We have reason, for example, to be suspicious of the first-person narrator of Edgar Allan Poe's "The Cask of Amontillado" (p. 61).

When a voice outside the story narrates, the story has a *third-person narrator*. An omniscient, or all-knowing, third-person narrator can tell readers what any character thinks and feels. For example, in Guy de Maupassant's "The Necklace" (p. 294), we know the feelings of both Monsieur and Madame Loisel. A limited third-person narrator sees the world through one character's eyes and reveals only that character's thoughts. In James Thurber's "The Secret Life of Walter Mitty" (p. 124), the narrator reveals only Mitty's experiences and feelings.

See also Speaker.

NONFICTION *Nonfiction* is prose writing that presents and explains ideas or that tells about real people, places, ideas, or events. To be classified as nonfiction, a work must be true. "Single Room, Earth View" (p. 437) is a nonfictional account of the view of Earth from space.

See also Autobiography, Biography, *and* Essay.

NOVEL A *novel* is a long work of fiction. It has a plot that explores characters in conflict. A novel may also have one or more subplots, or minor stories, and several themes.

NOVELLA A *novella* is a work of fiction that is longer than a short story but shorter than a novel.

OCTAVE *See* Stanza.

ONOMATOPOEIA *Onomatopoeia* is the use of words that imitate sounds. *Whirr, thud, sizzle*, and *hiss* are typical examples. Writers can deliberately choose words that contribute to a desired sound effect.

ORAL TRADITION The *oral tradition* is the passing of songs, stories, and poems from generation to generation by word of mouth. Many folk songs, ballads, fairy tales, legends, and myths originated in the oral tradition.

See also Myth.

OXYMORON An *oxymoron* is a combination of words, or parts of words, that contradict each other. Examples are "deafening silence," "honest thief," "wise fool," and "bittersweet." This device is effective when the apparent contradiction reveals a deeper truth, as in Act 2, Scene ii, line 184, of *Romeo and Juliet* (p. 730) when Juliet bids goodbye to Romeo: "Parting is such *sweet sorrow.*"

PARADOX A *paradox* is a statement that seems contradictory but actually may be true. Because a paradox is surprising, it catches the reader's attention.

PARALLELISM *See* Rhetorical Devices.

PENTAMETER *See* Meter.

PERSONIFICATION *Personification* is a type of figurative language in which a nonhuman subject is given human characteristics. William Wordsworth personifies daffodils when he describes them as "Tossing their heads in sprightly dance" (p. 568).

See also Figurative Language.

PERSUASION *Persuasion* is writing or speech that attempts to convince the reader to adopt a particular opinion or course of action.

PLOT *Plot* is the sequence of events in a literary work. In most novels, dramas, short stories, and narrative poems, the plot involves both characters and a central conflict. The plot usually begins with an *exposition* that introduces the setting, the characters, and the basic situation. This is followed by the *inciting incident*, which introduces the central conflict. The conflict then increases during the *development* until it reaches a high point of interest or suspense, the *climax*. All the events leading up to the climax make up the *rising action*. The climax is followed by the *falling action*, which leads to the *denouement,* or *resolution,* in which a general insight or change is conveyed.

POETRY *Poetry* is one of the three major types of literature, the others being prose and drama. Most poems make use of highly concise, musical, and emotionally charged language. Many also make use of imagery, figurative language, and special devices of sound such as rhyme. Poems are often divided into lines and stanzas and often employ regular rhythmical patterns, or meters. However, some poems are written out just like prose, while others are written in free verse.

See also Genre.

POINT OF VIEW *See* Narrator.

PROSE *Prose* is the ordinary form of written language. Most writing that is not poetry, drama, or song is considered prose. Prose is one of the major genres of literature and occurs in two forms: fiction and nonfiction.

See also Fiction, Genre, *and* Nonfiction.

PROTAGONIST The *protagonist* is the main character in a literary work.

See also Antagonist *and* Character.

PUN A *pun* is a play on words involving a word with two or more different meanings or two words that sound alike but have different meanings. In *Romeo and Juliet* (p. 730), the dying Mercutio makes a pun involving two meanings of the word *grave*, "serious" and "burial site": "Ask for me tomorrow, and you shall find me a grave man" (Act 3, Scene i, lines 92–93).

QUATRAIN A *quatrain* is a stanza or poem made up of four lines, usually with a definite rhythm and rhyme scheme.

REPETITION *Repetition* is the use of any element of language—a sound, a word, a phrase, a clause, or a sentence—more than once.

Poets use many kinds of repetition. Alliteration, assonance, rhyme, and rhythm are repetitions of certain sounds and sound patterns. A refrain is a repeated line or group of lines. In both prose and poetry, repetition is used for musical effects and for emphasis.

See also Alliteration, Assonance, Rhyme, *and* Rhythm.

RESOLUTION *See* Plot.

RHETORICAL DEVICES *Rhetorical devices* are special patterns of words and ideas that create emphasis and stir emotion, especially in speeches or other oral presentations. *Parallelism*, for example, is the repetition of a grammatical structure in order to create a rhythm and make words more memorable. In his "I Have a Dream" speech (p. 494), Martin Luther King, Jr., uses parallel statements beginning, "I have a dream that . . ."

Other common rhetorical devices include *restatement*, expressing the same idea in different words, and *rhetorical questions*, questions with obvious answers.

RHYME *Rhyme* is the repetition of sounds at the ends of words. *End rhyme* occurs when the rhyming words come at the ends of lines, as in "The Desired Swan Song" by Samuel Taylor Coleridge:

> Swans sing before they die—'twere no bad *thing*
> Should certain persons die before they *sing*.

Internal rhyme occurs when the rhyming words appear in the same line, as in the first line of Edgar Allan Poe's "The Raven" (p. 639):

> Once upon a midnight *dreary*, while I pondered, weak and *weary*,

Exact rhyme involves the repetition of words with the same vowel and consonant sounds, like *ball* and *hall*. *Slant rhyme* involves the repetition of words that sound alike but do not rhyme exactly, like *grove* and *love*.

See also Repetition *and* Rhyme Scheme.

RHYME SCHEME A *rhyme scheme* is a regular pattern of rhyming words in a poem. The rhyme scheme of a poem is indicated by using different letters of the alphabet for each new rhyme. In an *aabb* stanza, for example, line 1 rhymes with line 2 and line 3 rhymes with line 4. William Wordsworth's poem "I Wandered Lonely as a Cloud" (p. 568) uses an *ababcc* rhyme pattern:

I wandered lonely as a cloud	a
That floats on high o'er vales and hills,	b
When all at once I saw a crowd,	a
A host, of golden daffodils;	b
Beside the lake, beneath the trees,	c
Fluttering and dancing in the breeze.	c

Many poems use the same pattern of rhymes, though not the same rhymes, in each stanza.

See also Rhyme.

RHYTHM *Rhythm* is the pattern of *beats*, or *stresses*, in spoken or written language. Some poems have a very specific pattern, or meter, whereas prose and free verse use the natural rhythms of everyday speech.

See also Meter.

RISING ACTION *See* Plot.

ROUND CHARACTER *See* Character.

SATIRE A *satire* is a literary work that ridicules the foolishness and faults of individuals, an institution, society, or even humanity in general.

SCENE *See* Drama.

SCIENCE FICTION *Science fiction* is writing that tells about imaginary events involving science or technology. Many science-fiction stories are set in the future. Arthur C. Clarke's "If I Forget Thee, Oh Earth . . ." (p. 148) is set on the moon after a nuclear disaster on Earth.

See also Fantasy.

SENSORY LANGUAGE *Sensory language* is writing or speech that appeals to one or more of the senses.

See also Image.

SESTET *See* Stanza.

SETTING The *setting* of a literary work is the time and place of the action. Time can include not only the historical period—past, present, or future—but also a specific year, season, or time of day. Place may involve not only the geographical place—a region, country, state, or town—but also the social, economic, or cultural environment.

In some stories, setting serves merely as a backdrop for action, a context in which the characters move and speak. In others, however, setting is a crucial element.

See also Mood.

SHORT STORY A *short story* is a brief work of fiction. In most short stories, one main character faces a conflict that is resolved in the plot of the story. Great craftsmanship must go into the writing of a good story, for it has to accomplish its purpose in relatively few words.

See also Fiction *and* Genre.

SIMILE A *simile* is a figure of speech in which the words *like* or *as* are used to compare two apparently dissimilar items. The comparison, however, surprises the reader into a fresh perception by finding an unexpected likeness. In "Blackberry Eating" (p. 615), Galway Kinnell creates such a simile: "the ripest berries / fall almost unbidden to my tongue / as words sometimes do . . ."

SOLILOQUY A *soliloquy* is a long speech expressing the thoughts of a character alone on stage. In William Shakespeare's *Romeo and Juliet* (p. 730), Romeo gives a soliloquy after the servant has fled and Paris has died (Act V, Scene iii, lines 74–120).

See also Monologue.

SONNET A *sonnet* is a fourteen-line lyric poem, usually written in rhymed iambic pentameter. The *English*, or *Shakespearean*, sonnet consists of three quatrains (four-line stanzas) and a couplet (two lines), usually rhyming *abab cdcd efef gg*. The couplet usually comments on the ideas contained in the preceding twelve lines. The sonnet is usually not printed with the stanzas divided, but a reader can see distinct ideas in each. See the English sonnet by William Shakespeare on page 682.

The *Italian*, or *Petrarchan*, sonnet consists of an octave (eight-line stanza) and a sestet (six-line stanza). Often, the octave rhymes *abbaabba* and the sestet rhymes *cdecde*. The octave states a theme or asks a question. The sestet comments on or answers the question.

See also Lyric Poem, Meter, *and* Stanza.

SOUND DEVICES A *sound device* is a technique used by a poet to emphasize the sound relationships among words in order to create musical and emotional effects and emphasize a poem's meaning. These devices include *alliteration, consonance, assonance, onomatopoeia*, and *rhyme*.

SPEAKER The *speaker* is the imaginary voice assumed by the writer of a poem. In many poems, the speaker is not identified by name. When reading a poem, remember that the speaker within the poem may be a person, an animal, a thing, or an abstraction. The speaker in the following stanza by Emily Dickinson is a person who has died:

> Because I could not stop for Death—
>
> He kindly stopped for me—
>
> The Carriage held but just Ourselves—
>
> And Immortality.

STAGE DIRECTIONS *Stage directions* are notes included in a drama to describe how the work is to be performed or staged. These instructions are printed in italics and are not spoken aloud. They are used to describe sets, lighting, sound effects, and the appearance, personalities, and movements of characters.

See also Drama.

STANZA A *stanza* is a repeated grouping of two or more lines in a poem that often share a pattern of rhythm and rhyme. Stanzas are sometimes named according to the number of lines they have—for example, a *couplet*, two lines; a *quatrain*, four lines; a *sestet*, six lines; and an *octave*, eight lines.

STATIC CHARACTER *See* Character.

STYLE *Style* refers to an author's unique way of writing. Elements determining style include diction; tone; characteristic use of figurative language, dialect, or rhythmic devices; and syntax, or typical grammatical structures and patterns.

See also Diction and Tone.

SURPRISE ENDING A *surprise ending* is a conclusion that violates the expectations of the reader but in a way that is both logical and believable.

O. Henry's "The Gift of the Magi" (p. 246) and Guy de Maupassant's "The Necklace" (p. 294) have surprise endings. Both authors were masters of this form.

SUSPENSE *Suspense* is a feeling of uncertainty about the outcome of events in a literary work. Writers create suspense by raising questions in the minds of their readers.

SYMBOL A *symbol* is anything that stands for something else. In addition to having its own meaning and reality, a symbol also represents abstract ideas. For example, a flag is a piece of cloth, but it also represents the idea of a country. Writers sometimes use conventional symbols like flags. Frequently, however, they create symbols of their own through emphasis or repetition. In James Hurst's "The Scarlet Ibis" (p. 350), for example, the ibis symbolizes the character named Doodle. Both are beautiful and otherworldly.

TALL TALE A *tall tale* is a type of folk tale that contains some or all of these features: humor, hyperbole, far-fetched situations, highly imaginative language, and a hero who performs outrageous feats. Tall tales originated during the development of the American frontier and are a particularly American form of folk tale. "Pecos Bill: The Cyclone" (p. 1114) is an example of a tall tale.

TETRAMETER *See* Meter.

THEME A *theme* is a central message or insight into life revealed through a literary work.

The theme of a literary work may be stated directly or implied. When the theme of a work is implied, readers think about what the work suggests about people or life.

Archetypal themes are those that occur in folklore and literature across the world and throughout history. Ill-fated love, the theme of *Romeo and Juliet* (p. 730), is an example of such a theme.

TONE The *tone* of a literary work is the writer's attitude toward his or her audience and subject. The tone can often be described by a single adjective, such as *formal* or *informal, serious* or *playful, bitter* or *ironic.* When O. Henry discusses the young couple in "The Gift of the Magi" (p. 246), he uses a sympathetic tone.

See also Mood.

TRAGEDY A *tragedy* is a work of literature, especially a play, that results in a catastrophe, a disaster or great misfortune, for the main character, or *tragic hero.* In ancient Greek drama, the main character was always a significant person—a king or a hero—and the cause of the tragedy was a *tragic flaw,* or weakness, in his or her character. In modern drama, the main character can be an ordinary person, and the cause of the tragedy can be some evil in society itself. Tragedy not only arouses fear and pity in the audience but also, in some cases, conveys a sense of the grandeur and nobility of the human spirit.

Shakespeare's *Romeo and Juliet* (p. 730) is a tragedy. Romeo and Juliet both suffer from the tragic flaw of impulsiveness. This flaw ultimately leads to their deaths.

See also Drama.

TRIMETER *See* Meter.

UNDERSTATEMENT An *understatement* is a figure of speech in which the stated meaning is purposely less than (or "under") what is really meant. It is the opposite of *hyperbole,* which is a deliberate exaggeration.

UNIVERSAL THEME A *universal theme* is a message about life that can be understood by most cultures. Many folk tales and examples of classic literature address universal themes such as the importance of courage, the effects of honesty, or the danger of greed.

VERBAL IRONY *See* Irony.

VILLANELLE A *villanelle* is a nineteen-line lyric poem written in five three-line stanzas and ending in a four-line stanza. It uses two rhymes and repeats two refrain lines that appear initially in the first and third lines of the first stanza. These lines then appear alternately as the third line of subsequent three-line stanzas and, finally, as the last two lines of the poem.

VISUAL ESSAY A *visual essay* is an exploration of a topic that conveys its ideas through visual elements as well as language. Like a standard essay, a visual essay presents an author's views of a single topic. Unlike other essays, however, much of the meaning in a visual essay is conveyed through illustrations or photographs.

VOICE *Voice* is a writer's distinctive "sound" or way of "speaking" on the page. It is related to such elements as word choice, sentence structure, and tone. It is similar to an individual's speech style and can be described in the same way—fast, slow, blunt, meandering, breathless, and so on.

Voice resembles *style,* an author's typical way of writing, but style usually refers to a quality that can be found throughout an author's body of work, while an author's voice may sometimes vary from work to work.

See also *Style.*

TIPS FOR DISCUSSING LITERATURE

As you read and study literature, discussion with other readers can help you understand, enjoy, and develop interpretations of what you read. Use the following tips to practice good speaking and listening skills while participating in group discussions of literature.

Understand the Purpose of Your Discussion

When you discuss literature, your purpose is to broaden your understanding and appreciation of a work by testing your own ideas and hearing the ideas of others. Stay focused on the literature you are discussing, and keep your comments relevant to that literature. Starting with one focus question will help keep your discussion on track.

Communicate Effectively

Effective communication requires thinking before speaking. Plan the points that you want to make, and decide how you will express them. Organize these points in logical order, and cite details from the work to support your ideas. Jot down informal notes to help keep your ideas focused.

Remember to speak clearly, pronouncing words slowly and carefully so that others can understand your points. Also, keep in mind that some literature touches readers deeply—be aware of the possibility of counterproductive emotional responses, and work to control them. Negative emotional responses can also be conveyed through body language, so work to demonstrate respect in your demeanor as well as in your words.

Encourage Everyone to Participate

While some people are comfortable participating in discussions, others are less eager to speak up in groups. However, everyone should work to contribute thoughts and ideas. To encourage the entire group's participation, try the following strategies:

- If you enjoy speaking, avoid monopolizing the conversation. After sharing your ideas, encourage others to share theirs.
- Try different roles. For example, have everyone take turns being the facilitator or host of the discussion.
- Use a prop, such as a book or gavel. Pass the prop around the group, allowing whomever is holding the prop to have the floor.

Make Relevant Contributions

Especially when responding to a short story, a poem, or a novel, avoid simply summarizing the plot. Instead, consider *what* you think might happen next, *why* events take place as they do, or *how* a writer provokes a response in you. Let your ideas inspire deeper thought or discussion about the literature.

Consider Other Ideas and Interpretations

A work of literature can generate a wide variety of responses in different readers—and that can make your discussions exciting. Be open to the idea that many interpretations can be valid. To support your own ideas, point to the events, descriptions, characters, or other literary elements in the work that produced your interpretation. To consider someone else's ideas, decide whether details in the work support the interpretation he or she presents. Be sure to convey your criticism of the ideas of others in a respectful and supportive manner.

Ask Questions and Extend the Contributions of Others

Get in the habit of asking questions to help you clarify your understanding of another reader's ideas. You can also use questions to call attention to possible areas of confusion, to points that are open to debate, or to errors.

In addition, offer elaboration of the points that others make by providing examples and illustrations. To move a discussion forward, pause occasionally to summarize and evaluate tentative conclusions reached by the group members. Then, continue the discussion with a fresh understanding of the material and ideas you have already covered.

Manage Differing Opinions and Views

Each participant brings his or her own personality, experiences, ideas, cultural background, likes and dislikes to the experience of reading, making disagreement almost inevitable. As differences arise, be sensitive to each individual's point of view. Do not personalize disagreements, but keep them focused on the literature or ideas under discussion.

When you meet with a group to discuss literature, use a chart like the one shown to analyze the discussion.

Work Being Discussed:	
Focus Question:	
Your Response:	Another Student's Response:
Supporting Evidence:	Supporting Evidence:
One New Idea That You Considered About the Work During the Discussion:	

Tips for Discussing Literature ■ *R-21*

LITERARY CRITICISM

Criticism is writing that explores the meaning and techniques of literary works, usually in order to evaluate them. Writing criticism can help you think through your experience of a work of literature and can also help others deepen their own understanding. All literary criticism shares similar goals:

- **Making Connections** within or between works, or between a work of literature and its context
- **Making Distinctions** or showing differences between elements of a single work or aspects of two or more works
- **Achieving Insights** that were not apparent from a superficial reading
- **Making a Judgment** about the quality or value of a literary work

Critics use various **theories of literary criticism** to understand, appreciate, and evaluate literature. Some theories focus on the context of the work while others focus on the work itself. Sometimes critics combine one or more theories. These charts show a few examples of the many theories of criticism:

Focus on Contexts		Focus on the Work Itself
HUMAN EXPERIENCE	**Mythic Criticism** Explores universal situations, characters, and symbols called archetypes as they appear in a literary work	**Formal Criticism** Shows how the work reflects characteristics of the genre, or literary type, to which it belongs
CULTURE AND HISTORY	**Historic Criticism** Analyzes how circumstances or ideas of an era influence a work	
AUTHOR'S LIFE	**Biographical Criticism** Explains how the author's life sheds light on the work	

Examples of Literary Theories in Action

- **Mythic Criticism:** discussing how Robert Frost's "The Road Not Taken," p. 661, explores the archetypal situation of choice at a fork in the road
- **Historical Criticism:** showing how American frontier life led to the use of exaggeration in "Pecos Bill: The Cyclone," p. 1114
- **Biographical Criticism:** showing that Edgar Allan Poe's loss of his parents at an early age influenced the theme of "The Raven," p. 639
- **Formal Criticism:** showing how "The Scarlet Ibis," p. 350, displays short-story elements like plot, setting, character, symbol, and theme

Apply It To Your Reading

Choose one selection from this textbook and explore it using two different theories of literary criticism. Write an essay explaining how the unique focus of each theory helped you appreciate different aspects of the selection.

LITERARY MOVEMENTS

Our literary heritage has been shaped by a number of **literary movements**, directions in literature characterized by shared assumptions, beliefs, and practices. This chart shows, in chronological order, some important literary movements. While these movements developed at particular historical moments, all of them may still influence individual writers working today.

Movement	Beliefs and Practices	Examples
Classicism Europe during the Renaissance (c. 1300–1650)	• Looks to classical literature of ancient Greece and Rome as models • Values logic, clarity, balance, and restraint • Prefers "ordered" nature of parks and gardens	the clarity and restraint of Robert Frost's verse ("The Road Not Taken," p.661)
Romanticism Europe during the late 1700s and the early 1800s	• Rebels against Classicism • Values imagination and emotion • Focuses on everyday life	the celebration of the natural world in Rachel Carson's writings ("Silent Spring," p. 153)
Realism Europe and America from the mid–1800s to the 1890s	• Rebels against Romanticism's search for the ideal • Focuses on everyday life	the faithful rendering of Pueblo life in Leslie Marmon Silko's fiction ("The Man to Send Rain Clouds," p. 268)
Naturalism Europe and America during the late 1800s and early 1900s	• Assumes people cannot choose their fate but are shaped by psychological and social forces • Views society as a competitive jungle	the portrayal of characters as victims of social pressures and psychology in Guy de Maupassant's fiction ("The Necklace," p. 294)
Modernism World-wide between 1890 and 1945	• In response to WWI, questions human reason • Focuses on studies of the unconscious and the art of primitive peoples • Experiments with language and form	the experiments with language in E. E. Cummings's poetry ("maggie and milly and molly and may," p. 668)
Post-Modernism World-wide after 1945; still prevalent today	• Believes works of art comment on themselves • Finds inspiration in information technology	the self-commentary in Scott McLoud's work ("Understanding Comics," p. 172)

TIPS FOR IMPROVING READING FLUENCY

When you were younger, you learned to read. Then, you read to expand your experiences or for pure enjoyment. Now, you are expected to read to learn. As you progress in school, you are given more and more material to read. The tips on these pages will help you improve your reading fluency, or your ability to read easily, smoothly, and expressively.

Keeping Your Concentration

One common problem that readers face is the loss of concentration. When you are reading an assignment, you might find yourself rereading the same sentence several times without really understanding it. The first step in changing this behavior is to notice that you do it. Becoming an active, aware reader will help you get the most from your assignments. Practice using these strategies:

- Cover what you have already read with a note card as you go along. Then, you will not be able to reread without noticing that you are doing it.

- Set a purpose for reading beyond just completing the assignment. Then, read actively by pausing to ask yourself questions about the material as you read.

- Use the Reading Strategy instruction and notes that appear with each selection in this textbook.

- Stop reading after a specified period of time (for example, 5 minutes) and summarize what you have read. To help you with this strategy, use the Reading Check questions that appear with each selection in this textbook. Reread to find any answers you do not know.

✔ Reading Check

What common problem do many readers face?

Reading Phrases

Fluent readers read phrases rather than individual words. Reading this way will speed up your reading and improve your comprehension. Here are some useful ideas:

- Experts recommend rereading as a strategy to increase fluency. Choose a passage of text that is neither too hard nor too easy. Read the same passage aloud several times until you can read it smoothly. When you can read the passage fluently, pick another passage and keep practicing.

- Read aloud into a tape recorder. Then, listen to the recording, noting your accuracy, pacing, and expression. You can also read aloud and share feedback with a partner.

- Use the *Prentice Hall Listening to Literature* audiotapes or CDs to hear the selections read aloud. Read along silently in your textbook, noticing how the reader uses his or her voice and emphasizes certain words and phrases.

✔ Reading Check

In what ways will reading phrases rather than individual words affect your reading?

Understanding Key Vocabulary

If you do not understand some of the words in an assignment, you may miss out on important concepts. Therefore, it is helpful to keep a dictionary nearby when you are reading. Follow these steps:

- Before you begin reading, scan the text for unfamiliar words or terms. Find out what those words mean before you begin reading.
- Use context—the surrounding words, phrases, and sentences—to help you determine the meanings of unfamiliar words.
- If you are unable to understand the meaning through context, refer to the dictionary.

Paying Attention to Punctuation

When you read, pay attention to punctuation. Commas, periods, exclamation points, semicolons, and colons tell you when to pause or stop. They also indicate relationships between groups of words. When you recognize these relationships you will read with greater understanding and expression. Look at the chart below.

Punctuation Mark	Meaning
comma	brief pause
period	pause at the end of a thought
exclamation point	pause that indicates emphasis
semicolon	pause between related but distinct thoughts
colon	pause before giving explanation or examples

Using the Reading Fluency Checklist

Use the checklist below each time you read a selection in this textbook. In your Language Arts journal or notebook, note which skills you need to work on, and chart your progress each week.

Reading Fluency Checklist

- ☐ Preview the text to check for difficult or unfamiliar words.
- ☐ Practice reading aloud.
- ☐ Read according to punctuation.
- ☐ Break down long sentences into the subject and its meaning.
- ☐ Read groups of words for meaning rather than reading single words.
- ☐ Read with expression (change your tone of voice to add meaning to the word).

Reading is a skill that can be improved with practice. The key to improving your fluency is to read. The more you read, the better your reading will become.

✓ **Reading Check**

Why should you look up words you do not know when reading an assignment?

Tips for Improving Reading Fluency ■ R-25

TYPES OF WRITING

Writing is a process that begins with the exploration of ideas and ends with the presentation of a final draft. Often, the types of writing are grouped into modes according to form and purpose.

NARRATION

Whenever writers tell any type of story, they are using **narration.** Most narratives share certain elements, such as characters, a setting, a sequence of events, and, often, a theme. Following are some types of narration:

Autobiographical Writing Autobiographical writing tells a true story about an important period, experience, or relationship in the writer's life. Effective autobiographical writing includes

- A series of events that involve the writer as the main character
- Details, thoughts, feelings, and insights from the writer's perspective
- A conflict or an event that affects the writer
- A logical organization that tells the story clearly
- Insights that the writer gained from the experience

Types of autobiographical writing include personal narratives, autobiographical sketches, reflective essays, eyewitness accounts, and memoirs.

Short Story A short story is a brief, creative narrative. Most short stories include

- Details that establish the setting in time and place
- A main character who undergoes a change or learns something during the course of the story
- A conflict or a problem to be introduced, developed, and resolved
- A plot, the series of events that make up the action of the story
- A theme or message about life

Types of short stories include realistic stories, fantasies, historical narratives, mysteries, thrillers, science-fiction stories, and adventure stories.

DESCRIPTION

Descriptive writing is writing that creates a vivid picture of a person, place, thing, or event. Most descriptive writing includes

- Sensory details—sights, sounds, smells, tastes, and physical sensations
- Vivid, precise language
- Figurative language or comparisons
- Adjectives and adverbs that paint a word picture
- An organization suited to the subject

Types of descriptive writing include descriptions of ideas, observations, travel brochures, physical descriptions, functional descriptions, remembrances, and character sketches.

PERSUASION

Persuasion is writing or speaking that attempts to convince people to accept a position or take a desired action. Following are some types of persuasion:

Persuasive Essay A persuasive essay presents a position on an issue, urges readers to accept that position, and may encourage a specific action. An effective persuasive essay

- Explores an issue of importance to the writer
- Addresses an issue that is arguable
- Uses facts, examples, statistics, or personal experiences to support a position
- Tries to influence the audience through appeals to the readers' knowledge, experiences, or emotions
- Uses clear organization to present a logical argument

Forms of persuasion include editorials, position papers, persuasive speeches, grant proposals, advertisements, and debates.

Advertisements An advertisement is a planned communication meant to be seen, heard, or read. It attempts to persuade an audience to buy a product or service, accept an idea, or support a cause. Advertisements may appear in printed or broadcast form. An effective advertisement includes

- A memorable slogan to grab the audience's attention
- A call to action
- Persuasive and/or informative text
- Striking visual or aural images
- Informative details about price, location, date, and time

Several common types of advertisements are public-service announcements, billboards, merchandise ads, service ads, and political campaign literature.

EXPOSITION

Exposition is writing that relies on facts to inform or explain. Effective expository writing reflects a well-thought-out organization—one that includes a clear introduction, body, and conclusion. Here are some types of exposition:

Comparison-and-Contrast Essay A comparison-and-contrast essay analyzes the similarities and differences between or among two or more things. An effective comparison-and-contrast essay

- Identifies a purpose for comparison and contrast
- Identifies similarities and differences between or among two or more things, people, places, or ideas
- Gives factual details about the subjects
- Uses an organizational plan suited to the topic and purpose

Cause-and-Effect Essay A cause-and-effect essay examines the relationship between events, explaining how one event or situation causes another. A successful cause-and-effect essay includes

- A discussion of a cause, event, or condition that produces a specific result
- An explanation of an effect, outcome, or result
- Evidence and examples to support the relationship between cause and effect
- A logical organization that makes the explanation clear

Problem-and-Solution Essay A problem-and-solution essay describes a problem and offers one or more solutions to it. It describes a clear set of steps to achieve a result. An effective problem-and-solution essay includes

- A clear statement of the problem, with its causes and effects summarized for the reader
- The most important aspects of the problem
- A proposal of at least one realistic solution
- Facts, statistics, data, or expert testimony to support the solution
- A clear organization that makes the relationship between problem and solution obvious

RESEARCH WRITING

Research writing is based on information gathered from outside sources. A research paper—a focused study of a topic—helps writers explore and connect ideas, make discoveries, and share their findings with an audience. An effective research paper

- Focuses on a specific, narrow topic, which is usually summarized in a thesis statement
- Presents relevant information from a wide variety of sources
- Uses a clear organization that includes an introduction, body, and conclusion
- Includes a bibliography or works-cited list that identifies the sources from which the information was drawn

Other types of writing that depend on accurate and insightful research include multimedia presentations, statistical reports, annotated bibliographies, and experiment journals.

RESPONSE TO LITERATURE

When you write a **response-to-literature essay,** you give yourself the opportunity to discover *what, how,* and *why* a piece of writing affected you. An effective response

- Contains a reaction to a poem, story, essay, or other work of literature
- Analyzes the content of a literary work, its related ideas, or the work's effect on the reader
- Presents a thesis statement to identify the nature of the response
- Focuses on a single aspect of the work or gives a general overview
- Supports opinion with evidence from the work addressed

The following are just a few of the ways you might respond in writing to a literary work: reader's response journals, literary letters, and literary analyses.

WRITING FOR ASSESSMENT

One of the most common types of school **assessment** is the written test. When a test includes an essay, you are expected to write a response that includes

- A clearly stated and well-supported thesis
- Specific information about the topic derived from your reading or from class discussion
- A clear organization

In your school career, you will probably encounter questions that ask you to address each of the following types of writing: explain a process; defend a position; compare, contrast, or categorize; and show cause and effect.

WORKPLACE WRITING

Workplace writing is probably the format you will use most after you finish school. In general, workplace writing is fact-based and meant to communicate specific information in a structured format. Effective workplace writing

- Communicates information concisely
- Includes details that provide necessary information and anticipate potential questions
- Is error-free and neatly presented

Common types of workplace writing include business letters, memorandums, résumés, forms, and applications.

WRITING LETTERS

Writing Friendly Letters

A friendly letter is much less formal than a business letter. It is a letter to a friend, a family member, or anyone with whom the writer wants to communicate in a personal, friendly way. Most friendly letters are made up of five parts:

- the heading
- the salutation, or greeting
- the body
- the closing
- the signature

The purpose of a friendly letter is often one of the following:

- to share personal news and feelings
- to send or to answer an invitation
- to express thanks

Model Friendly Letter

In this friendly letter, Betsy thanks her grandparents for a birthday present and gives them some news about her life.

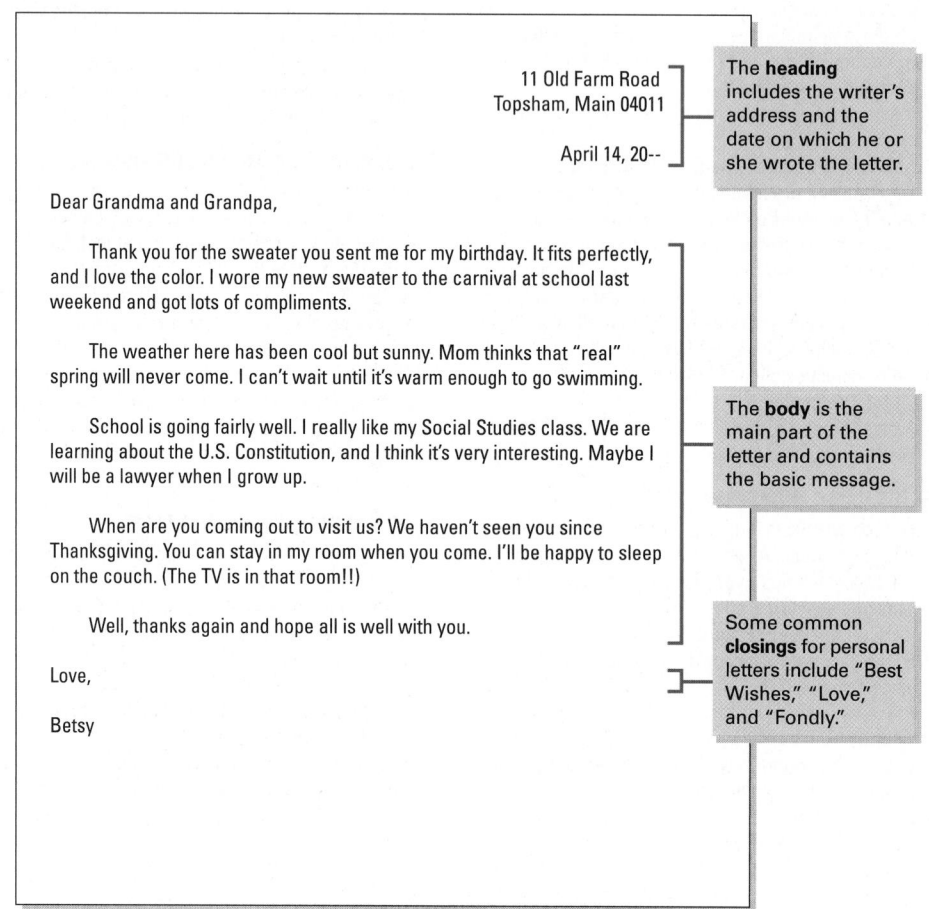

11 Old Farm Road
Topsham, Main 04011

April 14, 20--

The **heading** includes the writer's address and the date on which he or she wrote the letter.

Dear Grandma and Grandpa,

Thank you for the sweater you sent me for my birthday. It fits perfectly, and I love the color. I wore my new sweater to the carnival at school last weekend and got lots of compliments.

The weather here has been cool but sunny. Mom thinks that "real" spring will never come. I can't wait until it's warm enough to go swimming.

School is going fairly well. I really like my Social Studies class. We are learning about the U.S. Constitution, and I think it's very interesting. Maybe I will be a lawyer when I grow up.

When are you coming out to visit us? We haven't seen you since Thanksgiving. You can stay in my room when you come. I'll be happy to sleep on the couch. (The TV is in that room!!)

Well, thanks again and hope all is well with you.

Love,

Betsy

The **body** is the main part of the letter and contains the basic message.

Some common **closings** for personal letters include "Best Wishes," "Love," and "Fondly."

Formatting Business Letters

Business letters follow one of several acceptable formats. In **block format,** each part of the letter begins at the left margin. A double space is used between paragraphs. In **modified block format,** some parts of the letter are indented to the center of the page. No matter which format is used, all letters in business format have a heading, an inside address, a salutation, or greeting, a body, a closing, and a signature. These parts are shown and annotated on the model business letter below, formatted in modified block style.

Model Business Letter

In this letter, Yolanda Dodson uses modified block format to request information.

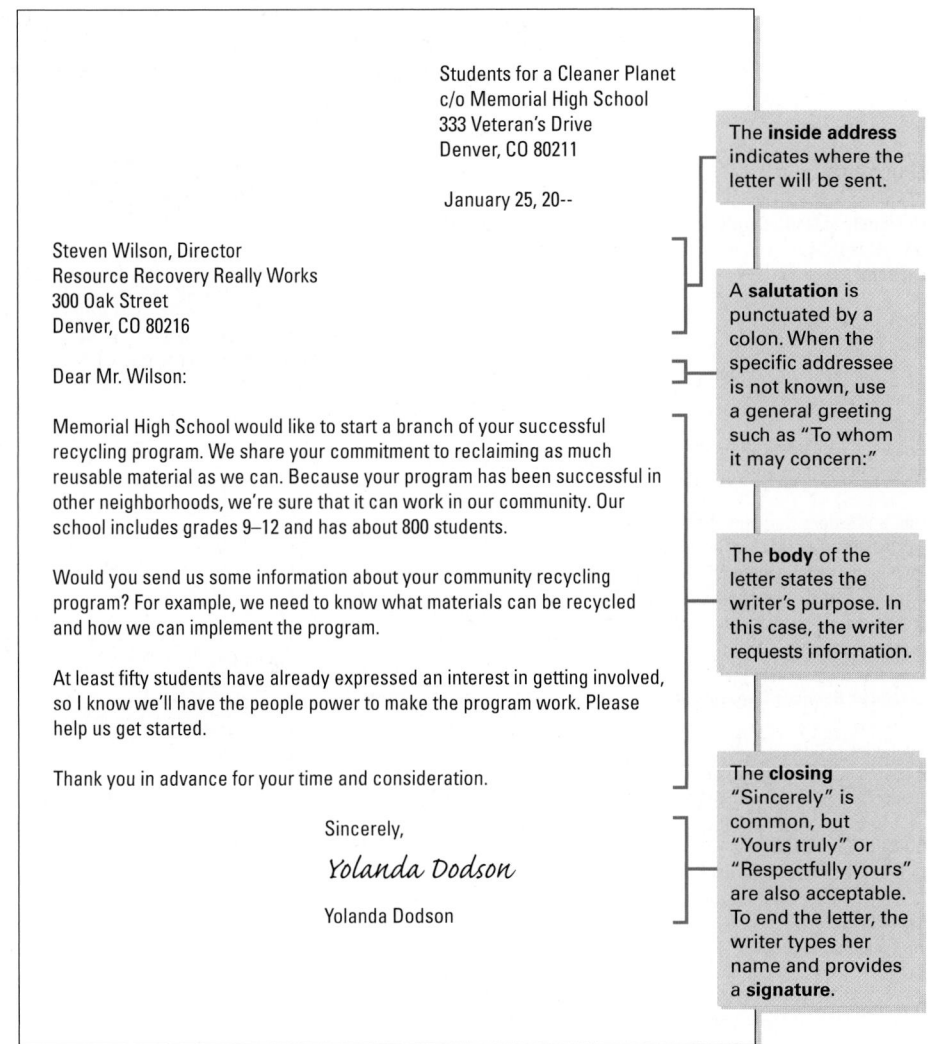

Students for a Cleaner Planet
c/o Memorial High School
333 Veteran's Drive
Denver, CO 80211

January 25, 20--

Steven Wilson, Director
Resource Recovery Really Works
300 Oak Street
Denver, CO 80216

Dear Mr. Wilson:

Memorial High School would like to start a branch of your successful recycling program. We share your commitment to reclaiming as much reusable material as we can. Because your program has been successful in other neighborhoods, we're sure that it can work in our community. Our school includes grades 9–12 and has about 800 students.

Would you send us some information about your community recycling program? For example, we need to know what materials can be recycled and how we can implement the program.

At least fifty students have already expressed an interest in getting involved, so I know we'll have the people power to make the program work. Please help us get started.

Thank you in advance for your time and consideration.

Sincerely,

Yolanda Dodson

Yolanda Dodson

The **inside address** indicates where the letter will be sent.

A **salutation** is punctuated by a colon. When the specific addressee is not known, use a general greeting such as "To whom it may concern:"

The **body** of the letter states the writer's purpose. In this case, the writer requests information.

The **closing** "Sincerely" is common, but "Yours truly" or "Respectfully yours" are also acceptable. To end the letter, the writer types her name and provides a **signature.**

Formatting Business Letters ■ R-29

WRITING A RÉSUMÉ

A résumé summarizes your educational background, work experiences, relevant skills, and other employment qualifications. It also tells potential employers how to contact you. An effective résumé presents the applicant's name, address, and phone number. It follows an accepted résumé organization, using labels and headings to guide readers. A résumé should outline the applicant's educational background, life experiences, and related qualifications using precise and active language.

Model Résumé

With this résumé, James, a college student, hopes to find a full-time job.

James H. McSweeney
1234 Greene Street, Apt. #3
Charlotte, NC 28223
jamesmcswe@email.com

EDUCATION

University of North Carolina; Charlotte, NC
Bachelor of Science in Administrative Information Management
Expected; June 20 _ _

WORK EXPERIENCE

P.E.S. Engineering; Charlotte, NC
Summer 2005
Intern
Designed a customized record management system for the engineers; trained in the data entry department.

Gen X Wireless Services; Paramus, NJ
2003–2005 (summers and breaks)
Receivables Management Representative
Handled incoming accounts-receivable calls for cellular phone accounts in the New York, New Jersey, and Connecticut markets; trained other representatives.

Computer Services Department; University of North Carolina, Charlotte, NC
Fall 2004
Computer Lab Technician
Assisted students in the use of software and hardware; responded to user questions and problems.

COMPUTER SKILLS
HTML, XML, Excel, Microsoft Access, and Microsoft Office

REFERENCES
Furnished on request

Put contact information such as name, address, telephone number, and e-mail address at the top of the résumé.

James uses heads with capital letters to identify each section of his résumé.

Entries on résumés should be short and to the point.

USING THE INTERNET

Introduction to the Internet

The Internet is a series of networks that are interconnected all over the world. The Internet allows users to have almost unlimited access to information stored on the networks. Dr. Berners-Lee, a physicist, created the Internet in the 1980s by writing a small computer program that allowed pages to be linked together using key words. The Internet was mostly text-based until 1992, when a computer program called the NCSA Mosaic (National Center for Supercomputing Applications) was created at the University of Illinois. This program was the first Web browser. The development of Web browsers greatly eased the ability of the user to navigate through all the pages stored on the Web. Very soon, the appearance of the Web was altered as well. More appealing visuals were added, and sound, too, was implemented. This change made the Web more user-friendly and more appealing to the general public.

Using the Internet for Research

Key Word Search

Before you begin a search, you should identify your specific topic. To make searching easier, narrow your subject to a key word or a group of key words. These are your search terms, and they should be as specific as possible. For example, if you are looking for the latest concert dates for your favorite musical group, you might use the band's name as a key word. However, if you were to enter the name of the group in the query box of the search engine, you might be presented with thousands of links to information about the group that is unrelated to what you want to know. You might locate such information as band member biographies, the group's history, fan reviews of concerts, and hundreds of sites with related names containing information that is irrelevant to your search. Because you used such a broad key word, you might need to navigate through all that information before you could find a link or subheading for concert dates. In contrast, if you were to type in "Duplex Arena and [band name]," you would have a better chance of locating pages that contain this information.

How to Narrow Your Search

If you have a large group of key words and still do not know which ones to use, write out a list of all the words you are considering. Once you have completed the list, scrutinize it. Then, delete the words that are least important to your search, and highlight those that are most important.

These **key search connectors** can help you fine-tune your search:

AND: Narrows a search by retrieving documents that include both terms. For example: *baseball* AND *playoffs*

OR: Broadens a search by retrieving documents including any of the terms. For example: *play-offs* OR *championships*

NOT: Narrows a search by excluding documents containing certain words. For example: *baseball* NOT *history of*

Tips for an Effective Search

1. Remember that search engines can be case-sensitive. If your first attempt at searching fails, check your search terms for misspellings and try again.

2. If you are entering a group of key words, present them in order from the most important to the least important key word.

3. Avoid opening the link to every single page in your results list. Search engines present pages in descending order of relevancy. The most useful pages will be located at the top of the list. However, read the description of each link before you open the page.

4. Some search engines provide helpful tips for specializing your search. Take the opportunity to learn more about effective searching.

Other Ways to Search

Using Online Reference Sites How you search should be tailored to what you are hoping to find. If you are looking for data and facts, use reference sites before you jump onto a simple search engine. For example, you can find reference sites to provide definitions of words, statistics about almost any subject, biographies, maps, and concise information on many topics. Here are some useful online reference sites:

Online libraries

Online periodicals

Almanacs

Encyclopedias

You can find these sources using subject searches.

Using the Internet ■ *R-31*

Conducting Subject Searches As you prepare to go online, consider your subject and the best way to find information to suit your needs. If you are looking for general information on a topic and you want your search results to be extensive, consider the subject search indexes on most search engines. These indexes, in the form of category and subject lists, often appear on the first page of a search engine. When you click on a specific highlighted word, you will be presented with a new screen containing subcategories of the topic you chose.

Evaluating the Reliability of Internet Resources

Just as you would evaluate the quality, bias, and validity of any other research material you locate, check the source of information you find online. Compare these two sites containing information about the poet and writer Langston Hughes:

Site A is a personal Web site constructed by a college student. It contains no bibliographic information or links to sites that he used. Included on the site are several poems by Langston Hughes and a student essay about the poet's use of symbolism. It has not been updated in more than six months.

Site B is a Web site constructed and maintained by the English Department of a major university. Information on Hughes is presented in a scholarly format, with a bibliography and credits for the writer. The site includes links to other sites and indicates new features that are added weekly.

For your own research, consider the information you find on Site B to be more reliable and accurate than that on Site A. Because it is maintained by experts in their field who are held accountable for their work, the university site will be a better research tool than the student-generated one.

Tips for Evaluating Internet Sources

1. Consider who constructed and who now maintains the Web page. Determine whether this author is a reputable source. Often, the URL endings indicate a source.

   • Sites ending in *.edu* are maintained by educational institutions.

   • Sites ending in *.gov* are maintained by government agencies (federal, state, or local).

   • Sites ending in *.org* are normally maintained by nonprofit organizations and agencies.

   • Sites ending in *.com* are commercially or personally maintained.

2. Skim the official and trademarked Web pages first. It is safe to assume that the information you draw from Web pages of reputable institutions, online encyclopedias, online versions of major daily newspapers, or government-owned sites produce information as reliable as the material you would find in print. In contrast, unbranded sites or those generated by individuals tend to borrow information from other sources without providing documentation. As information travels from one source to another, it could have been muddled, misinterpreted, edited, or revised.

3. You can still find valuable information in the less "official" sites. Check for the writer's credentials, and then consider these factors:

   • Do not be misled by official-looking graphics or presentations.

   • Make sure that the information is updated enough to suit your needs. Many Web pages will indicate how recently they have been updated.

   • If the information is borrowed, notice whether you can trace it back to its original source.

Respecting Copyrighted Material

Because the Internet is a relatively new and quickly growing medium, issues of copyright and ownership arise almost daily. As laws begin to govern the use and reuse of material posted online, they may change the way that people can access or reprint material.

Text, photographs, music, and fine art printed online may not be reproduced without acknowledged permission of the copyright owner.

CITING SOURCES AND PREPARING MANUSCRIPT

In research writing, cite your sources. In the body of your paper, provide a footnote, an endnote, or a parenthetical citation, identifying the sources of facts, opinions, or quotations. At the end of your paper, provide a bibliography or a works-cited list, a list of all the sources you cite. Follow an established format, such as Modern Language Association (MLA) Style.

Works-Cited List (MLA Style)

A works-cited list must contain accurate information sufficient to enable a reader to locate each source you cite. The basic components of an entry are as follows:

- Name of the author, editor, translator, or group responsible for the work
- Title of the work
- Place and date of publication
- Publisher

For print materials, the information required for a citation generally appears on the copyright and title pages of a work. For the format of works-cited list entries, consult the examples at right and in the chart on page R34.

Parenthetical Citations (MLA Style)

A parenthetical citation briefly identifies the source from which you have taken a specific quotation, factual claim, or opinion. It refers the reader to one of the entries on your works-cited list. A parenthetical citation has the following features:

- It appears in parentheses.
- It identifies the source by the last name of the author, editor, or translator.
- It gives a page reference, identifying the page of the source on which the information cited can be found.

Punctuation A parenthetical citation generally falls outside a closing quotation mark but within the final punctuation of a clause or sentence. For a long quotation set off from the rest of your text, place the citation at the end of the excerpt without any punctuation following.

Special Cases

- If the author is an organization, use the organization's name, in a shortened version if necessary.
- If you cite more than one work by the same author, add the title or a shortened version of the title.

Sample Works-Cited Lists

Carwardine, Mark, Erich Hoyt, R. Ewan Fordyce, and Peter Gill. *The Nature Company Guides: Whales, Dolphins, and Porpoises.* New York: Time-Life Books, 1998.

Whales in Danger. "Discovering Whales." 18 Oct 1999. <http://whales. magna.com.au/DISCOVER>

Neruda, Pablo. *"Ode to Spring." Odes to Opposites.* Trans. Ken Krabbenhoft. Ed. and illus. Ferris Cook. Boston: Little, Brown and Company, 1995.

The Saga of the Volsungs. Trans. Jesse L. Byock. London: Penguin Books, 1990.

List an anonymous work by title

List both the title of the work and the title of the collection in which it is found.

Sample Parenthetical Citations

It makes sense that baleen whales such as the blue whale, the bowhead whale, the humpback whale, and the sei whale (to name just a few) grow to immense sizes (Carwardine, Hoyt, and Fordyce 19–21). The blue whale has grooves running from under its chin to partway along the length of its underbelly. As in some other whales, these grooves expand and allow even more food and water to be taken in (Ellis 18–21).

Author's last name

Page numbers where information can be found

Writing Handbook

MLA Style for Listing Sources

Book with one author	Pyles, Thomas. *The Origins and Development of the English Language.* 2nd ed. New York: Harcourt Brace Jovanovich, Inc., 1971.
Book with two or three authors	McCrum, Robert, William Cran, and Robert MacNeil. *The Story of English.* New York: Penguin Books, 1987.
Book with an editor	Truth, Sojourner. *Narrative of Sojourner Truth.* Ed. Margret Washington. New York: Vintage Books, 1993.
Book with more than three authors or editors	Donald, Robert B., et al. *Writing Clear Essays.* Upper Saddle River, NJ: Prentice-Hall, Inc., 1996.
Single work from an anthology	Hawthorne, Nathaniel. "Young Goodman Brown." *Literature: An Introduction to Reading and Writing.* Ed. Edgar V. Roberts and Henry E. Jacobs. Upper Saddle River, NJ: Prentice-Hall, Inc., 1998. 376–385.
Introduction in a published edition	Washington, Margaret. Introduction. *Narrative of Sojourner Truth.* By Sojourner Truth. New York: Vintage Books, 1993. v–xi.
Signed article in a weekly magazine	Wallace, Charles. "A Vodacious Deal." *Time* Feb. 2000: 63.
Signed article in a monthly magazine	Gustaitis, Joseph. "The Sticky History of Chewing Gum." *American History* Oct. 1998: 30–38.
Unsigned editorial or story	"Selective Silence" Editorial. *Wall Street Journal* 11 Feb. 2000: A14.
Signed pamphlet	[Treat the pamphlet as though it were a book.]
Pamphlet with no author, publisher, or date	*Are You at Risk of Heart Attack?* n.p.n.d. [n.p.n.d. indicates that there is no known publisher or date.]
Filmstrips, slide programs, and videotapes	*The Diary of Anne Frank.* Dir. George Stevens. Perf. Millie Perkins, Shelley Winters, Joseph Schildkraut, Lou Jacobi, and Richard Beymer. Twentieth Century Fox, 1959.
Radio or television program transcript	"Nobel for Literature." Narr. Rick Karr. *All Things Considered.* National Public Radio. WNYC, New York. 10 Oct. 2002. Transcript.
Internet	National Association of Chewing Gum Manufacturers. 19 Dec. 1999. <http://www.nacgm.org/consumer/funfacts.html> [Indicate the date you accessed the information. Content and addresses at Web sites change frequently.]
Newspaper	Thurow, Roger. "South Africans Who Fought for Sanctions Now Scrap for Investors." *Wall Street Journal* Feb. 2000: A1+ [For a multipage article, write only the first page number on which it appears, followed by a plus sign.]
Personal interview	Smith, Jane. Personal interview. 10 Feb. 2000.
CD (with multiple publishers)	Simms, James, ed. *Romeo and Juliet.* By William Shakespeare. CD-ROM. Oxford: Attica Cybernetics LTD.; London: BBC Education; London: HarperCollins Publishers, 1995.
Signed article from an encyclopedia	Askeland, Donald R. "Welding." *World Book Encyclopedia.* 1991 ed.

GUIDE TO RUBRICS

What is a rubric?

A rubric is a tool, often in the form of a chart or a grid, that helps you assess your work. Rubrics are particularly helpful for writing and speaking assignments.

To help you or others assess, or evaluate, your work, a rubric offers several specific criteria to be applied to your work. Then, the rubric helps you or an evaluator indicate your range of success or failure according to those specific criteria. Rubrics are often used to evaluate writing for standardized tests.

Using a rubric will save you time, focus your learning, and improve the work you do. When you know what the rubric will be before you begin writing a persuasive essay, for example, you will be aware as you write of specific criteria that are important in that kind of essay. As you evaluate the essay before giving it to your teacher, you will focus on the specific areas that your teacher wants you to master—or on areas that you know present challenges for you. Instead of searching through your work randomly for any way to improve it or correct its errors, you will have a clear and helpful focus on specific criteria.

How are rubrics constructed?

Rubrics can be constructed in several different ways.

- Your teacher may assign a rubric for a specific assignment.
- Your teacher may direct you to a rubric in your textbook.
- Your teacher and your class may construct a rubric for a particular assignment together.
- You and your classmates may construct a rubric together.
- You may create your own rubric with criteria you want to evaluate in your work.

How will a rubric help me?

A rubric will help you assess your work on a scale. Scales vary from rubric to rubric but usually range from 6 to 1, 5 to 1, or 4 to 1, with 6, 5, or 4 being the highest score and 1 being the lowest. If someone else is using the rubric to assess your work, the rubric will give your evaluator a clear range within which to place your work. If you are using the rubric yourself, it will help you make improvements to your work.

What are the types of rubrics?

- A **holistic rubric** has general criteria that can apply to a variety of assignments. See p. R-37 for an example of a holistic rubric.
- An **analytic rubric** is specific to a particular assignment. The criteria for evaluation address the specific issues important in that assignment. See p. R-36 for examples of analytic rubrics.

Sample Analytic Rubrics

Rubric With a 4-point Scale

The following analytic rubric is an example of a rubric to assess a persuasive essay. It will help you evaluate focus, organization, support/elaboration, and style/convention.

	Focus	Organization	Support/Elaboration	Style/Convention
4	Demonstrates highly effective word choice; clearly focused on task.	Uses clear, consistent organization strategy.	Provides convincing, well-elaborated reasons to support the position.	Incorporates transitions; includes very few mechanical errors.
3	Demonstrates good word choice; stays focused on persuasive task.	Uses clear organizational strategy with occasional inconsistencies.	Provides two or more moderately elaborated reasons to support the position.	Incorporates some transitions; includes few mechanical errors.
2	Shows some good word choices; minimally focused on persuasive task.	Uses inconsistent organizational strategy; presentation is not logical.	Provides several reasons, but few are elaborated.	Incorporates few transitions; includes many mechanical errors.
1	Shows lack of attention to persuasive task.	Demonstrates lack of organizational strategy.	Provides no specific reasons or does not elaborate.	Does not connect ideas; includes many mechanical errors.

Rubric With a 6-point Scale

The following analytic rubric is an example of a rubric to assess a persuasive essay. It will help you evaluate presentation, position, evidence, and arguments.

	Presentation	Position	Evidence	Arguments
6	Essay clearly and effectively addresses an issue with more than one side.	Essay clearly states a supportable position on the issue.	All evidence is logically organized, well presented, and supports the position.	All reader concerns and counterarguments are effectively addressed.
5	Most of essay addresses an issue that has more than one side.	Essay clearly states a position on the issue.	Most evidence is logically organized, well presented, and supports the position.	Most reader concerns and counterarguments are effectively addressed.
4	Essay adequately addresses issue that has more than one side.	Essay adequately states a position on the issue.	Many parts of evidence support the position; some evidence is out of order.	Many reader concerns and counterarguments are adequately addressed.
3	Essay addresses issue with two sides but does not present second side clearly.	Essay states a position on the issue, but the position is difficult to support.	Some evidence supports the position, but some evidence is out of order.	Some reader concerns and counterarguments are addressed.
2	Essay addresses issue with two sides but does not present second side.	Essay states a position on the issue, but the position is not supportable.	Not much evidence supports the position, and what is included is out of order.	A few reader concerns and counterarguments are addressed.
1	Essay does not addresses issue with more than one side.	Essay does not state a position on the issue.	No evidence supports the position.	No reader concerns or counterarguments are addressed.

Points	Criteria
6 Points	• The writing is strongly focused and shows fresh insight into the writing task. • The writing is marked by a sense of completeness and coherence and is organized with a logical progression of ideas. • A main idea is fully developed, and support is specific and substantial. • A mature command of the language is evident, and the writing may employ characteristic creative writing strategies. • Sentence structure is varied, and writing is free of all but purposefully used fragments. • Virtually no errors in writing conventions appear.
5 Points	• The writing is clearly focused on the task. • The writing is well organized and has a logical progression of ideas, though there may be occasional lapses. • A main ideas is well developed and supported with relevant detail. • Command of the language is mature. • Sentence structure is varied, and the writing is free of fragments, except when used purposefully. • Writing conventions are followed correctly.
4 Points	• The writing is clearly focused on the task, but extraneous material may intrude at times. • Clear organizational pattern is present, though lapses may occur. • A main ideas is adequately supported, but development may be uneven. • Command of the language is mature. • Sentence structure is generally fragment free but shows little variation. • Writing conventions are generally followed correctly.
3 Points	• Writing is generally focused on the task, but extraneous material may intrude at times. • An organizational pattern is evident, but writing may lack a logical progression of ideas. • Support for the main idea is generally present but is sometimes illogical. • Sentence structure is generally free of fragments, but there is almost no variation. • The work generally demonstrates a knowledge of writing conventions, with occasional misspellings.
2 Points	• The writing is related to the task but generally lacks focus. • There is little evidence of organizational pattern, and there is little sense of cohesion. • Support for the main idea is generally inadequate, illogical, or absent. • Sentence structure is unvaried, and serious errors may occur. • Errors in writing conventions and spellings are frequent.
1 Point	• Writing is generally focused on the task, but extraneous material may intrude at times. • An organizational pattern is evident, but writing may lack a logical progression of ideas. • Support for the main idea is generally present but is sometimes illogical. • Sentence structure is generally free of fragments, but there is almost no variation. • The work generally demonstrates a knowledge of writing conventions, with occasional misspellings.
Unscorable	The paper is considered unscorable if: • The response is unrelated to the task or is simply a rewording of the prompt. • The response has been copied from a published work. • The student did not write a response. • The response is illegible. • The words in the response are arranged with no meaning. • There is an insufficient amount of writing to score.

Guide to Rubrics ■ R-37

STUDENT MODEL
Persuasive Writing

This persuasive letter, which would receive a top score according to a persuasive rubric, is a response to the following writing prompt, or assignment:

With the increased use of technology in the workplace, the skills that high-school graduates must possess have changed. Write a letter to your principal advocating new technology courses that could give high-school graduates a competitive edge.

Dear Principal:

I am writing to alert you to an urgent need in our school's curriculum. We need computer graphics courses!

Although you would have to find funds to buy the equipment, I've concluded that setting up this course would be well worth it. By adding this course, you would be adding many high paying career options for students. Computer graphics is a type of art, and businesses all around us involve art in some form. You see computer graphics in commercials, movies, news broadcasts, weather broadcasts, architectural design, and business presentations. Workers with computer graphics skills are well paid because they are in such high demand.

> The letter begins with an engaging introduction that clearly states the persuasive focus.

You may argue that the school already has computer science classes. Good point! I'm in a computer science class and it is mainly programming. Once we did have an assignment to design a graphic of a pumpkin. You wouldn't believe how much coding it takes to get a simple, animated drawing. In order to get a really creative image with definite lines, shading, lifelike colors, and texture, you need to use computer graphics software designed especially for that purpose. With software, you can make images that move and talk smoothly and environments with realistic colors and lighting. This is the same graphics software that businesses use for commercials, movies, and brochures. Students should be learning how to use this software.

> The author effectively counters an opposing argument to increase the persuasive power of her own argument.

Most important, computer graphics is a subject area that allows students to express their creativity. Adding a computer graphics course would have a positive effect on students. Course participants would enjoy doing their assignments, so they would earn good grades and turn in creative work. The energy and enthusiasm they would bring to their projects would catch the attention of the community at large. As a result, they would make the school and the principal look good.

> A positive argument that is well supported enhances the letter's persuasive appeal.

As you can see, adding a computer graphics course could be a very profitable idea for you, the students, and the community. You would be ensuring the success of the students who desire an art or computer career. You would be opening hundreds of different career pathways. Wouldn't it be great to know you were the reason for these students' success? Thanks for your time and consideration.

Sincerely,
Dawn Witherspoon

GRAMMAR, USAGE, AND MECHANICS

Parts of Speech

Nouns

A **noun** names a person, place, or thing. **Common nouns** name any one of a class of people, places, or things. **Proper nouns** name specific people, places, or things.

Common Noun	Proper Noun
city	Washington, D.C.

Exercise A Distinguishing Between Common and Proper Nouns. Write the one proper noun in each group, adding the necessary capitalization.

1. planet	neptune	star
2. jurassic period	dinosaurs	jaw
3. biology	high school	science 9
4. june	spring	month
5. dandelion	mothers	mothers' day

Pronouns

A **pronoun** is a word that stands for a noun or for a word that takes the place of a noun.

A **personal pronoun** refers to (1) the person speaking, (2) the person spoken to, or (3) the person, place, or thing spoken about.

	Singular	Plural
First Person	I, me, my, mine	we, us, our, ours
Second Person	you, your, yours	you, your, yours
Third Person	he, him, his, she, her, hers, it, its	they, them, their, theirs

Exercise B Identifying and Using Personal Pronouns. Write the personal pronoun or pronouns in each sentence. Then, write a new sentence, using the same personal pronoun or pronouns.

1. John does his homework before the game.
2. "Dad, can you take Reggie to the baseball game?" Jayne asked.
3. When the bus arrives, it is always late.
4. Patrick asked Sarah if she had his baseball glove.
5. Gregory brought his bat with him.

A **reflexive pronoun** ends in *-self* or *-selves* and adds information to a sentence by pointing back to a noun or pronoun earlier in the sentence.

As I said these words I busied *myself* among the pile of bones of which I have before spoken.

—"The Cask of Amontillado," p. 61

An **intensive pronoun** ends in *-self* or *-selves* and simply adds emphasis to a noun or a pronoun in the same sentence.

The best playground, however, was the dark alley *itself*.

—"Rules of the Game," p. 305

Exercise C Distinguishing Between Reflexive and Intensive Pronouns. Write the reflexive or intensive pronoun in each sentence. Then, label each one reflexive or intensive.

1. Mardi Gras itself has become an event.
2. It was originally intended to allow people to enjoy themselves before a time of fasting.
3. If you yourself have ever attended one, you know it is a week-long celebration.
4. Participants dress themselves in colorful costumes.
5. The mayor himself attends the festivities.

Demonstrative pronouns (*this, these, that,* and *those*) direct attention to a specific person, place, or thing.

These are the juiciest pears I have ever tasted.

A **relative pronoun** begins a subordinate (relative) clause and connects it to another idea in the sentence.

The poet *who* wrote "Fire and Ice" is Robert Frost.

The poet *whom* I admire is Frost.

An **interrogative pronoun** is used to begin a question. The five interrogative pronouns are *what, which, who, whom, whose.*

Exercise D Recognizing Demonstrative, Relative, and Interrogative Pronouns. Write the pronoun in each sentence. Then, label each one demonstrative, reflexive, or interrogative.

1. Mardi Gras is a carnival that is held before Lent.
2. This is the grand finale of a long carnival season.
3. Mardi Gras, which is a French tradition, was introduced to the United States in the 1700s.
4. This is a holiday in a few states.
5. Which of the states has a famous celebration?

An **indefinite pronoun** refers to a person, place, or thing, often without specifying which one.

Some of the flowers were in bloom.

Everybody chose something.

Grammar, Usage, and Mechanics ■ R-39

Answers
Grammar, Usage, and Mechanics

Exercise A
1. Neptune
2. Jurassic Period
3. Science 9
4. June
5. Mothers' Day

Exercise B
Make sure that students use the personal pronouns correctly in their sentences.
1. his
2. you
3. it
4. she, his
5. his, him

Exercise C
1. itself: intensive
2. themselves: reflexive
3. yourself: intensive
4. themselves: reflexive
5. himself: intensive

Exercise D
1. that: relative
2. This: demonstrative
3. which: relative
4. This: demonstrative
5. Which: interrogative

Exercise E

1. no one
2. somebody
3. someone
4. Many
5. everyone

Exercise F

1. occurred: intransitive
2. ruled: intransitive
3. overthrew: transitive
4. lived: intransitive
5. reflected: transitive

Exercise G

1. was links *mission* to *successful*
2. may be links *It* to *mission*
3. were links *men* to *aboard*
4. felt links *astronauts* to *concerned*
5. became links *correction* to *solution*

Exercise H

1. may have
2. should have
3. would
4. can
5. had

Exercise E Identifying Indefinite Pronouns. Write the indefinite pronoun or pronouns in each sentence.

1. Before 1900, no one moved Ferris wheels from place to place.
2. Eventually, somebody working for the Eli Bridge Company started making portable Ferris wheels.
3. This someone was William E. Sullivan.
4. Many were sold to carnivals that wanted to travel.
5. Now, everyone could enjoy a ride on a Ferris wheel.

Verbs

A **verb** is a word that expresses time while showing an action, a condition, or the fact that something exists.

An **action verb** indicates the action of someone or something.

An action verb is **transitive** if it directs action toward someone or something named in the same sentence.

Marcos accepted their bouquets . . .

—"Uncle Marcos," p. 133

An action verb is **intransitive** if it does not direct action toward something or someone named in the same sentence.

"He nodded and smiled a lot."

—"American History," p. 202

Exercise F Recognizing Transitive and Intransitive Verbs. Write the action verb in each sentence, and then label it transitive or intransitive.

1. The fall of the Shang dynasty occurred about 1000 B.C.
2. The last Shang monarch ruled unjustly.
3. The king of Chou overthrew him.
4. The people of Chou lived on the northwestern fringes of the Shang domain.
5. The Chou culture reflected the influence of the Shang civilization.

A **linking verb** is a verb that connects the subject of a sentence with a noun or pronoun that renames or describes the subject. All linking verbs are intransitive.

Life *is* a broken-winged bird . . .

—"Dreams," p. 567

Exercise G Identifying Linking Verbs. Write each sentence, underlining the linking verb. Then, draw a double-headed arrow to show which words are linked by the verb.

1. The *Apollo 13* mission was successful.
2. It may be the most famous lunar-landing mission.
3. These men were aboard during an explosion on the module.
4. The astronauts felt concerned after sensing the explosion.
5. A minor mid-course correction became the only solution.

A **helping verb** is a verb that can be added to another verb to make a verb phrase.

Nor *did* I suspect that these experiences could be part of a novel's meaning.

Exercise H Identifying Helping Verbs. Write the helping verb(s) in each sentence.

1. The *Apollo 13* mission may have been the most exciting in history.
2. The mission should have proceeded normally.
3. However, problems would arise from an electrical surge.
4. An electrical surge can cause an explosion and a fire.
5. The crew had quickly moved to the lunar module.

Adjectives

An **adjective** describes a noun or a pronoun or gives a noun or a pronoun a more specific meaning. Adjectives answer these questions:

What kind?	*blue* lamp, *large* tree
Which one?	*this* table, *those* books
How many?	*five* stars, *several* buses
How much?	*less* money, *enough* votes

The articles *the, a,* and *an* are adjectives. *An* is used before a word beginning with a vowel sound.

A noun may sometimes be used as an adjective.

diamond necklace   *summer* vacation

Exercise I Identifying Adjectives and the Words They Modify.
Identify each adjective in the following sentences. Then, indicate the word each adjective modifies and the question that it answers.

1. Small work boats were sailed extensively for pleasure in early colonial times.
2. The first pleasure schooner was built in 1816.
3. It was built specifically as a large, luxurious yacht.
4. American yacht clubs started around the 1840s.
5. Six members of the New York Yacht Club financed America's first racing yacht.

Adverbs

An **adverb** modifies a verb, an adjective, or another adverb. Adverbs answer the questions *Where? When? In what way?* or *To what extent?*

He could stand *there*. (modifies verb *stand*)

He was *blissfully* happy. (modifies adjective *happy*)

It ended *too* soon. (modifies adverb *soon*)

Exercise J Identifying Adverbs.
Identify each adverb and tell which question it answers: *Where? When? In what way?* or *To what extent?*

1. The Maya were very accomplished astronomers.
2. Their primary interest was in carefully observing Zenithal Passages.
3. A special event occurred when the sun crossed directly over the Mayan latitudes.
4. The sun travels annually to its summer solstice point, latitude 23⅓ degrees north.
5. Mayan cities were always located south of this point.

Prepositions

A **preposition** relates a noun or a pronoun that appears with it to another word in the sentence.

the scene *before* the end   stood *near* me

Exercise K Identifying Prepositions.
Write each sentence, replacing the underlined preposition with another preposition that makes sense.

1. Does the basketball season generally come before the football season?
2. The standard length of a basketball court is 94 feet, and the width is 50 feet.
3. A basket attached to a backboard hangs over each end of the court.
4. Her free throw hit the backboard above the basket, and she failed to score.
5. A player can advance the ball only with dribbling or with passing.

Conjunctions

A **conjunction** connects other words or groups of words.

A **coordinating conjunction** connects similar kinds or groups of words.

mother *and* father   simple *yet* stylish

Correlative conjunctions are used in pairs to connect similar words or groups of words.

both Sue *and* Meg   *neither* he *nor* I

A **subordinating conjunction** connects two complete ideas by placing one idea below the other in rank or importance.

You would know him *if* you saw him.

Exercise L Identifying Conjunctions.
Write the conjunction(s) in each sentence. Then, label each one coordinating, correlative, or subordinating. Write *none* if a sentence contains no conjunction.

1. The term *environment* refers to the surroundings of either an individual organism or a community or organisms.
2. The word *surroundings* refers to all living and non-living materials around an organism.
3. An organism is influenced not only by its immediate surroundings but also by physical forces.
4. When we use the word *environment*, we often think about the adverse effects of human activities.
5. After a ship struck a sandbar, an oil spill occurred.

Interjections

An **interjection** expresses feeling or emotion and functions independently of a sentence.

"*Oh*, my poor, poor, Mathilde!"

—"The Necklace," p. 294

Exercise M Supplying Interjections.
Write each sentence, adding an interjection that conveys the indicated emotion.

1. (disappointment) Look at the garbage left on the ground.
2. (delight) The park certainly is cleaner since the town provided more garbage cans.
3. (happiness) Here comes the recycling truck at last.
4. (pain) I stumbled on that tree root.
5. (annoyance) I missed the trash can.

Grammar, Usage, and Mechanics ■ R-41

Exercise I

1. Small, work—boats, what kind; early, colonial—times, which one
2. first—schooner, which one; pleasure—schooner, what kind
3. large, luxurious—yacht, what kind
4. American, yacht—clubs, what kind
5. Six—members, how many; first—yacht, which one; racing—yacht, what kind

Exercise J

1. very, To what extent?
2. carefully, In what way?
3. directly, Where?
4. annually, When?
5. always, When?

Exercise K

Sample answers:

1. Does the basketball season generally come <u>after</u> the football season?
2. The standard length <u>for</u> a basketball court is 94 feet, and the width is 50 feet.
3. A basket attached to a backboard hangs <u>above</u> each end of the court.
4. Her free throw hit the backboard <u>over</u> the basket, and she failed to score.
5. A player can advance the ball only by dribbling or <u>by</u> passing.

Exercise L

1. either . . . or, correlative
2. and, coordinating
3. not only . . . but also, correlative
4. When, subordinating
5. After, subordinating

Exercise M

Sample answers:

1. Sigh, look at the garbage left on the ground.
2. Wow! The park certainly is cleaner since the town provided more garbage cans.
3. Hooray! Here comes the recycling truck at last.
4. Ouch! I stumbled on that tree root.
5. Ugh, I missed the trash can.

Exercise A

1. F
2. F
3. F
4. S
5. S

Exercise B

1. RO, comma splice
2. RO, comma splice
3. S
4. RO, fused
5. S

Exercise C

1. basketball
2. ball
3. points
4. basketball
5. championships

Exercise D

Sample answers:

1. her mother
2. his teammate
3. Jerry
4. Tom
5. us

Exercise E

1. simple
2. simple
3. compound-complex
4. complex
5. compound-complex
6. compound-complex

Sentences, Phrases, and Clauses

Sentences

A **sentence** is a group of words with a subject and a predicate. Together, these parts express a complete thought.

> I closed my eyes and pondered my next move.
> — "Rules of the Game," p. 305

A **fragment** is a group of words that does not express a complete thought.

> The Swan Theater in London

Exercise A **Recognizing Sentence Fragments.** Write *F* if an item below is a fragment and *S* if it is a complete sentence.

1. An array of finely tuned instruments.
2. Will play any instrument in the band.
3. In the concert hall on the stage.
4. That's loud.
5. After you finish reading, I will practice the cello.

A **run-on** is two or more complete sentences run together without punctuation.

Exercise B **Recognizing Run-ons.** On your paper, write *S* if an item is a sentence and *RO* if it is a run-on. Indicate whether each run-on is a fused sentence or a comma splice.

1. Percussion instruments produce sound when struck or shaken, some examples are drums, rattles, and bells.
2. The marimba is a percussion instrument with wooden bars arranged like the keys on a piano, mallets are used to strike the bars and produce sound.
3. If you are near a beach, you can collect driftwood to make your own marimba.
4. Gather several pieces of driftwood test each one for sound quality by striking it in the center.
5. To make the marimba, place the driftwood pieces in order by tone, then attach the pieces side by side over two long support pieces.

A **direct object** is a noun or pronoun that receives the action of a transitive verb.

Exercise C **Recognizing Direct Objects.** Write the direct object in each sentence.

1. A YMCA instructor invented basketball in 1891.
2. In basketball, players put a ball through a basket to make points.
3. The winning team scores the most points.
4. Spectators first watched basketball in the nineteenth century.
5. Most states now hold championships in basketball.

An **indirect object** is a noun or pronoun that appears with a direct object and names the person or thing that something is given to or done for.

Exercise D **Supplying Indirect Objects.** Supply a logical indirect object in each sentence.

1. Pam told _____ the highlights of the basketball game.
2. At the beginning of the game, the center tipped _____ the jump ball.
3. A foul gave _____ a chance to score.
4. In the last 30 seconds of the game, the guard passed _____ the ball and he made a three-pointer.
5. As a result, the home team gave _____ another victory.

The Four Structures of Sentences

There are two kinds of clauses: independent and subordinate. These can be used to form four basic sentence structures: *simple, compound, complex,* and *compound-complex.*

A **simple sentence** consists of a single independent clause.

A **compound sentence** consists of two or more independent clauses.

The clauses in a compound sentence can be joined by a comma and a coordinating conjunction (*and, but, for, not, or, so, yet*) or by a semicolon (;).

A **complex sentence** consists of one independent clause and one or more subordinate clauses.

The independent clause in a complex sentence is often called the *main clause* to distinguish it from the subordinate clause or clauses.

A **compound-complex sentence** consists of two or more independent clauses and one or more subordinate causes.

Exercise E **Identifying the Structure of Sentences.** Identify each sentence as simple, compound, complex, or compound-complex.

1. South Africa is the southernmost country of Africa.
2. It is the most powerful and the wealthiest country of the region.
3. Gold and diamonds are mined in both South Africa and Namibia, but it was in South Africa that the biggest diamond in the world was found.

4. Although it is not as wealthy as South Africa, Mozambique is the site of the second biggest port in all of Africa.

5. Its capital, Maputo, is the city where the port is located; it is linked by rail with South Africa, Swaziland, and Zimbabwe.

6. Even though most people think of Africa as a desert, Zimbabwe has a hot, tropical climate, so mangoes, passion fruit, pineapples, and avocados grow well.

Phrases

A **phrase** is a group of words, without a subject and a verb, that functions in a sentence as one part of speech.

A **prepositional phrase** is a group of words that includes a preposition and a noun or a pronoun that is the object of the preposition.

outside my window   below the counter

Exercise F **Identifying Prepositional Phrases.** Write the prepositional phrase or phrases in each sentence. The number at the end of each sentence tells how many prepositional phrases the sentence has.

1. College basketball tournaments came into their own in 1939. (2)

2. Since that time, players have been setting records. (1)

3. Players are often named all-American for outstanding performances. (1)

4. A few players join professional teams after graduation from college. (2)

5. Some teams win medals at international games. (1)

An **adjective phrase** is a prepositional phrase that modifies a noun or a pronoun by telling *what kind* or *which one*.

The wooden gates *of that lane* stood open.

Exercise G **Identifying Adjective Phrases.** Write each sentence, underlining the adjective phrase or phrases in each. Then, draw an arrow from each phrase to the word it modifies.

1. There are several different kinds of Native American tribes in North America.

2. The culture of each tribe varies.

3. The tribes of western Louisiana and eastern Texas are the Caddo.

4. Farming provided their main source of food.

5. Also important was the annual hunt for buffalo.

An **adverb phrase** is a prepositional phrase that modifies a verb, an adjective, or an adverb by pointing out *where, when, in what way,* or *to what extent.*

"... I could sleep without closing my eyes ..."
—"The Most Dangerous Game," p. 215

Exercise H **Identifying Adverb Phrases.** Write each sentence, underlining the adverb phrase or phrases in each. Then, draw an arrow from each phrase to the word it modifies.

1. The Pawnee divided themselves into four different tribes.

2. Most of them lived in earth lodges.

3. One tribe, the Skidi Pawnee, became part of the Grand Pawnee in the early 1800s.

4. Religion was very important to this tribe.

5. In their religion, they paid homage to the morning star.

An **appositive phrase** is a noun or pronoun with modifiers, placed next to a noun or a pronoun to add information and details.

"It is a very great pleasure and honor to welcome Mr. Sanger Rainsford, *the celebrated hunter,* to my home."
—"The Most Dangerous Game," p. 215

Exercise I **Identifying Appositive Phrases.** Write the appositive phrase in each sentence. Then, write the word or words each appositive phrase renames.

1. Sugar cane, a plant with a strong stem, was used to make armor for Creek warriors.

2. Clubs, slings, lances, and bows and arrows—the usual weapons of war—were made of cane, rock, and other materials found in the area.

3. A war post, a cane stock painted red and hung with feathers and arrows, signified the start of a war party.

4. Those who wanted to enlist would hit the post as hard as they could with a war club, a piece of cane painted red.

5. Then, warriors would put themselves through a purification rite, a physically strenuous ceremony.

A **participial phrase** is a participle with its modifiers or complements. The entire phrase acts as an adjective.

"Try the settee," said Holmes, *relapsing into his armchair* ...
—"The Red-headed League," p. 1067

Grammar, Usage, and Mechanics ■ R-43

Exercise F

1. into their own, in 1939
2. Since that time
3. for outstanding performances
4. after graduation, from college
5. at international games

Exercise G

1. of Native American tribes (modifies *kinds*)
2. of each tribe (modifies *culture*)
3. of western Louisiana and eastern Texas (modifies *tribes*)
4. of food (modifies *source*)
5. for buffalo (modifies *hunt*)

Exercise H

1. into four different tribes (modifies *divided*)
2. in earth lodges (modifies *lived*)
3. in the early 1800s (modifies *became*)
4. to this tribe (modifies *important*)
5. to the morning star (modifies *paid*)

Exercise I

1. a plant with a strong stem (Sugar cane)
2. the usual weapons of war (Clubs, slings, lances, and bows and arrows)
3. a cane stock painted red and hung with feathers and arrows (war post)
4. a piece of cane painted red (war club)
5. a physically strenuous ceremony (purification rite)

Exercise J

1. Living in the Northwest (the Nootka and other tribes)
2. Hollowed-out (trees)
3. Fishing from these boats (the tribes)
4. Hunting whales with great skill (the Nootka tribe)
5. wearing armor carved from wood (Men)

Exercise K

1. planting crops—object of preposition
2. fighting the Sioux—direct object
3. hunting buffalo—object of preposition
4. decorating clothing and other costumes—object of preposition
5. Trading with Native Americans—subject

Exercise L

Make sure that students correctly use the infinitive phrases as the parts of speech indicated.

Exercise M

1. independent
2. independent
3. subordinate
4. independent
5. subordinate

Exercise N

1. which is also known as the Congo (adjective)
2. Because it has many tributaries (adverb)
3. so its levels are always high (adverb)
4. because it lies on the equator (adverb)
5. Besides whatever cooking and cleaning African women do (adverb)

Exercise J **Recognizing Participial Phrases.** Write the participial phrase in each sentence. Then, write the word or words it modifies.

1. Living in the Northwest, the Nootka and other tribes built their lives around fish and wood.
2. Hollowed-out trees were turned into boats.
3. Fishing from these boats, the tribes brought in abundant amounts of salmon and halibut.
4. Hunting whales with great skill, the Nootka tribe of Vancouver Island became well known for its catches.
5. Men, wearing armor carved from wood, had protection when fighting during their battles.

A **gerund phrase** is a gerund with modifiers or a complement, all acting together as a noun.

The baying of the hounds drew nearer, . . .

—"The Most Dangerous Game," p. 215

Exercise K **Identifying Gerund Phrases.** Write the gerund phrases in each sentence, and identify their functions.

1. Pilgrims learned about planting crops from the Wampanoags.
2. Advanced weapons made fighting the Sioux a successful effort for the Chippewa.
3. The Sioux became a tribe that lived by hunting buffalo.
4. Beads brought by the Europeans were used in decorating clothing and other costumes.
5. Trading with Native Americans allowed Europeans to survive.

An **infinitive phrase** is an infinitive (*to* and a verb) with modifiers, complements, or a subject, all acting together as a single part of speech.

I continued, as was my wont, *to smile in his face*, . . .

—"The Cask of Amontillado," p. 61

Exercise L **Writing Sentences With Infinitives.** Write a sentence for each infinitive phrase, using the infinitive phrase as the part of speech indicated.

1. to succeed in school (subject)
2. to call home (direct object)
3. to leave on vacation (adverb modifying adjective *happy*)
4. to travel to another state (predicate noun)
5. to go to the ceremony (appositive)

Clauses

A **clause** is a group of words with a subject and a verb.

An **independent clause** has a subject and a verb and can stand by itself as a complete sentence.

A **subordinate clause** has a subject and a verb but cannot stand by itself as a complete sentence; it can only be part of a sentence.

Exercise M **Identifying Independent and Subordinate Clauses.** Identify each clause as independent if the clause can stand alone or subordinate if the clause cannot stand alone.

1. weavers of this tribe make beautiful cloth
2. each one has a different pattern
3. because one has a different pattern
4. it is called "Gold Dust"
5. when Ghana elected its first president

An **adjective clause** is a subordinate clause that modifies a noun or a pronoun by telling *what kind* or *which one*.

Walter Mitty stopped the car in front of the building *where his wife went to have her hair done.*

—"The Secret Life of Walter Mitty," p. 124

An **adverb clause** modifies a verb, an adjective, an adverb, or a verbal by telling *where, when, in what way, to what extent, under what condition,* or *why*.

The hunter shook his head several times, *as if he was puzzled.*

—"The Most Dangerous Game," p. 215

A **noun clause** is a subordinate clause that acts as a noun.

. . . I discovered *that the intoxication had worn off* . . .

—"The Cask of Amontillado," p. 61

Exercise N **Recognizing Adjective, Adverb, and Noun Clauses.** Write the adjective, adverb, or noun clauses from each sentence. Label each one correctly.

1. The Zaire River, which is also known as the Congo, runs almost the whole length of the country.
2. Because it has many tributaries, it is an important source of transportation.
3. The river drains a vast area of rain forests, so its levels are always high.
4. The climate of the Democratic Republic of the Congo is hot and humid because it lies on the equator.

5. Besides whatever cooking and cleaning African women do, they also work in the fields and sell crops in the market.

Parallelism involves using similar grammatical structures to express similar ideas. Sentences with parallel structure contain repeated grammatical patterns or repeated types of phrases or clauses within a sentence.

> Marguerite has a great love *for art, for children,* and *for teaching.*

Exercise O **Correcting Faulty Parallelism.** Rewrite the sentences that lack parallel structure. If a sentence needs no revision, write *correct.*

1. As a boy, Frankin taught himself geometry, worked on his writing style, and newspapers.

2. He was a clever and creative youth.

3. He became a printer and worked with his brother before going to Philadelphia.

4. Because of his effort, and he was efficient, the British gave him the job of deputy postmaster of the Colonies.

5. Franklin later helped build a hospital, starting a university, and collect money for charities.

The Four Principal Parts of Verbs

Tenses are formed from principal parts and helping verbs.

A verb has four **principal parts**: the present, the present participle, the past, and the past participle.

Exercise A **Writing Sentences With Principal Parts of Verbs.** For each numbered item, write a sentence using the subject and the principal part of the verb indicated. Then, identify the tense of the verb in the sentence you have written.

1. We, past participle of *talk*

2. Mike, present participle of *wait*

3. People, present of *laugh*

4. I, past of *stop*

5. You, present participle of *help*

Pronoun Case

The **case** of a pronoun is the form it takes to show its use in a sentence. There are three pronoun cases: nominative, objective, and possessive.

The **nominative case** is used to rename the subject of the sentence. The nominative case pronouns are *I, you, he, she, it, we, you, they.*

> As the subject: *She* is brave.
>
> Renaming the subject: The leader is *she.*

The **objective case** is used as the direct object, indirect object, or object of the preposition. The objective case pronouns are *me, you, him, her, us, you, them.*

> **As a direct object:** Our manager praised her.
>
> **As an indirect object:** Give him the new product.
>
> **As an object of the preposition:** The coach gave pointers to me.

The **possessive case** is used to show ownership. The possessive pronouns are *my, you, his, her, its, our, their, mine, yours, his, hers, its, ours, theirs.*

Exercise B **Choosing Pronouns in the Correct Case.** Choose the pronoun that is the correct case to complete each sentence. Identify the case of the pronoun you choose.

1. School fund-raisers taught (we, us) how to sell products to the public.

2. When promoting a product to customers, a salesperson should provide an incentive for (they, them) to buy.

3. (Them, Their) buying often depends on how they react to the seller.

4. This year, my teammates and (I, me) are selling team-spirit banners.

5. Customers know that the sale helps (we, us) earn money for the team.

Subject and Verb Agreement

A singular verb must be used with a singular subject; a plural verb must be used with a plural subject.

> *Reegan is* going home now.
>
> Many *storms are* the cause of beach erosion.

In a sentence with combined singular and plural subjects, the verb should agree with the subject closest to it.

> Either the *cats* or the *dog is* hungry.
>
> Neither *Angie* nor her *sisters were* present.

Exercise C **Making Verbs Agree With Their Subjects.** Choose the verb in parentheses that agrees with the subject of each sentence.

1. Before 1940, most Hungarians (was, were) farmers.

2. Today, many people (works, work) in industry.

3. When thinking of the past, my uncle (remembers, remember) the restrictions of Communist party rule.

Grammar, Usage, and Mechanics ■ R-45

Exercise O

Sample answers:

1. As a boy, Franklin taught himself geometry, worked on his writing style, and read newspapers.

2. correct

3. correct

4. Because of his effort and efficiency, the British gave him the job of deputy postmaster of the Colonies.

5. Franklin later helped build a hospital, started a university, and collected money for charities.

Exercise A

Sample answers:

1. We have talked about many interesting subjects. (past perfect)

2. Mike is waiting to hear from his lawyer. (present progressive)

3. People laugh at her jokes. (present)

4. I stopped at the bank. (past)

5. You are helping the team deliver brochures to the neighborhood. (present progressive)

Exercise B

1. us (objective)

2. them (objective)

3. Their (possessive)

4. I (nominative)

5. us (objective)

Exercise C

1. were

2. work

3. remembers

4. has

5. elect

Exercise D

1. He, his

2. they

3. his or her

4. it

5. We, our

4. Since the fall of the communist government, a great change (has, have) occurred.

5. Today, the citizens (elects, elect) their leaders.

Antecedents are the nouns (or the words that take the place of nouns) to which pronouns refer.

A personal pronoun must agree with its antecedent in number and gender. *Number* indicates whether a pronoun is singular or plural.

Some pronouns and nouns also indicate one of three *genders*: masculine, feminine, or neuter.

Use a singular personal pronoun to refer to two or more singular antecedents joined by *or* or *nor*.

Use a plural personal pronoun to refer to two or more antecedents joined by *and*.

Exercise D **Making Personal Pronouns Agree With Their Antecedents.** Write the appropriate personal pronouns to complete each sentence.

1. One computer pioneer is Alan Kay. _____ is noted for _____ role in the development of the laptop computer.

2. Before Kay introduced graphics and animation, _____ had not been seen before on PCs.

3. In the 1970s, the average person did not have a computer in _____ home.

4. However, once the microprocessor was invented, _____ hastened the development of the PC.

5. Today, you and I don't even have to leave home. _____ can access the world through _____ PCs.

Degrees of Comparison

Most adjectives and adverbs have different forms to show degrees of comparison.

The three degrees of comparison are the *positive*, the *comparative*, and the *superlative*.

Use the comparative degree to compare two people, places, or things. Use the superlative degree to compare three or more people, places, or things.

Use *more* or *most* to form the comparative and superlative degrees of all modifiers with three or more syllables.

Memorize the irregular comparative and superlative forms of certain adjectives and adverbs.

The most commonly used irregular modifiers are listed in the following chart. Notice that some modifiers differ only in the positive degree. For instance, the modifiers *bad, badly,* and *ill* all have the same comparative and superlative forms (*worse, worst*).

IRREGULAR MODIFIERS		
Positive	**Comparative**	**Superlative**
bad	worse	worst
badly	worse	worst
far (distance)	farther	farthest
far (extent)	further	furthest
good	better	best
ill	worse	worst
late	later	last *or* latest
little (amount)	less	least
many	more	most
much	more	most
well	better	best

Exercise E Supplying the Comparative and Superlative Degrees

Write the appropriate comparative or superlative degree of the modifier in parentheses.

1. Although Shakespeare died nearly 400 years ago, his plays are among those (often) read and performed.
2. Even the (bad) actor will learn to recognize at least one Shakespearean character.
3. Shakespeare's popularity as a playwright is unequaled by even the (good) modern-day writer.
4. His plays still command some of the (large) number of ticket sales.
5. The movie *West Side Story* is one of the (successful) modern versions of Shakespeare's *Romeo and Juliet*.

Capitalization and Punctuation

Capitalization

Capitalize the first word of a sentence and also the first word in a quotation if the quotation is a complete sentence.

> I said to him, "My dear Fortunato, you are luck-ily met."
>
> —"The Cask of Amontillado," p. 61

Capitalize all proper nouns and adjectives.

> O. Henry   Ganges River   Great Wall of China

Capitalize a person's title when it is followed by the person's name or when it is used in direct address.

> Madame   Dr. Mitty   General Zaroff

Capitalize titles showing family relationships when they refer to a specific person, unless they are preceded by a possessive noun or pronoun.

> Uncle Marcos   Granddaddy Cain

Capitalize the first word and all other key words in the titles of books, periodicals, poems, stories, plays, paintings, and other works of art.

> *Odyssey*   "I Wandered Lonely as a Cloud"

Exercise A Capitalizing Proper Nouns, Proper Adjectives, and Titles Correctly. Copy the following sentences onto your paper, adding the missing capitals. Underline any titles that appear in italics.

1. New York City served as the first american capital, and president george washington was inaugurated there.
2. Throughout history, many influential new yorkers have entertained and educated us and helped us create a better american way of life.

3. Have you read the short story "rip can winkle," written by Washington Irving, who was born in New York city?
4. One of he most celebrated american poets, Walt Whitman, spent most of his life in brooklyn.
5. Colin Powell, the son of caribbean immigrants, grew up in the south bronx.

Punctuation

End Marks

Use a **period** to end a declarative sentence, an imperative sentence, an indirect question, and most abbreviations.

> Mr. Jabez Wilson laughed heavily.
>
> —"The Red-headed League," p. 1067

Use a **question mark** to end a direct question, an incomplete question, or a statement that is intended as a question.

> "What do you expect me to do with that?"
>
> —"The Necklace," p. 294

Use an **exclamation mark** after a statement showing strong emotion, an urgent imperative sentence, or an interjection expressing strong emotion.

> Free at last! Free at last!
> Thank God almighty, we are Free at last!
>
> —"I Have a Dream," p. 494

Exercise B Punctuating the Ends of Sentences.
Write the end mark required in each of the following sentences.

1. Backpacking is a popular type of hiking
2. Items that are packed must be as lightweight as possible
3. For crying out loud, you can't expect a backpacker to walk for 50 miles with 200 pounds of equipment
4. By carrying clothes, food, and plenty of water, a backpacker can spend many days in remote areas where these supplies would normally be unavailable
5. Where Anyplace you want

Commas

Use a **comma** before the coordinating conjunction to separate two independent clauses in a compound sentence.

> All at once . . . she came upon a superb diamond necklace, and her heart started beating with overwhelming desire.
>
> —"The Necklace," p. 294

Exercise E

1. most often
2. worst
3. best
4. largest
5. most successful

Exercise A

1. New York City served as the first American capital, and President George Washington was inaugurated there.
2. Throughout history, many influential New Yorkers have entertained and educated us and helped us create a better American way of life.
3. Have you read the short story "Rip Van Winkle," written by Washington Irving, who was born in New York City?
4. One of the most celebrated American poets, Walt Whitman, spent most of his life in Brooklyn.
5. Colin Powell, the son of Caribbean immigrants, grew up in the South Bronx.

Exercise B

1. Backpacking is a popular type of hiking.
2. Items that are packed must be as lightweight as possible.
3. For crying out loud, you can't expect a backpacker to walk for 50 miles with 200 pounds of equipment!
4. By carrying clothes, food, and plenty of water, a backpacker can spend many days in remote areas where these supplies would normally be unavailable.
5. Where? Anyplace you want.

Exercise C

1. The modern shopping mall was made possible by the automobile, the growth of the suburbs, and television advertising.

2. Some consist of one long or angled building, usually of one story, divided into several stores.

3. To get from store to store in an open mall, a customer must go outdoors.

4. correct

5. correct

Exercise D

1. requirements; as

2. week; trainees

3. aircraft; following

4. tall; payload

5. experience; but

Use commas to separate three or more words, phrases, or clauses in a series.

> My brothers and I would peer into the medicinal herb shop, watching old Li dole out onto a stiff sheet of white paper the right amount of insect shells, saffron-colored seeds, and pungent leaves for his ailing customers.
> —"Rules of the Game," p. 305

Use commas to separate adjectives of equal rank. Do not use commas to separate adjectives that must stay in a specific order.

> The big cottonwood tree stood apart from a small group of winterbare cottonwoods which grew in the wide, sandy arroyo.
> —"The Man to Send Rain Clouds," p. 268

> His present turned out to be a box of intricate plastic parts.
> —"Rules of the Game," p. 305

Use a comma after an introductory word, phrase, or clause.

> When Marvin was ten years old, his father took him through the long, echoing corridors . . .
> —"If I Forget Thee, Oh Earth . . . ," p. 148

Use commas to set off parenthetical and nonessential expressions.

> An evil place can, so to speak, broadcast vibrations of evil.
> —"The Most Dangerous Game," p. 215

Use commas with places, dates, and titles.

> Poe was raised in Richmond, Virginia.
> On September 1, 1939, World War II began.
> Dr. Martin Luther King, Jr., was born in 1929.

Use a comma to set off a direct quotation, to prevent a sentence from being misunderstood, and to indicate the omission of a common verb in a sentence with two or more clauses.

> Michele said, "I'm going to the game tonight."

Faulty:	She stifled the sob that rose to her lips and lay motionless.
Revised:	She stifled the sob that rose to her lips, and lay motionless.

> In the *Odyssey*, the Cyclops may symbolize brutishness; the Sirens, knowledge.

Exercise C Using Commas Correctly. Rewrite each sentence, inserting commas where necessary. If the sentence is written correctly, write *correct*.

1. The modern shopping mall was made possible by the automobile the growth of the suburbs and television advertising.

2. Some consist of one long or angled building usually of one story divided into several stores.

3. To get from store to store in an open mall a customer must go outdoors.

4. The enclosed mall is covered by a roof which can be eight stories tall.

5. Malls have become all-purpose entertainment centers where a person may shop or eat or go to the movies.

Semicolons

Use a **semicolon** to join independent clauses that are not already joined by a conjunction.

> The lights of cities sparkle; on nights when there was no moon, it was difficult for me to tell the Earth from the sky. . . .
> —"Single Room, Earth View," p. 437

Use a semicolon to join independent clauses separated by either a conjunctive adverb or a transitional expression.

> Edward Way Teale wrote nearly thirty books; moreover, he was also an artist and a naturalist.

Use semicolons to avoid confusion when independent clauses or items in a series already contain commas.

> Unable to afford jewelry, she dressed simply; but she was as wretched as a *déclassée*, for women have neither caste nor breeding—in them beauty, grace, and charm replace pride of birth.
> —"The Necklace," p. 294

Exercise D Using Semicolons Correctly. Decide where a semicolon is needed in each of the following sentences. Write the word before the semicolon, write the semicolon, and write the words after the semicolon.

1. Astronaut trainees work hard to fill the requirements as a result, they are physically and mentally ready for the arduous tasks that lay before them.

2. Applicants are physically tested and interviewed for a period of one week trainees are selected from those who score the highest.

3. Those applying as pilot astronauts must also complete 1,000 hours in a top-level flight post, such as command pilot in a high-performance jet aircraft following that, they must pass a spaceflight physical.

4. Pilot astronauts must be between 5'4" tall and 6'4" tall payload specialists have no height requirement.

5. To fit the requirements, an astronaut applicant must have the appropriate education, physical health and stature, and experience but, in most cases, an applicant may be of any age.

Colons

Use a **colon** in order to introduce a list of items following an independent clause.

> The authors we are reading include a number of poets: Robert Frost, Lewis Carroll, and Emily Dickinson.

Use a colon to introduce a formal quotation.

> I have a dream that one day this nation will rise up and live out the true meaning of its creed: "We hold these truths to be self-evident; . . ."
> —"I Have a Dream," p. 494

Exercise E **Using Colons Correctly.** Rewrite each item, adding colons where appropriate. Some items may require more than one colon. Write *correct* if an item needs no additional punctuation.

1. August 1, 1998

2. To whom it may concern

3. Meeting Friday, September 8, for Junior Space Camp

4. Place American Hills High School

5. Time 7 00 P.M.

Quotation Marks

A **direct quotation** represents a person's exact speech or thoughts and is enclosed in quotation marks.

> "This great nation will endure as it has endured, will revive and will prosper," said President Franklin D. Roosevelt.
> —"First Inaugural Address," p. 503

An **indirect quotation** reports only the general meaning of what a person said or thought and does not require quotation marks.

> I went up to her, put my arms around her, and said something to her.
> —from *A White House Diary*, p. 98

Always place a comma or a period inside the final quotation mark.

> "There," he said, "there's something for you."
> —"The Necklace," p. 294

Place a question mark or an exclamation mark inside the final quotation mark if the end mark is part of the quotation; if it is not part of the quotation, place it outside the final quotation mark.

> "That pig will devour us, greedily!"
> —"The Golden Kite, the Silver Wind," p. 362

> Have you ever read the poem "Dreams"?

Use single quotation marks for a quotation within a quotation.

> "'But,' said I, 'there would be millions of red-headed men who would apply.'"
> —"The Red-headed League," p. 1067

Use quotation marks around the titles of short written works, episodes in a series, songs, and titles of works mentioned as parts of a collection.

> "I Hear America Singing"   "Pride"

Exercise F **Using Quotation Marks With Other Punctuation Marks.** Copy the following sentences, adding quotation marks and any needed commas, colons, semicolons, or end marks. *Note:* Italics included in some of the sentences are a clue to which text should be in quotations.

1. Solomon was sent away without being admitted to the king, but he was so persistent that the king *had him shut up as a madman*!

2. Nineteenth-century locomotives powered by steam were created by expanding on these basic ideas. *Air expands as it heats. Steam has a lot of power.*

3. Was it really the Marquis of Worcester who first discovered the power of steam from observing *the motion of the lid of a teakettle of boiling water*?

4. Perhaps, but the author of "The First Locomotives" writes *it does seem far more likely that Solomon . . . would be the one to observe the effects of the steam upon the lid of a teakettle.*

Dashes

Use **dashes** to indicate an abrupt change of thought, a dramatic interrupting idea, or a summary statement.

> The streets were lined with people—lots and lots of people—the children all smiling, placards, confetti, people waving from windows.
> —from *A White House Diary*, p. 98

Exercise E

1. correct

2. To whom it may concern:

3. Meeting: Friday, September 8, for Junior Space Camp

4. Place: American Hills High School

5. Time: 7:00 P.M.

Exercise F

1. Solomon was sent away without being admitted to the king, but he was so persistent that the king "had him shut up as a madman"!

2. Nineteenth-century locomotives powered by steam were created by expanding on these basic ideas: "Air expands as it heats"; "steam has a lot of power."

3. Was it really the Marquis of Worcester who first discovered the power of steam from observing "the motion of the lid of a teakettle of boiling water"?

4. Perhaps, but the author of *The First Locomotives* writes, "It does seem far more likely that Solomon . . . would be the one to observe the effects of the steam upon the lid of a teakettle."

Exercise G

1. Blue and yellow macaws—which belong to the parrot family but are not actually called parrots—live in South America.

2. Nuts, fruits, seeds, and berries—these are the staple foods of the macaw diet.

3. Bonding between the pair is reinforced as the birds preen—groom each other's feathers.

4. When eggs are laid—usually only two at a time—the female incubates them.

5. Baby macaws—always hatched in pairs—are blind and featherless at hatching.

Exercise H

1. The sulphur-crested cockatoo has been kept as a pet (I have one) since the nineteenth century.

2. Its shrill voice (heard mostly early in the morning or when it becomes alarmed) can be trained to mimic the human voice.

3. Cockatoos that make the best pets are those that are bred in captivity. (They are calmer and easier to train.) Buying only birds that are captivity-bred also helps protect the birds of the wild.

4. A cockatoo will use the crest of feather on its head to show strong emotion (fear or aggression).

5. When buying a cockatoo, be sure to buy a large cage; cockatoos will grow to be over a foot (18-20 inches) long.

Exercise I

1. The all-powerful beak of a macaw is hinged to crush tough nuts that other birds are not able to eat.

2. From the top of the body to the tip of the tail, macaws can reach up to thirty-six inches.

3. correct

4. Cuckoo birds create a co-op with other species when raising their young.

5. A female cuckoo looks for an insect-eating host species like the one she was raised in.

Exercise J

1. one's

2. husband's

3. head of state's

4. Council of Ministers'

5. forests' and hills'

R50

Exercise G **Using Dashes Correctly.** Rewrite the following sentences, adding dashes where appropriate.

1. Blue and yellow macaws which belong to the parrot family but are not actually called parrots live in South America.

2. Nuts, fruits, seeds, and berries these are the staple foods of the macaw diet.

3. Bonding between the pair is reinforced as the birds preen, they groom each other's feathers.

4. When eggs are laid usually only two at a time the females incubates them.

5. Baby macaws always hatched in pairs are blind and featherless at hatching.

Parentheses

Use **parentheses** to set off asides and explanations only when the material is not essential or when it consists of one or more sentences.

> One last happy moment I had was looking up and seeing Mary Griffith . . . (Mary for many years had been in charge of altering the clothes which I purchased) . . .
>
> —from *A White House Diary*, p. 98

Exercise H **Using Parentheses.** Copy the following sentences, adding the necessary parentheses.

1. The sulphur-crested cockatoo has been kept as a pet I have one since the nineteenth century.

2. Its shrill voice heard mostly early in the morning or when it becomes alarmed can be trained to mimic the human voice.

3. Cockatoos that make the best pets are those that are bred in captivity. They are calmer and easier to train. Buying only birds that are captivity-bred also helps protect the birds of the wild.

4. A cockatoo will use the crest of feather on its head to show strong emotion fear or aggression.

5. When buying a cockatoo, be sure to buy a large cage; cockatoos will grow to be over a foot 18–20 inches long.

Hyphens

Use a **hyphen** with certain numbers, after certain prefixes, with two or more words used as one word, and with a compound modifier coming before a noun.

> seventy-six   Post-Modernist

Exercise I **Using Hyphens Properly in Words and to Clarify Sentences.** Rewrite the words that require hyphens. If no hyphen is needed, write *correct*.

1. The all powerful beak of a macaw is hinged to crush tough nuts that other birds are not able to eat.

2. From the top of the body to the tip of the tail, macaws can reach up to thirty six inches.

3. The tail is two thirds the length of the whole body.

4. Cuckoo birds create a coop with other species when raising their young.

5. A female cuckoo looks for an insect eating host species like the one she was raised in.

Apostrophes

Add an **apostrophe** and -*s* to show the possessive case of most singular nouns.

> Thurmond's wife   the playwright's craft

Add an apostrophe to show the possessive case of plural nouns ending in -*s* and -*es*.

> the sailors' ships   the Wattses' daughter

Add an apostrophe and -*s* to show the possessive case of plural nouns that do not end in -*s* or -*es*.

> the children's games   the people's friend

Use an apostrophe in a contraction to indicate the position of the missing letter or letters.

> You'll be lonely at first, they admitted, but you're so nice you'll make friends fast.
>
> —"Checkouts," p. 74

Exercise J **Using Apostrophes With Possessive Nouns.** Copy the underlined nouns, putting them into the possessive form.

1. In India, <u>one</u> personal life tends to be arranged around traditional extended families.

2. When a woman marries, she moves in with her <u>husband</u> family.

3. It is the <u>head of state</u> job to appoint the prime minister.

4. The <u>Council of Ministers</u> appointment is made by the president on the advice of the prime minister.

5. The <u>forests</u> and <u>hills</u> inhabitants are fewer than the cities' inhabitants.

Glossary of Common Usage

among, between

Among is usually used with three or more items. *Between* is generally used with only two items.

> *Among* the poems we read this year, Margaret Walker's "Memory" was my favorite.

> Mark Twain's "The Invalid's Story" includes a humorous encounter *between* the narrator and a character named Thompson.

around

In formal writing, *around* should not be used to mean *approximately* or *about*. These usages are allowable, however, in informal writing or in colloquial dialogue.

> Shakespeare's *Romeo and Juliet* had its first performance in *approximately* 1595.

> Shakespeare was *about* thirty when he wrote this play.

as, because, like, as to

The word *as* has several meanings and can function as several parts of speech. To avoid confusion, use *because* rather than *as* when you want to indicate cause and effect.

> *Because* Cyril was interested in the history of African American poetry, he decided to write his report on Paul Laurence Dunbar.

Do not use the preposition *like* to introduce a clause that requires the conjunction *as*.

> Dorothy Parker conversed *as* she wrote—wittily.

The use of *as to* for *about* is awkward and should be avoided.

> Rosa has an interesting theory *about* E. E. Cummings's unusual typography in his poems.

INDEX OF SKILLS

Page numbers in **boldface** *refer to pages where terms are defined.*

Literary Analysis

Acting and actors, 702

Acts of play, **704,** 706

Aesthetic qualities of poetry, **612**

Allegory, comparing symbolism and, **348,** 350, 351, 353, 354, 356, 357, 359, 360, 361, 363, 364, 366, 367, **R10**

Alliteration, **552, 590,** 596, 608, **R10**

Allusion, **R10**
   in contemporary interpretation, **1026,** 1037
   in dramatic speech, **782,** 810

Analogy, **492,** 495, 510, **R10**

Anecdote, **R10**

Antagonist, **936, 1048,** 1051, 1056, 1057, 1059, 1060, 1063, 1064, 1068, 1071, 1075, 1077, 1078, 1079, 1085, 1086, 1089, 1090, **R10**

Anticlimax, **R10**

Appeals to reason or emotion, **474,** 480, 488

Archetypal theme: ill-fated love, comparing, **856,** 859, 860, 861, 864, 867, 869, 871

Archetype, **856,** 871, **936, R10**

Articles, **386, 388**

Aside in dramatic speech, **705, 782,** 810, **R10**

Assonance, **552, 590,** 596, 608, **R10**

Atmosphere, **628,** 636, 648, **R10**

Attitude, voice and, **96,** 104, 114

Audience, **5,** author's purpose and, **1098,** 1102, 1108
   for drama, 702
   for leadership and heroism, 938
   for nonfiction, **5,** 14

Author's motive, **474,** 480, 488

Author's purpose, **5**
   in nonfiction, **5,** 14, **388,** 390, 395, 938
   in poetry, **1098,** 1102, 1108

Author's style in nonfiction, **388,** 398, **402,** 405, 406, 409, 412, 416, 417, 419, 420

Autobiography, **R10**

Autobiographical writing, **96,** 99, 103, 104, 109, 110, 113, 114

Ballad, **553, R10**

Bias, **388**

Biography, **R10**

Biographical writing, comparing, **450,** 455, 456, 458, 459, 462, 463

Blank verse, **756,** 758, 759, 761, 763, 764, 765, 767, 768, 771, 772, 775, 776, 778, 780, **R10**

Cause and effect, **424,** 434, 442

Chapters, **4**

Character, **R10**
   characterization of, **292,** 302, 316
   in drama, **704,** 706
   in fiction, **4,** 6, 10
   motives of, **832,** 834, 835, 837, 838, 842, 847, 848
   qualities of, **122,** 126, 129, 130, 135, 138, 140, 142
   in short story, **184,** 186, 190, 194, 196

Characterization, **R11**
   direct and indirect, **292,** 294, 295, 297, 299, 302, 306, 307, 308, 309, 312, 316
   in short story, **184**

Chorus, **705**

Circle, **936**

Climax, **R11**
   in drama, **704**
   in plot, **46,** 58, 68
   in short story, **184**

Comedy, **R11**
   in drama, **705, 882,** 886, 888

Comic relief, **814,** 830, **R11**

Comparison and contrast, **424,** 434, 442

Conflict, **R11**
   in drama, **704,** 718
   in fiction, **4,** 6
   in plot, **46,** 58, 68

in short story, **184, 200,** 205, 207, 208, 209, 211, 212, 216, 218, 222, 224, 225, 226, 228, 232, 234, 236

Connotation, **R11**

Consonance, **552, 590,** 596, 608, **R11**

Contemporary interpretations, comparing, **1026,** 1029, 1030, 1031, 1032, 1033, 1036, 1037, **R11**

Couplets, **552, R11**

Cultural context, 942, **944**

Cultural details, **937**

Culturally distinct values, **937**

Culture, 934

Deductive reasoning, **586**

Denotation, **R11**

Denouement, **R11**

Description, 394, **424,** 434, 442, **R11**

Descriptive essay, **389**

Descriptive nonfiction, **5**

Development, **R11**

Dialect, **320,** 323, 327, 330, 337, 340, **R12**

Dialogue, **R12**
   in drama, 702, **704,** 713, 717, **720, 728,** 732, 737, 743, 744, 745, 747, 748, 751, 752, 753, 754
   in short story, **320,** 323, 324, 327, 330, 337, 340

Diction, **R12**
   comic, **520,** 531
   in essays, 390, **402,** 412, 420

Direct characterization, **292,** 302, 316, **R12**

Drama, **702–706,** 708, 710, 711, 712, 714, 717, 718, **720, R12**

Dramatic effect, **704,** 711

Dramatic irony, **814,** 816, 819, 820, 825, 826, 828, 830, **882,** 888, **R12**

Dramatic monologue, **R12**

Dramatic poetry, **553, R12**

Reading Skills and Strategies

Vocabulary

ACADEMIC VOCABULARY

Writing

WRITING APPLICATIONS. *See also* **TIMED WRITING**

Critical Thinking

Critical Viewing

Research the Author

Listening and Speaking

INDEX OF FEATURES

INDEX OF FEATURES

Unit Introductions

Writing Workshops

INDEX OF AUTHORS AND TITLES

Nonfiction selections and informational texts appear in red. Page numbers in italic text refer to biographical information.

ACKNOWLEDGEMENTS

Houghton Mifflin Company "All Watched Over by Machines of Loving Grace" from *The Pill Versus The Springhill Mine Disaster* by Richard Brautigan. Copyright © 1968 by Richard Brautigan. "Blackberry Eating" from *Mortal Acts, Mortal Words* by Galway Kinnell. Copyright © 1980 by Galway Kinnell. "A Fable for tomorrow" from *Silent Spring* by Rachel Carson. Copyright © 1962 by Rachel L. Carson, copyright © renewed 1990 by Roger Christie. Reprinted by permission. **Houghton Mifflin Company and Oxford University Press, Inc. (Canada)** "Siren Song" from *Selected Poems, 1965-1975* by Margaret Atwood. Copyright © 1976, 1990 by Margaret Atwood. Reprinted by permission of Houghton Mifflin Co. and Oxford University Press, Inc. (Canada) **James R. Hurst** "The Scarlet Ibis" by James Hurst, published in the *Atlantic Monthly, July 1960*. Copyright © 1988 by James Hurst. Reprinted by permission of the author. **International Creative Management, Inc.** "Libraries Face Sad Chapter" by Pete Hamill from www.petehamill.com. Copyright © by Pete Hamill. Reprinted by permission of International Creative Management, Inc. **Japan Publications, Inc.** "Dragonfly catcher" and "Bearing no flowers" by Chiyojo and "Temple bells die out" by Basho from *One Hundred Famous Haiku* translated by Daniel C. Buchanan. Copyright © 1973 by Japan Publications. Used with permission of Japan Publications, Inc. **Lyndon B. Johnson Library** "A White House Diary" by Ladybird Johnson from *A White House Diary*. Used with permission of the Lyndon B. Johnson Library. **Adam Kirsch** "Chekhov in American" by Adam Kirsch from *The Atlantic Monthly, July 1997, Vol. 280, No. 1, Pages 110-112*. Copyright © 1997 by Adam Kirsch. Reprinted with permission of the author. **Alfred A. Knopf, Inc.** "Dream Deferred" from *The Collected Poems of Langston Hughes* by Langston Hughes. Copyright © 1994 by The Estate of Langston Hughes. "The News" from *Conscientious Objections* by Neil Postman. Copyright © 1988 by Neil Postman. "Dreams" from *The Collected Poems of Langston Hughes* by Langston Hughes. Copyright © 1994 by The Estate of Langston Hughes. "Uncle Marcos" by Isabel Allende translated by Magda Bogin from *The House Of The Spirits*. Copyright © 1985 by Alfred A. Knopf, A Division of Random House, Inc. Used by permisson of Alfred A. Knopf, a division of Random House, Inc. **Alfred A. Knopf Children's Books** "Pecos Bill: The Cyclone" from *Pecos Bill: Texas Cowpuncher* by Harold W. Felton. Copyright © 1949 by Alfred A. Knopf, a division of Random House, Inc. Copyright renewed 1976 by Harold W. Felton. Used by permission of Alfred A. Knopf Children's Books, a division of Random House, Inc. **Little, Brown and Company, Inc.** "Perseus" from *Mythology* by Edith Hamilton. Copyright © 1942 by Edith Hamilton; Copyright © renewed 1969 by Dorian Fielding Reid and Doris Fielding Reid.. "Pyramus and Thisbe" by Edith Hamilton from *Mythology*. Copyright © 1942 by Edith Hamilton. Copyright renewal © 1969 by Dorian Ffielding Reid and Doris Fielding Reid. Reprinted by permission of Little, Brown and Company Inc. **Liveright Publishing Corporation** "maggie and milly and molly and may" from *Complete Poems: 1904-1962* by E. E. Cummings, edited by George J. Firmage. Copyright © 1956, 1984, 1991 by the Trustees for the E. E. Cummings Trust. Reprinted by permission of Liveright Publishing Corporation. **Marie-Christine MacAndrew** "The Necklace" from *Boule de Suif and Selected Stories* by Guy de Maupassant, translated by Andrew MacAndrew, New York, NAL, 1964, pp. 143-151. Used by permission of Marie-Christine MacAndrew. **John McPhee** "Arthur Ashe Remembered" by John McPhee, first published in *The New Yorker, March 1, 1993*. Reprinted by permission of the author. **Methuen Publishing Ltd.** "The Inspector-General" from *The Sneeze: Plays And Stories* by Anton Chekhov, translated and adapted by Michael Frayn. Originally from *An Awl in a Sack* by Anton Chekhov, 1885. Reprinted with permission of Methuen Publishing Ltd. **National Aeronautics and Space Administration** "Space Shuttle Basics" from www.nasa.gov. "Robotics Education Project" from http://robotics.arc.nasa.gov. Used with permission. **The Estate of Charles Neider** "The Invalid's Story" by Mark Twain from *The Complete Sketches and Tales of Mark Twain*, edited by Charles Neider. Copyright © 1977 by Charles Neider. Reprinted by permission of the Estate of Charles Neider. **North Carolina Transportation Museum** "North Carolina Transportation Museum" by Staff from *North Carolina Transportation Museum*. Used with permission. Used with permission of the North Carolina Transportation Museum. **Northwestern University Press** "Sonnets on Love XIII" by Jean de Sponde from *Sonnets on Love and Death*, translated by David R. Slavitt. Evanston: Northwestern University Press, 2001, p. 29. Used by permission of Northwestern University Press. **W. W. Norton & Company, Inc.** "Alabanza: In Praise of Local 100" from *Alabanza* by Martin Espada. Copyright © 2003 by Martin Espada. "The War Against the Trees" from *The Collected Poems* by Stanley Kunitz. Copyright © 2000 by Stanley Kunitz. Used by permission of W. W. Norton & Company, Inc. **Naomi Shihab Nye** "Daily" by Naomi Shihab Nye from *Hugging The Jukebox*. Copyright © 1982 by Naomi Shihab Nye. All rights reserved. Reprinted by permission of the author. **Orchard Books, a division of Scholastic Inc.** "Checkouts" from *A Couple Of Kooks And Other Stories About Love* by Cynthia Rylant. Published by Orchard Books/ Scholastic, Inc. Copyright © 1990 by Cynthia Rylant. Reprinted by permission of Scholastic, Inc. **The Penguin Press, a division of Penguin Group (USA) Inc.** "Play Hard; Play Together; Play Smart" by Dean Smith and Gerald D. Bell with John Kilgo from *The Carolina Way* Copyright © 2004 by Dean E. Smith. Used by permission of The Penguin Press, a division of Penguin Group (USA) Inc. **Playbill Magazine** "On Summer" by Lorraine Hansberry, reprinted from *Playbill Magazine, June 1960*. © Playbill, Inc. All rights reserved. Used by permission of Playbill®. **Portfolio, an imprint of Penguin Group (USA) Inc.** "The Only Thing We Have to Fear" from *Nothing to Fear: Lessons in Leadership from FDR* by Alan Axelrod. Copyright © 2003 by Alan Axelrod. Used by permission of Portfolio, an imprint of Penguin Group (USA) Inc. **G.P. Putnam Sons, a division of Penguin Group (USA) Inc.** "Rules of the Game" from *The Joy Luck Club* by Amy Tan. Copyright © 1989 by Amy Tan. Used by permission of G.P. Putnam Sons, a division of Penguin Group (USA) Inc. **Random House, Inc.** "New Directions" from *Wouldn't Take Nothing For My Journey Now* by Maya Angelou. Copyright © 1993 by Maya Angelou. "Blues Ain't No Mockin Bird" from *Gorilla, My Love* by Toni Cade Bambara. Copyright © 1971, by Toni Cade Bambara. "Big Kiss: One Actor's Desperate Attempt to Claw His Way to the Middle" by Henry Alford. Used by permission of Random House, Inc. **Dr. Sally K. Ride** "Single Room, Earth View" by Sally Ride, published in the *April/May 1986* issue of *Air & Space/Smithsonian Magazine*, published by The Smithsonian Institution. Copyright © Dr. Sally K. Ride. Published by Washington Speakers Bureau. Used with permission of the author. **Riverhead Books, an imprint of Penguin Group (USA) Inc.** "Carry Your Own Skis" by Lian Dolan from *Satellite Sisters' Uncommon Senses* by Julie, Liz & Sheila Dolan and Monica & Lian Dolan. Copyright © 2001 by Satellite Sisters, LLC. Reprinted by permission of Riverhead Books, an imprint of Penguin Group (USA) Inc. **Scovil Chichak Galen Literary Agency, Inc.** "If I Forget Thee, Oh Earth…" from *Expedition To Earth* by Arthur C. Clarke. Copyright © 1953, 1970 by Arthur C. Clarke; Copyright © 1951 by Columbia Publications, Inc. Reprinted by permission of the author and the author's agents, Scovil Chichak Galen Literary Agency, Inc. **The Estate of May Swenson** "Analysis of Baseball" by May Swenson from *American Sports Poems*. Used by permission of the Literary Estate of May Swenson. **Third Woman Press** "Twister Hits Houston" by Sandra Cisneros from *My Wicked Wicked Ways*. Copyright © 1987 by Sandra Cisneros. All rights reserved. **The University of Georgia Press** "American History" from *The Latin Deli: Prose and Poetry* by Judith Ortiz Cofer. Copyright © 1992 by Judith Ortiz Cofer. Used with permission of The University of Georgia Press. **University of Pittsburgh Press** "Candle Hat" from *Questions About Angels* by Billy Collins. Copyright © 1991. Reprinted by permission of the University of Pittsburgh Press. **University Press of New England** "The Talk" from *A Summer Life* by Gary Soto. Copyright © 1990 by University Press of New England. Used with permission. **Viking Penguin, Inc.** "Old Man of the Temple" from *Under The Banyan Tree* by R. K. Narayan. Copyright © 1985 by R. K. Narayan. Used by permission of Viking Penguin, a division of Penguin Group (USA) Inc. **Vital Speeches of the Day** "Glory and Hope" by Nelson Mandela from *Vital Speeches of the Day, June 1, 1994*. Reprinted by permission of Vital Speeches of the Day. Used with permission. **Wesleyan University Press** "Slam, Dunk, & Hook" from *Magic City in Pleasure Dome: New and Collected Poems* by Yusef Komunyakaa. Copyright © 2001 by Yusef Komunyakaa. Reprinted by permission of Wesleyan University Press. **World Book Inc.** "Detective Story" by David Geherin from *The World Book Encyclopedia, Volume 5, pages 162-163*. Copyright © 2001. Reprinted with permission of World Book, Inc. **Writer's House, LLC.** "Meciendo ("Rocking")" by Gabriela Mistral translated by Doris Dana from *Selected Poems Of Gabriela Mistral*. "Meciendo (Rocking)" by Gabriela Mistral, translated and edited by Doris Dana from *Selected Poems Of Gabriela Mistral*. Copyright © 1961, 1964, 1970, 1971 by Doris Dana. Reprinted by permission of Writer's House, LLC on behalf of the estate of the author. **Writer's House, LLC. for the Estate of Martin Luther King Jr.** "I Have a Dream" by Dr. Martin Luther King, Jr. from *The Words Of Martin Luther King, Jr.* Reprinted by arrangement with the Estate of Martin Luther King Jr., c/o Writers House as agent for the proprietor, New York, NY. **The Wylie Agency, Inc.** "The Man to Send Rain Clouds" from *Storyteller* by Leslie Marmon Silko. Copyright © 1981 by Leslie Marmon Silko. Reprinted by permission of The Wylie Agency, Inc.

Note: Every effort has been made to locate the copyright owner of material reproduced in this component. Omissions brought to our attention will be corrected in subsequent editions.

CREDITS

Cover: *Play it Pretty for the People*, collage, Phoebe Beasley/Omni-Photo Communications, Inc.; **Title page:** *Play it Pretty for the People*, collage, Phoebe Beasley/Omni-Photo Communications, Inc.; **vii:** istockphoto.com; **viii–ix:** Images.com/CORBIS; **ix:** Canberra Bicycle Museum and Resource Centre, Australia; **x–xi:** Franklin McMahon/CORBIS; **xi:** The Granger Collection, New York; **xii–xiii:** ©Images.com/CORBIS; **xiii:** GK Hart/Vikki Hart/Getty Images; **xiv-xv:** The Grand Design/SuperStock; **xvi–xvii:** Getty Images; **xvii:** Camera Press/Retna, LTD; **xviii–xix:** Getty Images; **xx-xxi:** Robert Frerck/Woodfin Camp & Associates; **xxviii:** MCDonald Wildlife Photog./Animals Animals; **xxix:** Getty Images; **1:** Images.com/CORBIS; **2:** b. ©Paul Vismara/Stock Illustration Source, Inc.; **2:** t. Prentice Hall; **3:** Images.com/CORBIS; **4:** CALVIN AND HOBBES © 1994 Watterson. Reprinted with permission of UNIVERSAL PRESS SYNDICATE. All rights reserved.; **5:** Getty Images; **7:** Alberto Giacometti, *Man Pointing*, 1947. Bronze, 70 1/2 x 40 3/4 x 16

3/8". The Museum of Modern Art/Licensed by Scala-Art Resource, NY. Gift of Mrs. John D. Rockefller 3rd. ©2004 Artists Rights Society (ARS), New York/ADAGP, Paris.; **8:** ©Jonathan Nourok/PhotoEdit Inc.; **10:** Christooph Wilhelm/Getty Images; **11:** Getty Images; **15:** Michael S. Lewis/CORBIS; **16:** Getty Images **18:** Maria Ferrari/SuperStock; **21:** Images.com/CORBIS; **25:** Robert Maass/CORBIS; **26:** *The Oldest Inhabitant*, 1876, Julian Alden Weir, oil on canvas, 65 1/2 x 32" Signed, upper left. Butler Institute of American Art, Youngstown, Ohio; **26:** background Lee Snider/CORBIS; **29:** Erich Lessing/Art Resource, NY; **31:** Lee Snider/CORBIS; **33:** Lee Snider/CORBIS; **34:** Getty Images; **35:** Royalty-Free/CORBIS; **36:** CORBIS; **37:** Photo © Graham Ilott; **39:** Photo © Graham Ilott; **43:** inset Barnabas Kindersley/© Dorling Kindersley; **43:** background Getty Images; **44:** background Getty Images; **44:** inset Barnabas Kindersley/© Dorling Kindersley; **48–49:** ©The Stock Market/ZEFA; **53:** John Heseltine/© Dorling Kindersley; **54:** © Dorling Kindersley; **57:** Canberra Bicycle Museum and Resource Centre, Australia; **59:** © Dorling Kindersley; **60:** Bettmann/CORBIS; **61:** ©Photo Researchers, Inc.; **63:** *Keying Up—The Court Jester* (detail), 1875, William Merritt Chase, Courtesy of the Pennsylvania Academy of the Fine Arts, Philadelphia, Gift of the Chapellier Galleries.; **65:** istockphoto.com; **66:** Ed Bohon/CORBIS; **69:** Ed Bohon/CORBIS; **73:** t. No Credit Necessary; **73:** b. ©Precious Ngcobo; **74:** *Food City*, 1967, Richard Estes, Oil acrylic and graphite on fiberboard, 48" x 68", Collection of the Akron Art Museum, Akron , Ohio, Museum Acquisition Fund, Photo by Richman Haire, ©Richard Estes/Licensed by VAGA, New York, NY/Courtesy Marlborough Gallery, NY; **78:** ©Ron Giling/Peter Arnold, Inc.; **80:** ©Ron Giling/Peter Arnold, Inc.; **82:** Barnabas Kindersley/© Dorling Kindersley; **83:** Corel Professional Photos CD-ROM™; **93:** Images.com/CORBIS; **97:** ©Archive Photos; **98:** Bettmann/CORBIS; **98:** background Mike Ginsburg; **100:** m. Courtesy of The Peace Corps; **100:** t.r. CORBIS Sygma; **100:** l. Audio Visual Archives at the John F. Kennedy Library; **100:** b.l. Bettmann/CORBIS; **101:** Bettmann/CORBIS; **102:** Bettmann/CORBIS; **105:** istockphoto.com; **106:** Copyright© by Julia Alvarez/Bill Eichner. Reprinted by permission of Susan Bergholz Literary Services, NY. All Rights reserved.; **107:** Charles Gupton/CORBIS; **111:** Time Life Pictures/Getty Images; **112:** b. Bettmann/CORBIS; **112:** t. Getty Images; **115:** Bettmann/CORBIS; **123:** CORBIS; **124:** *The Man With Three Masks*, John Rush, Courtesy of the artist; **127:** *New Orleans Fantasy*, 1985 (detail) Max Papart, Lithograph, Courtesy of Nahan Galleries, New York; **128:** Hulton-Deutsch-CORBIS; **131:** *The Man With Three Masks*, (detail) John Rush, Courtesy of the artist; **132:** AFP/Getty Images; **133:** Images.com/CORBIS; **134–135:** Bettmann/CORBIS; **136:** Bettmann/CORBIS; **139:** Werner Forman/Art Resource, NY; **141:** *Still Life Reviving*, Remedios Varos, Collection of Beatriz Varo de Cano, Valencia, Spain. Donation of Walter Gruen and Anna Alexandra Varsoviano in memory of Isabel Gruen Varsoviano. Col. Museo de Arte Moderno, Reproduction authorized by the Instituto Nacional de Bellas Artes y Literature-CONACULTA; **143:** Werner Forman/Art Resource, NY; **147:** t. AP/Wide World Photos; **147:** b. Photofest; **148:** NASA; **150:** NASA; **153:** Corel Professional Photos CD-ROM™; **154–155:** Getty Images; **162:** David Young-Wolff/PhotoEdit Inc.; **165:** Prentice Hall; **172:** Pages 2–9 from Understanding Comics by Scott McCloud a 215 page analysis of comics in comics form. © and TM 1994 Scott McCloud; **173:** Pages 2–9 from Understanding Comics by Scott McCloud a 215 page analysis of comics in comics form. © and TM 1994 Scott McCloud; **174:** Pages 2–9 from Understanding Comics by Scott McCloud a 215 page analysis of comics in comics form. © and TM 1994 Scott McCloud; **175:** Pages 2–9 from Understanding Comics by Scott McCloud a 215 page analysis of comics in comics form. © and TM 1994 Scott McCloud; **176:** Pages 2–9 from Understanding Comics by Scott McCloud a 215 page analysis of comics in comics form. © and TM 1994 Scott McCloud; **177:** Pages 2–9 from Understanding Comics by Scott McCloud a 215 page analysis of comics in comics form. © and TM 1994 Scott McCloud; **178:** Pages 2–9 from Understanding Comics by Scott McCloud a 215 page analysis of comics in comics form.; **179:** t. Pages 2–9 from Understanding Comics by Scott McCloud a 215 page analysis of comics in comics form. © and TM 1994 Scott McCloud; **179:** b. Courtesy of Scott McCloud; **180–181:** Franklin McMahon/CORBIS; **182:** t. Eric Cator; **182:** b. ©Images.com/CORBIS; **183:** ©Images.com/CORBIS; **184:** www.CartoonStock.com; **185:** Prentice Hall; **187:** Wolfgang Kaehler/CORBIS; **188:** Christie's Images/CORBIS; **190:** Pearson Education/PH School Division; **191:** Pearson Education/PH School Division; **192:** Pearson Education/PH School Division; **194:** Alan Carey/Photo Researchers, Inc.; **197:** Franklin McMahon/CORBIS; **201:** Miriam Berkely/Authorpix; **202:** CORBIS; **204:** AP/Wide World Photos; **206:** Getty Images; **209:** Jonathan Nourok/PhotoEdit; **211:** Robert Harding World Imagery; **213:** AP/Wide World Photos; **214:** The New York Times; **215:** *Peering Through the Jungle*, Larry Noble, Sal Barracca & Associates; **216–217:** Ron Stafford/CORBIS; **218–219:** ©Royalty-Free/CORBIS; **221:** Sovfoto/Eastfoto; **222:** Paula Weidiger/CORBIS; **227:** Ann Shamel/Graphicstock; **228–229:** Corel Professional Photos CD-ROM™; **230:** Grace Davies/Omni-Photo Communications, Inc.;; **231:** Corel Professional Photos CD-ROM™; **232:** Corel Professional Photos CD-ROM™; **233:** l.t. Andy Crawford© Dorling Kindersley; **233:** l.b. Jane Burton/© Dorling Kindersley; **233:** r. The Imperial War Museum London, artist's name and title of the work; **234:** ©The Stock Market/John Dominis; **241:** ©Copyright 1986, 2001, Hawaiian Lifeguard Association. All Rights Reserved.; **241:** background CORBIS; **242:** ©Copyright 1986,2001, Hawaiian Lifeguard Association. All Rights Reserved.; **242:** background CORBIS; **245:** Bettmann/CORBIS; **246:** Jeff Spielman/Getty Images; **246:** t. Carved Tortoiseshell Comb, mid 19th century, England or France tortoiseshell, Cooper- Hewitt National Design Museum, Smithsonian Institution/Art Resource, NY, Bequest of Mrs. John Innes Kane, 1926-22-545, photo by Richard Goodbody; **249:** Corel Professional Photos CD-ROM™; **250:** *Hairdresser's Window*, 1907, John Sloan, oil on canvas, 1947.240, Wadsworth Atheneum, Hartford, CT. The Ella Gallup Sumner and Mary Catlin Sumner Collection Fund; **251:** Carved Tortoiseshell Comb, mid 19th century, England or France tortoiseshell, Cooper- Hewitt National Design Museum, Smithsonian Institution/Art Resource, NY, Bequest of Mrs. John Innes Kane, 1926-22-545, photo by Richard Goodbody; **253:** Corel Professional Photos CD-ROM™; **254:** E.O. Hoppe/Stringer/Time Life Pictures/Getty Images; **255:** David De Lossy/Getty Images; **257:** R. Ashenbrenner/Stock Boston; **258–259:** Kenneth Redding/Getty Images; ©Nancy Crampton; **267:** t ©Nancy Crampton; **267:** b. AP/Wide World Photos; **268–269:** Corel Professional Photos CD-ROM™; **271:** *Feast Day, San Juan Pueblo*, 1921, William Penhallow Henderson, National Museum of American Art, Smithsonian Institution; Given in Memory of Joshua C. Taylor/Art Resource, New York; **274–275:** Charles Weckler/Getty Images; **277:** Sheldon Collins/CORBIS; **278:** Historical Picture Archive/CORBIS; **289:** Franklin McMahon/CORBIS; **293:** Time Life Pictures/Getty Images; **294:** Christie's Images; **296:** Christie's Images; **298:** *The New Necklace*, 1910; William McGregor Paxton, Courtesy, Museum of Fine Arts, Boston. Reproduced with permission. ©2002 Museum of Fine Arts, Boston. All Rights Reserved. Zoe Oliver Sherman Collection, 22.644; **300:** Christie's Images; **303:** Christie's Images; **304:** Getty Images; **305:** Getty Images; **306:** Getty Images; **308:** Getty Images; **310:** Getty Images; **313:** *Chess Mates*, 1992, Pamela Chin Lee, Courtesy of the artist, Photo by John Lei/Omni-Photo Communications, Inc.; **314:** Getty Images; **317:** Getty Images; **321:** Nikky Finney; **322:** *Sharecropper*, Elizabeth Catlett, Courtesy The Estate of Thurlow E. Tibbs, Jr., ©Elizabeth Catlett/Licensed by VAGA, New York, NY; **325:** Clay Perry/CORBIS; **326:** t. Frank Greenaway/© Dorling Kindersley; **326:** b. Jim Zipp/Photo Researchers, Inc.; **331:** Frank Greenaway/© Dorling Kindersley; **332:** Bettmann/CORBIS; **333:** ©Hulton Getty/Archive Photos; **334:** *Sacramento Railroad Station* (detail), 1874, William Hahn, Fine Arts Museum of San Francisco, Gift of the M. H. de Young Endowment Fund, 54936; **338:** Foodpix; **341:** The Granger Collection, New York; **349:** t. Photo Courtesy James Hurst; **349:** b. Bassouls Sophie/CORBIS; **350:** inset *Scarlet Ibis*, John James Audubon, ©Collection of The New-York Historical Society; **350:** Corel Professional Photos CD-ROM™; **352:** Francois Gohier/Photo Researchers, Inc.; **355:** *Two Boys in a Punt*, N. C. Wyeth, Collection of Dr. and Mrs. William A. Morton. Photography courtesy of the Brandywine River Museum. ©2002 Brandywine Conservancy; **358–359:** *Scarlet Ibis*, John James Audubon, ©Collection of The New-York Historical Society; **362:** *The Nymph of the Lo River*, section of a handscroll. (H.91/2") Attributed to Ku K'ai-chih, Courtesy of the Freer Gallery of Art, Smithsonian Institution, Washington, D.C. #14.53; **365:** Robert Harding World Imagery; **372:** ©Pierre Tremblay/Masterfile; **375:** Eric Cator; **382:** Scala/Art Resource, NY; **383:** Christopher Felver/CORBIS; **384–385:** ©Images.com/CORBIS; **386:** b. ©Images.com/CORBIS; **386:** t. Marion Ettlinger; **387:** ©Images.com/CORBIS; **388:** PEANUTS reprinted by permission of United Feature Syndicate, Inc.; **389:** Beryl Goldberg Photographer ©; **391:** istockphoto.com; **392:** Greg Ryan & Sally Beyer; **394:** Ambient Images; **396:** istockphoto.com; **399:** ©Images.com/CORBIS; **403:** Courtesy of the author; **404:** *Don Nemesio*, 1977, Esperanza Martinez, Courtesy of the artist; **407:** *El Leñador*, 1934, Tom Lea, oil on canvas, 36 x 30, Collection of the Museum of New Mexico, Museum of Fine Arts, Gift of P.E.R.A.; **408–409:** Charles Place/Getty Images; **410:** Warner Books, Inc.; **413:** Charles Place/Getty Images; **414:** CORBIS; **415:** AP/Wide World Photos; **418–419:** Robert Frerck/Woodfin Camp & Associates; **421:** AP/Wide World Photos; **426:** Bob Krist/CORBIS; **428:** Getty Images; **430:** Getty Images; **432:** Getty Images; **435:** Getty Images; **436:** Bettmann/CORBIS; **437:** NASA; **440:** r. Clive Streeter/© Dorling Kindersley; **440:** l (1). © Dorling Kindersley; **440:** l(2). © Dorling Kindersley; **440:** l(3). © Dorling Kindersley; **443:** NASA; **447:** border NASA; **448:** border NASA; **451:** b. Thomas Victor; **451:** t. Time Life Pictures/Getty Images; **452:** *Lincoln Proclaiming Thanksgiving*, Dean Cornwell, The Lincoln Museum, Fort Wayne, Indiana, (#1153); **454:** *Peculiarsome Abe*, N.C. Wyeth, Children's Special Collections, The Free Library of Philadelphia; **457:** Courtesy of the Library of Congress; **460:** b. ©Allsport/Hulton Deutsch; **460:** t. istockphoto.com; **471:** ©Images.com/CORBIS; **475:** Photo Courtesy of ABC Radio Networks; **476:** inset Photo courtesy of Lian Dolan; **476:** istockphoto.com; **478:** ©Alamy Images; **482:** AP/Wide World Photos; **483:** Massimo Listri/CORBIS; **484–485:** Sandro Vannini/CORBIS; **486:** ©Alamy Images; **487:** The Granger Collection, New York; **489:** Sandro Vannini/CORBIS; **493:** Bettmann/CORBIS; **494:** Bettmann/CORBIS; **496:** CORBIS; **499:** CORBIS; **501:** CORBIS; **503:** Underwood & Underwood/CORBIS; **504–505:** Getty Images; **507:** t. Bettmann/CORBIS; **507:** b. National Collection of Fine Arts, Washington, DC; **508:** CORBIS; **511:** CORBIS; **515:** background. Bettmann/CORBIS; **515:** Franklin Delano Roosevelt Library, Hyde Park, NY; **516:** background. Bettmann/CORBIS; **517:** Bettmann/CORBIS; **517:** background. Bettmann/CORBIS; **518:** The Granger Collection, New York; **518:** background. Bettmann/CORBIS; **521:** t. Courtesy of the Author. Photo by Carolyn Soto.; **521:** b CORBIS; **522:** Jimmy dorantes/LatinFocus.com; **525:** *Young Brothers in the Hood*, 17x22, Tom McKinney, Courtesy of the artist; **526:** Deborah Davis/PhotoEdit; **529:** Henry Horenstein/StockBoston; **536:** Jose Luiz Pelaez, Inc. /CORBIS; **539:** Marion Ettlinger; **546:** istockphoto.com; **547:** ©Cloe Poisson/The Hartford Courant; **548–549:** The Grand Design/SuperStock; **550:** b. ©Images.com/CORBIS; **550:** t. Cheron Bayna; **551:** ©Images.com/CORBIS; **552:** LUCKY COW ©2003 Mark Pett. Dist. By UNIVERSAL PRESS SYNDICATE. Reprinted with permission. All rights reserved.; **553:** © Allan Davey/Masterfile; **555:** Paul & Lindamarie Ambrose/Getty Images; **556:** Paul & Lindamarie Ambrose/Getty Images; **557:** Photo courtesy of Pat Mora; **561:** The Grand Design/SuperStock; **565:** b. Bettmann/CORBIS; **565:** t. Time Life

PH Literature ©2007

Staff Credits: Ernie Albanese, Diane Alimena, **Rosalyn Arcilla,** Jasjit Arneja, Penny Baker, **Nancy Barker, Amy Baron,** Rachel Beckman, Betsy Bostwick, **Ellen Bowler,** Jennifer Brady, Evonne Burgess, Pradeep Byram, Rui Camarinha, **Pam Carey,** Lisa Carrillo, Jaime Cohen, Allison Cook, **Irene Ehrmann,** Leanne Esterly, Steve Frankel, Philip Fried, **Maggie Fritz,** Michael Ginsberg, **Elaine Goldman,** Patricia Hade, **Monduane Harris, Martha Heller,** Beth Hyslip, Vicki A. Kane, **Kate Krimsky,** Mary Sue Langan, Monica Lehmann, **Mary Luthi, George Lychock,** Gregory Lynch, Daniela Mastria, John McClure, Jim McDonough, Kathleen Mercandetti, Kerrie Miller, Karyl Murray, Ken Myett, Kim Ortell, Carolyn Pallof, Sal Pisano, Jackie Regan, Erin Rehill-Seker, Bruce Rolff, **Laura Ross,** Carolyn Sapontzis, Donna Schindler, Mildred Schulte, **Melissa Shustyk, Robert Siek, Rita Sullivan, Cynthia Summers,** Patrice Titterington, Elizabeth Torjussen, Jane S. Traulsen

Additional Credits: Susan C. Ball, William Bingham, Andrea Brescia, Donna Chappelle, Jennifer Ciccone, Jason Cuoco, Florrie Gadson, Judith Gaelick, Phillip Gagler, James Garratt, Allen Gold, Kristan Hoskins, Lisa Iozzia, Mohamed Kaptan, Barbara Kehr, Terry Kim, Stuart Kirschenbaum, Linda Latino, Julian Liby, Karen Mancinelli, Ginidir Marshall, Bill McAllister, Patrick J. McCarthy, Caroline McDonnell, Michael McLaughlin, Meg Montgomery, Gita Nadas, Lesley Pierson, Maureen Raymond, Rachel Ross, Lloyd Sabin, James Savakis, Donna Schindler, Debi Taffet, Elizabeth Torjussen, Ryan Vaarsi, Alfred Voto, Gina M. Wangrycht, Lindsay White

R-70 ◆ *Credits*

Zlata Filipović
Gary Blackwood
Cornelius Eady
Richard Mühlberger
Pat Mora
John Phillip Santos
Joao Magueijo
Anita Desai
Gary Soto
Frank Kermode
Joseph Bruchac
Walter Dean Myers
Arthur Miller
Rebecca Walker
Julius Lester
Dean Smith
Samantha Chang
Coleman Barks
Patricia McKissack
Marilyn Nelson
Berry
William L. Andrews
Jean Craighead George
John Kilgo
Richard Rodriguez
Wendy Doniger
Laurence Yep
Pat Mora
Judith Ortiz Cofer
Susan Power
W.S. Merwin
Gretel Ehrlich
Seamus Heaney
David Mamet
Jane Yolen
Richard Peck
Jon Scieszka
Burton Raffel
Anne Tyler
Jamaica Kincaid
Susan Vreeland
Jacqueline Woodson
Charles Johnson
Andrew Mishkin
Tim O'Brien
Wayson Choy
Cherie Bennett
David Henry Hwang
Nell Irvin Painter
Gretel Ehrlich
Walter Dean Myers
Chinua Achebe
Elizabeth McCracken
James Berry
Frank Kermode
Anita Desai
Cornelius Eady
C.J. Cherryh
Patricia McKissack
Arthur Miller
Gary Blackwood
Zlata Filipović
Elizabeth McCracken
Jean Craighead George
Jon Scieszka
Julius Lester
Walter Dean Myers
Dean Smith
Richard Mühlberger
Pat Mora
Jamaica Kincaid
Gretel Ehrlich